Irma S. Rombauer

Marion Rombauer Becker

Ethan Becker

Illustrated by John Norton

SCRIBNER

NEW YORK   LONDON   TORONTO   SYDNEY

SCRIBNER
1230 Avenue of the Americas
New York, NY 10020

Copyright 1931, 1936, 1941, 1943, 1946,
© 1951, 1952, 1953, 1962, 1963, 1975 by Simon & Schuster Inc.

Copyright renewed © 1959, 1964, 1969, 1971,
1974, 1979, 1980, 1981, 1990, 1991 by Simon & Schuster Inc.

Copyright © 1997, 2006 by Simon & Schuster Inc.,
The Joy of Cooking Trust, and The MRB Revocable Trust

Illustrations copyright © 2006 by John Norton

For information regarding special discounts for bulk purchases,
please contact Simon & Schuster Special Sales:
1-800-456-6798 or business@simonandschuster.com

Designed by Liney Li
Set in Frutiger
Manufactured in the United States of America

1   3   5   7   9   10   8   6   4   2

Library of Congress Cataloging-in-Publication Data is available.

ISBN-13: 978-0-7432-4626-2
ISBN-10:   0-7432-4626-8

To the four women of JOY:

My grandmother, Irma,

My mother, Marion,

My wife, Susan,

and my dear friend, Maggie

. . . To receive the full value of joy
you must have someone to share it with.

Mark Twain

CONTENTS

A Note from Julia Child ix

A Letter from Ethan Becker xi

Acknowledgments xv

Author's Note About Using This Book xvii

75 Years of JOY
A History of the *Joy of Cooking* 1

Nutrition 4

Entertaining 11

Menus 19

Beverages 28

Wine and Beer 44

Cocktails and Party Drinks 54

Appetizers and Hors d'Oeuvres 69

Brunch, Lunch, and Supper Dishes 95

Stocks and Soups 114

Salads 152

Sandwiches, Wraps, and Pizza 177

Egg Dishes 194

Fruits 208

Vegetables 240

Pasta, Noodles, and Dumplings 320

Grains 344

Shellfish **369**

Fish **393**

Poultry and Wildfowl **418**

Meat **462**

Game **523**

Stuffings **532**

Savory Sauces, Salad Dressings, Marinades, and Rubs **542**

Breads and Coffee Cakes **591**

Pancakes, Waffles, Fritters, and Doughnuts **643**

Pies and Pastries **661**

Cakes and Cupcakes **698**

Cookies and Bars **760**

Icings, Toppings, and Glazes **784**

Desserts **801**

Frozen Desserts and Sweet Sauces **828**

Candies and Confections **854**

Keeping and Storing Food **883**

Canning, Salting, Smoking, and Drying **888**

Freezing **910**

Jellies and Preserves **927**

Pickles and Relishes **943**

Know Your Ingredients **956**

Cooking Methods and Techniques **1045**

Index **1073**

A NOTE FROM
JULIA CHILD

The *Joy of Cooking* has always been a very important book. When it was first published, it made a great impression on American cooking. It is, and should continue to be, a staple in any good culinary collection, because Irma's voice is there with you in the kitchen giving guidance and encouragement and friendly tips and reminders. The whys and hows are carefully explained, and that's what makes JOY a fundamental resource for any American cook!

Julia Child
Santa Barbara, California
June 2004

A LETTER FROM ETHAN BECKER

Five years ago, as we looked to the next revision, Susan and I imagined being able to sit down with Mom and Granny Rom to ask for their direction on this most important project: JOY's 75th anniversary edition. We asked ourselves who held the position they once held as the country's culinary queens and, of course, the only person who came to mind was Julia Child. It was the spring of 2001 when we called and asked Julia to review and critique our vision of the anniversary edition of the *Joy of Cooking*. She answered with great enthusiasm and grace, "I'd love to, dear—for whatever it's worth."

Just a few months later, we sat around the table at her home in Santa Barbara, California. Our goal, we told her, was to bring Know Your Ingredients back to its full glory, to restore, expand, and revise the teaching text, and bring JOY's voice back loud and clear. We explained that our dream was to base the 2006 edition on the best-selling JOY ever published—the 1975 edition—the apex of the culinary knowledge that had been compiled and communicated by my mother and grandmother since 1931. On the dust jacket of the 1975 edition, Julia herself was quoted, ". . . it is number one on my list . . . *the* one book of all cookbooks in English that I would have on my shelf if I could have but one."

A few days later, we received a note from her that said, "Thanks for putting the joy back in JOY." We were thrilled. In the coming weeks, Julia reviewed revisions of some of the chapters and blessed our work with her approval. Our friendship with her was short-lived because of her failing health and eventual death, but knowing her and working with her was an honor and a privilege. We thank her for loving the *Joy of Cooking* enough to give some of her precious time.

There have been numerous others with whom we've worked to complete this project—family and friends, cooking teachers and food writers, editors and publishers—to mention just a few, and we thank all of them. JOY was never written without the help of many.

Our late cousin Elsa Hunstein, Granny Rom's favorite niece, and her husband, Jack, opened their home to us on two different visits, where we spent hours cooking, eating, talking, and laughing. She shared intimate memories of Granny Rom and Mom working on the JOYs that were published in the 1930s and '40s. From the time she was six years old, Elsa sampled recipes almost weekly at Aunt Irma's. One of her favorite dishes was borscht, and she loved the silver tureen in which it was served. My mother gave Elsa that tureen many years later when Granny Rom died. Then Elsa gave it to us just before she died in 2004. Thanks for everything, Elsa.

And when the test kitchen in New York had trouble with the "Rombauer Special" cake, one of Granny Rom's favorite cakes, we relied on the Hunstein kids to help us solve the problem, as Elsa had baked this cake for Jack year after year on his birthday. Julia, Mary, Jim, and Alice rose to the occasion by recalling their mom's wise counsel, "Don't bake this cake in hot, humid weather." Jim, of course, spoke from experience, as he baked this cake himself with memorable results. We have pictures.

Probably the greatest pleasure that has come out of this revision is the relationship we have established with Maggie Green (and her family). Maggie stepped into the position as one of JOY's primary editors with ease and confidence. She has not only persisted through the most challenging parts of this project, but has guided it much of the way. Her efforts, enthusiasm, and dedication to

JOY made this very difficult job much easier for everyone involved. She is one of the most organized and productive people on earth, and her infallible memory has made her the guardian angel of this revision. All of us are lucky that she has touched this book with her knowledge, experience, and attention to detail. Know Your Ingredients and Cooking Methods and Techniques, two of JOY's most important reference chapters, were her babies, and it shows. What ever would we have done without her?

Our fearless leader on this monumental project was Beth Wareham, director of Lifestyle Publications at Scribner. Thanks for your devotion to this project, your sense of humor, and your last nerve (it's in a jar on my desk). How will we ever forget the big chart; endless conversations about bizarre minutiae; the infinite list of adjectives; obsessing over hummus, cranberries, finger bowls, frog legs, and grilled pizza; and the many conversations about who is eating what in this country. It's been fun.

Our friends Arch and Shirley Corriher gave of their hearts to the heart of the *Joy of Cooking*, Know Your Ingredients. This indispensable chapter has been both restored and revised with expanded and updated information, thanks to contributions from the *CookWise* author and couple. And, while we did not personally consult him, we must thank Harold McGee for the hundreds of times we flipped through his fabulous book, *On Food and Cooking*, for hard-to-find answers to food questions.

Culinary historian and writer Anne Mendelson became part of the JOY family many years ago when she wrote *Stand Facing the Stove*, a book about the *Joy of Cooking*'s history and the women who wrote it. Her chapter on JOY's first seventy-five years is a valuable addition to this revision and celebration of JOY's anniversary.

Ikki and Polly Matsumoto, www.ikkimatsumoto.com, were kind enough to explore illustration styles. Ikki's illustrations in the 1975 edition reflect his incredible talent and precious hours of work with Mom, and they gave us a foundation for the illustrations in this book. Many thanks to John Norton, www.johnnortonart.com, for picking up where Ikki left off and pulling the book together with fresh, sophisticated art and lightning speed.

Our gratitude also goes to all the other experts who put their time and passion into this book to make it all it should be. Author and hunter Rebecca Gray worked on Game and Poultry and Wildfowl to teach us how to cook and *Eat Like a Wildman*. We appreciate her expertise on foraging, hunting, making maple syrup, and fishing. *Pie in the Sky* author Susan Gold Purdy, www.highaltitudebaking.com, went to great heights to ensure that our high-altitude cakes are not only delicious, but doable at every elevation. Her attention to detail and willingness to read chapters proved extremely valuable. Sproutmaster Gil Frishman, www.sproutpeople.com, contributed greatly to the information on Sprouting Grains and Beans, one of our favorite ways of gardening.

For all of us who love to cook on the grill or a campfire, we added a section on hearth cooking, in the Cooking Methods and Techniques chapter, thanks to expert and author William Rubel, www.williamrubel.com, who shared his passion and knowledge of *The Magic of the Fire*. Working with William was easy and rewarding. We thank Elizabeth Andress, director of the National Center for Home Food Preservation, www.homefoodpreservation.com, for the hard work she did updating our chapters on canning, freezing, and other methods of keeping food. She helped us bring back this incredibly important reference material to JOY.

Gratitude is also due to Dr. Walter Willett, coauthor of *Eat, Drink, and Be Healthy*, and chair of the Department of Nutrition at the Harvard School of Public Health, www.hsph.harvard.edu/nutritionsource. JOY's updated nutrition chapter is the result of his practical, sound information and advice. Our appreciation goes to Brian St. Pierre, who was kind enough to add up-to-date information about wine (and beer) with an open, inviting attitude that teaches but does not intimidate. His book *A Perfect Glass of Wine* led us to this outstanding teacher and writer, who also read each chapter of this tome to ensure that the family's voice was clear and present.

Susan and I also want to thank my brother, Mark; his wife, Jennifer; and their son, Joe, for their continued belief in us to do what is right for JOY. My son, John, must be acknowledged for tolerating Susan's constant requests for editing and input on a number of chapters and concepts. Hats off to the winemaker in our family, Koerner Rombauer; his late wife, Joan; daughter, Sheana; and son, KR, who promote JOY all year long at Rombauer Vineyards in St. Helena, California. The opportunity to sign books at their Chardonnay Extravaganza is an annual thrill.

We thank those who gave us recipes and ideas on a number of topics: Hector Gomez, Bonnie Scripps, Gina Gerardhi, our dear friends Alice and Matt MacLeid, and our ever-faithful friend and kindred spirit, Brenda Ward. Our appreciation goes to Cindi Menard-Marshall, who gave us her point of view on cooking as a mom on the go with three growing boys, and we thank her for her care of the business details in our lives. Warren Green gave freely of his time and expertise in Know Your Ingredients, and he was an understanding husband when he came home from a hard day's work to find Maggie and Susan with books, manuscripts, and laptops all over the kitchen. Thank you, Warren. Our friend Susan Collins, a lady and perfect hostess, recommended that we include information on working with a caterer. Not only is that an addition most of us need, it is a concept that has helped make this JOY even better and up-to-date. We also want to thank all the dietetic interns from Good Samaritan Hospital in Cincinnati, Ohio, who worked with Maggie. And we want to recognize Missy Lynn of Missy's Finest Jams & Jellies, who contributed her kitchen and knowledge to the jelly and jam testing.

There are two people who labored along side of me as I worked to keep the *Joy of Cooking* alive and growing during the 1980s. They gave greatly of their energy, knowledge, skills, and devotion to a revision that was completed but never printed, and I appreciate all they did. The world is not the same without them in it. Thank you to the regal Sasha Vereschagin and the spirited Patty Eiser.

This book could not have come to fruition without the faith of the leading ladies at Scribner, who saw we were moving in the right direction and helped us get where we wanted to go. What a team! Susan Moldow and Roz Lippel, thanks for working on many fronts on JOY's behalf. Carolyn Reidy, thank you for your continued belief in the book. Sarah Billingsley and Jill Vogel deserve a big pat on the back for hanging in there, and for all of their hard work. Thank you to *Cooking by the Book*'s Suzi O'Rourke and her staff for testing all of these recipes, a monumental task. And I want to express appreciation to my agent, Sam Pinkus—sounding board, supporter, and friend.

Last but not least, I want to thank my wife, Susan, who picked up the phone and called Julia, hired Maggie, and put together the first plan to make this JOY a revision of the 1975 edition. Pestiferous at times, but always persistent, she worked passionately not only for JOY's integrity, but also as a writer and editor on this revision. Susan did everything in her power to make this book a reality. I will always love her for this, as I do for so many, many other reasons.

Happy Anniversary, Granny Rom, Mom, and Pop. I hope you are pleased. We've worked long and hard to put "the joy back in JOY."

Ethan Becker
Half Moon Ridge
Citico, Tennessee
April 2006

P.S. Come visit Maggie, Susan, and me at www.thejoy kitchen.com!

ACKNOWLEDGMENTS

A special thanks to the chapter editors who worked with care and respect to make this *Joy of Cooking* a special revision indeed:

Elizabeth L. Andress, Melissa Clark, Arch and Shirley Corriher, Abby Dodge, Rebecca Gray, Maggie Green, Susan Gold Purdy, Anne Mendelson, Brian St. Pierre, Stephen Schmidt, Michele Scicolone, Marah Stets, and Walter Willett, M.D.

We must also thank the troops of dedicated people who have worked behind the scenes—recipe developers, copy editors (especially Judith Sutton), designers, typesetters, and some great cooks—for their endless contributions to the JOY:

Marilyn Abraham, Sue Anderson, Tamara Bigelow, Sarah Billingsley, Donna Capobianco Boland, Jeanine Botsko, Larry Catanzaro, David Cerpa, Howard Chapman, Anne Cherry, Helen Chin, Suet Chong, Joshua Cohen, Todd Coleman, David (The Kid) Cope, Sarah Copeland, Lauren Brown Costello, Mia Crowley-Hald, Jane Davis, Jennifer Davis, Linda Dingler, dix! Digital Prepress Inc., Tierney Dodge, David Domedion, Georgia Downard, Suzanne Fass, Hope Marie Flamm, Bobby Flay, Joyce Galletta, Melissa Gaman, Tom Gelinne, Temple Grandin, Reid Green, Gabrielle Guise, Kathy Hamilton, Jessica Harris, Jan Hazerd, Suki Hertz, Lauren Huber, Adrian James, Anne Jones, Jamaica Jones, Irene Kheradi, Liana Krissoff, Carl and Peggy Kroboth, Olga Leonardo, Abby Lupoff, Sandy MacGregor, Christine Malloy, Ann Mileti, Michael Mitchell, Gay Moldow, Hiromi Nobata, John Norton, Alexandra Noya, Maggie O'Dell, Ashley O'Neal, Joyce O'Neil, Brian O'Rourke, Amy Palma, Stacy Pearl, Elizabeth Perreault, Kim Pistone, Larry Placek, Lisa Porter, Andrea Potischman, Kathleen Rizzo, Rick Rodgers, Liliana Scali, Dianne Schwalb, Tracey Seaman, Tim Shaw, Martha Rose Shulman, Patrick J. Skerrett, Rian Smolik, Catherine Sprinkel, Moraima Suarez, Diana Thompson, James Togba, Judy Troy, Tracy Van Buskirk, Claire Van de Berghe, Lisa West, Russell White, Lisa Wolff, and Miriam Wysoker.

AUTHOR'S NOTE ABOUT USING THIS BOOK

WATCH FOR THESE SYMBOLS

➤   Pointers

▲   High-Altitude

( )   Optional

We present you first with a key to this book. Whenever we emphasize an important principle or tip, the arrow ➤ is a pointer to success. The triangle ▲ alerts you to high-altitude cooking methods, tips, and recipes. Parentheses indicate an optional ingredient—one that may enhance the recipe, but its omission will not prevent the success of the recipe. ➤ Note, too, the meaning of the following terms as we use them: Any meat, fish, or grain, unless otherwise specified, is raw, not cooked. Eggs are large or the 2-ounce size; milk is whole, fresh milk; butter is unsalted when specified; flour denotes the unbleached all-purpose variety; spices are ground; herbs are fresh; condensed canned soup is to be used undiluted.

In response to many requests from users of the JOY who ask "what are your favorites?" we have indicated these recipes by using word significant to our family. When you see a recipe that includes the word "Cockaigne" the recipe was one of Mom and Pop's favorites. Cockaigne, which in medieval times signified "Utopia, a mythical land of peace and plenty," and the name for their beloved Cincinnati home. "Becker" indicates recipes that I have developed over the last few years and reflect my personal way of cooking—I love short cuts that save time. Other recipes that include "Half Moon" are our current favorites, and are named for our Tennessee mountain home, Half Moon Ridge. And how could I forget? Recipes with "Rombauer" in the title are JOY classics or were some of Granny Rom's favorite creations.

When a recipe bears a classic title, you can be assured that it contains the essential ingredients or methods that created its name in the first place. For quick meals, look to our Brunch, Lunch, and Supper Dishes chapter and to the list in the Menus chapter, where you can find many recipes that are quickly made. The Menus chapter will also give you list after list of dishes for anything from picnics to wedding buffets, from holidays to backpacking.

The index, 1073, is your backdoor key to this book. This will lead you to such action terms as *simmer, braise,* and *sauté;* descriptive ones such as *rémoulade, chiffonade, brûlée,* and *mirepoix;* and to national culinary enthusiasms such as flavored vodkas, iced mochas, plank-roasted salmon, and individual molten chocolate cakes.

Other features of this book that we ask you to investigate include the chapter on Cooking Methods and Techniques, which gives you many clues to maintaining the appearance and nutrients in the food you are cooking. You will find this chapter a reliable cooking teacher, whether on the stove or the hearth. Know Your Ingredients is an encyclopedia of food within JOY that reveals vital characteristics of the ingredients you commonly use, how and why they react as they do, how to measure them and, when feasible, how to substitute one for another. In sections headed "ABOUT," you will find information relating to these food categories, including information about buying, storing, and serving.

Even more important, we hope that in answering the question "What will we have to eat?," you will find in Nutrition a stimulus to choose foods wisely. Using this information you may agree with Samuel Chamberlain, who said, "The gentle art of gastronomy is a friendly one. It hurdles language barriers, makes friends among civilized people, and warms the heart." Choose from our book what suits you as an individual, for your tastes and your pleasure, and join us in the joy of cooking.

E. B.

75 YEARS OF
JOY

A History of the
JOY OF COOKING

The Great Depression tightened its grip on a shaken nation in 1931, but not on the resolve of one strong-willed St. Louis woman confronting another sort of wound. Desolated by her husband's suicide in 1930, she forged her own new purpose in life. She spent more than a year assembling a collection of favorite recipes and sent it forth into the world, at her own expense, with a title that defied grief: *The Joy of Cooking*.

When Irma von Starkloff Rombauer (1877–1962) began her late-life career with the encouragement of her son, Edgar Jr., and her daughter, Marion, the major American cookbooks were mostly the work of what H. L. Mencken called "cooking-school marms" or "a vast and cocksure rabble of dietitians." Irma, the daughter of a cultured and politically active immigrant German family, was something else entirely. A complete amateur with no official credentials, she nonetheless knew that neophyte cooks somehow learn faster in the company of a friend. This small, chic, witty, and immensely forceful woman appointed herself that friend.

For several years she sold copies of her book out of her apartment, while rethinking the whole business of recipe writing. Eventually she hit on a novel format with the ingredients lists worked into the directions, now known as the action method. With the help of her husband's former secretary, Mary Whyte (later Mary Whyte Hartrich), she recast all her recipes in the new style and prepared an expanded edition published in 1936 by the Bobbs-Merrill Company of Indianapolis. It was a modest success.

These first JOY editions take us back to an America where chicken was expensive and veal cheap, most kitchen knives had to be scoured clean with lemon juice to keep from staining, "frosted" (frozen) vegetables were making a very slow entry into kitchens, home refrigerators didn't outnumber literal "iceboxes" cooled by blocks of ice, and milk was not homogenized. Electric mixers were a novelty; most people beat egg whites or whipped cream with a rotary eggbeater or wire whisk. Pureeing was done without blenders or food processors, by forcing the ingredients through a sieve with a wooden pusher or spoon. Many people had never encountered zucchini, broccoli, acorn squash, soy sauce, or fresh ginger. Goat cheese, fennel, fettuccine, bagels, yogurt, macadamia nuts, mangoes, hoisin sauce, extra-virgin olive oil, and cilantro were esoteric items known only to a few. Cherry tomatoes, Cornish hens, and butter wrapped in quarter-pound sticks lay some distance in the future, as did aluminum foil, household plastic bags, paper towels, and plastic wrap.

The only ethnic cuisines that most Americans had any exposure to were German, Italian, Chinese, and, in some states, Mexican. The favorite ways of serving vegetables (aside from simply boiled and buttered) were creamed or made into timbales or soufflés. For a backyard cookout—few people said "barbecue"—you needed to build a brick or stone fireplace. Mainstream cooks and hostesses might have had a qualm or two about putting garlic in the salad, but not about serving steak, cream sauces, variety meats like sweetbreads and tongue, butter-and-lard piecrusts, cheese omelets, gelatin salads, or condensed soups. Irma Rombauer's cooking wholeheartedly embraced all the important features of this landscape as well as her own family's traditional St. Louis German cooking.

Then as now, American food resisted easy generalizations, but in 1936, accommodating many diverse gastronomic preferences in a single cookbook was less of a stretch than it is today. And it was no stretch at all for Irma. She equally enjoyed old-fashioned dishes cooked from scratch and up-to-the-minute shortcuts using processed ingredients—like canned soups and evaporated or condensed milk—that some cooks thought were modern miracles while others looked down on them as inferior substitutes for homemade or fresh originals. The human bond represented by cooking meant more to her than fixed yardsticks of elegance or authenticity, and from the beginning, users of JOY felt that they were being addressed as friends, not pupils. They sensed the presence of a real person who could always take time to inject something extracurricular into the proceedings, whether it was a mention of her favorite comic-strip characters or literary quotations like Mark Twain's "Too much of anything is bad, but too much of good whiskey is barely enough."

The next JOY incarnation arrived in 1943, during the great national crisis of World War II. Irma wove together much of the 1936 edition with *Streamlined Cooking*, a short book of timesaving recipes that she had published in 1939, to produce an expanded edition that appealed to the broadest audience yet. This revision paid attention to developments like pressure cookers and a growing herbs-

and-seasonings vogue, introduced more culinary reference material and nutritional information, included a section of recipes that used unrationed substitutes for ingredients subject to wartime rationing (hence the first soybean recipes in JOY), and offered newly fashionable dishes like beef Stroganoff, vichyssoise, and guacamole. Just as important, Irma gave her own lively personality even freer rein, strengthening the sense of a friend speaking to friends as she patriotically held "our mighty weapon, the cooking spoon." Her efforts made JOY into a nationwide bestseller—indeed, as letters of thanks reached her from servicemen in the Pacific theater and harassed cooks on the home front.

In 1946, that edition was reissued with slight rearrangements to delete the war-rationing recipes, and in the same year Irma published a work for children, *A Cookbook for Girls and Boys.* She was already thinking ahead toward a more thorough updating of JOY for which she would call upon the talents of her daughter, Marion Rombauer Becker (1903–1976).

Marion had contributed artwork, recipe testing, and moral support to the first privately printed JOY. When Irma asked her to participate in the revision, she was living in Cincinnati with her husband, John William Becker, and their two young sons, Mark and Ethan. Like Irma, she was proud to call herself an amateur cook. But her skills and interests were a complement to her mother's, not a carbon copy. She held staunch beliefs about a range of issues extending far beyond the kitchen, from the nutritional importance of whole grains to the virtues of organic gardening and ecological awareness. Her years as the first professional director of the Cincinnati Modern Art Society honed her feeling for visual presentation as an aid to learning and steered her to the young artist Ginnie Hofmann, who was hired to supply a large number of unusually apt and informative line drawings for the new edition.

Irma, meanwhile, had made helpful contacts in the New York food world—especially her friend Cecily Brownstone of the Associated Press—that enabled her to keep abreast of new culinary fashions and kitchen resources. Mother and daughter together reshaped the book to embrace important postwar developments like the growing role of home freezers and other specialized appliances. New signs-of-the-times recipes included chicken cacciatore, bacon-wrapped prunes, plain brown rice, herring in sour cream sauce, homemade yogurt, and pizza (called Vegetable Shortcake). This JOY also provided bits of "desert island" information—e.g., how to pasteurize milk at home—that would prove a blessing to people in strange or isolated situations anywhere from city to wilderness.

Irma's part in the work was cut short by a series of strokes beginning in 1955. Along with the demands of her mother's illness, Marion was left to undertake the next revision with the aid of John, who contributed much editorial polish, wit, and culinary judgment. They produced not just a cookbook but an encyclopedic, though personable and entertaining, resource with strengthened desert-island elements and a new emphasis on background information. In this edition, Marion, who loved the sense of sharing pleasures with reader-friends as much as Irma, pointed to her family's special favorites with the designation "Cockaigne"—the name of the Beckers' beloved Cincinnati home, where she had created an eight-acre "wild garden" and model of ecological restoration.

This JOY would stand as one of the signal documents of the 1950s–1960s gourmet revolution, along with *The James Beard Cookbook, Mastering the Art of French Cooking, The New York Times Cookbook,* and *Michael Field's Cooking School.* It would, however, have a broader influence than any of these. It was the book that amateurs and professionals alike turned to when they needed to grind their own peanut butter, tackle chitterlings or a whole octopus, set up a campfire for cooking, deal with a then-exotic fruit like cherimoya, purify drinking water, or substitute honey for sugar without ruining a recipe. And it rightly judged that American cooks were ready to embark on dishes like fish quenelles, cassoulet, stuffed grape leaves, bolognese sauce, baked kasha, and French-style pâtés.

Because of serious author-publisher disagreements, though, the new edition was not published in a form acceptable to Marion until 1963 (a garbled version had appeared in 1962, the year of Irma's death). The next dozen years—a time of great fulfillment for Marion and John—saw JOY confirmed as the nation's reigning kitchen bible, perhaps the most remarkable American cookbook of the twentieth century.

The next revision was prepared in the shadow of advancing illness. From 1972 on, Marion underwent debilitating treatments for incurable cancer, and in 1974 she lost John to a brain tumor. With the support of loyal helpers, including Ethan and his wife, Joan, as well as illustrator Ikki Matsumoto, she soldiered on through all obstacles. In 1975, she saw to completion an edition that embodied many of her own concerns (for instance, about the often troubling course of modern agribusiness) and convictions while providing an even greater range of recipes and reference material. This edition also saw such new entries as granola, hoppin' or hopping John, bagna cauda, bulgur pilaf, pita-type flatbreads, and Chinese firepot. And it was the first to introduce kiwis and jicama, give practical directions for making tofu, discuss the uses of phyllo, and define kosher meat.

Intensely committed to continuity with JOY's past as a family legacy and document, Marion took pains to leave in place much that had been in the book since 1931, from tomato pudding, potatoes O'Brien, onion soufflé, and cinnamon star cookies to choice Irmaisms like, "A bit of tomato skin was once as out of place at a dinner table as a bowie knife." Her swan song struck an immediate chord with a huge audience ranging from suburban housewives to hippies on communes to the nation's most admired food writers, and it would prove the most durable of all JOY editions to date.

Marion died at the end of 1976, leaving JOY in the hands of Ethan and Mark. After some years of joint revision efforts, Ethan took over sole responsibility. The next decades saw large publishing-industry shifts—including the demise of Bobbs-Merrill—that impeded further progress for a long while, until at last JOY came under the Scribner imprint of Simon & Schuster. In 1997, Scribner published an edition that, unlike earlier ones, included commissioned recipes and other material from dozens of professional food writers. The new edition also broke with the past in deemphasizing the first-person comments and whimsical asides that had been crucial to Irma and Marion's approach. Yet they would have been the first to hail the valuable services that it performed: correcting past errors of fact in the light of more recent research; acknowledging the importance of appliances like food processors, microwave ovens (which Marion had had reservations about), and bread machines in contemporary American cooking; and—the most important change of all—taking account of exciting foods from other cultures, Cuban and Thai, Indian and Japanese. At the same time, the new version paid necessary attention to now indispensable ingredients or preparations (balsamic vinegar, Asian noodles, many chile pepper varieties, basmati rice, garam masala) and brought into the JOY fold such welcome recipe additions as grilled vegetables, gravlax, Mexican salsas, and Vietnamese phó.

In 1997, the year of that edition, Ethan married writer and artist Susan Cope. In the family tradition of looking toward future JOYs as soon as an updated version was completed, Ethan and Susan at once began working on a new revision for 2006.

It would not have escaped Irma Rombauer and Marion Rombauer Becker's notice that, like some past JOYs, the seventy-fifth-anniversary edition finds the United States confronting "times that try men's souls." They would have been proud to send forth another version of their enduring work to all people of good will, with a title that still defies grief.

NUTRITION

Food is a central part of our lives. It provides the body with fuel and raw materials for maintenance, growth, and repair. It draws together family and friends, anchors celebrations and rites of passage, and sometimes soothes the soul. It has the power to heal, and also to harm. And it is the heart of a vast commercial enterprise.

Throughout most of human history, the brief life span—during the Roman Empire, the average life expectancy at birth was just twenty-two years—meant that it didn't really much matter what you ate as long as you took in at least as many calories as you burned. It matters now. In many countries, amazing transformations in society, public health, and medicine have made life easier and longer. Today the average American reaches a ripe old age of seventy-seven years. That's more than long enough to develop a litany of diseases associated with getting older. It turns out, though, that most of these diseases aren't the inevitable consequences of aging. Instead, many are rooted in poor nutrition, lack of exercise, and other unhealthy habits.

There's a bright side to this: ➤ Combined with regular exercise and not smoking, a truly nutritious diet is your best bet for staying healthy or getting back to good health. Long-term studies from the Harvard School of Public Health show that this combination can prevent a stunning 80 percent of heart attacks, 90 percent of cases of type 2 diabetes, and 70 percent of colon cancers. A healthy diet can also help you avoid stroke, high blood pressure, high cholesterol, osteoporosis, constipation and other digestive woes, anemia, cavities, cataracts and other eye problems, and memory loss. The benefits aren't just for the future—a healthy diet can give you more energy,

help you control your weight, and make you feel better right now.

How you eat—the mood or spirit, the beauty of the table, and the company with whom you enjoy a meal—also matters. As a source of satisfaction and renewal, few daily rituals have the extraordinary potential of the act of preparing and sharing a meal. Whether you are feeding your family, friends, or even strangers, cooking can be an expression of affection and connection, both of which are good for the mind and the body. The conversation and social interaction are usually the best part of the meal.

NUTRITION 101

If a "healthy diet" has you picturing a parched chicken breast with salad for dinner, think again. You can choose foods—many found in this book—with a world of healthy flavors that please your palate, satisfy your hunger, and meet your body's needs.

Back in 1951, we listed these recommendations for a healthy diet: Two fruits and three vegetables daily. Some good protein from meat, dairy products, eggs, fish, and dried peas and beans. Baked goods made with whole grains and flavored with brown sugar or molasses. Good advice, but since then, we have learned a lot more about how diet affects health. Unfortunately, notions about what constitutes a healthy diet have varied wildly, tugged this way and that by food fads, food scares, ill-advised public policy, and the billions of dollars a year the food industry spends to influence our food choices. These have largely drowned out the voice of solid nutrition science. However, the Healthy Eating Pyramid developed by Dr. Walter Willett and his colleagues at the Harvard School of Public Health (www.harvard.edu/nutritionsource/pyramids.html) is a simple guide that can help you make better choices about what to eat. It encourages you to ➤ choose most of the foods you eat from the lower sections—whole grains, healthy oils, fruits, vegetables, beans, nuts, and seeds. You don't have to weigh your food or tally up fat grams. There are no complicated food exchange tables to follow, nor do you need to eat odd combinations or religiously avoid particular foods (with the exception of those containing trans fats).

You shouldn't eat by the book, or by the pyramid or pie chart, for that matter. Slavishly following any healthy eating guide takes all the fun out of eating. What is far more important is using aids like this to develop sensible eating habits. If a bacon cheeseburger or wedge of chocolate cheesecake beckons, relish it—once in a while. ➤ The goal is using common sense guided by some simple principles: 1) Choose fresh, nutritious foods according to guidelines based on solid science; 2) Handle and cook food properly; and 3) Eat sensible amounts. Most of the portion sizes given in this book are sensible—large enough, but not excessive. See What Is a Serving?, 10.

Most of us think in terms of foods, not nutrients. Yet in order to choose healthy foods, it helps to know a little about their components, some of which are better for you than others.

Very little of what we eat is wasted. Digestive enzymes take apart the proteins, fats, and carbohydrates in food, breaking them into amino acids, sugars, and fatty acids. The body has an amazing built-in system that rivals that of any computer. It balances and allocates with infallible and almost instant decisions what we take in, sending each substance on its proper course and making the most of what we give it. Our job is to help this system along, neither overloading nor shortchanging it.

FATS

No matter what our national fat phobia suggests, the human body needs fats and cholesterol. **Fats** are a prime source of energy. Certain kinds of fats protect the heart. **Cholesterol** helps make the "skin" around cells and the bile acids needed to digest food. It also provides the raw material for making vitamin D and hormones such as estrogen and testosterone. Body fat provides an essential energy storage depot, cushions and insulates organs and tissues, and regulates body temperature.

There are four main types of fats: saturated, monounsaturated, polyunsaturated, and trans fats. Understanding good and bad fats is actually simple: ➤ Monounsaturated and polyunsaturated fats are liquid at room temperature. Saturated and trans fats are solid rather than liquid.

First we'll look at **unsaturated fats,** which are good for the heart. They improve the body's cholesterol profile, can prevent potentially deadly irregular heartbeats, and keep blood from forming clots inside arteries.

Monounsaturated fats are liquid at room temperature. They are found in olive oil, peanut oil, and canola oil. Avocados and most nuts are other good sources.

We get essential **polyunsaturated fats** from corn oil, soybean oil, seeds, nuts, whole grains, and fatty fish such as salmon and tuna. The omega-3 fats are a particularly important type of polyunsaturated fat. They help with everything from normal brain and nerve development to healthy functioning of the immune system, heart, and blood vessels. These fats are also liquid at room temperature.

Saturated and trans fats, on the other hand, should be only a limited part of your diet or avoided altogether. **Saturated fats** are abundant in red meat, dairy products, and a few vegetable oils, like palm and coconut oils. At room temperature, saturated fats, such as the drippings from bacon or hamburgers, are solid rather than liquid. The saturated fats in butter, full-fat dairy products, and meat increase levels of LDL (bad cholesterol), and the more LDL in the bloodstream, the higher the chances of having a heart attack or stroke or of dying from heart disease. Try to limit your intake of saturated fats to 8 percent of our daily calories, or about 17 grams of saturated fat per day. That is the equivalent of 7 pats of butter, 3 glasses of regular milk, a cup of premium ice cream, or an 8-ounce steak.

Trans fats are doubly bad for the heart. They are created by heating liquid polyunsaturated vegetable oil in the presence of hydrogen and finely ground particles of nickel metal, a process that turns the oil into solid fat—margarine and vegetable shortenings. These processed fats not only raise LDL, but they also lower HDL (good cholesterol) and cause other changes inside arteries that help set the stage for heart disease. Trans fats are found in hard stick margarines and almost all fast food and commercially prepared baked goods. We recommend you avoid them whenever possible.

CARBOHYDRATES

The low-carb/no-carb craze once had the country in a tizzy over carbohydrates, and it turned bread, pasta, and even some fruits and vegetables from healthy staples into dietary demons. Thank goodness the craze has passed, although it did help highlight the real problem of too much of the wrong carbohydrates in the American diet.

Sugar and starch are the main digestible carbohydrates in food. The body converts both of them into the same thing—glucose (blood sugar), which every cell in the body uses for energy. Some foods contain carbohydrates that send blood-sugar levels skyward in a flash. Foods rich in **bad carbohydrates** include white bread and other baked goods made from highly refined white flour, white rice, sugary sodas and juices, and potatoes, especially French fries. Diets heavy on foods that cause quick, strong increases in blood-sugar levels have been linked to an increased risk for diabetes, heart disease, and excess weight.

Foods containing **good carbohydrates** that yield their sugars gradually, which increases blood sugar more slowly and to a lesser extent, are fruits, vegetables, whole wheat bread, whole-grain pastas, and whole grains such as brown rice, quinoa, oats, and bulgur. These foods deliver essential vitamins and minerals, fiber, and a host of important phytonutrients, and they have only slow, steady effects on blood sugar.

Fruits, vegetables, and whole grains all contain **fiber,** plant material that the body can't digest. Some fiber traps cholesterol-rich bile acids and carries them out of the body, which helps lower cholesterol levels in the bloodstream. Other fiber delays the digestion and absorption of sugars and starch, which smooths out the rise in blood sugar and insulin that occurs after eating carbohydrates. ➤ Twenty-five grams of fiber a day is a good target. Good sources include bran and whole-grain cereals, legumes, green peas and other vegetables, and fruits.

PROTEIN

Not counting water, three-quarters of your body weight is protein. It is in your skin, muscles, red blood cells, and the thousands of enzymes that keep you alive and active. But you can't store protein or its amino acid building blocks, so you need a daily supply. The latest guidelines call for 0.8 gram of protein per kilogram of body weight. That translates to 50 grams of protein for someone who weighs 140 pounds or 70 grams for someone weighing 190 pounds. Given the abundance of protein-containing foods, most Americans easily achieve this target.

Some **dietary protein** is complete, meaning it contains all the amino acids needed to make new protein. Some is incomplete, meaning it lacks one or more amino acids the body can't make from scratch or convert from other amino acids. Meat, poultry, fish, eggs, and dairy products are sources of **complete proteins,** while vegetable sources of protein are often incomplete. That's why it is wise to eat combinations that complement each other throughout the day, such as rice and beans, peanut butter and bread, or tofu and brown rice.

The protein from a steak is much the same as protein from salmon or black beans. What is different is the **protein package.** The steak comes with a hefty wallop of saturated fat. The salmon and beans are low in saturated fat, and the salmon delivers heart-healthy omega-3 fats, while the beans give you fiber along with plenty of vitamins, minerals, and phytonutrients.

VITAMINS AND MINERALS

Your body needs a baker's dozen of vitamins and at least sixteen minerals for its day-to-day operation. The body can't make vitamins and minerals, so they must come from food and supplements. A healthy diet that includes lots of fruits, vegetables, and whole grains delivers most of the **vitamins and minerals** you need. However, food can't deliver all the vitamin D that many people need, and older people and those with digestive problems may not be able to absorb enough vitamin B_{12} from food. Women who are pregnant or who plan to become pregnant need extra folic acid. So do people who regularly drink alcohol, since alcohol blocks the absorption and effects of folic acid.

A daily multivitamin is good insurance against deficiencies that might affect even the most informed people. A standard store brand that delivers the recommended daily value (DV) of vitamins and some minerals is fine. Look for one that has been certified by the U.S. Pharmacopeia (USP), an independent organization that sets manufacturing standards for drugs, dietary supplements, and other health-care products.

Sodium, an essential mineral in our diet, is on the other side of the nutritional ledger. The average American consumes 3,500 to 4,500 milligrams a day, but only 1,000 milligrams or so are needed to keep body systems in good working order. Much of this excess salt comes from processed foods. ➤ A salt-laden diet may cause a harmful increase in blood pressure, so it is prudent to avoid unnecessary salt.

CALORIES

Calories aren't nutrients, but a measure of energy. In practical terms, a food calorie is roughly the amount of energy a 150-pound person burns each minute while sleeping. Books and articles on dieting often talk about "fat calories" or "carbohydrate calories," but there is no real dif-

ference—200 calories from red meat, from ice cream, or from pasta all have similar results in the body. ➤ In the end, consuming too many calories and burning too few is what leads to weight gain.

To find out how many calories you need each day to keep your weight steady, multiply your weight by 15. (If you weigh 160 pounds, you need 160 x 15, or 2,400, calories a day.) ➤ If you'd like to *lose* weight, you can shed 1 pound a week by cutting back by 500 calories a day. You can accomplish the same thing by eating 250 fewer calories a day and walking briskly for 30 minutes each day.

How you get these calories—the ratio of carbohydrates to fats to protein—is up to you and your tastes. See Putting It Together, 7.

FLUIDS

You need to take in as much fluid every day as you lose through breathing, sweating, and elimination. We've long been told this means drinking eight 8-ounce glasses of water a day, yet that just isn't true. Fluid needs differ from person to person. The Institute of Medicine recommends letting thirst be your guide, and it says you can get your daily fluid from a variety of sources.

When it comes to slaking thirst, water can't be beat. It has 100 percent of what you need without a single calorie, and tap water costs less than a penny a glass. But if water isn't the beverage for you, there are other ways to get as much fluid as you need. Fruits and vegetables are full of water and have loads of minerals, vitamins, and fiber, with relatively few calories. Low-calorie beverages such as coffee, unsweetened tea, and low-calorie soda are good ways to quench your thirst. Whole milk, regular soda, juice, and other sugary beverages quench thirst too, but their calories can really add up.

ALCOHOL

Alcohol is both a tonic and a toxin. The difference lies mostly in the dose. A drink before a meal can improve digestion, and the occasional drink with friends can be a social pick-me-up. Moderate drinking helps raise levels of HDL, the good form of cholesterol, and also reduces the formation of clots that block arteries in the heart, neck, and brain. There is clear evidence that moderate alcohol consumption protects against heart disease and the most common type of stroke. At the same time, heavy drinking is a major cause of preventable death in most countries, and it can lead to a variety of health, emotional, and social problems.

So, if you enjoy alcohol, keep it moderate—one or two drinks a day for men, no more than one drink a day for women. If you don't like alcohol, don't feel compelled to start: You can get the same benefits by exercising more. And don't forget that alcohol isn't calorie-free. ➤ A 12-ounce beer contains about 150 calories, and a 5-ounce glass of wine and a $1^1/_2$-ounce shot of spirits contain 100 calories each.

PUTTING IT TOGETHER

These guidelines summarize the best thinking today on what constitutes a healthy diet. The blueprint includes:

- Eating more mono- and polyunsaturated fats and less saturated fat, and avoiding trans fats;
- Eating plenty of colorful vegetables and fruits (don't count potatoes—they're really a starch);
- Eating more whole-grain carbohydrates and fewer refined-grain carbohydrates;
- Choosing healthier sources of protein by trading red meat for chicken or turkey, fish, legumes, or nuts;
- Using alcohol in moderation, or not at all;
- Taking a daily multivitamin supplement for nutritional insurance;
- Maintaining a stable, healthy weight; and
- Exercising regularly.

How you put these together depends on what you like to eat. A healthy diet can include up to 35 percent to 45 percent of calories from fat (as long as most are unsaturated fats) or as little as 10 percent. Carbohydrates can contribute between 10 percent and 65 percent, with the majority coming from fruits, vegetables, and whole grains and a minimum from refined starches and added sugars. Calories from protein can range from 10 to 35 percent—just make sure to pay attention to the protein package.

MANAGING WEIGHT

Body weight sits at the center of an intricate web of health and disease. ➤ Next to whether or not you smoke, your weight is the most important measure of your future health. Keeping your weight in the healthy range (see www.nhlbisupport.com/bmi/bmicalc.htm) is always easier said than done. In our super-size-me culture, we are constantly bombarded by ads enticing us to buy more and eat more. At the same time, opportunities for physical activity seem to shrink by the year.

Most diets, sad to say, don't really work. People can initially lose weight with almost any kind of diet, no matter how outrageous, but precious few keep it off. One reason is that restricting certain (usually tasty) foods and focusing on a limited menu is no fun, and this creates cravings that lead to diet "indiscretions." Another reason is that many dieters ignore the importance of exercise in losing weight and keeping it off. A third reason is that people respond differently to different diets. Some lose weight on diet A but not diet B, while others gain on A and lose on B.

Instead of following a diet created for someone else, build your own. It should provide plenty of choices, have relatively few restrictions, and be as good for your heart, bones, and the rest of you as it is for your waistline. The elements of healthy eating described here, using many of the recipes in this book, can give you the foundation for such a plan.

HOW TO READ FOOD LABELS

Most packaged foods carry a food label that offers a host of useful information. To get the most out of these labels, it is helpful to understand a few of their nuances.

SERVING SIZE AND SERVINGS PER CONTAINER

These give the amount of the product that people are supposed to eat—which may not be how much you normally eat—and how many servings of that size are in the package. If a package contains 2 servings and you eat the whole thing, you will, of course, need to double the calories, fat, and so forth.

CALORIES AND CALORIES FROM FAT

The number of calories per serving is important. The calories from fat is less important than the breakdown of the types of fat.

Nutrition Facts		
Serving Size 1 cup (228g)		
Servings Per Container 2		
Amount Per Serving		
Calories 260	Calories from Fat 120	
		% Daily Value*
Total Fat 13g		**20%**
Saturated Fat 5g		**25%**
Trans Fat 2g		
Cholesterol 30mg		**10%**
Sodium 660mg		**28%**
Total Carbohydrate 31g		**10%**
Dietary Fiber 0g		**0%**
Sugars 5g		
Protein 5g		
Vitamin A 4%	•	Vitamin C 2%
Calcium 15%	•	Iron 4%

* Percent Daily Values are based on a 2,000 calorie diet. Your Daily Values may be higher or lower depending on your daily needs:

	Calories:	2,000	2,500
Total Fat	Less than	65g	80g
Sat Fat	Less than	20g	25g
Cholesterol	Less than	300mg	300mg
Sodium	Less than	2,400mg	2,400mg
Total Carbohydrate		300g	375g
Dietary Fiber		25g	30g

Calories per gram:
Fat 9 • Carbohydrate 4 • Protein 4

% DAILY VALUE
This shows how much of each listed component the food provides based on a 2,000-calories-per-day diet.

TOTAL FAT
Food labels must include the amount of trans fats, no longer requiring a hunt for terms like "partially hydro-genated oil" and "vegetable shortening" to find out if a product contains trans fats. The trans fat content should be 0%; for saturated fat and cholesterol, the lower the % Daily Value, the better. You can get an idea of the amount of heart-healthy unsaturated fat in the product by adding the grams of saturated and trans fats and subtracting that number from the total fat grams.

SODIUM
In general, less sodium is better. A good daily target is 2,000 milligrams or less.

TOTAL CARBOHYDRATE
If a product contains 24 grams of carbohydrates and 22 of them are listed as sugar, the odds are it won't make many healthy-eating lists. The more dietary fiber listed under carbohydrate, the better.

PROTEIN
This number helps you track your daily protein intake.

VITAMINS AND MINERALS
Anything that provides above 20% of a vitamin or mineral is considered a good source.

INGREDIENTS
These are listed from largest to smallest amount by weight. The shorter the list the better, and look for recog-nizable ingredients.

VEGETARIAN DIETS
Millions, if not billions, of people around the globe follow a vegetarian or near-vegetarian diet, either because meat is scarce or for religious, philosophical, and/or health rea-sons. In the United States, some vegetarians happily eat chicken, fish, eggs, and dairy products, drawing the line only at red meat; others eschew all animal products. Veg-etarian diets can be quite nutritious if they include plenty of vegetables, fruits, whole grains, beans, nuts, and seeds. Such variety, with appropriate combinations, usually pro-vides all essential nutrients and ample protein. Those who follow a vegan diet (no animal products) and some other vegetarians need to find other sources of vitamin B_{12}, such as tofu, fortified soy milk, or a vitamin supplement. Vege-tarian diets are okay for children too, but they will require a bit more planning and vigilance. If a vegetarian child is gaining weight, developing normally, and has plenty of

---

HEALTHY SUBSTITUTIONS

Reinventing a diet takes practice. Here are tips for getting more of what you need and less of what you don't.

Whole Grains
- Try whole-grain breads instead of white bread.
- Choose a whole-grain cold or hot breakfast cereal.
- Substitute whole wheat flour for half the white flour in pancake, muffin, and other baked goods recipes.
- Add a half cup or more cooked wheat or rye berries, wild rice, brown rice, or barley to your favorite soup.
- Make risottos, pilafs, and other such dishes with whole grains such as barley, brown rice, bulgur, millet, or quinoa instead of white rice.
- Buy whole-grain pasta or one of the newer whole-grain blends.

Unsaturated Fats
- Switch to olive, canola, peanut, or another healthful vegetable oil, instead of sautéing with butter.
- Make cakes, cookies, and quick breads with healthful oils or trans fat–free shortening.
- Use extra-lean ground meat (or, better yet, ground chicken or turkey) in place of regular ground beef, and pork tenderloin in place of pork loin or other fatty cuts of pork.
- Try skim or 1% milk in recipes calling for whole milk, and nonfat plain yogurt in those calling for sour cream.

Salt
- Use fresh or frozen poultry, fish, and lean meat instead of canned or processed versions.
- Buy fresh, frozen, or canned vegetables with no salt added.
- Buy low-sodium, reduced-sodium, or no-salt-added versions of convenience foods, when possible.
- Choose breakfast cereals that are lower in sodium.
- Cut back on frozen dinners, pizza, packaged mixes, canned soups, and broths, which often have a lot of sodium.
- Spice up your food with herbs, spices, citrus zest, and salt-free seasoning blends rather than salt.

energy, he or she is probably getting enough calories. Like adults, children who follow a vegetarian diet need extra vitamin B$_{12}$. Children who do not consume any dairy products need extra sources of calcium, such as broccoli, sweet potatoes, certain beans, and/or calcium-fortified orange juice or soy milk.

FOOD SAFETY

We take for granted that the food we buy in grocery stores or eat in restaurants is not contaminated by microbes or hazardous substances. This involves a large measure of faith that the U.S. Department of Agriculture, the Food and Drug Administration, and various state and local agencies are doing their jobs to ensure that our food has been grown, treated, transported, processed, and packaged safely. It also requires our own vigilance and effort. Bacteria, viruses, and other microbes are found naturally in raw foods. Some are extremely helpful—yeasts are necessary for making bread and wine; bacteria turn milk into cheese. Others spoil food or make us sick. The Federal Centers for Disease Control and Prevention estimate that food-borne diseases cause approximately 76 million illnesses, 325,000 hospitalizations, and 5,000 deaths in the United States each year.

Much of the trouble stems from improper storage and handling of food. Temperature control is a big problem. Most microbes are dormant or slow-growing in the refrigerator but proliferate at room temperature. ➤ Simple safety rules can help you avoid food poisoning: Keep meat, fish, poultry, dairy products, and other items refrigerated until it is time to cook them. Wash produce well. Keep raw foods and cooked foods separate. Keep hot foods hot and cold foods cold. Wash your hands, utensils, towels, dishrags, sponges, cutting boards, and work surfaces frequently and thoroughly. And cool and refrigerate leftovers as soon as possible.

Please also read the specific sections in this book for recommendations on proper handling and storage of eggs, poultry, meat, fish, and other foods that require special safety considerations.

ADDITIVES

What do a box of cold cereal and a package of hot dogs have in common? A sometimes dizzying list of additives in the ingredients section of their food labels. Additives serve several purposes. Some, like folic acid or calcium, are there for nutritional reasons. Others, like artificial color or emulsifiers, give the food a more appealing look, taste, or texture. Preservatives such as sodium benzoate or the ubiquitous butylated hydroxyanisole (BHA) and butylated hydroxytoluene (BHT) help keep food from spoiling. Artificial sweeteners, such as sorbitol, saccharine, and aspartame, add sweetness without calories.

The Food and Drug Administration classifies these substances as generally recognized as safe. The small amounts added to foods should pose no health risk. ➤ As a general rule, though, *the more additives a product contains, the lower its nutritional value.*

NONORGANIC AND ORGANIC FOODS

Most farmers in the United States use chemicals to protect their crops from insects, worms, weeds, fungi, and other pests. Foods treated with these chemicals often retain small amounts of their residue. The National Academy of Science has concluded that there is no evidence that pesticides or other toxicants in food contribute significantly to cancer risk. This doesn't mean, however, that pesticide residues don't influence cancer or other diseases at all—only that they play a minor role.

Washing produce carefully will rid it of chemicals clinging to the surface, but it won't touch those inside. The best way to ensure pesticide-free food is to buy organic produce. By definition, organic fruits, vegetables, and other foods have been grown without the use of chemical pesticides. Whether going organic is healthier in the long run has yet to be determined, and eating a generous amount of nonorganic fruits and vegetables is certainly better than avoiding them because of worries over pesticides. Still, organic foods, especially those raised locally, are likely to be more flavorful and have a smaller impact on the environment than mass-produced fruits and vegetables grown far away.

THE FUTURE OF FOOD

When the first JOY appeared in 1931, we were just beginning to glimpse some sweeping changes in what and how Americans would eat. Rural electrification projects were making it possible for millions of farm families to have refrigerators. Early highways and improvements in transportation threw open the possibility of transporting fresh food across the country. Yet we couldn't have imagined things we take for granted today—easy year-round access to fresh fruits and vegetables from around the world, ordering groceries over the Internet, legions of fast-food restaurants serving up assembly-line food that we gobble down, microwavable foods, and the epidemic of diabetes and obesity among both children and adults.

One of the least positive changes has been an emphasis on quantity of food over quality, along with a vast increase in our consumption of refined starches, sugars, and trans fats. This has been driven in part by convenience, as our hunger for time—blessed, unscheduled time to go for a walk, play with a child, or pursue a hobby—often outweighs our hunger for good food. One encouraging trend, however, is the growing awareness that healthy food is an important key to a longer, healthier life. We hope that another will be a return to the kitchen and family meals at the table.

A top priority for the future is finding ways to grow enough food to feed the world's population (now at 6.5 billion, with another 3 to 4 billion coming over the

WHAT IS A SERVING?

The concept of "a serving" can be a bit confusing. On the surface, it is what you serve yourself or are served—a bowl of cereal, a bag of chips, a steak. But the USDA and nutrition researchers use the term much more precisely, and not knowing their definitions can cause trouble if you try to follow most guidelines for healthy eating. Here are some standard serving sizes:

Fruits: 1 medium banana, apple, or orange; $\frac{1}{2}$ cup cut-up fresh, frozen, or canned fruit or berries ($\frac{1}{2}$ cup is about half a baseball); $\frac{1}{4}$ cup dried fruit; $\frac{3}{4}$ cup fruit juice

Vegetables: $\frac{1}{2}$ cup cut-up raw or cooked vegetables; 1 cup raw leafy vegetables; $\frac{3}{4}$ cup vegetable juice

Grains (1-ounce equivalents): 1 slice bread; 1 cup dry cereal; $\frac{1}{2}$ cup cooked rice, pasta, or cereal

Meat, poultry, and fish: 3 ounces (about the size of a deck of cards or the palm of your hand)

Beans and nuts: $\frac{3}{4}$ cup cooked beans; 3 tablespoons peanut butter; $1\frac{1}{2}$ ounces nuts or seeds

Dairy products: 1 cup milk or yogurt; $1\frac{1}{2}$ ounces low-fat or fat-free natural cheese; 2 ounces low-fat or fat-free processed cheese

The size of portions in restaurants and packaged goods has crept steadily upward over the years. To see just how much, try playing Portion Distortion, a game from the National Heart, Lung, and Blood Institute, at http://nhlbihin.net/portion. It challenges you to guess the calorie counts in portions of food today compared to twenty years ago.

next 75 years, mostly in poor urban areas of developing countries) while minimizing the environmental impact of food production. This isn't a matter of "environmentalism" but of necessity—pollution, deforestation, and soil depletion all diminish the Earth's capacity to yield healthy food. We depend on birds, frogs, insects, nematodes, and nonfood plants in ways that we don't rightly understand, and crowding them out or killing them off could have serious repercussions. Changes in farming and land use will probably produce enough calories to feed everyone, but the quality of the food will be a huge issue, as will the environmental impact of food production.

A trend that hits close to home is the food industry's fascination with so-called functional foods. These are foods containing "something extra" said to improve health—more vitamin C, antioxidants, flavonols, or other hot nutrients of the month. This has more to do with marketing than health. You can get all the nutrients you need for good health by eating foods that already exist.

Decoding the human genome offers incredible poten-tial for learning about diseases and ways to fight them. In the not-too-distant future, the Human Genome Project could also make it possible for your doctor to recommend a customized nutrition plan based on your genetic profile. A tailored diet could be extremely useful for people with—or at high risk for—high blood pressure, high cholesterol, diabetes, colon cancer, and other conditions. The average person, though, hopes to prevent many different diseases, yet he or she can eat only one diet. And imagine what would happen to the family meal (not to mention the family cook) if everyone had to follow a different diet.

It may seem as though food and its future are completely out of your hands. That isn't so. You can vote with your feet, wallet, or purse at your favorite grocery store and at restaurants. Ask the manager to carry more healthy foods or those grown locally. Let your legislators know that food safety, sustainable agricultural production, and the quality of our land, air, and water are important to you. If we are what we eat, we need to do everything we can to protect our precious food resources.

ENTERTAINING

When you are entertaining, try not to feel that something unusual is expected of you as a host. It isn't. Just be yourself. Nothing is more disconcerting to guests than the impression that their presence is causing a household commotion. Confine noticeable efforts for their comfort and refreshment to the period that precedes their arrival. Satisfy yourself that you have anticipated every possible emergency, then relax and enjoy your guests.

If, at the last minute, something does happen to upset your well-laid plans, rise to the occasion. The mishap may be the making of your party. Remember that way back in Roman times, the poet Horace observed, "A host is like a general: it takes a mishap to reveal his genius."

We are frequently asked what is the perfect number for a dinner party. While there is no ideal answer to the question, there is probably a workable minimum: If guests are close friends, any number under eight will do. However, first-time acquaintances must be able to establish small centers of mutual interest, and we suggest that this can only be engineered with any degree of success in groups of at least eight. Select friends you think will genuinely enjoy each other, whether or not they've ever met. Written invitations should go out two to three weeks in advance, but a telephone call or personalized e-mail is far more common today and perfectly acceptable for casual evenings. For a party on or near a major holiday, send invitations at least a month ahead of time.

THE MENU

If you are cooking the meal yourself, remember these two important rules: Plan foods that can be prepared ahead of time, so that you can spend more time at the table than over the stove, and never, ever, make a dish for company that you haven't made before and mastered.

Beyond that, let common sense prevail: Plan enough courses to show that you've gone to some trouble, but not so many that guests will feel overwhelmed. Offer a varied but well-balanced progression of dishes, considering the colors, textures, and flavors of each one and how they will fit together. Let the menu reflect the climate, serving lighter dishes in hot weather and heartier ones when it's cold. See Menus, 19. Follow the seasons, buying what's best and freshest in the markets. Unless you know your guests' food preferences well, avoid serving exotic animal parts or overly spicy foods; inquire discreetly about food allergies or vegetarian preferences if it's appropriate.

Don't hesitate to serve guests what you like to eat yourself. Serving something you enjoy and are confident making is part of sharing yourself—even if that something is meat loaf or spaghetti and meatballs. It is also perfectly acceptable to serve at least some commercially prepared food. We often present appetizers from the local deli or market: pâté, bread, and cheeses, with an assortment of olives. And no guest has been known to turn down cake from a bakery, or store-bought ice cream and cookies. Maybe you didn't make these foods, but you certainly made them possible.

TABLE DECOR

An inviting table is as important to a successful dinner as the food you present. Here are a few simple guidelines. Table decorations can be as natural or as whimsical as you like, but make sure they won't interfere with passing the serving dishes or with the guests' views of one another.

Floral centerpieces or decorations should have no detectable scent—and neither should you: Heavy perfumes of any kind will compete with the aromas and flavors of the food. Select flowers in heights that will not obstruct conversation across the table. We often let the food be the centerpiece and place small individual vases at each place setting. If guests bring flowers, put them in a vase on the sideboard or in the living room. Candles are always a pleasing touch for any dinner table, but use only dripless unscented candles. As with your flowers, make sure the candles are below or above eye level. One of the most important things to remember is that ➤ no matter what the decoration, it should be suited in color and scale to the foods served.

Although an attractive tablecloth adds to any party, for casual dinners, cloth or rush placemats look good on a wooden table. Cotton or linen napkins are essential for a formal dinner party. Fold napkins simply, even at the most formal dinners. Napkins should be folded into quarters and then in half into rectangles. The open corners should face the bottom left, making it easy for the seated diner to pick up the napkin by one corner, let it drop and unfold completely, and place it on his or her lap. A napkin folded into quarters and then in half to form a triangle is also simple and elegant. The napkin can be placed on top of the plate, open corners facing the guest, or to the left of the plate, top of the triangle pointing outward, underneath the fork or forks or beside them. Napkin rings are fine for everyday use. Salt and pepper sets should be placed on the table—at least one set for every four to six guests, small individual sets are inexpensive and elegant. Saltcellars, tiny shallow bowls filled with salt to pinch up with fingers or scoop with tiny spoons, may also be used.

TABLE SETTING

There are certain time-honored positions for tableware and equipment that result from the way food is eaten and served. So keep in mind these basic placements: ➤ Forks to the left except the very small fish fork, which goes to the right. ➤ Spoons, including iced-tea spoons, and knives to the right, with the sharp edge of the knife toward the plate. There is, of course, a practical reason for placing the knife at the diner's right, since right-handed persons, who predominate, commonly wield the knife with their favored hand, and do so early in the meal. Generally, having cut their food, the diner lays down the knife and transfers the fork to the right hand. ➤ Place flatware that is to be used first farthest from the plate. It is also better form never to have more than three pieces of flatware at either side. Bring in any other needed table utensils on a small tray as the course is served. The server is always careful to handle tableware by the handles only, including carving and serving spoons and forks, which are placed to the right of the serving dish.

Seafood forks are placed to the right of the knife

GLASSWARE

Separate glasses for white and red wine dress up a table setting but are hardly essential. A good-sized wineglass with a capacity of 8 or 9 ounces and a tulip-shaped bowl is fine for both. Clear long-stemmed glasses, uncut or etched, are best. Stemmed water glasses are elegant and should be used for formal dining, but tumblers are entirely acceptable for more casual meals. Usually both wine and water glasses are set on the table before the diners arrive, but no more than three wineglasses per setting should be positioned at the same time, no matter how many wines are being served. The wineglass to be used during the main course should be placed about a half inch above the point of the main-course knife. All other wineglasses are then

Beverage spoons are placed to the right of all other flatware, but small coffee spoons should rest on the saucer

Wine and water glasses are placed on a diagonal, with the main-course glasses about a half inch above the point of the main-course knife

placed on a diagonal from this point, according to when they will be used, as shown above. Wine is poured from the right. The water glass goblet is placed above the wineglasses. If you are setting out a tall tumbler for iced tea, lemonade, or another beverage in place of wine, place it where the main-course wineglass would normally sit.

SEATING

Experienced hosts swear that the key to a successful dinner is seating. Think about which friends may share similar hobbies or professions. Spouses should be seated apart unless it's a family occasion. Although "boy-girl-boy-girl" is one of the first seating rules everybody learns, strict alternation of men and women is often impossible—and may be impractical if you want to match guests with similar interests. ➤ Tradition holds that the guest of honor, if female, sits to the right of the host or, if male, sits to the left of the hostess. If a dinner party is hosted by a woman with a woman guest of honor, the two women sit at opposite ends of the table; the same rule applies to two men.

Place cards are helpful at a dinner of more than eight or ten. They go directly atop the napkin if it is centered on the plate, or just above the plate and in the center of the place setting if it is not. The hosts do not have place cards. For a smaller party, simply indicate where each guest should sit. Clear place cards with the first course so guests aren't wondering what to do with them, unless you're hosting a large party with guests unknown to one another—in which case they may be left on the table to ease mutual identification.

FORMAL DINING

Most of us look with amazement if not dismay at the menus of formal dinners of the past. Just reading the endless procession of appetizers, entrées, and sweets is likely to harden contemporary arteries.

First, plan your guest list and send out the invitations. Written invitations are always preferable and should go out 1–3 weeks in advance—at least a month ahead if your dinner party is near a holiday. Then plan the menu.

In choosing your menu the traditional order of courses is meant to guide, not rule: hors d'oeuvre, soup or other first course, seafood, meat or main course, salad, cheese course before, or instead of, dessert, dessert, and coffee, which may be accompanied by chocolates, small confections, and liqueurs.

When the guests come into the dining room, the table is all in readiness. ➤ The place settings forecast the menu through the first three courses. If more silverware is required, it is brought in separately later. A charger or service plate—a decorative plate larger than the dinner plate—is at each place. ➤ In order to ensure that each guest has sufficient elbow room, there should be at least thirty inches from the center of one service plate to the center of the next. The appetizer plate and then the soup bowl are set on top of it. The butter plate and its accompanying knife are to the left. The water glasses should be about two-thirds full; the empty wineglasses stand in place, see 12. Water and wine are poured from the right. The glasses may stay in place throughout the meal, but it is preferable to remove each wineglass after use. A third wineglass may be strung out on a diagonal with the others. If more than three wines are to be served, fresh glasses replace the used glasses as the latter are removed.

When the party is less formal, the host may prefer to pour the wines himself from a decanter or from a bottle. If the wine is chilled, he will wrap it in a napkin, and hold a napkin in the left hand to catch any drip from the bottle. The hostess on such occasions may pass relishes to the guest at her right, and the guests may continue to pass them on to one another. Also, relishes may be arranged at strategic places on the table, but must be removed with the soup.

Once the guests are seated, the server's steady but un-

Table setting for a meal that includes soup and dessert, with butter knives placed on each butter plate in a position identical to the main-course knife

obtrusive labor begins. ➤ There should be a plate, filled or unfilled, before each guest throughout the meal. The server usually removes a plate from the right and replaces it immediately with another from the left, so that the courses follow one another in unbroken succession. At such a dinner, second helpings are seldom offered. The service plate or charger remains in place through the first course or two—always underneath the appetizer or soup plate, for example—and is removed before another plate, such as the seafood or main course, is put down.

As to the setting and using of flatware or silverware, the simple rule for both host and guest is to work from the outside in. As each course is finished, its accompanying utensils should be removed with the used plate or bowl. Thus, the guest may be confident in using the knife or fork now found at the outside. See Table Setting, 12.

If the entrée and side dishes are to be presented to each individual diner, the service plates or chargers are again removed before the main course, and warmed dinner plates placed either in front of the host or in front of the guests.

If the meat course is to be served in the dining room, the platter is put before the host, who carves enough meat for all the guests before any further serving takes place. The server, who has replaced the host's service plate with a warm dinner plate, stands to the left of the host, holding a second warm plate on a napkin. When the host has filled the plate before him, the server removes it and replaces it with the empty hot plate he or she has been holding. Then, after taking the service plate in front of the guest of honor from the right, the server gives him the filled warm plate from the left, then returns to the host for another hot plate and waits to serve the plate being filled by the host for another guest.

Each guest then serves him- or herself from the serving platter or bowl offered by the server, who holds it in the palm of his or her left hand and may steady it with the right. The server should always make sure that the handles of the serving tools are toward the diner.

When all the guests have been attended to, the server passes the gravy or sauce and then the vegetables. Hot breads come next. During this course, the server also replenishes water and wine. The work of the server calls for calculated timing. It is easy to see why ➤ one server should not be called on to take care of more than six or eight guests—at most—if smooth going is expected.

A handsomely arranged fruit compote, passed during the meal course, can be used as an alternative to a salad. If a compote is substituted for a salad, a spoon is put on the right of the setting, instead of a salad fork on the left. A separate salad can be served after the meat course is removed. After the salad course is removed, any unused flatware, the butter plates, and salt and pepper are taken away. The server uses a folded napkin and brushes the crumbs lightly onto a plate or a crumb tray.

For courses requiring guests to use their fingers, such as lobster in the shell, fowl, or small cuts of meat, finger bowls are much appreciated. The finger bowl, partially filled with water, may have a scented geranium leaf, a fragrant herb or flower, or a thin slice of lemon floating in it. Finger bowls are often brought to the table on top of the dessert plates, with the dessert fork and spoon resting on the plate on either side of the bowl; the guest places the fork and spoon to either side of the plate and puts the finger bowl opposite the water glass, to the upper left. Finger bowls may be set, on a saucer or not, to the left of each diner's plate for fruit, a cheese course, or dessert, whichever ends the meal.

If coffee is served at the table, a demitasse (espresso cup) or small coffee cups and saucers are placed at this time to the right of each diner. The demitasse spoons are on the saucers, parallel to the handle, see 12. Coffee is poured from the right and cream and sugar passed on a small tray from the left. Liqueurs may be served with the coffee at the table or passed on a tray should the host and guests choose to move to the living room for conversation and coffee.

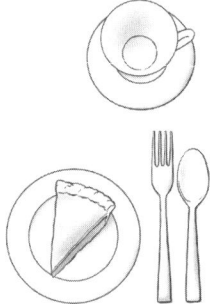

When no knife is set, as for pie and coffee,
the fork is placed on the right with the spoon.

INFORMAL DINING

The most traditional form of informal dining, and to our mind the most satisfying, is the sit-down **dinner party.** At good dinner parties, conversation flourishes, friendships

Table setting for an informal meal

are forged or reinforced, and good food and drink appreciated and discussed. In no other form of entertaining does the host so unequivocally display respect for the guests and convivial concern for their welfare.

Plan a menu that will favor advance preparation and require little last-minute fussing. ➤ Consider serving just three courses: a hearty stew or casserole, for instance, salad, and a simple dessert. Many dishes that can be prepared in advance will be found throughout this book. Five minutes before your guests are expected, everything should be organized and in readiness: appetizers, wine, and cocktails—which may be simple—on a convenient side table; plates warming in the oven, a warming drawer, or the dry cycle of the dishwasher; and the dining table completely set, needing only that last-minute ceremonial touch, the lighting of the candles.

Styles of serving food have evolved over the centuries, but in the dining rooms of the Western world today, they fall into two main categories: (1) platters or dishes of all the food are put in the middle of the table, and then passed; (2) the food is arranged on individual plates in the kitchen, with everyone given the same amount of the same food.

For most modern informal dinner parties, a combination of formal and informal styles of serving may be appropriate. Appetizers might be plated in the kitchen, for instance, and platters of the roasted meat or other main course passed around the table by servers or the guests themselves. In addition, certain courses might be arranged on a sideboard for buffet service. This is particularly appropriate when serving a mixed appetizer course or assorted desserts. If you are an accomplished carver, consider practicing your art at the table, impressing your guests with your deftness and offering each one the cut he or she prefers. If, on the other hand, you don't want your guests to see you wrestle with a turkey or a leg of lamb, carve it safely out of sight and quickly bring the prewarmed platter to the table. Unless the food was first plated in the kitchen, seconds are always offered. With any method of service, guests should ask for the salt, pepper, or any sauce or condiment they require, all of which will be left on the table; the person closest to the desired object passes it, choosing its route so it will pass through the fewest hands possible.

When dinner is finished, clear no more than two plates at a time, scraping and stacking them out of view of the guests. Resist the urge to do any extensive cleaning up while your guests are still present; your job and your pleasure as host is to spend as much time with them as possible. Resist, as well, the kind of good-intentioned rush to help that often turns a dinner's aftermath into a volunteer free-for-all. On the other hand, two hosts can share preliminary cleanup duties, and there's nothing wrong with accepting an unobtrusive dependable assist from one good friend who knows his or her way around your kitchen. In general, though, the more people who remain at the table at meal's end the better—and that includes you.

Before serving dessert, clear all plates, serving dishes, and condiments, including salt and pepper, from the table. Brush off crumbs with a tightly folded clean napkin, if needed. Set the dessert plates if you are using them. It is the American custom to take coffee or tea with dessert, while the European practice is to offer them afterward, accompanied perhaps by chocolate truffles, small cookies, or petits fours. Coffee and tea, like all drinks, are poured from the right, and cream and sugar are offered from the left; if the creamer and sugar bowl have been placed on the table, they are passed counterclockwise. Invite guests to have after-dinner beverages in the living room, if you wish; often, though, the conversation is at its best and most expansive during and after dessert, and guests would rather stay at the table. At this point in the evening, hostly duties taper off, limited to refilling guests' cups or liqueur glasses. For the host, these final moments are some of the best of the evening.

BRUNCH

The meal we call brunch is an easy one to prepare and a good way for beginners to practice their entertaining skills. Scones, muffins, bagels, and quick breads are all perfectly acceptable. Brunch may be served buffet-style or may more closely resemble a casual light lunch. Choose your menu carefully, keeping things simple and avoiding complicated egg dishes that might be difficult to prepare for a crowd, such as individual omelets or eggs Benedict. ➤ The popularity at brunch time of quiche lorraine and other make-ahead egg-based specialties such as frittatas and stratas (breakfast casseroles) is understandable. It is customary to serve something alcoholic with brunch, but keep this simple too: Champagne or white wine, mimosas, or a pitcher of bloody Marys or screwdrivers will usually suffice.

BUFFETS

Buffets are a good choice for large, casual get-togethers when dining table space is limited. Choose a colorful, varied array of foods and display them on a handsomely appointed table. Make sure you have ample backup portions of everything served so you can replenish dishes often. Plan generously, for guests are apt to take larger portions at buffets. ➤ Everything offered on a buffet should be easy to eat with a fork or with fingers—only minimal knife cutting, if any, should be required. Label any food that isn't easily identifiable with a small card placed beside the dish. Drinks should be set up away from the buffet table so as not to disrupt traffic. If you're having more than a dozen guests, set up a two-sided buffet line if space allows so that guests can serve themselves quickly and still have the chance to sample everything—and make sure that there are cutlery and plates for both lines.

If you do not have many casseroles or hot plates, restrict the number of hot foods to those you can serve quickly straight from the pot or a hot serving dish, or get more serving vessels from a party rental company. For dishes that must be kept cold, use ice packs instead of ice, which makes a mess as it melts, or pans specifically manufactured for freezing. Put the frozen packs on a rimmed tray or pan and arrange your platters on top.

Whether you are planning a picnic, holiday feast, or casual get-together, a **potluck,** where each guest brings a dish and all are presented buffet-style, is a resourceful way of creating a meal. Distribute assignments for prepared dishes evenly, depending on the occasion. We suggest category assignments, such as salads, hot side dishes (you may want to specify a vegetable or starchy side dish), main dishes, and desserts. If you know one guest makes a breathtaking coconut layer cake, request it. And don't forget to assign ice, beverages, and bread. Some hosts and hostesses prefer to provide the main dish and ask guests to bring accompaniments only. For a more casual gathering, it is fine for guests to bring and serve their dishes in disposable containers. If the party is a little fancier, warranting serving platters, remind guests to put their names on the bottom of the serving dishes for easy cleanup and return. Preheat the oven for guests who need to reheat their contributions before serving. A potluck is also a great place for a recipe exchange: Have guests bring enough copies of their recipes to distribute to all.

CHILDREN'S PARTIES

Entertaining is not just for adults. Children's parties are popular for toddlers to twelve-year-olds. The best children's parties bring together a manageable number of children for food and games. For very young children, it is best to invite a parent of each as well. For older children, estimate that one adult will be needed for every six to seven children. An afternoon event of approximately two to three hours allows time for games, playtime, and food. See 23 for menu ideas. Keep children's parties simple, and perhaps let the guests help with food preparation, making the kitchen the focus of the party. Decorating cupcakes with frosting, sprinkles, cinnamon hearts, and colored sugar or putting toppings on homemade pizzas provides food and fun in the same room. If children are to work in the kitchen, be sure to mention this in the invitation so they are dressed appropriately. Velvet dresses covered with flour are never a welcome surprise.

COCKTAIL PARTIES AND OPEN HOUSES

The cocktail party is an estimable but endangered social institution. Its demise may be blamed on factors as various as the regrettable decline of the art of conversation and flirtation and the growing acceptance that dinner by itself is sufficient diversion for an evening. We steadfastly defend the cocktail party, however, as an American invention and an uncomplicated and extremely pleasant means of entertaining. And we can't help pointing out that it is also a relatively easy way of entertaining business contacts and of discharging social obligations to those to whom you owe hospitality.

A good cocktail party begins with good liquor, wine, and beer (see Wine and Beer, 44, and Cocktails and Party Drinks, 54). Unless you plan to hire a professional bartender or the number of guests is so small that you or a guest volunteer can handle mixology duties without missing the fun, it's best to serve just one type of cocktail, made up in batches—pitchers of martinis or margaritas, for example. Or simply display exemplars of the four "basic" liquors—Scotch, bourbon, gin, and vodka—with an assortment of appropriate mixes and flavored syrups, a bucket of ice, glasses in several sizes, and an assortment of bar tools, and let guests serve themselves highballs and drinks on the rocks. Wine, both red and white, and beer should also be part of the bar, and there should always be something nonalcoholic available (see Beverages); sparkling mineral water and freshly squeezed orange juice are never out of place.

There must always be food at a cocktail party, of course, or the cocktails will quickly overwhelm the party. As a general rule, before dinner, two or three kinds of lighter party foods with cocktails will usually suffice. For a cocktail party without dinner, prepare five to seven more substantial hors d'oeuvres and finger foods. The food need not be complicated, nor even homemade. Store-bought pâtés and terrines or an assortment of well-chosen cheeses, 69–70, in either case served with crackers or sliced breads of good quality, will be sufficient for an informal gathering. More sophisticated cocktail parties call for elegant hors d'oeuvres or, perhaps, an attractive service of smoked salmon. In general, cocktail parties shouldn't last more than two hours, and those two hours should be found somewhere between 5 and 8 P.M.—never later, unless enough food is served to constitute a light dinner. A shorter cocktail period is appropriate if it is a prelude to another event—a dinner out with the same guests, for instance, or a concert or the theater. In that case, keep both drinks and food as simple as possible. Champagne and smoked salmon would be perfect.

A variation on the cocktail party, usually specific to the year-end holidays, is the **open house.** The same basic rules apply, but the event may run for three to four hours or even more, with the expectation that guests will drop by at their convenience during a prescribed period of time and rarely stay more than an hour or so. This means of entertaining is particularly appropriate for busy holiday weekends for which guests may be expected to have several invitations; it also permits the host to invite a larger number of people than might fit comfortably in the available space at one time. Because of the inevitable ebb and flow of guests, passed finger foods are inappropriate for an open house of any size and duration, and the food tends to be rather more substantial than at a simple cocktail party. A modified buffet table, 15, is more appropriate, preferably involving nothing that needs to be kept warm or cold. Baked ham, turkey, or a whole poached salmon make attractive and satisfying centerpieces for such occasions.

FAMILY MEALS

Never forget that your family is really the most important assembly you ever entertain. It is a fact that families who sit down to eat together are healthier and happier than those who don't. The success of family meals lies first in sharing the fun and responsibilities in planning the menu and shopping for ingredients. A well-stocked pantry, 884, is the foundation for cooking, making grocery store and market trips necessary only for perishable items such as meat, poultry, seafood, produce, and dairy products.

Planning a week of family dinners is a simple task. We cook one or two dishes that take time—say a roast turkey or large cut of beef—on the weekend and then, after its first appearance as a meal, convert the leftover meat into soups, sandwiches, casseroles, and pasta sauces throughout the week. We intersperse it with recipes that take under thirty minutes from start to finish, see Menus, 25, as well as with meals from the slow cooker, 99, and outdoor or indoor grill. Keep recipes simple when building a repertoire of family favorites, but ➤ do try out a new dish every few weeks. Invite children into the kitchen to help with age-appropriate tasks so they can share in the joy of cooking—such as tearing lettuce, cutting soft fruit, or peeling hard-cooked eggs.

LUNCH

Today, lunch is another endangered practice in the United States. Business people boast about "brown bagging" as an indication of professional dedication, or they spend lunchtime at the gym or doing errands; stay-at-home moms and dads are busy telecommuting and caring for children. Students and young professionals, alas, seem to prefer fast food to a more leisurely meal. This is a pity, because the **sit-down lunch,** even when it's simple and light, is an immensely civilized respite from the rigors of the day. The basic rules governing table settings, seating, and serving for a sit-down dinner party apply, 14, but ➤ a modern lunch should rarely have more than two or three courses—a modest appetizer, a simply prepared main course, and perhaps a light dessert—and two will frequently suffice. Multi-ingredient salads, medium-bodied soups (hot or cold), and fish or poultry dishes are suitable for lunch—and elegant sandwiches should not be forgotten. Alcoholic beverages are usually less appropriate at lunch than at dinner for a variety of reasons, but a token quantity of white or light red wine, depending on the food served, should be offered in most cases. On occasion, particularly over holidays when no one has work to do in the afternoon, a more elaborate lunch might be enjoyed, one with more courses and an array of wines. Or consider a **formal luncheon** with the help of servers or a caterer: it is a rare enough event that your guests won't soon forget it. See Formal Dining, 13.

OUTDOOR ENTERTAINING

The **backyard barbecue** offers perhaps the easiest and most comfortable way of cooking for friends and family during warm weather. As with any form of entertaining, however, the host should consider the guests' comfort and anticipate potential problems. What's the weather likely to be? If rain is possible, is there an indoor alternative? If it will be very hot, is there plenty of shade and plenty of drinking water? If swimming is a possibility, does everybody know, so that they can come equipped? What protection can you offer against insects if they're likely to be a problem (screened porches, citronella candles, insect repellent)? If the affair will go on after dark, are there outdoor lights, hurricane candles, or other adequate light sources? While the menu at a cookout should be simple, will there be something for the kids to eat (if there are kids) and something for those who might not favor meat? Plastic glasses and utensils and paper plates and napkins are perfectly acceptable, but if you'll be serving grownups on a terrace or on a porch, real glassware, silver, china, and a cloth tablecloth and napkins add undeniable flair to the proceedings—even if the food is corn on the cob, hot dogs, and spareribs.

For small groups of people, an excursion to the park, beach, or mountains with coolers, bags, and baskets of food and drink in hand for a **picnic** is casual entertaining at its best. Leave highly perishable foods at home or carry them in well-chilled coolers (deviled eggs and other dishes with mayonnaise—potato salad included—must be kept cool). Again, if appropriate, real wineglasses, silverware, and cloth napkins can add elegance to a picnic. Because you're not at home, it's a good idea to bring along a strictly practical ➤ "picnic kit" containing a corkscrew, a small sharp knife, a serving spoon, a can opener, a bottle opener, matches, a small salt-and-pepper set and other dried seasonings, a package of small napkins, a roll of paper towels, tablecloth clips, a screwdriver, plastic bandages, insect repellent, sun block, and safety pins.

For **tailgating** as well as backyard barbecues, you will want to prepare a portable grill, either charcoal or gas, as well as a few key grilling accessories: long-handled tongs for turning the meat, clean brushes to apply sauces, and heavy-duty oven mitts. Since you will probably tailgate in a parking lot or a field before a sporting event, this is not the time or place for dainty foods. Grilled beef, chicken, and sausages are favorites, served with beer and wine.

SUPPER AND COOKING CLUBS

A popular practice that has sprung from the dinner party is the supper or cooking club. Members are usually friends who share a love of creating menus, cooking, and eating and gather for regularly scheduled dinner parties.

There are two ways to organize a successful supper or cooking club event. The more common is to establish a theme—regional cooking, recipes from the same cookbook, or a season's best ingredients—and assign each member a dish. Club members rotate serving as host or hostess for each dinner. Occasionally such clubs may hold a progressive dinner, where each course is served at a different location, usually the various members' homes. As with any dinner party, a good number of guests is approximately eight.

AFTERNOON TEA

Like the sit-down luncheon, the tea party might seem to some unsuited to the modern world—too time-consuming, too much of an air of the raised pinkie about it. The truth is, though, that offering guests a well-brewed pot of tea is almost as easy as pouring them mugs of coffee. A proper afternoon tea is served between 4 and 6 P.M. Set a tea table as you would a buffet table, 15, putting out cups on their saucers and teaspoons to one side, along with small cloth napkins. No other silverware should be necessary unless you are serving jam, butter, or clotted cream to accompany scones or other baked goods. This may be the time to present butter molded into attractive designs. If you are offering a wide variety of sweet and savory foods, also set butter plates. You'll want to provide an array of foods, such as small tea cakes, pastries, muffins, and the traditional scones, 640, as well as tea sandwiches, 185, rolled and cut into a variety of shapes. It is elegant to arrange tea cakes and sandwiches on small plates or tiered stands, if you have them. At an informal tea party, the host pours the tea. For a more formal tea, the guest of honor "does the honors" and pours tea.

COOKING FOR LARGE PARTIES

At times we are called on to produce meals for larger groups, and it is then that we must be on our guard, for surprises are apt to pop up just when we want everything to go particularly well. To begin, ➤ cook dishes in several moderate-sized batches, rather than in one chunk, because, mysterious as it sounds, but true even for the experts, quantity cooking is not always a matter of indefinite multiplication. (Most of the recipes in this book make 4 to

6 servings and can be doubled for 8 to 12.) Please read comments on enlarging recipes, 1032.

Take into account the longer time needed in preparation—not only for peeling and washing of vegetables or drying salad greens, but for heating up large quantities. Even more important, you may be confronted with a sudden dearth of refrigerator space—discovering that the shelves are needed for properly chilling cold soups or cream pies just when they are also needed for keeping other sizable quantities of food at safe temperatures. ➤ Have coolers and ice at the ready. This warning is of special importance if you are serving stuffed poultry, creamed foods, ground meat, mayonnaise-based dishes, cream puffs, custards, or custard pies: these foods spoil readily, without showing any evidence of hazard.

If the meal is a hot one, plan to use recipes that will involve both the oven and top burners. Increase limited heating surfaces by supplementing them with electric skillets and woks, indoor grills or slow cookers, hot plates, and the age-old chafing dish, to hold food in good serving condition—above 140°F.

Stage a dress rehearsal—from the cooking equipment requirements right through to the way the serving dishes will be placed. Then, satisfied that the mechanical requirements are met, schedule the actual cooking of food so that enough can be done in advance to relieve the sink and the work surfaces of last-minute crowding and mess.

If a host is faced with a significant event where only a formal meal is appropriate, do not undertake this alone. Service help is a must. By service help we mean trained, experienced service and kitchen staff, paid or unpaid. Some turn to professional caterers at such a moment.

WORKING WITH A CATERER

Caterers, as well as service staff, are available when you are called upon to entertain a wedding party or other large group that requires extra help. Knowing how to work with a caterer to make the event a great success requires understanding your needs and the caterer's capabilities. Keep the kind of event and number of guests in mind. Do you need a bartender? Will you need to rent chairs, tables, glassware, silverware, and/or dishes? Do you need just food for a small group, or do you need servers as well to handle a crowd? Schedule a tasting of the proposed menu and make adjustments. Sometimes there is an additional fee for a tasting, but it is well worth the price. If you are hiring a caterer for formal dining, make sure he or she is skilled in the special service required for that type of entertaining. Have the caterer do a walk-through of the party area and especially the kitchen to make sure there is ample work space. Get a written agreement that details all costs, including food, service, and rentals. Agree upon a date for when you will confirm the guest count. The caterer will usually assign a "captain"—someone in charge of the event—and this is the person to whom you give a tip (usually 20 percent) at evening's end for the entire staff, from bartenders and servers to kitchen help.

A FINAL NOTE

Remember, even after all this instruction, never let the rules get between you, your guests, and the food. Long after the meal passes, your guests will remember only a wonderful day or evening spent in the pleasure of your company rather than a misplaced saucer, missing salad fork, or an empty water glass.

MENUS

When to eat is a matter of ever-changing habit and custom. What to eat varies from day to day, and differs with special occasions and holidays. Combining foods into a meal is planning a menu. In doing so recall the words of the French gastronome Brillat-Savarin: *Menu malfait, dîner perdu*—"A badly made menu means a lost dinner."

Good meals, whether simple or elaborate, or for family or friends, are built on balance and harmony of the food. When planning a meal, consider the season, climate, time of day, and of course any food preferences of those you are serving. When entertaining a group of people whose preferences you do not know, consider serving familiar foods that everyone loves.

Remember that our families can be our best company, and that almost any menu can be served to guests, depending on who's coming to dinner and what you can cook particularly well. The most important quality of a "company" meal should be the excitement of the unusual—for them.

Below are meal suggestions and lists of recipe ideas for holidays, special occasions, brunch, lunch, afternoon teas, and dinner. They are suggestions only. Your taste, girth, circumstances, market, mood—and we hope, your imagination—can change the menus. ➤ For further service suggestions, please read the chapter on Entertaining, 11, and ➤ if the meal or party includes more people than you usually cook for, see 17 for suggestions for the safe handling of food, and check the availability of cooking and serving equipment.

HOLIDAY DINNERS

THANKSGIVING

Stuffed Raw Vegetables, 79
Oyster Bisque, 141, or Pumpkin Soup, 129
Roast Turkey, 442, with Bread Stuffing with Giblets, 534, and Poultry Pan Sauce or Gravy, 546, or Crown Roast of Pork, 498
Mashed Cauliflower, 267, Root Vegetable Puree, 245, or Candied Sweet Potatoes, 302
Creamed Pearl Onions, 287
Green Beans with Slivered Almonds, 250
Baked Winter Squash II, 308, or Succotash, 272
Riced Potatoes or Potato Snow, 295, or Au Gratin Potatoes, 297
Molded Cranberry Salad, 175, or Whole Berry Cranberry Sauce, 221
Tart Greens with Apples, Pecans, and Buttermilk-Honey Dressing, 158, or Carrot, Apple, and Horseradish Salad, 167
Parker House Rolls, 610
Pumpkin Chiffon Cake, 710, Sweet Potato Pie, 686, Pumpkin Buttermilk Pudding, 823, or Mock Mincemeat Pie, 680
Mulled Wine, 67, or Mulled Cider, 68

CHRISTMAS

Stollen, 622, or Apple Strudel, 673
Oyster Stew, 140, Lobster Bisque, 140, or Oxtail Soup, 137
Herring Salad, 165, or Mixed Greens with Cheese Crisp, 158
Roast Stuffed Goose, 450, with Chestnut Dressing, 537, and Pan Sauce for Wildfowl, 547, Standing Beef Rib Roast, 471, with Yorkshire Pudding, 637, or Roast Fresh Ham or Leg of Pork, 499, or Lobster Americaine, 384
Brussels Sprouts with Chestnuts, 261
Roasted Shallots, 304
Roasted Carrots, 267
Kale and Potato Gratin, 278, or Chantilly Potatoes, 296
Roasted Garlic Flan, 207
Cloverleaf Rolls, 610
Bûche de Noël (Yule Log Cake), 737, Plum Pudding, 825, with Hard Sauce, 851, Warm Gingerbread, 724, with Buttered Cider Sauce, 845, Caramel Ice Cream, 832, or Ice Cream Sandwiches, 830, with Chocolate Cookies, 776, and Peppermint Stick Ice Cream, 832
Bourbon Balls, 879, or Cinnamon Stars, 774
Eggnog, 66, Syllabub, 67, or Glögg, 67

NEW YEAR'S EVE

Caviar, 86, or Salmon Pâté, 85
Fettuccine Alfredo, 327
Pan-Seared Duck Breasts with Fig and Red Wine Sauce, 449
Baked or Roasted Beets, 259

Creamy Leeks, 280
Broiled Stuffed Mushroom Caps, 284
Endive and Walnut Salad, 160
Baked Alaska, 843
Individual Molten Chocolate Cakes, 729, with Hazelnut
    Gelato, 834
Angel Cake, 705, with Mango Coulis, 853

NEW YEAR'S DAY
New Year's Soup, 146, Roasted Red Pepper Soup, 132, or
    Portuguese Greens Soup (Caldo Verde), 139
Wilted Greens, 160, or Bistro Salad, 160
New Potatoes Stuffed with Sour Cream and Caviar, 79
Chicken Liver Mousse, 81, or Salmon Mousse, 85
Braised Lentils with Sausage, 258
Hoppin' John, 356, or Red Beans and Rice, 256
Pan-Roasted Pork Tenderloin, 503, with Sauerkraut, 265
Louisiana-style Chayote, 269
Sautéed Greens with Garlic, 278
Pretzels, 619
Creamy Water-Bath Cheesecake, 744, Cream Roll, 736,
    or Baked Alaska, 843

VALENTINE'S DAY
Oysters on the Half-Shell, 372, with Mignonette, 568
Grilled or Broiled Figs with Prosciutto, 227
Asparagus with Orange and Hazelnuts, 250
Avocado Cups, 172, with Lobster Salad, 165
Spicy Walnut Vinaigrette, 574, or Spinach Salad with
    Grapefruit, Orange and Avocados, 159
Duxelles, 284
Roasted Fillet or Tenderloin of Beef, 472, with
    Mushroom-Wine Sauce (Marchand de Vin), 555
Roasted Chicken with 40 Cloves of Garlic, 425, or Spicy
    Maple-Roasted Quail, 460
Coeur à la Crème, 826, Frozen Grand Marnier Soufflé,
    809, Chocolate Terrine, 817, or White Chocolate
    Mousse with Toasted Almonds, 816, with Raspberry
    Sauce, 853, in a chocolate cup, 830

ST. PATRICK'S DAY
Potato Leek Soup, 130, or Salmon Chowder, 143
Colcannon, 296, or Boiled New Potatoes, 295
Corned Beef with Cabbage, 484, Shepherd's Pie, 102,
    Fish and Chips, 410, Irish Stew, 496, or Roasted
    Whole Salmon, 397
Irish Soda Bread, 629
Irish Coffee, 32
Pistachio Ice Cream, 832, with Hot Fudge Sauce, 847,
    or Chocolate Bread Pudding, 822, with Southern
    Whiskey Sauce, 852

PASSOVER
Hard-Boiled Eggs, 194
Matzo Ball Soup, 126
Gefilte Fish, 401

Glazed Parsnips, 289, or Parslied Carrots, 266
Chicken Tagine with Chickpeas, 435, Sweet-and-Sour
    Brisket, 481, or Herb-Roasted Whole Fish, 397
Spinach Salad with Grapefruit, Orange, and Avocado,
    159, or Endive and Walnut Salad, 160
Meringue Kisses, 771, or Strawberries Romanoff, 220

EASTER
Stuffed Raw Vegetables using Snow Peas, 79
Cream of Watercress or Purslane Soup, 145
Baked Goat Cheese and Mesclun Salad, 160
Boiled New Potatoes, 295
Cooked Cucumbers, 273
Natural–Dyed Easter Eggs, 207
Roasted Asparagus, 250
Baked Ham, 507, or Stuffed Butterflied Leg of Lamb, 491
Easter Bunny Biscuits, 639
Coconut Cake, 715

CINCO DE MAYO
Guacamole, 72
Jicama Salad, 167
Roasted Cactus Pad Salad, 265
Green Posole, 351
Refried Beans, 254
Baked Chiles Rellenos with Cheese, 293
Enchiladas Verdes, 104, Chicken and Cheese
    Tamales, 351, Chicken Chili Verde, 435, or
    Turkey in Red Mole, 444
Shrimp and Avocado Tostadas, 189
Sopapillas, 608, or Flan with Condensed Milk, 803
Sangria, 65, Margarita, 62, or Papaya-Mango
    Batidos, 40

MOTHER'S DAY
Mediterranean White Bean Soup, 133
Field Salad with Fresh Herbs, 158
Panfried Potatoes, 297
Braised Baby Artichokes and Peas, 248
Goat Cheese and Walnut Soufflés, 205
Wild Rice Pilaf with Sautéed Mushrooms, 363
Stuffed Boned Chicken, 446, or Fish en Papillote, 398
Lemon Sponge Custard, 805, or Strawberry Icebox
    Cake, 731

FATHER'S DAY
Caesar Salad, 159
Seared Pepper-Crusted Fish Steaks, 409, Broiled or
    Grilled Lamb Chops, 493, or Grill-Roasted Whole
    Chicken, 427
Twice-Baked Potatoes, 297, or Baked Polenta, 349
Grilled Mushrooms, 283, or Broiled Tomatoes, 312
Sticky Toffee Pudding, 823, New Orleans Bread
    Pudding, 822, or Bananas Foster, 826

SPECIAL OCCASION MENUS

SUPER BOWL PARTY
Seven-Layer Dip, 74
Scotch Eggs, 195, Fried Mozzarella Sticks, 77,
    or Fried Okra, 285
Buffalo Chicken Wings, 80
Crispy Potato Skins, 79
Nachos, 77
Beer Cheese Dip in a Bread Bowl, 73
Beer, Cheese, and Scallion Bread, 629
Chicken Tamale Pie, 102
Steak Wraps, 187, or Submarine or Hero Sandwich, 184
Stuffed Cabbage Rolls, 263
Chili Con Carne, 513
Chicken Jambalaya, 356
Black Bottom Cupcakes, 738, or Chocolate
    Sheet Cake, 722

WEDDING BUFFET
Champagne Punch, 65
Cold Vichyssoise, 130, Jellied Beet Soup, 127,
    or Cold Cucumber Soup, 147
Crudités, 78
Coconut Lime Salad, 226, or Asparagus Sesame
    Salad, 165
Pesto Cheesecake, 76, or Marinated Goat Cheese with
    Fresh Thyme, 77
Smoked Trout on Cucumber Rounds, 86, or Smoked
    Salmon Canapés, 87
Mushroom Triangles, 88
Miniature Turnovers with Caramelized Onions and Blue
    Cheese, 91
Cheese Puffs, 91
Brie Baked in Pastry, 92
No-Fail Boiled Shrimp, 385, with Cocktail Sauce, 568,
    or Tomatillo-Horseradish Sauce, 568
Beef Wellington, 468
Celery Root Rémoulade, 167
Florentines Cockaigne, 770
Chocolate Cream Caramels, 865, truffles, 858–859
Lemon Tarts, 688
Large or Wedding Cake, 703
Petits Fours, 738
Peppermint Wafers, 867

OUTDOOR ENTERTAINING IDEAS
Deep-Fried Plantains (Tostones), 294
Jamaican Jerk Chicken, 428
Baby Back Ribs, 505
Becker Buffalo Burgers, 531
Barbecue-Rubbed Grilled Bluefish, 404, with Spicy
    Tartar Sauce, 581
Grilled Shrimp or Fish Tacos, 189
Grilled or Roasted Corn, 271
Grilled Mushrooms, 283

Grilled or Broiled Fruit Kebabs, 214
Coconut Lime Salad, 226
Creamy Coleslaw, 161
Creamy Macaroni Salad for a Crowd, 172
Southern Corn Bread, 632
Banana Pudding, 807, Ice Cream Float, 39, Chocolate
    Sheet Cake, 722, or Mississippi Mud Cake, 723
Planter's Punch in Quantity, 66, Plugged Watermelon, 64,
    Old-Fashioned Lemonade or Limeade, 40,
    or Sweet Southern Iced Tea, 34

PICNIC
Pop's Deviled Eggs, 195
Fried Chicken, 429
Baked Beans, 255
American Potato Salad, 168
Spicy Watermelon Salad, 170
Dee's Corn and Tomato Salad, 272
Brownies Cockaigne, 762, Chocolate Chip Cookies, 766,
    or Butterscotch Icebox Cookies, 776

AFTERNOON TEA
Tea Sandwiches, 185, with Egg Salad, 164, Chicken
    Salad, 163, or spreads, 178–180, or Rolled
    Sandwiches, 187
Sweet Zucchini Bread, 628, or Banana Bread Cockaigne,
    628, with Nut Butter, 178
Classic Scones, 640, or Cream Scones, 640, with Lemon
    Curd, 756, or Crème Fraîche, 1014
Lemon Curd Bars, 765, Pecan or Angel Slices, 764,
    or Madeleines, 739
Petits Fours, 738
Sachertorte, 728
Chocolate Shortbread, 775, or Jelly Tots, 778
Tea, 33, or Herbal Tea, 35

VEGETARIAN
White Bean Dip with Rosemary and Garlic, 73
Tuscan Bread and Tomato Soup, 132
Gazpacho, 146
Mushroom Barley Soup, 131
Wonton Soup, 126

Baked Cheese Grits, 350
Millet Cakes with Parmesan and Dried Tomatoes, 352
Rye Berry Salad with Roasted Red Pepper Dressing, 361
Israeli Couscous Pilaf, 363

Vegetarian Chili, 254
Lentil and Rice Pilaf with Toasted Cumin Seeds, 355
Moroccan-Style Vegetable Stew, 246
Tomato Goat Cheese Quiche, 109
Curried Chickpeas with Vegetables, 257
Becker Portobello Pizzas, 282
Risotto with Mushrooms, 361
Tagliatelle with Wilted Greens, 328
Roasted Vegetable Lasagne, 340

Creamy Pasta with Chard and Tomatoes, 328
Szechuan-Style Hacked Tempeh, 318
Moo Shu Tempeh, 317

COOKING AND SUPPER CLUB MENUS

ITALIAN
Bagna Cauda, 78
Squash Blossoms Stuffed with Cheese and
      Herbs, 309
Fava Beans Roman-Style, 253
Fried Artichokes, 248
Tuscan Beans, 255
Risotto Milanese, 360
Pork Braised in Milk, 501
Pizza, 190–192
Tiramisu, 819, Espresso Granita, 839, Lemon Granita,
      839, with Biscotti, 774, or Almond Macaroons, 771

ASIAN
Summer Rolls, 92, with Thai Chile-Lime Dipping
      Sauce, 570, or Peanut Dipping Sauce, 570
Green Papaya Salad, 231
Vietnamese Beef Noodle Soup (Pho Bo), 137
Thai Fish Cakes, 410, with Nam Prik, 570
Spicy Peanut Sesame Noodles, 332
Indonesian Rice Table, 358
Grilled Duck Breast with Hoisin Ginger Sauce, 449
Ginger Melon Soup, 148
Green Tea Ice Cream, 832

INDIAN
Samosas with Potatoes and Peas, 89, with
      Tamarind Dipping Sauce, 237, or Apple or
      Green Tomato Chutney, 951
Raita, 567
Saag Paneer, 306
Coconut Chicken Curry, 431
Tandoori Chicken, 428
Dal, 258
Coconut Rice, 357
Naan, 608
Coconut Ice Cream, 833, with Fresh Mango
      Sauce, 853

EASTERN EUROPEAN
Beets in Sour Cream, 259
Cherry Soup, 148
Borscht, 129
Chicken Paprika, 431
Chicken Kiev, 438
Hungarian Goulash, 480
Pierogi, 341
Vareniki, 341
Bowties with Kasha (Kasha Varnishkes), 347
Sachertorte, 728
Palatschinken, 652

GREEK
Stuffed Grape Leaves (Dolmas), 82
Taramasalata, 75
Becker Gyro Sandwich, 188
Spinach and Feta Triangles, 89
Green Beans with Onions, Tomatoes, and Dill, 251
Lamb Kebabs, 494
Moussaka, 274
Grilled or Broiled Whole Fish, 403, with Tzatziki, 567
Phyllo Cups, 675, filled with Vanilla Frozen Yogurt, 835,
      and poached figs in Heavy Syrup, 212

MIDDLE EASTERN
Tabbouleh, 362
Hummus, 74
Baba Ghanoush, 74
Persian Rice, 357
Pita Salad (Fattoush), 159
Rice Pilaf, 355
Falafel Sandwich, 188
Couscous with Chicken, Lemon, and Olives, 363
Braised Lamb Shanks, 495
Baklava, 675
Baked Rice Pudding, 820, with rosewater and pistachios

NEW ORLEANS
New Orleans Beignets, 656
Red Beans and Rice, 256
Fried Green Tomatoes, 312
Oyster Po'Boy, 185
Shrimp or Crawfish Étouffée, 388
Chicken Jambalaya, 356
Muffuletta, 181
Chicken Étouffée, 436
Becker Barbecued Shrimp, 386
Blackened Fish Steaks or Fillets, 409
Chicken Gumbo, 136, or Seafood Gumbo, 141
Buttermilk Biscuits, 639
New Orleans Bread Pudding, 822
Bananas Foster, 826
Coffee Ice Cream, 832, sprinkled with crushed
      Praline, 876, or Pecan Buttermilk Pralines, 876
Café au Lait, 31

COCKTAIL PARTIES
For cocktail suggestions, see Cocktails and Party Drinks,
54.

Cheese Platter or Board, 70
Curried Nuts, 70
Crisp Spicy Pecans, 70
Spanish-Style Marinated Olives, 71
Scallop Seviche, 370
Rolled Sushi, 359
Rumaki, 83
Grilled or Broiled Shrimp Cockaigne, 84
Cheese Puffs, 91

Canapés, 86
Bruschetta with Tomatoes and Basil, 88

CHILDREN'S PARTIES
Stuffed Raw Vegetables using Snow Peas, 79, or Stuffed
    Celery, 79
Melon Baskets or Fruit Cup, 230
Cheese Straws, 91
Chicken Fingers, 80, with Honey Mustard Dipping
    Sauce, 566
Cocktail Tartlets, 90, filled with Shrimp Wiggle, 113,
    or pepperoni and mozzarella
Tea Sandwiches, 185, filled with Honey Butter, 179, or
    peanut butter and jelly, and cut into shapes with
    cookie cutters
Pigs in a Blanket, 91, or Corn Dogs, 185
Cheese Quesadillas, 77, or Cheese Enchiladas, 104
Yellow Cupcakes, 737, or Black Bottom Cupcakes, 738
Chocolate Mousse, 816, or Banana Pudding, 807
Ice Pops, 838, or Chocolate-Dipped Bananas, 218
Ice Cream Sandwiches made with White Chocolate
    Macadamia Monsters, 767, or Oatmeal Chocolate
    Chip Cookies, 768, or Peanut Butter Cookies, 767,
    with French Vanilla Ice Cream, 831, Chocolate Ice
    Cream, 832, or Caramel Ice Cream, 832
Shirley Temples or Roy Rogers, 64

PARTY PLATTERS
See About Party Platters, 69

Bread Sticks, 620
Deviled or Stuffed Eggs, 195
Cucumber slices spread with Red Onion Dip, 72
Spinach Dip in a Bread Bowl, 73
Hot Chorizo and Cheese Dip, 73
Crudités, 78, or Stuffed Raw Vegetables, 79
Broiled Stuffed Mushrooms Cockaigne, 78
Roasted Garlic and Parmesan Spread, 76, with
    Flatbreads, 607–608
Chutney Cheese Spread, 76, or Honey Yogurt Dip, 78,
    with slices of peach, apple, and pear
Stuffed Raw Vegetables using Cherry Tomatoes, 79, or
    tomatoes stuffed with Seafood Salad, 165
Miniature Quiches, 90, or Spinach and Feta
    Triangles, 89
Buffalo Chicken Wings, 80
Fish Kebabs,405, Fruit Kebabs, 214, or Chicken
    Kebabs, 427, with a table sauce, 564–570
Beef Satay, 81, or satay skewers, with Peanut Dipping
    Sauce, 570
Rolled Sushi, 359, and Pickled Ginger, 952
Egg Rolls, 92, or Summer Rolls, 92, with Nam Prik, 570,
    or Plum Dipping Sauce, 570
Sliced Roast Beef, 470, with No-Knead Light Rolls, 609,
    and Horseradish Cream, 565, or Cold Mustard
    Sauce, 566

Cheesecake, 743–746, served with Fresh Blueberry
    Sauce, 853, or Fruit Coulis, 853
Cheesecake Brownies, 763, or Mississippi Mud Cake, 723
Raspberry Streusel Bars, 764, or Pecan or Angel
    Slices, 764

BREAKFAST OR BRUNCH IDEAS
Lemon Poppy Seed Muffins, 635, or Herb Muffins, 635
Quiche Lorraine, 108
Muesli, 353, with Yogurt, 1029
Melon Cups with a fruit salad, 170
Dutch Baby, 652, or Baked French Toast, 648
Bacon Cornmeal Waffles, 647, or Belgian Waffles, 647
Silver Dollar Pancakes, 644, or Buckwheat
    Pancakes, 645
Sweet Cheese Blintzes, 651
Panfried or Lyonnaise Potatoes, 297
Hash Brown Potatoes, 298
Potato Pancakes, 298
Corned Beef or Roast Beef Hash, 107
Crab Strata, 98
Bagels and Lox, 184
Hangtown Fry, 202, or Eggs Benedict, 197
Crumb Cake, 630, Raspberry Danish Pinwheel, 625
Grand Marnier Souffléd Omelet, 203
Matzo Brei, 199
Egg Baked in a Muffin Tin, 199
Blended Juices, 38–39

LUNCH MENUS
Crab Cakes, 381
Tangy Coleslaw, 161
Sweet-and-Sour Spiced Gherkins, 946
Cold Lime Soufflé, 817, or Lime Sorbet, 836

Eggs Poached in Red Wine, 197
Field Salad with Fresh Herbs, 158
Flan, 803

Club Sandwich, 180, or Hot Roast Beef Sandwich, 182
American Potato Salad, 168
Apple Pie with Cheddar Crust, 690, with Vanilla Ice
    Cream, 831

Ham and Spinach Crepes, 650, or Crepes with Apples,
    Chicken, and Blue Cheese, 650
Green Salad, 158
Vanilla Pots de Crème, 804

Sautéed Boneless Chicken Breasts, 436, or Panfried Fish
    Fillets or Steaks, 407
Coconut Milk Pudding, 808, with Mango Sauce, 853

Cold Avocado Soup, 146
Lobster Salad Vinaigrette, 162
Orange Ice Milk, 834, served in Chocolate Cups, 830

Spinach Salad, 159
Cream of Mussel Soup (Billi-Bi), 140
Chocolate Shortbread, 775

Baked Potato Soup, 130
All-Rye-Flour Bread, 605
Asian Greens and Whole Herbs, 158
Raspberry Streusel Bars, 764

Provençal Vegetable Soup (Soupe au Pistou), 128
Beer Bread, 629
Fresh Berry Pie, 676, with Crème Fraîche

Bean Salad, 170, made with lima beans, served in Tomato
    Cups, 173
Greek Lemon Soup, 124
Ginger Thins, 770

Blender Borscht, 149
Pumpernickel Toast with Liptauer Cheese, 76
Instant Sorbet, 837, or Butterscotch Icebox
    Cookies, 776

FORMAL DINNER MENUS
Roast Duck à l'Orange, 448
Pommes Anna, 298
Tart Green Salad, 158
Coffee Bavarian Cream, 818

Grilled Venison Chops with Blue Cheese and Caraway
    Butter, 529
Wild Rice with Sautéed Mushrooms, 363
Sautéed Greens with Garlic, 278
Blueberry Pie, 677, with Butter Pecan Ice Cream, 833

Breaded Veal Cutlets (Wiener Schnitzel), 487, with Cold
    Mustard Sauce, 566
Spätzle, 335
Braised Red Cabbage, 264
Apple Brown Betty, 692, with Vanilla Sauce, 850, or Rum
    Raisin Ice Cream, 832

Grilled Cornish Hens in Spicy Port Marinade, 441
Warm Barley, Mushroom, and Asparagus Salad, 347
Belgian Endive au Gratin, 275
Lemon Soufflé, 809, and Tuiles, 781

Baked Goat Cheese and Mesclun, 160
Mushroom Ragout, 283, over Soft Polenta, 349
Rustic Sourdough Bread, 604, with Tapenade, 75
Pickled Red or Golden Beets, 949
Fresh Fruit Tart, 681, with Fresh Blueberry Sauce, 853

Creamy Cucumber Salad, 167
Fish Baked in Salt, 399, with Lemon Butter, 557
Stir-Fried Snow Peas, 290
Jasmine Rice, 367
Panna Cotta, 813, with Kumquat
    Compote, 225

Edamame and Carrot Salad with Rice Vinegar
    Dressing, 167
Grilled Duck Breast with Hoisin Ginger Sauce, 449
Spicy Soba Noodles, 333
Pink Grapefruit Sorbet, 836, with Sautéed Lychees, 229,
    or slices of star fruit

DINNER FOR FAMILY AND FRIENDS
Braised Stuffed Pork Chops Cockaigne, 504
Mushroom Walnut Noodle Kugel, 336
Green Beans, 250
Chocolate Mayonnaise Cake, 718

Oven-Fried Chicken with a Cornmeal Crust, 430
Southern-Style Greens, 277
German Potato Salad, 168
Mustard Pickle or (Chow-Chow), 947
Cobbler, 693, with Vanilla Ice Cream, 831

Tomato Soup, 132
Cabbage Rolls Stuffed with Kasha and Bulgur, 348
Dill Batter Loaf, 598
Lemon or Lime Chiffon Pie, 688

Johnny Marzetti Spaghetti Pie, 95
Caesar Salad, 159
French Vanilla Ice Cream, 831, with Butterscotch
    Sauce, 849

Mediterranean Short Ribs with Olives, 99
Mashed Celery Root, 268
Garlic-Braised Broccoli Rabe, 261
Chocolate Semifreddo, 841, made with Frangelico

Green Salad, 159
Shrimp Wiggle, 113
Mashed Potatoes, 295
Pineapple Upside-Down Cake, 691, with Pineapple Ice
    Milk, 834

Bread Sticks (Grissini), 620
Cannelloni, 340, with Chicken and Cheese Filling, 338,
    and White Sauce I, 550
Panned or Sicilian Spinach, 306
Hazelnut Gelato, 834, with Shortbread, 775

COOK FOR A DAY, EAT FOR A WEEK
Use these recipe suggestions to cook for a day, freeze, and
eat for a week. See 925.

King Ranch Chicken Casserole, 96
Chicken Rice Casserole, 96
Turkey Tetrazzini, 96
Tuna-Vegetable Casserole, 97
Bean, Tomato, and Sausage Gratin, 97
Hearty Meat Ragú, 101
Chicken or Turkey Potpie, 103
Beef Potpie, 103
Chicken Enchiladas, 104

Beef or Pork Enchiladas, 104
Cheese Quiche, 109
Vegetable Soup, 128
Minestrone, 128
Chicken Noodle Soup, 125
French Onion Soup, 129
Potato Leek Soup, 130
Tomato Soup, 132
U.S. Senate Bean Soup, 133
Mediterranean White Bean Soup, 133
Lentil Soup with Greens, 134
Becker Chicken Soup, 134
Beef Barley Soup, 136
Pasta and Beans, 329
Pastitsio, 336
Baked Manicotti or Jumbo Shells, 339
Any lasagne, 340–341
Chicken Chili Verde, 435
Brunswick Stew, 432
Kentucky Burgoo, 484
Chicken Cacciatore, 433
Chicken Curry, 434
Any beef stew (without potatoes), 479–481
Lamb Stew, 495
Irish Stew (without potatoes), 496
Lamb Curry with Tomato, 497
Italian Meatballs, 513
Swedish Meatballs, 513
Chili con Carne, 513
Any chili, 513–514
Tomato Sauce, 562
Marinara Sauce, 562
Tomato Meat Sauce, 563
Bolognese Sauce, 564

30-MINUTE RECIPES

When time is of the essence, these recipes will get dinner to the table in short order. For additional ideas, see Dishes Using Cooked Meat, Poultry, Fish, or Beans, 103, and About Quick Soups Cockaigne, 148.

Fried Rice, 357
Bean Burritos, 103
Becker Pork Hash, 108
Chicken or Turkey Chili Hash with Sweet Potatoes, 108
Chipped Beef and Gravy, 112
Welsh Rarebit, 112
Shrimp Wiggle, 113
Quick Chicken à la King, 113
Chicken Noodle Soup, 125
Butternut Squash Soup, 129
Chicken, Avocado, and Tomato Soup, 135
Tomato Soup, 132
Cream of Tomato Soup, 144
Oyster Stew, 140
Salmon Chowder, 143

Cream of Carrot Soup, 144
Cream of Asparagus Soup, 144
Baked Potato Soup, 130
Cold Avocado Soup, 146
Any gazpacho (if not chilled), 146–147
Steamed Mussels, 373
Steamed Clams, 375
Baked Soft-Shell Clams, 375
Thai Clam Pot, 376
Grilled or Broiled Shrimp or Scallops with Hoisin or Barbecue Sauce, 387
Becker Barbecued Shrimp, 386
Shrimp Scampi, 386
Broiled or Grilled Shrimp or Scallops, 386
Japanese Noodles in Broth, 333
Fettuccine with Butter and Cheese, 325
Stovetop Macaroni and Cheese, 325
Fettuccine with Fresh Herbs, 326
Fettuccine Alfredo, 327
Fettuccine with Smoked Salmon and Asparagus, 327
Spaghetti with Garlic and Oil (Aglio e Olio), 327
Linguine with White Clam Sauce, 328
Penne with Vodka Sauce, 328
Tagliatelle with Wilted Greens, 328
Creamy Pasta with Chard and Tomatoes, 328
Spaghetti Carbonara, 329
Pasta with Puttanesca Sauce, 563
Orecchiette with Sausage and Broccoli Rabe, 329
Baked Fish Fillets in White Wine, 397
High-Heat Roasted Fish Fillets, 398
Grilled or Broiled Whole Fish, 403
Broiled Fish Fillets with Lemon, 403
Broiled Fish Fillets with Tomatoes and Herbs, 406
Grilled Salmon Fillets with Chipotle Pepper Mayonnaise, 406
Panfried Fish Fillets or Steaks, 407
Panfried Spice-Crusted Fish Fillets, 408
Seared Pepper-Crusted Fish Steaks, 409
Mediterranean Boneless Chicken Breasts Baked in Foil, 439
Chicken Piccata, 436
Sautéed Breaded Boneless Chicken Breasts, 437
Sautéed Chicken Breasts with Mushroom Sauce, 437
Chicken Fingers, 430
Sautéed Steak with Red Wine Herb Sauce, 475
Steak Diane, 475
London Broil, 474
Peppered Steak with Cream Sauce, 474
Becker Mongolian Beef, 477
Sautéed Veal Scaloppine, 486
Veal Piccata, 486
Veal Marsala, 486
Veal Saltimbocca, 486
Sautéed Lamb Chops, 493
Grilled Pork Tenderloin , 503

Sautéed Pork Chops, 504
Chutney Turkey Burgers, 445
Patty Melt, 510
Sloppy Joe, 510
Becker Lamb Patties, 511
Ohio Farmhouse Sausage Chili, 514
Picadillo, 514
Croque Monsieur, 181
Monte Cristo, 181
Fried Soft-Shell Crab Sandwich, 183
Turkey and Avocado Wraps, 187
Ground Beef Tacos, 188
Bistro Salad, 160
Spinach with Seared Shrimp and Bacon, 163
South Carolina Skillet Shrimp, 385
Oregon Shrimp Salad, 163
Thai Beef Salad, 163
Taco Salad, 163
Chinese Chicken Salad, 164
Pasta Salad with Grilled Chicken, 172
Pasta Salad with Shrimp, 172
Huevos Rancheros, 196
Creamed Eggs au Gratin, 195
Curried Eggs, 195
Creamed Eggs with Asparagus Tips Cockaigne, 195
Spanish Omelet, 201
Frittata, 202
Hangtown Fry, 202
Western or Denver Omelet, 202
Savory Cheese-and-Herb-Filled Souffléd Omelet, 203

MENUS WITH GUEST PARTICIPATION

Many guests like to be where the action is, and the host or hostess is often hard pressed to find more to suggest than the last-minute pouring of the ice water. The ideas below can utilize willing guests in helping serve, or doing some at-table cooking, and in exploiting the guests' willingness to help, may reveal some special talents that add to the conviviality of the get-together.

I. Have a soup pot filled with hearty Lentil Soup, 134, US Senate Bean Soup, 133, or the soup of your choice with an assortment of salad makings and dressings or a large salad platter, such as Cobb Salad, 162, from which guests can select their choice. Have nearby an assortment of breads, rolls, cheese, and cookies or pies.

II. Prepare the ingredients for one of the following recipes, which give guests a choice of combinations: Beef Fondue, 110, Cheese Fondue, 110, Thai Clam Pot, 376, Pad Thai, 332, or Indonesian Rice Table, 358

III. And for tweens and teens, set up a hamburger feast, serving hamburgers, 510–511, with varied buns and toppings, and a platter of raw vegetables and Sour Cream Dip, 72. For dessert, serve assorted ice cream in cones, sundaes, or homemade milkshakes and malts, 40.

IV. Set up a pasta buffet. Cook the pasta shapes of your choice, including one tubular or shaped pasta and one noodle pasta. Lightly coat the pasta with olive oil, then cool and chill until ready to use. Prepare three sauces, Pesto, 569, Marinara, 562, and Flourless White Sauce, 551, and an assortment of toppings may also be prepared: grated Parmesan cheese, sliced black olives, grilled, shredded chicken, Sautéed Mushrooms, 283, or chunks of Italian cooked sausage. With a guest chef or willing guest in charge, have two sauté stations set up for preparing the pasta dish to order, allowing the guest to choose their pasta, sauce, and toppings of choice.

V. Grilled Pizza Crusts, 192, can be prepared ahead of time and when cool placed in a napkin-lined basket. Surround the basket with a choice of pizza sauces: Pesto, 569, olive oil, Tomato Sauce, 562, or Tapenade, 75. Offer bowls of precooked pizza toppings, 190, as well, allowing guests to create their own pizzas. Once topped, the pizza is returned to the grill to warm the crust and ingredients.

VI. With a guest chef, or a willing guest in charge, have two chafing dishes or sauté stations set up for omelets or crepe making. Read About Omelets, 200, for suggestions, and have on hand an assortment of fillings, such as chopped seafood, cooked chicken, shredded cheeses, Sautéed Mushrooms, 283, a large green salad, 158, with generous vegetable components, and cut Cheesecake Cockaigne, 743, with fresh berries and whipped cream or Chocolate Sauce Cockaigne, 847, or Hot Fudge Sauce, 847.

BACKPACKING MENU SUGGESTIONS

Whether you intend to travel far from civilization or just a few miles in the back country, food and equipment that are light in weight and low in bulk are crucial. Choose food that cooks in little or no time to conserve fuel, whether it be fuel hauled on your back or provided by nature on the spot. Always have sources of fire—lighters and wooden matches in a waterproof container. For ways to build fires, see 1056. For a flame that is controllable, acquaint yourself with the immense range of stoves and fuels available. Solid fuels stoves are the most reliable, and the fuel may also be used as a fire starter. Their drawbacks are toxicity in closed spaces. ➤ No stove should be used in tents or other unventilated spaces because of carbon monoxide and/or toxicity from fumes. Butane or propane stoves are extremely easy to use, but the fuel is bulky, and they are not very efficient at very low temperatures. Liquid gas stoves are by far the most efficient and will boil water fast. They do, however, require maintenance and can be cranky. If you are third-worlding it, there are liquid multi-fuel stoves that burn almost any liquid hydrocarbon.

Pretest your meals at home first; what tastes good at home will be excellent fare on the trail. Menu planning and prepackaging are essential for fast and foolproof trail cooking. Each meal for each person should be prepackaged with seasoning in resealable plastic bags with excess air removed. One day's meals, along with that day's munchies and extra beverage mixes, vitamin pills, and sundries should be placed in a large marked bag. Try to provide at least one course in each meal—or a large part of the main course—in a form that can be eaten without cooking, in case of a weather or fuel emergency or some other disaster. Always include the extra munchies in a separate bag.

If you are in very dry country where water is likely to be in short supply, remember that proteins require fairly large amounts of water to be utilized in the body, so increase carbohydrates. In cold weather you will benefit from foods heavy in fats. Also during cold weather you may wish to serve soups more often and coffee or tea less. Dried fruits, nuts, and candy-coated chocolate, known to hikers as "gorp," make good desserts and trail munchies, as do cookies, 760–783. See Fruit-Nut Pemmican, 212, Fruit Leather, 909, or Energy Bars, 765, for nourishing treats. If you plan your initial meals around sandwiches and later ones around tinned fish, freeze-dried meats, jerked meat—see Jerky, 905—instant rice, dried seaweed, dried mushrooms, instant potatoes, vegetable flakes, and Japanese-style quick-cooking noodles, you will have more time to enjoy the outdoors. You can also carry dry mixtures for pancakes, 643–660, or Granola, 353, or crackers, 93, biscuits, 637–640, or Bagels, 321. Some grains, such as couscous and bulgur, and pasta shapes, such as macaroni, are light to carry and cook quickly. See the grains chart, 364–368, or pasta chart, 321, for ideas. At high altitudes, be certain that all foods are easy to digest and blander than usual, for altitude sickness seems to be more prevalent when the expedition diet is highly spiced or difficult to digest. While you may not be able to avoid it altogether, be wary of too much MSG in preserved foods. Check the labels.

Always pack in the basic outdoor cooking tools: a sharp hunting knife and stainless steel soupspoon. Cookware sets made from aluminum or titanium are easily obtainable today. Pick outdoor cooking utensils that can also serve for storage of water or food.

After meals, be sure to carefully scrape clean and rinse all cooking and eating utensils. Dunk them first in soapy boiling water and then in clear boiling rinse water. Or, if water or fuel is scarce, scorch the insides and food-bearing surfaces over an open flame. Remember that even a mild case of dysentery can be disabling far from civilization. Wilderness water supplies should always be treated with suspicion. Boil water for at least 5 minutes, or treat it with a charcoal filter or iodine tablets according to the instructions that come with them.

BEVERAGES

Despite the considerable efforts of soft-drink advertisers, coffee and tea are still the most popular beverages around the world. Hot or cold, strong or mild, sweetened or plain, what has made them valued for so long—more than a thousand years—is caffeine, nature's own stimulant. Primitive man located the only sources of caffeine known to this day: tea, coffee, cola, chocolate, and yerba maté and its relatives. People have been tinkering with them ever since. Subsequent generations have adopted social rituals and created special equipment to enhance the cheer.

Other less rousing brews have been traditionally made from leaves, roots, bark, blossoms, and seeds. Find fresh herbs in the produce department at the grocery store or grow your own herbs, 989, if possible, and use them frequently, fresh or dried, to make herbed tea, 35, or infused sugar syrups, 43, which can enhance or form the basis of beverages of all types. And, of course, fresh fruit and fresh or bottled fruit juices make some of the most refreshing beverages of all.

The recipes in this chapter are nonalcoholic, except for a few variations under Coffee and Tea and one or two composite party drinks. For alcoholic drinks of all kinds, their preparation, and use, see Cocktails and Party Drinks, 54. Remember that, in any beverage you may brew, the quality of the water greatly affects results.

ABOUT COFFEE

Coffee has always thrived on adversity. In the Arab world, where the coffee plant was first cultivated commercially in the fifteenth century, coffee was widely consumed by the populace but condemned by Islamic leaders for its supposed intoxicating effects. Coffee was banned repeatedly as it traveled from Constantinople to Venice and then to Vienna and other European capitals. The beans were initially sold by pharmacists and eventually in cafés—which became notorious hotbeds of revolution and enlightened thinking. These days, coffee controversies continue as new studies appear, alternately decrying coffee as a health hazard or informing us that, no, it's all right to drink after all. For anyone in doubt, the best approach, as it is so often, is moderation.

Coffee beans are the seed of a fruit, which are picked green and do not acquire their familiar brown color and aroma until they are roasted. All commercial coffee beans belong to one of two main varieties, **arabica** or **robusta.** Arabica beans are the better of the two, producing the finest flavors when grown at high altitudes in semitropical climates in various countries near, but not at, the equator. Robusta beans require less care when grown and thrive in warmer, wetter areas, such as the lowlands of West Africa and islands in the Pacific. Generally, robusta is used more for dark-roasted styles of coffee.

For those who love coffee but are highly sensitive to caffeine or in whom it induces insomnia, we suggest decaffeinated coffee rather than a coffee substitute. It may also be helpful to remember that the caffeine content of coffees can vary: Robusta has almost twice the caffeine of arabica on average. Our other favorite source of caffeine, tea, has about one-third the caffeine of arabica coffee, depending on the strength of the brew.

BREWING COFFEE

There are several ways of preparing coffee, and guidance for most of them follows. The steeped coffee recipe, 30, is suggested for campers or others who happen to lack any equipment more specialized than a saucepan. Illustrated on the following page are the best devices for making coffee: Manual drip coffee is made with the **filter cone method,** which involves pouring hot water through measured ground coffee in a filter set inside a cone to drip into a glass pot or thermal carafe. **Electric drip coffeemakers** operate on the same principle as manual filter cones, but they pour the water over the coffee from a premeasured reservoir. In electric coffeemakers, look for power as expressed in wattage; the higher it is, the stronger the heater and, thus, the better the coffee. Some think that flat-bottomed basket-shaped filters allow the water to saturate the ground coffee more evenly than cone-shaped filters. For either method or filter shape, paper filters are convenient but **gold screen filters** are preferred, as they can go into the dishwasher and will withstand years of constant use. **Stovetop metal drip pots** have 3 separate chambers, top to bottom, for hot water, ground coffee, and brewed coffee. This can be an excellent brewing method, but beware of aluminum pots, which interact with the acids in coffee and with time can impart off flavors. **Plunger pots,** also called **French press pots,** make coffee with a thick texture that is preferred by some and is

Filter cone and glass pot, stovetop metal drip pot, plunger pot or French press, vacuum brewer

particularly appropriate to the flavors of dark-roasted beans. **Vacuum brewers** long required the use of the stovetop or a freestanding heat source, and their fragile bases were prone to messy, sometimes dangerous, breakage. Today's freestanding electric models make vacuum brewing far easier than it once was, and advocates praise the robust coffee produced by this method. Also shown are a **pump espresso machine, moka pot,** and **Neapolitan coffeepot**.

Whatever device you choose, ➤ follow the directions of its manufacturer carefully, especially as to the grind recommended—coarse, regular, or fine. In each case, to assure a full-bodied brew, ➤ use 1 to 2 level tablespoons of coffee for each ¾ cup (6 ounces) of fresh water; be sure to use soft, not softened or hard, water, 1026. Brewing a full or almost full pot of coffee usually gives the best results. Time your method consistently. And keep the coffeemaker scrupulously clean—coffee residue can create a bitter flavor in the next batch.

Electric coffeemakers should be cleaned every few months. Run a combination of 1 part vinegar to 4 parts water through the machine, or use a cleaning powder especially for the purpose. Run several cycles of fresh water through the machine to rinse it after cleaning.

Never boil coffee—with the exception of Turkish coffee.

Water between 200° and 205°F is ideal for extracting flavor without drawing acids. Note that at sea level, water boils at 212°F, so if making manual drip or steeped coffee, let the water sit for *several seconds* after boiling before adding it to the ground coffee. Remember that any moisture activates coffee; and never reuse coffee grounds. If you will not be serving the whole pot you brew within 10 to 15 minutes, ➤ transfer the coffee to a warmed thermal carafe to keep it warm. ➤ If using milk or cream, scald, 997, it in the microwave or on the stovetop or allow it to reach room temperature beforehand, so as to cool the coffee as little as possible.

GRINDING AND STORING COFFEE BEANS

In general, ➤ the shorter the brewing time, the finer the grind must be. Espresso requires a fine grind, resembling superfine sugar. French press coffee requires a coarse grind, resembling coarsely ground cornmeal. Drip coffee, which falls between the two, requires a regular grind, resembling granulated sugar. You can grind your coffee using the grinder at the market, or you may choose instead to grind your coffee at home. **Propeller-blade grinders** are the most popular. They are inexpensive and easy to use. Grind no more than 4 scoops at a time, and whirl in short bursts. **Burr mill grinders** have two notched

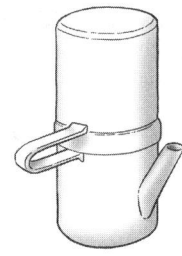

Pump espresso machine, moka pot, Neapolitan coffeepot

Propeller-blade grinder with view of blade, burr mill grinder

blades whose positions can be set to change the fineness of the grind. They are noisier and slower than propeller grinders, but you can grind larger amounts and obtain consistent results. Old-fashioned hand-cranked grinders are burr mills.

Always grind coffee in small quantities in a clean grinder. ➤ To clean your grinder, grind 2 to 3 tablespoons of uncooked rice and repeat. Wipe out grinder and lid with a dry paper towel. The rice gives the added benefit of sharpening the blades. ➤ The best way to store coffee beans, ground or whole, is in an opaque airtight canister at room temperature.

DRIP COFFEE

This is the method for manual drip coffee. If you have an electric drip coffeemaker, follow the manufacturer's directions, using the water-to-coffee proportions listed here. Place in drip filter:

2 tablespoons regular- to fine-grind coffee for each ³/₄ cup water

Bring water to a rolling boil, then remove it from the heat and wait about 15 seconds. Slowly drip just enough water over the ground coffee to moisten it thoroughly. Wait another 30 seconds or so, then pour in the rest of the water, in stages if necessary.

When the drip process is complete, serve coffee at once or keep it in a thermal carafe. Dripping coffee more than once through a filter does not strengthen the brew.

FRENCH PRESS POT COFFEE

To keep coffee as hot as possible, warm the pot with hot water before brewing and wrap the pot in a kitchen towel while it steeps. Place in the pot:

2 tablespoons coarse-grind coffee for every ³/₄ to 1 cup water

Bring water to a rolling boil, then remove it from the heat and let stand for a few seconds. Pour the water over the coffee and stir well. Place the lid on top, making sure that the plunger is fully extended. Let steep for 6 minutes, then slowly push the plunger all the way down, forcing the coffee grounds to the bottom of the pot.

VACUUM-METHOD COFFEE

Boiling water in the lower bowl of the vacuum coffeemaker is forced into the upper chamber, where it mixes with the coffee and then filters back into the lower bowl. If using an electric vacuum coffeemaker, follow manufacturer's directions, using the water-to-coffee proportions listed here. Allow:

1 to 2 tablespoons coarse- to fine-grind coffee for every ³/₄ to 1 cup water

Measure water into lower bowl. Place on heat. Add the ground coffee to the upper bowl. If your equipment has a vented stem, you can place it, already assembled, on the heat; if it does not have this small hole on the side of the tube above the hot water line, wait until the water is actively boiling before putting the upper bowl in place. Insert the upper bowl into lower one with a light twist to ensure a tight seal. When nearly all the water has risen into the upper bowl (some of it will always remain below), stir the water and coffee thoroughly. In 1 to 3 minutes (the finer grinds, the shorter the time) remove from heat and allow the coffee to run back into the lower bowl.

PERCOLATED COFFEE

This is the method for stovetop percolators; if you have an electric machine, follow the manufacturer's directions, using the water-to-coffee proportions listed here.
For every 1 cup of coffee, place in the percolator:

2 tablespoons regular-grind coffee ³/₄ to 1 cup cold water

When water boils, remove percolator from heat. Place the basket inside. Cover, return to heat, and percolate slowly, 6 to 8 minutes. Remove the coffee basket. Overpercolating does not make coffee stronger, it impairs its flavor.

STEEPED COFFEE

For every 1 cup of coffee, place in a pot:

³/₄ to 1 cup water 2 tablespoons regular- to fine-grind coffee

Bring water to a rolling boil, and remove it from the heat; wait about 15 seconds. Pour water over the ground coffee and stir for at least 30 seconds. Let stand, covered, in the pan 5 to 10 minutes, depending on the grind and the strength of brew desired. Pour the coffee off the grounds through a strainer and into another pot. To keep the coffee hot, place the pot in a pan of hot water.

COFFEE IN QUANTITY

30 to 35 servings

For large percolators, see Percolated Coffee, 30. For large coffee urns: Put in a cheesecloth bag large enough to allow for double expansion:

12 ounces regular-grind coffee

Bring to a boil:

4 to 5 quarts water

Pour into the coffee urn. Place the coffee-filled bag in it. Let stand, covered, in a warm place 7 to 10 minutes. Agitate the bag several times during this period. Remove the bag, cover the urn, and serve at once.

INSTANT COFFEE

We really can't regard the jiffy product as equal to the one that takes a few minutes longer to prepare.

For each serving, use:

1 teaspoon instant coffee

$^2/_3$ cup boiling water

To avoid foaming, add the water to the instant coffee. A better flavor is obtained by simmering gently in a small pan for about 2 minutes.

ABOUT ESPRESSO, CAPPUCCINO, AND CAFFÈ LATTE

The term **espresso** refers to the brewing method, not the coffee bean or degree of roast, and it's the brewing method that gives the fullest-bodied coffee by far. This Italian specialty, which, of course, is called *caffè espresso* on its home ground, is distinguished from any brew made by filtering, no matter how concentrated. A properly brewed cup of espresso measures $1^1/_2$ to 2 ounces. The coffee-to-water proportions for brewing espresso are roughly the same as for regular coffee, 2 tablespoons of finely ground coffee for each $^3/_4$ cup water. There are two ways to make espresso at home. A stovetop apparatus called the **moka pot,** 29, yields coffee that is roughly halfway between drip coffee and true espresso in body and flavor. To use, fill the bottom chamber with cold water to the level of the safety valve. Set the metal filter in it and fill it with dark-roasted coffee ground medium-fine. Screw on the upper chamber and set the pot over medium-low heat. After about 3 minutes, coffee will begin to hiss and dribble out the two holes at the sides of the tube in the upper compartment, and steam will rise from the spout. Turn off the heat and let the pot sit until all the water has been forced into the upper chamber. **Pump espresso machines,** 29, force hot water through finely ground coffee at a pressure high enough to achieve the syrupy consistency and pleasantly bittersweet flavor of true espresso. Follow the manufacturer's instructions for the particular machine, but in general it's a good idea to preheat the metal filter and its holder by running hot water through them and into the espresso cup. This also primes the pump. Be sure to use a sufficiently fine grind of coffee—preground coffee labeled "espresso" is often the best choice. Serve espresso after dinner, in demitasse cups or espresso glasses, and offer sugar—unrefined sugar, 1018, has the deepest flavor—alongside. Give the brew a tasty alcoholic kick with a dash of sambuca or Tía Maria.

Cappuccino, named for the brown robes of Capuchin monks, whose color it is thought to resemble, is the glory of the Italian coffee bar. In Italy you shouldn't expect powdered cinnamon or cocoa sprinkled over the top, though, for **cappuccino** is just espresso and steamed or scalded milk topped with satiny foam—with coffee, milk, and foam in equal proportions.

Caffè latte is 1 part espresso diluted with 4 parts scalded or steamed milk, with no foam on top. **Caffè macchiato** is espresso "marked" with just a tablespoon or two of foam. The dark-roasted milk **café au lait** of France is also popular in New Orleans, where the coffee is often brewed with chicory. Combine equal parts of strong coffee and hot milk. Add sugar to taste.

To prepare the milk and foam for cappuccino, **steam the milk** according to the manufacturer's instructions for your espresso machine or scald, 997, the milk in a saucepan, making certain it does not boil and whisking vigorously to create the foam. You want a warm combination of milk and foam that is a bit less than twice the volume of the milk you started with. Use a spoon to block the foam when pouring the milk into the espresso, then spread the foam gently on top. For caffè latte and café au lait, the milk should be hot but not too foamy; it can be heated in the microwave and then whisked lightly to produce just a small amount of foam.

TURKISH OR MIDDLE EASTERN COFFEE

Probably every nation of the eastern Mediterranean brews coffee with a simple method thought to have originated in the coffeehouses of Cairo in the fifteenth century: Presweetened very finely ground coffee is lightly boiled several times in a long-handled brass or copper vessel called a *cezve* in Turkish and *ibrik* or *briki* in Greek. The average content of the pot is 10 ounces of liquid, and it should never be filled to more than two-thirds capacity. The coffee is not filtered, but the grounds stay in the bottom of the pot; some sediment always finds its way into each cup, where it sinks to the bottom and remains. This is often dumped onto the saucer with one smart rap after the coffee is consumed and then used to tell fortunes.

To brew Turkish coffee, start with specially ground coffee—ground almost to a powder—available, along with the pots, at Greek or Middle Eastern markets, some supermarkets, and Internet retailers. You can use regular coffee and grind it at home, but this can be tricky, as even grinders with a "Turkish" setting often don't grind the coffee fine enough.

For each serving, place in the pot:

1/2 cup water
2 teaspoons very finely ground coffee
Sugar to taste
(Pinch of ground cardamom)

Bring to a frothing simmer over medium heat. Just as the coffee puffs and is about to boil over, remove the pot from the stove and pour a bit of foam into warmed cups. Return the pot to the heat for two or three brief boilings, removing it quickly each time as it is about to boil over. Divide the brewed coffee among the cups, distributing the remaining foam equally.

ABOUT FLAVORED COFFEES

Flavored coffees are extremely popular, but those commonly available tend to rely on chemical flavoring essences. In the kitchen, you have an array of natural flavorings for your coffee. Add any of the following to 1 pound ground coffee before brewing: 4 ounces ground chicory, 4 ounces cocoa nibs, 4 cracked cinnamon sticks, 4 star anise, 4 wholes cloves, 4 crushed cardamom pods, 4 vanilla beans split lengthwise in half and cut into pieces, or several large pieces of citrus zest. If you wish to prepare flavored coffee in advance, mix in one or more flavorings with the ground coffee and store in a tightly sealed container in the refrigerator or freezer for up to 1 month as some of these ingredients may spoil if left at room temperature for extended periods.

ABOUT COFFEE DRINKS

Coffee by itself or with nothing more than sugar and cream is probably the closest thing we have to a national beverage. Coffee blends well with alcohol and other flavorings to produce a variety of deliciously assertive and warming, or cooling, drinks. For coffee-chocolate combinations, see About Chocolate and Cocoa Beverages, 35, Brazilian Chocolate, 36, Kai, 37, Flying Mocha Monkey, 40, and Cocomoka, 42.

JAMAICAN COFFEE

1 serving

Stir together in a warmed mug:

1 ounce Jamaican dark rum
1 ounce Tía Maria
3/4 cup hot strong coffee

Top with:

Whipped cream

IRISH COFFEE

1 serving

Heat but do not boil, then pour into a warmed mug:

1 1/2 ounces Irish whiskey
1 to 2 teaspoons sugar

Fill to within 1/2 inch of the top with:

Hot coffee

Stir until the sugar is dissolved. Top with:

Whipped cream

CAFÉ DIABLO

8 servings

This festive coffee bowl requires a darkened room for the full dramatic effect.

Rinse and dry:

1 small orange

Stud it with:

20 whole cloves

Combine in a deep silver bowl:

Peel of 1 orange, thinly sliced
Peel of 1 lemon, thinly sliced
2 cinnamon sticks
10 small sugar cubes

Heat, but do not boil, then pour into the bowl:

3/4 cup brandy or 1/4 cup Cointreau

Place the bowl on a tray and bring the bowl, the orange, and a flameproof ladle to the table. Carefully ignite the brandy and ladle the liquid repeatedly over the peel and cinnamon until the sugar is melted. Pour into the bowl:

4 cups hot strong coffee

Now fill the ladle with:

1/4 cup Cointreau or 1/4 warm brandy

Set the studded orange in the brandy and carefully, ignite the brandy, then lower the flaming ladle into the bowl, allowing the orange to float. Ladle into demitasse cups.

For individual servings, and an easier version of this recipe, put a small sugar cube in a coffee spoon, saturate it with brandy, and ignite. When the sugar is melted, lower the spoon into a partially filled demitasse cup of hot coffee. Add a lemon twist and 1 or 2 cloves, then stir the mixture with a cinnamon stick. Or, simply stir a teaspoon of warmed light rum or whiskey into a small cup of hot coffee, adding a twist of lemon peel and sweetening to taste.

ICED COFFEE

Prepare any coffee any way you wish, 28–32, using for each serving:

2 1/2 to 3 tablespoons coffee and 3/4 cup water

Chill it or pour it hot over cubed ice in tall glasses. You may sweeten it with:

(Sugar or Sugar Syrup, 43, to taste)

Stir in:

(Milk or cream to taste)

Or top with:

(Whipped cream or vanilla ice cream)

ICED COFFEE VIENNESE

Prepare any **Iced Coffee, 32,** in a tall glass. Add **1 ounce light rum or brandy.** Top with **whipped cream.**

FROZEN COFFEE

For each drink, place in a blender:

$1/2$ cup Iced Coffee, 32
$1/4$ cup milk

Add, for each drink:

1 tablespoon sugar
Pinch of ground cloves
(1 ounce rum)

Add not less than:

1 cup crushed ice

Blend thoroughly. Serve in chilled tall glasses.

ABOUT TEA

Considering how many very different kinds of tea there are in the world—white, green, oolong, pekoe, black, gunpowder, jasmine, Earl Grey, and many more—it's astonishing to discover that they all come from just one type of plant, an evergreen shrub originally from southern China and northern India that would grow into a tall tree if its branches and leaves weren't so often ruthlessly pruned and picked. The tea plant, now cultivated in India and a dozen or so countries in Asia, and Africa, changed its character so completely as it adapted to each new environment that it now seems like a family made up of strikingly assorted individuals.

As if the natural variations weren't complicated enough, the processing, manufacture, grading, and blending, and the additions of blossoms, zests, or spices, all create further considerable differences in the finished product. Yet, most of these variations are intriguing and delicious, as well as refreshing.

There are three principal methods of processing tea leaves, resulting in white tea, green tea, black tea, and oolong tea. All start in more or less the same way. Tea leaves are brittle when fresh and must be "withered" to be made supple enough to handle. They are then rolled, twisted, and lightly broken, usually by machine. The essential oils that give tea its flavor come to the surface at this point. Tea picked and harvested before the tea leaves are fully open is called white. If development is stopped by "firing," or heating, the leaves, the tea is called green, even though its color may range from olive green to warm cream. All Japanese tea and most Chinese tea is green.

Until the 1830s, Americans drank only green tea, but consumption declined steadily after that to the point that it virtually ceased. Today, though, green tea is coming into fashion again, not only because of its delicate flavor but also for its apparent health benefits. It is packed with antioxidants that some researchers believe may help prevent cancer and heart disease.

Tea leaves turn black if their flavor-giving oils are exposed for a long period to air—usually very humid air—and allowed to oxidize. Oxidation darkens the color of the leaves and allows them to develop new flavor compounds—among them the astringent ones called polyphenols but commonly known as tannins. Black tea is the variety Americans drink most of the time.

The third way to process tea is to allow it to oxidize only partially, so that some of the fresh flavors of green tea and some of the deeper flavors of black tea are combined. This kind of tea, called oolong, is produced in China and Taiwan. Taiwan's former name, Formosa, is still used for the oolong produced there, which some connoisseurs consider to be the best.

Almost all tea sold commercially is blended, and there are often as many as twenty or more types in a blend—most of them black, sometimes from several countries, and often with a full-flavored tea such as Assam from India predominating. Much tea is flavored, and the most famous of these is Earl Grey, a blend of black tea flavored with oil of bergamot, a citrus fruit. Tea may be tumbled with flower petals, as green or oolong teas are for jasmine tea, or smoked, as for Lapsang souchong.

Most tea bags are filled with "fannings" or "dust"—two sorting grades that describe size, not quality. Although most packers use lesser-quality teas for bags than for loose tea, sometimes the fannings or dust can be quite good. The problem is that tea bags are rarely packed in airtight containers, and because the leaves are so finely chopped or pulverized, they grow stale more quickly than loose tea does.

Don't overlook tea's usefulness on the dining table in places such as flavored vodka, 58, marinade, 584, salad dressing, 972, and even ice cream, 832.

BREWING TEA

All you need to brew tea well is the best tea you can afford and hot or boiling water—the water being almost as important as the tea. Use cold water that is freshly drawn from the tap, soft—not softened, and not hard, 1026. If your tap water is of questionable quality, use a water filter installed on the tap or a freestanding filter pitcher; these are widely available and inexpensive.

Preheat the teapot with boiling water or very hot tap water. Water for brewing most teas should only just have arrived at a brisk rolling boil before being poured over the tea leaves, so they will open up for the fullest infusion and flavor; the exception is green tea, for which the water should be hot but not boiling (170° to 190°F).

Place tea leaves in a preheated pot, allowing 1 to 2 teaspoons tea leaves or 1 tea bag for each 1 cup water.

Tea leaves or bags should steep for at least 3 minutes and no more than 5; oolongs, Darjeelings, and delicate black teas usually require 3 to 4 minutes; other black teas need 4 to 5 minutes; green and white teas should steep for 1 to 2 minutes. Many green teas can be steeped more than once, but never steep black tea leaves more than once. Stir,

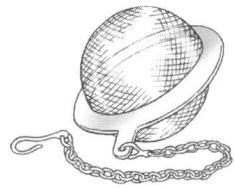

Tea ball

and serve the tea promptly. Milk is frequently added to black tea. On a chilly afternoon, we sometimes like to put a small decanter of rum or brandy on the tea tray for the cup that cheers.

To serve tea to a crowd, brew it in advance in a pot using twice as much tea as usual, then fill each cup or pot with half of this tea essence and half hot water.

Once the tea is brewed, it is simple to remove tea bags from the pot, of course. One possibility for decanting loose tea is to brew it in a separate pot or even in a clean saucepan set over very low heat and then to pour it through a strainer into the serving pot. Those who do not wish to trouble with a strainer may use a tea ball. The best tea ball is a globe of wire mesh, above, that usually shuts with a hinge. Any teapot should have a wide mouth, for getting tea in and out of the pot, and a handle that stays cool. Avoid pots of aluminum or any uncoated metal, which will interact with the tea and produce off flavors. We recommend a tea pot that contains a wide, deep inset basket, which gives plenty of room for the leaves to expand and can be lifted out as soon as the tea is ready. Individual metal tea filters are also useful. Look for one with a cylinder that extends to the bottom of the cup, which offers the most water-tea contact.

To keep tea warm both during and after brewing, you can wrap the teapot in a tea cozy or thick towel. Once you've removed the leaves, the tea can be transferred to a thermal carafe—less elegant than a teapot but a more practical way to serve it fresh and hot. ➤ Do not use a carafe you've previously put coffee in, however, or your tea will take on a coffee flavor.

In any case, ➤ stirring the brew just before serving in a preheated pot is imperative, since it circulates through the liquid the essential oils that contribute so much to tea's characteristic flavor.

SPICED TEA
8 servings
Combine in a saucepan and bring to a boil:
$^1/_2$ cup sugar
$^3/_4$ cup water
Remove from the heat and add:
$^1/_4$ cup strained orange juice
$^1/_2$ cup strained lemon juice
6 whole cloves
1 cinnamon stick

Meanwhile, prepare tea, above, using:
10 teaspoons black tea leaves
5 cups water
Pour the hot infusion into a heavy bowl. Pour the steeped tea over the mixture and serve at once in punch cups or teacups. Top with:
A slice of orange
1 cinnamon stick

CHAI
4 to 5 servings
Bring just to a boil in a medium saucepan:
3 cups water
1$^1/_2$ cups milk
$^3/_4$ cup sugar, or to taste
2 cinnamon sticks
16 cardamom pods, crushed
1 teaspoon whole cloves
$^1/_2$-inch piece fresh ginger, thinly sliced
$^1/_2$ teaspoon whole white or black peppercorns
Remove from heat, cover, and let stand for 20 minutes. Return to a simmer. Remove from heat and stir in:
2 tablespoons black tea leaves
Cover and let stand 2 minutes. Strain and serve at once, or let cool and serve over ice.

ICED TEA
We swell with pride when we recall that this beverage originated in our family's native town, St. Louis. The inventor was actually an Englishman who arrived at the concoction as an act of desperation. Hard water, 1026, produces murky iced tea.
Prepare tea, using twice the quantity of leaves indicated. Stir, strain, and pour over ice. Serve with:
Lemon slices
(Sprigs of mint)
(Sugar or Sugar Syrup, 43, to taste)
Commercially prepared and instant teas are also available, sometimes sweetened and flavored, if time is a factor.

SWEET SOUTHERN ICED TEA
6 to 8 servings
In the South, iced tea is sweet and strong—too dark to read the newspaper through.
Prepare tea, using:
4 cups water
6 to 7 tea bags
Stir in while hot:
1 cup sugar, or to taste
Transfer to a large pitcher and add:
2 to 4 cups water
Chill. Serve over ice with:
(Lemon slices)

FLAVORED ICED TEA

I. Pour strained hot tea over:

1 bunch mint, including stems
Zest strips of 1 lemon

Let stand at room temperature until cool, then chill. Strain, then pour the tea into tall glasses. Add ice cubes and:

Sugar or Sugar Syrup, 43, to taste
(Sprigs of mint)

II. Add to each serving of Iced Tea, above:

2 to 3 tablespoons Fruit Syrup, 43, or Herb Syrup, 43

Garnish the glasses with:

Slices of orange, lemon, or lime
(Sprigs of mint)

III. For each serving, pour over ice:

**$^1/_2$ cup lemonade or limeade or fruit juice such as
   pineapple, orange, cranberry, or mango nectar**
$^1/_2$ cup Iced Tea, 34

ABOUT HERBAL TEAS

From time immemorial, various plants, less stimulating than tea or coffee, have been used the world over to soothe and refresh. These are not really teas but rather infusions (the French call them *tisanes*), made with herbs, not tea leaves. An old herbalist recommended them for "wamblings of the stomach," and they are especially welcome shortly after dinner.

They range all the way from commonplace chamomile and mint to the South African rooibos, or redbush, shrub—whose green leaves turn red during the drying process and are the source of red tea. You can purchase specialty teas or ingredients at health food stores, ethnic markets, some specialty shops, and online.

Some of the homegrown herbs and spices that, singly or in combination, may become interesting beverages are the leaves, fresh or dried, of angelica, bergamot, comfrey, hyssop, lemon verbena, mints, sages, thymes; the blossoms of chamomile, clover, linden, orange, lemon, wintergreen, and elderberry; and the seeds of anise and fennel. Below are good general rules for quantity per cup of water in preparing these infusions. Devotees of infusions say, "Never use cream."

For strong herbs, allow per serving:

$^1/_2$ to 1 tablespoon fresh or $^1/_4$ to $^1/_2$ teaspoon dried

For mild herbs, allow:

Twice the above amounts

Or, for each of the following spices and herbs, allow for each cup:

1 star anise
6 chamomile flowers
$^1/_8$ teaspoon dried mint
$^1/_4$ teaspoon fennel seeds
$^1/_2$ teaspoon dried linden blossoms
3 tablespoons dried lemon verbena
1 stalk fresh lemongrass, finely chopped
3 thin slices fresh ginger

Never use a metal pot. Steep for 3 to 10 minutes in water

brought to a rolling boil, then strain. Serve with honey or lemon, if desired.

ICED HIBISCUS TEA

1 $^1/_2$ quarts

Bring to a boil in a large saucepan:

3 cups water

Add and stir until dissolved:

7 tea bags
$^1/_2$ cup dried hibiscus flowers
$^1/_2$ cup sugar

Let stand 10 minutes, then strain into a pitcher. Stir in:

3 cups ice water

Pour over ice in tall glasses. Garnish with:

Orange slices or raspberries

ABOUT CHOCOLATE AND COCOA BEVERAGES

Chocolate, an Aztec drink, comes to us, with the addition of sugar and spice, via Spain. In France, you can count on a milk base and cream incorporated into the drink. In Vienna, they add a generous topping of whipped cream. In Russia and Brazil, coffee is added, and in Mexico, we find in it cinnamon and even orange rind. In the United States, we like our hot chocolate and cocoa to be made with milk—especially if we are drinking it before bedtime.

Cocoa powder, from which most hot cocoa is made, does not dissolve instantly in liquid but tends to form lumps that must be smoothed by vigorous stirring. It helps to first combine the cocoa with sugar in the saucepan, or mix it in the blender with a small quantity of the liquid called for in the recipe. Don't confuse cocoa powder, which is unsweetened, with **instant cocoa,** which usually contains sugar, is precooked, and has an emulsifier added to make it dissolve readily in either a hot or a cold liquid. You will have a much better hot cocoa if you start with unsweetened cocoa powder, sweeten it to taste, and mix it with fresh milk. ➤ For quick preparation of hot or cold chocolate drinks, you may want to keep on hand Cocoa Syrup, 36, or Ganache for Hot Chocolate, 36. See About Chocolates and Cocoas, 969.

To fluff chocolate drinks just before serving, which inhibits the formation of the cream "skin" that often appears on top, use a wire whisk or an immersion blender. Serve the hot beverage in a deep narrow mug or cup so as to retain the heat and spoon whipped cream on top if desired. You can also add marshmallows or steep spices in the mix. Coffee-chocolate combinations are found in Brazilian Chocolate, 36, Kai, 37, Flying Mocha Monkey, 40, and Cocomoka, 42.

HOT COCOA

4 servings

The proportions suggested here will produce a cocoa richer in flavor but far less sweet than you will get from most commercial mixes. Skim or low-fat milk can be substituted for whole milk, as can half-and-half.

Stir together in a medium heavy saucepan:

$^1/_4$ cup unsweetened cocoa powder

4 to 6 teaspoons sugar

Vigorously stir in, first by tablespoons and then in a slow, steady stream:

3 cups milk

Heat over medium heat, stirring constantly and scraping the bottom of the pan, just until bubbles appear around the sides. Remove from the heat and stir in:

($^1/_2$ teaspoon vanilla or 2 teaspoons Kahlúa or Grand Marnier)

Top each serving with:

Ground nutmeg or cinnamon

Whipped cream or marshmallows

COCOA SYRUP

1 cup

This syrup is quick and easy to prepare, and its flavor far exceeds anything you can buy. It can be used to make hot and cold cocoa drinks alike.

Whisk together in a medium saucepan:

1 cup unsweetened cocoa powder

$^3/_4$ cup sugar

Add and stir to combine:

$^1/_2$ cup cold water

($^1/_2$ cup malted milk powder)

Bring just to a boil over medium heat, stirring constantly. Reduce heat to low and simmer 3 to 5 minutes. Remove from heat and let cool. Store it covered at room temperature several days, or refrigerate 2 to 3 weeks. To liquefy refrigerated syrup, heat on the stove or in the microwave.

QUICK HOT COCOA

For each 8-ounce cup of cocoa, use **2 tablespoons Cocoa Syrup, above.** Slowly stir in $^3/_4$ **cup milk** and **(2 tablespoons heavy cream).** Heat thoroughly, without boiling.

GANACHE FOR HOT CHOCOLATE

Enough for 6 servings

Ganache is a rich chocolate-cream icing or filling. Here we use it to make an extraordinary beverage, sweeter than hot cocoa. Top with whipped cream or marshmallows. Bring to a rolling boil in a medium heavy saucepan:

1 cup light or heavy cream

Immediately remove from the heat, and whisk in until smooth:

8 ounces bittersweet or semisweet chocolate, finely chopped

Strain the mixture through a fine-mesh sieve, pushing it through with a rubber spatula. Let cool, then refrigerate in a covered jar for up to 10 days.

QUICK HOT CHOCOLATE

1 serving

I. Stir together in a small saucepan or microwave bowl:

$^1/_4$ cup Ganache for Hot Chocolate, above

$^1/_4$ cup milk, water, or coffee

Heat over low heat, or in a microwave on high for 30 to 45 seconds, until warm but not boiling. Stir in:

($^1/_8$ teaspoon vanilla, or $^1/_2$ teaspoon Kahlúa or Grand Marnier)

Top with:

Ground nutmeg or cinnamon

II. Bring just to a boil in a small saucepan or microwave bowl:

$^1/_2$ cup half-and-half

Remove from heat, and whisk in until melted:

1 ounce semisweet or bittersweet chocolate, finely chopped

SPICED HOT COCOA

4 servings

In a medium, heavy saucepan stir together:

6 tablespoons unsweetened cocoa

6 tablespoons sugar

Vigorously stir in, first by tablespoons and then in a slow, steady stream:

3 cups milk

Heat over medium heat, stirring constantly and scraping the bottom of the pan, just until bubbles appear around the sides. Remove from the heat and stir in:

2 cinnamon sticks, crushed

6 whole cloves, crushed

1$^1/_2$-inch piece fresh ginger, peeled and sliced

Let stand, covered, for 30 minutes. Strain and top each serving with:

(Whipped cream)

SPICED HOT CHOCOLATE

1 serving

Prepare **Quick Hot Chocolate I or II, above,** omitting vanilla, liqueur, and nutmeg. Stir in spices for **Spiced Hot Cocoa, above.** Let stand, covered, for 30 minutes. Strain the chocolate into a saucepan and bring it back to a rolling boil. Top each serving with **(Whipped Cream, 973).**

BRAZILIAN CHOCOLATE

4 servings

Melt in a medium saucepan over very low heat:

1 ounce semisweet or bittersweet chocolate, chopped

$^1/_4$ cup sugar

$^1/_8$ teaspoon salt

Stir in:

1 cup boiling water

Heat on very low heat 3 to 5 minutes, and do not allow to boil. Add:

$^1/_2$ cup milk

$^1/_2$ cup hot cream

1$^1/_2$ cups hot strong coffee

Beat well with a whisk, and add:

1 teaspoon vanilla

Pinch of cinnamon

KAI
1 serving

This rich and delicious drink was a longtime staple of the British Royal Navy, meant to keep men on night duty nourished as well as wide awake. For those of us with more modest agendas, our version is a superb sustainer on a cold winter's day. For best results, use double-strength coffee or espresso, 31.

Place in a large mug and heat in the microwave for 30 seconds on high:

>   1/4 **cup half-and-half or heavy cream**

Meanwhile, mix together in a small bowl:

>   1 **tablespoon sugar**
>   2 **tablespoons malted milk powder**
>   1 **teaspoon unsweetened cocoa powder**

Remove the cream from the microwave and add the cocoa mixture, stirring constantly for about 30 seconds, until the cocoa and sugar are dissolved. Add, stirring well:

>   3/4 **cup hot strong coffee**

ICED CHOCOLATE
1 to 4 servings with Quick Hot Chocolate,
4 servings with Brazilian Chocolate

Prepare, then chill:

>   **Quick Hot Chocolate I or II, 37, or**
>   **Brazilian Chocolate, 36**

Serve over crushed ice. Top with:

>   **Whipped cream or coffee ice cream**

Garnish with:

>   **Grated sweet chocolate**

EGG CREAM
1 serving

A soda-fountain classic.

Combine in a blender or stir vigorously until foamy:

>   1 **cup very cold milk**
>   2 **tablespoons Cocoa Syrup, 36**

Pour into a tall glass and stir in:

>   1/3 **cup seltzer water**

ABOUT JUICES AND FRUIT BEVERAGES

The recipes that follow are designed mainly to whet the appetite, are excellent nonalcoholic additions to any party, and are good served before a meal. They fall into three styles: simple combinations that can in most cases be made using store-bought juices, though superior results will be had if freshly squeezed and pressed juices are used; combinations of fruits and vegetables that can be processed in a blender or juicers, with or without ice; and cooked fruit and vegetable juices.

For coaxing the juice from citrus fruit, there are electric or manual reamers or lever-type crushers. We recommend one that is large enough to handle grapefruit as well as oranges. Don't forget frozen concentrates, especially for strong-flavored, quick-chilling beverages.

Fresh herb, vegetable, and fruit **garnishes,** 55, do more than merely spruce up the appearance of a beverage. They can enhance its flavor and texture as well. Also important to the taste of a beverage is ice, 55.

Heighten the charm of cold drinks and beverages with **decorative** or **flavored ice cubes.** Fill an ice cube tray with water. Place one of the following in each section: a maraschino cherry, strawberry slice, square of lemon rind or pineapple, or small sprig of mint or thyme. Ordinary fruit juices also offer possibilities for enhancing beverages. Used sparingly, frozen cubes of orange juice, pineapple juice, lemonade, or limeade make flavorful additions to many drinks and punches.

To make a **Decorative Ice Mold** for punch, see 65.

TOMATO JUICE
4 servings

I. If using fresh tomatoes, combine in a large saucepan and simmer 30 minutes:

>   12 **medium ripe tomatoes, chopped**
>   2 **ribs celery with leaves, chopped**
>   1 **slice onion**
>   3 **sprigs parsley**
>   1/2 **bay leaf**
>   1/2 **cup water**

Strain into a pitcher. Season with:

>   1 **teaspoon salt**
>   1/4 **teaspoon paprika**
>   1/4 **teaspoon sugar**

Serve thoroughly chilled.

II. If using canned or bottled tomato juice, this juice can be served hot or chilled. Curry powder, a few cloves, a cinnamon stick or sprigs of tarragon, parsley, or some other herb may be steeped in the cocktail and then strained out before it is served.

Combine in a pitcher:

>   2 1/2 **cups tomato juice**
>   1 1/2 **tablespoons lemon juice**
>   1 **teaspoon grated celery**
>   1/2 **teaspoon grated onion**
>   1/2 **teaspoon grated horseradish**
>   3/4 **teaspoon salt**
>   1/4 **teaspoon sugar**
>   1/8 **teaspoon paprika**
>   **A dash of Worcestershire or hot pepper sauce**

ORANGE-TOMATO JUICE
4 servings

This mix is equally good with lemon or lime juice.

Combine in a small pitcher:

>   1 1/3 **cups tomato juice**
>   1 **cup orange juice**
>   1 **teaspoon sugar**
>   1 **tablespoon lemon or lime juice**
>   1/2 **teaspoon salt**
>   1/2 **cup crushed ice**

Serve chilled or over ice.

ORANGE-LIME JUICE

4 servings

Combine in a small pitcher:

2 cups orange juice

1 tablespoon lime juice or 2 tablespoons lemon juice

$^1/_8$ teaspoon salt

Serve chilled or over ice.

BROTH ON THE ROCKS

A salty-sweet refresher with a beautiful tangerine color. Be sure the broth is not too rich in gelatin, or it may congeal. For each serving combine equal quantities of:

Chicken broth or Beef Consommé

Tomato Juice, 37

Orange juice

Pour over ice cubes and add:

A squeeze of lemon juice

FRUIT JUICE COMBINATIONS

Good combinations are equal parts of:

Orange juice and pineapple juice

White grape juice and orange juice

Cranberry juice and lime juice, sweetened if desired, pineapple, or grapefruit juice

CITRUS JUICE MEDLEY

2 to 3 servings

Combine in a pitcher:

$^3/_4$ cup grapefruit juice

$^1/_4$ cup lemon juice

$^1/_2$ cup orange juice

$^1/_4$ cup sugar or Sugar Syrup, 43

Serve chilled or over ice, garnished with:

Sprigs of mint

PINEAPPLE-GRAPEFRUIT JUICE

4 servings

Prepare **Sugar Syrup, 43,** using:

$^1/_3$ cup sugar

$^1/_3$ cup water

Stir in:

$1^1/_4$ cups grapefruit juice

$^2/_3$ cup pineapple juice

$^1/_4$ cup lemon juice

Serve chilled or over ice.

RASPBERRY OR BLACKBERRY SHRUB

$2^2/_3$ cups syrup; enough for 8 to 12 shrubs

Shrubs are usually made with raspberries or blackberries gently accented with vinegar.

Prepare, using raspberries or blackberries:

Berry Syrup, 43

Stir into the syrup while still hot:

$^1/_3$ cup distilled white vinegar, or Red Raspberry Vinegar Cockaigne, 1025, or more to taste

Chill syrup. For each serving, pour into a 10- to 12-ounce glass filled with cracked or shaved ice:

$^1/_4$ to $^1/_3$ cup cold syrup, above

$^1/_4$ to $^1/_3$ cup water or half water and half vodka or rum

Stir well. Garnish with:

(Sprigs of mint)

CRANBERRY JUICE

4 to 6 servings

Combine in a medium saucepan and cook over medium heat until skins pop, about 5 minutes:

One 12-ounce bag cranberries

3 cups water

Strain through cheesecloth, into a medium saucepan, squeezing to extract all the juice from the berries. Bring to a boil and add:

$^1/_3$ to $^1/_2$ cup sugar

(6 whole cloves)

Cook for 2 minutes. Cool, and remove cloves, if using. Add:

$^1/_4$ cup orange juice or 1 tablespoon fresh lemon juice

Chill thoroughly. Garnish with:

Slices of lime

HOT CRANBERRY JUICE

4 servings

Heat well in a medium saucepan, but do not boil:

1 quart cranberry juice

1 lemon, thinly sliced

A few whole cloves

(A few star anise)

(Honey to taste)

Strain. Serve in mugs, garnished with:

Cinnamon sticks

MULLED CIDER

4 servings

Great on a frosty night.

Heat well, but do not boil:

1 quart apple cider

10 to 12 whole cloves or 4 to 5 crushed cardamom pods

1 cinnamon stick

Strain and serve in mugs.

ABOUT BLENDED JUICES

Pineapple, melon, berries, mango, and papaya, and carrots, beets, fennel, and parsley can be turned into nourishing, delicious beverages by processing in a blender or electric juice extractor. The only trouble in making these is that the enthusiast often gets drunk with power and whirls up more and more weird and intricate combinations, some of them quite undrinkable. Resist the temptation to become a sorcerer's apprentice.

Electric juice extractors, also called juicers, are capable of turning virtually any fruit or vegetable into juice. Those with a large feed tube are the most convenient. Juicers yield more juice than blenders, and with tastier results. Blenders work fine if you don't have a juicer, but with either appliance, always follow manufacturer's directions.

To make rich vegetable juices, process vegetables in the blender or juicer. If the juice seems too thick, dilute it with a little cold water. Sometimes a gray color results. If so, stir in lemon juice a little at a time. Serve immediately after adding the lemon juice, as the clear color may not last long. In general, fresh fruit juices don't keep well, so plan on drinking them within a day or so. We recommend that you serve chilled or poured over ice.

BEET-CARROT-GRAPE JUICE

2 to 4 servings

Process the following in a juice extractor:

5 small beets (about 1 pound), trimmed and washed
2 cups seedless black or red grapes
1 large carrot, peeled

TOMATO-CELERY-CARROT COOLER

2 to 4 servings

Process the following in a juice extractor:

2 large celery ribs
2 medium tomatoes, cored and quartered
2 large carrots, peeled

CELERY-APPLE-WATERMELON SPLASH

2 to 4 servings

Process the following in a juice extractor:

2 large celery ribs
2 medium apples
2 cups cubed seeded watermelon

PINEAPPLE JUICE

2 to 4 servings

Peel and core, 234:

1 pineapple

Cut into cubes. Process in a blender or juicer. Strain and serve with:

Sprigs of mint

ORANGE-MELON JUICE

2 to 4 servings

Combine in a blender or juicer until smooth:

$1^1/2$ cups seeded orange pulp
1 cup cubed melon, such as cantaloupe or honeydew
2 tablespoons lemon juice
$1/8$ teaspoon salt

PINEAPPLE-CUCUMBER COCKTAIL

2 to 4 servings

Combine in a blender until smooth:

1 cup unsweetened pineapple juice
1 cup diced ($1/2$-inch) peeled, seeded cucumber

$1/2$ cup watercress sprigs
2 sprigs parsley

TROPICAL JUICE

2 to 4 servings

Combine in a blender until smooth:

$1^1/2$ cups unsweetened pineapple juice
1 ripe banana
2 teaspoons honey
Juice of $1/2$ lime

Garnish with:

(Sprigs of mint)

FRUIT SODAS

Fruit "nectars," which are often more concentrated than fruit juices, are delicious served this way.

For each serving, pour over ice:

$1/2$ cup club soda or seltzer water
$1/2$ cup lemonade, limeade, orange, pineapple, cranberry, guava, apricot, or other juice or nectar
2 to 3 tablespoons any flavored Sugar Syrup, 43

ABOUT ICE CREAM DRINKS AND SMOOTHIES

Ice cream drinks are a favorite in our house, and most likely why we have altered our smoothie recipes to include yogurt, cream, milk, and soy milk as well as ice cream. However, a smoothie is truly a nondairy shake made with fruit and thickened with ice, bananas, or frozen fruits.

ICE CREAM SODA

1 serving

There are many possible combinations of fruit syrups and ice cream flavors. Lime or lemon syrup with vanilla ice cream is a classic.

Mix well in a tall glass:

2 tablespoons Fruit Syrup, 43, or Cocoa Syrup, 36

Add:

Dash of club soda
1 scoop vanilla ice cream

Fill the glass with:

Club soda

ICE CREAM FLOAT

1 serving

Add to a glass:

1 scoop or more vanilla ice cream

Fill the glass with:

Root beer, cola, or other soft drink

MILK SHAKE

2 servings

Process in a blender until smooth and frothy:

2 cups any flavor ice cream
2 cups milk
($1/4$ cup Cocoa Syrup, 36)

FRUIT MILK SHAKE
2 servings
Process in a blender until smooth:
    1 cup vanilla ice cream
    1 cup milk
    2 cups sliced ripe bananas, peeled peaches, or
        strawberries

FLYING MOCHA MONKEY
2 servings
Process in a blender until smooth:
    1 cup ice cubes
    ³/₄ cup milk or half-and-half
    ¹/₂ cup cooled double-strength coffee
    1 ripe medium banana
    1 tablespoon Cocoa Syrup, 36
    1 tablespoon sugar

STRAWBERRY SMOOTHIE
2 servings
Process in a blender until smooth:
    2 cups vanilla frozen yogurt or ice cream
    2 cups sliced strawberries
    (1 tablespoon honey)

TROPICAL SMOOTHIE
2 to 4 servings
Process in a blender until smooth:
    1 cup vanilla ice cream or frozen yogurt
    1 cup canned unsweetened coconut milk
        (stirred before measuring)
    1 cup diced pineapple or canned tropical fruit salad
    1 cup ice cubes
    1 ripe medium banana

CHOCOLATE CHERRY SMOOTHIE
2 servings
Process in a blender until smooth:
    1¹/₄ cups milk or half-and-half
    1 cup pitted sweet dark cherries
    1 cup ice cubes
    3 tablespoons Cocoa Syrup, 36

PAPAYA COCONUT SMOOTHIE
2 servings
Process in a blender until smooth:
    1 cup half-and-half
    1 cup canned unsweetened coconut milk
    (1 large egg white)
    1 ripe papaya, peeled, seeded, and chopped
    1 tablespoon Sugar Syrup, 43

PAPAYA-MANGO BATIDO
4 to 5 servings
Process in a blender until smooth:
    1 cup papaya nectar
    1 cup diced mango

    1¹/₂ cups milk
    1 cup crushed ice
    3 tablespoons lime juice
    ¹/₄ cup sugar

MANGO LASSI
2 servings
A popular yogurt drink in India.
Process in a blender until the ice is partially crushed:
    2 cups plain yogurt
    1 ripe mango, peeled, pitted, and chopped
    2 tablespoons sugar
    10 ice cubes
Pour with ice, into chilled mugs or glasses. Garnish with:
    Thin curls of mango peel

FRUIT KEFIR
4 to 6 servings
Kefir is a close relative of yogurt sold in liquid form.
Process in a blender until smooth:
    1 cup kefir, 1013
    1 cup milk
    2 to 2¹/₂ cups chopped ripe strawberries or peeled
        peaches, apricots, or mangoes
Refrigerate for about 24 hours. Stir before serving.

BREAKFAST SMOOTHIE
2 servings
Process in a blender until smooth:
    1 cup ice cubes
    ¹/₂ cup each raspberries and blueberries or 1 cup any
        diced soft ripe fruit
    ¹/₂ cup milk
    ¹/₄ cup vanilla yogurt
    ¹/₄ cup Granola, 353
    1 tablespoon sugar

ABOUT PARTY BEVERAGES
Most of the following recipes, unless otherwise indicated, will ➤ yield quantities to serve approximately 20 people. For best results, chill all ingredients before mixing. ➤ To make a Decorative Ice Mold for punch, see 65.

OLD-FASHIONED LEMONADE OR LIMEADE
8 servings
Orange, pineapple, raspberry, white grape juice, or other fruit juices may be combined with lemonade or limeade. Chilled tea added to these fruit juice combinations— about ¹/₃ cup for every cup of juice—gives these lemon-ades an invigorating lift. Frozen lemonade and limeade concentrates, diluted a little less than prescribed by the manufacturer, are quite acceptable.
Boil for 2 minutes:
    8 cups water
    1¹/₂ to 2 cups sugar

Refrigerate until cold, then stir in:

1 cup lemon or lime juice

Pour over ice cubes in tall glasses or into a pitcher of ice.

HERBED LEMONADE OR LIMEADE

8 servings

I. Prepare **Old-Fashioned Lemonade or Limeade, 40,** placing in the pan with the water and sugar one of the following: **2 to 3 sprigs rosemary,** or **a small bunch of mint or thyme,** or **a 6-inch piece of fresh ginger, thinly sliced.** Refrigerate until cold, then strain before combining with the citrus juice.

II. For a slightly sweeter version, for each serving, combine: **1 cup Old-Fashioned Lemonade or Limeade, 40,** and **2 tablespoons Herb Syrup, 43.** Or, to flavor a whole batch at once, add **1 cup plus 2 tablespoons Herb Syrup.**

PINK LEMONADE

For each serving, combine **1 cup Old-Fashioned Lemonade or Limeade, 40,** and **1 teaspoon grenadine.** Or, to color a whole batch at once, add **3 tablespoons grenadine.**

QUICK LEMONADE OR LIMEADE

1 serving

Flavored sugar syrups can be made in only a few minutes, store very well, and allow for speedy production of refreshing drinks. If making more than one serving at a time, combine liquids in a pitcher and pour over ice.

I. **$^1/_2$ cup water or club soda**
    2 tablespoons Lemon or Lime Syrup, 43

II. **$^1/_2$ cup water or club soda**
    (2 tablespoons orange, pineapple, white grape, or cranberry juice)
    1 tablespoon Lemon or Lime Syrup, 43

III. **$^1/_2$ cup water or club soda**
    1 tablespoon Lemon or Lime Syrup, 43
    1 tablespoon Herb Syrup, 43, or Berry Syrup, 43

POMEGRANATE SUNBURST PUNCH

15 servings

Prepare **Sugar Syrup, 43,** using:

1 cup sugar

1 cup water

Let cool, then transfer to a punch bowl and stir in:

1 liter club soda

4 cups ice water

24 ounces pomegranate juice

1$^1/_4$ cups lime juice

$^3/_4$ cup orange juice

Pour over ice in punch cups.

WATERMELON PUNCH

1 gallon

Prepare **Sugar Syrup, 43,** using:

1 cup sugar

1 cup water

Let cool. Seed and cut into cubes:

4 pounds watermelon

You should have 5 to 6 cups. Puree in a blender with the sugar syrup, in batches, then strain through a medium sieve into a punch bowl. Stir in:

1 liter club soda

1$^1/_4$ cups lemon juice

Just before serving, stir in:

1 quart strawberries, hulled and sliced

1 liter ginger ale

Serve over ice in tall glasses.

CRANBERRY-MANGO PUNCH

20 servings

Combine in a large punch bowl:

64 ounces raspberry-cranberry juice

1 quart mango nectar

1 liter club soda

One 750-ml bottle sparkling apple cider

Float on top:

Lime slices

(Decorative Ice Mold, 65, with raspberries and diced mango)

LEMONADE FOR 100 PEOPLE

Prepare **Sugar Syrup, 43,** using:

8 cups sugar

4 cups water

Chill the syrup. Add:

7$^1/_2$ cups lemon juice

Stir in:

16 quarts pineapple juice or six to eight 6-ounce cans frozen pineapple juice concentrate plus 4 gallons water

Add:

8 sliced seeded oranges

Chill. Serve over ice.

PINEAPPLE PUNCH

20 servings

Combine in a large bowl and stir well:

2 cups cooled strong tea

2 cups orange juice

$^3/_4$ cup lemon juice

2 tablespoons lime juice

1 cup sugar

Leaves from 12 sprigs mint

Refrigerate for 2 hours. Shortly before serving, strain the punch and add:

10 slices fresh pineapple or one 20-ounce can sliced pineapple, including juice

2$^1/_2$ liters ginger ale

2 liters club soda

Pour over large chunks of ice in a punch bowl.

FRUIT PUNCH

20 servings

Prepare **Sugar Syrup, 43,** using:

1¼ **cups sugar**

1¼ **cups water**

Add:

2½ **cups strong hot tea**

Cool, then add:

2½ **cups noncitrus juice, such as cherry, white grape, or strawberry**

1 **cup crushed pineapple**

1 **cup lemon juice**

2 **cups orange juice**

Add sufficient water to make 4 quarts of liquid. Chill for 1 hour. Immediately before serving, then add:

1 **liter club soda**

Pour over ice in a punch bowl.

FRUIT PUNCH FOR 50 PEOPLE

Prepare **Sugar Syrup, 43,** using:

2½ **cups sugar**

1¼ **cups water**

Reserve ½ cup syrup. Add to the remainder and stir well:

2 **cups orange juice**

2 **cups Fruit Syrup, 43**

2 **cups white grape juice, grapefruit juice, pineapple juice, or crushed pineapple**

1 **cup strong tea**

1 **cup lemon juice**

(1 **cup maraschino cherries with their juice**)

Cover and let stand 30 minutes or more to cool. Add enough ice water to make about 1½ gallons. At the last minute, add:

1 **liter club soda**

If you find the punch lacking in sweetness, add part or all of the reserved sugar syrup.

STRAWBERRY FRUIT PUNCH

15 servings

Prepare **Sugar Syrup, 43,** using:

3 **cups sugar**

3 **cups water**

Cool. Combine:

2 **quarts strawberries, sliced**

1 **liter club soda**

1 **cup sliced fresh or canned pineapple**

1 **cup mixed juice—pineapple, apricot, raspberry, etc.**

Juice of 5 large oranges

Juice of 5 large lemons

Add 2 cups of the sugar syrup, or to taste. Chill until cold. Transfer to a punch bowl. Float on top:

(**Sliced kiwi**)

GALA TOMATO PUNCH

20 servings

For a summer brunch in a shady corner of the patio. Combine:

4 **quarts Tomato Juice, 37**

4 **cups canned beef consommé**

Season with:

½ **cup lemon or lime juice, or to taste**

(**Slivered herb leaves or chiffonade, 989, of herbs**)

Chill and pour into a punch bowl that has been rubbed, with:

(**A garlic clove**)

Adorn with:

Decorative Ice Mold, 65, with mixed herbs

COCOMOKA HOT

18 servings

Like Irish coffee with a cocoa flavor, this warming concoction is perfect for a winter party since it can be made in a large pot and kept on the stove or in a slow cooker. Prepare, then combine in a pot:

9 **cups coffee, using 3 tablespoons coffee to each**

1 **cup water**

9 **cups Hot Cocoa, 35**

Bring to just under the boiling point. Remove from the heat and add:

1 **cup crème de cacao, warmed**

¾ **cup rum, warmed**

(¼ **cup honey**)

¼ **cup ground cinnamon or 2 tablespoons ground cardamom**

2 **tablespoons almond extract**

Stir. Sweeten to taste. Pour into hot mugs. Top with:

Whipped cream

Grated or ground nutmeg or grated sweet chocolate

COCOMOKA COLD

15 servings

Prepare, then chill well:

7 **cups coffee**

Whip until stiff:

2 **cups heavy cream**

If desired, whip an additional:

½ **cup heavy cream**

Reserve, chilled, to garnish the tops. Have ready:

2 **quarts chocolate ice cream, softened**

Pour the chilled coffee into a large chilled bowl. Add the whipped cream and half the ice cream. Beat until the ice cream is partly melted. Add:

¼ **cup rum or 1 teaspoon almond extract**

¼ **teaspoon salt**

Fold in the remainder of the ice cream. Pour into tall glasses. Garnish the tops with the reserved cream, if using. Sprinkle with:

Grated or ground nutmeg or grated sweet chocolate

ABOUT SUGAR SYRUP

A simple sugar syrup is a useful ingredient when sweetening cold beverages such as Iced Tea, 34, and Old-Fashioned Lemonade or Limeade, 40. Sugar syrup infused with fruits, herbs, or spices adds not only sweetness but flavor as well. Add flavored syrups to club soda and garnish with fresh fruit or herbs. Substituting flavored syrup for plain sugar syrup in a beverage adds more intense flavor and complexity. A wide assortment of flavored syrups can be easily made at home. All syrups should be stored in glass or plastic containers. Plain sugar syrup can be refrigerated for up to 6 months.

SUGAR SYRUP

2 cups

Combine in a saucepan:

>   2 cups sugar
>   1 cup water

Cook over low heat, stirring occasionally, until sugar is dissolved. Simmer, covered, for 5 minutes. Let cool, then chill until needed.

BERRY SYRUP

About 2 1/2 cups

Proceed as for **Sugar Syrup, above.** Once the sugar has dissolved, stir in **1 pint raspberries, blackberries, or blueberries, rinsed and stemmed if necessary, or 3 cups sliced strawberries.** Simmer, covered, for 10 minutes, stirring occasionally. Let cool. Strain through a fine-mesh strainer, pressing to extract the syrup. Discard fruit. Chill until needed.

FRUIT SYRUP

About 2 1/2 cups

Proceed as for **Sugar Syrup, above.** Once the sugar has dissolved, stir in **2 cups sliced or cubed peaches, plums, or pineapple.** Simmer, covered, for 10 minutes. Let cool. Strain and chill until needed.

LEMON OR LIME SYRUP

About 3 cups

Proceed as for **Sugar Syrup, above,** adding to the pan with the water and sugar **peel of 2 lemons or limes, cut into thin strips.** Once cool, add **1 cup lemon or lime juice.** Strain, and chill until needed.

HERB SYRUP

About 2 cups

I. Proceed as for **Sugar Syrup, above.** Once the sugar has dissolved, stir in **1 small bunch of lavender, rosemary, or lemon verbena.** Simmer, covered, for 10 minutes. Let cool. Strain and chill until needed.

II. Prepare **Sugar Syrup, above.** Remove the hot syrup from the heat and add **1 bunch mint or 3/4 cup mint leaves.** Cover and let stand 10 to 20 minutes. Strain and let cool. Chill until needed.

SPICED SYRUP

About 2 cups

Prepare **Sugar Syrup, above.** Remove the hot syrup from the heat and stir in one of the following: **1 1/2 teaspoons whole cloves, 4 cinnamon sticks, 6 star anise, or one 3-inch piece fresh ginger, thinly sliced.** Cover and let stand 20 to 30 minutes. Strain and let cool. Chill until needed.

ABOUT SOFT DRINKS

As a postscript, we'd like to offer a few words of caution regarding "soft drinks." Not the least of our concerns is the hard fact that synthetic fruit and cola drinks make up a disturbingly large part of most adults' and children's intake. The regular bottled or canned soft drinks are often a blend of caffeine, sugar, high-fructose corn syrup, flavoring, preservatives, and water. They are caloric unless made with a sugar substitute—and both incarnations are utterly devoid of nutritional value.

As to canned, bottled, or boxed "fruit drinks," the government has seen fit to identify several juice drink categories, ranging from those in which genuine fruit juice predominates to those that are entirely or almost entirely artificial. Close attention to the food labels is urgently recommended; see 7. Our suggestion is to make a practice of offering children unsweetened fruit juice in very small quantities—cut by as much as half with water—and soft drinks and sugar-sweetened juices only on occasion.

WINE AND BEER

ABOUT WINE

America is now the most sophisticated marketplace for a wider variety of the world's wines than any other country. The choices have been further broadened in the last few decades by the skill of American winemakers, who have combined ambition, science, and our temperate climate to produce a new generation of even better wines. Best of all, while beginning to take wine for granted, Americans have also democratized it, brushing away snobbery, arcane rules, and mythology.

Wine is simply fermented grape juice. Whether wine making is considered to be artful science, scientific art, or merely a sublime form of food processing, it's fairly basic: Grapes are crushed, the juice ferments, and its sugar is converted into alcohol, resulting in wine. It is, to a great extent, a natural beverage. The color of wine comes from the grape skins. White or pink wine (such as blanc de noir or rosé Champagne, Tavel or Bandol rosé from the South of France, rosados from northern Spain, and "white" Zinfandel from California) can be made from red grapes if the juice is separated from the skins soon after the grapes are crushed. Modern technology simply improves on old methods. While a hundred years ago, the winemaker would open the doors to the wine cellar and let in the cold night air of autumn to cool the wooden barrels, today wine is often made in stainless steel tanks that are cooled electronically in order to create maximum flavor.

These days, technology, good sanitation, and scientific progress generally ensure that wine is better made than ever before. The factors that affect quality are soil, the grapes, and the climate, and how they're managed—which is where the variables come in. As so often, people

are the wild cards. An ambitious winemaker can now produce good Chardonnay in Virginia, where Thomas Jefferson's vineyard was one of his few failures two hundred years ago; a brave winemaker in Lebanon has been making fine wine for several decades on the edge of a battlefield. Well-traveled winemakers use their air miles to share information face-to-face on an unprecedented scale. Others think of wine as a commodity and produce millions of gallons that all taste pretty much the same, and sell them at an inexpensive price. Few other products in the world encompass such a spread. The main thing is that most wine today is clean, sound, and palatable, and its sheer diversity means that somewhere in the world there's a wine for everyone who wants one.

Most of the world's wine regions now use the American system of identifying a wine. Known as "varietal labeling," it calls the wine by the name of the principal grape variety it's made from rather than naming it after the place where it was made. Exceptions are some parts of France, Italy, Spain, and Portugal, where regions such as Bordeaux, Burgundy, Chianti, Rioja, and Dão rely on hundreds of years of cultivation, history, and tradition for their identities.

In return, winemakers in the United States, Chile, Argentina, Australia, New Zealand, South Africa, and other places have adopted some European ideas and nomenclature. "Estate bottled" means wine made from grapevines owned by and close to the winery. "Reserve" usually refers to special small batches of wine kept separate and aged longer than the regular bottlings. Geographical designations, from broad areas such as "Northern California" or "Central Coast" down through smaller areas like the Napa Valley, and even on down to the specific vineyard, are also clues to a wine's identity. From country to country, the terms vary. They may be informal and relatively elastic, or legally required and quite definite, but one thing is certain: They may indicate quality, but they don't guarantee it. The name of the winery, and its style and standards, come closest to that ideal.

Some external aspects of the package matter, some don't. Vintage dates simply tell you when the grapes were picked and the wine made, not necessarily whether it's any good. A basic rule of thumb is, the more expensive it is, the more likely the weather was at its best during the vintage. A beguiling fancy label is of no importance. A screw cap or composite cork, seen increasingly, may seem plebeian, but it's actually a good example of efficiency in the service of flavor. Around the world, too many wines have been spoiled by infected corks, which give them a moldy stink, and so winemakers have turned to the more technically sophisticated aluminum-alloy screw caps to keep their wines clean and fresh. Twisting one off may take away a bit of the glamour of a popping cork, but it increases the odds of getting a decent wine.

Enjoying wine is a matter of taste, and taste it you should. Whatever your questions about wine, the answers are on the tip of your tongue. Many colleges and universities offer evening wine appreciation courses, and most cities usually have a wine society offering lectures, wine tastings, and wine-themed dinners. Informal opportunities for comparisons abound: Walk-around tastings are increasingly popular, often as fund-raisers. Another opportunity can come when organizing a large party—select two or three different wines of the same type for you and your guests to compare informally. If, for example, you've settled on Chardonnay as your favorite white wine, take whatever opportunity arises to taste various types from different places—there will surely be several you like within your budget. If you want to go further, find a professional mentor: Almost every state in America now has at least a few wineries that welcome visitors and offer educational tours and tastings. Other help may be just around the corner, at your local wine shop—discuss your preferences and budget, follow through, and you could be quietly launched on a delicious adventure.

Before you set off, it's worth taking a moment to deal with wine talk, which isn't quite the same as ordinary talk, and can even sound silly. Wine experts use professional shorthand in an attempt to describe their impressions. Fruit references are common, often making a wine sound more like salad than a beverage. Personifications can creep in (one wine may be "muscular," another "voluptuous," and so on). It's mainly an attempt to capture something elusive. Wine's job is to be enjoyable, and no one is an impartial judge of pleasure. At any rate, wine experts often disagree, sounding much like Lewis Carroll's Humpty Dumpty: "When I use a word, it means just what I choose it to mean. . . ." There's no more embarrassment in not knowing, or disagreeing with, a wine term than there is in not knowing that a Mozart quartet is in D major or whether Joe DiMaggio's record for hits in successive baseball games still stands. No one knows everything. A few simple ideas and key words are enough to aid memory and enjoyment.

Acidity: Various acids (citric, tartaric, malic) occur in grapes and wine. Balanced acidity makes a wine refreshing and crisp. Too much, and it tastes sour or harsh. Too little, and it's known as *flabby*—limp and dull.

Aftertaste: It may be harsh, mouth-puckering, or nearly nonexistent in a low-acid or characterless wine. Ideally, though, it should be refreshing, and linger.

Alcohol: Boldly flavored wines, such as Zinfandels, can balance a high amount of alcohol (13 to 14 percent). If wines, like whites and light reds, taste too strong and have a harsh aftertaste, the alcohol content is out of whack.

Body: The density, weight, and fullness of a wine in your mouth, coming from the alcohol and the components of the dissolved grape pulp, make the wine feel heavy or light as you drink.

Dry: Grapes contain fructose and glucose. These sugars are turned into alcohol by fermentation, which can be stopped while there is still sweetness in the wine (ranging from predominant to a hint) or go on to total dryness.

Fruit: The aroma and flavor of the grapes used, depending on their grape variety, can have hints of other fruits, such as apples, peaches, apricots, berries, or even tropical fruits—just a hint, but that helps to define each wine and adds to the complexity of its flavor. Many Chardonnays, matured in oak barrels, also acquire an additional aspect of butterscotch aroma and flavor from the wood. Opinion is divided over whether or not this is a virtue.

Oxidation: If overexposed to air, or cold, a wine's virtues fade. White wines darken and taste and smell like bruised fruit or old apples; reds taste stale, flat, and dried out.

Tannin: This occurs naturally in the seeds and skins of fruit, as a preservative, and has an astringent, mouth-puckering quality, most apparent in some young red wines. Tannins smooth out with aging.

Texture: This comes from tannins, which help determine whether wine feels smooth or rough going down.

Vintage: This is simply the year the grapes were harvested. Vintage wine isn't necessarily high quality. Most Champagne, for example, is a blend of different vintages, and better for it.

WINE AND FOOD

These days, for more and more Americans, wine is the alcoholic beverage of choice for most occasions, but the broadest use of wine is still with meals—it's no accident that most are known as table wines. Following is a rundown on the most popular types of wine, organized primarily by color—white, then red, and then several unique types—and grape variety or geographical identity and listed in descending order of popularity within their category. Also included are some thoughts on their flavors and the ways in which wine made from the same grapes may vary in different countries, as well as a few suggestions on their best matches with food. As always, though, your own taste is the final arbiter.

Deciding which wine to drink with which food is not as complicated a matter as it's sometimes made out to be. Certainly it matters, just as deciding which seasonings go best with different food matters. The simple and very pleasant truth is that there are usually several wines that go well with almost any dish. What is important is that their flavors complement each other, that the wine enhances the food in the same way that salt or pepper or oregano or a squeeze of lemon may. The most important thing to keep in mind is that complementary aspect: ➤ A thick chunk of medium-rare steak grilled over charcoal, for example, pairs best with a full-bodied red with pronounced flavor, ➤ while a quickly sautéed filet of white-fish matches well with a dry medium-bodied white wine for the same reason we squeeze a wedge of lemon onto the fish: acidity, which sharpens the delicate flavor of the fish. ➤ Hot and spicy food often goes best with refreshing, fruity, and rather simple red wines and rosés, which lighten the intensity of the heat. Balance is the key, and there is ample room to maneuver.

For information on cooking with wine, see 1027.

WHITE WINES

Most often, that "glass of white" handed across a bar, served at a party, or lubricating a convivial dinner is **Chardonnay,** the most popular wine in America and the most prevalent white wine in much of the rest of the world. Originally from the Burgundy region of France, it has been transplanted to so many different countries that it easily qualifies as one of the most successful agricultural immigrants in history.

Several generations later, its character has adapted to its circumstances. It's exalted, even considered noble, in the famed vineyards of Burgundy and some high-rent districts of California, Washington, and Australia. Only a short step down, there is a wide middleweight range of firmly reliable, dry, and full-flavored Chardonnays pouring forth from well-defined cool areas of America and Australia and small pockets of Chile, Italy, and South Africa. After that come medium-bodied, fairly good to barely average, straightforward wines from a lot of other less-favored, usually warmer, places around the world. More serviceable than subtle, these wines are deservedly inexpensive.

The usual descriptions of the flavor of the best of Chardonnays involve comparisons with the crisp similarities of apples and peaches, often with hints of mild honey, and light touches of vanilla or butterscotch, acquired during aging in oak barrels. When all these elements are in balance, they provide Chardonnay with an array of subtle but definite flavors that results in a delicious complexity all the way through to its aftertaste. At this level, these are wines for special occasions and ➤ rich food: lobster or any other shellfish cooked or dipped in butter; grilled scallops; roast fish such as sea bass, halibut, or Dover sole; salmon prepared almost any way; roast pork or veal with an abundance of herbs; and bouillabaisse and other rich fish stews.

Downward from that exalted station, budget and the occasion determine the best partners. Mid-priced Chardonnays from broad geographic areas such as Sonoma County in California, Columbia Valley in Washington, or Mâcon-Villages in southern Burgundy are also ➤ good wines for shellfish and full-flavored fish like flounder, bluefish, and tuna; barbecued chicken; and grilled pork chops. And they have enough body and acidity to stand up to Caesar salad and ceviche. Bargain versions of Chardonnay tend to be serviceable wines for fairly simple preparations of poultry and fish, and they do well on mixed-food occasions such as buffets, where they generally harmonize moderately well with a range of flavors.

More distinctive is **Sauvignon Blanc.** Its strikingly spicy, penetrating aromas and flavor are at once musky and tart. When it's balanced, Sauvignon Blanc is very crisp, refreshing, and lively, with a scent of fresh-cut grass and a clear zing of acidity. In New Zealand, the Loire Valley of France, and northeastern Italy, it is a highly distinctive and vibrant wine, while the extra sunshine of California and Washington (where it is also known as **Fumé Blanc**) mellow it out somewhat. Balanced Sauvignon Blanc is ➤ a fine partner for food cooked with herbs, such as fish with dill or oregano or chicken with sage or thyme. It also makes a good fit with chiles, lemongrass, ginger, garlic, and cilantro, so it's often a perfect match for Thai, Indian, and Mexican dishes.

Riesling is much misunderstood, thanks mainly to the Germans, who made it into a great wine while never explaining it very well to the rest of the world. Some of the problem is the sheer unfamiliarity of the language, making the wine labels a puzzle. But the biggest obstacles are built in. As a light table wine with a hint of sweetness, it's unfashionable in an age of dry wines, and the fact that the grape is often made into intensely sweet dessert-style wines creates further confusion among consumers. At its best, relatively dry German Riesling is ➤ terrific with lobster salad, cold cracked crab, chicken salad, cold meats, or on its own as a low-alcohol refresher. Much more clearcut, and more fashionable, are the bold Rieslings of Australia and New Zealand, which are made in a bone-dry style, with lemon-lime tartness and an assertive zing of alcohol. ➤ These are perfect wines for the spice and savor of Chinese, Thai, and Mexican fish dishes or stir-fries, grilled shellfish, and barbecued pork.

Pinot Grigio is not generally considered much of a match for most meals, but when it's good, it's quite pleasant as a drink—relatively low in acid, medium-bodied, and quite dry, with an appealing hint of fresh apricots in its aroma and flavor. It has become the fastest-growing white wine in America, and it almost immediately also became a victim of that success, with an ocean of uninteresting wines, mass-produced in California's hot San Joaquin Valley and in central Italy, pouring in to supply the demand. The first-rate exceptions are a handful of wines from the northeastern corner of Italy, the areas of Friuli and Alto Adige. And wines from the same grape made in the Alsace region of France and in Oregon, known as **Pinot Gris,** can provide more consistent pleasure, on their own or as ➤ good companions to light hot or cold fish dishes: salmon mousse, fish cakes, or gravlax, and pasta with pesto or cheese-based sauces.

Soave, made from a blend of native Italian grapes grown on the rolling hillsides near Verona, crisp and lightly lemony, was once Italy's most popular white wine, lauded as the perfect match for fish. As with Pinot Grigio, though, popularity led to expanded production and some instances of lowered standards, but Soaves labeled "Classico" possess an appealing citrus aroma and refreshing, tart flavor, ➤ a fine all-rounder for fish.

Albariño is considered to be Spain's best white wine, full-bodied and distinctively flavored, with a strong hint of peaches in its aroma and a crisp bite of acidity in every sip, quite refreshing and ➤ a good partner for Cajun-style seafood, spicy Mexican-style fish dishes like snapper with green peppers and onion, or shrimp in piquant salsa verde. It's also wonderful with dishes flavored with spicy sausages such as chorizo or linguiça, with combinations of seafood and spicy meat such as paella, or even with pepperoni pizza.

Many of the rest of the world's most popular white wines tend to be pleasant but light-bodied and one-dimensional, merely thirst quenchers or for casual drinking. They're usually inexpensive and worth sampling and comparing; constant experimentation and improvement in vineyards and wineries mean you're liable to encounter above-average wines from time to time. A few other white wines offer more, and are very much worth trying. **Gewürztraminer,** from the Alsace region of France, is immediately recognizable by its pronounced aroma, which combines scents of mixed spices and roses with a flavor likened precisely to lychees; indeed, ➤ the wine is often recommended with Chinese or Thai food because of this spiciness. Wines from the **Viognier** grape, originally from France's Rhône Valley but now widely planted in southern France, and turning up in California and Australia as well, are also prized for distinctive aromas and flavors (apricots, peaches, and mixed wildflowers is the usual characterization). **Semillon** from Washington or Australia has a subtle flavor comparable to figs or melons that, combined with a full-bodied aspect, ➤ makes it a utility wine, good company for a variety of foods.

RED WINES

Red wines tend to be heavier and bolder, their flavors boosted by higher percentages of alcohol and a prolonged soaking of crushed skins, pulp, and seeds with the wine as it ferments and gains color and character. Red wines are also usually the top wines of any given country, often requiring at least a few years of age to mellow into their most pleasant form. The grape skins, which provide the wines' color, also provide tannins—compounds that feel and taste dry and astringent (often compared to the mouth-puckering feel of strong tea or the sensation of chewing the skin of an apple or plum); too much tannin can make a wine seem harsh or overly dry. Tannin softens with age, however, eventually contributing a bracing firmness to a mature wine. In the case of wines that sell in several price categories, such as Merlot and Cabernet Sauvignon, the tannin is often much softer in the inexpensive versions, due to less precise techniques in the vineyard and winemaking—the wines are made quickly to sell quickly. A few comparative tastings are worthwhile.

For most people, the king of the hill is **Cabernet Sauvignon.** Like some mythical monster, its name doesn't even have to be pronounced in order to invoke its awesome powers: Just mention first growth Château Lafite or Château Margaux and a few other magical icons, Cabernets one and all, and you're immediately on the top shelf of international wine.

Cabernet Sauvignon is a very tannic wine to begin with, and most of the words used to describe it are almost disparaging—professionals refer to it as "hard," "angular," "austere," and other similarly charmless terms. In its original home, Bordeaux, and most other places, it tends to be blended with small amounts of other grapes (especially Merlot) to add aroma, spice, or fruitiness. Even then, when young, the wine can be somewhat rough, with mere hints of concentrated blackberry fruitiness in the flavor, astringent tannin, and vaguely herbal aromas. Cabernet may initially seem to be quite an unpromising wine, but after five years or so, it begins to soften, and the fruitiness comes to the fore. Over another five years, and often more, it mellows further and reveals even more nuances of flavor, as well as a smooth, persistent aftertaste. Tasting an older Cabernet, you suddenly realize what the fuss is about.

The top-ranked Bordeaux still set the standard, but they have become closely challenged by quite a few California wineries, who are in turn pursued by an increasing number of winemakers in Washington and Australia, with a few outriders from Italy. The high price tags on these wines clearly announce their status. Below the top tier, Cabernets range from merely expensive to everyday wines, and they come from many places: Bordeaux, California, Washington, Australia, and Chile generally offer the most consistently well-made wines. Good-value possibilities abound up and down this ladder, so explore at your most comfortable price level.

Generally, Cabernet Sauvignon is a wine that only comes into its own with food, when its firm, bracing quality creates a taste-for-taste counterpoint. ➤ The best food partners are assertive in terms of flavor and texture: roast lamb or grilled lamb chops, char-grilled steak, filet mignon, calf's liver with bacon and onions, venison, squab, and any red meat with a rich, reduced sauce.

Merlot is the other red wine of Bordeaux, also a fine wine, though mellower from the start, and also blended there, usually with a little Cabernet Sauvignon, to create some complexity. Its relative smoothness means that Merlot tends to be more ready to drink at an earlier age, which has led to its increasing popularity around the world in bargain versions, whose flavors are usually not complex. In the Pomerol and St.-Emilion regions of France, parts of Washington State, and the Napa and Sonoma Valleys in California, Merlot can be a smooth and lively fine wine, ➤ a splendid partner for roast lamb or duck, grilled steak, lamb or beef stew, and braised meat in reduced sauces. Chile weighs in just below this level with some decent good-value versions. Farther down the wine-and-food chain, Merlot's relatively low acidity makes it a good all-rounder for a wide range of meat prepared in different ways.

Zinfandel (the original, deep red wine, not to be confused with the pale version known as "white Zinfandel") was long known as "California's mystery grape," because no one knew where it had originated. Now the mystery has been solved by DNA analysis—it's descended from a southern Italian variety known as **Primitivo.** It has been a very successful transplant indeed, and its character has evolved enough in its new home for it to be considered California's own. Zinfandel tends to be robust in every way. It's bursting with ripe blackberry jam flavor, vibrantly acidic, and fairly high in alcohol, with a bracing jolt of astringent tannin. A well-made Zinfandel will be superb five years after the vintage date and can easily age for at least ten years; a decent bargain version will provide a lot of pleasure today. Its boldness and fruitiness makes Zinfandel ➤ a good match for hearty food such as roast pork with gravy or rich sauce, osso buco, and slow-braised lamb shanks, as well as pasta with spicy sausages, tomato-based chicken fricassees, and even first-rate cheeseburgers. Primitivo, incidentally, is an interesting wine in its own right, and making a comeback thanks to modern wine-making techniques; it's a more rustic wine, less polished than Zinfandel, but fine with hearty Italian home cooking.

For many winemakers and connoisseurs, **Pinot Noir** is the ultimate wine. If the Holy Grail were ever found, Pinot Noir would be the wine they'd drink from it. Originally from Burgundy in France, it has been celebrated for nearly a thousand years. A large part of its appeal comes from sheer sensual pleasure. Good Pinot Noir is smooth and relatively light (among the rapturous comparisons it evokes, "silky" is usually high on the list) but with a persistent, lingering flavor, a unique combination of delicacy and power often characterized as an iron fist in a velvet glove. It smells and tastes of violets and black cherries and musk, slightly earthy and tangy, and it stands alone among all other red wines, distinctive and different.

Technology, research, and ambition have ensured that good Pinot Noir can be made in various places around the world, but there aren't many. Burgundy is still the apex by a wide margin; California and Oregon have created a strong second rank with slightly more voluptuous wines, while New Zealand has a racy and slightly leaner style. Among these, there are no bargain versions, but there are plenty of good values.

The smooth texture and persistent yet delicate flavor of Pinot Noir accounts for one of its most enduring, ➤ classic food pairings: with rare roast beef. Dark-meat poultry is another favorite, especially duck and quail, while its lightness makes it a good red for turkey. The slightly gamy quality in the aroma and touch of earthiness in the flavor make it a good partner with dishes featuring mushrooms, such as a risotto or beef with morel sauce. Best of all is beef stew, as in *boeuf à la bourguignonne,* which is traditionally both made and served with Pinot Noir.

Syrah comes from the steep, terraced hillsides above the long reach of the Rhône River, which cuts through France from the Swiss Alps down to the Mediterranean Sea near Marseille. Its wines have been famous since the Middle Ages. In the early nineteenth century, Syrah was transplanted to Australia and became that continent's most esteemed and popular red wine, renamed **Shiraz.** The wines had a reputation as weighty and dark, but then in the last decades of the twentieth century, California, Washington, South Africa, and even Italy started producing lighter, more vibrant versions. Now even the old-timers back in France have lightened up a bit. Syrah is noted for a slightly peppery aftertaste, which makes it ➤ a splendid partner for grilled meat, pepper steak, venison, and roast leg of lamb.

Syrah is also a blending partner with other red grapes in the warmer southern part of the Rhône Valley. It's officially known in France as an "improving variety" and is included to firm up softer, more voluptuous wines, resulting in smooth, rich, and refreshing blends. **Syrah blends** have spread around the world. Some bottlings are expensive, some not, but most are good value anyway—the pricey versions are able to age well and tend to be more refined. The most famous from France are Châteauneuf-du-Pape and Gigondas, while Côte-du-Rhône Villages are the everyday renditions. In Australia, the mix of varieties is stated on the front label; in California and Washington, the wines often go under fanciful names, with clues to their style or the names of the grapes (Syrah, Grenache, and Mourvèdre) on the back label. ➤ They go nicely with a lot of different foods: grilled tuna, roast duck, barbecued pork or chicken, cioppino and other garlicky stews, cassoulet, duck curry, bacon cheeseburgers, and lasagna.

Barolo and **Barbaresco** are Italy's best red wines, bearing up for more than a century under the cliché of "the king of wines, the wine of kings." The hype isn't far off the mark. Only wines made in northwestern Italy from the Nebbiolo grape and grown in the best vineyards, on steep, vertigo-inducing hillsides, are entitled to these world-famous names. The wines are full-bodied but also complex, with aromas likened to violets, tar, and roses and flavors often cited as plum, cherry, and earthiness. These are wines for special occasions, ➤ best with flavorful preparations of beef such as pot roast or beef in a red-wine braise and oxtail stew, as well as osso buco and roast lamb. A step down from this exalted level, in price and complexity, yet still worthy, are Nebbiolo d'Alba and Nebbiolo delle Langhe.

Italy's best-known wine, on the other hand, has had a bumpy ride in the last century. **Chianti** is an ancient wine from Tuscany, an intriguing blend of Sangiovese and a few minor grapes. Chianti had become much less interesting by the mid-twentieth century, when its popularity curdled into excessive commercialization and careless winemaking. After thoughtful modernization of vineyards and wineries, though, a comeback finally took wing in the 1990s, and the wines of the heartland, known as Chianti "Classico," are again considered some of Italy's best. They're medium-bodied and firmly dry, with a light bite of cherry-like fruitiness and a tangy aftertaste. Like Tuscan food, they're known for a kind of rustic elegance, ➤ good with light meats without sauces such as roast loin of veal or rabbit; grilled chops; casseroled chicken, guinea hen, quail, and chicken livers.

Rioja, Spain's leading red wine, has enough unique aspects to set it apart from other notable wines of the world. It's a blend of grapes: Tempranillo provides smoothness and fruitiness and a lovely aroma of violets, Grenache gives it firmness, and a mixture of a few ancient varieties provides a touch of complexity. It's matured in barrels made of American oak, which gives it a pleasant hint of vanilla. Most important, it's often aged deep in the winery's own underground cellars until it's mature (many other reds are sold when two to three years old, for cash-flow reasons, with consumers expected to age them further at home); Rioja reserva isn't sold until it's at least four years old, and gran reserva, made only in very good vintage years, only goes on sale when it's six. Riojas tend to be smooth and mellow, ➤ a fine match with lamb; dark-meat birds like pheasant, squab, and duck; beef with caramelized onions; and Southern-style barbecued beef and pork.

Beaujolais isn't on everybody's list of notable wines, but it should be—the world needs more wines that are delicious, uncomplicated, and refreshing. From the region just south of Burgundy in France, it's made from the Gamay grape, with a flavor and texture that may remind you of thick jam. The most worthwhile, in terms of dependable flavors, are in two categories: Wines labeled Beaujolais-Villages tend to be light, informal, straightforwardly grapey and not terribly acidic, meant to be drunk within a year or two after the vintage date, good for picnics, brunches, or just drinking. The more serious versions carry the names of specific villages on the labels: Fleurie, Moulin-à-Vent, Morgon, Chiroubles, St.-Amour, Juliénas, Chénas, Côte de Brouilly, and Brouilly. "Serious" is a relative term here—these are appealing wines with fresh aromas, persistent fruity flavors, and just enough concentration to make ➤ a good match with rustic food like baked ham, shepherd's pie, or meat loaf. They are also smoothly attuned to hot, spicy dishes like Szechuan beef or Thai curries. Both styles are best lightly chilled, for about 30 to 45 minutes in the refrigerator.

The rest of the world's most popular reds offer a wide array of flavors and aromas. In fact, some of these wines are distinctive enough to break through into being fashionable at any time. Certainly that's begun to happen for **Barbera,** formerly an ordinary workhorse grape in Italy that's been groomed and reinvented as a would-be fine wine. It's still quite robust and tangy, ➤ a good match for any meat-and-tomato dish, sausages or chicken livers with herbs and onions, or mushroom-laden pizza. Italy gives us even more of what the rest of the wine-making world seems determined to leave behind, which is wines that are light, refreshing and, though simple, quite delicious: **Dol-**

cetto, **Valpolicella, Negroamaro,** and **Nero d'Avola,** for example. They're dry and go well with Mediterranean food. Another notable oddity is **Malbec,** undistinguished in its native France, but with a lively blackberry character in Argentina, where it's the leading red. Malbec is very good with beef.

ROSÉS

Pink wines, known often as rosés, made everywhere there are red grapes, are usually not really significant wines, but still worth consideration. Drawn off before the wine acquires color from the red grape skins while fermenting, they provide something to drink in the summer after the vintage, while people wait for the red wines to mellow. In general, wines labeled with a varietal name, such as Zinfandel rosé or Cabernet Sauvignon rosé, are liable to be drier and at least echo the flavor of the parent grape. They and the classic blended French versions from the southern Rhône area, such as Tavel and Bandol, also dry and often somewhat substantial, are ➤ excellent with barbecued spareribs or baked ham, as well as with Mexican and Indian food.

The best-known pink wine in America is, of course, **White Zinfandel,** California's own cheap and cheerful, somewhat sweet, quaffing wine, denigrated by many connoisseurs but selling millions of gallons every year anyway. Its success has spawned several other "white" wines from red grapes in the same style.

SPARKLING WINES

Sparkling wines are versatile, setting off celebrations, creating occasions, bracketing meals. Good **Champagne** is made mostly from the finest grape varieties, such as Chardonnay and Pinot Noir, and has considerable character and nuance under those cheerful bubbles. The types seen most often are **Brut,** usually a dry blend of those two grapes and some other members of the Pinot family; **Blanc de Noirs,** white wine from red Pinots, which has a coppery tinge; **Blanc de Blancs,** made from Chardonnay alone; and **Rosé,** a pretty pink style either made from red grapes or from white grapes with a little red wine added.

Real Champagne comes from France and is strictly regulated; California champagne doesn't and isn't, though some of those from Anderson Valley in Mendocino, the Carneros district of Napa and Sonoma, Russian River in Sonoma, and the hills between Napa and Sonoma are often quite good. On the label, look for the phrase "fermented in *this* bottle," which tells you that it was made by the classic Champagne method of individual bottling. Check the back label to see if it mentions Chardonnay or Pinot Noir varieties. Ask a good wine merchant for recommendations, and be prepared to pay a premium. Cheap "Champagnes" are never a bargain—every corner cut shows up in the glass, disagreeably.

Champagne is crisp, tart, and bracing. Its acidity cuts through salty or smoked flavors well, which is why ➤ it works with caviar and smoked salmon. It's excellent with most of the components of brunch and buffets, such as omelets, soufflés, corned beef hash, chicken hash, smoked sturgeon and other whitefish, and deep-fried shrimp or calamari. It's wonderful with Cantonese or Szechuan chicken and fish dishes, and a revelation with sushi, where the succession of small dishes can become a string of perfect matches, appetizing and appealing.

Other notable sparkling wines are Italy's light, lovely, and barely sweet **Prosecco,** a refreshing sipping wine and fine aperitif, and the sweet and faintly musky **Asti Spumante,** a popular after-dinner or dessert wine.

APPETIZER WINES

Once upon an indulgent time, Americans could, and did, choose from a wide array of wines designed to begin and end a meal, generally known as appetizer and dessert wines. They still exist, but they've steeply declined in our calorie- and alcohol-conscious culture. The best-known wine for openers is dry **sherry,** known as *fino* or *manzanilla* in Spain, a white wine prematurely matured by deliberate exposure to air and fortified with a bit of extra alcohol. The final result is bone-dry and assertive, with a slightly nutty flavor, ➤ best enjoyed the Spanish way, with snacks like salami, chorizo, or linguiça; stuffed or marinated mushrooms; stir-fried or grilled shrimp; or olives, almonds, and cashew nuts. **Sake,** the rice wine of Japan (now also produced in California), has evolved into a lighter drink that can be chilled (though traditionally served warm); it has many of the same flavor attributes as dry sherry.

DESSERT WINES

Every wine-producing country in the world makes sweet wines, sometimes against long odds and with great ingenuity: Grapes are left on the vine till they shrivel into moldy raisins, dried and semi-dried in barns, or even baked, and then made into intensely sweet wines. Other versions are only slightly fermented and then fixed in place with a jolt of brandy. Some have low alcohol, as little as 5 or 6 percent; some weigh in at a domineering 18 to 20 percent. Some are meant to accompany dessert, while some replace it—more a matter these days of personal preference than anything else.

Some basic limitations in matching wine and desserts are determined by temperature—frozen desserts dull the palate and crowd out other flavors—and texture—creamy puddings and soft custards can coat your tongue and block other flavors. Acidity, as in fruit salads, can throw off the flavor of a sweet wine. ➤ One good rule of thumb is to choose a dessert that's slightly less sweet than the wine. ➤ Another is not to pair two spectacular divas—a great wine should match a simple dessert, and vice versa; let one be the soloist, the other the accompanist.

Wine and salads are a whole different issue. Wine isn't usually recommended with salad, but if it's unavoidable, as in a buffet or a lunch featuring chilled seasonal seafood—crab salad say, or lobster—the usual advice is to ➤ make a salad dressing without vinegar, substituting lemon juice, which doesn't clash with the wine.

Among the wide array of sweeter wines, **Port** is still the most popular, a large family of robust and quite sweet wines of different intensity from Portugal, fortified with brandy, capable of aging for a long time, and made in ruby-red and tawny versions. ➤ Reds go well with bittersweet chocolate, either plain or in cakes or tarts, and blue cheese with walnuts, and are sensational with mince pie. ➤ Lighter and mellow, the amber tawnies are good with strong cheese and winners with pumpkin pie.

The rarest and most expensive of all dessert wines is **Sauternes,** the golden, richly sweet wine of southern Bordeaux in France, tasting of honey and apricots. It's the best-known example of the "late-harvested" wines, which are made from grapes left on the vines long after all other grapes have been picked, well into late autumn, when a beneficial mold known, ironically, as "noble rot" shrivels them into sweet raisins. Some sweet and very fine German **Rieslings** and Hungarian **Tokay** are also made this way. ➤ Simple fruit cakes and tarts are good partners. The ultimate late-harvest wines come from Canada, Michigan, and New York: **Ice wine** (or **Eiswein**) is made from several different varieties of grapes left on the vine until they freeze in early winter. When the ice is removed, the remaining grape juice is concentrated nectar, and it ferments into a wine that tastes much like exotic marmalade, or liquid fruitcake—unique, delicious, and ➤ dessert all by itself.

FRUIT AND OTHER GRAPE WINES

There is another category of wine, not in the mainstream but not to be overlooked: American wine made from nontraditional grapes or from other fruit. All fifty states now have wineries, and the assortment of offerings is astonishing. There are wines made from native American varieties such as Concord and Muscadine or Scuppernong, as well as from hybrid varieties such as Baco Noir, Seyval Blanc, and several others. There are also cranberry wines, blueberry wines, apple and peach wines, and as many more as there are types of fruit. Some are sweet, some dry. All are worth consideration, part of the fascinating diversity of the beverage.

WINE AND TEMPERATURE

Temperature has a lot to do with enjoying wine. Room temperature (an average of about 70°F) is too warm to bring out the maximum flavor of any wine. A good rule of thumb is to chill a little. Among reds, some Rhônes, Burgundies, Pinot Noirs from countries other than France, and light Zinfandels benefit from a slight coolness that increases their liveliness. Light red wines such as Beaujolais and Valpolicella taste fresher when well chilled. Rosés, which exist to refresh, need coldness to do the job, as do most still and sparkling white wines and sweet dessert wines; the one exception among whites is the relatively full-flavored Chardonnay, which should only be well chilled.

Here's a handy guide to the chill factor in refrigerators: ➤ The temperature of wine in a 750-milliliter bottle drops at a rate of between five to ten degrees an hour in a standard 41°F refrigerator (obviously, the cooler the wine is to begin with, the quicker the drop). If a wine goes in at 70°F, it will decline to 65°F in 30 minutes (slight coolness), 59°F in an hour (well chilled), 53°F in 90 minutes (cold).

Using the freezer isn't recommended. It isn't really much quicker, and you may forget the wine, which can freeze and crack the bottle, leaving you with a mess of wine slush. ➤ A safer and more efficient method is to put the bottle in a bucket filled with a mixture of half ice and half water. The combination chills the wine more quickly than ice alone, from room temperature to cold in 30 to 40 minutes. When entertaining, ➤ a good idea is to put the first white you'll be serving in an ice bucket and the second in the refrigerator, to give it a head start on cooling down, so that it will require very little time in the ice bucket after you've served the first.

WINE AND CHEESE

The long-standing partnership of wine and cheese is a natural—both are born of similar fermentations and often have similar types of acidity. More important, both offer endless variations of compatible flavors, creating a match-making game that everybody can win.

With all the possibilities, it's fair to wonder about which wine with which cheese, but it's really an opportunity rather than a problem. The conventional wisdom for pre-meal serving or as a snack has been ➤ young, fairly bland cheese with middle-of-the-road white wine, and in terms of flavors and the occasion, it makes sense. Consider light and fairly dry German, Washington, or California Rieslings; good-quality Pinot Gris or Pinot Grigio from anywhere; or Pinot Blanc from Alsace or Friuli in Italy.

After dinner, many people bring out strong red wines to combine with fine cheese and create a grand finale. The usual suspects are ➤ port and Stilton with Amarone and Gorgonzola, very old Rioja with Manchego, and Bordeaux with aged Cheddar or Gouda. Red wines are not terribly flexible with cheese, however, because their tannin can sometimes taste bitter with pungent or salty cheeses. Many sweet wines offer wider-ranging and more elegant possibilities, from the classic of Sauternes with Roquefort to late-harvest Rieslings with creamy Muenster, Taleggio, or ripe Brie. ➤ Fortified wines such as Marsala, Muscat de Beaunes de Venise, and aged tawny port are lovely with aged Parmesan and pecorino. Any of these combinations end a meal on a gracious note.

ABOUT BEER AND ALE

Beer may be the world's oldest alcoholic beverage, having been made for more than six thousand years. As it has flowed through such a long history, and in modern times been filtered through multiple layers of advertising, marketing, and urban legends, this commonplace beverage has accumulated quite a bit of lore, mythology, and firmly held beliefs. Is canned better than bottled? (Heads or tails?) Is draft better than bottled or canned? (Perhaps—in a clean, well-run bar, it will almost surely be fresher, and freshness counts.) Should the glass be chilled? (No, chilling diminishes flavor.) Beer or ale should be clear, not hazy. (Not necessarily: it may be unfiltered, or overchilled, when it acquires "chill haze," which goes away after a while.) What seems to be a simple quaff is actually fairly complicated in many ways.

Beer is fermented from grain, traditionally barley, but also occasionally wheat; in mass-market beer making, fairly neutral rice or corn is often added to the barley, producing a lighter, milder drink. The methods of handling the grains—a sequence of soaking, toasting, soaking again, draining, brewing, seasoning, and fermenting—involve hundreds of subtle variations among different brewers and are as important as the ingredients, which, importantly, include the water.

Anyone who has ever grown bean sprouts knows about germination, which is the first step in making beer. The grain is turned into malt by soaking it in water until it begins to sprout and then drying with hot air, most often lightly, but sometimes to a browned toastiness, which results in the darker color and fuller body and flavor of dark beers or stout and porter. The malt is then ground and combined with hops (resinous flower buds that add distinctive character, flavor, aroma, and stability) in hot water and boiled—it is a process that's much like making tea. The rather sweet, dense liquid that results is filtered and cooled, yeasts are added to start fermentation, and the brew is finally under way.

Although there are almost two dozen principal styles of beer, one predominates by a very wide margin. Most brews around the world are **lager**-style beer, familiar and fairly similar everywhere. The word "lager" refers to the ancient German practice of fermenting and storing beer in cold mountain caves, a technique that spread, with the advent of refrigeration, to other European countries and then to America in the mid-nineteenth century—where some confusion was created by the fact that lager beers were often marketed as Pilsener, Munich, or Dortmunder, in an attempt to borrow a degree of authenticity. That, and standardization, worked well enough: By the end of the last century, the United States had become the world's largest producer of beer, which flowed almost entirely from a few large brewers, each making more than the entire output of several European nations. The beers they produced, in the lager style, were all much the same, mass-produced by long, slow, cool fermentation, an easily controlled process that gives a consistent clean, soft, relatively mild flavor. Minor variations on this style are American dark beers, which may have a slightly richer but softer flavor, and **malt liquor,** higher in alcohol but without much distinctive taste.

Alternatively, some beers are so different and so unique in their distinctive flavors that they're off in a different category altogether—notably **ale, stout,** and **porter**. They begin with much the same ingredients, though the barley will be toasted darker for stout and porter (and sometimes ale), and they are created in somewhat similar fashion. Where they differ is when they come to life at fermentation. Instead of the well-mannered, somewhat restrained cool fermentations of lager beers, these brews are fermented briskly and briefly at high temperatures, which makes the fermenting yeasts and carbon dioxide bubbles float to the surface (this is why they are smoother and less bubbly than lager beer—the gas has dissipated). The process is known as top-fermentation, and it generally creates a fuller body and more complex, pronounced flavors, and even some fruitiness, one reason these are served at warmer temperatures than lager. Some experts even equate the differences between the two types of brews with the differences between red and white wine.

Top-fermentation led to the creation of a broad diversity of styles and flavors. Many, though, were too distinctive or offbeat to achieve large-scale popular success, and such beers nearly disappeared until they were revived by small independent, and enthusiastic, American craft brewers, whose microbreweries and brewpubs were created in the 1980s as a backlash against standardized taste. The best example of this sort of salvaging is porter, the nearly black brew that fueled the working class during England's Industrial Revolution, now back from the brink of extinction. British ales, either the dark, full style known as **brown ale** or the lighter versions known as **bitter** that are invariably the subject of jokes by Americans encountering them in British pubs ("This beer's warm and flat!"), are also the models for many American brewmasters. Belgium and Germany produce **wheat beers** flavored with fruit and sometimes herbs; northern France sends forth very strong ales that are meant to be aged, like fine wine. **Pale ale,** also sometimes called India Pale Ale, is an odd British specialty that became an American favorite in the nineteenth century and has managed to hang on to a shred of popularity. Heavily infused with hops, it is famous for a defiantly weedy, herbal aroma and taste. Part of the problem of ale's lack of mass popularity may be its quirky individuality, but that is surely also a large part of its appeal to adventurous palates. Every variation among this complicated family has its champions, and comparisons are basically unhelpful, given the multiplicity of differences. As with wine, the best idea is to taste and taste again.

Also as with wine, beers and ales have a definite place at the table with food. And they neatly fill a gap by matching up with some notoriously difficult foods that wine can't easily bridge. ➤ Smoked or salt-cured meats such as corned beef, pastrami, and ham, as well as a variety of sausages, spiced or mild, make a good fit with lager beer

and light and dark ale. ➤ Dark brown stout and oysters is a classic combination, but a platter of mussels steamed in wine with plenty of garlic and parsley snuggles up to stout well too. ➤ The British "plowman's lunch" of several kinds of strong cheese, bread, pickles or relish, and salad is a natural partner to dark beer or ale. ➤ Hot and spicy Mexican food, especially Tex-Mex specialties such as flautas, tacos, and chimichangas, as well as chili con carne and soups such as posole, may be the best match of all with first-rate lager beer.

In America, most beer and ale is served too cold to bring out its maximum flavor. The average refrigerator is set at about 40° to 41°F, which is just right for food safety and preservation, but ➤ the generally recommended serving temperature for lager beer is higher, merely well chilled, about 45°F. Premium beers, often labeled "export," and dark beers are more flavorful at a lightly chilled level, about 48°F. Stout, porter, and British bitter ales are best at what is known as "cellar temperature," about 54° to 55°F. Rather than invest in a fancy thermometer, it's more practical to simply ➤ remove beer or ale from the refrigerator 10 to 20 minutes before serving it.

Beer stein, Pilsner glass, ale glass, beer mug

WINE AND BEER COCKTAILS

Wine and beer drinks, made by combining wine and beer with mixers, can be refreshing as well as festive, which makes them ideal for parties. Note here that sparkling wine is called for in recipes where one might otherwise expect to see Champagne. A number of excellent Champagne-style sparkling wines are produced both here and abroad, including Spanish cavas and California and New York sparkling wines, and they can be better values than similarly priced Champagnes. As with cocktails made from other liquors, you do not need to use a bottle of the highest quality. However, ➤ you should select a wine or beer good enough to drink on its own.

KIR

1 serving

Canon Félix Kir was the mayor of the city of Dijon, in the Burgundy region of France, and a hero of the Resistance

Red wine glass, brandy snifter, white wine glass, all-purpose wineglass, champagne flute

during World War II. His favorite drink was then called *vin blanc cassis,* based on Aligoté, the everyday white wine of the region, and another local product, black currant liqueur. Locals renamed the beverage in his honor. Today Kir is most often made with Chardonnay. A **Kir Royale** replaces the white wine with Champagne.
Combine in a large wineglass and stir:

> **6 ounces chilled Chardonnay**
> **Dash of crème de cassis**

MIMOSA
1 serving
Our **Half Moon Pomosa** replaces the orange juice with pomegranate juice.
Pour into a chilled Champagne flute or wineglass:

> **2 ounces orange juice**

Fill the glass with:

> **Chilled sparkling wine**

BLACK VELVET
1 serving
Pour into a chilled Champagne flute or wineglass:

> **3 ounces chilled stout**

Fill the glass with:

> **Chilled sparkling wine**

CHAMPAGNE COCKTAIL
1 serving
I. Pour into a large Champagne flute:

> **$^1/_2$ teaspoon Sugar Syrup, 43**
> **$^3/_4$ ounce chilled brandy**

Fill glass almost to the top with:

> **Chilled sparkling wine**

Add:

> **2 dashes yellow Chartreuse**
> **2 dashes orange bitters**

II. Place in a champagne flute:

> **1 small sugar cube**

Drop onto the sugar cube:

> **1 or 2 drops Angostura bitters**

Fill the glass with:

> **Chilled dry sparkling wine**

WHITE WINE SPRITZER
1 serving
Combine over 1 or 2 ice cubes in a wine- or highball glass:

> **6 ounces chilled Riesling or other semidry white wine**
> **4 ounces club soda**

BELLINI
1 serving
Process in a blender until smooth:

> **$^1/_2$ ripe peach, peeled and pitted**

Push the pulp through a sieve to extract the juice. Pour the juice into a champagne flute, then fill with:

> **Chilled Prosecco or other sparkling wine**

SHANDY
1 serving
Combine in a large beer glass:

> **12 ounces lager**
> **4 ounces lemon-lime soda, ginger ale, or ginger beer**

Serve with:

> **A lime wedge**

COCKTAILS AND PARTY DRINKS

The preceding chapter on beverages has to do with nonalcoholic drinks. This one takes up the subject of liquor, from cocktails served before dinner to what may be offered late in the evening, and concludes with a selection of party drinks. Because when to serve what drinks is as important as any other aspect of menu building, and because to many the intricacies of mixing drinks are either debatable or a mystery, this section is explicit and detailed.

ABOUT COCKTAILS AND OTHER BEFORE-DINNER DRINKS

The cocktail is almost certainly an American invention, and it is undeniably in the American spirit of improvisation. Whatever mixtures you put together—and part of the fascination of cocktail making is the degree of inventiveness it seems to encourage—hold fast to a few general principles. ➤ The most important of these is to keep the quantity of the basic ingredients—gin, whiskey, rum, etc.—no more than about 60% of the total drink, never below half.

Cocktails often rely on intricate formulas designed to balance elements in an agreeable way. Adding too much vodka to a Bloody Mary is as misguided as putting too much salt in a stew. ➤ Remember, as a corollary, that cocktails are before-meal drinks. For this reason, they should be neither oversweet nor overloaded with cream, to avoid spoiling the appetite instead of stimulating it.

Illustrated here are some of the tools included in basic bar equipment: A **zester** and a **channel knife**, both designed to remove only the colored part of citrus rind for garnishing drinks; two of the many corkscrew styles available are the **Lever-style corkscrew** and the **waiter's corkscrew;** a **muddler** for smashing herbs or soft fruits, often

together with sugar; a **two-sided jigger,** typically with the standard $1\frac{1}{2}$-ounce jigger on one side and a 1-ounce pony on the other; and a **strainer.** Not illustrated here is a **blender,** indispensable for preparing frozen drinks. Your bar should also include a **citrus reamer,** 37, **cocktail shaker, ice bucket and tongs, bartender's glass** with a long spoon for stirring drinks, and a sharp paring knife.

In addition to various liquors, it is advisable for the home bartender to have on hand Sugar Syrup, 43, as well as a stock of bitters, club soda, tonic water, bitter lemon, ginger ale, cola, and fruit and tomato juice, along with lemons, oranges, limes, olives, cherries, sugar, and coarse salt. For garnishes, see 55. See Appetizers and Hors d'Oeuvres, 69, for suitable accompaniments for cocktails—and a steady head.

A stock of basic glasses of varying sizes and designs is useful for the home bartender, and sipping drinks from the right glasses adds to your guests' enjoyment. Shown left to right are: a **cocktail** or **martini glass,** which holds 5 to 7 ounces and has a long stem flaring into a bowl, bucket, or saucer shape; an **old-fashioned glass,** holding about 6 ounces; a **highball glass,** generally holding 8 to 12 ounces; and a **collins glass,** which holds 14 to 16 ounces.

Narrow **Champagne glasses** with either **curving (tulip)** or **flared sides (flute)** preserve the bubbles in drinks made with sparkling wine, releasing them slowly. **Silver** or **pewter cups** holding 10 to 12 ounces are highly favored by some for such drinks as mint juleps. Some people dislike drinks served in metal, but if straws are used, no metallic taste is noticeable. Some **punch glasses** or **cups,** 3 to 4 ounces, are frequently made of porcelain, an advantage when serving mulled or flaming drinks. Other useful specialty glasses are **margarita glasses,** which have broad rims designed to hold lots of salt, and 15-ounce **hurricane glasses,** which are ideal for serving piña coladas and other festive drinks served blended or over ice.

When making drinks, it helps to understand a few key terms. **Proof** simply designates alcoholic content: A 100-proof liquor has 50 percent alcohol, 200-proof has 100 percent, and so on. A drink served **neat** is served straight out of the bottle; a drink served **straight up** or **up** is shaken or stirred with ice before being strained into a glass with no ice; and a drink **on the rocks** is served over ice.

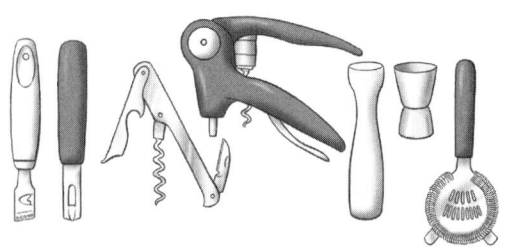

Zester, channel knife, waiter's corkscrew, Lever-style corkscrew, muddler, two-sided jigger, strainer

Glasses: Cocktail or martini, old-fashioned, highball, collins, Champagne, silver or pewter cup, punch, margarita, hurricane

Refrigerate mixers such as club soda, ginger ale, and tonic water, if possible before adding them to drinks. ➤ Similarly, chilling glasses in the refrigerator or freezer before using them will help to keep chilled drinks cold.

The cocktails that follow are some fundamental ones, listed according to their basic ingredients. ➤ All shaken or stirred cocktails should be shaken or stirred and strained into the glasses just before serving. ➤ Mix only one round at a time.

ABOUT GARNISHES FOR DRINKS

A garnish should enhance the appearance and flavor of a drink: sprigs of mint or rosemary, basil leaves, stalks of lemongrass, olives, cinnamon sticks, carrot, celery sticks, or cucumber sticks, strawberries, cherries, or pineapple wedges. Lemons, limes, and oranges add acidity and aromatic oils. To make **wedges,** cut lemons or limes lengthwise into 8 pieces. To make **citrus twists,** use a paring knife or vegetable peeler to remove roughly 1 1/2-inch-long strips of citrus rinds. Twist the rind over the drink, then drop it in. For **citrus swirls,** use a channel knife or vegetable peeler to cut 3- to 4-inch-long strips of zest from around the fruit. For **grated zest** to be mixed into or floated on top of drinks, use a fine-toothed grater or a zester to remove the colored part of the rind.

Frosting—sometimes called **rimming**—a cocktail or other glass with sugar or salt is another way to add flavor, texture, and eye appeal to drinks. ➤ To frost a glass, swab the outer edge of the rim with a wedge of lemon or lime from which the juice flows freely. Hold the glass at an angle and roll the rim in granulated sugar or coarse salt. Avoid coating the inside of the glass. Lift the glass and tap it gently, upside down, to remove any excess sugar or salt.

Some drinks, such as a mint julep, call for **muddling** herbs, soft fruits, or citrus slices, usually with sugar, which brings out more of their flavor and juices. Use a muddler, shown on 54, or large spoon to gently bruise and mash together these ingredients.

ABOUT ICE

Ice with which a drink is shaken, stirred, or served is an important ingredient. For the clearest and best-tasting cubes, start with filtered water, if possible, or let the water sit for an hour before freezing, as for an ice mold, 65.

Whenever drinks are shaken or stirred with ice or served on the rocks, use large **ice cubes** to avoid diluting the drinks. However, some drinks, such as the mint julep, are best served over **crushed** or coarser **cracked ice.** If too finely crushed, it will melt too quickly and may dilute the drink. Crushed ice can be made in a blender or in a countertop ice crusher. To crack ice by hand, place whole ice cubes in a sturdy zip-top plastic bag, wrap the bag in a kitchen towel, and give it several strong whacks with a rolling pin, hammer, or meat mallet. If you need a large quantity of cracked ice, make it in advance, and freeze. To make Decorative Ice Molds, see 65.

MEASUREMENTS FOR DRINKS

1 dash	=	6 drops
1/4 ounce	=	1 1/2 teaspoons
1/2 ounce	=	1 tablespoon or 3 teaspoons
1 ounce	=	2 tablespoons
1 1/2 ounces	=	3 tablespoons
2 ounces	=	1/4 cup
8 ounces	=	1 cup
16 ounces	=	2 cups or 1 pint
750 ml	=	25.4 ounces
1 quart	=	32 ounces
1 liter	=	33.8 ounces
1 lemon	=	1 to 3 tablespoons juice
1 lime	=	1 1/2 to 2 tablespoons juice
1 medium orange	=	4 to 6 tablespoons juice
1 medium grapefruit	=	10 to 12 tablespoons juice

ABOUT GIN AND GIN COCKTAILS

Gin is a spirit—that is, a distilled liquor. Much of its distinctive flavor comes from the juniper berry. Victorian novelists tended to assume that only the lower classes—footmen, scullery maids, and the like—had a taste for gin. The "bathtub" concoctions of the Roaring Twenties did nothing to enhance gin's repute. Recent generations, however, have recognized the fact that this liquor, regardless of its shady past and its possibilities as a straight drink, is probably the best mixing base ever invented.

Gin, or at least its precursor, was invented in Holland in 1650. Dutch gin, or *jenever*, retains a more pronounced flavor of juniper and other herbs and spices to this day. It is usually drunk straight and chilled, and the aged *jenevers* elicit as much reverence as fine whiskey. The British reformulated and lightened gin, and it is the London "dry" style that is most popular today. More perhaps than is the case with most other liquors, the quality of commercial gin varies: Its cost is a rough measure of its worth.

MARTINI

1 serving

Vermouth is not the enemy of the martini, it is its defining element. Good gin is a potent spirit with real flavor of its own, but it needs more than a whisper of vermouth to turn it into a cocktail. A classic martini is served straight up in a chilled cocktail glass, though a fashion for sipping the cocktail on the rocks has developed—perhaps with the intention of muting its strength. A pitted green olive is the traditional garnish, but there are those who prefer a lemon twist. Adding a dash of olive brine along with the olive makes a **Dirty Martini**. With a small pickled onion in the glass, the martini becomes a **Gibson**. When vodka takes the place of gin, the cocktail is a **Vodka Martini**.

I. Shake or stir well with ice:

    2¼ ounces gin
    ½ ounce dry vermouth

Strain into a chilled martini glass or over ice in an old-fashioned glass.
Add:

    1 small pitted green olive or a lemon twist

II. A formula we happen to prefer, perhaps closer to what the very first martini tasted like.

Shake or stir well with ice:

    2¼ ounces gin
    ½ ounce dry vermouth
    ½ ounce sweet vermouth

Strain over ice in an old-fashioned or martini glass and add:

    A dash of orange bitters
    1 small pitted green olive

GIN COCKTAIL

1 serving

In 1931, during Prohibition, when the first edition of JOY was published, most cocktails containing liquor were made with gin and ingenuity in the following proportions: an ample supply of the former and a good dose of imagination for the latter.

Shake or stir well with ice:

    2 ounces gin
    2 ounces orange juice
    ¾ ounce lemon juice
    (1 teaspoon Fruit Syrup, 43)
    A dash of bitters

Strain over ice into an old-fashioned glass.

GIN AND TONIC

1 serving

Use vodka in place of the gin for a **Vodka Tonic**.
Pour over ice in a highball glass:

    1½ ounces gin or vodka

Fill the glass with:

    Tonic water

Garnish with:

    A lime wedge

BRONX

1 serving

Shake with ice:

    1½ ounces gin
    A dash of dry vermouth
    A dash of sweet vermouth
    ½ ounce orange juice

Strain into a chilled cocktail glass and garnish with:

    An orange slice

GIMLET

1 serving

Replace the gin with vodka for a **Vodka Gimlet**.
For an **Orange Blossom**, add ½ to 1 ounce orange juice and (1 teaspoon Sugar Syrup, 43), and garnish with an **orange slice.**
Shake with ice:

    1½ ounces gin
    ¼ ounce lime juice

Strain into a chilled cocktail glass. Garnish with:

    A lime wedge

GIN FIZZ

1 serving

Add **1 large egg white** to the shaker with the other ingredients to make a **Silver Fizz**.
Shake with ice:

    1½ ounces gin
    1 ounce lime juice
    ½ ounce Sugar Syrup, 43

Strain into a chilled highball glass. Fill the glass with:

    Club soda

Stir and serve.

TOM COLLINS

1 serving

Substituting vodka for gin produces a **Vodka Collins**.
Shake with ice:

    1½ ounces gin
    ¾ ounce lemon juice
    ½ ounce Sugar Syrup, 43

Strain over crushed ice in a collins or highball glass, and fill with:

    Club soda

Garnish with:

    A lemon slice

SINGAPORE SLING

1 serving

This was invented in the early 1900s at the legendary Long Bar at the Raffles Hotel in Singapore. There are countless versions, the only constants being gin, cherry brandy, and grenadine. Some top it off with soda.

Shake well with ice:

1 ounce gin
$^1/_2$ ounce cherry brandy
4 ounces pineapple juice
$^1/_4$ ounce lime juice
A dash of Triple Sec
A dash of Bénédictine
A dash of grenadine
A dash of Angostura bitters

Strain over ice in a collins glass. Garnish with:

A pineapple slice or a maraschino cherry

NEGRONI

1 serving

Invented at the Casoni Bar in Florence, Italy, in the 1920s in honor of Count Camillo Negroni, this is one of the most elegant and sophisticated cocktails. A lower-proof version, known as the **Americano,** omits the gin and adds a few ounces of soda on top. A **Campari Cocktail** is a Negroni with Italian brandy substituted for the gin.

Pour over ice in a highball glass:

$1^1/_2$ ounces gin
$1^1/_2$ ounces Campari
$1^1/_2$ ounces sweet vermouth

Stir well or shake with ice and strain into a chilled cocktail glass. Garnish with:

An orange slice

PINK LADY

1 serving

Shake with ice:

$1^1/_2$ ounces gin
1 teaspoon grenadine
1 teaspoon light cream
(1 egg white)

Strain into a chilled cocktail glass and serve.

PIMM'S CUP

1 serving

A gin-based liqueur enhanced with fruits and herbs, Pimm's Number 1 is especially suited to summertime outdoor parties.

Pour over ice in a highball glass:

$1^1/_2$ ounces Pimm's Number 1

Fill the glass with:

Ginger ale

Garnish with:

A cucumber stick or a lemon wedge or an orange slice

ABOUT VODKA AND VODKA COCKTAILS

Vodka may look deceptively like water but it is actually a neutral spirit distilled from grain, usually barley or wheat, sometimes rye or corn, and occasionally potatoes, grapes, or even beets. Many consider vodka the perfect cocktail mixer because it doesn't impose much of its own flavor.

There are also available an increasing number of flavored vodkas, enhanced with lemon, lime, orange, vanilla, currants, or chile peppers, among other things, which are generally served straight and as cold as ice. Flavored vodkas are also quite easy to make at home, 58.

BLOODY MARY

1 serving

When tequila takes the place of vodka in a Bloody Mary, it becomes a **Bloody Maria;** made with gin, it is a **Ruddy Mary.** Replace the tomato juice with beef consommé or bouillon and omit the celery salt, salt, and pepper for a **Bullshot.** A Bloody Mary without any alcohol is, of course, a **Virgin Mary.**

Shake well with ice:

$1^1/_2$ ounces vodka
6 ounces Tomato Juice, 37
2 to 3 drops lemon juice
2 to 3 drops Worcestershire sauce
A drop of hot pepper sauce
Pinch of celery salt
Pinch of salt
Pinch of black pepper

Strain over ice in a highball glass. Garnish with:

Small celery stalk

BECKER BLOODY BULL SHOT

8 servings

Mix together in a pitcher:

32 ounces tomato or tomato vegetable juice, chilled
One 10- to 11-ounce can beef consommé, chilled

Pour over ice in each highball glass:

$1^1/_2$ ounces vodka (12 ounces total)
$^3/_4$ teaspoon fresh lime juice (2 tablespoons total)
A dash of hot sauce

Fill with the tomato-consommé mixture. Add and stir in:

Black pepper to taste

SCREWDRIVER

1 serving

Shake well with ice:

$1^1/_2$ ounces vodka
4 ounces orange juice

Strain over ice in a highball glass. Garnish with:

An orange slice

SALTY DOG

1 serving

Without the salty rim, this drink is called a **Greyhound.**
Shake well with ice:
  1^1/$_2$ **ounces vodka**
  6 **ounces grapefruit juice**
Frost the rim of a highball glass, 55, using:
  Grapefruit juice
  Coarse salt
Drop ice into the glass and strain in the drink.

SEABREEZE

1 serving

Stir with ice cubes in a highball glass:
  1^1/$_2$ **ounces vodka**
  4 **ounces cranberry juice**
  1 **ounce grapefruit juice**
Garnish with:
  A lime wedge

COSMOPOLITAN

1 serving

Omit the cranberry juice and double the amount of lime juice for a **Kamikaze.**
Shake well with ice:
  1 **ounce vodka**
  ^{1}/$_2$ **ounce Triple Sec**
  1 **ounce cranberry juice**
  ^{1}/$_4$ **ounce lime juice**
Strain into a chilled cocktail glass.

HARVEY WALLBANGER

1 serving

Pour over ice in a highball glass:
  1 **ounce vodka**
  6 **ounces orange juice**
Stir well, then top with:
  ^{1}/$_2$ **ounce Galliano liqueur**

MADRAS

1 serving

Pour over ice in a highball glass:
  2 **ounces vodka or rum**
  2 **ounces cranberry juice**
  2 **ounces orange juice**
Garnish with:
  A lime wedge or orange slice

WHITE RUSSIAN

1 serving

To make a **Black Russian,** omit the heavy cream.
Shake well with ice:
  1^1/$_2$ **ounces vodka**
  1^1/$_2$ **ounces heavy cream**
  1 **ounce Kahlúa or other coffee liqueur**
Strain over ice in an old-fashioned glass.

MOSCOW MULE

1 serving

Pour over ice in a chilled mug or highball glass:
  1^1/$_2$ **ounces vodka**
  ^{1}/$_2$ **ounce lime juice**
Fill the mug or glass with:
  Ginger beer (5 to 7 ounces)
Stir well.

JOY TEA

1 serving

Shake with ice:
  1^1/$_2$ **ounces Tea Vodka, below**
  1 **ounce water**
  ^{1}/$_2$ **ounce Sugar Syrup, 43**
Pour over ice in a highball glass. Garnish with:
  A lemon slice

ABOUT FLAVORED VODKA

Nothing compares to flavoring your own vodka. Use the bottle size called for in the recipe so that it can be stored in its original bottle after steeping. Wash citrus fruit before steeping. ➤ Avoid oversteeping or they will become bitter. After straining, store in the freezer indefinitely. Serve alone with a garnish or use in place of regular vodka in cocktails.

CITRUS VODKA

One 750-ml bottle

Drop the **peel of 1 medium orange or lemon,** cut into strips, into **one 750-ml bottle vodka.** Stir. Steep in the refrigerator for at least a week. Strain, return to the bottle, and store in the freezer.

TEA VODKA

One 750-ml bottle

Drop ^{1}/$_4$ **cup black tea leaves** into **one 750-ml bottle vodka.** Stir. Steep at room temperature for at least 2 hours, or up to 3 days. The vodka should be at least as dark as straw; the longer it sits, the darker it will get. Strain, return to the bottle, and store in the freezer.

BLACK PEPPER VODKA

One 750-ml bottle

Excellent served with rich hors d'oeuvres that contain sour cream, caviar, smoked salmon, or smoked sturgeon, and excellent used in place of vodka in a Bloody Mary, 57.
Drop ^{1}/$_2$ **cup whole black peppercorns** into **one 750-ml bottle vodka.** Allow to steep at room temperature for at least 4 hours, or up to 3 days. The vodka should be straw-colored; the longer it sits, the darker it will get. Strain, return to the bottle, and store in the freezer.

ABOUT WHISKEY AND WHISKEY COCKTAILS

Whiskey, or whisky, as it is spelled in Scotland and, usually, in Canada, is a distilled grain spirit, made mainly from barley, corn, rye, or wheat that is ground, soaked in water, and turned into a mash that is then fermented, distilled, and aged in oak barrels. The **Scotch** version gets its particular flavor from malted barley smoked over peat fires. Most Scotch is blended; that is, a percentage of malted barley liquor is mixed with a liquor made from another grain, often fairly neutral, which results in a milder drink. The increasingly popular **single-malt Scotch**, however, comes from a single distillery and is made exclusively from malted barley in small batches in old-fashioned pear-shaped copper stills, which result in strong and individualistic flavors, laden with overtones of smoke and malt. The yield of each malt distillery (there are only about 100 in Scotland today) has a character very much its own; few other spirits have such a range of flavor variations, of smokiness and earthiness, sometimes a hint of tar, once in a while even a suggestion of heather's spice. Single malts are expensive and their penetrating flavor overwhelms any other ingredients in a mixed drink. Scotch lovers sip single malts in brandy snifters like Cognac, straight or with a splash of water. Despite the fact that single malts are so popular, many blended Scotches are superb as well.

The heart of **bourbon whiskey** is corn. Some bourbons are mostly corn; some get by with the minimum of 51 percent that is required by law. The rest can be rye or barley or just about anything else. A whiskey with a corn content greater than 80 percent is called **corn whiskey**. Most bourbon is made in Kentucky, but legally it needn't come from Kentucky at all. Aged in charred oak casks, bourbon is somewhat sweeter and smoother than other whiskies. A very similar whiskey, made in a neighboring state, is called **Tennessee whiskey;** it is filtered through sugar maple charcoal, adding a layer of unique flavor. **Single-barrel bourbon,** Tennessee, and even Scotch whiskey is aged in one single barrel, with the barrel number and bottling date often noted on the label. They are by definition produced in very small batches and are increasingly sought after. Their cost encourages that they be served and savored as one does single-malt Scotch.

An American whiskey with a limited but steady popularity is **rye,** made predominantly from that grain, rather than corn or barley. There is also American whiskey sold without a specific type being specified; this is known generically as **blended whiskey. Canadian whiskey** is lighter than other examples of the spirit and comparatively mild. **Irish whiskey** is somewhat similar to Scotch, but there are several important differences in the method of manufacture: The barley is dried with coal instead of peat fires, a percentage of raw grain is used in the mash, and it's distilled more than once, making it a slightly milder, less smoky drink. The Irish claim to have invented whiskey, and this is probably the case, as even Scottish distillers admit it.

MANHATTAN
1 serving

This version might also be called a **Dry Manhattan.** A **Perfect Manhattan** uses a dash each of dry and sweet vermouth. A **Sweet Manhattan** is made with only sweet vermouth and garnished with a maraschino cherry. Scotch may replace the bourbon or rye in the formula, in which case it's called a **Rob Roy.**
Pour over ice in an old-fashioned glass:
> 1$^{1}/_{2}$ ounces bourbon, rye, or blended whiskey
> 2 dashes dry vermouth
> A dash of Angostura bitters

Stir well. This cocktail may also be shaken with ice and strained into a chilled cocktail glass. Garnish with:
> A lemon twist

OLD-FASHIONED
1 serving

Some like their old-fashioneds on the fancy side, adding a squeeze of lemon juice; a dash of curaçao, kirsch, or maraschino liqueur; or a spear of fresh pineapple—or substituting a fresh ripe strawberry for the time-honored cherry. Try also, a **Scotch Old-Fashioned.**
Put into an old-fashioned glass and stir:
> $^{1}/_{2}$ teaspoon Sugar Syrup, 43
> 2 dashes Angostura bitters
> 1 teaspoon water

Add and stir:
> Ice cubes
> 1$^{1}/_{2}$ ounces bourbon or rye

Garnish with:
> A lemon twist
> A thin orange slice
> A maraschino cherry

WHISKEY SOUR
1 serving

Try a **Gin, Rum,** or **Brandy Sour.**
Shake well with ice:
> 1$^{1}/_{2}$ ounces blended whiskey
> $^{3}/_{4}$ ounce lemon juice
> $^{1}/_{2}$ teaspoon Sugar Syrup, 43

Strain into a chilled old-fashioned glass. Garnish with:
> A lemon slice or a maraschino cherry

HIGHBALL OR RICKEY
1 serving

The following are classic results of using one's imagination: **Vermouth Cassis,** with a base of 1 ounce crème de cassis and 1$^{1}/_{2}$ ounces dry vermouth, and **Horse's Neck** or **Cooler,** with a long spiral of lemon peel draped over the edge of the glass and ginger ale substituted for club soda.
Put 2 large ice cubes into a 6-ounce glass and add:
> 1$^{1}/_{2}$ ounces whiskey, bourbon, Scotch, rye, or gin

Fill the glass with:
> Club soda

Stir lightly and serve.
For a **Rickey,** add before the club soda:
> $^{1}/_{2}$ to $^{3}/_{4}$ ounce fresh lime juice

With dry liquors, you may add:
> $^{1}/_{2}$ teaspoon Sugar Syrup, 43

SAZERAC
1 serving
Stir with ice:
  1½ ounces bourbon or rye
  ½ teaspoon Sugar Syrup, 43
  A dash of Peychaud or Angostura bitters
  A dash of Herbsaint, Pernod, or other anise-flavored
    liqueur
Pour over ice in an old-fashioned glass and garnish with:
  A lemon twist

RUSTY NAIL
1 serving
Pour over ice in an old-fashioned glass and stir:
  1½ ounces Scotch
  ½ ounce Drambuie

LYNCHBURG LEMONADE
1 serving
Shake well with ice:
  1 ounce Jack Daniel's
  1 ounce Triple Sec
  1 teaspoon Sugar Syrup, 43
  ¾ ounce lemon juice
Strain over ice in a highball glass. Top off with:
  Lemon-lime soda or lemonade

MINT JULEP
1 serving
This drink is superlative. And it is well, at this point, to remember that, as Voltaire put it, "The good is the enemy of
the best." Use only the best bourbon; tender, terminal
mint leaves for bruising; and very finely crushed ice. Chill a
highball glass or silver julep cup in the refrigerator.
Muddle, 55, in the chilled glass or cup:
  5 to 6 fresh mint leaves
  1 teaspoon Sugar Syrup, 43
  A dash of cold water
Fill the glass with:
  Crushed ice
Pour in:
  1½ ounces bourbon
Stir once, and garnish with:
  A mint sprig

HOT TODDY
1 serving
Put in an 8-ounce mug:
  1½ ounces whiskey, rum, or brandy
  1 teaspoon honey
  1 teaspoon lemon juice
  1 cinnamon stick
Fill mug with:
  Very hot water
Hang over the rim of the mug:
  ½ lemon slice, studded with 3 whole cloves

ABOUT RUM AND RUM COCKTAILS
Rum is distilled from the juice of sugarcane or from molasses made from sugarcane. As it is produced primarily in
the Caribbean and South America, it is hardly surprising
that rum is the traditional alcoholic component of tropical
drinks. What is perhaps more surprising is that the heavier,
more pungent rums (for instance, those of Jamaica) and
some of the lighter ones from the French islands of Guade-
loupe and Martinique can achieve great subtlety and complexity when well aged and can be served like fine brandy
in a snifter. Don't waste these fine rums in mixed drinks. In
general, light rums (also called white or silver) should be
used for cocktails and medium-bodied (also called amber
or gold) ones for punches and long drinks. Some people
like the taste and look of a frosted glass, 55, and consider it
the final fine touch to a rum cocktail.

CUBA LIBRE
1 serving
A Caribbean classic. Although any cola may be used, the
drink was made originally with and is indelibly associated
with Coca-Cola®.
Pour over ice in a highball glass:
  1½ ounces rum
  6 ounces cola
  ½ ounce lime juice
Stir, and garnish with:
  A lime slice

DAIQUIRI
1 serving
With grenadine substituted for the sugar syrup, this cocktail becomes a **Pink Daiquiri** or **Daiquiri Grenadine.**
Shake well with ice:
  1½ ounces light rum
  ½ ounce lime juice
  2 teaspoon Sugar Syrup, 43
Strain into a chilled cocktail glass.

FROZEN DAIQUIRI
1 serving
I. This is a formula that can be interestingly varied. For a
crowd, use a higher proportion of ice and rum and, instead of the lime juice and sugar syrup, a chunk of frozen
concentrated limeade fresh out of the can. For a frozen
fruit daiquiri, add 1 cup sliced fresh or frozen strawberries, sliced peaches or bananas, or cubed melon.
Process in a blender until smooth:
  1½ ounces light rum
  1 ounce Triple Sec
  1 ounce grapefruit or orange juice
  1 ounce lime juice
  1 ounce Sugar Syrup, 43
  6 to 8 ice cubes
Pour into a chilled wineglass.

II. *2 servings*
A slushier daiquiri is achieved by adding more ice cubes.
For a **Virgin Daiquiri,** simply omit the liquor.
Process in a blender until frothy and smooth:

> 1 cup sliced fresh or frozen berries, peaches, banana,
> or cubed melon
> 1¹/₂ ounces light rum
> 1 ounce Triple Sec
> 1 ounce lemon or lime juice
> 1 ounce Sugar Syrup, 43
> 6 to 8 ice cubes

PIÑA COLADA
1 serving
For a nonalcoholic **Niña Colada,** replace the rum with a
dash of grenadine.
Process in a blender until smooth and frothy:

> 1¹/₂ ounces dark rum
> 3 ounces pineapple juice
> 2 ounces cream of coconut
> 3 or 4 ice cubes

Pour into a goblet or highball glass. Garnish with:

> ¹/₂ slice pineapple

LONG ISLAND ICED TEA
1 serving
Pour over ice in a collins or tall highball glass:

> ¹/₂ ounce light rum
> ¹/₂ ounce gin
> ¹/₂ ounce vodka
> ¹/₂ ounce tequila
> A dash of Triple Sec
> ³/₄ ounce lemon juice

Stir well, then fill the glass with:

> Cola

Garnish with:

> A lemon slice

RUM ICED TEA
1 serving
Pour over ice in a highball glass:

> 8 ounces Flavored Iced Tea I, 35
> ¹/₂ ounce rum
> 2 teaspoons Sugar Syrup, 43

Stir, and garnish with:

> A lemon slice

PLANTER'S PUNCH
1 serving
Shake well with ice:

> 1¹/₂ ounces dark rum
> 6 ounces orange juice
> A dash of grenadine
> ³/₄ ounce lime juice
> 1 teaspoon Sugar Syrup, 43

Strain over ice in a highball glass. Garnish with:

> An orange slice

MAI TAI
1 serving
Shake well with ice:

> 1 ounce dark rum
> 1 ounce light rum
> ¹/₂ ounce curaçao
> ¹/₂ ounce orgeat or almond syrup
> A dash of grenadine
> ¹/₂ ounce lime juice

Strain into an old-fashioned glass, with or without ice.
Garnish with:

> A lime wedge and a mint sprig, or a skewer of fresh
> fruit

GROG
1 serving
Try using maple syrup or molasses instead of sugar syrup.
Stir together in an 8-ounce mug:

> 1 teaspoon Sugar Syrup, 43
> ¹/₂ ounce strained fresh lemon juice
> 1¹/₂ ounces dark rum

Fill mug with:

> Very hot tea or water

Garnish with:

> A lemon twist

Dust top with:

> A pinch of ground nutmeg or cinnamon

HOT BUTTERED RUM
1 serving
An old-time New England individual portion. Curious, isn't
it, that the Puritans made drinks like this one, which has
been said to make a man see double and feel single.
Place in a warmed 8-ounce mug:

> 1 teaspoon confectioners' sugar

Add:

> 2 ounces boiling water
> 2 ounces dark rum
> 1 tablespoon butter

Fill the mug with boiling water. Stir well. Sprinkle on top:

> Freshly grated or ground nutmeg

ABOUT TEQUILA AND TEQUILA COCKTAILS
Tequila is one of the fastest-selling spirits in the United
States, thanks largely to the popularity of a single cocktail,
the margarita. Tequila is distilled from the fermented sap
of the blue agave plant, usually mixed with neutral spirits
of various kinds. More perhaps than is the case with other
white liquors, the quality of commercial tequila varies. Its
cost is a rough measure of its worth, and there are some
very good premium tequilas being sold in the United
States. Technically tequila is a specific kind of **mezcal** from
a specific region of Mexico in much the same way that

Cognac is a superior type of brandy, and generic mezcal has long been seen as tequila's poor relation. There are now some premium mezcals being imported, however, which are superb.

TEQUILA SHOTS

Pour into a shot glass:

¹/₂ ounce tequila

Turn one hand sideways as if to shake hands and form it into a loose fist, then lick the portion between your thumb and the knuckle of the forefinger. Quickly sprinkle with:

Salt

Drink the tequila in one swallow, then immediately lick the salt off your hand and suck the juice from:

A lime wedge

Repeat the process as often as good sense allows.

MARGARITA

1 serving

Shake well with ice:

1¹/₂ ounces tequila
¹/₂ ounce Triple Sec or Cointreau
¹/₂ ounce fresh lime juice

Frost the rim of a cocktail or margarita glass, 55, using:

A lime wedge
Coarse salt

Drop the lime wedge into the glass, add ice, and strain in the drink.

FROZEN MARGARITA

Place the ingredients in a blender, increasing the lime juice to 1 ounce. Add **¹/₂ ounce Sugar Syrup, 43,** and **4 to 6 ice cubes.** Process until the ice has a slushy consistency. Strain into a chilled frosted cocktail or margarita glass.

GRAPEFRUIT HERB MARGARITA

1 serving

Shake well with ice:

3 ounces grapefruit juice
1¹/₂ ounces tequila
1 ounce fresh lime juice
¹/₂ ounce Herb Syrup, 43

Frost the rim of a margarita glass, using:

Lime juice
Coarse salt

Pour the drink over a glass of ice. Garnish with:

A grapefruit twist

TEQUILA SUNRISE

1 serving

Pour over ice in a highball glass:

1¹/₂ ounces tequila
6 ounces orange juice

Stir well. Pour over the top:

A dash of grenadine

Do not stir. Garnish with:

An orange slice

ABOUT BRANDY AND BRANDY COCKTAILS

This spirit is distilled from fruit, most commonly grapes. All wine-producing countries also make brandy (the word comes from the Dutch *brandewijn,* meaning burnt wine) but there is a definite hierarchy, led by **Cognac**—the world's most famous brandy, made only in the Cognac region of France, and prized for its lightness and finesse. **Armagnac** is a close cousin, made in the Armagnac region of France and similarly regulated. As a general rule, Armagnac tends to be more full bodied than Cognac. The letters V.S., V.S.O.P, and X.O. on Cognac and other brandy bottles carry no legal weight but are used by reliable producers as indicators of how long the brandy was aged before bottling—theoretically, the older the spirit, the smoother it will be. Once bottled, spirits don't age further. In general, V.S. (or sometimes "3-star") is the youngest, and the best spirit for mixed drinks. While we adhere firmly to the belief that "the better the liquor, the better the drink," we recommend reverentially sipping brandies of V.S.O.P. and X.O. quality on their own.

Spain, Portugal, and Germany, among other European countries, all produce high-quality brandies. A considerable quantity of brandy and some high-quality Cognac-style spirits are produced in California.

While brandy is distilled from wine, **marc** (as the French call it) and **grappa** (the Italian name) are distilled from the mush of grape skins and stalks that is left after wine is made. Unlike brandy, marc and grappa are usually colorless. They are fiery spirits, often with a rough finish, and were for centuries considered a cut-rate brandy substitute. Today, grappa in particular has become a fashionable and expensive substance, thanks in large part to the packaging and marketing savvy of Italian producers. At its best, grappa can be intensely aromatic and quite delicious.

Calvados, which comes from Normandy, France, may be considered one of the world's great brandies, but it is an apple brandy. (French law also permits a portion of pear spirits to be added.) At its best, it can rival Cognac and Armagnac; at its worst, it can be as harsh as poor-quality grappa. **Applejack** is an American-made apple brandy.

Another class of nongrape brandies are generally known by their French name, **eaux-de-vie,** or "waters of life." Colorless and very agreeable in flavor and aroma, though never very complicated, eaux-de-vie are served in snifters, which are sometimes chilled. The most popular varieties are **poire** or **poire Williams** (pear), **framboise** (raspberry), **mirabelle** or **slivovitz** (blue plum), and **kirsch** (cherry), but virtually any kind of fruit can be used.

Brandy cocktails may be served in sugar-frosted glasses, 55, with grenadine substituted for the citrus juice in preparing the glass for frosting.

BRANDY ALEXANDER

1 serving

Notoriously rich and sweet, best after dinner than before. Shake with ice:

1 ounce brandy
1 ounce dark crème de cacao
1 dash heavy cream

Strain into a chilled cocktail glass.

SIDECAR
1 serving

A sidecar with Armagnac instead of Cognac has been dubbed an **Armored Car.** Substitute light rum for half the Cognac and lime for lemon juice, and you've got a **Between the Sheets.**

Frost the rim of a cocktail glass, 55, with:

(Sugar)

Shake with ice:

1 ounce V.S. Cognac
$^1/_2$ ounce Triple Sec
$^3/_4$ ounce fresh lemon juice

Strain into the glass.

STINGER
1 serving

Shake with ice:

$1^1/_2$ ounces brandy
1 ounce white crème de menthe

Strain into a chilled cocktail or old-fashioned glass.

THE NIKOLASHKA

The drink of Grand Duke Nicholas's regiment, as recreated by our dear friend Sasha Vereschagin and our family. *Vashe zdorovie!* To health!

Slice as thin as possible:

1 lemon

Dredge one side of each lemon slice in:

Freshly ground coffee

Place coffee side up on a platter and sprinkle with:

$^1/_4$ teaspoon sugar

Grate over lemon slices until they appear peppered:

Milk, semisweet, or dark chocolate

Place a lemon slice in your mouth, chew for a few seconds, and quickly sip:

Cognac

ABOUT CORDIALS, LIQUEURS, AND CORDIAL AND LIQUEUR COCKTAILS

Cordials and liqueurs are made by infusing liquor, such as vodka, brandy, or whiskey, with other flavors. A common characteristic of almost all cordials and liqueurs is their sweetness. Cordials usually have one predominant flavor: caraway in **kümmel,** mint in **crème de menthe,** anise in **anisette,** cherry in **maraschino liqueur,** black currant in **crème de cassis.** Liqueurs have a more intricate flavor based on several ingredients or more—Chartreuse, Bénédictine, and Drambuie are examples. This is not a hard-and-fast rule, as demonstrated by two of the most popular liqueurs: **crème de cacao,** flavored with cacao and sometimes vanilla beans, and **curaçao,** an orange-flavored

liqueur. Cordials are used in small doses in mixed cocktails, while many liqueurs are taken on their own, as a softer, sweeter alternative to brandy. However, do not overlook the mixing potential of other liqueurs: a few drops, experimentally added, have touched off many a brave new cocktail. By themselves, serve liqueurs at room temperature or a little below, and in small quantities.

SCARLETT O'HARA
1 serving

Shake well with ice:

$1^1/_2$ ounces Southern Comfort
1 ounce cranberry juice
$^1/_2$ ounce lime juice

Strain into a chilled cocktail glass. Garnish with:

A lime twist

FUZZY NAVEL
1 serving

Pour over ice in a highball glass:

$1^1/_2$ ounces peach schnapps
4 ounces orange juice

Stir, then garnish with:

An orange slice

GRASSHOPPER
1 serving

Shake with ice:

1 ounce green crème de menthe
1 ounce white crème de cacao
1 ounce half-and-half

Strain into a chilled cocktail glass.

MUDSLIDE
1 serving

Process in a blender until smooth:

$^3/_4$ cup chocolate ice cream
2 ounces heavy cream
$1^1/_2$ ounces Kahlúa
1 ounce Irish cream
1 ounce vodka

Pour into a tall glass. Garnish with:

A maraschino cherry

ABOUT VIRGIN COCKTAILS

"Virgin," or nonalcoholic, drinks may be appreciated by adults and the underaged alike. In addition to those that follow here, many recipes in this chapter include nonalcoholic variations: see Bloody Mary, 57, Daiquiri, 60, Piña Colada, 61, Mulled Cider, 68, and Cooked Eggnog, 66. Also see the Beverages chapter, especially the juices, 37–39, and smoothies, 39–40, many of which are elegant alternatives to spiked drinks.

SHIRLEY TEMPLE

1 serving

For generations, this has been the first cocktail sampled by American children—named for a child movie star in the 1930s. The sweet grenadine in this drink is a hit with adults as well as children. Substituting cola for ginger ale produces a **Roy Rogers,** named after the TV movie cowboy of the 1940s and 1950s.

Stir together with ice in an old-fashioned glass:

    1 dash grenadine

    Ginger ale

Garnish with:

    A maraschino cherry

CRANBERRY COLLINS

1 serving

Stir together with ice in a highball glass:

    4 ounces sweetened cranberry juice

    ³/₄ ounce fresh lemon juice

Fill the glass with:

    Club soda

Garnish with:

    A lemon slice

ROCK SHANDY

1 serving

Angostura bitters do contain alcohol, but determining the amount held in a single dash brings to mind the similarly confounding question of how many angels can dance on the head of a pin.

Stir together with ice in a highball glass:

    4 ounces lemonade

    2 ounces club soda

    A dash of Angostura bitters

Garnish with:

    A lemon slice

ABOUT PLUGGED FRUIT

We had no luck when, much younger, we plugged a watermelon and cautiously tried to impregnate it with rum. Later we discovered we had been too impatient. Time does the trick—about 8 hours. For those fortunate ones who can easily come by an abundance of other kinds of fruit, we give the following formulas for picturesque and delightfully refreshing drinks.

COCONUT EXTRAVAGANZA

1 serving

This rather beguiling specialty, as well as the one that follows, is only feasible if you have at hand a fairly plentiful supply of the featured container. To remove the milk from a coconut, see 972.

Cut or saw off the top of:

    1 coconut, drained, 972

to produce an opening about 2¹/₂ inches in diameter.

Pour:

    The milk of a second coconut

into the coconut:

    2 ounces light rum

    ¹/₂ ounce apricot liqueur or Cointreau

    ¹/₂ ounce cream of coconut

Add:

    ³/₄ cup finely crushed ice

Stir, insert a straw, and serve.

PINEAPPLE TROPIC

1 serving

Slice off the top of and reserve the top for the lid:

    1 pineapple

Hollow out a cavity about the size of a highball glass. Pour into it:

    1¹/₂ ounces light rum

    1 ounce Fruit Syrup, 43, made with pineapple

Fill with finely crushed ice and stir well. Garnish with:

    Fresh fruit

Serve lidded, or cut a notch in the lid to insert a long straw.

PLUGGED WATERMELON

Remove and reserve a 3-inch-wide plug from:

    A whole watermelon

Pour in, a little at a time:

    As much vodka or rum as the fruit will hold

Return the plug to the fruit and seal with a piece of tape. Store in a cool place for several hours or more: It takes at least 8 hours for the liquor to be evenly distributed through the fruit, and overnight is better.

Slice and serve or make into watermelon balls and spoon into tall glasses. Add to each serving:

    A dash of fresh lime juice

ABOUT PARTY DRINKS

Most of the formulas in this section are of the punch bowl variety. The punch bowl tends to draw people together and animate social gatherings in ways that go beyond the effects of the alcohol it may contain. Punches and other party drinks can also be served in attractive pitchers. Most hot party drinks may be kept warm for the length of the party in a slow cooker set to its lowest heat; ➤ this is not recommended, however, for egg-based hot drinks.

Unless otherwise noted, in each of the recipes here, ➤ the quantity of liquid will equal approximately 5 quarts and will serve about 20 people, each one having two 4-ounce cups.

Fruit juices used in the concoction of party drinks should be fresh, but frozen unsweetened concentrates are acceptable as long as you dilute them only about half as much as the directions on the container prescribe.

In punch bowl drinks, it is wise to test the mix for flavor and sweetness before adding the soda or water and ice. Ideally, punch mixes should be allowed to blend for an hour or so; if served cold, they should be chilled in the refrigerator before club soda, water, or ice is added. With cold punches, be on the alert for dilution. Ice only two-thirds of the liquid at the outset and add the remainder just before the guests come back for seconds.

As for the ice itself, avoid small pieces; even regular-sized cubes can melt fairly quickly. Larger ice blocks can be made by freezing water in mixing bowls or other containers; when ready to use, dip the bottom of the bowl into cold water and invert onto a plate. Slide into the punch bowl. Best yet, decorative ice molds, below, are more unique and don't melt as quickly. ➤ Freezing fruit juice into cubes or blocks is advantageous because they will not water down the punch as they melt, but they must be used judiciously, for the juice can make the punch quite a bit sweeter or otherwise alter the balance. Most punches are traditionally mixed with plain rather than carbonated water. When carbonated water is a component, the drink is known as a **cup.**

Before taking leave of cold party drinks, we want to remind you that any of the drinks made of an alcoholic base plus fruit juice, 37–39, can also serve as the foundation for delectable punches and cups.

DECORATIVE ICE MOLD
1 ice ring
For an unclouded ice ring, use cold filtered water. Or let unfiltered tap water sit at room temperature for 1 hour before using; stir it well 4 or 5 times during this period to break up and expel the air bubbles in newly drawn tap water. Avoid molds that are too deep. They induce top heaviness in the final product and risk its turning turtle later.
Pour into a 4- to 6-cup ring mold:
> $^{1}/_{2}$ **inch water**

Freeze until slushy, then arrange in the mold, pressing gently into the ice:
> **Fresh strawberries, cherries, or raspberries or thin slices of lemon, lime, and orange**
> **Fresh mint, lemon thyme, or sweet woodruff**

Add enough water to come about halfway up the side of the berries or citrus slices, but not enough to float them. Freeze until the ingredients are frozen into position. Add water to cover the fruit and herbs and freeze. When ready to serve, dip the bottom of the mold in cold water for a few moments, and invert onto a plate. Slide the ice ring into a punch bowl to float in the drink. To make decorative ice cubes for individual drinks, see 37.

CHAMPAGNE PUNCH
Thirty-two 6-ounce servings
Peel, and crush, 234:
> **3 pineapples, cored and sliced**

Place in a large bowl and cover with:
> **1 pound (4 cups) confectioners' sugar**

Let stand, covered, for 1 hour. Add:
> **2 cups lemon juice**
> **2 cups brandy**
> **2 cups light rum**

> $^{1}/_{2}$ **cup curaçao**
> $^{1}/_{2}$ **cup maraschino liqueur**

Stir, and refrigerate for 4 hours. Just before serving, place in a punch bowl with ice. Stir and add:
> **Four 750-ml bottles chilled sparkling wine**

WHISKEY OR BRANDY CUP
Place in a large bowl:
> **2 cups crushed fresh pineapple**

Add:
> **1 quart strawberries, hulled and sliced**

Sprinkle over the fruit:
> **12 ounces (3 cups) confectioners' sugar**

Pour over:
> **2 cups dark rum**

Allow to stand, covered, for 4 hours. Add:
> **2 cups fresh lemon juice**
> $^{1}/_{2}$ **cup fresh orange juice**
> **1 cup grenadine**
> **Two 750-ml bottles bourbon or brandy**

Just before serving, place in a punch bowl with ice. Stir to blend and chill. Add:
> **2 liters chilled club soda or dry ginger ale**

SANGRÍA
6 to 12 servings
An adaptation of a favorite Spanish summer thirst quencher served iced from a pitcher.
Combine in a large pitcher, stirring to dissolve the sugar:
> **4 cups dry red wine**
> $^{3}/_{4}$ **cup brandy**
> $^{1}/_{2}$ **cup Cointreau**
> **6 tablespoons lemon juice**
> $^{1}/_{2}$ **cup sugar, or to taste**

Add:
> **2 oranges, thinly sliced**
> **1 lemon, thinly sliced**
> **1 cup pitted fresh or frozen sweet cherries**
> **1 cup sliced peaches**

Cover with plastic wrap and refrigerate for 2 hours.

FISH HOUSE PUNCH
About twenty 4-ounce servings
This potent colonial punch was first formulated at Philadelphia's Schuylkill Fishing Company. Just before the Revolutionary War, George Washington is said to have stopped by for a sample. Some recipes use strong tea instead of water.
Chill ingredients first, then mix in a punch bowl:
> $1^{1}/_{2}$ **cups Sugar Syrup, 43, or to taste**
> $1^{1}/_{2}$ **cups lemon juice**
> $1^{1}/_{2}$ **cups brandy**
> $1^{1}/_{2}$ **cups dark rum**
> $1^{1}/_{2}$ **cups peach liqueur or peach brandy**
> **3 cups club soda**

If peach brandy is used instead of peach liqueur, the amount of sugar syrup should be increased to taste.

PLANTER'S PUNCH

About twenty 4-ounce servings

Mix in a large pitcher or bowl:

6 cups pineapple juice
6 cups orange juice
1¹/₂ cups light rum
1¹/₂ cups dark rum
1 cup orange curaçao or Triple Sec
1 cup lime or lemon juice
1 cup Sugar Syrup, 43
¹/₂ cup grenadine

Fill tall glasses three-quarters full with:

Crushed ice

Pour punch mixture to within ³/₄ inch of top of each. Decorate with:

Pineapple wedges, orange slices, or maraschino cherries

Serve with straws.

BOWLE

About twenty-five 6-ounce servings

A German favorite made with any of a variety of fruits. Slice and place in a large bowl:

6 ripe unpeeled peaches, 8 unpeeled apricots, 1 pineapple, or 1 quart strawberries

Sprinkle over the fruit:

1¹/₄ cups confectioners' sugar

Pour over mixture:

2 cups Madeira or cream sherry

Allow to stand at least 4 hours, or longer. Stir, then pour over ice in a punch bowl. Add:

Four 750-ml bottles dry white wine

MAY WINE

About twenty-five 5-ounce servings

Another German drink, dedicated to springtime and featuring fresh sweet woodruff, or Waldmeister, 155, which, incidentally, may be grown in a shady corner of your backyard. Use the leaves before the plant's fragrant white flowers have bloomed, and let them stand in the wine for no more than 30 minutes. A Riesling will give best results. Place in a bowl in the order listed:

12 sprigs young sweet woodruff or Waldmeister
1¹/₄ cups confectioners' sugar
One 750-ml bottle Riesling
(1 cup brandy)

Cover and let stand for 30 minutes, no longer. Remove the woodruff. Stir thoroughly and pour over ice in a punch bowl. Add:

Three chilled 750-ml bottles Riesling
1 liter chilled club soda or one 750-ml bottle Champagne

Thinly sliced oranges, sticks of pineapple, and, most appropriate of all, sprigs of woodruff may be used to decorate the "Maitrank." Put a hulled strawberry in the bottom of each glass, to be eaten when the drink is finished.

RHINE WINE CUP

Twenty-six 6-ounce servings

Mix in a punch bowl:

1 cup Sugar Syrup, 43
2 cups fresh lemon juice
1 cup brandy
2 cups dry sherry
1 cup cold strong tea
Three 750-ml bottles Rhine wine
2 cups thinly sliced peeled, seeded cucumbers

Let stand for 20 minutes. Remove cucumber with a slotted spoon. Add ice and pour over it:

1 liter club soda

EGGNOG

About 18 servings

Some people like to add a little more spirit to the following recipes, remembering Mark Twain's observation that "too much of anything is bad, but too much whiskey is just enough." See About Egg Safety, 980.

Beat in a large bowl until light in color:

12 egg yolks

Gradually beat in:

1 pound confectioners' sugar

Add very slowly, beating constantly:

2 cups dark rum, brandy, bourbon, or rye

(These liquors may each form the basic ingredient of the nog or may be combined to taste.) Let stand, covered, in the refrigerator for 1 hour to dispel the eggy taste.

Add, beating constantly:

2 to 4 cups chosen liquor(s)
2 quarts (64 ounces) heavy cream
(1 cup peach brandy)

Refrigerate, covered, for 3 hours. Beat until stiff but not dry:

8 to 12 egg whites

Lightly fold into the eggnog. Serve sprinkled with:

Freshly grated nutmeg

COOKED EGGNOG

16 servings

Please read Cooking Eggs, 978, and About Egg Safety, 980. Lightly cooking this eggnog kills dangerous bacteria in the eggs. For a **nonalcoholic alternative,** 2 tablespoons vanilla or 1¹/₂ cups strong coffee can replace the spirits. Do not double this recipe.

Combine:

1 cup milk
1 cup heavy cream

Whisk in a medium bowl just until blended:

12 egg yolks
1¹/₃ cups sugar
1 teaspoon freshly grated or ground nutmeg

Heat in a large saucepan over medium-low heat:

2 cups milk
2 cups heavy cream

While whisking, slowly add part of the hot milk and cream mixture to the egg yolks. Then slowly pour the cream and egg mixture back into the saucepan, stirring constantly, until the mixture becomes a little thicker and reaches a temperature of about 175°F. Do not overheat or the mixture will curdle. Remove from heat and immediately stir in the combined 1 cup milk and 1 cup heavy cream. Strain through a fine mesh strainer into a storage container and cool. Chill thoroughly, uncovered, then stir in:

> 1/2 **cup brandy, Cognac, dark rum, or bourbon**

Cover and refrigerate for at least 3 hours, or up to 3 days. Serve sprinkled with:

> **Ground nutmeg**

SYLLABUB
8 to 10 servings

The original syllabub was made by milking a cow directly into a basin of wine or cider. Today a syllabub is a creamy milk-based concoction flavored with sherry or white wine and acidified with lemon juice. It remains a favorite Christmas drink in parts of the American South.

Combine in a 2-quart glass jar or glass or metal bowl:

> 3/4 **cup sugar**
> 3/4 **cup cream sherry**
> **Grated zest of 2 lemons**
> 1/4 **cup strained fresh lemon juice**
> 2 **tablespoons brandy or Cognac**
> 1 1/2 **teaspoons ground nutmeg**

Shake or whisk thoroughly. Cover tightly and refrigerate for at least 4, or up to 24 hours. Shake or whisk again to mix in any undissolved sugar, then strain through a fine-mesh sieve, pressing firmly on the zest before discarding it. Combine in a large bowl:

> 1 1/2 **cups chilled heavy cream**
> 1/2 **cup chilled milk**

Beat on high speed until very soft peaks form. Reduce the speed to low and slowly add the strained sherry mixture, followed by:

> 1/2 **cup chilled milk**

The syllabub will turn soupy. Serve at once, or cover tightly and refrigerate for up to 24 hours. The syllabub will separate upon standing, so gently whisk to combine.

Serve in cups or a punch bowl. Dust the top with:

> **Ground nutmeg**

TOM AND JERRY
20 servings

See About Egg Safety, 980.

Beat in a large bowl until stiff but not dry:

> 12 **egg whites**

Cover and set aside. Beat in a medium bowl until light:

> 12 **egg yolks**

Gradually beat in:

> 3/4 **cup confectioners' sugar**
> 2 **teaspoons ground allspice**

> 2 **teaspoons ground cinnamon**
> 2 **teaspoons ground cloves**

Fold the yolks into the beaten whites. Remove 2 tablespoons of the egg mixture into each of twenty 8-ounce mugs, and add to each:

> 1 1/2 **tablespoons brandy**
> 3 **tablespoons dark rum**

Fill each mug with:

> **Very hot water, milk, or coffee**

Stir vigorously until foamy. Dust the tops with:

> **Freshly grated or ground nutmeg**

GLÖGG
20 servings

Glögg, the traditional Swedish spiced Christmas drink, was originally mulled wine, but over the years it came to acquire a considerably stronger alcoholic kick. Swedes often make it with high-proof neutral alcohol—a personal antifreeze for icy Scandinavian winter nights—but brandy and aquavit or vodka give it a nice flavor.

Combine in a large nonreactive pot:

> **Two 750-ml bottles tawny port**
> **One 750-ml bottle brandy**
> 2 **cups aquavit or vodka**
> **Peel of 1 orange, cut into strips**
> 1 **cup raisins**

Tie up in a small square of cheesecloth:

> 4 **cinnamon sticks**
> 10 **whole cloves**
> 10 **cardamom pods**

Add to the pot, cover, and bring almost to a boil. Reduce the heat and simmer slowly for 1 hour. Discard spice package and orange zest. Holding the lid against the edge of the pot as a shield, hold a lighted long match near the rim of the pot until the alcohol fumes ignite. Let burn for 4 to 5 seconds, then extinguish by covering the pot. Ladle into warmed cups. Serve with small spoons for the raisins.

MULLED WINE
16 servings

Combine in a saucepan:

> **Four 750-ml bottles Merlot or other dry red wine**
> 6 **cinnamon sticks**
> **Peel of 4 oranges, each cut into 4 pieces**
> 3/4 **to 1 cup sugar**
> **(Star anise)**

Bring to a simmer, reduce the heat to low, and simmer, covered, for 20 to 30 minutes. Ladle into warmed mugs, placing a cinnamon stick and a piece of orange peel or slice in each one.

To make **Vin Brûlé**, a French variation, bring the same ingredients to a boil, covered, over high heat. Remove from heat, uncover, and carefully ignite with a long match. When the flames have died, ladle the wine into warmed mugs, garnishing them as above.

WASSAIL
Twenty-two 6-ounce servings

The best time to "come a-wassailing" is, of course, Christmas week. Wassail can also be made with a combination of beer and wine, preferably sherry, in which case the proportion should be roughly 4 of beer to 1 of sherry. Please read About Egg Safety, 980.

Core and bake, 216:

12 all-purpose apples

Combine in a saucepan and boil for 5 minutes:

4 cups sugar
1 cup water
1 tablespoon ground nutmeg
2 teaspoons ground ginger
$1/2$ teaspoon ground mace
6 whole cloves
6 allspice berries
1 cinnamon stick

Meanwhile, beat in a large bowl until stiff but not dry:

12 egg whites

Beat in another large bowl until light in color:

12 egg yolks

Fold the whites into yolks. Strain sugar and spice mixture into eggs, combining thoroughly, but gently. Bring almost to a boil in a large pot:

Four 750-ml bottles cream sherry or Madeira
2 cups brandy

Gradually add the hot wine to the spice and egg mixture, beginning slowly and whisking briskly with each addition. Toward the end of this process, add the brandy. Just before serving, while the mixture is still foaming, add the baked apples. Ladle into warmed mugs, placing a piece of baked apple in each mug.

MULLED CIDER
Twenty 6-ounce servings

This satisfying alternative to Mulled Wine, 67, is particularly good when the weather is cool. A nonalcoholic version can be made by omitting the rum.

Combine in a saucepan:

Five 750-ml bottles apple cider
$1^3/4$ cups light or dark rum
20 cinnamon sticks
Peel of 5 oranges, cut into 4 pieces each, or 5 small oranges, thinly sliced
5 tablespoons sugar

Bring to a simmer, reduce the heat to low, and simmer, covered, for 20 to 30 minutes. Ladle into warmed mugs, placing a cinnamon stick and a piece of orange peel or an orange slice in each one.

APPETIZERS AND HORS D'OEUVRES

The words "hors d'oeuvre" and "appetizer" are at most times interchangeable. The main difference is that hors d'oeuvres are served outside the meal and are typically finger foods, whereas appetizers can also be the first course of a meal. Call them what you will—both hors d'oeuvres and appetizers are eaten with drinks before the main meal. Served at a cocktail party, they can be a meal in themselves.

For cocktail parties and most other occasions, the simpler foods presented in the first part of this chapter will usually suffice: seasoned nuts and popcorn, dips, cheese spreads, raw and marinated vegetables, and olives. But when staging a special party, you may want to explore more complex and generally more substantial foods.

Many hors d'oeuvres are rich in fat or are combined with an oil or butter base, in part to buffer the impact of alcohol on the system. If, during preprandial drinking, the appetizer intake is too extensive, true enjoyment of the meal will be destroyed. ➤ Before a rich dinner, two or three hors d'oeuvres are usually plenty—a bowl of nuts or olives, crudités with a dip, perhaps a canapé. ➤ For a cocktail party without dinner to follow, offer five to six different appetizers, including at least two that involve meat or seafood and at least two that are hot. ➤ Allow six to eight pieces of appetizers or finger foods per person if a meal is to follow. If appetizers are the only food being served, allow for double that amount per person. In either case, aim for a selection that is balanced with respect to texture, flavor, and richness.

While we approve of serving imaginative combinations, it is important to remember that, unlike the opera overture, the hors d'oeuvre course should not forecast any of the joys that are to follow. For example, forget cheese balls or nachos if you are serving a cheesy potato gratin at dinner, and likewise skip battered fried shrimp if your entrée is a breaded veal cutlet.

When passing food at a cocktail party, ➤ choose self-contained bite-sized canapés or hors d'oeuvres unless you are furnishing plates. A table of such tidbits often looks more dramatic if the colors and textures of the foods accent the trays or table. Don't torture or obscure buffet food with fussy detailing. Set off plates of appetizers or hors d'oeuvres with plenty of attractively cut vegetables and garnishes of fresh herbs and greens.

Serve hot finger foods ➤ directly from the oven, or use a chafing dish or warming tray. ➤ Remove cold foods from the refrigerator just before serving, or, if they will have to be out for an extended time, set them on chilled platters over ice or replace platters frequently. Some trays are made to be chilled and hold their temperature for a long period of time. Cheeses should be presented at room temperature. ➤ Keep in mind, too, what the plated foods will look like as guests begin to dig in and empty spaces appear. It is often more sensible to arrange several small plates that are easily replaced or replenished than one big one that may be difficult to restore to its pristine glory.

ABOUT PARTY PLATTERS

Just by the clever placement of food on a tray, you can create a party platter in short order when a merry mob descends on you. Popular ingredients on party trays are meat, cheese, fresh fruit, vegetables, and condiments. On the side, serve dressings, relishes, dips, or sauces that complement the foods you offer, as well as an assortment of crackers or breads to accompany the food. For more party tray ideas, see Menus, 23.

Disposable platters are handy when taking a tray to a party. Antique or more formal platters are a nice touch on special occasions.

Arranging a tray is a fun and creative pursuit. Garnish a platter with romaine, red or green leaf lettuce, kale, or parsley. Next examine the space you have and the ingredients you need to arrange, and divide your tray into sections. Alternate foods according to their colors or shapes. "Paint" the tray with splashes of color using black and green olives, bell pepper or carrot or celery sticks, grape tomatoes, radishes, sliced boiled eggs, grapes, or artichoke hearts. Cocktail Meatballs, 82, can be made ahead in hors d'oeuvre size and reheated. Marinate and skewer Rumaki, 83, well ahead of the party. Cover, refrigerate, and broil when ready to serve.

Refer to the chart at right for party tray quantities. Also see About Antipasto, 80, for more meat and cheese suggestions, and Crudités, 78, for vegetable suggestions, as well as About Fruit Platters, 77. Following are ideas for party trays.

MEAT

Thinly slice and roll into slim tubes: turkey breast, smoked or peppered turkey, roast beef, honey or baked ham, Westphalian or Black Forest ham, prosciutto, corned beef, and/or pastrami. Cut into thick wedges: pepperoni, Lebanon bologna, salami, summer sausage, mortadella, cured smoked chorizo, sopressata, and/or pâtés.

CHEESE

Slice, cube, or cut into triangles: American, Cheddar, Monterey Jack, pepper Jack, Muenster, provolone, Swiss, Colby, mozzarella, Gouda, Havarti, Brie, Parmigiano-Reggiano, or Romano.

FRUIT

Leave whole on stem, cube, ball, or slice: berries, grapes, cherries, melon, kumquats, oranges, kiwi, pineapple, dates, figs.

CONDIMENTS AND GARNISHES

Distribute on the tray or place in bowls: dried apricots, sun-dried tomatoes, peperoncini, olives, almonds, flavored mayonnaise, 578, hot peppers, artichoke hearts, cashews, walnuts, pecans, pistachios, prunes, chutney, spicy mustard, horseradish, cornichons, pesto, tapenade, Honey Yogurt Dip, 78, and sprigs of herbs such as rosemary, savory, parsley, thyme, or sage.

ABOUT SERVING A CHEESE PLATTER OR BOARD

Rather than the simple cheese-based recipes later in this chapter, consider serving a cheese platter as an hors d'oeuvre. Buying and serving complementary cheeses is a carefree way to entertain. If serving with predinner drinks, keep in mind that cheese can be filling, so limit the variety and quantities. Serve 3 to 4 ounces of cheese per person if only fruit, bread, and cheese are on the menu. When other hors d'oeuvres are offered before dinner, 2 ounces per person will suffice. Choose at least three different varieties of cheese but no more than five. Cheeses with different shapes, textures, and flavor profiles add diversity to the cheese board. A good mix is one soft-ripened cheese, one double- or triple-cream cheese, a semi-soft cheese, an aged cheese, and a blue- or green-veined cheese. Serve the cheeses at room temperature—cheese is rarely good or at its peak when served cold. Arrange delicately flavored cheeses away from strong-flavored cheeses, and present a knife or cheese cutter for each cheese so as not to mix the flavors. When serving a whole wheel of cheese, the host makes the first cut into the cheese to prevent any hesitation a guest may have about beginning. Accessories such as wooden boards, platters, marble slabs, or flat wicker mats or baskets enhance serving. Avoid crowding cheeses—leave room for the guests to reach and slice the cheese easily. Add some pats of sweet butter to the cheese board along with plain toast, crackers, or crusty French bread; bread and crackers are best arranged in a separate

basket or platter. Salted, toasted, or spiced nuts, 70–71; almonds; celery or fennel; and apples, pears, grapes, strawberries, plums, melon, or fresh figs all make pleasant accessories, as do honey and chutneys. The Spanish Manchego cheese pairs particularly well with quince paste, or membrillo, 236, while pears are traditional with Stilton. See The Cheese Course in Desserts chapter, 827.

PARTY TRAYS—QUANTITIES		
Item	**15 People**	**25 People**
Meats	3 pounds	5 pounds
Cheese	1 pound	1 1/2 pounds
Bread	30 slices or	50 slices or
	15 rolls	25 rolls
Mayonnaise	1/2 cup	3/4 cup
Mustard	1/3 cup	1/2 cup
Horseradish	1/3 cup	1/2 cup
Leaf Lettuce	1 pound	1 1/2 pounds
Sliced Tomatoes	2 pounds	3 1/2 pounds
Sliced Onions	2/3 pound	1 pound
Vegetables	1 1/2 pounds	2 1/2 pounds
Relishes	1 pound	1 1/2 pounds
Dip	2 cups	3 cups
Fruit	3 pounds	5 pounds

ROASTED NUTS

4 cups

Preheat the oven to 350°F. Toss to coat:

> **1 pound unsalted mixed nuts (cashews, pecans, almonds, hazelnuts, peanuts, or walnuts)**
> **Salt and black pepper to taste**
> **2 tablespoons butter, melted**

Spread in an even layer on a parchment-lined baking sheet. Bake until lightly browned, about 7 minutes. Let cool before serving.

CURRIED NUTS

Prepare Roasted Nuts, above, adding along with the butter **1 tablespoon curry powder** and **1/8 teaspoon cayenne.**

ROSEMARY AND BROWN SUGAR NUTS

Prepare Roasted Nuts, above, adding, along with the butter, **3 tablespoons finely chopped rosemary, 2 tablespoons brown sugar,** and **2 tablespoons light corn syrup.** After removing the nuts from the oven, stir them occasionally until the coating dries, about 5 minutes. Cool completely before serving.

CRISP SPICY PECANS

2 cups

A mixture of whole almonds, walnuts, and pecans may also be used.

Preheat the oven to 325°F.

Combine in a small bowl:

3 tablespoons butter, melted
1 tablespoon sweet paprika
1$\frac{1}{2}$ teaspoons Worcestershire sauce
$\frac{1}{2}$ teaspoon ground red pepper

Set aside to cool. Beat with an electric mixer in a medium bowl until very foamy:

1 egg white
1 teaspoon salt

Gradually add and beat until soft peaks form:

6 tablespoons sugar

Fold in along with the butter mixture until well coated:

2 cups (8 ounces) pecan halves

Spread in a single layer on a baking sheet. Bake, stirring twice, until crisp and browned, about 30 minutes. Remove from oven and pour onto a large sheet of aluminum foil to cool, then break into clusters or individual nuts.

ROASTED CHESTNUTS

Preheat the oven to 425°F. To prevent them from exploding, prick **chestnuts** with a knife point or ice pick. Spread on a baking sheet and bake for 15 to 20 minutes. To peel, see 270.

TOASTED PUMPKIN OR SQUASH SEEDS

Delicious all by themselves or as a garnish for fall soups. A medium butternut squash will yield approximately $\frac{1}{4}$ cup seeds, a medium pumpkin much more.
Separate the fibers from:

Pumpkin or winter squash seeds

Put in a saucepan, cover with salted water, and bring to a boil. Reduce the heat and simmer 2 hours. Drain and dry on paper towels. Preheat the oven to 250°F. Spread the seeds on a baking sheet. For each $\frac{1}{4}$ cup seeds, add, tossing to coat:

$\frac{1}{4}$ teaspoon vegetable oil
$\frac{1}{8}$ teaspoon salt

Bake, stirring occasionally, until golden brown, about 1 hour. Cool completely.

TOASTED SUNFLOWER SEEDS

1 cup
Preheat the oven to 250°F.
Toss together, then spread on a baking sheet:

5$\frac{1}{2}$ ounces shelled sunflower seeds (1 cup)
1 tablespoon vegetable oil
$\frac{1}{2}$ teaspoon salt

Bake, stirring from time to time, until golden brown, about 1 hour. Cool completely.

POPCORN

5 cups
Keep unpopped corn tightly covered. One half cup corn equals about 1 quart when popped. Wire poppers used over coals or the stove call for no butter or oil for popping. These will process about $\frac{1}{4}$ cup of kernels at a time. For sweet popcorn additions, see 865.

Heat in a lidded 3-quart heavy-bottomed pot over high heat:

2 tablespoons vegetable oil
3 popcorn kernels

When the kernels start to pop, add and shake to coat:

$\frac{1}{2}$ cup popcorn

Cover and cook, shaking the pot, until the popping stops, about 2 minutes. Transfer to a large bowl. Sprinkle with:

Salt to taste
(Melted butter)

SAVORY ADDITIONS TO POPCORN

Make sure to butter the popcorn first so additions will stick. Shaking the popped corn and additions in a large paper bag makes mixing easy. Use one or more:

1 tablespoon melted butter
$\frac{1}{4}$ teaspoon ground red pepper
2 tablespoons grated Parmesan
$\frac{1}{4}$ teaspoon finely chopped rosemary
$\frac{1}{2}$ teaspoon garlic powder
$\frac{1}{2}$ teaspoon paprika

ABOUT OLIVES

Though the grading and typing of olives is taken very seriously by the producers, cooks should know that size does not necessarily have anything to do with quality. Olives offer a great variety of flavors, sizes, and colors—green olives can't compare in flavor or texture to the small, yellow Manzanilla fines or the almost black kalamata. Try various types in making up your hors d'oeuvre tray.

There are many stuffings for olives: blue cheese; a sliver of almond, garlic, or pimiento; a tiny slice of anchovy, smoked salmon, or prosciutto. For a real treat, put in a little foie gras, and close with a pistachio nut. For a more in-depth discussion of olives, see 1002.

SPANISH-STYLE MARINATED OLIVES

4 cups
Rinse in warm water, drain, and dry with paper towels:

2 cups brine-cured green olives
1 cup oil-cured black olives
1 cup brine-cured black olives

Place in a lidded container and add:

1 cup extra-virgin olive oil
3 garlic cloves, very finely minced
2 bay leaves
1 tablespoon finely chopped rosemary
(1 teaspoon grated lemon zest)
Pinch of crushed red pepper flakes

Stir to combine. Cover and refrigerate for at least 2 days, or up to 1 month. Remove bay leaves and serve at room temperature.

ABOUT DIPS

Dips offer an opportunity for endless flavor combinations. Creamy dips, such as Sour Cream Dip, 72, Spinach Dip in a

Bread Bowl, 73, and Hot Crab Dip, 74, are built on a number of bases, including sour cream, yogurt, soft cheeses, mayonnaise, and cream cheese. White Bean Dip with Rosemary and Garlic, 73, or any of the salsas, 571–572, and flavored mayonnaises, 578–582, also make great dips.

Prepare cold dips an hour ahead or even a day in advance to allow the flavors to blend. Cover and refrigerate until ready to serve. ➤ If a dip calls for plain yogurt, drain the yogurt by placing it in a sieve lined with cheesecloth or a coffee filter for about 30 minutes. The ingredients for hot dips can be assembled ahead, covered, and kept refrigerated until ready to cook. Serve cold dips in small bowls, hollowed-out large round loaves of bread, or vegetable containers, such as cabbage leaves or halved, seeded bell peppers. In warm weather, place the dip container in a bowl filled with crushed ice when serving. Accompany dips with an assortment of cut-up raw vegetables, crackers, breads, toast, chips, seafood, and/or cubes of cheese or meat. ➤ About 1 cup dip serves 4 people.

SOUR CREAM DIP
2 cups

Mix well in a large bowl:
> 1½ cups sour cream
> ½ cup mayonnaise
> 2 tablespoons chopped fresh chives or 2 teaspoons
>   dried chives
> 1 tablespoon grated onion
> ½ teaspoon dried dill
> ½ teaspoon salt
> ½ teaspoon white pepper

Serve chilled.

BECKER SOUR CREAM DIP
2 cups

Mix well in a large bowl:
> 2 cups sour cream
> 2 tablespoons soy sauce
> 2 teaspoons black pepper
> 2 garlic cloves, minced
> ½ teaspoon salt
> Grated zest of 1 lemon

Serve chilled. You can add:
> (3 to 4 scallions, thinly sliced)
> (1 tablespoon prepared horseradish)
> (½ cup Caramelized Onions, 287)

CLAM DIP

Prepare **Becker Sour Cream Dip, above,** stirring in **1 cup chopped drained canned clams** and **1 teaspoon Worcestershire sauce.**

SHRIMP DIP
1¾ cups

Combine in a small bowl:
> **One 4-ounce can cooked shrimp, drained**
> **⅔ cup sour cream**
> **⅓ cup mayonnaise**
> **3 tablespoons chili sauce**
> **2 teaspoons lemon juice**
> **1 teaspoon finely minced onion**

Refrigerate for at least 1 hour, or up to 24 hours. Serve chilled.

RED ONION DIP
2 cups

Melt in a large nonstick skillet over medium-high heat:
> **1 tablespoon butter**

Add and cook, stirring, for 5 minutes, or until softened:
> **3 small red onions, finely chopped (about 2 cups)**

Stir in:
> **2 teaspoons sugar**
> **½ teaspoon salt**

Cook, stirring, until the onions turn golden brown and are very soft. Add:
> **2 cups beef broth**
> **3 garlic cloves, minced**
> **(1½ tablespoons minced peeled fresh ginger)**
> **1 teaspoon fresh thyme leaves or about ½ teaspoon**
>   **dried thyme**

Boil, stirring occasionally, until almost all of the broth has evaporated, about 15 minutes; watch it carefully so that it doesn't burn. Transfer to a bowl and stir in:
> **1 teaspoon balsamic vinegar**

Let cool completely, then stir in:
> **1 cup sour cream**
> **Salt and black pepper to taste**

Chill for at least 1 hour.

GUACAMOLE
About 2 cups

Serve guacamole as a dip with tortilla chips or cut-up raw vegetables, as a filling for tacos, or as a topping for grilled poultry or fish. In place of Hass avocados, 1 very large or 2 medium smooth-skinned Florida avocados can be used, but the guacamole will be less flavorful.

Peel and pit:
> **4 medium ripe Hass avocados**

Place in a bowl and mash to a coarse consistency with fork or potato masher. Stir in:
> **¼ cup fresh lime juice (from 1 to 2 limes), or to taste**
> **¼ cup finely chopped onion or thinly sliced scallions**
> **¼ cup finely chopped cilantro or parsley**
> **(2 tablespoons extra-virgin olive oil)**
> **(1 to 2 jalapeño peppers, seeded and minced)**
> **1 tablespoon finely minced garlic**
> **1 to 2 dashes hot pepper sauce**
> **¾ teaspoon salt**

Taste and adjust seasoning; more lime juice and/or salt may be needed. Gently stir in:

    ($^1/_2$ **to 1 cup finely diced tomatoes**)

Serve at room temperature.

WHITE BEAN DIP WITH ROSEMARY AND GARLIC

3 cups

Heat in a medium saucepan over medium heat:

    $^1/_4$ **cup olive oil**

Add, reduce heat to low, and cook, stirring, for 5 minutes:

    2 garlic cloves, minced

    2 teaspoons minced rosemary

    $^1/_2$ **teaspoon white pepper**

Stir in:

    3 cups cooked white beans or two 14- to 16-ounce cans navy, Great Northern, or cannellini beans, rinsed and drained

Mash or process in a food processor until smooth. Serve warm or at room temperature drizzled with:

    (Extra-virgin olive oil)

TEXAS CAVIAR

8 cups

A great stand-in for salsa or bean salad, this can be eaten immediately or refrigerated overnight. The longer it sits, the better it gets.

Combine in a large bowl:

    Three 16-ounce cans black-eyed peas, rinsed and drained

    One 6-ounce jar pimientos, chopped, with juice

    (3 fresh or canned jalapeño peppers, chopped)

    1 cup chopped tomatoes

    (1 green bell pepper, seeded and chopped)

    3 garlic cloves, minced

    $^1/_2$ **cup sliced scallions**

    $^1/_4$ **cup chopped parsley**

    1 tablespoon chopped oregano

    1 tablespoon chopped cilantro

    1 tablespoon hot pepper sauce

    1 tablespoon Worcestershire sauce

    1 teaspoon black pepper

    1 cup basic Vinaigrette, 572

SPINACH DIP IN A BREAD BOWL

2 cups

Thaw and squeeze as dry as possible:

    One 10-ounce package frozen chopped spinach

Mince in a food processor:

    3 scallions, coarsely chopped

    1 to 2 garlic cloves, coarsely chopped

Add the spinach, along with:

    2 cups plain yogurt, drained, 1029, or sour cream

    2 tablespoons grated Parmesan

    (2 tablespoons sour cream if using yogurt)

    $^1/_8$ **teaspoon grated or ground nutmeg**

    Salt to taste

Pulse until smooth. Refrigerate for 1 hour or up to 24 hours. To make the bread bowl, slice off the top inch of:

    1 round loaf of bread (about 1 pound)

With a serrated knife remove the soft inner part of the loaf, leaving about 1 inch of thickness at sides and bottom. Tear the removed bread into chunks for dipping. Fill the hollow loaf with the dip just before serving.

BEER CHEESE DIP IN A BREAD BOWL

About 2 cups

Prepare a bread bowl as directed above, using:

    1 round loaf dark rye bread

Simmer in a medium saucepan over medium heat:

    1 cup beer

While the beer is heating, whisk together:

    1 tablespoon cornstarch

    1 tablespoon water

Add the cornstarch mixture to the beer and cook, whisking, until slightly thickened, about 2 minutes. Lower the heat and whisk in $^1/_2$ cup at a time, allowing each addition to melt before adding the next:

    2 cups Cheddar (8 ounces), grated

    1 ounce cream cheese, cut into pieces

    1 ounce blue cheese, crumbled

    $^1/_2$ **teaspoon Dijon mustard**

    $^1/_2$ **teaspoon Worcestershire sauce**

Pour the dip into the bread bowl and serve hot with pieces of the hollowed-out bread for dipping.

HOT CHORIZO AND CHEESE DIP

About 1$^2/_3$ cups

Melt in a medium saucepan over medium heat:

    1 tablespoon butter

Add and cook, stirring, until translucent, 2 to 3 minutes:

    $^1/_2$ **cup minced onion**

Add and cook until the fat is rendered, 4 to 6 minutes:

    4 ounces smoked chorizo, casing removed and diced

Pour off all but 1 tablespoon of fat from the pan. Add and cook, stirring, for 2 minutes to blend:

    1 tablespoon all-purpose flour

Remove from the heat and gradually whisk in:

    1 cup milk

Return to medium heat and cook, stirring frequently, until thickened, about 5 minutes. Reduce the heat to low and stir in $^1/_4$ cup at a time until melted:

    $^3/_4$ **cup Cheddar (3 ounces), grated**

Stir in:

    ($^1/_2$ cup diced roasted Anaheim peppers, 292, or other mild chiles, such as poblanos)

    $^1/_4$ **teaspoon salt**

Serve warm with:

    Corn or tortilla chips

HOT CRAB DIP

2 cups

Preheat the oven to 325°F. Butter a 2-cup ovenproof bowl. Puree in a food processor or mix in a bowl until smooth:

8 ounces cream cheese, softened
³/₄ cup mayonnaise
2 tablespoons minced onions
1 teaspoon drained prepared horseradish
1 teaspoon Worcestershire sauce
¹/₄ teaspoon salt

Fold in:

One 6-ounce can crabmeat, drained

Sprinkle with:

(Slivered almonds)

Bake until heated through, about 25 minutes.

BAKED ARTICHOKE DIP

About 2¹/₂ cups

Preheat the oven to 400°F. Combine in a medium bowl:

1 cup mayonnaise
1 cup grated Parmesan (4 ounces)
¹/₂ cup finely chopped onions

Pulse in a food processor until finely chopped:

One 13³/₄-ounce can artichoke hearts, drained

Stir into the mayonnaise-cheese mixture, along with:

1 tablespoon lemon juice or dry white wine
¹/₄ to ¹/₂ teaspoon black pepper

Scrape into a small baking dish or ovenproof crock. Sprinkle over the dip:

(3 tablespoons dry bread crumbs)
(1 teaspoon olive oil)

Bake until browned, about 20 minutes. Serve with:

Crackers or pita chips

SEVEN-LAYER DIP

20 servings

Spread evenly in a 13 x 9-inch glass dish:

One 16-ounce can refried beans

Mash together and spread over the beans:

3 large ripe Hass avocados, peeled and pitted
3 tablespoons lime juice

Mix together and spread over the avocado layer:

2 cups sour cream
One envelope (1¹/₄ ounces) taco seasoning

Layer in the order listed:

3 tablespoons chopped drained canned green chiles
One or two 5³/₄-ounce cans sliced black olives, drained
8 plum tomatoes, chopped (about 4 cups)
2 cups grated sharp Cheddar (8 ounces)
(Chopped cilantro or scallions)

Serve with:

Tortilla or pita chips

HUMMUS (CHICKPEA AND TAHINI DIP)

About 2 cups

You may substitute one 16-ounce can chickpeas, rinsed and drained. Use water to thin the puree as necessary. Pick over, rinse, and soak, 253:

³/₄ cup dried chickpeas

Drain and place in a pan with water to cover by 2 inches. Bring to a boil, reduce the heat, and simmer until very tender, about 1¹/₂ hours. Drain, reserving the cooking liquid. Transfer the chickpeas to a food processor or blender and add:

¹/₃ cup fresh lemon juice
3 tablespoons tahini (sesame paste)
2 garlic cloves, finely minced
(¹/₂ teaspoon ground cumin)
Salt

Puree until smooth, adding 2 to 3 tablespoons of the cooking liquid as needed to obtain a soft, creamy consistency. Transfer to a shallow serving bowl and garnish with:

1 tablespoon olive oil
1 tablespoon finely chopped parsley
Sprinkling of hot or sweet paprika

HALF MOON HUMMUS

About 3¹/₂ cups

This is the original Becker hummus recipe, named for our Tennessee mountain home, Half Moon Ridge. Combine in a blender:

2 cups strained cooked chickpeas, 253
²/₃ cup tahini (sesame paste)
³/₄ cup lemon juice
2 pressed garlic cloves
¹/₄ cup pitted black olives
1 teaspoon salt

Remove this mixture from blender and add:

3 tablespoons finely chopped parsley

BABA GHANOUSH (ROASTED EGGPLANT DIP)

About 3 cups

For a creamy, tangy twist, stir ¹/₂ cup yogurt into the finished eggplant puree. For a smoky flavor, roast the eggplants on a grill or open flame.

Preheat oven to 400°F. With a paring knife, pierce in several places each:

3 medium eggplants (about 4 pounds)

Place on a baking sheet and roast, 244, until skins are dark mahogany in color and flesh feels soft, 45 to 60 minutes. Let stand until cool enough to handle. Split the eggplants, scoop the flesh into a colander, and press to extract excess liquid. Transfer to a food processor and add:

2 tablespoons tahini (sesame paste)
1 to 2 garlic cloves, chopped
1 tablespoon lemon juice
2 teaspoons salt

Pulse until smooth. Taste and adjust the lemon juice and salt. Transfer to a shallow serving bowl and garnish with:

1 tablespoon olive oil
1 tablespoon finely chopped parsley
(Pitted black olives)

Serve with:

Warm pita bread

EGGPLANT CAVIAR

8 to 10 servings

Preheat the oven to 375°F. With a paring knife, pierce in several places:

2 medium eggplants (about 2 pounds)

Place on a baking sheet and roast, 244, until soft, 45 to 60 minutes. Let stand until cool enough to handle. Peel the eggplants and finely chop; set aside. Heat in a large skillet over medium heat:

$1/3$ cup olive oil

Add and cook, stirring occasionally, until soft:

2 medium onions, finely chopped
(1 green bell pepper, seeded and finely chopped)
2 tablespoons minced garlic

Add the chopped eggplant along with:

One 28-ounce can plum tomatoes, drained and finely chopped
$1/2$ teaspoons salt
Black pepper to taste

Bring to a boil, then reduce the heat to low and simmer, covered, for 1 hour. Remove the lid and continue to simmer, stirring frequently, until the excess liquid is evaporated; the mixture should be thick but not dry. Stir in:

2 tablespoons lemon juice

Taste and add salt if needed. Let cool, then cover and refrigerate for several hours.

TAPENADE (OLIVE CAPER PASTE)

About $2 3/4$ cups

An essential ingredient in this popular olive spread is the caper. Tapenade made without capers or with only a hint of them is sometimes called *Olivade*. Both are traditionally served with crusty bread or crudités, 78.

Combine in a food processor:

2 cups black olives, pitted
(3 anchovy fillets, rinsed and patted dry)
3 tablespoons drained capers
3 tablespoons olive oil
2 tablespoons lemon juice or brandy
2 garlic cloves, coarsely chopped
2 teaspoons fresh thyme leaves or 1 teaspoon dried thyme
Salt and black pepper

Pulse mixture to a coarse puree.

TARAMASALATA

About 2 cups

This rich, creamy mixture works as a dip or spread, usually served with pita bread or crackers. True *taram,* the salted and dried roe of gray mullet, may be difficult to find. Smoked cod or carp roe is a good substitute; rinse under cold running water to remove excess salt.

Prepare:

1 cup Riced Potatoes, 295

Toss the hot potatoes with:

2 tablespoons olive oil

Let cool. Beat with a mixer in a medium bowl:

$1/2$ cup smoked salmon or carp roe
1 tablespoon chopped onion

Beat in the potatoes, along with:

3 tablespoons lemon juice

Drop by drop beat in:

$1/2$ cup olive oil

until the mixture is the consistency of a heavy cream sauce. Add:

(1 tablespoon finely chopped parsley)
(1 tablespoon tomato puree)
Salt and black pepper

Refrigerate until ready to serve.

CREAM CHEESE BALL

One 5-inch ball

Blend well in a large bowl:

Two 8-ounce packages cream cheese, softened
$1/3$ cup grated Parmesan
$1/4$ cup mayonnaise
(2 tablespoons finely chopped onions)
(2 tablespoons finely chopped carrots)
(2 tablespoons finely chopped celery)
1 teaspoon drained prepared horseradish
$1/2$ teaspoon salt

Place mixture on a large piece of plastic wrap. Bring up the edges of the wrap and form mixture into a ball. Place in a small deep bowl to help it hold its shape and refrigerate for at least 1 hour. When it is firm, roll the cheese ball in:

1 cup chopped walnuts or pecans

Press the nuts to make them adhere. The cheese ball can be stored in the refrigerator for up to 3 days.

CHEDDAR CHEESE BALL

One 5-inch ball

Process in a food processor until smooth:

$2 1/2$ cups shredded sharp Cheddar (10 ounces)
3 ounces cream cheese
6 strips fried bacon, crumbled
2 tablespoons milk
1 tablespoon drained prepared horseradish
$1/8$ teaspoon salt

Proceed as for Cream Cheese Ball, above, rolling the ball in:

1 cup chopped walnuts or pecans

ROQUEFORT CHEESE BALLS

About 16 small balls

This recipe can also be made into one large cheese ball; see Cream Cheese Ball, 75, for the technique. Likewise any large cheese ball can be made into small balls.

Blend with a mixer in a large bowl:

> $^2/_3$ cup crumbled Roquefort ($5^1/_2$ ounces)
> 3 ounces cream cheese
> 2 tablespoons butter
> 1 teaspoon Worcestershire sauce or 1 tablespoon brandy
> 1 teaspoon paprika
> Pinch of ground red pepper

Shape into 1-inch balls. Roll in:

> $^1/_2$ cup finely chopped pecans
> (Chopped herbs or watercress)

Press the nuts to make them adhere.

LIPTAUER CHEESE SPREAD

1 cup

This is a Hungarian spiced cheese spread, delicious served with thinly sliced black or rye bread and radishes.

Blend well by hand or in the food processor:

> 8 ounces cream cheese, softened
> 2 teaspoons sweet Hungarian paprika

Stir in:

> 2 tablespoons finely minced onions
> 2 teaspoons drained capers, chopped
> ($^3/_4$ teaspoon caraway seeds)

Scrape into a small bowl.

BLUE CHEESE SPREAD WITH WALNUTS

$1^1/_4$ cups

This is delicious with sliced French bread, sliced apples or pears, and quartered fresh figs. If serving with apple or pear slices, sprinkle with lemon juice to prevent browning.

Puree in a food processor until smooth:

> 8 ounces cream cheese, softened
> $^1/_4$ cup crumbled blue cheese (2 ounces)
> (2 tablespoons port)

Scrape into a small bowl. Sprinkle with:

> 1 tablespoon chopped walnuts, toasted, 1001

CHUTNEY CHEESE SPREAD

$1^1/_2$ cups

Blend:

> 8 ounces cream cheese, softened
> 6 tablespoons mango chutney

Scrape into a small bowl. Sprinkle with:

> 1 tablespoon chopped walnuts, toasted, 1001

GARLIC CHEESE SPREAD

About 2 cups

Shred into a medium bowl:

> 8 ounces Havarti or Muenster

Add:

> 3 to 4 tablespoons mayonnaise
> 2 teaspoons finely minced garlic
> 1 tablespoon snipped chives
> (Pinch of salt)

Mix well, then taste and adjust the salt. Cover and refrigerate for at least 4 hours. Serve at room temperature.

ROASTED GARLIC AND PARMESAN SPREAD

$1^1/_4$ cups

Roast, 277, and allow to cool:

> 4 heads garlic

Squeeze the garlic pulp from the skins into a food processor bowl. Add:

> $^1/_2$ cup finely grated Parmesan (2 ounces)
> 3 tablespoons olive oil
> 2 tablespoons chopped thyme and/or basil
> Salt and black pepper

Process briefly to blend. Stir in by hand:

> ($^1/_4$ cup pitted Kalamata olives, finely chopped)

Spread on:

> Sliced crusty bread, toasted

Top with:

> Sliced grape tomatoes
> Minced herbs, such as basil or thyme

PESTO CHEESECAKE

20 servings

This was served at our wedding celebration in 1997.

Prepare:

> Pesto Sauce, 569

Preheat oven to 375°F. Lightly butter an 8-inch springform pan. Dust the bottom and sides of the pan with:

> Seasoned dry bread crumbs

In a large bowl, mix $^1/_2$ cup of the pesto with:

> 1 pound ricotta cheese
> $^1/_2$ cup sour cream
> 4 large eggs
> 1 teaspoon salt
> $^1/_2$ teaspoon grated lemon zest
> $^1/_2$ teaspoon grated or ground nutmeg
> $^1/_2$ teaspoon black pepper

Pour into the prepared pan. Bake in a water bath, 742, until set, 30 to 35 minutes. Remove from the water bath and transfer the pan to a rack to cool completely, then cover and refrigerate until cold, 6 to 12 hours. Slide a thin-bladed knife around the outside of the cake and remove the outer ring. Spread the remaining pesto around the sides of the cheesecake. Spread the top evenly with:

> $^1/_2$ cup sour cream

If desired, arrange on top:

> (12 sun-dried tomato halves in oil, drained and chopped)

Serve cold or at room temperature.

MARINATED GOAT CHEESE WITH FRESH THYME

8 to 10 servings

Goat cheese marinated in olive oil with herbs is a staple of the Mediterranean table and a favorite of ours.

Place in a shallow bowl:

$1/4$ cup olive oil

2 teaspoons chopped thyme

Add, turning to coat:

One 7-ounce log goat cheese

Cover and marinate in the refrigerator, turning once or twice, for at least 1 hour, or up to 5 days. Bring to room temperature before serving, about 30 minutes.

MARINATED MOZZARELLA

6 to 8 servings

Warm in a medium skillet over medium heat until fragrant:

1 cup olive oil

Add:

2 garlic cloves, thinly sliced

12 whole black peppercorns

3 large sprigs rosemary

$1/4$ teaspoon salt

Pinch of crushed red pepper flakes

Remove from the heat and let cool to room temperature. Remove and discard the rosemary sprigs. Combine in a bowl with:

12 ounces mozzarella, cut into 1-inch cubes

Pour the oil over and let stand at room temperature for several hours, or cover and refrigerate for up to 4 days. Bring to room temperature before serving.

FRIED MOZZARELLA STICKS

8 pieces

Please read About Deep-Fat Frying, 1046.

Cut into eight $3^1/2$ x $1/2$ x $1/2$-inch sticks:

One 8-ounce block mozzarella

Spread in a shallow dish:

$1/2$ cup all-purpose flour

Beat in a shallow bowl:

1 large egg

Spread on a plate:

$1/2$ cup seasoned dry bread crumbs

Dredge the mozzarella sticks lightly in the flour, shaking off the excess. One by one, dip in the egg, coating completely, then roll in the bread crumbs to coat. Put the sticks on a plate and freeze for 15 minutes. Meanwhile, heat to 365°F in a deep fryer or deep heavy pot:

3 inches vegetable oil

Fry the mozzarella sticks in 2 batches until golden brown, about 1 minute. Drain on paper towels. Serve hot with:

Marinara Sauce, 562

NACHOS

10 to 12 servings

Preheat the broiler. Spread on an 11- or 12-inch round heatproof platter (they can be slightly overlapping):

4 ounces tortilla chips (about 4 cups)

Sprinkle with:

$1^1/2$ cups grated Cheddar (6 ounces)

$1^1/2$ cups grated Monterey Jack (6 ounces)

(One $4^1/2$-ounce can chopped green chiles, drained)

Broil until the cheese is melted, 2 to 3 minutes. Top with your choice of:

Sour cream

Pinto or black beans, rinsed and drained if canned

Chopped scallions

Canned sliced jalapeños

Chopped cilantro

Serve immediately.

CHEESE QUESADILLAS

20 or 30 pieces

Lay out on a work surface:

Ten 6-inch flour tortillas

Divide among half of the tortillas:

2 cups shredded Monterey Jack or Cheddar (8 ounces)

(One $4^1/2$-ounce can chopped green chiles, drained, or $1/2$ cup chopped drained bottled red peppers)

($3/4$ cup chopped scallions)

(2 tablespoons minced cilantro or $1/2$ teaspoon dried oregano)

Salt and black pepper to taste

Top with the remaining 5 tortillas. Preheat the oven to 200°F, and place a baking sheet inside. Heat a medium skillet, preferably nonstick, over medium-high heat for 3 minutes. Brush lightly with:

Vegetable oil

Transfer 1 quesadilla to the skillet and cook until browned and crisp on the first side, about 2 minutes. Flip the quesadilla and cook until the second side is crisp, about 2 minutes longer. Transfer to the baking sheet in the oven and cook the remaining quesadillas in the same manner. Cut each quesadilla into 4 or 6 wedges and serve at once, topped with:

(Sour cream, Guacamole, 72, or Salsa Fresca, 571)

ABOUT FRUIT PLATTERS

Fruit offers a light, refreshing counterpoint to savory hors d'oeuvres. Keep the pieces large and arrange them according to size, color, and shape rather than tossing them together like a salad. Mix different styles on the same platter by combining cut melons, pineapple, or other fruit with some whole fruit with stems, like strawberries, small clusters of seedless grapes, or cherries on the stem. Use organic or washed fruit leaves for garnish, if available.

For a spicy arrangement, prepare a platter of sliced peeled honeydew melon, watermelon, cantaloupe, mango, and green apple. Just before serving, sprinkle with lime juice and a mixture of salt and chili powder. Also consider skewered fruits served with Honey Yogurt Dip, 78. Grilled fruits, such as pineapple, plums, peaches, and bananas, served on or with skewers or toothpicks, are another possibility, 214. Or serve a large basket of strawberries with a bowl of sour cream and another of brown sugar, or melon slices or figs wrapped in prosciutto, 227.

HONEY YOGURT DIP

2¹/₂ cups

This dip is perfect served with the fruit platter above. Blend:

    2 cups plain yogurt, drained, 1029
    ¹/₂ cup honey
    1 tablespoon minced mint
    1 teaspoon grated lemon zest

ABOUT VEGETABLES AS PARTY FOOD

Cooked or raw vegetables make some of the most colorful and appreciated foods for grazing. Put a bowl of cherry tomatoes next to a compatible dip or radishes next to a dish of coarse sea salt. Fill a stemmed glass with carrot, celery, or jicama sticks. Or make a crudité basket or platter, below.

CRUDITÉS

6 to 8 servings

The French word *crudités* refers to an assortment of sliced or whole raw vegetables. For visual effect, intersperse those with brighter colors (radishes, bell peppers, carrots) with those of a more subdued hue (celery, cauliflower, mushrooms). If the crudités are the centerpiece of a buffet of assorted dishes, offer several dipping options. Arrange in a shallow basket or on a platter:

    About 6 cups assorted vegetables—rinsed, seeded,
        and trimmed as needed: cauliflower florets,
        radishes, carrot sticks, celery sticks, cucumber
        spears, zucchini strips, mushrooms, turnips, snow
        peas, bell pepper strips, fennel strips, blanched
        green beans, romaine lettuce hearts, scallions,
        cherry tomatoes, strips of cooked beets

Garnish as desired with:

    Green and/or black olives
    Large parsley and/or rosemary sprigs

Set out one or more of the following for dipping:

    Tahini Dressing, 576
    Roasted Red Pepper Dressing, 574
    Roasted Garlic Dressing, 575
    Russian Dressing, 576
    Creamy Blue Cheese Dressing, 576
    Creamy Caraway Dressing, 577
    Curry Mayonnaise, 580
    Mayonnaise with Green Herbs, 580
    Chipotle Mayonnaise, 580
    Spinach Dip in a Bread Bowl, 73
    Aioli, 581

BAGNA CAUDA

About 1 cup

Bagna cauda means "hot bath" in Italian. Any vegetables that are good eaten raw are enhanced by a dip in a hot bath of this garlicky butter and olive oil mixture.
Prepare:

    Crudités, above

Place in a heavy fondue pot or other heavy pot:

    ¹/₂ cup (1 stick) butter
    ¹/₂ cup olive oil
    8 anchovy fillets, mashed
    2 garlic cloves, minced

Simmer gently 5 minutes, stirring occasionally. Add:

    ¹/₂ teaspoon black pepper

Use fondue forks or skewers to dip vegetables in the warm sauce.

MARINATED GREEN BEANS

2 cups

Prepare:

    2 cups green beans, blanched, 1054

Drain and toss with:

    Fresh Herb Vinaigrette, 572

Marinate in the refrigerator for up to 4 hours. Drain and serve chilled.

MARINATED MUSHROOMS

About 2¹/₂ cups

Combine, tossing well:

    10 ounces small whole white mushrooms or 1¹/₄ cups
        thinly sliced medium white mushrooms
    ¹/₂ cup basic Vinaigrette, 572, or Ginger Lemongrass
        Dressing, 575

Marinate, refrigerated, 1 hour or more. Drain, then sprinkle with:

    Chopped parsley, chives, or cilantro

Serve with toothpicks on:

    (Lettuce or watercress)

BROILED STUFFED MUSHROOMS COCKAIGNE

24 pieces

These can be frozen unbaked for up to 2 weeks, but for best results, cook them fresh. If frozen, thaw for 1 hour, then bake as directed. Serve warm.
Preheat the oven to 375°F. Clean, then remove and reserve the stems from:

    1¹/₄ pounds medium white mushrooms (about 32)

Count out 24 same-sized mushroom caps and toss with:

    2 to 3 tablespoons butter, melted, or olive oil

Slice the remaining caps. Chop the stems. Heat in a medium skillet over medium heat:

    2 tablespoons butter or olive oil

Add the sliced mushrooms and stems, along with:

    1 large shallot, minced
    (1 garlic clove, minced)
    ¹/₂ teaspoon dried thyme

Cook, stirring occasionally, for 5 minutes. Stir in:

$1/2$ cup dry bread crumbs
$1/4$ cup chopped pecans or other nuts
3 tablespoons snipped chives or chopped basil
2 tablespoons cream, broth, or dry vermouth or sherry

Transfer to a food processor and coarsely chop the mushrooms. Season with:

Salt and black pepper

Fill each mushroom cap with a heaping tablespoon of the filling. Place on a baking sheet. Sprinkle with:

2 to 3 tablespoons grated Parmesan

Bake until the tops are bubbling, about 15 minutes.

STUFFED RAW VEGETABLES

Hollowed-out vegetables make terrific cases for any number of fillings. When stuffing round vegetables such as cherry tomatoes and mushroom caps, first cut a small slice off the bottom of each vegetable to keep them from rolling around the tray. Fill the vegetable cases using a small spoon or pastry bag.

I. Blend:

1 tablespoon softened butter
1 tablespoon Roquefort
3 ounces softened cream cheese
Salt to taste
(1 teaspoon caraway, dill, or celery seeds)

Place this mixture in:

Celery or fennel ribs; snow peas, blanched, 1054;
**   Belgian endive leaves; cherry tomatoes; or**
**   scooped-out yellow squash or zucchini**

II. Fill vegetables with (For an elegant look, pipe the cheese mixture through a large pastry tube.):

Salmon Mousse, 85
Cream Cheese Spread, 179, or any sandwich
**   spread, 178–180**

Sprinkle with:

Paprika

III. Or fill vegetables with:

Guacamole, 72

IV. Or with:

Caviar on sour cream, with a little lemon juice

STUFFED CELERY

24 pieces

Prepare:

Twenty-four 3-inch-long pieces of celery

Using a knife, pastry bag, or sealed plastic bag with a cut corner, stuff the celery with any of the following:

Blue Cheese Spread with Walnuts, 76
Liptauer Cheese Spread, 76
Garlic Cheese Spread, 76
Guacamole, 72

Garnish with:

Chopped walnuts or minced parsley

NEW POTATOES STUFFED WITH SOUR CREAM AND CAVIAR

24 pieces

Small new potatoes are best, but large ones may be used. Place in a saucepan or pot:

Twelve $1/2$- to 2-inch new potatoes ($1/2$ pounds)

Add enough water to the pot to cover by 1 inch, then add:

1 tablespoon salt

Bring to a simmer over medium-high heat. Cook, uncovered, just until the potatoes are tender, about 20 minutes. Drain and let cool to room temperature. Peel the potatoes, if desired. Cut each potato in half. Using a melon baller, scoop a small crater out of each half. Cut a thin slice off the rounded side of each half so that the potatoes will sit flat. The potatoes can be covered with plastic wrap and set aside at room temperature for up to 4 hours. Just before serving, sprinkle the potatoes with:

Coarse kosher or sea salt

Have ready and spoon or pipe into each potato:

$1/2$ cup sour cream or crème fraîche
1 to 4 tablespoons caviar or other roe

Top each potato with $1/8$ to $1/2$ teaspoon caviar. Sprinkle generously with:

Snipped chives

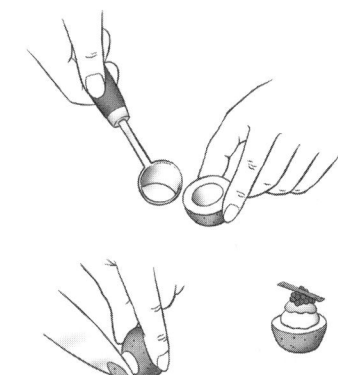

Scooping out the center of the potato with a melon baller;
cutting a thin slice off the rounded side of a potato half;
completed New Potato Stuffed with Sour Cream and Caviar

CRISPY POTATO SKINS

16 pieces

Use the leftover potatoes for Duchess Potatoes, 300, or Puffed Potatoes, 299.

Bake until tender:

Four 8-ounce baking potatoes

Let cool completely. Cut each potato lengthwise into quarters. With a teaspoon, scoop out most of the pulp, leaving a $1/4$-inch shell. Arrange the potato skins on a baking sheet, cut side up. Combine:

6 tablespoons butter, melted

1 tablespoon chili powder and/or 2 teaspoons finely minced garlic

Brush on the potato skins. Season generously with:

Salt

The potatoes can be covered loosely and refrigerated up to 12 hours. Shortly before serving, set a rack in the upper third of the oven and preheat the oven to 450°F. Bake the potato skins until very brown and crisp, about 30 minutes. Sprinkle with:

1 cup shredded Monterey Jack or Cheddar (4 ounces)
(8 slices bacon, cooked until crisp and crumbled)

Return to the oven until the cheese begins to brown, about 5 minutes. Serve at once, accompanied with:

(Sour cream or any salsa, 571)

ABOUT ANTIPASTO

Antipasto—or "what comes before the meal"—can be a snack with drinks or the basis of an entire meal. This ever-present constituent of Italian menus is an assortment of hard sausages, prosciutto, and other cured meats, with or without melon or figs; fish, such as anchovies, sardines and tuna; pickled onions, beets, peperoncini, marinated artichokes, cauliflower, and/or mushrooms; seasoned chickpeas; and cold eggplant in tomato puree. It may also include fresh tomatoes, fennel, hard and soft cheeses, and crusty breads. Other suggestions are listed below:

Salami
Cappicola
Prosciutto
Chunk white tuna in oil
Asiago
Provolone
Italian Fontina or Fontinella
Parmigiano-Reggiano
Marinated Mozzarella, 77
Marinated Mushrooms, 78
Marinated Artichokes
Roasted Red Peppers, 292
Spanish-Style Marinated Olives, 71
Assorted olives
Sliced Hard-Boiled Eggs, 194

BUFFALO CHICKEN WINGS

About 24 pieces

These were invented at the Anchor Bar in Buffalo, New York, in 1967.

Preheat the oven to 350°F. Remove the wing tips from:

1¹/₂ pounds (about 12) chicken wings

Cut each wing into 2 pieces at the joint. Mix on a plate:

¹/₃ cup all-purpose flour
1 teaspoon salt
¹/₂ teaspoon black pepper

Coat the wings with the flour mixture, shake off the excess, and set aside. Pour into a deep fryer or deep heavy pot:

1 inch vegetable oil

Heat over medium heat to 375°F, or until a corner of a wing held in the oil makes a lively sizzle. Add as many wings as will fit in a single layer and fry, turning once, until golden brown and cooked through, about 10 minutes. Drain on paper towels and keep warm on a baking sheet in the oven. Repeat with the remaining wings. Heat in a small saucepan over low heat until foaming:

3 tablespoons butter

Remove from the heat and stir in:

2 tablespoons red wine vinegar or cider vinegar
2 tablespoons hot pepper sauce, or to taste

Transfer the wings to a large bowl. Pour the sauce over them, and toss until evenly coated. Taste and adjust the seasonings. Serve hot with:

Celery sticks
Creamy Blue Cheese Dressing, 576

LEMON ROSEMARY CHICKEN ON SKEWERS

14–16 pieces

If using wooden skewers, either soak them in water for 1 hour or cover the exposed ends with foil. Alternatively, grill or broil the chicken unskewered, and skewer to serve. For another skewered chicken dish, prepare Beef Satay, 81, using chicken.

Stir together in a medium bowl:

3 tablespoons olive oil
2 teaspoons grated lemon zest
2 tablespoons lemon juice
1 teaspoon chopped fresh rosemary or ¹/₂ teaspoon dried rosemary
1 teaspoon minced garlic
¹/₂ teaspoon salt
¹/₄ teaspoon black pepper

Remove the tenders, if attached, from:

2 boneless, skinless chicken breast halves

Cut each breast half crosswise into 7 to 8 strips. Add the chicken to the marinade and stir to coat. Cover and refrigerate 1 to 2 hours. Prepare a medium-hot grill fire or preheat the broiler. Thread the chicken pieces, including the tenders, onto 16 skewers. Grill or broil, turning once, just until cooked through, about 2 minutes on each side. Serve hot or at room temperature.

CHICKEN FINGERS

About 12 pieces

Please read About Deep-Fat Frying, 1046.

Whisk together in a large bowl:

¹/₂ cup milk
1 large egg
1 tablespoon vegetable oil
1 tablespoon water

Stir together on a plate:

¹/₂ cup seasoned dry bread crumbs
¹/₂ cup cornmeal
¹/₂ cup all-purpose flour
1 teaspoon salt
¹/₂ to 1 teaspoon ground red or black pepper

Coat in the milk mixture, then roll one at a time in the crumb mixture:

1 pound chicken breast tenders

Place the tenders in a single layer on a baking sheet covered with wax or parchment paper. (The chicken can be refrigerated for several hours.) Heat to 375°F in a deep fryer or large deep heavy pot:

2 inches vegetable oil

Add one-third of the tenders and cook until golden brown, about 2 minutes on each side. Drain on paper towels. Fry the remaining tenders in 2 more batches. Serve with any of the following sauces or dips:

Creamy Blue Cheese Dressing, 576, Marinara
Sauce, 562, Ranch Dressing, 576, or
Honey Mustard Dipping Sauce, 566

CHICKEN LIVER MOUSSE

About 2 1/4 cups

Heat in a large skillet over medium-low heat:

1 tablespoon vegetable oil

Add:

1/2 cup finely chopped shallots (about 2 large)

Cook until softened, 3 to 5 minutes. Add:

**1 1/2 cups diced Golden Delicious apple (about
1 medium)**

Cook, stirring constantly, until softened, 5 to 7 minutes. Transfer to a food processor, then heat in the same skillet until the foam subsides:

1/4 cup (1/2 stick) butter

Add:

**1 pound chicken livers, tendons trimmed, halved,
rinsed, and patted dry**

Salt and black pepper

Cook over high heat until the livers are brown on the outside but still pink in the center, about 2 minutes on each side. Remove the pan from the heat. Pour in:

3 tablespoons Calvados or Cognac

Ignite with a match. Return the pan to the heat and swirl until the alcohol has burned off. Transfer to the food processor. Add:

1/4 cup heavy cream

Process until smooth. With the machine running, drop in, one piece at a time:

1/4 cup (1/2 stick) butter, cubed and chilled

Taste and adjust seasonings. Scrape mousse into a small crock or bowl and smooth the top with a spatula. Press plastic wrap directly on the surface and refrigerate until firm, at least 2 hours. Serve cold or at room temperature.

FIVE-SPICE RIBS

6 to 8 servings

This recipe is designed for the oven but the ribs can also be grilled, 1057.

Cut off and discard the green tops, then thinly slice the tender inner bulbs:

**2 stalks lemongrass, 994, or 1 tablespoon ground
lemongrass**

Place in a blender or food processor along with:

3 tablespoons sugar

2 tablespoons chopped shallots or scallion

2 tablespoons minced garlic

2 tablespoons fish sauce

2 tablespoons soy sauce

2 tablespoons toasted sesame oil

2 tablespoons vegetable oil

2 tablespoons five-spice powder

**1 teaspoon chili garlic paste or 1/4 teaspoon crushed
red pepper flakes**

Process until finely pureed, then transfer to a large bowl. Rinse, pat dry, and add:

3 pounds pork spareribs, cut into individual ribs

Turn to coat each rib thoroughly. Cover and refrigerate for 8 to 24 hours. Preheat the oven to 325°F. Lightly brush a large broiling pan or with baking sheet with vegetable oil. Arrange the ribs meaty side down on the pan and bake 45 minutes. Turn the ribs and bake until completely tender, 45 minutes to 1 hour longer. Serve, sprinkled with:

(2 tablespoons sesame seeds, toasted)

BEEF SATAY WITH PEANUT SAUCE

6 to 8 servings

You can substitute chicken for the beef in this recipe. To cut and cook the chicken, see Lemon Rosemary Chicken on Skewers, 80. Soak the bamboo skewers in water for 1 hour before putting over fire.

Process in a blender or food processor until smooth:

1/2 cup canned unsweetened coconut milk

1/3 cup minced shallots

2 tablespoons brown sugar

2 tablespoons soy sauce

1 tablespoon minced garlic

1 teaspoon ground cumin

1 teaspoon ground coriander

Place in a shallow dish:

**1 pound boneless beef sirloin, cut across the grain
into thin strips about 3 x 1 1/2 inches**

Add the marinade and toss to coat the beef strips thoroughly. Cover and let stand for 1 hour at room temperature, or refrigerate for up to 24 hours. Combine in a medium saucepan:

1 cup canned unsweetened coconut milk

1/2 cup creamy peanut butter

4 teaspoons light brown sugar

1 tablespoon fish sauce

1 tablespoon soy sauce

1 tablespoon Thai massaman curry paste

1/2 teaspoon curry powder

Whisk in thoroughly:

1/2 cup hot water

Simmer, stirring occasionally, over low heat until the flavors are well blended, 15 to 20 minutes. Prepare a medium-hot grill fire or preheat the broiler. Stir into the peanut sauce:

2 teaspoons lime juice

Keep warm while you cook the meat. Thread a 6-inch-long bamboo skewer through each strip of meat. Lightly brush the meat on both sides with:

Vegetable oil

Grill or broil, turning once, until browned, 2 to 3 minutes. Serve immediately, passing the warm peanut sauce on the side for dipping.

COCKTAIL MEATBALLS

About 70 meatballs

Preheat the oven to 350°F. Combine:

2 pounds ground beef round
1 cup crushed cornflakes
$^1/_3$ cup catsup
2 tablespoons soy sauce
3 tablespoons minced onion or 2 tablespoons dried onion
$^1/_4$ cup finely chopped parsley
3 garlic cloves, minced
$^1/_4$ teaspoon black pepper
2 eggs

Form into meatballs 1 inch in diameter. Arrange in a 13 x 9 x 2-inch baking pan. Combine in a medium saucepan:

1 tablespoon brown sugar
16 ounces jellied cranberry sauce (1$^1/_2$ cups)
1 tablespoon lemon juice
One 12-ounce bottle chili sauce

Stir over medium heat until cranberry sauce melts. Pour over meatballs in pan. Bake, uncovered, 30 minutes.

STUFFED GRAPE LEAVES (DOLMAS)

About 30 pieces

For a vegetarian version, omit the lamb, double the amount of rice, and add **$^1/_2$ cup dried currants** and **2 tablespoons pine nuts** to the filling mixture; pour an additional 1 cup water into the pan before cooking. Please read About Leaf Wrappings, 1051.

Drain:

Two 8-ounce jars grape leaves in brine

Separate the leaves, place in a large bowl, and cover with boiling water. Let soak for 1 hour, changing the water twice (use cold water) to remove excess salt. Drain and gently pat dry. Combine well:

1 cup finely ground lamb
2 cups finely chopped onion
$^1/_4$ cup finely chopped parsley
$^1/_4$ cup finely chopped dill
$^1/_2$ cup uncooked white rice

Line a Dutch oven with several grape leaves, using the small or torn ones. Stuff the remaining large whole leaves, reserving a few leaves for the top. One at a time, place each leaf vein side up on a plate. Put a heaping tablespoon of stuffing on the leaf near the stem end. Fold the stem

Making stuffed grape leaves

end over the stuffing, then fold in the two sides and roll up the leaf like a small cigar, tucking in the edges to make a neat package. Place seam side down in the prepared pot. Pack the leaves in a single layer, then repeat with a second layer. Drizzle over the top:

3 tablespoons olive oil

Pour in:

2 cups chicken or beef broth or water

Cover the top with the reserved grape leaves and weight with a heatproof plate. Cover the pan and simmer over low heat until the rice is cooked, 30 to 40 minutes. Serve hot or cold.

STEAK TARTARE

6 servings

The essential ingredient for this classic dish is top-quality fresh lean beef, preferably tenderloin, although top round or sirloin may be substituted. There is a slight risk of ingesting dangerous bacteria when eating uncooked meat or eggs; using the freshest meat and keeping it cold helps the flavor and texture and lowers the possibility of contamination. Prepare just before serving.

Place in a food processor:

1$^1/_2$ pounds beef tenderloin, well trimmed and cut into $^1/_2$-inch cubes

Pulse until the meat is chopped into $^1/_8$-inch pieces, about 7 to 10 seconds; do not overprocess. Use a fork and spoon to transfer the meat to a chilled platter or individual plates and gently form into 6 individual mounds. If desired, make a spoon-shaped indentation on top of each mound and crack and separate:

6 eggs

Place a yolk in each indentation. (Reserve whites for another use.) Divide and arrange in small mounds around each serving:

$^1/_2$ cup minced onions
$^1/_2$ cup minced shallots
$^1/_2$ cup minced parsley
$^1/_4$ cup minced drained capers
(8 to 12 anchovy fillets, minced)

Serve immediately, passing separately:

Lemon juice

Worcestershire sauce

Dijon mustard

Hot pepper sauce

Salt and black pepper

Serve with:

Thin-sliced pumpernickel or toasted French bread

RUMAKI

36 pieces

Assemble ahead of time on the day you serve them and bake just before needed. You can also make these using whole water chestnuts in place of the liver.

Rinse, trim, and cut into quarters:

8 ounces chicken livers

Whisk together in a medium bowl:

2 tablespoons soy sauce

2 tablespoons sake or dry sherry

1 tablespoon grated peeled fresh ginger

2 teaspoons light brown sugar

Add the livers and toss until coated. Cover and marinate in the refrigerator for 1 to 2 hours. Preheat oven to 400°F. Have ready:

18 slices bacon, cut in half

36 very thin slices rinsed canned water chestnuts (from one 8-ounce can)

Lay 1 piece of chicken liver and 1 slice water chestnut on each piece of bacon, roll up, and secure with a toothpick speared through the overlapping ends of the bacon and out the other side. Place on a rimmed baking sheet. Bake for 10 minutes. Turn the oven to broil and cook until the bacon is crisp and the livers are cooked through, about 2 minutes. Drain briefly on paper towels, then transfer to a platter and serve hot.

SALAMI ROLLS

About 24 pieces

You can also mince the scallions and tomatoes and mix this by hand.

Process in a food processor until smooth:

4 ounces cream cheese, softened

2 to 3 sun-dried tomato halves, drained

2 tablespoons chopped scallion greens

Black pepper to taste

Lay out on a work surface:

12 very thin slices salami (about 3 ounces)

Spread the cream cheese mixture thinly over the salami. Roll each slice into a cylinder and cut in half. Stand the pieces on end in a platter, alone or with other rolled meats.

SMOKED TURKEY AND ARUGULA ROLLS

32 pieces

Stir together:

$1/3$ cup mayonnaise

4 teaspoons Pesto Sauce, 569

Have ready:

32 arugula leaves or small watercress sprigs

Lay out on a work surface:

10 ounces thinly sliced smoked turkey breast

Carefully spread a thin layer of the mayonnaise over each slice. Cut each slice in half on the diagonal, then in half the opposite way, to form 4 triangles. Top each with an arugula leaf (or small watercress sprig) and roll up to form a cone with a little green peeking out. Arrange seam side down on a platter, alone or with other rolled meats.

BEEF AND SCALLION ROLLS (NEGI MAKI)

About 30 pieces

To make slicing easier, freeze 30 minutes to 1 hour:

$1^1/4$ pounds boneless beef sirloin, trimmed of fat

Meanwhile, trim and cut into 2-inch lengths, then divide into 15 bundles (approximately 2 to 3 pieces each):

8 to 10 scallions, including green tops

Cut the beef into 15 very thin slices. Place each slice between 2 sheets of plastic wrap and pound lightly with the bottom of a small skillet to an even thinness. (If the beef should tear, patch it with another piece on top.) Roll a piece of beef snugly around each scallion bundle, wrapping it 2 to 3 times, and secure the roll by threading a wooden toothpick lengthwise through the meat.

Heat in a large skillet over high heat:

$1^1/2$ tablespoons vegetable oil

Add the rolls seam side down and sear. Once the seams have sealed, turn to brown the rolls on all sides. After about 2 minutes, when the beef has changed color, add:

2 tablespoons sake

2 tablespoons soy sauce

1 tablespoon sugar

Reduce the heat slightly and cook for 1 minute, shaking the pan to keep the rolls from sticking. Transfer the rolls to a plate and let cool slightly, then to remove the toothpicks (twist one in place, then pull out gently). If there is a lot of sauce left in the skillet, reduce over high heat to 2 tablespoons. Just before serving, return the rolls to the skillet over high heat and shake to glaze them with the sauce. Slice each roll crosswise in half and serve warm.

ABOUT SEAFOOD PARTY FOODS

Fish and shellfish hors d'oeuvres are easy to prepare, since most of the work can be done ahead of time. No-Fail Boiled Shrimp, 385, for example, can be cooked a day ahead for presentation as Shrimp Cocktail, 370. Coconut Shrimp, 84, can be served on a tray sprinkled with coconut flecks. You can turn Grilled or Broiled Shrimp or Scallops, 386, or any of the variations into an hors d'oeuvre by threading the seafood on skewers before grilling. Oysters and clams should be opened as close to serving time as possible. Make sure you buy the freshest shellfish and store carefully before cooking. See Shellfish, 369.

GRILLED OR BROILED SHRIMP COCKAIGNE

5 dozen pieces

Shell, leaving the tails on, and devein, 385:

2 pounds jumbo shrimp

Combine in a large bowl:

1 garlic clove, minced

1 cup olive oil

¹/₂ cup sweet white wine, such as Riesling or Sauternes

1 tablespoon lemon juice

3 tablespoons basil and parsley chopped together

1 teaspoon salt

¹/₄ teaspoon black pepper

Add the shrimp, turning to coat. Cover and marinate in the refrigerator for several hours. Prepare a grill fire medium high or preheat the broiler. Grill or broil the shrimp, turning once, until opaque throughout, about 10 minutes. Serve at once with:

Lemon Butter, 557

flavored with:

1 large garlic clove, minced

BAKED HONEY SHRIMP

About 50 pieces

Mix together in a small bowl:

1 tablespoon chopped parsley

1 teaspoon grated lemon zest

Cover and refrigerate until ready to use. Whisk together in a medium bowl:

2 tablespoons lemon juice

¹/₂ cup olive oil

2 tablespoons soy sauce

2 tablespoons honey

2 tablespoons Cajun seasoning

1 tablespoon chopped parsley

¹/₄ teaspoon ground red pepper

Add:

2 pounds large shrimp, peeled and deveined

Toss well in the dressing. Cover and marinate in the refrigerator for 1 hour, stirring occasionally. Position a rack in the center of the oven and preheat to 450°F. Transfer the shrimp to a baking pan or sheet large enough to hold them in one layer. Bake until firm, 5 to 10 minutes. Sprinkle with the reserved lemon zest and parsley mixture.

CAJUN POPCORN SHRIMP

12 to 15 servings

This recipe can also be made with clams, oysters, or, as is traditionally done in Louisiana, with crayfish. This treat will be scooped up and eaten as easily as a handful of popcorn, so make sure you have plenty.

Stir together in a medium bowl:

1 cup all-purpose flour

1 teaspoon sugar

1 teaspoon salt

¹/₂ teaspoon onion powder

¹/₂ teaspoon garlic powder

¹/₂ teaspoon white pepper

¹/₂ teaspoon black pepper

¹/₂ teaspoon ground red pepper

¹/₂ teaspoon dried thyme

Make a well in the center of the mixture. Gradually pour in, whisking constantly:

1¹/₂ cups milk

2 large eggs, lightly beaten

Let stand for 30 minutes. Meanwhile, heat to 365°F in a deep fryer or deep heavy pot:

4 inches vegetable oil

Stir into the batter:

2 pounds small shrimp, peeled, or larger shrimp, peeled, deveined, and cut into ¹/₂-inch pieces

Remove with a slotted spoon and lightly toss with:

2 to 3 cups dry bread crumbs or fine cornmeal

In batches, add the shrimp to the hot oil and fry until crisp and lightly browned, 2 to 3 minutes. With a slotted spoon, transfer to paper towels to drain. Serve with:

Garlic Mayonnaise, 581

BEER-BATTER SHRIMP

About 60 pieces

Shell, leaving the tails:

2 pounds medium shrimp

Cut the shrimp down the back, devein without cutting through, then open, and press flat. Prepare:

Fritter Batter for Vegetables, Meat, and Fish, 658

Add the shrimp and let stand for 30 minutes. Heat to 365°F in a deep fryer or deep heavy pot:

2 inches vegetable oil

Remove the shrimp one at a time from the batter and fry in small batches, turning twice to ensure they are golden brown and crisp on all sides, 3 to 4 minutes. Transfer to paper towels to drain. Serve as is, or with:

Rémoulade Sauce, 581, Becker Cocktail Sauce, 568, Tartar Sauce, 581, or Fruit Salsa, 572

COCONUT SHRIMP

Prepare **Beer-Batter Shrimp, above,** substituting ¹/₂ cup **orange juice** for the beer. After dipping the shrimp in the batter, press them into a mixture of **3 cups shredded unsweetened dried coconut** and **1 cup dry bread crumbs.** Fry and serve as is or with **Fruit Salsa, 572.**

ANGELS ON HORSEBACK

24 pieces

Preheat the oven to 400°F. Butter and lightly toast in oven:

Twenty-four 2-inch bread rounds (cut from 8 slices firm white bread)

Leave the oven on. Shuck, 371, or drain if shucked:

24 medium oysters

Cut in half:

12 slices bacon

Spread one side of each bacon slice lightly with:

(Anchovy paste)

Wrap a slice of bacon (anchovy side in) around each oyster and secure with a toothpick. Place on a baking sheet. Bake until the bacon is cooked, about 10 minutes. Drain on paper towels, and remove toothpicks. Place the oysters on the toasts and sprinkle with:

3 tablespoons minced parsley

OYSTERS ROCKEFELLER

24 pieces

Preheat oven to 450°F. Shuck, 371, leaving the oysters on the half-shell:

24 medium oysters

Process in a food processor just until minced:

1^1/$_2$ cups well-drained cooked spinach

^{1}/$_3$ cup fresh bread crumbs, 961

^{1}/$_4$ cup chopped scallions

2 tablespoons chopped parsley

^{1}/$_2$ teaspoon salt

4 drops hot pepper sauce

Add:

^{1}/$_4$ cup (^{1}/$_2$ stick) butter, softened

1 tablespoon Pernod or anisette, or to taste

Process for 10 seconds more. Cover a baking sheet with:

Coarse kosher or sea salt

Nestle the oysters in the salt to steady them. Spoon 1 heaping teaspoon of the spinach mixture over each oyster. Bake until plumped, about 10 minutes. Broil until the tops are browned, about 2 minutes.

CLAMS CASINO

24 pieces

This treatment is also quite tasty with oysters.

Preheat the broiler. Combine in a bowl and mix well:

^{1}/$_4$ cup (^{1}/$_2$ stick) butter, softened

1 scallion, finely chopped

1^1/$_2$ tablespoons minced parsley

1 tablespoon lemon juice

^{1}/$_4$ teaspoon salt

Shuck, 371, leaving on the half-shell:

24 cherrystone clams

Spoon about 1 teaspoon of the butter mixture on top of each clam. Top with:

6 slices cooked bacon, crumbled

Broil until the butter is bubbling, about 3 minutes.

SALMON PÂTÉ

4 to 6 servings

Combine in a small saucepan:

4 ounces skinless salmon fillet, cut into bite-sized pieces

^{1}/$_2$ cup dry white wine

1 tablespoon olive oil

2 tablespoons Cognac or other brandy

Salt and black pepper

Bring to a boil over medium heat and cook until the salmon is opaque, about 5 minutes. Drain, discarding the wine. Melt in another small saucepan over medium heat:

3 tablespoons unsalted butter

Add and cook, stirring, until opaque, 3 to 5 minutes:

4 ounces sliced smoked salmon

Let cool. Puree the salmon in a food processor with:

3 tablespoons unsalted butter, softened

Using a fork, combine the fresh salmon and smoked salmon mixtures in a bowl until well blended. Taste and adjust the seasonings. Cover and refrigerate for at least 12 hours. About 30 minutes before serving, remove the pâté from the refrigerator. Serve on:

Thin slices of toast

SALMON MOUSSE

3 cups

This mousse can also be piped through a pastry bag onto sliced bread, into Cucumber Cups, 173, or onto cucumber slices.

Pour into a small saucepan:

^{1}/$_4$ cup lemon juice

1 envelope (2^1/$_4$ teaspoons) unflavored gelatin

Let stand for 5 minutes to soften the gelatin. Place over low heat and stir until dissolved, 1 to 2 minutes. Let cool to lukewarm. Stir into the gelatin:

^{1}/$_4$ cup mayonnaise

^{1}/$_4$ cup sour cream

Combine in a food processor:

15 ounces canned red salmon, drained, skin and bones removed

^{1}/$_4$ cup chopped dill

1 shallot, minced

1 tablespoon drained capers or chopped cornichons

1 teaspoon sweet paprika

Ground red pepper or white pepper to taste

Pulse briefly just until combined; do not overprocess. Add the gelatin mixture and pulse once or twice just to combine. Beat until stiff peaks form:

^{3}/$_4$ cup heavy cream

Gently fold into the salmon mixture. Oil a decorative fish mold or a stainless steel bowl. Transfer the salmon mixture to the oiled container and smooth the top. Cover and refrigerate until firm, 2 to 3 hours. To unmold, submerge two-thirds of the mold in very hot water for 10 seconds. Top the mold with a platter and immediately invert the mousse onto the platter. Garnish with:

Watercress sprigs, thinly sliced cucumber, or lemon wedges

SMOKED SALMON ROLLS

18 pieces

Combine in a bowl:

3 ounces cream cheese, softened

2 tablespoons minced dill

1 tablespoon minced scallion
1 teaspoon lemon juice
Spread thinly over:
   6 ounces thinly sliced smoked salmon
Roll up the pieces of salmon, then cut into $^{1}/_{2}$-inch slices. Cover and refrigerate for up to 1 day before serving.

SMOKED TROUT ON CUCUMBER ROUNDS
About 75 pieces
For a more decorative effect, score cucumbers with a fork or peel lengthwise, creating a striped look, 173.
Cut each into 30 to 40 slices and lay out on baking sheets:
   2 cucumbers
Stir together:
   $^{1}/_{2}$ cup sour cream
   4 teaspoons drained prepared horseradish, or to taste
Using a measuring spoon, dollop about $^{1}/_{4}$ teaspoon of the horseradish cream onto the center of each cucumber slice. Divide among the cucumber slices:
   8 ounces smoked trout fillets, skinned and broken into almond-sized pieces
These can be stored for up to 3 hours in the refrigerator, lightly covered with dampened paper towels. Before serving, garnish with:
   Sprigs of dill
Serve on a tray, garnished with:
   Lemon wedges

CAVIAR
A lady was once moved to ask plaintively why caviar is so expensive, to which a helpful maître d' replied, "After all, madam, it is a year's work for a sturgeon." The best caviar is the roe of the sturgeon, and the most sought-after caviar, **Beluga** and **Osetra** (or *Oscietre*), comes from the Caspian Sea. A third type, **Sevruga,** is taken from a smaller Caspian sturgeon. At present, bans have gone into effect to protect the wild sturgeon and trade of its caviar has been prohibited by several international organizations. Today sturgeon are farm-raised for caviar in California and the Pacific Northwest region. While American caviar does not have the cachet—and some would argue the flavor— of Caspian caviar, it is more reasonably priced.

Spoonbill or paddlefish roe comes from fish native to the Mississippi and Tennessee Rivers. It is small, silvery, rich, and flavorful. There are other fish roe that, unlike spoonbill roe, look nothing like caviar but are nevertheless enjoyed in their own right, from the large, robustly flavored orange roe of salmon to the small, firm, and mild-tasting golden roe of whitefish.

Buy caviar only from a reputable source, and read labels carefully. The eggs should be shiny, translucent, gray, and large-grained. If at all possible, taste before buying. No caviar should taste excessively salty or truly fishy. ➤ As fresh caviar spoils in a few hours in temperatures of 40°F or above, always serve it on ice. Caviar may be kept, un-opened, at 35°F for a month. Once opened, it should be eaten within a day or two.

To serve individual portions, heat the back of a metal spoon, press it into an ice cube, and fill the depression with caviar using a plastic spoon or a special caviar spoon. ➤ Never allow caviar to touch metal or to be served on it. If you spread it on canapés, or blini, be careful not to bruise the eggs. The classic accompaniments are lemon wedges, parsley, and black bread, pumpernickel, or toast. Although hard-cooked egg whites and yolks and onions— all finely minced and separately arranged—are frequently used as a garnish, connoisseurs consider them less suitable than the simpler lemon and parsley. Other ways to serve caviar are with potatoes or simply mixed half and half with sour cream. Caviar should be accompanied by either chilled dry white wines or, preferably, Champagne, vodka, or Black Pepper Vodka, 58. See Caviar Butter, 559.

ABOUT CANAPÉS
Canapés are dainty hors d'oeuvres with their own built-in bread, cracker, or pastry base. They resemble small open-faced tea sandwiches and are eaten in one or two bites. Canapés built on toast have four components: base, spread, main ingredient, and garnish. The base may be cut into any number of shapes—a square, triangle, or circle, or a more decorative shape—by using the widely available canapé cutters. The spread is typically a very thin layer of plain or seasoned butter, mayonnaise, or cream cheese mixture, and is essential to keep the bread from drying out and to fix the main ingredient to the base. The main ingredient or combination of ingredients is placed in a single layer on top. Very thinly sliced meat, shellfish, smoked fish, vegetable, or cheese is common. Finally, the garnish adds eye appeal but should not overshadow the canapé. It can be a fresh herb leaf or sprig or a sliver of any colorful, complementary ingredient. Small crackers, miniature tartlet shells, 90, baked miniature phyllo shells, or miniature choux, 671, or puff paste shells, 670, are used in canapés with pastry. For more inspiration, see About Pastry Party Foods, 88, and About Tea Sandwiches, 185.

OPEN-FACED TEA SANDWICHES (CANAPÉS)
About 32 small sandwiches
Using the bread suggestions below, have ready:
   Thirty-two $^{1}/_{4}$-inch-thick slices baguette, 2 x 2 x $^{1}/_{2}$-inch crustless squares Challah, 600, or Egg Bread, or 2 x 2 x $^{1}/_{4}$-inch squares any dense dark bread (black bread, pumpernickel, etc.)
   About 5 tablespoons butter, softened, or $^{2}/_{3}$ cup mayonnaise or other spread
Spread one side of each bread slice with about $^{1}/_{2}$ teaspoon butter or 1 teaspoon mayonnaise or spread. Cover with any one of the following:
   Thinly sliced strawberries and sour cream or crème fraîche (egg bread or challah)

Brie, chopped mango chutney, toasted sliced almonds, and butter (dark bread)

Blue cheese, thinly sliced pears, and butter (baguette)

Thinly sliced smoked salmon, tiny dill sprigs, and Russian Horseradish Cream, 581 (baguette or dark bread)

Sliced poached shrimp, parsley or tarragon leaves, and Mayonnaise with Green Herbs, 580 (baguette)

Flaked crabmeat, thinly sliced avocado, and mayonnaise (baguette)

Caviar, minced onions, and butter (pumpernickel)

Sliced chicken or turkey breast, thinly sliced Granny Smith apples, and Curry Mayonnaise, 580 (baguette, egg bread, or challah)

Sliced roast beef, cilantro leaves, and Chipotle Mayonnaise, 580 (baguette)

CHEESE PUFF CANAPÉS

16 pieces

Preheat the broiler. Beat in a medium bowl until very stiff:

3 egg whites

Fold in:

1¹/₂ cups shredded Gruyère or Swiss (6 ounces)
1¹/₂ teaspoons Worcestershire sauce
1¹/₂ teaspoons Dijon mustard
³/₄ teaspoon paprika

Toast, then arrange on a baking sheet:

Four 4-inch square slices white bread, crusts removed and quartered

Spread with the cheese mixture and place under the broiler until the cheese is puffed and brown.

MARINATED HERRING ON TOAST

Drain:

Marinated herring

Place fillets on:

Squares or rounds of toast

Cover with:

Thin slices red onion

Sprinkle with:

Chopped parsley or watercress

Serve promptly.

SMOKED SALMON CANAPÉS

Salmon for canapés should be sliced across the grain as thin as possible. It is delicious when garnished with cucumber or egg. The thin slices of salmon also make an ideal lining for cocktail tarts.

I. Place on crackers or squares of toast:

Thinly sliced smoked salmon

Dust with:

Black pepper

Sprinkle with:

Lemon juice

II. Or top each with a slice of:

Stuffed olives

Brush the canapés with:

Mustard

III. Or top the salmon with:

Guacamole, 72

IV. Or garnish with a mixture of:

Minced hard-cooked egg yolk, dill, red onion, and capers

ANCHOVY TOASTS

16 pieces

Soak for 10 minutes in cold water to cover:

4 ounces anchovy fillets, drained

Pat dry, and mince. Combine well with:

3 tablespoons olive oil
1 tablespoon red wine vinegar
3 tablespoons chopped parsley
2 garlic cloves, minced
Black pepper to taste

Preheat the broiler. Place on a baking sheet:

16 slices French bread, cut from a baguette

Broil until golden. Spread with the anchovy mixture and broil until warm, about 1 minute. Serve immediately.

BEEF OR PORK TENDERLOIN CANAPÉS

About 90 pieces

Served on thin slices of baguette, a little beef or pork tenderloin goes a long way. A wide variety of flavored spreads can be applied; some are suggested below.

Prepare:

Roasted Filet or Tenderloin of Beef or Pork, 472

Meanwhile, thinly slice:

3 baguettes

Spread the slices evenly with:

1¹/₄ to 1¹/₂ cups Snail Butter, 559, Maître d'Hôtel Butter, 559, flavored butter, 558, honey mustard, whole-grain mustard, or flavored mayonnaise, 578

Cut the meat lengthwise into quarters and thinly slice each quarter. Top each piece of bread with a slice of filet. If desired, top with any of the following:

Sprigs of parsley, dill, or watercress, capers, sliced or diced raw or roasted, 244, yellow or red bell peppers, minced onions, or Caramelized Onions, 287

HAM BISCUITS

20 to 24 biscuits

Preheat the oven to 425°F. Prepare the dough for:

Rolled Biscuits, 638

adding, if desired:

(¹/₄ cup snipped fresh chives)

Roll out the dough into a circle or rectangle about ¹/₂ inch thick. Cut into 2-inch rounds, hearts, or diamonds with a biscuit or cookie cutter. Place 1 inch apart on ungreased baking sheets and brush the tops with:

Melted butter

Bake until golden on top, about 15 minutes. Prepare:

Honey Mustard Dipping Sauce, 566

Or have ready for spreading:

$^1/_4$ cup ($^1/_2$ stick) butter

When the biscuits are cool enough to handle, split them, spread with the honey mustard or butter, and make sandwiches with:

12 ounces thinly sliced ham or prosciutto

Serve warm or at room temperature.

TURKEY BISCUITS WITH CHUTNEY BUTTER

20 to 24 biscuits

Cress or Arugula Butter, 558, Nut Butter, 178, or any other flavored butter can be substituted for the chutney butter. Prepare the biscuits for Ham Biscuits, above. While the biscuits are baking, stir together:

$^1/_2$ cup (1 stick) butter, softened
3 tablespoons mango chutney
Pinch of curry powder
Pinch of salt

Cool biscuits, split them, spread with the chutney butter, and make sandwiches with:

12 ounces sliced turkey breast

Serve warm or at room temperature. Or, to serve hot, heat on a baking sheet in a 350°F oven about 10 minutes.

BRUSCHETTA WITH TOMATOES AND BASIL

32 pieces

From the Italian word meaning "roasted over coals," bruschetta, in its simplest form, it is nothing more than grilled bread rubbed with garlic cloves and brushed with olive oil. However, bruschetta also serves as the foundation for a wide variety of toppings. A single bruschetta makes a good first course, while two or three will make a nice lunch when accompanied with a simple salad. Before putting the tomato mixture on top of the grilled or broiled bread, you can melt a slice of mozzarella and then top with the tomato mixture, substituting chopped fresh oregano for the basil. To serve as an hors d'oeuvre, cut each bruschetta into quarters.

Prepare a medium-hot grill fire or preheat the broiler. Grill or broil until golden brown, on each side:

8 thick slices crusty bread

Remove from the heat and rub on both sides with:

2 large garlic cloves, halved

Brush with:

3 to 4 tablespoons olive oil

Combine:

4 medium tomatoes, diced
$^1/_2$ cup slivered basil leaves
Salt and black pepper

Divide the tomato mixture among the bruschetta.

ABOUT PASTRY PARTY FOODS

Pastry is a perfect choice for hors d'oeuvres that can be at least partially prepared in advance. The pastry dough can be rolled, cut, shaped, and frozen, then removed from the freezer at the appropriate time, filled, and baked. Phyllo pastries can be completely assembled and then frozen to be baked straight from the freezer. **Choux paste,** 671, can be frozen in its uncooked state and thawed overnight in the refrigerator. The morning of the party, pipe the paste into shapes and bake. For specific details on handling choux paste, phyllo, and puff pastry, see 661.

MUSHROOM TRIANGLES

32 to 36 triangles

Combine in a small bowl:

$^1/_2$ ounce dried porcini or shiitake mushrooms
1 cup hot water

Let stand for 30 minutes. Lift the mushrooms out of the soaking liquid and strain the liquid through a fine-mesh sieve lined with a dampened paper towel; reserve the liquid. Finely chop the mushrooms. Melt in a medium skillet over medium heat:

2 tablespoons butter

Add and cook, stirring constantly, for 1 minute:

2 tablespoons minced shallots
1 teaspoon minced garlic

Add the chopped dried mushrooms, along with:

6 ounces cremini, shiitake, or button mushrooms, coarsely chopped

Cook, stirring occasionally, until the mushrooms begin to wilt, about 3 minutes. Add:

3 tablespoons reserved mushroom soaking liquid
2 tablespoons minced parsley
$^1/_2$ teaspoon salt
$^1/_4$ teaspoon black pepper, or to taste

Cook, stirring occasionally, until the mixture is almost dry, about 5 minutes. Transfer to a bowl and let cool completely. If desired, stir in:

(2 ounces soft goat cheese)

Preheat the oven to 375°F. Melt in a small saucepan:

$^1/_4$ cup ($^1/_2$ stick) butter

Lay on a work surface and cover with a damp towel:

8 sheets phyllo dough, thawed if frozen

Remove 1 sheet and brush it with melted butter. Lay another sheet over the first and cut the sheets lengthwise into 8 or 9 strips. Working with 1 strip at a time, spoon 1 teaspoon of the filling onto the bottom left corner of the strip. Fold the bottom end over the filling to meet the right-hand edge, making a triangle, then continue to fold, as if folding a flag, all the way to the top. Place on a lightly oiled baking sheet. Repeat with the remaining strips. Brush the tops with melted butter. Repeat with the remaining phyllo and filling. Bake until golden brown, about 15 minutes. Serve hot.

SPINACH AND FETA TRIANGLES

32 to 36 triangles

Melt in a small skillet over medium heat:

2 tablespoons butter

Add and cook, stirring, for about 5 minutes:

¹/₄ cup minced onions

Add:

**One 10-ounce package frozen chopped spinach,
thawed and well drained (about 1 cup)**

Cook until the liquid has evaporated, about 5 minutes. Transfer to a medium bowl and cool. Stir into the spinach:

1 cup crumbled feta (4 ounces)
1 teaspoon lemon juice
¹/₂ teaspoon black pepper

Lay on a work surface and cover with a damp towel:

8 sheets phyllo dough, thawed if frozen

Proceed as for Mushroom Triangles, above, substituting the spinach mixture for the mushroom filling.

PARTY PIROSHKI

18 piroshki

Grease or line with parchment paper and sprinkle with cornmeal 2 baking sheets. In a large skillet over medium heat, warm:

1 tablespoon vegetable oil

Add:

1 cup chopped onion

Cook until softened, 5 to 6 minutes. Add:

1 pound ground beef
¹/₂ teaspoon salt

Cook until the meat browns, about 5 minutes. Add:

1 cup beef broth
¹/₂ teaspoon ground black pepper
1 teaspoon sugar
¹/₂ cup rice

Bring to a simmer, cover, reduce heat to low, and cook for about 25 minutes, until rice is tender. Cool mixture, then refrigerate until cold. Preheat oven to 425°F. Have ready:

**2 recipes Food Processor Puff Pastry, 669, or one
17¹/₂- to 18¹/₂-inch package frozen puff pastry**

Roll dough out into two 18- by 8-inch rectangles. Using about 1¹/₃ cups filling for each rectangle, spread filling along the edge of the dough, leaving an inch along the edge. Roll dough over and seal with a small amount of water. Trim excess dough. Brush with:

Egg Wash, 799

Carefully transfer each roll to a prepared baking sheet and chill in freezer until firm. Preheat the oven to 350°F. Bake until golden brown, about 20 minutes. Cool, then slice into ³/₄-inch slices. Filled dough may be frozen and baked while still frozen in a 350°F oven for about 30 minutes.

SAMOSAS WITH POTATOES AND PEAS

About 60 samosas

Samosas are traditionally made with a soft pastry. Here they are conveniently made with phyllo. They freeze well when tightly wrapped in plastic, and they can be baked frozen—simply add 5 minutes to the baking time.

Drop into boiling salted water to cover:

1¹/₂ pounds boiling potatoes (6 to 8 potatoes)

Cover and cook until tender, 25 to 30 minutes. Drain, peel, and mash in a medium bowl.

Heat in a medium skillet over high heat:

1 tablespoon vegetable oil

Add and heat until they pop:

1 teaspoon black or yellow mustard seeds

Add and cook for 20 seconds more:

3 garlic cloves, thinly sliced

Stir the garlic mixture into the mashed potatoes, along with:

1 cup frozen peas, thawed
1 small onion, finely chopped (about ¹/₂ cup)
¹/₄ cup chopped cilantro
1 serrano or jalapeño pepper, seeded and minced
2 tablespoons lemon juice
1¹/₄ teaspoons salt

Preheat the oven to 375°F. Grease 2 baking sheets. Unroll on a dry work surface:

1 pound phyllo dough, thawed if frozen

Cover with a damp towel. Melt:

¹/₂ cup (1 stick) butter

Remove 1 sheet of phyllo and lay it on the work surface, with a long side facing you. Brush lightly with melted butter, lay a second sheet on top, and brush it with melted butter. Cut the sheets vertically into 2¹/₂-inch-wide strips (the last strip will be only 2 inches). Cover the strips with a sheet of wax paper or plastic wrap and cover that with a damp towel. Working with 1 strip at a time, scoop up a rounded teaspoon of the potato mixture and pat it over the bottom right-hand corner of the strip, so that it fills the entire corner, not just the center. Fold the corner to the other side to make a triangle and continue folding to the end of the strip, as if folding a flag. Place on a baking sheet and brush the top with melted butter. Repeat with the remaining phyllo and filling. Bake until lightly browned about 15 minutes. Serve immediately.

SAMOSAS WITH GROUND BEEF

About 60 samosas

Heat in a large skillet:

2 tablespoons canola or other vegetable oil

Add and cook, stirring, over medium heat until limp, about 3 minutes:

1 medium onion, chopped (about 1 cup)

Add:

1 teaspoon minced garlic
1 teaspoon minced peeled fresh ginger
³/₄ teaspoon ground coriander

$^1/_2$ teaspoon turmeric

$^3/_4$ teaspoon salt

Cook, stirring for 2 minutes. Add:

1 pound lean ground beef

Cook, stirring, until the meat is cooked through, about 5 minutes. Add:

$^1/_2$ **cup water**

Simmer until evaporated, 3 to 4 minutes. Stir in:

$^1/_4$ **cup chopped cilantro**

2 serrano or jalapeño peppers, seeded and minced

Fill and bake as for Samosas with Potatoes and Peas, above.

MINIATURE TARTLET SHELLS OR TURNOVERS

24 shells or turnovers

Prepare:

Cream Cheese Pastry Dough, 666

To make **tartlet shells,** form the dough into 24 balls, using 1 tablespoon for each. Press each ball into the bottom and up the sides of one cup of an ungreased 24-cup mini muffin pan, allowing the dough to extend $^1/_8$ inch above the top of the cup. Refrigerate at least 20 minutes, or for up to 8 hours. Preheat the oven to 425°F.

Prick the bottom and sides of each shell with a fork. Bake until the edges are brown, the bottoms feel firm and dry, and the sides have shrunk slightly from the cups, 18 to 20 minutes. When cool, remove the shells from the pan and fill and bake as directed in the recipes below.

To make **turnovers,** divide the dough in half, flatten each half into a disk, wrap in plastic, and refrigerate for at least 1 hour, or for up to 24 hours.

On a floured surface, roll one half of the dough $^1/_8$ inch thick into a 12-inch-wide circle. Cut the dough using a 3-inch round cookie or biscuit cutter. Transfer to a large baking sheet lined with parchment paper and refrigerate. Set the scraps aside. Roll and cut the other half of the dough in the same way. Gather the scraps from both batches into a ball, roll out, and cut into additional rounds, making 24 altogether.

Place the filling in the center of the rounds as directed in the recipes below. Generously moisten the edges of each round with cold water and fold in half. Firmly press the edges with your fingers, then press with the tines of a fork. Prick the top once with a fork. Arrange on a baking sheet lined with parchment paper. Refrigerate for at least 1 hour, or for up to 8 hours. Preheat the oven to 425°F. Combine in a small bowl and beat with a fork:

1 large egg white

Pinch of salt

Lightly brush the top of each turnover with the egg wash. Bake until golden brown, 12 to 15 minutes.

COCKTAIL TARTLETS

24 tartlets

Preheat the oven to 425°F. Prepare tartlet shells following the instructions in Miniature Tartlet Shells or Turnovers, above. Place the baked shells on a baking sheet lined with parchment paper. Have ready about 1$^1/_4$ cups of any of the following:

Chipped Beef and Gravy, 112

Shrimp Wiggle, 113

Ratatouille Provençale, 274

Creamed Mushrooms, 283

Creamed Spinach, 305

Creamed Chicken or Turkey, 445

Finely crumbled cooked sausage and shredded cheese

Finely diced ham and diced cheese

Fill shells with 1 teaspoon of filling. Bake until heated through, 8 to 10 minutes.

MINIATURE QUICHES

24 quiches

Preheat the oven to 425°F. Have ready:

$^1/_4$ **cup finely chopped ham, cooked broccoli, or roasted red peppers**

Combine in a medium bowl and whisk until thoroughly blended:

2 large eggs

$^1/_2$ **cup heavy cream**

$^1/_3$ **cup grated Parmesan (1$^1/_2$ ounces)**

2 teaspoons grated onion or shallot

$^1/_4$ **teaspoon salt**

$^1/_8$ **teaspoon black or white pepper**

Have ready Miniature Tartlet Shells or Turnovers, above. Place the baked shells on a baking sheet lined with parchment paper. Place $^1/_2$ teaspoon of the finely chopped ingredients in the bottom of each shell, then fill to the brim with the egg mixture. Bake until the filling is set and puffed, 12 to 15 minutes.

MINIATURE TURNOVERS WITH SUN-DRIED TOMATOES AND PESTO

24 turnovers

Prepare and bake the turnovers following the instructions in Miniature Tartlet Shells or Turnovers, above.

Place in a strainer set over a bowl and allow to drain for 30 minutes:

$^1/_2$ **cup Pesto Sauce, 569**

Place pesto in a medium bowl and combine well with:

$^3/_4$ **cup crumbled goat cheese (3 ounces)**

4 oil-packed sun-dried tomatoes, drained and finely chopped

(3 tablespoons pine nuts or walnuts, finely chopped)

Salt and black pepper to taste

Place 1 teaspoon filling in the center of each dough round.

MINIATURE TURNOVERS WITH CARAMELIZED ONIONS AND BLUE CHEESE

24 turnovers

Prepare and bake the turnovers following the instructions in Miniature Tartlet Shells or Turnovers, 90.

Combine in a medium skillet and set over medium heat:

1¹/₂ cups finely chopped onions

2 tablespoons olive oil

¹/₈ teaspoon salt

Cook, stirring frequently, until the onions are very brown but not scorched, 20 to 30 minutes. Scrape into a bowl and cool to room temperature.

Add to the onions and thoroughly mix:

1 cup crumbled blue cheese (4 ounces)

3 tablespoons finely chopped walnuts

³/₄ teaspoon finely chopped fresh rosemary or

¹/₄ teaspoon crumbled dried rosemary

Place 1 teaspoon filling in the center of each dough round.

STUFFED CHOUX PUFFS

24 puffs

Prepare:

¹/₂ recipe Choux Paste, 671

Form into twenty-four 1-inch puffs on a baking sheet. Bake as directed and cool. Have ready:

1 to 1¹/₂ cups Egg Salad, 164, Shrimp Salad, 165, Curried Chicken or Turkey Salad, 164, Chicken Liver Pâté, 440, Salmon Mousse, 85, or Lobster Salad, 165

For **salad fillings**, split the puffs, place 1 to 2 tablespoons filling on each bottom, and replace pastry tops. For the **creamy fillings,** you can use the same method or pierce the bottoms of the unsplit puffs and pipe filling into the bottom of the puffs using a pastry bag fitted with a large plain tip.

CHEESE PUFFS (GOUGÈRES)

About 48 puffs

Pass these on a tray and serve with Champagne.

Preheat the oven to 400°F. Stir:

1 cup grated Gruyère (4 ounces)

into:

1 recipe Choux Paste, 671

Pipe as directed for Profiteroles, 673. Sprinkle with:

About ¹/₂ cup grated Gruyère (2 ounces)

Bake for 15 minutes. Reduce the oven to 350°F and bake until brown and firm, 10 to 15 minutes more.

PIGS IN A BLANKET

16 pieces

Kids love helping to roll this classic favorite.

Preheat the oven to 375°F. Carefully unroll:

One 8-ounce can refrigerated crescent roll dough

Cut and separate into 4 equal rectangles, ignoring the corner-to-corner perforations. Cut each rectangle into four 3-inch-long strips. Brush each strip lightly with:

Dijon mustard

Top each strip with:

1 cocktail frank (16 franks total)

Roll the dough up around each frank, pushing together at the seam to seal. Place seam side down on an ungreased baking sheet, about 2 inches apart. Bake until the dough is puffy and golden brown, about 15 minutes. Serve with:

Honey Mustard Dipping Sauce, 566, or mustard

PUFF PASTRY CHEESE STRAWS

About 100 pieces

Please read About Puff Pastry, 668.

Unbaked straws can be frozen in a covered container, the layers separated by sheets of wax paper, for up to 1 month. Bake (without thawing) as needed.

Have ready:

One 17¹/₂-ounce package frozen puff pastry sheets, thawed, or 1 pound Food Processor Puff Pastry, 669

If using frozen puff pastry, unfold the two sheets and stack on top of each other. If using food processor pastry, roll the dough on a lightly floured work surface into a 16-x-10-inch rectangle. Turn the dough so a short end faces you. Lightly brush the bottom two-thirds of the rectangle with water, then sprinkle evenly with:

³/₄ cup grated Parmesan (3 ounces)

¹/₈ to ¹/₄ teaspoon ground red pepper, or to taste

Lay a sheet of plastic wrap over the cheese and roll over lightly with the pin to stick the cheese to the dough. Remove the wrap and set aside. Fold the top third of the dough down over the center and bring the bottom third over the top third. Roll again into a 16 x 10-inch rectangle. Again brush the bottom two-thirds with water and sprinkle evenly with:

³/₄ cup grated Parmesan (3 ounces)

¹/₈ to ¹/₄ teaspoon ground red pepper, or to taste

Roll over the cheese and fold the dough as before. Wrap the dough in plastic and refrigerate for at least 1 hour, or for up to 24 hours. Position racks in the lower and upper thirds of the oven and preheat the oven to 375°. Line 2 large baking sheets with parchment paper. With an open end to your right, again roll the dough into a 16 x 10-inch rectangle. Cut the dough lengthwise in half. Cut each half crosswise into strips slightly wider than ¹/₄ inch. Twist each strip about 3 times and transfer to a baking sheet, spacing the strips just ¹/₂ inch apart). Bake for 15 minutes, then reverse the positions of the sheets and rotate front to back. Bake until golden brown and crisp, 10 to 15 minutes longer. Set on the sheets on wire racks to cool.

QUICK CHEESE STRAWS OR WAFERS

24 pieces

Please read about Puff Pastry, 668.

The dough keeps for up to a week in the refrigerator or freezer and is quickly sliced or formed into small balls to be baked for unexpected guests.

Preheat the oven to 350°F. Place in a food processor:

$^1/_2$ cup (1 stick) unsalted butter, softened
8 ounces sharp Cheddar or blue cheese, cut into
    chunks

Add:

1$^1/_2$ cups all-purpose flour
$^1/_4$ teaspoon salt
$^1/_4$ to $^1/_2$ teaspoon ground red pepper
1 teaspoon Worcestershire sauce

Process until the mixture comes together. Wrap dough in plastic and chill for 30 minutes. Divide the dough into 4 equal pieces. Roll each piece out between 2 sheets of wax paper to $^1/_8$ inch thick. Cut into 6 x $^1/_2$-inch strips. Twist, if desired, and arrange on 1 or 2 ungreased cookie sheets. Or, if desired, use a cookie press fitted with a houndstooth or star dispenser to push the dough out onto an ungreased cookie sheet into individual wafers. Bake until crisp and lightly browned, about 15 minutes. For a darker color, cook a bit longer. Let cool completely on the sheet on a rack.

BRIE BAKED IN PASTRY

28 servings

Please read About Puff Pastry, 668.

Thaw:

One 17$^1/_2$-ounce package frozen puff pastry sheets

Unfold the two squares. On a lightly floured surface, roll out each into a 12-inch square. Center 1 sheet in a 9-inch pie pan. Top with:

One 2.2-pound Brie wheel (8 inches in diameter)

If desired, spread the top of the cheese with:

(3 to 4 tablespoons sweet fruit chutney, finely
    chopped, or sweet preserves)

Fold the edges of the pastry up and over the Brie, pleating the excess and trimming it to 1 inch over the top rim of the cheese. Cut the second pastry sheet into a circle the diameter of the Brie, using the top of the cheese box as a template. Lay the pastry circle on top of the Brie. Gently roll the top and bottom edges together, and crimp to seal. Refrigerate for at least 30 minutes, or up to 24 hours. Preheat the oven to 400°F. Stir together in a small bowl:

1 large egg yolk
1 tablespoon milk

Gently brush the egg wash over the pastry. Bake for 10 minutes. Reduce the oven temperature to 350°F and bake until golden and puffy, 30 to 40 minutes. Let stand for 1 hour and transfer to a plate. Cut a small wedge and partially remove it, then set out the Brie with a knife, surrounded by:

Sliced fresh or dried fruit
Sliced French bread

EGG ROLLS

About 20 egg rolls

Please read About Deep-Fat Frying, 1046. Serve hot with several choices for dipping: soy sauce, Chinese hot mustard, and Sweet-and-Sour Mustard Sauce, 564.

Heat in a large skillet or wok over high heat:

3 tablespoons vegetable oil

Add and stir-fry until slightly wilted, 2 to 3 minutes:

1$^1/_2$ cups shredded carrots
1$^1/_2$ cups finely chopped celery
5 cups finely shredded cabbage
$^3/_4$ cup finely chopped scallions

Add and stir-fry for 2 minutes:

Two 8-ounce cans water chestnuts, rinsed, drained,
    and chopped
12 ounces bean sprouts, rinsed and drained
3 garlic cloves, minced
One 3-inch piece fresh ginger, peeled and grated
$^3/_4$ teaspoon sugar

Remove from the heat and set aside to cool, then stir in:

1$^1/_2$ cups finely diced cooked shrimp (about 6 ounces)
1$^1/_2$ cups finely diced cooked pork (about 6 ounces)

Have ready:

About twenty 6-inch square wonton wrappers

Arrange 1 wrapper on a work surface so that one corner is facing you. Spoon about 3 tablespoons of the filling about one-third of the way up the wrapper, leaving a 1-inch border on the left and right sides. Fold the bottom point over the filling, then fold in the left and right sides so that they overlap slightly. Roll up to enclose the filling, moistening the last point with a little water to seal. Place on a tray, and repeat with the remaining wrappers and filling. Egg rolls can be wrapped in plastic wrap and refrigerated overnight or frozen for up to 1 month; thaw overnight in the refrigerator before proceeding.

Heat to 375°F in a deep fryer or large deep pot:

4 inches vegetable oil or peanut oil

Fry the egg rolls in batches, turning once, until golden, 2 to 3 minutes. Remove and drain on paper towels.

SUMMER ROLLS

8 rolls or 16 pieces

Bring to a rapid boil in a medium saucepan:

4 cups water
1 bundle cellophane, vermicelli, or rice stick noodles
    (about 2$^1/_2$ ounces), broken in half

Boil until the noodles are just firm to the bite. Transfer the noodles to a colander, and rinse under cold water. Add to the still-boiling water:

16 medium shrimp in the shell

Boil until they turn pink, about 2 minutes. Drain in a colander and rinse under cold water. Peel, cut lengthwise in half, and rinse under cold water to remove the veins. Drain on paper towels.

Have ready:

4 large leaves red-leaf or Boston lettuce, torn
    lengthwise in half and central ribs removed
1 large carrot, shredded
1 cup bean sprouts, rinsed
$^1/_2$ cup mint leaves
$^1/_2$ cup cilantro leaves

16 chives, chopped
Eight 12-inch round sheets rice paper

Lay a damp kitchen towel in front of you and set out a large bowl of hot water (115° to 120°F). Dip 1 sheet of rice paper into the hot water, being sure to immerse it completely to make it pliable. Quickly remove it and place on the towel. Place a piece of lettuce along the bottom edge of the sheet, about 2 inches from the edge. Top the lettuce with one-eighth each of the cooked filling, then with 4 shrimp halves. Fold the sides of the rice paper over the filling, then roll up tightly into a neat cylinder. If the rice paper starts to tear, use 2 sheets for each roll. Immerse them as directed on package, then overlap 2 sheets in the middle by 4 inches. Set seam side down on a large platter and cover with a damp towel. Repeat with the remaining rice paper and filling ingredients. To serve, cut each roll in half on the diagonal. Serve immediately or the rice paper will toughen. Pass for dipping:

Peanut Dipping Sauce, 570

POT STICKERS

About 50 dumplings

Combine:

2 pounds ground pork
4 garlic cloves, minced
A 1-inch piece of fresh ginger, peeled and minced
$1/4$ cup minced raisins or dried apricots
1 cup minced cilantro sprigs
2 scallions, minced
$1/2$ teaspoon salt
$1/2$ teaspoon black pepper
2 tablespoons oyster sauce
$1^1/2$ teaspoons chili paste
$1^1/2$ teaspoons toasted sesame oil

Peel apart:

About 50 round wonton wrappers

Brush the edges of the wrappers with:

1 egg, beaten

Assemble in batches so the egg does not dry out. Place a rounded teaspoonful of filling in the center, fold over, and press the edges together. Cook in small batches in a large pot of boiling water, 7 to 8 minutes; set the boiled pot stickers aside to drain. Heat in a wide skillet:

1 tablespoon peanut oil

Sear the pot stickers until browned on the bottom, adding more oil as necessary. Serve with:

Dipping Sauce, 564

FRIED WONTONS

30 wontons

Please read About Deep-Fat Frying, 1046. Prepare **Wontons, 342, or Vegetable Wontons, 342.** Heat to 350°F in a wok, deep fryer, or large deep pot **4 inches vegetable or peanut oil.** Add a batch of wontons and fry, making sure wontons don't stick to the bottom, until the skins are golden and crisp, 2 to 3 minutes. Remove with a long-

handled strainer and set on paper towels to drain. Repeat the process until all the wontons have been fried, keeping the fried wontons warm in a 200°F oven. Serve with **Sweet-and-Sour Mustard Sauce, 564.**

ABOUT CRACKERS AND BREAD

Transform store-bought bagels and flatbreads into delicious chips with a brush of olive oil. Add aromatic herbs or seeds, a sprinkle of cheese, and heat in the oven. Homemade chips and crackers may sound time-consuming, but rest assured you and your guests will love the results. See also Pita Bread, 607.

BAGEL CHIPS

Preheat the oven to 450°F. Thinly slice:

Bagels

Lay out on a baking sheet and brush one side with:

Olive oil

Sprinkle with:

Coarse kosher or sea salt
(Garlic powder or salt)
Cracked black pepper
(Dried herbs, such as thyme, oregano, rosemary, or basil)

Bake for 5 to 7 minutes, until golden brown. Transfer to a wire rack to cool. Break into smaller pieces, if desired. Store in an airtight container after completely cooled.

PITA CHIPS

Prepare **Bagel Chips, above,** substituting **pitas** for the sliced bagels by splitting the pitas in half, then cutting each half into quarters.

SODA CRACKERS

About 100 crackers

Combine in a medium bowl:

$1^1/2$ cups all-purpose flour
1 envelope ($2^1/4$ teaspoons) active dry yeast
$1/4$ teaspoon salt
$1/4$ teaspoon cream of tartar

Combine in a small bowl:

$2/3$ cup hot water
$1/2$ teaspoon honey
2 tablespoons vegetable shortening

Add the liquid to the dry ingredients and beat with a wooden spoon until smooth. If the dough is sticky, beat in a little more flour. Turn the dough out onto a floured surface and knead until smooth and elastic, about 5 minutes. (Or mix and knead the dough in a heavy-duty stand mixer fitted with a dough hook.) Place the dough in a greased bowl and turn once to coat. Cover and refrigerate for at least 1 hour, or overnight. Preheat oven to 425°F. Grease 2 large baking sheets. On a floured surface, roll the dough into an 18 x 6-inch rectangle. Fold into thirds, as if you were folding a business letter, and roll out again into a rectangle of the same size. Cut into squares or shapes. Prick dough all over with a fork, and transfer to a greased baking sheet. Sprinkle with:

Salt

(Poppy, sesame, or caraway seeds)

Bake until crisp and brown, 10 to 20 minutes, depending on thickness of dough. Cool on wire racks.

POTATO OR SARATOGA CHIPS

4 servings

Please read About Deep-Fat Frying, 1046.

Properly fried potato chips are light, without any greasy feel. It helps to use a deep-fat fryer with a basket, and it's important not to let the chips brown too quickly, or they'll be limp once removed from the fat: It should take them about 3 minutes to turn from white to gold. Since many conditions affect how rapidly anything cooks and browns, from altitude to the condition of the ingredient, adjust the temperature as necessary to get the timing right with the first few, then continue with the rest.

A mandoline produces thin, even slices for regular chips. For waffled potato chips, use the waffle-cut attachment on the mandoline.

Soak in cold water for 2 hours, changing the water twice:

1 pound baking potatoes, peeled and sliced as thin as possible

Drain and dry very well between dish towels.

Heat to 380°F in a deep fryer or deep heavy pot:

3 inches vegetable or olive oil

Slowly drop a handful of potatoes at a time into the oil, and stir them several times with a spoon to prevent them from sticking to one another. Cook until golden, 2 to 3 minutes. Transfer to paper towels to drain. Sprinkle with:

Salt

ROOT VEGETABLE CHIPS

6 servings

Other root vegetables can also be turned into chips, providing varied flavors and colors.

Peel, then slice as thin as possible with a sharp knife, mandoline, vegetable peeler, or food processor any combination of the following, about 1½ pounds total:

Celery root, carrots, parsnips, rutabagas, sweet potatoes, red or golden beets, lotus root

Place the sliced vegetables in cold water to prevent discoloring. Heat to 375° in a deep fryer or deep heavy pot:

3 inches vegetable or olive oil

Drain the vegetables and pat them dry. Fry each type of vegetable separately in batches. Add just a handful at a time, so as not to overcrowd, and stir the slices to prevent them from sticking. Cook until golden brown, about 2 to 3 minutes; the time will vary slightly for each vegetable. Transfer to paper towels to drain. Season with:

Salt

TORTILLA CHIPS

48 chips

Cut into quarters:

12 corn tortillas, homemade, 609, or store-bought

Heat to 375°F in a medium skillet:

½ inch vegetable oil

Add as many tortilla quarters as will fit in a single layer and fry, turning once, until browned and crisp. Transfer to paper towels to drain. Repeat with the remaining tortillas. Sprinkle immediately with:

Salt

BRUNCH, LUNCH, AND SUPPER DISHES

several precooked or quick-cooking foods, one of which is generally rice or pasta, bound together with a sauce. This sauce is sometimes made with canned condensed soup, a product that JOY has sung the praises of as a timesaver since its introduction in the 1930s. Since the American casserole first took shape, with its delectable gratinéed topping of bread or cracker crumbs, grated cheese, and butter, uncountable variations on this basic theme have been created, a testament to its delicious flexibility. Because they are served in the dish in which they are heated, it is wise to wipe off the edges and exposed surfaces of casseroles before cooking so they do not show any browned spilled-over areas when served.

Avoid assembling casseroles more than 24 hours in advance of baking. Bake them just until heated through and bubbling, and serve as soon as they come out of the oven. Many cooked casseroles can be covered and refrigerated for up to 3 days or frozen up to 3 months, then reheated. ➤ For large groups—a casserole makes an excellent self-service dish on a buffet—be sure to bake them in ➤ wide shallow dishes to ensure quick, even heating and provide plenty of topping for each serving. ➤ Generously grease the baking dish.

How we love this grab-bag chapter, for the ease and speed with which most of its dishes, elegant or ordinary, can be prepared; for its tricks with precooked food; for its wonderful mix of familiar and new; and for the stimulus it gives to the attractive serving of leftovers. In this chapter, too, are last-minute ways to combine staples from your pantry—dried, preserved, canned, or frozen, many of them perked up with onions, cheese, herbs, or fruit—great emergency fare for unexpected guests. There are recipes for casseroles, quiches and stratas, slow-cooker meals and fondues, burritos and savory pies, and all manner of one-pot meals, including one of our favorites, Becker Pork Hash, 108.

There are some similar combinations in the Egg Dishes, 194, Grains, 344, and Pancakes, Fritters, and Doughnuts, 643, chapters. From many of these recipes, attractive meals can be prepared in less than half an hour's time. Keep in mind that many fresh fish and shellfish recipes are almost as easily and rapidly cooked as those involving a processed food. Other quick dishes are found in almost every chapter. Refer especially to Sandwiches, Wraps, and Pizza, 177, and Ground Meats, 509. Be sure to check the Leftovers section, 994, for more ideas and suggestions.

Care in cooking and skill in seasoning and presentation can make even a can of tuna memorable. The large gratin dish, the individual lidded baking dish, or one of the cases for food, 111, as well as garnishes all lend distinction in making a quick dish a gracious one.

ABOUT CASSEROLES

The casserole has come to mean a favorite type of dish that graces American tables. They consist of a mixture of

JOHNNY MARZETTI SPAGHETTI PIE

6 to 8 servings

This pasta casserole, made famous at Marzetti's restaurant in Columbus, Ohio, contains ground beef, tomatoes, and pasta, but we like to add mushrooms, olives, and/or mozzarella. Any type of dried pasta can be used.
Combine in a large heavy saucepan or pot:

> **1 1/2 pounds ground beef**
> **1 large onion, chopped**
> **(1 large green bell pepper, chopped)**
> **2 teaspoons minced garlic**

Place over medium-high heat and cook, breaking up the beef with a spoon, until it is browned and the vegetables are softened, about 10 minutes. Add:

> **One 28-ounce can diced tomatoes, with 1/2 cup juice**
> **One 15-ounce can tomato sauce**
> **1 teaspoon dried oregano**
> **1 bay leaf**
> **Salt and black pepper to taste**

Bring to a boil, reduce the heat to medium-low and simmer uncovered, stirring frequently, for 20 minutes. Preheat the oven to 350°F. Stir into the beef mixture:

> **1 pound spaghetti, ziti, or other pasta, cooked and well drained**
> **1 cup shredded sharp Cheddar (4 ounces)**

Transfer to a 13 x 9-inch baking dish. Mix together well, then sprinkle over the top:

> **1 cup fresh or dry bread crumbs**
> **1 cup shredded sharp Cheddar (4 ounces)**

Bake until the top is lightly browned and the casserole is bubbling, about 30 minutes. Let stand for 5 minutes before serving.

KING RANCH CHICKEN CASSEROLE

6 to 8 servings

Preheat the oven to 375°F. Lightly grease a 13 x 9-inch baking dish. Have ready:

> **12 corn tortillas, cut into quarters**
> **3 to 4 cups cubed cooked chicken**
> **1 large onion, chopped**
> **2 cups shredded American cheese (8 ounces)**

Combine in a large bowl:

> **One $10^3/_4$-ounce can condensed cream of chicken soup**
> **One $10^3/_4$-ounce can condensed cream of mushroom soup**
> **$1^3/_4$ to 2 cups chicken broth (depending on amount of chicken)**
> **One 10-ounce can tomatoes and green chiles, drained, or 1 cup canned diced tomatoes plus one 4-ounce can chopped green chiles, drained**

Layer half of the tortillas, chicken, onion, and cheese in the prepared baking dish in the order listed. Pour half of the soup mixture over the top. Repeat. Bake until browned on top and bubbling, 45 to 50 minutes.

CHICKEN RICE CASSEROLE

8 servings

Also a favorite treatment for cooked turkey. Use any type of cooked brown, white, or wild rice. For enhanced flavor, toast nuts, 1001, if desired.

Preheat the oven to 400°F. Grease a 13 x 9-inch baking dish. Melt in a large saucepan over medium heat:

> **6 tablespoons ($^3/_4$ stick) butter**

Stir in and cook until softened, about 5 minutes:

> **8 ounces mushrooms, sliced (3 cups)**

Stir in until well blended:

> **$^1/_2$ cup all-purpose flour**

Slowly add while whisking:

> **2 cups chicken broth**
> **$1^1/_2$ cups milk or half-and-half**

Bring to a boil, reduce heat, and cook until sauce is thickened and smooth, about 5 minutes. Mix in:

> **4 cups chopped cooked chicken**
> **3 cups cooked rice**
> **$^1/_2$ cup chopped walnuts, almonds, or pecans**

Pour into the prepared dish. Mix together and sprinkle on top:

> **$^1/_2$ cup dry bread crumbs**
> **2 tablespoons grated Parmesan**
> **1 tablespoon butter, melted**

Bake until the sauce is bubbling and the topping is golden brown, 25 to 35 minutes.

QUICK CHICKEN RICE CASSEROLE

Prepare as for **Chicken Rice Casserole, above,** substituting for the sauce **two $10^3/_4$-ounce cans condensed cream of chicken or mushroom soup** mixed with **1 cup milk or half-and-half.** Add chicken, rice, and nuts and bake as directed.

TURKEY TETRAZZINI

8 servings

If you are using leftover pasta, you will need about 4 cups. Cooked chicken may be substituted for the turkey. Preheat oven to 400°F. Grease a 13 x 9-inch baking dish. Cook in a large pot of boiling salted water until tender:

> **8 ounces spaghetti, macaroni, or egg noodles**

Meanwhile, melt in a saucepan over medium heat:

> **6 tablespoons ($^3/_4$ stick) butter**

Stir and cook until softened, about 5 minutes:

> **8 ounces mushrooms, sliced ($2^1/_2$ cups)**

Stir in until well blended:

> **$^1/_2$ cup all-purpose flour**

Slowly add while whisking:

> **2 cups chicken broth**
> **$1^1/_2$ cups milk or half-and-half**

Bring to a boil, reduce heat, and cook until sauce is thickened and smooth, about 5 minutes. Mix in:

> **4 cups chopped cooked chicken**
> **$^1/_2$ cup slivered or sliced almonds, toasted, 1001**

Gently mix in the cooked spaghetti. Pour into the prepared dish and sprinkle with:

> **$^1/_2$ cup grated Parmesan**

Bake until the sauce is bubbling and the cheese is golden brown, 25 to 35 minutes.

QUICK TURKEY TETRAZZINI

Prepare as for **Turkey Tetrazzini, above,** substituting for the sauce **two $10^3/_4$-ounce cans condensed cream of chicken or mushroom soup** mixed with **$^1/_2$ cup chicken broth** and **$^1/_2$ cup milk or half-and-half.** Add chicken, almonds, and noodles. Bake as directed above.

QUICK TUNA CASSEROLE

4 to 5 servings

Mom always said this was "An excellent emergency dish." Preheat the oven to 375°F. Grease a shallow $1^1/_2$- to 2-quart baking dish. Place in a mixing bowl and break into chunks with a fork:

> **12 ounces canned or pouch tuna, drained**

Stir in until just combined:

> **2 cups cooked egg noodles or elbow macaroni (about 4 ounces uncooked)**
> **One $10^3/_4$-ounce can condensed cream of mushroom soup**
> **1 cup frozen green peas, thawed, or one 8-ounce can green peas, drained**
> **$^3/_4$ cup milk**
> **($^1/_4$ cup chopped pimientos or minced red bell pepper)**
> **(2 tablespoons minced scallions or onion)**
> **(1 teaspoon Worcestershire sauce or red pepper sauce)**

Turn this mixture into the prepared dish. Mix together and sprinkle on top:

> **$^1/_2$ cup dry bread crumbs, fine cracker crumbs, or crushed cornflakes**

(^{1}/$_3$ cup grated Parmesan)
    2 to 3 tablespoons butter, melted
Bake until top is bubbling and browned, 25 to 35 minutes.

TUNA-VEGETABLE CASSEROLE

4 to 6 servings

Preheat the oven to 375°F. Grease a 1^1/$_2$- to 2-quart shallow baking dish. Melt in a medium saucepan over medium heat:

^{1}/$_4$ **cup (^{1}/$_2$ stick) butter**

Add:

^{3}/$_4$ **cup sliced mushrooms**
    (^{1}/$_4$ **cup finely diced red or green bell pepper**)
    ^{1}/$_4$ **cup finely chopped onion**

Cook, stirring occasionally, until the vegetables are just tender, about 5 minutes. Stir in:

^{1}/$_4$ **cup all-purpose flour**

Cook for 1 minute. Gradually whisk in:

2^1/$_2$ **cups milk**

Bring the sauce to a boil, whisking, then turn the heat down and simmer for 10 minutes. Remove from the heat and add, whisking until hot:

^{3}/$_4$ **cup to 1 cup shredded Cheddar (3 to 4 ounces)**
    12 **ounces canned or pouch tuna, drained and broken
        into chunks**

Add and stir together well:

2 **cups cooked egg noodles (4 ounces uncooked)**
    ^{1}/$_4$ **cup minced parsley**
    Salt and black pepper to taste

Pour the mixture into the prepared baking dish. Mix together and sprinkle over the top:

^{1}/$_2$ **cup dry bread crumbs, fine cracker crumbs,
        or crushed cornflakes**
    2 **tablespoons butter, melted**

Bake until browned on top, 25 to 35 minutes.

SALMON, POTATO,
AND SPINACH CASSEROLE

6 servings

Cod is a tasty substitute for salmon in this casserole. Have ready:

2 **cups White Sauce I, 550**
    **Four 10-ounce packages chopped frozen spinach,
        thawed**

Drain spinach thoroughly. Transfer to a bowl and stir in ^{1}/$_2$ cup of the sauce. Boil:

1^1/$_2$ **pounds red potatoes, peeled**

Reduce heat. Simmer gently until potatoes are tender when pierced with the point of a knife, 20 to 30 minutes, depending on their size. Drain well, return to the pot, cover, and let sit off the heat for 5 minutes. Uncover. Preheat the oven to 425°F. Grease a 2-quart baking dish. When the potatoes are cool enough to handle, slice into ^{1}/$_4$-inch-thick rounds. Arrange in the bottom of the prepared dish and season with:

Salt and black pepper to taste

Spread the spinach in an even layer over the potatoes. Top with a layer of:

1 **pound skinless salmon fillets, sliced ^{1}/$_2$ inch thick**
    Salt and black pepper to taste

Spread the remaining 1^1/$_2$ cups white sauce over the top. Dot with:

2 **tablespoons butter, cut into small pieces**

Bake until the top is lightly browned and the casserole is bubbling, 25 to 30 minutes. Let stand for 5 minutes before serving.

BEAN, TOMATO, AND SAUSAGE GRATIN

8 servings

This hearty casserole is great for a crowd. It keeps well for 3 to 4 days in the refrigerator and freezes well too. The bean and tomato mixture can be made ahead, and then the gratin assembled and baked before serving.

Soak for 6 hours or overnight in water to cover by 2 inches:

2 **cups pinto or borlotti beans, rinsed and picked over**

Drain the beans. Transfer to a large pot and add:

8 **cups water**
    1 **onion, halved, each half stuck with 1 clove**
    2 **garlic cloves, minced**
    1 **Bouquet Garni, 960**
    (**A Parmesan rind**)

Bring to a boil, then reduce the heat, cover, and simmer gently for 1 hour. Add:

Salt to taste

Simmer for another 30 to 60 minutes, until the beans are tender. While the beans are simmering, prepare:

Tomato Meat Sauce, 563

using sausage and cooking just up to the point that the browned pancetta and sausage are returned to the pot. Remove the bouquet garni from the beans, and drain the beans in a strainer set over a bowl. Measure 2 cups of the cooking liquid and combine in a separate bowl with the beans. Add the beans and their liquid to the meat sauce. Bring to a simmer, then cover and cook over low heat for 30 minutes, stirring often, until thick and flavorful. Preheat the oven to 400°F. Grease a 3- to 4-quart baking dish. Stir into the beans:

2 **to 3 tablespoons slivered basil leaves or chopped
        parsley**

Spoon the beans and tomatoes into the baking dish. Mix together, then sprinkle over the top:

^{1}/$_2$ **cup fresh or dry bread crumbs**
    1 **tablespoon olive oil**
    ^{1}/$_2$ **cup grated Swiss or Gruyère (2 ounces)**

Bake until the top is lightly browned and the casserole is bubbling, about 30 minutes.

CROQUE MONSIEUR CASSEROLE

4 servings

This casserole has all the elements of the famous French sandwich of the same name, 181—toasted bread layered with ham and cheese, topped with a rich cheese sauce, and baked until browned on top.

Preheat the oven to 375°F. Grease a 2-quart baking dish. Prepare:

2 cups Mornay Sauce, 551

Lightly toast:

8 slices white bread

Brush lightly with:

2 tablespoons butter, melted

Arrange half the toasted bread in the bottom of the baking dish, cutting the bread if necessary to fit. Top with:

8 ounces sliced Swiss or Gruyère
8 ounces sliced ham

Top with the remaining toast. Pour the Mornay sauce over the toast and spread it evenly to cover. Bake until bubbling and browned, 20 to 30 minutes. Let stand for 10 minutes before serving.

ABOUT STRATA

This dish, also referred to as a **breakfast casserole,** is made in layers. The layers are bread and, generally speaking, cheese and meat or vegetables, all soaked in a milk and egg mixture. Stratas can be assembled and refrigerated overnight, then baked the next day, leaving you nothing to do but brew the coffee.

SAUSAGE AND MUSHROOM STRATA

6 to 8 servings

Place in a large skillet:

1¹/₂ pounds bulk sausage

Cook over medium-high heat, stirring, until no longer pink, about 10 minutes. Tilt the skillet and spoon out all but 2 tablespoons of fat. Add:

8 ounces mushrooms, sliced (about 2¹/₂ cups)
(4 to 6 shiitake mushroom caps, sliced)
¹/₂ cup chopped onion

Cook, stirring, until the onion is translucent and the juices released by the mushrooms have mostly evaporated, about 10 minutes. Set aside. Have ready:

One 8-ounce loaf French or Italian bread, cut into
1-inch cubes or slices (about 6 cups)
2 to 3 cups (8 to 12 ounces) shredded Swiss or
Cheddar

Generously grease a 13 x 9-inch baking dish. Scatter half of the bread cubes or slices over the bottom of the dish. Cover with the sausage mixture and all but ¹/₂ cup of the shredded cheese. Top with the remaining bread and sprinkle with the reserved cheese. Whisk together in a medium bowl until thoroughly blended:

2¹/₂ cups milk
5 eggs

¹/₄ teaspoon salt
¹/₄ teaspoon black pepper

Slowly pour the egg mixture over the bread cubes, moistening them evenly. Press down with a spatula until the egg mixture rises to the top and the top layer of bread appears well soaked. Cover and refrigerate for 2 to 24 hours. Preheat the oven to 350°F. Bake until the strata is puffed and a knife inserted into the center comes out clean, about 45 minutes.

HAM AND VEGETABLE STRATA

6 to 8 servings

Prepare **Sausage and Mushroom Strata, above,** substituting this mixture for the sausage-mushroom mixture.

Melt in a large skillet over moderate heat:

2 tablespoons butter

Add:

1 large onion, chopped

Cook, stirring frequently, until the onion is translucent but not brown, about 7 minutes. Stir in:

2 cups diced ham
2 cups chopped cooked broccoli or asparagus or one
10-ounce package frozen chopped broccoli or cut
asparagus, thawed and drained

Cook, stirring, for 2 minutes, then remove from heat. Proceed as above.

CRAB STRATA

6 servings

Trim the crusts from:

4 slices white sandwich bread

Generously grease an 8 x 8-inch baking pan. Line the bottom of the pan with the bread, trimming it as necessary to fit. Cut the trimmings into small cubes and scatter over the top of the bread, along with:

6 to 8 ounces canned or cooked crabmeat (1¹/₂ to
2 cups)
³/₄ cup shredded Swiss (3 ounces)

Whisk together in a bowl until thoroughly blended:

2 cups half-and-half
4 eggs
¹/₂ cup milk
¹/₂ small onion, grated
1 teaspoon prepared mustard
¹/₂ teaspoon salt
¹/₈ teaspoon ground red pepper

Drizzle over the bread, moistening it evenly. Let stand for 15 minutes, or cover and refrigerate for up to 3 hours. Preheat the oven to 325°F. Sprinkle the top of the strata with:

³/₄ cup shredded Swiss (3 ounces)

Bake in a water bath, 801, until a knife inserted in the center comes out clean, about 1 hour. Let stand for 15 minutes, then cut into squares.

ABOUT SLOW-COOKER MEALS

The beauty of a slow cooker is its ability to cook food un-attended yet safely. Dishes that are traditionally cooked slowly—that is, for more than $1\frac{1}{2}$ hours on the stove or in the oven—work well in the slow cooker: ➤ soups, stews, braises, pot roasts, ragouts, pasta sauces, and bean dishes. Tough cuts of meat, including chuck, round, shoulder, and neck, and bone-in dark meat poultry are all perfect candidates for the slow cooker.

Slow cookers vary in design but all consist of an outer heating element, a crockery insert, and a lid. They come in two basic shapes, cylindrical and oval, and range in capacity from $1\frac{1}{2}$ to 7 quarts. ➤ A 4- to 5-quart model will nicely accommodate recipes serving 4 to 8; when cooking for larger groups, a $6\frac{1}{2}$- to 7-quart model is optimal. Recipes with a large yield can be halved or otherwise reduced to fit smaller models, and vice versa. The larger oval models can hold roasts and whole poultry. Newer models often have timers, including a stay-warm feature to hold food at a safe serving temperature once the cooking is complete. For non-timer models, you can use a freestanding electric timer, but ➤ never allow the food to stand for longer than 2 hours before the cooking element is turned on or after it is turned off.

Many slow-cooker recipes call for simply putting all the raw ingredients into the pot. ➤ If you find the resulting flavors a bit too bland, take time to brown meats and sauté vegetables such as onions, carrots, and celery. It takes less than 15 minutes, and this quick investment will be repaid many times over in the flavor of the final dish.

For the most efficient cooking, fill the insert no less than half full and no more than two-thirds full. ➤ Most low settings cook food at just under a boil, high settings, at just above. Follow the cooking times and settings in your recipe. Avoid opening the lid while cooking unless the recipe instructs you to do so. Every time the lid is opened, ➤ heat is released, and you'll need to add 20 minutes or so to the cooking time.

To adapt standard recipes for the slow cooker, estimate 2 hours on low or 1 hour on high in a slow cooker for every 30 minutes of cooking time in the original recipe. Just as for a stew or roast, brown the meat and sauté the vegetables to maximize flavor. Vegetables, ➤ especially root vegetables, cook more slowly than meat and should be placed in the bottom of the slow-cooker so they can heat directly in the cooking liquid. To compensate for the steam that will collect, decrease the liquid called for in the oven or stovetop recipe by $\frac{1}{2}$ cup. ➤ Add dairy-based ingredients such as milk, cream, or cheese only during the last 30 minutes, as they will curdle if cooked too long. ➤ Use a combination of light and dark poultry meat whenever possible, as dark has more flavor and will not dry out as much as white meat. ➤ If cooking fish or shellfish, add in the final minutes of cooking.

PORK SHOULDER WITH MUSTARD AND ROSEMARY SAUCE
8 to 10 servings

Trim the excess fat from:
   1 bone-in pork shoulder roast (about $7\frac{1}{2}$ pounds)
Season the meat with:
   1 teaspoon salt
   $\frac{1}{2}$ teaspoon black pepper
Heat over medium heat in a heavy pot large enough to hold the meat:
   1 tablespoon vegetable oil
Add the meat and brown well on all sides, about 10 minutes. Transfer the meat to a 7-quart oval slow cooker. Pour off all but 1 tablespoon of fat from the pot. Return the pot to medium heat and add:
   1 medium onion, chopped
   1 medium carrot, chopped
   2 garlic cloves, chopped
Cook, stirring occasionally, until the vegetables soften, about 5 minutes. Add:
   $1\frac{1}{2}$ cups chicken broth
   1 cup dry white wine
   $1\frac{1}{2}$ teaspoons dried rosemary
Bring to a boil, stirring to release the browned bits in the bottom of the pot. Pour over the meat. Cover and turn the slow cooker to the low setting. Cook without opening the lid, until the meat is very tender, 5 to 6 hours. Transfer the meat to a deep platter and tent with aluminum foil to keep warm. Pour the cooking liquid into a large heatproof bowl. Let stand for 5 minutes, then skim the fat from the surface, 123. Melt in a medium saucepan over medium-low heat:
   $\frac{1}{4}$ cup ($\frac{1}{2}$ stick) butter
Whisk in and let bubble without browning for 2 minutes:
   $\frac{1}{4}$ cup all-purpose flour
Whisk in the cooking liquid and bring to a boil over high heat. Reduce the heat to medium and cook until lightly thickened, about 10 minutes. Whisk in:
   2 to 3 tablespoons Dijon mustard to taste
Adjust the seasoning with:
   Salt and black pepper
Slice the meat, which should literally fall off the bone, and discard the skin. Pour half of the sauce over the meat, transfer the remaining sauce to a bowl or sauceboat, and serve with buttered noodles.

MEDITERRANEAN SHORT RIBS WITH OLIVES
6 servings

This ragout of succulent short ribs in a fragrant sauce, accented with herbs and olives, is one of the best examples of what a slow cooker can do.
Pat dry:
   5 pounds beef short ribs (preferably English-style)
Season with:
   1 teaspoon salt
   $\frac{1}{2}$ teaspoon black pepper

Heat in a large skillet over medium-high heat:

1 tablespoon olive oil

Add the short ribs in batches and brown on all sides, being careful not to crowd the pan, about 8 minutes. Using tongs, transfer to a 5- to 7-quart slow cooker. Pour off all but 2 tablespoons of fat from the skillet, and add:

1 large onion, chopped
1 medium carrot, chopped
1 medium celery rib, chopped
4 garlic cloves, chopped

Cook, stirring occasionally, until the vegetables soften, about 5 minutes. Stir in:

2 cups dry red wine or water

Bring to a boil, stirring to release the browned bits in the bottom of the skillet. Transfer to the slow cooker. Stir in:

2 cups beef broth
1 teaspoon dried rosemary
1 teaspoon dried basil

Cover and turn the slow cooker setting to low. Cook, without opening the lid, until the meat is very tender, about 6 hours. Using tongs, transfer the short ribs to a deep platter, and cover with aluminum foil to keep warm. Pour the cooking liquid into a large glass bowl. Let stand 5 minutes, then skim the fat from the surface. Melt in a medium saucepan over medium-low heat:

7 tablespoons butter

Whisk in and let bubble without browning for 2 minutes:

$1/3$ cup plus 2 tablespoons all-purpose flour

Whisk in the cooking liquid and bring to a boil over high heat. Reduce the heat to medium and cook at a brisk simmer until lightly thickened, about 10 minutes. During the last 5 minutes, add:

$1/2$ cup brine-cured black olives, pitted and coarsely chopped

Season to taste with:

Salt and black pepper

Pour the sauce over the meat. Sprinkle with:

Chopped parsley

CHICKEN AND SWEET POTATO FRICASSEE

4 servings

For a warming lunch or supper entrée, this combination of lightly savory, mellow flavors is very satisfying.

Rinse and pat dry:

$2^{1}/_{2}$ pounds chicken parts

Season with:

$1/2$ teaspoon salt
$1/4$ teaspoon black pepper

Heat a large skillet over medium heat. Add and heat:

1 tablespoon vegetable oil

Add the chicken parts to the skillet, skin side down, and cook until the skin is golden, about 3 minutes. Transfer to a plate. Pour off all but 1 tablespoon fat from the skillet, and add:

6 ounces smoked ham, cut into $1/2$-inch cubes

Cook, stirring often, until lightly browned. Add:

1 medium onion, finely chopped
1 medium carrot, finely chopped
1 medium celery rib, finely chopped

Cook, stirring occasionally, until the vegetables soften, about 5 minutes. Add:

2 cups chicken broth

Bring to a boil, stirring to release the browned bits in the bottom of the skillet. Pour into a 4- to 5-quart slow cooker. Add:

3 cups water
2 medium sweet potatoes, peeled and cut into cubes

Place the chicken on top of the sweet potatoes; the liquid does not have to cover the chicken. Turn the slow cooker to the low setting. Cook, without opening the lid, until the chicken is tender, about 4 hours. During the last 15 minutes, add:

$1/3$ cup heavy cream
($1/4$ cup chopped parsley)

Season to taste with:

Salt and black pepper

SPICY SEAFOOD STEW

6 servings

Seafood loses its flavor and texture with lengthy cooking, making it an unlikely candidate for the slow cooker. The solution? Use the slow cooker to create a savory base for a stew, and add the seafood just before serving.

Heat in a medium skillet over medium heat:

1 tablespoon olive oil

Add and cook until the onion is translucent, 3 minutes:

1 medium onion, chopped
1 medium celery rib, chopped
1 jalapeño pepper, seeded and finely chopped
2 garlic cloves, finely chopped

Transfer to a 4- to 5-quart slow cooker. Stir in:

One 28-ounce can tomatoes, crushed, with their juice
2 cups bottled clam juice
$1/2$ cup dry red or white wine or additional clam juice
1 teaspoon dried oregano
$1/4$ teaspoon crushed red pepper flakes

Cover and turn the slow cooker to the low setting. Cook, without opening the lid, until the stew base is well flavored, about 4 hours. Turn the setting to high. Add:

1 pound skinless cod fillets, cut into 1-inch cubes
8 ounces medium (31 to 35 count) shrimp, peeled and deveined

Cover and cook until the fish is opaque, 12 to 15 minutes. Season with:

Salt and black pepper to taste
($1/4$ cup chopped basil or parsley)

SPICY SEAFOOD STEW WITH ORZO

Prepare **Spicy Seafood Stew, above.** After $3^{1}/_{2}$ hours of cooking, stir in **$1/3$ cup orzo** and turn the setting to high. Cover and cook for 15 minutes. Add the cod and shrimp and continue as directed.

SLOW-COOKER VEGETARIAN CHILI

8 servings

Pick over, rinse, and soak overnight, 253, or use quick-soak method, 253:

1 pound dried pinto beans

Drain and place in a 4- to 5-quart slow cooker. Heat in a large skillet over medium heat:

2 tablespoons olive oil

Add and cook, stirring often, until the vegetables soften, about 10 minutes:

1 large onion, chopped
1 green bell pepper, seeded and chopped
1 red bell pepper, seeded and chopped
2 medium carrots, chopped
2 medium celery ribs, chopped
2 jalapeño peppers, seeded and chopped
2 garlic cloves, chopped

Add, stirring to coat the vegetables:

1 tablespoon chili powder

Add and bring to a boil:

2 cups water
One 6-ounce can tomato paste

Stir well. Pour into the slow cooker. Stir in:

4 cups water
2 teaspoons salt

Cover and turn the slow cooker to the low setting. Cook, without opening the lid, until the beans are tender, about 6 hours. During the last 30 minutes, stir in:

10 ounces fresh or thawed frozen corn kernels
    (about 2 cups)

Remove the insert from the slow cooker or transfer all into a large bowl. Let stand 10 minutes before serving.

HEARTY MEAT RAGÙ

2¹/₂ quarts sauce

This recipe makes a large batch of chunky meat-and-vegetable tomato sauce. Serve with pasta such as ziti or penne. Freeze leftovers for another meal.

Pat dry and cut into 1-inch cubes:

2 pounds boneless stewing beef, such as chuck,
    short-rib meat, or bottom round

Heat in a large skillet over medium-high heat:

2 tablespoons olive oil, or as needed

Add the meat in batches and brown on all sides, being careful not to crowd the pan. With a slotted spoon, transfer to a 4- to 5-quart slow cooker. Pour off all but 2 table-spoons of fat from the pan (or add more if needed). Add:

1 large onion, finely chopped
1 medium carrot, finely chopped
1 medium celery rib with leaves, finely chopped
4 garlic cloves, chopped

Cook, stirring occasionally, until the vegetables soften, about 5 minutes. Add:

1 cup dry red wine

Bring to a boil, stirring to release the browned bits in the bottom of the skillet. Pour into the slow cooker. Stir in:

One 28-ounce can tomatoes, crushed, with juice
One 28-ounce can crushed tomatoes in puree
1¹/₂ teaspoons dried basil
1¹/₂ teaspoons dried oregano
¹/₂ teaspoon crushed red pepper flakes

Cover and turn the slow cooker to the low setting. Cook, without opening the lid, until the meat is very tender, 6 to 7 hours. Season to taste with:

Salt and black pepper

ABOUT SAVORY PIES

When we think about comfort food, a category that always comes to mind is pie—meat, fish, and vegetable pastries, including not only potpie and shepherd's pie, but also samosas, tamales, and piroshki. The old-fashioned way, and our favorite style, is to top your savory pie with homemade biscuit dough, 637, or piecrust, 665. However, there are many options for premade crusts at your market, such as refrigerated piecrust, frozen biscuit dough, puff pastry, and phyllo dough.

HAMBURGER PIE

4 to 5 servings

This old-time favorite is found in the JOY library's *Streamlined Cooking*, a 1939 cookbook that Irma wrote to feature recipes using newly available convenience foods. The toast "crust" that tops this pie is rarely seen today. It is easy and delicious.

Preheat the oven to 350°F. Combine in a large skillet over medium-high heat:

1 pound lean ground beef
1 medium onion, chopped

Cook, breaking up the beef with a spoon, until it is browned and the onion softened, about 10 minutes. Stir in:

2 tablespoons all-purpose flour
2 teaspoons chili powder

Cook, stirring, 1 minute. Stir in:

One 14¹/₂-ounce can tomatoes, with their juice
One 15¹/₄-ounce can corn, drained, or one 10-ounce
    package frozen corn, thawed

Bring to a simmer, breaking up the tomatoes with a spoon, and cook 3 minutes. Stir in:

³/₄ teaspoon salt
(1 to 2 teaspoons minced garlic)
(1 teaspoon brown sugar)

Transfer the mixture to a 9-inch glass pie pan or 8 x 8-inch baking dish. Set aside. Trim the crusts from:

6 slices white sandwich bread

Spread one side of the slices with:

2 tablespoons butter, softened

Cut the bread slices into quarters. Arrange the quarters buttered side up over the meat mixture, overlapping the pieces by about ¹/₂ inch and covering the mixture completely. Gently press the bread down to anchor it to the filling. Bake until the crust is browned, about 30 minutes.

CHICKEN TAMALE PIE

8 to 10 servings

This is an update of a recipe from JOY's 1943 edition, in which the filling is completely enclosed in a cornmeal crust. We find it delicious. This dish can be baked 3 days ahead, cooled, and kept covered in the refrigerator, then reheated in a 300°F oven for 25 minutes.

Brown in a large skillet over medium-high heat:

> 1¹/₂ pounds ground chicken or ground turkey

If necessary, tilt the skillet and spoon out any fat. Stir in:

> 3 cups salsa
> ¹/₂ cup pimiento-stuffed green olives
> 1 tablespoon chili powder
> 1 tablespoon ground cumin
> ¹/₂ teaspoon ground cinnamon

Bring to a simmer. Reduce the heat to low and simmer gently, stirring occasionally, for 10 minutes. Remove from the heat. Preheat the oven to 400°F. Bring just to a boil in a small saucepan:

> 1¹/₃ cups water
> 1 cup vegetable or chicken broth

Cover and remove from the heat. Whisk together in a large bowl:

> 2 teaspoons baking powder
> 1¹/₂ teaspoons salt
> ¹/₃ cup vegetable oil

Stir in, mixing until all the cornmeal is coated with the oil:

> 3 cups cornmeal

Add the reserved stock mixture and stir well. Let the batter stand for 5 minutes, then mix in:

> 2 eggs

Reserve 1¹/₂ cups of the batter. Spread the remaining batter evenly over the bottom and sides of a greased 13 x 9-inch baking dish. Spoon in the chicken filling. Cover with:

> 3 cups grated Cheddar (12 ounces)

Stir into the reserved batter:

> ¹/₄ cup hot water

Spread in a thin, even layer over the top of the pie. (The batter will blend with the cheese.) Bake until browned, 40 minutes. Let stand 15 minutes before cutting.

CORN BREAD TAMALE PIE

6 servings

Sauté in a large skillet over medium-high heat:

> 1 pound ground beef
> 1 medium onion, chopped

When the meat is browned and the onion translucent, about 10 minutes, add:

> 1 cup canned black beans, rinsed and drained
> 1 cup drained canned or frozen corn
> 1 cup tomato sauce
> 1 cup water or beef or chicken broth
> (¹/₂ cup diced green bell pepper)
> 1 tablespoon chili powder
> ¹/₂ teaspoon ground cumin

> 1 teaspoon salt
> ¹/₄ teaspoon black pepper

Simmer 15 minutes. Set aside. Preheat the oven to 425°F. Whisk together in a medium bowl:

> ³/₄ cup cornmeal
> 1 tablespoon all-purpose flour
> 1 tablespoon sugar
> 1¹/₂ teaspoons baking powder
> ¹/₂ teaspoon salt

In a small bowl, whisk together until well blended:

> 1 egg
> ¹/₃ cup milk
> 1 tablespoon vegetable oil

Pour the wet ingredients over the dry and whisk until well combined. Spread the meat mixture in a greased 3-quart casserole and cover with the corn bread topping. The topping will disappear into the meat mixture but will rise during baking and form a layer of corn bread. Bake until the corn bread is brown, 20 to 25 minutes.

SHEPHERD'S PIE

4 servings

Finely chopped or ground lamb covered with mashed potatoes is a favorite pub food in England and Ireland. Substituting chopped or ground beef for the lamb makes the dish **Cottage Pie.**

Place in a large pot of cold water over medium heat:

> 1¹/₂ pounds all-purpose potatoes, peeled and quartered

Bring to a boil and cook until tender, about 15 minutes. Drain, reserving ¹/₂ cup of the cooking water. Transfer the potatoes to a bowl and mash with a fork or potato ricer or masher, adding the reserved cooking water along with:

> 1 tablespoon butter
> Salt and white pepper to taste

Beat with a wooden spoon until fluffy. Set aside. Preheat the oven to 400°F. Combine in a large skillet:

> 3 tablespoons vegetable oil
> 1 medium onion, chopped
> 1 carrot, chopped
> 1 celery rib, chopped

Cook over low-medium heat, stirring occasionally, until the vegetables are tender but not brown, 10 to 15 minutes. Increase the heat to medium and add:

> 2 cups finely chopped cooked lamb or 1 pound raw ground lamb

If using cooked lamb, cook, stirring, until the meat begins to brown, about 5 minutes. If using raw lamb, cook, breaking up the meat with a spoon, until the lamb loses its pink color, 5 to 10 minutes. Spoon off excess fat. Stir in:

> 1 tablespoon all-purpose flour

Cook, stirring, for 2 minutes. Add:

> ³/₄ cup beef or chicken broth
> ¹/₂ teaspoon dried thyme or 1¹/₂ teaspoons chopped fresh thyme

$^{1}/_{2}$ **teaspoon dried rosemary or 1** $^{1}/_{2}$ **teaspoons**
    chopped fresh rosemary
Pinch of grated or ground nutmeg
Salt and black pepper to taste

Reduce the heat to low and cook, stirring occasionally, until thickened, about 5 minutes. Transfer to a greased 9-inch pie plate or 8 x 8-inch baking dish. Spread the mashed potatoes over the top, making peaks with a fork. Scatter over the top:

2 tablespoons butter, cut into small pieces

Bake until the potatoes are browned and the dish is heated through, 30 to 35 minutes. Let cool slightly, then serve directly from the baking dish.

CHICKEN OR TURKEY POTPIE

6 to 8 servings

Leftover or store-bought, precooked chicken or turkey breast is perfect here.
Prepare:

Creamed Chicken or Turkey, 445, made with $^{1}/_{2}$ **cup**
    flour, or Quick Creamed Chicken or Turkey, 446

Prepare the dough for:

Rolled Biscuits, 638, Buttermilk Biscuits, 639, Quick
    Drop Biscuits, 639, $^{1}/_{2}$ **recipe Basic Pie or Pastry**
    Dough, 665, or $^{1}/_{2}$ **recipe Deluxe Butter Pie or**
    Pastry Dough, 665

Set aside. Position a rack in the upper third of the oven. Preheat the oven to 400°F. Grease a 13 x 9-inch baking dish. Heat in a large skillet over medium-high heat:

2 tablespoons butter

Add and cook, stirring often, about 5 minutes:

1 medium onion, chopped
3 medium carrots, sliced
2 small celery ribs, sliced

Stir the vegetables into the creamed chicken, along with:

$^{3}/_{4}$ **cup frozen peas, thawed**
3 tablespoons minced parsley

Pour the mixture into the prepared dish. If using rolled biscuit dough, cut the dough into biscuits and arrange on top of the chicken, overlapping the biscuits if necessary. If using drop biscuit dough, simply drop the dough in walnut-sized pieces on top. If using pie dough, roll it out into the shape of the dish, place on top of the chicken, and tuck the edges down in against the dish sides. Brush the top with:

2 tablespoons beaten egg ($^{1}/_{2}$ **large)**

Bake until the sauce is bubbling and the topping is browned, 30 to 40 minutes.

BEEF POTPIE

6 to 8 servings

Prepare:

Beef Stew, 479
$^{1}/_{2}$ **recipe Basic Pie or Pastry Dough, 665,** $^{1}/_{2}$ **recipe**
    Deluxe Butter Pie or Pastry Dough, 665,
    Rolled Biscuits, 638, Buttermilk Biscuits, 639, or
    Quick Drop Biscuits, 639

Position a rack in the upper third of the oven. Preheat the oven to 400°F. Grease a 13 x 9-inch baking dish and add the stew. If using rolled biscuit dough, cut the dough into biscuits and arrange on top of the stew, overlapping the biscuits if necessary. If using drop biscuit dough, simply drop the dough in walnut-sized pieces on top. Roll the dough out into the shape of the dish, place on top of the stew, and tuck the edges down in against the sides of the dish. Brush the top with:

2 tablespoons beaten egg ($^{1}/_{2}$ **large)**

Bake until the pie is bubbling and the crust is nicely browned, 30 to 40 minutes.

DISHES USING COOKED MEAT, POULTRY, FISH, OR BEANS

There was a time when the following quick dishes depended on leftovers. Not anymore. Today our grocery stores offer a huge variety of cooked meats, poultry, and seafood—some already chopped. But whether you are using leftovers or store-bought, these recipes are as tasty as they are easy.

BEAN BURRITOS

8 burritos

Preheat the oven to 350°F. Wrap in foil and warm in the oven for 10 minutes:

Eight 10-inch flour tortillas

Have ready:

Two 16-ounce cans refried beans or 4 cups Refried
    Beans, 254
2 to 4 cups shredded Cheddar or Monterey Jack
    (8 to 16 ounces)
$^{1}/_{2}$ **to 1** $^{1}/_{2}$ **cups finely chopped onions**
($^{1}/_{4}$ **to** $^{1}/_{2}$ **cup chopped seeded fresh jalapeño peppers**
    or drained canned sliced jalapeños)

Remove tortillas from the oven and slip 1 tortilla out of the foil, leaving the rest wrapped. Place the tortilla on a work surface. Spread with $^{1}/_{2}$ cup refried beans, leaving a 1-inch border all around. Sprinkle with $^{1}/_{4}$ to $^{1}/_{2}$ cup cheese, 1 to 3 tablespoons onions, and, if using, 1 to 2 tablespoons peppers. Fold 1 inch of tortilla over from the bottom. Then, fold sides in and roll up. Place seam side down on a baking sheet lined with aluminum foil. Make 7 more burritos in the same way and heat in the oven. Serve with:

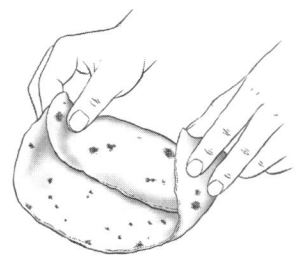

Folding a burrito

1 small head romaine or iceberg lettuce, cut into thin
  strips
1^1/$_2$ cups sour cream
1 cup salsa

CHICKEN BURRITOS

Prepare **Bean Burritos, above,** but use only 2 to 3 cups refried beans. Before rolling up, place **2 to 4 tablespoons
chopped or shredded cooked chicken** in a line across the
center of each burrito.

BURRITOS CON CARNE

A great use of leftover pork, pot roast, or other beef.
Prepare **Bean Burritos, 103,** but use only 2 to 3 cups refried
beans. Before rolling up, place 2 to 4 tablespoons of one
of the following in a line across the center of each burrito,
leaving a 1-inch border on both sides:

Pulled Pork, 500
MacLeid's Rockcastle Chili, 513
Picadillo, 514
Shredded pot roast
Sloppy Joe filling, 510
Any leftover pork or beef roast, shredded

CHICKEN ENCHILADAS
4 to 6 servings
If time is of the essence, use 4 to 5 cups store-bought enchilada sauce instead of freshly cooked sauce. Serve with
sour cream and chopped scallions if desired.
Combine in a large skillet:

2 large onions, chopped
4 medium jalapeño peppers, seeded and chopped
2 tablespoons finely chopped garlic
2 tablespoons vegetable oil

Cook over medium-high heat, stirring frequently, until the
onions are translucent and just beginning to brown
around the edges, about 7 minutes. Stir in:

^{1}/$_4$ cup chili powder
2 teaspoons ground cumin
^{1}/$_2$ teaspoon ground red pepper

Cook for 1 minute, stirring constantly. Add:

Two 28-ounce cans diced tomatoes, drained

Cook for 3 minutes, stirring frequently. Cool and thoroughly puree the mixture in a blender or food processor. In
a medium bowl, combine ^{1}/$_2$ cup of the sauce with:

2^1/$_2$ cups shredded cooked chicken

Set aside. Preheat the oven to 400°F. Set out:

12 corn tortillas

Lightly brush on both sides with:

Vegetable oil

Arrange the tortillas, slightly overlapping, on a large baking sheet lined with aluminum foil. Cover the baking sheet
tightly with a second sheet of aluminum foil. Bake until
the tortillas are soft and pliable, about 5 minutes. Pour
^{1}/$_2$ cup of the sauce over the bottom of a 13 x 9-inch bak-

ing dish. To make each enchilada, spoon about 2^1/$_2$ tablespoons of the chicken mixture down the center of a tortilla, then roll the tortilla up into a cylinder. Arrange the
enchiladas seamside down in the baking dish. Cover with
the remaining sauce, then sprinkle with:

1 cup shredded Cheddar or Monterey Jack (4 ounces)

Bake until the sauce begins to bubble, about 10 minutes.

CHEESE ENCHILADAS

Prepare **Chicken Enchiladas, above,** substituting 2^1/$_2$ cups
additional shredded Cheddar or Monterey Jack, or a combination of the two, for the chicken.

BEEF OR PORK ENCHILADAS

Prepare **Chicken Enchiladas, above,** substituting **2^1/$_2$ cups
shredded leftover pot roast or leftover pork roast** for the
chicken.

ENCHILADAS VERDES
4 to 6 servings
Prepare:

**^{1}/$_2$ recipe (2^1/$_2$ cups) Roasted Tomatillo Spinach
  Sauce, 568**

Combine in a bowl:

2^1/$_2$ cups shredded cooked chicken
^{1}/$_2$ cup sour cream
2 tablespoons finely chopped scallions
2 tablespoons chopped cilantro
^{1}/$_4$ teaspoon salt

Preheat the oven to 400°F. Set out:

12 corn tortillas

Lightly brush on both sides with:

Vegetable oil

Arrange the tortillas, slightly overlapping, on a large baking sheet lined with aluminum foil. Cover the baking sheet
tightly with a second sheet of aluminum foil. Bake until
the tortillas are soft and pliable, about 5 minutes. To make
each enchilada, spoon about 3 tablespoons of the chicken
mixture down the center of a tortilla, then roll the tortilla
up into a cylinder. Arrange the enchiladas seamside down
in a lightly oiled 13 x 9-inch baking dish or other shallow
baking dish large enough to hold them in one layer. Cover
with the reserved sauce. Bake until the sauce begins to
bubble, about 10 minutes. Serve with:

Sour cream

CHOP SUEY OR CHOW MEIN
4 servings
These Chinese-American dishes are JOY classics and
can be made with cooked pork, chicken, beef, or sea-
food. They differ in that Chop Suey is served over rice,
Chow Mein over fried noodles. Please read about Stir-
Frying, 1042.
Heat in a deep heavy skillet:

2 tablespoons vegetable oil

Add and stir-fry over medium-high heat for 3 minutes:

$^1/_2$ cup sliced celery with leaves

$^1/_2$ cup sliced scallions

Add and stir-fry for 2 to 3 minutes:

2 cups cooked pork, cut into $^1/_4$-inch-wide 2-inch strips

1 green bell pepper, coarsely chopped

1 cup coarsely chopped mushrooms

1 cup bean sprouts, rinsed

Add:

Jellied juices (as much as cooks out) from a roast or a bit of Meat Glaze, 117 (up to 1 cup)

1 cup Consommé, 123, or canned beef consommé ($^1/_2$ cup slivered seeded tomato, or $^1/_2$ cup diced red bell pepper)

Season with:

Salt and black pepper to taste

1 tablespoon soy sauce

3 tablespoons dry sherry

The sauce may be thickened with:

(1 tablespoon cornstarch, mixed well with 3 tablespoons warm water)

Stir in and boil for 1 minute. Serve immediately over:

Cooked rice or chow mein noodles

SWEET-AND-SOUR PORK, CHICKEN, OR TURKEY

4 to 6 servings

Though especially well suited to pork, this dish can also be made with poultry. For a vegetarian version, use 1$^1/_2$ pounds firm tofu, diced, and vegetable broth.

Mix together in a small bowl or glass measuring cup:

$^1/_2$ cup chicken broth

2 tablespoons soy sauce

2 tablespoons cornstarch

Melt in a large skillet or pot over medium-low heat:

2 tablespoons butter

Stir in:

1 large onion, diced

1 large red or green bell pepper, diced

$^1/_2$ teaspoon ground ginger

$^1/_2$ teaspoon salt

$^1/_4$ to $^1/_2$ teaspoon ground red pepper

Cover and cook, stirring occasionally, until the vegetables are crisp-tender, 7 to 10 minutes. Add:

One 20-ounce can pineapple chunks, with their juice

$^3/_4$ cup chicken broth

$^1/_3$ cup distilled white or cider vinegar

$^1/_3$ cup sugar

Stir in the reserved cornstarch mixture. Raise heat to high and bring to a simmer, stirring. Add:

3 to 4 cups diced cooked pork, chicken, or turkey

Return to a simmer, then turn the heat down as low as possible and cook, uncovered, 10 minutes to blend the flavors. Serve over:

Cooked rice or chow mein noodles

MEAT CURRY

4 servings

This dish is especially tasty when sprinkled with any or all of the following: chopped peanuts or cashews, toasted coconut, 972, or chopped fresh cilantro.

Heat in a large skillet over medium heat:

2 tablespoons butter

2 tablespoons vegetable oil

Add:

2 to 3 cups diced cooked beef, pork, lamb, or veal

2 medium apples, peeled, cored, and diced

1 large onion, diced

Cook, stirring frequently, until well browned and the apples are beginning to fall apart, about 15 minutes.

Add and cook, stirring, 1 minute:

1 tablespoon curry powder

1 tablespoon all-purpose flour

Add:

1$^1/_4$ cups beef broth

($^1/_2$ cup dark or golden raisins)

Bring to a simmer and cook, stirring, until lightly thickened, about 5 minutes. Serve with:

Cooked rice

CHICKEN OR TURKEY CURRY

4 servings

Melt in a medium saucepan over medium heat:

2 tablespoons butter

Add:

1 large onion, chopped

Cook, stirring occasionally, until the onion is translucent, about 7 minutes. Add and cook, stirring, 1 minute:

2 tablespoons all-purpose flour

1 tablespoon curry powder

$^1/_2$ teaspoon ground ginger

$^1/_4$ teaspoon ground cinnamon

Remove the pan from heat and whisk in:

One 13$^1/_2$-ounce can unsweetened coconut milk

1$^1/_4$ cups chicken broth

One 8-ounce can crushed pineapple with juice

Place the pan over medium-high heat and bring to a boil, stirring constantly. Boil until the sauce is reduced to about 1$^1/_2$ cups and is lightly thickened, about 10 minutes. Stir in:

2 to 3 cups diced cooked chicken or turkey

Cook over the lowest possible heat, stirring now and then, for 5 minutes to blend the flavors. Season to taste with:

Salt and white or ground red pepper

Serve over:

Cooked rice

If desired, sprinkle with:

(Chopped cilantro and/or minced seeded fresh or canned chiles)

HOT CHICKEN SALAD

4 servings

This recipe multiplies well for serving a large crowd.

Preheat the oven to 350°F. Combine:

2 cups cubed cooked chicken
1 cup finely diced celery
$^1/_2$ cup mayonnaise
$^1/_2$ cup White Sauce I, 550, or $^1/_3$ cup canned condensed cream of chicken soup mixed with 3 tablespoons milk
$^1/_2$ cup sliced almonds, toasted, 1001
2 tablespoons lemon juice
1 tablespoon chopped chives
$^1/_4$ teaspoon dried tarragon
$^1/_2$ teaspoon salt

Transfer to 4 greased individual gratin dishes or a greased shallow 9-inch baking dish. Bake, until heated through, about 15 minutes. Garnish with:

Chopped parsley or small sprigs of thyme

HAM LOAF

4 servings

Think of this as a ham sandwich in the form of a delicious savory meat loaf.

Place in a food processor and pulse until coarsely ground:

2 cups diced ham

Add:

$^1/_2$ cup seasoned dry bread crumbs
2 eggs
2 to 3 teaspoons prepared mustard, to taste

Pulse just until well mixed. Let stand for 10 to 30 minutes to blend the flavors. Preheat the oven to 375°F. Grease a 8$^1/_2$ x 4$^1/_2$-inch loaf pan. Pack the ham mixture into the prepared pan. Bake until firm, about 30 minutes.

HAM CAKES WITH PINEAPPLE AND SWEET POTATOES

6 servings

Prepare the mixture for **Ham Loaf, above,** and shape into six 3-inch cakes. Preheat the oven to 375°F. Drain, reserving the juice:

One 20-ounce can pineapple slices in juice

Place a large skillet, preferably nonstick, over medium-high heat. Add and heat:

1 tablespoon vegetable oil

Place 6 pineapple rings in the skillet and cook, turning once, until lightly browned, about 3 minutes per side. Transfer the slices to a shallow baking dish large enough to hold them in one layer. Set aside. Add to the skillet and heat:

3 tablespoons vegetable oil

Carefully place the ham cakes in the skillet and cook the cakes until the undersides are browned, 3 to 5 minutes. Turn and cook 3 to 5 minutes longer. Place 1 cake on each pineapple slice. Return the skillet to medium heat and add:

1 tablespoon vegetable oil

When the oil is hot, add:

Two 16-ounce cans sweet potatoes, drained and sliced
$^1/_4$ cup packed dark brown sugar
$^1/_8$ to $^1/_4$ teaspoon ground cloves

Cook, turning the potatoes gently with a spatula, until glazed, about 3 minutes. Place a chunk of potato on each ham cake and scatter remaining potatoes over the bottom of the baking dish. Pour the reserved pineapple juice into the baking dish. Bake until the juices are thick and bubbling, about 30 minutes, basting the ham cakes several times just before serving.

FISH LOAF

4 to 6 servings

Preheat the oven to 375°F. Grease a 8$^1/_2$ x 4$^1/_2$-inch loaf pan. Place in a food processor and process to crumbs:

3 slices white sandwich bread, torn into pieces

Transfer to a bowl. Add to the processor and pulse until finely chopped:

1 medium onion, quartered
2 celery ribs, cut into 1-inch chunks

Add and pulse just until mixed:

1 egg
3 tablespoons butter, melted

Add the bread crumbs, along with:

18 ounces canned drained or pouch tuna
2 tablespoons lemon juice
1 teaspoon dried basil or oregano
$^1/_2$ teaspoon red pepper sauce
$^1/_2$ teaspoon salt
$^1/_4$ teaspoon black or white pepper

Pulse just until mixed, leaving the tuna in slightly coarse pieces. The mixture can be covered and refrigerated up to 24 hours at this point. Pack the mixture into the prepared pan. Bake until heated through, 30 to 40 minutes. Let stand 20 minutes. Serve cut into thick slices, with:

Tartar Sauce, 581, Horseradish Cream, 565, or Cheese Sauce, 551

BEAN AND RICE CAKES

4 servings

These unusual bean cakes gain distinction from a rich and crunchy sesame crust.

Combine in a skillet over medium-low heat and cook until the vegetables have softened, about 5 minutes:

3 tablespoons butter or vegetable oil
$^1/_4$ cup finely chopped onion
$^1/_4$ cup finely chopped green bell pepper
$^1/_4$ cup finely chopped celery

Transfer to a bowl. Add and mix well (use 2 eggs if mixture is dry or yolk is small):

One 15$^1/_2$-ounce can chickpeas, rinsed, drained, and coarsely mashed
1 cup cooked rice
1 or 2 eggs, well beaten
2 tablespoons finely chopped parsley

(2 tablespoons chopped well-drained pimientos)
$^1/_4$ teaspoon salt
$^1/_4$ teaspoon black pepper

Form the mixture into 8 small patties and set aside. Have ready in three shallow bowls or pie plates:

$^1/_4$ cup all-purpose flour
1 egg, beaten with a pinch of salt
1 cup sesame seeds

One at a time, dredge the cakes in flour, then coat with beaten egg, and then roll in sesame seeds. Set on a plate. Heat over medium heat in a 10- to 12-inch skillet:

2 to 3 tablespoons vegetable oil

Add the cakes to the skillet and cook, turning once, until the seeds are golden and crisp, 2 to 4 minutes per side.

VEGGIE BEAN BURGERS

6 servings

Heat in a large skillet over medium heat:

2 teaspoons olive oil

Add and cook, stirring until softened:

1 cup chopped onions
4 garlic cloves, minced

Add and cook over low heat for 5 minutes:

$^1/_2$ cup grated carrots
1 teaspoon chili powder
$^1/_2$ teaspoon ground cumin

Remove from the heat and let cool. Mash in a large bowl:

Two 15$^1/_2$-ounce cans black, pinto, kidney, or
     chickpeas, rinsed and drained
2 tablespoons Dijon mustard
2 tablespoons soy sauce
2 tablespoons catsup
2 tablespoons minced parsley

Stir in the vegetable mixture. Add:

1$^1/_2$ cups cooked brown rice
(1 cup chopped mushrooms)

Season to taste with:

Salt and black pepper
(Pinch of ground red pepper)

Form the mixture into six 3- to 4-inch patties. Heat in a nonstick skillet:

1 teaspoon vegetable oil

Add the burgers and cook over medium-low heat, for 5 to 8 minutes per side, until browned and crisp.

ABOUT HASH

An Irish cook praised for her hash declared: "Beef ain't nothing. Onions ain't nothing. Seasoning's nothing. But when I throw myself into my hash, that's hash!" There are two styles of hash: one made with gravy and one cooked dry, perhaps the more commonplace today.

To prepare gravy-style hash, add cooked meat and vegetables to a hot gravy, prepared or leftover. Use about half as much gravy as other ingredients. Have the gravy or sauce at a boiling point when adding the other ingredients, but ➤ never allow it to boil once the meat is added.

Reduce the heat at once and warm through. Serve over toast or noodles, or with rice or eggs. For this venerable combination, see Old-Fashioned Beef or Lamb Hash in Gravy, 108, and Becker Pork Hash, 108.

"Sautéed" or "browned" hash is a relatively dry mixture of onions, potatoes, and cooked meat or poultry sautéed in a skillet until browned and crisp. If it is made with raw potatoes, a loose, crumbly mixture results; if made with cooked potatoes, the hash can be compressed into a more or less cohesive cake, slid onto a serving plate, and cut into wedges. The first two recipes below use the same ➤ basic formula: 1 large onion, 1 pound potatoes, or potatoes and other vegetables, and 2 to 3 cups (1 to 1$^1/_2$ pounds) cut-up cooked meat or poultry. Using this formula, you can create your own terrific hashes.

CORNED BEEF OR ROAST BEEF HASH

4 to 5 servings

If you make this with leftovers from New England Boiled Dinner, 484, you can replace half the potatoes with other root vegetables.

Heat in a heavy 12-inch skillet over medium-high heat:

3 tablespoons vegetable oil

Stir in:

1 large onion, chopped

Cook, stirring with a spatula, until the onion is just beginning to brown, 3 to 5 minutes. Stir in:

1 pound peeled cooked or raw potatoes, cut into
     $^1/_2$-inch dice (about 3 cups)

If the potatoes are cooked, simply toss to coat with oil. If they are raw, cook, stirring frequently, until about half-tender, 5 to 7 minutes. Add:

2 to 3 cups cooked corned beef or roast beef cut into
     $^1/_2$-inch cubes

Cook, stirring, until the potatoes and meat are browned around the edges, about 5 minutes. Stir in:

3 tablespoons beef or chicken broth or water, or
     2 tablespoons catsup, tomato sauce, chili sauce,
     or meat gravy mixed with 2 tablespoons broth
     or water
($^1/_2$ teaspoon dried thyme or rubbed sage)
Salt and black pepper to taste

Turn the heat down to medium. Cook, stirring frequently, until all the ingredients are nicely browned, 5 to 10 minutes. For a cake, firmly press the hash into a cake with the back of the spatula, then cook, pressing occasionally, until the bottom is well browned, 10 to 15 minutes. Loosen the bottom of the cake with the spatula, then slide or invert onto a serving plate and cut into wedges. Sprinkle with:

(2 tablespoons chopped parsley)

Serve with:

(Fried Eggs, 196, or Poached Eggs, 196)

CHICKEN OR TURKEY CHILI HASH WITH SWEET POTATOES

4 to 5 servings

This can also be made entirely with white potatoes.
Heat in a heavy 12-inch skillet over medium-high heat:

> 3 tablespoons vegetable oil

Stir in:

> 1 large onion, chopped
> 1 cup chopped green bell peppers, jalapeño peppers,
>   or poblano peppers, or a combination

Cook, stirring with a spatula, until just beginning to brown, about 3 minutes. Stir in:

> 1½ cups peeled diced cooked or raw potatoes
>   (about 8 ounces)
> 1½ cups peeled diced cooked or raw sweet potatoes
>   (about 8 ounces)

If the potatoes are cooked, simply toss to coat with oil. If they are raw, cook, stirring frequently, until they are about half-tender, 5 to 7 minutes. Add:

> 2 to 3 cups shredded or cubed cooked chicken or
>   turkey

Cook, stirring, until the potatoes and poultry are browned around the edges, about 5 minutes. Stir in:

> 3 tablespoons chicken or turkey broth or water
> 1 to 3 teaspoons chili powder (to taste)
> Salt and black pepper to taste

Turn the heat down to medium. Cook, stirring frequently, until all ingredients are nicely browned, 5 to 10 minutes. For a cake, firmly press the hash into a cake with the back of the spatula, then cook, pressing occasionally, until the bottom is well browned, 10 to 15 minutes. Loosen the bottom of the cake with the spatula, then slide or invert onto a serving plate and cut into wedges. Sprinkle with:

> (2 tablespoons chopped cilantro)

OLD-FASHIONED BEEF OR LAMB HASH IN GRAVY

4 to 6 servings

Melt in a large saucepan over medium heat:

> 2 tablespoons butter

Add and cook, stirring occasionally, until tender and golden, about 10 minutes:

> 1 large onion, chopped

Stir in:

> 8 ounces mushrooms, sliced
> 2 cups leftover or store-bought beef gravy
> ½ cup diced ham
> 1 teaspoon minced garlic
> ¼ teaspoon dried thyme or rubbed sage

Bring to a simmer, then turn the heat down to low and simmer gently until the gravy is thick enough to coat a spoon heavily, 10 to 15 minutes. Add and bring to a simmer:

> 2 cups diced cooked potatoes

Add:

> 3 cups diced cooked beef or lamb

Cook, without allowing the gravy to simmer, until the meat is just warmed through. Serve on:

> Hot toast, Roll Cases, 111, or Toast Baskets, 111

BECKER PORK HASH

3 to 4 servings

A favorite family use for leftover roast pork that has survived the late-night refrigerator raids. Also excellent made with leftover roast beef, chicken, or turkey.
Melt in a large skillet over high-medium heat:

> 2 tablespoons butter

Add:

> 3 medium carrots, diced
> 1 large onion, chopped

Cook, stirring, until the carrots are crisp-tender and the onion translucent, 5 to 7 minutes. Add:

> 1½ cups leftover pork pan juices or chicken broth
> ¼ cup port or Marsala
> 1 tablespoon soy sauce

Whisk in, blending well:

> Two 10¾-ounce cans condensed cream of chicken or
>   cream of mushroom soup

Reduce the heat and simmer, stirring occasionally, until thick, 5 to 10 minutes. Add and heat through, without simmering:

> 2 to 3 cups cubed cooked pork
> (One 10-ounce package frozen petite peas)

Season to taste with:

> Black pepper

Serve over:

> Buttered fine egg noodles or toast

ABOUT QUICHES

The most famous of savory custards is quiche, a custard containing small bits of vegetables, fish, meats, and/or cheese baked in a tart or pie crust. The basic proportions are ➤ 3 to 4 whole eggs for every 2 cups of milk. Using cream in place of milk or replacing one whole egg with 2 yolks gives you a richer, more custardy quiche. Quiche is traditionally prepared in a prebaked shell brushed with egg yolk to help prevent it from becoming soggy. For a more elegant presentation, it can also be baked in individual tart shells.

For a quick preparation, mix the custard filling and other ingredients the day before, refrigerating the covered containers. Then, when ready, all you need do is fill the prebaked shell and pop in the oven.

Cooked quiche can be refrigerated up to 3 days or frozen, tightly wrapped, up to 3 months but must be thawed overnight in the refrigerator before reheating.

QUICHE LORRAINE

6 servings

Traditional Quiche Lorraine does not contain cheese, so omit it if you prefer to stick with tradition.

Preheat the oven to 375°F. Bake, 664, in a 9-inch quiche, tart, or pie pan:

> **¹/₂ recipe Basic Pie or Pastry Dough, 665, or Pat-in-the-Pan Butter Dough, 666**

While still warm, brush the baked crust with:

> **Beaten egg yolk**

Chop into 1-inch lengths:

> **4 ounces bacon**

Cook over medium heat in a heavy skillet, turning often, until most of the fat is rendered but the bacon is not yet crisp. Drain on paper towels. Whisk together:

> **2 cups milk or cream**
> **3 eggs**
> **¹/₄ teaspoon salt**
> **¹/₈ teaspoon black pepper**
> **Pinch of grated or ground nutmeg**
> **1 teaspoon chopped chives**

Sprinkle the bacon in the bottom of the pie shell, followed by:

> **(¹/₂ cup diced Swiss)**

Pour the custard mixture over it. Bake 35 to 40 minutes, or until the top is golden brown.

CHEESE QUICHE

6 servings

Preheat the oven to 375°F. Bake, 664, in a 9-inch quiche, tart, or pie pan:

> **¹/₂ recipe Basic Pie or Pastry Dough, 665, or Pat-in-the-Pan Butter Dough, 666**

While still warm, brush the baked crust with:

> **Beaten egg yolk**

Place the pan on a baking sheet. Sprinkle onto the crust:

> **1¹/₂ cups shredded Cheddar or Swiss (6 ounces)**

Whisk together thoroughly in a medium bowl until no streaks of egg white remain:

> **1 cup heavy cream**
> **3 eggs**
> **¹/₂ small onion, grated**
> **¹/₈ teaspoon grated or ground nutmeg**
> **¹/₂ teaspoon salt**
> **¹/₄ teaspoon white or black pepper**

Pour the mixture evenly over the cheese in the pastry shell. Bake until the filling is puffed around the sides and a knife inserted in the center comes out clean, 30 to 40 minutes. Let stand 10 minutes before slicing.

ADDITIONS TO QUICHE

To prevent the egg filling from becoming watery, cook and thoroughly drain vegetables, meat, and seafood before adding to quiches. Use 1¹/₂ cups total:

> **Onions, thinly sliced**
> **Broccoli, chopped**
> **Mushrooms, chopped**
> **Tomatoes, chopped and drained**
> **Spinach, chopped**
> **Ham, chopped**

> **Chicken, cooked and diced**
> **Shrimp, peeled, deveined, and cooked**
> **Chopped tarragon, chives, or basil**

TOMATO AND GOAT CHEESE QUICHE

6 servings

Prepare and fit into a 9-inch quiche, tart, or pie pan:

> **¹/₂ recipe Basic Pie or Pastry Dough, 665, or Pat-in-the-Pan Butter Dough, 666**

Brush the dough with:

> **Beaten egg yolk**

Refrigerate. Set a rack in the lowest position in the oven. Preheat the oven to 400°F. Seed, core, and quarter:

> **1 pound tomatoes**

Crumble and blend with the back of a wooden spoon until smooth in large bowl:

> **4 to 6 ounces soft fresh goat cheese**
> **³/₄ cup half-and-half or heavy cream**
> **¹/₂ cup milk**

Add and whisk until smooth:

> **3 eggs**
> **1 tablespoon chopped parsley**
> **1¹/₂ teaspoons chopped thyme or 3 tablespoons chopped basil**
> **¹/₄ teaspoon salt**
> **Black pepper to taste**

Arrange most of the tomato quarters in the prepared pastry shell like the spokes of a wheel. Fill in the center with the remaining tomato quarters. Pour the cheese mixture over the tomatoes. Bake until the top is golden brown, 40 to 45 minutes. Let rest for 10 minutes before slicing.

LEEK TART

6 servings

Prepare and fit into a 9-inch quiche, tart, or pie pan:

> **¹/₂ recipe Basic Pie or Pastry Dough, 665, or Deluxe Butter Pie or Pastry Dough, 665**

Brush the dough with:

> **Beaten egg yolk**

Refrigerate. Melt in a medium skillet over medium heat:

> **2 tablespoons butter**

Add:

> **2 pounds leeks, white and tender green parts only, cut into ¹/₄-inch slices**
> **¹/₂ teaspoon salt**
> **Black pepper to taste**

Cover and cook, stirring occasionally and reducing the heat as the leeks cook, until they are very soft, about 30 minutes. Meanwhile, preheat the oven to 400°F. Beat together until well combined:

> **2 eggs**
> **¹/₂ cup heavy cream or half-and-half**
> **¹/₄ teaspoon grated or ground nutmeg**
> **Salt and black pepper to taste**

When the leeks are done, add to the custard. Transfer to the prepared pastry shell. Bake until the top is golden and the custard is set, 20 to 30 minutes. Let rest for 10 minutes.

CHEESE CUSTARD PIE OR FLAN

8 servings

In Switzerland our family had a vile-tempered cook named Marguerite. Her one idea, after being generally disagreeable, was to earn enough to buy a small chalet on some high peak where she could cater to mountain climbers. If she has attained her ideal, many a climber will feel it worthwhile to scale a perilous peak to reach her kitchen. Her cheese pie was always served in a solitary state. Its flavor varied with Marguerite's moods and her supply of cheese, and was never the same twice, as she had no written recipe, but this recipe reflects all the delicious memories we have.

Preheat the oven to 375°F. Bake, 664, in a 9-inch quiche, tart, or pie pan:

¹/₂ recipe Pat-in-the-Pan Butter Dough, 666

While still warm, brush the baked crust with:

Beaten egg yolk

Bring to just under a simmer:

1³/₄ cups heavy cream

Reduce the heat and add, stirring until melted:

2 cups grated Swiss or Cheddar (8 ounces)

Add:

¹/₂ teaspoon salt
¹/₄ teaspoon paprika
¹/₂ teaspoon grated onion
Pinch of ground red pepper

Remove from the heat and beat in one at a time:

3 eggs

Fill the piecrust. Bake until the custard is firm, about 35 to 40 minutes.

ABOUT FONDUE

From *fondre,* the French word for "melt," the term "fondue" has several meanings. Fondue originated in Switzerland as a way of using up hardened cheese. These days fondue refers to food cooked in a central pot at the table. **Cheese fondue** is a classic dish consisting of melted cheese combined with white wine, kirsch, and seasonings. Bite-sized chunks of bread are dipped into the hot cheese mixture. Fondue bourguignon or **beef fondue** is a variation where raw beef slices are dipped in a pot of hot oil, and served with various savory sauces. Because of the hot oil, it is particularly important to use a stable heavy pot and caution for this type of fondue. Yet another version is **dessert fondue,** a rich chocolate sauce, 848, into which assorted fruits, pieces of cake, or even marshmallows are dipped.

Because fondue is a "communal" meal, here are some guidelines. ➤ To eat fondue spear a morsel of bread, meat, fruit, or cake using a fondue fork and dip it into the pot. Twirl the food gently in the cheese, oil, broth, or sauce. Hold the fork over the pot for a moment before you put it in your mouth. This allows drippings to go back into the pot and allows time for cooling. ➤ When you put the food in your mouth, try not to touch the fork with your lips or tongue because the fork does go back in the pot, not to

mention that the fork may be hot. Or you can use a table fork to slide the morsel off the fondue fork, then eat it with the second fork, but this may be more cumbersome than necessary. Never make fondue in advance.

Other similar recipes include Mongolian Hot Pot, 137, Hot Chorizo and Cheese Dip, 73.

CHEESE FONDUE

4 to 5 servings

The cheese or combination of cheeses used must be natural, not processed. Kirsch is traditional, but a nonsweet liquor such as Cognac or applejack can be substituted. Measure all ingredients and have them ready to add, for the pot must be stirred constantly from the time the wine is hot enough for the cheese until the fondue is ready to eat, about 10 minutes of cooking. Never make fondue in advance. Have ready a breadbasket or bowl filled with crusty French or Italian bread cut into 1 x 1 x ³/₄-inch pieces, making sure that each piece has one side of crust. The guests, each equipped with a heatproof-handled fork—preferably two- or three-tined—spear the bread from the soft side and dip the impaled bit into the well-warmed cheese. The fondue will at first be on the thin side, but will thicken as the process progresses. There is seldom much left by the time another 10 minutes has elapsed. Serve with fresh fruit and tea.

Tear into bite-sized pieces:

1 loaf white crusty French or Italian bread

Rub the interior of a medium stainless steel pot or fondue pot with:

1 garlic clove, peeled and halved

Discard the garlic. Add to the pot:

1¹/₄ cups Swiss Fendant or other dry white wine

Bring to a simmer over medium heat. Add gradually, stirring constantly:

1 pound Gruyère or Emmanthaler, cubed
Pinch of grated or ground nutmeg

Cook, stirring with a wooden spoon, until the cheese is melted (the cheese and wine will not yet be blended). Mix together thoroughly in a small bowl:

1 tablespoon cornstarch
2 tablespoons kirsch, Cognac, or applejack

Stir into the cheese mixture. Continue to stir and simmer until the mixture is smooth, about 5 minutes. Season to taste with:

Salt and black pepper

If the fondue is too thick, add up to:

¹/₄ cup Swiss Fendant or other dry white wine

Quickly transfer to a fondue pot or chafing dish set over a flame. The cooking continues on low heat while the guests take over as described above.

BEEF FONDUE

6 servings

This dish is traditionally cooked at the table in a special fondue pot that narrows at the top to keep the butter or oil from spattering; it can also be cooked in an electric skillet because the butter is clarified, which keeps it from popping. We love this dish inordinately. It gives the host or hostess an easy time, both from the cooking angle and from the entertaining one, as the guests quickly reveal their individual characteristics. They are all there—hoarder, co-operator, kibitzer, boss. Don't try to get more than 5 or 6 guests around one heat source. Allow $1/3$ to $1/2$ pound beef for each person. Use caution when working with the hot butter or oil, and advise guests not to eat off a fondue fork fresh from the hot pot.

Cut into 1-inch cubes:

> **About 3 pounds beef tenderloin**

Arrange on a platter, and garnish with:

> **Parsley sprigs**

Have ready, at room temperature or slightly warmed, several of the following accompaniments:

> **Mustard with capers**
> **Creamy Horseradish Dressing, 578**
> **Andalouse Sauce, 580**
> **Curry Mayonnaise, 580**
> **Watercress Dressing, 573**
> **Bitter Orange Marmalade, 941**
> **Marchand de Vin, 555**

Melt in an electric skillet or a fondue pot:

> **1 cup clarified unsalted butter, 557, or peanut oil**

When the butter is brownish, announce the rules of the game: Ask each guest to dip no more than 2 pieces of meat at a time, so as not to crowd the pot and lower the cooking temperature. If a skillet is used, each person impales the cubes on his fork, releases the meat into the pan, and worries it around the hot fat until it's done to his liking; if he prefers rare, the time is short. If a fondue pot is used, the meat must stay on the fork during the cooking, or it will be irretrievably lost—but, according to an old Swiss custom, the loser gets a consolation prize: the right to kiss the miss or mister on the left! Each guest arranges on his plate an assortment of sauces—like oil paints on an artist's palette—into which he then dips the hot browned meat. Serve with crusty French bread or rolls and a tossed salad with green grapes or avocado slices.

BROTH FONDUE

4 to 6 servings

Cooking thin strips of beef, chicken, and vegetables in a simmering broth makes another excellent fondue.

Bring to a simmer:

> **4 cups beef or chicken stock**
> **2 large garlic cloves, minced**
> **$2/3$ cup wine or rice wine vinegar**
> **2 teaspoons granulated sugar**
> **($1/4$ cup chopped green onions or chives)**

Cut into thin strips and bring to the table on a platter:

> **2 pounds boneless, skinless chicken breasts**
> **2 peeled potatoes**

And:

> **1 bunch broccoli, cut into florets**
> **1 pound whole button or shiitake mushrooms, trimmed**

Have ready at room temperature or slightly warmed several of the following accompaniments:

> **Sour cream with fresh herbs**
> **Any Flavored Mustard, 1000**
> **Creamy Horseradish Dressing, 578**
> **Herb, Watercress, Chipotle Pepper, or Curry Mayonnaise, 580**
> **Nam Prik, 570, or Chile Oil, 590**

Ask each guest to limit himself to two pieces of meat or vegetable at a time, so as not to crowd the pot and lower the cooking temperature. Each person impales the cubes on his fork and holds them in the broth until they're done to his liking, about 3 to 5 minutes. The fork will be very hot, so either slide the meat off it, using a dinner fork, or eat the fondue meat without letting your lips or tongue touch the hot tines. Biting only the food, not the fork, is considered proper fondue etiquette.

ABOUT DISHES IN CREAM SAUCE

We have long ago left behind the era of trenchers: thick bread slices soaked with sauce. But none of us has lost the taste for creamed foods served on toast or in bread or pastry containers. Buttered noodles, mashed potatoes, rice, or couscous may be substituted for bread or pastry.

BREAD AND PASTRY CASES FOR DISHES IN CREAM SAUCES

I. ROLL CASES

Preheat the oven to 300°F. Hollow out from the top, leaving a $1/2$-inch-thick wall all around:

> **Small or large rolls**

Brush the hollows generously with:

> **Melted butter**

Arrange on a baking sheet and bake until completely crisp, 20 to 30 minutes.

II. TOAST BASKETS

Allow two of these delicious and utterly charming containers per serving.

Preheat the oven to 275°F. Trim the crusts from:

> **Sliced white sandwich bread**

Spread lightly on both sides with:

> **Softened butter**

Press one slice each into the cups of a standard muffin tin ($1/3$-cup capacity per cup), letting the corners of the slices protrude crown-like beyond the cups. Toast until completely crisp, 20 to 30 minutes.

III. Try any of the following instead of cases:

> **Savory Crepes, 649**
> **Waffles, 646**
> **Rosettes, 657**
> **Cream Biscuits or Shortcakes, 639**
> **Popovers, 637**

WELSH RAREBIT

6 servings

Our correspondence is closed on the subject of rarebit versus rabbit. We stick to "rarebit," because "rabbit" already means something else. We can only answer the controversy with a story. A stranger trying to calm a small crying boy: "I wouldn't cry like that if I were you." Small boy: "You cry your way and I'll cry mine."

Melt in the top of a double boiler over simmering water:

1 tablespoon butter

Stir in and heat until warm:

1 cup beer, ale, milk, or cream

Gradually, stir in:

4 cups shredded sharp Cheddar or Colby (1 pound)

Cook, stirring constantly with a fork, until the cheese is melted. Stir in:

1 egg, well beaten
1 teaspoon Worcestershire sauce
1 teaspoon salt
$1/2$ teaspoon sweet paprika
$1/4$ teaspoon dry mustard
($1/4$ teaspoon curry powder)
Pinch of ground red pepper

Cook, stirring, until slightly thickened, about 1 minute. Serve at once on top of:

12 slices white, rye, or other bread of your choice, toasted, or 18 crackers

THE MACKIE

Prepare **Welsh Rarebit, above,** topping toasted slices of white bread with **sliced tomatoes** and **crisp bacon** before covering with the cheese mixture.

BLUSHING BUNNY

Prepare **Welsh Rarebit, above,** substituting **tomato juice or canned condensed cream of tomato soup** for the beer or milk.

CREAMED MUSHROOMS ON TOAST

4 servings

Prepare:

Creamed Mushrooms, 283

Serve on or in:

Hot buttered toast, Patty Shells, 670, or Toast Baskets, 111

CHIPPED BEEF AND GRAVY

4 servings

Sliced dried beef is sold in the canned meat section of most supermarkets. Do not salt this dish.

Pull apart into bite-sized pieces:

8 ounces sliced dried beef

Melt in a medium saucepan over medium heat:

3 tablespoons butter

Add and cook until the onions are golden:

3 tablespoons minced onion
(3 tablespoons minced green bell pepper)

Sprinkle with:

3 tablespoons all-purpose flour

Remove from the heat. Add slowly, whisking constantly until well blended:

2 cups milk

Add the beef and return to the heat. Simmer until the sauce thickens enough to coat a spoon heavily, about 10 minutes. Serve on:

Hot buttered toast

CHICKEN OR TURKEY DIVAN

4 servings

Preheat the oven to 400°F. Butter an 8- or 9-inch square baking dish. Place in the baking dish:

4 slices hot buttered toast

Arrange on the toast:

2 boneless, skinless chicken breast halves, cooked and thinly sliced, or 12 ounces thinly sliced cooked turkey breast

Spoon over the chicken or turkey:

One 10-ounce package frozen chopped broccoli or cut asparagus, thawed and drained, or 2 cups cooked chopped broccoli or cut asparagus

Sprinkle with:

$1/4$ teaspoon salt

Cover with:

2 cups Mornay Sauce, 551

Sprinkle with:

$1/3$ cup grated Parmesan

Bake until the sauce is browned and bubbling, 25 to 35 minutes. Serve at once.

SEAFOOD DIVAN

Prepare **Chicken or Turkey Divan, above,** substituting **12 ounces canned or pouch tuna, drained and broken into chunks, or 12 ounces cooked shrimp or fresh or canned crabmeat or imitation crab** for the poultry. If you wish, stir **3 to 4 tablespoons well-drained chopped pimientos** into the Mornay sauce.

CHICKEN À LA KING

8 servings

The classic enrichment of egg yolks and cream can be omitted. Cooked turkey or shrimp may be substituted for the chicken.

Melt in a large saucepan over medium heat:

6 tablespoons ($3/4$ stick) butter

Stir in and cook until softened, about 5 minutes:

8 ounces mushrooms, sliced

Add, whisking until well blended:

$1/3$ cup all-purpose flour

Slowly add, whisking constantly:

2 cups chicken broth
$1 1/2$ cups milk or half-and-half

Bring to a boil, then reduce the heat and cook, stirring, until thickened and smooth, about 5 minutes. Mix in:

4 cups chopped cooked chicken

$^1/_4$ cup chopped drained pimientos

For a more velvety sauce, whisk in a medium bowl:

2 egg yolks

$^1/_3$ cup heavy cream

Gradually stir 2 cups of the hot broth mixture into the egg yolk mixture to temper the egg yolks. Slowly pour the egg mixture back into the remaining chicken and stir thoroughly. Return to low heat and bring to a gentle simmer, stirring constantly; do not boil. The sauce should thicken slightly. Serve in or over any of the following:

Patty Shells (Bouchées), 670

Cooked rice

Toast

Sprinkle with:

($^1/_4$ cup sliced or slivered almonds, toasted)

(2 tablespoons minced parsley)

QUICK CHICKEN À LA KING

Substitute **two 10$^3/_4$-ounce cans condensed cream of chicken or mushroom soup mixed with $^1/_2$ cup chicken broth and $^1/_2$ cup milk or half-and-half** for the sauce. Add cooked chicken and pimientos and heat through.

SHRIMP WIGGLE

4 servings

An updated version of an American classic, printed in JOY's original 1931 edition.

Melt in a medium saucepan over moderate heat:

3 tablespoons butter

Add and cook, stirring, until tender and translucent but not brown, about 7 minutes:

$^1/_4$ cup minced onion

Stir in and cook, stirring, 1 minute:

3 tablespoons all-purpose flour

Remove from the heat. Add, whisking until well blended:

1$^1/_2$ cups milk

$^1/_2$ cup bottled clam juice

2 teaspoons catsup or cocktail sauce

Whisk until well blended. Return to heat and simmer, stirring frequently, until reduced by one-quarter and thick enough to coat a spoon heavily, about 10 minutes. Add:

1$^1/_2$ cups cooked peeled shrimp, deveined (about 6 ounces)

1 cup frozen peas, thawed

Heat to the first bubble of a simmer, then remove from heat, cover, and let stand 5 minutes. Season with:

(1 teaspoon sherry)

($^1/_2$ teaspoon lemon juice)

Salt to taste

$^1/_4$ teaspoon white, black, or ground red pepper

Serve on:

Hot buttered toast, Roll Cases, 111, or Toast Baskets, 111

STOCKS AND SOUPS

Now and always, a pot of soup simmering on the stove epitomizes home cooking. In the old days, when a "soup bunch" of vegetables and herbs cost a nickel and bones were free from the butcher, home cooks routinely made stocks and soups from scratch.

Because not everyone wants to bother with the painstaking methods often required to extract soup stock, and because soups are such an interesting addition to or base for meals, have on hand a supply of canned, dried, or frozen bases. They bring quick and revivifying soups into the range of even the most casual cook. No one can afford to be without a varied store of these consistently good, and often excellent, products.

ABOUT STOCKS

Antique dealers may respond hopefully to dusty bits in attics, but true cooks palpitate over more curious odds and ends: mushroom stems and tomato skins, poultry carcasses, celery leaves, fish heads, and knucklebones. These are just a few of the treasures for the stockpot—that magic source from which comes the telling character of the cuisine. You will note in most recipes for soups, sauces, gravies, or aspics the insistent call for stocks. In France, stocks are called *fonds,* signaling their importance as the foundations for many dishes. While they need not always be heavily reduced, ➤ do experiment by tasting the wonderful difference when these liquids replace water. ➤ When stocks are specified in long-cooking recipes, they are always meat stocks, as vegetable and fish stocks deteriorate in flavor if simmered longer than 30 minutes. The characteristics of any good stock are flavor, body, and clarity. Of the three, flavor is paramount.

MEAT AND POULTRY STOCKS

Stock making is an exception to almost every other kind of cooking. Rather than seek out things young and tender, remember that meat from mature animals will be most flavorsome. Remember, too, that instead of making every effort to keep juices within the materials you are cooking, you want to extract and trap every vestige of flavor from them—in liquid form. ➤ Starting to cook in cold water, which draws out juices, is the first step on the way to your goal. ➤ Bones should be disjointed or cracked and trimmed of excess fat.

In making dark stocks, first browning or roasting a portion of the meaty bones will add flavor, but before proceeding further, pour off any grease that develops. ➤ For a sturdy meat stock, allow only 2 cups of water to every cup of lean meat and bone, which may be used in about equal weights. When this much meat is used, only a few vegetables are needed to give flavor to the soup.

Gelatin gives a stock body and a rich, smooth texture. ➤ Beef or veal bones such as knucklebones, shoulder bones, and oxtails contain a large amount of natural gelatin, which plays a very important role in meat stock. In making ➤ poultry stock, back, neck, and wing bones are good sources of gelatin. If too large a proportion of bones is used, however, the stock may become gluey. ➤ Raw and cooked bones should not be mixed if a clear stock is desired. Nor, ➤ for clear stock, should any starchy or oily foods be added to the stockpot. Starchy foods also tend to make a stock deteriorate rapidly.

The most flavorful stocks are made with raw ingredients and enough cold water just to cover the bones. Additional water is needed only when it evaporates to below the level of the ingredients before the stock is done. Follow the recipes for ideal ratios of liquids to solids, but the principle is simple: ➤ Keep the solids covered while cooking. After adding the seasonings or aromatics called for, simmer the stock ➤ partially covered, with the lid at an angle, until you are sure you have extracted all the goodness from the ingredients, at least 2 hours, and as long as 12 hours if raw bones are used. If you are short on time, make Slow-Cooker Stock, 118, or Becker Express Stock, 120. Essential to retaining the maximum flavor of the extracted juices is ➤ a steady low heat for the simmering of the brew. When preparing ingredients for stock making, chop bones and vegetables to size according to their cooking times—large for long-cooking and small for quick-cooking—to allow their flavors to be fully extracted.

The most important tool for making stock is the most obvious—a stockpot. The best type is narrow, tall, and heavy-bottomed, to allow the stock to simmer gently without too much evaporation and to facilitate skimming. An 8- to 10-quart stockpot is ideal for making 2- to

4-quart batches of stock, but a smaller pot can be called into service for lesser quantities. Just be sure the pot is large enough to accommodate all of the solids with room to cover them with 2 inches of water. Dutch ovens or wide soup pots also work, as long as you add more water whenever the level drops below the solids. ➤ Avoid aluminum pots, which may react with the ingredients and affect the clarity and flavor of the stock.

The clarity of a stock is more than an aesthetic concern. ➤ The secret to a clear stock is to start with cold water and allow it to come slowly to a boil, then immediately lower the temperature to the slightest simmer. As stock heats, a heavy scum will rise to the surface. ➤ If a clear stock is wanted, it is imperative to skim any impurities, froth, or fat that rises to the surface and to be especially vigilant during the first 30 minutes of simmering. This removes impurities from the meat and bones that would otherwise cloud your stock. Do not allow the stock to boil or the scum that forms on the surface of the stock will be incorporated into the liquid.

Simmering stock past the recommended cooking time can produce an unpleasant bitter taste. A stock should be strained when all the flavor and essence have been fully extracted from the meat, bones, and vegetables. If in doubt, retrieve a meaty bone from the simmering stock. If the meat still has some flavor, allow the stock to simmer for longer. If the meat is tasteless and the bone joints are falling apart, it is time to strain the stock. ➤ If a stock tastes weak after straining, remove and discard the fat, then simmer the stock briskly to reduce it and concentrate the flavor. This technique, known as **reduction,** 116, produces a more deeply flavored stock.

SEASONING STOCK

Seasoning ingredients ➤ should be added sparingly, about half an hour after the stock has begun to simmer and the scum has been removed. ➤ Never salt heavily at the beginning of stock making. The considerable reduction involved both in the original cooking and in sub-sequent cooking—if the stock is used as an ingredient—makes it almost impossible to judge the amount you will need, and even a very little extra salt can easily ruin your results. If stocks are stored, the salt and seasoning are apt to intensify, and if wine is used in dishes made from stock, the salty flavor will be increased. Vegetable stocks, 119, are an exception to the rule.

Use herbs discreetly—in a Bouquet Garni, 960, a bundle of parsley, thyme, and bay leaves tied together or bundled in a square of cheesecloth—and whole spices such as peppercorns, cloves, allspice, cinnamon, and coriander, but not too much. Add mace, paprika, and cayenne in only the stingiest pinches. For a quick-cooking stock, there is no need to tie the seasonings in a bundle—they may simply be tossed in with the vegetables. An onion stuck with two or three cloves is classic. Carrots, celery, mushrooms, and leeks are also commonly used. Add 2 or 3 rinds of Parmesan cheese to stock for flavor and body.

Purists may insist on using only fish stock in a fish soup or beef stock in a beef stew, but chicken and vegetable stocks can be used for both fish soup and beef stew. Certainly, full-flavored beef stock or savory white veal stock is still worth making if you have the time.

STRAINING AND STORING STOCK

When the stock has finished cooking, strain it through a fine-mesh sieve, a colander lined with a double layer of damp cheesecloth, dampened paper towels, or a coffee filter into another pot or a large heatproof container, then discard the solids. To keep the stock clear, ladle it out, leaving any solids at the bottom of the pot or use a stockpot with a spigot. Pressing heavily on the solids while straining may cloud the stock. Do not let the stock sit out at room temperature for long, as it is a good breeding ground for bacteria. To cool, place the stockpot uncovered in the sink and partially immerse in ice water. Stir it a few times, and once it cools ➤ cover tightly and refrigerate. The grease will rise in a solid mass, which is also a protective coating. Do not remove it until just before you

Straining, cooling, and storing stock

reheat the stock for serving or use. See About Drippings, 981.

To remove fat from stock that is to be used immediately, lay a paper towel flat on the surface of the stock, and when it has absorbed as much fat as it will hold, discard it. Repeat as necessary. Or roll a paper towel and use one end to skim over the surface to remove the fat; when the end becomes coated with fat, cut off the used part with scissors and repeat the process. Alternatively, use a baster with the bulb as a suction device for grease removal. Or, for degreasing small quantities of stock, use a gravy or fat separator.

Stocks keep 3 to 4 days refrigerated. If refrigerating for longer, after 3 days skim the solidified fat from the surface and boil the stock for 10 minutes, then let cool and refrigerate for another 3 to 4 days.

Stocks can be frozen for up to 6 months. Transfer the stock to pint or quart plastic containers or resealable plastic freezer bags and freeze. ➤ Small amounts of stock can also be frozen in ice cube trays and the cubes stored in a resealable plastic bag. See Reducing Stocks or Glazes, below, for other storage possibilities.

Keep in the freezer resealable plastic "stock bags." Use one to store bones from roasted poultry or meat, another for raw bones. Toss in unwanted dinner leftovers, such as the lone drumstick. ➤ Note that raw and cooked bones should not be mixed in storage or in stock nor should very greasy foods be added. Reserve in their own bag any fish bones, light-fleshed fish, and shellfish shells and leftovers for fish stock. Vegetable trimmings and vegetable cooking liquids can be refrigerated or frozen. Store separately and use sparingly certain strongly flavored waters in which you have cooked cabbage, carrot, turnip, and fresh bean or, if the stock is to be a clear one, those from starchy vegetables. Bring the liquids to a boil before combining with other ingredients.

CLARIFYING STOCK

For extra-sparkling Consommé, 123, Aspic, 174, and Jellied Soup, 127, you may wish to clarify stock. This technique removes cloudiness; the second method also strengthens the flavor, and the result is more commonly known as consommé. ➤ Be sure the stock to be clarified is completely free of fat, 123, and never let it boil.

I. Allow for each quart of stock:

1 egg white, slightly beaten
1 eggshell, crumbled

If the stock has not been fully cooled and is still lukewarm, also add a few ice cubes for each quart. Stir the egg whites, shells, and ice, if using, into the stock well. Bring the stock very, very slowly, without stirring, to a simmer. As the stock heats, the eggs will bring a heavy, crusty foam more than an inch thick to the top. Do not skim this, but push it very gently away from one side of the pot. Through this small opening, you can watch the movement of the simmering stock, to make sure it never boils. Continue

simmering for 10 to 15 minutes. Remove the pot carefully from the heat and let it stand for 10 minutes to 1 hour.

Line a sieve with slightly dampened cheesecloth and place it over a bowl. Push the scummy crust to one side and ladle the stock carefully into the sieve, straining it through the cloth. Cool uncovered. Store covered tightly and refrigerated.

II. *About 6 cups*

The vegetables give this a more intense flavor than method I. It can be used in recipes calling for clarified stock or served on its own as a clear broth, or consommé.

Combine in a food processor:

1 small unpeeled onion, quartered
1 small carrot, cut into 2-inch pieces
1 small rib celery, cut into 2-inch pieces
2 tablespoons packed parsley leaves
$^1/_2$ teaspoon thyme leaves

Pulse until coarsely chopped. Add:

1 pound boneless, skinless chicken breasts, fat trimmed and cut into 2-inch pieces, or 1$^1/_2$ pounds beef round or rump steak, fat trimmed and cut into 1-inch pieces

Pulse until chopped. Remove to a medium bowl. Add:

3 large egg whites

Stir together well. Thoroughly degrease. Warm in a soup pot over low heat:

8 cups Poultry Stock, 117, Household Beef Stock, 117, or Brown Beef Stock, 117

Whisk in the vegetable mixture. Very slowly bring to a simmer, without boiling, and occasionally stirring and scraping the bottom of the pot to prevent burning, until the egg foam rises to the surface, about 30 minutes. (Be careful not to stir after the broth reaches a simmer.) When the egg foam starts to solidify, make a small hole in the center with a wooden spoon. Continue to simmer very gently until the egg foam mixture is solid, about 30 minutes more. Remove the pot from the heat. Line a sieve with a slightly dampened cheesecloth and place it over a large bowl or other container. Gently move the foam to the side of the pot and ladle the consommé into the sieve, straining it into the saucepan. Cool and store as above.

REDUCING STOCKS OR GLAZES

Glazes, also known as glace de viande, are meat stocks cooked down very slowly, uncovered, until they are syrupy and thick enough to coat a spoon. ➤ This **reduction** usually involves cooking the stock down to about 10 to 15 percent of the original amount of liquid. It will last for months tightly covered in the refrigerator or freezer. When we have time to make them, these potent glazes are most valuable for seasoning and finishing sauces, soups, and other dishes. See About Glazes, 582, and About Brown Sauces, 554.

MEAT GLAZE

Prepare:

> **Brown Beef Stock, below, Light Veal Stock, below,
> or Brown Poultry Stock, 118**

Degrease the stock well and place it in a medium saucepan over medium-high heat. Allow the stock to simmer vigorously, skimming off any foam. When the stock begins to get thicker, lower the heat to avoid burning. The glaze is ready when it coats the back of a spoon, 2 to 4 hours. Remove from the heat, transfer to a bowl or other container, and let cool. The glaze will solidify and feel rubbery to the touch. Cover and refrigerate, or cut into small squares equivalent to 1 tablespoon or more and freeze in a resealable plastic freezer bag.

BROWN BEEF STOCK

4 to 8 cups

Please read Meat and Poultry Stocks, 114.
Preheat the oven to 425°F. Place in a lightly oiled roasting pan and roast for 15 minutes:

> **5 pounds meaty beef bones**

Add:

> **2 medium unpeeled onions, quartered**
> **2 carrots, cut into 2-inch pieces**
> **2 celery ribs, cut into 2-inch pieces**

Roast, stirring occasionally to prevent the vegetables from burning, until the bones are well browned, about 40 minutes longer. Transfer to a stockpot. Carefully pour off the fat from the roasting pan, keeping the caramelized cooking juices, and add to the pan:

> **2 cups cold water**

Scrape up any browned bits, then add the liquid to the stockpot, along with:

> **Cold water to cover**

Bring slowly to a boil over medium heat, and reduce the heat at once. Simmer gently, partly covered, skimming often to remove scum, about 30 minutes. Add:

> **1 leek, split lengthwise and cut into 2-inch pieces**
> **1 Bouquet Garni, 960, including 1 whole clove**

Simmer, uncovered, for 6 to 8 hours, skimming often and adding water as needed to cover. Strain and cool uncovered, then refrigerate covered. Remove the fat when ready to use.

HOUSEHOLD BEEF STOCK

About 4 cups

Place in a large saucepan:

> **2 cups leftover cooked lean meat and bones**
> **Cold water to cover**

Bring just to the boiling point, then turn down the heat and simmer, uncovered, 30 minutes, skimming often to remove the scum. Add:

> **1 cup chopped vegetables and herbs: carrots, turnips, celery, parsley, etc.**
> **1 small unpeeled onion, chopped**
> **1 cup chopped tomatoes**

> **4 black peppercorns**
> **¹/₂ teaspoon sugar**
> **¹/₂ teaspoon salt**
> **¹/₈ teaspoon celery seeds**

Continue to simmer, with pot partly covered, about 2 hours, adding water to keep the ingredients covered as necessary, and skimming as needed. Strain the stock, and cool uncovered, then refrigerate covered. Remove the fat before using.

LIGHT VEAL STOCK

About 8 cups

Please read Meat and Poultry Stocks, 114. For **Brown Veal Stock,** begin with roasting as for Brown Poultry Stock, 118, substituting the veal for the chicken.
Blanch 5 minutes, using method II, 1054:

> **4 pounds veal knuckles**

Drain and add:

> **Cold water to cover**

Bring slowly to a boil. Then reduce the heat at once and simmer, uncovered, about 30 minutes, skimming often to remove scum. Add:

> **1 medium unpeeled onion, chopped**
> **3 celery ribs, chopped**
> **1 medium carrot, chopped**
> **1 Bouquet Garni, 960**
> **8 white peppercorns**
> **6 whole cloves**

Continue to simmer, partly covered, skimming often, 2¹/₂ to 3 hours, or until reduced by about half. Strain stock and cool uncovered, refrigerate covered. Remove the fat before using or freezing.

POULTRY STOCK

About 10 cups

Please read Meat and Poultry Stocks, 114. Combine in a stockpot over medium heat:

> **4 to 5¹/₂ pounds poultry parts, or one 4- to 5¹/₂-pound whole bird**
> **Cold water to cover**

Bring slowly to a boil, reduce the heat at once, simmer, uncovered, about 30 minutes, skimming often. Add:

> **1 unpeeled onion, coarsely chopped**
> **1 carrot, coarsely chopped**
> **1 celery rib, coarsely chopped**
> **8 black or white peppercorns**
> **1 Bouquet Garni, 960**
> **(2 whole cloves)**

Simmer, partly covered, for 3 to 4 hours, adding water to cover, if necessary, and skimming. Strain and cool uncovered, then refrigerate covered. Remove the fat when ready to use.

BROWN POULTRY STOCK

About 6 cups

Please read Meat and Poultry Stocks, 114.

Preheat oven to 425°F. Lightly grease a roasting pan. Place in the prepared pan:

Poultry and vegetables for Poultry Stock, above

Roast, stirring occasionally, until well browned, about 1 hour. Remove the chicken and vegetables to a stockpot. Add to the roasting pan:

1 cup water

Scrape up any browned bits, and add the liquid to the stockpot, along with:

Water and 1 Bouquet Garni, 960

Continue as directed.

SLOW-COOKER STOCK

Place in a 6-quart slow cooker all the ingredients for:

**Poultry Stock, 117, Brown Beef Stock, 117,
    or Vegetable Stock, 119**

Cook on low for 8 to 10 hours for chicken, a minimum of 6 hours for beef, and no more than 4 hours for vegetable stock. Strain and cool uncovered, then refrigerate covered. Remove fat when ready to use.

HOUSEHOLD POULTRY STOCK

3 to 20 cups

Try this stock when you have leftover cooked chicken, duck, or turkey. Use poultry from the smallest 3-pound bird to the largest 25-pounder. Use the large quantities for larger carcasses.

Break into small pieces and put in a pot:

**1 cooked chicken, duck, or turkey carcass
Cold water to cover**

Bring slowly to a boil, then reduce heat at once. Simmer, uncovered, about 30 minutes to 1 hour, skimming often to remove scum. Add:

**1 to 2 celery ribs, chopped
1 to 2 large unpeeled onions, quartered
1 to 2 carrots, chopped
4 to 8 black peppercorns
1 Bouquet Garni, 960**

Continue to simmer, uncovered, 1 to 1½ hours. Strain and cool uncovered, then refrigerate covered. Remove the fat before using.

LAMB STOCK

About 7 cups

Do not use in recipes calling for poultry or other kinds of meat, as the distinctive lamb character will overpower other flavors. Prepare **Brown Beef Stock, 117,** omitting the beef and using instead **2 pounds lamb shoulder chops, well trimmed.** Reduce the onions, carrots, celery, and water by half; omit the leek. Proceed as directed, simmering for 3 hours.

GAME STOCK

About 8 cups

Proceed as for **Brown Beef Stock, 117,** replacing the beef bones with **5 pounds venison or other game bones.** Replace the 2 cups of water with **1 cup dry red wine** and add **8 juniper berries.** Add to the bouquet garni **several stems fresh thyme and rosemary.** Proceed as directed.

FISH STOCK AND FUMET

Fish stock is prepared like any basic stock. Ingredients are covered with cold water and gently simmered. **Fumet,** a more intense version, is made by first "sweating," or cooking in a small amount of oil, the fish bones and diced vegetables to extract and release their flavor. White wine and water are added and the ingredients simmered to produce a robust, concentrated liquid. ➤ When clarity of the stock is important, choose a fish stock, the lighter and clearer of the two, over a fumet.

Fish stocks and fumets require less time—about 30 to 45 minutes—over relatively higher heat than when making meat or poultry stocks. Fish heads and bones work best, and these can be obtained at the fish counter. Ask for them if you don't see any on display, or order ahead. They must smell fresh, and be sure to rinse the head and bones, removing all traces of blood and viscera before using them in stock. Fish heads are particularly flavorful, but for mild-tasting all-purpose stock, ➤ avoid heads or trimmings from oily strong-flavored fish like herring, mackerel, skate, or mullet, 413–417. ➤ Use salmon only for stock to be used in salmon sauce.

If bones are unavailable, use inexpensive whole fish such as porgies. Shells from crab, shrimp, and lobster are delicious additions to fish stock and can be collected in the freezer until you have enough to make stock. See Shrimp Stock, 119. For Express Fish Stock, see 120.

About 10 cups

Combine in a stockpot over medium heat:

**2 pounds fish heads and bones, or whole fish,
    cleaned, scaled, rinsed well, and drained
1 small unpeeled onion, sliced
1 large leek, thoroughly cleaned and sliced
(½ fennel bulb, sliced)
(1 to 2 garlic cloves)
(1 cup dry white wine)
(1 teaspoon fresh lemon juice)
Cold water to cover
1 Bouquet Garni, 960**

Bring to a boil, reduce the heat, and simmer gently, uncovered, skimming often, 20 to 30 minutes. Strain and cool uncovered, then refrigerate covered.

FUMET

Melt **2 tablespoons butter** in a stockpot over medium-low heat. Cook the vegetables about 5 minutes. Add the fish heads and bones and cook, stirring once or twice, until they begin to turn opaque, 5 minutes more. Be sure not to let the vegetables or fish brown. Add the wine, lemon juice, cold water, and bouquet garni and proceed as directed for **Fish Stock, 118.**

SHRIMP STOCK
About 5 cups

Please read Fish Stock and Fumet, 118. For a clear stock, omit the tomato paste.

Heat in a stockpot over medium-high heat:

    2 tablespoons vegetable oil

Add and cook, stirring occasionally, until the shells are bright pink and aromatic, about 5 minutes:

    4 cups raw shrimp shells (from about 2 pounds
        shrimp), well rinsed and drained
    1 small unpeeled onion, thinly sliced
    1 small carrot, thinly sliced
    1 rib celery, thinly sliced

Stir in:

    (2 tablespoons tomato paste)

Add:

    Cold water to cover
    1 bay leaf
    1$\frac{1}{2}$ teaspoons lightly crushed black peppercorns
    (Splash of Pernod or $\frac{1}{4}$ teaspoon fennel seeds)

Bring almost to a boil, reduce the heat, and simmer gently, partially covered, for 20 minutes, skimming occasionally. Strain, pressing down on the shrimp shells to extract all the liquid. Let cool uncovered, then refrigerate covered.

DASHI
About 4 cups

One of the bases of traditional Japanese cuisine and an essential component of Miso Soup, 125, this stock is made quickly from two ingredients—kombu, or kelp, and *katsuobushi,* or dried bonito flakes, also referred to as smoky fish flakes—both of which can be found in Asian markets or health food stores. Dashi should not be boiled or cooked for too long, and it does not freeze well. If reheating, do not boil.

Combine in a saucepan over high heat:

    One 5 x 4-inch piece kelp (kombu)
    4$\frac{1}{2}$ cups cold water

Bring almost to a boil. Immediately remove from the heat and stir in:

    $\frac{1}{3}$ cup dried bonito flakes *(katsuobushi)*

Let stand until the flakes begin to sink, 2 to 3 minutes. Remove the kombu. Strain at once. Let cool uncovered, then refrigerate covered. Use within 4 to 5 days.

ABOUT VEGETABLE STOCKS

In making vegetable stock, your goal is to draw all the flavor out of the vegetables. Use 1$\frac{1}{2}$ to 2 times as much water as vegetables. Prepare vegetables as you would for eating—wash, scrape, or peel, as needed, and remove bruised or bad portions. Onions are the exception: The skins may be left on to give color to the stock. Beyond the standard recipes below, vegetable stock allows for much improvisation. Good additions include potatoes, corncobs, fresh herbs, ginger, garlic, leeks, and a few tablespoons of uncooked lentils. Cooking liquids from vegetables are always welcome. ➤ For quicker preparation and greater flavor, chop the vegetables in a blender or food processor.

Balance the amount and kinds of vegetables with other flavors, and when possible, ➤ tailor the ingredients to suit the recipes the stock will be used in. For example, a stock accented with ginger and garlic is good in many Asian recipes. Stock made with cabbage, cauliflower, and broccoli would be a real asset to Borscht, 129, but a calamity in chicken soup. We find green peas or snow peas, except in pea soups, a deadening influence. Too many carrots or parsnips tend to oversweeten the pot; we like to add a small turnip to the stock to offset the sweetness of the carrot. ➤ Vegetables to avoid include eggplant and most strong greens.

There are several ways to bring up the flavor of vegetables used in stock. One is to sauté them gently in butter; another is to cook them in meat stock. You may always add a bit of color, if no discernible flavor, to stock by adding a small amount of Caramelized Sugar, 1019.

In general, 5 cups vegetables to 6 cups water makes about 3 to 4 cups stock. Vegetable stocks do not require more than an hour and a half to cook. In fact, their delicate flavors deteriorate if overcooked. We do not recommend reducing vegetable stock.

VEGETABLE STOCK
About 4 cups

Heat in a stockpot over medium-high heat:

    1 tablespoon vegetable oil or butter

Add and cook, stirring, until softened:

    $\frac{1}{2}$ cup finely chopped onion and skins
    2 cups diced celery, including leaves
    (1 cup shredded lettuce)
    $\frac{1}{4}$ cup chopped carrots
    $\frac{1}{4}$ cup chopped turnips
    $\frac{1}{4}$ cup chopped parsnips
    (Mushroom trimmings or tomato skins)
    $\frac{1}{2}$ teaspoon salt
    1 Bouquet Garni, 960
    A dash of white pepper
    A dash of ground red pepper

Add:

    Cold water to cover

Bring to a boil, partially cover, and simmer about 1$\frac{1}{2}$ hours, or until the vegetables are very tender. Strain, pressing down on the vegetables, and cool uncovered. Then refrigerate covered. Remove the fat before using.

RICH VEGETABLE STOCK
About 4 cups

Heat in a large skillet over medium-high heat:

    2 tablespoons vegetable oil

Add and cook, stirring occasionally, until well browned:

8 ounces mushrooms or mushroom stems (about
3 cups)
1 unpeeled onion, quartered
2 carrots, cut into 2-inch pieces
4 garlic cloves, peeled and smashed
1 small turnip, peeled and cut into 2-inch pieces

Remove the vegetables to a stockpot, then deglaze the hot skillet by adding:

1 cup cold water

Scrape up any browned bits, then add the liquid to the pot, along with:

Cold water to cover
1 Bouquet Garni, 960, including a pinch of crushed red
pepper flakes

Simmer gently, uncovered, until the vegetables are very tender, 45 to 60 minutes. Skim if necessary. Strain, pressing down on the vegetables to extract the juices. Let cool uncovered, then refrigerate covered.

ABOUT STORE-BOUGHT STOCKS

When there is not time enough to prepare stock or broth from scratch the best solution is store-bought stock or broth, consommé, or clam juice. These pantry staples can be used straight out of the package, or you can boost their flavor. Sauté carrot, onion, or celery, add them to the stock, and simmer a few minutes, then strain. Reduced or low-sodium products are preferable, because the lesser amount of sodium and MSG leaves the cook free to adjust the seasonings. However, most store-bought broths are less than ideal candidates for sauces, which depend on complex, full-flavored stocks as their base. Taste a variety of store-bought broths until you find one you like, and keep in mind that price is not necessarily indicative of flavor. Concentrated stock bases generally contain less sodium and preservatives and have good flavor for soups. We do not recommend using bouillon cubes. See also About Quick Soups Cockaigne, 148, for soup recipes based on canned soups.

BECKER EXPRESS STOCK

About 4 cups

Omit the giblets if using beef broth or consommé.
Combine in a heavy saucepan:

Three 14^1/$_2$-ounce cans reduced-sodium chicken broth
or beef broth or consommé
(Any chicken giblets, trimmings, or bones on hand)
Ingredients for 1 Bouquet Garni, 960 (not wrapped)

Cut into 1-inch pieces and pulse in a food processor until finely chopped, then add to the pan:

1 small unpeeled onion
1 small carrot
1 small celery rib, with leaves
(1 leek, white part only, thoroughly cleaned,
or 3 scallions, trimmed)
(1 small garlic clove)

(^{1}/$_2$ cup dry white wine)
(1 tablespoon soy sauce)

Bring almost to a boil over medium-high heat, then reduce the heat and simmer gently for about 30 minutes, skimming any scum. Strain and cool uncovered, then refrigerate covered. Remove the fat when ready to use.

EXPRESS FISH STOCK

About 3 cups

A reliable fish stock using bottled clam juice.
Heat in a medium heavy skillet over medium-low heat:

1^1/$_2$ teaspoons olive oil

Add and cook, stirring, until soft:

1 cup finely chopped unpeeled onions or leeks,
thoroughly cleaned
^{1}/$_2$ cup finely chopped carrots

Add: ·

^{1}/$_2$ cup dry vermouth or dry white wine

Stir for about 1 minute, then stir in:

Four 8-ounce bottles clam juice
(Fish trimmings)
(^{1}/$_4$ small lemon)
1 Bouquet Garni, 960

Simmer for 20 minutes, skimming and stirring occasionally. Strain and cool uncovered, then refrigerate covered.

COURT BOUILLON

About 8 cups

Court bouillons are seasoned liquids that are cooked only a short time (*court* is French for "short"); their composition varies. They are not actual broths or stocks in themselves, but rather prototypes that may develop into them. Sometimes they are used only as a blanching or cooking medium, then discarded, as in the cooking of vegetables, where their purpose is to preserve color in the vegetable or leach out undesirable flavors from it. Sometimes they are a liquid storage medium for food cooked in them, as in Vegetables à la Grecque, 246. Use as a poaching liquid or a hot marinade in which fish is soaked before cooking. When used in the cooking of delicately flavored fish, they become—after the fish is removed—a fumet or fish stock, 118. You may refrigerate this court bouillon for several days and use it again for poaching another fish, or strain and use in place of fish stock in any recipe.
Rub:

3 pounds fish, cleaned and scaled

with:

Fresh lemon juice

Meanwhile, in a large saucepan, bring to a boil:

8 cups water

Add:

^{1}/$_2$ bay leaf
^{1}/$_4$ cup chopped onion
^{1}/$_2$ cup chopped celery
1 small onion, studded with 2 cloves
^{1}/$_2$ cup sherry vinegar or 1 cup dry white wine

1 teaspoon salt
(Several sprigs parsley or 1 Bouquet Garni, 960)

When the mixture is boiling, plunge in the fish and at once reduce the heat. Simmer the fish uncovered, 30 minutes, or until tender. Remove bay leaf, drain and serve.

ABOUT BROTHS

After all this, you may be asking, what is homemade broth? A broth is a clear soup made from meat, poultry, fish, shellfish, or vegetables. Unlike stock, broth is eaten "as is," like a soup, though it can also be used as a component in recipes. Because broth does not have the gelatin content of a stock, it is not a candidate for reduction, or to make complex sauces or Meat Glaze, 117. Broth should have an eye-appealing golden or amber color as well as a balanced flavor and delicate aroma. Choose meaty bones for making broth; in the case of poultry or chicken broth, stewing hens or mature game birds make the most flavorful broth. There are no set rules on the vegetables to select for a vegetable broth, but a nice combination includes carrots, turnips, parsnips, leeks, celery, mushrooms, and tomatoes. Broth lends itself to many additions such as ginger, lemongrass, garlic, shallots, or wild mushrooms. For garnishes for clear soups, see 150.

CHICKEN BROTH

About 12 cups

Combine in a stockpot over medium heat:

One $3^1/_2$- to 4-pound chicken, cut into parts
Cold water to cover

Bring almost to a boil, reduce the heat, and simmer gently for 30 minutes, skimming often. Pulse in a food processor until finely chopped:

1 medium unpeeled onion, cut into eighths
1 carrot, cut into 2-inch pieces
1 celery rib, cut into 2-inch pieces

Add vegetables to the pot. Simmer, uncovered, until the chicken is cooked, about 40 minutes longer. Remove the chicken and reserve. Strain and let cool uncovered, then refrigerate covered. Remove the fat when ready to use.

BEEF BROTH

About 4 cups

Combine in a stockpot over medium heat:

$1^1/_2$ pounds boneless beef chuck, cut into 1-inch cubes and pulsed in a food processor until coarsely chopped
5 cups cold water

Bring almost to a boil, then reduce the heat and simmer gently for 30 minutes, skimming often to remove scum. Add:

1 medium unpeeled onion, cut into 1-inch chunks
1 large leek, thoroughly cleaned and chopped
1 carrot, cut into 2-inch pieces
1 tablespoon tomato paste
5 parsley stems

$^1/_2$ teaspoon dried thyme
3 black peppercorns, lightly crushed
1 whole clove

Simmer, uncovered, for 1 hour. Strain and let cool uncovered, then refrigerate covered. Remove the fat when ready to use. The broth will separate, so whisk before using.

CLAM BROTH

About 2 cups

Please read About Clams, 374. The broth is delicious hot. It can also be frozen until slushy and served in small glasses with wedges of lemon. The clams themselves may be used in various seafood dishes, 369.

Place in a pot:

24 littleneck clams, scrubbed
$1^3/_4$ cups water, chicken stock or broth, or tomato juice
$^1/_2$ cup chopped unpeeled onion
1 celery rib with leaves, chopped
A pinch of ground red pepper

Cover tightly and steam the clams until the shells open. Remove the clams and strain the broth through a double layer of moistened cheesecloth to remove any sand. If desired, heat the broth and dilute with warm cream or rich milk. Season to taste with:

Salt and black pepper

Top with a spoonful of:

(Unsweetened whipped cream or sour cream)

and/or sprinkle with:

(Snipped chives)

VEGETABLE BROTH

About $3^1/_2$ cups

Serve strained or unstrained, hot or cold.
Melt in a large saucepan over medium heat:

3 tablespoons butter

Add and cook gently for 5 minutes:

3 cups or more chopped vegetables for stock

Do not let the vegetables brown. Add:

4 cups boiling water or a combination of boiling water and tomatoes or tomato juice

Simmer the broth, partially covered, 1 hour. Season to taste with:

Salt and black pepper
(1 tablespoon soy sauce)

MUSHROOM BROTH

About 6 cups

Pulse in a food processor until fine:

12 ounces mushrooms

Combine in a large saucepan with:

6 cups Poultry Stock, 117, Chicken Broth, above, or beef consommé

Simmer, partially covered, 15 minutes. Strain, if you like, or thicken, 123. Serve very hot. Add to each cup:

1 teaspoon dry sherry (2 tablespoons total)

ABOUT SOUPS

No one can afford to be without a supply of store-bought stocks and broths for making soups. But not everyone has the time to start from scratch. There is no doubt that homemade stocks and broths are the basis of the very best soups but soup is relatively simple to make, and is often the perfect use of leftovers. Most soups freeze well, below, and are easily thawed and warmed for a quick meal.

Some soups are served hot, some cold, and some either way. To serve soup piping hot, use heated bowls or cups, tureens, or lidded bowls. Cold soups should be very well chilled and served in chilled bowls or dishes—especially jellied soups, which tend to break down more rapidly, being relatively light in gelatin. Cold soups, when not jellied, may be prepared quickly by using a blender and chilling briefly in the freezer. But no matter by what method it is made, ➤ soup should complement or contrast with what is to follow if being served as an appetizer. On informal occasions, soups may be chilled in a tall jug or pitcher and served directly from it into chilled cups or bowls. ➤ Consider 1 cup of soup an appetizer, 1½ to 2 cups a main course. There are some classic dishes—New England Boiled Dinner, 484, and Hungarian Goulash, 480—that occupy the middle ground between soups and stews.

Some soups in this chapter are pureed to make them smooth; others are partially pureed to give them a creamier texture. A **food processor** is especially good to puree thick soups. Beware of overloading, as liquids can leak out the bottom or overflow. Depending on the size of your food processor, it may be best to puree a soup in batches. Or you can puree the solid ingredients with just enough liquid to keep the blade from sticking, then return the puree to the pot and stir or whisk to blend. A **blender** works well for pureeing thinner soups. ➤ When blending hot soup, do not fill the blender more than one-third full. Wrap a dish towel around the lid and start on a low speed, then gradually increase the speed. A **hand-held immersion blender** is exceptionally convenient. Immerse in the soup, turn it on, and stir it around the soup until you achieve the desired texture. The solid ingredients must be very soft for the immersion blender to work, and it will never create a completely silken texture, but it is an excellent tool for soups that are only partially pureed, such as some bean soups. A **food mill** is useful when a soup has been cooked until the ingredients are quite soft. The food mill purees and strains simultaneously. Interchangeable disks help the cook control the final texture of the soup.

Soups keep very well tightly covered in the refrigerator, most improving in flavor as they sit. Fruit soups and soups made with meat, poultry, milk, cream, eggs, vegetables, or legumes will keep for up to 3 days. The exception is soup made with fish or seafood; the delicate flavors have the finest quality as soon as they are cooked. Refrigerate soup when it has completely cooled, and cover tightly. ➤ All soups can be frozen if they don't contain eggs, seafood, or cheese. Freeze in tightly sealed labeled containers that ➤ allow 1½ inches of headroom for expansion. Soups that contain chunks of vegetables that do not freeze well— root vegetables, for example—can be pureed after thawing, then heated with enough stock or milk to loosen. In busy households, it may be useful to freeze main-dish soups in individual portions.

▲ Above 2,500 feet, soups need longer cooking times than called for in these recipes, as liquid boils at a lower temperature.

COLORING SOUPS

If a soup has been cooked with tomato skins, roasted onion skins, or caramelized onions, and if the amount of meat used is substantial, it should have a good, rich color. A shake of soy or tamari sauce, a dab of miso or store-bought demiglace also enhances color. Caramelized Sugar, 1019, may be added if necessary. We prefer it to commercial soup coloring, which can overwhelm a delicately flavored soup with its pervasive telltale aroma. Also read About Vegetable Stocks, 119.

SEASONING SOUP

Soup is as flavorful as the stock or broth on which it is based. ➤ Please read About Stocks, 114, and Seasoning Stock, 115. The addition of wine to soup frequently enhances its flavor, but ➤ do not oversalt soups to which wine is added, as wine intensifies saltiness. ➤ Add the wine after the initial cooking period, when it is in the simmering stage, to allow the alcohol to cook off and the flavor to integrate. A strongly flavored soup prepared with beef or oxtail is improved by the addition of dry red wine, and a dry white wine adds zest to a fish, crab, or lobster bisque or chowder. ➤ Add ¼ to ½ cup wine to 1 quart soup. Fortified wine, such as a medium-dry sherry or Madeira, blends well with veal or chicken soup and should be added just before serving, while ruby or tawny port may be added to robust game soups and stocks. To add wine to soups containing cream or eggs, see individual recipes. ➤ Do not boil a soup after adding wine.

Beer adds a tang to bean, cabbage, and vegetable soups. ➤ Use 1 cup for every 3 cups soup. Add the beer,

Hand-held immersion blender, food mill

at room temperature, just before serving. Heat the soup through, but ➤ do not boil.

To bring up the flavor of soup vegetables, sauté them gently in butter—see Consommé Brunoise, 124—or cook them in meat stocks. When you add vegetables to soup as a garnish the trick is not to soften them to the point where they release their juices, but to keep them full of flavor. If the vegetables you are using as a garnish are strong, like peppers or onions, blanch them first. No matter what the soup, a small quantity of salt pork, a ham hock, or a few slices of bacon will add flavor and depth.

REMOVING FAT FROM SOUP

As for stocks, see 116, there are three simple methods for removing fat from soup. Chill the soup, the fat will solidify and it is then easy to spoon it off. Or float a paper towel on the surface of warm soup, and when it has absorbed as much fat as it will hold, discard. Or roll up a paper towel and use one end to skim over the soup surface to remove the fat, as shown. When the end becomes drenched with fat, cut off the used part with scissors and repeat the process, as shown.

Remove fat from soup
with a rolled paper towel

THICKENERS FOR SOUPS

Egg yolks are one of the richest and best of soup thickeners, but must be added just before serving. Take care that the soup is not too hot. Please read About Egg Safety, 980.

I. Allow for each cup of soup:

1 egg yolk, beaten with 1 tablespoon cream or sherry

To avoid curdling, add a small quantity of the hot soup to this beaten mixture before incorporating it into the soup. When using egg- or cream-based thickeners, keep the soup below the boiling point after their addition.

II. Allow for each cup of soup:

2 riced hard-boiled egg yolks, 194

Add at the last minute, and do not allow the soup to boil.

III. A good soup thickener for those whose diet does not include flour. Allow:

3 tablespoons grated raw potato

for each cup of soup. Grate the potato directly into the soup about 15 minutes before it has finished cooking. Simmer until the potato is tender and acts as a thickener.

IV. This method is good for soups cooked with starchy vegetables such as dry beans, peas, or lentils. This mixture will thicken about 3 cups strained boiling soup. Blend:

1 tablespoon butter, melted
1 tablespoon all-purpose flour

with a small amount of:

Cold water, stock or broth, or milk

Stir into the boiling soup and simmer at least 5 minutes before serving.

V. To thicken a soup with flour, make a paste of it with a cold liquid. Allow for each cup of soup:

1½ teaspoons all-purpose flour

Make paste of the flour with about twice as much:

Cold stock or broth, milk, or water

Pour the paste slowly into the boiling soup, stirring constantly. Simmer, stirring, 5 to 10 minutes.

VI. Make a Roux, 543. For each cup of soup, allow:

1½ teaspoons butter
1½ teaspoons all-purpose flour

Pour the soup into the mix, stirring constantly until smooth and boiling.

VII. You can also **puree leftover cooked vegetables** as thickeners for soup. Additional thickenings for soup include dry bread crumbs, heavy cream or sour cream, and White Sauce, 550. **Noodles, dumplings, and cooked grains** such as rice give an effect of body to a clear soup. Stir uncooked grains into soup for the last hour of cooking. For a light thickening of each cup of liquid, allow approximately:

1 teaspoon barley
1 teaspoon rice
1 teaspoon oatmeal
½ teaspoon tapioca

SERVING SOUP OR BROTH MEAT

Any poultry or meat that is immersed in ➤ cold water and simmered for a long period is bound to give its best flavor to the cooking liquor. But some nutritional value remains in the meat, and it may be heightened in flavor by serving it, when removed from the soup, with one of these sauces:

Horseradish Sauce, 552
Mustard Sauce, 552
Quick Tomato Sauce, 562
Brown Onion Sauce, 555
Salsa Verde, 567

ABOUT CLEAR SOUPS

When making these soups, a full-bodied homemade stock or broth is strongly recommended. You can intensify the flavor of a stock by reducing it, 116. Or simmer it with sautéed chopped vegetables—finely diced carrots, celery, and onions—and fresh herbs, then strain them out.

CONSOMMÉ

The most classic and pure example of a clear soup, intensely flavorful consommé makes an elegant start to a

formal dinner party. For a clear consommé, the stock must be completely free of fat.
Prepare:

Poultry Stock, 117, or Brown Beef Stock, 117

and clarify it by method I, 116. This will give you a clear thin consommé. For more flavor, clarify the stock by method II. Before serving, add:

(3 tablespoons Marsala)

CONSOMMÉ BRUNOISE

6 cups
Melt in a saucepan over medium-low heat:

2 tablespoons butter

Add and cook gently:

2 celery ribs, finely diced
2 small carrots, finely diced
1 small turnip, peeled and finely diced
1 small onion, finely diced

Allow enough time to let the vegetables absorb the butter, but do not let them brown. Add:

2 cups Consommé, 123

and cook, covered, until the vegetables are almost tender. Add:

2 tablespoons fresh or frozen peas
2 tablespoons finely diced green beans

Add to the vegetables:

4 cups hot Consommé

Remove fat and season with:

Salt and black pepper to taste

Just before serving, add:

(2 tablespoons finely chopped chervil)

CONSOMMÉ MADRILENE

About 4 cups
Heat to a boil:

2 cups tomato juice
2 cups Poultry Stock, 117
$^1/_2$ teaspoon grated onion
A strip of lemon zest

Strain into a tureen. Flavor with:

1 tablespoon fresh lemon juice, 2 teaspoons dry sherry, or 2 teaspoons Worcestershire sauce

Garnish with:

Sour cream
Red caviar

EGG DROP SOUP

2 cups
A classic JOY recipe whose infallible directions were given to Irma by her dear friend, the late Cecily Brownstone. A food writer for the Associated Press, Cecily gave JOY its first review in a national publication in the early 1930s.
Heat in a small saucepan until boiling vigorously:

2 cups Poultry Stock, 117, or Brown Beef Stock, 117, or broth

Reduce the heat so the broth simmers. Break into a cup:

1 egg, at room temperature

Beat it with a fork, just long enough to combine the yolk and white. When the fork is lifted high, the egg should run off the tines in a watery stream. Now, ➤ with the broth simmering, hold the cup in one hand, 5 inches above the rim of the saucepan. Pour a little of the beaten egg slowly in a fine stream into the broth; with a fork in the other hand, make wide circles on the surface of the broth to catch the egg as it strikes and draw it out into long filmy threads, 3 or 4 times, so as not to disturb the simmering. Or have a helper pour the egg through a strainer instead of from a cup. Simmer about 1 minute. Season with:

Salt and black pepper to taste

Serve at once in warmed cups with:

(A generous squeeze of lemon juice)

GREEK LEMON SOUP (AVGOLEMONO)

About 4 cups
Bring to a rolling boil in a medium saucepan:

3 cups Poultry Stock, 117, or Chicken Broth, 121
$^1/_2$ cup long-grain white rice

Reduce the heat, cover, and simmer until the rice is tender, about 20 minutes. Whisk in a medium bowl just until combined and uniform in color:

2 eggs
$^1/_4$ cup fresh lemon juice or any dry white wine

Stir in 2 tablespoons of the hot stock. Gradually pour the eggs into the hot but not boiling soup, stirring constantly. Season with:

(1 to 2 tablespoons fresh lemon juice)
Salt and black pepper

Serve in hot cups, garnished with:

Chopped parsley or snipped dill

ITALIAN PARMESAN AND EGG SOUP (STRACCIATELLA)

About 3 cups
Bring to a simmer in a medium saucepan:

3 cups Poultry Stock, 117, Chicken Broth, 121, or other light stock or broth

Meanwhile, whisk together until blended:

1 egg
$1^1/_2$ tablespoons grated Parmesan
1 tablespoon dry bread crumbs
2 tablespoons chopped parsley
1 small garlic clove, finely minced

Stir this mixture rapidly into the simmering stock and stir until the egg is set, 30 to 60 seconds. Garnish with:

Freshly grated or ground nutmeg or grated lemon zest

GARLIC SOUP WITH EGGS (SOPA DE AJO)

About 4 cups
Heat in a soup pot over medium-low heat:

3 tablespoons olive oil

Add and cook, stirring, 10 to 15 minutes:

1 head garlic, separated into cloves and peeled (about 16 cloves)

With a slotted spoon, remove the garlic to a small bowl.

Cook in the oil over medium-high heat, turning once, until golden, 1 to 2 minutes on each side:

4 slices French or country bread

Remove from the pot and rub on both sides with:

1 (raw) garlic clove, halved

Stir into the pot:

1 tablespoon sweet or hot paprika

¼ teaspoon cumin seeds

Stir in the cooked garlic, along with:

4 cups Poultry Stock, 117, Chicken Broth, 121, or water

½ teaspoon salt

¼ teaspoon black pepper

Bring to a boil, reduce the heat, and simmer until the garlic is tender, about 20 minutes. Preheat the oven to 400°F. With a slotted spoon, remove the garlic from the pot, and mash with a fork. Return it to the pot, then bring the soup to a low simmer. Set 4 ovenproof bowls or crocks on a baking sheet and fill with the soup. One at a time, break into a small bowl, then slide into a bowl of soup:

4 eggs

Bake just until the egg whites are set (the yolks should still be runny), about 3 minutes. Top each serving with a garlic crouton, allowing the soup to soak into the bread.

ROASTED GARLIC SOUP

6 cups

This garlic soup, a family favorite, was discovered by my son John while he was traveling in Spain. The soup is even richer served in individual ovenproof bowls, topped with cheese and browned under the broiler.

Roast, using method II, 277:

6 heads garlic, unpeeled

Set garlic aside and reserve the roasting juices. Pour into a large saucepan:

Three 14- to 16-ounce cans chicken broth

Squeeze the roasted garlic into the broth, and whisk until blended. Bring to a simmer, then whisk in:

3 slices white bread, crusts removed, torn into small pieces

¼ teaspoon salt

¼ teaspoon hot paprika

Black pepper to taste

Reserved juices from roasted garlic

(Juice of ½ lemon)

Simmer for 5 minutes. Serve topped with:

Grated Parmesan or shredded Manchego

MISO SOUP

About 4½ cups

Please read About Miso, 998.

Soak in cold water for 10 minutes:

(1½ teaspoons dried seaweed [*wakame*] bits)

Drain, squeeze out the excess liquid, and divide the seaweed among 4 soup bowls. Heat in a medium saucepan over high heat:

1 teaspoon vegetable oil

Add and cook, stirring, until slightly browned:

2 to 3 shiitake mushroom caps, thinly sliced

1 small leek, white part only, thinly sliced on a diagonal

Pinch of salt

(½ teaspoon sake)

Cook, stirring, about 1 minute. Stir in:

4 cups Dashi, 119

1 teaspoon soy sauce

Cook over medium-low heat just until warmed through. Place in a small bowl:

3 to 3½ tablespoons red miso

Add about ¼ cup of the warm dashi and whisk to dissolve the miso, then whisk this mixture back into the soup. Divide among the soup bowls:

(2 ounces firm tofu, cut into small cubes [about ⅓ cup])

Ladle the broth and vegetables into the bowls.

BECKER QUICK MISO SOUP

2½ cups

At our house, this is a traditional sickbed treat.

Bring to a boil over medium-high heat:

2 cups Chicken Broth, 121

Stir in:

2 tablespoons instant miso, or 1 tablespoon fresh

(1 or 2 finely sliced mushrooms)

(1 or 2 finely chopped scallions)

Boil for 1 minute. Garnish each serving with:

A thin slice of lemon

Black pepper

(1 teaspoon Port)

(Dash of hot pepper sauce)

CHICKEN NOODLE SOUP

About 4 cups

If you use homemade chicken stock or broth, add some of the cooked chicken to the soup.

Bring to boil in a medium saucepan:

4 cups Poultry Stock, 117, Chicken Broth, 121, or other light stock or broth

Stir in:

1 cup fine egg noodles or 2 ounces small pasta, such as orzo or ditalini

Cook until noodles or the pasta are tender but firm. Stir in:

2 tablespoons chopped parsley or dill

Salt and black pepper to taste

CHICKEN RICE OR BARLEY SOUP

About 4 cups

Bring to a simmer in a medium saucepan:

4 cups Poultry Stock, 117, Chicken Broth, 121, or other light stock or broth

½ teaspoon salt

Stir in:

3 tablespoons long-grain rice or 2 tablespoons
    pearl barley

Simmer until tender, about 15 minutes for rice, 30 to 45
minutes for barley.

CHICKEN SOUP WITH RAVIOLI
OR TORTELLINI

Substitute 8 ounces **ravioli** or **tortellini** for the rice or barley in the recipe above. Simmer until pasta is tender but
firm, 5 to 10 minutes.

MATZO BALL SOUP

7 1/2 cups

Beat in a medium bowl with an electric mixer on medium
speed for 1 minute:

4 eggs
(2 to 3 tablespoons chicken fat)
1 teaspoon salt

Stir in:

2 tablespoons snipped dill
(1/2 cup finely diced fennel)
(4 teaspoons snipped fresh chives or dried minced
    chives or 2 tablespoons chopped parsley)
1/3 cup plus 1 tablespoon soda water

Fold in until well blended:

1 cup matzo meal
1/4 teaspoon black pepper
(1 teaspoon curry powder)
(1 to 2 teaspoons finely chopped peeled fresh ginger
    or 1 teaspoon ground ginger)

Cover and refrigerate for 1 to 4 hours. With wet hands,
form the matzo mixture into 2-inch balls. Drop gently, one
at a time, into a large pot of boiling salted water. Cover, reduce the heat, and simmer for 25 minutes. When the
matzo balls are almost cooked, heat in a soup pot:

6 cups Poultry Stock, 117, Chicken Broth, 121, or other
    light stock or broth

Season with:

1 1/4 teaspoons salt
(1/4 teaspoon black pepper)

Add the matzo balls to the stock. Ladle the stock into
warmed bowls, with 2 matzo balls in each bowl.

KREPLACH SOUP

7 1/2 cups

Prepare one of the following fillings:

I. Heat in a small skillet:

1 tablespoon vegetable oil

Add:

1/2 cup minced onion
8 ounces ground beef

Cook, stirring, until the onions are soft and beef is no
longer pink.

Season with:

3/4 teaspoon salt and black pepper

II. Or combine:

1 1/2 cups minced onion, sautéed in 1 tablespoon
    vegetable oil
1 cup finely chopped cooked chicken
1 raw egg yolk
3/4 teaspoon salt
1 tablespoon chopped parsley

Prepare:

1/2 recipe Fresh Pasta Dough, 324

This will make about 20 kreplach. Do not allow the dough
to dry before cutting it into 3-inch squares. Put about
1 1/2 teaspoons of filling in the center of each square, as
shown. Fold the dough over the filling, making a triangular shape. Press the edges carefully with a fork to seal them
completely. Place the kreplach on a flour-dusted kitchen
towel and let dry for 30 minutes, then turn over and dry
for 30 minutes longer. Drop the kreplach into:

About 4 quarts rapidly boiling broth or salted water

and simmer gently 7 to 10 minutes; drain well.
Meanwhile, heat:

6 cups well-seasoned strong broth

Serve the kreplach in the broth.

Filling and folding kreplach

WONTON SOUP

7 cups

Assemble and set aside:

Wontons or Vegetable Wontons, 342

Bring to a simmer in a soup pot:

5 cups Poultry Stock, 117, Chicken Broth, 121,
    or (if using vegetable wontons) reserved
    mushroom-soaking liquid, if any, plus 4 to 5 cups
    Vegetable Stock, 119

Season with:

1¹/₄ teaspoons salt or soy sauce

Cover and keep warm. Bring a large pot of water to a simmer. Drop in the wontons in 2 or 3 batches and simmer gently until done, about 3 minutes. Drain, then divide among 6 to 8 bowls. Ladle the hot broth over the wontons. Garnish with:

Grated carrots
Chopped scallion greens

ABOUT JELLIED SOUPS

These delicious chilled soups were once served more than they are today, but they remain a warm-weather treat and are overdue for a revival. Any clear broth, especially consommé, can be served this way. Stock made from veal knuckles and beef bones, 117, may jell enough naturally to be served without added gelatin. Watch the salt content of these soups. If you prepare them in advance, their saltiness is intensified.

JELLIED SOUP

Allow:

1 envelope (2¹/₄ teaspoons) unflavored gelatin
(2 teaspoons fresh lemon juice)

for each:

2 cups clarified stock, 116, or Consommé, 123

Heat the stock to a simmer. Stir in the gelatin until dissolved, remove from the heat, and cool to room temperature. Stir in the lemon juice, and if using:

(A few drops of Worcestershire sauce)

Add, after soup is cooled and partially set:

(Fresh parsley leaves)
(Thin slices carrot, blanched)

For rapid chilling, place the soup in a wet bowl set on cracked ice and water, or put the bowl in the freezer for a few minutes but no longer. Freezing would destroy the texture. Chill until firm but wobbly. Gently break up the soup before serving in small cups.

JELLIED TOMATO SOUP

About 4 cups

Combine:

1 envelope (2¹/₄ teaspoons) unflavored gelatin
¹/₂ cup cold water

for 5 minutes to soften the gelatin. Heat to a boil, then strain:

2 cups tomato juice
2 cups Poultry Stock, 117, Chicken Broth, 121, or other light stock or broth
A piece of lemon rind

Dissolve the gelatin in the hot stock. Cool, then flavor to taste with any of the following:

¹/₂ to 1 teaspoon fresh lemon juice, or
¹/₂ to 1 teaspoon Worcestershire sauce, or
¹/₂ to 1 tablespoon dry sherry

Pour soup into a wet bowl. Chill until firm but wobbly. Stir gently to break up the soup before serving. Garnish with:

Lemon slices, sour cream, chopped chives, mint, small nasturtium leaves, chopped olives, hard-cooked riced eggs, horseradish, sprigs of parsley, watercress, or dill

JELLIED BEET SOUP

5 cups

Combine in a saucepan and simmer, covered, until the beets are tender, about 20 minutes:

1 pound beets, peeled, cut in half if large
4 cups water
1 thick-sliced unpeeled onion
1 Bouquet Garni, 960

Meanwhile, combine:

1 envelope (2¹/₄ teaspoons) unflavored gelatin
¹/₂ cup cold water

for 5 minutes to soften the gelatin. Strain the hot beet liquid mixture through a fine-mesh sieve lined with cheesecloth into a large glass, measure and reserve the beets. You should have 2 cups; add more water if necessary. Stir the gelatin into the hot liquid until dissolved, then pour into a bowl. Dice the beets, then stir them in, along with:

¹/₂ to 1 teaspoon red wine vinegar or fresh lemon juice

Chill until firm but wobbly, about 4 hours. Gently break up the soup with a spoon before serving. Garnish each serving with:

(1 teaspoon caviar)
1 teaspoon sour cream
Snipped dill

ABOUT THICK SOUPS

Puree, cream, bisque, velouté, potage—to the connoisseur, each of these is a quite distinctive embodiment of the indispensable thick soup. If you like to attach a label to your creations, know that a **puree** is a soup that gets its major thickening from the vegetables or other food put through a food mill or blender and has butter swirled into it at the very last moment. By omitting the butter or lessening the amount and adding cream, and sometimes egg yolk, you get a **cream** soup. If that soup has a shellfish base, and only if it has, you may call it a **bisque.** If you add both eggs and cream and a Velouté Sauce, 552, to a puree base, you achieve a **velouté soup. Potages,** the most variable of soups, are likely to have the phrase *du jour* added, meaning that they are both the specialty of the day and, from the cook's point of view, seasonal and convenient to compose. Potages, which tend to be hefty, taste best when their vegetables are first braised in butter and are then put through a food mill before serving. For ways to thicken soups, see 123.

Here are a few practical hints that will help you make the most of thick soups. Be sure to scrape the puree off the bottom of the strainer. ➤ If you use a food processor or blender, first blanch, 1054, or steam any vegetables with strings, like celery, or skins, like peas. After butter, cream, or eggs are ➤ added, never allow the soup to reach a boil: If you are not serving it at once, reheat it over very low heat or in a double boiler.

When making the soup, cut ingredients uniformly to ensure even cooking, and bear in mind that some vegetables, such as potatoes or carrots, take longer to cook than others. These should be added first, then followed by vegetables such as celery, onions, and green beans. Leave quick-cooking greens, such as spinach and chard, for last.

Thick soups should not be served as the first course of a heavy meal. The wonderful thing about them is that they are nearly a meal in themselves. Balanced by a green salad or fruit, they make a complete lunch or light supper.

VEGETABLE SOUP (SOUPE PAYSANNE)
About 7 cups
Heat in a large saucepan:
   2 tablespoons olive oil or butter
Add and cook on medium heat until slightly softened:
   $^1/_2$ cup diced carrots
   1 cup diced onions
   1 cup diced celery
Add:
   4 cups hot stock or water, or broth
   2 cups chopped tomatoes
   (1 cup diced peeled potatoes)
   (1 cup diced peeled turnips)
   2 tablespoons chopped parsley
   1 teaspoon salt
   $^1/_4$ teaspoon black pepper
Cover and cook about 35 minutes, then add:
   (1 cup chopped cabbage or spinach)
Cook about 5 minutes more. Add:
   2 tablespoons chopped parsley
   Salt and black pepper to taste

MINESTRONE
About 12 cups
Heat in a large soup pot over medium heat until the bacon has released its fat, 2 to 3 minutes:
   2 tablespoons olive oil
   2 slices bacon or 1 ounce pancetta, chopped
Add and cook, stirring, until the greens are beginning to wilt, 5 to 10 minutes:
   $1^1/_2$ cups chopped onions
   $^3/_4$ cup chopped carrots
   $^3/_4$ cup minced celery, including leaves
   $^1/_2$ small head green cabbage, chopped
   3 chard leaves, chopped
   2 garlic cloves, minced
   One 4-inch sprig fresh rosemary or 1 teaspoon dried rosemary
   $^1/_4$ cup packed basil leaves, chopped
   $^1/_4$ cup packed parsley leaves, chopped
Cover and cook until the vegetables are tender, about 10 minutes. Stir in:

   One 14-ounce can whole tomatoes, drained and crushed
Cook, stirring, over medium-high heat for 3 to 5 minutes. Stir in:
   One $15^1/_2$- to 19-ounce can cannellini, Great Northern, or other white beans, rinsed and drained, or 1 to 2 cups cooked beans, 253, half of them mashed
   10 cups Poultry Stock, 117, Chicken Broth, 121, or water
   2 teaspoons salt
   (2 x 3-inch rind Parmesan)
Bring to a boil, reduce heat, and simmer, partly covered, 30 minutes. Remove the rosemary sprig, stir in:
   4 ounces orzo or elbow macaroni (1 cup)
Simmer for 15 minutes. Season with:
   Salt and black pepper to taste
Drizzle over each serving:
   Extra-virgin olive oil
   (Grated Parmesan, Romano, or Asiago)

PROVENÇAL VEGETABLE SOUP (SOUPE AU PISTOU)
About 3 quarts
Heat in a large soup pot, over medium heat:
   2 tablespoons olive oil
Add and cook, stirring, until tender but not browned, 5 to 10 minutes:
   1 medium onion, chopped
   1 small leek, thoroughly cleaned and chopped
   1 medium carrot, chopped
   1 large rib celery, chopped
Stir in:
   2 medium ripe tomatoes, peeled, seeded, and chopped
   1 small potato, peeled and chopped
   8 cups water
   2 teaspoons salt
   (Pinch of saffron threads)
Bring to a boil, reduce the heat, and simmer until the potatoes are tender, about 30 minutes. Stir in:
   One $15^1/_2$- to 19-ounce can cannellini, Great Northern, or other white beans, rinsed and drained, or 1 to 2 cups cooked beans, 253
   2 small handfuls broken thin spaghetti or macaroni
   1 small zucchini, quartered lengthwise and sliced
   $^1/_2$ cup 1-inch pieces green beans
Simmer just until the pasta is tender. Meanwhile, prepare:
   Pistou, 569
without seasoning it. Stir the pistou into the soup, along with:
   1 teaspoon black pepper
Serve hot, at room temperature, or cold.

BEET SOUP (BORSCHT)

About 5 cups

For a meat version, see 138, and for our quick blender version, see 149.

Heat in a soup pot over medium-low heat:

1 tablespoon butter

Add and cook, stirring, until softened, about 8 minutes:

2 cups very finely chopped beets
$^1/_2$ cup very finely chopped carrots
1 cup very finely chopped onions

Add, and bring to a simmer, simmer 30 minutes:

2 cups Brown Beef Stock, 117, Poultry Stock, 117, or Vegetable Stock, 119, or broth
1 cup very finely shredded green cabbage
1 tablespoon red wine vinegar or sherry vinegar

Season with:

Salt and black pepper to taste

Serve hot or cold. Garnish each serving with a dollop of:

Sour cream

BUTTERNUT SQUASH SOUP

About 8 cups

Almost any winter squash can be substituted. For faster preparation, use three 10- to 12-ounce packages frozen cooked squash puree.

Prepare Baked Winter Squash, 308, using:

1 medium to large butternut squash (about 3$^1/_2$ pounds)

Heat in a soup pot over medium-low heat:

3 tablespoons butter or vegetable oil

Add and cook, stirring, until the leeks are tender but not browned, 5 to 10 minutes:

2 large leeks, white part only, chopped
4 teaspoons minced peeled fresh ginger

Scrape the cooled squash flesh from the skin and stir it in along with:

4 cups chicken or vegetable stock or broth

Bring to a simmer. Cook for 20 minutes, stirring and breaking up the squash. Puree the soup in a blender or food processor until smooth. Return to the pot and stir in:

2 cups chicken or vegetable stock or broth
1$^1/_2$ teaspoons salt

Heat through. Serve garnished with:

Chopped parsley or cilantro
Soup Croutons, 151
(Squash seeds, toasted, 1009)

PUMPKIN SOUP

About 5 cups

Heat in a soup pot over medium heat:

1 tablespoon butter or olive oil

Add and cook until translucent, about 8 minutes:

1 cup minced onions
$^1/_2$ cup minced celery

Stir in:

3 cups canned pumpkin or 2 pounds fresh pumpkin, cooked
3 cups scalded milk, 997, or chicken stock or broth
($^3/_4$ cup heavy cream or half-and-half if you are using the chicken stock)
($^1/_2$ cup finely julienned ham)
1 tablespoon sugar or 2 tablespoons brown sugar
($^1/_2$ teaspoon ground ginger)
($^1/_2$ teaspoon ground cinnamon)
Salt and black pepper to taste

Heat through, but do not boil. Puree and reheat.

WINTER MELON SOUP

About 8 cups

In China, the outside of the vegetable called winter melon is delicately carved, and serves as the soup tureen.

Soak in warm water for 20 minutes:

4 dried shiitake mushrooms, 282

Drain and chop. Then heat in a large saucepan with:

4 cups chicken stock or broth
$^1/_3$ cup diced cooked chicken
1 cup small peeled shrimp
1 pound peeled, seeded winter melon, cut into 1-inch squares (about 3$^1/_2$ cups)
1 small leek, chopped
One 5-ounce can sliced bamboo shoots, rinsed, drained, and diced
1 teaspoon grated, peeled fresh ginger

Bring to a boil, then cover, lower the heat, and simmer about 15 minutes. Just before serving, add:

$^1/_3$ cup diced ham

FRENCH ONION SOUP

About 8 cups

Heat in a soup pot over medium-low heat until the butter is melted:

2 tablespoons butter
2 tablespoons olive oil

Add and stir to coat:

5 medium onions, thinly sliced
Pinch of dried thyme

Cook over medium heat, stirring occasionally and keeping an eye on the onions so they do not scorch. As soon as they start to brown, about 15 minutes, reduce the heat to medium-low and continue to cook, covered, stirring, until they are a rich brown, about 40 minutes. Stir in:

2 tablespoons dry sherry or Cognac

Increase the heat to high and cook, stirring constantly, until the sherry has evaporated. Stir in:

3$^1/_2$ cups Household Beef Stock, 117, Beef Broth, 121, Rich Vegetable Stock, 119, Vegetable Broth, 121, or Brown Poultry Stock, 118

Bring to a boil, reduce the heat, and simmer, partially covered, for 20 minutes. Season with:

1 teaspoon salt, or to taste
$^1/_4$ teaspoon black pepper, or to taste

Place 8 ovenproof soup bowls or crocks on a baking sheet. Ladle the hot soup into the bowls and top each with:

1 to 3 slices French bread, toasted (8 to 24 slices total)

Sprinkle each bowl with:

3 tablespoons grated Gruyère or Swiss (1 1/2 cups total)

Broil until the cheese is melted and brown.

POTATO LEEK SOUP

About 8 cups

Melt in a soup pot over low heat:

3 tablespoons unsalted butter

Add and cook, stirring, until tender but not browned, about 20 minutes:

6 medium leeks, chopped

Stir in:

1 1/4 pounds all-purpose potatoes, peeled and thinly sliced

6 cups Poultry Stock, 117, Chicken Broth, 121, Vegetable Stock, 119, Vegetable Broth, 121, or water

Bring to a boil, reduce heat, and simmer until the potatoes are soft, about 30 minutes. Puree until smooth. For a finer texture, push through a sieve. Season with:

Salt and white or black pepper to taste

Thin, if necessary, with:

Additional stock or water

VICHYSSOISE

7 1/2 cups

This famous leek soup may be served hot or very cold. Yes, the last "s" is pronounced. Be sure to process the soup to a velvety smoothness.

Prepare **Potato Leek Soup, above.** Add **1/2 to 1 cup heavy cream or a combination of milk and cream.** Reheat gently, or chill and serve cold. Garnish with **(snipped chives).**

BAKED POTATO SOUP

8 cups

Heat in a soup pot over medium-high heat:

3 tablespoons butter or olive oil

Add and cook, stirring, until soft:

1 medium onion, chopped

Add and bring to a simmer:

5 cups peeled and cubed baked potatoes

6 cups Poultry Stock, 117, Chicken Broth, 121, Vegetable Stock, 119, or Vegetable Broth, 121

Stir in:

1 1/2 cups heavy cream

1/2 cup sour cream

Heat through; do not boil. Season with:

Salt and black pepper to taste

Serve garnished with any of the following:

(Crumbled crisp bacon)

(Snipped chives)

(Grated Cheddar or Parmesan cheese)

GREEN PEA SOUP

About 5 cups

Have ready:

One 1-pound bag thawed petite peas or 16 ounces fresh peas

Melt in a soup pot over medium-low heat:

2 tablespoons butter

Add and sauté gently until the onion is tender:

1 head Boston lettuce, shredded

1 medium onion, diced

1/2 cup chopped celery, including leaves

2 sprigs parsley, chopped

Add 2 cups of the peas, along with:

2 1/2 cups Poultry Stock, 117, Chicken Broth, 121, or other light stock or broth

10 to 12 snow peas or sugar snap peas

(1 bay leaf)

Simmer, covered, until the peas are very soft. Discard the bay leaf. Process soup in a food processor or blender until smooth. Combine and simmer the remaining peas in:

1 1/2 cups Poultry Stock, 117, or Chicken Broth, 121

Add to the processed soup. To bind the soup, if desired, see Thickeners for Soups IV, 123. Season with:

Salt and black pepper to taste

Serve with:

Butter Dumplings, 335, or Soup Croutons, 151

Or top with:

Sour cream

2 teaspoons chopped mint

CABBAGE SOUP

About 8 cups

Heat in a soup pot over medium-low heat:

2 tablespoons olive or other vegetable oil

Add and cook, stirring, until tender but not browned, 5 to 10 minutes:

2 small leeks, white part only, chopped

2 medium onions, diced

2 tablespoons finely chopped garlic

Stir in and bring to a boil:

4 cups Poultry Stock, 117, Chicken Broth, 121, or other light stock or broth

2 cups water

2 large carrots, sliced

(1/4 teaspoon caraway seeds, or, if garnishing with Roquefort, 1 teaspoon)

(2 small potatoes, peeled and diced)

Reduce the heat and simmer until the potatoes are mostly cooked, about 15 minutes. Stir in:

4 cups shredded green cabbage

Simmer until the cabbage is wilted, about 15 minutes, adding a little water to cover if necessary. Stir in:

1 teaspoon salt

1/4 teaspoon black pepper, or to taste

1/4 cup chopped parsley

Sprinkle each serving with:

(Crumbled Roquefort or other blue cheese)

BEAN SOUP WITH VEGETABLES (GARBURE)
9 to 10 cups
Soak, 253:
1 cup dried flageolet, navy, or fava beans, rinsed and picked over
You may blanch, 1054, or not, depending on its maturity:
2 pounds green or white cabbage
Cut the cabbage into fine shreds. Drain the beans, and put in a soup pot, along with:
1¹/₂ cups sliced peeled potatoes
1 cup sliced carrots
1 cup sliced peeled turnips
¹/₄ cup sliced leeks, white parts only
¹/₂ onion, sliced
(A ham hock)
A sprig of thyme
Cover with:
8 to 10 cups water
Bring to a boil, reduce the heat, and simmer for 1 to 1¹/₂ hours, adding water if neccessary. Add:
1 pound smoked beef sausage or kielbasa, sliced into ¹/₂-inch rounds
1 teaspoon salt
¹/₂ teaspoon black pepper
Simmer for 30 minutes, or until the sausage is cooked.

VEGETABLE STEW
About 6 cups
Heat in a soup pot over medium-high heat:
4 tablespoons (¹/₂ stick) butter or ¹/₄ cup olive oil
Add and cook, stirring, until softened, about 5 minutes:
4 cups sliced okra
2 cups diced celery
1 small onion, diced
(1 green bell pepper, diced)
Add:
2 large tomatoes or 1 cup canned tomatoes, chopped
1 teaspoon brown sugar
¹/₄ teaspoon paprika, or to taste
4 cups boiling water
Bring to a boil, reduce the heat, and simmer gently until the vegetables are tender, about 30 minutes. Season to taste with:
Salt and paprika
Stir in one or more of the following:
(1¹/₂ cups diced cooked chicken, ham, or fish)
(6 slices fried bacon, crumbled)
(Hot pepper sauce to taste)
Serve with:
Cooked rice

MUSHROOM BARLEY SOUP
About 6 cups
Blend in a soup pot over high heat:
3¹/₂ tablespoons olive oil
1 tablespoon unsalted butter (or additional olive oil)

Add:
1¹/₂ pounds mushrooms, sliced and tough stems removed
¹/₂ cup chopped shallots
Cook, stirring often, until the mushrooms are wilted, about 5 minutes. Add:
3 tablespoons dry sherry or Madeira
1 tablespoon chopped fresh thyme or 1 teaspoon dried thyme
Reduce the heat to low and cook, stirring and scraping brown bits off the bottom of the pot, for 5 minutes. Stir in:
4¹/₂ cups Household Beef Stock, 117, or Beef Broth, 121
³/₄ cup pearl barley
¹/₂ to 1 teaspoon salt
¹/₂ teaspoon black pepper
Bring to a boil, reduce the heat, cover, and simmer until the barley is tender, about 1 hour. Serve garnished with:
Chopped parsley or whole thyme leaves

HOT-AND-SOUR SOUP
About 5 cups
Combine in a medium bowl and let stand until mushrooms are softened, about 20 minutes:
(10 dried wood ear or cloud ear mushrooms)
4 dried shiitake mushrooms (8 if not using wood ears)
(10 tiger lily buds)
1¹/₂ cups hot water
Meanwhile, combine and stir in a small bowl:
5 tablespoons rice vinegar
3 tablespoons soy sauce
1 tablespoon cornstarch
Add, turning to coat:
4 ounces center-cut pork chops, cut into ¹/₄-inch-wide strips.
Remove the mushrooms and lily buds from the soaking liquid and strain the liquid through a fine-mesh sieve lined with a dampened paper towel; reserve. Slice the mushrooms into strips and cut the lily buds in half, discarding any tough pieces. Pour the reserved mushroom liquid into a soup pot and add:
4 cups Poultry Stock, 117, Brown Poultry Stock, 118, Chicken Broth, 121, Vegetable Stock, 119, or Vegetable Broth, 121
Bring to a boil. Add the mushrooms and lily buds, reduce the heat, and simmer for 3 minutes. Meanwhile, stir together in a small bowl:
3 tablespoons cornstarch
3 tablespoons water
Add to the soup and simmer, whisking constantly, until slightly thickened. Add the meat, along with:
4 ounces firm tofu, well drained and diced
³/₄ to 1 teaspoon black pepper
Bring back to a simmer, then stir in:
1 egg, well beaten

Remove from the heat and add:

1 tablespoon toasted sesame oil

Serve garnished with:

Sliced scallion greens

Pass rice vinegar and chili oil at the table.

TOMATO SOUP

About 6 cups

Fresh tomatoes can be grilled, 243, or roasted, 244, to add a smoky flavor.

Heat in a soup pot, over medium-low heat:

2 tablespoons olive oil

Add and cook, stirring, until tender but not browned, 5 to 10 minutes:

1 medium onion, coarsely chopped

Stir in:

3 pounds tomatoes, peeled, 311, seeded, and chopped, with their juices, or two 28-ounce cans tomatoes, chopped, with their juice

Simmer until the tomatoes are covered in their own liquid, about 25 minutes. Puree the soup until smooth. Return to the pot and stir in:

$^3/_4$ teaspoon salt

$^1/_4$ teaspoon black pepper

Heat through.

ROASTED RED PEPPER SOUP

About 8 cups

Roast, 292:

6 large red bell peppers

Peel, seed, and cut the flesh into long strips. Or, drain and cut into strips:

(Two 7-ounce jars roasted red peppers)

Heat in a soup pot over medium-low heat:

3 tablespoons olive oil

Add and cook, stirring, until tender but not browned, 10 to 15 minutes:

2 cups chopped onions

1 cup diced carrots

1 cup chopped fennel or celery

Stir in the roasted peppers along with:

6 cups Poultry Stock, 117, Chicken Broth, 121, or other light stock or broth

3 tablespoons white rice

2 tablespoons chopped fresh basil or 2 teaspoons dried basil

1 tablespoon chopped fresh rosemary or 1 teaspoon dried rosemary

1 to 1$^1/_4$ teaspoons fennel seeds

$^1/_8$ teaspoon crushed red pepper flakes

Bring to a boil, reduce the heat, and simmer, partially covered, until the peppers and rice are very tender, about 30 minutes. Puree the soup until smooth. Return the soup to the pot and stir in:

$^1/_2$ cup heavy cream

2 to 3 drops balsamic vinegar

Salt and black pepper to taste

Serve hot or cold, with Croutons, 974.

TUSCAN BREAD AND TOMATO SOUP (PAPPA AL POMADORO)

About 4 cups

Have ready:

2 or 3 slices stale crusty white bread

(Or, if your bread is fresh, preheat the oven to 200°F and dry the bread in the oven for 15 to 20 minutes.) Rub the bread on both sides with:

1 garlic clove, halved

Heat in a soup pot over medium heat:

3 tablespoons olive oil

Add and cook, stirring, about 10 minutes:

1 medium red onion, coarsely chopped

Meanwhile, coarsely chop:

4 large garlic cloves, peeled

$^1/_3$ cup packed basil leaves

Reduce heat to medium-low, stir in the garlic and basil, and cook until the garlic barely colors, 2 to 3 minutes. Add:

1$^1/_2$ pounds tomatoes, peeled, 311, seeded, and coarsely chopped, or one 28-ounce can tomatoes, drained and chopped

Pinch of crushed red pepper flakes

Cook, stirring, over medium-high heat until thick and fragrant, about 5 minutes. Stir in:

2 cups Poultry Stock, 117, Chicken Broth, 121, or other light stock or broth

Bring to a boil and boil for 2 minutes. Add:

Salt and black pepper

Break up bread in the bottom of soup bowls. Ladle in the hot soup and top each serving with:

4 basil leaves, torn

Drizzle of extra-virgin olive oil

Parmesan shavings

Serve hot or at room temperature.

TORTILLA SOUP

About 4 cups

Sliced chard or shredded cooked chicken can be added for a more substantial version.

Heat a medium cast-iron or other heavy skillet or griddle over medium heat until hot. Place in the skillet:

1 to 2 jalapeño peppers

2 large garlic cloves, unpeeled

Roast, turning occasionally, until the peppers are blistered and blackened on all sides and the garlic is soft to the touch, 10 to 15 minutes. When cool enough to handle, peel the garlic. Place in a food processor or blender with the jalapeño peppers. Pulse to coarsely chop. Add:

One 28-ounce can tomatoes, drained

Process until coarsely pureed. Heat in a soup pot over medium heat:

1$\frac{1}{2}$ **teaspoons vegetable oil**

Add and cook until browned, 8 to 10 minutes:

$\frac{1}{2}$ **small onion, thinly sliced**

Increase the heat to medium-high and add the tomato mixture. Cook, stirring, until the mixture is darkened and slightly thickened, about 5 minutes. Reduce the heat to medium-low and stir in:

3 cups Poultry Stock, 117, Chicken Broth, 121, or other light stock or broth

Simmer, stirring occasionally, for 15 minutes. Season with:

$\frac{1}{2}$ **to 1 teaspoon salt**

Just before serving, bring the soup to a boil over medium-high heat and add:

8 ounces tortilla chips, 94

Stir to coat the chips well, then boil rapidly, stirring gently and often, until the chips are softened but still chewy and the soup is thick, 2 to 3 minutes for thinner chips, 4 to 5 minutes for thicker chips. Garnish with:

$\frac{1}{4}$ **cup finely crumbled queso fresco or grated Monterey Jack**

(2 tablespoons chopped cilantro)

(2 tablespoons sour cream)

ABOUT HEARTY BEAN AND LEGUME SOUPS

Bean and legume soups are easy to prepare in large batches, require little attention while cooking, and freeze well. The ingredients are easily kept in the pantry. Some packaged dried legumes do not require soaking. Follow directions on the label. Please read About Dried Legumes, 253.

To puree legume soups use a blender, food processor, immersion blender, or food mill; the food mill will also remove the skins. If a legume soup becomes too thick, thin it with tomato juice, water, milk, or stock.

For other soups with beans, see Minestrone, 128, and Provençal Vegetable Soup, 128. ➤ We do not recommend the use of a pressure cooker for legume soups.

U.S. SENATE BEAN SOUP

About 6 cups

There's a reason this soup has been on the menu of the U.S. Senate restaurant every day since 1901.
Soak, 253:

1$\frac{1}{4}$ **cups small dried white beans, such as navy or Great Northern, rinsed and picked over**

Drain and place in a soup pot, along with:

1 small ham hock

7 cups cold water

Bring to a boil, reduce the heat, and simmer until the beans are tender, about 1$\frac{1}{4}$ hours. Remove the ham hock (leave the soup at a gentle simmer). Discard the bone, skin, and fat; dice the meat. Return it to the pot and add:

1 large onion, diced

3 medium celery ribs with leaves, chopped

1 large potato, peeled and finely diced

2 garlic cloves, minced

1$\frac{1}{2}$ **teaspoons salt**

$\frac{1}{2}$ **teaspoon black pepper**

Simmer until the potato pieces are quite soft, 20 to 30 minutes. Remove from the heat and mash with a potato masher until the soup is a bit creamy. Stir in:

2 tablespoons chopped parsley

MEDITERRANEAN WHITE BEAN SOUP

About 6 cups

Soak, 253:

1 cup dried white beans, such as Great Northern or cannellini, rinsed and picked over

Drain and place in a soup pot, along with:

$\frac{3}{4}$ **teaspoon dried rosemary**

8 garlic cloves, chopped or sliced

7 cups water

Bring to a boil, reduce the heat, and simmer until the beans are tender, 1 to 1$\frac{1}{2}$ hours. Stir in and heat through:

$\frac{1}{2}$ **cup chopped tomatoes**

$\frac{1}{4}$ **cup chopped parsley**

$\frac{1}{4}$ **cup olive oil**

4 teaspoons red wine vinegar

2 teaspoons salt

$\frac{1}{2}$ **teaspoon black pepper**

BLACK BEAN SOUP

About 7 cups

Soak, 253:

1 pound dried black beans, rinsed and picked over

Drain, reserving the liquid. Add enough water to the reserved liquid to make 8$\frac{1}{2}$ cups. Melt in a soup pot over medium heat:

3 tablespoons butter

Add and cook, stirring, until onion is translucent:

1 cup chopped celery, including leaves

$\frac{1}{2}$ **cup chopped onion**

$\frac{1}{2}$ **cup chopped carrots**

Add and cook, stirring, until fragrant, about 1 minute:

(1 garlic clove, minced)

(1 teaspoon sugar)

($\frac{1}{2}$ teaspoon ground cumin)

($\frac{1}{4}$ teaspoon dried thyme)

(Pinch of ground red pepper)

Stir in the reserved bean soaking liquid and the beans, and add:

A ham bone, or a 2-inch cube salt pork

(1 bay leaf)

Bring to a boil, reduce the heat, and simmer, covered, 2$\frac{1}{2}$ to 3 hours, until the beans are tender. Discard the bones or salt pork, and bay leaf, if using. Puree half of the soup in a food processor or blender, and stir back into the pot. Stir in:

(1 cup diced smoked ham)

2 teaspoons salt, or to taste

1 teaspoon black pepper

Serve over:

(Cooked rice)

Garnish with:

($\frac{1}{2}$ cup chopped scallions)

LENTIL SOUP

About 10 cups

Heat in a large soup pot over medium-low heat:

3 tablespoons olive oil

Add and cook, stirring, until the vegetables are tender but not browned, 5 to 10 minutes:

3 medium carrots, peeled and diced

3 medium celery ribs, diced

1 large onion, diced

3 garlic cloves, minced

(4 slices bacon or 2 ounces pancetta, diced)

Stir in:

2 cups dried lentils, rinsed and picked over

One 14$\frac{1}{2}$-ounce can diced tomatoes, drained

1 teaspoon dried thyme

8 cups water

Bring to a boil, reduce the heat, and simmer until the lentils are tender, 30 to 45 minutes. Stir in:

1$\frac{1}{2}$ teaspoons balsamic vinegar

2 teaspoons salt (1 teaspoon if using bacon)

1 teaspoon black pepper

LENTIL SOUP WITH SAUSAGE AND POTATO

After the lentils have been cooking for 30 minutes, add **1 large potato, peeled and diced,** and cook for 10 minutes. Add **6 ounces smoked chorizo or kielbasa, sliced,** and **$\frac{1}{2}$ cup water.** Simmer until the potatoes are tender and the sausage is just heated through, about 5 minutes.

LENTIL SOUP WITH GREENS

Trim, remove the center rib if tough, wash, and dry **1 bunch kale or spinach (about 10 ounces).** Stack, roll up tightly, and cut the leaves crosswise into strips. Add to the finished soup and cook until tender but still bright green.

SPLIT PEA SOUP

About 6 cups

Combine in a soup pot:

A small ham hock or a hambone

2 cups green split peas, rinsed and picked over

8 cups cold water

Bring to a boil, reduce the heat, and simmer for 1 hour. Stir in:

1 large carrot, diced

1 large celery rib, diced

1 medium onion, diced

2 garlic cloves, minced

1 Bouquet Garni, 960

Simmer until the ham hock and peas are tender, about 1 hour more. Season with:

Salt and black pepper to taste

Remove from heat and remove the ham hock or ham bone. Discard the bone, skin, and fat; dice the meat. Return it to the soup. For a thicker soup, simmer to the desired consistency. Stir to blend before serving. Garnish with:

Soup Croutons, 151

GEORGIA PEANUT SOUP

About 6 cups

Melt in a soup pot over medium-low heat:

2 tablespoons butter

Add and cook, stirring, until tender but not browned, about 5 minutes:

2 medium celery ribs, minced

1 medium onion, minced

1 garlic clove, minced

Stir in:

2 tablespoons all-purpose flour

Reduce the heat to low and cook, stirring, for 5 minutes. Whisk in:

4 cups hot Poultry Stock, 117, or Chicken Broth, 121

Simmer, stirring often, until the soup begins to thicken, about 5 minutes. Stir in:

1$\frac{1}{2}$ cups natural peanut butter

1 cup heavy cream or half-and-half

1$\frac{1}{2}$ teaspoons salt

$\frac{1}{2}$ teaspoon ground red pepper

$\frac{1}{2}$ teaspoon hot pepper sauce

Heat through, but do not boil. Stir in:

2 teaspoons lime juice

Serve garnished with:

3 tablespoons chopped dry-roasted peanuts

$\frac{1}{4}$ cup chopped scallions

ABOUT POULTRY AND MEAT SOUPS

Many of these robust soups can be served as a full meal. The poultry soups in this section are made with chicken. All chicken, especially white meat, becomes dry and stringy with overcooking, so if you reheat the soup, do so gently, just until hot. All the meat soups here require long simmering. This allows economical cuts of meat to become tender and impart their full flavor to the soup.

BECKER CHICKEN SOUP

About 7 cups

The flavor of this soup can be enhanced by first browning the chicken pieces and vegetables in vegetable oil. The curry powder is my wife Susan's secret ingredient.

Place in a soup pot over medium heat:

2 to 2$\frac{1}{2}$ pounds chicken parts

3 carrots, diced

3 celery ribs, diced

(2 parsnips, peeled and diced)

3 to 4 garlic cloves, roughly chopped

1 large yellow onion, diced

1 Bouquet Garni, 960

8 cups Poultry Stock, 117, or Chicken Broth, 121, or water

Bring to a boil, reduce heat to a simmer, and cook for 1 hour and 15 minutes, skimming the foam occasionally. Turn off the heat and remove the chicken pieces to a platter to cool. Remove the bouquet garni and skim fat from the broth. Discard the chicken skin and bones and dice or shred the meat. Add the meat to the soup. Reheat, and stir in:

> (^{1}/$_4$ cup chopped parsley)
> (1^1/$_2$ teaspoons curry powder, or to taste)

Season with:

> **Salt and black pepper to taste**

CHICKEN RICE SOUP (ASOPAO DE POLLO)
About 9 cups
Combine in a small bowl:

> 1^1/$_2$ **teaspoons garlic powder**
> 1^1/$_2$ **teaspoons onion powder**
> 1^1/$_2$ **teaspoons dried oregano**
> ^{3}/$_4$ **teaspoon salt**
> ^{3}/$_4$ **teaspoon black pepper**

Rub the spices into the skin of:

> **3 pounds chicken parts**

Heat in a soup pot over medium-low heat:

> **3 tablespoons vegetable oil**

Add and cook, stirring until tender but not browned, 5 to 10 minutes:

> **1 medium onion, diced**
> **1 medium green bell pepper, cored, seeded, and diced**
> ^{1}/$_2$ **cup diced ham**
> **1 Scotch bonnet pepper or 2 jalapeño peppers, seeded and diced**
> **2 garlic cloves, minced**

Stir in the chicken, along with:

> **6 cups water**
> **One 14^1/$_2$-ounce can diced tomatoes, drained**
> **(2 teaspoons ground annatto seeds, 958)**

Bring to a boil, reduce the heat, and simmer, partially covered, for 25 minutes. Stir in:

> ^{1}/$_2$ **cup long-grain white rice**

Simmer until the chicken and rice are cooked, about 20 minutes. Turn off the heat, remove the chicken, and let cool slightly. Discard the skin and bones, and dice or shred the meat. Return it to the soup and stir in:

> **1 cup fresh or thawed frozen peas**
> ^{1}/$_2$ **cup chopped cilantro**
> ^{1}/$_2$ **cup pimiento strips or sliced pimiento-stuffed green olives**
> **Salt to taste**

Simmer gently 2 to 3 minutes.

THAI CHICKEN AND COCONUT SOUP
About 6 cups
Bring to a boil in a soup pot:

> **3 cups Poultry Stock, 117, Chicken Broth, 121, or other light stock or broth**
> 2^2/$_3$ **cups unsweetened coconut milk**

Reduce the heat and stir in:

> **2 small Thai peppers or 3 jalapeño peppers, seeded and sliced**
> **3 tablespoons fish sauce, 982, or soy sauce**
> **1 teaspoon minced peeled fresh ginger**
> ^{1}/$_8$ **teaspoon salt**

Simmer for 10 minutes. Stir in:

> **1 pound boneless, skinless chicken breasts, thinly sliced**
> **2 tablespoons fresh lime juice**

Simmer, stirring occasionally, until the chicken is cooked through, about 5 minutes. Serve garnished with:

> **Chopped cilantro**

COCK-A-LEEKIE
About 7 cups
Combine in a soup pot and bring to a boil:

> **2 pounds chicken thighs**
> **6 cups cold water**

Skim the scum from the surface. Add:

> ^{1}/$_4$ **cup pearl barley**
> **1 teaspoon salt**

Simmer, uncovered, until the chicken is cooked and the barley is tender, 30 to 40 minutes. Turn off the heat and remove the chicken to a platter to cool slightly. Discard the bones and skin, and shred the meat. If you want to degrease the stock, remove the surface fat. Melt in a large skillet over medium-high heat:

> **2 tablespoons butter or 1 tablespoon butter plus 1 tablespoon vegetable oil**

Add and cook, stirring, until tender, about 10 minutes:

> **5 medium leeks, diced (about 5 cups)**

Add the leeks to the soup, along with:

> **12 pitted prunes**

Simmer for 10 minutes. Return the chicken to the pot and simmer 5 minutes longer. Season with:

> **Salt and black pepper to taste**

Garnish each bowl with:

> **1 pitted prune, chopped**

CHICKEN, AVOCADO, AND TOMATO SOUP
5 cups
Inspired by our friend Hector Gomez, owner of Los Amigos restaurant in Maryville, Tennessee.
Bring to a boil in a large saucepan:

> **4 cups Poultry Stock, 117, Chicken Broth, 121, or other light stock or broth**

Stir in just before serving:

> **1 cup cooked chicken, shredded or diced**

Garnish with:

> **1 avocado, pitted, peeled, and diced**
> ^{1}/$_4$ **cup diced yellow or sweet onion**
> ^{1}/$_4$ **cup diced tomatoes**
> **(2 red radishes, slivered)**

Season with:

> **Salt and black pepper to taste**

CHICKEN GUMBO

About 10 cups

Combine in a large plastic or paper bag:

1¹/₂ teaspoons salt

2 teaspoons ground red pepper

1 teaspoon black pepper

1 teaspoon garlic powder

Add and shake until completely coated:

3 pounds chicken parts

Add and shake again:

¹/₂ cup all-purpose flour

Heat in a Dutch oven or other large heavy pot over medium heat:

2 to 4 tablespoons vegetable oil

Brown the chicken pieces on all sides, 5 to 10 minutes. Remove to a platter. Pour off the fat in the pot, and set the pot aside. Heat in a medium heavy saucepan:

¹/₂ cup vegetable oil

Whisk in:

¹/₂ cup all-purpose flour

Cook, stirring constantly with a wooden spoon over medium heat until the roux turns dark mahogany brown, about 30 minutes. Meanwhile, combine in a small bowl:

1 cup sliced okra

¹/₂ cup chopped celery

¹/₂ cup chopped onion

¹/₂ cup chopped green bell peppers

Remove the roux from the heat and stir until it stops bubbling, 1 to 2 minutes. Very carefully add the roux and vegetable mixture to the Dutch oven. Whisk in:

8 cups Poultry Stock, 117, Chicken Broth, 121, or other light stock or broth

Bring to a boil, whisking. Reduce the heat and add the chicken. Simmer until the chicken is cooked through, about 30 to 45 minutes. The breast pieces will cook faster. Remove the chicken from the pot. Stir into the pot:

12 ounces andouille, chorizo, or other smoked sausage, cut into thin slices or small cubes

1 tablespoon chopped garlic

Simmer until the sausage is cooked through, about 10 minutes. Discard the chicken skin and bones, and shred the meat. Stir the chicken into the pot, along with:

¹/₂ cup chopped scallions

1 tablespoon filé powder

Salt to taste

Hot pepper sauce

Serve over:

Cooked rice

Garnish with:

Chopped scallions

MULLIGATAWNY SOUP

About 7 cups

Heat in a soup pot over medium heat:

¹/₄ cup (¹/₂ stick) butter or vegetable oil

Add and cook, stirring, until softened:

¹/₂ cup diced onion

1 carrot, diced

2 celery ribs, diced

Add and cook, stirring, about 3 minutes:

1¹/₂ tablespoons all-purpose flour

2 teaspoons curry powder

4 cups Poultry Stock, 117, Chicken Broth, 121, or other light stock or broth

1 bay leaf

Boil, reduce the heat, and simmer 15 minutes. Add:

¹/₄ cup diced tart apples

¹/₂ cup cooked rice

¹/₂ cup diced cooked chicken or lamb

1 teaspoon salt

¹/₄ teaspoon black pepper

¹/₈ teaspoon dried thyme

¹/₂ teaspoon grated lemon zest

Simmer 15 minutes longer, then remove bay leaf. Immediately before serving, stir in:

¹/₂ cup heavy cream or unsweetened coconut milk

Heat through, but do not boil.

BEEF BARLEY SOUP

8 cups

Season:

1 pound stew beef, cut into 1¹/₂-inch cubes

with:

1 teaspoon salt

¹/₂ teaspoon black pepper

Heat in a soup pot or Dutch oven over medium-high heat:

1 tablespoon vegetable oil

Add the beef to the pot, in batches if necessary, without crowding and brown on all sides. Remove from the pot and set aside. Proceed, using the same pot as for:

Mushroom Barley Soup, 131

Return the beef to the pot with the stock and seasoning.

POT-AU-FEU (FRENCH SIMMERED BEEF AND VEGETABLES)

10 to 15 servings

Prepared with chicken alone, this becomes **Poule-au-Pot.** Combine in a large soup pot:

4 quarts Brown Beef Stock, 117, Beef Broth, 121, Poultry Stock, 117, Chicken Broth, 121, or water, or a combination of any of these

One 4-pound boneless rump, bottom round, or chuck roast, or 4 pounds brisket, rolled if necessary and tightly tied

(4 beef marrow bones, wrapped in cheesecloth)

2 onions, each stuck with 2 cloves

2 carrots, chopped

2 celery ribs, chopped

Bring to a boil, reduce the heat to low, and simmer, partially covered, skimming occasionally, for 1¹/₂ hours. Add:

One 3- to 4-pound chicken, trussed, 421

Simmer, partially covered, skimming occasionally, for 30

minutes. Tie loosely in bundles of cheesecloth and add to the pot:

4 medium carrots, cut into 1-inch pieces
4 medium leeks, cut into 1-inch pieces
2 medium turnips, peeled and cut into 1-inch pieces
3 medium celery ribs, cut into 1-inch pieces
(1 cabbage, cut into thin wedges)

Add:

1 pound smoked sausage
1 Bouquet Garni, 960

Simmer, covered, 30 to 45 minutes. Remove and reserve the meat and bundled vegetables. Strain the broth and return it to the pot; keep warm over very low heat. Slice the beef and sausage. Cut the chicken into 8 serving pieces. Arrange the meats and vegetables on an ovenproof platter. Cover with aluminum foil and keep warm in a 200°F oven. Skim the fat. Season with:

Salt and black pepper to taste

Heat the broth, and ladle into warmed bowls. Pass the meat platter after the broth, accompanied with:

Dijon or coarse-grain mustard
Coarse salt
Cornichons
(Toasted sliced French bread)

VIETNAMESE BEEF NOODLE SOUP (PHO BO)
4 servings

The meat is easier to slice thin if placed in the freezer for about 20 minutes. After slicing it, allow it to come to room temperature while you prepare the soup.

Heat in a large soup pot over medium-high heat:

1 tablespoon vegetable oil

Add and cook, stirring, until fragrant:

$1/4$ cup thinly sliced peeled fresh ginger
1 medium onion, sliced

Add and cook, stirring, until no longer pink, 5 minutes:

$3^1/2$ pounds oxtails, cut into 2-inch pieces

Stir in:

$3^1/2$ quarts cold water

Bring to a boil, skimming off the impurities. Stir in:

1 cinnamon stick
6 star anise
1 tablespoon salt
1 teaspoon soy sauce
(One 1-inch piece Chinese rock sugar)

Reduce the heat and simmer the soup for $2^1/2$ to 3 hours, skimming as needed. About 30 minutes before the broth is ready, soak in cold water to cover:

12 ounces dried rice stick noodles *(banh pho)*

Bring a large pot of water to a boil. Drain the rice stick noodles and cook in the boiling water for $1^1/2$ to 2 minutes. Drain. Strain the broth into another pot, and skim the fat off the surface. When ready to serve, bring the broth to a boil over high heat. Meanwhile, divide the noodles among heated soup bowls. Divide among 4 bowls:

12 ounces raw round steak, very thinly sliced
2 serrano peppers, thinly sliced
24 basil leaves, halved
$1/4$ cup 2-inch pieces scallion, halved lengthwise

Fill each bowl with boiling broth and serve. If the broth is added at the table, diners have the pleasure of watching it cook the beef. Pass a plate of:

2 cups bean sprouts, 3 tablespoons coarsely chopped basil, lime wedges, 3 coarsely chopped serrano peppers

MONGOLIAN HOT POT
6 to 8 servings

The meat is easier to slice thin if placed in the freezer for 20 minutes first. This is a wonderful party dish; see About Fondue, 110.

For the dipping sauce, puree in a blender:

$1/2$ cup rice vinegar
$1/3$ cup sugar or $1/4$ cup honey
$1/2$ cup soy sauce
$1/3$ cup red miso or rinsed fermented black beans
$1/4$ cup toasted sesame oil
1 tablespoon minced peeled fresh ginger
2 teaspoons chili oil, or more to taste
3 garlic cloves, chopped

Pour the sauce into individual serving bowls and garnish with:

3 scallions, chopped
Chopped cilantro
Snipped chives

Arrange decoratively on a platter:

2 pounds beef sirloin steak or lamb loin, fat trimmed and very thinly sliced
3 cups sliced Napa cabbage
8 ounces firm tofu, cut into 16 pieces
8 ounces spinach, trimmed, washed, and dried

Bring the sauce and platter to the table. Bring to a boil:

8 to 10 cups Brown Beef Stock, 117, or Beef Broth, 121

Pour the hot stock into a hot pot, fondue pot, or electric skillet at the table and keep at a simmer. With chopsticks or forks, diners should hold the meat or vegetables in the simmering stock until done, then dip it into the sauce and eat. When the ingredients on the platter are almost consumed, combine and let stand for 10 minutes:

4 ounces dried rice stick noodles, broken into small pieces
6 cups hot water

Drain the noodles and add to the hot stock. Pour the remaining sauce into the serving bowls and ladle the stock and noodles into the bowls.

OXTAIL SOUP
About 4 cups

Heat in a soup pot:

2 tablespoons olive oil or butter

Add and brown:

2 pounds oxtails, cut into 2-inch sections
$1/2$ cup sliced onion

Add:

8 cups water
$1^1/2$ teaspoons salt
4 whole black peppercorns

Bring to a boil, reduce the heat, and simmer, partially uncovered, about $4^1/2$ hours. Add water as necessary to keep the meat covered. Strain the stock and chill, then remove the fat, 123. If desired, remove the meat from the bones and dice; refrigerate. To serve, reheat the stock and add:

1 cup diced celery
$1/2$ cup diced carrots
$1/2$ cup peeled, seeded, and chopped tomatoes
$1/4$ cup dry sherry or Madeira or $1/2$ cup dry red wine
$1/4$ cup barley
$1/4$ cup chopped parsley
1 teaspoon dried thyme, marjoram, or basil
1 bay leaf

Simmer until the vegetables are tender, about 30 minutes. Discard the bay leaf. Brown in a skillet:

1 tablespoon all-purpose flour

Add and stir until blended:

2 tablespoons butter

Slowly add the stock, then add the reserved meat and vegetables. Season with:

Salt and black pepper to taste

Remove bay leaf and serve the soup with:

Lemon slices

BORSCHT WITH MEAT

About 5 cups

Preheat oven to 400°F. Scrub:

3 to 4 medium beets (12 ounces)

Wrap the beets in aluminum foil and roast on a baking sheet until they are tender, about 1 hour. While the beets are roasting, lightly dredge:

1 pound boneless beef chuck, cubed

in:

All-purpose flour

Heat in a soup pot over medium-high heat:

2 tablespoons vegetable oil

Add the meat and brown on all sides. Add:

$4^1/2$ cups Brown Beef Stock, 117, Beef Broth, 121, or water
One 28-ounce can whole tomatoes, drained and chopped

Bring to a boil, reduce the heat, and simmer, partially covered, until the meat is almost tender, about 30 minutes. Stir in:

2 cups shredded green or red cabbage
1 medium onion, chopped
2 medium carrots, sliced
2 medium celery ribs, sliced
$1^1/2$ teaspoons tomato paste

Simmer, partially covered, until the vegetables and meat are tender, about 30 minutes. Peel the beets, then slice and cut into thin strips. Stir the beets into the soup, along with:

2 tablespoons red wine vinegar
2 teaspoons fresh lemon juice
2 garlic cloves, minced
Salt and black pepper
($1^1/2$ teaspoons sugar)

Simmer, partially covered, for 15 minutes. Thin the soup with water if necessary. Garnish with:

Sour cream
(Snipped dill)

MOCK TURTLE SOUP

About 12 cups

Put in a stockpot:

5 pounds veal bones

Add and bring to a boil:

14 cups water

Add:

4 cups chopped celery, including leaves
2 cups canned whole tomatoes, crushed, with juice
2 cups chopped carrots
1 cup chopped onions
One 6-ounce can tomato paste
1 tablespoon salt
$1/2$ teaspoon dried thyme
6 black peppercorns, crushed
6 whole cloves
2 bay leaves

Bring to a boil, reduce the heat, and simmer, partially covered, skimming occasionally to remove scum, 3 to $3^1/2$ hours. Strain broth into a soup pot. Skim the fat off the top. Heat in a 12-inch skillet over medium-high heat:

1 tablespoon vegetable oil

Add and cook, stirring, until the meat is no longer pink:

2 pounds ground beef
2 garlic cloves, minced
2 teaspoons salt

Add the meat to the stock, with:

4 teaspoons sugar
1 teaspoon Worcestershire sauce

Bring to a boil, reduce the heat, and simmer about 15 minutes, skimming occasionally to remove scum. Meanwhile, remove 1 cup of the stock and let cool. Blend with:

6 tablespoons Browned Flour, 544

Stir this paste into the simmering soup. Let simmer 5 minutes more. Season with:

Salt and black pepper to taste

Add:

2 lemons, thinly sliced

Reheat through; do not boil. Serve garnished with:

3 hard-boiled eggs, 194, sliced

SCOTCH BROTH
About 6 cups

Combine in a soup pot:

6 cups water
1¹/₂ pounds boneless lamb shoulder, trimmed of fat
    and cut into ¹/₂-inch pieces

Bring to a boil, reduce the heat, and simmer for 10 minutes, skimming to remove scum. Stir in:

¹/₂ cup pearl barley
3 medium leeks, white part only, chopped
1 large carrot, diced
1 large celery rib, diced
¹/₂ teaspoon salt

Bring to a boil, reduce the heat, and simmer, partially covered, until the meat is tender, about 1¹/₂ hours. Add water as needed. Spoon off the fat from the surface and season with:

Salt and black pepper to taste
2 tablespoons chopped parsley

PORTUGUESE GREENS SOUP (CALDO VERDE)
About 10 cups

A family favorite, and an inspiration to use fresh, frozen, or canned greens in many of our soups.
Heat in a large soup pot over medium-low heat:

1¹/₂ tablespoons olive or other vegetable oil

Add and cook, stirring, until tender but not browned, 5 to 10 minutes:

1 medium onion, chopped
2 garlic cloves, minced

Stir in:

8 cups Poultry Stock, 117, Chicken Broth, 121, or other
    light stock or broth
4 medium potatoes, peeled and thinly sliced
1¹/₂ teaspoons salt
¹/₂ teaspoon black pepper

Bring to a boil, reduce the heat, and simmer until the potatoes are soft, about 20 minutes. Remove the pot from the heat. Using a potato masher, lightly mash the potatoes in the pot. Heat in a medium skillet over medium-high heat:

(¹/₂ teaspoon vegetable oil)

Add and cook, stirring, until browned:

6 ounces Portuguese linguiça, chorizo, or other
    smoked sausage, thinly sliced

Add to the pot. Pour 1 cup of the soup into the skillet, scrape up the browned bits, and return the liquid and browned bits to the soup. Simmer 5 minutes. Stir in:

4 cups shredded kale, chard, or collard leaves (from a
    6- to 8-ounce bunch), washed and dried

Simmer 5 minutes. Stir in:

2 tablespoons fresh lemon juice

PEPPER POT
About 9 cups

Cook in a large saucepan until translucent:

4 slices bacon, cut into small pieces

Add and cook, stirring, about 5 minutes:

¹/₃ cup minced onion
¹/₂ cup minced celery
2 green bell peppers, minced
(1 teaspoon dried marjoram or summer savory)

Add:

8 cups Brown Beef Stock, 117, Poultry Stock, 117, or
    Beef Broth, 121
1 bay leaf
¹/₂ teaspoon ground pepper

Bring to a boil, and add:

12 ounces ready-to-cook honeycomb tripe, washed
    and cut into fine shreds

Bring just to a boil, reduce the heat, and simmer gently, covered, until the tripe is tender, 1¹/₂ to 2 hours. Add:

1 cup peeled and diced potatoes

Gently simmer, uncovered, until the potatoes are tender. Remove the bay leaf. Meanwhile, melt in a small skillet:

2 tablespoons butter

Stir in until blended:

2 tablespoons all-purpose flour

Add a little of the soup and bring to a boil, then pour into the soup. Season with:

Salt and black pepper to taste

Stir in:

¹/₂ cup warm cream

Heat through, but do not boil.

ABOUT FISH AND SEAFOOD SOUPS

Fish and seafood lend themselves to hearty but quick soups because they provide full flavor in a brief time. ➤ They are easy to overcook, so remove from the heat as soon as the fish or shellfish is cooked. When served, the fish and shellfish are often presented on the side.

In the preparation of delicate shellfish **bisques,** the shrimp or lobsters are often poached separately, then minced or pounded in a mortar before incorporation into a separate stock, cream, and egg base. The poaching stock may then be used as a Court Bouillon, 120, for cooking other fish. Bisques, as well as oyster, clam, and mussel soups and stews, need so little heat that the stock bases are warmed first and the shellfish then just heated through in them, preferably in a double boiler, ➤ over, not in, boiling water. Serve fish soups at once. If you must hold or reheat, be sure to do so in a double boiler ➤ over, not in, simmering water.

Use frozen or canned fish if you must, but remember that ➤ the fragrant, distinctive, and elusive charm of **fishermen's soups** and stews can only be captured if the fish that go into them are freshly caught. Bouillabaisse, 142, can only be approximated in this country, even if its ingredients are just off the hook, for its unique flavor depends on the use of fish native to the Mediterranean alone: a regional rockfish, high in gelatin content, for example, that gives a slightly cloudy but still thin texture to the soup, and numberless finny tidbits too small for market. We offer a free translation of bouillabaisse into American, realizing fully that we have succeeded only in changing poetry to rich prose.

A certain amount of freewheeling must be the rule, too, in concocting **chowders** of both ocean and freshwater fish. These are milk-based and often have potatoes added. Whatever fish you use, see that it is ➤ as fresh as possible, and experiment with combinations of those that are most easily available.

Fish Stock, 118, can be made very quickly, but if a supply of fish bones and heads are not on hand, note the alternatives, 120. In some cases, a light chicken stock may be substituted for fish stock as well. With the exception of most chowders, which tend to sit well overnight, generally fish soups are best eaten as soon as they are cooked.

CHARLESTON CRAB OR SHE-CRAB SOUP
About 4 cups
Melt in a large saucepan over low heat:
2 tablespoons butter
Whisk in:
2 tablespoons all-purpose flour
Cook, whisking, until the flour smells toasted but is not browned, about 3 minutes. Remove the pan from the heat and slowly whisk in:
3 cups milk
Return to the heat, bring to a simmer, and cook over medium-low heat whisking constantly, until thickened and smooth. Reduce the heat to low and stir in:
**1 pound lump crabmeat, picked over for shells and
    cartilage, preferably with roe**
1 tablespoon dry sherry
1 teaspoon salt
1 teaspoon Worcestershire sauce
($\frac{1}{2}$ teaspoon hot pepper sauce, or to taste)
$\frac{1}{8}$ teaspoon ground mace
Adjust the seasonings. Heat gently just until the crab is warmed through. Garnish with:
Thinly sliced scallion greens

LOBSTER BISQUE
About 7 cups
Prepare and remove the meat and coral from:
2 medium lobsters, boiled, 383
Dice the body meat. Mince the tail and claw meat. Crush the shells and combine them with the tough ends of the claws in a large pot with:
**$2\frac{1}{2}$ cups Poultry Stock, 117, Chicken Broth, 121,
    Fish Stock, 118, or Clam Broth, 121**
4 ribs celery with leaves, sliced thin
1 unpeeled onion, sliced
6 whole black peppercorns

2 whole cloves
1 bay leaf
Bring to a boil, reduce the heat, and simmer for 30 minutes. Strain the stock. Force the reserved coral roe, if any, through a fine sieve. Combine in a soup pot with:
$\frac{1}{4}$ cup ($\frac{1}{2}$ stick) butter, softened
Blend in:
$\frac{1}{4}$ cup all-purpose flour
Gradually whisk in:
3 cups hot milk
$\frac{1}{4}$ teaspoon ground nutmeg
Bring just to a boil over medium heat, whisking constantly. Add the reserved stock. Simmer, covered, 5 minutes. Remove the bisque from the heat and stir in:
Reserved lobster meat
1 cup hot but not boiling cream
Season with:
Salt and black pepper to taste
Serve at once, garnished with:
Minced parsley
Paprika

CREAM OF MUSSEL SOUP (BILLI-BI)
About 4 cups
Place in a large soup pot:
3 pounds small mussels, scrubbed and debearded, 373
$1\frac{1}{2}$ cups dry white wine
$\frac{1}{3}$ cup chopped shallots
5 sprigs parsley
3 sprigs thyme
Cover and steam over medium heat until the mussels are open; discard any that do not open. Remove the mussels and set aside. Strain the cooking liquid through a sieve lined with several layers of dampened cheesecloth or paper towels into a medium saucepan. Bring to a simmer. Remove the mussels from their shells. Whisk together in a small bowl:
1 cup heavy cream or half-and-half
1 egg yolk
Gradually whisk about 1 cup of the cooking liquid into the egg mixture, then whisk back into the saucepan. Heat through, but do not boil. Season with:
Salt and white or red pepper to taste
($1\frac{1}{2}$ teaspoons curry powder)
Garnish with the reserved mussels and sprinkle with:
Snipped chives

OYSTER STEW
About 4 cups
Combine in the top of a double boiler set directly on medium-low heat:
2 to 4 tablespoons butter
**1 tablespoon minced onion or leek, or 1 small garlic
    clove, minced, or $\frac{1}{2}$ cup minced celery**
Cook, stirring, until the butter is melted and the onion is

tender but not browned, about 5 minutes. Remove from the heat and stir in:

1 to 1¹/₂ pints shucked oysters, coarsely chopped, with their liquor

1¹/₂ cups milk

¹/₂ cup heavy cream

¹/₂ teaspoon salt

¹/₈ teaspoon white pepper or paprika

Place the top of the double boiler over, not in, boiling water. When the milk is hot, and the oysters float, add:

2 tablespoons chopped parsley

OYSTER BISQUE

Before adding the parsley above, remove the soup from the heat and pour a small quantity over **2 beaten egg yolks.** Mix well, then slowly return this mixture to the hot soup. Heat over low heat for 1 minute; do not allow to boil. Serve at once.

SEAFOOD GUMBO

About 9 cups

Melt in a soup pot over medium heat:

2 tablespoons butter

Stir in and cook, stirring, until golden, about 10 minutes:

1 cup chopped onions

Stir in until blended:

3 tablespoons all-purpose flour

Whisk in until smooth:

1¹/₂ cups tomato puree

4 cups Fish Stock, 118, Poultry Stock, 117, or Chicken Broth, 121

Add:

8 ounces peeled shrimp, cut up

8 ounces lump crabmeat, picked over for shells and cartilage

10 ounces sliced okra or frozen sliced okra

Reduce the heat and simmer until the okra is tender, 15 to 20 minutes. Add:

16 shucked oysters

Salt and black pepper to taste

Heat just until the oysters are plump. Sprinkle with:

Chopped parsley

(Ground red pepper)

Filé powder

Serve over:

Cooked rice

CARIBBEAN CALLALOO

About 12 cups

Place in a soup pot and cook, stirring, over medium heat until almost crisp:

3 slices bacon, cut into 1-inch pieces

Leaving the bacon in the pot, pour off all but 1 teaspoon of the fat. Add and cook, stirring, until the onion is tender but not browned, 5 to 10 minutes:

1 medium onion, chopped

1 garlic clove, minced

3 scallions, thinly sliced

8 ounces ham, cubed

Stir in:

1 pound callaloo, spinach, or chard, trimmed and coarsely chopped

5 cups Poultry Stock, 117, Chicken Broth, 121, or other light stock or broth

¹/₄ teaspoon dried thyme

Cover, bring to a boil, then reduce heat and simmer for 5 minutes. Remove the lid, and add:

8 ounces lump crabmeat, picked over for shells and cartilage, or sliced peeled raw shrimp

8 ounces white fish fillets (tilefish, cod, grouper, orange roughy, or sea bass)

¹/₂ teaspoon salt

8 ounces sliced okra or frozen sliced okra

1 cup unsweetened coconut milk

Black pepper

Simmer until the okra and fish are cooked, about 10 minutes. The fillets will break up as they cook.

LOUISIANA COURT BOUILLON

About 7 cups

Heat in a large skillet over medium heat:

3 tablespoons vegetable oil

Add and cook, stirring, until lightly browned, about 5 minutes:

3 tablespoons all-purpose flour

Add and cook, stirring, just until softened, about 3 minutes:

¹/₂ cup diced green bell pepper

¹/₂ cup diced celery

¹/₂ cup diced onions

2 garlic cloves, minced

¹/₂ teaspoon dried thyme

Stir in:

One 28-ounce can plum tomatoes, drained and coarsely chopped

2 cups Fish Stock, 118 or Clam Broth, 121

Bring to a boil, reduce the heat to medium-low, and simmer for 10 minutes. Stir in:

1 pound white fish fillets, cut into 2-inch pieces

4 ounces small shrimp (about 12), peeled

Cover and cook until the fish is opaque throughout, about 3 minutes. Season to taste with:

2 teaspoons Worcestershire sauce, or

1 teaspoon salt

³/₄ to 1¹/₄ teaspoons hot pepper sauce

Stir in:

¹/₂ to ³/₄ cup cooked long-grain rice

BOUILLABAISSE

About 10 cups (4 to 6 servings)

Heat in a large saucepan over medium heat until the butter is melted:

1 tablespoon olive oil
1 tablespoon butter

Add and cook, stirring occasionally, until the vegetables are tender but not browned, 5 to 10 minutes:

1 medium leek, halved lengthwise, and cut into
  $^1/_2$-inch pieces
1 small fennel bulb, quartered, cored, and thinly sliced
1 celery rib, cut into thin diagonal slices
1 bay leaf
(1 star anise or $^1/_4$ teaspoon anise seeds or fennel
  seeds)
(Peel of $^1/_2$ orange)
$^1/_4$ teaspoon saffron threads
$^1/_2$ teaspoon salt

Add and cook, stirring, for 2 minutes:

3 garlic cloves, minced

Reduce the heat if the bottom of the pan begins to scorch. Add:

1 tablespoon tomato paste

Cook, stirring, for 1 minute. Stir in:

$^1/_2$ cup dry white wine

Bring to a gentle boil and cook for 3 minutes. Stir in:

4 cups Fish Stock, 118, or Clam Broth, 121
1$^1/_2$ cups canned tomatoes with juice, crushed
$^1/_2$ teaspoon ground red pepper
$^3/_4$ teaspoon salt

Bring to a boil, reduce the heat, cover, and simmer for 20 minutes. Remove from the heat. The broth can be made a day in advance and refrigerated. Remove the star anise, orange peel, and bay leaf before continuing with the recipe. Bring just to the smoking point in a large soup pot over high heat:

2 tablespoons olive oil

Add:

12 littleneck clams, scrubbed

Cook, stirring, for 2 to 3 minutes. Reduce the heat if necessary to keep the oil from smoking. Add the reserved broth. Bring to a boil, reduce the heat, cover, and simmer for 3 minutes. Stir in:

12 ounces monkfish, sea bass, red snapper, or
  halibut fillets, or a combination, cut into
  1$^1/_2$-inch pieces

Cook, covered, for 1 minute. Stir in:

12 sea scallops (about 8 ounces)

Cook just until the seafood is done, 2 to 3 minutes more. Discard any clams that are not open. Stir in:

(1 to 2 tablespoons anisette or Pernod)

Serve over:

Sliced toasted French bread

topped with:

Rouille, 582

Pass the remaining rouille separately.

NEW ENGLAND CLAM CHOWDER

4$^1/_2$ cups

Serve this traditional chowder with Cream Biscuits, 639, or homemade Soda Crackers, 93.

I. Prepare for steaming, 374:

5 pounds quahogs or other hard-shell clams

Place in a large soup pot and add:

1 cup water
(Scraps of onion and celery with thyme and bay leaf)

Cover and steam over high heat until the clams are completely open, 10 to 20 minutes. Remove the clams to a bowl, discarding any that do not open. Pour the cooking liquid through a fine-mesh sieve lined with cheesecloth and set aside. Remove the clams from their shells, holding them over the bowl to catch any juices. Coarsely chop into $^3/_8$-inch pieces. Strain the juices into the rest of the reserved cooking liquid. Melt in a soup pot:

2 tablespoons butter or bacon fat

Add and cook, stirring, until the onion is translucent:

1 medium onion, cut into $^1/_2$-inch dice
1 tablespoon butter
$^1/_2$ teaspoon chopped thyme
1 bay leaf

Add and stir until blended and lightly colored:

1 tablespoon all-purpose flour

Add the reserved cooking liquid and:

2 cups diced ($^1/_2$-inch) new potatoes

Bring almost to a boil, reduce the heat, and simmer until the potatoes are tender, about 12 minutes. Remove bay leaf. Stir in the chopped clams, along with:

1 cup heavy cream

Simmer for 5 minutes; do not boil. Season with:

Black pepper to taste
1 tablespoon chopped parsley

II. For quicker preparation, use canned clams. Proceed as above, omitting the quahogs and beginning with cooking the onion. When the onion is translucent, add along with the potatoes:

3 cups Fish Stock, 118, Clam Broth, 121,
  Poultry Stock, 117, or Chicken Broth, 121

Stir in with the cream:

1 cup chopped drained canned clams

MANHATTAN CLAM CHOWDER

About 10 cups

Prepare for steaming, 374:

10 to 12 pounds quahogs or other hard-shell clams

Place clams in a large pot and add:

2 cups water

Cover and steam over high heat until the clams are completely open, 10 to 20 minutes. Remove the clams to a bowl, discarding any that do not open. Pour the cooking liquid through a fine-mesh sieve lined with cheesecloth and set aside. Remove the clams from the shells and finely chop. Heat in a large skillet over medium heat:

2 tablespoons vegetable oil, butter, or bacon fat

Add and cook, stirring, until tender but not browned, 5 to 10 minutes:

> **2 medium onions, chopped**
> **1/2 green bell pepper, diced**
> **1 large celery rib, diced**

Stir in the reserved cooking liquid, along with:

> **One 28-ounce can tomatoes, chopped**
> **3 cups Fish Stock, 118, or Clam Broth, 121**

Bring to a boil. Stir in:

> **1 pound potatoes, cut into 1-inch dice**

Reduce the heat and simmer until the potatoes are tender, about 20 minutes. Stir in the chopped clams and season with:

> **1/2 teaspoon black pepper**
> **2 tablespoons chopped parsley**

RHODE ISLAND CLAM CHOWDER

Use **3 tablespoons olive oil** in place of the vegetable oil or other fat, as above. When the potatoes are tender, add **6 ounces Portuguese linguiça or smoked chorizo, thinly sliced, and 1/4 to 1/2 teaspoon crushed red pepper flakes.** Simmer over low heat for 10 minutes. Add the chopped clams and seasoning and continue as directed.

SALMON CHOWDER
About 5 cups

Simmer but do not boil in a small saucepan, whisking occasionally, until reduced to 2/3 cup:

> **1 cup heavy cream**

Meanwhile, melt in a soup pot over medium heat:

> **1 tablespoon butter**

Add and cook, stirring, until the leeks are tender but not browned, 5 to 10 minutes:

> **2 medium leeks, white part only, chopped**
> **1/4 cup dry vermouth**
> **1 garlic clove, minced**

Stir in:

> **3 cups Fish Stock, 118, or Clam Broth, 121**
> **2 red or white new potatoes, diced**
> **1/2 teaspoon salt**

Bring to a boil, reduce the heat, and simmer until the potatoes are tender, 10 to 15 minutes. Reduce the heat to low. Add the cream, along with:

> **12 ounces salmon fillet**
> **1/4 teaspoon black or white pepper**

Simmer just until the salmon is cooked, 8 to 10 minutes. Break apart the fillet with a spoon. Garnish with:

> **Small dill sprigs**

FISH CHOWDER
12 to 14 cups

Use firm fish such as salmon, monkfish, cod, or wolffish. Cook in a large soup pot, over low heat, stirring, until beginning to crisp, 10 to 15 minutes:

> **4 ounces salt pork or 4 slices bacon, diced**

Add and cook, stirring, until the onions are tender but not browned, 10 to 15 minutes:

> **1/4 cup (1/2 stick) butter**
> **2 large onions, chopped**
> **3 bay leaves**
> **1 tablespoon chopped thyme**

Stir in:

> **3 large boiling potatoes, peeled, halved lengthwise, and cut into 1/4-inch slices**
> **3 cups Fish Stock, 118, or Clam Broth, 121**

Bring to a boil, reduce the heat, and simmer until the potatoes are tender, about 20 minutes. Remove the bay leaves and stir in:

> **31/2 pounds boneless, skinless fish fillets**
> **2 cups heavy cream**

Simmer (do not boil) until the fish is cooked through and beginning to flake, 8 to 10 minutes. The fish will come apart in large chunks. Season with:

> **Salt and black pepper to taste**
> **2 tablespoons chopped parsley and/or chervil**

CORN CHOWDER
About 6 cups

Cook, stirring, in a soup pot over medium-low heat until beginning to crisp, 10 to 15 minutes:

> **4 slices bacon, chopped**

Leaving the bacon in the pan, spoon off all but 2 tablespoons of fat. Add and cook, stirring, until tender and slightly browned, 10 to 15 minutes:

> **1 small onion, chopped**
> **2 medium celery ribs, diced**

Meanwhile remove the kernels from:

> **6 small ears corn**

Set the kernels aside and add the cobs to the pot, along with:

> **41/2 cups milk**
> **2 medium potatoes, diced**

Submerge the corncobs in the milk. Bring the milk almost to a boil, reduce the heat, and simmer, covered, until the potatoes are tender, 10 to 15 minutes. Remove the cobs. Stir in the reserved corn kernels, with:

> **11/2 teaspoons salt**
> **1/2 teaspoon white or black pepper**

Simmer gently until the corn is tender, about 5 minutes. Remove from the heat. With a slotted spoon, remove 11/2 cups solids from the soup and puree until smooth. Return to the soup and add:

> **1 tablespoon butter**

Let stand until the butter is melted, then stir and serve.

ABOUT CREAM SOUPS

These rich, smooth soups can be served at lunch or dinner as first courses. Like appetizers, they act as a stabilizer for the cocktails that have just been consumed or as a buffer against the wines that are to come. For everyday cream soups, cook the vegetables directly in the stock, puree with an immersion blender or in a food processor or blender, and then stir in milk or cream. The soup is usually served without straining. However, ➤ if seafood or poultry is pureed, it tends to be unpleasantly stringy, so strain those soups. ➤ All cream soups, whether thickened with egg or not, are ruined by boiling, so be sure to heat just to the boiling point, or cook them in the top of a double boiler ➤ over boiling water. Reheat them the same way. Many cream soups are equally good hot or cold; when serving cold, adjust the seasoning before serving.

CREAM OF CAULIFLOWER SOUP
About 8 cups
Melt in a soup pot over medium heat:
   4 tablespoons (¹/₂ stick) butter
Add and cook, stirring, until tender but not browned:
   1¹/₂ cups minced celery
   1 cup coarsely chopped onions
Stir in:
   **1¹/₂ pounds cauliflower, trimmed and coarsely
      chopped**
Cover and cook 5 minutes, stirring occasionally. Stir in:
   ¹/₄ cup all-purpose flour
Turn the heat to high. Slowly stir in and bring to a boil:
   **4 cups Poultry Stock, 117, Chicken Broth, 121, or other
      light stock or broth**
Reduce heat to medium-low and simmer, partially covered, until the cauliflower is very tender, about 25 minutes, stirring occasionally. Using a food processor or an immersion blender, process until smooth. Return the soup to the pot and stir in:
   ¹/₂ to 1 cup heavy cream, half-and-half, or milk
Heat through, but do not boil. Add:
   A pinch of grated or ground nutmeg
   Salt and white or black pepper
Serve garnished with:
   (Grated cheese such as Cheddar or Swiss)

CREAM OF ASPARAGUS SOUP
About 5 cups
Prepare **Cream of Cauliflower, above.** Omit the celery. Replace the cauliflower with **1¹/₂ pounds asparagus, trimmed and chopped into 1-inch pieces,** and cook until tender, about 10 minutes. Continue as directed, omitting the nutmeg.

CREAM OF BROCCOLI SOUP
About 7 cups
Prepare **Cream of Cauliflower, above.** Replace the cauliflower with **1¹/₂ pounds broccoli, trimmed and chopped.** Continue as directed, omitting the nutmeg.

CELERY ROOT SOUP
About 8 cups
Prepare **Cream of Cauliflower, above.** Replace the cauliflower with **2 pounds celery root, peeled and cut into ¹/₂-inch dice.** Continue as directed, omitting the nutmeg.

CHESTNUT SOUP
About 6 cups
Prepare **Cream of Cauliflower, above.** Reduce the celery to ¹/₂ cup. Replace the cauliflower with **1 pound Boiled Chestnuts, 270, or vacuum-packed or canned chestnuts, coarsely chopped.** Continue as directed, omitting the nutmeg.

CREAM OF TOMATO SOUP
About 6 cups
Prepare **Tomato Soup, 132.** Stir in **¹/₄ cup heavy cream** and **(1 tablespoon Pesto, 569).** Gently heat through.

CREAM OF CARROT SOUP
About 6 cups
Heat in a soup pot over medium-low heat until hot:
   ¹/₄ cup water or stock
   (1 tablespoon butter)
Add and cook, partially covered, stirring occasionally, until tender but not browned, 5 to 10 minutes:
   1 medium onion, coarsely chopped
   1 tablespoon minced peeled fresh ginger
   (¹/₂ teaspoon curry powder)
Stir in:
   **4 cups Poultry Stock, 117, Chicken Broth, 121, or other
      light stock or broth**
   1 cup orange juice
   1¹/₂ pounds carrots, sliced
Bring to a boil, reduce the heat, and simmer until the carrots are tender, 15 to 20 minutes. Using a food processor or blender, process until as smooth as desired. Return the soup to the pot and stir in:
   ¹/₄ to ¹/₂ cup heavy cream or half-and-half
   ¹/₂ to 1 teaspoon salt
   ¹/₈ teaspoon black pepper
Heat through, but do not boil. Garnish with:
   Chopped parsley or snipped dill or chives
Serve with:
   Soup Croutons, 151, or crackers

CREAM OF MUSHROOM SOUP
About 4¹/₂ cups
The flavor of mushrooms is more pronounced if they have begun to color.
Melt in a soup pot:
   2 tablespoons butter
Add and cook, stirring, until they release their juices:
   8 ounces mushrooms with stems
Add:
   **2 cups Poultry Stock, 117, Chicken Broth, 121, or
      other light stock, or water**
   ¹/₂ cup chopped tender celery
   ¹/₄ cup sliced onion
   2 tablespoons chopped parsley
Bring to a boil, reduce the heat, and simmer, covered, 20 minutes. Using a blender or food processor, puree the soup until smooth. Prepare:
   White Sauce IV, 550

Pour the puree slowly into the cream sauce, then cook, stirring, until the soup is hot; do not boil. Season with:

¹/₂ teaspoon salt

¹/₈ teaspoon paprika

(¹/₈ teaspoon grated or ground nutmeg)

(3 tablespoons dry white wine)

Serve topped with:

(Sour cream or unsweetened whipped cream)

and garnished with:

Sprigs of parsley or chopped chives or arugula

SCALLION AND MUSHROOM SOUP

About 7 cups

Beat with a wooden spoon until light and fluffy:

¹/₄ cup (¹/₂ stick) unsalted butter, softened

Add and stir together well:

5 bunches scallions, very finely chopped

Remove to a soup pot and season with:

1 teaspoon salt

¹/₂ teaspoon black pepper

Cook, covered, over low heat for about 10 minutes. Do not brown the scallions. Remove the pot from the heat. Stir in:

2 tablespoons all-purpose flour

Cook for 1 minute. Whisk in:

4 cups Poultry Stock, 117, Chicken Broth, 121, or other light stock or broth

Bring to a boil, whisking, over medium heat. Reduce the heat and simmer for 10 minutes. Wipe clean, remove the tough ends of the stems, and very thinly slice:

12 ounces mushrooms

Remove the soup from the heat and stir in two-thirds of the mushrooms. Immediately push through a sieve or food mill. Stir in:

¹/₄ to ¹/₂ cup half-and-half, cream, or buttermilk

Gently heat the soup until hot, then stir in the remaining mushrooms. Ladle into warmed bowls. Top each serving with:

Sprinkle of ground red pepper

Dollop of sour cream

CREAM OF ONION SOUP

About 4 cups

Melt in a soup pot over medium heat:

3 tablespoons butter

Add and cook, stirring, until golden brown, about 20 minutes:

2 cups chopped onions

Stir in:

1 tablespoon all-purpose flour

¹/₂ teaspoon salt

Cook, stirring, 1 to 2 minutes. Add:

3 cups Poultry Stock, 117, Chicken Broth, 121, or other light stock or broth

1 cup heavy cream or half-and-half or milk

Simmer, covered, until the onions are very tender, 15 to

20 minutes; do not boil. Add a small amount of hot soup to:

4 egg yolks, beaten

then add the egg mixture to the soup. Heat through, but do not boil. Season to taste with:

Salt and paprika

Ground nutmeg or Worcestershire sauce

Divide among the 4 cups:

4 teaspoons chopped parsley

Pour the hot soup over it.

CREAM OF SPINACH SOUP

About 7 cups

Fresh spinach is best for this soup, but you can substitute three 10-ounce packages frozen chopped spinach, thawed and drained.

Heat in a soup pot, over medium-low heat:

2 tablespoons butter or 1 tablespoon butter plus 1 tablespoon vegetable oil

Add and cook, stirring, until tender but not browned:

¹/₄ cup minced onion

Stir in:

2 tablespoons all-purpose flour

Cook, stirring constantly, over medium heat for 2 minutes. Do not brown the flour. Gradually whisk in:

2 cups milk

2 cups Poultry Stock, 117, Chicken Broth, 121, or clam juice

Simmer over low heat, stirring occasionally, until slightly thickened, about 10 minutes. Stem and wash thoroughly:

2 pounds spinach

Place in a large pot and cook, covered, over medium heat until wilted, about 5 minutes. Immediately drain in a colander, rinse with cold water, then press out the excess water. Add the spinach to the soup and remove from the heat. Process in a blender, in batches if necessary, until smooth. Return to the soup pot and stir in:

(³/₄ to 1 cup heavy cream or half-and-half)

Heat just until hot; do not boil. Season with:

1 teaspoon salt, or to taste

(¹/₄ teaspoon grated or ground nutmeg)

¹/₄ teaspoon black pepper

CREAM OF WATERCRESS OR PURSLANE SOUP

About 6 cups

Combine in a soup pot and bring to a boil:

5 cups Poultry Stock, 117, Chicken Broth, 121, or other light stock or broth

3 tablespoons brown or white rice

(2 teaspoons minced peeled fresh ginger)

Simmer until rice is tender, about 35 minutes. Stir in:

1 medium bunch watercress or purslane (about 7 ounces), chopped or pureed

¹/₂ cup hot heavy cream, half-and-half, or milk

1 tablespoon chopped parsley

Simmer the soup about 5 minutes; do not boil. Stir a small quantity of the soup into:

2 eggs, well beaten

Add this to the rest of the soup, stirring it in slowly. Heat the soup about 5 minutes; do not boil. Serve at once.

CHEDDAR CHEESE SOUP

About 6 cups

Melt in a soup pot over medium heat:

6 tablespoons (¾ stick) butter

Add and cook, stirring, until tender but not browned, 5 to 10 minutes:

1 cup diced onions
1 cup diced celery
¾ cup diced carrots

Sprinkle with:

¼ cup all-purpose flour

Cook, stirring, for 3 to 4 minutes more. Slowly whisk in:

4 cups Poultry Stock, 117, Chicken Broth, 121, or other
light stock or broth

Bring to a boil, whisking constantly. Reduce the heat to a simmer. Cook until thickened, about 45 minutes. Puree until smooth. Bring to a simmer, and stir in:

1 cup heavy cream or half-and-half
2 cups Cheddar, grated (8 ounces)
1 teaspoon dry mustard

Reduce the heat to low and stir until the cheese is melted. Do not let the soup boil: if the soup is too hot, the cheese will separate or curdle. Season to taste with:

(Hot pepper sauce)
(Worcestershire sauce)
Salt and black pepper

If you prefer a thinner soup, thin with additional:

(Stock or cream)

Garnish with:

Soup Croutons, 151
Finely chopped smoked ham
Chopped cooked broccoli

MILK TOAST

1 serving

While not exactly a soup, this dish brings the same kind of cozy comfort to the young or the ailing.

Toast lightly on both sides:

A ¾-inch-thick slice of bread

Spread it lightly with:

Butter

Sprinkle it with:

(Salt)

Place it in a bowl and pour over it:

1 cup hot milk or cream

NEW YEAR'S SOUPS

Served just before parties break up, these are also known as hangover soups, or *Lumpensuppe*, and are sometimes helpful for the morning after.

I. **French Onion Soup, 129,** with the addition of **1 cup dry red wine.**

II. **Lentil Soup, 134,** with **sour cream** and **sausage.**

ABOUT COLD SOUPS

Cold vegetable soups make refreshing first courses or light main courses. Any of these is always welcome on a buffet table. Place the serving bowl in a large bowl of ice to keep the soup cool on particularly hot days. For other cold soups, see Vichyssoise, 130, Blender Borscht, 149, and Cherry Soup, 148.

COLD AVOCADO SOUP

About 4 cups

This is one of the quickest, easiest, and most impressive soups we have ever served. Enjoy!

Puree in a food processor until smooth:

2 ripe Hass avocados (about 1 pound)
1 small garlic clove, minced

Add and process to blend:

2 cups buttermilk
4 teaspoons fresh lime juice
¼ teaspoon salt
Pinch of ground red pepper

Remove to a bowl and refrigerate until cold. Thin if necessary with:

(¼ to ½ cup buttermilk, cream, or milk)

Taste and adjust the seasonings. Ladle the soup into chilled bowls and garnish with any of the following:

Salsa Fresca, 571
2 tablespoons sour cream or plain yogurt
8 ounces lump crabmeat, picked over for shells and cartilage
Mayonnaise
Thin slices of lime

GAZPACHO

About 6 cups

Finely chop, but do not puree, in a food processor or blender:

1 medium cucumber, peeled, seeded, and coarsely chopped
1 medium green bell pepper, cored, seeded, and coarsely chopped

Remove to a large bowl. Finely chop in the processor:

1 small onion, coarsely chopped
⅓ cup packed parsley leaves

Remove to the bowl. Add to the processor and finely chop:

2½ pounds ripe tomatoes, peeled, 311, seeded, and coarsely chopped

Remove to the bowl. Add:

1 cup tomato juice
3 tablespoons red wine vinegar
3 tablespoons olive oil
2 garlic cloves, minced

(1 jalapeño pepper, seeded and minced, or a dash of
hot pepper sauce)
2 teaspoons salt

Stir well. Refrigerate for at least 2 hours. Serve in chilled
bowls.

BECKER BLENDER GAZPACHO
About 12 cups

One of our most requested recipes.

Combine in a large stainless steel bowl:

One 46-ounce can tomato or tomato vegetable juice
One 10^1/$_2$-ounce can condensed beef consommé,
undiluted
Juice of 1 lemon or lime or 1 tablespoon red wine
vinegar
2 tablespoons chopped basil
(2 tablespoons chopped thyme)
(1 tablespoon soy sauce)
1 to 2 garlic cloves, minced
^{1}/$_4$ to ^{1}/$_2$ teaspoon hot pepper sauce

Process in batches in a blender, until finely chopped (do
not puree), and add to the bowl:

1 cucumber, peeled, seeded, and coarsely chopped
3 large carrots, cut into chunks
^{1}/$_2$ head small purple cabbage, cored and cut into
chunks
2 celery ribs, cut into chunks, or 1 bunch watercress,
tough stems trimmed
^{1}/$_2$ to 1 cup chopped parsley (omit if using watercress)
1 bunch scallions, trimmed, or 1 medium onion, cut
into chunks
(^{1}/$_2$ red or green bell pepper)

Season with:

Salt and black pepper to taste

Cover and chill until very cold, 1 to 2 hours. Serve in chilled
bowls and pass:

Croutons, 974

WHITE GAZPACHO
About 9 cups

We were served this refreshing summer soup dining with
cousin Koerner Rombauer and his late wife, Joan, at the
Culinary Institute of America's Greystone Restaurant in
Napa Valley. It combines the best flavors of traditional
Spanish gazpachos with something new and pleasantly
different. Thanks for the inspiration, Chef!

Process in a food processor, in batches if necessary, until
smooth:

2 pounds seedless green grapes
1 European hothouse (seedless) cucumber,
peeled and cut into chunks
4 scallions, chopped
2^1/$_2$ cups half-and-half
1^1/$_4$ cups plain yogurt
2 ounces cream cheese

2 tablespoons white wine vinegar
2 tablespoons olive oil

Remove to a bowl. Season with:

^{1}/$_4$ cup snipped dill
Salt and white pepper or ground red pepper

Cover and chill. Serve garnished with:

Chopped toasted almonds
Snipped chives

COLD CUCUMBER SOUP
About 3 cups

Combine in a medium bowl:

2 tablespoons olive oil
1 teaspoon salt
^{1}/$_4$ teaspoon white pepper
^{1}/$_4$ to 1 cup chopped walnuts
1 garlic clove, minced
2 tablespoons chopped dill

Add and toss gently to coat:

1^1/$_2$ cups very thinly sliced peeled, seeded cucumbers

Refrigerate, covered, for 2 to 6 hours. When ready to
serve, stir in:

1 to 1^1/$_2$ cups plain yogurt or sour cream

The soup should have the consistency of heavy cream. If
necessary, it can be thinned with a small amount of:

(Light stock or broth, milk, cream, or water)

ABOUT FRUIT SOUPS

Fruit soups can be served as a dessert or chilled as a summertime prelude to the entrée. You can mix fresh and
dried fruits, and use one variety or a combination, cooked
until they can be pureed easily. ➤ If the soup is served at
the beginning of the meal, go easy on the sugar. Fruit
soups are also refreshing when made from frozen fruits.

WINTER FRUIT SOUP
About 6 cups

Combine in a large saucepan and let stand for 45 minutes:

^{3}/$_4$ cup dried apricots or peaches, quartered
^{3}/$_4$ cup prunes, pitted and quartered
3 tablespoons raisins
2 tablespoons dried currants
2 cinnamon sticks
Grated zest of 1 orange
3 tablespoons quick-cooking tapioca
4 cups apple juice, cranberry juice, or water

Stir in:

Up to ^{1}/$_4$ cup sugar

Bring to a boil, reduce heat to low, and simmer, stirring occasionally, until fruit has softened and the soup is thickened, about 30 minutes. Add:

2 apples, peeled, cored, and cut into 1-inch pieces

Cook until the apples are tender, about 8 minutes. Let cool
slightly, and remove the cinnamon sticks. Serve warm or
cold, garnished with:

Sour cream or heavy cream
(Toasted sliced almonds)

CHERRY SOUP

About 6 cups

Have ready:

2 pounds cherries, stemmed and pitted, or 4 cups thawed frozen or canned cherries, drained

Reserve half the cherries and place half in a soup pot with:

2 cups Gewürztraminer or medium-dry white wine
2 cups water

Bring to a boil, reduce the heat, and simmer until the cherries are soft, about 15 minutes. Puree in a food processor or blender until smooth. Stir together in a small bowl:

$1/4$ cup sugar
4 teaspoons cornstarch

Add 3 tablespoons of the puree to the cornstarch and sugar and stir well. Return the puree paste to the pot and cook over high heat, whisking, until thickened, about 5 minutes. Reduce the heat and stir in the reserved cherries, with:

1 teaspoon grated orange zest
1 tablespoon fresh orange juice
1 tablespoon fresh lemon juice

Simmer until warmed through. Taste. If not sweet enough, add additional:

(Sugar)

If too sweet, add additional:

(Fresh lemon juice)

Serve warm or cold, garnished with:

Sour cream or plain yogurt
Mint sprigs

GINGER MELON SOUP

About 8 cups

Puree in a food processor until smooth:

2 medium ripe, sweet cantaloupes, or muskmelons, seeded and cut into chunks

Pour into a large bowl and stir in:

1 cup fresh orange juice
$1/4$ cup fresh lime juice
2 tablespoons fresh lemon juice

Refrigerate until cold, about 2 hours. To serve, prepare:

$1/2$ cup minced or grated peeled fresh ginger

Using a cheesecloth or your hands, squeeze out the ginger juice into a small bowl. Stir 1 tablespoon juice into the soup. Serve in chilled bowls, garnished with:

Thinly sliced kiwifruit or strawberries
Mint sprigs

ROSE HIP SOUP

About 4 cups

Be sure the bushes from which you gather the rose hips were not sprayed.

Wash, pat dry, and crush in a nonreactive pan:

2 cups fresh or dried rose hips
4 cups water

Bring to a boil, reduce heat, and then simmer, covered,

about 45 minutes. Strain through a sieve lined with several thicknesses of cheesecloth into a saucepan. Add enough:

Raspberry juice, peach nectar, or fresh orange juice

to make about 4 cups liquid in all. Mix:

1 tablespoon arrowroot

with a small quantity of the liquid and:

$1/3$ cup honey

Return to the pan and bring to a simmer, stirring until the soup begins to thicken. Chill well. Serve garnished with:

Sour cream or whipped cream

ABOUT QUICK SOUPS COCKAIGNE

We suggest here a process, rather than a recipe, for achieving very special results. Mingle canned or frozen soups with the liquids that are precious by-products of cooking vegetables, to make a quick soup. Or, if you have on hand some leftover bones, lean poultry, or meat trimmings, build a soup base. See Becker Express Stock, 120. And remember that most fish soups, 139, are quick soups, even when you start with raw materials. There is also the possibility that you are harboring some refrigerator scraps that could be easily transformed into a quick cream soup, see About Cream Soups, 143. Before processing, heat them with a few mushrooms or a few leaves of spinach, lettuce, or cress; after processing, enrich them with a small amount of milk and cream. If you grow fresh herbs, now is the time to gather a few. Use parsley lavishly, dried herbs discreetly.

Words of caution: ➤ Normally we dilute ready-prepared soups considerably less than their manufacturers recommend, whether we use home-cooked stocks, milk, or—less desirably—just plain water. But we find that the more concentrated the soup, the more likely it is to taste oversalted. Test your mix and correct this tendency. ➤ Be sure, too, if you puree uncooked vegetables, that they are tender enough not to spoil the texture of your soup with stringy fibers or bits of hull. Add to a clear soup a canned consommé or chicken broth, diluted as suggested above, or one of several quickly confected egg drops, 124. If you fancy a more filling dish, turn to Blender Borscht, 149, or Cold Cucumber Soup, 147. Then perhaps a naive house-guest will say, as did a restaurant diner: "I like your soup du jour, but why is it different every day?"

QUICK BEEF STEW

About 6 cups

Heat in a large skillet over high heat:

1 tablespoon vegetable oil

Add and cook until browned:

1 pound boneless beef sirloin, cut into 1-inch cubes

Transfer the beef to a soup pot. Add to the skillet:

$1/2$ cup dry red wine

Cook over high heat, stirring and scraping, until reduced by half. Pour over the beef. Add:

One 8-ounce can tomato sauce
One $10^{1}/_2$-ounce can condensed French onion soup

1 cup water

1 tablespoon Worcestershire sauce

One 24-ounce bag frozen vegetables

1 teaspoon salt

Heat to a boil, reduce the heat, cover, and simmer 10 minutes, or until the vegetables are tender. Stir in:

$^1/_4$ cup chopped parsley

BLENDER BORSCHT

4 to 5 cups

For three generations, the Rombauer-Becker family continues to stock the refrigerator with the ingredients of this cold borscht. For a quick, chilled soup when unexpected guests arrive, open and toss in a blender and it's ready to serve.

I. Combine in a blender:

One 10$^1/_2$-ounce can condensed consommé

One 10$^3/_4$-ounce can condensed cream of chicken soup

One 15-ounce can beets, with liquid

(1 garlic clove, minced)

Half of the liquid from the beets may be drained if a thick soup is desired. Blend until smooth and chill. Serve with a garnish of:

Sour cream and chopped Fines Herbes, 982

II. Process until smooth in a blender or food processor:

2 cups tomato juice

One 15-ounce can beets, with liquid

3 small dill pickles

3 tablespoons minced onion

A drop of hot pepper sauce

(1 garlic clove, minced)

Chill. Serve garnished with:

4 hard-boiled eggs, 194, thinly sliced

Sour cream

Chopped dill or fennel

ROMBAUER BORSCHT

About 4 cups

Combine in a saucepan:

One 15-ounce can diced beets, with liquid

One 10$^1/_2$-ounce can condensed consommé

1 tablespoon chopped onion

1 cup water

Cook for 5 minutes. Add:

1 tablespoon fresh lemon juice

$^1/_2$ teaspoon salt

Garnish each portion with a dollop of:

Sour cream

QUICK CREAM OF CAULIFLOWER SOUP

About 3$^1/_2$ cups

Melt in a large saucepan over medium-high heat:

2 tablespoons butter

Add and cook, stirring, about 4 minutes:

$^1/_4$ cup chopped onion

2 small ribs celery with leaves, minced

Add:

One 14$^1/_2$-ounce can chicken broth

1 cup mashed or riced cooked cauliflower

Heat to a boil. Add:

1 cup half-and-half

Heat through, but do not let boil after adding cream. Season with:

Salt and black pepper to taste

Garnish with:

Chopped parsley

(A light grating of nutmeg or a pinch of ground coriander)

QUICK CHEESE SOUP

About 4 cups

Combine in a large saucepan and stir over low heat until the cheese is melted. Do not let boil:

One 10$^3/_4$-ounce can condensed cream of celery soup

One 10$^3/_4$-ounce can condensed Cheddar cheese soup

1$^1/_4$ cups water or milk

$^1/_2$ cup shredded Cheddar (2 ounces)

Add:

(1 tablespoon chopped onion)

($^1/_4$ teaspoon Worcestershire sauce)

Garnish with:

Chopped parsley

QUICK TOMATO CORN CHOWDER

3 cups

Combine in a medium saucepan and heat through over medium heat, but do not boil:

One 10$^3/_4$-ounce can condensed tomato soup

1$^1/_4$ cups milk

$^1/_2$ cup canned cream-style corn

$^1/_2$ teaspoon sugar

(1 teaspoon curry powder)

Season to taste with:

Salt and black pepper

QUICK CREAM OF MUSHROOM SOUP

About 4 cups

Pour into a large saucepan:

Two 10$^1/_2$-ounce cans condensed consommé

Add:

One 10$^3/_4$-ounce can condensed cream of mushroom soup

1 cup milk

Add and reconstitute:

1 ounce dried mushrooms, 282

Heat, stirring until hot, and serve.

QUICK FRESH TOMATO CREAM SOUP

About 3 cups

One way to use surplus garden tomatoes. Peel, 311, seed, and chop coarsely, then drop into a blender:

1 pound very ripe tomatoes (about 2$^1/_2$ cups)

Add and blend briefly:
>   1 cup heavy cream
>   1 tablespoon chopped parsley
>   1 tablespoon chopped basil

Season with:
>   Salt and black pepper to taste

Chill. Serve with:
>   Lemon slices

ABOUT GARNISHES FOR SOUP

Adding meatballs instead of chopped herbs or watercress to the same clear soup can change the temper of a meal. Scan the parade of garnishes and breads below to determine your pacesetter du jour. If serving an informal buffet, arrange a group of garnishes around a tureen to give your guests a choice of rich, lean, or green. Whip up some satisfying dumplings, 334, for hungry children. Tempt a finicky appetite with an egg drop, 124. ➤ Be sure none of the garnishes are chilled, unless the soup is a cold one.

For individual servings, dress up the soup bowls with garnishes. The most popular soup garnish for clear or thick soups is a lemon slice. Unsprayed flowers such as calendula, violets, or nasturtium lend color to pale cream soups. Bits of vegetables and tofu add visual interest to clear soups. Strengthen the color of a bowl of shrimp bisque with a whole shrimp garnished with an avocado slice and parsley. Float tiny raw mushroom caps filled with sour cream on a spinach soup.

FOR CLEAR SOUPS

Drop into the soup:
>   Thin lemon or orange slices
>   Thin avocado slices drenched in lemon
>   Minced parsley, chives, watercress, onion, mint, basil, or chervil, tarragon, or dill, floated on the surface or sprinkled on a dab of whipped cream
>   Green or snow peas, thawed frozen petite peas, or sugar snap peas
>   Thin slices of cooked celery root
>   Consommé Brunoise, 124
>   Noodles
>   Potato Gnocchi, 335
>   Wontons, 342
>   Kreplach, 126
>   Dumplings, 334
>   Ravioli, 339
>   Farina Balls Cockaigne, 334
>   Spätzle, 335
>   Nöckerlen, 653
>   Meatballs for Soup, 151 or Sausage Balls for Soup, 151
>   Pesto, 569
>   Cubes of tofu
>   Bean sprouts
>   Finely julienned vegetables
>   Cooked rice or barley
>   Port or Madeira
>   Sliced scallions
>   Thinly sliced greens such as spinach, escarole, or kale

FOR CREAM SOUPS

Garnish with:
>   Unsweetened whipped cream or sour cream and a dusting of finely chopped mixed herbs
>   Herbs and Greens for Soup, below
>   Shredded toasted blanched almonds or cashews

FOR THICK SOUPS

Garnish with:
>   Thin orange, lemon, or lime slices
>   Sliced small hard sausages
>   Sliced hard-boiled eggs, 194
>   Soup Croutons, 151
>   Sour cream
>   Meatballs for Soup, 151
>   Potato Gnocchi, 335
>   Julienned strips of cooked ham or chicken or chunks of cooked seafood
>   Grated cheese
>   Pesto, 569

BREADS TO SERVE WITH SOUPS

>   Fancy shapes cut from toasted white, rye, or whole wheat
>   Melba Toast
>   Toasted rye sticks
>   Plain or toasted Garlic Bread, 641, or other herbed bread
>   Crackers, hot and plain, or spread with herb butters, or cheese spreads
>   Quick Cheese Straws or Wafers, 91
>   Hush Puppies, 633
>   Corn Dodgers Cockaigne, 633, or Corn Zephyrs Cockaigne, 633
>   Soup Croutons, 151
>   Small Choux Paste Puffs, 671
>   Turnovers, 695
>   Soda Crackers, 93

HERBS AND GREENS FOR SOUPS

Always use the freshest and most tender of greens—being sure to remove stems and coarse midribs of lettuce, sorrel, or parsley—alone or in combination with whatever fresh herbs you have on hand that are compatible with the flavor of your soup. Allow:
>   1 to 2 tablespoons chopped fresh herbs
> $1/2$ cup shredded spinach, watercress, or arugula

for each:
>   2 cups soup

Add the herbs to a small quantity of the soup and chop in a food processor or blender until fine. Combine the blended herbs with the remaining soup. If you have no blender, mince a combination of herbs very, very fine.

FRITTER GARNISH

½ cup batter, enough for about 3 cups garnish
Please read About Deep-Fat Frying, 1046.
Beat until light in a small bowl:

1 egg

Add and stir until smooth:

¼ teaspoon salt
⅛ teaspoon paprika
½ cup all-purpose flour
2 tablespoons milk

Push the batter through a colander into deep fat heated to 365°F. Fry until golden brown. Drain on paper towels. Place in the soup just before serving.

MEATBALLS FOR SOUP

About twelve 1-inch meatballs
A superb main dish may be had by adding these to vegetable soup. Prepare ½ **recipe German Meatballs, 512.** You can use more bread if desired. Mix the ingredients lightly with a fork. Shape them without pressure into 1-inch balls and drop into boiling soup or stock. Simmer until done, about 10 minutes.

SAUSAGE BALLS FOR SOUP

About sixteen 1-inch meatballs
Good in pea, bean, or lentil soup.
Combine:

8 ounces bulk sausage
1 egg white
2 teaspoons minced parsley
½ teaspoon minced basil
¼ teaspoon minced rosemary
3 tablespoons browned bread crumbs, 960

Roll this mixture into 1-inch balls. Drop into boiling stock. Reduce the heat at once and simmer until done, about 30 minutes. Skim fat from the soup before serving.

SOUP CROUTONS

For other croutons, see 974.
To retain the crispness of these ever-popular diced toasts, serve them in individual dishes and let the guests add them to their soup. Or, use them diced small, so they are much like buttered toasted crumbs, to garnish spinach, noodles, or game. They may be flavored by sautéing in:

Butter and olive oil

or dusting them with:

Grated cheese

while still hot.

Iceberg, Boston, Green Leaf

SALADS

For virtually everyone, salad nowadays has assumed a legitimately high priority, and it often takes first place on the menu. However, some are still inclined to prefer a green salad in its traditional location, between entrée and dessert, mainly because it creates a clean break between savory and sweet. But the presentation of a light salad as an appetizer can spark the appetite before the main course and be a lifesaver for a host or hostess whose pièce de résistance has, in fact, resisted and is not as ready for dinner as the guests are.

Keep the rest of the menu in mind when preparing your salad and its dressing. A rich, heavy entrée demands a tart green salad. Other salads, especially those made from one or several vegetables, beans, or legumes, can replace side dishes. Tangy coleslaw and creamy potato salad go well with casual meals, cookouts, and impromptu suppers where hearty, uncomplicated foods are served.

Innovative combinations of salad greens with grilled or roasted meat, fish, shellfish, or vegetables serve as full-fledged entrées in our quest for healthful and lighter ways of eating. See Combination Salads, 162.

ABOUT SALAD GREENS

Buy the freshest greens with crisp leaves, free of brown spots. Use greens as soon as possible after buying them. If you have to store them, remove any leaves that are wilted or show signs of decay and take off any rubber or metal bands holding them together. Store them in the vegetable bin of your refrigerator in an open plastic bag. If the greens wilt slightly, they can often be revived by soaking them in ice-cold water for 3 to 5 minutes, then drying them well.

Enjoy the full range of lettuces and cultivated greens listed below. To cook greens, see the Vegetables chapter, 240.

ICEBERG OR CRISPHEAD LETTUCE
The heads are large, firm, crisp, brittle, and tightly packed. Outer leaves are medium green, inner ones pale green and chunky. The leaves can be torn, shredded, or sliced like cabbage. They add "crunch" and do not readily wilt.

BUTTERHEAD LETTUCE
The heads are smaller, less compact, and softer than iceberg. The leaves are delicate, the outer ones dark green, the inner light green to yellowish, and "buttery" to the taste. Familiar varieties include **Boston, buttercrunch, Limestone,** and **Red Tip,** but the aristocrat of the line is undoubtedly **Bibb.** The subtly sweet, buttery flavor of these lettuces both combines well with stronger-flavored greens and is lovely on its own.

LOOSE-LEAF LETTUCE
Mild and mellow, these lettuces have sprawling crisp leaves with sweet and refined flavors; they may have ruffled edges and/or red tips. There are many varieties of loose-leaf lettuces, including **green leaf, red leaf,** and **oak leaf.** They are wonderful to eat on their own and also blend well with stronger-tasting greens. They are used as a bed for fruit or molded salads or on party platters.

MÂCHE
This green is also called **rapunzel, feldsalat, lamb's lettuce,** and **corn salad** because it often grows in cornfields. Delicate, sweet, and nutty, it is expensive because it is highly perishable. The clusters are small, made up of smooth green leaves. Mâche can be cooked like spinach.

Oak Leaf, Mâche, Red Leaf

Romaine Lettuce, Arugula, Belgian Endive

ROMAINE LETTUCE OR COS
The elongated heads are made up of long stiff leaves, which are usually medium dark to dark green on the outside and greenish-white near the center; there is also a **red romaine.** This lettuce's more pungent flavor enlivens a tossed salad. Tear the leaves and discard the fibrous ribs. The tender, paler inner leaves are best.

ARUGULA OR ROCKET
Also called **Italian cress,** arugula has tender dark-green leaves, and a pungent peppery bite. Some varieties have smooth-edged leaves, others have serrated leaves. The spiciness of arugula intensifies as it ages. Arugula is delicious alone or as an accent in mixed green salads.

BELGIAN OR FRENCH ENDIVE OR WITLOOF CHICORY
Another bitter salad component, they look rather like young unshucked ears of corn. The outer of the closely packed greenish-white leaves may, like celery ribs, serve as receptacles for hors d'oeuvres. Belgian endive blends well with tart greens like radicchio and arugula and contrasts equally well with soft, delicate lettuces like Boston or Bibb.

CABBAGE
All types of cabbage are candidates for salad, but **Chinese, celery, Napa,** and **Savoy** cabbages, as well as **bok choy,** tend to be sweeter and more delicate than familiar red, white, or green cabbage. Slaw, 161, it is important to remember, can be made of the red and Chinese varieties as well as the conventional green cabbage. The most commonly available Chinese cabbage has oblong heads with pale ruffled leaves and crunchy ribs. **Bok choy** or **pak choi** has tender loose dark green leaves atop wide white fleshy stems. Baby bok choy is a miniature, delicately flavored

bunch of leaves with small stalks about 4 inches long. The yellow-flowering shoots are delicious too.

CELERY LEAVES
Chopped celery ribs appear in many kinds of salads, but the leaves are also tasty and leave a hint of pepper on the tongue. The pale whitish green ones at the heart of the celery are best.

CELTUCE
Also known as stem or asparagus lettuce, this is an Asian lettuce grown for its thick, succulent stalk. It tastes a bit like water chestnuts. Very young leaves can be used like lettuce in salads.

Watercress, Curly Endive, Dandelion Greens

CRESSES
Common cresses, which belong to the mustard family, are spicy and peppery additions to any tossed salad. The most widely available type is **watercress,** which has dime-sized dark green glossy leaves on sprigged stems; use only the leaves and tender portions of the stems. Do not confuse **garden cress** with watercress. Garden cress has very tiny leaves, and it is frequently combined in sandwiches and hors d'oeuvres with baby mustard greens, 154. **Curly cress** leaves are lacy, like those of flat-leaf parsley, but extremely pungent. **Upland cress** is similar to watercress, but if grown in hot weather, it becomes so strong as to be nearly inedible. It is a good idea to taste any of these before adding them to a salad.

CURLY ENDIVE AND FRISÉE
These two types of chicory are sometimes confused with each other. **Curly endive** has coarse, spiky green leaves,

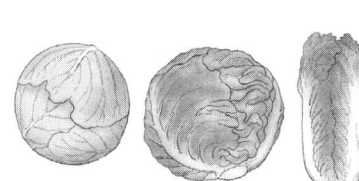

Green, Red, Chinese, Napa and Savoy cabbages, Bok Choy, Celery, Celtuce

dark at the bottom and pale on top. It adds a bitter flavor and a somewhat prickly texture to a tossed salad. **Frisée** has small, tender, lacy green leaves that are very pale at the center of the head, with a mild tartness and a more delicate taste than other chicories.

DANDELION GREENS

Now cultivated, these are very tart greens with jagged-edged leaves that look like arrows. Young, tender leaves less than 6 inches long are less tart and are ideal in salads. Both raw and cooked, dandelion greens have a rich, bracing flavor. See About Foraging for Wild Greens, 156.

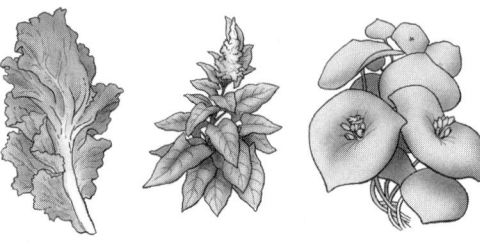

Escarole, Good King Henry, Miner's Lettuce

ESCAROLE OR BROAD CHICORY

Eaten both raw and cooked, the leaves of this member of the chicory family are broader, paler, and less crimped than curly endive, above. The taste is less bitter, though the sturdy leaves do have a pronounced tartness and a firm, chewy texture.

GOOD KING HENRY

Good King Henry tastes like and can be treated as spinach both served raw in salads and cooked. Its spade-shaped leaves are often the first greens of spring, and its flowering tips are also edible. Good King Henry mixes nicely with tender red-leaf lettuces.

MINER'S LETTUCE

The small, fleshy, triangular leaves are tender and mild, with a buttery flavor. The flowers are also edible.

MIZUNA

Of Japanese origin, mizuna, one of the most delicately flavored of the mustards, has dark green, feathery leaves that are delightful tossed with light dressing flavored with sesame oil. Related is **mibuna,** which is similar in flavor but

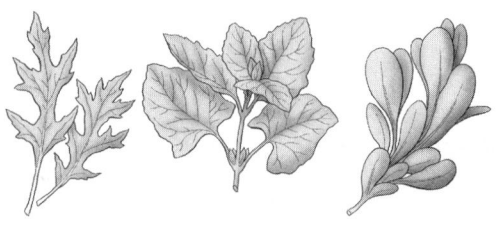

Mizuna, Orache, Purslane

slightly stronger, with a distinctive appearance of long, narrow, densely packed stems that explode into a spray of leaves. Mizuna is often an ingredient in mesclun, 155.

ORACHE

The arrow-shaped leaves of this green have a mild spinach flavor, and orache is sometimes called **mountain spinach.**

PURSLANE

Although considered a weed in most of the United States, this green has been eaten for centuries. It resembles a small creeping jade plant. Purslane has juicy stalks and oval leaves with a tart lemony flavor. The leaves of the cultivated **Goldgelber** variety are large and golden green. Snap the stems into sprigs and use them in salad.

RADICCHIO

Two readily available varieties of this red-leaved chicory are **rosso,** with a round head that resembles a small cabbage, and **Treviso,** with elongated leaves. Beautiful magenta in color with ivory streaks, they have a pleasantly bitter, slightly peppery flavor. Radicchio combines well with most salad greens and adds stunning color to any salad.

SORREL

Best in spring, when young, tender, and mild, sorrel is wonderful in salads. Use it discreetly, because its sour flavor can be overwhelming and it has a high concentration of oxalic acid. Also see Sorrel, 304.

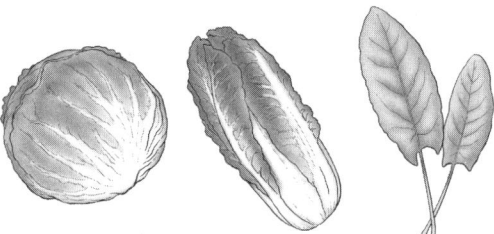

Round Radicchio, Oblong Radicchio, Sorrel

SPINACH

Whether curly, crinkled, or flat (the latter is more delicate in flavor), spinach leaves are a versatile, valuable salad green. Include the stems, chopping them neatly—and if the pink roots are still attached, drop them in too for their crunch. Spinach leaves are often sandy, so wash thoroughly, repeating a second time if necessary.

TATSOI

A ground-hugging member of the mustard family, also called **spoon mustard,** tatsoi has rounded, thick leaves and stalks that add flavor and crunch to salads.

YOUNG LEAFY GREENS

Fully grown leafy green vegetables such as **broccoli rabe, mustard greens,** and **chard,** as well as **beet** and **turnip greens,** are commonly cooked before eating, but younger

Curly-leaf Spinach, Flat-leaf Spinach,
Tatsoi, Amaranth

greens of the same varieties are more delicate in texture and flavor and can be eaten raw in salads. Young green-leaf **amaranth,** also known as **Chinese spinach,** is tender with an intense spinach-like taste. The red varieties have the same flavor and brighten a salad nicely. The Japanese green **komatsuna,** also known as **mustard spinach,** has thick, dark green leaves. Its flavor combines cabbage with the bite of mustard. The young stalks are delicious.

MESCLUN

Mesclun is a mixture of salad greens that is also called **spring mix** or **baby greens.** The term "mesclun" comes from the French word for mixture, and the idea comes from the practice of gathering a variety of young field greens and mixing them in a salad. A good mesclun has a variety of flavors, textures, and colors, striking a balance between strong-flavored greens such as arugula and mizuna and more subtle greens such as baby lettuces. To make your own mesclun, choose a selection from the Salad Greens Guide, below, picking one or two each from the mild, slightly tart, and tart greens.

HERBS AND EDIBLE FLOWERS

To add flavor and color to salads, add herb leaves or blossoms whole, tear them into bite-sized pieces, or cut them into ribbons. The following herbs are mild enough to be added to salads in quantity as you would any other salad green: **angelica, basil, chervil, cilantro, dill, fennel fronds, lemon balm, lovage, marjoram, mint, parsley, sage, salad burnet, sweet cicely,** and **tarragon.** These herbs are more pungent and should be used as garnishes: **ambrosia, anise, anise hyssop, caraway, chives, epazote, garlic, garlic chives, hyssop, mitsuba, oregano, perilla (shiso), rosemary,**

savory, and **thyme.** Try any of the following colorful flowers: **clove pinks, elderberry, lavender** (sparingly), **lemon, mustard, nasturtium, rose, rosemary, scented geranium, shungiku, sweet woodruff,** and **violets.** Use only unsprayed flowers. You may want to gently rinse and pat the blooms dry. If the blossoms are small, add them whole; separate larger blooms into petals. Also see Growing Culinary Herbs, 989, and Using Herbs, 992.

PEA SHOOTS

The first 3 to 5 inches at the tip of a snow pea vine, including the tendrils, leaves, pods, and sometimes flowers, are the pea shoot. These are popular in Asian cooking and now appear in our markets. Freshly picked, they are crisp, with a light pea flavor. They are exquisite in salads and, though delicate, hold their own with stronger flavors.

SPROUTS

The long translucent sprouts emerging from alfalfa, radish, mung bean, and other sprouted seeds are embryonic roots and stalks. The smallest sprouts are preferable for salads, adding crunch, texture, and flavor. To sprout your own beans, seeds, or grains, see 1011.

SALAD GREENS SUBSTITUTIONS

MILD GREENS	MILDLY TART GREENS
Butterhead lettuces	Belgian endive
Celery leaves	Collards
Celtuce	Curly endive
Crisphead lettuces	Dandelion greens
Loose-leaf lettuces	Escarole
Mâche	Frisée
Romaine lettuces	Garden cress

Komatsuna, Pea shoots, Kale, Collards

MILDLY TART GREENS
Kale
Mizuna
Purslane
Shungiku
Watercress

TART GREENS
Arugula
Broccoli rabe
Curly cress
Curly endive
Escarole
Mustard greens
Radicchio
Radish leaves
Tatsoi
Turnip greens
Upland cress

CABBAGE
Bok choy
Baby kale

CABBAGE
Komatsuna
Napa cabbage

ASIAN GREENS
Bok choy
Komatsuna
Mizuna
Mustard greens
Pea Shoots
Shungiku
Tatsoi

SPINACH
Amaranth
Baby beet greens
Baby chard
Young dandelion greens
Good King Henry
Komatsuna
Miner's lettuce
Young mustard greens
Orache

ABOUT FORAGING FOR WILD GREENS

Wild edibles such as young purslane, miner's lettuce, wild mustard, peppergrasses, dandelion, sorrels, chickweed, cheese mallows, shepherd's purse, ramps, wild watercress, winter cress, spiderwort, and some flower buds like the day lily, 659, can be gathered by a knowledgeable and experienced forager and used raw in salads. In using wild greens, it is prudent to use them when they are young and tender, and to add them in relatively small amounts to more conventional greens, because many of them contain oxalates and other substances that may be dangerous to ingest in quantity. Be very sure you can identify the greens you propose using, and wash them with great care.

Dandelion is easy to identify and easy to handle if it is cut off at the root crown so that the leaf cluster holds together. Its slightly acid taste complements that of beetroot. After the dandelions flower, the mature leaves are tough and quite bitter. Edible varieties of sorrel are numerous, the best being *Rumex acetosella,* **sheep sorrel,** and *R. acetosa.* The leaves have a pleasantly sour taste and when cooked also make an esteemed garnish for seafood. **Winter cress,** or *Barbera vulgaris,* is, as its name implies, highly resistant to cold and widely distributed; it resembles mustard greens in flavor. The rosettes of smooth dark green leaves may be gathered as new growth either in early spring or late fall.

Wild mint and **Jerusalem artichoke,** though not, of course, a green, are exceptionally good accompaniments to salads composed of wild greens.

ABOUT PACKAGED GREENS

Packaged cut lettuces and salad mixtures tend to be more expensive than lettuce or greens sold in heads or bunches. Examine the contents carefully for wilted or yellowed leaves. To refresh and crisp packaged greens, soak in ice-cold water for 3 to 5 minutes, then drain and dry thoroughly and refrigerate 30 minutes before dressing.

ABOUT PREPARING GREENS FOR SALADS

Salad ingredients prepared too far in advance suffer a loss of nutritive value and arrive at table looking discouragingly limp. Take care in washing not to bruise them; see that they are well chilled, crisp, and—especially—dry. It is usual to tear rather than cut most greens, which might bruise the more tender leaves; iceberg lettuce, cabbage, and other especially crisp greens can be sliced or shredded with a stainless steel knife.

To clean greens, separate leaves, discard any that are discolored, wilted, or tough, and place in a large bowl or sink full of cold water. Swish around for 30 seconds or so, then lift them from the water so that the dirt and grit remain in the water. Repeat the process until the water is clear. Spinach, which is sandy, may take two or three rinses.

To clean iceberg lettuce, remove the core, either by cutting around the core using a sharp knife or by pounding the core quite hard on a cutting board, and twist it loose for easy removal. Hold upside down under running water and invert to drain.

Dry greens by letting them drain in a colander, then wrapping them lightly in a soft absorbent towel until dry, then chilling in the refrigerator until crisp. Salad spinners are a wonderful convenience. Overcrowding a salad spinner, however, will both bruise the greens and hinder the device's ability to dry them adequately. Fill the spinner only about half to two-thirds full. Alternatively, place the greens in a tea towel and swing the towel around to sling off the water—just be sure to do this outside.

To dry loosely bunched lettuces such as Bibb, wash while still in head form, invert to drain, then place in the refrigerator on a tea towel, cover with another towel, and chill for several hours. Gravity and capillary action will render them dry and crisp.

Once they are washed and dried, ➤ store greens in whole form, tearing or cutting them only when you are about to make the salad. Place them in the vegetable storage bin, in an open plastic bag, with a dry paper towel.

ABOUT DRESSING SALADS

Place the greens in an ample bowl and give them a preliminary light coating of oil. ➤ About 1 tablespoon of oil will suffice for a medium-sized head of lettuce, or 2 cups of salad greens. Toss repeatedly by lifting the leaves gently with your hands or a large salad fork and spoon until each leaf is completely coated. This conditions the greens against the wilting actions of the vinegar. Follow up with more oil, then vinegar—in all, about one-quarter of the amount of oil—salt to taste, and further tossing. If a salad is mixed following this principle, it will stay crisp, although it is usually eaten too quickly to prove it.

Add the dressing as close to serving time as possible, since vinegar and salt cause lettuces to release juices and moisture and turn limp. ➤ For a picnic or for transporting, wash and drain the greens (iceberg will stay crisp the longest), and put them in a large plastic bag. Take the dressing along in a separate container. Just before serving, pour the dressing into the bag and gently toss it until the salad greens are coated. Serve from the bag or turn out into a large bowl.

The choice of oil is important. First, in order of excellence is olive oil, preferably extra virgin. If you find extra-virgin olive oil too strong, try combining it with pure or light olive oil or any blander vegetable oil. Nut oils, such as those made from walnuts and hazelnuts, are particularly good in salads, especially when highlighted by toasted bits of the nuts themselves. Toasted nut oils can be quite strong and should be mixed with light-flavored vegetable oil for salads. In this last group are grapeseed, safflower, and canola oils, which impart relatively little flavor and thus are versatile both on their own and to temper more strongly flavored oils. Whichever oil you choose, it should complement, not overpower, the greens.

Your choice of an acidic ingredient will depend on your taste buds, but good red or white wine vinegar or fresh lemon juice is the usual accompaniment to oil. A small amount of balsamic vinegar can be added as a seasoning, but it can be overpowering if it is the sole acidic ingredient. Various kinds of herb vinegars are frequently chosen, but you may prefer to mix fresh herbs with the greens themselves or add dried herbs separately to the dressing. For a discussion of vinegars, see 1024. ➤ The classic oil-to-vinegar proportions are 3 parts oil to 1 part vinegar. Remember the old admonition: "Let the salad maker be a spendthrift for oil, a miser for vinegar, a statesman for salt, a madman for mixing." To which we would add: an abolitionist for moisture.

As a general rule, thick, creamy dressings work better with heartier, stronger greens, and simple dressings often match up best with complex salads with many ingredients. Your dressing should enhance the salad by summoning forth its special flavor and texture and adding a bit of tartness. ➤ Allow 1½ to 2 cups loosely packed washed and dried greens and 2 to 3 tablespoons dressing per person (less for vinaigrettes, and more for creamy dressings). ➤ Figure ½ cup vinaigrette or ¾ cup creamy-style dressing for 4 servings. We have suggested or included within the recipes suitable dressings for the individual salads in this chapter. See also 572.

ABOUT SALAD BOWLS

Bowls made of glass, glazed pottery, or hard, greaseproof plastic are our first choices for preparing and serving salad.

Well-seasoned wooden bowls have acquired an untouchable sacredness with some gourmets that we think is misplaced. If the surface of a wooden salad bowl is protected by a varnish, the flavors·of the oil, vinegar, and herbs will not penetrate it, and you might just as well wash it in the usual way. An untreated wooden surface will certainly absorb some of the dressing used, but the residue left after wiping the bowl tends to become rancid. This rancidity can noticeably affect the flavor of a salad. To remove a buildup of oil, use a stiff pad to scrub the bowl with salt and lemon juice. Rinse and repeat as necessary until clean, then apply a thin, even coat of mineral oil. Lettuce and cabbage leaves can also be used as bowls, 172.

ABOUT ADDITIONS TO GREEN SALADS

The simplest way to enhance a green salad is to add condiments or seasonings to the salad while or after you toss it with the dressing. Be sure to give the greens a few extra tosses to integrate the additions well. ➤ With a light coat of dressing on the greens, small accents such as croutons, nuts, cheese, and olives will cling to the salad and are less apt to fall to the bottom of the bowl. For more substantial additions like grilled chicken, sliced beef, or the multiple ingredients of a Greek salad, everything gets tossed together at once. After the dressings and all additions are incorporated, you may find that salting your salad is unnecessary. Following are some popular additions:

Tomatoes are a colorful and tasty salad ingredient but it is ➤ unwise to add cut-up tomatoes to a tossed salad, as their juices will thin the dressing. Instead prepare them separately and use them to garnish the salad bowl; or cut the tomatoes into vertical wedges. Cherry, grape, or pear tomatoes can be left whole, but even cut in half, they release little juice.

Croutons, 974, are valued as much for their crunchy texture as for their flavor. Add at the last minute to prevent them from becoming soggy. Do not include if the salad is served alongside a starchy dish, such as pasta or rice.

Nuts and seeds add crunch and can complement the greens and the dressing. Toasting them first, 1001, significantly enhances their flavor.

Raw vegetables: Thinly sliced, shredded, grated, or julienned, such as carrots, turnips, cabbage, celery, cucumbers, onions, bell peppers, fennel, and mushrooms mix with the greens and do not fall to the bottom of the bowl.

Garlic is perhaps the most influential seasoning. There are two ways of giving a salad a delicate touch of this pungent flavor. Halve a clove of garlic and rub the inside of a salad bowl with the cut sides; then discard the clove. Or rub a rather dry crust of bread on all sides with a halved clove of garlic (this is called a **chapon**) and place it in the salad bowl under the greens. Add the dressing and toss the salad lightly to distribute the flavor; remove the chapon, and serve the salad at once. The chapon itself can be served to a garlic lover. For a slightly stronger flavor, mash a clove of garlic at the bottom of the salad bowl with the other seasonings, and add the dressing to the bowl before the greens.

Other additions may include:

Sliced avocados
Cooked crumbled bacon
Sliced or crumbled cheese
Grilled and sliced chicken or beef
Chickpeas, kidney beans, or other cooked legumes
Fresh herbs
Chopped hard-boiled eggs, 194
Thinly sliced ham or other cured meats
Flaked smoked or cured fish (salmon, trout, mackerel)
Whole or sliced marinated artichoke hearts
Pitted olives
Orange or grapefruit slices (peel and pith removed)
Dried fruit (raisins, currants, cranberries, cherries)
Sliced apples
Sliced mangoes
Sliced pears
Thinly sliced scallions or red onions
Bean sprouts
Sliced fresh or canned hearts of palm, 288
Cheese Crisp, below

CHEESE CRISP

I. *Makes 1 large crisp*

Toss together in a small bowl:

$^1/_2$ **cup grated Gruyère**
1 tablespoon grated Parmesan

Sprinkle in an even layer in a large nonstick skillet to form an 8-inch disk. Cook over medium heat, spooning off the fat, until lightly browned, about 4 minutes. Using a spatula, carefully lift the pancake onto a paper towel–lined baking sheet and blot dry.

II. *Makes 8 crisps*

Preheat the oven to 300°F. Have ready:

$^1/_2$ **cup grated Parmesan**

Using 1 tablespoon cheese per chip, sprinkle into 3$^1/_2$-inch rounds on a large nonstick baking sheet or a baking sheet lined with parchment paper and lightly coated with olive oil. Bake until the chips are golden and have stopped bubbling, 10 to 15 minutes. Transfer to a paper towel–lined platter.

GREEN SALAD

4 to 6 servings

Combine in a salad bowl:

2 large heads Boston or Bibb lettuce, torn into bite-sized pieces
1 tablespoon chopped parsley
1 tablespoon snipped chives

Toss well to coat with:

$^1/_2$ **to $^3/_4$ cup Vinaigrette, 572**

TART GREEN SALAD

4 to 6 servings

Combine in a salad bowl:

2 bunches arugula, tough stems trimmed and torn into bite-sized pieces
3 Belgian endives, cores removed and cut crosswise into 1$^1/_2$-inch-slices
1 small head radicchio, torn into bite-sized pieces

Toss well to coat with:

$^1/_2$ **to $^3/_4$ cup Fresh Herb Vinaigrette, 572**

TART GREENS WITH APPLES AND PECANS

4 to 6 servings

Prepare:

Buttermilk Honey Dressing, 578

Combine in a salad bowl:

4 cups bite-sized pieces arugula
1 small head radicchio, torn into bite-sized pieces
2 Belgian endives, cores trimmed and removed and leaves sliced lengthwise into long strips

Place in another bowl:

1 Granny Smith or other tart apple, cored and very thinly sliced

Stir the dressing well, then add just enough to both the greens and the apple to moisten, and toss to coat. Divide the greens among salad plates. Top with the apple and:

$^1/_2$ **cup pecan halves, toasted, 1001**

FIELD SALAD WITH FRESH HERBS

4 to 6 servings

Combine in a salad bowl:

1 cup herb leaves (any combination of chervil, sage, tarragon, dill, basil, marjoram, parsley, and/or mint)
4 cups bite-sized pieces slightly tart salad greens, any combination

Toss well to coat with:

$^1/_3$ **to $^1/_2$ cup Vinaigrette, 572**

ASIAN GREENS AND WHOLE HERBS

4 to 6 servings

A perfect accompaniment to rich meats (like lamb and beef) and fish (tuna or mackerel). Top with grilled fish, 402, or meat, 467, for a main-course salad.

Prepare:

Ginger Lemongrass Dressing, 575

Combine in a salad bowl:

10 to 12 cups Asian greens (if tiny and young, leave whole)
2 red bell peppers, cut into thin strips
$^1/_2$ **cup cilantro leaves**
$^1/_4$ **cup mint leaves**
$^1/_4$ **cup basil leaves**

Stir the cooled dressing well. Add just enough to moisten the salad and toss gently to coat.

MIXED GREENS WITH CHEESE CRISP

4 servings

Prepare:

Cheese Crisp I or II, 158

Place in a salad bowl:

6 cups bite-sized pieces mild and slightly tart salad greens

Toss well to coat with:

$^1/_4$ to $^1/_3$ cup Vinaigrette, 572

Divide among 4 salad plates. Break the cheese crisp into pieces, distributing it equally among the salads.

CAESAR SALAD

6 servings

Top with strips of grilled chicken breast, shrimp, or sliced beef. Any of these toppings make for an entrée. Adding the optional egg or mayonnaise will keep the dressing emulsified. If you omit the egg, combine the dressing well before adding it to a salad. Please read About Egg Safety, 980.

Mash together in a small bowl until a paste is formed:

2 garlic cloves, peeled

$^1/_2$ teaspoon salt

Whisk in:

2 tablespoons fresh lemon juice

(1 large egg or 1 tablespoon mayonnaise)

1 teaspoon Worcestershire sauce

(3 to 4 anchovy fillets, mashed to a paste)

Salt and black pepper to taste

Add in a slow, steady stream, whisking constantly:

$^1/_2$ cup extra-virgin olive oil

Place in a salad bowl:

2 heads romaine lettuce, torn into bite-sized pieces

Toss with the dressing and:

Croutons, 974

Sprinkle with:

$^1/_4$ cup grated Parmesan

GREEK SALAD

4 to 6 servings

Combine in a salad bowl:

2 large or 3 small heads Boston, romaine, or iceberg lettuce, torn into bite-sized pieces

8 cherry tomatoes, halved, or 8 tomato wedges

$^1/_2$ cup crumbled feta

6 thin slices red onion

$^1/_2$ cucumber, peeled and sliced

8 Kalamata olives, pitted

$^3/_4$ cup sliced celery hearts

4 scallions, cut into 1-inch pieces

8 radishes, sliced

One 2-ounce can anchovy fillets, drained, rinsed, and halved lengthwise

Whisk together:

6 to 7 tablespoons extra-virgin olive oil

2 tablespoons fresh lemon juice or red wine vinegar

1 teaspoon finely minced garlic

1 teaspoon dried oregano

Salt and black pepper to taste

Pour the dressing over the salad and toss well.

PITA SALAD (FATTOUSH)

6 to 8 servings

Toss together in a colander:

1 small cucumber, peeled, seeded, and cut into $^1/_2$-inch cubes

1 teaspoon salt

Let stand to drain for 30 minutes. Preheat the oven to 350°F. Split open and place on a baking sheet:

Two 7-inch pita breads

Bake until crisp and lightly browned, about 10 minutes. Break into bite-sized pieces. Press the excess water out of the cucumber, rinse and blot dry. Combine the cucumber in a medium bowl with:

$^1/_2$ head romaine lettuce, torn into bite-sized pieces

3 medium tomatoes, chopped

6 scallions, finely chopped

$^2/_3$ cup chopped parsley

$^1/_4$ cup chopped cilantro

2 tablespoons finely chopped mint

Whisk together in a small bowl:

$^1/_3$ cup extra-virgin olive oil

$^1/_4$ cup fresh lemon juice

1 garlic clove, crushed

$^1/_2$ teaspoon salt

$^1/_4$ teaspoon black pepper

Pour the dressing over the salad and toss well. Add the pita toasts and toss again.

SPINACH SALAD

4 servings

Cook in a skillet over medium-high heat until crisp:

4 slices bacon

Drain on paper towels, cool, and crumble. Combine well:

$^1/_4$ cup cider vinegar

2 tablespoons olive or vegetable oil

(2 teaspoons yellow mustard seeds)

(2 teaspoons minced parsley)

1 teaspoon minced onion

1 teaspoon sugar

Wash well and place in a salad bowl:

1 large bunch baby spinach

Pour the dressing over the spinach and toss. Sprinkle with the crumbled bacon and garnish with:

2 or 3 hard-boiled eggs, 194, sliced into rounds

SPINACH SALAD WITH GRAPEFRUIT, ORANGE, AND AVOCADO

2 to 4 servings

Toss together in a salad bowl:

6 cups baby spinach leaves

2 to 3 pinches of salt

3 to 4 tablespoons Tangerine Shallot Dressing, 575

Divide the spinach among salad plates and arrange on top:

>**1 grapefruit, peeled and sectioned, 223**
>**1 navel orange, peeled and sectioned, 223**
>**1 avocado, pitted, peeled, and sliced**

Sprinkle with:

>**(Sesame seeds, toasted, 1001)**

Season with:

>**Black pepper to taste**

ENDIVE AND WALNUT SALAD
4 servings

Whisk together in a salad bowl:

>**1 tablespoon red wine vinegar**
>**1 tablespoon minced shallot**
>**¹/₂ teaspoon Dijon mustard**
>**Salt and black pepper to taste**

Add in a slow, steady stream, whisking constantly:

>**2 tablespoons walnut oil**
>**2 tablespoons vegetable oil**

Add:

>**4 Belgian endives, cores removed and cut crosswise into ¹/₂-inch slices**
>**¹/₂ cup walnut halves, toasted, 1001**
>**(¹/₄ cup crumbled Gorgonzola or other blue cheese)**

Toss well to coat.

ABOUT WARM OR WILTED SALADS

Exceptions prove the rule, and we justify the formulas for wilted greens in this section as applying to semicooked rather than raw salads—and thus outside our previous insistence on crispness of leaf.

These salads make impressive first courses or entrées. Serve warm salads immediately, because they can become soggy. For other warm salads, see Spinach with Seared Shrimp and Bacon, 163, Thai Beef Salad, 163, and Hot Slaw, 161.

WILTED GREENS
4 servings

Cook in a large skillet until crisp:

>**4 to 5 slices bacon**

Drain on paper towels, cool, and crumble. Pour all but 2 tablespoons of the bacon drippings out of the pan. Alternatively, heat in the same pan:

>**2 tablespoons butter or vegetable oil**

Add:

>**¹/₄ cup cider vinegar**
>**(2 to 3 teaspoons sugar)**

Add the bacon and, if desired:

>**(2 teaspoons yellow mustard seeds)**
>**(1 teaspoon minced onion)**

Meanwhile, place in a salad bowl:

>**2 large bunches flat spinach, young mustard, dandelion greens, or butter lettuce**

Pour the hot dressing over the spinach and toss. Serve at once, garnished with:

>**2 hard-boiled eggs, 194, sliced or chopped**

BISTRO SALAD
6 servings

Cook in a large skillet until crisp:

>**8 ounces thick-cut bacon, cut crosswise into ¹/₂-inch strips**

Drain on paper towels. Pour the fat into a glass measuring cup and add:

>**Enough extra-virgin olive oil to make ¹/₂ cup total**

Set aside. Add to the skillet and cook until softened, about 2 minutes:

>**2 shallots, thinly sliced**

Add and cook until softened and fragrant, about 1 minute:

>**2 garlic cloves, minced**

Add and cook 30 seconds, scraping up the browned bits in the pan:

>**3 tablespoons red wine vinegar**

Whisk in the reserved bacon fat mixture. Stir in:

>**1 tablespoon minced parsley**
>**1 teaspoon thyme leaves**
>**Salt and black pepper to taste**

Meanwhile, place in a salad bowl:

>**2 large heads frisée, torn into bite-sized pieces**

Toss with the bacon and:

>**Croutons, 974**

Toss well with just enough of the hot dressing to coat. Divide among 6 salad plates and top with:

>**6 poached eggs, 196, well drained and trimmed**
>**(Minced parsley)**

BAKED GOAT CHEESE AND MESCLUN
4 servings

A delicious appetizer salad. For a lunch or supper entrée, double the bread crumb mixture and cut the entire goat cheese log into 8 slices, serving 2 rounds of goat cheese per salad.

Preheat the oven to 400°F. Grease a small baking dish. Place in a salad bowl and refrigerate:

>**5 cups mesclun or baby mixed greens**
>**1 cup packed coarsely chopped mixed herbs, such as parsley, sage, dill, and tarragon**

Stir together in a shallow bowl:

>**1 cup fine dry bread crumbs**
>**1 teaspoon dried thyme**

Pour into another shallow bowl:

>**¹/₄ cup extra-virgin olive oil**

Cut four ¹/₂-inch slices from:

>**One 3- to 4-ounce log goat cheese**

Coat each round first with the olive oil and then with the bread crumbs. Place in the baking dish and bake until golden brown and lightly bubbling, about 6 minutes. Meanwhile, prepare:

Vinaigrette, 572

Toss the greens with just enough vinaigrette to coat and divide among 4 salad plates. Place a round of baked cheese in the center of each salad.

ABOUT COLESLAW

Slaw is traditionally made with red or green cabbage, or a combination. Or substitute napa cabbage or bok choy, 262. When time is short, packaged shredded cabbage or broccoli can be used instead. One 16-ounce bag is roughly equivalent to 8 cups.

CREAMY COLESLAW

This creamy slaw is the American favorite. However, if you choose, dress your slaw with $1/2$ to 1 cup Vinaigrette, 572.

6 to 8 servings

Remove the outer leaves and core from:

1 small head green or red cabbage (about 2 pounds)

Finely shred or chop by hand or in a food processor (you should have 8 to 10 cups). Place in a deep bowl. Pour just enough over the cabbage to moisten it:

Creamy Dressing for Coleslaw, 578

Toss well to coat. Season with:

Salt and black pepper to taste

If desired, stir in any of the following:

(1 to 2 teaspoons dill, caraway, or celery seeds, or a combination)

(2 tablespoons chopped parsley, chives, or other herb)

(3 to 4 strips crisp bacon, crumbled)

(1 cup pineapple chunks)

($1/2$ cup grated carrots)

($1/2$ cup coarsely chopped onions, bell peppers, or pickles)

BECKER COLESLAW

4 to 6 servings

One of the most requested recipes from the JOY kitchen, and a Becker original.

Combine in a large bowl:

2 cups diced green cabbage

1 cup diced red cabbage

$1/2$ cup diced carrot

($1/2$ cup diced red radish)

$1/4$ cup diced celery

$1/2$ cup chopped parsley

2 to 3 dashes hot pepper sauce

Grated zest of one lemon

Combine, then toss with the salad, one of the following:

$1/2$ cup Balsamic Vinegar, 1024, and $1/2$ cup mayonnaise, or $3/4$ cup Balsamic Vinaigrette

Cover and refrigerate until chilled.

TANGY COLESLAW

6 servings

Combine:

$3/4$ to 1 cup mayonnaise

4 scallions, chopped

2 teaspoons rice or cider vinegar

$1/8$ teaspoon Worcestershire sauce

$1/4$ teaspoon salt

$1/8$ teaspoon black pepper

$1/4$ teaspoon sugar

Place in a large bowl, dress, and toss lightly:

3 cups shredded cabbage

3 cups shredded watercress or arugula

1 carrot, grated

($1/4$ to $1/2$ green bell pepper, cut into strips)

SPICY CHINESE SLAW

6 to 8 servings

This is from our dear friend Bruno. He and his wife, Helen, cook most of the meals when they come to visit. This slaw will stay fresh for 2 to 3 days in the refrigerator if it lasts through the meal.

Slice into 2-inch matchsticks one of the following:

2 to 3 kohlrabi, peeled, or

5 small cucumbers, peeled and seeded, or

6-inch piece daikon (or 3 cups) radish or

3 cups shredded cabbage

Place mixture in a glass bowl and toss with:

4 tablespoons salt

Let stand to drain, 30 to 45 minutes. Rinse the vegetables under cool running water to wash off the salt. Drain well, place in a bowl, and stir in:

2 tablespoons minced garlic

$1 1/2$ teaspoons minced red chile pepper, or

2 tablespoons crushed red pepper flakes

1 tablespoon sugar

1 tablespoon rice wine vinegar

$1 1/2$ tablespoons extra-virgin olive oil

$1 1/2$ to 2 tablespoons toasted sesame oil

Salt to taste

Marinate for a minimum of 1 hour. Serve at room temperature or chilled.

HOT SLAW

4 to 6 servings

Cook in a large skillet over low heat until crisp:

6 slices thick-cut bacon or 8 ounces finely diced salt pork

Remove and drain on paper towels, then crumble the bacon. Add to the fat in the skillet:

3 tablespoons cider vinegar

2 tablespoons water

1 tablespoon brown sugar

(1 teaspoon caraway or celery seeds)

Salt to taste

Bring to a boil, then reduce the heat to a simmer and stir in:

3 cups shredded red or green cabbage

(1 large cooking apple, peeled, cored, and grated)

Simmer for 2 minutes. Serve hot, garnished with the crumbled bacon.

ABOUT COMBINATION SALADS

Also known as **main-course salads,** these are served as an entrée and typically contain generous quantities of meat, fish or seafood, chicken, or cheese, either served on top of the greens or bound with mayonnaise or vinaigrette. Most of the various components can be prepared ahead, then chilled, and the salad assembled just before serving.

CHEF'S SALAD

4 to 6 servings
Place on a large platter:
   About 10 cups bite-sized pieces lettuce
Prepare:
   ³/₄ cup Vinaigrette, 572, Creamy Blue Cheese Dressing, 576, or Thousand Island Dressing, 576
or as needed. Drizzle just enough to lightly coat the lettuce. Arrange on top:
   1 cup thin strips cooked chicken or turkey breast
   4 ounces ham, cut into thin strips, or prosciutto, very thinly sliced and rolled into cigar shapes
   5 ounces Swiss, Cheddar, Gruyère, or other firm cheese, cut into thin strips
Garnish with:
   2 tomatoes, cut into wedges
   2 or 3 hard-boiled eggs, 194, quartered
   12 black olives, pitted
   ¹/₂ cup minced parsley
   Salt and black pepper to taste

COBB SALAD

4 to 6 servings
Prepare:
   Creamy Blue Cheese Dressing, 576, Roquefort or Blue Cheese Vinaigrette, 573
Line a platter with:
   1 head Bibb lettuce, separated into leaves
Arrange in rows on top of the lettuce:
   1 large bunch watercress, coarsely chopped
   1 avocado, pitted, peeled, and diced
   4 cups diced cooked chicken or turkey breast
   4 to 6 slices bacon, cooked and crumbled
   3 hard-boiled eggs, 194, diced
   3 medium tomatoes, coarsely chopped
   (¹/₄ cup finely snipped chives)
   ¹/₄ cup crumbled Roquefort or other blue cheese
Lightly drizzle vinaigrette over the salad and serve, passing the remaining vinaigrette separately.

SALADE NIÇOISE

4 to 6 servings
Cook in a large pot of boiling salted water until tender, about 20 minutes:
   6 small new potatoes

Remove with a slotted spoon and let cook. Meanwhile, add to the pot and boil until bright green but still crisp, 2 to 3 minutes:
   1 pound green beans, trimmed
Cool in an ice bath and drain well. Place in a medium bowl. Cut the cooled potatoes into ¹/₂-inch slices and add to the beans. Whisk together in a small bowl:
   3 tablespoons red wine vinegar
   2 teaspoons Dijon mustard
   Salt and black pepper to taste
Add in a slow, steady stream, whisking constantly:
   6 tablespoons extra-virgin olive oil
Drizzle one-quarter of the dressing over potatoes and beans and gently toss to coat. Arrange on a large platter:
   1 head Boston lettuce, separated into leaves
   2 large tomatoes, cut into 8 wedges each
Drizzle another quarter of the dressing on top. Arrange the green beans and potatoes on the platter, along with:
   5 hard-boiled eggs, 194, halved
   6 ounces canned or pouch tuna, drained and flaked
Drizzle remaining dressing. Scatter over top:
   ¹/₂ cup Niçoise olives
   ¹/₄ cup minced parsley
   2 tablespoons drained capers
   (2 to 4 anchovy fillets, rinsed and patted dry)
Sprinkle with:
   Salt and black pepper to taste

LOBSTER SALAD VINAIGRETTE

4 to 6 servings
Prepare:
   Basil Vinaigrette, 573
Combine in a salad bowl:
   2 cups watercress, tough stems trimmed
   2 cups mesclun, mixed greens, baby romaine, or baby spinach leaves
   1¹/₂ cups thinly sliced Belgian endive
Toss well with just enough vinaigrette to coat. Divide the greens among salad plates. In the same bowl, toss together, adding just enough vinaigrette to coat:
   10 to 12 ounces cooked lobster meat, 382, cut into ¹/₂-inch chunks, crab, or shrimp
   1 avocado, pitted, peeled, and diced
   (¹/₂ red bell pepper, diced)
   (¹/₂ yellow bell pepper, diced)
Spoon over the greens, and garnish with:
   2 plum tomatoes, peeled, seeded, and diced
   2 cups Croutons, 974

CRAB LOUIS

4 servings
Line a platter or a salad bowl with:
   Boston or Bibb lettuce leaves
Place on top:
   About 1 cup thin strips Boston, Bibb, or red-leaf lettuce

Heap on top of these:

    2 cups lump crabmeat, picked over for shells and cartilage

Pour over the crab:

    1 cup Sauce Louis, 581

Garnish with:

    (2 hard-boiled eggs, 194, sliced)

    Snipped chives

SPINACH WITH SEARED SHRIMP AND BACON

4 servings

Peel, seed, and cut into thin strips:

    2 bell peppers, preferably 1 each red and yellow, roasted, 292; or 1/2 cup thin strips rinsed and drained jarred roasted peppers

Heat in a medium skillet over medium heat until hot:

    2 tablespoons olive oil

Add:

    1 pound medium shrimp, peeled, tails left on, and deveined if desired

    Salt and black pepper to taste

Cook until the shrimp are firm and pink, 3 to 4 minutes each side. Remove from the pan, cool, and chill. Meanwhile, return the skillet to the heat and cook until crisp:

    8 slices bacon

Drain on paper towels, cook, and crumble. Prepare:

    Sherry Vinaigrette, 573 or Vinaigrette, 572

Place in a salad bowl:

    4 cups bite-sized pieces spinach

Add the peppers, shrimp, and bacon. Stir the dressing well and add just enough to moisten the ingredients.

OREGON SHRIMP SALAD

4 servings

This was inspired by our favorite salad at the Mallory Hotel in Portland, Oregon, a home away from home.

Line 4 plates with:

    Torn iceberg lettuce

Place on top of each, cavity facing up:

    1/2 avocado, peeled and pitted (2 total)

Place in the cavity:

    1/4 cup cooked tiny shrimp

Divide among the plates, surrounding the avocado:

    1 hard-boiled egg, 194, quartered

    1/2 large carrot, sliced

    6 pitted black olives

    6 slices cucumber

Drizzle each with a few tablespoons:

    Vinaigrette, 572, or Sauce Louis, 581

Or serve on the side:

    Cocktail Sauce, 568

Garnish with:

    Lemon slices

    Finely sliced red cabbage

THAI BEEF SALAD

6 servings

Prepare a medium-hot grill fire or preheat the broiler. Grill, 467, or broil, 465:

    1 1/2 pounds boneless beef steak

Meanwhile, combine in a salad bowl:

    3 bunches watercress, tough stems trimmed

    1 1/4 cups mint leaves

    1 1/4 cups cilantro leaves

    2 bunches radishes, thinly sliced

    1 medium red onion, thinly sliced

    2 tablespoons grated lemon zest

Cover and refrigerate until ready to serve. Prepare:

    Thai Vinaigrette, 575

Slice the beef into 1/2-inch-thick strips. Add beef and dressing to watercress mixture. Toss to coat and combine.

TACO SALAD

8 to 10 servings

Layer in a 5- to 6-quart glass bowl or serving dish in the order listed:

    One 13 1/2-ounce bag tortilla chips, broken into bite-sized pieces

    Meat from Ground Beef Tacos, 188

    12 ounces Cheddar, grated (about 3 cups)

    1 small head iceberg or romaine lettuce, thinly sliced

    3 scallions, chopped, or 1 small onion, diced

    1 large tomato, coarsely chopped

    1 cup tomato salsa or Salsa Fresca, 571

Serve with:

    (Sour cream)

    (Guacamole, 72)

CHICKEN OR TURKEY SALAD

4 servings

A traditional party dish, generous main-dish servings for 50 will require 25 cups diced cooked chicken, from four to five 5-pound roasters or 12 to 13 pounds boneless, skinless chicken breasts. If you substitute turkey, you will need five 3-pound boneless breasts. Chicken salad should taste of chicken, the other ingredients being present only to enhance flavor and add variety of texture. So always keep the proportions of at least ➤ twice as much chicken as the total of your other ingredients. Be sure to include plenty of both dark and light meat for the best flavor. For the ultimate chicken or turkey salad, roast, smoke, or grill the poultry. Since the meat is usually combined with mayonnaise, be careful to refrigerate this salad, particularly if you make it in advance.

Combine in a medium bowl:

    2 cups diced cooked chicken or turkey

    1 cup diced celery

    (1 cup halved seedless grapes)

    (1/4 cup coarsely chopped toasted, 1001, almonds, walnuts, or pecans)

Mix in:
> $^1/_2$ to $^3/_4$ cup mayonnaise
>   Salt and black pepper to taste

Serve on a bed of:
>   Lettuce leaves

Garnish with:
>   (1 tablespoon chopped parsley or tarragon)

CHICKEN SALAD VARIATIONS

Follow the recipe for Chicken Salad, 163. You can substitute cooked duck, turkey, or veal for the chicken. Remember to keep the proportions to twice as much meat or poultry as the other ingredients.

>   Chicken, celery, and hard-boiled eggs, 194
>   Chicken, bean sprouts, and water chestnuts
>   Chicken, cucumber, and walnuts
>   Chicken, Boiled Chestnuts, 270, celery, and, if desired, roasted red pepper or pimientos
>   Chicken and parboiled oysters
>   Chicken and fruit, such as seedless grapes, chopped fresh pineapple, and pomegranate seeds, and sliced almonds

CURRIED CHICKEN OR TURKEY SALAD

4 servings

Combine in a medium bowl:
>   2 cups diced cooked chicken or turkey
> $^1/_4$ cup chopped toasted, 1001, walnuts, almonds, or cashews
> $^1/_4$ cup dark or golden raisins
>   3 scallions, chopped
>   1 apple, cored, peeled, and coarsely chopped
>   2 celery ribs, thinly sliced

Mix in:
> $^1/_2$ to $^3/_4$ cup Curry Mayonnaise, 580
>   Salt and black pepper to taste

Serve on a bed of:
>   Lettuce leaves

CHINESE CHICKEN SALAD

4 to 6 servings

Combine in a large bowl:
>   4 cups thin strips cooked chicken
>   One 11-ounce can mandarin oranges, drained and juice reserved
> $^2/_3$ cup sliced scallions
> $^1/_2$ cup chopped roasted peanuts

Whisk together well in a small bowl:
>   About $^2/_3$ cup reserved mandarin orange juice
> $^1/_2$ cup peanut oil
>   2 tablespoons fresh lemon juice
>   (1$^1/_2$ teaspoons chili oil, or to taste)
>   1 teaspoon soy sauce
>   1 teaspoon minced peeled fresh ginger
> $^1/_2$ teaspoon salt, or to taste

> $^1/_4$ teaspoon ground Szechuan peppercorns or black pepper

Pour $^2/_3$ cup dressing over the chicken mixture and toss to combine. Taste and adjust the seasoning. Serve the salad over:
>   4 cups shredded Napa cabbage

Top with:
> $^1/_2$ cup chopped unsalted roasted peanuts
>   1 cup chow mein noodles

HAM SALAD

4 servings

Finely chop the ham and boiled eggs if using on sandwiches. Combine in a bowl:
>   2 cups cubed cooked ham
> $^1/_4$ cup finely chopped dill or sweet pickles or pickle relish
> $^1/_4$ cup mayonnaise
>   (3 hard-boiled eggs, 194, finely chopped)
>   2 tablespoons minced onion
>   (1 tablespoon fresh lemon juice)
> $^1/_2$ teaspoon Dijon mustard
> $^1/_8$ teaspoon black pepper

Cover and refrigerate until chilled.

EGG SALAD

3 to 4 servings

Combine in a medium bowl:
>   6 hard-boiled eggs, 194, finely chopped
> $^1/_4$ to $^1/_3$ cup mayonnaise
>   (2 tablespoons minced onion)
>   (2 tablespoons minced celery)
>   ($^1/_4$ teaspoon curry powder)
>   Salt and black pepper to taste

Cover and refrigerate until chilled.

TUNA SALAD

4 servings

Flake with a fork:
>   1 cup canned or pouch tuna

Flake it with a fork. Add:
> $^1/_2$ to 1 cup diced celery or cucumber

In a small bowl, whisk together:
>   2 tablespoons olive oil
>   2 tablespoons lemon juice

or use:
> $^1/_4$ cup mayonnaise

Add:
>   (1 tablespoon chopped chives)
>   (1 tablespoon chopped parsley)

Combine the mixture and oil or mayonnaise with a fork.

BECKER TUNA SALAD

4 servings

We sometimes replace the mayonnaise in this recipe with an additional $^1/_4$ cup vinaigrette.

Combine in a large bowl:

> 6 ounces canned or pouch tuna, drained
> 1/2 cup chopped red or green cabbage
> 1/2 cup diced carrots
> 1/2 cup diced celery
> 1/4 cup chopped parsley
> (1/4 cup chopped radishes)
> 2 to 3 dashes hot pepper sauce
> Grated zest of 1/2 lemon
> 1/4 cup Balsamic Vinegar, 1024
> 1/4 cup mayonnaise

Cover and refrigerate until chilled.

LOBSTER OR SHRIMP SALAD

2 servings

Combine in a medium bowl:

> 2 cups chopped or shredded cooked lobster meat or
> cooked medium shrimp, halved lengthwise
> 1/4 to 1/2 cup sour cream or mayonnaise
> (2/3 cup thinly sliced seeded, peeled cucumber)
> (1 hard-boiled egg, 194, chopped)

Stir in:

> (1 tablespoon finely snipped chives)
> (1 tablespoon minced parsley)
> (1 teaspoon minced tarragon)
> 1/4 teaspoon grated lemon zest
> 1 teaspoon fresh lemon juice
> Salt and black pepper to taste

Serve immediately on chilled plates lined with:

> Boston lettuce leaves or mixed greens

Garnish with:

> Snipped chives or chopped parsley

SEAFOOD SALAD

I. *2 to 3 servings*

Combine:

> 1 cup lump crab or lobster meat, picked over for shells
> and cartilage
> 1/2 cup diced seeded cucumber
> 1/4 cup extra-virgin olive oil
> 1 tablespoon fresh lemon juice
> 1 tablespoon finely snipped chives
> Salt and black pepper to taste

II. *4 to 6 servings*

Combine:

> 1 pound lump crabmeat, cooked shrimp, lobster meat,
> or salmon
> 1/2 cup mayonnaise
> (1/2 cup diced celery)
> 2 tablespoons fresh lemon juice
> 2 tablespoons drained capers

HERRING SALAD

20 to 24 servings

Cut into 1/4-inch cubes:

> Three 12-ounce jars pickled herring (not in cream),
> well drained

Dice all 1/4-inch and combine in a large bowl:

> 3 cups diced peeled apples
> 1 1/2 cups diced cooked beets, 258
> 1 cup shredded blanched almonds
> 1/2 cup diced onion
> 1/2 cup diced dill pickles
> 1/2 cup diced cold boiled potatoes
> 2 hard-boiled eggs, 194, diced
> 2 celery ribs, diced

Mix together, pour over salad and mix well:

> 1 cup red wine vinegar or dry red wine
> 1 cup sugar
> 2 tablespoons prepared horseradish
> 2 tablespoons chopped parsley

Shape the salad into a mound on a platter, or place it in a serving bowl. Garnish with:

> (Riced hard-boiled eggs)
> (Pickles and olives)
> (Anchovies)
> (Sprigs of parsley)

ABOUT VEGETABLE SALADS

The variety of textures and tastes in vegetables make these salads a welcome alternative to crisp green salads or slaws. Almost any vegetable makes an interesting salad when steamed or blanched and paired with a dressing. Try green beans, snap peas, artichokes, asparagus, or leeks with Spicy Walnut Vinaigrette, 574, Tangerine Shallot Dressing, 575, or any of the vinaigrettes on pages 572–575.

ARTICHOKE HEART SALAD

Freshly cooked or canned artichoke hearts are delicious cut up and added to green salads or aspics, or sliced in half or quarters and used as groundwork for an attractive individual salad plate. We like to dress them with:

> Vinaigrette, 572, or Fresh Herb Vinaigrette, 572

ASPARAGUS SESAME SALAD

4 to 6 servings

Cook:

> 1 1/2 pounds asparagus, cut into 2-inch pieces

Meanwhile, whisk together in a small bowl:

> 3 tablespoons toasted sesame oil
> 2 1/2 tablespoons sugar
> 4 teaspoons white wine vinegar or rice vinegar
> 4 teaspoons soy sauce
> 4 teaspoons sesame seeds, toasted, 1001

Toss the asparagus with the dressing while warm. Serve warm or chilled.

ABOUT AVOCADO SALADS

Please read About Avocados, 218. To prepare avocado cups, cut the fruit in half lengthwise and, using a large knife, cut around the fruit in a circular motion with the blade moving around the pit within. Twist the avocado

 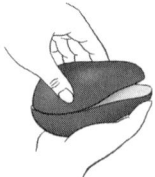 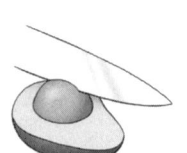  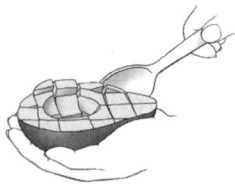

Making avocado cups or dicing an avocado

open by gently rotating the two halves. To remove the pit, firmly tap it with a knife, embedding the sharp edge of the blade in the pit, twist, and lift it out, as shown. Scoop the avocado cup from the peel with a large spoon. Or, for a carefree method of dicing or slicing, hold the pitted avocado half in your hand and score the pulp into cubes or slices before scooping.

To prevent the fruit from darkening after cutting, sprinkle with lemon or lime juice. ➤ To store a cut avocado, allow the seed to remain embedded, spread the edges with lemon juice or mayonnaise, cover well with plastic wrap, and refrigerate.

AVOCADO AND CITRUS SALAD

4 servings

Section, 223:

1 large grapefruit

2 large oranges

Cut crosswise on a slight angle into ¼-inch slices:

2 avocados, pitted and peeled

Marinate the avocado for 5 minutes in:

½ cup Celery Seed Dressing, 574, or Poppy Seed–Honey Dressing, 574

Alternate the avocado and citrus slices on a bed of:

1 small head romaine lettuce, shredded

AVOCADO AND MANGO SALAD

4 servings

Halve:

1 lemon

Halve, pit, peel, and thinly slice lengthwise:

2 avocados

Gently rub the slices with the lemon halves. Slice vertically into segments:

1 ripe mango or papaya, peeled and seeded

Whisk together in a small bowl:

½ cup extra-virgin olive oil

2 tablespoons fresh lemon juice

Salt and black pepper to taste

Toss with half of the dressing:

2 cups arugula leaves

½ cup thinly sliced red onion

Divide among chilled salad plates. Alternate the slices of avocado and mango around the arugula. Spoon as much of the remaining dressing over the slices as desired.

CREAMY BEET SALAD

4 to 6 servings

Cut into ¾-inch cubes and place in a medium bowl:

4 medium beets (about 1½ pounds), cooked, 258, peeled and cut into ½-inch cubes

Pour over the warm beets and toss to coat evenly:

½ recipe Creamy Horseradish Dressing, 578

Garnish with:

(Snipped dill)

PICKLED BEET SALAD

4 to 6 servings

Drain, reserving the liquid:

2½ cups cooked or canned beets

(Two 15-ounce cans sliced beets)

Place the beets in a heatproof jar or serving bowl. Combine in a saucepan and bring to a boil:

1 cup cider vinegar

1 cup reserved beet juice

¼ cup sugar

10 whole black peppercorns

6 whole cloves

2 bay leaves

1 teaspoon salt

(1 green bell pepper, cored, seeded, and sliced)

(1 small onion, sliced)

(1 teaspoon prepared horseradish)

Remove from the heat, cover, and let stand for 30 minutes. Bring the marinade back to a boil, then pour over the beets. Cover and refrigerate at least 12 hours before serving on:

Watercress, tough stems trimmed

CARROT AND RAISIN SALAD

6 to 8 servings

Combine in a medium bowl:

4 large carrots, coarsely grated (3 cups)

½ cup raisins

½ cup coarsely chopped pecans or unsalted peanuts

2 teaspoons grated lemon zest

1 tablespoon fresh lemon juice

¾ teaspoon salt

Black pepper to taste

Cover and toss salad with:

1 cup sour cream or ½ cup sour cream plus ½ cup mayonnaise

CARROT, APPLE, AND HORSERADISH SALAD
4 to 6 servings
Stir together well:
> 3 large carrots, coarsely grated (2 cups)
> 1 large tart apple, peeled, cored, and coarsely grated
> $1/2$ cup sour cream or plain yogurt
> 2 to 3 tablespoons grated peeled fresh horseradish or drained prepared horseradish
> 2 tablespoons chopped parsley
> 2 tablespoons snipped chives
> 1 teaspoon fresh lemon juice
> 1 teaspoon sugar

Cover. Refrigerate until chilled, 1 hour. Season with:
> Salt and black pepper to taste

EDAMAME AND CARROT SALAD WITH RICE VINEGAR DRESSING
8 servings
Combine in a medium bowl:
> One 10-ounce bag shelled edamame, cooked (2 cups)
> 3 large carrots, coarsely grated (2 cups)
> $1/2$ cup thinly sliced scallions
> (2 tablespoons chopped cilantro)

Whisk or shake together in a bowl or jar:
> 2 tablespoons rice vinegar
> 2 tablespoons fresh lemon juice
> 1 tablespoon peanut or vegetable oil
> 1 garlic clove, minced

Add to the salad, tossing to coat evenly. Season with:
> Salt and black pepper to taste

CELERY ROOT RÉMOULADE
4 to 6 servings
Peel and cut into $1/4$-inch rounds:
> 2 medium celery roots

Cook in boiling salted water for 3 to 4 minutes. Drain and let cool, then cut into very thin strips. Place in a shallow bowl and cover with:
> Rémoulade Sauce, 581

allowing about $1/2$ cup sauce for every 2 cups celery root. Cover and chill well. Serve on a bed of:
> Watercress, tough stems trimmed

ABOUT CUCUMBER SALADS
Please read About Cucumbers, 272. Be sure to select firm, hard cucumbers for salads. Seedless European cucumbers, long and usually wrapped in plastic, are a good choice. If the skin has not been waxed, it is edible. If you wish to make the cucumbers more decorative, leave them unpeeled and score them with a fork, as shown, 173; before slicing remove the setting by cutting lengthwise and scraping the seeds out with a spoon.

MARINATED CUCUMBERS
4 servings
I. Combine in a medium bowl:
> $1/4$ cup rice vinegar or white wine vinegar
> (4 teaspoons sesame seeds, toasted, 1001)
> 2 teaspoons sugar

Add and toss to coat:
> 1 large cucumber, peeled, halved crosswise and cut into thin strips or slices

Cover and refrigerate until chilled, about 1 hour.
II. Layer in a bowl, sprinkling with salt:
> $1^1/2$ to 2 cups peeled sliced cucumbers

Place a weighted plate on top, cover, and refrigerate 2 hours. Rinse the cucumbers under cold water, drain, and pat dry. Place in a bowl and toss with:
> $1/4$ cup cider vinegar
> 1 tablespoon sugar, dissolved in
> 1 tablespoon water
> Salt and black pepper

Chill 1 to 2 hours. Serve garnished with:
> Chopped dill
> Thinly sliced Bermuda onion

CREAMY CUCUMBER SALAD
4 servings
Toss together in a colander:
> 2 medium cucumbers, peeled and thinly sliced
> 2 teaspoons salt

Let stand to drain for 45 minutes. Press the excess water out of the cucumbers and place in a bowl. Add:
> $2/3$ cup sour cream or plain yogurt
> 1 teaspoon fresh lemon juice

and toss well. Garnish with:
> 1 teaspoon chopped dill, basil, or tarragon

HEARTS OF PALM SALAD
I. Cut lengthwise into strips:
> Chilled canned hearts of palm

Serve on:
> Romaine lettuce leaves

Garnish with:
> Chopped parsley
> Paprika
> Stuffed olive slices
> Green or red bell pepper rings

Serve with:
> Vinaigrette, 572, Creamy Blue Cheese Dressing, 576, or Mayonnaise, 579

II. Dice:
> Fresh hearts of palm, 288

Sprinkle with:
> Fresh lemon juice

Serve with:
> Lime Vinaigrette, 573, or Sauce Louis, 581

JICAMA SALAD
6 to 8 servings
Peel, halve lengthwise, and cut into matchsticks:
> 1 medium jicama (about 1 pound)

Cut into $1/4$-inch slices:

**2 small cucumbers, peeled, halved lengthwise,
    and seeded**

Cut both ends off:

3 medium navel oranges

Stand the oranges on a cutting board and cut away the peel and all the white pith. Halve lengthwise, then cut crosswise into ¼-inch slices. Toss the jicama, cucumbers, and oranges in a large bowl, along with:

6 radishes, thinly sliced
1 small red onion, thinly sliced
⅓ cup fresh lime juice

Let stand for 20 minutes, then season with:

Salt to taste

Spoon the salad onto a platter and drizzle the accumulated juices on top. Sprinkle with:

2 teaspoons ground chile pepper
⅓ cup chopped cilantro

ORANGE AND ONION SALAD (SICILIAN SALAD)

4 to 6 servings

Cut both ends off:

**3 small fennel bulbs, trimmed, halved, and thinly
    sliced crosswise**
1 small red onion, thinly sliced
½ cup pitted black olives, halved

Add and toss well:

3 tablespoons thinly sliced mint leaves
2 tablespoons extra-virgin olive oil, or to taste
4 teaspoons fresh lemon juice
Coarse salt and black pepper to taste

Arrange in the center of the platter. Garnish with:

1 tablespoon thinly sliced mint leaves

THREE-PEA SALAD

6 servings

For a main-course salad, add sautéed shrimp.
Prepare the dressing for:

Asparagus Sesame Salad, 165

Cook in a large pot of boiling salted water for 2 minutes:

1 cup sugar snap peas

Add:

½ cup snow peas
½ cup fresh or frozen tiny peas, thawed

Cook 1 minute. Drain and rinse under cold water. Pat dry. Toss the peas in a bowl with the dressing and:

6 cups (8 ounces) pea shoots or bean sprouts

ABOUT POTATO SALAD

Potato salad is best prepared from scrubbed potatoes that are cooked in their jackets until just soft enough to pierce with a fork. Peel and dress while still warm. For mayonnaise- and cream-based dressings, allow the potatoes to cool slightly. Small red waxy potatoes hold their shape and don't crumble when sliced or diced, but medium-sized mature Idahos are satisfactory for potato salads. ➤ For hot-weather picnics, use a vinaigrette, to avoid the chance of dangerous spoilage.

POTATO SALAD

4 servings

I. Boil in salted water until tender:

1 pound waxy potatoes

Drain; when cool enough to handle, slice. Marinate in:

⅓ cup Vinaigrette, 572, heated

Serve warm or cold. Just before serving, fold in gently:

1 tablespoon chopped parsley
1 tablespoon chopped chives or grated onion

II. Cook and slice the potatoes as above. Marinate in:

3 tablespoons Vinaigrette, 572, or chicken broth

Chop or slice and add a mixture of any of the following:

**Hard-boiled eggs, 194, onions, olives, pickles, celery
    with leaves, cucumbers, and/or capers**

along with:

1 to 2 teaspoons salt
Paprika
Pinch of ground red pepper
(2 teaspoons prepared horseradish)

Refrigerate for at least 1 hour. Add:

**¼ cup mayonnaise, Boiled Salad Dressing, 577,
    or sour cream**

Refrigerate 1 hour longer. Before serving, toss in:

(Coarsely chopped watercress)

AMERICAN POTATO SALAD

6 to 8 servings

Customize potato salad with sweet pickle relish, black olives, crumbled bacon, mint, pimientos, coarse-grain mustard, or halved grape or cherry tomatoes.
Boil in salted water until tender:

2 pounds waxy potatoes

Drain. Peel if desired and cut into bite-sized pieces. Toss the warm potatoes in a medium bowl, with:

1 celery rib, diced
2 tablespoons minced onion or 2 scallions, minced
(¼ cup minced parsley)
(3 hard-boiled eggs, 194, diced)
¾ cup mayonnaise
2 tablespoons red wine vinegar
(1 tablespoon coarse-grain or yellow mustard)
(1 tablespoon sweet pickle relish)
Salt and black pepper to taste

Cover and refrigerate until chilled.

GERMAN POTATO SALAD

6 servings

Boil in salted water until tender:

2 pounds waxy potatoes

Drain, peel, and slice. Cook in a skillet:

**4 slices bacon, minced, or 2 tablespoons bacon
    drippings**

Remove bacon from pan and set aside. Add to the bacon fat and cook until golden:

$^1/_4$ to $^1/_2$ cup chopped onion
$^1/_4$ cup chopped celery

Add:

$^1/_4$ cup chopped dill pickle

In a small saucepan, heat to a boil:

$^1/_4$ cup water or chicken broth
$^1/_2$ cup cider vinegar
$^1/_2$ teaspoon sugar
$^1/_2$ teaspoon salt
$^1/_8$ teaspoon paprika
($^1/_4$ to $^1/_2$ teaspoon dry mustard)

Combine all the ingredients in skillet, and fold into the potatoes. Serve at once warm, garnished with:

Chopped parsley or chives

ABOUT TOMATO SALADS

Please read About Tomatoes, 311. In preparing tomatoes for salad, always cut out the core. Good texture is as important as good flavor. Homegrown or vine-ripened tomatoes are infinitely superior to those picked green and allowed to mature on their way to the supermarket. Use the latter for Cold Stuffed Tomatoes, 173, where they can be somewhat redeemed with a spicy filling. Plum or Roma, the pear-shaped Italian variety, which has a distinctive mellow flavor, makes an excellent substitute. Another way to deal with out-of-season tomatoes is to choose, instead, grape tomatoes. Halved or whole, these small varieties also lend themselves to decorative uses. Tomatoes are most flavorful served at room temperature.

TOMATO SALAD

6 to 8 servings

Arrange, overlapping, around or across a chilled platter:

6 large tomatoes, cut into $^1/_2$-inch-thick slices or wedges

If desired, alternate with the tomato slices:

(1 red, Bermuda, or Vidalia onion, thinly sliced)

Drizzle over the tomatoes:

$^1/_2$ cup extra-virgin olive oil and splash of balsamic vinegar, or Vinaigrette, 572

Sprinkle with:

$^1/_4$ cup minced parsley or basil
Salt and black pepper to taste

TOMATO AND MOZZARELLA SALAD (INSALATA CAPRESE)

4 to 6 servings

Arrange, alternating the slices, on a platter:

4 large ripe tomatoes, cut into $^1/_2$-inch slices
12 ounces mozzarella, cut into $^1/_4$-inch slices

Sprinkle with:

$1^1/_2$ cups basil leaves, chopped

Drizzle over the salad:

$^1/_2$ cup extra-virgin olive oil

Sprinkle with:

Salt to taste

BREAD AND TOMATO SALAD (PANZANELLA)

6 to 8 servings

Preheat the oven to 350°F. Spread on a baking sheet:

5 cups 1-inch bread cubes (from a 1-pound fresh or stale loaf Italian or French bread)

Bake, shaking the pan once or twice, until browned, 10 to 15 minutes. Meanwhile, whisk together in a small bowl:

$^1/_3$ cup extra-virgin olive oil
$^1/_3$ cup red wine vinegar
3 tablespoons fresh lemon juice
3 tablespoons minced parsley
1 teaspoon minced garlic
Salt and cracked black pepper

Toss the croutons in a salad bowl with:

2 cucumbers, seeded and cut into $^1/_2$-inch cubes
2 large tomatoes, cut into $^1/_2$-inch cubes
1 medium red onion, cut into $^1/_2$-inch cubes
$^1/_3$ cup pitted and halved black olives
$^1/_3$ cup torn basil leaves

Add the dressing and toss well. Remove to a large platter or bowl. Sprinkle with:

($^1/_2$ cup Parmesan shavings)

Serve at once.

ABOUT FRUIT SALADS

Fruit salads can be served as a first course, a side, a main dish when mixed with protein, or a last course instead of dessert. ➤ To prevent browning, toss fruit with a lightly acidic solution, see Acidulated Water, 957, or sprinkle with lemon juice. Make fruit salads as close to serving time as possible. Choose fruits with a hard, crisp texture when it is necessary to mix the salad in advance.

Using fresh fruits in season, 208, or high-quality dried fruits will ensure the best salads. As a general rule, ➤ keep dressings fairly tart for fruit salads served with a meal.

Add nuts, crisp vegetables, chicken, beef, pork, or seafood. As a change from the usual base of salad greens, serve them where suitable in baskets, cups, or cases as described on 230. See more fruit salads in the Fruit chapter, 224.

WALDORF SALAD

4 servings

The addition of $^1/_2$ cup miniature marshmallows is popular with children. Combine in a medium bowl:

1 cup diced celery
1 cup diced cored, peeled apples
$^1/_2$ cup coarsely chopped walnuts
($^1/_2$ cup seedless red grapes, halved)

Stir in:

$^1/_2$ to $^3/_4$ cup mayonnaise

Serve at room temperature or chilled.

SPICY WATERMELON SALAD

4 to 6 servings

Stir together in a small bowl:

$1/2$ teaspoon chili powder
$1/2$ teaspoon salt, or to taste
$1/8$ teaspoon ground red pepper, or to taste

Toss together in a serving bowl:

6 cups $1/2$-inch pieces seeded watermelon
$1/2$ small red onion, diced
1 small jalapeño pepper, seeded and diced
3 tablespoons fresh lime juice, or to taste
2 tablespoons chopped cilantro or parsley

Sprinkle with the spice mixture and toss well. Serve at room temperature.

PEAR, WALNUT, AND ENDIVE SALAD

6 servings

Prepare:

Vinaigrette, 572, using walnut oil

Toss with enough vinaigrette to moisten:

4 Belgian endives, or 1 head frisée, trimmed
2 large bunches watercress, tough stems trimmed

Divide and arrange on 6 plates:

1 large Comice pear or Granny Smith apple, cored and sliced
(6 fresh figs, halved)

Sprinkle with:

$1/2$ cup walnuts, toasted, 1001
12 ounces Gorgonzola, Roquefort, or feta, crumbled
(Additional vinaigrette)

MELON CUPS

Cut a small cantaloupe or other melon in half, 230. Remove the seeds and scallop or zigzag the edges, if desired, for a more decorative effect. Refrigerate until cold. Just before serving, fill with:

Chicken or Turkey Salad, 163, Curried Chicken or Turkey Salad, 164, or a fruit salad, 169–170

ABOUT BEAN SALADS

The mild flavor and chewy texture of cooked legumes is a perfect backdrop for a variety of stick-to-the-ribs salads. To cook dried legumes, see 253. ➤ As a general rule, 1 cup dried beans yields 3 cups cooked beans. Canned beans can easily be substituted for dried; rinse and drain before using. ➤ One 16-ounce can of beans, drained, equals $1 1/2$ to 2 cups beans.

BEAN SALAD

4 to 6 servings

Kidney, navy, or lima beans are the basis of this salad, but it is excellent made with lentils or edamame.

Place in a bowl:

$2 1/2$ to 3 cups cooked beans, rinsed and drained if canned

($1/2$ cup diced red onion)
(2 tablespoons chopped parsley)

Toss with:

$1/4$ cup Vinaigrette, 572, or $2/3$ cup Thousand Island Dressing, 576

Season with:

Salt and black pepper to taste

Garnish with:

Chopped chives or parsley

THREE-BEAN SALAD

4 to 6 servings

Combine in a large bowl:

2 cups cooked kidney beans
1 cup $1/2$-inch pieces cooked green beans
1 cup $1/2$-inch pieces cooked yellow wax beans
$1/2$ cup chopped green bell pepper
$1/2$ cup chopped onion

Prepare:

Sweet-and-Sour Vinaigrette, 574

Pour the dressing over the bean mixture and toss well to coat. Cover and refrigerate for at least 6 hours, or overnight. Serve cold.

BLACK BEAN SALAD

6 to 8 servings

Prepare:

Basil Vinaigrette, 573, or Vinaigrette, 572

Dress in a serving bowl until thoroughly coated:

3 cups cooked black beans
$1 1/2$ cups corn kernels, rinsed and drained if canned
8 ounces cherry tomatoes, halved
1 cup chopped red onion

Garnish with:

Fresh cilantro or basil

CHICKPEA SALAD

4 servings

Roast your own peppers or use drained, canned ones. Combine in a medium bowl:

2 cups cooked chickpeas
2 red bell peppers, roasted, 292, peeled, and diced, or $1/2$ cup diced bottled roasted red peppers
$1/2$ small red onion, minced
$1/4$ cup minced parsley
$2 1/2$ tablespoons fresh lemon juice
2 tablespoons extra-virgin olive oil
2 teaspoons Dijon mustard
1 to 2 garlic cloves, minced
Salt and black pepper to taste

Line a platter with:

4 cups shredded chicory, escarole, or romaine lettuce

Spoon the chickpea salad on top.

WARM LENTIL AND POTATO SALAD
8 servings
Combine in large bowl:
>   4¹/₂ cups warm cooked green or brown lentils, 257
>   1 pound warm boiled waxy potatoes, 295, cut into
>   small cubes
>   ¹/₂ cup thinly sliced scallions
>   ¹/₂ cup chopped parsley

Whisk together in a small saucepan:
>   ¹/₄ cup extra-virgin olive oil
>   3 tablespoons sherry vinegar
>   1 garlic clove, minced
>   ¹/₂ teaspoon salt
>   ¹/₈ teaspoon black pepper

Heat, stirring, until warm. Pour over the salad and serve.

ABOUT GRAIN AND RICE SALADS

Grain salads are best made with freshly cooked or leftover rice or other grains and dressed while still warm, if possible, so that the rice or grain soaks up the maximum amount of flavor. Please read Grains, 344. ➤ As a general rule, use 3 cups cooked grains for roughly an equal amount of all the other ingredients, and use about ¹/₂ cup dressing.

RICE SALAD WITH CHICKEN AND BLACK OLIVES
6 to 8 servings
This recipe can be used as a blueprint for many other rice salads. Stir together in a medium bowl:
>   1¹/₂ cups diced cooked chicken
>   ¹/₂ cup diced peach (about 1 medium)
>   ¹/₂ cup coarsely chopped pitted black olives
>   ¹/₂ cup diced red or yellow bell peppers
>   ¹/₂ cup Fresh Herb Vinaigrette, 572
>   3 cups cooked long-grain white rice

Toss well. Serve warm, at room temperature, or chilled.

WILD RICE SALAD WITH SAUSAGE
4 to 6 servings
Whisk together in a small bowl:
>   2 tablespoons white wine vinegar or champagne
>   vinegar
>   1 tablespoon Dijon mustard
>   ¹/₃ cup olive oil
>   Salt and black pepper

Cook in a skillet over medium heat, breaking up lumps with a spoon:
>   1 pound sweet Italian sausage, casings removed

Drain on paper towels. Let cool, then remove to a large bowl. Add and mix well:
>   2¹/₄ cups cooked wild rice, rinsed and drained
>   2¹/₄ cups cooked long-grain white rice
>   3 ribs celery with leaves, thinly sliced
>   (2 cups seedless green or red grapes, halved)

Add the dressing and toss well to coat. Taste and adjust the seasonings. Serve at room temperature.

BROWN RICE SALAD WITH DATES AND ORANGES
4 to 6 servings
Stir together in a large bowl:
>   3 cups cooked brown rice
>   16 dates, pitted and diced
>   2 large navel oranges, sectioned, 223, each segment
>   cut into thirds
>   2 scallions, minced
>   ¹/₄ cup dark or golden raisins
>   ¹/₄ cup minced parsley
>   ¹/₄ cup extra-virgin olive oil
>   2 tablespoons fresh lemon juice
>   ¹/₄ teaspoon ground cinnamon
>   ¹/₄ teaspoon ground cumin
>   Pinch of crushed red pepper flakes
>   Salt to taste

Serve at room temperature.

ABOUT PASTA SALADS

When cooking pasta for a salad, cook it al dente—tender yet still firm to the bite. Rinse in cool water to rid them of excess starch and to stop the cooking, then mix with the dressing. If adding vegetables or chopped fresh herbs, stir in just before serving to maintain texture and color.

In general, ➤ 8 ounces dry pasta will yield 3 to 4 cups of cooked pasta, enough for 6 to 8 servings. Pasta salads can be made ahead and refrigerated but are best served at room temperature. Before serving, taste, adjust the seasoning, and add more dressing if needed.

Try substituting different fresh herbs, mixing in yellow and red tomatoes, or adding diced or shredded cheese, or diced cooked meat, such as ham, chicken, or lamb, to the mix. Use macaroni, penne, fusilli, wagon wheel, farafelle, or other short pastas. ➤ If you prefer a creamy pasta salad, substitute ¹/₂ cup mayonnaise for the vinaigrette. Small vegetable- or cheese-filled pastas such as tortellini or ravioli can also be the basis of a tasty pasta salad.

PASTA SALAD
4 to 6 servings
Place in a large bowl while still warm:
>   8 ounces elbow macaroni, penne, or other pasta,
>   cooked al dente, rinsed, and drained

Combine with:
>   3 tablespoons extra-virgin olive oil
>   3 tablespoons white wine vinegar
>   (2 tablespoons chicken stock or broth)
>   Salt and black pepper

or:
>   ¹/₂ cup Fresh Herb Vinaigrette, 572

Let cool to room temperature. Stir in:
>   24 cherry or grape tomatoes, halved
>   (¹/₂ cup finely diced red onion)
>   12 black olives, pitted and chopped
>   ¹/₄ cup minced basil

(¹/₄ cup minced parsley)

2 tablespoons minced mint

1 teaspoon finely grated lemon zest

Adjust the seasonings. Serve at room temperature.

PASTA SALAD WITH PESTO

8 to 12 servings

Cook in a large pot of boiling salted water for 2 minutes:

1 large bunch broccoli, cut into small florets

2 medium carrots, diced

³/₄ cup fresh or frozen peas

Remove the vegetables with a large strainer and cool under cold running water. Return the water to a boil. Add and cook until al dente:

1 pound penne

Drain and rinse under cold running water. Combine the pasta and cooked vegetables in a large serving bowl, along with:

1 red or yellow bell pepper, finely diced

1 medium red onion, finely diced

Toss with:

Pesto, 569

PASTA SALAD WITH GRILLED CHICKEN

8 to 10 servings

Add the avocado just before serving.

Combine well in a large serving bowl:

3 boneless, skinless chicken breast halves (about 1 pound), grilled, 427, and cut into thin strips

1 pound fusilli pasta, cooked until al dente, rinsed, and drained

1 large avocado, pitted, peeled, and finely diced

3 medium tomatoes, seeded and chopped

4 scallions, thinly sliced

2 garlic cloves, finely minced

¹/₄ cup drained capers

¹/₄ cup chopped basil, cilantro, or parsley

¹/₄ cup extra-virgin olive oil

2 tablespoons fresh lemon juice

Salt and black pepper to taste

PASTA SALAD WITH SHRIMP

8 servings

Toss together in a large bowl:

1 pound penne pasta, cooked al dente, rinsed, and drained

¹/₃ cup extra-virgin olive oil

1 garlic clove, minced

Add:

1 pound medium shrimp, boiled, 385, peeled, and deveined

4 red bell peppers, roasted, 292, peeled, and cut into strips, or 1 cup bottled roasted red peppers cut into strips

¹/₂ cup pitted black olives

¹/₂ cup chopped parsley

¹/₄ cup pine nuts, toasted, 1001

Pinch of ground red pepper

Salt and black pepper to taste

Toss well to coat and combine.

CALICO MACARONI SALAD

5 servings

Whisk together in a medium bowl:

1¹/₂ tablespoons fresh lemon juice or 2 tablespoons red wine vinegar

1 tablespoon vegetable oil

Add:

4 ounces (1 cup) elbow macaroni, cooked al dente, rinsed, and drained

Cover and chill for 2 to 3 hours. Add to the salad and toss well:

1 teaspoon minced onion or 2 tablespoons chopped chives

1 cup diced celery

1 cup minced parsley

¹/₂ cup chopped pimiento-stuffed olives

³/₄ teaspoon salt

Black pepper to taste

3 tablespoons sour cream

Or substitute for the mixture above:

5 tablespoons Pesto, 569

CREAMY MACARONI SALAD FOR A CROWD

Sixteen to twenty ¹/₂-cup servings

Combine in a bowl:

1 pound (4 cups) elbow macaroni, cooked al dente, rinsed, and drained

1 red bell pepper, cored, seeded, and diced

1 green bell pepper, cored, seeded, and diced

2 carrots, diced

1 small red onion, diced

¹/₂ cup chopped parsley

Add and toss to coat:

Creamy Dressing for Coleslaw, 578

ABOUT VEGETABLE AND FRUIT CUPS

Salads presented in bright, colorful fresh vegetable or fruit cups are feasts for the eyes as well as the palate. Use hollowed-out avocados, tomatoes, artichokes, melons, or lettuce and cabbage leaves.

STUFFED ARTICHOKES

Prepare and cook, 247:

Artichokes

Chill, then remove the inedible choke and leaves around it, 247. Fill with:

Tuna Salad, 164, Seafood Salad, 165, or Ratatouille Provençale, 274

AVOCADO CUPS

Halve and pit, 165:

Avocados

Sprinkle with:
> **Fresh lemon juice**

Fill the hollows with:
> **Seafood Salad I or II, 165, using lump crabmeat or**
> **lobster meat, or Shrimp Salad, 165**

CUCUMBER CUPS

Peel or, for a more decorative effect, if the cucumbers are not waxed, score the skin with a fork, shown below.
> **Small cucumbers, chilled**

Cut the cucumbers lengthwise in half, scoop out the seeds, and fill the halves. Alternatively, slice the whole cucumbers crosswise into 2- to 3-inch pieces and hollow the pieces from one end, leaving enough on the bottom to prevent the filling from falling out.

Fill with:
> **A chicken salad, 163–164, any seafood salad,**
> **164–165, a rice salad, 171, or other**
> **small-grain salad**

Serve the cucumbers on:
> **Shredded lettuce or watercress**

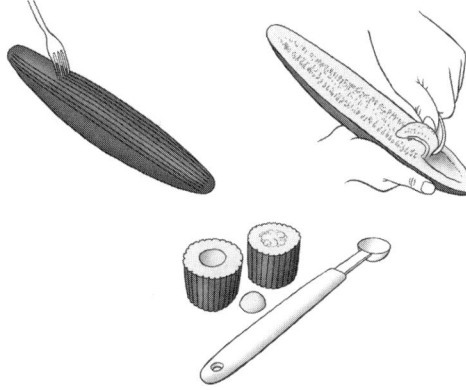

Scoring and seeding cucumbers and making cucumber cups

COLD STUFFED TOMATOES

Almost any finely chopped salad goes well in tomatoes. Whether or not to peel the tomatoes before stuffing is a personal choice these days, but there was a time when a bit of tomato skin was as much out of place at a dinner table as a bowie knife. Peeled tomatoes are more delicate and best used to hold loosely packed vegetable salads, such as the cucumber and asparagus salads listed below.

To prepare tomato cups, peel them, 311, if you choose. Slice off the round top of each tomato. Hollow them out, being careful to leave a wall thick enough to support the filling. Invert and drain for 20 minutes. Chill them and fill the hollows with one of the suggested fillings below. You can also cut the tomatoes crosswise in half in a zigzag fashion and fill them sandwich-style as shown below, or fill the hollowed-out halves separately.

FILLINGS FOR STUFFED TOMATOES:
> **A rice salad, 171**
> **Couscous with Pine Nuts and Raisins, 362**
> **A coleslaw, 161**
> **Tabbouleh, 362**
> **Seafood Salad, 165**
> **Lobster or Shrimp Salad, 165**
> **Egg Salad, 164**
> **A chicken salad, 163–164**
> **Tuna Salad, 164**
> **Cottage cheese or soft cream cheese flavored with**
> **fresh herbs, 179**
> **A cucumber salad, 167**
> **Asparagus Sesame Salad, 165**

ABOUT MOLDED SALADS

Molded salads can be prepared a day or so in advance and kept chilled in the refrigerator. These salads depend on gelatin to hold their shape, so ➤ please read about Gelatin, 987. Molds may be filled dry, but a jellied mixture is more readily removed when the molds have been moistened with water. If the mixture is not a clarified one, you may lightly brush the mold with oil. Be sure to sample your salad before pouring it into the mold, and season to taste. ➤ Undersalt if it is to be held for 24 hours, as too much salt will loosen the jelly. ➤ Never freeze molded salads.

Before adding ingredients to gelatin, drain them well and chill. ➤ One envelope (2¼ teaspoons) gelatin will thicken 2 cups liquid with or without 1½ cups solids. To intensify the flavor of a molded fruit salad, substitute 1 to 2 tablespoons of sweet wine or liquor for the liquid in the recipe; add it when the gelatin has dissolved and the liquid has cooled.

Certain ingredients naturally come to rest either at the top or bottom of a jelling salad, and you can achieve interesting layered effects by manipulating nuts, fruits, and vegetables of different weights and porosity. Put them in a very slightly jelled mixture—of egg-white consistency—and let them find their own levels. Apple cubes, banana slices, grapefruit sections, pear slices, strawberry halves, nuts, and marshmallows will all float in gelatin, while fresh orange slices, fresh grapes, and canned apricots, cherries, peaches, pears, canned pineapple, plums, and raspberries will settle lower in the mold. ➤ Fresh or frozen pineapple, kiwi, papaya, honeydew, figs, or ginger—and their juices—cannot be added to a gelatin salad. They contain enzymes that inhibit jelling. Canned pineapple has been cooked and may be used; or boil fresh pineapple and its juice before using.

Many of the recipes that follow can be made either in a large mold or in individual molds. Use ring molds if you wish to fill the centers. ➤ To unmold gelatins or aspics, have ready a chilled plate. Moisten its surface, which will prevent the molded salad from sticking and enable you to center the mold more easily. Use a thin knife at several points around the edge of the mold to release the vacuum. Dip the mold in warm water for 5 to 10 seconds. Dry the outside of the mold, cover with the serving plate, and invert. Shake or tap to release the salad. If the mold does not release, shake the mold lightly, holding it tightly against the serving plate.

ABOUT ASPICS

Please read About Gelatin, 987.

The most delicious aspics of all are reduced chicken and veal stocks, 117. Clarified strong meat, fish, and fowl stocks with added gelatin are next in favor—but the average home cook seldom clarifies their own. Instead, they depend on canned consommé for their aspics. ➤ Dry wine and liquor are fine additions to your aspic: 1 or 2 tablespoons per cup of liquid is sufficient to heighten the flavor. Substitute the wine for part of the liquid called for in the recipe, ➤ and add it when the gelatin has been dissolved and the liquid is beginning to cool. Dry white wine or dry sherry goes well with savory aspics such as chicken and veal.

We have omitted clarifying the stock, 116, opting for ease of cooking rather than an absolutely clear aspic.

BASIC SAVORY ASPIC

6 to 8 servings

Please read About Gelatin, 987. In addition to meat, poultry, or seafood, ingredients such as chopped raw celery, pitted olives, or toasted nuts make nice additions to this aspic.

Combine in a medium bowl and let stand for 5 minutes:

1 envelope (2¼ teaspoons) unflavored gelatin
¼ cup cold water

Add and stir until the gelatin is dissolved:

¼ cup boiling seafood, poultry, or meat stock
or broth

Stir in:

1½ cups cold seafood, poultry, or meat stock or broth
2 tablespoons white wine vinegar or 1½ tablespoons fresh lemon juice, or to taste
Salt to taste

Chill the aspic. When it is the consistency of raw egg whites, stir in:

1½ cups diced savory ingredients of your choice—such as cooked shrimp, lobster, or other seafood if using seafood stock; cooked chicken or turkey if using poultry stock; cooked beef or lamb if using meat stock

Wet a 4-cup mold or bowl. Pour in the aspic, cover, and refrigerate until set, about 3 hours. Unmold the aspic, 173, onto a platter and surround with:

Lettuce leaves

Serve cold, with or without:

Mayonnaise, Russian Horseradish Cream, 581, or plain yogurt

TOMATO ASPIC

8 to 10 servings

I. Please read About Gelatin, 987. Simmer in a medium saucepan for 30 minutes:

4 cups tomato juice
½ cup tomato puree
½ cup chopped onion
2 celery ribs, chopped
2 tablespoons fresh lemon juice
(1 tablespoon balsamic vinegar)
2 teaspoons sugar
2 teaspoons dried basil or tarragon or 2 tablespoons minced fresh herbs
1 teaspoon salt
1 teaspoon whole black peppercorns
1 whole clove
1 bay leaf

Combine in a large bowl and let stand for 5 minutes to soften the gelatin:

2 envelopes (4½ teaspoons) unflavored gelatin
½ cup cold water

Strain the hot tomato juice mixture. Pour enough of it into the gelatin to make 4 cups. Add water if necessary to bring it to 4 cups. Chill the aspic. When it is the consistency of raw egg whites, add 1 to 1½ cups of any combination of the following:

1 avocado, pitted, peeled, and cut into ½-inch cubes
1 cup diced yellow bell peppers
1 jalapeño pepper, seeded and minced
1 cup lump crabmeat, flaked, picked over for shells and cartilage
1 tablespoon chopped cilantro or basil

Wet a 6- to 8-cup mold or bowl, pour in the aspic, cover, and refrigerate until set, 6 to 8 hours. Unmold the aspic, 173, onto a platter and garnish with:

Sliced vegetables, such as bell peppers or scallions

II. QUICK TOMATO ASPIC

8 servings

Please read About Gelatin, 987.

Combine in a large bowl and let stand 5 minutes:

1 envelope (2¼ teaspoons) unflavored gelatin
2 tablespoons cold water

Add and stir to dissolve:

2 tablespoons boiling water

Add:

One 10¾-ounce can condensed tomato soup

Heat:

2 cups tomato juice

Dissolve in it:

One 3-ounce package lemon- or lime-flavored gelatin

Add to the gelatin mixture, along with:

⅛ teaspoon salt

Wet a 6- to 8-cup mold or bowl, pour in the aspic, cover, and refrigerate until set, about 3 hours. Unmold the aspic, 173, onto a platter.

GELATIN FRUIT SALAD
6 servings

Please read About Gelatin, 987. Do not use fresh or frozen pineapple, or the gelatin will not set.
Combine in a large bowl and let stand 5 minutes to soften the gelatin:

1 envelope (2¼ teaspoons) unflavored gelatin
½ cup cold water

Add and stir to dissolve:

1 cup boiling water or fruit juice

Add:

4 to 6 tablespoons sugar, or less if is using sweetened
    fruit juice
⅛ teaspoon salt
¼ cup fresh lemon juice

Let cool to room temperature, then chill. When the mixture is the consistency of raw egg whites, stir in:

1½ cups drained cut-up fruit

Wet a 4-cup mold or bowl, pour in the gelatin mixture, cover, and refrigerate until set, about 3 hours. Unmold the salad, 173, onto a platter. Serve with:

Cream (Chantilly) Mayonnaise, 580

GOLDEN GLOW SALAD
8 to 10 servings

Please read About Gelatin, 987. Drain, reserving the juice:

1 cup canned crushed pineapple

Heat to a boil:

Reserved pineapple juice plus enough water to yield
    1¾ cup
½ teaspoon salt

Dissolve in the hot liquid:

One 3-ounce package lemon-flavored gelatin

Cool, then chill. When the gelatin mixture is the consistency of egg whites, stir in the pineapple, and:

2 cups grated or ground carrots
(½ cup chopped pecans)

Wet a 3- to 4-cup mold or bowl, pour in the gelatin mixture, cover, and refrigerate until set, about 4 hours. Unmold the salad, 173, onto a platter lined with:

Lettuce leaves

Serve with:

Mayonnaise, sour cream, or plain yogurt

MOLDED CRANBERRY SALAD
6 to 8 servings

Please read About Gelatin, 987. Combine in a large bowl:

1 envelope (2¼ teaspoons) unflavored gelatin
3 tablespoons cold water

Let stand 5 minutes.
Meanwhile, cook:

2 cups cranberries

in:

1 cup boiling water, orange, or cranberry juice

until the skins pop. Add and cook, stirring to dissolve the sugar, for 5 minutes:

½ cup sugar
¼ teaspoon salt

Add the gelatin mixture. Cool, then chill. If desired, when the gelatin it is about to set, fold in:

(⅔ cup drained canned crushed pineapple)
(½ cup diced celery)
(⅓ cup chopped pecans)

Wet a 6-cup mold or bowl, pour in the gelatin mixture, cover, and refrigerate until set, about 4 hours. Unmold the salad, 173, onto a platter. Serve with:

Mayonnaise

PINEAPPLE ORANGE GELATIN SALAD
6 to 8 servings

Please read About Gelatin, 987. Chicken stock and mustard make this gelatin salad a wonderful addition to a menu, especially where ham or turkey is the main attraction. Do not use fresh pineapple, or the gelatin will not set.
Bring to a boil:

½ cup water
½ cup chicken stock or broth

Whisk together in a medium bowl:

One 3-ounce package pineapple-flavored gelatin
¾ teaspoon dry mustard
⅛ teaspoon ground ginger

Add the boiling stock and lightly whisk until the gelatin is dissolved. Stir in:

1 cup cold water
¾ teaspoon Dijon mustard

Cool, then chill until the gelatin is as thick as raw egg whites, 1 to 1½ hours. Fold in:

¾ cup drained canned pineapple chunks
¾ cup drained mandarin orange sections
4 teaspoons chopped mint

Wet a 3- to 4-cup bowl or mold, then pour in the gelatin mixture and refrigerate until set, about 3 hours. Unmold, 173, or serve from the bowl.

ABOUT SAVORY MOUSSES

Please read About Molded Salads, 173, and About Gelatin, 987. Mousses differ from the previous gelatin salads in their lack of transparency—due to the inclusion of one or two additional ingredients: cream and egg. A **mousseline** may be either a kind of pastry or, as in this section, a mousse confected with whipped cream. For Salmon Mousse, see 85.

CUCUMBER MOUSSE
4 servings

Please read About Gelatin, 987. Combine in a small saucepan and let stand 5 minutes to soften the gelatin:

1¼ teaspoons unflavored gelatin
3 tablespoons cold water

Stir to dissolve the gelatin over low heat. Add:

2 teaspoons cider vinegar or fresh lime or lemon juice
1 teaspoon minced onion

$^3/_4$ **teaspoon salt**

$^1/_4$ **teaspoon paprika**

Chill until gelatin is the consistency of raw egg whites. Drain well:

1 cup peeled, seeded, grated cucumbers

Whip in a medium bowl until stiff:

$^1/_2$ **cup heavy cream**

Gradually fold the gelatin mixture into the cream. Fold in the cucumbers. Rinse four 4-ounce ramekins or molds with cold water, fill them with the mousse. Chill until firm, about 3 hours. Unmold the mousse, 173, onto a plate.

LOBSTER MOUSSE

8 to 10 servings

Please read About Gelatin, 987. Combine in the top of a double boiler or a heatproof bowl and let stand for 5 minutes to soften the gelatin:

1 envelope (2$^1/_4$ teaspoons) unflavored gelatin

$^1/_4$ **cup cold water**

Place the double-boiler top on its base or set the bowl over, not in, boiling water and stir to dissolve the gelatin. Remove from the heat.

Combine in a medium bowl:

$^3/_4$ **cup minced celery**

1$^1/_2$ cups cooked lobster meat, 382

($^2/_3$ cup minced apple)

Season with:

Salt and paprika

Combine in a medium bowl:

$^3/_4$ **cup mayonnaise**

3 tablespoons fresh lemon juice

(A few drops of hot pepper sauce)

Stir in the gelatin. Whip until stiff, then fold into the gelatin mixture:

$^1/_3$ **cup heavy cream**

Fold the lobster mixture into the gelatin-cream mixture. Place the mousse in an oiled 9-inch ring mold. Chill until set, about 3 hours. Unmold the mousse, 173, onto a platter. Garnish with:

Watercress

Thin lemon slices

SANDWICHES, WRAPS, AND PIZZA

People on the move keep green the legend of Lord Sandwich, whose mania for gambling, from which he didn't want to be disturbed long enough to eat, gave the world the convenient concoction that bears his name. Though the Earl was probably responsible for the name, he certainly didn't invent it, as almost every culture has assembled something similar.

Sandwiches range greatly in size and complexity. Don't neglect the Tea Sandwiches, 185–187, where many smaller versions are found.

ABOUT BREAD FOR SANDWICHES

The number of sandwiches to a loaf of bread is hard to gauge exactly because the size and shape of sandwiches as well as breads vary. However, ➤ from a loaf of sandwich bread weighing anywhere from 1 to 1^1/$_2$ pounds, you can expect 18 to 20 slices. Besides sandwich bread, there are numerous other breads available for making sandwiches: tortillas, lavash, or other flatbreads work well for wraps. Pita, ciabatta, foccacia, croissants, brioche, and baguettes are good choices for stuffed sandwiches. Trimmed and cut sandwich or cocktail party breads, or sweet quick breads, are the perfect base for dainty tea sandwiches. Don't be afraid to experiment with breads and fillings, but do consider the flavor of both when improvising. Canapés, 86, are best made using a thin slice of firm bread. ➤ Have all spreads at room temperature to avoid pulling or tearing the bread.

To avoid raggedy sandwiches, use a finely textured bread. Otherwise, try freezing ordinary bread before cutting. This procedure makes for more practical handling throughout, particularly in preparing rolled shapes, which should be thin and made of fresh bread. Other sandwiches are easier to make if the bread is one day old. Remember, though, that all bread that has been frozen dries out quickly after thawing and that precautions should be taken to keep the sandwiches as moist as possible.

ABOUT PREPARING AND KEEPING SANDWICHES

A few preliminary steps help toward serving sandwiches in prime condition. Have ready foil, moistened and wrung-out paper towels, plastic wrap, plastic bags, or wax paper for wrapping the sandwiches immediately. When preparing sandwiches in advance, especially sandwiches that include watery materials like lettuce, be sure that any moist or juicy filling is put on bread that is spread to the edges with a firm layer of butter or mayonnaise, so that the bread will not get soggy. Most sandwiches are best served within 4 hours of being made, especially if they contain greens, tomatoes, or other fresh vegetables. ➤ When making sandwiches to be eaten later (as for a lunch box), keep them from becoming too soggy by packing additions like tomato, lettuce, and pickle slices in separate plastic bags. The extras can be added to the sandwiches just before eating. For lunch box or brown bag sandwiches, use less perishable spreads and fillings, such as cheese, cold cuts, nut butters, jelly, honey butter, or cream cheese spreads. When making sandwiches in quantity, ➤ save time by setting up an assembly line. Line up the bread slices in a row. Place dabs of mayonnaise or butter on one row, then fill the next. Do the final spreading by bringing fillings and butters to the edges of the bread. If you need to make a large number of sandwiches in advance, arrange them on a tray, separating the layers with wax paper. Cover with a final layer of wax paper. Lay slightly moistened paper towels on top to introduce moisture. Wrap the tray loosely with plastic wrap and refrigerate.

FILLINGS AND DRESSINGS FOR SANDWICHES AND WRAPS

ROAST BEEF
Basic: lettuce/sliced tomatoes/mustard or mayonnaise
Watercress/red onion/mayonnaise/black pepper
Lettuce/Swiss/Green Goddess Dressing, 576
Red Onion Marmelade, 949/Thousand Island
    Dressing, 576
Sun-dried tomatoes/Roasted Red Pepper Dressing, 574
Lettuce/Swiss/mustard
Roasted red peppers
Lettuce/feta/Garlic Mayonnaise, 581

ROAST PORK
Basic: lettuce/sweet pickles/mustard or mayonnaise
Coleslaw, 161/Barbecue Sauce, 586
Arugula or watercress/tomatoes/Garlic Mayonnaise, 581
Thinly sliced red onion/Apple or Green Tomato Chutney,
    951, or Fruit Salsa, 572/butter

HAM
Basic: lettuce/sliced tomatoes/Swiss cheese/mustard
Cheddar/sweet pickles/mustard or butter
Swiss/Chow-Chow, 947/mustard
Cranberry sauce/butter
Havarti or cream cheese/Apple or Green Tomato Chutney, 951
Gruyère/Garlic Butter, 559
Lettuce/Brie/mustard

SLICED CHICKEN OR TURKEY
Basic: lettuce/sliced tomatoes/mayonnaise
Stuffing/Whole Berry Cranberry Sauce 221, or cranberry sauce
Lettuce/bacon/Cheddar/mayonnaise or Thousand Island Dressing, 576
Shredded lettuce/chopped tomato/Hummus, 74
Radicchio and prosciutto/Garlic Mayonnaise, 581
Thinly sliced cucumbers/thinly sliced onion/butter or Garlic and Walnut Sauce, 568
Sprouts/sliced avocados/Honey Mustard Vinaigrette, 573
Grilled onions/Barbecue Sauce, 586
Sun-dried tomatoes/sliced black olives/Pesto Sauce, 569

CHICKEN OR TURKEY SALAD
Basic: lettuce/sliced tomatoes
Thinly sliced radishes and scallions/butter
Bibb or Boston lettuce/sliced avocados
Sliced scallions/chopped cashews/mango chutney
Sliced green grapes/butter or Orange Butter, 559

EGG SALAD OR TUNA SALAD
Basic: lettuce/sliced tomatoes
Sun-dried tomatoes/Tapenade, 75
Lettuce/thinly sliced green and black olives
Roasted red peppers, 292
Bibb or Boston lettuce/bacon
Thinly sliced avocados/sliced tomatoes
Watercress/thinly sliced red onion

PEANUT BUTTER (OR OTHER NUT BUTTER)
Basic: jelly
Bacon/hot pepper jelly
Sliced bananas/marshmallow cream
Honey/butter or cream cheese
Bacon and/or Cheddar/apple butter
Cheddar or Swiss cheese/butter

VEGETABLES
Basic: Mozzarella/Fresh Herb Vinaigrette, 572
Prosciutto/Garlic Mayonnaise, 581
Sprouts/mango chutney
Watercress or arugula/cream cheese or Andalouse Sauce, 580
Monterey Jack/Salsa Verde Cruda, 571
Lettuce/Red Onion Marmalade, 949

GRILLED OR FRIED FISH
Basic: lettuce/sliced tomatoes and onions/mayonnaise or Tartar Sauce, 581

Frisée and/or arugula/Tapenade, 75
Shredded lettuce/sliced radishes/Salsa Verde Cruda, 571 (in flour tortillas)
Watercress/Corn and Tomato Relish, 949
Grilled onion/mustard or mayonnaise
Boston or Bibb lettuce/sliced cucumbers/Thousand Island Dressing, 576

CHEESE
Basic: lettuce/sliced tomatoes/mayonnaise or mustard
Lettuce/Red Onion Marmalade, 949
Watercress/sliced tomatoes/sliced avocados/Rémoulade Sauce, 581
Arugula/sliced tomatoes/sliced red onion/mayonnaise
Alfalfa sprouts/Hummus, 74
Frisée/Piccalilli, 947
Roasted red peppers/mayonnaise
Sweet pickles/sliced onion/butter

ABOUT NUT BUTTERS

Nut butters made in the food processor have an appealing coarse texture and a fresh, rich flavor. Walnuts and pecans produce light-textured butters with a relatively loose consistency. Peanuts, cashews, and almonds produce denser butters. If you use salted nuts, do not add salt. Prepare the nuts in the processor until they are finely chopped and the mixture looks blended and creamy, stopping and scraping down the sides of the work bowl as needed.

NUT BUTTER
1 1/2 to 1 3/4 cups
Place one of the following in a food processor:
   3 cups roasted peanuts
   3 cups roasted cashews
   3 cups walnut or pecan pieces, toasted, 1001
   3 cups blanched whole almonds, toasted, 1001
   3 cups hazelnuts, toasted and peeled, 1001
Process until the nuts gather into a ball, 2 to 3 minutes. Break up the ball with a spoon, then add, unless using salted nuts:
   (1/4 teaspoon salt)
Process until the nuts release their oil and a butter forms. This generally takes 1 to 3 minutes but may take as long as 5 minutes, particularly if you are using almonds. Store the butter, covered, at room temperature up to 2 days or refrigerate up to 2 weeks.

FLAVORED NUT BUTTERS
About 1 1/2 cups
When making these, start with cold unsalted butter and be careful not to overprocess, or the butter will melt.
I. SAVORY WALNUT BUTTER
Combine in a food processor and process until smooth:
   1 1/2 cups (about 6 ounces) walnut pieces, toasted
   1/2 cup (1 stick) cold unsalted butter, cut into pieces
   2 tablespoons Worcestershire sauce

Season with:

About ¼ teaspoon salt

Black pepper to taste

II. ROSEMARY PECAN BUTTER

Combine in a food processor and process until smooth:

1¼ cups (about 5 ounces) pecan pieces, toasted

½ cup (1 stick) cold unsalted butter,
cut into pieces

1 tablespoon finely chopped rosemary

1 tablespoon light or dark brown sugar

Season with:

¼ to ½ teaspoon salt

Black pepper to taste

III. CURRIED MACADAMIA BUTTER

Combine in a food processor and process until smooth:

1⅓ cups (6 ounces) salted dry-roasted
macadamia nuts

½ cup (1 stick) cold unsalted butter, cut into pieces

1 tablespoon honey

½ teaspoon curry powder

Season with:

Salt to taste

HONEY BUTTER

Mix equal quantities of:

Honey

Softened butter

Season with:

Salt to taste

If necessary, chill until firm enough to spread.

CREAM CHEESE SPREADS

1¼ to 1½ cups

Cream cheese is the perfect emergency binder for the many taste provokers that follow. All of these can be used at once or refrigerated, covered, up to one week.

Rub a bowl with:

1 garlic clove, halved

Add and mash until soft:

8 ounces cream cheese, softened

2 tablespoons heavy or sour cream

Add one or more of the following:

2 tablespoons minced onion

¼ cup chopped parsley, dill, cilantro, or chives

⅓ cup minced celery or green bell pepper

¾ cup chopped green or black olives

2 tablespoons drained prepared horseradish

3 tablespoons minced scallions

6 slices crisp bacon, crumbled

2 tablespoons anchovy or fish paste

¾ cup shredded salted almonds or other nuts

¾ cup chopped toasted, 1001, almonds or pecans

1 to 2 tablespoons chive blossoms or marigold petals

¼ cup chopped ripe or pimiento-stuffed olives

1 tablespoon caviar

¾ cup diced ham

Season with:

(Salt, paprika, and/or ground red pepper)

CUCUMBER CREAM CHEESE SPREAD (BENEDICTINE)

About 1½ cups

Made famous at Benedict's restaurant in Louisville, Kentucky, this became a tradition during May for the Kentucky Derby. This recipe is easily doubled.

Grate on the large holes of a grater:

1 medium cucumber, peeled and seeded

½ medium onion

Wrap in cheesecloth or a kitchen towel and squeeze to remove excess moisture. Measure ¼ cup each drained cucumber and onion and combine in a medium bowl. Add:

8 ounces cream cheese, softened

Pinch of ground red pepper

Salt to taste

(Dab of green food coloring)

Combine with a wooden spoon or process until fluffy.

PIMIENTO CHEESE

About 4 cups

This rich, spicy cheese spread appeared in some fashion in JOY from 1931 until the 1960s. The 1936 edition declared it "a grand cheese spread for hot or cold sandwiches."

Combine in a medium bowl:

One 4-ounce jar chopped pimientos, drained

1 cup mayonnaise

1 garlic clove, minced

1 tablespoon lemon juice

1 teaspoon dry mustard

½ teaspoon Worcestershire sauce

¼ teaspoon ground red pepper

Beat with a wooden spoon or an electric mixer at medium speed until blended. Add:

2 cups grated Cheddar (8 ounces)

2 cups grated Colby (8 ounces)

Beat until the consistency of cottage cheese.

SWEET TEA SPREADS

Use at once or covered and refrigerated up to 3 days; bring to room temperature before spreading.

I. ALMOND GINGER CREAM CHEESE SPREAD

1⅓ cups

Combine in a bowl and beat until smooth:

8 ounces cream cheese, softened

¾ cup finely chopped toasted almonds

¼ cup minced candied ginger

II. ORANGE PECAN CREAM CHEESE SPREAD

1½ cups

Combine in a bowl and mix until smooth:

8 ounces cream cheese, softened

¾ cup finely chopped toasted pecans

¼ cup orange marmalade

¼ teaspoon salt

III. CHUTNEY NUT CREAM CHEESE SPREAD
1 1/2 cups

Combine in a bowl and mix until smooth:

    8 ounces cream cheese, softened

    1/2 cup finely chopped toasted almonds or cashews

    1/3 cup mango chutney, finely chopped, or more to taste

Taste and add if desired:

    2 to 3 tablespoons mango chutney, finely chopped

    (Ground red pepper)

DEVILED HAM OR CHICKEN SPREAD
About 1 1/2 cups

Use as a sandwich spread or serve in a crock with crackers. Combine in a food processor and process to a paste:

    1 1/2 cups diced cooked chicken or ham

    5 tablespoons butter or mayonnaise

    3 tablespoons chicken broth

    2 tablespoons chopped parsley

    (3/4 teaspoon Dijon mustard)

    1/4 teaspoon paprika

    Salt and black or white pepper to taste

CHICKEN OR HAM SALAD SPREAD
About 1 1/4 cups

Use as a sandwich spread or serve in a crock with crackers. Chop very fine:

    1 cup diced cooked chicken or ham

Transfer to a bowl and mix in:

    1/2 cup mayonnaise

    1/4 cup chopped pecans

    1/4 cup chopped bread-and-butter pickles or chopped green olives

    2 tablespoons finely chopped celery

    Pinch of ground red pepper

    Salt to taste

GRILLED CHEESE SANDWICH
1 sandwich

Especially good with sliced tomatoes, sprouts, bacon, or ham. We like ours with mayonnaise. To garnish your sandwich, pull apart while hot and cheese is melted. Make a sandwich of:

    2 slices white sandwich bread

    2 slices American cheese, or other cheese

Butter both sides of the bread with:

    1 1/2 teaspoons softened butter

Cook the sandwich slowly in a skillet or on a griddle on one side until golden brown. Turn and brown the second side. Serve at once.

WAFFLE SANDWICH
1 sandwich

Lay out on a work surface:

    White or whole wheat sandwich bread, preferably sliced thin

Spread lightly with:

    Softened butter

Cut off the crusts. Make sandwiches with:

    Cheese spreads, 179, or other sandwich fillings, 177–178

Trim sandwich to fit the sections of a waffle iron. Heat the iron, place sandwich in the iron, and bake until crisp.

BLT
4 sandwiches

This was Granny Rom's favorite sandwich. Lay out on a work surface:

    8 slices white sandwich bread, toasted

Spread lightly with:

    Mayonnaise (about 3 tablespoons total)

Divide among 4 slices:

    2 medium tomatoes, sliced

    8 lettuce leaves

    12 slices bacon, cooked until crisp

    Salt and black pepper to taste

Top with the remaining 4 slices toast, press together gently, and cut in half if desired.

CLUB SANDWICH
4 sandwiches

An all-American meal, and a JOY favorite since 1931. Lay out on a work surface:

    12 slices white bread, lightly toasted

Spread lightly with:

    Mayonnaise

Divide among 4 of the slices:

    Lettuce leaves

    8 ounces thinly sliced turkey breast or chicken

Top with another 4 slices toast, mayonnaise side down. Spread the tops with:

    Mayonnaise

Divide among the sandwiches:

    Lettuce leaves

    1 medium tomato, thinly sliced

    12 slices crisp bacon

    (1/2 cucumber, peeled, seeded, and very thinly sliced)

Top with the remaining 4 slices toast, mayonnaise side down. Run 4 toothpicks through each sandwich midway between the center and each corner. Cut the sandwiches into triangles between the toothpicks.

TWIN SANDWICH
1 sandwich

Place on a large plate:

    1 thin slice ham

Cover one half with:

    1 thin slice American or Cheddar

Fold the ham over the cheese. Heat a nonstick skillet or griddle over medium heat. Place the package in the skillet and cook on each side for 1 minute, or until the ham is sizzling and the cheese is melted. Have ready:

2 slices sandwich bread, toasted

Place the hot ham and cheese on 1 slice of toast. Top with:

1 or 2 slices tomato

Cover with the remaining toast. Serve warm.

REUBEN SANDWICH

4 sandwiches

For a **Rachel,** substitute turkey for the corned beef. Preheat the oven to 400°F. Lay out on a work surface:

8 slices rye bread, toasted

Spread thinly with:

Softened butter
Russian Dressing, 576

Divide among 4 slices:

About 1¼ pounds thinly sliced lean corned beef
About 12 ounces well-drained sauerkraut
4 slices Swiss

Cover with remaining slices of bread. Spread the top of each sandwich with:

Softened butter

Arrange the sandwiches, buttered side down, on a baking sheet and butter the tops. Bake until golden brown. Serve hot with:

Dill or sweet-and-sour pickles

CROQUE MONSIEUR

6 sandwiches

Preheat the broiler. Lay out on a work surface:

12 slices home-style white bread or French Bread, 601

Spread one side of 6 of the slices with:

Softened butter (3 tablespoons total)
(Dijon mustard)

Top with:

6 thin slices ham (about 4 ounces)

Cover with the remaining slices of bread. Place the sandwiches under the broiler until golden. Turn the sandwiches over and cover with:

1 cup grated Gruyère (about 4 ounces total)

Broil until the cheese is bubbling and golden. Cut into halves or quarters and serve warm.

CROQUE MADAME SANDWICH

Prepare **Croque Monsieur, above.** When the sandwiches are almost golden, remove from the broiler and use a paring knife to cut a small round out of each top piece of the cheese-covered bread, exposing the ham. Reserve the rounds. Break **1 small egg** into each hole and place under the broiler until the eggs are set, 2 to 3 minutes. To serve, top the eggs with the cheese-covered rounds.

MONTE CRISTO

Prepare **Croque Monsieur, above,** substituting **very thinly sliced chicken** for the ham and **Swiss cheese** for the Gruyère.

CUBAN SANDWICH

4 sandwiches

Traditionally pressed with a sandwich iron, you can achieve the same effect with two heavy skillets. Crusty bread with a soft inside is best for this sandwich. French or Italian bread can be substituted for the Cuban bread. Preheat the oven to 400°F. Split lengthwise in half:

One 24-inch-long loaf Cuban bread

Spread the bottom half lightly with:

Softened butter

Spread the other half generously with:

Coarse-grain mustard

Layer on the bottom half:

8 ounces thinly sliced ham
8 ounces thinly sliced Swiss or Muenster
8 ounces thinly sliced pork butt or loin, 498
Sliced dill pickles

Cover with the top half of the bread and slice crosswise into 4 sandwiches. Wrap each sandwich tightly in aluminum foil. Place sandwiches in a grill pan or large cast-iron skillet and place a heavy ovenproof skillet on top to press them down. Grill the sandwiches until very hot and the cheese is melted, 20 to 25 minutes. Carefully unwrap and serve hot.

PROSCIUTTO, MOZZARELLA, AND BASIL PANINI

4 sandwiches

Panini means, literally, "little sandwiches" in Italian, but in this country the word has come to mean the type of sandwich that is pressed and heated until the bread is crisp. A countertop electric grill makes wonderful panini, but if not, place a skillet on the stovetop and weigh them down with a panini press or second skillet. Preheat the grill or heavy skillet to high. Split:

4 pieces ciabatta bread, each about 5 x 4 inches

Drizzle the inside of both halves lightly with:

Olive oil
Balsamic vinegar

Divide evenly among the bottom halves:

16 thin slices prosciutto (about 8 ounces)
8 ounces mozzarella, thinly sliced
16 basil leaves

Sprinkle with:

Salt and black pepper to taste

Cover with the top halves. Grill the sandwiches for 4 minutes, or until the cheese melts and the bread is crisp. Press with grill top or second skillet, and grill for 2 minutes, then turn over and grill for an additional 2 minutes. Serve hot.

MUFFULETTA

6 servings

Combine well in a small bowl:

1 cup finely chopped green olives
1 cup finely chopped black olives
½ cup olive oil

$^1/_3$ cup finely chopped parsley

2 teaspoons minced fresh oregano or about
   $^3/_4$ teaspoon dried oregano

1 garlic clove, minced

$^3/_4$ cup chopped roasted red bell pepper, 292

Juice of $^1/_2$ lemon, or to taste

Cover. Refrigerate for at least 8 hours. Split horizontally:

1 large round loaf (8 to 9 inches) Italian or
   French bread

Remove some of the soft inner bread, creating a cavity inside each half. Drain the olive mixture, reserving the marinade. Brush the insides of both halves of the loaf generously with the marinade, then spread half of the olive mixture in the bottom half. Add in layers:

About 4 ounces thinly sliced salami

About 4 ounces thinly sliced cappicola or ham

About 4 ounces thinly sliced provolone

(1 cup coarsely chopped tomatoes)

About 2 cups shredded lettuce

Top with the remaining olive salad. Cover with the top half of the loaf, and wrap tightly in plastic. Place on a large plate, cover with another plate, and weight with several pounds of canned goods. Refrigerate for at least 30 minutes, or up to 6 hours. To serve, cut into wedges.

CHEESE TOAST

4 sandwiches

Preheat the broiler. Lay out on a baking sheet:

4 slices white bread, toasted

Spread tops with:

2 tablespoons butter, softened

Sprinkle with:

1 cup grated sharp Cheddar (about 4 ounces)

(4 slices crisp bacon, crumbled)

(1 plum tomato, diced)

Broil for 2 to 3 minutes, until the cheese browns.

TUNA MELT

4 sandwiches

Preheat the broiler. Lay out on a work surface:

4 slices rye, toasted

Divide among the slices:

Tuna Salad, 164

Top with:

1 cup grated Monterey Jack, Cheddar, Fontina, or
   American cheese

Broil until the cheese is melted and golden, 1 to 2 minutes.

ENGLISH MUFFIN PIZZA

1 to 2 servings

Split in half:

1 English muffin

Toast the flat sides under the broiler. Spread the untoasted sides with:

1 tablespoon Quick Tomato Sauce, 562, chili sauce,
   or catsup

Sprinkle with:

$^1/_4$ teaspoon dried oregano

Top each with:

$^1/_4$ cup grated Cheddar, mozzarella, or Swiss

Over all:

1 teaspoon olive oil

Broil until the cheese is melted and beginning to brown.

HOT BROWN

4 servings

Developed at the Brown Hotel in Louisville, Kentucky, in 1920, this delight remains on the menu to this day.

Preheat the broiler. Divide among 4 small gratin dishes:

4 slices white toast, cut into quarters

Top with, dividing the turkey evenly:

8 ounces thinly sliced turkey

Pour over the top:

1 to 1$^1/_3$ cups Mornay Sauce, 551

Top with, dividing the ingredients evenly:

8 slices tomato

8 slices crisp bacon

Broil until bubbling. Serve immediately.

HOT ROAST BEEF SANDWICH

4 sandwiches

Leftover turkey or meat loaf are delicious substitutions for the roast beef. Served with mashed potatoes and peas, this is an American classic.

Slice:

Cold roast beef

Prepare:

1$^1/_2$ to 2 cups Quick Brown Sauce, 556,
   or warmed canned beef gravy

Add:

1 tablespoon finely minced dill pickle or
   $^1/_2$ cup chopped green olives

Lay out on a work surface:

6 slices of white or dark bread

Blend until soft:

2 tablespoons butter

$^1/_4$ teaspoon prepared mustard or 1 teaspoon
   prepared horseradish, drained

Spread the bread with this mixture. Dip the beef slices in the hot gravy. Place them between the slices of bread. Serve the sandwiches on a hot platter, covered with remaining gravy.

PASTRAMI AND CORNED BEEF TRIPLE-DECKER SANDWICH

4 triple-decker sandwiches

Lay out on a work surface:

12 slices rye bread

Generously spread 8 of the slices with:

Russian Dressing, 576

Arrange on top of 4 of the coated slices, dividing evenly:

8 to 12 ounces sliced pastrami

³/₄ to 1 cup Coleslaw, 161

Top with the remaining 4 coated slices, dressing side up. Cover with:

8 to 12 ounces sliced corned beef

Finish the sandwiches with the remaining 4 slices bread.

BRAUNSCHWEIGER SANDWICH

4 sandwiches

Lay out on a work surface:

8 slices pumpernickel or rye bread

Generously spread 4 of the slices with:

Prepared horseradish, drained

Spread the other 4 slices with:

Spicy mustard

(Mayonnaise)

Layer on top of the horseradish-spread slices:

8 ounces Braunschweiger or other liverwurst, thinly sliced

Thinly sliced red onion

(Sliced cucumber)

(8 slices crisp bacon)

Cover with the remaining bread.

MEAT LOAF SANDWICH

4 sandwiches

Lay out on a work surface:

8 slices sandwich bread

Generously spread 4 of the slices with:

Green Goddess Dressing, 576, or Thousand Island Dressing, 576

Arrange on top of the dressing:

4 slices Meat Loaf, 512

Sliced onion

Lettuce leaves

Top with the remaining 4 slices bread.

MIXED VEGGIE SANDWICH

4 sandwiches

Lay out on a work surface:

8 slices sandwich bread

Generously spread 4 of the slices with:

Feta Dressing, 576, or mayonnaise

Arrange on top of the dressing:

1 avocado, peeled, pitted, and sliced

¹/₂ medium cucumber, peeled and sliced

4 slices Vidalia or other sweet onion

4 slices tomato

¹/₂ cup packed alfalfa sprouts

Top with the remaining 4 slices bread.

LOBSTER ROLL

4 sandwiches

The classic New England seashore sandwich.

Combine:

1¹/₃ cups cooked lobster meat

¹/₂ cup finely diced celery

(1 tablespoon finely chopped parsley)

1 tablespoon lemon juice

¹/₄ teaspoon salt

Black pepper or ground red pepper to taste

Stir in:

About ¹/₃ cup mayonnaise or to taste

Divide the mixture among:

4 hot dog buns or brioche or challah rolls, toasted and buttered

Serve while the bread is still warm.

CLAM ROLL

6 sandwiches

Prepare:

Fried Clams with Bread Crumb or Cracker Coating, 377

Divide among:

6 hot dog buns, toasted

Serve with:

Tartar Sauce, 581

FRIED SOFT-SHELL CRAB SANDWICH

4 sandwiches

Lay cut side up on a work surface:

4 hamburger buns, split and toasted

Combine:

¹/₃ cup mayonnaise

1 tablespoon lemon juice

Spread the mixture on both halves of the buns. Divide among the bottom halves:

1 medium tomato, thinly sliced

Prick with a pin in six or eight places on each side:

4 fresh or frozen soft-shell crabs, 379

Season with:

Salt and black pepper

Roll until well coated in:

¹/₂ cup all-purpose flour

(1 teaspoon crab boil seasoning)

Heat a large skillet over medium-high heat until hot:

¹/₂ cup vegetable oil

Carefully place the crabs in the skillet and cook, turning once with tongs, until golden brown, 3 to 4 minutes per side. Place the crabs on the bottom halves of the buns. Top with:

Boston, Bibb, or any lettuce leaves

Cover with the top halves of buns, press together gently, and serve.

FRIED EGG SANDWICH

1 serving

Preheat the broiler. Prepare:

1 or 2 over-medium to well-done Fried Eggs, 196

Season with:

Salt and black pepper to taste

(Crushed red pepper flakes to taste)

Toast:

2 slices bread or 1 English muffin, split

Cover 1 slice of bread or bottom half of the muffin with:

1 to 2 tablespoons grated Cheddar or Swiss

Broil until the cheese is melted.

Garnish, if desired, with:

(Catsup)

(Lettuce)

(Bacon or thinly sliced ham)

Cover with egg and remaining toast or top of the muffin.

WESTERN EGG SANDWICH

1 sandwich

Mix together:

1 large egg, well beaten

2 tablespoons milk

2 tablespoons chopped cooked ham or bacon

1 tablespoon minced onion

1 tablespoon finely chopped green or red bell peppers

Salt and black pepper to taste

Melt in a medium skillet, preferably nonstick, over medium heat:

1 teaspoon butter

Pour the egg mixture into the hot pan and cook until almost set. Flip it over and cook for 1 minute more.

Serve on:

1 large kaiser roll or hard roll, split and warmed

BAGELS AND LOX

2 sandwiches

The combination of bagels, cream cheese, and smoked salmon is a Jewish classic.

Cut in half horizontally, and toast if desired:

2 bagels

Spread the bottom halves with:

¼ cup cream cheese

Top the cream cheese with:

2 thin slices Bermuda or red onion

2 thin slices ripe tomato

4 paper-thin slices (about 2 ounces) lox or other smoked salmon

Serve either open-faced or as a sandwich.

SUBMARINE OR HERO SANDWICH

4 sandwiches

The hero—also known as a submarine, bomber, grinder, wedge, zep, or hoagie—is essentially a long, wide roll filled with deli meats and cheese. To help blend the flavors, compress the sandwiches by wrapping them tightly in foil.

Split lengthwise in half:

One 24-inch loaf Italian or French bread

Moisten the inside of the loaf generously with:

Olive oil

Red or white wine vinegar

Layer on half of the bread a combination of 3 or more sandwich meats:

About 1 pound sliced salami, prosciutto, mortadella, and/or cappicola or ham

Stack on top of the meat:

4 to 8 ounces sliced provolone

(7 ounces sliced pickled hot peppers)

(1 onion, thinly sliced)

(1 tomato, thinly sliced)

2 cups finely shredded lettuce

Cover with the top half of the bread. Serve immediately, or wrap tightly in aluminum foil and let stand for 30 minutes, under weights such as heavy cans or bricks if desired, before serving. Cut into 4 sandwiches.

SAUSAGE AND PEPPER SUB

4 sandwiches

Cook slowly in a large skillet over medium heat until browned and cooked throughout:

4 sweet or hot Italian sausages, pricked several times with a fork or paring knife

Remove the sausages to a plate. Pour off all but 2 tablespoons of the fat in the pan. Add:

2 tablespoons olive oil

1 large onion, thinly sliced

3 garlic cloves, minced

1 large red bell pepper, cut into thin strips

1 large green bell pepper, cut into thin strips

(1 teaspoon dried oregano)

Salt and black pepper to taste

Cook over low heat, stirring often, until the peppers are very soft, about 25 minutes. Stir in, if desired:

(1 tablespoon balsamic vinegar)

Return the sausages to the pan and heat through, about 3 minutes. Spoon the mixture into:

Four 6-inch hero rolls, split and warmed

Gently press the sandwiches together and serve.

MEATBALL SANDWICH

4 sandwiches

Prepare:

Tomato Sauce, 562, or Quick Tomato Sauce, 562

Italian Meatballs, 513

Preheat the broiler. Divide the meatballs and sauce among:

Four 6-inch hero rolls, split

Top with:

6 ounces provolone, thinly sliced

Place the sandwiches on a baking sheet and place under the broiler until the cheese melts, 1 to 2 minutes.

PHILLY CHEESE STEAK

4 sandwiches

Preheat the oven to 350°F. Wrap in aluminum foil and warm in the oven:

Four 6-inch hero rolls, split

Heat in a large nonstick skillet over medium heat until hot but not smoking:

3 tablespoons vegetable oil

Add:

2 medium onions, thinly sliced
(1 small green bell pepper, cut into thin strips)

Cook, stirring, until the vegetables are soft, 10 to 15 minutes. Add:

1 pound beef sirloin, sliced into $1/8$- to $1/4$-inch strips

Cook, stirring, until the meat is no longer pink, about 5 minutes. Season to taste with:

Salt

Hot pepper sauce

Divide the beef mixture among the bottom halves of the rolls (set the tops aside). Top equally with:

1 cup shredded provolone or mozzarella

Place in the oven for 2 to 3 minutes to melt the cheese. Cover with the top halves of the rolls, press together gently, and serve hot.

OYSTER PO'BOY

4 sandwiches

Originating in New Orleans, the po'boy is a large sandwich made with French bread. Popular stuffings include fried shrimp, hot Italian sausage, ham, or, as here, deep-fried oysters. The sandwiches are served plain or dressed with mayonnaise, lettuce, and tomato.

Please read about Deep-fat Frying, 1046. Heat to 375°F in a deep fryer or deep heavy pot:

$1^1/2$ inches vegetable oil

Meanwhile, combine:

$1/2$ cup yellow cornmeal

1 teaspoon salt

1 teaspoon black pepper

Dredge in mixture:

24 oysters, shucked

Shake gently to remove the excess cornmeal, then deep-fry in batches of 6, turning occasionally, until golden brown and just cooked through, 1 to 2 minutes. With a slotted spoon, remove to paper towels to drain. Halve crosswise, then lengthwise:

Two 15-inch loaves soft-crusted French or Italian bread

Spread the cut sides generously with:

Mayonnaise, Tartar Sauce, 581, Rémoulade, 581, or Becker Cocktail Sauce, 568

Divide among the bottom halves of the bread:

1 large tomato, sliced thin

About 1 cup shredded lettuce

Top with the oysters, cover with the top halves of the bread, and press together gently. Serve warm.

HOT DOGS

4 hot dogs

An American beach and backyard grill classic, hot dogs can be dressed with a variety of condiments. Since most are precooked, all you do is heat them up.

Place in a saucepan and simmer in water to cover for 5 minutes; or grill and broil until well seared, about 3 min-

utes each side; or slice lengthwise almost all the way through, open up to flatten, and cook in a teaspoon or two of butter in a skillet until browned, about 4 minutes each side:

4 wieners or frankfurters

Meanwhile, toast:

4 hot dog buns, split

Spread each bun with:

2 teaspoons butter (8 teaspoons total)

Place the hot dogs in the prepared buns. Serve with your choice of **catsup, mustard, Green Tomato Relish, 948, Piccalilli, 947, chopped red or white onion, Chili Con Carne, 513, sweet relish, and Tart Corn Relish, 948.**

HOT DOG VARIATIONS

GERMAN DOG: Top each hot dog with about **3 tablespoons prepared sauerkraut.**

CHEESE DOG: Top each hot dog with **1 or 2 slices American** or **2 tablespoons cheese spread.**

MEXICAN DOG: Top each hot dog with **2 tablespoons Salsa Fresca, 571, $1/2$ jalapeño pepper, coarsely chopped,** and **1 tablespoon grated Monterey Jack.**

CHEESE CONEY: Top with **Cincinnati Chili Cockaigne, 514, shredded Cheddar, diced onion,** and **yellow mustard.**

CORN DOGS

16 corn dogs

Please read about Deep-Fat Frying, 1046. Whisk until smooth:

1 cup plus 2 tablespoons yellow cornmeal

$1/2$ cup all-purpose flour

2 tablespoons sugar

1 teaspoon salt

$3/4$ cup buttermilk

2 tablespoons milk

1 egg

$1/2$ teaspoon baking soda

Let batter rest 10 minutes to thicken. Preheat the oven to 225°F. In a heavy, deep pot, heat to 375°F:

Vegetable oil to a depth of 3 inches

Meanwhile, impale on wooden skewers:

16 wieners or frankfurters

Pour batter into a tall cup and dip each skewered wiener in batter, turning to coat evenly. Fry corn dogs, turning skewers for even cooking, until browned, 3 to 4 minutes. Keep warm in oven until all are fried. Serve with:

Catsup and mustard

HAMBURGERS

See About Ground Meat and Hamburger, 509.

ABOUT TEA SANDWICHES

Tea sandwiches are small, delicate sandwiches made with a variety of fillings. This sandwich is made fancier when constructed into shaped, finger, ribbon, or rolled sand-wiches. When preparing a platter of tea sandwiches, only a surprisingly few are needed for an attractive presenta-tion. A combination of tea sandwiches and canapés gives variety to the tray. But keep in mind that alternating rows of similarly cut sandwiches with contrasting fillings on a small or medium plate or tray are more attractive than sparsely arranged sandwiches on a large platter. When buying bread for tea sandwiches, remember that ➤ most 1-pound loaves of sliced sandwich bread contain 18 to 20 slices. Tea sandwiches require a bit of time and handiwork, but they can be successfully stored for up to 24 hours. Arrange the sandwiches on a tray, top with wax paper, and then cover with a slightly moistened paper towel. Wrap the tray in plastic wrap and refrigerate until ready to serve. Please read About Bread for Sandwiches, 177. For further inspiration, see About Canapés, 86.

HEARTY TEA SANDWICHES

About 36 sandwiches

Have ready:

5 tablespoons butter, softened, or $^1/_3$ cup mayonnaise

Lay out on a work surface:

18 slices white or wheat sandwich bread

Spread one side of each slice with about 1 teaspoon butter or mayonnaise to the edges of the bread. Cover half of the bread with any filling below; slice meats and vegetables about $^1/_8$ inch thick.

Peeled European cucumbers and butter (best on white bread)

Red onion, minced parsley, and butter or mayonnaise

Cheddar, minced cilantro, minced mango chutney, and butter

Watercress, minced scallions, and butter

Tomatoes, basil, and mayonnaise or Garlic Mayonnaise, 581

Ham, orange marmalade, and butter (best on wheat bread)

Roast beef, horseradish, and butter or mayonnaise

Chicken or turkey breast, minced mango chutney, and butter

Finely chopped Lobster Salad, 165, and mayonnaise or butter

Finely chopped Egg Salad, 164, small capers, and mayonnaise or butter

The filling should reach the edges of the bread. Top with remaining bread, spread side down, making 8 to 9 large sandwiches. Gently press the sandwiches with your hand. Using a serrated knife, trim off the crusts and any protrud-ing filling. Cut each sandwich into triangular quarters or 4 lengthwise fingers.

TEA SANDWICHES WITH SPREADS

About 36 small sandwiches

Lay out on a work surface:

18 slices white or wheat sandwich bread

Spread half of the slices with:

1 cup Nut Butter, 178, Flavored Nut Butter, 178, Cream Cheese Spread, 179, Cucumber Cream Cheese Spread, 179, Pimiento Cheese, 178, Deviled Ham or Chicken Spread, 180, or Chicken or Ham Salad Spread, 180

Cover with the remaining slices, making 9 large sand-wiches. Gently press sandwiches and, using a serrated knife, trim off the crusts, then cut each sandwich into rec-tangular or triangular quarters or into 4 fingers. Spread the cut edges of the sandwiches lightly with:

(Mayonnaise or softened butter)

And roll in:

(Finely minced nuts or minced parsley)

SHAPED TEA SANDWICHES

18 to 36 sandwiches

Prepare 9 large sandwiches as described in Tea Sand-wiches with Spreads, above, but do not trim the crusts. Using biscuit or cookie cutters, cut the sandwiches into as-sorted shapes, cutting them as close to each other and to the crusts as possible in order to minimize waste. The number of sandwiches you will get depends on the size and shape of the cutters you use.

TEA SANDWICHES ON SWEET BREAD

50 to 60 sandwiches

Have ready:

Two $7^1/_2$ x $3^5/_8$ loaves Brown Bread, 629, each cut into about twenty-five $^1/_4$-inch-thick slices (50 slices total), or 1 loaf Pumpkin Bread, 628, or Date Nut Bread, 627, cut into about thirty $^1/_4$-inch-thick slices

$1^1/_4$ to $1^1/_2$ cups Nut Butter, 178, Honey Butter, 850, Almond Ginger Cream Cheese Spread, 179, or Orange Pecan Cream Cheese Spread, 179

Spread half of the slices with the filling. Cover with the re-maining slices, and press gently. Using a sharp knife, trim the sandwiches to make squares. Cut brown bread sand-wiches into rectangular or triangular halves; cut pumpkin bread or date nut bread sandwiches into rectangular or tri-angular quarters or into 4 lengthwise fingers each.

RIBBON SANDWICHES

48 sandwiches

Have ready:

8 slices dark bread

16 slices white bread

Spread the dark bread slices and 8 of the white bread slices with:

$1^1/_4$ to $1^1/_2$ cups Nut Butter, 178, Flavored Nut Butter, 178, Cream Cheese Spread, 179, Cucumber Cream Cheese Spread, 179, Pimiento Cheese, 178, Deviled Ham or Chicken Spread, 180, or Chicken or Ham Salad Spread, 180

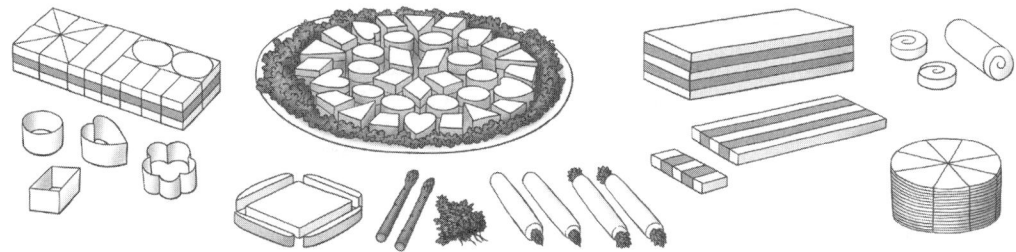

Making ribbon and pinwheel sandwiches

Top the spread slices of white bread with the dark slices, spread side up. Top with the remaining white bread slices. Gently press the sandwiches and, using a serrated knife, trim the crusts from each sandwich, then cut each sandwich lengthwise into 4 fingers.

ROLLED SANDWICHES
About 18 large or 36 small sandwiches
A generous quantity of filling is required in order to ensure that the bread will not crack or tear when rolled. If using cucumber cream cheese spread, tuck **a couple of watercress sprigs** into each sandwich, allowing the leafy tops to protrude from each end, before rolling. Rolled sandwiches with sprigs of cress or parsley projecting—placed like the spokes of a wheel—make a charming border for a platter. Using a serrated knife, cut the crusts from:

>**18 slices white or whole wheat sandwich bread**

Firmly flatten each slice with a rolling pin. Spread to the edges to ensure the rolls will be well sealed:

>**1¼ to 1½ cups Nut Butter, 178, Flavored Nut Butter, 178, Cream Cheese Spread, 179, Cucumber Cream Cheese Spread, 179, Pimiento Cheese, 179, Deviled Ham or Chicken Spread, 180, or Chicken or Ham Salad Spread, 180**

Roll up each slice tightly. Wrap each in plastic and refrigerate for several hours so the sandwiches will hold their shape when served. Serve whole or cut in half.

ABOUT WRAPS AND PITA SANDWICHES
Virtually any sandwich filling can be used for a wrap or pita sandwich; see Fillings and Dressings for Sandwiches and Wraps, 177. Flatbread designed specifically for wraps is sold in most supermarkets. Eight-inch flour tortillas warmed can be substituted. Layer ingredients for wraps methodically, leaving as little space between them as possible and a bare border of at least 1 inch all around the edges of the bread; the filling should be no thicker than about ½ inch. To roll, fold up the exposed edge of the bread closest to you, fold over the right and left sides, and then roll up. Place the wrap seam side down and, if desired, cut in half on the diagonal.

Cut off about one-fifth of each pita bread to make an opening to the pocket for stuffing. You may wish to toss the filling with dressing before inserting it into the pocket, or spread the inside of the pocket with the dressing first. Pita bread is less likely to tear when stuffed if slightly warmed in a dry skillet or on a grill.

TURKEY AND AVOCADO WRAPS
4 sandwiches
Lay out on a work surface:

>**Four 8-inch wrap breads or flour tortillas**

Divide among them, leaving a 1-inch border all around:

>**12 ounces sliced roasted turkey breast**
>**1 avocado, peeled, pitted, and thinly sliced**
>**2 medium carrots, grated**
>**1 medium tomato, chopped**
>**2 scallions, finely chopped**
>**(1 cup sprouts, such as alfalfa)**
>**Salt and black pepper to taste**

Drizzle over the filling:

>**Tahini Dressing, 576, Creamy Blue Cheese Dressing, 576, or Tangerine Shallot Dressing, 575**

Roll as in About Wraps and Pita Sandwiches, above.

STEAK WRAPS
4 sandwiches
Lay out on a work surface:

>**Four 8-inch wrap breads or flour tortillas**

Spread with equal portions of:

>**1 head Roasted Garlic, 277**

Divide among them, leaving a 1-inch border all around:

>**1 small head Boston lettuce leaves, washed and dried**
>**1 small red onion, very thinly sliced**
>**1 medium tomato, coarsely chopped**
>**1 pound sirloin, top round, flank steak, or strip steak, grilled or broiled, and sliced ¼ inch thick**
>**Salt and black pepper to taste**

Drizzle with:

>**Horseradish Cream, 565**

Roll as in About Wraps and Pita Sandwiches, above.

GRILLED VEGETABLE WRAPS
4 sandwiches
Please read about Grilling Vegetables, 243. Grill until soft:

>**2 red bell peppers, halved**
>**2 green bell peppers, halved**

**1 small eggplant, cut lengthwise into $^1/_2$-inch-thick
    slices**
2 medium red onions, cut into thick slices
**1 medium zucchini or yellow summer squash,
    cut lengthwise into $^1/_2$-inch-thick slices**
8 mushrooms, wiped clean

Cool. Chop vegetables into $^1/_4$-inch pieces. Combine in a
bowl with:

2 tablespoons chopped basil, parsley, or cilantro
Salt and black pepper to taste
**About $^1/_4$ cup Mojo, 566, Andalouse Sauce, 580,
    or Vinaigrette, 572**

Divide among them, leaving a 1-inch border all around:

Four 8-inch wrap breads or flour tortillas

Roll as in About Wraps and Pita Sandwiches, 187.

BECKER GYRO SANDWICH

4 sandwiches

Heat until warm:

4 pita breads

Open the pita breads and divide among them:

12 Becker Lamb Patties, 511

Garnish with:

Chopped sweet onion
Chopped tomatoes
Shredded romaine or iceberg lettuce

Spoon into the sandwiches:

Tzatziki, 567

FALAFEL SANDWICH

4 sandwiches/12 falafel patties

Soak for at least 12 hours, or overnight, 253:

$1^1/_4$ cups dried chickpeas, picked over and rinsed

Stir together:

$^1/_3$ cup tahini (sesame paste)
$^1/_3$ cup cold water
4 teaspoons fresh lemon juice
Pinch of salt

Drain thoroughly. Place in a food processor and finely
chop. Add:

$^1/_2$ cup chopped onion
$^1/_4$ cup packed parsley leaves
2 garlic cloves, chopped
2 teaspoons ground cumin
$1^1/_2$ teaspoons salt
$^1/_2$ teaspoon ground coriander
$^1/_2$ teaspoon baking soda
$^1/_4$ teaspoon ground red pepper
$^1/_2$ teaspoon turmeric

Process until the mixture is coarsely pureed. Remove to a
bowl and stir in:

2 tablespoons all-purpose flour

With wet hands, form the chickpea mixture into 12 balls.
Let stand for 15 minutes.
Heat in a deep skillet until hot:

$^1/_2$ inch vegetable oil

Fry the chickpea patties, in batches, turning occasionally
until golden, 6 to 8 minutes. Drain on paper towels. Divide
the falafel among:

4 pita breads

Drizzle with half of the tahini sauce, then top with:

$1^1/_2$ cups shredded lettuce
$^3/_4$ cup diced tomatoes
$^3/_4$ cup diced peeled cucumbers
($^1/_4$ cup diced red onion or sliced scallions)

Drizzle with the remaining sauce.

ABOUT TACOS, TOSTADAS, AND FAJITAS

The foundation of any taco, tostada, or fajita is a corn or
flour tortilla. The flour tortilla is most commonly used for
burritos, 103, soft tacos, and **fajitas.** Baked or fried flat
and crisp and served with toppings, the flour or corn tortilla becomes a **tostada.** Corn tortillas are typically folded
and fried, then used for **tacos.** Commercially prepared
taco shells are also available.

To heat tortillas ➤ on the stovetop, place on an ungreased griddle or skillet until they bubble slightly. Turn
and heat the other side. To heat ➤ in a microwave, wrap
in plastic wrap and heat for 20 seconds for 1 to 2 tortillas,
1 to 2 minutes for 10 to 12 tortillas. To warm ➤ in the
oven, wrap tightly in foil and bake in a preheated 350°F
oven for 10 minutes.

To fry tortillas, ➤ heat $^1/_2$ inch vegetable oil in a skillet.
Fry one at a time, turning once, until crisp; drain on paper
towels. Fried tortillas are best served immediately, but they
can be kept briefly in the oven. Wrap in paper towels or a
kitchen towel and keep warm in a 200°F oven.

Avocado slices or Guacamole, 72, would be a great addition to any of the taco recipes.

GROUND BEEF TACOS

12 tacos

Heat in a medium skillet over medium heat:

2 tablespoons vegetable oil

Add:

$^3/_4$ cup chopped onion

Cook, stirring often, until softened, 4 to 5 minutes. Increase the heat to medium-high and add:

1 pound ground beef

Cook, breaking up the meat with a wooden spoon, until it
is no longer pink, about 3 minutes. Stir in:

1 to 3 garlic cloves, minced
1 tablespoon chili powder
2 teaspoons ground cumin
(2 teaspoons ground coriander)
Salt to taste

Cook, stirring, for 30 seconds. Add:

1 cup tomato sauce
**Minced fresh jalapeños, chopped drained canned
    jalapeños, or chile or hot pepper sauce to taste**

Cook, stirring occasionally, over low heat for 10 minutes.
Meanwhile, place in separate serving bowls:

2 cups shredded lettuce

1 cup shredded Monterey Jack, Cheddar, or queso fresco (4 ounces)

Salsa Fresca, 571

Sour cream

Have ready:

Twelve 6-inch corn or flour tortillas, or 12 taco shells

Transfer the meat mixture to a serving bowl. Place the taco shells in a basket. Allow guests to assemble their own tacos, or layer each shell with some of the ground meat mixture, lettuce, and cheese, and top with generous dollops of salsa and sour cream.

SHREDDED CHICKEN TACOS

12 tacos

Preheat the oven to 350°F. Remove the skin from:

1½ pounds chicken drumsticks and/or thighs

Rub the meat with:

½ cup Chile-Garlic Spice Paste, 589

Place in a roasting pan and roast until the meat pulls away from the bone easily, about 1 hour. Let stand until cool enough to handle. Pull the meat off the bones (reserve the pan drippings) and shred. Put the meat in a medium bowl and mix with enough of the pan drippings just to moisten it.

Spoon the chicken into:

Twelve 6-inch corn or flour tortillas, or 12 taco shells

Top with dollops of:

Salsa Fresca, 571

Sour cream

SHREDDED PORK TACOS

Fill the **taco shells** with shredded pork prepared as directed for **Pulled Pork, 500.** Top with **lettuce, tomato, avocado, guacamole,** and/or **sour cream.**

BLACK BEAN TACOS

Fill the taco shells with **Refried Beans, 254.** Sprinkle the filling in each taco with about **2 tablespoons grated Monterey Jack or Cheddar** and **chopped onion** and **chopped cilantro** if desired.

GRILLED FISH TACOS

12 tacos

Please read about Skewer Cooking, 1049.

Place in a shallow baking dish just large enough to hold the fish in a single layer:

2 pounds swordfish, halibut, monkfish, or other firm fish steaks or fillets, cut into 1-inch cubes

Mix well:

⅓ cup fresh lime juice

3 tablespoons chopped cilantro or oregano

1 to 2 tablespoons minced jalapeños or other chile peppers

1 teaspoon salt

1 teaspoon black pepper

Pour the marinade over the fish, cover, and refrigerate for at least 1 hour, or up to 3 hours. Prepare a medium-hot grill fire. Have ready:

Twelve 6-inch corn or flour tortillas, or 12 taco shells

Remove the fish from the marinade and thread it onto skewers. Grill or broil, turning the skewers once, until the fish is opaque in the center, 4 to 5 minutes on each side. Slide the fish off the skewers onto a platter. Place on the table along with

2 cups shredded lettuce

1 cup thinly sliced radishes

Corn, Tomato, and Avocado Salsa, 571

Place the taco shells in a basket. Allow guests to assemble their own tacos, or layer each taco with the fish, lettuce, and radishes, and top with a generous dollop of the salsa.

GRILLED SHRIMP TACOS

Prepare **Grilled Fish Tacos, above,** substituting **1½ pounds medium shrimp, peeled, deveined, and marinated for 1 hour,** for the fish. Grill or broil the shrimp until opaque in the center, 3 to 4 minutes each side.

SHRIMP AND AVOCADO TOSTADAS

4 tostadas

Whisk together in a large bowl:

¼ cup vegetable oil

2 tablespoons lime juice

2 tablespoons minced cilantro

1 teaspoon ground cumin

1 teaspoon ground coriander

Salt to taste

Hot pepper sauce to taste

Add:

1 pound medium shrimp, cooked, 385, peeled, and deveined

1 cup cooked or canned corn kernels

1 cup grated Monterey Jack or queso fresco (4 ounces)

1 ripe avocado, peeled, pitted, and coarsely chopped

2 tomatoes, chopped

½ cup minced red onion

Salt to taste

Hot pepper sauce to taste

The mixture can be refrigerated up to 24 hours. When ready to serve, spoon the shrimp mixture into:

4 Corn Tortillas, 609, fried

Top with:

2 cups shredded lettuce

Garnish with:

Cilantro sprigs

CHICKEN, TURKEY, OR BEEF TOSTADAS WITH BLACK BEANS

4 tostadas

Combine in a large bowl:

3 cups shredded lettuce

1½ cups diced cooked chicken, turkey, or beef

1 cup grated Monterey Jack or queso fresco
(4 ounces)
1 cup cooked, 253, or canned black beans,
rinsed if canned, drained
1 small red or yellow bell pepper, chopped
Add and toss to coat:
About $^1/_2$ cup Lime Vinaigrette, 573, or
$^3/_4$ cup Guacamole, 72
Spoon the mixture into:
4 corn tortillas, fried, 609
Serve immediately with:
Sour cream
Salsa Fresca, 571

STEAK FAJITAS

12 fajitas

Place in a baking dish or roasting pan just large enough to
hold it:
1$^1/_4$ pounds skirt or flank steak
Whisk together:
$^1/_4$ cup fresh lime juice
2 scallions, thinly sliced
3 garlic cloves, minced
(3 tablespoons minced cilantro)
1 tablespoon vegetable oil
$^1/_2$ teaspoon salt
$^1/_2$ to 1 teaspoon crushed red pepper flakes
$^1/_2$ teaspoon ground cumin
Pour the marinade over the steak, turning to coat. Cover
and refrigerate 12 to 24 hours, turning several times.
When ready to cook the steak, prepare a medium-grill fire
or preheat the broiler. Meanwhile, heat in a large skillet
over medium-high heat:
2 tablespoons vegetable oil
Add and cook, stirring, until tender:
2 medium onions, sliced
2 red or green peppers, cut into strips
$^1/_2$ teaspoon salt
$^1/_2$ teaspoon black pepper
Remove from the heat and cover to keep warm. Remove
the steak from the marinade (discard the marinade) and
grill or broil 3 to 4 minutes on each side for medium-rare.
Transfer to a platter and let stand 5 minutes. Have ready:
Twelve 6-inch Flour Tortillas, 608, warmed
Slice the steak across the grain on the bias into thin strips.
Serve with the tortillas and:
Salsa Fresca, 571, Roasted Tomato-Chipotle Salsa,
572, or other salsa of choice
(Guacamole, 72)
Sour cream
To assemble, place some steak and sautéed peppers and
onions on each tortilla, top as desired, and roll.

CHICKEN FAJITAS

Prepare **Steak Fajitas, above,** substituting 1$^1/_4$ **pounds
boneless, skinless chicken breasts or thighs** for the steak. If
broiling or sautéing, cut the chicken into chunks or strips.
Marinate the chicken 1 to 6 hours. Broil or sauté the cut-
up chicken, 419, until firm to the touch and cooked
through, 10 to 12 minutes. Or grill the chicken breasts or
thighs whole, then cut into strips.

SHRIMP FAJITAS

Please read About Skewer Cooking, 1049. Prepare **Steak
Fajitas, above,** substituting 1$^1/_4$ **pounds peeled and deveined shrimp** for the steak. Marinate for 30 minutes to 1
hour. Broil, 386, or sauté the shrimp until pink, slightly
curled, and opaque throughout, 4 to 5 minutes. Or, to
grill, thread onto bamboo skewers that have been soaked
in water for 1 hour.

ABOUT PIZZA, CALZONE, AND STROMBOLI

In its simplest form, **pizza** is a round of yeast dough rolled
to any thickness, topped with assorted ingredients and
baked. The simplest pizza is made with tomato sauce and
cheese; the most simple variation is white pizza, without
tomato sauce. A **calzone** is like a turnover, made by rolling
a round of pizza dough, topping half of the dough with ingredients, and folding the other half over to encase them;
it is sealed around the edges and baked. Calzones are
served individually. **Stromboli** is made with dough rolled
into a rectangle, filled with an assortment of ingredients,
sealed, and baked. It is sliced to serve.

TOPPINGS OR FILLINGS FOR
PIZZA OR CALZONES

Topping a pizza is a matter of taste. In Russia, pizza may be
topped with red herring or *mackba* (a mixture of sardines,
salmon, mackerel, tuna, and onions). Indians top pizza
with pickled ginger, minced mutton, and paneer. In Japan,
squid and *"mayo jaga"* (mayonnaise, potato, and bacon)
are popular. The "Double Dutch" is a favorite in the
Netherlands: double cheese, double onions, and double
beef. The important thing to remember is that some toppings must be precooked to release excess fat or liquid to
prevent a soggy pizza. Listed below are a few of America's
favorite toppings.

MEATS AND SEAFOOD

Cooked pepperoni, canned anchovies, ham, Canadian
bacon, prosciutto, Italian sausage, ground beef, breakfast
sausage, bacon, chicken, venison, duck, crayfish, fish,
shrimp, clams.

VEGETABLES AND FRUIT

Cooked mushrooms, onions, artichoke hearts, eggplant,
spinach, potatoes, broccoli; grilled vegetables, Roasted
Red Peppers, 292, Caramelized Onions, 287, Roasted Garlic, 277; uncooked sun-dried tomatoes, pineapple, green
peppers, jalapeños and other chile peppers, pitted black
or green olives, sliced fresh tomatoes.

CHEESES

Mozzarella, goat, feta, provolone, ricotta, Parmesan, Gorgonzola, blue cheese, pecorino romano.

HERBS, FRESH OR DRIED

Sage, rosemary, oregano, basil, thyme, Pesto Sauce, 569.

PIZZA WITH TOMATO SAUCE AND MOZZARELLA

Two 12-inch pizzas

This is the classic American **pizza,** a medium thick crust topped with tomato sauce and cheese. Prepare through the first rise:

> **Basic Pizza Dough, 607, or two 1-pound packages pizza dough**

Preheat the oven to 475°F. Grease 2 baking sheets and dust with cornmeal, or place a baking stone in the oven and preheat it for 45 minutes. Punch the dough down, and divide it in half if using homemade dough. Roll each piece into a ball and let rest, loosely covered with plastic wrap, for 10 to 15 minutes. One at a time, flatten each ball of dough on a lightly floured work surface into a 12-inch round, rolling and stretching the dough as necessary. Place each round on a prepared baking sheet, or, if using a baking stone, place one round of dough at a time on a baker's peel, below, dusted with cornmeal. Lift the edges and pinch to form a lip on both rounds. Brush the top of the dough with:

> **Olive oil**

Use your fingertips to push dents in the dough, and let rest for about 10 minutes. Spread in an even layer over both pizzas, leaving a 1/2-inch border all around:

> **1/2 cup Italian Tomato Sauce, 562**

Sprinkle with:

> **1 1/2 cups mozzarella, shredded (6 ounces)**
> **(1/2 cup coarsely chopped basil)**
> **Salt and black pepper to taste**

If baking the pizzas on baking sheets, place one pan on the bottom rack. If using a baking stone, slide the pizza off the peel onto the baking stone. Bake one pizza at a time until the crust is browned and the cheese is golden, about 12 minutes.

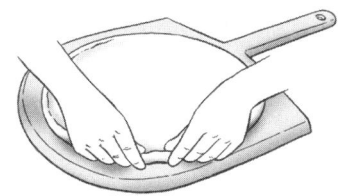

Lifting and pinching edges of pizza dough to form a lip

PIZZA MARGHERITA

Prepare the pizzas as directed, omitting the tomato sauce and topping the cheese with **ripe tomato slices.**

PEPPERONI PIZZA

Prepare the pizzas as directed, omitting the basil and topping with **thin pepperoni slices** as desired.

PIZZA WITH MUSHROOMS, PEPPERS, AND ONION

Prepare the pizzas as directed, scattering **1 1/4 cups thinly sliced mushrooms, 2 green bell peppers, thinly sliced,** and **1 onion, thinly sliced,** over the tomato sauce before adding the cheese.

PIZZA WITH ITALIAN SAUSAGE AND ONION

Remove the casings from **12 ounces hot or mild Italian sausages,** and brown in a skillet over medium heat, breaking up the lumps of meat, about 5 minutes. Drain the sausage. Prepare the pizzas as directed, topping them with the sausage and **1 onion, very thinly sliced.**

PIZZA WITH MUSHROOM, SAUSAGE, AND PEPPERONI

Remove the casings from **8 ounces Italian sausages with fennel** and brown in a skillet over medium heat, breaking up the lumps of meat, about 5 minutes. Drain the sausage. Prepare the pizzas as directed, topping with the sausage, **1 1/4 cups thinly sliced mushrooms,** and **about 24 slices pepperoni.**

SEATTLE PIZZA

Prepare the pizzas as directed, omitting the basil and topping them with **very thin slices prosciutto** or **thin slices Canadian bacon, halved,** and **canned pineapple chunks, well drained.**

PIZZA WITH PROSCIUTTO, ARTICHOKES, AND OLIVES

Prepare the pizzas as directed, topping them with **very thin slices prosciutto, drained marinated artichoke hearts, quartered,** and **Kalamata or other brine-cured black olives, pitted and sliced.**

PIZZA WITH GRILLED EGGPLANT, MUSHROOMS, AND SUN-DRIED TOMATOES

Remove the casings from **12 ounces hot or mild Italian sausages** and brown in a skillet over medium heat, breaking up the lumps of meat, about 5 minutes. Prepare the pizzas as directed, topping them with the sausage, **1 small eggplant, grilled, 243, and thinly sliced;** 3/4 cup **thinly sliced mushrooms; 1 red onion, very thinly sliced,** and **8 oil-packed sun-dried tomatoes, drained and thinly sliced.**

WHITE PIZZA WITH FRESH TOMATOES, BASIL, AND FETA CHEESE

Prepare the pizzas as directed, omitting the tomato sauce and mozzarella, topping instead with **very thinly sliced tomatoes** and **3 ounces feta, crumbled.**

WHITE PIZZA WITH CARAMELIZED ONIONS, BLACK OLIVES, AND ROSEMARY

Prepare the pizzas as directed, omitting the tomato sauce and mozzarella, topping instead with **1¹/₂ cups Caramelized Onions, 287,** and **sliced pitted Kalamata or other brine-cured black olives;** substitute **4 teaspoons finely chopped fresh rosemary or 2 teaspoons dried rosemary** for the basil.

WHITE PIZZA WITH FRESH CLAMS AND GARLIC

Prepare the pizzas as directed, omitting the tomato sauce, mozzarella, and basil and topping instead with **24 shucked littleneck clams** and **3 garlic cloves, minced;** season with **about 2 teaspoons salt.** When each pizza comes out of the oven, sprinkle it with **about 1 tablespoon chopped parsley.**

WHITE PIZZA WITH SPICY SHRIMP AND ROASTED RED PEPPERS

Prepare the pizzas as directed, omitting the tomato sauce, mozzarella, and basil and topping instead with **24 cooked peeled medium shrimp, coarsely chopped; 2 roasted bell peppers, 292, cut into thin strips;** ¹/₂ **teaspoon crushed red pepper flakes,** and ¹/₂ **teaspoon dried thyme.**

WHITE PIZZA WITH PORTOBELLO MUSHROOMS AND GOAT CHEESE

Prepare the pizzas as directed, omitting the tomato sauce, mozzarella, and basil, topping instead with **2 sautéed portobello mushrooms** or **10 to 15 button mushrooms, thinly sliced and sautéed; 1 red onion, thinly sliced and sautéed with 3 minced garlic cloves,** and ¹/₂ **teaspoon dried thyme. Top with 4 ounces fresh goat cheese, crumbled.**

WHITE PIZZA WITH CHICKEN AND BROCCOLI

Prepare the pizzas as directed, omitting the tomato sauce, mozzarella, and basil, topping instead with **2 boneless chicken breasts, grilled or sautéed, and cut into small bite-sized pieces; 2 cups well-drained blanched broccoli florets; 1 onion, very thinly sliced,** and **1 cup shredded mozzarella (about 4 ounces).**

WHITE PIZZA WITH POTATOES AND SAGE

Prepare the pizzas as directed, omitting the tomato sauce, mozzarella, and basil, topping instead with **8 ounces broiled or roasted thinly sliced potatoes, 2 tablespoons coarsely chopped fresh sage or 2 teaspoons dried sage,** and **2 tablespoons extra-virgin olive oil.**

ABOUT GRILLED PIZZA

Grilled pizza is simple to make and has a crisp yet chewy crust. Both charcoal and gas grills work well. A large grill is more convenient than a small one, but if your grill cannot accommodate a 12-inch round, simply divide the dough and make smaller pizzas. ➤ Hardwood lump charcoal results in more of a wood-fired pizza flavor.

Prepare the dough as for Pizza with Tomato Sauce and Mozzarella, 191. Use two spatulas or a baker's peel, 191, to transfer each round of dough to the grill. Watch for the dough to firm up as the bottom cooks. When it is firm enough, about 5 minutes, flip it over, leave it on the grill, and top with your selected ingredients; or place it cooked side up on a floured counter (to prevent sticking), add the toppings, and then return to the grill. ➤ Use less topping on a grilled pizza than one baked in an oven to ensure heating throughout. ➤ To cook and heat the topping and to melt the cheese, cover the grill.

Making grilled pizza crusts can be the basis for a festive party. Make smaller crusts for individual pizzas. Grill both sides of the dough, and have a basket full of crusts alongside a variety of toppings when guests arrive. Each person tops his or her own, and you heat them on the grill.

Another grilling method that produces an incredibly crisp crust requires a pizza stone. Place the stone in a covered grill and preheat for 45 minutes to 1 hour. A gas grill should be preheated to high, and a charcoal grill needs a hot fire. Place each uncooked pizza on the stone, and time the baking as you would using an oven, checking every 5 to 10 minutes.

Prepare as directed:

Basic Pizza Dough, 607, or two 1-pound packages refrigerated pizza dough

Prepare a hot charcoal fire, setting the grill rack 3 to 4 inches above the coals, or preheat a gas grill to medium-high. Meanwhile, punch the dough down, and divide it in half if using homemade dough. Roll each piece into a ball and let rest, loosely covered with plastic wrap, for 10 to 15 minutes. Remove the plastic wrap from one ball of dough. Flatten it on a lightly floured work surface into a 12-inch round, rolling and stretching the dough as necessary. Lift the edge and pinch to form a lip. Use your fingertips to push dents in the surface of the dough to prevent bubbling, and let rest for about 10 minutes.

Grill the pizza about 5 minutes until the crust is lightly browned on the bottom and the dough has firmed up. Flip, then top as for Pizza with Tomato Sauce and Mozzarella, 191, or use any of the topping combinations, 190–191, remembering less is more when topping a grilled pizza. Grill, preferably covered, for about 5 minutes, until the bottom is browned, the toppings are hot, and the cheese has melted. Repeat with the remaining balls of dough.

CALZONES

Eight 8-inch calzones

The possibilities for calzone fillings are many, including toppings used in any of the pizza recipes. You will need about 4 cups of filling or ¹/₂ cup per calzone. Cooked dry ingredients will prevent the bottoms of the calzones from becoming mushy.

Prepare through the first rise:

Basic Pizza Dough, 607, or two 1-pound packages
    refrigerated pizza dough
Preheat the oven to 450°F. Lightly grease 2 baking sheets. Divide the dough in eight balls. Place on a lightly floured work surface, sprinkle with flour, and cover with a kitchen towel or plastic wrap. Let stand for 20 minutes. Meanwhile, coarsely chop:

2 to 2½ cups filling

Mix with:

1½ to 2 cups shredded mozzarella (6 to 8 ounces)

Shape each ball of dough into a thick disk and let stand for about 5 minutes, then roll each disk into an 8-inch round. Divide the filling among the rounds, placing it on one half of each. Fold the dough over, making a half-circle, moisten the edges with water, and tightly seal with your fingertips. Place the calzones on the baking sheets and transfer to the oven. Reduce the oven temperature to 400°F and bake the calzones until nicely browned, about 25 minutes. Serve hot or at room temperature, with:

Marinara Sauce, 562

STROMBOLI

Two 12-inch stromboli

Prepare through the first rise:

Basic Pizza Dough, 607, or two 1-pound packages
    refrigerated pizza dough

Preheat the oven to 400°F. Lightly grease 2 baking sheets. Divide the dough in half if using homemade dough. Form each piece into a ball. Place on a lightly floured work surface, sprinkle with flour, and cover with a kitchen towel or plastic wrap. Let stand for 20 minutes. Shape each ball of dough into a thick disk and let stand for about 5 minutes, then roll each one into an 8 x 12-inch rectangle. Spread with:

¼ cup Italian Tomato Sauce, 562, or Marinara, 562

Top with, leaving a ½-inch border:

10 ounces sliced provolone

6 ounces sliced salami

4 ounces sliced pepperoni

Starting from a long side, tightly roll each rectangle up into a 12-inch log. Pinch the ends closed and place the logs seam side down on the baking sheets.

Bake the stromboli until firm and lightly browned, about 20 minutes. Cut into 1-inch slices, and serve hot or at room temperature.

EGG DISHES

It is not surprising that the egg, so elegant a package, should turn out to hold a small treasure of balanced nutrients—proteins, fats, and minerals. Eggs and egg dishes may be acceptably served at any meal, fried, scrambled, boiled, poached, baked, or incorporated into omelets or a soufflé. Almost unlimited variations of meat, vegetables, or fish may also accompany or be folded into them. ➤ For more about eggs, see 976.

No egg dish really succeeds, however, unless the eggs are very fresh and are cooked with due respect. JOY's basic admonition about cooking eggs has always been, "Eggs cook with a very low degree of heat, so treat them gently. They like the consideration and will respond by being tender." ➤ In only one type of preparation should the heat be high and brief—for omelets. ➤ Otherwise, dishes in which eggs predominate invariably do best if gently cooked and carefully timed. In combining eggs in custards, soufflés, and sauces, let them partially cook in the stored heat in the pan, and very carefully put them back on direct heat to maintain a satisfactory texture.

ABOUT SOFT-BOILED, HARD-BOILED, AND CODDLED EGGS

To help prevent the shells from cracking, you can prick a small hole in the end of the shell with a clean thumbtack or pushpin. You never want to actually boil eggs, but rather use one of the following techniques.

Soft-boiled eggs require very precise timing. For that reason, we recommend using a ➤ **boiling water start**—water is boiled then reduced to a simmer, at which point the eggs are placed in the water and timing begins. For soft-boiled eggs, boil, then reduce to a simmer:

Water

to cover:

Unshelled eggs

Using a tablespoon, gently place the eggs in the water, time the eggs from that moment, and maintain a simmer throughout the following cooking times: 4 minutes for large eggs, $3^1/_2$ minutes for small and medium, and $4^1/_2$ minutes for extra-large or jumbo. ➤ Eggs cooked right out of the refrigerator will require an additional 2 minutes.

To serve a soft-boiled egg in an eggcup, place the egg in wide end down. Use a table knife or teaspoon to crack off the top third of the shell, and season with salt and pepper. Alternatively, spoon the egg out of the shell, using a napkin to protect your hand from the heat, and serve in a small bowl. Soft-boiled and coddled eggs may be served shelled, in the ways suggested for Poached Eggs, 196.

Hard-boiled eggs can also be cooked with the boiling-water start method, but ➤ to simplify hard-boiling eggs, we use the **cold water start.**

Place in a pot in a single layer:

Unshelled eggs

Cover them by 1 inch with:

Cold water

Put the pan over high heat and bring to a boil. Promptly remove the pot from the heat, cover, and let the eggs stand: 15 minutes for large eggs, 12 minutes for small and medium eggs, 18 minutes for extra-large and jumbo eggs. Again, ➤ eggs that are not room temperature will require an additional 2 minutes. When cooking is complete, run cold water over eggs to stop cooking.

To shell hard-boiled eggs, crack the shell and roll the egg between the palms of your hands to free the thin tough skin from the egg and make shelling easier. If eggs are very fresh, they are more difficult to shell. If you want to slice the eggs smoothly, dip your knife blade into water before slicing. ➤ Hard-boiled eggs are best stored in their shells in the refrigerator. A peeled hard-boiled egg should be used within a few days.

To coddle eggs, lower unshelled eggs carefully into boiling water with a tablespoon. Cover the pan and remove from the heat. Allow 6 to 8 minutes for delicately coddled eggs. If you want the eggs to remain shapely when opened, turn them several times within the first few minutes of coddling so that the white of the egg solidifies evenly in the air space and the yolk is centered. Or use an egg coddler—a specially designed cup with a screw-on top. Fill a saucepan with enough water to reach the rim of the egg coddler and bring to a boil over high heat. Butter the insides of the egg coddler and break in:

1 egg

Top with:

($^1/_2$ teaspoon butter)
(2 teaspoons light or heavy cream)
Salt and black pepper

Screw top on tightly. Set the coddler in the pan, on a rack

or folded towel, cover, and immediately reduce the heat to a simmer. Simmer for 6 to 8 minutes for a medium-set egg.

CREAMED EGGS AU GRATIN

2 to 4 servings

Preheat the oven to 350°F. Heat until blended in a small skillet, over low heat:

1 tablespoon butter
1 tablespoon olive oil

Add and cook, stirring, until softened but not browned, about 5 minutes:

$1/4$ cup minced shallots or onions

Remove to a bowl. Add and mix gently:

4 hard-boiled eggs, 194, chopped or sliced
1 cup White Sauce I, 550
2 tablespoons chopped herbs of your choice
1 teaspoon Dijon mustard
$1/2$ teaspoon minced garlic
Salt and black pepper to taste

Transfer to a baking dish. Sprinkle with:

$3/4$ cup fresh bread crumbs
1 tablespoon butter, cut into small pieces

Bake until heated through and browned, 15 to 20 minutes. If desired, place briefly under the broiler to brown and crisp the crumbs.

CURRIED EGGS

Prepare **Creamed Eggs au Gratin, above.** Add to the sautéing onions **1 teaspoon curry powder.** Garnish with **sliced and chopped almonds** and **parsley.**

CREAMED EGGS WITH ASPARAGUS TIPS COCKAIGNE

Prepare **Creamed Eggs au Gratin, above.** Add to the sauce **$3/4$ cup asparagus tips, cooked and drained** (see About Asparagus, 249).

DEVILED OR STUFFED EGGS

The blandness of hard-boiled eggs is a challenge to adventurous cooks. Here are a few suggestions to enliven this basic ingredient with supplies from your pantry shelves. Prepare and peel:

Hard-boiled eggs, 194

Cut the eggs lengthwise in half, or across. For a barrel-shaped container, slice off both ends. Remove the yolks carefully, so as not to damage the whites. Crush the yolks without packing them and moisten them with:

Vinaigrette, 572, or mayonnaise; heavy cream or sour cream; soft butter with vinegar and sugar to taste; fresh lemon juice or sweet pickle juice

Season to taste with one or more of the following:

Salt and paprika
(A little dry mustard or prepared mustard)
(Catsup or chili sauce)
(A dash of ground red pepper, curry powder, or hot pepper sauce)
(Worcestershire sauce)

EXOTIC ADDITIONS TO THE YOLKS

Anchovy or sardine paste
Chopped braunschweiger or cooked foie gras, 449
Minced Sautéed Chicken Livers, 440
Chutney
Caviar, 86
Chopped or finely diced smoked salmon
Curry powder
Guacamole, 72
Salsa, 571–572
Sliced scallions or shallots
Deviled Ham or Chicken Spread, 180
Jalapeños or other hot peppers
Crumbled blue cheese
Chopped chives, tarragon, chervil, parsley, basil, or dill

Put the filling in the whites using a small spoon or, for elaborate effects, a pastry tube. Chill 30 minutes before serving.

Garnish with:

Sliced olives, truffles, or capers

POP'S DEVILED EGGS

8 stuffed eggs

Pop loved to make deviled eggs. His favorite recipe is still a family treat.

Prepare and peel:

4 hard-boiled eggs, 194

Prepare them as for

Deviled Eggs, above

Mix with the yolks:

2 tablespoons mayonnaise
1 teaspoon chili sauce
($1/2$ teaspoon curry powder)
$1/8$ teaspoon black pepper
$1/8$ teaspoon celery salt
$1/8$ teaspoon dry mustard

Stuff the egg whites as above.

SCOTCH EGGS

6 servings

Please read about Deep-Fat Frying, 1046. Prepare:

12 ounces ground sausage or Herbed Pork Sausage, 516
6 hard-boiled eggs, 194, peeled

Place on a plate:

$1/4$ cup all-purpose flour

Beat in a shallow bowl:

1 large egg

Spread on another plate:

$1^1/2$ cups fresh or dry bread crumbs

Wet your hands with cold water before coating each egg to prevent the sausage from sticking to your hands. Shape the sausage into 6 patties. Mold each patty around a hard-boiled egg. Roll each egg in the flour to coat and shake off the excess, dip in the beaten egg, and then roll in the bread crumbs to coat.

Heat to 350°F in a deep heavy pot:

3 inches vegetable oil

Fry the eggs in two batches until the sausage is golden brown, about 6 minutes. Let stand for 5 to 10 minutes and serve hot, at room temperature, or chilled, with:

Mayonnaise

Mustard

FRIED EGGS

2 to 4 servings

Use enough butter or other fat to generously coat the bottom of the pan. A nonstick skillet makes it easy to turn the eggs and to slide them onto a plate. If you like tender whites, use medium heat. For whites with brown edges, use medium-high to high heat. Cooking a **sunny-side up** egg in a generously greased pan will give you a yolk that is barely thickened around the edges and quite runny. For an egg that is slightly more cooked on top, use the larger amount of butter called for in the recipe and baste it as it cooks with the hot fat from the pan or simply cover the pan during cooking. For those who prefer whites that are done and yolks that are runny—**over easy** or **over medium**—when the whites are firm, insert a slotted spatula under the egg, supporting the yolk area, and cautiously turn it in the skillet. Cooking the second side will take only a matter of moments. Fried eggs **over hard** or **well** are cooked a bit longer on the second side, until the yolk is nearly set.

Melt in a large nonstick skillet over medium-low heat:

1 to 3 tablespoons butter or other fat

When the butter is sizzling but not brown, break into the skillet:

4 eggs

Season with:

Salt and black pepper to taste

To get a firm white, cook, covered if desired, until the whites are completely set and the yolks are just barely beginning to thicken around the edges, about 3 minutes if covered, 4 to 5 minutes if uncovered.

ADDITIONS TO FRIED EGGS

It is often the extras that give punch to eggs, especially for brunch and lunch dishes.

Serve the eggs on a small mound of:

Cooked rice, noodles, potatoes, or rounds of toast, or on top of a **green salad, 158–159**

Top with any of these sauces:

Quick Tomato Cheese Sauce, 562

White Sauce I, 550, seasoned with mustard or curry powder, herbs, onion, celery, green peppers, capers, anchovies, and/or cheese

Black Butter, 557, or Brown Butter, 557

A mushroom or onion sauce

EGGS IN A BASKET

2 servings

Kids get a big kick out of this dish, especially when they get to make the basket.

Using a 2¹/₂-inch biscuit cutter or small glass, cut a hole out of the center of:

2 slices sandwich bread

Melt in a large skillet over medium heat:

2 tablespoons butter, plus more as needed

Add the bread and cook for about 30 seconds. Crack into the holes:

2 eggs

Do not worry if some of the white remains on top of the bread or runs out from underneath. When the eggs begin to set, 2 to 3 minutes, flip the bread and eggs, using a spatula. Add more butter as needed. Fry the other side until the eggs are done to your liking. Grill the rounds of bread in butter and serve them as well.

HUEVOS RANCHEROS

4 servings

This classic Mexican dish can be served with any variety of salsas, meats—especially chorizo—and, always, refried beans.

Heat and keep warm:

2 cups Salsa, 571–572

Heat in a large nonstick skillet, over medium-high heat until hot:

1 to 2 tablespoons vegetable oil

Add 1 at a time and quick-fry for 2 to 3 seconds each side:

4 corn tortillas

Remove to paper towels to drain, then wrap in foil and keep warm in a 200°F oven. Set the skillet over medium-low heat and add a bit more oil if needed. Break into the skillet:

4 to 8 eggs

Let cook until set, sunny-side up or as desired. Cover the pan for a minute or so for the most even cooking. Season with:

Salt and black pepper to taste

Set a tortilla on each of 4 warmed plates and top with 1 or 2 eggs. Spoon a generous ¹/₂ cup of the warm salsa around each serving. Serve immediately, sprinkled with:

Finely crumbled queso fresco, farmer's cheese, or feta (Chopped cilantro)

POACHED EGGS

2 to 4 servings

Poached eggs are cooked in simmering liquid until the yolks are thick yet still liquid in the center. They can be poached in water, stock, sauce, milk, heavy cream, or soup, as in Garlic Soup with Eggs, 124. In some classic recipes, such as Eggs en Meurette, 197, an aromatic poaching liquid is thickened and used as a sauce for the eggs.

Although there are various rings and egg poaching sets available, all that is really necessary to poach eggs are a saucepan and a slotted spoon. The challenge when poaching eggs is to prevent them from spreading when they are added to the poaching liquid. For best results, use very fresh eggs, which best hold their shape. Adding vinegar and salt to the water helps the white to set more quickly. Use scissors or a small knife to trim away any thin streamers of white.

Bring to a rolling boil in a large nonstick skillet:

2 to 4 inches of water

Reduce heat until the water is barely simmering. Add:

1 tablespoon vinegar
¹/₂ teaspoon salt

Have ready:

4 eggs

One at a time, break each egg into a small bowl or cup, bring the edge of the bowl level with the surface of the water, and slide each egg in gently. Simmer until the whites are set, about 3 minutes. With practice, you will be able to judge the right degree of doneness. Remove the eggs with a large slotted spoon, and drain well before serving. If cooking for several people or a crowd, prepare eggs in advance. Transfer the finished eggs to a wide shallow bowl of water warmed to 150°F and hold for up to 30 minutes. They can also be poached well ahead of time and refrigerated for up to 24 hours. Transfer the poached eggs to a bowl of cold water the moment they are done and refrigerate. When ready to reheat and serve, with a slotted spoon, transfer the eggs to a large pan of 150°F water, cover, and let stand for at least 5 minutes, or up to 20 minutes. Return the pan to very low heat if the temperature of the water drops below 145°F.

POACHED EGGS MORNAY

Prepare **Poached Eggs, 196.** Arrange them in a shallow buttered baking dish. Cover with **Mornay Sauce, 551,** sprinkle with **Au Gratin II or III, 961,** and brown quickly under a hot broiler.

EGGS FLORENTINE

Prepare **Poached Eggs, 196.** Cover the bottom of a shallow buttered baking dish with **Creamed Spinach, 305.** Arrange the poached eggs on the spinach and proceed as for Poached Eggs Mornay, above.

EGGS BENEDICT

2 to 4 servings

For variations on a theme, place the eggs on top of Creamed Spinach, 305, or Fried Green Tomatoes, 312. Prepare and drain well, and keep warm:

4 Poached Eggs, 196

Place on warmed plates or a warmed serving platter:

2 English muffins, split, toasted, and buttered

Cover with:

4 thick slices ham or Canadian bacon, warmed

Top with the well-drained eggs, then top the eggs with:

¹/₂ cup Hollandaise Sauce, 560, or more if desired

Serve immediately, passing extra sauce on the side.

POACHED EGGS BLACKSTONE

2 to 4 servings

Prepare and keep warm:

4 Poached Eggs, 196

Fry in a large skillet until crisp:

4 slices bacon

Remove to paper towels to drain and cool, then crumble. Reserve the drippings in the pan.

Dredge:

Four ¹/₂-inch-thick tomato slices

in:

Flour for dusting
Salt and white pepper to taste

Cook them in the bacon fat until lightly browned. Place on warmed plates, and sprinkle with the bacon. Top each tomato slice with a poached egg. Generously top the eggs with:

Hollandaise Sauce, 560, or Béarnaise Sauce, 561

EGGS POACHED IN RED WINE (EGGS EN MEURETTE)

4 servings

Melt in a wide saucepan over medium heat:

¹/₄ cup (¹/₂ stick) butter

Reduce the heat to medium-low and add:

1 cup chopped carrots
1 cup chopped celery
1 cup chopped onions
4 garlic cloves, peeled and crushed
¹/₂ cup chopped ham or pancetta

Cook, stirring occasionally, until the vegetables are thoroughly softened, about 15 minutes. Add:

2¹/₂ cups dry red wine and 1¹/₂ cups Poultry Stock, 117, or broth or 4 cups dry red wine
1 Bouquet Garni, 960

Bring to a simmer and cook for 30 minutes. Strain, discard the solids, and return the liquid to the saucepan. Boil until reduced to 1 cup, 10 to 20 minutes, then remove from heat. Meanwhile, heat in a small skillet over medium heat:

2 tablespoons butter

Add and cook until lightly browned:

1 cup sliced mushrooms
2 tablespoons chopped shallots

Set aside. Prepare and keep warm:

8 Poached Eggs, 196
Beurre Manié, 545

Bring the reduced liquid to a simmer and whisk in the Beurre Manié bit by bit to thicken the sauce. Add the sautéed mushrooms. Season with:

¹/₄ teaspoon salt
¹/₈ teaspoon black pepper
(Dash of red wine vinegar)
(Dash of brandy)

Cook over low heat until the sauce is heated through; do not let the sauce boil. Arrange on a serving platter:

Eight 3-inch rounds of bread, toasted and buttered

Top with the well-drained poached eggs. Pour the sauce around the eggs and garnish with:

Minced parsley

EGGS WITH SMOKED SALMON

A genial winter breakfast or luncheon dish.
Toast and butter:

Slices of light rye or pumpernickel bread

Place on the toast:

Very thin slices of smoked salmon

Top with:

Poached or Fried Eggs, 196

Cover with:

**(Hollandaise Sauce, 560, or Scandinavian Mustard Dill
Sauce, 566)**

Sprinkle with:

Snipped dill

SCRAMBLED EGGS

For soft and creamy scrambled eggs, beat the eggs until the whites and yolks are completely blended and cook them over low heat. The addition of a small amount of milk or half-and-half will keep the eggs tender. A heavy-bottomed skillet is best for even cooking, but a nonstick surface makes cooking and cleanup easier. Infrequent stirring will produce large curds; constant stirring results in smaller, creamier curds. For fluffier eggs, beaten egg whites, 978, may be added to whole eggs in the proportion of 1 additional white to each 3 whole eggs. Remove the eggs from the pan just before they reach the desired consistency, as the residual heat will continue to cook them briefly.

1 to 2 servings

I. This method gives you tender eggs with large curds.
Beat with a fork or whisk until completely blended:

3 eggs
$1/4$ teaspoon salt
(2 tablespoons milk or cream)
($1/8$ teaspoon paprika)

Melt in a 10-inch skillet, preferably nonstick, over medium-low heat:

$1^{1}/_2$ tablespoons unsalted butter

Pour in the eggs and, with a wooden spoon or heatproof rubber spatula stir slowly and constantly, pushing the eggs to the center of the pan and scraping the bottom and sides. When the eggs begin to thicken, after about 2 minutes, continue stirring until not quite cooked to the desired consistency. Stir in:

**(1 tablespoon softened unsalted butter
  or heavy cream)**

Sprinkle with:

(Pinch of black pepper)

II. A slower but foolproof alternative. Melt in a double boiler over, not in, boiling water:

$1/2$ tablespoon unsalted butter

Have ready:

The seasoned egg mixture in I, above

When the butter is hot, pour in the egg mixture. Stir with a wooden spoon until the eggs have thickened into soft creamy curds. Serve in:

Prebaked Tartlet Shells, 666, or Bouchées, 670

ADDITIONS TO SCRAMBLED EGGS

Up to 1 tablespoon per egg of the following ingredients may be stirred into the egg mixture before scrambling. The additions should be at room temperature.

Chopped herbs
Grated or ground nutmeg or ground mace
Grated or crumbled hard cheese
**Cottage cheese, farmer's cheese, or cubed cream
  cheese**
**Roasted, 292, or sautéed red, green, or yellow bell
  peppers**
Finely chopped scallions
Sautéed or Caramelized Onions, 287
**Peeled, seeded, and chopped tomatoes sautéed with
  basil**
Cooked asparagus tips (see About Asparagus, 249)
Sautéed sliced mushrooms
Sautéed sliced zucchini and shallots
Chopped cooked, drained spinach
Crumbled cooked bacon, sausage, or diced ham
**Strips of smoked salmon or crabmeat, seasoned with
  a dash of curry powder**

SCOTCH WOODCOCK

4 servings

Preheat the oven to 200°F. Toast:

Four $1/2$-inch-thick slices bread

Spread with:

4 teaspoon Anchovy Butter, 558, or anchovy paste

Keep warm in the oven. Mix together thoroughly in a small heavy saucepan:

4 egg yolks
$2/3$ cup half-and-half or heavy cream
$1/4$ teaspoon salt, or to taste
Black or white pepper to taste

Cook over low heat, stirring constantly with a wooden spoon or heatproof rubber spatula until you see the first signs of thickening along the bottom of the pan, about 10 minutes. At this point, begin to stir quite briskly and cook until thick and smooth, like a cheese sauce, 3 to 5 minutes more. Do not let it come near the simmer, or it will turn into scrambled eggs. Remove from the heat and immediately stir in:

2 tablespoons cold butter, cut into small pieces
2 tablespoons minced parsley
Ground red pepper to taste

Spoon over the warm anchovy toast and serve.

MATZO BREI

1 serving

If making a large quantity for a crowd, use 2 pans and keep the cooked matzo brei warm in a 200°F oven.
For each serving, use:

2 unsalted matzos
1 large egg, well beaten

Hold the matzos briefly under hot running water to wet both sides without making them soggy. Drain and tear into $2^1/_2$- to 3-inch pieces and set in a bowl. Add the egg and gently stir to coat the matzo. Season with:

Salt to taste

Heat in a large skillet:

$^1/_8$ inch vegetable oil or chicken fat

Using a large spoon or spatula, spread the matzo mixture in the skillet in a very thin layer. Cook, turning the pieces as they brown, until medium-brown and crispy. Serve warm, passing the salt shaker or cinnamon sugar.

BAKED EGGS

Baked eggs served in individual ramekins, casseroles, or cocotte dishes always have great eye appeal. If you wish to eliminate the butter or cream, simply cover each dish with aluminum foil. **Shirred eggs,** also referred to as *oeufs sur le plat* or *oeufs au miroir,* are baked in small gratin dishes directly on an oven rack, sometimes under the broiler, not in a water bath.

Four-ounce ramekins, which hold 1 egg, are commonly used to bake eggs, but you can use something larger—6-ounce custard cups, ovenproof coffee cups, small bowls, or muffin tins. For tender, evenly cooked eggs, we recommend baking them in a water bath, 801. The eggs should be cooked until the whites are just set but the yolks are still soft and runny. ➤ Take care not to overcook or hurry the eggs. The ramekins will retain heat and continue to cook the eggs after they are removed from the oven.

1 serving

Preheat the oven to 350°F. Grease ramekins or other ovenproof dishes. For each serving, break into a ramekin:

1 egg

Season lightly with:

Salt

Drizzle over the top:

1 teaspoon heavy cream or melted butter

Bake in a water bath, 801, about 15 minutes. Garnish with:

(Chopped sautéed chicken livers, well seasoned, or ham and herbs or Tomato Sauce, 562)

ADDITIONS TO BAKED EGGS

I. **Sautéed mushrooms, 283, or asparagus tips**
Chopped tomatoes
Creamed Spinach, 305, Creamed Mushrooms, 283, or Creamed Onions, 287
Chicken or Turkey Chili Hash with Sweet Potatoes, 108
Crumbled cooked bacon or sausage or chopped anchovies

II. Place in the bottom of the baking dish before egg:
A round of toast covered with Gruyère

III. Before baking, cover with:
Cheese Sauce, 551, or Tomato Sauce, 562

EGGS BAKED IN A MUFFIN TIN

12 servings

These are good ways to serve baked eggs to a crowd.

I. Preheat the oven to 350°F. Lightly grease a muffin tin, preferably nonstick, with:

Softened butter

Have ready:

12 eggs

Sprinkle into each muffin cup:

1 tablespoon grated Parmesan ($^3/_4$ cup total)
2 tablespoons diced ham (1$^1/_2$ cups total)

Crack 1 egg into each muffin cup. Bake in a water bath, 801, until the whites are just set but the yolks are still soft and runny, 13 to 14 minutes. Remove each egg with a small spatula and transfer to a plate.

II. Preheat the oven to 350°F. Lightly grease a muffin tin, preferably nonstick, with:

Softened butter

Have ready:

12 eggs

Cook in a skillet or broil until lightly browned but still soft:

18 slices bacon

Line the sides of each muffin cup with 1$^1/_2$ strips of bacon. Place in each cup:

(1 tablespoon chili sauce; $^3/_4$ cup total)

Crack an egg into each muffin cup. Pour over each egg:

1 teaspoon melted butter (4 tablespoons total)

Sprinkle with:

Salt and paprika to taste

Bake in a water bath, 801, described above. Place the eggs on:

12 rounds of toast or warm slices of drained canned pineapple

Garnish with:

Chopped parsley

EGGS IN A NEST

4 servings

Delicious unadorned or with Tomato Sauce, 562.
Preheat the oven to 375°F. Have ready:

4 eggs

Mix together:

2 cups Mashed Potatoes, 295
5 tablespoons milk
$^1/_2$ cup chopped ham or crumbled cooked bacon
3 tablespoons chopped parsley
$^1/_4$ teaspoon paprika
Salt to taste

Spread the mixture in the bottom of a greased baking dish. Make 4 large hollows in it with a tablespoon. Break 1 egg into each hollow. Sprinkle the top with:

Au Gratin I, 961
Bake until the eggs are set but not hard, about 22 minutes.

ABOUT OMELETS

Andrew Carnegie once counseled: "Put all your eggs in one basket. Then watch that basket!" When the container is a skillet and the objective an omelet, his advice is especially apt. The name "omelet" is loosely applied to many kinds of egg dishes, but there are four basic types of omelets: French, firm, flat, and souffléed. All are made from beaten eggs cooked so that the exterior is firm and smooth while the inside remains somewhere between runny and barely moist.

The classic omelet, the **French omelet,** is rolled or folded, typically around some sort of savory filling. The **firm omelet** is easier to make—perfect for the novice—as it is cooked into a fairly firm cake before being folded in half. A **flat omelet,** called a **frittata** in Italy, is made much like a large pancake. A **souffléd omelet** is made puffy and light by beating the egg whites until airy.

Since omelet making is so rapid, see that you have ready everything you are going to serve the omelet with or on, and be sure you have your diners captive.

The success of all omelets demands that ➤ the pan and the fat be hot enough to bind the base of the egg at once so as to hold the softer egg above, but not so hot as to toughen the base before the rest of the egg cooks.

Eggs, therefore, and any food incorporated with them, must be room temperature before being put into the pan. ➤ To warm eggs to room temperature, place in a bowl of hot tap water for 5 minutes. More omelet failures are due to eggs being used directly from the refrigerator than to any other cause. There is always, too, the problem of salting. As salt tends to toughen the egg structure, it should, in general, be added to the fillings or garnishes you choose to fold into the omelet.

Glazing omelets makes them look prettier but tends to toughen them. ➤ To glaze an omelet, brush it with butter. Or, if you want a really sophisticated job, put the omelet on a warm broilerproof serving dish, coat it lightly with about ¼ cup of thin Mornay Sauce, 551, and run it under the broiler for 1½ to 2 minutes. Or, if it is a sweet omelet, sprinkle it with sugar and run it under the broiler briefly.

Omelet purists contend that one pan should be used solely for their specialty. But we find an all-purpose 10- to 12-inch nonstick skillet perfect for omelet preparation. An omelet is easiest to manage when prepared in the proper size pan. For a 2-egg omelet, an 8- to 10-inch pan is best. A 3- to 5-egg omelet needs a 12-inch pan.

Filling omelets is not necessary, but the results are splendid. ➤ About ½ to ¾ cup of cooked filling is required for a 3-egg omelet. Herbs or finely grated cheese may be added to the beaten eggs before cooking. For other fillings, ➤ see Additions to Scrambled Eggs, 198, and Fillings for Omelets, 201.

FRENCH OMELET (ROLLED OR FOLDED)
1 serving

For French omelets both rolled and folded, the eggs should be beaten only enough to thoroughly blend the whites and yolks, not enough to incorporate air or make them frothy. Using a fork rather than a whisk to beat the eggs helps ensure that you do not overbeat them.

When making more than one omelet, beat the total number of eggs you will need, then use a ladle or measuring cup to pour 3½ ounces, or about ½ cup, for each 2-egg omelet. Keep the butter and filling ingredients by the stove and move quickly, as you make the omelets one by one. Serve them as they are ready, or keep them warm in a 200°F oven and serve when all are finished. If you have more than 4 to make, use another pan, or even two. Attention to more than one pan at a time is a skill that needs to be developed, so practice before your debut. Stagger the cooking so the omelets are not all at the same stage at once.

Beat with a fork until the whites and yolks are blended:

2 large eggs
⅛ teaspoon salt
Pinch of black pepper

Melt in an 8- to 10-inch skillet, preferably nonstick, over medium-high heat:

1 tablespoon unsalted butter

Tilt the skillet to coat the sides and bottom thoroughly. You can also use nonstick cooking spray or a combination of butter and oil. When the butter is hot and has reached the point of fragrance, but is not brown, pour in the eggs. Meanwhile, agitate the pan forward and backward with the left hand. Keep the egg mass sliding as a whole over the pan bottom. With a dinner fork, quickly swirl the eggs with a circular motion, as shown. Hold the fork so the tines are parallel to, but not scraping, the base of the pan.

Preparing a rolled French omelet

At this point the heat in the pan may be sufficient to cook the eggs, and you may want to lift the pan from the heat as you gently swirl the eggs, as illustrated, in circular scrolls from the edges to the center. Pay no attention to the ridges formed by the fork. The rhythm of the pan and the stirring is like a child's trick of patting the head while rubbing the stomach. Have ready a hot serving plate, which helps to inflate the omelet; choose a heat-resistant one if you plan to glaze; see About Omelets, 200. Whether you fill your omelet or leave it plain, grasp the handle of the pan so the left palm is up, as shown. Tip the pan down away from the handle and, with the fork, flip about one-third of the omelet over, away from the handle, as shown in the center. If the omelet shows any tendency to stick, discard the fork and give the pan handle a sharp rap or two with the fist, as sketched. The omelet will flip over without the use of a fork and will start to slide. Slant the pan to 90 degrees or more until the omelet makes a second fold in sliding out of the pan and lies with its ends folded under on the plate—ready to serve. Glaze and garnish, if you wish, and serve at once.

FILLINGS FOR OMELETS

Herbs or finely grated cheese may be added to the beaten eggs before cooking or more substantial fillings may be placed in the middle of the omelet just before it is rolled. Use $1/3$ to $1/2$ cup filling at room temperature for a 2-egg omelet:

> Ratatouille Provençale, 274
> Creamed Mushrooms, 283
> Guacamole, 72, and Salsa Fresca, 571
> Ricotta or goat cheese mixed with tomatoes and herbs
> Chopped olives and sour cream
> Creamed Chicken, 445
> Chopped ham and grated cheese
> One part red or black caviar to 2 parts sour cream
> Duxelles, 284
> Caramelized Onions, 287
> Sautéed zucchini or asparagus tips
> Diced leftover cooked meat or seafood

FIRM OMELET

4 servings

For the beginner, the texture of this omelet is a little more manageable.
Beat with a fork until blended:

4 eggs

Beat in:

$1/4$ **cup milk, cream, or stock**
$1/2$ **teaspoon salt**
($1/8$ **teaspoon paprika**)

Melt in a skillet:

$1^1/2$ **tablespoons butter**

When the butter is fairly hot, add the egg mixture and cook over low heat. Lift the edges with a spatula and tilt

the skillet to permit the uncooked mixture to run to the bottom, or stick the egg mixture with a fork in the soft spots to permit the heat to penetrate the bottom layer. When it is all an even consistency, fold the omelet over and serve it. For a festive occasion, before serving, fold into the omelet any fillings for omelets, above.

SPANISH OMELET

4 servings

Heat in an 8- to 10-inch skillet over medium-high heat:

$1/2$ **cup olive oil**

Add:

1 cup peeled thinly sliced potatoes

Turn them constantly until well coated with the oil. Reduce the heat and turn them occasionally, about 20 minutes. Meanwhile, heat in a large heavy skillet:

2 tablespoons olive oil

Add and cook about 5 minutes:

$1/2$ **cup thinly sliced onion**
$1/2$ **cup julienned strips green bell pepper**

Add:

1 garlic clove, minced
$1/3$ **cup chopped peeled, seeded, and drained tomato**
Salt and black pepper to taste

Continue to cook about 15 minutes. Add the potatoes to the onion mixture, and keep hot. Prepare:

4 French Omelets, 200

Fill each omelet with 2 tablespoons of the filling and top each with 2 more tablespoons filling.

EGG WHITE OMELET

1 serving

Choose a moist, full-flavored filling for this omelet, such as smoked salmon and Neufchâtel cheese, sautéed or roasted peppers, 292, or sautéed mushrooms, or sun-dried tomatoes and Caramelized Onions, 287. Please read About Omelets, 200. Beat with a fork until well blended:

3 large egg whites
2 teaspoons chopped herbs, such as parsley, chives, tarragon, and/or dill
$1/8$ **teaspoon salt**
Pinch of ground black pepper

Heat in 6- to 8-inch skillet over medium-high heat:

1 tablespoon vegetable oil

When the oil is hot but not smoking, pour in the egg whites, tilting the skillet so that they cover the bottom. As the omelet begins to set on the bottom, lift the edges with a pancake turner and tilt the skillet to allow the uncooked egg mixture to run onto the bottom of the skillet. When the omelet is an even consistency, place any filling on the bottom half and fold the omelet in half, forming a half-moon shape. Remove with a spatula. Serve immediately.

FRITTATA

3 servings

Flat omelets and their Italian counterparts, frittatas, are made with vegetables, meats, or other savory ingredients mixed into the eggs. You may use any of the Fillings for Omelets, 201, except the creamed or sauced ones, ➤ allowing about 1 cup of filling to 3 eggs. Frittatas are served hot or at room temperature cut in wedges like pizza. ➤ To avoid sticking, use a well-seasoned 10- to 12-inch cast-iron skillet or a nonstick pan with a heat-proof handle, and make sure the bottom and sides of the pan are well greased before adding the eggs.

Have ready:

> 1¹/₂ to 2 cups additions, such as diced cooked
> vegetables, cheese, chicken, seafood, or ham—
> in any combination

Beat with a fork until blended:

> 6 eggs

Stir in the filling and:

> Salt and black pepper

How much salt and pepper you add will depend on how highly seasoned your filling is. Heat a 10-inch skillet over medium heat, and add:

> 1¹/₂ tablespoons olive oil

Pour in the egg mixture and proceed as in the basic French Omelet, 200, until the bottom of the frittata is set and the top is still creamy. To finish cooking the top, place the frittata in a 350°F oven or under the hot broiler for a few seconds until the top is firm. A traditional frittata is not browned. Serve at once on a hot platter, or serve at room temperature.

ARTICHOKE FRITTATA FOR A CROWD

8 servings

Serve as an appetizer to keep a small crowd happy while dinner is cooking.

Drain and cut lengthwise in half:

> Two 13³/₄-ounce cans (3¹/₄ cups) artichoke hearts

Drain and slice into ¹/₄-inch strips:

> 4 ounces (about ²/₃ cup) roasted red peppers

Set aside. Whisk together:

> 12 large eggs
> 1¹/₄ cups half-and-half
> 1 cup grated Parmesan
> ¹/₂ cup chopped basil
> 1 teaspoon salt
> Black pepper to taste

Melt in a 12-inch ovenproof greased or well-seasoned cast-iron skillet over medium heat:

> 3 tablespoons unsalted butter

Add and cook, stirring, until softened and lightly browned, about 10 minutes:

> 2 medium leeks, chopped
> 1 large garlic clove, finely chopped

Add the artichokes and red peppers along with:

> 2 tablespoons unsalted butter

Swirl to melt the butter and coat the pan. Cook the frittata over medium-low heat until the center is almost set, about 18 minutes. Preheat the broiler. Broil the frittata 7 inches from the heating element until browned, about 5 minutes. Cool to warm, and serve directly from the skillet in thin slices.

HANGTOWN FRY

4 servings

Dredge:

> 12 oysters, shucked, 371

in:

> ¹/₂ cup all-purpose flour
> Salt and black pepper to taste

Cook until crisp in an 8- to 10-inch skillet, preferably nonstick, over medium heat:

> 4 slices bacon

Remove the bacon and drain on paper towels. Pour the excess grease out of the skillet and set it over high heat. Add:

> 2 tablespoons butter

Add the breaded oysters and fry them until golden and crisp, about 2 minutes per side. Crumble the bacon into the skillet, then add:

> 5 eggs, lightly beaten
> ¹/₄ teaspoon salt
> ¹/₈ teaspoon black pepper

Reduce the heat to medium and let cook, undisturbed, for about 5 seconds, then use a wooden spatula to slowly move the eggs toward the center, tilting the pan to allow the uncooked eggs to run to the bottom of the pan. Stop moving the eggs as they set. Flip the omelet and cook the other side for a few seconds, or brown under the broiler. The omelet should still be a bit soft in the center.

WESTERN OR DENVER OMELET

2 servings

Please read About Omelets, 200. Melt in an 8- to 10-inch skillet, preferably nonstick, over medium heat:

> 1 tablespoon butter

Add and cook, stirring, until soft, about 10 minutes:

> ¹/₃ cup minced onion
> ¹/₃ cup minced green bell pepper

Add and cook, stirring, for another 5 minutes:

> ¹/₃ cup finely diced ham

Meanwhile, mix together:

> 4 eggs
> 1 tablespoon milk
> ¹/₈ teaspoon salt
> ¹/₈ teaspoon black pepper

Pour the eggs over the cooked vegetables and ham in the hot pan. Let cook, undisturbed, for about 5 seconds, then use a wooden spatula to slowly move the eggs toward the center, tilting the pan to allow the uncooked eggs to run to the bottom of the pan. Stop moving the eggs as they set. Flip the omelet and cook the other side for a few seconds, or brown under the broiler. The omelet should still be a bit soft in the center. Divide the omelet in half, and serve on warmed plates.

POTATO OMELET (TORTILLA ESPAÑOLA)

6 servings

Please read About Omelets, 200. Heat in a 10- to 12-inch skillet, preferably nonstick, over medium heat:

2 tablespoons olive oil

Add:

1 large onion, cut into ⅛-inch slices
Salt and black pepper to taste

Cook, stirring, until the onion is soft and golden, about 10 minutes. Remove to a large bowl. Heat in the same skillet over medium-high heat:

¼ cup olive oil

Add:

1 pound red-skinned potatoes, peeled and cut into
⅛-inch slices

Cook until golden brown, 10 to 12 minutes. Remove the potatoes to paper towels to drain. Set the pan aside with the oil in it. Add to the onions and mix well:

6 large eggs
½ teaspoon salt

Sprinkle the potatoes with:

Salt and black pepper to taste

Add the potatoes to the egg mixture and toss to coat the slices well with the egg. Return the skillet to high heat and heat the oil remaining in the pan. When it is hot, add the egg mixture and immediately reduce the heat to low. Let the omelet cook for 3 to 4 minutes, undisturbed, until the bottom is golden and the egg are two-thirds to three-quarters set. Shake the pan from time to time to make sure the omelet does not stick. If it does, slide a spatula under it to free it from the pan. Cook the top under the broiler until the top is firm. Shake the omelet to loosen it from the pan and slide onto a plate. Cut into wedges and serve hot or at room temperature.

SOUFFLÉD OMELET

4 servings

A properly executed souffléd omelet has a lovely brown, firm, dry exterior enveloping a soft, creamy, airy center. For a 4-egg omelet, you will need an ovenproof 10- to 12-inch pan for a full rise. We especially like sweet fillings, such as fruit or preserves, with these omelets, but cheese or herb fillings are also delicious. Please read About Omelets, 200.

Preheat the oven to 375°F. Whisk until thick and light:

4 large egg yolks
3 tablespoons sugar

In a large bowl, beat just to firm peaks, 978:

4 large egg whites
Pinch of salt

Fold the yolk mixture gently into the whites. Melt in a 10-inch ovenproof skillet over medium heat:

1 to 2 tablespoons butter

When the foam has subsided, pour the egg mixture into the pan, spread evenly, and smooth the top. Shake the pan after a few seconds to discourage sticking, then cover the pan with a lid whose underside has been buttered to prevent sticking. Reduce the heat and cook for about 5 minutes. Remove the lid and place the skillet in the oven until the top of the omelet is set, 3 to 5 minutes. Fold the omelet in half, if desired, slide it out onto a warmed plate, and sprinkle with:

(Confectioners' sugar)

JAM-FILLED SOUFFLÉD OMELET

Prepare **Souffléd Omelet, above.** Before folding the omelet, fill it with **2 tablespoons warm apricot jam mixed with 1 teaspoon rum or brandy,** or **2 tablespoons raspberry jam mixed with 1 teaspoon fresh lemon juice.**

GRAND MARNIER SOUFFLÉD OMELET

Prepare **Souffléd Omelet, above.** Add to the egg yolks **3 tablespoons Grand Marnier.** If desired, after sprinkling the omelet with confectioners' sugar, heat **3 tablespoons brandy or Grand Marnier;** do not boil. Pour the warm brandy over the omelet and flambé, 1055.

APPLE-FILLED SOUFFLÉD OMELET

4 servings

Melt **1 tablespoon butter** in a small skillet over medium heat. Add **⅓ cup Golden Delicious apple slices** and sauté until brown, about 2 minutes. Add **1 tablespoon brandy (preferably apple).** Let it boil briefly, then set aside. Prepare **Souffléd Omelet, above,** arranging the apple slices on the surface before putting the omelet in the oven.

SAVORY CHEESE-AND-HERB-FILLED SOUFFLÉD OMELET

Prepare **Souffléd Omelet, above,** omitting the sugar and instead seasoning the yolks with **salt and black pepper to taste.** Before putting the omelet into the oven, sprinkle the top with **2 tablespoons chopped herbs (chives, parsley, or chervil, or a combination)** and **¼ cup grated cheese of your choice.** Serve the omelet with **Tomato Sauce, 562, or Salsa Fresca, 571.**

ABOUT SOUFFLÉS

The soufflé is considered the prima donna of the culinary world. The timbale, 206, is her more even-tempered relative. With closer cultivation, both become quite tractable and are great glamorizers for leftover foods. ➤ Cooked foods are best for use in both soufflés and timbales, as they will release less moisture than will raw ones.

Soufflés have a duration as evanescent as a "breath,"

which is what this French word means. Some last a bit longer than others, though all have a built-in limit for holding their puff. These tours de force, often based on a white sauce with egg yolks and whipped whites, are easy to make if certain pointers are carefully heeded. The white sauce should be a rather thick one, ➤ heated just to a boil. Remove it from the heat and let stand for 30 seconds before the room-temperature eggs and any other ingredients—also at room temperature—are added. Instead of white sauce, some soufflés are made with other thick sauces or purees. Whatever the base, it can be made up to 2 days in advance and held in the refrigerator. About 1 hour before you plan to serve the soufflé, ➤ warm the base to lukewarm and proceed with the recipe.

The air trapped inside the foam of well-beaten egg whites is responsible for the lightness of soufflés. It expands in the oven and forces the mixture to rise. Proper beating of the whites, 978, is crucial to the success of any soufflé. The egg whites should be ➤ stiff but not dry. Once the whites have reached stiff peaks, immediately incorporate them into the base, first stirring in a quarter of the whites to lighten the base and then folding in the rest as gently as possible so as not to deflate the mixture. See Folding in Egg Whites, 978. ➤ Soufflés can always be made lighter by adding an extra egg white for every 2 whole eggs.

Soufflé molds are nice, but any straight-sided deep baking dish will do. Eight-ounce ramekins are ideal for individual soufflés to be served as a first course or as the main course of a luncheon, brunch, or light supper. To make one large, impressive soufflé, use a 6-cup soufflé dish for one made with 4 to 5 egg whites, enough for 4 servings, or an 8-cup dish for one made with 6 to 7 egg whites, enough for 6 servings.

To prepare a soufflé dish for baking, grease the bottom and sides well with butter and then coat the buttered surface with a thorough dusting of flour, dry grated cheese, bread crumbs, cornmeal, or sugar, depending on the flavor of your soufflé. Tilt the mold in all directions until the bottom and sides are well coated, then invert the mold and tap out any excess. The mold can be prepared some hours ahead.

Be sure the oven is heated to the indicated temperature. A soufflé needs quick bottom heat. Place the oven rack in the lower third of the oven.

Fill the mold no more than three-quarters full. Before baking, run your thumb around the inside rim of the dish, making a 1-inch-deep groove (make a ½-inch groove for individual molds), or moat, in the soufflé mixture. This will promote an even rise and give the cooked soufflé a top-hat appearance. For the fluffiest soufflés, bake them as soon as they are assembled, but they can sit at room temperature, covered with an inverted bowl, for up to an hour before baking.

A soufflé is most fragile as it first rises, so be sure to keep the oven door closed during the first half of baking

time. ➤ Test for doneness when it has risen 3 to 4 inches above the rim of the mold and the crust is golden. When a skewer inserted in the center comes out clean, the soufflé is done. Or, touch the top lightly with your hand. If it feels firm with a slight wobble in the middle, it is done. A soufflé can be served slightly moist and creamy inside, or firm and dry all the way through. If you prefer a drier soufflé, bake it a bit longer—but not too long, or it will begin to deflate.

Soufflés can also be baked in a water bath, 801, until risen and brown. This will take 5 to 10 minutes longer. They will not rise as high, and their texture will be more dense and custard-like, but they will hold their loft longer after baking, giving the cook a little breathing space.

Once baked, a soufflé should be served immediately. It will begin its inevitable fall within a minute or two of leaving the oven. Soufflés are sometimes accompanied by a sauce, which can be passed separately or spooned into a hole created in the center of the soufflé.

CHEESE SOUFFLÉ COCKAIGNE

4 to 6 servings

Please read About Soufflés, 203. Preheat the oven to 350°F. Generously butter a 6-cup soufflé dish or four 8-ounce ramekins. Dust the insides with:

¼ to ½ cup dry bread crumbs or grated Parmesan

Shake out the excess. Bring to a boil in a large saucepan:

1 cup White Sauce II, 550

Remove from the heat and let stand for 30 seconds. Add, stirring well:

5 tablespoons grated Parmesan
2 tablespoons shredded Gruyère

Add one at a time, mixing well after each addition:

3 egg yolks, beaten

Beat until stiff but not dry, 978:

4 egg whites

Fold into the cheese mixture. Pour into the prepared soufflé dish or ramekins. If desired, top the soufflés with:

(Paper-thin slices aged Swiss)

Bake 25 to 30 minutes, or until risen and set.

HAM AND CHEESE SOUFFLÉ

Proceed as for **Cheese Soufflé Cockaigne, above.** Add ¾ cup finely chopped smoked ham and 1 tablespoon chopped onion to the egg yolk mixture before adding the whites.

BLUE CHEESE–PARMESAN SOUFFLÉ

Proceed as for **Cheese Soufflé Cockaigne, above.** Use 2 tablespoons crumbled blue cheese in place of the Gruyère.

SPINACH SOUFFLÉ
6 servings

Please read About Soufflés, 203. Preheat the oven to 350°F. Generously butter an 8-cup soufflé dish or six 8-ounce ramekins. Dust the insides with:

   $^{1}/_{4}$ to $^{1}/_{2}$ cup dry bread crumbs or grated Parmesan

Shake out the excess. Combine in a large bowl:

   1$^{1}/_{2}$ cups White Sauce II, 550, at room temperature or
      slightly warmed
   $^{3}/_{4}$ teaspoon salt
   $^{1}/_{8}$ teaspoon grated or ground nutmeg or
      ground red pepper
   Pinch of white pepper

Combine in a medium bowl:

   6 large egg yolks
   $^{3}/_{4}$ cup grated Parmesan and/or Swiss

Beat in $^{1}/_{2}$ cup of the sauce, then combine the mixture with the rest of the sauce, beating vigorously to blend. Add:

   1$^{1}/_{2}$ cups cooked spinach, squeezed dry and finely
      chopped

Beat until stiff but not dry, 978:

   6 large egg whites
   Pinch of salt

Stir one-quarter of the whites into the soufflé base to lighten it, then fold in the rest. Pour into the prepared soufflé dish or ramekins. Bake until risen and golden brown on top, 40 to 45 minutes for a large soufflé, 20 to 25 minutes for individual soufflés. Serve immediately.

MUSHROOM SOUFFLÉ

Proceed as for **Spinach Soufflé, above.** Substitute $^{1}/_{2}$ to 1 cup grated Gruyère for the Parmesan and 1$^{1}/_{2}$ cups sautéed finely chopped mushrooms for the spinach. Add 1$^{1}/_{2}$ teaspoons chopped marjoram or rosemary to the sauce.

BROCCOLI OR CAULIFLOWER SOUFFLÉ

Proceed as for **Spinach Soufflé, above.** Substitute $^{3}/_{4}$ cup grated Cheddar for the Parmesan and 1$^{1}/_{2}$ cups finely chopped cooked broccoli or cauliflower for the spinach. Use the ground red pepper rather than nutmeg, and add 1 teaspoon dry mustard.

CARROT SOUFFLÉ

Proceed as for **Spinach Soufflé, above.** Substitute 1$^{1}/_{2}$ cups pureed cooked carrots for the spinach. Add 1 tablespoon minced thyme or dill to the white sauce.

CORN SOUFFLÉ

Proceed as for **Spinach Soufflé, above.** Substitute 1$^{1}/_{2}$ cups fresh corn kernels for the spinach. Use the ground red pepper rather than nutmeg in the sauce. Serve with a spoonful of **Pesto, 569.**

GOAT CHEESE AND WALNUT SOUFFLÉ
8 servings

Easily made ahead. Refrigerate for up to 3 days, and re-heat to serve.

Please read About Soufflés, 203. Preheat the oven to 350°F. Generously butter eight 6-ounce ramekins or custard cups. Combine:

   $^{3}/_{4}$ cup walnuts, toasted, 1001, and finely chopped
   $^{1}/_{4}$ cup cornmeal

Sprinkle the insides of the ramekins with the cornmeal mixture, tilting them in all directions until completely coated. Scatter any nuts that do not adhere over the bottoms of the dishes. Melt in a saucepan over medium heat:

   3 tablespoons unsalted butter

Stir in until smooth:

   $^{1}/_{4}$ cup all-purpose flour

Cook, stirring, for 1 minute. Remove from the heat and stir in:

   $^{2}/_{3}$ cup milk

Return to the heat and, stirring briskly, bring to a boil until the mixture is very thick. Scrape into a bowl. Add and mash until the cheese is melted:

   10 ounces fresh goat cheese

Beat in:

   4 large egg yolks
   2 garlic cloves, very finely minced
   $^{1}/_{4}$ teaspoon dried thyme
   $^{1}/_{4}$ teaspoon salt
   $^{1}/_{4}$ teaspoon white pepper

Beat until stiff but not dry, 978:

   5 large egg whites
   $^{1}/_{4}$ teaspoon cream of tartar

Stir one-quarter of the whites into the soufflé base to lighten it, then fold in the rest. Pour into the prepared ramekins and smooth the tops. Place the ramekins in a water bath, 801. Bake until a skewer inserted in the center comes out almost clean, about 30 minutes. Let stand for 15 minutes in the water bath, then invert the soufflés onto a greased baking sheet. The soufflés can be served immediately or cooled, covered tightly with plastic wrap, and refrigerated for up to 3 days. Before serving, heat the soufflés in a 425°F oven, 5 to 7 minutes.

SWEET POTATO SOUFFLÉ
6 servings

This soufflé is superlative with cold or hot ham.

Please read About Soufflés, 203. Preheat the oven to 350°F. Generously butter an 8-cup soufflé dish or six 8-ounce ramekins. Dust the insides with:

   $^{1}/_{4}$ cup flour

Shake out the excess. Prepare:

   3 cups mashed Baked or Boiled Sweet
      Potatoes, 301

While the potatoes are still warm, add and beat with a fork until fluffy:

   3 tablespoons butter

$^1/_2$ teaspoon salt
$^1/_2$ teaspoon grated lemon zest
2 egg yolks, beaten
(Pinch of grated or ground nutmeg)
Fold in:
$^1/_2$ to $^3/_4$ cup drained crushed pineapple or applesauce
Cool slightly. Beat until stiff but not dry, 978:
2 egg whites
Fold into the soufflé base. Pour into the prepared soufflé
dish and smooth the top. Bake about 35 minutes.

CRAB OR TUNA SOUFFLÉ

4 servings
Please read About Soufflés, 203. Preheat the oven to
325°F. Generously butter an 8-cup soufflé dish or six
8-ounce ramekins. Dust the insides with:
$^1/_4$ to $^1/_2$ cup dry bread crumbs or grated Parmesan
Shake out the excess. Prepare:
1 cup White Sauce II, 550
When it is smooth, stir in and heat through:
$^3/_4$ to 1 cup flaked lump crabmeat or tuna
$^1/_4$ cup finely chopped carrots
$^1/_4$ cup finely chopped celery
(2 tablespoons chopped parsley)
Remove from the heat. Stir $^1/_2$ cup of the sauce into:
3 egg yolks, beaten
Return this mixture to the remaining sauce and stir well to
combine. Season with:
$^1/_2$ teaspoon salt
$^1/_2$ teaspoon paprika
$^1/_2$ teaspoon grated or ground nutmeg
$^1/_2$ teaspoon dry mustard
Fresh lemon juice, Worcestershire sauce, catsup,
or hot pepper sauce to taste
Let cool slightly. Beat until stiff but not dry, 978:
3 egg whites
Stir one-quarter of the whites into the soufflé base to
lighten it, then fold in the rest. Pour into the prepared
soufflé dish and smooth the top. Bake until firm, about 35
minutes. Serve with:
Tomato Sauce, 562, Sauce Nantua, 552,
or Anchovy Sauce, 552

ABOUT TIMBALES

Once a virtually indispensable mainstay of that sterling
American institution, the ladies' luncheon, the timbale is a
soufflé with a more equable disposition and greater stam-
ina. Often referred to as a **savory mousse**, a timbale is a savory custard cooked in an individual dish and served
unmolded. It can be coated or served with a sauce.

Butter individual or larger molds lightly and fill them
about two-thirds full with the timbale mixture. ➤ Bake in
a water bath, 801. The water should be as high as the filling in the molds. ➤ Check the heat occasionally to make
sure the water around the mold never boils—just simmers.

It is wise to protect the top of the timbale with parchment
paper.

Bake the timbales in a ➤ moderate oven, about 325°F,
for 20 to 50 minutes, depending on the size of the mold.
They are done when a knife blade inserted in the center of
the mold comes out clean. They are then ready to invert
onto a serving platter or individual plates.

BASIC TIMBALE CUSTARD

4 servings
Preheat the oven to 325°F. Combine in a bowl and beat
with a whisk:
$1^1/_2$ cups warm heavy cream or $^1/_2$ cup cream
plus 1 cup Chicken Broth, 121, or stock
4 eggs, at room temperature
$^3/_4$ teaspoon salt
$^1/_2$ teaspoon paprika
($^1/_8$ teaspoon grated or ground nutmeg or celery salt)
(1 tablespoon chopped parsley)
(A few drops onion or lemon juice)
To bake and unmold, see About Timbales, above. Serve
with:
Creamed vegetables
Garnish with:
Crisp cooked crumbled bacon
Parsley

SPINACH, BROCCOLI, OR CAULIFLOWER TIMBALES

5 to 6 servings
Preheat the oven to 325°F. Prepare **Basic Timbale Custard,
above**. Add **1 to $1^1/_2$ cups well-drained cooked spinach,
broccoli, or cauliflower, chopped or put through a food
mill**, and **($^1/_2$ cup grated cheese)** to the timbale mixture.
Adjust the seasoning if necessary. Proceed as directed.

MUSHROOM TIMBALES

5 to 6 servings
Preheat oven to 325°F. Prepare **Basic Timbale Custard,
above**. Add **2 cups drained and finely chopped sautéed
mushrooms** to the timbale mixture. Proceed as directed.

ASPARAGUS TIMBALES

4 servings
Adding bread crumbs will give you a less custard-like timbale that is especially tolerant of improvisation with leftover pureed vegetables or small amounts of soups.
Preheat the oven to 325°F. Lightly butter four 4-ounce
ramekins and line the bottoms with wax or parchment
paper. Stir together in a large bowl until well combined:
$1^1/_2$ cups chopped cooked and seasoned
asparagus
2 large eggs
$^1/_3$ cup lightly packed fresh bread crumbs
$^1/_4$ cup grated Swiss, Cheddar, or Parmesan
$3^1/_2$ tablespoons heavy cream

1 tablespoon grated onion
1 tablespoon chopped parsley
$^1/_2$ teaspoon salt
$^1/_8$ teaspoon black pepper
(Dash of hot pepper sauce)

Fill the ramekins three-quarters full and place them in a water bath, 801. Bake until set and golden brown and a knife inserted in the center comes out clean, 35 to 40 minutes. Let cool for 10 minutes. Run a knife around the inside edge of each ramekin and invert the timbales onto serving plates.

ROASTED GARLIC FLAN

6 servings

These individual flans can be served on a bed of greens as a first course or alongside roasted or grilled meats, fish, or poultry.
Preheat the oven to 350°F. Butter six 4-ounce ramekins. Roast, 277:

2 heads garlic

Squeeze the cloves from the skins and mash into a paste. Combine 3 to 4 tablespoons of the garlic paste (reserve excess for another use) in a food processor with:

3 large eggs
1 teaspoon salt
$^1/_2$ teaspoon black pepper

Pulse until smooth. Add and process just until mixed:

1$^1/_2$ cups heavy cream

Pour the mixture into the prepared ramekins. Place the ramekins in a water bath, 801. Bake until set and golden brown and a knife inserted in the center comes out clean, 35 to 45 minutes. Let cool for about 5 minutes. Run a knife around the inside edge of each ramekin and invert the flans onto serving plates.

ABOUT COLORING EASTER EGGS

Often a child's first memorable experience in the kitchen is coloring Easter eggs. Store-bought dyes are tempting with their fizzy tablets, stickers, and transfers, but using food coloring and ingredients from your kitchen gives beautiful and bright results. You and your children will be surprised and delighted as red cabbage turns an egg blue, or skins from a red onion change a white egg to orange. The longer it rests in the dye, the darker the color. To add designs, attach stickers or small strips of masking tape to the eggs or carefully stretch rubber bands around them before dyeing, or write or draw on eggs with a white crayon before dropping them into the dye.

NATURAL DYE

Makes 4 cups

You can prepare half this recipe for less dye.
Please read about Hard-Boiled Eggs, 194. Place in a pot:

4 cups water
2 tablespoons white vinegar

Add one of the following dyeing agents:

4 cups chopped beets for pink
4 cups boiled red cabbage for blue
3 tablespoons turmeric powder for yellow
Skins from 12 red onions for burnt orange to orange
Skins from 12 large yellow onions for brown

Bring to a boil, reduce the heat, and simmer 30 minutes. Strain each dye through a sieve lined with a coffee filter into a bowl or cup. Add hard-boiled eggs to the dye and soak them until they have reached the color you desire. Air-dry the eggs on a rack or a cookie sheet lined with paper towels.

FOOD COLORING DYE

Mix one dye per cup or bowl. Let cool, then gently lower the eggs into the dye with a spoon. When the egg has reached the desired color, remove it and air-dry the eggs on a rack or a cookie sheet lined with paper towels. Mix yellow and blue to make green, red and yellow to make orange, and blue and red to make purple.
For each color, mix:

40 ($^1/_2$ teaspoon) to 45 drops food coloring
2 teaspoons white vinegar

Add:

1 cup hot water

FRUITS

"It was not a watermelon that Eve took," observed Mark Twain. "We knew it because she repented." In salads or sauces, stuffings or salsas, fresh fruit makes a wonderful accompaniment to grilled chicken, pork, or fish. Poached, sautéed, baked, and grilled fruit makes excellent sides and garnishes. See ideas for fresh fruit platters in Appetizers and Hors d'Oeuvres, 69. And don't forget that a light fruit dessert—or just fruit itself, perhaps with cheese—can be a happy ending for all concerned.

ABOUT FRESH FRUITS

Pomologists have long worked to hybridize the most popular fruits in order to extend the harvest, earlier and later; to produce plants more resistant to disease and adverse climate; and to improve shipping and keeping characteristics. Unfortunately, much of this effort has been carried forward with little regard to flavor or juiciness. Today some small growers are reviving flavorful heirloom fruit varieties, which are available at specialty produce markets and farmers' markets.

Should you undertake to grow your own fruit, choose seeds or plants expressly labeled "for the home garden." Such fruit has been developed with an eye to immediate consumption rather than shelf life, and so comprises varieties with more flavor and delicate texture than those commercially propagated.

When buying fruit, rather than shopping from a list, see what looks freshest at the market. For the very best quality, shop local farmers' markets and roadside stands for locally grown fruits in their peak seasons. Farmers as well as produce managers are typically delighted to share a taste of their fruits when asked, so when possible, sample before buying. Aroma is another sign of fruit that is ripe and flavorful. Choose fruit that is bright, plump, and free of bruises, blemishes, and wrinkles. "Fruit specials" can be too far out of date to be a bargain, and may include pieces that are below standard in size or quality.

If the fruit you are buying has been shipped from considerable distances, chances are that it was picked before it ripened. This has become the norm to ensure the fruit ships in a firm state and ripens as it travels, a practice that has lessened the flavors of many varieties. Peaches, apricots, and nectarines will get softer, but the taste will not improve. Those that do ripen after picking are avocados, bananas, mangoes, melons, papayas, pawpaws, pears, persimmons, pineapples, and some tropical exotics. If purchased underripe, these fruits should be stored at room temperature out of the sun. ➤ To ripen, put each variety in its own partly closed paper bag, the individual fruits (except for bananas and melons) wrapped in paper towels. ➤ Adding an apple or banana to the bag will speed the process, because these fruits emit a harmless gas that enhances ripening. Examine fruit often and remove any fruit that shows any sign of spoilage: mold, softness, or leakage. Spoilage is infectious and will quickly ruin surrounding fruits.

Some ripe fresh fruit can be stored in the refrigerator at temperatures between 35° and 40°F with the protection of a plastic bag—apples, cherries, and grapes, for instance. Store blueberries, strawberries, and raspberries in the refrigerator in the containers they were bought in. Most fruit, though, should be left at room temperature until ripe. After that, freshness can be extended in the refrigerator. Whole fruit will last slightly longer than cut fruit. Citrus fruits—grapefruit, lemons, limes, oranges, and tangerines—will last in an open plastic bag in the refrigerator for up to 1 month. Apricots, kiwifruit, papayas, peaches, and nectarines will keep up to a week in the refrigerator, and melon (canteloupe and honeydew), guava, mangoes, and pears for 2 to 3 days. Mature bananas lose flavor when chilled. Do not wash fruit before storing; the moist tissues of fruit are susceptible to molds and should be kept as dry as possible during storage.

➤ Wash fruit quickly under cold running water just before serving or using in a recipe. Washing with soap or detergent will remove only the surface contaminants from fruits that have been waxed, such as apples. To remove fungicide or pesticide residues trapped in the skin, peel, then rinse. Organically grown fruits can also be waxed with food-grade wax, such as carnauba or beeswax, and so may also need to be thoroughly washed or peeled.

Apricots, peaches, nectarines, and most varieties of plums can be peeled by being dipped into boiling water, or **blanching.** Drop the fruit—no more than 3 or 4 pieces at a time—into a large pot of boiling water. Leave the fruit in the water for 15 to 30 seconds, then transfer to a bowl of

A SEASONAL GUIDE TO FRUITS

JANUARY
blood oranges, grapefruit, guava, mandarins, kiwi, kumquats, oranges, pears, quinces, tamarind, tangerines

FEBRUARY
avocados, blood oranges, grapefruit, oranges, pears, tamarind, tangerines

MARCH
avocados, blood oranges, grapefruit, guava, oranges, tamarind

APRIL
avocados, grapefruit, oranges, papayas, rhubarb, tamarind

MAY
apricots, avocados, blueberries, cherries, tamarind, mangoes, oranges, papayas, peaches, raspberries, rhubarb

JUNE
apricots, blackberries, blueberries, boysenberries, cherries, lychees, melons, nectarines, passionfruit, peaches, mangoes, papayas, raspberries, strawberries

JULY
apricots, blackberries, blueberries, cherries, currants, lychees, mangoes, melons, nectarines, peaches, raspberries, strawberries

AUGUST
blackberries, blueberries, cherries, currants, figs, gooseberries, huckleberries, lychees, mangoes, melons, nectarines, peaches, plums, raspberries, strawberries

SEPTEMBER
apples, dates, figs, gooseberries, grapes, huckleberries, mangoes, melons, nectarines, peaches, pears, plums, raspberries, strawberries

OCTOBER
apples, cranberries, dates, figs, gooseberries, grapes, kumquats, pears, persimmons, plums, pomegranates, quince, raspberries, star fruits

NOVEMBER
apples, clementines, cranberries, dates, grapefruit, grapes, kiwi, kumquats, mandarins, oranges, pears, persimmons, pomegranates, quince, star fruits, tamarind, tangerines

DECEMBER
blood oranges, clementines, dates, grapefruit, guava, kiwi, kumquats, oranges, pears, persimmons, pomegranates, prickly pear, star fruits, tamarind, tangerines

ice water. The skin should slip off easily. If not, repeat the blanching process or peel the fruit with a knife or vegetable peeler.

SEASONAL FRUIT

With produce shipped to supermarkets from around the globe, many fruits are available year-round, regardless of when they are in season in this country. In a well-stocked market, you will usually find apples, avocados, bananas, coconuts, grapefruit, grapes, kiwis, lemons, limes, oranges, pears, pineapples, and plantains at any time of the year. Some fruits only appear when they are in peak season. The chart above is a general guide to when certain fruits are at their height of ripeness and flavor in the United States. (Keep in mind that the season will be longer or shorter in some regions.)

If fruit lacks flavor, pair it with candied citrus peels, fresh or candied ginger, or spices, or add a little lemon or lime juice to cooked fruits and fruit fillings. Vary the flavor of a particular fruit by steeping it in the juices of other fruits or in liqueur, or by blending it with others in a puree. You can glaze poached fruit with contrasting fruit jellies, especially those of apple and quince, which are high in pectin. Or combine canned, frozen, and fresh fruits—cold or warm and laced with brandy or liqueur—in what the French call a **compôte composée.**

FRUIT SUBSTITUTIONS

When a fruit called for in a recipe is unavailable, by all means substitute another. The following are botanical categories of fruits, virtually interchangeable in a recipe:

Pome fruits: Apples, pears, or quinces are interchangeable.

Stone fruits: Apricots, cherries, nectarines, peaches, or plums are interchangeable.

Berries: Interchange blackberries, raspberries, or other caneberries. Blueberries, huckleberries, cranberries, currants, gooseberries, Cape gooseberries, elderberries, or grapes are interchangeable.

Citrus: Oranges, mandarins, grapefruit, pomelos, lemons, limes, or any other in this group are interchangeable.

Melons: All melons are interchangeable.

ANTIBROWNING SOLUTION FOR FRESH FRUITS

Apples, apricots, avocados, bananas, nectarines, peaches, pears, plums, quinces, and some exotic fruits darken to varying degrees when cut and exposed to air. Solutions that are used in both canning and freezing can be successfully applied to fresh fruits peeled slightly in advance of serving. Acid, in the form of citrus juice or vinegar, mixed with water creates an antibrowning solution. **To prevent browning,** toss cut fruit with sufficient lemon or lime juice to coat lightly. Or briefly soak in a solution of 4 cups water and 1 tablespoon lemon juice or vinegar.

FRUIT SALAD OR FRUIT CUP

8 to 10 servings

Sweetened fresh fruit may be served in small bowls, glass cups, or melon baskets, 230. To frost containers, see 55. Combine:

    **2 oranges, peeled, seeded, and cut into
        bite-sized chunks**
    1 tablespoon fresh lemon juice
    $^1/_3$ cup honey or sugar
    2 large apples, cut into bite-sized chunks
    1 large pear, cut into bite-sized chunks
    1 large banana, sliced

Or combine 1 cup each of 4 of the following fruits:

    Apricots, cut into bite-sized chunks
    Kiwis, peeled and sliced
    Strawberries, hulled and halved or quartered
    Raspberries, blueberries, or blackberries
    Sweet cherries, pitted
    Melon or watermelon balls, 230
    Peaches or nectarines, cut into bite-sized chunks
    Plums, seeded and cut into bite-sized chunks
    Seedless green or red grapes

AMBROSIA

6 servings

Canned mandarin orange sections and pineapple chunks can be substituted for the fresh oranges and pineapple. Peel and section, 223, into a bowl:

    6 oranges

Add and gently combine:

    3 bananas, sliced
    $^1/_2$ pineapple, peeled, cored, and diced ($2^1/_2$ to 3 cups)
    $^1/_2$ to 1 cup shredded sweetened dried coconut
    ($^1/_2$ to 1 cup miniature marshmallows)
    ($^1/_4$ cup orange liqueur, sherry, or port)

If you have not used marshmallows, stir in:

    ($^1/_4$ to $^1/_2$ cup sugar)

Cover and refrigerate at least 3 hours or up to 12, to blend the flavors.

MACÉDOINE OF FRESH FRUITS

8 servings

The following fruit and wine or liqueur combinations should be made with ripe, perfect, pared, seeded, and sliced seasonal fruits. Favorites for this dessert are strawberries, raspberries, peeled seedless green grapes, peaches, apricots, kiwifruit, oranges, grapefruit, melons, cherries, and nectarines. Be sure to prick the fruit to allow the marinade to soak in. If you use raw apples or pears, marinate the slices for several hours in wine or liqueur or

they will be too hard in texture. Some good marinating combinations are:

    **Brandy with oranges or with cherries and
        clove-studded peaches**
    Port with melon
    Kirsch with strawberries
    Grand Marnier with grapes

Layer in a glass bowl:

    4 cups sliced seasonal fruits, 209

Sprinkle with:

    Confectioners' sugar

Stir gently until the sugar is almost dissolved. Add:

    **2 to 4 tablespoons brandy, kirsch, Grand Marnier,
        or Southern Comfort**

Serve chilled over vanilla ice cream or pound cake.

FRUIT FOOL

4 servings

Long ago the word "fool" was a term of endearment. We have an old-fashioned fondness for recipes in which fruit is combined with cream.

I. FRESH FRUIT FOOL

Puree in a food processor or blender and set aside in a medium bowl:

    **2 cups blackberries, blueberries, raspberries,
        or strawberries**
    $^1/_4$ to $^1/_3$ cup confectioners' sugar
    1 tablespoon fresh lemon juice

Combine. Whip until the mixture holds firm peaks, 973:

    $1^1/_4$ cups heavy cream
    1 tablespoon sugar
    $^1/_2$ teaspoon vanilla

Gently fold the berry puree into the whipped cream. Pour into a glass bowl and chill thoroughly.

II. COOKED FRUIT FOOL

Whip in a medium bowl until stiff peaks form:

    $^1/_2$ cup heavy cream, sweetened to taste

Fold in:

    **1 cup applesauce or rhubarb, berry, apricot, currant,
        or other fruit puree**
    **$1^1/_2$ teaspoons grated lemon zest or $^1/_4$ teaspoon
        almond extract**

Transfer to a serving bowl. Chill thoroughly. Before serving, sprinkle the top with:

    Macaroons, 771, crumbled

Or serve with:

    Ladyfingers, 740

ABOUT CANNED AND FROZEN FRUITS

A wide assortment of delicious canned fruits—apricots, blueberries, sweet cherries, grapefruit, mandarin oranges, peaches, pears, plums, and pineapple—is available at virtually any supermarket, while other canned fruits, such as gooseberries, tart cherries, kumquats, guavas, lychees, and mangoes may require a visit to a specialty shop or online retailer. Most canned fruits are packed in light or heavy sugar syrups, but some are also available in their own juices; check the label. Fruits for commercial or home canning are picked in a riper state than those sold fresh, which explains why canned apricots (not to mention canned tomatoes) often taste better than their fresh counterparts bought out of season.

The roster of frozen fruits is limited, in most supermarkets, to blueberries, raspberries, strawberries, peaches, and, sometimes, mangoes. These are available both sweetened and unsweetened and are referred to as dry-pack or IQF (Individually Quick Frozen). Sweetened frozen fruits are particularly useful for quick dessert sauces. Thaw and, if desired, puree in a blender or food processor, straining through a sieve if seedy. Add sugar to dry-pack frozen fruits to make excellent dessert sauces as well. ➤ Dry-pack frozen fruits may also be substituted for fresh fruit in any recipe where the fruit is cooked or baked. ➤ Measure before thawing, and add while still frozen.

ABOUT RAISINS AND OTHER DRIED FRUITS

The high caloric and nutritional values of dried fruits can be readily grasped once you realize that ➤ it takes $5^1/2$ pounds of fresh apricots to yield 1 pound dried. When fruits are dried without cooking, their subsequent contact with the air—as well as the enzymatic activity that takes place within them—tends to darken the pulp. A sulfur dioxide solution is often used to lessen darkening. Some people prefer to avoid this; if you are interested in drying your own fruits, see 907.

Apples, apricots, cherries, cranberries, currants, dates, figs, and grapes are among the fruits most often dried. They must all be ➤ stored covered airtight in a cool, dark place. Under most household shelf conditions, they are likely to keep for several months. This is especially true of the increasingly numerous dried fruits that are treated and tightly packaged so as to remain plump and soft. All varieties must be watched for insect infestation. For dried plums, or prunes, see 235.

Raisins, which of course are simply dried grapes, divide into **seedless,** those that grow without seeds, and **seeded,** which have had the seeds removed. As their flavors are quite different, it is wise to use the specific type called for in recipes. Muscats, very aromatic and sweet, are usually available around the end-of-year holidays and used for baking into rich cakes and confections. The common dark and golden raisins sold at supermarkets are both dried Thompson seedless grapes and are interchangeable in recipes. Sultanas are larger, paler, and more acidic. They are most often found in specialty stores, as are Monukkas, which are large, dark, and sweet. Both are delicious eaten fresh. **Dried currants** are tiny raisins—traditionally dried Zante or Black Corinth grapes.

Raisins and currants are both improved, unless they are very fresh, by **plumping,** especially when used in short-cooking recipes. This can be done by soaking them in the liquid part of the batter in which they are to be cooked—

such as the liquid called for in cakes—for 10 to 15 minutes before use. Raisins and currants may also be plumped by washing briefly, draining, spreading on a baking sheet, and heating, tightly covered, in a 350°F oven until they puff up and are no longer very wrinkled.

When **cooking dried fruits,** do not soak them first unless the processor so directs on the package or you are directed in the recipe. The less water used, the more natural sugars will be retained within the fruit. If you must soak fruit such as dried apples, cover with boiling water and soak just until tender. Use the soaking water in the recipe, if applicable. ➤ Allow 1 pound dried for $3^1/2$ to 4 pounds fresh apples and proceed as for any apple recipe.

Dried fruits are often messy to cut or chop. For a cleaner, easier cut, put dried fruit in the freezer for about 40 minutes. Or spray your knife or shears, or food processor blade, with cooking spray. Dipping the knife or shears in hot water will also help. A food processor can be used to chop a quantity of dried fruit: use quick on-off pulses. Should the fruit begin to stick together, add up to 2 tablespoons of sugar to help separate it. When baking with dried fruit, use a portion of the flour called for in the recipe to flour the fruit before chopping.

Candied, or glacéed, fruits have been cooked in a sugar syrup, then drained and, to varying degrees, dried. The fruits most commonly found in stores are lemon, orange, and citron rind; cherries; ginger; and pineapple. ➤ Candied and preserved fruits can sometimes be substituted in recipes for dried fruits. If large amounts of candied fruits are used, allow for their extra sugar content. With preserved fruits, compensate for both sugar and liquid.

Dried fruits are an elegant note on a cheese platter. Should any of the fruits become dried out, steam them ➤ lightly sprinkled with wine or water—in the top of a double boiler—over boiling water. Or, in the case of dates, prepare them for stuffing by steaming 10 to 15 minutes in a colander over boiling water, until tender enough to pit. Stuff each one with a hazelnut or almond, or with fillings suggested under Candies and Confections, 879.

DRIED FRUIT COMPOTE

3 cups; 6 to 8 servings
Eat this at breakfast or serve as a dessert with cookies, cake, or custard, or on top of ice cream.
Combine in a medium heavy saucepan:

>   **1 pound dried fruit, one kind or mixed**
>   **3 cups water**
>   **(Zest of 1 lemon or orange removed in strips with a**
>   **vegetable peeler)**
>   **(1 cinnamon stick)**

Bring to a gentle simmer, cover, and cook until the fruit is plumped, 25 to 35 minutes, adding more water if necessary to keep the fruit covered. Add:

>   **$1/2$ to 1 cup sugar**

Simmer, uncovered, 5 minutes longer, stirring to dissolve sugar. Serve warm or chilled.

FRUIT-NUT PEMMICAN

2 cups

This quite palatable, albeit sticky, substance is the modern outdoorsman's version of the old suet-parched corn-fruit concoction that sustained both Indians and frontiersmen in earlier times. These ingredients may be changed to fit individual preferences. For a tasty variation, use pecans as the only nuts. Package for the trail in plastic bags.

Combine in a food processor and coarsely grind:

$\frac{1}{3}$ **cup raisins**
$\frac{1}{3}$ **cup dried apricots**
$\frac{1}{3}$ **cup dried apples**
$\frac{1}{3}$ **cup pecans or almonds**
$\frac{1}{3}$ **cup toasted soybeans or hulled sunflower seeds**
$\frac{1}{3}$ **cup peanuts**

Combine with:

2 tablespoons honey

ABOUT COOKED FRUITS

A good reason for eating fruits raw is to retain their maximum nutritional value, but you can minimize the loss of vitamins and natural sugars in cooking by using as little water as possible and by cooking briefly. Fruits may be baked, 213; broiled or grilled, 214; sautéed, 214; steamed, 1050; microwaved, 1063; or poached in a liquid, below. Below are three basic syrups ideal for poaching various fruits.

Because of their acidity, fruits discolor when cooked in aluminum or iron pots and pans. Use stainless steel, enameled cast-iron, or nonstick pots and pans. ➤ When peeling, paring, or slicing, use a stainless steel knife to avoid discoloration.

POACHING LIQUIDS FOR FRUITS

When making syrups for fruit, keep in mind that **wine** can be used instead of water, or mixed half and half with water. Another flavorful adaptation is using **fruit juices** as the liquid in the syrup—even the juice of a fruit you are not using in the dish. Syrups can also be reduced for a thicker consistency when desired.

I. THIN SYRUP

For apples, grapes, and rhubarb. Combine in a saucepan and heat, stirring to dissolve sugar:

1 cup sugar
3 cups water
Dash of salt

II. MEDIUM SYRUP

For apricots, cherries, grapefruit, pears, and prunes. Use:

1 cup sugar
2 cups water
Dash of salt

III. HEAVY SYRUP

For berries, figs, peaches, and plums. Use:

1 cup sugar
1 cup water
Dash of salt

SPICED SYRUP FOR FRESH FRUITS

Enough for 1 to 1$\frac{1}{2}$ pints fruit

Tie in a cheesecloth bag:

1$\frac{1}{2}$ teaspoons whole cloves
1$\frac{1}{2}$ teaspoons whole allspice berries
1 cinnamon stick

Combine in a saucepan, add the spice bag, and bring to a boil:

1$\frac{1}{2}$ cups sugar or packed brown sugar or 2 cups honey
1 cup cider vinegar
1 cup water

Boil 5 minutes. Remove the spice bag and discard. Drop the prepared fruit into the boiling syrup. Cool and serve.

SPICED SYRUP FOR CANNED FRUITS

Drain and reserve the syrup from:

Canned peaches, apricots, pears, or pineapple

Measure the syrup and simmer until slightly reduced with:

$\frac{1}{4}$ **to $\frac{1}{2}$ as much wine vinegar**

Allow for every 2 cups of juice and vinegar:

1 stick cinnamon
$\frac{1}{2}$ **teaspoon cloves without heads**
(2 or 3 small pieces gingerroot)

After simmering about 10 minutes, add fruit. Remove pan from heat and let fruit cool in the liquid. Strain out the spices and serve hot or cold with meat.

ABOUT POACHED FRUIT

Fruit should always be poached rather than stewed. ➤ Drop it into a simmering liquid, preferably a syrup, just until the fruit is barely tender. Remove the fruit from the heat immediately so it will not continue to cook and get mushy, or set the pot in a sink of cold water. Reserve the cooking liquid and set aside to cool. Top the cooked fruit before serving or store the liquid for later use. Soft, juicy fruits, such as peaches, should be poached in a single layer in a skillet in a heavy syrup, above. By adding the sugar late in the cooking, you will need less of it to sweeten the same quantity of fruit than if you had used it from the start. This method will keep the skin soft.

Apples and other hard fruits ➤ should be poached in simmering water or a thin syrup, above. If using water, sugar should be added after poaching. Watch closely to avoid overcooking. Poached fruit makes a refreshing addition to a meat course. Poached fruit can be stored up to 2 days in the refrigerator before serving. You can use the syrup again for a compatible fruit—it will keep refrigerated for up to 1 week.

POACHED FRUIT

6 servings

Please read About Poached Fruit, above. Combine in a large saucepan:

4 cups water
1$\frac{1}{2}$ cups sugar

Add one or more of the following:

    2 cinnamon sticks

    One 2-inch piece fresh ginger, thinly sliced

    $^1/_2$ vanilla bean, split lengthwise, or 1 tablespoon vanilla

    Zest of 1 lemon, lime, or orange removed in strips with a vegetable peeler

Set the pot over low heat and bring to a simmer, then cover and cook 5 minutes. Add any of the following:

    12 large or 18 small apricots, halved and pitted

    6 large or 9 small bananas, halved crosswise

    4 to 5 cups sweet cherries, pitted

    6 large peaches or nectarines, peeled, halved, and pitted

    6 pears, peeled, halved, and cored

    1 large pineapple, peeled, cored, and cut into rings, 234

    18 small plums or 12 large plums, halved and pitted

Raise the heat to high and bring to a simmer. Cook, uncovered, stirring the fruit frequently, until tender when pierced with a knife, 5 to 10 minutes.

Transfer to a serving dish or storage container, or remove the fruit to a dish or container and boil the syrup down until reduced by half, then pour it over the fruit. Serve warm, at room temperature, or chilled.

POACHED THIN-SKINNED FRUIT

6 to 8 servings

Bring to a boil in a large saucepan:

    2 cups water

Add:

    1 quart (4 cups) unpeeled peaches, pears, apricots, or nectarines, whole or sliced

Reduce the heat at once and simmer the fruit until nearly tender. Add:

    $^1/_2$ to $^3/_4$ cup sugar

During the last few minutes of cooking, add:

    (1 vanilla bean, split lengthwise, or 1 teaspoon vanilla)

Transfer the fruit to a container and strain the juices over it.

POACHED THICK-SKINNED FRUIT

6 to 8 servings

If necessary remove the seeds from:

    4 cups halved and pitted plums, blueberries, or pitted cherries or other thick-skinned fruit

You may prick the fruit before dropping it into a large saucepan of:

    1 to 1$^1/_2$ cups boiling water

Reduce the heat at once and simmer until nearly tender. Add:

    $^1/_2$ to 1 cup sugar

Cook a few minutes longer. If cooking blueberries, lemon juice is a good addition. Transfer fruit to a container, strain the juices over the fruit, and stir gently to avoid clumping.

TANGY POACHED FRUIT

4 to 6 servings

These are perfect as a garnish for ham or pork. Combine in a large saucepan:

    2$^1/_4$ cups sugar or packed brown sugar or 3 cups honey

    1$^1/_2$ cups water

    $^3/_4$ cup cider vinegar

    2 cinnamon sticks

    1$^1/_2$ teaspoons whole cloves

    1$^1/_2$ teaspoons whole allspice berries

Bring to a simmer over medium heat and simmer, covered, for 5 minutes. Add any of the following:

    4 small to medium apples, peeled, quartered, and cored

    4 peaches, peeled, halved, and pitted

    4 nectarines, peeled, halved or quartered, and pitted

    4 pears, peeled, halved, and cored

    12 small plums or 8 large plums, halved and pitted

    1 small pineapple, peeled, cored, and cut into rings, 234

Simmer the fruit gently, turning frequently, until translucent and very tender, 10 to 20 minutes, depending on the fruit. Transfer the fruit to a storage container and strain the syrup over it. Cover and refrigerate until cold.

BAKED FRESH FRUIT COMPOTE

4 servings

Use this also as a garnish for custard or vanilla pudding. Preheat the oven to 350°F. Peel:

    8 small peaches, nectarines, plums, apples, or pears

or use:

    3 cups pineapple chunks or 8 rings

Place the fruits whole or in thick slices in a baking dish. In a medium saucepan, combine and heat but do not boil, then stir and pour over the fruits:

    $^2/_3$ cup red wine or water

    $^2/_3$ cup sugar

    $^1/_2$ stick cinnamon

    4 whole cloves

    $^1/_8$ teaspoon salt

    $^1/_2$ lemon or lime, seeded and thinly sliced

Bake either covered or uncovered until tender when tested with a fork. If cooked uncovered, it must be basted every 10 minutes. Turn the fruit after the first two bastings for more rapid and even cooking, if desired.

ADDITIONS TO BAKED FRUITS

I. To be served as a meat garnish. After baking, fill centers of halved fruit with:

    Mint, currant, or cranberry jelly

    Boiled pearl onions, minced peeled fresh ginger, and crème fraîche

    Crumbled corn bread and dried fruit

II. As dessert, fill the centers of halved fruit with:

> A mixture of Roquefort or blue cheese, cream cheese, and chopped almonds, pecans, hazelnuts, or walnuts, sweetened ricotta, grated lemon zest, and ground cinnamon

ABOUT GRILLED OR BROILED FRUIT

Grilling fruit gives it a luscious outdoor flavor by caramelizing the sugars in the fruit. Place cut fruit around whatever meat, poultry, or fish is on the fire. For smaller pieces, thread on skewers, putting soft fruits and firmer fruits on separate skewers as they will not finish cooking at the same time. When broiling, allow 3 to 6 inches between the fruit and the source of the heat, depending on the thickness of the fruit and its sugar content. Very sweet fruit may turn black if broiled too close to the heat.

Grilled fruits make a delicious quick garnish for grilled meats as well as a terrific dessert. Grill tender fruits only until the surface is lightly charred.

GRILLED OR BROILED FRUIT

4 to 6 servings

I. Lightly brush one of the following with vegetable oil:

> 6 large or 8 small apricots, halved and pitted
> 4 large or 6 small bananas, peeled
> 6 large fresh figs, stemmed and halved lengthwise
> 4 peaches, halved and pitted
> 4 nectarines, halved and pitted
> 4 pears, peeled, halved, and cored
> 6 large juicy plums, halved and pitted
> 6 pineapple rings (about $1/2$ inch thick)

Arrange in a single layer, halved fruits cut side down, on a very hot grill. Cook until lightly charred, 2 to 3 minutes. Turn and cook 2 to 3 minutes longer. Serve at once.
II. Prepare the fruit as above and place, hollow side up, in a shallow baking pan. Sprinkle lightly with:

> Salt
> Ground cinnamon

Broil in the oven until light brown.

GRILLED OR BROILED FRUIT KEBABS

8 to 12 servings

Combine in a large bowl:

> 1 cup grapefruit juice
> Grated zest and juice of 1 lemon
> $1/2$ cup honey
> 3 tablespoons orange liqueur or orange juice
> (1 tablespoon finely chopped mint)

Add, turning to coat, and marinate 30 minutes:

> 3 pears, peeled, cored, and cut into 1-inch pieces
> 2 cups cubed pineapple
> 2 apples, peeled, cored, and cut into 1-inch pieces
> 2 bananas, cut into 1-inch pieces
> 2 grapefruits, peeled and separated into sections

Prepare a medium-hot grill fire or preheat your grill or broiler. If using wooden skewers, soak them under water for 30 minutes before using. Grill or broil until lightly browned, about 5 minutes total, turning once and basting with the marinade.

FRUIT BRÛLÉ

4 to 6 servings

Often made only with seedless green grapes but also delicious with a mix of fruits and other berries.

Spread in a 9-inch round baking dish or glass pie plate:

> $3^{1}/2$ cups raspberries, blackberries, blueberries, hulled strawberries, pitted cherries, seedless green or red grapes, or diced mangoes, peaches, nectarines, or pineapple

Mix together, then spread evenly over the fruit:

> 1 to $1^{1}/2$ cups sour cream
> 1 teaspoon vanilla

Cover and refrigerate until thoroughly chilled, or for up to 8 hours. Preheat the broiler. Dust the cream evenly with:

> 1 cup packed brown sugar

so that none of the cream shows through. Place the dish about 6 inches beneath the heating element and broil until the sugar caramelizes, 1 to 2 minutes. Watch closely so that the sugar does not scorch. Serve at once.

SAUTÉED FRUIT

4 to 6 servings

Melt in a wide skillet, preferably nonstick, over medium-high heat:

> 3 tablespoons butter

Sprinkle into the pan in an even layer:

> $1/3$ cup white or brown sugar

Cook until the mixture turns golden brown. Add any of the following, arranging halved fruits cut side down:

> 6 large apricots, halved and pitted
> 6 large or 8 to 12 small figs, stemmed and halved lengthwise
> 4 peaches, peeled, halved, and pitted
> 4 nectarines, peeled, halved or quartered, and pitted
> 4 medium pears, peeled, halved, and cored
> 6 large plums, halved and pitted
> 4 pineapple rings (about $1/2$ inch thick), halved

Cook 2 minutes, periodically shaking the skillet to keep the fruit from sticking. Turn the fruit and cook, again shaking the skillet, just until it is warmed through and has begun to release its juices. Serve at once with the pan juices drizzled over. Sprinkle with, if desired:

> (Ground cinnamon)

SAUTÉED FRUIT TO SERVE WITH MEAT

4 servings

Melt in a wide skillet, preferably nonstick, over medium-low heat:

> 3 tablespoons butter or bacon drippings

Add and cook, stirring for 5 minutes, or until tender:

> 1 cup finely sliced onions

Then proceed as for:
Sautéed Fruit, 214
Add with the sugar:
Pinch of salt
Pinch of paprika

ABOUT PUREED FRUIT

Unsweetened fruit purees are delicious on meat and fish. They pair well with savory dishes, especially roasted meat, or can be served on their own as a sweet treat. Fruit purees can add body and flavor to sauces and dressings, or they can be a sauce in and of themselves; see fresh fruit sauces, 853. Combine fresh or cooked fruit purees with lightly sweetened whipped cream for a luscious Fruit Fool.

Most fruits are tender enough to be pureed raw after you have removed the peel, pit, seeds, or core. Cut into small pieces before pureeing to ensure even results. ➤ Firm fruit such as apples, rhubarb, quince, some pears, and dried fruits must be cooked before pureeing. Combine peeled and sliced fruit with a small amount of water and cook in a covered pan over gentle heat until very tender when pierced with a knife. Then process in a blender, food processor, or food mill. **To puree very tender fruits,** such as banana and overripe pears, just force through a sieve. Strain fruits with tiny seeds, or ones that are stringy, through a sieve. Sugar can help intensify the flavor of purees. Fresh lemon juice will help preserve color and brighten the flavor of fruit purees. Add water or fruit juice as necessary to thin purees to the desired consistency.

Serve pureed fruit hot or cold with one of the following:

GARNISHES FOR PUREED FRUITS
Grated lemon zest or ground cinnamon
Heavy cream and nutmeg
Chopped walnuts or almonds, toasted, 1001, and
**   marmalade**
Crushed dry macaroons and whipped cream
Sour cream or yogurt mixed with sugar, rum, and nuts
Bread or cake crumbs browned in butter
Slivered almonds
Chopped mint

FLAMBÉED FRUITS

For best results, use at least 2 ounces of liquor, and ➤ have fruit at room temperature or you may not get any effect at all. Heat the fruit ➤ gently in a covered chafing dish or electric skillet. ➤ Warm the liquor, too, but do not boil it. Sprinkle the fruit lightly with sugar and, after pouring the warm liquor over the warm fruit, re-cover the pan for a moment before lighting. Stand back!
This recipe makes 6 servings as a sauce, but only 3 if used as a main dessert dish. Caramelize, 1019, lightly over low heat:
3 tablespoons sugar
Add:
3 tablespoons butter
or melt the butter first and substitute brown sugar, stirring

until dissolved. Cook over very low heat for 4 to 5 minutes. Add 2 of the following:
3 split bananas, mangoes, peaches, or pears
**   or 3 slices pineapple**
Simmer until tender, basting occasionally. Since the banana will cook more rapidly than the rest of the fruit, it should be added later. Flambé the fruit with:
2 ounces brandy, dark rum, or liqueur

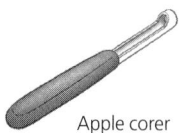
Apple corer

ABOUT APPLES

Although apples are in the market year-round, they are at their peak in the fall, 209. So, when the trees begin to turn red and gold and the air becomes crisp, go looking for the best eating apples of the year—at orchards, markets, and roadside stands. Select apples with smooth skins, and inspect carefully for dents and soft spots, signs of bruising. For fast ripening, keep apples at room temperature. Refrigeration in plastic bags keeps apples for the longest period, but they also keep well in a cold, dry place (32° to 40°F). Store apples so they are not touching each other. If you receive a windfall from a friend's orchard and want to reserve some of it, let fruit stand in a cool, dark place for 24 hours, then inspect for blemishes. Wrap each fruit in paper and store in slotted boxes in a cold, dark, airy place. With long storage, apples lose flavor and become mealy.

Among firm, long-keeping apples, only **Red Delicious** is unsuited to cooking. **McIntosh** and the similar **Empire** and **Macoun,** all fine-grained and soft, do not hold their shape when cooked, but they do very well for salads and applesauce. **Cortlands,** while similar to these three when eaten raw, are firmer and more flavorful when cooked and may be baked whole or used in pies or tarts. Cortlands have the added distinction of not browning quickly when cut, which makes them good apples for fruit salads or for slicing and presenting on a cheese tray. **Fuji, Gala,** and **Braeburn** are known for their sweetness and are best eaten raw or in salads. Finally, **Granny Smiths,** the firmest and most tart of all dessert apples, give off a great deal of juice when cooked but are wonderful for applesauce, sautéed apple rings, and tarte Tatin.

The most versatile of all-purpose apples is **Golden Delicious,** which, despite its name, is an entirely separate variety from **Red Delicious.** Sweet and aromatic when raw, it becomes even more so when cooked, holds its shape beautifully, and exudes little juice. **Rome Beauty,** another common all-purpose apple, has a rich texture when cooked, making it a particularly good choice for baking whole. Other all-purpose apples worth seeking out include: **Newtown/Pippin, Mutsu/Crispin, Northern Spy, Spygold, Spitzen-**

burg, Baldwin, Jonathan, Stayman Winesap, Gravenstein, Grimes Golden, Pink Lady, Ida Red, Jonagold, and **Rhode Island Greening**—an early American variety, richly flavored and tart, which is perhaps the best of all for cooking.

Peel apples with a paring knife, vegetable peeler, or apple peeler, as you prefer. To core apples, use an apple corer, shown, 215—a must if apples are to be served whole or cut into rings—or cut the fruit into quarters, then cut away the core with a paring knife. Pair apples with sausage, pork, or ham. Apples are particularly complemented by cinnamon, cloves, nutmeg, mace, rosemary, sage, coriander, lemon and orange zest, vanilla, dark rum, brandy, bourbon, almonds, and quinces. An apple with disappointing flavor can be improved somewhat in cooking by the addition of lemon juice, but nothing can really compensate for a lack of natural tartness. Should apples seem dry after peeling, ➤ simmer their cores and skins in water. Drain and reduce the liquid and use it to moisten the apples during cooking.

APPLE RINGS
4 servings
Core and cut crosswise into $^3/_8$-inch slices:
2 large all-purpose apples, such as Golden Delicious or Rome Beauty
Melt in a large skillet over medium heat:
2 tablespoons butter or bacon drippings (or as necessary)
Add a single layer of apple rings to the skillet. Cook until the bottoms are golden, about 3 minutes, then turn and cook the apples until just tender when pierced with a fork. Set aside on a platter. Cook the remaining rings in batches, adding more butter to the skillet if necessary. When all are done, sprinkle with:
1 to 3 tablespoons sugar
Ground cinnamon

HONEY APPLES
4 servings
An excellent way to use a dull-flavored apple. Heat in a small deep saucepan:
1 cup honey
$^1/_2$ cup cider vinegar
Peel, core, and thinly slice:
2 apples
Drop the apples in batches into the simmering mixture, then skim out with a slotted spoon when translucent, about 2 minutes. Serve hot or cold.

SAUTÉED APPLES AND BACON
4 servings
A fine breakfast or brunch dish. If you omit the bacon, sauté the apples in 3 tablespoons butter instead.
Peel, core, and cut into $^1/_2$-inch wedges or chunks:
4 large all-purpose apples, such as Golden Delicious or Rome Beauty
Cook in a large heavy skillet over medium heat until crisp:

8 slices bacon
Transfer the bacon to a dish lined with paper towels and keep warm. Pour all but 2 to 3 tablespoons of the bacon fat out of the skillet. Add the apples and cook over high heat, stirring frequently, until they are tender, translucent, and beginning to brown, 7 to 10 minutes. Sprinkle with:
2 to 4 tablespoons sugar or brown sugar
Surround apples with the bacon. Garnish with:
Sprigs of parsley

APPLESAUCE
4 to 6 servings
Canned applesauce can also be flavored and/or seasoned in any of the ways found in the recipes below, and served warm or cold. Please read About Pureed Fruit, 215.
I. Peel, core, and chop:
3 pounds apples such as McIntosh or Empire
You should have about 6 cups. Combine the apples in a heavy-bottomed saucepan or pot with:
$^1/_2$ cup water
(2 tablespoons lemon juice)
(One 3-inch cinnamon stick)
Cover and simmer, stirring occasionally, until the apples are soft and falling apart, 20 to 30 minutes. Stir in:
$^1/_2$ to $^3/_4$ cup sugar or packed brown sugar
Raise the heat to medium and cook, uncovered, stirring frequently, until the applesauce thickens. If you would like a smooth sauce, puree in a food processor or blender.
II. Prepare **Applesauce** as above, using only:
White sugar
Puree the sauce with:
2 tablespoons unsalted butter
1 teaspoon vanilla
Serve with:
Custard Sauce, 846, or Fresh Strawberry or Raspberry Sauce, 853

SEASONED APPLESAUCES
I. Add to fresh or canned applesauce, and serve warm:
Grated lemon zest or fresh lemon juice
Ground cinnamon
1 or 2 teaspoons melted butter
$^1/_2$ teaspoon vanilla or a few drops of almond extract
II. For a good variation to be served with pork, add **1 or 2 tablespoons prepared horseradish.**
III. For a festive version especially good with roast ham or turkey, add to **2 cups Applesauce, above:**
1 cup pureed apricots or raspberries, or
1 cup canned crushed pineapple plus 1 teaspoon crushed preserved ginger, or
2 cups Cranberry Sauce, 221, flavored with grated orange zest

BAKED APPLES
6 servings
Golden Delicious, Pippins, Granny Smith, and other firm apples, 215, hold their shape when baked.

I. Preheat the oven to 350°F. Wash well, core, and arrange in a deep baking dish or heavy pot:

6 large all-purpose apples

Divide evenly among the hollows:

¹/₂ to ³/₄ cup sugar or packed brown sugar
2 tablespoons butter

Sprinkle with:

(¹/₂ to 1 teaspoon ground cinnamon)

Pour into the pan:

²/₃ cup water, apple juice, or cider

Cover tightly with foil or a lid and bake until the apples are nearly tender when pierced with a fork but not mushy, 20 minutes. Uncover and bake the apples, basting frequently with the cooking juices, until soft but still firm enough to hold their shape, 20 minutes longer. If the juices are thin, remove the apples to a serving dish and reduce the juices in the pan, then pour over the apples. Serve hot or chilled.

II. A richer dish than the above. This may be assembled up to 8 hours ahead, refrigerated, uncovered, and then baked before serving.

Preheat the oven to 300°F. Wash well, core, and peel:

6 large all-purpose apples

Pour into a small bowl:

1¹/₄ cups sugar

Place in another bowl:

1 cup heavy cream or 6 tablespoons melted butter

Roll each apple in the cream, then roll in the sugar until coated. Reserve leftover liquid. Place in a 9 x 13 x 2-inch baking dish. Combine in a bowl, then stuff into the hollows of the apples:

¹/₂ cup raisins, chopped figs, or chopped dates
¹/₂ cup chopped walnuts or pecans
(Grated zest of 1 lemon or ¹/₂ orange)

Mix together the leftover cream and sugar, then stir in:

1 teaspoon ground cinnamon
(¹/₂ teaspoon grated or ground nutmeg)
(¹/₄ teaspoon ground cloves)

Spoon as much of this mixture into the hollows of the apples as they will hold, then pour the rest into the bottom of the pan, along with:

1 cup water, apple juice, cider, dark rum, or brandy

Bake, uncovered, without basting, until the apples are tender when pierced with a fork but still hold their shape, about 1 hour. Serve warm with the pan syrup, accompanied with:

Heavy cream, sour cream, crème fraîche,
or vanilla ice cream

BAKED APPLES STUFFED WITH SAUSAGE
6 servings

A three-star winter dish, best eaten by the fire.
Preheat the oven to 350°F. Wash:

6 large baking apples, such as Ida Red
or Golden Delicious

Cut a slice from the tops. With a spoon, scoop out the cores and pulp, leaving ³/₄-inch-thick shells. Cut the pulp away from the cores and chop it. Combine with:

1 cup well-seasoned sausage meat or sliced small
link sausages

Put the apple shells in a baking dish and sprinkle with:

(2 tablespoons brown sugar)

Fill heaping full with the sausage mixture. Bake, uncovered, until the apples are tender when pierced with a fork but still hold their shape and the sausage is cooked, 30 to 40 minutes.

ABOUT APRICOTS

Fresh apricots have a beautiful blush and should be firm in texture. Avoid if wilted or shriveled, if tinged with green or lacking aroma. The skin is tender, and is generally left on, whether the fruit will be eaten raw or cooked. Apricots are delicious in a fruit salad, 210. They can also be sautéed, 214, baked, 213, or grilled, 214. Orange complements apricots, and apricots complement grilled poultry, pork, or seafood.

SPICY APRICOT SAUCE
2 cups

Combine in a medium skillet and cook, stirring, until the vegetables are tender, about 5 minutes:

1 to 2 tablespoons vegetable oil
1 medium sweet onion, chopped
(1 red bell pepper, cored, seeded, and chopped)
1 to 2 jalapeño peppers, seeded and chopped
2 garlic cloves, minced

Add:

1¹/₂ cups halved and pitted fresh apricots, 1¹/₂ cups
canned apricots, or ¹/₂ cup diced dried apricots
1 cup water
2 tablespoons brown sugar
2 tablespoons cider vinegar
2 teaspoons Dijon mustard
1 teaspoon soy sauce

Simmer until the apricots soften and the sauce thickens, about 15 minutes. Cool, then process to a smooth paste in a blender or food processor, if desired. Add:

¹/₄ teaspoon salt
¹/₈ teaspoon ground red pepper

COOKED DRIED APRICOTS
10 servings

In a more or less cooked-down or glazed state, they enliven a whole galaxy of filled cakes, open tarts, torten, and frozen desserts.

Place in a heavy pan:

1 pound dried apricots
3 cups water

Simmer the fruit about 35 minutes. Add:

¹/₂ to 1 cup sugar

Heat until the sugar is dissolved, about 5 minutes longer. You may puree, 215, the fruit.

ABOUT AVOCADOS

A native of the Americas, this fruit is available year-round, principally in two varieties: the dark, bumpy **Hass avocado,** grown in California, and the larger green, smooth-skinned **Fuerte avocado** from Florida. For most purposes, including guacamole, choose Hass avocados, which have a deeper flavor and richer, smoother texture than Fuerte avocados in part because they contain twice as much fat. However, Fuerte avocados do very nicely in salads and sandwiches, which benefit from their lighter flavor and moister texture. Look also for the delightful miniature seedless **cocktail avocados,** also known as *avocaditos,* sold at specialty stores and some supermarkets. Serve them with a flavored mayonnaise, 578, at your next cocktail party.

To test an avocado for ripeness, hold it in your hand and apply even, gentle pressure. If it yields slightly, it is ready to eat. Never buy an avocado that feels soft or that has loose, puffy or indented skin; it will prove slimy and bitter. Like bananas, avocados do not ripen on the tree. Buy them slightly underripe, and ripen at home. Even the hardest avocados will ripen within 2 to 4 days at room temperature, and often within just 1 day if placed in a paper bag. Once ripened, store avocados in the refrigerator and use within 2 days.

To **cut an avocado,** see 165. The flesh of avocados darkens when exposed to air. Tossing or rubbing the cut fruit with lemon or other citrus juice slows the process but does not stop it, so it is best to slice avocados just before serving. ➤ Avocados become bitter when subjected to high heat, so add to soups and other hot foods only at the last minute as a garnish. For salad combinations and other ways to serve an avocado, see 165. For Guacamole, see 72.

ABOUT BANANAS

Bananas are called the "humblest fruit," but they are one of the most popular fruits around the world, delicious, nutritious, digestible, inexpensive, and always available. Add to that their nutritive value, and you have an incomparable fruit. They are picked green, and ripen best off the tree. They appear at markets year-round in varying stages of ripeness. For poaching, sautéing, baking, and grilling, firm-ripe bananas are preferable because they will hold their shape. For banana breads and cakes, use very ripe bananas. **Red bananas** can also be used for baking. Serve with fish, poultry, or pork instead of rice or mashed potatoes, or sprinkled with confectioners' sugar for dessert. **Dwarf** or **finger** bananas are great for lunch boxes. Also see About Plantains, 293.

Ripen bananas at room temperature, enclosed in a paper bag if you wish to hasten the process. Bananas that become overripe can be refrigerated; though the skins will blacken, their interiors remain palatable for up to 3 days.

Peeled bananas may also be successfully frozen, but use them immediately after partially thawing in the refrigerator. Once cut, they darken rapidly unless sprinkled with citrus juice. There are a number of ways to prepare **frozen bananas** and enjoy them even without thawing. A favorite for kids of all ages is **Banana Snow:** Place chunks of frozen bananas in a blender with a little milk and sugar, and blend until smooth. Or cut bananas into chips, spread out on a piece of foil, wrap them securely, and freeze. Munch on them as snacks. You can also mash up the pulp of ripe bananas with a mixture of lemon juice, honey, and cinnamon before freezing. Another frozen treat—which kids really enjoy—is Chocolate-Dipped Bananas, below.

CHOCOLATE-DIPPED BANANAS

12 servings
Peel and cut crosswise in half:
 6 ripe bananas
Insert firmly a wooden craft stick into the cut end of each half. Freeze on a sheet of foil for at least 1 hour. Prepare:
 A double recipe of Quick Chocolate Fondue
 Sauce II, 848
Remove the bananas from the freezer and dip them one by one into the chocolate, twirling to ensure complete coverage. Serve at once, or let set on wax paper, then return to the freezer in a plastic bag for later.

BAKED BANANAS

4 servings
 I. Preheat the oven to 375°F or prepare a hot grill fire. Place in a shallow baking dish or on the grill:
 4 bananas in their skins
Bake or grill, turning occasionally, until the skins are black and have begun to split, about 20 minutes. Serve hot, in their skins. On opening, sprinkle with:
 (Fresh lemon or lime juice)
 (Salt or confectioners' sugar)
 II. A candied version. Preheat the oven to 375°F. In a small saucepan, melt together and boil about 5 minutes:
 $1/2$ cup dark brown sugar
 $1/4$ cup water
Peel, slice in half lengthwise and then once crosswise, and place in a buttered shallow dish:
 $1^1/2$ to 2 slightly underripe bananas
Sprinkle with:
 Salt
Add to the cooled syrup:
 Juice of $1/2$ lemon or 1 lime
Pour the syrup over the bananas and bake about 30 minutes, turning the fruit after the first 15 minutes. Serve on hot dessert plates, sprinkled with:
 Rum
 Chopped candied ginger

HONEY-GRILLED BANANAS

4 servings
Prepare a medium-hot grill fire. Cut lengthwise in half:
 4 ripe firm bananas, peeled

Cut each half crosswise on the diagonal into 3 pieces. Heat until thin:

> 1/4 **cup honey**

Toss the bananas with the honey in a shallow bowl until coated. This can be done 1 to 2 hours in advance. Arrange the bananas crosswise on the grill. Grill until lightly browned, then turn and grill just until the second side is marked. Arrange on a platter and sprinkle with:

> **Ground cinnamon**
> **(Ground ginger or chopped candied ginger)**

CURRIED TROPICAL CHUTNEY

6 to 8 servings

Excellent with fish, poultry, or pork; with Jamaican Rice and Peas, 356; or with tortillas.
Heat in a large pot:

> **3 tablespoons vegetable oil**

Add and cook, stirring, until softened, 3 to 5 minutes:

> **3 cups chopped onions**
> **3 garlic cloves, minced**
> **1 red bell pepper, chopped**
> **1 jalapeño pepper, seeded and chopped**

Add:

> **2 tablespoons curry powder**
> **1 teaspoon salt**
> 1/4 **teaspoon crushed red pepper flakes**

and stir for 1 minute. Stir in:

> **1 cup packed dark brown sugar**

Add:

> **5 cups sliced bananas**
> **1 cup canned crushed pineapple, with its juice**
> 1/2 **cup chopped dried fruit, such as apricots, dates,**
> **or mango**
> **1 tablespoon fresh minced peeled ginger**
> 1/2 **cup white or cider vinegar**

Reduce the heat to medium-low and simmer until thickened, about 25 minutes. Cool slightly, and add:

> **Juice of 1 lime**
> **(1 cup chopped cilantro)**

ABOUT BERRIES

Good color, firm flesh, and plumpness in berries denote prime condition. Always inspect the bottom of the box for signs of staining, and look carefully for any sign of mold. Remove any crushed or damaged berries before storing. Remember, though, that in preserving, ripe berries contain more pectin. Store ripe berries, covered and unwashed, in the refrigerator. Do not crowd or press them.

Wash berries just before using. To keep from bruising them, tip them into a colander, immerse it in a sinkful of cool water and move gently from side to side, then lift out and drain. Scatter the berries over paper towels and let air-dry. Many berries freeze well, 210, for use out of season.

BERRY CONES

Kids love this unusual and attractive way to serve berries. Mom and Pop were first introduced to Berry Cones in Puerto Rico, where they were greeted beside a waterfall by children with wild berries in leaf cones. We recommend using Parchment Cones, 787, or ice cream cones, 780. The tray was a boxtop with holes. Glorify your tray with colored paper or aluminum foil.

Berry cones

FRESH SELF-GARNISHED BERRIES

4 servings

Wash and stem or hull as necessary:

> **1 quart berries**

If they are very large, slice strawberries in half lengthwise. Puree 1 1/2 cups of the berries in a food processor or blender with:

> 1/2 **to** 3/4 **cup confectioners' sugar**
> **2 tablespoons fresh lemon juice**
> **(2 tablespoons orange or raspberry liqueur**
> **or crème de cassis)**

Strain out the seeds. Refrigerate for up to 12 hours. Serve whole berries chilled. Garnish with the puree.

BERRIES COCKAIGNE

A real family favorite that is as delicious and elegant as it is simple to prepare. Strawberries are our preference.
Arrange:

> **Unhulled berries**

on a plate around mounds of:

> **Brown sugar**

Pass a dish of:

> **Sour cream, yogurt, whipped cream, or crème fraîche**

Strawberry huller

ABOUT STRAWBERRIES

Strawberries are grown in temperate climates, and most varieties are a ruddy red. The very large cultivated fruit is usually less flavorsome than the medium to small local berries available from late spring through early summer.

➤ Aroma is an excellent sign of ripeness and flavor. No one, however, has really experienced paradise on earth until he has plucked and eaten a clutch of fully ripe wild strawberries warmed by mountain sunshine. These wild berries, *fraises des bois,* can be spotted at some farmers' markets and specialty stores in early to midsummer.

To hull a strawberry, remove its leafy top and pale cone-shaped core by cutting around it with the point of a paring knife, or scoop it with a strawberry huller, 219. Always hull after washing, not before.

FRESH STRAWBERRY VARIATIONS

Serve whole or sliced strawberries in one of the following ways:

I. Simmer for 10 minutes equal parts of:

   Orange juice
   Strawberry juice
   1/4 cup sugar or to taste

Cool and chill the syrup. Season with:

   (Orange liqueur or kirsch)

II. Or cover chilled strawberries with:

   Chilled pineapple juice
   Confectioners' sugar to taste

III. Or sprinkle lightly with:

   Fresh lemon juice
   Confectioners' sugar

Garnish with:

   Mint leaves

IV. Or toss sliced berries with:

   Balsamic vinegar

Top with:

   Sweetened crème fraîche or sour cream

V. Wash and dry thoroughly:

   2 pints strawberries, whole

Temper, 857:

   1 pound bittersweet or semisweet chocolate

Hold by stems, dip into chocolate. Place on wax paper. Refrigerate 20 minutes.

STRAWBERRIES ROMANOFF

6 to 8 servings

Hull and slice lengthwise into a shallow bowl:

   1 1/2 quarts strawberries

Sprinkle over them:

   1/2 cup fresh orange juice
   2 tablespoons sugar

Stir gently to mix. Cover and refrigerate for 2 to 3 hours. Soften at room temperature for 10 minutes:

   1 pint vanilla ice cream

Drain the strawberries and remove to a glass serving bowl. Add and toss until blended:

   4 to 6 tablespoons Grand Marnier or strained fresh
      orange juice
   1/4 cup confectioners' sugar, sifted

Whip until soft peaks form:

   1/2 cup cold heavy cream

Blend the ice cream and cream together very lightly with a spoon. Serve at once.

STRAWBERRIES ROMBAUER

6 to 8 servings

A real classic.

Hull and cut in half and mix:

   2 quarts strawberries
   Sugar to taste

Whip slightly:

   1 pint ice cream
   1 cup whipped cream

Add:

   6 tablespoons Cointreau

Blend the ice cream and strawberries lightly.

ABOUT BLUEBERRIES

If the seeds are small, it's blueberries you have. If they are many and large, it's huckleberries. The difference is why the blueberry is preferred, both for eating out of hand and for cooking. Look for plump, deep-colored berries with a whitish sheen, or "bloom." The intensely flavored wild blueberries sometimes found in late summer and early fall are also available frozen.

FRESH BLUEBERRY SYRUP

About 1 cup

Delicious with pancakes, waffles, and pound cake, and also with venison and duck, if the sugar is decreased.

Bring to a boil in a small saucepan:

   1/4 cup water
   1/4 cup sugar

Add:

   1 cup blueberries
   One 1-inch piece cinnamon stick
   1/2 teaspoon grated lemon zest
   (1 tablespoon dark rum or port)

Reduce the heat to medium-low and simmer 10 minutes, or until thickened.

ABOUT BLACKBERRIES AND RASPBERRIES

All the fruits under this heading belong to one species—*Rubus*—grow on canes, and have similar characteristics. **Raspberries,** of which there are only a few species, come in four colors: red, amber, purple, and black. Raspberries are most plentiful, least expensive, and of most reliable quality in early and late summer. The most fragile of all berries, they must be handled and washed with great care, 219. There are hundreds of species of **blackberries,** which are truly tart—whether wild or domestic—and usually require sugar to make them palatable. Raspberry-blackberry hybrids, sometimes known collectively as caneberries, include **boysenberry, marionberry, loganberry, youngberry,** and **tayberry.** Most caneberries are commonly used in jams and preserves, cobblers, and pies.

BLACKBERRY FLUMMERY

4 to 6 servings

This can be eaten for breakfast, with oatmeal and milk, or as a dessert, topped with sweetened cream.

Combine in a large saucepan:

1 quart blackberries
¹/₂ cup hot water
2 tablespoons to ¹/₂ cup sugar
3 tablespoons cold water
¹/₄ teaspoon ground cinnamon
Dash of salt

Bring to a boil over medium-high heat, then reduce the heat and simmer, stirring gently, 5 minutes. Blend into a paste:

3 tablespoons water
2 tablespoons cornstarch

Stir into the berry mixture and cook, stirring until thick, about 3 minutes. Cool, then refrigerate until chilled.

RASPBERRY PUREE

1 cup

For desserts, poultry, and game birds.

Puree, preferably in a food mill or food processor:

1 (12-ounce) package frozen raspberries in light
   syrup, partially thawed
1¹/₂ teaspoons fresh lemon juice

Strain to remove the seeds. Add:

Sugar to taste

RASPBERRY SYRUP

1 cup

Combine and bring to a boil over low heat:

2 cups sugar
¹/₂ cup water

Add:

2 cups fresh or unthawed frozen raspberries

Stir until the sugar is dissolved, about 5 minutes. Add:

(2 teaspoons orange liqueur, framboise, or kirsch)
(¹/₂ teaspoon grated orange zest, vanilla,
   or almond extract)

Drain in a strainer lined with cheesecloth set over a bowl for 1 to 2 hours. Pour the syrup into a saucepan and reduce syrup by half.

ABOUT CRANBERRIES

Cranberries are most often made into relishes, but they can also be turned into liquid or molded sauces. The tartness of cranberries lends itself to sweet and savory flavors and is delicious with pork, game birds, and venison, in addition to turkey. You can buy cranberries several weeks ahead and refrigerate them in their original plastic bag. They can also go directly into the freezer in their bag and stay frozen for up to 1 year. Wash and dry them after thawing. Fresh cranberries are available in markets from October through early January. To prepare for cooking, pick over, removing any shriveled berries or twigs, then rinse.

CRANBERRY SAUCE AND JELLIED SAUCE

6 to 8 servings

Wash and pick over:

4 cups cranberries (1 pound)

Place in a saucepan over medium heat and cover with:

2 cups boiling water

As soon as the water comes to a boil again, cover the pan. Boil 3 to 4 minutes, until the skins burst. Put the berries through a ricer, 294, or puree in a blender or food processor. Put the puree in a saucepan and stir in:

2 cups sugar

Bring to a rolling boil. For cranberry sauce, immediately remove from the heat. If you want to mold the mixture for cranberry jelly, boil 5 minutes, skim, and pour into a wet mold. The cooking periods indicated are for firm berries; very ripe berries require a few minutes less.

WHOLE BERRY CRANBERRY SAUCE

6 to 8 servings

Combine, bring to a boil, and stir until the sugar is dissolved:

2 cups sugar
2 cups water

Boil the syrup 5 minutes. Add:

4 cups cranberries (1 pound)

Simmer the berries in the syrup very gently, uncovered, without stirring, until the berries are translucent, about 5 minutes. Skim off any foam. Add, if desired:

(2 teaspoons grated orange zest)

Pour the berries into 1 large or several individual molds that have been rinsed in cold water. Chill until firm. Unmold to serve.

COOKED CRANBERRY RELISH

About 2¹/₂ cups

Combine in a large skillet:

One 12-ounce package cranberries (3 cups)
1 cup sugar
¹/₃ cup water
(2 teaspoons grated orange zest)
¹/₃ cup orange juice

Bring to a simmer and simmer, uncovered, over medium heat until the cranberries pop and the relish is somewhat thickened, 7 to 10 minutes. Add, if desired:

(¹/₂ cup slivered almonds)

Let cool and serve, or refrigerate for up to 1 day.

ADDITIONS TO CRANBERRY SAUCE

Prepare **Cooked Cranberry Relish,** above, adding to the relish as desired:

Coarse black pepper
Ground cinnamon
Ground cloves
Minced peeled fresh ginger or ground ginger
Five-spice powder
Fresh or dried thyme or rosemary

3 tablespoons port, bourbon, dry red wine, cherry or pomegranate juice, or raspberry or balsamic vinegar

Dried cherries

Currants or raisins

Diced apples

Minced shallots

Pecans or walnuts

Sweeten with:

Maple syrup or molasses

For a Southwestern flair, add:

$^1/_2$ cup finely minced jalapeño peppers

$^1/_3$ cup chopped cilantro

UNCOOKED CRANBERRY RELISH

About 2 $^1/_2$ cups

Pick over:

One 12-ounce package cranberries (3 cups)

Cut into eighths, removing any seeds:

1 navel orange, unpeeled

Place half of the cranberries and half of the orange in a food processor and pulse until the mixture is evenly chopped but not pureed. Transfer to a medium bowl. Repeat with the remaining cranberries and orange. Stir in:

1 cup sugar, or to taste

Cover and refrigerate at least 2 days, or up to 2 weeks.

ABOUT GOOSEBERRIES

There is limited cultivation of gooseberries in this country, and most of the commercial crop is canned. Prime season for fresh berries is early summer. The common varieties are the size and shape of marbles, translucent, and green when underripe, amber, pink, or purplish when ripe. The berries are generally harvested when underripe and sour and used in recipes that cook them with sugar. When fully ripe, though, gooseberries are sweet enough to eat uncooked. To "top and tail" a gooseberry means to pinch off the stem at the top end and the blossom remnant at the tail end. Gooseberry fool is a classic of English cuisine. Do not confuse gooseberries with Cape gooseberries, 238, which are an unrelated species and react differently in cooking. See also Gooseberry Jelly, 932. To cook gooseberries, see Poached Thick-Skinned Fruit, 213.

GOOSEBERRY CHUTNEY

About 1 $^1/_2$ cups

The flavors will intensify over time. Excellent on a cheese plate, but try also with ham, pork, or duck.

Combine in a large saucepan:

3 to 4 cups fresh gooseberries, topped and tailed, or frozen gooseberries, thawed

1 small onion, chopped

1 cup sugar

$^1/_2$ cup water

Bring to a simmer and simmer until the berries soften, about 8 minutes. Add:

1 cup cider vinegar

1 tablespoon ground ginger or 1 tablespoon minced peeled fresh ginger

$^1/_2$ teaspoon dry mustard

$^1/_4$ teaspoon salt

$^1/_4$ teaspoon ground red pepper

Simmer, stirring often, until thick, about 40 minutes. Cool and refrigerate in jars; this also freezes well.

ABOUT CURRANTS

Currants are in peak season from mid-June through August. These fresh, tiny, round, shiny berries divide into two principal types, **red currants** and **black currants**. **White currants** are a less acidic variety of red. Black currants are much less common than red. Currants are very tart and seedy and are generally cooked. Red currants make one of the world's most beloved jellies, while black currants, somewhat sweeter and fuller in flavor, make delicious jams as well as the liqueur crème de cassis. Currants are generally sold in clusters still attached to their stems. Use a fork or your fingers to gently free them.

RED CURRANT SAUCE

About 1 cup

A warm dessert sauce or glaze for roasted meats or turkey.

Wash and stem:

1 cup red currants

Whisk together in a small saucepan over medium heat:

$^1/_2$ cup sugar

1 tablespoon cornstarch

$^1/_2$ cup water

Bring to a boil, stirring constantly. Add the currants and:

$^1/_4$ cup red currant jelly

Stir just until the jelly is melted. Serve warm.

ABOUT MULBERRIES AND ELDERBERRIES

Though not related, both of these fruits grow on trees and are primarily foraged, though both sometimes show up at farm stands in summer. **Mulberries,** which look similar to blackberries, are sweet but tart in flavor and make delicious syrups, sorbets, and preserves. **Elderberries** are small, purplish aromatic berries that grow in sprays. Freeze the sprays on baking sheets, then shake them over a deep bowl—the berries will drop off. Elderberries are used primarily to make wine, jelly, and jam, since they are much too tart to eat raw.

ELDERBERRY VINEGAR

$^2/_3$ cup

Deep in color and with a slightly musky flavor, this is good in vinaigrettes or to flavor sauces for game. This can be made using $^1/_4$ cup dried elderberries and 1 cup vinegar. Preheat the oven to 350°F. Place in a baking dish:

2 cups elderberries, stemmed

Cover with:

White or cider vinegar

Bake until the berries pop, about 1½ hours. Let the mixture stand at room temperature or chill for 12 to 24 hours, then strain. Add:

(Sprigs of mint or tarragon)

and store in a jar, refrigerated, for up to 6 months.

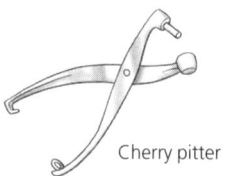

Cherry pitter

ABOUT CHERRIES

Cherries are available in two sharply contrasting types: sweet and tart. The peak season for **sweet cherries** runs from late May through August. Two principal kinds of sweet cherries are found in markets: the familiar red **Bings** and the golden **Rainiers** or **Queen Annes.** In purchasing either type, select those that are plump, glossy, and firm. The darkest-red Bings are the ripest; Rainiers and Queen Annes should have a rose blush. Sweet cherries can be refrigerated for 3 to 4 days. They are delicious in a fruit salad, 210, and are also excellent poached, below. Cherries have an affinity for spirits, including kirsch and maraschino liqueur, both made from the fruit, as well as dark rum, 60, brandy, 62, and amaretto. They're also delicious paired with almonds, basil, tarragon, cinnamon, vanilla, and chocolate.

   Sour cherries, or "pie cherries," which are extremely tart, are available in some markets June to August. Cooking and sugar mellow them wonderfully. The **Early Richmond cherry** is the first pie cherry of the season. Widely cultivated varieties derive from the **Morello.** The colorless **Montmorency** is the most frequently available. Select and store sour cherries as for sweet cherries. The canned cherries in grocery stores are good pie substitutes in the off season. Included in this fruit category—by courteous extension—is the **Sorinaw cherry:** not a cherry at all but a tropical fruit that resembles it and is now grown rather extensively in Florida. It makes a spicy and delicious jelly. Cherries are most easily and neatly pitted with a cherry pitter, above. For a classic dessert, see Cherries Jubilee, 826.

POACHED CHERRIES

I. For preparing a compote of sour cherries, see Poached Thick-Skinned Fruit, 213.

II. Cook until tender but still shapely:

   Pitted sweet cherries

For each pound cherries, have ready:

   ½ cup currant jelly

melted in:

   ¼ cup kirsch or other liqueur

Drain the cherries. Reserve the juice for pudding sauce or basting meats or in baking. Shake the drained cherries in the jelly mixture until well coated. Chill and serve.

MACERATED CHERRIES WITH HERBS
4 servings

Serve as a side dish to grilled or roasted poultry or pork, or as a dessert with ice cream and pound cake.

Mix together in a medium bowl:

   1 pound sweet cherries, stemmed, pitted, and halved
   3 to 4 tablespoons fresh lemon juice
   ¼ cup sugar
   2 tablespoons chopped basil, mint, or tarragon
   ¼ teaspoon black pepper

Let marinate for at least 15 minutes at room temperature, stirring once or twice, or up to 2 days in the refrigerator. Serve at room temperature.

Rasp grater, citrus juicer, citrus reamer

ABOUT CITRUS FRUITS

Choose citrus fruits that feel firm in the hand and heavy for their size. Most citrus fruits can be stored in the refrigerator for 2 to 3 weeks. When they appear at the market, citrus fruits are usually equipped with a thin coating of wax. The wax is harmless, but it is undesirable if you are grating the zest. Remove the wax by lightly scrubbing with a brush under running water.

   When grating or zesting, ➤ do not take off more than the highly colored outer coating. The best tool for removing strips of zest is a zester or a vegetable peeler. A rasp grater shaves off the zest in very fine shreds. Or you can use a box grater.

   To extract citrus juice easily, first roll the fruit firmly beneath your palm over a hard surface, exerting pressure. Cut the fruit crosswise in half, and if juicing only one fruit, remove the juice with a citrus reamer. When juicing several fruits, use a citrus hand press or an electric juice extractor.

   To section a small or average-sized citrus fruit, hold it over a bowl to catch all the juices, and use a sharp knife to remove the rind, including the pulpy white skin. Peel it around and around like an apple so that the cells are exposed. Loosen the sections by cutting between the fruit and the membrane. Lift out each segment (sometimes called a **supreme**) in one piece and remove any seeds.

   To section larger fruits like grapefruit into supremes, slice off the top and bottom of the fruit, down to the flesh. Stand the fruit on a cutting board and use a serrated knife to cut off the rind in even slices. Trim away any remaining white membrane. Free each segment by cuttting down against the membrane on either side. Lift out the segment

Sectioning small or average-sized citrus fruits

and remove any seeds. Squeeze all the juice from the membranes into a bowl.

WINTER FRUIT SALAD
3 to 4 servings
Section or peel and cut into bite-sized pieces:
1 grapefruit
1 navel orange
Place the fruit and all juices in a bowl. Gently stir in:
1 to 2 cups seedless red grapes, halved
Cover and refrigerate until chilled. As close to serving time as possible, add:
1 apple, quartered, cored, and thinly sliced
1 banana, sliced
Coat with citrus juices to prevent discoloration, 209.

CITRUS SALAD
6 servings
Grate 3 tablespoons zest from:
4 navel oranges
Place the zest in a medium bowl. Section the oranges, or peel and cut into bite-sized pieces. Add the oranges and their juices to the bowl with the zest. Section or peel and cut up, removing seeds:
2 grapefruits
2 tangelos or 3 mandarins
Combine with the oranges. Gently stir in:
Sugar to taste
(2 tablespoons orange liqueur)
Cover and refrigerate until chilled and ready to serve. If desired, sprinkle with:
(Chopped mint)

ABOUT LEMONS AND LIMES
Both of these fruits are quite indispensable, and we discuss them more fully in Know Your Ingredients, 956. The juiciest lemons are those with thin, smooth, yellow skins. **Meyer lemons,** a lemon-tangerine cross, are less tart and pungent and may be added to tossed salads and fruit cups. They may also be used in any way that ordinary lemons are or may be preserved, below. ➤ A squirt of lemon juice can enhance the natural flavor of any ingredient, just as a dash of salt does.

The most common limes are **Persian limes.** In a pinch,

lime juice can be substituted for lemon juice as a seasoning. The small **Key limes** have a tart, complex flavor that some find indispensable for Key Lime Pie, 688. Small **Makrut** limes, long known as *Kaffir,* have a strong fragrance and sour juice. The rind and leaves are used as a flavoring for curries, as well as dried; the juice is acrid. Fresh Makrut leaves are more intense and fragrant than dried. For general use of limes in beverages, see 55. For use to stop discoloration of fresh fruits and vegetables, see 209.

Fresh **citrons,** which so resemble bumpy lemons that we put them here rather than in citrus, can be found at farmers' markets in citrus-growing areas in the fall. Large and typically pear-shaped, the fruit is cultivated for use as a table decoration—it is highly aromatic and will perfume an entire room—and for its thick rind, which is candied and used in cakes and desserts. Supermarket candied citron is so often dried out and tasteless it has given the fruit an ill-deserved bad reputation. Fine-quality candied citron can be found at Middle Eastern and Indian markets or through Internet retailers, where it is often sold in uncut halves. It is tender, spicy, and thoroughly delicious.

SALT-PRESERVED LEMONS
1 quart
Prepare these pickles to flavor a seafood soup or stew, vegetable salad, lamb casserole, poached chicken, or stuffing. Preserved lemons will keep for 1 year as long as they are completely covered with salted juice and not contaminated by bacteria. For this reason, always remove the lemons from the jar with clean dry tongs.
Wash, dry, remove stems, and set in a warm 200°F oven for 5 minutes to dry thoroughly:
2 pounds lemons
Measure:
$\frac{1}{3}$ cup coarse salt
Spoon 2 tablespoons of the salt into a sterilized wide-mouth quart jar. Roll the lemons on the counter to release their juice. Quarter a lemon lengthwise, stopping $\frac{1}{2}$ inch from the bottom so the quarters fan out but remain attached at one end. Gently open the lemon and sprinkle the 8 cut surfaces with $\frac{1}{2}$ teaspoon of the salt. Carefully squeeze the lemon juice into a bowl. Close the lemon, pack into the jar, and add the juice. Continue with the remaining lemons, sprinkling each layer with $1\frac{1}{2}$ teaspoons salt. If the juice does not cover the lemons when all are in the jar, add:
Fresh lemon juice to cover
Leave a $\frac{1}{2}$-inch space at the top of the jar. Force out air bubbles by sliding a narrow spatula between the lemons and the side of the jar—slowly turn the jar while moving the spatula up and down, forcing up any bubbles. Then be sure the lemons are still covered with liquid and there is only a $\frac{1}{2}$-inch headspace. Wipe the rim of the jar. Fold a square of plastic wrap to make 4 layers and place over the top, then tightly cap the jar.

Place the jar on a saucer in a warm place to cure for 1 month. Each day, turn the jar upside down to redistribute the salted juice. After the curing period, refrigerate or keep in a cool, dry place. To use, run the lemons under running water.

ABOUT ORANGES

Usually varieties of **Valencia** are classified as "juicers," and various types of **navel** oranges are considered "eaters," but some Valencias are virtually seedless, faintly sweet, and very good eating. In our household if we have fruit of interesting flavor in either category, we often cut it in half right across the middle and section each half into thirds or fourths, then proceed to eat the slices over a plate. The process is untidy but it lets us ingest the fibrous parts of the pulp, as well as the juice. For the same reason, when we ream or squeeze oranges for juice, we prefer not to use a fine strainer. **When giving an orange to a child,** roll to make juices release, then cut a cone-shaped section from the top, leaving a hole the size of a nickel. Sucking the juice from the orange is easy and fun with little mess.

Highly desirable for table use is the **blood orange,** with dark red flesh, available from December through March. For special uses, the most venerable but harder to find is the **Seville,** or **bitter orange.** Bitter oranges make superb marmalade and lend piquancy to meat and fish dishes and to various drinks. For milder but still intriguing character, add a few tablespoons of the chopped orange zest to beef or lamb stews.

Mandarins have loose, easily peeled rinds and juicy flesh. The canned versions are wonderful. **Tangerines** are old favorites, but increasingly popular today is the **clementine. Satsumas** are a separate sweet seedless variety. **Tangors,** mandarin-orange crosses, have the flattened look, loose skins, and juiciness of mandarins but taste like oranges. **Temple** is a common variety, in season from January through March.

Tangelos are mandarin-grapefruit crosses. **Minneolas** are instantly recognizable by their fiery orange rind and prominent knobby neck. They are juicy, but also quite tart, and some prove seedy. Its peak season is from December through April. **Ugli fruits** are large, bumpy-skinned, yellowish tangelos with a decided grapefruit flavor. However, they are much sweeter and juicier.

All members of the mandarin family are delicious in fruit salads, 210, but difficult to section. Instead, section and cut segments in half with a serrated knife and remove the seeds. Mandarins are not suitable to most cooking purposes. If you want to add mandarin to a hot dish, do so at the last minute.

Kumquats are the size of robins' eggs. They're not, strictly speaking, a citrus fruit but are generally classed as one because of their citrusy taste. They are edible in their entirety, both rind and flesh. There are two principal types: an elongated oval variety, which has a sweet rind but sour

flesh, and a slightly larger round variety, whose rind and flesh are both sweet. The oval variety is more common at markets. Both may be eaten raw, either out of hand or sliced in a fruit salad, 210, though the oval variety is delicious when candied, 880, made into preserves, 939, served as a compote, below, or otherwise cooked with sugar.

ORANGES IN SYRUP
About 9 cups
Wash and dry, grate the zest from, and set aside:
    1 large navel orange
Combine the zest in a small saucepan with:
    1 cup sugar
    ¹⁄₂ cup currant jelly
    ¹⁄₄ cup water
Bring to a boil over medium-high heat, stirring constantly, then turn the heat down as low as possible and simmer 10 minutes. Remove the syrup from the heat and let cool to tepid, then stir in, if desired:
    (2 tablespoons Cognac or other brandy)
Set aside. Slice off the peel as for sectioning, 223 (but do not separate the segments), from the zested orange and:
    5 large navel oranges
Cut the oranges crosswise into ¹⁄₄-inch-thick slices. Arrange them in slightly overlapping rows in a large shallow dish and pour the syrup over them. Cover and refrigerate 12 to 24 hours. Serve with:
    Drop Butter Wafers, 766, or Tuiles, 766

KUMQUAT COMPOTE
6 servings
Spoon this bright and versatile compote over pork, firm white fish, foie gras, yogurt, ice cream, or panna cotta. Cover with cold water and bring to a boil:
    2 cups kumquats
Drain. Slice the kumquats into rings and remove any seeds. Combine in a medium saucepan and bring to a boil over medium-high heat:
    2 cups water
    1 cup sugar
Add the kumquats and simmer until tender and the sugar is dissolved, about 5 minutes. Remove to a bowl, and boil to reduce the syrup by half. Strain the syrup over the kumquats, cover, and refrigerate until chilled.

ABOUT GRAPEFRUIT

White, pink, and ruby red grapefruit have their peak season from January to June. Marvelous in a tossed salad, with its tart, bracing flavor, grapefruit also makes an excellent garnish for rich foods like avocados, roasted meats, fatty fish, and shellfish. For all such purposes, section the fruit, 223. For a garnish, warm the fruit slightly and/or sweeten it very lightly by tossing it with sugar or honey.

Pomelo, or **shaddock,** is an ancestor of today's grapefruit. This large citrus fruit is at least grapefruit-sized, or bigger. It can be round or pear-shaped, with firm white or pink flesh. The **Chandler,** the most common pomelo, has delicious sweet pink flesh, usually with few seeds. Pomelos are traditionally served in segments, 223. Pomelo-grapefruit crosses offer us **Oroblanco** and **Melogold,** supersweet fruits with no bitterness or seeds. Look for these cantaloupe-sized fruits from winter through spring.

BROILED GRAPEFRUIT
4 servings
This old-fashioned grapefruit recipe can be served as a first course, for dessert, or for breakfast. Pink grapefruit is preferred, for its appealing color and sweetness.
Adjust the broiler rack so the grapefruit will be about 4 inches below the heating element. Preheat the broiler. Cut horizontally in half:
 2 grapefruits, preferably pink or red
Remove any large seeds. If desired, snip out the tough centers. Loosen each section by cutting along the membranes and skin with a grapefruit knife or small serrated knife. Place the halves on a small rimmed baking sheet. Sprinkle each half with:
 1 tablespoon sugar ($^1/_4$ cup total)
 (Pinches of ground ginger or ground star anise)
Broil the grapefruit until the tops begin to brown, about 5 minutes. For garnish, place in the centers of the grapefruit and serve at once:
 (4 small raspberries or strawberries)

SWEETENED GRAPEFRUIT
4 servings
Peel and section, 223:
 2 large grapefruits
Place the fruit and juice, if any, in a bowl and refrigerate until chilled. Fifteen minutes before serving, divide the fruit among 4 glass bowls and sprinkle lightly with:
 Confectioners' sugar or honey
Immediately before serving, add to each bowl:
 1 tablespoon Cointreau or orange liqueur
  ($^1/_4$ cup total)
Or fill each bowl one-quarter full with:
 Chilled orange juice

CHILLED GRAPEFRUIT CUPS
Chill:
 Grapefruit
Cut into halves. Loosen the pulp from the peel with a sharp-toothed, grapefruit, or steak knife, or remove the seeds and cut out the tough fibrous center with a grapefruit corer. Five minutes before serving, sprinkle with:
 Confectioners' sugar
Add to each half immediately before serving:
 (1 tablespoon curaçao or a mint leaf)

ABOUT COCONUT
Coconuts are a large nut, or stone, from the *Cocos nucifera* palm tree. While not botanically a fruit, coconut deserves a place here because of its use in delicate fruit

dishes, such as Ambrosia, 210. ➤ To substitute packaged flaked unsweetened coconut for fresh, use $1^1/_3$ cups firmly packed for each 1 cup grated fresh coconut. To grate fresh coconut, use the large holes of a box grater. Sweetened flaked coconut will yield much sweeter results. Also see Know Your Ingredients, 956.

COCONUT LIME SALAD
5 servings
Serve this salad beside grilled fish. Mango and papaya are great additions.
Combine in a large bowl:
 2 cups grated fresh coconut
 1 cup seeded and grated cucumber
 $^1/_2$ cup chopped cilantro
 Grated zest and juice of 1 lime
 1 jalapeño pepper, seeded and minced
 $^3/_4$ teaspoon salt
 $^1/_4$ teaspoon black pepper
 2 tablespoons olive oil
Let stand 15 minutes before serving.

ABOUT DATES
In the desert regions of North Africa and the Middle East, the date palm was traditionally put to almost total use—as food and fiber. Long before the advent of cane sugar, it was a valuable sweetener. It dominated Arab culture just as the bison did among Plains Indians in the United States—shaping, regulating, and limiting a lifestyle.
    The California date industry began in the early 1900s. Date varieties now cultivated in the United States—**Medjool, Deglet Noor,** and **Khadrawy**—are all of Arabic origin. Fresh dates are in season in the fall. They have a milder flavor than dried and a delicate texture, and they are delicious paired with creamy cheeses.
    About half of the fruit is sugar, which accounts for the grayish crystallization that shows up on both fresh and dried dates. It also explains why eating only a few brings on a surfeit, and why, served as a garnish for a fruit dessert tray, they are often stuffed with cream cheese and nuts, with a fondant made piquant with almond paste and spices, or with a tangy marmalade.
    Dates are sold whole, pitted or unpitted, and chopped. Dates are easier to slice or chop ➤ if first frozen for 1 hour. Because they are high in sugar, dates keep well, about a month at room temperature, several months in the refrigerator, and up to 1 year in the freezer.

STUFFED DATES
30 pieces
Combine in the top of a double boiler:
 30 pitted dates
 $^1/_4$ cup brandy
 2 tablespoons orange juice
Cover and cook over simmering water, about 15 to 20 minutes. Cool, and peel while still warm. Stuff with:
 30 blanched whole almonds

Mix together in a small bowl:

¹/₄ cup sugar

1 teaspoon ground cinnamon

Grated zest of 1 orange

Roll the stuffed dates in the spiced sugar and let them dry for 2 hours. Pack the dates layered between sheets of wax paper or aluminum foil in an airtight tin. Let them dry for several days before eating. Stored airtight, these will keep for up to 3 months, longer if refrigerated.

ABOUT FIGS

A fig tree marked the foundation of Rome, and Buddha meditated his way toward perfect knowledge beneath one. There are hundreds of varieties of the fruit, in a multitude of shapes, sizes, and colors. In the United States, all figs are grown in California. Most are dried, but the availability of fresh figs has increased. The two principal varieties of California figs are the green **Calimyrnas** and the purple-black **Missions,** similar in flavor but different in texture: Calimyrnas are firm and slightly chewy, Missions soft and tender. Choose figs that are plump and with taut skins. Ripe figs can be stored for 3 or 4 days on a plate covered with plastic wrap. Fresh figs are generally eaten raw but they are also delicious sautéed, 214, or baked, below. If using hard dried figs, increase the water to 3¹/₂ cups and soak the figs in the water for at least 3 hours, or overnight, before cooking. Grilled figs make an excellent accompaniment for grilled chicken, lamb, or pork, as well as a dessert, served with crème fraîche, mascarpone, or vanilla ice cream. Also excellent are fig fritters. Drizzle with warm honey. Follow the recipe for Fruit Fritters, 658, using 12 large whole figs.

BAKED FIGS WITH RICOTTA

4 servings

Preheat the oven to 350°F. Combine in a small saucepan and bring to a boil, stirring to dissolve the sugar:

¹/₃ cup sugar

3 tablespoons water

Remove the syrup from the heat and add:

¹/₂ cup sweet or dry Marsala

Quarter from the top down almost to, but not through, the bottoms:

8 large fresh figs

Press up from the bottom to spread the figs open, and place in a shallow baking dish. Spoon the Marsala syrup over the figs. Bake until the figs are tender, about 20 minutes. Meanwhile, mash together:

¹/₃ cup ricotta cheese

¹/₃ cup heavy cream

1 teaspoon sugar

Place the figs in serving dishes, dab some of the cheese mixture into the center of each, and spoon the syrup around them. Serve warm or at room temperature, garnished with, if desired:

(Shaved or grated bittersweet or semisweet chocolate or chopped almonds)

GRILLED OR BROILED FIGS WITH PROSCIUTTO

32 pieces

Prepare a medium-hot grill fire or preheat the broiler. Quarter:

8 large fresh figs

Wrap with:

4 ounces thinly sliced prosciutto or serrano ham, cut into strips

Brush each with:

Olive oil

Grill or broil until just warm, 1 minute per side. Serve immediately, drizzled with:

(Balsamic vinegar)

FIG COMPOTE WITH LEMON AND GINGER

6 to 8 servings

Excellent with yogurt, as part of a cheese plate, or alongside roast duck.

Combine in a medium saucepan:

1 pound dried figs, stems removed

3 cups water

Zest of 1 lemon, removed in strips

One 2-inch piece fresh ginger, peeled and thinly sliced

Simmer, cover, and cook until the figs are plumped, 25 to 35 minutes. Add more water if necessary. Add:

³/₄ cup sugar

2 tablespoons fresh lemon juice

Simmer, uncovered, 5 minutes longer. Remove from the heat and stir in:

(1 to 2 tablespoons Cognac, brandy, or ruby port)

Serve warm or chilled. The compote can be kept in the refrigerator, covered, up to 1 month.

ABOUT GRAPES

There are thousands of varieties of grapes, but only a small percentage are sweet and crisp enough to be eaten straight or used in cooking. A few of the wine-grape varieties, known as *vinifera,* are also good eating, especially the pale-green **Thompson seedless** and **Perlette.** Several seedless red varieties of vinifera have also been developed and are increasingly popular, notably **Red Flame** and **Ruby Seedless.** These seedless varieties are the best for cooking and in salads.

Labrusca are grapes native to America. They have thicker skins that slip easily from the pulp, so they are often referred to as slip-skins. Fox grapes are the principal American species. These grapes are sweet, with a musky flavor and aroma that is described as "foxy." **Concords** are an example of fox grapes. Look for them, and many other hybrids ranging in color from palest green or yellow through red to darkest purple, from July through October.

The second native American species are the **muscadines,** of the vine *rotundifolia.* Most are sweet, and some are even muskier and more richly aromatic than the foxes. **Scuppernongs** are the best-known muscadine; they are so sweet their jelly can taste like honey. At their peak in September and October, they are usually too fragile to ship but are often found in local markets.

When buying grapes, taste one. Grapes can be stored, refrigerated in a perforated plastic bag, for up to a week. See other grape recipes in Salads, 152, Desserts, 801, and Pies and Pastries, 661.

GRAPES AND SAUSAGES

4 servings

Preheat the oven to 500°F. Prick all over with a fork to prevent bursting:

1¹/₂ pounds sweet Italian sausages

Heat in a large heavy skillet over medium heat:

2 tablespoons olive oil or butter

Add the sausages and cook, turning occasionally, until browned, about 20 minutes. Mix in a baking pan:

12 ounces seedless grapes, halved if large

2 teaspoons minced rosemary

Lay the sausages over the grapes. Roast about 20 minutes. Season with:

Salt and black pepper to taste

(A dash of balsamic vinegar)

PICKLED GRAPES

About 2 cups

Pairs well with roasted meat, and great in salads or on a cheese plate, especially with goat cheese. Or try pickled grapes instead of olives in a vodka martini.

Place in a large jar or bowl:

2 cups seedless grapes

6 garlic cloves, peeled

Combine in a saucepan and bring to a simmer over medium heat, stirring until the sugar is dissolved:

1¹/₂ cups white or cider vinegar

1 cup sugar or packed brown sugar

2 tablespoons grated peeled fresh ginger

1 teaspoon salt

1 teaspoon ground coriander

10 whole cloves

(1 jalapeño pepper, seeded and finely chopped,
or 1 teaspoon crushed red pepper flakes)

Pour over the grapes. Let stand at least 1 hour, or overnight, or cover tightly, once cool, and refrigerate for up to 3 months.

ABOUT GUAVAS

Guavas range in color from white to dark red and in size from that of a walnut to that of an apple. They are delicious when pureed, baked, or served fresh, alone or in combination with other fruits such as bananas or pineapple. The simplest way to enjoy guavas is to cut them in half and eat the flesh with a spoon. To add to a fruit salad, 210, peel with a vegetable peeler, slice crosswise, and scrape out the pulp and seeds. Guavas can be poached, 212. See also Apple Cake Cockaigne, 691, or prepare guava jelly with cream cheese.

GUAVAS IN LIGHT RUM SYRUP

4 servings

Peel and halve:

4 ripe but firm guavas

Remove the seeds and soft pulp with a spoon, and reserve. Combine in a medium saucepan:

2 cups sugar

2 cups water

¹/₂ cup fresh lemon juice

(1 tablespoon dark rum, or to taste)

1 teaspoon minced fresh ginger

2 whole cloves

Add the guava seeds and pulp and bring to a boil over medium heat. Lower the heat and simmer for 3 minutes. Strain into a second saucepan, pressing down on the pulp to extract all of the juice. Add the guava halves to the saucepan and bring to a boil. Lower the heat and simmer for 3 to 5 minutes, until guavas are tender but not mushy when pierced with a fork. Remove the guavas to a plate to cool slightly; reserve ¹/₂ cup of the poaching liquid. Serve the guavas warm, at room temperature, or chilled, drizzled with the reserved poaching liquid and topped with:

Whipped cream

(Grated lemon zest)

ABOUT KIWIS

Also known as Chinese gooseberries, kiwis come from California and New Zealand and are available year-round. Select firm fruits without wrinkles. The hairy dull brown exterior does not prepare one for the fruit's vivid green translucency when sectioned, or the lovely intricacies of pattern the seeds reveal when it is sliced. Kiwis are highly decorative and can be added to a fruit salad, 210, or served with a little lime juice. The flesh never darkens, even if cut hours in advance. When cooked, it turns an olive color.

KIWI SHRIMP SALAD

4 servings

Prepare:

Vinaigrette, 572, using lemon and fresh mint

Cook in a large saucepan over medium-high heat, stirring, until toasted and golden, about 3 minutes:

1 cup whole buckwheat or quinoa

Stir in:

2 cups boiling chicken stock or broth or water

¹/₂ teaspoon salt

Cook over low heat, covered, until the liquid is absorbed, about 15 minutes. Let stand, covered, for 5 minutes. Combine in a large bowl:

4 kiwis, peeled and sliced
1 bunch radishes, sliced
1 bunch scallions, sliced
8 ounces large shrimp, cooked, 385, peeled, and deveined

Toss with ½ cup of the vinaigrette. Arrange the buckwheat, kiwi mixture, and:

1 head butter lettuce, torn into bite-sized pieces

on a large platter. Drizzle with the remaining vinaigrette.

ABOUT LYCHEES (OR LITCHIS)

The deep red shells of these walnut-sized fruits contain a highly perfumed flesh that is a bit like fragrant jelly. Fresh lychees are available at Asian markets and some supermarkets. Select bright red or brownish-red fruits. Pale fruits are underripe, very brown ones past their prime. Store the fruit at room temperature in a loosely closed plastic bag. Peel lychees with your fingers. Lychees are usually served unpitted because the flesh does not hold its shape well when cut away from the seed. Add to a fruit cup, 210. Lychees are available canned, but the flavor is not so hauntingly aromatic.

SAUTÉED LYCHEES

3 to 4 servings
Heat in a large skillet over medium heat until the butter is melted and the ginger fragrant:

3 tablespoons butter
3 tablespoons brown or turbinado sugar
1 teaspoon minced peeled fresh ginger

Add:

2 cups peeled and seeded fresh lychees or canned lychees

Cook, stirring occasionally, about 5 minutes. Add, if desired, and serve over pound cake or scoops of ice cream:

(2 tablespoons light or dark rum)
(½ teaspoon ground cinnamon)

ABOUT MANGOES

When chilled and eaten raw, they are as good as any peach-pineapple-apricot mousse you can concoct—rich and sweet but never cloying. A perfectly ripe mango gives slightly when squeezed, much like a ripe avocado. The seed, which extends the length of the fruit, makes cutting up a mango a challenge. To peel and cut a mango, see below.

Serve sliced mangoes with prosciutto and lime wedges as a first course. They are also delicious sautéed, 214, in a fruit salad, 210, or serve sliced on vanilla ice cream. Fruit Salsa, 578, is delicious with tortilla chips or as an accompaniment to fish, poultry, or meat. Use them in chutneys and for poaching or baking. If you want to freeze mangoes, see Freezing Fruit Purees, 918.

MANGOES AND CUCUMBERS

About 2 cups
Combine in a bowl:

1 mango, peeled, pitted, and diced
1 cucumber, peeled, seeded, and diced
3 tablespoons chopped red onion
1 tablespoon fresh lime juice

MANGO WITH CILANTRO

About 1 cup
Combine in a medium bowl:

1 mango, peeled, pitted, and chopped
½ teaspoon grated lemon zest
2 tablespoons fresh lemon juice
1 tablespoon chopped cilantro

Let stand 15 minutes at room temperature. Serve with grilled fish and seafood.

ABOUT MEDLARS

In the south of Europe and in the southern United States these 2-inch fruits, which resemble crab apples, are eaten fresh-plucked. In England, far north in their range, they are always overtaken by frost and look shabby indeed, although their flavor is desirable, especially for jellies.

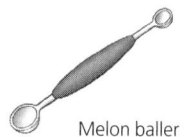

Melon baller

ABOUT MELONS

Melons are available in such variety it is difficult to list them all by name. A distinction is usually made between

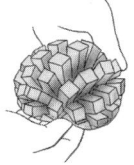
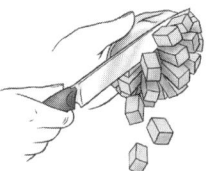

Peeling and dicing a mango

winter, or smooth-skinned, melons and **summer** melons, whose skin is netted, the patterns raised and of a light color. Summer melons come into season as their name implies; winter melons actually ripen in fall. Choose melons that are heaviest for their size, with no soft spots, mold, or cracks. Winter melons should be aromatic at the stem end. In order for it to be sweet, the fruit must have matured on the vine. If it did, you will see that the scar at the stem end is slightly sunken and well callused. The more fragrant the melon, the sweeter it will be.

America's **cantaloupe, muskmelon, nutmeg,** and **Persian** melons are all in the summer or netted group. **Honeydew** and **Santa Claus,** or **Christmas,** are winter melons. **Canary** and **Crenshaw** melons are also in this group with a slightly wrinkled skin, and **casabas** have distinct wrinkles. All winter melons ripen slightly after picking.

Watermelons are a breed apart. The flesh may be red, pink, orange, or gold; it may have seeds or be seedless. Some are the size of a small cantaloupe. If selecting a whole melon, pick one that is symmetrical with a dull sheen on the rind, and check underneath to make sure it is yellowish—a sign it ripened on the ground. A watermelon, if truly ripe, will respond by giving up a thin green shaving if scraped with a fingernail. A cut piece of watermelon should be fragrant through the plastic wrap, and the flesh should appear dense and firm.

Melons are usually eaten raw, and they may be served singly or in combination. They can be served from one end of a meal to the other, from salads to desserts.

Store melons for several days between 50° and 70°F, away from sunlight. Chill lightly just before serving. Seal the fruit in plastic or foil in your refrigerator. Melons can be cut into decorative shapes, below, and they respond favorably to lime or lemon juice or a sprinkling of fresh or powdered ginger, or white pepper.

MELON BASKETS OR FRUIT CUPS
8 to 10 large servings
Cut a thin slice off the bottoms of the melons to keep them from wobbling, then cut into halves or make into baskets or cups, as shown:
4 cantaloupes or 1 large watermelon
Remove the seeds. Using a melon baller, remove and reserve 1 to 2 cups of the flesh for the baskets or cups. Store the leftovers in the refrigerator for another use. Next, scallop the edges. Chill the fruit and combine the following ingredients:

2 cups peeled, sliced seeded or seedless oranges
2 cups peeled, sliced fresh peaches or strawberries
2 cups diced pineapple, fresh or canned
1 cup blueberries or sliced kiwi
1 to 2 cups reserved melon balls
(Sugar, to taste)
Chill thoroughly. Just before serving, fill the melons or cups with the fruit. Pour over each:
(1 tablespoon orange liqueur or rum)
Top with:
(Lemon and Orange Sorbet, 836, or Orange Sherbet, 837)

MELON AND PROSCIUTTO
4 to 6 servings
I. One of summer's most refreshing first courses. Cut in half and scoop out the seeds from:
1 cantaloupe, honeydew, or Crenshaw melon
Slice each half into 6 wedges and remove the rind. Place 2 or 3 wedges on each plate. Cut into wide strips:
8 ounces thinly sliced prosciutto or serrano ham
Drape the ham over the slices. Top with:
(Parmesan shavings)
(Fresh lemon juice)
Serve at once, and pass the pepper mill.
II. To grill, prepare as above but cut melon wedges into 2-inch chunks. Wrap each piece of melon with ham and secure with a toothpick. Grill 4 inches from the heat for 2 to 3 minutes per side. This is one of our favorites.

WATERMELON AND GOAT CHEESE
4 servings
Prepare:
A 2-pound piece watermelon, rind removed, seeded, and cut into bite-sized squares
Arrange on a platter and top with:
Slices of goat cheese (from a 4-ounce log)
Black pepper
Drizzle with:
Extra-virgin olive oil

ABOUT PAPAYAS
Papayas grow up to 20 inches in length. When fully ripened, the flesh develops orangey tones and the greenish rind turns soft and yellow. Their milky juice, when chilled, makes a pleasant drink, and their black seeds, which contain pepsin, are used for garnish, eaten raw, or dried and used for seasoning like a mild mustard. Papain, the tenderizer, is made from the enzymes of the papaya leaves. ➤ Because of this enzyme, do not use papaya in any gelatin mixture.

Use underripe fruits for cooking. Process them as for summer squash, 306. If serving papayas raw, chill and sprinkle with lime or lemon juice. To eat as a melon, halve and scrape out the seeds and strings. It's excellent in fruit salads, too.

Melon baskets

SAUTÉED PAPAYA

4 to 6 servings

Serve as a side dish with grilled fish or chicken.
Peel, halve, seed, and cut into ¹/₂-inch dice:

1 ripe papaya

Heat in a large skillet, preferably nonstick, over high heat:

1 tablespoon butter or vegetable oil

Add the papaya and spread it out into a single layer. Once it has begun to brown, about 1 minute, toss or stir, then season with:

Salt and black pepper to taste

Cook for another minute or so, until lightly browned. Add:

Juice of ¹/₂ lime

Serve immediately.

GREEN PAPAYA SALAD

4 servings

Combine in large bowl:

2¹/₂ cups shredded peeled green papaya
1 cup green beans, quartered lengthwise
2 plum tomatoes, seeded and cut into strips

Mix:

2 tablespoons fish sauce
2 tablespoons fresh lime juice
1 tablespoon chopped cilantro
1 tablespoon chopped basil
1 tablespoon chopped mint
¹/₂ teaspoon minced garlic
1 teaspoon crushed red pepper flakes

Toss with the papaya mixture. Sprinkle with, if desired:

(Crushed peanuts)

Serve with:

Lime wedges

ABOUT PASSION FRUIT

This fruit was named by sixteenth-century Jesuits, who found its flower emblematic of the Passion of Christ. It is available in many markets year-round. Sometimes called the *purple granadilla,* this egg-sized fruit is at its best when a little overripe and wrinkled-looking. Passion fruit can be stored whole in the refrigerator for several days. The sweet, aromatic pulp is inseparable from the seeds. To prepare, slice off the top of the fruit and spoon out the pulp. The seeds are edible, but remove them by rubbing the pulp through a fine mesh sieve. To make a dessert sauce, puree, 215, diluting the pulp slightly with water, and sweeten to taste.

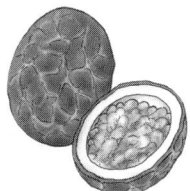

ABOUT PAWPAWS

Also known as Poor Man's Banana or Hoosier Banana, the pawpaw is the largest edible fruit native to America. Pawpaws often occur as clusters of up to nine individual fruits. The ripe fruit is soft and thin-skinned. These smoky-tasting native fruits should be picked and eaten after the first heavy frost, or when they fall from the tree. The domestication process of this fruit is well under way in the United States, and some believe they will be as readily available one day as kiwis and mangoes are today. Pawpaw jam, chutney, sauce, and frozen pulp are available through online sources. Pawpaws can be ripened at room temperature and will keep up to 3 weeks even fully ripe in the refrigerator. The fruits can also be frozen whole, as can the pureed fruit. To make pawpaw puree, remove the skin and the two rows of inedible seeds and puree in a food processor.

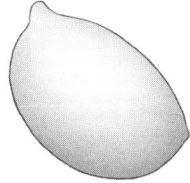

PAWPAW PUDDING

6 to 8 servings

Serve like a savory corn pudding or a sweet pudding, either as a side dish to poultry or with a dollop of whipped cream.

Preheat the oven to 350°F. Grease a 9 x 13-inch baking pan. Combine in a large bowl:

2 cups packed brown sugar
1¹/₂ cups self-rising flour
1 teaspoon baking powder
¹/₂ teaspoon grated or ground nutmeg

Make a well in the dry ingredients and add:

3 eggs

Stir to combine eggs and flour mixture, then add:

2 cups pawpaw pulp
1¹/₂ cups milk
¹/₂ cup (1 stick) butter, melted

Mix well. Pour into the greased baking pan and bake until the center is set, about 50 minutes.

ABOUT PEACHES AND NECTARINES

There are two varieties of peaches—freestone and clingstone—named for the ease or difficulty of removing the pit from the flesh. The mostly yellow-fleshed **freestone peaches** are favorites for eating fresh, out of hand, and for canning and drying. **Clingstones,** with white or yellow flesh that clings to the pit and a somewhat sharper flavor, are excellent for cooking, especially poaching, or simply sautéed with a little butter and sugar. Choose firm, but not hard, well-colored fruit without any flattened brownish bruises which betray areas of decaying flesh underneath. ➤ Discard peach pits, as their almondlike kernels are high in deadly prussic acid.

Although their smooth skin and their flavor strongly suggest a cross between a peach and plum, **nectarines** are in fact simply a variety of peach, resulting from what botanists call "bud variation," and they also are either clingstone or freestone.

Peaches and nectarines do not ripen once picked. If you keep peaches that are slightly hard at room temperature, preferably in a paper bag, for a day or two, they will soften, but not sweeten. A large quantity of peaches may be peeled by blanching, 1054. For peaches marinated in spirits, see Macédoine of Fresh Fruits, 210.

FILLED PEACHES

8 servings

Peel, halve, and pit:

4 chilled freestone peaches

Place in a bowl. Stir together in another bowl:

2 to 3 cups chilled berries

$1/3$ cup sugar

$1^1/2$ to 2 tablespoons lemon juice

Pour the berries over the peaches. Serve with:

Whipped cream

BAKED STUFFED PEACHES

4 or 8 servings

A delightful simple dessert that can be assembled up to 3 hours before baking and refrigerated.

Preheat the oven to 350°F. Peel, halve, and pit:

4 large freestone peaches, or 8 canned peach halves

Place the peaches in a baking dish large enough to hold them in one layer. Mix together to dissolve, then sprinkle over the peaches:

$1/2$ cup orange juice

$1/4$ cup confectioners' sugar

Toss gently with your hands until the peaches appear evenly coated. Turn the peach halves pitted side up in the dish. Pulse in a food processor until the almonds are in very fine pieces:

$1/3$ cup slivered almonds, toasted, 1001

$1/4$ cup packed dark brown sugar

$1/4$ teaspoon grated orange zest

Add:

1 tablespoon cold butter, cut into pieces

Pulse until the mixture is crumbly. Divide the almond mixture evenly among the hollows of the peaches. If canned peaches are used, sprinkle with a little lemon juice. Bake until the pan juices are bubbly, 15 to 20 minutes. Serve warm.

GLAZED NECTARINES

4 or 8 servings

Roasting whole nectarines in a tangy raspberry vinegar glaze turns their skins a lovely russet color. Serve with poultry, pork, venison, or game.

Preheat the oven to 425°F. With the tip of a knife, slash on 4 sides to prevent the skin from bursting:

4 nectarines

or cut in half for 8 servings. Place in a 9-inch pie pan and set on a baking sheet. Combine:

1 cup raspberry vinegar

1 cup packed light brown sugar

2 tablespoons butter

Heat, stirring, over low heat until the sugar is dissolved and the butter melted. Pour over the nectarines. Bake for 20 minutes, basting once. Turn the nectarines and bake 5 minutes more. Transfer the nectarines to a serving dish and cover with foil to keep warm. Pour the glaze back into the saucepan and boil over high heat until reduced and thickened. Stir in:

$1/4$ teaspoon black pepper, or to taste

Pour over the nectarines and serve.

ABOUT PEARS

Pears are available during the cool-to-cold months of the year. As summer ends, we find red-skinned **Bartletts**, sweet and juicy but perishable. Apt to come next are the tiny but sugar-sweet **Seckels**, ideal for pickling and canning. In November, a dazzling array of hardier fall varieties arrives, all of which can be bought far into the winter months. These include the squat teardrop-shaped green or red **Anjou**, firm in texture and mild in taste; the russet **Bosc**, which is crisp and applelike when still flecked with green, soft and sweet when fully ripe; and the ruddy **Comice**, whose juicy flesh makes it the queen of dessert pears. In some markets you may also find **Winter Nellis**, a pear generally reserved for cooking.

Most pears can be tested for ripeness by squeezing; they should give slightly. Like bananas and avocados, pears are picked slightly green. ➤ If you plan to cook them, do so when they are still firm. To prepare, peel if desired and cut lengthwise in half. Scoop out the core with a teaspoon or melon baller, and, if desired, cut out the fibrous string that runs from core to stem. The two halves may be quartered lengthwise, sliced, or diced. **To prepare whole pears for poaching,** peel, leaving the stem attached, then cut a thin slice off the base so that the pear will stand upright when served.

All types of pears seem to be congenial company for cheese. If serving them cut, toss with lemon juice to prevent discoloration, 209. Pears are an excellent addition to a fruit salad, 210. For cooking, choose Anjou, Bosc, or Winter Nellis. Pears are delicious poached, 212, either in a lightly flavored syrup, 212, or, if to be served with meat, a spiced syrup, 212. If very firm, they may take as long as 20 minutes to cook. Pears can also be sautéed, 214; used to make a baked fruit compote, 213; or combined with other fruits in kebabs, 214. Canned pears gain distinction when broiled, 214, or steeped in a spiced syrup, 212. Dried pears are a bit too bland to be used by themselves in a dried fruit compote, 211, but are excellent combined with other fruits.

Asian pears, sometimes called **apple pears,** are round with dull gold skins and might almost be mistaken for apples. Choose fruits that are firm, without wrinkling or shriveling. Asian pears have a very crisp flesh, and are best eaten raw and unpeeled. Thin wedges are delicious in a tossed green salad, 158, or a fruit salad, 210. Whole crosswise slices are especially attractive on a cheese platter—the seeds form a star pattern.

POACHED PEARS IN RED WINE

6 servings

Combine in a saucepan or pot just large enough to hold the pears in one layer on their sides:

> 1 1/2 **cups dry red wine**
> **1 cup sugar**
> **One 2-inch strip lemon peel (removed with a**
>   **vegetable peeler)**
> **2 tablespoons fresh lemon juice**
> **1 cinnamon stick**
> **6 whole cloves or 4 cardamon pods, lightly crushed**

Bring to a boil, then reduce the heat to low and simmer, covered, for 5 minutes. Peel and slice 1/2 inch from the bottom of:

> **6 whole pears**

Add the pears to the pot, keeping the liquid at a low simmer. Poach uncovered until tender, 10 to 20 minutes, turning frequently. The pears can be set aside at room temperature in the poaching liquid, covered, for up to 12 hours, or refrigerated for up to 3 days. The longer they sit, the more deeply they will color; turn them periodically to tint them evenly. Serve the pears upright on the plate. They are delicious warm, at room temperature, or chilled, with a few spoonfuls of the poaching liquid and:

> **(Custard Sauce, 846)**

For an elegant presentation, remove the pears from the syrup and boil the syrup over high heat until reduced to about 2/3 cup of thick glaze. Strain to remove the spices. Serve the pears on plates, drizzled with the glaze.

STUFFED PEARS

4 or 8 servings

Preheat the oven to 350°F. Peel, halve, and core:

> **4 pears**

Place in a baking dish large enough to hold them in one layer. Pour over:

> 1/2 **cup honey**
> **2 tablespoons lemon juice**

Toss with your hands until the pears are coated, then turn cavity side up in the dish. Mix together in a small bowl:

> 1/4 **cup golden raisins**
> **2 tablespoons chopped walnuts or pecans**
> **2 tablespoons sugar**
> **1 tablespoon lemon juice**

Stuff into the hollows of the pears. Dust generously with:

> **Sugar**
> **Ground cinnamon**

Cover with foil and bake until the pears are nearly tender, 20 to 30 minutes. Uncover and bake until the pears have begun to brown and the juices have thickened, 10 to 15 minutes longer, basting once or twice. Serve warm, at room temperature, or chilled. The pears can be refrigerated, covered, for 1 day; if desired, reheat in 350°F oven for 10 to 15 minutes.

ABOUT PERSIMMONS

Brilliant-orange persimmons, 235, come to market in the fall and remain available through much of the winter. The common market type is Asian, called **Kaki,** which subdivides into two varieties, the large astringent acorn-shaped **Hachiya** and the smaller nonastringent pincushion-shaped **Fuyu.** Hachiyas are edible only when extremely ripe and almost as soft as jelly; otherwise, they are far too astringent. Fuyus may be eaten ripe and soft, but they are also pleasant even when underripe, hard and crisp. Neither Hachiyas nor Fuyus are likely to be fully ripe at the market, but both can be ripened at home sealed in a plastic bag with a ripe apple. There is also a native **American persimmon,** generally gathered in the wild in the Midwest and South. Like Hachiyas, American persimmons are inedibly astringent unless very ripe and soft, usually after the first frost.

To prepare, remove the core, then cut the fruit lengthwise in half and slice or cut into wedges. Ripe persimmons are ➤ delicious raw, in salads or pureed, and also in fruit cups, salads, puddings, ice creams, sherbets, and cookies. To make persimmon puree, remove and discard any seeds, then scrape the flesh from the skin with a spoon and force through a sieve or food mill, or puree in a food processor. The pulp can be frozen for later use. ➤ Four persimmons equal about 1 pound of fruit.

PERSIMMONS IN VINAIGRETTE

4 to 6 servings

A surprising sweet-and-tangy side for roast meats.

Core, peel, and thinly slice:

> **6 Fuyu persimmons**

Toss with:

> 1/4 **cup Vinaigrette, 572, Fresh Herb Vinaigrette, 572,**
>   **or Lime Vinaigrette, 573**

SAUTÉED PERSIMMONS

4 servings

Heat in a large skillet over medium-high heat:

> **1 tablespoon olive oil**

Add:

> **3 cups cubed Fuyu persimmons**

Cook, stirring until browned. Add:

> 1/4 **cup chopped chives**
> **Salt and black pepper to taste**
> **(Chopped fresh sage or** 1/4 **teaspoon dried sage)**
> (1/8 **teaspoon ground cinnamon and/or nutmeg)**

ABOUT PINEAPPLES

Among the important discoveries of Christopher Columbus was the pineapple—an immediate success in Europe—and transplanted as far away as India and China. The first pineapples grown in England in a nobleman's "stove-house" were graciously rented to his friends as table decorations. So beloved is this fruit that in many Southern homes it was carved above the door as a symbol of hospitality.

A small, compact crown usually denotes the finest fruit. As neither skin nor fruit color indicates ripeness, a dull, solid sound when a finger is flicked against the side of the fruit, along with protruding "eyes" and a delicious aroma, are perhaps the most reliable tests for ripeness. Store at room temperature, away from sunlight. Pineapple lends itself magnificently to all kinds of combinations, but watch for one thing: ➤ be sure to cook fresh pineapple before combining it with any gelatin mixture.

Pineapple contains an enzyme, bromelain, that breaks down gelatin. As heat disables the enzyme, canned or cooked pineapple may be used in any gelatin dish. The enzyme also makes fresh pineapple juice an effective ingredient in a marinade for meat. But ➤ do not add uncooked pineapple to cottage cheese or yogurt or to a meat or poultry salad until the last moment, for it quickly turns dairy products watery and meat and poultry mushy.

To prepare pineapple slices, trim the sharp points of the crown. Grasp firmly and slice off the skin with wide downward strokes, cutting off the "eyes." Cut off the crown. The fruit may then be sliced crosswise or into wedges or flat slices from top to bottom. Trim out the core.

Raw pineapple is incomparable, whether eaten on its own or added to a fresh fruit salad, 210. Cooked pineapple is equally delicious. Pineapple is also excellent poached in spiced syrup, 212, sautéed, 214, used to make a baked fruit compote, 213, grilled, 214, or served on a kebab with other fruits, 214. Canned pineapple rings, when broiled, 214, or steeped in spiced syrup, 212, make a good quick meat garnish. Dried pineapple is generally processed with a great deal of sugar. For use in a dried fruit compote, use unsweetened dried pineapple. Don't forget one of our childhood favorites, Pineapple Upside-Down Cake, 691.

PINEAPPLE TIDBITS

I. *8 servings*

This dish must be made with very ripe pineapple. Trim two-thirds from the leafy top of:

1 chilled ripe pineapple

Cut the fruit into 8 lengthwise wedges. Cut off the core and place each part so that it will resemble a boat, as sketched. Pare the skin in 1 piece, leaving it in place, and cut the pulp downward into 5 or 6 slices, retaining the boat shape, as shown below. Serve each boat on an individual plate, with a small mound of:

Confectioners' sugar

Add:

5 or 6 large unhulled strawberries for each serving

Peeling and serving pineapple

II. A Texas girl named Beth taught us to prepare a pineapple this way. Divide a chilled pineapple into small sections by cutting it down to the core, diagonally, with a sharp knife. Impale each section with a pick and let the guests serve themselves, as shown, above.

III. Pineapple can make an attractive edible centerpiece. Cut off the top and bottom of a ripe pineapple and reserve them. Insert a long sharp knife about ½ inch from the outer edge so the fruit is entirely loosened but the pineapple as a whole retains its shape. Leaving the fruit in this cylindrical shell, cut it in about 12 long pie-shaped wedges. Set it back on its base and use the top for a lid. Let guests remove the long spears with a two-pronged fork.

FILLED PINEAPPLE

8 to 10 servings

Cut in half and hollow out:

1 pineapple

Chill the pineapple shells. Cube the cut-out pineapple. Halve, seed, remove the rind, and cut into cubes:

1 cantaloupe or small honeydew melon

Combine the pineapple chunks and melon in a bowl with:

1 cup raspberries or sliced hulled strawberries

(3 tablespoons chopped mint)

(3 tablespoons orange, melon, or maraschino liqueur)

Heap the mixture in the pineapple baskets and serve.

FRESH PINEAPPLE CUP

6 servings

Peel, core, and dice:

1 pineapple

Chill the pineapple. Meanwhile, combine in a small saucepan:

1 cup sugar

⅓ cup water

Bring to a boil, stirring to dissolve the sugar, and boil for 1 minute. Cool and chill the syrup. Add to the syrup:

½ cup orange juice

3 tablespoons fresh lime juice

Place the pineapple in glasses or bowls and pour the syrup mixture over it.

ABOUT PLUMS

Meaty Japanese plums, which peak in August, comprise the most common market types, including the dark purple **Friar,** green **Kelsey,** and red-fleshed **Santa Rosa** and **Elephant Heart.** European plums, which are harvested in the fall, are generally smaller, oval rather than round, and more meaty than juicy. They include the various **prune plums,** which are indeed dried for prunes but also make excellent cakes and tarts. The luscious **greengages, Damsons,** and **Mirabelles** are generally reserved for preserving, as are **native American** plums. Choose aromatic, soft plums. A whitish bloom or film on the surface is natural. Plums can be stored, 208, at room temperature for 3 to 5 days, depending on how ripe they are. Expect the skins of plums to detach, wholly or partially, when the fruit is cooked. Small chunks of raw plums give a delicious dimension to savory stews and braises; mix them in at the end and cook just enough to soften.

   Prune plums are small purplish-black freestone plums. They are good for eating or cooking and are commonly dried to make prunes because their high sugar content and firmness battle successfully against the twin hazards of drying out and interior decay. Dried prunes are sometimes sold, and labeled, as dried plums.

STEWED PRUNES

I. *8 servings*
If the label calls for soaking, please read about Raisins and Other Dried Fruits, 211. Otherwise, cover with cold water in a saucepan:

   1 pound pitted prunes

Bring to a boil, then reduce the heat and simmer gently about 20 minutes. Add, if desired:

   (^{1}/4 cup or more sugar)

Cook about 10 minutes longer. If desired, add for this second cooking period:

   (^{1}/2 lemon, sliced)

   (1 cinnamon stick)

Serve warm or chilled.

II. *6 servings*
Tea intensifies the flavor of stewed prunes. The cooked prunes will keep for at least 2 weeks in the refrigerator, improving in flavor.

Combine with just enough water to cover in a medium heavy saucepan:

   1 pound pitted prunes

Bring to a simmer, then reduce the heat to low, cover, and cook for 20 minutes. Gently stir in:

   ^{1}/2 cup sugar

   ^{1}/2 cup orange juice

Add:

   2 bags Earl Grey tea

Cover and cook until all the prunes are tender, about 10 minutes more. Remove from the heat and refresh the flavor by blending in another:

   ^{1}/2 cup orange juice

Discard the tea bags, and remove the fruit and syrup to a container. Cover and refrigerate for at least 3 hours before serving. Accompany with:

   Heavy cream, crème fraîche, sour cream, or yogurt

WINE PLUM SAUCE
About 1 cup

A deeply flavored sauce for roast chicken or duck.

Combine in a saucepan and bring to a boil over medium-high heat:

   8 ounces red or purple plums (5 to 8), pitted and sliced

   1 cup dry red wine

Boil until reduced to a syrup, about 15 minutes. Cool, then puree in a blender or food processor or press through a food mill. Return the puree to the pan, and stir in:

   ^{1}/4 cup honey

   ^{1}/4 cup chicken or vegetable stock or broth

   1 tablespoon soy sauce

Simmer until thickened, about 10 minutes. Season with:

   Salt and black pepper to taste

ABOUT POMEGRANATES

By eating a single seed of the pomegranate, below, offered her by the wily Pluto, Persephone was obliged to return periodically to the infernal regions, leaving earth for six months in the cheerless embrace of each winter. We have always wondered, since our own first encounter with the crimson cells enclosing seed and luscious pulp, how Persephone managed to eat only one.

   Avoid pinkish, dull-looking fruits. Pomegranates dry out quickly at room temperature—for example, when part of a table decoration—but they can be stored for 2 weeks or longer in the refrigerator.

   The simplest way to remove the seeds from a pomegranate is to cut it lengthwise into quarters and pull the seeds off the papery membranes. The seeds may be stored, tightly covered, in the refrigerator for 1 to 2 days. The jewel-like seeds make a beautiful garnish for salads, including a fruit salad, 210, braised meat dishes, rice pilafs, and desserts. If you use pomegranates for jelly, do not bruise the seed kernels, for an unpleasant flavor develops. If you live where the fruit is available ripe and in abundance, you may feel it is sacrilegious to eat them any way but plain, or chilled, with yogurt.

   The refrigerated, commercial pomegranate juice is superb. But if you prefer juicing your own, the easiest way to juice a pomegranate is to cut the fruit in half crosswise and ream it using a hand or electric citrus press.

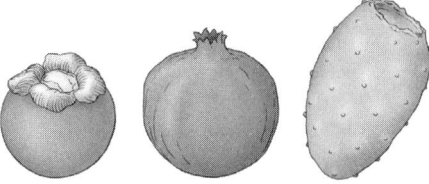

Persimmon, Pomegranate, Prickly pear

POMEGRANATE MOLASSES

1 cup

This dark, tangy syrup can be used as a base for a cooling spritzer. Brush it over light meats and poultry before grilling or after sautéing. Stir a little into salad dressing. Use it for sweetening tropical fruits, or spoon it over cakes and desserts. Extracting the juice is a nuisance, so this syrup is a labor of love—the reward is wonderfully rich flavor and that it keeps for several months.

Roll on the counter to free the juices:

> **5 pounds pomegranate, or 2 cups pomegranate juice**
> **8 ounces lemons (2 or 3)**

Cut the pomegranates in half. Peel off the rinds, and pull the fruit apart into manageable chunks. To extract the juice, see above. Juice the lemons. Strain the lemon juice into a deep heavy saucepan. Ladle the clear pomegranate juice into the pan and add:

> **$1/2$ cup sugar**

Stir over low heat, until the sugar dissolves, then simmer, uncovered, until the liquid is reduced to 1 cup, about 2 hours. Cool, and pour into a sterilized jar.

ABOUT PRICKLY PEARS

The American cactus that bears the prickly pear, 235, also known as the **cactus pear,** was long ago transported to the shores of the Mediterranean, where it is now as much at home as in its native Southwest. Most varieties are egg-shaped, with thick purplish-red or green skins and scarlet flesh. At their prime, prickly pears are juicy and taste faintly of melon. The large hard seeds are edible. Choose fruits that give slightly in the hand but be careful of the fruit's hair-like spines. You may want to wear leather gloves when handling. As with fruits like fresh pineapple, these contain an enzyme that will ruin a gelatin dish, see 234.

To prepare a prickly pear, cut off the top and bottom, then slit the skin lengthwise and peel it off. Prickly pear pulp is usually eaten raw in salsas, but the juices can be boiled into a paste or syrup. The fresh juice can be used to flavor mixed drinks, vinaigrettes, salsas, or fruit salads, or pureed and made into a dessert sauce.

MELON WITH PRICKLY PEAR SAUCE

6 servings

This sauce combines deliciously with cantaloupe or Crenshaw melon.

Wearing plastic gloves, peel:

> **3 ripe prickly pears (about 1 pound)**

Cut into 1-inch chunks, and puree in a food processor until smooth. Combine in a bowl with:

> **3 tablespoons fresh orange juice**
> **2 tablespoons fresh lemon juice**
> **2 tablespoons sugar**

Cover and chill for at least 1 hour. Remove the seeds and rinds from:

> **3 pounds ripe melon**

Set a melon wedge on each plate, and spoon a ribbon of sauce over it.

ABOUT QUINCES

Quinces must be cooked before eating; their flesh is hard and astringent when raw. When cooked, however, quinces taste of apples and pears. The flesh of most quince varieties turns anywhere from pink to red during cooking. If you wish to deepen the color, cover the pan during cooking. Ripe quinces have a fuller flavor, but slightly underripe fruits are higher in pectin and preferred by some for jelly, jam, and preserves. Ripe quinces can be stored for 3 weeks in the refrigerator.

To prepare quinces, peel, then cut the fruits lengthwise into quarters or eighths. Both flesh and core are extremely hard. Cut out the core bits from each wedge with a paring knife, being sure to cut deeply enough to remove all grainy whitish material. The flesh may darken, but using lemon juice can prevent this.

Quinces are delicious poached, 212, in a medium to thick syrup, 212.

BAKED QUINCES

4 servings

Preheat the oven to 350°F. Wash, cut into halves, and core:

> **4 quinces**

Rub with:

> **Butter**

Place in a baking dish and bake, covered, for approximately 1 hour. Pierce with a knife. If the flesh is still very firm, continue baking and checking for up to 1 more hour, until tender but not mushy. Remove from the oven and scoop out most of the flesh, reserving the rinds for presentation. Mix the pulp with:

> **$1/3$ cup fine dry bread crumbs**
> **$1/4$ cup chopped nuts**
> **1 cup brown sugar**
> **A grating of lemon zest**
> **A pinch of salt**

Stuff the quinces with the mixture. Bake about 15 minutes longer, or until tender. Serve hot or chilled.

QUINCE PASTE (MEMBRILLO)

About 2 pounds

Traditional in Spain with a cheese platter, accompanied by nuts and pears, and wine.

Combine in a heavy large saucepan and bring to a simmer over medium heat:

> **2 to 4 medium quinces (2 pounds), peeled, cored, and sliced**
> **1 cup water**

Cover, reduce the heat slightly, and simmer until the quinces are soft, about 40 minutes. Puree the quinces in a food processor or food mill, then return to the pan. Stir in:

> **3 cups sugar**

Simmer over medium-low heat, stirring occasionally, until the mixture is very thick and pulls away from the sides of the pan, about 2$\frac{1}{2}$ hours. Spread the paste in a $\frac{1}{2}$-inch layer on a greased baking pan or cookie sheet, and let dry overnight at room temperature. Cut the paste into squares or other desired shapes with a biscuit or cookie cutter. Continue to dry, turning the pieces occasionally, until the surface dries out completely.

ABOUT RHUBARB

Only by the wildest stretch of botanical definitions can rhubarb, the stem of a plant, be included in this chapter, but its tart flavor and customary uses make it a reasonable facsimile of fruit. Hothouse rhubarb is tender and sweet and never needs peeling. Field-grown rhubarb is in season only in spring. Whichever type, choose crisp, firm stalks, preferably no more than an inch wide. If any leaves are attached, cut them off before storing and discard. ➤ Never eat the leaves; they contain poisonous oxalic acid.

To prepare rhubarb, rinse well. Cut off and discard 1 inch from the base of the stalks, then cut the remainder of the stalks into $\frac{1}{2}$- to 2-inch pieces. Should the stalks be tough, peel them like celery to remove the strings before cooking. Rhubarb makes a delectable sweet or savory compote. It can be sautéed and served as a side dish, or used in baking. Baked rhubarb pairs well with peaches, lemon, apples, pears, and berries.

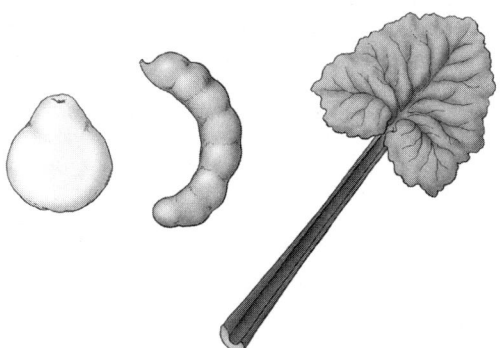

Quince, Tamarind, Rhubarb

POACHED RHUBARB

3 servings

Versatile poached rhubarb is delicious with pork or duck, or spooned over vanilla ice cream. You can also serve it as a dessert by increasing the sugar and garnishing with a dollop of crème fraîche. Try adding balsamic vinegar; cinnamon, cloves, or fresh or ground ginger; or sautéed shallots or onions to sharpen the flavor.

Combine in a medium heavy saucepan:

   4 cups diced rhubarb (about 6 stalks)
   $\frac{1}{4}$ to $\frac{1}{2}$ cup sugar

Let stand at room temperature until the rhubarb exudes some juice, at least 15 minutes. Bring the mixture to a boil over medium-high heat, stirring constantly. Reduce the heat to low, cover, and simmer, stirring occasionally, until the rhubarb is tender and the liquid thickened, 10 to 12 minutes. Remove from the heat and let cool, without stirring. Refrigerate for at least 2 hours, or up to 2 days. The compote will thicken when chilled.

RHUBARB RELISH

6 to 8 servings

Try this on poultry.

Combine in a medium saucepan and bring to a boil over high heat:

   2 cups diced rhubarb (3 stalks)
   $\frac{1}{2}$ cup sugar
   Grated zest of 1 orange
   $\frac{1}{3}$ cup fresh orange juice
   $\frac{1}{4}$ cup chopped shallots or red onion
   $\frac{1}{2}$ teaspoon chopped peeled fresh ginger
   $\frac{1}{4}$ teaspoon ground cardamom
   1 jalapeño pepper, seeded and chopped

Reduce the heat and simmer until the rhubarb softens, about 12 minutes.

ABOUT TAMARINDS

The 2- to 6-inch brownish pods that are the fruit of the graceful tamarind tree can be found in Asian and Latino markets as well as some supermarkets. The fibrous brown spicy pulp scraped from the pods has a date-apricot flavor. Some eat the pulp raw, but it is more commonly used in making curries, sauces, marinades, chutneys, relishes, drink syrups, and tea. Tamarind extract is sold as a thick paste used to acidify and flavor sweet-sour preserves, sauces, soups, and drinks. The pulp can also be bought in plastic-wrapped bricks at Asian markets. Kept in a plastic bag, the pulp can be stored on a shelf for many months or in the refrigerator or freezer more or less forever. To use it, combine 1 tablespoon with $\frac{1}{3}$ cup hot water, knead with your fingers until a viscous, brownish liquid forms, and then strain to remove the seeds and fibers. Strained tamarind concentrate is available in jars. If you need a substitute, combine:

   1 tablespoon lime juice
   1 tablespoon molasses
   1 teaspoon Worcestershire Sauce

TAMARIND DIPPING SAUCE

This tangy dip adds a kick to Seafood or Pork Shumai, 343, Vegetable Wontons, 342, or frittered vegetables, 658.

Soak 15 minutes:

   $\frac{2}{3}$ cup hot water
   2 tablespoons tamarind pulp

Strain the soaking liquid into a blender. Add:

   $\frac{1}{4}$ cup raisins
   $\frac{1}{4}$ cup pitted dried or fresh dates
   $\frac{1}{2}$ cup packed brown sugar
   2 tablespoons chopped cilantro

2 teaspoons salt
2 teaspoons chili garlic sauce
1 teaspoon ground cumin
1 teaspoon ground ginger or $\frac{1}{2}$ teaspoon minced
    peeled fresh ginger

Blend until smooth. Strain once more.

ABOUT TROPICAL EXOTICS

These fruits are becoming increasingly available, particularly at specialty markets and through online retailers.

ACEROLA

The habitat, size, and color of this fruit are indicated by its common aliases, **Barbados cherry** and **West Indian cherry.** Shallow grooves in the bright red skin indicate the positions of the three pits. This citrus fruit has a raspberry flavor when eaten raw and is suggestive of tart apple when cooked.

BREADFRUIT AND JACKFRUIT

Both relatives of the mulberry and fig, these fruits are structurally similar. Breadfruits may weigh up to 9 pounds and jackfruits as much as 90 pounds. Breadfruit, shown above, a native of the Pacific Islands, has a high starch content, thus the name; some sugar; and little water—only 10 percent. Jackfruits are native to India and have, when ripe, a flavor that conjures pineapples, berries, and caramel.

CAPE GOOSEBERRY OR GROUND CHERRY

These small yellow-green or orange berries, like their relative the tomatillo, grow inside papery husks. The flesh is sweet, with a gooseberry or melon flavor. Before using, pull off the husks and rinse well—the skins are sticky. Cape gooseberries can be added to a fruit salad, 210, dipped in chocolate, or poached in a lemon-flavored syrup, just until softened, about 3 minutes.

CARAMBOLA OR STAR FRUIT

Available from Florida in fall and winter, this semi-tropical fruit is readily identifiable by its translucent golden skin and five prominent ridges, which, when the fruit is sliced, make the points of a star. The flesh is crisp and tart-sweet. Ripe fruits can be refrigerated for up to 1 week. To serve, rinse, pat dry, and slice crosswise. Star fruits can be grilled, added to a fruit salad, 210, or a savory salad, 152, since they complement any foods that pair well with pineapple, such as chicken, shrimp, and avocado, as well as cilantro.

CERIMAN OR MONSTERA

This fruit is known to most of us as monstera, or split-leaf philodendron, a houseplant with long, perforated leaves. Unless we are in subtropical climates, we seldom see the 8- to 10-inch cylindrical pine cone–like fruit with its pineapple-banana flavor. A single fruit ripens over a 3- to 4-day period, and ➤ the lower sections, which break apart at the base of the stem, should be eaten only when fully ripe. The rind will turn yellow. To keep the top sections unbruised until ripened, place the fruit stem end up

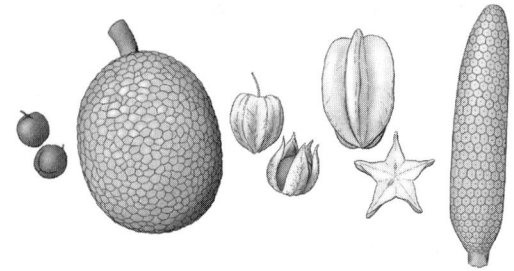

Acerola, Breadfruit, Cape Gooseberry,
Starfruit, Monstera

in a jar, and pluck off the segments as they ripen. Or wrap the fruit in plastic and set aside at room temperature until the entire rind is loose; peel, then pull the creamy flesh off the core with a fork. Serve plain or with vanilla ice cream.

CHERIMOYA OR CUSTARD APPLE

The nineteenth-century German naturalist Alexander von Humboldt, who traveled widely in Latin America, declared that this fruit—with its custard texture and flavor of tropical fruits—was worth a trip across the Atlantic. Cherimoyas resemble artichokes in size and shape, and the pattern of their greenish skins suggests artichoke leaves. The fruit must be tree-ripened but still firm when picked. The fruit bruises easily. When ripe, cherimoyas yield to gentle pressure in the hand, like a ripe peach. Refrigerate ripe fruits for no longer than a day or two.

Cherimoyas are generally cut into wedges and scooped from the skin with a spoon (discard the large black seeds) or blended into drinks, sherbets, and sorbet. A spritz of lemon or lime juice brings out their flavor. The fruit may also be added, peeled and diced, to a fruit salad, 210. If the salad does not include a citrus fruit, toss the cherimoya with lemon juice to prevent discoloration, 209. Other fruits of the *Annona* family are the **sweetsop** or **sugar apple** and the **soursop.**

DURIAN

Fruits of this famous tree, native to Southeast Asia, weigh up to 20 pounds and have been described as "smelling like Hell, and tasting like Heaven." They are highly favored by certain wild animals, and tales abound of Malays who gather durians, only to be gathered in turn by elephants. Durian can be eaten raw or mixed into drinks or ice cream. The large seeds are roasted and eaten like nuts.

FEIJOA

Often called **pineapple guava,** a sobriquet that aptly reflects the feijoa's delicious and complex flavor, this fruit is dark green and about 2 inches long, with a white interior. The flesh has the slightly granular texture of a ripe pear; the jellylike center is filled with tiny edible seeds. Feijoas are used chiefly for jellies and preserves, and are also deli-

Cherimoya, Durian, Feijoa, Genip, Jujube

cious split in half, topped with dabs of cream cheese, and eaten with a spoon. They may also be added to a fruit salad, 210. Remove the bitter skin with a vegetable peeler, then cut the fruit into cubes or quarters. Toss the flesh with lemon juice to prevent discoloration, 209.

GENIP OR MAMONCILLO
These grape-sized, lime-green Caribbean fruits grow in clusters and come to market in summer. They are mostly pit, but their orange-pink flesh is sweet and reminiscent of grapes. Peel off the tough skin with your fingers, then eat out of hand, spitting out the large pits.

JUJUBE OR CHINESE DATE
These fruits, long prized in China, resemble dates in size and taste and also have a single pit in the center. They are available fresh in Chinese markets in the fall. Look for orange-red fruits just beginning to spot with brown. Though most often served raw like dates, jujubes can be poached, 212, and combined with other poached fruits to make an intriguing compote. Puncture their tough skins in several places with a skewer before cooking so that the syrup can penetrate. Dried jujubes can be found in Chinese markets year-round.

KIWANO OR AFRICAN HORNED CUCUMBERS OR HORNED MELON
These small, spiky orange fruits suggest exotic sea creatures. Actually, they are relatives of melons and cucumbers, and their orange-green flesh is cucumber-like in both taste and texture. Cut off the rind and slice the flesh into chunks for green salads or fruit salads.

LOQUAT
These olive-sized fruits, yellow and loosely clustered, mature in the springtime. They are hard to find in markets outside their growing areas, as they bruise easily. Depending on the variety, the orange flesh is somewhat sour but pleasant, and tastes of cherries. Loquats can be refrigerated for up to 3 days. To eat out of hand, simply slice or snap off the stem, if still attached, and enjoy, discarding the toxic brown seeds and the tough bit at the blossom end. To add to a fruit salad, 210, slice lengthwise in half and remove the seeds. The fruits may be poached, 212, or made into jam or jelly.

MANGOSTEEN
This 2- to 3-inch-diameter fruit has a most exquisite milky juice and a floral flavor akin to lychees. Its sections—5 to 6 in number—may be easily scooped out and eaten with a spoon, and it can also be made into preserves.

SAPODILLA
Sapodilla is an evergreen tree whose sap produces chicle gum, from which chewing gum is sometimes made. The fruit has a rather grainy but entirely edible flesh, with a texture somewhat like moist brown sugar. The seeds must be removed, after which the raw pulp may be eaten fresh or used in puddings and other desserts. A sprinkling of lemon juice helps. A close relative, the **sapote,** has similar traits and makes excellent sherbet.

TAMARILLO OR TREE TOMATO
This ovoid fruit has smooth red-yellow skin, edible black seeds, and red-yellow flesh that tastes sweet and somewhat acidic. It is a relation of the tomatillo. Ripe tamarillos can be refrigerated, tightly wrapped, up to 10 days. To prepare, remove the skin and the outer layer of flesh to get at the succulent flesh that holds the seed. Cut in half to scoop out the pulp and eat it plain, or add to savory sauces, 542, or mash into Guacamole, 72.

Kiwano, Loquat, Mangosteen, Sapodilla, Tamarillo

VEGETABLES

When it comes to cooking vegetables, many cooks seem to suffer from arrested development. Delicious meat is accompanied by something indescribable that turns out to be a vegetable that has come through a siege. It is drained of all life force and has despairingly surrendered to the inevitable.

It is this life force that is of the utmost importance, for the loss of vitamin and mineral content through careless cooking robs the vegetable of all flavor and virtually reduces it to a nutritional zero. That's why we encourage you to buy—or grow—the best varieties possible and do very little to them. They will reward you in return with vitamins, phytochemicals, minerals, fiber, and, often, protein.

If you are lucky enough to have the space to grow your own vegetables, you can choose seeds specifically listed for the home garden, seeds that usually produce a harvest of superior texture and flavor. Grow them in organically enriched soil, and control their moisture requirements through mulching and watering during dry periods when they need a boost. The longer it takes vegetables to mature, the coarser their cell structure. These slowpokes and overdeveloped vegetables will demand a longer cooking period and incur consequent loss of nutritive value, color, texture, and flavor.

Few things would make us happier than to branch out at this point with instructions on how our readers might successfully produce for themselves at least the basic repertory of garden vegetables, but the subject is too broad for inclusion here. On the other hand, because culinary herbs can be grown in small outdoor areas or even in window pots on a year-round basis, and because fresh herbs so greatly enhance the flavor of vegetables and other foods, we do give explicit instructions for their culture in Know Your Ingredients, 989.

There is also a renewed interest in the oldest source of supply, foraging—the collecting of greens, 278, and of fruits, roots, and blossoms in the wild. This enterprise is not without peril for the uninitiated. We have included those wild vegetables we have found, on close inspection, to be most palatable and trouble-free. Even some of these have toxic elements when raw that must be carefully broken down by heating or leaching; see About Mushrooms, 281, and About Wild Greens, Shoots, and Roots, 278. Where the use of regional names might produce dangerous confusion, we have identified edible varieties with scientific names and specific descriptions. We recommend using a field guide to edible wild plants while gathering. And be sure that plants taken from roadside habitats have not been coated with poisonous sprays.

On your more conventional quests, trips to the market, use the tests for ripeness we describe under individual vegetable listings. If store stocks are uneven, give preference to commonplace vegetables in peak condition over the exotic vegetable that appears in decline. Care in cooking, piquancy in seasoning, and ingenuity in combining familiar varieties can compensate for the more ordinary choice. But the choices are constantly increasing. It is amazing how many once-unattainable vegetables are now available at the farmers' market, the supermarket, and through Internet retailers.

Give preference to domestically raised vegetables in their peak season. Even better, try to buy vegetables from your own part of the country—they will not have been stressed by being shipped a long distance, they will be much more flavorful, and their nutrients will be intact. Baby vegetables are popular and increasingly available in supermarkets, farmers' markets, and from Internet retailers. Baby vegetables are either a specific variety or a vegetable picked before it reaches maturity. All baby vegetables are tender and delicate in flavor, and have the same nutritional values as their larger-sized counterparts. Use them in recipes that call for the mature vegetables, but decrease the cooking time.

When time does not permit preparing fresh vegetables of any description, the next best bets are—in order of preference—frozen, canned, and dried. To retain nutritive values in vegetables, see 241.

After any vegetable cookery involving moisture, save the cooking liquids to use in sauces or as stocks. The nutritional benefits can be substantial.

For vegetable combinations, often protein-enriched, consult Brunch, Lunch, and Supper Dishes, 95, where you will discover a host of recipes in which cooked vegetables make up the principal ingredient.

STORING VEGETABLES

Certain vegetables and fruits should not be stored together. Apples give off an ethylene gas that makes carrots bitter, and onions hasten the spoilage of potatoes. ➤ Do not wash vegetables until you are ready to use them, as the added moisture and the inevitable nicking of skin and/or leaves hasten spoilage. Cut the leaves from all root vegetables at once, for the flow of sap will continue to the leaf at the expense of the root. We have found that most vegetables—lettuces, cabbages, celery, and beans—keep best if stored in plastic bags in the refrigerator vegetable crisper. They benefit from moderate humidity. However, there are exceptions. For storing watercress and mushrooms, see 151 and 282. ➤ Potatoes, onions, and garlic are best kept in dry, cool air, in a cellar or unheated pantry, if possible. Dried peas and beans should be held in a dry, cool pantry, sealed in a plastic bag or airtight canister. To ripen tomatoes and sweet potatoes, store in dry air at room temperature.

PREPARING VEGETABLES FOR COOKING

Prepare vegetables as close to cooking time as possible. Most thin-skinned vegetables can simply be washed and cooked unpeeled. If vegetables are to be peeled before cooking, trim them as lightly as possible unless the recipe indicates otherwise. Also, unless the individual processing requires it, never soak vegetables after peeling or cutting. Those vegetables that tend to brown after peeling may be sprinkled with lemon juice, 209. ➤ Whether you cook vegetables whole or peeled and cut, see that the pieces are uniform in size so they will all cook through in the same length of time.

When slicing round vegetables like potatoes, first cut a thin slice off one side of the vegetable so that it rests flat on the cutting surface. Whatever the object to be sliced, hold it as shown. Many chopping and slicing devices are available, including the mandoline, but nothing can replace a relaxed skilled wrist and a sharp knife. Acquire this indispensable trick, and you will be forever grateful. Practice with a mushroom, which is yielding and not slippery, and work up to an onion, which can be both resistant and evasive and requires a special procedure, 286.

The point of the knife is ➤ never lifted from the cutting board but instead acts as a pivot. The cutting edge, in turn, is never lifted above the joints of the fingers that hold the vegetable. The handle end of the knife is raised high enough to be eased gently up and down, its wide blade

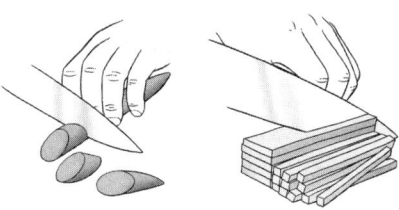

Diagonal cuts, fine julienne

guided by the knuckles of the hand holding the vegetables. As the slicing progresses, the holding hand inches a slow retreat, without releasing its grasp on the object.

If a vegetable like celery or zucchini is to be sliced on the diagonal, the two guide fingers are set at an angle, as shown. But the knife hand continues its relaxed accurate slicing while the other makes way without losing control of the vegetable.

Vegetables gain appeal when cut into special shapes. Think of the irresistible charm of vegetables floating like flowers in a Japanese lacquered bowl. The French, adept at presentation, disguise the same old carrots, beans, and potatoes under a mass of impressive modifiers. As chiffonade, they are thinly or finely shredded. As **brunoise, small dice, medium dice,** or **large dice,** they are sliced respectively into cubes from $\frac{1}{8}$ to $\frac{1}{4}$ to $\frac{1}{2}$ to $\frac{3}{4}$ inch, which later we call just plain **diced.** As **julienne,** or **allumette,** they are longer and thinner, about 2 to 3 inches long and $\frac{1}{8}$ inch thick. **Battonet** is a long rectangular cut, most often used for French fries. When they are round in shape and small, you may call them **pearls;** if they are elliptical, **olivette** at $\frac{3}{8}$ inch, **noisette** at $\frac{1}{2}$ inch, and **Parisienne** if about 1 inch at their widest diameter. To make **julienne (matchsticks)** or **dice** of any dimension, start by trimming the vegetable into as squared a shape as possible. Cut the shape into slices, then stack the slices a few at a time and cut into sticks. To make dice, cut the sticks into cubes. Use whatever scraps are left over in stocks, unless they are starchy ones; those can be cooked in soups.

RETAINING NUTRIENTS, FLAVOR, AND COLOR DURING VEGETABLE COOKING

Probably the greatest loss of vitamins, especially of vitamin C (from one-quarter to one-half) occurs when mash-

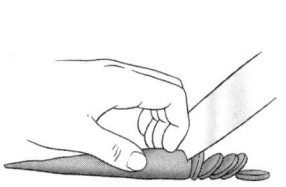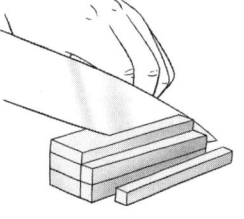

round cuts, dicing

ing and pureeing vegetables. Some vegetables may simply be scrubbed, then steamed or baked unpeeled, minimizing vitamin loss—provided the cooking is not overly prolonged.

Some enthusiasts go so far as to insist that vegetables are best if not cooked at all. No one method of vegetable cooking can claim complete superiority. Pressure-cooking, like stir-frying and steaming, is both quick and efficient, as is steaming with only the water that adheres to the vegetables after rinsing, plus a small quantity of butter or oil. Other methods are discussed at length in the following pages.

Boiling green vegetables uncovered is the surest way to retain bright color. Both steaming and stir-frying also promote good color, provided the vegetables are not kept covered after the point of palatable tenderness. Color should never be maintained by the addition of baking soda, for this not only destroys nutrient values but makes the vegetable mushy. Color may also be lost through cooking in hard acidic water, 1026. Never cook green vegetables in cast-iron pans or those lined with tin.

Since older vegetables tend to lose their natural sugars, they often profit from adding a pinch of sugar during cooking, as well as by dressing them with seasoned butters, herbs, spices, and/or sauces. Dried legumes and canned vegetables in particular profit greatly from both rinsing and bold seasoning. But vegetables in their prime are best simply tossed in butter or olive oil, allowing not more than 1 to 2 teaspoons per cup so that the full flavor of the vegetable prevails.

STEAMING VEGETABLES

Steamed vegetables are cooked over briskly simmering water in a tightly covered pot. A collapsible metal steaming basket is particularly convenient because it expands to fit the contours of your pan. When steaming only one or two servings of vegetables, fit the basket, partially expanded, into a small pot; when steaming a large quantity, fit the basket, fully expanded, into a large pot. Also available are bamboo steamers and large stockpots that come with a perforated steaming insert, to be placed over simmering water. These are useful when steaming a large quantity of vegetables or large vegetables, like artichokes. ➤ When using any of these, be sure that the water does not reach the vegetables. Throughout cooking, keep the heat sufficiently high to generate not only steam but also pressure; steam should spew from beneath the pot lid. When steaming a vegetable that requires prolonged cooking, such as artichokes or whole small potatoes, check periodically to make sure the water has not boiled away. If it has, replenish with boiling water.

BOILING VEGETABLES

Properly done, boiling is one of the easiest methods of vegetable preparation. Bring the water to a rolling boil and add a generous teaspoon of salt per quart. Drop in the vegetables and cook, uncovered, until done to taste. Start timing the moment the vegetables hit the water. For best color and texture, green vegetables should be cooked in a large quantity of boiling water, roughly 4 quarts for the first pound of vegetables and an additional 1 to 2 quarts for each additional pound. Not all green vegetables cook in 5 to 7 minutes, but that is when their color begins to deteriorate. Some very delicate vegetables such as haricots verts may be cooked just after the water returns to the boil. Drain at once in a colander. ➤ Root vegetables such as carrots, potatoes, and turnips require different treatment. Place the vegetables in a pot large enough to hold them comfortably and add enough cold water to cover by 1 inch. Bring the water to a boil over high heat, then adjust the heat to maintain the water at a gentle simmer. Cook, either covered or not, until the vegetable is tender, or as indicated in the recipe. To drain, pour the contents of the pot into a colander or, if the vegetable is very soft, transfer the pieces to a colander with a slotted spoon or skimmer.

STIR-FRYING VEGETABLES

Asian cooks are justifiably partial to this method of cooking vegetables, which preserves freshness of flavor and crisp texture.

The labor-intensive part of this method is the preparation. For best results, the vegetables must be finely sliced into uniform size or thickness. Those that tend to stringiness, like celery, are cut on the diagonal. Stem ends and midribs should be removed from coarse-leaf vegetables such as bok choy and sliced separately, also on the diagonal. The vegetables are then grouped so the longer-cooking ones go into the wok or pan first.

For 4 servings, allow about 1 pound of kale, cabbage, okra, celery, or celery cabbage; about 1½ pounds of spinach or chard; and about ¾ pound of beans. Use about 1 to 2 tablespoons of cooking oil—peanut oil or light sesame oil are great favorites—per pound of vegetables. Heat the pan well, then put in the cooking oil and heat until almost smoking. You may add a slice or two of garlic or fresh ginger to flavor the oil; cook briefly and discard before the vegetables are put into the pan. Add the vegetables and stir rapidly with a large flat spatula, coating them with oil, until they show signs of wilting slightly. Some cooks like to season at this point with a dash of soy sauce and stock before clapping on the lid to maintain succulence. Lower the heat. When the vegetables are just tender, you may stir in a small quantity of additional stock if needed, or Chinese-Style Sauce for Vegetables, 557. ➤ Cover the pan briefly until the sauce reaches the boiling point, and serve at once.

If meat and vegetables are to be cooked together, the meat is cooked first. Remove it from the pan to cook the vegetables, and then add it to the vegetables for reheating. To ensure crispness, serve immediately.

BRAISING VEGETABLES

Slow-cooking in a flavorful liquid such as stock or broth is ideal for vegetables like carrots, turnips, green beans, asparagus, rutabaga, and Brussels sprouts. The vegetables are first cooked for a short period of time in hot butter or another fat, then simmered partially covered in the cooking liquid until they are soft and the liquid is reduced to a sauce-like consistency. Onions, mushrooms, garlic, and, frequently, bacon or ham are added for an additional layer of flavor.

Braising can be done on top of the stove or in the oven. Either requires a heavy pot. This helps to retain heat and caramelize the juices of a sweet vegetable, like carrots, yielding deep and delicious flavor. Finishing the dish with lemon juice, mustard, butter, or heavy cream adds a final element of flavor.

DEEP-FRYING VEGETABLES

The French have made the fried potato famous as **French fries,** 299; the English as **chips,** 410. The Italians, by using either a beaten-egg coating or a batter, produce their famous fried food mixtures as **fritto misto,** 658. And the Japanese, who learned the technique from Portuguese sailors, prepare fried delicacies today as **tempura,** 657.

Since success depends so largely on the ➤ quality of the fat and on preventing its excess absorption, ➤ please read about Deep-Fat Frying, 1046. If the vegetables are wet, ➤ dry with paper towels before applying any coating. It is also best to let the coating dry for about 10 minutes before immersing the food in the fat, which should be heated to between 350° and 375°F. Cook until the vegetables are golden.

Vegetables suitable for this type of cooking are green beans; sliced eggplant; whole mushrooms; green or red peppers cut vertically into wide strips; rounds of cucumber, squash, zucchini, or sweet potato; sliced lotus root or bamboo shoots; onion rings or very young green onions; asparagus tips; cauliflower or broccoli florets; and artichoke hearts or peeled stems. As a general rule, the thinner the slices of vegetable, the crisper they will turn out when fried.

MICROWAVING VEGETABLES

For speed of cooking and maximum preservation of nutrients, the microwave oven is matchless. Resulting colors and flavors are vibrant and, with careful attention, textures can be too. Timing in these recipes is for food cooked on a turntable in a 750- to 1050-watt oven. In the range of times given, the shorter cooking time is for the higher wattage. A turntable is essential for even cooking. If your oven has no built-in turntable, turn the dish and stir the vegetables at regular intervals. Generally, a 2-quart baking dish is called for here. An 8 x 8 x 2-inch square glass dish is ideal, with a lid or microwave-safe plastic wrap sealed all around the dish except at one corner, where it is folded back or left slightly ajar to make a vent. For liquid, use vegetable, chicken, or beef stock or broth or lightly salted water.

No matter what the recipe timing says, as soon as you can smell the vegetables, stop the heating and taste a piece, because they are close to ready. The importance of letting the vegetable stand to finish cooking cannot be overemphasized. Microwaving works best for vegetables in quantities of about 1 pound; otherwise the cooking can be uneven. Nevertheless, it is often faster to microwave two successive batches and mix them together than it is to cook a vegetable in one batch by a slower method. No matter which way you have cooked the vegetable, you can use the microwave to melt butter or make a simple sauce right in the serving dish; see Creamy Microwave Cheese Sauce, 551.

PRESSURE-COOKING VEGETABLES

The pressure cooker offers another fast way of steaming vegetables. It is a boon for dense vegetables like roots and winter squashes, but not for green vegetables, which are almost invariably overcooked. We do not recommend pressure-cooking any vegetable that requires less than 5 minutes of conventional cooking. The quantity of food in the pot does not affect timing; so the pressure cooker offers an advantage when there is a quantity of potatoes, for example, to prepare. Follow the manufacturer's booklet regarding timing. Also note within this chapter which vegetables *cannot* be pressure-cooked. After cooking vegetables, cool the cooker at once by placing it under cold running water, or as directed by the manufacturer.

GRILLING VEGETABLES

Here are three simple ways to cook vegetables with a grill or over an open fire. For the first, use frozen or washed and sliced vegetables. Place them on a square of heavy-duty aluminum foil and season with salt, pepper, and perhaps herbs and spices. You can add olive oil or butter as well. Wrap completely, 1051. Place the foil-wrapped vegetables in a grill, under or on the hot coals, for 10 to 15 minutes. If placed on the grate of the grill, allow additional time to cook. This is a form of steaming the vegetables and it works well with any vegetable that steams well—potatoes, carrots, or green beans, for example. Carrots and other hard vegetables may take twice as long as they would on the stovetop when cooked by this method.

For the second method, cut vegetables into thick slices, large pieces, or leave whole. Brush the cut surfaces with oil or vinaigrette to protect from drying and promote browning. Place directly on a greased grill rack above a hot fire. Tomatoes, eggplant, summer squash, mushrooms, bell peppers, and fennel are all excellent grilled by this method. Cook until the vegetables are soft and slightly charred. The time will vary depending on the vegetable and how it is cut.

The third way is skewered, or en brochette. Cut the vegetables into similar-sized chunks or leave smaller vegetables whole (grape or cherry tomatoes and small button mushrooms, for example). Brush the vegetables with oil and slide onto skewers. Place on a greased grill rack above the coals and cook until tender.

To cook vegetables in embers on the hearth, see 1059.

ROASTING VEGETABLES

The oven offers intense heat for cooking chunks or slices of vegetables, taking advantage of the vegetables' natural sugars and creating flavor through browning or caramelizing these sugars. Chunks or slices of vegetable are tossed with oil or melted butter, and placed in a single layer on a baking sheet. Season and cook the vegetables in a hot oven, at least 425°F, until the vegetables are lightly browned. Stir once or twice during roasting. Serve warm, or at room temperature, or use in recipes as directed.

ABOUT VEGETABLES FOR A ROAST

To cook vegetables for a roast, it is better to prepare them separately. If they are placed in the roasting pan, the moisture they release tends to make the oven steamier than is desirable for roasting meat. Root vegetables, such as potatoes, carrots, onions, and turnips, profit by separate cooking. Steam them, 242, until partially tender. Finish cooking them in butter in a ➤ heavy covered pan over low heat until tender, then uncover the pan, raise the heat, and allow to brown. Pile the vegetables around the roast on a platter, or serve separately, glazed with the pan sauce or gravy.

ABOUT BUTTERED AND SAUCED VEGETABLES

Practically any vegetable may be served with butter or a sauce. Buttered and sauced vegetables are generally cooked by steaming or boiling. ➤ Drain them well. The amount to allow for finishing depends largely on the richness of the sauce. Use only 1 to 2 teaspoons of butter or vinaigrette per cup of cooked vegetables, but up to 1/4 cup of a milk-based cream sauce. If the vegetable is heated in the sauce, allow about 2 to 3 tablespoons for each cup of vegetables, using a bit less if it is a rich dressing made with cream or sour cream—more, perhaps, if based on cream soup. Consider, too, if the vegetable is to be presented in individual deep dishes, in which case it can be very saucy, or from a serving bowl onto flat dinner plates, in which case it should be dry enough not to run into other foods on the plate.

If you are cooking the vegetable in a sauce, allow enough sauce to just cover the vegetables. Such casseroles are often finished off Au Gratin, 961.

You may add to vegetable butters and sauces, if not already so indicated in the recipe, citrus juices and pinches of grated zest, 971; fresh or dried herbs; curry powder, dry or prepared mustard, or chili powder; horseradish; or grated cheese—and don't forget onions. Brown Butter, 557, and Brown Butter Crumb Sauce, 557, are simple and classic.

Chutneys, relishes, salsas, and dipping sauces (see Sauces, 542) are also delicious with vegetables, particularly those that are roasted or deep-fried. Such condiments are generally served on the side in separate small bowls or dishes, rather than directly on the vegetables.

ABOUT STUFFED VEGETABLES

Tomatoes, peppers, squashes, cucumbers, onions, cabbage leaves, and mushrooms all make decorative and delicious vegetable cases. Fill them with other prepared vegetables, contrasting in color or flavor, or enhance milder ones with a highly seasoned meat, seafood, or cheese stuffing or with a creamed mixture. Raw foods that need long cooking should not be used in vegetable stuffings.

Some vegetable cases are blanched prior to stuffing; see recipes under individual vegetables for when this is necessary. After draining, place the filled cases on a rack in a baking pan containing about 1/4 inch of water, or as directed in the recipe.

Heat the cases through in a 400°F oven, unless otherwise indicated, before serving. If you want to serve them Au Gratin I or II, 961, you may find they have better color if you run them first under a broiler and then bake as above. With Au Gratin III, the cheese will probably brown the tops sufficiently in the baking alone without the use of a broiler.

ABOUT MASHED AND PUREED VEGETABLES

Potatoes, the vegetable most commonly mashed or pureed, are handled in a special way, described on 294–295. ➤ Other vegetables may be coarsely mashed or finely pureed, as you prefer, in a food mill or ricer, 294. For a lumpier texture, mash with a potato masher or with a fork, large spoon, or slotted spoon. For a fine puree, whirl the vegetables in a food processor or, in small batches, in a blender. If the vegetables prove too thick, thin the mixture with milk, cream, or melted butter, which are generally called for in pureed mixtures anyway.

ABOUT COOKING FROZEN VEGETABLES

Please read About Thawing and Cooking Frozen Vegetables, 922. Frozen vegetables are a boon to the busy household; there is virtually no preparation time involved. When cooked properly, frozen vegetables rival their fresh counterparts, especially out of season. The secret to preparing frozen vegetables is to cook them until just tender, retaining as many of the vitamins, bright colors, and fresh flavors as possible. Cook frozen vegetables, except spinach and corn on the cob, without thawing. Leafy vegetables such as spinach cook more evenly if thawed just enough to separate the leaves before cooking. Corn on the cob should be partially thawed before cooking, so that the cobs will be heated through by the time the corn is cooked.

Frozen vegetables are usually cooked on the stovetop, in a microwave oven or pressure cooker, or in an electric skillet. For the stovetop, use a pan that is large enough for the vegetables to lie flat. In general, it's best to use as little water as possible. With the exception of corn on the cob and lima beans, use $\frac{1}{2}$ cup of water for every 2 cups of vegetables. Use 1 cup of water for every 2 cups of lima beans. Corn on the cob should be cooked with enough water to cover completely.

If using a microwave, follow the package instructions and, as with fresh vegetables, cook a pound or less at a time. For an electric skillet, place the hard-frozen vegetable—except for spinach and corn on the cob, which must be partially thawed, as noted above—in the skillet and then cover. Cook at 350°F until steam escapes. Reduce the temperature to 300°F and cook until the vegetables are tender.

To pressure-cook frozen vegetables, allow half as long as for the regular pressure-cooking times given for fresh vegetables, but use the same amount of water.

ABOUT REHEATED AND CANNED VEGETABLES
Leftover and canned cooked vegetables can still be delicious and make versatile supporting players in a meal. Reheat the vegetables in a steamer basket or in a pan with a few teaspoons of water or stock, if needed. Sautéing and browning in a little butter or olive oil is also an excellent treatment. Try serving leftover vegetables in a salad, tossed with a vinaigrette. Making leftover vegetables into soufflés, 203–206, omelets, 200–201, or frittatas, 202, both glamorizes and stretches them.

▲ COOKING VEGETABLES AT HIGH ALTITUDES
In baking or roasting vegetables at high altitudes, use approximately the same temperatures and timing given for sea-level cooking. When cooking vegetables at high altitudes by any process involving moisture, both more liquid and a longer cooking time are needed, as liquids boil at lower temperatures. Frequently the cooking time can be lessened if the vegetables are thinly sliced or cut into small pieces. To avoid tough stems and overcooked leaves with leafy vegetables, remove the midribs and use in the stockpot.

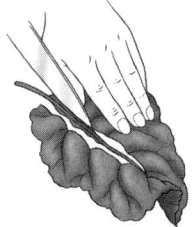

Deribbing or cutting stems from greens

Use these adjustments as an approximate timing guide: For each 1,000 feet of elevation, add to the cooking time given in the recipes about 10 percent for whole beets, carrots, and onions and about 7 percent for green beans,

squash, green cabbage, turnips, and parsnips. In cooking frozen vegetables at high altitudes, whole carrots and beans may require as much as 5 to 12 minutes additional cooking, while other frozen vegetables may need only 1 to 2 more minutes.

When pressure-cooking vegetables at high altitudes, you will have to increase the liquid in the cooker by $\frac{1}{4}$ to $\frac{1}{2}$ cup for every 2 cups of vegetables, depending on their respective cooking times. As with other vegetable cooking at high altitude, sliced or shredded vegetables, as well as peas, corn, and spinach, may cook almost as rapidly as at sea level at 15 pounds pressure. But you may find that with some of the leafy greens, 10 pounds of pressure and a slightly longer cooking period give a better result. This is also true of asparagus, celery, turnips, and cauliflower. Don't be surprised if whole potatoes, beets, yams, and beans need considerably more time than at sea level.

As always, we recommend you consult the manufacturer's instructions. Your county extension office will test the gauge on your pressure cooker and may have a pressure chart for your area.

GLAZED ROOT VEGETABLES
A simple technique, with attractive results. Vegetables prepared with this method are suitable for garnishing and require no further saucing.
Combine in a heavy saucepan:

> **2 cups vegetables: peeled onions, carrots, turnips, parsnips, rutabaga, salsify, potatoes, or sweet potatoes cut into $\frac{1}{2}$-inch pieces**
> **1 cup Light Veal or Poultry Stock, 117, or chicken broth**
> **2 tablespoons butter**
> **2 teaspoons sugar**
> **$\frac{1}{2}$ teaspoon salt**

Bring to a simmer, then cover, reduce the heat, and simmer until the vegetables are nearly done and the liquid has been almost absorbed. Uncover and continue to cook, shaking the pan constantly over medium-high heat, until the vegetables are coated with a golden glaze.

ROOT VEGETABLE PUREE
4 to 6 servings
The potatoes lend this puree a light texture and delicate flavor.
Place in a large saucepan:

> **8 ounces all-purpose or baking potatoes, peeled and thickly sliced**

Add water to cover generously, bring to a boil, and cook for 5 minutes. Add:

> **1 pound carrots or parsnips, peeled and cut into thick slices, or 1$\frac{1}{2}$ pounds celery root, salsify, turnips, or rutabaga, peeled and diced**

Continue to cook until the potatoes and other vegetables are completely tender, about 25 minutes. Drain and return the vegetables to the pan. Over low heat, mash the vegetables with a potato masher or beat with a hand-held mixer until smooth. Or, for the smoothest texture, puree in a blender or food processor. Mix in:

> 1/2 cup milk or heavy cream
> 1 1/2 tablespoons butter, softened
> 1/2 teaspoon salt
> 1/4 teaspoon white pepper

Taste and adjust the seasonings, and heat through. If desired, top with:

> Nut Butter, 178, or Brown Butter, 557

ROOT VEGETABLE BRAISE

4 servings

Serve this robust, savory stew in soup plates with Garlic Bread, 641, or surround it with mashed potatoes. In addition to the vegetables listed, you can also use fennel, salsify, artichoke hearts, and Jerusalem artichokes.

Heat in a large skillet or Dutch oven over medium heat:

> 1 1/2 tablespoons olive oil
> 1 tablespoon butter
> 1 bay leaf
> 1 large sprig thyme

Add:

> 2 onions, diced

Cook, stirring occasionally, until the onions begin to brown, about 12 minutes. Add and cook, stirring, for 3 minutes:

> 4 large mushrooms, thickly sliced
> 2 garlic cloves, minced

Pour in:

> 1/2 cup dry white wine

Increase the heat and boil, scraping the bottom of the pan, until the liquid is reduced to a syrup, about 5 minutes. Add:

> 8 ounces turnips, peeled and cut into 1-inch cubes
> 8 ounces rutabaga, peeled and cut into 1-inch cubes
> 1 pound celery root, peeled and cut into 1-inch cubes
> 1 tablespoon all-purpose flour
> 1/2 teaspoon salt

Stir the vegetables, then pour in:

> 2 1/2 cups chicken stock or broth

Bring to a boil, then reduce the heat and simmer, covered, until the vegetables are tender, 20 to 25 minutes. Remove the bay leaf. Mix together and pour into the stew:

> 3 tablespoons heavy cream
> 1 tablespoon Dijon mustard

Stir well, and season with:

> Black pepper to taste
> Thyme leaves or chopped parsley

VEGETABLES À LA GRECQUE

These mixed vegetables, left whole if small or cut into attractive shapes, 241, become aromatic as the result of simmering in a court bouillon of highly seasoned oil and water. They are served at room temperature so that the oil will not solidify. They make convenient hors d'oeuvres, ad-

ditions to salads or an antipasto tray, or garnishes, as they keep well if covered and refrigerated.

Prepare:

> 1 to 2 pounds mixed vegetables

Suitable choices include artichoke hearts; julienned carrots; cauliflower florets; celery or fennel pieces; trimmed green beans; leeks halved lengthwise; whole mushrooms; pearl onions; strips of bell peppers; and whole olives. Cucumber and eggplant slices or strips are delicious, but these should have excess moisture removed; see 273.

Squeeze over the cut vegetables to prevent browning:

> Juice of 2 lemons

Reserve 2 of the lemon shells. Prepare one of the following marinades:

I. Place in a medium stainless steel or enameled saucepan:

> 4 cups water
> 1/3 to 1/2 cup olive oil
> (3 shallots, peeled)
> 2 garlic cloves, peeled
> 1 teaspoon salt

Add the following herbs and spices, tied in a cheesecloth bag:

> 6 sprigs parsley
> 2 teaspoons fresh thyme leaves or 1/2 teaspoon dried thyme
> 12 whole black peppercorns
> (3 coriander seeds or 1/4 teaspoon dried oregano)
> (1/8 teaspoon fennel or celery seeds)

Add 2 of the reserved lemon halves for flavor. Bring to a boil, then remove from the heat, cover, and let stand to infuse for about 15 minutes. Remove the spice bag and garlic. Bring the court bouillon again slowly to a simmer. Add the vegetables, and cook until tender. Drain, reserving the marinade, and place vegetables in a bowl. Let the marinade cool, and cover the vegetables with the marinade to store in the refrigerator. Bring to room temperature to serve. After the vegetables have been eaten, use the marinade for sauces.

II. Combine in a medium stainless steel or enameled saucepan:

> 2 cups olive oil
> 1 cup dry white wine
> 1/2 to 3/4 cup water
> 1/2 cup cider vinegar
> 2 lemons, sliced
> 2 garlic cloves, peeled
> 3 sprigs parsley
> 6 whole black peppercorns
> 1/4 teaspoon salt

Prepare the court bouillon and cook the vegetables, as in I.

MOROCCAN-STYLE VEGETABLE STEW

6 servings

This meatless entrée (vegetarian if made with vegetable broth) boasts both summer and winter squash—zucchini and butternut. Serve over a bed of couscous.

Heat in a large Dutch oven over medium heat:

2 tablespoons butter or olive oil

Add and cook, stirring, until softened, 2 to 3 minutes:

2 medium onions, chopped

Stir in:

1¹/₂ cups chicken or vegetable stock or broth

Simmer, stirring often, over medium-low heat until the onions are very tender, about 20 minutes. Meanwhile, mix in a large bowl:

1 teaspoon ground cumin
³/₄ teaspoon chili powder
¹/₂ teaspoon ground cardamon
¹/₂ teaspoon ground cinnamon
¹/₂ teaspoon grated or ground nutmeg
Pinch of ground cloves

Stir in:

1 small butternut squash (1¹/₂ pounds), peeled, halved, seeded, and cut into ¹/₂-inch cubes
1 large baking potato, peeled, halved, and cut into ³/₄-inch slices

Add the squash mixture to the onions, along with:

3 medium carrots, cut into ¹/₄-inch slices
¹/₄ cup raisins
5 garlic cloves, minced

Bring to a simmer, then reduce the heat to medium-low. Cover first with a sheet of aluminum foil placed directly on the surface of the vegetables, then with the lid. Simmer gently until the vegetables are completely tender, about 25 minutes.

Stir in:

2 medium zucchini, halved lengthwise and cut into ¹/₃-inch slices
One 15-ounce can chickpeas, rinsed and drained
¹/₃ cup halved and pitted black oil-cured olives
1 teaspoon salt
¹/₄ teaspoon black pepper

Simmer, covered, until the zucchini is tender, about 10 minutes. Stir in:

¹/₄ cup chopped parsley or cilantro
3 tablespoons fresh lemon juice
Several drops of hot pepper sauce

ABOUT ARTICHOKES

Artichokes, one of springtime's earliest vegetables, are the immature flower buds of a thistle plant; they are sometimes called globe artichokes. The edible parts are the base of the leaves and the saucer-shaped piece above the stem—generally called the "heart." Trimmed hearts can be prepared at home and are also available frozen and canned. Select tightly closed artichokes that feel heavy for their size. Store in a plastic bag in the refrigerator vegetable crisper. Before cooking, wash each artichoke, holding the stem end and plunging rapidly and repeatedly in a bowl of water.

For the true artichoke lover, baby artichokes are a dream come true. With the outer leaves removed and the stem trimmed, they can be steamed, sautéed, or breaded and fried and eaten whole. Baby artichokes may be hard to find, but are available through Internet retailers.

The mature vegetable, after cooking, is most frequently served one to each diner and eaten with the fingers. The leaves are removed singly and dipped into melted butter or a sauce, the lower end of the leaf being simply drawn through the teeth to extract the tender edible portion, and the leaf then discarded. Continue this procedure until a light-colored cone of young leaves appears. Pull this up with one movement. Then, with a spoon, knife, or grapefruit spoon, cut out cleanly the fuzzy center and discard it. Eat the remaining heart with a fork, dipping each piece first into the butter or sauce. Artichoke hearts, with bottoms neatly trimmed, make delicious salad material, as well as bases for stuffing.

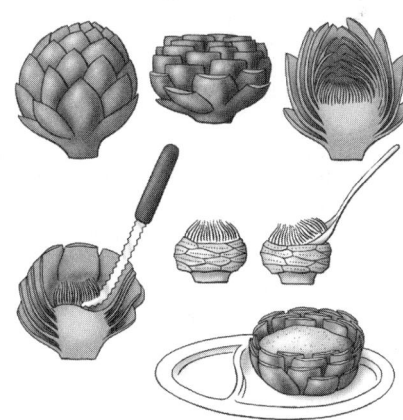

Trimming an uncooked artichoke and removing the choke

Artichokes contain the acid cynarin, which causes wines and foods served with them to taste sweet. When serving a special wine, it is best to keep artichokes off the menu, although we did enjoy a Pinot Noir with artichokes and grilled meat. Artichokes go well with the sharp flavors of lemons, oranges, vinegars, black olives, and capers, ham and garden peas, garlic, shallots, parsley, sage, tarragon, fennel, basil, and oregano.

To microwave, place 2 medium artichokes in a 2-quart baking dish. Add 2 tablespoons water, cover, and cook on high until tender enough to pierce all the way through the bottom with a fork, 5 to 8 minutes. Let stand, covered, for 5 minutes.

Large artichokes can be pressure-cooked with 1 cup water at 15 pounds pressure for 10 minutes, small ones 8 minutes.

UNCORED ARTICHOKES

To prepare, wash:

Artichokes

Cut off the stems with a knife. If desired, slice off the top one-quarter of each artichoke. Snip off the thorny tops of the remaining leaves. Snap off the tough bottom row of leaves by bending them backward. To avoid discoloration, rub the cut surfaces with:

Fresh lemon juice

Place upside down in a steamer basket over 1 to 2 inches of boiling water, first adding to the water, if desired:

(1 onion, sliced, or 1 garlic clove, smashed)
(2 celery ribs with leaves)
(1$\frac{1}{2}$ tablespoons fresh lemon juice, dry white wine, or distilled white vinegar)
(2 tablespoons vegetable oil)
(A bay leaf)

Steam, 242, covered, until the bottoms feel tender when pierced with a paring knife, about 45 minutes. Drain and serve hot or chilled with:

Melted butter, Mayonnaise, 579, Hollandaise Sauce, 560, White Sauce I, 550, or Sauce Vinaigrette, 550

ARTICHOKE HEARTS

I. Wash:

5 medium artichokes

Leave the stems attached. Snap off all the outer leaves until you reach the pale inner cone of leaves, and cut it off. Lay each artichoke on its side and cut lengthwise into quarters through the stem. Using a sharp spoon, scrape off the fuzzy choke. Peel the dark green skin off the stem quarters. Steam, 242, or simmer in water to cover until tender, about 20 minutes. Serve hot with:

Brown Butter, 557, or Hollandaise Sauce, 560

II. Cooked frozen or canned artichoke hearts, well drained, may be sautéed until hot in:

Butter or olive oil

to which you may add:

(Minced garlic, shallots, or onions)

Season with:

Salt and paprika
Fresh lemon juice

Serve hot or cold.

STUFFED ARTICHOKES

Clean and trim as described above:

Artichokes

Part the center leaves and pull out the prickly pinkish leaves in the center. Using the tip of a spoon or a grapefruit spoon, scrape out the fuzzy choke; be careful not to cut into the bottom. Steam as above, but upright on the steamer rack. Drain well, and serve warm (if the artichokes are too hot when filled, the hollandaise may separate), the centers filled with:

Hollandaise Sauce, 560

Or fill the centers with:

$\frac{1}{2}$ cup cooked cocktail shrimp or small chunks of lobster

heated in:

Newburg Sauce, 561

You may also serve these artichokes cold and stuffed with Chicken Salad, 163, or Lobster Salad, 165. Incidentally, the very tender leaves, usually discarded in the preparation, make delectable flavorings for an omelet or a casserole if trimmed and cooked.

FRIED ARTICHOKES

4 servings

Prepare as for Artichoke Hearts, above:

4 medium artichokes

As you work, drop them into a bowl of water and:

Fresh lemon juice

Heat in a large skillet over medium-high heat until hot:

1 cup olive oil

Meanwhile, drain the artichokes and pat them dry. Mix in a shallow bowl:

$\frac{1}{2}$ cup all-purpose flour
Salt and black pepper to taste

Lightly beat together in a second shallow bowl:

2 large eggs

Toss the artichokes in the seasoned flour to coat them, then dip them into the eggs, turning to coat. When the oil is hot, fry several at a time, turning often, until golden and tender, 5 to 6 minutes. Drain briefly on paper towels, then pile them on a platter and season with:

Salt

Serve with:

Lemon wedges

BRAISED BABY ARTICHOKES AND PEAS

4 to 6 servings

Rinse and thoroughly dry:

24 walnut-sized baby artichokes

Pull off all tough outer leaves and trim the stems flush with the bottoms. Heat in a medium deep skillet over medium-high heat:

2 tablespoons olive oil

Add and cook, stirring, until it browns around the edges, 7 to 10 minutes:

1 small onion, chopped

Add the artichokes and cook, shaking the pan to toss them, until they are browned all over, about 10 minutes. Stir in:

2 large garlic cloves, minced
2 tablespoons butter
2 tablespoons chicken stock or broth or water

Bring to a simmer, cover, reduce the heat, and cook gently until the artichokes are nearly tender, 15 to 20 minutes, stirring occasionally. Add more liquid if needed. Add:

2 cups fresh green peas or frozen peas, thawed

Cook until the peas are tender, about 10 minutes. Season with:

Salt and black pepper to taste

Stir in:

2 tablespoons shredded basil leaves
2 teaspoons fresh lemon juice

JERUSALEM ARTICHOKES (SUNCHOKES)

Vegetable nomenclature abounds in double or doubtful terms—endive, chicory, pepper, yam, and "wild rice," for example—but "Jerusalem artichoke" should get some sort of prize in the misnomer sweepstakes. It is not even a thistle, like the true artichoke, but the tuber of a sunflower; and "Jerusalem" is a corruption of the Italian *girasole*, or "turn-to-the-sun," as sunflowers, like heliotropes, are obliged to do.

Select the smoothest tubers (some varieties are scarcely knobby), with tight-fitting skins of uniform color, firm, and free of discoloration or mold. Store in an open plastic bag in the refrigerator crisper. They can be eaten raw or prepared as for Saratoga Chips, 94, or as below.

When cut, the flesh of Jerusalem artichokes discolors quickly. Toss pieces with an acidic dressing immediately if you plan to serve them in salad, or keep in acidulated water (4 cups cold water mixed with 1 tablespoon vinegar) for up to 30 minutes before cooking. Be careful not to overcook; if cooked beyond tender, they will again become tough.

With their neutral flavor, Jerusalem artichokes, like potatoes, are compatible with most flavors. They are especially good with lemon, butter, cream, garlic, and tarragon and can also be glazed like carrots, 266. Or cut into halves and pressure-cook 10 minutes at 15 pounds.

6 servings

Wash and peel:

1 1/2 pounds Jerusalem artichokes

Steam, 242, or drop them into a saucepan of boiling water. To prevent discoloration, add:

1 teaspoon mild vinegar or dry white wine

Cook, covered, until just tender. Test with a fork after 15 minutes. Drain.

Meanwhile, melt:

2 to 3 tablespoons butter

Add:

2 tablespoons chopped parsley
2 drops hot pepper sauce

Pour over the artichokes and serve. Or cream them, 244.

ABOUT ASPARAGUS

The Romans used to say, if they wanted something in a hurry, "Do it in less time than it takes to cook asparagus." The peak season for asparagus is spring and early summer, but today it shows up in markets throughout the year. Choose taut, firm stalks without a trace of wrinkling. To maintain freshness, stand bundles with their cut ends in shallow water, or wrap in moist paper towels and put in a plastic bag in the refrigerator. Pencil-thin asparagus are simply thin stalks of common green asparagus—a thin stalk is not indicative of tenderness or age. White asparagus is a thick variant grown by heavy fertilization and deep mulching.

Before cooking asparagus, rinse thoroughly and snap off the stem ends where they become tough. You can simply bend the stalk until it snaps between the tough and tender sections. White asparagus must be peeled before cooking. Some also prefer to peel green asparagus, but it's not necessary. Starting just below the tip, strip off the skin with a vegetable peeler.

Asparagus has affinities for parsley, tarragon, soy sauce, sesame, garlic, ginger, lemon, cream, hard-cooked eggs, Parmesan, and, of course, butter.

To microwave, place 1 pound trimmed spears in a 2-quart baking dish. Add 2 tablespoons stock or lightly salted water, cover, and cook on high until crisp-tender, 4 to 9 minutes, rearranging the stalks every 3 minutes. Let stand, covered, for 2 minutes.

We do not recommend pressure-cooking.

ASPARAGUS

4 to 6 servings

I. Wash:

2 pounds asparagus

Snap off the lower part of the stalks where they break easily. Tie the asparagus in serving bunches with kitchen string.

Bring 1 cup water to a boil in an asparagus steamer or in the bottom part of a double boiler. Stand the asparagus in the water and cook the asparagus, tightly covered, until tender, about 5 minutes. The inverted double boiler top may be used as a lid. Drain well, reserving the liquid for White Sauce, if using, and place on a platter. Cover to keep warm. Add:

1/2 teaspoon salt

Melt in a medium skillet:

1/3 cup (5 1/3 tablespoons) butter or Brown Butter, 557

Add and cook, stirring, until coated, for 1 minute:

1 cup dry bread crumbs

Pour over the tips of the asparagus. Or serve them with:

**1 cup White Sauce I, 550, made with half cream and
    half asparagus liquid, or Hollandaise Sauce, 560**

II. For real speed, slice diagonally 1/4 inch thick:

Asparagus

Stir-fry, 242, and garnish with:

Buttered bread crumbs, 960

III. If asparagus must be held, both the color and the texture are improved if this recipe is used—although we do not guarantee the nutritive value.

Arrange in no more than 3 or 4 layers in a large skillet:

2 pounds asparagus

Season with:

1/2 teaspoon salt

Cover with cold water, then with parchment paper. Bring to a boil, then reduce the heat at once and simmer until tender, 5 to 10 minutes. Turn off heat and keep lukewarm in pan for up to 15 minutes until ready to serve, then drain well.

ROASTED ASPARAGUS

3 to 4 servings

Preheat the oven to 500°F.

Snap off the stem ends from:

1 pound asparagus, rinsed

Arrange the spears in a single layer in a shallow baking sheet. Drizzle very lightly with:

Extra-virgin olive oil

Toss the spears to coat lightly. Roast until just tender, 6 to 8 minutes. Sprinkle with:

Extra-virgin olive oil

(2 tablespoons minced parsley, tarragon, and/or chives)

Salt and black pepper to taste

Serve hot or at room temperature, garnished with:

Lemon wedges

STIR-FRIED ASPARAGUS

4 to 6 servings

Please read Stir-Frying Vegetables, 242.

Snap off the stem ends and cut into 2-inch pieces:

2 pounds asparagus, rinsed

Heat a wok or skillet over high heat, then add:

2 tablespoons peanut or vegetable oil

Stir the oil in the pan, then add the asparagus, along with:

1 tablespoon slivered peeled fresh ginger

Stir-fry for 2 to 3 minutes, then add:

2 garlic cloves, slivered

$1/8$ teaspoon salt

Stir-fry for 1 minute, then add:

$1/4$ cup chicken stock or broth

Cover, reduce the heat slightly, and cook until the asparagus is tender, about 5 minutes. If desired, serve sprinkled with:

($1\frac{1}{2}$ tablespoons white or black sesame seeds, toasted, 1011)

($1/4$ teaspoon toasted sesame oil)

ASPARAGUS WITH ORANGE AND HAZELNUTS

3 to 4 servings

Steam, 242, or boil, 242:

1 pound asparagus, rinsed and bottoms snapped off

Combine in a large skillet:

2 tablespoons butter

$1/4$ cup hazelnuts, toasted, 1001, and chopped

$1\frac{1}{2}$ tablespoons grated orange zest

Juice of $1/2$ orange

Cook over medium heat until the butter is melted and slightly browned. Add the cooked asparagus and toss several times to heat through. Season to taste with:

Salt and black pepper

Serve warm.

ABOUT BAMBOO SHOOTS

In Asian dishes, these slightly acidic shoots complement mushrooms and meat. Canned shoots, readily available in the Asian section of the grocery store, are most commonly used. Simply rinse and slice them before cooking. If you are fortunate and find fresh shoots, they must be young and tender. They are usually available only in winter and are hard to find even then. Unpeeled fresh shoots will keep for a week in the refrigerator. *To use,* peel away the outer leaves, cut off and discard the base, and cook the edible inner core, whole or sliced, in boiling water for 10 to 15 minutes. If the shoots taste bitter, boil in fresh water for 5 more minutes.

ABOUT FRESH BEANS

Beans are a large and diverse family of vegetables, as adaptable in the soil as they are in the kitchen, and an important part of the human diet for thousands of years. Fresh beans are of two broad types: those with edible pods and fresh shell beans, of which only the beans inside are eaten. In the former group are common **green beans,** or **snap beans.** These were once called string beans, because their strings had to be removed, but today they have been hybridized so that most varieties are stringless and need only have the stem ends snipped off. **Haricots verts** are a slimmer and more tender version of green beans. Other edible-pod beans are the slightly tart yellow **wax beans,** the richly flavored broad **Romano beans,** and the delightful Asian **yard-long beans.** Fresh shell beans include **cranberry beans, English runner beans, lima beans, flageolet,** and **fava** or **European broad beans.** Shell these beans raw, 252. Or, if the beans inside are under pea size, slice the whole pods into 2 or 3 pieces and prepare as for snap beans. Cook edible **soybeans** in their pods, as described on 252. To avoid toughening fresh beans, add salt to their liquid only once half cooked.

Edible-pod beans are available year-round. Choose plump, firm beans with a bright color and store in a partially closed bag in the vegetable crisper. Edible-pod beans have a great affinity with butter, bacon, and chopped toasted nuts, especially almonds and hazelnuts. Especially good herbs for beans are dill, mint, chives, parsley, and basil.

To microwave edible-pod beans, cut 1 pound tender beans into $1\frac{1}{2}$-inch pieces. Place in a 2-quart baking dish. Add $1/4$ cup lightly salted water, cover, and cook on high until tender but still crisp, 9 to 13 minutes, stirring twice. Let stand, covered, for 2 minutes. *To microwave shell beans,* see About Fresh Shell Beans, 252.

Pressure-cook green beans 3 minutes at 15 pounds pressure.

GREEN BEANS

4 to 5 servings

This vegetable lends itself to endless variations. One of our very favorite ways of serving cooked green beans is to make them into a salad; see 170.

Wash:

1 pound green beans

Snip off the stem ends. You may then sliver them, cut them on the diagonal, or leave them whole.

Steam, 242, or drop them into a saucepan of boiling water. Cook, uncovered, until barely tender, no longer—6 to 10 minutes. Drain, place on a serving plate, and season with:

Salt and black pepper to taste

Drizzle with:

(1 tablespoon butter, melted)

Or use one of the garnishes or sauces suggested below.

ADDITIONS TO GREEN BEANS

To garnish or sauce, use for 1 pound of beans:

1 tablespoon butter or Brown Butter, 557, $^{1}/_{4}$ cup buttered bread crumbs, or 2 tablespoons crumbled crisp cooked bacon and drippings

adding:

$^{1}/_{2}$ teaspoon celery or dill seed, 1 teaspoon minced summer savory or basil, or 2 teaspoons chopped chives

Or garnish with:

Anchovy Butter, 558, or Almond (Amandine) Garnish, 957

Or add:

$^{1}/_{2}$ cup Sautéed Mushrooms, 283

$^{1}/_{3}$ to $^{1}/_{2}$ cup sour cream

2 tablespoons chopped parsley

Or add:

2 tablespoons wine vinegar

$^{1}/_{4}$ teaspoon Dijon mustard

1 tablespoon Worcestershire sauce

A drop of hot pepper sauce

Or add:

2 tablespoons butter

$^{1}/_{4}$ cup slivered almonds, toasted, 1001

($^{1}/_{4}$ cup sliced canned water chestnuts)

If the beans are not to be served at once, reheat in:

A White Sauce, 550, canned cream of chicken or mushroom soup seasoned with herbs, or Quick Tomato Sauce, 562

GREEN BEAN CASSEROLE

6 servings

I. Preheat the oven to 350°F. Wash and trim the stem ends from:

1 pound green beans

Place in a greased 8 x 8 x 2-inch baking dish. In a medium bowl, mix:

One 10$^{3}/_{4}$-ounce can condensed cream of tomato soup

3 tablespoons prepared horseradish

1 teaspoon Worcestershire sauce

$^{1}/_{4}$ teaspoon salt

$^{1}/_{4}$ teaspoon paprika

Pour over beans and bake, covered, about 1 hour.

Top with:

Au Gratin III, 961

Heat in broiler until the cheese is melted.

II. Preheat the oven to 350°F.

Wash and trim the stem ends from:

1 pound green beans

Place in a buttered baking dish. Mix in bowl:

$^{3}/_{4}$ cup milk

One 10$^{3}/_{4}$-ounce can condensed cream of mushroom soup

$^{2}/_{3}$ cup canned French-fried onion rings

Salt and black pepper to taste

Pour over beans and bake, uncovered, about 30 minutes. Sprinkle with:

$^{1}/_{2}$ cup canned French-fried onion rings

Bake until browned, 5 to 10 minutes.

GREEN BEANS, POTATOES, AND SMOKED MEAT

8 servings

Place in a medium pot:

One 4- to 8-ounce piece of smoked meat— ham, Canadian bacon, or smoked sausage— or a ham bone

Add water to cover, bring to a simmer, and simmer 30 minutes.

Bring to a boil and add:

1 pound green beans, trimmed

4 medium boiling potatoes, peeled and halved

(1 onion, chopped)

Simmer, covered, until the beans are very tender, 10 to 15 minutes. Drain, and season with:

Salt and black pepper to taste

Chop the pork, if desired, and toss with the beans. Serve garnished with:

Lemon wedges

GREEN BEANS WITH ONIONS, TOMATOES, AND DILL

4 servings

Heat in a large skillet or a Dutch oven over medium heat:

2 tablespoons olive oil

Add and cook until the onions have wilted, about 4 minutes:

1 medium onion, finely chopped, or 1 bunch scallions, white part only, finely chopped

1 large garlic clove, thinly sliced

$^{1}/_{4}$ teaspoon dill seeds

Add:

1 pound green beans, trimmed

2 large tomatoes, peeled and finely chopped, or one 14-ounce can diced tomatoes, with their juice

$^{1}/_{4}$ cup water, vegetable stock or broth, or tomato juice

1 tablespoon chopped dill

1 tablespoon chopped parsley

Simmer, covered, until the beans are very tender, about 25 minutes. Season with:

   1/4 teaspoon salt, or to taste

Serve hot or at room temperature.

STIR-FRIED YARD-LONG BEANS

4 servings

Yard-long beans are available in Asian markets and some specialty-produce markets. They are related to black-eyed peas and share their earthy flavor. Stir-fry to keep their firm, crunchy texture. Select thin, dark green beans, as opposed to lighter-colored beans, for best flavor. This recipe also works well, with shorter cooking time, for green beans. Please read Stir-Frying Vegetables, 242.

Heat a wok or large skillet over high heat for 30 seconds. Add:

   2 tablespoons vegetable oil

Swirl the pan to coat it with the oil, and heat until the oil is fragrant. Add and stir-fry until the beans are bright green, 5 to 6 minutes:

   1 pound yard-long beans or green beans, trimmed
      and cut into 1-inch pieces
   1 tablespoon minced peeled fresh ginger
   2 teaspoons minced garlic
   1/4 teaspoon salt

Do not allow the garlic to burn. Add:

   1/4 cup chicken stock or broth or water

Lower the heat to medium, cover, and simmer until the beans are tender, 8 to 10 minutes for yard-long beans, 2 to 5 minutes for green beans.

ABOUT FRESH SOYBEANS (EDAMAME)

The edible vegetable type is available fresh and frozen. The fuzzy pods should still be green. Cook in boiling salted water until tender, approximately 3 to 5 minutes. Dust with coarse salt. These can be eaten as an informal cold snack, in the Japanese manner: scraped from the pod with your teeth, or use the shelled beans in any recipe for lima beans, below. Shelled cooked beans may also be spread in a greased pan, dotted with butter, and roasted in a 350°F oven until brown, about 40 minutes.

ABOUT FRESH SHELL BEANS

To shell beans in the pod, cut a thin strip from the inner edge of the pod to which the beans are attached. The beans will pop out easily. One pound in the pod will yield 2 servings. Be aware that ➤ both limas and favas can be toxic when eaten raw, and some people are allergic to favas. Shell beans always taste richer when seasoned with something from the onion family, and they are delicious with tomatoes, carrots, peppers, ham, sausages, mild cheeses, chile peppers, garlic, and herbs including summer savory, marjoram, sage, parsley, celery, thyme, and bay. For that famous combination called Succotash, see 272.

The following beans, whether canned, frozen, or fresh, may be substituted for one another in most recipes: Fordhooks or baby limas, Sieva types, and favas.

To microwave shell beans, place 1 pound shelled beans in a 2-quart baking dish. Add 2/3 cup water, cover, and microwave on high for 5 to 7 minutes, stirring occasionally. *Pressure-cook* shell beans with 3 times as much water as beans. For small beans, cook at 15 pounds of pressure for 30 minutes; cook larger beans at 15 pounds of pressure for 40 minutes.

LIMA BEANS

6 servings

I. Steam, 242, or place in a wide skillet and cover with water by 1 inch:

   4 cups fresh lima beans (about 4 pounds in the pod)

Bring to a boil. Add:

   1 tablespoon butter

Simmer for 15 minutes. Add:

   1 teaspoon salt

Simmer, covered, until tender, up to 20 minutes more, depending on the age of the beans. Drain and add to the steamed or boiled beans:

   1 1/2 tablespoons fresh lemon juice
   1 tablespoon butter or olive oil
   1 tablespoon chopped parsley, chives, or dill

Or dress them with:

   Sour cream, at room temperature, and white pepper

Or toss them with:

   Sautéed Onions, 287, Creamed Mushrooms, 283,
      or a sprinkling of crisp cooked bacon

II. Place in a heavy saucepan:

   4 cups fresh lima beans (about 4 pounds in the pod)
   2 tablespoons peeled, 311, seeded, and finely diced
      tomatoes
   1 small garlic clove, thinly sliced

Add water to barely cover. Cover the pan and simmer about 15 minutes. Add:

   2 tablespoons butter
   1 tablespoon chopped parsley
   1/2 teaspoon salt

Continue cooking, covered, until the beans are tender.

LIMA BEANS AND MUSHROOMS

6 servings

Have ready:

   2 cups cooked or canned lima beans, drained,
      rinsed if canned
   1/2 recipe Sautéed Mushrooms, 283

Melt in a large skillet over medium heat:

   1 tablespoon butter

Whisk in until well blended:

   1 tablespoon all-purpose flour

Slowly whisk in:

   1/2 cup chicken stock or broth
   1/2 cup half-and-half or heavy cream

Bring to a simmer, whisking constantly, and cook 1 minute. Add the beans and mushrooms and heat through. Stir in:

> **(1 tablespoon sherry)**
> **1 tablespoon chopped fresh basil or $^1/_2$ teaspoon dried basil**
> **Salt and black pepper to taste**

Transfer to a shallow baking dish and cover with:

> **($^1/_2$ cup Au Gratin I or II, 961)**

Place under a preheated broiler until the crumbs are brown.

FAVA BEANS ROMAN-STYLE

4 to 6 servings

The skin covering individual fava beans may be bitter and tough, and many prefer to remove it, though the process is admittedly painstaking. To remove the skin, plunge shelled fava beans into boiling water for 30 to 60 seconds, lift out, drop into cold water to cool, and then drain. To peel, run a thumbnail along a bean, cutting the skin, then pinch to pop the bean out of its skin.

Shell, then, unless very small, blanch and peel, as described above:

> **3 pounds fava beans (1$^1/_2$ cups)**

Or use:

> **1$^1/_2$ cups frozen fava beans, thawed**

Heat in a large skillet or Dutch oven over medium heat:

> **$^1/_4$ cup extra-virgin olive oil**

Add:

> **$^1/_2$ cup finely chopped onions**
> **(2 slices bacon, diced)**
> **1 tablespoon chopped parsley**

Cook, stirring, until the onions have softened, about 4 minutes. Add the beans, along with:

> **$^3/_4$ cup chicken stock or broth or water**
> **1 teaspoon salt**
> **Black pepper to taste**

Simmer uncovered, stirring occasionally, until the beans are tender, 10 to 20 minutes. By the time the beans are done, the liquid there should be just a little sauce to coat them. If necessary, reduce the liquid over high heat. Taste for salt and pepper before serving, and stir in:

> **2 tablespoons fresh lemon juice**

ABOUT BEAN SPROUTS

The threadlike **mung bean sprouts** common in Asian cooking add delicate crunchiness to stir-fried dishes. Asian markets and some groceries often also carry **soybean sprouts,** which are thicker and longer and have yellow heads. Unlike mung bean sprouts, which can be enjoyed raw, soybean sprouts should be cooked briefly—either stir-fried, steamed, or parboiled for 1 minute—to rid them of enzymes that inhibit digestibility. They remain crunchy despite the cooking. Various **sprouted legumes** are also available—more bean than sprout in most cases—and are excellent in salads. Sprouts contribute texture and color to rice; add them, without stirring, for the last few minutes of cooking. Be sure sprouts are fresh when you buy them, with no wilting or browning. Refrigerate in a plastic bag in the refrigerator crisper. Before using, rinse and spin dry in a salad spinner. To sprout beans, seeds, and grains, see 1011.

STIR-FRIED BEAN SPROUTS

4 servings

Please read Stir-Frying Vegetables, 242. Rinse in cold water, snapping off any dark ends:

> **1 pound bean sprouts**

Have ready:

> **3 scallions, cut into 1-inch pieces**
> **2 teaspoons distilled white or rice vinegar**
> **1$^1/_4$ teaspoons salt**
> **1 teaspoon soy sauce**

Heat a wok or medium skillet over high heat. Add and swirl until very hot but not smoking:

> **$^1/_4$ cup peanut oil**

Add the bean sprouts and stir-fry for 30 seconds. Add the scallions and stir-fry for another 30 seconds. Add the salt and soy sauce and stir-fry for 30 seconds more. Add the vinegar and stir-fry for a final minute. Serve immediately.

ABOUT DRIED LEGUMES

Dried peas and beans, being rather on the dull side, respond readily—like a good many dull people—to the right company. Mix them with tomatoes, onions, chiles, meat, and cheese for stimulating dishes. They are more unpredictable than one would think. Their cooking time depends on the locality in which they were grown and on their age—usually two unknowns for the cook—and the type of water used in cooking them; see Water, 1026. Rinse, then pick over, removing any woody bits or pebbles.

Except for lentils and split peas, dried legumes generally must be soaked before cooking. Soak overnight in 3 to 4 times as much water as beans. ➤ Remove any that float. ➤ If time does not allow for soaking, use the quick-soak method: Cover beans with cold water in a large saucepan, bring to a boil, and simmer for 2 minutes. Remove from the heat and let stand, tightly covered, 1 hour. Before cooking, drain and discard the soaking liquid.

To cook dried legumes, bring them just to a boil in water to cover generously. Reduce the heat, cover, and ➤ simmer until tender. Chickpeas are usually the toughest of the lot and may take up to 3 hours simmering. Dried limas, after soaking, and lentils, which don't require soaking, may cook in as little as 30 minutes. Remember that 1 cup of dried beans, peas, or lentils will expand to 2 to 2$^1/_2$ cups after cooking. Do not add tomatoes, citrus, vinegar, molasses, or any other acidic ingredients until near the end, after the beans are tender; acid, like salt, prevents the beans from softening. This principle is conveniently applied in reverse when you make Boston baked beans: the precooked beans do not turn mushy when baked for hours in the oven because the added molasses and tomatoes keep the skins firm.

Canned beans can be substituted in recipes that call for cooked beans, though they may be softer and less flavorful. Since brands vary in quality, it is worth comparing different ones. Rinsing canned beans may improve the taste and remove excess salt. Put the beans in a colander and run cold water over them, then drain well. ➤ For 2 cups cooked beans, you will need a 19- to 20-ounce can. Fifteen- or 16-ounce cans hold 1½ to 1¾ cups of beans.

There are dozens of varieties of dried beans and peas available in stores. They include **broad, black** or **turtle, cranberry, scarlet runner, red, kidney, black-eyed peas** (also known as **cowpeas** or **field peas**), **soybeans, pinto, chickpeas** or **garbanzos, flageolets, borlotti, lentils, Great Northern, navy, cannellini,** and **adzuki** beans, from which Japanese bean paste is made. Each variety has, for the connoisseur, its own slightly different but satisfying charm.

Times for pressure cooking vary according to the size of the bean. Check manufacturer's instructions. ▲ At high altitudes, dried beans take more time to rehydrate and cook. The difference begins to be noticeable above 3,500 feet; the cooking time may be as much as doubled.

BOILED BEANS

5 servings
Soak, above:

    **1 pound dried kidney, navy, or other red, black, or
       white beans, rinsed and picked over**
Drain and place in a heavy saucepan. Cover with water. Add:

    6 tablespoons (¾ stick) butter
    ⅓ cup chopped onion
    3 whole cloves
    2 teaspoons salt
    ¼ teaspoon black pepper
    ¼ teaspoon dried thyme
Bring to a simmer, reduce the heat slightly and simmer, covered, until nearly tender, 1 to 1½ hours. Stir from time to time. Add and cook, uncovered, about 20 minutes longer:

    1 cup dry red wine or chicken stock
When the beans are tender, serve hot, with or without their cooking liquid, garnished with:

    Chopped chives or parsley

REFRIED BEANS (FRIJOLES REFRITOS)

6 servings
A classic side dish with enchiladas, burritos, or chiles rellenos. The beans are easier to mash if they are warm.
Heat in a large skillet over medium-high heat:

    2 tablespoons vegetable oil, bacon drippings, or lard
Add:

    1 medium onion, chopped
Cook, stirring often, until deep golden brown, about 10 minutes. Add:

    4 garlic cloves, minced
Cook, stirring, for 1 minute. Add 1 cup at a time, mashing each addition to a coarse puree with a potato masher or the back of a large spoon before adding the next:

    **4 cups cooked black beans or pinto beans
       (about 1⅓ cups dried; 253), undrained if canned**
Stir in:

    1 cup reserved bean cooking liquid or water
Cook, stirring often, over medium to low heat until the beans are a little soupier than you would like to serve them—they will thicken as they sit. The whole mashing and cooking process should take 10 to 15 minutes. Season with:

    Salt to taste
Serve warm, with:

    **Crumbled queso fresco or feta or grated Parmesan
    Tortilla chips**

VEGETARIAN CHILI

8 servings
Heat in a large saucepan over medium heat:

    2 tablespoons olive oil
Add:

    1 cup chopped carrots
    1 cup chopped red bell peppers
    1 cup chopped green bell peppers
    1 cup chopped onions
    2 garlic cloves, minced
Cook, stirring, until the onions are golden, 12 to 15 minutes. Add:

    **1 to 2 fresh green chile peppers such as jalapeños,
       seeded and finely chopped, or 1 chipotle pepper
       in adobo sauce, minced**
    **1 tablespoon chili powder or ground ancho chile
       powder**
    1 tablespoon ground cumin
Cook, stirring, for 2 minutes. Stir in:

    **One 28-ounce can tomatoes, coarsely chopped,
       with their juice**
    **One 16-ounce can kidney beans, rinsed and
       drained, or 1½ cups cooked beans
       (about ½ cup dried; 253)**
    **One 16-ounce can cannellini or Great Northern beans,
       rinsed and drained, or 1½ cups cooked beans
       (about ½ cup dried; 253)**
    **One 16-ounce can black beans, rinsed and drained, or
       1½ cups cooked beans (about ½ cup dried; 253)**
    1 cup tomato juice, or as needed
    Salt to taste
Bring to a boil. Reduce the heat to medium-low and simmer, uncovered, stirring occasionally and adding more tomato juice or water as needed, until the flavors are blended, about 45 minutes. Taste and adjust the seasonings. Ladle into bowls and serve with:

    Sour cream
    Salsa Fresca, 571
    Chopped cilantro

CARIBBEAN RED BEAN STEW WITH PORK

4 to 6 servings

This is a tasty way to stretch a small amount of meat.

Soak, 253:

> 1¹/₂ cups dried red kidney, pinto, or small red beans, rinsed and picked over

Drain. Combine in a large saucepan with:

> 8 cups water
> 1 small onion
> 1 leafy celery top
> 1 bay leaf
> 1 garlic clove, peeled
> 1 cinnamon stick

Bring to a boil, then reduce the heat and simmer, covered, until the beans are tender, 1 to 1¹/₂ hours. Drain, reserving 4 cups of the cooking liquid. Discard the vegetables, bay leaf, and seasonings. Heat in a large saucepan over medium heat:

> 1 tablespoon olive oil

Add, in batches if necessary, and brown on all sides:

> 1 pound boneless pork loin or chops, cut into
>   1-inch cubes

Add:

> 2 cups cubed peeled sweet potato
> 1 large onion, diced
> 1 green bell pepper, cored, seeded, and diced
> 1 tablespoon coarsely chopped garlic
> 1 teaspoon salt

Cook, stirring, until the onions are golden, 12 to 15 minutes. Stir in:

> 2 teaspoons hot paprika or 1 teaspoon ground
>   red pepper

Add the cooked beans and the reserved cooking liquid and bring to a boil. Reduce the heat and simmer, uncovered, until the pork is tender and the stew is thick, about 1 hour.

BAKED BEANS

6 servings

Baked beans are as traditional in Sweden as they are in Boston. Please read About Dried Legumes, 253.

Soak, 253:

> 1¹/₂ cups dried white beans or navy beans, rinsed and
>   picked over

Drain, then cover with water in a large saucepan. Bring to a boil, then simmer slowly, covered, until tender, 45 minutes to 1 hour.

Preheat the oven to 250°F.

Drain the beans, reserving the cooking water. Combine the beans in a greased casserole with:

> ¹/₂ cup boiling water or beer
> ¹/₄ cup chopped onion
> 3 tablespoons molasses
> 3 tablespoons catsup
> 1 tablespoon dry mustard
> (1 tablespoon Worcestershire sauce)

> (1 teaspoon curry powder)
> 1 teaspoon salt
> (¹/₂ teaspoon vinegar)

Top with:

> 4 ounces sliced salt pork

Bake, covered, 4 to 4¹/₂ hours; uncover for the last hour of cooking. If they become dry, add a little:

> Chicken stock or broth or reserved bean water

BAKED BEANS WITH BACON

Preheat the oven to 350°F.

Place in a greased 9 x 9-inch baking dish:

> 3 cups canned beans (one 28-ounce can)

approximately:

> ¹/₄ cup catsup or chili sauce
> ¹/₄ cup minced onion
> 2 tablespoons molasses
> 2 tablespoons brown sugar
> (1 tablespoon cider vinegar)
> (3 drops hot pepper sauce or 1 tablespoon prepared
>   mustard)
> (2 tablespoons bacon drippings)

Stir lightly to combine. Cover the top with:

> 6 slices bacon

Bake, covered, about 30 minutes. Uncover and bake about 30 minutes more.

TUSCAN BEANS

6 to 8 servings

Tuscans love beans so much that the rest of Italy calls them *mangia fagioli*, "the bean eaters."

Soak, 253:

> 1 pound (about 2 cups) dried cannellini, pinto, or
>   cranberry beans, rinsed and picked over

Drain. Combine in a large pot with:

> 12 fresh sage leaves or 1 teaspoon dried sage
> 3 garlic cloves, halved
> 1 tablespoon extra-virgin olive oil

Add water to cover by 3 inches. Bring to a boil, then reduce the heat, partially cover, and simmer gently until tender, about 45 minutes. Drain the beans and season to taste with:

> Salt and black pepper

Serve hot, warm, or at room temperature, drizzling over each portion:

> About 1 teaspoon extra-virgin olive oil
>   (2 to 3 tablespoons total)

MASHED FAVA BEANS

4 servings

Spread this puree on crostini, or use as a dip for pita chips, 93, or raw vegetables. Lima or white beans can be substituted; they will need to be cooked a bit longer.

Soak, 253:

> 1¹/₄ cups dried fava beans, rinsed and picked over

Drain. Use your fingertips or a small paring knife to peel

off the tough outer skins. Combine the beans in a large saucepan with water to cover by 2 inches. Stir in:

1 garlic clove, halved

1 bay leaf

¹/₂ teaspoon fresh oregano leaves or ¹/₄ teaspoon dried oregano

¹/₂ teaspoon fresh thyme leaves or ¹/₄ teaspoon dried thyme

¹/₄ teaspoon crushed red pepper flakes

Bring to a boil, then reduce the heat to a simmer and cook, partially covered, until the beans are very tender, 30 to 45 minutes. Drain and let cool slightly. Discard the bay leaf, and combine the beans in a bowl with:

1 cup chopped celery

¹/₄ cup coarsely chopped parsley

3 tablespoons extra-virgin olive oil

1 tablespoon fresh lemon juice

1 garlic clove, finely minced

¹/₂ teaspoon salt

¹/₈ teaspoon black pepper

Stir and mash with a fork until blended and the beans are coarsely mashed.

RED BEANS AND RICE

6 to 8 servings

A Southern classic, much loved, though humble, and even celebrated in song.

Soak, 253:

1 pound (about 2 cups) dried red kidney, pinto, or small red beans, rinsed and picked over

Combine in a large pot:

8 cups water

2 smoked ham hocks (1 to 2 pounds)

1 cup finely chopped celery

1 cup finely chopped onions

1 cup finely chopped green bell peppers

2 teaspoons finely chopped garlic

2 bay leaves

1 teaspoon dried thyme

1 teaspoon dried oregano

1 teaspoon white or black pepper

¹/₂ teaspoon ground red pepper

Bring to a boil, then reduce the heat and simmer, covered, stirring occasionally, until the ham hocks are tender, 1 to 1¹/₂ hours. Remove the ham hocks and let cool.

Drain the beans, add them to the pot, and return to a boil. Reduce the heat and simmer, covered, until the beans are tender, 30 minutes to 1 hour. Add water as needed to keep the beans covered.

Remove the meat from the ham hocks and add it to the pot, along with:

1 pound smoked andouille or smoked kielbasa sausage, cut diagonally into ¹/₂-inch slices

Warm through. Remove the bay leaves. Serve over:

Cooked rice

BRAZILIAN BLACK BEANS

6 servings

The texture of this spicy dish falls in between a soup and a stew. Cook it down if you prefer it thicker.

Soak, 253:

1 pound (about 2 cups) dried black beans, rinsed and picked over

Drain and transfer to a soup pot. Add:

4 cups water

Bring to a boil, then reduce the heat and simmer, partially covered, stirring occasionally, for 1¹/₂ hours.

Meanwhile, if you'd like, pierce in several places with a fork:

(8 ounces fresh hot sausage)

Cook in a medium skillet over medium heat until firm and no longer pink. Let cool, then slice into ¹/₄-inch rounds. Heat in a medium skillet (use the same skillet if you cooked the sausage) over medium heat:

¹/₄ cup olive oil

Add:

1 onion, chopped

1 green bell pepper, cored, seeded, and chopped

4 garlic cloves, minced

Cook, stirring, until the vegetables are tender but not browned, 7 to 10 minutes. Add:

1 teaspoon ground cumin

³/₄ teaspoon crushed red pepper flakes

³/₄ teaspoon ground cardamom

Stir and cook for 1 minute, then remove from the heat. After the beans have cooked for 1¹/₂ hours, add the cooked vegetables. Cook, uncovered, until the beans are very tender, about 30 minutes more. Add:

³/₄ cup orange juice

¹/₄ cup dry sherry

1 to 2 teaspoons salt, or to taste

Return the sausage, if using, back to the pan and cook for 15 minutes more (or longer to thicken, if desired). Serve with:

Sour cream

BLACK-EYED PEAS AND GREENS

4 servings

This dish is inspired by two Southern specialties—collards cooked with salt pork and black-eyed peas cooked with a ham hock.

Soak, 253:

1¹/₂ cups dried black-eyed peas, rinsed and picked over

Drain the peas and combine in a large pot with:

6 cups water

1 smoked ham hock (about 12 ounces)

1 small onion

1 small carrot, peeled

1 leafy celery rib

1 bay leaf

1 garlic clove, peeled

Bring to a boil, then reduce the heat and simmer, covered, until the peas are tender, about 45 minutes.

Drain, reserving about 1 cup of the cooking liquid. Discard the bay leaf, onion, garlic, and celery. Return the peas to the pot, along with the reserved cooking liquid. Shred the meat from the ham hock and add it. Cut the carrot into small chunks and add it. Stir in:

> 1 head escarole or bunch collard greens or chard, coarsely chopped

Bring to a boil, then reduce the heat and simmer, covered, until the greens are tender, 10 to 15 minutes. Stir in:

> 1 tablespoon red wine vinegar
> $1/2$ teaspoon salt, or to taste
> $1/4$ teaspoon black pepper

Serve warm or at room temperature.

CURRIED CHICKPEAS WITH VEGETABLES

4 servings

This quick skillet dish makes a perfect meatless entrée. Heat in a large skillet over low heat until sizzling:

> $1/4$ cup vegetable oil
> 2 teaspoons cumin seeds

Add:

> 1 tablespoon minced peeled fresh ginger
> 1 tablespoon minced garlic

Cook, stirring, for 1 minute; do not brown. Stir in:

> 2 teaspoons curry powder

Cook for 1 minute. Stir in:

> $1^3/4$ cups cooked chickpeas (about $2/3$ cup dried, 253), or canned chickpeas, rinsed and drained
> 2 cups cubed peeled sweet potatoes
> 2 cups cauliflower florets
> 1 cup green beans, cut into 1-inch pieces
> 1 cup chicken or vegetable stock or broth
> $1/2$ to 1 teaspoon salt
> Black pepper to taste

Cover and cook over medium heat until the vegetables are tender, about 10 minutes.

Stir together in a small bowl:

> 1 cup plain yogurt
> 2 tablespoons all-purpose flour

Add to the vegetables, along with:

> 1 tablespoon finely chopped seeded jalapeño pepper

Cook, stirring, over low heat until thickened and heated through; do not boil. Serve the vegetables garnished with:

> $1/4$ cup chopped roasted unsalted cashews or peanuts
> 2 tablespoons shredded unsweetened dried coconut, toasted, 972

OVEN-ROASTED CHICKPEAS

4 servings

Coated with olive oil and garlic and roasted until golden brown, these chickpeas are great as a snack, tossed into a salad, or sprinkled over rice pilaf.

Preheat the oven to 350°F.

Toss to coat and combine:

> 2 cups cooked chickpeas (about $2/3$ cup dried, 253), or canned chickpeas, rinsed and drained
> $1/4$ cup olive oil, preferably extra-virgin
> 2 garlic cloves, finely minced

Spread in a 13 x 9-inch baking pan. Bake, stirring often, until the chickpeas are golden, 30 to 40 minutes.

Sprinkle with:

> $1/2$ teaspoon salt

Serve warm.

ABOUT LENTILS

Lentils have a slightly stronger flavor than other legumes. The olive-drab lentils sold everywhere are sometimes called green, other times brown, and are actually shades of both; they cook to a somewhat soft texture and mild taste. French green lentils (Le Puy are the finest example) are about half the size of the more common lentils, are a much darker green, and have a deeper flavor. Lentils adapt well to a variety of seasonings. Add a pinch of dried thyme and/or oregano, a chopped carrot, a leafy green celery top, or even a slice of fresh ginger as they cook. Plainly cooked lentils make a perfect side dish, or you can use them in salads and side dishes, combined with cooked vegetables and/or rice, if desired. The yield from 1 pound ($2^1/2$ cups) dried lentils is about $7^1/2$ cups cooked. These recipes can be halved. Brown lentils become very soft when cooked. The smaller plump green lentils hold their shape. *Pressure-cook* 1 cup lentils with $2^1/2$ cups of water at 10 pounds of pressure for 20 minutes.

I. *8 servings*

If you omit the meat flavorings, serve the lentils with Roast Pork, 498, and Applesauce, 216.

Combine in a large saucepan:

> 2 cups brown or green lentils, rinsed and picked over
> 3 sprigs parsley or a celery rib with leaves
> $1/4$ cup sliced onion
> $1/2$ bay leaf
> (A piece of corned beef, smoked sausage, salt pork, or ham hock)
> (1 whole clove)
> (1 garlic clove, peeled)

Cover with:

> 4 cups water

Bring to a boil, then reduce the heat and simmer, covered, until the lentils are tender, 20 to 40 minutes. Stir occasionally and add boiling water if necessary.

Drain and serve with:

> Quick Tomato Sauce, 562

Or serve as a puree, 244.

II. *4 servings*

To serve as a salad, toss with a vinaigrette, 572, and garnish with hard-cooked egg slices. Serve hot or at room temperature.

Rinse and pick over:

> **1 cup brown or green lentils**

Heat in a saucepan or skillet over medium heat:

> **$1/4$ cup olive oil**

and cook, stirring, until golden brown:

> **1 onion, minced**

Add the lentils and stir to coat with oil. Add:

> **$3^{1}/_{2}$ cups boiling water**

Cover the pan and simmer until the lentils are tender, 20 to 40 minutes. Season to taste with:

> **Salt and black pepper**

Serve hot or at room temperature.

III. *6 to 8 servings*

Combine in a large saucepan:

> **1 pound (about $2^{1}/_{2}$ cups) brown or green lentils, rinsed and picked over**
> **8 cups water**
> **$1/2$ small onion**
> **1 garlic clove, peeled**
> **1 bay leaf**

Bring to a boil, then reduce the heat and simmer, uncovered, until the lentils are tender, 20 to 30 minutes. Drain and let cool. Remove the onion, garlic, and bay leaf. Season with:

> **Salt and black pepper to taste**

Serve as a side dish or use in another recipe.

INDIAN LENTIL PUREE (DAL)

4 to 6 servings

Dal is the Hindi word for both an array of legumes used in Indian cooking and this preparation of legumes. If the dal is pureed, it is "wet" and eaten with rice; if not pureed, it is "dry" and eaten with bread. A pureed dal may be thick or thin, as the cook chooses.

Rinse, pick over, and place in a large saucepan:

> **1 cup yellow split peas or red lentils**

Add:

> **2 cups water**
> **1 small onion, sliced**
> **$3/4$ teaspoon minced garlic**
> **1 teaspoon minced peeled fresh ginger**
> **$1/2$ teaspoon turmeric**

Bring to a boil, then reduce the heat and simmer, covered, until the legumes are tender, 20 to 25 minutes. Stir in:

> **1 cup water**
> **$3/4$ teaspoon salt**

Simmer, partially covered, until the dal is thickened to the consistency of split pea soup, about 20 minutes. Stir in:

> **2 serrano or jalapeño peppers, seeded and finely chopped**
> **1 plum tomato, diced**
> **2 tablespoons chopped cilantro**

Serve with:

> **Cooked rice**

BRAISED LENTILS WITH SAUSAGE

6 servings

This is a New Year's dish from northern Italy. It is made with *cotechino,* a juicy, lightly spiced fresh pork sausage, and lentils braised in a tomato sauce. The recipe can be made 1 day ahead.

Bring 3 quarts water to a gentle simmer in a pot large enough to hold the sausage. Pierce in several places with a fork:

> **$1^{1}/_{2}$ to 2 pounds cotechino sausage or fresh andouille sausage**

Add to the pot, adjust the heat so the water stays just below a simmer, and cook, covered, until an instant-read thermometer inserted in the center of the sausage registers 160°F, about 45 minutes. Turn off the heat and keep warm in the water. Meanwhile, bring 10 cups water to a boil in a large saucepan. Add:

> **1 pound (about $2^{1}/_{2}$ cups) brown or green lentils, rinsed and picked over**

Reduce the heat and simmer, partially covered, until barely tender, about 20 minutes. While the lentils cook, heat in a large skillet over medium heat:

> **3 tablespoons extra-virgin olive oil**

Add:

> **1 medium red onion, minced**
> **1 medium carrot, minced**
> **1 small celery rib with leaves, minced**
> **1 large bay leaf**

Cook, stirring, until golden brown, about 10 minutes. Stir in:

> **1 large garlic clove, minced**
> **2 teaspoons chopped fresh marjoram, or $1/2$ teaspoon dried oregano**

Cook for 30 seconds. Stir in:

> **One 14- to 16-ounce can whole tomatoes, drained and crushed**
> **1 cup chicken stock or broth**

Cook over medium-high heat until very thick, 10 to 15 minutes.

Drain the lentils, stir into the tomato mixture, and cook about 10 minutes. Remove the bay leaf. Season with:

> **Salt and black pepper to taste**

Mound the lentils on a serving platter. Cut the hot sausage into $1/4$-inch slices and arrange the slices over the lentils.

BEETS

Once, to paraphrase Gertrude Stein, "a beet was a beet was a beet," a crimson finger- and apron-stainer, earthy and sweet. Now markets also carry varieties that are gold, orange, white, or candy-striped (chioggia). They can be perfectly round or long and slender, no bigger than the tip of your thumb or as big as your fist. When selecting beets, choose a bunch with small leaves that are not yellowing or tattered. The greens are an indication of freshness of the beet; if they look moist and fresh, the beet will be too. If beets are sold without leaves, avoid any that look dry, cracked, or shriveled. Cut off the leaves, leaving 1 to 2 inches of stem on the beets, and store the beets and leaves separately in open plastic bags in the refrigerator crisper. The greens will keep only a day or two, but the roots will keep at least 1 week.

They are delicious hot or cold, sliced or whole if small, as a side dish or in a salad. Scrub beets just before cooking but do not remove the skin; leave the rootlets, or tails, in place. Beets go well with lemon and orange, vinegar, cream, onions, walnuts, parsley, caraway seeds, dill, tarragon, and mustard.

To microwave, place 5 medium unpeeled beets in a 2-quart baking dish. Add $1/4$ cup lightly salted water, cover, and cook on high until tender when pierced with a thin skewer, 12 to 18 minutes, stirring every 5 minutes. Let stand, still covered, for 3 minutes.

Pressure-cook whole unpeeled $2^1/2$-inch beets with $1^1/2$ cups liquid at 15 pounds pressure for 15 minutes, small beets with 1 cup liquid for 12 minutes. Cool the cooker at once.

STEAMED OR BOILED BEETS
4 servings
Trim:

1 pound beets

leaving 2 inches of stem. If the tops are young, reserve; see Beet Greens, 278. Wash the beets. Steam them, 242, or place in a saucepan, cover with boiling water, and cook gently, covered, until tender. Allow 30 to 40 minutes for young beets, 1 hour or more for old beets; add boiling water if needed.

When the beets are done, cool them slightly and slip off the skins. If small, serve whole. If larger, slice. Season with:

Salt and black pepper to taste

Then either pour over them:

Melted butter

and sprinkle with:

Chopped parsley

or serve the beets in:

White Sauce II, 550, made with half orange juice and
half water instead of milk

adding:

3 tablespoons brown sugar
2 teaspoons grated orange zest

SWEET-AND-SOUR (HARVARD) BEETS
6 servings
For a cold version of sweet-and-sour beets, see Pickled Beet Salad, 166.
Slice or dice:

1 pound, 12 ounces cooked, above, or canned beets
(about 3 cups)

Stir in the top of a double boiler until smooth:

$1/2$ cup sugar
$1/2$ cup cider vinegar or dry white wine
1 tablespoon cornstarch
$1/2$ teaspoon salt
2 whole cloves

Cook over simmering water, stirring, until clear. Add the beets and let them stand over the hot water, off the heat, for about 30 minutes. Just before serving, reheat the beets just until heated through, and add:

2 tablespoons butter
(1 tablespoon orange marmalade)

or:

($1/2$ teaspoon cider vinegar)

BEETS IN SOUR CREAM
6 servings
Combine in the top of a double boiler:

3 cups sliced cooked, above, or canned beets
$1/2$ cup sour cream
1 tablespoon prepared horseradish, or to taste
1 tablespoon fresh lemon juice or white vinegar
1 tablespoon chopped chives
Salt to taste
(1 teaspoon grated onion)

Heat these ingredients over hot water, being careful not to overheat and curdle the sour cream. Serve immediately.

BAKED OR ROASTED BEETS
4 servings
Convenient when the stovetop is crowded. Serve hot or at room temperature.
Preheat the oven to 350°F.
Place in an 8-inch square baking pan:

1 pound beets, stems trimmed to 1 inch

Add $1/2$ cup water. Cover the pan tightly with aluminum foil and bake until the beets are easily pierced with a thin skewer or knife tip, about 45 minutes for small beets, 1 hour for medium, and $1^1/4$ hours for large beets.
Slip off the skins, and leave the beets whole or slice into rounds or wedges. Season with:

Salt and black pepper or paprika to taste

Toss with:

2 tablespoons melted butter or olive or walnut oil
1 tablespoon minced parsley, chives, or dill
Fresh lemon or lime juice to taste

BREADFRUIT
If ever you are stranded on a desert island, remember that, like Robinson Crusoe, you can eat raw any breadfruit that has a seed. ➤ All seedless varieties must be cooked. Breadfruit is 6 to 8 inches in diameter and greenish brown or yellow when ripe. The slightly fibrous meat is light yel-

low and sweet. You may remove the center core with its seed, if it has one, before or after cooking. Season and serve as you would sweet potato.

6 servings

I. To boil, choose mature firm fruit, with its rind still green in color.

Drop:

4 cups diced peeled and cored breadfruit

into a saucepan of boiling water, reduce the heat, and simmer, covered, until tender, about 1 hour. Drain, season with salt and black pepper, and serve.

II. To bake, preheat the oven to 375°F.

Place in a baking pan:

1 unpeeled breadfruit

Add enough water to the pan to prevent burning. Bake until tender, about 1 hour. Pull out the stem and core and discard. Cut the fruit in half. Season with:

Salt and black pepper or sugar and butter

III. To steam, peel and core:

1 breadfruit

Cut into halves or quarters, and steam, 242, 2 hours. Drain.

Season to taste with:

Butter

Salt and black pepper

You may also steam ³/₄-inch-thick breadfruit slices, roll them in flour, and fry in deep fat, 243, until golden brown.

BROCCOLI

Choose heads that are dark green with a purple or blue haze. Yellowish heads are overly mature and should be avoided. Store in an open plastic bag in the refrigerator crisper up to 3 days. The vegetable variously sold as purple broccoli, purple cauliflower, and broccoflower closely resembles broccoli in shape and flavor.

Snap or cut the florets off the thick center stalks. If some florets are much larger than others, cut them to match the rest. Use a paring knife to cut off the tough, fibrous skin of the stalks down to the tender flesh. Slice the stalks into pieces about ¼ to ½ inch thick. If desired, cut broccoli apart in larger bunches, leaving 1 to 2 inches of peeled or unpeeled stalk and stem.

Cooked broccoli is delicious hot or at room temperature. It has affinities with lemon, orange, butter, olive oil, nut oils, garlic, capers, olives, sweet peppers, cheeses, hard-boiled egg, dill, and marjoram.

To microwave, cut 1 pound broccoli as above and place in a baking dish. Salt lightly and add 2 tablespoons water. Cover and cook on high about 5 minutes, stirring after 3 minutes. Let stand, uncovered, for 2 minutes before serving.

Pressure-cook broccoli for about 2 minutes at 15 pounds pressure.

STEAMED BROCCOLI

4 to 6 servings

Prepare, above:

2 pounds broccoli

Steam, 242, until barely tender, 5 to 10 minutes. Season with:

¹/₂ teaspoon salt

Sprinkle with:

Buttered bread crumbs, 960, melted butter, or fresh lemon juice

(¹/₄ cup chopped salted almonds or walnuts)

Or top with:

Au Gratin II, 961

Or serve with one of the following sauces:

Vinaigrette, 572

Hollandaise Sauce, 560

Cheese Sauce, 551

Onion Sauce, 551

Midwestern Cream Dressing, 577

Egg-Thickened Velouté, 554

DEEP-FRIED BROCCOLI

4 to 6 servings

Use one batch of batter for every pound of broccoli. Please read about Deep-Fat Frying, 1046.

Prepare but undercook slightly:

Steamed Broccoli, above

Cool and pat dry. Reserve the stalks for another purpose. Dip the florets into:

Fritter Batter for Vegetables, Meat, or Fish, 658

Deep-fry the broccoli in vegetable oil or melted shortening, heated to 375 °F until golden brown. Serve with:

Curry Mayonnaise, 580, or Mustard Mayonnaise, 580

BROCCOLI STIR-FRY

4 servings

Please read about Stir-Frying Vegetables, 242.

Prepare, cooking it until crisp-tender:

Steamed Broccoli, above

Drain and set aside. Stir together in a small bowl until smooth:

2 tablespoons water

2 teaspoons cornstarch

Combine in a small bowl:

¹/₃ cup Shaoxing wine or dry sherry

3 tablespoons soy sauce

2 tablespoons light brown sugar

1 teaspoon toasted sesame oil

Place a wok or large skillet over high heat. When hot, add and swirl until very hot but not smoking:

3 tablespoons vegetable oil

Add:

4 slices peeled fresh ginger

4 large garlic cloves, crushed

Stir and press with the back of the spoon until the garlic is lightly golden, then remove and discard the ginger and garlic. Add the broccoli and stir-fry until lightly coated with oil. Pour the wine mixture down the side of the pan, and toss to blend well. Reduce the heat to medium, cover, and cook for 30 seconds. Stir the cornstarch mixture, add it to the wok, and stir to combine thoroughly. Cook, uncovered, until the sauce thickens, 1 to 2 minutes.

BROCCOLI CHEESE CASSEROLE
4 to 6 servings
Position a rack in the upper third of the oven. Preheat the oven to 425°F. Butter a shallow 2-quart baking dish. Sprinkle into the dish:
2 tablespoons dry bread crumbs
Fold together gently in a bowl:
Steamed Broccoli, 260
Mornay Sauce, 551, made with Cheddar
Spread evenly in the baking dish and cover the top with:
Au Gratin I or II, 961
Bake until bubbling around the edges and browned, about 20 minutes.

BROCCOLI RABE
A distant cousin of broccoli, broccoli rabe—also called **rapini**—has a mustardy bite and is somewhat bitter, though the bitterness is lessened if it is blanched. Strip the slightly stringy skins off the stalks with a paring knife, if desired. Select fresh-looking bright green bunches and store in an open plastic bag in the vegetable crisper up to 5 days.

GARLIC-BRAISED BROCCOLI RABE
4 servings
Bring 4 quarts water to a rolling boil in a stockpot, and add:
1¹⁄₂ tablespoons salt
Meanwhile, cut into 1-inch pieces:
1 bunch broccoli rabe (about 1 pound), stems peeled, if desired
Add to the boiling water and boil for 2 minutes, then drain and cool slightly. Squeeze the moisture out of the leaves. Heat in a large skillet over medium heat:
2 tablespoons extra-virgin olive oil
Add:
1 garlic clove, thinly sliced
(1 small dried red chile pepper)
Add the broccoli rabe and cook, stirring occasionally, until tender, about 4 minutes. Remove and discard the chile. Season with:
Salt and black pepper to taste

BRUSSELS SPROUTS
These small green gems are among the most prevalent of winter cabbage types, valued for their nutty crunch and ability to combine well with various flavorings. If you find Brussels sprouts still attached to their stalks, choose a small stalk: It will be young and its sprouts sweet. When sprouts are sold loose, select those that are heavy for their size and tightly closed, without any touch of yellow or signs of drying. Store Brussels sprouts in the refrigerator crisper either in their original package or in a closed plastic bag.

Before cooking, pull off damaged or loose outer leaves and trim the stems. Rinse and drain. To cook sprouts quickly and most evenly, slice them in half from top to bottom. If cooking whole, cut an X in the base of each sprout. Brussels sprouts can be steamed, boiled, baked, or sautéed. Brussels sprouts pair well with almonds, bacon, butter, Parmesan, chestnuts, cream, garlic, and vinegar.

To microwave, place 4 cups whole sprouts in a 2-quart baking dish. Add ¹⁄₄ cup stock or lightly salted water, cover, and cook on high until tender when pierced with a thin skewer, 6 to 8 minutes, stirring after 2 minutes. Let stand, covered, for 3 minutes.

Pressure-cook Brussels sprouts about 3 minutes at 15 pounds pressure.

4 to 6 servings
If wilted, pull the outer leaves from:
1 pound Brussels sprouts
Cut off the stems. Cut an X in the base of each. Steam, 242, 8 to 10 minutes. Or drop them into a pot of rapidly boiling water, reduce the heat, and simmer, uncovered, until barely tender, about 10 minutes. Do not overcook; drain. Drizzle with:
1 to 2 tablespoons butter, melted
2 to 3 tablespoons grated Parmesan and chopped parsley, 1 tablespoon fresh lemon juice, or a grating of nutmeg
Or sauté in the butter:
1 tablespoon grated onion or 2 tablespoons dry bread crumbs plus ¹⁄₄ teaspoon dry mustard
Or, best of all, serve with lots of:
Hollandaise Sauce, 560

BRUSSELS SPROUTS WITH CHESTNUTS
6 servings
If fresh chestnuts are not available, use vacuum-packed ones. Canned chestnuts are soft, and they add little to the finished dish.
Melt in a large skillet over medium heat:
2 tablespoons butter or bacon drippings
Add:
4 shallots, halved, or 12 small boiling onions, peeled
1 pound fresh chestnuts, peeled, 270
Roll the chestnuts around the pan, then cook, gently shaking the pan occasionally, until both the shallots and chestnuts are lightly browned, about 10 minutes. Add and bring to a boil:
1 pound Brussels sprouts, trimmed and halved
1 cup chicken or vegetable stock or broth or water
1 bay leaf
1 sprig fresh thyme or ¹⁄₄ teaspoon dried thyme
3 sprigs parsley

(3 tablespoons dry port or dry sherry)
$^1/_4$ teaspoon salt
$^1/_8$ teaspoon black pepper

Reduce the heat to medium, cover, and simmer until the Brussels sprouts are tender, about 15 minutes. Remove the bay leaf, thyme sprig, if used, and parsley sprigs before serving.

BECKER BRUSSELS SPROUTS

2 to 4 servings
This family favorite will surprise people who think they don't like Brussels sprouts. We have many delighted converts, even children.

Trim, and slice lengthwise in half:

12 Brussels sprouts

Heat in a medium skillet over medium-low heat:

**3 tablespoons butter or 1$^1/_2$ tablespoons butter plus
1$^1/_2$ tablespoons olive oil**

Add and cook, stirring, until beginning to brown:

1 to 2 garlic cloves, crushed

Remove the garlic and discard. Place the sprouts cut side down in the garlic butter, cover, and cook over low heat until tender, 15 to 20 minutes. Arrange the sprouts on a warm platter and drizzle any remaining butter on top. Serve with, if desired:

(Grated Parmesan)

BURDOCK

From Japan, burdock is a slender root that has mildly sweet white flesh. It is nice in salads, and it is always part of a mixed vegetable tempura when it is in season. Look for burdock in Asian groceries. Select firm, crisp roots with no soft spots. They will probably have dirt clinging to them. Wrap, unwashed, in moist paper towels, place in a plastic bag, and keep in the refrigerator crisper.

When ready to cook, rinse off the soil. Scrub gently with a stiff brush. Snip off any hairy roots. Burdock can be cooked any way carrots can, 266, so slice or cut accordingly. Because the flesh quickly discolors when cut, drop the pieces into cold water with a splash of cider vinegar or lemon juice. (Sometimes burdock that has been out of the ground for a while turns bitter—soaking in the acidulated water for an hour or so should eliminate this.) With its neutral flavor, burdock is a useful addition to stews. Depending on the dish, allow 2 to 4 ounces per serving.

4 servings
Prepare as for Carrots Vichy, 266:

2 cups thinly sliced burdock

Allow to cook until tender, about 45 minutes. Season with:

Salt and black pepper to taste

ABOUT CABBAGE

Cabbages have evolved into perhaps the most diverse extended family in the vegetable world, and they have been challenging cooks to keep up on every step of that long and winding road. Cabbage is good braised, steamed, fried, or sautéed. It is excellent stuffed or served raw in salads or slaw. When pickled, it is Sauerkraut, 265. The recipes below—which, you will note, are many, as befits a vegetable so available, versatile, and inexpensive—demonstrate a variety of international responses to its virtues.

The firm old standbys are the **head cabbage,** including many varieties of green or red, and the soft-leaved, crinkly **Savoy.** Head cabbage is available year-round. Choose heads weighing under 2 pounds, with firm, unblemished leaves. Stored in the refrigerator, head cabbage will keep for several weeks. Savoy cabbage can be used in any recipe for head cabbage, though it is milder in taste and texture. Select firm, crisp heads. Savoy cabbage must be stored in the refrigerator.

Bok choy, also called **pak choi,** is a mild-flavored Asian cabbage. Select brightly colored, firm bunches of bok choy. Very small bunches are labeled "baby bok choy." Store in the refrigerator.

Chinese cabbages have oblong heads with thin, juicy, full-flavored leaves. The Chinese cabbage we usually see in the supermarket is the pale green **Napa cabbage.** It is referred to as "hearted" or "barrel shaped" to distinguish it from the less common "cylindrical" **Michihli cabbage,** also known as **celery cabbage.** Select and store as for bok choy.

Allow 1 pound raw cabbage for 2 cups cooked. To avoid long boiling, which renders the outer leaves of a whole head limp and waterlogged, we recommend quartering the head and boiling gently, uncovered, 15 to 20 minutes. Better still, shred the cabbage first, and cook only 7 to 10 minutes. You may prefer to stir-fry, 242, shredded cabbage, which retains crispness. *To shred cabbage,* cut the head into eighths through the core. Shred on the cheese-shredding side of a box grater, and discard the core; or shred in a food processor fitted with a shredding disk, first cutting out the core. Don't forget that cabbage lends itself to stuffing, as do the leaves; see Stuffed Cabbage Rolls, 263, Cabbage Rolls Stuffed with Kasha and Bulgur, 348, as well as the recipes here. Do not freeze cooked cabbage; when thawed, it is usually watery and unpleasant.

Cabbage is especially good accompanying rich meats or salted and smoked meats, game, and all root vegetables. It goes well with red wine, sage, thyme, caraway, dill, fennel, horseradish, apples, onions, chestnuts, juniper berries, and sour cream.

To microwave, spread 1 pound shredded cabbage in a 2-quart baking dish. Add 2 tablespoons stock or lightly salted water, cover, and cook on high until tender but still crisp, 8 to 12 minutes, stirring after 4 minutes. Let stand, covered, for 2 minutes. One pound cabbage, cut into 2-inch-thick wedges, can be cooked the same way; cook until tender, 12 to 14 minutes, rearranging the pieces after 5 minutes. Let stand, covered, for 3 minutes.

Pressure-cook 2- to 3-inch wedges of cabbage 3 to 5 minutes at 15 pounds pressure.

CABBAGE
4 servings
Remove the outer leaves, core, and cut into 8 wedges:
   One 2-pound cabbage
Drop it into a pot of rapidly boiling water, reduce to a simmer, and cook, uncovered, until tender but still crisp, about 30 minutes. Drain. Sprinkle with:
   1 teaspoon salt
Place in a serving dish and pour over it:
   ¼ cup (½ stick) butter, melted
Sprinkle with:
   (Bread crumbs, caraway seeds, poppy seeds, minced chiles, or a few drops fresh lemon juice plus 1 tablespoon chopped parsley)
Or place the cooked cabbage in a baking dish and cover with:
   Au Gratin III, 961
Heat through in a 350°F oven.

CREAMED CABBAGE
6 servings
This method makes young cabbage very delicate and is a great help in disguising the age of a mature one.
Bring to a boil in medium saucepan:
   ¾ cup milk
Gradually add:
   3 cups very finely shredded cabbage
Boil for 2 minutes. Drain, and discard the milk.
Drop the cabbage into a saucepan of hot:
   White Sauce I, 550
Season with:
   1½ teaspoons prepared horseradish
   1 teaspoon salt
   ¼ teaspoon white or black pepper
   ¼ teaspoon grated or ground nutmeg
Simmer for 3 minutes. Sprinkle with:
   1 teaspoon caraway seeds, toasted, 1001
Serve at once, with, if desired:
   (Broiled, grilled, or panfried sausages)

CABBAGE, POTATOES, AND HAM
4 servings
Put in a large pot with water to cover generously:
   1 pound smoked ham hocks or neck bones
Bring to a simmer and simmer for about 1 hour, until the meat is nearly tender.
Bring the water to a boil and add:
   One 2-pound cabbage, trimmed, cored, and quartered
   4 medium boiling potatoes, peeled and halved
Reduce the heat and simmer, covered, until the vegetables are tender, 20 to 25 minutes.
Drain, and season with:
   Salt and black pepper to taste
Serve on a large platter, garnished with:
   Lemon wedges
   Chopped parsley

SAUTÉED CABBAGE
4 servings
Preheat the oven to 375°F. Shred, 262:
   One 2-pound cabbage, outer leaves and core removed
Cook in a large skillet over medium heat until crisp:
   4 slices bacon
Remove the bacon to paper towels to drain. Add the cabbage to the fat remaining in the pan, along with:
   ¾ cup chopped onion
   1 teaspoon salt
   ¼ teaspoon paprika
Increase the heat to medium-high and cook, stirring, until the cabbage is crisp-tender. Transfer to a greased 8 x 8 x 2-inch baking dish. Spread over the top:
   1 cup sour cream
Bake until the sour cream is set, about 20 minutes. Sprinkle with:
   ½ teaspoon caraway seeds, toasted, 1001
and the crumbled bacon.

STUFFED CABBAGE ROLLS
12 rolls
Stuffed cabbage makes a satisfying cold-weather party dish—wonderful with potato pancakes or mashed potatoes. The rolls are even better when prepared 2 to 3 days in advance, and they can be frozen for up to 1 month.
Combine in a large bowl:
   1 pound ground beef, chicken, or turkey
   1 large egg
   ½ cup seasoned dry bread crumbs
   ½ cup uncooked long-grain white rice
   ½ cup water
   1 large carrot, grated
   1 onion, finely chopped
   1 garlic clove, minced
   1 teaspoon salt
   ¼ teaspoon black pepper
Bring 4 quarts water to a rolling boil in a stockpot. Add:
   1½ tablespoons salt
Cut out the core with a small, sharp knife, then drop cored side down into the water:
   1 Savoy or green cabbage (about 2 pounds)
Boil for 5 to 10 minutes, then remove from the pot and carefully remove the softened outer leaves. Return the cabbage to the simmering water to continue to soften as you begin to fill the leaves. (Alternatively, freeze the whole cabbage for 24 hours, then thaw and separate the leaves.) Trim off enough of the center rib of each leaf to make the leaf supple enough to roll. Wrap the meat mixture in the leaves as shown, folding the sides first. Roll up the leaf loosely, as the rice will expand. Repeat with more leaves until all the filling is used. Either tie the rolls with string, or place seam side down to cook.
Chop enough of the remaining cabbage leaves to make 1 cup. Heat in large heavy pot or Dutch oven over medium-high heat:

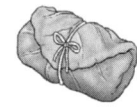

Making stuffed cabbage rolls

3 tablespoons vegetable oil

Add the chopped cabbage, along with:

1 medium onion, chopped

Cook, stirring, until golden brown. Add:

$^1\!/_2$ cup dry white wine

Bring to a boil, then reduce the heat to low and simmer 5 minutes. Add:

One 28-ounce can crushed tomatoes in puree

1 cup water

($^1\!/_2$ cup raisins)

$^1\!/_4$ to $^1\!/_2$ cup packed brown sugar

8 gingersnaps (2 inches across), crumbled

Juice of 1 large lemon

2 chunks sour salt or $^1\!/_2$ teaspoon ground sour salt

Bring to a boil. Place the cabbage rolls seam side down in the sauce; if the sauce does not cover the rolls, add a little water. Reduce the heat, cover, and simmer for 1$^1\!/_2$ hours, shaking the pan every 30 minutes to prevent sticking. Serve hot with:

Sour cream

BRAISED RED CABBAGE

4 servings

An old favorite with turkey, pork, or game.

Quarter, core, and thinly shred:

1 medium red cabbage (about 2 pounds)

Place the cabbage in a large bowl and cover with cold water. Place in a large heavy skillet or Dutch oven over low heat:

**2 slices bacon, diced, or 2 tablespoons butter or
vegetable oil**

If using bacon, cook until it has rendered most of its fat. If using butter or oil, heat until fragrant. Add and cook, stirring, until golden:

$^1\!/_4$ cup finely chopped onion

Lift the cabbage out of the water and add it to the pan, along with:

1 large green apple, peeled, cored, and thinly sliced

$^1\!/_4$ cup red wine or cider vinegar

2 tablespoons honey or sugar

$^3\!/_4$ teaspoon salt

($^1\!/_8$ to $^1\!/_4$ teaspoon caraway seeds)

Cover and cook over low heat, stirring occasionally, until the cabbage is very soft, 1 to 1$^1\!/_2$ hours, adding boiling water if the mixture becomes dry during cooking. Or, if liquid is left when the cabbage is done, uncover the pot and cook gently until it is absorbed.

STIR-FRIED BOK CHOY WITH MUSHROOMS

4 to 6 servings

Please read Stir-Frying Vegetables, 242. Place in a small bowl:

6 dried shiitake mushrooms

Pour over the mushrooms:

$^1\!/_2$ cup boiling water

Let soak for 20 minutes, stirring occasionally. Lift the mushrooms from the bowl, reserving the liquid, and cut into $^1\!/_4$-inch slices. Strain the soaking liquid and reserve 2 tablespoons. Pour the reserved soaking liquid into a small bowl and stir in:

1 tablespoon Shaoxing wine or dry sherry

2 teaspoons cornstarch

$^3\!/_4$ teaspoon white pepper

Combine in another small bowl:

1 cup chicken broth or stock

$^1\!/_2$ teaspoon salt

$^1\!/_2$ teaspoon sugar

Heat in a wok or a large skillet over high heat:

3 tablespoons peanut or vegetable oil

Add the reserved mushrooms and:

**1$^1\!/_2$ to 2 pounds bok choy, cut crosswise into
2-inch pieces**

Stir-fry until the bok choy is wilted, 3 to 4 minutes. Add the chicken stock mixture, cover, and steam until crisp-tender, 1 to 2 minutes. Stir in the reserved cornstarch mixture and bring to a boil, stirring often. Add:

2 teaspoons toasted sesame oil

Stir well and serve immediately.

STIR-FRIED NAPA CABBAGE AND CARROTS

4 servings

Combine in a small bowl and stir well to mix:

2$^1\!/_2$ tablespoons soy sauce

1 teaspoon toasted sesame oil

**($^1\!/_2$ teaspoon chili-garlic paste or $^1\!/_4$ teaspoon crushed
red pepper flakes)**

Salt and black pepper to taste

Set aside. Heat a wok or large skillet over high heat. Add and stir-fry for a few seconds, without allowing the garlic to brown:

1 tablespoon peanut or vegetable oil

2 garlic cloves, minced

1 tablespoon minced peeled fresh ginger

Add and stir-fry for 3 minutes:

2 cups shredded carrots

Add and stir-fry until tender, about 3 minutes:

**1 medium Napa cabbage (about 2 pounds), thinly
sliced (9 cups)**

Add the soy sauce mixture and heat through, stirring to coat vegetables thoroughly. Serve immediately, sprinkled with:

Minced cilantro or parsley

SAUERKRAUT
6 servings

The healthful quality of sauerkraut was recognized in 200 B.C., when, as history records, it was doled out to the laborers working on that largest and longest of public works, the Great Wall of China. To retain its full strong flavor, sauerkraut should be served uncooked or barely heated through. But for milder flavor, cook for a long time, as in this recipe. Sauerkraut is traditionally served with frankfurters, sausages, roast pork, and spareribs. For a vegetarian main dish, serve with roasted root vegetables, 244, and Applesauce, 216.

Heat in a large ovenproof skillet over medium heat:

> 2 tablespoons butter, bacon drippings,
>   or vegetable oil

Add and cook, stirring frequently, until translucent, 7 to 10 minutes:

> 1/2 cup sliced onion or shallots

Add and cook, stirring, for 5 minutes:

> 4 cups (2 pounds) fresh, 265, or store-bought
>   sauerkraut, drained

Peel, grate, and add:

> 1 medium potato or tart apple
> 1 to 2 teaspoons caraway seeds

Cover the sauerkraut with:

> Boiling vegetable stock or water
> 1/4 cup dry white wine

Cook, uncovered, for 30 minutes. Meanwhile, preheat the oven to 325°F.

Cover the skillet and bake for about 30 minutes. Season with:

> (1 to 2 tablespoons brown sugar)

CACTUS PADS

The oval green pads of the prickly pear cactus, also called **nopales,** are used fresh in salsas and salads and are also sold pickled and canned. The fresh pads can be stewed, fried, or baked. They are available year-round in Latino markets and some specialty groceries. Choose pads that are bright colored and somewhat stiff. Select those that are about 4 inches wide and under 1/4 inch thick, without spines. (If you can only get them with spines, remove them with pliers.) Store in an open plastic bag in the refrigerator crisper.

Use a vegetable peeler to trim the edges and any eyes where spines were. Cut off the thick base and discard. Rinse the pads well. Cactus pads can be oiled and slowly grilled whole (flavorful but a little chewy). Usually, however, they are cut into 1/4- to 1/2-inch squares and boiled until tender: Bring a saucepan of salted water to a boil and drop in the pieces, adding a handful of coarsely chopped scallion greens, if desired, to reduce the mucilaginous quality. Boil, uncovered, for 10 to 15 minutes, depending on the thickness. Drain and rinse several times in cold water, until they are no longer sticky.

Some markets sell packages of cactus pads that have already been diced. They are fine if they are fresh and not discolored. Cactus pads have affinities with chiles, garlic, and salty cheeses.

ROASTED CACTUS PAD SALAD
4 cups; 8 servings

Preheat the oven to 375°F. Trim:

> 7 fresh medium cactus pads

Cut into 3/4-inch squares. Place on a baking sheet and toss with:

> 1 tablespoon olive oil

Spread on a baking sheet and sprinkle with:

> Salt to taste

Roast, stirring occasionally, until the cactus is tender and all the liquid it exuded has evaporated, about 20 minutes. Let cool.

Combine the cactus in a bowl with:

> 1 1/2 cups Salsa Fresca, 571
> 1 tablespoon olive oil

Season with:

> 1/2 teaspoon salt, or to taste

Line a serving bowl with:

> Several leaves romaine lettuce

Add the salad. Sprinkle with:

> 2 tablespoons crumbled Mexican queso añejo or
>   dry feta or grated Parmesan

CARDOONS

Cardoons are a plant in the thistle family, as are artichokes. The thick, fleshy stalks look like very large, coarse, matte-gray celery. The tender stalks are eaten, rather than the fruit head. Select crisp, unbruised stalks—the smaller, the better. Wrap the base of the stalks in a moist paper towel and store in an open plastic bag in the refrigerator crisper.

Before cooking, discard the tough outer stalks, wash well, and trim off any leaves. Scrape off strings with a vegetable peeler. Cut the stalks into 2- to 3-inch pieces, stopping where the stalk becomes tough. Because cardoons tend to darken, boiling them in water with lemon juice is the preferred basic cooking method; ➤ steaming is not recommended. If the pieces are tender, you can serve them raw with a dipping sauce. Cooked cardoons are delicious sautéed in butter or oil and sprinkled with grated Parmesan, and they are delectable when coated with Fritter Batter for Vegetables, 658, and deep-fried, 243.

Cardoons have affinities with butter, cream, lemon, and hollandaise sauce.

4 servings

Bring to a boil in a large saucepan:

> 8 cups water
> Juice of 1/2 lemon
> 1 tablespoon salt

Prepare, as directed above:

> 1 pound cardoons

Boil gently, uncovered, adding more boiling water if the pieces become exposed. For crisp-tender cardoons, boil for 30 to 45 minutes; for thoroughly tender pieces, boil for up to 1 hour. Drain well.

ABOUT CARROTS

Cultivated carrots are thought to be descended from Queen Anne's Lace, and the sturdiness of that weed hints at the staunchness of this vegetable, both in the refrigerator and in the pot. The great quantity of beta-carotene in carrots sometimes actually increases during storage, and the vegetable grows sweeter when cooked to softness, making it an indispensable flavoring agent of soups and stews and a good friend of cooks who are not too attentive to timing.

Carrots are always available. ➤ Avoid carrots tinged with green, any that are cracked, those with softness or mold at the stem end, and any that are rubbery or shriveled. Before storing, cut off the green tops. Since carrots are in the parsley family, their tops can be used to season a soup in the same way as the herb. Store carrots in a closed plastic bag in the refrigerator crisper. They will keep for 2 to 3 weeks.

Peel carrots using a vegetable peeler. If small, they may be served whole. If large, they are more attractive if cut into rounds, diced, or julienned. Carrots go well with onions, celery, olives, mushrooms, brown sugar, raisins and currants, lemon and orange, thyme, dill, mint, parsley, chervil, ginger, and nutmeg.

To microwave, spread 2 cups sliced carrots in a 1-quart baking dish. Add 2 tablespoons lightly salted water, cover, and cook on high 5 to 8 minutes. Let stand, covered, for 3 minutes.

Whole large (1¼-inch diameter) carrots can be *pressure-cooked* with 1 cup liquid at 15 pounds pressure for 4 to 8 minutes. Sliced carrots take approximately 2½ minutes at 15 pounds. Cool the cooker at once.

CARROTS

4 servings
Peel and slice:
   1 pound carrots
Steam, 242, or place them in a saucepan with enough boiling water or stock to cover by 1 inch and cook, covered, until tender, 12 to 20 minutes. Cook only 5 to 10 minutes for sliced carrots. If necessary, add a small quantity of boiling water. Drain off any liquid that remains after cooking.
   Serve with:
   Butter and chopped parsley, orange marmalade, or White Sauce I, 550
Or add to 3 cups cooked carrots:
   2 tablespoons butter
   2 tablespoons sugar, brown sugar, honey, or orange marmalade

(¾ **teaspoon ground cumin, coriander, or cardamom,**
   ¼ **teaspoon each ground cinnamon and grated or ground nutmeg, or 2 teaspoons caraway seeds)**
Simmer the carrots in this mixture until well glazed.
Or use the glaze for:
   Candied Sweet Potatoes, 302

CARROT PUREE

Prepare **Root Vegetable Puree, 245,** using **1 pound carrots,** peeled and cut into thick slices.

CARROTS VICHY

4 servings
Place in a medium saucepan:
   2½ cups thinly sliced carrots (1 pound)
   ½ **cup cold water**
   2 tablespoons butter
   1 tablespoon sugar
   ¼ **teaspoon salt**
   (1 teaspoon fresh lemon juice)
Bring to a boil over high heat, then reduce the heat and simmer, covered, until tender, about 12 minutes. Uncover the pan, increase the heat, and boil off the liquid, about 5 minutes. Sprinkle with:
   Chopped parsley, tarragon, dill, or chervil

BRAISED CARROTS

4 servings
Place in a skillet or sauté pan that is wide enough to hold the carrots in a single layer:
   1 pound carrots, quartered lengthwise
   ½ **cup water or chicken or beef stock or broth**
   1½ tablespoons butter
   1 teaspoon sugar or brown sugar
   ½ **teaspoon salt**
Bring to a simmer, then reduce the heat and simmer, covered, until the carrots are tender and most of the liquid has been absorbed, 15 to 20 minutes. Uncover and cook for a few minutes more, then season with:
   1 tablespoon chopped parsley, chervil, or tarragon
   Black pepper to taste
Or top with:
   Grated Gruyère or Parmesan or Orange Butter, 559

GLAZED CARROTS

Serve as a side dish or to garnish a roast.
Prepare:
   Braised Carrots, above
Increase the sugar to 1½ tablespoons and the butter to 2 to 3 tablespoons. Add:
   1 tablespoon brandy
Cook the carrots, covered, until a syrupy glaze forms on the bottom of the pan. Uncover and roll the carrots around in the pan until they are well coated. Turn them into a serving dish and garnish with:
   Chopped mint or parsley

ROASTED CARROTS

4 servings

The carrots may be left whole, if desired.

Preheat the oven to 400°F. Toss together:

> 1¹/₂ pounds carrots, peeled and cut into large chunks
>
> Olive or vegetable oil to lightly coat
>
> ¹/₈ teaspoon dried thyme or several sprigs fresh thyme
>
> Salt and black pepper to taste

Spread the carrots in a single layer on a rimmed baking sheet. Roast until golden and tender, about 1 hour.

ABOUT CAULIFLOWER

Cauliflower has a pleasantly nutty, mild cabbage taste that matches well with other flavors, especially aromatic spices and sauces. Select heads that feel firm and whose florets are creamy white, tightly packed, and without brown discoloration. Small brown blemishes may be pared off with only cosmetic damage. Store in the original wrapper or in a plastic bag in the refrigerator crisper.

To prepare as florets, cut the florets off the central stalk, then cut any large florets into halves or quarters. If cooking a whole head, cut out the tough end of the stem, removing the leaves, and soak in cold salted water, stem up, for 10 minutes.

Milder in flavor than broccoli, cauliflower still has similar affinities; see 260. It is especially good with cheese sauce, sautéed almonds, brown butter, ham, celery, curry, and nutmeg. Cauliflower is also excellent served raw with a dipping sauce or in salads.

To microwave, spread 2 cups florets in a 1-quart baking dish, add 1 tablespoon lightly salted water, cover, and cook on high for 3 to 5 minutes, stirring after 2 minutes. Let stand, covered, for 2 minutes. Or place a whole head in a 2-quart casserole with 2 tablespoons water, cover, and cook the same way.

Pressure-cook whole cauliflower about 7 minutes at 15 pounds pressure.

STEAMED CAULIFLOWER

4 servings

Cut out the tough end of the stem of:

> 1 cauliflower

You may leave it whole or cut into florets. Steam, 242, stem down if whole, until barely tender, up to 15 minutes if whole, 6 to 10 minutes if in florets. Place in a serving dish. For Cauliflower Polonaise, toss with:

> Brown Butter Crumb Sauce, 557
>
> (Chopped nuts sautéed in butter)

Or cover with one of the following:

> Hollandaise Sauce, 560
>
> White Sauce I, 550, with crumbled bacon or chopped ham
>
> Lemon Butter, 557
>
> Mornay Sauce, 551

MASHED CAULIFLOWER

4 servings

Cut out the tough end of the stem of:

> 1 cauliflower

Cut into florets. Place in a large pot and add:

> 2 garlic cloves, peeled and chopped
>
> 1 cup chicken or vegetable stock or broth or water
>
> ¹/₂ teaspoon salt

Bring to a simmer and simmer until the cauliflower is tender, about 10 minutes. Add:

> ¹/₂ cup heavy cream, half-and-half, or whole milk
>
> 1 tablespoon butter

Mash, or puree in a food processor. Season with:

> Black pepper to taste
>
> (Minced chives)
>
> (1 tablespoon chopped parsley or tarragon)

SCALLOPED CAULIFLOWER

4 servings

Preheat the oven to 350°F. Butter a 2-quart shallow baking dish. Prepare, cutting into florets before cooking:

> Steamed Cauliflower, above

Spread in the prepared dish. Spoon over:

> 2 cups White Sauce I, 550, mixed with ¹/₄ teaspoon grated or ground nutmeg or 1 tablespoon Dijon mustard

Sprinkle over the top:

> ¹/₂ cup plain or buttered fresh bread crumbs, 960
>
> ¹/₃ cup grated Parmesan, Gruyère, or aged Cheddar

Bake until bubbly and browned on the top, about 25 minutes. Serve sprinkled with:

> Paprika or ground red pepper

CAULIFLOWER AND POTATO CURRY

4 servings

This is a popular vegetable curry combination. You can substitute peas for the spinach, if desired.

Cook for 5 minutes in a saucepan of boiling water:

> 1 cauliflower (2 to 3 pounds), cut into florets

Remove from the water with a slotted spoon and transfer to a bowl. Add to the boiling water and cook for 5 minutes:

> 2 medium boiling potatoes, peeled and cut into ¹/₂-inch cubes

Drain, rinse under cold water, and drain well again; transfer to the bowl of cauliflower. Process in a food processor until minced but not pureed:

> 1 large tart apple, peeled, cored, and sliced
>
> 3 large garlic cloves
>
> One 2-inch piece fresh ginger, peeled and sliced
>
> (2 hot chile peppers, such as jalapeño or serrano, seeded and sliced)

Heat in a Dutch oven over medium heat:

> ¹/₄ cup vegetable oil, clarified butter, 557, or Ghee, 557

Add:

2 medium onions, coarsely chopped

and the apple mixture and cook, stirring, until the onions are softened and starting to color, 5 to 7 minutes. Add:

2 tablespoons curry powder
1 tablespoon all-purpose flour

Cook, stirring, for 3 to 5 minutes to lightly brown the curry powder and flour. Add:

One 14-ounce can unsweetened coconut milk
1/2 cup water or vegetable or chicken stock or broth
1 teaspoon salt

Bring to a boil over high heat, stirring, then add the reserved cauliflower and potatoes, and:

One 16-ounce can chickpeas, rinsed and drained

Reduce the heat to medium, cover, and cook for 15 minutes. Stir in, cover, and cook until wilted, about 3 minutes:

10 to 12 ounces spinach, stemmed, washed, and
torn into pieces, or one 10-ounce package frozen
peas

Season with:

Salt and black pepper to taste

Serve the curry over:

Cooked rice

Garnish with, if desired:

(Golden raisins)
(Chopped cashews)

CELERY

Celery is available year-round. Select a compact bunch that is heavy for its size, with fresh-looking leaves. Keep in a plastic bag in the refrigerator crisper. To prepare, separate the stalks and rinse them well, giving a light scrub to the bases, where grit often gathers. Trim off the ends of the stalks and discard any thick outer stalks that are bitter or tough. When the celery is chopped or thinly sliced, the strings are imperceptible, but if the stalks are to be cooked whole or in large pieces, you may wish to strip off the strings. Should stalks be limp after storage—or should you want them to be super-crisp, for serving raw—soak them in ice water until they firm up.

Celery is excellent raw, especially the paler center stalks, called the heart. The green leafage, usually discarded, is well worth reserving: Chopped fine, it adds considerable flavor to soups, stews, or stocks.

Celery is a flavorful addition to stir-fries and goes well with every sort of cheese; cream, lemon, dill, chives, and parsley—and who can resist a rib filled with peanut butter or plain or flavored cream cheese?

To microwave, cut 1 pound celery stalks into 2- to 3-inch pieces. Place in a 2-quart baking dish. Add 2 tablespoons stock or lightly salted water, cover, and cook on high until tender but still crisp, 8 to 12 minutes, stirring after 4 minutes. Let stand, covered, for 2 minutes.

Pressure-cook celery about 1 1/2 minutes at 15 pounds pressure.

4 servings

Wash, trim, and cut in 1/2-inch pieces:

1/2 bunch celery (2 to 3 cups)

Steam, 242, or drop it gradually into:

1 cup boiling water

Cook, covered, until tender, about 6 minutes, allowing it to absorb the water. Should there be any liquid, drain the celery and reserve the liquid for the sauce. Brown the celery in:

Seasoned butter

Or drop the celery into:

1 cup White Sauce I, 550, made with cream and
celery liquid

Season the sauce with:

Curry powder, or celery, or dill seeds, or freshly grated
nutmeg, or herbs

ABOUT CELERY ROOT (CELERIAC)

This type of celery is grown for its knobby root, prized for its succulent, subtly sweet flavor when cooked. It can be tough and woody if too old; peak season is autumn and winter. It can be difficult to peel, so cut into quarters and use a sharp peeler or paring knife first. Select small to medium knobs that feel heaviest for their size. Any stalks on top should be crisp and fresh. Leave on stalks and store in a plastic bag in the refrigerator crisper.

Celery root is delicious raw when cut very fine and tossed with a flavorful dressing. Let sit several hours to tenderize and "mellow" the vegetable. It can also be cooked like or with potato to use in potato salad. Celery root's affinities are the same as those of celery, above, and are also complemented by mustard, celery seeds, and apples. To prepare, scrub well with a stiff brush under cold running water. Cut off any roots. When peeling, have ready a bowl of acidulated water, 957, to drop the pieces in, because the flesh discolors when exposed to the air. *Pressure-cook* celery root about 5 minutes at 15 pounds pressure.

STEAMED CELERY ROOT

4 to 6 servings

Scrub well, peel, and cut into 1/2-inch cubes:

3 small or 2 medium celery roots (1 1/2 pounds)

Steam, 242. Or add to a saucepan of boiling water, reduce the heat, and simmer, uncovered, until tender, 6 to 10 minutes; drain. Toss with:

2 tablespoons butter
1 teaspoon fresh lemon juice
(1 teaspoon chopped parsley, chives, thyme, tarragon,
dill, or sage)

MASHED CELERY ROOT

4 servings

A delicious accompaniment to roasted meats.
Mash together:

2 cups Root Vegetable Puree, 245,, prepared using
2 medium celery roots (about 1¹/₂ pounds total),
peeled, quartered, and thinly sliced
1 cup mashed cooked potato, 295

Add to the hot vegetables:

2 tablespoons butter
Salt and black pepper to taste

BAKED CELERY ROOT
4 servings

These can also be served like baked potatoes. Surprisingly, the skin sometimes turns out tender enough to eat.
Position a rack in the center of the oven. Preheat the oven to 350°F. Trim, scrub, and pat dry:

2 medium celery roots

Brush with:

2 tablespoons olive oil

Place in an 8 x 8-inch square baking pan and roast, uncovered, until tender all through when pierced with a thin skewer, about 1 hour. Turn with tongs after 30 minutes. To serve, slice the roots in half, then slice each half into thirds. Mash the centers just enough to absorb butter or a sauce, and drizzle with:

4 to 6 tablespoons (¹/₂ to ³/₄ stick) butter, melted,
Lemon Butter, 557, or Brown Butter, 557

Sprinkle with:

Salt to taste
Minced parsley

ABOUT CHAYOTE

It doesn't look like much, but pear-shaped, pale green chayote, a tropical summer squash, has a firm texture and a hint of sweetness. Also called **mirliton** and **christophene,** it has deep lengthwise ridges and a long, flattish, central seed. The harder the squash, the better the flavor. Chayote can be stored in a plastic bag in the refrigerator crisper; it also freezes well. Chayote is especially good with cheese, and it is delicious halved and steamed and stuffed with Sautéed Mushrooms, 283, and grated cheese.

Unless the chayote is very small or you plan to stuff it, peel with a vegetable peeler, working under running water to prevent being irritated by the sticky substance just under the skin, which disappears in cooking. Cut off the stem, halve the squash lengthwise, and remove the seed. Cook the squash in halves or quarters, or cut the halves crosswise into ³/₄-inch slices.

To microwave, place 1 chayote, peeled and cut into ¹/₄-inch-thick slices, in a 2-quart baking dish. Add 3 tablespoons stock or lightly salted water, cover, and cook on high until tender or crisp-tender, 5 to 6 minutes, stirring after 2 minutes. Let stand, covered, for 2 minutes.

Pressure-cook whole chayotes at 15 pounds pressure for 6 to 8 minutes; diced, 2 minutes.

BOILED CHAYOTE
4 servings

Peel, halve, remove seeds from, and cut crosswise into ³/₄-inch slices:

1 pound chayotes (2 medium)

Drop into boiling water to cover. Reduce heat and simmer until tender, 10 to 20 minutes. Drain.
Toss with:

Butter, salt, and black pepper to taste,
Black Butter, 557, or Mornay Sauce, 551,
or grated Parmesan or dry Jack

LOUISIANA-STYLE CHAYOTE
6 servings

Boil in salted water to cover until tender but firm, about 6 to 10 minutes:

3 chayotes, halved and pitted

Drain and set upside down on a rack to cool. Scoop out the insides, leaving ¹/₃-inch-thick shells. Pat the shells dry and place in a 13 x 9-inch baking dish. Chop the pulp. Preheat the oven to 375°F.
Heat in a large nonstick skillet over high heat:

1 tablespoon olive or vegetable oil

Add and cook, turning once or twice, until bright pink, 1 to 2 minutes:

6 large shrimp (about 3 ounces), peeled and deveined, if desired

Remove the shrimp with a slotted spoon and let cool. Add the squash pulp to the pan, along with:

¹/₃ cup finely diced red bell pepper
¹/₃ cup chopped parsley
¹/₄ cup finely diced ham
1 large scallion, chopped
1 garlic clove, minced
1 teaspoon chopped fresh thyme or ¹/₄ teaspoon dried thyme
Salt and black pepper to taste
Pinch of ground red pepper

Cook over medium-high heat until no liquid remains, about 4 minutes. Meanwhile, finely chop the shrimp. Remove the filling from the heat and stir in the shrimp. Divide among the 6 squash shells and sprinkle with:

3 to 6 tablespoons dry bread crumbs

Bake until heated through and browned on top, about 35 minutes.

ABOUT CHESTNUTS

Chestnuts are equally delicious served as a vegetable, as an accompaniment to roasted meats, or as a sweet compote, or dessert. Fresh chestnuts are available from October through January. *To choose fresh chestnuts,* squeeze the nuts firmly between thumb and forefinger. The shells should feel rigid and unyielding. Refrigerate in a plastic bag. Chestnuts are always cooked before being eaten.

Chestnuts are also available dried, canned, or vacuum-packed year-round.

A handful of cooked whole chestnuts can be added to braised cabbage dishes (they are especially good with Brussels sprouts), and they are a classic ingredient in stuffings, 532. ➤ One pound of fresh chestnuts yields a little more than 8 ounces peeled, or 2 cups. If available, 8 ounces vacuum-packed cooked peeled chestnuts can be substituted in any recipe.

To peel, cut an X on the flat side of each nut. Drop into a pot of boiling water, let the water return to a boil, and boil for 5 minutes. Turn off the heat. Remove a few nuts at a time and peel off the outer shell and the inner membrane or skin. If some resist peeling, return them to the pot to soak longer, or reboil if necessary. Now the chestnuts are ready to be cooked.

BOILED CHESTNUTS

6 servings

I. To prepare as a vegetable, peel and skin, above:

1½ pounds fresh chestnuts (3 cups peeled)

or use:

12 ounces shelled dried chestnuts, soaked overnight in water to cover

Use the soaking water for cooking the nuts. Bring 8 cups water to a boil in a large saucepan. Add the chestnuts, along with:

3 ribs celery, coarsely chopped
1 small onion, coarsely chopped
1 tablespoon salt
(1 tablespoon vinegar)
(⅛ teaspoon anise seeds)

Simmer gently, uncovered, until the nuts can be pierced easily with the point of a paring knife, 30 to 40 minutes. Drain well, and discard the celery and onion.

Toss with:

2 to 3 tablespoons butter
Salt and black or white pepper to taste

II. To prepare as a compote, peel and skin, above:

1 pound fresh chestnuts (2 cups peeled)

Add to a saucepan of boiling water, reduce the heat, and simmer, uncovered, until cooked as above. Drain, reserving ½ cup of the liquid. Combine the liquid in a saucepan with:

½ cup sugar
(½ cup raisins)
(½ cup chopped nuts)
1 teaspoon grated lemon zest
1 teaspoon grated orange zest
3 tablespoons fresh lemon juice
3 tablespoons fresh orange juice
2 whole cloves
1 cinnamon stick
¼ teaspoon ground ginger

Bring to a simmer and simmer gently, uncovered, until the syrup is slightly reduced, about 10 minutes. Add the chestnuts and cook at the barest simmer until reduced to a syrup, about 25 minutes. Allow to stand for 30 minutes, then serve warm as a garnish for roasted poultry, pork, or ham.

ABOUT CORN

Fresh corn brightens a meal and is one of the most loved of all vegetables. It is at its peak in summer and ideally, it is eaten very close to picking. If this isn't possible, remember that many hybrids, whether the kernels are yellow, white, or "butter and sugar" (a combination of white and yellow), remain sweet while shipped and stored. Available almost year-round, these hybrids are delicious and can rival freshly picked summer corn. If corn is sold in the husks, the husks should be bright green and the silk pale and fresh looking. The kernels should appear plump and moist. Also available in some supermarkets and in Asian markets are finger-sized cobs, meant to be eaten whole, good in stir-fries and stews. Store corn in the husk or its original wrapping in the vegetable crisper of the refrigerator.

To prepare corn, first remove the husks and silks. To remove the kernels from the cob, use a sharp knife and large cutting board. Cut off the stem end to create a flat base. Hold the ear tip end up and cut downward, removing two or three rows at a time. Press along the rows with the dull side of a knife to retrieve the richly flavored juices and the heart of the kernels. Or, to remove only the creamy corn pulp, run the tip of a knife down through the center of each row of kernels, opening the kernels. Then, with the back of the knife, scrape down the cob and press out all the pulp. ➤ One ear of corn yields approximately ½ cup kernels or 3 to 4 tablespoons creamy pulp.

Sweet corns taste delicious uncooked in salads and salsas. Corn goes well with butter, bacon, cream, cheese, chile peppers, chili powder, basil, parsley, cilantro, and lime. In the following recipes, corn can be fresh, canned, or frozen except when otherwise noted.

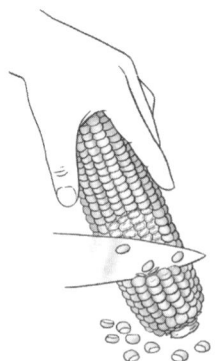

Cutting the kernels from an ear of corn

CORN ON THE COB

Allow 1 to 3 ears per person, depending on appetites.

I. Remove the husks and silk from:

Ears of fresh corn

Drop them one at a time into a large pot of rapidly boiling water. Cover and cook until hot and tender, 2 to 8 minutes, depending on maturity. Remove from the water with tongs. Serve with:

Salt and black pepper, butter, (Garlic Butter, 559)

II. Remove the husks and silk from:

Very young freshly picked corn

In a large kettle that you can cover tightly, bring to a rolling boil:

Enough water to cover corn generously

Slip the ears into the water one by one. Cover the kettle and remove from the heat at once. Allow the corn to remain in the hot water for about 5 minutes or until tender. Drain and serve at once.

GRILLED OR ROASTED CORN

I. Please read Grilling Vegetables, 243. Soak ears of corn in their husks in cold water for 2 to 3 hours before putting them on the grill or on hot coals. Do not worry about removing the silks; they will come off later with the husks. Lay the ears in the husks, directly on a hot grill rack. Cook, turning the ears with a pair of tongs so that they roast evenly on all sides, about 25 minutes, depending on the heat. Or roast the corn in their water-soaked husks for 8 to 15 minutes in a 450°F oven. Serve with:

Salt, black pepper, and butter

II. To intensify the taste of grilled corn and to caramelize the sugar in sweet corn, remove the husks and silks and lay the ears on a grill rack over very hot coals. Grill, turning the ears to brown them evenly, for 5 to 7 minutes.

III. This method steams the ears inside foil wrappers. Remove the husks and silks from the corn. Rub lightly with:

Basic Flavored Butter, 558, or vegetable oil

Sprinkle with:

Salt and black pepper to taste

Wrap each ear in a piece of aluminum foil. Place on the grill, or place directly in hot ashes, and cook, turning a few times, 8 to 10 minutes. Or roast in the oven at 450°F for 8 to 10 minutes.

SAUTÉED CORN (FRIED CORN)

4 servings

Cut the kernels from:

6 ears corn (about 3 cups)

Melt in a medium skillet over medium heat:

2 tablespoons butter

Add the corn and cook, stirring often, until heated through, 3 to 4 minutes. Season with:

Salt and black pepper to taste

Stir in any of the following:

Minced parsley
1 tomato, seeded and chopped
Chopped tarragon, basil, cilantro, thyme, or marjoram
Pinch of chili powder

Diced seeded jalapeño or serrano peppers, chopped roasted, 292, poblano peppers, or chopped Anaheim peppers
1 or 2 slices bacon, cooked and crumbled

CREAMED CORN

4 servings

Cut and then scrape from the cob:

5 ears corn (about 2½ cups)

Melt in a medium nonstick skillet over low heat:

1 tablespoon butter

Add and cook, stirring, until softened, 3 to 4 minutes:

(¼ cup thinly sliced scallions or chopped shallots)

Add the corn, along with:

1 cup heavy cream

Cook over low heat, stirring once or twice, until thickened, about 2 minutes. Season to taste with:

Salt and black or red ground pepper

CORN PUDDING

6 servings

This can be mixed a day ahead and baked when needed. The addition of vanilla was inspired by our editor Maggie Green.

Position a rack in the center of the oven. Preheat the oven to 350°F. Butter a 1½-quart baking dish.

Mix together in a large bowl:

2 cups fresh, frozen, or canned corn kernels, drained
¾ cup milk or half-and-half
2 large eggs, well beaten
2 tablespoons butter, melted and cooled
1 tablespoon all-purpose flour
1 teaspoon salt
(1 teaspoon vanilla)

Pour into the prepared baking dish. Place in a larger pan of water, 801, and bake for 30 to 45 minutes, until the center is set.

ADDITIONS TO CORN PUDDING

3 poblano or New Mexico chile peppers, roasted, 292, peeled, seeded, and chopped
1 cup shredded Monterey Jack, Muenster, or sharp Cheddar (4 ounces)
2 teaspoons minced garlic
1 small onion, diced and sautéed

SOUFFLÉED CORN PUDDING

Prepare:

Corn Pudding, above

adding only the egg yolks to the corn mixture.

Beat until stiff but not dry, 978:

2 egg whites

Fold them into the corn mixture. Bake the pudding until set. Serve at once.

CHEESE-CHILE CORN SQUARES

About 9 servings

Preheat the oven to 350°F. Generously butter a 9-inch square baking pan.

Combine:

    1¹/₂ cups fresh, frozen, or canned corn kernels, drained

    4 cups shredded Monterey Jack (about 1 pound)

    6 large eggs, well beaten

    3 jalapeño peppers, seeded and finely chopped

    2 tablespoons chili powder

    Salt and black pepper to taste

Scrape the mixture into the prepared pan. Bake until the top is nicely browned, about 30 minutes.

Let cool until it firms sufficiently to be cut, then cut into 3-inch squares.

SUCCOTASH

4 servings

Succotash takes its name from the Narragansett word *msickquatash,* meaning "boiled kernels of corn." This is entirely acceptable made with canned or frozen vegetables. You can also break with tradition and add a cup of cooked kidney beans.

Combine in a medium saucepan over medium heat and cook, stirring occasionally, until heated through:

    1 cup cooked corn kernels

    1 cup cooked lima beans or finely chopped green beans

    2 tablespoons butter

    ¹/₂ teaspoon salt

    ¹/₈ teaspoon paprika

    Chopped parsley or thyme to taste

FRESH CORN FRITTERS

4 servings

The author of the following account graciously permitted us to use it when we told him how much it pleased us.

"When I was a child, one of eight, my father frequently promised us a marvelous treat. He, being an amateur arboriculturist, would tell us of a fritter tree he was going to plant on the banks of a small lake filled with molasses, maple syrup, or honey, to be located in our backyard. When one of us children felt the urge for this most delectable repast, all we had to do was to shake the tree—the fritters would drop into the lake, and we could fish them out and eat fritters to our hearts' content. Mother was a good cook, and she duly developed this fabulous fritter." The following is, we hope, a faithful transcription of her recipe.

Scrape from the cob into a bowl:

    2¹/₂ cups corn kernels (about 5 ears)

Stir in:

    1 large egg yolk, well beaten

    2 teaspoons all-purpose flour

    ¹/₄ teaspoon salt

Whip in a medium bowl until stiff but not dry, 978:

    1 large egg white

Fold into the corn mixture.

Heat in a large nonstick skillet over high heat:

    2 tablespoons butter or vegetable oil

Drop in the batter a heaping tablespoon at a time, without crowding. Reduce the heat to medium and cook, turning once, until browned on both sides, 2 to 3 minutes per side. Do not overcook. Serve immediately.

DEE'S CORN AND TOMATO SALAD

4 servings

Few things symbolize summer as well as corn and tomatoes, and they combine colorfully and deliciously in this dish from our friend Dee Schmid.

Cut from the cob:

    3 cups corn kernels (about 6 ears)

Combine in a bowl with:

    1 large tomato, diced

    ¹/₂ red onion, diced

    1 to 2 tablespoons chopped basil

Barely moisten with:

    Vinaigrette, 572

Serve, chilled or at room temperature, within 2 to 3 hours, garnished with:

    Basil leaves

ABOUT CUCUMBERS

At their best, they are crisp and juicy and thirst-quenching, deserving to be immortalized as "cool as a . . ." (we all know the rest). Among the slicing varieties of cucumbers are the thin-skinned **American** slicing and the very long virtually seedless **European** greenhouse or hothouse cucumbers, and **Japanese** slicing types. Pickling cucumbers, by contrast, are short and have been bred to keep their crispness and to absorb liquid especially well. **Gherkins, cornichons,** and **Kirbys** are pickling cucumbers. To pickle cucumbers, see 945.

A cucumber fit for use is firm, with no soft spots, bruises, cuts, or withered places. It should have a lustrous skin—do not be misled by the heavy waxy finish that has been applied to those in many markets. If the skin is not waxed, it is edible. Store in the refrigerator crisper.

Peel the cucumber with a vegetable peeler or paring knife. Slice it in half lengthwise. Use the tip of a spoon to scrape out the seeds, 173, if desired. If you leave the skin on, an attractive finish for slicing is made by running a fork down the length of the cucumber, scoring it all around. If a sample of a cucumber tastes bitter, cut off the ends, peel it, and place in a bowl. Sprinkle cider vinegar all over it, then add a pinch each of salt and sugar and toss. Let stand for 30 minutes, then rinse well.

Cucumbers are delicious raw with salt and go well with sour cream, yogurt, raw onions, garlic, mint, chives, lemon, dill, sesame seeds, vinegar, and fresh tomatoes. Some people who are allergic to cucumbers find they can enjoy them if they are seeded and cooked. The texture and flavor of a cooked cucumber is tender and mild. Cook cucumbers as you would zucchini, remembering that the flesh is considerably more watery.

COOKED CUCUMBERS

2 servings

Prepare:

2 cups peeled cucumber strips

Drop them into a small saucepan of boiling water, reduce the heat, and simmer until nearly tender, 3 to 5 minutes. Drain well, and return to the pan. Season with:

Salt and white pepper to taste

Grated or ground nutmeg or 1 teaspoon chopped dill, chives, parsley, or dill or celery seeds

Stir in:

1 tablespoon butter or 2 tablespoons heavy cream

Reheat briefly, and serve at once.

Or serve with:

Lemon Butter, 557, with capers, or Fresh Tomato Sauce, 563, with basil, or Onion Sauce, 551

ABOUT EGGPLANT

In this country, the eggplants most commonly available are inky purple and teardrop- or globe-shaped. However, there are also **white eggplants,** and it is from these varieties the vegetable gets its name (*aubergine,* the common term for it in Europe, is a corruption of its Arabic name; in Italian, it's known as *melanzana,* from its undeserved Latin name meaning "apple of madness"). **Asian eggplants** are pale purple or lightly striped, small, and elongated. Although they can be used in recipes calling for standard eggplant, Asian eggplants are tastiest baked, grilled, or sautéed.

Select eggplants that are heavy for their size, with taut, glossy skin, a fresh, green cap and stem, and no soft spots, cuts, or bruises. As a rule, small to medium eggplants weighing 1 pound or less are the choicest, being the youngest and having the fewest seeds. Store in a cool, dry place and use as soon as possible. Refrigeration is not recommended.

Eggplant has a blotter-like capacity for oil or butter. Salting and draining serves to compact the flesh, helping it to absorb less oil when cooking and giving the cooked vegetable a firm, creamy texture. Trim off the stem and cap. Unless your recipe says otherwise, peel off the skin with a thin sharp knife. Cut into slices, cubes, or halves as called for. ➤ Eggplant discolors quickly when cut and should be sprinkled or rubbed with lemon juice. Generously sprinkle the pieces with salt. Place cubes in a colander, slices or halves on a baking sheet, and let stand for 30 to 60 minutes. Then rinse quickly and, working in small batches, press the eggplant to remove the juice. ➤ One pound of eggplant equals 3 to 4 cups diced.

Eggplant goes well with lamb, tomatoes, mushrooms, onions, peppers, cheese, cream sauces, oregano, marjo-

ram, soy sauce, and garlic. Microwaving and pressure-cooking are not recommended.

BAKED EGGPLANT SLICES

4 to 6 servings

Preheat the oven to 400°F.

Peel:

2 medium eggplants (about 1 pound each)

Cut into $1/2$-inch-thick slices. Brush the slices on both sides with:

Softened butter, olive oil, or vegetable oil

Season to taste with:

Salt and black pepper

Place on a baking sheet and bake until tender, about 15 minutes, turning once. Garnish with:

Chopped parsley or basil

FRIED EGGPLANT

4 servings

These coatings make the eggplant crisp on the outside and softly creamy inside.

I. Please read Deep-Frying Vegetables, 243.

Peel and cut into $1/2$-inch slices or sticks:

1 medium eggplant

Dip them in:

Fritter Batter for Vegetables, 658

Fry them until golden in vegetable oil to cover, heated to 365°F. Drain on paper towels and sprinkle with:

Salt to taste

Serve hot.

II. Peel and cut into $1/2$-inch slices or sticks:

1 medium eggplant

Whisk together in a shallow bowl:

3 large eggs

1 tablespoon olive oil

Dredge the eggplant in:

$1/3$ cup all-purpose flour

Shake off the excess, dip in the egg mixture, letting the excess drip off, and dredge in:

$1 1/4$ cups fresh bread crumbs

Arrange the eggplant slices on a rack and let dry for 30 minutes. Heat in a large skillet over medium-high heat:

$1/4$ cup olive oil

Add as many eggplant slices as will fit without crowding and cook for 4 to 5 minutes on each side. Transfer to a plate. You may have to add more oil to fry the remaining batches. Season with:

Salt and black pepper to taste

EGGPLANT PARMIGIANA

4 to 6 servings

Prepare:

Fresh Tomato Sauce, 563

Fried Eggplant II, above

Position a rack in the upper third of the oven. Preheat the oven to 425°F.

Coat a 17 x 12-inch rimmed baking sheet with half of the

tomato sauce. Arrange the fried eggplant slices in a single layer, or slightly overlapping if necessary, on the baking sheet. Top with the remaining tomato sauce and:

2 teaspoons dried oregano
$1/4$ teaspoon black pepper

Combine and sprinkle over the eggplant:

$1^1/2$ cups shredded mozzarella (6 ounces)
$2/3$ cup grated Parmesan

Sprinkle over the top:

2 teaspoons chopped parsley

Bake until the cheese is melted and bubbly, about 15 minutes. Serve at once.

ROASTED WHOLE EGGPLANT

Roasting eggplant produces a tender pulp that can be used for all kinds of dips. You can also roast whole eggplants on a hot grill, allowing them to char for a distinctive smoky flavor, or cook them over embers in the hearth, 1060. A 1-pound eggplant will yield about $1^1/2$ cups pulp. Preheat the oven to 400°F. Make several slits with a knife tip in:

1 eggplant

Fill the cuts with:

Garlic slivers

Set in a baking dish. Bake until the eggplant has collapsed, 30 minutes to 1 hour, depending on size.
Remove to a colander so that any juices can drain off, then cut in half and scoop out the pulp. Leave it coarse or mash it to a puree. Use for eggplant dips, such as Baba Ghanoush, 74, or season to taste with any of the following:

Extra-virgin olive oil, melted butter, or toasted
sesame oil
Chopped herbs, such as marjoram or basil
Fresh lemon juice or any vinaigrette, 572
Plain yogurt
Salt and black pepper

RATATOUILLE PROVENÇALE

8 servings

Served on a platter that shows off its contrasting colors, this dish looks like a colorful Cubist still life.
Heat in a large skillet or Dutch oven over high heat:

$1/4$ cup olive oil

Add and cook, stirring, until golden and just tender, 10 to 12 minutes:

1 medium eggplant (about 1 pound), peeled and
cut into 1-inch chunks
1 pound zucchini, cut into 1-inch chunks

Remove the vegetables to a plate and reduce the heat to medium-high. Add and cook, stirring, until the onions are slightly softened:

2 tablespoons olive oil
$1^1/2$ cups sliced onions

Add and cook, stirring occasionally, until the vegetables are just tender but not browned, 8 to 12 minutes:

2 large red bell peppers, cut into 1-inch squares
3 garlic cloves, finely chopped

Season with:

Salt and black pepper to taste

Add:

$1^1/2$ cups peeled, 311, seeded, chopped fresh tomatoes
or one 14-ounce can diced tomatoes, drained
2 to 3 sprigs fresh thyme or $1/2$ teaspoon dried thyme
1 bay leaf

Reduce the heat to low, cover, and cook for 5 minutes. Add the eggplant and zucchini and cook until everything is tender, about 20 minutes more. Taste and adjust the seasonings. Stir in:

$1/4$ cup chopped basil
(Pitted black olives, chopped)

MOUSSAKA

6 to 8 servings

This moussaka is topped with a mixture of yogurt and eggs, which is lighter than the traditional Greek béchamel, or white sauce. Greek cheeses and yogurt can be found in Greek markets and delicatessens specializing in Mediterranean and Middle Eastern foods. Because kefalotyri cheese is quite salty, we like to combine it with Parmesan. Slice lengthwise about $1/3$ inch thick:

2 to $2^1/2$ pounds eggplant (2 large or 3 medium)

Salt the slices generously and place on a baking sheet. Let stand for 30 minutes to an hour.
Meanwhile, heat a large skillet over medium-high heat, and add:

1 pound minced or ground lamb or lean beef

Cook, stirring, until the meat has browned and rendered its fat, about 5 to 10 minutes. Season with:

Salt and black pepper to taste

Using a slotted spoon, transfer the meat to a bowl. Pour off the fat from the pan. Add 2 tablespoons water to the pan and, using a wooden spoon, stir and scrape up any browned bits. Add the meat. Return the pan to medium heat, add, and heat:

2 tablespoons olive oil

Add and cook, stirring, until tender, about 5 minutes:

1 large onion, chopped

Add and cook, stirring, until fragrant, about 30 seconds to a minute:

2 large garlic cloves, minced

Stir in:

One 14-ounce can diced tomatoes, with their juice
1 heaping tablespoon tomato paste
$1/2$ teaspoon sweet paprika
Rounded $1/4$ teaspoon ground cinnamon
$1/8$ teaspoon ground allspice
$1/2$ teaspoon sugar
1 bay leaf
$1/2$ cup hot water, or enough to just barely cover
the meat
Salt and black pepper to taste

Bring to a simmer, then reduce the heat to low, cover, and simmer 45 minutes to an hour, stirring occasionally. The mixture should be thick and very fragrant.

Cook uncovered for another 5 to 10 minutes, until the liquid in the pan is just about gone. Remove from the heat and remove the bay leaf. Taste and adjust the seasonings. Let cool slightly, then stir in:

$1/2$ cup chopped parsley
1 large egg, well beaten

Set aside while you cook the eggplant. Preheat the broiler. Brush 2 baking sheets with olive oil. Rinse the eggplant slices and pat dry. Place on the baking sheets and brush with:

Olive oil

One sheet at a time, place under the broiler, about 2 inches from the element, and broil for 3 to 5 minutes, or until the slices are lightly browned and softened. Remove from the heat and allow to cool. (You can also bake the eggplant slices in a 450°F oven for 10 to 15 minutes, until lightly browned and softened.)

Preheat the oven to 350°F. Grease a 3-quart baking dish or gratin dish. Make an even layer of half the eggplant in the bottom of the dish, and spread all of the sauce over the eggplant. Top with the remaining eggplant. Bake for 30 minutes.

Meanwhile, beat together:

4 large eggs
$1 1/4$ cups plain yogurt, preferably Greek, drained, 1029
A pinch of paprika
Salt (about $1/2$ teaspoon) and black pepper to taste

Pour over the eggplant. Sprinkle evenly over the top:

$1/2$ cup mixed grated Greek kefalotyri and
  Parmesan, or Parmesan only

Return to the oven and bake for another 25 to 30 minutes, until golden. Serve warm.

EGGPLANT RELISH (CAPONATA)

About 4 cups

A hearty Italian accompaniment for fish, poultry, or meat, as well as a spread to be served with pita bread, crackers, or crostini.

Peel and cut into $1/2$-inch cubes:

1 medium eggplant (about 1 pound)

Sprinkle generously with:

Salt

Place in a colander, and let stand 30 to 60 minutes. Rinse and pat dry. Heat in a large heavy skillet over medium heat:

2 tablespoons olive oil

Add and cook, stirring often, until softened, about 4 minutes:

1 cup finely chopped celery

Add and cook, stirring often, until the onion is soft and lightly colored, about 5 minutes:

1 medium onion, finely chopped
1 garlic clove, minced

With a slotted spoon, remove the vegetables to a bowl. Add to the skillet:

2 tablespoons olive oil

Add the eggplant cubes and cook, stirring constantly, until lightly browned, 5 to 7 minutes. Add the celery mixture, along with:

$1 1/2$ cups canned plum tomatoes, drained and
  coarsely chopped
12 green olives, pitted and coarsely chopped
$1 1/2$ tablespoons drained capers
2 tablespoons red wine vinegar
1 tablespoon tomato paste
2 teaspoons sugar
1 teaspoon minced fresh oregano or $1/4$ teaspoon
  dried oregano
1 teaspoon salt
Black pepper to taste

Bring to a boil, then reduce the heat to low and simmer, uncovered, until thickened, about 15 minutes.

Taste and adjust the seasonings with additional salt, pepper, and/or vinegar if needed. Remove to a serving bowl, let cool, and garnish with:

2 tablespoons minced parsley

Serve at room temperature.

ABOUT ENDIVE, ESCAROLE, AND RADICCHIO

Some are smooth, some frizzy, a few are white, and many are pale shades of green, but all members of the chicory family have in common firm leaves and a refreshing touch of bitterness. See also Salad Greens, 152, for they are eaten raw too. Cooking tames the bitterness slightly and softens the leaves, yielding a perfect counterpoint to rich meats. All can be torn into pieces or sliced into ribbons and sautéed like chard, 277. Because Belgian endive and radicchio have compact heads, they also can be baked, roasted, or grilled. Radicchio adds gorgeous red color to the plate.

These greens go well with strong cheeses such as Roquefort or fontina, salty meats like ham and bacon, capers, olives, red bell peppers, and hard-boiled eggs. Store as you would salad greens, 152.

BELGIAN ENDIVE AU GRATIN

4 servings

Many people are surprised that Belgian endive can be cooked as a vegetable. It is an excellent accompaniment to grilled fish or meats.

Position a rack in the center of the oven and preheat the oven to 325°F. Lightly butter an 8-inch square baking dish. Have ready:

8 medium Belgian endives, any bruised outer leaves
  removed, and halved lengthwise
3 tablespoons unsalted butter, cut into pieces
2 tablespoons fresh lemon juice

Place half the endive in the prepared baking dish and top

with half with butter and juice. Repeat to make a second layer. Pour over the top:

¼ cup boiling chicken stock or broth or water

Cover and bake for 45 minutes.

Uncover and sprinkle over the top:

½ cup fresh bread crumbs

2 tablespoons grated Parmesan

Increase the oven temperature to 375°F and bake until the endive is browned, about 20 minutes more.

BRAISED RADICCHIO

4 to 6 servings

Braised radicchio can be finely chopped and tossed with fresh pasta.

Cook in a large skillet over medium heat until curled, 3 minutes:

1 tablespoon extra-virgin olive oil

2 ounces lean pancetta or bacon, chopped

Increase the heat to high, add, and cook, stirring, for 1 minute:

1 medium onion, finely chopped

½ small carrot, finely chopped

Add:

1 pound radicchio, any wilted leaves trimmed and cut into 4 to 6 wedges each

Cook, turning often, until the radicchio is wilted and nicely browned on all sides. Add:

½ cup dry white wine

Simmer over medium heat until the wine is evaporated, turning the radicchio once or twice. Pour in:

½ to ⅔ cup chicken stock or broth

2 tablespoons heavy cream

Simmer for about 3 minutes, scraping up any browned bits in the pan. Season with:

Salt and black pepper to taste

FENNEL

The anise-flavored fennel bulbs, which can be found in most supermarkets, may be eaten raw with dips or in salads, as a substitute for celery, or roasted, braised, grilled, or sautéed, or the fronds used discreetly for seasoning. Fennel is especially delicious with fish. It is particularly complemented by tomatoes, oranges, apples, walnuts, cheeses, lemon, and dill.

Fennel does not store well and never for more than 2 or 3 days. To cook, trim the stalks off and pull away the tough outer layers on the bulb. Cut out the core, except when slicing, which should be done lengthwise, from core to fronds. The core holds the slices together.

ROASTED FENNEL

4 to 6 servings

Preheat the oven to 375°F.

Trim the stalks from and slice:

2 medium fennel bulbs

Brush a baking pan with:

1 tablespoon olive oil

Arrange the fennel slices in a single layer in the pan. Brush the tops with:

2 tablespoons olive oil

Roast for about 15 minutes, then turn and roast until the slices can be pierced with a knife and are lightly browned, 15 to 20 minutes more. Season with:

Salt and white pepper to taste

Serve hot or at room temperature, sprinkled with:

Fresh lemon juice or finely shredded Parmesan

ABOUT FIDDLEHEAD FERNS

The new shoots, or "fiddleheads," of the ostrich fern have a flavor reminiscent of asparagus and artichoke—some say with a touch of green beans. They are available at specialty produce stores and farmers' markets in the spring. Choose ferns that are bright green and tightly coiled or curled in crosiers. They are also available canned. To prepare, trim the "tail" to the same thickness as the coil. Immerse the ferns in cold water, swirl and rub off any brown fuzz, and then rinse well. Steam, 242, just until tender, 10 to 15 minutes. Serve (on toast, if desired) with melted butter and lemon juice or with Hollandaise Sauce, 560. Fiddleheads may also be deep fried.

Caution: Some people are allergic to ferns. ➤ Do not pick fiddleheads in the wild, since, although many ferns send up the coils, only the ostrich fern is safe for eating.

ABOUT GARLIC

Garlic is available all year, with peak season in the spring. Choose plump, firm heads with tight, papery skins that may be white, purplish, or tinged with red. Store at room temperature away from light. Avoid cloves with brown spots or green sprouts—they are past their prime. Garlic maintains its freshness when frozen as a paste. The bunches of **green garlic** you may find at the farmers' market are harvested before the bulb is grown—just as many varieties of scallions are onions harvested before the onion has formed. Store green garlic as you would scallions, but use as you would garlic. **Elephant garlic** is not true garlic but a type of leek. Its cloves are the size of brazil nuts, and their flavor is very mild. Read more about garlic, 1003.

To peel, lay the clove on a board, and press down gently but firmly with the side of a large knife. The skin will split and is easily pulled off. Or use a tubular rubber garlic peeler, available in kitchen supply stores. *To mince,* slice a peeled clove lengthwise without cutting completely through it, then cut through once or twice horizontally and chop crosswise into very fine pieces. *To mash to a paste,* hold the knife blade almost flat against minced garlic and crush the pieces while pulling the knife back and forth through the pulp until it becomes as smooth as you can make it. A pinch of salt worked into the paste is a tasty foundation for vinaigrettes. Pressing garlic with a garlic press is recommended when raw garlic will be of a very smooth mixture and even mincing and mashing is not fine enough. When cooking garlic in oil, be careful not to burn it, which makes it strong and acrid.

ROASTED GARLIC

4 to 6 servings

To eat this as a first course, squeeze the pulp from each clove and spread on slices of buttered toasted French bread. Serve with assorted olives and fresh goat cheese, if desired. Or use in Roasted Garlic and Parmesan Spread, 76.

I. Preheat the oven to 325°F. To expose the cloves, cut the top third from:

4 large heads garlic

Drizzle over the cut portions of the heads:

2 tablespoons olive oil

Wrap each head tightly in aluminum foil, place in a baking dish, and bake until the garlic is soft and tender, 45 minutes to 1 hour. Serve hot or at room temperature.

II. Preheat the oven to 325°F. To expose the cloves, cut the top third from:

4 large heads garlic

Place in an 8 x 8-inch baking dish and add:

Chicken stock or water to come one-third up the sides of the heads

Drizzle over the top:

2 tablespoons olive oil or chicken stock

Place on each head:

(1 sprig fresh thyme)

Cover with aluminum foil and bake until the garlic is soft and tender, about 1 hour. Serve hot or at room temperature.

ABOUT CULTIVATED GREENS

Cultivated greens are available in a variety of types, with flavors from mild to pungent. Greens are chock-full of the nutrients for which dark green vegetables are celebrated—vitamins A and C, minerals such as iron, and numerous phytochemicals. **Chard,** or **Swiss chard,** is in peak season during the summer and can be found with leaf veins and midrib in a rainbow of colors: crimson, orange, yellow. Chard is versatile and has a mild yet slightly bitter flavor (similar to beets). Chard ribs can be cooked like asparagus, 249, and are excellent with any cream sauce or in a gratin. **Beet greens** are milder in flavor. They are typically sold attached to a beet, 259. **Turnip greens** are slightly sweet and tender when young but grow to be tough and strong-tasting as they age. Their peak season is in the fall and winter. **Kale** is a close relative of collards. Kale grows well in colder temperatures and can withstand frost—which helps it produce even sweeter leaves. It is available year-round, but it is most flavorful and abundant during the winter. Select deep-colored bunches with small leaves. The tough center stalk should be removed before cooking. **Collard greens** are at their peak in the winter, and the best collards are found in crisp bunches with roots still intact. Like kale, collard greens are sweetest after the first frost. **Mustard greens,** also at their peak in the winter, usually have a hot and pungent "mustardy" flavor, and are generally cooked in combination with other greens.

Store greens, unwashed, in a plastic bag in the refrigerator crisper. Use within a few days, as the leaves are prone to wilting. Before cooking, all greens need to be washed thoroughly in several changes of cold water to remove grit and dirt. Fill a sink with water. Put the greens in a colander or sieve and submerge. Swish the leaves around for 30 seconds or so, then lift the colander gently out of the water. Drain the sink, refill, and repeat the cleaning process as necessary to remove all dirt.

The old-fashioned custom is to cook greens for an hour or more, with bacon, salt pork, or ham hocks and serve them with vinegar. We prefer to retain color and nutrients by using the following methods. Leaves can be cooked whole, or to reduce the cooking time—when the greens are unusually large and mature—derib or strip the leafage from the midribs, 245. The leafy parts can be torn into 2- to 3-inch pieces, or stacked and rolled, and then sliced crosswise into 1-inch ribbons.

Steaming and greens don't mix. An acid in the greens is activated by heat. The reason for cooking in a large quantity of water rather than steaming is to wash away the acid, which would otherwise destroy the chlorophyll and turn the greens from a deep green to a dingy gray.

Greens have affinities with garlic, bacon, red pepper flakes or sauce, vinegar, salt pork, soy sauce, and mustard.

To microwave, remove the stems, and, if they are large and tough, the midribs from 1 1/4 pounds greens. Place the leaves in a 3-quart baking dish with the water that clings to them from rinsing. Cover and cook on high until tender, 7 to 10 minutes, stirring after 3 minutes. Let stand, covered, for 2 minutes. *Pressure-cook* beet greens 3 minutes at 15 pounds.

Most greens are edible raw when they're young. See Salads, 152.

SOUTHERN-STYLE GREENS

8 servings

Two or more types of greens can be cooked together if desired. In the South these greens are traditionally drained and served with vinegar and hot pepper sauce and the cooking liquid, or pot liquor, which is soaked up with Southern Corn Bread, 632.

Combine in a large pot and bring to a boil:

10 cups water

5 ounces salt pork or bacon, diced, or 1 pound ham hocks or smoked pork neck bones

Reduce the heat slightly and boil gently, partially covered, for 1 hour. Wash well:

3 pounds any greens

Derib the leaves if necessary, 245, then tear or cut the leaves into small pieces. Add to the pot, along with, if desired:

(1 small dried red chile pepper, seeds removed, or 1/2 teaspoon crushed red pepper flakes)

Reduce the heat and simmer, partially covered, just until the greens are tender, 15 to 45 minutes, depending on the type, stirring occasionally. Serve with:

Vinegar or hot pepper sauce

SAUTÉED GREENS WITH GARLIC

4 to 6 servings

Remove the stems and midribs from:

2 medium bunches red or green chard, kale, or beet greens (about 1½ pounds)

Cut any stems and ribs into ½-inch pieces. Coarsely chop the leaves. Rinse well, but do not dry.

Heat in a large skillet over medium-low heat until the oil is fragrant and the garlic is just beginning to color:

2 tablespoons extra-virgin olive oil

2 garlic cloves, thinly sliced

(1 small dried red chile pepper, crumbled, or ¼ to ½ teaspoon crushed red pepper flakes)

Add the stems and ribs and season to taste with:

Salt

Cook, stirring occasionally, until nearly tender, about 2 minutes. Add the leaves and cook, partially covered, until both the leaves and stems are tender, 3 to 5 minutes more. Season with:

Juice of ½ lemon or 1½ tablespoons red wine vinegar

Taste again for salt. Serve in a bowl, surrounded with:

Lemon wedges

Or, instead of the salt and lemon, dot with:

Soy sauce or tamari

KALE AND POTATO GRATIN

6 servings

Preheat the oven to 350°F. Butter a 2-quart shallow baking dish.

Steam, 242, until almost tender, 8 to 10 minutes:

1 large bunch kale (about 1 pound), washed well and sliced and deribbed, 241

Meanwhile, peel and cut into ⅛-inch rounds:

4 medium Yukon Gold or all-purpose potatoes (about 1¼ pounds)

2 small onions

Drain the kale and let stand until cool enough to handle. Press out the excess water and coarsely chop.

Build up alternating layers of potatoes, onions, and kale (2 layers of each) in the baking dish, beginning and ending with potatoes and dotting each onion layer with:

2 tablespoons butter, cut into pieces

(1 teaspoon minced tarragon)

½ teaspoon salt

¼ teaspoon black pepper

Pour over the top:

1½ cups milk or half-and-half

Cover and bake until the potatoes are tender and almost all the liquid is absorbed, 30 to 45 minutes. Run under the broiler, if desired, to brown the top.

BEET GREENS

I. Beet greens may be prepared like Spinach, 305. If you are serving the greens with the beets, put the beets in a ring and serve the greens in the center, dressed with melted butter, and garnish with Horseradish Sauce, 552.

II.

4 servings

Heat in a large skillet over medium heat:

2 tablespoons butter or vegetable oil

Add and cook, stirring, until the greens are wilted, about 5 minutes:

4 cups chopped beet greens, including stems

1 tablespoon grated fresh horseradish

1 teaspoon grated onion

½ tablespoon Dijon mustard

⅛ teaspoon salt

Add:

¼ cup water

Cover and simmer until the greens are tender, 10 to 15 minutes. Uncover and cook, stirring, until all liquid has evaporated. If desired, remove from the heat and stir in:

(½ cup sour cream)

ABOUT WILD GREENS, SHOOTS, AND ROOTS

If you are in earnest about collecting edible wild foods, try to find a local expert. If such a person is not available, the best advice comes from a reliable field guide to edible plants, such as Lee Allen Peterson's *A Field Guide to Wild Edible Plants* or Robert Henderson's *The Neighborhood Forager: A Guide for the Wild Food Gourmet*.

Wild greens can harbor concentrations of oxalates, nitrates, and other toxic elements. Such irritants are lessened by cooking and can be eliminated entirely by parboiling before a final cooking. ➤ Sample all wild greens sparingly. Remember, too, that all plants have seasons when they are succulent and periods when they are inedible, and that they all need careful washing to remove grit.

COOKING WILD GREENS

The greens listed here are those most popularly collected. Prepare as for Spinach, 305: young chickweeds, lamb's-quarters, purslane, mustards, miner's lettuce that is past salad stage (with tougher leaves), tiny plantains, bladder campion, cleavers, and nettles. All these will cook down by at least half. Nettles, which have to be handled before cooking with tongs or impervious gloves, may be used as blanched shoots all winter if the roots are dug and grown in boxes of soil in a cool cellar. Prepare these also as for spinach. Before foraging, consult a local expert on wild foods or a reliable field guide to wild edible plants.

Parboil the plants listed below for about 5 minutes, then drain and cook for 10 minutes or so in fresh boiling water: dandelion leaves picked before the plant flowers, young sour and curly dock, young chicory leaves, evening primrose, and escaped comfrey. Most of these, even after parboiling and cooking, will remain slightly bitter, and you may want to mix them with other less bitter cooked greens, such as purslane.

COOKING WILD SHOOTS
There are certain wild shoots that bring rave reviews—wild asparagus, of course, and its cousin, stalks of bellwort. The latter are usually too scarce to consider cropping and should be left in the wild. This does not hold for such prevalent shoots as cattails, fireweed, burdock, and the escaped Japanese butterbur or fuki, which grow in such thriving colonies that they are easy to locate. The roots of burdock and butterbur may be used (see 262), as well as the stems, which should be very carefully peeled prior to cooking. All of the above may be prepared as for Asparagus, 249.

Then there are poke shoots, which must be cut very young, for both leaf and root are poisonous before cooking. The shoot should be parblanched, 1054, in two changes of water, then cooked a third time in fresh water until tender.

COOKING WILD ROOTS
Preparation of certain water-grown roots is for the hearty forager, or for those who still like to feel the squish of mud between their toes in their gathering of wild edibles. Bulrushes and cattails can be dug year-round. Use the root stalks. Scrape off and remove the hairs. Parboil at least 10 minutes, then boil in fresh water or roast for over an hour. Roasting in coals takes from 2 to 3 hours. Arrowhead tubers, dug in the fall, should be treated like potatoes, 294. Boil the long spongy roots of the yellow spatterdock water lily about 30 minutes. You may also eat the unopened flowers of the fragrant white water lily, sautéed briefly in butter, or the seeds of both the spatterdock and the white water lily, which can be fried like popcorn. Among water plants, the young leaves of pickerelweed are the quickest to prepare, needing only about 8 minutes of boiling. Or chop the raw leaves and put in salad.

Among the land-based roots, Jerusalem artichokes, also found in cultivated forms, 249, are favorites. Cooked in the same ways are groundnut roots, butterbur and burdock roots, and—after their runners are removed—the roots of the day lily. To prepare the buds and flowers, see 994. The first-year roots of evening primrose may also be prepared as for Jerusalem artichokes if they are first parboiled 10 minutes. Spring beauty corms, which are sometimes found as sods in old lawns, may be treated like potatoes—but patience and Lilliputian appetites are necessary prerequisites.

SAUTÉED MILKWEED PODS
4 servings
Cook in a pot of boiling water (be certain all the pods are thoroughly immersed for about 5 minutes, or until tender):

30 small milkweed pods, less than 4 inches, and preferably 1¹⁄₂ inches in length

Drain. Heat in a large skillet:

2 tablespoons olive oil
Add and cook, stirring, until fragrant:

3 medium garlic cloves, minced
Add the milkweed pods. Season to taste with:

Salt and black pepper
Cook, stirring occasionally, a few minutes more until the pods are tender. Stir in:

¹⁄₄ cup grated Parmesan

JICAMA
The uninspiring appearance of jicama—like a rough, brown-skinned turnip—belies its sweet, crisply juicy white flesh. It is a favorite for the raw vegetable tray and salad bowl, as well as a fine substitute for water chestnuts in stir-fries, or with Panfried Potatoes, 297. Select small to medium tubers that are uniformly hard and heavy for their size, with no sign of shriveling or drying. Store unpeeled and unwrapped in the refrigerator. Scrub well, then use a sharp paring knife to peel. Remove the thin, fibrous layer beneath the skin. Cut into slices, wedges, cubes, or matchsticks. Try sprinkling jicama with lime, lemon, or orange juice.

KOHLRABI
Kohlrabi means cabbage turnip in German. The part of the kohlrabi most often eaten is the thickened part of the stem. This knob has a mild, sweet cabbage flavor and is very crisp. Unless young, kohlrabi is frequently too fibrous in texture to be worth preparing. Snip off the stalks and store them with the bulbs in a loosely closed plastic vegetable bag in the refrigerator crisper.

Kohlrabi has special affinities with white sauce, tomatoes, cream, cheese, chives, and parsley.

Unless very small, the bulbs must be peeled. Shredded, kohlrabi is wonderful in salads or on raw vegetable trays, or used to make Spicy Chinese Slaw, 161. The stalks are nippy, like radishes, and can be chopped for salads.

To microwave, spread 1 pound sliced kohlrabi in a 2-quart baking dish. Add ¹⁄₄ cup stock or lightly salted water, cover, and cook on high until tender but still crisp or completely tender, 6 to 8 minutes, stirring after 3 minutes. Let stand, covered, for 2 minutes.

4 to 8 servings
I. Wash:

16 small kohlrabi
Cut off the stalks, if attached, and cut into 1-inch pieces. Peel the knobs and slice ¹⁄₄ inch thick. Drop the slices and the stalks into a pot of rapidly boiling water and cook, uncovered, until barely tender, about 10 minutes. Drain and toss with:

Butter or olive oil
Drops of fresh lemon juice or vinegar
Salt and black pepper to taste
II. Boil the stalks and knobs in separate pots, as above.

After draining well, chop the tops until very fine or puree in a food processor. Combine them with the knobs. Prepare:

White Sauce I, 550

Add, if desired:

(A grating of nutmeg)

When the sauce is smooth and hot, add the kohlrabi.

ABOUT LEEKS

Looking like enormous scallions with flat leaves, leeks are part of the onion family, milder and sweeter than any others in the clan. Leeks, like other onion types, make a wonderful seasoning. When pureed in soups and stews, they add thickening as well as flavor. They may also be cooked as a side dish. Because they grow buried in dirt, ➤ they must be carefully washed to free the interlacing leaves from grit. Only the white portion and the pale green portion of the leaves are used. Store in an open plastic bag in the refrigerator crisper.

To wash, cut off and discard the dark green leaves. Trim off the roots, leaving the root pad attached. Starting at the leaf end, split the leek lengthwise two-thirds of the way toward the root; or, if cooking the leek in halves, split all the way. Hold the leek under running water, spreading the layers with your fingers, until all grit is washed away.

Leeks are compatible with many foods, but they taste especially good with lemon, butter, cheese, cream, fennel, potatoes, garlic, ham, dill, nutmeg, parsley, and chives.

To microwave, cut 6 to 8 leeks in half lengthwise and place in a baking dish. Salt lightly and add $1/4$ cup water or stock. Cover and cook on high for 8 to 10 minutes, stirring after 4 minutes. Let stand, uncovered, for 2 minutes before serving.

Pressure-cook whole leeks 2 to 4 minutes, depending on size, at 15 pounds pressure.

BRAISED LEEKS

4 servings

These leeks can be served with a simple finishing touch of olive oil or butter and chopped herbs, turned into a succulent gratin, grilled, or served cold with a mustard or shallot vinaigrette. The leftover braising liquid is excellent to use in risottos and soups.

Bring to a simmer in a large skillet:

**3 cups chicken stock or broth or 3 cups water
plus 1 teaspoon salt**

Trim, halve lengthwise, and wash, above:

4 large or 6 medium leeks

Add the leeks to the simmering liquid, cover, and simmer until tender when the cut sides are pierced with a knife, about 15 minutes. Turn the leeks several times as they cook so that they do not dry out.

When done, carefully remove each leek, draining off the excess liquid, and place cut side up on a platter. Drizzle or sprinkle over the top:

**Vinaigrette, 572, butter, extra-virgin olive oil,
or herb-flavored olive oil**
Chopped chervil, chives, tarragon, and/or parsley
Salt and black pepper to taste

CREAMY LEEKS

4 servings

Melt in a large skillet over medium-low heat:

$2^{1}/_{2}$ tablespoons butter

Add and cook for 2 to 3 minutes:

4 cups julienned leeks (about 3 large leeks)

Add:

**1 cup chicken stock or broth or 1 cup water
plus $1/2$ teaspoon salt**
1 sprig fresh thyme or $1/4$ teaspoon dried thyme

Cover and simmer until the leeks are tender, about 5 minutes. Uncover, increase the heat to medium-high, and add:

$1/4$ cup dry white wine

Boil until the liquid is reduced by half, 10 to 15 minutes. Stir in:

**2 tablespoons heavy cream
($1/2$ teaspoon curry powder or a pinch of grated
or ground nutmeg)**

Cook until the cream is absorbed. Season to taste with:

Salt and black pepper

If you used curry, serve the leeks garnished with:

Finely snipped chives

If you used nutmeg, serve with:

Chopped parsley or chervil

LEEKS VINAIGRETTE

4 servings

Use thin leeks for this classic French first course. The cooking liquid is turned into a mustard vinaigrette.

Have ready:

16 slender leeks (about $3/4$ inch thick)

Heat in a large skillet over medium-high heat until hot but not smoking:

$1/4$ cup olive oil

Add the leeks and cook, turning, until golden brown, about 10 minutes. Stir in:

1 cup chicken stock or broth
$1/4$ cup dry red wine

Cook, covered, turning occasionally, until the leeks are tender when pierced, about 8 minutes. Transfer to a serving platter. Add to the skillet:

$1/4$ cup chicken stock or broth
2 teaspoons red wine vinegar, or to taste

Cook, stirring, about 3 minutes. Remove from the heat and stir in:

2 teaspoons minced parsley
1 teaspoon Dijon mustard
Salt and black pepper to taste

Pour the vinaigrette over the leeks and let cool. Serve at room temperature, garnished with:

Snipped chives

ABOUT COOKED LETTUCE

In their enthusiasm, home gardeners often find themselves with sudden surpluses of lettuce and wish they had rabbits instead of children—failing to realize that a crisp nibble is not the only approach to this vegetable. Try these delectable alternatives after making sure that the leaves at hand are not bitter: Cook lettuce as a cream soup, 143; cream it like Spinach, 305; cook with peas, 256; stuff it like Cabbage, 263; or use to wrap whole fish or fillets for steaming. For more information on lettuces, see Salads, 152.

BRAISED LETTUCE

6 servings

A highly flavored and unexpected vegetable to serve with roasted meats.

Combine in a large skillet and cook, uncovered, over low heat for 10 minutes:

**1 thick or 2 thin slices bacon (about 2 ounces),
    finely diced, or 2 tablespoons olive oil**
³/₄ cup diced onions
³/₄ cup diced carrots

Meanwhile, drop into a large pot of boiling water and cook for 2 minutes:

**3 large heads butter lettuce, washed and outer
    leaves removed**

Drain, then cut lengthwise in half.

Set the lettuces cut side down over the vegetables and add enough water to come slightly less than halfway up the sides. Season to taste with:

Salt and black pepper

Bring to a boil, then reduce the heat, cover, and simmer for 15 minutes.

Remove the lettuce with a slotted spoon to a warmed platter. Keep warm. Boil down the liquid, uncovered, over high heat to a syrupy sauce, and pour over the lettuce.

ABOUT LOTUS ROOT

The lotus plant is a tropical water lily. Its buds, flowers, leaves, and seeds can all be eaten. Blanch the ¹/₂-inch oval seeds first and push out the bitter center portion with a wooden pick. Use these vitamin-rich seeds in soups or stews, or in sweet dishes. The leaves, either fresh or dried, make vegetable, meat, or rice wrappings. But it is the crisp stem or root that is most important. Plump, oblong, and jointed, it is perforated with holes—a crosswise slice looks like Swiss cheese and can be stir-fried or stuffed and steamed. Lotus roots are in Asian markets year-round. Select firm, buff-colored pieces without soft spots, blemishes, or bruises. Size has no effect on texture or flavor. Store the roots in a cool, dark place, as you would potatoes. The flesh darkens rapidly when exposed to the air, so have a bowl of acidulated water, 957, ready. Peel off the skin, then slice and drop into the water. Cook quickly.

STIR-FRIED LOTUS ROOT

4 servings

Cook in a saucepan of boiling water for 12 minutes, or until softened:

2 cups sliced peeled lotus root (8 ounces)

Drain. Heat in a large skillet over medium-high heat:

2 tablespoons vegetable oil

Add and stir-fry, 242, for 30 seconds:

1 tablespoon chopped peeled fresh ginger
2 scallions, chopped

Add the lotus, along with:

2 tablespoons dry sherry
1 tablespoon soy sauce
1 teaspoon toasted sesame oil
1 teaspoon sugar
¹/₄ teaspoon crushed red pepper flakes

Cook, stirring until the sauce thickens, about 5 minutes. Garnish with:

Sesame seeds, toasted, 1001
Chopped scallions

ABOUT MUSHROOMS

There is nothing simple about these uncomplicated-looking fungi. For example, although they're mostly water, they have more protein and vitamin B than most plants. For another, they manage to contribute both elegance and earthiness to any dish. They gratify many of us, too, with their almost total lack of calories. But they trick us, while cooking, with their sly habit of absorbing considerable amounts of butter, oil, or cream.

In addition to common button mushrooms, several wild mushrooms are now cultivated and available in specialty groceries and supermarkets. When a costly mushroom is needed to flavor a dish, buy one or two, depending on the intensity of its flavor, then fill in with neutral-tasting button mushrooms. **White button,** or commercial, mushrooms are rounded, plump, creamy, and quite mild. If they are very small, use them whole.

Wild mushrooms are more flavorful than cultivated mushrooms. **Chanterelles,** or **girolles,** resemble a curving trumpet. They are available in grocery stores and by foraging for them. See below for foraging information. Their golden or orange-brown caps and slender stems can hint of apricots or be delicately earthy. They have an affinity with cream, whether over toast, pasta, chicken, or polenta. The similarly shaped black mushrooms variously called **black trumpets, horns of plenty,** or **trumpets of death** are closely related and similar in taste but have thinner flesh. They too are available in grocery stores and by foraging. Both are gathered from summer into winter. There is a slightly toxic (causes nausea) look-alike known as a **Jack O'Lantern,** so ➤ take care not to pick the orange, trumpet-shaped mushrooms that grow on wood.

Cremini, or Italian browns, are the same as button mushrooms, only grown outdoors and bigger. They have light brown caps and more developed flavor.

Enoki are as slender as bean sprouts with tiny dots of caps. They are a pretty salad ingredient, adding a faintly sweet taste. They are also delicious barely heated and served in broth. To use, trim off the spongy base and separate the strands.

Morels are small, with dark brown conical, spongelike caps, and are available in specialty grocery stores and by foraging in the spring. There are black and yellow morels, which are both edible and highly prized. There is a false morel that is very poisonous, but it doesn't look that similar to its edible cousin. The honeycombed surface that allows morels to soak up sauces can also harbor sand and tiny creatures. Rinse morels in a bowl of water, being sure to pat them dry thoroughly before using. Morels have a special affinity with tender young vegetables.

Oyster mushrooms may be cultivated or wild. They grow in clusters of small fan-shaped caps with short stems, cream colored to grayish brown. Their texture is smooth, and their flavor can have a touch of the sea.

Porcini, also called **cèpes** or **boletes,** look something like large button mushrooms with very thick stalks and reddish-brown caps. They are among the tastiest of all mushrooms, something to enjoy simply in a risotto or sauté of mixed mushrooms. Brush large ones with olive oil and lemon juice and broil or grill as you would meat.

Portobellos are cultivated mushrooms, cremini grown large. They are generous in size (up to 6 inches wide), meaty, and robustly flavored. Their open gills and large flat caps make them naturals for grilling and broiling. They are also useful in sautés.

Shiitakes are brown or brown-black and umbrella shaped. They are cultivated on logs and have a distinctive earthy taste. Save the tough stems for stock, 114.

Wood or **cloud ear** mushrooms are the dark, very thin, almost crunchy mushrooms that give so many Chinese dishes a subtle woodsy taste. Unlike other fresh mushrooms, these should look damp. They are available in Asian markets and some supermarkets.

Choose mushrooms that are heavy for their size, with dry, firm caps and stems—nothing damp or shriveled, no dark or soft spots—and all close to the same size. If the gills are open, the mushrooms are more mature and their flavor will be stronger, and with a wild mushroom, this may be a plus. Open-gilled mushrooms should be used as soon as possible. To store, wrap unwashed mushrooms in a loosely closed paper bag or wrap loosely in paper towels. Leave packaged mushrooms unopened. Store on a refrigerator shelf, not in the crisper (too much moisture hastens spoilage), for 1 or 2 days.

Wipe mushrooms with a damp cloth to clean. Or, if they are truly grimy, rinse them quickly under cold running water and pat dry. Never soak fresh mushrooms—their delicate tissues absorb water. If desired, slice $1/8$ inch off the bottom of the stems. If only caps are called for in a recipe, cut the stems off flush with the cap, but do not discard the flavorful stems. Either chop them fairly fine, toss

them until lightly browned in a little butter, and add them to the dish or use within a day for making stock, 114, or (except for shiitake stems) in Duxelles, 284.

Mushrooms go well with cream, lemon, garlic, black pepper, shallots, onions, cheese, peas, dill, chervil, parsley, tarragon, basil, oregano, and capers. A channeled button or white mushroom is a fine garnish. To carve curving lines on the rather firm but spongy-textured mushroom evenly with a sharp knife requires considerable skill, but the point of a curved grapefruit knife makes it quick and easy.

Dried mushrooms add intense mushroom flavor to a sauce, soup, stew, or gravy. To reconstitute, soak dried mushrooms in hot water to cover until softened, at least 15 minutes, then lift out of the soaking liquid, and remove the hard stems. Strain the soaking liquid through a sieve lined with a damp coffee filter, paper towel, or cheesecloth to remove sand or grit. Both the softened mushrooms and soaking liquid can be used. ➤ Three ounces dried mushrooms reconstituted equals 1 pound fresh.

FORAGING FOR WILD MUSHROOMS

If you plan to forage for wild mushrooms, ➤ be aware that a number of poisonous mushroom types, during various stages of development, resemble edible forms. The quite innocent-looking and rather widely distributed **amanitas** include varieties so deadly that they are frequently assumed to have furnished the murderous potions so useful to the princely houses of the early Renaissance. Although many mushrooms are poisonous, few are deadly; and many more simply don't taste very good. In sober truth, though, ➤ there is no simple way to identify harmless mushrooms and other related fungi. Even the experts often prefer to examine up to ten specimens of a single variety before announcing a verdict.

The novice should remember that there are bold mushroom hunters and old mushroom hunters, but no bold old mushroom hunters, and begin his or her collecting with a safe and obvious—if not very thrilling—family like the **puffballs,** which have neither stems nor gills. They are edible if they grow above ground and the flesh inside is white throughout. *Lycoperdon giganteum* varies from marble to watermelon size, and *Lycoperdon craniforme* resembles a skull slightly shriveled even when in prime eating condition. If you are a novice forager, it is always best to go the first time with an experienced true expert and a good field guide. Then stick to picking only those mushrooms you can identify 100 percent. Wild mushrooms should not be eaten raw.

BECKER PORTOBELLO PIZZAS

If the caps you have are small, these are wonderful appetizers; if large, a main course.
Preheat the oven to 350°F. Lightly oil a baking sheet. Remove the stems from:

   Portobello mushrooms

Arrange the mushrooms stem side up on the baking sheet. Layer the caps with:

Finely chopped garlic
Thinly sliced plum tomatoes
Diced smoked ham or hard salami

Top with:

Grated Parmesan, Romano, or provolone
Black pepper
**A sprinkling of thyme, oregano, or basil, preferably
    fresh chopped leaves**

Bake until the mushrooms are softened, about 30 minutes. Then place under the broiler until the cheese is melted and lightly browned.

GRILLED MUSHROOMS

6 servings

The best mushrooms for grilling are portobellos and shiitakes.

Prepare a medium-hot grill fire. Remove the stems from:

**6 large portobello mushrooms or 12 large shiitake
    mushrooms**

Brush the caps on both sides with:

Olive oil

Season with:

Salt and black pepper to taste

Place the mushrooms stem side up and grill, turning once, until tender, 5 to 8 minutes each side. Place on a large platter and garnish with:

2 tablespoons chopped parsley

Grill or toast:

6 or 12 thick slices Italian bread

Rub with:

2 peeled garlic cloves

Brush lightly with:

Olive oil

Arrange the toast around the mushrooms, or place 1 mushroom on each slice of toast.

SAUTÉED MUSHROOMS

4 servings

Thinly slice to uniform thickness:

1 pound any fresh mushrooms

Heat in a very large skillet over high heat until hot:

2 tablespoons butter
1 tablespoon vegetable oil

or:

3 tablespoons clarified butter, 557

Add the mushrooms and shake the pan so the mushrooms are coated, without scorching. Add:

(1 garlic clove, peeled)

Cook over medium-high heat, uncovered, shaking the pan frequently. At first the mushrooms will seem dry and will absorb the fat. Continue to shake the pan for 3 to 4 minutes, depending on the size of the slices, until the mushrooms begin to color and release their juice. Remove the garlic, if you used it. (If you are holding the mushrooms

to add to other food, do not cover, as this will draw out their juices.) Season to taste with:

Salt and black pepper

If using as a garnish or vegetable, serve on:

Toast rounds
Grilled tomatoes or eggplant

or on a bed of:

Puree of Peas, 290

CREAMED MUSHROOMS

4 servings

A very rich side dish or sauce, or an opulent first course when spooned over toast.

Heat in a large skillet over medium heat:

2 tablespoons butter
2 tablespoons olive oil

Add and cook, stirring, until translucent, about 5 minutes:

$^1/_2$ cup finely diced onion

Add:

1 pound any fresh mushrooms, thinly sliced

Increase the heat to medium-high and cook, stirring often, until the mushrooms release and then reabsorb their juices, about 5 minutes. Add:

1 cup heavy cream or crème fraîche
2 garlic cloves, minced
**1$^1/_2$ teaspoons fresh thyme leaves or $^1/_4$ to
    $^1/_2$ teaspoon dried thyme**
Salt and black pepper to taste

Reduce the heat to medium and simmer until the sauce is slightly thickened. Taste and adjust the seasonings, then add:

1 tablespoon chopped parsley

MUSHROOM RAGOUT

4 servings

Serve over pasta, polenta, rice, garlic-rubbed croutons, or in popovers. For more intense flavor, soak $^1/_2$ ounce dried mushrooms, then chop and add with the fresh mushrooms; use the strained soaking water for part of the liquid.

Heat in a large saucepan over medium-high heat:

1 tablespoon olive oil

Add and cook, stirring, until golden, about 6 minutes:

1 onion, finely chopped

Remove the onion to a bowl. Heat in the same pan over medium heat:

1 tablespoon olive oil

Add and cook until they begin to release their liquid:

1 pound any fresh mushrooms, thickly sliced

Add the onion, along with:

2 garlic cloves, finely chopped
**1 teaspoon chopped fresh rosemary or $^1/_4$ teaspoon
    dried rosemary**
Salt and cracked black peppercorns to taste

Cook until the mushrooms begin to brown, another 3 to 4 minutes. Stir in:

1 tablespoon tomato paste

Increase the heat to high and cook, stirring, for 1 to 2 minutes more. Add:

1½ cups vegetable or chicken stock or broth or water

Reduce the heat to medium-low and simmer for 10 minutes. Gradually stir in:

2 tablespoons cold butter, cut into pieces

Stir in:

1½ teaspoons balsamic vinegar

Garnish with:

(Grated Parmesan)

Chopped parsley

DEEP-FRIED MUSHROOMS

4 servings

Choose mushrooms with 1- to 1½-inch caps.

Please read Deep-Frying Vegetables, 243.

Cut off the stems ¼ to ½ inch below the caps:

1 pound white button mushrooms

Sprinkle with:

Fresh lemon juice to taste

Salt to taste

Dip in:

Fritter Batter for Vegetables, Meat, and Fish, 658

and deep-fry in oil heated to 365°F until golden brown. You may hold the mushrooms, covered with a paper towel on a baking sheet, for a very short time in a 200°F oven. Just before serving, dust with:

Chopped parsley or thyme

Serve with:

Tartar Sauce, 581

BROILED STUFFED MUSHROOM CAPS

4 small servings

Place the broiler rack 2 to 4 inches from the heat source and preheat the broiler. Remove the stems from:

12 medium button or cremini mushrooms

Brush with:

Melted butter or olive oil

Season to taste with:

Salt

Broil stem side down for 2½ minutes. Remove from the broiler, turn over, and fill the caps with any one of the following:

Cream cheese, or fresh goat cheese mixed with minced garlic and herbs

Snail Butter, 559

Maître d'Hôtel Butter, 559

Shrimp or Lobster Butter, 559

Creamed Spinach, 305

Broil until the filling is hot and bubbling, another 2 minutes. Serve plain or on:

(Thin slices of toast)

DUXELLES

About ½ cup

This mushroom flavoring is delicious in scrambled eggs or omelets, stuffed under the skin of chicken, folded into mashed potatoes, or even on toast. It is important to squeeze all the moisture out of the chopped mushrooms, or they will not brown properly.

Chop very fine or pulse in a food processor until they resemble coarse sand:

8 ounces mushrooms

Squeeze about ¼ cup of the mushrooms at a time in dampened cheesecloth or a thin cotton towel, wringing them very hard to extract their juices. The mushrooms will be in a solid lump if you have squeezed hard enough.

Heat in a medium skillet over medium-high heat until the foam subsides:

1½ tablespoons butter

1 teaspoon vegetable oil

Add and cook briefly, until softened:

2 tablespoon finely minced shallots or scallions (white part only)

Add the mushrooms and cook, stirring often, until they have begun to brown and there is very little liquid left, 5 to 6 minutes. Stir in:

1 tablespoon dry sherry or Madeira

Cook until completely evaporated. Add:

(¼ cup heavy cream)

Salt and black pepper to taste

Pinch of dried thyme or grated or ground nutmeg

Let cool. Refrigerate in a covered container for up to 10 days or freeze for up to 3 months.

BECKER DUXELLES

About 1 cup

An especially luxurious variation.

Prepare **Duxelles, above,** using **2 tablespoons butter** and **3 tablespoons olive oil.** Substitute **½ cup very finely chopped onion** for the shallots and cook until translucent. Add **2 garlic cloves, minced.** Omit the dry sherry, and add **2 tablespoons port or dry red wine, ½ teaspoon black pepper, (¼ teaspoon grated lemon zest),** and **(salt).**

TRUFFLES

So precious are these nubbly, odd-looking fungi that in southern Europe, where they are found, they are usually locked in a safe until they can be sold. Truffles, an underground flowering of a fungus typically harvested from around oak or hazelnut trees, defy cultivation. They are rooted out by trained pigs or dogs. Too bad we haven't invented a truffle Geiger counter, but we know in general where to start digging—truffles are symbiotic with oaks. And another hint: the season is October to March. There are said to be at least 70 species of truffles in all, but in the culinary canon the only two that really matter are the **black truffle** (*Tuber melanosporum*), harvested primarily in France and a bit in Italy and Spain, and the **white truffle**

(*Tuber magnatum pico*), found mostly in the Piedmont region of Italy. The two types are vastly different in character: Black truffles have a nutty character and a faint but distinct aroma; they are usually cooked or at least marinated or macerated (typically in Cognac) before use. Black truffles are often added to pâtés and terrines (especially of foie gras) and are frequently combined with eggs and potatoes. White truffles are positively pungent. In Italy, it is against the law to carry them on public transportation. White truffles are almost never cooked but instead are shaved raw over pasta, risotto, fonduta (the Piemontese version of fondue), egg dishes, and salads. They are often stored (briefly) nestled in closed containers of risotto rice, to which they impart a vivid truffle flavor; the truffle can then be used elsewhere, as it does not give all its flavor to the rice. Fragments are often used to flavor olive oil; a few drops can impart quite a bit of truffle flavor. The terms **Périgourdine, Piémontaise,** and **Lucullus** are often applied to truffled dishes.

Less expensive than classic black and white truffles are the so-called **summer truffle** (*Tuber aestivum*), a pleasant but mild-flavored black variety, and a musky white variety (*Tuber gibbosum*), sometimes called **Oregon truffle,** found in northern California and southern Oregon.

Truffles sold in jars or cans vary widely in quality but can be quite good. If you are so fortunate as to be able to buy a fresh truffle, choose one that is firm to the touch, with a pronounced aroma. Spongy, bland-smelling truffles are old. *To clean fresh truffles,* brush them lightly with a soft kitchen brush or wipe them gently with a soft cloth. Do not wash them unless they are coated with dirt.

Place thin slices of truffle on the food to be cooked with them and store overnight in a closed container in the refrigerator. Add truffles to dishes at the end of cooking or after cooking.

ABOUT OKRA

Okra is the young seedpod of a plant related to hollyhocks and hibiscus. It can be cooked whole or sliced, with distinctly different results. Whole pods, stems removed, may be steamed or sautéed for just 3 to 5 minutes. The pods emerge tender but still crisp. Alternatively, for soup or stew, the pods may be cut into slices so they release their sweet mucilaginous sap for a natural thickening.

Okra is in the market year-round. If possible, choose pods no more than 2 inches long. Pods should be heavy for their size, plump, and blemish free, with stems intact. Store up to 3 days in a closed plastic bag in the vegetable crisper. Wash and dry okra before cooking. *To serve whole,* trim off the stem, being careful not to cut a hole in the pod, exposing the seeds. *To slice,* cut off the whole top end and slice. Do not cook okra in an unlined aluminum, iron, or copper pot.

Okra goes well with tomatoes, peppers, onions, garlic, ham, hot sauce, curry powder, and lemon, lime, or vinegar. Pickling okra reduces its sticky juices.

Pressure-cook okra cut into 1-inch pieces 4 minutes at 15 pounds pressure.

STEWED OKRA

2 to 3 servings
Wash and cut off the stems:
   2 cups okra (7 ounces)
Add ⅛ inch of water to a large skillet and bring to a boil. Add the okra and simmer, covered, until tender, about 5 minutes. Drain if necessary, and season to taste with:
   Salt and black pepper
Serve hot with:
   2 tablespoons butter
   (Dash of hot pepper sauce)
or:
   Hollandaise Sauce, 560
Or cool and toss with:
   Vinaigrette, 572

FRIED OKRA

10 to 12 servings
In a medium bowl, combine:
   ½ cup cornmeal
   ½ teaspoon salt
   ½ teaspoon garlic powder or onion powder
   ¼ teaspoon cayenne
   ⅛ teaspoon ground black pepper
Dredge:
   ½ pound whole okra
in:
   ¼ cup all-purpose flour
Dip in:
   1 egg beaten with 1 teaspoon water
Then dip into cornmeal mixture. Heat to 365°F in a large skillet:
   2 inches vegetable oil
Add okra to oil in batches, frying until golden, about 2 minutes. Remove okra with a slotted spoon and drain on paper towels. Serve with:
   Green Tomato Chutney, 951, Ranch Dressing, 576,
      or Creamy Horseradish Dressing, 578

ABOUT ONIONS

An elderly cousin of ours maintained that onions are the secret of health; to which our grandfather liked to rejoin, "But how on earth can you keep the secret?" For various suggestions to disguise their outspokenness and exploit their potential, please read About Onions as Seasoning, 1002, where you will also find a full discussion of this marvelous family with the qualities each member contributes.

Poet Carl Sandburg contended that life itself is like an onion: It has a bewildering number of layers; you peel them off, one by one, and sometimes you cry. There are many shapes and sizes of onion, but generally only three colors—white, red, or yellow. Onions fall into one of two categories depending on when they are harvested: fresh or spring onions and storage or dry onions.

Fresh or **spring onions** are onions that were once harvested just in the spring but are now sold year-round as **green onions, scallions, bunching onions,** or **spring onions.** They are either picked when very young or are a variety of onion that does not form a bulb when grown. They have a soft flesh, small bulbs, long green stalks, and usually a mild or sweet taste. The green stalks as well as the white portion are edible. These varieties can be used uncooked, grilled, or sautéed. The white parts of these onions are a good substitution for shallots.

Storage or dry onions are lower in water and higher in sulfur than fresh or spring onions and store well when harvested in a cool, dry spot for months. Available year-round, storage onions have a firm flesh and dry, crackly outer skins. The flavor can be pungent and in general they're best if cooked before eating. **Yellow onions** are the most flavorful and preferable for general cooking uses. Yellow onions turn a rich brown and become sweeter and milder when cooked, giving dishes such as French Onion Soup, 129, its dark color and sweet flavor. Many people find them too pungent to eat raw. **White onions** are popular cooking onions, often called for in dishes in which yellow onions would be too strong. They're slightly more prone to mold than yellow onions, so store them in a dry, well-ventilated place. **Red onions** are sweet enough to eat raw, and they're often used to add color to salads and other dishes. They are also excellent grilled or lightly sautéed. Specific onion varieties include the milder **Bermuda onions,** which are white or yellow; **Spanish onions,** which are white or yellow; and the strong-flavored **globe onions,** red, white or yellow. **Pearl onions** or **cipolline** are a type of tiny storage onion, and are delicious cooked whole, pickled, added to stews, creamed, or glazed. *To peel pearl onions,* pour boiling water over them and let cool. Cut off the roots, pull off the skin, and then cut a shallow X in the root end.

Sweet onions are juicy and mild in flavor, best eaten raw or lightly cooked. These are the onions of choice for slicing raw on burgers and sandwiches and in salads. They have a higher water content and so don't store well. There are several different varieties, often named after the region in which they're grown: **Vidalia, Granos, Walla Walla, Sweet Imperial, Texas Spring Sweet, Oso Sweet,** and **Maui.**

To prepare onions without tears, you may drop them into rapidly boiling water for about 10 seconds, then dry and chill them, after which the skins should slip off easily. Or peel them under running water. To keep the irritants diluted and prevent tears, you can chop them in a food processor, but then it, of course, must be cleaned. A skilled wrist and a sharp knife are the best method to prevent tears.

Peel the onion, leaving the tuft at the root end intact; the root will prevent the onion from falling apart. Cut the onion in half from stem to stern. Place one half cut side down. Start slicing it perpendicular to the root end in $1/8$-inch parallel cuts, leaving about $1/2$ inch of the root end intact. Then turn your knife so the blade is parallel to the work surface and again make $1/8$-inch parallel incisions to the $1/2$-inch demarcation at the root end. Finally, make $1/8$-inch slices from the top perpendicular to the longitudinal slices, starting at the stem end of the onion. The onion will fall into dice. *To remove onion odors,* you may rub your hands—and the cutting board—with a slice of lemon or a little powdered mustard, then rinse in water.

Dicing an onion

When used to flavor a dish, onions are generally cooked in a small amount of fat or oil over moderate heat until tender and translucent but not browned, a process that takes about 5 to 7 minutes, depending on the size of the onion pieces. If you cook onions over low heat so that they wilt without browning, they are said to be **sweated.** At this stage, their taste is gentle but not sweet. **Browned** onions are cooked over moderate heat until golden, 10 to 15 minutes, depending on the amount. Be sure they are evenly sliced so they all cook at the same time, with none remaining raw and harsh. So-called caramelized onions are cooked very slowly for as long as 1 hour until they are soft and very brown, and half of their original volume. When browning or caramelizing, be careful not to allow the onions to turn black. This brings on an acrid flavor caused by the breakdown of their sulfur component.

Onions have affinities with sugar, cream, bacon, mushrooms, potatoes, cheese, tomatoes, oranges, walnuts, dill, caraway, thyme, sage, mint, parsley, and chervil.

STEAMED ONIONS
5 servings

Steam, 242, until tender, 30 minutes or more:
>   **10 small unpeeled yellow or white onions (about 1$1/2$ pounds total)**

Replenish water if necessary.

Peel, and then toss with:
>   **1 cup fresh buttered bread crumbs, 960**

or with:
>   **$1/4$ cup ($1/2$ stick) butter, melted**
>   **1 teaspoon sugar**
>   **$1/2$ teaspoon ground cinnamon or cloves**
>   **$1/2$ teaspoon salt**

CREAMED PEARL ONIONS

4 servings

This dish can be assembled 1 day ahead, covered, and re-frigerated, then baked when ready to serve.

Preheat the oven to 350°F. Drop into a large saucepan half-filled with cold water:

1 pound pearl onions

Bring to a boil and boil for 1 minute. Using a slotted spoon, remove the onions and peel, then return to the boiling water. Simmer until tender, about 10 minutes. Drain, reserving $1/3$ cup of the cooking liquid. Transfer the onions to a shallow greased 2-quart baking dish.

Melt in a small saucepan over medium heat:

$1^1/2$ tablespoons butter

Stir in:

$1^1/2$ tablespoons all-purpose flour

Cook, stirring occasionally, over low heat until fragrant but not colored, about 3 minutes. Add the reserved cooking liquid, along with:

$1/2$ cup milk

$1/2$ cup half-and-half or additional milk

$1/2$ teaspoon salt

$1/4$ teaspoon black or white pepper

($1/8$ teaspoon grated or ground nutmeg)

Bring to simmer and cook, whisking constantly, 3 minutes. Pour the mixture over the onions and sprinkle with:

(1 cup shredded Swiss; about 4 ounces)

Bake until bubbly, about 15 minutes.

OVEN- OR FIRE-BAKED WHOLE ONIONS

I. Preheat the oven to 375°F.

Peel:

Large yellow onions (6 ounces each)

Place on a rack in a baking pan over $1/4$ inch of water. Bake until very soft, about $1^1/2$ hours. Cut a slice from the root end of each onion, and remove and discard the outer shells. Pour over the onions:

Melted butter to taste

Season to taste with:

Salt and paprika

Cover with:

(Grated Parmesan or chopped parsley)

II. Please read about Fireplace or Hearth Cooking, 1060. Cook in a bed of embers for about 45 minutes:

Whole onions

The outer skin forms a protection. When the onions are tender, puncture the skin to let the steam escape. Scoop out the centers and season to taste with:

Salt and black pepper

Garnish with:

(Sour cream)

GRILLED SWEET ONIONS

4 servings

Large red onions can be used when sweet onions are un-available. These are great with hamburgers.

Prepare a medium-hot grill fire.

Peel and slice into 1-inch-thick rounds:

3 large sweet onions

Thread each slice onto a skewer so they will not fall apart.

Rub with:

$1/4$ cup olive oil

Salt and black pepper to taste

Grill until nicely browned, turning once, about 6 minutes each side. Remove the skewers. Serve plain or with:

Fresh Herb Vinaigrette, 572, Aïoli, 581,
or Lemon and Parsley Butter, 559

SAUTÉED ONIONS

2 to 4 servings

Cooked quickly over high heat, onions emerge lightly browned—crisp on the outside and moist on the inside—perfect for topping mashed potatoes, ham, burgers, or steak.

Heat in a large skillet over high heat:

2 tablespoons olive oil, butter, or a combination

Add:

4 medium yellow onions (about 1 pound total), halved and thinly sliced or cut into $1/2$-inch or larger squares

Cook, stirring frequently, until lightly browned around the edges, about 10 minutes. Season well with:

Salt and black pepper

(Dash of balsamic vinegar)

CARAMELIZED ONIONS

About 4 cups

Caramelized onions are the basis for many stews and sauces, and are an excellent side dish, topped with Parmesan cheese. These cook down to half their original volume and can be refrigerated for a few days or frozen.

Heat in a very large skillet over medium-high heat until the butter is melted:

2 tablespoons butter

2 tablespoons olive oil

Add:

3 pounds yellow or white onions, thinly sliced

Sprinkle with:

1 teaspoon salt

Cook, stirring constantly, 15 minutes. Reduce the heat to low and continue cooking, stirring occasionally, until the onions are soft and brown, about 40 minutes. If the residue from the juices has built up in the pan, add:

$1/2$ cup dry white wine or water

Stir and scrape the pan to dissolve the browned bits. They will immediately mix into the onions, darkening them further. Remove from the heat and season well with:

Salt and black pepper

(Grated Parmesan)

SCALLOPED ONIONS WITH CHEESE

6 servings

Peel and slice crosswise into ¼-inch rings:

6 large white Spanish or sweet onions (about 4 pounds)

Pour into a large skillet:

8 cups milk

Add the onions and bring to a simmer, then reduce the heat and simmer gently until tender, about 30 minutes. Drain. Meanwhile, preheat the oven to 350°F.

Place in a buttered baking dish:

4 slices buttered toast

Arrange the onions on the toast. Sprinkle with:

½ cup shredded American or Cheddar

Beat well in a small bowl:

1 large egg

1 cup milk

½ teaspoon salt

⅛ teaspoon paprika

Pour over the onions. Dot the top with:

1 tablespoon butter

Bake about 20 minutes, until bubbling. Sprinkle with:

Crumbled crisp cooked bacon

Chopped parsley

FRENCH-FRIED ONION RINGS

4 servings

Try dusting the hot onions with ground red pepper as well as salt. Please read about Deep-Fat Frying, 1046.

Peel, cut crosswise into ¼-inch slices, and separate into rings:

4 large white Spanish or sweet onions (about 3 pounds)

Combine:

1½ cups milk

1½ cups water

Soak the onions in the liquid for 1 hour. Remove the onion rings and drain on paper towels, then dredge in:

Fritter Batter for Vegetables, Meat, and Fish, 658

Pick up a group of the rings on a fork and let excess batter drip off; add them, one by one, to oil heated to 365°F, and fry until light brown. Drain on paper towels. Sprinkle with:

Salt

BAKED ONIONS STUFFED WITH SAUSAGE

4 servings

Peel, but do not cut off the stem or root ends:

4 large yellow onions or Spanish onions (about 2½ pounds)

Place in a large pot and add 4 quarts water. Add:

1½ tablespoons salt

Bring to a simmer, then reduce the heat and gently simmer, partially covered, until the onions are tender enough to be pierced by a skewer but still feel slightly resistant, 15 to 20 minutes. Remove the onions from the pot with a slotted spoon and let stand until cool enough to handle.

To hollow the onions, slice off the top quarter of each onion at the stem end, reserving the tops. Using a small knife or grapefruit spoon, make several cuts into the center of each onion, going about two-thirds of the way down to the bottom and cutting to within 3 or 4 of the outermost layers. When the center of the onion has been well scored and the interior layers feel loose, hollow out the center with a teaspoon and set aside, leaving a wall 3 layers (about ¼ inch) thick. Coarsely chop the centers, along with the reserved onion tops. If there is a hole in the wall of an onion, simply patch it with a piece scraped from the middle.

Position a rack in the center of the oven. Preheat the oven to 375°F. Butter a baking dish just large enough to hold the onions. Arrange the scooped-out onions in the baking dish.

Crumble into a medium skillet and brown well over medium heat:

½ cup (about 4 ounces) fresh pork sausage

Without draining off the fat, add the chopped onion tops and cook, stirring, until golden and very soft, about 10 minutes. Meanwhile, squeeze dry and finely chop:

One 10-ounce package frozen spinach, thawed, or 8 ounces fresh spinach leaves, steamed, 242

Add the spinach to the sausage mixture, reduce heat to low, and cook slowly for 5 minutes. Pour in:

⅔ cup heavy cream

Cook for about 1 minute more; the mixture should be quite thick. Remove from the heat and stir in:

3 to 4 tablespoons fresh bread crumbs, or enough to make the stuffing hold its shape on a spoon

Stir in:

⅛ teaspoon grated or ground nutmeg

(⅛ teaspoon ground sage)

Salt and black pepper to taste

Pile the sausage stuffing into the onions. Sprinkle with:

2 tablespoons fresh bread crumbs

1 tablespoon butter, cut into small pieces

Bake until lightly browned, 20 to 25 minutes. Let stand for a few minutes before serving.

HEARTS OF PALM

Not all palm "hearts" are edible. Most of those eaten in this country are taken from the palmetto, and the same variety furnishes almost all the canned product. The hearts are harvested while the palms are tiny. A whole trimmed palm heart resembles a large off-white carrot. It is composed of layers of rings, like an onion. The flavor of canned hearts, most commonly used, resembles that of canned artichoke hearts; fresh hearts taste something like asparagus.

Most fresh hearts are sent to market trimmed of their fibrous exterior layer. Select fresh hearts that are moist at both ends and have no signs of cracking, dehydration, or separation of layers. Hearts generally weigh between 2 and 3 pounds trimmed. Fresh hearts are very perishable, so store in a closed plastic bag in the refrigerator crisper.

Rinse fresh hearts, and, if necessary, peel away any fibrous material to reach the tender white heart. *To prepare raw for salads,* slice crosswise into rounds $^{1}/_{4}$ to $^{1}/_{2}$ inch thick and soak in ice water for 1 hour. Drain and pat dry. The crunchy pieces can be dressed with vinaigrette and served on a bed of greens or added to a mixed salad. For more ideas, see Salads, 152. To cook, steam, 242, the hearts whole until tender when pierced with a knife, 7 to 9 minutes. Slice and serve at once with a squeeze of lemon, a drizzle of melted butter or olive oil, and a little chopped parsley or garlic. Or drop into a bowl of ice water to stop the cooking, then slice and finish later in any way you would asparagus or artichoke hearts.

To roast, wrap the heart in heavy foil. Roast in a 400°F oven until tender, about 20 minutes. Peel off the outside layer. Slice the heart and serve with lemon juice and salt.

PARSLEY

There was a time when parsley, in some American households, was regarded mostly as a decorative plant—like asparagus fern—and was seldom used as an herb except for an occasional light sprinkling over boiled potatoes. Now we know, and appreciate, the refreshing taste that our parents may have been missing. **Curly parsley** is tightly bunched and bright green, while **Italian parsley** is dark green with flat leaves and a more pronounced flavor.

The so-called **Hamburg parsley,** or **turnip-rooted parsley,** can sometimes be found in markets. It makes an interesting change from more common root vegetables and is cooked similarly, 245.

DEEP-FRIED PARSLEY

Please read about Deep-Fat Frying, 1046. When parsley takes the following form, it is irresistible. Care is the watchword, though: ➤ It becomes limp if the fat is not hot enough, olive green if the fat is too hot. The finished result should be at once crisp and a bright dark green. To achieve both objectives, use at least 2 to 3 inches of fat and fry no more than 1 cup of parsley at a time. The parsley must first be carefully stemmed, washed, and placed between towels until absolutely dry.

Put in a frying basket:

    Tiny sprigs of curly parsley

Immerse the basket in fat that has been heated to between 400°F and 425°F and leave it 1 to 2 minutes, or until the hissing stops. Remove and drain on paper towels.

ABOUT PARSNIPS

Parsnips are a winter root vegetable. Like carrots, which they resemble, these cream-colored roots are prized for their sweetness. When cooked, they have a creamy texture, and they make a velvety puree (try mixing some with mashed potatoes, to accompany roast beef or pork). Select small to medium roots (large parsnips can have woody cores) that are unblemished. Store in a closed plastic bag in the refrigerator crisper.

Parsnips have affinities with cream, butter, tarragon, chives, hazelnuts, and nutmeg.

Peel with a vegetable peeler and trim the stem ends before using. The dense core will soften when cooked unless it is fibrous, in which case halve or quarter the parsnip to cut out and discard. Cut into cubes, slices, or matchsticks.

To microwave, follow the instructions for carrots, 266.

Pressure-cook parsnips at 15 pounds pressure for 10 minutes.

OVEN-BRAISED PARSNIPS
4 servings

Parsnips, which are drier than most root vegetables, turn chewy and tough when dry-roasted but stay moist when braised. Allow them to color a little at the end, once they are cooked.

Preheat the oven to 375°F.

Peel and quarter lengthwise:

    1$^{1}/_{2}$ pounds parsnips

Combine in a shallow baking dish with:

    $^{3}/_{4}$ cup water or chicken stock or broth
    2 tablespoons butter, cut into small pieces
    $^{1}/_{2}$ teaspoon salt

Cover and bake until tender, 20 to 25 minutes. Give the pan a shake once or twice during baking. Uncover, increase the oven temperature to 400°F, and bake until the parsnips begin to color, about 10 minutes more. Serve with:

    Black pepper to taste
    Chopped parsley, tarragon, or chives

FRENCH PARSNIPS

Prepare as for Carrots Vichy, 266.

GLAZED PARSNIPS
4 to 6 servings

For maple-glazed parsnips, add 3 tablespoons maple syrup at the end of cooking, and cook about 1 minute more.

Peel and cut in half crosswise:

    1$^{1}/_{2}$ pounds parsnips

Combine the parsnips in a large skillet with:

    1 cup water
    3 tablespoons butter
    2 teaspoons sugar
    1 teaspoon salt
    $^{1}/_{4}$ teaspoon white pepper

Bring to a simmer, then reduce the heat, cover, and simmer until tender, 10 to 15 minutes.

Uncover, increase the heat to high, and boil the cooking liquid down to a syrupy glaze that coats the parsnips, stirring often. Be careful not to scorch. If desired, toss with:

    (Chopped parsley)

PARSNIP PUREE

Prepare **Root Vegetable Puree, 245,** substituting **1 pound parsnips** for the carrots. Add **1 small, fresh piece of peeled**

fresh ginger. Remove the ginger before mashing the vegetables. Top with **Nut Butter, 558,** made with cashews.

ABOUT GREEN PEAS

For many people, lilacs and robins are welcome, cheering signs that spring is here once again. Good enough, certainly, but best of all is the appearance of peas, bright green, lightly sweet, and thoroughly delicious. Fresh green peas can be found in markets throughout the year but are at their peak from spring through early summer. Fresh peas come in two ways: those with an edible pod—such as snow peas and sugar snap peas—and those without, where only the pea, or seed, is eaten from the pod. When buying **green peas,** select medium-sized pods that are bright green, firm, and filled end to end with fat peas. Avoid those that are blemished and puffy. Store peas in a closed plastic bag in the refrigerator crisper.

To shell green peas, first rinse them. Snap off the stem and pull it down the stem side—a string will come with it, unlocking the pod. Press the pod at the seam, opening it, and the peas will pop out. No need to rinse them. ➤ One pound of well-filled pea pods will yield about 1¼ to 1½ cups hulled peas. Frozen peas are often the equal of fresh peas found in markets and can be substituted for fresh in any recipe. Peas go well with cream, mint, parsley, chervil, sage, thyme, carrots, onions, peanuts, mushrooms, and ham.

To microwave, place 2 cups fresh peas in a 1-quart baking dish. Add ¼ cup stock or lightly salted water, cover, and cook on high until tender, 4 to 6 minutes, stirring after 3 minutes. Let stand, covered, for 3 minutes. *Pressure-cook* peas 2 minutes at 15 pounds pressure.

Snow peas are thin and flat, cook very quickly, and are a staple of stir-fries. They are a nice addition to salads when blanched, then slivered. **Sugar snap peas** are plump because they contain peas of a good size. However, the pods are as sweet and tender as those of snow peas. Most sugar snap peas and snow peas must have their strings removed. Snow peas may need just the string removed from the seam side, but sugar snaps will probably need strings from both sides removed. *To microwave,* cook as for fresh peas.

In Asian markets and some grocery stores, look for a bin or box containing small dark green leaves on slender stalks, some with fine tendrils and white blossoms. These are **pea shoots,** the new growth of a variety of snow pea. Choose the smallest and brightest shoots with the thinnest stalks. Pea shoots are usually eaten raw as a garnish or in salad but can be briefly cooked as for any delicate green. They are perishable and are best used the day you bring them into the kitchen. To store, plunge the ends into a jar of water and refrigerate.

GREEN PEAS
2 servings

Young peas, with good reason, have always brought forth paeans of praise—but how to cope with the older ones,

with their often dismayingly tough skins? Try Braised Peas or Puree of Peas, below.
Wash, then shell:

1½ pounds green peas (2 to 2¼ to cups shelled)
Steam them, 242, or cook in a skillet in ⅛ inch boiling water. There is a tradition, which you may choose to follow, that one must add to peas:

(A pinch of sugar)
Two or three pods may also be cooked with the peas for flavor. Simmer 3 to 10 minutes, depending on the maturity of the peas, adding more water if the pan becomes dry. When the peas are tender, drain them if necessary. Remove the pods. Season with:

1 to 2 tablespoons butter or cream
(1 teaspoon chopped parsley or mint)
Salt and black pepper to taste

PUREE OF PEAS
2 servings

Cook:
One 10-ounce package frozen peas (2 cups)
Drain and puree in a food processor or blender with:
3 to 5 tablespoons heavy cream
For a smooth texture, force the puree through a sieve with the back of a spoon or rubber spatula. Season to taste with:

Salt
(Pinches of sugar)
(Minced mint)

PEAS AND CARROTS

Disdainfully dubbed "Keys and Parrots" by a cousin of ours, a devout antivegetarian, but a classic just the same. Combine in any proportion:

Hot cooked carrots, well drained
Hot cooked green peas, well drained
Pour over them:
Melted butter
Season with:
Salt and black pepper to taste
Sprinkle with:
Chopped parsley

PEAS AND MUSHROOMS

Prepare as for **Peas and Carrots, above,** substituting for the carrots **Sautéed Mushrooms, 283,** but omit additional butter.

STIR-FRIED SNOW PEAS
4 to 6 servings

This dish also can be made with sugar snaps; they will need to cook a bit longer. Please read about Stir-Frying Vegetables, 242.
Remove the stems and strings from:

1 pound snow peas

Heat a wok or large skillet over high heat. Add and heat until almost smoking:

1 tablespoon peanut oil or vegetable oil

Add:

1 tablespoon minced peeled fresh ginger

Stir-fry for 30 seconds, then add the peas and stir-fry vigorously until all are shiny and coated with oil. Sprinkle with:

1 tablespoon chopped lemon basil or regular basil
$^1/_2$ teaspoon salt

Stir-fry until the peas are hot, another minute or two.

PEAS WITH PROSCIUTTO AND ONIONS

4 to 6 servings

Heat in a large skillet over medium heat:

3 tablespoons olive oil

Add and brown lightly:

24 pearl onions, peeled

Add:

3 tablespoons water

Cover and cook over low heat until the onions are tender, about 5 minutes. Stir in:

2 cups fresh green peas or one 10-ounce package
frozen baby peas, thawed
4 ounces prosciutto or ham, finely diced
1 to 2 teaspoons water, if using fresh peas
Salt and black pepper to taste

Cover and cook until the peas are tender, 5 to 8 minutes if using fresh peas, 3 to 5 minutes if using frozen.

ABOUT PEPPERS

"Pepper" is one of the confusing designations so frequent in vegetable cookery. Is it a "pepper" or is it a "chile"? Aside from the bell pepper we treat as a vegetable, the words "pepper" and "chile" are used interchangeably. Chock-full of vitamin C, peppers add texture, vibrant color, and, often, heat to a dish. The larger, milder varieties are perfect for stuffing. Store fresh unwashed peppers in the refrigerator, wrapped in paper towels, for up to 2 weeks. ➤ Never overcook peppers, as they become bitter. Remember, ➤ a chile pepper grows hotter as it ripens.

The most common kind of sweet pepper, **bell peppers** can be dark green, red, bright orange, bright or pale yellow, or dark purple. Roasting changes their flavor and softens their flesh. The perfect stuffing pepper, bells are also used in soups, stews, salads, relishes, sauces, and casseroles. Fleshy sweet-to-hot **pimiento peppers** (also called pimientos) are usually available only in the red-ripe stage and commercially canned.

Anaheim peppers are light lime green to red, taste of bell peppers and apples, and are likely the ones you find in a can labeled "green chiles." Anaheims range from mild to hot, depending on the specific variety. They can be roasted, 292, and peeled and used in stews and sauces, stuffed, or eaten raw in salads. Dried, Anaheims are known as the **New Mexico chile.** Pale yellow to orange-red crisp **banana peppers** are sweet to very piquant, easy to grow, and hard to roast. Use raw or pickled.

Cayenne, the most commonly grown pepper in the world, is dried and kept whole, ground into powder for cooking and spice blends, or used in bottled hot sauces. Named for their large round pods, **cherry peppers** are usually pickled whole in their green and red stages. They range from mild to hot and have many seeds, a slightly sweet taste, and tough skin.

Reputed to be the hottest of all chiles, the lantern-shaped **habanero pepper** packs an incredible punch. Usually green, yellow orange, or bright orange, habaneros are used in salsas, sauces, and condiments. Fresh **jalapeños** are available virtually everywhere and vary from mild to very hot. (When mature jalapeños are smoked and dried, they are known as **chipotles.**) This bright green pepper is used in many dishes, from raw salsas to soups and stews, and even stuffed and fried.

Best known as the pickled pepper used in Italian dishes, **peperoncini** are mildly piquant pale green to red peppers that are rarely found fresh in markets but are popular with many home gardeners.

The **poblano pepper** is dark green and rich-tasting, with a varying amount of heat. Use them roasted and peeled in soups, sauces, and stews or whole as an edible vessel for pork or cheese filling, as in chiles rellenos. When dried, poblanos are usually called **ancho chiles.** The extremely hot **Scotch bonnet peppers** are bright yellow, orange, green, or red and can be distinguished from the habanero—the two are often confused—by their stouter shape and sweeter flavor. These flavorful chiles are used extensively in hot sauces and condiments. The tapered, bullet-shaped **serrano** is prized for its consistent heat level and pure, fresh chile taste. Mostly sold green, though greenish yellow to red peppers can sometimes be found, serranos are used fresh, pickled, or roasted. A staple in Mexican cooking, they are often simply called **chiles verdes,** or **green chiles.**

The pale green to yellow-orange to red hot **Tabasco pepper** is most often encountered commercially packed into vinegar as a condiment or as a hot sauce. Its heat is intense. There are many different peppers in the Asian markets labeled **"Thai peppers,"** perhaps the most common being the small, elongated, intensely hot, pointy green to red peppers sold with their stems attached.

To cut peppers into pieces, ➤ use a small sharp knife to cut around the stem. Lift out the top with the core and seeds. Slice off a bit of the bottom, then cut lengthwise down one side. Open the pepper into one flat piece. Set the pepper skin side down on the cutting surface, scrape away any remaining seeds, and cut away the membranes, then slice the pepper. To cut a pepper into rings, cut out the stem as above, then slice crosswise. Cut away the membranes and seeds from each slice.

Note: ➤ Chiles contain a substance called capsaicin, which can severely irritate your skin and eyes. ➤ Wear gloves when handling chiles, and wash your hands in soapy water immediately afterward.

ABOUT DRIED PEPPERS

Drying increases the heat of an already hot pepper and concentrates flavor. **Ancho peppers** are dried poblanos. **Chiles de Arbol** are fiery hot, pointy, and bright red, used in hot sauces and ground into powder. The round cranberry-red **cascabel peppers** are rich and spicy and perfect for salsas, sauces, soups, and stews. **Chipotle peppers** are dried smoked jalapeños. The smooth-skinned, dark, translucent cherry-red **guajillo pepper,** medium hot to very hot, is the workhorse of the Mexican kitchen, used in sauces, soups, stews, and moles. **Mulato chiles** are a very dark black red and are often confused with anchos. But once tasted, the difference is clear: These dried peppers are more intensely flavored and less sweet. The **New Mexico pepper** (called Anaheim when fresh) is the one most often strung in wreaths (*ristras*) or swags and is mild to hot. But these translucent-red chiles are not just for decoration; they are delicious in soups, stews, and sauces and make a wonderful pure ground chile powder. The nearly black **pasilla** adds a uniqueness (and medium amount of heat) to soups, stews, sauces, and moles. **Pequín chiles** are little red ovals that have relentless heat and are best in salsas and sauces or fried whole as a garnish.

To rehydrate dried chile peppers, toast or stove-roast first, below, if desired. ➤ Cover them with hot, not boiling, water, submerge them in the bowl with a saucer, and let them soak until soft, about 15 to 20 minutes. ➤ Longer soaking leaches out flavor. You can also use the soaking liquid in the recipe if appropriate, but taste it and make sure it is not bitter. To grind dried chiles, see 1007.

ABOUT ROASTING PEPPERS

Roasting fresh peppers removes the skin, softens the flesh, and adds a delicious smoky flavor. ➤ Once they are blistered, lay fresh peppers in a bowl and cover with plastic wrap or plate for 10 minutes. The remaining heat will create steam, which will loosen the skin. ➤ Do not rinse the peppers after roasting, because the smokiness lies at the surface. ➤ Rather, scrape off the skins with a knife. Since peppers are usually roasted whole, make a slit down one side and run the tip of a small knife around the stem. Remove the top—the core and seeds will come with it—then scrape away any remaining seeds and cut away the membranes. ➤ Roasting and peeling can be done a day or two in advance. Put the peppers in an airtight container and refrigerate. Roasted peppers can also be frozen for up to 1 month, but leave the skins on in that case and peel when thawed. Frozen peppers will lose texture but are good in sauces.

To roast fresh peppers in the oven, line a rimmed baking sheet or broiler pan with aluminum foil. Place the whole peppers on the foil and brush with olive oil. Broil, turning with tongs (forks pierce the skin and releases juices) as needed, until blistered or partially blackened all over. *To roast on the stovetop,* place whole peppers directly in the flames of a gas burner on its highest setting. ➤ Turn frequently and let the peppers blister all over or partially char to black. *To grill-roast fresh peppers,* set whole peppers on a rack over the ash-covered coals of a hot but dying fire—medium-high or high on a gas grill. Grill on the first side until blistered or charred, then flip, and repeat until the whole pepper is done. This can also be done on the hearth, 1060.

For small fresh chiles, roast in a dry cast-iron skillet or griddle over high heat. Shake or move them around the skillet or griddle until their skins are charred and blistered. These chiles are usually not peeled after roasting.

Many cooks quickly toast or stove-roast dried chiles before rehydrating. As in toasting bread, a bit of intense heat deepens the flavors. Put dried chiles in a dry cast-iron skillet or on a griddle. Cook whole chiles over medium heat. To expose more of the flesh to direct heat, press the chiles with a spatula, ➤ then turn and press again until you can smell them—this will take only a few seconds. When the pods are lightly browned in places, remove from the heat. When cool, break off the stems, shake out the seeds, and discard. For large dried chiles, first remove the stem, slit down one side, open the pod, shake out the seeds, and break the chiles into pieces that will lie flat. Then roast as for whole dried chiles.

GREEN PEPPERS AND ONIONS
4 servings

A sterling accompaniment to cold meat.
Heat in a large skillet over medium heat:

   3 tablespoons butter, ham or bacon fat, or olive oil
Add and cook, stirring, until softened, about 10 minutes:

   6 medium onions (about 1½ pounds total), thinly sliced
Add and cook, stirring, 5 minutes:

   3 large green bell peppers, cored, seeded, and cut into ¾-inch-wide strips
Add:

   2 tablespoons chicken stock or broth or water
   Salt and black pepper to taste
Cover and simmer until the onions are tender, about 10 minutes. Serve with, if desired:

   (Quick Tomato Sauce, 562)

ABOUT STUFFED PEPPERS

To prepare a whole fresh pepper for stuffing, slice off the top ½ inch, then scrape out seeds and membrane with a spoon. ➤ If the pepper will not stand straight, level the bottom by cutting a off thin slice—without creating a hole, or the juices and stuffing will run out. Huge peppers should be halved lengthwise through the stem. ➤ Do not remove the halved stem (it helps hold in the stuffing), but scrape out the seeds and membrane.

Steam the peppers on a rack over boiling water, 242,

until nearly tender, about 10 minutes. Proceed with your recipe. Or fill the pepper cases with desired ingredients (see Stuffings, 532). Bake in a 350°F oven until the filling is hot, 20 to 30 minutes. If you desire, cover the filling with Au Gratin I, II, or III, 961, and run briefly under the broiler until the top is golden.

STUFFED BELL PEPPERS
4 servings
An American classic. Create a vegetarian version by substituting ¹/₂ pound firm tofu, drained and crumbled, for the beef.
Preheat the oven to 375°F. Grease a baking dish in which the peppers will fit snugly. Prepare for stuffing, 292:
   4 medium bell peppers
Steam, 242, for 10 minutes. Set aside. Heat in a large skillet over medium heat:
   2 tablespoons olive or vegetable oil
Add and cook, stirring and breaking the beef up with a spoon, until it is lightly colored, about 10 minutes:
   8 ounces ground beef
   ¹/₂ cup finely chopped onion
   ¹/₂ teaspoon dried thyme
Add:
   1 cup cooked rice
   1 medium tomato, peeled, 311, seeded, and finely chopped, or ¹/₂ cup canned diced tomatoes, drained
   2 large eggs, well beaten
   1 garlic clove, minced
   1 teaspoon dried basil or oregano, crumbled
   (Worcestershire sauce or crushed red pepper flakes to taste)
   Salt and black pepper to taste
Fill the peppers with the meat mixture and set them in the baking dish. Sprinkle over the tops:
   Au Gratin II, 961
Bake until the peppers are tender and the filling hot and firm, about 25 minutes. If necessary, brown the tops under the broiler.

BELL PEPPERS STUFFED WITH RICE
4 servings
Preheat the oven to 350°F. Oil a baking dish that will hold the peppers snugly.
Prepare for stuffing, 292:
   4 medium bell peppers
Steam, 242, until nearly tender, about 10 minutes. Set aside.
Combine in a bowl:
   1¹/₂ cups cooked rice
   ¹/₂ cup grated or shredded Parmesan, Cheddar, or Monterey Jack, or more if desired
   ¹/₂ cup stock or broth, heavy cream, or tomato sauce
   ¹/₂ teaspoon curry powder, dried basil, or dried oregano

   Salt and black pepper to taste
   (A pinch of ground red pepper)
Fill the pepper cases. Bake until the filling is piping hot, about 25 minutes.
If desired, cover the tops with:
   (Au Gratin I or II, 961)
and brown briefly under a broiler.

BAKED CHILES RELLENOS WITH CHEESE
6 servings
Wrap a chile relleno in a large warm flour tortilla for a Tex-Mex sandwich.
Preheat the over to 350°F.
Roast, 292:
   6 medium poblano peppers
Peel the charred skin from the peppers. Make a long slit in the side of each pepper and carefully remove the seeds and veins. Pat dry and place on a baking sheet.
Mix together:
   2 cups coarsely shredded queso fresco, Monterey Jack, or mild Cheddar (about 8 ounces)
   2 large scallions, minced
Form the cheese mixture into 6 ovals, then stuff an oval into the center of each pepper and gently reshape them.
Bake for about 15 minutes to thoroughly heat through.
Serve with:
   Warmed salsa
   Chopped cilantro

ABOUT PLANTAINS
This 9- to 12-inch variety of banana, unlike its smaller cousins, ➤ must be cooked before eating. Plantains can be prepared in their green state as well as when semi-ripe or quite mature, when the skins often become black and mottled. Cooked chopped ripe plantains make a more than acceptable component of soups, stews, and omelets.
   Peel and then remove the fibrous strings from plantains before cooking, as they will darken. Green plantains are very hard. Peel them wearing gloves or under running water to keep from staining your hands. Yellow or half-ripe plantains are creamy and have a delicate taste. They are best boiled and served like potatoes. Soft brown to black fully ripe plantains, which taste like bananas, are best baked whole or cut into thick slices and fried. Plantains can be ripened at room temperature. Available year-round, plantains have affinities with butter, lime juice, rice, and tropical fruits.

PLANTAINS
I. Cut into 2-inch-thick pieces:
   Green or yellow half-ripe plantains (unpeeled)
Slit the skin along each of its ridges, then pull off the peel, starting from a corner of each section. Place at once in rapidly boiling water, and simmer 30 minutes. Season with salt and pepper and serve with butter.

II. Cut off the top and bottom, slit the skin lengthwise, and peel:

   Brown-black ripe plantains

Arrange in a single layer in a greased baking dish. Bake in a 400°F oven until the flesh is fork-tender, about 40 minutes. Serve with butter as you would a baked potato, also sprinkling with fresh lime juice and hot pepper sauce, if desired.

GOLDEN SAUTÉED PLANTAIN SLICES

4 servings

Best served hot, these can be reheated if needed in a skillet or the oven. Especially good with fried chicken, baked ham, or Mojo, 566.

Cut off the ends, slit the skin lengthwise, and peel:

   4 small ripe plantains

Cut into ¼-inch slices.

Heat in a large nonstick skillet over medium-low heat:

   2 tablespoons butter

   1 tablespoon vegetable oil

Add only as many plantain slices as will fit in a single layer and cook, turning once, until golden on both sides, 6 to 8 minutes. Remove to a plate and keep warm while you fry the remaining slices.

Sprinkle with:

   Coarse salt to taste

   (Black pepper to taste)

   (Fresh cilantro)

DEEP-FRIED PLANTAINS (TOSTONES)

6 servings

Serve these with rice, 354, beans, 256, and any type of roast chicken or pork. Don't forget the hot sauce. Please read about Deep-Fat Frying, 1046.

Cut off the ends, slit the skin lengthwise, and peel:

   4 small brown-black ripe plantains

Cut into ¼-inch-slices.

Heat to 325°F in a deep fryer or deep heavy pot:

   2 inches vegetable oil

Deep-fry the plantain slices a few at a time until golden, about 3 minutes per side. Drain well on paper towels.

Place the fried slices in a single layer on a baking sheet and flatten each slice with a meat mallet to an even ⅛-inch thickness. Reheat the oil to 350°F, and refry the plantain slices a few at a time until golden and crisp, 2 to 3 minutes. Drain well on paper towels and serve immediately, sprinkled with:

   Coarse salt to taste

ABOUT POTATOES

Of all the odd facts about food—and there are many—consider this: It took more than a century for the potato to be accepted in Europe after its introduction from South America, and even longer than that to make its way to North America, when it was finally brought over by Irish immigrants. Today the potato is a leading fresh food crop!

Potatoes fall into three groups. **Boiling potatoes** are relatively high in moisture and low in starch. These waxy potatoes hold their shape when cubed or sliced, so they are chosen for potato salads, gratins, and stews. They may also be mashed or fried. **Baking potatoes** are low in moisture and high in starch. When cooked, their flesh is dry and fluffy, exactly right for baking, frying, and mashing. Baking potatoes also give body to soups, such as Vichyssoise, 130, as they fall apart in cooking. The best bakers are the **russet potatoes,** sometimes called **Idaho,** identifiable by their rough (and very tasty) brown skins and elongated shape. They also make the best mashed potatoes, and they are excellent for frying and for potato soufflés. **All-purpose potatoes,** typically roundish, usually with a dull brown skin, are moderate in moisture and starch content and good for any cooking method. The **Yukon Gold** has thin, smooth golden skin and yellow flesh. Other all-purpose potatoes include **Kennebec** and **Katahdin.**

New potatoes are "just-dug" potatoes, usually small in size, of any variety. They are generally boiled, steamed, or roasted whole in their skins. Many **heirloom potatoes** are now being raised. Popular heirloom boiling potatoes are **Yellow Finn, Bintje, Butterfinger,** and **Russian Banana;** among the bakers, **Russet Burbank** and **Lemhi Russet;** and among the all-purpose, **fingerling, Red Gold,** and **Peruvian Blue.**

Select potatoes that are firm and heavy for their size, with taut skin and no cuts, dark spots, cracks, mold, or other sign of spoilage. If there is a greenish cast to the potato or a green patch on it, avoid it—the green part was exposed to the sun and will be bitter (even mildly toxic). Avoid those that have sprouted; they will be soft and can have an off taste. Don't use frost-bitten potatoes, which are watery and have a black ring under the skin when cut. Store potatoes, unwashed and loose, in a cool, dry dark place. Refrigeration is not recommended. After storing, should you find your potatoes have turned green or begun to sprout, cut off the green or sprout with ¼ inch of the flesh beneath it (or discard the potatoes).

Potatoes have great affinities with butter, heavy or sour cream, cheese, chives, dill, onions, garlic, parsley, chervil, rosemary, sage, oregano, bacon, and mushrooms. They are often combined and mashed with other cooked vegetables in varying proportions, such as: 2 parts celery root to 1 part potato, 1 part turnips to 1 part potato, or 1 part avocado to 3 parts potato. Skins provide flavor and nutrients, but if peeling is called for, the most efficient method is to use a swivel peeler. Flesh exposed to air will turn brown, so drop peeled potatoes into a bowl of cold water.

A potato ricer, which has a perforated bowl for holding the boiled potatoes and two long handles that, when squeezed together, force the potatoes through holes in the bottom of the cup, is the best tool for preparing light, even-textured mashed potatoes. Look for a sturdy metal ricer with at least a 2-cup bowl; a good ricer should come with two disks with different-sized perforations that can be inserted into the cup. One has smaller holes for finely riced potatoes. The other disk has larger holes that can be used to press out spätzle or to remove excess moisture from cooked greens or other vegetables. An electric mixer is no doubt the most used tool to mash a potato and does a fine job. A potato masher, fork, or food mill takes more elbow grease but can do the job. The food processor leaves potatoes with an unappetizing gluey texture. A mandoline, shown below, makes quick work of cutting raw potatoes uniformly, whether paper-thin slices for Potatoes Anna, 298, or perfect shoestring potatoes for frying.

To microwave, arrange 4 medium baking potatoes, peeled and quartered, in a 2-quart baking dish. Cover and cook on high until tender, 9 to 12 minutes, stirring after 5 minutes. Let stand, covered, for 3 minutes. Mash a microwaved potato immediately if your goal is a fluffy texture.

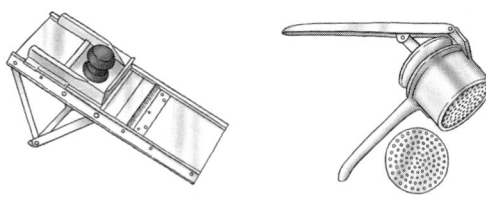

Mandoline and ricer

Pressure-cook whole large (2½-inch-diameter) potatoes with 1½ cups liquid at 15 pounds pressure for 15 minutes; 1½-inch-diameter potatoes need just 1 cup liquid and 10 minutes cooking; small new potatoes need 1 cup liquid and 2½ minutes; and ¾-inch-thick slices need 1 cup liquid and 5 minutes cooking.

In the following recipes we have tried to give this delicious vegetable the careful attention it deserves. ➤ Be sure, if a potato type is specified, to use that type only.

BOILED POTATOES (POMMES ANGLAISE)
6 servings
Peel:

2 pounds potatoes (any type)

If in haste, cut them into quarters. Cook, covered in salted water (½ teaspoon salt for each 4 cups water), letting water come to a boil, until tender, 20 to 40 minutes. Drain well. (If desired, reserve the **potato water** for a thick soup base or for use in bread making.)

If you like your potatoes mealy, place a folded towel over the pot for 5 minutes; or shake the pot gently several times. Remove the towel, which will have absorbed excess steam. Roll the potatoes in:

(2 to 3 tablespoons butter, melted)
(3 to 4 tablespoons chopped parsley or chives)

BOILED NEW POTATOES
4 servings
Few vegetables are as ingratiating as small new potatoes, especially when they are served in their tender skins so that all their delicate goodness is held until the moment they are eaten.
Cook:

12 small new potatoes, washed

in water, covered, letting water come to a boil, until tender, 10 to 20 minutes. If desired, remove the skins.
Serve with:

Chopped parsley, mint, or chives

Or melt in a skillet:

3 to 6 tablespoons butter

Add the potatoes and shake them gently over low heat until well coated. Serve sprinkled with:

Salt and black pepper to taste
Chopped parsley or chopped dill or fennel sprigs

Or add to the butter in the pan:

3 to 4 tablespoons grated fresh horseradish

and shake the potatoes until coated. This last is particularly choice with cold cuts.

RICED POTATOES (POTATO SNOW)
6 servings
A fine foil for meat with a rich gravy or sauce.
Cook:

Boiled Potatoes, above

When they are tender and dried, put them through a food mill or a ricer, directly into the serving dish. Do not touch the mound with a spoon, or you will compact the potatoes. Pour over them:

(2 tablespoons butter, melted)

Sprinkle with:

Salt to taste

MASHED POTATOES
6 servings
Baking, or russet, potatoes make the best mashed potatoes. A food mill or ricer ensures a smooth puree. Mashed potatoes are best when served at once, for they lose some fluffiness when held or reheated. They can be kept hot for up to 30 minutes by covering the (heatproof) serving bowl with aluminum foil and placing it in a larger pan of hot water over a low burner. Or put them in a buttered dish, pour a thin layer of cream on top, and keep in a warm oven.
Boil, above, or microwave, above, until tender:

2 pounds potatoes (about 6 medium), peeled and cut into large chunks

Include in the pan or microwave dish:

(2 garlic cloves, thinly sliced)
(1 onion slice or 2 scallions, white part only, chopped)
(1 small rib celery with leaves)
(1 small bay leaf or 1 sprig thyme or parsley)

Drain thoroughly. Remove any large pieces of vegetables

or herbs. Return to the pan, and shake over medium heat until mealy and dry. Cover to keep hot.

Heat in a small pan over low heat:

^{1}/$_3$ **cup heavy cream, half-and-half, milk, or buttermilk**

3 tablespoons butter

Be careful not to let the mixture boil. Meanwhile, quickly puree or mash the hot potatoes, working out every lump. Whip with a fork while pouring in the hot cream and butter, then whip the mixture until fluffy, about 30 seconds more. Stir in:

Salt and black or white pepper to taste

Serve at once, topped with:

1 to 2 tablespoons butter, softened

ADDITIONS TO MASHED POTATOES

1 head Roasted Garlic, 277

2 pinches saffron threads, crushed and steeped in 2 tablespoons warm water or chicken stock or broth for 10 minutes

^{1}/$_2$ **cup Duxelles, 284**

^{1}/$_2$ **cup chopped Caramelized Onions, 287**

^{1}/$_3$ **cup chopped basil, parsley, chervil, or thyme**

^{1}/$_2$ **cup grated Swiss, Gruyère, or Cheddar or ^{1}/$_2$ cup soft goat cheese**

MASHED POTATOES WITH CABBAGE AND SCALLIONS (COLCANNON)

6 to 8 servings

This is an Irish favorite. The British often fry it and call it "bubble and squeak," after the look of it and the noise it makes when cooking.

Place in a large saucepan or Dutch oven:

2 pounds Yukon Gold or other all-purpose potatoes, peeled and cut into 1^1/$_2$-inch chunks

Add cold water just to cover. Pile on top of the potatoes:

2 bunches scallions, white part only, sliced

1 small green cabbage (about 1 pound), cored and chopped into 1-inch pieces

Bring to a boil, then cover, reduce the heat to maintain a gentle boil, and cook until the potatoes are fork-tender, about 20 minutes. Drain and return the potatoes, cabbage, and scallions to the pot. Mash the mixture over low heat, adding:

^{1}/$_2$ **cup milk or half-and-half, warmed**

^{1}/$_4$ **to ^{1}/$_2$ cup (^{1}/$_2$ to 1 stick) butter, softened**

^{3}/$_4$ **teaspoon salt**

^{1}/$_4$ **teaspoon black pepper**

When the mixture is coarsely mashed, taste and adjust the seasonings.

CHANTILLY POTATOES

6 to 8 servings

The use of whipped heavy cream is what makes a dish **Chantilly.**

Preheat the oven to 375°F. Prepare:

3 cups Mashed Potatoes, above

Whip until stiff:

^{1}/$_2$ **cup heavy cream**

Season it to taste with:

Salt and white pepper

A few grains of ground red pepper

Fold in:

^{1}/$_2$ **cup grated Parmesan (1^1/$_2$ ounces)**

Shape the potatoes into a mound on an ovenproof plate. Cover the potatoes with the whipped cream mixture. Bake until the cheese is melted and the top is lightly browned.

CREAMED POTATOES

6 servings

Should you wish to delay serving this dish, place the potatoes in a buttered casserole and set aside until ready to serve. Cover with Au Gratin III, 961, and bake in a 400°F preheated oven until heated through.

Prepare:

2 pounds Boiled New Potatoes, 295

Drain, and dry the potatoes over very low heat. Peel and cut into ^{1}/$_2$-inch dice. Serve at once in:

White Sauce II, 550

flavored with, if desired:

(Dill seeds)

SCALLOPED POTATOES

6 servings

I. Preheat the oven to 350°F. Drop into boiling water:

3 cups very thinly sliced peeled boiling potatoes

Add:

1 teaspoon salt

Parboil about 8 minutes. Drain well. Grease a 10-inch round baking dish. Place the potatoes in it in 3 layers, sprinkling each layer with flour and dotting with butter, using in all:

2 tablespoons all-purpose flour

3 to 6 tablespoons butter

There are many tidbits you can put between the layers. Try, if you like:

(^{1}/$_4$ cup finely chopped chives or onions)

(12 well-drained anchovies, chopped, or 3 slices bacon, cooked until crisp and crumbled, reduce the salt below)

(^{1}/$_4$ cup finely chopped bell peppers)

Heat in a small saucepan:

1^1/$_4$ cups milk or cream

Season with:

1^1/$_4$ teaspoons salt

^{1}/$_4$ **teaspoon paprika**

(^{1}/$_4$ teaspoon dry mustard)

Pour the mixture over the potatoes. Bake about 35 minutes, testing for tenderness with a fork.

II. Preheat the oven to 350°F.

Layer in a greased 10-inch round baking dish:

3 cups very thinly sliced peeled boiling potatoes

Heat in a medium saucepan:

One 10^3/$_4$-ounce can condensed cream of mushroom
  or cream of celery soup
1^1/$_2$ cups milk or cream
Stir in:
  ^{1}/$_4$ cup shredded Swiss or Cheddar
  (^{1}/$_2$ cup Sautéed Mushrooms, 283)
Pour the mixture over the potatoes. Bake about 1 hour,
testing for doneness with a fork.

AU GRATIN POTATOES

6 to 8 servings

Use a suitable proportion of milk to half-and-half, depending on the desired richness of the final product.
Preheat the oven to 350°F. Rub a 12-inch gratin dish or a
shallow 3-quart baking dish with:
  1 garlic clove, halved
Let dry, then coat with:
  1 tablespoon butter, softened
Combine in a large saucepan or Dutch oven:
  **2^1/$_2$ pounds baking potatoes, peeled and very thinly
    sliced**
  3 cups milk or half-and-half or a combination
  1 teaspoon salt
  ^{1}/$_4$ teaspoon black pepper
  Pinch of grated or ground nutmeg
Bring to a gentle simmer over medium heat, then cook
and stir gently until the liquid thickens slightly, about
5 minutes.
Pour the mixture into the prepared dish. Press down on
the top layer to submerge the potatoes. Sprinkle with:
  Au gratin I, II, or III, 961
using Swiss or Gruyère.
Bake until the top is golden and the potatoes are tender,
45 minutes to 1 hour.

BAKED POTATOES

We have always liked the snug phrase "baked in their
jackets" to describe this process. But we are told that at
least one young cook, after encountering it, asked her
grocer where she could find the potato jackets!
The best baked potatoes are flaky when served, so start
with mature baking types like russets. Although boiling
and all-purpose potatoes can be used—and will need only
about half as much baking time—they will never have the
desired quality. Wrapping potatoes in foil inhibits flakiness, because too much moisture is retained. In fact, to
draw moisture out of baking potatoes, they are sometimes cooked on a bed of rock salt.
Preheat the oven to 400°F. Scrub:
  Baking potatoes
Pierce them in 6 or 8 places with a fork, and place directly
on the oven rack. Bake until tender when pierced with a
fork, 40 to 60 minutes, depending on size. When done,
serve at once with:
  Butter or sour cream or Cheese Sauce, 551
  Chopped chives or parsley

TWICE-BAKED POTATOES

6 servings

Preheat the oven to 400°F. Prepare:
  6 Baked Potatoes, above
Cut them lengthwise in half, or leave them whole, cutting
only a small ellipse from the flat top. Scoop out the potato
pulp into a bowl leaving a ^{1}/$_2$-inch thick shell. Add to it:
  3 to 4 tablespoons butter
  3 tablespoons hot milk or ^{1}/$_2$ cup sour cream
  (2 tablespoons minced scallion)
  1 teaspoon salt
If you plan to serve these with fish, also add for piquancy:
  1 tablespoon prepared horseradish
Beat until smooth. Whip until stiff but not dry, 978:
  (2 large egg whites)
Fold them into the potato mixture. Fill the potato shells.
Sprinkle the exposed potato with:
  ^{1}/$_2$ cup grated Parmesan
  Paprika
  (Crumbled cooked bacon)
  (Chopped scallions)
Broil until the cheese is browned.

PANFRIED OR LYONNAISE POTATOES

4 servings

Boil, 295:
  8 small new potatoes
While they are still hot, peel and slice thin. Heat in a large
heavy skillet over medium-high heat:
  2 tablespoons butter
  2 tablespoons vegetable oil
Add the potatoes and cook, stirring occasionally, until
golden brown. Meanwhile, heat in a small skillet:
  2 tablespoons butter or beef drippings
Add and cook, stirring, until softened:
  ^{1}/$_2$ cup thinly sliced onion
Gently mix the potatoes and onions together. Season
with:
  Salt and black pepper to taste
Sprinkle with:
  Chopped parsley

BROWNED OR FRANCONIA POTATOES

4 servings

We love browned potatoes but have an aversion to the
hard-crusted, grease-soaked variety so often served. Boil
these first to ensure a tender crust.
Boil in salted water to cover until they are not quite done,
so there is resistance to a fork:
  **6 scrubbed all-purpose potatoes, about 2 inches
    in diameter**
Drain. Meanwhile, preheat the oven to 350°F.
Heat in a small heavy ovenproof skillet until hot:
  3 tablespoons butter
  3 tablespoons vegetable oil

Add the potatoes, cover, and bake for about 20 minutes, turning occasionally for even browning. Sprinkle with:

   2 tablespoons finely chopped parsley

Bake, uncovered, about 10 minutes more.

POTATOES ANNA (POMMES ANNA)

6 to 8 servings

A beautiful presentation for a beautiful dish is the lidded copper potatoes Anna (*pommes Anna*) pan, about 8 inches in diameter and $3^{1}/_{2}$ inches high. The lid, which has side handles, fits down into it to a $1^{1}/_{2}$-inch depth during baking, then is reversed to hold the potatoes for serving. You can substitute a heavy lidded ovenproof skillet. A mandoline, 295, or an inexpensive plastic version, often called a v-slicer, makes slicing the potatoes a breeze. Position a rack in the center of the oven and preheat the oven to 425°F. Have ready:

   1 cup (2 sticks) butter, clarified, 963, or $^{3}/_{4}$ cup
   ($1^{1}/_{2}$ sticks) melted butter

Pour the butter into a 10-inch cast-iron skillet or *Pommes Anna* pan to a depth of $^{1}/_{4}$ inch. Set over low heat and layer in:

   $2^{1}/_{2}$ to 3 pounds baking potatoes, peeled and sliced
   $^{1}/_{8}$ inch thick

Build the bottom layer carefully with overlapping, nicely shaped slices. As you assemble, sprinkle each layer with:

   Salt and black pepper to taste
   (Melted butter)

When all the potatoes are layered in the pan and the bottom has formed a light crust, lightly butter or oil a skillet slightly smaller than the pan and press it firmly on top of the potatoes to compress them. Cover the pan tightly with foil, or cap with the *Pommes Anna* pot lid. Put the pan in the oven over a baking sheet to catch drips. Bake for 20 minutes, remove the cover, and press down firmly on the potatoes again. Bake, uncovered, until the sides are visibly browned and crisp, 20 to 25 minutes more. Holding the skillet or lid firmly against the potatoes, tilt the pan and pour off any melted butter that has not been absorbed. To serve, loosen edges from the pan with a knife, then invert the potatoes onto a plate and slice into wedges.

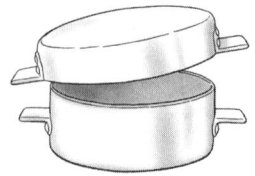

Pommes Anna pan

HASH BROWN POTATOES

4 servings

Combine with a fork:

   3 cups finely diced all-purpose potatoes

   1 tablespoon chopped parsley
   1 teaspoon grated onion
   $^{1}/_{2}$ teaspoon salt
   $^{1}/_{4}$ teaspoon black pepper

Heat in a 9-inch skillet:

   3 tablespoons bacon drippings, oil, or other fat

Spread the potato mixture in the pan, and press it with a broad knife or a spatula into a cake. Cook the potatoes slowly, shaking them from time to time to keep them from sticking and being careful not to splatter. When the bottom is brown, cut the potato layer in half and turn each half with 2 spatulas. Drizzle evenly over the potatoes:

   $^{1}/_{4}$ cup heavy cream

Brown the second side, and serve the potatoes piping hot.

POTATO PANCAKES

About twelve 3-inch cakes

Use baking or all-purpose potatoes—their starch content helps hold the potato shreds together.

Wrap in a clean dish towel and wring to squeeze out as much moisture as possible:

   2 cups coarsely grated peeled potatoes

Combine in a bowl with:

   3 large eggs, well beaten
   $1^{1}/_{2}$ tablespoons all-purpose flour
   1 tablespoon grated onion
   $1^{1}/_{4}$ teaspoons salt

Heat in a large, heavy skillet over medium-high heat until hot:

   $^{1}/_{4}$ inch or more vegetable oil or butter

Place spoonfuls of the potato mixture into the skillet, in batches, and form them into 3-inch patties about $^{1}/_{4}$ inch thick. Brown on the bottom, reducing the heat to medium if necessary to prevent scorching. Turn and brown the second side until crisp, 3 to 5 minutes each side. Drain briefly on paper towels. Serve with:

   Applesauce, 216
   Sour cream or Yogurt Cheese, 1030
   Snipped chives

If you want to hold the cooked pancakes until all are cooked, place them on a rack on a baking sheet in a 200°F oven. Then serve all of them at once after draining on paper towels to remove any excess fat.

PAN-BROILED GRATED POTATOES

4 servings

Very good and quick—next best to a potato pancake.

Wash, then grate on the large side of a box grater, skin and all:

   3 medium-sized baking potatoes ($1^{1}/_{2}$ pounds total)
   2 tablespoons grated onion

Melt in a very large skillet over medium-low heat:

   2 tablespoons butter
   2 tablespoons vegetable oil

Spread the potatoes in the skillet to a depth of about

¼ inch. Cook, covered, until the bottom is brown. Turn with a spatula and brown the other side.
Season with:

Salt and black pepper to taste

SOUFFLÉED OR PUFFED POTATOES

6 servings

According to legend, which we like to believe, Louis XIV, on campaign against the Dutch, as befits a major monarch traveling in an exquisite little palace on wheels, had sent a courier ahead to his chef, detailing just what he desired for dinner. The roads were nearly impassable, the hour grew late, and the chef, who had managed to keep most of the elaborate menu in reasonably prime condition, found to his consternation as the king's party clattered into the courtyard that his *pommes frites* had gone utterly limp. In a frenzy, he immersed the potatoes in the hot fat a second time, madly agitated the pan, and behold!—the dish that was to make him rich and famous.

There were several more coincidences that the cook may not have been aware of: His potatoes must have been old, so that the starch content was just right to make them puff. He must have had a very systematic apprentice who cut the potatoes all "with the grain" and to a very uniform thickness, as shown. In his relief at having something to serve, he evidently didn't mind a 10 percent failure, for even experts who make this dish daily count on that great a percentage of dud spuds. The duds, by the way, are acceptable as French fries, just not so glamorous as the puffs.

Restaurants famous for this dish age their own potatoes to the point where you can no longer pierce or scrape the skin off with your fingernail, but must use a knife to pierce it. Please read about Deep-Fat Frying, 1046.
Scrub:

8 large mature baking potatoes

Slice the potatoes lengthwise into ⅛-inch slices that are of uniform thickness. (In restaurants this accuracy is produced by a mandoline, 295, or other slicing machine.) Once you have these long even slices, you can cut them into the classic polygonal shape, as shown, or even into triangles, circles, or fancy ovals with crimped edges. Soak the slices for at least 25 minutes in ice water. Drain and dry

them thoroughly. Meanwhile, heat to 275°F in a deep fryer or deep heavy pot:

3 inches rendered beef kidney fat (suet)
or vegetable oil

Working in batches, drop in the potato slices one by one. Do not crowd the pan. The slices will sink. This next admonition is not without danger for the unskilled! When, after a few seconds, the slices rise, use a continuous shaking motion with the pot, which will set up a wavelike action to keep the floating slices bathed in the fat. Continue to cook them, turning them at least once, until they begin to turn transparent toward the centers and show a marked difference in texture at the cut edges to a depth of about ¹⁄₁₆ inch. Drain on paper towels. If you do not want to use them at once, they may be refrigerated up to 4 hours before the second cooking, but bring them to room temperature before immersing in the hot fat the second time. If you want to proceed at once, let them cool and drain for about 5 minutes.

Just before you are ready to serve, heat the fat to 385°F. Drop the potato slices again one by one into the fat, again agitating the pan as described. The once-fried slices should puff at once, although they always retain a seam wherever you have made an original perimeter cut. Cook to a golden brown. Drain on paper towels. Salt and serve the puffed ones at once, preferably in a basket as shown, to keep them crisp. If they are not crisp enough, return them to the fat for a few seconds. Drain again.

NEVER-FAIL FRENCH FRIES

4 to 6 servings

For crisp, golden fries, use starchy baking potatoes and a two-stage frying operation. After the first frying, you may keep the potatoes at room temperature for up to 2 hours. Fry for the second time just before serving. Please read about Deep-Fat Frying, 1046.
Soak in a bowl of cold water to cover for 30 minutes:

4 large baking potatoes, peeled and cut into
2¼ x ⅜ x ⅜-inch strips

Drain and dry on paper toweling to remove excess starch and surface moisture. Meanwhile, heat to 350°F in a deep fryer or deep heavy pot:

3 inches peanut or other vegetable oil

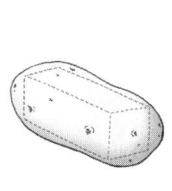 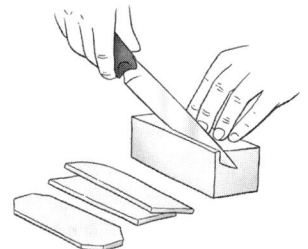 

Preparing Souffléed or Puffed Potatoes

Using a frying basket, if you have one, drop in the potatoes in batches, about 1 cup at a time, and fry until all the sputtering ceases, about 2 minutes. Skim out the rather limp potatoes with a slotted spoon and drain on paper towels. Let cool for at least 5 minutes before the second frying; the potatoes can be held for up to 2 hours.

For the second frying, heat the oil to 365°F. Fry until the potatoes are golden brown and crisp, 2 to 3 minutes, then drain on paper towels. Never cover them, or they will get flabby. Sprinkle with salt and serve at once.

SHOESTRING POTATOES

A mandoline, 295, or other vegetable slicer makes perfect shoestrings, but you can also use a knife or a food processor to cut the potatoes. They should brown in 2 to 3 minutes during the second frying; do not let them brown faster, or they will end up limp.

Cut the potatoes into strips no more than $^3/_{16}$ inch thick, and cook as above.

OVEN "FRENCH-FRIED" POTATOES

4 servings
Rutabagas and turnips also can be cooked this way.
Preheat the oven to 450°F.
Peel and cut lengthwise into $^1/_2$-inch-thick strips:
   4 medium baking potatoes (about 1 pound)
Soak in cold water for 10 minutes, then drain and dry well between towels. Toss the potatoes with:
   2 tablespoons vegetable or olive oil, bacon drippings, or melted butter
Spread on a baking sheet and bake, turning several times, until golden, 30 to 40 minutes. Turn the potatoes onto paper towels to drain briefly, then sprinkle with:
   $^1/_2$ teaspoon salt
   (Paprika or black pepper to taste)

DUCHESS POTATOES

8 servings
Prepare:
   4 cups Riced Potatoes, 295 (use 8 medium potatoes)
Add while still hot:
   $^1/_4$ cup ($^1/_2$ stick) butter
   2 large egg yolks, beaten
   (A dash of dry mustard)
   Salt and black pepper to taste
Allow to cool briefly.
Preheat the oven to 400°F. Butter a baking sheet.
Shape the potato mixture into eight 2-inch flat cakes on a floured work surface. Place on the buttered baking sheet. Brush with:
   1 large egg, well beaten
Bake until golden, about 20 minutes. Serve at once.
Note: If you want to use the potato mixture as a garnish, do not allow it to cool. Transfer it to a pastry bag fitted with a large fluted tip and pipe it at once in wavy scallops around the edge of a plank or a heat-resistant serving platter. Then brown it in the oven.

POTATO CROQUETTES

4 servings
Place in a bowl:
   2 cups Mashed Potatoes, 295
Beat in:
   1 large egg
Add any of the following, if desired:
   ($^1/_2$ cup sautéed chopped onions or sliced mushrooms)
   (5 scallions, thinly sliced)
   (2 tablespoons chopped thyme, parsley, or chives or 2 teaspoons dried chopped thyme or marjoram)
Divide into 8 portions and shape into small cakes. Dust lightly with:
   Flour
Dip in:
   1 large egg, well beaten
and then in:
   1 cup fresh bread crumbs or $^1/_2$ cup sesame seeds
Heat in a large nonstick skillet over medium-high heat:
   2 tablespoons butter, olive oil, or vegetable oil
Add the croquettes and fry until nicely browned, about 5 minutes on each side. Drain on paper towels. Serve hot.

ABOUT LEFTOVER POTATOES

Not inappropriately is an unresponsive person called a "cold potato." Held over after cooking, potatoes lose their texture and that subtle down-to-earth flavor. However, the following suggestions are more than acceptable treatments for salvaging them.

LEFTOVER GERMAN-FRIED POTATOES

4 servings
Heat in a skillet over low heat:
   2 or more tablespoons vegetable oil
Add:
   2 cups sliced boiled potatoes
   1 or more teaspoons minced onion
   Salt and paprika to taste
Cook the potatoes, turning frequently, until lightly browned.

LEFTOVER POTATOES O'BRIEN

6 servings
Preheat the oven to 350°F.
Dice:
   6 medium boiled potatoes
Combine with:
   1 green bell pepper, cored, seeded, and chopped
   1 onion, minced
   ($^3/_4$ cup grated or shredded cheese)
   1 tablespoon all-purpose flour
   Salt and black pepper to taste
   A few grains of ground red pepper
Place in a shallow greased baking dish. Pour over the top:
   1 cup hot milk

Cover with:
Au Gratin II or III, 961
Bake until browned, about 30 minutes.

LEFTOVER POTATO CAKES
Season:
Mashed Potatoes, 295
with any of the following, adding for each cupful:
(1 large egg, beaten)
(Chopped parsley)
(Chopped celery or celery seeds)
(Grated onion or ¼ cup chopped sautéed onions)
(A grating of nutmeg)
Shape into little cakes and dip in:
All-purpose flour, bread crumbs, or crushed cornflakes
Melt in a skillet:
Butter or other fat
Brown the cakes on both sides, turning once.

LEFTOVER AU GRATIN POTATOES
Preheat the oven to 400°F.
Dice:
Boiled potatoes
Prepare:
White Sauce I, 550, or Cheese Sauce, 551
making half as much sauce as there are potatoes.
Combine the potatoes and sauce. Add, if desired:
(Chopped parsley, minced onion, or minced chives)
Put the mixture in a greased baking dish. Cover with:
Au Gratin II or III, 961
Bake until browned.

ABOUT SWEET POTATOES AND YAMS
There are many distinct types of sweet potatoes available, ranging from a brown-skinned type with dry pinkish flesh to a coppery- or purple-skinned sweeter variety with moister deep orange flesh. This orange sweet potato is affectionately, if mistakenly, called a yam in many parts of the country, and is the type purchased as canned "yams."

Choose sweet potatoes that are firm, heavy for their size, and free of soft spots, dark spots, or mold. Store wrapped in a cool, well-ventilated, dark, dry place. Sweet potatoes lend themselves to most of the cooking methods used for white potatoes and are enhanced by fruits and fruit flavorings. Some particularly good pairings are with orange, pineapple, apples, pecans, sweet spices, butter, cream, brown sugar, and maple sugar and syrup. Or contrast the sweetness of these potatoes with chile peppers, bell peppers, cilantro, scallions, tomatoes, garlic, lemon, and lime. They reheat better than leftover white potatoes.

True **yams** are an unrelated tropical tuber with crisp, bland white to yellow flesh. Available in Latino groceries, they can be boiled, baked, fried, or prepared in any other way potatoes are—except pureed, which overemphasizes their sticky qualities.

Scrub well. If peeling is necessary, it is easiest to do so after cooking. When peeling orange sweet potatoes, be sure to remove not only the skin but also the pale fibrous layer just beneath.

To microwave, pierce as many as 4 whole medium potatoes in several places each. Place on a paper towel on the turntable in a spoke pattern. Cook on high until tender, 5 to 9 minutes for 2 potatoes, 10 to 13 minutes for 4 potatoes, turning them over and rearranging after 5 minutes. Cover with a towel and let stand for 5 minutes.

Pressure-cook whole large sweet potatoes with 1 cup liquid at 15 pounds pressure for 10 minutes. Cool the cooker at once.

BOILED SWEET POTATOES
Scrub sweet potatoes, drop them into boiling water to cover, and cook, covered, until tender, 25 to 35 minutes. Peel and salt before serving.

MASHED SWEET POTATOES
4 to 6 servings
Boil as above until thoroughly tender:
2 pounds sweet potatoes, scrubbed
Drain and let stand until cool enough to handle. Remove the skins, then mash, rice, or put through a food mill into a bowl. Add:
¼ cup (½ stick) butter, softened, or to taste
Salt to taste
Thin with:
Warm heavy cream or fresh orange, tangerine, or fresh lemon juice
If desired, season additionally with any of the following:
½ cup chopped pineapple, or to taste
½ cup pecans or ¼ cup black walnuts, toasted, 1001
3 tablespoons diced crystallized ginger or ½ teaspoon ground ginger
2 tablespoons light or dark brown sugar
1 tablespoon bourbon or dry sherry
1 teaspoon grated orange or lemon zest
Pinch of ground cloves or ½ teaspoon cinnamon
Beat the potatoes with a fork, whisk, or electric mixer until light. Serve immediately, or reheat at serving time at 375°F in a buttered baking dish.
Garnish with:
Fine shreds of orange zest

BAKED SWEET POTATOES
Preheat oven to 400°F. Scrub and pat dry.
Sweet potatoes
Pierce the skin in several places. For soft skin, rub the potatoes with butter or oil. Place in a single layer on a baking sheet lined with aluminum foil. Bake until soft and tender when pierced with a small knife, about 45 to 60 minutes, depending on the size. Serve with:
Honey Butter, 179, or softened butter, brown sugar, and cinnamon

TWICE-BAKED SWEET POTATOES

6 servings

Southerners use lots of butter, some brown sugar, nutmeg, and black walnuts, and replace the sherry with 2 tablespoons bourbon whiskey. Marshmallows may be substituted for the bread crumb and butter topping. These are a matter of taste.

I. Bake as above:

3 large sweet potatoes, scrubbed

Reduce the oven temperature to 375°F. Cut the potatoes lengthwise in half and scrape out most of the pulp into a bowl, leaving ¼-inch shells. Add to the pulp:

2 tablespoons butter, softened

¼ cup hot cream or ¾ cup crushed pineapple

½ teaspoon salt

(1 tablespoon dry sherry)

Beat with a fork until fluffy. Fill the shells and place on a baking sheet. Cover the tops with:

Au Gratin I, II, or III, 961

Bake the potatoes until browned, about 20 minutes.

II. Bake, as above:

3 large sweet potatoes, scrubbed

Halve lengthwise and scoop out the pulp, leaving ¼-inch shell. Mash or puree the flesh, then season as for Mashed Sweet Potatoes, 301, and beat until light. Fill the shells. Serve immediately, or dot with butter and broil until a light crust is formed, about 5 minutes.

CANDIED SWEET POTATOES

4 servings

Cook, covered, in boiling water until nearly tender:

5 medium sweet potatoes

Meanwhile, preheat the oven to 375°F.

Drain the potatoes, peel, and cut lengthwise into ½-inch slices. Place in a shallow greased baking dish. Season with:

Salt and paprika to taste

Sprinkle with:

¾ cup packed brown sugar

1½ tablespoons fresh lemon juice

½ teaspoon ground ginger

(½ teaspoon grated lemon zest)

Dot with:

2 tablespoons butter

Bake, uncovered, about 20 minutes, until glazed.

DEEP-FRIED SWEET POTATOES

4 servings

Please read about Deep-Fat Frying, 1046.

Cook in boiling water for 10 minutes:

4 large sweet potatoes, scrubbed

Peel, then cut into long strips about ⅜ inch thick. Heat to 365°F in a deep fryer or deep heavy pot:

3 inches vegetable oil

Deep-fry the strips in batches, about 1 cup at a time, until golden brown. Drain on paper towels. Sprinkle to taste with:

(Brown sugar)

Salt

Grated or ground nutmeg

Offer a dipping sauce, if desired:

(Chipotle Mayonnaise, 580, Peanut Dipping Sauce, 570, or Thai Hot Sauce [Nam Prik], 570)

SWEET POTATOES AND APPLES

6 servings

This is exceptionally good with roast pork, baked ham, or game. For a different version, omit the sugar and substitute ½ cup Cooked Dried Apricots, 217, or crushed pineapple for the apples.

Cook, covered, in boiling water until nearly done:

6 medium sweet potatoes

Meanwhile, cook, covered, until nearly tender in a very little boiling water:

1½ to 2 cups thinly sliced all-purpose apples

If the apples are not tart, sprinkle them with:

Fresh lemon juice

Preheat the oven to 350°F. Drain the sweet potatoes, peel, and cut them into ½-inch slices. Drain the apples, reserving ½ cup of the cooking liquid, if desired.

Grease a 9 x 9-inch baking dish and place it in alternate layers of apples and sweet potatoes, sprinkling each layer with a portion of:

½ cup packed brown sugar, or more to taste

(2 tablespoons raisins)

(2 tablespoons chopped pecans)

A dash of ground cinnamon or grated lemon zest

Dot the top with:

¼ cup (½ stick) butter

Pour the reserved apple cooking liquid or ½ cup water over the top. Cover and bake until tender, about 45 minutes.

SWEET POTATO AND PEANUT STEW

6 servings

Omit the ground beef or turkey for a vegetarian version. Heat in a large heavy saucepan over medium heat:

¼ cup peanut oil

Add:

1 onion, chopped

1 bell pepper, cored, seeded, and chopped

1 jalapeño or serrano pepper, seeded and minced

Cook, stirring, until the vegetables are tender but not browned, 7 to 10 minutes. Add:

4 garlic cloves, minced

1 packed tablespoon minced peeled fresh ginger

Cook for another 2 to 3 minutes, then stir in:

1 tablespoon chili powder

1 teaspoon ground cumin

½ teaspoon crushed red pepper flakes

Cook for 1 minute, and add:

2 sweet potatoes, peeled and cut into 1½-inch pieces

⅓ cup tomato paste

Add enough water to barely cover the vegetables and mix well. Bring to a boil, then lower the heat, cover, and simmer for 45 minutes, stirring occasionally. While the stew cooks, heat in a medium skillet over high heat:

1 teaspoon peanut oil

Add:

12 ounces ground beef or turkey

Cook, breaking up the meat with a spoon, until browned. With a slotted spoon, transfer to a plate and set aside. After the stew has cooked for 45 minutes, add the meat along with:

2 small zucchini (1 inch in diameter), sliced

Cook for another 15 minutes. Place in a small bowl:

¹/₂ cup peanut butter (chunky or smooth)

Add 1 cup of the stewing liquid, stirring until smooth, then add the peanut butter mixture to the stew. Mix well and cook another 15 minutes.

Season with:

Salt and black pepper to taste

Serve plain or with:

Cooked rice or couscous, 362

ABOUT RADISHES

Used to add color, crunch, and a peppery bite to salads, radishes were once so esteemed as a stimulant for the appetite that people used to start their day with a handful. In addition to the **table** or **small red radishes,** including **cherry belle,** try the carrot-shaped **icicles,** or **French Breakfast** types, which are milder. The name French Breakfast refers to the French custom of starting the day with radishes, dipped in a bit of sweet butter. After rinsing, serve radishes well chilled with a dish of coarse salt. If radishes are not thoroughly crisp, they can be revived by soaking in ice water.

Asian radishes are larger; round or oval and green or white, they can weigh upwards of a pound. Their flesh may be white, green, rose, or all three colors. They are served raw. The jumbo, carrot-shaped, juicy white radishes called **daikon** in Japan and **mooli** in India are mild in flavor and a central part of the daily diet—often pickled, added to soup, or grated and cooked with other vegetables and spices. **Black radishes,** black on the outside and snow white on the inside, are turnip-shaped with flesh that is pungent and relatively dry. They are a favorite for slicing or adding to mixed vegetable salads dressed with sour cream. Any radish can be cooked as for turnips, 313, or prepared as for Celery Root Rémoulade, 167. Use daikon in Spicy Chinese Slaw, 161.

To prepare, choose firm, flawless roots with bright, crisp greens. Trim the leaves from the roots and store separately in perforated plastic vegetable bags in the refrigerator crisper. The leaves, which have a shorter keeping life than the roots, are as tasty and nutritious as turnip greens. Cook them the same way, 277, or add them to a tossed salad. Radishes have affinities with scallions, chives, salt, parsley, sherry, rice vinegar, and lemon.

To boil or to steam radishes, cook as for turnips, 313.

RED RADISHES WITH SCALLIONS

4 servings

Trim the leaves and any excessively long roots from:

2 bunches red radishes, well scrubbed

Cut any especially large ones in half or into quarters. Melt in a large skillet over medium heat:

1 tablespoon butter

Add and cook, stirring, until softened, 2 to 3 minutes:

2 bunches scallions, white part and 1 inch of green, cut into ¹/₂-inch pieces

Add the radishes, along with:

¹/₂ cup chicken stock or broth

Cover the pan and simmer until the radishes are tender, 3 to 4 minutes. Uncover, increase the heat to medium-high, and boil rapidly to reduce the pan juices while shaking the pan back and forth a few times. Season with:

Salt to taste

ABOUT RUTABAGA

These roots are the size of grapefruits and have brown and purplish skins. They will keep for several weeks, unwrapped, in a cool, dry room or in the refrigerator. Rutabagas may be cooked in the same ways as their close relative turnips, 313, though rutabagas will generally take longer to become tender. Their golden flesh has a sharp, turnip-like flavor. It pairs well with butter, cream, ginger, lemon, sage, thyme, and parsley. Contrary to expectations, the tough skin and wax can be stripped off with a vegetable peeler, though it is necessary to go over the same spot several times to penetrate to the heart of the vegetable. Alternatively, the vegetable can be cut in half, placed cut side down on a work surface, and peeled with a knife. ➤ Do not use the leaves.

BOILED RUTABAGA

4 servings

Trim off any leaves, peel, and dice:

1 medium rutabaga (2 cups)

Drop into a saucepan of boiling water and cook, uncovered, until tender, 15 to 25 minutes.

Drain well. Season with:

¹/₂ teaspoon salt

Serve with:

Melted butter

to which you have added generously:

Fresh lemon juice

Chopped parsley

Or mash the rutabagas and add them in any proportion to mashed potatoes, with:

Chopped parsley, sour cream, and nutmeg

RUTABAGA PUREE

4 servings

Prepare:

Boiled Rutabaga, above

After draining, puree in a food processor with:

¹/₄ cup heavy cream
2 tablespoons brown sugar
1 teaspoon ground ginger

Or season generously with:

Black pepper

and top with:

(Orange Butter, 559)

ABOUT SALSIFY

There are two vegetables called salsify, **true salsify,** or **oysterplant,** which resembles a large beige carrot covered with tiny rootlets, and **black salsify,** or **scorzonera,** a long, thin, black-skinned root that looks like a stick. The roots are almost identical in texture and flavor, with white to cream-colored flesh hinting of the sea. Select only firm, unblemished roots, and store in an open plastic vegetable bag in the refrigerator crisper.

Salsify has affinities with lemon, parsley, chives, hollandaise sauce, butter, walnuts, and vinegar.

To avoid discoloration, put cut pieces in acidulated water, 957, then steam, 242, unpeeled salsify for about 10 minutes. Or, if peeled, cook in acidulated water, as in Salsify with Herbs, below. Peeled cooked salsify is delicious mashed with butter, salt, pepper, and a pinch of mace or nutmeg (see Root Vegetable Puree, 245). It also can be prepared as for parsnips, 289, or turnips, 319.

SALSIFY WITH HERBS

4 servings

Combine in a bowl:

Juice of 2 lemons
2 cups water, or as needed to cover

Peel, cut into 3-inch lengths, and immediately put into the water:

2 pounds salsify

Bring to a boil in a medium saucepan:

8 cups water
2 tablespoons fresh lemon juice
1 tablespoon all-purpose flour
1 teaspoon salt

Drain the salsify and add to the pan. Boil, uncovered, until tender when pierced with a knife, 10 to 20 minutes. Drain, then toss with:

2 tablespoons butter or olive oil
1¹/₂ tablespoons chopped parsley
1¹/₂ tablespoons chopped tarragon
2 teaspoons snipped chives
Fresh lemon juice or white wine vinegar to taste

ABOUT SHALLOTS

These members of the onion family, 285, are the size of small boiling onions, with copper, gold, or gray-brown skin. Their flesh can be white, yellow, or pink. Most often what appears to be one round shallot will be two or more sections; simply pull them apart. The flavor of a shallot is milder than that of onions. Select firm bulbs that fill their skins and have no sprouts on top. Cut off the stem and trim the root, but leave the root pad attached. *To chop or slice shallots,* cut lengthwise, peel off the skin, and cut as you would an onion, 286.

Shallots are typically used as a seasoning, 1004, as for onions, but are delicious cooked whole like small boiling onions, 286. Shallots go well with butter, white and red wine, and vinegar.

ROASTED SHALLOTS

4 servings

A delectable accompaniment for simply cooked fish, poultry, meat, and main-dish vegetables.

Preheat the oven to 450°F.

Peel:

1 pound shallots

Brush the bottom of a baking dish that will hold the shallots in a single layer with:

Olive or walnut oil

Brush the shallots with oil and arrange in the dish. Roast for 15 minutes, shaking the dish once or twice to move the bulbs around.

Use tongs to turn the shallots over and roast until they can easily be pierced, 4 to 5 minutes more. Sprinkle with:

Salt and white pepper to taste

CRISPY SHALLOTS

About ¹/₂ cup

Use these crisp, sweet shallots atop Asian noodles, stir-fries, rice, and sautéed greens. They will keep for a month at room temperature in a tightly covered container.

Heat in a small heavy pan until hot but not smoking:

¹/₂ cup peanut oil
¹/₈ teaspoon turmeric

Drop in:

4 large shallots, sliced into thin rounds

Simmer in the oil until they turn very light gold, then stir in:

¹/₂ teaspoon sugar

Cook until the shallots just begin to brown, another 3 to 4 minutes. Remove with a slotted spoon and drain thoroughly on paper towels. When dry, store in a covered container.

SORREL

Sorrel has long thin bright green leaves and a piercingly sour flavor. It is used more as a seasoning than a vegetable, though sorrel ribbons are delightful in salads. It is in season spring, summer, and fall, but its leaves are most tender in spring. Choose the smallest and crispest leaves, with no wilting, soft spots, or tears. Store in an open plastic bag in the refrigerator crisper.

Rinse and rip off the stems at the base of the leaves (the stems can be fibrous). Strip mature leaves from the midribs, but keep tender leaves whole. Before use, sorrel is customarily cut crosswise into thin ribbons. Be sure to use a nonreactive pan and knife when cooking sorrel. Because it is heavy in oxalic acid, it is usually parblanched, 1054, for 3 minutes and drained before cooking as for spinach, below, or chard, 277, and it is often combined with them rather than being served by itself. See Salads, 154.

ABOUT SPINACH

Spinach is one of the most delectable of greens, with a distinctive taste that seems to divide people into definite "yes" and "no" camps. For us on the positive side, it's a special treat as a garnish with other foods, where its presence may be heralded by the title **Florentine.** If you get a bunch with an astringent taste, counteract the mild bitterness with a pinch of sugar. To use in a salad, see 154. Spinach has affinities with butter, cream, cheese, eggs, lemon, vinegar, garlic, dill, parsley, basil, nutmeg, onion, mushrooms, bacon, and anchovies.

Wash spinach thoroughly by swishing in a sinkful of cool water, then lifting it out. If there is grit in the bottom of the sink, change the water and repeat. Twist off the pink root ends, if attached. If the spinach is mature, with large, crinkly leaves, tear off the stems at the base of the leaves; if the spinach is young, or it is baby spinach, leave the tender stems attached. Use leaves whole, stack and cut crosswise into ribbons, or tear into small pieces.

To microwave, place 1 pound rinsed leaves in a 3-quart baking dish. Cover and cook on high until tender, 5 to 7 minutes, stirring after 3 minutes. Let stand, covered, for 5 minutes.

Pressure-cook spinach 1 minute at 15 pounds pressure.

BOILED SPINACH

3 to 4 servings

This treatment is for mature spinach.

If the spinach is young and tender, cook as for Wilted Spinach, below. Wash and trim:

1 pound mature spinach

Bring 2 cups water to a rapid boil in a large saucepan. Add the spinach, reduce the heat, and simmer, covered, until tender, about 5 to 7 minutes. Drain the spinach well. If desired, process briefly in a food processor or chop the spinach as fine as you like it.

While the spinach cooks, if desired, melt in a small skillet over medium heat:

2 tablespoons butter or bacon drippings

Add and cook, stirring, until softened:

2 tablespoons diced red bell pepper
2 tablespoons minced onion
1 garlic clove, minced

Add:

Fresh lemon juice to taste
Salt and black pepper to taste

Serve the spinach topped with the seasonings. Other garnishes for spinach include:

Sliced hard-boiled egg, 194
Crumbled crisp cooked bacon

Fine buttered croutons, 974
Hollandaise Sauce, 560
Au Gratin II or III, 961

CREAMED SPINACH

4 servings

I. Prepare:

Boiled Spinach, above

Process in a food processor or chop to a fine puree. Rub a medium skillet with:

(1 clove garlic, peeled)

Turn the heat to medium. Add and melt:

2 tablespoons butter

Add and cook, stirring, until golden:

2 tablespoons finely chopped onion

Stir in until blended:

1 tablespoon all-purpose flour or 2 tablespoons
  Browned Flour, 544

Slowly stir in:

$1/2$ cup hot cream or chicken stock or broth
$1/2$ teaspoon sugar

When the sauce is smooth and hot, add the spinach, stir, and cook 3 minutes. Season with:

Salt and black pepper to taste
(Grated or ground nutmeg or grated zest of
  $1/2$ lemon)

Serve garnished with:

Diced hard-boiled egg, 194
Crumbled crisp cooked bacon

II. Place in a food processor:

$3/4$ cup milk
(1 thin slice onion)
3 tablespoons butter, softened
2 tablespoons all-purpose flour
$1/2$ teaspoon salt
$1/8$ teaspoon paprika
A grating of nutmeg or lemon zest
($1/2$ clove garlic)

Process until smooth. Add:

10 to 12 ounces spinach, washed and trimmed

Pulse until the spinach is finely chopped.

Transfer the mixture to a heavy skillet and stir over low heat until it bubbles and the flour is cooked, about 3 minutes. Serve with:

Buttered bread crumbs, 960
4 slices bacon, cooked until crisp and crumbled
2 hard-boiled eggs, 194, sliced

WILTED SPINACH

2 to 3 servings

This can also be made with chard, or a combination of spinach and chard. Combined with ricotta cheese, it makes an excellent filling for ravioli.

Wash thoroughly but do not dry:

12 well-packed cups trimmed spinach leaves

Coarsely chop, then place in a large skillet. Season with:

Salt to taste

Cook, stirring frequently, over medium heat until completely wilted but still bright green, about 5 minutes. Remove to a serving dish and toss with:

Extra-virgin olive oil

Dash of white or red wine vinegar,
or fresh lemon juice

Black pepper to taste

Or serve plain, with:

Garlic and Walnut Sauce, 568

PANNED OR SICILIAN SPINACH

2 to 3 servings

Heat in a large heavy skillet over medium heat:

1¹/₂ tablespoons olive oil

Add:

2 to 3 garlic cloves, minced

Reduce the heat to medium-low and cook until the garlic is just beginning to color, 30 to 60 seconds. Add:

1 pound fresh spinach, washed and trimmed,
or two 10-ounce packages frozen spinach

If using fresh spinach, cover the pan and cook over high heat until steam appears, then reduce the heat and simmer, covered, until tender, 2 to 3 minutes. If using frozen, follow the package instructions. Season with:

Salt and black pepper to taste

To turn this into **Sicilian Spinach**, add:

(2 or more anchovies, chopped)

Or serve the spinach with a bowl of:

Nam Prik (Thai Hot Sauce), 570,
or Ginger Soy Sauce, 571

SAAG PANEER

4 servings

Saag paneer, which literally translates as spinach cheese, is a typical Indian combination of vegetables and fresh cheese. Our stir-fried recipe is a variation on the traditional pureed recipe. Be sure to use a nonstick pan to fry the cheese.

In a medium heavy saucepan, bring to a boil:

4 cups whole milk

Remove the pan from the heat and add:

3 tablespoons fresh lemon juice

Stir until the milk curdles and separates into bits of solid curd floating in the liquid whey. Let stand for 5 minutes, then pour through a fine-mesh sieve lined with a double layer of cheesecloth, set over a bowl. Let stand until cool enough to handle, then pull the edges of the cloth together over the curd and squeeze out as much liquid as possible. Flatten the curd, still in the cheesecloth, to a thickness of ¹/₂ to 1 inch. Set it on a plate and top with another plate. Weight with a can and let stand for 20 minutes, then cut the cheese into ¹/₂-inch cubes.

Coarsely chop:

1¹/₄ pounds spinach, washed and trimmed

Heat in a large nonstick skillet over medium-high heat:

¹/₄ cup vegetable oil

Add and cook, stirring, until lightly browned, about 15 seconds:

1 teaspoon cumin seeds

Add the cheese cubes and cook, shaking the pan every now and then to turn the cubes, until golden brown, 3 to 4 minutes. Remove the cheese and set aside.

Add to the oil in the pan:

1 medium onion, thinly sliced

Cook, stirring, until softened and translucent, 3 to 4 minutes. Add and stir for 1 minute:

4 garlic cloves, thinly sliced

2 small dried red chile peppers

Add as much chopped spinach as will comfortably fit into the pan, cover, and cook until wilted enough to add more spinach. Add a few more handfuls of spinach, cover, and let wilt. Continue until all the spinach is wilted.

Sprinkle with:

¹/₂ teaspoon salt

Cook, uncovered, until all the water is evaporated. Fold in the fried cheese, remove the chile peppers, and serve hot.

ABOUT SQUASHES

More than most vegetables, squashes are a family of individuals; easy cross-pollination accounts for their myriad diversity. These plants divide into summer and winter types. We often call for special varieties in the recipes that follow, but others may be substituted as long as they belong to the respective type.

SUMMER SQUASH

Whether green, yellow, or white, long, round, or scalloped, these (also known as **marrows**) are all thin-skinned and easily punctured with a fingernail—the shopper's furtive assurance and the proprietor's despair. They should be firm and heavy for their size. Avoid any with a skin that is tough or a wrinkled or black stem. Unless the squash is to be stuffed, always choose smaller specimens. If they are young, there is no need to peel or seed them. Should only harder-rind older squash be available, do both.

Summer squash do not store well. A limited number of the more popular varieties can be found all year at the market. America's favorite summer squash is **zucchini.** Try also the closely related **cocozelle,** a long and slender Italian zucchini; the **cousa,** a Middle Eastern zucchini; and the large, narrow **English zucchini** with pure white fine-textured flesh. Prepare these squashes as for cucumber or eggplant. **Pattypan squash** are 2- to 3-inch disks with scalloped edges. **Yellow crooknecks** are heritage American squash with bright yellow, bumpy skin and slender curved necks. **Straightneck yellow squash** has the same flavor but looks like yellow zucchini.

Summer squashes are excellent with summer flavors, especially tomatoes, onions, peppers (both sweet and hot), garlic, oregano, marjoram, basil, parsley, dill, rosemary, sage, and tarragon, as well as lemon, cheese, butter, olive oil, and capers.

To prepare summer squash, wash and cut into small pieces. If the squash is very tender or small it may be left whole.

To microwave, place 2 cups slices in a 1-quart baking dish, cover, and cook on high just until tender, 2 to 4 minutes, stirring after 2 minutes. Let stand, covered, for 1 minute. Summer squash is too delicate for a pressure cooker.

WINTER SQUASH

These are of many colors and shapes. Except for butternut, they have hard-shelled skins. Choose the others for their hard rinds; watery spots indicate decay. Store whole squash unwrapped in a cool, dark, dry place. Store cut pieces wrapped in plastic in the refrigerator for up to 3 days.

Winter squash remain in the market from fall to early spring. The most common varieties are the dark green or orange **acorn squash; butternut squash; and spaghetti squash,** with yellow fibers that look and can be used like spaghetti. Most of the other available winter squash—**banana, Hubbard, buttercup** or **turban, Cushaw,** and **delicata**—have soft, sweet, rich flesh suggestive of butternut squash. Unless you are baking the squash whole, remove the seeds and stringy portions. Peel and cut into small pieces.

Pumpkin is the name given to orange winter squash with rounded shapes and orange flesh. Americans think of this squash first as pie, 686, and next as soup, 129, but it is also surprisingly delicious as a vegetable. Cook by any recipe calling for a winter squash.

Because squash is bland in flavor, it benefits from imaginative treatment. It may be cut lengthwise into "boats" and scooped out, or cooked and the centers filled with succulent cargo. For fillings, see Stuffings, 532. If the squash is a tender summer type, you may combine the removed portion with the filling, which may include vegetables, bread crumbs, nuts, mushrooms, or cooked meat. Winter squash are delicious baked, mashed, and added to soups, stews, gratins, and savory tarts or combined with other vegetables in purees. They retain their quality when frozen mashed. All squash are tasty with butter, cream, garlic, spicy cheeses, thyme, sage, mushrooms, pork, and toasted nuts.

To prepare winter squash, scrub the squash. If baking whole or in pieces, leave the skin on. For all other cooking techniques, peel the squash by cutting it in half, or into pieces if large. Cutting into the thick hard shell of winter squash can be difficult. Use a strong sharp knife; some people prefer serrated. Have someone steady the squash for you or set the squash on a thick towel. Cut slowly and deliberately, plunging in the tip of the knife first, then pulling down on the rest of the blade. Rather than try to saw your way through, lift the knife out and start again from the other side. Remove the seeds and strings, and peel with a vegetable peeler or a paring knife. Cut the squash into chunks, cubes, or slices. On average, 1 pound untrimmed squash yields a generous 13 ounces edible flesh or 1¾ cups cooked puree.

To microwave a whole acorn squash, pierce in 4 or 5 places with a sharp knife. Place on a paper towel and cook on high until tender, 7 to 10 minutes, turning the squash after 4 minutes. Cover with a cloth and let stand for 5 minutes before cutting. *To microwave spaghetti squash,* see 308. For peeled, cubed squash, place in a 2-quart baking dish. Cover and cook on high until tender, about 6 minutes, stirring after 3 minutes. Let stand, covered, for 2 minutes. For slices, place in a 2-quart baking dish, cover, and cook on high until tender, about 7 minutes, stirring after 3 minutes. Let stand, covered, for 2 minutes.

Winter squash can be *pressure-cooked* if cut into 1-inch-thick cubes or slices. Cook with 1½ cups liquid at 15 pounds pressure for 12 minutes. Cool the cooker at once.

STEAMED SUMMER SQUASH

4 servings

Please read Summer Squash, 306.
Wash and cut into small pieces:

> **2 cups diced any summer squash: zucchini, yellow crookneck, or pattypan**

Or, if very tender, the squash may be left whole. Steam, 242, until tender. Drain very well. Sprinkle generously with:

> **Grated Parmesan and melted butter**

SUMMER SQUASH CASSEROLE

6 servings

Try this with whatever summer squash is available.
Preheat the oven to 350°F. Lightly butter a 10-inch gratin dish.
Steam, 242, until tender, about 10 minutes:

> **1¼ pounds yellow squash, cut into ½-inch cubes, or pattypan squash, quartered**

Remove to a medium bowl. Heat in a small skillet:

> **1 tablespoon butter or olive oil**

Add and cook, stirring, until softened:

> **½ small onion, finely diced**

Add to the squash, along with:

> **⅔ cup diced Monterey Jack, Swiss, or Brie**
> **⅓ cup sour cream or crème fraîche**
> **2 tablespoons grated Parmesan**
> **1 tablespoon white vermouth or dry white wine**
> **1 teaspoon ground coriander**
> **Salt and white pepper to taste**

Spread into the prepared dish. Sprinkle over the top:

> **Au Gratin II or III, 961**

Bake until bubbling and golden, about 35 minutes.

SAUTÉED SUMMER SQUASH

4 servings

Prepare:

    3 cups diced any summer squash

Heat in a large skillet:

    3 tablespoons butter or olive oil

Add and cook, stirring, until golden:

    1 cup minced onions

Add the squash and season with:

    $^{1}/_{2}$ teaspoon salt

    $^{1}/_{4}$ teaspoon white pepper

Cover and cook until the squash is tender, about 6 minutes, shaking the pan occasionally to prevent sticking. Remove the lid and cook 3 minutes longer to evaporate juices. Serve sprinkled with any of the following:

    Chopped parsley or basil

    Grated Parmesan

    2 large cloves garlic, finely chopped

    1 tablespoon grated lemon zest

or drizzled with:

    Quick Tomato Sauce, 562

STUFFED BAKED SUMMER SQUASH

4 servings

Please read Summer Squash, 306.

Preheat the oven to 350°F. Wash:

    4 small summer squash

Halve them and scoop out the pulp, leaving $^{1}/_{2}$-inch shells. Melt in a small skillet:

    2 tablespoons butter

Add and cook, stirring, until softened:

    2 tablespoons chopped onion

Add the squash pulp, along with:

    $^{1}/_{2}$ teaspoon salt

    $^{1}/_{4}$ teaspoon paprika

    A dash of nutmeg or cloves

Stir and cook until hot. Remove from the heat. Add:

    1 large egg, beaten

    $^{1}/_{2}$ cup dry bread crumbs

    $^{1}/_{2}$ cup grated cheese

Rub the squash shells with:

    (Butter or pan drippings)

Fill them with the stuffing. Place on a rack in a baking dish over $^{1}/_{8}$ inch of water or stock. Sprinkle the tops with:

    Au Gratin II or III, 961

Bake the squashes until tender, about 20 to 25 minutes, depending on their size.

DEEP-FRIED ZUCCHINI

Please read about Deep-Fat Frying, 1046.

Wash, dry, and cut into $^{1}/_{4}$- to $^{1}/_{2}$-inch slices:

    Zucchini

Dry well. Dip in:

    Fritter Batter for Vegetables, 658

Fry in oil heated to 365°F, in batches if necessary, until golden. Serve at once.

SPAGHETTI SQUASH

The long fibers of this variety of winter squash really do resemble spaghetti when cooked, making it a blessing for anyone who wants to add more vegetables to their diet, or those on wheat-free diets, as it's a delicious base for pasta sauces. Pierce with a knife several times and bake like potatoes or boil (without peeling) in water to cover, 20 to 30 minutes.

To microwave, pierce with a knife tip in several places, place it on the turntable, and cook on high until tender when pressed with your fingers, about 15 minutes. If you do not have a turntable, rotate the squash every 5 minutes during the cooking time. Let cool for 10 minutes before cutting the squash.

Halve the cooked squash and remove the seeds, then scrape the strands into a bowl, separating them with a fork to make "spaghetti." Spaghetti squash has an affinity for butter, cream, or olive oil, grated Parmesan, red pepper flakes, and sauces typically used on pasta, 321.

BAKED WINTER SQUASH

Please read Winter Squash, 307.

  I. Preheat the oven to 375°F.

Scrub:

    Acorn squash or other small winter squash

Deeply pierce each squash in 4 to 5 places with a knife. Set in a baking dish or on a rimmed baking sheet. Bake until the flesh is tender when pierced with a thin knife, 45 minutes to 1$^{1}/_{2}$ hours, depending on the size and type.

Cut in half through the stem end, scoop out seeds and strings, and serve with butter, salt and pepper, and finely chopped herbs such as chives, oregano, and thyme.

II. Preheat the oven to 375°F.

Cut into halves, quarters, or slabs:

    Large winter squash

Remove any seeds and strings. Arrange the squash cut side up on a rimmed baking sheet. Add $^{1}/_{4}$ inch water to the pan and cover with aluminum foil. Bake until the squash is tender when pierced with a thin skewer, 30 to 45 minutes. Halfway through baking, if desired, uncover the pan, brush the squash with butter or vegetable oil, and sprinkle with brown sugar and nutmeg or another spice. Serve in the shell, or as desired.

MASHED WINTER SQUASH

Please read Winter Squash, 307.

  I. Prepare:

    Baked Winter Squash I or II, above

Scrape the squash from the skin and mash the pulp with a spoon, fork, or potato masher. For each 1 cup mashed squash, add:

    1 tablespoon butter

    1 teaspoon brown sugar or maple syrup

    $^{1}/_{4}$ teaspoon salt

    $^{1}/_{8}$ teaspoon ground ginger, or more to taste

    ($^{1}/_{8}$ teaspoon ground cinnamon)

Beat well with enough:

Warm heavy cream or orange juice

to make it a soft, smooth puree. Serve sprinkled with:

(Raisins or chopped nuts)
($^1/_4$ cup well-drained crushed pineapple)

II. Or, for a savory puree, add to each 1 cup mashed squash:

1 tablespoon butter or olive oil
(1 small garlic clove, minced)
1 tablespoon chopped parsley or $^1/_2$ teaspoon minced sage
Salt and black pepper to taste

Beat in with a spoon, adding enough to make a smooth, soft puree:

Warm milk or cream

Serve plain, or top with:

(Sautéed Onions, 287, fine shreds of lemon zest, mascarpone or sour cream, or grated Parmesan or Swiss)

BAKED ACORN SQUASH WITH PEAR AND APPLE

4 servings

Preheat the oven to 325°F. Grease a baking pan large enough to hold the squash.

Place cut side down in the baking pan:

2 medium acorn squash, halved and seeds and strings removed

Add $^1/_4$ inch hot water to the pan, and bake for 45 minutes. Meanwhile, mix in a medium bowl:

2 large apples, peeled, cored, and diced
1 ripe pear, peeled, cored, and diced
$^1/_4$ cup dried currants or raisins
2 tablespoons dark brown sugar
Grated zest of 1 small orange
$^1/_4$ teaspoon ground cinnamon
$^1/_8$ teaspoon grated or ground nutmeg

Melt in a large skillet over medium heat:

2 tablespoons butter

Add the apple mixture and cook, stirring, until the fruit is golden brown, about 5 minutes. Stir in:

$^1/_4$ cup apple cider or orange juice
(1 tablespoon bourbon or dark rum)

Simmer, stirring often, until the fruit is tender, about 8 minutes. Remove from the heat. Remove the squash from the oven. Pour off the water from the pan and turn the squash cut side up. Fill with the apple mixture. Bake until the squash is tender, about 15 minutes more.

BAKED BUTTERNUT SQUASH STUFFED WITH SAUSAGE AND APPLES

4 servings

Preheat the oven to 375°F. Grease a baking dish large enough to hold the squash comfortably. Halve lengthwise and remove the seeds and strings:

2 butternut squash (about 1 pound each)

Arrange cut side up in the baking dish and brush lightly with:

1 tablespoon vegetable oil

Cover with a lid or aluminum foil and bake until almost tender, 30 to 40 minutes. Remove from the oven and let the squash cool slightly. Keep the oven on.

Prepare:

Bread Stuffing with Sausage and Apples, 533

When the squash has cooled, scoop out most of the flesh, leaving $^3/_8$-inch-thick shells. Lightly mix the squash pulp into the stuffing mixture, breaking up the squash as little as possible.

Pile the stuffing into the squash halves. Dot each half with:

1 tablespoon butter, cut into small pieces
1 tablespoon dark brown sugar

Bake, uncovered, until piping hot and brown and crusty on top, 20 to 25 minutes. Let cool for several minutes before serving.

ABOUT SQUASH BLOSSOMS

If you grow squash, you may wonder why so many blossoms fall off without maturing. These are male flowers, not needed for seed development. Male blossoms are long and slender; female blossoms are round at their base. They can be harvested after they close and drop, but it is preferable to pick them off the plant while still fresh. The choicest blossoms are unsprayed zucchini. It is best to pick the flowers just before using. However, flowers can be kept in a closed storage container in the refrigerator for 1 day if necessary. Squash blossoms (taken from both summer and winter squash) also are available at specialty markets. Do not wash unless the blossoms are dusty. Remove the stem and calyx—the outer green whorl of the flower at the top of the stem—if they seem tough. Remove pistils if stuffing. Inspect for insects.

Squash blossoms are decorative as well as delicious when stuffed with soft cheese, like ricotta or mozzarella, with the mixture for Ground Turkey or Chicken Loaf, 445. Open each flower and put in only a small amount of stuffing, to allow the petals to close again. Place the stuffed blossoms side by side on a greased baking dish and bake in a 350°F oven until thoroughly heated, about 20 minutes. Serve alone or as a platter garnish. Squash blossoms also make fine sweet or savory fritters, 659.

Partially opened squash blossoms may be sautéed in butter or olive oil and served as a side dish. Do not brown.

SQUASH BLOSSOMS STUFFED WITH CHEESE AND HERBS

4 servings

Serve these with a light tomato sauce, 562, beneath them.

Remove the pistils, leaving the stems on:

12 large squash blossoms

Mince together:

1 garlic clove, peeled
¼ teaspoon salt
Transfer to a small bowl and mix with:
¾ cup fresh goat cheese, ricotta, or shredded
    mozzarella or Monterey Jack
½ cup grated Parmesan
1 tablespoon chopped parsley
1 tablespoon chopped basil or 2 teaspoons
    chopped thyme
Black pepper to taste
Carefully open the petals of each blossom and stuff about 1 tablespoon of the mixture into the base. Twist the tops of the petals together. Dip the blossoms one at a time into:
1 large egg, lightly beaten
Then coat with:
Flour
Shake off any excess. Heat in a medium skillet over medium heat:
½ inch olive oil
Fry the blossoms 3 or 4 at a time, turning occasionally, until golden, 2 to 4 minutes. Drain briefly on paper towels. Serve right away.

ABOUT TARO

This versatile plant has leaves similar to the inedible elephant ears we grow in the garden, and a potato-like root that becomes grayish or violet when cooked. "Taro" is the umbrella name for a number of starchy tropical roots; **dasheen** is one variety. The roots are used as a vegetable or as the base for puddings and confections. A common taro has brown skin and white or lavender flesh. Taro leaves can be boiled as for spinach, 305; young leaves require 3 to 5 minutes and mature leaves 10 to 15. Select firm roots with no soft spots or blemishes. *To bake,* remove loose fibers and parboil for 15 minutes, then time as for potato baking, 297, but keep the oven at 375°F or lower.
➤ Uncooked taro may prove irritating to the skin, so handle it in water to which you add 1 tablespoon baking soda for every quart of water. *To boil taro,* treat as for Boiled Potatoes, 295. Taro may also be fried as for Saratoga Chips, 94. Do not soak the slices—merely dry for 30 minutes on paper toweling.

POI

About 5 cups
This native Hawaiian dish is an acquired taste, a little like sauerkraut but with a pureed texture.
Cut into 1-inch cubes:
2½ pounds taro roots, peeled and boiled as above
Mash in a wooden bowl with a wooden potato masher until a starchy paste forms. Work in gradually with your hands:
2½ cups water
To remove lumps and fibers, force the poi through a fine-mesh sieve lined with several thicknesses of cheesecloth.

Serve, or let stand 2 to 3 days in a cool place until it ferments and has a sour taste.

TARO CAKES

10 cakes
Bring a large saucepan of salted water to a boil. Wash, peel, and cut into 1-inch dice:
1 pound taro root
Boil until tender, about 25 minutes. Cool, then mash until smooth.
Heat in a small skillet over medium heat:
2 tablespoons olive oil
Add and cook, stirring, until soft:
1 cup finely chopped sweet onions
(1 jalapeño pepper, finely chopped)
Mix into the mashed taro, along with:
1 teaspoon salt
2 tablespoons chopped cilantro
2 tablespoons chopped parsley
Shape the mixture into ten 2-inch cakes. Roll each cake in:
¼ cup dry bread crumbs (2½ cups total)
Heat to 365°F in a large skillet:
1 inch vegetable oil
Fry the cakes, in batches, until golden on both sides, about 2 minutes. Serve immediately.

TOMATILLOS

Tomatillos look like small, shiny, green, yellow-green, or lavender tomatoes encased in parchment-paper husks. They are picked underripe and have a lemony tang. This tang lends sprightliness to sauces in Mexican cooking. Tomatillos may be sporadically available at the supermarket, but they are always for sale in Latino groceries. Select fruits that are firm and fill their husks, avoiding any that have come out of them. Store them, unwashed and un-husked, loose in the refrigerator crisper—they will keep for weeks.

Tomatillos go well with tomatoes, avocados, chile peppers, cilantro, lime, fish, and seafood. Try Roasted Tomatillo Spinach Sauce, 568, Chicken Chili Verde, 435, or Tomatillo Salsa, 571. *To prepare,* peel off and discard the husks, wipe off the sticky covering, and trim out the cores. Do not peel. Tomatillos can be quartered and added raw to salads, but even when a Mexican salsa is called *cruda,* or raw, the tomatillos are cooked because cooking intensifies their flavor.

To boil, bring 8 cups water and 2 teaspoons salt to a rolling boil in a large saucepan. Add 1 pound prepared tomatillos and cook just until softened, 3 to 5 minutes, depending on size. To steam, 242, cook, just until softened, 5 to 10 minutes, depending on size.

The flavor of tomatillos is greatly enhanced by *roasting* on a hot dry griddle in the manner of chile peppers, 292, cooking until the skin is slightly charred and the fruits have softened. *To broil,* place on a rimmed baking sheet 4 inches under a very hot broiler until they blister, darken, and soften on one side, about 4 minutes; turn them over and broil the other side for 5 to 6 minutes.

ABOUT TOMATOES

The late Southern humorist Lewis Grizzard said, "It's difficult to think anything but pleasant thoughts while eating a homegrown tomato." We couldn't agree more. Unfortunately, the opportunity to eat homegrown tomatoes only comes along once a year, from midsummer to the first frost—peak tomato season in most parts of America. When they are in season, pick or buy them ripe off of the vine. You can ripen a tomato that is green or partially green by letting it sit, or use it to make Fried Green Tomatoes, 312.

Salad tomatoes are small to medium in size and tend to be moderately juicy. Large beefsteak tomatoes (one of the largest varieties) are usually served sliced. In season, they are meaty, rich, and juicy, not to mention dark and deep in color. In most sections of the country, large field-grown tomatoes are not available during the colder months, being supplanted by hydroponic or hothouse-grown kinds. We find most of these disappointingly mushy in texture. Try instead the meaty pear-shaped plum tomatoes, Romas, which tend to have better flavor than round tomatoes out of season. They are particularly valued in cooking because their flesh is thick, meaty, and almost dry. Sometimes they are called paste or Roma tomatoes (the best-known variety) because they are the ones used to make classic tomato paste. They contribute a tangy-sweet flavor not just to pasta sauces but to soups, gratins, stews, or any other cooked tomato dish. You can also use plum tomatoes raw in uncooked sauces, in salads, and whenever juiced tomatoes are called for—just skip the juicing step called for in a particular recipe. Or use cherry, grape, or the tiny ultrasweet currant tomatoes, which are well flavored throughout the year. At the height of the season (midsummer to late frost) look at farmers' markets for so-called heritage or heirloom varieties of tomatoes, which come in a rainbow of colors and many shapes, with delightfully distinctive flavors to match.

Do not be confused by market tomatoes that are "vine-ripened" and are still on a portion of the vine. The tomatoes were harvested by snipping the vine with the green tomatoes still attached and offer little more value for the cost.

When shopping for any tomatoes, select firm, bright specimens that feel heavy for their size. Scarring around the stem end is harmless but attached stems and leaves should look fresh. If a tomato has a pronounced tomato smell, grab it. Homegrown tomatoes should be picked when they are fragrant. Try to eat them the same day they are picked if possible. Store ripe tomatoes at room temperature for as long as 5 or 6 days in a single layer out of sunlight with the stem side down. If you can't consume them quickly enough and they continue to ripen, store them in the refrigerator, and use as soon as possible.

Fruit of mature size but still green in color may be ripened on a windowsill but will lack the flavor and some of the nutritive value of its vine-ripened counterpart. Immature small-sized tomatoes will not ripen satisfactorily after harvesting. Use them, if at all, for pickling, 943.

Prepare tomatoes stuffed, for salads, 173, and as cases for vegetables, 313.

Tomatoes have great affinities with butter, olive and nut oils, cheese in any form, onions, garlic, basil, oregano, sage, thyme, dill, parsley, rosemary, cilantro, peppers, walnuts, olives, and capers.

To peel tomatoes, stroke the skin with the dull edge of a knife blade until the skin wrinkles; or cut an X in the skin on the bottom of each tomato. Lower one by one into a pot of boiling water for about 15 seconds. Lift them out with a sieve and drop into a bowl of ice water to stop the cooking. Pull off the skin with the tip of the knife. If the skin sticks, return the tomato to the boiling water for another 10 seconds and repeat. ➤ To peel a large quantity of tomatoes, see Blanching I, 1054. If a recipe can use a touch of smoky flavor and you have gas burners, an easier way to peel tomatoes is to hold the tomato on a long-handled fork over a burner, turning it until the skin splits. ➤ Do not plunge in water, but after cooling, peel as above.

Peeling tomatoes

When you use fresh tomatoes in cooking, their juiciness is seldom an asset. ➤ To avoid watery results, slice the tomatoes across the equator; then, holding it above a bowl, squeeze the tomato to eject excess juice and seeds. When recipes call for strained canned tomatoes, force the pulp through a strainer or sieve, to make the most of its thickening and seasoning power; and watch your brand—find the most flavorful, undiluted, highest-quality canned tomatoes possible.

To microwave, place tomato halves in a round dish, cover, and cook on high: 2 to 4 minutes for 2 medium tomatoes, 10 to 13 minutes for 4 medium tomatoes, rearranging once halfway through. Let stand, covered, for 2 minutes.

To process for canning, see 888.

STEWED TOMATOES

4 servings

Quarter:

> 6 large tomatoes, peeled, 311, or 2^1/$_2$ cups
>   canned tomatoes

Place them in a heavy saucepan over low heat. You may add:

> (^{1}/$_2$ cup chopped celery)
> (1 teaspoon minced onion)
> (2 or 3 whole cloves)

Cook about 20 minutes for fresh tomatoes, 10 for canned. Stir occasionally to keep them from scorching. Season with:

> ^{3}/$_4$ teaspoon salt
> ^{1}/$_4$ teaspoon paprika
> 2 teaspoons white or brown sugar
> ^{1}/$_8$ teaspoon curry powder or 1 teaspoon
>   chopped parsley or basil
> 1 tablespoon butter

The tomatoes may be thickened with:

> (^{1}/$_2$ cup dry bread crumbs, 960)

FRIED GREEN TOMATOES

6 servings

This is for those of us who love homegrown tomatoes and can't wait for them to ripen. A true early-summer delight.
Core, then cut crosswise into ^{1}/$_2$-inch slices:

> 6 large green tomatoes

Combine in a shallow bowl:

> 2 cups fine cornmeal
> 1 cup all-purpose flour
> 1 teaspoon paprika
> Salt and black pepper to taste
> (1 tablespoon chopped parsley)
> (1 tablespoon chopped thyme)

Dip the tomato slices one at a time into:

> 1 cup milk

and then coat with the cornmeal mixture, shake off the excess, and set on a plate. Heat in a large skillet until hot enough to sizzle a drop of water:

> 1 inch vegetable oil or bacon drippings

Add as many tomatoes as will fit in a single layer and fry until golden and crisp, turning once. Drain on paper towels. Repeat with the remaining tomatoes, adding oil as needed. Serve immediately, plain or with:

> (Ranch Dressing, 576, Garlic Mayonnaise, 581,
>   or Rémoulade Sauce, 581)

TOMATOES PROVENÇALE

4 servings

If necessary, cut a thin slice from the bottom of each tomato so that it will stand upright.
Preheat the oven to 350°F. Lightly oil a 13 x 9-inch baking dish. Combine in a small bowl:

> ^{1}/$_2$ cup fresh bread crumbs
> 2 tablespoons grated Parmesan

> 2 tablespoons chopped flat-leaf parsley
> 2 tablespoons chopped basil
> 2 cloves garlic, finely chopped
> 2 teaspoons extra-virgin olive oil

Halve crosswise, then gently squeeze the seeds from:

> 4 medium firm-ripe tomatoes

Arrange cut side up in the baking dish and season with:

> Salt and black pepper to taste

Spoon the bread crumb mixture over the tomatoes, gently patting it into a dome on each. Drizzle over the tops:

> Olive oil

Bake until the bread crumbs are golden and the tomatoes are softened, about 50 minutes.

BROILED TOMATOES

4 servings

Serve as a side dish or place on thin slices of toast rubbed with garlic for warm open-faced sandwiches.
Preheat the broiler. Lightly oil a rimmed baking sheet. Core and cut into slices ^{1}/$_2$ to 1 inch thick:

> 4 large tomatoes, ripe but not too soft

Season with:

> 1 teaspoon salt
> ^{1}/$_4$ teaspoon black pepper

Place on the baking sheet and sprinkle with, if desired:

> (^{1}/$_2$ cup grated Parmesan)

Drizzle with:

> 2 tablespoons olive oil

Broil about 5 inches from the heat until golden on top and heated through, about 5 minutes. If made without cheese, serve with:

> Rémoulade Sauce, 581

SLOW-ROASTED TOMATOES

2 to 4 servings

Baking tomatoes for a long time at low heat concentrates their flavor to a rich tomato sauce. Toss with pasta or use on a pizza.
Preheat the oven to 250°F. Spread out on a rimmed baking sheet lined with parchment paper:

> 4 to 5 large ripe tomatoes, cut into ^{3}/$_4$-inch slices

Combine:

> 1 teaspoon confectioners' sugar
> 1 teaspoon salt
> 1 teaspoon black pepper

Sprinkle over the tomatoes. Drizzle with:

> Olive oil

Sprinkle with:

> Chopped basil, thyme, or other herb of your choice

Bake for 2 hours. Let cool to room temperature.

TOMATOES CREOLE

4 servings

Melt in a large skillet:

> 2 tablespoons butter

Add and cook, stirring, until softened:

1 large onion, minced

Add:

6 fresh tomatoes, peeled, 311, seeded, and sliced or
   2 cups drained seeded canned tomatoes

2 tablespoons minced celery

1 green bell pepper, cored, seeded, and cut into
   thin strips

Cook, stirring until tender, about 12 minutes. Add:

$^3/_4$ teaspoon salt

$^1/_4$ teaspoon paprika

$2^1/_2$ teaspoons brown sugar

($^3/_4$ teaspoon curry powder)

Strain the juice from the vegetables, set the vegetables aside, and cover to keep warm. Add enough:

Heavy cream

to the juices to make $1^1/_2$ cups liquid. Stir in:

Kneaded Butter, 545

Return to skillet and simmer, stirring the sauce until thick and smooth. Combine with the vegetables and cook, stirring, until heated through. Serve hot on:

Toast

with:

Cooked bacon

Or use the mixture to fill pepper cases, 292, or squash cases, 308.

SCALLOPED TOMATOES

8 to 10 servings

An old-fashioned way to make use of the summer's bounty of fresh tomatoes. For a more substantial dish, mix 1 cup finely diced ham or cooked chicken with the tomatoes.

Preheat the oven to 350°F. Grease a 10-inch shallow round baking or quiche dish or pie pan. Peel, 311, halve, seed, then cut into $^1/_4$-inch dice:

3 pounds tomatoes (about 4 cups)

Melt in a large skillet over medium heat:

2 tablespoons butter

Stir in:

$1^1/_2$ cups fine dry bread crumbs

Cook, stirring constantly, until fragrant and nicely toasted, 3 to 6 minutes. Scrape the crumbs into a mixing bowl and set aside. Return the skillet to medium heat and add:

3 tablespoons butter

Heat until the foam begins to subside, then add:

1 cup finely chopped onions

1 large red or green bell pepper, cored, seeded,
   and finely chopped

Cook, stirring occasionally, until tender and just beginning to color, about 10 minutes. Add the vegetables to the crumbs, along with:

1 tablespoon sugar

$^3/_4$ teaspoon salt

$^1/_2$ teaspoon black pepper

Mix well. Distribute half of the crumb mixture over the bottom of the baking dish. Cover evenly with the tomatoes and sprinkle lightly with:

Salt and black pepper

Sprinkle the remaining crumb mixture evenly over the top. Bake until the tomatoes are bubbly in the center and the top is richly browned, about 40 minutes.

Sprinkle with:

Chopped parsley

HOT STUFFED TOMATOES

To prepare cases for hot food, cut large hollows in the stem ends of firm but ripe (unpeeled) tomatoes. Salt and invert them on a rack to drain about 15 minutes. To prepare for cold foods, see 173.

Fill the tomato cases with any of the cooked foods listed below and cover with:

Au Gratin I, II, or III, 961

Place the cases on a rack in a baking pan over $^1/_2$ inch water and bake in a preheated 350°F oven 10 to 15 minutes. If they are very ripe, you may bake them in well-greased muffin tins to keep them shapely.

For fillings, try:

Goat cheese, mozzarella, or ricotta and minced herbs

Cooked ground lamb, pine nuts, and rice

Cooked sausage and mushrooms

Salmon or tuna and capers

Cooked long-grain white rice, wild rice, or bulgur,
   seasoned with salt and brown sugar

Creamed green peas or mushrooms with parsley

Creamed Spinach, 305

Creamed Corn, 271, and crumbled crisp cooked bacon

ABOUT TURNIPS

Those in the know choose turnips as an accompaniment to game. They make a good change, if browned, to serve instead of potatoes around a roast, 244. A favorite German peasant dish, **Himmel und Erde** (Heaven and Earth), is made of mashed turnips, potatoes, and seasoned apples, combined in any proportion. Small mild turnips are sometimes eaten raw.

All turnips consist of a lower stem and taproot. They have white flesh and are best when freshly harvested and purchased during cool, not hot, weather. Select firm, unblemished roots that are heavy for their size—the smaller, the milder and sweeter. Store in an open plastic bag in the refrigerator crisper, up to 1 week. If the greens are attached, remove and store separately. If tender, they can be cooked like greens, 277.

Turnips can be cooked and served any way potatoes are; cook until soft. Do not cook for too long, however, or an overcooked cabbagey flavor and texture will dominate. Turnips have affinities with cream, butter, lemon, nutmeg, garlic, sharp cheeses, crisp bacon, thyme, parsley, and chervil.

To prepare, wash, and to avoid bitterness, peel past the dark line separating rind from the white center. Cut into slices, wedges, cubes, or matchsticks. One pound of turnips will yield about 2 cups cooked. The earthy taste of cooked rutabagas and older turnips makes it possible to use them interchangeably in recipes.

To microwave, place 1 pound turnips, peeled and cut into $1/2$-inch cubes, in a 2-quart baking dish. Add 3 tablespoons stock or lightly salted water, cover, and cook on high until tender, 7 to 9 minutes, stirring after 3 minutes. Let stand, covered, for 3 minutes.

Pressure-cook whole turnips 8 to 12 minutes at 15 pounds pressure.

COOKED TURNIPS
4 servings
Large mature turnips are better suited to the second cooking method.
 I. Peel and slice or dice:
> **1 pound turnips**
Steam, 242, until tender, 7 to 12 minutes. Season to taste with:
> **Salt and black pepper**
and dress with:
> **Butter**
> **Fresh lemon juice or vinegar or**
> **Quick Tomato Sauce, 562**
Or mash or cream as for potatoes.
 II. Peel and slice or leave whole if small:
> **1 pound turnips**
Drop them into rapidly boiling water to cover. Add:
> **$1/2$ teaspoon salt**
> **$1/2$ teaspoon sugar**
Cook, uncovered, until tender, about 10 minutes if sliced, 15 to 25 minutes if whole. Serve as in I.

BRAISED TURNIPS
4 servings
Cook in boiling water, uncovered, over high heat for about 6 minutes:
> **$1^1/2$ pounds turnips, peeled, left whole if small,**
> **quartered if large**
Drain.
Melt in a large heavy skillet over high heat:
> **3 tablespoons butter**
Add the turnips and cook, stirring, until coated with butter, about 5 minutes. Add:
> **1 cup chicken stock or broth, or as needed**
> **$1/2$ teaspoon salt, or more to taste**
> **Black pepper to taste**
The stock should come about $3/4$ inch up the side of the turnips; add more stock or water if needed. Reduce the heat, cover the skillet, and simmer until the turnips are tender but still slightly resistant to the tip of a sharp knife, 10 to 20 minutes.

Remove the turnips to a serving dish. Boil the cooking liquid over high heat until reduced to a thin, syrupy glaze. Pour it over the turnips and serve immediately.

TURNIP PUREE
4 to 6 servings
Mashed potatoes soften the aggressive edge that turnips can have. You can simply boil the turnips and mash them, but they taste better if braised first. Keep the puree hot and work quickly, as reheating deflates the light texture. Prepare:
> **Braised Turnips, above**
adding, if desired:
> **1 leek, white part only, thoroughly cleaned and**
> **chopped**
Puree until smooth. Beat the puree into:
> **1 to 2 cups warm Mashed Potatoes, 295**
Add:
> **Softened butter to taste or $1/4$ cup heavy cream**
> **1 tablespoon chopped parsley**
> **1 teaspoon minced thyme**
> **Salt and black pepper to taste**
Whip with a fork until fluffy, about 30 seconds. Pile into a warmed serving bowl and top with:
> **1 to 2 tablespoons butter, softened**

ABOUT WATER CHESTNUTS
Water chestnuts are not chestnuts at all but rather an enlarged tip of a stem of watergrass. Fresh water chestnuts have a seductive delicacy not found in the blandly straightforward crunch of the canned. Choose firm water chestnuts without soft spots or signs of yellowing; refrigerate them in a paper bag for up to 2 weeks. Store opened canned water chestnuts in a plastic container in the refrigerator. If they have a metallic taste, boil for 1 minute and drain.

Water chestnuts grow in muddy water; fresh ones must be washed before you peel them. Their crisp white flesh will discolor, so drop the peeled pieces into a bowl of water if not cooking at once. Water chestnuts can be eaten raw but become more flavorful and remain crispy with cooking. Slice and add to stir-fries or chop and mix into ground meat or grains prior to cooking. For use in salads, boil them for 5 minutes, drain, and chill.

STIR-FRIED WATER CHESTNUTS
4 servings
Please read about Stir-Frying Vegetables, 242. Stir-fry shrimp or diced chicken breasts with the red peppers to turn this colorful dish into a main course.
Drop into a pot of boiling water and cook for 5 minutes if fresh, 1 minute if canned:
> **8 ounces fresh water chestnuts, peeled and sliced, or**
> **two 8-ounce cans sliced water chestnuts, rinsed**
> **and drained**
Drain well and pat dry. Combine in a small bowl:
> **3 tablespoons soy sauce**
> **2 teaspoons minced or crushed garlic**
> **2 teaspoons minced peeled fresh ginger**
> **2 teaspoons toasted sesame oil**

1 teaspoon sugar
1 teaspoon chili-garlic paste or $^1/_4$ teaspoon crushed
   red pepper flakes
Heat in a wok or large skillet over medium-high heat until
very hot:
1 tablespoon vegetable oil
Add:
2 large red bell peppers, cut into matchsticks
Stir-fry for 2 minutes. Stir in:
1 pound snow peas, trimmed
Stir-fry until tender but still crisp, about 2 minutes. Add the
water chestnuts and stir-fry until all the vegetables are tender, another 1 to 3 minutes. Stir in the soy sauce mixture,
increase the heat to high, and cook, stirring to coat thoroughly, until the sauce is slightly reduced, about 2 minutes
more. Stir in, if desired:
(1 cup bean sprouts)
Serve hot, sprinkled with:
2 tablespoons minced cilantro
1 scallion, minced

WATERCRESS

Usually thought of only as salad and sandwich material,
watercress not only adds a distinctive flavor to soups and
vegetables but lends piquancy to other cooked greens. ➤
Never overcook it, as it becomes stringy. Serve it pureed
as a garnish with grilled meat and fish. See Cream of Watercress Soup, 145.

ABOUT YUCA

Also called **cassava** or **manioc,** this root known as yuca in
Spanish has a rich, buttery taste. It is from this root that
tapioca is processed. The texture is that of a rather flaky
boiled potato and it is tasty in stews, served with garlicky
olive oil or fresh salsa. Its shiny barklike brown skin con-
ceals hard pure-white flesh that turns yellowish and almost translucent when cooked. Yuca does not store well,
so make sure it smells fresh and has no mold or cracks
when you buy it. Keep it at cool room temperature and
cook it as soon as possible. Or freeze peeled raw chunks
tightly wrapped in plastic for up to 1 month.

Yuca is higher in calories than potatoes and quite filling
in small portions; it provides much potassium and some
iron. Scrub and cut the tapered root into chunks, slit the
skin with a paring knife, and then use the blade to peel
away the skin and its under-layer in one piece. Halve the
chunks lengthwise and pull out the thin, fibrous core that
runs down the center of the root. Rinse well and hold in
cold water.

YUCA WITH CITRUS AND GARLIC

6 servings
Use a paring knife to remove the outer peel and fibrous
underlayer from:
3 pounds yuca, scrubbed and cut into 3-inch sections

Rinse well, and place in a pot of cold water to cover. Add:
$^1/_2$ teaspoon salt
Bring to a boil, then reduce the heat and simmer, covered,
until the yuca is easily pierced with a fork, about 30 minutes. Meanwhile, heat in a large skillet:
2 tablespoons vegetable oil
Add and cook, stirring, until translucent, about 4 minutes:
1 small onion, minced
Stir in:
6 cloves garlic, minced
$^1/_3$ cup fresh grapefruit or lemon juice
$^1/_3$ cup fresh orange juice
$^1/_4$ teaspoon salt
Cook gently until the garlic is tender, 10 to 15 minutes.
Stir in:
2 tablespoons chopped parsley or cilantro
1 teaspoon crumbled dried oregano
Drain the yuca, combine with the sauce, and serve immediately.

ABOUT TOFU, TEMPEH, AND OTHER VEGETARIAN PROTEINS

TOFU

Tofu is the humble soybean's leap toward culinary art, especially in the cuisines of China and Japan. Also called
bean curd and **dofu,** regular tofu is made like cheese, by
coagulating soy milk until it forms curds, which are broken
up and then pressed. But, unlike cheese, tofu rarely stands
on its own. Instead, it soaks in the flavors of the soup,
sauce, marinade, or dressings in which it is served.

Tofu is as perishable as dairy foods and highly susceptible to bacterial contamination, so keep the tofu refrigerated ➤ and wash your hands and work surfaces after
preparing it.

When buying tofu, check the expiration date. You can
leave it in its original package, but it is better to open the
package, discard the liquid, and pour in fresh water;
change the water daily. It will keep for up to a week, depending on its freshness when purchased. Because of the
risk of contamination, ➤ it is best to avoid tofu sold from
open tubs, even if it is refrigerated.

Regular tofu is labeled soft, firm, or extra firm. Extra
firm and firm hold together better when cooked, when
sliced or cubed, and they release less moisture which may
dilute a sauce or soup. If you press soft tofu, below, you
can substitute it for firm.

Another type of tofu is called "silken." It is aseptically
packaged and is labeled soft, medium, firm, or extra firm.
All are much more fragile than regular tofu. Made more
like yogurt than like cheese, silken tofu is coagulated from
soy milk and not pressed. Silken tofu is delicate, cannot be
pressed, and is *not* interchangeable with regular tofu. It
can be carefully cut into cubes, and makes a welcome garnish for clear soups. Silken tofu purees beautifully in a
food processor or blender. Pureed soft silken tofu has the

consistency of yogurt and can be used in salad dressings, sauces, dips, cream soups, and puddings. Refrigerate pureed tofu and stir well before using. Be aware that it will darken slightly to a beige or grayish color as it stands, so use it with ingredients that will mask the color. For a dessert topping, use brown sugar or maple syrup instead of white sugar. You may add 1 to 2 teaspoons fresh lemon or lime juice to any recipe containing pureed tofu to perk up the taste.

Make tofu firm by pressing it under a weight; the curd becomes denser and chewier and holds together better when sliced or cubed.

To press a 1-pound block of tofu, cut it horizontally to make two slabs, each about 1 inch thick. Place a sheet of aluminum foil over a cutting board large enough to hold both slabs side by side. Allow the water to drain off by placing one end of the board over the edge of the sink or on a baking sheet and propping up the other end with a $1/4$-cup measure. Place the tofu on the board and cover with another sheet of foil. Place a second cutting board or similarly shaped weight over the tofu and let stand for 10 minutes. The sides of the tofu should bulge very slightly, but be careful not to overweight soft tofu before it has compacted, or it may split. After 10 minutes, add more weight, evenly distributed; a cast-iron skillet or Dutch oven with two or three large cans, or several nested heavy skillets will do the job. Check the weighted tofu for firmness after 30 minutes; if desired, turn the slabs over, replace the weight, and press for an additional 15 to 30 minutes. Refrigerate pressed tofu in a bowl of water; it will not reabsorb water and can be kept for 2 to 3 days if you change the water daily. While some recipes call for pressed tofu, this extra step is not essential, it just adds textural refinement.

Freezing pressed tofu removes even more moisture. The thawed tofu can be cut into cubes and used like other tofu, but the dryness makes it chewier and better able to absorb marinades and sauces. It can be crumbled over salads or soups, and the crumbles can mimic the texture of hardboiled egg whites in a mock egg salad. Pressed firm or extra-firm tofu works best, but soft tofu can also be frozen.

Pressed or not, tofu can be cut into cubes or slices and sautéed in oil to brown and crisp it before adding to stir-fries or stews. The flexibility of tofu—its ability to take on so many textures and flavors—should not detract from the ease of cooking it simply. It is excellent cubed and tossed into stir-fried vegetables, 242, or in miso soup, 125. Tofu is, after all, a convenience food—one that provides all the nutrients of soybeans with very little preparation.

Smoked tofu is exceptionally convenient, because it tastes good straight from the package, like a semifirm smoked cheese. Slice it for a sandwich or mix cubes of it into a chopped vegetable salad.

Please note that ➤ tofu package sizes vary widely. In the following recipes, you can use any size package that closely approximates the weight indicated.

TOFU OR SOYBEAN CURD
About 1 $1/2$ cups

Bean curd, a valuable complete-protein product of delicate cheeselike consistency, must be processed from the freshly made hot soy milk, not store-bought soy milk. Prepare:

4 cups Soy Milk, 1023

Have ready two 1-quart plastic freezer boxes of the type that nest. Perforate the bottom and lower portion of one with holes about $1/4$ inch in diameter as though on a 1-inch grid.
For a solidifier, combine:

1 cup water
1$1/2$ teaspoons epsom salts or calcium sulfate; or use 2$2/3$ tablespoons lemon juice, or 2$1/4$ tablespoons cider vinegar

Heat the soy milk with:

6 cups water

to boiling point, then remove from the heat.
Add one-third cup of the solidifier solution. Stir gently and completely. Gently stir in another $1/3$ cup of solidifier, and cover the pot for 3 minutes to await the forming of the curds. Sprinkle the remaining solution over the milk and gently stir the surface. Cover for 3 minutes, or for 6 minutes if using epsom salts or calcium sulfate. If curds do not form during this period, add:

(A little more dissolved solidifier)

Line the perforated quart container with a generous square of moist thin muslin and place the container in the sink. Gently ladle in the soy curd mixture and fold the ends of the cloth over the top. Partly fill the other plastic container with water to use as a 1-pound weight. Let set 10 to 15 minutes or until the whey no longer is expressed. The whey can be saved for stock. Submerge in cold water the perforated container with the wrapped curd. Very gently unwrap the curd under water and let it sit undisturbed for 3 to 5 minutes to firm up. It is highly perishable; store it refrigerated in water for only a few days. Use squares of drained tofu as a soup garnish, in salads, or as a dressing. For other suggestions, see *The Book of Tofu,* by William Shurtleff and Akiko Aoyagi.

TOFU BURGERS
6 servings

This flavorful mixture can also be baked as a loaf in a greased loaf pan at 350°F for 40 to 45 minutes.
If using dried mushrooms, soak in warm water to cover until softened, about 20 minutes:

1 ounce dried mushrooms

Drain, discarding the liquid, and squeeze out the excess water from the mushrooms or rinse:

4 ounces fresh shiitake mushrooms

Chop the mushrooms, discarding the tough centers and stems. Heat in a large skillet over medium heat:

2 to 3 teaspoons toasted sesame oil

Add the shiitakes, along with:

1 cup finely chopped broccoli florets and stems

$^1/_3$ cup finely chopped red bell pepper

$^1/_4$ cup sliced scallions

2 teaspoons finely chopped peeled fresh ginger

$1^1/_2$ teaspoons minced garlic

Cook, stirring, until tender, 4 to 5 minutes. Stir in:

8 ounces regular or smoked tofu, finely chopped

1 cup cooked brown rice

$^2/_3$ cup dry bread crumbs

2 large eggs, lightly beaten

1 tablespoon soy sauce

Remove to a food processor and pulse several times, until a spoonful of the mixture can be pressed into a ball. Shape the mixture into 6 patties, using about $^1/_2$ cup for each.

Cook in a lightly greased skillet over medium heat until browned, 3 to 5 minutes per side. Serve as for Hamburgers, 510.

TOFU SALAD

2 servings

Use this in a sandwich, with fresh tomatoes, or heap on a green salad.

Cube:

8 ounces extra-firm tofu, pressed if desired, 316

Mix with:

$^1/_4$ to $^1/_3$ cup mayonnaise

1 to 2 teaspoons Dijon mustard

$^1/_4$ cup minced red onion

$^1/_4$ cup minced celery or fennel

$^1/_4$ cup minced carrot

2 tablespoons chopped parsley, cilantro, basil, or mint

(2 teaspoons chopped cornichons or capers)

($^1/_8$ teaspoon curry powder, chili powder, or turmeric)

(Pinch of ground red pepper)

($^1/_2$ teaspoon fresh lemon juice or white wine vinegar)

Salt and black pepper to taste

Refrigerate until cool, about 1 hour.

TEMPEH

Tempeh is a high-protein cake made from partially cooked and fermented soybeans. As the soybeans ferment, they become bound together in a slab. Packaged and sold refrigerated, tempeh has a sharp flavor and firm texture. Grains such as millet, wheat, or rye may be added to tempeh to soften the flavor. Tempeh is perishable, so check the freshness date and store refrigerated. Unused tempeh can be stored in the refrigerator in an airtight container for up to a week. A slight white mold on tempeh is normal, but ➤ sliminess or signs of yellow, green, or red mold are not desirable, nor is a strong smell of ammonia. Tempeh must be cooked before eating, and is usually cut into slices, strips, and cubes or crumbled before cooking. It substitutes well for meat with marinades, sauces, stir-frying, or sautéing and pairs well with mushrooms.

MOO SHU TEMPEH

6 servings

Mandarin pancakes are delicate and delicious. They are available at Chinese markets and some supermarkets, but warm flour tortillas will substitute nicely.

Combine and let stand until the mushrooms are softened, 15 to 20 minutes:

1 ounce dried shiitake mushrooms

$^1/_4$ ounce dried wood ear or cloud ear mushrooms

$1^1/_2$ cups hot water

Drain, reserving the liquid, and squeeze out the excess water from the mushrooms. Slice the mushrooms, discarding the tough centers and stems.

Combine in a bowl:

8 ounces tempeh, cut into thin strips

1 tablespoon soy sauce

Meanwhile, warm loosely covered, in a 300°F oven, about 10 or 15 minutes:

12 Mandarin pancakes

Combine in another bowl:

3 tablespoons soy sauce

3 tablespoons dry sherry

1 tablespoon cornstarch

1 teaspoon sugar

Set aside.

Heat in a wok or large skillet over medium heat:

1 teaspoon toasted sesame oil

Add:

3 large eggs, lightly beaten

Cook, without stirring, until set but still moist. Remove the egg pancake and cut into small pieces; set aside.

Heat in the wok or skillet:

1 tablespoon toasted sesame oil

Add the tempeh and stir-fry until lightly browned. Add the mushrooms, along with:

One 8-ounce can bamboo shoots, rinsed, drained, and sliced

$^1/_4$ cup sliced scallions

2 teaspoons minced peeled fresh ginger

Stir-fry for 2 to 3 minutes. Strain the mushroom soaking liquid through a fine-mesh sieve lined with dampened paper towels, measure it, and add water as needed to make $^3/_4$ cup. Add the soy sauce–cornstarch mixture and pour into the wok and boil, stirring, until thickened, about 1 minute. Gently stir in the egg pieces.

Remove the pancakes from the oven and spread each pancake with:

2 to 3 tablespoons plum sauce ($1^1/_2$ to $2^1/_4$ cups total)

Top each with about $^1/_3$ cup of the tempeh mixture and then with:

1 scallion, trimmed (12 total)

Roll up, then fold up the bottom end for eating.

SZECHUAN-STYLE "HACKED" TEMPEH
4 servings

Tempeh replaces the chicken in this traditional dish. Served chilled, it is tossed with a peanut sauce.
Combine in a bowl and let stand for 30 minutes:

> **One 8-ounce package tempeh, cubed**
> **2 tablespoons soy sauce**
> **2 to 3 tablespoons minced peeled fresh ginger**
> **1 teaspoon minced garlic**
> **$^1/_2$ teaspoon Szechuan peppercorns, cracked**

Heat in a wok or large skillet over medium heat:

> **1 tablespoon vegetable oil**

Add the tempeh mixture and cook, stirring, until browned. Let cool, then refrigerate until chilled.
Combine and arrange on a serving platter:

> **2 cups sliced seeded peeled cucumbers**
> **$^1/_2$ cup chopped red bell pepper**
> **$^1/_4$ cup sliced scallions**

Spoon the tempeh mixture over the vegetables. Stir together until smooth, then drizzle over the tempeh mixture:

> **$^1/_4$ cup smooth peanut butter**
> **2 tablespoons soy sauce**
> **2 tablespoons rice vinegar**
> **1 tablespoon dry sherry**
> **3 to 4 teaspoons toasted sesame oil**
> **1 teaspoon chili paste**
> **2 tablespoons water**

Garnish with:

> **$^1/_2$ cup chopped red bell peppers**
> **$^1/_4$ cup sliced scallions**
> **$^1/_4$ cup chopped salted peanuts**

Toss just before serving. If desired, serve with:

> **Chilled cooked rice noodles**

TVP (TEXTURED VEGETABLE PROTEIN)

The high protein content of soybeans has inspired American manufacturers to make it available in rather anonymous forms, without the distinct character of tofu or tempeh, for use as a meat substitute known as **textured vegetable protein,** or **TVP.** TVP is made from compressed defatted soy flour. The granules swell to twice their volume when cooked, taking on the texture of ground meat. To equal the volume of 1 pound ground meat, soak 1 cup textured vegetable protein; use it alone or in combination with ground meat in meat loaves, spaghetti sauce, chili, tacos, Sloppy Joes, or any other recipe where ground meat is used. A meat loaf made with textured vegetable protein will be softer than one made with meat but will firm up to meat texture if refrigerated overnight. Such loaves, like meat loaf, freeze well.

Textured soy concentrate or protein, or **TSP,** is defatted soy flour concentrate processed to remove the natural bean sugars that cause gas. The product is extruded into chunks and dried. Rehydrate the chunks in hot stock or water and add to stews, curries, or other saucy dishes as they simmer to absorb the seasonings.

TEX-MEX STYLE DINNER LOAF
6 servings

The flavor of this loaf is even better the next day. Leftovers make terrific sandwiches.
Soak in $^1/_2$ cup boiling water until softened, 15 to 20 minutes:

> **1 ancho chile pepper**

Preheat the oven to 350°F. Grease a 9 x 5-inch loaf pan.
Drain the chile, and squeeze out the excess water. Chop the chile, discarding the seeds and membranes. Combine with:

> **1 cup textured vegetable protein**
> **One 15-ounce can Italian or Mexican-style tomato sauce**
> **One 15-ounce can black beans, rinsed and drained**
> **$^3/_4$ cup water**
> **1 large egg, beaten**
> **$^1/_4$ cup raisins**
> **1 small onion, chopped**
> **1 small fresh jalapeño pepper, seeded and minced, or 2 canned chile peppers, drained and chopped**
> **$^3/_4$ cup dry bread crumbs**
> **$^1/_3$ cup all-purpose flour**
> **$^1/_4$ cup finely chopped cilantro**
> **2 teaspoons salt**
> **1 teaspoon ground cumin**

Pack the loaf mixture into the pan. Cover loosely with aluminum foil and bake for 45 minutes.
Uncover and bake until set, 30 minutes. Let stand in the pan on a rack for 5 minutes, then invert onto a serving platter.

SEITAN

Also called **wheat gluten** or **wheat meat,** seitan is another protein-rich meat substitute, but made with wheat instead of soy. It was invented by Buddhist monks centuries ago to bring the texture and protein of meat to their vegetarian diet. It is made by kneading and washing a dough made of high-protein wheat flour to develop the gluten and remove its starch and bran. Seitan swells, absorbs flavor, and becomes firm with cooking. You can shortcut the process of making seitan at home by starting with a packaged mix or buying ready-to-use seitan in jars or refrigerated tubs or packages. Seitan is commonly sold in the liquid it was cooked in, and may be sold flavored.

Seitan should be prepared in a way that will disguise its gray color, but ➤ lengthy cooking brings out a bitter taste. Small chunks or cutlets can be panfried or lightly battered and deep-fried for appealing crispness. Thin slices can be simmered in a sauce and will indeed have the texture of braised meat. Chop seitan in a food processor or grind in a meat grinder and use it like ground beef in spaghetti sauce and Sloppy Joes. ➤ It should be avoided by anyone sensitive to gluten, especially those with celiac disease.

To prepare gluten or seitan from flour, knead into a stiff dough:

4 cups whole-grain or unbleached flour

1¹/₂ to 3 cups lukewarm water

Roll it into a ball and submerge it in water for 2 hours. Then, still keeping the dough ball under water, work the starch out of it by kneading. At intervals, pour off the starchy water. Replace the water you pour off and continue to knead, repeating this operation until the water is almost clear. The gluten is then ready to cook. Form the starch-free dough into a loaf and cut it into ¹/₂-inch slices. Put into a 3-quart pan for which you have a tight lid:

¹/₄ cup vegetable oil

You may flavor the gluten at this point by sautéing until clear and golden:

1 finely sliced medium-sized onion

Put the gluten slices into the pan and cover with:

Boiling water

Simmer, closely covered, for 1 hour and drain. Store refrigerated and closely covered. The gluten slices can then be further cooked by dipping them in:

Egg Wash, 799

then:

Potato or rice flour

Brown slowly in an oiled pan. Or cover with:

Undiluted condensed tomato, cream of mushroom, or celery soup

Place in a preheated 350°F oven about 20 minutes or until thoroughly heated.

ROOT VEGETABLE AND SEITAN STEW

8 servings

Vary the vegetables for the stew depending on availability and preference. Turnips, rutabagas, kohlrabi, and fennel are other delicious choices.

Heat in a large Dutch oven or heavy pot over low heat:

2 tablespoons vegetable oil

Add:

1 cup sliced onions

1 cup sliced leeks

Cook, uncovered, stirring occasionally, until caramelized, 20 to 30 minutes. Stir in:

4 cups chopped mixed mushrooms, such as portobellos, shiitake, and/or oyster mushrooms

5 garlic cloves, minced

1 teaspoon salt

Cook for 3 to 4 minutes, then stir in:

3 tablespoons all-purpose flour

Cook for 1 minute. Cut into 1-inch cubes and add:

1 medium baking potato

1 medium parsnip, peeled

1 small butternut squash, peeled and seeded

1¹/₂ cups chopped unpeeled Jerusalem artichokes (sunchokes)

Add:

1 cup sliced carrots

Stir in:

3¹/₂ cups vegetable stock or broth

¹/₂ cup white wine or additional vegetable stock

¹/₂ teaspoon dried rosemary

¹/₂ teaspoon dried thyme

2 or 3 pinches of grated or ground nutmeg

Bring to a boil, then reduce the heat and simmer, covered, for 20 minutes. Stir in:

1¹/₂ cups halved small Brussels sprouts

1¹/₂ cups chopped plum tomatoes

1 pound seitan, cut into 1-inch cubes

Simmer, covered, for 20 minutes. Season with:

Salt and black pepper to taste

Serve over:

(Hot cooked bulgur, 365, or brown rice, 367)

PASTA, NOODLES, AND DUMPLINGS

From linguine to lo mein, from spätzle to soba, pasta, noodles, and dumplings make up one of the largest and richest categories of our cooking history. Certainly Italy has made the greatest contribution. Italy's influence on our love affair with noodles is so great that the Italian word *pasta* has become part of our everyday language. In this chapter, we generally use "pasta" to refer to noodles of Italian origin and "noodles" when referring to European and Asian dishes.

Those concerned about calories should keep portion sizes within reasonable limits, use tomato or other vegetables sauces rather than cream sauces, and add only small amounts of meat or cheese.

ABOUT PASTA AND NOODLES

Although fresh and dried pasta and noodles are different, one should not necessarily be considered better than the other. **Dried pasta** is usually made from durum wheat and water. It comes in a wide variety of shapes, from long, thin spaghetti to short, hollow ziti. Dried pasta is convenient, inexpensive, reliable, and always available.

Fresh pasta, either flat strands like fettuccine or stuffed pieces like ravioli, is typically made with eggs and all-purpose flour. **Homemade pasta** is sublime. Though it is somewhat time consuming to make, you can control the ingredients and shape or fill it to suit your own taste. If you do have access to fresh pasta, buy sheets of it and cut to make your own ravioli or tortellini. ➤ Fresh pasta cooks faster than dried pasta.

Egg noodles are another form of pasta. They are usually made with eggs and all-purpose flour and cut into short, wide to narrow strips. Egg noodles are typically available

dried, though they are very good when fresh and homemade. Asian noodles come in many varieties. The most common are made from wheat, buckwheat, or rice, and they may be fresh or dried. They are typically cut into long strands (see About Asian Noodles, 330).

ABOUT COOKING PASTA

Figure on 2 ounces pasta per person for first-course servings and at least 4 ounces for main-course servings. ➤ One pound pasta serves 6 to 8 as a first course or 4 as a main course. ➤ Allow the same amount of noodles for a main course, and 1 to 2 ounces per person when served as a side dish.

To avoid pasta or noodles sticking together, cook all types of pasta in a large quantity of boiling salted water. ➤ Allow 4 to 6 quarts water per 1 pound pasta. ➤ Use about 1 tablespoon salt per each 2 to 3 quarts water. Cooking more than 2 pounds of pasta at once invites uneven cooking and would require too big a pot to make for safe draining.

Since pasta cooks quickly and is at its best as soon as it is cooked, have everything ready before you start—the sauce, a large colander set in the sink for draining, and, if possible, a serving bowl or dishes warming in the oven. Once the salted water is rapidly boiling, add the pasta all at once; long strands that do not fit under the water should be allowed to soften for a few seconds, then pressed down and stirred in. Give the pasta a stir, partially cover the pot, and let it return to the boil. ➤ Do not cover the pot completely, or it will boil over. When the water is boiling again, uncover. Stir the pasta often to keep it from sticking together.

No matter which pasta you are cooking, ➤ do not overcook. The timing can be gauged only by lifting a piece from the pot and tasting it—not once, but several times. The perfect state is **al dente**—or literally, to the tooth—reached when ➤ no taste of raw flour remains but the pasta still offers slight resistance to the bite. Start testing fresh pasta and very thin shapes after about 30 seconds, spaghetti and linguine after 4 minutes, and macaroni and other short, tubular shapes after 8 minutes. Once the pasta is done, ➤ immediately scoop out and reserve a small amount of the hot cooking water in case the sauce needs thinning. Empty the pot into the colander and quickly shake the colander to rid ➤ the pasta of most of the water. The pasta should not be bone-dry, or the surface starch will cause it to stick together. ➤ Rinse only if you want to separate the pieces (for example, for lasagne) or if it is to be eaten cool in a salad. The starch that clings to unrinsed pasta helps the sauce meld with the hot pasta.

Immediately combine the drained pasta with its sauce, over heat for maximum flavor, or simply toss the hot pasta and sauce in a warmed serving bowl. ➤ Use some of the reserved cooking water to thin the sauce if needed. The starch in the hot water extends the sauce and brings body to it, while the salt in the cooking water helps season it. It is especially useful to loosen sauces based on garlic and olive oil or sautéed vegetables with the cooking water; adding more oil instead would make the sauce too heavy.

ABOUT SAUCES FOR PASTA

Sauces for pasta can be as simple as melted butter or as complex as a long-simmered ragu of assorted meats, tomatoes, vegetables, and seasonings.

Garlic and oil, or *aglio e olio*, 327, is a classic. Uncomplicated vegetable sauces are made by adding zucchini, cauliflower, broccoli rabe, bell peppers, beans, or other vegetables to this olive oil base. Other typical additions include anchovies, crushed red pepper flakes, and fresh herbs. Pesto Sauce, 569, the classic sauce of Genoa, and Pistou, 569, from Provence, are made by mixing fresh basil, cheese, and pine nuts with olive oil and garlic.

Marinara sauce, 562, is simply olive oil and garlic with chopped tomatoes; its many variations include Puttanesca, 563, with olives and capers, and Red Clam Sauce, 328. In northern Italy, where butter prevails, you will likely come across egg pasta tossed with nothing more than butter, cream, and a little grated Parmesan; the sauce for Fettuccine Alfredo, 327, is made with just these three ingredients. Many meat-based sauces contain very little tomato. Bolognese, 564, a ragu from Bologna, will typically include veal, beef, butter, and a little milk or cream. Tuscan beef sauces are flavored with olive oil and often red wine. Rome is famous for its lamb ragu. The classic Neapolitan meat sauce is based on pork and tomatoes.

Most tomato sauces invite improvisation, but no matter what other ingredients eventually find their way into the sauce, ➤ the best begin with good tomatoes—ripe with deep flavor and a balance of sweet and acid. When fresh tomatoes are unavailable, choose good-quality canned whole tomatoes for best flavor. Cans of crushed and pureed tomatoes can contain tomato paste, which will affect taste. Do not assume imported canned tomatoes are best; several brands of domestic tomatoes are as good as or even better than imported varieties.

MATCHING PASTA AND SAUCES

There are hundreds of different pasta shapes. With all these possibilities, it helps to remember a basic rule for pairing pasta and sauce, ➤ the chunkier, more robust and rustic the sauce, the bolder the pasta shape. Match large shapes such as penne and wide, thick rigatoni with sauces with big flavors and bite-sized chunks of vegetables or meats. Ethereal angel hair is best with light sauces. Hearty bean and vegetable soups are best with bite-sized pasta such as tubetti, ditalini, elbows, or small shells. Cream or butter sauces go best with fresh egg pasta. ➤ Remember that pasta is meant to be moistened with sauce, not swimming in it: you want to taste the pasta as well as the sauce.

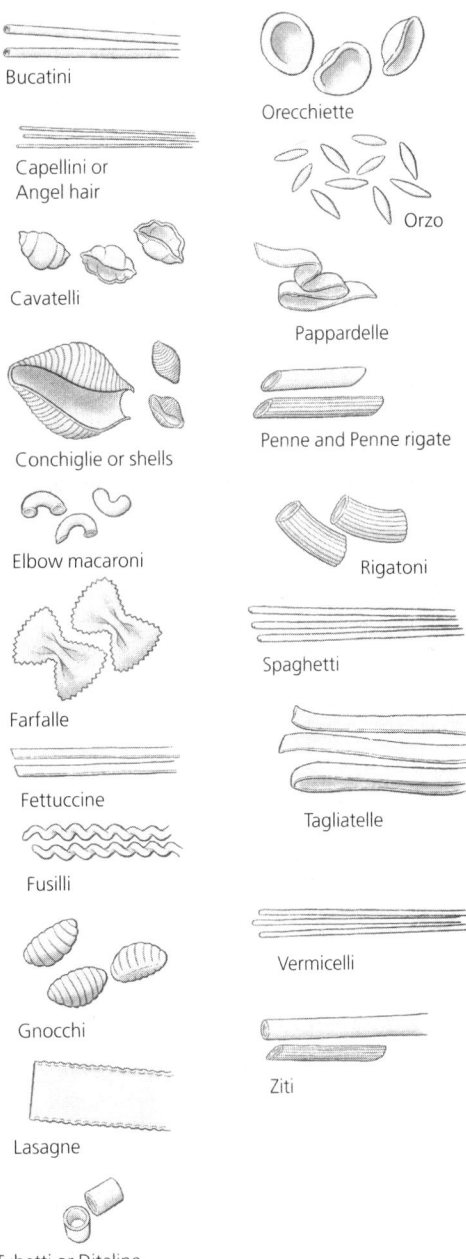

Bucatini

Capellini or Angel hair

Cavatelli

Conchiglie or shells

Elbow macaroni

Farfalle

Fettuccine

Fusilli

Gnocchi

Lasagne

Tubetti or Ditaline

Orecchiette

Orzo

Pappardelle

Penne and Penne rigate

Rigatoni

Spaghetti

Tagliatelle

Vermicelli

Ziti

SUGGESTED PASTA SAUCES

The following are not the only sauces to enhance a pasta, so search our sauce chapter for others that may appeal to your ingenuity: Roasted Red Pepper Sauce, 549, Oyster Sauce, 552, Tomato Sauce, 562, Piquant Sauce, 556, Sun-Dried Tomato Sauce, 562, Tomato Sauce with Meatballs, 564, Quick Tomato Sauce, 562, Fresh Tomato Sauce, 563, Grilled Tomato Sauce, 563, Amatriciana Sauce, 563,

Puttanesca Sauce, 563, Tomato Meat Sauce, 563, Bolognese Sauce, 564, Pesto Sauce, 569, and Sun-Dried Tomato Pesto, 569. You can find pasta inspiration in other chapters as well, such as Mixed Shellfish in Tomato Sauce, 369, and Thai Clam Pot, 376, in Shellfish; Italian Pot Roast, 477, and Hungarian Goulash, 480, in Meat; and Creamed Chicken, 445, and Woodcock in Rosemary Cream Sauce, 461, in Poultry and Wildfowl.

COMMERCIALLY PREPARED PASTA SAUCE

Prepared sauces are convenient for quick pasta meals. Look for the simplest versions, with the fewest preservatives, and avoid those that are heavy with thickeners and sugar. Try several different kinds until you find one you like.

Simple additions that can boost the flavor of a store-bought sauce are:

A drizzle of good olive oil and a sprinkling of black pepper
A handful of mushrooms, sliced and sautéed, 283
A few pitted olives and drained capers
A can or pouch of tuna, drained
Chopped anchovies
A mixture of minced herbs, such as parsley, basil, thyme, and/or rosemary
Minced garlic and/or onion sautéed in olive oil
Crumbled browned Italian sausage or ground beef

ADDITIONS TO PASTA

Pasta is the perfect starting point for a quick and easy meal. For an easy supper, stir in a few of the following:

Extra-virgin olive oil
Goat cheese, ricotta, or other soft cheese
Chopped herbs such as oregano, thyme, marjoram, parsley, or mint
Grated lemon zest or fresh lemon juice
Chopped sun-dried tomatoes, olives, or capers
Chopped smoked salmon
Chopped garlic or mild onions
Grated hard cheese, such as Romano or Parmesan
Chopped ham, prosciutto, or salami
Chopped anchovies or canned tuna
Italian Meatballs, 513
Melted butter, heavy cream, plain yogurt, or crème fraîche
Gorgonzola and chopped walnuts
Vegetables such as sautéed zucchini, chunks of roasted eggplant, slices of roasted red bell peppers, cooked or thawed frozen peas, and sautéed mushrooms

ABOUT CHEESE FOR PASTA

The combination of pasta and cheese in even the simplest arrangements, such as Fettuccine with Butter and Cheese, 325, can be so superb that it's little wonder the two ingredients are linked in our minds. For the best flavor, buy cheese in chunks, and grate it over the dish just before serving.

Using one of the many low-cost graters on the market, grating cheese is simple. For the coarsest texture, desirable for a robust dish, ➤ use the largest holes of a box grater; the finest gratings are made with a small hand-held grater/zester, perfect for fragile pastas with delicate sauces.

Do not feel obliged, however, to serve grated cheese with every pasta dish. Some pasta dishes are better without it, such as most seafood pasta dishes, where cheese can overwhelm the delicate flavors of many fish and shellfish. Highly seasoned sauces such as those containing olives, capers, or crushed red pepper do not need cheese.

Parmesan cheese is a hard, dry cow's milk cheese with a salty, nutty flavor. True **Parmigiano-Reggiano** is made in a small designated area of Emilia-Romagna, in northern Italy. Parmigiano-Reggiano usually reaches its peak at about two years. Other Parmesans are made in the United States, Argentina, and Australia, and some are quite good. Use Parmesan grated in savory dishes and stuffings or over pasta or soup. Freeze the rinds and use later to enrich broths of soups. Parmesan is also a fine eating cheese. Try it cut into chunks or as an appetizer drizzled with good balsamic vinegar, or for dessert with nuts and fresh or dried fruits. **Grana Padano, dry Jack,** and **Asiago** are good substitutes.

Pecorino means sheep's milk cheese; it is made in almost every area of Italy. The cheese can be hard, salty, and sharp—mainly used for grating over finished pasta dishes (**Pecorino Romano,** sheep's milk cheese from Rome and Sardinia, is the best known); or semifirm, with a nutty flavor, ideal for eating. If Pecorino Romano is not available, try another sharp cheese, such as Parmigiano-Reggiano or Asiago. American **Romano** is made from cow's milk and is good for grating. Sheep's and cow's milk is also used to make **ricotta,** a soft, fresh cheese, excellent for stuffed pasta dishes and in desserts.

ABOUT LEFTOVER PASTA

Leftover pasta, with or without sauce, can be reheated in a skillet or casserole or used in a frittata, 202. Cooked in a skillet with a little olive oil or butter over medium heat, the pieces turn crisp, brown, and chewy. Add a bit of water to guard against scorching or sticking. Serve the pasta for a quick meal with cooked garlicky greens, fried eggs, a sauce, or just a sprinkle of cheese.

Most leftover tomato sauces and cooked pastas can be combined in Leftover Pasta Casserole, 323, for a delicious second night's dinner. Improvise by adding some browned ground meat or sausage, grated cheese, or cooked vegetables.

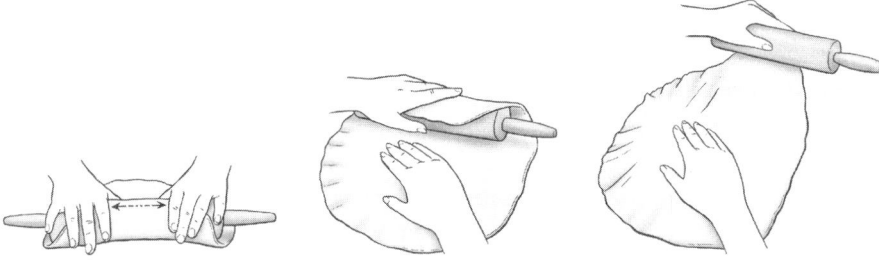

Rolling pasta by hand

PANFRIED LEFTOVER PASTA

1 to 2 servings

Heat **1 tablespoon olive oil** in a medium skillet until hot. Add **1 cup cooked spaghetti or 1½ cups cooked penne or other short pasta with sauce.** Cook, stirring occasionally, until the pasta is lightly golden, about 6 minutes. Season to taste with **salt and black pepper.**

LEFTOVER PASTA CASSEROLE

4 servings

Preheat the oven to 375°F. Butter an 8- to 9-inch square baking dish. Heat:

> **3 cups pasta sauce, such as Marinara, 562, Tomato Meat Sauce, 563, or Puttanesca, 563**

Toss 4 cups leftover pasta, such as spaghetti, penne, or ziti, with the sauce. Pour the mixture into the dish. Sprinkle with:

> **¼ cup fine dry bread crumbs**
> **¼ cup grated Parmesan or other cheese**

Season to taste with:

> **Salt and black pepper**

Dot with:

> **1 to 2 tablespoons butter**

Bake until the top is browned, about 30 minutes.

ABOUT MAKING FRESH PASTA

Fresh egg pasta has a light, delicate texture and a rich flavor. It is more absorbent than dried pasta and cooks faster. Fresh pasta is generally made with unbleached all-purpose flour. Whole eggs, egg whites, and/or water are used to moisten the flour, and sometimes seasonings such as salt and olive oil are added. Fresh pasta dough is easy to make

by hand, or you can mix it in a food processor or mixer. Either way, it should be kneaded for 10 minutes. To roll the dough, you will need either a long wooden rolling pin or a pasta rolling machine, available in many kitchenware stores. Avoid automatic pasta machines, which mix and then extrude the finished pasta—pasta rolled by hand or through a hand-cranked pasta machine has a more satisfying texture. You can flavor and color homemade pasta with pureed spinach, fresh herbs, spices, citrus zest, tomato paste, or squid ink, which can be purchased in many fish markets.

ROLLING OUT AND CUTTING FRESH PASTA

The key to light, resilient pasta is gently stretching and pulling the sheet of dough as you roll it thinner and thinner. Whether with a rolling pin or a hand-cranked pasta machine, ➤ work with only a quarter of the pasta dough at a time, leaving the rest loosely covered.

WORKING BY HAND

Lightly flour a large surface and use a rolling pin to roll out one piece of the dough at a time, repeatedly giving it a quarter turn as the circle grows. Continue, flipping the dough over occasionally, until it reaches the desired thickness. ➤ For ribbon pastas, such as fettuccine, the dough should be about ⅛ inch thick, thin enough to detect the outline of your hand through it. ➤ For filled pasta, the sheets should be as thin as paper—sheer enough to see your hand clearly through it.

WORKING WITH A PASTA MACHINE

Set the machine's rollers at the widest setting. Work with one piece of dough at a time. Lightly flour the dough and

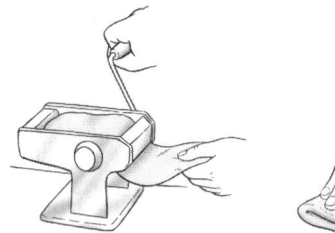
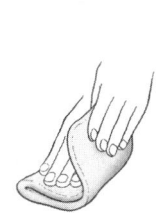
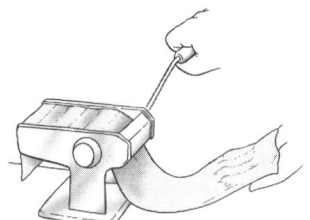

Making pasta with a pasta machine

pass it through the rollers 3 times, folding it over onto it-self before rolling it each time. Sprinkle flour on the dough any time it threatens to stick. ➤ Guide the dough as it comes out of the rollers with the palm of your hand, held flat to protect the dough from being punctured by your fingers. To make the dough thinner, set the rollers one notch closer together and repeat the rolling process an-other 2 or 3 times. Stop flouring the dough when it is no longer sticky. ➤ The dough should go from lumpy and even holey to a satiny sheet. As this happens, begin to stretch the dough gently as it emerges from the rollers. Continue to notch the rollers closer together and roll the pasta through them until you reach the desired thick-ness. For more information, consult the manufacturer's instructions.

CUTTING AND MAKING PASTA SHAPES

For filled pasta, such as ravioli or cannelloni, trim the pasta sheets into long strips approximately 4 inches wide or leave as wide as the strips come from the machine. For **cannelloni,** cut the strips crosswise into 4-inch squares. Fill the pasta while it is still fresh and moist enough to fold and seal. **For ribbons and unfilled shapes,** let the pasta sheet dry on a lightly floured counter until it feels leathery but not at all stiff, about 20 minutes. ➤ Use a sharp knife, pizza cutter, or a pastry wheel to cut it into ribbons, strips, or squares or create crimped edges for lasagna. Separate the strips and dry the cut pasta further in an airy space on large baking sheets covered with aluminum foil and dusted with flour or drape them over a pasta drying rack until no longer moist but still flexible. ➤ Once cut, fresh pasta should rest for at least an hour before cooking.

Farfalle: Cut the pasta into rectangles about 1$\frac{1}{2}$ x 1 inch—use a pastry wheel if you have one—and pinch each one together at the center.

Fettuccine: Cut long strands a little wider than $\frac{1}{8}$ inch.

Lasagne: Cut rectangles about 8 x 4 inches.

Pappardelle: Cut ribbons about $\frac{3}{4}$ inch wide.

Tagliatelle: Cut ribbons less than $\frac{3}{8}$ inch wide.

STORING FRESH PASTA

To store fresh pasta ribbons and similar shapes, dust with flour to prevent sticking and roll a few strands at a time into loose coils. Place the coils on wire racks to dry further until ready to cook. Or, to store them in the refrigerator, line large baking sheets with aluminum foil. Spread out the pieces so that they do not touch. Refrigerate, lightly covered with a lint-free cloth. Turn the pieces occasionally. Use within 24 hours.

For longer storage, let the pasta coils dry completely—they will break with a snap—and store in plastic bags. ➤ Make sure they are thoroughly dry before placing them in plastic bags, or they will turn moldy. Once dried, home-made pasta will keep for several days. It will become brittle and break easily, so handle carefully.

To freeze fresh fettuccine and other ribbons, line large baking sheets with aluminum foil. Arrange the coils on the sheets and freeze for 1 to 2 hours, until firm. Handling them carefully, put the frozen coils into heavy-duty freezer bags and store them in the freezer for up to 1 month. To freeze shapes such as farfalle or ravioli, spread out the pasta on the sheets so that the pieces do not touch, and freeze overnight. Then carefully put the pieces into heavy freezer bags and seal, leaving some air in the bags to pro-tect the pasta from being crushed. ➤ Pasta can be cooked while it is still frozen.

FRESH PASTA DOUGH

About 1 pound; 8 first-course or 4 main-course servings
Please read About Making Fresh Pasta, 323.
Mound on a clean counter:
    2 cups unbleached all-purpose flour
Make a well in the center and add to the well:
    3 large eggs or 4 or 5 large egg whites (about $\frac{2}{3}$ cup)
    ($\frac{1}{2}$ teaspoon salt)
    (1 teaspoon extra-virgin olive oil)
Beat the eggs lightly with a fork, drawing in some flour as you go, until the eggs are mixed and slightly thickened. Using the fingertips of one hand, gradually incorporate the flour into the eggs and blend everything into a smooth, not too stiff dough. If the dough feels too dry and crumbly, add a little water as needed. If it is too sticky, add a little more flour. Use a dough scraper to lift and turn the dough if it sticks.

Alternatively, process the ingredients in a food proces-sor just until blended, 15 to 20 seconds, being careful not to overwork the dough.

Knead the dough until satiny and very elastic, about 10 minutes, or pulse for 15 to 20 seconds then remove from the processor and knead for 10 minutes. Divide the dough into 4 pieces, and wrap the pieces loosely in plastic wrap or cover with an inverted bowl. Let the dough rest at room temperature for 60 minutes before rolling it out.

SPINACH PASTA

About 1 pound; 8 first-course or 4 main-course servings
Cook, 305, **10 ounces fresh spinach, trimmed and washed, or frozen spinach.** Drain, squeeze very dry, and mince it very fine. You should have about $\frac{1}{2}$ cup. Prepare **Fresh Pasta Dough, above,** reducing whole eggs to 2 (or 3 egg whites), and adding the spinach to the flour with the eggs.

HERB PASTA

About 1 pound; 8 first-course or 4 main-course servings
Place in a towel $\frac{1}{2}$ **cup minced strong herbs (sage, rose-mary, thyme, oregano, or marjoram) or 1$\frac{1}{2}$ cups minced mild herbs (basil, chives, parsley, or scallions)** and squeeze well to extract the moisture. Prepare **Fresh Pasta Dough, above,** adding herbs to the flour with the eggs.

WHOLE WHEAT PASTA
About 1 pound; 8 first-course or 4 main-course servings
Prepare **Fresh Pasta Dough, 324,** substituting **1 cup whole wheat flour** for the same amount of all-purpose flour. This dough may need a little more liquid; if it seems dry and crumbly, add 1 to 2 teaspoons water and knead until blended and smooth.

FRESH EGG NOODLES
About ³/₄ pound; 2 to 3 main-course servings
Some of the first noodle dishes served in the United States arrived with Dutch and German settlers. These are rich and savory egg noodles.
Combine in a large bowl:
   1¹/₂ cups all-purpose flour
   ¹/₈ teaspoon salt
Cut in with a pastry blender or your fingers to form fine crumbs:
   1 tablespoon plus 1 teaspoon cold unsalted butter
Make a well in the center of the ingredients. Lightly beat together and add to the well:
   2 large eggs
   2 large egg yolks
Using a fork, gradually mix the flour mixture into the eggs, and continue to mix until the dough comes together. Divide the dough into quarters.
   Alternatively, cut the butter into very small pieces and place in a food processor with the flour and salt. Pulse 2 or 3 times to mix. Add the eggs and pulse again to mix. The dough should just form a ball around the blade; do not overmix. Let the dough rest for 30 minutes.
   Please read Rolling Out and Cutting Fresh Pasta, 323. Roll out the dough and cut into fine threads, about ¹/₈ inch wide, or thick ribbons, about ¹/₂ inch wide, then cut into 2-inch lengths.

PENNSYLVANIA DUTCH EGG NOODLES
About 1 pound; 8 first-course servings
This is an all-purpose German-style noodle.
Mix together in a large bowl or on the counter, then shape into a mound:
   2 cups all-purpose flour
   (1 teaspoon salt)
Make a well in the center of the flour. Lightly beat together and pour into the well:
   1 large egg
   4 large egg yolks
Beat the eggs with a fork, drawing in some flour as you do so, until they are slightly thickened. Using the fingertips of one hand, gradually incorporate the flour and blend everything into a smooth, not too stiff dough, adding as needed:
   1 to 2 tablespoons water
Alternatively, combine the ingredients in a food processor and process just long enough to blend, 15 to 20 seconds, being careful not to overmix the dough. Once the dough

has come together, turn it out onto a lightly floured surface, and knead to form a soft dough, about 5 minutes, adding more flour if necessary to keep the dough from sticking.
   Divide the dough into 4 pieces, and wrap the pieces loosely in plastic or cover them with an inverted bowl. If you have time, let the dough rest 30 minutes before rolling it out.
   Please read Rolling Out and Cutting Fresh Pasta, 323. Roll out the dough and cut into fine threads, about ¹/₈ inch wide, or thick ribbons, about ¹/₂ inch wide, then cut into 2-inch lengths.

BOILED PASTA OR EGG NOODLES
8 first-course or 4 main-course servings
Please read About Cooking Pasta, 320. Bring to a rolling boil in a large pot:
   4 to 6 quarts water
   2 to 3 tablespoons salt
Drop in:
   1 pound pasta or noodles
Return to a boil and cook, stirring frequently, until tender but still firm. Drain in a large colander. Toss it immediately with the sauce to prevent the pasta from sticking together, or rinse the pasta if it is to be used cold.

FETTUCCINE WITH BUTTER AND CHEESE
8 first-course or 4 main-course servings
Please read About Cooking Pasta, 320. Cook in a large pot of boiling salted water:
   1 pound fettuccine or tagliatelle
I. Drain the pasta and toss with:
   ¹/₂ cup (1 stick) unsalted butter, softened,
      or ¹/₃ cup olive oil
   Black pepper to taste
   1¹/₂ cups grated Parmesan (6 ounces)
II. While the pasta cooks, boil in a large skillet until reduced by half:
   1¹/₂ cups chicken stock or broth
Stir in:
   3 tablespoons unsalted butter
Season to taste with:
   Salt and black pepper
Drain the pasta and toss with the stock mixture in the skillet, along with:
   1¹/₂ cups grated Parmesan (6 ounces)

STOVETOP MACARONI AND CHEESE
4 to 6 main-course or 8 to 10 side-dish servings
Very creamy, very cheesy. A large pot is essential in this recipe.
Please read About Cooking Pasta, 320. Cook in a large pot of boiling salted water:
   2 cups (8 ounces) elbow macaroni
Drain and return to the pot. Add:
   ¹/₄ cup (¹/₂ stick) unsalted butter, cut into small pieces

Stir until well blended. Add and stir well:

> One 12-ounce can evaporated milk
> 3 cups extra-sharp Cheddar, shredded (12 ounces)
> 2 large eggs, lightly beaten
> 1 teaspoon dry mustard dissolved in 1 teaspoon
>   hot water
> $^1/_2$ teaspoon salt, or to taste
> $^1/_4$ teaspoon ground red pepper, or to taste

Set the pot over very low heat and cook, stir constantly, until the sauce is smooth and the pasta is steaming, 5 to 10 minutes. The sauce should thicken noticeably. Increase the heat slightly if the sauce is still soupy after 5 minutes, but watch it very carefully. Do not overheat, or the sauce will curdle.

BAKED MACARONI AND CHEESE

4 to 6 main-course or 8 to 10 side-dish servings

An especially good rendition of a timeless classic. The sauce can be made ahead and combined with the just-cooked macaroni before baking, or the entire casserole can be assembled a day in advance.

Please read About Cooking Pasta, 320. Preheat the oven to 350°F. Grease a deep 1$^1/_2$-quart baking dish. Prepare:

> 2 cups White Sauce I, 550

Stir in:

> $^1/_2$ medium onion, minced
> 1 bay leaf
> $^1/_4$ teaspoon sweet paprika

Simmer gently, stirring often, for 15 minutes. Have ready:

> 2$^1/_4$ cups grated sharp Cheddar or Colby
>   (9 ounces)

Remove the sauce from the heat, discard the bay leaf, and stir in two-thirds of the cheese. Reserve the rest. Season with:

> Salt and black pepper to taste

Meanwhile, cook in a large pot of boiling salted water just until tender:

> 2 cups (8 ounces) elbow macaroni, small shells,
>   or tubetti

Drain and remove to a large bowl. Stir in the sauce. Pour half of the mixture into the baking dish and sprinkle with half of the remaining cheese. Top with the rest of the macaroni and then the remaining cheese. Sprinkle over the top:

> $^1/_2$ cup Buttered Bread Crumbs, 960

Bake until the bread crumbs are lightly browned, about 30 minutes. Let stand for 5 minutes before serving.

MACARONI AND CHEESE FOR A CROWD

16 servings

Please read About Cooking Pasta, 320. You can crumble blue cheese into this dish as well.

Cook in a large pot of boiling salted water:

> 4 cups (1 pound) elbow macaroni, small shells, or
>   tubetti

Preheat the oven to 325°F. Grease two 9-inch square baking pans. Have ready:

> 4 cups sharp cheese, such as Cheddar, Gruyère,
>   or Asiago, grated (1 pound)
> 1$^1/_2$ cups dry bread crumbs

Mix together half of the cheese and 1 cup of the crumbs with:

> $^1/_4$ cup ($^1/_2$ stick) butter, melted

Drain the macaroni and mix with:

> 7 large eggs, beaten
> 1$^3/_4$ cups milk
> (1 cup finely chopped celery)
> ($^1/_2$ cup sliced pitted black olives)
> ($^1/_3$ cup chopped roasted red bell pepper, 292,
>   or pimientos)
> ($^1/_3$ cup chopped green bell pepper)
> 3 tablespoons finely chopped onion
> 1 teaspoon salt
> $^1/_2$ teaspoon white or black pepper, or to taste

Stir in the remaining cheese and crumbs. Divide the mixture between the baking pans. Cover with the bread crumb mixture. Bake about 25 minutes, or until the egg mixture sets and the top is golden brown.

FETTUCCINE WITH FRESH HERBS

8 first-course or 4 main-course servings

Please read About Cooking Pasta, 320. Cook in a large pot of boiling salted water:

> 1 pound fettuccine or tagliatelle

Meanwhile, rub a warmed serving bowl with:

> 1 garlic clove, halved

Combine in the bowl:

> 3 to 4 tablespoons extra-virgin olive oil
> 1 cup loosely packed basil leaves, finely chopped
> 1 cup finely snipped chives or chopped scallion greens
> $^1/_4$ cup oregano or marjoram leaves, finely chopped
> 1 cup grated Parmesan (4 ounces)
> Salt and black pepper to taste

Drain the pasta, reserving $^1/_2$ cup of the cooking water. Toss the pasta with the herb mixture, adding the reserved cooking water as needed.

STRAW AND HAY (PAGLIA E FIENO)

8 first-course or 4 main-course servings

This quick but luxurious dish gets its name from the mix of green spinach fettuccine and golden egg fettuccine.

Please read About Cooking Pasta, 320. Cook in a large pot of boiling salted water:

> 8 ounces spinach fettuccine
> 8 ounces egg fettuccine

Meanwhile, melt in a large skillet over medium heat:

> 1 tablespoon butter

Add and cook for 1 minute:

> 4 ounces prosciutto, chopped

Add, bring to a boil, and boil for 2 minutes:

> 1 cup heavy cream

Stir in and cook 2 minutes more:

1 cup fresh or frozen tiny peas

Season with:

Salt and black pepper to taste

Turn off the heat, and drain the pasta and add it to the skillet, along with:

1 cup grated Parmesan (4 ounces)

Toss well.

PASTA PRIMAVERA

8 first-course or 4 main-course servings

Any seasonal vegetables can be added—just make sure they are all cut into about the same size. Try sugar snap peas, artichokes, green beans, scallions, or zucchini. Please read About Cooking Pasta, 320. Bring to a rolling boil in a large pot:

4 to 6 quarts water

2 tablespoons salt

Add and cook for 1 minute:

6 asparagus, trimmed, stalks diced,
**   tips left whole**

1 small bunch broccoli, cut into very small florets,
**   stems reserved for another use**

Remove the vegetables with a sieve and rinse under cold water to stop the cooking. Keep the cooking water warm. Heat in a large skillet over medium heat:

2 tablespoons olive oil

3 tablespoons butter

Add and cook, stirring, until softened, about 5 minutes:

1 large onion, finely chopped

2 medium carrots, finely chopped

Add the blanched asparagus and broccoli, along with:

$^3/_4$ cup fresh or thawed frozen peas

Salt and black pepper to taste

Cook, stirring, until all the vegetables are tender. Meanwhile, return the vegetable cooking water to a boil. Add and cook, until tender but firm:

1 pound fresh or dried fettuccine or tagliatelle

While the pasta is cooking, stir into the vegetables and simmer gently until slightly reduced:

1 cup heavy cream

Drain the pasta and add it to the sauce, along with:

12 basil leaves, chopped

$^1/_2$ cup grated Parmesan (2 ounces)

Toss to coat over low heat. Serve hot.

FETTUCCINE ALFREDO

8 first-course or 4 main-course servings

Please read About Cooking Pasta, 320. Cook in a large pot of boiling salted water:

1 pound fettuccine or tagliatelle

Just before the pasta is cooked, melt in a large skillet over medium heat:

$^1/_2$ cup (1 stick) butter

Drain the pasta and add it to the skillet, along with:

1 cup heavy cream

1 cup grated Parmesan (4 ounces)

Salt and black pepper to taste

Toss over low heat until the pasta is well coated.

FETTUCCINE WITH SALMON AND ASPARAGUS

8 first-course or 4 main-course servings

Use green spinach fettuccine for an especially attractive dish. Please read About Cooking Pasta, 320. Bring to a rolling boil in a large pot:

4 to 6 quarts water

2 tablespoons salt

Add and cook until tender but firm, 1 to 4 minutes, depending on their thickness:

1 pound asparagus, tough ends trimmed and cut into
**   1-inch pieces**

Scoop out the asparagus with a sieve and rinse under cold water to stop the cooking. Add to the boiling water and cook until tender but firm:

1 pound spinach fettuccine

Meanwhile, melt in a large skillet over medium heat:

3 tablespoons butter

Add the asparagus and cook, stirring, just to coat with butter, about 1 minute. Stir in and heat through:

1 cup heavy cream

Grated zest of 1 lemon

Drain the pasta and add it to the skillet, along with:

4 ounces smoked salmon, cut into thin strips, or
**   cooked fresh salmon, cut into small pieces**

$^1/_4$ cup snipped chives

$^1/_4$ cup chopped parsley

(2 to 3 tablespoons capers, drained)

Salt and black pepper to taste

Toss to combine and serve hot.

SPAGHETTI WITH GARLIC AND OIL (AGLIO E OLIO)

8 first-course or 4 main-course servings

A simple sauce of olive oil and garlic is one of the purest ways of enjoying good spaghetti or other thin pasta strands. Please read About Cooking Pasta, 320. Cook in a large pot of boiling salted water:

1 pound spaghetti or linguine

Meanwhile, heat in a large skillet over medium heat:

3 tablespoons olive oil

Add:

3 large garlic cloves, thinly sliced

(1 dried red chile pepper)

Cook, stirring, until the garlic is pale blond, about 2 minutes. Discard the chile pepper, if you used it. Drain the spaghetti, reserving $^1/_2$ cup of the cooking water. Add the hot pasta and cooking water to the garlic mixture and toss to combine. Season to taste with:

Salt and black pepper

LINGUINE WITH WHITE CLAM SAUCE
8 first-course or 4 main-course servings

If you want to use canned clams, add four 6½-ounce cans of clams with their juices to the cooked pasta. Please read About Cooking Pasta, 320. Heat in a large pot over medium-high heat:

1 tablespoon olive oil

Add and cook, stirring, until the onion softens, 3 to 5 minutes:

1 small onion, chopped
1 garlic clove, sliced
½ teaspoon dried oregano
3 tablespoons chopped parsley
(Pinch of crushed red pepper flakes)

Increase the heat to high and add:

4 pounds small clams (such as littlenecks), scrubbed
1 cup dry white wine

Cover the pan and cook until the clams open. Remove the clams from the broth, discarding any unopened ones; pour the broth into a bowl. Working over a bowl to catch the juices, shuck the clams, 374; if the clams are sandy, rinse them in the broth as you go. Put the clams in a small bowl. Add the clam juices to the broth, strain, and reserve. Heat in a large skillet:

2 tablespoons olive oil

Add and cook, stirring, for a few minutes:

1 large garlic clove, minced
¼ cup chopped parsley

Add the broth and simmer until reduced to about 1 cup. Meanwhile, cook in a large pot of boiling salted water:

1 pound linguine or spaghetti

Stir the clams and any liquid into the broth. Whisk in:

2 tablespoons cold butter

Add the drained pasta to the sauce, and toss to coat. Season with:

Salt and black pepper to taste

LINGUINE WITH RED CLAM SAUCE

Proceed as for **Linguine with White Clam Sauce, above,** up to the oil, garlic, and parsley mixture. When the garlic is barely colored, add **1 cup drained whole tomatoes, chopped.** Simmer, stirring, for 3 minutes. Continue as directed.

PENNE WITH VODKA SAUCE
8 first-course or 4 main-course servings

Please read About Cooking Pasta, 320. Heat in a large skillet over medium heat:

3 tablespoons butter or olive oil

Add and cook, stirring, until softened, about 5 minutes:

1 onion, finely chopped

Add and cook, stirring, until just starting to color, about 1 minute:

2 large garlic cloves, finely minced

Stir in:

One 28-ounce can whole plum tomatoes, drained and chopped

¼ cup vodka
¼ teaspoon crushed red pepper flakes

Simmer briskly for 10 minutes. Stir in and heat through:

½ cup heavy cream

Meanwhile, cook in a large pot of boiling salted water:

1 pound penne

Stir into the sauce:

(12 basil leaves, chopped)
Salt and black pepper to taste

Drain the pasta and add to the sauce:

(½ cup grated Parmesan)

Toss well.

TAGLIATELLE WITH WILTED GREENS
8 first-course or 4 main-course servings

Make this dish as spicy as you like by using more or fewer chile peppers.

Please read About Cooking Pasta, 320. Cook in a large pot of boiling salted water:

1 pound tagliatelle or fettuccine

Meanwhile, heat in a large skillet over medium heat:

3 tablespoons olive oil

Add and cook, stirring, until barely browning:

¼ cup minced onion
4 garlic cloves, chopped
1 to 3 hot chile peppers, seeded and chopped

Increase the heat to high and drop in:

3 big handfuls arugula or mixed tart salad greens, 158
Salt and black pepper to taste

Cook, stirring, until the greens are wilted. Drain the pasta and toss it with the greens, adding:

½ cup grated Romano or crumbled fresh goat cheese

CREAMY PASTA WITH CHARD AND TOMATOES
4 first-course or side-dish servings

Please read About Cooking Pasta, 320. Heat in a large saucepan over medium-high heat:

1 tablespoon olive oil

Add and cook, stirring occasionally, until soft and golden, 2 to 3 minutes:

¼ cup chopped onion
2 garlic cloves, minced
¼ to ½ teaspoon crushed red pepper flakes

Add and cook, stirring occasionally, until most of the liquid is evaporated, about 5 minutes:

2 large ripe tomatoes, peeled, 311, and chopped, or
1 cup chopped drained canned tomatoes

Add and cook, stirring, until the chard has wilted, about 2 minutes.

1 pound chard, trimmed and cut crosswise into ½-inch strips

Add:

¾ cup heavy cream
Salt and black pepper to taste

Cook 2 minutes, or until bubbling. Remove from the heat. Meanwhile, cook in a large pot of boiling salted water

8 ounces fresh or dried fettuccine or egg noodles

Drain the pasta, add to the sauce, and toss well to coat. Add and toss in:

³/₄ cup grated Parmesan (3 ounces)

PASTA AND BEANS (PASTA E FAGIOLI)
8 first-course or 4 main-course servings

This version of pasta and beans is more a thick stew than a soup. If you prefer it thinner, add more stock or broth, or even water. Please read About Cooking Pasta, 320. Heat in a large saucepan over medium heat:

2 tablespoons extra-virgin olive oil

Add and cook, stirring, until the onion is golden brown, about 5 minutes:

1 medium onion, finely chopped
1 carrot, finely chopped
1 celery rib with leaves, finely chopped
2 tablespoons minced parsley

Stir in:

2 large garlic cloves, minced

Cook for 1 minute, then add:

Two 15¹/₂-ounce cans cannellini, Great Northern, or pinto beans, rinsed and drained

Partially mash the beans with the back of a spoon. Add:

2 cups chicken stock or broth, or as needed

Bring to a simmer, partially cover, reduce the heat, and simmer for 5 minutes. Stir in:

1 cup elbow macaroni
Salt to taste

Cook until the macaroni is tender, about 15 minutes. Thin the sauce, if needed, with additional stock or water. Season to taste with:

Black pepper

Just before serving, stir in:

¹/₄ cup grated Romano (2 ounces)

Ladle into bowls and serve, passing:

Additional grated cheese

SPAGHETTI CARBONARA
8 first-course or 4 main-course servings

Please read About Cooking Pasta, 320. Cook in a large pot of boiling salted water:

1 pound spaghetti or linguine

Meanwhile, combine in a small skillet and cook, stirring occasionally, until the bacon is crisp:

2 tablespoons olive oil
6 slices bacon, chopped

Add:

¹/₃ cup dry white wine

Simmer until the wine has evaporated. Beat together:

3 large eggs
Salt and black pepper to taste
²/₃ cup mixed grated Parmesan and Romano (3 ounces)

Drain the pasta and return it to the hot pot. Immediately add the cheese mixture and the hot bacon and fat, stirring to coat thoroughly; the heat of the pasta will cook the eggs.

ORECCHIETTE WITH SAUSAGE AND BROCCOLI RABE
8 first-course or 4 main-course servings

Please read About Cooking Pasta, 320. Heat in a large skillet over medium heat:

¹/₄ cup olive oil

Remove the casings from and add:

4 fresh Italian sausages (about 1 pound)

Cook, breaking the meat up with a spoon, until nicely browned, about 5 minutes. Stir in and cook for 1 minute:

3 large garlic cloves, finely minced
¹/₄ teaspoon crushed red pepper flakes

Stir in:

1 large bunch broccoli rabe, trimmed and coarsely chopped, or 1 to 1¹/₂ pounds broccoli, trimmed, stems peeled, and coarsely chopped
Salt and black pepper to taste

Cover and cook just until tender, about 5 minutes. Meanwhile, cook in a large pot of boiling salted water:

1 pound orecchiette or cavatelli

Drain the pasta, add it to the skillet, and toss over low heat. Serve sprinkled with:

Grated Romano

PAPPARDELLE WITH GRILLED TOMATO SAUCE
4 to 6 main-course or 8 to 10 side-dish servings

Please read About Cooking Pasta, 320. Prepare:

Grilled Tomato Sauce, 563

Meanwhile, cook in a large pot of boiling salted water:

1 pound pappardelle

Drain the pasta and toss with the sauce. Season to taste with:

Salt and black pepper

Sprinkle with:

Grated Romano or Parmesan

BUTTERED EGG NOODLES
6 to 8 side-dish servings

Please read About Cooking Pasta, 320. Cook in a large pot of boiling salted water:

1 pound egg noodles

Drain and return to the pot. Add:

¹/₂ cup (1 stick) butter, melted
Salt and black pepper to taste

Toss to coat.

POPPY SEED NOODLES

Prepare **Buttered Egg Noodles, above.** Toss with **2 tablespoons poppy seeds, or to taste,** and **(1 teaspoon sugar)** along with the salt and pepper.

EGG NOODLES WITH BROWN BUTTER AND NUTS

6 to 8 side-dish servings

Please read About Cooking Pasta, 320. Cook in a small pan over medium heat until the butter is golden brown:

$1/2$ **cup (1 stick) butter**

Add any one or all of the following:

$1/3$ **cup chopped toasted nuts, 1001, such as cashews, peanuts, pecans, almonds, pine nuts, or walnuts**

1 teaspoon minced garlic

3 tablespoons chopped fresh herbs or 1 teaspoon dried, such as thyme, basil, chives, parsley, oregano, and/or tarragon

Grated zest of 1 small lemon

Meanwhile cook in a large pot of boiling salted water:

1 pound egg noodles

Toss the noodles with the sauce. Season to taste with:

Salt and black pepper

EGG NOODLES WITH GARLIC AND BREAD CRUMBS

6 to 8 side-dish servings

Please read About Cooking Pasta, 320. Cook in a large pot of boiling salted water:

1 pound egg noodles

Meanwhile, melt in a medium skillet and cook until the foam subsides:

$1/4$ **to** $1/2$ **cup ($1/2$ to 1 stick) butter**

Add:

1 cup dry bread crumbs

1 to 2 garlic cloves, minced

Cook, stirring, until the bread crumbs begin to brown. Stir in:

1 tablespoon chopped parsley

Drain the noodles and toss with the bread crumb mixture. Season to taste with:

Salt and black pepper

EGG NOODLES WITH COTTAGE CHEESE

6 to 8 side-dish servings

Please read About Cooking Pasta, 320. Cook in a large pot of boiling salted water:

1 pound egg noodles

Drain and return to the pot. Add:

$1/2$ **cup (1 stick) butter, melted**

2 cups (16 ounces) cottage cheese

Salt and black pepper to taste

Heat through over low heat. Serve garnished with:

(Crumbled crisp bacon)

Chopped parsley or snipped dill

EGG NOODLES WITH SOUR CREAM AND CHIVES

6 to 8 side-dish servings

Please read About Cooking Pasta, 320. Melt in a medium saucepan over medium-low heat:

$1/2$ **cup (1 stick) butter**

Add:

8 ounces sour cream or plain yogurt

$1/4$ **cup minced onion**

2 tablespoons finely snipped chives

2 tablespoons chopped parsley

1 garlic clove, minced

Cook, stirring occasionally, about 5 minutes; do not boil. Meanwhile, cook in a large pot of boiling salted water:

1 pound egg noodles

Drain the noodles and toss with the sauce. Season to taste with:

Salt and black pepper

ABOUT ASIAN NOODLES

In more than two thousand years of making noodles, cooks in China, Japan, Thailand, Vietnam, and other Asian countries have come up with a wondrous variety of recipes. Today, many of these—panfried noodles, sesame noodles, pad Thai, and lo mein—are American favorites.

Asian noodles are best categorized by the type of flour or starch with which they are made. ➤ When looking for substitutes, choose noodles in the same starch family. The most common Asian noodles are made with wheat or rice; some are made from mung bean starch or buckwheat.

Asians prefer noodles long and uncut, especially when served at birthday celebrations, because they symbolize longevity. Eating noodles in Asia can be a noisy affair: it is not impolite to slurp them up. When boiled, Asian noodles are cooked without salt until very tender. ➤ Before stir-frying, panfrying, or adding to soup, rinse boiled noodles under cold water and toss with a little oil to prevent clumping.

Chinese Egg Noodles: Chinese egg noodles are made with wheat flour and eggs. The best are pale yellow in color (an unnaturally bright yellow indicates color additives). Chinese egg noodles are popularly known as *mein*. Regular *mein*, about $1/8$ inch thick, resemble spaghetti and are used for stir-frying (as in lo mein), for panfrying, or in cold noodle dishes. Egg noodles are also available thin or extra thin for soups. Flat fettuccine-like noodles are best stir-fried or boiled and topped with a sauce.

Dried Rice Noodles: Noodles made with rice flour and water are among the most popular of all Asian noodles. They are sold in two basic styles—rice sticks and rice vermicelli. Thin, flat, and translucent, rice stick noodles are most commonly used in pad Thai and other stir-fried dishes and soups. Delicate, thin rice vermicelli are used in soups, salads, and stir-fries.

Soba, or Japanese Buckwheat Noodles: Enjoyed in northern Japan, these thin, brownish dried noodles are made from wheat flour and buckwheat. The noodles are expensive, but there is no real substitute for their slightly nutty, appealing taste (in some recipes udon or Chinese wheat flour noodles can be substituted). Often a course unto itself, soba is traditionally served cold in a square wooden bento box with a dipping sauce made of dashi (Japanese seaweed broth), 119, seasoned with soy sauce and mirin.

Japanese Udon: Long, plump white noodles made of wheat flour, salt, and water, udon come both flat and round, dried and fresh. Typically served in broth and sprinkled with chopped scallions and shichimi, 1012, these hearty noodles also work well in stews and casseroles.

CHICKEN LO MEIN
4 to 6 first-course or 3 main-course servings
Fresh Chinese egg noodles are traditional in this dish, but any spaghetti-like noodles work. Almost any combination of meat and vegetables can be added.

Please read Stir-Frying, 1048, and About Asian Noodles, 330. Stir together in a medium bowl:

1 teaspoon cornstarch
$1/2$ teaspoon salt
1 teaspoon toasted sesame oil

Cut across the grain to make very thin slices (more easily done if the chicken is partially frozen):

1 boneless, skinless chicken breast (about 6 ounces)

Toss in the cornstarch mixture and let marinate for 10 to 20 minutes. Stir together in a small bowl:

$1/4$ cup chicken stock or broth
2 tablespoons oyster sauce
1 tablespoon soy sauce
$1^1/2$ teaspoons sugar

Cook in a pot of boiling unsalted water just until tender:

6 ounces Chinese egg noodles or spaghetti

Drain in a colander and cool under cold running water. Drain again and toss thoroughly with:

1 teaspoon toasted sesame oil

Heat a wok or large skillet over high heat. When hot, pour in:

$1/3$ cup peanut oil

Swirl the oil around the pan until very hot but not smoking. Add the chicken and stir-fry, flipping it in the oil to separate the slices, and cook just until white. Drain in a sieve or colander and discard the oil. Heat the pan again until hot. Pour in:

3 tablespoons peanut oil

Swirl and heat until very hot but not smoking. Add:

4 ounces bok choy, cut into 3-inch pieces ($2^1/2$ cups)
$1/4$ cup canned bamboo shoots, rinsed, drained, and sliced
3 scallions, cut into 2-inch pieces
$1/4$ cup sliced mushrooms
1 teaspoon finely minced garlic

Stir-fry until the vegetables are well coated with oil, about 45 seconds. Pour the stock mixture down the side of the pan; stir and cover to steam the vegetables in the sauce for 1 minute. Uncover, add the noodles and chicken, and stir and toss for about 30 seconds. Add:

($1/4$ cup bean sprouts)

Stir for about 30 seconds. Serve immediately.

BEEF CHOW FUN
4 main-course servings
Chow fun usually implies panfried broad rice noodles. This dish is typical noodle-house fare.

Please read Stir-Frying, 1048, and About Asian Noodles, 330. Soak in hot water to cover until softened, about 10 minutes:

8 ounces $1/2$-inch-wide dried rice noodles

Stir together well in a medium bowl:

2 teaspoons soy sauce
1 teaspoon cornstarch

Stir in:

1 teaspoon toasted sesame oil

Cut across the grain to make very thin slices (more easily done if the meat is partially frozen):

8 ounces flank steak

Toss in the soy mixture and marinate for 20 to 30 minutes. Stir together in a small bowl:

$1/2$ cup chicken stock or broth
$1/4$ cup oyster sauce
2 tablespoons Shaoxing wine or dry white wine
2 tablespoons soy sauce
2 teaspoons sugar

Stir together well in a cup:

2 teaspoons cornstarch
2 tablespoons cold water

Drain the noodles well. Heat a wok or large skillet over high heat. When hot, pour in:

$1/4$ cup peanut oil

Swirl the oil around the pan until very hot but not smoking. Add the noodles and stir and toss occasionally until some surfaces brown slightly. Remove to a plate, and discard the oil. Heat the pan again until hot. Pour in:

$1/4$ cup peanut oil

Swirl the oil around the pan until very hot but not smoking. Add the beef and stir-fry, flipping it in the oil to separate the slices, about 20 seconds. Drain in a colander. Heat the pan again. When hot, pour in:

2 tablespoons peanut oil

Swirl until very hot but not smoking. Add and stir briefly:

2 teaspoons fermented black beans, lightly mashed
2 teaspoons finely minced garlic
4 teaspoons finely minced peeled fresh ginger

Add and toss for 1 minute:

8 ounces green beans, trimmed and cut into 2-inch pieces

Add and stir-fry for 1 minute:

3 red chile peppers (or $1/2$ red bell pepper, for less heat), cut into thin strips
$1/2$ cup 2-inch pieces scallion

Stir in the stock mixture and stir and toss to coat the vegetables and heat through. Return the beef and noodles to the pan and stir-fry to mix thoroughly. Stir the cornstarch mixture, and slowly add it, stirring. Continue to stir until the sauce is thickened and the noodles are glazed and shiny. Stir in:

1 teaspoon toasted sesame oil

Remove to a serving dish. Top with:

¼ cup chopped cilantro

SPICY PEANUT SESAME NOODLES

6 to 8 first-course or 4 main-course servings

Served at room temperature as an appetizer, lunch, or light supper, this dish is a delight with soft noodles, a creamy, spicy sauce, and the crunch of cucumbers. And because it is made ahead, it is perfect party or potluck fare.

Please read About Asian Noodles, 330. Combine in a food processor and blend thoroughly:

1 cup unsalted peanut butter

¼ cup rice vinegar or white vinegar

2 tablespoons light soy sauce

1 teaspoons dark soy sauce

1 garlic clove, chopped

1 to 3 serrano or other chile peppers, seeded and chopped

1½ tablespoons sugar or honey

1 teaspoon salt

¼ cup toasted sesame oil

1 tablespoon chili oil

½ cup freshly brewed black tea

The sauce can be covered and refrigerated for 1 to 2 days. Allow to return to room temperature and stir well before using. Cook in a large pot of boiling unsalted water until soft:

1 pound Chinese egg noodles or spaghetti

Drain in a colander and rinse under cold water until cool. Toss thoroughly with:

2 teaspoons toasted sesame oil

Place in a serving dish. Add:

(2 boneless, skinless chicken breast halves, poached, 1050, cooled, and shredded, or 4 cups shredded cooked chicken)

Top with the sauce and stir together gently. Or serve on individual dinner plates and top with 3 to 4 generous tablespoons sauce per serving. Garnish with:

Thin strips peeled, seeded cucumber

Cilantro leaves

Coarsely chopped unsalted peanuts

PAD THAI

8 first-course or 4 main-course servings

There are many versions of this Thai specialty. You can replace the shrimp with an equal amount of thinly sliced chicken, pork, or lobster. Please read Stir-Frying, 1048, and About Asian Noodles, 330. Soak in hot water to cover until softened, 20 to 30 minutes:

6 ounces rice stick noodles

Drain; cover and set aside. Stir together well in a medium bowl:

1 teaspoon cornstarch

1 teaspoon toasted sesame oil

Add and toss to coat:

8 ounces large shrimp, peeled, deveined, and split lengthwise in half

Marinate for 15 to 20 minutes. Stir together in a small bowl:

2 tablespoons Thai fish sauce (nam pla)

2 tablespoons soy sauce

¼ cup fresh lime or lemon juice

3 tablespoons sugar

Heat a wok or large skillet over high heat until hot. Pour in:

1 tablespoon peanut oil

Swirl the oil around the pan until very hot but not smoking. Add the shrimp and stir-fry 30 to 45 seconds. Drain the shrimp in a colander. Reheat the pan until hot. Pour in:

2 tablespoons peanut oil

Swirl briefly, then slowly pour into the pan and cook, stirring vigorously, until set:

3 eggs, well beaten

Remove to a plate. Heat the pan again until hot. Pour in:

2 tablespoons peanut oil

Swirl until very hot but not smoking. Add and stir-fry until the garlic browns very slightly:

½ cup 1½-inch pieces scallion (white part only)

1 to 2 small green chiles, seeded and chopped

1 small garlic clove, finely minced

Add the noodles and stir until well coated. Add the fish sauce mixture and stir well, then add the shrimp and eggs and stir well. In the order listed, stir in:

½ cup fresh bean sprouts

⅓ cup roasted peanuts, coarsely chopped

¼ cup basil leaves, cut into thin strips

¼ cup cilantro leaves

(2 teaspoons dried shrimp, 976, finely ground)

½ teaspoon crushed red pepper flakes

Garnish with:

Lime wedges

SPICY SZECHUAN NOODLES

8 first-course or 4 main-course servings

A pork and noodle dish in the Szechuan style, with plenty of fresh ginger, garlic, and chile peppers. Please read About Asian Noodles, 330.

Stir together well in a small bowl:

½ cup chicken stock or broth

1 tablespoon soy sauce

2 tablespoons Chinese black bean sauce

2 teaspoons sugar

Heat a wok or large skillet over high heat. When it is hot, pour in:

2 tablespoons peanut oil

Swirl the oil around the pan until very hot but not smoking. Add and stir-fry briefly, until the garlic browns very slightly:

2 tablespoons finely minced peeled fresh ginger

1 tablespoon finely minced garlic

1 to 2 tablespoons coarsely chopped chile peppers

¼ cup coarsely chopped canned bamboo shoots

Add:

>**1 pound ground pork**

Stir-fry, breaking up the meat, until the pork is well separated and no longer pink but not browned. Meanwhile, cook in a large pot of boiling unsalted water until softened:

>**1 pound Chinese egg noodles or spaghetti**

Add the stock mixture to the pork, stir well, and cook for 1 to 2 minutes. Add and stir-fry briefly:

>**1/2 cup 2-inch pieces scallion**

Remove the pan from the heat. Drain the noodles and pour into a large bowl. Pour the sauce over the noodles. Season with:

>**1/2 teaspoon toasted sesame oil**

Stir well. Garnish with:

>**1/4 cup finely chopped scallion**

JAPANESE NOODLES IN BROTH

4 to 6 servings

Simplicity itself—freshly cooked noodles in a flavorful broth garnished with scallions and spice. Cooking the noodles first and then reheating them in boiling water guarantees that they will not get soft and mushy sitting in the broth. The Japanese seven-spice mix, 1012, that is traditionally sprinkled on top of the broth is available in Japanese markets.

Please read About Asian Noodles, 330.

Bring to a boil in a large pot over high heat:

>**8 cups chicken stock or broth**
>**1/4 cup soy sauce**
>**2 tablespoons sugar**
>**1 tablespoon salt**

Cook in a large pot of boiling unsalted water until softened:

>**1 pound dried udon noodles**

Drain, and divide among individual soup bowls. Sprinkle with:

>**2 cups 2-inch pieces scallions**

Ladle 1 1/2 to 2 cups seasoned broth into each bowl. Sprinkle over to taste:

>**Seven-spice mix (shichimi), 1012, or Five-spice powder, 982**

JAPANESE NOODLES IN DASHI

4 to 6 servings

Proceed as for **Japanese Noodles in Broth, above,** substituting for the chicken stock or broth **8 cups Dashi, 119, 5 tablespoons soy sauce, 2 tablespoons sugar,** and **2 tablespoons mirin.**

MOON-VIEWING NOODLES

4 to 6 servings

Traditionally eaten on the first full moon in September. Prepare **Japanese Noodles in Broth, above,** Top each bowl of noodles with **1 poached egg, 196 (4 to 6 eggs total).**

COLD SOBA NOODLES

4 servings

This is the classic way to eat buckwheat noodles—chilled but accompanied by hot and spicy condiments, creating an appealing contrast.

Please read About Asian Noodles, 330. Combine in a medium saucepan and bring to a gentle boil over medium heat:

>**2 1/2 cups Dashi, 119**
>**1/2 cup plus 2 tablespoons soy sauce**
>**1/4 cup mirin**
>**1 teaspoon sugar**

Stir in:

>**3 cups dried bonito flakes, 960**

Remove from the heat. After the flakes are wet, about 15 seconds, strain the liquid and let cool to room temperature. (The dipping sauce will keep, covered, in the refrigerator, for up to 24 hours.) Using scissors, cut into fine shreds:

>**1 sheet nori, 1011**

Arrange on a plate:

>**2 tablespoons wasabi paste, 1026**
>**1/2 cup sliced scallions**
>**1/3 cup grated radishes**

Cook in a large pot of boiling unsalted water until nearly tender:

>**8 ounces soba noodles**

Drain in a colander and rinse under cold water until cool, swishing the noodles with your hand to rinse well. Divide the noodles among 4 bowls. Sprinkle each serving with nori shreds. Divide the dipping sauce into 4 little bowls and place beside each serving. Place the plate with wasabi on it within easy reach.

SPICY SOBA NOODLES

6 to 8 servings

Toss cooked soba with all fresh herb pastes or dressings.

Please read About Asian Noodles, 330. Stir together well in a large bowl:

>**1/2 cup soy sauce**
>**3 1/2 tablespoons mirin or sake**
>**3 tablespoons Chinese black vinegar or Worcestershire sauce**
>**2 1/2 tablespoons sugar**
>**1 tablespoon safflower or corn oil**

Add and toss to coat thoroughly:

>**2 boneless, skinless chicken breast halves, poached, 1050, cooled, and shredded**
>**6 ounces snow peas, trimmed and blanched, 1054**
>**1 red bell pepper, cut into 2-inch-long thin strips**
>**1 yellow bell pepper, cut into 2-inch-long thin strips**

Combine in a food processor or blender and finely chop:

>**4 to 6 garlic cloves, peeled**
>**2 jalapeño peppers, seeded and coarsely chopped**
>**1 cup cilantro leaves**
>**1/2 cup parsley leaves**
>**1 tablespoon toasted sesame oil**

Cook in a large pot of boiling unsalted water until nearly tender:

12 ounces soba noodles

Drain in a colander and rinse under cold water until cool, then drain well and pour into a large bowl. Add the garlic mixture to the noodles and toss to coat thoroughly. Stir the chicken and vegetable mixture and arrange attractively atop the noodles.

ABOUT DUMPLINGS

One of winter's comforts when combined with stew or soup, dumplings are light and fluffy, akin to biscuits or cake. They are cooked on top of a stew, potpie, or casserole, and served directly out of the pot or dish. The secret to making dumplings light and fluffy is to keep them steaming on top of ➤ simmering liquid, and to ➤ be sure the temperature of the stock or broth, gravy, or water in which you are cooking them never exceeds a simmer, or the dumplings may become soggy or even disintegrate.

Most dumplings are bound together by egg, and the protein in the egg must not be allowed to toughen through overheating. Use ample liquid in a wide cooking vessel, giving each ball or drop of dough a chance to expand. ➤ Never crowd the pot. The minute the batter is floating in the liquid, ➤ cover the pot to capture the steam and ➤ do not lift the lid until the dumplings are done. This is easier if you cover the pot with a tight-fitting heat-resistant glass lid or pie pan, so you can watch the swelling of the batter. When the dumplings look fluffy, test them for doneness as you would a cake, by inserting a wooden toothpick and seeing that it comes away clean. Serve as soon as they are done, or they will become heavy. Some good additions to dumpling dough are parsley or other herbs, cheese, or grated onion.

European dumplings such as Spätzle, 335, and Gnocchi, 335, are similar to fresh pasta in taste and texture. These dumplings are often simmered in water or broth, then tossed with butter or a sauce. They are done about a minute after they float to the surface, or when they are tender and cooked through. You can usually cook these dumplings in advance. To prevent them from turning soft and sticky, ➤ drain them well, lightly coat them with oil or melted butter, and store them in a single layer, covered, in the refrigerator for up to 2 days.

DUMPLINGS

2 cups

Please read About Dumplings, above. Whisk together:

1 cup cake flour
2 teaspoons baking powder
1/2 teaspoon salt

Break into a 1-cup measure:

1 egg

Add until the cup is half full:

Milk

Beat well and stir the liquid slowly into the dry ingredients.

Add more milk if necessary but keep the batter as stiff as possible. You may add:

(1/4 cup finely chopped parsley, or 1 tablespoon fresh chopped herbs, or 1/2 teaspoon grated onion)

Bring just to a boil in a large saucepan:

2 or 3 cups stock or broth

To drop dumpling batter from a spoon easily, dip the spoon in stock first; then dip the spoon in the batter, fill it, and drop the batter into the stock. Continue doing this until the dumplings are barely touching. Then cover them and simmer 10 minutes. They should be served at once.

FARINA BALLS COCKAIGNE

6 servings

A favorite of Mom's, these remain after many tests the queen of dumplings. Though usually served in soup, they may be simmered in stock or broth or boiling water, then served with gravy. Or they may be drained, placed in a greased baking dish, and covered with a cup of White Sauce I, 550, to which you may add onion juice and parsley or chopped chives. Sprinkle the top with 1/4 cup grated Parmesan, dot it with butter, and bake in a 350°F oven for about 15 minutes. Please read About Dumplings, above.

Bring to a boil in a medium saucepan:

2 cups milk

Add, stir, and simmer until thick, about 5 minutes:

1/2 cup farina
1 tablespoon butter
1/2 teaspoon salt
1/8 teaspoon paprika
(1/8 teaspoon grated or ground nutmeg)

Remove from the heat and beat in vigorously one at a time:

2 large eggs, at room temperature

The heat of the mixture will thicken the eggs. Moisten your hands with cool water. Shape the dough a generous teaspoon at a time into small balls and drop into simmering stock or broth. Cook, covered, about 2 minutes.

CORNMEAL DUMPLINGS

4 to 6 servings

We believe that dumplings reached their peak in a small Kentucky town when we were served chicken with dumplings—the latter light as thistledown. "Oh, yes," said the hotel proprietress wearily, "they are always like that when our cook is drunk."

Please read About Dumplings, above. Bring to a simmer in a wide saucepan:

5 to 6 cups beef or chicken stock or broth

Meanwhile, sift together into a bowl:

3/4 cup all-purpose flour
1/2 cup cornmeal
2 teaspoons baking powder
1/2 teaspoon salt

Cut in with a fork or pastry blender:

1 tablespoon cold butter

Whisk together:

1 large egg

$^1/_3$ cup milk

Stir into the dry ingredients just until blended. Gently drop teaspoonfuls of the batter into the simmering stock, tightly cover the pan, and simmer the dumplings for about 20 minutes. Serve them in the stock.

BUTTER DUMPLINGS (BUTTERKLÖSSE)

4 servings

Please read About Dumplings, 334. Beat until soft in a medium bowl:

2 tablespoons butter, softened

Beat in:

2 large eggs, lightly beaten, at room temperature

Stir in:

6 tablespoons all-purpose flour

$^1/_4$ teaspoon salt

Meanwhile, bring to a simmer in a wide saucepan:

5 cups stock, broth, or soup

Salt and black pepper to taste

Drop the batter from a teaspoon into the simmering stock, cover, and simmer the dumplings about 8 minutes.

POTATO DUMPLINGS (KARTOFFELKLÖSSE)

6 to 8 servings

These are light and tender, especially good with a roast and gravy. They are traditional with Sauerbraten, 478. Many cooks like to put a tiny sprig of parsley in the center of each dumpling.

Please read About Dumplings, 334. Cook in a large pot of boiling water until tender:

6 medium baking potatoes, scrubbed

Drain, cool, and peel. Push them through a potato ricer or force through a sieve with the back of a spoon. Combine with:

2 large eggs

$^1/_2$ cup all-purpose flour

1$^1/_2$ teaspoons salt

Stir with a fork just until the ingredients are blended and fluffy. Gently shape into 1-inch balls. Bring to a simmer in a large pot:

4 to 6 quarts water

2 tablespoons salt

Drop the balls into the water and cook for about 10 minutes. Drain. Stir together:

$^1/_2$ cup (1 stick) butter, melted, or $^1/_2$ cup hot bacon

drippings

1 cup dry bread crumbs

Sprinkle the crumbs over the dumplings and serve.

POTATO GNOCCHI

About 200 gnocchi;

18 first-course or 10 main-course servings

Here is ingenuity at its best—light but substantial and delicious, amiably matched with other flavors, well worth the

effort. It is traditional to cook and sauce potato gnocchi like pasta and eat them as a first course or one-dish meal. Preheat the oven to 400°F. Scrub well:

2 pounds all-purpose or boiling potatoes

Prick each potato in a dozen places with a fork. Bake directly on an oven rack until easily pierced with a fork, about 1 hour. While the potatoes are still hot, split them lengthwise and scoop out the pulp. Push it through a potato ricer or force through a sieve with the back of a spoon. There should be about 2$^2/_3$ packed cups. Combine the potatoes in a bowl with:

1$^1/_3$ cups all-purpose flour

1 teaspoon salt

$^1/_4$ teaspoon grated or ground nutmeg

Stir vigorously, then turn out onto a work surface and knead until smooth and blended. Bring 3 to 4 inches of well-salted water to a simmer in a large pot. Have ready:

3 tablespoons butter, melted, or olive oil

Roll about 2 tablespoons of the dough into a $^3/_4$-inch-thick cylinder. Cut into $^3/_4$-inch pieces. Roll each piece against the tines of a fork while pressing a small dent on the opposite side with your finger. Test the gnocchi by dropping a few into the simmering water and cooking until they float, about 2 minutes. They should hold a firm shape and be chewy to the bite. If they are too soft or dissolve in simmering water, knead into the dough:

(Up to 3 tablespoons all-purpose flour)

(Some beaten egg)

Both of these have binding properties. Test again. When the dough is right (keep the water hot), roll it into three or four $^3/_4$-inch-thick ropes. Cut the ropes into $^3/_4$-inch pieces, shape the dough on the fork as below, letting them drop onto a lightly floured baking sheet. Bring the water back to a simmer. Drop one-third to half of the gnocchi into the pot and simmer, uncovered, until they float, then remove with a slotted spoon or skimmer to a wide bowl. Drizzle some of the melted butter over the gnocchi. Toss to coat. Repeat until all the gnocchi are done. Serve hot with:

Additional melted butter and grated Parmesan, a

tomato sauce or ragù, 562, or Pesto Sauce, 569

To make gnocchi ahead, spread the uncooked gnocchi on a lightly floured baking sheet and refrigerate, covered with plastic wrap, for up to 12 hours. To keep them longer, freeze the gnocchi on the baking sheet until hard, then remove to a freezer bag or container; they will keep frozen for up to 1 month. Cook directly from the freezer, adding about 1 minute to the cooking time.

SPÄTZLE

4 to 5 side-dish servings

These German egg dumplings are often served alongside a goulash or stew and are particularly welcome next to roasted veal. Substituting milk for the water produces a richer, if slightly denser, dumpling. Boiled spätzle are also delicious when sautéed in a buttered skillet until the edges of the spätzle are crisp.

Please read About Dumplings, 334. Combine in a bowl:

1¹/₂ cups all-purpose flour
¹/₂ teaspoon baking powder
³/₄ teaspoon salt
Pinch of grated or ground nutmeg

Beat together:

2 large eggs
¹/₂ cup water or milk

Add to the flour mixture. Beat well with a wooden spoon to create a fairly elastic batter. Bring to a simmer in a large saucepan:

6 cups salted water, chicken stock, or chicken broth

Drop small bits of the batter from a spoon into the bubbling liquid, or force the batter through a spätzle machine or colander to produce strands of dough that will puff into irregular shapes. The spätzle are done when they float to the surface. They should be delicate and light, although slightly chewy. If the first few taste heavy and dense, add a few more drops of water or milk to the batter before continuing. Lift the cooked spätzle from the saucepan with a strainer or slotted spoon. Serve as a side dish, sprinkled with:

Melted butter or ¹/₃ cup Browned bread crumbs, 960

Or remove to a shallow baking dish, and preheat the broiler. Top the spätzle with:

¹/₄ cup grated mild cheese

Broil until the cheese is melted, about 1 minute.

ABOUT BAKED PASTA AND NOODLE DISHES

You can easily bake delicious casseroles by tossing cooked fresh or dried pasta or noodles with sauces, meats, vegetables, or cheese. Try classics like pastitsio, or kugel, or improvise by adding leftovers or other ingredients you have on hand. These are good served hot or just warm. If assembled in advance and refrigerated before baking, ➤ be sure to add at least 15 minutes to the baking time. If the top of the casserole is browning too quickly, or if you like a moister baked pasta ➤ cover the baking dish with foil for all or part of the cooking time. Let the baked dish stand for 10 minutes before serving. For baked pastas with fillings, such as lasagne or cannelloni, see pages 339–341.

PASTITSIO

8 to 12 servings

This Greek casserole is a little time-consuming to prepare, but it can be done in stages. In fact, it tastes best when assembled ahead and refrigerated for a day before baking. Please read About Cooking Pasta, 320. Have ready:

3³/₄ cups White Sauce I, 550

Heat in a medium saucepan over medium heat:

1 tablespoon olive oil

Add and cook, stirring, until beginning to soften, about 5 minutes:

1 large onion, chopped

Add:

1 pound ground lamb or beef
1¹/₂ teaspoons minced garlic

Cook, stirring to break up the meat, until no longer pink. Stir in:

One 14¹/₂-ounce can whole tomatoes, coarsely
    chopped, with their juice
¹/₂ cup dry red wine
1 tablespoon tomato paste
1 teaspoon ground cinnamon
1 teaspoon dried oregano
1¹/₂ teaspoons salt
¹/₂ teaspoon black pepper

Simmer, uncovered, for 15 to 20 minutes. Cool slightly and stir in:

¹/₄ cup parsley leaves, minced

Meanwhile, cook in a large pot of boiling salted water until slightly undercooked:

1 pound elbow macaroni, penne, or other small pasta

Drain and toss with:

1 tablespoon olive oil

Combine the pasta and meat sauce. (The pasta mixture and the white sauce can be covered and refrigerated for up to 2 days before assembling.) Preheat the oven to 375°F. Grease a 13 x 9 x 2-inch baking dish. Spoon the pasta mixture into the dish. Place the white sauce in a large bowl and mix in:

4 large eggs, beaten
¹/₂ cup grated Parmesan (2 ounces)
¹/₂ cup crumbled feta

Pour the white sauce over the pasta. Sprinkle with:

¹/₂ cup grated Parmesan (2 ounces)

Bake until set and golden, 35 to 40 minutes. Let stand for 10 minutes before cutting.

MUSHROOM-WALNUT NOODLE KUGEL

10 to 12 side-dish servings

This kugel or baked pudding can be served as a side dish with meat or poultry or as a main dish for brunch or lunch. If you prefer a dish without a crunchy top, bake covered with foil. Please read About Cooking Pasta, 320. Preheat the oven to 350°F. Grease a 13 x 9 x 2-inch baking pan. Heat in a large skillet over medium-high heat:

¹/₂ cup vegetable oil

Add and cook, stirring, until golden brown, about 10 minutes:

2 medium onions, thinly sliced

With a slotted spoon, remove to a bowl. Add to the oil remaining in the skillet:

1 large portobello mushroom cap, cut into
    1-inch pieces
8 ounces button mushrooms, sliced
Salt and black pepper to taste

Cook, stirring, until the mushrooms are browned, about 10 minutes. Set the pan aside. Meanwhile, cook in a large pot of boiling salted water:

12 ounces egg noodles

Drain and place in a bowl. Add and stir together well:

5 large eggs, well beaten

Stir in the onions and mushrooms, with the oil from the skillet, along with:

³/₄ cup coarsely chopped walnuts

Pour the noodle mixture into the baking pan. Bake until the noodles are lightly browned, about 35 minutes. Let stand 10 minutes before serving.

SWEET NOODLE KUGEL

12 to 14 side-dish servings

Some varieties of noodle kugel are served at most traditional Jewish holiday meals, and there are countless recipes for them. This one is wonderful hot, warm, or cold. Please read About Cooking Pasta, 320. Preheat the oven to 325°F. Grease a 13 x 9 x 2-inch baking pan. Stir together in a large bowl:

2 cups sour cream
1 pound cottage cheese
1 pound cream cheese, softened
3 large eggs
¹/₂ cup sugar
2 teaspoons vanilla
1 teaspoon ground cinnamon
¹/₂ teaspoon salt

Cook in a large pot of boiling salted water until slightly undercooked:

1 pound egg noodles

Drain, add to the cheese mixture, and stir together well. Pour into the baking pan. Bake for 1¹/₂ hours. Meanwhile, stir together in a small bowl with a fork or your fingers:

¹/₂ cup packed dark brown sugar
¹/₂ cup chopped walnuts
2 tablespoons all-purpose flour
2 teaspoons ground cinnamon
2 tablespoons butter, softened

Sprinkle over the top of the casserole. Bake for 30 minutes more. Let stand 10 minutes before serving.

ABOUT STUFFED PASTA

Pasta or noodle dough stuffed or layered with a homemade filling is an impressive dish, whether served with a sauce or floating in a rich broth as a soup. Though making stuffed pasta requires some work, the advantage over store-bought is that you can use fresh ingredients, the filling can be seasoned to taste, and unique combinations can be created, such as fresh whole wheat pasta, 325, with a mushroom filling or spinach pasta, 324, with cheese filling.

To save time, buy ready-made fresh pasta sheets and cut and fill them as if they were homemade. Large dried pasta shapes such as jumbo shells and manicotti are also excellent when stuffed.

In most cases, ➤ the filling and the sauce can be prepared a day in advance and refrigerated until you are ready to stuff the pasta. Stuffed pastas are typically matched with cream, white sauce, butter, meat, or tomato sauces. Match the pasta to the sauce according to your taste and the rest of the menu. For soups, bite-sized tortellini are ideal.

ABOUT FILLINGS FOR PASTA

Pasta fillings are made from cheese, vegetables, meat, or poultry. Leftovers from a roast or stew can be ground, seasoned, and quickly turned into a pasta filling.

When making filled pasta, ➤ the dough must be filled and shaped while it is still moist, so it is best to have the filling prepared before making the pasta. All of these fillings can be made at least 24 hours in advance. Roll the pasta thin enough so you can see your hand through it and keep the sheets moist by covering them with plastic wrap as you work. ➤ Please read Rolling Out and Cutting Fresh Pasta, 323. For ravioli or tortellini, if the pasta is a little dry, it may be difficult to seal. Dip your fingertip in water and run it halfway around the edge of each piece of dough before pressing the edges together.

Pastas stuffed with firm meat fillings or others that are essentially dry can be stored in the refrigerator overnight and will freeze well.

BOILED STUFFED PASTA

Bring to a boil in a large pot:

4 to 6 quarts water
2 tablespoons salt

Add:

1 pound fresh or frozen stuffed pasta

Be careful not to overcrowd the pot; cook the pasta in batches if necessary. Reduce the heat and simmer gently, uncovered. Most filled pastas will float to the surface when they are done. Frozen pasta will require an extra minute or two.

CHEESE FILLING

About 2 ¹/₄ cups

A basic filling for fresh pastas, such as ravioli or tortellini. This is also good as a stuffing for dried pastas such as manicotti or jumbo shells. If you like, add some finely chopped prosciutto. Pasta stuffed with this filling is complemented by tomato sauces, 562–564, meat sauces, 563–564, or a simple butter sauce, 557.

Beat in a bowl until fluffy:

15 ounces ricotta

Beat in one at a time:

2 large eggs

Add:

1 tablespoon chopped parsley
¹/₂ cup grated Parmesan (2 ounces)
Salt and black pepper to taste

MUSHROOM FILLING

About 2 ³/₄ cups

Try it in ravioli, tortellini, or lasagne with a white, tomato, meat, or butter sauce. Please read About Fillings for Pasta, above.

Rinse and soak in hot water to cover:

Generous ¹/₃ cup dried mushrooms, such as porcini

Heat in a large skillet over medium heat:

2 tablespoons olive oil

Add and cook, stirring, until the onion is browned:

1 medium onion, finely chopped

2 bay leaves

Lift the mushrooms from the soaking liquid, reserving the liquid, squeeze dry, and finely chop. Add the mushrooms to the skillet, along with:

12 ounces any kind of fresh mushrooms, coarsely chopped

Cook, stirring, for 2 minutes. Add, bring to a boil, and cook until the pan is almost dry:

¹/₃ cup dry red wine

2 tablespoons tomato paste

2 garlic cloves, minced

Strain the mushroom soaking liquid through a sieve lined with dampened paper towels into the skillet. Let it boil until evaporated. Do the same with:

¹/₂ cup chicken stock or broth

Add:

Salt and black pepper to taste

Remove from the heat and let cool; remove and discard the bay leaves. Blend in:

¹/₂ to 1 cup grated Parmesan (2 to 4 ounces)

The filling can be covered and refrigerated up to 3 days.

MEAT AND SPINACH FILLING

About 2 cups

Our favorite filling for ravioli, this is also good for tortellini. Please read About Fillings for Pasta, 337. Serve the pasta with Butter and Cheese Sauce, 325, Bolognese Sauce, 564, or a tomato sauce, 562. For cheese filling, see 337. Combine in a bowl:

¹/₂ cup pureed cooked spinach

1 cup cooked ground veal or lean pork

2 large eggs

¹/₄ cup fresh bread crumbs, 961, lightly toasted

¹/₂ cup grated Romano or Parmesan (2 ounces)

¹/₂ teaspoon dried basil or marjoram

(¹/₂ garlic clove, minced)

2 teaspoons finely chopped parsley

Salt and black pepper to taste

Stir in:

Enough stock or broth, cream, or gravy to form a stiff paste

CHICKEN AND CHEESE FILLING

About 4 cups

Our favorite cannelloni filling. White Sauce I, 550, is the best complement to the filling. Please read About Fillings for Pasta, 337.

Melt in a large skillet:

2 tablespoons butter

Add and cook, stirring, until lightly browned:

¹/₂ cup finely chopped onions

10 ounces mushrooms, finely chopped

Stir in and cook about 5 minutes:

10 ounces fresh spinach, trimmed and rinsed, or frozen spinach, cooked, 305, and drained, squeezed very dry, and minced

2 cups minced cooked chicken

¹/₄ teaspoon grated or ground nutmeg

Salt and black pepper to taste

Let cool. Add:

One 15-ounce container ricotta

2 tablespoons grated Parmesan

Mix thoroughly, and season to taste.

MEAT FILLING

About 4 cups

Use to fill ravioli, tortellini, or cannelloni. You can omit the pork, and add 6 more ounces of poultry. Serve the pasta with White Sauce I, 550, Amatriciana Sauce, 563, Tomato Meat Sauce, 563, Vodka Sauce, 328, or Roasted Red Pepper Sauce, 549. Please read About Fillings for Pasta, 337. Heat in a medium skillet over medium-high heat:

1 to 2 tablespoons butter or olive oil

Add and cook, stirring often, until the meat is browned and cooked through, 4 to 5 minutes:

4 to 5 ounces boneless, skinless turkey or chicken breast, thinly sliced

One 1-inch-thick pork loin chop (8 to 9 ounces), boned, trimmed, and thinly sliced, or 6 to 7 ounces ground pork

2 tablespoons finely chopped onion

¹/₄ teaspoon salt

¹/₄ teaspoon black pepper, or to taste

Stir in:

¹/₄ cup dry white wine

Bring to a boil, scraping up the browned bits on the bottom of the pan. Remove from the heat and cool. Have ready:

1¹/₂ cups grated Parmesan (6 ounces)

Scrape the meat mixture into a food processor. Add 1 cup of the cheese, along with:

4 ounces mortadella or other salami, chopped

3 ounces prosciutto, chopped

Pinch of grated nutmeg

Salt and black pepper to taste

Process until finely chopped and well blended. Stir in the remaining cheese. Taste and adjust the seasonings; there should be just a hint of nutmeg. The filling can be covered and refrigerated for up to 2 days.

WINTER SQUASH FILLING

About 1 ³/₄ cups

Use this filling to make ravioli or tortellini. Serve with a butter sauce, 557, or Nut Butter, 558. Please read About Fillings for Pasta, 337.

Preheat the oven to 375°F. Line a baking pan with foil. Cut lengthwise in half:

1 medium butternut squash (1½ pounds)

Scoop out the seeds and membranes. Place the halves cut side down in the pan. Bake 1 hour, or until tender when pierced with a knife. Let cool slightly, then scoop out the squash. Pass the squash through a ricer or food mill, or puree it in a food processor until smooth. You should have about 1½ cups. Mix the squash with:

½ cup grated Parmesan (2 ounces)
⅛ teaspoon grated or ground nutmeg
Salt to taste

RAVIOLI

40 ravioli

Please read About Fillings for Pasta, 337. Have ready:

Fresh Pasta Dough, 324, cut into 4-inch-wide sheets
1¼ cups filling, 337–339

On the bottom half of a sheet of pasta, place ½ teaspoon mounds of the filling spaced 1 inch apart. Dip your finger in water and run it around each mound of the filling. Fold over the unfilled half of the pasta sheet, taking care to cover each mound so that no air is trapped. With the side of your hand, press firmly between the mounds of filling

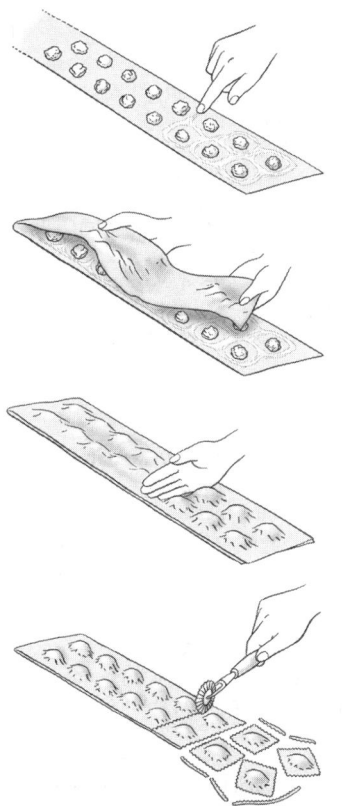

Making ravioli

to seal. Use a pizza cutter or pastry wheel to cut the sheet into squares or rectangles, checking that each piece is well sealed. Place the ravioli, not touching one another, on baking sheets dusted with flour. Let stand 45 minutes to 1 hour at room temperature, turning the pieces occasionally, before cooking. Repeat with the remaining pasta and filling. To cut round ravioli, use a cookie cutter or biscuit cutter.

TORTELLINI

48 tortellini

Tortellini are traditionally filled with meat, but a mushroom, winter squash, or cheese filling is also good. Please read About Fillings for Pasta, 337. Prepare:

Fresh Pasta Dough, 324, cut into 4-inch-wide sheets
1½ cups filling, 337–339

Using a cookie or biscuit cutter, cut the pasta into 2-inch rounds. Place ¼ teaspoon filling in the center of each round. Dip your finger in water and run it halfway around the filling. Fold each round in half and firmly press the edges to seal. Then bring the "tails" of each half circle together, overlapping them, and pinch them together. Lay on a baking sheet and let stand 45 minutes to 1 hour before cooking.

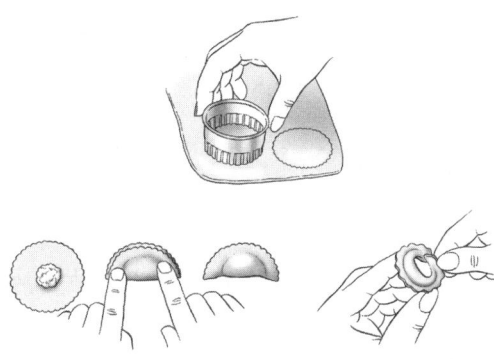

Making tortellini

ABOUT BAKED STUFFED PASTA

Baked stuffed pasta dishes range from stuffed shells to lasagne made with sheets of fresh or dried pasta. Since the pasta is cooked twice in these recipes, boil it only long enough to be pliable and barely tender. Please read About Fillings for Pasta, 337.

BAKED MANICOTTI OR JUMBO SHELLS

6 to 8 servings

Please read About Fillings for Pasta, 337.
Have ready:

3 cups Tomato Sauce, 562
2¼ cups Cheese Filling, 337, or Meat and Spinach Filling, 338

Preheat the oven to 350°F. Lightly grease a shallow 3-quart baking dish. Cook in a large pot of boiling salted water until barely tender:

8 ounces manicotti or jumbo shells

Drain. Using a small spoon, fill the pasta with the filling. Arrange the pieces side by side in the baking dish. (At this point, the dish can be covered and refrigerated for up to 24 hours.) Spoon the tomato sauce over the pasta and sprinkle with:

1 cup shredded mozzarella (4 ounces)
6 tablespoons grated Parmesan or Romano

Cover with aluminum foil and bake until heated through, about 40 minutes. Let stand for 15 minutes before serving.

CANNELLONI

8 servings

Please read About Fillings for Pasta, 337.
Have ready:

2 cups White Sauce I, 550
Chicken and Cheese Filling, 338, or 1¹/₂ recipes of Mushroom Filling, 337

Mix 1 cup white sauce into filling mixture. Set aside. Preheat the oven to 350°F. Grease a 13 x 9 x 2-inch baking or lasagne pan. Cook in a large pot of boiling salted water until barely tender:

Fresh Pasta Dough, 324, cut into 4-inch squares

Drain the pasta and place it in a bowl of ice water to cool. Separate the pasta and blot it dry. Spread a thin layer of sauce over the bottom of the prepared pan. Spread about ¹/₄ cup of the filling along one edge of each pasta square. Roll up the filled pasta to form a tube shape, and place seam side down in the pan. Spoon on the remaining sauce and sprinkle with:

¹/₄ cup grated Parmesan (2 ounces)

Bake 25 minutes, or until browned and bubbling. Let stand for 15 minutes before serving.

LASAGNE

8 to 12 main-course servings

Tomato Meat Sauce, 563, or Tomato Sauce with Meatballs, 564, can also be used for this lasagne. No-boil noodles can be used. Please read About Fillings for Pasta, 337.
Have ready:

5 cups Tomato Sauce, 562
15 ounces ricotta
1 pound mozzarella, thinly sliced or shredded
¹/₂ cup plus 2 tablespoons grated Parmesan (4 ounces)

Preheat the oven to 375°F. Grease a 13 x 9 x 2-inch baking or lasagne pan. Cook in a large pot of boiling salted water until barely tender:

1 pound lasagne

Drain the pasta and place it in a bowl of ice water to cool. Remove the pasta and blot it dry. Spread a thin layer of sauce over the bottom of the prepared pan. Arrange a single layer of pasta, slightly overlapping, in the bottom of

the pan. Spread with one-third of the ricotta. Scatter one-quarter of the mozzarella over the ricotta and sprinkle with 2 tablespoons of the Parmesan. If using Tomato Sauce with Meatballs, slice the meatballs and layer them with the remaining ingredients. Reserve 2 cups of the sauce for the top of the lasagne, and spoon about 1 cup sauce into the pan. Add another layer of pasta, and continue layering until you have 4 layers of pasta with 3 layers of filling. Spread the reserved 2 cups sauce over the top layer of pasta. Sprinkle the remaining mozzarella over the sauce, along with the remaining Parmesan. Bake until well browned and bubbly, about 45 minutes. Let stand for 15 minutes before serving.

LASAGNE BOLOGNESE

8 to 10 main-course servings

Prepare the white sauce and meat sauce a day or so ahead, if you like. Please read About Fillings for Pasta, 337.
Have ready:

8 cups Bolognese Sauce, 564
6 cups White Sauce I, 550
1 cup grated Parmesan, Romano, Asiago, or dry Jack (4 ounces)

Preheat the oven to 350°F. Grease a 13 x 9 x 2-inch baking or lasagne pan. Cook in a large pot of boiling salted water until barely tender:

1 pound spinach lasagne

Drain the pasta and place it in a bowl of ice water to cool. Separate the pasta and blot it dry. If necessary, warm the bolognese sauce. Spread a thin layer of bolognese sauce over the bottom of the prepared pan. Cover with a layer of pasta, overlapping the noodles slightly. Spread a thin layer of white sauce over the noodles and top with a thin layer of meat sauce. Sprinkle with 1¹/₂ tablespoons of the cheese. Top with another layer of pasta. Repeat, and top the final layer of pasta with 1 cup white sauce and ¹/₄ cup of the cheese. Loosely cover with aluminum foil and bake for 40 to 50 minutes, until well browned and bubbly. Let stand for 15 minutes before serving.

ROASTED VEGETABLE LASAGNE

8 to 12 main-course servings

The vegetables in this meatless lasagne can be prepared a day ahead and stored in the refrigerator. It is important to roast the vegetables in a single layer so that they brown. Please read About Fillings for Pasta, 337.
Have ready:

3 cups Tomato Sauce, 562
4 cups shredded mozzarella (1 pound)
¹/₂ cup grated Parmesan (about 2 ounces)

Preheat the oven to 450°F. Grease a 13 x 9 x 2-inch baking or lasagne pan. Slice in ¹/₂-inch slices:

2 eggplants (about 3 pounds), quartered lengthwise
6 medium zucchini (about 3 pounds)

Pour over the vegetables and toss to coat:

1/2 cup olive oil
1 teaspoon salt
1/2 teaspoon black pepper

Divide the vegetables between 2 roasting pans or baking sheets, spreading them in a single layer. Roast for 20 minutes. Toss the vegetables and continue to roast until well browned and soft, about 20 minutes more. Transfer the vegetables to a large bowl. Reduce the oven temperature to 375°F. Cook in a large pot of boiling water until barely tender:

1 pound lasagne

Drain the pasta and place it in a bowl of ice water to cool. Separate the pasta and blot it dry. Stir together well in a medium bowl:

15 ounces ricotta
2 large eggs
1/2 cup grated Parmesan (2 ounces)
1/2 teaspoon salt, or to taste
Black pepper to taste
(Grated or ground nutmeg to taste)

Spread a thin layer of sauce over the bottom of the prepared pan. Cover with a layer of pasta, slightly overlapping. Spread with one-third of the ricotta mixture. Sprinkle one-quarter of the mozzarella and grated Parmesan over the ricotta. Spoon one-third of the roasted vegetables on top and then 1/2 cup of sauce. Add another layer of pasta and continue layering the lasagne until you have 4 layers of pasta and 3 layers of filling. Spread the remaining sauce on top and sprinkle with the remaining mozzarella and Parmesan. Cover the pan with aluminum foil and bake for 30 minutes. Uncover and continue to bake until golden and bubbly, about 15 minutes more. Let stand for 15 minutes before serving.

ABOUT FILLED DUMPLINGS

Meat, cabbage, mushrooms, and cheese are just a few of the ingredients used in northern European countries to make filled dumplings. Some are wrapped in pastry and baked, while others are fried and served with melted butter or sour cream and dill. Asian dumplings typically consist of a thin dough wrapper filled with meat, fish, or vegetables and can be steamed, boiled in soup, or fried; see 342.

VARENIKI

36 dumplings

These slightly sweet Russian cheese dumplings are served with butter and sour cream for a first course or as a meal. Have ready:

Fresh Pasta Dough, 324, cut into 4-inch-wide sheets

Combine well in a medium bowl:

6 ounces cottage or farmer's cheese, drained
1 large egg, beaten
2 teaspoons butter, melted
2 teaspoons sugar
1/2 teaspoon salt
1/4 teaspoon grated or ground nutmeg

With a biscuit cutter, cut the dough into 3 1/2-inch circles. Place 1 heaping teaspoon filling in the center of each circle, fold over to form a half circle, and pinch the edges together; if necessary, moisten the edges with a little water to help them stick. Arrange the dumplings in a single layer on a lightly floured baking sheet. Bring to a boil in a large pot:

4 to 6 quarts salted water

Add the dumplings in batches to avoid overcrowding, reduce the heat, and simmer until the dumplings float, 2 to 3 minutes. Carefully remove with a strainer or slotted spoon to a warmed bowl. Repeat with the remaining dumplings. Pour over:

2 to 4 tablespoons butter, melted

Serve with:

Sour cream

PIEROGI

18 to 20 pierogi

These central European dumplings are made with a wide variety of fillings, including blueberries, cheese, and buckwheat groats. The fillings can be prepared in advance and refrigerated. Have ready:

Potato and Cheese Filling, below, or Sauerkraut Mushroom Filling, 342, or cheese filling for Vareniki, above

Prepare dough for:

Fresh Egg Noodles, 325

Roll the dough to a thickness of 1/16 inch. With a biscuit cutter, cut the dough into 3 1/2-inch circles. Place 1 tablespoon filling in the center of each circle, fold over to form a half circle, and pinch the edges together; if necessary, moisten the edges with a little water to help them stick. Arrange the dumplings in a single layer on a lightly floured baking sheet. The dough scraps can be rolled out again and reused once. Bring to a boil in a large pot:

4 to 6 quarts salted water

Add the pierogi in batches to avoid overcrowding, reduce the heat, and simmer until the dumplings are tender, 5 to 7 minutes. Carefully remove with a strainer or slotted spoon to a buttered bowl. Repeat with the remaining pierogi. (The pierogi can be cooled, then frozen for up to 1 month.) If desired, cook the boiled pierogi in batches until crisp in a large skillet over medium heat in:

Butter

Season to taste with:

Salt and black pepper

Serve with:

Sautéed sliced onions
Sour cream or cottage cheese
Fresh bread crumbs, browned in butter, 960

POTATO AND CHEESE FILLING

2 1/2 cups

Cook in boiling salted water until tender:

1 pound all-purpose potatoes, peeled

Drain and mash or rice the potatoes. Mix in:

    3 tablespoons butter
    $^1/_2$ cup grated Cheddar or Parmesan (2 ounces)
    ($^1/_2$ cup minced onion, sautéed)
    Salt and black pepper to taste

Allow to cool completely before using.

SAUERKRAUT MUSHROOM FILLING

2 cups

Heat in a large skillet over medium heat:

    2 tablespoons butter or olive oil

Add and cook, stirring, until soft:

    1 cup chopped onions

Add and cook, stirring, until tender:

    1 cup sliced mushrooms, such as button, portobello,
        cremini, or shiitake, or a combination

Remove to a bowl and stir in:

    1 cup sauerkraut, drained
    Salt and black pepper to taste

Allow to cool completely before using.

WONTONS

30 wontons

Homemade wontons are fun and easy to prepare, especially with the readily available premade wrappers. Once assembled, they can be frozen for later use. When cooking wontons, be sure to keep the water at a low simmer to prevent them from opening.

Please read About Filled Dumplings, 341. Pulse in a food processor until finely chopped:

    8 ounces boneless, skinless chicken breast,
        deveined peeled raw shrimp, or ground pork,
        or a combination

Transfer to a bowl, and stir to combine with:

    1 tablespoon cornstarch
    1 tablespoon soy sauce
    1 tablespoon Shaoxing wine or dry sherry
    1 teaspoon toasted sesame oil
    $^1/_2$ to 1 teaspoon chili oil
    1 teaspoon sugar
    $^1/_2$ teaspoon salt
    $^1/_8$ teaspoon black pepper

Add:

    8 canned water chestnuts, minced (about $^1/_4$ cup)
    2 tablespoons chopped scallion
    2 teaspoons minced peeled fresh ginger

In a small bowl, stir together:

    1 large egg
    1 tablespoon water

Working in batches of 10, lay out the first batch of:

    30 square wonton wrappers

Arranging them so that one point is facing you. Lightly brush each wrapper with egg wash. Place 1 teaspoon filling in the center of each wrapper, as shown. Fold the wonton in half by bringing the bottom corner up to meet the top corner, forming a triangle. Seal by pressing the edges

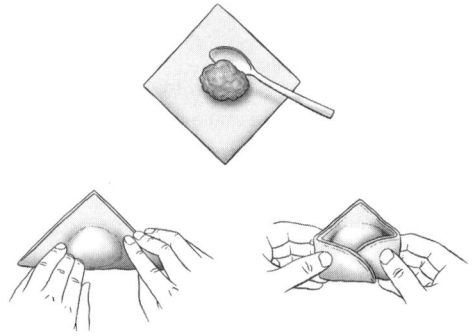

Making wontons

firmly, squeezing all the air out. Then, bring the two outside points to meet at the center and press to seal. If necessary, moisten the tops with egg wash. To cook, see Wonton Soup, 126, or Fried Wontons, 93.

VEGETABLE WONTONS

30 wontons; 4 to 6 servings

Fresh or dried mushrooms can be used in this filling.

Please read About Filled Dumplings, 341. Soak for 30 minutes:

    6 medium dried shiitake mushrooms

In:

    2 cups hot water

Lift out the mushrooms, and strain the soaking liquid through a sieve lined with a dampened paper towel and reserve the soaking liquid for later use. Remove the mushroom stems, and thinly slice. Or thinly slice:

    8 fresh shiitake mushrooms, stems discarded
        (about 1$^1/_2$ cups sliced)

Heat in a large skillet over medium heat:

    1 tablespoon vegetable oil

Add the mushrooms, along with:

    2 cups chopped fresh white mushrooms
        (about 5 ounces)
    8 ounces firm tofu, drained and crumbled
    2 scallions, chopped
    $^1/_2$ cup thinly sliced Napa cabbage
    1 tablespoon minced peeled fresh ginger

Cook, stirring, until the vegetables are wilted, about 5 minutes. Remove to a bowl and let cool, then season with:

    2 tablespoons soy sauce
    1 tablespoon toasted sesame oil
    1 tablespoon Shaoxing wine or dry sherry
    (1 teaspoon chili oil)
    1 teaspoon sugar
    $^1/_2$ teaspoon salt
    $^1/_8$ teaspoon black pepper

Fill and shape the wontons, as directed for Wontons, above.

SEAFOOD OR PORK SHUMAI

32 dumplings

Please read About Filled Dumplings, 341. Combine in a large bowl and mix well:

1 pound sea bass or other mild white fish fillets, finely chopped, or a combination of fish, shrimp, and scallops, finely chopped, or ground pork

1 large egg

2 tablespoons minced peeled fresh ginger (about a 2-inch piece)

2 tablespoons minced cilantro

2 tablespoons minced scallion

1 tablespoon toasted sesame oil

1 tablespoon fresh lemon juice

2 teaspoons rice wine vinegar

Salt and black pepper to taste

Have ready:

32 round wonton wrappers

Place a wonton wrapper on a work surface and place 1 tablespoon filling in the center. Pick the wrapper up so that it partially surrounds the filling, pleating the edges of the

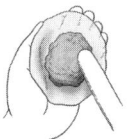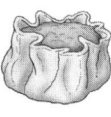

Making shumai

wrapper so that it resembles a cup, as shown above; the filling should be exposed at the top and level with the wrapper. Tap the dumpling against the work surface to flatten the bottom. Place on a plate and repeat with the remaining wrappers and filling. Place half the dumplings, without touching each other, in an oiled steamer basket. Bring 1 inch of water to a boil in a large pot, put the basket on top, cover, and cook 10 minutes, or until the dumplings are cooked through. Remove to a plate and keep warm. Cook the remaining dumplings in the same way. Serve hot with:

Soy sauce, Sweet-and-Sour Mustard Sauce, 564, Thai Hot Sauce, 570, or Nuoc Cham, 570

GRAINS

When our ancestors made the transition from living always on the move, hunting and gathering, to a less transient life it was because they learned to cultivate grain. The need to grow, tend, and defend their crops anchored people to one place, marking the beginning of civilization. Grains are powerhouses of nutrition providing complex carbohydrates, protein, fat, fiber, B-complex vitamins, minerals, phytochemicals, and antioxidants. And they are a joy to cook with. Grains combine easily with other foods and grace many tables as main courses, side dishes, or ingredients in soups and salads.

All true grains are fruits of grasses; whole grain kernels are sometimes called berries. Most grains are similar in structure to the wheat kernel, sketched in cross-section below, composed of three basic parts: the bran, the germ, and the endosperm. The outer, or bran, layers contain

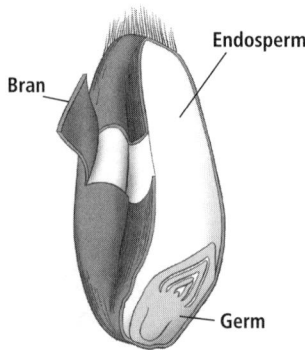

The three basic parts of a grain kernel

most of the grain's vitamins, minerals, and fiber. The germ, which is only a small part of the kernel, nonetheless contains most of the protein and all of the fat. The endosperm is largely starch, with some protein. Most of the nutritional content and rich, nutty flavor are in the bran and germ. However, it is common practice when processing grain to extend shelf life by removing the bran and the germ, leaving only the endosperm. White rice, for example, is endosperm only, as is the part of the wheat that is ground into white flour. Grains may be enriched with B vitamins and iron to replace what was lost in processing, but the vitamin E and fiber found in whole grains are not typically replaced. Nutritionally, whole grains are the best choice.

Most grains have similar nutritional and cooking properties. This chapter contains a separate discussion of each grain with recipes and cooking information. Buckwheat, quinoa, amaranth, and couscous (a pasta made from hard durum wheat) are covered here too. Though they are not true grains, botanically speaking, they are very similar in preparation and cooking use.

ABOUT BUYING AND STORING GRAINS

Whole grains such as wheat berries and brown rice still have the high-fat germ intact; therefore they are more prone to rancidity than their refined cousins such as white rice or pearl barley. Any whole or refined grain, or meal, may be prone to insect infestation. ➤ Buy grains in small quantities and store them in tightly covered containers in a cool, dry pantry or the refrigerator or freezer. With the exception of wheat germ and buckwheat, ➤ most grains can be stored for up to 6 months in the pantry and for up to one year in the freezer. Signs of rancidity are an off odor before cooking or a bitter taste when cooked. If the grains clump together, it may be a sign of spoilage, and at that point, unfortunately, it is best to discard the grain.

If insect infestation occurs in your pantry, it is not enough to kill the insects you can see. Immediately throw away any opened containers of grain, meal, or flour, even if they are tightly wrapped, and thoroughly vacuum and clean the storage area. ➤ For a period of several weeks or months after an infestation, use the pantry to store only packages that are still sealed in their original packaging. Any opened containers should be stored in the refrigerator or freezer.

PRESOAKING WHOLE GRAINS

Grains should be rinsed and picked over for bits of chaff or debris before cooking. Put in a bowl, cover with cold water, and rake the grains with your fingers. Let any debris rise to the surface, and remove it, then drain well. Grains bought loose from bulk bins should be rinsed twice.

To shorten cooking time, soak hard whole grains covered by 2 inches of water for 8 hours, or overnight. Or, to speed the soaking process, simmer the grain in water for 2 minutes, remove from the heat, and allow to stand, covered, for 1 hour. Alternatively, microwave the grain and water in a covered casserole on high for 10 minutes and then on medium for 5 minutes; let stand, covered, for 1 hour. Grains can be cooked in their soaking liquid.

ABOUT COOKING GRAINS

Most grains must be added ➤ slowly to sufficient rapidly boiling water and ➤ stirred in, so that each individual grain is surrounded and quickly penetrated by the hot liquid. The water must be kept at a boil throughout as the grain is added. With grains that tend to gumminess, this slow addition to the boiling water allows the outer starch layers to stabilize and keeps the granules separated after swelling. Some grains are simply combined with liquid, salt, and perhaps a little fat, covered, and simmered until done. For most grains, ➤ you must leave the lid in place during cooking to keep the heat and steam inside the pot.

For fluffier results, use a very wide saucepan, Dutch oven, or deep skillet with a tight lid. Fine-textured and small grains, such as cornmeal, teff, and amaranth, tend to stick to the pan and scorch if not stirred often. A double boiler or the microwave reduces this risk as well as the need for constant stirring. Cooking grains such as rice and barley in the oven yields consistently fluffy results when using a wide heavy-lidded casserole dish.

Other appliances can be used to cook whole grains. A rice cooker is a convenient and reliable appliance for cooking whole grains, especially brown rice, whole wheat berries, or rye. Most rice cookers work with a timer and produce excellent results. Feel free to experiment, using the same quantity and ratio of grain and water found on the Grains Cooking Chart, 364–368. A pressure cooker is also effective for cooking most grains, especially the longer-cooking grains such as wheat berries and hulled barley, where the cooking time may be cut in half. Consult the manufacturer's manual for specific instructions.

Whole grains are done when they are tender yet chewy; the degree of tenderness desired may vary depending on how they will be served. Most grains benefit from being fluffed after cooking. Use a fork to reach to the bottom of the pan and gently pull the grains to the top; repeat this action several times. If not serving at once, keep covered. ➤ Most grains also profit from resting in the covered pan for 5 to 10 minutes, either before or after fluffing. This allows the grain to absorb the last bits of moisture. Most recipes in this chapter indicate precise amounts of liquid, but grains may also be cooked in more liquid than called for and drained—a helpful technique when cooking other ingredients in the same pot, as in Warm Barley, Mushroom, and Asparagus Salad, 347. ➤ Count on 4 to 6 servings for each cup of uncooked grain.

The Grains Cooking Chart, 364–368, gives you basic methods for cooking grains in recipes, as well as ideas for using grains.

ABOUT FLAVORING GRAINS

Toasting grains before cooking brings out their fragrance and enhances the flavor of some grains. **To toast grains on the stovetop,** spread them in a heavy saucepan or skillet and heat over medium heat, stirring often, until their aroma is released; be careful not to scorch very small grains such as amaranth, millet, and teff. ➤ Heating a little oil or butter in the pan before you toast the grains will add flavor and help keep the kernels separate, promoting a fluffy texture in the cooked dish; this technique is used in making pilafs, 355. **To toast grains in the oven,** spread them on a baking sheet and toast in a preheated 350°F oven for about 10 minutes, stirring once.

Another way to enhance the flavor of grains is to ➤ cook the grain in stock or broth instead of water. Add olive oil or butter to the liquid for extra flavor and richness. When making breakfast cereals, apple juice or milk can be used. Substitute any of these for part or all of the water. Most grains cooked in plain water need about 1/8 teaspoon salt per serving. Some grains, such as cornmeal and buckwheat, need as much as 1/4 teaspoon. Grains that require longer cooking times, such as wild rice and barley, can be simmered with chopped onions, mushrooms, carrots, or celery; the vegetables will cook long enough to become tender. When preparing faster-cooking grains such as buckwheat or rice, simmer the chopped onions or other vegetables in the water for 10 to 15 minutes before adding the grain.

Dried currants, raisins, and other dried fruits cut into small pieces can be cooked with any grain and are especially good for breakfast cereals. Whole spices such as a small piece of cinnamon stick, a few lightly cracked cardamom pods, or a couple of whole bay leaves add flavor to grains. Or sprinkle chopped fresh herbs over the grains after cooking, then stir in before serving.

ABOUT COMBINING GRAINS

Two or three grains in one dish yield more flavor and texture. Do this with grains that are cooked in roughly the same amount of time and with similar amounts of liquid. Some examples are brown rice and pearl barley; bulgur and buckwheat; cornmeal and amaranth; hulled barley and wheat berries. When combining grains that require different amounts of cooking, add to the pot sequentially; they will need a little less water together than they do separately because there is less evaporation. If grains are to be added to the pot sequentially, be sure to choose a pot big enough to hold both grains, and water if needed, 1/4 cup at a time, toward the end of cooking.

Our favorite combination is **wheat berries and brown rice:** Stir 1/2 cup wheat berries into 1 cup boiling water and 1/2 teaspoon salt. Simmer, covered, for 20 minutes, then stir in 1/2 cup brown rice. Continue simmering, covered, until both grains are tender, about 40 minutes. Flavor with butter and soy sauce.

ABOUT SERVING GRAINS

Any grain can be served as a side dish, but there are great possibilities for grains beyond a supporting role on the dinner plate. ➤ Stir 1/2 to 1 cup of a cooked grain into soup a few minutes before it is finished. Alternatively, stir 1/4 to 1/3 cup uncooked grain into soup in time for the grain to cook in the simmering broth; this will also thicken the soup. Grains are delicious stirred into cooked vegetables, as in Amaranth with Tomatoes or Mushrooms, below.

Any grain can be turned into a wonderful salad. See About Grain Salads, 171, and recipes under Barley, below, and Rice, 354, for specific preparations. Toss the grain with the dressing while it is still warm or at room temperature for the best absorption and least stickiness.

ABOUT BREAKFAST CEREALS AND GRAINS

In America, ready-to-eat cereals are found in every supermarket and are shouted about on TV. They are either exploded into puffs under high steam, pressed and dried into myriad forms, or malted, sugared, and shattered into flakes. You pay as much for all the processing and for the expensive packaging to retain crispness as you pay for the cereals themselves. While it does take more time to cook whole grains or to make up cereal snacks, there is no question of the increased nutritive value and superb flavor.

Grain combinations supplemented with seeds, nuts, and/or dried fruits—raisins, dates, prunes, and apricots—have long been popular in health and vegetarian circles and prized by campers and climbers for their high energy potential. Snackers love these mixtures for their delicious flavors but should watch their intake because of the high calorie content. If the grains are toasted before being added to the other ingredients, the mix is often called Granola, 353; if the grains are mixed raw, the term is usually Muesli, 355.

Any cooked grain makes a nutritious hot breakfast cereal. See the entries under amaranth, oats, and teff on the Grains Cooking Chart, 364–368, and individual recipes under About Oats, 353, and About Cornmeal, Hominy, and Grits, 348. Also consider buckwheat groats, millet, and spelt, or whole wheat couscous, all of which can be cooked as directed in the basic methods detailed in the chart, with additional water if desired, and served with warmed milk or butter and honey or brown sugar. ➤ For a porridge consistency, use three times the amount of water or milk called for and cook the grain twice as long; drain and serve.

ABOUT STORING AND REHEATING COOKED GRAINS

Most cooked grains can be refrigerated for up to 3 days—or a few days longer if cooked in plain water, not with stock or other perishable ingredients. ➤ Cooked grains reheat beautifully. **In the microwave,** spread portions on individual plates, cover with plastic wrap, and cook on high for 1 to 2 minutes per serving. To reheat a bowlful, sprinkle the surface lightly with water, cover with plastic wrap or a lid, and heat on high for about 1 1/2 minutes per cup; stir before serving. **To reheat on the stovetop,** pour 1/8 inch of water into a saucepan, add the grain, stir, and simmer, covered, over medium heat until hot. Or heat 1 to 2 tablespoons vegetable oil for every 3 cups cold cooked grain in a skillet; add the grain and cook, stirring, until heated through. Or quickly transform leftover grains into spoon bread, 633, a delicious side dish, especially accompanying roasted poultry or meat.

ABOUT AMARANTH

It must be noted that amaranth is not technically a grain, but it is rich in iron, magnesium, phosphorous, calcium, folicin, zinc, and amino acids. These tiny gold seeds flecked with black have a pleasantly crunchy texture and taste a bit like sesame seeds, with a peppery bite. When cooked, the seeds turn shiny and resemble small-grain brown caviar. ➤ Because they are so small, they clump together and tend to stick to the pot, so use a nonstick saucepan if possible. Amaranth is good cooked in soups or mixed with other grains: 1/3 cup amaranth with 2/3 cup toasted quinoa, 353, simmered in 2 cups water for 15 to 20 minutes yields a tempting blend.

AMARANTH WITH MUSHROOMS

4 to 6 servings
Cook:
    1 cup amaranth, above
Combine with:
    Sautéed Mushrooms, 283

ABOUT BARLEY

Barley is perhaps most familiar in soups such as Mushroom Barley, 131, or Beef Barley, 136, or Scotch Broth, 139. But barley's roasted-nut flavor and pleasing chewy bite also make it especially welcome as a side dish or in salads. Barley is sold three ways: pearl, Scotch, and hulled. The off-white oval kernels commonly sold as **pearl barley** have had their husk, bran, and germ removed, leaving only the starchy endosperm. This strips the grain of much of its nutrition but makes it faster-cooking and gives it a smoother texture than Scotch or hulled barley. **Scotch,** or **pot, barley** has more of the bran left on, and therefore more fiber, potassium, and B vitamins are retained. It should be presoaked, 344, and has a chewier texture than pearl barley. **Hulled, whole,** or **hull-less barley** is the most nutritious, with only the inedible outer husk removed. ➤ It, too, can be presoaked and requires longer cooking. It is chewier and grittier than pearl or Scotch barley. Barley is also processed into two quick-cooking forms: **barley grits,** 364, and **rolled barley,** or **barley flakes,** which look like rolled oats and can be cooked the same way. These are generally used to make breakfast cereal.

BARLEY "RISOTTO" WITH MUSHROOMS

6 to 8 first-course or 4 main-course servings

This is not a real risotto because it is not made with rice, but it is prepared the same way.

Heat in a large deep skillet over medium heat until the foam subsides:

¼ cup (½ stick) butter

Add and cook, stirring, until tender but not brown, about 7 minutes:

1⅓ cups finely chopped onion

Stir in and cook until softened:

8 ounces shiitake mushrooms, stems removed, caps diced

Add and stir until glazed with butter:

1 cup pearl barley

Add and cook, stirring, until the liquid is absorbed, about 3 minutes:

⅔ cup dry white wine
1 tablespoon mashed or finely minced garlic
(½ teaspoon salt)
½ teaspoon black pepper

Meanwhile, bring to a boil, then reduce the heat to a gentle simmer:

8 cups chicken broth

Stir 2 cups of the broth into the barley. Cook at a moderate to brisk simmer, stirring occasionally, until the broth is almost absorbed, 8 to 9 minutes. Add the remaining stock ½ cup at a time, allowing each addition to be absorbed before adding the next and stirring often; it will take 4 to 5 minutes for each addition to be absorbed and a total of 45 to 55 minutes for the barley to become tender. If you run out of stock before the barley is done, finish cooking with hot water. Stir in, if serving as a main course:

(½ to 1 cup grated Parmesan)

Garnish with:

2 to 3 tablespoons chopped parsley or
1 to 2 teaspoons chopped thyme

This can be made up to 4 days ahead. Let cool completely, then cover and refrigerate. Reheat in a skillet over low heat, adding a little water and stirring frequently.

WARM BARLEY, MUSHROOM, AND ASPARAGUS SALAD

4 to 6 servings

Cook:

1 cup pearl barley, 364

Meanwhile, heat in a small skillet over medium heat:

3 tablespoons olive oil

Add:

2 shallots, minced

Cook, stirring, until softened, about 2 minutes. Add:

1 cup mushrooms, sliced

Cook, stirring, until the mushroom liquid is evaporated, 3 to 5 minutes. Stir in:

½ teaspoon grated lemon zest
1 tablespoon fresh lemon juice

1 tablespoon minced parsley
Salt and black pepper to taste

Remove from the heat. When the barley is tender, add and cook until bright green and tender, about 2 minutes:

6 ounces asparagus, cut diagonally into 1-inch pieces (1½ cups)

Drain thoroughly, add the mushroom mixture, and adjust the seasoning. Serve warm.

ABOUT BUCKWHEAT

Botanically, **buckwheat** is a seed, not a grain, and has no relation to wheat. It is therefore safe for those on a gluten-free diet to eat and is high in protein, calcium, B vitamins, and phytonutrients. Its delicate nutty flavor is found in buckwheat flour used in breads and pancakes, and in breakfast cereal made from the cracked form. **Kasha** is simply roasted or toasted buckwheat, and has a more intense nutty flavor than raw buckwheat. Both natural buckwheat and kasha are available whole or cracked to various degrees of fineness. Cooking them whole yields chewy, separate kernels; cracked versions yield a porridge that can range from grainy to smooth. ➤ Kasha is commonly mixed with an egg and toasted in the pan before cooking to keep the grains firm and separate. Skip this step if microwaving. As with other grains, cooking buckwheat in broth will add flavor, 345.

BOW TIES WITH KASHA (KASHA VARNISHKES)

8 side-dish or 4 main-course servings

Kasha varnishkes is a traditional eastern European dish. It can be turned into a salad by adding blanched asparagus, broccoli, or other fresh vegetables and tossing with a vinaigrette. Rigatoni or small shells may be substituted for the bow tie pasta. This dish can be made 1 to 2 days in advance and reheated, uncovered, in a 350°F oven.

Combine in a large nonstick skillet and cook over medium-high heat, stirring frequently, until the onions are browned, about 10 minutes:

2 to 3 tablespoons rendered chicken fat, 981, or vegetable oil
2 large onions, cut into ½-inch pieces
(2 cups sliced button, shiitake, or portobello mushrooms)
1 garlic clove, minced
Salt and black pepper to taste

Transfer to a large bowl. Wipe out the skillet and set aside. Meanwhile, cook in a large pot of boiling salted water until al dente:

1½ cups (6 ounces) bow tie pasta

Drain and toss with the onion mixture. In nonstick skillet, cook:

Kasha with Egg, 366

using:

1 cup whole kasha (roasted buckwheat)

1 egg

2 cups chicken broth

Stir in the pasta mixture. Taste and adjust the seasoning. If the mixture is dry, add:

($^1/_4$ cup chicken broth or water)

Sprinkle with:

2 tablespoons chopped parsley

CABBAGE ROLLS STUFFED WITH KASHA AND BULGUR

6 servings

Use Savoy cabbage, and almost any grain can be used as stuffing.

Parboil as directed for Stuffed Cabbage Rolls, 263:

1 head Savoy or white cabbage

Remove 12 outer cabbage leaves. Reserve the remaining cabbage for another use. Heat in a large skillet over medium heat:

1 tablespoon olive oil

Add and cook, stirring, until the mushrooms are tender, about 10 minutes:

2 cups chopped mushrooms

1 large leek, chopped (about 1$^1/_2$ cups)

$^1/_2$ cup chopped red bell pepper

1 garlic clove, finely minced

Add:

2 teaspoons grated lemon zest

2 teaspoons fresh thyme leaves or $^1/_2$ teaspoon dried thyme

$^1/_2$ teaspoon salt

$^1/_4$ teaspoon black pepper

Transfer to a bowl; set the skillet aside. Beat in a medium bowl:

1 egg

Stir in until blended:

1 cup whole kasha (roasted buckwheat)

Heat the skillet used to cook the vegetables over high heat. Add the kasha mixture and cook, stirring, until the grains are toasted and separate, 2 to 3 minutes. Add half of the mushroom mixture, along with:

$^1/_2$ cup bulgur

3 cups boiling chicken or vegetable broth

Bring to a boil, then cover and cook over medium-low heat until the liquid is absorbed, 8 to 10 minutes. Transfer to a bowl and cool. Wipe out the skillet. Add remaining mushroom mixture, along with:

One 28-ounce can whole tomatoes, coarsely chopped, with their juice

Bring to a boil, then simmer, uncovered, over low heat for 20 minutes. Add:

$^1/_2$ teaspoon salt

$^1/_8$ teaspoon black pepper

Place about $^1/_3$ cup of the grain filling on each leaf and roll up, 264. Secure each roll with a wooden toothpick and place seam side down in the simmering sauce. Cover and cook over low heat, basting occasionally with the sauce,

until the filling is cooked through and the cabbage leaves are tender, about 45 minutes. Remove to a serving dish. If necessary, boil the sauce until slightly thickened, about 10 minutes (cover the rolls with aluminum foil), then spoon over the cabbage rolls.

BUCKWHEAT PILAF

About 3$^1/_2$ cups; 4 to 6 servings

Heat in a large saucepan over medium-low heat:

1 to 2 tablespoons butter or vegetable oil

If desired, add and cook, stirring, until softened, about 2 minutes:

(1 garlic clove, minced, or 2 tablespoons minced shallot or onion)

Add and cook, stirring, until toasted and golden, about 3 minutes:

1 cup whole buckwheat

Stir in:

2 cups boiling chicken broth or water

$^1/_2$ teaspoon salt

Cook over low heat, covered, until the buckwheat is tender and the liquid is absorbed, about 15 minutes. Let stand, covered, for 5 minutes. Fluff before serving.

BULGUR

See About Wheat Berries, Cracked Wheat, Bulgur, and Couscous, 362.

ABOUT CORNMEAL, HOMINY, AND GRITS

Dent corn, named for the indentation in each kernel, is raised for drying and processing as **cornmeal** or **hominy.** It is starchier and less sugary than **sweet corn,** 270, which is eaten off the cob. **Cornmeal** is dried and ground dent corn. Most cornmeal on the market is hulled and degerminated before grinding, then enriched to replace the nutrients removed in processing. Whole-grain cornmeal, however, contains some or all of both the bran and germ. It has a higher fiber and mineral content and richer flavor than degerminated cornmeal. It is usually stone-ground. **Coarse, medium,** and **fine** cornmeal can be used interchangeably in any recipe unless otherwise specified, as can **yellow, white,** and **blue cornmeal.** It is extremely versatile, used in both baking and cooking; favorite cornmeal dishes include Corn Bread, 632, Indian Pudding, 823, Spoon Bread, 633, and Chicken Tamale Pie, 102. Simmer cornmeal in water to make Cornmeal Mush, 349, or Polenta, 349.

To prevent lumps when making polenta or cornmeal mush, ➤ add the cornmeal in a thin, steady stream to the pot of boiling water or stock, whisking constantly, and continue to stir frequently as it cooks. Alternatively, mix the cornmeal with cold liquid before adding it gradually to boiling liquid. Use any grind of cornmeal to make polenta or mush; it is sometimes labeled "polenta" or "polenta meal." Cooking time will vary depending on the grind. Polenta can be spread in a pan and allowed to cool, then sliced and browned, 349. Packaged logs of cooked polenta ready for slicing and browning can be found in most supermarkets.

Hominy is corn that has been treated with slaked lime or lye to loosen the hulls and partially cook the kernels, which are then washed and dried. Dry hominy is available whole or cracked. ➤ It requires soaking and cooking. Cooked whole hominy is available frozen and canned. Hominy comes in a rainbow of colors: white, yellow or golden, blue, and red. Whole white hominy is sometimes sold under the Mexican name *posole,* which is also the name of a stew in which hominy is used, 351. If dry hominy is not available, you can use dry giant white corn in its place. Freshly slaked hominy is ground fine or coarse to make **masa,** the dough for corn tortillas. It is also dried first and then ground into flour, or **masa harina.**

Grits are a favorite dish throughout the American South. Grits can be made from ground dried corn or hominy, and are ground and packaged in several ways: **old-fashioned grits** are coarsely ground, **quick-cooking grits** are more finely ground, and **instant grits** are already cooked and dried. **Stone-ground grits** contain the germ and thus have a shorter shelf life but more nutrients and a much richer flavor than degerminated grits. Grits are deliciously cooked plain, served topped with butter or a fried egg, 196, or baked in a casserole, as in Baked Cheese Grits, 350.

CORNMEAL MUSH
3 to 3 1/2 cups; 4 to 6 servings
Bring to a boil:
    4 cups water or 2 cups each water and milk
Meanwhile, stir together in the top of a double boiler:
    1 cup white or yellow cornmeal
    1/2 cup cold water
    1 teaspoon salt, or to taste
Gradually stir in the boiling liquid. Stir until smooth. Cover and cook over boiling water, stirring often, until the cornmeal loses its raw taste, 30 minutes. Spoon into bowls and drizzle over the top:
    Melted butter
    Molasses, pure maple syrup, sorghum, or honey

SOFT POLENTA
About 4 cups; 4 to 6 servings
Bring to a boil in a large saucepan:
    4 cups water
    3 tablespoons butter
Pour in very slowly, whisking constantly:
    1 cup yellow cornmeal
Reduce the heat to low and cook, stirring frequently with a wooden spoon, until the polenta is thick and comes away from the sides of the pan as it is stirred and the cornmeal has lost its raw taste, 30 to 40 minutes. Stir in:
    2 tablespoons to 1/2 cup grated Parmesan
    1 teaspoon salt, or to taste

BECKER FIVE-MINUTE POLENTA RUSTICA
About 4 cups; 4 servings
Melt in a large saucepan:
    3 tablespoons butter
Add and cook until translucent:
    1/2 cup finely chopped onion
Add and bring to a boil:
    4 cups chicken broth
Slowly add, whisking constantly:
    1 cup yellow cornmeal
Cook, whisking, over low heat for 5 minutes. Stir in:
    1/2 to 1 cup grated Parmesan
    1/4 teaspoon salt, or to taste

BAKED POLENTA
6 servings
Heat in a large saucepan over medium heat:
    2 tablespoons butter or olive oil
Add and cook, stirring, until translucent, about 5 minutes:
    1/2 cup finely chopped onion
Stir in and bring to a boil:
    3 cups water or 1 1/2 cups each chicken broth
        and water
Stir together in a bowl:
    2 cups water or 1 cup each chicken broth and water
    1 1/2 cups yellow cornmeal
Gradually stir into the boiling water. Cook, stirring constantly, over low heat for 15 minutes. Remove from the heat. Meanwhile, preheat oven to 350°F. Lightly butter a shallow 2-quart baking dish. Have ready:
    4 ounces Swiss or Gruyère, thinly sliced
    4 ounces mozzarella, thinly sliced
    1/2 cup grated Parmesan
Pour half of the polenta into the baking dish. Smooth with a spatula. Cover the polenta with half of the cheese. Spread the remaining polenta on top and cover with the remaining cheese. Pour over:
    1/2 cup heavy cream, half-and-half, or milk
Bake until the top is browned and bubbly, 35 to 45 minutes. Let stand for 10 minutes before serving.

FRIED OR TOASTED POLENTA
4 servings
Serve as an appetizer with roasted peppers, 292, or mushrooms, 283, or as an accompaniment to soups and stews or braised meats. Cooked polenta can be stored in the refrigerator for up to 1 day before toasting.
Prepare:
    Soft Polenta, above
decreasing the butter to 2 tablespoons and using 2 tablespoons Parmesan. Lightly oil a 13 x 9-inch baking pan. Spread the polenta in an even layer in the pan and let cool slightly. Cover and refrigerate until cold and firm, at least 1 1/2 hours. When ready to fry or toast, cut the polenta into 3-inch squares, then cut the squares into triangles.

I. FRIED POLENTA

Heat on a griddle or in a large heavy skillet:

$^{1}/_{4}$ **cup olive oil or 4 tablespoons butter**

Carefully transfer the polenta to the pan, without crowding (cook in batches if necessary), and brown on both sides. Drain on paper towels.

II. TOASTED POLENTA

Preheat the oven to 425°F. Lightly brush a nonstick baking sheet with:

Olive oil

Carefully transfer the polenta to the baking sheet. Bake until the bottom is browned, about 15 minutes. Carefully turn over the polenta. Bake until the second side is browned, about 10 minutes. Serve with:

Fresh Tomato Sauce, 563, Piquant Sauce, 556, or Tomato Meat Sauce, 563

LOW COUNTRY CREAM-STYLE GRITS

3 cups; 4 to 6 servings

Bring to a boil in a heavy-bottomed saucepan:

3 cups water
3 tablespoons unsalted butter
$^{1}/_{2}$ **teaspoon salt**

Stir in:

$^{3}/_{4}$ **cup old-fashioned grits**

Return to a boil, then reduce the heat to medium-low and simmer, stirring occasionally, until the grits have absorbed most of the water and are very thick, about 10 minutes. Add:

$^{3}/_{4}$ **cup broth or water**

Simmer about 10 minutes, until most of the liquid has been absorbed. Stir in $^{1}/_{2}$ cup at a time:

1 to 2 cups milk, cream, or half-and half, depending on consistency desired

cooking until the grits are soft but not runny, about 1 hour.

BAKED CHEESE GRITS

4 servings

Melt in a large saucepan over medium heat:

$^{1}/_{4}$ **cup ($^{1}/_{2}$ stick) unsalted butter**

Add and cook, stirring, until translucent, about 5 minutes:

$^{1}/_{2}$ **cup chopped onion**

Stir in and cook for 1 minute:

1 garlic clove, finely minced

Add and bring to a boil:

5 cups water

Stir in:

1 cup old-fashioned grits
1 teaspoon salt

Cover and cook over low heat, stirring occasionally, until the consistency of runny oatmeal, 20 to 30 minutes. Preheat the oven to 350°F. Butter a 2-quart casserole or soufflé dish. Add to the grits:

2 cups grated Cheddar (8 ounces)

Whisk together until blended:

$^{1}/_{2}$ **cup milk**
2 eggs
$^{1}/_{4}$ **teaspoon ground red pepper**

Gradually stir into the grits. Transfer to the casserole and smooth the top. Bake until a toothpick inserted in the center of the grits comes out clean, 50 to 60 minutes.

SOUFFLÉED CHEESE GRITS

Prepare **Baked Cheese Grits, above,** but separate the eggs and whisk just the yolks with the milk and ground red pepper; stir into the grits. Beat the egg whites until soft peaks form, then fold into the grits just before spooning them into the casserole. Bake as directed.

SHRIMP AND GRITS

4 servings

Peel and devein if desired, reserving the shells:

1$^{1}/_{2}$ pounds medium shrimp

Set the shrimp aside. Place the shells in a saucepan with:

2$^{1}/_{2}$ cups water

Bring to a boil, reduce the heat, and simmer until the liquid is reduced by half. Strain the liquid into a bowl, pressing on the shells. Discard shells and set broth aside. Cook in a large skillet over medium heat until the fat is rendered, 5 to 7 minutes:

4 ounces bacon, cut crosswise into $^{1}/_{2}$-inch pieces

Stir in and cook until lightly browned:

1 medium onion, minced

Stir in and cook until fragrant:

1 garlic clove, minced

Stir in and cook, stirring, until lightly browned, about 1 minute:

2 tablespoons all-purpose flour

Add the reserved shrimp and cook, stirring, until pink, about 3 minutes. Slowly stir in the reserved broth, then stir in:

(1$^{1}/_{2}$ cups peeled, 311, seeded, and chopped tomatoes or one 14$^{1}/_{2}$-ounce can whole tomatoes, drained and chopped)
$^{1}/_{4}$ **teaspoon salt**
$^{1}/_{8}$ **teaspoon ground red pepper**

Simmer, stirring occasionally, until the shrimp are cooked through and the liquid is slightly thickened. Stir in:

$^{1}/_{4}$ **cup heavy cream or half-and-half**

Heat just until hot. Stir in, if desired:

(2 tablespoons chopped parsley)

Serve over:

3 cups Low Country Cream-Style Grits, above, or cooked old-fashioned grits

BAKED HOMINY

4 to 6 servings

Preheat the oven to 375°F.

Heat in a medium skillet over medium heat:

1 tablespoon vegetable oil

Add and cook, stirring, until the onion is softened:

1 cup chopped onion

¹/₂ cup chopped baked ham or peeled apples

Stir in:

2¹/₂ cups cooked dry hominy, 365, drained canned
    hominy, or thawed frozen hominy

One 14¹/₂-ounce can diced tomatoes

¹/₂ teaspoon salt

¹/₈ teaspoon black pepper

Remove from the heat. Combine:

1 cup fine fresh bread crumbs

1 cup grated Cheddar (about 4 ounces)

Spoon half of the hominy into a 2-quart casserole. Sprinkle with half of the bread crumb mixture. Spoon the remaining hominy mixture on top and sprinkle with the remaining bread crumb mixture. Dot the top with:

1 tablespoon butter, cut into small pieces

Bake until the top is browned, about 15 minutes.

GREEN POSOLE

8 to 10 servings

In place of the dry hominy, you can use two 1-pound cans hominy, drained; increase the chicken broth to 3 quarts.

Bring to a boil in a large pot:

1 pound dry hominy

4 quarts water

Cover and simmer 2 hours, or until the kernels are tender and have begun to splay. Drain over a bowl and reserve the hominy and:

4 cups of the cooking liquid

Simmer in water to cover for 10 to 15 minutes, or until tender, turning halfway through the cooking:

1 pound tomatillos, husked and rinsed

Drain the tomatillos and place in a blender. Alternatively, place directly in the blender:

(Two 13-ounce cans tomatillos, drained)

Add to the blender:

1 small bunch sorrel or watercress, stemmed
    and coarsely chopped

6 serrano or 3 jalapeño chiles or more to taste, seeded
    and coarsely chopped

Blend until smooth. Pulverize in a spice mill:

¹/₂ cup hulled pumpkin seeds, toasted, 100, and cooled

Sift into a bowl. Stir in:

³/₄ cup chicken broth

Mix well. Heat in a large heavy soup pot or Dutch oven over medium heat:

2 tablespoons vegetable oil

Add and cook, stirring often, about 5 minutes:

1 large onion, chopped

Add:

3 large garlic cloves, minced

Stir for about 30 seconds, until fragrant. Drizzle in a bit of the pumpkin seed mixture. Cook, stirring constantly, until the mixture thickens, about 5 minutes. Turn heat to medium-high and pour in the tomatillo mixture. Cook, stir-

ring, until the mixture is thick and bright green, about 5 minutes. Add the hominy and reserved 4 cups cooking liquid, along with:

3 garlic cloves, minced

8 cups chicken broth

Bring to a boil. Cover, reduce the heat, and simmer for 1 to 2 hours, until the hominy is very tender. Add:

1 tablespoon salt, or more to taste

(1 pound red-skinned potatoes, diced)

(2 large epazote sprigs, chopped)

Simmer another 20 minutes, or until the potatoes, if using, are tender. Stir in:

(3 cups shredded cooked chicken)

Simmer 15 minutes, partially covered. Taste and adjust the seasonings. Stir in:

1 cup chopped cilantro

Serve, passing separately:

1 small red onion, minced

2 avocados, peeled, pitted, and diced

6 corn tortillas, toasted or fried until crisp, 94, and
    crumbled

8 leaves romaine lettuce, cut crosswise into
    thin slivers

CHICKEN AND CHEESE TAMALES

16 tamales; 4 servings

Tamales are like individual corn breads stuffed with chicken, meat, beans, or cheese or, sometimes, a sweet mixture. They are wrapped in corn husks or banana leaves and baked or steamed. (If neither is available, you can use 6 x 8-inch pieces of parchment paper.) Please read About Wrap Cookery, 1051.

Put into a large saucepan and add water to cover:

About 4 ounces dried corn husks

Bring to a boil. Remove from the heat, place a plate or other weight on the corn husks to keep them submerged, and let stand until soft and pliable, 1 to 2 hours. Combine on a plate:

1 teaspoon ground cumin

1 teaspoon chili powder

1 teaspoon salt

¹/₂ teaspoon ground red pepper

Coat with the seasoning:

2 boneless, skinless chicken breast halves
    (about 12 ounces)

Melt in a large skillet over low heat:

2 tablespoons butter

Add and cook, stirring, until tender but not browned:

³/₄ cup thinly sliced onion

Remove the onion to a medium bowl. Increase the heat to medium, add the chicken to the skillet, and brown lightly on both sides. Then cover and cook over low heat until cooked through, about 10 minutes. Remove to a plate and let cool. Finely shred the chicken. Add to the onion, along with:

2 tablespoons minced seeded jalapeño peppers

Set aside. Stir together in a large bowl until blended:

3 cups (1¹/₂ pounds) masa harina, 349

2¹/₄ teaspoons baking powder

Beat in another large bowl with an electric mixer on high speed until fluffy, about 2 minutes:

³/₄ cup to 1 cup (6–8 ounces) lard or vegetable shortening

Gradually add the masa mixture, beating on high speed. Slowly beat in:

2 to 2¹/₄ cups chicken broth, heated until very warm

Continue beating until the dough is the consistency of fluffy mashed potatoes, about 2 minutes. The dough is ready when ¹/₂ teaspoon dropped into a glass of cold water floats. Season with:

1¹/₂ teaspoons salt, or to taste

Drain the corn husks and pat dry. Set aside 16 of the biggest ones. Have ready:

1¹/₂ cups grated Monterey Jack (6 ounces)

Place a steamer insert or an expandable steamer in a deep stockpot, or use a tamal steamer. Fill the bottom of the pot or steamer with 1 to 2 inches of water (it should not touch the bottom of the steamer insert or rack). Line the bottom and sides of the pot or steamer with two-thirds of the remaining corn husks.

To form the tamales, lay one corn husk rough side up on a work surface, with the pointed end closest to you. Spread ¹/₄ cup dough into a 4-inch square on it, leaving at least a 1¹/₂-inch border at the pointed end and a 1-inch border along the other three sides. Spoon 2 tablespoons of the chicken mixture in a line down the middle of the masa, then sprinkle with 1¹/₂ tablespoons of the cheese. Fold over the left and right sides to enclose the filling (if the husk is too small to enclose the filling, wrap with another husk), then fold the pointed end over and loosely tie around the middle with kitchen string to secure. Stand the tamale in the steamer, open end up. As you form the rest of the tamales, pack them into the steamer, as they need room to expand.

Cover the tamales with the remaining corn husks. Cover the pot, bring to a boil, and steam over medium heat until a husk peels away easily from the filling, 1 to 1¹/₄ hours. Add more boiling water to the pot if necessary.

Remove from the heat and let stand, covered, for 5 minutes before serving. Or let cool completely, and re-

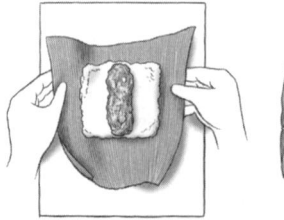

Making tamales

frigerate for several days or freeze for up to 1 month. Reheat in the steamer before serving.

COUSCOUS

See About Wheat Berries, Cracked Wheat, Bulgur, and Couscous, 362.

FARRO

See About Wheat Berries, Cracked Wheat, Bulgur, and Couscous, 362.

ABOUT MILLET

Unlike the millet sold as birdseed, the grain marketed for human consumption has been hulled. Tiny, rounded, and pale gold or red, cooked millet makes a fluffy side dish that resembles couscous, with a delicate flavor and a slightly crunchy texture. It can also be cooked as a porridge, stirred into soups, or served as a salad or stuffing. ➤ Its flavor becomes fuller and richer when the grain is toasted first. Millet goes well with garlic, chile peppers, and Parmesan. It can be cooked with other grains and seeds, especially quinoa or white rice, both of which cook in less time than millet.

MILLET CAKES WITH PARMESAN AND DRIED TOMATOES

4 to 6 servings

Delicious served under roasted chicken, game, or meats. Or serve with cooked greens as a vegetarian entrée. Prepare:

¹/₄ cup diced sun-dried tomatoes, loose or packed in olive oil

If loose, cover with water and soak 30 minutes, then drain. If packed in oil, blot with paper towels. Heat in a large skillet or large wide saucepan over medium heat:

2 tablespoons olive oil

Add and cook for 1 minute:

¹/₄ cup finely chopped onion

Add:

¹/₃ cup millet

¹/₃ cup long-grain white rice

Cook, stirring, over medium heat until the onion and millet are golden, about 4 minutes. Add:

1 garlic clove, minced

Cook 30 seconds. Add the dried tomatoes, along with:

2 cups chicken broth

Bring to a boil, then cover and cook over medium-low heat until the liquid is absorbed and the millet is soft, 25 to 30 minutes. Uncover and stir briskly to soften the millet. Cool slightly. Add:

¹/₄ cup grated Parmesan

1 egg, beaten

Stir until well blended. Dampen your hands with cold water and shape approximately ¹/₃-cup portions of the millet mixture into small patties about 3 inches in diameter and ¹/₂ inch thick. Place on a platter and refrigerate until thoroughly chilled, at least 1 hour. Heat in a large skillet until hot:

$^1/_8$ to $^1/_4$ inch olive or vegetable oil

Fry the millet cakes until browned on the first side, about 4 minutes. Turn and brown the other side.

ABOUT OATS

Oats deserve attention for their nutritional value, especially for their fiber, half of which is the insoluble type that aids digestion and the other half the soluble type that lowers cholesterol. Oats can be purchased in two basic forms: **rolled oats** and **oat groats.** Rolled oats have been steamed and then flattened into flakes. They are available as "old-fashioned oatmeal," "quick-cooking oatmeal," and "instant oatmeal," all of which can be cooked in 5 minutes or less. Oat groats are hulled oat berries that are either steel-cut (also called Irish oatmeal or Scotch oats) or crushed. Oat groats take longer to cook than rolled oats and yield a delightfully chewy porridge. All cooked oatmeal is excellent for breakfast with raisins, dried cherries or blueberries, fresh fruit, and cinnamon or nutmeg, topped with brown sugar or maple syrup and milk or cream. All oats are whole grains and still have the bran. **Oat bran** is the outer layers of the oat kernel only; it is sold crushed and is cooked as a cereal.

GRANOLA

About 9 cups

Preheat the oven to 300°F. Scatter over a large rimmed baking sheet and toast in the oven about 15 minutes, stirring frequently:

3 cups old-fashioned rolled oats

Mix in a large bowl:

$1^1/_2$ cups wheat germ

($^1/_2$ cup dry milk powder)

1 cup coarsely chopped almonds

1 cup shredded or flaked sweetened coconut

$^1/_2$ cup sesame seeds

1 cup hulled sunflower seeds

Heat in a small saucepan over low heat for 5 minutes:

$^1/_2$ cup vegetable oil

$^1/_2$ cup honey or maple syrup

Stir the honey mixture into the wheat germ mixture. Combine with the toasted oats. Spread in a thin layer on the baking sheet (use 2 pans if necessary) and toast, stirring frequently, 45 minutes, or until all the ingredients are toasted. Let cool, then store in a tightly sealed container at room temperature for up to 5 days or in the refrigerator for up to 1 month.

THREE-GRAIN APPLE CINNAMON GRANOLA

About 9 $^1/_2$ cups

Preheat the oven to 300°F. Combine on a large rimmed baking sheet:

2 cups old-fashioned rolled oats

1 cup barley flakes

1 cup rye flakes

Bake, stirring frequently, until toasted, about 15 minutes. Add and stir to combine:

2 cups chopped walnuts

$^1/_2$ cup wheat germ

$^1/_2$ cup hulled sunflower seeds

Bake for 10 minutes. Let cool slightly, then pour into a large bowl (leave the oven on) and stir in:

$^1/_2$ cup soy flour or dry milk powder

1 tablespoon ground cinnamon

Heat, stirring, in a small saucepan until blended:

$^2/_3$ cup honey

$^1/_2$ cup vegetable oil

$1^1/_2$ teaspoons vanilla extract

Add to the dry ingredients and stir until coated. Spread on the baking sheet. Bake, stirring frequently, for 20 minutes. Stir in:

1 cup chopped dried apples

$^1/_2$ cup raisins

Let cool, then store in a tightly sealed container for up to 5 days or in the refrigerator for up to 1 month.

MUESLI

2 cups; 2 to 4 servings

Muesli, also called **Swiss oatmeal,** was developed in the late nineteenth century by a Swiss physician for his patients. Eat it at room temperature or warmed, with milk, yogurt, cream, or sliced fruit on top.

Stir together in a large bowl:

1 cup old-fashioned rolled oats

1 cup boiling water

Stir in:

$^1/_2$ cup raisins

$^1/_3$ cup chopped walnuts or unblanched almonds

$^1/_4$ cup flaked or shredded dried sweetened coconut

$^1/_4$ cup chopped dried apricots

1 to 2 teaspoons brown sugar, or to taste

ABOUT QUINOA

Quinoa, pronounced "keen-wa," is not truly a grain, but is cooked and eaten as a grain. Cultivated in the Andes by Inca farmers for thousands of years, quinoa cooks fast, is high in minerals, and is one of the best sources of plant protein. ➤ Always rinse quinoa under cold running water until the water runs clear. When cooked, quinoa uncoils and becomes translucent. Toast quinoa before cooking, with or without butter, for the best flavor; it is especially good with toasted pecans or other nuts and makes a delicious pilaf. Quinoa is tasty combined with amaranth or substitute quinoa for bulgur or rice in pilafs and salads.

QUINOA PILAF

About 3 cups; 4 servings

Proceed as for **Buckwheat Pilaf, 348,** using **1 cup quinoa, rinsed and drained,** in place of the buckwheat. Increase the cooking time to about 17 minutes.

ABOUT RICE

"May your rice never burn" is a popular Chinese New Year's greeting. "May it never be gummy" is ours. Like flour, rice may have more or less moisture and starch in its makeup. Besides that variability, the type must also be reckoned with. **White rice** has been processed to remove the outer coating of bran and the oily germ. It cooks quickly and has excellent keeping qualities, remaining fresh for a year or longer at ordinary shelf temperatures. **Brown rice,** by contrast, is a whole grain, with the bran and germ still attached. Although more valuable nutritionally than highly refined white rice, it is much slower to tenderize. Because it retains the oily germ, it is prone to rancidity. Store brown rice in the refrigerator and use it within a few months.

Parboiled rice, commercially referred to as converted, is a specially processed white rice. It is less prone to becoming sticky or clumpy when cooked than white rice, and it is enriched with B vitamins. It also requires a bit more liquid and a slightly longer cooking time than white rice but shares the same long shelf life. **Instant rice,** which can be either white or brown, has been cooked and dehydrated before packaging. It is not as flavorful as conventional rice, but it is convenient because it cooks in just a few minutes.

The size of the grain has an effect on the cooked rice's texture. Use **short-** or **medium-grain** rices—which are oval in shape and cook up tender and moist, and sometimes intentionally sticky—in paella, risotto, sushi, and puddings. Use for thickening soups and sauces. Some medium-grain rices are **Arborio, Japanese,** and **Chinese sticky rice. Long-grain** rice has a long, slender shape and is best for salads, soups, pilafs, and main dishes where each grain needs to be separate and fluffy.

There are numerous varieties of **aromatic rice,** which have a pronounced nutty or floral fragrance when cooked. **Basmati** is a long-grain white or brown rice. Its name means in Sanskrit "Queen of Fragrance," and it has an alluring aroma and flavor. Basmati gives Indian pilafs their distinctive fluffy texture and aroma. **Jasmine,** another long-grain white rice, is dense when cooked, almost like medium-grain rice. It has a subtle perfumed aroma. Domestically grown jasmine rice need not be rinsed; imported rice should be. Several American hybrid aromatic rices have become more widely available. These include **Texmati,** a white or brown basmati grown in Texas; **Wehani,** a long-grain brown rice from California; and **Louisiana Pecan,** a white rice named for its nutlike aroma.

Red and **black rice** come in various grain sizes and may be aromatic or not. Often the bran has been left on. **Thai black rice** turns purplish and sticky when cooked; it is deeply flavorful and is often cooked with coconut milk to make a pudding.

Wild rice is not true rice: The seed comes from an American grass. It needs its own recipes; see 363.

Some imported rice, and any rice bought in bulk, should be rinsed before cooking. However, in recipes such as risotto, where a creamy consistency is desired, or with parboiled rice, to which vitamins and minerals have been added during processing, rinsing is not recommended.

See the chart, 367, for **stovetop** and **microwave** steaming methods, and the recipes that follow for several rice pilafs. ➤ Rice can also be cooked like pasta. Bring a large pot of salted water to a boil, add the rice, and boil until tender. Drain and serve. **Electric rice cookers** are ingenious devices that make preparing white or brown rice a snap. Most rice cookers have a large cooking chamber (often with a nonstick lining) that rests above an electric heating element. Follow the manufacturer's instructions.

Do not stir except as directed in recipes. The biggest disaster for rice is constant removal of the lid or stirring during cooking. ➤ To keep rice white when cooking it in hard water, add 1 teaspoon lemon juice or 1 tablespoon vinegar to the water.

BAKED WHITE RICE
4 servings
This foolproof recipe is easily doubled.
Preheat the oven to 350°F. Heat in a 2-quart flameproof casserole over medium heat:
    1 tablespoon butter or olive oil
Add, and cook, stirring, until softened, 3 to 5 minutes:
    (¹⁄₂ cup chopped onion)
Add and stir until well coated:
    1 cup long-grain white rice
Add:
    2 cups chicken broth or water
    ¹⁄₄ teaspoon salt
Bring to a boil. Cover, put in the oven, and bake until rice is tender and the stock has been absorbed, 20 to 25 minutes. Let stand, covered, for 5 minutes before serving.

ROMBAUER ITALIAN RICE
4 to 6 servings
This recipe was called "Italian Rice (Risotto)" in the 1931 JOY. It's less demanding, and yields good results.
Melt in a medium saucepan:
    ¹⁄₄ cup (¹⁄₂ stick) butter
Add and cook for 1 minute, stirring to coat:
    1 cup Arborio or other short-grain rice
Slowly add:
    4 cups hot chicken or vegetable broth
    ¹⁄₂ cup grated Parmesan
Stir in:
    ¹⁄₄ teaspoon paprika
    Pinch of saffron
    Pinch of cayenne
Transfer to the top of a double boiler set over boiling water. Cover and cook for 45 minutes, until rice is tender and liquid is absorbed, stirring several times. Season to taste.

BAKED BROWN RICE WITH MUSHROOMS

4 to 6 servings

Pearl barley can be substituted for the brown rice; increase the stock to 3 cups.

Preheat the oven to 350°F. Heat in a 2-quart flameproof casserole or sauté pan over medium-high heat:

3 tablespoons butter or olive oil

Add and cook, stirring, until the mushrooms are lightly browned, about 8 minutes:

1 $\frac{1}{2}$ cups coarsely chopped mushrooms

$\frac{1}{2}$ cup chopped onions

1 garlic clove, finely chopped

Add and stir until coated with fat:

1 cup long-grain brown rice

Add:

2 $\frac{1}{4}$ cups chicken or vegetable broth

$\frac{1}{4}$ teaspoon salt

$\frac{1}{8}$ teaspoon black pepper

Bring to a boil. Cover, transfer to the oven, and bake until the liquid is absorbed and rice is tender, about 45 minutes. Let stand, covered, for 10 minutes before serving.

RICE PILAF

4 to 6 servings

Pilafs call for cooking rice briefly in butter or oil before adding water or broth, a technique that ensures that the grains will be fluffy and separate.

Melt in a large saucepan over medium-low heat:

2 tablespoons butter

Add and cook, stirring, until golden, about 8 minutes:

$\frac{1}{2}$ cup chopped onions

Add and stir until well coated, about 3 minutes:

1 cup long-grain white rice, or basmati rice

Stir in:

2 cups water or chicken broth

($\frac{1}{2}$ teaspoon salt if using water)

Bring to a boil. Stir once, cover, and cook over low heat until the liquid is absorbed and the rice is tender, about 15 minutes. Let stand, covered, for 5 minutes before serving. Sprinkle with:

2 tablespoons chopped toasted walnuts, 1001, or

2 tablespoons chopped parsley

LENTIL AND RICE PILAF WITH TOASTED CUMIN SEEDS

6 servings

Serve this as a side dish or, topped with a variety of cooked vegetables, as a main course.

Bring a medium saucepan of water to a boil. Stir in:

$\frac{1}{2}$ cup lentils, picked over and rinsed

Boil, uncovered, for 10 minutes; drain. Heat in a large saucepan over low heat:

2 tablespoons vegetable oil

Add and cook just until sizzling, about 1 minute:

1 garlic clove, finely chopped

$\frac{1}{2}$ teaspoon cumin seeds

Add the lentils, along with:

1 cup long-grain white rice

Cook, stirring, until coated, about 1 minute. Add:

2 cups chicken broth

$\frac{1}{4}$ teaspoon salt, or to taste

Bring to a boil. Stir once, cover, and cook over medium-low heat until the broth is absorbed and the rice and lentils are tender, about 15 minutes. Uncover and let stand for 5 minutes. Sprinkle over the pilaf before serving:

$\frac{1}{4}$ cup toasted chopped walnuts, 1001

SPICED VEGETABLE PILAF WITH CASHEWS

4 to 6 servings

Heat in a large, wide saucepan or deep skillet over medium heat:

2 tablespoons vegetable oil

Add and cook, stirring, until golden brown, 10 to 15 minutes:

2 cups thinly sliced onion

Add and stir to coat with the oil:

1 cup white basmati rice

$\frac{1}{2}$ cup diced carrot

1 cup small cauliflower florets

2 garlic cloves, minced

2 whole cardamom pods

1 cinnamon stick

1 thin slice peeled fresh ginger

Add:

2 cups water

$\frac{3}{4}$ teaspoon salt

Bring to a boil. Stir once, cover, and cook over medium-low heat until the liquid is absorbed and the rice is tender, about 20 minutes. Quickly uncover the pan and place on top of the rice:

1 cup fresh or thawed frozen peas

Cover again and let stand for 10 minutes. Remove the cardamom, cinnamon stick, and ginger. Fluff the rice and mix in the peas with a fork. Spoon into a serving dish and top with:

$\frac{1}{2}$ cup coarsely chopped dry-roasted unsalted cashews or peanuts

BECKER RICE AND NOODLE PILAF

10 to 12 servings

Combine in a large wide saucepan or deep skillet over medium heat and stir until the noodles are toasted and brown:

3 tablespoons butter

1 tablespoon vegetable oil

2 shallots, minced

4 ounces (2 $\frac{1}{2}$ cups) fine egg noodles

2 cups long-grain white rice

Add and bring to a boil:

4 cups chicken broth

Reduce heat to low, cover, and simmer gently for 20 minutes. Allow to stand, covered, 5 minutes before serving. Fluff with a fork.

SPANISH RICE

4 to 6 servings

Preheat the oven to 350°F. Combine in a 10-inch ovenproof skillet or flameproof casserole and cook, stirring, over medium heat until the onions are golden, about 5 minutes:

1 tablespoon vegetable oil
2 slices bacon, minced
¹/₂ cup chopped onion
¹/₂ cup chopped green bell pepper
1 garlic clove, minced

Add and stir until well coated:

1 cup long-grain white rice

Add and bring to a boil:

1³/₄ cups chicken broth
1 cup chopped drained canned tomatoes
¹/₂ teaspoon sweet or hot paprika
¹/₄ teaspoon salt
¹/₄ teaspoon black pepper

Stir once, cover, transfer to the oven, and bake until the liquid is absorbed and the rice is tender, about 25 minutes. Uncover and let stand 5 minutes before serving.

HOPPIN' JOHN

6 to 8 servings

Southerners traditionally serve Hoppin' John, a rice pilaf made with black-eyed peas and ham, on New Year's Day. Rinse, pick over, and soak, 253–254:

8 ounces dried black-eyed peas (about 1¹/₄ cups)

Drain and rinse thoroughly. Place in a pot and add:

1¹/₂ cups chopped onions
(1 tablespoon minced garlic)
4 ounces smoked ham, diced
¹/₂ teaspoon dried thyme
¹/₂ teaspoon crushed red pepper flakes
2 large bay leaves
3 cups water

Bring to a simmer and simmer gently, uncovered, just until the peas are tender, 30 to 50 minutes (depending on the age of the peas). Drain, reserving the cooking liquid (set the pot aside). Discard the bay leaves. Transfer the peas and ham to a bowl and season with:

Salt and black pepper to taste

Cover and set aside. Add to the reserved cooking liquid, to make 2¹/₂ cups:

¹/₂ to 1¹/₄ cups chicken broth

Preheat the oven to 325°F. Set the pot you used to cook the peas over medium heat and add:

2 tablespoons butter
2 to 4 slices bacon, diced

Cook, stirring, until the bacon has rendered most of its fat and begun to crisp. Stir in:

1¹/₄ cups long-grain white rice
1 teaspoon salt

Cook, stirring to coat the rice with fat, about 1 minute. Add the pea cooking liquid and the peas and bring to a simmer. Stir once, then cover, and bake until the rice has absorbed all the liquid, 20 to 25 minutes. Sprinkle with:

¹/₄ cup minced parsley

Toss lightly with a fork to fluff the rice and mix the ingredients. Let stand uncovered for 10 to 30 minutes before serving. Hoppin' John can be made 1 day ahead, covered, and refrigerated. Bring to room temperature, then bake, covered and without stirring, in a 275°F oven just until warmed through.

JAMAICAN RICE AND PEAS

6 to 8 servings

Serve with a Caribbean dish such as Jamaican Jerk Chicken, 428.

Rinse, pick over, and soak, 253–254:

1 cup dried pigeon peas or black-eyed peas

Drain and place in a pot, along with:

2 garlic cloves, minced
3 cups water

Bring to a boil, then reduce the heat and simmer, covered, until the beans are almost tender, about 40 minutes. Stir in:

One 13¹/₂-ounce can unsweetened coconut milk
2 sprigs thyme
2 scallions, trimmed
1 Scotch bonnet or habanero chile
2 teaspoons salt
¹/₂ teaspoon black pepper

Bring to a boil. Stir in:

2 cups long-grain white rice

Return to a boil. Stir once, reduce the heat to low, cover, and simmer until the rice is tender and has absorbed the liquid, about 20 minutes. Remove from the heat and let stand, covered, 10 minutes. Remove the thyme sprigs, scallions, and chile pepper, and fluff with a fork before serving.

CHICKEN JAMBALAYA

6 to 8 servings

Try adding ham and either chicken or shrimp. Season:

2¹/₂ pounds chicken parts

with:

Salt and black pepper to taste

Heat in a large skillet or large Dutch oven over medium heat:

2 tablespoons butter or vegetable oil

Add the chicken and cook, turning often, until browned on all sides, about 10 minutes. Add to the skillet and brown:

12 ounces andouille sausage or chorizo, sliced, or smoked ham, diced

Remove to a plate. Add to the drippings in the skillet and cook, stirring, until softened, about 8 minutes:

1 cup chopped onion
1 medium green bell pepper, cored, seeded, and diced

1/2 **cup diced celery**
1 **garlic clove, minced**

Cook for 2 minutes, stirring to coat:

1 **cup long-grain white rice**
2 **tablespoons tomato paste**
1/4 **to 1 teaspoon ground red pepper**

Stir in:

2 **cups boiling water**
One 14 1/2-**ounce can whole tomatoes, chopped,**
   with their juice
1/4 **cup chopped parsley**
3/4 **teaspoon salt**
1/4 **teaspoon dried thyme**
1/8 **teaspoon black pepper**
1 **bay leaf**

Return the chicken and andouille to the skillet. Cook, covered, over medium-low heat until the water is absorbed and the chicken is cooked through, about 20 minutes. Cook, uncovered, until the sauce thickens, 5 to 8 minutes.

FRIED RICE

4 servings

This is a delicious way to use leftover rice. The variations are endless: Add about 1/2 cup cut-up cooked vegetables (broccoli, carrots, green beans, squash, or sweet potatoes); thawed frozen green peas; diced or slivered cooked chicken or pork; or chopped cooked shrimp or fish to the rice. For additional flavor, sprinkle with toasted sesame seeds, chopped peanuts, or cashews.

Whisk together:

4 **eggs**
1/2 **teaspoon salt**

Heat a large nonstick skillet or wok over medium heat until hot. Pour in, tilting the skillet to coat:

1 **tablespoon vegetable or peanut oil**

Add the eggs all at once. As the eggs set, push the edges toward the center and tilt the skillet to redistribute uncooked egg. When completely set, break the egg into clumps and remove to a bowl. Pour into the skillet and heat:

2 **tablespoons vegetable or peanut oil**

Add and cook, stirring to coat the rice with oil, about 3 minutes:

3 **to 4 cups cold cooked rice (1 to 1** 1/3 **cups uncooked)**
1 **teaspoon minced peeled fresh ginger**

Stir in the cooked eggs, along with:

1/2 **cup thinly sliced scallion**

Serve with toasted sesame oil or soy sauce for drizzling.

PERSIAN RICE

4 to 6 servings

Traditionally Persian rice is cooked slowly in a heavy pot over direct heat so that a delicious crust, called *tah dig,* forms on the bottom. The crust is lifted out and served either on top of the soft cooked rice or in a separate dish. In this simplified version, the rice is baked in a nonstick skillet

and inverted like a large pancake, with the crisp rice on top and the soft cooked rice underneath.

Preheat the oven to 350°F. Bring to a boil in a large pot:

4 **quarts water**
1 **tablespoon salt**

Stir in:

2 **cups white basmati rice**
1 **cinnamon stick**
3 **whole cloves**
3 **black peppercorns**
1/4 **teaspoon cardamom seeds (from about 3 pods)**

Cook uncovered, stirring occasionally, until the rice is almost tender, about 10 minutes. Drain and let stand in a sieve until ready to use. (Leave the spices in the rice.) Melt in a large ovenproof nonstick skillet over medium heat:

1/2 **cup (1 stick) butter**

Spoon off 3 tablespoons of the butter and reserve. Add to the skillet:

1 **cup thinly sliced onions**
1/4 **teaspoon saffron threads**

Cook, stirring, until the onions are golden, about 8 minutes. Spread the onions in an even layer in the skillet. Stir into the cooked rice:

2 **tablespoons diced dried apricots**
2 **tablespoons dried sweet or sour cherries or**
   golden raisins
Salt to taste

Spoon the rice over the onions. Smooth the top of the rice with the back of a large spoon and press down very firmly to pack it. Drizzle the reserved butter evenly over the top. Cover with a double layer of aluminum foil, pressing down on the top and crimping the edges. Transfer to the oven and bake for 1 hour. Let stand, covered, for 10 minutes. Uncover the rice and invert a large round platter over the skillet. Protecting your hands with a dish towel, turn the skillet and platter over, allowing the rice to drop onto the platter. Sprinkle with:

1/4 **cup chopped pistachios**

COCONUT RICE

4 to 6 servings

Bring to a boil in a large saucepan:

1 **cup canned unsweetened coconut milk**
1 **cup water**
1 **cup jasmine rice**
1 **thin slice peeled fresh ginger**
3/4 **teaspoon salt**

Stir once, cover, and cook over very low heat until the liquid is absorbed and the rice is tender, about 20 minutes. Sprinkle over the cooked rice:

1/3 **cup shredded sweetened coconut, toasted, 1001**
(Cilantro leaves)

INDONESIAN RICE TABLE

6 to 8 servings

The traditional Indonesian rice table, or *rijsttafel,* is a sociable feast at which many aromatic dishes are presented with rice. It's basically a sit-down buffet with a multitude of variations. This version is a good beginning.

Heat in a large saucepan but do not allow to boil:

4 cups canned unsweetened coconut milk

Add:

2 cups shredded coconut, sweetened or unsweetened

Melt in another large saucepan over medium heat:

1 tablespoon butter

Add and cook, stirring, until golden brown, about 8 minutes:

¹/₂ cup finely chopped onions

Add:

1 garlic clove, finely chopped

1¹/₂ tablespoons curry powder

(1 tablespoon chopped peeled fresh ginger)

Add the coconut milk mixture, along with:

1 cup milk or chicken broth

Transfer 3 tablespoons of this liquid to a small bowl and stir in until smooth:

1 tablespoon all-purpose flour

1 tablespoon cornstarch

Return this mixture to the sauce and heat, stirring, until thickened. Season to taste with:

Salt and black pepper

Transfer half the sauce to another saucepan and keep warm. Add to the remaining sauce and heat through:

3 cups cooked diced chicken, shrimp, fish, veal, sweetbreads, or mushrooms, alone or in combination

Have ready:

3 to 4 cups cooked rice

The ceremony of serving this dish is part of its charm. Pass the rice first. Spread it generously over your plate, forming a base or "table." Next pass the food in the sauce. Follow this with a platter of:

Thinly sliced onions

Hard-boiled eggs, chopped, 194

Chopped peanuts or toasted, 1001, almonds

Shredded coconut, sweetened or unsweetened

Chutney, raisins, and preserved ginger or kumquats

Sautéed Bananas, 214, halved

Mixed pickles

Finally, pass the extra heated sauce.

SEAFOOD AND SAUSAGE PAELLA

10 servings

Paella is most often made with either seafood and sausage or with chicken and rabbit. Paella can be made over an open fire, 1056. Use a full-flavored stock and Spanish fresh chorizo. Paella is made with medium-grain rices such as Arborio or Valencia. Paella should never be stirred while the rice is cooking.

Peel and devein, reserving the shells:

1 pound medium shrimp

10 jumbo shrimp

Set the shrimp aside and combine the shells in a 3- or 4-quart pot with:

1 onion, quartered

2 garlic cloves, crushed

1 carrot, sliced

1 Bouquet Garni, 960

6 cups fish or chicken broth or water

Bring to a boil, then reduce the heat and simmer 45 minutes, until fragrant. Strain through a strainer lined with cheesecloth and discard the solids. Set the shrimp aside. Season the broth with:

1¹/₂ teaspoons salt, or to taste

Meanwhile, scrub:

24 littleneck clams, 374

Place in a medium pot or large saucepan and add:

1 cup dry white wine

2 garlic cloves, crushed

2 tablespoons chopped onion

Bring to a boil, then reduce the heat, cover tightly, and cook 5 to 6 minutes, until all the clams have opened. Remove from the heat, and when they are cool enough to handle, remove the clams from their shells and set aside. Strain the broth through a fine-mesh strainer lined with cheesecloth into a bowl and combine with enough of the shrimp broth to measure 7 cups. Set the clams aside. Season the broth to taste with:

Salt

The broth should be very well seasoned. Transfer to a saucepan and stir in:

About ³/₄ teaspoon saffron threads, crumbled

Set aside. Heat a medium skillet over medium-high heat and add:

1 teaspoon olive oil

1 pound fresh Spanish chorizo or mild Italian sausage

Cook, turning the sausages until browned and blistered on all sides and cooked through, about 10 minutes. Remove from the heat and cut into ¹/₂-inch slices. Set aside. Season to taste with salt:

1¹/₂ pounds monkfish fillets or a combination of monkfish and halibut or yellowtail steaks, cut into 2-inch pieces

Set a 12-inch or larger paella pan or braising pan or a 15-inch nonstick skillet over medium-high heat, or set it over hot coals in a kettle barbecue at least 21 inches in diameter. Add and heat:

2 tablespoons olive oil

Add the fish and sear until the surface is opaque, about 1 minute per side. Remove to a platter. Add all the shrimp to the pan and cook, stirring, just until the surfaces turn pink, about 1 minute. Remove to the platter. Add to the hot pan:

¹/₃ cup olive oil

1 medium onion, chopped

Cook, stirring, until the onion begins to color. Meanwhile, bring the reserved broth to a simmer. Stir into the onion:

8 garlic cloves, minced

1 red bell pepper, roasted, 292, peeled, and cut into strips, or 2 pimientos, cut into strips

Cook, stirring, for 30 seconds to 1 minute, taking care that the garlic does not burn. Stir in and cook until fragrant, 2 to 3 minutes:

3 tomatoes, halved, seeded, and grated against the large holes of a grater

1 tablespoon sweet paprika, preferably Spanish

$^1/_2$ teaspoon salt

Stir in the chorizo, then stir in until the rice is coated with oil, 3 to 4 minutes:

3 cups medium-grain Valencia Arborio rice

1 bay leaf, crumbled

1$^1/_2$ cups fresh or thawed frozen peas or lima beans

1$^1/_2$ cups 2-inch pieces green beans, preferably romano beans, blanched, 250

Add the simmering broth. Add, pushing them down into the broth:

18 mussels, scrubbed and debearded

Arrange the clams, shrimp, and monkfish over the top, without pushing them down into the broth. Cook uncovered, at a moderate bubble, without stirring or poking, for 20 to 25 minutes, or until the broth has been absorbed. Remove from the heat, cover with foil or kitchen towels, and let sit undisturbed for 10 to 15 minutes. Serve with:

Aïoli, 581

PLAIN JAPANESE RICE (GOHAN)

6$^1/_2$ cups

This plain rice is the base for all sushi (vinegared rice) dishes. Use Japanese short- or medium-grain rice. Adding kelp (*kombu*) to the cooking pot will enhance the flavor of the rice.

Place in a bowl with cold water to cover:

3 cups Japanese short- or medium-grain rice

Stir vigorously, then drain the rice. Repeat until the water remains clear. This usually takes several rinsings. Drain the rice well after the final rinse and place in a heavy straight-sided pot, along with:

3 cups plus 2 tablespoons cold water

(One 1-square-inch piece kelp [kombu])

Let the rice stand for 10 minutes. Cover the pot with a tight-fitting lid and bring to a boil over high heat. Do not remove the lid; instead, watch for the lid to begin to dance. This should take about 5 minutes. Reduce the heat to medium and continue to cook until the water is absorbed, about 5 minutes. Increase the heat to high again for 30 seconds to dry the rice. Remove the pot from the heat and let stand, still tightly covered, for at least 10 minutes, or for up to 30 minutes. Use the following amounts to make less rice:

1 cup rice and 1 cup plus 1$^1/_2$ tablespoons water yields a generous 2 cups

2 cups rice and 2 cups plus 2 tablespoons water yields a generous 4 cups

SUSHI RICE (SHARI)

6 cups

This is the vinegared rice essential to sushi. Use warm freshly cooked rice, which will better absorb the seasoned vinegar. If it is refrigerated, it will turn hard and crusty. Combine in a small saucepan:

1 cup rice vinegar

2 tablespoons sugar

1 teaspoon salt

Heat, stirring, just until the sugar and salt are dissolved. Set the seasoned vinegar aside. Prepare:

Plain Japanese Rice, above

Remove the hot rice to a wide bowl. Toss the rice with a spatula or spoon while fanning it with a piece of stiff cardboard to cool it. When steam no longer rises from the rice, gradually add 6 tablespoons of the seasoned vinegar, 1 tablespoon at a time, gently folding and tossing with the spatula. Taste and continue to add, again 1 tablespoon at a time, up to 6 tablespoons more seasoned vinegar, or to taste. Cover with a dampened cloth until ready to use.

ROLLED SUSHI (MAKI-ZUSHI)

10 rolls; 5 to 10 servings

This makes 5 crab or tuna rolls and 5 vegetable rolls. If the nori is not toasted, cook each sheet for a few seconds on both sides under the broiler or over a gas flame until its color becomes greenish and it is soft enough to roll. Prepare:

Sushi Rice, above

Have ready:

10 sheets toasted nori (*yaki nori*)

If necessary, cut the nori sheets into 7 x 5-inch rectangles. Have ready:

1 tablespoon wasabi paste, or 1 tablespoon wasabi powder mixed to a paste with 2 teaspoons cold water

2$^1/_2$ to 5 ounces lump crabmeat, five 7 x $^1/_4$-inch imitation crab sticks, or five 7-inch-long, $^1/_4$-inch-thick strips sushi-grade raw tuna (2$^1/_2$ to 5 ounces total)

1 cucumber, peeled, seeded, and sliced into ten 7 x $^1/_4$-inch strips

1 avocado, peeled, pitted, and sliced lengthwise into 20 strips, dipped in fresh lemon juice

2 scallions, trimmed and cut into 10 pieces

1$^1/_2$ tablespoons unhulled sesame seeds, toasted, 1001

$^1/_2$ cup radish sprouts, or dill or cilantro sprigs

Place a bamboo sushi mat on the work surface with the slats running horizontally. Lay 1 nori sheet shiny side down on the mat with a long side closest to you. Spread $^1/_2$ cup rice across the entire surface, leaving a 1-inch border at the top of the nori sheet. Spread a line of wasabi paste across the center of the rice, if desired.

To make each crab or tuna roll, place $1/2$ to 1 ounce crab-meat, 1 strip imitation crab, or 1 strip tuna across the strip of wasabi paste. Add 1 long strip of cucumber or 2 short strips placed end to end, 2 strips of avocado placed end to end, and a few strips of scallion.

To make each vegetable roll, sprinkle the wasabi paste with sesame seeds. Top with 1 long strip of cucumber or 2 short strips placed end to end, 2 slices of avocado placed end to end, and a few strips of scallion. Top with radish sprouts (or herb sprigs).

Beginning with the edge closest to you, roll up each nori sheet, using the sushi mat to squeeze along the length of the sheet to compress it into a compact roll. Continue rolling and squeezing to the end of the nori sheet. The roll should be as tight as possible. Lay the rolls seam side down on a tray, cover with plastic wrap, and refrigerate until ready to serve.

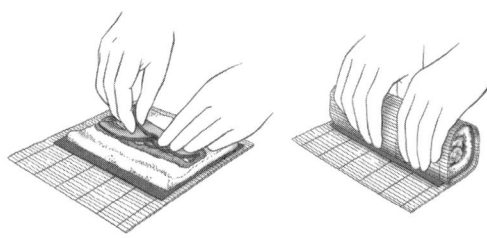

Rolling maki-zushi

To serve, cut each roll into 8 equal pieces. Serve with:
Pickled ginger, 952
Soy sauce
Wasabi paste
Diners can mix the soy sauce with wasabi to taste for dipping.

ABOUT RISOTTO

Risotto, the classic rice dish of northern Italy, is surprisingly easy to prepare. The essential ingredients are rice, broth, and butter or oil. The technique is not difficult: ➤ Stir simmering stock or broth into rice until it cooks to a creamy consistency. Use only medium-grain rices such as **Arborio, Vialone Nano,** or **Carnaroli rice** or **American medium-grain rice**—these contain the starch essential to the texture of risotto. The rice expands as it absorbs the hot broth and the friction of the constant stirring softens the outer layer of the grain, resulting in a creamy consistency. Medium-grain rices have a firm center or core that remains **al dente,** or firm to the bite. Risotto is typically prepared with chicken stock or broth, but a flavorful vegetable broth, 121, can be used.

To ensure success, ➤ use a wide shallow heavy-bottomed saucepan with plenty of space for stirring. ➤ Cook the risotto at a simmer, ➤ adding consistent amounts of hot broth, usually $1/2$ to 1 cup each time. ➤ If the simmering broth begins to run low, add water to the remaining broth and heat to simmering. ➤ Taste the rice frequently while cooking to gauge its tenderness and creaminess, and anticipate about 20 minutes total cooking time once the stock is first added. Let the risotto stand off the heat for a few minutes before serving.

If desired, when half of the stock has been used and the rice is still quite firm, the risotto can be removed from the heat, allowed to cool, and refrigerated, covered, for up to 2 days. To finish the risotto, reheat and continue. The result will not be quite as creamy, but it will still be delicious.

RISOTTO (RISOTTO IN BIANCO)

6 first-course or 4 main-course servings
Pour into a saucepan, heat, and maintain at a bare simmer:
8 cups chicken broth
Heat in a large heavy saucepan over medium-low heat:
2 tablespoons butter or olive oil
Add and cook, stirring, until soft but not browned:
1 cup minced onions
Stir in:
2 cups Arborio or other risotto rice or American medium-grain rice
Continue to stir the rice until it is thoroughly coated in fat and almost entirely opaque, 3 to 5 minutes. Add:
$1/2$ cup dry white wine
Stir until absorbed. Start stirring in the broth 1 cup at a time, waiting for each cup to be absorbed before adding the next. Stir the risotto continuously and maintain a simmer. When 6 cups stock have been absorbed, begin adding the remaining stock $1/2$ cup at a time and start tasting the rice. Take the risotto off the heat when the rice is tender but still has some "bite"; it should be creamy, not stiff. Fold in:
1 tablespoon butter
Gently fold in:
$2/3$ to 1 cup grated Parmesan
Season to taste with:
Salt and black pepper

RISOTTO MILANESE

6 first-course or 4 main-course servings
A traditional accompaniment to braised meat, especially Osso Buco, 489, or lamb shanks.
Combine and let stand for 10 minutes:
3 generous pinches saffron threads
1 cup hot chicken broth
Pour into a saucepan, heat, and maintain at a simmer:
9 cups chicken broth
Melt in a large heavy saucepan over medium-low heat:
3 tablespoons butter
Add and cook, stirring, until soft and translucent but not browned:
1 cup minced onions
Stir in:
2 cups Arborio or other risotto rice or American medium-grain rice

Continue to stir the rice until it is thoroughly coated and almost entirely opaque, 3 to 5 minutes. Add:

¹/₂ cup dry white wine

Stir until absorbed. Add the saffron mixture and simmer, stirring often, until absorbed. Add the chicken stock 1 cup at a time, waiting for each cup to be absorbed before adding the next. Stir continuously and maintain a simmer. The risotto is done when the rice is tender but firm; it should be creamy, not stiff. Fold in:

1 to 1¹/₂ cups grated Parmesan (4 to 6 ounces)

Season to taste with:

Salt and ground pepper

If desired, serve with:

(Grated Parmesan)

RICE AND PEAS (RISI E BISI)

8 to 10 first-course or 6 to 8 main-course servings

Proceed as for **Risotto Milanese, above,** adding with the onion **2 ounces pancetta, minced.** Omit the saffron, but use the 10 cups total broth. When half the stock has been absorbed, add **1¹/₂ pounds fresh or thawed frozen peas, ¹/₂ cup coarsely chopped parsley, 2 tablespoons chopped fennel tops or 1 teaspoon ground fennel seeds.** Continue cooking. Finish with the cheese, **2 tablespoons butter,** and **a generous amount of black pepper.**

RISOTTO WITH MUSHROOMS

6 to 8 first-course or 4 to 6 main-course servings

One of the most satisfying main-course versions, but also good as a side dish with game and dark-meat poultry.

Soak in hot water to cover for 20 minutes:

¹/₂ cup dried porcini mushrooms

Drain the soaking liquid through a mesh sieve lined with a damp paper towel, reserving the liquid, and chop coarsely. Heat in a large skillet over medium-high heat:

2 tablespoons olive oil

Add the porcini and:

1 pound any kind of fresh mushrooms, sliced

2 shallots, minced

Cook until lightly browned. Add the mushroom soaking liquid and boil until it has evaporated. Add:

¹/₄ cup dry white wine

Boil until it has evaporated. Prepare:

Risotto Milanese, above, omitting the saffron

Fold the mushrooms into the risotto for the last 10 minutes of cooking. Fold in with the cheese:

(1 tablespoon butter)

ABOUT RYE

Though the stuff of robust breads and whiskey, **rye** has a surprisingly mild flavor as a whole grain. Labeled **rye berries** or **rye grain,** the long gray-brown kernels take time to simmer to chewy softness, 368. Rye is a good source of thiamine, iron, and phosphorus, and it is a favorite among dieters because it promotes a feeling of fullness. Substitute rye berries in a wheat berry salad or serve warm as a bed for roasted poultry. Also available are **rye flakes** or **rolled rye,** which look like rolled oats and can be cooked the same way. Rye flakes are generally used to make breakfast porridge or Granola, 353.

RYE PILAF

About 2¹/₂ cups; 4 servings

Proceed as for **Buckwheat Pilaf, 348,** using in place of the buckwheat **1 cup rye berries.** Increase the liquid to 2¹/₂ cups, and increase the cooking time to 80 to 85 minutes.

RYE BERRY SALAD WITH ROASTED RED PEPPER DRESSING

4 to 6 servings

Cook until tender, 368:

1 cup rye berries

Drain and transfer to a large bowl. Add just enough:

Roasted Red Pepper Dressing, 574

to moisten. Stir to coat. Stir in:

1 large carrot, diced

2 small celery stalks with leaves, diced

6 to 8 radishes, diced

1 medium zucchini, diced

¹/₂ fennel bulb, diced

1 small yellow bell pepper, cored, seeded, and diced

¹/₂ small red onion, finely diced

2 tablespoons minced cilantro

Salt and black pepper to taste

Add enough additional dressing to coat. Taste and adjust the seasonings. Serve at room temperature.

SPELT

See About Wheat Berries, Cracked Wheat, Bulgur, and Couscous, 362.

ABOUT TEFF

The size of celery seeds, tiny teff smells like molasses while cooking; it has a light, nutty flavor and crunchy texture. Rich in protein, calcium, and iron, the kernels have a high bran-to-endosperm ratio, which makes them high in fiber. Teff is best known as the staple grain of Ethiopia, where the flour is turned into a spongy flatbread called *injera.* In the United States, teff is sold as a flour, a pasta, and a whole grain. The kernels naturally clump together. Serve it as a side dish or as breakfast porridge, topped with warmed milk, or stir cooked teff into other cooked grains to enhance their flavors. Teff cooked like a porridge (3 parts water to one part teff) can be spread in a baking pan while warm, refrigerated, cut into squares or triangles, then baked or fried like Polenta, 349.

ABOUT TRITICALE

A hybrid of wheat (*triticum* in Latin) and rye (*secale* in Latin), triticale was developed in Scotland over a century ago. It is an excellent source of fiber, B vitamins, and magnesium. Triticale berries are a little larger than wheat berries and milder in taste but can be soaked and cooked the same way, below, and substituted in any wheat berry recipe. Toast them first in a skillet or in the oven to bring out more of their subtle flavor.

ABOUT WHEAT BERRIES, CRACKED WHEAT, BULGUR, AND COUSCOUS

Whole wheat kernels are called **wheat berries.** The wheat berries most often available in markets are hard red winter wheat. However, the berries of **spelt** and **kamut,** both types of wheat, are also available, as are the berries of **farro,** an Italian strain of spelt (whose English name is **emmer**). Spelt and farro have a wheaty flavor; farro is softer, faster cooking, and stickier, than spelt. Kamut berries, when cooked, are yellow beige and much larger than other wheat berries, and they make a colorful contrast to other wheat berries or grains in pilafs and salads. All wheat berries can be used interchangeably in recipes. The sturdy texture of the berries makes them a welcome addition to salads made with softer grains or beans.

Milled wheat berries are called **cracked wheat.** If the milling is coarse, the wheat can be cooked like white rice and used in salads and pilafs; if finely ground, it can be added for texture to bread doughs and batters. Either way, cracked wheat tastes better toasted. When wheat berries are steamed, dried, and then milled, the result is **bulgur,** available in fine, medium, and coarse grinds. Bulgur is a central ingredient in Tabbouleh, below.

Couscous is a tiny pasta typically made from coarsely ground semolina—the hard-wheat flour generally used for dry pasta—but it can be made from other flours, such as whole wheat or spelt. Although not a grain, couscous is interchangeable with bulgur and other tiny grains in many soups and salads, and so it is included here. Couscous is also the name of a Moroccan stew that is a mainstay of North African cuisines and is eaten throughout the Mediterranean. The couscous commonly sold in the United States has been presteamed and dried before packaging and is typically simply reconstituted in boiling water; it may be labeled **quick-cooking, precooked,** or **instant.** Couscous that is not presteamed comes in different granulations and requires cooking. **Israeli couscous,** also called pearl pasta, is roughly the size of barley. It can be cooked in a generous amount of boiling salted water, as for other pasta, 320, and is especially good in a pilaf, 355.

TABBOULEH
8 to 10 servings
Tabbouleh is a popular Middle Eastern salad. Try adding chopped cucumbers, red onions, dill, basil, and/or crumbled feta cheese.
Prepare, 365:
   1 cup medium-grain bulgur
Drain, put in a large bowl, and add:
   4 large tomatoes, finely chopped
   2 cups chopped parsley leaves, finely chopped

   1 cup mint leaves, finely chopped
   (1 cup purslane, finely chopped)
   1 bunch scallions, finely chopped, or 1 medium onion, finely chopped
Stir in:
   (¹/₂ teaspoon ground allspice)
   ¹/₄ teaspoon black pepper
Whisk together:
   ¹/₃ cup fresh lemon juice
   ¹/₃ cup extra virgin olive oil
Add to the tabbouleh and toss to coat. Taste for seasoning. Spoon onto a platter and surround with:
   1 head romaine lettuce, leaves separated and ribs removed

WHEAT BERRIES WITH SAUTÉED ONIONS AND DRIED FRUITS
4 to 6 servings
Heat in a large skillet over medium heat:
   2 tablespoons butter or olive oil
Add and cook, stirring, until golden, 8 to 10 minutes:
   1 cup chopped onions
Stir in:
   1 cup mixed dried fruits, such as diced dried apricots or pitted prunes, dark or golden raisins, or dried currants, cherries, or cranberries
Stir in:
   3 cups cooked wheat, spelt, or kamut berries, or a combination of cooked berries, cooked millet, and cooked brown and/or wild rice
   1 cinnamon stick
   ¹/₂ cup chicken broth or water
Cover and cook over low heat, stirring once or twice, about 10 minutes. Season with:
   Salt and black pepper to taste
If desired, sprinkle with:
   (¹/₄ cup chopped toasted, 1001, blanched almonds, walnuts, or pecans)

COUSCOUS WITH PINE NUTS AND RAISINS
6 to 8 servings
Bulgur can also be used in this recipe, or mix couscous and bulgur together for a tasty variation.
Toss together in a large bowl:
   3 cups cooked couscous (about 1¹/₃ cups uncooked)
   ¹/₄ cup Lime Vinaigrette, 573
Add and toss to combine:
   ¹/₄ cup pine nuts, toasted, 1001
   1 yellow bell pepper, very finely diced
   6 dried apricots, chopped
   3 tablespoons golden raisins
   2 tablespoons dried currants
   2 tablespoons chopped cilantro or snipped chives
Season to taste with:
   Salt

COUSCOUS WITH CHICKEN, LEMON, AND OLIVES

4 servings

An amalgamation of two classic Moroccan chicken stews, one with olives and one with preserved lemon. If you can't find preserved lemon, make your own, 224.

Combine in a large resealable plastic bag:

4 pounds chicken parts, skinned, if desired
2 large garlic cloves, minced
2 tablespoons olive oil
1 teaspoon cracked coriander seeds
¹/₂ teaspoon ground ginger
¹/₂ teaspoon black pepper
¹/₂ teaspoon ground cumin
¹/₂ teaspoon paprika
A pinch of crushed saffron threads or ¹/₈ teaspoon powdered saffron
1 teaspoon salt

Refrigerate 30 minutes to 1 hour, moving the chicken around in the bag from time to time. Remove the chicken pieces. Heat in a Dutch oven or other large heavy pot:

2 tablespoons vegetable oil

Add the chicken, without crowding, and brown on both sides; cook in batches if necessary. Remove to paper towels to drain. Pour any excess fat out of the pot. Return the chicken to the pot and add:

2 cups water

Bring to a simmer over medium-high heat, skimming off any foam that rises with a slotted spoon. Add:

1 large leek, thinly sliced
A few sprigs each parsley and cilantro

Reduce the heat, cover, and simmer gently for 30 to 45 minutes, until the chicken is tender. Add:

1 preserved lemon, cut into thick slices
²/₃ cup oil-cured green olives, pitted and cut in half

Simmer another 10 to 15 minutes, until the chicken is falling off the bone. Meanwhile, cook, 365, omitting the optional butter or oil:

2¹/₂ cups couscous

Transfer to a large serving bowl and toss with:

1 tablespoon olive oil

Arrange the chicken, preserved lemons, and olives on top of the couscous. Bring the liquid in the pot to a boil and reduce by half. Stir in:

¹/₄ cup fresh lemon juice, or more to taste
2 tablespoons chopped parsley
2 tablespoons chopped cilantro

Taste and adjust the seasonings. Pour the sauce over the chicken and sprinkle with:

2 tablespoons chopped parsley
2 tablespoons chopped cilantro

ISRAELI COUSCOUS PILAF

4 servings

Heat in a saucepan over medium heat:

2 tablespoons butter or vegetable oil

Add and cook, stirring, until softened but not browned:

1 shallot or garlic clove, minced

Stir in:

1 cup Israeli (not quick-cooking) couscous

Cook, stirring, until lightly browned, about 3 minutes. Add:

1³/₄ cups water or chicken or vegetable broth
¹/₂ teaspoon salt

Bring to a boil, then reduce heat and simmer, covered, until couscous is tender but still firm and the liquid has evaporated, 15 to 18 minutes.

ABOUT WILD RICE

Wild rice is the seed from a grass native to the Great Lakes region. Most of the wild rice commonly available is now cultivated. ➤ It is a good idea to cover wild rice with cold water before cooking so that bits of hull will float free and can then be skimmed off. The nutty flavor and chewiness of wild rice make it a good match with any rice or barley. For cooking instructions, see 368.

WILD RICE WITH SAUTÉED MUSHROOMS

4 to 6 servings

Cook:

1 cup wild rice

While the rice is cooking, prepare:

Sautéed Mushrooms, 283, any combination

Stir the cooked wild rice into the mushrooms, along with:

Salt and black pepper to taste

Cover and reheat, if necessary, over medium heat, until heated through. Sprinkle with:

¹/₄ cup chopped parsley
(¹/₄ cup sliced almonds, toasted, 1001)

GRAINS COOKING CHART

Grain	Amount of Liquid (unless otherwise indicated, water, stock, or broth can be used)	Other Ingredients (use less salt if liquid contains salt)	Method	Yield
Amaranth 1 cup	2 cups for chewy kernels 3 cups for porridge consistency	Pinch of salt	Bring amaranth, liquid, and salt to a boil. Reduce heat to low and simmer, covered, 20 to 25 minutes. **To microwave:** Combine amaranth, liquid, and salt. Microwave, covered, on high 5 minutes, then on medium-low for 15 to 20 minutes. Let stand, covered, 5 minutes.	2½ to 3 cups; 3 to 4 servings
Barley, grits 1 cup	4 cups water	1 teaspoon salt Butter, brown sugar, maple syrup; milk	Bring water and salt to a boil. Stir in grits. Reduce heat to low, cover; simmer until water is absorbed, about 45 minutes. Serve topped with butter or brown sugar or syrup and milk.	4 cups; 4 to 6 servings
Barley, pearl 1 cup	3 cups for firm, chewy texture 4 cups for softer texture 2¾ cups if microwaving	½ to ¾ teaspoon salt	Bring barley, liquid, and salt to a boil. Reduce heat to low and cook, covered, until barley is tender and liquid is absorbed, about 30 minutes. If barley is tender before liquid is absorbed, drain excess water. **To microwave:** Combine barley, liquid, and salt. Microwave, covered, on high 5 minutes, then on medium-low 40 to 45 minutes. Let stand, covered, 5 minutes.	Scant 4 cups; 4 to 6 servings
Barley, rolled or flaked 1 cup	2 cups	¼ to ½ teaspoon salt Brown sugar, maple syrup, honey; milk	Bring liquid and salt to a boil. Stir in barley. Reduce heat to low and simmer, covered, 5 to 7 minutes; stir occasionally. Remove from the heat and let stand 2 minutes. Top with brown sugar, syrup, or honey and milk.	2½ cups; 2 servings
Barley, Scotch, hulled 1 cup	4 cups	½ to ¾ teaspoon salt	Soak barley at least 8 hours, or overnight, then cook as for pearl barley until tender, 1 to 1½ hours. Drain if necessary.	3 cups; 3 to 4 servings
Buckwheat, whole 1 cup	2 cups	¼ to ½ teaspoon salt (1 to 2 tablespoons butter or oil)	Bring liquid, salt, and butter to a boil. Stir in buckwheat. Reduce heat to low, cover; simmer until buckwheat is tender and most liquid is absorbed, about 15 minutes. Let stand, covered, 5 minutes. Fluff with a fork. **To microwave:** Cook liquid, salt, and butter, covered, on high for 5 minutes. Stir in buckwheat; microwave, covered, on medium until liquid is absorbed, about 15 minutes. Let stand, covered, 5 minutes; fluff with a fork and let stand 5 minutes more.	3 cups; 3 to 4 servings

Grain	Liquid	Seasoning	Directions	Yield
Bulgur—slightly chewy for salads, 1 cup	2½ cups boiling	¼ to ½ teaspoon salt	Place bulgur in a bowl. Stir in boiling liquid and salt. Cover with an inverted plate and let stand until liquid is absorbed, about 30 minutes. Drain. Press out excess moisture or squeeze dry in a dish towel.	3 cups; 4 servings
Bulgur—soft and fluffy, 1 cup	2 cups	¼ to ½ teaspoon salt	Bring liquid to a boil. Stir in bulgur and salt. Reduce heat to low, cover, and simmer 15 minutes. Drain if necessary.	3 cups; 4 servings
Bulgur—soft and slightly sticky, 1 cup	2 cups	1 tablespoon butter or oil, ½ teaspoon salt	Heat butter over medium heat. Add bulgur; cook, stirring, until lightly toasted and coated with butter, 1 minute. Add liquid and salt. Bring to a boil, reduce heat to low, simmer, covered, until bulgur is tender and liquid is absorbed, about 20 minutes.	3½ cups; 4 servings
Couscous, quick-cooking, 1¼ cups	1½ cups	(1 tablespoon butter or oil) ¼ to ½ teaspoon salt	Bring liquid, butter, and salt to a boil. Remove pan from heat, stir in couscous, cover, and let stand until liquid is absorbed, 10 minutes. Fluff with a fork.	3 cups; 3 to 4 servings
Couscous, whole wheat or spelt, quick-cooking, 1¼ cups	1½ cups	As for quick-cooking couscous	Proceed as for quick-cooking couscous, simmering couscous for 3 minutes before removing pan from heat to let stand.	3½ cups; 3 to 4 servings
Farro, see Wheat berries				
Grits, old-fashioned, 1 cup	5 cups water	1 teaspoon salt, Butter	Bring water and salt to a boil. Stir in grits, reduce heat to low, cover; simmer until water is absorbed, 15 to 20 minutes. Serve with butter. **To microwave:** Combine grits, water, and salt. Microwave on high until liquid is absorbed, about 11 minutes, stirring after 7 minutes. Let stand, covered, 5 minutes.	4¼ cups; 4 to 6 servings
Hominy, dry, whole or cracked, 1 cup	Water to cover by 2 inches		Soak at least 8 hours, or overnight, in water to cover. Drain. Add water to cover by 2 inches; bring to a boil. Reduce heat to low, cover; simmer until tender, 1½ to 2 hours. Drain.	3 cups; 3 to 4 servings
Kamut, see Wheat berries				

Grain	Liquid	Seasonings	Cooking Instructions	Yield
Kasha with Egg, whole or coarse- or medium-grind 1 cup	2 cups boiling	1 large egg or egg white, well beaten 1/4 to 1/2 teaspoon salt	Stir together kasha with egg until well coated. Heat a skillet over high heat. Add kasha to skillet; cook, stirring, until grains are toasted and separate, 2 to 3 minutes. Reduce heat to low; add boiling liquid and salt. Stir, cover, and simmer until liquid is absorbed and kasha is tender not mushy, 8 to 11 minutes for ground kasha, and 10 to 15 minutes for whole kasha.	4 cups; 4 to 6 servings
Kasha, whole 1 cup	2 cups	1/4 to 1/2 teaspoon salt (1 to 2 tablespoons butter or oil)	Cook or microwave as for buckwheat, simmering or microwaving for about 10 minutes.	4 cups; 4 to 6 servings
Kasha, ground, coarse or medium 1 cup	2 cups	1 to 2 tablespoons butter or oil 1/4 to 1/2 teaspoon salt	Heat butter, add kasha, and cook, stirring, until grains are toasted, 3 minutes. Stir in liquid and salt. Bring to a boil, reduce heat to low, and simmer, covered, until tender, 8 to 11 minutes.	4 cups; 4 to 6 servings
Millet 1 cup	2 1/2 cups	1/2 teaspoon salt	Bring liquid and salt to a boil. Stir in millet, reduce heat to low, cover, and simmer 20 minutes. Let stand, covered, 5 minutes.	3 1/2 cups; 4 to 6 servings
Oats, old-fashioned rolled 1 cup	2 cups water	(1/3 cup raisins) Pinch salt; (1 teaspoon vanilla, 1/2 teaspoon ground cinnamon, and/or 1/4 teaspoon grated or ground nutmeg) Brown sugar, maple syrup	Bring water to a boil in a medium saucepan. Stir in oats, raisins, if using, and salt. Reduce the heat and simmer, uncovered, for 3 to 5 minutes. Stir in other flavorings as desired, and serve topped with brown sugar or syrup.	2 1/2 cups; 2 to 3 servings
Oats, quick-cooking 1 cup	2 cups water	As for old-fashioned rolled oats	Prepare as for old-fashioned rolled oats.	2 cups; 2 to 3 servings
Oats, steel-cut (Scotch oats; Irish oatmeal) 1 cup	4 cups water 1 cup water to 1/4 cup oats if microwaving	As for old-fashioned rolled oats, increasing salt to 1/2 teaspoon	Bring water to a boil in a medium saucepan; stir in oats and salt. Cook, stirring, for 3 minutes. Reduce heat and simmer, uncovered, 20 minutes; stir and scrape bottom of pan often to discourage sticking. Stir in other ingredients, such as raisins, and simmer 10 minutes. Serve with brown sugar or syrup. **To microwave:** Combine water, oats, 1 teaspoon butter, and a pinch of salt. Microwave on medium-high; stir every 3 minutes, until liquid is absorbed, about 12 minutes. Let stand, covered, 3 minutes.	3 cups; 3 to 4 servings

Grain	Liquid	Salt/Butter	Method	Yield
Oats, steel-cut (Scotch oats; Irish oatmeal), soaking method, 1 cup	4 cups water	As for old-fashioned rolled oats, increasing salt to 1/2 teaspoon	Bring water to a boil. Remove from heat; stir in oats and salt. Cover and let stand overnight. Cook over low heat 7 to 10 minutes; stir often and add other ingredients such as raisins in the last 5 minutes.	3 2/3 cups; 3 to 4 servings
Quinoa, 1 cup	2 cups	1/4 to 1/2 teaspoon salt (1 tablespoon butter or oil)	Rinse quinoa, 353. Bring liquid, salt, and butter to a boil. Stir in quinoa. Reduce heat; simmer, covered, until quinoa is tender and liquid is absorbed, 15 to 17 minutes. **To microwave:** Microwave quinoa, liquid, salt, and butter, covered, on high 5 minutes, then on medium-low 15 minutes. Let stand, covered, 5 minutes. Fluff with a fork.	3 1/2 cups; 4 servings
Rice, converted white, 1 cup	2 1/4 cups	As for long-grain white rice	Proceed as for long-grain white rice, simmering for about 25 minutes.	4 cups; 4 to 6 servings
Rice, long-grain brown, 1 cup	2 1/4 cups for chewy rice 2 1/2 cups for softer, slightly stickier rice	As for long-grain white rice	Proceed as for long-grain white rice, simmering for 35 minutes. Let stand, covered, 10 minutes; uncovered 10 minutes. Fluff with a fork. **To microwave:** Proceed as for long-grain white rice, cooking on medium-low for 40 to 45 minutes.	3 to 3 1/2 cups; 4 servings
Rice, long-grain white, 1 cup	1 3/4 cups for drier, firm rice 2 cups for moist, tender rice	(1 tablespoon butter or oil) 1/4 to 1/2 teaspoon salt	Bring liquid, butter, and salt to a boil. Add rice and stir once with a fork. Cover and cook over very low heat until all liquid is absorbed, 15 to 18 minutes; do not lift cover before the end of cooking. Let stand, covered, 5 to 10 minutes. **To microwave:** Microwave rice, liquid, butter, and salt, covered, on high 5 minutes, then on medium 15 minutes. Let stand, covered, 5 minutes.	3 to 3 1/2 cups; 4 servings
Rice, medium- or short-grain brown, 1 cup	2 cups	As for long-grain white rice	Proceed as for long-grain white rice, simmering for 40 to 45 minutes.	3 cups; 4 servings
Rice, medium- or short-grain white, 1 cup	1 3/4 cups	As for long-grain white rice	Proceed as for long-grain white rice, cooking over low, not very low, heat.	3 cups; 4 servings

Grain	Liquid	Salt	Instructions	Yield
Rye berries 1 cup	3 cups 2¾ cups if microwaving	½ teaspoon salt	Bring liquid and salt to a boil. Stir in rye berries. Reduce heat to low; simmer, covered, until some berries have burst and all are tender, 45 to 60 minutes. Drain. **To microwave:** Microwave berries, liquid, and salt, covered, on high 10 minutes, or until boiling, then on medium-low until some berries have burst and all are tender, 45 to 60 minutes. Drain.	2 to 2½ cups; 4 servings
Spelt, see Wheat berries				
Teff 1 cup	2½ cups for firm grains 3 cups for porridge consistency	1 teaspoon salt	Bring liquid and salt to a boil. Gradually stir in teff. Reduce heat to low and simmer, covered, until tender, about 15 minutes. **To microwave:** Combine teff, liquid, and salt. Microwave, covered, on high 5 minutes, or until boiling, then on medium 15 minutes. Let stand 5 minutes.	2½ to 3 cups; 2 to 4 servings
Triticale 1 cup	4 cups	¼ to ½ teaspoon salt	Cook as for wheat berries.	2 to 3 cups; 4 servings
Wheat berries 1 cup	3 cups	¼ to ½ teaspoon salt	Soak berries at least 8 hours, or overnight, 344, in 3 cups water. Add salt and bring berries, with soaking liquid, to a boil. Reduce heat and simmer, uncovered, until tender but chewy, 45 to 60 minutes. *For unsoaked berries,* bring liquid and salt to a boil. Stir in berries, reduce heat, and simmer, uncovered, until tender but chewy, 1¼ to 1½ hours. Drain if necessary.	Scant 2¼ cups; 4 servings
Wild rice 1 cup	3 cups	1 teaspoon salt	Rinse and drain rice. Bring rice, liquid, and salt to a boil. Stir once, reduce heat to low, and simmer, covered, until rice is tender and most kernels are splayed, revealing white interior, 35 to 55 minutes. Drain excess liquid; or, if liquid evaporates before rice is done, add a little more.	Scant 3 cups; 4 servings

SHELLFISH

Nothing brings the fragrances of the ocean into our kitchens like cooking shellfish. When we speak of shellfish, we are usually talking about members of two major groups: **crustaceans** and **mollusks.** (Though turtle and frog legs are not shellfish by our definition, they have landed in this chapter for cooking and handling instructions.)

Crustaceans have legs and sometimes claws, and include **crabs, lobsters, shrimps,** and **crayfish.** Most crustaceans are sold alive, frozen, or cooked. Lobsters are most commonly sold alive, so be sure to buy from a clean tank and choose active lobsters. Shrimp is mostly available at the supermarket as "fresh raw" shrimp that has been brought to the store frozen and then sold thawed. To check for freshness, smell the shellfish and if there are any off odors or smell of ammonia, don't buy it. When you do buy, cook the same day. If you purchase shrimp frozen, use the same test after thawing and before rinsing and cooking. Peeled, deveined, and cooked shrimp are also readily available.

Most edible **mollusks** live within a protective shell that helps detect food or enemies, and controls water flow in and out. Mollusks include **oysters, clams, scallops, mussels, conch, whelk,** and **snails.** The most advanced of the mollusks, the **cephalopods,** include **squid, octopus,** and **cuttlefish.** Buy mollusks alive in shells that are closed tight, and keep on ice and cover with a damp cloth. ➤ Remember, when cooking bivalves such as mussels, oysters, scallops, and clams in the shell always to discard any that do not open when cooked. All mollusks can be steamed.

Most shellfish come from salt water and are either wild or farmed. Some shellfish, especially shrimp, comes to us from all over the world. Many shellfish, such as clams and mussels, must be sold alive unless they are cooked. Properly handled, many shellfish can live for short periods out of the water and, although they are never as flavorful as they are when first harvested, their quality can remain fairly high. Recipes for mussels, oysters, and clams are fairly interchangeable, and exciting dishes may be created by combining mollusks and crustaceans.

Some mollusks, however, come with a caveat. ➤ Eaten raw, there is a small but present risk of contaminants in oysters and clams that can cause illness. ➤ It is imperative that these shellfish be purchased from a reputable source. If in doubt, ask to see the tag that, by law, must be affixed to each container of oysters, clams, mussels, and scallops in the shell. The tag will state the date and location of harvest as well as the harvester's registration or identification number.

MIXED SHELLFISH IN TOMATO SAUCE
4 to 6 servings
To make this moist enough to serve over pasta, add extra tomatoes or $1/2$ cup of the pasta cooking water.
Combine in a large heavy skillet over medium-high heat:
> **3 tablespoons olive oil**
> **1 small dried chile pepper**
> **3 garlic cloves, coarsely chopped**

Cook, stirring, until fragrant. Discard the garlic and pepper. Add:
> **3 cups peeled, seeded, and chopped or canned crushed tomatoes**
> **1 teaspoon chopped fresh rosemary or $1/2$ teaspoon dried rosemary**
> **Salt and black pepper to taste**

Reduce the heat to medium and cook, stirring occasionally, until the tomatoes break up. Stir in:
> **$1^1/2$ to 2 pounds mixed shellfish—peeled shrimp, cleaned squid, 389, mussels, scrubbed and debearded, 373, and/or hard-shell clams, scrubbed, 374, cooked whelk, 390, and/or octopus, 389—cut into bite-sized pieces**

Cover the pan, reduce the heat to medium-low, and cook 5 to 10 minutes, until the shellfish have cooked and the mussels or clams, if using, have opened. Garnish with:
> **Chopped parsley or basil**

SHELLFISH STEW WITH MUSHROOMS AND GREENS
4 servings
Combine in a large heavy saucepan:
> **$1/4$ cup olive oil**
> **2 cups chopped mixed mushrooms**
> **1 tablespoon minced garlic**

Cook, stirring, over medium heat, until the mushrooms begin to soften, about 5 minutes. Add:
> **1 cup coarsely chopped greens, such as dandelion, kale, chard, or collards**

2 cups liquid (see About Liquids for Cooking
Shellfish, 371)

Increase the heat and cook until the greens are softened and the liquid has been reduced by half, about 10 minutes. Stir in:

1½ to 2 pounds mixed shellfish—peeled shrimp, cleaned squid, 389, mussels, scrubbed and debearded, 373, and/or hard-shell clams, scrubbed, 374, cooked whelk, 390, and/or octopus, 389—cut into bite-sized pieces

Cover the pan, reduce the heat to medium-low, and cook until the shellfish are cooked and the mussels and clams, if using, have opened, 5 to 10 minutes. Season with:

Salt and black pepper to taste

Spoon the shellfish, mushrooms, and greens into serving bowls and pour some of the cooking juices over them. Drizzle with:

Extra-virgin olive oil

ABOUT RAW SHELLFISH

The beauty of raw shellfish lies in its delicate flavors and textures. This is especially true of oysters, which vary considerably in flavor and texture. ➤ Remember, whenever you eat raw shellfish, it must be impeccably fresh and properly chilled; raw shellfish can cause illness if not handled with care.

Buy your shellfish from a reputable source. Avoid buying from parked trucks, temporary roadside stands, or other itinerant "shops." ➤ Care should be taken when gathering shellfish yourself; the Coast Guard should be consulted first—information is posted online. As long as the water is regularly tested and contains no more than the legal limit of harmful bacteria, your risks are minimal.

SCALLOP SEVICHE

4 servings

Seviche is raw shellfish or fish marinated in an acidic dressing. Though not technically cooked, the shellfish turns opaque and firms up because of the acid. Be sure to use only the freshest shellfish or fish. You can take this basic recipe in many directions. Garnish with parsley if you use lemon juice, or with scallions if you add soy sauce. For a spicy kick, add ½ teaspoon or more crushed red pepper flakes or diced jalapeño, habanero, or Scotch bonnet pepper. For sweetness, add diced red or yellow bell pepper, top with minced fresh or sliced pickled ginger or diced red onions, or surround with Tomato Concassé, 563.

Combine in a medium bowl:

1 pound sea or bay scallops, side "hinge" removed, 377, and cut into ⅛- to ¼-inch slices or small chunks

½ cup fresh lemon or lime juice, or a combination

(1 tablespoon soy sauce)

Refrigerate and stir occasionally until the scallops are opaque, about 1 hour, or for up to 90 minutes. Drain and season with:

Salt and black pepper to taste

Garnish with:

Minced parsley, cilantro, chives, or scallions

A squeeze of lemon or lime

SHRIMP SEVICHE

Substitute for the scallops **1 pound cooked, peeled medium-to-large shrimp, cut into ¼-inch bits.** Reduce the lemon and lime juices to 3 tablespoons each and refrigerate for no more than 1 hour. Drain, then stir in the salt, pepper, and herbs as directed and finish with a squeeze of fresh lemon or lime.

SHELLFISH COCKTAILS

Serve these well chilled, the shrimp preferably hanging from the rims of martini glasses or arranged on a platter of ice. For clams and oysters, open and arrange the raw shellfish on the half-shell in a circle on a large platter or tray of ice; place the dipping sauces in the center. You may also pour the sauce over the seafood or toss the seafood in the sauce and serve on lettuce leaves, in endive spears, or on a bed of watercress. If serving individually, allow about ⅓ cup seafood per person, or 5 to 6 mollusks or shrimp, with about ¼ cup sauce.

For shellfish:

No-Fail Boiled Shrimp, 385

Raw oysters

Raw hard-shell clams

Cooked crab legs in the shell

Cooked lobster, cracked into pieces and left in the shell

For sauces:

Rémoulade Sauce, 581

Becker Cocktail Sauce, 568

Mignonette Sauce, 568

Tomatillo-Horseradish Sauce, 568

Serve with:

Oyster crackers

Quick Cheese Straws or Wafers, 91

Soda Crackers, 93

Matzo

Rye or rice crackers

Garlic Bread, 641

Endive or radicchio leaves

CRAB COCONUT COCKTAIL

4 servings

Whisk together in a large bowl:

2 cups unsweetened coconut milk

3 to 4 tablespoons hot pepper sauce

Juice of 2 limes

¼ cup chopped cilantro

2 tablespoons honey

½ teaspoon salt, or to taste

¼ teaspoon black pepper

Cover and let sit for 15 minutes. Gently fold in:

1½ pounds lump crabmeat, picked over for shells
    and cartilage
1 ripe mango, peeled, pitted, and chopped
1 Belgian endive, core removed and sliced crosswise
1 head radicchio, sliced

Stir gently to combine. Divide the mixture among 4 plates.
Garnish with:

(9 to 12 Deep-Fried Plantains, 294, or tortilla chips
    per plate)
(Cilantro leaves)

LOBSTER AVOCADO COCKTAIL

4 servings

Whisk together in a medium bowl:

½ cup fresh lime juice
2 teaspoons honey
2 tablespoons prepared horseradish, drained
1 tablespoon Worcestershire sauce
1 teaspoon hot pepper sauce
1 tablespoon chopped tarragon
Salt and black pepper to taste

Add:

Meat from a cooked 2-pound lobster, 383,
    coarsely chopped
1 ripe avocado, pitted, peeled, and chopped
¼ cup chopped watercress

Stir together gently. Serve in martini glasses, bowls, or:

(Avocado Cups, 172)

ABOUT LIQUIDS FOR COOKING SHELLFISH

In many shellfish recipes, some liquid is needed to begin or
finish the cooking. You can choose from a variety of liquids or combine them as you like. Generally speaking,
these are, in order of preference:

Fish Stock, 118
Express Fish Stock, 120
Water from steaming shellfish, strained, and reduced
    for more flavor if desired
Shrimp Stock, 119, Poultry Stock, 117, or Vegetable
    Stock, 119
Bottled clam juice
Dry white wine
Water

ABOUT OYSTERS

Although edible at any time, these shellfish are best in flavor when they are not spawning. Most oysters spawn during summer months, but southern oysters spawn all
throughout the year; they are often mild and sweet and
do not have the crisp flavor of northern types. Oysters in
the shell should be alive. If they have broken shells or gape
and do not close quickly in handling, discard them. These
mollusks have one shallow and one deep half-shell, and it
is in the deeper shell that they are served raw or baked.
Some canny diners have been known to ask for them on
the shallow shell in restaurants, in the hope of getting
them absolutely freshly opened.

Of the numerous species of oyster, four regional types
are important in America: the **Eastern oyster,** the **Pacific
oyster,** the **European flat oyster,** and the **Olympia
oyster.** Within these major species fall the musical names
that reflect this bivalve's geographic diversity: **Wellfleet,
Kumamoto, Chincoteague, Blue Point, Belon, Westcott Bay,
Malpeque, Apalachicola, Breton Sound, Mad River,** and
Marennes. An oyster's flavor depends on the waters it
comes from: Salinity, mineral content, and temperature
contribute to its texture and taste.

"He was a bold man," declared Jonathan Swift, "that
first ate an oyster." And, in our opinion, he must have
been quite a determined character just to shuck it. ➤ **To
open oysters,** first provide yourself with a strainer and a
bowl in which to catch the juices. Later you may pour the
strained liquor over the oysters before serving them on the
half-shell—bedded down in coarse salt if served hot or on
cracked ice if cold. When preparing oysters in a sauce, add
the oyster liquor to it.

Now back to the actual opening of the shells. Hold a
well-scrubbed oyster, deep shell down, in a folded napkin
in the palm of one hand, working over a strainer set over a
bowl. Insert the edge of an oyster knife into the hinge of
the shells. Turn the knife to pry and lift the upper shell
enough to cut through the hinge muscle, then run the
knife between the shells, without cutting into the oyster,
to open.

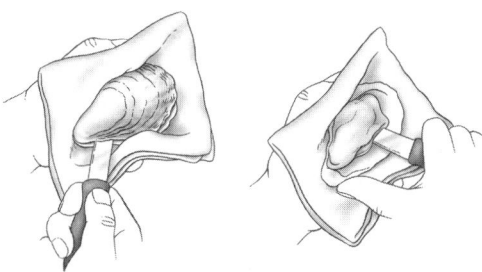

Shucking an oyster

Until you develop the knack, shucking is not easy.
Should you grow slightly desperate, you may be willing to
sacrifice some flavor for convenience. If so, place the oysters in a 400°F oven for 5 to 7 minutes, depending on size,
then drop them briefly into ice water and drain. They
should open more easily, but cooking can toughen the
muscle that attaches the oyster to its shell, making it more
difficult to pry the meat from the shell. A better idea is to
have your fish seller do the shucking for you, as close to
serving time as possible. But do remember to ask to have
the oyster liquor and shells reserved!

However you open an oyster, complete the release of
the flesh from the shell by using a knife, and ➤ examine
each oyster with your fingers to be sure no bits of shell are
adhering to it. If you are using the oysters out of the shell,

drop them into the strainer, reserving the juice. If the oysters are sandy, you may rinse them in a separate bowl, allowing ➤ ¹/₂ cup cold water to each quart of shucked oysters. Pour it over the oysters, then strain carefully, and reserve the water. Before using the oyster liquor and the rinse water in a sauce, be sure to ➤ strain through doubled cheesecloth to free it of grit. ➤ Before using oysters in any fried or creamed dish, dry them carefully with an absorbent towel.

If oysters have been bought in bulk, already opened, be sure, again, to free them of any bits of shell. They should be plump and creamy in color, and the liquor clear, not cloudy, and free from sour or unpleasant odors. If oysters burst during cooking, it means they may have been previously soaked in fresh water to plump them, and their flavor, as well as their texture, ruined. Allow ➤ 1 quart undrained shucked oysters for 6 servings. It is hard to estimate amounts for oysters on the shell, as they vary in size—6 moderate-sized Eastern oysters would equal about 20 of the tiny West Coast Olympia oysters.

To store oysters in the shell, refrigerate, preferably at 39°F, in a bowl or mesh bag, not directly on ice; keep dry. Store shucked oysters at the same temperature, covered by their liquor, in a closed container. The container may be set in crushed ice, up to about three-quarters of its height. If you bought them fresh, shucked oysters may be stored in this way up to three days.

For other oyster suggestions, see Appetizers and Hors d'Oeuvres, 83. For other cooked oyster suggestions and oyster soups, see Hangtown Fry, 202, Cajun Popcorn Shrimp, 84, Angels on Horseback, 84, Oyster Stew, 140, Oysters Rockefeller, 85, and Seafood Gumbo, 141.

OYSTERS ON THE HALF-SHELL
Allow 5 to 6 oysters per serving
Scrub well, then chill and open just before serving:
> **Oysters**
Arrange them in the half-shell on cracked ice on serving plates. Place in the center small glasses of one or more of these sauces:
> **Mignonette Sauce, 568**
> **Becker Cocktail Sauce, 568**
> **Tomatillo-Horseradish Sauce, 568**
> **Lorenzo Dressing, 574**
Or serve them with:
> **Lemon wedges and grated fresh horseradish**
and:
> **Buttered brown bread**

BROILED OYSTERS
Allow 6 oysters per serving
Preheat the broiler, with the rack 5 inches below the heating element. Scrub well, then open, 371, leaving the oysters in the half-shell:
> **Oysters**

Place on a thick bed of coarse salt in a metal pie plate or on a baking sheet. Broil about 2 minutes, until the edges curl. Garnish with:
> **Minced parsley or Lemon Butter, 557**
Serve with:
> **Lemon wedges and grated fresh horseradish**

GRILLED OYSTERS
Allow 6 oysters per serving
You may grill many oysters in their shells right on the coals without toughening them, but if you have the smaller Eastern or Olympia oysters, put them on a piece of foil in which you have punched holes before placing them on the grill.
I. Please read About Oysters, 371. Prepare a hot grill fire. Scrub:
> **Oysters**
Grill until the shells pop open. Season and serve with:
> **Lemon wedges**
> **Melted butter**
II. Prepare a medium-hot grill fire. Open, 371, leaving them on the half-shell:
> **Scrubbed oysters**
Sprinkle them with:
> **Gremolata, 989**
Heat for a few minutes on the grill.

FRIED BREADED OYSTERS
4 servings
Please read About Oysters, 371. Bread:
> **24 large oysters, shucked, 371, and patted dry**
as for **Fried Clams, Oysters, Shrimp, or Scallops with Bread Crumb or Cracker Coating, 377.** When the bread crumbs have absorbed as much moisture from the oysters as possible, heat in a large skillet over medium-high heat:
> **6 tablespoons vegetable oil**
> **¹/₄ cup (¹/₂ stick) butter**
Add the oysters and cook, in batches if necessary, turning gently once or twice, until golden.
Serve at once with:
> **Tartar Sauce, 581, or Mayonnaise with Green Herbs, 580**

BAKED OYSTERS ON THE HALF-SHELL
4 servings
Please read About Oysters, 371.
Preheat the oven to 475°F. Scrub well, then open, leaving the oysters in the half-shell and reserving the liquor:
> **24 large oysters**
Use the reserved liquor to prepare:
> **A double recipe of sauce for Creamed Oysters, 373**
Cover each oyster with 1 tablespoon sauce. Sprinkle them with:
> **Dry bread crumbs**
Bake about 10 minutes, or until the bread crumbs are golden. Sprinkle with:
> **Chopped chervil or parsley**

SCALLOPED OYSTERS

6 servings

Please read About Oysters, 371. Preheat the oven to 350°F. Butter a deep casserole. Have ready:

1 quart shucked oysters, with their liquor

Mix together:

2 cups coarsely crushed soda crackers
1 cup dry bread crumbs
³/₄ cup (1¹/₂ sticks) butter, melted

Combine in a small bowl:

1 cup heavy cream
Pinch of grated or ground nutmeg or ground mace
Salt and black pepper to taste
(Celery salt to taste)

Place a thin layer of the crumb mixture in the bottom of the casserole. Cover it with half of the oysters. Pour over half of the cream mixture. Follow with three-quarters of the remaining crumbs and the rest of the oysters. Pour the remaining cream over the oysters and cover with the remaining bread. Bake until crumbs are golden and sauce bubbles, 20 to 25 minutes.

CREAMED OYSTERS

4 servings

Please read About Oysters, 371. Drain, reserving the liquid:

1 pint shucked oysters

Pat the oysters dry. Melt in a medium saucepan over medium heat:

2 tablespoons butter

Add and stir until blended:

2 tablespoons all-purpose flour
¹/₂ teaspoon salt
¹/₈ teaspoon paprika or ground red pepper
(¹/₂ to 1 teaspoon curry powder)

Cook for 2 to 3 minutes. Slowly stir in:

1 cup reserved oyster liquor or fish stock, or a
**   combination of oyster liquor or stock and**
**   cream or milk**

Continue stirring until the sauce is smooth and hot. Add the oysters and heat through, 1 to 2 minutes; do not allow the sauce to boil. Season with:

1 teaspoon fresh lemon juice or ¹/₂ teaspoon
**   Worcestershire sauce**

Serve the oysters at once in:

Bread Cases, 111, or Patty Shells, 670

or on:

Hot buttered toast

Sprinkle generously with:

Chopped parsley

ABOUT MUSSELS

Sweet, delicious, and abundant, these mollusks were once known as "the oysters of the poor." ➤ These sweet delicious mollusks do deteriorate rapidly and, if uncooked, may be the cause of illness. **To store,** do not use a sealed plastic bag, where the mussels will suffocate. Best is a bowl or mesh bag, in the refrigerator, covered lightly with a damp towel. Ice is not necessary; ➤ mussels stay alive for days at 40°F.

To test mussels for freshness, try to slide the two halves of the shell across each other. ➤ If they budge, the shell is probably filled with mud, not mussel. Discard any mussels with broken shells or shells that will not close when tapped or after you put them into the freezer for a minute or two.

Both fresh and canned mussels can be sandy. **To remove sand,** soak in cool water until the mussels release their grit. Then scrub the shells with a stiff brush under running water. Some mussels are distinguished by a **beard,** a tangle of dark fibers that enables them to cling to rocks, which is usually removed before cooking. Debeard, if necessary, just before cooking, as the mussels will die soon after it is removed. ➤ Simply pull or clip off the dark, fibrous strands.

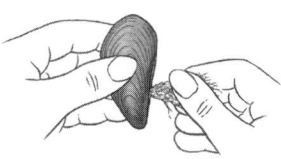

Removing the beard from a mussel

Mussels may be steamed, then removed from the shell and served much like oysters or clams, or served with a sauce, shell and all. It is permissible—no doubt because it is necessary—to separate the shells with your hands to eat. Some suggest that a half-shell be used to spoon up the liquor to the last drop. ➤ For 4 servings, allow about 1 quart undrained shucked mussels or 3 quarts (about 6 pounds) of mussels in the shell.

STEAMED MUSSELS

4 servings

If you wash the mussels well, above, you can steam them in their own juices and serve them with the broth, and crusty bread to mop it up with. You can also add cut-up pieces of smoked sausage, such as linguiça or chorizo, to the pot, or use about a cup of chopped tomato in place of or along with the wine.

Wash and debeard, above:

4 to 6 pounds mussels

Place them in a large pot and add:

¹/₂ cup dry white wine
¹/₂ to 1 cup minced parsley, chervil, or basil
2 tablespoons chopped garlic

Cover the pot, place it over high heat, and cook, shaking the pot occasionally, until most of the mussels have opened, 8 to 10 minutes. Use a slotted spoon to remove the mussels to a serving bowl, then strain the cooking liquid over them through cheesecloth or a fine-mesh strainer. Drizzle over the mussels:

1 tablespoon extra-virgin olive oil
Juice of 1 lemon

BUTTERED BAKED MUSSELS

Allow 10 to 12 per serving

Please read About Mussels, 373. Preheat the oven to 450°F. Place in a large pan in a single layer:

Mussels, scrubbed and debearded, 373
2 tablespoons olive oil

Heat in the oven just until the shells open; do not over-cook. Remove the upper shell from each mussel, working over a bowl to catch the liquor. If any has escaped to the pan, strain and add it to the liquor in the bowl. Serve the mussels on their lower shells with:

Melted butter or melted Garlic Butter, 559
(Squeeze of lemon)

and the liquor in small cups or glasses for rinsing; see Steamed Clams, 375.

GRILLED MUSSELS

Please read About Mussels, 373. Proceed as for **Grilled Oysters I, 372,** using mussels in place of oysters.

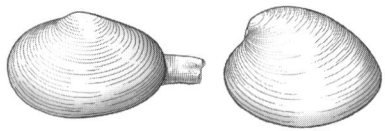

Soft-shell clam   Hard-shell clam

ABOUT CLAMS

There are dozens of varieties of clams, but all fall roughly into two distinct types: **soft-shell** and **hard-shell.** Clams are sold fresh, in the shell, shucked, or canned. If in the shell, ➤ test to see that they are tightly closed or, if slightly open, that they close tightly at once upon being touched. ➤ Discard any that have broken shells. Store in a bowl or mesh bag in the refrigerator, covered lightly with a damp towel. Do not store in a sealed plastic bag, where they will suffocate. Ice is not necessary; ➤ clams stay alive for days at 40°F.

Eight quarts of clams in the shell will yield about 1 quart shucked. ➤ Allow about 1 quart of unshucked clams per person for steamed clams, 6 to 8 medium-sized clams if served shucked.

Canned clams are perfectly acceptable in a pinch and should be a pantry staple. They are sold minced, chopped, or whole and are a good substitute for fresh in chowders and sauces. Look for preservative-free brands.

SOFT-SHELL OR LONGNECK CLAMS

Found mostly north of Cape Cod, **soft-shell** or **longneck clams** are the preferred type to be steamed whole and are also referred to as **"steamers."** On the West Coast, the predominant soft-shelled clams are the **razor** and **geoduck** (pronounced "gooey-duck"). All soft-shell clams are sandy. **To remove sand** before shucking, ➤ they should be scrubbed and washed in several changes of cold water, then soaked in a cold brine of $1/3$ cup salt per 1 gallon of water for 3 to 12 hours. It may even be necessary later to put the cooked clams under cold running water to rid them completely of sand. They are easily opened by running a short sharp knife along the edge of the top shell. Work over a bowl, as for oysters, to trap the juices. Cut the meat from the bottom shell. Slit the skin of the neck, or siphon, and pull off the neck skin.

Although they are easy to shuck, ➤ soft-shell clams are never eaten raw. The small varieties are usually steamed or deep-fried. ➤ **To eat clams,** lift them out of the shell by the neck, dip into the broth to remove possible sand, and then dip into the butter. All of the clam except the neck sheath is edible.

HARD-SHELL CLAMS

Hard-shell clams include **quahogs** (pronounced "ko-hogs"), **littlenecks, top necks, count necks, cherrystones, Manila clams, mahogany clams, chowder clams, sea clams, hard clams,** and **cockles,** among others. **Surf clams,** large triangular mollusks found on the East Coast, are the sandiest of all clams. They may be used in chowders, broth, or cocktails, but their sweetness should be counteracted with salt. The **Pacific butter clam** is distinguished from its Atlantic counterparts by its small size—even when adult—and its rarity, but makes up for both in succulence. Another West Coast variety is the sweet and tender **pismo.**

The large strong-flavored hard-shells such as quahogs are preferred for chowders, the smaller ones for eating on

Shucking a clam

the half-shell. Scrub the clams under running water. Hard-shelled clams are not sandy and do not need to be soaked. Hard-shells are difficult to open, but ➤ if they are covered with water for 5 minutes and then gently picked up, you may be able to insert a knife quickly in the opening. Or, if you are using them in a cooked dish and do not mind a small loss in flavor, place them in a baking pan in a moderate oven until they open. After opening, cut through the muscle holding the shells together. ➤ Open the stomachs with sharp shears and scrape out and discard the contents. Large hard-shell clams have a tough upper portion that may be separated from the tender portion, then chopped or ground, and used in various dishes: creamed; scalloped; made into fritters, 657; or used in chowders, 142–143.

STEAMED CLAMS

4 to 8 servings

Please read About Clams, 374. You can steam any clam you like, but soft-shell clams are the traditional steamers. In large part, soft-shell clams are steamed because it is difficult to purge them entirely of sand. After steaming, the resulting broth gives you a flavorful dip in which you can rinse the clams before eating. Steam as many or as few as you like.
Scrub and soak, above:

4 to 8 pounds soft-shell clams

Place the clams in a large pot with an inch or so of water. Cover the pot, turn the heat to high, and cook the clams, shaking the pot occasionally, until they are all open, 5 to 10 minutes. Overcooking makes clams tough. Meanwhile, melt in a small saucepan over low heat:

1 cup (2 sticks) butter

When the clams are cooked, remove them to a large bowl. Strain the broth, then taste and season to taste with:

Salt and black pepper

Pour the butter into separate dishes for each diner. Serve the broth in cups along with the clams and garnish with:

Lemon wedges

The broth is delicious to drink, but, to avoid any residue of sand, don't entirely drain the cup.

BAKED SOFT-SHELL CLAMS

4 servings

Please read About Clams, 374. Preheat the oven to 425°F. Scrub and soak, above:

36 soft-shell clams

Line a baking sheet with a bed of rock salt or crumpled foil to keep the clams steady, and arrange them in the pan. Bake about 15 minutes, until the shells open. Remove the top shells carefully, over a bowl. Serve on the half-shell on individual plates with:

Melted butter or melted Basic Flavored Butter, 558
Becker Cocktail Sauce, 568
Tomatillo-Horseradish Sauce, 568

Garnish with:

Lemon wedges

BROILED CLAMS ON THE HALF-SHELL

Allow 6 to 8 medium clams per person

Please read About Clams, 374. Preheat the broiler. Line a baking dish or pan with a bed of rock salt or crumpled foil to keep the clams steady.
Arrange on the foil:

Cherrystone clams on the half-shell

Top each clam with:

A dash of Worcestershire sauce
A 1- to 1$\frac{1}{2}$-inch square of bacon
A thin slice of lemon

Broil the clams until they bubble, about 4 minutes. Squeeze the hot lemon juice on the clam before eating.

CLAMBAKE

Whatever the size of your bake, buy the clams the day before. Scrub, above, them well to remove sand. ➤ Store the clams in a cool place. Rinse and drain them just before using. A big bake is described in I; a smaller one, often more practical, in II, with amounts proportionately cut.

In addition to the food, you will need seaweed for a clambake. Rockweed is best, because its little sacks full of water provide a lot of steam. If there is no rockweed on the beach, use any seaweed you can find. If making version I, you will also need enough driftwood (or cordwood) to build a large fire, about 15 large rocks, and a large canvas tarp to place on top of the food so the heat and steam are trapped inside the pit.

About 20 servings

I. Please read About Clams, 374. Dig a pit about 2 feet deep, 2 feet wide, and 3 feet long in the sand. Line the bottom of the pit with large smooth stones, then build a big fire on top of the stones. Feed the fire to keep it going for 1 to 2 hours, then allow it to burn down until all the wood has burned to coals, about 2 hours.

Have ready:

3 pounds potatoes or sweet potatoes, scrubbed
8 quarts littleneck or cherrystone clams,
rinsed and drained, 374
2 dozen ears corn in the husk, silks removed
2 pounds large onions, peeled
(8 quarts mussels, scrubbed and debearded, 373)
12 chicken thighs
(3 pounds spicy sausages, wrapped in cheesecloth)

When the fire is all coals, spread out the coals and cover the stones with a 6- to 8-inch-thick layer of seaweed, preferably rockweed. Stack the potatoes, clams, corn, onions, mussels, chicken, and sausage, in this order, on top of each other on the coals, adding thin layers of seaweed in between. You may wrap ingredients in cheesecloth to make large bundles.

Add:

Twelve 1-pound live lobsters

Top with a 3- to 4-inch layer of seaweed. If using seaweed other than rockweed, pour about 8 cups seawater over the last layer of seaweed. Cover the pit completely with a large canvas tarp that has been thoroughly soaked with seawater. Cover the tarp with rocks to hold it in place. During the steaming, the tarp will puff up, which is a sign of a satisfactory "bake." Cook 1 to 1½ hours. To test, lift the tarp carefully at one corner, so as not to get sand into the pit, and see if the clams have opened. If so, the whole feast should be cooked to just the right point. Remove the food packets and lobsters from the pit and serve hot, with plenty of paper towels and:

>**Melted butter**

8 servings

II. A more domesticated "bake" can be prepared in a 20-quart stockpot on a stove or outdoor grill.

Soak enough seaweed to line the bottom of the pot with a 4-inch layer in cold water for 45 minutes, then rinse several times to remove all the sand.

Put the seaweed in the pot, and add about:

>**4 cups water**

and bring to a boil. Add:

>**8 potatoes**
>**6 to 8 pounds chicken parts, cut into serving pieces and wrapped in cheesecloth**

Cover, reduce the heat, and simmer gently 30 minutes. Add:

>**Eight 1½-pound live lobsters**

Cover and cook 8 minutes more. Place on the lobsters:

>**8 ears corn, shucked**

Cook 10 minutes, covered. Add:

>**48 soft-shell clams, well scrubbed**

Cover and steam until the clams open, 5 to 10 minutes longer. Serve with:

>**Melted butter**

STIR-FRIED CLAMS OR MUSSELS WITH OYSTER SAUCE

4 servings

Use littleneck clams or mussels for this stir-fry.

Please read About Clams, 374, or About Mussels, 373. Have ready:

>**4 pounds littleneck clams, rinsed and drained, 374, or mussels, scrubbed and debearded, 373**

Heat a wok or large skillet over high heat. Pour in and heat:

>**2 tablespoons peanut or other vegetable oil**

Add:

>**1 tablespoon minced garlic**
>**1 teaspoon minced peeled fresh ginger**

and the clams or mussels. Cover and cook 2 minutes. Uncover and cook, stirring, until the mollusks open, a few minutes more. Add:

>**2 tablespoons soy sauce**
>**2 tablespoons oyster sauce**
>**1 tablespoon dry sherry or dry white wine**
>**2 tablespoons chopped scallions**

Cook, stirring, for about 30 seconds. If the mixture seems dry, add:

>**¼ to ½ cup liquid, 371**

Garnish with:

>**Minced scallions, chives, or cilantro**

Serve with:

>**Cooked rice**

THAI CLAM POT

4 to 6 servings

Here are clams at their spiciest and most delicious. Japanese somen noodles are a tasty alternative to Italian pasta. Please read About Clams, 374. Have ready:

>**8 garlic cloves, thinly sliced**
>**8 scallions, cut into 2-inch lengths, then cut lengthwise in half**
>**1 to 2 teaspoons crushed red pepper flakes**
>**1 cup mirin combined with 1 cup water**
>**3 pounds littleneck clams, rinsed and drained, 374**
>**1 cup basil leaves, cut into thin strips**
>**2 tablespoons fish sauce**

When ready to cook, bring a large pot of water to a boil. Add and cook until tender:

>**8 ounces angel hair pasta or thin somen noodles**

Immediately drain in a colander and rinse lightly to remove starch. While the noodles are cooking, heat a heavy pot large enough to hold the clams over high heat, and add:

>**2 tablespoons peanut oil**

Heat, stirring, until very hot. Add the garlic, scallions, and red pepper flakes. Stir for about 15 seconds. Standing back, add the mirin mixture, then cover and bring to a boil. Add the clams, cover, and return to a boil, then reduce the heat to medium and cook just until the clams have opened, 7 to 8 minutes, shaking the pot 3 or 4 times to ensure they cook evenly. Add the basil, cover, and cook for 30 to 45 seconds. Add the fish sauce and stir. Divide the noodles among individual bowls, add the clams, and pour the broth over them.

FRIED SHELLFISH WITH FLOUR COATING

4 servings

When you fry with no liquid in the coating you get a very light, translucent crust.

Heat to 365°F in a deep-fat fryer or deep heavy pot over medium-high heat:

>**2 inches vegetable oil**

Have ready:

>**1½ to 2 pounds mixed shellfish, such as shucked clams, 374, and oysters, 371; shrimp, peeled, deveined, and butterflied, 385; scallops, side "hinge" removed, 377; and/or squid, cleaned, 390, and cut into pieces**

Pour into a shallow bowl:

>**1½ cups milk or buttermilk**

Mix in a second shallow bowl:

>**2 cups all-purpose flour**
>**1½ teaspoons salt**
>**1 teaspoon black pepper**

Dip the shellfish in the milk and drain thoroughly, then coat with the seasoned flour, shaking off the excess. Add a few pieces at a time to the oil, without crowding, and cook until golden brown, stirring occasionally (large pieces may need to be turned). Drain on paper towels. Serve with:

> Lemon wedges and hot pepper sauce, Tartar Sauce, 581, Aïoli, 581, a flavored mayonnaise, 578, or Marinara Sauce, 562

FRIED CLAMS, SHRIMP, OR OYSTERS WITH CORNMEAL COATING

4 servings

Sprinkle with spices, such as cumin, chili powder, or curry powder, after frying, if desired.
Please read about Deep-Fat Frying, 1046. Heat to 365°F in a deep-fat fryer or deep heavy pot over medium-high heat:

> **2 inches vegetable oil**

Have ready:

> **1¹/₂ to 2 pounds clams or clam strips; shrimp, peeled and deveined, 385; or shucked oysters, 371**

Pour into a shallow bowl:

> **1 cup milk or buttermilk**

Mix in a second shallow bowl:

> **1¹/₂ cups cornmeal**
> **¹/₂ cup all-purpose flour**
> **1¹/₂ teaspoons salt**
> **Ground black or red pepper to taste**

Dip the shellfish in the milk and drain thoroughly, then coat with the seasoned cornmeal, shake off excess, and place on a rack or wax paper. Add a few pieces at a time to the oil, without crowding, and cook until golden brown, stirring occasionally (large pieces may need to be turned). Drain on paper towels. Serve with:

> Lemon wedges and hot pepper sauce, Tartar Sauce, 581, Aïoli, 581, or a flavored mayonnaise, 578

FRIED CLAMS, OYSTERS, SHRIMP, OR SCALLOPS WITH BREAD CRUMB OR CRACKER COATING

4 servings

Please read about Deep-Fat Frying, 1046. Remove from the shell, clean, and have ready:

> **1¹/₂ to 2 pounds shellfish such as shucked clams, 374, and oysters, 371; shrimp, peeled and deveined if desired, 385; or scallops, side "hinge" removed, below**

Whisk together in a shallow bowl:

> **3 large eggs**

Mix in a second shallow bowl:

> **2 cups dry bread crumbs, panko, or cracker crumbs**
> **Salt and black pepper to taste**

Dip the shellfish in the eggs, then coat with the seasoned crumbs and shake off excess. Place on a rack or baking sheet lined with wax paper and refrigerate for 1 to 2

hours. Heat to 365°F in a deep-fat fryer or deep heavy pot over medium-high heat:

> **2 inches vegetable oil**

Add a few pieces of the shellfish at a time, without crowding, and cook until golden brown, stirring occasionally (large pieces may need to be turned). Drain on paper towels. Serve with:

> Lemon wedges and hot pepper sauce, Tartar Sauce, 581, Aïoli, 581, or a flavored mayonnaise, 578

SHRIMP, SCALLOPS, SQUID, CLAMS, OR OYSTERS TEMPURA

4 servings

Add some cut-up vegetables such as asparagus, green beans, mushrooms, or zucchini to this mixture, and you have a complete tempura meal.
Please read about Deep-Fat Frying, 1046. Prepare in a medium bowl:

> **Tempura Batter, 658**

Heat to 365°F in a deep-fat fryer or deep heavy pot over medium-high heat:

> **2 inches vegetable oil**

Remove from the shell, clean, and have ready:

> **1¹/₂ to 2 pounds shellfish such as shrimp, peeled, deveined, and butterflied, 385; scallops, side "hinge" removed, below; shucked clams and oysters, 371; squid, cleaned, 390, and cut into pieces**

Be sure to dry the pieces well. Test the oil by dripping a few drops of batter into it: it should sink slightly, then rise and puff quickly, but not color immediately. Working in batches, dip the shellfish 1 piece at a time into the batter and add to the oil without crowding. Fry, undisturbed, for about 1 minute, then turn and fry for another minute, or until the shellfish is opaque and the batter crisp but barely colored. Remove to paper towels to drain. Serve with:

> Lemon wedges or Ginger Soy Sauce, 571

ABOUT SCALLOPS

These beautiful mollusks, known on French menus as **coquilles St. Jacques,** are emblematic of the shrine of St. James in Santiago de Compostela, Spain. Pilgrims who visited ate the mollusks as penance—surely not a rigorous one—and afterward fastened the shells to their hats. Scallops are also responsible for the cooking term "scalloped," which originally meant seafood creamed, heated, and served in a shell. The scallops available in our markets are almost never the whole mollusk but instead are the edible sections of its adductor muscle, which controls its movement.

If you do get scallops in the shell, wash and scrub them thoroughly. Since scallops gape naturally, they are easy to shuck. Open the shell with any sharp knife, then scoop out the muscle (and red or white roe, if any). ➤ Discard all else in the shell. Whether processed in the shell or shucked, **remove the "hinge"** attached to the side of the muscle.

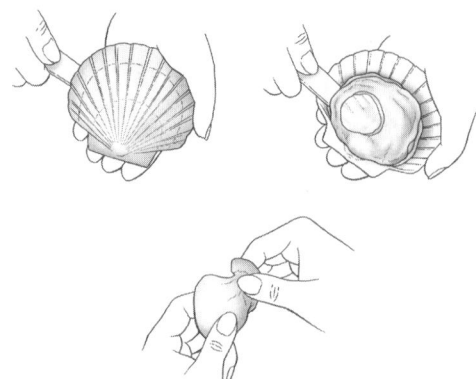

Shucking a scallop and removing the "hinge"

Many people prefer the small, tender, creamy pink or tan **bay scallops** to the larger, firmer, whiter, and also quite delicious **sea scallops.** If only sea scallops are available, they may be sliced horizontally through the middle before or after after cooking into 2 or 3 slices, for use in salads, seviches, stir-fries, creamed dishes, or sauces. **Calicos** are the tiny scallops—smaller than the last joint on your pinkie—usually sold in supermarkets, frequently at very appealing prices. They are more sweet and delicate, but ➤ use extreme care not to overcook them. They are so small that they need only 1 to 2 minutes' cooking by most methods. Keep them tender, and they are worth eating; overcook them, and they turn to rubber.

To test scallops for freshness, see that they have a sweet odor. Those that are sold shucked may be soaked in a bath of water and preservatives which extends their shelf life and artificially increases their weight. ➤ Make every effort to buy unsoaked, or "dry" scallops. They have a cleaner taste, and brown better when sautéed because they contain less water. Be suspicious of any sea scallops that are pure white, a good indication that they have been soaked; the natural color of sea scallops ranges from white to off-white to pale shades of orange, pink, and tan. Individually quick frozen (IQF) sea scallops can be a good buy and usually retain most of their flavor.

For sautéing, broiling, or frying, ➤ allow about ⅓ pound of sea scallops or ¼ pound of bay scallops per serving. Cooked scallops may be used in any recipe for fish salads, or they may be skewered and grilled. Scallops are successfully combined in dishes with more robustly flavored shellfish like shrimp and crab. See also seafood suggestions in Brunch, Lunch, and Supper, 95.

POACHED SCALLOPS

4 servings

Bring to a simmer in a large skillet:

    Enough water to cover scallops
    3 sprigs parsley
    1 bay leaf

Add:

    2 pounds shucked bay or sea scallops, side "hinge" removed, 377

Simmer until tender, 3 to 5 minutes. Remove and discard the herbs, remove the scallops, and keep warm. Turn the heat to high, and reduce the liquid by half. Season to taste and spoon over the scallops.

SCALLOPS MEUNIÈRE

4 servings

Dry between towels:

    1 pound shucked bay or sea scallops, side "hinge" removed, 377

Dip them in:

    Bound Breading or Coating, 961

Let them dry on a rack about 15 minutes. Heat in a large heavy skillet:

    2 tablespoons butter
    2 tablespoons vegetable oil

Add the scallops and cook, turning bay scallops frequently and sea scallops just once, until evenly browned on both sides, about 3 to 5 minutes for bay scallops, 5 minutes for sea scallops. Just before the scallops are done, sprinkle with:

    Fresh lemon juice
    Finely chopped parsley
    Salt and black pepper to taste

Serve with:

    Tomatoes Provençale, 312

SEA SCALLOP GRATIN (COQUILLES ST. JACQUES AU GRATIN)

2 servings

The sauce can be prepared several hours in advance and refrigerated; bring to a simmer before proceeding.

Please read About Scallops, 377. Combine in a bowl and mix well:

    2 tablespoons unsalted butter, melted
    ½ cup fresh bread crumbs
    3 tablespoons grated Parmesan
    1 tablespoon minced parsley
    1 teaspoon chopped thyme
    ⅛ teaspoon salt
    Black pepper to taste

Melt in a medium skillet over medium heat:

    1 tablespoon butter

Add:

    2 shallots, minced
    2 garlic cloves, minced

Cook, stirring, until softened but not browned, about 2 minutes. Add:

    8 ounces small mushrooms, quartered
    1 teaspoon salt

Cook, stirring occasionally, until the mushrooms are softened, about 7 minutes. Add:

    ¼ cup dry white wine

Increase the heat and simmer until the wine has almost evaporated, about 3 minutes. Add:

1 cup heavy cream

Bring to a gentle boil and boil until thickened, about 5 minutes. Preheat the broiler. Reduce the sauce to a simmer and add:

12 ounces shucked scallops, side "hinge" removed, 377, and cut horizontally in half

Cook until the scallops are no longer translucent, about 1 1/2 minutes. Remove from the heat and stir in:

1 teaspoon fresh lemon juice

Spoon the mixture into scallop shells or individual gratin dishes. Sprinkle the bread crumb mixture over the scallops and sauce. Broil until golden brown on top and bubbling around the edges, about 1 1/2 minutes.

ABOUT ABALONE

This delicious shellfish comes to our markets from Mexico and Japan, canned or frozen, shelled, pounded, and ready to cook. Wild American abalone, native to the Pacific Ocean off Alaska and California, is in dwindling and controlled supply, but baby varieties are farmed in Hawaii and California. Still, abalone is rare and always expensive. **If you get it in the shell,** remove the edible portion by running a knife between the shell and meat. Trim off the dark part. ➤ Abalone needs prodigious pounding to tenderize it. Leave it whole or cut it in 1/4-inch strips before ➤ pounding with an even, not too hard, motion. The meat is ready to cook when it looks like Dalí's limp watch. **For steaks,** slice against the grain and then pound. Bread if you like in dry crumbs or in Bound Breading or Coating, 961, and sauté. Or poach, 399, as for any fish. Beat and chop abalone for chowder. ➤ Allow 1 pound for 2 to 3 servings.

SAUTÉED ABALONE

2 to 3 servings

Cut into 3/8-inch-thick steaks across the grain and pound:

1 pound abalone

Dip in:

Bound Breading or Coating, 961

Melt in a heavy skillet over medium-high heat:

2 tablespoons vegetable oil or Clarified Butter, 557

Add the abalone and cook 1 to 2 minutes on each side.

ABOUT CRABS

Recipes for cooking crabmeat apply to almost all species of edible crab, but the type of crab or the part of the crab from which the meat is taken may make a difference in color, taste, and texture. ➤ All crabs must be sold live or cooked. If the crab feels slimy, it should be scrubbed. ➤ Cooked crabmeat is all nonperishable until opened. For crab dishes made with cooked or canned crab. If using canned or fresh lump crabmeat, ➤ be sure to pick it over for small bits of shell and cartilage. To prepare crab shells for restuffing, select large perfect shells and scrub them well with a brush. Place them in a large kettle and cover with hot water. Add 1 teaspoon baking soda. Drain, rinse, and dry. The shells are now ready for refilling.

BLUE CRABS

These denizens of the Atlantic, comically skittish on land, efficiently beautiful swimmers in the water, furnish most of the fresh crabmeat in the market. Lump or backfin meat, taken from the body, is white in color and choice for looks. Other grades include flake and claw. If possible, buy fresh-picked rather than pasteurized crabmeat; the flavor is noticeably better. ➤ Picked crabmeat should be stored in the refrigerator or frozen.

If taken live, blue crabs fall into two classifications, hard-shell and soft-shell, which are prepared and eaten quite differently. Uncooked soft-shells, crabs that have shed their old, hard shells, are bought alive and packed in straw, paper, or seaweed. They will not be very active, but they should have a fresh smell. Soft-shells can also be purchased cooked or frozen. Store live crabs in the refrigerator, on ice; ➤ use as quickly as possible.

Hard-shell blue crabs are those caught between their periodic sheddings of carapace, or "lid," when the carapace has hardened. To cook and eat them, see Poached (or Boiled) Hard-Shell Crabs, 381. They also make great additions to soups and sauces when cleaned and added to simmering liquid; discard when cooking is done.

To parboil live blue crabs to retrieve the meat, plunge them into boiling water for 30 seconds, until dead, then remove and rinse under cold water. When removing the meat, reserve the tomalley if desired as well as the shells and lower sections of the legs to replace the shrimp or lobster shells in Shrimp or Lobster Butter, 559. **To remove the meat from parboiled or fully cooked blue crabs,** turn the crab onto its back and lift the pointed apron at the base away from the body with a firm hold at the wide end. Then slowly twist off the apron, removing the intestinal vein as well. As you can see from the illustration, the fe-

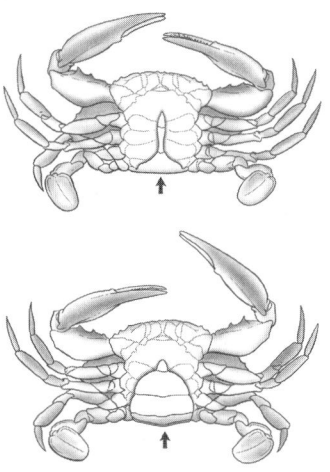

Male crab and female crab

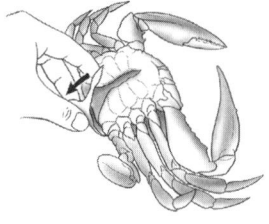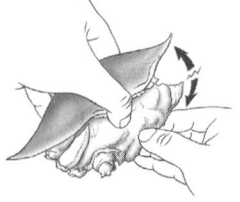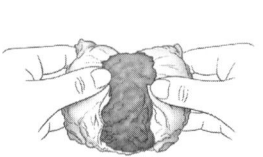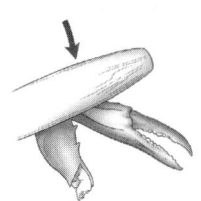

Cleaning a hard-shell crab

male has a wider fringed apron than the male. Pull off the large claws at the body, then gently crack the claws with a mallet or rolling pin and pull out the meat. Remove the legs, then bend each one to break at the joint and remove the upper leg meat. Pull off the top shell, then clean out and discard the stringy gills found under both sides of the shell. Break the body in two and pick out the meat, discarding any bits of shell or cartilage, and remove the tomalley and roe.

To prepare soft-shell crabs for cooking, wash them in several changes of cold water. Snip off the eyes and mouth with scissors. Lift the tapering points on each side of the top shell and pull out and discard the gills and sand bags. Turn the crab on its back, lift the pointed flap called the "apron," and, with a firm hold at the wide end, slowly twist and pull it off. Almost every part of a soft-shell crab is edible. They are usually broiled, breaded, and sautéed, or deep-fried, as in the recipes that follow.

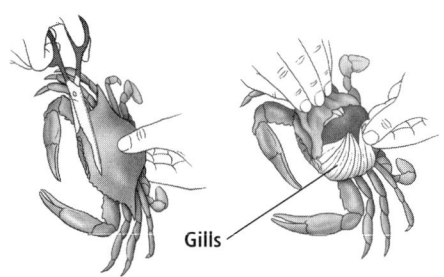

Gills

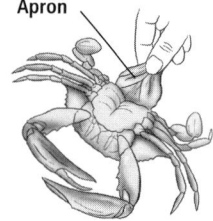

Apron

Cleaning a soft-shell crab

DUNGENESS CRABS
Native to the West Coast, this is a large crab prized for its sweet lobster-like meat. These crabs are difficult to keep alive, so, like king and snow crabs, they are usually pre-cooked and frozen. They are best in 2½- to 3-pound size.

Rock crabs are an East Coast relative of the Dungeness crab, with brownish flesh. Dungeness crabs do not need to be cleaned, and can be eaten like hard-shell blue crabs.

KING CRABS
Mostly from Alaskan waters, king crabs are huge and pinkish in color. Consisting mainly of leg meat, they are almost always sold frozen. Slit the underside of the leg shell with a cross-shaped cut before broiling, steaming, or grilling. **Snow crab,** smaller and less expensive than king crab, is also sold cooked and frozen.

STONE CRABS
From Florida, with pale flesh and a very delicate texture and flavor, stone crabs have become so rare that now when one is caught only one claw may be removed, then the crab must be returned to its habitat, where, hopefully, it will grow another claw—as crabs are quite capable of doing. Sold cooked and chilled, stone crabs need no preparation. Crush or crack the claw shell with a hammer and pick out the meat.

DEEP-FRIED SOFT-SHELL CRABS
Allow 2 to 3 crabs per serving
For panfried soft-shell crabs, see Fried Soft-Shell Crab Sandwich, 183.
Please read about Deep-Fat Frying, 1046. Dry between paper towels:
   Soft-shell crabs, cleaned, above
Dip them in:
   Bound Breading or Coating, 961
Heat to 365°F in a deep-fat fryer or deep heavy pot over medium-high heat:
   2 inches vegetable oil
Add the crabs a few at a time, without crowding, and fry 3 to 5 minutes, or until golden brown, turning once. Drain on paper towels. Sprinkle well with:
   Salt and black pepper
Serve with:
   **Tartar Sauce, 581, Rémoulade Sauce, 581,
      parsley, or Brown Butter, 557**

GRILLED, BROILED, OR ROASTED SOFT-SHELL CRABS

4 servings

Prepare a medium-hot grill or preheat the broiler. Make sure the grill rack is clean and place it about 4 inches from the heat, or put the broiler rack 2 or 3 inches from the broiler heat. Or preheat the oven to 500°F.

Mix in a small bowl:

¼ cup (½ stick) butter, melted, or olive oil

(1 teaspoon minced garlic)

(A pinch of ground red pepper)

Salt and black pepper to taste

Brush the butter mixture over both sides of:

8 soft-shell crabs, cleaned, 380, and patted dry

Grill or broil until firm, about 4 minutes each side, taking care not to burn the shells, especially the claws. They do not turn red, as other crabs do. Or place in a roasting pan and bake, without turning, about 10 minutes. Serve with:

Lemon or lime wedges and hot pepper sauce,
or Lemon Butter Sauce, 558

STEAMED BLUE CRABS

About 5 to 10 crabs per person

The traditional and delightfully messy way to serve these crabs is to dump them onto the center of a table covered with newspapers. Hand out small hammers, pliers, nut-crackers, seafood forks, and nut picks. A roll of paper towels on the table is always an asset.

Please read Blue Crabs, 379. Fit a tall fitted rack or slotted lift-out basket into a very large stockpot. Pour into the pot:

2 cups cider vinegar

Add water to come two-thirds of the way up to the bottom of the rack or basket. Bring the vinegar and water to a boil. Rinse quickly under cold water:

24 live blue crabs

Arrange in no more than 6 layers on the rack, sprinkling each layer with:

1 tablespoon coarse salt (up to 6 tablespoons total)

(1 tablespoon crab boil seasoning—up to
6 tablespoons total)

Reduce the liquid to a rapid simmer, cover the pot tightly, and steam the crabs until they turn bright pink and their legs can be pulled from the sockets fairly easily, 15 to 20 minutes. Serve with:

Melted butter

Lemon wedges

POACHED (OR BOILED) HARD-SHELL CRABS

The preparation here is basic. From a 5-ounce hard-shell crab, you can expect about 1½ ounces of meat. Serve the crabs whole, with melted butter and lemon juice or wedges, or use the cooked crabmeat in other recipes.

Bring a large pot of salted water to a boil (allow 1 tablespoon salt for each quart of water).

Using tongs, slide into the water, one at a time, so as not to disturb the boil:

Live hard-shell crabs, rinsed or scrubbed, 379

Reduce the heat at once to a simmer and cook about 15 minutes. Remove the crabs to a platter.

Serve the crabs whole, with:

Melted butter

To eat, open the tail flap on the belly side and pull it against the carapace, removing both. Sometimes a sharp knife will be necessary to complete this job. Take out and discard the spongy substance under the shell and split the bodies in half to pick out the meat, discarding the gills, intestines, and sand bags. Claw meat can be released with a nutcracker.

CRAB CAKES

8 small or 4 large crab cakes

Allow time to refrigerate the cakes after you shape them so that they will hold together when you cook them.

Heat in a small skillet over medium heat:

2 tablespoons butter or olive oil

When the butter foam has subsided or the oil is hot, add:

½ cup minced scallions

(1 tablespoon minced red bell pepper)

1 teaspoon minced garlic

Cook, stirring, until the scallions are tender but not browned, about 10 minutes. Set aside. Gently mix in a large bowl:

1 pound lump crabmeat, picked over for shells
and cartilage

1 egg, lightly beaten

¼ cup mayonnaise

1 tablespoon Dijon mustard

(¼ teaspoon ground red pepper)

Salt and black pepper to taste

(1 teaspoon crab boil seasoning)

¼ cup minced parsley, cilantro, or dill

2 tablespoons fresh bread crumbs

Add the sautéed vegetables and mix well. Place on a plate:

1 to 2 cups fresh bread crumbs, toasted, 1001

Shape the crab mixture into 8 small or 4 large cakes. One at a time, coat each cake in the bread crumbs, pressing lightly to make sure the crumbs adhere. Place the cakes on a rack or on a plate lined with wax paper. Refrigerate for 1 to 2 hours. Heat in a large skillet over medium heat:

¼ cup butter (½ stick) or ¼ cup Clarified Butter, 557,
or vegetable oil

When the fat is hot, add the cakes without crowding—cook them in 2 batches if necessary. Adjust the heat so that the fat is sizzling but not burning the bread crumbs, and cook, turning the cakes until both sides are nicely browned. Smaller cakes need a total of 8 to 10 minutes, larger ones 12 to 15 minutes. If cooking in batches, keep the finished cakes warm in a 300°F oven while you complete the cooking. Serve hot with:

Lemon wedges, Aïoli, 581, flavored mayonnaise, 578,
or Salsa Fresca, 571

ABOUT LOBSTERS

The **American** or **Northern lobster,** with its great delicious claw and tail meat, is shown. It is caught from Canada to the Carolinas, and is often referred to as Maine lobster. Very similar but somewhat smaller is the **European lobster.**

The **spiny** or **rock lobster,** or **langouste** (called crayfish in Australia and New Zealand), is shipped from Florida, California, Australia, South Africa and the Mediterranean. It has extra-long antennae but no claws, and most of the meat is in the heavy tail.

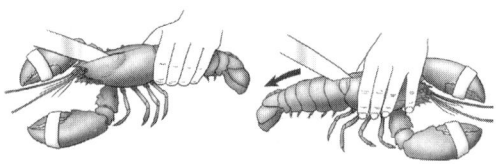

To halve the lobster, cut forward through the head and back through the body and tail.

The Americans and Europeans, a mottled dark blue green when caught, are most delicious, we think, served hot. The **spinys,** which usually reach us frozen, may be tough, especially if they weigh over 10 ounces. Fresh meat is preferred for cold dishes. They vary in color from tan through reddish orange to maroon, with lighter spotting and variable spininess.

Rarely encountered on this side of the Atlantic because it is native to European waters, the **Norwegian lobster,** a relative of the spiny, is known in France as **langoustine** and is famous in Italy as **scampo** (usually referred to in the plural, **scampi**).

Of whatever kind, most lobsters require about the same cooking time and may be cut and cleaned as shown on 383. But as the lobster ritual is more complicated for the American type, we will discuss it in further detail below.

Among connoisseurs, the female lobster is considered finer in flavor. Look for soft, leathery, finlike appendages on the underside, just where the body and tail meet. In the male, these appendages are bony. On opening the female lobster, you may find a delicious **roe** or **coral** that reddens

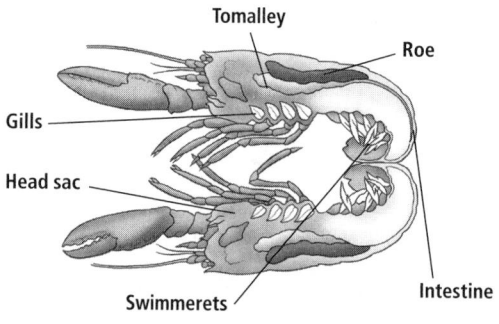

A halved lobster

[Labels: Tomalley, Roe, Gills, Head sac, Swimmerets, Intestine]

Spiny or rock lobster   American or Northern lobster

in cooking. Eat with the meat or use as a garnish or to color a sauce. The flesh of the male stays firmer when boiled. The greenish substance in both of them is the **liver,** or **tomalley,** not attractive but delicious.

Allow 1 lobster per serving. Buy active live lobsters weighing from 1¼ to 2½ pounds. ➤ A 2½-pound lobster will yield about 2 cups of cooked meat. Some people say that larger lobsters are tough, but that is not the case. In fact, there is a good argument to be made that a 3-pound lobster contains more edible meat than two 1½-pound lobsters. The larger a lobster gets, the more meat it has in those difficult-to-reach parts of the claw and the body that make lobster eating so much fun. Yes, some lobster meat is occasionally tough and stringy, but this is usually the result of overcooking; size has nothing to do with it.

To store live lobsters until ready to use, place them in the refrigerator or on a bed of moist seaweed or newspaper, not directly on ice or in water. The claws should be plugged with a small piece of wood or held together with rubber bands. Before cooking, test to make sure your lobsters are still active and that the tail snaps back if it is stretched out when you pick up the lobster. Make sure, too, that your crustaceans are clean. Grasp each one firmly at the back and rinse under cool running water.

If you buy preboiled lobster in the shell, make sure that the color is bright red and that it has a fresh seashore aroma. ➤ Most important of all, the tail—as with the uncooked lobster—when pulled, should roll back into place under the body. This means the lobster was alive, as it should have been, when cooked.

When a whole lobster is served, it lies on the plate with head and tail intact, arched shell up. The claws may be detached before serving and drained of excess moisture. Pick up the lobster in your fingers, turn it soft side up, and arch it until the tailpiece separates from the body. Remove the tail flippers by bending them back until they too crack off. Now lift the tailpiece downside up, insert the lobster fork at the point where the flippers broke off, and push the meat out through the open end.

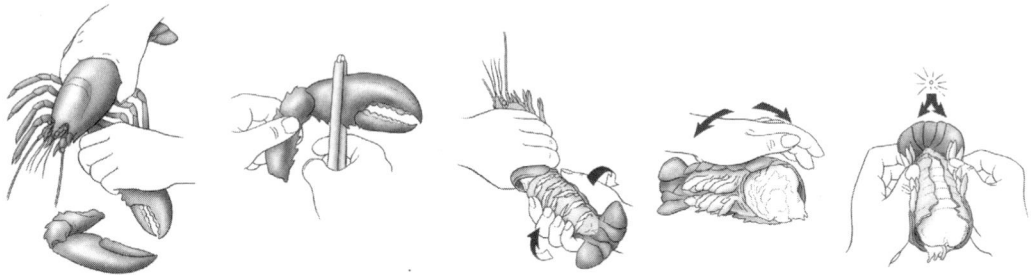

Snap and crack the claws off the lobster; twist and crack off the lobster tail; and peel off the shell

Having freed the tail meat, grasp the chest portion in both hands to release the contents as shown to the left.

To remove cooked lobster meat from the large claws, crack them with a nutcracker or a mallet. Place it on a flat surface, the lighter underside up. Using a mallet, hit the shell at the inner hump. This will crack it so that the meat in the entire larger pincer claw is released. Crack off the small pincer shell, and its meat will slide out.

To eat the leg meat, break off the legs, insert the broken end of each in your mouth, and suck out the contents—quietly. Large lobsters will yield a lot of leg meat. To re-move the tail, ➤ twist it off where it meets the body. Split the underside of the tail down the center, and pull it apart. Pull the meat from the tail; it will come out in one large piece. You may want to keep the lobster shells to make Lobster Butter, 559.

STEAMED LOBSTER
The easiest method of preparation for the home cook.

I. Please read About Lobsters, above. Set a rack or a colan-der in the top of a deep stockpot (at least 12 inches deep and 16 to 18 inches wide) with 1½ inches water boiling furiously.
Add:

1½- to 2½-pound lobsters

Weight the cover to keep in the steam and the lobsters. Lower the heat. Steam about 12 minutes for 1½-pound lobster, plus about 2 minutes for each additional ½ pound. Serve with:

Melted butter
Lemon wedges

II. To cook large lobsters often used for salads, hors d'oeuvres, or sauced dishes, prepare as for I, using:

A 2½- to 3-pound lobster

After the cooking period, drain and plunge the lobster into cold water to arrest further cooking. For how to eat a lobster, see above.

BOILED (OR POACHED) LOBSTERS
Please read About Lobsters, 382. Place in a large heavy pot enough water so the lobsters will be completely covered when you plunge them in. Add for each quart of water:

1 tablespoon salt

Bring water to a rolling boil. Carefully immerse, headfirst because of splashing:

½- to 2½-pound lobsters

Allow the water to return to a boil, then reduce the heat at once and simmer the lobsters about 5 minutes for 1½-pound lobsters, plus about 2 to 3 minutes for each additional pound, until they are bright red. Drain.
Serve with small bowls filled with:

The juices from the pot or melted butter

and:

Lemon wedges

Provide each person with plenty of napkins and a bib. For how to eat a lobster, see above.

GRILLED OR BROILED LOBSTER
2 servings

Lobsters can be killed before cutting by lowering them into boiling water for 2 minutes. If you don't parboil them, preparing the lobster may be easier for both of you if you put them into the freezer for a few minutes, until they are still. Please read About Lobsters, 382. Prepare a medium-hot grill or preheat the broiler. Prepare:

Two 1¼-pound live lobsters

by severing the vein behind the head of each one with a sharp, heavy knife: Place the lobster belly-down on a cut-ting board; hold it firmly in place. Find the crosshatch right behind the lobster's head, plunge the point of the knife straight down, shown below. Quickly cut through the head; this will kill the lobster instantly. Cut forward through the head and back through the body and tail.

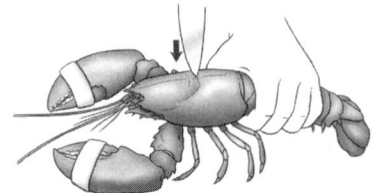

To kill a lobster without cooking it, pierce it behind the head with a sharp, heavy knife

The lobster can then lie flat for serving. Beyond a doubt edible is the delicious black roe, or coral, which turns into the so-called red coral during cooking, and the greenish-brown liver, or tomalley. If broiling the lobsters, you may prepare a stuffing by removing and mixing together the **coral** and **tomalley** with:

(2 tablespoons fresh bread crumbs, toasted, 100)
(2 teaspoons fresh lemon juice or dry sherry)

Replace it in the cavities. Brush the exposed lobster meat and the stuffing, if using, with:

Melted butter or olive oil

Season with:

Salt and black pepper to taste

If grilling or broiling unstuffed, place shell side down on the grill or shell side up on a baking sheet and cook about 10 minutes, brushing with:

Melted butter

to keep the meat moist. If broiling stuffed, place shell side down on a baking sheet and broil about 10 minutes. Serve with:

Lemon wedges
Melted butter

LOBSTER AMERICAINE (OR ARMORICAINE)

2 servings

This method of cooking lobster is good enough to credit regional inventiveness on both sides of the Atlantic. Please read About Lobsters, 382. Have ready:

¹/₂ cup fish stock, 118

Place on a rimmed baking sheet, to reserve the juices that result from cutting:

Two 1¹/₂-pound live lobsters

Split lengthwise in half as for Grilled or Broiled Lobster, 383. Cut off the claws. Cut the tail into 3 or 4 pieces, at the segmentations. Remove and discard the grain sac from the head. Reserve the coral, if any, and the tomalley for the sauce. Have ready two large heavy skillets. In one, melt:

3 tablespoons butter

Add and cook over medium heat, stirring, until softened:

1 cup Mirepoix, 998
¹/₂ cup chopped shallots

Meanwhile, combine in another large skillet and heat until fragrant:

¹/₂ cup olive oil
1 garlic clove

Add the cut-up lobster still in the shell, and cook, stirring frequently, until the shells are red and the flesh is firm, about 4 minutes. Add the lobster to the mirepoix in the first skillet. Reserve the oil in the second skillet and discard the garlic; set the skillet aside. Flambé, 1055, the lobster mixture in:

2 tablespoons brandy

Remove from the heat. Add to the second skillet, bring to a simmer, and simmer about 5 minutes:

1 cup dry white wine
¹/₂ cup tomato puree

3 tomatoes, peeled, seeded, and chopped, or 3 canned plum tomatoes, seeded and chopped

Add the lobster pieces, still in the shell, to the tomato sauce, along with:

1 teaspoon chopped tarragon

Add any juices from the lobster, the coral, if any, and the tomalley. Simmer about 15 minutes. Season with:

Salt and black pepper to taste

If desired, thicken the sauce slightly with:

(Kneaded Butter, 545)

Serve the lobster with the hot sauce poured over it, garnished with:

Chopped parsley

BAKED STUFFED LOBSTER

2 servings

Please read About Lobsters, 382. Preheat the oven to 375°F. Toss together in a medium bowl:

1¹/₂ cups browned bread crumbs, 960
¹/₄ cup chopped parsley
1¹/₂ teaspoons minced garlic
¹/₄ teaspoon salt
¹/₄ teaspoon black pepper
2 tablespoons olive oil

Split lengthwise in half, as for Grilled or Broiled Lobster, 383, working on a rimmed baking sheet to collect the juices:

Two 1¹/₂- to 2-pound live lobsters

Remove the head sacs and tail veins. Turn the lobsters cut side up on the baking sheet. Lightly press the bread crumb mixture into the chest cavities and tails. Using a fork, bring some of the flavorful tomalley up into the stuffing, and moisten the stuffing of each lobster with 1 tablespoon of the lobster juices. Pour into the baking sheet:

³/₄ cup dry white wine

Bake the lobsters for 30 to 35 minutes, basting the claws two or three times with the pan juices. If the stuffing looks dry, moisten it again with pan juices, but do not add more than a teaspoon or two, or the stuffing will become soggy. The lobsters are done when the stuffing is very hot and browned on top and the tail meat feels firm when pressed with your finger.

LOBSTER THERMIDOR

2 servings

Prepare:

2 Boiled (or poached) Lobsters, 383, about 1¹/₂ pounds each

Remove and crack the claws; extract the meat. Remove the tails, keeping the tail shells intact, and remove the meat, discarding the vein. Remove the body meat, tomalley, and coral, if any. Cut the tail and claw meat into ¹/₂-inch chunks. Press the tomalley and any coral through a sieve. Prepare:

Mornay Sauce, 551

and adding the tomalley and coral and:

1 teaspoon Dijon mustard
(1 to 2 tablespoons dry sherry)

Fill the tail shells or 1-cup ramekins with one-third of the sauce. Add the lobster meat and cover it with the rest of the sauce. If desired, sprinkle the tops with a mixture of:

(Grated Parmesan cheese and melted butter)

Preheat the broiler. Run the lobsters or ramekins under the broiler until the sauce is golden brown.

LOBSTER NEWBURG

4 servings

Please read About Lobsters, 382. Prepare:

Newburg Sauce, 561

Stir:

2 cups boiled diced lobster meat

into the butter with the shallots. Serve on:

Hot buttered toast

ABOUT SHRIMP

There are two important things to understand about shrimp: first, there are many varieties. Second, almost all shrimp, now a global commodity, is frozen when caught, and is sold still frozen or thawed. The most common shrimp in supermarkets these days are almost always farm-raised and almost always from Asia.

Shrimp are sold by size or count per pound. **U-10** shrimp, under 10 per pound, are huge; **51/60** count, with 51 to 60 shrimp per pound, are quite small. Given that it is best to peel shrimp yourself (the shells make excellent stock when boiled with a cup or so of water; they'll keep, frozen in a plastic bag, for later use), it makes sense to buy the largest shrimp you can afford. Stay with those in the **16/20** or **26/30** count per pound range for a good combination of economy, size, and relative ease of peeling.

Let us also remind you of the miniature shrimp from our West Coast and from Scandinavia—widely used as hors d'oeuvres. Jumbo-sized varieties—sometimes called **prawns**—are shrimp so large that 2 or 3 are sufficient for a serving. These are perfect for grilling. In spite of slight differences in flavor and texture, all shrimp, including freshwater varieties, may be substituted for one another if size is taken into consideration for serving amounts and cooking time. If you are grilling, broiling, or boiling shrimp, it is ➤ best to buy and cook them in their shells, for it protects the meat from drying out and helps retain maximum flavor.

To test shrimp for freshness, see that they are dry and firm. ➤ For 3 servings, allow about 1 pound of shrimp in the shell or ½ pound cooked peeled shrimp. In buying, remember that 2 to 2½ pounds of shrimp in the shell gives only about 1 pound cooked, shelled shrimp, or 2 cups. To prevent curling and toughening, ➤ drain shrimp at once after boiling. Peeling is easy either before or after cooking. A slight tug releases the body shell from the tail.

The "vein" of a shrimp can impart a bitter taste, so deveining is recommended, especially for large shrimp, though not mandatory. **To devein shrimp,** make a shallow cut down the back of a peeled shrimp and pull out the vein with the tip of a small-pointed knife or deveining tool

Peeling a shrimp

while holding the shrimp under running water. **To butterfly shrimp,** lay the shrimp peeled or unpeeled on its side on a work surface. Starting about ¼ inch from the tail, make a cut along the inside curl of the shrimp (through the legs), without cutting the shrimp or shell in half, or make a cut down the back of the shrimp. With your fingers, open the shrimp and flatten it with the palm of your hand so it lies almost flat.

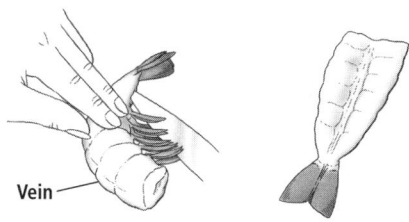

Vein

Butterflying shrimp

For more shrimp recipes, see Hors d'Oeuvres and Appetizers, 69, Pasta, 320, and Brunch, Lunch, and Supper Dishes, 95.

SOUTH CAROLINA SKILLET SHRIMP

2 servings

Our dear friend Julie, from Edisto Island, South Carolina, taught us to cook shrimp in the most simple and foolproof fashion. It takes fresh shrimp, a skillet, and little time and delivers the sweetest essence of the shellfish. Eat your fill with a cold glass of Chardonnay or Champagne.

Place in a large nonstick skillet:

1 pound shrimp in their shells

No matter their size, cover and cook in their own juices on medium to medium-high heat for 2 minutes. Remove the lid. Stir and cook an additional 2 minutes or until shells are pink. Put on ice or serve hot. Cover the table with newspaper, get a roll of paper towels, and serve with:

Melted butter

Lemon wedges

NO-FAIL BOILED SHRIMP

4 servings

If desired, simply cook the shrimp in plain water.

Please read About Shrimp, above. Combine in a large saucepan:

2 celery ribs, cut into 2-inch lengths
1 medium onion, cut into eighths
1 small lemon, quartered
$^1/_2$ bunch parsley
8 whole black peppercorns
2 bay leaves
1 tablespoon salt
$^1/_2$ teaspoon ground red pepper
10 cups water

Bring to a boil, then reduce the heat and simmer, uncovered, for 10 minutes. Strain the liquid and return it to the pan. Add:

2 pounds shrimp (any size), preferably in their shells

Return the liquid to a boil, reduce the heat, and simmer, uncovered, for exactly 2 minutes. Drain the shrimp, remove to a platter, and let cool. Serve with any one or more of the following:

Becker Cocktail Sauce, 568
Rémoulade Sauce, 581
Tartar Sauce, 581
Tomatillo-Horseradish Sauce, 581

BECKER BARBECUED SHRIMP

2 servings

Crusty bread dipped in the sauce is so tasty it's almost possible to ignore the shrimp. To double the recipe, prepare two batches in separate pans.

Please read About Shrimp, 385. Grind in a spice mill or coffee grinder:

2 teaspoons dried rosemary
1 teaspoon dried oregano
1 teaspoon crushed red pepper flakes
1 teaspoon sweet paprika
1 teaspoon whole black peppercorns
1 teaspoon salt

Melt in a large skillet over medium heat:

$^1/_4$ cup ($^1/_2$ stick) butter

Add the spice mixture and:

4 garlic cloves, minced

Cook, stirring, for 2 minutes. Add and cook for 4 to 5 minutes, stirring once or twice:

16 to 20 medium-to-large shrimp, peeled and deveined

Remove the shrimp to a bowl. Add to the pan:

$^1/_2$ cup chicken broth
$^1/_2$ cup beer

Bring to a boil over high heat and cook for 1$^1/_2$ to 2 minutes. Turn off the heat and return the shrimp to the pan to heat through. Season with:

2 tablespoons minced parsley
2 tablespoons fresh lemon juice

SHRIMP SCAMPI

6 servings

In the 1950s, Italian-American restaurants transformed the name of the main ingredient into the method. This dish is still found today, under this name, as far away as Tokyo. At any rate, it deserves to be a classic, equally delicious made with the same amount of bay scallops, 378, cut-up cleaned squid, 390, or cooked octopus, 390, or whelk, 390.

Please read About Shrimp, 385. Combine in a large skillet:

$^1/_2$ cup olive oil
1 tablespoon minced garlic

Cook, stirring occasionally, over very low heat until the garlic is golden, about 10 minutes; do not rush it. Increase the heat to medium-high and add:

1$^1/_2$ to 2 pounds large or extra-large shrimp, peeled and deveined

Cook until the shrimp turn pink on the bottom, and turn them over. Add:

$^1/_4$ cup minced parsley
(1 teaspoon minced garlic)

Cook until the shrimp are firm and pink, about 5 minutes total. Sprinkle with:

1 tablespoon fresh lemon juice
Minced parsley

GRILLED OR BROILED SHRIMP OR SCALLOPS

4 servings

Since shrimp and scallops cook in just about the same amount of time and complement each other nicely, you can cook some of each if you like. It is important not to overcook them.

Prepare a medium-hot grill or preheat the broiler. If grilling, place the grill rack or broiler rack as close to the heat as possible. Toss to coat in a shallow bowl:

1$^1/_2$ to 2 pounds large shrimp, peeled and deveined, 385, or sea scallops, side "hinge" removed, 377, or a combination
2 tablespoons olive oil
(1 tablespoon sherry vinegar)

If grilling, to keep the shellfish from falling into the fire, it is advisable to use a wire-mesh grill basket or skewers. Grill or broil, turning shrimp after the first side becomes pink, 2 minutes or so; or turn scallops when the first side becomes opaque, 2 to 3 minutes. Season liberally with:

Salt and black pepper

Grill or broil until the second side is pink or opaque; test one of the shrimp or scallops by cutting into it to make sure it is cooked through. Serve with:

Lemon wedges, minced parsley or cilantro, and extra-virgin olive oil or Scandinavian Mustard Dill Sauce, 566

GRILLED OR BROILED SHRIMP OR SCALLOPS WITH CHILI PASTE

4 servings

If you like fiery food, use more red pepper; if you prefer milder food, omit it altogether—the chili powder will add plenty of flavor by itself.

Prepare a medium-hot grill fire or preheat the broiler. Place the grill or broiler rack as close to the heat source as possible. Mix together in a large shallow bowl:

1 tablespoon minced garlic
1 tablespoon chili powder, or to taste
$^1/_2$ teaspoon ground red pepper, or to taste
1 tablespoon peanut, olive, or other vegetable oil,
**   or as needed to make a moist paste**
Salt and black pepper to taste

Add and toss to coat well:

1$^1/_2$ to 2 pounds large shrimp, peeled and deveined,
**   385, or sea scallops, side "hinge" removed, 377,**
**   or a combination**

Follow the cooking instructions for Grilled or Broiled Shrimp or Scallops, 386. Serve hot or at room temperature with:

Lime wedges
Minced parsley or cilantro or Orange Oil, 590

GRILLED OR BROILED SHRIMP OR SCALLOPS BASQUE-STYLE

4 servings

Prepare a medium-hot grill fire or preheat the broiler. Place the grill or broiler rack as close to the heat source as possible. Mix together in a serving bowl:

$^1/_3$ cup fresh lemon juice
$^1/_3$ cup extra-virgin olive oil
1 tablespoon minced garlic
$^1/_4$ to $^1/_2$ teaspoon hot pepper sauce, or to taste
$^1/_2$ cup coarsely chopped herbs (any combination of
**   parsley, sage, thyme, basil, marjoram, oregano,**
**   and/or chervil)**
Salt and black pepper to taste

Toss in a shallow bowl to coat the shellfish:

1$^1/_2$ to 2 pounds large shrimp, peeled and deveined,
**   385, or sea scallops, side "hinge" removed, 377,**
**   or a combination**
2 tablespoons olive oil

Follow the cooking instructions for Grilled or Broiled Shrimp or Scallops, 386. Add the hot shellfish to the herb mixture, toss gently, and serve immediately.

BROILED SHRIMP OR SCALLOPS WITH PERSILLADE

4 servings

Persillade, a mixture of chopped parsley and garlic, often combined with bread crumbs, is wonderful on broiled seafood.

Preheat the broiler. Mince together:

1$^1/_2$ cup fresh bread crumbs
$^1/_2$ cup parsley leaves
1 garlic clove, peeled

Season with:

Salt and black pepper to taste

Toss in a shallow roasting pan to coat the shellfish:

1$^1/_2$ to 2 pounds large or extra-large shrimp, peeled
**   and deveined, 385, or sea or bay scallops, side**
**   "hinge" removed, 377, or a combination**
2 tablespoons olive oil

Place under the broiler as close to the heat source as possible. Turn shrimp after the first side becomes pink, 2 minutes or so; or turn scallops when the first side becomes opaque, 2 to 3 minutes. Spread the bread crumb mixture all over the shellfish, then broil about 4 inches from the heat source just until the bread crumbs are browned, 3 to 4 minutes. Serve with:

Lemon wedges

GRILLED OR BROILED SHRIMP OR SCALLOPS WITH HOISIN OR BARBECUE SAUCE

4 servings

Take care not to burn the sauce once you brush it on—move the shellfish to a cooler part of the grill or lower the broiler rack.

Prepare a medium-hot grill fire or preheat the broiler. Place the grill rack about 4 inches from the heat on a grill or place the broiler pan 2 or 3 inches from the heat source.

Combine in a shallow bowl:

1$^1/_2$ to 2 pounds large shrimp, peeled and deveined,
**   385, or sea scallops, side "hinge" removed, 377,**
**   or a combination**
2 tablespoons soy sauce
1 tablespoon sake or dry white wine

Remove the shellfish from the soy mixture, pat dry, and place on the grill or under the broiler. Grill or broil until beginning to brown, about 2 minutes. Turn, then brush the top side with:

Hoisin sauce or catsup-based barbecue sauce, 586

Grill or broil for 2 minutes more. Turn again, move the shellfish to a cooler part of the grill or adjust the broiler rack down a notch, and brush again with sauce. Turn and brush every minute or so for 3 to 4 minutes, until the shellfish has developed a nice glaze and is cooked through. Serve hot or at room temperature, garnished, if you like, with:

(Minced scallions or chopped walnuts)

DEEP-FRIED SHRIMP

3 servings

Please read about Deep-Fat Frying, 1046. Shell and devein, 385:

1 pound shrimp

Combine in a bowl:

$^2/_3$ cup milk
$^1/_4$ teaspoon salt
$^1/_8$ teaspoon paprika

Soak the shrimp in the milk 30 minutes. Drain well. Sprinkle with:

Fresh lemon juice
Salt

Roll in:

Cornmeal

Let dry on a rack for 15 minutes. Fry in deep fat heated to 375°F until golden brown. Drain on paper towels. Serve hot with:

Fresh lemon juice or Mayonnaise, 579, seasoned with pureed chutney

SHRIMP FRIED IN BATTER

12 servings

Please read About Deep-Fat Frying, 1046. Prepare:

Fritter Batter for Vegetables, Meat, and Fish, 658

Peel and devein, 385, leaving the tails on:

1 pound shrimp

Dip a few shrimp at a time in the batter, holding them by the tail—do not cover the tails with batter—and fry in deep fat heated to 375°F until golden brown. Drain on paper towels. Serve with:

Lemon wedges
Becker Cocktail Sauce, 568
Tartar Sauce, 581

SHRIMP TEMPURA

2 servings

Please read about Deep-Fat Frying, 1046. Heat to 365°F in a deep fryer or deep heavy pot over medium-high heat:

3 inches vegetable oil

Peel and devein, 385, leaving tails:

1 pound raw shrimp

Butterfly the shrimp, 385. Dry the pieces well.
Prepare just before frying:

Tempura Batter, 658

Dip each shrimp in the batter and place in the oil one at a time. Let fry, undisturbed, for about 1 minute. Turn and fry about 1 minute more. Drain on paper towels and serve immediately with:

Soy sauce
Ginger Soy Sauce, 571

BAKED STUFFED JUMBO SHRIMP

4 servings

Position a rack in the upper third of the oven. Preheat the oven to 450°F. Have ready:

14 jumbo shrimp (2 pounds or more) in the shell

Butterfly, 385, 12 of the shrimp. Season lightly with:

Salt and black pepper

Peel the remaining shrimp and coarsely chop. Combine with:

1$^1/_2$ cups fine fresh bread crumbs

6 tablespoons ($^3/_4$ stick) butter, melted
$^1/_4$ cup chopped parsley
2 teaspoons minced garlic
$^1/_4$ teaspoon salt
$^1/_4$ teaspoon black pepper

Arrange the shrimp in a single layer in a shallow baking dish and then top with the stuffing mixture, pressing it lightly, so it adheres. Pour around the shrimp, to just cover the bottom of the baking dish:

$^3/_4$ to 1 cup dry white wine

Bake the shrimp until piping hot, 10 to 12 minutes; be careful not to overcook. Spoon a bit of the juices from the baking dish over each shrimp and serve immediately.

VANILLA COCONUT SHRIMP

6 to 8 servings

Heat in a large skillet over medium-high heat:

$^1/_4$ cup olive oil

Add:

1 cup finely chopped shallots

Cook until the shallots begin to brown, 3 to 4 minutes. Add:

1$^1/_2$ cups dry white wine
1 vanilla bean, split lengthwise, seeds scraped out

Bring to a simmer and reduce the wine by half, about 5 minutes. Add:

1 cup chicken, vegetable, or fish stock or broth
One 14$^1/_2$-ounce can coconut milk
2 to 3 teaspoons minced peeled fresh ginger
$^1/_4$ teaspoon salt
$^1/_4$ teaspoon black pepper

Bring to a simmer and reduce the sauce by half, about 7 minutes. Add:

1$^1/_2$ pounds large shrimp, peeled and deveined, 385

Cook about 10 minutes, turning the shrimp once, until just cooked thoroughly. Remove the vanilla bean. Add:

$^1/_4$ cup chopped basil

Serve over:

Cooked rice or angel hair pasta

SHRIMP OR CRAWFISH ÉTOUFÉE

4 to 6 servings

Have ready:

3 pounds medium to large shrimp, peeled and deveined, 385, or 3 to 4 pounds crawfish, 389

Toss with:

1 teaspoon paprika
1 teaspoon dried thyme
1 teaspoon salt
$^1/_2$ teaspoon ground black pepper
$^1/_2$ teaspoon dried basil
$^1/_4$ teaspoon ground red pepper

Set aside. In a large, flat-bottomed pot or skillet, stir together over medium heat:

3 tablespoons vegetable oil
3 tablespoons flour

Cook, stirring constantly, until the roux is almost as dark as milk chocolate, about 20 minutes. Stir in:

1 cup chopped onions
$1/2$ cup chopped celery
$1/4$ cup chopped red bell peppers
$1/4$ cup chopped green bell peppers
$1/4$ cup chopped andouille sausage or smoked ham

Cook, stirring, until the vegetables are golden brown, 5 to 6 minutes. The roux will continue to darken to a deep mahogany color. Add:

2 tablespoons chopped garlic
$1/4$ teaspoon dried sage, crumbled
$1/4$ teaspoon dried thyme

Stir well and cook for 1 minute more. Stir in:

2 cups chicken stock
2 tablespoons tomato paste
1 tablespoon Worcestershire sauce
$1/4$ teaspoon hot red pepper sauce, or to taste

Stirring constantly, bring the sauce to a simmer. Add the spice-coated shrimp or crawfish to the skillet and bring the liquid back to a simmer. Reduce the heat so the sauce bubbles gently, cover, and cook until the shrimp or crawfish are just firm and pink, and are curled, about 10 minutes. Add:

$1/2$ cup finely chopped scallions
$1/4$ cup chopped fresh parsley

Season to taste with:

Salt and ground black pepper
Hot red pepper sauce

Serve with:

Cooked rice

ABOUT CRAYFISH OR CRAWFISH (ÉCREVISSES)

One of the thrills our great-grandparents had was to find in Missouri streams the crayfish they had so relished in Europe. These crustaceans, looking like miniature lobsters, were brought to the table in great steaming crimson mounds, garnished with dill or swimming in their own juices—that is, *à la nage*. By the way, a single Australian crayfish is so large it suffices for one serving.

If you are preparing these crustaceans for an hors d'oeuvre, cook as below but only until the water is boiling well, after they are all immersed, then remove from the heat and let them cool in the liquid. Shelled, they lend themselves to all kinds of combinations and sauces, but the connoisseur usually wants them for themselves alone.

When buying live crayfish, be sure to sort out dead ones. If frozen, the crayfish should be whole and individual. Live crayfish can be stored in the refrigerator, covered with damp cloth or paper towel, for no more than a day or two.

BOILED CRAYFISH

Allow about 1 dozen per serving

Have ready:

Fresh or frozen crayfish

If using fresh crayfish, rinse well in several changes of cold water. If they have been kept in fresh running water before you buy them, they need not be eviscerated. If they have not, clean them while still alive: Grasp the middle tail fin, give a long firm twist, and pull to remove the stomach and intestinal vein. Fill a large pot with water and season with:

1 leek, white part only, chopped
Parsley sprigs
1 carrot, chopped
(3 tablespoons white or cider vinegar)

Bring to a boil. Drop the crayfish one by one into the boiling water at a rate that will not disturb the boil and cook not longer than 5 to 7 minutes, until shells turn red. Serve in the shell, with plenty of:

Melted butter

seasoned with:

Minced dill

Crayfish are eaten with the fingers; be sure to serve with napkins and finger bowls. Separate the tail from the body, and crack open the tail by holding it between your thumbs and forefingers of both hands and forcing it back against the curve of the shell.

ABOUT OCTOPUS, SQUID, AND CUTTLEFISH

These inkfish belong to the category of odd-looking sea creatures that must be eaten to be appreciated. They all have long, edible arms and a body that can be formed into a natural sack for stuffing, as well as an ink-expelling sac, which the creature uses to create an escape screen in the water.

Freezing and thawing is common before sale for all inkfish, and does not diminish quality significantly, so long as they remain plump, shiny, and fresh smelling. You may keep them frozen for up to three months. **To thaw,** move to the refrigerator the day before cooking. **Octopus** is generally sold somewhere at between 1 and 4 pounds, with 2 being ideal. Look for small **squid** and **cuttlefish** (8 inches long or less), as they are more tender. Squid is also known as *calamari,* its Italian name. ➤ Allow about $1/2$ pound per serving.

Cuttlefish, similar to squid when cooked, is imported from Europe, is only available occasionally, and costs

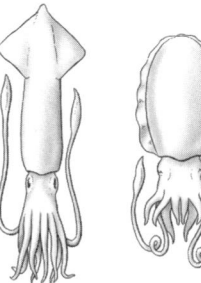

Squid and cuttlefish

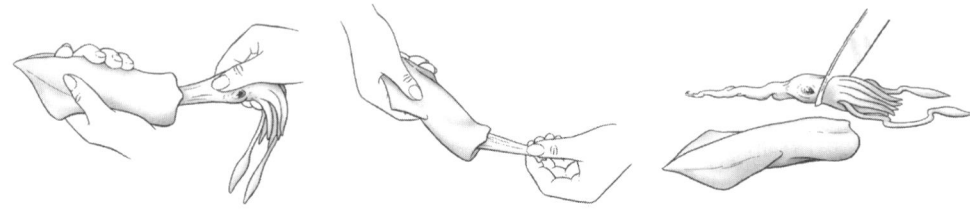

Cleaning a squid

more. Small squid and cuttlefish are tender and can be cooked briefly. They are typically boiled for salads, or breaded or battered and deep-fried. Octopus is tougher and should be precooked until tender before sautéing, grilling, or frying. It need only be partially cooked (for about 30 minutes) if it will be braised. **To precook octopus,** simmer it in water to cover with 1 tablespoon salt, 1 bay leaf, 2 crushed garlic cloves, and a few black peppercorns. Test for tenderness after 45 minutes by piercing it with a knife; ➤ it is ready when the knife meets little resistance, which may take up to 2 hours.

Inkfish are generally sold cleaned, but if necessary, cleaning is easy. **To clean fresh octopus,** trim off the mouth and eyes, taking care not to pierce the ink sac, which lies close by. Cut off the head, turn it inside out, and rinse away its contents. Remove the hard beak from the body by pushing it through the opening at the end of the body. Massage under running water to remove all mud from the suckers. The skin is edible but most will come off during cooking. **To clean squid,** grasp the head and innards by reaching far up inside the body, and pull gently, removing the translucent quill or beak as well. Cut off the tentacles just below the eyes. Use a dull knife blade to scrape out the innards and the purplish skin from the body. Rinse the body and tentacles. Leave the body whole for stuffing (the tentacles can be chopped and used in the stuffing), or cut the body into rings and the tentacles into like-sized pieces. ➤ **Clean cuttlefish** as for squid, except first slice the body lengthwise to make it easier to remove the innards. You may need to cut the cuttlebone out with a knife. ➤ The small gray ink sac of squid or cuttlefish can be carefully cut away and its contents used to lend a saline flavor and inky black color to soups, stews, sauces, pasta, or risotto.

GRILLED SQUID
4 servings
Any of the flavor treatments suggested for shrimp and scallops in the recipes above can be used on squid.
Prepare a hot grill fire. Place the grill rack as close to the heat as possible.
Toss in a shallow bowl to coat:
> **2 pounds cleaned squid, tentacles cut off, bodies halved lengthwise, above**
> **2 tablespoons extra-virgin olive oil**
> **(1 tablespoon sherry vinegar or other vinegar)**

When the fire is good and hot, place the squid on the grill and cook about 1 minute, 2 at most, until the surface facing the flame is firm and seared. Turn and cook another 1 to 2 minutes. Be careful—overcooking will make the squid tough. Serve immediately with:
> **Lemon wedges and minced parsley, Green Sauce, 567, or Lemon Oregano Vinaigrette, 573**

STUFFED SQUID
6 servings
Clean, above:
> **Twelve 5-inch squid**
Chop the tentacles and set aside.
Preheat the oven to 325°F. Prepare:
> **¹⁄₂ recipe Rice Dressing for Cornish Hens, 441, or ¹⁄₂ recipe Parsley and Bread Crumb Stuffing for Fish, 535**
Mix in the chopped tentacles. Stuff each squid body with 2 tablespoons stuffing. Tie each pouch closed at the top with kitchen twine. Place in a single layer in a baking dish. Combine:
> **¹⁄₄ cup olive oil**
> **¹⁄₄ cup tomato sauce or crushed canned tomatoes**
> **¹⁄₂ cup dry white wine**
> **¹⁄₂ cup water**
> **¹⁄₄ cup finely chopped parsley**
Pour over the squid. Bake about 1 hour and 15 minutes, or until the squid is tender. Serve hot or cold.

ABOUT CONCH AND WHELK
Conch and whelk, though similar in appearance, are different members of the mollusk family. They are in fact large marine snails. ➤ It is now illegal to harvest live conch in U.S. waters—they are on the endangered species list. Most conch comes from the Caribbean islands. You can order legally harvested, usually farmed, conch from Internet retailers. It should be cooked and frozen. If you have a live conch, ➤ poach in boiling water for 3–5 minutes. Once cooked, you can easily grab the meat with a fork or skewer and pull out a substantial—4 ounces or so—piece of meat. Conch and whelk can be cooked the same ways. Both are tender and delicious when raw or cooked minimally; more often their meat is cooked long enough so it toughens and then becomes fairly tender again, like squid.

Conch and whelk can be braised, stewed, or fried (as in fritters). Because of their mild, sweet clam-like flavor, both can be substituted for clams in chowder and pasta, or marinated in salads.

CONCH (OR WHELK) SALAD
4 servings

Trim all the orange and dark flesh from:

4 conchs or whelks (2 cups), cut into chunks

Bring a large saucepan of water to a boil. Add the conch and boil 30 minutes. Drain.

Combine in a large bowl:

1 cup chopped tomatoes
$^1/_2$ cup chopped red onion
$^1/_2$ cup chopped red bell pepper
$^1/_2$ chopped cucumber
1 jalapeño pepper, seeded and chopped
$^1/_4$ cup chopped cilantro or mint
$^1/_3$ cup fresh lime juice
2 tablespoons olive oil
Salt and black pepper to taste

Add the conch and toss to mix. Serve over:

Romaine leaves

ABOUT IMITATION CRAB AND LOBSTER (SURIMI)

Surimi, often sold as imitation crab legs or lobster chunks, is a processed form of white fish fillets (usually, but not always, Pacific pollack), shaped and colored to look like crabmeat, which it does—right down to the dyed pinkish red edges. Surimi is best used as a substitute for crab in mayonnaise-based recipes such as salads, creamy dips, and soups. See Seafood Salad, 165, Hot Crab Dip, 74, or Rolled Sushi, 359.

ABOUT TURTLES

In the United States, only farm-raised freshwater turtles and limited species of wild freshwater turtles can legally be used for food. ➤ Sea turtle populations have been protected by the Endangered Species Act since 1973, and the **diamondback terrapin**—once prized for its tender flesh in soup—is now protected by state laws all along the eastern seaboard. The turtles most frequently caught or farmed and consumed in temperate North America are **freshwater turtles,** such as the **snapping turtle,** which abound in lakes and streams from North Dakota to Florida. Aptly named as to disposition, they are quite a different kettle of fish: short-tempered and capable of inflicting nasty bites.

We ➤ do not recommend attempting to prepare live turtles in the domestic kitchen. Most of us are content to eat the highly prized, gelatinous meat of turtles diced and found cooked and canned or frozen raw, from an Internet purveyor or seafood market. See About Freezing, 923, for thawing instructions.

TURTLE SOUP
4 to 6 servings

Melt in a heavy saucepan over medium heat:

2 tablespoons butter

Add and brown, about 7 minutes:

1 pound canned or thawed turtle meat, cut into $^1/_2$-inch chunks

Season with:

Salt and black pepper to taste

Add:

1 onion, chopped
3 celery ribs, chopped
3 garlic cloves, finely chopped
1 jalapeño pepper, finely chopped
$^1/_2$ cup chopped green bell pepper
1$^1/_2$ teaspoons dried thyme
$^1/_2$ tablespoon dried oregano
2 bay leaves

Cook until the vegetables soften, about 5 minutes. Add:

4 cups beef or veal stock or broth

Bring to a boil, then reduce the heat and simmer 25 minutes. Meanwhile, melt in a small saucepan:

$^1/_4$ cup ($^1/_2$ stick) butter

Stir in:

$^1/_4$ cup all-purpose flour

Cook, stirring, over medium heat until brown, about 8 minutes. Gradually whisk the roux into the soup and simmer another 20 minutes, whisking occasionally. Add:

1$^1/_2$ cups chopped peeled tomatoes
$^3/_4$ cup dry sherry
1 tablespoon hot pepper sauce
1$^1/_2$ teaspoons Worcestershire sauce
Juice of $^1/_2$ lemon

Simmer 10 minutes. Add:

Salt and black pepper to taste

Garnish with:

Watercress
Chopped hard-boiled egg, 194

ABOUT SNAILS

The Romans, who were passionate about snails, grew them on ranches where they were fed special foods like bay leaves, wine, and spicy soups as preseasoning. Some things haven't changed—today most snails are farmed. If you gather them yourself, follow these directions: For 10 days to 2 weeks, feed them on lettuce leaves, removing the old leaves and furnishing new ones every few days. Then, ➤ scrub your wild snails—or purchased ranch-raised snails—until all slime is removed. Put the snails into a large stainless steel or enameled pot. To prepare enough acidulated water, 957, to cover about 50 snails, mix:

Water
$^1/_4$ cup vinegar
$^1/_2$ cup salt

Rinse them, and repeat this entire process two more times, or until the acidulated water remains clear. Discard any snails whose heads have not by this time popped out of their shells, and drain. Cover the snails with boiling water and cook for 5 minutes. Drain and cool, then remove the snails from the shells with a small fork; reserve the shells. Hold the upper part of each snail with your thumb and forefinger and score the lower part of the body so you can pull out the swollen intestinal tube. Discard it. Simmer the snails in a court bouillon of:

1 part water or light stock and 1 part dry white wine

about 3 hours, or until tender. Add during the last 30 minutes of cooking:

1 Bouquet Garni, 960
2 garlic cloves

Allow the snails to cool in the court bouillon. Drain.

SNAILS

Allow 6 to 9 snails per serving

I. Prepare snails as described above. Dry the snails and shells with a cloth. Place in each shell a generous dab of:

Snail Butter, 559

Replace the snails in their shells. Pack them firmly in the shell, so generously covered that only the herbed butter is visible at the opening. You may refrigerate the snails for later use, or bake them at once. Preheat the oven to 425°F. Arrange the snails on a pan lightly sprinkled with water just long enough to get them piping hot—a matter of a few minutes. Serve in heated snail dishes.

II. For canned snails, the following effects a small miracle of resuscitation. Prepare to fill 48 snail shells:

3 recipes of Snail Butter, 559

Combine in a medium saucepan:

1 cup canned consommé
1 cup dry white wine
1/2 bay leaf
1 garlic clove

Bring to a boil and boil until reduced to 1 cup. Set aside. Meanwhile, wash the snail shells well and drain. Put in a colander:

48 canned snails

Pour 4 cups warm water over them, and drain well. Simmer the snails briefly in the hot reduced consommé and wine. Drain. Pack the snails and butter into the shells as described above. Heat and serve as above.

III. Replace the snail shells with:

Sautéed Mushrooms, 283

Fill each mushroom cap with one or more snails, depending on size. Coat the snails with:

Snail Butter, 559

and run under a hot broiler briefly, until heated.

ABOUT FROG LEGS

Light pink, meaty frog legs, often compared to chicken in texture and flavor, should be gently cooked to preserve their sweetness. They are primarily found frozen, skinned and ready to use, imported from Asia. Fresh frog legs are harvested in the South and Midwest in the spring and summer and many people go frog digging during this time. **If the frogs are not prepared,** cut off and discard the feet; then cut off the hind legs—the only part of the frog used—close to the body. Separate and wash the legs in cold water. Begin at the top and strip off the skin like a glove. Through an experiment with a twitching frog leg, Galvani discovered the electric current that bears his name. Should you prefer keeping your kitchen and your scientific activities separate and distinct, chill the frog legs before skinning. ➤ Allow 2 to 3 large or 6 small frog legs per person.

BRAISED FROG LEGS

4 servings

Clean:

8 large frog legs

Roll them in:

Seasoned Flour, 962

Melt in a large skillet:

6 tablespoons Clarified Butter, 557

Add and cook until soft:

1/2 cup chopped onion

Brown the frog legs in the butter. Reduce the heat and add:

3/4 cup boiling chicken stock or broth

Cover tightly and cook the frog legs until tender, about 10 minutes.

Meanwhile, melt in a medium skillet:

6 tablespoons (3/4 stick) butter

Add and toast in the butter:

1 1/4 cups seasoned dry bread crumbs
(3/4 cup finely chopped hazelnuts)

Add:

1 teaspoon fresh lemon juice

Roll the frog legs in the bread crumbs and serve them garnished with:

Chopped fennel sprigs

or, if you used hazelnuts, with:

Chopped parsley

DEEP-FRIED FROG LEGS

Please read about Deep-Fat Frying, 1046. Clean:

Frog legs

Dip them in:

Bound Breading or Coating, 961

Let dry on a plate or rack for 1 hour. Fry the frog legs in 3 inches of deep fat heated to 365°F until golden. Drain. Serve with:

Tartar Sauce, 581

FISH

With its ample coastline, bays, lakes, rivers, and streams, much of this country enjoys stocks of wonderful fresh fish, and increasingly, one can find a wide selection of high-quality fish in even the most landlocked areas. From beachside fry shacks to elegant restaurants to the home kitchen, the preparation and presentation of fish is as varied as the many fish species available at markets and caught by those who fish recreationally. Few things can compare to the taste of fish you've just caught yourself. But whether you catch them or buy them, wild fish often have more flavor than farm-raised fish, and so may be worth the higher price. Of course, anglers should check with local officials to confirm that the waters they fish in are clean and the fish safe to eat.

In the market, a trustworthy fishmonger is an invaluable resource in the selection of a fish, as well as an appropriate method of cooking it. However, in any shopping environment, those armed with knowledge of how to buy fish and how to substitute similar varieties, see 413, can do very well.

Recent concerns about the levels of mercury and pesticides in fish would seem to contradict the advice to eat it frequently, yet most studies have indicated that the benefits outweigh the potential dangers for all except very young children and pregnant or breast-feeding women. The four fish that may contain the highest levels of mercury are shark, swordfish, king mackerel, and tilefish. Often the darker areas of a fish's flesh contain higher concentrations of toxins (as do the roe and liver), and these can be trimmed off or not eaten.

Consuming a wide variety of fish from a variety of sources, rather than sticking to one favorite type, is advis-able in terms of safety and nutritional diversity, because different fish offer different nutritional benefits, and small quantities of toxins found in a particular type of fish can build up if consumed frequently.

BUYING AND STORING FISH

There are some simple rules that will help you bring home high-quality fish. First, ➤ buy or catch the fish the day you are going to eat it, or at most the day before. If your plans change and you find you are not going to cook it, freeze it. Wrap the cleaned and rinsed fish tightly in plastic wrap, then wrap again. See directions for freezing fish and cooking frozen fish, below.

When buying fish, remember that a whitish dry or chalky appearance on the surface of the flesh may indicate moisture loss or freezer burn, and that in some stores, ➤ thawed frozen fish is sold with no indication that it should be used at once and never refrozen. Whenever possible, ask; otherwise, trust your instincts. Good fish has firm, unmarred flesh, and good ocean fish smells like fresh seawater. The surface of the fish should be bright, clear, and almost translucent. It should not have spots of pink (which are usually bruises) or brown (which indicate spoilage), and there shouldn't be any areas of deep red or brown or oily, faintly rainbow-colored areas. In whole fresh fish, look for red gills, bulging clear eyes, an undamaged layer of scales, firm flesh when pressed, and no browning anywhere. Again, the smell should be sweet. The best whole fish look alive, as though they just came out of the water.

After buying fresh fish, keep it on ice or in a cooler on the way home if possible. Home refrigerators are not cold enough for maximum preservation, so ➤ it's best to store fillets and steaks in their original wrapping on ice in the refrigerator. Whole fish may be kept directly on ice if drainage is provided to prevent it from soaking up water. A large colander full of ice placed over a bowl works well. The length of fish storage depends largely on the condition in which it reaches you. The sooner it is used the better.

FROZEN FISH

Since large fishing boats go out for weeks at a time, fish that is frozen on board these ships will be fresher than any that has merely been chilled. As long as the freezing has been fast, and the thawing gradual, frozen fish can be of very good quality (in fact, much of what is served in sushi restaurants has been frozen). Ask or look on the package for "once frozen" to avoid fish that has already been thawed and refrozen.

Buy only solidly frozen packages. They should not be torn or misshapen or show evidence of refreezing. Frozen fish should be thawed in the refrigerator or cooked while still frozen. Fish sticks or individually breaded portions should not be thawed before cooking. ➤ Use thawed fish immediately, and do not refreeze. It may be cooked in the same way as its fresh counterpart. ➤ If cooked from a frozen state, fish is best baked, broiled, or cooked en papillote, 398, or in aluminum foil. Double the cooking time given for fresh fish. ➤ Remove the skin from frozen fish before cooking it.

PREPARING FISH FOR COOKING

The most important factor in fish cookery is to keep the fish as fresh as possible. Then, whether your fish is large or small, choose the cooking method most likely to retain its juiciness, and, no matter what its size or type, ➤ never overcook it. Leaner fish, such as halibut and grouper, will require more fat in cooking and are delicious prepared with a marinade, 584–586. Fattier fish, such as bluefish and mackerel, are strongly flavored and can handle a heavier sauce. ➤ Always rinse fish and pat it dry before cooking.

SMALL FISH

To clean fish such as smelts, sardines, anchovies, or sprats, snap down on the head and pull it off in a downward direction; some of the innards will come out along with it. Use your finger to open the fish from the front and remove the remaining innards, then grasp the backbone between your fingers and pull it out. You will be left with two tiny fillets joined by the skin.

Small fish may be **butterfly-filleted.** In this technique, the head and tail are removed, after which the flesh is cut cleanly away from both sides of the backbone and the dorsal fin; the ventral, or belly, fin is removed by slot-cutting around it. The meat is then cut off in a single piece, freeing it from the backbone, and flattened out ready for rinsing, drying, and cooking.

LARGE FISH

If fish are 2 pounds or over, bake, steam, or poach or cut into steaks, below. Fish of this size and somewhat smaller ones can also be filleted. You will sometimes see suggestions for slashing the skin of whole large fish before cooking. This is suitable chiefly for firm-fleshed fish, to hasten heat penetration and allow seasonings to flavor the flesh, or when, as with a whole turbot, the surface area of skin is extensive and it might otherwise split.

To clean a fish that is to be cooked whole, begin by spreading several layers of newspaper covered with three layers of brown paper on a steady work surface. If the fish needs scaling, first cut off the fins with scissors so they will

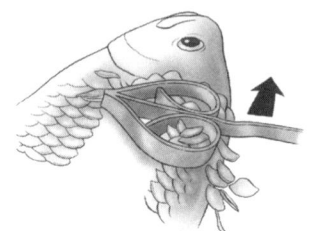

Scaling a fish

not nick you while you work. Wash the fish briefly in cold water—scales are more easily removed from a wet fish. Grasp the fish firmly near the base of the tail. If it is very slippery, you may want to hold it with a cloth or wear rubber gloves. Beginning at the tail, ➤ press a rigid sharp knife blade or a scaler at a slight angle to raise the scales as you strip them off. Work against the "nap" up toward the head, in short strokes, to minimize flying scales. Be sure to remove the scales around the back of the head and the fins. After scaling, discard the first layer of brown paper with the scales on it.

Next, **draw or gut the fish.** Cut down the entire length of the belly from the vent, or base, near the tail, to the head, and remove the entrails. These are all contained in a pouchlike integument that is easily freed from the flesh, so gutting the fish need not be a messy job. If you are removing the head, cut above the collarbone and break through the backbone by snapping it off on the edge of the work surface. The pectoral fins, if they were not previously cut off, should come away with the head. Then remove the tail by slicing through the body just above it. Wrap and discard the entrails, keeping the choicer trimmings—especially the head—for Fish Stock, 118.

To cut a fish into steaks, or darnes, begin at the head end and cut evenly, as shown below, into cross-sections at least 1 inch thick.

If you are preparing fish for stuffing, you can remove the dorsal fin in such a way as to remove unwanted bones. First cut down either side of its full length, then give a quick pull forward toward the head to release it and, with it, the bones attached to it. Wash the fish in cold running water, removing any blood, bits of viscera, or membrane. ➤ Be sure the blood line under the backbone has been removed. Dry the fish well. It is ready for cooking unstuffed or stuffed.

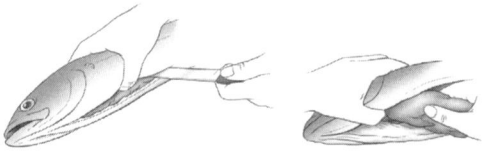

Gutting a roundfish

Removing the head and tail   Cutting into steaks or darnes

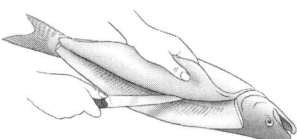

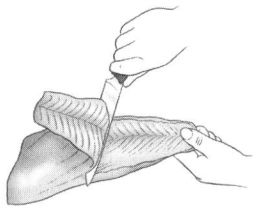

Filleting a roundfish   Skinning a fillet

To fillet a roundfish (the eyes are on either side of its head and it yields one fillet from each side), whether a 1-pound mackerel or an 8-pound mahimahi, you need not scale the fish, remove its fins, or gut it. Place it on a work surface on several layers of brown or waxed paper. First cut all around the back of the head and just above the tail, then all down the back. Then, slice down at a slight angle behind the collarbone. Holding the knife blade parallel to the fish, with the cutting edge toward the tail and the point toward the cut along the back, cut with a sliding motion along the backbone until you have freed the fillet all the way to the tail. It should come off in one piece. Repeat on the other side to remove the second fillet.

To skin the fillets, place each fillet skin side down. Holding the tail end firmly with your free hand, cut through the flesh of the fillet about $^1/_2$ inch from the tail end. Then flatten the knife against the skin, with the blade pointing toward the top of the fillet, and work the knife forward, as shown, keeping it flat and close against the skin while your other hand continues to hold the skin taut.

An exception to the above procedure must be made with flatfish, which, rather disconcertingly, have both eyes on their upper side, and are skinned and filleted in a special way. Shaped like a flat oval, these fish yield four fillets each. All of them, including turbot, which is less flat than most, can be cooked using recipes for sole or flounder.

FILLETING FISH

You may turn large steaks into two small fillets by cutting along the inside of the skin and the bone of one fillet, as shown. Repeat on the other side. Cut off the thin ends if desired.

To gut a flatfish, cut around the head, making a V-shaped notch. Pull the head away from the body, twisting it. The guts will come away with the head.

To fillet a flatfish, ➤ you may want to first skin the fish (sometimes white skin is not removed): Cut a gash through the skin above the tail. Peel back about $^3/_4$ inch of the skin. Grasp the released skin firmly in one hand and hold the tail flat with your other hand while you pull the skin steadily toward the head. When skinned, ➤ a flatfish reveals a lengthwise indentation down the center that separates the sets of fillets on each side. Cut through the flesh on either side of the spine on the first side. Slip the knife under one fillet, close to the bone, and cut the fillet loose from the backbone, working toward the outside edge of the fish. Repeat with the second fillet, then turn the fish over and repeat on the other side. Discard the unusable entrails, and, unless the fish is a strong-flavored or oily one, keep the bone structure, skin, heads, and tails for Fish Stock, 118.

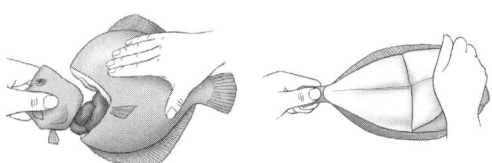

Gutting a flatfish for fillets

ABOUT COOKING FISH

Many of our fish recipes call for cooking in baking dishes. Service is simplified if such dishes are attractive enough to appear on the table. This way, the fish—which is fragile—undergoes less handling, and you have fewer dishes to clean up later. ➤ Allow per serving 1 pound whole small fish, or 4 ounces if the head, tail, and fins have been removed; 8 ounces fish steak; or 8 ounces fillet.

To test fish for doneness, you can insert a thermometer at an angle into the thickest portion of the flesh. For well done, cook fish to an internal temperature of 145°F. ➤ Fish is done enough for most people when the internal temperature reaches 120°F to 135°F.

The general signs of doneness are: a firming up of the flesh, the beginnings of flakiness, and an opaque look throughout. When you suspect that a piece of fish has nearly finished cooking, take a thin-bladed knife and gently poke between the flakes of fillets or steaks. If you like your salmon or swordfish just underdone or your tuna

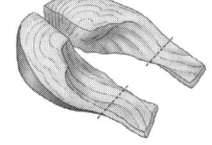

Cutting large steaks into fillets

medium-rare, learn what it looks like inside. Remove the fish just before it reaches the stage at which you want to eat it, as it will continue to cook if placed on a hot plate.

If you don't have a thermometer, stick a wooden toothpick into the thickest part of the fish; if it meets little resistance and comes away clean, in all likelihood it is done. A "rule of finger" for doneness in a soft-fleshed fish is to press it as you would a cake to see if the flesh will return to its original shape. Good cooks know through experience how long to cook their fish, but even they will watch the proceedings with a vigilant eye to guard against over-doneness.

Many fish that are mild in flavor profit by a complementary sauce. If, on the contrary, the fish is strong in flavor, many expert cooks ➤ discard the butter or cooking oil in which it has been cooked. Otherwise, you can deglaze the pan, 546.

If cooked fish is to be served cold, keep it refrigerated until the very last minute. If serving buffet-style, place it over cracked ice. ➤ To keep a whole fish warm, put it on a heated serving platter in an oven set as low as possible. Leave the door ajar. For fillets, treat as for a whole fish, but cover them with a damp warm paper towel or cloth. ➤ Be sure that any sauce served on the fish is very hot. **To keep a sauced fish warm,** use an uncovered double boiler, or place the baking dish in a pan of boiling water and hold uncovered.

To minimize fish tastes and odors, ➤ use lemon, wine, vinegar, ginger, scallions, or garlic in the marinating or cooking. To remove the odor of fish from utensils and dishcloths, use a solution of 1 teaspoon baking soda to 4 cups water. Pans can be washed in hot suds, rinsed and dried, and then rinsed with a little vinegar, and again with water. To remove the odor of fish from your hands, rub them with lemon juice, vinegar, or salt before washing.

To prepare other dishes based on cooked fish and shellfish, see Brunch, Lunch, and Supper Dishes, 95, and Appetizers and Hors d'Oeuvres, 69. For About Fish and Seafood Soups, see 139. To smoke fish, see 907. A great variety of sauces suitable for fish are coupled with individual recipes in this chapter. Others may be found in Sauces, 542.

There are any number of attractive ways to serve and garnish fish. Handsome foundations for cold dishes are salmon, lake trout, halibut, turbot, Dover sole fillets, walleyed pike, and carp. In summer, a mixed vegetable salad or salsa makes a refreshing accompaniment to grilled fish. See Salads, 152, and Sauces, 542. An attractive garnish for fish is delicious, colorful Deep-Fried Parsley, 289.

Following are the descriptions of cooking procedures especially appropriate for fish, such as roasting, steaming, poaching, braising, microwaving, grilling, broiling, plank-roasting, sautéing, panfrying, and deep-frying, each followed by recipes for that type of cooking method. Instructions for curing and pickling and recipes suited to specific kinds of fish complete the chapter.

ABOUT ROASTING OR BAKING FISH

Roasting (or baking) is a highly recommended way of cooking fish: it preserves nearly intact the subtle, distinctive, and delicate fresh flavor of a fish. Roasting at 350°F or even lower allows more leeway in cooking times and better preserves the fish's moisture. High heat is faster, of course, and it delivers a nice crust to fish, as well as adds flavor by browning.

You will find higher- and lower-heat recipes here; they allow you to minimize preparation time and fat content, cook the fish without constant attention, and, if desired, add vegetables to the dish. Generally, ➤ roasting is best for whole fish, steaks, and thick fillets. You can roast any fish whole—size is no limit. Very large fish roast just as well as one-pounders, maybe better, because the longer cooking time allows the skin to become crispy. Thin steaks and fillets can also be roasted long enough to brown, but thin fillets may dry out before they brown and are better cooked under the broiler, 402.

Lightly greased fish is set in an amply large baking dish, or on an oiled rack in the dish that is high enough to clear not only the juices from the fish, but also those that may accumulate if it is basted. The dish should be placed a little higher than the oven center. Line the pan with aluminum foil if you wish for easier cleanup. Firmer-fleshed fish will require longer roasting, as will stuffed fish. Try to turn the fish only once, if at all, and use two spatulas to minimize the risk of it breaking apart. To test for doneness, see About Cooking Fish, 395.

ABOUT SERVING WHOLE FISH

To bone a whole cooked roundfish, remove the skin from one side of the fish with your hands or a fork. With a narrow blade, cut a line down the middle of the exposed side from

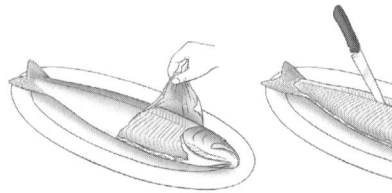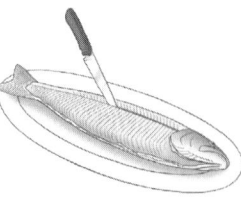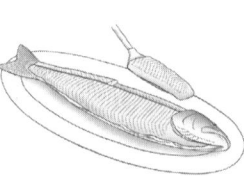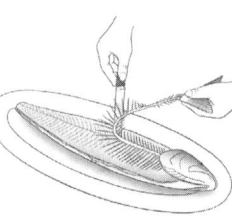

Serving a whole roundfish

head to tail. From both sides of this line, cut pieces 2½ to 3 inches wide and lift them away from the bone structure. Now, beginning at the tail and holding down the bottom fillet with the knife or the back of a fork, free the backbone. The exposed lower fillet is now ready to be served.

To bone a whole cooked flatfish, use a knife or spatula to pull away the small bones along the top and bottom edges. Cut along the midline of the fish to separate the two fillets on the top side. Starting at the backbone, pull each of these fillets up away from the bones, and put on the serving plate. Cut through the backbone at the head, then lift it up and discard it. Separate the two bottom fillets and place them on the serving plate.

ROASTED WHOLE FISH
6 servings
A larger fish may be used, but it will require longer roasting, 1045.
Preheat the oven to 325°F. Scale, clean, 394, and pat dry:
>One 3-pound fish, such as red snapper, tilefish,
>haddock, grouper, char, or salmon

If the fish has a tough skin, slash it in several places. Place it on a greased rack in a baking dish. Brush generously with:
>Clarified Butter, 557, or olive oil

If the fish is lean, you may bard it, 455. If it is not barded, baste it frequently as it cooks with:
>Clarified Butter, 557, or olive oil

Bake about 30 minutes, or until firm and opaque throughout, 395. Serve on a hot platter, garnished with:
>Slices of lemon
>Sprigs of parsley or basil
>(Hot Stuffed Tomatoes, 313)
>(Almond Garnish, 957)

Suitable sauces are:
>Shrimp Sauce, 552, or Mustard Sauce, 552

and, for very mild fish:
>Lorenzo Dressing, 574, Fruit Salsa, 572, or Green
>Sauce, 567

ROASTED STUFFED WHOLE FISH
6 servings
Stuffing for fish should not be so bold in seasoning as to overwhelm the naturally delicate fish flavor. If you bone the fish before stuffing, be sure to leave the skin intact.
Preheat the oven to 325°F. Scale, clean, 394, and pat dry:
>One 3-pound fish, such as red snapper, tilefish,
>haddock, grouper, char, or salmon

Stuff with:
>1½ cups Bread Stuffing with Oysters, 533, Parsley and
>Bread Crumb Stuffing for Fish, 535, or Green Herb
>Dressing for Fish or Poultry, 536

or with a combination of:
>Butter or olive oil, fresh bread crumbs,
>and sliced almonds

Place the fish on a greased rack in a baking dish and bake about 40 minutes, or until firm and opaque throughout. Serve with:
>Onion Sauce, 551, Cream Sauce, 553, Lemon and Parsley
>Butter, 559, Hollandaise, 560, or Béarnaise, 561
>Lime or lemon wedges

ROASTED WHOLE SALMON
8 to 10 servings
This recipe also works well on the grill. Follow the directions below, and grill over indirect heat, 1057. A 7-pounder is the largest salmon that will fit comfortably into a standard oven or a 22½-inch kettle grill.
Preheat the oven to 475°F. Scale, clean, 394, and pat dry:
>One 7-pound salmon

Rub inside and out with:
>2 tablespoons olive oil
>Salt and black pepper to taste

Stuff with:
>1 small lemon, sliced
>Several sprigs thyme

Loosely wrap the head and tail of the fish in aluminum foil. Place on a greased rack set in a baking dish and roast until firm and opaque throughout, about 45 minutes.

Remove the fish to a serving platter with two spatulas. Remove the foil. Cut the skin around the head and tail, and down the top of the back, and gently pull off the skin. Use a blunt knife to push out the line of little bones that run along the top of the back. Then push out the bones that run along the bottom of the belly. Gently cut off the brown flesh. Garnish the platter with:
>Chopped parsley and thyme
>Lemon wedges

BAKED FISH FILLETS IN WHITE WINE
4 servings
Preheat the oven to 350°F. Place in a greased baking dish:
>1½ pounds skinned sole, flounder, or other
>white-fleshed fish fillets

If the fillets are large, they may be cut in half. Pour over them:
>1 cup dry white wine
>(2 tablespoons dry sherry)

Bake until firm and opaque throughout, 25 to 30 minutes. Serve drizzled with the liquid from the dish, which you may boil to reduce slightly. Season with:
>Salt and black pepper to taste

Garnish with:
>Lemon wedges
>(Sautéed Mushrooms, 283)

SOLE DUGLÉRÉ
4 servings
Preheat the oven to 350°F. Dry well between paper towels:
>2 pounds skinned sole fillets

Sprinkle with:

>   2 tablespoons fresh lemon juice

Melt in an ovenproof skillet:

>   3 tablespoons butter

Add:

>   1/4 cup finely chopped shallots
>   1/4 cup finely chopped mushrooms
>   2 tablespoons very finely chopped parsley

Add the fish and:

>   1 cup dry white wine

Bring to a boil. Reduce the heat at once and cover pan with buttered parchment paper. Transfer the pan to the oven and bake about 10 minutes, or until the fish is firm and opaque throughout. Meanwhile, peel, 311, seed, and dice:

>   1 pound tomatoes

Remove the fish to a buttered baking dish; reserve the stock. If necessary, reduce the stock to about 1/2 cup. Use it to prepare:

>   White Wine Sauce for Fish, 552

replacing the stock and wine in the recipe. Preheat the broiler. When the sauce thickens, add the tomatoes. Pour the sauce over the fish. Sprinkle the top generously with:

>   Grated Parmesan

Mixed with:

>   A dash of paprika

Run under the broiler until the sauce colors.

HIGH-HEAT ROASTED FISH FILLETS

4 servings

This technique works with most fillets. Fillets from flatfish such as flounder or sole will be cooked in 3 to 5 minutes. Fillets of cod and other delicate white fish will be done at a rate of about 8 minutes per inch of thickness; those of sturdier white fish, such as red snapper, or dark-fleshed fish, such as mackerel, at 9 to 10 minutes per inch of thickness. To avoid overcooking, remove the fish from the oven just as the last traces of remaining translucence begin to disappear.

Preheat the oven to 500°F. Lightly grease a rimmed baking sheet or shallow roasting pan with a little oil or butter. Lay in the pan:

>   1 1/2 to 2 pounds skinned fish fillets in 1 to 4 pieces, rinsed and patted dry

Brush with:

>   1 tablespoon olive oil or melted butter

Season with:

>   Salt and black pepper to taste

Roast, undisturbed, until firm and opaque throughout. Serve with:

>   Minced parsley and lemon wedges, Champagne or White Wine Sauce for Fish, 552, Onion Sauce, 551, White Butter Sauce, 558, a flavored butter, 558, or a flavored oil, 590, or a Vinaigrette, 572

SLOW-ROASTED FISH FILLETS

4 servings

You can drizzle almost anything over these fillets: Orange Oil, 590; soy sauce warmed with a little sesame oil and several drops of vinegar; Pesto Sauce, 569, thinned with oil or broth; or Fresh Tomato Sauce, 563. You can even top them with Mashed Potatoes, 295. The gentle cooking ensures that the fish remains moist and tender.

Preheat the oven to 325°F. Coat a shallow baking dish with:

>   1 teaspoon olive oil

Place in the dish, skin side up:

>   2 thick skin-on fish fillets, such as salmon, cod, halibut, or swordfish, about 12 ounces each and 1 1/4 inches thick at the thickest point, rinsed and patted dry

Place the fish in the oven. After 15 minutes, check the internal temperature with an instant-read thermometer. When the temperature reaches 125°F, remove the fish from the oven and let stand for 3 minutes. Or, flake a bit of fish off the fillet and check that it is opaque throughout. Remove the skin and turn the fillets over.

MOLDED FILLED FISH FILLETS (PAUPIETTES)

4 Servings

Preheat the oven to 350°F. Have ready:

>   8 skinned sole or bluefish fillets or other very thin fillets

Butter 4 individual 8-ounce molds or ramekins. Line each mold with 2 fillets, crisscrossing them at the bottom and extending up the sides. The fillets must be long enough, when folded over, to overlap at the top. Combine in a bowl and blend with a fork:

>   1/4 cup (1/2 stick) butter, melted
>   1 1/2 cups fresh bread crumbs, 961
>   1/4 cup chopped celery
>   1 tablespoon chopped parsley
>   1 teaspoon chopped onion
>   1/4 teaspoon salt
>   (1/8 teaspoon dried basil)

Fill the molds with this filling, and fold the ends of fillets over the top. Place the molds in a pan of hot water, 742. Bake until firm and opaque throughout, about 30 minutes. Unmold the paupiettes onto a hot platter. Garnish with:

>   Lemon wedges
>   Sprigs of parsley or watercress

Serve with:

>   Lemon Butter, 557, Oyster Sauce, 552, Hollandaise, 560, or Anchovy Sauce, 552

FISH EN PAPILLOTE

For a party, make individual packets ahead of time and refrigerate. Let them sit at room temperature for 10 to 15 minutes before baking.

Preheat the oven to 450°F. For each serving, place on a heart-shaped piece of parchment paper, 1053:

**2 medium skinned pompano, perch, snapper,
or trout fillets**

Cover with:

Shrimp Sauce, 552

Dot with:

1 tablespoon butter

Close the parchment paper and fold and crimp the edges. Bake about 15 minutes, until the paper is browned and puffed and the fish is firm and opaque throughout. Serve immediately.

COD BOULANGÈRE

4 servings

Preheat the oven to 350°F. Cook in a medium saucepan of boiling water until tender but not mushy, 15 to 20 minutes:

16 small potatoes, peeled

Meanwhile, cook in a small saucepan of boiling water:

12 pearl onions, peeled

Place in a buttered shallow baking dish:

**One center-cut cod fillet (about 24 ounces) or
a small cod, scaled, cleaned, 394, and
patted dry**

Arrange the potatoes and onions around it and sprinkle with:

A pinch of thyme

Salt and black pepper to taste

Bake until firm and opaque throughout, 20 to 30 minutes, brushing frequently with:

Melted butter

Serve in the baking dish, garnished with:

Chopped parsley

Lemon slices

FISH BAKED IN SALT

4 servings

Baking fish in coarse salt is one of the finest, simplest, and most flavorful ways to prepare it, for the salt crust acts as a moist "oven," enveloping the entire fish and baking it gently and evenly.

Preheat the oven to 500°F. Cover the bottom of a baking dish that is just large enough to hold the fish with a 1/2-inch layer of:

Coarse salt

Rinse and pat dry:

**One 2- to 3-pound center-cut fish fillet, such as
salmon, or one 2- to 3-pound whole fish, such as
red snapper, grouper, porgy, tilefish, rockfish, or
other white-fleshed fish, cleaned, 394, but not
scaled**

Lay the fish on the salt and pour enough salt over and around it to cover all of its surfaces by at least 1/4 inch. Bake for 30 minutes. Poke through the salt into the thickest part of the fish with a thermometer. The fish is done at

130°F; it will likely take 10 to 15 minutes more to reach this temperature. Remove the pan from the oven and let stand for 5 minutes.

Remove the fish to a platter and brush off all the salt (some of it will have caked, but it will come off easily). Remove to a serving plate and remove the skin (it, too, will come off easily). Serve garnished with:

Lemon wedges

and drizzle over the top:

Extra-virgin olive oil

or serve with:

**Champagne or White Wine Sauce, 553, Onion Sauce,
551, or Lemon Butter, 557**

FISH BAKED IN A COVERED DISH

4 servings

Cooking time depends on the shape of the fillets.

Preheat the oven to 350°F. Combine:

2 tablespoons butter, softened

1/8 teaspoon black pepper or paprika

A grating of nutmeg

Rub the mixture over:

**2 pounds skinned haddock, grouper, tilapia, or other
white-fleshed fish fillets**

Place the fish in a baking dish. Cover tightly with a lid or aluminum foil and bake until firm and opaque throughout, 20 to 25 minutes. You may add while cooking:

(2 tablespoons dry white wine)

Place the fish on a hot platter and keep warm. Sauté in a small saucepan:

3 tablespoons butter

Add:

2 tablespoons capers

1 teaspoon chopped parsley

1 teaspoon chopped chives

2 teaspoons fresh lemon juice

Salt and black pepper to taste

Pour the sauce over the fish.

FISH BAKED IN FOIL

2 servings

Please read Foil Cookery, 1052. Preheat the oven to 500°F. Scale and clean:

1 pound or less small whole fish, fillets or steaks

Rub with:

Flavored Butter, 558

Place each fish or fillet on a piece of buttered aluminum foil large enough to envelop the fish with a generous fold. Place on a baking sheet and bake until firm and opaque throughout, 10 to 15 minutes.

ABOUT STEAMING AND POACHING OR BRAISING FISH

Steaming is one of the better ways to cook a delicate lean fish if you want to retain flavor. Poaching fish—sometimes called **braising** in fish cookery—runs a close second.

A steamer tray is designed to hold the fish above the water level. A fish poacher is a special cooking vessel with a rack that holds the fish either just above or immersed in liquid. ➤ A poaching rack is always greased before the fish is placed on it. Fish may be poached in fumet, 118, Court Bouillon, 120, or Express Fish Stock, 120, depending on the flavor you wish to impart and/or the degree of whiteness you desire. If you are chiefly concerned with preserving the true flavor of the fish, salted water may well be all you care to use. ➤ Allow 1 tablespoon of salt for every 2 quarts of water.

If a fumet or light stock is used for the steaming or poaching liquid, you may want to use some of it, either as is or reduced, in the sauce. **To reduce the cooking liquid,** strain it into a wide saucepan and simmer until it has thickened to the desired consistency (if it goes too far, you can always add a little water).

Court bouillons are not used in sauces because they are apt to contain too much vinegar and salt. If you want to reuse the poaching liquid, after you are finished cooking, boil it for 2 minutes, then cool, strain, and refrigerate up to 3 days or freeze indefinitely. It pays to brighten it a bit with fresh herbs, spices, and vinegar every time you use it.

Please read Poaching, 1050. Small fish or fish fillets or steaks are started in boiling liquid, large fish or pieces in cold liquid, because ➤ immersing a fish of any considerable size in boiling water will cause the skin to shrink and split. In either case, when the liquid reaches the boiling point, ➤ immediately reduce it to a simmer for the remainder of the cooking period. Allow 5 to 8 minutes per pound, depending on the size of the fish.

Without a poacher, there is the problem of keeping the top of the fish constantly bathed in liquid or steam. This problem can be solved by the use of parchment, or poaching, paper, 1050, or by wrapping the fish loosely in cheesecloth. The latter procedure is a great help, after cooking, in lifting the fish out of the pan.

If a large pan is not available, cut a whole fish crosswise in two and place it in the smaller pan, with the halves side by side. The fish can be reassembled on a platter later and the cut masked with a sauce. Whatever pan you use, add several onion and lemon slices, a chopped carrot, and a few celery ribs. Fill the pan with the liquid of your choice, to within an inch of the top of the pan. If you use a cloth wrapping, baste the fish with the cooking liquid as it simmers on the stove or in the oven, ➤ making sure that the cloth is always completely soaked. The top of the fish will then cook as quickly as the bottom.

After cooking, the fish is sometimes allowed to cool in the liquid. We do not recommend this practice, as it leads to overcooking and waterlogging. ➤ If the fish is to be served cold, it is easier to remove the skin and trim the fish while it is still warm.

POACHED FISH
4 servings

This easy method consistently results in a moist piece of fish, and it works as well with a whole fish, a section of a whole fish, or a sizable fillet. Try it with cod, sturgeon, turbot, bass, char, or halibut, as well as salmon. If you want to poach steaks, see Fish Steaks Poached in White Wine, below.

Place in a pot large enough to hold it comfortably:

> **One 3-pound salmon, scaled and cleaned, one 2- to 3-pound center-cut piece salmon, or one 2- to 3-pound center-cut salmon fillet**

Cover with cold water. Add:

> **1 tablespoon salt**

Bring to a boil over high heat, then immediately remove from the heat. Let stand for 10 minutes. Remove the fish from the water, drain, and serve or refrigerate until ready to serve. Before serving, bring the fish to room temperature, and peel off the skin. Season with:

> **Salt and black pepper to taste**

Garnish with:

> **Herb sprigs**

Serve with one or several of the following:

> **Any flavored mayonnaise, 578, thinned with sour cream, Scandinavian Mustard Dill Sauce, 566, Paprika Sauce, 553, Asian Black Bean Sauce, 570, or Orange and Ginger Sauce, 549**

FISH STEAKS POACHED IN WHITE WINE
4 servings

Use any fish steaks you like in this recipe: salmon, cod, sturgeon, turbot, and halibut are all good. If you prefer, you can poach the fish in Court Bouillon, 120.

Please read About Steaming and Poaching or Braising Fish, 399. Combine in a deep skillet or casserole large enough to hold the fish in a single layer:

> **2 cups dry white wine**
> **2 cups water**
> **2 tablespoons rice, sherry, or white wine vinegar**
> **1 teaspoon salt**
> **10 whole black peppercorns**
> **10 coriander seeds**
> **2 whole cloves**
> **1 bay leaf**
> **1 garlic clove**
> **Several sprigs parsley, thyme, or tarragon or**
> **¹/₂ teaspoon dried**

Bring to a boil, uncovered, over high heat, then reduce the heat and simmer for 5 minutes. Gently place in the poaching liquid:

> **1¹/₂ to 2 pounds fish steaks (4 small or 2 large), rinsed**

Cover the pan and adjust the heat so that the liquid is gently simmering. Cook for 8 minutes, then check for doneness, 395. Remove the fish when the flesh is still slightly translucent. Serve hot, at room temperature, or chilled, with:

mayonnaise, 578–581, Vinaigrette, 572–575,
or Mousseline Sauce, 561

BRAISED WHOLE FISH WITH RED WINE SAUCE

4 to 6 servings

Ideal fish for this dish are red snapper or grouper, which are found easily in larger sizes; striped or black sea bass and salmon are other possibilities. Serve with plenty of crusty bread for mopping up the sauce.

Please read About Steaming and Poaching or Braising Fish, 399. Soak in hot water to cover:

1 to 2 tablespoons dried porcini mushrooms

Meanwhile, heat over low heat in a deep skillet, casserole, or roasting pan large enough to hold the fish:

$^1/_4$ cup vegetable oil

Prepare:

1 cup Seasoned Flour, 962

Coat with the seasoned flour:

One 3- to 5-pound red snapper or other fish, scaled, cleaned, and patted dry

Increase the heat under the pan to high and heat the oil until hot. Add the fish and brown for about 5 minutes on each side, turning carefully only once and making sure that a nice dark crust develops.

Remove the fish to a platter. Pour the fat from the pan and wipe it out with paper towels. Reheat the pan over medium heat. Add:

2 tablespoons olive oil or butter

8 ounces mushrooms, sliced

Cook, stirring, for a minute or two. Lift the porcini from the soaking water, and strain the water through cheesecloth. Chop the porcini and add them, along with 2 tablespoons of the soaking water, to the cooking mushrooms. Add:

1 cup chopped onions

1 teaspoon minced garlic

1 teaspoon fresh thyme leaves or a scant $^1/_2$ teaspoon dried thyme

Salt and black pepper to taste

Cook, stirring occasionally, until the onions have softened, about 8 minutes. Add the remaining porcini water, along with:

1 cup dry red wine

1 bay leaf

Bring to a boil, stir, and reduce the heat to medium-low. Set the fish in the pan, cover, and cook gently until the fish is firm and opaque throughout, 15 to 20 minutes for a 3-pound fish, 25 to 30 minutes for a 5-pound fish. Carefully remove the fish to a platter.

If the sauce is too thin, boil, stirring over high heat, until reduced to the desired consistency. Remove the bay leaf, spoon the sauce over the fish, and serve garnished with plenty of:

Minced parsley

POACHED QUENELLES

4 to 6 servings

Once encountered, never forgotten is the texture of a well-made quenelle. Success lies not only in the mixing but in the very shaping. Use any delicate white-fleshed fish and poach in either fish stock or water.

Have ready a well-buttered wide-bottomed pan or large skillet. Combine in a food processor:

$1^1/_2$ pounds fresh cleaned or shelled pike, sole, shrimp, or lobster

Place the ground mixture in a large bowl and set into a large bowl of ice. With a wooden spoon, work it to a smooth paste. Gradually work in by small additions:

2 egg whites

Season with:

Grated nutmeg

Salt

White Pepper

Dash of Cognac

Dash of cayenne or hot pepper sauce

Mix well. At this point, the quenelle mixture should be very firm. Still over ice, add gradually and mix well with the spoon:

2 to $2^1/_2$ cups well-chilled whipping cream

The consistency should be that of a firm whipped cream. The classic method of shaping uses two spoons of equal size. Run one spoon under hot water and scoop up the quenelle mixture. Use the other spoon over top to form the quenelle and smooth the surface. It will double in size when cooked. Put in the buttered pan. Repeat until the pan is full. Boil:

Fish stock or water

Cover the quenelles halfway with the boiling liquid and simmer gently for 8 to 10 minutes. As the undersides cook, the quenelles will rise and turn over. Remove with a slotted spoon.

Serve with:

Newburg Sauce, 561, Poulette Sauce, 554, or Cream Sauce, 553

GEFILTE FISH

10 servings

Fillet and skin, 395:

3 pounds mixed lean and fat fish, 413: whitefish, bluefish, jack, salmon, pike, and/or carp

Combine the fish in a food processor with:

1 large onion

1 rib celery

$^1/_4$ cup chopped parsley

Pulse until finely ground. Remove the fish mixture to a bowl and stir in:

3 eggs, beaten

3 tablespoons matzo meal or crushed crackers

1 tablespoon salt

1 tablespoon black or white pepper

1 tablespoon sugar

Add, folding in slowly to create a fluffy texture:

$^{3}/_{4}$ to 1 cup ice water

Dip your hands in chilled water and shape the mixture into 1-inch balls. Bring to a boil in a large pot:

4 quarts Fish Stock or Fumet, 118

Gently drop the fish balls into the stock (there should be enough room for them to puff up), cover, and simmer 1$^{1}/_{2}$ hours. Add:

1 carrot, sliced

Simmer, uncovered, 30 minutes longer. With a slotted spoon, remove the balls and layer in a large baking dish with high sides. Reserve the stock. Sprinkle:

2 envelopes (4$^{1}/_{2}$ teaspoons) unflavored gelatin

over:

$^{1}/_{2}$ cup cold water

and allow it to soften for 5 minutes. Stir the gelatin into 8 cups of the stock until dissolved. If there is any stock left over, it can be frozen. Pour the mixture over the fish balls. Cover and refrigerate until set, about 2 hours. Serve the fish cold with some of the jelly, along with:

Grated horseradish

Sprigs of dill

FILLETS OF SOLE FLORENTINE

6 servings

Please read About Steaming and Poaching or Braising Fish, 399. Poach, 1050:

6 sole or other white-fleshed fish fillets

Preheat the broiler. Spoon into the bottom of a deep oven-proof platter:

1$^{1}/_{2}$ cups Creamed Spinach, 305

Arrange the drained poached fillets on top. Cover with:

1 cup seasoned White Sauce II, 550

Sprinkle over it:

Au Gratin III, 961

Run under the broiler until the crumbs are browned.

ABOUT MICROWAVING FISH

For simple fish dishes that are most like steamed fish, in very small quantities, the microwave does a credible job. The rules are straightforward: Get used to cooking fish in your microwave, so that you can get a sense of how long the cooking will take (the alternative is opening the oven door every 30 seconds). ➤ Cook small portions, never more than a pound, and preferably less. Do not use a lot of liquid. And keep added ingredients few—the more you include, the more likely that half the dish will be done and the other half not.

MICROWAVED FISH FILLETS

2 servings

Flaky white fish such as cod, perch, or trout works beautifully in this basic recipe.

Arrange on a plate with the thickest edge toward the outside:

8 to 12 ounces fish fillets, up to 1 inch thick, preferably in 2 pieces, rinsed and patted dry

Season with:

Salt and black pepper to taste

Sprinkle with:

1 tablespoon fish stock or broth, Court Bouillon, 120, dry white wine, or fresh lemon or lime juice

Cover with another plate or plastic wrap. Microwave on high for 3 minutes, 2 minutes if you are using flounder or other flatfish, 4 minutes if the fillets approach an inch in thickness. To check for doneness, see 395. If the fish is nearly done, cover it and let it stand for a minute to finish cooking. If it needs more time, continue to microwave in 1- to 2-minute bursts, to avoid overcooking. Drizzle over the fish:

Extra-virgin olive oil

Serve with:

Lemon wedges

ABOUT GRILLING AND BROILING FISH

"Ruling a large kingdom," observed Lao-tzu, "is like cooking a small fish." What he meant was that both should be discreetly handled, and the treatment never overdone. We have usually respected the old philosopher's advice. But in grilling and broiling fish, we have discovered that they taste even better when they are subjected to quite high, rather than gentle, heat. Grilling and broiling are ideal techniques for cooking many fish. The intense heat complements the flavor of the fish by charring its surface; often, little more added flavor is needed. In grilling, the heat is beneath the food; in broiling, it is from above.

Delicate white fish and thin fillets are virtually impossible to grill. Best for grilling are thick steaks such as swordfish, salmon, tuna, and small firm whole fish such as mackerel, pompano, and red snapper—as well as, of course, many shellfish.

When grilling, make sure the grill grates are clean, and brush the fish and grate with olive oil. Use a medium-hot fire. To test the heat of a charcoal fire or grill, see 1058.

Grills vary, but the rack is usually about 4 inches above the fire. If cooking fillets, start grilling the fish skin side down. If the skin sticks to the grill rack, do not worry. A grilling basket can make grilling fillets easier. If the fillet is not too large, you can cover the grill and not turn the fish during cooking at all.

When broiling, use a ➤ lightly oiled baking sheet. If the fish is to be turned, a wire basket may also be conveniently used in the oven broiler pan. Grease the basket with olive oil, and the fish with olive oil or Clarified Butter, 557. A lean fish may be floured before dotting with butter.

Fillets, flat, and split fish are usually placed about 2 to 3 inches from the source of heat. If unskinned, place them skin side down. It is not necessary to turn them, but it is advisable to baste several times during the cooking period.

If thick fish steaks or large fish are being broiled, place the rack about 6 inches from the source of heat. They may take as long to cook as 5 or 6 minutes to a side.

Good fish for broiling include: halibut or salmon steaks,

sole, and its cousins, split herring, mackerel, and sea trout. For swordfish steaks, be sure to baste with plenty of butter, as they tend to become dry. Melted butter, lemon wedges, and parsley adequately garnish broiled fish.

In addition to the recipes here, rub fish with Mediterranean Garlic Herb Paste, 589, before grilling or serve simply grilled or broiled fish with any of the following, choosing richer sauces for leaner fish and vice versa: Flavored Butters, 558, Flavored Oils, 590, Lemon Butter Sauce, 558, White Butter Sauce, 558, Tomato Concassé, 563, or Fresh Tomato Sauce, 563, Green Sauce, 567, vinaigrettes, 572, Fruit Salsa, 572, Roasted Tomatillo Spinach Sauce, 568, or Roasted Red Pepper Sauce, 549.

GRILLED OR BROILED WHOLE FISH
4 servings

Please read About Grilling and Broiling Fish, 402. Brush:

> **Four 1- to 1½-pound fish, scaled, cleaned, 394,**
> **and patted dry**

with:

> **1 tablespoon olive oil**

Sprinkle with:

> **Salt and black pepper**

Place them on the grill or under the broiler. Grill or broil until firm and opaque throughout and browned on the first side, 3 to 6 minutes; turn and cook the other side until browned, 3 to 5 minutes more. Serve immediately, with:

> **Lemon wedges, several drops of vinegar,**
> **or Tart Corn Relish, 948**

GRILLED OR BROILED WHOLE FISH WITH BACON
4 servings

If you catch your own trout, there is nothing better, but if you are shopping, fresh mackerel is the tastier and less expensive choice.

Please read About Grilling and Broiling Fish, 402. Sprinkle:

> **4 mackerel or trout (1 to 1¼ pounds each), scaled if**
> **necessary, cleaned, 394, and patted dry**

with:

> **Salt and black pepper to taste**

Wrap each fish in:

> **1 or 2 slices bacon**

Place the fish on the grill or under the broiler. Cover the grill if possible and cook for 3 to 4 minutes, taking care not to burn the bacon. Move the fish to a cooler part of the grill or lower the broiler rack if necessary. Turn and continue to cook, then turn again if necessary. The fish is done when the bacon is crisp and the flesh is firm and opaque throughout, 12 to 15 minutes.

GRILLED WHOLE RED SNAPPER WITH GINGER-SOY VINAIGRETTE
4 servings

Please read About Grilling and Broiling Fish, 402. This recipe can be adapted for broiling. Toast in a small dry skillet over medium-high heat:

> **¾ cup coriander seeds**
> **2 tablespoons crushed red pepper flakes**

Grind the spices coarsely with a spice mill. Season with:

> **Salt and black pepper to taste**

Rub the spice mixture all over, inside and out:

> **2 red snapper or other fish (1½ to 2 pounds each),**
> **scaled, cleaned, and patted dry**

Place the fish on the grill, and cover the grill if possible. Cook, undisturbed, until the side of the fish facing the heat is brown and blistered, about 8 minutes. Turn carefully and cook until the meat near the bone is firm and opaque throughout, 8 to 10 minutes. Serve immediately, with:

> **2 cups Ginger Soy Sauce, 571**

GRILLED WHOLE TROUT STUFFED WITH PESTO
4 servings

This recipe can be adapted for broiling. Trout are among the easiest fish to grill whole.

Please read About Grilling and Broiling Fish, 402. Prepare:

> **1½ cups Pesto Sauce, 569, or Pistou, 569**

Prepare a medium-hot grill fire. Make sure the grill rack is oiled. Sprinkle:

> **4 small trout (about 12 ounces each), cleaned, 394,**
> **and patted dry**

with:

> **Salt and black pepper to taste**

Place one-quarter of the pesto in the body cavity of each trout. Place the trout on the grill rack and grill for 4 to 5 minutes per side, or until golden brown and blistered on the outside and opaque throughout.

BROILED FISH FILLETS WITH LEMON
4 servings

This recipe can be adapted for grilling. This is a basic recipe, useful for many types of fish. Substitute butter for the olive oil if you like. When broiling fillets of oily fish such as bluefish or mahimahi, use 1 or 2 teaspoons of fresh lemon juice or vinegar in place of the oil.

Please read About Grilling and Broiling Fish, 402. Preheat the broiler. Oil a baking sheet or shallow roasting pan. Place on the oiled pan:

> **1½ to 2 pounds fish fillets, skin on or off, in 1 or more**
> **pieces, rinsed and patted dry**

Brush lightly with:

> **1 to 2 tablespoons olive oil or melted butter**

Sprinkle with:

> **Salt and black pepper to taste**

Place the fish under the broiler and broil undisturbed for 4 minutes. Fillets that are ½ inch thick or less are done as soon as the exterior turns opaque. If they are thicker, check after 6 minutes. Fish up to 1 inch thick probably will be done at this point; thicker fillets will need another couple of minutes and should be basted with a little more oil. Those over 1 1/2 inches thick should be turned and cooked another 5 or 6 minutes until firm and opaque throughout. Sprinkle with:

2 teaspoons fresh lemon juice

Serve with:

Minced parsley and lemon wedges

BROILED FISH FILLETS WITH HERBS

This recipe can be adapted for grilling.

Please read About Grilling and Broiling Fish, 402. Prepare **Broiled Fish Fillets with Lemon, above.** Stir **2 tablespoons chopped herbs** (any combination of **parsley, chervil, basil, thyme, and/or fennel**) into the olive oil. If the fillets are 1/2 inch thick or less, spread this paste on them before broiling. Rub thicker fillets with some olive oil and spread the herb paste on them 3 or 4 minutes before they are done.

BROILED FISH FILLETS WITH SEASONED BREAD CRUMBS

This recipe can be adapted for grilling.

Please read About Grilling and Broiling Fish, 402. Heat in a skillet over medium heat until the oil is hot or the butter is melted and the foam has begun to subside:

3 tablespoons olive oil or butter

Add:

3/4 cup fresh bread crumbs, 961

Salt and black pepper to taste

Cook, tossing, until the crumbs have darkened and become crisp, about 1 minute. Drain on paper towels.

Prepare:

Broiled Fish Fillets with Lemon, 403

If the fillets are 1/2 inch thick or less, omit the olive oil or butter and spread the bread crumb mixture on them before broiling. Rub thicker fillets with some olive oil or melted butter and spread the bread crumb mixture on them 3 to 4 minutes before they are done. Serve with:

Parsley and lemon wedges or any of the suggested accompaniments on 403

GRILLED OR BROILED FISH STEAKS

4 servings

Steaks should be at least 1 inch thick so that they will not cook too quickly; if possible, buy 2 large ones rather than 4 small ones. Consider serving this (or any grilled or broiled fish) with Vinaigrette, 572, slightly warmed in the microwave or over low heat. Please read About Grilling and Broiling Fish, 402. Prepare a medium-hot grill fire or preheat the broiler. Brush:

1 1/2 pounds fish steaks such as tuna, salmon, or swordfish (2 large or 4 small), at least 1 inch thick, rinsed and patted dry

with:

1 tablespoon olive oil

Sprinkle with:

Salt and black pepper to taste

Place them on the grill or under the broiler. Grill or broil until firm and opaque throughout and browned on the first side, 3 to 6 minutes. Turn and grill the other side until browned, 3 to 5 minutes more. Serve immediately, with:

Lemon wedges, several drops of vinegar, any of the suggested accompaniments on 403, or Tart Corn Relish, 948

BARBECUE-RUBBED GRILLED BLUEFISH

4 servings

This recipe can be adapted for broiling. This dish borrows the robust flavors of Southern barbecue in the form of a spice rub. As the fish cooks, the rub forms a dense, flavorful crust on the outside, leaving the inside moist and tender. Also try this with other firm fish such as mahimahi, salmon, or red mullet.

Please read About Grilling and Broiling Fish, 402. Prepare a medium-hot grill. Make sure the grill rack is oiled. Prepare:

Sweet Spice Rub, 588

Rub generously over both sides of:

4 skinless bluefish fillets (8 ounces each), about 1 1/2 inches thick

Place the fillets on the grill rack and grill for 8 to 10 minutes per side, or until opaque throughout. Remove and serve at once with:

Spicy Tartar Sauce, 581

GRILLED FISH STEAKS WITH TOMATO-OLIVE RELISH

4 servings

This recipe can be adapted for broiling.

Please read About Grilling and Broiling Fish, 402. Prepare a medium-hot grill fire. Mix well in a small bowl:

2 ripe tomatoes, diced

1 large red onion, diced

1/2 cup pitted black olives, cut in half if desired

1/4 cup olive oil

1/4 cup fresh lemon juice

1/4 cup chopped basil

1 teaspoon minced garlic

Salt and black pepper to taste

Brush:

4 swordfish, salmon, or tuna steaks (6 to 8 ounces each), 1 inch thick, rinsed and patted dry

with:

2 tablespoons vegetable oil

Sprinkle with:

Salt and black pepper to taste

Place on the grill rack and grill over a medium fire for 5 to 6 minutes per side, or until opaque throughout. Serve with the relish.

GRILLED TUNA WITH PICKLED GINGER, SOY SAUCE, AND WASABI

4 servings

This recipe can be adapted for broiling.

Please read About Grilling and Broiling Fish, 402. Prepare a medium-hot grill fire. Brush:

4 tuna steaks (10 to 12 ounces each), about 2 inches thick, rinsed and patted dry

with:

¼ cup vegetable oil

Sprinkle with:

Salt and black pepper to taste

Place on the grill rack and grill over a medium-hot fire, turning once, 4 to 5 minutes per side for rare, 5 to 7 minutes per side for medium-rare, or 7 to 9 minutes per side for medium. Serve, accompanying each serving with a small dish containing:

2 to 3 tablespoons soy sauce (½ to ¾ cup total)
Wasabi paste
Pickled Ginger, 952

ABOUT SHAD ROE

Shad roe is a sac of millions of tiny eggs held together by a membrane. The two crescent-shaped parts are usually divided and one half will serve one person; it is very rich and filling. The flavor is like nothing else, delicate and not very fishy; the texture is dense and chewy. It is only available in the early spring when the shad are running. Be careful not to overcook, for it continues to cook after being removed from the heat. It should be darker in the center, not uniformly pink throughout.

BROILED SHAD ROE

2 servings

Preheat the broiler. Gently separate the 2 parts and pat dry:

1 pair shad roe

Place on a greased rack in the broiler pan and sprinkle with:

Fresh lemon juice

Drape the roe with:

4 slices uncooked bacon

Broil 5 to 7 minutes, until firm and springy to the touch. If the roe is large, you may have to turn it, baste it with the drippings, and continue to cook until firm. Serve on:

Warm toast

Garnished with:

Lemon and Parsley Butter, 559
Chopped parsley

FISH KEBABS

4 servings

Please read About Grilling and Broiling Fish, 402, and Skewer Cooking, 1049. Prepare a medium-hot grill fire or preheat the broiler. Rinse, pat dry, and cut into 1½-inch cubes:

1½ to 2 pounds thick fish steaks or fillets

Whisk together in a small bowl:

½ cup balsamic vinegar
¼ cup fresh lemon juice
1 teaspoon minced garlic
½ teaspoon sugar
Salt and black pepper to taste

Set aside. Whisk together in a large bowl:

⅓ cup olive oil
¼ cup fresh lemon juice
⅓ cup chopped basil
Salt and black pepper to taste

Add the fish and toss to coat. Add and toss to combine:

2 nectarines or peaches, pitted, quartered, and each quarter halved crosswise
2 red bell peppers, cored, seeded, quartered, and each quarter halved crosswise
2 red onions, cut into 8 wedges each

Thread the fish, nectarines, bell peppers, and onions onto 4 (or 8, if you prefer) metal or wooden skewers (if you use wood, it is best to soak them in water first, 1049); do not crowd. Thread any leftover basil on the skewers as well. Grill or broil the skewers, turning as each side browns and brushing occasionally with any remaining marinade, 10 to 15 minutes. Remove from the grill, drizzle with the balsamic vinegar mixture, and serve immediately.

TERIYAKI-GRILLED FISH STEAKS

4 servings

The secret to succulent teriyaki is to apply the glaze bit by bit toward the end of the grilling process so that it browns but does not burn. The technique also works well with eel, and boneless chicken breasts or thighs.

Please read About Grilling and Broiling Fish, 402. Combine in a small saucepan:

⅔ cup soy sauce
½ cup mirin
1 tablespoon sugar

Cook, stirring, over medium heat until the sugar is dissolved. Increase the heat slightly and cook, stirring occasionally, until foamy. Reduce the heat and simmer, stirring constantly, until the mixture is reduced by half. Let cool. (The whole recipe makes enough for about 10 servings; leftover sauce can be stored in the refrigerator for up to 1 month.)

Place in a baking dish:

4 salmon, tuna, or other fish steaks (6 to 8 ounces each), at least 1 inch thick, rinsed and patted dry

Add, turning to coat the fish:

1 cup sake

Cover and marinate in the refrigerator for about 15 minutes, turning 2 or 3 times.

Meanwhile, prepare a hot grill fire or preheat the broiler. Make sure the grill rack is oiled and place it about 4 inches from the heat on a grill, or place an oven rack 2 to 3 inches from the broiler heat. Remove the fish from the sake and pat dry. Place on the grill rack or broiler pan and sprinkle very lightly with:

Coarse salt

Grill or broil for 2 minutes, until the fish begins to brown. Turn and grill or broil for 2 minutes more. Move the fish to a cooler part of the grill, or move the broiler rack down a notch. Brush the fish with the teriyaki glaze and grill or broil, with the glazed surface facing the heat, until the glaze dries, about 1 minute. Brush the other side and grill or broil, again with the glazed surface toward the heat, until the glaze dries. The fish should be done or nearly so. To check for doneness, see 395. If it needs another few minutes, repeat the brushing and cooking procedure once or twice. Serve with additional teriyaki sauce.

BROILED FISH FILLETS WITH TOMATOES AND HERBS

4 servings

This recipe can be adapted for grilling.

Please read About Grilling and Broiling Fish, 402. Combine in a bowl:

2 very ripe beefsteak tomatoes, cored, seeded, and cut into 1/2-inch dice

5 tablespoons olive oil

3 tablespoons soy sauce

2 tablespoons fresh lemon juice

1 1/2 cups fresh basil leaves

2 teaspoons finely chopped mint

1/2 teaspoon cracked black pepper

Cover the salsa and let stand for 30 to 40 minutes. Preheat the broiler. Generously brush all sides of:

4 firm fish fillets (6 to 7 ounces each), such as salmon, black sea bass, or haddock

with:

2 tablespoons olive oil

Season well with:

Salt and black pepper

Brush:

Eight 1/2-inch-thick onion slices

with:

Olive oil

Season with:

Salt and black pepper to taste

Place the fish on a broiler pan and overlap 2 onion slices on each fillet. Broil about 8 inches from the heat until the onions have wilted and caramelized, 12 to 15 minutes. Do not worry if the onions char here and there, but if they start to blacken, cover with foil. Check the fish for doneness: it should be opaque throughout. Remove the fish to plates and serve with the tomato salsa.

GRILLED SALMON FILLETS WITH MAYONNAISE

4 servings

This recipe can be adapted for broiling.

Please read About Grilling and Broiling Fish, 402. Prepare a medium-hot grill fire. Sprinkle:

4 salmon fillets (8 ounces each), rinsed and patted dry

with:

Salt and black pepper to taste

Place on the grill rack and grill for 5 to 6 minutes per side, or until opaque throughout. Serve with:

Sauce Louis, 581, Chipotle Mayonnaise, 580, or Watercress Mayonnaise, 581

PLANK-ROASTED FISH

4 servings

This cooking method is adaptable to many seasonings. Try coating the fish with Dijon mustard and brown sugar or prepared horseradish.

Soak for at least 6 hours:

A 6 x 12-inch plank of untreated hardwood

Preheat the oven to 450°F or prepare a hot grill fire.

Lightly rub the plank with vegetable oil, and place in its center, skin side down:

4 firm fish fillets or steaks (6 to 7 ounces each), such as salmon, black sea bass, trout, halibut, or monkfish

Brush the fish with:

3 to 4 tablespoons olive oil or melted butter

Season to taste with:

Salt and black pepper

Place the plank in the oven or on the grill, and cover the grill. Cook until fish is opaque throughout, about 20 minutes. Serve with:

Lemon wedges

(Puttanesca Sauce, 563, or Mustard Sauce, 552)

ABOUT SAUTÉING AND PANFRYING FISH

Sautéing and panfrying involve cooking fish on the stovetop in a small amount of fat, as opposed to deep-fat frying, 1046, in which the fish is submerged in fat. ➤ Always be sure to use a fat that can withstand the heat at which the fish will be cooked—vegetable oils, Clarified Butter, 557, or a mixture of half oil and half butter all work well. ➤ After rinsing the fish, dry well to reduce splattering. You might also want to use a splatter screen or inverted colander placed over the pan.

Sautéing fish involves cooking fillets or steaks in a small amount of fat and is best suited to firm-fleshed fish. Pan juices may accompany the fish or be incorporated into a sauce. Whole fish can be panfried, a process that combines elements of both sautéing and deep-frying. The heat is generally high, as it is the oil that cooks the fish, not the pan heat, but the oil does not cover the fish, so the fish may have to be turned once to cook through. This method can produce a nice crusty exterior. Place the fish in the pan when the fat begins to sizzle. Reduce the heat slightly. When the bottom is completely cooked, turn the fish and cook until the second side is done. Quite large fish may be sautéed on both sides until seared, then placed in a preheated 375°F oven about 10 minutes for finishing.

Turning delicate fillets can be challenging, and a wide spatula will help. Or you can brown one side, then simply place a lid on the pan to steam-cook the top of the fish, or use an ovenproof pan and brown the top under the broiler. Keep in mind that ➤ the thinner or smaller your piece of fish, the higher the heat at which you can sauté or panfry it. ➤ Cook fish that has been breaded at a lower temperature to avoid overbrowning or burning the coating.

If breading the fish, you can dip it in a bowl of milk, cream, or buttermilk before dredging in the flour or meal to help the coating adhere. Making a coating for fish that will be fried can be as simple as adding salt and pepper to cornmeal or flour. ➤ Or use a mixture of both using this rule: 3 parts cornmeal to one part flour. Seasoning your breading is a matter of personal taste. Besides the traditional addition of salt and pepper, try chili powder, minced herbs, white pepper, curry powder, red pepper flakes, or coarsely ground black pepper. Mix in a little grated Parmesan cheese for a real treat. Also see Seasoned Flour, 962.

PANFRIED WHOLE FISH
2 servings

This basic recipe for panfrying fish is useful for every fish from tiny smelts or sardines to mid-sized butterfish, bluegills, crappie, and sunfish all the way up to croaker and porgy. Allow 1 pound of whole fish per person.

If you do not wish to soak the fish in milk first, simply coat it well with cornmeal or flour before cooking it.

Pour into a shallow dish:

1 cup milk or cream, or as needed to cover

Add and soak for 15 minutes in the refrigerator:

1 to 2 pounds small fish, scaled and cleaned

Mix in a shallow bowl:

1 cup seasoned cornmeal or all-purpose flour
Salt and black pepper to taste

Lift the fish out of the liquid and coat it with the seasoned cornmeal; set on a plate. Heat a large nonstick skillet over medium-high heat for 2 to 3 minutes. Add:

$^1/_2$ cup olive, peanut, or canola oil mixed with melted
butter, bacon drippings, or lard

Heat until the fat is hot. Add the fish and fry, turning once, until browned on each side, adjusting the heat so that the fat is always bubbling but not burning. Usually the fish is done when each side is golden, but check the interior of larger fish to make sure no blood remains and the flesh is firm and opaque throughout. Drain well on paper towels, and serve hot or at room temperature with:

Minced parsley and lemon wedges or
Salsa Fresca, 571, or Tartar Sauce, 581

Or keep the fish warm while you make this light sauce: Pour off all but 1 tablespoon fat from the skillet, and add:

1 tablespoon minced shallots or 1 teaspoon
minced garlic

Cook, stirring, over medium heat until softened, about 30 seconds. Add:

(1 teaspoon minced tarragon or $^1/_2$ teaspoon dried
tarragon)
1 cup dry white wine, fish stock or broth, or water

Increase the heat to medium-high and cook, stirring, until the liquid is reduced by half, about 5 minutes. Stir in:

1 tablespoon fresh lemon juice or any light
(not red) vinegar

Cook for another 30 seconds. Taste and adjust the seasonings, and serve with the fish.

PANFRIED FISH FILLETS OR STEAKS
4 servings

Please read About Sautéing and Panfrying Fish, 406. Heat a large nonstick skillet over medium-high heat for 3 minutes. Meanwhile, lightly brush:

$1^1/_2$ to 2 pounds skin-on salmon or other fish steaks or
fillets (2 large or 4 small), rinsed and patted dry

with:

2 tablespoons olive oil

Lay the fish skin side down in the skillet and cook, undisturbed, until the skin is brown and the flesh is firm and opaque throughout, 4 to 5 minutes. Sprinkle with:

Salt and black pepper

Turn the fish and cook for 1 to 2 minutes for medium-rare, 3 to 4 minutes for almost cooked through, or 5 minutes or more for well-done. If desired, serve with:

(Fresh Tomato Sauce, 563)

Garnish with:

Minced parsley
Lemon wedges

BREADED PANFRIED FISH FILLETS
4 servings

Best for flounder, sole, or other flatfish, this basic technique is also fine for frying thicker fillets, such as cod. A few rules to keep in mind: Use the biggest skillet you have, do not skimp on the fat, and cook in batches if necessary, keeping the first batch warm while cooking the second batch.

Please read About Sautéing and Panfrying Fish, 406. Preheat the oven to 200°F. Heat a large nonstick skillet over medium heat for 3 to 4 minutes. Meanwhile, mix:

1 cup seasoned cornmeal or all-purpose flour
Salt and black pepper to taste

Coat with the seasoned flour, shaking off the excess, and set aside:

1 to $1^1/_2$ pounds thin (less than $^1/_2$ inch thick) white-
fleshed fish fillets (about 8), such as flounder
or sole, skinned, rinsed, and patted dry

Add to the skillet and heat:

$^1/_4$ cup ($^1/_2$ stick) butter, $^1/_4$ cup vegetable oil,
or a combination

Add 3 or 4 of the fillets, without crowding, increase the heat to high, and fry, shaking the pan from time to time, until the bottom of the fish is nicely browned, and the flesh is firm and opaque throughout, about 3 minutes.

Turn and brown the other side. Remove the fillets to a plate and keep warm in the oven. Cook the remaining fillets, replacing the fat if it has burned. When all the fish is cooked, garnish with:

> Minced parsley
> Lemon wedges

PANFRIED SPICE-CRUSTED FISH FILLETS

4 servings

This recipe produces an almost deep-fried crust and as much spicy flavor as you like. Use firm-fleshed fish such as catfish, dogfish, blackfish, grouper, or red snapper. Please read About Sautéing and Panfrying Fish, 406.
Mix together in a shallow bowl:

> 1 1/2 cups all-purpose flour
> 1 1/2 cups water
> 1 tablespoon (or more) curry powder, Garam Masala, 987, chili powder, or other spice mixture of your choice
> Salt and black pepper to taste

Rub:

> 1 1/2 pounds fish fillets in 2 or 4 pieces, rinsed and patted dry

with:

> Fresh lime or lemon juice or vinegar

Heat a large skillet over medium heat. Pour in:

> 1/8 inch peanut, corn, or canola oil

and heat until hot. Dip each of the fillets in turn into the spice batter, let the excess drip off, and place in the skillet. Increase the heat to medium-high and cook, turning once, until nicely browned on both sides, adjusting the heat as needed to keep the oil bubbling but not burning. Drain on paper towels. Serve with:

> Minced cilantro
> Lime wedges

MARINATED FLOUNDER FILLETS

6 servings

Please read About Sautéing and Panfrying Fish, 406. Place in a shallow baking dish:

> 2 pounds flounder fillets

Add:

> 1 cup tarragon vinegar

Turn fillets to coat, and marinate 10 minutes. Mix:

> 1/2 cup yellow cornmeal
> 1/2 cup all-purpose flour
> 1/4 teaspoon salt
> 1/8 teaspoon black pepper

Drain the fillets, and coat in the cornmeal mixture. Melt in a large skillet over medium-high heat:

> 4 tablespoons (1/2 stick) butter

Add the fillets and cook until golden brown, about 4 minutes on each side. Serve with:

> Ravigote Sauce, 553, or Shrimp Sauce, 552

BREADED SMELTS

2 servings

Please read About Sautéing and Panfrying Fish, 406.
Clean, 394, rinse thoroughly, and wipe dry:

> 12 smelts

Sprinkle with:

> Fresh lemon juice

Let stand, covered, for 15 minutes. Dip the smelts in:

> Heavy cream

Dredge in:

> Flour or cornmeal or Seasoned Flour, 962

Melt over medium heat in a large skillet:

> 1/4 cup (1/2 stick) butter

Cook the smelts, in batches if necessary, in the butter, turning occasionally, until both sides are golden brown and the flesh is firm and opaque, about 6 to 8 minutes.

BROOK TROUT MEUNIÈRE

4 servings

Please read About Sautéing and Panfrying Fish, 406.
Clean, 394:

> 4 brook trout, about 8 ounces each

Cut off the fins; leave the heads and tails on. Dredge in:

> Seasoned Flour, 962

Melt over medium-high heat in a large skillet:

> 1/4 cup Clarified Butter, 557

Add the trout and cook, turning once, until firm and nicely browned. Remove to a hot platter. Add to the drippings in the pan:

> 3 tablespoons butter

Let it brown. Cover the fish with:

> Chopped parsley

Pour the browned butter over the fish. Garnish with:

> Lemon wedges

PANFRIED SKATE WITH BLACK BUTTER

4 servings

Please read About Sautéing and Panfrying Fish, 406.
Preheat the oven to 200°F. Mix:

> 1 cup all-purpose flour
> Salt and black pepper to taste

Coat with the flour:

> 2 skate fillets, halved crosswise

Heat a nonstick skillet large enough to hold the skate in a single layer over medium heat. Add and heat until the foam subsides:

> 2 tablespoons butter
> 1 tablespoon olive oil

Add the skate, increase the heat to high, and brown quickly on both sides; the skate is done when you can begin to separate the segments, which should take about the same amount of time as it does to brown it. Remove the skate to a platter and keep warm in the oven. Wipe out the skillet and return to medium heat. Add:

> 3 tablespoons butter

Cook until the milk solids fall to the bottom of the pan and turn dark brown, then stir in:

2 tablespoons drained capers
1 tablespoon white wine vinegar

Cook about 10 seconds. Pour the sauce over the skate and garnish with:

Minced parsley

SEARED PEPPER-CRUSTED FISH STEAKS

4 servings

Searing requires very little fat and a very hot pan, in which the exterior of the fish browns quickly while the interior remains moist and rare, even translucent. Use this technique for the freshest of thick fish steaks such as tuna or swordfish. These are two fish that can be treated like meat and may make the most devoted steak eaters enjoy eating a creature of the sea.

Please read About Sautéing and Panfrying Fish, 406. Press:

2 tablespoons coarsely cracked black peppercorns
or a mixture of cracked black, white, pink,
and green peppercorns

onto both sides of:

4 tuna or swordfish steaks (6 to 8 ounces each)

Heat a large cast-iron or other heavy skillet over medium-high heat for 5 minutes. Add the steaks to the pan, increase the heat to high, and sear them for 2 minutes on each side. At this point, smaller tuna steaks will be rare; cook thicker steaks, such as swordfish, for another 2 minutes each side. (Alternatively, sear them on one side, then move the pan, without turning the fish, to a hot broiler and broil until cooked as desired.) Remove to a warmed platter and reduce the heat to medium.

Add to the pan:

1 cup dry red wine
1 tablespoon minced shallots

Cook, stirring, until the wine is reduced by about one-third and the shallots are softened, about 2 minutes. Stir in:

1 to 2 tablespoons butter, softened
1 teaspoon salt

until the butter is incorporated. Add:

1 teaspoon minced fresh tarragon or a pinch of dried
tarragon, or 2 tablespoons minced parsley

Spoon the sauce over the fish and serve.

BLACKENED FISH STEAKS OR FILLETS

4 servings

The original blackened fish was redfish, the spice mixture and accompanying technique were created in New Orleans. Make this dish with any firm-fleshed steaks or fillets, such as swordfish, red snapper, grouper, or catfish. But do not make the dish unless your stove has a functional exhaust fan. And turn off the smoke detectors.

Please read Blackening, 1049. Prepare:

Cajun Dry Rub, 587

Place a large cast-iron skillet over high heat. Turn on the exhaust fan. Have ready:

¹⁄₂ cup Clarified Butter, 557, or olive oil
4 firm-fleshed fish fillets or steaks (6 to 8 ounces),
rinsed and patted dry

When the pan is quite hot, after 5 to 10 minutes, brush both sides of the fish with a little of the butter or oil, then lay it in the spice mixture, turning to coat. Place in the pan and drizzle a little butter or oil over each. Cook, turning once, for 3 to 6 minutes, depending on the thickness of the fish, or until the flesh is firm and opaque throughout. Reduce the heat if necessary to keep the spice mixture from burning. Serve with:

Lemon wedges

ABOUT DEEP-FRYING FISH

Please read About Deep-Fat Frying, 1046. Fish cook very quickly when deep-fried and should be at room temperature, and proper oil temperature is critical. ➤ If you are deep-frying large pieces of fish, a temperature of 350°F ensures that the fish cooks through before its exterior becomes too brown; smaller pieces can be fried at higher temperatures, up to 380°F. Make sure the oil is deep enough that the fish is covered completely. When you deep-fry whole fish, you must have a suitably large vessel and plenty of oil. To test for doneness, you'll need to cut into a piece of the fish. If you are frying several pieces, fry a "tester" first to establish a frying time, then just keep the temperature of the oil and size of the fish or fillets consistent as you cook. When deep-frying a whole fish, it will rise to the surface when done. For a discussion about coatings, see About Sautéing and Panfrying Fish, 406.

DEEP-FRIED FISH

Allow about ¹⁄₃ pound fish per serving

Use firm-fleshed fish—catfish, snapper, blackfish, dogfish, grouper, and the like are best. Please read about Deep-Fat Frying, 1046.

Have ready:

1-inch chunks of fish

Dip them in:

Fritter Batter for Vegetables, Meat, and Fish, 658,
or Bound Breading or Coating, 961

Fry in deep fat heated to 370°F for 5 to 8 minutes, or until golden brown. Drain on paper towels. Serve very hot, with:

Lemon Butter Sauce, 558, Tartar Sauce, 581,
or Russian Horseradish Cream, 581

SOUTHERN-STYLE DEEP-FRIED FILLETS

4 servings

Catfish is king in this recipe. Please read about Deep-Fat Frying, 1046.

Heat to 350°F in a deep-fat fryer or deep heavy pot over medium-high heat:

2 inches vegetable oil

Mix:

1 cup cornmeal
(1 tablespoon chili powder)
Salt and black pepper to taste

Coat with the seasoned cornmeal, patting and pressing the cornmeal onto the fish:

1½ to 2 pounds fish fillets, rinsed and patted
    thoroughly dry

Add fish one fillet at a time to the hot oil, without crowding, and increase the heat to high to maintain the temperature. Cook the fish in batches if necessary—it will not take long. Stir once or twice just to keep the fillets from sticking. Remove the fillets when they are golden brown, and drain on paper towels. Serve immediately, with any or all:

Hush Puppies, 633
Tartar Sauce, 581, Becker Cocktail Sauce, 568,
    or Tomatillo-Horseradish Sauce, 568
Lemon wedges
Sliced tomatoes

FISH AND CHIPS

4 servings

Dogfish, now being sold as "cape shark" or "sand shark," in fact is classic for fish and chips. Any white-fleshed fish is suitable, but firmer fillets, such as haddock or halibut, are less likely to fall apart than delicate fish such as cod.

Please read about Deep-Fat Frying, 1046. Cut into thick uniform strips slightly larger than French fries:

4 large peeled baking potatoes

Soak in cold water for 30 minutes.
Stir together in a medium bowl:

1 cup all-purpose flour
1 teaspoon baking powder
1 teaspoon salt
½ teaspoon black pepper
(½ teaspoon ground cinnamon)

Add and stir until smooth:

1 cup milk or water, or a combination
1 large egg

Set aside. Heat to 330°F in a deep-fryer or deep heavy pot over medium-high heat:

3 inches peanut or vegetable oil

Drain and dry the potatoes. Drop the potatoes about 1 cup at a time into the hot oil and fry until the spattering ceases, about 2 minutes. Remove with a slotted spoon and drain on a brown paper bag or paper towels. When finished with the potatoes, increase the temperature of the oil to 365°F. Stir the batter. Dip into it one piece at a time, letting the excess batter drip off:

1½ pounds dogfish or other white-fleshed fish fillets
    (6 or 8), rinsed and patted thoroughly dry

and slip carefully into the oil. Increase the heat if necessary to maintain the temperature. The fish is done when golden brown. Drain on paper towels.

To finish the chips, fry the potatoes in small batches until golden brown, 2 to 3 minutes. Drain on paper towels. Arrange the potatoes and fish on a platter and serve with:

Warmed malt or cider vinegar
Lemon wedges
Tartar Sauce, 581, or Spicy Tartar Sauce, 581

MARINATED DEEP-FRIED FISH

3 servings

This yields very tender, moist fish, lightly crisp on the outside.

Please read about Deep-Fat Frying, 1046. Skin and cut into 2- to 2½-inch pieces:

1½ pounds fish steaks, such as cod, halibut, catfish,
    or whitefish

Marinate for 30 minutes in:

6 tablespoons dry white wine or 2 tablespoons fresh
    lemon juice

Drain and pat dry. One at a time, dip each piece in:

6 tablespoons cream

and then in:

Seasoned Flour, 962

Fry the fish in deep fat heated to 370°F until golden, about 7 minutes. Serve with:

Tartar Sauce, 581

THAI FISH CAKES

4 servings

These are fragrant, spicy, crisp, and fresh-tasting. Serve with a spicy, vinegary coleslaw, 161, or Creamy Cucumber Salad, 167.

Please read about Deep Fat Frying, 1046. Combine in a food processor:

1 shallot, chopped
2 garlic cloves, chopped
A ½-inch piece peeled fresh ginger or galangal, 587,
    coarsely chopped
2 tablespoons fish sauce
1 teaspoon grated lime zest
1 teaspoon crushed red pepper flakes
½ teaspoon salt
1 teaspoon sugar

Add:

1 pound white-fleshed fish fillets, rinsed and
    patted dry
1 large egg

Process to a paste. Add:

2 tablespoons chopped cilantro
2 scallions, coarsely chopped

Pulse the machine a few times to combine. Remove to a bowl. Heat to 370°F in a deep-fat fryer or deep heavy pot over medium-high heat:

2 inches vegetable or peanut oil

Knead the fish mixture until it is smooth, then shape it into 1-inch balls. Gradually add them to the hot oil, and increase the heat to high to maintain the temperature. Cook, in batches if necessary, until nicely browned, 2 to 3 minutes. Drain on paper towels. Serve, garnished with:

Minced cilantro
Lime wedges

WHITEBAIT OR SMELTS

Please read about Deep-Fat Frying, 1046, and Preparing Fish for Cooking, 394. Pick over, and wash if necessary:

Whitebait

Roll in:

Seasoned Flour, 962

Fry 2 to 3 minutes, depending on size, in deep fat heated to 375°F. Garnish with:

Lemon slices

ABOUT CURING AND PICKLING FISH

Some commercially cured fish—smoked, dried, salted, or pickled—come both preserved and ready for serving. Haddock and several kinds of herring are usually cold-smoked, 906. They are salted and smoked over a smoldering fire to the dry stage, but they have not been cooked. Whitefish, chub, and salmon are usually hot-smoked, 906, so they have cooked in the heat of the smoking fire and can be used as is. Haddock, when smoked, becomes **finnan haddie.** A smoked herring is known as a **kipper**—actually a general term for any smoked fish. ➤ Store all smoked fish refrigerated in covered containers. If you smoke your own fresh fish, 907, cook before serving.

Cod, mackerel, and herring are often salted and air-dried, and must be soaked in water, skin side down, for several hours before cooking. If soaking in fresh running water is not practical, change the water frequently during the soaking period. For ways to cook, see Cod, 414. Fish was often pickled in the days before refrigeration, and in eighteenth-century English and American cookbooks, you will find recipes for "caveaching" fish in spices, oil, and vinegar. We imagine there is a relationship between the French *escabeche* and its Spanish equivalent, *seviche,* in word derivation and method. Nowadays herring and mackerel are usually reserved for pickling, although Pickled Fish, below, can be used for small fish like fresh anchovies, sardines, young mullet, and whiting.

CURED SALMON (GRAVLAX)

15 servings

This traditional Swedish method of curing salmon is easy to do at home. The fish must be impeccably fresh. Gravlax keeps well, covered and refrigerated, for several days. Please read About Curing and Pickling Fish, above.

Leaving the skin on, cut into 2 fillets:

One 4- to 5-pound salmon

Mix together:

$2^1/_2$ cups sugar
$1^1/_2$ cups salt
1 tablespoon black pepper

Rub the fillets all over with this mixture. Lay on the flesh side of one of the fillets:

2 cups coarsely chopped dill, including stems

Sprinkle with:

2 tablespoons brandy, aquavit, plain or lemon-flavored vodka, 58, or other spirits

Lay the other fillet flesh side down on top of the dill-covered fillet. Sprinkle the outside with the remaining dill and sugar mixture, and wrap in plastic wrap or cheesecloth. Place on a platter, cover with another platter, and top the whole package with 3 or 4 pounds of weights. Refrigerate for 2 to 4 days. Twice a day, open the package and baste the fish all over with the juices it has exuded. Flip the fish over and rewrap and weight it. The gravlax is done when the flesh is opaque. Thinly slice. Serve with:

Scandinavian Mustard Dill Sauce, 566, or Mustard Mayonnaise, 580, thinned with cream or sour cream

SEVICHE

6 servings

Seviche is raw fish or shellfish marinated in citrus juice. Though the fish is technically not cooked, it turns opaque and firms up due to the acid in the marinade so that it doesn't seem raw. Fish options here include grouper, halibut, flounder, and snapper. Please read About Curing and Pickling Fish, above.

Remove the skin and any bones from:

1 pound very fresh firm-fleshed fish fillets

Cut into small cubes, about $^3/_8$ inch, and place in a glass or stainless-steel bowl. Stir in:

$^1/_2$ cup fresh lemon juice
$^1/_2$ cup fresh lime juice

Cover with plastic wrap and refrigerate, stirring occasionally, until the fish is opaque throughout (break open a piece to check it), 4 to 6 hours. Thoroughly drain the fish. (It can be refrigerated at this point for up to 18 hours before serving, if desired.) Mix the drained fish with:

1 cup tomato juice
$1^1/_2$ tablespoons olive oil
1 medium ripe tomato, diced
1 small onion, finely diced
$^1/_4$ cup coarsely chopped green olives
2 tablespoons chopped cilantro
1 to 2 jalapeño peppers, seeded and minced
1 teaspoon dried oregano
$^1/_2$ teaspoon salt, or to taste
$^1/_2$ to 1 teaspoon sugar, to taste

Taste and adjust the seasonings and refrigerate until serving time. Serve garnished with:

Cilantro sprigs
Diced avocado

PICKLED FISH (ESCABÈCHE)

6 servings

Any mild, firm-fleshed white fish works well here.

Please read About Curing and Pickling Fish, above. Combine in a small saucepan:

1 cup white wine vinegar

1 cup water
1 tablespoon minced garlic
1 tablespoon sugar
1 teaspoon ground cumin
1 small jalapeño or other chile pepper,
    seeded and minced
Salt and black pepper to taste
Bring to a boil over high heat, then remove from the heat.
Mix:
    $^{1}/_{2}$ cup all-purpose flour
    1 teaspoon salt
    1 teaspoon cracked black peppercorns
Coat with the seasoned flour:
    1 pound skinned cod, snapper, or halibut fillets
Heat in a large skillet over medium-high heat until hot but
not smoking:
    $^{1}/_{4}$ cup vegetable oil
Fry the fillets until golden brown and completely opaque
at the center, 3 to 4 minutes on each side. Remove to a
wide shallow bowl. Pour the vinegar mixture on top and
sprinkle with:
    $^{1}/_{4}$ cup chopped cilantro
    Juice of 2 limes
Serve at room temperature.

CODFISH BALLS OR CAKES

4 servings
Please read Cod, 414. Have ready:
    1 cup flaked desalted salt cod
Rice or mash:
    6 medium potatoes, or half potatoes and half
        parsnips, boiled
Combine the fish and vegetables in a medium bowl. Beat
in one at a time:
    2 eggs
Add and beat until fluffy:
    2 tablespoons heavy cream
    (1 teaspoon minced onion)
    (1 teaspoon dry mustard)
    (1 teaspoon Worcestershire sauce)
    Salt and black pepper to taste
Shape the mixture into balls or patties, and use one of the
following cooking methods:
 I. Form the mixture into 2-inch cakes. Dip in flour and
    cook in butter in a hot skillet until brown. Serve at once.
 II. Form the mixture into patties. Bake in a greased pan in a
    375°F oven about 3 minutes. Dot with butter and serve.
Serve with:
    Mustard Sauce, 552, or Anchovy Sauce, 552

CREAMED FINNAN HADDIE

Place in a saucepan:
    Smoked haddock
Barely cover with:
    Milk

Soak 1 hour. Slowly bring the milk to a boil. Simmer 20
minutes. Drain the fish, flake, and remove the skin and
bones. Combine the fish with very hot:
    White Sauce I, 550
using about two-thirds as much sauce as you have fish.
Add for each cup of flaked fish:
    1 hard-boiled egg, chopped
    1 teaspoon chopped green bell pepper
    1 teaspoon chopped pimiento
Serve the fish on:
    Toast rounds
Sprinkle with:
    Fresh lemon juice
    Chopped chives or parsley

SALT HERRING AND POTATOES

4 servings
Soak overnight in water or milk to cover:
    2 large salt herring
Drain and split them. Remove and discard the skin and
bones. Cut the fillets into 1-inch-wide pieces. Preheat the
oven to 375°F. Slice very thin:
    6 potatoes, peeled
    2 medium onions
Butter a baking dish. Arrange the potatoes, onions, and
herring in alternate layers, beginning and ending with potatoes. Cover the top with:
    Au Gratin, 961
Bake 45 minutes, or until potatoes are tender.

HERRING AND APPLES

Prepare **Salt Herring and Potatoes, above.** Substitute
tart apples for the onions and **fresh herring** for the salt
herring. Season each layer of herring with **salt and black
pepper.**

SARDINE TOAST

4 servings
Skin and bone, 394:
    12 canned sardines
Mash 6 of them with:
    1 teaspoon minced onion
    2 teaspoons butter
    $^{1}/_{2}$ teaspoon prepared mustard
    1 teaspoon fresh lemon juice
Spread:
    6 narrow toast strips
with this mixture. Place a whole sardine on each toast, and
run under the broiler. Before serving, garnish with:
    (Finely chopped fennel)
    A grinding of black pepper

KEDGEREE

4 servings
Bring to a boil in a medium saucepan:
    1 cup heavy cream

Add:

¹/₄ teaspoon ground red pepper
¹/₄ teaspoon turmeric
¹/₂ teaspoon salt

Simmer for 2 minutes. Add and heat through:

3 cups cooked long-grain, basmati, or jasmine rice

Meanwhile, thinly slice, keeping the white and green parts separate:

4 scallions

Fold the scallion whites into the rice mixture, along with:

2 smoked trout fillets (about 8 ounces total), at room temperature, broken into 1-inch pieces

Remove the kedgeree to a 5-cup soufflé dish or casserole. Top with the scallion greens and:

3 large hard-boiled eggs, chopped

Alternatively, butter the dish, pack it with the kedgeree, and unmold onto a serving plate, then top with the scallion greens and chopped eggs.

COMMONLY COOKED FISH

Generally how a fish is cooked is determined by the thickness and overall size of the cut and whether it is a saltwater or freshwater fish. The firmer-flesh, often bigger cuts of saltwater fish can tolerate almost any way you wish to cook then, from grilling to poaching. The generally smaller and more ➤ delicate freshwater fish are often easiest to broil or panfry. Two other aspects to consider are the oiliness of the fish and whether it has come out of warmer freshwater. ➤ Oily fish are strong in flavor and best suited to smoking and grilling. Warmwater fish are also strong flavored, and panfrying or deep-frying is the best way to cook them. The most commonly cooked fish are listed below with more detailed information on how best to cook them.

ANCHOVY

Anchovies are strong flavored and lean, with soft dark-colored flesh. Canned or salted anchovies should be rinsed and used as a flavoring. White anchovies, cured in vinegar and imported from Spain, are particularly delicate tasting (no need to rinse them). Grilling is typical for whole fresh fish, though broiling may be easier if they are very small. Fresh anchovies can also be used in Pickled Fish, 411. Anchovies are a saltwater fish.

ARCTIC CHAR

A relative of salmon and trout, with a similar fat content and flavorful pink to ivory-colored firm flesh, Arctic char is well suited to all preparations. Most of the char in the markets is farmed. **Dolly Varden** and **grayling** are similar fish. Arctic char is a freshwater fish.

BASS

Lean and relatively free of bones, true ocean-caught bass have wonderfully sweet, fairly firm white flesh and are ideal to serve whole or in fillets. **Black sea bass** are popular in markets and among fishermen. They are usually sold at 2 or 3 pounds, though they can be larger. Take particular care to avoid overcooking sea bass, as it will toughen. **Striped bass** (often called **rockfish** in the Chesapeake) is anadromous—it lives in salt water but spawns in fresh water—and, whether wild or farmed, is similarly delicate. Gaining popularity here, **branzino**, also known as **sea bass,** has long been prized in the Mediterranean for its white, firm, mildly sweet flesh that is reminiscent of scallops. Panfry in olive oil.

Groupers are also part of the large family of bass. Grouper is found in the southern Atlantic and Pacific, in greater quantity in the summer. It shows up as meaty white fillets in most markets. Lean and flavorful, the firm, flaky flesh stands up to most treatments, including cooking in liquid. Groupers are saltwater fish.

Smallmouth and **largemouth bass** are among the most popular freshwater sportfish in America. Their moderately firm flesh is suited to broiling, grilling, panfrying, roasting, and sautéing. Smallmouth are the better of the two for eating, as they live in colder water.

BLACKFISH (TAUTOG)

A popular sport fish, blackfish is seen in some East Coast markets in the summer. The sturdy, lean white flesh should be skinned (the skin can be bitter) before broiling, sautéing, poaching, or grilling. It is a saltwater fish.

BLOWFISH (PUFFER FISH, SEA SQUAB)

An edible saltwater fish from a family of mostly poisonous varieties (including **fugu,** consumed as a delicacy in Japan and handled only by experts who are able to remove the toxic innards), blowfish have mild, lean, meaty white flesh that should be cooked quickly to avoid dryness. The fillets resemble chicken drumsticks. Blowfish can be used as a substitute for scallops, shrimp, or frog legs.

BLUEFISH

Popular among fishermen and sold in markets on the East Coast in the summer, this strong-flavored, oily saltwater fish should be well cleaned as soon as it is caught and kept very cold. The dark-colored, rich flavorful flesh is soft, but whole fish can be carefully grilled, and fillets can be broiled, panfried, deep-fried, or sautéed.

BUTTERFISH (PACIFIC POMPANO)

A close relative of pompano, these small saltwater fish are best served whole, skin on; their silver skin needs no scaling. Butterfish are flavorful and moderate in fat content, with meaty, off-white flesh, and are delicious panfried.

CARP

These great, languid, soft-finned freshwater fish can be admired swimming in koi (carp) ponds or in the tanks from which they are sold live in Chinatowns. The fish should always be skinned before cooking. Carp is classic in Gefilte Fish, 401.

CATFISH (CHANNEL CAT, BULLHEAD)

Now mostly farmed, catfish has a clean, mild flavor and firm yet flaky white flesh that is ideal for panfrying, deep-frying, grilling, broiling, or sautéing.

CHILEAN SEA BASS (PATAGONIAN TOOTHFISH)

Not really a bass, this delicious white-fleshed saltwater fish became so popular during the late 1990s that it was overfished in the South American waters where it is found. Since the fishery is hard to regulate, and it is difficult to determine if you are buying Chilean sea bass via the black market, many conscientious chefs, markets, and home cooks have stopped buying and serving them.

COD

While supplies of Atlantic cod have dwindled, **pollack, hake, whiting, cusk,** and **haddock** are also all in the cod family—most of which tend toward delicacy of flavor and firm to moderately firm white flesh that cooks to large flakes (hake has soft flesh). **Scrod** is a term for any fish in this family weighing no more than 2 pounds. Prepare any way but grilled, as the flesh is too delicate. **Salt cod,** which has been salt-cured and sun-dried until it is quite stiff, is a popular ingredient in Portuguese, French, Spanish, and Italian cooking. Look for thick, white, firm fillets. **To desalt,** soak the fish in several changes of fresh water in the refrigerator for 18 to 24 hours before using. **To flake salt cod,** put the desalted fish in cold unsalted Court Bouillon, 120, to cover, and bring to a boil, then ➤ reduce the heat and simmer 20 to 30 minutes. Drain, skin, bone, and flake. One pound dried salt cod will yield about 2 cups flaked fish.

Smoked split haddock, **finnan haddie,** originated in Scotland, though it is now also made in Canada, Denmark, and New England. Finnan haddie can be roasted, or creamed, 412, broiled, basted in butter, or simmered in milk, which tempers its strong flavor. Fish in the cod family are saltwater fish.

CROAKER (SPOT, SPOTFIN)

Fish in this family have a firm texture with light-colored, very lean flesh and a sweet flavor. They are saltwater fish, and suitable for many preparations, from panfrying and deep-frying to cooking in liquid and roasting.

DORY

A flatfish with a pronounced lower jaw and a black spot on both sides said to represent the thumbprint of St. Peter, dory is also known as St. Pierre. The European **John dory** is the most well known, though there is also an **American dory.** The firm, lean, delicious white flesh should be prepared as fillets, as the fish is bony. Dory are saltwater fish.

DRUM (REDFISH, RED CHANNEL FISH, BLACK DRUM)

Red drum or **redfish** are the drums most likely to be found commercially. All have sweet, mild white flesh low in fat. Drum is best suited to panfrying, deep-frying, grilling, and cooking in liquid. Drums are saltwater fish.

EEL

Eel is a saltwater fish that believes in long journeys. It spawns in the Sargasso Sea in the western Atlantic, and from there travels back to its freshwater haunts in this country or in Europe to feed and grow up in the rivers and streams frequented by its parents. The young eel, or **elver,** still only 2 or 3 inches long after its immense journey, is transparent and yellowish. Broil, grill, or cook in liquid. Little eels, as well as larger ones, can be cooked, smoked, or pickled to make a delicious addition to an hors d'oeuvre selection or Antipasto, 80.

Most cooks prefer to buy eel skinned, but for the intrepid, we offer the following method: Keep the eel alive until ready to skin, they kill it with a sharp blow to the head. Do not be alarmed if the eel continues to move after it is dead; the movement is only muscle contractions. Slip a noose around the eel's head and hang the other end of the cord on a hook, high on the wall. Cut the eel skin all around about 3 inches below the head, so as not to penetrate the gallbladder, which lies close to the head. Peel the skin back, pulling down hard—if necessary, with a pair of pliers—until the whole skin comes off like a glove. Clean the fish by slitting the white belly and removing the gut, which lies close to the surface of the belly. Cooked, the rich flesh of eel is firm with a delicate flavor.

FLOUNDER (WINTER)

The delicate white flesh of this saltwater flatfish, usually sold filleted, is sometimes marketed as sole. It can be prepared as for other flatfish fillets. The fish sold as **gray sole** is actually a flounder with an elongated shape and firmer flesh. Large flounder fillets are often called **lemon sole.**

FLUKE (SUMMER FLOUNDER)

A common catch for recreational fishermen, these saltwater fish can be up to 5 pounds, and their thick, flaky white fillets are particularly able to absorb the flavors of other ingredients. Fluke is wonderful marinated or sauced and can be grilled, panfried, sautéed, or roasted.

HALIBUT

Atlantic halibut are larger than any other flatfish sold in this country. The fish is usually sold in steaks that divide into four segments around the central bone. The firm, flaky white flesh is lean, with a delicate flavor, and can withstand cooking in soups and stews. **Pacific halibut** is similar, though more often sold as fillets and not quite as flavorful. **California halibut** is actually a flounder (see Flounder, above).

HERRING

A small, rich saltwater fish with dark, strong-flavored flesh, herring occasionally passes for sardines in the market, but it is more often found preserved or smoked. Fresh herring can be seen in markets in the spring, and these are good grilled, broiled, roasted (as in the variation for Salt Herring and Potatoes, 412), or even coated in oatmeal and fried. Herring has innumerable tiny fine bones. If you split a herring down the center of the back with a sharp knife, lever up the backbone, and carefully pull it out, most of these small bones will come with it. After cleaning, you may cook herring in one piece or split it in two.

Kippered herring have been salted, split, and cold-smoked until they take on a reddish hue (though this is sometimes artificially produced with red food coloring). More lightly salted and briefly smoked, whole silver-colored **bloaters,** so called for their slightly plumped, or bloated, look, can be eaten cold with bread and butter, or broiled in butter.

Marinated herring comes in various disguises. **Rollmops** are fresh boned herring that are rolled, often around a piece of cucumber, held together with a toothpick, and pickled. **Bismarck herring** are flat fillets cured, skin-on, in vinegar, often with onions, sometimes sweetened. **Matjes,** or **virgin,** herring come in a sweet-sour brine of vinegar and sugar.

JACK

The firm, flavorful white flesh of the fish in this family is sometimes very strong tasting. There are 21 species of jack, all saltwater fish. Little edible jacks (under 5 pounds) can be cooked like bluefish; grilling is great. Not all jacks are worthy of eating, and some can carry the disease ciguatera.

LING COD

Unrelated to cod, this saltwater fish has lean, slightly green flesh that becomes white and delicate flavored when cooked. It is firm enough for grilling, soups, and stews.

MACKEREL

Mackerel are in the same family as tuna, though much smaller. **Atlantic mackerel** are the most common and have a softer texture and stronger flavor than **Spanish mackerel** or **king mackerel.** King mackerel is often sold as steaks. All are wonderful panfried, broiled, grilled, or in escabèches, 411. Acid cuts through the oily, strong flavor of this tan-fleshed fish. Especially quick to develop a fishy smell, mackerel should be kept very cold at all times. Mackerel are saltwater fish.

MAHIMAHI (DOLPHINFISH, DORADO)

Unrelated to dolphin, fished mostly in the South Atlantic and Pacific, and an exciting catch for fishermen, mahi-mahi are most plentiful in the warmer months. Their firm, flavorful, off-white flesh holds up to all cooking techniques except deep-frying.

MARLIN

Marlin has lean flesh that resembles tuna and can be prepared accordingly. Currently, this large saltwater game fish is in decline, and many conscientious chefs, markets, and home cooks have stopped buying and serving marlin.

MONKFISH (ANGLERFISH, LOTTE)

With mild, dense white flesh, monkfish is sometimes called "poor man's lobster." The tails or tail fillets of this lean saltwater fish are usually covered with a thin gray membrane, which should be removed with a knife before cooking. Monkfish can be grilled, broiled, roasted, sautéed, or cooked in liquid.

MULLET

Delicious when locally caught and extremely fresh, both **striped mullet** and **silver mullet** weigh between 1 and 4 pounds. Firm enough to stand up to grilling, they are best prepared by any method using direct heat or by hot-smoking. Mullet are saltwater fish.

ORANGE ROUGHY

Imported skinless orange roughy fillets from Australia and New Zealand have firm, lean white flesh. They can be pan-fried or cooked with moist heat. It has mild flavor and is a suitable substitute for more expensive cod or fillet of sole. A saltwater fish, orange roughy is sturdy enough for most preparations, except grilling.

PANFISH

This category was made up to pay tribute to the little fish, usually freshwater, that we catch as children: **sunfish** (sometimes called **bream**), **bluegills, crappies, bullhead,** and **rock bass.** They account for the greatest proportion of sportfishing in the United States and can be caught in lakes and ponds everywhere. If you don't "catch and release," panfry them.

PERCH

Only two true perch are seen with any regularity. **Walleye** (sometimes erroneously referred to as walleye pike) has relatively few bones and a delicate flavor, and its sweet, lean flesh can be roasted, panfried, or gently cooked in liquid. **Yellow perch** is a popular sport fish with firm, lean flesh that should be skinned before panfrying or braising. Perch are freshwater fish.

PIKE

A sweet, lean freshwater fish, typically used in Gefilte Fish, 401, the **Northern pike** can get up to 20 pounds. The larger the pike, the easier it is to find and remove its many bones. **Musellunge,** the largest member of the family, is a popular game fish. Very low in fat, this fish's moderately firm flesh is best for panfrying, roasting, and sautéing.

POMPANO

Ranging from 1 to 3 pounds, whole silver-skinned pompano are best grilled or panfried. **Yellowtail** is a Pacific saltwater fish and is also a favorite at sushi restaurants (where it is called **hamachi**). One of the world's great sport fish, pompano is perfect for grilling whole, roasting, cooking in liquid, and sautéing.

PORGY

Also known as **sea bream** (the French **dorade** or Italian **orato**) or **scup,** the lean, flaky flesh of these saltwater fish makes up for their boniness with mild, subtle flavor. Cook and season gently so their flavor is not overwhelmed.

RED MULLET

Unrelated to true mullet, these European saltwater imports have firm, lean, well-flavored white flesh that can be prepared by most methods but is best panfried or grilled.

ROCKFISH

This family of saltwater fish encompasses a variety of Pacific fish (not to be confused with the colloquial name used in the Chesapeake for striped bass). Their very lean white flesh cooks to small flakes and is perfect for cooking in liquid or deep-frying.

ROE AND MILT

The eggs of female fish are known as **roe,** or **hard roe;** the male fish's sperm is known as **milt,** or **soft roe,** as its texture is creamy rather than grainy. Both types are used in cooking, and the roe of certain fish is more valued than the fish itself; see Caviar, 86.

Shad roe is considered choice. It should be cooked until pale red in the center; overcooked, it is hard, dry, and tasteless. Hard roe to be cooked and served on its own should be pricked with a needle to prevent the membrane from bursting and splattering the little eggs. If pepper is used in seasoning, white pepper is preferable for its less intrusive flavor and appearance.

You may serve the roe or milt of other fish such as herring, mackerel, flounder, salmon, carp, or cod as in the recipe for Broiled Shad Roe, 405. The milt of salmon must have the vein removed.

Roe may be served as a luncheon dish or an appetizer or as stuffing or garnish for the fish from which it comes. Or it may be used raw, as it is on sushi (particularly **cod, flying fish [tobiko], herring** or **salmon roe,** or the delicacy known as **uni, sea urchin roe,** which must be served very fresh), as an hors d'oeuvre, or as in Marinated Herring.

When buying roe, look for unpasteurized lightly salted roe that has been kept refrigerated.

SABLEFISH (ALASKA COD, BLACK COD)

Sometimes mistakenly called **butterfish,** this saltwater fish is not actually a cod. It has a flavorful, rich, fairly firm flesh that cooks to large white flakes, and its high fat content makes it ideal for smoking. The black skin should be removed before cooking.

SALMON

One of the country's most popular and affordable fish, salmon is suited for almost every cooking technique (though it is too high in fat to benefit from deep-frying). Salmon can be broken down into Atlantic and Pacific varieties. Its flesh ranges from pale coral to vermilion in color. There are five species of Pacific salmon and most are wild, including the prized Alaskan varieties, which include **Chinook** or **king salmon, coho** or **silver salmon,** and **sockeye,** and these boast a rich, full-flavored flesh that is more distinctive than that of farmed salmon. Salmon is also wonderful both hot- and cold-cooked and cured, as in Cured Salmon, 411. Salmon are anadromous—they live in both fresh water and salt water.

SARDINES

Sardines are actually members of the herring family. Imported European sardines are fatter and more flavorful than those caught in the American Atlantic, which are more often canned. Rinse off the scales and pull out the gills and innards of whole fresh sardines, then cook them as is, or cut their backbones out for stuffing. Serve with lemon wedges, or use another type of acid in the cooking, such as vinegar, to cut through the fatty, full flavor of their dark tan meat. Sardines are saltwater fish.

SHAD

A herring relative prized for its roe, **American shad** has sweet, rich, soft flesh that is best purchased filleted, preferably by an expert who can navigate around its many small bones. Plank-roasting, 406, is a traditional way to prepare whole shad, which is available in the spring. Shad are anadromous, meaning they live in both salt water and fresh water.

SHARK

Shark is usually sold as steaks, with sweet white flesh. The rough gray skin is usually removed. The firm meat stands up to most cooking methods. Look for light-colored shark meat with no odor of ammonia, and avoid overcooking, as it is lean and therefore prone to dryness. **Mako shark,** sometimes misnamed **bonito,** is the most common.

SKATE (RAY)

You can buy skate and ray filleted and skinned, or fillet them yourself as you would a flatfish, 395. The firm, lean, flavorful meat is a good candidate for panfrying or deep-frying. Always serve hot, as skate develops a sticky texture with cooling because of its cartilaginous skeleton. Skate are saltwater fish.

SMELTS

Often sold as **whitebait** or **rainbow smelt** when very small, smelts are mild and sweet. **Eulachon,** small, short-lived smelt, are stronger flavored and richer. These small whole fish are ideal for panfrying or deep-frying. Smelts are freshwater fish.

SNAPPER

True snappers are justifiably favored for their sweet flavor and generally firm texture, which is well suited to grilling. Other fish of lesser quality are often sold as snapper. The popular red-skinned **red snapper** has lean white flesh with a touch of sweetness that cooks to large flakes. **Yellowtail snapper,** which are gray with a yellow stripe that runs from head to tail, are milder and have pinkish flesh. Snapper are saltwater fish.

SOLE

Dover sole, also called **channel sole,** is imported from Europe and correspondingly costly. This firm sole has a delicate flavor that is so popular that imposters such as the inferior **Pacific flounder** are sometimes marketed as Dover sole. Remove the tough skin before cooking; grill (whole fish only), pangrill, sauté, roast, or cook in liquid (gently and briefly). The flatfish caught in American waters and referred to as sole is actually flounder; true sole is found only in European salt waters. Classic recipes calling for sole can be prepared with any firm white fish. Sole are saltwater fish.

SWORDFISH

Unless you've seen the extremely long sword of this fish displayed on the wall of a seafood restaurant or store, you are not likely to encounter it, as these large fish are sold in pieces, the most common being symmetrical steaks, with four sections of meat with concentric markings or whorls, around the central vertebra. Firm and flavorful, swordfish is an ideal candidate for cooking with high heat—grilling, broiling, roasting, or panfrying. Currently, this large salt-water game fish is in decline, and many conscientious chefs, markets, and home cooks have stopped buying and serving swordfish.

TILAPIA

Most tilapia at the market has been farm-raised, and fillets may have been frozen. Tilapia is a mild, round, all-purpose saltwater fish that has lean, fairly firm flesh. Poach or roast or deep-fry.

TILEFISH

A firm white saltwater fish with lean, delicately flavored flesh, tilefish, available on the East Coast year-round, is sold filleted or in steaks and is usually very affordable. Any cooking method except grilling works well.

TROUT

Though farmed trout varies, it can be quite good. While freshly caught brook trout is sought after, lake trout can vary from flavorful to unctuous. Particularly rich specimens respond well to hot-smoking. When **rainbow trout** head out to sea, they become **steelhead trout** and are said to gain in flavor. All trout, including **brown, cutthroat,** and **golden,** are suited to grilling (very carefully, in a fish basket, if you have one), broiling, panfrying, and roasting. Except for steelhead, trout are freshwater fish.

TUNA

Widely distributed and of widely differing characteristics, tuna range in size from the **bluefin**—a magnificent game fish that can weigh up to 1,500 pounds—to the far smaller **albacore,** whose processed meat often ends up in cans or pouches of "white" or "light" tuna.

The almost translucent red meat of bluefin tuna is en-joyed raw in sushi or sashimi and as tuna tartare, and it is firm enough to be cooked with intense heat (grilling, pan-frying, or searing). Red at the center is a good way to enjoy its flavor, provided the fish is very fresh. When preparing tuna, you may want to trim away any dark streaks, which are strong flavored. Currently, bluefin tuna is in decline.

A close second to bluefin, **bigeye tuna** is prized for its rich taste and bright red flesh. **Skipjack** are usually under 10 pounds and have strong-flavored flesh. While most skipjack is canned, it is possible to find small whole fish in markets. **Bonito,** not to be confused with shark, is a more affordable fish that resembles skipjack in taste, though it has much lighter-colored flesh. **Yellowfin** also shows up frequently, usually as loins from which steaks can be cut (this is preferable to buying precut steaks, as they will be fresher), and is used in sushi. Tuna is a saltwater fish.

TURBOT

A prized European saltwater flatfish that inspired the cre-ation of the French cooking vessel called a *turbotière* to accommodate its diamond shape, true turbot has firm and delicate white flesh and is very expensive.

WEAKFISH

Weakfish is actually a drum but does not resemble red or black drum in shape. It is also called **sea trout** and **spotted sea trout,** with reason, as it is an excellent food fish, finely textured and delicate flavored like trout. Weakfish is a salt-water fish.

WHITEBAIT

Minnow-sized freshwater fish of any variety are some-times given this name, but technically, whitebait are a Pacific Coast variety of **smelts,** 416. Their skinny, near-translucent bodies are wonderful deep-fried and eaten whole as a crispy snack.

WHITEFISH

Occasionally found in fish markets but more commonly caught by fishermen, this very distant salmon relative has silver skin and rich, mild-flavored meat that takes well to smoking. It is too rich to deep-fry. Whitefish is a freshwater fish.

WOLFFISH

The white, fairly firm, meaty, flavorful flesh of wolffish, sold in fillets or steaks, cooks into large flakes. Although it is firm enough to grill (but brush well with oil to minimize sticking), most other techniques work well too, especially sautéing and roasting.

POULTRY AND WILDFOWL

The chicken is a world citizen: Turkey, ducks, and geese, along with the many game birds that migrate from continent to continent, are also international favorites. And each nation has learned to cook them in a manner distinctively its own. The worldly cook will not be content with only fried chicken and roasted turkey, but also will welcome into the kitchen some of the specialties that enliven our global cuisine: Coq au Vin from France, Chicken Cacciatore from Italy, Tandoori Chicken from India, and Satay Chicken from Indonesia.

Properly defined, the term "poultry" means a farm-raised bird, while the term "wildfowl" means a bird harvested in the wild. Today these two categories of birds have been further refined: Poultry also includes specialty birds available online or by ordering through your local meat department, such as **domestic duck** and **goose, guinea hen, ostrich, emu,** and **squab.** Wildfowl or game birds include species that are primarily hunted and are not usually available commercially, such as **wild duck, goose,** and **turkey,** which are very different birds from their farm-raised counterparts, as well as **pheasant, partridge, grouse, quail, dove, pigeon, woodcock,** and **snipe.** Pheasant, quail, and some European species of partridge and grouse can be purchased but are included in the game bird category as they are more often a hunter's quarry.

Whether you purchase your bird or hunt it, you will have to assess its quality and potential and consider the application of cooking techniques that will be most suitable and rewarding. ➤ See, for example, Dry-Heat, 1045, for ways to cook young birds. For most poultry or wildfowl of questionable age, consult Moist-Heat Processes, 1049, or marinate them to tenderize them.

ABOUT BUYING POULTRY

Look for plump, meaty birds, and check the "sell by" date on the package. If the package contains an unusual amount of liquid, feels sticky, or has even the faintest off odor, the contents are suspect regardless of the expiration date. Avoid bruised poultry. Chicken skin should be either yellow or white; the color is not an indication of fat content. Refrigerate raw poultry immediately, and keep your poultry separate from other foods.

When shopping for poultry, remember ➤ you will get about ³/₄ of a pound of cooked or edible meat from 1 pound of boneless poultry; and about ¹/₂ pound from 1 pound of bone-in poultry. You will get about 1 cup of cooked meat per pound from a whole chicken. If you chop the meat, a 3-ounce portion yields about ²/₃ cup.

Many folks swear by the superior flavor of a **freshly killed turkey.** Fresh turkeys are available, but you will find the cost a little higher since they have to be specially handled. For that reason, speak to your butcher and ask about when and how to order a fresh turkey.

Free-range and organic poultry are widely available. By USDA standards, free-range chickens and turkeys must have access to the outdoors. There are differing regulations for organic poultry, and those regulations can vary from state to state. Generally, though, to be considered organic, poultry must be raised without antibiotics and fed organically grown feed; according to the USDA, "Poultry or inedible poultry products must be from animals that have been under continuous organic management beginning no later than the second day of life."

ABOUT STORAGE AND SAFE HANDLING OF POULTRY

Store poultry at the back of the refrigerator, on the bottom shelf, and ➤ cook or freeze within 2 days of purchase. Assuming a freezer temperature of 0°F or lower, poultry will remain safe to eat for several months, but for the best taste and texture, cook it within 1 month.

Frozen poultry must be ➤ thawed thoroughly before cooking, either in the refrigerator or in cold water, so always buy frozen poultry, especially large birds such as turkey, well in advance.

In the case of birds that are to be roasted whole, under-thawing is disastrous. The birds will cook through on the outside while the center remains virtually raw. Should a refrigerator-thawed whole bird prove to be stiff and icy on the day you plan to roast it, transfer it to cold water to finish defrosting. Never refreeze poultry that you have partially thawed or completely thawed at home. We do not advocate buying uncooked ready-stuffed poultry.

To thaw in the refrigerator, set the bird, still in its original packaging, on a baking sheet and allow 1 day for every 6 pounds. **To thaw in cold water,** leave the poultry in its original packaging, place it in cold water, and weight it with a heavy pot to keep it submerged. Defrost for 1 to 8 hours, depending on the weight, turning the bird and

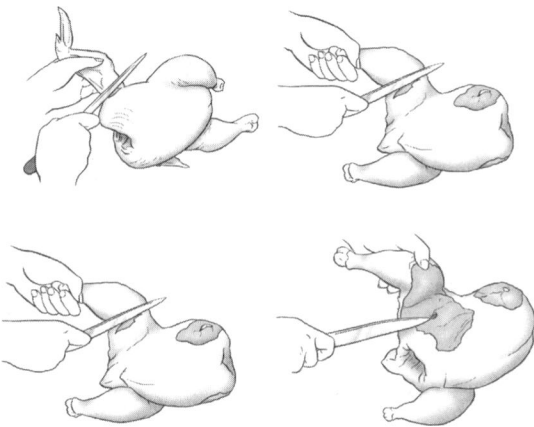

Cutting off the wings and legs; separating the drumstick and thigh

changing the water frequently. Poultry can appear to be thawed before it really is. Do not assume it is fully defrosted until the flesh feels soft and pliable to the touch and the legs and wings move freely at the joints when wiggled. ➤ Thawed frozen poultry is highly susceptible to spoilage and must be cooked promptly.

The undercooking of poultry is rarely the cause of salmonella poisoning. *Salmonella enteridis* is completely eradicated at 160°F, the lowest temperature at which most find chicken or turkey palatable. The usual way salmonella and other bacterial infections are caused is by eating uncooked or lightly cooked food that has come into contact with infected raw poultry or its juices, most commonly as residue on cutting boards, counters, or knives. ➤ To reduce the chance of contamination, never store poultry next to uncooked or unwrapped food that will be eaten raw, such as salad greens, fresh fruit, or bread. And ➤ after cutting up or handling raw poultry, always wash your hands, cutting board, counter surface, knives, and poultry shears, in hot sudsy water before preparing other foods. ➤ If you wipe your hands on your apron or a dish towel, replace them promptly with clean ones.

ABOUT CUTTING UP POULTRY

With a little practice and a sharp knife, you can easily cut a whole chicken, duck, turkey, or goose into serving pieces. By cutting up a bird yourself, you not only save money, you ensure you have precisely the right parts, cut just the way you want them. ➤ Using paper towels to hold the bird will give you a sure grip.

Wrap and freeze the back, neck, heart, and gizzard for later use. These are excellent for stock. Whole poultry can be cut into six, eight, or ten pieces.

To cut a whole bird into parts, grasp the bird by one wing, letting its weight tug against the skin at the wing joint, as shown, above, and clip through the skin, flesh, and joint, severing the wing from the body. Use the same method to sever the second wing. For easier eating, you may want to transform the wings into mock legs. Just cut off the wing tips and straighten the two remaining sections with your hands. Pull them into a straight line to look like a small double leg. **To cut off the legs,** force them outward and down, as shown. Where the leg joins the body, insert a knife to cut the ligaments. When the leg is loosened, cut a long gash and continue to cut down toward the back, leaving as much skin as possible on the leg. **To separate the drumstick from the thigh,** flex the leg and crack the ball joint. Place the leg on a cutting board and, with the inner side up, cut at the thin line of skin separating the drumstick and thigh.

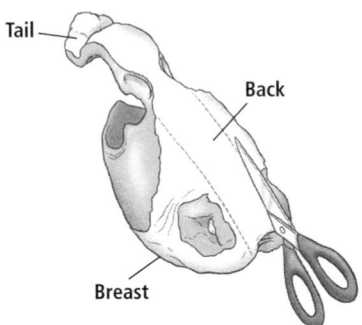

Separating the breast from the back

With the wings and legs severed, you are ready to cut up the carcass. To **separate the back from the breast,** cut through the rib bones on either side of the backbone with poultry shears or a sharp knife. Leave the breast in one piece or cut it into 2 or 4 pieces with the poultry shears. The back has little meat except for two choice "oysters" near the fatty flap at the end of the spine.

To butterfly a whole bird, cut through the ribs on either

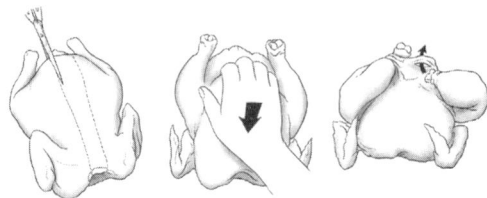

Butterflying a chicken

side of the backbone with shears and remove the bone, as shown. Turn the bird breast side up, place your palm on the breastbone, and press hard to flatten the bird completely. To keep the legs in place during cooking, make ¹/₂-inch slits on either side of the breast tip, then insert the ends of the drumstick into the openings.

To split a whole bird, remove the backbone and flatten as for butterflying. Place skin side down and pry out the breastbone and attached cartilage with your fingers. Cut in half where the breastbone has been removed.

To prepare a boneless, skinless breast, locate the wishbone at the wide end of the breast, scrape it free with the tip of a knife, and pull it out. Place the breast skin side up on your work surface and press down firmly with the heel of your hand to break the membrane covering the breastbone. Flip the breast and, using the point of a paring knife, cut around the shoulder bones attached to the breastbone at the wide end of the breast and remove them. Free the breastbone and cartilage from the flesh with your fingers, then pull them out. Slip your fingers or the paring knife beneath the rib bones and free them from the flesh. Remove the skin and reserve, along with the bones, for stock. Cut the breast in half, and pull or cut out the long white tendon that runs through each half.

To make cutlets or strips, start with a boneless, skinless breast. If possible, to ensure even slices, freeze the breast until it is firm and icy, about 2 to 4 hours. Using a very sharp knife, slice the meat parallel to where the breastbone was, angling to make the longest slices possible, and about ¹/₂ inch wide. For a uniform thickness, pound the strips gently between two sheets of waxed paper.

Boning a chicken breast

ABOUT BONING WHOLE POULTRY

Boning a whole bird so that it can be stuffed and shaped into an impressive facsimile of its original self for a special occasion is much less difficult than you might suspect. ➤ During the entire boning job, be careful not to pierce the skin except for the initial incision. The unpierced skin acts as protection, encasement, and insulation through the cooking period. ➤ Always keep the tip of the knife toward the skeleton and close to the bone.

Begin by placing the bird breast down on a cutting board. Make an incision down the entire length of the backbone, through both skin and flesh. Using a sharp knife (a boning knife, if possible), work as close to the carcass as you can cut, pushing the skin and flesh back as you cut. Work first toward the ball-and-socket joint of the

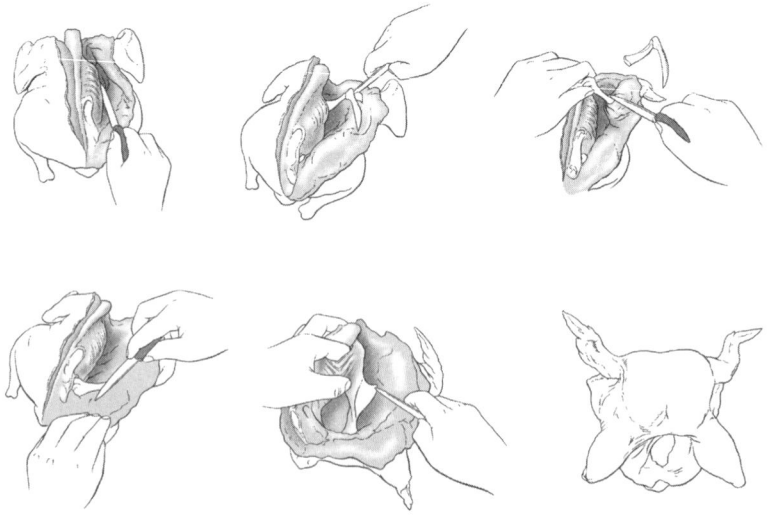

Boning a whole bird

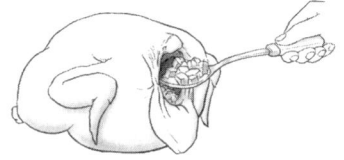 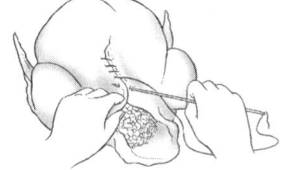 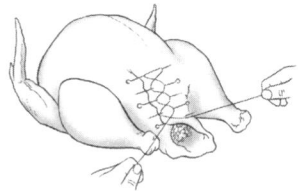

Stuffing and trussing a whole turkey

shoulder, cutting it free and boning the shoulder blade. Pull the wing bone through from the inside, bringing the skin with it. Bone the meat from the wing and reserve it. Then begin on the ball-and-socket joint, cutting it free and boning the shoulder blade. Reserve the meat. After you have freed and reserved the meat from both wings and legs, continue to work the meat free first from one side of the body, then from the other, until the center of the breastbone is reached. ➤ Here great care is needed to free the skin without piercing it, as it is very thin at this point. You should now be able to get the whole skeleton out in one mass. Wash the skin and flesh in cold running water and pat dry with paper towels. To stuff a boned chicken, see 446.

ABOUT BRINING POULTRY

Brining—that is, soaking poultry in a solution of water and salt—helps the bird retain moisture and seasons the meat throughout. ➤ Remember: The longer you brine, the saltier the meat. Always use a nonreactive or plastic bucket or container large enough to hold water to completely cover your bird and small enough to fit in the refrigerator. ➤ Do not brine self-basting or kosher turkeys, as they have already been treated with salt. Use 1 cup table salt or 2 cups kosher salt per each gallon of water. If preparing a large bird such as turkey, brine for 12 to 24 hours, always in the refrigerator. If your poultry is smaller, decrease the time in the brine accordingly. You can also experiment with adding flavors to your brine: peppercorns, allspice, brown sugar, apple juice, or even ingredients associated with soup-making—chunks of onion and carrot and herbs. Discard the brine after the soaking; it cannot be reused.

Brined poultry can be stuffed. However, in that case,

make sure to rinse the bird, inside and out, a few times after removing it from its brine before stuffing it. ➤ Reduce or omit the salt in the stuffing and if using the pan drippings for gravy or sauce; residual brine may make your stuffing and gravy oversalty.

ABOUT STUFFING AND TRUSSING POULTRY

Always ➤ wait until just before roasting to stuff a bird. This may not be convenient, but it is the only safe procedure. Contamination is frequent in prestuffed poultry. Even if refrigerated, the cold may not fully penetrate the stuffing.

Your task will be easier if you place the bird in a large pan before stuffing it. Have the stuffing hot or at least room temperature, and ➤ pack it loosely in the body and neck cavities—only about three-quarters full—as it will expand during cooking. Sew both cavities closed with a trussing needle and twine. Or cover the neck cavity with the neck skin and secure with a small skewer or toothpicks and secure the body cavity with small skewers and lacing. You can find trussing kits at most grocery stores. You can also loosen the breast skin with a spoon or your fingers and place more stuffing or some butter and fresh herbs between the skin and flesh.

Trussing is rarely a must, but gives the bird a handsome shape and makes handling the bird easier when turning during roasting. Fasten the legs close to the body by tying the ends of the drumsticks together. Turn the wings back, pass the string around them, and tie it.

ABOUT CARVING POULTRY

After removing it from the oven, allow small poultry to rest 10 to 15 minutes, a large bird such as a turkey 20 to 40 minutes, to make the meat juicier and slicing easier. Always ➤ take all the stuffing out of the bird before you

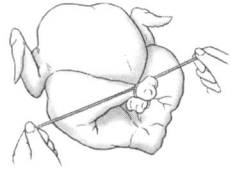  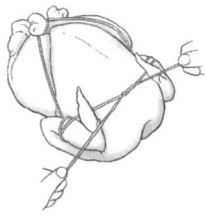

Performing a simple truss on a chicken

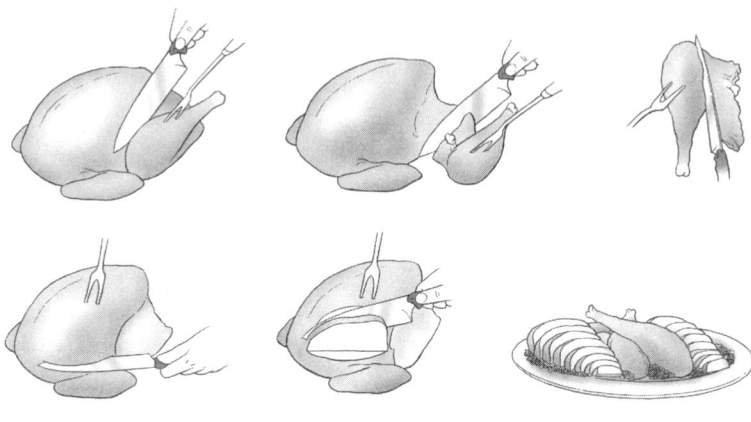

Carving a bird

begin to carve. If the bird is to be carved at the table, be sure the heated serving platter is large enough, and garnish it lightly with fresh herbs and roasted vegetables.

There is a subtle art to carving, and a keen-edged knife and two-tined long-handled fork are the fundamental tools for mastering it. Place the bird breast side up on the platter. Insert the fork firmly into the knee joint, pulling the leg away from the body. Slice the thigh away from the body until the ball-and-socket hip joint is exposed. To sever the thigh joint, make a twisting movement with the knife and continue to hold the knee joint down firmly with the fork. Cut the joint between the thigh and drumstick. Repeat on the other side. Arrange attractively on the serving platter.

If a large bird is being carved, some slices of meat may be cut from the thigh and the drumstick at this point. Proceed to remove the wings in a similar manner. If the bird is large, divide the wings at the second joint. To slice the breast, begin at the area nearest the neck and thinly slice across the grain, down the entire length of the breast. With a large bird such as a turkey, carve only one side to begin unless more is needed at the first serving.

In carving a duck or goose, you will find the leg joint more difficult to sever because it is much farther under the bird and somewhat recessed. Here for the inexperienced carver or the impatient one, poultry shears are a valuable and most welcome addition to the weaponry.

ABOUT ROASTING POULTRY

There are differences of opinion as to whether to salt poultry before roasting. While not really necessary, we prefer to salt and pepper the bird inside and out. Salting brings up another step many chefs and home cooks swear by, brining, 421, soaking your bird in salt water. Whether or not you salt or brine, rub birds well with melted unsalted butter or oil and place on a greased rack in an ➤ uncovered roasting pan in the center of the oven.

Small chickens and Cornish hens will cook and brown best when roasted in a shallow roasting pan or on a rimmed baking sheet. Roast all other birds in a deep roasting pan. Using a rack in the roasting pan promotes air circulation, for more even cooking. Any bird weighing less than 10 pounds can be roasted on a sturdy wire cooling rack in the pan. Heavier birds should be roasted on a roasting rack. A V rack is particularly convenient for roasting a bird using the turned roasted method as it will hold the bird in place.

The biggest challenge facing the cook when roasting any bird—and especially turkeys—is how to cook two kinds of meat at the same time and keep both of them moist and tender—the softer meat of the breast and the tougher, fattier leg and thigh meat. We have found two methods for solving this problem, and either can be used for roasting any bird. The first method is easiest when handling a very large bird.

The **shield and baste** technique is the easiest and most traditional when roasting a large bird like a turkey: Shield the breasts from the high heat coming from above, and baste constantly to add moisture. To begin, rub the bird well with melted unsalted butter or olive oil or a combination of the two, and place on a greased rack. Do not cover the pan. Cover the entire top surface of the fowl with cheesecloth that has been soaked in melted unsalted butter or olive oil, or a combination. ➤ After the first half hour of cooking, for birds of all sizes, baste both over and under the cloth about every half hour with pan drippings. If necessary, the cloth may be removed during the last half hour of cooking to brown the breasts.

Another method for cooking light and dark meat evenly is **turned roasting.** Here the poultry is roasted on its side and turned every 20 to 30 minutes during cooking, exposing the dark meat to the reflected glare of the hot oven roof while keeping the sensitive breast turned toward the relatively cooler oven walls. This permits the dark meat to cook fully while keeping the breast tender and juicy. Since larger birds can be hard to handle, turn them only from side to side every 30 minutes. Utilizing a V rack with any type of whole poultry makes this method much safer. If not using the rack, crumple foil and tuck under the bird to stabilize. We caution you to be careful, of course. Silicone gloves or heavy-duty oven mitts will protect your hands, and sturdy tongs will help lift and balance the bird as you handle it. ➤ Use extreme caution if you choose to use the turning method for a bird weighing over 15 pounds. See 424 for a turned chicken recipe; 442 for turkey.

Timing when a bird is done involves many factors: the age of the bird and its fat content, its size, and whether it is stuffed. Using a thermometer is the most reliable method. Insert it into the inner thigh muscle, taking care that the tip is not in contact with the bone. ➤ Cook until the internal temperature has reached 165°–170°F. The bird will finish cooking out of the oven as it "stands" or "rests" with a final temperature of 180°F. ➤ The center of the stuffing should reach at least 165°F. If not using a thermometer, ➤ allow 20 to 25 minutes per pound for **birds up to 6 pounds.** ➤ For birds between **7 and 15 pounds,** allow 15 to 20 minutes per pound. ➤ For turkeys weighing **over 16 pounds,** allow 13 to 15 minutes per pound. In any case, ➤ add about 5 minutes to the pound if the bird you are cooking is stuffed. If the poultry has finished cooking and ➤ the stuffing is still not at 165°F, remove it and bake in a buttered baking dish in the oven while the bird rests.

Other tests for doneness are to prick the skin of the thigh to see if the juice runs clear or to jiggle the drumstick to see if the hip joint is loose. Sometimes with a young bird the meat close to the bone remains reddish brown even after adequate cooking. The bone marrow in immature fowls has not yet fully hardened, and the red blood cells frequently seep into the adjacent meat, causing it to look rare. See temperature chart, 1036.

Some people like to use an even, **slow heat** throughout the cooking period, placing the bird in a preheated 325°F oven and not basting at all. This method has gained popularity because it is carefree. Some find the flavor superior when the meat is **sealed by high heat** at the outset. Preheat the oven to 450°F, and after placing the bird in the oven, reduce the heat to 350°F.

Just a word about **baking or roasting chicken parts.** For some odd reason, the term "baked chicken" usually implies a dish prepared with chicken parts. Baking is certainly the easiest technique for cooking chicken parts and it produces excellent results. If you are preparing drumsticks and/or thighs only, you can bake them just until the juices run clear or, if you prefer, until the meat falls off the bones. Breast, though, should be removed from the oven as soon as the flesh is no longer pink to prevent the meat from drying out. ➤ When using a recipe, always follow the prescribed baking times, but remember that ➤ boneless chicken cooks quicker than bone-in. Also see chicken parts in About Chicken, right.

ABOUT CHICKEN

As a general rule, ➤ figure on 1 pound of bone-in chicken per person for an 8-ounce serving. **Poussins** are the smallest chickens available and the perfect choice for a single serving. Also referred to as **baby chickens** or **squab broilers,** they are simply very young chickens. **Rock Cornish hens,** 440, are larger than poussins and smaller than chickens. The most common chicken available in markets is the **broiler/fryer,** sometimes labeled simply as "whole chicken." These are usually between 3½ and 4¾ pounds. Larger chickens—generally weighing between 5 to 7 pounds—are sold as **roasters.** They can be roasted whole or cut up, as well as cooked in a fricassee or stew. A **capon** is a castrated young male chicken. His loss is the epicure's gain—it causes him to swell to a weight of 8 to 10 pounds, enough for 8 or more generous servings. Traditionally these birds are fed milk and bread the last 10 days of life, making the meat extremely white and tender. Reserve them for roasting. **Stewing hens,** sometimes called fowls, are older than the usual young chicken that goes to the market but their meat is highly flavorful. While not best for roasting or frying, hens are perfect for moist-heat cooking in fricassees, stews, and soups.

When a recipe calls for **chicken parts,** use a broiler/fryer or any whole chicken, weighing between 3¼ and 5 pounds. See About Cutting Up Poultry, 419. If you cut apart a roaster, be aware that ➤ the larger parts will need to cook longer. And roaster parts are not suitable for frying or broiling. Also keep in mind that ➤ boneless chicken parts cook quicker than bone-in parts.

A variety of chicken parts is available at the supermarket. A cut-up whole chicken is sold in a package of parts that consists of 2 drumsticks, 2 thighs, 2 breast halves, 2 wings, and maybe the giblets. Other choices include quartered whole chickens; whole or split bone-in chicken breasts; boneless, skinless breasts; chicken tenders; whole legs (drumsticks and thighs in one piece); drumsticks; thighs; boneless, skinless thighs; wings; and wing "drumettes" (the meaty first and second wing joints). Increasingly popular are "value" packs containing larger amounts of a single part—perfect for entertaining, large families, or freezing. See About Storage and Safe Handling of Poultry, 418. For cooking chicken livers, see 440.

Ground chicken and **turkey** are widely available. Both are mild and take on the flavors they are cooked in—perfect for meatballs or as an addition to other ground meats. See About Ground Turkey and Chicken, 445.

POACHED CHICKEN OR TURKEY
4 to 6 servings
An excellent way to prepare large amounts of chicken for such dishes as Chicken à la King, 112, enchiladas, or pot pies. Please read About Poaching, 1050.
Place in a Dutch oven:

> **3½ pounds chicken or turkey parts or 1½ pounds boneless, skinless chicken or turkey breast**

2 carrots, cut into 2-inch pieces
2 stalks celery, cut into 2-inch pieces
1$^3/_4$ to 2 cups chicken stock or broth
1 medium onion, quartered
1 Bouquet Garni, 960

Add additional water to cover the pieces by 2 inches. Bring to a simmer, reduce heat so the broth liquid barely bubbles. Partially cover and cook until the meat releases clear juices when pierced with a fork, 25 to 30 minutes for chicken or turkey parts, 8 to 12 minutes for boneless, skinless chicken or turkey breast. Remove the meat and let cool. If using chicken parts, remove and discard the skin and bones. Cut or shred the meat into bite-sized pieces. Skim the fat with a spoon. Strain vegetables and discard. If not using immediately, broth can be cooled and frozen, 115–116.

ROAST CHICKEN
4 to 8 servings
Please read About Roasting Poultry, 422, and About Carving Poultry, 421.

I. Position a rack in the center of the oven. Preheat the oven to 450°F. Remove the neck and giblets from:

1 whole chicken

Truss, 421, the chicken if desired. Place breast side up on a rack set in a roasting pan. If desired, place in the cavity:

(3 to 6 sprigs parsley, tarragon, thyme, rosemary, or sage or 1 lemon, halved)

Rub the chicken with:

2 to 3 tablespoons melted butter or olive oil

Sprinkle with:

Salt and black pepper to taste

Place the chicken in the oven, reduce the heat to 350°F, and roast about 20 minutes per pound, basting periodically. Transfer to a platter and let stand 10 to 15 minutes before carving. The chicken is done when the thigh registers 180°F. If desired, prepare:

(Poultry Pan Sauce Gravy, 546)

II. Use these proportions for a chicken weighing about 4 pounds. Double the ingredients for a larger bird. Combine:

2 teaspoons minced fresh rosemary or thyme or $^3/_4$ teaspoon dried, crumbled
(1 teaspoon grated lemon zest)
2 to 3 medium garlic cloves, minced
$^1/_4$ teaspoon crushed red pepper flakes
$^1/_2$ teaspoon salt

Being careful not to tear it, loosen the skin around the breast, thighs, and drumsticks with your fingers and spread the herb mixture under the skin. Then roast as directed above, or follow the recipe for **Turned Roast Chicken,** below.

III. Prepare the smaller amount of vegetables and other ingredients for a 4- to 5-pound chicken, the larger amount for a bigger bird.

Toss together in a large roasting pan:

2 to 3 large boiling potatoes, peeled and quartered

2 to 3 medium carrots, halved lengthwise and cut into 1-inch pieces
2 to 3 medium onions, quartered lengthwise
2 to 3 medium ribs celery, cut into 1-inch pieces
2 to 3 tablespoons melted butter or vegetable oil
$^1/_2$ to $^3/_4$ teaspoon dried thyme
$^1/_2$ to $^3/_4$ teaspoon salt
Black pepper to taste

Set the chicken on a rack over a roasting pan, then roast as above or following the recipe for **Turned Roast Chicken,** below. Stir the vegetables every time you baste the chicken. Add the vegetables midway through roasting; they will take about 45 minutes to become tender and browned. If done before the chicken, remove, then reheat while the chicken rests. Pour into the pan to deglaze it:

($^1/_3$ to $^1/_2$ cup hot chicken stock or broth)

Scrape the browned bits off the pan, then pour over the vegetables.

TURNED ROAST CHICKEN

Please read About Roasting Poultry, 422. Prepare **Roast Chicken, above,** but place the chicken on its side on the rack. Roast for 20 minutes. Grasp the chicken at both ends, protecting your hands with silicone gloves or heavy-duty oven mitts, and, if needed, use a set of sturdy tongs to help balance the bird as you turn it breast side down. Baste and roast 20 minutes longer. Continue to turn and baste until the chicken is cooked. To brown the breast, you may roast the chicken breast side up for the last 20 to 30 minutes. Let stand for 10 to 15 minutes before carving.

ROAST CHICKEN WITH STUFFING
6 to 10 servings
Please read About Stuffing and Trussing Poultry, 421, and About Roasting Poultry, 422. Position a rack in the center of the oven. Preheat the oven to 450°F. Prepare and have hot or at room temperature:

$^1/_2$ recipe Basic Bread Stuffing or a variation, 532,
$^1/_2$ recipe Basic Corn Bread Stuffing or a variation, 534, or $^1/_2$ recipe Mashed Potato Stuffing, 537

Remove the neck and giblets from:

One 6- to 8-pound chicken

Loosely pack the stuffing into the body and neck cavities. Truss, 421, the bird, if you desire. Roast as directed for **Roast Chicken,** above, or **Turned Roast Chicken,** above. The stuffing may increase the total roasting time by 30 to 40 minutes. Let stand 10 to 15 minutes before carving.

ROAST CHICKEN STUFFED UNDER THE SKIN
4 servings
Please read About Stuffing and Trussing Poultry, 421, and About Roasting Poultry, 422. Position a rack in the center of the oven. Preheat the oven to 400°F. Prepare:

Spinach Ricotta Stuffing, 538, or Duxelles, 284

Remove the neck and giblets from:

One 3$^1/_2$- to 4-pound chicken

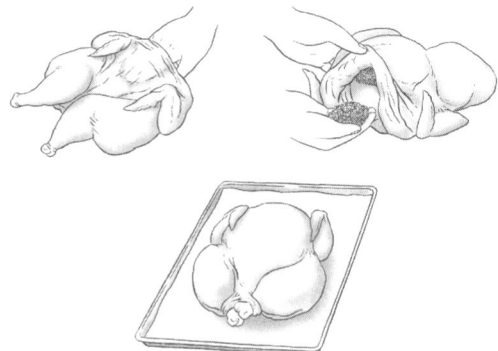

Preparing roast chicken stuffed under the skin

Butterfly the bird, 420. Insert your hand at the wing end of the breast and loosen the skin over the breast and around the thighs and drumsticks. Generously pack the stuffing under the skin, first pushing it over the drumsticks and thighs and then over the breast, 425. Cut a ¹/₂-inch slit in the skin on either side of the breast, about 1 inch from the tip, and slip the ends of the drumsticks into the openings, 425. Smooth the stuffing with your hands to give the bird a plump but natural shape. Place the bird skin side up on rack in a shallow roasting pan. Brush with:

1 to 2 tablespoons melted butter or olive oil
Roast, basting often, until the thigh registers 165°–170°F on a thermometer, 423, about 45 to 50 minutes. Let rest for 15 to 20 minutes before serving.

ROAST CHICKEN WITH 40 CLOVES OF GARLIC

4 servings
Because it is cooked in a covered casserole, the flesh ends up moist and succulent but will not brown.
Remove the neck and giblets from:

One 3¹/₂- to 4-pound chicken
Rub the skin with:

Olive oil
Mix, then rub into the cavity and on the skin:

1 teaspoon dried thyme
1 teaspoon dried sage
¹/₂ teaspoon salt
¹/₂ teaspoon dried rosemary
¹/₂ teaspoon black pepper
Place in the cavity:

1 lemon, quartered
Truss, 421, if desired. Arrange the chicken breast side up in a flame-proof casserole, cover, and refrigerate for 2 to 24 hours to infuse with flavor. Position a rack in the center of the oven. Preheat the oven to 375°F. Add to the casserole:

3 garlic heads, cloves separated but not peeled
1³/₄ cups chicken stock or broth, or as needed
1 cup dry white wine, or as needed

Bring to a boil on the stovetop. Cover the casserole with a lid or foil and transfer to the oven. Roast for 25 minutes. Increase the oven temperature to 450°F, uncover the casserole, and roast the chicken until the thigh registers 165°–170°F on a thermometer, 30 to 45 minutes more. Make sure there is always some liquid in the bottom of the casserole; add a little more wine or stock if needed.

Remove the chicken and garlic from the casserole and keep warm. Skim as much fat as possible from the pan juices with a spoon. If the pan juices are watery or weak in flavor, boil them down over high heat to concentrate. Transfer the juices to a saucepan. If you wish, peel 6 or more of the garlic cloves and mash to a paste, then stir into the sauce and boil for 1 minute. Remove the sauce from the heat and stir in:

(2 tablespoons minced parsley or finely shredded
basil or 2 teaspoons minced thyme, tarragon,
or rosemary)
Season with:

Salt and black pepper to taste
Cut the chicken into serving pieces and arrange on a platter. Spoon the pan juices over it and scatter the garlic cloves around it.

CHICKEN BREASTS BAKED ON A BED OF MUSHROOMS

4 to 6 servings
Position a rack in the center of the oven. Preheat the oven to 400°F. Trim any excess fat from:

6 bone-in or boneless chicken breast halves
(with skin)
Season with:

1 teaspoon dried thyme
Salt and black pepper to taste
Lightly oil a baking pan or shallow baking dish just large enough to hold the chicken pieces in a single layer. Remove the stems from:

6 large portobello mushrooms or 12 to 18 large
shiitake or button mushrooms
Or cut into ¹/₄-inch slices:

Enough smaller mushrooms to cover the bottom of
the pan
Arrange the mushrooms in the pan and distribute over all:

2 cups dry white wine, or as needed
1 tablespoon minced garlic
Salt and black pepper to taste
Lay the chicken breasts skin side up on top of the mushrooms. Brush lightly with:

Olive oil
Bake, uncovered, until the chicken skin turns golden brown, about 20 minutes. Check to make sure there is some liquid in the pan; if not, add more wine. Baste the chicken with pan juices and turn it over. Bake until the chicken registers 165°F on a thermometer, 10 to 20 minutes more.

Using a slotted spoon, remove the chicken and mushrooms to a platter, arranging the chicken skin side up on the mushrooms. Pour the pan juices into a small saucepan and skim off the fat with a spoon. Add:

$^1\!/_2$ cup chicken stock or broth
$^1\!/_2$ cup heavy cream

Boil over high heat until reduced to about 1 cup, with a slightly syrupy consistency. Taste and adjust the seasonings. Spoon some of the sauce over the chicken and pass the rest separately. Sprinkle the chicken with:

(2 tablespoons minced parsley)

BAKED CHILI-GARLIC CHICKEN

4 servings

Place in a shallow baking dish:

$3^1\!/_2$ to $4^1\!/_2$ pounds chicken parts

Using about 2 tablespoons per piece, coat the chicken on all sides with:

1 cup Chili-Garlic Spice Paste, 589

Cover and refrigerate for 2 to 24 hours. Position a rack in the center of the oven. Preheat to 350°F. Lightly oil a shallow roasting pan or baking sheet. Arrange the chicken skin side down in the pan. Roast for 20 minutes. Turn skin side up and roast until the thigh releases clear juices when pricked with a fork and registers 180°F on a thermometer, about 20 minutes more. To crisp the skin, run the chicken briefly under a hot broiler.

GINGER SPICE BAKED CHICKEN

Prepare **Baked Chili-Garlic Chicken, above,** substituting **1 cup Asian Ginger Spice Paste, 589,** for the chili paste.

THAI CURRY BAKED CHICKEN

Prepare **Baked Chili-Garlic Chicken, above,** substituting **1 cup Thai Green Curry Paste, 589,** for the chili paste.

ABOUT BROILING CHICKEN

Small whole chickens or small pieces are best for broiling. By the time larger pieces are done, the skin will have charred and the kitchen filled with smoke. Buy the smallest chicken you can find and split it or divide it into parts, or buy the smallest chicken parts available. Another alternative is to broil Cornish hens: Split them, removing the backbones, and serve a half or two halves to each person.

Broiling chicken should be a slow process. As a general rule, the chicken should be placed bone side up 6 to 8 inches beneath the preheated broiler element and broiled for 15 minutes, then turned and broiled for 10 to 15 minutes on the skin side. ➤ Always broil the bone side first, or the skin will become soggy. When ovens with very hot broilers are used, it may be necessary to move the chicken farther from the heat to prevent charring.

Rubs and pastes tend to burn on broiled chicken. Marinades, glazes, and sauces also tend to blacken. ➤ To use a marinade, choose one that does not include sugar, molasses, honey, jelly, or jam. ➤ Any garlic to be used in a marinade should be put through a garlic press or minced almost to a paste. When using any of the above, apply

separately to each side of the chicken shortly before that side is cooked through.

Always ➤ broil chicken in a two-piece broiling pan with a slotted or perforated broiling tray, which allows the dripping fat to drain away and collect in the pan below. If broiled in a flat baking pan, on a rack set in a pan, or in a ridged disposable foil pan, the fat will be directly exposed to the heat and will smoke and may even catch fire.

BROILED CHICKEN

4 servings

Preheat the broiler. If broiling a whole chicken, cut the bird in half, removing the backbone, 419, and make a shallow incision on the inside of each leg at the drumstick/thigh joint to help the heat penetrate. Arrange skin side down on a broiler tray:

One $3^1\!/_2$- to 4-pound chicken or $3^1\!/_2$ pounds chicken parts

and brush the exposed side with:

2 tablespoons melted butter or olive oil

Sprinkle liberally with:

Salt and black pepper

Place pan 8 inches beneath broiler for 12 to 15 minutes. Turn chicken skin side up and brush with:

1 to 2 tablespoons melted butter or olive oil

Sprinkle with:

Salt and black pepper to taste

Broil the second side until skin is browned and crisp and thigh registers 170°F on a thermometer, 423, 15 to 20 minutes for a split chicken, 8 to 10 minutes for chicken parts. If the skin begins to char before the chicken is done, move the pan farther from the heat. Remove to a platter and let stand 10 to 15 minutes.

To make a pan sauce, pour in the broiling pan while scraping with a spoon:

($^1\!/_2$ cup chicken stock or broth)

Skim the fat and place the pan on two burners over medium heat. Boil until the juices are reduced. Spoon sauce over chicken and sprinkle with:

2 tablespoons minced parsley

BROILED BARBECUED CHICKEN

Prepare **Broiled Chicken, above.** About 2 minutes before the chicken is fully cooked, brush both sides with **1 cup Barbecue Sauce, 586, or Barbecue Sauce for Poultry, 586.** Return to the broiler skin side up and broil until the skin and sauce have charred slightly and the flesh is done. Serve with additional barbecue sauce.

BROILED TERIYAKI CHICKEN

Prepare **Broiled Chicken, above.** Rub the pieces with vegetable oil before broiling and omit the salt and pepper. Prepare **Teriyaki Marinade, 586,** and simmer, stirring, in a small saucepan over medium heat until slightly thickened. About 2 minutes before the chicken is fully cooked, brush both sides with about $^3\!/_4$ cup of the sauce. Return to the broiler skin side up and broil until the skin is lightly charred. Serve with additional sauce.

BROILED LEMON GARLIC CHICKEN
4 servings
Combine in a large bowl:
> $1/4$ **cup fresh lemon juice**
> $1/4$ **cup olive oil**
> **1 to 2 tablespoons pressed or minced garlic**
> **1 tablespoon Dijon mustard**
> $1/2$ **teaspoon dried thyme**
> **1 teaspoon salt**
> **1 teaspoon black pepper**

Prepare:
> **Broiled Chicken, 426**

omitting the salt, pepper, butter or oil. Place chicken parts in the marinade, turning to coat. Refrigerate, covered, for 1 to 3 hours. Cook as for Broiled Chicken, 426. Brush with the reserved marinade. Remove the chicken to a platter. Prepare a pan sauce, if desired, by boiling the remaining pan juices and marinade until reduced, stirring occasionally to loosen any browned bits from the pan.

ABOUT GRILLING CHICKEN
Skin-on chicken tends to drip fat and may catch fire when grilled directly over hot coals. For this reason, grill skin-on chicken over direct heat only until its skin begins to crisp and render fat, then move off the direct heat, cover, and cook using indirect heat; see About Grilling, 1057. As a rule of thumb, ➤ chicken parts require about 10 minutes over direct heat to brown nicely, then 10 to 25 minutes with indirect heat to cook through. ➤ White meat cooks more quickly than dark, and small parts, of course, more quickly than large. Because they cook quickly and release little fat, boneless, skinless chicken breasts, thighs, and kebabs can be grilled over direct heat from start to finish, though ➤ they will require close attention to prevent overcooking. If your grill does not have a lid, cook the chicken over a cooler fire and be sure to reserve a cool spot to which the chicken can be ➤ quickly pulled in case of flare-ups.

Rubs and pastes tend to burn on grilled chicken, just as on broiled chicken. Marinades, glazes, and sauces also tend to blacken. To use a marinade, choose one that does not include sugar, molasses, honey, jelly, or jam. Any garlic to be used in a marinade should be put through a garlic press or minced almost to a paste. When using any of the above, apply separately to each side of the chicken shortly before that side is cooked through.

Although the recipes in this section are written for use with a **charcoal grill,** almost all can be adapted for **gas grilling.** If using a gas grill, turn both burners on high for about 10 minutes to preheat the grill, then turn off one of the burners to create a spot for indirect-heat cooking.

GRILL-ROASTED WHOLE CHICKEN
4 servings
Roasting a chicken on the grill produces perfectly cooked meat and a delicious smoked taste.
Prepare a hot grill. Remove the neck and giblets from:
> **One $3^1/2$- to $4^1/2$-pound chicken**

Generously rub the neck and body cavities and sprinkle the skin with:
> **Salt and black pepper**

Truss, 421, if desired. Brush the chicken all over with:
> **2 tablespoons melted butter or olive oil**

Open the vents on the bottom of the grill completely. If using charcoal, let it heat until covered with white ash. Divide the coals in half and push half to each side of the grill. Replace the grill rack and arrange the chicken breast side up on the rack midway between the two piles of coals. Cover the grill and open the cover vents all the way. After 45 minutes, if desired, brush the chicken with:
> **($1/2$ to 1 cup Barbecue Sauce, 586, or Barbecue Sauce for Poultry, 586)**

Roast until the thigh registers 170°F on a thermometer, 60 to 80 minutes. Let the chicken rest for 10 to 15 minutes before carving.

CHICKEN KEBABS
4 to 6 servings
Soak wooden or bamboo skewers in water for at least 30 minutes before use. Almost any vegetable will work, but firm vegetables such as carrots, potatoes, cauliflower, and broccoli should first be steamed until nearly tender. Please see About Grilling Chicken, above, and About Skewered Cooking, 1049. Prepare in a large bowl:
> $3/4$ **cup Fresh Herb Vinaigrette, 572, Black Pepper Vinaigrette, 573, or Lemon-Oregano Vinaigrette, 573**

Pour half of the marinade into a medium bowl. Add, turning to coat, and marinate in the refrigerator for at least 30 minutes, and up to 2 hours:
> **4 boneless, skinless chicken breast halves or 6 boneless, skinless chicken thighs, cut into 1-inch cubes, 420**

When you are ready to grill, add to remaining marinade:
> **1 large red onion, cut into 1-inch chunks**
> **16 small mushrooms**
> **16 cherry tomatoes**
> **1 red, yellow, or green bell pepper, cut into 1-inch squares, or 2 small zucchini or summer squash, halved lengthwise and sliced $1/2$ inch thick**

Lightly oil the grill rack and prepare a medium-hot charcoal fire. Remove the chicken from the marinade and thread it onto skewers, leaving a little space between the pieces to allow for even cooking. If you thread the pieces onto 2 parallel skewers for each kebab, they will stay put when turned. Skewer the vegetables in the same manner. Spread the hot coals in one side of the grill. Cover the grill and heat the rack for 5 minutes. Arrange the skewers on the hot rack over the coals, and place the skewers of vegetables on the other side of the grill, away from direct heat. Place strips of aluminum foil under the exposed ends of the skewers. Grill for 4 minutes, then turn and grill until the vegetables are crisp-tender and browned along the edges, and the chicken is opaque in the center and browned on the outside, 3 to 4 minutes more.

GRILLED LEMON CHICKEN

4 servings

Please read About Grilling Chicken, above. Prepare:

A double recipe of Lemon-Oregano Vinaigrette, 573

Place in a shallow baking dish:

4 bone-in chicken breast halves (with skin)

Add half the vinaigrette, turning to coat. Cover and marinate, refrigerated, for 1 hour. Prepare a medium-hot fire. Place the chicken skin side down on grill rack, cover the grill, and cook until the skin is crisp and golden brown, 8 to 10 minutes. Move the chicken to the opposite side of the grill, turning it skin side up. Move chicken off direct heat, cover the grill, and cook until the meat is opaque throughout and registers 165°–170°F on a thermometer, 10 to 15 minutes more. If using a broiler, cook 10 minutes, skin side down, then 10 minutes skin side up. Spoon the remaining vinaigrette over the chicken before serving.

JAMAICAN JERK CHICKEN

8 servings

Chicken, pork, and fish all can be cooked in the popular Jamaican marinade known as "jerk." The cornerstone of all jerk dishes is a vinegary, intensely hot paste of dried herbs and habanero peppers, which are about fifty times hotter than jalapeños. If you cannot find them, a habanero-based hot sauce makes a good substitute. You can cook the chicken immediately after brushing it with the jerk paste, or marinate it, covered and refrigerated, for up to 12 hours. Please read About Grilling Chicken, 427. Prepare:

Jamaican Jerk Paste, 588

Brush the jerk mixture over:

8 whole chicken legs or 8 bone-in chicken breast halves

Lightly oil the grill rack and prepare a medium-hot charcoal fire. Spread the hot coals on one side of the grill. Arrange the chicken pieces skin side down on the side of the grill away from the coals. Cover the grill and cook for 20 minutes. Turn the chicken and cook 15 to 20 minutes more.

TANDOORI CHICKEN

4 servings

In Indian cooking, "tandoori" refers to cut-up chickens, meat kebabs, and flatbreads that are cooked in a tandoor, a fiercely hot charcoal-fired vertical oven. Before cooking, the chicken and meat are usually marinated in an aromatic mixture of yogurt and spices. This marinade is tinted with a natural dye, sometimes turmeric, which gives tandoori chicken its characteristic orange-yellow color. An excellent tandoori-style chicken can be prepared in a covered grill using a very hot fire. To ensure that the outside does not char before the chicken cooks through, use the smallest chicken parts you can find, or cut a 3½- to 4-pound chicken into parts yourself. See About Cutting Up Poultry, 419. Two split Cornish hens also work well. In lieu of grilling, you can roast the chicken on a lightly oiled baking sheet in a 500°F oven for 25 to 30 minutes, but be prepared for a smoky kitchen. Turn on the exhaust fan and turn off the smoke detectors.

Please read About Grilling Chicken, 427.

Prepare in a large bowl:

Tandoori Marinade, 584

Remove the skin from:

3½ pounds chicken parts

Add the chicken pieces to the marinade, turn to coat, cover, and refrigerate for 4 to 6 hours.

Prepare a hot charcoal fire. Spread the hot coals on one side of the grill. Cover the grill and heat the rack for 5 minutes. Arrange the chicken parts skin side up over the coals, cover the grill, and cook for 15 minutes. Move the chicken to the side of the grill away from the coals, turning it skin side down, cover the grill, and cook 10 to 15 minutes more.

ASH-ROASTED CHICKEN THIGHS

3 to 6 servings

This is a technique for all seasons—the grill's hot coals in summer and a campfire or fireplace in winter, 1059. Be sure to bury the chicken in the embers surrounding the fire, not directly under it. This recipe can be multiplied to serve many people, but wrap only 2 thighs per packet to guarantee easy handling.

Remove the skin from:

6 bone-in chicken thighs

Sprinkle generously with:

Salt and black pepper

Have ready:

¼ cup minced parsley

6 garlic cloves, thinly sliced

1 lemon, very thinly sliced

Cut a sheet of wide heavy-duty foil about 18 inches long. Place 2 thighs in the center, sprinkle with one-third of the parsley and garlic, and top with 2 or 3 lemon slices. Cover with a second sheet of foil of the same size. Crimp the edges to seal securely, then roll the edges in toward the center to make an 8- to 9-inch square packet. Wrap the packet in a third sheet of foil to seal completely. Repeat, making 3 packets in all.

Prepare a hot charcoal fire. Push the coals to one side of the grill and arrange the chicken packets in a single layer over the bottom of the grill, then scatter the coals in an even layer over the packets. Cook for 35 minutes.

Remove the packets from the coals with tongs and let stand for 10 minutes. Open the foil carefully to avoid being burned by the steam.

ASH-ROASTED CHICKEN HOBO PACKS

4 servings

These packets—also known as "hobo packs"—can contain just about any combination of meat and vegetables. Combine in a large bowl and toss well:

12 unpeeled garlic cloves
1 lime, thinly sliced
$^1/_3$ cup chopped cilantro or parsley
$^1/_4$ cup olive oil
1 teaspoon minced chile pepper
Salt and black pepper to taste

Add to mixture and turn to coat:

4 boneless, skinless chicken breast halves or thighs
8 small new potatoes

Place 2 chicken breasts and 4 potatoes in the center of a sheet of wide heavy-duty aluminum foil about 18 inches long. Cover with a second sheet of foil. Crimp the edges of the two sheets to seal securely, then roll in the edges 3 to 4 inches toward the center. Wrap the package completely in a third sheet of foil to double-seal. Repeat to make a second package.

Prepare a hot charcoal fire. Clear a space in the grill and lay the packages in the space. Pile the hot coals over and around the packages. Cook for 30 to 40 minutes. Remove with tongs and let stand 10 minutes. Open carefully to avoid being burned by steam.

ABOUT FRYING CHICKEN

You can cook fried chicken in a variety of ways, including baking it in the oven. Fried chicken is defined not so much by the cooking process as by the result, which should be juicy, succulent chicken covered in a crispy crust that is not at all greasy.

When panfrying chicken, it should go into sizzling hot fat. Monitor the chicken, turning it several times to get an even color. The following recipes call for frying in butter or vegetable oil or shortening; also try a combination of lard and butter.

In preparing any recipe for fried chicken, ➤ the skin can be removed prior to coating, which substantially reduces the fat content. All fried chicken is good both hot and cold, but chicken held at room temperature will be crisper and juicier than if refrigerated. ➤ The crust will best retain its crispness if you drain the chicken not on a rack but on paper towels or a brown paper bag.

PANFRIED (OR SAUTÉED) CHICKEN

4 servings

The quickest and simplest of all fried chicken recipes. Because it is not coated with flour, the chicken does not have a true crust, but the skin is deliciously brown and crispy. Please read About Frying Chicken, above. Season:

$3^1/_2$ to $4^1/_2$ pounds chicken parts

generously with:

Salt and black pepper

Heat in a large heavy skillet over medium-high heat:

1 tablespoon butter
1 tablespoon vegetable oil

Cooking in batches if necessary, arrange the chicken pieces skin side down in a single layer in the skillet. Fry until the chicken is nicely browned on the first side and detaches easily from the skillet, about 5 minutes. Turn the chicken with tongs and cook until nicely browned on the second side, about 5 minutes more. Reduce the heat to medium and continue to cook the chicken, turning often, until the thigh juices run clear when pricked with a fork, about 20 minutes more. Remove the chicken to a platter. Prepare in the pan:

(Poultry Pan Sauce Gravy, 546)

FRIED CHICKEN

4 servings

This chicken has the crackling crisp skin and distinctive mahogany color that are the hallmarks of the dish as prepared by the best Southern cooks. The optional buttermilk marinade promotes tenderness. Use a seasoned cast-iron skillet if possible, for it allows the chicken to achieve the prized deep color without charring. Fry in batches if necessary. Frying the chicken in vegetable shortening rather than oil gives the crust a snapping crispness.

Please read About Frying Chicken, above. Separate:

$3^1/_2$ to $4^1/_2$ pounds chicken parts

into legs, thighs, and drumsticks and cut each breast half diagonally in half through the bone. If you'd like to marinate the chicken, stir together in a large bowl:

($1^1/_2$ cups buttermilk)
(1 teaspoon salt)
($^1/_2$ teaspoon black pepper)

Add the chicken and turn to coat well. Cover and refrigerate for 2 to 12 hours, and drain before coating.

Combine in a sturdy paper or plastic bag and shake to mix:

2 cups all-purpose flour
2 teaspoons salt
1 teaspoon black pepper
(Pinch of ground red pepper)

Shake the chicken a few pieces at a time in the bag until well coated, and let dry on a rack at room temperature for 15 to 30 minutes. Place in a deep heavy skillet, preferably cast iron, over medium-high heat:

$^1/_2$ inch vegetable shortening

When the oil is hot enough, a small corner of a chicken piece dipped into the fat will cause vigorous bubbling. Gently place the chicken skin side down in the hot fat in a single layer. Cover and cook for 10 minutes, or until browned on the first side; check after 5 minutes and move the pieces if they are coloring unevenly or turn the heat down if the chicken is browning too quickly. Turn the chicken with tongs and cook, uncovered, until the second side is richly browned, 10 to 12 minutes more. Remove the chicken to a baking sheet lined with paper towels or a brown paper bag. If not serving immediately, keep the chicken warm in a barely warm oven.

You may pour the fat out of the pan, retaining the browned bits, and prepare with milk:

(Meat Pan Gravy, 546)

EXTRA-CRISPY FRIED CHICKEN

4 servings

Try this recipe if plain fried chicken is not crusty enough to suit your taste. There is almost as much crust as there is meat.

Please read About Cutting Up Poultry, 419, and About Frying Chicken, 429. Have ready:

3¹/₂ to 4¹/₂ pounds chicken parts

Separate the legs into thighs and drumsticks; cut each breast half diagonally in half through the bone. Sprinkle very generously with:

Salt and black pepper

Whisk thoroughly in a medium bowl:

2 eggs

¹/₂ cup milk

1 teaspoon salt

Mix together on a plate:

1¹/₂ cups all-purpose flour

2 teaspoons salt

2 teaspoons black pepper

Heat in a deep-fat fryer or deep heavy pot to 350°F:

2 to 3 inches vegetable oil or shortening

Toss the breast pieces in flour mixture, then remove to the egg mixture and turn until thoroughly moistened on all sides. One at a time, lift the pieces out of the egg, letting the excess drip off. Roll in the flour mixture again until completely coated, and slip into the hot fat. Fry for 10 minutes, turning the pieces several times with tongs and keeping the fat between 320° and 360°F. Remove the pieces to a baking sheet lined with paper towels or a brown paper bag, and hold in a warm oven. Repeat the procedure with the thighs and drumsticks, frying the pieces for 15 minutes. Serve with:

(Rémoulade Sauce, 581, or warm honey)

OVEN-FRIED CHICKEN WITH CORNMEAL CRUST

4 servings

Please read About Cutting Up Poultry, 419, and About Frying Chicken, 429. Have ready:

3¹/₂ to 4¹/₂ pounds chicken parts

Whisk in a large bowl:

Yogurt or Buttermilk Marinade, 585

adding:

(1 teaspoon grated lemon zest)

¹/₄ cup fresh lemon juice

2 tablespoons finely minced shallots

1 tablespoon finely minced fresh thyme or rosemary or 1 teaspoon dried

2 teaspoons salt

2 teaspoons chili powder

Add the chicken and turn to coat. Cover and refrigerate for 2 to 4 hours. Position a rack in the center of the oven. Preheat the oven to 425°F. Lightly oil a baking sheet. Combine in a wide shallow bowl:

²/₃ cup grated Parmesan or aged Monterey Jack

¹/₂ cup dry bread crumbs

¹/₂ cup cornmeal

3 tablespoons minced parsley

1 teaspoon chili powder

1 teaspoon salt

¹/₂ teaspoon black pepper

Whisk together in a shallow bowl:

2 eggs

2 tablespoons butter, melted

Remove chicken from the marinade and shake off the excess. Dip the chicken in the egg mixture, then coat with the cornmeal mixture, patting with your fingers to make the crumbs adhere. Arrange the chicken skin side up on the baking sheet. (The chicken can be prepared to this point up to 3 hours in advance and kept, uncovered, in the refrigerator.) Drizzle over the chicken:

(2 to 3 tablespoons melted butter or olive oil)

Oven-fry 35 to 40 minutes. Serve hot or cold.

CHICKEN FINGERS

3 to 5 servings

With a dipping sauce, these make nice hors d'oeuvres, and of course children love them.

Read About Cutting Up Poultry, 419, and About Frying Chicken, 429. Have ready:

4 boneless, skinless chicken breast halves

Trim fat. Peel off the tenders on the underside and remove the white tendons. Cut the chicken breasts crosswise into 6 pieces each. Combine in a wide shallow bowl:

2 cups dry bread crumbs

(¹/₂ cup grated Parmesan)

1 tablespoon minced parsley or 1 teaspoon paprika

1 teaspoon salt

¹/₂ teaspoon black pepper

Whisk together in a shallow bowl:

2 large eggs

2 teaspoons water

Dip the chicken fingers and tenders into the egg mixture, then coat with the bread crumb mixture, patting with your fingers to make the crumbs adhere. Heat in a heavy 10 to 12 inch skillet over medium-high heat until hot:

3 tablespoons vegetable or olive oil

Add as many pieces of chicken to the skillet as will fit without crowding and cook until nicely browned on both sides, 4 to 5 minutes. Remove to a plate, add more oil to the skillet if needed, and cook the remaining chicken in the same manner. Serve with:

(Honey Mustard Dipping Sauce, 566, or Ginger Soy Sauce, 571)

ABOUT CHICKEN FRICASSEES, STEWS, AND OTHER BRAISED DISHES

The world's cuisines boast a wealth of fricassees, stews, and ragouts made with chicken. Definitions of these dishes overlap, but all involve braising browned or plain chicken in stock or water, often with vegetables or other additions. The liquid becomes a flavorful sauce or gravy, which can be thickened after cooking with flour or egg yolks or enriched with cream. Most braised chicken dishes can be served with couscous, 362, rice, 353, noodles, 325, Boiled Potatoes, 295, or Späetzle, 335.

COQ AU VIN

4 servings

When the old rooster, or *coq,* lost his crow, he would find himself the main ingredient in this classic French country fricassee. Commonly made with red wine, but if you would like to try a white, choose one that is fruity, such as Riesling or Chardonnay.

Have ready:

3¹/₂ to 4¹/₂ pounds chicken parts

Season with:

Salt and black pepper to taste

Cook in a Dutch oven over medium-high heat until browned:

4 ounces thick-cut bacon, cut crosswise into
   ¹/₄-inch strips

Remove to a plate. Add as many pieces of chicken to the pot as will fit and cook until brown on both sides, about 7 minutes. Remove to a plate. Brown the remaining pieces. Pour off all but 3 tablespoons of the fat. Add:

1 cup chopped onions
¹/₂ cup chopped carrots

Cook, stirring occasionally, about 10 minutes. Stir in:

3 tablespoons all-purpose flour

Reduce heat to low. Cook, stirring constantly, until the roux just begins to turn light brown, about 5 minutes. Stir in:

3 cups dry red wine
1 cup chicken stock or broth
2 tablespoons tomato paste
2 bay leaves
¹/₂ teaspoon dried thyme
¹/₂ teaspoon dried marjoram or oregano, crumbled

Increase the heat to high and bring the sauce to a boil, stirring constantly. Return the bacon and chicken, with any accumulated juices, to the pot. Return the sauce to a boil, then reduce the heat so that the liquid barely simmers, cover, and cook until the thigh registers 180°F on a thermometer, 25 to 35 minutes.

Meanwhile, heat in a wide skillet over medium-high heat:

3 tablespoons butter

Add:

(1 to 2 cups pearl onions, peeled)

Cook, stirring often, until lightly browned and just tender, 5 to 8 minutes. Add:

8 ounces mushrooms, sliced

Cook, stirring, until the mushrooms release their juices.

Remove from the heat. Remove the chicken to a platter and cover with aluminum foil. Discard the bay leaves. Bring the sauce to a boil over high heat and reduce until syrupy, using a spoon to skim off the fat as it accumulates. Add the mushrooms and onions with the pan juices to the sauce and heat through. Season with:

Salt and black pepper to taste

Pour the sauce over the chicken. Garnish with:

(2 to 3 tablespoons minced parsley)

COCONUT CHICKEN CURRY

4 to 6 servings

Have ready:

2 pounds chicken thighs or breasts

Season with:

Salt and black pepper to taste

Heat in a large skillet or wok, over high heat:

2 tablespoons vegetable oil

Add chicken. Brown on both sides. Remove from pan. Add:

1 cup chopped onions
1 large carrot, sliced
¹/₂ cup peas, thawed if frozen
2 scallions, chopped
1 jalapeño pepper, seeded and chopped
1 tablespoon finely chopped peeled fresh ginger
2 to 3 garlic cloves, finely chopped

Cook until the vegetables are soft, about 5 minutes. Add and bring to a boil:

1¹/₂ cups unsweetened coconut milk
¹/₂ cup golden raisins
1 tablespoon curry powder
1 teaspoon salt

Add the chicken, reduce the heat, and simmer 20 minutes for breasts, 25 minutes for thighs, or until the sauce is thickened and the chicken is cooked. Serve with:

Cooked rice

CHICKEN PAPRIKA (PAPRIKÁS CSIRKE)

4 servings

Especially good made with Hungarian sweet paprika, 1006.

Have ready:

3¹/₂ to 4¹/₂ pounds chicken parts

Season generously with:

Salt and black pepper

Heat in a wide heavy skillet over medium-high heat:

2 tablespoons butter or lard

Add the chicken to the skillet without crowding and cook, turning once, until golden, about 5 minutes per side. Remove the chicken to a plate and brown the remaining chicken. Add to the fat in the skillet:

3 cups very thinly sliced onions

Reduce the heat slightly and cook, stirring, until the onions begin to color, about 10 minutes. Sprinkle with:

¹/₄ cup sweet paprika
2 tablespoons minced garlic

1 bay leaf
$^1/_2$ teaspoon salt
$^1/_2$ teaspoon black pepper

Bring to a boil, stirring constantly. Return the chicken, with any accumulated juices, to the skillet. Reduce the heat so that the liquid barely bubbles, cover, and cook, turning the chicken once or twice, until the thigh registers 180°F on a thermometer, 20 to 30 minutes.

Remove the chicken to a platter and cover to keep warm. Discard the bay leaf. Let the sauce stand briefly, then skim the fat off the surface with a spoon. Boil the sauce over high heat until very thick, almost pasty. Remove the skillet from the heat and whisk into the sauce:

1 to 1$^1/_2$ cups sour cream

Return the sauce to high heat and boil until thickened. Season with:

Salt and black pepper to taste
Several drops of fresh lemon juice

Pour sauce over chicken and serve.

SESAME CHICKEN

4 servings

Bring a large pot of water to a boil over high heat. Add:

3 bone-in chicken breast halves, skin on

When the water returns to a boil, turn the heat down to low and simmer the chicken until no longer pink, 8 to 10 minutes. Remove to a plate and let cool. Thoroughly combine in a medium bowl:

$^1/_4$ cup toasted sesame paste (tahini) or smooth
    peanut butter
2 to 3 tablespoons toasted sesame oil (enough to
    liquify the sesame paste or peanut butter)

Add:

2$^1/_2$ tablespoons light soy sauce
1 tablespoon distilled white vinegar
1$^1/_2$ teaspoons to 1 tablespoon hot chili oil, or to taste
2 teaspoons minced peeled fresh ginger
1 teaspoon sugar
1 scallion, finely chopped

Remove the chicken skin and bones, and tear the meat along the grain into rough shreds 2$^1/_2$ inches long and $^1/_2$ inch thick. Place in a serving bowl. Pour the sesame paste sauce over the chicken shreds and mix thoroughly to coat. Prepare:

1 medium cucumber, halved, seeded, and cut
    into $^1/_4$-inch slices

If desired, cover the chicken and cucumbers separately and refrigerate for up to 24 hours. Bring to room temperature before serving. To serve, pile the cucumber slices on top of the chicken.

CHICKEN OR TURKEY FRICASSEE

4 to 5 servings

Have ready:

3$^1/_2$ to 4$^1/_2$ pounds chicken or turkey parts

Separate the legs into thighs and drumsticks; cut each breast half diagonally in half through the bone. If you wish, remove the skin. Sprinkle the chicken with:

Salt and black or white pepper to taste

Heat in a heavy large skillet over medium heat:

$^1/_4$ cup ($^1/_2$ stick) butter

Place only as many chicken pieces in the pan as will fit without crowding and cook, turning once, until pale golden, 3 to 5 minutes on each side. Remove the chicken to a plate and brown the remaining pieces in the same manner. Add to the fat in the pan:

1$^1/_2$ cups chopped onions

Cook, stirring occasionally, until tender but not browned, about 5 minutes. Stir in:

$^1/_3$ cup all-purpose flour

Cook, stirring, for 1 minute, then reduce heat to medium-low and whisk in:

1$^3/_4$ cups chicken stock or broth or water

Whisking constantly, bring to a boil over high heat. Add:

8 ounces mushrooms, sliced
3 medium carrots, diced
2 large or medium ribs celery, diced
$^1/_2$ teaspoon dried thyme
1 teaspoon salt
$^1/_2$ teaspoon white or black pepper

Return the chicken pieces, with any accumulated juices, to the pan and bring to a simmer. Reduce the heat so that the liquid barely bubbles. Cover tightly and cook until the thigh registers 180°F on a thermometer, 20 to 30 minutes. Skim off the fat from around the sides of the pan with a spoon. Stir in:

($^1/_4$ to $^1/_2$ cup heavy cream)

Season with:

Salt and white or black pepper to taste
Several drops of fresh lemon juice

The sooner the chicken is served, the juicier it will be. However, the dish can be made ahead. To serve within 1 hour, simply cover the pan and slide to a warm corner of the stove. Or, cover and refrigerate for up to 3 days.

CHICKEN AND DUMPLINGS

4 to 5 servings

Prepare:

Chicken Fricassee, above

Push the chicken pieces down so that they are submerged in the sauce. Drop in spoonfuls over the top:

Dumplings, 334, or Cornmeal Dumplings, 334

Cover and cook as directed for the dumplings.

BRUNSWICK STEW

8 to 10 servings

This Southern specialty has many variations. It may be made with chicken, pork, rabbit, squirrel, or a combination. Tomatoes, lima beans, and corn are usually part of the mix as well. For a delicious twist, remove the cooked chicken from the pot, cover the chicken with foil, and prepare Cornmeal Dumplings, 334, in the sauce.

Have ready:

5 pounds chicken parts

Season with:

Salt and black pepper to taste

($^1/_2$ teaspoon ground red pepper)

Heat in a Dutch oven over medium-high heat:

2 tablespoons bacon fat or vegetable oil

Add the chicken pieces, in batches, and brown on all sides. Remove them to a plate. Pour off all but 2 tablespoons of the fat in the pot. Reduce the heat to medium and add:

1 cup chopped onions

1 cup chopped celery

Cook, stirring occasionally, until just tender, 5 to 7 minutes. Return the chicken, with the accumulated juices, to the pot. Add:

3 cups fresh or frozen lima beans

(2 cups Pulled Pork, 500, or smoked ham cut into $^1/_2$-inch chunks)

$1^1/_2$ to 2 cups chopped peeled seeded fresh tomatoes or chopped seeded canned tomatoes

1 cup Barbecue Sauce, 586

1 cup tomato puree

1 cup chicken stock or broth or water

(1 tablespoon minced garlic)

2 bay leaves

Salt and black pepper to taste

Ground red pepper to taste

Bring to a boil over high heat. Reduce the heat to low, cover, and simmer gently until the chicken is nearly tender, 35 to 45 minutes. Add:

3 cups fresh or frozen corn

Simmer, uncovered, for 10 minutes more. Skim off any fat with a spoon. Discard the bay leaves. Season the stew with:

Salt and black pepper to taste

Several drops of Worcestershire sauce

Several drops of hot pepper sauce

Sprinkle with:

(Minced parsley)

(Browned bread crumbs, 960)

CHICKEN CACCIATORE

4 servings

"Cacciatore" means hunter's style in Italian, and there are countless versions of this dish, some made of rabbit. Polenta, 349, is a traditional companion.

Season:

$3^1/_2$ to $4^1/_2$ pounds chicken parts

with:

Salt and black pepper to taste

Heat in a large heavy skillet over medium-high heat:

3 tablespoons olive oil

Add the chicken pieces, in batches, and brown on all sides. Remove to a plate. Pour off all but 2 tablespoons of the fat in the pan. Reduce the heat to medium and add:

1 cup chopped onions

1 bay leaf

$1^1/_2$ teaspoons chopped fresh rosemary or $^1/_2$ teaspoon dried rosemary, crumbled

1 teaspoon minced fresh sage or $^1/_2$ teaspoon dried sage, crumbled

Cook, stirring, until the onions are golden brown, about 5 minutes. Add:

1 large garlic clove, minced

Cook about 30 seconds more, being careful not to brown the garlic. Return the chicken to the skillet and pour in:

$^1/_2$ cup dry red or white wine

Boil over medium-high heat until all the wine is evaporated, turning the chicken and scraping up the browned bits on the bottom with a wooden spoon. Add:

8 ounces canned tomatoes, chopped, with their juice

$^3/_4$ cup chicken stock or broth

Bring to a boil, then reduce the heat to low, cover, and simmer gently for 25 minutes. Add:

($^1/_2$ cup oil-cured black olives, pitted and sliced)

8 ounces mushrooms, sliced

Cook, covered, for 10 minutes. Uncover and boil the pan juices over high heat until slightly thickened. Taste and adjust the seasonings.

CHICKEN MARENGO

8 servings

This was the dish served to Napoleon after he had fasted through his victory at Marengo. Composed of findings from the nearby countryside, the dish was such a success that from there on in, Napoleon's chef had to prepare it after every battle. It is a good buffet casserole which profits by a day's aging, refrigerated.

Have ready:

6–8 pounds chicken parts

Sauté until delicately colored:

1 thinly sliced onion

in:

$^1/_2$ cup olive oil

then remove. Add the chicken pieces and brown on all sides. Add:

$^1/_2$ cup dry white wine

2 crushed garlic cloves

$^1/_2$ teaspoon thyme

1 bay leaf

Sprigs of parsley

1 cup chicken stock

2 cups Italian-style tomatoes

Cover the pot and simmer about 1 hour, until tender. When the meat is done, remove it to a platter. Strain the sauce and reduce it about 5 minutes and season to taste in:

$^1/_4$ cup butter

Juice of 1 lemon

Arrange chicken quarters, mushrooms, onions, and:

1 cup pitted black olives

in a deep earthenware casserole. Sprinkle over all:

1 jigger brandy

Add the sauce and reheat in a 350°F oven. Remove bay leaf. Garnish with:

Chopped parsley

Serve with:

Cooked rice

COUNTRY CAPTAIN

4 servings

This dish has become a favorite in America, although it probably got its name not from the sea captain who brought the recipe back to our shores, but from the Indian officer who first made him acquainted with it. So said the late Cecily Brownstone, a great family friend; this is her time-tested formula.

Preheat the oven to 350°F. Have ready:

$3^1/_2$ to $4^1/_2$ pounds chicken parts

Coat the pieces with:

Seasoned Flour, 962

Brown in:

$^1/_4$ cup butter

Remove, drain, and place in a casserole. Simmer gently in the pan drippings until golden:

$^1/_4$ cup finely diced onions
$^1/_2$ cup finely diced green pepper, seeds and membranes removed
Minced garlic clove
$1^1/_2$ to 3 teaspoons curry powder
$^1/_2$ teaspoon thyme

Add:

2 cups stewed or canned tomatoes

Simmer until the pan is deglazed. Pour this sauce over the chicken and bake uncovered, about 40 minutes or until the chicken is tender. During the last 5 minutes of cooking, add:

3 tablespoons currants

Serve with:

Cooked rice

Garnish with:

Toasted slivered almonds

CHICKEN CURRY

4 servings

Remove the skin from:

$3^1/_2$ to $4^1/_2$ pounds chicken parts

Heat in a wide heavy skillet over medium-high heat:

2 tablespoons vegetable oil

Add and cook, stirring occasionally, until browned, 7 to 10 minutes:

1 large onion, thinly sliced

Add and cook, stirring, for 30 seconds:

2 teaspoons minced garlic
2 teaspoons minced peeled fresh ginger
$1^1/_2$ teaspoons Garam Masala, 987
1 teaspoon turmeric

Add the chicken, in batches, and cook, turning once, until golden, 2 to 3 minutes on each side. Stir in:

$^1/_2$ cup plain low-fat yogurt

Increase the heat to high and cook, stirring occasionally, until the yogurt has reduced and thickened and the oil separates into pools, 3 to 5 minutes. Stir in:

1 cup water
2 tablespoons chopped cilantro
1 serrano or jalapeño pepper, quartered lengthwise
$^3/_4$ teaspoon salt

Simmer, covered, and cook until the thigh releases clear juices when pierced with a fork, 30 to 40 minutes. Remove the chicken to a platter and cover to keep warm. If the sauce is thin, boil over high heat to reduce and thicken it. Pour over the chicken. Serve with:

Cooked rice
Curried Apricot Chutney, 950

BASQUE CHICKEN

4 servings

Have ready:

$3^1/_2$ to $4^1/_2$ pounds chicken parts

Heat in a Dutch oven over medium-high heat:

3 tablespoons olive oil

Add the chicken, in 2 batches, and lightly brown on both sides. Remove the chicken to a plate. Pour off all but 3 tablespoons of the fat in the pot. Return the chicken to the pot and add:

2 pounds red and/or yellow bell peppers, cut into $^1/_2$-inch-wide strips
4 small jalapeño peppers, seeded and minced
8 ounces ham, cut into $^1/_2$-inch dice
$^1/_4$ cup chopped garlic
$^3/_4$ teaspoon salt
$^1/_2$ teaspoon ground black pepper

Place the pot over low to medium heat, cover tightly, and cook at a quiet sizzle, turning and stirring often, until the thigh registers 180°F on a thermometer, and the peppers are soft, about 45 minutes.

Meanwhile, prepare the sauce. Heat in a large saucepan over medium-high heat:

2 tablespoons olive oil

Add:

2 to 3 cups chopped onions

Cook, stirring often, until tender but not browned, about 7 minutes. Add:

2 pounds fresh tomatoes, peeled, seeded, and chopped, or one 28-ounce can whole tomatoes, seeded and crushed, with their juice
$^1/_2$ teaspoon salt
$^1/_2$ teaspoon black pepper

Bring to a boil. Reduce the heat to medium. Simmer, stirring often, until the sauce has thickened, about 20 minutes. Skim off any excess fat from the chicken with a spoon. Season both the chicken and sauce with:

Salt and black pepper to taste

Serve over:

Cooked rice

CHICKEN AND RICE (ARROZ CON POLLO)
4 servings
Season:
> **3¹/₂ to 4¹/₂ pounds chicken parts**

with:
> **Salt and black pepper**

Heat in a Dutch oven over medium-high heat:
> **2 tablespoons vegetable or olive oil**

Add the chicken in batches, and brown on both sides. Remove the chicken to a platter. Pour off all but 3 tablespoons of the fat from the pan. Reduce the heat to medium-low and add:
> **2 cups chopped onions**
> **(1 green bell pepper, diced)**
> **4 ounces ham, finely diced (about ¹/₂ cup)**

Cook, stirring occasionally, until the onions are tender but not brown, about 5 minutes. Add:
> **2 cups medium- or long-grain white rice**

Cook, stirring, until the grains are coated with fat. Add:
> **1 tablespoon minced garlic**
> **1 tablespoon paprika**
> **1 teaspoon salt**
> **¹/₂ teaspoon black pepper**

Cook, stirring, for 1 minute. Add:
> **3 cups chicken stock or broth**
> **(¹/₂ teaspoon dried oregano)**
> **(¹/₄ teaspoon loosely packed saffron threads)**

Bring to a boil over high heat, scraping the bottom of the pan with a wooden spoon to loosen the browned bits. Place the chicken pieces in the rice and pour in any accumulated juices. Cover the pan and simmer over medium-low heat for 20 minutes. Stir in:
> **1 cup unthawed frozen peas**
> **¹/₃ cup drained pimientos or roasted red peppers, cut into thin 1-inch-long strips**
> **¹/₄ cup chopped green olives**

Cover and cook until the rice is tender, about 10 minutes more. Taste and adjust the seasonings.

CHICKEN TAGINE WITH CHICKPEAS
4 servings
Remove the skin, rinse, and pat dry:
> **3¹/₂ to 4¹/₂ pounds chicken parts**

Heat in a skillet or Dutch oven over medium-high heat:
> **2 tablespoons butter**

Brown chicken on both sides. Remove to a plate. Add to the pan:
> **2 cups chopped onions**
> **¹/₂ cup chopped scallions**

Cook 5 to 7 minutes. Stir in:
> **One 15- to 19-ounce can chickpeas, rinsed and drained**
> **1 cup water**
> **1 tablespoon minced garlic**
> **1 teaspoon ground ginger**
> **³/₄ teaspoon salt**

> **¹/₂ teaspoon ground cinnamon**
> **¹/₂ teaspoon black pepper**
> **¹/₈ to ¹/₄ teaspoon ground red pepper**

Return the chicken to the pan and coat. Bring to a boil. Reduce the heat to a simmer. Cover tightly and cook, turning the chicken once or twice, until the thigh registers 180°F on a thermometer, 35 to 45 minutes. Remove from the heat and stir in:
> **¹/₂ cup chopped parsley and/or cilantro**

Season with:
> **Salt and black pepper to taste**

CHICKEN CHILI VERDE
4 servings
Serve with rice, beans, or corn tortillas or used as a filling for burritos, tacos, or enchiladas. You can make a quicker version with 2 to 3 cups chopped leftover chicken or turkey and 2 cups canned chicken broth.
Have ready:
> **2¹/₂ pounds chicken parts**

Combine in a medium pot with:
> **4 cups chicken stock or broth or 4 cups water plus 1 teaspoon salt**

Bring to a boil, then reduce to a simmer. Cook, partially covered, for 30 minutes. Remove from the heat. Remove the chicken from the broth. Let stand until cool. Remove the skin and bones, keeping the meat in the largest chunks. Skim the fat. Heat in a skillet or Dutch oven over medium heat:
> **2 tablespoons vegetable oil**

Add:
> **1 cup chopped onions**
> **¹/₄ cup chopped celery**
> **1 tablespoon finely chopped garlic**

Cook, stirring occasionally, until the vegetables are tender, about 5 minutes. Sprinkle with:
> **2 teaspoons chili powder**
> **1 teaspoon ground cumin**
> **¹/₂ teaspoon dried oregano**
> **¹/₂ teaspoon salt**

Cook, stirring, about 1 minute, then remove the pan from the heat. Add:
> **1 cup drained chopped canned tomatillos, or 4 large or 6 medium fresh tomatillos, husked, 310, rinsed, and diced**

Separate the leaves and stems of:
> **1 large bunch cilantro**

Finely chop the leaves and stems separately. Add the stems to the pan. Add 2 cups of the chicken stock, along with:
> **3 Anaheim or poblano peppers, roasted, 292, peeled, and chopped, or one 7-ounce can diced green chiles, drained**
> **(2 jalapeño peppers, seeded and finely chopped)**

Bring to a simmer and simmer gently, uncovered, for 10 minutes. Add the chicken and ¹/₂ cup of the chopped cilantro leaves, along with:
> **2 tablespoons fresh lime juice**

Simmer for 5 to 10 minutes to heat through. Season with:

Salt to taste

Serve garnished with the remaining cilantro leaves.

CHICKEN ÉTOUFFÉE

4 to 6 servings

This is a classic Cajun chicken fricassee.

Please read About Roux, 543. Have ready:

4 to 5 pounds chicken parts

Mix together:

1 teaspoon paprika

1 teaspoon dried thyme

1 teaspoon salt

$1/2$ teaspoon dried basil

$1/2$ teaspoon black pepper

$1/4$ teaspoon ground red pepper

Rub the spice mixture all over the chicken pieces. Pour into a brown paper bag:

1 cup all-purpose flour

Shake chicken in the bag to coat with flour; remove and shake off the excess. Reserve the flour. Heat in a wide heavy skillet or Dutch oven over medium heat:

3 tablespoons vegetable oil

Brown the chicken on both sides. Remove to a plate. Pour off all but about 3 tablespoons of the fat in the skillet. Reduce the heat to medium, and stir in 3 tablespoons of the reserved flour. Cook, stirring constantly, until the roux is almost as dark as milk chocolate, up to 20 minutes. Stir in:

1 cup chopped onions

$1/2$ cup chopped celery

$1/4$ cup chopped red bell peppers

$1/4$ cup chopped green bell peppers

$1/4$ cup chopped andouille sausage or smoked ham

Cook, stirring, 5 to 6 minutes. The roux will continue to darken. Add:

2 tablespoons finely chopped garlic

$1/4$ teaspoon dried sage, crumbled

$1/4$ teaspoon dried thyme

Stir well and cook for 1 minute more. Stir in:

2 cups chicken stock or broth

3 tablespoons tomato paste

1 tablespoon Worcestershire sauce

$1/4$ teaspoon hot pepper sauce, or to taste

Bring to a simmer, stirring constantly. Return the chicken pieces, with juices, to the skillet and bring the liquid to a simmer. Cover and cook, turning occasionally, until the thigh registers 180°F on a thermometer, about 30 minutes. Remove the chicken to a plate. Skim the fat from the sauce. Add:

$1/2$ cup finely chopped scallions

$1/4$ cup chopped parsley

Boil until the sauce is thickened. Season generously with:

Salt and black pepper

Hot pepper sauce

Return the chicken to the pan and heat through. Serve with:

Cooked rice

ABOUT BONELESS, SKINLESS CHICKEN BREASTS

Boneless, skinless chicken breasts are low in fat, quick and easy to prepare, and amenable to a wide range of cooking treatments, including sautéing, frying, grilling, poaching, and baking. The important thing to remember is that ➤ they are easy to overcook. Cook them just to the point where they release clear juices when pricked with a fork, or they will be disappointingly dry and firm. ➤ You will find they are easier to cut in strips or pieces if they are partially frozen. You can save money by preparing this cut yourself from bone-in, skin-on chicken breasts. See About Cutting Up Poultry, 419.

SAUTÉED BONELESS CHICKEN BREASTS

2 to 4 servings

Sautéed, this chicken should be a rich nut-brown on the outside, tender and juicy inside. The secret to success is high heat. If the oil is hot enough, the chicken will take only about 4 minutes per side to cook through. Serve with a sauce made in the pan, see 546–549.

Please read About Boneless, Skinless Chicken Breasts, above. Have ready:

4 boneless, skinless chicken breast halves
(about $1/2$ pounds)

Trim any fat around the edges. If you wish, remove the white tendon running through each tenderloin. Sprinkle on both sides with:

Salt and black pepper to taste

Spread on a plate:

$1/4$ cup all-purpose flour

Coat the chicken on both sides with the flour; shake off the excess. Heat in a heavy 10- to 12-inch skillet over medium heat until fragrant and nut-brown:

$1/2$ tablespoons butter

Add:

$1/2$ tablespoons olive oil

Swirl the butter and oil together. Sauté for exactly 4 minutes. Using tongs, turn the chicken and cook until firm to the touch, 3 to 5 minutes more.

CHICKEN PICCATA

2 to 4 servings

Prepare and keep warm in a 200°F oven:

Sautéed Boneless Chicken Breasts, above

Remove all but about 1 tablespoon of the fat in the skillet. Heat the remaining fat over medium heat, and add:

2 to 3 tablespoons minced shallots or scallions

Cook, stirring, until wilted, about 1 minute. Increase the heat to high and add:

1 cup chicken stock or broth

Bring to a boil, scraping the bottom of the skillet with a wooden spoon to loosen the browned bits. Add:

3 to 4 tablespoons fresh lemon juice

2 tablespoons drained small capers

Boil until the sauce is reduced to about $1/3$ cup, 3 to 4 minutes. Add any accumulated chicken juices and reduce again to $1/3$ cup. Remove from the heat and swirl in:

2 to 3 tablespoons butter, softened

Pour the sauce over the chicken and serve immediately.

SAUTÉED CHICKEN BREASTS WITH MUSHROOM SAUCE

2 to 4 servings

Prepare and keep warm in a 200°F oven:

Sautéed Boneless Chicken Breasts, 436

Remove all but about 2 tablespoons of the fat. Heat the remaining fat over medium heat, and add:

2 to 3 tablespoons minced shallots or scallions

Cook, stirring, until wilted, about 1 minute. Increase the heat to high and add:

8 ounces mushrooms, thinly sliced

Cook, stirring, until softened and lightly browned, 2 to 3 minutes. Add and bring to a boil:

$1/3$ cup sweet or dry sherry

Boil until the sherry is nearly evaporated, 1 minute. Add:

1 cup heavy cream

$1/2$ cup chicken stock or broth

Boil until the sauce is thick enough to lightly coat a spoon, about 5 minutes. Stir in:

2 tablespoons finely chopped parsley

Pinch of grated or ground nutmeg

Salt and black pepper to taste

Several drops of fresh lemon juice

Spoon the sauce over the chicken and serve immediately.

SAUTÉED BREADED BONELESS CHICKEN BREASTS

2 to 4 servings

Please read About Boneless, Skinless Chicken Breasts, 436. Have ready:

4 boneless, skinless chicken breast halves (about $1^1/2$ pounds)

Trim any fat around the edges. You may remove the white tendon running through each tenderloin. One at a time, place the breasts between sheets of wax paper and pound with a mallet or rolling pin to flatten.

Combine in a wide shallow bowl:

1 cup dry bread crumbs

($1/4$ cup grated Parmesan)

(1 tablespoon minced parsley or basil or 1 teaspoon dried rosemary, thyme, or oregano, crumbled)

1 teaspoon salt

$1/2$ teaspoon black pepper

Whisk together in a shallow bowl:

1 large egg

1 teaspoon water

Spread on a plate:

$1/4$ cup all-purpose flour

Coat the chicken with the flour and shake off the excess. Dip in the egg mixture, then coat with the bread crumb

mixture, patting with your fingers to make the crumbs adhere. Set aside on a plate. Heat in a heavy skillet over medium-high heat:

$1/3$ cup olive oil

Add the chicken and cook until lightly browned, 2 to 3 minutes each side. Add more oil if the pan looks dry. Drain on paper towels. Serve immediately or at room temperature.

CHICKEN PARMIGIANA

2 to 4 servings

This Italian-American classic can be assembled early in the day, refrigerated, and baked when needed. Use your favorite store-bought sauce if time is short. Prepare:

Sautéed Breaded Boneless Chicken Breasts, 436

Position a rack in the center of the oven. Preheat the oven to 350°F. Lightly oil a 13 x 9-inch baking pan or similar shallow baking dish. Have ready:

$1^1/2$ cups Tomato Sauce, 562

Spoon $1/2$ cup of the sauce into the baking pan. Arrange the chicken breasts over the sauce, slightly overlapping them. Sprinkle with:

3 to 4 tablespoons grated Parmesan

Spoon over the remaining sauce. Top with:

6 ounces mozzarella, thinly sliced

$1/2$ cup grated Parmesan

Cover the pan with aluminum foil and bake until heated through, 20 to 30 minutes. If you wish to brown the top, remove the foil and run the dish briefly under a hot broiler. Serve hot, sprinkled with:

(Chopped parsley)

CHICKEN CORDON BLEU

2 to 4 servings

Please read About Boneless, Skinless Chicken Breasts, 436. Trim any fat around the edges. You may remove the white tendon running through each piece from:

4 boneless, skinless chicken breast halves (about $1^1/2$ pounds)

One at a time, place the chicken breasts between sheets of wax paper and pound with a mallet or rolling pin until about $3/8$ inch thick. Season with:

Salt and black pepper to taste

Cover one half of each chicken breast with:

1 thin slice ham or prosciutto (4 total)

Leaving space around the edges, top the ham slice with:

1 thin slice Gruyère or other Swiss cheese (4 total)

Fold each chicken breast in half over the ham and cheese and press the edges firmly together to seal. A $1/8$-inch cut along the folded edge of the breast will help prevent the packet from opening during cooking. Combine in a wide shallow bowl:

1 cup dry bread crumbs

$1/4$ cup minced parsley

1 teaspoon salt
$^1/_2$ teaspoon black pepper

Whisk together in a shallow bowl:

1 large egg
1 teaspoon water

Spread on a plate:

$^1/_4$ cup all-purpose flour

Press both sides of each packet in the flour, then dip in the egg mixture and coat with the bread crumb mixture, patting with your fingers to make the crumbs adhere. Set aside on a plate. Heat in a heavy skillet over medium-high heat until fragrant and nut-brown:

1$^1/_2$ tablespoons butter

Add:

1$^1/_2$ tablespoons olive oil

Stir the butter and oil together. Place the packets in the skillet and cook until browned on both sides, 3 to 4 minutes each. Drain on paper towels and serve immediately.

SAUTÉED STUFFED CHICKEN BREASTS

2 to 4 servings

Please read About Boneless, Skinless Chicken Breasts, 436. Season and stuff as for **Chicken Cordon Bleu, 437,** but do not bread:

4 boneless, skinless chicken breast halves
(about 1$^1/_2$ pounds)

with:

4 thin slices ham or prosciutto
4 thin slices Gruyère or other Swiss cheese

Heat in a large heavy skillet over medium-high heat:

3 tablespoons butter

Add the chicken and cook, turning once, until cooked through and the cheese is beginning to melt, about 2 to 3 minutes per side. Remove to a plate and cover to keep warm. Add to the fat in the pan:

12 mushroom caps
$^1/_4$ cup finely minced shallots

Cook, stirring, until the mushrooms have wilted and begun to release their juices, about 3 minutes. Add:

$^1/_2$ cup dry white wine
$^1/_2$ cup chopped seeded peeled tomato

Simmer until most of the liquid has evaporated. Add:

$^1/_2$ cup heavy cream

Simmer until the sauce thickens slightly, 1 to 2 minutes. Return the chicken breasts to the pan and heat through turning once or twice; do not let the sauce boil. Add:

2 tablespoons finely chopped parsley
Salt and black or white pepper to taste

Serve at once, over:

Cooked rice or Buttered Noodles, 329

CHICKEN KIEV

4 to 8 servings

This classic consists of thin pounded boneless, skinless chicken breasts rolled around seasoned butter, breaded, and fried. The key to success is to seal the chicken packets tightly and to bread them so that the butter does not leak out during cooking. You may want to prepare the chicken a day ahead.

Read About Frying Chicken, 429, and About Boneless, Skinless Chicken Breasts, 436. Using the back of a wooden spoon or an electric mixer, cream together in a medium bowl:

1 cup (2 sticks) unsalted butter, softened
2 tablespoons fresh lemon juice or 2 teaspoons grated lemon zest
1 tablespoon minced parsley
(1 tablespoon finely snipped fresh chives or 2 teaspoons dried chives)
1 teaspoon minced garlic
$^1/_2$ teaspoon salt
$^1/_4$ teaspoon black pepper

Shape the butter into a 6 x 3-inch cake on a sheet of wax paper. Wrap in the paper and refrigerate for 2 hours. Trim any fat around the edges. You may remove the white tendon running through:

8 boneless, skinless chicken breast halves
(about 3 pounds)

One at a time place the breasts between sheets of wax paper and gently pound with a mallet or a rolling pin until $^1/_4$ inch thick. Season on both sides with:

Salt and black pepper

Cut the chilled butter crosswise into 8 fingers. Arrange the chicken tender side up on a work surface. Place 1 finger of butter crosswise on each breast about one-third of the way up from the narrow end. Fold the narrow end over the butter, as shown, then roll up the butter in the breast, tucking in the sides to enclose completely, as shown. Combine in a bowl:

2 cups dry bread crumbs
1 teaspoon salt
1 teaspoon black pepper

Whisk together in a shallow bowl:

2 large eggs
2 teaspoons water

Spread on a plate:

$^1/_2$ cup all-purpose flour

Coat the chicken packets in the flour, being sure to cover the ends, roll the packets in the egg mixture, and then coat on all sides with the bread crumb mixture, patting with your fingers to make the crumbs adhere. Place the rolls on a rack seam-side down, cover loosely

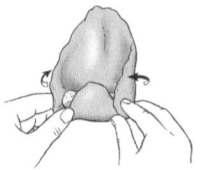 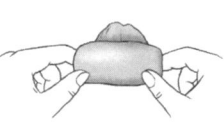

Preparing Chicken Kiev

with foil or parchment paper, and refrigerate for 1 to 8 hours.
Heat in a large skillet over medium-high heat to 350° to 365°F:

> $^1/_2$ **cup vegetable oil**

Arrange the rolls seam side down in the skillet and cook until the first side is nut-brown, 2 to 3 minutes. Turn to brown on all sides, about 1 minute per side.

BAKED STUFFED BONELESS CHICKEN BREASTS

4 to 8 servings

Please read About Boneless, Skinless Chicken Breasts, 436. Position a rack in the center of the oven. Preheat the oven to 350°F. Heat in a skillet over medium-high heat:

> **2 to 3 tablespoons butter**

Add and cook, stirring, until tender but not brown, about 5 minutes:

> $^1/_3$ **cup finely chopped onion**

Stir in and cook for 30 seconds:

> **1 teaspoon minced garlic**

Remove the mixture to a bowl, and stir into:

> $^1/_2$ **recipe Italian Bread Stuffing, 533**

Stir in:

> $^1/_3$ **to** $^2/_3$ **cup chicken stock or broth**

The stuffing should be just moist enough to hold together in a ball when squeezed firmly in the hand; do not over-moisten. Taste and adjust the seasonings.
Trim any fat around the edges. You may remove the white tendon running through each tenderloin from:

> **8 boneless, skinless chicken breast halves**
>   **(about 3 pounds)**

One at a time, place the chicken breasts between sheets of wax paper and pound with a mallet or a rolling pin until about $^3/_8$ inch thick. Season both sides with:

> **Salt and black pepper to taste**

Lightly oil a 13 x 9-inch baking pan. Lay the breasts smooth side down and place $^1/_4$ cup stuffing on the center of each chicken breast and press lightly to compact. Bring the ends of the chicken up over the stuffing. Secure with toothpicks or string. Lay the packets seam side down in the baking pan and brush with:

> **Olive oil**

Season with:

> **Salt and black pepper to taste**

Bake until the chicken is lightly browned and feels firm when pressed, 20 to 30 minutes.

BAKED STUFFED BONELESS CHICKEN BREASTS SICILIAN-STYLE

Prepare **Baked Stuffed Boneless Chicken Breasts, above.**
Reduce the bread crumbs in the bread stuffing to $1^1/_2$ cups, and add to the finished stuffing:

> $^1/_4$ **cup oil-cured black olives, pitted and chopped**
> $^1/_4$ **cup raisins, chopped, or dried currants**
> $^1/_4$ **cup pine nuts or finely chopped walnuts**

> **(3 to 4 anchovy fillets, rinsed, dried,**
>   **and finely chopped)**
> **2 tablespoons drained small capers**

MEDITERRANEAN BONELESS CHICKEN BREASTS BAKED IN FOIL

4 servings

Please read about Cooking en Papillote, 1052, and About Boneless, Skinless Chicken Breasts, 436.
Position a rack in the center of the oven. Preheat the oven to 450°F. Trim any fat around the edges. You may remove the white tendon running through:

> **4 boneless, skinless chicken breast halves**
>   **(about 1** $^1/_2$ **pounds)**

Season on both sides with:

> **Salt and black pepper**

Combine in a small bowl:

> **10 brine-cured black olives, finely chopped**
> **8 oil-packed sun-dried tomatoes, cut into thin strips**
> **3 tablespoons olive oil**
> **2 tablespoons finely shredded basil or minced parsley**

Tear four 18-inch pieces of heavy-duty aluminum foil or parchment paper. Lightly oil one side of each. Lay one chicken breast on the oiled side. Spoon the tomato mixture over the breasts. Loosely fold over the chicken, then crimp the edges of the packets to seal tightly. Place the packets on a baking sheet and bake for 20 minutes, until puffed. Remove from the oven and let stand for 5 minutes. To avoid being burned by steam, open carefully.

STIR-FRIED GARLIC CHICKEN

3 to 4 servings

Please read About Stir-Frying, 242.
In a medium bowl, mix together thoroughly:

> **1 tablespoon cornstarch**
> **1 tablespoon Chinese cooking wine or dry white wine**
> **2 teaspoons light soy sauce**
> **2 teaspoons oyster sauce**
> **1 teaspoon salt**
> **1 teaspoon sugar**

Cut into $1^1/_2$ x $^1/_2$-inch pieces:

> $1^1/_2$ **pounds boneless, skinless chicken breasts or**
>   **thighs**

Toss in the soy sauce mixture. Cover with plastic wrap and let stand for 20 to 30 minutes. Have ready:

> **4 teaspoons finely minced garlic**
> **1 tablespoon finely minced peeled fresh ginger**
> $^2/_3$ **cup chicken stock or broth**
> $^1/_2$ **cup snow peas, trimmed**
> **1 medium onion, cut into** $^1/_4$**-inch slices**
> **3 scallions, sliced lengthwise, then cut into 2-inch**
>   **sections**

Mix well in a small bowl:

> **1 tablespoon hoisin sauce**
> **1 tablespoon catsup**
> **1 tablespoon toasted sesame oil**

1 1/2 teaspoons dark soy sauce
1/2 teaspoon crushed red pepper flakes

Heat a wok or large skillet over high heat until hot. Add:

2 tablespoons peanut oil

Add the minced garlic and ginger and stir briefly until the garlic is very slightly browned. Add the chicken and quickly stir and flip it in the oil to separate the pieces. Toss and cook for about 3 minutes. Add the chicken stock and stir until the stock is heated through. Add the snow peas and onions, stir once, cover, and cook for 2 minutes. Add the hoisin sauce mixture and stir gently until all the chicken pieces are thoroughly coated. Sprinkle with the scallions, stir gently, and immediately remove to a serving dish.

SAUTÉED CHICKEN LIVERS

3 to 4 servings

The trick to sautéing chicken livers is to cook them in small batches in a very hot pan using an ample quantity of fat. This ensures that they will brown lightly and cook evenly. Turn into a colander and rinse lightly:

1 pound chicken livers

Remove the connective strings, separating the lobes. Pat as dry as possible. Season generously with:

Salt and black pepper

Heat in a large skillet over high heat until lightly browned and fragrant:

3 tablespoons butter, or as needed

Add half of the livers to the skillet and quickly spread them out in a single layer with a slotted spoon or spatula. Cook undisturbed for 1 minute, then nudge them over onto their uncooked side and cook until firm and beginning to release juices into the pan, 1 to 2 minutes more. Remove the livers to a plate and cook the remaining livers in the same manner, adding more butter if needed.

Add to the fat remaining in the skillet:

1/2 cup very finely minced shallots or onion

Cook, stirring, until brown and crisp around the edges, about 2 minutes. Stir in:

1/2 cup dry white wine or apple juice

Bring to a boil, scraping the bottom of the skillet with a wooden spoon to loosen the browned bits, and boil until the liquid is reduced by half. Add:

1/2 cup chicken stock or broth

Boil again until reduced by half and slightly syrupy. Return the livers, with their accumulated juices, to the skillet and heat, stirring, just until the sauce bubbles. Remove from the heat and stir in:

2 tablespoons minced parsley

Season with:

Salt and black pepper to taste
Several drops of vinegar

FRIED CHICKEN LIVERS

3 to 4 servings

Remove membranes from, separate into lobes, and pat dry:

1 pound chicken livers

Combine:

1/2 cup all-purpose flour
1 teaspoon garlic salt
1 teaspoon black pepper

Toss the livers in the mixture to coat. Heat in a large heavy skillet:

1 inch vegetable oil

Add the livers to the hot oil in batches, without crowding, and fry until browned on the first side, about 3 minutes. Turn and brown the other side. Drain on paper towels, and serve immediately.

CHICKEN LIVER PÂTÉ

8 servings

Cut into small pieces and place in the freezer:

1 1/2 cup (1 stick) butter

Melt in a large skillet over medium-low heat:

2 tablespoons butter

Add:

2 large shallots, finely chopped

Cook, stirring, until softened, 2 to 3 minutes. Add:

**1 small Golden Delicious apple, peeled, cored,
    and grated**

Cook, stirring constantly, until softened, about 3 minutes. Remove to a food processor. Rinse and pat dry:

1 pound chicken livers, trimmed and halved

Heat in the same skillet until the foam subsides:

1 tablespoon butter

Add the chicken livers and season with:

Salt and black pepper to taste

Cook over high heat until brown on the outside but still pink in the center, about 2 minutes on each side. Remove the pan from the heat. Pour in:

3 tablespoons Calvados or Cognac

If using electric heat, ignite with a match; if using gas heat, carefully tilt the pan to catch the flame. Return the pan to the heat and swirl until the alcohol has burned off. Add to the food processor along with:

2 tablespoons heavy cream

Process until smooth. With the machine running, drop in the pieces of chilled butter one at a time. Taste and adjust the seasonings. Scrape into a small crock or bowl and smooth the top with a spatula. Press plastic wrap directly on the surface and refrigerate until firm, at least 2 hours. Serve cold or at room temperature.

ABOUT CORNISH HENS

Like iced tea and peanut butter, Cornish hens, or Rock Cornish hens, are an American invention, and a surprisingly recent one, dating only from the mid-1960s. Although sometimes referred to as "game hens," these birds are simply a cross between the White Rock and Cornish breeds of chicken, which are naturally small. Cornish hens weigh between 1 and 2 pounds, with 1 1/4 pounds being the average. ➤ Choose the smallest Cornish hens you find when you want to serve a whole bird per person.

➤ A large Cornish hen, roasted whole or split and broiled or grilled, makes a perfect dinner for 2 people. To broil, use any of the broiled chicken recipes on pages 426–427.

ROAST CORNISH HENS

4 servings

Please read About Cornish Hens, 440, and About Roasting Poultry, 422. Position a rack in the center of the oven. Preheat the oven to 400°F. Lightly oil a rimmed baking sheet or shallow roasting pan large enough to allow several inches of space between the birds. Remove the neck and giblets:

   4 small Cornish hens or 2 large hens, split

Arrange the birds breast side up on the pan. Mix together:

   1¹/₂ teaspoons dried thyme
   1 teaspoon salt
   1 teaspoon black pepper

Rub half of the mixture into the body cavities of the hens. Brush the skin with:

   2 to 3 tablespoons melted butter or olive oil

Sprinkle with the remaining seasoning.

Roast until the thickest part of the thigh releases clear juices when pricked and registers 170°F on an instant-read thermometer, 30 to 35 minutes for small hens, 40 to 50 minutes for larger ones. Remove the birds to a platter and let stand for 10 minutes. Prepare:

   (Poultry Pan Sauce Gravy, 546)

GLAZED STUFFED CORNISH HENS

6 servings

Please read About Cornish Hens, 440. Position a rack in the center of the oven. Preheat the oven to 400°F. Remove the neck and giblets:

   6 small Cornish hens

Sprinkle the body and neck cavities and skin with:

   Salt

Stuff with ¹/₂ cup of one of the following stuffings:

   Wild Rice Stuffing, 540, Rice Stuffing with Almonds, Raisins, and Middle Eastern Spices, 539, Couscous Stuffing with Dried Apricots and Pistachios, 539, Wild Rice and Porcini Stuffing, 540, or Rice Stuffing with Chorizo and Hot Chile Peppers, 539 (a scant 3 cups total)

Tie the legs together. Arrange the birds breast side up on a rack set in a shallow roasting pan. Roast for 25 minutes. Heat in a small saucepan over low heat and stir until smooth:

   ¹/₃ cup jelly, seedless jam, or strained preserves or marmalade
   2 tablespoons soy sauce or balsamic vinegar

Set aside. Remove the birds from the oven and brush generously with the glaze. To prevent smoking, pour ¹/₈ inch of water into the roasting pan. Return the birds to the oven and roast until the thickest part of the thigh registers 180°F on a thermometer, 15 to 25 minutes. Remove the birds to a platter and let stand for 10 minutes.

BROILED CORNISH HENS

Prepare **Broiled Chicken, 426,** or any of its variations, using **2 Cornish hens (1¹/₂ to 1³/₄ pounds each),** prepared as for whole chicken.

GRILLED CORNISH HENS IN SPICY PORT MARINADE

4 servings

Please read About Cornish Hens, 440, and About Grilling Chicken, 427. Combine in a large shallow baking dish:

   2 cups ruby port
   ¹/₂ cup red wine vinegar
   ¹/₄ cup olive oil

Combine and coarsely grind:

   2 teaspoons juniper berries
   1 teaspoon coriander seeds
   1 teaspoon fennel seeds
   1 teaspoon cracked black peppercorns

Add the spices to the baking dish, along with:

   1 small onion or 2 scallions, coarsely chopped
   3 garlic cloves, lightly crushed
   1 tablespoon peeled minced fresh ginger

Using a knife or poultry shears, butterfly, 420:

   4 small Cornish hens

Place in the marinade and turn to coat. Marinate in the refrigerator, covered, preferably overnight; turn the hens frequently to distribute the marinade evenly. Half an hour before grilling, remove the hens from the refrigerator. Prepare a medium-hot grill fire.

Spread the hot coals in the center of the grill. Arrange the hens skin side down in a ring around the coals. Cover the grill and open the vents completely. After 10 minutes, turn the hens and move them directly over the coals. Cook for 15 minutes more. Turn again and cook for 5 minutes more. The hens are done when the thigh registers 180°F on a thermometer.

ABOUT TURKEY

Benjamin Franklin wrote in a letter to his daughter, "I wish the bald eagle had not been chosen as the representative of our country. . . . The turkey is a much more respectable character and, withal, a true original native of America." Perhaps Ben would have been pleased that the turkey has taken first place in the feasts of his countrymen.

The whole turkeys available at supermarkets generally weigh between 10 and 25 pounds. Those weighing under 18 pounds are usually hens, while those weighing more are almost always toms. There is no appreciable difference in quality between female and male turkeys, so select a size according to the number of people you will be serving, ➤ allowing about 1 pound per person, plus, if you wish, a margin for leftovers. Even though most turkeys labeled "fresh" have actually been held for several weeks at temperatures ranging from 0° to 26°F, see About Buying Poultry, 418, "fresh" tastes markedly better than frozen turkeys and are worth their higher price. Whether or not a turkey labeled "organic," "free-range," or "natural" is worth the money is up to you. For information about wild turkeys, see 456.

Self-basting turkeys have been injected with broth or vegetable oil or butter plus seasonings and flavor enhancers to increase moistness and improve the flavor. If the solution makes up 3 to 8 percent of the total weight, the label may read simply "basted," "marinated," or "added flavoring." If the solution is more than 8 percent by weight, the precise percentage and the method of preparation must be stated on the packaging.

Many turkeys and whole turkey breasts are sold with a **pop-up "thermometer."** It is our experience that they are not trustworthy indications of doneness, as they often pop up too early or too late. ➤ The most reliable **test for doneness** is when the thigh registers 180°F and the stuffing 165°F on a thermometer. Insert it into the thickest part of the thigh, not touching the bone. Remove the bird when the temperature reaches 170°F, and let it "stand" or "rest" for 20 to 40 minutes. During this time, the temperature will continue to rise and will finish cooking with its final temperature reaching 180°F.

The **gravy recipes** we offer are guaranteed to produce smooth, delicious results. Quick Turkey Gravy, 547, is made entirely in the roasting pan. Giblet Gravy, 546, requires the preparation of a giblet stock, but this can be done ahead, even a day or two before roasting. The browned bits and sticky brown glaze remaining in the roasting pan when the bird is done are the basis of perfect gravy, so be certain not to discard any of these precious elements when skimming the fat from the juices.

At our house, we feel that if we do not have leftovers, we have not had a true Thanksgiving. **Leftover turkey** can be put to many uses besides the usual sandwiches and salads. For some excellent ideas, see Creamed Chicken or Turkey, 445, Potpie, 103, Casseroles, 95–98, and Croquettes, 659. Or turn the turkey into an elegant salad by tossing cubes or strips of meat with a relish, salsa, or chutney, and serving on a bed of mixed greens.

The carcass, meanwhile, can be recycled to make an excellent turkey stock. See About Stocks, 114.

ROAST TURKEY

10 to 25 servings

If you do not stuff your bird, you may fill the cavity with a handful or two of chopped onions, carrots, and celery and a few sprigs of parsley, sage, or thyme to subtly flavor both the meat and the juices, making for a better gravy.

Please read About Stuffing and Trussing Poultry, 421, About Roasting Poultry, 422, and About Carving Poultry, 421.

Position a rack at the lowest level of the oven. Preheat the oven to 325°F.

If you want to stuff the bird, have hot or at room temperature:

Bread Stuffing or Dressing or a variation, 532–533, or Corn Bread Stuffing or a variation, 534–535

Remove the giblets and neck from:

1 turkey (10 to 25 pounds)

Rub the body, neck cavities, and skin with:

Salt

Loosely pack the body and neck cavities with the stuffing, and skewer or sew the openings closed, 421. If desired, truss, 421. Set the turkey breast side up on a rack in a roasting pan. Brush the skin all over with:

3 to 6 tablespoons melted butter, depending on the size of the turkey, or as needed

basting every 30 minutes with additional melted butter or the pan drippings, until a thermometer plunged into the thickest part of the thigh registers 170°F, 12 minutes per pound if the bird is not stuffed, 12 to 15 minutes per pound if it is.

To be safe to eat, stuffing must register at least 165°F. If the bird is done but the stuffing is not, remove the stuffing from the bird and bake it in a buttered casserole while the bird rests.

Remove the turkey to a platter and let rest for 20 to 40 minutes before carving.

Meanwhile, you may make:

(Quick Turkey Gravy, 547, or Giblet Gravy, 546)

TURNED ROAST TURKEY

12 to 15 servings

This high-heat roasting technique delivers a beautifully browned, intensely flavorful bird, and it only requires attention to a few details. Because the turkey must be flipped from side to side every 30 minutes, a bird that weighs less than 15 pounds is easiest to handle. The pan or rack must be nonstick. To keep the drippings from burning, the pan must be heavy-gauge.

Please read About Turkey, 441, About Stuffing and Trussing Poultry, 421, About Roasting Poultry, 422, and About Carving Poultry, 421.

Position a rack at the lowest level of the oven. Preheat the oven to 425°F. If you plan to stuff the bird, have ready:

Bread Stuffing or Dressing or a variation, 532–533, or Corn Bread Stuffing or a variation, 534–535

Remove the giblets and neck from:

1 turkey (12 to 15 pounds)

Generously rub the body, neck cavities, and skin with:

Salt

Loosely pack the body and neck cavities with the stuffing, and truss, 421. Place the turkey on a rack in a heavy nonstick roasting pan and brush all over with:

4 to 5 tablespoons vegetable oil

Turn the turkey onto its side. If it topples over, prop it up with crumpled aluminum foil. Roast for 30 minutes. Remove the turkey from the oven. Wearing silicone gloves or heavy-duty oven mitts to protect your hands, grasp the turkey at both ends. You might find a set of sturdy tongs helpful for lifting and balancing the bird. Turn it onto its other side, again propping it up with foil if necessary. Baste all the exposed skin with pan drippings, then roast for 30 minutes. Turn and baste twice more so that the turkey roasts twice on each side and until a thermometer plunged into the thickest part of the thigh registers 170°F, 10 to 30 minutes more. Stuffing must register at least 165°F. If the bird is done but the stuffing is not, remove the stuffing from the bird and bake it in a buttered casserole while the bird rests. Remove the turkey to a platter and let stand loosely covered with aluminum foil, for at least 20 minutes before carving. If desired, make:

(Quick Turkey Gravy, 547, or Giblet Gravy, 546)

ROAST BRINED TURKEY

10 to 25 servings

Please read About Brining Poultry, 421, About Turkey, 441, About Stuffing and Trussing Poultry, 421, About Roasting Poultry, 422, and About Carving Poultry, 421. Remove the giblets and neck from:

1 turkey (10 to 25 pounds)

Combine in a plastic or nonreactive container large enough to hold the turkey and stir until the salt dissolves:

2 cups table salt or 4 cups kosher salt

2 gallons water

Submerge the turkey in the brine and refrigerate for 12 to 24 hours. Position a rack at the lowest level of the oven. Preheat the oven to 325°F. Remove the turkey from the brine. Thoroughly rinse inside and out, then pat the skin and both cavities dry. Place in the cavity:

1 onion, peeled and quartered

1 carrot, cut into 1-inch chunks

1 small rib celery, cut into 1-inch chunks

(1 teaspoon dried thyme or 8 sprigs fresh thyme)

There is no need to close the cavities. Truss, if desired, 421. Brush the turkey skin all over with:

4 to 6 tablespoons ($^1/_2$ to $^3/_4$ stick) butter, melted

Place breast-side down on a V rack in a roasting pan, or prop it up with crumpled aluminum foil. Pour $^3/_4$ cup water into the roasting pan. Roast for 2 hours if it weighs 18 pounds or less, $2^1/_2$ hours if it weighs between 18 and 21 pounds, or 3 hours if it weighs more than 21 pounds. Baste the back and legs once or twice with:

2 to 3 tablespoons butter, melted

Remove the turkey from the oven. Wearing heat-resistant mitts or protecting your hand with paper towels, grasp the turkey at both ends and turn breast side up. Return the turkey to the oven and roast, basting once or twice with the pan drippings, until a thermometer inserted into the thickest part of the thigh registers 170°F, 30 to 90 minutes more, depending on the turkey's size. If the turkey approaches doneness before the breast has browned, increase the oven temperature to 400°F for the last 5 to 10 minutes of roasting. Remove the turkey to a platter and let stand for 20 to 40 minutes before carving. Meanwhile, make:

(Quick Turkey Gravy, 547, or Giblet Gravy, 546)

GRILL-ROASTED BRINED TURKEY

12 servings

It is fun to grill-roast a whole turkey outdoors, and the results are excellent. Turkeys in the range of 11 to 14 pounds work better than larger ones. You can omit the brining, but that step yields an especially moist, well-seasoned bird and is worth the effort. This method is not appropriate for stuffed birds. Please read About Brining Poultry, 421, and About Grilling, 427.

Remove the neck and giblets from:

One 11- to 14-pound turkey

Combine in a clean bucket or other container large enough to hold the turkey, and stir until the salt dissolves:

2 cups table salt or 4 cups kosher salt

2 gallons water

Submerge the turkey in the solution. If the turkey is not completely covered, prepare additional brine using a ratio of $^1/_4$ cup table salt or $^1/_2$ cup kosher salt to 4 cups water. Refrigerate the turkey for 4 to 6 hours.

Remove the turkey from the brine. Thoroughly rinse inside and out, then pat the skin and both cavities dry. Arrange the turkey breast side down on a V rack or wire rack set inside a large disposable roasting pan. If you are using a flat rack, you may need to prop the turkey up with crumpled aluminum foil. Brush the back and legs with:

2 tablespoons melted butter

Pour $^1/_2$ cup water into the roasting pan.

Open the bottom vents of the grill completely. Ignite a thick layer of charcoal briquettes and heat until covered with white ash, then push half the coals to each side of the grill. Replace the grill rack and set the turkey, in the pan, in the center of the rack. Cover the grill and open the cover vents completely. Roast for 1 hour.

Meanwhile, about 40 minutes into roasting, heat more charcoal in a chimney starter. After 1 hour of roasting, remove the turkey from the grill, remove the grill rack, stir up the coals, and add half of the new hot coals to each pile. Replace the grill cover. Protecting your hands with towels or mitts, grasp the turkey at both ends and turn breast side up. Baste the breast with:

2 tablespoons melted butter

If the pan is dry, add more water. Return the turkey to the center of the grill, replace the lid, and cook until a meat thermometer inserted into the thickest part of the thigh registers to 180°F, 60 to 80 minutes more. Remove the turkey to a platter and let stand for at least 20 minutes.

Meanwhile, if you wish, prepare:

(Quick Turkey Gravy, 547, or Giblet Gravy, 546)

DEEP-FRIED TURKEY

12 servings

Before filling the fryer with oil, determine the amount you will need by filling the pot with water and submerging the turkey in it. Dry the pot well before adding the oil. A 40-quart pot usually takes 6 gallons of oil to cook a 12-

pound turkey. As the cooked turkey is quite heavy, this is a cooking technique that is best performed by two people. Heat to 350°F in an outdoor propane turkey fryer, 40-quart capacity:

6 gallons peanut oil

If desired, use a hypodermic meat injector (available at gourmet shops and online retailers), to infuse the bird with seasoning. Fill the needle with:

(8 cups Lemon-Oregano Vinaigrette, 573)

and inject the marinade in several places all over:

A 12-pound turkey

Rub the skin all over with:

Cajun Dry Rub, 587, Coffee Spice Rub, 588, or Toasted Whole Spice Rub, 588

Wearing silicone gloves or mitts, place the turkey in the cooking basket and carefully lower into the hot oil. is advisable as the oil will spit and pop as the cold turkey enters the hot oil. Bring the temperature back to 350°F and cook for about 42 minutes, or 3½ minutes per pound. Use long-handled tongs or a coat hanger to locate the handle of the cooking basket. Slip the lifting rod back under the handle to remove the turkey from the oil. Hold it over the pot and let the excess oil drain, then place the basket and turkey on a rimmed baking sheet.

ABOUT TURKEY PARTS

Allow about ¾ pound bone-in turkey per person. A **whole turkey breast** with bone and skin generally weighs between 4 and 7 pounds. For Thanksgiving or some other festive occasion, you might want to consider a "hotel-style" whole turkey breast, which comes with the wings intact and a packet of giblets for making gravy. A **boneless half turkey breast,** with or without the skin, is often called **turkey London broil** at the supermarket, a perfect cut for broiling or outdoor grilling. Slices of boneless, skinless turkey breast are sometimes called **turkey cutlets** or, if sliced very thin, **turkey scaloppine.** These can be used in any recipe calling for boneless, skinless chicken breasts or veal cutlets or scaloppine. Finally, supermarkets sometimes carry packages of **turkey tenderloins** or **tenders,** the 4- to 6-ounce strips of breast meat located on either side of the breastbone. These cuts are perfect for skewering, stir-frying, or sautéing.

Whole **turkey legs, turkey drumsticks,** and **turkey thighs** are all available in individual packages. The legs can be baked, braised, or used to make delicious soups and stews. **Turkey wings** are usually sold whole. They roast and grill well and make excellent stock. The meaty first and second joints can be prepared in the same ways as chicken wings.

The **giblets** are the gizzard, heart, and liver of any fowl. Although these morsels are lumped together under the same rubric, they are rarely cooked together except in the making of giblet gravy. Gizzards and hearts require long, slow braising in order to become tender. Poultry livers, by contrast, respond best to quick cooking and should be served while still pink and creamy on the inside. Generally speaking, only chicken giblets are sold in bulk at the supermarket, though turkey gizzards and hearts sometimes show up at holiday time. The gizzards and hearts usually come mixed together. The livers come in plastic tubs.

COOKING TURKEY PARTS

Please read About Cutting Up Poultry, 419. Preparing a turkey breast or turkey legs separately gives each cut the kind of cooking treatment that it responds to best. Roast, grill, broil, poach, or sauté the breast just until it has lost all traces of pink—to an internal temperature of around 160°F. Roast the legs to an internal temperature of at least 170°F, or braise until the meat is so tender it separates from the bone. Thighs should reach 180°F.

ROAST TURKEY BREAST

5 to 9 servings

Position a rack in the center of the oven. Preheat the oven to 350°F. Have ready:

1 whole turkey breast (4 to 7 pounds)

Season both the skin and bone sides generously with:

Salt and black pepper

Arrange the breast skin side up on a rimmed baking sheet or in a shallow roasting pan. Brush the skin with:

2 tablespoons melted butter

Roast until the meat releases clear juices when pricked with a fork and the thickest part registers 160°F on a thermometer, about 15 to 20 minutes per pound. Let stand for 20 minutes before carving. If desired, prepare:

(Quick Turkey Gravy, 547, Giblet Gravy, 546, or Poultry Pan Sauce Gravy, 546)

TURKEY IN RED MOLE

6 servings

Pass plenty of hot corn tortillas when serving this version of mole, Mexico's classic fiesta dish.

Prepare:

Red Mole, 549

Preheat the oven to 325°F.

Have ready:

One 2-pound boneless turkey breast half or 2 to 2¼ pounds bone-in turkey thighs

Heat a large heavy skillet over medium-high heat until hot. Add and heat until hot:

1 tablespoon vegetable oil

Add the turkey and brown on all sides. Remove from the pan and place into the mole. Cover, put in the oven, and cook until a thermometer inserted in the thickest part of the meat registers about 160°F for a breast half, or 180°F for thighs, about 40 minutes. Remove the turkey from the mole, and cut into pieces or thick slices. Serve with a generous amount of the sauce and a garnish of:

Parsley leaves

Sesame seeds, toasted, 1001

ABOUT GROUND TURKEY AND CHICKEN

For many, ground turkey and chicken make tasty, healthful substitutes for ground beef, particularly in highly sea-soned dishes like chili and tacos. ➤ When substituting ground poultry for beef in milder dishes, you may want to increase the seasonings.

CHUTNEY TURKEY BURGERS

4 burgers

For the simplest turkey burgers, simply shape a pound of ground turkey into 4 patties, season to taste with salt and pepper, and grill, broil, or panfry, then serve on buns with thick slices of red onion. For added moisture and flavor, we suggest combining the meat with other ingredients, as the following recipe prescribes.

Stir together in a small bowl:

> $1/2$ **cup prepared chutney**
> **1 tablespoon Dijon mustard**
> **2 teaspoons lemon juice**

Combine in another bowl:

> **1 pound ground turkey**
> **3 tablespoons prepared chutney**
> **2 scallions, minced**
> **1 teaspoon cumin**
> **1 teaspoon coriander**
> **Salt and black pepper to taste**

Shape into 4 patties and grill, broil, or panfry, turning once, just until cooked through, 4 to 5 minutes on each side. Meanwhile, spread the chutney mixture over:

> **8 thick slices sourdough bread, toasted**

Top 4 slices of the bread with:

> **Arugula leaves**
> **Thinly sliced red onion**

Place the burgers on top, and add:

> **Salt and pepper to taste**

Top with the remaining bread.

GROUND TURKEY OR CHICKEN LOAF

4 servings

Position a rack in the center of the oven. Preheat the oven to 350°F.

Lightly oil a 8 x 4-inch or $8^1/2$ x $4^1/2$-inch loaf pan. Heat in a medium skillet over medium heat:

> **1 tablespoon olive oil**

Add and cook, stirring, 5 to 7 minutes:

> $1/2$ **cup chopped onion**
> **1 garlic clove, minced**

Remove to a medium bowl and add:

> **1 pound ground turkey or chicken**
> **1 large egg**
> $1/4$ **cup grated Parmesan**
> **2 tablespoons milk**
> **2 tablespoons dry bread crumbs**
> **1 tablespoon tomato paste**
> **1 tablespoon chopped fresh basil or 1 teaspoon**
>   **dried basil**

> $1^1/2$ **teaspoons salt**
> $1/2$ **teaspoon black pepper**

With your hands, thoroughly combine, then pat the mixture into the prepared pan. Bake until the center feels firm when pressed, about 35 minutes. Let stand for 10 minutes, then, if desired, unmold onto a platter. Serve hot.

TURKEY OR CHICKEN MEATBALLS

4 servings

Prepare the mixture for:

> **Ground Turkey or Chicken Loaf, above**

Form into 1-inch balls and roll in:

> $1/2$ **cup cornmeal**

Heat in a large heavy skillet over medium-high heat until hot but not smoking:

> **2 tablespoons olive oil**

Add the meatballs and brown, about 10 minutes. Serve with a vegetable or with pasta and a tomato sauce, 562.

ABOUT CREAMED CHICKEN OR TURKEY

Creamed chicken or turkey—white or dark meat in a rich cream sauce—can be served over rice or pasta, on toast, or in pastry shells, or used as the base for a potpie, or casserole.

CREAMED CHICKEN OR TURKEY

4 to 6 servings

I. Prepare:

> **Poached Chicken or Turkey, 423**

Melt in a large saucepan over medium-low heat:

> **4 tablespoons ($1/2$ stick) butter**

Add and whisk until smooth:

> $1/3$ **cup all-purpose flour (for a creamed dish),**
>   **or $1/2$ cup (for a potpie or casserole)**

Cook, whisking constantly, for 1 minute. Remove the pan from the heat. Add 2 cups of the cooking broth and whisk until smooth. Whisk in:

> $1^1/2$ **cups milk or half-and-half**

Increase the heat and bring the mixture to a simmer, whisking constantly. Remove the pan from the heat, scrape the inside of the saucepan and whisk vigorously to break up any lumps. Return the pan to the heat and, whisking, bring to a simmer and cook for 1 minute. Stir in the cooked poultry, bring to a simmer, and cook for 1 minute more. Remove from the heat and season to taste with:

> **Fresh lemon juice**
> **Salt and white or black pepper**
> **Grated or ground nutmeg**

II. Prepare recipe I, using 4 cups cooked chicken or turkey. In making the sauce, replace the poaching broth with:

> **2 cups canned chicken broth**

QUICK CREAMED CHICKEN OR TURKEY

4 to 6 servings

Combine in a large saucepan **3 to 4 cups bite-sized pieces Poached Chicken or Turkey, 423,** two **10³/₄-ounce cans cream of chicken soup,** and **1 cup milk.**

Heat through and serve.

STUFFED BONED CHICKEN

10 to 12 servings

Have ready:

   ¹/₃ recipe Chicken Farce, 541

Bone, 420, making sure to leave the skin intact:

   One 6-pound chicken

Preheat the oven to 450°F. Before stuffing the chicken, tie it off securely at the neck, wing ends, and legs. Sew the opening under the tail shut. If filling, shape the stuffing so that, when you have sewn the seam down the back, the bird will resemble its former self. Be sure not to pack the stuffing or fill the skin too tightly, or it may burst during cooking as the stuffing swells. Sew the seam closed. Brush the bird generously all over with:

   Clarified Butter, 557, allow about ¹/₂ pound butter

Prick the chicken all over with a sharp skewer and repeat this operation after every basting. Set the bird on a rack in a roasting pan, place in the hot oven, and reduce the heat at once to 350°F. After 40 minutes of cooking, begin basting at 10-minute intervals and continue until the center reaches a temperature of 170°F, about 2 hours in all. The chicken may be served hot but it is unusually delicious when served cold. Chill at least 24 hours to allow the seasonings to develop. If serving chilled, slice very thin with a hot serrated knife.

GALANTINE OF TURKEY

15 main-course servings or 30 hors d'oeuvre servings

A galantine of fowl is an extravagant production that begins with the boning process. The skin of the bird eventually becomes the covering of an oversized, luxuriant sausage that contains the meat of the bird combined with eggs, spices, and other meats. When a galantine finally appears in all its glazed and truffled splendor, no one will suspect how it began, for in no way does it resemble any bird ever seen. After making the first slit down the spine, it is ➤ essential to keep the rest of the skin intact. Any cuts must be patched by sewing.

Bone, 420:

   One 12- to 15-pound turkey

Reserve the meat, including that cut from the drumsticks and the breast. Make a stock, 114, of the bones. Reserve half the breast meat for filling and cut into ¹/₂-inch strips. Grind also and combine with the breast meat:

   1 pound boneless lean veal
   1 pound boneless lean pork

Season the mixture with:

   ¹/₄ cup brandy or dry sherry or Madeira

   1 tablespoon salt
   2 teaspoons Worcestershire sauce
   1 teaspoon grated or ground nutmeg
   Black pepper to taste
   Dash of hot pepper sauce

Add:

   8 large eggs, beaten
   ¹/₂ cup finely chopped parsley

Mix into a smooth paste. Spread a large piece of rinsed cheesecloth on a work surface. If the cheesecloth is thin, use a double or triple layer. Place the turkey skin in the center of the cloth, outer side down. Pat the meat mixture onto it in an even rectangular shape, extending it all the way to the edges. Arrange in neat alternating rows down the center:

   Strips of cooked ham or tongue

and the reserved strips of turkey breast. Make a center row of:

   Small black truffles, 284, or pitted canned
      black olives

Sprinkle over the whole:

   ³/₄ cup pistachios
   ¹/₄ cup finely chopped parsley

Starting at the long side farthest away from you, pull the cloth toward you gently to roll the filled turkey skin into a sausage shape. You do not want the cloth inside the turkey roll, but keep manipulating it until it forms an outside casing. You may need an extra helping hand. Tie the cloth securely at both ends. The roll should be smooth and even. Also tie it lengthwise.

Place it seam side down on a rack in a large pot, over:

   Mirepoix, 998

Add:

   Enough Poultry Stock, 117, to cover

Cover the pot and bring to a boil, then immediately reduce the heat and simmer very gently 1¹/₂ to 2 hours, until the roll is firm to the touch and internal temperature has reached 175°F. Carefully remove it to a platter. You can serve it hot, sliced, with buttered toast. Or let it cool, still wrapped, on the platter. When it has cooled to at least 70°F—not before—remove the wrapping, cover with plastic wrap or foil, and refrigerate until thoroughly chilled. Glaze with:

   Savory Aspic, 174, minus the savory ingredients

made from the reserved poaching broth. Serve thinly sliced with:

   Buttered toast

ABOUT DUCK

Virtually all commercially sold domesticated ducks are descendants of **mallards.** Domestic ducks such as **Long Island,** or **Pekin,** duck have a reputation for being fatty. Actually, though, nearly all of the fat is under the skin or at the openings of the body and neck cavities. The meat itself is fairly lean. Since you can, if you cook the bird with care, render, 981, most of the fat out of the skin, leaving the skin crisp and delicious. Duck should not be reserved only for special occasions.

Ducks generally weigh between 3 and 5½ pounds. As duck has both a heavy frame and a high fat content, ➤ allow about 1⅓ pounds to 1½ pounds per serving. Indeed, most restaurants serve a half duck per person. Formerly, ducks usually came to market frozen, but many supermarkets now carry fresh ducks wrapped in such a way as to permit storage of a week or longer. If you buy one of these, check the expiration date on the package and be sure to cook it by that date.

In recent years, specialty breeds, particularly **moulard** and **Muscovy** ducks, have become available. These ducks have a meatier flavor than the domesticated supermarket type, and Muscovy ducks, in particular, have considerably larger breasts. These ducks must be special-ordered and are expensive. Producers offer both whole birds and separately packaged breasts and legs, 448. Cook specialty ducks as you would supermarket ducks, allowing a little extra time if the ducks or parts are large.

ABOUT ROASTING DUCK OR GOOSE

Please read About Duck, 446, About Roasting Poultry, 422, and About Goose, 450. If you are cooking a harvested wild duck, please read About Harvested Wildfowl, 453. Pull out large pieces of fat from the openings of the body and neck cavities. These birds ➤ must be pricked frequently, but lightly, all over to allow excess fat to escape but be sure to insert the skewer or knife tip only into the skin, without puncturing the meat itself. You may also hasten the cooking with the old Chinese trick of placing several metal forks in the cavity to intensify the heat at that point. ➤ As a general rule when roasting duck or goose, place the bird in a 450° preheated oven, lower the heat to 350° and proceed as for chicken, allowing about 20 minutes to the pound for an unstuffed duck, 25 minutes per pound for a gosling. Large geese take about 15 minutes per pound. ➤ Add 20 to 30 minutes if the duck or goose is stuffed.

ROAST DUCK

2 to 4 servings

Please read About Duck, 446. Preheat the oven to 450°F. Remove the neck and giblets from:

One 4½- to 5½-pound duck

Pull out all large pieces of fat from the openings of the body and neck cavities. Rub with:

A halved garlic clove

or sprinkle with:

Paprika

To stuff the bird, please read About Stuffing and Trussing Poultry, 421. Have hot or at room temperature:

Sausage Dressing with Apples, 537, Apple and Prune Dressing, 537, or Sauerkraut Dressing for Game, 539

Loosely pack the stuffing into the body and neck cavities. Truss, 421, if desired. Set the bird on a rack in a roasting pan. Put into the oven and reduce the heat at once to 350°F. Cook about 20 minutes to the pound for an unstuffed bird, 25 minutes for a stuffed one, or until the thigh registers 180°F on a thermometer. Let stand 10 to 15 minutes before carving as for Crispy Roast Duck, below. Make:

Poultry Pan Sauce Gravy, 546

Serve with:

Polenta, 349

or, if the duck has not been stuffed, with:

Crushed pineapple, Poultry Pan Sauce Gravy, 546, or Herbed Pan Sauce, 547

CRISPY ROAST DUCK

2 to 4 servings

Slow-roasting in a very low oven ensures that the delicate breast meat will remain moist and that the skin will be crispy and without fat.

Please read About Duck, 446. Position a rack in the center of the oven. Preheat the oven to 250°F. Remove the neck and giblets from:

One 4½- to 5-pound duck

Pull out all large pieces of fat from the openings of the body and neck cavities. Rub the body cavity and sprinkle the skin with:

Salt

Prick the skin all over in 20 to 30 places. Place the duck breast side down on a V rack in a large roasting pan.

Roast for 3 hours, giving the skin a few extra pricks every hour or so. Drain the fat out of the roasting pan, turn the duck breast side up, and increase the oven temperature to 350°F. Roast for 45 minutes more. The skin should be nice and crispy. Remove the duck to a platter and let stand for 10 minutes. Meanwhile, prepare:

(Poultry Pan Sauce Gravy, 546

To serve 2, cut the duck in half through the breastbone. To serve 4, first cut off the legs and separate them at the thigh/drumstick joint. Cut off the wings and cut them in half. Cut each breast half from the bone, then divide each part in half. Serve each person a drumstick or thigh, half a wing, and a piece of breast meat.

CRISPY ROAST DUCK WITH QUICK ORANGE SAUCE

2 to 4 servings

Please read About Duck, 446. Prepare **Crispy Roast Duck, above.** After cooking and cutting into pieces, combine in a small saucepan:

½ cup orange marmalade

2 tablespoons soy sauce

2 tablespoons orange liqueur

1 tablespoon white wine vinegar

Bring to a boil over medium heat and cook just until the

sauce is the consistency of light syrup. If it becomes too thick, dilute it with stock or water. Season with:

Salt and black pepper to taste

Serve with the duck.

FRUIT-AND-HONEY-GLAZED ROAST DUCK

2 to 4 servings

Preheat the oven to 450°F. Prepare and cook **Roast Duck, 447** (unstuffed), removing it from the oven just before it is done. Lift the rack holding the duck onto a rimmed baking sheet and pour the fat out of the pan, then return the duck on its rack to the pan. If you wish to make pan gravy, transfer the duck to a clean pan. Combine in a small bowl and mix well:

1 cup apricot, cherry, or peach preserves
$^{1}/_{2}$ cup honey
(1 tablespoon brandy)
(1 tablespoon orange liqueur)

Coat the duck with this glaze, and return it to the oven until the glaze caramelizes, 10 to 15 minutes. Let stand 10 to 15 minutes before carving.

ROAST DUCK À L'ORANGE (BIGARADE)

2 to 4 servings

Prepare **Roast Duck, 447** (unstuffed). When it is done, remove it to a platter and keep warm. Prepare **Sweet-Sour Orange Pan Sauce, 548**, using the pan juices.

CHINESE ROAST DUCK

2 to 4 servings

With its crispy, lacquered-looking skin, this is similar to the famous Pekin duck but requires much less time and effort. Please read About Duck, 446. Remove the neck and giblets from:

One 4$^{1}/_{2}$- to 5-pound duck

Pull out the large pieces of fat from the openings of the body and neck cavities.

Combine in a pot large enough to hold the duck and bring to a boil:

5 cups water
$^{1}/_{2}$ cup soy sauce
$^{1}/_{4}$ cup honey

Place the duck in the boiling mixture for 1 minute, turning it with 2 wooden spoons to coat it evenly. Remove the duck from the pot (discard the liquid), drain, and pat dry. Place the duck on a rack set on a baking sheet. Refrigerate, uncovered, for 24 hours. Or set the duck in front of an electric fan in a cool location for 2 to 3 hours to dry the skin well. Position a rack in the lower third of the oven. Preheat the oven to 425°F. Place the duck breast side up on a V rack in a roasting pan. To prevent the fat from smoking, pour 2 cups water into the pan. Roast the duck for 20 minutes, then turn breast side down and roast for 20 minutes more. Remove from the oven, and reduce the oven temperature to 350°F. Pour all the fat and water out of the roasting pan, then turn the duck breast side up. Prick the duck skin all over with a knife tip or metal skewer, being careful not to pierce the meat. Stir together in a small bowl:

$^{3}/_{4}$ cup orange juice
$^{1}/_{4}$ cup rice vinegar
3 tablespoons soy sauce
2 tablespoons honey
($^{1}/_{2}$ teaspoon five-spice powder, 982)

Brush the duck with the orange juice mixture. Roast for 20 minutes. Turn the duck breast side down, brush again with the mixture, and roast for 20 minutes. Turn the duck breast side up again, give it another brushing, and roast for 20 minutes more. Let the duck rest for 10 minutes, then carve as directed for Crispy Roast Duck, 447.

ABOUT DUCK PARTS

Ducks are entirely dark meat, yet their breasts and legs are quite different. The breast is tender and very lean, while the legs are firm and tough. This means that the breast, although delicious when roasted on the whole bird to the well-done stage, is, to many, even better when cooked separately to just rare or medium-rare. The legs, by contrast, require thorough cooking, whether roasted on the whole bird or prepared on their own.

Boneless duck breasts, with or without skin, and duck legs can be bought from specialty producers and in many supermarkets. If you wish to prepare them yourself, see About Cutting Up Poultry, 419. Carefully trim any clinging bits of fat and membrane—nearly invisible when the breast is raw—is unsightly once the breast is cooked. You can cook the wings or chop them up and combine them with the carcass and giblets to make duck stock. Follow the directions for Poultry Stock, 117.

PAN-SEARED DUCK BREASTS

6 servings

Boneless, skinless duck breasts are similar to a lean boneless steak and are always served rare or medium-rare. In addition to being pan-seared, they can be broiled or grilled.

Please read About Duck Parts, above. Have ready:

6 boneless, skinless duck breast halves

Combine in a nonreactive bowl:

3 tablespoons raspberry or fruit-flavored vinegar
2 tablespoons olive oil
2 tablespoons honey
2 tablespoons minced onion, shallots, or scallions
1 tablespoon minced garlic
$^{1}/_{2}$ teaspoon dried marjoram or oregano
$^{1}/_{2}$ teaspoon dried sage, crumbled
$^{1}/_{2}$ teaspoon dried thyme
$^{1}/_{2}$ teaspoon salt
$^{1}/_{2}$ teaspoon black pepper
$^{1}/_{4}$ teaspoon ground allspice

Add the duck breasts to the marinade. Turn to coat, then cover and refrigerate for 2 to 12 hours.

Remove the duck breasts from the marinade, scrape off the solids, and pat dry. Brush both sides of the breasts and a large heavy skillet with:

> **Olive oil**

Heat the skillet over medium-high heat until the oil begins to smoke. Add the duck breasts and cook until the first side is lightly browned, 2 to 3 minutes. Turn and cook for 2 to 3 minutes more.

PAN-SEARED DUCK BREASTS WITH FIG AND RED WINE SAUCE

6 servings

This sauce can be made a week ahead and kept in a covered container in the refrigerator. If possible, use the large Calimyrna figs rather than the smaller, darker Mission figs. Combine in a medium saucepan:

> **2 cups fruity dry red wine, such as Zinfandel**
> **$1/4$ cup duck or chicken stock or broth**
> **2 tablespoons sugar**
> **$1/2$ teaspoon dried thyme**
> **One 2-inch strip lemon zest**
> **1 large garlic clove, minced**
> **1 bay leaf**
> **Pinch of ground cloves or allspice**

Bring to a boil over high heat, stirring occasionally. Add:

> **16 dried figs, stems removed**

Return the mixture to a boil. Reduce the heat, cover, and simmer gently until the figs are very soft but still retain their shape, about 45 minutes. If the liquid reduces to less than 1 cup before the figs are soft, add a little water.

Remove from the heat, and remove the lemon zest and bay leaf. Puree 3 of the figs with $1/3$ cup of the poaching liquid in a food processor or blender, then stir this mixture back into the remaining figs. If needed, thin the sauce with wine, stock, or water. Prepare:

> **Pan-Seared Duck Breasts, 448**

Warm the sauce through and serve with the duck.

GRILLED DUCK BREASTS WITH HOISIN GINGER SAUCE

4 servings

Grilling duck breast presents a challenge. The fat renders out as it cooks and causes flare-ups. Move the duck to other areas of the grill as flare-ups occur.

Please read About Grilling, 1057. Prepare a low-heat grill fire. Combine in a small bowl and mix well:

> **$1/2$ cup hoisin sauce**
> **$1/4$ cup rice vinegar**
> **1 tablespoon minced peeled fresh ginger**

Have ready:

> **4 boneless duck breasts, skin on**

Sprinkle with:

> **Salt and black pepper to taste**

Arrange the duck breasts skin side down on the grill rack and grill for about 6 minutes. Turn and cook for 5 to 7 minutes more until medium-rare and firm to the touch. Remove to a platter and let stand for 10 minutes, then thinly slice on the diagonal. Spoon the sauce over the slices and serve.

ABOUT FOIE GRAS

Foie gras is French for fat liver, and it is, indeed, the liver of a duck or goose that has been enlarged to stupendous proportions by means of special feeding and production techniques. Foie gras is very mild in taste, more like butter than liver.

Fresh foie gras must be special-ordered or bought online and is always very expensive. Usually it is sold whole, but you can sometimes buy either the larger or the less desirable smaller lobe separately. It is packaged in Cryovac and will keep for quite some time, though not indefinitely. In handling foie gras, remember that it is largely fat. It will chip and crumble if cut when too cold and will simply melt away to nothing if cooked too much. To prepare foie gras for cooking, leave it at room temperature for about 1 hour to soften slightly. Carefully pull apart the 2 lobes with your hands and pull out as much of the connective matter as you can with your fingers. Don't be overzealous, or you will end up breaking the foie gras. In traditional practice, foie gras is deveined, but this complicated procedure is quite unnecessary if you plan to slice and pansear the foie gras (the usual method of preparation in America) rather than to poach, steam, or bake it whole. If you would like to draw excess blood from the foie gras, submerge it in water and ice and refrigerate for 1 hour. Once foie gras has been cleaned, it can be tightly wrapped in plastic and refrigerated for a day before cooking.

Before slicing chilled foie gras, let it stand at room temperature for 1 hour. (If you are proceeding directly from cleaning to slicing without an intermediary soaking, it has already softened enough.) Provide yourself with a pitcher filled with very hot water, a stack of paper towels, and a thin sharp knife. Cut each lobe crosswise into slices over $1/2$ inch thick, dipping the knife in hot water each time and thoroughly wiping the knife clean after each cut. Arrange the slices in a single layer on a baking sheet lined with wax paper. If you are not going to cook the foie gras at once, cover it with another sheet of wax paper, and refrigerate it for up to 12 hours.

Cold foie gras is traditionally served with a very sweet white wine, such as Sauternes, but hot foie gras is equally good with other sweet or semi-sweet whites wines, especially German Riesling.

PAN-SEARED FOIE GRAS

8 to 10 first-course servings

Pan-seared foie gras is always served rare and creamy in the center. It cooks in a flash and must be served at once, so have all ingredients, cooking equipment, and serving plates—as well as your guests—assembled before you begin. Pan-seared foie gras is usually served on a bed of something—we suggest polenta, sautéed fresh corn, or finely diced mangoes and peaches—but it is equally delicious served simply on small thin rounds of toasted brioche or corn bread.

Clean, and, if you wish, soak, as above:

1 whole duck foie gras (at least 12 ounces)

If it has been chilled, let the foie gras stand at room temperature for 1 hour. Cut into slices a little more than $^1/_2$ inch thick. Season to taste with:

Salt and black pepper

Have ready a large plate on which to put the foie gras slices as they are cooked and a bowl into which you can drain excess sautéing fat. Brush a wide heavy skillet with a thin film of:

Vegetable oil

Heat the skillet over very high heat until the oil begins to smoke. Place 4 to 6 slices foie gras in the skillet and cook just until the foie gras pulls in slightly on the underside and releases fat into the pan, about 15 seconds. Turn the slices with a spatula and cook about 15 seconds on the second side. Remove the foie gras to the plate and pour the fat into the bowl. Repeat until all the foie gras is cooked, leaving about 2 tablespoons of fat in the skillet. Pour in:

$^1/_2$ cup port or Madeira

Bring to a boil, scraping the bottom of the skillet with a wooden spoon to loosen the browned bits, and boil over the highest heat until nearly evaporated. Add:

$^1/_2$ cup apple juice or cider

Boil until reduced by half and syrupy. Add:

2 tablespoons veal glaze, 582, dissolved in $^1/_3$ cup warm water, or 1 cup rich veal or duck stock, reduced to $^1/_3$ cup

1 tablespoon wine vinegar or strained fresh lemon juice

Boil the sauce until slightly syrupy, then remove from the heat. Moisten the foie gras with the sauce, and serve at once.

ABOUT GOOSE

Goose is entirely dark meat and it tastes very much like well-done roast beef. In seventeenth-century England, certain cuts of roast beef were known, fancifully, as goose.

Dressed geese generally weigh 9 to 12 pounds. Buy the largest one you can find, as there is a great deal of skin, fat, and bone in proportion to meat. Except at holiday time, most geese come to market frozen, a process that they withstand quite nicely.

Goose is famously fatty—a single bird may release a quart or more of fat into the pan during roasting—but, as with all poultry, the fat is under the skin, not in the meat itself, which is lean. Please read About Roasting Duck or Goose, 447, and About Roasting Poultry, 422. Before roasting, goose should be scalded and dried to tighten the

skin so that it squeezes out fat during cooking. The end result is crisp, fairly lean skin as irresistibly delicious as that of Pekin duck.

To scald a goose, bring a large pot of water to a rapid boil. Protecting your hands with rubber gloves, submerge the neck end of the goose in the boiling water for 1 minute. Then submerge the tail end for 1 minute. Drain the goose, and pat as dry as possible, inside and out. Set the goose breast side up on a flat rack set in a roasting pan and refrigerate, uncovered, for 24 to 48 hours to dry the skin.

Goose really should be stuffed. The stuffing does not absorb fat, and since there is relatively little meat on a goose, a stuffing is needed in order to amply serve 8 people. Goose is carved in the same basic way as chicken and turkey, see About Carving Poultry, 421, but its leg and wing joints are located closer to the back and are harder and tighter. In other words, goose is best carved in the kitchen rather than at the table (but do exhibit it at the table first), for disjoining the bird is inevitably a bit of a struggle. While you are at it, you might consider making up individual plates of meat, skin, stuffing, and gravy in the kitchen, rather than bringing everything out to the dining room in serving dishes. That way, you can portion out the scarce meat and prized skin evenly and round out servings with generous helpings of stuffing.

If the goose fat left in the pan after the bird has been roasted is a golden color, not browned or burned, it is delicious. Don't throw it out. Strain into a clean container and keep it to use in place of lard to make Confit, 451, or for frying most anything—especially potatoes.

ROAST STUFFED GOOSE WITH GIBLET GRAVY

8 servings

Note that the drying of the skin, essential for crispness, requires 1 to 2 days.

Please read About Goose, above, About Roasting Poultry, 422, and About Roasting Duck and Goose, 447. Remove and reserve the neck and giblets from:

One 10- to 12-pound goose

Snip the wing tips off and reserve them with the giblets. Pull out any lumps of fat from around the cavities. Using small pliers, pull out any quills in the skin. Using a skewer or knife tip, prick the skin all over, especially over the thighs and breast. Avoid puncturing the meat.

Meanwhile, using the reserved neck, giblets, and wing tips, prepare:

Giblet Gravy, 546

up through the step where it is thickened with roux. Let cool, then cover and refrigerate.

Position a rack in the center of the oven. Preheat the oven to 325°F. Have hot or at room temperature:

Bread Stuffing with Sausage and Apple, 533, Bread Stuffing with Toasted Nuts or Chestnuts and Dried Fruit, 533, or Herbed Mashed Potato Stuffing, 537

Loosely pack the body and neck cavities of the goose with stuffing and skewer or sew openings closed, 421. Bake any leftover stuffing in a buttered baking dish until it reaches 165°F on a thermometer, about 35 minutes. Place the goose breast side down on the rack in the roasting pan and roast for 1½ hours. Remove from the oven and spoon out most of the fat in the roasting pan, being careful not to discard the juices and browned bits. Turn the goose breast side up and roast until the flesh of the drumsticks feels soft when pressed and the skin has puffed around the breast and tops of the thighs, 1¼ to 1½ hours longer. For ➤ extra-crispy skin, transfer the goose, still on its rack, to a rimmed baking sheet. Increase the oven temperature to 400°F and roast the goose for 15 minutes more. Remove the goose to a cutting board and let stand for 30 minutes, covered loosely with aluminum foil. Carefully pour, then spoon, the fat out of the pan, leaving all the juices and browned particles in the pan. Set the pan on two burners over medium heat. Pour in:

   ½ cup Madeira or port

Bring to a simmer, all the while scraping the bottom of the pan to loosen the browned bits. Combine the drippings and reserved gravy base in a saucepan and bring to a simmer over medium heat. Simmer, stirring occasionally, for 5 minutes to blend the flavors. Season with:

   Salt and black pepper to taste

Remove the stuffing from the goose and carve the meat. Cut any skin that becomes detached from the meat into strips. Serve the stuffing, meat, and skin with the gravy.

GOOSE CONFIT

12 first-course or 6 main-course servings

Since confit is now made solely for its taste, this recipe uses only enough salt to flavor the meat. which means that the confit should not be kept longer than a month in your refrigerator. A classic ingredient in cassoulet, 496, goose confit is traditionally prepared with legs only, but this recipe starts with a whole goose because that is what most home cooks are likely to have. Of course, 4 to 6 goose legs can be substituted, as can 8 to 10 duck legs. To cut up a goose, please see About Cutting Up Poultry, 419.

Cut into 6 pieces:

   One 10- to 12-pound goose

Combine:

   ⅓ cup kosher salt
   2 tablespoons black pepper
   2 teaspoons dried thyme
   ¼ teaspoon ground allspice

Rub the mixture evenly over the goose pieces. Place them in a shallow pan, cover tightly, and refrigerate for 1 to 3 days. Combine in a large, heavy pot:

   2 medium onions, sliced
   10 unpeeled garlic cloves
   10 sprigs fresh thyme or 1 teaspoon dried thyme
   7 pounds goose fat or lard

Heat, stirring, over low heat until the lard melts. Remove

from the heat. Slip the goose pieces into the fat. They should be completely submerged. If they are not, add:

   1 to 3 pounds additional lard or solid vegetable shortening

The fat should be kept at a very lazy bubble, about 200°F. If necessary, place the pot on a heat diffuser, 1062. Cook, uncovered, over the lowest possible heat until the goose legs feel tender when pierced with a knife, 1½ to 2 hours. Remove to a plate. Increase the heat to medium-high and cook the fat 5 to 10 minutes. Strain through a very fine sieve and discard the solids. Place the goose in a crock or in the wiped-out cooking pot and cover with the strained fat. Let cool to room temperature, then cover and refrigerate.

The goose will keep for up to 1 month if you make sure the meat is always well covered with the fat. Remelt some of the fat from the pot and cover the meat. To serve confit, broil or panfry it slowly until it is heated through and the skin is crisp.

ABOUT GUINEA HEN

Guinea hen or **guinea fowl,** also known as **African pheasant,** has been commercially raised for centuries in many parts of the world. The tender flesh is light and delicate, with a taste similar to that of pheasant, to which it is related. Any recipe for pheasant or chicken will work equally well with guinea fowl. This bird is very lean and may be barded, 455, before roasting. It is also delicious braised, stewed, or sautéed. Guinea fowl generally weigh between 1 and 4 pounds. ➤ Allow one small bird per person; split or quarter larger ones to serve 2 or 4.

ROAST GUINEA HEN WITH CHILE BUTTER

4 servings

The hens may be prepared up to 2 hours before cooking time and refrigerated until ready to roast.

Preheat the oven to 450°F. Heat in a small skillet over medium heat:

   2 tablespoons olive oil

Add and cook, stirring, until softened:

   ½ cup minced shallots or scallions
   4 garlic cloves, finely chopped

Remove to a small bowl and let cool. Stir in:

   ¼ cup (½ stick) butter, softened
   ½ teaspoon ground cinnamon
   ½ teaspoon ground cumin
   1½ tablespoons chili powder
   2 tablespoons minced fresh cilantro and/or parsley
   1 tablespoon fresh lemon juice
   Salt and black pepper to taste

Have ready:

   One 3- to 3½-pound guinea hen

Being careful not to tear it, loosen the skin around the breast and thighs, then force the butter under the skin with your fingertips. Rub any remaining butter on the outside of the bird. Place it breast side down on a V rack in a roasting pan and roast for 20 minutes. Reduce the oven temperature to 350°F and turn the bird breast side up. Add to the pan, if desired:

   (^{1}/4 to ^{1}/2 **cup dry white wine**)

Roast, basting often with the pan juices, until a thermometer inserted in the thickest part of the thigh registers 180°F and the juices from the thigh run clear when the skin is pierced, 25 to 30 minutes more. Transfer to a cutting board, cover loosely with aluminum foil, and let stand for 10 minutes before carving. Carve, 421, and pour the pan juices over the meat.

ABOUT SQUAB

Squab, or **pigeonneau,** are farm-raised young (usually under 4 weeks) domestic **pigeons** that have not yet learned to fly. Their meat is dark, rich, tender, and succulent. In order to best appreciate its flavor and texture, ➤ squab should be served medium-rare, at which stage the juices run pink and the meat remains slightly rosy and moist. If cooked longer, the meat takes on a distinctive liver flavor. Squab adapts well to many cooking methods. It can be roasted or braised whole, or split and broiled, grilled, or sautéed. Always begin cooking squab by browning the breast so that the thin layer of fat beneath the skin bastes the meat as it cooks. ➤ Squab generally weigh ^{3}/4 to 1 pound—enough to serve 1 person. They may also be split for an appetizer for 2.

BROILED SQUAB

2 servings

Preheat the broiler. Grease the broiler pan. Butterfly, 420:

   2 squab (about 1 pound each)

Lay the squab skin side up on the broiler pan. Brush well with:

   2 tablespoons melted butter

Broil the squab 4 inches from the heat, turning once, until the juices from the thigh are light pink when the skin is pierced, 15 to 20 minutes. Season to taste with:

   Salt

   Hot or sweet paprika

Serve on:

   (**Buttered toast**)

Pour any pan drippings over the squab. Serve immediately, garnished with:

   Chopped parsley

GRILLED SQUAB

Prepare a medium-hot grill fire, 1059. Proceed as for **Broiled Squab, above,** substituting **olive oil** for the butter. Grill the squab starting skin side down. If desired, serve each one topped with a slice of **flavored butter, 558–560.**

SALMI OF SQUAB

2 to 3 servings

A true salmi is a laborious two-step French preparation for wild duck, pheasant, partridge, or woodcock. First the bird is roasted until barely rare. Then the meat is cut from the bones and the carcass is crushed using a duck press or large mortar and pestle to release the juices. These juices form the basis for the sauce, which is enriched with demi-glace, Cognac, and even truffles. The meat and sauce are warmed tableside in a chafing dish with great ceremony and served at once. Needless to say, the dish is rarely presented in its original form today. This is a much simpler version. Other game birds can be substituted.

Remove the backbone and split in half at the breastbone, 419:

   2 squab (about 1 pound each)

Season on both sides with:

   Salt and black pepper to taste

Heat in a large skillet over medium-high heat:

   2 tablespoons olive oil

Add the squab skin side down, in batches if necessary, and cook until crispy and brown, 4 to 5 minutes. Turn over and cook for 2 to 3 minutes more. Remove to a plate. Add to the pan and cook, stirring, until they begin to brown, about 8 minutes:

   1 pound mushrooms, preferably cremini, sliced

Remove the mushrooms and set aside. Add to the pan:

   1 tablespoon olive oil

   ^{1}/2 cup sliced shallots

   1 tablespoon fresh thyme or 1 teaspoon dried thyme

Reduce the heat to medium and cook, stirring, until the shallots are softened, about 2 minutes. Add and cook, stirring to loosen the browned bits, until almost evaporated:

   3 tablespoons Cognac or other brandy

Add and cook until reduced by half:

   1^1/2 cups dry red wine

Add and cook until reduced by half:

   1^1/2 cups game, beef, or chicken stock or broth

Return the squab to the pan and simmer until the meat begins to fall from the bone, 20 to 25 minutes, turning the birds halfway through cooking. Remove the pan from the heat and transfer the birds to a plate to cool slightly; set the pan aside. Pull off and discard the skin of the birds, then pull the meat from the bones and add it to the pan. Add the reserved mushrooms and reheat over medium heat. Stir in:

   (**2 tablespoons butter**)

   Salt and black pepper to taste

   2 tablespoons chopped parsley

Heat for 2 to 3 minutes more, and serve over:

   Toasted Polenta, 349, or cooked pasta

HOME-SMOKED CHINESE-STYLE SQUAB

4 servings

You can smoke any small bird this way, but be careful not to overcook it, or the meat will dry out.

Please read About Smoking Food, 905. Combine in a large shallow pan:

Grated zest of 1 lemon
Grated zest of 1 orange
$^1/_2$ cup light soy sauce
$^1/_3$ cup oyster sauce
2 tablespoons honey
1 tablespoon chopped cilantro
1 teaspoon finely chopped peeled fresh ginger
2 garlic cloves, finely chopped
1 bay leaf
$^1/_2$ teaspoon black pepper

Add to the pan, turning to coat:

4 squab (about 1 pound each), whole or backbone removed and split, 420

Marinate, covered and refrigerated, for 6 hours to 12 hours, turning occasionally. Prepare a covered grill for hot-smoking, 906. Hot-smoke the squab until the juices from the thigh run slightly pink when the skin is pierced, 45 minutes to 1$^1/_2$ hours, depending on how hot the fire is. Baste with the marinade every 15 minutes and add 8 to 10 coals to the fire halfway through the cooking time to maintain an even heat. Serve immediately.

ABOUT OSTRICH AND EMU

Although classified as poultry, ostrich and emu taste and are cooked very much like venison. Both of these farm-raised birds have deep red meat that is extremely low in fat, especially saturated fat, and has very little cholesterol. The main difference between the two is that the meat of the emu, which is a smaller animal, is finer grained. Although the different cuts of ostrich and emu can be confusing, ➤ the most tender portions are the cuts referred to as the fan fillet, inside strip, tenderloin, and oyster; next in tenderness are the tip, top loin, and outside strip. The tougher cuts come from the leg area. ➤ Use any recipes for lean venison or for beef in preparing ostrich or emu. The best cooking methods are sautéing or quickly grilling to medium-rare. As with venison and buffalo, overcooking turns the meat dry and tough. For grilling, rub the meat with a little olive oil and season with salt and pepper.

EMU OR OSTRICH FILLETS

In a large cast-iron skillet or Dutch oven, heat:

2 tablespoons olive oil

Add, in batches if necessary:

24 ounces ostrich or emu, cut into 6 fillets

and sear for 3 minutes per side for medium rare. Serve with:

Herbed Pan Sauce, 547, Onion Sauce, 551, or Basic Cream Sauce for Game, 549

ABOUT WILDFOWL

The birds referred to as "wildfowl" were once exclusively taken in the wild. Today, however, there are species of wildfowl available farm-raised. Unless you hunt or have generous friends who do, you will be working with the latter type, for, by law, only farm-raised wildfowl or species hunted in Europe and imported to the United States may be sold in supermarkets and other shops. Whether bought or harvested from the wild, wildfowl are, without exception, leaner than chicken and turkey. For this reason, barding, 455, is often advisable for wildfowl.

Ideally, the criterion for doneness should be internal temperature, but the flesh of some wildfowl, particularly smaller birds, is thin, making thermometers impractical to use. Instead, the cook is advised to ➤ observe the approximate cooking times we recommend, and if necessary, prick the meat or cut into it carefully near the beginning of the period to determine how much more time is required. Remember that it will continue to cook when removed from the heat source and that ➤ all game is better—distinct and flavorful—on the rare side. Meat can always be returned for continued cooking; it is impossible to undo overcooking. When game, whether fowl or animal, is overcooked, it tastes like liver.

Suggestions are given in individual recipes for those combinations of foods which are classic with game. ➤ Let us recommend, as particularly compatible accompaniments, a dressing of chestnuts or wild rice; a salad of chicory or watercress; a dish of gooseberry or quince conserve; and a sour cream, heavy cream, or wine sauce, classically seasoned with juniper berries.

ABOUT HARVESTED WILDFOWL

We lived for years under a major flyway and looked forward to the days when the hunters in our family sought out the birds in the surrounding marshes and fields. On their return, dinner parties were held in profusion. The children usually clamored for the mild-tasting plump little quail, leaving the rare-cooked ducks to their more sophisticated elders.

The purpose of hunting has always been to provide sustenance and meat for the table. Consequently, ➤ a hunter's ethic usually dictates that any shot bird must be eaten. Rarely is there an instance when that ethic should be overruled, but there is one: Wild birds by definition lead an uncontrolled, nonmanaged life and reveal little history until shot and inspected during preparation. What the bird has been feeding on, how old it is, and how those both affect the overall health of the bird is not known at the point of pulling the trigger. ➤ If the bird appears sickly—discolored meat or putrid odor—it is prudent to discard it. This is not to say that just because a bird is old or has been eating fish it should be returned to the field or marsh for reentry into the food chain. But ➤ when in doubt, throw it out.

To a larger extent, ➤ proper care immediately after shooting and the condition of the bird (cleanly shot and undamaged by the retrieve) determine the cooking method and ultimate excellence of flavor in wild birds. Birds should be field-dressed (gutted) sooner rather than later and placed in a cool, dry place such as an ice chest. As soon as is practical, birds should be put whole, even in the feathers, into a refrigerator. Cooling is an essential part of good game care.

ABOUT PREPARING HARVESTED WILDFOWL

Although hanging wild game birds is still widely done in Europe, it is a fading practice here in the United States. Hanging meat is an aging process that breaks down tissue, thus tenderizing it and, some say, enhancing flavor. In the United States, our palates prefer the flavor of aged, tenderized beef and we still hang and age all large animals, including venison. But although hanging birds for days or weeks does tenderize the meat and intensify flavor, for most of us it is not necessary or a priority. Hanging takes time, is adversely affected by fluctuating temperatures, and can invite spoilage. ➤ The benefits of hanging can better be accomplished by simply refrigerating the whole bird for a couple of days. Even that is unnecessary for small birds such as quail, dove, woodcock, and snipe; it is effective primarily for large goose or pheasant.

PLUCKING AND SINGEING

Unless you intend to skin the bird, plucking is necessary, and dry-plucking game birds is preferable and ➤ easier to do if the bird is chilled. Scalding or soaking before plucking breaks down the fatty tissues in the skin too rapidly if the birds will subsequently be held, even a short time, before cooking or freezing. Pull the feathers by hand, taking care not to tear the skin as you do, from the body down to the knee joint on the legs, and to near the first joint of the wings. (If you intend to use only the breast meat, it is necessary to remove only the feathers from the breast area—see below.) After plucking the bird, remove all pinfeathers (the immature feathers embedded in the skin). Pinfeathers do not affect taste, but they are unattractive. Use a pair of pliers, or grasp each pinfeather between your forefinger and the tip of a knife, then pull. Some pinfeathers may also be removed during the singeing process.

After removing the coarser feathers, it is likely those remaining are downy or small. You can then ➤ singe the bird to remove these last unsightly feathers. Hold it by the legs and singe the pinfeathers over a gas flame, or use a small propane torch. Although tedious, even a candle will work. Turn the bird so that all parts of the skin are exposed to the heat.

DRAWING AND DRESSING

Breasting-out birds is especially for small game birds such as dove, band-tail pigeon, quail, and woodcock, which involves only the breast meat. Thus the entire bird need not be plucked and dressed. To "breast-out" a bird, remove the feathers from the breast and, with a sharp knife, cut each breast away from the breastbone and ribs. (This is much like boning a chicken breast, 420, only here you are working on a whole bird to remove just the breast.) Often it is not necessary to keep the breast skin; see individual recipes.

To prepare whole birds, cut off the head, pull down the neck skin, and cut off the neck close to the body. Now simply cut off the feet and wings with a cleaver or poultry shears. For wild turkey or pheasant, see About Wild Turkey, 456, before removing the legs.

Lay the bird breast side up and, taking great care not to pierce the innards, make a shallow incision across the carcass just below the breastbone. Make a second incision, cutting from the anus up to the breastbone incision so the cuts form a T shape. Insert your fingers into the cavity between the organs and breastbone and pull free the internal organs, stomach, and intestines, if not already removed in the field. Explore carefully to ensure the removal of every bit of the viscera from the cavity, as well as surplus fat, which may prove to be too strong in flavor. ➤ Among the edible viscera of a wildfowl is the heart, which is fine as is. The liver and gizzard, although edible, are so only with some careful surgery, and you may feel they are not worth the effort.

Should you choose to use the giblets, be sure to remove the veins, arteries, thin membrane, and blood from around the heart and discard them. Cut the green sac, or gallbladder, away from the liver very carefully and discard it. It is better to leave a small piece of liver attached to the sac than to cut the sac so close to the liver as to risk puncturing it, for the bitterness of its fluid will ruin whatever it touches. Cut away any portion of the liver that may be discolored. ➤ Sever the intestines from the gizzard and remove the membrane and fat from it. Then cut a shallow slit along the indented curve of the gizzard, being careful not to cut so deeply as to pierce the lining of the inner sac. Push against the outside of the opened gizzard with the thumbs to force out the sac. Discard it. Wash and dry the giblets. Keep them well refrigerated, and use or cook them as soon as possible. See Variety Meats, 518, Stuffings, 532, and Savory Sauces, 542, for the many ways to use giblets.

Turn the fowl over and remove the oil sac at the base of the tail by scooping out an oyster shape above the heart-shaped area called the croupion or—by the irreverent, the parson's or pope's nose.

Before cooking, ➤ look the bird over carefully and remove any shot with a pointed utensil. ➤ Do not use livers or gizzards that have been penetrated by shot. Cut out meat that has discolored near the shot or any dog-damaged areas. After plucking and dressing, ➤ wash the bird thoroughly inside and out under running water and pat dry with paper towel. This should be done both before cooking and when preparing for the freezer in order to remove any blood. Blood is often the cause of the "gamy taste" complaint, and it can make the meat bitter. ➤ Wildfowl should not be soaked and should be completely wiped dry before cooking or freezing. Exceptions are fish-feeding ducks like diving ducks, which, if they must be used, can be parblanched for 30 minutes before cooking.

COOKING HARVESTED WILDFOWL

The interior of the bird may be salted or rinsed with 2 tablespoons lemon juice, brandy, or sherry. If the bird is to be roasted unstuffed, place in it an apple, an onion, a carrot, parsley, a few celery ribs, and sprigs of rosemary or some juniper berries. Discard before serving.

Age and diet of any bird or animal can affect the flavor and determine how it should be cooked. In wildfowl age is only relevant in the larger birds—turkey, goose, and pheasant (see 456, 457 for determining age). With any duck or smaller bird, age is not a consideration. In general, braise rather than roast older birds.

In many cases, only the breasts of wildfowl are served, as the legs are tough and the leg tendons so numerous as to be impossible to remove. A good use for the legs is as an appetizer or hors d'oeuvre when made in a confit using domestic duck fat, 451. Or simmer the legs with the carcass for game stock, 118. This is most useful, because wildfowl produce little juice during cooking, and the stock can be used to bring up the flavor of a sauce. If game stock is not available, veal stock is the best substitute.

BARDING WILDFOWL

Recommendations on the advisability of barding are given in the recipes. **To bard,** use bacon, pancetta, prosciutto, or thin 1/8- to 1/4-inch slices of pork fat or fatback, cut into small squares or lengths. As you truss the fowl, 421, slip pieces of bacon or fat into place on either side between the breast and legs to cover the breast. Alternatively, cover the entire trussed bird—legs and all—with bacon or fat and tie securely, making sure all exposed surfaces are blanketed. After cooking, discard the barding. Bear in mind that ➤ the barding fat will prevent the surface from browning. To remedy this, you may remove the barding halfway through the cooking process, but, if so, baste with butter or olive oil until the bird is done.

An alternative to barding is to rub the bird all over with butter or drizzle with olive oil before roasting. A flavored butter, 557–60, may be used to baste the bird and boost the flavor at the same time. Gently loosen the skin around the breast and thighs of the bird and work the softened butter under the skin—this is best on birds duck-size or larger—and then over the outside of the bird before roasting. See Roasted Guinea Hen with Chile Butter, 451. Butter not only helps keep the bird moist but it also promotes attractive browning of the skin.

ABOUT WILD DUCKS

Flavor depends very much on the way ducks have been feeding. The shallow-water or dabbler types may have been feasting in nearby grain fields and may be very succulent. These include **mallard, black duck, pintail, baldpate or widgeon, gadwall, teal, shoveler,** and **wood duck.** Diving ducks, which thrive on aquatic vegetation, include **redhead, ruddy, bufflehead, golden-eye, scaup canvasbacks,** and **ring-neck.** Sometimes these varieties feed on fish or shellfish, a diet that will alter their flavor. The red and American **mergansers** or other habitual fish eaters will taste of their feed and are not the most delicious for eating. ➤ Their breast meat can be diced, parboiled in milk, and sautéed in butter and herbs for a fine appetizer.

Wild ducks are not usually stuffed, but their interiors may be greased to help retain juices. They may be rubbed with ginger or lemon juice or splashed with Calvados or brandy. Celery, grapes, fresh herbs, or sliced apples in the cavity also impart a nice flavor to the meat. ➤ Discard these additions before serving.

Cooking time varies with type. It may be as long as 25 minutes for a big mallard and only 12 minutes for teal.

ROAST WILD DUCK

4 servings

This cooking method may be the hunter's ideal. The juices are red and flow freely when the duck is carved.
Please read About Wildfowl, 453, and About Wild Ducks, above. Preheat the oven to 500°F. Rinse, and pat thoroughly dry inside and out:

> **2 wild ducks such as mallards, pintail, or black ducks,
> at room temperature**

Rub the insides with:

> **Butter**

Fill the cavities loosely with:

> **A few peeled onions or peeled, cored, and chopped
> apples, or 1 cup drained sauerkraut**

Bard the ducks, above. Place the ducks on a rack in a roasting pan, place in the oven, and reduce the heat to 350°F. Roast, uncovered, only until rare, 20 minutes or so. If there is a need, degrease the drippings. Then add:

> **Wine and stock**

Reduce, then remove from the heat and add:

> **Sour cream**

Heat through, but do not boil. Serve the ducks at once with the sauce and:

> **Braised celery, 243**

BLACK DUCK FRICASSEE

4 servings

Please read About Preparing Harvested Wildfowl, 454. Rinse, pat dry, and heat a large skillet over medium-high heat, until hot. Add, skin side down:

> **Breasts from 4 breasted-out black ducks or
> other wild ducks, 454**

Cook, turning once, until the skin is crisp and browned and the meat is cooked to medium-rare, about 15 minutes. Remove the duck to a platter and cover to keep warm. Pour off all but 2 tablespoons of the fat from the pan and add:

> **2 tablespoons olive oil
> 2 onions, chopped
> 4 carrots, sliced
> 1 leek, chopped**

Cook, stirring, until the onions are translucent, about 8 minutes. Add:

2 cups chicken stock or broth

2 teaspoons chopped thyme

Bring to a boil, then reduce the heat to medium-low and simmer until the liquid has reduced by half, about 10 minutes. Whisk in:

$^1\!/_4$ cup ($^1\!/_2$ stick) unsalted butter

2 large tomatoes, peeled, seeded, and chopped

Return the duck breasts to the pan and heat until warmed through, 2 to 3 minutes. Season to taste with:

Salt and black pepper

Chopped thyme

ABOUT WILD TURKEY

Even "wild" turkeys that are farm-raised are quite different in flavor and texture from their supermarket relatives. They have more leg meat and less breast meat than the domestic kind, and like many other game birds, all of their meat, including the breast, is dark. Despite its leanness, wild turkey is succulent and rich in flavor: imagine a cross between domestic turkey and squab. Fresh wild turkeys generally appear in the market only at Thanksgiving and Christmas. Frozen ones are sometimes available; thaw them slowly in the refrigerator to maintain juiciness.

It has been estimated that 50 percent of the wild turkey harvested annually are yearlings. This is good, since old birds can be tough and should probably be smoked or deep-fried. ➤ To determine if you have young tom, hold it by the lower mandible and shake hard; if the beak breaks with the motion, the bird is not old.

It is rare to find wild turkeys, whether farm-raised or harvested in the wild, at more than 15 pounds in the feathers, and the younger hens—often considered the best—generally weigh only 6 to 10 pounds. ➤ Figure 1 to 1$^1\!/_2$ pounds per person.

If you plan to roast a wild turkey and want the leg meat to be as tender as possible, ➤ it is important to remove the tendons, and this is best accomplished before the feet are removed. To do this, cut around the knee joint, then bend the joint to snap it. Wiggle the leg, loosen the joint, and pull on the foot. Most of the tendons should slide out; any ends of the tendons that remain can usually be pulled out with pliers. We also recommend barding the breast, 455, before roasting to keep the lean meat moist. If you spit-roast the bird, baste it frequently.

WILD TURKEY ROASTED IN A BAKING BAG

6 to 10 servings

It was a hunter's wife of our acquaintance who discovered that roasting wild turkey in a bag would keep it from losing precious juices. Roast with or without stuffing, as you desire.

Please read About Wildfowl, 453. Preheat the oven to 375°F. Have ready a 23$^1\!/_2$ x 19-inch roasting bag. Rinse and pat dry:

1 wild turkey (6 to 10 pounds)

Rub with:

Salt and black pepper to taste

Stuff with:

(Basic Bread Stuffing, 532, or Bread Stuffing with Sausage and Apples, 533)

or:

(3 ribs celery, cut into 1-inch pieces)

(1 onion, quartered)

Tie the legs together. Insert a meat thermometer in the center of the thigh muscle. Put the turkey in the roasting bag, tie the bag closed, and place it in a roasting pan. Roast until the thermometer registers 165°F and the juices from the thigh are just slightly pink when the skin is pierced, about 10 minutes per pound if unstuffed, 12 minutes per pound if stuffed. Remove the turkey from the oven and let stand for about 20 minutes before removing from the roasting bag and carving. If you would like a gravy, carefully transfer the juices in the bag to a saucepan. Mix together in a small bowl:

(2 tablespoons cornstarch)

(2 tablespoons water)

Whisk this into the juices, and whisking constantly, bring to a boil. Season with:

(Salt and black pepper to taste)

BRAISED WILD TURKEY OR WILD GOOSE

5 to 6 servings

Please read About Preparing Harvested Wildfowl, 454. Rinse, pat dry, and cut into serving pieces, 419, then set aside:

One 5- to 6-pound wild turkey or wild goose

Heat in a Dutch oven over medium heat, until hot:

5 tablespoons butter

Add:

1$^1\!/_2$ cups small white onions

$^1\!/_4$ pound finely diced salt pork

Cook until the onions are golden, about 10 minutes. Using a slotted spoon lift out the onions and pork; discard the pork. In batches, if necessary, brown the cut-up bird on both sides in the remaining fat. Add:

Juice of $^1\!/_2$ lemon

$^1\!/_2$ teaspoon ground allspice

(A few slivers of peeled fresh ginger)

Cover and simmer gently about 30 minutes, stirring occasionally. Add the onions and:

2 cups dry red wine

Simmer, covered, until the turkey is tender, about 45 minutes longer. Remove the turkey and onions to a platter. To thicken the pan gravy slightly, stir in:

Dry bread crumbs, toasted, 960

Serve with:

Fresh Egg Noodles, 325

Apricots or crabapples

POTTED WILDFOWL

Allow ¹/₂ pound per person

A good way to preserve any extra wildfowl, such as the legs.

Please read About Preparing Harvested Wildfowl, 454. Prepare:

A young wild goose or other wildfowl, cleaned

as for:

Goose Confit, 451

Serve hot or cold.

ABOUT PHEASANT

Pheasant, which has been **farm-raised** for centuries in both Europe and America, is one of the most popular of game birds. The pinkish-white meat of farm-raised birds has a very mild, delicate flavor and more texture than chicken, although it is one "exotic" meat that really does resemble chicken.

Whole pheasants ➤ weigh between 2 and 4 pounds and will serve 2 people. The small bones of a pheasant mean a high ratio of meat to bone. The leg and thigh meat is a bit darker, firmer, and stronger in flavor than the breast meat. These birds, although smaller than chickens, ➤ can be used in most chicken recipes with the understanding that, in spite of the thin coating of fat protecting the breast meat of farm-raised pheasant, it is quite a bit leaner than chicken, so the cook must avoid overcooking, which renders the meat dry and tasteless. Barding the breast, 455, before roasting will keep it moist.

Wild pheasant has a rich, distinct flavor. We hope your pheasant is young, with a flexible breastbone, gray legs, and a large pointed terminal feather in its wings. If it is a cock, it should have rounded, not sharp or long, nubs for spurs. That means it is young; you may roast or broil it. ➤ It is important when roasting wild pheasant to remove the leg tendons before the feet have been taken off. For determining the age of the bird and/or removing the leg tendons, see About Wild Turkey, 456. Barding is usually advisable too.

To give the bird both flavor and tenderness, ➤ the pheasant should be kept in the refrigerator in the feathers for about 3 days. An old bird should be barded and either braised or used in another moist-heat recipe.

Alternatively, wild pheasant can be cut up before cooking and the tougher thighs and legs braised or stewed, the more tender breast meat grilled, sautéed, or roasted.

ROAST PHEASANT

2 servings

The regal pheasant under glass, considered the ultimate in elegant dining in an earlier era, was served beneath a glass dome, which helped keep it moist between oven and table. The bird was stuffed with wild rice and mushrooms and served with Hunter's Sauce, 555. These and other options are given below.

Please read About Wildfowl, 453. Preheat the oven to 400°F. Rinse and pat dry:

1 young pheasant (2 to 3 pounds)

Season inside and out with:

Salt and black pepper to taste

Stuff with:

(Chestnut Stuffing, 537, Sausage Stuffing, 537, or Wild Rice and Mushroom Stuffing, 540)

Bard the bird, 455, if desired, or brush with:

(3 tablespoons butter, melted)

Place it on a rack in a roasting pan, set the pan in the oven, and reduce the oven temperature to 350°F. Roast until the juices from the thigh run clear when it is pierced, 35 to 40 minutes if unstuffed, 1¹/₂ hours if stuffed. Let stand about 20 minutes before carving. Remove the barding fat, if used, and carve. Serve with:

(Hunter's Sauce, 555)

PHEASANT BRAISED WITH GIN AND JUNIPER

2 servings

Slow braising guarantees a moist bird. Use a good-quality gin for optimum flavor.

Rinse and pat dry:

1 young pheasant (2 to 3 pounds)

Season inside and out with:

Salt and black pepper

Tie the legs together. Bard, 455, wrapping the bird completely in:

2 to 4 ounces bacon or thinly sliced pork fat

and tying the fat securely around the bird. Heat in a Dutch oven over medium-high heat:

2 tablespoons vegetable oil

Add the pheasant and cook, turning occasionally, 5 to 10 minutes. Remove it to a plate. Add to the pot and cook, stirring, until golden, 3 to 5 minutes:

¹/₂ cup sliced shallots

Add the pheasant, along with:

1 cup chicken stock or broth

²/₃ cup gin

¹/₄ cup dry sherry

¹/₂ teaspoon crushed juniper berries

2 bay leaves

Bring to a boil, then cover the pan, reduce the heat to low, and simmer until the pheasant is tender and the juices from the thigh run clear when it is pierced, 35 to 40 minutes. Remove the pheasant to a platter and keep warm.

Strain the sauce, then skim off the fat, remove the bay leaves, and return the sauce to the pot. Boil over medium-high heat until slightly thickened, 3 to 5 minutes. Stir in:

3 tablespoons minced parsley

(2 tablespoons butter)

Salt and black pepper to taste

Remove the barding fat from the pheasant, and carve. Spoon the sauce over the meat and serve.

BRAISED PHEASANT WITH APPLES

2 to 3 servings

Delicious anytime, but especially evocative of autumn. Rinse and pat dry:

1 young pheasant (2 to 3 pounds)

Place in a heavy pot large enough to hold the pheasant comfortably:

2 tablespoons butter

and heat over medium heat until the butter begins to color. Add the pheasant and lightly brown on all sides, 5 to 7 minutes. Remove the pot from the heat. Turn the pheasant breast side up, and drape over the breast and thighs:

3 slices bacon

Scatter around the pheasant:

**3 Golden Delicious apples, peeled, cored, and cut into
$^1/_2$-inch dice (3 cups)**

Stir the apples to coat with fat, then sprinkle with:

2 tablespoons brandy or Calvados

1 tablespoon fresh lemon juice

$^1/_4$ teaspoon dried thyme

Bring to a simmer, then cover tightly and simmer over low heat until the pheasant releases clear juices when its skin is pierced, 45 minutes to 1 hour. Transfer the pheasant to a platter and cover with foil to keep warm. Transfer the apples to a small bowl. Place the pot over high heat and boil the pan juices until reduced to $^1/_2$ cup. Remove from the heat. Whisk together in a medium bowl:

1 cup sour cream

1 tablespoon all-purpose flour

Slowly whisk in the pan juices. Pour the sauce back into the pot, add the apples, and cook over low heat, stirring gently, until the sauce comes to a simmer and thickens slightly. Do not boil, or the sauce may curdle. Season to taste with:

Salt and black pepper

Serve the pheasant with the sauce, accompanied by:

Wild Rice, 354, or Gnocchi, 335

ABOUT PARTRIDGE AND GROUSE

Most **farm-raised partridge** in America today is the variety known as **chukar partridge.** These are small birds, appreciated for their tender, tasty, lean breast meat, which is similar to that of pheasant but a little firmer and less delicate. Farm-raised partridges generally weigh a bit less than 1 pound apiece, so ➤ serve 1 bird per person. They can be roasted as for grouse, below, or cut into serving pieces and grilled, sautéed, or braised.

In addition to wild chukar partridge, there is another wild partridge species in America known as **Hungarian partridge**—and just to confuse things, the partridge name is also given in the North to the ruffed grouse and in the South to quail.

Grouse, a close cousin of partridge, is not farmed and remains a true game bird; any found in U.S. markets is imported. It is considered by many to be the finest of game birds, often with more flavorful meat than partridge. In the United States we hunt **ruffed, spruce, sage, ptarmigan,** and **sharptail grouse,** and the unlikely sounding grouse called **prairie chicken.** Grouse may range from a pound or so for a ruffed grouse to 5 or 6 pounds for the large sage grouse; whatever the size of the bird, ➤ about 1 pound per person is a generous helping of this rich and delicious bird.

Although the age of a grouse or partridge may have little or no effect on the flavor or texture of the meat, diet can. Both grouse and partridge are fairly liberal in their dietary habits, but survival certainly comes first and the birds eat whatever is available in their habitat. For ruffed grouse, native to the forests of the northern United States and Canada, this means that in the fall they are often found in apple orchards or feeding on other fruits such as wild grapes. This diet makes the ruffed grouse particularly delectable. Spruce grouse, as their name implies, live in and eat spruce needles and have the bad reputation of tasting "sprucey." In the late fall and winter months, when their feed is limited, they do depend heavily on spruce and are less tasty than in the early fall. In general, no matter the species, ➤ early season birds that are still well fed and eating a range of optimal foods are preferable for the hunter's table.

Although wild chukar and Hungarian partridge are different from grouse in flavor, they are similar in size and diet and consequently ➤ most grouse and partridge recipes are interchangeable.

ROASTED GROUSE

4 servings

Please read About Wildfowl, 453. Preheat the oven to 400°F. Rinse and pat dry:

4 grouse (about 1 pound each)

Season inside and out with:

Salt and black pepper to taste

Divide among the cavities:

1 small apple, quartered

1 small onion, quartered

1 rib celery, cut into 4 pieces

Bard the birds, 455. Place them on a rack in a roasting pan, set the pan in the oven, and reduce the oven temperature to 350°F. Roast, basting often, until the juices from the thigh are light pink when the skin is pierced, 25 to 35 minutes. Remove the birds to a platter and cover to keep warm. Prepare:

**Pan Sauce for Wildfowl, 547, or Poultry Pan Sauce
    Gravy, 546**

Remove the barding fat. Serve with:

(Uncooked Cranberry Relish, 222)

BAKED MARINATED PARTRIDGE
OR GROUSE

2 to 3 servings

Please read About Preparing Harvested Wildfowl, 454. Rinse, pat dry, cut up, or split:

1 partridge or grouse

Place in a deep baking dish.

Combine in a bowl:

> **2 cups port, or as needed**
> **1 small onion, quartered**
> **1 garlic clove, sliced**
> **1 small bay leaf**
> **³/₄ teaspoon salt**
> **¹/₂ teaspoon black pepper**

Pour over the bird. Be sure the marinade covers the bird; add more port if necessary. Cover and refrigerate 24 hours.

Preheat the oven to 325°F. Remove the bird from the marinade and pat dry with paper towels. Reserve the marinade. Put into a casserole or a Dutch oven just large enough to hold the partridge in one layer and melt:

> **2 tablespoons butter**

Add the bird and turn to coat. Bake, uncovered, 45 minutes, turning several times. Strain the marinade and pour it over the partridge. Return to the oven for about 30 minutes, until tender. Remove the partridge to a platter, and cover to keep warm. Pour the pan juices into a small saucepan and boil over high heat until reduced to about 1 cup of sauce with a slightly syrupy consistency. Season with:

> **Drops of lemon juice**

Pour the sauce over the partridge. Serve with:

> **Wild Rice, 354, Kasha, 347, or Fresh Egg Noodles, 325**

ROASTED SHARPTAIL GROUSE, PTARMIGAN, OR PRAIRIE CHICKEN

Allow 1 bird per person

Preheat the oven to 300°F. Rinse and pat dry:

> **Grouse**

You may lard the breasts, 464, with thin strips of:

> **Salt pork**

or bard them, 455. Or you may stuff with:

> **(Small apples, peeled onions, or ribs of celery)**

Place on a rack in a roasting pan and roast until cooked to rare—the meat should be pale pink. Allow 30 to 45 minutes, and, if you are not barding, baste frequently with:

> **Melted butter or the pan drippings**

Remove from the oven and increase the temperature to 500°F. Remove the bacon, if you barded the birds. Brush the birds with:

> **Melted butter or oil**

Dredge lightly in:

> **Flour**

Place in the 500°F oven until brown. Let rest about 15 minutes before serving. Make:

> **Poultry Pan Sauce Gravy, 546, or Pan Sauce for**
> **Wildfowl, 547**

Serve with:

> **Cranberry Sauce, 222**

ABOUT SMALL GAME BIRDS

The birds discussed here are of many kinds: **quail, woodcock, coots** (these are not the sea ducks that are called coot, but small rail-like birds), **wild doves, band-tail pigeon, snipe, rails, curlews,** and **gallinules.** They are grouped together on the basis of size and therefore similar treatment and the fact that they are served one or more to a person. Small birds are usually used as fresh as possible, although they remain edible as long as the legs are flexible. Plucking such small birds for roasting is very labor-intensive, particularly because ➤ a serving size is usually at least 2 birds per person. However, if you are planning an event and choose to roast whole birds, they should, like all game birds, be dry-plucked; see 454. ➤ Small birds should be barded, 455, or you may wrap them in fig or grape leaves. All lend themselves to roasting and skewering or broiling; allow from 3 to 10 minutes. Any special peculiarities or classic combinations are listed in individual recipes.

Small birds produce very little pan drippings. Pour what there is on a crouton, or on a piece of crisp scrapple. Or combine the drippings with a Demi-Glaze Sauce, 554, and wine or lemon, or use them to make Hunter's Sauce, 555, Orange and Ginger Sauce, 549, or Champagne or White Wine Sauce, 553.

ABOUT QUAIL

Quail is one of the sweetest and most tender of all game birds and also, since it is widely farm-raised, one of the most readily available. Quail is sold both fresh and frozen (in which form it is quite acceptable). It is the smallest game bird commonly eaten in the United States, weighing between 4 and 8 ounces, with only a few ounces of breast meat per bird. ➤ Two quail make a main course, one an appetizer. We love quail served hot off the grill or spit, to be picked up and eaten with the fingers, but they can be roasted whole or cut up and then broiled or sautéed.

"Boned" or "semiboned" quail has the backbone and breastbone removed, but the tiny wing and leg bones remain. This product is widely available and, from both a cook's and a diner's standpoint, very convenient.

Sometimes called partridge in our deep South, **wild quail** has delicious white meat. In the United States, we hunt **bobwhite, California, Mountain,** and **Gambel's quail** and all are about the same size as their farm-raised cousins. Like all wild birds, wild quail have unpredictable diets and can taste stronger than those purchased from the grocery store. Please read About Small Game Birds, above.

Whether bought or shot wild in a covey from horseback, quail can be treated identically in the kitchen. Serve with quince preserves and curried rice; watercress and lemon wedges; green grapes; or baked pears, the centers stuffed with pimientos. If you broil the quail, brush it with Anchovy Butter, 558.

SPICY MAPLE-ROASTED QUAIL

4 main-course or 8 first-course servings

Serve these as an appetizer on their own or as a main course accompanied by sautéed greens and rice. The marinade may be used with Cornish hens, chicken, and pork tenderloin as well.

Rinse and pat dry:

8 quail

Season inside and out with:

Salt and black pepper to taste

Whisk together in a shallow bowl:

$1/3$ cup maple syrup

$1/4$ cup soy sauce

2 tablespoons red wine vinegar

2 tablespoons chili-garlic paste

8 cloves garlic, finely chopped

$1/2$ teaspoon five-spice powder, 982

Add the quail, turning to coat. Marinate, covered and refrigerated, for 4 to 8 hours. Preheat the oven to 475°F. Drain the quail, reserving the marinade, and place on a rack in a roasting pan. Fold the wingtips under the birds and tie the legs together. Roast for 10 minutes. Reduce the oven temperature to 400°F and roast, basting twice with the reserved marinade, until the juices from the thigh are slightly pink when the skin is pierced and the flesh is still juicy, about 10 minutes more. Cover loosely with aluminum foil and let stand for 5 minutes before serving.

ROASTED SMALL GAME BIRDS

3 to 6 servings

Please read About Small Game Birds, 459. Preheat the oven to 450°F. Rinse, pat dry, and bard, 455:

6 small game birds

It is not necessary to stuff them, although a few peeled grapes or bits of celery or parsley may be tucked inside and discarded later. Place in a roasting pan. Roast the birds about 5 minutes. Reduce the heat to 350°F and roast them 5 to 15 minutes longer, according to size. Timing in general varies from 8 to 10 minutes for woodcock to 10 to 15 minutes for unstuffed quail to 15 to 18 minutes for stuffed quail. Remove barding and let stand about 15 minutes before serving.

BROILED SMALL GAME BIRDS

3 to 6 servings

Please read About Small Game Birds, 459. Preheat the broiler. Rinse, pat dry, and bard, 455:

6 small game birds

Place them on the broiler pan and broil, turning frequently, for 12 to 20 minutes, according to size. The barding may be removed toward the end of the cooking period and the birds browned briefly. Prepare:

Poultry Pan Sauce Gravy, 546, Pan Sauce for Wildfowl, 547, or Pan Sauce with Leeks, Orange, and Rosemary, 548

Serve the birds on:

Croutons, 974

Pour the gravy over them. Garnish with:

Chopped parsley

BRAISED SMALL GAME BIRDS

3 to 6 servings

For this recipe, the birds can be skinned and in parts. Please read About Small Game Birds, 459. Preheat the oven to 350°F.

Melt in a Dutch oven:

2 tablespoons butter

Rinse, pat dry, and add:

6 small game birds

Lightly brown on all sides. Add:

$1/2$ cup boiling stock or wine

Mirepoix, 998

Cover the birds with parchment paper and transfer to the oven. Bake 15 to 20 minutes. Remove the birds to a platter and cover to keep warm. Make:

Poultry Pan Sauce Gravy, 546

Add to the gravy, if desired:

(2 tablespoons fresh lemon juice, brandy, or sour cream)

Serve on:

Croutons, 974

Garnish with:

Chopped parsley

SKEWERED SMALL BIRDS

Please read About Small Game Birds, 459, and About Grilling, 427. Rinse, pat dry, and wrap in buttered grape or fig leaves:

Small birds

or bard them, 455, with very thin slices of:

(Pancetta or prosciutto)

Prepare a hot grill fire. Roast skewered on the grill 10 to 15 minutes until browned. To finish for serving, you may remove the leaves or barding and roll the birds in dry bread crumbs, baste with drippings, and heat in a 350°F oven 5 minutes longer.

ABOUT DOVES, SNIPE, RAILS, AND BAND-TAILED PIGEONS

Allow 2 birds per person

All of these birds have dark meat with a fine flavor. **Dove** is usually more tender than **pigeon, rail,** or **snipe.** Please read About Small Game Birds, 459.

Prepare:

Roasted, above, or Broiled Small Game Birds, above

Serve garnished with:

Almond-stuffed olives

or with a:

Compote of Red Sour Cherries, 213

DOVES AND NOODLES

6 servings

Please read About Small Game Birds, 459. For this recipe, the doves can be skinned and cut into serving pieces. Rinse, pat dry, and place in a large pot:

12 doves, whole or cut up

Add water to cover, bring to a boil, and simmer until the doves are tender, 10 to 15 minutes. Drain, discard skin, if any, and season with:

Salt and black pepper to taste

Let cool. When cool, take the meat off the bones and reserve. Preheat the oven to 350°F.

Melt in a medium saucepan over medium heat:

2 tablespoons butter

Add:

1 small onion, chopped

1 garlic clove, minced

Cook, stirring, until soft. Remove from the heat, and mix in:

1 cup sour cream

One 10 3/4-ounce can condensed cream of
mushroom soup

1/4 teaspoon salt

1/8 teaspoon black pepper

Combine the sauce in a 13 x 9 x 2-inch baking dish with:

4 cups cooked egg noodles (8 ounces dried)

Mix in the dove meat. Cover with foil and bake for 30 to 40 minutes, until bubbling. Sprinkle with:

Chopped parsley and/or mint

DOVE AND WILD RICE PILAU

4 servings

Please read About Small Game Birds, 459. Rinse and pat dry:

12 doves, cleaned

Preheat oven to 375°F. Soak in hot water until plump, about 30 minutes:

1 cup raisins

Drain. Cook in a skillet over medium heat:

6 slices pancetta or bacon

Remove from pan and discard all but 1 tablespoon of the fat. Chop into 1-inch pieces. Add to pan:

1 cup chopped celery

Cook until softened, about 5 minutes. Remove the celery to a large mixing bowl. Add raisins and pancetta, and stir in:

2 1/2 cups cooked wild rice

1 tablespoon butter

1 teaspoon salt, or to taste

1 teaspoon black pepper, or to taste

4 eggs, beaten

Stuff the doves with this mixture. Combine:

1 cup balsamic vinegar

3 tablespoons mustard powder

Brush each bird with the mixture and place them in a shallow baking dish. Sprinkle each bird with:

Olive oil

Bake, uncovered, 30 minutes, basting frequently with vinegar and mustard mixture. Drizzle with basting juices.

ABOUT WOODCOCK

American woodcock is a true epicurean delight and the game bird aficionado's favorite bounty. Its dark, rich meat is like no other and ➤ should always be prepared rare. It is meant for a sophisticated and game-savvy palate, occasionally being served "in the round"—whole bird with entrails and head—and, as a somewhat acquired taste, is best reserved for the woodcock fancier. Smaller than its European cousin, it is a migratory bird that is only available in the wild, and there are small limits on the number that can be taken each day. Although it is particularly protein-packed and therefore filling, ➤ one bird per person is barely a meal—so often the hunter returns with only enough woodcock to serve as an appetizer or hors d'oeuvre. Please read About Small Game Birds, 459.

WOODCOCK IN ROSEMARY CREAM SAUCE

2 to 4 main-course servings or 8 to 10 first-course servings

Serve this with toothpicks for an hors d'oeuvre or over angel hair pasta as a main course.

Rinse, pat dry, and breast out, 454, or, if boned, slice into strips:

4 woodcock, dove, or squab

Heat in a large skillet over high heat:

2 tablespoons olive oil

Add the woodcock strips and cook, stirring, for about 1 minute. The meat should still be pink. Using a slotted spoon, remove to a warm platter. Add to the pan:

3 tablespoons Armagnac

1 tablespoon juniper berries, crushed or ground

and stir with a whisk, making sure to scrape the bottom. Add:

1/2 cup heavy cream

Bring to a boil and boil until thickened and reduced by half. Whisk in:

1 tablespoon chopped rosemary

Season with:

Salt and black pepper to taste

Pour the sauce over the meat.

MEAT

A novice approaching the meat counter may arrive, and remain, in a state of confusion. The friendly, informative butcher of times past has often been succeeded by an unseen presence that mysteriously slices, grinds, and wraps behind a partition or, more recent, by binfuls of packaged meat cuts straight from the processing plant, where new procedures of boning and packing save transportation costs and safeguard sanitation. Whatever the merits of prepackaging—and skillful aging is not likely to be one of them—some cuts look bafflingly similar but react to cooking in totally unexpected ways. In this chapter, we hope to provide you with the skill and expertise to choose the right cut for the type of dish in mind.

Tender cuts, which generally lie in the sections of the animal where the least movement and stress occur, respond to **dry-heat processes:** roasting, grilling, broiling, pan-broiling, sautéing, deep-frying, and stir-frying. For further details, see Cooking Methods and Techniques, 1088, for both these processes and those for the tougher cuts. The latter, with more connective tissue, demand long, slow cooking with **moist-heat processes:** braising, stewing, fricasseeing, pot-roasting, and poaching. In all but the last, the temperature of the cooking liquid ➤ should never go above 180°F. For ways to counteract toughness, see Cooking Tough Meats, 464, About Mincing, Grinding, Pounding, and Macerating Meat, 464, and Seasoning Meat, 463.

▲ In high altitudes, roasting meat needs no time adjustment up to 7,000 feet; after that, a longer cooking period may be needed.

For the thawing and cooking of frozen meats, please see 463.

A sharp blade makes working with meat easier and safer. For a discussion of knife sharpening, see 1070.

There is more about meat than cuts, grades, and cooking methods that must be considered. How the animals are fed, how long the meat has been held and at what temperature, whether or not it was treated with preservatives, and when it was packaged—all are factors for which you must rely partly on your experience but mostly on the integrity of the packager. Read the label carefully, ask questions, and stay informed.

ABOUT MEAT GRADES AND BUYING

Most American consumers benefit from two forms of protection legislated by the U.S. Department of Agriculture in the meat market. First, all meat sold in interstate commerce is subject to government inspection for wholesomeness and cleanliness; ➤ do be cautious in purchasing locally butchered meats not subject to these rigid federal sanitation regulations. Second, meats sold by wholesale packing companies are graded and stamped according to nationally uniform federal standards of quality for tenderness, juiciness, and flavor by government-employed "graders" who work at the packing plant. We are especially concerned here with grading, for the quality of the meat is as important in our choice of cooking method as is the cut (where the meat lies on the animal's body). U.S. grading falls into eight main categories, as described below, but **Choice** and **Select** are the two grades of interest to most consumers.

PRIME

This grade represents about 2 percent of graded beef or lamb, and generally commandeered by restaurants and some specialty markets. Prime grade meat is abundantly marbled or flecked with fat; it is tender, well flavored, and fine-textured.

CHOICE

Usually the highest grade available in the supermarket. Choice is meat of high quality but has somewhat less marbling with fat than prime. The more tender cuts may be roasted, grilled, or broiled. The meat should be a bright red color with some marbling.

SELECT

Still a relatively tender grade but with a higher ratio of lean meat to fat. The encasing layer of fat may be thin, and the meat is less juicy and flavorful. Oven-roasting by the constant-heat method may be satisfactory for more tender sections, but moist-heat cooking should usually prevail.

Standard, Commercial, Utility, Cutter, and **Canner** are given to meat with a coarser appearance than other grades and no marbling. These grades are mainly ground or used in processed meat products. Although we are always being assured that the protein value of meat from older animals is comparable to that from the younger, more tender ones, we know that they rarely match in eating quality. Definite exceptions apply to meats for stocks, 114, and for soups, 134. Both have more flavor if made from the meat of more mature animals. Be aware that some meats are sold without a grade and are in fact in the Select category. ➤ If the meat looks good to you, ask about it. **Kosher** meats are processed according to rabbinical law, and **halal** meat is processed according to Islamic law. According to the USDA, the term **"natural"** on a label means only that the meat has been minimally processed and contains no artificial flavorings, colorings, preservatives, or other synthetic ingredients. All fresh meat falls into this category. However, increasingly the term "natural" is coming to mean that the meat was raised with no antibiotics and no growth hormones. Read the label carefully. An **"organic"** certification means that the animal ate 100 percent organically raised feed. **Grass-fed** animals have been raised on grass, silage (fermented grass), or cornstalks.

When purchasing meat, bear in mind that ➤ cuts with the smallest percentage of bone and fat make the best buys, and that while price per pound may go down for bonier cuts with more fat, the amount you need per serving goes up. It may surprise you to know that the cost of sirloin steak is comparable per portion to unboned chuck, that center-cut pork chops are cheaper per serving than loin or rib chops, and that spareribs can be twice as expensive per serving as center-cut pork chops.

SERVING SIZES

When buying **trimmed meat,** ➤ allow $^1/_4$ to $^1/_3$ pound per serving for boneless cuts. This category includes ground beef, lamb, and veal; boneless stew meat; boned roasts and steaks; flank and strip steak; tenderloin; and most variety meats. When buying meat with **some bone,** ➤ allow $^1/_3$ to $^1/_2$ pound per serving. These cuts include rib roasts, bone-in steaks and chops, and hams. For **bony cuts,** ➤ allow $^3/_4$ to 1 pound per serving. In this bracket are short ribs; spareribs; shanks; shoulder, breast, and plate cuts; brisket; and hocks.

STORING MEAT BEFORE COOKING

Ground meat, fresh sausage, and organ meats are among the most perishable types, in terms of both flavor retention and safety. Cook them within 24 hours of purchase. If ground meat is to be stored in amounts over a pound, make sure it is loosely covered and so placed in a container that is no more than 2 inches high, thereby allowing the chill of the refrigerator to penetrate it quickly. Diced and cubed uncooked meat should be used within 48 hours. Steaks and chops will hold for 2 to 4 days, roasts for 3 to 5 days. As a general rule, the larger the cut of meat, the longer it will keep. Some cuts of meat are Cryovac packaged and the date on the package will indicate when it is best cooked by.

Prepackaged cured or smoked meat and sausages may be stored refrigerated for a week in their original wrappers. Once the package is opened, exposed surfaces should be protected. In checking for spoilage, be sure meat is not slimy to the touch, and that there is no off odor on the surface or where the bone meets the flesh.

Any meat that cannot be cooked within the recommended time should be frozen (see Keeping and Storing Food, 883). Assuming the freezer is 0°F or lower, the quality of beef, lamb, and veal steaks or roasts will keep for 1 year; pork chops and roasts 4 to 8 months; ground meat 3 months; and sausage for less than 3 months.

We recommend bringing large roasts to room temperature before cooking, but most other cuts of meat can be cooked straight from the refrigerator. Thaw frozen meat completely in the refrigerator. Steaks and chops will thaw in 1 day; larger roasts may take up to 3 days. Make sure to contain the juices from thawing meats. When storing and handling raw meat, ➤ take care to avoid cross-contaminating other foods, especially those eaten uncooked, such as salad greens or fruits.

SEASONING MEAT

If you are salting the meat, do so at the start of cooking. Pepper is a different matter. The taste of freshly ground pepper fades during cooking. We recommend peppering the meat twice: once before cooking, so that the flavor penetrates the surface slightly, and again before serving.

There are other ways to accent flavor. **In dry-heat cooking methods,** meat may be rubbed with garlic, onion, herbs, and/or spices about a half hour before cooking. Any bits of garlic remaining on the surface of the meat should be discarded before cooking, as it may scorch and turn bitter. Alternatively, make small incisions over the surface of a large cut of meat and stuff slivers of garlic or bits of onion, anchovies, or a mix of spices and herbs into the meat. These little flavor packets will perfume the surrounding meat. **In moist-heat methods,** the addition of herbs or wine to the cooking liquid will lessen the need for salt. Delicacy of flavor may be preserved in meat heavy with fat by pouring off or skimming excess grease after the first half hour of cooking.

Spice rubs and pastes, see About Dry Rubs and Pastes, 587, can be rubbed on immediately before cooking or up to a day in advance and kept refrigerated. The spice rub or paste will give the meat a highly flavorful, slightly crunchy crust, while the interior retains the original flavor of the meat.

Marination is the process of enhancing the tenderness and flavor of meat by soaking it in a liquid containing some form of seasoning and almost always an acid, such as vinegar, wine, lemon juice, buttermilk, or yogurt. Because marination is also used for foods other than meat, it is discussed fully in About Marinades, 584. Brining, 421, is also an excellent method to make pork moist and more flavorful.

COOKING TOUGH MEATS

Tenderness in raw meats depends not only on the age of the animal, but on its breed and the way it was fed. Toughness is due both to the presence of connective tissues and to a lack of fat. **Larding, below,** and **Barding, 455,** can help to make up somewhat for lack of fat, but the best way to convert stringy to more tender tissue is very long and very slow covered moist heat cooking. See Pot-Roasting, Stewing, and Braising Meat, 466. Grinding and mincing make chewing easier. If the texture of the meat is basically tough, however, it will remain so, and it should never be used in dishes like stroganoff, stew, or, for that matter, even in those so commonplace as hamburger.

Any meat can be made more palatable by seasonings and by added fats or dressings. Pounding and scoring are a help in cuts that are normally treated by dry-heat methods, such as sautéing and panfrying.

We cannot say much for the method of sprinkling meat with papain, a papaya derivative, which tenderizes but may adversely affect the meat flavor. If you care to try out a commercial meat tenderizer, sprinkle it on both sides of the meat, allowing 1 teaspoon of tenderizer per pound. Prick the meat all over with a fork after applying the tenderizer. The tenderizer should be applied just before the meat is put on to cook.

ABOUT MINCING, GRINDING, POUNDING, AND MACERATING MEAT

The results of mincing and grinding meat are quite different. **Minced meat** remains separate in further preparation, but ground meat, especially if ground 2 or 3 times, tends to clump together. ➤ Always handle ground meat lightly to avoid a dense finished texture.

Pounding, which breaks down the tough fibers of meat, may be done with a **wooden, metal,** or **rubber mallet, a macerating mallet,** or the flat side of a **cleaver.** If you are inexperienced at using a cleaver, hold it in both hands, and ➤ be sure the handle projects beyond the board or table surface, so that you don't bang your fingers. If you slightly moisten the mallet or cleaver and strike with a glancing motion, the meat is less likely to stick. When pounding something delicate, like veal scallops, put the meat between sheets of plastic wrap or a fold of parchment paper. These precautions will keep the meat intact even when pounded paper-thin. A chef friend has suggested that if you find a very thin piece of meat too measly looking, it can be pounded and then folded over for the cooking to make it more presentable when served.

All work surfaces and equipment should be cleaned with hot water and detergent and carefully dried after any of these procedures since salmonella and other dangerous bacteria thrive in equipment and on surfaces not properly sanitized. And again, be especially careful about keeping raw and cooked food separated, to avoid cross-contamination.

ABOUT LARDING

Larding, or inserting of strips of pork fat or bacon into lean cuts, helps give meat juiciness and flavor. This process has become more useful now that the trend in meat production is toward less marbled meat. **To prepare lardoons,** see the recipe below. Allow about 2 to 3 ounces of pork fat for 1 pound of meat. Insert short ones near the surface, and put them in across the grain of the meat. Or cut long ones so that they will protrude slightly at either end of a chunk of meat, and force them in parallel to the grain, so they will show up when the meat is sliced. It is important for attractiveness to cut all lardoons in uniform square-cut thicknesses, varying from ⅛ to ½ inch. Insert with **larding needles,** which are of two types. Those used in surface larding are very thin pinpointed models with a flexible top that can easily be pried open to insert the lardoons and then pressed tightly against the lardoon to hold it as the needle is drawn completely through the meat at a shallow angle, shown below. The second type has a blade like a pen point, which elongates the entire length of the shaft and remains open all along the top. This type is used for both making and inserting the lardoon.

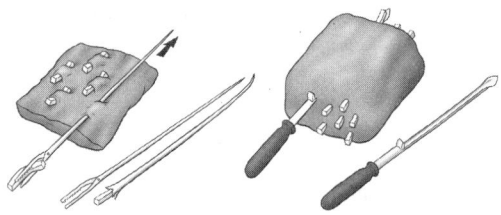

Inserting short and long lardoons
into meat with larding needles

A quicker way to lard meat is to cut the pieces of fat into ½- to ¾-inch-wide strips and cut a point on one end of each. Place the fat in the freezer until stiff. Then cut slits in the meat and push in the frozen strips of fat like tacks or needles. For another method of preventing meat from drying out, see Barding, 455.

LARDOONS
Enough for 2½ pounds of meat
Please read About Larding, above.

Lardoons may be blanched briefly to release salt, then dried. They may also be frozen before insertion into meat, see above.

I. Rub:

   4 ounces pork fatback, salt pork, or slab bacon
with, if desired:

   (A halved garlic clove)
Cut the pork into small uniform strips from ⅛- to ½-inch-thick. Dip into:

   Black pepper
   Ground cloves

II. Cut into lardoons
  ¼ pound salt pork or fatback or slab bacon
Marinate in:
  A few tablespoons of brandy
Just before using, sprinkle with:
  Grated or ground nutmeg
  Chopped parsley or chives

BROWNING MEAT

Browning gives meat a richer, more pronounced, more interesting flavor and texture. Browning occurs naturally when dry-heat cooking methods such as grilling, broiling, sauteing, or roasting are used. But when using moist-heat cooking methods such as braising, stewing, or potroasting, the meat is browned first.

Heat a heavy-bottomed pan large enough to hold the meat comfortably until hot enough to sizzle but not hot enough to scorch. Turn the meat so that all sides brown. Done properly, browning takes time; expect a large piece of meat, like a roast, to take 15 to 20 minutes; smaller chunks of stew meat may take 10 to 15 minutes. ➤ Do not crowd the pan—it lowers the heat, causes steam to form, and results in gray rather than browned meat. See Pot-Roasting, Stewing, and Braising Meat, 466.

SAUTÉING OR PANFRYING MEAT

Since this technique is used for many foods other than meat, a full description will be found on 1048. It is a popular and quick method of cooking thin, tender, or breaded cuts of meat.

PAN-BROILING MEAT

This method of broiling can be convenient for cooking steaks or chops up to 2 inches thick. Slowly heat a heavy skillet—preferably cast-iron—until the edge of a steak lightly touched to the skillet will sizzle briskly, not hiss sharply. Greasing the pan is unnecessary for meats that are marbled or for ground beef with normal fat content; for lean meat, you may rub the skillet with a small amount of fat. Let the meat cook, uncovered, sizzling briskly, for about 5 minutes. When the meat is seared and brown on the bottom, turn and sear for a few minutes on the other side. Avoid long cooking, which toughens the meat. ➤ Pour off any fat that accumulates, or the meat will wind up fried or sautéed rather than pan-broiled.

BROILING MEAT

Please read about Broiling, 1046, and, if applicable, about Spit-Cooking, 1059, and Outdoor Grilling, 1057. Choose tender cuts, such as beef steaks or lamb chops for broiling. Flank steaks are also broiled, but must be cooked rare, to avoid toughening. Consult your stove manufacturer's instructions before broiling to determine if preheating is required and whether the oven door should be left partially open. Cut off excess fat and score the remaining fat about

every 2 inches around the edges of the meat to keep it from curling. Center the meat in the pan—which should be cold, to prevent sticking—and adjust the broiler rack so that the top surface of the meat is 3 to 5 inches from the heat source. If the pan is hot, grease it or the meat. Broil until the top side is well browned, then turn and broil until the second side is browned. Only one turn is required for a 1-inch-thick steak or chop, and the chop should be about 2 inches from the heat. For 2-inch-thick meats, lower the rack so the surface of the meat is 4 inches from the heat source and turn more frequently. ➤ Broiling time depends on thickness, fat content, whether or not the meat was aged, and the degree of doneness desired. Approximate timings for various meats are given in the individual recipes.

ROASTING MEAT

Please read About Meat Grades and Buying, 462, for types of meat appropriate for roasting. In choosing meat for this dry-heat process and deciding which variation of the procedure to follow, the important factors are ➤ the tenderness of the cut and the amount of marbling. Temperatures and timings are given in the individual recipes. Please read Timing and Doneness, 467. For gravy-making methods, read about sauces made by degreasing and deglazing, 546, or About Gravies and Pan Sauces, 546.

For Prime and Choice grades, place the roast fat side up on a rack in shallow greased pan in a preheated oven. Setting the meat on a **roasting rack**—either a V rack, or flat grid-type rack—keeps it off the bottom of the pan and promotes even browning by allowing the hot, dry oven air to circulate around the entire roast. ➤ As soon as you close the oven door, reduce the heat and time the cooking from that point. For Prime meats, the fat content makes basting unnecessary. All Choice-grade cuts profit from basting, 466, and may benefit from larding, 464, or barding, 455.

If you are dealing with the next lower grade, Select, be forewarned that because of less marbling you may be taking a chance if you oven-roast rather than pot-roast or braise meat of this type. Dry roasting is not recommended for Select cuts weighing less than 4 pounds. For Select grade cuts above 4 pounds, use constant-heat roasting rather than high-heat roasting. Place the meat in a preheated oven—350°F for pork, 325°F for beef and lamb—and keep the temperature steady during the entire roasting process. Larding, 464, barding, 455, and basting, 466, may prove helpful. In short, everything possible should be done to accentuate whatever tenderness the leaner grades may have. ➤ One of the tricks is never to roast less-tender cuts to more than medium-rare and to ➤ carve the meat in very thin slices diagonally across the grain.

Another constant-heat roasting method for meats, uses lower heat for a longer period. The oven should remain ➤ at least 275°F at all times, for unwanted organisms may not otherwise be destroyed, no matter how long the cooking. Dry-roasting is not recommended for meat lower than Select grade. These tougher meats should be prepared by long, slow moist-heat cooking. See Pot-Roasting, Stewing, and Braising Meats, below.

BASTING

Basting helps retain the juiciness of roasting meat by moistening its surface from time to time with melted fat, meat juice, sauces, or marinades. Since roasting, like broiling, is a dry-heat process, the meat remains uncovered and no water or stock is used, for these liquids form steam and change the process to moist heat cooking. No basting is necessary for well-marbled meats with a high fat content, but all the less-marbled cuts profit from basting.

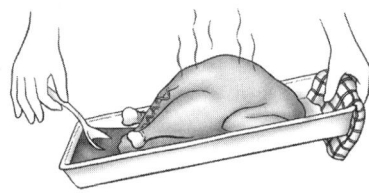

Basting meat with a bulb baster and spoon

Before roasting, brush the pan with a little fat to prevent the drippings from charring, which would result in a bitter taste in the juices used later for gravy. ➤ Basting should begin after about the first half hour of cooking and should be repeated as often as necessary to prevent drying—at intervals of 10 minutes or more, depending on the size of the roast, its leanness, the oven temperature, and the stage of the roasting process. The best utensil for basting is a **bulb-type baster** that suctions up the pan drippings, to which other melted fat may have been added. Or a long-handled, large spoon may be used. Very lean meats profit by larding, 464. Barding, 455, results in an effective form of self-basting.

POT-ROASTING, STEWING, AND BRAISING MEAT

All three methods benefit less tender cuts, such as chuck, shoulder, top or bottom round, blade, brisket, and rump roast. The cooking is done by simmering meat in varying amounts of liquid in a closed pot or casserole for relatively long periods. **Pot-roasting** may be used for cuts up to 4 or 5 pounds, and **stewing** for meat in smaller chunks. Cuts of various sizes may be **braised** using less liquid than for a stew and a somewhat longer simmering period. Braising is invariably preceded by browning. The ideal type of container for all three methods is a heavy pot, such as a Dutch oven, with a tight-fitting cover.

For moist-heat cooking in general, we recommend the following procedure. Before it is browned, the meat may simply be wiped dry, or it may be dredged with flour, 961, or it may be marinated, 463, then wiped dry. For browning, we prefer olive oil or a vegetable oil that complements the flavor, ➤ using only enough to cover the bottom of the pot and to prevent sticking. In a Dutch oven or heavy skillet, heat the fat slowly until a piece of meat sizzles briskly when it touches the pot. It is important not to crowd the pot—which would lower the heat, cause steam to form, and result in graying rather than browning. ➤ Turn the meat frequently so it browns slowly. For flavoring, diced vegetables such as onions, celery, and carrots may be added to the fat when the meat is partially colored. Or, to control the cooking more easily, vegetables may be sautéed separately until translucent and then combined with the meat. Onions sautéed or caramelized separately will add intense flavor and attractive color to the stew.

After browning meat, pour off excess fat. You may leave 1 or 2 tablespoons of fat in the pot and set the meat on a bed of Mirepoix, 998. Or, for pot-roasting, place the meat on a rack inside the pot. Then add the stock or other liquid, and bring to a boil. In pot-roasting and braising, add liquid to a depth of ¼ to ½ inch. For a stew, the liquid should barely cover the meat. As soon as the liquid reaches a boil, reduce the heat at once to maintain a simmer ➤ and cover the pot tightly. If necessary, replenish the liquid from time to time with boiling stock or water. Turn the meat occasionally to keep it moist.

When cooking on top of the stove, the vegetables you will serve with the meat may be added to the pot during the last 45 minutes of cooking—about ¼ pound of vegetables to ¾ pound of meat. Very mature vegetables may profit from a brief blanching beforehand. For oven stews, it is preferable to cook the vegetables separately on top of the stove and add them to the casserole toward the very end of the cooking period.

A **slow-cooker** is an effective tool for pot-roasting, stewing, and braising. Brown the meat first on the stove-top, then follow the manufacturer's instructions. To adapt a recipe for the slow-cooker, see 99. You can short-cut the entire process by pressure-cooking, but the high heat produces a less desirable result. Time benefits stewing, braising, and pot-roasting; many cooks say that pot roasts, stews, and braises taste even better the day after they are made.

To roast in the oven after browning, place the pot in a preheated low oven for the remainder of the cooking, ➤ keeping the temperature constant throughout. The temperament of the oven and the degree of heat retention of your pot will determine the correct temperature—300° to 325°F—for long, slow, steady cooking.

The best cuts for pot-roasting come from the chuck and rump, and the chuck is the more desirable of the two. Most cuts from the round are too lean and may dry out when braised. The exception is ➤ bottom round rump roast, which makes first-rate pot roast. Boneless cuts are easier to handle and serve than bone-in pot roasts, but make sure the boneless roast is tied into a neat, compact shape before cooking, as any loose or excessively thin parts will overcook before the whole roast is tender. A pot roast is done when it is **fork-tender,** meaning that the meat easily separates and shreds when a fork is twisted in the meat. The meat should still be somewhat moist. If the meat has been cooked gently enough, there may even still be a faint tinge of pink in the center. If the meat is still tough and hard, let it cook a little longer to dissolve the collagen in the meat, until fork-tender. Avoid the common mistake of overcooking a pot roast until it becomes coarse, dry, and stringy.

For the cooking method known as **à blanc**—sometimes used for veal, pork, or poultry in stews—raw meat without browning is placed directly in boiling water rather than browned and the heat reduced ➤ almost at once to a simmer as the meat changes color. This more gentle method yields tender meat and rich stock.

The gravy for braised or pot-roasted meat should not be thick but should have good body. ➤ Always allow a stew or pot roast to stand at least 5 minutes off the heat so that the fat will rise and can be skimmed off before serving. If made some hours in advance, the meat can be removed from the pot and the gravy cooled and defatted more easily. You may thicken the gravy with a small amount of flour paste, 544, or kneaded butter, 545, or cornstarch. To reheat leftover meat, see 469.

GRILLING MEAT

There is no finer treatment for a thick, tender steak than to cook it on the grill. The exterior will be charred and crisp with a juicy interior. ➤ An inch and a half is a good thickness for grilled meats. As thin cuts will dry out quickly; extra-thick cuts will char outside before they cook through. We prefer to cook without a cover, since covering the grill tends to overwhelm the meat with smoky flavor. (To smoke meats, see 905.) The grill rack should be 4 to 6 inches above luminous coals (for a discussion of direct and indirect heat, see 1059). Grilled meats also benefit from marinating, 584, spice rubs, 587, and Basting, 466, with sauces. Also see Grilling, 1057.

BARBECUING MEAT

A very American pursuit, **barbecuing** is the outdoor equivalent of slow-roasting. The best barbecues allow wood or hardwood charcoal to burn in a separate chamber from the meat, which is then slow-cooked by the heat and smoke. The effect can be replicated on a grill, provided it is covered and the meat is not placed directly over hot coals, but rather to the side for indirect heat, 1059.

TIMING AND DONENESS

The following chart gives you the final temperatures the meat should reach after it has been removed from the oven and allowed to **rest** or **stand** for 5 to 10 minutes after cooking. During this resting or standing time, the meat continues to cook—known as **carry-over cooking**—and the final temperatures seen on the chart will be reached. Because of carry-over cooking, ➤ meat should be removed from the oven when the meat thermometer registers 5 to 10 degrees less than chart specifies for final temperatures. Most of our recipes factor this in and are written accordingly.

INTERNAL TEMPERATURES FOR COOKING MEAT AFTER CARRY-OVER COOKING		
Fresh ground beef, veal, lamb, pork		160°F
Beef, veal, lamb (roasts, steak, chops)	Rare	135°F
	Medium-rare	145°F
	Medium	160°F
	Well-done	170°F
Fresh pork (roasts, steaks, chops)	Well	160°F
	Well-done	170°F
Ham, uncooked		160°F
Ham, fully cooked, reheat		140–145°F

Timings and temperatures for varying degrees of doneness are given in the individual recipes. But meat timings are approximate at best, for there are many factors that make precision impossible—the temperature of the meat at the outset of cooking, its shape and thickness, the fat and bone content, the matter of aging. We recommend, therefore, ➤ the use of a thermometer for more accurate results. If using a **meat thermometer,** insert it into the center of the meat, away from fat or bone, with the top of the thermometer as far as possible from the heat source. The meat thermometer is left in the meat during cooking. An **instant-read thermometer** is a low-cost tool. When inserted into the thickest part of the meat (without touching bone), the temperature will register quickly. Instant-read thermometers are not meant to be left in the meat during cooking. The more expensive **continuous-read thermometer** can be left in the meat for the duration of the cooking. When measuring the temperature of thin foods, such as pork chops or hamburger patties, insert the thermometer probe in through the side, so the sensing area is in the center of the food.

If you have no thermometer, there are a couple of time-honored **tests for doneness. Press the surface** of the roast with your finger; if the meat is soft yet resilient, if it dents easily and at once resumes its shape, it is cooked to medium-rare. If it remains firm under finger pressure, it is well-done. Another test is to make a small incision in roasted, grilled, or broiled meats, and check the center. Rare meat produces red juice; medium-rare, pink; well-done, colorless juice. And again, ➤ once meat is removed from the heat source, it will continue to cook and the temperature will rise.

The following are some general rules related to the timing of meats. Ovens must be preheated for roasting; in broiling, consult stove manufacturer's instructions.

To ensure internal temperatures high enough to destroy bacteria, ➤ 275°F is the minimum oven heat for roasting meats, except for pork, 497, no matter how long the meat is cooked—even up to 12 hours of roasting. For comparative periods of moist-heat cooking, a simmering temperature of 180°F suffices because of the more penetrating quality of the heat.

COOKING MEAT EN CROÛTE

Meat cooked in a crust, or *en croûte,* lends itself particularly well to buffet service: hot, it remains in a good serving condition for half an hour, and, hot or cold, it is a conversation piece. There are two ways to proceed. The roasted meat—which may be beef, lamb, or ham—may be precooked to within 30 to 45 minutes of doneness and cooled somewhat before the encasing dough is applied; then the wrapped meat is baked only long enough to brown the pastry and finish cooking the meat.

An alternate method wraps uncooked meat in the dough, and the roast or ground meat pâté is baked long enough to cook the meat thoroughly while the crust browns. For meats that are not precooked, it is essential that the dough covering be vented in several places to allow steam to escape and to prevent the crust from buckling, see Beef Wellington, below.

Often the tough croûte or dough covering is not eaten but serves merely as a medium to preserve aroma and juices. If you prefer a latter-day American variety of edible crust, you may use Deluxe Butter Pie Pastry Dough, 665, Brioche, 614, or Food Processor Puff Pastry Dough, 669. Or use a stiff bread dough, which will need to be punched down once before rolling out. The recipe given here is for the traditional nonedible croûte—heavy in egg to lend the tensile strength necessary to cover big pieces of meat securely.

I. FOR PARTIALLY COOKED MEATS

Preroast the meat to within 30 or 45 minutes of doneness. Remove from the oven and let it cool to room temperature. Make a covering of one of the doughs mentioned above, or the following.

Have all ingredients at room temperature and combine in a large bowl:

> **4 cups all-purpose flour**
> **1½ teaspoons salt**
> **1 cup vegetable shortening**

Mix to the consistency of coarse cornmeal. Make a well in the center and work in, one at a time:

> **3 to 4 large eggs**

And then:

> **½ cup water**

Turn the dough out and knead until smooth. Roll into a ball and let rest, covered, 1 hour at room temperature. Roll the dough into a large ⅛-inch-thick sheet. Place the meat on the dough, top surface down, and fold the dough neatly over the meat. Bring the edges of the dough together and seal the seams with:

> **1 egg white, beaten**

Turn the covered meat seam side down and brush off any excess flour. At this point, you may use scraps of dough or puff pastry, 669, to decorate the log. Put the meat in a preheated 450°F oven. Reduce the heat at once to 350°F. Allow the crust to bake until it is browned. For even browning, glaze the log with beaten egg at the end of baking. You may also brush the crust with butter after you remove it from the oven.

II. FOR UNCOOKED MEATS

Prepare the dough as above, or use one of the above-mentioned doughs. Fold the dough up around the meat and decorate it, if desired. Cut a series of steam vents in the dough, as for a covered pie, 469. Bake the meat in a preheated 300°F oven for 2 to 3 hours, depending on size. Hams and legs of lamb may be boned and stuffed before baking. Precook any stuffing you may use, as the heat may not penetrate it sufficiently to cook it through.

BEEF WELLINGTON

6 to 8 servings

In the classic method, the beef is roasted twice—once before being wrapped in pastry and once after—with the often unfortunate result of either overcooked beef or undercooked pastry. In our method, we skip the preliminary roasting and instead wrap the uncooked meat in pastry. This method promises moist, rosy-centered beef surrounded by crisp pastry crust. A roast of uniform thickness is crucial to success.

Position a rack in the center of the oven. Preheat the oven to 400°F. Season:

> **1 center-cut fillet of beef roast (about 3 pounds),**
> **well trimmed, 472**

with:

Salt and black pepper

Combine in a medium bowl:

**5 ounces (¹⁄₂ cup) foie gras or duck, goose, or
chicken liver mousse or Pâté Maison, 518,
mashed until smooth**

1¹⁄₂ cups Duxelles, 284, cooled

3 tablespoons Madeira, sherry, or vermouth

Spread the pâté mixture over the entire roast. Roll out to a
¹⁄₄-inch-thick square large enough to wrap easily around
the meat with some overlap, about 14 x 14 inches:

**Brioche Dough, 614, or 1 pound Food Processor Puff
Pastry Dough, 669, lightly chilled, or a 14 x 10-inch
sheet frozen puff pastry, thawed and softened**

Lightly whisk together:

1 large egg

1 tablespoon water

1 tablespoon milk

Place the beef in the center of the dough. Gently pull the
pastry up and around the roast, wrapping it in a neat package. Trim off any excess dough and seal the edges by
brushing them with the egg wash and pressing them together. Lightly grease a baking sheet. Place the wrapped
beef seam side down on the pan and brush the top with
egg wash. Use the dough trimmings to make decorative
leaves or scrolls, if desired. Cut 2 or 3 small evenly spaced
neat holes in the top of the pastry to allow steam to escape
and to allow you to insert a meat thermometer without
breaking the crust. Bake until the crust is golden brown
and a thermometer inserted in the thickest part of the
roast registers 120° to 125°F for rare, 125° to 130°F for
medium-rare, or 135° to 140°F for medium, 55 minutes to
1 hour 10 minutes (the temperature will continue to rise by
5 to 10 degrees out of the oven). If the pastry begins to get
too brown during baking, cover it loosely with aluminum
foil. Remove the roast from the oven and let stand, uncovered, for 15 to 20 minutes. Slice the roast at the table,
using a serrated knife to cut ³⁄₄-inch-thick slices. If desired,
consult savory sauces, 542, for sauce ideas, or serve with:

**(Mushroom Wine Sauce, 555, or Red Wine and
Marrow Sauce, 555)**

MEAT PASTRIES AND MEAT PIE TOPPINGS

How we'd relish judging an international competition of
cooks turning out their native meat pastries! The doughs
would range from the resilient to the flaky, with fillings
running a full gamut of flavor. They would include wontons, 342, ravioli, 339, kreplach, 126, piroshki, 89, potpies, 103, and shumai, 343. It is in such homely functional
dishes, varied according to the season and by the individual cook, that the true cuisine of a country dwells. Many of
the smaller specialties call for precooked fillings, which,
once encased, need only a brief cooking of the dough and
reheating of the filler, by simmering in broth, deep-frying,
sautéing, or baking. Pastry-covered meats can fit into the
menu in many ways, depending on their size, from hors
d'oeuvre or soup garnishes to a one-dish meal. The prize

for the heartiest would go to the English with their Steak
and Kidney Pie, 483. Usually the one most common on
American tables is the potpie, 103—stewed meat heated
in gravy, sometimes with vegetables, covered in various
fashions with a dough topping.

One method is to place unbaked biscuits or dumplings
on top of a stew, spacing them widely enough to allow
steam to escape. ➤ The two essentials in making a meat
pie are first, to have enough tastily seasoned gravy to almost cover the cooked meat, and second, to ensure that
steam does not produce a soggy crust. One sure-fire procedure to prevent sogginess is the following.

I. Use:

Any unsweetened Pastry Dough, 665–670

Roll out and cover the casserole or smaller individual
dishes in which you will serve the meat pie. Since pie
dough shrinks in baking, you must cut it slightly larger
than the dish, and prick the dough with a fork. Bake the
pastry in a baking sheet at 425°F for 15 or 20 minutes,
until golden brown. This separate baking means you will
have to cover your casserole in some other way as the
stew itself heats—with a piece of foil placed lightly on top,
or with a loose-fitting lid. Just before serving, when the
casserole has been heated through, place the prebaked
crust on top. Serve at once.

II. If you prefer an unbaked dough topping on the stew
and heat the meat mixture and bake the dough at the
same time, proceed as follows.

Preheat the oven to 350°F. Fill baking dish with stew
and gravy to 1 inch from the top. Place over it a generous
round of dough. To allow for shrinkage, first brushing
under the surface with beaten egg white to help make it
impervious to steam. ➤ Be sure to slash steam vents in the
dough covering. Bake 45 minutes to 1 hour, until the stew
is thoroughly heated and the crust golden. You may brush
the crust with butter before serving.

STORING COOKED MEAT

It is wise to promptly cover meat that is left over and to refrigerate it, tightly covered, as soon as it cools slightly. Do
not store ➤ meat in hot gravy in quantities larger than
3 cups. Drain off the gravy and allow it to cool separately if
the amounts are larger. ➤ If meats are stuffed, remove
the stuffing and store it separately.

REHEATING COOKED MEAT

For convenience, you may sometimes be obligated to
prepare roasted meat in advance, to be reheated just before serving. Although this procedure is not always satisfactory because of the tendency of meat—especially large
roasts—to become dry on reheating, it can be done if
there is no other solution to your problem of time. Simply
bring the preroasted meat to room temperature and warm
through in a preheated moderate oven.

Reheat sliced or sauced meats, gravy-style meats such
as stew, or hash by first heating the sauce separately, just

to the point of boiling. Then add the meat and ➤ reduce heat to low at once. When the meat is thoroughly heated, serve immediately. Another method for warming sliced roasted meat is suggested on 469.

ABOUT MEAT CUTS
We show, 473, the side of a beef, which is very similar to that of other four-legged mammals except for proportion of bone to meat. Also see 490, 497, and 485, for lamb, pork, and veal.

With all four-legged animals, the areas along the central spine portion that more or less hangs between the shoulder blade and the hip socket—the areas with the least active musculature—are the most tender. They can be counted on to cook by the dry-heat methods: roasting, broiling, grilling, and panfrying. Those areas just contiguous sometimes respond to dry heat, but most of the meat up through the shoulder and foreshank in front and from the rump to the hind shank, where the muscles are active, will need slow, moist cooking to break down the connective tissues. This is particularly true as you descend from Prime to Select grades, 462.

There are, of course, other differences in cuts and major differences in cooking procedures. They are noted in the recipes and in the sections on beef, veal, pork, and lamb.

ABOUT ECONOMICAL USE OF LARGE CUTS OF MEAT
If you are shopping for a household of two, there are times when you may look longingly at the weekly special on meat. How tempting the standing rib roast of beef, the rump of beef, the leg of spring lamb, the loin of pork, the round of veal, or the half or whole ham! But unless you are planning to have guests, it seems like far more meat than you care to buy. However, by taking advantage of special sale prices and planning ahead by freezing a part of the cut for future use, it is an economy to buy the large piece. You can still have your delicious small roast—or steaks from the ham or veal, chops from lamb or pork, short ribs from beef. Then the remainder of the roast may be used in many interesting leftover dishes; see Brunch, Lunch, and Supper Dishes, 95.

ABOUT BEEF
Beef is far and away the most popular American meat. Most beef is processed at a young age to ensure tenderness, though it is less flavorful than meat from older animals. Please read the general remarks in the beginning of the chapter and, to identify the various beef cuts, please read About Meat Cuts, above, About Fillet or Tenderloin of Beef, 472, and About Beef Steak Cuts, 472. The recipes that follow are those involving dry-heat first, then moist-heat methods. For ground beef recipes, see 509–515; for cooked and leftover beef recipes, see Brunch, Lunch, and Supper Dishes, 95.

BONELESS ROAST BEEF
For convenience and ease of carving, there are boneless cuts that are excellent for roasting. The most tender are the **tenderloin** or **fillet,** the **rolled rib roast** or **rib eye**—a boneless version of the standing prime rib—and the **strip loin roast,** sometimes called the **top loin** or **shell roast.** Less tender but more economical, and just as flavorful if not overcooked, are the **bottom sirloin, eye round, top round,** and **sirloin tip.**

ROAST BEEF
2 to 3 servings to the pound
Please read Roasting Meat, 465. These directions are for the large, tender cuts we think of as Sunday dinner roast beef. Count on 2 servings per pound for bone-in roasts, 3 servings per pound for boneless roasts. The most tender are the standing rib roast and the rolled rib roast. The sirloin tip roast, eye of round, or rolled rump may be cooked the same way if they are of Prime or Choice grade. If you choose a standing rib roast, have your butcher remove the shoulder bone and chine bone, and then have him or her tie the chine back to keep the contour of the meat and to protect the eye of the roast during cooking.

Preheat the oven to 550°F. Having removed the roast from the refrigerator 2 hours before, place the meat fat side up on a rack in a greased shallow roasting pan. Do not cover, and don't add liquid. Put the roast in the oven, immediately reduce the heat to 350°F, and roast 18 to 20 minutes to the pound for medium-rare. A rolled roast will require 5 to 10 minutes longer to the pound. A thermometer should read between 125° and 130°F for rare and 135° to 140°F for medium. Let rest. To make gravy, see About Gravies and Pan Sauces, 546, and Meat Pan Gravy, 546. To carve, steady the roast with a meat fork and slice the meat off the bones in one chunk. Then set the roast fat side up and cut it vertically into slices as thick or as thin as you like. A second method, shown below, is to set

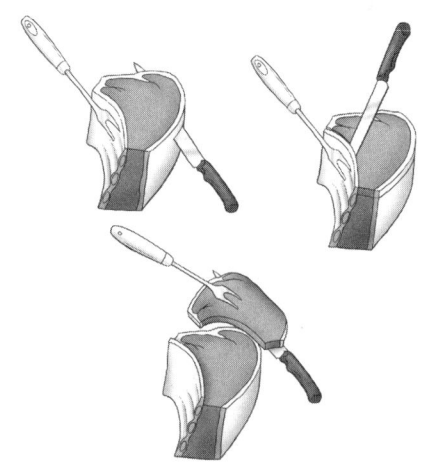

Carving a roast

the roast on its side and cut it horizontally from the fat side toward the rib into thicker slices, removing the rib bones one at a time with a vertical cut as you carve off the slices.

ABOUT MAKING A JUS

A simple method for boosting the flavor and enhancing the juiciness of roast beef is to make a quick **jus**, or **juice**, with the pan drippings as soon as the roast comes from the oven. Remove the cooked roast from the roasting pan and set it aside, loosely covered, to rest. Pour off any excess grease from the pan drippings.

Place the roasting pan over medium heat and add:

$^1/_2$ to $^3/_4$ cup of any flavorful stock, 117–120, preferably beef or mushroom, or low-sodium canned stock

Bring the liquid to a boil and scrape the bottom of the pan with a wooden spoon until all the roasting particles are dissolved. Season with:

Salt and pepper to taste

and drizzle the jus over the sliced beef. Bear in mind that a jus does not preclude the use of a more robust sauce—it simply enhances it.

ROAST STRIP SIRLOIN FOR A CROWD

24 to 30 servings

Preheat the oven to 550°F. Trim the excess top fat from:

One 18- to 22-pound eye of the strip sirloin

Place fat side up on a rack in a greased shallow roasting pan in the oven. Reduce the heat at once to 350°F. Roast, uncovered, about 1 hour for rare, or until a thermometer registers between 125° and 130°F for rare to medium-rare.

ROAST EYE OF ROUND, TOP ROUND, OR BOTTOM SIRLOIN

6 to 8 servings

Economical large cuts such as eye of round, top round, and round sirloin tip roasts are full-flavored but less pricy than the luxury cuts. Because they are lean, they are best cooked only to medium-rare.

Preheat the oven to 325°F. Prepare:

1 eye of round, top round, or bottom sirloin roast (3 to 3$^1/_2$ pounds)

Place the meat fat side up in a greased shallow roasting pan. Roast, uncovered, about 1 hour 30 minutes, or until a thermometer inserted in the thickest part of the meat reaches 125° to 130°F for rare. Remove the meat to a platter, cover loosely with foil, and let stand 15 to 20 minutes before carving into thin slices. To make gravy, see About Gravies and Pan Sauces, 546. Or serve with:

Horseradish Sauce, 552, or Sauce Perigeux, 555

STUFFED BUTTERFLIED EYE OF ROUND OR TOP ROUND ROAST

8 to 10 servings

Preheat the oven to 425°F. Heat in a medium skillet over medium heat:

2 tablespoons olive oil

Add and cook, stirring, until softened, 5 minutes:

2 medium onions, chopped

Add and cook, stirring, until heated, about 5 minutes:

1 cup finely chopped pancetta or ham (about 4 ounces)
1 cup cooked spinach, well drained and chopped
$^1/_3$ cup chopped black olives
2 garlic cloves, chopped
2 tablespoons chopped fresh basil or 2 teaspoons dried basil
2 teaspoons chopped parsley
1 teaspoon black pepper
$^1/_2$ teaspoon salt

Let cool, then stir in:

$^2/_3$ cup fresh bread crumbs

Have ready:

1 boneless beef eye of round or top round roast (about 4 pounds), well trimmed

Make a long straight cut down the center of the roast just to the center of the meat. Then, starting inside that cut and holding the knife at a slight angle, make a cut to the left and a cut to the right, both about 1$^1/_2$ inches deep. (This is called a Y cut, because if you could see a cross-section of the meat, it would look like an inverse Y.) Open out the meat and cover it with the spinach mixture. Reshape the meat and tie it at 1$^1/_2$-inch intervals. Toss together:

6 garlic cloves, finely sliced lengthwise
1 teaspoon chopped fresh thyme or scant $^1/_2$ teaspoon dried thyme
1 teaspoon salt
$^1/_2$ teaspoon black pepper

Make slits in the roast and insert the seasoned garlic slices. Rub the meat with:

2 tablespoons olive oil

Place the roast on a rack in a roasting pan and roast until a thermometer inserted in the thickest part of the meat reads 125° to 130°F for rare, 135° to 140°F for medium-rare, or 150° to 155°F for medium, 25 to 45 minutes (the temperature will continue to rise 5 to 10 degrees out of the oven). Remove the roast from the oven, cover loosely with aluminum foil, and let stand for 15 to 20 minutes before carving. Cut into $^3/_4$-inch slices and serve.

STANDING BEEF RIB ROAST, OR PRIME RIB FOR A CROWD

25 to 30 servings

The most luxurious and traditional cut of beef for roasting is the standing rib roast, also called a rib roast or prime rib. A full standing rib roast contains 7 rib bones, which act as a natural roasting rack and give the roast its impressive appearance. When buying less than a full rib roast, ask for a roast cut from the more tender loin end, or small end. Most markets will remove the backbone, or chine bone, to promote even cooking and make carving easier. The thick layer of fat that covers the roast should be trimmed to no more than 1/4 inch.

Preheat the oven to 450°F. If desired, season with:

Salt and black pepper

Pat dry:

One 7 rib beef roast (18 to 20 pounds), trimmed

Place the rib side up in a shallow greased roasting pan. Roast 30 minutes. Flip the meat over and roast until the desired temperature is reached, see 467, on a thermometer inserted in the thickest part of the roast, about 2 hours 15 minutes for medium-rare. Remove the meat to a platter, cover loosely with aluminum foil, and let stand for 15 to 20 minutes before carving. If desired, make a jus as directed on page 471. Carve the roast into 1/8- to 1/2-inch slices. Drizzle the jus over the slices. If desired, serve with:

Sauce Chasseur, 555, Horseradish Cream, 565, Béarnaise Sauce, 561, or Meat Pan Gravy, 546

ABOUT FILLET OR TENDERLOIN OF BEEF

The choicest and most tender cut, the fillet or tenderloin can be used in many ways. **To trim a whole tenderloin,** first trim off the fat and sinew. Loosen the fat at the small, or tail, end and tear this off, as well as the fat near the thicker end, and the tougher, gristly flesh, the **chain,** that hangs along the side of the meat. With a sharp pointed knife, remove the thin, tough, blueish sinew underneath, known as the **silverskin. To cook the fillet whole,** tuck the thin end under the roast to equalize thickness, and tie with kitchen twine. Or you may simply cut off about 6 inches of the end and save it for Beef Stroganoff, 476, Sukiyaki, 476, stir-fries, 476, kebabs, 494. We do not cook our tenderloins past medium, and we always use a dry-heat method such as roasting, grilling, sauteing, or browning.

There is some confusion about classic fillet cuts for steaks. Perhaps the drawing above will help clarify the situation. Beginning and extending not quite halfway through the heavy end of an entire fillet is the **head,** or **tenderloin butt.** In the second half of the heavy end lies the **chateaubriand,** usually cut thick enough for a double or triple portion. If you divide the remainder of the fillet into 4 sections, as shown, you have first the **fillet** steaks, next the **tournedos,** then the **filet mignons,** or small fillets, and finally a tip section that is usually cubed for brochettes or beef kebabs, 494. The cuts vary from 2 to 3 inches in thickness for chateaubriand to 1 1/2 to 2 inches for fillets and 1 inch for tournedos. Cooking times, therefore, vary proportionately.

ROASTED FILLET OR TENDERLOIN OF BEEF
10 to 12 servings

If roasting less than a whole tenderloin, buy a piece from the butt, or thicker, end. The roasting time will be about the same as for a whole tenderloin. Be sure to use a shallow roasting pan just big enough for the fillet.

Preheat the oven to 425°F. Lightly oil a roasting pan. Pat dry:

1 fillet of beef (about 5 pounds), trimmed and tied

Mix together and rub the entire surface with:

2 tablespoons olive oil or softened butter

1/2 teaspoon salt

1 teaspoon black pepper

Place the tenderloin in the roasting pan and roast until a thermometer inserted in the thickest part of the roast reads 125° to 130°F for rare, 135° to 140°F for medium-rare, or 150° to 155°F for medium, 25 to 45 minutes. Cover the roast loosely with aluminum foil and let stand for 15 to 20 minutes. Remove the strings and cut the tenderloin into 1/2-inch slices. If desired, serve with:

Béarnaise Sauce, 561, Sauce Marchand de Vin, 555, Horseradish Sauce, 552, or Sauce Bordelaise, 555

GRILLED FILLET OR TENDERLOIN OF BEEF
10 to 12 servings

Those who find fillet of beef too bland have not tasted it cooked over a charcoal fire. Searing the meat over a hot fire, then pushing the coals to the side, covering the grill, and finishing it over indirect heat gives it a deliciously crusty exterior with a tender, moist interior. You can be somewhat less fastidious when trimming a tenderloin for grilling, since a little external fat will simply add to the wonderful charbroiled flavor.

Prepare a very hot charcoal fire. Season:

1 fillet of beef (about 5 pounds), trimmed

with:

2 teaspoons cracked black peppercorns

Brown the beef well on both sides, about 10 minutes per side. Remove the meat from the grill and push all the coals to one side of the grill. Place the meat on the side without the coals, cover the grill, leaving the vents open a bit, and cook, turning once or twice, until a thermometer inserted in the thickest part of the meat reads 135° to 140°F for medium-rare, or the desired temperature is reached. See chart on page 467. Remove the meat to a platter, cover loosely with aluminum foil, and let stand for 15 to 20 minutes before carving. Cut the tenderloin into 1/2-inch slices. If desired, serve with:

Chimichurri, 566, or Horseradish Cream, 565

ABOUT BEEF STEAK CUTS

As the large and increasing number of steakhouses shows, no meat is more popular. At home when celebrating, the cry is usually, "Let's have steak." This term covers many cuts, but, by definition, a steak is a slab of meat cut anywhere from 3/4 to 3 inches thick, cut across the muscle

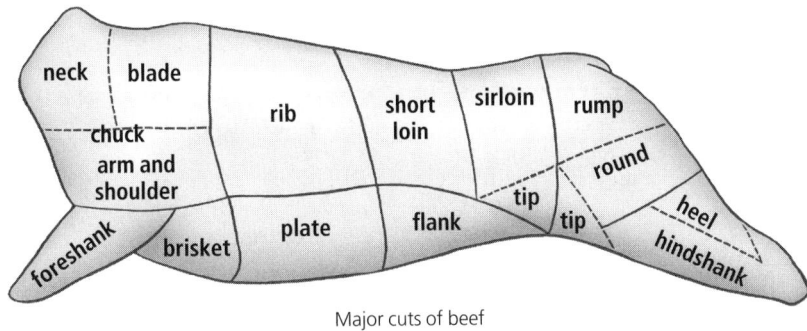

Major cuts of beef

grain and intended for cooking methods that use high heat: grilling, broiling, pan-broiling, or sautéing.

The most tender steaks come from the **rib, short loin, and sirloin** sections of the cow, see above. Less tender but more flavorful steaks come from the front- and hind quarters. Most Prime or Choice-grade steaks will be more tender than the Select grade.

Porterhouse and **T-bone steaks** come from the **short loin.** Both have a large T-shaped bone. The porterhouse is the larger of the two and has a larger section of tenderloin. Short-loin steaks with no tenderloin section are called **top loin, strip loin, shell,** or **strip steaks. Delmonico** is the more colloquial name and, when sold boneless, these steaks are often referred to as **Kansas City steak, New York strip steak,** and **boneless club steak.** For steaks from the tenderloin alone, see About Fillet or Tenderloin of Beef, 472.

Rib steaks, prime rib, and **boneless rib-eye steaks,** sometimes called **Spencer steaks,** are cut from the rib section of beef.

The sirloin is the hip section between the short loin and the rump. From this section come many desirable cuts of meat. The best steaks come from the top portion of the sirloin and are sold as **top sirloin,** sometimes called **top butt sirloin, hip sirloin,** or **center-cut sirloin.** From the bottom sirloin, or **bottom butt,** comes the increasingly popular **tri-tip,** or **triangle steak.**

Flavorful **top round steaks** come from the hind leg or rump. Other popular round steaks from the rump or round are the **bottom round** and **round tip steaks,** also called **knuckle steaks.** ➤ For grilling or broiling, avoid the tough **eye-of-the-round** steaks, or remember that they are best braised.

You might consider the often overlooked **blade steak,** from the chuck, or shoulder, section. Inexpensive and tender, this steak has a line of tough connective tissue down the middle that can be removed after cooking. **Flank steak** is a lean, flat, boneless cut from the underside of the beef. It has tremendous flavor but must be cooked quickly and thinly sliced across the grain. **Skirt steak** is a long thin cut also from the underside, but it is more tender, with more fat than the flank steak.

The easiest way to check for doneness in a steak is to make a small cut in the thickest part and take a peek at the inside. For bone-in steaks, cut right near the bone. Pull the steak from the heat when it appears just short of the desired doneness, so if you like your steak medium-rare, stop cooking when it still looks somewhat rare inside. A thick steak will continue to cook for a few minutes after you remove it from the heat, and the juices will be redistributed, giving it the perfect degree of doneness. We also judge doneness by feel. This takes some practice, but you can start by feeling a raw steak—it will be soft. Steaks cooked to rare are less yielding but remain quite soft. At medium-rare, the meat will feel springier with a slight bit of firmness. The meat continues to firm up (and toughen) as it cooks; a well-done steak will feel hard and unyielding. With steaks over 1½ inches, you can insert a thermometer several inches into the side of the steak without hitting any bone; look for 120° to 130°F for rare, 130° to 135°F for medium-rare, 140° to 150°F for medium, and 155° to 165°F for medium-well. Steaks cooked past medium tend to be dry and tough, especially if the beef is lean.

To serve with steak, try Red Wine and Sour Cherry Pan Sauce, 548, Horseradish Sauce, 552, Bordelaise Sauce, 555, Anchovy Butter, 558, Garlic Butter, 559, or Chimichurri, 566.

GRILLED OR BROILED STEAK

4 servings

Cooking times for grilling and broiling are approximate and depend on the many variables of steaks and cooking temperatures. Please read About Beef Steak Cuts, 472.

Prepare a medium-hot grill fire or preheat the broiler and broiler pan. If broiling, position the broiler pan 4 to 5 inches from the heating element. Pat dry:

4 beef steaks or 2 larger steaks, 1¼ to 2 inches thick

Season both sides with:

Salt and black pepper to taste

If desired, rub with the cut side of:

(1 garlic clove, halved)

Grill or broil the steaks, turning them once just past the halfway point in the cooking time. Thicker steaks may require broiling farther from the heat or moving the steaks to a cooler section of the grill to complete the cooking. Let rest 5 minutes before serving.

GRILLED OR BROILED FILLET STEAK

For fillet steak cuts, please see About Fillet or Tenderloin of Beef, 472. The thickness of these steaks vary, and therefore so do the cooking times, but these steaks are usually served quite rare.
Flatten slightly:

Fillet steaks, 1 to 2 inches thick
and surround each one with a strip of bacon secured by a wooden toothpick. Spread with:

Softened butter
Broil as for:

Grilled or Broiled Steak, above
When done, remove the bacon. Serve the steaks on:

Croutons, 974
Serve with:

Béarnaise Sauce, 561, or lemon slices and chopped parsley
and:

Broiled Stuffed Mushroom Caps, 284, and Potatoes Anna, 298, or Duchess Potatoes, 300

PAN-BROILED STEAK

4 servings

Pan-broiling, or dry-skillet cooking, is a simple and convenient method for cooking any steak up to 2 inches thick. It is especially useful for steaks less than ³/₄ inch thick. As an added advantage, pan-broiling is an excellent method for achieving a crisp, browned crust. The high heat used for pan-broiling creates smoke and splattering, so use your exhaust fan.

Pan-broiling is best done in a well-seasoned heavy skillet or griddle. Specially designed ridged cast-iron pans are ideal but not necessary. The steaks should be patted dry and seasoned immediately before cooking. With a well-seasoned skillet or grill pan, additional oil or fat is unnecessary when cooking well-marbled steaks. For leaner cuts, we recommend a light coating of oil. Pat dry:

4 small beef steaks, or 2 large steaks, ³/₄ to 1¹/₂ inches thick
If the meat is very lean, brush it with:

Olive oil
Season both sides of the steaks to taste with:

Salt and black pepper
Heat a large heavy skillet, griddle, or grill pan over medium-high heat. Use 2 skillets if the steaks are large. Once the pan is hot, sear uncovered, without crowding, about 5 minutes. Turn and sear the other side for 3 to 4 minutes for rare, 5 to 8 minutes for medium. Make a small incision and check the center. The interior should be slightly less done than desired, for it will continue to cook somewhat off the heat. Turn the steaks more than once if one side gets too brown before they are done. Pour off any fat that accumulates during cooking. If it is allowed to

remain the steaks will be fried, and not broiled. For sauce ideas, see 546.

PEPPERED STEAK WITH CREAM SAUCE (STEAK AU POIVRE)

4 servings

Green peppercorns can easily be substituted for some or all of the black peppercorns, but use caution: Green peppercorns tend to pop when heated.
Pat dry:

2 to 4 boneless beef strip steaks, 1¹/₂ to 2 inches thick
Press into the steaks, working the seasonings into both sides of the meat with the heel of your palm or the flat side of a cleaver:

¹/₄ cup cracked black peppercorns
1 tablespoon salt
Heat a large heavy skillet, preferably cast iron, over high heat. Once the pan is hot, sear the steaks, without crowding, for 6 to 7 minutes on each side. Cook each side 1 minute more for medium. Remove the steaks to a platter and let stand, loosely covered. Pour off any excess fat from the pan and set the pan over medium-high heat. To make the sauce, add:

¹/₄ cup chopped shallots or onion
Cook, stirring, just until barely softened, about 15 seconds. Remove pan from heat and carefully add:

¹/₄ cup brandy
If the brandy flames, let it burn itself out. Return pan to heat and cook until the liquid is almost evaporated. Add:

1 cup beef or veal stock or broth
Boil until reduced by half, about 5 minutes. Add:

¹/₄ cup heavy cream
Bring to a boil and cook until reduced by half, about 4 minutes. Add:

2 tablespoons chopped parsley
Salt and cracked black peppercorns to taste
Serve immediately over the steaks.

LONDON BROIL OR BROILED FLANK STEAK

4 to 6 servings

London broil is a cooking method, not a cut of meat, and refers to a quick pan-broiling over high heat and thinly slicing the meat across the grain before serving. Flank steak is the traditional cut for London broil. It is well flavored and easy to cook, and there is no waste. Other lean, tougher steak cuts, such as shoulder and round are ideal for cooking this way. For best results, never cook London broil beyond medium-rare, or it will become tough and dry out.
Pat dry:

1 boneless beef flank steak, not less than ³/₄ inch thick
If desired, rub each side with the cut side of:

(1 large garlic clove, halved)
Season with:

(1 teaspoon dried oregano)
Salt and black pepper to taste

Heat a large heavy skillet or grill pan over high heat or place an ovenproof skillet or small roasting pan under the broiler and turn on broiler. Once the pan is hot, sear or broil the steak on one side for 4 to 5 minutes. Turn it over and sear or broil the other side for 3 to 4 minutes. Make a small incision and check the center: It should be slightly less done than desired. Remove the steak to a platter and let it stand for 5 minutes, then carve it diagonally across the grain into $1/4$-inch slices.

PLANK STEAK

Please read about Planking or Plank-Roasting, 1055. Preheat the broiler. Brush the plank with:

Vegetable oil

Preheat it. Place in the center of the plank:

A $1/2$- to 2-inch-thick steak

Brush with:

Melted butter

Season with:

Salt and black pepper to taste

Place 4 inches from the broiler and broil to desired doneness, flipping the steak after 2 minutes for a thinner steak, 3 minutes for a 2-inch-thick steak. Serve with:

**Green Peas, 290, Broiled Tomatoes, 312,
and Grilled Mushrooms, 283**

SAUTÉED STEAK

4 servings

Sautéing is especially well suited for tender steaks such as fillet, sirloin, and strip. The steak is browned in a small amount of fat over medium-high heat, not as high as panbroiling. This technique produces steaks with an evenly browned exterior and lends itself to the making of tasty pan sauces. For more sauce ideas, please read About Gravies and Pan Sauces, 546. Sautéing becomes panfrying when more fat is added to the pan, as in the case of regional specialties like Chicken-Fried Steak, below.

Pat dry:

4 boneless beef steaks, $3/4$ to $1 1/4$ inches thick

Season both sides with:

Salt and black pepper to taste

Heat in a large heavy skillet over medium-high heat:

1 tablespoon olive oil

Sauté for about 5 minutes each side for medium-rare, or to the desired doneness. Remove the steaks to a warmed platter and let stand for 5 minutes before serving. Meanwhile, if desired, pour off all but 1 tablespoon of fat from the pan and make a pan sauce, 546–549, to serve with the steak.

STEAK DIANE

4 servings

This recipe also works nicely with medallions of pork.

Prepare:

Sautéed Steak, above

While the steaks stand, pour off any fat in the pan and return the pan to medium-high heat. Add and heat:

2 tablespoons butter

Add and cook, shaking the pan, until softened, about 2 minutes:

$1/2$ cup chopped shallots or scallions (white part only)

Stir in:

$1/4$ cup beef stock or broth

$1/4$ cup brandy

1 tablespoon Dijon mustard

2 teaspoons fresh lemon juice

1 teaspoon Worcestershire sauce

Salt and black pepper to taste

Boil for 1 to 2 minutes, scraping up any browned bits. Add any juices from the steaks. If desired, remove from the heat and add bit by bit, swirling the pan until melted:

(2 tablespoons butter)

Stir in:

2 tablespoons chives

2 tablespoons chopped parsley

Pour the sauce over the steaks and serve immediately.

CHICKEN-FRIED STEAK

4 servings

This dish is battered and fried like Southern fried chicken. Using the flat side of a cleaver or a meat mallet, pound to $1/3$ inch thick:

1 beef round or rump steak (about $1 1/2$ pounds)

Cut into 4 serving pieces. Mix in a shallow bowl:

1 cup all-purpose flour

2 teaspoons black pepper

$1 1/2$ teaspoons salt

$3/4$ teaspoon ground red pepper

Whisk together in a second shallow bowl:

$1/4$ cup milk

1 large egg

Coat each steak with the seasoned flour, dip into the egg mixture, coat with the seasoned flour again, and shake off any excess. Let dry on a rack for 15 minutes. Heat in a large heavy skillet over medium-high heat:

$1/2$ inch vegetable oil, vegetable shortening, or lard

Add the steaks and fry, turning once, until golden brown, 2 to 3 minutes each side. Remove to a warmed platter and cover loosely. Pour off all but 2 to 3 tablespoons of fat from the pan and set over heat. Add and cook, stirring, about 5 minutes:

1 onion, thinly sliced

Add and cook, stirring, for 2 to 3 minutes:

2 tablespoons all-purpose flour

Stir in and bring to a boil, scraping up any browned bits:

1 cup milk

Reduce the heat and simmer until thickened, 3 to 5 minutes. Season with:

Salt and black pepper to taste

(Dash of hot pepper sauce)

Pour over the steaks.

COOKING BEEF CUBES, STRIPS, AND TIPS

A quick way to cook beef is to cut any tender steak into cubes or strips and sauté or stir-fry over high heat. In addition to being convenient, such dishes are popular with those who enjoy the taste of beef but prefer to avoid a large slab of steak. Because the beef is cooked quickly over high heat, ➤ success depends on starting with naturally tender cuts, such as fillet, top loin, or sirloin. For Beef Stew, see 479.

BEEF STROGANOFF

4 to 6 servings
Cut into thin 2 x ¼-inch strips:

2 pounds fillet of beef, top loin, or sirloin tip
Season with:

Salt and black pepper to taste
Heat in a large skillet over medium-high heat:

2 tablespoons olive or vegetable oil
Add the meat in batches, cooking just until browned, about 2 minutes. Remove to a plate and melt in skillet:

3 tablespoons butter
Add and cook, stirring until softened, about 3 minutes:

1 onion or 2 shallots, chopped
Add, and cook, stirring, until the liquid the mushrooms release evaporates, about 8 minutes:

1 pound mushrooms, sliced
Add:

2 cups beef broth or stock
(2 tablespoons Cognac)
Simmer about 10 minutes, then stir in:

1 cup sour cream
1 tablespoon Dijon mustard
Salt and black pepper to taste
Add any accumulated juices from the cooked meat. Simmer—do not boil—until the meat is heated through but still medium-rare, about 2 minutes. Stir in, if desired;

(2 tablespoons chopped dill)
Serve immediately, with:

Fresh egg noodles, 325

BEEF AND VEGETABLE STIR-FRY

4 to 6 servings
This basic stir-fry recipe can be varied with different combinations of vegetables and seasonings. Any cut of lean tender beef can be used. Lean pork, lamb, or chicken can be substituted for the beef. Please read about Stir-Frying, 1048.
Mix in a medium bowl:

¼ cup soy sauce
2 tablespoons Chinese rice wine or dry sherry
1 tablespoon water
1 tablespoon sugar
1 tablespoon cornstarch
2 teaspoons toasted sesame oil
Add and toss to coat:

1 pound boneless beef steak, sliced across the grain into 2 x ½-inch strips

Marinate for at least 20 minutes. Have ready:

1 medium onion, chopped
2 bell peppers, preferably 1 green and 1 red, chopped
1 cup mushroom caps, sliced
4 scallions, cut into 2-inch lengths
Combine in a small bowl:

2 tablespoons minced peeled fresh ginger
1 tablespoon minced garlic
(½ to 1 teaspoon chili oil, or more to taste)
Remove the beef from the marinade. Add to the marinade, then set aside:

⅓ cup chicken stock or broth or water
Heat in a wok or large heavy skillet over high heat until very hot but not smoking:

2 tablespoons peanut oil
Add ginger mixture and stir-fry until fragrant but not browned, about 30 seconds. Add beef and stir-fry, stirring to separate the slices, until browned, about 2 minutes. Remove the beef, ginger, and garlic to a plate. Wipe out the pan and reheat over high heat until hot. Add:

1 tablespoon peanut oil
Heat until hot but not smoking. Add the onion, peppers, and mushrooms and stir-fry until crisp-tender, about 2 minutes. Add the scallions. Return the meat to the pan, along with any accumulated juices and the marinade mixture. Toss for 10 seconds over high heat. Garnish with:

(2 tablespoons chopped cilantro or scallions)

SUKIYAKI

6 to 8 servings
Japan's famous "friendship dish" is prepared ceremoniously at table in an electric skillet or wok—or, less festively, in the kitchen in a wok or heavy skillet. The orderly cooking ritual lasts about 15 minutes, as one after another of the uniformly sliced ingredients are taken from a beautifully arranged platter and stir-fried.
For easy slicing, freeze for 20 minutes:

2 pounds boneless beef (sirloin tip, eye of round, or fillet)
Slice ⅛ inch thick against the grain, and arrange on a platter. Also arrange attractively on the platter, in diagonally cut uniform slices:

½ cup thinly sliced onions
6 scallions, thinly sliced
2 cups thinly sliced mushrooms
2 cups thinly sliced Napa cabbage or watercress
Canned bamboo shoots, rinsed and thinly sliced
½ cup fresh or dried lily buds, soaked 30 minutes if dried, and drained
½ cup ¾-inch cubes firm tofu, 315
Combine in a small bowl:

¼ cup soy sauce
½ cup chicken stock or broth
1 teaspoon sugar
Heat the wok or skillet over medium heat. Add:

3 tablespoons peanut or vegetable oil

If a single skillet is used, cook only half the amount on the platter at one time, sharing that batch, and then cooking the "seconds" later; or use 2 pans. Add the beef and cook, turning frequently, without browning, about 3 minutes. Remove the meat to a separate platter and then stir-fry in sequence the onions, scallions, mushrooms, and cabbage and lily buds. The sautéing of the onions to almost golden, followed by the gradual addition of the other vegetables, should take about 7 minutes in all. As the other vegetables are being added, pour in, a little at a time, the soy sauce mixture. This procedure produces a fast-rising steam but not enough moisture to waterlog the vegetables. Return the meat and accumulated juices to the pan, add the bamboo shoots and tofu, and stir-fry about 4 minutes more. The vegetables should retain their crispness and color. Season to taste. Serve at once over:

Cooked rice

BECKER MONGOLIAN BEEF

4 servings

Stir together in a small bowl:

2 tablespoons tamari sauce

2 dashes hot pepper sauce

1 tablespoon cornstarch

1 tablespoon rice wine vinegar

Heat in a large skillet over medium heat:

2 tablespoons peanut oil

Add and cook, stirring, for about 2 minutes:

One 1-inch piece fresh ginger, peeled

and cut into thin strips

4 garlic cloves, thinly sliced

With a slotted spoon, remove the garlic and ginger to a small bowl. Increase the heat to medium-high and brown in batches:

1 pound beef sirloin tip or strip steak, cut into

thin strips

Remove to a plate as each batch is browned. When all the meat is browned, return it to the skillet, along with the cornstarch mixture, garlic, and ginger. Cook, stirring, over medium heat 3 to 4 minutes, until the sauce has thickened. Stir in:

3 bunches scallions, sliced into matchsticks

or julienne, 241

Remove from the heat, cover, and let stand 5 minutes to wilt the scallions. Serve over:

Cooked rice

BEEF POT ROAST

6 to 10 servings

The key to a moist and tender pot roast is to cook the meat at a bare simmer. Please see Pot-Roasting, Stewing, and Braising Meat, 466.

Pat dry:

1 boneless beef pot roast (3 to 5 pounds)

If the meat is lean, you may lard it, 464. Season with:

Salt and black pepper

Heat in a large Dutch oven over medium-high heat:

2 to 3 tablespoons vegetable oil

Add the roast and brown on all sides, about 20 minutes. Do not let it scorch. Remove the meat to a plate. Pour off all but 2 tablespoons of fat from the pot and add:

2 cups chopped onions

$^{1}/_{2}$ cup chopped celery

$^{1}/_{2}$ cup chopped carrots

(1 turnip, chopped)

Cook, stirring occasionally, just until the vegetables begin to color, about 5 minutes. Add:

1 cup beef or chicken stock or broth, dry red wine,

beer, or water

Bring to a boil and add:

1 bay leaf

$1^{1}/_{2}$ teaspoons chopped fresh thyme or

$^{1}/_{2}$ teaspoon dried thyme

Return the roast to the pan, cover. On the stovetop reduce the heat to its lowest setting, so that the liquid just barely simmers. Cook, turning the roast every 30 minutes or so, until tender. Flat roasts will take $1^{1}/_{2}$ to $2^{1}/_{2}$ hours; round or oblong roasts can take as long as 4 hours. Make sure there is always some liquid in the pot; add more as needed. When the meat is fork-tender, remove it to a platter and cover with aluminum foil to keep warm. Skim off any fat from the surface of the liquid, and strain the liquid, making sure to remove the bay leaf. Serve the pan juices as is, or to thicken the sauce, bring the liquid to a boil. For each cup liquid, stir together in a separate bowl and whisk in:

1 tablespoon all-purpose flour

1 tablespoon unsalted butter, softened

Simmer, stirring constantly, until thickened. Serve with the beef.

ITALIAN POT ROAST (STRACOTTO)

8 to 10 servings

A classic of Italian home cooking. The braising juices can be used to sauce pasta, and leftover stracotto makes excellent hot sandwiches on chewy rolls, moistened with the pan sauce. Please see Pot-Roasting, Stewing, and Braising Meat, 466.

Mince together:

3 large garlic cloves

$^{1}/_{4}$ cup packed parsley leaves

4 fresh sage leaves or 1 teaspoon dried sage

1 tablespoon chopped fresh rosemary or 1 teaspoon

dried rosemary

Set aside half the mixture, and mix the rest with:

1 tablespoon olive oil

$^{1}/_{4}$ teaspoon black pepper

Make about 10 deep slits in:

1 boneless beef pot roast (4 to 5 pounds)

Stuff the slits with the herb and oil mixture. Heat in a large Dutch oven over medium-high heat:

3 tablespoons olive oil

Add the roast and brown on all sides, about 20 minutes. Do not let it scorch. Remove the roast to a plate and pour off all but 2 tablespoons of the fat. Sprinkle the roast with:

1 teaspoon salt

Return the pot to the heat and add:

1 onion, chopped
1 carrot, chopped
1 celery rib with leaves, chopped
4 ounces mushrooms, thinly sliced
1 bay leaf

Cook, stirring, until the onion is lightly browned. Stir in the remaining herb mixture and cook for 30 seconds. Add and boil until the pot is almost dry:

$^1/_2$ cup dry red wine
2 tablespoons tomato paste

Stir in and boil until reduced to less than $^1/_2$ cup:

1 cup dry red wine
1 cup beef or chicken stock or broth

Add the roast, along with:

One 28-ounce can whole tomatoes, drained and crushed
1 cup dry red wine
1 cup beef or chicken stock or broth

Bring to a gentle simmer and cover the pot. Reduce the heat to its lowest setting, so that the liquid just barely simmers, and cook for about $2^1/_2$ hours. Turn the roast every 30 minutes or so. When the meat is tender, remove it to a platter and cover it with aluminum foil to keep warm. Skim off any fat from the surface of the liquid and remove the bay leaf. Taste and adjust the seasonings. If the sauce seems thin, boil it down for a few minutes. Slice the meat about $^1/_4$ inch thick and moisten it with the braising liquid. Serve with:

Soft Polenta, 349

SAUERBRATEN
6 servings

This is a classic JOY recipe, in the book since 1931.
Pat dry:

1 boneless beef pot roast (about 3 pounds)

Rub thoroughly into the meat:

Black pepper to taste
(1 garlic clove, halved)

Place the meat in a deep crock or glass bowl. Combine in a saucepan and heat, stirring, to dissolve the sugar; do not boil:

2 cups white vinegar or white wine vinegar
2 cups water
$^1/_2$ cup sliced onion
2 bay leaves
1 teaspoon black peppercorns
$^1/_4$ cup sugar
(2 teaspoons caraway seeds)

Pour the hot marinade over the beef; more than half should be covered. Cover and refrigerate 2 to 4 days, turning occasionally. (The longer you leave it, the more sour

the meat.) When ready to cook, drain the meat, saving the marinade. Heat in a Dutch oven:

2 tablespoons vegetable oil

Brown the meat on all sides, as for Beef Pot Roast, 477. Then cook as directed, using the reserved marinade in place of the stock. When the meat is tender, sprinkle it with:

$^1/_4$ cup packed brown sugar

and cook 5 to 10 minutes more, or until the sugar is dissolved. Remove the meat to a platter and cover to keep warm. Skim the fat from the cooking liquid. Thicken stock with:

All-purpose flour, see Meat Pan Gravy, 546

Stir in and heat through, but do not boil:

1 cup heavy cream or sour cream

We like the gravy "straight." Some cooks add:

(Raisins, catsup, and ground gingersnaps)

Serve with:

Potato Dumplings, 335, Potato Pancakes, 298,
or Pennsylvania Dutch Egg Noodles, 325

FRENCH POT ROAST (BOEUF À LA MODE)
6 servings

A pot roast deluxe, because it is so elegantly presented. The meat is sliced very thin and covered with the sauce, and the platter is garnished with beautifully arranged vegetables.
Put in a deep bowl:

1 boneless beef pot roast (about 3 pounds)

Pour over the meat:

Red Wine Marinade, 584

Cover and marinate in the refrigerator for up to 24 hours. Drain the meat and pat dry. Heat in a Dutch oven over medium-high heat:

$^1/_4$ cup vegetable oil

Brown the meat on all sides. Remove, to a plate, and brown in the same pot:

1 pound veal shanks (2 or 3 shanks)

Pour off the excess oil, return the beef to the pot, and add:

5 cups beef stock or broth

Bring to a boil, then reduce the heat to low and simmer, covered, until tender, $3^1/_2$ to 4 hours. Toward the last hour of cooking, degrease the simmering liquid and add:

1 cup sliced carrots
1 cup sliced onions

Just before serving, stir in:

1 cup sautéed mushrooms, 283

Cut the roast into thin slices, remove and shred the shank meat. Serve garnished with the vegetables and spoon the cooking liquid over all.

BOILED BEEF (BOEUF BOUILLI)
6 servings

Bring to a boil in a Dutch oven:

6 cups beef stock or broth or water

Put in:

3 pounds lean stewing beef or pot roast in one piece

Bring to a boil and skim off the fat. Add:

1 onion, stuck with 3 whole cloves

1 bay leaf

1 cup sliced carrots

1 cup sliced celery with leaves

1 to 1^1/$_2$ teaspoons salt

(1 turnip, sliced)

Cover, reduce the heat, and simmer gently until the meat is tender, 3 to 4 hours. Remove the meat to a platter and cover to keep warm. Strain the broth, then skim off the fat. Melt in the same pot:

^{1}/$_4$ cup (^{1}/$_2$ stick) butter

Add and brown lightly:

^{1}/$_2$ cup chopped onion

Stir in until blended and cook 1 minute, until smooth:

2 tablespoons all-purpose flour

Slowly stir in 2 cups of the broth. Season the sauce with:

2 tablespoons grated fresh or prepared horseradish

Salt

(Sugar)

(Vinegar or fresh lemon juice)

If using prepared horseradish, use less vinegar or lemon juice and season to taste. Cut the meat into thin slices against the grain and reheat very briefly in the hot gravy. Garnish with:

Chopped parsley

BEEF STEW

6 to 8 servings

Well-browned beef and slow-simmered stock or wine provide the undertones of meaty flavor, while ingredients such as pungent herbs, fresh vegetables, and spices create sharper flavors throughout the dish. As with so many full-flavored, slow-cooked dishes, beef stews are better 1 or 2 days after being made. Reheat stews gently, adding a bit more liquid if necessary. Serve in wide bowls with pasta, rice, potatoes, fresh bread, dumplings, or biscuits.

The best beef stew is made with **shoulder, chuck, short rib, cross-rib, brisket, blade,** and **bottom round. Shank,** or **shin,** meat can also be used, but it adds much more texture than flavor. We recommend buying steaks or roasts and trimming and cutting them yourself into ^{1}/$_2$- to 3-inch cubes. Packaged precut meat labeled "beef stew meat" is often more expensive per pound, and you never know what cut of beef you are getting. The smaller the cube, the faster the stew will cook. Small cubes will also give the stew a thicker, more homogeneous character, while large chunks maintain their shape. Large or small, it should be considered done when tender enough to cut with a fork. Through altering the vegetables or the proportions, the recipe variations are limitless. For a fresher flavor, add more vegetables or herbs toward the end of the cooking. Trim and pat dry and cut into 2-inch cubes:

2 pounds boneless beef stew meat, such as chuck, short-rib meat, or bottom round

Season with:

^{1}/$_2$ to 1 teaspoon dried herbs (thyme, marjoram, savory, oregano, and/or basil)

^{1}/$_2$ teaspoon salt

^{1}/$_2$ teaspoon black pepper

Dredge in:

^{1}/$_2$ cup all-purpose flour

Shake off any excess flour. Heat in a Dutch oven over medium-high heat:

2 tablespoons olive or vegetable oil, bacon fat, or beef drippings

Add the meat in batches and brown on all sides, being careful not to crowd the pot or scorch the meat. Remove with a slotted spoon. Pour off all but 2 tablespoons of fat from the pot (or add more if needed). Add:

1 onion, chopped

1 carrot, chopped

1 small rib celery, chopped

4 garlic cloves, chopped

Cover and cook, stirring often, over medium heat until the onions are softened, about 5 minutes. Add:

2 bay leaves

^{1}/$_2$ to 1 teaspoon dried herbs, same as above

^{1}/$_2$ teaspoon salt

^{1}/$_2$ teaspoon black pepper

Add enough to cover the meat at least halfway:

2 to 3 cups beef or chicken stock or broth, dry red or white wine, or beer

Bring to a boil, then reduce the heat, cover, and simmer gently until the meat is fork-tender, 1^1/$_2$ to 2 hours. Add:

2 to 3 carrots, cut into chunks

3 to 4 boiling potatoes, peeled and cut into chunks

(2 turnips, peeled and cut into chunks)

(2 parsnips, peeled and cut into chunks)

Cover and cook until the vegetables are tender, 35 to 40 minutes. Remove the pot from the heat, skim off any fat from the surface, and remove the bay leaves. Taste and adjust the seasonings. Thicken the sauce by whisking into the stew:

(1 to 1^1/$_2$ tablespoons Kneaded Butter, 545)

And simmering, stirring, until thickened. Garnish with:

Chopped parsley

FRENCH BEEF STEW (BOEUF BOURGUIGNONNE)

6 servings

Based on local ingredients and local wine, this robust stew typifies the earthy, full-flavored cooking of Burgundy, France. Choose a light, dry red wine such as Pinot Noir (the grape of Burgundy) or Beaujolais and marinate the beef refrigerated overnight for the most flavor.

Cut into 2-inch cubes:

2 to 3 pounds boneless beef stew meat, such as shoulder chuck

Place the meat in a large bowl and add:

2 cups dry red wine

^{1}/$_4$ cup olive oil

1 onion, chopped
1 carrot, chopped
1 garlic clove, chopped
1 bay leaf
2 tablespoons chopped parsley
1 teaspoon chopped fresh thyme
    or $^1/_2$ teaspoon dried thyme
1 teaspoon cracked black peppercorns
$^1/_2$ teaspoon salt

Stir to combine and coat the meat. Cover and marinate in the refrigerator for at least 1 hour, or up to 24 hours, turning the meat occasionally. Drain the beef, reserving the marinade, and pat dry. Strain the marinade and reserve the liquid and the vegetables separately. Heat a large Dutch oven over medium-high heat. Add and brown:

4 ounces bacon, diced

Remove the bacon, leaving the fat in the pan. You should have 2 tablespoons. If not, add vegetable oil as needed. Return the pot to medium-high heat. Add the beef in batches and brown on all sides, being careful not to overcrowd the pot. Remove with a slotted spoon. Add the reserved vegetables and cook until lightly browned, about 5 minutes. Stir in:

2 tablespoons all-purpose flour

Cook, stirring, until beginning to brown, about 1 minute. Stir in the marinade, then return the beef and bacon to the pot. Add:

2 cups small boiling onions, peeled

Bring to a boil. Reduce the heat to low and cook, covered, until the meat is fork-tender, 1 to 1$^1/_4$ hours. Add:

2 cups mushrooms, quartered (about 8 ounces)

Cover and cook until tender, about 20 minutes. Skim off the fat from the surface. Add:

$^1/_4$ cup chopped parsley
Salt and black pepper to taste

If you wish, thicken the sauce by whisking in:

(1 to 1$^1/_2$ tablespoons Kneaded Butter, 545)

And simmering, stirring, until thickened.

BEEF STEW WITH MUSTARD, HERBS, AND WHITE WINE (BEEF DAUBE)

6 to 8 servings

The word *daube* comes from *daubière,* the French word for a covered casserole. This is a refreshing change from the heavier flavors that we associate with beef stew.
Pat dry and cut into 3-inch cubes:

2 pounds boneless beef stew meat

Dredge in:

Seasoned flour, 962

Heat in a Dutch oven over medium-high heat:

3 tablespoons olive oil

Add the meat in batches and brown on all sides, being careful not to crowd the pot or scorch the meat. Remove with a slotted spoon and set aside. Pour off all but a light film of fat from the pot. Add:

3 cups dry white wine

Bring to a boil, scraping up any browned bits on the bottom of the pot. Reduce the heat and gently simmer, uncovered, until the wine is reduced by about half, 7 to 10 minutes. Add and whisk to blend:

2 tablespoons Dijon mustard

Return beef and accumulated juices to the pot and add:

One 16-ounce can plum tomatoes, with juice
3 medium onions, halved and sliced
3 garlic cloves, halved
1 Bouquet Garni, 960

Cover and simmer over low heat until the meat is fork-tender, 2 to 3 hours. Remove and discard the bouquet garni. With a slotted spoon, remove the beef, onions, and tomatoes to a platter. Increase the heat to high and boil the sauce until slightly thickened and reduced by one-third, about 10 minutes. Reduce the heat to medium, return the beef and vegetables to the sauce, and reheat gently.

BELGIAN BEEF STEW (CARBONNADE FLAMANDE)

4 to 6 servings

Pat dry and cut into 1$^1/_2$-inch cubes:

2 pounds boneless beef stew meat

Toss with:

Seasoned flour, 962

Heat in a large Dutch oven:

1 tablespoon butter

Add and cook, stirring, until browned:

$^1/_2$ cup thinly sliced onion

Remove with a slotted spoon and reserve. Add to the pot:

1 tablespoon butter

Add the meat in batches and brown on all sides, then drain off any excess fat. Remove the meat. Combine in the pot and bring to a boil:

1 cup flat beer
1 garlic clove, chopped
$^1/_2$ teaspoon sugar
$^1/_2$ teaspoon salt

Return all the meat to the pot, reduce the heat, and add the onions. Cover and simmer gently 2 to 2$^1/_2$ hours, until the meat is tender. Remove the meat to a platter, strain the sauce, and add:

($^1/_2$ teaspoon vinegar)

Serve the meat with the sauce and:

Boiled New Potatoes, 295, garnished with parsley
    or dill

HUNGARIAN GOULASH (PIRKILT)

6 servings

In beef goulash, the meat is always browned before simmering. A knowing friend claims that shinbone meat with its high gelatin content makes a glorious goulash. But variations using veal, pork, or lamb, alone or in combination, may be cooked à blanc—that is, without browning. Vegetables are sometimes added for the last hour of cooking. Six small peeled potatoes may be added during the last half hour of cooking, but they will soak up the gravy, which to some is the best part of the goulash. Some cooks use very little water, others prefer stock, sour cream, or red wine.

Pat dry and cut into 1-inch cubes:

2 pounds boneless beef stew meat, or 1 pound beef plus 1 pound lean veal

Toss with:

Seasoned flour, 962

Melt in a Dutch oven:

¼ cup (½ stick) butter or ¼ cup vegetable oil or bacon drippings

Add the meat in batches and brown on all sides. Add and cook, stirring, until translucent:

1½ cups chopped onions

Add:

About 1 cup boiling beef or chicken stock or broth or tomato juice

(1 green bell pepper, cored, seeded, and diced)

1 teaspoon salt

1 to 3 teaspoons sweet Hungarian paprika

Use just enough stock to keep the meat from scorching, and add more gradually during cooking if necessary. Cover the pot and simmer the meat for 1½ hours or until tender. Let rest and skim fat before serving.

BEEF BRISKET WITH SAUERKRAUT

6 to 8 servings

Trim and pat dry:

3 pounds trimmed beef brisket

Heat in a large Dutch oven:

3 tablespoons bacon fat or vegetable oil

Add, if desired, and brown lightly:

(¼ cup chopped onion)

Add the meat to the pot and place over it:

2 pounds sauerkraut, rinsed and drained

(1 large apple, cored and quartered)

2 cups boiling beef stock or broth or water

Reduce the heat and simmer, covered, 3 to 3½ hours, or until the meat is tender. Season to taste with:

Salt and black pepper

(Caraway seeds)

Garnish with:

Sour cream

SWEET-AND-SOUR BRISKET

6 to 8 servings

You can serve this immediately, but it is much better if prepared a day ahead and chilled, as in this recipe.

Preheat the oven to 350°F. Pat dry:

3½ pounds trimmed first-cut or thin-cut beef brisket

Spread with:

3 garlic cloves, minced

Black pepper to taste

Heat in a flameproof roasting pan over medium-high heat:

1 tablespoon vegetable oil

Brown the brisket, about 3 minutes each side. While it is searing, scatter around it:

2 large onions, sliced

Remove the brisket, reduce the heat to medium, and cook the onions until very brown, about 4 minutes more. Add:

½ cup dry red wine

½ cup beef stock or broth

Cook for 1 minute, scraping up the browned bits. Stir in:

1 cup chili sauce

½ cup cider vinegar

½ cup packed dark brown sugar

1 bay leaf

Taste the sauce and adjust the seasoning. Return the meat to the pan and spoon the sauce over it. Cover the pan tightly with aluminum foil, and roast until the brisket is fork-tender, 2 to 3 hours. Remove the pan from the oven, uncover, and let cool in the pan, then refrigerate overnight. Remove the bay leaf, slice the meat, and return it to the sauce. Reheat in a 350°F oven for 25 to 30 minutes.

SMOKED BRISKET

10 to 12 servings

Rub:

4 to 5 pounds beef brisket, trimmed of excess fat

with:

Beef Brisket Rub, 588, Southern Barbecue Dry Rub, 587, or Peppery Dry Rub, 587

Wrap in plastic wrap and refrigerate for at least 2 hours, or overnight. Bring to room temperature before smoking. Heat your smoker or, if using a grill, prepare it for cooking over indirect heat, 1059. For a smokier flavor, add to the smoker or grill:

Soaked hickory or mesquite chips, or a combination

Smoke the brisket until the meat is fork-tender, 4 to 5 hours. If grilling, you may baste every 30 minutes or so with:

(Basic Mop, 587, or Beer Mop, 587)

Allow the brisket to rest for 15 to 30 minutes. Slice and serve with:

Barbecue Sauce, 586

CHUCK ROAST IN FOIL

12 servings

Foil-cooked meats often have a pasty look about them, but here the onion soup mix gives great vigor of color and flavor, despite the fact that the meat is not browned first. Try this for casual entertaining.

Preheat the oven to 300°F. Place:

One 7-pound bone-in chuck roast

on a double thickness of heavy-duty foil large enough to envelop it. Combine:

1 to 2 packages dried onion soup

½ teaspoon black pepper

Sprinkle the meat with half this mixture, then turn over

and sprinkle with the remaining mix. Wrap the roast carefully in the foil, sealing it tightly so that no juices can escape. Place in a roasting pan, and bake 3½ to 4 hours. If your company is informal, do not cut the foil until you are at table and ready to carve. The sudden burst of fragrance adds to the anticipation. Serve with:

   Mashed Potatoes, 295, or Spätzle, 335

SWISS STEAK

6 servings
Preheat the oven to 300°F. Pat dry:

   One 2-pound bottom round steak, ³/₄ inch thick
Rub with:

   ½ garlic clove
Pound into both sides of the steak with a mallet, 464:

   As much seasoned flour, 962, as the steak will hold
Cut into serving pieces or leave whole. If leaving whole, gash the edges to prevent curling. Heat in a Dutch oven:

   2 tablespoons vegetable oil
Sear the steak on one side until browned. Turn it over, brown the second side, then add:

   ½ cup finely chopped onion
   ⅓ cup each chopped carrots, bell peppers, and celery
      (1 cup total)
Do not allow the vegetables to brown. Season to taste and bring to a boil:

   1 cup beef stock or broth
   (½ cup hot tomato sauce)
Cover and bake 1½ to 2 hours, or until the meat is tender. Remove the steak to a hot platter. Strain and degrease the pan juices, and make:

   Meat Pan Gravy, 546
Pour the gravy over the steak and serve with:

   Mashed Potatoes, 295

FLANK STEAK WITH DRESSING

4 to 6 servings
The sharper the seasonings, the more "deviled" the effect.
Have ready:

   One 2- to 3-pound flank or round steak
Trim the edges. Season with and pound in:

   1 teaspoon salt
   ⅛ teaspoon paprika
   ¼ teaspoon mustard
   (⅛ teaspoon ground ginger)
   (1 teaspoon Worcestershire sauce)
Melt:

   ¼ cup butter or bacon drippings
Add and sauté until golden:

   2 tablespoons chopped onion
Add and stir until well blended, about 2 minutes:

   1 cup bread crumbs
   ¼ teaspoon salt
   A few grains paprika
   2 tablespoons chopped parsley

   3 tablespoons chopped celery
   1 slightly beaten egg
Spread this dressing over the steak. Roll the steak up loosely and tie it at 2-inch intervals. Preheat oven to 300°F. Heat in a large skillet on high heat:

   3 tablespoons vegetable oil
Brown the rolled steak on all sides in the hot oil. Put the steak in a roasting pan, Dutch oven, or casserole. Reduce the heat in the skillet and stir into the oil:

   2 tablespoons flour
Add:

   1 cup water or stock
   1 cup tomato juice or dry red wine
   ¼ teaspoon salt
When thickened, pour this mixture over the steak. Bake covered about 1½ hours. Add seasoning if required.

BRAISED SHORT RIBS

4 servings
Beef short ribs are the meaty ends of the beef ribs from the rib, chuck, and brisket portion. Short ribs are sold in slabs of varying lengths and widths. Unlike back ribs, which are more bone than meat, short ribs offer a good amount of beefy-tasting meat. Before trimming the excess external fat, it is best to brown the ribs before cooking to render more fat and intensify the meat flavors. There are two cuts of short ribs, **English** and **flanken**. English-cut ribs have one section of rib bone; flanken-cut ribs have multiple bone segments; either style will work. By substituting different dry rubs or herb pastes, 587, for the herbs and salt and pepper in this basic recipe, you can produce a host of variations. You can also change the vegetables and the braising liquid.
Preheat the oven to 350°F. Pat dry:

   3 pounds beef short ribs, excess fat trimmed
Season with:

   1 teaspoon salt
   1 teaspoon black pepper
   ½ teaspoon dried herbs (marjoram, oregano, rosemary, savory, thyme, or sage)
Heat in a Dutch oven or large heavy ovenproof skillet over medium-high heat:

   2 tablespoons vegetable oil, beef fat, or bacon fat
Add the ribs in batches, being careful not to crowd the pot, and brown well on all sides. Remove the ribs with a slotted spoon. Pour off all but about 2 tablespoons fat from the pot. Add and cook, stirring, over medium heat just until the vegetables begin to color, about 10 minutes:

   2 cups chopped onions
   ½ cup chopped celery
   ½ cup chopped carrots
   3 tablespoons chopped garlic
   1½ teaspoons black pepper
   ½ teaspoon salt
   Pinch of dried herbs (the same herb used to season the meat)

Add and bring to a boil:

1¹/₂ cups beef or poultry stock or broth

Return the short ribs to the pot. Add:

2 to 3 bay leaves

Cover and bake until the ribs are tender and the meat pulls away easily from the bone, 1¹/₂ to 2 hours. Remove the ribs to a platter and cover to keep warm. Skim off any fat from the surface of the liquid, and reduce over high heat until the sauce is syrupy. Serve the ribs with the sauce.

BEEF ROLLS, ROULADES, ROULADEN, OR PAUPIETTES

Thin strips of pounded meat, poultry, or fish rolled around vegetables or other fillings are known variously as **beef rolls, roulades, paupiettes, braciole,** or **rouladen,** among other names. They may be further wrapped in salt pork or bacon. To make them with beef, use:

**Thin strips of pounded round or flank steak, 3 x 4
    inches**

Season with:

Salt and black pepper

Place on each strip about 2 tablespoons of one of the following fillings:

**Well-seasoned smoked or cooked sausage with
    chopped parsley or dill pickle**

Julienned ham, carrot, and celery

**Seasoned cooked rice, chopped stuffed olives,
    or seedless green grapes with lemon zest**

Roll up the meat and tie with string near both ends, or wrap as for cabbage leaves, shown on 1051. Dredge in:

All-purpose flour

Brown in:

Bacon drippings or rendered salt pork

Place in a Dutch oven and add for every 6 rolls:

2 cups beef stock, broth, or dry red wine

2 to 3 tablespoons tomato paste

Cover and cook slowly in a preheated 300°F oven, or simmer over direct heat, about 1 hour and 15 minutes.

BEEF BRACIOLE

4 servings

Braciole, an Italian specialty, is best made from thin slices of beef rump, top round, or bottom round. Pork cutlets can be substituted for the beef in this dish. The individual slices are stuffed, rolled, tied, and braised in a combination of wine, stock, and tomatoes. Stuffings vary slightly from household to household, so feel free to improvise.

Purchase from a butcher or slice from a roast:

**Four ¹/₄-inch-thick slices rump, bottom round, or top
    round steak (4 to 5 ounces each)**

Using the flat side of a cleaver or a flat mallet, pound the slices to about ¹/₈ inch thick, taking care not to tear the meat. Trim any excess fat and pat dry. Season lightly with:

Salt and black pepper

For the stuffing, mix together:

1 cup fresh bread crumbs from day-old bread

4 ounces ground beef, veal, or pork

¹/₂ cup grated Parmesan

¹/₄ cup chopped parsley

¹/₄ cup finely chopped prosciutto or boiled ham

1 large egg, lightly beaten

Spread the meat evenly with the stuffing, leaving at least a 1-inch border all around. Roll up, tucking in the sides to form a tight, neat packet. Tie securely with string, both crosswise and lengthwise. Dredge the rolls in:

¹/₂ cup all-purpose flour

Shake off the excess. Heat in a large heavy skillet over medium-high heat:

2 tablespoons olive oil

Add the meat packets and brown carefully on all sides. Remove the rolls with a slotted spoon, and pour off all but 2 tablespoons of fat from the pan. Add to the pan:

¹/₂ cup finely chopped onion

¹/₄ cup finely chopped carrot

2 teaspoons minced garlic

Cover and cook over medium heat for 5 minutes. Add:

¹/₂ cup beef stock or broth

¹/₂ cup tomato puree or 2 tablespoons tomato paste

1 bay leaf

Bring to a boil. Return the beef rolls to the pan, reduce the heat, cover, and simmer until the beef is fork-tender, 1 to 1¹/₂ hours. Remove the rolls to a platter and cover to keep warm. Discard the bay leaf. Skim off the fat from the surface of the liquid. Reduce, if necessary, over high heat just until syrupy. Season with:

Salt and black pepper to taste

Remove the strings from the rolls and cut into 1-inch slices, or leave whole. Pour the sauce over the meat.

STEAK AND KIDNEY PIE

6 to 8 servings

Classic recipes for this old English favorite often call for beef kidneys. If they are used, they must be blanched, 519, and the cooking time must be increased to ensure tenderness. If you'd rather not use kidneys, substitute the same amount of sliced mushrooms. Rather than encasing the stew in dough, we recommend a topping only.

Preheat the oven to 350°F. Cut into ¹/₂-inch-thick cubes:

1¹/₂ pounds boneless round steak or other steak

Wash, remove the membranes, and thinly slice:

12 ounces veal or lamb kidneys

Melt in a large saucepan or skillet over medium-high heat:

3 tablespoons butter or beef fat

Add the kidneys and:

¹/₂ cup chopped onion

Cook, stirring, about 5 minutes. Meanwhile, dredge the beef cubes in:

Seasoned flour, 962

Add the beef cubes to the pan, in batches if necessary, and brown on all sides. Add:

2 cups beef stock or broth

1 cup dry red wine or beer

Bring to a boil, then reduce the heat and simmer, stirring occasionally, 1 hour. Preheat the oven to 425°F. Transfer the meat mixture to a 9 x 9-inch baking dish. Cover with:

¹⁄₂ recipe Deluxe Butter Pie or Pastry Dough, 665, rolled to an 11-inch circle

Bake 15 to 20 minutes, until the crust is browned.

KENTUCKY BURGOO

10 servings

This classic JOY recipe was resurrected at the insistence of Maggie Green, our editor in Kentucky. The accent for burgoo is on the first syllable. This thick, long-simmered potpourri, a catch-as-catch-can mixture of meats, fowl, and garden gleanings—with squirrel thrown in, in some authentic local versions—has an assortment of Old World forebears. In Spain, it is known as **Olla Podrida;** in Ireland, it surfaces as **Mulligan Stew.** But in Kentucky it came into its own as the local solution to feeding the multitudes; it was made, in amounts to serve several hundreds, in huge hog-butchering kettles over an outdoor fire, providing an occasion for great socializing, a "stirring" overnight vigil. This simplified version can be varied according to your preference or to what meat is available—lamb or veal may be used as well. It makes good sense, too, to freeze this seasonal dish in meal-sized packages.

Combine in a large Dutch oven:

12 ounces lean beef stew, meat cubed
12 ounces boneless pork shoulder, cubed
3¹⁄₂ quarts water or stock or broth

Bring slowly to a boil. Reduce the heat at once and simmer about 1¹⁄₂ hours. Add to the pot:

One 3¹⁄₂-pound chicken, cut into serving pieces

Bring again to a boil, then reduce the heat and simmer about 1 hour more, or until the meat is falling from the bones. Remove the chicken and remove the skin and bones. Return the meat to the pot and bring to a boil. Add:

2¹⁄₂ cups quartered peeled, 311, ripe tomatoes
1 cup fresh or frozen lima beans
¹⁄₂ jalapeño or serrano chile, diced
2 green bell peppers, diced
2 cups diced potatoes
1 cup diced carrots
1 cup diced okra
³⁄₄ cup diced onion
¹⁄₂ cup diced celery
1 tablespoon Worcestershire sauce
1 bay leaf

Reduce the heat, and simmer gently, stirring frequently as the sauce thickens, 45 minutes or more. Add:

2 cups corn (from about 4 ears)

Simmer 15 minutes more, or until all the vegetables are soft. Season to taste with:

Salt and black pepper

Serve in deep bowls, garnished with:

Chopped parsley

CORNED BEEF

8 to 10 servings

The term "corned" is a reference to the kernel-sized crystals of salt used to cure large cuts of beef brisket. Spices such as garlic, allspice, black pepper, and bay leaves were also added. In most supermarkets, corned beef is sold in vacuum-sealed bags that contain some of the brine and seasonings used during curing; it needs to be cooked before serving. Corned beef makes great sandwiches, and, of course, there is Corned Beef Hash, 107.

I. Wash under running water to remove the surface brine:

One 4-pound corned beef brisket

Bring enough water to cover the brisket to a boil in a large pot. Add the meat and:

20 black peppercorns
2 bay leaves

Simmer, covered, until a fork can easily penetrate to the center, about 3 hours. If desired, add to the pot for the last 15 to 30 minutes of cooking:

(1 head green cabbage, cut into wedges)

Remove the meat and let stand for 15 minutes. Drain the cabbage, if using, and keep warm. Cut the brisket into thin slices against the grain and remove to a platter. Serve with:

Horseradish Cream, 565, or prepared horseradish
Coarse whole-grain mustard and or
    hot English-style mustard
Boiled Potatoes, 295

Serve leftover corned beef cold in sandwiches with the above condiments, or, better still, serve as a hot corned beef sandwich or in a Reuben, 181.

II. For a dramatic candied corned beef. Combine and mix:

1 tablespoon brown sugar
1 tablespoon water
1 teaspoon soy sauce
2 teaspoons paprika
¹⁄₂ teaspoon ground ginger

After cooking the corned beef as above, place on a baking sheet, coat it with the glaze, and bake in a preheated 350°F oven 15 minutes, or until the topping is set.

NEW ENGLAND BOILED DINNER

10 to 12 servings

This is a delectable dinner if composed only of beef, onions, and cabbage, but for authenticity, we include additional vegetables as well. Some devotees of this dish add about 8 ounces salt pork to the corned beef for the last 2 hours of cooking.

Prepare:

Corned Beef I, above, without the cabbage

When it is tender, remove the beef to a platter. Add to the simmering stock and cook 30 minutes:

3 small parsnips, peeled and quartered
6 large carrots, quartered
3 large turnips, peeled and quartered, or 1 rutabaga,
    peeled and quartered

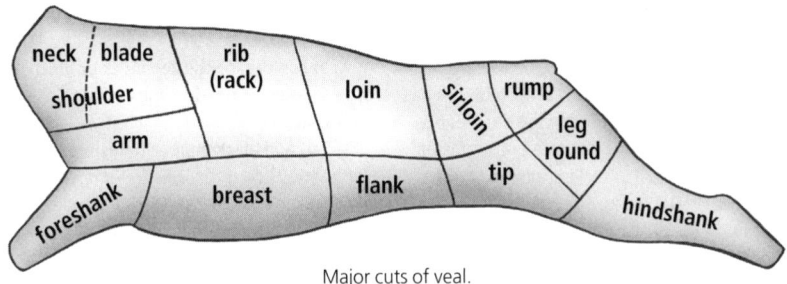

Major cuts of veal.

Add:

10 small or pearl onions, peeled

6 medium potatoes, peeled and quartered

Simmer 15 minutes longer. Add and simmer until tender, about 10 to 15 minutes longer:

1 head cabbage, cut into wedges

Reheat the meat in the stock. Serve it on a platter, surrounded by the vegetables, reheated if desired. Garnish with:

Chopped parsley

RED FLANNEL HASH

Beets give this hash its color and its name.

Prepare:

Corned Beef Hash, 107

Add:

2 to 3 beets, cooked, 258, peeled, and cut into $^{1}/_{2}$-inch cubes to the other vegetables

ABOUT VEAL

Veal is young beef, 4 to 6 months old. Look for meat that is very pale, with white, creamy fat. The bones should be white on the outside and bright red at the center. Veal that is reddish in color has likely come from older calves who were fed grain rather than milk. Reddish veal will have a stronger flavor and tougher exterior and is good for stews or braises. To improve older veal, blanch briefly, starting in cold water; or soak refrigerated in milk overnight; or marinate in lemon juice for 1 hour. We use the palest of meat for roasts, chops, and scaloppine. Veal needs a careful cooking approach, as it is lacking in fat and may toughen quickly. Since it also has a higher proportion of connective tissue, veal should not be broiled; ➤ long, slow, covered cooking is best. Large cuts of veal need some moisture, and the meat should be covered at least part of the cooking time.

VEAL ROAST

6 to 8 servings

Position a rack in the center of the oven. Preheat the oven to 350°F. Pat dry:

One 3- to 4-pound boneless veal shoulder, leg (top round), loin, or rib roast

Tie the roast in a neat, compact shape and rub with:

2 tablespoons olive or vegetable oil

Season generously with:

Salt and black pepper

Place the veal fat side up on a rack in a shallow roasting pan. Roast until a thermometer inserted in the thickest part of the meat registers 145° to 150°F for medium, 1$^{1}/_{4}$ to 1$^{3}/_{4}$ hours (the temperature will continue to rise about 5 degrees out of the oven). Remove the roast to a platter, cover loosely with aluminum foil, and let stand for 15 to 20 minutes. Set the roasting pan over high heat and pour in:

$^{1}/_{3}$ cup dry white wine

$^{1}/_{3}$ cup chicken stock or broth

Bring to a boil, scraping up the browned bits with a wooden spoon, and boil for 1 minute. Slice the veal and arrange the meat on the platter. Drizzle the sauce over the veal and serve.

STUFFED ROASTED VEAL

15 to 20 servings

This is a beautiful presentation and a perfect company dish. Have the butcher prepare the breast for stuffing by slicing a horizontal pocket along the bones (between the meat and bones) and cutting through the rigid cartilage between the rib bones from underneath the breast (not the meat side) without cutting into the meat. This cracks the bones, which will make carving the roast easier. You will need a pan that is at least 17 x 11$^{1}/_{2}$ inches to accommodate the entire veal breast.

Prepare:

Basic Bread Stuffing, 532

Preheat the oven to 325°F. Pat dry:

One 12- to 14-pound whole veal breast

Season with:

Salt and black pepper

Fill the pocket with the stuffing, spreading it in an even layer. Place the breast in a large roasting pan. Brush with olive oil. Roast, uncovered, until the inside is no longer pink when you make a small incision near the bone, 2$^{1}/_{2}$ to 3 hours. Remove the meat to a platter and let stand for 15 to 20 minutes. Skim the fat from the pan juices, and add:

2 cups dry white wine or chicken stock or broth

Set the roasting pan over high heat and bring to a boil. Reduce the heat and simmer until the sauce is reduced by half. Slice the veal and spoon the sauce over the slices.

COLD VEAL IN TUNA SAUCE (VITELLO TONNATO FREDDO)

4 servings

This is a classic Italian dish of cold sliced veal served with a tuna mayonnaise–style sauce. It is best when the veal is cooked ahead and well chilled. You can use any cut of veal that is easily sliced, preferably a boneless loin roast. The sauce is also good over roasted turkey or pork.

Refrigerate until cold:

1 to 1¹/₂ pounds cooked veal roast

Prepare:

Tuna Sauce, 567

Cut the veal into thin slices and arrange on plates or a platter. Spoon a generous amount of the tuna sauce over the slices and serve with:

Lemon wedges

VEAL SCALLOPS AND CUTLETS

A **scallop** is a thin slice of meat, usually round or oval in shape, cooked by quickly sautéing. Called **scaloppine** in Italian, these are usually pounded to ¹/₄- to ¹/₈-inch thickness, dredged in flour, quickly cooked, and served with a pan sauce. The most prized meat for veal scallops comes from the long round muscle of the leg freed from its membrane and tough connective tissue. Cutlets, also cut from the round of the leg, are usually cut ¹/₂ to ³/₄ inch thick, with the small round bone intact. After the bone is removed they are often pounded, especially if used in recipes calling for rolling or stuffing. Sometimes veal from the rib section is treated in similar fashion. Whether you call them **scallops, cutlets,** or **Schnitzels,** they may be sautéed with or without breading. Trim off any fat, and if any membrane adheres, slash it in a number of places so the meat will not curl up during cooking. Do not crowd the pan, or the meat will steam in its own juices.

SAUTÉED VEAL CUTLET OR SCALOPPINE

4 servings

Serve simply, as in this recipe, or try any of the variations that follow. Please read Veal Scallops and Cutlets, above. Preheat the oven to 180°F. Have ready an ovenproof platter. Season:

1 pound boneless veal cutlets or scallops (8 to 12), pounded to slightly less than ¹/₄ inch

with:

Salt and black pepper

Dredge in:

¹/₂ cup all-purpose flour

Shake off the excess. Heat in a large skillet over high heat:

1 tablespoon olive oil, or as needed

1 tablespoon butter, or as needed

Brown the cutlets in batches, being careful not to crowd the pan; cook quickly, 30 to 60 seconds each side. Remove to the platter as browned and keep warm in the oven, and add more oil and butter to the pan as needed. Add to the

pan and bring to a boil, scooping up the browned bits with a wooden spoon:

¹/₂ cup veal or chicken stock or broth or ¹/₄ cup stock plus ¹/₄ cup dry white wine

Season with:

Salt and black pepper to taste

Simmer 10 to 15 minutes to reduce liquid. Pour the sauce over the veal and serve garnished with:

(Sautéed Mushrooms, 283)

VEAL PICCATA

4 servings

Please read Veal Scallops and Cutlets, above.

Prepare:

Sautéed Veal Cutlet or Scaloppine, above

above, omitting the stock, and keep warm in the oven. Add to the pan:

¹/₄ cup dry white wine and ¹/₃ cup fresh lemon juice

Bring to a boil, scraping up the browned bits with a wooden spoon. Reduce the heat and simmer until slightly reduced, about 5 minutes. Turn off the heat and quickly whisk in:

¹/₄ cup (¹/₂ stick) butter, softened

2 tablespoons chopped parsley, and salt and black pepper to taste

Spoon the sauce over the scaloppine and serve immediately.

VEAL MARSALA

4 servings

Prepare:

Veal Scaloppine, above, omitting the stock

Set the veal aside; do not keep warm in the oven after browning. If desired, add to the pan and cook, stirring, until softened for 2 to 3 minutes:

(¹/₂ cup sliced mixed mushrooms)

Add:

²/₃ cup dry Marsala

Bring to a boil, scraping up the browned bits with a wooden spoon. Reduce the heat and simmer until the wine is reduced to about ¹/₂ cup. Whisk in:

2 tablespoons butter, softened

Continue to simmer until the sauce becomes thicker and velvety. Return the veal to the pan, along with:

2 tablespoons chopped parsley

Simmer just so the meat warms through, about 1 minute. Remove from the heat and serve immediately.

VEAL SALTIMBOCCA

4 servings

Saltimbocca means "jump into the mouth," which is precisely what these delicious stuffed and sauced cutlets do. Prosciutto and sage is the traditional stuffing, but a slice of cheese is often added as well. The Italians make saltimbocca with veal cutlets, but turkey breast is also very good. Please read Veal Scallops and Cutlets, above.

Season:

1 pound veal scallops (8 to 12), pounded to
$^{1}/_{8}$ inch thick

with:

Salt and black pepper to taste

Lay the scaloppine out flat, and top each with:

1 paper-thin slice prosciutto (about 2 ounces total)
2 large fresh sage leaves (8 to 12 total)

Roll the veal around the filling and secure with toothpicks. Heat in a large heavy skillet over medium-high heat:

1 tablespoon olive oil
1 tablespoon butter

Add the veal packets and cook, turning once, until lightly browned, about 1$^{1}/_{2}$ minutes on each side. Remove to a platter and cover with aluminum foil to keep warm. Add to the hot pan:

$^{1}/_{2}$ cup dry white wine

Bring to a boil, scraping the bottom of the pan with a wooden spoon to loosen the browned bits, and boil until the wine is almost evaporated. Add:

1 cup chicken or veal stock or broth
1 tablespoon lemon juice, or as needed

Boil over high heat until reduced to about $^{1}/_{2}$ cup. Remove the skillet from the heat and stir in:

2 tablespoons butter, softened

Taste and adjust the seasonings, adding a bit more lemon juice to taste. Pour the sauce over the veal packets.

VEAL PARMIGIANA

4 servings

Please read Veal Scallops and Cutlets, 486. Prepare **Chicken Parmigiana, 437,** substituting **1 pound veal scallops** for the chicken cutlets.

VEAL FRANCESE

4 servings

Also known as **Veal Dorato,** for its deep golden color. Please read Veal Scallops and Cutlets, 486.

Preheat the oven to 180°F. Have ready an ovenproof platter. Dredge:

1 pound veal scallops (8 to 12), pounded to slightly
less than $^{1}/_{4}$ inch thick

in:

$^{1}/_{2}$ cup all-purpose flour

Shake off the excess. Beat together in a bowl until frothy and thick:

3 large eggs
6 tablespoons grated Parmesan
1$^{1}/_{2}$ tablespoons chopped parsley
$^{1}/_{2}$ teaspoon salt
$^{1}/_{4}$ teaspoon black pepper

Heat in a large skillet over medium-high heat:

1$^{1}/_{2}$ tablespoons olive oil, or as needed
1$^{1}/_{2}$ tablespoons butter, or as needed

Working in batches, dip the floured veal into the egg batter and place in the pan, being careful not to crowd the

pan. Cook until browned, 1$^{1}/_{2}$ to 2 minutes on each side. Remove to the platter as browned and keep warm in the oven. Add more oil and butter to the pan as needed. Return all the scallops to the pan and sprinkle with:

Juice of 1 large lemon ($^{1}/_{4}$ to $^{1}/_{3}$ cup)

Reheat, either covered or uncovered, and cook for 1 minute more. Serve with:

Chopped parsley
Lemon wedges

BREADED VEAL CUTLETS (WIENER SCHNITZEL)

4 servings

This Austrian specialty is made with breaded veal cutlets; the Germans make it with pork cutlets. Viennese friends insist that true Wiener Schnitzel is deep-fried; others contend that it is sautéed. But most traditional Viennese recipes put up to $^{3}/_{4}$ cup butter in the sauté pan, which virtually gives a deep-fat rather than a sautéed result. Although there are many variations, we suggest the following. Please read Veal Scallops and Cutlets, 486.

Preheat the oven to 180°F. Have ready an ovenproof platter. Season:

1 pound boneless veal cutlets (8 to 12), pounded to
slightly less than $^{1}/_{4}$ inch thick

with:

Salt and black pepper

Spread on a plate:

$^{1}/_{2}$ cup all-purpose flour

Beat together in a shallow bowl:

2 large eggs
1 tablespoon milk

Spread on another plate:

2 cups fresh bread crumbs

Dredge the veal lightly in the flour mixture and shake off the excess. Dip into the egg mixture, then coat with the crumbs, pressing down on the crumbs slightly to help them adhere to the veal. Heat in a large skillet over medium-high heat:

3 tablespoons vegetable oil or butter, or a
combination, or as needed

Cook the cutlets in batches, being careful not to crowd the pan, until nicely browned, 1 to 1$^{1}/_{2}$ minutes each side. Remove to paper towels to drain as they brown, then keep warm on the platter in the oven, and add more oil or butter to the pan as needed. Sprinkle the cutlets with:

Salt and black pepper to taste

Serve with:

Lemon wedges or rolled anchovies

If you cap these cutlets with a fried egg, you may call it **Wiener Schnitzel à la Holstein.**

PAPRIKA SCHNITZEL (OR CUTLET)

4 to 5 servings

Trim and remove the bone from:

One 1$^{1}/_{2}$-pound veal cutlet, $^{1}/_{4}$ to $^{1}/_{2}$ inch thick

Pound to ⅛ inch thick. Dredge one side only in:

Seasoned flour, 962

Heat in a large skillet on medium-high heat:

¼ cup (½ stick) butter

Add, if desired, and cook, stirring, until lightly browned:

(½ cup or more sliced onions)

Remove the onions to a bowl. Add the meat to the pan, seasoned side down, and cook until lightly browned. Turn, then sprinkle with:

1 teaspoon paprika

1 cup chicken stock or broth

and the reserved onions. Set over very low heat, cover, and simmer until the veal is tender, about 25 minutes. Stir in:

½ cup sour cream

Heat through, but do not boil. Season with:

Salt and black pepper to taste

Garnish with:

Chopped parsley, capers, or anchovies

Serve with:

Applesauce, 216, Creamed Spinach, 305, Spätzle, 335, or Buttered Egg Noodles, 329

VEAL CORDON BLEU

6 servings

Prepare **Chicken Cordon Bleu, 437,** substituting for the chicken **veal scallops, pounded thin and cut into about 12 three-inch squares.**

VEAL CHOPS AND MEDALLIONS

Veal chops are cut from the rib or loin. **Rib chops** have one curved bone; **loin chops** are a T-bone shape, with the loin muscle on one side and the tenderloin on the other. Both have a thin layer of fat around the edges. You can trim this fat, but we like to leave at least ¼ inch to keep the chops moist during cooking. **Veal shoulder chops,** or **blade steaks,** as they are sometimes called, are a bit tougher and generally reserved for braising. **Medallions** are individual round steaks cut from the boneless loin, which has been trimmed of fat and connective tissue. What remains is a perfectly clean, solid piece of tender meat.

The best techniques for cooking veal chops are grilling or sautéing; broiling is not recommended. Chops for grilling are best cut about 1½ inches thick so that the center remains pink and juicy while allowing time for the meat to cook near the bone. Pan-fried chops are ideal if cut 1 inch thick; they do not burn or dry out. Veal medallions are generally sliced about ¾ inch thick and cook very quickly in a hot skillet. Grilled veal chops can be cooked and served simply with a wedge of lemon, or try an herb or spice rub or serve with a vinaigrette, chutney, relish, or other sauce or condiment. Panfried chops and medallions are perfect for making pan sauces that can be made in just a few minutes after the meat is cooked. You also can make a sauce ahead and reheat it gently either in the skillet or in a separate pan. See the Sauces chapter, 542, for ideas.

BRAISED VEAL SHOULDER CHOPS

4 servings

These chops may also be browned and then simmered slowly, covered, on top of the stove until done, about 15 to 20 minutes.

Preheat the oven to 325°F. Heat in a large skillet on medium-high heat:

2 tablespoons butter

2 tablespoons vegetable oil

Add and brown on both sides:

4 veal shoulder chops, ¾ inch thick

Remove the chops to a Dutch oven, arranging them in an overlapping pattern. Add to the hot fat in the skillet and cook, stirring until limp:

2 tablespoons chopped scallions or shallots

Add, stirring, until the liquid reduces, about 5 minutes:

⅔ cup dry white wine

⅔ cup chicken stock or broth

1 tablespoon chopped fresh basil

Salt and black pepper to taste

Pour the pan juices over the chops, cover, and bake about 20 minutes, basting occasionally, until juices begin to thicken and bubble. Serve with:

Quick Tomato Sauce, 562, Mushroom Wine Sauce, 555, or Madeira Sauce, 555

GRILLED VEAL CHOPS

4 servings

Prepare a medium-hot grill fire. Pat dry:

4 rib or loin veal chops, 1¼ to 1½ inches thick

Rub with:

2 tablespoons olive oil

Sprinkle with:

Salt and black pepper

Place the chops over the hottest area of the grill and sear for 2 minutes on each side. Move the chops to a cooler spot and finish cooking, 8 to 10 minutes, turning halfway through the cooking time. The chops should be well browned and give only slightly when pressed firmly with a finger and should measure 125°F on a thermometer. Remove to a platter or plates and serve with:

Lemon wedges

SAUTÉED VEAL CHOPS

4 servings

Pat dry:

4 rib or loin veal chops, cut 1 inch thick

Season with:

Salt and black pepper

Heat in a large skillet over medium-high heat:

2 tablespoons butter

Add the chops and sear both sides, each about 2 minutes. Reduce the heat to medium and cook for 3 to 5 minutes, turning the chops halfway through cooking. Remove to plates and let stand. Increase the heat to high and add to the pan:

¹/₂ cup veal or chicken stock or broth

Boil, stirring, until syrupy, 1 to 2 minutes. Spoon over the chops and serve.

VEAL STEWS AND BRAISED VEAL

The best cuts of veal for stewing and braising are the tougher, more flavorful ones, including the neck, chuck, shoulder, breast, sirloin, and shank. For stews, buy or cut cubes of meat from the neck, chuck, or shoulder. For braising larger cuts, look for whole pieces of boneless chuck, shoulder, or veal breast, which can be braised on the bone or boneless, rolled and tied into a loaf—ideal for stuffing. Veal shanks should be cut into thick crosswise slices to expose the bone marrow, which is considered a special treat in the Italian braised veal dish Osso Buco, below. The best are the hind shanks, as they are meatier and more tender than the smaller foreshanks. Please see Pot-Roasting, Stewing, and Braising Meat, 466.

WHITE VEAL STEW (BLANQUETTE DE VEAU)

6 servings

As the name suggests, this is prepared without browning the veal.

Cut into 2-inch pieces:

1¹/₂ pounds boneless veal shoulder

1¹/₂ pounds boneless veal breast

Blanch, 1054, the veal in salted water about 2 minutes. Drain and rinse well under cold running water. Put the meat in a Dutch oven and add:

5 cups veal or chicken stock or broth

1 large onion, studded with 1 whole clove

1 carrot, chopped

1 inner celery rib, chopped

1 Bouquet Garni, 960

Bring to a simmer and cook, uncovered, 1¹/₄ to 1¹/₂ hours, until the veal is tender. Remove and discard the vegetables and bouquet garni. Add:

24 small white or pearl onions, peeled

2 cups button mushroom caps

Simmer about 10 minutes, stirring occasionally. Blend together in a small bowl:

¹/₄ cup all-purpose flour

¹/₄ cup (¹/₂ stick) butter, softened

Gradually add to the stew and simmer another 10 minutes. Remove from the heat. Lightly beat in a small bowl:

3 large egg yolks

Stir in:

¹/₂ cup warm heavy cream

Stir about ¹/₄ cup of the hot cooking liquid into the eggs and cream, then return the mixture to the pot and stir until thoroughly blended. Add:

2 to 3 tablespoons fresh lemon juice

Season to taste with:

Salt and black pepper

Garnish with:

Chopped parsley

BRAISED VEAL SHANKS (OSSO BUCO)

4 servings

Literally translated, *osso buco* means bone with a hole, and in veal shanks, that hole contains marrow, 522. If possible, choose veal hind shank, which is meatier than those from the foreshank.

Preheat the oven to 325°F. Pat dry:

8 slices veal shank, 1¹/₂ inches thick

Heat in a large Dutch oven over medium-high heat:

2 tablespoons olive oil

Add the shanks in batches and brown well on all sides, adding more oil as needed. Remove to a plate. Reduce the heat to medium-low and add to the pot:

1 small carrot, chopped

1 small onion, chopped

¹/₂ celery rib, chopped

4 garlic cloves, minced

1 small Bouquet Garni, 960

Cook, stirring, until the vegetables are softened. Return the shanks to the pot, arranging in a single layer. Add:

1 cup dry white wine

1 cup veal or chicken stock or broth, or as needed

Black pepper to taste

The liquid should reach about halfway up the shanks. Increase the heat to high and bring to a boil. Cover, place in the oven, and braise for 1 hour. Turn the slices over and add if needed to keep the level halfway up the shanks:

(1 to 2 cups veal or chicken stock or broth)

Braise until the meat is tender, about 1 hour more. Turn off oven, remove the shanks to an ovenproof serving platter and keep warm in the oven. Spoon off any fat from the braising juices, strain the juices into a saucepan, and boil over high heat until slightly thickened. Before serving, stir in:

Gremolata, 989

Salt and black pepper to taste

Spoon the sauce over the meat and serve with:

Risotto Milanese, 360, or Soft Polenta, 349

And scoop the marrow from the bones with a marrow spoon to eat or spread on bread or toast.

ABOUT LAMB AND MUTTON

Most lamb comes to market between 5 and 7 months of age, with a dressed weight of 50 to 65 pounds. The smallest lamb, sometimes referred to as **hothouse** or **milk-fed** lamb, can be less than 4 weeks old and weigh as little as 8 pounds. Lambs of this size are generally roasted whole. Other small lambs, between 20 and 50 pounds, are often sold under the name of **spring** or **Easter** lamb, but are available year-round.

Mutton is meat from sheep over 1 year old and is larger, darker in color, and richer in flavor than lamb. ➤ Mutton tends to have more fat than lamb and should be well trimmed before cooking. Prepare mutton according to lamb recipes, allowing extra cooking time for larger cuts.

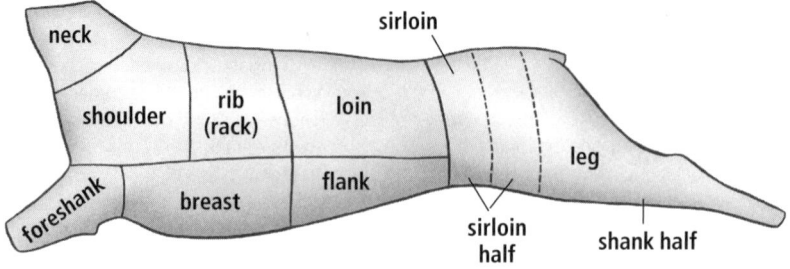

Major cuts of lamb

Lamb is graded Prime, Choice, and Select. Marbling with fat is not a factor in grading lamb as it is with beef. Less than 10 percent is graded Prime. Look for meat that is moist and bright; color may range from pinkish rose to pale red, depending on the age of the animal. The fat should be waxy white.

Large lamb cuts are covered with a white membrane called the **fell,** which some cooks want removed before cooking because they feel it has a strong flavor. It does hold the meat together, and with larger cuts, it is best left on. The fat is best trimmed away. Leave only a few streaks to baste the meat as it cooks.

Some cuts of lamb—**leg, chops, rack,** and **loin**—are tender enough for dry-heat cooking methods such as roasting, broiling, sautéing, or grilling. Lamb cooked this way is best rare or medium-rare. To determine doneness, insert a thermometer into the thickest portion of the meat without touching bone. The temperature ➤ for medium-rare lamb is 145°F, for medium is 160°F and well done 170°F. See Internal Temperatures for Cooking Meat After Carry-Over Cooking, 467. Bear in mind that the internal temperature of large cuts will rise about 5 degrees as the meat rests after cooking. Less tender cuts, including the **shoulder, shanks,** and **breast,** are best braised or stewed until tender. Please see Pot-Roasting, Stewing, and Braising Meat, 466.

Lamb stands up well to assertive seasonings, from pungent herbs to spice rubs and curry sauces.

LEG OF LAMB

Naturally tender and extremely flavorful, leg of lamb is best roasted, whole, boneless, or stuffed. Boned and butterflied leg of lamb and smaller, thinner cuts from the leg, such as lamb steaks, leg chops, or kebabs, can be grilled, broiled, or sautéed. The flavor and texture of lamb are best ➤ when it is not cooked past medium. Tender, lean leg meat does not hold up well to the long cooking of a stew.

Leg of lamb comes in several forms. Most common is the **whole leg on the bone,** which we prefer because the flavor is enhanced by the bone. These generally weigh from 7 to 9 pounds untrimmed, but may weigh 5 pounds or less. ➤ Figure on 8 to 10 ounces per person of bone-in lamb. Each leg has 3 bones: the hip or pelvis, the thigh, and the shank. The butcher will remove all or some of

these. If you want a bone-in leg, we recommend asking the butcher to remove the hip bone to make carving easier. If you do this at home, trim the lamb of its exterior fat and cut around the side of the bone so that you can pull the meat out as flat as possible on either side of the bone. A fully boneless leg is most often opened out as a butterflied leg of lamb—perfect for stuffing and rolling or simply grilling or broiling flat like a large steak. ➤ When buying a boneless leg, allow 6 to 8 ounces per person.

As a general rule when cooking leg of lamb, figure on 10 to 13 minutes per pound for a large leg (over 7 pounds), 8 to 9 minutes per pound for a smaller leg (5 to 7 pounds).

You have a choice when **carving a bone-in leg of lamb.** For large, thin, flat slices, grab the shank, or narrow end, of the roast with a towel, paper towel, or heavy cloth napkin and raise it at an angle off the platter. With a sharp carving knife held parallel to the bone, begin cutting away from you to carve flat, 1/4-inch-thick slices from the meatiest part of the leg. Continue until you reach the leg bone. Turn the leg over and use the same slicing method until you reach the bone again. Finally, carve away any meat left attached to the bone. If the hip bone is still attached, again hold the shank with the meatiest part of the leg facing up. Or, with a sharp carving knife, start at the shank end and make vertical slices down to the bone. Then turn the knife parallel to the bone and cut the slices free from the bone. Continue slicing toward the wide end of the leg. Rotate the leg as you go to carve the meat off all sides. As you reach the hip bone, carve around it.

ROAST LEG OF LAMB
10 servings

A simply seasoned roast leg of lamb needs no sauce—though some people insist on a bit of mint jelly or Mint Sauce, 565. Some enjoy Lemon Egg Sauce, 561, or Caper Sauce, 554, served on the side. Please read Leg of Lamb, above.

Preheat the oven to 450°F. Pat dry, trim, and prepare:

   1 whole bone-in leg of lamb (7 to 8 pounds)

Combine in a small bowl:

   1 tablespoon black pepper

   2 teaspoons salt

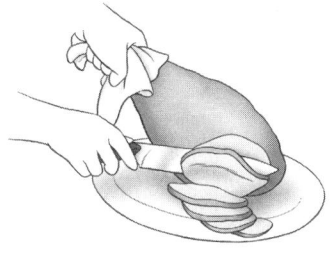

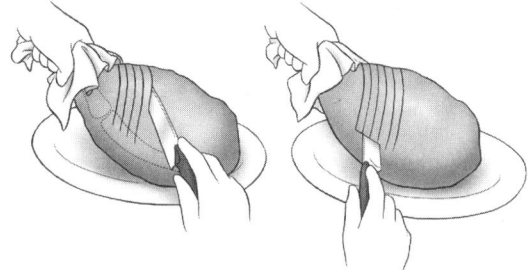

Carving method 1   Carving method 2

Carving leg of lamb

1 teaspoon finely minced fresh rosemary or
    $^1\!/_2$ teaspoon finely crumbled dried rosemary

Rub the wide end of the leg with half of the seasoning mixture. Add to the remaining seasoning mixture and toss to coat:

**2 large garlic cloves, cut lengthwise
    into slivers or slices**

Cut 15 to 20 evenly spaced slits in the roast, and insert the seasoned garlic slivers. Rub the surface of the roast with:

3 tablespoons olive oil

Rub any remaining seasoning mixture over the roast, and arrange it meatier side up on a rack in a roasting pan. Place it in the oven and immediately reduce the oven temperature to 325°F. Roast until a thermometer inserted in the thickest part of the meat reads 140°F for medium-rare, or 160°F for medium, 1$^1\!/_4$ to 1$^3\!/_4$ hours (the temperature will rise about 5 degrees out of the oven). Remove from the oven, cover loosely with aluminum foil, and let stand for 15 to 20 minutes.

STUFFED BUTTERFLIED LEG OF LAMB

8 to 10 servings

Please read Leg of Lamb, 490.

Preheat the oven to 375°F. Pat dry:

**1 butterflied leg of lamb (4 to 5 pounds), trimmed to
    an even thickness of 2 to 2$^1\!/_2$ inches**

Season the boned side of the meat with:

(2 tablespoons chopped garlic)
1$^1\!/_2$ teaspoons salt
1 teaspoon black pepper

Spoon onto the seasoned surface:

**4 cups Spinach, Mushroom, and Ground Meat Stuffing,
    538, made with ground lamb or pork, or 5 cups
    Couscous Stuffing with Dried Apricots and
    Pistachios, 539**

Starting from a longer side, roll up the lamb to enclose the stuffing. Tie the leg securely at 2-inch intervals to give it a snug, compact, cylindrical shape. You may need to sew the small end closed with a trussing needle or secure it with small skewers. With the point of a paring knife, make

20 to 25 slits about 2 inches apart over the surface of the lamb. Push into the slits:

3 garlic cloves, cut lengthwise into slivers

Rub the surface with:

3 tablespoons olive oil
1 teaspoon salt
$^1\!/_2$ teaspoon black pepper

Place the leg seam side down on a rack in a roasting pan and roast 1 hour. Carefully flip the leg over, return to the oven, and roast until a thermometer inserted in the thickest part of the meat reads 140°F for medium-rare, 30 to 45 minutes longer (the temperature will rise about 5 degrees out of the oven). Remove from the oven, cover loosely with aluminum foil, and let stand for 10 to 15 minutes. Just before serving, remove the string and cut the lamb into $^1\!/_2$- to $^3\!/_4$-inch-thick slices (the roll may come apart). Pass separately, if desired:

Piquant Sauce, 556

GRILLED OR BROILED
BUTTERFLIED LEG OF LAMB

8 to 10 servings

Pat dry:

**1 butterflied leg of lamb (4 to 5 pounds), trimmed to
    an even thickness of 2 to 2$^1\!/_2$ inches**

Rub the entire surface with:

**$^1\!/_2$ cup Peppery Dry Rub, 587, or West Indies Dry Rub,
    588**

or a mixture of:

**3 tablespoons minced fresh rosemary or 1 tablespoon
    dried rosemary**
2 tablespoons minced garlic
1 teaspoon salt
1 teaspoon black pepper

Place on a baking sheet, cover, and marinate in the refrigerator for at least 1 hour, or up to 24 hours. Position the broiler pan 4 to 5 inches away from the heating element and preheat the broiler and broiler pan, or prepare a medium-hot grill fire. Place the lamb boned side down on the broiler pan or boned side up on the grill rack. Cook, turning once, until well seared but still juicy and pink on the inside, about 12 minutes on each side. Cook for a few minutes more each side for medium. Let stand for 6 to 8 minutes, loosely covered with aluminum foil, then cut into ½-inch-thick slices. Serve with:

(Red Onion Marmalade, 567, or Roasted Tomato–Chipotle Salsa, 572)

RACK OF LAMB

The rack is the rib section of the lamb, extending from the shoulder to the loin, with the rib lamb chops left in one piece. There are usually 7 rib bones, although some butchers include an eighth rib from the shoulder end. ➤ An average trimmed rack weighs between 1¼ and 2½ pounds and feeds 2 or 3 people, figuring 2 to 3 chops per person. With the smaller rack, or for especially large appetites, figure on ➤ 3 to 4 chops per person.

Trimming a rack of lamb so that the ends of the rib bones are exposed is called **Frenching.** Place the rack bone side down on a cutting board and, with a sharp knife held perpendicular to the rib bones, make a long cut through the fat layer about 2 inches from the end of the bones and above the eye meat. Angle the knife into the cut and slide the knife away from the eye meat toward the ends of the bones. Keep the blade flush with the bones and remove the layer of fat covering them. Cut out the meat between the bones. Scrape the exposed bone free of any fat or tendon, which will otherwise burn during roasting.

ROASTED RACK OF LAMB
3 to 4 servings

Browning the rack of lamb before roasting gives it a brown exterior and helps melt any untrimmed fat. If you choose to skip this step, add 5 to 8 minutes to the cooking time. Preheat the oven to 425°F. Pat dry:

1 rack of lamb (7 or 8 ribs), trimmed, leaving a thin layer of fat on the surface
Season with:
1 teaspoon salt
½ teaspoon black pepper

Heat a large heavy ovenproof skillet over high heat. Add the lamb meat side down and brown well, about 2 minutes. Turn it and brown the other side, about another 2 minutes. Pour off any fat in the pan, then set the lamb bone side down in the skillet and place in the oven. Roast until a thermometer inserted in the thickest part of the meat registers 125°F for rare, or 135°F for medium-rare, about 15 to 20 minutes (the temperature will rise about 5 to 10 degrees out of the oven). Remove from the oven, cover loosely with aluminum foil, and let stand for 5 to 10 minutes. Cut between the bones and serve 2 or 3 chops per person, with:

(Red Wine and Sour Cherry Pan Sauce, 548, or Red Onion Marmalade, 567)

ROASTED RACK OF LAMB WITH MOROCCAN SPICE RUB

Have ready a rack of lamb as for **Roasted Rack of Lamb, above.** Combine **2 tablespoons olive oil, ¼ cup chopped mint, 2 tablespoons chopped parsley, 1½ teaspoons ground ginger, ½ teaspoon ground allspice, ½ teaspoon ground cinnamon, ½ teaspoon paprika, ½ teaspoon ground coriander, ½ teaspoon salt, ½ teaspoon black pepper, ¼ teaspoon ground red pepper,** and **⅛ teaspoon ground cloves** in a small bowl and mix well. Rub the paste all over the unseasoned lamb and marinate for 30 to 60 minutes in the refrigerator. Do not brown the lamb. Roast as directed.

ROASTED LOIN OF LAMB
4 servings

The two lamb loins run along either side of the backbone, starting at the last rib and extending to the hindquarters, or **sirloin.** If they are still attached to the backbone, the loins are referred to as the **saddle.** A single boned and trimmed loin ranges in size from ¾ pound for New Zealand or baby lamb to 2 pounds for average domestic lamb. For a special meal, order a boneless loin of lamb and roast it to medium-rare. To avoid drying out the very small loins and to have enough to serve 4 to 6 people, if the boneless loins are under 1 pound, buy 2 and have the butcher tie them together into one compact cylinder. Roast as for one whole 2-pound loin. Even when roasting a single whole loin, tie it with butcher twine so that it holds its shape. We recommend leaving a ¼-inch layer of fat on the roast to keep it moist while roasting. Rubbing the roast with olive oil before roasting is also a good idea. Preheat the oven to 425°F. Pat dry:

1 boneless loin of lamb (1½ to 2 pounds), trimmed and tied at 1½-inch intervals
Season with:
1 teaspoon salt
½ teaspoon black pepper

Heat a large heavy ovenproof skillet over high heat. Add the lamb and brown on all sides, about 3 minutes. Place the skillet in the oven and roast until a thermometer inserted in the thickest part of the meat registers 125°F for rare, or 135°F for medium-rare, about 25 minutes (the temperature will rise 5 degrees out of the oven). Remove from the oven, cover loosely with aluminum foil, and let stand for 5 to 10 minutes. Remove the strings and cut the lamb into ¾- to 1-inch-thick medallions. If desired, serve with:

(Red Wine and Sour Cherry Pan Sauce, 548, or Sauce Marchand de Vin, 555)

ABOUT LAMB CHOPS AND STEAKS

The most popular, and most expensive, lamb chops are the loin and rib chops, prized for their tenderness. **Rib chops** are recognizable by a "handle" of rib bone. **Loin chops** are more compact and somewhat meatier, resembling a tiny

T-bone steak. Either can be grilled, broiled, pan-broiled, or sautéed; as with all tender cuts of lamb, however, they are best when not cooked past medium. Chops at least ³/₄ inch thick are preferable; thinner ones are easy to overcook. ➤ Figure on 2 or 3 chops per person, depending on size.

Chops from the arm and shoulder are labeled as **shoulder, arm,** or **blade.** Unlike rib and loin chops, these less expensive cuts have lines of fat laced through the muscle and varying amounts of connective tissue. Shoulder and arm chops are often braised to tenderize them. We have also had good luck marinating them before grilling or broiling. While never as tender as rib or loin chops, they have excellent flavor and will not dry out when cooked past medium. ➤ Allow one 6- to 8-ounce chop per person, a bit more if the chops have a lot of bone.

Leg chops tend to be larger than rib and loin chops and less fatty than shoulder chops. Many consider chops from the upper leg, or sirloin, among the best cuts of lamb; these can be grilled or braised. They will not be as tender as rib and loin chops, but they have a marvelous rich flavor. Leg chops vary from market to market, however, ➤ so you should specify that you want steaks from the sirloin and not the smaller, less tender leg parts. Large steaks from farther down the leg are recognizable by the cross section of leg bone, much like a ham steak. These can be cooked by dry-heat methods such as grilling or broiling, although they may be a bit chewy. ➤ Figure on 6 to 8 ounces leg meat per serving, a bit more if the steaks have a lot of bone.

BROILED OR GRILLED LAMB CHOPS

4 servings
Make sure the chops are close enough to the heat to brown well but 3 to 4 inches is ideal.
Preheat the broiler and broiler pan or prepare a medium-hot grill fire. Pat dry:

    8 lamb chops, about 1 inch thick
Rub both sides with:

    2 tablespoons olive oil
    1 teaspoon salt
    ¹/₂ teaspoon black pepper
Place the chops on the broiler pan or grill rack and cook for 5 minutes on each side for medium-rare. Cook for 1 minute more for medium. Serve immediately, with, if desired:

    Aïoli (Garlic Mayonnaise), 581, Anchovy Butter, 558,
        or Roasted Tomato–Chipotle Salsa, 572

SAUTÉED LAMB CHOPS

4 servings
Pat dry:

    8 lamb chops, about 1 inch thick
Season with:

    1 teaspoon salt
    ¹/₂ teaspoon black pepper

Heat in a large heavy skillet over medium-high heat until the butter begins to turn light brown:

    1 tablespoon butter
    1 tablespoon olive oil
Arrange the lamb chops in the pan. Sauté the chops for 4¹/₂ to 5 minutes on each side for medium-rare. Sauté for 1 minute more for medium. Serve immediately with:

    Herb Pan Sauce, 547, Pan Sauce with Leeks, Orange,
        and Rosemary, 548, or chopped parsley

BRAISED LAMB SHOULDER CHOPS

4 servings
Unlike tender rib and loin chops, these flavorful chops fare best when braised, in a mixture of wine and stock.
Pat dry:

    4 lamb shoulder chops, about ³/₄ inch thick
Season with:

    1 teaspoon salt
    ¹/₂ teaspoon black pepper
Heat in a large heavy skillet over high heat until the butter begins to turn light brown:

    1 tablespoon butter
    1 tablespoon olive oil
Brown the lamb chops evenly, about 2 minutes each side. Remove the chops and pour off all but about 1 tablespoon fat from the pan. Place the pan over medium heat and add:

    3 garlic cloves, coarsely chopped
    1 teaspoon dried herbes de Provence or
        ¹/₂ teaspoon dried thyme, rosemary, and basil
Cook, stirring, until the garlic is soft but not brown. Add:

    1 cup dry white wine
Bring to a boil, then reduce the heat and simmer, scraping up any browned bits on the bottom of the pan, until reduced by half. Add and reduce again by half, or until slightly thickened:

    ¹/₂ cup lamb stock, or chicken stock or broth
    1 cup tomato puree
Return the chops to the pan. Reduce the heat to low, cover, and simmer, turning once, until the chops are tender, 40 to 45 minutes. Remove from the heat and skim off any fat from the surface of the sauce. Add:

    (¹/₂ cup halved, pitted black olives)
Taste and adjust the seasonings. Garnish with:

    Chopped parsley

ABOUT KEBABS

Please read about Skewer Cooking, 1049. Shish kebab originated as a Turkish dish of skewered marinated lamb grilled over a charcoal fire, but today we cube and skewer just about anything from beef, poultry, pork to vegetables and call them kebabs. Create your own versions by using marinades or glazes such as Teriyaki Marinade, 586, or Orange Molasses Glaze, 583. The meat and vegetables are first lightly oiled, to prevent sticking, and then seasoned. As with all tender cuts, beef kebabs should not be cooked beyond medium, or they will become tough and dry.

For any meat kebabs, the meat is cut into 1¹/₂-inch cubes, which are marinated, refrigerated, for 2 to 3 hours, then wiped dry and threaded on skewers, close together if the meat is to be rare, widely spaced for well-done; bits of bacon or bay leaf may be inserted between the pieces of meat to add flavor. Kebabs are grilled or broiled about 3 inches from the heat source, about 8 to 12 minutes total according to taste. ➤ If using wooden or bamboo skewers, soak them in water for at least 30 minutes before grilling to prevent them from burning.

Kebabs lend themselves perfectly to picnics— presoaked in a savory marinade, they can be grilled over an open fire and served straight from the skewers on Flatbread, 607. Or the grilled cubes may be slipped off the skewers onto a bed of rice, kasha, or bulgur, or served on parsley, watercress, or shredded lettuce.

Alternate meat cubes with an assortment of vegetables such as grape or cherry tomatoes, green pepper slices, mushrooms, and onions, or with pineapple or stuffed olives. The vegetables can be skewered separately and cooked at the side of the grill, where the heat is less intense.

LAMB KEBABS

Follow the procedure described above, using one of these marinades:

> **Yogurt or Buttermilk Marinade, 585**
> **Tandoori Marinade, 584**
> **Balkan Marinade, 585**

BEEF KEBABS

4 servings

Please read About Kebabs, 493.

Prepare:

> ¹/₄ **recipe Peppery Dry Rub, 587**

Cut into cubes:

> **One 1- to 1¹/₂-pound boneless beef top loin,**
> **sirloin, fillet, or top round steak**

Combine the beef in a bowl with:

> **1 medium bell pepper, cut into pieces**
> **1 onion, cut into small wedges**

Coat with the rub. Cover and marinate in the refrigerator for 2 to 24 hours. Preheat the broiler and broiler pan or prepare a medium-hot grill fire. If broiling, position the broiler pan 3 to 4 inches from the heating element. Thread the meat and vegetables onto skewers. Broil or grill for 8 to 10 minutes, turning the skewers occasionally. Make a small incision in a cube of meat and check the center: It should be slightly less done than desired, for it will continue to cook somewhat off the heat. Serve immediately with:

> **Rice Pilaf, 355, or Couscous, 362**

ABOUT LAMB STEWS AND BRAISES

Lamb stew meat generally comes from the shoulder, neck, breast, shank, or leg. Of these, meat from the shoulder and neck has the best flavor; leg meat is the mildest, but it can become dry when stewed or braised. The whole shoulder is also often available, boned and rolled, and can be braised slowly as for a pot roast, 477, or barbecued, 467. Shoulder chops are ideal for braising, see 1051. Lamb neck pieces are another fine choice for slow, moist cooking; although they are less meaty than some cuts, the flavor is tremendous. Unlike roasted and sautéed lamb, stewed and braised lamb—even chops, 492—should be cooked gently in a bit of wine, stock, or tomato juice, or some combination of these, until the meat is well-done and tender. In addition to the recipes that follow, lamb can be substituted for beef, pork, and veal in any slow-cooked stew or braise. Please see Pot-Roasting, Stewing, and Braising Meat, 466.

BRAISED SHOULDER OF LAMB

8 servings

Lamb shoulder has great flavor and becomes tender when braised. Most markets sell boneless lamb shoulder roasts rolled and tied. If you prefer a bone-in shoulder roast for more flavor, cook it until the meat falls off the bone.

Preheat the oven to 425°F. Pat dry:

> **1 lamb shoulder (4 to 5 pounds boneless, rolled and**
> **tied, or 8 to 9 pounds bone-in)**

Season with:

> **1 teaspoon salt**
> ¹/₂ **teaspoon black pepper**

Heat in a Dutch oven over high heat:

> **2 tablespoons olive oil**

Add the lamb and brown on all sides. Remove the lamb from the pot, reduce the heat, and remove all but 2 tablespoons of fat from the pot. Add:

> **1 medium onion, chopped**
> **1 celery rib, chopped**
> **1 carrot, diced**
> **1 small turnip or parsnip, peeled and diced**
> **1¹/₂ teaspoons salt**
> **1 teaspoon black pepper**
> ¹/₂ **to 1 teaspoon mixed spices (ground coriander,**
> **cumin, turmeric, or fenugreek, saffron threads**
> **or powder, and/or curry powder)**

Cook slowly, scraping up any browned bits, until the vegetables are starting to soften, about 10 minutes. Meanwhile, bring to a boil in a small saucepan over high heat:

> **2 cups beef, lamb, or vegetable stock or broth**
> **1 cup tomato puree**

Return the lamb to the pot with the vegetables. Add the boiling stock mixture, along with:

> **1 bay leaf**

Cover the pot, bring to a simmer, and place in the oven. Immediately reduce the oven temperature to 325°F, and cook until the meat is fork-tender, 2 to 2¹/₂ hours (up to 3¹/₂ hours if bone-in). Remove the meat from the sauce and keep warm. Skim off the fat from the surface of the sauce and remove the bay leaf. Taste and adjust the seasonings. Cut the strings from the meat and serve it in chunks or slices, with plenty of sauce. If desired, serve with:

(Mashed Potatoes, 295, or Au Gratin Potatoes, 297)

BRAISED STUFFED SHOULDER OF LAMB

10 to 12 servings

Preheat the oven to 300°F. Rub:

1 boned shoulder of lamb (8 to 9 pounds)

with:

(A halved garlic clove)

Salt and black pepper

or insert slivers of garlic under the skin if desired. Prepare about:

**¹/₂ recipe Spinach, Mushroom and Ground Meat
    Stuffing, 538, or 3 cups Bread Stuffing, 532**

Lay out the lamb, boned side up, and spread the stuffing on the meat. Roll up from a long side like a jelly roll and secure with kitchen string, or fasten with spiral skewers, 1049. Heat in a large skillet:

3 tablespoons vegetable oil or butter

Brown the lamb on all sides. Place in a roasting pan:

1 cup vegetable stock or broth

Put the browned roast in it, cover, and cook about 45 minutes. For added flavor, you may put some of the bones in the pan. After the meat has cooked about 45 minutes, add to the roasting pan:

3 cups diced celery, carrots, onions, and potatoes

1 cup vegetable stock or broth

Cover and continue to cook about 1 hour longer, or until the internal temperature of the meat registers 175° to 180°F. Pour off and reserve most of the liquid. Glaze the meat and vegetables by baking uncovered about 10 minutes longer. Meanwhile, skim the fat from the reserved cooking liquid, and pour it into a saucepan, and simmer to reduce it somewhat. Season with:

Salt and black pepper to taste

Slice the meat and serve with the sauce.

BRAISED LAMB SHANKS

4 servings

Lamb shanks are the shin portion of the legs. Foreshanks are the meatiest and the most available. Front or back, most lamb shanks are cut longer than the more familiar veal shanks and have enough meat attached so that one per person gets a satisfying portion. The shank contains a good deal of connective tissue, which, when cooked by the slow, moist heat of a braise, produces a velvety sauce. Substitute lamb shanks in any recipe for braised veal shank or beef ribs or oxtail.

Preheat the oven to 300°F. Trim most of the external fat from:

4 meaty lamb shanks (about 3 to 4 pounds)

Season with:

1 teaspoon salt

¹/₂ teaspoon black pepper

Heat in a large Dutch oven over high heat:

2 tablespoons olive oil

Add the shanks and brown on all sides, about 5 minutes. Remove the shanks and keep warm. Pour off the fat from the pot. Add:

2 tablespoons olive oil

2 onions, halved and thinly sliced

2 tablespoons chopped garlic

Reduce the heat to medium, cover, and cook, stirring often, until the onions are quite soft. Sprinkle with:

**1 tablespoon chopped fresh mint or 1 teaspoon
    dried mint**

1 teaspoon ground coriander

1 teaspoon ground cumin

¹/₂ teaspoon black pepper

Pinch of ground cinnamon

Pinch of ground allspice

Stir well to coat the onions. Add:

2 cups chicken or lamb stock or broth or water

1 cup dry white wine

¹/₃ cup tomato puree

Increase the heat and bring to a boil. Return the lamb shanks to the pan, cover, and bake until the meat is almost falling off the bone, 1 to 1¹/₂ hours. Add:

2 cups carrots, sliced

**2 cups diced, peeled winter squash, such as
    butternut or Hubbard**

Cover and bake until the vegetables are tender, about 15 minutes more. Remove the meat and vegetables to a platter and cover with aluminum foil to keep warm. Skim off the fat from the surface of the sauce. Add:

2 tablespoons fresh lemon juice

**2 to 3 tablespoons chopped fresh mint or
    2 tablespoons dried mint**

(2 teaspoons Harissa, 569, or to taste)

Taste and adjust the seasonings. Pour the sauce over the meat and vegetables. Serve with:

Orzo, Rice Pilaf, 355, braised lentils, or white beans

LAMB STEW (NAVARIN PRINTANIÈRE)

8 to 10 servings

Cut into 1¹/₂-inch pieces:

1 pound boneless shoulder of lamb

1 pound boneless breast of lamb

Dredge the meat in:

Seasoned flour, 962

Heat in a large heavy skillet:

2 tablespoons vegetable oil

Add the meat, in batches, and brown on all sides. Remove the meat as it browns to a Dutch oven. Pour off the fat. Add to the pan:

2 cups light stock or broth

(2 tablespoons tomato paste)

Bring to a boil, stirring to release any browned bits. Pour

over the meat and simmer, covered, about 1 hour. Skim off the fat from the cooking liquid, and add to the pot:

2 cups cubed peeled new potatoes
6 carrots, cut into chunks
3 turnips, peeled and cut into chunks
18 small onions, peeled

Simmer, covered, about 1 hour longer, or until the lamb is tender. Skim off any fat and gently stir in:

1 cup cooked fresh or frozen peas
1 cup cooked sliced green beans

Heat through, serve at once, sprinkled with:

Finely chopped parsley

IRISH STEW

4 to 6 servings

The potatoes in this recipe are cut in two different ways because they serve different purposes. The sliced potatoes break down and thicken the stew without the addition of flour. The halved potatoes cook just to tender and add soft bite to the stew. As in a French blanquette, the meat is not browned here.

Preheat the oven to 325°F. Heat in a Dutch oven over medium heat:

2 tablespoons vegetable oil or butter

Add and cook, stirring, without browning, until softened:

2 medium onions, chopped

Stir in:

3 pounds boneless lamb stew meat, cut into 1-inch
**   cubes, or 3 pounds lamb shoulder chops**
2 teaspoons fresh thyme or ³/₄ teaspoon dried thyme
Salt and black pepper

Stir in:

2 medium boiling potatoes, peeled and sliced
3 cups chicken stock or broth, dark stout, or water

Add:

4 medium potatoes, peeled and halved

Cover tightly and bake for 1 hour. Remove from the oven and stir in:

4 medium carrots, cut diagonally into slices

Cover, return to the oven, and bake until the meat is fork-tender, 45 to 60 minutes more. Skim the fat from the top of the stew, and season to taste with:

Salt and black pepper to taste

Serve sprinkled with:

Chopped parsley

CASSOULET

About 15 servings

With a thicker texture than a Pot-au-Feu, 36, this dish from the south of France always has one solid pivot—white beans. Cassoulet is usually made with fresh pork and sausage, but often with mutton and duck or partridge. Goose fat is a frequent component; as is an onion stuck with cloves. Vegetables vary seasonally. Garlic is essential. For this recipe, you almost need a routing sheet. If, however, you follow the directions, you can proceed with

the utmost self-confidence. The beans are soaked and then cooked with meats and other trimmings. The pork is first roasted for a while before the lamb joins it. Then the meats that have been cooking with the beans are taken from the bone and sliced before being returned to the beans. This way, the flavors unite in a single casserole and make a final triumphant appearance under a crust of golden crumbs.

Soak, 253:

1 pound dried flageolet, broad, or Great Northern
**   beans, rinsed and picked over**

Preheat the oven to 350°F. Pat dry and roast for about 2¹/₂ hours:

One 3-pound boneless pork loin or shoulder roast, 498

Meanwhile, heat in a large heavy skillet:

1 tablespoon oil

Add and brown on all sides:

One 3-pound boneless lamb shoulder roast, rolled and
**   tied, with the reserved bones**

Add the lamb and bones to the roasting pan with the pork and roast about 1¹/₂ hours longer. Meanwhile, place in a pot of cold water to cover and bring just to a boil:

1 ham shank
1 pound salt pork

Drain. Drain the beans, reserving the soaking liquid. Combine the liquid in a large pot with enough water to make 4 quarts. Bring to a boil and skim off the foam. Add the beans, the ham shank, salt pork, and:

1 Bouquet Garni, 960
3 garlic cloves
1 medium onion, studded with a few whole cloves

Simmer, covered, about 1¹/₂ hours. After the pork has roasted a total of 2¹/₂ hours, remove the lamb bones and reduce the oven temperature to 300°F. Pour over the meat:

Tomato Sauce, 562, or 2²/₃ cups tomato puree

and bake, covered, about 30 minutes more. After the beans have cooked 1¹/₂ hours, add:

8 ounces hard Italian sausage, kielbasa, or hard salami

Simmer about 1 hour longer, until the beans are tender but still intact. Remove both the pork roast and the lamb from the sauce, and reserve the sauce and drippings. Slice the meat. (Leave the oven on.) Drain the cooked beans, adding the juice to the tomato sauce. Trim as necessary and slice the ham, sausage, and salt pork into bite-sized pieces. Layer all the meats with the beans in a large casserole. Skim the fat from the combined sauce and stir into the casserole. Top with:

1 cup buttered dry bread crumbs, 960
2 tablespoons butter, cubed

Increase oven temperature to 350°F and bake about 1 to 1¹/₂ hours to blend the flavors; the crumbs should turn a golden color.

LAMB CURRY WITH TOMATO

4 servings

This fiery hot red curry has a rich, reduced tomato sauce. Eat it with a flatbread such as pita. For a milder dish, reduce the red pepper to ¼ teaspoon.

Drain, reserving the juice, and coarsely chop:

One 28-ounce can whole tomatoes

Heat in a Dutch oven over medium heat:

¼ cup vegetable oil

Add and cook, stirring, until softened and evenly golden brown, 5 to 7 minutes:

1 medium onion, thinly sliced

Increase the heat to medium-high, add, and cook, stirring, for 30 seconds:

2 teaspoons ground cumin

2 teaspoons ground coriander

1½ teaspoons minced garlic

1½ teaspoons grated peeled fresh ginger

1 teaspoon turmeric

½ teaspoon ground red pepper

Add ½ cup of the chopped tomatoes and ¼ cup of the tomato juice, along with:

1½ pounds boneless lamb stew meat, trimmed and cut into 1- to 1¼-inch cubes

Simmer, stirring occasionally, until the liquid is reduced and thickened slightly, 5 to 7 minutes. Stir in the remaining tomatoes and juice. Season with:

¾ teaspoon salt

Cover, reduce the heat to maintain a simmer, and cook until the lamb is tender, 45 to 60 minutes. Remove the meat with a slotted spoon and keep warm. Skim any fat from the surface of the liquid, increase the heat, and simmer briskly until the sauce is thickened. Return the meat to the sauce to heat through, and stir in:

(2 tablespoons chopped cilantro)

ABOUT PORK

Someone once observed that a pig resembles a saint, in that he is more honored after death than during his lifetime. American pork is not the same meat it used to be. In response to market demands, pork has turned from a fatty rich meat to a lean one, which raises problems for cooks—the fat used to keep pork moist as it cooked; now it can easily dry out, becoming tough and tasteless. Pork producers feed their livestock a diet of grain supplemented with protein, vitamins, and minerals and bring them to market at approximately 5 to 6 months old.

To get the most flavor from today's pork, we endorse cooking pork to ➤ a final internal temperature of 160°F for tender, juicy roasts and chops. The tendency to cook pork until gray and dry came from a fear of trichinosis, once associated with eating uncooked pork. ➤ But trichinosis is destroyed at 137°F—well below our recommended temperature. Cooked pork may be pink even when the meat is cooked to the correct internal temperature. A pink color is also often a result of ingredients added to the pork, or the cooking method used, such as smoking. ➤ Never taste raw pork, including bacon and sausage, in any form. After handling, wash your hands and any knife, utensil, or surface the pork may have touched.

The cuts of fresh pork sold in markets are standardized. The most popular are from the **loin**—the meat that runs along either side of the backbone, starting in the shoulder blade area and running all the way to the leg. Retail cuts from the loin include **rib** and **loin roasts** and **chops,** the **tenderloin,** and **back** and **country-style ribs.** Country-style ribs are cut from the shoulder blade end of the loin. Back ribs are cut from the center section of the loin and also from the shoulder end.

The **shoulder** is the large front arm and shoulder blade section. It is sometimes sold cut in half, yielding **shank** and **shoulder end** pieces of about equal weight. **Picnic shoulder roasts,** from the arm, are delicious roasted fresh, but they are most often smoked as hams. The upper part of the shoulder is known as the **pork butt** or **Boston butt.** A whole **Boston-style shoulder** is flavorful, meltingly tender, and very juicy from its higher proportion of fat. It is a great cut for braising, which keeps it moist and tender.

The **leg** is available fresh and is sometimes called **fresh ham.** The **whole bone-in leg** is also available **boneless and tied** as well as cut into **bone-in** and **boneless roasts** or **leg steaks. Spareribs** and **bacon** come from the underside of the pig.

Pork has no grades, because producers breed the animals with such consistency. When buying pork, ➤ look for meat that is moist and pink, not gray or red. Expect

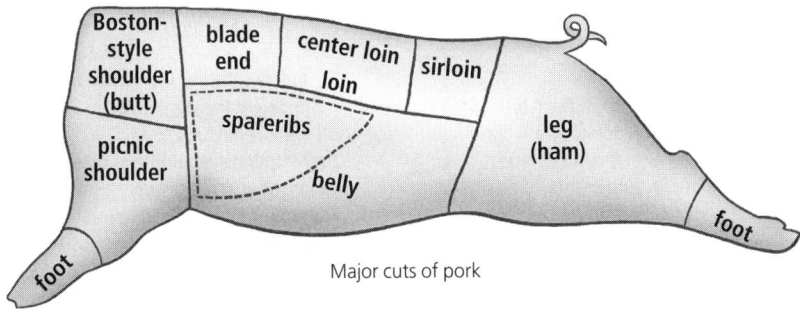

Major cuts of pork

little marbling, and choose cuts with a fine-grained texture. Any exterior fat should be smooth and white. It will keep well wrapped in plastic for 2 to 4 days in the refrigerator.

Dry-heat cooking methods, such as roasting, grilling, sautéing, panfrying, and stir-frying are reserved for naturally tender cuts from the loin and tenderloin. For best results, cook these cuts to medium, with a faint blush of pink. Tougher shoulder and leg cuts are cooked to tenderness by the slow, moist heat of braising or stewing—although they can be slow-roasted in the oven if basted frequently. Pork is also made moist and delicious by brining, 421.

Try seasoning with rubs, 587, and marinades, 584. Pork is quite tasty with fruit, including apples, plums, cherries, and, especially for ham, peaches or pineapple.

BONELESS PORK ROAST

6 to 8 servings

Boneless pork loin is best slow-roasted, but it is difficult to give exact cooking times, since pork loins vary in diameter. In general, a 3-pound boneless pork loin should take 1¼ to 1½ hours total cooking time. If the roast is very small, less than 2 inches in diameter, check the internal temperature after it has cooked at 250°F for 30 minutes. Otherwise, begin checking at 45 minutes. For the best results, test for doneness with a thermometer. After roasting, make a quick pan sauce by adding stock or wine to the pan, or simply serve the meat with the degreased pan juices.

Preheat the oven to 500°F. Mix together:

   1 tablespoon olive oil
   1 tablespoon dried thyme, sage, oregano, or rosemary
   1 teaspoon salt
   ½ teaspoon black pepper

Rub evenly over the entire surface of:

   1 boneless center-cut pork loin roast (about 3 pounds)

If desired, dredge in:

   (Seasoned Flour, 962)

Place the meat on a rack in a roasting pan. Roast for 10 minutes. Reduce the oven to 250°F and roast until a thermometer inserted in the thickest part of the meat registers 150° to 155°F, 1 to 1½ hours (the temperature will continue to rise about 5 to 10 degrees out of the oven). Remove to a cutting board, cover loosely with aluminum foil, and let stand for 10 minutes. To make the pan gravy, skim off the fat from the pan juices. If desired, place the pan over medium-high heat and add:

   (½ to 1 cup chicken stock or broth or dry white wine)

to make about 1 cup liquid. Boil, scraping up any browned bits, until slightly thickened. Cut the meat into ¼- to ½-inch slices and spoon the pan juices or pan sauce over.

BONE-IN PORK LOIN ROAST

6 servings

Pork loin roasted on the bone has more flavor than a boneless loin but needs to cook slightly longer. For easy carving, have the butcher cut through the backbone. **Rack of pork,** a rib roast on the bone with the chine bone completely removed, is also available. You can substitute any of the rubs or seasoning mixtures for boneless pork loin roast, 587–588, for the one given here.

Preheat the oven to 450°F. Rub:

   1 bone-in center-cut pork loin roast (about 5 pounds)

all over with:

   (Peppery Dry Rub, 587)

Place the roast in a roasting pan (there is no need for a roasting rack, because the roast rests on the backbone). Roast the pork for 15 minutes, then reduce the temperature to 250°F and cook until a thermometer inserted in the thickest part of the meat registers 155°F, about 1 to 1¼ hours more. Remove the roast to a cutting board, cover loosely with aluminum foil, and let stand for 15 minutes. Skim the fat off the pan juices. If desired, add stock to the pan juices and boil to thicken as in Boneless Pork Roast, above. Slice the roast and serve with the pan juices or pan sauce.

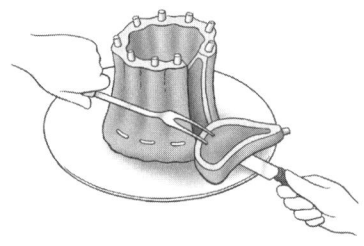

Carving crown roast of pork

CROWN ROAST OF PORK

12 to 15 servings

Most butchers will prepare a crown roast for you from two racks, but make sure the roasts used are of uniform size so that it cooks evenly. Crown roasts are usually cooked stuffed, but sometimes we prefer to bake the stuffing separately in a casserole.

Prepare and place in greased casserole:

   Basic Bread Stuffing, 532, Bread Stuffing with
      Sausage and Apples, 533, Bread Stuffing with
      Toasted Nuts or Chestnuts and Dried Fruit, 533,
      or Sweet Potato and Apple Stuffing, 538

Preheat the oven to 350°F. Mix together:

   2 tablespoons vegetable or olive oil
   4 teaspoons dried thyme
   4 teaspoons ground allspice
   2 teaspoons salt
   1 teaspoon black pepper

Rub the mixture all over the surface of:

1 crown roast of pork (8 to 10 pounds)

Place in a roasting pan and roast for 15 minutes. Reduce the oven temperature to 250°F and roast until a thermometer inserted in the thickest part of the meat registers 155°F, 2 to 3 hours (the temperature will continue to rise 5 degrees out of the oven). After the pork has roasted for 1½ hours, fill the center with the stuffing if desired, or place the stuffing in a separate buttered baking dish. Bake until heated through. Remove the finished roast to a cutting board, cover loosely with aluminum foil, and let stand for 15 minutes. Skim the fat off the pan juices and add to the roasting pan:

½ cup Madeira or dry white wine

Bring to a simmer, scraping up the browned bits on the bottom of the pan. Remove to a saucepan and add:

1½ cups chicken stock or broth

Bring to a boil, then boil to concentrate the flavor if the juices taste thin and weak. If you want to thicken the juices to make gravy, reduce the heat and add the simmering juices, whisking until smooth:

(2 tablespoons cornstarch, dissolved in 2 tablespoons cold water)

Bring to a boil to thicken, and adjust the seasoning. Serve the sauce with the roast, cut into chops, and the stuffing.

PORK ORLOFF COCKAIGNE

6 to 8 servings

I fell in love with Veal Orloff while a student at Le Cordon Bleu in Paris. Back in Cincinnati, I had a difficult time finding a good veal roast and improvised on a classic with pork roast. Substituting pork for the veal makes a wonderful dish that is a standout on its own.

Prepare:

Boneless Pork Roast, 498

While the loin is in the oven, prepare:

1½ recipes Duxelles, 284

When the roast is done, spread a thin layer of duxelles on a serving platter. Slice the roast. Spread the pork slices with duxelles and reassemble the roast on the platter. Finish with a line of duxelles down the top of the roast. Garnish with:

Chopped parsley or chopped watercress

Serve with:

Boiled New Potatoes, 295

BONELESS ROAST PORK FLORENTINE

6 to 8 servings

Simple but elegant, this Italian classic is equally delicious served warm or cold.

Preheat the oven to 500°F. Mix together:

4 large garlic cloves, crushed
4 teaspoons chopped rosemary
(1 teaspoon fennel seeds, crushed)
½ teaspoon salt
½ teaspoon black pepper

Make several deep incisions in:

1 boneless center-cut pork loin roast (about 3 pounds)

Stuff the incisions with the garlic mixture, and spread any remaining mixture over the surface of the meat. Rub with:

1 to 2 tablespoons olive oil

Place the meat on a rack in a roasting pan and roast for 10 minutes. Reduce the oven temperature to 250°F and roast until a thermometer inserted in the thickest part of the meat registers 155°F, 1 to 1½ hours. Remove the roast to a cutting board, cover loosely with aluminum foil, and let stand for 10 minutes. Skim the fat from the pan juices. Slice the meat and serve with the pan juices.

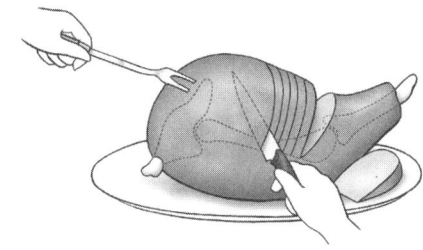

Carving a whole ham

ROAST FRESH HAM OR LEG OF PORK

15 to 20 servings

A whole pork leg, also known as fresh uncured ham, is perfect for feeding a large crowd and great for holidays. Cooking times are approximate because the weight of fresh hams is variable. If your fresh ham weighs more than 20 pounds, increase the cooking time accordingly. Plan on about 1 pound per person, less if there are numerous side dishes. Ask your butcher to remove most of the skin, leaving that around the shank. Score the fat and meat deeply and rub with seasonings to obtain a crisp, savory crust. Preheat the oven to 425°F. If the butcher has not done so, remove the skin up to but not including the shank from:

1 bone-in pork leg/fresh ham (15 to 20 pounds)

Score the fat and meat 1 to 1½ inches deep in a diamond pattern, 1 to 1½ inches apart. Mix together:

2 tablespoons olive or vegetable oil
1 tablespoon salt
2 teaspoons dried sage, thyme, savory, oregano, or crumbled rosemary
2 teaspoons black pepper

Rub this mixture over the entire surface of the pork. Scatter in a large roasting pan:

2 large onions, halved
4 carrots, quartered
4 celery ribs, quartered
1 bay leaf

Place the pork on the bed of vegetables. Roast for 1½ hours. Pour over the meat:

2 cups dry white wine

Roast, basting every 20 to 30 minutes and adding water if

necessary so the pan doesn't scorch, until a thermometer inserted in the thickest part of the meat registers 150° to 155°F (the temperature will continue to rise 5 to 10 degrees out of the oven) for well-done. Remove the ham to a large platter, cover loosely with aluminum foil, and let stand for 30 to 60 minutes. Pour off the fat from the pan. Make:

> Meat Pan Gravy, 546

To carve the meat, cut it into slices starting at the shank end, keeping the knife perpendicular to the bone. Then make one long slice with your knife along the bone to separate the slices from the leg. Arrange the slices on a platter and serve with the pan juices or gravy, if desired.

PULLED PORK

Serves 12

In many parts of the country, this is what is meant by barbecue. Pulled pork is pork shoulder cooked until it is tender enough to be shredded with a fork. After being pulled apart, it can be mixed with a sauce and served on a bun with Coleslaw, 161.

Trim the excess fat from:

> 1 boneless Boston butt or pork shoulder blade roast
> (about 4 pounds)

Rub with:

> Southern Barbecue Dry Rub, 587

The meat can be cooked at once, or wrapped in 2 layers of aluminum foil and refrigerated for up to 24 hours. Position a rack in the center of the oven. Preheat the oven to 325°F. Heat a large Dutch oven or other heavy ovenproof pot large to hold the meat over medium heat. Add and heat:

> 2 tablespoons lard or vegetable oil

Add the meat and brown well on all sides. Cover the pot tightly with a lid or foil, place in the oven, and bake until the meat is tender enough to be shredded with a fork, 3 to 3½ hours. Skim the fat from the pan juices. Shred the meat with a fork and mix with the pan juices. Stir in:

> 1½ to 2 cups barbecue sauce, 586–587

ROAST SUCKLING PIG

8 to 12 servings

Our editor is always roasting pigs in a pit in her Manhattan backyard. This is her favorite recipe. A 15- to 20-pound pig, while large, yields just enough meat for 8 to 12 people. The meat will melt in your mouth.

Order a few days ahead and have the butcher prepare the pig for you by cleaning it well and removing all organs, including the kidneys, eyeballs, and lower lids. A 20-inch roasting pan is ideal. Do not use a disposable aluminum pan, as it will collapse. The day before or just before roasting, prepare 12 cups of one of the following stuffings:

> 1½ recipes Basic Bread Stuffing, 532, 1 recipe Bread
> Stuffing with Toasted Nuts or Chestnuts and Dried
> Fruit, 533, 1½ recipes Sweet Potato and Apple
> Stuffing, 538, or 3 recipes Couscous Stuffing with
> Dried Apricots and Pistachios, 539

Position a rack in the lowest part of the oven. Preheat the oven to 450°F. Generously oil a 20-inch-long roasting pan. If the pan is smaller (no smaller than 17 inches), have ready a loaf pan and lots of heavy-duty aluminum foil.

Place in the sink:

> 1 suckling pig (15 to 20 pounds)

Check to make sure that no bristles or hairs remain; if any do, shave them off with a razor blade or singe them with a flame. Rinse the pig well inside and out and pat dry. On a work surface, turn the pig on its back and fill the cavity loosely with the stuffing. Truss with string or skewers about 2 inches apart. Skewer legs into position, pulling forelegs forward and bending hindlegs into a crouching stance. Turn the pig over. Slash the skin on either side of the backbone in long parallel diagonal cuts about 2 inches apart, to prevent the skin from swelling and bursting during cooking and to release the fat and allow it to baste the meat. Avoid cutting below the layer of fat into the meat. Put a block of wood or ball of aluminum foil in its mouth to hold it open. Mix together and rub over the entire pig:

> ½ cup olive oil
> 2 tablespoons salt
> 1 tablespoon black pepper

Place the pig in the roasting pan, resting it on its haunches and keeping it upright. If your pan is too small, arrange the pig diagonally in the pan and prop its head up with the loaf pan under its chin. Slip heavy-duty aluminum foil extending out from the roasting pan under the head and loaf pan to catch the juices and let them flow back into the pan during cooking. If the pig has a tendency to lean, prop it up with balls of aluminum foil. Cover the ears and tail with pieces of foil. If desired, pry open the pig's mouth with a screwdriver and prop open with a ball of aluminum foil or a wooden block. Place the pig in the oven, uncovered, and roast for 30 minutes. Reduce the oven temperature to 350°F, and pour into the roasting pan:

> 3 cups dry white wine

Baste the pig all over with:

> ½ cup olive oil

Roast until a meat thermometer inserted in the thickest part of the rump reads 150° to 155°F, 2 to 2½ hours more (the temperature will continue to rise 5 to 10 degrees out of the oven). Baste the pig every 20 minutes with the wine and pan juices. Place the pig on a platter and let stand for 30 to 60 minutes. Skim off the fat from the pan juices. Place the roasting pan over medium-high heat and add:

> 2 cups chicken stock or broth

Bring to a simmer, stirring to scrape up the browned bits on the bottom of the pan. Serve with the pan juices or pour the juices into a saucepan and make a gravy. Mix together and whisk into the simmering juices:

> ¼ cup cornstarch
> 3 tablespoons cold water

Bring to a boil, whisking, to thicken, and cook down until it is flavorful. Season with:

Salt and black pepper to taste

Remove the foil from the pig's ears and tail. Gently roll it on its side and remove the string and/or skewers. Return the pig to its right-side-up position. Remove the foil ball or wooden block, if using, and place in the pig's mouth:

(1 apple, lemon, or lime)

and in the eyes:

(Prunes, grapes)

Garnish the platter with:

A bed of watercress or other greens, Apples Stuffed with Sausages, 217, or Tomatoes Provençal, 312

After presenting the pig at the table, carve it by removing the forelegs and hindquarters and arranging these on a platter. Cut the skin into squares. Remove the loin meat and cut into slices. Separate ribs. Arrange the slices and skin on the platter and let the guests pick at the rest. Pass platter with the gravy.

ABOUT BRAISING AND STEWING PORK

Braising and stewing are moist-heat cooking methods used for less tender cuts of pork from the shoulder and leg. The cuts from either end of the loin—the blade end or the sirloin end—are best cubed and stewed. Like most braised and stewed dishes, pork prepared this way often tastes better the next day. For more information on braising and stewing, see Pot-Roasting, Stewing, and Braising Meat, 466.

PORK BRAISED IN MILK

6 servings

You can also use the Boston butt, shoulder, or sirloin roast. Use boneless or bone-in, but with bone-in pork, the sauce will have enormous flavor.

Heat in a Dutch oven over medium heat:

1 tablespoon butter

Add:

One 2^1/$_2$-pound boneless pork loin or 3-pound bone-in pork loin roast, or other cut

Brown the meat evenly on all sides, about 10 minutes total. If the butter browns too much, reduce the heat. Add:

1 cup milk

Bring to a boil, then reduce the heat to low, cover the pot tightly, and simmer for 1^1/$_2$ to 2 hours more, turning the meat occasionally, until it is very tender when pierced with the tip of a sharp knife. Remove the meat to a cutting board and let stand. Spoon off the fat from the surface of the sauce and bring to a boil. Cook until browned and thickened slightly, about 5 to 10 minutes. To thin the sauce, stir in a couple of tablespoons of water. Season with:

Salt and black pepper to taste

Slice the meat and arrange on a platter. Season with salt and pepper, spoon the sauce over the meat with all the clusters of milk, and serve.

BRAISED PORK WITH SAUERKRAUT

8 servings

The addition of fresh cabbage to the traditional pairing of pork and sauerkraut gives this dish another dimension of flavor.

Mix together:

2 teaspoons sweet paprika

1 teaspoon salt

1 teaspoon black pepper

^{1}/$_2$ teaspoon dried sage

^{1}/$_2$ teaspoon dried thyme

^{1}/$_4$ teaspoon dry mustard

Pat dry and rub all over with the spice mix:

1 pork shoulder, Boston, butt, or blade roast (4 pounds), excess fat trimmed

Marinate the meat for 2 to 24 hours in the refrigerator. Preheat the oven to 325°F. Heat in a large Dutch oven over medium heat:

2 tablespoons olive oil or bacon fat

Add the meat and brown on all sides. Remove to a plate. Pour off all but 2 tablespoons of fat from the pot and add:

4 cups shredded cabbage

2 cups thinly sliced onions

^{1}/$_2$ cup diced carrots

^{1}/$_2$ cup thinly sliced leeks, white part only

Cover the pan and cook, stirring occasionally, until the vegetables are softened and the cabbage is wilted, about 10 minutes. Add:

1 tablespoon minced garlic

Cook for 1 minute more. Add:

1 pound sauerkraut, rinsed and drained

1 cup chicken stock or broth

One 12-ounce bottle dark beer

1 teaspoon caraway seeds

1 teaspoon dried savory

2 bay leaves

Bring to a boil. Return the meat to the pot, nestling it into the cabbage mixture, and cover the pot. Braise in the oven for 2 hours. Check the meat; it should be fork-tender. If not, cook for 30 to 60 minutes more. Remove the meat from the pot and remove the bay leaves. Skim off any fat from the pan juices. Slice and serve with the vegetables and juices.

LATIN ROASTED PICNIC SHOULDER

12 to 15 servings

The picnic shoulder is among the tastiest of pork roasts. Here it is seasoned with oregano and garlic. Brushing it with water during roasting makes the crisp, brittle skin tender enough to eat.

Mash to a paste using a mortar and pestle or very finely chop with a knife:

12 large garlic cloves

2 tablespoons salt

Remove to a small bowl and stir in:

2 tablespoons dried oregano

1 tablespoon black pepper

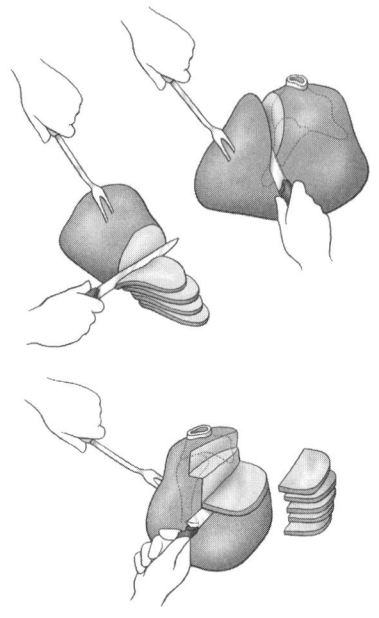

Carving a picnic shoulder

Moisten with:

1 to 2 tablespoons red wine vinegar

With a paring knife, cut deep slits into the exposed fleshy ends of:

1 pork picnic shoulder (about 7 pounds)

Push some of the paste into the pockets with your fingers. Loosen the skin in several places and spread the rest of the paste underneath the skin and then over the surface of the roast where there is no skin. Wrap the roast in foil and refrigerate for 25 to 48 hours. Preheat the oven to 325°F. Unwrap the roast and place on a rack in a roasting pan. Roast to an internal temperature of 185°F, about 4 to 4½ hours, brushing the skin every 15 to 20 minutes with cold water to keep it soft. Remove the roast to a cutting board, cover loosely with aluminum foil, and let stand for 20 minutes. Meanwhile, skim off the fat from the pan juices and add:

1 cup chicken stock or broth ½ cup stock or broth plus ½ cup dry white wine

Bring to a boil, scraping up the browned bits on the bottom of the pan, and boil for 2 to 3 minutes to dissolve the roasting particles. Remove the skin from the meat and cut it into strips or squares. Slice the meat, arrange on a platter, and pour the sauce over it. Arrange the skin around the meat and serve.

PORK ADOBO

6 servings

Adobo is a marinade of chile peppers, paprika, and vinegar commonly used with pork. This is a style of adobo popular in New Mexico; it can also be made with beef. In the Southwest, this stew would be served with rice and sopapillas, 608, but flour or corn tortillas can be substituted.

Cover with boiling water in a small bowl:

4 dried ancho or 6 dried New Mexico (red Anaheim) chile peppers

Let soak for 20 minutes. Drain the peppers, reserving the water. Slit the peppers open and discard the stems and seeds. Put the peppers and ¼ cup of the soaking liquid in a food processor or blender. Add:

⅓ cup cider vinegar

4 garlic cloves, peeled

1 teaspoon salt

1 teaspoon cumin seeds

½ teaspoon dried oregano

½ teaspoon black pepper

¼ teaspoon ground coriander

Pinch of ground cinnamon

Process to a smooth paste. Pour the paste into a large bowl and add:

3 pounds Boston-style pork shoulder or butt, boned, trimmed, and cut into 2-inch cubes, 4 pounds country-style ribs, trimmed, or 3½ pounds pork shoulder blade steaks

Toss to coat the meat with the marinade. Cover and refrigerate for at least 12 hours, or up to 3 days, turning the meat occasionally. Heat in a large Dutch oven over medium heat:

2 tablespoons vegetable oil

Add and cook, stirring often, until softened but not browned, about 5 minutes:

1 cup chopped onions

Add the pork, with all the marinade, along with:

1½ cups peeled, seeded, 311, chopped tomatoes

Reduce the heat, cover, and simmer until the pork is tender, 1½ to 2 hours. Remove the meat to a serving bowl and keep warm. Spoon off the fat from the sauce, then boil the sauce over high heat to thicken. Taste and adjust the seasonings. Pour the sauce over the meat and stir to coat it.

ABOUT PORK TENDERLOIN

Pork tenderloin was traditionally sold only as part of a bone-in loin roast beside the backbone. Now it is widely available as a separate cut. Tenderloin is very low in fat—nearly as low as skinless chicken breasts—and very tender, with good flavor. It cooks quickly and is best suited to pan-frying, pan-roasting, broiling, grilling, sautéing, and deep-frying. It can also be oven-roasted; because the cut lacks fat, the best temperature is 500°F. Lower temperatures dry out the meat before it is cooked through and browned.

Tenderloin can be cooked whole or cut into slices and pounded thin into cutlets. Cut these slices from the thicker end of the tenderloin and save the narrow end for pan frying or pan-broiling in one piece. Tenderloin is also perfect cut into cubes or strips for kebabs, satays, or stir-fries. Butterfly the tenderloin, either whole or cut into pieces (see Country-Fried Pork Tenderloin with Gravy, below), for even quicker cooking. Because tenderloin is so lean, take care not to overcook it—it should always remain juicy with a pale pink color. Cook a whole one as you would a loin roast, to an internal temperature of 150° to 155°F, let stand for a few minutes, and serve. Sliced or cut-up tenderloin cooks in just a few minutes. Tenderloins are generally sold prepackaged with 2 in each package. ➤ The best tenderloins are the smaller ones, about 8 to 12 ounces each, generally enough for 2 to 3 servings.

PAN-ROASTED PORK TENDERLOIN

4 servings

A savory fruit sauce makes a fine accompaniment.
Pat dry:

2 pork tenderloins (8 to 12 ounces each)

Season with:

Salt and black pepper

Heat in a large skillet over high heat:

1¹/₂ teaspoons butter
1¹/₂ teaspoons olive oil

Brown the pork well on all sides. Reduce the heat to medium and cook, turning once or twice, until thermometer inserted in the thickest part of the meat reads 155°F (the temperature will continue to rise 5 to 10 degrees off the heat). Remove to a plate, cover loosely with aluminum foil, and let stand for 5 to 10 minutes before slicing. If desired, pour off all the fat from the skillet, place over medium-high heat, and make:

(Herb Pan Sauce, 547; Orange and Ginger Sauce, 549;
or Pan Sauce with Leeks, Orange, and Rosemary,
548)

Bring to a boil, scraping up any browned bits from the bottom. Slice, spoon the sauce over the tenderloin, and serve.

COUNTRY-FRIED PORK TENDERLOIN WITH GRAVY

12 pieces

This spicy pork dish is sometimes served at breakfast, but also makes a tasty sandwich or main course.
Combine in a small bowl:

1 tablespoon sweet paprika
1¹/₂ teaspoons salt
1¹/₂ teaspoons black pepper
¹/₂ teaspoon garlic powder
¹/₂ teaspoon dried sage
¹/₂ teaspoon dried oregano
¹/₂ teaspoon dry mustard
¹/₂ teaspoon ground red pepper

Pat dry:

2 pork tenderloins (about 12 ounces each), cut into
6 pieces each

Butterfly each piece by making a lengthwise cut through one side of the meat, holding the knife parallel to the work surface, without cutting all the way through the meat. Leave ¹/₂-inch of the meat intact on the opposite side to form a hinge. Fold each piece open like a book and flatten it with your hand. Rub with the spice mixture and marinate for 30 to 60 minutes in the refrigerator. Heat in a large skillet over medium-high heat:

¹/₄ inch vegetable oil

Dredge the tenderloin pieces in:

¹/₂ cup all-purpose flour

Shake off the excess. Add to the skillet in batches and fry until browned on one side, 3 to 4 minutes. Turn over and fry on the other side for 3 to 4 minutes. Remove the pork to a platter and cover to keep warm. For the gravy, pour off all but 2 tablespoons of the fat from the pan. Add:

1 cup milk

Heat just to a boil, scraping up any browned bits on the bottom of the pan. Pour the gravy over the pork. Serve with:

Biscuits, 637–640

for breakfast, or on soft rolls for lunch.

GRILLED PORK TENDERLOIN

4 servings

Grill tenderloin whole or in medallions, or cut into large cubes for kebabs; anything smaller dries out too quickly. The sauce for grilled tenderloin can be a barbecue sauce, a flavored butter, or a dry rub, condiment, dipping sauce, vinaigrette, glaze, or salsa. See 542 for ideas.
Prepare a medium-hot grill fire. Pat dry:

2 pork tenderloins, whole or cut into
1-inch-thick medallions

Rub with:

1 tablespoon olive or vegetable oil

Season with:

Salt and black pepper

Grill whole tenderloins for 8 to 10 minutes on each side, or until a thermometer inserted in the thickest part of the meat reads 155°F (the temperature will continue to rise 5 to 10 degrees off the grill); let stand, loosely covered with aluminum foil, for 5 to 10 minutes before slicing. Medallions will take about 2 minutes on each side.

ABOUT PORK CHOPS, STEAKS, AND CUTLETS

Although the terms "chops," "steaks," and "cutlets" are somewhat interchangeable when referring to pork, you can most often expect a **chop** to be a single-serving, thick cut of meat from the pork loin with the bone in—but these are also sold boneless. **Steak** is used a bit more loosely to refer to any thick slice of meat, and **cutlets** are thinner boneless cuts from the loin or leg. **Pork chops** cut from the loin have a variety of names. Starting at the shoulder end are pork **loin blade chops** (also called **blade steaks**). Next, from the center section, come **rib chops** and **loin chops,** the latter containing the tenderloin and resembling a small T-bone or porterhouse beef steak. The most tender pork chops are cut from the **center** section of the pork loin; these are sold in varying thicknesses. After the center section come the **sirloin chops,** which are larger and sometimes cut thin for cutlets. Pork steaks can be cut from the leg, shoulder, or loin. The leg offers **tip, top, bottom,** and **eye steaks** from different muscles and, for a larger steak, a whole crosswise **center slice.**

Pork chops from the loin are best cooked by dry-heat methods—panfrying, pan-broiling, sautéing, or grilling. Braising works for blade and sirloin chops and for shoulder and leg steaks, but not for classic pork loin chops, which can easily become overcooked and tough when cooked in liquid. Look for pork loin chops that are about 1 inch thick. For pork chops for stuffing, we suggest $1\frac{1}{2}$ to 2 inches, and for cutlets, $\frac{1}{4}$ to $\frac{1}{2}$ inch thick. We also sometimes find **pork loin medallions,** which are slices of boneless center loin cut any thickness. Sauté quickly if thin or cook slowly, covering and reducing the heat after browning, if 1 inch or thicker. Panfry or sauté pork chops and medallions, if you want a sauce, for pan sauces are easily put together right in the skillet, dissolving the caramelized juices into the sauce, after the meat has cooked. Or you can prepare a sauce ahead and have it ready to reheat. See 542 for sauce and gravy ideas.

PORK CHOPS
4 servings
I. SAUTÉED PORK CHOPS
Pat dry:
    4 center-cut pork loin chops (bone-in or boneless),
        1 inch thick
Season with:
    Salt and black pepper
Heat in a large skillet over high heat:
    $1\frac{1}{2}$ teaspoons butter
    $1\frac{1}{2}$ teaspoons olive or vegetable oil
Add the chops and brown for 1 minute on each side. Reduce the heat to low, cover the pan, and cook the chops on each side for 5 minutes if bone-in, 4 minutes if boneless. They should be browned on the outside but slightly pink in the center. Remove to a warmed platter or plates. Increase the heat to high and boil down the pan juices. If desired, make a pan sauce or reheat a prepared sauce such as **Sauce Marchand de Vin, 555,** in the juices.

II. BAKED PORK CHOPS
Recommended for thick chops.
Preheat the oven to 350°F. Pat dry:
    4 pork chops (bone-in or boneless)
Season with:
    Salt and black pepper
After searing as above, bake, covered, about 1 hour. During the last half hour, you may add one of the following and sprinkle over the chops:
    (3 tablespoons minced scallions and celery)
    (1 minced garlic clove)
    ($1\frac{1}{2}$-inch piece peeled, minced, and ginger, mashed in
        1 tablespoon vinegar)
    (3 orange slices or $\frac{1}{2}$ cup orange juice)

III. GRILLED PORK CHOPS
Try a relish or salsa such as Fruit Salsa, 572, Red Onion Marmalade, 567, or Mojo, 566.
Prepare a medium-hot grill fire. Pat dry:
    4 center-cut pork loin chops (bone-in or boneless),
        $\frac{3}{4}$ to $1\frac{1}{2}$ inches thick
Rub with:
    2 tablespoons olive or vegetable oil
Season with:
    Salt and black pepper
Grill over hot coals for 5 to 8 minutes each side for bone-in, or 4 to 6 minutes on each side for boneless, depending on thickness.

BREADED PORK CHOPS OR CUTLETS
4 servings
Thin pork chops or thin slices of pork loin make tender, juicy breaded chops. Add other herbs or spices to the bread crumbs for more flavor.
Prepare **Breaded Veal Cutlets, 487,** substituting for the veal:
    4 pork loin chops or thin slices pork loin

BRAISED STUFFED PORK CHOPS COCKAIGNE
6 servings
Preheat the oven to 350°F. Cut from the bone:
    6 pork rib chops, about $1\frac{1}{2}$ inches thick
Trim off the excess fat, and cut a large gash or pocket in one side of each chop. Pat dry, and stuff with:
    Italian Bread Stuffing, 533
Skewer closed with toothpicks. Sear the chops in a hot skillet, and place in a lidded baking dish with:
    Milk or chicken stock or broth, about $\frac{1}{4}$ inch deep
Cover and bake about 1 hour and 15 minutes, or until tender. Prepare:
    Meat Pan Gravy, 546
Or serve with:
    Cranberry Sauce, 221

SWEET-AND-SOUR PORK
6 servings
Cut into 2-inch-long $\frac{1}{2}$-inch-thick strips:
    2 pounds lean boneless pork shoulder or loin
In a wok or large skillet over medium-high heat, brown the meat in:
    2 tablespoons vegetable oil
Remove meat and drain on paper towels. Add and cook, stirring, until the sauce is slightly thickened and clear:
    1 cup pineapple juice
    $\frac{1}{2}$ cup water or chicken stock or broth
    $\frac{1}{2}$ cup cider vinegar
    $\frac{1}{4}$ cup packed dark brown sugar
    2 tablespoons cornstarch
    2 tablespoons soy sauce
    2 teaspoons Worcestershire sauce
Add the meat, reduce the heat, and simmer, covered, about 1 hour, or until tender. Add:

1½ cups pineapple chunks
1 small green bell pepper, thinly sliced
(¼ cup sliced onion)

Cook, uncovered, about 10 minutes. Serve over:

Cooked rice

ABOUT PORK RIBS

Spareribs come from the side or underbelly of the pig. They have the least amount of meat of the three types but are very flavorful; plan on 1 pound of spareribs per person. (St. Louis–style ribs are further trimmed spareribs with the breastbone removed.) Back ribs are cut from the loin section, or the back, of the pig, and are sometimes called **loin back ribs.** These are meatier than spareribs and not as fatty. **Baby back ribs** are simply a narrower slab of back ribs cut from the rib end; they are sometimes called **riblets.** A whole rack of back ribs weighs between 1½ and 1¾ pounds; count on 1 pound of back ribs per person. **Country-style ribs** are the meatiest of all ribs, with much less bone than the other types; they are even sometimes sold boneless. Like back ribs, they are cut from the loin section of the pig. Figure on 8 to 12 ounces of country-style ribs per person.

Ribs can be baked, grilled, or braised. The two most important factors in cooking ribs well are time—plenty of it—and temperature—very low. Baked ribs are best cooked at 300° to 325°F. On the grill, ribs fare best over indirect heat, with the coals pushed to the sides. Ribs are considered done when you can just loosen or wiggle the bone from the meat with little effort and the meat is very tender. Ribs take seasonings well and are delicious sauced or covered with a spice rub. If using a sauce when grilling, baste only during the last 30 minutes of cooking; most sauces contain some type of sugar or sweetener and tend to burn. Ribs sauced in the gentler heat of the oven can be brushed from the beginning of cooking.

BARBECUED SPARERIBS

6 servings

I. Outdoors

Pat dry:

2 sides pork spareribs (about 6 pounds)

Rub both sides with:

⅔ cup Southern Barbecue Dry Rub, 587

Refrigerate for 1 to 2 hours, or, for a stronger flavor, wrap in plastic and refrigerate for 12 to 24 hours. Prepare a large charcoal fire. When the coals are covered with a light ash, push them to one side of the grill. Open the bottom vents of the grill completely. Wrap 2 cups hickory smoking chips in aluminum foil, poke small holes in the foil with a fork, and lay the package on the coals. Arrange the rib slabs side by side on the grill rack as far from the charcoal as possible and cover with the lid, leaving the top vent two-thirds open. Cook the ribs for 2 to 2½ hours, turning them every 30 minutes. If the fire threatens to die out, add a few more briquettes as far away from the ribs as possi-

ble. The ribs are done when the bones begin to pull away from the meat and feel loose when twisted. Immediately wrap the ribs in aluminum foil and let stand for 15 minutes. If you wish, swab the ribs lightly and/or pass with:

Barbecue Sauce, 586–587

II. Indoors

Position a rack in the center of the oven. Preheat the oven to 350°F. Prepare:

Barbecued Spareribs, above

Roast the ribs for 45 minutes, then turn them meat side up and roast until the ribs are nicely browned and very tender, 45 to 60 minutes more. Remove from the oven and let stand for 15 minutes. Slice between the bones and serve as above.

BABY BACK RIBS

4 servings

Pat dry:

2 racks baby back pork ribs (4 pounds)

Rub with:

Southern Barbecue Dry Rub, 587, Peppery Dry Rub, 587, Coffee Spice Rub, 588, Sweet Spice Rub, 588

Place in a roasting pan and pour in:

One 12-ounce bottle beer

Cover and marinate, refrigerated, 8 hours, or overnight. Prepare:

A barbecue sauce or mop, 586–587

Preheat the oven to 350°F. Cover the ribs with foil and bake for 1½ hours. To finish the ribs in the oven, reduce the temperature to 300°F, drain the fat from the pan, and continue baking, basting every 10 to 15 minutes with the sauce or mop until tender, about 1 hour. To finish them on the grill, prepare a medium-hot grill fire. Baste the ribs with the sauce, then place meaty side up on the grill, close the lid, and grill until tender, 30 to 45 minutes, basting every 10 to 15 minutes.

COUNTRY-STYLE RIBS
BAKED IN BARBECUE SAUCE

6 to 8 servings

After 4 hours of cooking, these ribs become fall-apart tender and deeply infused with the flavor of the sauce.

Position a rack in the center of the oven. Preheat the oven to 300°F. Arrange in a large baking dish:

4 pounds country-style ribs

Whisk together in a bowl:

1½ cups Barbecue Sauce, 586–587, or Ray's Mustard Barbecue Sauce, 586

1 cup orange juice

Pour the sauce over the ribs and turn them to coat. Cover with aluminum foil and bake for 3 hours. Uncover, increase the oven temperature to 350°F, and bake the ribs for 1 more hour, turning them once after 30 minutes. Remove the ribs to a platter and let stand for 15 minutes. Spoon off the fat from the sauce and serve the ribs with the sauce.

ABOUT DESALTING HAM AND OTHER CURED MEAT

Today, because of the prevalence of refrigeration, **ham** and **Canadian bacon, tongue, corned beef, pastrami,** and **salt pork** are subjected to much weaker brining than formerly. But all of these salted meats, while relished for their pungent flavors are, like brined vegetables, less valuable nutritionally than when they are fresh. If the meat has been heavily pickled, or aged, like country hams, below, be sure to soak 12 hours, allowing 1 quart of water to 1 pound of cured meat. Or ➤ blanch, 1054, before cooking. After blanching, put the meat into rapidly boiling water, bring to boil again, and ➤ at once reduce heat to a simmer. Cook ➤ uncovered until tender. Time indications are noted in the individual recipes.

ABOUT HAM

Someone once defined eternity as a ham and two people. The definition probably dates from the days when the term ham applied only to the small mountain of meat we now call a **whole ham,** which is technically the entire back leg portion of the hog, cured or smoked. **Fresh ham** is a hind leg that has not been smoked or cured. It is treated as a pork roast. Today the term "ham" is used for a variety of pork cuts from the back leg or the front shoulder that have been processed through salt-curing and sometimes smoking and aging.

Hams are usually labeled "partially cooked" or "fully cooked." Whichever you buy, ➤ follow the instructions on the label scrupulously. Partially cooked hams—sometimes labeled "cook before eating"—need to be roasted to an internal temperature of 160°F. Fully cooked hams—also called "ready to eat" or "ready to serve"—can be eaten as is, with no further preparation, but they will taste better and have a more appealing presentation if baked and glazed, as in Baked Ham, 507, with an internal temperature of 140° to 145°F.

Although most hams in this country are smoked, you may also find milder, less expensive hams that have been precooked by other methods. Heavy cold-smoking is used for expensive specialty hams, such as the domestic **Smithfield** and the European **Westphalian.** This process does not cook the ham but does destroy microorganisms, and also dries and flavors the meat, resulting in the characteristic firm texture of the top-quality hams. Cold-smoked hams are drier, with a deeper color and richer flavor, owing to the lengthy aging process; they are often enjoyed sliced paper-thin and eaten raw.

Both **partially** and **fully cooked hams** come in several sizes and shapes. A whole ham, a 10- to 15- pound hind leg of pork with the bone intact, is the most flavorful and least wasteful cut. ➤ It will serve 20 to 30 people generously, probably with leftovers. The best have a short plump shape, with a stubby rather than elongated shank, or pointed end. For smaller meals, you can buy a section of a whole ham, either the rounded part called the **rump half**

or **butt portion,** which is the upper thigh of the animal, or the lower **shank half.** The rump half is somewhat more meaty but relatively difficult to carve. ➤ Either section can weigh from 4 to 7 pounds—enough to serve 10 to 12 people. Smaller steaks and ham roasts are also available cut from the center of the leg. These **center ham slices or roasts** generally weigh under 2 pounds and are quick to cook and serve; see Broiled Ham Steak, 507.

Spiral-cut hams are fully cooked cured hams that are presliced so that they hold together for a dramatic presentation but are very easy to serve. Besides the typical ham from the hind leg, there are other bone-in hams that tend to cost less while providing excellent taste. A **picnic ham** is the smoked arm section of the shoulder. Although flavorful, it is slightly tougher than ham from the hind leg. Because it contains more fat, bone, and skin in proportion to lean meat, ➤ you should figure on almost a pound of picnic ham per serving. Another shoulder ham, known as **Boston butt, cottage ham,** or **daisy ham,** comes from the Boston-style shoulder, and although tender and tasty, it may be quite fatty. ➤ A long narrow piece will usually serve 3 or 4 people. Cut into slices, it makes a delicious alternative to bacon. It may be broiled, sautéed, roasted, or simmered.

Fully cooked hams are available in many boneless forms: whole, in halves, or in chunks of various sizes. Such hams are meant to be eaten sliced for sandwiches. The deli hams found thus packaged are made with lean cured meat with most of the external fat removed and may contain added water and phosphates. The best contain no added water or other ingredients and are simply labeled "ham." Others, in descending order of quality, are "ham with natural juices," "ham with water added," and "ham-and-water product."

The wide assortment of **canned hams** offers the instant convenience one needs when the house is suddenly flooded with unexpected guests. When you buy canned hams, ➤ check the label for perishability and suggested refrigeration. Most larger canned hams must be kept under refrigeration before being opened and can be stored thus for a few months. Some smaller canned hams can be stored without refrigeration.

Country ham, sometimes called **Kentucky, Virginia,** or **Tennessee ham,** is dry-cured and heavily salted and requires soaking followed by long simmering.

Ham should be served warm or cold but never chilled. Do not worry if a rainbow incandescence appears on sliced ham—it is merely light refraction on a thin fatty film. For best results, ➤ uncanned whole hams should not be stored for more than a week in the refrigerator before cooking; small portions should be kept no longer than 3 to 5 days. Sliced ham is best used within 2 days.

Prosciutto means ham in Italian, and these Italian hams have exquisite flavor. The hogs are specially raised on a diet of chestnuts or, in the Parma region, on the whey from the local Parmesan cheese production. The hind legs are dry-cured and air-dried for a minimum of 10 months, giving the meat a firm, dry quality. Prosciutto needs no cooking and, in fact, can become tough and dry if cooked. Instead, it is added at the end of cooking for flavor and is commonly served sliced paper-thin with sliced melons or figs, or used sparingly to season soups and stews.

The name **serrano ham** comes from the Spanish for mountain ham—*jamon serrano*. Similar to prosciutto from Italy, serrano hams are from the mountainous regions of Spain, where the raw hams are cured by air-drying. The best serrano ham is rich in flavor and firm in texture and should be eaten alone as an appetizer or used in small quantities to flavor cooked dishes.

A heavily spiced and smoked cured ham, **tasso** is a Creole and Cajun specialty made primarily from pork shoulder. Tasso is first cured with a salt brine, then rubbed with a pungent mix of spices and cold-smoked until it becomes quite dry. The resulting ham is often chopped and added for flavor to gumbo, jambalaya, étoufée, or other Louisiana dishes. Tasso is available in specialty markets and through Internet retailers.

Ham hocks are pieces of lower leg with bone, lean meat, fat, and rind. They are most often found salted and heavily smoked, although fresh ones are sometimes available. They are a great contribution to slow-cooked stews and bean soups, adding an earthy, smoky flavor and enriching the texture of the cooking liquid.

BAKED HAM

Allow 1/3 pound per person.
Please read About Ham, 506, to determine the type of ham and the number of servings.
I. Ham labeled "Cook Before Eating"
Preheat the oven to 325°F. Place the ham on a rack, in a shallow roasting pan. For a whole 10- to 15-pound ham, allow 18 to 20 minutes per pound; for a half—5 to 7 pounds—about 20 minutes per pound; or for a shank or butt portion weighing 3 to 4 pounds, about 35 minutes to the pound. In all cases, cook uncovered until the internal temperature reaches 160°F. Remove the rind and excess fat and serve with:
    Raisin Sauce, 565, Barbecue Sauce, 586,
      or English Cumberland Sauce, 565
Or, if you prefer an attractive, quick finish, glaze as directed below.
Suggested accompaniments are:
    Scalloped Potatoes, 296, or Pureed Chestnuts, 244
II. Ham labeled "Fully Cooked" or "Ready to Eat"
Preheat the oven to 325°F. To heat the ham, place it on a rack in a shallow roasting pan, and bake uncovered. For a whole ham, allow 15 to 18 minutes to the pound; for a half, 18 to 24 minutes per pound. The ham will be ready when the internal temperature reaches 140°F. To glaze the ham, remove it from the oven about 30 minutes before it is done, and increase the oven heat to 425°F. Remove all the rind but a collar around the shank bone. Slash the fat

in the top of the ham in a diamond pattern, and cover the surface with:
    1 1/3 cups packed brown sugar
    2 teaspoons dry mustard
moistened with:
    3 tablespoons cider vinegar, prune juice, wine,
      or ham drippings
Stud the fat at the intersections of the diamonds with:
    Whole cloves
Or decorate with:
    Alternating half pineapple rings studded with
      cranberries and stars cut from preserved
      orange peel
Return the ham to the oven, reduce the oven heat to 325°F again, and cook about 30 minutes. Place on a platter. Garnish with:
    Slices of jellied cranberry sauce topped with thin
      orange or pineapple slices
or with:
    Mashed Sweet Potatoes, 301

COUNTRY HAM

Allow about 1/3 pound per person.
To prepare a country ham, soak it in cold water to cover for 24 to 36 hours. Then scrub it well, using a stiff brush to remove any mold, and rinse thoroughly. Place in a pot of simmering water to cover:
    1 country ham
Simmer 20 minutes to the pound, or until the meat reaches an internal temperature of 150°F. Add to the water for the last quarter of the cooking time:
    4 cups cider
    1/4 cup packed brown sugar
Preheat the oven to 425°F. Drain the ham, and remove the skin while the ham is still warm, being careful not to tear the fat. Partially trim the fat. Dust the ham with a mixture of:
    2 teaspoons black pepper
    1 cup cornmeal
    1/2 cup brown sugar
Place on a rack in a roasting pan and bake until glazed. Serve warm or cold sliced very, very thin.

BROILED HAM STEAK

Traditional accompaniments are Fresh Corn Fritters, 272, and Broiled Tomatoes, 312. Allow 1/3 pound ham per person.
Preheat the broiler. Slash in several places the fat edge of:
    1 ham steak, about 1 inch thick
Place it on the broiler rack 3 inches below the heating element and broil 8 to 12 minutes on each side. If desired brush it toward the end of cooking with a mixture of:
    1 teaspoon dry mustard
    1 tablespoon fresh lemon juice
    1/4 cup grape jelly, melted

COUNTRY HAM STEAK
WITH RED-EYE GRAVY

4 servings

A Southern classic served over hot biscuits.
Melt in a large skillet over medium-high heat:

   1$^{1}/_{2}$ teaspoons butter

Add:

   1 fully cooked $^{3}/_{4}$- to 1-inch-thick country ham steak (1$^{1}/_{2}$ to 2 pounds)

Cook the steak until nicely browned, 3 to 5 minutes on each side. Remove to a platter and season with:

   Black pepper to taste

Return the skillet to the heat. Add:

   1 cup coffee

to the skillet and boil, stirring, until it turns slightly red. Add:

   $^{1}/_{2}$ cup heavy cream

Reduce the heat and simmer until slightly thickened, about 10 minutes. Season to taste with:

   Salt and black pepper

Serve the ham with the gravy.

STEWED PORK NECK BONES

Add to salted boiling water to partly cover:

   Pork neck bones

Reduce the heat and simmer, covered, until tender, about 1$^{1}/_{2}$ hours. Vegetables may be added to the stew for the last 30 minutes of cooking.

STEWED PORK HOCKS

Add to salted boiling water:

   Pork hocks

Reduce the heat and simmer, covered, 1$^{1}/_{2}$ to 3 hours. You may add potatoes for the last 30 minutes of cooking or sliced greens or cabbage for the last 20 minutes. Or drain the hocks, cool, and marinate for 2 hours or more in:

   (Herbed French Dressing)

Serve cold with a salad.

ABOUT BACON

Bacon is made from trimmed hog bellies that have been cured in a brine and smoked until partially cooked. It is a fatty cut, and the fat is integral to its flavor and texture. Most bacon sold in the supermarket is sliced, thick or thin. Unsliced **slab bacon** is ideal for thick pieces to use for larding, see 464, or for *lardons,* the French term for bacon that has been diced or sliced, blanched, and fried until crisp.

   Canadian bacon, which bears little resemblance to standard bacon, actually comes from the meatier, leaner loin and is more thoroughly trimmed before curing. Although most Canadian bacon is brined and smoked and so closely resembles ham, it is also sold uncooked. Slice the cooked variety as you would regular ham, for cold cuts or panfrying. The uncooked variety comes rolled in cornmeal and is typically baked; try, instead, grilling thick slices.

   Pancetta is the Italian version of bacon. Most commonly sold in a tight roll secured in a natural casing, it may also be found in slabs. Pancetta is cured with salt and spices but is not smoked, so it is moister and has a mellower flavor than bacon. ➤ If you substitute bacon for pancetta, blanch it first in boiling water to subdue the smoky flavor.

   The belly of the pig also yields **fatback,** unprocessed fat from the pig belly, usually used for rendering into fat for cooking or for larding meats. Because it is not cured or smoked, fatback has a pure, mellow flavor. **Cracklings** are little pieces of fatback that are fried until crispy, and they are sometimes baked into corn bread. **Salt pork** is from the belly or the knuckle or shoulder. It is a heavily salted, unsmoked product prized for its fat, which is commonly rendered for cooking. A piece of salt pork added to a soup, stew, or pot of beans during cooking lends a richness to the entire dish. Soak before using to cut down the saltiness. Bacon is a fine substitution for salt pork, without first presoaking.

   Sliced bacon with a good proportion of lean striping, cured without excessive salt, is best. We prefer thick sliced bacon, and especially enjoy the black-peppered bacon. When separating raw bacon slices, remove 2 or 3 slices at a time and then separate into singles. Allow 2 or 3 slices per person. **To oven-broil bacon,** begin with a cold pan. Or, if you are sautéing it, start with a cold pan. These methods prevent curling and work better than weighted covers or specialized gadgets. ➤ Keep heat low to medium and check frequently; bacon can burn in seconds.

BAKED BACON

The preferred method for cooking bacon in quantity.
Preheat the oven to 350°F. Place on the cold rack of a broiler pan or on a rack on a rimmed baking sheet:

   Slices of bacon

(If the slices of bacon are hard to separate, place the entire block of strips you will need in a slightly warm pan and slide them apart as they heat.) Bake until crisp, 15 to 20 minutes. No turning is necessary. Drain on paper towels.

SAUTEED BACON

When cooking bacon, cook to your own personal taste; the longer bacon cooks, the more fat is rendered out of it. Place in a large cast-iron or other heavy skillet:

   Slices of bacon

Do not overlap the slices. Place the pan over medium-low heat and slowly cook until the bacon is browned. Turn it often and monitor the heat to avoid burning it. Remove to paper towels to drain. If cooking in batches, pour all of the accumulated grease into a coffee mug between each batch. This will prevent excess popping and splattering.

BROILED BACON

Preheat the broiler. Arrange on a cold broiler pan:

   Slices of bacon

Position the broiler pan 4 to 6 inches from the heating element. Cook, turning often, until browned and crisp, 10 to 15 minutes. Remove to paper towels to drain.

MICROWAVED BACON

Since microwaves vary in power and efficiency, the method below provides only an approximate time. Practice to find the timing and desired degree of doneness for your own oven.

Spread 3 or 4 layers of paper towels on a plate and arrange on the towels:

Slices of bacon

Place in the microwave oven and cook on high for 3 minutes. Touch the bacon and, if it is not crisp enough, continue cooking, checking for doneness every 30 seconds. Pat the surface of the bacon with paper towels and serve.

GOAT OR KID

You can find the meat of a young goat, or kid, at Hispanic, Greek, Italian, and West Indian meat markets, especially around Easter, and premium markets occasionally sell it as well. It is labeled **chevron** by U.S. government ruling.

Most kid comes to market under 4 months of age, with a dressed weight of between 12 and 30 pounds. ➤ The smaller the animal, the more subtle tasting and tender the meat. Use kid in any stewed or braised lamb or beef recipe, such as Lamb Curry with Tomato, 497, or Beef Stew with Mustard, Herbs, and White Wine, 480, or Roast Mountain Goat or Bighorn Sheep, 530.

JAMAICAN CURRIED GOAT

4 to 6 servings

Considered by many the national dish of Jamaica, this curry is fiery-hot when made with the Caribbean habanero pepper or Scotch bonnet. Milder jalapeño peppers provide good flavor and less heat. Lamb or pork can be substituted for the goat.

Combine in a large bowl and toss to coat evenly:

2 pounds boneless goat meat, trimmed and cut into
1-inch cubes
2 tablespoons curry powder
2 chile peppers, seeded and minced
2 garlic cloves, minced
1 teaspoon salt
1 teaspoon black pepper

Cover and refrigerate for at least 1 hour, or up to 12 hours. Remove the meat from the bowl, reserving any juices that may have accumulated, and pat dry. Heat in a Dutch oven over medium-high heat:

3 tablespoons vegetable oil

Add the meat, in batches if necessary, and brown on all sides, 5 to 6 minutes. Remove the browned meat with a slotted spoon. Add to the pot and cook over medium heat, stirring often, until the onion begins to brown, about 5 minutes:

1 medium onion, chopped
1 rib celery, chopped

Add the goat, reserved marinade juices, and:

2½ cups vegetable stock or broth or water
1 bay leaf

Bring to a boil, then cover and simmer over low heat for 1 hour. Add:

3 to 4 potatoes, peeled and cut into 1-inch chunks

Cover and cook until the potatoes and meat are fork-tender, 35 to 45 minutes. Remove from the heat and skim off any fat from the surface. Taste and adjust the seasonings, remove the bay leaf, and serve with:

Cooked rice

ABOUT GROUND MEAT AND HAMBURGER

Merchants of the German port of Hamburg, through centuries of trade with Estonians, Latvians, and Finns, had acquired the Baltic taste for scraped raw beef, but it was not until the St. Louis World's Fair in 1904 that broiled, bunned beef was introduced to the rest of the world by the Germans of South St. Louis as hamburger. Americans quickly latched on to the hamburger as their all-time favorite; for a bustling people it offered a combination of convenience, economy, and tasty nourishment that seemed just what the doctor ordered.

Ground beef is by far the most popular ground meat in America. Different cuts contain varying levels of fat and flavor. According to federal ruling, ground beef sold as **"hamburger"** must contain no more than 30% fat, though most supermarkets and butcher shops sell several grades of ground beef labeled according to the degree of leanness. **Ground sirloin** contains about 15% fat, **ground round** approximately 20%, and **ground chuck** nearly 30%. The leanest ground beef is often the most expensive. The fat content is an important consideration in buying ground beef, for the range of fat not only affects the nutrition profile but also the choice of cooking method. ➤ To ensure safe cooking and the elimination of foodborne pathogens potentially present in ground meats, we recommend cooking all ground meat dishes to an internal temperature of 160°F.

Beef can be ground at home in a food processor or in a meat grinder. The best cuts of beef for this purpose are chuck, sirloin, or round. Before the meat is ground, remove any gristle and tendons. Cut into cubes and place in food processor bowl. Pulse the processor on and off to prevent the beef cubes from becoming overprocessed. Stir the meat after several pulses. Use caution, as the food processor will grind the beef quickly, making it easy to overprocess the meat, resulting in ground beef that has a pasty texture. The best results occur when the meat is ground just until the larger chunks are broken down into pieces that are no smaller than ¼ inch.

When buying ground beef, remember that **ground chuck** has the best flavor and is the best for hamburgers, while the leaner, **ground round** can be used for meat loaf and meatballs. Always decide before you put the meat into the pan how thick you want the finished hamburger and shape it accordingly. ➤ Never compact it in the pan by pressing down on it with a spatula.

Ground turkey and chicken, which have become recent favorites, are discussed in Poultry, 445. Other ground meats include veal, pork, and lamb. Ground veal should be almost white or very pale pink. Veal contains very little fat and for meatballs, burgers, and meat loaf is generally combined with either beef or pork to make up the difference. Ground pork should be nicely pink. Very pale or white pork is high in fat and is not recommended for meatballs and meat loaf; it can be used for pâtes and terrines, 517. Ground lamb should be pale red or dark pink and is generally ground from the shoulder.

Store any uncooked ground meat for no more than 24 hours in the refrigerator. In our kitchen, we buy large packs and divide them into small portions and freeze. It is easy, convenient, and economical.

HAMBURGERS
4 burgers
It is a mistake to make burgers with lean beef, for they need some fat for flavor and moistness. The ideal burger is made from ground chuck.
Divide the meat into 4 equal portions and form each into a patty about 1 inch thick:
1¼ pounds ground beef chuck
Sprinkle with:
Salt and black pepper
Cook, flipping once, by grilling over a hot fire, broiling under a preheated broiler, or cooking in a preheated skillet over medium-high heat. For all three methods, it will take about 3 minutes on each side for rare, 4 minutes for medium, or 5 minutes on each side for well-done. Place the burgers in or between:
4 hamburger buns or other rolls, split,
  or 8 slices bread
Add your choice of:
Mayonnaise
Mustard
Sliced tomato
Lettuce
Sliced onion
Dill pickles
Tomato catsup or other catsup of your choice, 951
Green Tomato Relish, 948
Piccalilli, 947
Chow-Chow, 947
Serve at once.

CHEESEBURGERS
Top the burgers, after flipping them, with **slices of American cheese or other cheese of your choice.** For a **Bacon Cheeseburger,** top each cooked cheeseburger with **2 or 3 slices crisp bacon.**

CHILI BURGERS
Top the cooked burgers with ½ to ¾ cup Chili Con Carne, 513, and 3 tablespoons minced onions.

BARBECUE BURGERS
Top the cooked burgers with ¼ to ½ cup Barbecue Sauce, 586.

BECKER BURGERS
4 burgers
The traditional way of serving these in our household is as open-faced sandwiches on whole wheat toast, with the pan juices poured over the burgers.
Divide into 4 equal portions and form each into a burger about ¾ inch thick:
1½ pounds lean ground chuck
Heat in a heavy skillet over medium-high heat:
2 tablespoons olive oil
Add the burgers and cook for 2 minutes. Turn and cook on the other side for 4 minutes for medium-rare. Sprinkle the burgers generously with:
Black pepper
and then:
2 tablespoons soy sauce
2 tablespoons port
Several drops of hot pepper sauce
Remove the skillet from the heat, cover, and let stand for 5 minutes before serving.

PATTY MELT
4 servings
Prepare:
Caramelized Onions, 287
using:
1 large red onion, cut into rings
1 tablespoon olive oil
Season:
1½ pounds ground chuck
with:
Salt and black pepper
Form into 4 burgers. Heat in a large griddle pan or cast-iron skillet over medium-high heat:
3 tablespoons butter
Cook the burgers to the desired doneness, adding more butter if necessary. Meanwhile, toast:
8 slices rye bread
Place each burger on a slice of toast, and top the burgers with the onions and:
8 slices Swiss or American cheese
Top with the remaining toast. Return the sandwiches to the skillet and heat over medium-low heat, turning once, until the cheese melts. Serve immediately.

SLOPPY JOE
6 servings
The Sloppy Joe—known as **"loosemeat"** in certain parts of the country—dates from the 1950s. Why "Joe," it is

not possible to say with surety, but "sloppy" is obvious enough.

Heat in a large skillet over medium heat:

    1 tablespoon vegetable oil

Add:

    1 small onion, finely diced
    1 small red or yellow bell pepper, finely diced
    4 garlic cloves, minced
    2 large celery ribs, finely diced
    (1 teaspoon fresh thyme leaves)
    Salt and black pepper to taste

Cook, stirring frequently, until the onion is softened but not browned, about 10 minutes. Transfer to a plate. Add to the skillet and increase the heat slightly:

    1¼ pounds ground beef chuck or sirloin

Cook, breaking up any lumps with a wooden spoon, just until browned, 3 to 4 minutes. Add the onion mixture, along with:

    ½ cup chili sauce or catsup
    ½ cup beer or water
    3 tablespoons Worcestershire sauce
    Hot pepper sauce

Partially cover and simmer, stirring occasionally, until the sauce is slightly thickened, about 15 minutes. Meanwhile, toast:

    6 large rolls or six 6-inch lengths French bread, split

Sprinkle the Sloppy Joe mixture with:

    3 tablespoons minced scallion greens

Spoon onto the bottom halves of the rolls and cover with the tops. Serve hot.

BECKER LAMB PATTIES

12 two-inch patties

Perfect to pass at a party. If you like lamb, you'll love these either sautéed or grilled.

Combine in a large bowl and mix well, using your hands:

    1 pound ground lamb
    Grated zest and juice of ½ lemon
    2 teaspoons sherry
    2 teaspoons soy sauce
    1½ garlic cloves, finely minced
    1 teaspoon dried thyme, crumbled
    1 teaspoon salt
    1 teaspoon black pepper
    2 dashes hot pepper sauce

Shape the mixture into 2-inch patties. Heat in a large skillet over medium-high heat:

    2 tablespoons olive oil

Add the patties and fry for 2 minutes, then flip and sprinkle with additional:

    Soy sauce

Fry for 1 minute more. Remove the skillet from heat, cover, and let stand for 1 minute. Serve with:

    French bread or toast rounds

GROUND MEAT PATTIES

About 15 patties

Mix together in a large bowl with your hands:

    2 pounds ground chicken, veal, or lamb
    ½ cup soft bread crumbs
    1 large egg
    ½ cup chopped onion
    1½ teaspoons grated lemon zest
    1 teaspoon salt
    1 teaspoon ground coriander
    1 teaspoon grated or ground nutmeg
    1 teaspoon curry powder
    ½ teaspoon black pepper

Shape the mixture into 15 large patties, and let rest for 15 minutes. Place the patties in a greased broiler pan and place under a preheated broiler about 10 minutes per side, or until lightly browned. Or, heat in a large skillet over medium heat:

    (2 tablespoons butter)
    (1 tablespoon olive oil)

Cook the patties, in batches, about 10 minutes per side. Serve with:

    Rice Pilaf, 355
    Chopped mint

ABOUT MEAT LOAF AND MEATBALLS

Although proportions of beef, veal, and pork are specified in the following recipes, they may be varied, provided the total amount of meat remains the same. Be sure to ➤ cook thoroughly if pork is used. Handle ingredients for meat loaf ➤ lightly, mixing with a two-tined fork or your hands. Do not overcook; it should be firm but not dry.

Meat loaf may be mounded on a flat greased pan or put into a greased ring mold or loaf pan, which will give a juicier result. It may also be baked in 2 layers with a stuffing between. Individual meat loaves take only about 20 to 30 minutes and—for attractive service—may be baked in greased muffin tins and glazed. You may pour about ½ cup of catsup in the bottom of the pan before filling it with the meat; or you may pour about 2 tablespoons of chili sauce over the meat loaf when it is half baked. This gives it a good flavor and a light crust. You may cover the loaf with a piece of foil, but remove the foil during the last quarter hour of baking.

If baked in a ring mold, it may be served hot, filled with green peas or some other vegetable and surrounded by browned potatoes. Or serve it cold, filled with potato or some other vegetable salad. Don't neglect to use for sandwiches and for picnics.

Meat loaf is highly suited to being either frozen raw for cooking later or cooked and frozen, then reheated. Wrap in plastic and aluminum foil before freezing.

Meatballs are similar to meat loaf in everything but form. Meatballs can be simmered in stock or browned and then added to a sauce or gravy. Uncooked meatballs can be frozen on a baking sheet, then placed in a plastic bag when firm and kept frozen for up to 3 months. ➤ Any meat loaf recipe can be used for meatballs. For meat loaf and meatballs made with turkey or chicken, see 445.

MEAT LOAF
8 servings

I. Preheat the oven to 350°F. Lightly grease a 9 x 5-inch loaf pan. Combine in a large bowl:

12 ounces ground beef chuck
12 ounces ground beef round
1¹/₂ cups finely chopped onions
1 cup quick-cooking rolled oats or dry bread crumbs
²/₃ cup catsup
²/₃ cup chopped parsley
3 large eggs, lightly beaten
1 teaspoon dried thyme
1 teaspoon salt
¹/₂ teaspoon black pepper

Knead the mixture with your hands just until well blended. Fill the loaf pan with the meat mixture, mounding the top. Place the pan on a baking sheet and bake until the meat loaf is firm to the touch and has shrunk from the sides of the pan or a thermometer inserted in the center reads 160°F, 1 to 1¹/₄ hours. Pour off the excess fat and let stand for 15 minutes before serving.

4 servings

II. Preheat the oven to 350°F. Combine in a large bowl:

1 pound ground beef round
1 to 2 tablespoons horseradish
2 tablespoons catsup or chili sauce
1 teaspoon salt
¹/₄ teaspoon black pepper
6 slices bacon, diced
2 cups chopped onions
1 cup cracker crumbs
1 large egg

Mix with your hands until blended. Shape into a loaf. Roll in:

¹/₄ cup cracker crumbs

Place in a shallow baking pan. Pour into the pan:

¹/₂ cup stock or broth

Bake, basting occasionally, until the meat loaf is firm to the touch or thermometer inserted in the center reads 160°F, about 1 hour. Make:

(Meat Pan Gravy, 546)

Or serve with:

Catsup, 951

ADDITIONS TO MEAT LOAF

Other ingredients can be added for flavor and texture. If you are experimenting, first mix a very small batch and fry a patty of the mixture to taste before mixing and cooking an entire loaf. To one 8-cup recipe, you can add vegetables such as:

¹/₂ cup finely grated carrots, potatoes, or sweet potatoes

¹/₂ cup thinly sliced sautéed mushrooms, 283, or cooked rice
¹/₄ cup coarsely chopped almonds, pecans, or walnuts
2 teaspoons chili sauce or hot pepper sauce
2 teaspoons Worcestershire sauce
1 tablespoon Dijon mustard
1 tablespoon drained prepared horseradish
1 tablespoon chopped thyme, basil, oregano, dill, or snipped chives

GERMAN MEATBALLS OR KÖNIGSBERGER KLOPS
About ten 2-Inch Balls

This is a very old family favorite. When we visited Cousin Elsa and her family in St. Louis, she prepared this for us, just as Granny Rom had prepared it for her as a child. Good old-fashioned German comfort food. Enjoy!

Soak in water, milk, or stock to cover:

One 1-inch-thick slice of bread

Have ready:

1¹/₂ pounds ground meat: beef, veal, pork, or a combination

Beat well and add to the meat:

2 eggs

Melt:

1 tablespoon butter

Sauté until golden:

¹/₄ cup finely chopped onions

Add to the meat. Wring the liquid from the bread. Add bread to the meat, along with:

3 tablespoons chopped parsley
1¹/₄ teaspoons salt
¹/₄ teaspoon paprika
¹/₂ teaspoon grated lemon rind
1 teaspoon lemon juice
1 teaspoon Worcestershire sauce or a grating of nutmeg

A few minced anchovies or ¹/₄ herring may be added at this time to the mixture or later to the gravy. Combine ingredients well. Do this lightly with the hands rather than with a fork or spoon. Shape lightly into 2-inch balls. Drop into:

5 cups boiling vegetable stock

Simmer, covered, about 15 minutes. Remove from the stock. Measure the stock. Make gravy out of it, 549, by using for every cup of stock:

2 tablespoons butter
2 tablespoons flour
Salt and pepper to taste

Cook and stir until smooth. Add:

2 tablespoons capers, or 2 tablespoons chopped pickles, lemon juice, or cultured sour cream
2 tablespoons chopped parsley

Reheat the meatballs in the gravy. Serve with a platter of:

Boiled Noodles, 325, or Spätzle, 335

Cover generously with:

Buttered Bread Crumbs, 960

ITALIAN MEATBALLS

About eight 2-inch meatballs

Combine in a large bowl:

1 pound ground beef
1 garlic clove, minced
$^1/_2$ cup chopped parsley
$^1/_2$ cup grated Parmesan
1 medium onion, finely chopped
$^1/_2$ cup fresh bread crumbs
1 large egg, beaten
(3 tablespoons dry red wine)
2 tablespoons tomato paste
1 teaspoon salt
$^1/_4$ teaspoon black pepper
$^1/_2$ teaspoon dried oregano

Mix with your hands. Scoop out the mixture in heaping tablespoons and form into 2-inch balls. Dredge the meatballs in:

$^1/_2$ cup all-purpose flour

Heat in a large skillet over medium heat:

2 tablespoons olive oil

Brown the meatballs in batches. Place in a baking pan and cook in a preheated 375°F oven for 10 minutes, or, if desired, finish as for:

Tomato Sauce, 562

SWEDISH MEATBALLS

About ten 2-inch meatballs

The trick to making authentic Swedish meatballs is to beat the ground meat with water until fluffy and smooth. Serve these as an hors d'oeuvre or as a main course accompanied by mashed potatoes and cranberry sauce.

Melt in a small heavy skillet over medium-high heat:

1 tablespoon butter

Add and cook, stirring until soft, 1 to 2 minutes:

1 tablespoon minced onion

Set aside. Combine in the bowl of an electric mixer, and let stand until soft, about 1 to 2 minutes:

$^2/_3$ cup fresh bread crumbs
1 cup water

Add the onions, along with:

12 ounces lean ground beef
12 ounces lean ground pork
2 large egg yolks
1 teaspoon salt
$^1/_4$ teaspoon black pepper
$^1/_4$ teaspoon grated or ground nutmeg
$^1/_4$ teaspoon ground allspice

Beat on low speed until smooth, then turn the mixer to high speed and beat until the mixture is light in color and fluffy, about 10 minutes. Shape the meat into 1-inch balls. Heat in a large skillet over medium heat:

$^1/_4$ cup ($^1/_2$ stick) butter

Brown the meatballs in batches, then remove and drain on paper towels before transferring to a platter. Cover to keep warm. Reduce the heat to low and add to the skillet:

2 tablespoons all-purpose flour

Cook, stirring, until lightly browned. Slowly add:

2 cups beef stock or broth

Cook, whisking, until the gravy is thick and smooth. Strain, if desired, and pour the gravy over the meatballs.

CHILI CON CARNE

6 to 8 servings

Pat dry:

3 pounds boneless beef chuck, trimmed and cut into $^1/_2$-inch cubes

Season with:

1 to 2 teaspoons salt

Heat in a large skillet over medium-high heat:

2 tablespoons olive oil

Add:

2 cups chopped onions
10 garlic cloves chopped
2 to 6 jalapeño peppers, seeded and minced
$^1/_2$ teaspoon salt

Cook, stirring often, until the vegetables are softened, 6 to 8 minutes. Add the meat and brown, pouring off excess fat, if desired. Stir in:

$^1/_2$ cup chili powder, 968

Cook for 2 minutes. Add:

One 28-ounce can whole tomatoes, with their juice
1 tablespoon red wine vinegar
4 cups water

breaking the tomatoes with the back of a spoon. Season to taste with:

Salt

Simmer, uncovered, stirring occasionally, until the meat is tender and the sauce is reduced and thickened, about 1$^1/_2$ to 2 hours.

CHILI WITH MEAT AND BEANS

8 to 10 servings

Stir **6 cups cooked black or pinto beans (1 pound dried beans; 253)** into **Chili con Carne, above,** and heat through.

MACLEID'S ROCKCASTLE CHILI

8 to 10 servings

This is a Saturday-night staple on Rockcastle River Gorge camping trips. Camp chef and good friend Matt MacLeid has also prepared it for us on the firepit at our Tennessee mountain home.

Cook in a large skillet until the cracklings are golden brown:

8 ounces bacon, diced

Remove the bacon using a slotted spoon. Cook briefly in the drippings:

1$^1/_2$ pounds beef round steak, coarsely ground or chopped in a food processor
6 to 12 large garlic cloves, coarsely chopped
2 large onions, coarsely chopped

Add, scraping up the browned bits on the bottom of the pan, and stir until the foam disappears:

One 12-ounce bottle dark beer

Remove all to a Dutch oven or other large pot. Stir in:

One 32-ounce can whole tomatoes, with their juice
One 16-ounce can kidney beans, with their liquid
One 16-ounce can Great Northern beans, with
**   their liquid**
One 16-ounce can pinto beans, with their liquid
6 tablespoons ancho chile powder
2 tablespoons ground cumin
1 tablespoon black pepper
1¹/₂ cups water or one 12-ounce bottle dark beer

Simmer for about 3 hours, covered, stirring occasionally to prevent sticking. Season to taste with:

Salt and black pepper
Hot pepper sauce

CINCINNATI CHILI COCKAIGNE

6 servings

There are hundreds of so-called original recipes for John Kiradjieff's Cincinnati Chili that he served in Cincinnati's first chili parlor, The Empress. We particularly like this version of our hometown obsession, and we can guarantee without question that it is not one of myth.

Bring to a boil in a large pot:

4 cups water

Add:

2 pounds ground beef chuck

Stir until separated, and reduce the heat to a simmer. Add:

2 medium onions, finely chopped
5 to 6 garlic cloves, crushed
One 15-ounce can tomato sauce
2 tablespoons cider vinegar
1 tablespoon Worcestershire sauce

Stir in:

10 whole black peppercorns, ground
8 whole allspice berries, ground
8 whole cloves, ground
1 large bay leaf
2 teaspoons salt
2 teaspoons ground cinnamon
1¹/₂ teaspoons ground red pepper
1 teaspoon ground cumin
¹/₂ ounce unsweetened chocolate, grated

Bring to a boil, then reduce the heat to a simmer and cook for 2¹/₂ hours. Cool, uncovered, and refrigerate overnight. Before serving, skim off all or most of the fat and discard. Discard the bay leaf. Reheat the chili. For a 2-Way, serve over:

Cooked spaghetti

For a 3-Way, top with:

Cheddar, grated

For a 4-Way, sprinkle on top of the cheese:

Chopped onions

For a 5-Way, top all with:

Cooked red kidney beans, 253

Traditional sides include:

Oyster crackers
Hot pepper sauce

OHIO FARMHOUSE SAUSAGE CHILI

4 to 6 servings

A delicious "warmer-upper" after a fine tramp in the woods on a chilly day.

Brown in a large skillet:

1 pound bulk pork sausage
1 large onion, chopped

Toward the end of the browning, add:

1 celery rib, diced

When the celery is softened, add:

One 28-ounce can diced tomatoes, with their juice
2 cups tomato juice or chicken broth, or a mixture of
**   the two**
1 to 2 tablespoons maple syrup or molasses
2 teaspoons ground cumin
1¹/₂ teaspoons ground sage
¹/₂ teaspoon black pepper

Simmer for 20 minutes. Add and simmer 15 minutes more:

3¹/₂ to 4 cups cooked red kidney beans, 253,
**   drained and rinsed**

PICADILLO

4 servings

This dish is sometimes served as is, with bowls of garnishes such as grated cheese, shredded lettuce, guacamole, and chopped tomatoes on the side. It is also a tasty filling for tortillas—enchiladas, tacos, tostados—as well as a stuffing for chile peppers, as in Baked Chiles Rellenos with Cheese, 293.

Cook in a large skillet, mashing down to crumble the meat, until the beef starts to brown:

1 pound ground beef
1 cup fresh chorizo

If a lot of fat is released, drain the meat on paper towels and return to the pan. Add:

1 onion, chopped
1 garlic clove, minced

Cook for a few minutes, then add:

1 cup chopped tomatoes
1 tablespoon vinegar
1 teaspoon ground cinnamon
¹/₄ teaspoon ground cumin
Pinch of sugar
Pinch of ground cloves
1 bay leaf

Simmer, covered, for 30 minutes. Add:

¹/₂ cup raisins
(¹/₂ cup slivered blanched almonds)
(¹/₂ cup pitted black olives, chopped)

Cook, uncovered, for 10 to 15 minutes. Remove bay leaf before serving.

INDIAN GROUND BEEF WITH POTATOES AND SPICES (KEEMA ALU)

4 servings

This dish of beef, tomatoes, and potatoes makes a satisfying meal when paired with cooked lentils and pita bread. Heat in a large cast-iron or other heavy skillet over medium-high heat:

3 tablespoons vegetable oil

Add and cook, stirring, until golden brown:

1 medium onion, finely chopped

Add and cook briefly, stirring, just until well mixed:

2 teaspoons minced garlic
2 teaspoons grated peeled fresh ginger
2 teaspoons ground cumin
2 teaspoons ground coriander
1 teaspoon turmeric
$^1/_4$ teaspoon ground red pepper, or to taste

Combine with the mixture:

1 pound lean ground beef or turkey
$^1/_2$ cup chopped lightly drained canned tomatoes
$^3/_4$ teaspoon salt

Cook, stirring, until the meat is no longer pink and all the liquid is evaporated, 8 to 10 minutes. Add:

12 ounces boiling potatoes, peeled and cut into $^1/_2$-inch cubes
1 cup water

Cover, reduce the heat to low, and simmer until the potatoes are tender, 15 to 20 minutes. Uncover, increase the heat, and cook until all the water is evaporated. Taste and adjust the seasonings. Sprinkle with:

2 tablespoons chopped cilantro
(1 serrano or jalapeño pepper, cut into thin strips)

If desired, serve with:

(Pita bread, Dal, 258, or Raita, 567)

ABOUT SAUSAGE

Sausage is one of the oldest of processed foods; 3,000 years ago, grinding meat into sausage was an established Mediterranean custom. Both the product and the concept traveled well over the centuries, proliferating around the world into countless varieties. Sausages are now available made of chicken, turkey, or duck, as well as the more common pork or beef, and a wide range of other ingredients, from sun-dried tomatoes to mushrooms.

Sausages, no matter what meat they are made of, fall into three main classes. **Fresh sausages** are made from raw meat and sold raw, to be cooked before eating. These are usually based on ground or chopped meat, with a slightly coarse texture, combined with spices and herbs. Sausages of this type can be bought in casings or in bulk. You can find fresh **country-style** or **breakfast sausage, Italian sausage,** and fresh **bratwurst** and **kielbasa,** among others, in the market. Because they are raw, these sausages are quite perishable; they should be refrigerated immediately and cooked within 2 days.

Precooked sausage can be smoked or cooked by other methods. The texture of sausages in this category range from very fine emulsified types, such as **hot dogs, bologna,** and **knockwurst,** to coarser types like **smoked kielbasa** and **cooked salami.** Boudin blanc, a fine-textured **white sausage** made from veal and chicken, and **boudin noir,** a **blood sausage,** are examples of sausages that are cooked but not smoked. All precooked sausages in this category are completely safe to eat as is, but most are vastly improved if heated through before eating. Since these sausages are perishable, they should be refrigerated immediately and eaten within 3 to 5 days of purchase, or by the use-by date.

Partially dry and **fully cured sausages** may be made of raw meat, as in **salami,** but are cured with salt and dried to prevent bacterial growth. **Fully cured sausages,** such as **dry salami** or **pepperoni,** will keep unrefrigerated for several months but will become hard. **Semidry partially cured types,** such as **summer sausage, thuringer,** and **Spanish chorizo,** are more perishable but will keep in the refrigerator for 2 to 3 weeks. Both types can be sliced and eaten cold, and they are used to flavor hot dishes, such as paella, 358, and pizza, 191.

Fresh raw sausage is best panfried, grilled, or broiled. We like fine-textured precooked sausages, such as frankfurters, poached in hot water. Coarser-textured smoked sausages, such as kielbasa, are best panfried, grilled, broiled, or even baked, but they dry out easily. All sausages are fantastic when grilled. Cook over medium-hot coals with the flames kept at a minimum. You can poach raw sausages before grilling, and do not prick sausages before or during cooking, as this causes flare-ups. Smoked sausages and poached fresh sausages should take no more than 7 to 10 minutes on the grill. Turn frequently for even browning. If you must microwave precooked sausages, it is best to submerge them in water or stock in a closely covered container to keep the skin from turning tough. Fresh sausages in casings will burst if microwaved.

Never taste raw or fresh sausage, whether bought or homemade, because of the danger of trichinosis. After handling raw sausage, always wash your hands and any utensils or surfaces you have used. ➤ For 4 servings, allow about 1 pound of freshly ground sausage meat, or slightly less for the more aged and drier types.

MAKING SAUSAGE AT HOME

It is quite easy to make fresh country-style homemade sausage, especially with a food processor. The advantage of making your own sausage is that you control everything: the amount of fat and salt, the quality and type of meat, the spice blend—the ultimate flavor. But when making sausage at home, remember these rules for safety and hygiene: ➤ Do not taste the raw meat mixture. Instead, fry a small patty and taste that to check the seasoning. ➤ Keep the meat refrigerated before and between all steps. Do not leave any meat sitting in the grinder.

➤ Wash all utensils and equipment at once, even if you are only going to take a short break. ➤ Wash your hands frequently. ➤ If fresh sausage will not be eaten within 3 days, freeze it.

COUNTRY SAUSAGE

About 2 pounds

Please read Making Sausage at Home, 515.

At butchering time in our valley, the popular man is the one who knows how to flavor the sausage—not too much of this and just enough of that. This process has to be played by ear, for uncooked meat cannot be tasted to correct the seasoning, and the strength of spices is so variable. The best way to learn is to mix a small batch and cook up a sample for the always hungry helpers to test.

Cut into strips if using a meat grinder, or into 1-inch cubes if using a food processor:

1¹/₂ pounds pork butt, chilled
8 ounces pork fatback, trimmed of rind and chilled

Grind the meat and fat together in the meat grinder fitted with a ¹/₄-inch plate, or coarsely chop in the food processor. Mix together in a large bowl with:

2 teaspoons salt
2 teaspoons coarsely ground black pepper
1¹/₂ teaspoons dried sage or thyme
¹/₂ teaspoon dried marjoram
¹/₄ teaspoon dried savory, crumbled
¹/₈ teaspoon ground ginger
(Pinch of ground cloves)
Pinch of ground red pepper, or to taste
¹/₄ cup cold water

Using your hands, knead and squeeze the mixture until well blended. Leave in bulk or form into patties as needed. If not using it immediately, the sausage can be refrigerated for up to 3 days or frozen for up to 2 months. To sauté fresh sausage patties, start them in a cold ungreased pan over medium heat, and drain the fat as it accumulates in the pan. Cook until well-done and medium brown on both sides.

HERBED PORK SAUSAGE

About 12 ounces

Please read Making Sausage at Home, 515. This is the ideal wrap for Scotch Eggs, 195.

Combine in a bowl and mix thoroughly:

12 ounces ground pork
1 large egg
1 tablespoon chopped parsley
(1 teaspoon grated lemon zest)
1 teaspoon salt
³/₄ teaspoon chopped fresh savory or ¹/₄ teaspoon dried savory
³/₄ teaspoon chopped fresh sage or ¹/₄ teaspoon dried sage
³/₄ teaspoon chopped fresh thyme or ¹/₄ teaspoon dried thyme

¹/₄ teaspoon black pepper
¹/₄ teaspoon ground coriander
¹/₄ teaspoon grated or ground nutmeg

Shape and cook or store as for Country Sausage, above.

CHICKEN AND APPLE SAUSAGE

About 2 pounds

Please read Making Sausage at Home, 515. This sausage can be used as a substitute for Country Sausage, above. Although it has less than half the fat of conventional breakfast sausage, it remains juicy if not overcooked. Serve these sausages with French Toast, 648, smothered with Apple Rings, 216.

Bring to a boil in a small saucepan and boil down to 2 or 3 tablespoons syrup:

1 cup apple cider

Let cool. Meanwhile, remove the bones from:

2¹/₄ pounds chicken thighs

Reserve the skin. Cut the chicken into strips if using a meat grinder or 1-inch cubes if using a food processor. Grind the chicken and skin together in a meat grinder fitted with a ³/₈-inch plate, or coarsely chop by hand or in a food processor, along with:

1¹/₂ ounces dried apples

Mix the chicken and apple mixture with the syrup in a large bowl. Add:

2¹/₂ teaspoons salt
1 teaspoon black pepper
1 teaspoon dried sage
¹/₂ teaspoon dried thyme
¹/₈ teaspoon ground cinnamon
¹/₈ teaspoon ground ginger

Using your hands, knead and squeeze the mixture until well blended. Shape and cook or store as for Country Sausage, above.

WHITE SAUSAGE (BOUDIN BLANC)

About 1¹/₂ pounds

Delicate and perishable

Please read Making Sausage at Home, 515. Have ready and tied at one end:

Sausage casings, 1 inch in diameter

Mince:

4 ounces leaf lard or pork fatback

Grind once in a meat grinder fitted with the finest blade or in a food processor:

8 ounces pork loin, cut into strips
¹/₂ pound chicken or rabbit breast, cut into strips

Combine with the minced fat in a bowl and add:

2 teaspoons salt
1 teaspoon white pepper
¹/₄ teaspoon ground cinnamon
¹/₈ teaspoon ground cloves
¹/₈ teaspoon grated or ground nutmeg
¹/₈ teaspoon ground ginger

Grind or process again with:

2 cups chopped onions

Soak together:

¹/₂ cup fresh bread crumbs

in:

¹/₄ cup warm cream

Add to the crumbs:

3 large eggs, beaten

Add the meat mixture and blend. Fill the casings only about three-quarters full, twisting and tying with kitchen string at 6-inch intervals. Without overcrowding, put the sausages in a wire basket and plunge them into a pot of boiling water. Reduce the heat at once to 190°F, and cook at this temperature about 20 minutes. Should any sausages rise to the surface of the liquid, puncture them to release the air and prevent bursting. Cool. Brush with:

Melted butter

and grill until golden brown.

PAN-BROILED SAUSAGE

4 servings

Please read Making Sausage at Home, 515.
Heat in a large heavy skillet over medium heat. Add:

1 teaspoon oil

8 raw or precooked sausages

Cover and cook, turning often, until evenly browned. Precooked sausages will take 5 to 6 minutes to brown and warm through; raw sausages will take 10 minutes or so to cook through completely and brown.

BOILED SAUSAGE

4 servings

Serve with Braised Red Cabbage, 264, or Sauerkraut, 265. Please read Making Sausage at Home, 515.
Bring 8 to 12 cups water to a boil in a medium pot. Add:

8 smoked or precooked sausages, such as frankfurters or white knockwurst

Simmer about 10 to 15 minutes. Drain and serve on:

Rolls

Accompany with:

(Mustard)

Or serve them alongside:

Braised Red Cabbage, 264, or Sauerkraut, 265

PORK SCRAPPLE OR GOETTA

About 6 servings

If you use cornmeal, call it **scrapple;** if you use oats, call it **goetta.** Please read Making Sausage at Home, 515.
Combine in a large pot and bring to a boil:

6 cups water

1 onion, sliced

6 whole black peppercorns

(1 small bay leaf)

Add:

2 pounds pork neck bones or spareribs

Reduce the heat and simmer until the meat falls from the bones, about 1¹/₂ hours. Strain, reserving the liquid. There should be about 4 cups. Add additional water or light stock if necessary. Using this liquid in place of boiling water, prepare:

Cornmeal Mush, 349

Or, for goetta, substitute **1 cup old-fashioned oatmeal** for the cornmeal, and, reduce the liquid by 1 cup. Remove all the meat from the pork bones and chop or grind it fine. Add it to the cooked mush. Season with:

1 teaspoon salt

2 teaspoons or more grated onion

(¹/₂ teaspoon dried thyme or sage)

A grating of nutmeg

A little ground red pepper

Pour the mixture into a loaf pan that has been rinsed with cold water. Refrigerate until cold and firm. To serve, slice and sauté slowly in:

Melted butter or drippings

ABOUT PÂTÉ

Pâtés and terrines are the stars of a cold buffet, and they are basically no harder to make than meat loaf. What distinguishes them is the sometimes-luxurious quality of their ingredients. The typical richness of a pâté can come from ground liver, cream, eggs, spices, or even truffles. The texture may be smooth, if all the meat is finely ground, or patterned, if the more colorful ingredients, such as green pistachios or strips of ham, are diced to show decoratively when the loaf is sliced. Endless combinations are possible to develop your own *pâté maison*. Lean meats, such as rabbit, can also be used, but they require the addition of lard or another animal fat.

The ingredients of pâtés and terrines should be very fresh. Handle liver with care; remove the gallbladder, if present, and all veins and blood. Wash thoroughly in cold water before using. Some of the meats can be bought ground, or you can ask your butcher to grind them for you. If you grind or puree your own, keep the meat well chilled, and keep everything impeccably clean, washing and drying the equipment thoroughly before and after each use.

Cook pâtés and terrines until the juices run clear when pierced with a skewer, or to an internal temperature of 160°F. Set on a rack to cool. The temperature will continue to rise by 5 to 10 degrees. Let cool to room temperature, then place the pâté or terrine on a baking sheet (with sides to catch any juices) and weight it to give it a compact texture: Simply place a board or smaller loaf pan directly on the pâté and place several cans on top. Refrigerate until firm, at least 12 hours, but preferably for 3 or 4 days to mature. A properly made, properly refrigerated pâté or terrine will safely keep 7 to 8 days in the refrigerator.

For chicken liver pâté, see 440.

PÂTÉ MAISON

10 servings

The texture and robust country flavors a pâté maizon, or pâté de campagne, make for a great first course when it is sliced and served with cornichons, the tangy small French pickles. Our version has a slightly smoky flavor from the bacon.

Preheat the oven to 325°F. Line the bottom and sides of a 9 x 5-inch loaf pan with:

12 to 16 slices bacon

Combine in a large bowl:

1 pound ground veal
1 pound ground calf's or chicken livers
2 large eggs, lightly beaten
¹/₂ cup heavy cream
1 tablespoon finely chopped garlic
2 teaspoons dried thyme
1¹/₂ teaspoons salt
1¹/₂ teaspoons black pepper
1 teaspoon grated or ground nutmeg
1 teaspoon sweet paprika
¹/₂ teaspoon ground sage

Mix until well combined. Heat in a small saucepan:

¹/₃ cup brandy or Cognac

If using electric heat, ignite with a match; if using gas heat, carefully tilt the pan to catch the flame. Pour the flaming brandy into the meat mixture and mix well to combine. Fill the lined loaf pan with the mixture and spread evenly. Place over the top:

5 or 6 slices bacon

Butter a piece of aluminum foil and place on top of the bacon to seal. Place a dish towel in a 13 x 11-inch roasting pan. Fill the pan about halfway with water and place the loaf pan in this water bath. Bake until the juices run clear and a thermometer inserted in the center registers 160°F, 1¹/₂ to 2 hours. Remove to a rack to cool completely. Place a small board or another loaf pan on top of the foil and weight with 2- or 3-pound cans. Refrigerate until firm, at least 12 hours, or up to 4 days. To serve, remove the bacon from the top of the pâté. Run a sharp knife around the edges, and turn the pâté out onto a serving platter or cutting board. Remove the bacon from the bottom and sides of the pâté, and slice the pâté into approximately ³/₄-inch slices. Serve with:

Cornichons
Dijon mustard
Sliced French bread

ABOUT VARIETY MEATS

Variety, we know, is the spice of life. And variety meats provide welcome relief from the weekly round of beef, pork, veal, chicken, and fish. They include **organ meats** like **sweetbreads, brains, kidney,** and **liver; muscle meats** like **heart, tongue,** and **tripe; bony meats** like oxtails or **knucklebones** and their **marrow** centers; and **extremities** such as **ears, feet,** and **heads.** Time was when most of these tidbits

were ours almost for the asking simply because most Americans had built-in prejudices against them. But in recent years, the American passion for travel has resulted in more cosmopolitan tastes in food, and more of us have learned to appreciate the odds and ends from which European cooks prepare some of their most celebrated dishes. There are practical reasons, too, to serve these: with the exception of **calf's liver** and **sweetbreads,** now in the higher-priced bracket, they are still gentle to a fragile budget.

Although variety meats are rarely prepared at home, it is not difficult to do so. We recommend ordering ahead from a full-service meat market or shopping for them at ethnic markets. ➤ It is essential that variety meats be fresh, as they are highly perishable. Use them at once.

ABOUT LIVER

Liver from young animals is preferred, as it is mildest and tenderest. Real calf's liver is delicate, delicious, and fairly expensive. It is paler in color than the redder, more mature "baby beef" liver. Choose the palest liver you can find, for it will have the mildest flavor. Often baby beef liver is labeled calf's liver in the supermarket. For true calf's liver, ask your butcher or buy it from a reputable gourmet supermarket.

Beef liver from a full-grown animal is dark red, almost brown, and the strength of color corresponds to the strength of flavor. Lamb liver is also tender but less flavorful. Pork liver, (➤ which must be cooked until no pink shows) is strong in taste, though very tender, and well worth the added effort of trimming out the tough fibers. Sheep, pork, and older beef livers should be soaked for several hours in a spicy marinade or in milk, after which time the liquid should be discarded. For pâtés and recipes using duck, goose, or chicken, see Poultry, 418.

Most recipes call for liver sliced ¹/₄ or ¹/₂ inch thick, however, thick slices over 1 inch may be successfully broiled, as for steak. **To prepare any liver for cooking,** wipe it first with a damp cloth, then remove the membrane and veining; the membrane can be peeled easily from fresh liver. ➤ Never toughen liver by cooking it too long or over excessive heat. ➤ Never cook beyond the point of tenderness. Liver has a natural affinity for Madeira, white wine, sour cream, nutmeg, and thyme. Sometimes the drippings in which liver has cooked are bitter; test them by tasting before you use them as sauce. Some good sauces to serve with liver are Béarnaise Sauce, 561, Barbecue Sauces, 586, Sauce Lyonnaise, 555, and Butter Sauces, 557. ➤ Allow 1 pound liver for 4 servings.

SAUTÉED CALF'S LIVER

4 servings

This classic presentation reminds us that simplicity is often the best approach. However, you may augment and garnish this basic recipe as you please.

Remove the membrane and cut into ¼-inch-thick slices:

1 pound calf's liver

Season to taste with:

Salt and black pepper

Dredge both sides with:

All-purpose flour

Heat in a large heavy skillet over medium-high heat:

**2 tablespoons vegetable oil or butter, or a
combination, or as needed**

Add the liver in batches, and brown quickly on both sides, 1 to 2 minutes; do not overcook. Do not crowd the skillet, and add more oil or butter as needed. Remove to a warmed platter when the liver is done.

LIVER AND ONIONS

4 to 6 servings

Prepare **Sautéed Calf's Liver,** above.

Heat in a large skillet over medium-low heat:

3 tablespoons olive oil

Add:

**3 to 4 large onions (1½ to 2 pounds total),
halved and thinly sliced**

Generous sprinkling of salt and black pepper

Cover and cook, stirring often, over low heat until the onions are very soft but not colored, 20 to 30 minutes. Spoon the liver over the cooked onions and serve immediately.

SWEETBREADS

To paraphrase Shakespeare's Puck, "What foods these morsels be!" Sweetbreads are the thymus or sometimes pancreatic glands of young animals. Veal sweetbreads are those most favored, but beef sweetbreads are sometimes incorporated into mixtures such as meat pies, pâtés, and terrines.

Like all organ meats, ➤ sweetbreads are highly perishable and should be prepared for use as soon as purchased. First soak them ➤ at least 1 hour in a large quantity of cold water to release any blood, changing the water 2 or 3 times. Next they must be blanched: Cover them with cold acidulated water, 957. Bring slowly to a boil and simmer uncovered for 2 to 5 minutes, depending on size. Drain. Firm them by plunging them at once into cold water. When cool, drain again and trim by removing cartilage, tubes, connective tissue, and tougher outer membranes. Refrigerate, weighted, for several hours if you plan on using them whole. If not, slice or break them into smaller sections, being careful not to disturb the very fine membrane that surrounds the smaller units.

After these preliminary processes, poach, braise, boil, cream, or sauce them. ➤ Allow 1 pair for 2 servings.

4 to 6 servings

Cut into ¼-inch-thick slices:

**1 pound sweetbreads, soaked, blanched, firmed,
trimmed, and weighted**

Whisk together in a shallow bowl:

1 large egg, lightly beaten

2 to 3 teaspoons water or milk

Spread in a second shallow bowl:

¾ cup dry bread crumbs

Spread in a third shallow bowl:

½ cup all-purpose flour

Pat the sweetbread slices dry and season with:

Salt and black pepper

Dredge the slices lightly with the flour and shake off the excess. Slide the flour-coated slices through the egg mixture, making sure the entire surface is covered, then coat with the bread crumbs, pressing the crumbs with your fingers so they adhere. Handle very gently so that the coating does not crack. Heat in a medium skillet over medium-high heat:

⅛ to ¼ inch olive oil

Add the sweetbread slices in batches and cook until brown on the first side, about 1½ to 2 minutes. Turn and brown on the other side, about 30 seconds. Do not overcook.

ABOUT BRAINS

We do not recommend eating the brains of cows, sheep, or pigs, nor any part of the spinal column, because of bovine spongiform encephalopathy (BSE) known as Mad Cow Disease.

ABOUT KIDNEYS

Calf and veal kidneys are the most tender and delicious. Those of lamb are somewhat soft and flat in flavor, but they are especially suitable for grilling. They should not be washed or soaked in water, as they will absorb it. Simply split and remove the cores and membranes.

Large beef kidneys tend to be hard and strong in flavor and need soaking for 2 hours in cold salted water. ➤ The white membranes should be snipped from all kidneys before they are washed. Removal of the membranes is easier if you first sauté the kidneys in fat for 1 minute. Discard the fat. Off flavors may be withdrawn by blanching, 1054, in acidulated water, 957, for 20 minutes; or, after soaking and drying, the kidneys can be sautéed briefly over brisk heat and allowed to cool partially before further cooking.

To prepare kidneys for broiling, butterfly. Keep them from curling during cooking ➤ by skewering them open. Expose the cut side to the heat first.

Calf, veal, and lamb kidneys should be cooked as short a time as possible over medium heat. ➤ Do not overcook: The center should be slightly pink. If kidneys are to be flambéed, never flame for more than 1 minute; longer exposure to such high heat will toughen them. Kidneys are often mixed with other ingredients, as in a stew of mushrooms and wine or in a creamy sauce of mustard and shallots. In any case, ➤ never allow them to boil in a sauce, as this only hardens them. Pour the hot sauce over them, or toss them in it for a moment or two. ➤ Allow 1 medium veal or calf kidney, 2 or 3 lamb kidneys, 1/2 beef kidney, or 1 small pork kidney per person.

SAUTÉED KIDNEYS WITH MUSTARD
3 to 4 servings
This traditional French dish pairs the pungent mustard from the French city of Dijon with capers and a bit of cream.
Prepare as above:

3 veal or 6 lamb kidneys

Cut veal kidneys crosswise into 1/2-inch slices or lamb kidneys lengthwise in half. Season with:

Salt and black pepper

Heat in a large heavy skillet over medium heat:

2 tablespoons butter or vegetable oil

Add the kidneys in batches and brown, about 1 1/2 minutes on each side. Remove to a plate and keep warm. If all the fat is gone, add to the pan:

(2 tablespoons butter or vegetable oil)

Add and cook, stirring until softened, 3 to 4 minutes:

1/2 cup chopped shallots or onion
1 teaspoon chopped garlic

Add:

1/2 cup dry white wine
1/2 cup chicken stock or broth
1 teaspoon chopped rosemary or thyme

Bring to a boil, scraping up the browned bits on the bottom of the pan, and reduce to about 1/3 cup. Turn off the heat. Stir in and mix thoroughly:

2 tablespoons heavy cream
1 tablespoon chopped drained capers
1 1/2 teaspoons Dijon mustard

Season to taste with:

Salt and black pepper

Return the kidneys and their juices to the pan and stir gently to coat with the sauce. Serve with:

Hot cooked rice

ABOUT TONGUE
Lucky indeed is the cook with the gift of tongues! No matter from which source—beef, calf, lamb, or pork—smaller tongues are usually preferable. The most commonly used and best flavored, whether fresh, smoked, or pickled, is beef tongue. For prime texture, it should be under 3 pounds.

Scrub the tongue well. If it is smoked or pickled, you may wish to blanch it first, 1054, in simmering water for about 10 minutes; drain and immerse in cold water. After draining, cook as in the recipe below.

If the tongue is to be served hot, drain, plunge it into cold water for a moment so you can handle it, and skin and trim it by removing the roots, small bones, and gristle. Return it very briefly to the hot cooking water to reheat before serving. If the tongue is to be served cold, allow it to cool just enough to handle comfortably. It skins easily at this point, ➤ but not if you let it get cold. Trim and re-

turn it to the pot to cool completely in the cooking liquid. It is attractive served in Aspic, 174.

To carve tongue, cut through at the bump parallel to the base. But toward the tip, ➤ better-looking slices can be made if the cut is diagonal.

BOILED FRESH, SMOKED, OR PICKLED BEEF TONGUE
6 to 8 servings
To remove some of the brine or smoky taste from a pickled or smoked tongue, blanch it first as described above.
Place in a large pot:

1 fresh, smoked, or pickled beef or calf's tongue (about 3 pounds)

Add:

2 medium onions, halved
1 large carrot, peeled
3 or more ribs celery with leaves
6 whole black peppercorns
2 bay leaves

Barely cover these ingredients with boiling water. Bring to a boil, then reduce the heat to a simmer. Skim off the scum on the surface after the first 5 minutes, and simmer the tongue, uncovered, until tender, 2 1/2 to 3 hours. Let the tongue cool in the liquid until it can be handled. Skin and trim the tongue. Return the tongue to the liquid and reheat it. Slice and serve hot with:

Piquant Sauce, 556

Or, refrigerate the sliced tongue in its liquid until cold and serve with:

Russian Horseradish Cream, 581, or coarse-grain or smooth French-style mustard

ABOUT HEART
Heart, which is firm and rather dry, is best prepared by slow-cooking. It is a muscle, not an organ meat. Before cooking, wash it well, removing fat, arteries, veins, and blood, and dry carefully. ➤ A 4- to 5-pound beef heart will serve 6; a veal heart will serve 1.

BAKED STUFFED HEART
3 servings
Preheat the oven to 325°F. Prepare as directed above:

One 4- to 5-pound beef heart or 3 veal hearts

Tie with a string to hold its shape, if necessary. Wrap in cheesecloth or foil and tie. Place over the heart:

4 slices bacon

Place on a rack in a baking dish and pour over it:

2 cups stock or broth

Cover the dish tightly and bake until tender—for beef, 3 to 4 hours, depending on size; for veal, about 2 hours. Remove the heart to a plate and cool slightly. Increase the oven temperature to 400°F. Heat in a double boiler until warm, then fill the heart(s) with:

3 cups Apple Dressing, 537

To allow for expansion, do not pack the dressing. Sprinkle the heart(s) with:

Paprika

Return to the 400°F oven long enough to heat through. If desired, use the drippings for:

Meat Pan Gravy, 546

ABOUT TRIPE

Tripe is the muscular lining of the four stomachs of ruminants. It includes **plain or smooth tripe** from the first stomach, **honeycomb,** the most available, along with the fatter, partially honeycombed **gras double,** second stomach; **feuillet or manyplies,** from the third stomach; and **reed,** from the fourth stomach.

Honeycomb tripe is the most delicate variety and today comes in either refrigerated plastic pouches or large sheets. Fresh tripe has usually already been blanched and parboiled. After cutting it into pieces, wash thoroughly. It is now ready to season and cook. ➤ Since tripe is very perishable, it should be kept refrigerated and used as soon as possible.

If you start from scratch, cooking tripe is a long, drawn-out affair. Fresh whole tripe calls for a minimum of 12 hours of cooking, with some time-honored recipes demanding as long as 24. **To prepare fresh tripe,** trim if necessary. ➤ Rinse it thoroughly, soak overnight, and then blanch, 1054, for 30 minutes in salted water. Rinse well again, drain, and cut for cooking. When cooked, the texture of tripe should be like that of soft gristle. More often, alas, ➤ because the heat has not been kept low enough, it has the consistency of wet shoe leather.

Tripe is sometimes pickled after cooking and served hot or cold in a marinade. Pickled tripe may also be found in the market.

SPANISH-STYLE TRIPE
6 servings

Cut into 1¹/₂-inch-wide strips and wash well:

2 pounds blanched and parboiled tripe

Boil, covered, about 2¹/₂ hours in salted water. Drain. Heat in a large skillet:

2 tablespoons olive or vegetable oil

Add and cook, stirring, until golden:

1 cup chopped onions
2 garlic cloves, minced

Add:

2 cups tomato puree
1 small green bell pepper, cored, seeded, diced
¹/₂ teaspoon dried thyme, basil, or oregano
1 bay leaf
¹/₂ teaspoon salt
Black pepper to taste

Cover and simmer about 15 minutes. Add the tripe and:

(¹/₂ cup minced cooked ham)
(¹/₂ cup sliced mushrooms)

Simmer 15 minutes more. If the sauce is too dry, add:

(¹/₄ to ¹/₂ cup dry red wine)

Serve with:

Cooked rice

BRAISED OXTAILS (OXTAIL STEW)
4 servings

The tough, coarse-grained oxtail meat takes the gentle, slow heat of a braise to soften the high amount of connective tissue present. This results in a tender dish with rich beef flavor and a velvety sauce. Oxtails are usually sold in 1- to 3-inch cross sections; because of the amount of bone, you should buy at least 1 pound per person. Pieces from the very narrow tip of the tail yield almost no meat at all and are best saved for the stockpot.

Preheat the oven to 350°F. Heat in a large heavy skillet:

4 tablespoons (¹/₂ stick) butter or ¹/₄ cup
    beef drippings
1 tablespoon olive oil

Dredge:

4 pounds oxtails, cut into sections

in:

Seasoned Flour, 962

Brown and place all in pan and add:

3 cups Brown Beef Stock, 117, or 1¹/₂ cups stock plus
    1¹/₂ cups tomato juice, or as needed
1 teaspoon salt
10 whole black peppercorns

Bring to a boil, then transfer to a casserole. Cover and bake until oxtails are tender, 4 to 5 hours, adding more stock if needed. During the last 45 minutes of cooking add:

2 cups chopped onion
1¹/₂ cups chopped carrots
1 cup chopped celery
4 garlic cloves, chopped
2 tablespoons chopped parsley

Strain the stock from the oxtails and skim off most of the fat. Use some of the stock for:

Meat Pan Gravy, 546

Season to taste with:

Salt and black pepper

Combine the meat, vegetables, and gravy.

CHITTERLINGS
6 to 7 servings

We were well along in years before we discovered that the name of this dish had an "e," an "r," a "g," and 3 syllables, and still farther along before we found these were the base for the andouillette sausage the French set such store by. Just after slaughter, the intestines of a young pig are emptied while still warm, turned inside out, and scraped clean. Wash in cold water, and soak, refrigerated, in cold salted water to cover for 24 hours. Wash them again in 5 or 6 changes of water. Remove excess fat, but leave some for flavor. If not preparing your own, they are available cleaned and soaked.

Put in a large pot with water to cover:

    10 pounds chitterlings, cleaned and cut into
        2-inch lengths
    $1/4$ cup sliced onions
    2 tablespoons chopped parsley
    2 tablespoons white wine vinegar
    (3 dried chile peppers)
    2 teaspoons salt
    1 teaspoon each ground cloves
    1 teaspoon mace
    1 teaspoon allspice
    $1/2$ teaspoon black pepper
    $1/2$ teaspoon dried thyme
    1 garlic clove
    1 bay leaf

Bring slowly to a boil. Cover and reduce the heat and simmer 3 to 4 hours. Stir occasionally to prevent sticking. During the last 30 minutes of cooking, you may add:

    ($1/4$ cup catsup)
    Salt and black pepper to taste

Serve with:

    Corn Bread, 632, or Black-Eyed Peas and Greens, 256

SAUTÉED CHITTERLINGS

Prepare **Chitterlings, above,** omitting the vinegar and catsup. When the chitterlings are tender, drain and dry well.

Dredge them in **Seasoned Flour, 962.** Cook gently in **butter** until a delicate brown.

ABOUT MARROW

Marrow is high in flavor, nutrients, and fat. A classic ingredient in French cuisine, it is found in the center of the long leg bones of animals, generally beef. Marrow bones should be fresh, clean, and free of blood. Marrow itself is slightly off white. It should be firm and kept well chilled.

Marrow can be prepared in several different ways. The marrow can be removed from split large bones. Use a cleaver to crack the bone, and pull it apart; remove the marrow from the center. Cut the marrow into $1/2$-inch slices and soften in the top of a double boiler over ➤ simmering, not boiling, water. You can also gently poach the slices in stock for $1 1/2$ to 2 minutes. Once cooked, marrow is slightly firm to the touch. Serve the poached slices on small toast rounds for an appetizer. ➤ Marrow must not be overcooked, as it is very fatty and simply melts and disintegrates under too much heat.

Alternatively, shorter 3-inch marrow bones can be poached for $1 1/2$ to 2 minutes in water, stock, or Court Bouillon, 120, or seasoned with salt and pepper and baked in a preheated 300°F oven for about 1 hour. Serve, with marrow spoons or other long spoons, with toast rounds and an accompaniment such as chutney.

GAME

Game cooking has had an enduring and important role in America's culinary history. For most urbanites, the craft of stalking and vivid excitement of the chase may be merely hearsay, but more of us than ever now track down purveyors of game in the yellow pages or on the Internet, or ride forth to the butcher shop or specialty section of the supermarket and come home with "something for the pot." The gustatory pleasures of game cookery—the robust flavors, unique textures, and sheer healthfulness—are, or should be at least on occasion, unmissable.

Even in the kitchen, though, wild game is sometimes unpredictable. It is important to remain flexible, adventuresome, and thoughtful when preparing wild foods—and they should not be cooked so that diners exclaim, "It tastes just like chicken!" Nor should game be masked, as it sometimes is, with elaborate, overpowering sauces. We should celebrate its differences and enhance them.

The renewed interest in game has been encouraged partly by gastronomic exploration and partly by the realization that the meat of most game is significantly lower in saturated fat than that of their domestic counterparts. As the demand for game has increased, however, the definition of game has changed. ➤ The term used to mean only animals or birds caught in the wild; today, "game" includes birds and animals once hunted in the wild that are now raised domestically, such as rabbit, deer, or quail.

Game is both ranched and farmed. Ranched game is raised under free-range conditions, developing a more complex flavor and less body fat than farmed animals. Farmed game is typically milder to the taste and somewhat fattier. Game raised by either method is usually more tender than wild game and, although lacking the assertive character of animals from the wild, may be more consistently pleasing in flavor. It is also far more convenient—both because of availability and it comes to market already dressed and often already cut into serving pieces.

Hunting remains a popular sport in almost every state in the union. ➤ If you choose to hunt, remember that proper handling of game will greatly enhance its flavor; if you're a novice, contact your local cooperative extension service or state and federal fish and wildlife agencies for information on proper handling of game before you hunt. When cooking wild game, follow the recommendation for its farm-raised counterpart, ➤ but remember that wild game is almost always leaner and often must be basted, 466, so that it does not dry out, and it will generally cook more quickly than farm-raised animals.

ABOUT BUYING GAME

Not every supermarket carries game. Many meat departments and butcher shops can special-order it on a few days' notice. There are also internet companies that will deliver game to your door. ➤ In judging the quality of game, use the same standards as for other meats and poultry. While fresh products are generally preferred, properly frozen game is far superior to a poorly handled fresh specimen. For best results, ➤ thaw frozen game slowly in the refrigerator, see About Storing Meat Before Cooking, 463.

ABOUT PREPARING GAME

The hunter must become familiar with season, limit, and holding laws as well as how to clean, cut, and store the prize of the effort. ➤ Quick cooling, scrupulous cleaning, and careful processing greatly enhance the flavor of the animal. Undesirable "gaminess" is often just the result of improper care and handling before cooking.

Those who handle animals, fish, and birds in the wild need to be aware of the potential risks involved for contaminating the flesh with organisms that cause disease during dressing, handling, and transporting it. ➤ Any raw game meat or fish can contain harmful bacteria such as *E. coli* or *enteridis*. They live in the intestines of the animals. Parasites are another concern in wild game as well as fish. ➤ To guard against diseases, such as trichinosis, 497, in bear, boar, and venison; tularemia, 524, in rabbit, and salmonellosis, 905, the hunter should wear gloves when handling raw meat and observe proper cooking temperatures before consuming. But whether dressing small or large game the procedure is basically similar—field-dress, skin, cool, and hang or freeze as quickly as possible. It is important, too, to ➤ remove the fat of wild animals as soon as possible, as it turns rancid quickly. And keep any loose hairs away from the flesh, or rinse them off, for the oils in the hair produce off flavors.

Edible variety meats, 518, should be used at once in camp cooking or frozen right away. With **larger game,** the logistics of butchering are similar to those of domestic cattle, 473. The ease of further preparation depends on the skill of your shot. If the animal is gut-shot, damaged areas of the meat must be trimmed by scraping or cutting to remove all traces of blood. Spilled intestinal contents can also lead to a "gamy" taste if they adhere to the flesh. If possible, wash the area with salt water and dry well.

Immediately ➤ after the kill, the animal should be **field-dressed**—or have its body opened and the internal organs removed—to bleed out the carcass and aid in rapid loss of body heat. A sharp knife with a small to medium blade works best.

Start where the breastbone ends and make a 3- to 4-inch downward cut in the skin of the abdomen. Be careful not to cut into any internal organs. You can insert two fingers of your free hand into the slit to hold the skin up and away from the intestines as you cut. Hold the knife blade outward so as not to pierce the intestines, and use just the knife tip so that you cut only the skin.

Continuing to guide with your free hand as you go, cut almost to the end of the gut cavity, where the meat of the hindquarters begins. When this long slit is made, roll the skin back about 3 or 4 inches on either side of the cut, keeping the loose hairs away from the flesh. At this point, the internal organs and intestines will protrude. Before trying to remove them, hold the hind legs apart and continue a skin-deep cut down the center around one side of the genitals and all the way to the anus. Cut around the opposite side of the genitals, and remove them.

Next cut the diaphragm from the body wall: The diaphragm is the muscle that separates the heart and lungs from the other internal organs. Cut close to the body wall, following the ribs down one side, across the backbone, and up along the ribs on the other side to the starting point. If the animal has been correctly lung- or heart-shot, a large amount of blood will pour out of the chest cavity, bleeding out the carcass. Free the heart and lungs by reaching forward until you feel the esophagus and windpipe; cut them as far forward of the lungs as possible. Free the intestines by cutting around the anus and pulling them through to the inside. This is easier if you split the pelvic bone with a heavy knife. You will need a small ax for moose or elk. Some hunters prefer not to split the pelvic bone or chest cavity until the animal is butchered. This helps keep flies, yellow jackets, and contamination out of the body cavity if you have to drag the carcass a long distance.

The internal organs can now be removed in their entirety by rolling the carcass onto its side and spilling them out onto the ground. If you have to trim away any connective tissue, be very careful not to cut the two tenderloins, which lie alongside the backbone below the rib cage.

Be careful ➤ not to cut into the musk glands in the lower belly or rupture the thin-walled bladder. Locate it by tracing the tube that leads to the outside. Grasp the tube, pinching it together to close off the bladder. After further freeing the bladder, retain your grasp on the tube as you

ease out the bladder fully. Cut away the liver, kidneys, and heart. Put in a plastic bag for easy carrying.

Work, if possible, in such a way that after the removal of the internal organs, you will merely have to wipe the cavity with a dry cloth. If fluids from internal organs or blood have touched the flesh, or the flesh has been bullet-pierced, though, scrape or cut the areas as cleanly as possible. Do not allow any blood to remain, as it will produce off flavors. Wipe such areas with snow or water or, if available, salt water. Dry carefully.

Hang the carcass to cool quickly. To shorten cooling time, the body cavity can be propped open with sticks. On a hot day, bags of ice can be put into the body cavity. Leave the ice in the bags.

Small game like birds, squirrel, and rabbit should also be field-dressed immediately after shooting. The procedure is similar to that above, but much easier. Cool the carcass as quickly as possible. Do not pack carcasses close together, which will slow down cooling. ➤ Small animals should be skinned as soon as possible, 525.

After cleaning game, cool to below 40°F as quickly as possible, then keep cool, preferably for a minimum of 24 hours, before butchering. Beef is better if allowed to age for a week or 10 days at 34° to 38°F, and the same is true for venison. ➤ Large game animals are prepared and processed like beef, small game like poultry.

If the meat is to be canned, spices should be used sparingly and vegetables omitted altogether. White pepper retains a better flavor than black pepper in meat products. If you like, you can place 1 teaspoon salt in each empty quart jar—this amount flavors but does not help to preserve the meat. ➤ Canned game must be pressure-processed as described in Canning, 888.

ABOUT COOKING GAME

The most common error in cooking game is overcooking it, because game is lower in fat than other meats and cooks more quickly. Like all meat, it continues cooking even after it has been removed from the heat source. Game meats raised domestically do not necessarily need to stew for hours in order to become tender. ➤ In general, the red meat of venison and buffalo is best when cooked only to medium-rare. More specific cooking instructions follow with the recipes. Also see the recipe for game stock in the Soups chapter, 118.

ABOUT SMALL GAME

Small game caught in the wild should be dressed as soon as possible, see About Preparing Game, 523. ➤ It is advisable to handle wild meat, especially when you are dressing it, with gloves to prevent against the danger of tularemia infection. Be guided in your choice of recipe by the age of the animal, using a moist-heat process, 462, for older animals.

Small game animals—**rabbit, squirrel, opossum, porcu-**

pine, raccoon, woodchuck, beaver, armadillo, muskrat—are often the young hunter's first quarry and as such have long been part of America's culinary tradition. Small game remains plentiful in the United States, but as rural life with its legacy of hunting declines, so does the need to have a repertoire of recipes for these animals. ➤ Know that small game can be cooked following most recipes for chicken. And we have included here some classic, and not so classic, recipes for rabbit, which is widely available to non-hunters, and these can be used for other types of small game as well.

RABBIT AND HARE

Although rabbit and hare are now widely available commercially, both are still much hunted. The **snowshoe rabbit,** which is actually a hare, and probably the one most commonly found in the kitchen, is the smallest of the hares, with a total weight of between 3 and 4 pounds. The largest native hare is the **Arctic hare,** which weighs between 6 to 15 pounds. Generally speaking, hare, which is dark meat, is tough and bony, especially the snowshoe, and should be at least marinated for a long time or stewed slowly. Generally, "hanging" and aging rabbits and hare after the animal has gone through rigor mortis does not have much effect on the tenderness. ➤ Rabbit is rich and strong in flavor and is the main course in millions of meals every year in the United States.

To dress rabbit or hare, don gloves to avoid possible tularemia infection. Sever the front legs at the joint as shown, below, by the dotted line. Cut through the skin around the hind legs the same way. Tie the feet together securely, and hang the rabbit on a hook. ➤ Working from the dotted line, pull the skin off the legs toward the hind feet, stripping it inside out like a glove. Then pull the remaining skin over the body and forelegs. Sever the head and discard it with the skin. Slit the rabbit down the front. Remove the entrails and discard them, except for the heart and liver. ➤ Wash the carcass inside and out with acidulated water, 957. Rinse and dry carefully.

To cut apart a rabbit for cooking, you basically cut the rabbit into five pieces: Lay skinned and cleaned rabbit on its back and cut off the two hindquarters (back legs and thighs). Next remove the two forequarters (right and left front legs and ribs). What remains is the back strap—the loin meat that runs along the backbone, below the ribs, stomach and above the hindlegs.

Skinning a rabbit or hare

SAUTÉED RABBIT
2 servings
If a rabbit is young (2 to 3 pounds with fur), prepare as for **Panfried (or Sautéed) Chicken, 429.** Serve with **Apricot preserves, 937.**

FRICASSEE OF RABBIT
4 servings
Cut into serving pieces, above:
   A rabbit
Dredge with:
   Seasoned flour, 962
Melt in a large skillet or Dutch oven:
   ¹/₄ cup (¹/₂ stick) butter
Or render, 981:
   4 ounces diced salt pork
Add:
   ¹/₄ cup chopped shallots or onion
   (1 cup cut-up mushrooms)
Cook, stirring until soft. Using a slotted spoon, remove the shallots and mushrooms to a bowl. Brown rabbit, in batches if necessary, in the fat remaining in the pan. If desired, flambé, 1055, the rabbit with:
   (¹/₄ cup brandy)
When the flames subside, add:
   1¹/₂ cups stock or dry white wine
Tie in a cheesecloth bag:
   1 piece of lemon rind
   3 whole black peppercorns
   2 sprigs parsley
   2 ribs celery with leaves
Add to the pan, cover, and simmer the meat until done, 1 hour or more, or put in a 300°F oven for about 2 hours. Do not let the liquid boil at any time. Ten minutes before you remove the rabbit from the pan, take out the seasoning bag and add the shallots and mushrooms. Place the rabbit on a hot serving dish. Thicken the sauce with:
   Beurre Manié, 545

RABBIT À LA MODE OR JUGGED HARE (HASENPFEFFER)
4 servings
Cut into serving pieces, above:
   A rabbit
Place the pieces in a crock, jar, or bowl and add:
   Cooked Marinade for Game, 585
Marinate in the refrigerator for 24 to 48 hours. Preheat the oven to 350°F. Drain the rabbit, and reserve the marinade. Pat the pieces of rabbit dry and dredge them in:
   Seasoned flour, 962
Heat in a large skillet:
   3 tablespoons bacon fat
Add the rabbit, in batches if necessary, and brown until golden. Remove the browned rabbit to an ovenproof casserole. Add to the skillet and cook, stirring, until the onions are tender:

2 tablespoons butter

1 cup finely chopped onions

Add the onions to the casserole, along with the reserved marinade, and bring to a boil on top of the stove. Remove from the heat at once, cover, and place in the oven. Cook about 2 hours, or until the meat is tender.

BRAISED MARINATED RABBIT WITH PRUNES

4 servings

Combine in a large bowl:

3 cups dry red wine

3 tablespoons olive oil

1 cup thinly sliced red onions

$^1/_2$ cup finely diced carrots

2 teaspoons fresh thyme leaves or $^3/_4$ teaspoon dried thyme

2 large bay leaves

Add, turning to coat:

One 3- to 3$^1/_2$-pound rabbit, cut into serving pieces, giblets reserved if desired

Cover and marinate in the refrigerator from 6 to 24 hours. Heat in a Dutch oven or casserole over medium-high heat:

2 tablespoons olive oil

Add and cook, stirring until lightly browned, about 15 minutes:

1 cup pearl onions, peeled

8 ounces small mushrooms

Remove with a slotted spoon and set aside. Add to the pot and lightly brown:

5 slices bacon, diced

Remove with a slotted spoon to paper towels to drain. Remove the rabbit from the marinade (reserve the marinade) and pat dry. Season with:

Salt and black pepper

Add the rabbit pieces to the pot and lightly brown. Remove to a plate. Reduce the heat to low, and cook, stirring, until starting to color slightly:

1 tablespoon all-purpose flour

Strain the marinade through a fine-mesh sieve into the pot, and whisk to blend with the flour. Bring to a boil and add the bacon and rabbit. Reduce the heat, cover, and simmer for 25 minutes. Add the reserved pearl onions and mushrooms, along with:

12 ounces pitted prunes

Cover and simmer until the rabbit is tender, about 20 minutes more. Remove the rabbit, vegetables, and prunes to a deep serving dish and cover to keep warm. If the sauce is thin, boil over high heat until slightly thickened, 5 to 8 minutes. Finely chop the giblets, if using, and add to the pot, along with:

2 tablespoons raspberry vinegar

(2 teaspoons red currant or apricot preserves)

Salt and white pepper to taste

Simmer, stirring, for 5 minutes more. Pour the sauce over the rabbit and serve immediately.

RABBIT WITH MUSTARD (LAPIN À LA MOUTARDE)

4 servings

Serve this French bistro classic on a bed of sautéed cabbage or with buttered noodles.

Mix together in a small bowl:

$^1/_3$ cup Dijon mustard

1 tablespoon fresh thyme leaves, or 1 teaspoon dried thyme

Generously brush it over:

One 3- to 3$^1/_2$-pound rabbit, cut into 8 serving pieces

Season to taste with:

Salt and black pepper

Heat in a large skillet over medium heat:

3 tablespoons olive oil

Add the rabbit pieces, in batches if necessary, and lightly brown, about 5 minutes on each side. Remove the rabbit to a platter. Reduce the heat to medium-low, add to the pan, and cook, stirring, until lightly browned:

2 tablespoons chopped shallots

Add and bring to a boil, scraping up the browned bits:

1$^1/_2$ cups chicken or vegetable stock or broth

1 cup dry white wine

($^1/_2$ cup heavy cream)

Reduce the heat and simmer for about 5 minutes. Return the rabbit to the pan, cover, and cook gently until tender but still moist, about 45 minutes. Remove the rabbit to a platter and cover to keep warm. Strain the sauce carefully through a fine-mesh sieve into a saucepan. Stir in:

1 tablespoon chopped parsley, chives, tarragon, or chervil

(2 teaspoons yellow mustard seeds, lightly toasted)

Bring to a boil over high heat and cook until the sauce is reduced to about 2 cups, about 6 minutes. Season with:

2 to 3 drops fresh lemon juice

Salt and black pepper to taste

Spoon the sauce over and around the rabbit.

CASSEROLED RABBIT AND SAUSAGE

4 servings

Skin, and cut into serving pieces, 525:

1 rabbit

Place in a large skillet and add:

1 pound fresh pork sausage or 3 smoked pork sausages

1 cup beer

$^1/_4$ cup cider vinegar

1 cup chicken consommé, stock, or broth

1 cup browned bread crumbs, 960, or $^1/_4$ cup raw rice

1 teaspoon caraway seeds

1 teaspoon grated lemon zest

1 teaspoon brown sugar

Salt and black pepper to taste

Bring to a boil. Reduce heat, cover, and simmer gently for approximately 2 hours. Skim off the fat, and make:

Poultry Pan Gravy, 546

Remove the rabbit to a platter and serve with the gravy.

RABBIT WITH CHILI

4 servings

Cut into serving pieces:

1 rabbit

Heat in a large skillet:

2 tablespoons olive oil

Add the rabbit, in batches if necessary, and brown on both sides with:

1 garlic clove, minced

Add to a pot of:

Vegetarian Chili, 254

Cover and simmer gently until tender, about 2 hours. Just before serving, preheat the broiler. Sprinkle the chili with:

2 tablespoons grated Cheddar or Jack cheese

Place under the broiler until the cheese is golden.

ABOUT LARGE GAME

No matter the method of handling large game, certain preparations are basic, see About Preparing Game, 523. Game shot in an unsuspecting moment is more tender and will also deteriorate less quickly than game that is chased. ➤ Immediate and careful gutting, immediate removal of all hair near exposed flesh, and prompt skinning are essential, 523. ➤ In dressing game, be careful not to cut into the musk glands in the lower belly. ➤ Care must be taken to remove all fat from any of these game animals, as it grows rancid quickly and should not be used to grease pans or for sautéing or browning. The livers and heart, after cooling, are often eaten at the campsite. As with all game, the lushness of the season and the age of the animal contribute to the decision as to how to cook it. For marinades for game, see 585. Yogurt or Buttermilk Marinade, 585, or any milk-based marinade will lessen the gamy flavor of antlered animals.

For sauces for game, see 222. Cabbage, turnips, chestnuts, wild rice, and mushrooms are classic game accompaniments, as are brandied fruits, 215.

VENISON

Please read About Large Game, above. We usually use the term "venison" to mean deer meat, but the word— derived from the Latin *venari,* "to hunt"—properly refers to all large antlered game animals, including **elk, caribou,** and **antelope,** as well as **deer.** Currently all four of these are raised commercially in America. In general, their meat is more tender and less strong than that of their wild counterparts. Differences in species, age, and methods of rearing and processing may account for differences in taste and texture, ➤ but all venison is lean red meat. Deer remains the most popular and common of venisons and is both farmed and ranched extensively, domestically and abroad. Much of the venison available today is the meat of farm-raised **red deer** from New Zealand. **Fallow deer** is also farm-raised. Other varieties, including **axis** and **sika deer,** are ranched, roaming freely on large-game compounds. Farm-raised deer are more uniform in size and flavor than wild or ranched deer, but the latter are leaner, and their flavor may be more complex.

Antelope meat is delicately flavored, a bit lighter than other venison and closer to veal. It is best cooked and served simply. Both **nilgai** (or nilgi) and **black buck antelope** are ranched in Texas; the former is larger and has a milder flavor. **Caribou,** which have been domesticated in Alaska for years, has juicy and flavorful meat. **Elk** is considered by some connoisseurs to be the best venison of all and is sometimes compared to prime beef.

COOKING VENISON

Venison of any type, unfortunately, is all too easy to ruin in the kitchen. Since there is very little intramuscular fat or marbling, the meat loses moisture quickly in the heat of the oven or skillet; without fat to coat its proteins, it quickly turns tough and chewy. Remember this simple axiom for cooking venison: ➤ Cook the tender cuts from the saddle, loin, tenderloin, and hind leg over high heat for a short time, and stew or braise the tougher cuts from the shoulder or neck. As with lamb or beef, ➤ the most tender and most popular cuts are the center and top portions, sold in the form of steaks, chops, or strip loins. In addition, many processors bone, trim, and butcher the hind leg, referred to as the Denver leg, into a convenient assortment of 7 or 8 cuts, all of which make excellent steaks, medallions, and small roasts.

All naturally ➤ tender cuts are best broiled, sautéed, or grilled quickly to rare or medium-rare. Venison should remain crimson; if it's gray, it's overcooked. ➤ Tougher cuts of venison, such as the shoulder, neck, and stew meat of commercially raised game, or large roasts from wild animals, should be seared over high heat to brown, then slowly roasted in a 225° to 250°F oven or braised until tender, 466. It is not necessary to marinate commercially raised venison, ➤ but wild venison often benefits from marinating, which increases tenderness and enhances flavor. Red wine marinades are traditional, but yogurt or buttermilk marinades, 585, offset the stronger flavor of wild venison, and the milk proteins tenderize the meats quite efficiently. Do not overmarinate; 1 hour at room temperature or up to 24 hours in the refrigerator is usually sufficient. ➤ Ground venison is best when combined with a little ground beef or pork or beaten eggs to keep it moist when grilled. Venison burgers without additions may be cooked by quickly browning them over high heat (either on a grill or in a pan), and then cooking them covered in a little broth or wine. To prepare cured venison, see Jerky, 905.

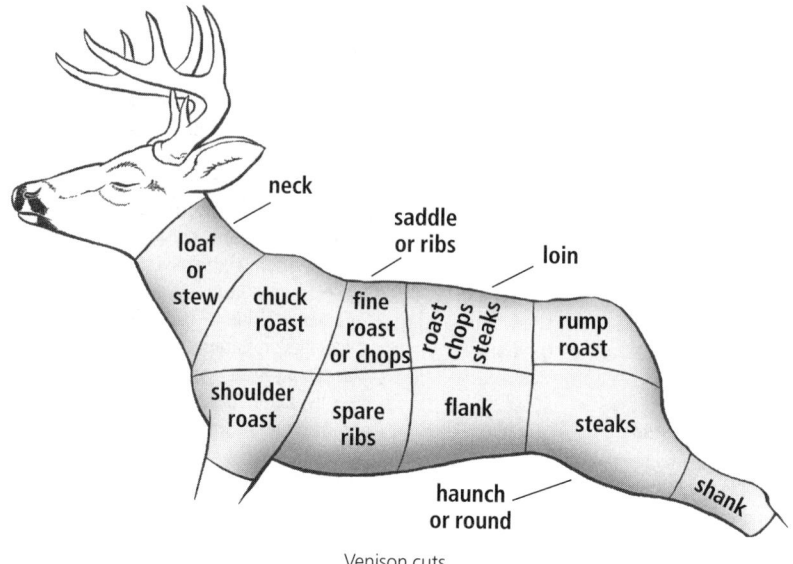

Venison cuts

VENISON BURGER

To make this lean meat moist, combine:

4 parts ground venison
1 part fresh pork sausage

Cook as for **Hamburgers, 510,** but allow extra time to ensure the meat is no longer pink. Serve with:

Salsa Fresca, 571, or a flavored mayonnaise, 578

ROASTED LEG OF VENISON

8 to 12 servings if boneless, 6 to 8 servings if on the bone

This recipe works equally well with venison saddle or rib roast and is perfect served with Mashed Potatoes, 295. Preheat the oven to 450°F. Melt in a saucepan over low heat:

¹/₂ cup (1 stick) butter

Add and cook for 5 to 6 minutes, without browning:

1 tablespoon minced garlic
2 tablespoons chopped fresh parsley
1 teaspoon dried sage
1 teaspoon dried oregano

Season with:

Salt and black pepper to taste

Remove from the heat. Place on a rack in a roasting pan:

One 6- to 8-pound boneless or bone-in venison roast

Pour the butter mixture over the meat, and roast for 20 minutes. Reduce the oven temperature to 325°F and add to the pan:

2 cups finely chopped onions
2 cups dry red wine

Roast, basting often, until a meat thermometer inserted in the thickest part of the roast registers 130° to 140°F for medium-rare, about 12 minutes per pound if boneless, 15 minutes per pound if on the bone. Remove the roast to a platter and cover to keep warm. Set the roasting pan over medium-high heat and add:

3 cups game or chicken broth

Boil, scraping up any browned bits, until the sauce is reduced to 1¹/₂ to 2 cups. Strain through a fine-mesh sieve into a saucepan. Set over high heat and add:

¹/₂ cup red currant jelly
¹/₄ cup Cognac or other brandy

Skim off any fat and boil for 2 to 3 minutes, until slightly thickened. Season with:

Salt and black pepper to taste

VENISON POT ROAST

Use the less tender cuts of venison, including all shoulder and blade roasts as well as cuts from wild venison, either in a single large piece or cut into small ones; be sure to remove all fat. Please read Cooking Venison, 527. Place the meat in a **marinade, 584,** cover, and refrigerate for 12 to 24 hours, turning it from time to time. Remove from the marinade (reserve the marinade) and pat dry. Prepare as for **Beef Pot Roast, 477,** adding some of the reserved marinade to the cooking liquid, if desired. Discard the rest. Cook as directed until tender; the length of time will depend on the size and shape of the cut of venison.

SAUTÉED VENISON STEAKS

6 servings

Use steaks cut from the loin or tender portion of the leg for this recipe.

Gently pound and flatten with a mallet or the bottom of a small heavy pan to an even thickness of about ¹/₂ inch:

6 venison loin steaks (6 to 7 ounces each)

Heat in a heavy skillet over medium heat:

3 tablespoons olive oil

Add and quickly brown:

4 garlic cloves, slightly crushed

Remove and discard the garlic. Increase the heat to high and very quickly brown the meat, 2 to 3 minutes each side. Season well on both sides with:

Salt and black pepper

Remove to a plate and cover. Add to the pot and simmer, uncovered, until the tomatoes are reduced to a pulp:

   2 pounds ripe tomatoes, seeded and chopped
   1 to 2 tablespoons chopped oregano
   Pinch of crushed red pepper flakes

Stir in and bring to a simmer:

   **$1/4$ cup chopped pitted black olives or 2 tablespoons
      drained capers**
   $1/2$ cup dry white wine

Season with:

   Salt and black pepper to taste

Pour over the steaks and serve immediately.

VENISON BLACK BEAN CHILI

10 to 12 servings

Soak, 253:

   2 cups dried black beans, rinsed and picked over

Or use:

   **Three $15^{1}/2$-ounce cans black beans, rinsed and
      drained**

If using dried beans, drain, place in a large pot, and bring to a boil. Reduce the heat and simmer for 1 to 2 hours, until the beans are tender but are still slightly firm. Heat in a Dutch oven over medium heat:

   2 tablespoons olive oil

Add and cook, stirring, until soft, about 15 minutes:

   2 medium onions, chopped
   1 rib celery, chopped

Add and cook, stirring, until softened, a few minutes:

   8 garlic cloves, chopped

Remove to a small bowl. Add to the pot and heat:

   2 tablespoons olive oil

Add and brown, in batches if necessary, over medium heat, 10 to 15 minutes:

   4 pounds boneless venison, cut into $1/2$-inch cubes

Return the onion mixture to the pot and add:

   $1/3$ cup chili powder
   3 tablespoons dried oregano
   2 tablespoons ground cumin
   1 tablespoon ground coriander
   2 teaspoons salt
   $1/2$ to 1 teaspoon ground red pepper

Stir to mix, and cook another 5 minutes. Add:

   **One 28-ounce can plum tomatoes, crushed,
      with their juice**
   $3^{1}/2$ cups hot chicken stock or broth

Bring to a boil. Stir well, reduce the heat, and simmer uncovered for 2 hours or until the meat is fork-tender. Stir in the beans and heat through. Season with:

Salt and black pepper to taste

Serve with:

   Brown Rice or Wild Rice

Garnish with:

   Chopped parsley
   1 cup sour cream, mixed with grated zest of 1 lemon

BECKER VENISON MEDALLIONS

4 servings

Place one at a time between sheets of wax paper and gently pound until $1/4$ inch thick:

   1 pound venison medallions

Season to taste with:

   Salt and black pepper

Melt in a large heavy skillet over medium heat:

   6 tablespoons ($3/4$ stick) butter

Add the medallions, in batches if necessary, and cook until browned, 1 to 2 minutes per side. Remove the meat to a platter and set aside. Add to the pan:

   3 tablespoons port or Madeira

with any juices from the meat, and warm the sauce for about 1 minute. Pour over the medallions, and serve with:

   Toast Points, 111

GRILLED VENISON CHOPS WITH BLUE CHEESE AND CARAWAY BUTTER

4 servings

Slather lots of butter and cheese on the chops—the extreme leanness of venison meat affords the great luxury of adding fat to the cooking process.

Whip in a mixer or food processor until soft:

   $1/2$ cup (1 stick) unsalted butter

Add:

   1 tablespoon crumbled blue cheese
   1 teaspoon caraway seeds
   A few drops of Worcestershire sauce
   Salt and black pepper to taste

Blend well. Remove to a sheet of plastic wrap, shape into a log, and wrap tightly. Chill for at least 1 hour, or overnight. Heat in a large skillet:

   3 tablespoons olive oil

Add and cook for 2 to 3 minutes per side, depending on thickness:

   4 venison chops

Transfer the chops to plates, slice off two or three pats of the butter per chop, and put on top of the meat to melt.

WILD SHEEP AND GOATS

Please read About Large Game, 527. Wild sheep and goats live in rugged terrain in the western part of the United States and Canada. They are plentiful, but one species of the bighorn sheep is currently considered endangered. There are four kinds of wild sheep that are called bighorn: **Rocky Mountain, desert, Dall's,** and **stone sheep.** ➤ The **desert bighorn** is on the endangered list (not from overhunting, but from loss of habitat). However, the numbers on other bighorns are sufficient to be huntable and are carefully controlled, with the fees from hunting licenses (which are substantial) going to increase their habitat and help them prosper. ➤ Wild sheep and goat are both delicious; the meat is distinct and flavorful yet mild. Best cooked on the bone, the meat has a texture like lamb. Any goat—from the mountain goats we hunt to the domestic goats of the Caribbean—can be used in the recipe below.

ROAST MOUNTAIN GOAT OR BIGHORN SHEEP

6 servings

Preheat the oven to 500°F. Season:

One 6- to 8-pound leg of goat or sheep, boned

with:

Salt and black pepper

Cover the inside of the roast with:

2 garlic cloves, sliced

1 tablespoon chopped fresh rosemary

6 thick slices bacon, preferably slab bacon

Roll up the meat and cinch the twine around the rolled meat 6 or 7 times to hold it together. Lay on top of the meat:

3 thin slices prosciutto

Roast 30 minutes. Remove the roast, and add to the pan:

1 onion, sliced into rings

1 cup veal stock or chicken stock or broth

1 cup dry red wine

1 tablespoon Worcestershire sauce

1/2 teaspoon dried basil

Return the roast to the pan. Reduce the oven temperature to 425°F. Roast until the internal temperature is 125°F for rare, 30 to 45 minutes. Remove to a warm platter. Mix:

1/4 cup all-purpose flour

1/4 cup water

Whisk into the juices in the pan and cook, stirring, over medium heat until thickened. Whisk in:

1/4 cup plum preserves or jam

Slice the meat thin and serve the sauce on the side.

BOAR

Please read About Large Game, 527. Boar, which has been hunted extensively in Europe for centuries, is a cousin of the domesticated hog, but its meat is leaner and more flavorful. In America, boar can be many things, from imported **Russian boar** to **razorback hogs** that have escaped into the wild to the native **American wild pig** called **peccary** or **javelina**. Boar can range in flavor from very mild and delicate to distinctly pungent, depending on their age and size, the season, and the animal's diet. In general, younger animals are preferred for flavor and tenderness. Wild boar may be prepared like pork, and it is sold in familiar pork cuts. The most popular cuts come from the loin or saddle; tougher, less expensive cuts, such as the hind leg, are best braised or stewed. ➤ Because boar can carry trichinosis, cook thoroughly. Substitute boar for pork in Boneless

Roast Pork Florentine, 499, Pork Braised in Milk, 501, or Braised Pork with Sauerkraut, 501.

LEMON-ROSEMARY BOAR CHOPS

4 servings

Season:

4 wild boar loin chops

to taste with:

Salt and black pepper

Combine in a small bowl:

Juice of 2 lemons

1/2 cup olive oil

1/4 cup chopped rosemary

2 cloves garlic, chopped

1 teaspoon Dijon mustard

Place the boar chops in a shallow baking dish and add the marinade, turning to coat. Cover and marinate, refrigerated, for 1 to 4 hours. Prepare a hot grill fire, 1056, or heat a large skillet over high heat. Sear the chops on the grill or in the pan for 2 minutes on each side, until browned. If grilling, move the chops to an area away from direct heat. If cooking in a skillet, reduce the heat to medium-low and cover the pan. Cook 10 minutes longer for medium-rare, 15 for medium, or longer for well-done, until the temperature in the thickest part of a chop registers 150° to 170°F. Remove to a platter. Let rest for 10 minutes. Drizzle with:

Extra-virgin olive oil

Serve with:

2 lemon wedges

ABOUT BEAR

Please read About Large Game, 527. All bear is edible. ➤ Remove all fat and bone from bear meat and freeze or render. If rendered at once, it is prized for cooking; if held, it is good only for boot grease. Tough, strongly flavored bear may be improved by refrigerating at least 24 hours in an oil-based marinade before cooking. Cook, after marination, as for Beef Pot Roast or Stew, 477–481. ➤ Bear can carry trichinosis, so be sure the meat is always well cooked through.

BRAISED BEAR

4 to 6 servings

Heat in a large skillet or Dutch oven:

1/4 cup corn oil

Brown in batches:

4 pounds boneless bear meat, cut into 2-inch cubes

Remove to a platter and set aside. Add to the pan:

1 tablespoon butter

When the butter has melted, add and cook, stirring, until softened, about 5 minutes:

2 carrots, sliced

1 small onion, chopped

1 rib celery, chopped

Add the browned meat, along with:

2 cups dry red wine

1 cup chicken stock or broth

Bring to a boil, then reduce to a simmer. Add:

20 garlic cloves

1 bay leaf

1 teaspoon dried thyme

Cover the pan with foil, pressing it down so there is no space between the liquid and foil and the foil is tight over the sides of the pan. Cover with a lid and simmer until a skewer comes out of a piece of meat easily, about 2 to 3 hours. Skim off any fat. Remove the meat to a plate and discard the bay leaf. Puree the vegetables with the cooking liquid, in batches if necessary, in a food processor or blender. Pour back into the pan and boil over high heat to reduce by one-third. Whisk in:

$^{1}/_{4}$ cup ($^{1}/_{2}$ stick) butter, cut into pieces

If the sauce is too thick, you may add and simmer until the desired consistency:

Additional stock or wine

Season with:

Salt and black pepper to taste

Return the meat to the sauce and heat through.

BUFFALO (BISON)

American buffalo, or bison, is an animal indigenous to North America that once roamed in huge herds over the plains of this country, providing both food and shelter for Native Americans. Buffalo is now raised for meat on numerous ranches around the United States, and the meat has significant advantages over beef. It is high in protein and extremely low in cholesterol (approximately 30 percent less than beef), and it has about half the calories and fat of beef. It is also delicious, not unlike beef. Buffalo may be used in virtually any beef recipe. ➤ It cooks more quickly than beef. Regardless of the cooking method, ➤ buffalo meat should be cooked only rare to medium-rare; well-done meat will prove dry, chewy, and flavorless. The best cuts are steaks, chops, and roasts from the rib, loin, and sirloin. Trim any visible fat before cooking buffalo. ➤ If grilling buffalo steaks or chops, cook them quickly at least 6 inches from the heat source, basting with a glaze or marinade to keep the meat moist. Ground buffalo, like ground venison, can be combined with a little ground pork, or beef, to add fat and moisture, if desired.

BUFFALO RIB ROAST WITH ORANGE MOLASSES GLAZE

10 to 14 servings

Carefully trim, removing all but a thin layer of fat:

One (7- to 9-pound) boneless buffalo rib or
     top sirloin roast

Tie securely, if desired, and place on a rack in a roasting pan. Prepare:

Orange Molasses Glaze, 583

Generously brush the roast with glaze. Let stand for 1 hour at room temperature, or cover and refrigerate for up to 24 hours. Bring to room temperature before roasting. Reserve any remaining glaze to baste the meat while it roasts. Preheat oven to 450°F. Roast the meat for 15 minutes. Reduce the oven temperature to 325°F and roast, basting occasionally with the glaze, until a meat thermometer inserted into the thickest part of the roast registers 120° to 130°F for rare, about 8 to 10 minutes per pound, or 130° to 140°F for medium-rare, about 10 to 12 minutes per pound. Be careful not to overcook. Remove the roast to a cutting board and cover to keep warm. Add to the roasting pan:

$1^{1}/_{2}$ cups beef stock or broth

$^{3}/_{4}$ cup dry red wine

Bring to a boil, scraping up the browned bits, and boil until slightly thickened and reduced to about 2 cups. Strain the sauce through a fine-mesh sieve and season to taste with:

Salt and black pepper

Slice the roast and serve with the sauce.

BECKER BUFFALO BURGERS

4 servings

If you find ground buffalo too dry, add ground beef, sausage, or beaten eggs. We love these just the way they are. Mix in a medium bowl:

1 pound ground buffalo

$^{1}/_{2}$ sweet onion, diced

1 tablespoon soy sauce

1 teaspoon hot pepper sauce

Generous grind of black pepper

Form into 4 patties and place on a plate. Allow to rest in the refrigerator, covered, at least 15 minutes, and up to 2 hours. Grill to desired degree of doneness.

STUFFINGS

"No more turkey," announced the little boy at the Thanksgiving dinner table, "but I'd like another helping of that bread he ate." Though not all stuffings are made of bread, all, if delicately and interestingly put together, are quite delicious enough to lure a budding gourmet away from even the most tradition-hallowed main dish. Some of the makings are celery, spices, herbs, oysters, giblets, sausage, mushrooms, olives, nuts, and fruits, as well as the essential members of the onion family. They enrich the bread crumbs, rice, potatoes, chestnuts, and other cereals that bind **stuffings, dressings**, and **farces** together. **Forcemeats** ("farce" is the French term) include such favorites as Sausage and Fennel Stuffing, 541, and Chicken Farce, 541. As with other stuffings, there is a great deal of variance in how forcemeat stuffings are prepared, but all must be thoroughly cooked before serving.

ABOUT BREAD STUFFINGS

Is there a difference between stuffing and dressing? Some say not, but here we will refer to **stuffing** as anything cooked in the bird, meat, or fish; and **dressing** as that cooked separately in a baking dish. The big difference worth mentioning is that we do not recommend using eggs in stuffing, but we do use them in dressing to bind the ingredients. ➤ We also caution you to cook pork for stuffings or dressings. ➤ Stuffing is cooked when it reaches an internal temperature of 165°F. ➤ Allow approximately $1/2$ cup stuffing for each pound of raw bird or fish. ➤ Serving size is about $3/4$ cup per person.

When bread crumbs are called for in a recipe, we recommend using day-old bread, whether Italian or French bread, homemade white bread, whole wheat, or corn bread. Whatever the bread, if it is stale and/or toasted, a dry, firm stuffing results. If it is fresh and not toasted, the stuffing will be moist and dense.

The quality of the crumbs used is very important, so check, 960–961, to differentiate between fresh and dry. ➤ Never grind bread to make crumbs, as the stuffing will be too compact. Plain unseasoned packaged bread crumbs or bread cubes can be used in any recipe that calls for fresh. ➤ If you use them, increase the stock called for in the recipe by one-third. ➤ A 1-pound loaf of bread yields about 10 cups of fresh bread cubes or 6 cups fresh bread crumbs, including the crust, which should be used unless otherwise specified in the recipe.

If you prefer a dry stuffing, add only as much stock as will enable the bread to barely stick together when firmly grasped in the hand. For a moister texture, add enough melted butter so that the bread holds together readily when pressed. In many of the recipes that follow, a reduction in the amount of butter is given with an increase in stock or broth for the benefit of those who want to add more moisture but not fat.

If made in advance, ➤ stuffings can be refrigerated up to one day but should be stored separately from the meat, fowl, or fish. To take off the chill, remove the stuffing from the refrigerator about 20 minutes before using, or preheat the stuffing until lukewarm over low heat or in a 300°F oven. It is important, too, ➤ to stuff food just before cooking; ➤ to mix, stir, and pack stuffings lightly so as not to compact them; and ➤ to allow space when stuffing, so the mixture can expand and stay light. Should there be extra stuffing that does not fit in the cavity of the fish, fowl, or meat, cook it separately in a greased baking dish. If the bird is done before the stuffing, remove the bird from the oven, scoop the stuffing into a buttered casserole, and continue to bake it in the hot oven while the bird rests.

Dressing baked in a dish can be assembled ahead and go directly from the refrigerator to the oven. To bake dressing, spread it in a layer 2 to 3 inches deep in a buttered baking dish. Ladle over the top $1/2$ cup stock, broth, or milk for every 4 to 5 cups of stuffing. ➤ For a softer dressing, cover with aluminum foil; for a crispy brown crust, dot the top with butter and bake uncovered. For either, bake in a preheated 350°F oven for 30 to 45 minutes. When baking the dressing and meat, fish, or fowl at the same time, occasionally baste the dressing with the pan drippings.

Remove all the stuffing before carving. For instructions on preparing a bird for stuffing, see About Stuffing and Trussing Poultry, 421.

BASIC BREAD STUFFING
8 to 10 cups
This recipe and the variations that follow yield enough to stuff a 14- to 17-pound turkey, and to make a small side casserole as well. To stuff a roasting chicken or 6 to 8 Cor-

nish hens, halve the recipes. For a larger turkey, increase the ingredients by half. Please read About Bread Stuffings, 532.

Preheat the oven to 400°F. Toast on a large baking sheet, stirring several times, until golden brown, 5 to 10 minutes:

1 pound sliced firm white sandwich, French, or Italian bread, including crusts, cut into ¹/₂-inch cubes (10 cups lightly packed bread cubes)

Turn into a large bowl. Heat in a large skillet over medium-high heat until the foam subsides:

¹/₄ to ¹/₂ cup (¹/₂ to 1 stick) unsalted butter

Add and cook, stirring, until tender, about 5 minutes:

2 cups chopped onions
1 cup finely chopped celery

Remove from the heat and stir in:

¹/₄ to ¹/₂ cup minced parsley
1 tablespoon minced fresh sage or 1 teaspoon dried sage
1 tablespoon minced fresh thyme or 1 teaspoon dried thyme
³/₄ teaspoon salt
¹/₂ teaspoon black pepper
¹/₄ teaspoon grated or ground nutmeg
¹/₈ teaspoon ground cloves

Add to the bread cubes and toss until well combined. Stir in, a little at a time, until the stuffing is lightly moist but not packed together:

¹/₃ to 1 cup chicken stock or broth, or as needed

Adjust the seasonings. If you desire a firm dressing and are baking in a dish, stir in:

(2 large eggs, well beaten)

Spoon the stuffing into the bird(s) or moisten with additional stock and bake separately in a dish, 532. Stuffing is done when it reaches an internal temperature of 165°F.

BREAD STUFFING WITH TOASTED NUTS OR CHESTNUTS AND DRIED FRUIT

Use 9 to 11 cups cooked fresh chestnuts or vacuum-packed, canned, or frozen; do not use chestnuts packed in syrup, which are too sweet. Prepare **Basic Bread Stuffing, 532.** Add **¹/₂ to 1 cup walnuts, pecans, or Brazil nuts, toasted, 1001, and coarsely chopped** or **1¹/₂ cups cooked, canned, or frozen chestnuts, coarsely chopped,** and **1 cup dried fruit (such as raisins, cranberries, cherries, or diced prunes).** Toss the bread with the seasonings and bake as above.

BREAD STUFFING WITH OYSTERS

Prepare 10 to 12 cups **Basic Bread Stuffing, 532.** Add **24 shucked, 371, or 1 pint raw oysters, drained, and liquor reserved.** Toss the bread with the seasonings. Add reserved oyster liquor to moisten. Stuffing is done when it reaches an internal temperature of 165°F; see Poultry and Wild-fowl, 418. To bake stuffing in a dish, see 532.

BREAD STUFFING WITH SAUSAGE AND APPLES

14 to 16 cups

Twelve ounces of brown-and-serve sausages, thawed and cut into small pieces, can be substituted for bulk sausage. Cook pieces with the apples, using butter in place of sausage drippings. Please read About Bread Stuffings, 532.

Cook in a large skillet over medium-high heat. Break up the meat with a spoon, until it is no longer pink, 8 to 10 minutes:

1 pound bulk pork sausage

Remove to a paper towel–lined plate to drain. Pour off all but 2 tablespoons of the fat and return the skillet to the heat. Add and cook, stirring, until tender:

4 cups diced peeled green apples, such as Granny Smith

Prepare:

Basic Bread Stuffing, 532

Add the sausage and apples when tossing the bread with the seasonings. Spoon the stuffing into the bird, or moisten with additional stock and bake separately in a dish, 532. Stuffing is done when it reaches an internal temperature of 165°F.

BREAD AND MUSHROOM STUFFING

10 to 12 cups

Please read About Bread Stuffings, 532.

Heat in a medium skillet over medium-high heat until the foam subsides:

2 tablespoons unsalted butter

Add and cook, stirring, until tender and the liquid the mushrooms release has evaporated:

1 pound button or wild mushrooms, sliced

Prepare:

Basic Bread Stuffing, 532

Add the mushrooms when tossing the bread with the seasonings. Spoon the stuffing into the bird, or moisten with additional stock and bake separately in a dish, 532. Stuffing is done when it reaches an internal temperature of 165°F.

ITALIAN BREAD STUFFING

4 cups

This stuffing may be used to stuff boneless chicken breasts, 420, or a whole roasted chicken, or, if doubled, a 12- to 15-pound turkey. ➤ If using as a stuffing, do not use the eggs. Please read About Bread Stuffings, 532.

Heat in a small skillet over medium-high heat until the foam begins to subside:

3 to 4 tablespoons butter

Add and cook, stirring, until tender but not browned, about 5 minutes:

²/₃ cup finely chopped onion

Stir in and cook for 30 seconds:

1 teaspoon minced garlic
Transfer to a bowl and stir in:
2 cups dry bread crumbs
1/2 cup grated Parmesan
(1 large egg, beaten)
1/4 cup finely chopped parsley
1/2 teaspoon dried rosemary, crumbled
1/2 teaspoon dried sage, crumbled
1/2 teaspoon salt
1/2 teaspoon black pepper
Stir in, adding enough to make the stuffing just moist enough to hold together in a crumbly ball when squeezed firmly in your hand:
1 to 1 1/2 cups chicken stock or broth, or as needed
(1 large egg)
Spoon the stuffing into the bird, or moisten with additional stock and bake separately in a dish, 532. Stuffing is done when it reaches an internal temperature of 165°F.

APPLE AND CHERRY BREAD STUFFING

About 7 cups
Perfect for pork. Please read About Bread Stuffings, 532.
Heat in a large skillet over medium heat until the butter foams:
1/4 cup (1/2 stick) butter
1 tablespoon olive oil
Add and cook, stirring, until translucent, about 5 minutes:
2 ribs celery, chopped
1 medium onion, chopped
Remove from the heat and add:
4 cups cubes dried white or whole wheat bread or
corn bread cubes or plain croutons
1 large apple, diced and peeled
3/4 cup dried tart cherries
1/2 cup port or Madeira
1/4 cup raisins
(1 tablespoon minced rosemary)
1 teaspoon black pepper
1/2 teaspoon salt
If baking as a dressing in a dish, add:
(1 large egg)
Moisten with up to:
1/2 cup chicken stock or broth, or as needed
Spoon the stuffing into the bird, or moisten with additional stock and bake separately in a dish, 532. Stuffing is done when it reaches an internal temperature of 165°F.

BREAD STUFFING WITH GIBLETS

About 8 cups
This light, mild-flavored stuffing can be varied by adding chopped nuts, sautéed mushrooms, 283, and other ingredients if you use the lesser amount of celery. Please read About Bread Stuffings, 532.
Chop:
Turkey or chicken giblets: gizzard, heart, and liver
Melt in a medium skillet over medium heat:

1/4 cup (1/2 stick) butter
Add the giblets and:
1/2 cup chopped onion
Cook, stirring occasionally, about 2 minutes, then cover and cook, stirring occasionally, for 10 minutes, until the onions are soft. Transfer to a large bowl and toss with:
6 cups cubed crustless day-old or slightly toasted
white or whole wheat bread or corn bread
1/4 to 1 cup chopped celery
1/4 cup chopped parsley
1 teaspoon crumbled dried tarragon or basil
3/4 teaspoon salt
1/2 teaspoon paprika
1/8 teaspoon grated or ground nutmeg
Add:
About 1/2 cup milk, stock or broth, or melted butter to
moisten the dressing very lightly, or as needed
If cooking in a baking dish, add:
(2 to 3 large eggs, well beaten)
Add:
(1 1/2 cups chopped nuts: Brazil or pine nuts, pecans,
or walnuts)
and one of the following:
1 cup sausage meat, cooked and browned
1 cup or more sliced mushrooms sautéed with onion
1 cup chopped or whole drained oysters
1 cup chopped soft-shell clams
1 cup chopped cooked shrimp
Spoon the stuffing into the bird, or moisten with additional milk, stock, or both and bake separately in a dish, 532. Stuffing is done when it reaches an internal temperature of 165°F.

BASIC CORN BREAD STUFFING

About 8 cups
A regional variation that is now widely traveled. Any corn bread will work in this recipe. However, if you are making corn bread from scratch, choose Southern Corn Bread, 632, which is unsweetened. Please read About Bread Stuffings, 532.
Preheat the oven to 400°F. Toast on a large baking sheet, stirring several times, until golden brown, 5 to 10 minutes:
1 recipe Southern Corn Bread, 632, or other corn
bread, cubed (8 cups)
Turn into a large bowl. If you like a crumbly texture, break up the cubes with your fingers. Heat in a large skillet over medium-high heat until the foam subsides:
1/4 to 1/2 cup (1/2 to 1 stick) unsalted butter
Cook, stirring, until tender, about 5 minutes:
2 cups chopped onions
1 cup finely chopped celery
(1 green bell pepper, cored, seeded, and cut into
small dice)
(1 red bell pepper, cored, seeded, and cut into
small dice)
(2 garlic cloves, minced)

Remove from the heat and stir in:

$^1/_4$ to $^1/_2$ cup minced parsley

1 teaspoon dried sage or 1 tablespoon minced fresh sage

$^3/_4$ teaspoon salt

$^1/_2$ teaspoon black pepper

Add to the bread cubes and toss until well combined. Stir in, a little at a time, until the stuffing is lightly moist but not packed together:

$^1/_3$ to 1 cup chicken stock or broth, or as needed

Adjust the seasonings. If you desire a firm dressing and are baking in a separate dish, stir in:

(2 large eggs, well beaten)

Spoon the stuffing into the bird, or moisten with additional stock and bake separately in a dish, 532. Stuffing is done when it reaches an internal temperature of 165°F.

CORN BREAD STUFFING WITH SAUSAGE AND BELL PEPPERS

12 to 14 cups

Prepare **Basic Corn Bread Stuffing, 534,** with the optional green and red bell peppers. Add **1 pound hot or mild bulk sausage, cooked,** and (**$^1/_4$ teaspoon ground red pepper).** Toss the bread with the seasonings.

CORN BREAD STUFFING WITH OYSTERS

10 to 12 cups

Omitting the garlic, prepare **Basic Corn Bread Stuffing, 534.** Add **24 shucked, 371, or 1 pint raw oysters, drained, and liquor reserved,** and **(1 to 2 cups pecans, toasted, 1001, and coarsely chopped).** Toss the bread with the seasonings. Add reserved oyster liquor to moisten.

CORN BREAD STUFFING WITH CUMIN AND HOT CHILE PEPPERS

10 to 12 cups

Two 4-ounce cans diced mild green chile peppers can be substituted for the poblano or Anaheim peppers.

Prepare, using the optional bell peppers and garlic:

Basic Corn Bread Stuffing, 534

Add:

4 poblano peppers or 8 Anaheim peppers, roasted, 292, peeled, seeded, and chopped

3 jalapeño peppers, roasted, 292, peeled, seeded, and chopped

1 teaspoon ground cumin

1 teaspoon dried oregano

1 cup frozen, canned, or cooked fresh corn kernels

Toss the bread with the seasonings and bake as directed.

DRY DRESSING

About 5 cups

This name was given by a family cook, Sarah Brown, to a dressing she frequently made, which is by no means dry. Chopped pecans, oysters, and olives may be added. Please read About Bread Stuffings, 532.

Melt in a small skillet over medium heat:

2 tablespoons butter

Add and cook, stirring, until barely tender, 5 minutes:

$^1/_2$ cup chopped onion

Add:

$3^1/_2$ to 4 cups fresh white or whole wheat bread crumbs

About 1 cup chopped celery

Season with:

Salt to taste

$^1/_4$ teaspoon paprika

Remove from the heat. Stuff the bird with half the dressing. Melt:

$^3/_4$ to 1 cup ($1^1/_2$ to 2 sticks) butter

Pour half of it onto the dressing in the cavity of the bird. Stuff with the remaining stuffing and pour the remaining butter onto it. Spoon the stuffing into the bird, or moisten with additional stock and bake separately in a dish, 532. Stuffing is done when it reaches an internal temperature of 165°F.

HAM DRESSING FOR TURKEY

About 6 to 7 cups

Pulse until coarsely ground in a food processor:

10 ounces smoked ham, cut into $^1/_2$-inch cubes

You should have about $1^1/_2$ cups. Transfer to a large bowl. Add and toss well:

4 cups fresh bread crumbs

One 8-ounce can crushed pineapple, undrained

1 cup golden raisins

1 cup chopped walnuts or pecans

Sweeten to taste with:

$^1/_4$ to $^1/_2$ cup honey

Spoon the stuffing into the bird, or moisten with additional stock and bake separately in a dish, 532. Stuffing is done when it reaches an internal temperature of 165°F.

PARSLEY AND BREAD CRUMB STUFFING FOR FISH

About 2 cups

This delicate, buttery stuffing can be used to stuff a range of seafood, from sole fillets to whole baked trout. Because fish cooks quickly, the bread for fish stuffings should be finely crumbed and the vegetables finely chopped. This recipe makes enough to stuff 4 servings, or 2 pounds fish fillets or steaks or 3 to 4 pounds of whole fish. Please read About Bread Stuffings, 532. See Preparing Fish for Cooking, 394, unless using for Roasted Stuffed Whole Fish, 397.

Melt in a medium skillet over low heat:

6 tablespoons ($^3/_4$ stick) butter

Add and cook, stirring, until tender but not browned, about 10 minutes:

$^1/_2$ cup finely chopped onions

$^1/_2$ cup finely chopped celery

Remove from the heat and stir in:

1¹/₂ **cups fresh bread crumbs**

3 tablespoons finely chopped parsley

(2 tablespoons drained small capers)

(¹/₂ teaspoon dried tarragon or dill)

Season with:

¹/₂ **teaspoon fresh lemon juice**

¹/₄ **teaspoon salt**

¹/₄ **teaspoon black pepper**

BACON STUFFING FOR FISH

About 2 cups

A savory stuffing for rich-tasting fish such as trout, salmon, bluefish, and mackerel. In a large skillet, cook, until crisp, **12 slices bacon.** Remove the bacon and drain. Omitting the butter and using the bacon fat to cook the vegetables, prepare **Parsley and Bread Crumb Stuffing for Fish, above.** Finish the stuffing by adding the crumbled bacon. Stir into the stuffing **(3 tablespoons chopped pecans).**

CRABMEAT STUFFING FOR FISH

About 2¹/₂ cups

A rich stuffing well suited for fish fillets such as cod, sole, and salmon. Prepare **Parsley and Bread Crumb Stuffing for Fish, 535,** reducing bread crumbs to 1 cup and increasing lemon juice to 1 teaspoon. Add to the vegetables ¹/₄ **cup finely chopped green bell pepper.** Add ¹/₂ **cup chopped freshly cooked or well-drained lump crabmeat, or lobster, picked over for shells and cartilage,** and ¹/₄ **teaspoon dry mustard.**

SEAFOOD DRESSING

2¹/₂ cups

This dressing has the consistency of a bread pudding and a smoky bacon flavor. Spread it on top of thick fish fillets or steaks before baking—thin pieces of fish will overcook by the time the stuffing is cooked through—or use it as a filling for bell peppers or other vegetable cases, 244. Please read About Bread Stuffings, 532. See Preparing Fish for Cooking, 394, unless using for Roasted Stuffed Whole Fish, 397.

Melt in a skillet over medium heat:

2 tablespoons butter

Add and cook, stirring, until the vegetables are tender but not browned, 7 to 10 minutes:

³/₄ **cup chopped celery**

¹/₂ **cup chopped onion**

2 slices bacon, minced

Add and cook, stirring, 1 minute longer:

1 cup fresh bread crumbs

Remove from the heat and let cool 10 minutes. Combine in a medium bowl:

1 cup cooked or canned crabmeat, picked over for shells and cartilage, or 1 cup chopped cooked peeled shrimp

(2 large eggs, well beaten)

Stir in the bread crumb mixture. Then stir in:

1 tablespoon dry sherry

¹/₂ **teaspoon grated lemon zest**

¹/₈ **teaspoon ground ginger**

Stuffing is done when it reaches an internal temperature of 165°F. To prepare separately as dressing, see 532.

OYSTER DRESSING FOR FISH

2¹/₂ cups

This makes enough for a 4-pound whole fish. See Preparing Fish for Cooking, 394, unless using for Roasted Stuffed Whole Fish, 397.

Melt in a small skillet over medium-high heat:

6 tablespoons (³/₄ stick) butter

Add and cook, stirring until golden brown, 10 to 12 minutes:

¹/₄ **cup chopped onion**

Transfer to a large bowl and add, stirring gently to mix:

2 cups dry bread crumbs

1 cup drained whole or chopped oysters

(¹/₂ cup well-drained chopped spinach)

2 tablespoons drained capers

1 tablespoon chopped parsley

³/₄ **teaspoon salt**

¹/₄ **teaspoon paprika or ground red pepper**

Stuffing is done when it reaches an internal temperature of 165°F. To prepare separately as dressing, see 532.

GREEN HERB DRESSING
FOR FISH OR POULTRY

About 1¹/₂ cups

This has a tempting pistachio-green color and lightly tangy flavor. Multiply the recipe as necessary if stuffing a bird. Or, if stuffing fish, see Preparing Fish for Cooking, 394, unless using for Roasted Stuffed Whole Fish, 397.

Melt in a small skillet over medium heat:

2 tablespoons butter

Add and cook, stirring. Heat until translucent, about 5 minutes:

2 tablespoons chopped shallots

Remove from the heat and cool slightly. Combine in a food processor:

(1 large egg)

¹/₂ **cup chopped tender inner celery stalks with leaves**

¹/₂ **cup parsley leaves**

¹/₄ **cup watercress leaves**

¹/₂ **teaspoon salt**

¹/₂ **to 1 teaspoon minced fresh basil or tarragon or**

¹/₄ **teaspoon dried**

Add the shallot mixture and pulse until a paste forms. Tear into small crumbly pieces:

2 slices white sandwich bread, crusts removed

Place in a medium bowl, add the herb paste, and blend lightly with a fork. Add:

¹/₄ **cup pistachios or seedless green grapes, quartered**

Stuffing is done when it reaches an internal temperature of 165°F. To prepare separately as dressing, see 532.

SAUSAGE DRESSING

About 2 1/2 cups

Delectable with duck, pheasant, turkey, or pork.
Cook in a skillet over medium heat, breaking up the meat with a spoon, until browned:

4 ounces bulk breakfast or Italian sausage

Drain off the fat. Add:

2 cups cracker crumbs or 1 cup fresh bread crumbs plus 1 cup corn bread crumbs
(1/2 cup chopped tart apple)
1/2 cup chopped celery
1/4 cup minced onion
1/4 teaspoon salt
1/8 teaspoon paprika

Remove from the heat and moisten with:

1/2 cup chicken or meat stock or broth

Spoon stuffing into bird, or moisten with additional stock and bake separately in a dish, 532. Stuffing is done when it reaches an internal temperature of 165°F.

CHESTNUT DRESSING

About 4 1/2 cups

A creamy stuffing with a rich chestnut flavor particularly good with duck or goose. You can substitute vacuum-packed cooked chestnuts (about 10 ounces) here.
Rice, mash, or puree in a food processor:

2 1/2 cups Boiled Chestnuts I, 968

Combine in a bowl with:

1 cup dry bread crumbs or cracker crumbs
1/2 cup chopped celery
1 small onion, grated
1/2 cup (1 stick) butter, melted
(1/4 cup raisins)
1/4 cup heavy cream
2 tablespoons chopped parsley

Season with:

1/2 to 1 teaspoon salt
1/8 to 1/4 teaspoon black pepper

Spoon the stuffing into the bird or bake separately in a dish, 532. Stuffing is done when it reaches an internal temperature of 165°F.

ONION AND SAGE DRESSING

About 5 cups

Melt in a large skillet over medium heat:

2 tablespoons butter or olive oil

Add, stirring:

2 cups chopped onions

Transfer to a bowl and add:

3 cups dry bread crumbs
1/4 cup cooked pork sausage
2 teaspoons chopped fresh sage or 3/4 teaspoon dried sage

(1 large egg, well beaten)
1/2 cup (1 stick) butter, melted
3/4 teaspoon salt
1/8 teaspoon paprika
1/2 teaspoon poultry seasoning
(1 cup chopped tart apple or 1/2 cup sliced olives)

Moisten slightly with:

Stock or broth

Spoon stuffing into bird, or moisten with additional stock and bake separately in a dish, 532. Stuffing is done when it reaches an internal temperature of 165°F.

APPLE DRESSING

6 cups

Combine:

6 cups sliced peeled all-purpose apples, such as Golden Delicious
1 cup dried currants or raisins
2 tablespoons fresh lemon juice
1 tablespoon brown sugar
(1 tablespoon chopped sage)
Salt and black pepper to taste

Spoon the stuffing into the bird, or moisten with additional stock and bake separately in a dish, 532. Stuffing is done when it reaches an internal temperature of 165°F.

APPLE AND PRUNE DRESSING

About 4 1/2 cups

Excellent with roasted pork, goose, turkey, or duck.
Combine in a bowl:

3 cups diced white bread (crusts removed)
1 cup diced peeled apples
3/4 cup chopped pitted prunes
1/2 cup chopped walnuts or pecans
1/2 cup (1 stick) butter, melted, or 1/2 cup bacon drippings
1 tablespoon fresh lemon juice
1 teaspoon salt
1/2 teaspoon paprika

Spoon the stuffing into the bird, or moisten with additional stock and bake separately in a dish, 532. Stuffing is done when it reaches an internal temperature of 165°F.

MASHED POTATO STUFFING

5 to 6 cups

This surprisingly light stuffing, which can be made from leftover mashed potatoes, is excellent baked on its own and served with roasted chicken, roast beef, or baked ham, but it also makes a very good stuffing for turkey, goose, pork, or capon.
Heat in a large skillet over medium heat:

1/4 cup (1/2 stick) butter or 1/4 cup olive oil

Add and cook, stirring occasionally, until tender and beginning to caramelize, 10 to 15 minutes:

3 cups thinly sliced onions

Turn into a large bowl and mix with:

4 cups Mashed Potatoes, 295
$^1/_2$ to 1 cup unseasoned bread crumbs
$^1/_2$ cup minced parsley
**$^1/_2$ to 1 cup milk or chicken stock or broth, or a
    combination**
**2 tablespoons minced fresh sage or 2 teaspoons
    dried sage**
**1$^1/_2$ teaspoons minced fresh thyme or $^1/_2$ teaspoon
    dried thyme**
(1 large egg, beaten)
Salt and black pepper to taste

Use as a stuffing, or turn into a buttered large shallow
baking dish and dot with:

2 tablespoons butter, cut into small pieces

Sprinkle with:

Grated Parmesan

Stuffing is done when it reaches an internal temperature
of 165°F. To prepare in a pan, bake in a 350°F oven until
golden brown, 30 to 45 minutes.

SWEET POTATO AND APPLE STUFFING
About 8 cups

Serve this with Pork Crown Roast, 498, roasted turkey, or
baked ham.

Put in a large pot and add water to cover:

2 pounds sweet potatoes, scrubbed

Bring to a boil, then reduce the heat and simmer, covered,
until tender. Drain. When cool enough to handle, remove
the skins and mash the potatoes in a large bowl.

Heat in a large skillet over medium-high heat until the
foam subsides:

2 tablespoons butter

Add and cook, stirring, until the vegetables are softened,
about 5 minutes:

1$^1/_2$ cups chopped onions
$^1/_2$ cup chopped celery
$^1/_2$ teaspoon salt
$^1/_4$ teaspoon black pepper

Add and cook, stirring, until the apples are tender but still
hold their shape, 3 to 4 minutes:

**2 cups diced peeled apples, such as Granny Smith or
    Golden Delicious**
$^1/_2$ cup apple cider
$^1/_4$ teaspoon ground cinnamon
$^1/_4$ teaspoon grated or ground nutmeg
$^1/_4$ teaspoon ground cloves

Stir into the sweet potatoes, along with:

2 cups unseasoned bread crumbs

Adjust the seasonings and moisten, if needed, with:

($^1/_4$ cup chicken or vegetable stock or broth)

Use as a stuffing, or turn into a buttered large shallow
baking dish and dot with:

$^1/_4$ cup ($^1/_2$ stick) butter, cut into small pieces

Stuffing is done when it reaches an internal temperature
of 165°F.

SWEET POTATO AND SAUSAGE STUFFING
About 9 cups

This makes enough to stuff a 14- to 17-pound turkey.
Cook until browned **8 ounces bulk sausage** in a large skillet
over medium-high heat, breaking up the meat with a fork.
Remove it from the pan. Prepare **Sweet Potato and Apple
Stuffing, above,** cooking the vegetables in the sausage
drippings instead of butter and adding the cooked
sausage with the **bread crumbs.**

SPINACH, MUSHROOM,
AND GROUND MEAT STUFFING
About 8 cups

Vary the meat in this stuffing depending on what it is
going into. To stuff veal breast, Crown Roast of Pork, 498,
or lamb, use the same ground meat. For small birds, try
bulk, Italian, or breakfast sausage.

Heat in a very large skillet over medium-high heat until the
foam subsides:

6 tablespoons ($^3/_4$ stick) butter

Add and cook, stirring occasionally, until tender but not
browned, about 7 minutes:

3 cups finely chopped onions

Add and cook, stirring, until wilted:

1 pound mushrooms, finely chopped

Squeeze almost dry:

**1$^1/_4$ to 1$^1/_2$ pounds fresh spinach, cooked, 305, and
    coarsely chopped, or two 10-ounce packages
    frozen chopped spinach, thawed**

Stir into the vegetable mixture and cook until all the liquid
is evaporated and the pan looks dry.

Turn the mixture into a large bowl and stir in:

1$^1/_2$ pounds ground veal or pork, or a combination
2 cups fine fresh bread crumbs
1 cup finely chopped parsley
1$^1/_2$ teaspoons dried thyme
1 teaspoon salt
1 teaspoon black pepper
$^1/_2$ teaspoon grated or ground nutmeg
2 large eggs, beaten

Stuff as indicated in recipes in Meats, Poultry and Wildfowl, or Pasta, depending on use.

SPINACH-RICOTTA STUFFING
About 2 cups

Stuff this well-seasoned mixture under the skins of
chicken parts or under the skin of a flattened butterflied
whole bird.

Heat in a medium skillet over medium heat:

2 teaspoons olive oil

Add and cook, stirring, until softened, about 5 minutes:

$^1/_2$ cup finely chopped onion
1 teaspoon minced garlic

Meanwhile, squeeze almost dry, and place in a medium
bowl:

12 ounces spinach, cooked, 305, and coarsely
   chopped, or one 10-ounce package frozen
   chopped spinach, thawed

Add the onion to the spinach, then mix in:

1 cup ricotta
1/2 cup fresh bread crumbs
2 tablespoons grated Parmesan
2 teaspoons olive oil
1/2 teaspoon salt
1/4 teaspoon black pepper
Pinch of grated or ground nutmeg

Stuff as indicated in recipes in Meats, Poultry and Wild-fowl, or Pasta, depending on use.

STUFFING FOR CROWN ROAST OF PORK

About 2 1/2 cups

Combine in a large bowl:

2 1/2 pounds pork sausage, cooked
1/2 cup dry bread crumbs
1/2 cup chopped celery
1/4 cup chopped onion

Moisten with:

2 to 4 tablespoons milk

Season to taste with:

Dried savory or sage
Paprika

Add the stuffing for the last hour of roasting, 1046.

SAUERKRAUT STUFFING FOR WILDFOWL

5 cups

When used as a stuffing for roast duck, this delicious stuffing tastes like Alsatian braised sauerkraut.

Combine:

4 cups drained Sauerkraut, 265, or commercial
   sauerkraut
1 cup chopped onions
1 chopped peeled Granny Smith apple
(1 cup chopped canned water chestnuts)
(1/4 cup dried currants)
(2 tablespoons brown sugar)
1 teaspoon minced garlic
1/4 teaspoon dried thyme
Salt and black pepper to taste

Lightly spoon the stuffing into the bird before cooking or warm in a 350°F oven for 10 minutes, then serve as a side. Stuffing is done when it reaches an internal temperature of 165°F.

COUSCOUS STUFFING WITH DRIED APRICOTS AND PISTACHIOS

About 4 cups

Use as a stuffing for small birds such as Cornish hens, poussins, or squab, or serve as a side dish for roasted or grilled lamb. For a sweeter stuffing, replace some of the apricots with finely diced dates.

Melt in a large saucepan over medium heat:

2 tablespoons butter

Add and cook, stirring, until tender, about 5 minutes:

1/2 cup finely chopped onion
1/2 cup finely chopped carrots

Stir in:

1 1/2 cups chicken stock or broth
1/2 cup finely chopped dried apricots
(1 tablespoon chopped Salt-Preserved Lemons, 224)
1/4 teaspoon salt
1/4 teaspoon black pepper
Pinch of ground cinnamon
Pinch of ground ginger

Bring to a boil, and stir in:

1 cup quick-cooking couscous

Remove from the heat, cover, and let stand for 5 minutes. Fluff with a fork and stir in:

1/2 cup chopped pistachios, whole pine nuts, or
   slivered almonds, toasted, 1001
1/4 cup minced parsley

Spoon the stuffing into the bird before cooking, or serve immediately as a side. Stuffing is done when it reaches an internal temperature of 165°F.

RICE STUFFING WITH CHORIZO AND HOT CHILE PEPPERS

About 6 cups

This is wonderful in chicken. One 4-ounce can diced mild green chiles can be substituted for the poblano or Anaheim peppers. If using as a stuffing, omit the optional egg.

Heat in a large skillet over medium-high heat:

2 tablespoons olive oil

Add and cook, stirring, until tender, about 5 minutes:

1 cup finely chopped onions
1 tablespoon minced garlic

Add and cook, stirring, until no longer pink, about 10 minutes:

1 1/4 pounds chorizo, casings removed

Transfer to a large bowl and add:

2 cups cooked white rice
(1 large egg, lightly beaten)
2 poblano peppers or 4 Anaheim peppers,
   roasted, 292, peeled, seeded, and chopped
1 cup chopped scallions
1/4 cup minced cilantro
1/4 teaspoon salt, or to taste
1/4 teaspoon black pepper, or to taste

Spoon into the bird before cooking, or bake separately in a large, shallow buttered dish, covered, at 350°F for 20 to 30 minutes. Stuffing is done when it reaches an internal temperature of 165°F.

RICE STUFFING WITH ALMONDS, RAISINS, AND MIDDLE EASTERN SPICES

About 4 cups

This intensely flavored, aromatic stuffing goes well with Cornish hens, partridge, or quail. Baked in a casserole, it also makes a good side dish with grilled chicken or fish.

Heat in a large skillet over medium heat:

2 tablespoons olive oil

Add and cook, stirring, until tender, about 5 minutes:

1 cup chopped onions

Add and stir until well blended:

1 cup medium- or long-grain rice
1 tablespoon minced garlic
¹⁄₂ teaspoon ground cumin
¹⁄₂ teaspoon ground coriander
¹⁄₂ teaspoon turmeric
¹⁄₂ teaspoon sweet paprika
¹⁄₂ teaspoon ground ginger
1 teaspoon salt
¹⁄₂ teaspoon black pepper

Stir in and bring to a simmer:

1¹⁄₂ cups (2 cups if using long-grain rice)
chicken stock or broth

Reduce the heat to low, cover, and simmer until the rice is tender and all the liquid is absorbed, about 20 minutes. Turn the mixture into a large bowl and let cool slightly, then stir in:

¹⁄₄ cup golden raisins
¹⁄₄ cup diced pitted prunes
¹⁄₄ cup slivered almonds, toasted, 1001
1 teaspoon grated lemon zest
2 tablespoons fresh lemon juice

If baking as a dressing, add:

(1 large egg, well beaten)

Adjust the seasonings. Spoon into the bird before cooking, or bake separately in a dish, 532. Stuffing is done when it reaches an internal temperature of 165°F.

WILD RICE DRESSING FOR GAME
About 3 to 4 cups

Combine in a medium saucepan:

3¹⁄₂ cups chicken stock or broth
1 chicken, game bird, or turkey heart and gizzard, finely diced
1 chicken, game bird, or turkey neck, chopped into 1-inch pieces
1 teaspoon salt (if stock is unsalted)

Bring to a boil, then reduce the heat and simmer, covered, 15 minutes. Uncover the pan, raise the heat to high, and bring to a rolling boil. Stir in:

1 cup wild rice

Turn the heat down to low, cover, and simmer until tender, 30 to 50 minutes. Stir in about 5 minutes before the rice is done:

(1 liver, finely diced)

Discard the neck pieces and set the rice aside. Melt in a large skillet over medium heat:

¹⁄₄ cup (¹⁄₂ stick) butter

Add and cook, stirring, until barely soft, about 3 minutes:

1 cup chopped mushrooms
¹⁄₄ cup chopped celery

2 tablespoons chopped shallots
(1 tablespoon chopped green bell pepper)

Add the hot rice and mix well. You may also add one or more of the following:

¹⁄₄ cup chopped black or green olives
¹⁄₄ cup chopped nuts
¹⁄₄ cup canned sliced water chestnuts

Spoon the stuffing into the bird before cooking, or bake separately in a dish, 532. Stuffing is done when it reaches an internal temperature of 165°F.

WILD RICE AND PORCINI STUFFING
About 3 cups

This is the perfect stuffing or accompaniment to wild game birds, venison, or braised beef. Use the strained mushroom soaking liquid as part of the liquid to cook the rice if you like. A wild rice blend can be substituted.

Combine in a small bowl and let soak for 20 minutes:

1 ounce dried porcini mushrooms
1 cup hot water

Lift the mushrooms from the soaking liquid and coarsely chop. Place in a large bowl. Meanwhile, heat in a medium skillet over medium-high heat until the foam subsides:

2 tablespoons unsalted butter

Add and cook, stirring, until softened, about 5 minutes:

¹⁄₂ cup finely chopped onion
¹⁄₄ cup finely chopped celery
¹⁄₄ cup minced shallots
1 tablespoon minced garlic

Stir into the mushrooms, along with:

2 cups cooked wild rice
(¹⁄₄ cup chopped fresh or frozen cranberries)
¹⁄₄ cup minced parsley
1¹⁄₂ teaspoons minced fresh thyme or ¹⁄₂ teaspoon dried thyme
¹⁄₂ teaspoon dried sage

Season with:

Salt and black pepper to taste

Spoon into the bird, or bake separately in a dish, 532. Stuffing is done when it reaches an internal temperature of 165°F.

APRICOT OR PRUNE DRESSING
About 5 cups

Have ready:

1¹⁄₂ cups dried apricots or pitted prunes

If using apricots, cover with boiling water and let stand until softened, 10 to 20 minutes, then drain well. Cut the apricots or prunes into strips. Combine with:

3 cups cooked rice, or 4 cups bread crumbs
¹⁄₂ cup chopped green bell pepper or celery
¹⁄₄ cup (¹⁄₂ stick) butter, melted
¹⁄₂ teaspoon salt
¹⁄₈ teaspoon black pepper

Moisten lightly with:

¹/₄ to ¹/₂ cup chicken stock or broth

Spoon into the bird, or bake separately in a dish, 532. Stuffing is done when it reaches an internal temperature of 165°F.

CHICKEN FARCE

Enough for three 6-pound chickens

A sumptuous stuffing for boned chicken or galantines, 446.

Finely grind in a food processor, in 2 or 3 batches:

About 3¹/₂ pounds boneless, skinless chicken breasts and/or thighs

3 cups mushrooms

Transfer to a large bowl and add, mixing well:

2 cups pistachios

8 or 9 large eggs, beaten

1¹/₃ cups dry sherry or brandy

1¹/₃ cups (2²/₃ sticks) butter, cut into small pieces

¹/₂ cup sautéed mushrooms, 283

(¹/₄ cup sliced black truffles)

2 tablespoons chopped parsley

1 teaspoon grated onion

1¹/₂ tablespoons salt

¹/₄ teaspoon black pepper

Spoon into the birds before cooking. Stuffing is done when it reaches an internal temperature of 165°F.

SAUSAGE AND FENNEL STUFFING

3 cups

Use this tasty meat loaf–like mixture to stuff a 6- to 7-pound chicken or capon.

Melt in a small skillet over low heat:

1¹/₂ tablespoons butter

Add and cook, stirring, over medium heat until tender and lightly browned, 15 to 20 minutes:

1 chicken heart, cut into small dice

1 chicken gizzard, peeled and cut into small dice

Add and cook, stirring, 2 to 3 minutes:

(1 chicken liver, cut into small dice)

2 teaspoons fennel seeds

1 tablespoon minced fresh rosemary or 1 teaspoon dried rosemary

³/₄ teaspoon salt

¹/₄ teaspoon black pepper

Turn into a large bowl and stir in, mixing well:

1 pound bulk sausage

1¹/₂ cups dry bread crumbs

If baking as a dressing, add:

(2 large eggs, beaten)

Use as a stuffing, or bake separately in a dish, 532. Stuffing is done when it reaches an internal temperature of 165°F.

SAVORY SAUCES, SALAD DRESSINGS, MARINADES, AND RUBS

Sauces are not only the hallmark of a good cook—they are an indication of the cook's aesthetic sense as well. There is nothing synonymous about them with the bogeyman. On the whole, they are simple and an area of cooking in which it is easy to excel.

Historically, most classic French sauces were known as "mother sauces," or *fonds de cuisine,* foundations of cooking. There was sauce béchamel, or white sauce; velouté sauce; brown sauce, also known as sauce espagnole; and hollandaise sauce. Most other sauces were variations of them, and they are all good enough to still be with us, but they're now only a part of the story.

Every region of the world has sauces of its own, in many ways quite different from anything the French would have once recognized. Many of these have traveled to America, where they've been adopted, sometimes adapted, and used in new ways. A sauce is no longer required to be discreetly smooth or mild, though it still needs to be a good partner—to enhance the food it accompanies by adding complementary flavor and texture and often visual appeal as well. If that means crossing culinary borders and integrating different ideas and cuisines, so be it. Even the classics started that way.

For hot sauces, basic prerequisites haven't changed, however: ➤ Remove sauces-in-progress from the heat before stirring in fresh ingredients, and ➤ always, if using eggs and if such ingredients are cold, **temper** the eggs by mixing them first in a separate container with a small quantity of the hot liquid before returning both to the saucepan. Other pointers for infallible sauce making will be found in each sauce category.

The sauces that follow are grouped into two general classes, hot and cold, although a few can be served both ways. It must be noted here, too, that temperatures should not be carried to extremes: cold sauces should be served, for the most part, cool, not chilled, and hot ones generally lukewarm. As to the content of this chapter, the sequence runs as follows: **gravies and pan sauces; white sauces; velouté sauce; brown sauces,** or **gravies; quick sauces,** which are simpler to make than the classic versions; **butter sauces,** including **flavored butters; hollandaise and béarnaise sauces; tomato sauces; table sauce; dipping sauces** and **condiments; vinaigrettes** and **salad dressings; mayonnaise; glazes; marinades; barbecue sauces; dry rubs and pastes; flavored oils** and **decorative sauces.**

For Au Gratin, see 961; Tomato and other catsups, see 951; Mustards, see 996; Flavored Vinegars, see 1024; and Horseradish, see 993. For sweet sauces of all types, see Dessert Sauces, 884.

ABOUT SAUCE TOOLS

Saucepans, if possible with sloping sides, are the most important tools in hot sauce making. They are excellent for reducing or cooking down sauces to concentrate flavor, as they allow sauces to boil down quickly, and the slanted sides facilitate whisking and stirring. Avoid aluminum, which may react with some ingredients.

Simple tools within easy reach of the stove smooth the process and encourage the addition of interesting ingredients to sauces. ➤ **Whisks** are vital for emulsified sauces such as hollandaise and mayonnaise and make lumps vanish in roux-based sauces and gravies. For adding flavorings, keep **measuring spoons** handy. **Kitchen shears** with a self-releasing hinge are easy to keep clean; snip herbs quickly, right into the sauce. A **box or rotary grater** or a **rasp-type zester** is convenient for adding a quick grating of cheese, lemon zest, or nutmeg. Also have ready a good-quality **fine-mesh sieve** for straining.

By all means use wooden or silicone **spoons** for the fragile sauces that may be broken down by a whisk. A **sauce spoon** with a pointed end will easily scrape the pan edges clean and help prevent lumping. If you use a metal spoon, make sure it is stainless steel, so as not to discolor a delicate sauce. A flat wooden, rubber, plastic, or silicone **spatula** is useful for scraping sauces from bowls or saucepans.

A double boiler is used to make some sauces—a stainless steel bowl set over a saucepan of water works well as an improvised double boiler.

Electric blenders and food processors are great labor-savers when making emulsified sauces and many condiments. They can, however, change the texture and flavor of a sauce somewhat, as they whip in a good deal of air, which tends to make a thickened sauce foamy and less intense and some sauces a little lighter in color.

ABOUT SAUCES IN QUANTITY

If you are making roux-based gravies or sauces in large amounts, ➤ it will take considerably longer to get rid of the raw flour taste after the liquid has been added to the roux than when you are making only 1 or 2 cups, for immediate use. We advise heating these large amounts ➤ uncovered in a low oven for 30 to 45 minutes and straining the sauce before serving, to remove any crusting or lumps. If you stir the sauce from time to time, it may not be necessary to strain it.

➤ When doubling the ingredients in any sauce recipe, taste before adding the full amount of seasoning. It is easy to overdo it.

KEEPING SAUCES

You can keep white sauces, veloutés, tomato sauces, brown sauces, and gravies in the refrigerator up to 4 to 5 days. To store, strain the sauce, pour it into a container, and cover with a piece of plastic wrap pressed directly against the surface, or thin layer of fat, vegetable oil, or sherry. You can also freeze these sauces in ice cube trays and then, after removing the cubes from the tray, keep the cubes in the freezer in a resealable plastic bag, taking out as many as you need for immediate use. They can be melted in a double boiler—4 large cubes melt down to about ½ cup sauce. You can also freeze Hollandaise Sauce, 560, and Béarnaise Sauce, 561, but be very careful when reheating; see 560. Do not freeze mayonnaise; it will separate.

Except for the sauces listed above, in general, do not try to keep sauces made with eggs, cream, or milk for more than 2 or 3 days in the refrigerator. Vinaigrettes can be kept for up to 1 week in the refrigerator, although those made with fresh herbs are best soon after they are made.

SAUCE INGREDIENTS

Many sauces are based on some sort of pan drippings or juices, because most pan residues—except from strong fish or variety meats—are desirable sauce ingredients. They may result from sautéing, roasting, braising, or browning. ➤ Making pan gravy is described in detail in About Gravies and Pan Sauces, 546.

Stocks, 114, are invaluable sauce ingredients, too, especially when reduced to a glaze, 116. Where possible, the stock should reflect the food it is to flavor: chicken stock for chicken, lamb stock for lamb. Although meat stocks, including poultry and game stocks, are often combined in sauce making—favorites being those of chicken and veal—fish and shellfish stocks, 118, should be reserved only for fish or shellfish dishes. Meat and poultry stocks always make better sauce ingredients if refrigerated 24 hours and then defatted, 116.

When pan drippings or juices or stocks are scanty, turn—with discretion—to wine. ➤ Please read Wine and Spirits for Cooking, 1027. Strong game sauces sometimes support stronger liquors such as rum, brandy, or Madeira,

but whiskey is not recommended. ➤ In any wine sauce, add egg, milk, cream, or butter after the wine has been incorporated.

Many sauce recipes begin by sautéing a mix of aromatic vegetables, spices, herbs, and/or other savory ingredients to develop a **flavor base.** See 957.

ABOUT THICKENERS FOR SAUCES

Sauces not made by deglazing, 546, with liquids or reduction, 161, are generally thickened just enough to lightly coat food, or to coat "the back of a spoon." This is a frequent directive in recipes for such types of sauce; it means simply that the sauce is thick enough that when a spoon is dipped into it, the back of the spoon will be coated with some sauce. If the sauce is not yet thick enough, the liquid will simply run right off. Do not add powdered thickeners such as flour or cornstarch directly to the hot liquid, or lumps that cannot be smoothed will form. ➤ First mix the starch with hot fat or a cold liquid, then stir it into the sauce. More suggestions for thickening are found in Thickeners for Soups, 123.

ROUX

The most common thickener for savory sauces is a roux: a mixture of fat and flour, usually in equal amounts. The fat lubricates and smooths the flour so it does not form lumps when combined with the liquid. The fat may be butter, chicken or other poultry fat, rendered meat drippings, oil, or margarine. A roux is made by melting or heating the fat, adding the flour, and cooking over low heat while whisking or stirring constantly. If a roux cooks too quickly, the resulting mixture will be grainy. (If the fat floats to the top, the roux has separated; if this happens, there is nothing to do but to throw out the roux and start over.)

There are three types of roux: white, blond, and brown. White roux, used to make white sauce, or béchamel, is cooked just until the butter and flour are evenly incorporated and should be removed from the heat before the roux begins to color, 3 to 5 minutes. Blond roux, used in velouté sauces and some cream soups, is cooked until it begins to give off a faint nutty aroma and turns an ivory color, 6 to 7 minutes. Brown roux, basic to Cajun and Creole cooking, is cooked the longest—15 to 20 minutes, sometimes more—until it is a dark brown and has a strong nutty fragrance. The longer you cook a roux, the less it will thicken a sauce or other mixture. Heat eventually breaks down the starch in the flour.

Whether making a white, blond, or brown roux, let it cool slightly before slowly whisking in the milk, stock, or other liquid. If you have made the roux in advance, it is important to first warm either it or the liquid to be added to it. Avoid combining a very hot roux and very hot liquid, which would spatter and cause burns, or a cold roux and cold liquid, which would become lumpy. Once the roux and liquid are combined, whisk constantly until the sauce is thickened and comes to a simmer. Once it has thickened, use gentle cooking to reduce the sauce to the desired consistency. Any trace of a floury taste should disappear after several minutes of slow simmering. If lumps do appear, strain the sauce through a fine-mesh sieve before proceeding with the recipe.

You may find it a time-saver to make roux in advance and store it in the refrigerator. It will keep in the freezer for several months if you proceed as follows. When the roux has been cooked to the desired color and is still soft, measure 1 tablespoon roux into each section of an ice cube tray, and freeze. Transfer the frozen cubes to a resealable plastic bag and store in the freezer. To thicken a sauce, drop the cubes into the hot sauce—2 cubes will thicken approximately 1 cup liquid—until the desired thickness is achieved.

FILÉ POWDER

Filé powder is made from ground sassafras leaves. For thickening and flavor, add filé to gumbos, 136. The powder has a tendency to become stringy when heated, so add after the gumbo is removed from the heat. Filé does not reheat well, so thicken only the portion of gumbo that will be served.

FLOUR

Sometimes called whitewash, flour mixed with water is pressed into emergency service to thicken gravies and sauces, but the results are never so palatable as when a roux is used. Whisk together 1 part flour and 2 parts cold water or stock to make a smooth paste. Stir as much of the paste as needed into the boiling stock or pan drippings or juices. Let the sauce heat until it thickens, and ➤ simmer at least 3 minutes more to reduce the raw taste of the flour, stirring frequently with a whisk. Cake and pastry flours have lower protein contents and will produce a smooth gravy in less time. If you use instant flour, 986, it can be mixed into the gravy or sauce without first being mixed with water.

BROWNED FLOUR

This is a variant used in gravies that enhances color and flavor. The slow—but inexpensive—procedure by which it is made is worth trying. The flour, when ready, will be golden brown and smell nutty and baked. Place about **1 cup of all-purpose flour** in a dry heavy skillet, and ➤ stir constantly over low heat, scraping the flour from the sides and bottom of the pan. Or heat the flour in a very heavy pan in a 200° to 250°F oven, shaking the pan periodically so the flour browns evenly. Do not let it get too dark, or, as with brown roux, it will become bitter and lose its thickening power altogether. ➤ Even properly browned flour has only about half the thickening power of regular flour. It can be stored in a tightly covered jar in a cool place and used in flour paste, above.

CORNSTARCH

Cornstarch is an excellent thickening agent. With almost twice the thickening power of flour, cornstarch gives a glossy, translucent appearance to sauces. If introduced directly into a hot liquid, lumps are formed which cannot be smoothed. Mix a small amount of cold liquid with the cornstarch to form a **slurry.** Whisk the slurry into a simmering sauce at the last minute. Cornstarch thickens almost immediately, allowing you to easily judge the amount needed. ➤ One tablespoon cornstarch will thicken about 1½ to 2 cups liquid. Overheating will thin a cornstarch-thickened sauce.

ARROWROOT

Of all the thickeners, arrowroot makes the most delicately textured sauces. It performs much like cornstarch when dissolved in cold liquid and whisked in at the last moment to thicken a sauce, making it shiny and glossy, but it has a bit more thickening power than cornstarch, and it is less likely to thin out if overheated. ➤ However, arrowroot should be used only when the sauce is to be served within 10 minutes of preparation. It will not hold, nor will it reheat. Since the flavor of arrowroot is neutral and it does not have to be cooked to remove rawness, as does flour, and since it thickens at a lower temperature than either flour or cornstarch, it is ideal for use in egg-based and other sauces that should not boil. Allow 2½ teaspoons to 1 cup liquid.

POTATO STARCH

Preferred by some cooks to flour as a thickener in certain delicate sauces. Mix it with a cold liquid and add to simmering stock. When it is used, less simmering is required than for flour, and the sauce gains some transparency. ➤ But if overheated, the sauce will thin out. And the sauce should be served soon after it has thickened, as potato starch has no holding power. One tablespoon of potato starch will moderately thicken 1 cup of liquid. It is usually stocked in the kosher foods section of the grocery store.

TAPIOCA FLOUR

Tapioca is derived from the cassava root. It is used for thickening sauces, clear fruit glazes, and fruit fillings, particularly those intended to be served cold or frozen, as it does not break down when frozen the way flour-thickened sauces do. Beware of boiling a liquid that has been thickened with tapioca flour, though; if boiled, it will become stringy. Once the liquid begins to simmer, remove it from the heat and let it sit for 15 minutes, stirring only once or twice during the first 5 minutes, and the sauce will set. Use 1 tablespoon tapioca flour per cup of liquid. Tapioca flour is available in well-stocked supermarkets, health food stores, and on the Internet. Pearl tapioca is used to make pudding, 821.

EGG YOLKS

Egg yolks not only thicken but also enrich a sauce. ➤ Never add them directly to hot liquid. Always temper the yolks by mixing them first in a separate bowl with a small quantity of hot liquid. Then incorporate a little more of the hot liquid. Off the heat, stir this mixture into the remainder of the hot liquid, and then stir over low heat until the sauce thickens. ➤ Do not allow the sauce to boil, or it will curdle. If this happens, it is sometimes possible to restore the sauce's smoothness by plunging the pot into cold water and stirring it vigorously, or by beating in a small amount of chilled cream, and/or by straining it. Unless you can control the heat source very precisely, it is generally safer to add egg yolks to a mixture in a double boiler ➤ over—not in—boiling water. Two or three egg yolks with $1/4$ to $1/3$ cup heavy cream will thicken $1^1/2$ cups of liquid.

Egg yolks added very slowly to melted butter or oil with constant stirring will produce an emulsion that is quite thick. Suitably seasoned, this becomes the base for hollandaise or mayonnaise.

REDUCTION
Another classic way to thicken sauces and intensify their flavor. Béchamel and sauce espagnole may be thickened during very slow simmering by the evaporation of liquid to achieve more richness and subtlety. If you intend to thicken a sauce by reduction, season ➤ after you have brought it down to the right consistency, or you may find it overseasoned or unpleasantly salty. There are a good many recipes for tomato sauces that demand long cooking and reducing. Unless you keep these sauces—or, in fact, any thickened sauces—over very low heat, they will cook too fast, and flavor and color will be impaired. ➤ Some reduced sauces, to be perfect in texture, should be strained before serving.

BUTTER SWIRLS
Swirled in bit by bit, butter finishes off many fine, rich sauces, both white and brown, after straining, if any, and final heating. But after swirling, the sauce must be served at once, ➤ and it can't be reheated. In addition to improving the flavor, the butter also very slightly thickens the sauce. To finish a sauce with butter after straining, if any, and heating, add ➤ cold unsalted butter bit by bit, moving the pan in a circular motion so that the butter makes a visible spiral in the hot sauce as it melts. Remove the pan from the heat before the butter is fully melted, and continue to swirl. ➤ Do not use a spoon to stir it. About 1 tablespoon butter is generally used to finish 1 cup of sauce. Flavored butters, 558, can also be used when their flavors are appropriate.

KNEADED BUTTER, OR BEURRE MANIÉ
Although it is a magic panacea for thickening thin sauces at the end of the cooking process, kneaded butter should not be used for sauces which require long simmering. After adding kneaded butter, ➤ do not boil the sauce. Simmer only long enough to dispel the floury taste. To make it, work 2 tablespoons softened butter and 2 tablespoons flour together with your fingers, as though you were making pastry. Form into pea-sized balls and drop

into the hot liquid, whisking constantly until the ingredients are well blended and the sauce thickens. This amount will be sufficient for 1 cup of thin liquid.

BREAD CRUMBS AND GROUND NUTS
Finely ground bread crumbs and finely ground nuts, especially almonds, can be used to add texture and thickness to sauces. Pesto, 569, is thickened with ground pine nuts, and bread crumbs add body to the spicy Mediterranean mayonnaise known as Rouille, 582.

CREAM AND CRÈME FRAÎCHE
Heavy cream can be used as a thickener if it is first simmered to reduce its volume. This can be done directly in the sauce, as in a gravy or pan sauce, or done separately and then added to the sauce. In either case, use a large heavy-bottomed pan so that the cream will not boil over, and let the cream simmer until it is reduced by about half its original volume. Reduced cream can be used in large amounts for white sauces or in small doses to add a satiny finish to almost any other sauce. **Crème fraîche** can be spooned directly into a simmering sauce to add body, richness, and a subtle tangy flavor. While it is as thick as sour cream or clotted cream to begin with, crème fraîche will not separate if the sauce is boiled down.

PUREES
Purees of cooked vegetables, fruits, and rice are an excellent way to add body and flavor to a sauce. The puree can be very smooth or slightly chunky. Starchy vegetables, such as potatoes or white beans, will make a sauce quite thick, while other vegetables and fruits, such as roasted peppers, stewed onions, or pureed apples, will thicken it only slightly.

SERVING SAUCES
Gravy boats and various small spouted containers are traditional ways to serve hot or cold sauces, but there are other attractive ways to serve them. Cold sauces and dips with a mayonnaise or sour cream base may be presented in a crisp hollowed-out cabbage, 1052, or individually in tomato or pepper cases, 173. When presenting cold shrimp or poached salmon with a delicately flavored Mayonnaise, 578, or Rémoulade Sauce, 581, serve the sauce in a large seashell.

Hot sauces may be served in ramekins and other small heatproof containers. Miniature individual pitchers and pots are appropriate when hot lobster, artichokes, or asparagus is on the menu. Sauces on the buffet table may be kept hot in small saucepans, placed over a candle, or in chafing dishes. Like the food it accompanies, sauce, if it is meant to be hot, must be kept hot. However, ➤ any sauce that is worth its salt won't keep indefinitely on a buffet table or in a chafing dish.

Cold sauces and Flavored Butters, 558, may be kept chilled on a mound of crushed ice; sauces in containers and molds and pats of seasoned butter may be placed directly on the ice. Don't use ice cubes—the butter would slip down between them.

ABOUT GRAVIES AND PAN SAUCES

Gravies and pan sauces are made from the pan drippings of roasted, fried, or sautéed meat or poultry. They are the quick and lively descendants of the brown sauce. While a traditional gravy is thickened with flour, a pan sauce is not. Residues, juices, and scrapings from sautéing, broiling, roasting, or browning, known as *fonds,* are the precious base for many delectable pan sauces to be served with poultry, meat dishes, and fish. When the roast is done, remove it from the pan and **degrease** the pan. There are several ways to do this quickly. One is to pour all the juices into a heatproof glass container and submerge it in cold water. The fat will rise at once and can be spooned off. Another way, if there is more fat than stock, is to use a baster: Tip the pan and siphon off the good juices from underneath the top layer of grease. Pour off the grease and return the juices to the roasting pan. You can also use a gravy or fat separator. To **deglaze,** add 1/4 cup or more liquids such as water, wine, or stock and reduce it, 1055, stirring and scraping the solidified juices from the bottom and sides. The addition of wine, stock, or other flavorful liquids will heighten aroma and flavor. Use the stock appropriate to your meat or poultry or the wine you are drinking with it. Gravies and pan sauces can be thickened with cream, kneaded butter, roux, or cornstarch, or finished with a butter swirl. ➤ See About Thickeners for Sauces, 543. If you use a roux, pour off the cooking juices and make the roux directly in the pan, then whisk the juices back in. To be sure there is enough gravy to go around for a big occasion, you can expand your yield by using warm stock and melted butter, or bacon fat, to multiply the recipe accordingly.

MEAT PAN GRAVY
About 1 cup

If desired, you may strain the drippings first and remove excess fat, then return some of the fat to the pan to absorb the flour. If you want to use a thickener other than flour, please see About Thickeners for Sauces, 543, for the correct amount to add for the amount of liquid below.
Remove the meat or poultry from the pan and place it on a platter, and keep warm. Pour off all but:

   2 tablespoons drippings or fat
from the pan. Blend into them:

   1 to 2 tablespoons all-purpose flour
Whisk until the roux is well combined and smooth. Stirring constantly, add:

   **The degreased pan juices plus enough stock, wine,
      beer, cream, milk, or water to make 1 cup**
Simmer until thickened, up to 10 minutes. Season to taste with:

   Salt and black pepper
   **(Minced fresh or crumbled dried herbs, such as thyme,
      rosemary, or sage)**
   (Grated lemon zest)
Strain the gravy, if desired, and reheat before serving.

POULTRY PAN SAUCE OR GRAVY
1 cup

These proportions are for a chicken weighing around 4 pounds. For a larger bird, double all ingredients.
After removing the chicken to a platter, pour into the roasting pan:

   1/4 cup dry white wine, sherry, port, Madeira, or water
Place the roasting pan on two burners over medium-high heat. Bring the juices to a simmer and, using a wooden spoon, scrape up the browned bits in the bottom of the pan. Pour the mixture into a heatproof glass container and let the fat rise to the top, then skim off the fat with a spoon and discard. (You can also use a gravy separator.) Return the mixture to the roasting pan or pour it into a small saucepan. Add the juices that have accumulated around the chicken, along with:

   3/4 cup chicken stock or broth
Bring to a simmer. If you wish to thicken the sauce into a gravy, mix to a smooth paste:

   (1 tablespoon unsalted butter, softened)
   (1 tablespoon all-purpose flour)
Whisk the paste bit by bit into the simmering sauce and cook until thickened. Season with:

   Several drops of fresh lemon juice or vinegar
   Salt and black pepper to taste

GIBLET GRAVY
4 cups

If increasing this recipe by half or doubling it, you may need to buy extra giblets.
Rinse and pat dry:

   1 turkey neck, heart, and gizzard
Chop the neck into 2-inch pieces. Cut the heart lengthwise in half, and divide the gizzard at the lobes. Heat in a wide heavy saucepan over medium heat:

   2 tablespoons vegetable oil
Add the turkey parts to the pan, then scatter around them:

   1/2 to 1 cup chopped onions
Cook, without stirring, until the turkey parts are richly browned on the first side, 5 to 10 minutes; reduce the heat slightly if the ingredients begin to burn. Turn and brown the second side in the same manner. Add:

   4 cups chicken or turkey stock or broth
   1/2 cup dry white or red wine
   (1/4 cup finely chopped carrots)
   (1/4 cup finely chopped celery)
   (2 small sprigs parsley)
   1 large bay leaf
   1/2 teaspoon dried thyme or 2 to 3 sprigs fresh thyme

(4 whole cloves or allspice berries or pinch of ground
      cloves or allspice)

Partially cover the pan and simmer very slowly until the
meat is tender, about 1 hour. Add and simmer until firm,
about 5 minutes:

(1 turkey liver, rinsed)

Strain the stock through a fine sieve and add enough
water to measure 4 cups. Finely chop the neck meat, cut
the giblets into tiny dice, and add to the stock. Discard the
vegetables. Heat in a large saucepan over medium-high
heat until foaming:

3 tablespoons unsalted butter

Add and cook, whisking constantly, for 1 minute:

$^1/_3$ cup all-purpose flour

Remove the pan from the heat. For an especially silky gravy,
transfer the stock to a saucepan and bring it to a furious
boil, then pour it all at once into the roux, whisking as you
pour. Otherwise, simply whisk the warm stock into the
roux, blending thoroughly. Whisking constantly, bring the
gravy to a simmer over medium heat and cook for 1
minute. Remove from the heat and cover. If you will be finishing and serving the gravy within 30 minutes to 1 hour,
let it stand at room temperature; otherwise, refrigerate it.

When the turkey is done, transfer it to a platter and
keep warm. Remove the rack from the roasting pan. If the
juices have evaporated, leaving only fat and browned bits
on the bottom of the pan, carefully pour out the fat and
discard it, retaining all browned bits. If there are juices, tilt
the pan and skim off as much fat as possible with a spoon.
Set the pan on two burners over medium heat. Pour in:

$^1/_2$ cup sherry, Madeira, port, dry white wine, or water

Bring to a simmer, scraping the bottom of the pan with a
wooden spoon to loosen the browned bits. Pour the drippings into the gravy. Place the gravy over medium heat
and simmer, stirring occasionally, for 5 minutes to blend
the flavors. Season with:

Salt and black pepper to taste

Pour into a gravy boat.

QUICK TURKEY GRAVY

4 cups

To prepare more than 4 cups, you may increase all the ingredients by half or double the recipe.

After roasting the turkey, remove the rack from the roasting pan. If the juices have evaporated, leaving only fat and
browned bits on the bottom of the pan, carefully pour out
the fat and discard it, retaining all browned bits. If there
are juices, tilt the pan and skim as much fat as possible
with a spoon. Set the pan on two burners over medium
heat. Pour in:

4 cups chicken stock or broth

Bring to a simmer, scraping the bottom of the pan with a
wooden spoon to loosen the browned bits. Reduce the heat
and simmer slowly for 5 minutes. Mix to a smooth paste:

$^1/_4$ cup water

3 tablespoons cornstarch

Whisking constantly, gradually pour this mixture into the
simmering broth, then simmer, whisking, for 1 minute.
Season to taste with:

(Sherry, port, or Madeira)

Salt and black pepper

Pour into a gravy boat.

PAN SAUCE FOR WILDFOWL

$^1/_2$ cup

This sauce is very rich, so a little goes a long way. Double all
the ingredients for a larger group. Use when roasting one
or more game birds that have been barded, 455, with
bacon, pancetta, or salt pork.

Transfer the bird(s) to a platter and keep warm. Beat together:

1 large egg yolk

$^1/_2$ cup heavy cream

Pour off the fat from the roasting pan. Add to the pan:

2 tablespoons brandy

Cook over low heat on two burners if necessary for
1 minute, stirring with a wooden spoon to loosen and dissolve any browned bits. Add the egg yolk and cream mixture and stir until thickened, but do not allow the sauce to
boil. Season well with:

Salt and black pepper

SAUSAGE GRAVY FOR BISCUITS

$2^1/_2$ cups

Brown in a large skillet, breaking up the meat with a
spoon:

8 ounces bulk sausage

Using a slotted spoon, remove to a paper towel–lined
plate. Pour off all but 2 tablespoons drippings from the
pan. If necessary, add enough:

Butter

to make 2 tablespoons. Stir in:

2 tablespoons all-purpose flour

Whisk until the roux is well combined and smooth. Stirring
constantly, add:

2 cups milk

Simmer, whisking, for 5 minutes, or until thickened. Season with:

$^1/_2$ teaspoon salt

1 teaspoon black pepper, or to taste

2 dashes hot pepper sauce

Fold the reserved sausage into the sauce before pouring it
over Biscuits, 637–640, or serve it sprinkled on top.

HERB PAN SAUCE

$^2/_3$ cup

A bright and lively sauce for lamb, pork, or chicken. The
mustard will make the sauce thinner, so omit it if you prefer a thicker sauce. This sauce can also be made without
pan drippings, in which case cook the shallots first in oil or
butter.

After panfrying lamb chops, pork chops, or chicken

breasts, remove them to a platter and keep warm. Pour off most of the excess fat and set the pan over medium heat. Add:

¹/₂ cup minced shallots

Cook, stirring, until softened but not browned. Turn the heat to medium-high and add:

²/₃ cup chicken stock or broth, apple cider, or dry white wine

Stir with a wooden spoon to loosen and dissolve any browned bits, then bring to a boil and add:

(4 teaspoons Dijon mustard)
1 tablespoon fresh lemon juice, white wine vinegar, or Cognac, or to taste
2 bay leaves
Salt and black pepper to taste

Cook, stirring occasionally, until slightly reduced and thickened, 1 to 2 minutes. Add and cook until reduced by about half, 1 to 2 minutes:

(¹/₂ cup heavy cream)

Strain the sauce through a fine-mesh sieve, if desired, and stir in:

2 tablespoons minced parsley, thyme, and/or rosemary

Swirl in bit by bit, 545:

About 1¹/₂ teaspoons butter

Arrange the meat on plates, spoon the sauce over, and garnish with:

Herb sprigs

SWEET-SOUR ORANGE PAN SAUCE

2 cups

For game birds. To turn this into a true **Bigarade Sauce** for duck or goose, use the zest and juice from a Seville, or bitter, orange and omit the lemon juice.

Using a vegetable peeler, remove the zest from:

1 navel orange

Cut the zest into slivers about ¹/₈ inch wide and 1 inch long. Place in a saucepan, add 4 cups cold water, and bring to a boil over high heat; cook 1 minute. Drain the zest in a sieve, rinse with cold water, drain again, and pat dry. Transfer the roasted bird(s) to a platter and keep warm. Pour off the fat from the roasting pan. Pour into the pan:

1 cup game, 118, or chicken stock or broth

Set the pan over medium heat over two burners if necessary and bring to a simmer, scraping the pan bottom with a wooden spoon to dissolve the brown bits. Remove the pan from the heat and set aside. Combine in a small heavy saucepan and cook over low heat, stirring, until a light brown, caramel color:

2 tablespoons white wine vinegar
2 tablespoons sugar

Add the contents of the roasting pan and cook 4 to 5 minutes. Stir together:

2 teaspoons cornstarch
1 tablespoon water

Stir into the sauce and simmer, 1 minute. Stir in the orange zest, whisking, along with:

¹/₂ cup fresh orange juice
2 tablespoons orange liqueur or thawed orange juice concentrate
1 tablespoon fresh lemon juice
Salt and black pepper to taste

Heat until hot, but do not allow the sauce to simmer. Spoon the sauce over the bird(s) and garnish with:

Orange sections

PAN SAUCE WITH LEEKS, ORANGE, AND ROSEMARY

¹/₃ cup

After panfrying steak, lamb chops, pork chops, or chicken breasts, remove them to a platter and keep warm. Pour off all but about 1 teaspoon fat from the pan, and set the skillet over medium heat. Add:

1 small leek, white part only, thinly sliced

Cook, stirring, until just starting to soften and brown. Add:

¹/₃ cup fresh orange juice

Bring to a boil, stirring with a wooden spoon to loosen and dissolve any browned bits, and cook for 2 to 3 minutes. Add:

¹/₃ cup chicken stock or broth
Two 2-inch strips orange zest
1 sprig rosemary

Cook, stirring often, until the sauce is reduced by about half and thickened, 4 to 5 minutes. Discard the zest and rosemary. Season with:

Salt and black pepper to taste

Swirl in bit by bit, 545:

About 5 teaspoons butter

Arrange the meat on plates, spoon the sauce over, and sprinkle with:

2 teaspoons minced parsley

RED WINE AND SOUR CHERRY PAN SAUCE

¹/₂ cup

After panfrying steak, pork chops, or chicken breasts, remove them to a platter and keep warm. Pour off all but 1 teaspoon fat from the skillet and set the pan over medium-high heat. Add and cook, stirring, until just starting to soften and brown:

¹/₃ cup finely diced red onions

Meanwhile, combine and set aside:

¹/₂ cup chicken stock or broth or water
¹/₃ cup dried tart cherries

Add to the onions:

¹/₄ cup dry red wine

Bring to a boil, stirring with a wooden spoon to loosen and dissolve any browned bits, and cook for 1 minute. Add the stock and dried cherries, along with:

One 2-inch strip lemon zest
1 teaspoon light brown sugar
¹/₂ teaspoon balsamic vinegar
¹/₂ teaspoon thyme leaves

Bring to a boil over high heat and cook, stirring often, until reduced by half and thickened, about 2 minutes. Discard the zest. Stir in any juices from the meat. Season with:

> **Salt and black pepper to taste**
> **(A few drops of fresh lemon juice)**

Swirl in bit by bit, 545:

> **About 1½ teaspoons butter**

Arrange the meat on plates and spoon over the sauce.

ABOUT PAN SAUCES MADE WITHOUT DRIPPINGS

Pan sauces can be made without pan drippings; instead the recipe usually begins with sautéing shallots or onions, then proceeds as for standard pan sauces. Layers of flavor come from successive additions of aromatic ingredients and liquids such as wine, stock, or juice. These simple sauces are almost always left unthickened. The key to success is to simmer the stock or other liquid until it is well reduced, but do not overcook. Feel free to add seasonings—and a swirl of butter at the last minute will add richness and give a beautiful sheen.

An alternative is to gently heat a vinaigrette, either in the skillet after cooking the meat, poultry, or fish or in a separate saucepan. Vinaigrettes are a quick and flavorful way to sauce anything from roasted meats to grilled vegetables.

ORANGE AND GINGER SAUCE

1½ cups

Serve this with poultry, wildfowl, or poached fish.
Melt in a large saucepan or skillet over medium heat:

> **1 tablespoon unsalted butter**

Add and cook, stirring, until very lightly browned:

> **³⁄₄ cup chopped mushrooms**
> **¹⁄₄ cup chopped shallots or scallions**

Add:

> **1 cup dry white wine**
> **2 tablespoons chopped peeled fresh ginger**

Increase the heat to high and boil until reduced by half.
Add and boil until reduced by half:

> **(3 cups chicken stock or broth)**
> **³⁄₄ cup fresh orange juice**

Add:

> **³⁄₄ cup heavy cream**

Cook until sauce is reduced and coats the spoon. Strain through a fine-mesh sieve. Stir in:

> **1 tablespoon grated orange zest**
> **Fresh lemon juice to taste**
> **Salt and black pepper to taste**

BASIC CREAM SAUCE FOR GAME

½ cup

For venison or dark-meat birds, this is also good with sautéed wild mushrooms or over pasta.
Combine in a medium saucepan:

> **1 cup heavy cream**
> **1 tablespoon lightly crushed juniper berries**
> **1 tablespoon chopped thyme, rosemary, or basil**

Bring to a rolling boil, stirring very occasionally with a whisk only to prevent boiling over. Reduce the heat slightly and reduce by half. Season with:

> **Salt to taste**

ROASTED RED PEPPER SAUCE

1 cup

Serve this deeply flavored, almost sweet sauce with roasted or grilled meats, chicken, fish, or pasta.
Heat in a heavy skillet over medium heat:

> **2 tablespoons olive oil**

Add and cook, stirring often, until lightly browned, 5 to 7 minutes:

> **1½ cups chopped onions**

Stir in:

> **3 large red bell peppers, roasted, 292, and coarsely chopped, or 2 cups chopped drained canned roasted red peppers**
> **2 tablespoons minced garlic**
> **1 tablespoon sweet paprika**
> **¹⁄₄ teaspoon ground cinnamon**
> **¹⁄₈ to ¹⁄₄ teaspoon ground red pepper**

Cook, stirring, for 1 minute. Add:

> **1½ cups beef stock or broth plus 1 cup water or 2½ cups water**

Bring to a boil, then reduce the heat, partially cover, and very slowly simmer for about 1 hour. Puree the sauce in a blender or food processor. Season with:

> **Salt and black pepper to taste**

BURGUNDY SAUCE (SAUCE BOURGUIGNONNE)

Scant 1 cup

For veal, venison, or beef.
Combine in a medium saucepan and bring to a boil:

> **2 cups dry red wine, preferably Burgundy**
> **¹⁄₄ cup finely chopped mushrooms**
> **2 shallots, minced**
> **¹⁄₄ teaspoon chopped fresh thyme or a pinch of dried thyme**
> **A few sprigs parsley**
> **1 bay leaf**

Reduce the heat slightly and reduce by half. Strain the sauce into a saucepan. When ready to serve, bring to a simmer and add:

> **1 to 1½ tablespoons kneaded butter, 545**
> **Salt and black pepper to taste**
> **(A dash of ground red pepper)**

Simmer for 1 minute, remove the bay leaf, and adjust the seasonings.

RED MOLE

5 cups

Serve with chicken or turkey. Leftover sauce can be frozen, 994, but to regain the smooth texture, you may need to process it in the blender before reheating it.

Heat a medium heavy skillet or griddle, preferably cast iron, over medium heat until hot. Add:

8 unpeeled large garlic cloves

Roast, turning occasionally, until soft, about 15 minutes. Let cool, then peel.

Meanwhile, remove the stems and seeds from:

8 medium dried ancho peppers (4 ounces)

Tear the peppers into flat pieces. Lightly toast the peppers in the hot skillet, pressing them flat with a metal spatula, for about 10 seconds on each side. Remove to a bowl, add hot water to cover, and submerge them with a plate. Let soak for about 30 minutes. Drain the peppers, and place in a blender, along with the garlic. Add:

^{2}/$_3$ cup Poultry Stock, 117, or chicken stock or broth

1^1/$_2$ teaspoons dried oregano

^{1}/$_2$ teaspoon black pepper

^{1}/$_8$ teaspoon ground cloves

Process the mixture until smooth, then press it through a medium-mesh sieve into a bowl. Heat in a Dutch oven over medium heat until hot:

1^1/$_2$ tablespoons vegetable oil

Add:

^{1}/$_2$ cup whole unblanched almonds

Cook, stirring constantly, until lightly toasted, about 3 minutes. With a slotted spoon, remove the almonds to the blender. Add to the hot oil remaining in the pan:

1 small onion, thinly sliced

Cook, stirring occasionally, until nicely browned, about 8 minutes. With the slotted spoon, remove the onion to the blender. Add to the hot pan:

^{1}/$_4$ cup raisins

Cook, stirring constantly, until puffed, about 30 seconds. Scoop the raisins into the blender. Add:

2 slices white bread, toasted and torn into
    pieces

1 cup chicken stock or broth

^{1}/$_2$ cup drained canned tomatoes, chopped

^{1}/$_4$ cup chopped unsweetened chocolate or
    2 tablespoons unsweetened cocoa powder

^{1}/$_4$ teaspoon ground cinnamon

Process until very smooth. Heat in the Dutch oven over medium heat until hot:

1 tablespoon vegetable oil

Add the reserved ancho mixture and cook, stirring, until it darkens and becomes very thick, about 5 minutes. Stir in the almond mixture and cook until very thick, about 5 minutes. Stir in:

4 cups chicken stock or broth

Bring to a boil, then reduce the heat to low, partially cover, and simmer, stirring often, about 45 minutes. Season with:

Salt to taste

1 tablespoon sugar, or to taste

ABOUT WHITE SAUCE (SAUCE BÉCHAMEL)

This basic sauce is prized for its unassertive character and smooth texture, useful not only for creaming foods like vegetables and fish but as a base for many other sauces.

➤ Make a little thicker than you think it should be, because it is easier to thin it out than to thicken it. For creamed dishes, use 1 cup sauce for every 2 cups solids, and use a light hand with the seasoning until you taste the mixture. The sauce can be refrigerated or kept warm in the top of a double boiler for up to an hour. Place a piece of wax paper or plastic wrap directly on the surface of the sauce to prevent a skin from forming.

I. WHITE SAUCE

1 cup

Melt in a medium saucepan over medium-low heat:

2 tablespoons butter

Whisk in until well blended and smooth, about 1^1/$_2$ minutes:

2 tablespoons all-purpose flour

Remove the pan from the heat and slowly whisk in:

1 cup milk

Return the pan to heat and bring to a simmer, whisking constantly to prevent lumps. Continue to cook, whisking, until the sauce is smooth and hot and has thickened, 1 to 2 minutes. Season to taste with:

Salt and black or white pepper

Grated or ground nutmeg

Note: For better consistency, scald the milk, 997, before adding it to the roux. For improved flavor, add to the milk before scalding:

(1 thick onion slice stuck with 2 whole cloves)

(1 bay leaf)

then cover and let stand for 15 minutes; remove the cloves and bay leaf, if used, and whisk into the roux. You may also vary the flavor of the sauce with one or more of the following:

1 teaspoon fresh lemon juice

^{1}/$_2$ teaspoon Worcestershire sauce

1 teaspoon sherry

2 tablespoons chopped parsley

2 tablespoons chopped chives

II. THICK BÉCHAMEL

1 cup

To use in soufflés.

Prepare **White Sauce I, above**, using **3 tablespoons butter, 3 tablespoons all-purpose flour**, and **1 cup milk.**

III. BINDING BÉCHAMEL

1 cup

For croquettes.

Prepare **White Sauce I, above**, using **3 tablespoons butter, ^{1}/$_3$ cup all-purpose flour**, and **1 cup milk.**

IV. THIN BÉCHAMEL

1 cup

Use as a quick base for a cream soup, adding pureed vegetables.

Prepare **White Sauce I, above**, using **1 tablespoon butter, 1 tablespoon all-purpose flour**, and **1 cup milk.**

The finished sauce should be just thick enough to coat the back of a spoon.

NO-CREAM WHITE SAUCE

2 cups

Homemade stock and a puree of rice produce the look and feel of heavy cream. Add seasonings and herbs to make it a sauce on its own to serve with fish, chicken, pasta, or rice, or use as an ingredient in casseroles and soups.

Heat in a medium saucepan over medium heat:

2 tablespoons olive oil

Add and cook, stirring, until softened:

1/2 cup chopped onions

Add and cook, stirring constantly, for 2 minutes:

1/3 cup rice, preferably medium- or short-grain

Add:

2/3 cup chicken stock or broth, or vegetable stock or broth

1 cup dry white wine

Bring to a simmer, then cover, reduce the heat, and simmer gently until the liquid is almost absorbed and the rice is very soft, about 35 minutes. Let cool slightly, then transfer to a blender or food processor and puree until smooth. With the machine running, add until the desired consistency is reached:

Up to 1½ cups more stock

Blend in until smooth:

(1 tablespoon chopped tarragon)

Season with:

1 tablespoon fresh lemon juice

Salt and black pepper to taste

FLOURLESS WHITE SAUCE

1 cup

This sauce is based on reduced stock and heavy cream. The result is not as thick as traditional white sauce, but it is rich and creamy. Use a saucepan large enough to allow the cream to foam up, and whisk the sauce from time to time to keep it from becoming grainy. Do not boil the cream longer than recommended, or it will lose its delicacy and curdle. Use this in place of white sauce in any of the variations, except for use in soufflés, casseroles, gratins, and croquettes.

Bring to a boil in a small heavy saucepan over high heat:

2 cups Poultry Stock, 117, or chicken stock or broth

Boil until reduced to 1/2 cup, then set aside.

Meanwhile, boil in a small heavy saucepan over medium-high heat, whisking to prevent boiling over, until reduced by half:

1 cup heavy cream

Whisk the cream into the hot stock and add:

Salt and white pepper to taste

MORNAY SAUCE (CHEESE SAUCE)

As versatile as it is delicious, this basic sauce is excellent with poached or baked eggs; steamed vegetables; poached poultry, fish, or seafood; and filled crêpes. If desired, the sauce can be smoothed over these foods and browned in the oven or under a broiler. It also makes ele-

gant macaroni and cheese. Using equal parts Gruyère and Parmesan is traditional, but any aged cheese, alone or in combination, is very good. Try Swiss, Cheddar, or blue cheeses such as Gorgonzola, Roquefort, and Stilton.

I. *1 cup*

Prepare:

White Sauce I, 550

When it is smooth and hot, reduce the heat to low and stir in:

1/4 cup firmly packed finely grated cheese

Cook, stirring, just until the cheese is melted, or the cheese may turn stringy. Season with:

Salt to taste

Pinch of ground red pepper

Pinch of grated or ground nutmeg or mace

Note: Should the sauce become stringy, bring it just to a simmer and whisk in:

(A few drops of dry white wine or fresh lemon juice)

then remove from the heat.

II. *1½ cups*

This richer version is good with broccoli and baked potatoes.

Prepare:

White Sauce I, 550

When smooth and hot, reduce the heat to low and stir in:

1 cup grated cheese (4 ounces)

Season with:

1/2 teaspoon salt

1/8 teaspoon paprika

A few grains of ground red pepper

(1/4 teaspoon dry mustard)

Stir until the cheese is melted.

CREAMY MICROWAVE CHEESE SAUCE

2 cups

Use mild Cheddar, extra sharp Cheddar, or Vermont white Cheddar.

Combine in a microwave-safe bowl:

1 cup whole-milk yogurt

4 ounces cream cheese, softened

1 cup shredded Cheddar (4 ounces)

1 tablespoon fresh lemon juice

1 tablespoon butter

1/2 teaspoon salt

1/2 teaspoon black pepper

2 dashes hot pepper sauce, or to taste

Microwave on high power for 1½ minutes. Let sit for 2 minutes, then whisk and microwave again on high power for 1½ minutes. Let sit for 2 minutes, then whisk until smooth. If necessary, return to the microwave for 1 minute more.

ONION SAUCE (SAUCE SOUBISE)

3/4 cup

For fish, veal, sweetbreads, lamb, or main-course vegetables.

Combine in a medium heavy 1-quart saucepan:
   1 large onion, chopped
   2 tablespoons chicken stock or broth
Cover and cook over low heat, stirring occasionally, until the onions are tender but not browned, about 25 minutes. Stir in:
   White Sauce I, 550
and cook for 15 minutes, stirring frequently. Strain through a fine-mesh sieve into a small saucepan (reserve the onions for soup if desired). The sauce will be thick. Set over low heat and slowly whisk in until the desired consistency is reached:
   2 to 4 tablespoons heavy cream or milk
Add:
   Salt and white pepper to taste
   Pinch of grated or ground nutmeg

MUSTARD SAUCE

1 cup

For broiled fish or ham.
Prepare **White Sauce I, 550.** When the sauce is smooth and hot, stir in **2 to 4 tablespoons Dijon, grainy French, or brown English mustard to taste.** Season as directed.

WHITE WINE SAUCE FOR FISH

1¼ cups

Also good with chicken breasts.
Combine in a small saucepan:
   ¼ cup dry white wine
   ¼ cup fish or chicken stock or broth
   1 bay leaf
   2 whole cloves
   2 black peppercorns
   (1½-inch piece fresh ginger, peeled and thinly sliced)
   1 teaspoon chopped shallot
Bring to a boil over medium heat and reduce by half. Strain and add to:
   White Sauce I, 550

SHRIMP SAUCE (SAUCE NANTUA)

1½ cups

Sauce Nantua is classically made with crayfish butter. Instead of the shrimp butter here, you may add 1 tablespoon finely ground cooked shrimp blended into a smooth paste with 1 tablespoon butter. Serve with fish, over toast, or as a substitute for hollandaise over poached eggs and salmon or with Eggs Florentine, 197.
Prepare:
   White Sauce I, 550
When the sauce is smooth and hot, reduce the heat to low and add:
   ½ cup heavy cream
Rub through a fine-mesh sieve into the sauce:
   2 tablespoons Shrimp Butter, 559
Bring just to a boiling point. Season with:
   Salt and black pepper to taste

Garnish with:
   Finely chopped cooked shrimp

OYSTER SAUCE

2 cups

For fish if made without the Worcestershire sauce; with it, serve over pasta or with eggs.
Prepare:
   White Sauce II, 550
Season well with:
   Salt
   (1 teaspoon Worcestershire sauce)
Just before serving, add:
   1 cup finely chopped poached, 1050, oysters and juice (from 1 pint raw whole oysters)
   3 tablespoons chopped parsley
Bring just to a simmer over medium heat.

ANCHOVY SAUCE

1 cup

Lightly salty, just the thing for fish and bland vegetables. Blend together well **White Sauce I, 550, and 3 to 5 anchovy fillets, rinsed and pounded to a paste, or 1 to 2 teaspoons anchovy paste.**

HORSERADISH SAUCE (SAUCE ALBERT)

1⅓ cups

A happy complement to corned beef, pot roast, or grilled salmon. Also good on a cold roast beef or steak sandwich.
Prepare:
   White Sauce I, 550
Remove it from the heat and stir in:
   3 tablespoons prepared horseradish
   2 tablespoons heavy cream
   1 teaspoon sugar
   1 teaspoon dry mustard
   1 tablespoon vinegar
Reheat, but do not boil. Serve immediately.

ABOUT VELOUTÉ SAUCE

The difference between white sauce and velouté sauce is primarily one of ingredients—the techniques are almost identical. Instead of milk, a velouté, named for its velvety texture, is made with any "white" or light-colored stock—chicken, veal, fish, even vegetable—and it uses a blond roux, 543. The resulting sauce is more ivory colored than béchamel and slightly translucent. Allowing the sauce to simmer gently for an extra 15 minutes removes any trace of floury taste. The sauce can be refrigerated or kept warm in the top of a double boiler after straining. Stir occasionally to prevent a skin from forming and whisk the butter in just before serving.

VELOUTÉ SAUCE

1¾ cups

Heat in a small saucepan over medium heat, stirring occasionally, until hot:

2¹/₂ **cups white veal stock, 117, chicken stock or broth,
fish stock or broth, or vegetable stock or broth**

Meanwhile, melt in a medium saucepan over low heat:

3 **tablespoons butter**

Stir in:

3 **tablespoons all-purpose flour**

Cook over low heat, stirring constantly with a wooden spoon or spatula, until the roux has a nutty aroma and is ivory colored, about 6 minutes. Remove from the heat and let cool for 2 minutes.

Gradually whisk the warm stock into the roux, along with:

(¹/₄ **cup minced mushrooms)**

Return the saucepan to the heat and bring the sauce slowly to a simmer, whisking to prevent lumps. Cook over medium-low heat, stirring often and skimming any skin that forms on the surface, until thick enough to coat the back of a spoon, about 20 minutes; do not boil. Strain through a fine-mesh sieve, if desired. Season with:

Salt and white pepper to taste

Just before serving, whisk in:

(1 **to 2 tablespoons unsalted butter, softened, or any
flavored butter, 558–560, softened)**

CREAM SAUCE (SAUCE SUPRÈME)

3 cups

Best with chicken or vegetables.

Prepare:

Velouté Sauce, above

adding to the saucepan along with the stock:

³/₄ **cup heavy cream**

Just before serving, whisk in:

2 **tablespoons heavy cream**

(2 **tablespoons unsalted butter, softened)**

CHAMPAGNE OR WHITE WINE SAUCE

1¹/₄ cups

Few of us may have to worry about what to do with left-over Champagne, but should that dilemma ever be yours, there is no better way than this to solve it and make a light but rich sauce for fish or chicken.

Prepare:

¹/₂ **recipe Velouté Sauce, above**

using fumet to replace the stock, if desired, if serving with fish.

Have ready:

¹/₂ **cup (1 stick) butter, cut into 6 pieces**

Combine in a medium saucepan and boil until reduced almost to a glaze:

1 **cup Champagne or dry white wine**

¹/₄ **cup minced shallots**

Remove from the heat and, stirring with a wooden spoon, add the butter piece by piece so that it softens but does not liquefy and the sauce retains a creamy texture. Add:

1¹/₂ **teaspoons chopped tarragon**

Meanwhile, heat the velouté sauce until hot but not boiling. Whisk in the butter mixture. Serve at once.

PAPRIKA SAUCE (SAUCE HONGROISE)

1¹/₂ cups

For fish, poultry, or veal.

Melt in a medium saucepan over medium-low heat:

1 **tablespoon butter**

Add and cook, stirring, until golden, about 7 minutes:

1 **medium onion, finely chopped**

Add and stir for 1 minute. Gradually add, stirring constantly, until heated through:

2 **tablespoons mild Hungarian paprika**

1 **cup heavy cream**

¹/₃ **cup Velouté Sauce, above**

Season to taste with:

Salt and black pepper

CURRY SAUCE

2 cups

Melt in a medium saucepan over medium-low heat:

¹/₄ **cup (¹/₂ stick) butter**

Add and cook, stirring, until tender:

¹/₄ **cup finely chopped onion**

Stir in and cook, stirring, without browning, for 5 to 6 minutes:

2¹/₂ **tablespoons all-purpose flour**

¹/₂ **to 2 teaspoons curry powder**

A pinch to ¹/₄ teaspoon saffron threads

Slowly add, stirring constantly:

1 **cup chicken stock or broth**

1 **cup heavy cream**

¹/₂ **teaspoon grated lemon zest**

Bring to a simmer and simmer until well blended. Stir in:

(4 **teaspoons chopped mango chutney)**

If you like a hot curry, liven up the sauce with dashes of:

(**Hot pepper sauce, ground red pepper,
or ground ginger)**

Add:

(**A few drops of dry sherry)**

RAVIGOTE SAUCE

1 cup

Serve lukewarm over fish, light meats, variety meats, or poultry.

Combine in a small saucepan:

2 **shallots, very finely chopped**

1 **tablespoon tarragon vinegar**

Bring to a boil and cook, stirring constantly, about 3 minutes, until vinegar has almost evaporated. Add:

1 **cup Velouté Sauce, 552**

Simmer gently about 10 minutes, stirring frequently. Season to taste with:

Salt and black pepper

Cool the sauce to lukewarm, then add:

1¹/₂ **tablespoons chopped parsley**

1 **tablespoon chopped drained capers**

2 **teaspoons chopped chives**

¹/₂ **teaspoon chopped tarragon**

EGG-THICKENED VELOUTÉ (SAUCE ALLEMANDE)

1¹/₂ cups

An enriched velouté, to be used with poached chicken or vegetables. It becomes **Poulette Sauce** if, as a final step, you add finely chopped parsley. Or if, at the last minute, you add a generous tablespoon of chopped drained capers, you have **Caper Sauce,** which goes well with fish or lamb. ➤ Do not let it boil after the egg is added, or it will curdle.

Prepare:

1¹/₂ cups Velouté Sauce, 552

Stir in:

³/₄ cup strong chicken stock or broth

Blend well and cook over medium-low heat, stirring occasionally, until reduced by one-third, about 10 minutes. Remove from the heat and add:

1 large egg yolk, beaten with 2 tablespoons
   heavy cream

Stir the sauce over low heat until slightly thickened. Just before serving, stir in:

1 tablespoon fresh lemon juice
1 tablespoon butter
Salt and black pepper to taste
Pinch ground nutmeg

ABOUT BROWN SAUCES

Espagnole is the fundamental brown sauce, and with either it or Demi-Glace Sauce, below, as a starting point, the possibilities are legion. This mother sauce is the head of a large and elite family, a clan that is diverse, rich, sophisticated, and rewarding, held in the highest regard by cooks and cheerful eaters alike. They may be more time-consuming than other sauces, but their flavor and texture are incomparable. For the most complex and compelling sauces, different liquids (wine, stock, or juice, for example) and savory ingredients (onions, chopped ham, and herbs, to name a few) are added at intervals and allowed to cook down and concentrate before the next is added. If it is necessary to save time by adding the liquids and ingredients all at once, the resulting sauce will not offer as many luscious layers of flavor.

The best brown sauces begin with good stock, preferably homemade, but if you find the flavor of either your stock or your sauce a bit pale, try adding a spoonful or two of Meat Glaze, 117, to the sauce as it simmers. The wines used in these sauces should be of good quality, especially any that are added close to the end of cooking. Do not attempt to produce brown sauces that are as thick as béchamels, 550, or veloutés, 552; they will only be sticky and unappealing. Stop cooking when the sauce has reached the consistency of heavy cream. Stir with a spoon rather than a whisk—whisking lightens the color by incorporating air. A swirl of butter at the end will add a sheen to these sauces while enriching their flavor. Herbs, spices, and mushrooms are frequent additions to any brown

sauce. Brown sauces can be refrigerated for 4 to 5 days or frozen for 3 months and are best stored in the refrigerator topped with a thin film of sherry.

BROWN SAUCE (SAUCE ESPAGNOLE)

5 cups

Melt in a large heavy saucepan or a Dutch oven:

¹/₂ cup (1 stick) butter or ¹/₂ cup beef or
   veal drippings or bacon fat

Add:

1 cup Mirepoix, 998

or:

¹/₂ cup finely chopped onions
¹/₄ cup finely chopped carrots
¹/₄ cup finely chopped celery

Cook, stirring, until the vegetables begin to color. Add:

¹/₂ cup all-purpose flour

Cook, stirring until the flour is thoroughly browned. Stir in:

10 whole black peppercorns
2 cups drained, peeled, and finely chopped canned
   tomatoes or 2 cups tomato purée
¹/₂ cup coarsely chopped parsley

Add:

8 cups Brown Beef Stock, 117

Increase the heat to high and bring to a boil, then reduce the heat and simmer until reduced by half, 2 to 2¹/₂ hours. Stir occasionally and skim off the fat as it rises to the top. The sauce should be the consistency of heavy cream, no thicker.

Strain the sauce through a fine-mesh sieve into a bowl. Stir occasionally as the sauce cools to prevent the formation of a skin. If necessary, thin with additional stock or water. If you are using this sauce as is, season with:

Salt and black pepper to taste

DEMI-GLACE SAUCE

4¹/₂ cups

Serve with filet mignon or game or use as a base for other sauces.

Combine in a large heavy saucepan or Dutch oven over medium heat:

4 cups Brown Sauce, above
4 cups Brown Beef Stock, 117, or Brown Poultry
   Stock, 118
¹/₂ cup chopped mushrooms

Bring to a simmer, then reduce the heat slightly and simmer gently, uncovered, skimming often to remove fat and scum, until reduced by half, 2 to 2¹/₂ hours. Strain through a fine-mesh sieve into a clean saucepan. Stir in over very low heat:

¹/₂ cup dry port, Madeira, or dry sherry
Salt and black pepper to taste

Just before serving, whisk in, small pieces at a time:

(2 to 4 tablespoons butter, preferably unsalted,
   softened)

MADEIRA SAUCE

1 cup

Dry sherry or port may be substituted for the Madeira. A wonderful accompaniment for game or fillet of beef.
Bring to a simmer in a medium saucepan:

1 cup Brown Sauce, above

Simmer until reduced by one-quarter. Add:

¹/₄ cup Madeira
(1 teaspoon Meat Glaze, 117)

Swirl in bit by bit, 545:

About 1 tablespoon butter

Note: You can also make this in the pan in which you cooked the meat. Remove the meat to a platter and keep warm. Pour off the fat from the pan, and deglaze, 546, the pan with the Madeira. Simmer until it is reduced by half, then add the brown sauce and cook 10 minutes before finishing as described above.

SAUCE PÉRIGUEUX

1 cup

For croquettes, shirred eggs, and chicken.
Prepare:

Madeira Sauce, above

Just before adding the butter, stir in:

1 tablespoon chopped black truffles

Season to taste. Very similar is **Sauce Périgourdine,** but there the truffles are finely diced instead of chopped and a dice of foie gras is added as well.

BROWN ONION SAUCE (SAUCE LYONNAISE)

Generous 1 cup

An inspired choice for leftover meat, our version of this classic is more of an onion relish than a true sauce. For a more saucelike result, add the stock as directed.
Melt in a medium saucepan:

2 tablespoons butter

Add and cook, stirring, until golden brown:

2 onions, finely chopped

Add:

¹/₃ cup dry white wine or 2 tablespoons cider vinegar
1 tablespoon chopped thyme

If you use the wine, simmer until reduced by half. Add:

1 cup Brown Sauce, 554

Bring to a simmer and simmer for 15 minutes. For a thinner sauce, add:

(Up to 1 cup beef stock)

Just before serving, add:

1 tablespoon finely chopped parsley
Salt and black pepper to taste

HUNTER'S SAUCE (SAUCE CHASSEUR)

2 cups

Traditionally served with game, this sauce is also delectable with roasted meats or poultry, steaks, or chops.
Melt in a medium heavy saucepan over medium heat:

2 tablespoons butter, preferably unsalted

Add and cook, stirring, until softened:

2 tablespoons minced shallots

Add and cook, stirring, until lightly browned, about 5 minutes:

1 cup sliced mushrooms

Add and simmer, uncovered, until reduced by half:

¹/₄ cup dry white wine
2 tablespoons brandy

Add and cook, stirring occasionally, for 5 minutes:

1 cup Brown Sauce, 554, or Demi-Glace Sauce, 554
¹/₂ cup tomato puree
Salt and black pepper to taste

Just before serving, stir in:

1 tablespoon minced parsley
(1 tablespoon minced chervil or tarragon)

Swirl in bit by bit, 545:

(About 2 tablespoons butter)

RED WINE AND MARROW SAUCE (SAUCE BORDELAISE)

Scant 1 cup

Serve with steak, sweetbreads, chops, or game. This sauce is also delicious, though a little less rich, without the poached marrow.
Combine in a small heavy saucepan over medium-high heat:

¹/₄ cup sherry vinegar or red wine vinegar
1 shallot, minced
1 sprig thyme
1 sprig parsley
¹/₂ bay leaf
4 whole black peppercorns

Bring to a simmer, uncovered, until reduced by three-quarters. Add:

¹/₂ cup dry red wine

Simmer until again reduced by three-quarters. Strain through a fine-mesh sieve into a medium saucepan. Place over medium heat and stir in:

1 cup Brown Sauce, 554, or Demi-Glace Sauce, 554

Simmer, uncovered, for 15 minutes. Just before serving, stir in:

¹/₄ cup diced beef marrow, poached in simmering water for a few minutes and drained
2 teaspoons minced parsley
Salt and black pepper to taste

MUSHROOM WINE SAUCE (MARCHAND DE VIN)

1¹/₂ cups

Serve with grilled or roasted meat.
Melt in a medium skillet over medium heat:

2 tablespoons butter

Add and cook, stirring, 2 minutes:

1 cup thinly sliced mushrooms

Add:

$^1/_2$ cup hot beef or brown chicken stock
$^1/_2$ cup dry red wine or Madeira
Simmer 10 minutes. Add:

1 cup Brown Sauce, 554, or Demi-Glace Sauce, 554
Simmer 20 minutes, until reduced by about a third.
Season with:

Salt and black pepper to taste
(Juice of $^1/_2$ lemon)

PEPPER SAUCE (SAUCE POIVRADE)

2$^1/_3$ cups
The traditional sauce to serve with venison.
Heat in a medium saucepan over medium-high heat:

$^1/_4$ cup vegetable oil
Add and cook, stirring, until browned, about 15 minutes:

1 carrot, chopped
1 onion, chopped
(Game bones, trimmings, and giblets, if available)
Add:

$^1/_4$ cup red wine vinegar or strained marinade, if the
game was marinated before cooking
3 sprigs parsley
1 bay leaf
A pinch of dried thyme
Simmer until reduced by two-thirds. Add:

3 cups Brown Sauce, 554
Bring to a boil, then reduce the heat and simmer 1 hour.
Add:

10 whole black peppercorns
and simmer 5 minutes. Strain the sauce into another
saucepan, pressing on the solids, and add:

$^1/_4$ cup vinegar or strained marinade
Simmer gently 30 minutes more. Add:

$^1/_2$ cup dry red wine
Salt to taste
and enough:

Cracked black peppercorns
to make a hot sauce.

PIQUANT SAUCE

1 cup
Excellent for hearty meats.
Melt in a small saucepan over medium heat:

1 tablespoon butter
Add and cook, stirring, until lightly browned:

2 tablespoons minced onion
Add:

2 tablespoons dry white wine
2 tablespoons white wine vinegar or rice vinegar or
fresh lemon juice
Cook until the liquid is almost evaporated. Add:

1 cup Brown Sauce, 554, or Demi-Glace Sauce, 554
Bring to a simmer and simmer 5 minutes. Just before serving, add:

1 tablespoon chopped parsley or chopped mixed
parsley, tarragon, and chervil

1 tablespoon chopped sour pickles
1 tablespoon chopped drained capers
Salt and black pepper to taste

ABOUT QUICK SAUCES

Not only do canned broths perform a valuable impromptu
role as strengtheners and flavoring for sauces: canned
soups may be used to furnish the very foundations for
sauce as well. The results, of course, are not so subtle and
delicate as roux-based sauces carefully constructed from
fresh meat or poultry stock, but an impressive savings in
time goes far toward offsetting loss of quality. Taste these
mixtures before salting and adding final seasoning.

  I. For chicken, fish, and vegetables.
2 cups
Heat until hot:

One 10$^3/_4$-ounce can condensed cream of chicken soup
$^1/_2$ cup chicken stock or broth
$^1/_2$ cup milk
  II. For beef or pork hash.
1$^1/_4$ cups
Melt in a small saucepan over medium-low heat:

1 tablespoon butter
Add and cook, stirring, until soft and translucent:

1 garlic clove, chopped or crushed
Stir in:

One 10$^3/_4$-ounce can condensed cream of
mushroom soup
$^2/_3$ cup canned beef consommé
  III. For creaming vegetables.
2 cups
Heat until hot:

One 10$^3/_4$-ounce can condensed cream of celery soup
2 tablespoons butter
$^3/_4$ cup chicken stock or broth
$^1/_4$ cup chopped chives

QUICK BROWN SAUCE

1$^1/_4$ cups
Serve as you would a brown gravy.
Rub a medium saucepan with:

($^1/_2$ garlic clove)
Melt in the pan over medium heat:

2 tablespoons butter
Stir in until blended:

2 tablespoons all-purpose flour
Cook, stirring, until lightly browned and nutty smelling,
about 7 minutes. Stir in:

One 10$^3/_4$-ounce can beef consommé
Bring to a boil, whisking constantly. Season to taste with
one or more of the following:

Black pepper or paprika
Fresh lemon juice, catsup, or chili sauce
Dry sherry or Worcestershire sauce
Fresh or dried herbs

QUICK MUSHROOM SAUCE

1 1/2 cups

For roast meat, chicken, and casseroles.

Melt in a medium skillet:

1 tablespoon butter

Add and cook, stirring, until lightly browned:

4 ounces mushrooms, sliced

Add:

Quick Brown Sauce, above

Heat through.

QUICK À LA KING SAUCE

2 cups

Melt in a medium saucepan:

1 tablespoon butter

Add and cook, stirring, until tender:

1 green bell pepper, minced

Add:

**One 10 3/4-ounce can condensed cream of
     mushroom soup**
1/2 cup milk

Heat through. Add:

1 pimiento, cut into strips
(2 tablespoons dry sherry)

CHINESE-STYLE SAUCE FOR VEGETABLES

1/4 cup

For about 1 pound vegetables. Delicious mixed with chicken or tofu and vegetables and served over rice.

Blend until smooth in a small bowl:

1 tablespoon cornstarch
3 tablespoons cold water

Add:

4 teaspoons soy sauce
1 1/2 teaspoons rice wine vinegar
1 teaspoon brown sugar
1/2 teaspoon salt
(2 teaspoons finely grated peeled fresh ginger)

Pour over vegetables that are cooking. Stir well until the whole mixture comes to a boil.

ABOUT BUTTER SAUCES

A few well-loved sauces depend almost entirely on butter. For these, nothing less than the freshest butter will do—unsalted is best, because it will not interfere with any other seasonings. The simplest of these, Brown Butter (Beurre Noisette), below, and Lemon Butter (Beurre Meunière), below, are nothing more than seasoned butter cooked until it begins to brown and take on a marvelous nutty flavor. The slightly more complicated White Butter Sauce (Beurre Blanc), 558, derives its smoothness from whisking in the butter so that it blends into and thickens the sauce without melting outright. These are usually served warm as simple sauces for sautéed, grilled, broiled, or steamed foods.

CLARIFIED OR DRAWN BUTTER

There needn't be mystery nor mystique about this substance: it is merely melted butter with the water and milk solids removed. But, because it is used in so many different ways—among others as a sauce for cooked lobster, for extra-smooth hollandaise and béarnaise sauces, and as a baking ingredient—here is the recipe. One cup (2 sticks) will yield 3/4 cup of clarified butter.

Melt in a saucepan over low heat without stirring:

Butter, cut into small pieces

Remove from the heat and skim off the foam. Let stand a few minutes, allowing the milk solids to settle to the bottom. Carefully pour the clear yellow liquid into a heat-proof container, leaving the solids behind.

GHEE

About 1 3/4 cups

Cook over the lowest heat, keeping it below a simmer:

1 pound butter

This can take 10 minutes to 1 hour, until color is golden and brown milk solids have settled at the bottom of the pan. At this slow rate, the milk solids settle nicely. Strain the ghee through cheesecloth or a fine-mesh strainer.

BROWN BUTTER (BEURRE NOISETTE)

5 tablespoons

Make this quickly in the same skillet you cooked fish in and serve it over the fish, or make it separately to use as a sauce for green vegetables.

Melt in a small skillet over medium-low heat:

4 to 5 tablespoons butter, preferably unsalted

Cook slowly until the butter becomes light brown and smells nutty, shaking the pan or stirring occasionally so it cooks evenly. Watch as the butter begins to foam; it can burn easily. Remove the butter from the heat and stir in:

1 teaspoon white wine vinegar or fresh lemon juice
Salt and black pepper to taste

Serve immediately.

BLACK BUTTER (BEURRE NOIR)

Delicious against the light flavor of sautéed fish such as sole, cod, or skate.

Prepare **Brown Butter** as above, allowing it to cook until it is dark brown.

LEMON BUTTER (BEURRE MEUNIÈRE)

Prepare, using lemon juice, **Brown Butter, above.** Stir in

1 tablespoon finely chopped parsley

BROWN BUTTER CRUMB SAUCE
(SAUCE POLONAISE)

1/2 cup

A traditional topping for vegetables, especially cauliflower.

Prepare **Lemon Butter, above.** Increase the heat to medium, add, and cook, stirring, until evenly golden brown:

1/4 cup fine dry bread crumbs

Add:

1 teaspoon salt, or to taste

$^1/_2$ teaspoon black pepper, or to taste

Toss thoroughly with the vegetable you are serving and:

Finely chopped hard-boiled egg

WALNUT BUTTER

$^1/_2$ cup

Lovely with squash or squash ravioli.

Cook in a small saucepan 2 minutes, or until the butter is lightly browned:

$^1/_2$ cup (1 stick) unsalted butter

$^1/_2$ cup coarsely chopped walnuts

Use immediately.

WHITE BUTTER SAUCE (BEURRE BLANC)

$^1/_2$ cup

Rich yet refined, white butter sauce, or beurre blanc, can be varied by substituting stock for all or part of the wine, by adding herbs or citrus zest, or by replacing all or part of the butter with a flavored butter, below. Beurre blanc is traditionally served with fish, especially shad, but it is also good on chicken breasts, squab, asparagus, artichokes, and leeks. Adding a small amount of cream before adding the butter helps keep the sauce stable and less likely to separate.

Combine in a small skillet over medium heat:

6 tablespoons dry white wine

2 tablespoons white wine vinegar

3 tablespoons minced shallots

Salt and white pepper to taste

Bring to a simmer and simmer, uncovered, until reduced by three-quarters. Stir in:

1 tablespoon heavy cream

Remove from the heat and add 1 piece at a time, whisking constantly, until the sauce is creamy and pale:

$^1/_2$ cup (1 stick) cold butter, preferably unsalted, cut into at least 8 pieces

Add each piece before the previous one has completely melted, or the sauce will separate. If you need a bit more heat to soften the butter, set the pan briefly over very low heat. Strain through a fine-mesh sieve, if desired. Season to taste with:

Salt and black pepper

Use immediately.

LEMON BUTTER SAUCE (LEMON BEURRE BLANC)

Prepare **White Butter Sauce, above,** replacing the white wine vinegar with **2 tablespoons fresh lemon juice** and adding, along with the shallots **the grated zest of 1 small lemon.**

HERBED BUTTER SAUCE

Prepare **White Butter Sauce, above.** Stir in **2 tablespoons mixed very finely chopped fennel fronds, parsley, chives,** basil, chervil, and/or tarragon, or 1 tablespoon mixed dried herbs.

ABOUT FLAVORED BUTTERS (BEURRES COMPOSÉS)

These garnishes are quick, tasty, and simple to make by blending herbs and other flavorings into plain butter. The main thing is to use fresh high-quality butter, preferably unsalted. Most flavored butters can be prepared more quickly and taste almost as good as melted butter sauces. Some flavored butters, such as shrimp and lobster, are used to flavor and finish sauces as well as being served by themselves.

These reach the table in solid form, being allowed to melt on the hot fish, meat, or vegetables for which they are designed. Some can also be used in place of plain butter for bread or rolls.

The butter can be used immediately while still soft, or rolled into cylinders in wax or parchment paper, plastic wrap, or aluminum foil and refrigerated for 1$^1/_2$ to 2 hours or frozen for several weeks, then sliced into thin rounds to garnish dishes just before serving. But herbed butters ➤ should not be refrigerated longer than 24 hours, as the herbs deteriorate quickly. You can form the butter into fancy shapes and molds, see 964, or smooth the butter into a small bowl or ramekin that just holds it and run a fork over the top in a decorative swirl or crosshatch; serve at room temperature. Allow about 1 tablespoon butter per serving.

BASIC FLAVORED BUTTER

$^1/_4$ cup

Cream with a fork or wooden spoon in a small bowl:

$^1/_4$ cup ($^1/_2$ stick) butter, softened

Gradually stir in flavorings as desired, along with:

Salt and white pepper to taste

NUT BUTTER

$^1/_4$ cup

Often used to finish cream sauces, and delicious on sautéed chicken and delicate fish.

Pulse in a food processor or pound with a mortar and pestle until very fine but not a paste:

$^1/_4$ cup toasted whole blanched almonds, hazelnuts, pistachios, walnuts, or pecans, 1001

If the nuts seem too dry, add:

1 teaspoon water

Stir into:

Basic Flavored Butter, above

ANCHOVY BUTTER

$^1/_4$ cup

For broiled fish, steak, and lamb chops and as a canapé spread.

Combine:

Basic Flavored Butter, above

1 teaspoon anchovy paste

$^1/_4$ teaspoon fresh lemon juice, or to taste

Salt and ground red pepper to taste

BERCY BUTTER

$^1/_4$ cup

For fish or broiled meats. Also a good topping for a simple omelet.

Combine in a small saucepan and simmer until the wine has reduced by about three-quarters:

   2 teaspoons finely chopped shallot

   $^2/_3$ cup dry white wine

Cool. Add to:

   Basic Flavored Butter, above

along with:

   2 teaspoons finely chopped parsley

CAVIAR BUTTER

$^2/_3$ cup

A lovely fish garnish.

Cream together with a fork or wooden spoon in a small bowl:

   $^1/_2$ cup (1 stick) butter, softened

   $^1/_4$ cup black caviar or salmon roe

   1 tablespoon fresh lemon juice

   Salt to taste if necessary

LEMON AND PARSLEY BUTTER (MAÎTRE D'HÔTEL BUTTER)

$^1/_4$ cup

Delicious over grilled or broiled steak.

Combine:

   Basic Flavored Butter, 558

   1 tablespoon finely chopped parsley

   1 to 1$^1/_2$ tablespoons fresh lemon juice

GARLIC BUTTER

$^1/_4$ cup

For vegetables, steaks, chops, chicken, fish, shellfish, snails, and bread. Blanched garlic has a sweeter, milder flavor than raw garlic. It can also be melted before serving. If desired, blanch in boiling water before serving for 5 to 6 minutes:

   1 to 3 garlic cloves, peeled

Mash to a paste. If using raw garlic, mash with:

   ($^1/_2$ teaspoon salt)

Prepare:

   Basic Flavored Butter, 558

Add the garlic paste and:

   (1 teaspoon minced herbs, such as oregano, marjoram, basil, chervil, or parsley, or a combination)

SNAIL BUTTER

$^1/_3$ cup

A milder, more interesting form of garlic butter but with the same uses—most traditionally for snails. Also good with grilled fish or for sautéing shrimp.

Combine:

   Basic Flavored Butter, 558

   2 tablespoons minced shallots or scallions (white part only)

   1 to 2 garlic cloves, mashed to a paste with $^1/_2$ teaspoon salt

   1 tablespoon minced parsley

   Black pepper to taste

   (1 tablespoon fresh lemon juice)

   (1 tablespoon minced celery)

ORANGE BUTTER

$^1/_4$ cup

For fish and vegetables.

Combine:

   Basic Flavored Butter, 558

   Finely grated zest of 1 orange

   1 tablespoon strained fresh orange juice, or to taste

   Pinch of ground red pepper

   Salt to taste

SHRIMP OR LOBSTER BUTTER

$^1/_4$ to $^1/_3$ cup

Delicately pink and deliciously flavored. Use for finishing cream sauces served with fish or by itself with the shellfish used in making the butter. The recipe is easily doubled. Spread on a baking sheet and dry in a 250°F oven for 20 to 30 minutes:

   Shells (uncooked or cooked) from 1 pound shrimp or crayfish or from one 1$^1/_2$- to 2-pound lobster, well rinsed and drained

Break up the shells as fine as possible with a wooden mallet or rolling pin. Melt in the top of a double boiler over simmering water:

   $^1/_2$ cup (1 stick) unsalted butter

Add the shells and cook over the simmering water for 10 minutes. Set aside for 20 minutes to allow the flavors to infuse. Pour into a fine-mesh sieve set over a bowl; let stand for up to 20 minutes to strain out all the butter. Place the bowl in a larger bowl of ice water to cool quickly, or refrigerate until chilled. Skim off the butter when the mixture has solidified; discard any liquid.

GREEN BUTTER

About $^1/_3$ cup

Use for broiled fish, steamed vegetables, or chicken, or to give white or cream sauces a light green color and some added zing.

Blanch in a saucepan of boiling water for 5 minutes:

   2 shallots, chopped, or 1 tablespoon chopped onion

   1 teaspoon fresh tarragon leaves

   1 teaspoon fresh chervil leaves

   1 teaspoon fresh parsley leaves

   6 to 8 spinach leaves

Drain and plunge into a bowl of ice water to cool, then drain and pat dry in a towel. Then pound to a paste in a mortar, or grind to a paste in a small food processor. Gradually blend in:

> **¹/₄ cup (¹/₂ stick) butter, softened**
> **Salt to taste**

ABOUT HOLLANDAISE, BÉARNAISE, AND OTHER EGG-THICKENED SAUCES

Smooth and velvety, delicious and rich, these sauces transform the plainest and simplest cooked vegetables or broiled or roasted meat or fish into superb dishes. As emulsified sauces—meaning the state where one liquid is suspended in another in tiny globules—both are close cousins of mayonnaise, though they are served hot. A professional chef will make these sauces over low direct heat, but don't try this unless you are prepared to act out a new definition of "stir crazy." We strongly recommend using a double boiler or—better yet—a stainless steel bowl set over a saucepan holding about 1¹/₂ inches of water. The advantage of the bowl is that its shape gives you plenty of room to whisk air into the sauce, making a lighter, more voluminous sauce. Whichever method you choose, ➤ the water in the bottom pan should simmer, not boil, and ➤ the water should not touch the bottom of the bowl or pan above. Remove the bowl or top of the double boiler from the heat if you feel that the sauce is getting too hot; whisk until the sauce cools slightly, then put it back over the heat to continue.

The most critical stage in making hollandaise or béarnaise is the initial whipping and cooking of the egg yolks. Begin by whisking the yolks and liquid (lemon juice or water) off the heat until light and frothy. Then, over the barely simmering water, continue to whisk vigorously to warm the yolks. They will become pale yellow, thicker, and expand to three or four times their original volume.

Remove the yolks from the heat and ➤ add the warm—not hot—melted butter, very very slowly at first. Use clarified butter for a smoother sauce. ➤ Whisk constantly, and as the sauce begins to thicken, add the butter in a steady trickle. Scrape the sides and bottom of the bowl or pan as you go to keep the sauce smooth. Do not let the sauce or butter cool too much as you whisk, or the butter will begin to harden and thicken; add a few drops of warm water if this happens. If at any point the sauce looks as if it is about to separate, immediately whisk in a few tablespoons of cold heavy cream or water. If it separates, all is not lost: simply whisk another yolk in a clean bowl, then slowly whisk this yolk into the broken sauce to re-form the emulsion. Some of our friends freeze hollandaise or béarnaise just as they do roux-based sauces. If frozen, it must be reheated in a double boiler ➤ over—not in—hot water, stirring briskly to preserve consistency.

Several other egg-thickened sauces are also included in this chapter: Newburg Sauce, 561, Lemon Egg Sauce, 561, Mousseline Sauce, 561, and Sweet-and-Sour Mustard Sauce, 564.

HOLLANDAISE SAUCE

Generous 1 cup

Melt over low heat:

> **10 tablespoons (1¹/₄ sticks) butter**

Skim the foam off the top and keep warm.
Place in the top of a double boiler or in a large stainless steel bowl:

> **3 large egg yolks**
> **1¹/₂ tablespoons cold water**

Off the heat, beat the yolks with a whisk until light and frothy. Place top of the double boiler or bowl over—not in—barely simmering water and continue to whisk until the eggs are thickened, 3 to 5 minutes, being careful not to let the eggs get too hot. Remove the pan or bowl and whisk to cool the mixture slightly. Whisking constantly, very slowly add the butter, leaving the white milk solids behind. Whisk in:

> **¹/₂ to 2 teaspoons fresh lemon juice**
> **(Dash of hot pepper sauce)**
> **Salt and white pepper to taste**

If the sauce is too thick, whisk in a few drops of warm water. Serve immediately, or cover and keep the sauce warm for up to 30 minutes by placing the pan or bowl in warm (not hot) water.

BLENDER HOLLANDAISE

¹/₂ cup

Easy but less flavorful and paler in color than handmade hollandaise. ➤ Do not make in a smaller quantity than given here—there will not be enough heat to cook the eggs properly.
Combine in a blender:

> **3 large egg yolks**
> **1¹/₂ to 2 teaspoons fresh lemon juice**
> **A pinch of ground red pepper**
> **¹/₂ teaspoon salt**

Heat until bubbling:

> **¹/₂ cup (1 stick) butter**

Remove from the heat. Blend the egg yolks on high for 3 seconds; with the blender still running, pour in the butter in a steady stream. By the time all the butter is poured in—about 30 seconds—the sauce should be finished. If not, blend on high about 5 seconds longer. If the sauce is too thick, add a few drops of warm water. Serve at once for up to 30 minutes or keep warm by immersing the blender container in warm water.

QUICK WHOLE-EGG HOLLANDAISE

1 cup

Even paler in color than Blender Hollandaise, but it does avoid the problem of what to do with those extra whites.
Place in a bowl and whisk until thoroughly blended and pale yellow:

> **3 large eggs**
> **4 to 5 tablespoons fresh lemon juice**
> **3 tablespoons water**

In a heavy nonstick skillet, melt over low heat:

6 to 7 tablespoons butter

Slowly add the egg mixture, stirring constantly until the sauce has thickened and a spoon dragged along the bottom of the pan leaves a trail. Do not overcook. Add:

$^1/_2$ teaspoon salt

MOUSSELINE SAUCE

1$^1/_2$ cups

Use with fillet of beef and scallops.
Whip into soft peaks, 973:

$^1/_4$ cup heavy cream

Prepare:

1 cup Hollandaise Sauce, 560

Fold the whipped cream into cooled Hollandaise. Serve warm or cold.

BÉARNAISE SAUCE

1 cup

Heavenly on grilled meat and fish, especially filet mignon, béarnaise is also at home with eggs.
Combine in a small saucepan:

3 tablespoons dry white wine
3 tablespoons tarragon vinegar or white wine vinegar
1 shallot, minced
6 sprigs tarragon, leaves removed, chopped, and reserved
8 whole black peppercorns, lightly crushed

Bring to a simmer and simmer, uncovered, until reduced by two-thirds. Remove the tarragon sprigs and reserve the liquid. Melt over low heat:

10 tablespoons (1$^1/_4$ sticks) butter

Skim any foam off the top and keep warm. Place in the top of a double boiler or in a large stainless steel bowl:

3 large egg yolks
1$^1/_2$ teaspoons cold water

Off the heat, whisk the egg mixture until light and frothy. Place the top of the double boiler or the bowl over—not in—barely simmering water and whisk until the eggs are thickened, 3 to 5 minutes, being careful not to let the eggs get too hot. Remove the pan or bowl and whisk to cool the mixture slightly. Whisking constantly, very slowly add the melted butter, leaving the white milk solids behind. Whisk in:

Tarragon leaves and reduced liquid to taste

Season with:

Salt and white pepper to taste

If the sauce is too thick, thin it slowly with a few drops of the reserved liquid or warm water. Serve immediately, or keep the sauce covered until serving to prevent a skin from forming. Serve warm.

BLENDER BÉARNAISE SAUCE

$^3/_4$ cup

Combine in a small saucepan over low heat and simmer until reduced to about 1 tablespoon:

2 tablespoons dry white wine
2 tablespoons tarragon vinegar
1 tablespoon minced shallot
$^1/_2$ teaspoon chopped tarragon
4 whole black peppercorns, lightly crushed

Strain through a fine-mesh sieve and let cool. Stir the liquid to taste into:

Blender Hollandaise, 560, made with water instead of lemon juice

Stir in:

$^1/_2$ teaspoon minced tarragon, or more to taste

Taste and adjust the seasonings. Serve immediately.

FRESH HERB BÉARNAISE SAUCE

$^3/_4$ to 1 cup

Using fresh mint makes a **Paloise Sauce**.
Prepare **Béarnaise Sauce, above**, or **Blender Béarnaise Sauce, above**, substituting for the tarragon **minced cilantro, parsley, basil, thyme, chives, sage, or mint.**

NEWBURG SAUCE

1$^1/_2$ cups

Melt in a wide saucepan over medium heat:

$^1/_4$ cup Lobster Butter, 559, or unsalted butter

Add and cook, stirring, until translucent:

2 teaspoons finely chopped shallots or mild onion

Add and cook until the mixture is reduced to about $^1/_4$ cup:

$^1/_4$ cup dry sherry or Madeira

Remove from the heat. Beat together in a small bowl until thoroughly blended:

1 cup heavy cream
3 large egg yolks

Beat in the butter mixture 1 tablespoon at a time. When all the butter has been added, return the mixture to the saucepan, place over very low heat, and stir constantly just until the sauce thickens enough to coat the back of a spoon; do not overheat. Season with:

Salt and white pepper to taste
($^1/_2$ teaspoon fresh lemon juice, or to taste)

Use at once.

LEMON EGG SAUCE (AVGOLEMONO SAUCE)

2$^1/_4$ cups

This favorite Greek sauce is good with lamb or green vegetables, or it can be added to soups, stews, and casseroles—anything, say the Greeks, that is not made with garlic or tomatoes.
Bring to a simmer and keep warm:

1 cup vegetable or chicken stock or broth

Beat with an electric mixer in a bowl until thickened:

3 large eggs

Beat in:

$^1/_4$ cup fresh lemon juice

Beat half of the hot stock into the egg mixture, then whisk this mixture back into the remaining stock. Cook, stirring constantly, over medium-low heat until the sauce is thick and creamy and coats the back of the spoon; do not let the sauce boil, or it will curdle. Remove from the heat and season to taste with:

Salt and black pepper

Serve immediately.

ABOUT TOMATO SAUCES

Although tomatoes originated in the Americas, our most popular tomato sauces have made long round trips to our kitchens. From Italy we get our rich family of pasta sauces and pizza toppings, and from England and Asia we have adopted our most famous condiment, catsup, 950. Mexico provides our native continuity with bright and fresh salsas, 571–572. Tomatoes can be used raw or cooked, pureed or coarsely chopped, as a backdrop for other ingredients or on their own, to produce a range of vibrant sauces. Their sharp flavor and juicy texture make them ideal for creating sauces without the broth or stock that so many other sauces depend on.

Most tomato sauce recipes invite improvisation, but no matter what other ingredients eventually find their way into the sauce, the best sauces begin with good fresh or canned tomatoes. Peeling, 311, is a matter of preference and tradition. Do not assume that imported canned tomatoes are best; several brands of domestic tomatoes are as good as and sometimes better than imported varieties.

The faster a tomato sauce is cooked, the fresher and brighter its flavor; hence we prefer using a wide skillet that lets liquids evaporate quickly. On the other hand, when generous amounts of aromatic vegetables and other seasonings enter a recipe, a longer simmer is required, and a saucepan encourages flavors to unfold and meld together. Meat-based tomato sauces often cook longer still, and then a Dutch oven or large saucepan works well.

Tomato paste and sugar are optional ingredients. The first, if high-quality and used in small quantities, boosts tomato flavor, while a little of the second smooths out excess acidity.

If using on pasta, 3 cups of tomato sauce will be enough for about 1 pound of pasta. Tomato sauces need not be restricted to pasta and pizza—use them on meats, poultry, fish, and vegetables. Top baked chicken breasts with Marinara, below, or Tomato Concassé, 563, or pair Puttanesca Sauce, 563, with sautéed pork medallions.

Tomato sauce can be kept in the refrigerator for up to 4 days or frozen for up to 3 months.

TOMATO SAUCE

2²/₃ cups

Heat in a large skillet over medium heat:

2 tablespoons olive oil

Add:

1 small onion, finely chopped
1 small carrot, finely chopped
1 celery rib with leaves, finely chopped
2 tablespoons finely chopped parsley

Cover, reduce the heat to low, and cook, stirring occasionally, until the vegetables are very soft, 15 to 20 minutes. Add and cook, stirring, for about 30 seconds:

2 small garlic cloves, minced
1 tablespoon chopped basil, rosemary, sage, or thyme

Stir in:

1³/₄ pounds ripe tomatoes, peeled, 311, seeded, and coarsely chopped, or one 28-ounce can whole tomatoes, with their juice
2 teaspoons tomato paste
³/₄ teaspoon salt, or to taste
¹/₄ teaspoon black pepper, or to taste

Simmer, uncovered, crushing the canned tomatoes with the side of a spoon to break them up, until the sauce is thickened, 15 to 20 minutes. Pass through a food mill if desired.

SUN-DRIED TOMATO SAUCE

Soak ¹/₂ cup sun-dried tomatoes (not in oil) in boiling water to cover until softened, about 20 minutes. Drain well and finely chop. Add to **Basic Tomato Sauce, above,** along with the garlic and basil.

MARINARA SAUCE

2¹/₄ cups

Combine in a large saucepan and bring to a simmer over medium-low heat:

2 pounds ripe tomatoes, peeled, 311, seeded, and coarsely chopped, or one 28-ounce can whole tomatoes, with their juice
¹/₃ cup olive oil
3 garlic cloves, halved
6 sprigs basil
6 sprigs parsley

Simmer, uncovered, crushing the tomatoes with the side of a spoon to break them up, until the sauce is thickened, about 10 minutes. Pass through a food mill, and season with:

Salt and black pepper to taste

QUICK TOMATO SAUCE

3 cups

Heat in a large skillet over medium heat:

1 tablespoon olive oil

Add and cook until softened:

¹/₂ small onion, minced

Stir in:

One 28-ounce can whole tomatoes, with their juice
¹/₄ cup tomato paste
2 teaspoons dried herbs, such as basil, oregano, or thyme, or a mix
1 teaspoon sugar
1 teaspoon salt

Bring to a boil, then reduce the heat and simmer gently, uncovered, crushing the tomatoes with the side of a spoon to break them up until thickened, 15 to 20 minutes. Puree in a blender or food processor, if desired.

FRESH TOMATO SAUCE

6 cups

Make this easy sauce when you can get juicy, ripe tomatoes. It's good on bruschetta as well as over pasta. If serving with pasta, you might toss the hot pasta with small cubes of fresh mozzarella cheese before adding the tomato sauce and sprinkle each portion with 1 to 2 teaspoons balsamic vinegar.

Drain in a colander for 20 minutes:

5 large ripe tomatoes, seeded and finely diced

Remove to a large bowl and stir in:

$1/2$ cup basil, oregano, or parsley leaves, finely chopped
($1/2$ cup pitted black oil-cured or brined olives)
3 tablespoons olive oil
2 garlic cloves, finely minced
(1 small fresh chile pepper, seeded and minced)
Salt and black pepper to taste

Let stand for at least 30 minutes. Serve at room temperature.

GRILLED TOMATO SAUCE

$3 1/2$ cups

Prepare a medium-low grill fire or preheat the broiler. Brush:

12 ripe plum tomatoes or 6 large round tomatoes

with:

2 tablespoons olive or other vegetable oil

Place the tomatoes on the grill or under the broiler. Turn with tongs as the skin chars. When charred all over, cool, then puree in a food processor or blender. Remove to a bowl and stir in:

$1/4$ cup extra-virgin olive oil
2 tablespoons chopped basil
Salt and black pepper to taste

TOMATO CONCASSÉ

1 cup

This is a wonderful condiment for grilled chicken or fish. Prepare only as much as you need of this basic preparation, as it does not keep well.

Peel, seed, and juice, 311:

2 large ripe tomatoes

Dice the pulp very fine.

AMATRICIANA SAUCE

2 cups

Combine in a large, heavy skillet over medium heat:

$1/2$ cup olive oil
6 to 8 ounces pancetta or bacon, cut into $1/4$-inch dice

Cook, stirring, until the pancetta has rendered most of its fat and turned deep golden brown, about 10 minutes. Remove with a slotted spoon and reserve. Pour off all but $1/4$ cup of the fat from the pan. Return the pan to medium heat, add, and cook, stirring until golden brown:

1 large onion, finely chopped

Add:

1 large garlic clove, minced
1 dried red chile pepper

Cook, stirring, for 1 minute, crushing the pepper with the back of the spoon and being careful not to burn the garlic. Increase the heat to high and add:

$1 1/2$ pounds ripe tomatoes, peeled, 311, seeded, and chopped, or one 28-ounce can whole tomatoes, with their juice

Stir in the pancetta and simmer, crushing the canned tomatoes with the side of a spoon to break them up, until thickened, about 5 minutes. Season with:

Black pepper to taste
Crushed pepper flakes to taste

PUTTANESCA SAUCE

3 cups

This spicy, savory, and exciting, puttanesca, or "streetwalker's" sauce, is ready in minutes. Ideal for busy cooks.

Heat in a large skillet over medium heat:

$1/4$ cup olive oil

Add:

2 large garlic cloves, minced
1 dried red chile pepper

Cook, stirring and crushing the pepper with the back of a spoon, just until the garlic is pale blond, about 30 seconds. Stir in and cook for about 30 seconds:

1 cup oil-cured black olives, pitted and chopped
6 anchovy fillets, soaked in water for 5 minutes and drained
$1/2$ teaspoon dried oregano

Stir in:

$1 1/2$ pounds ripe tomatoes, peeled, 311, if desired, seeded, and chopped, or one 28-ounce can whole tomatoes, with their juice

Simmer, uncovered, crushing the canned tomatoes with the side of a spoon to break them up until the sauce is thickened, about 5 minutes. Stir in:

3 tablespoons packed minced parsley
2 tablespoons drained capers

Season with:

Salt and black pepper to taste

TOMATO MEAT SAUCE

8 cups

Heat a large heavy casserole or skillet over medium heat. Add:

$1/4$ cup olive oil
(2 ounces pancetta or bacon, diced)

If using pancetta or bacon, cook, stirring, until it renders its fat, about 3 minutes. Add:

1 pound ground beef or sweet Italian sausages, casings removed and crumbled

Cook, stirring, until the meat loses its pink color, about 5 minutes. Pour off all but 2 tablespoons of fat from the pan. Add and cook, stirring, until tender, about 5 minutes:

1 medium onion, chopped

Add and stir until fragrant, about 30 seconds:

2 to 4 garlic cloves, minced

Stir in and cook, stirring, for 2 minutes:

1 tablespoon tomato paste

Add:

Two 28-ounce cans whole tomatoes, with their juice
(1 teaspoon fresh thyme or oregano leaves or
   ¹/₂ teaspoon dried)
1 teaspoon salt
¹/₂ teaspoon black pepper
¹/₈ teaspoon sugar

Cook, uncovered, crushing the tomatoes with the side of a spoon to break them up, until they have cooked down and smell very fragrant, about 15 minutes. Cover and cook over low heat for 30 minutes, stirring often, until the sauce is thickened. Stir in:

2 to 3 tablespoons slivered basil or chopped parsley
Salt and black pepper to taste

BOLOGNESE SAUCE

4¹/₂ cups

With beef as the main ingredient and surprisingly little tomato, the many subtle tastes in this sauce come together beautifully. Serve over tagliatelle or other wide noodles. Heat in a large saucepan over medium-low heat:

3 tablespoons olive oil
(1 ounce pancetta or bacon, finely chopped)

If using pancetta or bacon, cook, stirring, until it releases its fat but is not browned, about 8 minutes. Increase the heat to medium and add:

1 large carrot, minced
2 small celery ribs, minced
¹/₂ medium onion, minced

Cook, stirring, until the onions are translucent, about 5 minutes. Add and brown:

1¹/₄ pounds coarsely ground beef skirt steak or
   ground chuck

Stir in:

³/₄ cup chicken or beef stock or broth
²/₃ cup dry white wine
2 tablespoons tomato paste

Reduce the heat to low and simmer gently, partially covered, skimming occasionally and adding 2 tablespoons at a time from time to time as the sauce simmers:

1¹/₂ cups whole milk

Cook until the sauce is the consistency of a thick soup, about 2 hours. Remove from the heat and let cool. Cover and refrigerate for up to 24 hours. Skim the fat off the top before reheating.

TOMATO SAUCE WITH MEATBALLS

Enough for 1 pound pasta

Prepare **Tomato Sauce, 562,** or **Quick Tomato Sauce, 562** and **Italian Meatballs, 513.** Brown the meatballs as directed, then transfer them to the simmering tomato sauce and simmer 15 to 20 minutes, until cooked through.

ABOUT TABLE SAUCES, DIPPING SAUCES, AND CONDIMENTS

Every country has its own special sauces that at mealtime are pulled from a cool place or prepared fresh and brought to the table. Some of these sauces, such as pesto, 569, and chimichurri, 566, go over food. Some, such as Wasabi Soy Sauce, 571, and Peanut Dipping Sauce, 570—and, in most cases, sweet-and-sour sauces—are for dipping. While we have received wonderful inspirations for these sauces, most of the recipes remain simple.

Use these as garnish for soups or stews, on steamed vegetables, with grains and beans, with pasta, grilled dishes, tortilla chips, breads, or crackers—or, best of all, put them out on the table so your guests can help themselves.

ASIAN SWEET-AND-SOUR SAUCE

Generous 3 cups

Serve over a dish of chicken, vegetables, and rice. Melt in a medium heavy saucepan:

2 tablespoons butter

Add:

1 cup chicken stock or broth
³/₄ to 1 cup diced green bell peppers
6 slices canned pineapple, diced

Bring to a simmer, then reduce the heat, cover, and simmer 5 minutes. Add:

³/₄ cup pineapple juice
¹/₂ cup rice vinegar
¹/₂ cup sugar
¹/₂ teaspoon salt
¹/₄ teaspoon ground ginger

Simmer, stirring constantly, until reduced to about 3 cups, about 35 minutes.
Meanwhile, stir together in a small bowl:

2 tablespoons cornstarch
¹/₂ cup chicken stock or broth
2 tablespoons soy sauce

Stir into the sauce and simmer 5 minutes to thicken.

SWEET-AND-SOUR MUSTARD SAUCE

2¹/₂ cups

Serve cold or at room temperature with any cold meat, as a sandwich condiment, or for dipping vegetables. Or thin the hot sauce with a bit of cream and serve with chicken or pork. A little goes a long way, so this is enough for up to 12 servings.
Mix:

2 cups heavy cream

with:

2 large egg yolks

Combine in the top of a double boiler over—not in—boiling water:

¹/₂ cup sugar
1 tablespoon all-purpose flour
4 teaspoons dry mustard

Whisking constantly, gradually add the cream mixture, and cook, whisking, until thick, 7 to 8 minutes. Gradually stir in:

¹/₂ cup distilled white vinegar

Cook 3 to 4 minutes longer.

MINT SAUCE

2¹/₂ cups

A tradition with roasted lamb. The sauce is thin and sprightly—a refreshing change from sweet jelly.

Stir together in a bowl until the sugar has dissolved:

1¹/₂ cups malt or other strong vinegar

1 cup sugar

Stir in:

1 cup loosely packed minced mint

Let stand for 2 hours. The sauce will keep, covered and refrigerated, for up to 2 days.

CHERRY SAUCE

1¹/₄ cups

For ham, roast pork, or game.

Combine in a blender or food processor and puree:

1 cup drained canned pitted sour cherries

¹/₂ cup plum preserves

2 teaspoons soy sauce

¹/₄ teaspoon dry mustard

Remove to a small saucepan and stir in:

(¹/₄ cup finely chopped walnuts)

Heat before serving.

RAISIN SAUCE

1¹/₂ cups

For ham or tongue.

Combine in a small saucepan:

2 tablespoons butter

2 tablespoons all-purpose flour

Add:

1¹/₂ cups apple cider or apple juice

¹/₂ cup raisins

Bring to a boil, stirring constantly. Reduce the heat and simmer 10 minutes, or until thickened. Add:

1 teaspoon grated lemon zest

(1 to 1¹/₂ teaspoons prepared mustard)

ENGLISH CUMBERLAND SAUCE

A relish to be served with game such as venison, elk, or goose, or with cold ham. The sauce may be served warm or cold.

I. *2 cups*

Combine in a medium saucepan:

1¹/₂ cups port or dry red wine

1 tablespoon brown sugar

1 teaspoon dry mustard

¹/₄ teaspoon ground ginger

¹/₄ teaspoon salt

¹/₄ teaspoon ground cloves

A few grains of ground red pepper

(¹/₂ cup raisins)

(¹/₂ cup slivered almonds)

Bring to a boil and boil for 2 minutes. Reduce the heat and simmer, covered, for 6 minutes. Meanwhile, mix together:

2 teaspoons cornstarch

2 tablespoons cold water

Stir into the sauce and simmer about 2 minutes. Stir in:

¹/₄ cup red currant jelly

1 tablespoon mixed grated orange and lemon zest

¹/₄ cup orange juice

2 tablespoons fresh lemon juice

For a rather exquisite final touch, you may add:

(2 tablespoons Grand Marnier)

II. *³/₄ cup*

If the jelly is very stiff, it may have to be diluted with a tablespoon or so of hot water while melting it over low heat. Combine and blend well:

¹/₂ cup red currant jelly, melted

1 tablespoon port or red wine

1 tablespoon confectioners' sugar

1 teaspoon prepared mustard

Grated zest of 1 orange

Grated zest of 1 lemon

Juice of 1 lemon

HORSERADISH CREAM

1¹/₃ cups

A particular delight with hot roast beef, but also good with cold meats.

Beat in a medium bowl to stiff peaks:

¹/₂ cup heavy cream

Gradually, beat in:

3 tablespoons fresh lemon juice or distilled white or cider vinegar

2 tablespoons grated fresh or drained prepared horseradish

¹/₄ teaspoon salt

Pinch of ground red pepper

Chill for 30 to 60 minutes. Stir gently before serving.

CUCUMBER ALMOND SAUCE

2 cups

Mostly for aspics, but also very good with cold meat or fish, especially salmon.

Beat in a medium bowl to stiff peaks:

³/₄ cup heavy cream or sour cream

If using heavy cream, slowly beat in:

(2 tablespoons distilled white vinegar or fresh lemon juice)

Season with:

¹/₄ teaspoon salt

¹/₈ teaspoon paprika

Add:

1 large cucumber, peeled, seeded, minced, and drained well

1/4 cup slivered almonds
(1 tablespoon finely chopped chives or dill)
Use immediately.

COLD MUSTARD SAUCE

1 2/3 cups

For cold meats or broiled sausages.
Whip until soft peaks form:
   1/2 cup evaporated milk, 997, or heavy cream
Fold into it:
   2 tablespoons Dijon mustard
Season to taste with:
   Salt and paprika

HONEY MUSTARD DIPPING SAUCE

About 2/3 cup

This simple sauce is especially good with fried chicken or fish.
Stir together well in a small bowl:
   6 tablespoons honey
   1/4 cup Dijon mustard
   Ground red pepper to taste
Serve at room temperature. The sauce will keep, covered and refrigerated, for up to 1 month.

SCANDINAVIAN MUSTARD DILL SAUCE

Generous 1/2 cup

Traditional with Gravlax, 411, this can also be served with other smoked, grilled, sautéed, or poached fish.
Whisk together in a medium bowl until smooth:
   6 tablespoons Swedish or Dijon mustard
   1/4 cup snipped dill
   2 to 4 tablespoons sugar
   1/4 cup fresh lemon juice or red wine vinegar, or to taste
   Salt and black pepper to taste
   Generous pinch of ground cardamom
Cover and let stand for 2 to 3 hours to allow the flavors to develop. Serve at room temperature or chilled. The sauce will keep, covered and refrigerated, for up to 2 days.

BAVARIAN APPLE AND HORSERADISH SAUCE

1 cup

Delightfully simple, and a marvelous accompaniment for hot sausages, pork, cold boiled beef, or cold poached fish.
Stir together well in a medium bowl:
   1/3 cup grated fresh or drained prepared horseradish
   1/3 cup finely grated peeled tart green apple
   2 1/2 tablespoons fresh lemon juice
   1/2 teaspoon sugar
   1/2 teaspoon salt
Cover and let stand for 15 to 30 minutes to allow the flavors to develop.
Stir in:
   1/4 cup sour cream

Garnish with:
   1 teaspoon minced parsley
   (1 teaspoon snipped dill)
Serve immediately.

MOJO

1 cup

This popular table sauce in Cuba and throughout the Caribbean is a colorful version of a vinaigrette. Unlike most vinaigrettes, it is briefly cooked to bring out the full flavor of the garlic. Serve with grilled beef, chicken, pork, or fish, or use as a marinade for any of these. Mojo is best served fresh, but the sauce will keep, covered and refrigerated, for up to 3 days.
Heat in a saucepan over medium heat:
   1/2 cup olive oil
Add and cook until fragrant but not browned, 20 to 30 seconds:
   8 garlic cloves, minced
Remove from the heat and let cool 5 minutes.
Carefully stir in and bring to a boil:
   3/4 cup fresh lime, sour orange, grapefruit, or pineapple juice
   3/4 teaspoon ground cumin
   Salt and black pepper to taste
Let cool, and serve at room temperature.

CHIMICHURRI

1 1/4 cups

A spicy hot Argentinian sauce, served with grilled or roasted meat.
Whisk together thoroughly in a small bowl:
   1/2 cup olive oil
   1/4 cup red wine vinegar
Stir in:
   1 small onion, finely chopped
   1/3 cup finely chopped parsley or cilantro
   4 garlic cloves, finely chopped
   (1 tablespoon finely chopped oregano)
   Salt to taste
   1/4 teaspoon ground red pepper, or to taste
   1/4 teaspoon black pepper, or to taste
Cover and let stand for 2 to 3 hours to allow the flavors to develop. The sauce will keep, covered and refrigerated, for up to 2 days.

MEXICAN HOT SAUCE

1 cup

Good with Huevos Rancheros, 196—or anything you'd serve with hot sauce. This may be served by itself, but it also combines excellently with a hot cream sauce or hot or cold mayonnaise.
Combine in a medium saucepan and bring to a simmer:
   3 large fresh tomatoes, peeled, 311, quartered, and seeded, or 3/4 cup drained chopped canned tomatoes

6 tablespoons chili sauce

6 tablespoons rice or cider vinegar

3 tablespoons grated fresh or drained prepared
   horseradish

2 teaspoons prepared mustard

1 teaspoon minced onion

$3/4$ teaspoon curry powder

$3/4$ teaspoon salt

$1/2$ teaspoon sugar

$1/4$ teaspoon black pepper

Pinch of ground red pepper

1 garlic clove, sliced

Simmer until fairly thick. Strain. Add:

1 teaspoon dried or 1 tablespoon fresh herbs

PARSLEY-CHILE SAUCE

$3/4$ cup

Serve over grilled beef.

Mix in a small bowl or in a food processor until smooth:

$1/2$ cup extra-virgin olive oil

$1/4$ cup balsamic vinegar

$1/4$ cup chopped parsley

2 teaspoons minced chile pepper, or to taste

1 teaspoon minced garlic

Salt and black pepper to taste

GREEN SAUCE (SALSA VERDE)

$3/4$ cup

This classic Italian tart green sauce—not to be confused with Tomatillo Salsa, 571—is traditionally served with braised meats, fried calamari, and grilled fish.

Combine in a food processor:

$2/3$ cup parsley leaves

2 tablespoons drained capers

(6 anchovy fillets)

$1/2$ teaspoon finely chopped garlic

$1/2$ teaspoon prepared mustard

$1/2$ teaspoon red wine vinegar or 1 tablespoon fresh
   lemon juice

$1/2$ cup extra-virgin olive oil

Salt to taste

Blend to a uniform consistency, but do not process to a puree. Adjust the seasonings. The sauce will keep, covered and refrigerated, for up to 1 week. Serve at room temperature.

TUNA SAUCE

2 cups

Serve with cold poached veal or chicken or with grilled or roasted vegetables. Replace some of the lemon juice with lime juice for a wonderful tang.

Combine in a food processor or blender:

One 6-ounce can tuna packed in oil, drained

1 cup mayonnaise

5 anchovy fillets, finely chopped, or 2 teaspoons
   anchovy paste

3 tablespoons drained capers

3 tablespoons fresh lemon juice

Black pepper to taste

Process until smooth, 30 seconds to 1 minute, scraping down the sides as needed. Remove to a bowl, cover, and refrigerate. To serve, thinly slice the cold meat or chicken and arrange, overlapping, on a platter. Pour the sauce over and sprinkle with:

Chopped parsley

RED ONION MARMALADE

$1 1/2$ cups

Wonderful with roasted meats, and a good alternative to cranberry sauce with roast turkey.

Combine in a medium saucepan over low heat:

4 large red onions, halved lengthwise and cut into
   $1/4$-inch slices (about 6 cups)

$1/2$ cup dry red wine

$1/2$ cup red wine vinegar

$1/3$ cup packed light brown sugar

$1/4$ cup honey

Cook, stirring, until the sugar is dissolved, then simmer, stirring often, until the consistency of marmalade, about $1 1/2$ hours. Stir in:

1 tablespoon orange juice

1 tablespoon fresh lemon juice

Cook, stirring, until blended. Let cool. The marmalade will keep, covered and refrigerated, for up to 3 weeks. Serve at room temperature.

TZATZIKI

2 cups

A cool companion for fried food, and a fine dip on its own.

Stir together:

1 cup plain yogurt

$1/2$ cucumber, peeled, seeded, and finely diced

1 tablespoon olive oil

1 tablespoon chopped dill

1 tablespoon chopped mint

1 tablespoon red wine vinegar or fresh lemon juice

1 garlic clove, minced

$1/2$ teaspoon salt

RAITA (INDIAN YOGURT SALAD)

$1 3/4$ cups

Serve this cooling condiment alongside spicy meats, fish, poultry, or vegetarian entrées—raita is a principal source of protein in an Indian vegetarian meal. It is best served fresh, but it can be prepared ahead and refrigerated, covered, for up to 2 hours.

Stir together well in a small bowl:

1 cucumber, peeled, halved, seeded,
   and finely chopped

1 cup plain yogurt or $1/2$ cup yogurt plus
   $1/2$ cup sour cream

1 tablespoon finely chopped mint

¼ teaspoon ground cumin
¼ teaspoon salt
(1 small jalapeño pepper, seeded and diced)

BECKER COCKTAIL SAUCE

1 cup

This wonderful recipe makes a lively dunking sauce for seafood or small sausages. For a contemporary version, add finely chopped cilantro, red onions, green chile peppers, and/or fresh lime juice.
Stir together well in a small bowl:

½ cup catsup
½ cup chili sauce
¼ cup finely grated fresh horseradish

Stir in:

(1 tablespoon tamari or soy sauce)
(1 to 2 garlic cloves, minced)
Hot pepper sauce to taste
Black pepper to taste
Zest of one lemon
Fresh lemon juice to taste

The sauce will keep, covered and refrigerated, for up to 1 week. Serve at room temperature.

TOMATILLO-HORSERADISH SAUCE

2 cups

This sauce makes a showstopping shrimp cocktail or a memorable Bloody Mary.
Preheat the oven to 350°F.
Combine in a roasting pan:

12 tomatillos, husked and rinsed
1 large red onion, coarsely chopped
4 garlic cloves, chopped
2 jalapeño peppers, chopped
2 tablespoons canola oil
Salt and black pepper

Cook until all the vegetables are soft, 20 to 25 minutes. Transfer to a food processor and process until smooth. Add:

3 tablespoons rice vinegar
¼ cup drained prepared horseradish
¼ cup chopped cilantro

Pulse to combine. Season with:

Salt and black pepper to taste

Refrigerate for at least 1 hour before serving.

MIGNONETTE SAUCE

½ cup; enough for 24 oysters

Classic with oysters on the half-shell, this sauce is good with any raw shellfish. For **Raspberry Mignonette Sauce,** substitute ½ cup raspberry vinegar and add lemon juice to taste.
Mix together in a small bowl:

½ cup red wine vinegar
4 teaspoons finely chopped shallots
1 tablespoon finely chopped parsley

¾ teaspoon salt
2 teaspoons cracked black peppercorns

Serve chilled or at room temperature.

CHAMPAGNE MIGNONETTE

Substitute ¼ cup Champagne and ¼ cup champagne vinegar for the red wine vinegar in **Mignonette Sauce, above.**

ROASTED TOMATILLO SPINACH SAUCE

5 cups

Serve with Enchiladas Verdes, 104. You can use this technique with almost any vegetable to create a range of vibrant sauces: Simply roast the vegetables until they are soft and beginning to caramelize and then puree the hot vegetables in a blender or food processor along with all their cooking juices, a bit of stock, and seasonings to match.
Preheat the oven to 400°F. Spread in a single layer in an oiled baking pan:

2 pounds tomatillos, husked and rinsed
2 medium poblano or Anaheim peppers,
     halved and seeded
1 large onion, quartered
12 garlic cloves, peeled

Roast until very soft, 40 to 45 minutes. Transfer the vegetables, including the pan juices, to a blender or food processor, and add:

1¼ cups coarsely chopped spinach
⅓ cup chopped cilantro
¼ cup chicken or vegetable stock or broth,
     or as needed
Salt and black pepper to taste

Pulse until smooth, adding more stock if necessary to make a medium-bodied sauce. Reheat gently in a small saucepan and serve or store, covered and refrigerated, for up to 2 days. Reheat before serving.

CAVIAR SAUCE

1⅓ cups

For smoked salmon or new-potato hors d'oeuvres or baked potatoes.
Combine:

1 cup sour cream
½ cup red caviar
1 teaspoon grated onion or shallot
1 tablespoon drained capers
1 teaspoon chopped chives or snipped dill
Salt to taste

GARLIC AND WALNUT SAUCE

1⅓ cups

Delicious with cucumbers, tomatoes, red beans, asparagus, spinach, and beets. You can increase the amount of spices, if desired.
Combine in a food processor and process until finely ground:

1 cup walnuts, toasted, 1001
3 small garlic cloves, coarsely chopped
Remove to a bowl. Add and stir well to combine:
3 tablespoons minced cilantro
2 teaspoons fresh lemon juice or red wine vinegar
¼ teaspoon ground coriander
¼ teaspoon ground red pepper, or to taste
¼ teaspoon turmeric
(¼ teaspoon ground fenugreek)
Thin the sauce to the consistency of light cream with:
About ¾ cup chicken or vegetable stock or broth
Serve at room temperature.

PISTOU

¾ cup

The French version of pesto, made without nuts, this is delicious with fish and a great addition to soups and stews.
Combine in a blender and puree until smooth:
2 cups basil leaves
2 garlic cloves, chopped
½ cup olive oil
Remove to a bowl and stir in:
⅓ cup coarsely grated Parmesan
¼ teaspoon black pepper
The sauce will keep, covered and refrigerated, for up to 2 days. Serve at room temperature.

PESTO SAUCE

1 cup

Pesto must be made with fresh basil, but it can be made in advance. If freezing it (up to 3 months), add the nuts and cheese after thawing. This is also excellent with almonds or hazelnuts in place of the pine nuts; it may require 1 to 2 tablespoons additional oil in that case.

I. Combine in a food processor and process to a rough paste:
2 cups loosely packed basil leaves
½ cup grated Parmesan
⅓ cup pine nuts
2 medium garlic cloves, peeled
With the machine running, slowly add:
½ cup olive oil, or as needed
If the pesto seems dry (it should be a thick paste), add a little more olive oil. Season to taste with:
Salt and black pepper
Use immediately, or pour a very thin film of olive oil over the top, cover, and refrigerate for up to 1 week.

II. For a more robust texture, use a mortar and pestle. Pound the basil in the mortar. Add the garlic and pine nuts and pound. Add the cheese and pound until the mixture forms a thick paste. Add the oil very slowly, pounding constantly. Season to taste.

SUN-DRIED TOMATO PESTO

1⅓ cups

Spread this on bruschetta or pizza; toss it with pasta; or serve it with grilled poultry, seafood, or pasta.

Combine in a small saucepan with water to cover:
⅓ cup chopped oil-packed sun-dried tomatoes
1 garlic clove, peeled
6 basil leaves
Bring to a boil, then remove from the heat and let stand for 20 minutes. With the machine running, drop through the feed tube of a food processor:
1 large garlic clove, peeled
1 cup packed basil leaves
¼ cup olive oil
⅓ cup grated Parmesan
Drain the tomato mixture, reserving the liquid. Add the tomato mixture to the processor and finely chop. Season to taste with:
Salt and black pepper
Blend in ⅓ cup of the reserved soaking liquid.

PICADA

⅔ cup

From Spain—this is not really a sauce, but a condiment to be stirred directly into stews, soups, and sauces a few minutes before they are done. Picadas destined to be used with meat, poultry, or game dishes often include a bit of chocolate; those to be used with fish sometimes have fish roe or livers added.
Heat in a small skillet over medium heat:
1 tablespoon extra-virgin olive oil
Add and toast on both sides:
One ½-inch-thick slice French or Italian bread
Crumble the bread and place in a mortar or small food processor or blender. Add and pound with the pestle or process:
½ cup mixed whole blanched almonds, skinned hazelnuts, and pine nuts or all almonds, toasted, 1001, and coarsely chopped
2 garlic cloves, halved
Salt to taste
(¼ teaspoon black pepper)
(Pinch of toasted saffron threads)
Remove the mixture to a bowl and work in with a fork, making a thick paste:
3 tablespoons extra-virgin olive oil, or as needed
1 teaspoon finely chopped parsley
Let stand until the picada holds together as a thick paste, about 30 minutes. It will keep, covered and refrigerated, for up to 2 days.

HARISSA

½ cup

This fiery pepper paste from North Africa is stirred into seafood stews, soups, herb salads, and vegetable dishes, tossed with black olives, and used as an ingredient in sauces for brochettes, tagines, and couscous.
Toast in a small dry skillet over medium heat, shaking the pan often to prevent burning, until very aromatic, 2 to 3 minutes:

1 teaspoon caraway seeds
1 teaspoon coriander seeds
$^1/_2$ teaspoon cumin seeds

Remove from the heat and let cool, then grind to a fine powder in a spice mill or coffee grinder or with a mortar and pestle. Add and grind until smooth:

2 garlic cloves, quartered
Salt to taste

Add and grind until well combined:

3 tablespoons sweet paprika
1 tablespoon crushed red pepper flakes
1 tablespoon olive oil

The harissa will be very thick and dry. To store, transfer the paste to a small jar and cover with:

Olive oil

It will keep, covered and refrigerated, for 6 months.

THAI HOT SAUCE (NAM PRIK)

$^1/_4$ cup

Nam prik, which translates as "pepper water," is the traditional table sauce of Thailand, where there are any number of variations on the recipe. It is served with vegetables, stirred into soups, and used as a sauce for rice, noodles, meat, or fish. The sauce is best if allowed to stand for a day or two, and it keeps well for several weeks in the refrigerator. If dried shrimp and fish sauce are not available, add more fresh or dried chile peppers and lime juice.

Combine in a small food processor or a mortar and process or pound to a paste:

18 tiny dried shrimp, chopped
4 small dried red chile peppers, seeded if desired and crumbled
4 garlic cloves, chopped
2 tablespoons fresh lime juice
1 tablespoon fish sauce, 982 (*nam pla*)

Stir in:

3 small red or green serrano peppers, seeded if desired and finely chopped
Chopped cilantro to taste
(A little brown sugar)

Cover and refrigerate for at least 1 day before serving.

PLUM, PEACH, OR APRICOT DIPPING SAUCE

$^3/_4$ cup

A dipping sauce or marinade for egg rolls, spareribs, and Chinese dishes.

Combine in a blender or food processor and puree:

$^1/_2$ cup plum, peach, or apricot preserves
$^1/_4$ cup mango chutney
1 tablespoon rice vinegar or cider vinegar

THAI CHILE-LIME DIPPING SAUCE

Generous $^3/_4$ cup

Pass this fiery sauce as a dip for grilled meats or fish. Mince together:

6 jalapeño peppers, seeded
6 garlic cloves, peeled

Place in a small bowl and stir in:

6 to 8 tablespoons fresh lime juice
Salt to taste

Let stand at room temperature until ready to serve.

PEANUT DIPPING SAUCE

$1^3/_4$ cups

Some version of this sauce is served all over Southeast Asia, with the small skewers of meat and chicken known as *satays,* or with many other dishes from spring rolls to grilled meats. Thin it with a bit of rice vinegar for a Thai-style salad dressing or marinade.

Heat in a small saucepan over medium heat:

2 teaspoons vegetable oil

Add and cook, stirring, until golden brown, about 1 minute:

4 garlic cloves, minced
1 teaspoon minced peeled fresh ginger
$^1/_2$ teaspoon crushed red pepper flakes, or to taste

Add and cook, stirring, until thickened, about 4 minutes:

1 cup water
2 tablespoons soy sauce
2 tablespoons fresh lime juice
$^2/_3$ cup chunky peanut butter, preferably unsweetened
1 tablespoon light brown sugar, or to taste
(3 tablespoons chopped unsalted roasted peanuts)

Remove from the heat and stir in:

(1 tablespoon finely chopped mint)

Serve warm or at room temperature. The sauce will keep, covered and refrigerated, for up to 1 week.

NUOC CHAM

Scant 1 cup

This all-purpose sauce is nearly always on the table in Vietnam, both at home and in restaurants. Use as a dipping sauce for spring rolls or to dress a salad of shredded cabbage.

Combine in a small bowl and let stand for 5 minutes:

1 hot fresh Asian chile or jalapeño pepper, preferably red, seeded and finely chopped
6 tablespoons fresh lime juice or 2 tablespoons lime juice plus $^1/_4$ cup rice vinegar

Stir in:

2 tablespoons fish sauce, 982 (*nuoc nam*)
3 tablespoons sugar, or to taste
2 tablespoons coarsely shredded carrot
(1 tablespoon coarsely shredded daikon radish)
3 to 5 garlic cloves, finely chopped

Serve at room temperature. The sauce will keep, covered and refrigerated, for up to 6 days.

ASIAN BLACK BEAN SAUCE

$^1/_2$ cup

This sauce can be rubbed on fish or shellfish before steaming or served as a condiment with the finished dish.

Mash to a paste with a fork in a small bowl:

3 tablespoons fermented black beans

Add and stir in:

2 scallions, finely chopped

2 tablespoons soy sauce

2 tablespoons dry sherry

4 garlic cloves, finely chopped

2 teaspoons peanut or other vegetable oil

2 teaspoons toasted sesame oil

2 teaspoons finely chopped peeled fresh ginger

Salt and cracked black peppercorns to taste

Serve at room temperature. The sauce will keep, covered and refrigerated, for up to 6 days.

WASABI SOY SAUCE

½ cup

This pungent dipping sauce is for strong-tasting fish and beef. Wasabi soy sauce is best eaten right away, for it loses its pungency as it sits.

Place in a small bowl:

1 tablespoon finely grated wasabi root, 1026

Or mix together with a fork to make a smooth paste:

1 tablespoon wasabi powder, 1026

2 to 3 drops lukewarm water

Cover, and let stand for 10 minutes to allow the flavors to develop. Stir in:

½ cup dark soy sauce, preferably low-sodium

Serve individually in small shallow bowls.

GINGER SOY SAUCE

Use for fish, chicken, or meat.

Prepare **Wasabi Soy Sauce, above,** substituting **1 tablespoon grated peeled fresh ginger** for the wasabi.

ABOUT SALSAS

Salsa means "sauce" in both Italian and Spanish, and in these countries, the word can apply to everything from creamy white sauce to brown gravy. Still, when we hear the word "salsa," it is usually the tomato-and-chile-based type that spring to mind. Like catsup, salsas can go over just about anything on the plate. Although some ingredients can be cooked, salsas should be made with the freshest ingredients possible and served soon after being made at room temperature.

In many instances, we recommend rinsing the chopped raw onions under cold water, and sometimes sprinkling with citrus juice, before combining them with the other ingredients. Rinsing mellows the onion, preventing any biting aftertaste that could overpower the other flavors of the sauce. The tomatoes can be seeded, 311, but that is not traditional for salsas.

When removing the blender's or food processor's lid after grinding mixtures that include chile peppers, avert your face—chile fumes are powerful.

For an extra dimension, mix a splash of light tequila or dark rum into a salsa.

For most recipes, allow 2 to 4 tablespoons per serving.

SALSA FRESCA

2 cups

This recipe for Mexican salsa is easily doubled or tripled, but try to make only as much as you will use immediately, as it loses its texture on standing and the chile pepper heat increases. Variations use either scallions or white or red onions, water instead of lime juice, and sour orange juice instead of lime juice. Any sort of fresh chile pepper can be used—each contributes its distinctive character. Precise amounts are less important than the happy marriage of flavors, so taste as you go. Salsa fresca complements everything from tacos to hot grilled foods and cool vegetables. In American-style Mexican food, this type of chunky salsa is sometimes called **pico de gallo.**

Combine in a medium bowl:

½ small white or red onion or 8 slender scallions, finely chopped, rinsed, and drained

2 tablespoons fresh lime juice

2 large ripe tomatoes or 3 to 5 ripe plum tomatoes, seeded if desired and finely diced

¼ to ½ cup chopped cilantro (leaves and tender stems)

3 to 5 serrano or jalapeño peppers or ¼ to 1 habanero pepper, or to taste, seeded and minced

(6 radishes, finely minced)

(1 medium garlic clove, minced)

Stir together well. Season with:

¼ teaspoon salt, or to taste

Serve immediately.

TOMATILLO SALSA (SALSA VERDE CRUDA)

2 cups

This intensely fresh, pungent, herbal salsa is especially good with fish, chicken, roasted vegetables, and eggs. It should be served within an hour of preparing; if left to sit, the raw onion will overpower the sauce.

Combine in a food processor or blender and coarsely puree, leaving the mixture a little chunky:

8 ounces tomatillos, husked, rinsed, and chopped

1 small white or red onion, chopped

3 to 5 serrano or jalapeño peppers, seeded and chopped

(1 garlic clove, peeled)

¼ cup cilantro sprigs

Remove to a medium bowl and stir in enough cold water to loosen the mixture to a saucelike consistency. Stir in:

½ teaspoon salt, or to taste

(¾ teaspoon sugar)

Serve immediately.

CORN, TOMATO, AND AVOCADO SALSA

3½ cups

Cook in boiling salted water to cover for 1 minute:

2 ears corn, husked and silk removed

Drain and remove the kernels. Place the corn kernels in a medium bowl, along with:

16 cherry tomatoes, halved and seeded if desired
1 ripe avocado, chopped
$^1/_2$ small red onion, finely diced, rinsed, and drained
1 garlic clove, finely chopped
1 to 3 jalapeño peppers, seeded and finely chopped
$^1/_4$ cup chopped basil
2 tablespoons vegetable oil
$^1/_4$ cup fresh lime juice, or to taste
$^1/_2$ teaspoon salt
$^1/_4$ teaspoon black pepper

Stir together well. This salsa will keep, covered and refrigerated, for up to 1 day.

ROASTED TOMATO–CHIPOTLE SALSA

2 cups

Ripe tomatoes take on a deeper flavor when roasted. This salsa is particularly good with grilled chicken, fish, or lamb and with tacos or enchiladas.

Prepare a medium-low grill fire or preheat the broiler.

Place on the grill or broiler pan:

6 medium ripe tomatoes, halved, seeded if desired

Grill or broil (broil as close to the heat as possible), turning as needed, until the skins are blackened in spots and slightly softened, about 5 minutes on each side on the grill, slightly less time in the broiler. When cool enough to handle, peel and coarsely chop the tomatoes. Put them in a medium bowl, and stir in:

1 small onion, finely chopped, rinsed, and drained
$^1/_4$ cup coarsely chopped cilantro
3 tablespoons fresh lime juice, or to taste
2 tablespoons olive oil
2 garlic cloves, finely chopped
1$^1/_2$ teaspoons finely chopped canned chipotle pepper, or to taste
1 teaspoon ground cumin
Salt to taste

Serve immediately.

FRUIT SALSA

3 cups

Use this as a basic recipe for fruit salsas—wonderful with just about any food, but particularly with grilled or sautéed fish. Basil or parsley can stand in for the cilantro, and pineapple or guava juice is a good alternative to the orange juice.

Combine in a large bowl:

1 small red onion, chopped, rinsed, and drained
$^1/_4$ cup fresh lime juice

Add:

1$^1/_2$ cups coarsely chopped peeled mango, papaya, pineapple, peaches, or apricots
1 small red bell pepper, cut into thin strips
$^1/_4$ cup coarsely chopped cilantro
($^1/_4$ to $^1/_3$ cup cooked or rinsed and drained canned small black beans)
1 garlic clove, minced

$^1/_4$ cup fresh orange juice
1 jalapeño or other small chile pepper, seeded and finely chopped

Stir together well. Season with:

Salt and cracked black peppercorns to taste

The salsa will keep, covered and refrigerated, for up to 1 day.

ABOUT VINAIGRETTES AND SALAD DRESSINGS

These are salad and fruit dressings of two very different types. Vinaigrettes are mixtures of oil and vinegar (or other acidic liquids, such as citrus juice or wine) and flavorings, while a richer class of dressings are thicker emulsions, often egg-based, such as mayonnaise. Whether simple or rich and complex, salad dressings, with the rarest exceptions, should never repeat in their composition the materials they grace.

Vinaigrettes are best made just before use. The classic proportions are 3 to 4 parts oil to 1 part of an acid, such as lemon juice, lime juice, or vinegar, with salt and pepper to taste. Vinaigrettes have many other uses, including as marinades for meats, poultry, and game. They may be mixed in a bowl or the ingredients placed in a jar with a tight-fitting lid or blended in a food processor or blender for a more thoroughly emulsified result. In all cases, mix the ingredients, except the oil, first, then slowly pour in the oil with the processor running. Constantly beating, whisking, or shaking, in any case, is a prerequisite. Please read About Salads, 152, About Oil, 1023, and About Vinegar, 1024. For heavier dressings, see Dips, 71.

VINAIGRETTE

1 cup

This dressing can become part of the salad making if you like. See About Dressing Salads, 156.

If garlic flavor is desired, mash to a paste:

(1 small garlic clove, peeled)
(2 to 3 pinches of salt)

Remove to a small bowl. Add:

$^1/_2$ teaspoon salt
$^1/_8$ teaspoon ground black pepper
$^1/_4$ cup red wine vinegar or fresh lemon juice
(1 teaspoon minced shallot)
($^1/_4$ to $^1/_2$ teaspoon prepared mustard)

Whisk until blended. Add gradually, whisking constantly after each addition:

$^3/_4$ cup olive or walnut oil

If made in advance, cover and refrigerate. Shake well before using.

FRESH HERB VINAIGRETTE

The fresh herbs should be added just before the vinaigrette is to be used.

Prepare **Vinaigrette, above,** then add $^1/_4$ cup minced or finely snipped herbs such as **basil, dill, parsley, chives, and/or thyme.**

BASIL VINAIGRETTE

Prepare **Vinaigrette, 572**, then add $\frac{1}{2}$ **cup thinly sliced basil leaves** or $\frac{1}{4}$ **cup each basil and snipped chives.**

BLACK PEPPER VINAIGRETTE

Prepare **Vinaigrette, 572**, then add **1 to 2 teaspoons cracked black peppercorns** and **1 teaspoon finely grated lemon zest.**

LIME VINAIGRETTE

Prepare **Vinaigrette, 572**, substituting $\frac{1}{4}$ **cup fresh lime juice** for the vinegar and adding ($\frac{1}{4}$ **teaspoon toasted cumin seeds**).

HORSERADISH DRESSING

$\frac{1}{2}$ cup

Prepare $\frac{1}{2}$ **cup Vinaigrette, 572.** Beat in **1 tablespoon grated fresh or drained prepared horseradish, or more to taste.** Let stand for 30 minutes before serving.

AVOCADO DRESSING

$\frac{3}{4}$ cup

Great for sliced tomatoes. For a perfectly smooth dressing, make in the blender or food processor.
Peel, and mash in a small bowl $\frac{1}{2}$ **avocado.** Gradually add $\frac{1}{2}$ **cup Vinaigrette, 572.** Whisk until smooth. Use immediately.

ROQUEFORT OR BLUE CHEESE VINAIGRETTE

$1\frac{1}{4}$ cups

Prepare **Vinaigrette, 572.** Beat in $\frac{1}{4}$ **to** $\frac{1}{3}$ **cup crumbled Roquefort or other blue cheese, or to taste.**

PARSLEY LIME VINAIGRETTE

$\frac{3}{4}$ cup

Whisk together in a small bowl:
  2 tablespoons fresh lime juice
  2 tablespoons red wine vinegar
  2 tablespoons chopped parsley
  1 tablespoon Dijon mustard
  2 teaspoons ground cumin
  $1\frac{1}{2}$ teaspoons honey
  Salt and cracked black peppercorns to taste
Add in a slow, steady stream, whisking constantly:
  $\frac{1}{2}$ cup olive oil

LEMON OREGANO VINAIGRETTE

$\frac{3}{4}$ cup

Also a delicious marinade for chicken, fish, or pork.
Bring to a boil in a medium saucepan, and reduce to $\frac{1}{4}$ cup:
  2 cups fresh lemon juice
Set aside. Heat in a small skillet:
  1 tablespoon olive oil
Add and cook, stirring, until soft:
  $\frac{1}{2}$ shallot, chopped
  1 garlic clove, chopped

Remove to a blender and add the reduced lemon juice and:
  1 teaspoon honey
Blend until smooth. With the blender running, gradually add:
  $\frac{1}{2}$ cup olive oil
Season with:
  Salt and black pepper to taste
  2 tablespoons chopped oregano

HONEY MUSTARD VINAIGRETTE

Generous $\frac{1}{2}$ cup

Whisk together in a small bowl:
  2 tablespoons fresh lemon juice
  1 tablespoon white wine vinegar
  1 tablespoon honey, or to taste
  1 teaspoon coarse-grain mustard, or to taste
  Salt and black pepper to taste
Add in a slow, steady stream, whisking constantly:
  6 tablespoons extra-virgin olive oil
Taste and adjust the seasonings.

SPINACH OR WATERCRESS DRESSING

2 cups

Excellent over salad greens or on cucumbers and with shrimp.
Whisk together in a small bowl:
  2 tablespoons fresh lemon juice
  1 tablespoon tarragon vinegar
  $\frac{1}{2}$ teaspoon salt
  $\frac{1}{8}$ teaspoon black pepper
Add in a slow, steady stream, whisking constantly:
  $\frac{1}{2}$ cup olive oil
Stir in:
  2 cups watercress or baby spinach leaves, finely chopped

SOUTHWEST DRESSING

$\frac{1}{2}$ cup

Whisk together in a small bowl:
  $\frac{1}{2}$ cup minced cilantro
  $\frac{1}{4}$ cup fresh lime juice
  1 teaspoon ground cumin
  $\frac{1}{2}$ teaspoon chili powder, or to taste
  Salt and black pepper to taste
Add in a slow, steady stream, whisking constantly:
  $\frac{1}{4}$ cup olive oil

SHERRY VINAIGRETTE

1 cup

Whisk together in a small bowl:
  $\frac{1}{4}$ cup sherry vinegar
  1 tablespoon Dijon mustard
  1 tablespoon chopped shallot
  1 teaspoon chopped thyme
  $\frac{1}{2}$ to 1 teaspoon crushed red pepper flakes

Add in a slow, steady stream, whisking constantly:
   ¾ cup olive oil

SWEET-AND-SOUR VINAIGRETTE

1 cup
Whisk together in a small bowl:
   ⅓ cup tarragon or red wine vinegar
   ⅓ cup sugar
   ¾ teaspoon minced fresh tarragon or ¼ teaspoon
      dried tarragon
   ¾ teaspoon salt
   ¼ teaspoon black pepper
Add in a slow, steady stream, whisking constantly:
   ⅓ cup vegetable oil

LORENZO DRESSING

1⅔ cups
For oysters or green vegetables.
Combine in a food processor or blender and blend:
   ¼ cup red wine vinegar
   1 tablespoon Dijon mustard
   1 teaspoon sugar
   ½ teaspoon salt
   ½ teaspoon black pepper
With the machine running, add in a slow, steady stream,
processing until thick:
   ⅔ cup extra-virgin olive oil
Remove to a bowl and stir in:
   ¼ cup chili sauce
   ¼ cup minced watercress
   ¼ cup crumbled crisp cooked bacon
   2 tablespoons minced shallots

ANCHOVY DRESSING

½ cup
For a leaf lettuce salad. Add some grated Parmesan for a
quick Caesar dressing.
Prepare:
   ½ cup Vinaigrette, 572
Beat in:
   1 tablespoon anchovy paste, or more to taste

CELERY SEED DRESSING

2 cups
Add to fruit salads just before serving.
Combine in a small bowl, whisking constantly:
   ½ cup sugar
   1 teaspoon dry mustard
   1 teaspoon salt
   1 to 2 teaspoons celery seeds
Add:
   1 tablespoon grated onion
Gradually add, whisking constantly:
   1 cup vegetable oil
   ⅓ cup rice vinegar or cider vinegar
Garnish the salad with:
   (A few small sprigs lemon thyme)

POPPY SEED–HONEY DRESSING

⅔ cup
This dressing is an old favorite for salads that combine
greens and fruit.
Whisk together in a small bowl until smooth:
   ¼ cup honey
   3 tablespoons cider vinegar or other fruit vinegar
   1 small shallot, minced
   2 teaspoons Dijon mustard
   1 teaspoon poppy seeds
   Salt and black pepper to taste
Gradually add, whisking constantly:
   2 tablespooons olive oil
Taste and adjust the seasonings.

SPICY WALNUT VINAIGRETTE

1 cup
Delicious over mixed greens with goat cheese or a grilled
chicken breast and spinach salad.
Whisk together in a small bowl:
   1 shallot, minced
   3 tablespoons balsamic vinegar, or to taste
   2 tablespoons minced walnuts
   2 teaspoons Dijon mustard
   Salt to taste
   Hot pepper sauce to taste
Add in a slow, steady stream, whisking constantly:
   ⅓ cup extra-virgin olive oil
   ⅓ cup walnut oil
Taste and adjust the seasonings.

PARMESAN VINAIGRETTE

1¼ cups
Ideal for a crunchy green salad or sliced fresh tomatoes.
Whisk together in a small bowl:
   ⅓ cup balsamic vinegar
   3 tablespoons grated Parmesan
   1½ teaspoons whole black peppercorns or fennel
      seeds, lightly crushed
   1 shallot, minced
   1 garlic clove, minced
   Salt and black pepper to taste
Add in a slow, steady stream, whisking constantly:
   ¾ cup olive oil
Taste and adjust the seasonings. Use immediately, or cover
and refrigerate.

ROASTED RED PEPPER DRESSING

1¼ cups
Mash together to a paste:
   1 garlic clove, peeled
   ¼ teaspoon salt
Transfer to a blender or food processor and add:
   One 6½-ounce jar roasted red peppers, drained
   6 tablespoons olive oil
   2 tablespoons fresh lemon juice

2 tablespoons white wine vinegar
3 tablespoons chopped shallots
1 tablespoon ground cumin
Salt and black pepper to taste
Pinch of ground red pepper
Blend until smooth.

TANGERINE SHALLOT DRESSING

1 1/3 cups

This dressing is especially good on any salad with chicken or drizzled over grilled chicken.
Mash together to a paste:

1 garlic clove, peeled
2 to 3 pinches of salt

Remove to a small bowl. Add and whisk until well blended:

1/4 cup fresh tangerine or clementine juice
2 tablespoons fresh lemon juice
1 small shallot, minced

Add in a slow, steady stream, whisking constantly:

2/3 cup vegetable oil

Taste and adjust the seasonings.

APRICOT DRESSING

1 cup

Especially good on salads of Asian greens or any salads with pork or lamb.
Whisk together in a medium bowl until smooth:

1/4 cup apricot nectar
3 tablespoons balsamic vinegar
3 tablespoons minced dried apricots
3 tablespoons coarsely chopped parsley
1 to 2 teaspoons minced garlic
2 teaspoons coarse-grain mustard
1 teaspoon sugar
Salt and cracked black peppercorns to taste

Add in a slow, steady stream, whisking constantly:

1/4 cup olive oil

Taste and adjust the seasonings.

GINGER LEMONGRASS DRESSING

1 cup

Combine in a small saucepan and bring to a boil over high heat:

2 stalks lemongrass, coarsely chopped
2 tablespoons minced peeled fresh ginger
2/3 cup distilled white vinegar
2/3 cup water
3 tablespoons sugar

Reduce the heat to low and simmer, uncovered, stirring occasionally, until reduced by about half, about 20 minutes. Strain into a small bowl. Whisk in:

2 tablespoons toasted sesame oil
2 tablespoons vegetable oil
2 tablespoons soy sauce
(2 tablespoons fish sauce [*nam pla*])

Cool to room temperature.

THAI VINAIGRETTE

1 1/4 cups

This also makes a good marinade for fish or chicken.
Whisk together in a small bowl:

1/2 cup fresh lime juice
(3 tablespoons fish sauce [*nam pla*])
1 tablespoon soy sauce
1 1/2 teaspoons sugar
1/4 teaspoon crushed red pepper flakes, or to taste
Salt and black pepper to taste

Add in a slow, steady stream, whisking constantly:

1/2 cup vegetable oil

JAPANESE STEAKHOUSE GINGER DRESSING

1 1/2 cups

Combine in a blender and process until thick and smooth:

1/2 cup coarsely chopped carrots
1/4 cup coarsely chopped celery
1/4 cup peanut oil
1/4 cup rice wine vinegar
2 tablespoons chopped peeled fresh ginger
2 tablespoons coarsely chopped onion
2 tablespoons sugar
1 tablespoon soy sauce
2 teaspoons catsup
2 teaspoons fresh lemon juice
1 teaspoon salt
1/2 teaspoon black pepper
2 dashes hot pepper sauce

ROASTED GARLIC DRESSING

3/4 cup

Preheat the oven to 400°F. Place on a piece of heavy-duty aluminum foil:

1 head garlic, top third cut off and loose skin removed
2 shallots, loose skin removed

Sprinkle with:

2 tablespoons olive oil

Wrap and seal tightly. Place on a baking sheet and cook for 1 hour. Remove the package from the oven, carefully open, and let cool. When cool enough to handle, squeeze the garlic and shallots from their skins into a small food processor or a blender. Add and process to a puree:

2 tablespoons extra-virgin olive oil
1 tablespoon fresh lemon juice
1 tablespoon white wine vinegar
1 teaspoon Dijon mustard
1 teaspoon thyme leaves
1 teaspoon minced rosemary
Salt and black pepper to taste

With the machine running, add in a slow, steady stream, processing until smooth:

6 tablespoons olive oil

Taste and adjust the seasonings. Use immediately, or cover and refrigerate.

TAHINI DRESSING

1 cup

Tahini, sesame seed paste, is a staple of Middle Eastern cooking. This dressing goes especially well with Falafel, 188, and salads that include chickpeas, and it makes a great dip for crudités.

Whisk together in a small bowl:

$1/2$ **cup tahini (sesame seed paste)**
$1/2$ **cup water**
2 tablespoons fresh lemon juice
Pinch of salt
Ground red pepper to taste

RUSSIAN DRESSING

$1^1/_3$ cups

Drizzle over arranged salads, eggs and shellfish, or in chicken salad.

Combine:

1 cup mayonnaise
1 tablespoon grated fresh or drained prepared horseradish
(3 tablespoons caviar or salmon roe)
(1 teaspoon Worcestershire sauce)
$1/4$ **cup chili sauce or catsup**
1 teaspoon grated onion
(1 tablespoon minced parsley)

Chill before using.

THOUSAND ISLAND DRESSING

$1^1/_2$ cups

An obvious relative of Russian dressing, Thousand Island is great on a wedge of iceberg lettuce. It also makes a good sandwich spread.

Stir together in a small bowl until well blended:

1 cup mayonnaise
$1/4$ **cup chili sauce or catsup**
1 hard-boiled egg, 194, chopped
2 tablespoons pickle relish or minced gherkins
1 tablespoon minced onion
1 tablespoon finely snipped chives
1 tablespoon minced parsley
Salt and black pepper to taste

Taste and adjust the seasonings. Use immediately, or cover and refrigerate.

RANCH DRESSING

1 cup

The original version was created at the Hidden Valley Guest Ranch in Santa Barbara in the 1950s. If you prefer a thicker dressing, stir in $1/3$ to $1/2$ cup sour cream or mayonnaise.

Combine in a blender or food processor until smooth:

1 garlic clove, peeled
2 to 3 pinches of salt

Remove to a bowl. Add and whisk until well blended:

$3/4$ **cup buttermilk**

2 to 3 tablespoons fresh lime juice
1 tablespoon minced cilantro or parsley
1 tablespoon snipped chives
Salt and black pepper to taste

Taste and adjust the seasonings. Use immediately, or cover and refrigerate.

GREEN GODDESS DRESSING

$1^3/_4$ cups

For fish or shellfish, especially crab or shrimp, or vegetable salads.

Combine:

1 cup mayonnaise
1 garlic clove, minced
3 anchovy fillets, minced
$1/2$ **cup sour cream**
$1/4$ **cup finely minced chives or scallions**
$1/4$ **cup minced parsley**
1 tablespoon fresh lemon juice
1 tablespoon tarragon vinegar
$1/2$ **teaspoon salt**
Black pepper to taste

Taste and adjust the seasonings. Use immediately, or cover and refrigerate.

CREAMY BLUE CHEESE DRESSING

$2^1/_4$ cups

Good-quality blue cheese, such as Roquefort, turns this into a truly distinctive dressing. Use on a wedge of iceberg lettuce, stuffed into celery stalks, or as a burger topping.

Combine in a food processor or blender and process until smooth:

1 cup mayonnaise
$1/2$ **cup sour cream**
$1/4$ **cup finely chopped parsley**
1 to 2 tablespoons fresh lemon juice or red wine vinegar
1 teaspoon minced garlic
6 dashes Worcestershire sauce
Salt and black pepper to taste
Pinch of ground red pepper, or to taste

Add and process to the desired consistency:

4 ounces Roquefort or other blue cheese

Taste and adjust the seasonings. Use immediately, or cover and refrigerate.

FETA DRESSING

$3/4$ cup

Serve with a Greek-style salad, over steamed vegetables or sliced tomatoes, or as a dip for crudités. The amount of oil needed will depend on how dry the cheese is and how the dressing is to be used.

Combine in a blender or food processor and process until smooth:

4 ounces feta, crumbled (1 cup)
2 tablespoons red wine vinegar

1 teaspoon minced oregano
Salt and black pepper to taste

With the machine running, add in a slow steady stream, processing until smooth:

2 to 4 tablespoons extra-virgin olive oil

Taste and adjust the seasonings. Use immediately, or cover and refrigerate.

GOAT CHEESE DRESSING

1¼ cups

Excellent for pasta salad—combine with the pasta while it is still hot.

Whisk together in a small bowl:

¾ cup buttermilk
2 teaspoons white wine vinegar
1 teaspoon Dijon mustard
1 teaspoon minced thyme
1 teaspoon minced parsley
Pinch of grated lemon zest
¾ teaspoon salt
Black pepper to taste

Stir in:

4 ounces soft fresh goat cheese, mashed

Taste and adjust the seasonings. Use immediately, or cover and refrigerate.

YOGURT HERB DRESSING

½ cup

Vary this all-purpose creamy dressing by using different herbs, such as dill, thyme, oregano, or mint; by substituting chives for the shallots; or by adding a generous pinch of curry powder, ground cumin, or ground red pepper.

Whisk together in a small bowl:

6 ounces yogurt
2 to 3 tablespoons minced shallots
2 tablespoons finely minced herbs
2 teaspoons Dijon mustard
Salt and black pepper to taste

CREAMY CARAWAY DRESSING

1¼ cups

You can make this dressing with equal parts yogurt and sour cream instead of crème fraîche. Delicious over green beans or crisp greens, or in a potato salad.

Whisk together in a small bowl:

¾ cup sour cream or crème fraîche
¼ cup fresh lemon juice
1 tablespoon caraway seeds, lightly toasted, 1001
1½ teaspoons coarse-grain mustard
1½ teaspoons chopped shallot
½ teaspoon chopped thyme

Add in a slow, steady stream, whisking constantly:

1 tablespoon extra-virgin olive oil

Season to taste with:

Salt and black pepper

Use immediately, or cover and refrigerate.

BOILED SALAD DRESSING

1 cup

The term "boiled," while traditionally used, is inaccurate: "double-boiled" comes closer. This classic JOY recipe is recommended for vegetable and potato salads, slaw, tomato salad, aspics, or fruit salad. Keep refrigerated.

Mix together in a small bowl:

2 tablespoons all-purpose flour
1 to 2 tablespoons sugar
½ to 1 teaspoon dry mustard
½ teaspoon salt
¼ teaspoon paprika

Whisk in:

½ cup cold water

Whisk together in the top of a double boiler:

1 large egg or 2 large egg yolks
¼ cup white wine vinegar

Whisk in the flour mixture, and whisk the dressing over—not in—simmering water until thick and smooth.

Whisk in:

2 tablespoons butter, softened

Chill the dressing before using. Thin with:

(Sour cream)

MIDWESTERN CREAM DRESSING

½ cup

This is a legacy from early farming days, when oil was too rare to be used on salads. It is particularly good on soft leaf lettuces and in potato salads and slaws.

Whisk together in a small bowl:

¼ cup cider vinegar or white wine vinegar
¼ cup sugar
1 tablespoon milk
1 tablespoon heavy cream
2 teaspoons celery seeds or poppy seeds
Salt and cracked black peppercorns to taste

Use immediately, or cover and refrigerate.

CREAMY DIJON DRESSING

1½ cups

If you use yogurt in this dressing, it's best to use milk rather than buttermilk, since both would make the dressing too acidic. Good for crudités or with fish or chicken.

Whisk together in a small bowl until well blended:

1 cup sour cream or plain yogurt
½ cup buttermilk or milk
2 tablespoons Dijon mustard, or to taste
1 tablespoon minced parsley
1 tablespoon snipped chives
1 tablespoon snipped dill
Pinch of sugar
Salt and black pepper to taste

Use immediately, or cover and refrigerate.

CREAM CHEESE VINAIGRETTE

²/₃ cup

Serve this dressing over a green salad or one made with a mix of vegetables.

Process in a food processor until smooth:

3 ounces cream cheese, softened

Add and process to blend:

1 teaspoon finely minced onion

¹/₂ teaspoon prepared mustard

¹/₂ teaspoon salt

Black pepper to taste

2 tablespoons chopped parsley

With the machine running, add in a slow, steady stream, processing until smooth:

¹/₄ cup vegetable oil

1¹/₂ tablespoons white wine vinegar

CREAM CHEESE OR YOGURT DRESSING FOR FRUIT SALAD

1¹/₄ cups

This dressing firms up somewhat on sitting, so pour it over fruit right after preparing it. If using nonfat yogurt, add an extra 1 to 2 tablespoons.

Mash with a fork in a small bowl, then beat until smooth:

3 ounces cream cheese, softened, or 6 tablespoons plain yogurt

Slowly beat in:

³/₄ cup heavy cream

2 tablespoons currant jelly

1 tablespoon fresh lemon juice

CURRY DRESSING FOR FRUIT SALAD

1 cup

Combine in a small bowl:

2 tablespoons white wine vinegar or rice vinegar

1 tablespoon fresh lemon juice

1 teaspoon sugar

¹/₄ to ¹/₂ teaspoon curry powder

1 cup sour cream

HONEY DRESSING FOR FRUIT SALAD

About 1 cup

Combine:

¹/₂ cup honey

¹/₂ cup fresh lime juice

(A pinch of ground ginger)

BUTTERMILK HONEY DRESSING

1¹/₃ cups

Whisk together in a small bowl:

¹/₄ cup rice vinegar

¹/₄ cup sour cream

¹/₄ cup buttermilk

3 tablespoons honey

1 teaspoon minced garlic

1 scallion, minced

Pinch of ground red pepper

Salt and black pepper to taste

Add in a slow, steady stream, whisking constantly:

¹/₂ cup olive oil

CREAMY HORSERADISH DRESSING

²/₃ cup

Whisk together in a small bowl:

4 teaspoons red wine vinegar

1 teaspoon salt

Gradually whisk in until well blended:

¹/₄ cup olive oil

2 tablespoons vegetable oil

Stir in:

¹/₄ cup heavy cream

2 tablespoons drained prepared horseradish

Salt and white pepper to taste

CREAMY DRESSING FOR COLESLAW

1 cup

Stir together until well blended:

³/₄ cup mayonnaise

¹/₄ cup cider vinegar or rice vinegar

1 to 2 tablespoons sugar

CREAMY PARMESAN DRESSING

About 2¹/₂ cups

Called Half-and-Half Dressing in previous editions of JOY, this vinaigrette is delicious served on tossed salad, combination salads, or hearts of lettuce.

Combine:

1 cup mayonnaise

1 cup Vinaigrette, 572

¹/₂ cup grated Parmesan

1 teaspoon minced garlic

(1 teaspoon mashed anchovy)

ABOUT MAYONNAISE AND FLAVORED MAYONNAISES

If you are accustomed to store-bought mayonnaise, your first taste of homemade will be a surprise. Homemade mayonnaise is an elegant sauce, and it is at its best when made by hand. The flavor is bright with lemon juice or vinegar and rich with fresh oil. That is reason enough, but there's an added attraction: Homemade mayonnaise can be made quickly.

Mayonnaise, like hollandaise and béarnaise, is an **emulsion**—a stable semi-liquid mixture in which one liquid is suspended in tiny globules throughout another liquid. The oil you choose will be the predominant flavor in your mayonnaise. Strongly flavored olive oil, for example, will make a pungent mayonnaise. For general use, a balance of fruity and mild oils, such as olive and vegetable, is most satisfying. Usually 3 parts mild to 1 part fruity oil is about right, although sometimes it can be half-and-half. The oil must be very fresh. One tinge of rancidity, and the mayonnaise will be all but inedible, so taste the oil before you start.

Making mayonnaise in a food processor or blender is quick and practically foolproof. The result also has a greater volume and a fluffier texture, but it cannot duplicate the smoothness and the rich sheen of the hand-beaten product. ➤ Ingredients at room temperature emulsify more readily than cold ones, so start by bringing the eggs to room temperature or by briefly covering the eggs in their shells with hot water to warm them. If the oil was refrigerated, bring it to room temperature. ➤ To be certain of success, bear in mind that you need 3 times as much oil as other liquid ingredients, including egg yolks. Rinse your bowl with hot water and dry thoroughly.

Problems with mayonnaise are simple to fix. If the mayonnaise starts to separate, place a fresh egg yolk in a small clean bowl and slowly add the separated mayonnaise, drizzling it and whisking it in as you first did with the oil. You may need to add more oil to compensate for the extra yolk. If the mayonnaise is too thick for your taste, thin it with a little water or cream.

Mayonnaise can be flavored in many ways. Add herbs, spices, flavored vinegars, and/or dry mustard to the yolks at the start. Lemon juice and wine vinegar are classic, but other citrus juices and most other vinegars can also be used. If you know you will be adding liquid flavorings, use 1 to 2 tablespoons extra oil to make a thicker mayonnaise.

Homemade mayonnaise can be kept tightly covered in the refrigerator for 1 to 2 days, but it will lose some of its sheen after a few hours. Mayonnaise does not freeze well. When serving homemade mayonnaise and any food containing it, keep track of the time it spends outside the refrigerator. Because raw eggs contain microorganisms that start multiplying above 40°F, the maximum time mayonnaise should be out of the refrigerator is 2 hours—or, when the temperature is 85°F or above, 1 hour. When the risk of salmonella in raw eggs is a concern, use pasteurized eggs, 977.

To perk up store-bought mayonnaise, fold in an equal amount of sour cream or beat an equal amount of chilled heavy cream and fold it in. If you use prepared mayonnaise, beating in 1 to 2 tablespoons good olive oil until all trace of it has disappeared will make the mayonnaise stiffer and heavier and improve its flavor. Sour cream, according to taste, can also do wonders for commercial mayonnaise—if well incorporated. Please note that commercial "salad dressing" is not mayonnaise, and these suggestions will not work if it is used. Any of the flavored mayonnaises starting below can be made with store-bought mayonnaise.

MAYONNAISE
1 cup

This is our basic mayonnaise, from which all of our variations can be prepared. It can be whisked to a lighter consistency by gradually adding an appropriately flavored stock, vegetable juice, or even spirits. Use a ceramic, glass, or stainless steel bowl—old aluminum or copper will react with the acid and affect the color and flavor of the sauce. Whisk together in a medium bowl until smooth and light:

> **2 large egg yolks, at room temperature**
> **1 to 2 tablespoons fresh lemon juice or**
> > **white wine vinegar**
> **1/4 teaspoon salt**
> **Pinch of white pepper**

Whisk in by drops until the mixture starts to thicken and stiffen:

> **1 cup vegetable oil, at room temperature**

As the sauce begins to thicken—when about one-third of the oil has been added—whisk in the oil more steadily, making sure each addition is thoroughly blended before adding the next. Should the oil stop being absorbed, whisk vigorously before adding more. Stir in:

> **(Up to 1 1/2 teaspoons Dijon mustard)**
> **Salt and white pepper to taste**

Serve immediately, or refrigerate for up to 2 days.

BLENDER MAYONNAISE
1 1/2 cups

Blender mayonnaise differs from the above recipe in that it uses a whole egg. If your beating arm is rather weak, we suggest you try this method as the emulsifying is produced by the action of the blender. You can also make this version in a food processor; use the plastic blade if you have one, as it seems to make a slightly lighter sauce.

Put in a blender:

> **1 large egg, at room temperature**
> **1 teaspoon dry mustard**
> **1 teaspoon salt**
> **A dash of ground red pepper**
> **1 teaspoon sugar**
> **1/4 cup olive or vegetable oil**

Cover and blend on high until thoroughly combined. With the blender running, slowly add:

> **1/2 cup vegetable oil**

and then:

> **3 tablespoons fresh lemon juice**

until thoroughly blended. Slowly add:

> **1/2 cup vegetable oil**

and blend until thick. You may have to stop and start the blender occasionally to scrape down the sides.

YOGURT MAYONNAISE
1 3/4 cups

A marvelously tangy light sauce to use in all the ways you would use mayonnaise.

Combine:

> **1 cup Mayonnaise, above, or Blender Mayonnaise,**
> > **above**
> **3/4 cup plain yogurt**
> **Salt and white pepper to taste**

CREAM (CHANTILLY) MAYONNAISE

2 cups

Serve with fruit salad.

Prepare:

    1 cup Mayonnaise, 579, or Blender Mayonnaise, 579

Shortly before serving, fold in:

    ¹/₂ cup heavy cream, whipped

CURRY MAYONNAISE

Generous 1 cup

Superb with cold vegetables, eggs, fish, poultry, and meats, this makes an interesting binder for a fruit, chicken, or shellfish salad.

Stir together in a small skillet over low heat for 30 to 60 seconds, until fragrant:

    2 tablespoons curry powder

    2 tablespoons mild vegetable oil

Let cool, then whisk into:

    1 cup Mayonnaise, 579, or Blender Mayonnaise, 579

Add:

    1 teaspoon fresh lime juice

    1 teaspoon honey

    ¹/₄ teaspoon salt

    (1 tablespoon chopped mango chutney)

    (1 tablespoon chopped kumquat)

    (1 tablespoon slivered almonds)

CREAM CHEESE MAYONNAISE

1 cup

A traditional French sauce for cold asparagus that contains no eggs and relatively little oil. It is also delicious with grilled chicken. However, it does have a tendency to separate. To prevent this, serve well chilled. If necessary, whirl for a minute or two in the food processor, then serve at once.

Process in a food processor until smooth and creamy:

    5 ounces cream cheese or Neufchâtel

    (¹/₄ teaspoon sweet or hot paprika)

With the machine running, add in a slow, steady stream:

    5 tablespoons mild vegetable oil, at room temperature

Add in a slow, steady stream:

    1¹/₂ tablespoons fresh orange juice

    1¹/₂ tablespoons fresh lemon juice

Add:

    ¹/₂ teaspoon salt

    ¹/₂ teaspoon white pepper

Stop the machine and scrape down the sides. Taste and adjust the seasonings. Transfer to a bowl, cover, and chill. The mayonnaise will keep, covered and refrigerated, for 1 week.

For a true **Sauce Parisienne**, stir in before serving:

    (2 tablespoons chopped chervil)

MUSTARD MAYONNAISE

1¹/₄ cups

For cold poultry, meats, fish, and strong-flavored vegetables, and traditional with cracked crab. Yellow mustard is lightest and best for fish and seafood; stronger Dijon suits poultry and meats.

Combine:

    1 cup Mayonnaise, 579, or Blender Mayonnaise, 579

    ¹/₄ cup prepared mustard

    Salt and black pepper to taste

CHIPOTLE MAYONNAISE

Generous 1 cup

A zesty sauce for grilled meat and poultry.

Combine:

    1 cup Mayonnaise, 579, or Blender Mayonnaise, 579

    2 tablespoons chopped cilantro

    1 tablespoon minced canned chipotle peppers

    1 tablespoon adobo sauce from the peppers, or to taste

    1 tablespoon fresh lime juice

    1 teaspoon minced garlic

    Salt and black pepper to taste

MAYONNAISE WITH GREEN HERBS

1 cup

Beautiful and delicious with cold shellfish, fish, and vegetables and with cold poached meats.

Combine:

    1 cup Mayonnaise, 579, or Blender Mayonnaise, 579

    2 to 3 tablespoons minced herbs, such as tarragon, basil, chervil, chives, parsley, and/or oregano

    Salt and black pepper to taste

Cover and refrigerate for 30 minutes before serving.

TOMATO AND RED PEPPER MAYONNAISE (ANDALOUSE SAUCE)

1¹/₂ cups

For hard-boiled eggs or crudités.

Combine:

    1 cup Mayonnaise, 579, or Blender Mayonnaise, 579

    1 small plum tomato, peeled, 311, seeded, and finely diced

    1 red bell pepper, roasted, 292, finely diced, or 1 pimiento, drained and finely diced

    Salt and white pepper to taste

SOUFFLÉED MAYONNAISE

2 cups

For fish or as a masking for broiled tomatoes.

Combine in a medium bowl and beat well:

    ¹/₂ cup Mayonnaise, 579, or Blender Mayonnaise, 579

    ¹/₄ cup pickle relish

    2 tablespoons chopped parsley

    1 tablespoon fresh lemon juice

    ¹/₄ teaspoon salt

    A few grains of ground red pepper

Beat until stiff but not dry, 978:
>**2 large egg whites**

Fold into the mayonnaise mixture.
Spread the sauce evenly on hot cooked fish or sliced tomatoes. Broil until the sauce is puffed and golden.

WATERCRESS MAYONNAISE

1 cup

Excellent with cold fish dishes, especially salmon.
Combine:
>**$^3/_4$ cup Mayonnaise, 579, or Blender Mayonnaise, 579**
>**$^1/_4$ cup finely chopped watercress**
>**1 tablespoon fresh lemon juice**
>**Salt and black pepper to taste**

MAYONNAISE FOR FRUIT SALAD

1$^1/_2$ cups

Delicious with fruit salad, a salad of shaved fennel and orange segments, or one of radicchio and arugula. Also good with fruit gelatin.
Combine:
>**1 cup Mayonnaise, 579, or Blender Mayonnaise, 579**
>**$^1/_2$ cup pineapple juice**
>**1 teaspoon grated orange zest**
>**1 tablespoon orange Curaçao**

TARTAR SAUCE

1$^1/_3$ cups

A good standby for fried fish. Try replacing the parsley with other herbs, such as tarragon or chives.
Combine:
>**1 cup Mayonnaise, 579, or Blender Mayonnaise, 579**
>**1 hard-cooked egg, finely chopped**
>**1 tablespoon chopped drained sweet pickle relish**
>**1 tablespoon chopped drained capers**
>**1 tablespoon finely chopped parsley**
>**(1 tablespoon chopped green olives)**
>**1 teaspoon Dijon mustard**
>**1 teaspoon minced shallot**
>**(Ground red pepper or hot pepper sauce to taste)**
>**Salt and black pepper to taste**

You may thin the sauce with:
>**(A little wine vinegar or fresh lemon juice)**

SPICY TARTAR SAUCE

Generous 1$^1/_4$ cups

Mix well in a medium bowl:
>**$^3/_4$ cup Mayonnaise, 579, or Blender Mayonnaise, 579**
>**$^1/_4$ cup chopped parsley**
>**3 tablespoons fresh lime juice**
>**2 tablespoons pickle relish**
>**2 tablespoons Dijon mustard**
>**1 teaspoon minced garlic**
>**4 to 8 dashes hot pepper sauce**
>**Salt and black pepper to taste**

SAUCE LOUIS

2 cups

Especially relished with stuffed artichokes, shrimp, or crab; see Crab Louis, 162.
Combine:
>**1 cup Mayonnaise, 579, or Blender Mayonnaise, 579**
>**$^1/_4$ cup heavy cream**
>**$^1/_4$ cup chili sauce**
>**1 teaspoon Worcestershire sauce**
>**$^1/_4$ cup finely chopped red, yellow, or green bell pepper**
>**$^1/_4$ cup finely chopped scallions**
>**2 tablespoons fresh lemon juice**
>**Salt and black pepper to taste**

REMOULADE SAUCE

1$^1/_2$ cups

This French classic is marvelous with salads, vegetables, cold meats, poultry, and shellfish.
Combine:
>**1 cup Mayonnaise, 579, or Blender Mayonnaise, 579**
>**1 tablespoon minced cornichons (sour gherkins)**
>**1 tablespoon drained small capers**
>**1 tablespoon chopped parsley**
>**1$^1/_2$ teaspoons chopped tarragon**
>**1 small garlic clove, minced**
>**$^1/_2$ teaspoon Dijon mustard**
>**Salt and black pepper to taste**
>**(1 hard-boiled egg, 194, finely chopped)**

RUSSIAN HORSERADISH CREAM

1$^3/_4$ cups

Piquant and suave, this is superb with cold beef, tongue, ham, game, and root vegetables.
Blend together thoroughly in a bowl:
>**1 cup Mayonnaise, 579, or Blender Mayonnaise, 579**
>**$^1/_2$ cup sour cream**
>**3 to 4 tablespoons grated fresh or drained prepared horseradish**

Add to taste:
>**1 to 2 teaspoons cider vinegar**
>**$^1/_4$ teaspoon salt, or to taste**
>**(Pinch of sugar)**

AÏOLI (GARLIC MAYONNAISE)

1 cup

Very popular in France, where it is sometimes referred to as *"beurre de Provence."* Spread on a sandwich as you would mayonnaise, use as a dipping sauce for crudités, or serve over cold poached salmon, grilled and roasted meats, cold boiled potatoes, or frittatas.
Mince:
>**4 to 6 garlic cloves**

that give the sauce its name. Place in a bowl and whisk together with:

2 large egg yolks, at room temperature
$^1/_8$ teaspoon salt
White pepper to taste
Very slowly, and whisking constantly, add, as for Mayonnaise, 579:
    1 cup olive oil
Whisk in:
    1 teaspoon fresh lemon juice
    $^1/_2$ teaspoon cold water
(If the sauce fails to thicken, see 543.)

POTATO-GARLIC MAYONNAISE (SKORDALIA)

Both the Greeks and Spanish use the trick of cutting the richness of mayonnaise by replacing some of it with a smooth potato puree. It is also delicious with almonds. Both versions are delicious in soups or served with grilled meats.

I.

1$^3/_4$ cups

Also good for binding dishes such as crab cakes.
Prepare:
    Aïoli, above
Whisk in:
    $^1/_2$ cup lukewarm cooked potatoes,
        mashed with a fork
blending well, but not more than necessary. Add:
    Salt and/or fresh lemon juice to taste
If the sauce is too thick, whisk in a compatible stock.

II.

1$^1/_2$ cups

Also an excellent dip.
Prepare:
    Aïoli, above
adding after the sauce has thickened:
    $^1/_4$ cup ground almonds
    1 small boiled potato, riced, or $^1/_4$ cup fresh
        bread crumbs
    1 tablespoon fresh lemon juice
    2 tablespoons chopped parsley
    $^1/_4$ teaspoon salt, or more to taste

ROUILLE (RED PEPPER GARLIC MAYONNAISE)

$^2/_3$ cup

Strongly flavored, rouille is served on toast with fish soups, especially bouillabaisse, 142.
Process in a food processor or pound together in a bowl or mortar to a smooth paste:
    $^1/_2$ roasted red bell pepper, 292, or 1 pimiento, drained
    1 small fresh red chile, blanched in boiling water until
        tender, or a dash of hot pepper sauce
    $^1/_4$ cup fresh bread crumbs, soaked in water and
        squeezed dry
    2 mashed garlic cloves
    $^1/_4$ teaspoon salt

Very slowly add, as for Mayonnaise, 579:
    $^1/_4$ cup olive or vegetable oil
Just before serving, thin the sauce with:
    2 to 3 tablespoons of the soup you are serving

ABOUT GLAZES

The term "glaze" is among the trickiest in the cooking vocabulary. However, we have postponed the explanation of sweet glazes—by all odds the more confusing—to the dessert chapters. Here we deal only with the simpler topic of savory glazes: the maskings and coatings that impart so much color and glamour to meats, fish, salads, and vegetables. Basically, glazing consists of decorative touches that also add flavor.

Savory glazing—particularly with meats and vegetables—can have several meanings. Before sorting them out, we may as well remind you of "deglazing," which has already been described in this chapter, 546. The juices captured in this effortless way from sautéed, broiled, browned, or roasted foods, may be used just as they are, or reduced or as the liquid in roux-based sauces. But meats may be glazed also by the use of Meat Glaze, 117, a substance yielded by a lengthy process of reduction. It is potent and delectable, but, like all other powerful essences, it must be used with moderation.

You can glaze vegetables by letting the butter in which they have been cooked combine with their reduced juices. This is best done over carefully controlled heat; often a little sugar or honey is added, see 245.

To glaze a sauce can mean to run it under a broiler until it turns golden brown. To glaze an hors d'oeuvre can mean to apply an aspic coating to it. You may coat eggs or fish with a rich white sauce, 550—a procedure that is then referred to as napping or glazing them.

A glaze is also a liquid that adds luster and gloss to foods, and it is this type of glaze you'll find here. The sheen comes from some form of melted sugar. Glazes should be thick enough to paint on the food without dripping. A quick final coating of glaze is often brushed on just before serving, and some glazes can be passed as dipping sauces at the table. In addition to being sweet, glazes are typically fruity and/or spicy.

The first six glazes below are best for baked ham, 507, and roasted poultry, 422. Apply the glaze during the last 15 to 45 minutes of cooking, the timing depending on the heat of the oven, the sweetness of the sauce, and the size of the piece of meat. To glaze a large ham, remove it from the oven about 45 minutes before it is done. Score the fat on top in any pattern, stud with whole cloves, if desired, and brush with the glaze, then return to the oven. Depending on size, wait until 15 to 30 minutes before the end of cooking to glaze poultry—the smaller the bird, the shorter the time. These glazes can be used to cook turkey parts as well.

BROWN SUGAR GLAZE

³/₄ cup

Mix together in a bowl with your fingers, breaking up any lumps:

> **³/₄ cup packed light brown sugar**
> **2 teaspoons dry mustard**

Slowly stir in until of spreading consistency:

> **Fresh orange juice**

CRANBERRY GLAZE

1¹/₂ cups

Stir together until of spreading consistency:

> **1 cup canned cranberry sauce**
> **¹/₂ cup packed brown sugar**
> **2 tablespoons fresh lemon juice**

MARMALADE GLAZE

Briefly heat if necessary to make it of spreading consistency:

> **³/₄ cup orange, lemon, ginger, pineapple, or any desired marmalade**

MUSTARD GLAZE

¹/₂ cup

Stir together:

> **¹/₂ cup packed light brown sugar**
> **¹/₄ cup yellow mustard**
> **2 tablespoons honey or light molasses**

PINEAPPLE GLAZE

²/₃ cup

Stir together:

> **¹/₂ cup finely chopped fresh or drained canned crushed pineapple**
> **³/₄ cup packed light brown sugar**
> **¹/₂ teaspoon ground ginger**

BOURBON GLAZE

2–3 cups

Combine:

> **¹/₂ to 1 cup dry red wine**
> **¹/₂ to 1 cup bourbon**
> **1 cup packed brown sugar**
> **6 cloves, smashed**
> **2 tablespoons grated orange zest**

HONEY GLAZE FOR MEAT OR ONIONS

¹/₂ cup

Combine:

> **¹/₄ cup honey**
> **¹/₄ cup soy sauce**
> **1 teaspoon prepared mustard**

RUM–BROWN SUGAR GLAZE

¹/₂ cup

Enough for 24 large shrimp or 1¹/₂ pounds of fish.
Combine in a small saucepan:

> **1 cup dark rum**
> **³/₄ cup packed light brown sugar**

Bring to a simmer, stirring to dissolve the sugar, and simmer until reduced by half.
Add:

> **1 teaspoon coarse black pepper**
> **Pinch of salt**

Brush on while grilling. Finish the dish by dousing with:

> **Juice of 2 limes**

The glaze will keep, covered and refrigerated, for several days.

ORANGE MOLASSES GLAZE

3 cups

Paint this dark, rich glaze on large cuts of beef, pork, ham, spare ribs, or game several hours before roasting and then baste generously with it as it cooks.
Heat in a medium saucepan over medium heat:

> **1 tablespoon olive oil**

Add and cook, stirring, until just beginning to color:

> **1¹/₄ cups finely minced onions**
> **3 tablespoons finely minced garlic**

Stir in and bring to a boil:

> **1 tablespoon cracked black peppercorns**
> **¹/₂ cup balsamic vinegar**
> **2 cups fresh orange juice**
> **1 tablespoon grated orange zest**
> **¹/₂ cup light or dark molasses**
> **1 tablespoon coriander seeds, crushed (toasted, if desired)**
> **¹/₄ cup yellow mustard seeds**
> **1 teaspoon salt**

Reduce the heat and simmer, uncovered, until the glaze is thickened and coats the back of a spoon, about 30 minutes. Let cool to room temperature. This glaze will keep, covered and refrigerated, for 3 to 4 days.

CHIPOTLE PEPPER GLAZE

1¹/₂ cups

This is a basic all-purpose sauce that can be used as a glaze or marinade, or as you would catsup or barbecue sauce. It can also be added to vinaigrettes and mayonnaises.
Heat in a large saucepan over medium-high heat:

> **1 tablespoon olive oil**

Add and cook, stirring, until lightly colored:

> **1 cup chopped onions**
> **2 teaspoons minced garlic**

Stir in:

> **³/₄ cup dry white wine**
> **³/₄ cup vegetable or poultry stock or broth**
> **¹/₂ cup fresh orange juice**
> **¹/₂ cup dried apricots**
> **2 large dried New Mexico peppers, seeded and torn into small pieces**
> **1 to 2 canned chipotle peppers, coarsely chopped**

Cover, reduce the heat, and simmer until the chiles are very soft, about 30 minutes. Let cool slightly.

Puree the chile mixture in a blender, along with:

> **¹⁄₄ cup pure maple syrup**
> **2 tablespoons Dijon mustard**

Season with:

> **Salt to taste**

Depending on its intended use, thin with additional:

> **(Stock, broth, or orange juice)**

Let cool to room temperature. The sauce will keep, covered and refrigerated, for up to 2 weeks.

ABOUT MARINADES

Never underestimate the power of a marinade. These aromatic seasoned liquids are used to flavor meat, poultry, fish, or vegetables before cooking. Because almost all contain some type of acid, such as wine, vinegar, citrus juice, or other fruit juice, they act to tenderize the surfaces of meat, fish, and poultry and to encourage the transfer of flavors.

Marinade containers ➤ should be made of food-grade plastic, glazed ceramic, glass, or a nonreactive metal such as stainless steel. Large resealable plastic bags are convenient, disposable containers for marinating. Less marinade is needed to cover if the meat, poultry, or fish is placed in a container just large enough to hold it. Stir or turn the meat occasionally during the process.

Marinades are a means of spreading flavor by immersion. The soaking period may vary from only a few minutes to many hours. Stronger, spicier marinades make bland food more interesting, but perhaps the most important function of a marinade is to tenderize foods.

Marinades may be cooked or uncooked. The cooked ones more effectively impart their flavors to food, and are preferable if marinating is to exceed 12 hours. The liquid should be cooked ahead and thoroughly chilled before the food is coated. The amount of vinegar should be reduced slightly if meat is to be marinated longer than 24 hours. Meat, poultry, and some shellfish also benefit from brining, 962.

The effects of marinating are hastened by higher temperatures, but so is the danger of bacterial activity. ➤ Refrigerate foods while they marinate.

Both cooked and uncooked marinades may be used to finish a sauce, so long as they have not been in contact with raw meat, poultry, or fish. So do not discard a marinade before deciding whether you want to incorporate it in your sauce. Pepper Sauce, 556, for venison is an example. And dishes such as Hasenpfeffer, 251, and Sauerbraten, 178, are cooked in the marinade, which is then converted into a proper sauce just before serving. Never, however, ➤ use the marinade for meat, poultry, or fish for basting cooked food or as a sauce without first bringing it to a boil to kill any harmful bacteria from the raw food.

Avoid marinating tender foods such as boneless chicken breasts, vegetables, or fish for more than 2 to 3 hours, or they may turn stringy, even mushy. Cubed meat is soaked just 2 to 3 hours; a 5- to 10-pound piece 12 to 24 hours, usually overnight. Marinating 12 hours or more cuts the cooking time significantly. Sprinkling salt over the food before placing it in the marinade ensures that the food will be seasoned evenly. If the food needs to be browned, drain and pat dry after marinating—wet food will not brown properly.

Allow about ¹⁄₂ cup of marinade for every pound of food. Vinaigrettes, 572–575, and some glazes, 582–583, also make delicious marinades.

MARINADES FOR VEGETABLES

Marinated vegetables are usually served cold as hors d'oeuvres or salads. Suitable for the short-term marinating of vegetables are:

> **Vinaigrette, 572–575, seasoned with herbs**
> **Ravigote Sauce, 553**

See also **Vegetables à la Grecque, 246.**

LEMON MARINADE

¹⁄₄ cup

For lamb, poultry, or stronger fish.

Combine:

> **2 to 3 tablespoons fresh lemon juice**
> **1 small garlic clove, finely minced**
> **¹⁄₂ teaspoon grated lemon zest**
> **¹⁄₂ teaspoon turmeric**
> **¹⁄₂ teaspoon ground ginger**

RED WINE MARINADE

Generous 2 cups

A cooked marinade, excellent for red meat.

Combine in a medium saucepan and simmer over low heat for 2 minutes:

> **2 cups dry red wine**
> **1 small red onion, thinly sliced**
> **2 garlic cloves, finely minced**
> **3 sprigs parsley**
> **2 sprigs thyme**
> **6 whole black peppercorns, cracked**
> **1 small bay leaf**
> **2 whole cloves**

Remove from the heat and season to taste with:

> **Salt**

Cool before using. The marinade will keep, covered and refrigerated, for up to 1 week.

TANDOORI MARINADE

1¹⁄₃ cups

In Indian cooking, chicken and lamb are marinated in an aromatic mixture of yogurt and spices before they are cooked in a tandoor, a fiercely hot vertical charcoal-fired oven. The acidity in the yogurt tenderizes the exterior of the meat and can actually overtenderize if left for more than 4 hours. The marinade is traditionally tinted with a

natural dye, which gives to tandoori chicken its characteristic orange-yellow color.
Heat in a small skillet over medium heat:

> 2 to 3 tablespoons vegetable oil

Add and cook, stirring, until fragrant, about 2 minutes:

> 1 teaspoon ground coriander
> 1 teaspoon ground cumin
> 1 teaspoon ground red pepper
> 1 teaspoon Garam Masala, 987, or $^1/_4$ teaspoon ground cinnamon
> $^1/_2$ teaspoon turmeric

Transfer to a small bowl and let cool completely.
Whisk together thoroughly in a small bowl:

> 1 cup plain yogurt
> 2 teaspoons finely minced garlic
> 2 teaspoons finely minced peeled fresh ginger
> $^1/_2$ teaspoon salt
> (1$^1/_2$ teaspoons red food coloring)

Stir in the cooled spices and use immediately.

BALKAN MARINADE

$^3/_4$ cup

For lamb or pork. Do not let the meat marinate for longer than 2 hours.
Crush together in a bowl:

> 1 tablespoon dried oregano
> 1 tablespoon dried rosemary
> 1 teaspoon salt
> 1 teaspoon black pepper

Whisk in:

> Grated zest of 2 lemons
> Juice of 2 lemons
> 2 to 4 garlic cloves, minced
> $^1/_4$ cup olive oil
> (1 tablespoon balsamic vinegar)
> (1 teaspoon dried thyme)
> (3 to 4 drops hot red pepper sauce)

The marinade will keep, covered and refrigerated, for up to 1 week.

YOGURT OR BUTTERMILK MARINADE

2 cups

Excellent for any meat, poultry, or game.
Combine:

> 2 cups plain yogurt or buttermilk
> 2 garlic cloves, finely minced

Season to taste with:

> Curry powder or ground cinnamon, ginger, or cardamom
> Salt and black pepper

COOKED MARINADE FOR GAME

8 cups

Use for venison, mutton, or hare.
Heat in a large skillet over medium-high heat:

> 1$^1/_2$ cups vegetable oil

Add and cook, stirring, until the onions are golden:

> 1 cup chopped celery
> 1 cup chopped carrots
> 1 cup chopped onions

Add:

> 3 cups red wine vinegar or cider vinegar
> 2 cups water
> $^1/_2$ cup coarsely chopped parsley
> 3 bay leaves
> 1 tablespoon dried thyme
> 1 tablespoon dried basil
> 1 tablespoon whole cloves
> 1 tablespoon whole allspice berries
> A pinch of ground mace
> 1 tablespoon crushed black peppercorns
> 6 garlic cloves, crushed

Bring to a boil, then reduce the heat and simmer for 1 hour. Strain and cool. The marinade will keep, covered and refrigerated, for up to 1 week.

BEER MARINADE

1$^2/_3$ cups

For beef or pork.
Combine:

> 1$^1/_2$ cups flat beer
> 1 tablespoon dry mustard
> 1 teaspoon ground ginger
> $^1/_2$ teaspoon salt
> 3 tablespoons soy sauce
> $^1/_8$ teaspoon hot pepper sauce
> 2 tablespoons sugar or honey
> $^1/_4$ cup orange marmalade
> 2 garlic cloves, minced

BECKER CHICKEN MARINADE

1 cup

Whisk together in a bowl until well blended:

> $^1/_4$ cup red wine vinegar
> $^1/_4$ cup red wine
> $^1/_4$ cup olive oil
> 2 tablespoons balsamic vinegar
> 2 tablespoons chopped thyme
> 1 tablespoon chopped rosemary
> 2 teaspoons salt
> 2 teaspoons soy sauce
> 2 teaspoons black pepper
> 4 to 6 garlic cloves, minced
> Juice of $^1/_2$ lemon
> Grated zest of 1 lemon
> 3 dashes hot pepper sauce

BECKER PORK MARINADE

1$^3/_4$ cups

Whisk together in a bowl until well blended:

> $^1/_2$ cup soy sauce
> $^1/_4$ cup red wine

1/4 cup olive oil
3 to 4 tablespoons hot pepper sauce
2 tablespoons sherry vinegar
2 teaspoons minced peeled fresh ginger
2 teaspoons black pepper
4 to 6 garlic cloves, minced
Grated zest of 1 lemon
Juice of 1/2 lemon

TERIYAKI MARINADE

Scant 2 cups

For meat, poultry, or firm-fleshed fish. Marinate 2 to 4 hours (no more than 2 for fish), and baste with the marinade during cooking.
Combine:

1 cup soy sauce
1/2 cup vegetable oil
3 tablespoons brown sugar
3 garlic cloves, smashed
1 tablespoon grated peeled fresh ginger
2 tablespoons sherry

ABOUT BARBECUE SAUCES AND MOPS

Barbecue sauces are made with a variety of ingredients. Whether based on catsup, mustard, or vinegar, they add distinction and style to the food being cooked. Several regions of the United States boast their own style; mustard or vinegar-based sauces predominate in the Carolinas and Virginia. Memphis and Kansas City sauces are tomato-based with varying levels of sweetness and spiciness. And Texas sauces may incorporate local ingredients such as ground chile peppers.

Barbecue sauce is typically a finishing touch added near the end of cooking, applied as a glaze. Consider the oven, grill, or broiler temperature, the sweetness of the sauce, and the size of what you are cooking to determine when to add the sauce. When cooking at high temperatures, either under the broiler or on the grill, apply the sauce during the last 15 minutes of cooking. Like any condiment, the sauce should complement rather than obscure the smoky flavor of the meat. Be sure to serve extra sauce at the table.

Many cooks like to baste the meat with a tangy, very flavorful liquid, called a "mop" or mopping sauce, to keep the meat moist while it is cooking. Most mops are made with vinegar, and can be as simple as the Basic Mop, 587, or can have some of the vinegar replaced by beer, wine, or lemon juice. Other common flavorings include whiskey, vegetable oil, herbs, or garlic. ➤ Mops should be brushed on grilling food once it is cooked on the outside.

BARBECUE SAUCE

4 cups

Combine in a medium saucepan and bring to a simmer over medium heat, stirring often:

1 1/2 cups catsup
1 cup cider vinegar or red wine vinegar

1/4 cup Worcestershire sauce
1/4 cup soy sauce
1 cup packed light or dark brown sugar
2 tablespoons dry mustard
1/4 cup chili powder, or to taste
1 tablespoon grated peeled fresh ginger or
    1 teaspoon ground ginger
2 garlic cloves, minced
2 tablespoons vegetable oil
3 lemon slices

Simmer, stirring often, for 5 minutes. Remove the lemon slices, if desired. The sauce will keep, covered and refrigerated, for up to 2 weeks.

RAY'S MUSTARD BARBECUE SAUCE

3 cups

Our friend Chuck Martin's Uncle Ray Smith concocts this classic central South Carolina sauce. Delicious with fried chicken, as a basting sauce for ribs, or with pulled pork.
Combine in a medium saucepan and bring to a slow simmer over medium-low heat:

1 1/2 cups prepared yellow mustard
1/2 cup catsup
1/2 cup cider vinegar
1/2 cup vegetable oil
1/4 cup grated onion
1/4 cup honey
4 garlic cloves, minced
Juice of 1 lime
2 tablespoons Worcestershire sauce
1 1/2 tablespoons black pepper

Simmer, stirring often to prevent sticking, about 15 minutes. The sauce will keep, covered and refrigerated, for about 1 month.

BARBECUE SAUCE FOR POULTRY

2 1/2 cups

Enough for 2 whole chickens, with enough left over to pass at the table. Make sure that the extra sauce has not come into contact with raw poultry.
Heat in a medium saucepan over medium-low heat:

3 tablespoons vegetable oil

Add and cook, stirring, until golden:

1 medium onion, chopped
1 garlic clove, minced

Add and bring to a simmer:

1 cup catsup
1 cup water
3 tablespoons soy sauce or Worcestershire sauce
2 tablespoons cider vinegar or red wine vinegar
1 red bell pepper, chopped
1/2 cup diced celery
2 to 4 tablespoons brown sugar
1 teaspoon prepared mustard
1/2 teaspoon salt

Simmer gently, stirring occasionally, for 30 minutes. Puree the sauce in a food processor or blender, then add:

> 1/4 cup fresh lemon juice

NORTH CAROLINA-STYLE BARBECUE SAUCE

1 1/2 cups

Mix in a bowl:

> 3/4 cup distilled white vinegar
> 3/4 cup cider vinegar
> 1 tablespoon hot pepper sauce, or more to taste
> 1 tablespoon sugar
> 2 teaspoons crushed red pepper flakes
> Salt and black pepper to taste

WESTERN NORTH CAROLINA BARBECUE SAUCE

3 cups

Prepare **North Carolina-Style Barbecue Sauce, above,** decrease sugar to 1 tablespoon, and add **3/4 cup catsup** or **tomato juice.** Mix and store as directed.

BASIC MOP

2 cups

For 4 to 5 pounds of pork ribs or 2 whole chickens. Whisk together in a bowl until the salt dissolves:

> 2 cups distilled white vinegar
> 1 tablespoon coarse salt
> 1 teaspoon black pepper, or to taste
> 1 teaspoon crushed red pepper flakes, or to taste

Stir in:

> 1 small onion, thinly sliced
> 1 jalapeño pepper, thinly sliced

Use the same day.

BEER MOP

8 cups

For a 5- to 6-pound brisket.

Combine in a saucepan and bring to a simmer:

> 1 large red onion, chopped
> 4 garlic cloves, chopped
> 2 serrano chiles, chopped
> Six 12-ounce bottles dark beer
> 1 cup cider vinegar
> 1/2 cup packed dark brown sugar
> 2 bay leaves
> Salt and black pepper to taste

Simmer for 15 minutes. Remove from heat, remove the bay leaves, and cool before using.

ABOUT DRY RUBS AND PASTES

A dry rub is a compatible blend of herbs and/or spices that is rubbed on food before grilling, sautéing, or roasting. ➤ For the most intense flavor, you can grind the ingredients, as directed, by hand with a mortar and pestle, or with a spice mill or coffee grinder. When a dry rub is moistened with oil or ground fresh ginger or garlic, it becomes a paste, which clings nicely to the food. Pastes are best ground in a blender or food processor.

To use a dry rub or paste, simply rub the mixture over the entire surface of the food, using enough pressure to make sure that an even layer adheres. Naturally a mild mixture can be applied more thickly than one that is spicy or hot. (Wash your hands well after rubbing, as some spices can irritate the skin.)

Although a rub or paste smeared on just before cooking still adds flavor, it's best when applied to the food up to 24 hours before cooking so the flavors will be more than skin-deep. Turn the food several times as it sits, and leave the seasoning in place for cooking. (Some seasonings produce a handsome dark finish and some create a tasty crunchy crust, especially during grilling or sautéing.) You can keep any unused pastes refrigerated for up to a week in tightly covered small jars, but ➤ discard any that have come into contact with raw poultry, fish, or meat. Unused rubs will keep at room temperature, tightly sealed for 6 weeks. Most pastes will keep, covered and refrigerated, up to 1 week.

PEPPERY DRY RUB

1 3/4 cups

Fantastic on steak and other red meats.

Stir together well in a small bowl:

> 1 cup coarsely cracked black peppercorns
> 2 tablespoons coarsely cracked white peppercorns
> 1 tablespoon ground coriander
> 1 to 2 tablespoons crushed red pepper flakes
> 2 tablespoons packed brown sugar
> 1/4 cup salt

CAJUN DRY RUB

1/4 cup

This mix, best known as "blackening spice," can be rubbed on chicken, fatty fish, steaks, or vegetables before blackening, 1049, broiling, grilling, or sautéing in a cast-iron pan. It will transform into a tangy, deeply caramelized crust as the food cooks. Expect the spices to smoke some during cooking.

Mix together:

> 1 teaspoon dried thyme
> 1 teaspoon dried oregano or marjoram
> 1 tablespoon paprika
> 1 teaspoon ground red pepper
> 1 teaspoon coarsely cracked black or white peppercorns
> 1 teaspoon coarse salt

SOUTHERN BARBECUE DRY RUB

2 cups

Southern barbecue chefs rub spice mixtures like this one onto pork or beef before starting the long, slow cooking that will transform it into barbecue.

Stir together well:

¼ cup packed brown sugar
½ cup sweet or hot paprika
¼ cup chili powder
2 tablespoons ground red pepper
2 tablespoons ground cumin
1 teaspoon ground mace
¼ cup salt
¼ cup cracked black peppercorns

COFFEE SPICE RUB

Generous 1 cup
Delicious on steak.
Mix well:

¼ cup ancho chile powder
¼ cup finely ground espresso-roast coffee beans
2 tablespoons sweet paprika
2 tablespoons dark brown sugar
1 tablespoon dry mustard
1 tablespoon salt
1 tablespoon black pepper
1 tablespoon dried oregano
1 tablespoon ground coriander
2 teaspoons ground ginger
2 teaspoons chile de árbol or other pure ground chile pepper powder

TOASTED WHOLE SPICE RUB

About 2 cups
This rub is delicious with duck, game hen, and pork.
Combine in a large dry skillet and toast over medium heat, shaking the pan often to prevent burning, until fragrant, 2 to 3 minutes:

2 cinnamon sticks
8 cardamom pods
½ cup coriander seeds
¼ cup white peppercorns
¼ cup cumin seeds
1 tablespoon whole cloves
1 tablespoon whole allspice berries
2 small dried red chile peppers
4 whole star anise

Remove from the heat and let cool to room temperature, then grind to a fine powder in a spice mill or coffee grinder or a blender, or with a mortar and pestle.

SWEET SPICE RUB

1¼ cups
This makes enough spice mixture for several uses. Rub on chicken, beef, lamb, or pork as well as salmon and bluefish.
Mix well:

¼ cup sweet paprika
¼ cup packed brown sugar
¼ cup ground cumin
¼ cup black pepper
¼ cup coarse salt

BEEF BRISKET RUB

½ cup
For a 5- to 6-pound brisket.
Combine:

¼ cup ancho chile powder or other pure ground chile pepper
2 tablespoons sweet paprika
1 tablespoon ground cumin
1 tablespoon dry mustard
1 tablespoon salt
2 teaspoons ground red pepper

WEST INDIES DRY RUB

1¾ cups
This rub goes well on poultry, pork, lamb, or beef.
Combine in a small dry skillet over medium heat and toast, shaking the pan often to prevent burning, until fragrant, 2 to 3 minutes:

¼ cup cumin seeds
¼ cup coriander seeds

Remove from the heat. Let cool, then grind to a fine powder in a spice mill or coffee grinder or a blender, or with a mortar and pestle. Transfer to a small bowl and add:

¼ cup curry powder
¼ cup white pepper
¼ cup ground ginger
¼ cup salt
2 tablespoons ground allspice
2 tablespoons ground red pepper

JAMAICAN JERK PASTE

1¼ cups
The cornerstone of all jerk dishes is the vinegary, intensely hot paste of dried herbs and habanero or Scotch bonnet peppers. If you cannot find either of these peppers, a habanero-based hot sauce makes a good substitute. This is traditional with pork or chicken.
Combine in a food processor or blender and puree:

⅓ cup fresh lime juice
10 habanero or Scotch bonnet peppers or
    ¼ cup habanero-based hot sauce
2 tablespoons distilled white vinegar
(2 tablespoons fresh orange juice)
3 scallions, coarsely chopped
2 tablespoons dried basil
2 tablespoons dried thyme
2 tablespoons yellow mustard seeds or
    1 tablespoon dry mustard
2 teaspoons ground allspice
1 teaspoon ground cloves
1 teaspoon salt
1 teaspoon black pepper

The mixture should have the consistency of thick tomato sauce. If necessary, thin with additional:

(Lime juice, vinegar, or orange juice)

MEDITERRANEAN GARLIC HERB PASTE
1¹/₂ cups

This is wonderful on grilled and roasted vegetables, fish, lamb, and beef.

Combine in a blender or food processor and coarsely puree, leaving the mixture a little chunky:

> 2 cups mixed fresh herb leaves (parsley, sage, rosemary, thyme, basil, and/or oregano)
> 10 garlic cloves
> 1 tablespoon crushed red pepper flakes
> ¹/₄ cup coarsley cracked black peppercorns
> 2 tablespoons salt
> ¹/₂ cup olive oil

MUSTARD PASTE
²/₃ cup

This is equally delicious on roasted lamb, beef, rabbit, and chicken, and it gives the meat a gilded finish.

Stir together well in a small bowl:

> ¹/₂ cup Dijon or brown mustard
> 2 tablespoons dry white wine
> (1 garlic clove, minced)
> 1 tablespoon minced fresh herbs or 1 teaspoon dried (use rosemary for lamb, thyme for beef, or tarragon for chicken or rabbit)
> 1 teaspoon minced peeled fresh ginger or ¹/₄ teaspoon ground ginger

Use immediately.

CHILE-GARLIC SPICE PASTE
2 cups

This paste is good with poultry, firm-textured fish, shrimp, and vegetables.

Combine in a blender or food processor until smooth:

> ³/₄ cup minced jalapeño peppers
> ¹/₂ cup garlic cloves
> ¹/₂ cup olive oil
> 2 tablespoons grated lemon or lime zest
> 2 tablespoons cracked black peppercorns
> 1 tablespoon salt
> 2 tablespoons chili powder

ASIAN GINGER SPICE PASTE
2¹/₃ cups

This fragrant herb paste suits poultry and game birds, full-flavored fish, pork, beef, and roasted vegetables.

Combine in a blender or food processor and coarsely puree, leaving the mixture a little chunky:

> ¹/₂ cup minced peeled fresh ginger
> ¹/₃ cup toasted sesame oil
> 1 tablespoon crushed red pepper flakes
> ¹/₄ cup chopped cilantro
> ¹/₄ cup chopped mint
> ¹/₄ cup chopped fresh basil
> 2 tablespoons salt
> 2 tablespoons cracked white peppercorns

THAI GREEN CURRY PASTE
1 cup

This fragrant, spicy paste is excellent on meats and seafood, or stir it into soups, pasta, rice, and other grain dishes.

Combine in a small dry skillet over medium heat and toast, shaking the pan often to prevent burning, 2 to 3 minutes:

> 2 teaspoons coriander seeds
> 1 teaspoon cumin seeds
> 1 teaspoon fennel seeds
> 1 teaspoon whole black peppercorns

Remove from the heat and let cool to room temperature, then grind to a fine powder in a spice mill or coffee grinder or a blender, or with a mortar and pestle. Transfer to a small bowl. Combine in a blender or food processor and process until finely chopped, about 4 minutes:

> ¹/₃ cup tightly packed cilantro leaves
> Two ¹/₄-inch slices peeled galangal or ginger
> 1 stalk lemongrass, bottom third only, chopped
> 12 serrano peppers or 6 jalapeño peppers, seeded and chopped
> 2 large shallots, chopped
> 4 garlic cloves, chopped
> Grated zest of 1 lime
> (1 teaspoon shrimp paste)
> 1¹/₂ teaspoons salt
> 1 teaspoon grated or ground nutmeg

Add the spices. With the machine running, slowly pour in:

> ¹/₄ cup peanut oil

RED CURRY PASTE

Prepare:

> **Thai Green Curry Paste, above**

Substitute **fresh or reconstituted, 292, dried red chiles** for the green chiles.

MOROCCAN HERB PASTE (CHARMOULA)
1¹/₂ cups

Charmoula is used to flavor fish before or after grilling, roasting, or baking. Its consistency is between that of a paste and a marinade.

Stir together well in a small bowl:

> ¹/₃ cup finely chopped parsley
> ¹/₃ cup finely chopped cilantro
> 2 tablespoons olive oil
> 2 tablespoons fresh lemon juice
> 2 garlic cloves, finely chopped

Grind to a fine powder in a spice mill or coffee grinder or a blender, or with a mortar and pestle:

> 1 teaspoon coriander seeds
> 1 teaspoon cumin seeds
> 12 white or black peppercorns
> 1 teaspoon crushed red pepper flakes
> (Generous pinch of saffron threads, toasted and crumbled)

Add to the herb mixture, along with:

1 medium onion, finely chopped
1 teaspoon hot or sweet paprika
Salt and ground red pepper to taste

Stir together well, then drizzle over the top:

Olive oil

ABOUT FLAVORED OILS

Oils infused with the flavors of herbs, spices, or fruits are a refreshing alternative to butter and other fats. Flavored oils are simple to make and add depth of flavor as well as moisture and a sensual touch to finished dishes. They are not for cooking, but for seasoning, just as you would drizzle olive oil over cooked vegetables, noodles, or pastas. The purest and easiest technique is a cold infusion—such as Orange Oil, below.

Allow $1/2$ to 3 tablespoons per serving. Flavored oils must always be refrigerated, and most will hold their quality for at least 1 week. Prepare only as much as you will use in that time. For optimum flavor, bring the amount of oil you will be serving to room temperature. ➤ Any leftover warmed oil that has been prepared with fresh (that is, not dried) ingredients must be discarded.

ORANGE OIL
About 1 cup

Use in vinaigrettes or drizzle over poached shellfish or grilled fish, chicken, or vegetables just before serving. Or stir into hot tomato soup. You may substitute lemon, lime, grapefruit, or a combination of zests for the orange zest.

You can use these proportions to make an infused oil with any fresh ingredients, unless they are unusually bland or strong. You may have to experiment with amounts, or infuse for a shorter time; do not leave fresh ingredients in oil for more than 4 days. Combine in a sterilized, 890, 8- to 10-ounce jar:

Grated zest of 3 oranges (about $1/4$ cup)
1 cup mild olive, walnut, peanut, or other mild oil

Cover and shake the jar gently, then let steep in the refrigerator for up to 4 days. Strain the oil through a dampened paper coffee filter (paper towels can taste of chemicals). The oil can be kept, covered and refrigerated, for up to 1 week, no longer.

BASIL OIL
$3/4$ cup

Measure and place in refrigerator:

1 cup mild olive oil

Bring a pot of water to boil. Have ready a bowl of ice water. Blanch for 10 seconds in the boiling water:

2 cups tightly packed sweet basil leaves

Remove them quickly with a strainer and dunk in the ice water, swishing them around to be sure they're all cold. Remove from the water and squeeze gently to remove the excess water. Roughly chop the basil and put it in a blender. Add the refrigerated oil and:

$1/4$ teaspoon kosher salt

Blend until the basil is pureed. The mixture will be very frothy. Let the puree settle for about 30 minutes. Strain through a fine mesh strainer lined with cheesecloth, very gently pushing down on the solids to extract the oil. For the best flavor, let the oil come to room temperature before using. Use immediately or refrigerate for up to 1 week.

CHILE OIL
Scant $1/2$ cup

Exceedingly hot—use sparingly. A few drops are superb in dipping sauces for dumplings or in dressings for Asian vegetable dishes.

Coarsely chop in a blender or spice grinder:

1 cup dried chile peppers, preferably Thai

Transfer to a stainless steel saucepan and add:

$3/4$ cup peanut oil

Heat over medium heat until large bubbles appear. Remove from the heat, cover, and let sit for 4 to 6 hours. Strain the oil through a dampened paper coffee filter into a sterilized, 890, jar or bottle. This will keep, covered and refrigerated, for up to 1 week.

BREADS AND COFFEE CAKES

The importance of bread was probably realized in tandem with the delight of it. Bread is one of our oldest foods, and perhaps the most fundamental. Transforming flour and water into bread is not only something like shaking hands with our history, but it's also, as every baker discovers, a return to real flavor, a fulfilling joy.

Begin, if you like, with whole wheat and go on from there to more cunning triumphs. Try a sourdough rye, 605, or a long crusty French loaf, 601, or a hearty country bread, 606. Or fashion thin, brittle Italian bread sticks, 620, feather-light brioches, 614, buttery Danishes, or a braided Christmas coffee cake, 622, kneading bread by hand or with the help of an electric mixer and a dough hook, 592. And do not forget quick breads such as biscuits, corn bread, and scones. The delicious flavors and textures of homemade breads always repay the effort it takes to make them.

ABOUT YEAST BREAD

If you have never made yeast bread before, behold one of the great dramas of the kitchen. Do not be intimidated by the process. All breads are made from just a handful of simple ingredients: **Yeast,** 1028, the rising agent, is generally sold today as **active dry** granules, sold in packets or jars. (For **fresh,** or **"compressed," yeast,** and **instant** or **quick-rising yeast** which require slightly different handling, see 1029.) Yeast is a living organism. As it feeds on the flour in the dough and multiplies, it releases carbon dioxide. It is this gas that causes the dough to rise. ➤ The process is virtually fail-proof, as long as one simple rule is observed: The yeast must not be exposed to too much heat. If it is, it will die, and the bread will not rise at all. In

most recipes, the yeast is dissolved in water or milk warmed to 105° to 115°F, sometimes with a pinch of sugar to activate the yeast. ➤ At this temperature, the liquid will feel warm but not hot. If in doubt, gauge the temperature with a thermometer—or simply use liquid warmed only to tepid. ➤ The yeast will not be harmed by the cooler temperature; it will just take a bit longer to work. Also, when yeast, either active dry or quick-rising, 1029, is mixed directly into the dry ingredients without first being dissolved, as in Fast White Bread, 597, liquids up to 130°F, the temperature of hot tap water, can be used to bind the dough.

Flour is the main ingredient of bread. In most recipes, the flour used is either all-purpose flour or bread flour. They are ideal for bread because they're rich in two proteins that, when combined with liquid and stirred or kneaded, produce gluten, an elastic web that traps the gas released by the yeast. Gluten gives structure to the bread, and gives bread its texture. **Bread flour** has an especially high protein content and is therefore preferred in the making of hearty breads such as Rustic French Bread, 603. **All-purpose flour,** which has slightly less protein than bread flour, will produce satisfactory results in all recipes and is better for some rolls and breads that are more delicate in texture. (Individual recipes will indicate which flour is better.) **Whole wheat flour** is usually used in combination with all-purpose or bread flour, to keep the loaf from being too heavy; see Whole Wheat Breads, 599. Delicious breads may be made with other flours or grains, such as **rye, oats, cornmeal,** or **rice flour.** For differences in flours, see 982. Some flours that have little or no gluten-producing capabilities are usually used in combination with all-purpose or bread flour.

Water and **milk** are the typical liquids used to bind the flour into a dough and to create steam when the bread is baked. Water tends to produce a chewy bread, milk a more tender and cakelike one. Most breads made with milk, such as White Bread, 596, can be made with water instead. The resulting loaf will be chewier. Do not, however, substitute water for milk in rolls, holiday breads, or coffee cakes, or the breads will be coarse and tough. For the effects of soft and hard water in baking, see 1026.

Many recipes call for shortening, oil, or butter. Even a small amount of **fat** makes bread more tender, by "shortening" the gluten strands created. A large amount makes bread so tender and close-grained that it has nearly the texture of cake. And, of course, some fats, particularly butter, add delicious flavor.

When a large amount of butter is used in a bread dough—whether a sponge dough or a conventional one, as for Brioche, 614—the point at which the butter is added is critical. When butter and flour are added to a dough at the same time, the butter coats the flour and inhibits its capacity to absorb moisture. This, in turn, inhibits the formation of gluten and results in a crumbly, cakelike texture. In a few breads, such as Stollen, 622, this is desirable. Generally speaking, however, a chewy texture is desired. In that case, the basic dough—yeast, liquid, flour, and so on—must be mixed and kneaded and the butter kneaded into this dough at the end. Kneading butter into a stretchy dough can be messy—unless, of course, the task is dispatched with a mixer fitted with a dough hook.

Eggs, like fat, promote tenderness in bread. Eggs also make breads light and puffy, which is one of the reasons that they are often used in rich breads, like challah, 600, which otherwise would tend to be dense. Fat and, to a lesser extent, eggs inhibit the action of yeast, and thus buttery, egg-rich doughs are slow to rise.

Finally, **salt** and **sugar** are added for flavor. Salt is a yeast inhibitor, but it is never added to bread in quantities large enough for that to be an issue. In small quantities, sugar is a yeast promoter, but in larger quantities (over $1/3$ cup per pound, or approximately 4 cups of flour), sugar slows yeast down. If more than $1/2$ cup sugar is used, the dough will hardly rise at all unless special procedures are followed. This is why even the sweetest breads are never as sweet as cake. There are quite a few other ingredients, too, that can bring bread depth and variety. For some adlibbing with nuts and raisins, herbs, and sprouts, see Additions to Yeast Doughs, 596.

MIXING BREAD DOUGH

To prepare the yeast, dissolve active dry yeast in liquid between 105° and 115°F and let stand 3 to 5 minutes. (If using compressed fresh yeast, dissolve it in liquid at 85°F and let stand, without stirring, 8 to 10 minutes.) ➤ A small quantity of sugar helps activate the yeast, ➤ but do not use more than called for. Formerly, milk was always scalded to kill bacteria. Now, with pasteurization, this operation is no longer necessary. However, warming the milk does help dissolve the sugar and melt the fat.

Batters are the simplest of all doughs, requiring little handling. Strong beating, with a heavy-duty electric mixer or by hand, develops the gluten content of the dough and takes the place of kneading. When the batter comes away from the sides of the bowl, the dough has been beaten enough. Batter breads are more porous and dry out faster than the kneaded type. For mixing directions, see Crumpets, 619.

The **conventional** or **straight** dough method, as given for White Bread, 596, is still our favorite for texture, storage qualities, and appearance. Also, and incidentally, we find the kneading a healthy outlet for frustrations. Use a good-sized bowl, and start by stirring some of the flour into the combined lukewarm liquid, shortening, and dissolved yeast mixture. Gradually mix in half the required flour and beat about 1 minute. Then, as you add the rest of the flour, lay aside the spoon and mix by hand. When the dough begins to leave the sides of the bowl, turn it out onto a lightly floured board or pastry cloth. ➤ To flour a board lightly and evenly, allow about 1 tablespoon flour for each cup of flour in the recipe—less for a very light

dough. A damp towel placed under the board will keep it from slipping. Turn the dough several times to make it easier to handle. ➤ Cover the dough with a clean cloth and let it rest 10 to 15 minutes before kneading.

With the **mixer method,** using a heavy-duty electric mixer, you can shorten preparation time by blending the active dry yeast at the very outset with part of the flour and other dry ingredients, as outlined for Fast White Bread, 597. Mixer breads are also quick to rise because very warm liquid is used, which speeds the rise. Combine part of the flour, the yeast, sugar, and salt in the mixer bowl and blend briefly at low speed. Add the liquids, heated to 120° to 130°F, and softened or melted fat and beat as indicated in the recipe. If eggs are called for, add them at this time with an additional cup of flour, beating them in as indicated in the recipe. Gradually add enough flour to make a soft dough. Then, if kneading by hand, turn the dough out and let rest, as above. Otherwise, knead with a dough hook until the dough is smooth and elastic, about 10 minutes. A stand mixer with a sturdy motor is needed for these breads; a hand-held mixer is not powerful enough.

KNEADING YEAST DOUGH

Generally speaking, doughs vary in moisture content and only experience can tell you exactly how much flour to add during the kneading process. Hence, some variations in amounts are indicated in the individual recipes. Kneading makes dough smooth and elastic by developing the gluten, an elastic cellular web formed when flour is combined with liquid. Yeast causes the dough to ferment, which produces carbon dioxide; this gas gets trapped as bubbles in the gluten strands, and the dough rises. Kneading may be done mechanically, as described below, but because the process is sensual and relaxing, many prefer to knead by hand. Even the sensualists, however, may find that kneading by machine is preferable for certain very wet or sticky doughs, such as rye dough.

Kneading may be done on a countertop or on a pastry or bread board. ➤ A damp towel placed under the board will keep it from slipping. You may want to grease your fingertips to prevent sticking. As the gluten develops in the flour through continued strong, rhythmic kneading, the dough becomes smooth and elastic. When the dough is first turned out on the work surface, it will be slightly sticky, 593. The first kneading, of about 10 minutes, must be thorough, but not heavy or rough.

Overkneading and long, slow risings will result in a coarse-textured bread. Fold the dough over toward you, then press it away from you with the floured heel of your hand, as shown; give it a quarter turn, fold it, and press away again. More flour may be necessary, on your hands and the board, to overcome stickiness. In the beginning of the process, to keep your hands from sticking, grasp the dough lightly and do not press too hard. ➤ Initially very soft doughs, like Brioche, 614, are not really kneaded but

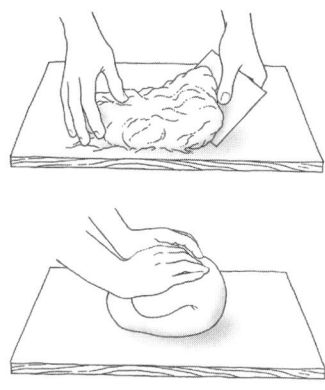

Kneading yeast dough

more peeled off the work surface and folded over onto themselves, shown above. Using a pastry scraper will help with these soft doughs.

Repeat the kneading process until the dough becomes smooth, elastic, and satiny. Air blisters will appear just under the surface coating, or "cloak." The dough at this point should no longer stick to the work surface or your hands. ➤ To test, slowly and gently stretch a small piece of dough, turning it in a circular motion as you pull so that it stretches evenly. The dough should hold together without tearing until it forms a sheer membrane, thin enough to let light come through. (Alternately, you may test the temperature of the dough with an instant-read thermometer; the center of the dough should register 77° to 80°F.)

A heavy-duty or stand (at least 300-watt) electric mixer equipped with a **dough hook** significantly reduces the time and physical labor involved in mixing and kneading doughs. ➤ Bear in mind that the motor can burn out if the dough is too tough (this is usually caused by an inadequate amount of liquid) or if too much dough is mixed at once. Refer to the manufacturer's instructions for guidance.

The dough can be mixed and kneaded from start to finish using the dough hook, but some bakers find it quicker to dispatch the initial mixing of dough with the paddle attachment and then to change to the hook when the dough reaches a firmer consistency. ➤ A large batch of dough may require a little kneading by hand to become truly smooth. Never walk away and leave a mixer unattended. It may "walk" off the countertop, or the dough may climb up the hook and gum up the gears. Either water or flour can be added during mixing to achieve the proper consistency. As a general rule, the correct amount of flour has been added when the dough cleans the sides of the bowl.

Some **food processors** are not strong enough to mix and knead bread dough, and many processors that *do* have the strength do not have the capacity to handle doughs made with more than 3 or 4 cups of flour. Be sure to check the manufacturer's instructions. Those instructions also tell you which blade to use.

To mix dough in a food processor, combine the lesser amount of flour called for in the recipe, the remaining dry ingredients, and the fat (softened in the case of butter) in the work bowl and process until well mixed, about 20 seconds. Dissolve the yeast in the warm liquid (105° to 115°F) and then combine it with the remaining liquids and any eggs, at refrigerator temperature (about 40°F; ➤ the food processor tends to overheat doughs, which is why cold ingredients are used.) With the machine running, add the liquid ingredients through the feed tube. Process until the dough cleans the sides of the bowl, 45 to 60 seconds, stopping the machine once or twice and adding a little flour if the dough seems sticky. ➤ *Do not process for longer than 60 seconds in all, or the gluten may begin to break down.* ➤ If, for some reason, the dough appears to require more kneading after 60 seconds, finish it by hand.

You may also process the yeast with the flour, without first dissolving it, and then proceed as above. This technique works best with quick-rise yeast.

PROOFING YEAST DOUGH

When the dough has been kneaded, grease a large clean bowl evenly, put the dough into it, and turn the dough over ➤ so that the entire surface is lightly greased. Cover the bowl with plastic wrap or a clean cloth. Set the dough to rise, or **proof.**

Generally speaking, yeast dough should rise in a draft-free place at a temperature of about 75° to 85°F. If the room is cold, you can place the dough in the bowl on a

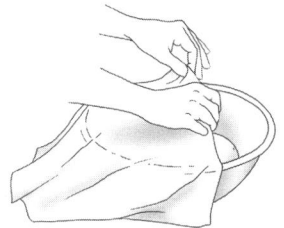

Covering the dough to rise, testing for properly risen dough, punching down the dough

rack ➤ over a pan of warm water; near, but not on, a radiator; or in an oven heated for less than 1 minute, until you can just feel warmth, and then turned off—a quite ideal rising cabinet. ➤ Be sure to remove the bread before preheating the oven to bake it.

The first time the dough rises it should be allowed to double in bulk, or a bit more, if the loaf is to have a moist crumb, which generally takes 1 to 2 hours. ➤ Never allow a dough to rise so much that it begins to deflate, as this may result in a bread that is coarse and dry. To make sure the dough has risen sufficiently, press it firmly with your fingertips. When it has doubled in bulk, ➤ the imprint of your fingertips will remain in the dough, 593.

Now punch down the dough with your fist, as illustrated on 593. Fold the edges of the dough to the center, and turn the dough bottom (smooth side) up in the bowl. Now you are ready for the second kneading, if one is indicated in the recipe. Its purpose is to give a finer grain. It lasts only a few minutes and may be done in the bowl. Then let the dough rise again, covered, until it has ➤ almost, but not quite, doubled in bulk.

▲ At high altitudes, use active dry or compressed fresh yeast for bread recipes in this book. ➤ unless specifically called for, avoid instant or rapid-rise yeast. It is fine for quick-rise sea-level baking, but is less successful at altitude because reduced air pressure encourages rapid yeast expansion; quick-rising yeast can make bread rise too fast, sacrificing flavor and texture.

▲ Yeast bread dough rises more rapidly above 3,000 feet and may become overproofed it is not watched carefully. To remedy this, you can reduce the quantity of yeast slightly and/or punch down your dough more often, giving it at least 3 rises. Or, let it rise in a warm place twice, then once overnight in the refrigerator; finally, bring to room temperature to shape for the last rise. Above 3,500 feet, preventing overproofing by allowing dough to rise until not quite double in volume for the first 2 or 3 rises and then only about one-third (not double) its volume for the final rise before baking. For other high-altitude hints, see page 746.

SHAPING YEAST DOUGHS

Yeast breads divide into two basic types: those baked in a pan, like White Bread, 596, and those baked free-form, like French Bread, 601. Each type requires a different shaping procedure. (Rolls are shaped variously according to type; consult individual recipes.)

Punch down the dough for a final time, and if necessary, divide it into the number of pieces called for in the recipe. Shape the portions lightly into mounds. Place them on a lightly floured work surface, cover with a clean cloth as shown below, and allow to rest 10 minutes.

For a pan-baked bread, get your pan(s) ready. Different types of bread pans promote distinctive crusts; to choose an appropriate pan, see About Bread Crusts, 595. Unless the recipe indicates otherwise, the pan(s) should be greased.

Begin to form the loaf by throwing down onto the board one of the pieces of dough which has been resting. You may use a rolling pin or your palm to press it evenly. Start with a circle and fold the two opposite sides toward the center to make a rectangle before shaping the loaf. You may prefer to treat yours instead like a thick scroll, as shown, using the heel of your hand to press it together as you complete the roll. Then, with your hands at either end of the roll, compress the ends and seal the loaf as shown below on the left, folding under any excess as you slide the dough, seam side down, into the greased pan. ➤ It is important that the finished dough contact the short ends of the pan so they support the dough as it rises.

Cover the pan with a clean cloth. The dough will eventually fill in the corners of the pan. While it is rising—to almost, but not quite, double in volume—preheat the oven. When ready to bake, the loaf will be symmetrical and ➤ a slight impression will remain when you press the loaf lightly with your fingertips, as shown. Do not permit a loaf to overrise, or an air space may form beneath the top crust. To bake, see specific directions in the recipes; for pan placement in the oven, see 1063.

Some loaves are not baked in a pan. These loaves, such as Rustic Sourdough, 604, are not supported by the sides of a pan, therefore they must be formed especially tight if the loaf is to hold its shape. Thus the shaping of free-form loaves is something of an art and the knack comes with practice. Do not be too critical of your results. Even professional bakers with years of experience find that their free-form loaves always sprawl a bit.

Divide the dough into the number of pieces as directed by the recipe. On a lightly floured work surface, shape the pieces into mounds. Cover with a clean cloth and let rest for 15 minutes. Prepare a baking sheet or sheets, as indicated in the recipe.

Covering the dough to rest, forming the loaf, and shaping pan-baked bread

To form a round loaf, place the dough on a lightly floured work surface. Holding your hands and fingers straight, as though to make a karate chop, wedge your hands at a 45-degree angle just beneath the loaf on either side, with the sides of your hands resting on the work surface. ➤ You are now, in effect, holding the loaf in a V. Exert pressure on the lower portion of the loaf so that a small portion of dough is tucked underneath the loaf and the surface of the loaf tightens. Rotate the loaf a quarter turn and repeat. Keep pressing and rotating until the loaf is round and the surface becomes smooth and taut. This will take 3 to 5 minutes, depending on the size of the loaf and your efficiency in shaping. Let the loaf rest for about 10 minutes, loosely covered with a clean cloth, and then ➤ give it a few more turns to tighten the loaf. Transfer to a baking sheet.

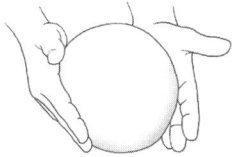

Forming a round loaf

SCORING LOAVES

Most round and long loaves are **scored,** or cut across the top, before baking. Scoring is both to aid rising and for decoration. If bread is baked without scoring, the pressure of the expanding dough may tear the crust in an irregular pattern—or, worse, the dough may be trapped by the crust and rise very little. Slashes may be made with a *lame* (a tool used by professional bakers), a single-edged razor blade, or a very sharp knife. Always hold the slashing tool at a 45-degree angle—never straight up and down—and cut about 1/2 inch into the dough.

For round loaves, you may make a single crescent-shaped cut about two-thirds of the way around the top of the loaf. Or you may make a crisscross pattern by making about 6 slashes, 1 inch apart, across the top of the loaf and then 6 more slashes perpendicular to or diagonal to these. Mark baguettes with 6 crosswise slashes or with 3 lengthwise diagonal slashes, two running from the ends of the loaf almost to the center and the third running down the middle of the loaf between the other two. ➤ Regardless of the loaf or slash pattern, never cut into the

sides or the ends of the loaf, or you will release the surface tension and the loaf will not hold its shape.

ABOUT BREAD CRUSTS

People have passions for different kinds of crust. ➤ The pan you choose will affect the crust. A standard aluminum bread pan, either bare metal or nonstick, will promote a thin, golden crust. Glass, dark-finished aluminum, ceramic, and enamel pans will all produce a thick, dark crust. ➤ Remember that glass and enamel pans require a lower temperature; see 1067.

Milk, either used in the dough or brushed on toward the end of the baking period, gives a good all-over brown color. Cream or butter may also be brushed on about 5 to 10 minutes before the end of baking for color. For a glazed crust, you may brush the top toward the end of baking with French Egg Wash, 799. To keep the crust soft, brush the crust with butter after the bread is baked and out of the pan, then cover it with a damp clean cloth.

For a hard, crunchy crust, mimic the steam injectors used in professional ovens. ➤ Preheat a baking pan on the bottom rack of the oven.

As soon as you put the bread in the oven, pour 2 cups of hot water or ice cubes into the heated pan. ➤ Brushing breads when partially baked with salted water will also harden crusts. Allow 1 teaspoon salt to 1/2 cup water.

If you are really determined to have a crusty loaf, you may want to invest in a baking stone and/or plain quarry tiles, which provide an intense heat necessary to crust formation. Place the baking stone or tiles on the middle oven rack. ➤ For an even better effect, you can also lean unglazed tiles around the sides of the oven. Baking stones and tiles take a long time to get hot, so ➤ preheat the oven and the tiles for at least 45 minutes before baking. Make the bottom crust of a free-form loaf especially thick and crisp by baking it directly on a stone or tiles. Give the loaf its final rise on a rimless baking sheet or baker's peel, 191, liberally dusted with cornmeal, then carefully slide the loaf directly onto the stone or tiles.

TESTING BREADS FOR DONENESS

To test for doneness, note if the loaf has shrunk from the sides of the pan. Or test by removing the loaf and tapping the bottom with your finger; if the loaf makes a hollow sound, it is done. Or test with an instant-read thermometer inserted into the center; it should read 195°F or above. If necessary, return the loaf to the oven, in or out of the pan, for a few minutes until it is finished.

Exceptions to these rules are especially dense, moist breads, such as country breads made with starters, such as All–Rye-Flour Bread, 605, and Sourdough Rye Bread, 605. These breads must be baked to an internal temperature of 200° to 210°F. And even when they have reached this temperature, look done (hard golden brown or darker crust), and sound hollow when tapped, these breads still

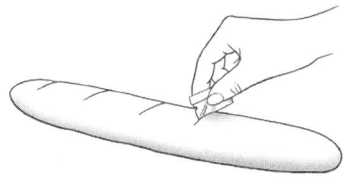

Scoring a baguette

need more time in the oven in order to evaporate moisture. Otherwise, the crust will soften and lose its crackle as it cools. ➤ Turn the oven off and let the loaves remain in the oven for 10 minutes. This cool-down technique will dry the bread without overbaking or burning it.

▲ At 5,000 feet and above, some breads, such as basic white, benefit from raising the baking temperature about 25 degrees above that at sea level; baking times at altitude may stay the same as sea level or take slightly longer. At 10,000 feet, the rise is enhanced if you preheat the oven 25 to 50 degrees above the baking temperature, then reduce the heat at least 25 degrees (or to temperature in recipe) when bread is put in the oven.

COOLING AND STORING BREAD

When the bread has finished baking, remove it at once from the pan and place it on its side on a wire rack. ➤ Let the bread cool completely before wrapping, storing, or freezing. There should be no warmth radiating from the loaf. If it is wrapped while still warm, condensation may encourage mold. ➤ Do not cut into a loaf until it has been out of the oven for at least 20 minutes, and wait an hour if possible (less for rolls and small breads). Bread always tastes best after it has cooled to an internal temperature of 85°F or less. Most breads stored in a bread box, a ventilated drawer, or a loosely closed paper bag will remain fresh for 3 to 5 days. (Bread boxes and drawers should be periodically wiped with a mild baking soda or bleach solution to kill mold spores.) Bread stored in a plastic bag or wrapped in plastic wrap will remain fresh somewhat longer, though the crust will soften. ➤ Never refrigerate bread—refrigeration dries bread out. If you need to store bread for a prolonged period, freeze well-wrapped loaves for up to 3 months. ➤ Once thawed, frozen bread goes stale very quickly, so do not thaw more than you can consume within a day or so.

ADDITIONS TO YEAST DOUGHS

Raisins, dates, dried fruits, candied citron, nuts, hulled sesame or roasted hulled sunflower seeds, briefly sautéed onions, dried or fresh herbs, bean or grain sprouts, toasted wheat germ, milk solids, and brewer's yeast—ingredients often called "improvers"—are added to yeast doughs for flavor and increased nutritional values. Improvers are seldom used in greater quantity than up to about one-quarter of the weight of the flour called for in the recipe. ➤ Some of the flour called for may be used to dust the fruits to keep them from sticking together. Before adding any of the above improvers, thoroughly mix the first addition of wheat flour to develop the gluten.

Any bread in which wheat flour is lacking will be deficient in the elasticity that the gluten of wheat provides. Therefore, when replacing wheat flour with other flours or grains in any of our recipes, please observe the following guidelines: ➤ When substituting buckwheat, barley, cornmeal, millet meal, white or brown rice flour, leftover

cooked grains, or any combination of these, use wheat flour for at least half of the flour called for in the recipe. ➤ If substituting bran or soy flour, use wheat flour for at least three-quarters of the flour called for. ➤ Coarse grains like rolled oats, grits, or bran must be pulverized in a blender or coffee/spice grinder before being added to bread, and whole grains and cracked grains must be cooked first. ➤ When adding cooked grains, decrease the liquid called for in the recipe by one-third to one-half.

Recipes for the allergy-prone, omitting wheat and using all rye or rice, can be found in the USDA Home and Garden Bulletin No. 147, "Baking for People with Food Allergies."

CORNELL TRIPLE-RICH FLOUR FORMULA

The work of Dr. Clive McCay at Cornell University in the 1930s did much to raise the standard of nutrition for large segments of the world's population. He discovered that the addition of certain ingredients in their natural forms to enriched unbleached bread flours significantly increases their nutritive value. Use this formula in your favorite bread, cookie, muffin, or cake recipe.

When you measure, first put in the bottom of each cup of flour called for:

1 tablespoon soy flour
1 tablespoon dry milk powder
1 teaspoon wheat germ

Then fill the cup with flour as called for in the recipe.

WHITE BREAD

Two 9 x 5-inch loaves
This perfect white bread has appeared in every JOY edition since 1931. It is an even-grained all-purpose bread that stales slowly and cuts well for sandwiches.

Combine in a small saucepan and heat until warm (105° to 115°F):

1 cup milk
2 tablespoons sugar
1 tablespoon vegetable shortening or lard
1 tablespoon butter
1 tablespoon salt

Combine in a large bowl and let stand until the yeast is dissolved, about 5 minutes:

$^{1}/_{4}$ cup warm (105° to 115°F) water
1 package (2$^{1}/_{4}$ teaspoons) active dry yeast

Have ready:

5 to 6 cups all-purpose or bread flour

Add the lukewarm milk mixture to the dissolved yeast. Stir in 3 cups of the flour and beat 1 minute, then stir or work in 2 more cups flour. Toss the dough onto a floured board and knead until it is smooth, elastic, and full of bubbles, gradually adding more flour until the dough no longer sticks to your hands. Place the dough in a greased bowl, turn the dough over once, and cover with a cloth. Let rise in a warm place (75° to 85°F) until doubled in bulk, at least 1 hour.

Punch down the dough and, if time permits, allow it to rise until doubled once more, then punch it down again. Divide the dough in half, shape into 2 loaves, and place in greased 9 x 5-inch loaf pans. Brush with oil, then cover with a clean cloth and let rise again until almost doubled in bulk. Preheat the oven to 450°F. To achieve the kind of crust you like, see 595. Bake the bread 10 minutes. Reduce the heat to 350°F and bake about 30 minutes longer. Bake until the crust is golden brown and the bottom sounds hollow when tapped, 595. Remove the loaves at once from the pans and cool completely on a rack.

FAST WHITE BREAD

One 9 x 5-inch loaf
A quick and easy yeast bread designed to work with quick-rise yeast; regular active dry yeast works too.
Stir together in a large bowl or the bowl of a heavy-duty mixer:

2 cups bread flour
1 tablespoon sugar
1 package (2^1/$_4$ teaspoons) active dry or quick-rise yeast
1^1/$_2$ teaspoons salt

Add:

1 cup very warm (115° to 125°F) water
2 tablespoons butter or margarine, melted or softened

Mix by hand or on low speed for 1 minute. Add ^{1}/$_4$ cup at a time until the dough is moist but not sticky:

1 to 1^1/$_4$ cups bread flour

Knead for about 10 minutes by hand or with the dough hook on low to medium speed, until the dough is smooth and elastic. Transfer the dough to an oiled bowl and turn it over to coat with oil. Cover the bowl loosely with plastic wrap and let rise in a warm place (75° to 85°F) until doubled in bulk, 40 to 45 minutes. Grease a 9 x 5-inch loaf pan. Punch down the dough, form it into a loaf, and place seam side down in the pan. Oil the surface and cover loosely with a clean cloth. Let rise in a warm place until doubled in bulk, 20 to 45 minutes. Preheat the oven to 450°F. Bake the loaf for 10 minutes. Reduce the heat to 350°F and bake about 30 minutes more. Bake until the crust is golden brown and the bottom sounds hollow when tapped, 595. Remove the loaf from the pan to a rack and let cool completely.

MILK BREAD

One 9 x 5-inch loaf
The milk, egg, and butter give this bread a delicate rich flavor, tender crumb, and soft golden brown crust. The dough is also easily shaped into rolls.
Combine in a large bowl or the bowl of a heavy-duty mixer and let stand until the yeast is dissolved, about 5 minutes:

3 tablespoons warm (105° to 115°F) water
1 package (2^1/$_4$ teaspoons) active dry yeast

Add:

1 cup warm (105° to 115°F) milk
5 tablespoons butter or margarine, melted
3 tablespoons sugar
1 large egg
1 teaspoon salt

Mix by hand or on low speed for 1 minute. Gradually stir in:

2 cups all-purpose or bread flour

Gradually add until the dough is moist but not sticky:

1^1/$_2$ to 2 cups all-purpose or bread flour

Knead for about 10 minutes by hand or with the dough hook on low to medium speed until the dough is smooth and elastic. Transfer the dough to an oiled bowl and turn it once to coat with oil. Cover loosely with plastic wrap or a clean cloth and let rise in a warm place (75° to 85°F) until doubled in bulk, about 1 hour.
Grease a 9 x 5-inch loaf pan. Form the dough into a loaf and place seam side down in the pan. Brush the surface of the dough with oil, cover loosely with plastic wrap, and let rise in a warm place until doubled in bulk, 1 to 1^1/$_2$ hours. Preheat the oven to 375°F. Brush the top of the loaf with:

Melted butter or milk

Bake until the crust is deep golden brown and the bottom of the loaf sounds hollow when tapped, 595, 35 to 45 minutes. Remove the loaf from the pan to a rack to let cool completely.

CINNAMON RAISIN BREAD

One 9 x 5-inch loaf
Prepare:

Dough for Milk Bread, above

Let rise once. While the dough is rising, place in a small saucepan with enough cold water to cover by ^{1}/$_2$ inch:

^{1}/$_2$ to 1 cup raisins

Bring to a boil, then drain well and let cool. Stir together:

^{1}/$_4$ cup sugar
1 tablespoon ground cinnamon

Grease a 9 x 5-inch loaf pan. Punch down the dough. Using a rolling pin, roll the dough into an 8 x 18-inch rectangle about ^{1}/$_2$ inch thick. Brush the surface of the dough with:

1^1/$_2$ teaspoons butter, melted

Sprinkle all but 2 teaspoons of the cinnamon sugar over the dough, then spread the raisins evenly over the surface. Starting from one 8-inch side, roll up the dough tightly, like a jelly roll. Pinch the seam and ends closed. Place seam side down in the pan. Cover loosely with oiled plastic wrap and let rise in a warm place until doubled in bulk, 1 to 1^1/$_2$ hours. Preheat the oven to 375°F.
Whisk together and brush over the top of the loaf:

1 egg
Pinch of salt

Sprinkle the top of the dough with the remaining cinnamon sugar. Bake until the crust is deep golden brown and the bottom of the loaf sounds hollow when tapped, 595, 40 to 45 minutes. Remove the loaf from the pan to a rack. While the bread is still hot, brush the top with:

2 teaspoons butter, melted

Let cool completely.

CHEESE BREAD

Two 9 x 5-inch loaves

For variation, add a sprinkling of minced fresh or dried herbs, such as thyme or marjoram, with the cheese. You may also add chopped onions or garlic or minced scallions, pimientos, or green olives when you roll up the loaves. For a pleasant variation, use whole wheat flour for half of the white and 2 tablespoons honey instead of the sugar.

Heat until warm (105° to 115°F):

1$^1/_2$ cups milk

Add to it and stir until the butter mostly melts:

$^1/_3$ cup sugar

$^1/_4$ cup ($^1/_2$ stick) butter, softened

1 tablespoon salt

Remove from the heat. Combine in a large bowl and let stand until the yeast is dissolved, about 5 minutes:

$^1/_2$ cup warm (105° to 115°F) water

2 packages (1$^1/_2$ tablespoons) active dry yeast

Stir in the milk mixture. Add and beat until smooth:

1 large egg

1$^1/_2$ cups shredded sharp Cheddar (6 ounces)

Beat in well:

3 cups all-purpose flour

Add and continue beating and stirring until the dough begins to leave the sides of the bowl:

2 to 3 cups all-purpose flour

Knead the dough about 10 minutes. Transfer the bread to an oiled bowl and turn it to coat with oil. Cover loosely with plastic wrap and let rise in a warm place (75° to 85°F) until doubled, about 1 hour. Grease two 9 x 5-inch loaf pans. Punch down the dough, divide it in half, and shape into 2 loaves. Place in the loaf pans and let rise again until nearly doubled, about 1 hour.

Preheat the oven to 375°F. Brush the loaves, if desired with:

(Melted butter)

Bake about 30 minutes. Bake until the crust is golden brown and the bottom sounds hollow when tapped, 595. Remove from the pans to a rack to cool completely.

HERB BREAD

If fresh herbs are available, mince them and triple the amounts suggested for the dry herbs given below.

Prepare:

Milk Bread, 597, or Whole Wheat Bread, 599

For each loaf, add to the dough before kneading:

1 teaspoon celery seeds

1 teaspoon caraway seeds

1 teaspoon dried dill or dill seeds

or:

$^1/_2$ teaspoon dried marjoram or basil

$^1/_4$ teaspoon dried thyme

1 tablespoon chopped parsley

($^1/_2$ teaspoon dried oregano)

or:

$^1/_4$ teaspoon ground ginger

1 teaspoon dried thyme

1 teaspoon dried savory, crumbled

1 teaspoon dried rosemary, crumbled

or:

1 teaspoon grated or ground nutmeg or ground cloves

1 teaspoon dried rosemary, crumbled

1 teaspoon dried dill

1 tablespoon chopped sage

DILL BATTER LOAF

One 9 x 5-inch loaf

This is an updated version of the Dill Batter Loaf that has been a longtime JOY favorite. Fresh dill can now be found year-round in most supermarkets and is much preferable to dried dill or dill seeds.

Combine in a small bowl and let stand until the yeast is dissolved, about 5 minutes:

$^1/_2$ cup warm (105° to 115°F) water

1 package (2$^1/_4$ teaspoons) active dry yeast

Combine in a large bowl or the bowl of a heavy-duty mixer:

3 cups bread flour

$^1/_2$ cup finely chopped onions

3 tablespoons chopped fresh dill, or 1 tablespoon dried dill or dill seeds

2 tablespoons sugar or honey

(1 tablespoon wheat germ, toasted)

1 teaspoon salt

Add the yeast along with:

1 cup large-curd cottage cheese

1 large egg

Mix by hand or on low speed until the dough comes together, adding additional flour or warm water if needed. Knead for about 10 minutes by hand or with the dough hook on low to medium speed until the dough is smooth and elastic. Transfer to an oiled bowl and turn it once to coat with oil. Cover loosely with plastic wrap and let rise in a warm place (75° to 85°F) until doubled in bulk, 1 to 1$^1/_2$ hours.

Grease a 9 x 5-inch loaf pan. Punch down the dough, form into a loaf, and place seam side down in the pan. Cover with oiled plastic wrap and let rise in a warm place until doubled in bulk, about 1 hour.

Meanwhile, preheat the oven to 350°F. If desired, brush the top of the loaf with:

1 egg, lightly beaten, or 1 tablespoon melted unsalted butter

Sprinkle lightly with:

$^1/_2$ teaspoon coarse salt or a few dill seeds

Bake until the crust is deep golden brown and the bottom

of the loaf sounds hollow when tapped, 595, 35 to 40 minutes. Remove the loaf from the pan to a rack and let cool completely.

WHOLE WHEAT BREAD

Three 9 x 5-inch loaves

Feather-lightness is, of course, by no means a prime objective in making whole wheat and other whole-grain breads, yet such loaves should have substance without being dense. Whole wheat bread is made the same way as white bread but with whole wheat flour substituted for some of the white flour. Bakers tend to disagree about the ideal proportions of whole wheat flour to white; we favor one part whole wheat to two parts white. Any of the white bread recipes on pages 591–597 can be adapted for whole wheat bread.

Please read About Whole Wheat Flour, 985.

Combine in a large bowl, and let stand until the yeast is dissolved, about 5 minutes:

$^{1}/_{4}$ **cup warm (105° to 115°F) water**
1 package (2$^{1}/_{4}$ teaspoons) active dry yeast

Add, and mix well:

1 large egg, beaten
$^{1}/_{4}$ **cup ($^{1}/_{2}$ stick) butter, melted**
2$^{1}/_{2}$ cups lukewarm (85°F) water
1$^{1}/_{2}$ teaspoons salt
$^{1}/_{4}$ **to $^{1}/_{2}$ cup sugar, honey, or maple syrup**

Add:

4 cups whole wheat flour
4 cups all-purpose flour

To knead, proof, and shape, follow the instructions on 592–595, allowing the dough to rise in a large oiled bowl until doubled, about 1 hour, and once in 2 greased 9 x 5-inch loaf pans until doubled, about 45 minutes.

Preheat the oven to 350°F.

Bake about 45 minutes. Bake until the crust is golden brown and the bottom sounds hollow when tapped, 595. Remove the loaves to a rack to cool completely.

SPROUTED WHOLE WHEAT BREAD

Prepare **Whole Wheat Bread, above,** using **2 packages (1$^{1}/_{2}$ tablespoons) yeast.** Mix with the 2 cups warm water before adding **2 cups ground sprouted wheat, soybeans, lentils, wheat berries, or chickpeas, 1010.**

WHOLE WHEAT SANDWICH BREAD

Two 9 x 5-inch loaves

Prepare **White Bread, 596,** substituting **2 cups whole wheat flour** for 2 cups of the white flour and using **2 packages (4$^{1}/_{2}$ teaspoons) active dry yeast.**

SUGAR-FREE WHOLE WHEAT BREAD

Two 9 x 5-inch loaves

Prepare **White Bread, 596,** omitting the sugar and substituting **2 cups whole wheat flour** for 2 cups of the white flour.

FAST WHOLE WHEAT BREAD

One 9 x 5-inch loaf

Prepare **Fast White Bread, 596,** substituting **1 cup whole wheat flour** for 1 cup of the bread flour.

ALL–WHOLE-WHEAT BREAD COCKAIGNE

Two 8$^{1}/_{2}$ x 4$^{1}/_{2}$-inch loaves

A heavier, coarser bread.

Combine in a large bowl and let stand until the yeast is dissolved, about 5 minutes:

$^{1}/_{4}$ **cup warm (105° to 115°F) water**
1 package (2$^{1}/_{4}$ teaspoons) active dry yeast
1 tablespoon brown sugar

Combine:

6 cups whole wheat flour
$^{1}/_{2}$ **cup dry milk powder**

Combine:

2 cups warm (105° to 115°F) water or milk
1 tablespoon salt
1 to 3 tablespoons melted butter or bacon fat
4 to 6 tablespoons molasses or honey

Stir into the yeast mixture. Gradually mix in the flour. Knead briefly, adding flour if necessary. Allow the dough to rise, covered, once in a large oiled bowl until doubled, about 1$^{1}/_{2}$ hours, and once in 2 greased 8$^{1}/_{2}$ x 4$^{1}/_{2}$-loaf pans, about 1 hour.

Preheat the oven to 350°F. Bake about 45 minutes. Bake until the crust is golden brown and the bottom sounds hollow when tapped, 595. Remove to a rack to cool completely.

CRACKED-WHEAT BREAD

Two 9 x 5-inch loaves

If your cracked wheat is a coarse grind, put it in the blender to get a finer grind. Try making this good bread with cooked grains other than cracked wheat.

Cook:

1 cup finely ground cracked wheat

in:

3 cups boiling water

for 10 minutes or until the moisture is absorbed. Remove from heat and stir in:

$^{3}/_{4}$ **cup milk**
3 tablespoons sugar or honey
2 tablespoons butter or vegetable shortening
1 tablespoon molasses
1 tablespoon salt

Let cool. Meanwhile combine in a large bowl and let stand until the yeast is dissolved, about 5 minutes:

$^{1}/_{4}$ **cup warm (105° to 115°F) water**
2 packages (1$^{1}/_{2}$ tablespoons) active dry yeast

Stir in the cooked cereal mixture, then gradually beat in:

4 cups all-purpose flour
2 cups whole wheat flour

Turn the dough out onto a floured board and knead about 10 minutes. Place in an oiled bowl, cover, and let rise in a warm place (75° to 85°F) until doubled in volume, about 1 hour.

Punch down the dough, knead a few times, and divide in half. Place in 2 greased 9 x 5-inch loaf pans and let rise, covered, until again doubled in volume, about 45 minutes. Preheat the oven to 350°F.

Bake about 35 to 40 minutes. Remove the loaves to a rack to cool completely.

OAT BREAD COCKAIGNE

Two 9 x 5-inch loaves

Heat to 105° to 115°F:

  2 cups milk

Place in a large bowl:

  1 cup old-fashioned rolled oats

Pour the milk over, and add:

  ¹/₂ cup packed brown sugar
  ¹/₄ cup vegetable oil
  2 teaspoons salt
  (¹/₂ teaspoon ground ginger)

Cool to lukewarm. Meanwhile, combine in a small bowl and let stand until the yeast is dissolved, about 5 minutes:

  ¹/₄ cup warm (105° to 115°F) water
  2 packages (1¹/₂ tablespoons) active dry yeast

Add the yeast mixture to the oats, then stir in:

  1 or 2 large eggs, lightly beaten
  ¹/₄ to ¹/₂ cup wheat germ
  1 cup soy flour
  2 cups whole wheat or rye flour

Gradually stir in:

  3 to 4 cups all-purpose flour

To knead, 592, and proof, 593, allow the dough to rise once in a large oiled bowl until doubled, about 1¹/₄ hours, and once in 2 greased 9 x 5-inch loaf pans until doubled, about 50 minutes.

Preheat the oven to 350°F. Bake about 1 hour. Bake until the crust is golden brown and the bottom sounds hollow when tapped, 595. Remove the loaves to a rack to cool completely.

BUTTERMILK POTATO BREAD

Two 9 x 5-inch loaves

This dough can also be used to make rolls.

Prepare:

  ³/₄ cup freshly cooked potatoes—riced through a
  potato ricer or mashed with a fork and still warm

Place the still-warm potatoes in a large bowl or in the bowl of a heavy-duty mixer and stir in:

  ¹/₂ cup (1 stick) unsalted butter, very soft

Add and mix well:

  2 cups room-temperature (72° to 75°F) buttermilk
  2 packages (1¹/₂ tablespoons) active dry yeast
  2 large eggs, lightly beaten
  2 tablespoons sugar
  2¹/₂ teaspoons salt

Gradually stir in until the dough is moist but not sticky:

  6¹/₄ to 6¹/₂ cups bread flour

When the dough comes together, knead for 10 to 12 minutes by hand or with the dough hook on low to medium speed until the dough is smooth, soft, and elastic. Transfer the dough to an oiled bowl and turn it once to coat with oil. Cover with plastic wrap and let rise at room temperature (72° to 75°F) until doubled in volume, 1 to 1¹/₂ hours. Grease two 9 x 5-inch loaf pans. Punch down the dough, divide it in half, and form into 2 loaves. Place seam side down in the pans. Cover with oiled plastic wrap and let rise until nearly doubled in volume, about 1 hour.

Preheat the oven to 375°F. Brush the top of the loaves with:

  1 egg, lightly beaten with a pinch of salt

If desired, sprinkle with:

  (1 tablespoon poppy seeds)

Bake the loaves until the crust is golden brown and the bottoms sound hollow when tapped, 595, 40 to 45 minutes. Remove to a rack and let cool for at least 30 minutes before serving.

CHALLAH

1 braided loaf

This traditional Jewish Sabbath egg bread is similar to Brioche, 614. It is particularly good at breakfast.

Combine in a large bowl or the bowl of a heavy-duty mixer and let stand until the yeast is dissolved, about 5 minutes:

  ¹/₂ cup warm (105° to 115°F) water
  1 package (2¹/₄ teaspoons) active dry yeast

Add:

  ¹/₂ cup bread flour
  2 large eggs, lightly beaten
  2 large yolks, lightly beaten
  3 tablespoons vegetable oil
  3 tablespoons sugar
  1¹/₄ teaspoons salt

Mix by hand or on low speed until thoroughly blended. Gradually stir in:

  2¹/₂ cups bread flour

Knead for about 8 minutes by hand or with the dough hook on low to medium speed until the dough is smooth and elastic and no longer sticks to your hands or the bowl. Transfer the dough to an oiled bowl and turn it once to coat with oil. Cover with plastic wrap or a clean cloth and let rise in a warm place (75° to 85°F) until doubled in bulk, 1 to 1¹/₂ hours.

Punch down the dough, knead briefly, and return to the bowl. Refrigerate, covered, until it has nearly doubled in volume (a three-quarter rise is sufficient), 2 to 12 hours. The dough is now ready to be shaped.

Divide the dough into 3 pieces. On an unfloured work surface, roll into balls. Let rest, loosely covered with plastic wrap, for 10 minutes.

Grease a baking sheet and sprinkle it with:

  Cornmeal

Roll each ball into a 13- to 14-inch-long rope, about 1¹/₂ inches thick and slightly tapered at the ends. Dust the

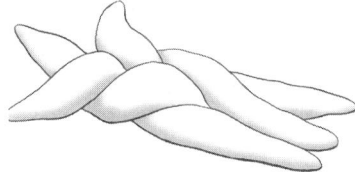 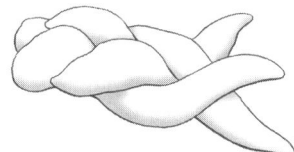 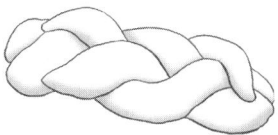

Braiding three-strand challah

3 ropes with flour, so they will be more distinctly separated when baked. Place the ropes side by side and pinch the top ends together. Braid the entire length of dough strands until you reach the other ends. Tuck both ends of the braid underneath the loaf and set it on the baking sheet.

Whisk together and brush over the top of the loaf:

> **1 egg**
> **Pinch of salt**

(Reserve the egg wash.) Loosely cover the braid with lightly oiled plastic wrap and let rise in a warm place until not quite doubled, about 45 minutes.

Preheat the oven to 375°F. Brush the loaf again with egg wash. If desired, sprinkle with:

> **(1 tablespoon poppy or sesame seeds)**

Bake until the crust is golden brown and the bottom of the loaf sounds hollow when tapped, 595, 30 to 35 minutes. Let cool completely on a rack.

FRENCH BREAD

2 baguettes

French cookbooks ignore French bread, and the French leave the making of this characteristic loaf to the commercial baker. Why? Because the baker alone has the traditional wood-fired stone hearth with its evenly reflected heat that is necessary to produce the genuine article. We regard French bread as uniquely delicious.

Combine:

> **4 cups all-purpose flour**
> **2 teaspoons salt**
> **1 package (2¹/₄ teaspoons) active dry yeast**

Make a well in the center of these ingredients. Pour in:

> **1¹/₂ cups water, at room temperature**

Stir thoroughly, by hand or in a heavy-duty mixer, until dough is soft and elastic, about 12 minutes on low speed. Cover dough with a clean cloth, or put in an oiled bowl, turn it once to coat with oil, and cover with plastic wrap. Let rise in a warm place (75° to 85°F) until doubled in bulk, about 2 hours. Punch down the dough. To make the traditional baguette shape for French bread, divide in half on a floured board and pat into 2 equal rectangles. Form each into a baguette by rolling the dough away from you, as shown below. Continue rolling, pressing outward with your hands and tapering the dough toward the ends until you have a long, thin loaf. Place the loaves on a greased baking sheet. ➤ If you are setting more than one loaf on a baking sheet, bear in mind that the loaves will double in

size, so leave plenty of space—at the least the size of a whole loaf—in between. Cover the loaf (or loaves) with a floured clean cloth. You can give the loaf additional support by encircling it with a lightly greased 1-inch band of aluminum foil. Remove the foil after the bread has risen halfway. Let rise in a warm place until somewhat less than doubled. Score, 595, the tops of the loaves.

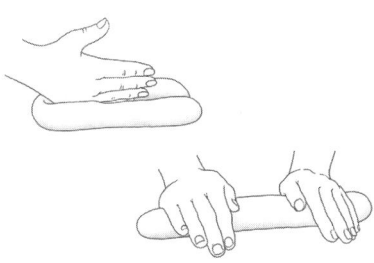

Forming a baguette

Preheat the oven to 400°F.

In the bottom of the oven, preheat a baking pan. Fill with 1 cup hot water; it should steam. Bake the bread on the oven's center rack for 15 minutes, then reduce the heat to 350°F and bake about 30 minutes longer. Bake until the crust is golden brown and the bottom sounds hollow when tapped, 595. Five minutes or so before the bread is finished, brush the loaves with:

> **1 egg white, beaten with 1 tablespoon cold water**

Let cool completely on a rack.

ABOUT SPONGE AND MIXED STARTERS

A **starter** is a fermented batter or dough that is used in place of yeast to make bread rise. The linchpin of all starters is long, slow fermentation, which encourages certain biological processes that give flavor both to the starter and to the bread. There are three basic types: **sponge** and **mixed starters,** and **sourdough starters.**

Breads like Stollen, 622, and Panettone, 621, which are made with large amounts of butter, egg, and/or sugar, are often started with a **sponge.** To mix the sponge, combine the dissolved yeast, liquid, and a portion of the flour called for in the recipe into a light batter. When the batter has fermented—it sometimes takes as long as 1 hour—it will have become foamy and spongy. Because the sponge is warm, wet, and free of inhibitors such as fat and salt, it provides an ideal growth medium for the yeast. Add the remaining flour and other ingredients to the sponge in the order indicated in the recipe.

SPONGE STARTER

1 cup

Sponge starters, called *poolishes* in France and *bigas* in Italy, are the quickest to make. Any starter can be made into a sponge starter simply by increasing the proportion of water. This recipe is for a sponge starter made with commercial yeast and requires only 6 hours fermentation. You can ripen the starter even more quickly by letting it rise in a warm place, but we recommend slow rising at room temperature for more flavor. Other than the straight dough method, this is the quickest way to make bread and will result in loaves with some of the rustic qualities—including crustiness and a hearty crumb—that make starter-raised breads so inviting.

Some bakers make sponge starters by combining all of the liquid called for in a bread recipe with one-quarter of the flour. The other ingredients are then combined with the sponge after the sponge has risen.

Combine in a medium bowl and let stand until the yeast is dissolved, about 5 minutes:

$\frac{1}{2}$ **cup lukewarm (100°F) water**
$\frac{1}{2}$ **teaspoon active dry yeast**

Add:

$\frac{3}{4}$ **cup bread flour**

Stir rapidly with a wooden spoon until you notice elastic strands pulling away from the sides of the bowl, about 2 minutes. Cover the bowl tightly with plastic wrap and let rise at room temperature, about 70°F, until bubbly and tripled in volume, about 6 hours. Or let the starter rise for about 14 hours in the refrigerator. (If making bread with a sponge that has just come out of the refrigerator, use warm water (105° to 115°F) for making the dough.) When the starter has tripled in volume and begins to collapse slightly, it must be used immediately to make bread.

MIXED STARTER

2 cups

A mixed starter is made from a piece of raw dough saved from a previous batch of bread that is mixed with more flour and water and allowed to rise again. Mixed starters tend toward sourness, though they are not as sour as sourdough starters and are sometimes not sour at all. (This branch of bread baking is not an exact science.) Any kind of bread can be made with a starter instead of yeast. However, starters are used today primarily in so-called country or hearth-style breads—crusty, free-form loaves made only with flour, water, yeast, and salt—because the essential characteristic of these breads is their deep, rich flavor. ➤ Once the starter has tripled in volume and begun to collapse slightly, it must be used immediately to make bread

or be fed with $\frac{3}{4}$ cup flour and $\frac{1}{2}$ cup water to keep the yeast from starving and the starter from weakening. When you are ready to bake, knead the leftover dough with flour and water, let it rise, and work this starter into your bread dough. When this dough has risen—just before you shape it into loaves—pinch off a 6-ounce piece of dough and reserve it for the next time. More and more flavor will develop in your breads as you keep repeating the process.

If making this starter for the first time, include an additional $\frac{1}{3}$ cup water and $\frac{2}{3}$ cup flour in your first batch of bread to compensate for the piece of dough you are going to remove before baking. If you continue to use leftover bread dough for making your breads, you will notice that the bread dough takes longer and longer to rise. This is because after several generations, the yeast weakens. While this slow fermenting will improve the flavor of your bread, there comes a point where the rising simply takes too long. At this point, dissolve $\frac{1}{8}$ teaspoon yeast in 1 teaspoon warm water and add this to your mixed starter before setting it aside to rise.

Remove from a fully risen batch of bread dough and reserve tightly wrapped for a day or two in the refrigerator (or in the freezer for up to 3 months):

$\frac{3}{4}$ **cup (after deflating; 6 ounces) dough**

When ready to make bread, bring the reserved dough to room temperature if it has been frozen. Place it in a large bowl or the bowl of a heavy-duty mixer and add:

$\frac{2}{3}$ **cup warm (105° to 115°F) water**
1$\frac{1}{2}$ **cups bread flour**

Mix by hand or on medium speed for 2 minutes. Knead by hand for 7 to 10 minutes or with the dough hook on medium speed for 3 minutes. Transfer the dough to an oiled bowl and turn it once to coat. Cover tightly with plastic wrap and let rise in a warm place (75° to 80°F) for 4 to 6 hours, until slightly more than doubled in volume or refrigerate for 8 to 12 hours, bringing it to room temperature before using. The starter is now ready to use in a bread recipe or can be refrigerated overnight before using.

SOURDOUGH STARTERS

This term brings to mind at once the hardbitten pioneer whose sharing of the bread "starter" was a true act of friendship. Of course, the best European breads and many other famous doughs, such as San Francisco sourdough, are also based on flour and water mixtures fermented in various ways to trap natural yeast. In kitchens where yeast baking has been going on for centuries, these organisms are plentiful in the air, and success is assured. But in an uninitiated streamlined kitchen, we recommend beginning a sourdough with yeast, especially in winter. Made with flour, liquid, and a commercial or wild yeast, it ferments in as little as 8 to 12 hours or as long as 5 days, after which time it must be "fed" with additional flour and water. This process results in more texture and flavor in the loaves eventually made from it. In general, a sponge starter is thinner, and more liquid, and is the quickest to make and use.

Here are some guidelines for the care and feeding of starters. The consistency of the feeding cycle is very important. Microorganisms develop a "memory" of their own and prefer regular intervals between feedings. However, you may refrigerate a starter for months without feeding it. It will go dormant, the acids will dissolve the gluten, and a grayish liquid, called the liquor, or "hootch," will separate from the flour and float on top. To reactivate the starter, merely pour off the liquid, throw out some of the dormant starter, and build it back as described in Sourdough Starter, below. It should begin to bubble and percolate within 2 to 4 days and be ready for baking.

The standard feeding of a starter doubles it in volume, so that if you have 2 cups starter, you will build it first to 4 cups, then to 8, and so on. If you eventually have more starter than you can use, give some away or throw some out. When making bread, always leave enough starter behind so you can build it back up in time for your next batch. You may also freeze a starter, but you must give it at least 24 hours first in the refrigerator, then at room temperature for at least 2 hours to reactivate it.

It is not usually necessary to sterilize your starter crock, jar, or container to prevent contamination. The dominant bacteria and yeast in a starter tend to fend off invaders. However, if the starter becomes discolored or foul smelling, it should be discarded.

It is best to use the starter for making bread 4 to 8 hours after the last feeding at room temperature. If you use the starter just before feeding, the yeast may be hungry and less active; if you use your starter just after feeding, you will have diluted it somewhat and it may rise a bit more slowly. Starter kept at room temperature must be fed twice daily at 12-hour intervals. If you find that you are using the starter infrequently, keep it covered in the refrigerator and feed it just once a week.

SOURDOUGH STARTER

I. For kitchens lacking yeast spores in the air.
Combine in a large wide-mouthed crockery or glass jar:

> **2 cups lukewarm (85°F) water**
> **1 package (2¹/₄ teaspoons) active dry yeast**
> **2 cups all-purpose flour**

Stir with a wooden spoon—never use metal. Let stand uncovered at 80° to 90°F for 4 to 7 days, or until the starter bubbles and emits a good sour odor. During this period, stir down once a day; if a crust develops, stir it down also. Use at once, or refrigerate until ready to do so. To replenish, discard all but 1 cup of the starter. (Any excess, unless reactivated, may become rancid.) Add to the cupful:

> **¹/₂ cup lukewarm (85°F) water**
> **¹/₂ cup all-purpose flour**

Let stand overnight until fermented and bubbling, then use or refrigerate. To build, add:

> **1 cup lukewarm (85°F) water**
> **1 cup all-purpose flour**

II. For kitchens laden with yeast spores from previous bread making, follow the directions in I, above, omitting the yeast and using:

> **1 cup lukewarm (85°F) milk**
> **1 cup all-purpose flour**
> **¹/₂ cup sugar**

To replenish, add these 3 ingredients in these amounts to 1 cup starter.

ABOUT BREADS MADE WITH SPONGE OR SOURDOUGH STARTERS

Such breads require more time and commitment than those made by the conventional straight dough method, but they are becoming increasingly popular as more home cooks discover the joys of freshly baked European-style breads and seek to re-create them at home. The following recipes include breads made with sponge starters and sourdough starters. Starters are really quite simple to make once you get used to the additional steps required—and once you make one, you can keep it on hand and replenish it indefinitely.

RUSTIC FRENCH BREAD

2 round loaves or thick baguettes or 4 thin baguettes
Raised with a sponge starter, 602, these free-form loaves have rustic qualities—including crustiness and a moist, chewy crumb.
Combine in a medium bowl and let stand until the yeast is dissolved, about 5 minutes:

> **¹/₂ cup lukewarm (80 to 90°F) water**
> **¹/₂ teaspoon active dry yeast**

Add:

> **³/₄ cup bread flour**

Stir rapidly with a wooden spoon until elastic strands pull away from the sides of the bowl, about 2 minutes. Cover the bowl tightly with plastic wrap and let rise at room temperature until bubbly and tripled in volume, about 6 hours; or let rise for about 14 hours in the refrigerator. (If the sponge has just come out of the refrigerator, use warm water [105° to 115°F] for making the dough.)
Pour the sponge into a large mixing bowl or the bowl of a heavy-duty mixer, and stir in:

> **2 cups room-temperature (72° to 75°F) water**
> **4¹/₂ cups bread flour, or as needed**

Sprinkle in:

> **1 tablespoon salt, preferably fine sea salt**

Mix until the dough cleans the sides of the bowl. If necessary, adjust the consistency of the dough by adding flour or water. The dough should feel sticky to the touch but should not actually stick to your hands. Knead for about 10 minutes by hand, or with the dough hook on low to medium speed until the dough is smooth and elastic. Transfer the dough to an oiled bowl and turn it once to coat with oil. Cover the bowl with plastic wrap and let rise until doubled in bulk, about 3 hours in a warm place (75° to 80°F) or about 6 hours at cooler room temperature.

Divide the dough in half and shape each half into a round loaf, 595, or divide the dough into 4 parts and shape into thin baguettes, 601. Place the shaped loaves on 2 floured baking sheets. Cover with plastic wrap and let rise at room temperature until doubled in bulk, 2 to 4 hours.

Set the racks in the lower and center levels of the oven. Place a baking pan on the lower level. Preheat the oven to 450°F. If using a baking stone, preheat it on the center oven rack for 45 minutes.

Score, 595, the tops of the risen loaves. Place the loaves on the center rack. Pour 2 cups boiling water into the pre-heated pan on the lower rack. Bake thin baguettes for about 30 minutes, thick baguettes for about 35 minutes, or round loaves for about 40 minutes. The loaves should be browned and the bottoms sound hollow when tapped; the internal temperature should be 210°F. To further set the crust, turn off the oven and leave the baked loaves in the oven for 5 to 10 minutes.

Let cool completely on a rack.

RUSTIC SOURDOUGH BREAD

2 round loaves or thick baguettes or 4 thin baguettes

Because of the time needed for making the sourdough starter, you will need to plan your baking at least 3 days in advance when making II, but the results are worth it. For whole wheat sourdough bread, substitute 2 cups whole wheat flour for 2 cups of the bread flour.

I. Prepare:

Rustic French Bread, above

substituting:

2 cups Sourdough Starter I, 603

for the sponge starter, and reducing the water to:

1³/₄ cups (use warm water if the starter is cold from the refrigerator)

II. Combine in a large bowl or the bowl of a heavy-duty mixer:

2 cups Sourdough Starter II, 603
1¹/₂ cups lukewarm (85°F) water
4 cups bread flour

Mix by hand or on low speed until a sticky dough forms. Cover the bowl with oiled plastic wrap and refrigerate the dough for 12 to 14 hours, letting it rise until almost doubled.

Let the dough stand at room temperature for 2 hours. Add:

¹/₂ cup bread flour
4 teaspoons salt, preferably fine sea salt

Knead by hand for 7 to 10 minutes or with the dough hook on low to medium speed until smooth and elastic but still sticky to the touch. Cover loosely with plastic wrap and let rest for 10 minutes.

Shape, let rise, and bake the dough as directed for Rustic French Bread, above.

III. Prepare:

Rustic French Bread, 603

substituting:

2 cups Mixed Starter, 602

for the sponge and reducing the water to:

1³/₄ cups (use warm water if the starter is cold from the refrigerator)

Remember to save ³/₄ cup (6 ounces) of the risen dough for the next batch.

WHITE BREAD MADE WITH A SPONGE STARTER

2 round loaves or thick baguettes or 4 thin baguettes

This sponge-based version of basic white bread is more flavorful than that made by the straight dough method, 592.

Mix in a large bowl or the bowl of a heavy-duty mixer until the dough cleans the sides of the bowl:

1 cup Sponge Starter, 602
2 cups room-temperature (72° to 75°F) water
4¹/₂ cups bread flour

Sprinkle in:

1 tablespoon salt, preferably fine sea salt

If necessary, adjust the consistency of the dough by adding flour or water. The dough should feel sticky to the touch but not actually stick to your hands. Knead for about 10 minutes by hand or with the dough hook on low to medium speed until the dough is smooth and elastic. Transfer the dough to an oiled bowl and turn it once to coat with oil. Cover the bowl with plastic wrap and set aside to let rise until doubled in volume, about 3 hours in a warm place (75° to 80°F) or about 6 hours at cooler room temperature.

Divide the dough in half and shape, 594, each half into a round loaf or thick baguette, or divide it into 4 parts and shape into thinner baguettes. Place the shaped loaves in baskets or on floured clean cloths or in oiled pans as directed. Cover with oiled plastic wrap and let rise at room temperature until doubled in volume, 2 to 4 hours.

Preheat the oven to 450°F. If using a baking stone, pre-heat it on the center oven rack for 45 minutes. To bake loaves directly on the hot stone, you will need a baker's peel or a flat, thin baking sheet sprinkled with cornmeal for the transfer—flip the risen loaves onto the peel, spacing them several inches apart.

Score, 595, the risen loaves. Spritz the preheated oven with water from a spray bottle, wait 1 minute, and quickly slide in the loaves. Wait 2 minutes and spritz the oven walls again. Bake thin baguettes for about 30 minutes, thick baguettes for about 35 minutes, or round loaves for about 40 minutes. The loaves should be browned and the bottoms of the loaves should sound hollow when tapped, 595. To further set the crust, turn off the oven and leave the baked loaves in the oven for 5 minutes. Let cool completely on a rack.

WHITE BREAD MADE WITH A MIXED STARTER

Prepare **White Bread made with a Sponge Starter, 604,** substituting **2 cups Mixed Starter, 602,** for the sponge starter and reducing the water to 1$^3/_4$ cups (use warm water if the starter is cold from the refrigerator). This dough will be firm enough that free-form loaves should not lose their shape prior to baking. Remember to save $^3/_4$ cup (6 ounces) of the risen dough for the next batch.

WHOLE WHEAT BREAD MADE WITH A MIXED STARTER

2 round loaves or 4 thin baguettes

Prepare **White Bread with a Mixed Starter, 604,** substituting **2 cups whole wheat flour** for 2 cups of the bread flour and using a total of 2 cups bread flour.

ALL-RYE-FLOUR BREAD

2 flat round loaves

Rye flour lacks the gluten-producing proteins of wheat flour, so a loaf made of all rye has a dense, heavy texture, similar to that of pumpernickel.

Combine in a large bowl and let stand until the yeast is dissolved, about 5 minutes:

    $^1/_2$ **cup warm (105° to 115°F) water**
    2 packages (1$^1/_2$ tablespoons) active dry yeast

Add:

    2 cups lukewarm (85°F) milk
    2 tablespoons butter, softened or melted
    1 tablespoon sugar or honey
    2 teaspoons salt

Stir in:

    2 cups rye flour

Let this sponge rise, covered, about 1 hour.

Gradually stir in:

    3 cups rye flour
    (1 large egg, beaten)
    (2 tablespoons caraway seeds)
    (2 tablespoons sesame seeds)

Let rise, covered, about 2 hours.

Sprinkle a board with:

    1 cup rye flour

Knead the dough, incorporating the flour, about 10 minutes. Divide in half and form into round loaves, 595. Put on a well-greased baking sheet and grease the tops of the loaves. Cover with plastic wrap, and allow to rise about 2 hours more.

Preheat the oven to 350°F.

Bake about 1 hour. Turn the oven off and let the loaves remain in the oven for 10 minutes. Bake until the crust is golden brown and the bottom sounds hollow when tapped, 595. Cool completely on a rack.

SOURDOUGH RYE BREAD

2 round or 2 long loaves

The best-flavored rye breads call for a sourdough starter, 603. For this recipe, first you make a sourdough starter,

using part of a package of yeast. The following day, you make two sponges, using the rest of the yeast.

To prepare the sourdough starter, combine in a bowl and work together lightly:

    $^1/_2$ **cup medium rye flour**
    $^1/_4$ **cup water**
    1 teaspoon active dry yeast

Cover tightly with plastic wrap and keep in a warm place (about 85°F) for 24 hours.

Stir into the starter:

    1 cup medium rye flour
    $^3/_4$ **cup water**

Cover and allow to ferment, about 4 hours longer. For the first sponge, stir into the starter:

    1$^3/_4$ cups medium rye flour
    $^3/_4$ **teaspoon active dry yeast**
    $^1/_4$ **cup water**

Let rise, covered with a damp clean cloth in a warm place until doubled in volume. For the second sponge add:

    1$^3/_4$ cups rye flour
    1$^3/_4$ cups all-purpose flour
    $^1/_2$ **teaspoon active dry yeast**
    1 cup water

Mix until smooth. Cover with a damp clean cloth and let rise until doubled in volume, about 1 hour.

Add:

    1$^3/_4$ cups all-purpose flour
    1 cup water
    1 tablespoon caraway seeds
    1 tablespoon salt

Mix until smooth, then let the dough rest, covered, 20 minutes.

Turn the dough out onto a floured board and knead into it:

    1$^1/_2$ to 2 cups all-purpose flour

until you have a rather firm dough—one that will not flatten or spread. Divide in half and shape it into 2 long or 2 round loaves, 595. Place them on a greased baking sheet and allow to rise, but not double in volume—too much rising will result in a flat loaf.

Preheat the oven to 425°F.

Place a baking pan containing about $^1/_4$ inch water in the oven. Bake the loaves 50 to 60 minutes. You may have to replenish the water, but remove the pan after 20 minutes. As soon as the bread is done, spread the tops with:

    Melted butter

or, if you wish a glazed crust, spread with:

    Salted water (1 teaspoon salt to $^1/_2$ cup water)

Cool completely on a rack.

RYE BREAD WITH A SPONGE STARTER

2 round loaves

Use medium rye flour, which is darker and has more rye flavor than the more common white rye flour. Before beginning, please read About Sponge and Mixed Starters, 601.

Combine in a medium bowl and let stand until the yeast is dissolved, about 5 minutes:

> $^1/_2$ **cup warm (105° to 115°F) water**
> $^1/_2$ **teaspoon active dry yeast**

Add:

> $^3/_4$ **cup bread flour**

Stir rapidly with a wooden spoon until you notice elastic strands pulling away from the sides of the bowl, about 2 minutes. Cover the bowl tightly with plastic wrap and let rise at room temperature until bubbly and tripled in volume, about 6 hours; or let the starter rise for about 14 hours in the refrigerator. (If the sponge has just come out of the refrigerator, use warm water [105° to 115°F] for making the dough.)

Scrape the sponge into a large mixing bowl or the bowl of a heavy-duty mixer and stir in:

> $2^1/_2$ **cups room-temperature (72° to 75°F) water**
> $3^1/_2$ **cups medium rye flour**
> $3^1/_2$ **cups bread flour**

Stir rapidly with a wooden spoon or mix on medium speed for about 2 minutes. Adjust the consistency of the dough by adding more bread flour or water. Work in by hand for 2 minutes or with the dough hook on the mixer:

> **4 teaspoons salt**

Knead by hand or with the dough hook on low to medium speed until the dough is smooth, elastic, and firm, about 7 minutes. Transfer the dough to an oiled bowl and turn it once to coat with oil. Cover the bowl tightly with plastic wrap and let rise in a warm place (75° to 85°F) for 1$^1/_2$ hours. The dough will rise only very slightly; do not leave it longer, or it will overferment the starter, which will make the bread heavy (yeast cells eat rye flour very quickly).

Divide the dough in half and shape, 595, each half into a round loaf. Place the loaves on greased baking sheets sprinkled with:

> **Cornmeal**

as free-standing loaves. Cover with oiled plastic wrap and let rise in a warm place for 1$^1/_2$ hours.

Set the racks in the lower and center levels of the oven. Place a baking pan on the lower level. Preheat the oven to 450°F. If using a baking stone, preheat it on the center oven rack for 45 minutes.

Place the loaves on the center rack. Pour 2 cups boiling water into the preheated pan on the lower rack. Bake until well browned and the bottom of the loaves sound hollow when tapped, 595, about 45 minutes. Let cool completely on a rack.

TUSCAN LOAF
2 oval loaves

This bread is satisfying on its own, but also ideal for Bruschetta, 88, or as a foundation for bread soups. If you have tasted them, you know: The breads of Tuscany contain no salt. The leisurely risings ensure two things: You build the bread around your own schedule, and the slow risings yield a bread full of deep wheat flavor.

Mix in a large bowl or the bowl of a heavy-duty mixer for 1 minute:

> **2 cups lukewarm (85°F) water**
> **1 cup whole wheat flour**
> $^3/_4$ **cup all-purpose flour**
> **1 package (2$^1/_4$ teaspoons) active dry yeast**

Cover the bowl with plastic wrap and let rise at room temperature for 8 to 12 hours. Stir in:

> $2^1/_2$ **cups all-purpose flour**
> **1 tablespoon olive oil**

Adding up to 1 cup more flour as needed, mix until a soft, slightly sticky dough forms. Knead by hand for 15 minutes or with the dough hook on low to medium speed for 7 minutes. The dough should be very elastic but still a bit sticky.

Transfer the dough to an oiled bowl and turn it once to coat with oil. Cover the bowl with plastic wrap and let rise at room temperature until doubled in volume, about 2 hours.

Punch down the dough and knead briefly. Shape into an oval loaf by stretching and tucking dough underneath itself, as for a round loaf, see Shaping, 594. Lightly oil a baking sheet and sprinkle with:

> **Cornmeal**

Transfer the loaf to the baking sheet, brush the surface with oil, and cover with plastic wrap. Let rise at room temperature until more than doubled, about 1$^1/_2$ hours. The loaf is ready to bake when the imprints of your fingers remain if the dough is gently pressed.

Preheat the oven to 425°F. Set a baking pan on the lowest oven rack.

Score, 595, the top of the risen loaf in a crosshatch pattern and place the baking sheet in the oven. Immediately add 1 cup hot water to the baking pan and shut the oven door. Bake until the bottom of the loaf sounds hollow when tapped, 595, about 40 minutes. Let cool completely on a rack.

SALT-RISEN BREAD
Three 9 x 5-inch loaves

This unusually good formula relies for its leavening on the fermentation of a salt-tolerant bacterium in cornmeal. The cornmeal must be stone-ground. Do not attempt this bread in damp, cold weather, and protect the batter well from drafts. Under the best of circumstances, it may prove to be erratic. We have had success setting a covered heavy bowl in water heated by an electric skillet or on a heating tray, or in a warming drawer.

Measure into a large jar or bowl:

> $^1/_2$ **cup stone-ground cornmeal, preferably white**
> **1 tablespoon sugar**

Heat and pour over the cornmeal:

> **1 cup milk**

Let stand overnight or longer, covered, in a warm place, preferably 90° to 95°F, until the mixture ferments: it should be light and have a number of small cracks over the surface. (If it isn't light in texture, the bread will not rise properly.)

Combine in a large bowl:

¹/₃ cup vegetable shortening or lard
2 tablespoons sugar
1 tablespoon salt

Pour in:

3 cups warm (105° to 115°F) milk

Stir in:

3¹/₂ cups all-purpose flour

Stir in the corn mixture. Place the bowl in a pan of warm water for 1 to 2 hours, replenishing the water as necessary to keep it warm, until bubbles work up from the bottom. Stir in:

5 cups all-purpose flour

Knead in on a work surface until smooth but not stiff:

2 to 2¹/₂ cups all-purpose flour

Divide the dough among 3 greased 9 x 5-inch loaf pans. Cover and let rise until doubled in bulk. Watch carefully—if it oversizes, it may sour.

Preheat the oven to 400°F.

Bake the bread for 10 minutes. Reduce the heat to 350°F and bake 25 to 30 minutes more. Bake until the crust is golden brown and the bottom sounds hollow when tapped, 595. Remove from the pans to a rack to cool completely.

PIZZA DOUGH

Two 12-inch crusts

As you become an avid pizza baker, you will no doubt come up with your own style of crust and your own favorite toppings For our favorite toppings, see 190–192. For baking instructions, see 191.

Combine in a large bowl or the bowl of a heavy-duty mixer and let stand until the yeast is dissolved, about 5 minutes:

1¹/₃ cups warm (105° to 115°F) water
1 package (2¹/₄ teaspoons) active dry yeast

Add:

3¹/₂ to 3³/₄ cups all-purpose flour
2 tablespoons olive oil
1 tablespoon salt
(1 tablespoon sugar)

Mix by hand or on low speed for about 1 minute. Knead for about 10 minutes by hand or with the dough hook on low to medium speed until the dough is smooth and elastic. Transfer the dough to a bowl lightly coated with olive oil and turn it once to coat with oil. Cover with plastic wrap or a clean cloth and let rise in a warm place (75° to 85°F) until doubled in bulk, 1 to 1¹/₂ hours.

Preheat the oven to 475°F. Grease 2 baking sheets and dust with cornmeal; or place a baking stone in the oven and preheat it for 45 minutes.

Punch down the dough and divide it in half. Roll each piece into a ball and let rest, loosely covered with plastic wrap, for 10 to 15 minutes. Prepare the desired toppings, 190–192.

One at a time, flatten each ball of dough on a lightly floured work surface into a 12-inch round, rolling and stretching the dough. Place each dough circle on a prepared baking sheet, or, if using a baking stone, place them on rimless baking sheets or baker's peels dusted with cornmeal. Lift the edges and pinch to form a lip. To prevent the filling from making the crust soggy, brush the top of the dough with:

Olive oil

Use your fingertips to push dents in the surface of the dough, to prevent bubbling, and let rest for about 10 minutes. The pizza is now ready to be topped and baked.

FOCACCIA

Two 8- or 9-inch round or square breads

A popular Italian flatbread, seasoned with olive oil, salt, and herbs.

Prepare:

Pizza Dough, above

Divide in half and roll each piece out to a ¹/₂-inch-thick round. Transfer to well-oiled 8- or 9-inch round cake pans or square baking pans. Let rise, covered with oiled plastic wrap, for 1¹/₂ hours. Preheat the oven to 400°F. Ten minutes before baking, press the dough with your fingertips to make indentations all over the dough. Drizzle with:

Up to ¹/₂ cup olive oil

Top with:

2 tablespoons grated cheese, such as romano,
Parmesan, or Asiago
1 teaspoon dried herbs, such as rosemary, dill, basil,
thyme, or oregano, or 2 teaspoons fresh herb
leaves or minced herbs
¹/₄ teaspoon coarse salt
(Slices of sun-dried tomatoes, olives, Caramelized
Onions, 287, or diced roasted potato)

Bake until golden brown, about 25 minutes. Remove from the pans to a rack. Serve warm or at room temperature, as is, or sliced open horizontally to use as a sandwich bread.

PITA BREAD

8 pitas

Also called pocket bread, this is excellent for sandwiches and scooping up dips and sauces—especially Hummus, 74, or Baba Ghanoush, 74, or even Guacamole, 72. You can substitute whole wheat flour for any portion of the white flour, according to your preference, although the dough may then require additional water to be soft and pliable. You may also spray the top of the rolled-out pita rounds with water and sprinkle with sesame seeds before baking.

Combine in a large bowl or the bowl of a heavy-duty mixer:

3 cups bread flour
1¹/₂ tablespoons sugar
1¹/₂ teaspoons salt
2 packages (1¹/₂ tablespoons) active dry yeast

Add:

2 tablespoons butter, melted

1¼ cups room-temperature (72° to 75°F) water

Mix by hand or on low speed for about 1 minute. Knead for about 10 minutes by hand or with the dough hook on low to medium speed until the dough is smooth, soft, and elastic. Add flour or water as needed; the dough should be slightly tacky but not sticky. Transfer the dough to an oiled bowl and turn it once to coat with oil. Cover with plastic wrap and allow to rise at room temperature until doubled in volume, 1 to 1½ hours.

Set a rack in the lower level of the oven and place a pizza or baking stone on the rack. Preheat the oven to 450°F for 45 minutes. (If you do not have a pizza or baking stone, preheat the oven, place an inverted baking sheet on the rack, and heat the baking sheet for 5 minutes.)

Meanwhile, punch down the dough. Divide equally into 8 pieces, and roll the pieces into balls. Cover and let rest for 20 minutes.

On a very lightly floured surface, roll out each ball of dough into a thin round, about 8 inches in diameter and ⅛ inch thick. Spray the stone or baking sheet with a mist of water, wait 30 seconds, and then place as many dough rounds as will fit without touching each other directly on the hot surface. Bake until the dough rounds puff into balloons, about 3 minutes, then bake 30 seconds longer and immediately remove the breads to a rack to cool. If you leave the breads in the oven too long, they will become dry and will not deflate to flat disks. Bake the remaining rounds.

NAAN

4 oval breads

This delicious soft Indian flatbread is traditionally baked in red-hot tandoor ovens, but at home use a baking stone.

Combine in a large bowl or the bowl of a heavy-duty mixer:

2 cups bread flour

½ teaspoon salt

1⅛ teaspoons active dry yeast

Add:

¾ cup yogurt or buttermilk, at room temperature

2 tablespoons butter, melted, or vegetable oil

1 teaspoon to 1 tablespoon water, as needed

Mix by hand or on low speed until a soft ball of dough is formed. Knead for about 10 minutes by hand or with the dough hook on low to medium speed, until the dough is smooth and elastic. Transfer the dough to an oiled bowl and turn it once to coat with oil. Cover with plastic wrap and let rise at room temperature for about 1½ hours.

Set a rack in the lowest level of the oven and place a pizza or baking stone on the rack. Preheat the oven to 475°F for 45 minutes. (If you do not have a pizza or baking stone, preheat the oven, place an inverted baking sheet, preferably heavy-gauge, on the rack, and heat the baking sheet for 5 minutes.)

Meanwhile, punch down the dough and divide equally

into 4 pieces. Roll into balls, cover, and let rest for 10 minutes.

Roll out each ball of dough on a floured surface to an oval 8 to 10 inches long and ¼ inch thick. Brush the tops with:

1 to 2 tablespoons butter, melted

If desired, sprinkle on top:

(2 tablespoons minced scallions or 2 teaspoons sesame or poppy seeds)

Place as many dough ovals as will fit without touching each other directly on the baking stone or sheet and bake until each oval is puffy and just beginning to turn golden, 6 to 7 minutes. Remove from the oven. If desired, drizzle over the baked bread:

(Melted butter)

Fold the naan in half, place in a cloth-lined basket, and keep covered. Bake the remaining dough. Serve warm.

SOPAPILLAS

12 breads

Serve it as a snack or as a dessert. Please read About Deep-Fat Frying, 1046.

Whisk together in a medium bowl until well blended:

2 cups all-purpose flour

1 tablespoon baking powder

1 tablespoon sugar

¾ teaspoon salt

Add and stir until a soft dough forms:

¾ cup warm water

1 tablespoon vegetable oil

With lightly floured hands, knead the dough just until smooth and slightly elastic, about 1 minute. (If kneaded too much, the dough will be difficult to roll out later.) Place the dough in an oiled plastic bag and refrigerate for 1 to 2 hours. Divide the dough into 12 pieces. Flatten each piece with your hand into a 3- to 4-inch round. Cover with plastic wrap and let rest 10 to 15 minutes. On a lightly floured work surface, roll each piece into a very thin round 7 to 8 inches in diameter. Poke a hole in the center of each round with your finger.

Heat to 375°F in a pot or skillet at least 10 inches wide:

2 to 3 inches lard or vegetable oil

Slip 1 round at a time into the hot oil and fry until puffy and light brown, about 1 minute per side, turning with tongs. Drain on paper towels. Drizzle with:

Honey

Or sprinkle with:

Confectioners' sugar

FLOUR TORTILLAS

Eight 6- to 8-inch tortillas

Flour tortillas, an unleavened bread, are surprisingly easy to make.

Combine in a large bowl or the bowl of a heavy-duty mixer:

2 cups bread flour

1 teaspoon baking powder

1 teaspoon salt
$^1/_4$ cup vegetable shortening or lard
$^3/_4$ cup hot (115° to 130°F) water

Mix by hand or on low speed until the dough comes together. Knead by hand or with the dough hook on low to medium speed until smooth, 4 to 6 minutes.

Divide the dough equally into 8 pieces and roll them into balls. Cover and let rest for 20 minutes.

Roll out each ball of dough into a 6- to 8-inch round about $^1/_8$ inch thick. If a dough round is resistant, move to the next piece and return later to finish rolling.

Heat a large cast-iron or nonstick skillet over medium heat. Slide the tortillas into the skillet one by one, cooking until brown spots appear, about 30 seconds on the first side, 15 seconds once flipped. Cover the cooked tortillas to keep warm while you cook the rest. Serve warm.

CORN TORTILLAS
Sixteen 5-inch tortillas

This dough dries out quickly; the unused portion should be kept covered until used, but you may always readjust the consistency by kneading it with additional water if necessary—extra kneading does not harm the finished product.

Mix in a bowl with your hands, adjusting the quantity of water as necessary to form a soft dough:

2 cups masa harina, 984
1$^1/_4$ to 1$^1/_3$ cups hot (120° to 125°F) water

Cover with plastic wrap and let rest at least 30 minutes. Knead the rested dough, adjusting the consistency with additional water or masa as necessary, until it is soft, smooth, and pliable but neither sticky nor crumbly.

Place 2 heavy ungreased skillets on the stove, or use a griddle large enough to cover two burners. Adjust the heat under 1 skillet (or one side of the griddle) to medium-low and the second to medium-high.

Form the dough into 1$^1/_2$-inch balls. Keep covered with a damp clean towel while you press the tortillas. Place a dough ball between 2 pieces of heavy plastic or wax paper. Using a tortilla press or the bottom of a heavy (unheated) skillet, press the dough firmly, turning it 180 degrees and pressing again as necessary, until it is uniformly $^1/_{16}$ inch thick. (If the tortilla crumbles when you pick it up, the dough is too dry; if it sticks to the plastic, the tortilla is too thin or the dough is too wet. Adjust the consistency of the rest of the dough accordingly before continuing to shape the tortillas.)

Lay the tortilla in the cooler of the 2 skillets until it begins to release itself from the pan but the edges have not begun to curl, about 20 seconds. Flip the tortilla over onto the hotter skillet and cook until the underside is lightly browned in spots, 20 to 30 seconds. Flip the tortilla over and finish browning the first side. If the pan is hot enough and the dough properly moist, the tortilla should puff up like a pillow (you may encourage this by pressing it with your fingers or the back of a spatula). When it is browned,

remove the tortilla to a clean towel (it will deflate) and cover it. Form and cook the remaining tortillas, stacking the hot tortillas on top of each other and covering the stack each time. Serve warm. (Reheat leftovers wrapped in foil in the oven or wrapped in wax paper in the microwave until soft and pliable.)

ABOUT YEAST ROLLS

There is little difference in bread- and roll-making, so if you are a novice, ➤ please read About Yeast Bread, 591. The visual appeal of delicately formed crusty or glazed rolls is a stimulant to the appetite. For varied shaping suggestions, see the illustrations throughout this chapter.

Professional cooks weigh the dough to keep the rolls uniform in size for good appearance and even baking. If you do not use muffin pans, place the rolls at regular intervals over the entire baking sheet. Parchment paper or a silicone baking liner saves having a pan to wash and also cuts the grease build-up that can result in a discolored pan and uneven browning.

You may use any of the additions to yeast dough, 596, or coffee cake, 621, to vary the flavor. Sprinkle the tops with poppy, celery, fennel, caraway, or lightly toasted sesame seeds, depending on the rest of your menu.

To bake, follow the individual recipes. ➤ Remove the rolls at once from the pan to a cooling rack. ➤ To reheat, sprinkle them lightly with water, wrap in aluminum foil, and heat, covered, in a 400°F oven until warm.

NO-KNEAD LIGHT ROLLS
Fifteen 2-inch rolls

These are the rolls we remember from childhood: light as a feather and served in a special soft linen napkin. Although they require no kneading, the dough is best chilled at least 2 hours and up to 12. Since this recipe is not heavy enough in sugar to retard the rising action, the dough should be baked after the chilling period.

Combine in a small bowl and let stand until the yeast is dissolved, about 5 minutes:

$^1/_4$ cup warm (105° to 115°F) water
1 package (2$^1/_4$ teaspoons) active dry yeast

Combine in a large bowl:

$^1/_4$ cup ($^1/_2$ stick) butter or $^1/_4$ cup vegetable shortening
2 tablespoons sugar
1$^1/_4$ teaspoons salt

Pour over these ingredients and stir until they are melted and dissolved:

1 cup hot water

Let cool to lukewarm, then stir in the yeast. Beat in:

1 large egg

Stir in and beat until a soft dough forms:

About 2$^3/_4$ cups all-purpose flour

Put the dough in a large greased bowl and turn to coat with oil. Either cover with foil and refrigerate for 2 to 12 hours, or cover with a clean cloth and let rise until doubled in bulk.

Punch down the dough. Divide the dough into 15 pieces and shape into round rolls. Place in greased muffin cups. Let rise until about doubled in volume, about 45 minutes if the dough was chilled, or 30 if not.
Preheat the oven to 425°F.
Bake until golden, 15 to 18 minutes. Remove to a rack to cool.

PARKER HOUSE ROLLS
Thirty 2-inch rolls
This is a basic not-too-sweet dough that can be used for variously shaped dinner rolls.
Heat until warm (105° to 115°F):
   1 cup milk
Add and stir until the sugar is dissolved:
   2 tablespoons butter, softened
   1 tablespoon sugar
   ³/₄ teaspoon salt
Combine in a large bowl and let stand until the yeast is dissolved, about 5 minutes:
   2 tablespoons warm (105° to 115°F) water
   1 package (2¹/₄ teaspoons) active dry yeast
When the milk mixture has cooled to lukewarm, stir it into the yeast. Beat in, if desired:
   (1 large egg)
Have ready:
   3¹/₃ to 3²/₃ cups all-purpose flour
Stir in part of the flour, then knead in the rest, using only enough to form a dough that can be handled easily. Place in an oiled bowl. Brush the top with:
   Melted butter
Cover and let the dough rise in a warm place until doubled in bulk.
Roll the dough out into a 30-inch-long log and cut into 1-inch pieces. Roll each piece into a ball and flatten into a 2-inch round. Dip the handle of a knife or wooden spoon in flour and use it to make a deep crease across the middle of each roll. Fold the rolls over on the crease and press the edges together lightly. Place about 2 inches apart in rows on greased baking sheets. Let rise in a warm place until light, about 35 minutes. Preheat the oven to 425°F. Bake until golden brown, about 15 minutes. Remove to a rack to cool.

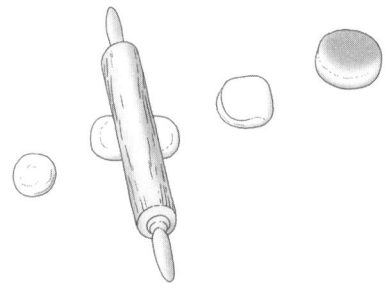

Forming Parker House Rolls—
a baked Parker House roll is at far right

CLOVERLEAF ROLLS
Twenty-four 2-inch rolls
Prepare:
   Dough for Parker House Rolls, above
After the first rising in the bowl, punch down the dough. Grease 2 muffin pans. Divide the dough into 24 pieces. For each roll, divide one piece of dough into 3 pieces, roll into small balls, and place in a muffin cup, as shown. Brush the tops with:
   Melted butter
Let rise, covered, in a warm place until about doubled in volume, about 30 minutes. Preheat the oven to 425°F. Bake until golden brown, 15 to 18 minutes. Remove to a rack to cool.

Shaping Cloverleaf Rolls

HOT CROSS BUNS
18 buns
These originated in medieval England, to commemorate Good Friday.
Prepare:
   Dough for Parker House Rolls, above,
      or Milk Bread, 597
increasing the sugar to ¹/₄ cup and using the egg. Add with the sugar:
   ¹/₄ cup currants or raisins
   (2 tablespoons finely chopped candied citron)
   ¹/₄ teaspoon ground cinnamon
   ¹/₈ teaspoon grated or ground nutmeg
After the first rising, punch down the dough, shape into 18 balls, and place about 1¹/₂ inches apart in rows on greased baking sheets. Cover and let rise until almost doubled in volume.
Preheat the oven to 425°F. Bake about 20 minutes, until golden brown. Decorate with the traditional cross, using:
   Milk Glaze, 799

JOINED FINGER ROLLS
18 rolls
Prepare:
   Dough for Milk Bread, 597
After the first rise, divide the dough into 18 pieces (about 1 ounce each). Grease a baking sheet. On an unfloured surface, roll the dough pieces into balls. Then, working

from the center outward, elongate them into plump oblong-shaped rolls, about 3 inches long, 1$\frac{1}{2}$ inches wide at the center, and slightly tapered at the ends. Place the rolls in straight lines and about $\frac{1}{2}$ inch apart on the baking sheet so they join together during rising.

Whisk together:

1 egg

Pinch of salt

Brush over the tops of the rolls (reserve the remaining egg wash). Cover with oiled plastic wrap and let rise in a warm place (75° to 85°F) until doubled in volume, about 1 hour. Preheat the oven to 425°F.

Brush the finger rolls again with the egg wash. If desired, sprinkle with:

(Coarse or granulated sugar)

Bake until the crust is golden brown, about 15 minutes. Serve freshly baked and warm, or reheat in a 400°F oven for 4 to 6 minutes.

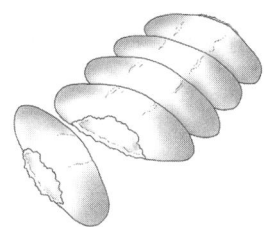

Joined Finger Rolls

PALM LEAF ROLLS (SOUR CREAM ROLLS)

About 36 rolls

Sweet enough for a dessert if you add a bit more sugar. Serve with coffee and fruit.

Combine in a small bowl and let stand until the yeast is dissolved, about 5 minutes:

$\frac{1}{4}$ cup warm (105° to 115°F) water

1 package (2$\frac{1}{4}$ teaspoons) active dry yeast

Stir together in a large bowl until blended:

3 cups all-purpose flour

1$\frac{1}{2}$ teaspoons salt

Cut in until reduced to pea-sized bits:

$\frac{1}{2}$ cup (1 stick) butter

Stir in:

2 large eggs, beaten

1 cup sour cream

1 teaspoon vanilla

Blend in the dissolved yeast. Cover and chill for 2 hours or more.

Have ready:

1 cup Vanilla Sugar, 1019

or a mixture of:

1 cup sugar

2 teaspoons ground cinnamon

Sprinkle a work surface with half the sugar mixture. Divide the dough in half. Roll one half into a 6 x 18-inch rectangle. Fold as shown on the left below, bringing the ends to within about $\frac{3}{4}$ inch of each other. Repeat this folding as shown in the right foreground and again as shown in the rear. Slice into $\frac{1}{4}$-inch-thick "palm leaves," and arrange 1 inch apart on a greased baking sheet. Repeat this process with the other half of the dough, first sprinkling the board with the remaining sugar mixture. Let rise, covered with plastic wrap, about 20 minutes.

Preheat the oven to 375°F. Bake until golden brown, about 20 minutes. Remove to a rack to cool.

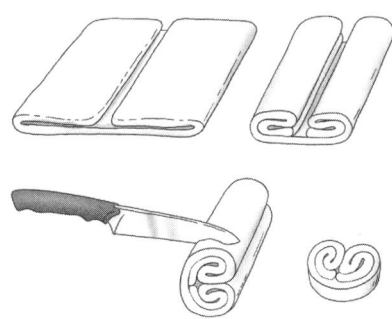

Folding and cutting Palm Leaf Rolls

BUTTERMILK ROLLS (FAN-TANS)

24 rolls

These rolls need not be buttered—perfect for a buffet.

Heat until warm, about 110°F:

1$\frac{1}{2}$ cups buttermilk

Pour $\frac{1}{3}$ cup of the buttermilk into a glass measure. Add and let stand until dissolved, about 5 minutes:

1 package (2$\frac{1}{4}$ teaspoons) active dry yeast

Pour the remaining buttermilk into a large bowl. When the yeast has dissolved, add to the buttermilk, along with:

$\frac{1}{4}$ cup sugar

2 teaspoons salt

$\frac{1}{4}$ teaspoon baking soda

Beat well, then stir in:

2 cups all-purpose flour

2 tablespoons melted butter

Add another:

2 cups all-purpose flour

Knead until smooth. Place the dough in an oiled bowl and turn it to coat with oil. Cover with a clean cloth and let rise until slightly more than doubled in volume, about 1 hour. Punch down the dough, knead lightly for 1 minute, and divide in half. Roll each part into half a 9 x 18-inch rectangle about $\frac{1}{8}$ inch thick. Let rest 10 minutes.

Brush the dough with:

2 tablespoons butter, melted

One at a time, cut each rectangle lengthwise into 6 strips, 1$\frac{1}{2}$ inches wide. Stack them and cut the stack into 1$\frac{1}{2}$-inch-wide pieces, with a string, as shown below, or using a dough scraper. Place the rolls in buttered muffin tins, cut edges up. Let rise in a warm place (75° to 85°F) until doubled in size.

Preheat the oven to 425°F. Bake 15 to 20 minutes, until well browned. Remove to a rack to cool.

Making Buttermilk Rolls (Fan-Tans)

KOLATCHEN
About thirty-six 2-inch rolls
Prepare:

Dough for Palm Leaf Rolls, 611, or Milk Bread, 597

Roll the dough into 2-inch balls and place about 2 inches apart on greased baking sheets. The dough will be very sticky; flour your hands as necessary. Have ready one or more of the following:

Prune, Apricot, Date, or Fig Filling, 624, jam
     or chopped fruit (1¹/₂ to 2¹/₄ cups total)

Press an indentation into the center of each roll, making a ¹/₄-inch rim. Fill each one with 2 teaspoons to 1 tablespoon of the fillings. Cover and let rise about 40 minutes. Preheat the oven to 375°F. Bake the rolls about 20 minutes. Remove to a rack to cool. If desired, sprinkle with:

(Confectioners' sugar)

OVERNIGHT ROLLS
About 48 rolls
This sweet dough is good for rolls, buns, and coffee cakes.

Stir in a saucepan over low heat until the shortening melts:

1 cup milk
¹/₂ cup vegetable shortening or lard

Let cool. Meanwhile, combine in a large bowl and let stand until the yeast is dissolved, about 5 minutes.

2 tablespoons warm (105° to 115°F) water

1 package (2¹/₄ teaspoons) active dry yeast
2 teaspoons sugar

Beat the milk mixture into the yeast mixture, along with:

¹/₂ cup sugar
3 large eggs, beaten
1 teaspoon salt

Gradually stir in

4¹/₂ cups all-purpose flour

Beat the dough about 5 minutes. Place in an oiled bowl and turn to coat with oil. Cover with foil and refrigerate for 12 to 24 hours. Divide the dough into 3 portions. Roll each one into a circle about 9 inches in diameter. Brush the circles with:

2 tablespoons butter, melted

and dust each circle with a mixture of:

¹/₄ cup sugar
1 teaspoon ground cinnamon

or top with:

³/₄ cup any coffee cake filling, 623–624

Cut each circle into 16 wedges.

Roll up each piece beginning at the wider end, stretching the dough a bit as you roll it. Brush the tips with:

Egg Wash, 601

Arrange the rolls 2 inches apart on greased baking sheets, seam side down, and let rise until doubled in volume, about 1¹/₂ hours.

Set a rack in the center of the oven. Preheat the oven to 375°F. Bake the rolls one sheet at a time until browned, 15 to 18 minutes. Take care—they burn easily. Remove to a rack to cool.

FILLED PINWHEEL ROLLS
About 30 rolls
Prepare:

Dough for Overnight Rolls, above

Let rise, covered and refrigerated, until doubled in volume. Punch down the dough. Divide the dough in half and roll each piece to ¹/₄-inch thickness. Cut into 4-inch squares. Spread the squares generously with:

¹/₂ cup (1 stick) butter, softened

Sprinkle with a mixture of:

3 tablespoons sugar
1 tablespoon ground cinnamon

Place in the center of each square:

1 teaspoon raisins and nuts or 1 teaspoon plum,
     apricot, or raspberry jam (about 1 cup total)

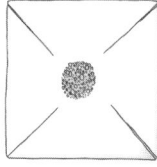   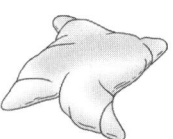

Forming Filled Pinwheel Rolls

Cut diagonally into the dough from each corner to within ³/₄ inch of the center. Fold every other point toward the center, as shown below, overlapping and sealing the points with a little water.

Place on greased baking sheets and let rise slightly, about 15 minutes.

Preheat the oven to 425°F. Bake until puffed, about 18 minutes. Remove to a rack to cool.

BUTTERMILK POTATO ROLLS
About 48 rolls

Prepare:

Dough for Buttermilk Potato Bread, 600

Preheat the oven to 425°F. Let rise once, then punch down. Shape and let rise as for Cloverleaf Rolls, 610.

If desired, glaze the tops of the rolls with:

(French Egg Wash, 799)

Sprinkle with:

(Poppy seeds)

Bake until browned, 15 to 18 minutes. Remove at once to a rack to cool.

CHEESE ROLLS
About 48 rolls

Prepare **Dough for Cheese Bread, 598.** Shape and bake as for **Overnight Rolls, 612.**

CARAMEL BUNS (SCHNECKEN)
Twenty-two 3-inch rolls

Prepare dough for:

Overnight Rolls, 612

Let rise, covered, until doubled in volume. Punch down the dough and roll into an 11 x 17-inch rectangle on a floured board. Spread generously with:

¹/₄ cup (¹/₂ stick) butter, melted

Sprinkle with a mixture of:

¹/₄ cup packed brown sugar
1¹/₂ teaspoons ground cinnamon

Add:

1 cup raisins
1 cup pecans
1 teaspoon grated lemon zest

Starting from the long side, roll up the dough as you would a jelly roll, then cut the roll into 1¹/₂-inch slices.

Bring to a simmer in a medium saucepan over medium heat, stirring to dissolve the sugar:

¹/₄ cup honey
¹/₄ cup (¹/₂ stick) butter
¹/₂ cup packed light brown sugar

Add:

¹/₂ cup pecans

Fill the bottom of each muffin cup with 1 tablespoon caramel. Lay the slices of dough over the caramel. Let rise about 30 minutes.

Preheat the oven to 350°F. Bake about 20 minutes, until golden brown. Watch closely for signs of scorching. Remove from the oven and invert the rolls onto a rack set over a baking sheet, allowing the honey mixture to drip over the rolls.

STICKY BUNS
Eight 4-inch buns

The ultimate sticky bun, chewy and decadent.

Prepare:

Dough for Yeasted Coffee Cake, 621

Butter a 13 x 9-inch baking pan. Bring to a boil in a small saucepan over medium heat, stirring to dissolve the sugar:

1 cup packed dark brown sugar
¹/₂ cup (1 stick) butter
¹/₄ cup honey

Remove from the heat and stir in, if desired:

(2¹/₂ cups chopped pecans)

Pour the hot syrup into the baking pan and spread it evenly. Let cool.

Using a rolling pin, roll out the dough to a 16 x 12-inch rectangle. Brush with:

1 tablespoon butter, melted

Sprinkle with:

¹/₃ to ¹/₂ cup packed dark brown sugar
2 teaspoons ground cinnamon

Starting from a long side, roll up the dough into a cylinder. Cut crosswise into 8 slices. Arrange the slices cut side down in the prepared pan, spacing them evenly. Cover

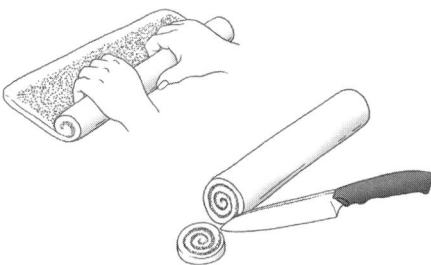

Preparing Sticky Buns

with oiled plastic wrap and let rise at room temperature until doubled in volume, about 1 hour.

Preheat the oven to 350°F. Bake until the buns are golden brown and the syrup is bubbling hot, about 30 minutes. Let the buns cool in the pan for 5 minutes, then invert the pan onto a rimmed baking sheet; you may want to line the sheet with aluminum foil. Serve warm or at room temperature, pulling the sticky buns apart at the seams.

BEAR CLAWS
6 claws
Prepare:
> **Dough for Yeasted Coffee Cake, 621,**
> > **or ¹⁄₂ recipe Danish Pastry Dough, 624**

Cut the dough into 3 pieces. Roll each into an 18 by 9-inch rectangle. Brush each one with:
> **2 tablespoons butter, melted**

Mix together:
> **¹⁄₂ cup chopped walnuts**
> **¹⁄₄ cup chopped dates**
> **2 tablespoons sugar**
> **¹⁄₂ teaspoon ground cinnamon**

Sprinkle over the dough. Fold the dough lengthwise into thirds, pinching the edges together to hold in the filling. Cut into 6 rectangles. Place them seam side down on a greased baking sheet. Make 3 slashes in each, to resemble claws. Brush with:
> **3 tablespoons butter, melted**

Cover and let rise, 45 minutes.
Preheat the oven to 375°F. Bake 25 minutes, or until golden. If desired, drizzle with:
> **(Translucent Sugar Glaze, 799)**

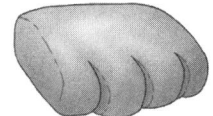

Bear claw

WHOLE WHEAT ROLLS
About forty 2-inch rolls
Prepare:
> **Dough for Whole Wheat Bread, 599, or Oat Bread**
> **Cockaigne, 600**

Let rise once, shape into 2-inch rolls, and let rise again, covered until almost doubled in size, about 1 hour.
Preheat the oven to 425°F. Brush the tops of the rolls with:
> **¹⁄₄ cup (¹⁄₂ stick) butter, melted**

Sprinkle with, if desired:
> **(Coarse salt, chopped nuts, or sesame seeds)**

Bake until browned, 12 to 18 minutes. Remove to a rack to cool.

RYE ROLLS
About 36 rolls
Prepare:
> **Dough for All-Rye-Flour Bread, 605**

Let rise once, then shape into rolls. Sprinkle the tops with:
> **Coarse salt**

Let rise, covered, until doubled, about 1 hour.
Preheat the oven to 375°F. Bake until browned, about 20 minutes. If desired, halfway through the baking time, brush with:
> **(Melted butter or heavy cream)**

Remove to a rack to cool.

OAT ROLLS
Thirty-six 2-inch rolls
An agreeable variation on an old-time favorite formula.
Prepare:
> **Dough for Oat Bread Cockaigne, 600**

Let rise once, then shape into rolls and let rise until doubled in volume, about 1¹⁄₂ hours.
Preheat the oven to 375°F. Bake until browned, about 15 minutes. Remove to a rack to cool.

BRIOCHE
1 loaf or 10 brioches
This classic is a simple yeast dough that is enriched with eggs and lots of butter; use it for loaves, 594, plain rolls, and rolls stuffed with fruit, meat, or cheese, or bake in special brioche tins, available at gourmet stores and on-line. The high butter content gives the impression that the dough is wetter than it actually is, leading to the temptation—which you must resist—to add more flour. This dough is easily braided, following directions for Challah, 600.

Combine in a large bowl or the bowl of a heavy-duty mixer and let stand until the yeast is dissolved, about 5 minutes:
> **¹⁄₃ cup warm (105° to 115°F) whole milk**
> **1 package (2¹⁄₄ teaspoons) active dry yeast**

Add:
> **1 cup all-purpose flour**
> **3 large eggs, lightly beaten**
> **1 tablespoon sugar**
> **1 teaspoon salt**

Mix by hand or on low speed. Gradually stir in:
> **1 cup all-purpose flour**

Mix for about 5 minutes, until all the ingredients are blended. Knead by hand for about 15 minutes or with the dough hook on low to medium speed for 7 to 10 minutes, until the dough cleans the sides of the bowl. Because this is a rather sticky dough, kneading by hand requires a particular technique: Slap the dough down on the work surface, lift half of it up with both hands (part of it will remain stuck to the table, which is fine), and slap it down over onto itself. Repeat this until the dough is smooth and elastic and no longer sticky. Add:
> **³⁄₄ cup (1¹⁄₂ sticks) unsalted butter, softened**

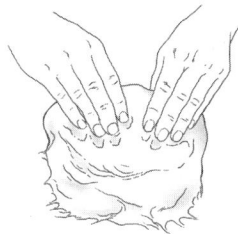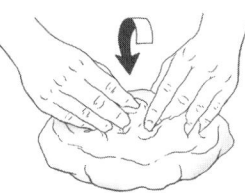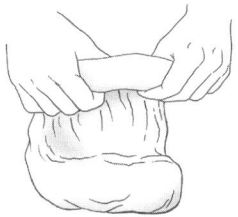

Kneading Brioche

Vigorously knead in the butter until it is completely incorporated and the dough is once again smooth. Place the dough in a buttered large bowl, cover with plastic wrap, and let rise in a warm place (75° to 85°F) until doubled in volume, about 1½ hours.

Punch down the dough and knead briefly. Refrigerate, covered, for 4 to 12 hours. If the dough has doubled, punch it down and shape it. If it has not yet doubled, let it finish rising in a warm place, then punch it down, refrigerate for 30 minutes, and shape.

Preheat the oven to 375°F. With a knife that has been dipped in water, cut four or five ½-inch-deep incisions in the top of the dough. This will help the dough rise evenly without tearing or losing its shape during baking. Brush the risen dough again with egg wash. Bake until deep golden brown and a knife inserted in the center of one brioche comes out clean and the crust is deeply golden, about 20 minutes for buns and 35 to 40 minutes for a loaf. Unmold the brioches onto a rack and let cool. Serve slightly warm or cool.

BRIOCHE AU CHOCOLAT
30 brioches

A favorite French after-school treat.
Prepare:

Dough for Brioche, 614, or Danish Pastry Dough, 624

Roll the dough into an 18 by 15-inch rectangle. Cut into 3-inch squares. Place on each square:

A generous sliver of dark or semisweet chocolate

Fold the dough over the chocolate like an envelope, or roll up like a cigar around the chocolate. Brush with, if desired:

(French Egg Wash, 799)

Place on ungreased baking sheets, cover with oiled plastic wrap, and allow to rise until doubled, about 40 minutes.

Preheat the oven to 400°F.
Bake the brioche until golden, about 15 minutes.

BRIOCHE À TÊTE (TOPPED BRIOCHE)
10 rolls

A *brioche à tête,* literally, with a head, has a small topknot that sits on a larger base. These are traditionally baked in fluted molds that flare at the top.

Roll the dough on an unfloured work surface into a ball. Cover with plastic wrap and let rest for 10 minutes.

Butter ten 4-ounce fluted brioche molds, muffin cups, deep tartlet pans, or ramekins. Divide the dough equally into 10 pieces and roll each piece into a ball. Shape the dough by using the edge of your hand (like a karate chop) to divide each ball partially, without separating, into 2 parts, one twice as big as the other. Set each piece of dough into a mold with the larger (base) part on the bottom; push the top section down so that it is deeply nestled in the base. Whisk together and brush over the dough:

1 egg
Pinch of salt

Cover loosely with oiled plastic wrap and let rise in a warm place (75° to 85°F) until doubled in volume, about 1 hour. Bake about 20 min, until deeply golden.

SECTIONED BRIOCHE LOAF
1 large loaf

Brioche is such a luxurious treat that it is worth making the extra effort to give it a dramatic shape. Here the dough is divided into quarters and each quarter rolled into a round. The rounds are nestled together in a loaf pan, and the result is an especially pretty loaf.

Butter a 9 x 5-inch loaf pan. Divide the brioche dough

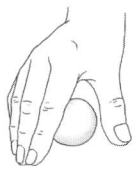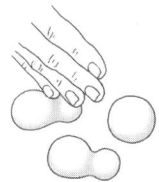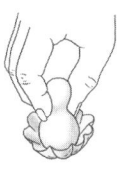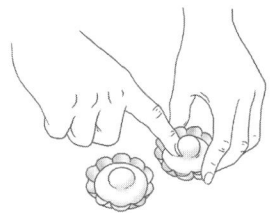

Forming Brioche à Tête

equally into 4 pieces. Roll each piece into a ball, cover with plastic wrap, and let rest for 10 minutes.

Stand the balls of dough on their sides in the loaf pan so they are touching. Whisk together and brush over the top:

1 egg
Pinch of salt

Reserve the remaining egg wash. Cover the brioche loosely with oiled plastic wrap and let rise in a warm place (75° to 85°F) until the dough doubles in volume and fills the pan, about 1 hour. Preheat the oven to 375°F. Brush the loaf again with the egg wash. Bake until golden brown and a knife inserted in the center of the loaf comes out clean, about 30 minutes. Unmold the loaf onto a rack. Serve slightly warm or cool.

Making a Sectioned Brioche Loaf

CROISSANTS

Eighteen 3 ¹/₂-inch-long croissants

Croissant is the French word for crescent. Rich, somewhat troublesome, but unequaled by any other form of roll, a croissant can be made plain or baked with a filling, such as jam, almond paste, or even a savory ingredient such as ham or cheese. Filled with chocolate, it is called *pain au chocolat*, chocolate bread.

If you wish, divide this recipe in half and use half to make croissants and half to make Pains au Chocolat, 617.

Place on a work surface:

1 ¹/₂ cups (3 sticks) cold unsalted butter

Measure:

3 tablespoons all-purpose flour

Sprinkle the butter with a little of the flour and begin to beat it with a rolling pin. Scrape the butter from the work surface and the rolling pin as needed and fold it over itself into a heap. Continue to work the butter until it is a smooth and malleable mass. Knead the remaining flour into the butter with your hands, working quickly to keep the butter cold. Place the butter on a sheet of plastic wrap and shape it into a 9 x 6-inch rectangle. Wrap and refrigerate the butter while you make the dough.

Whisk together in a small bowl and let stand until the yeast is dissolved, about 5 minutes:

1 cup warm (105° to 115°F) whole milk

1 package (2 ¹/₄ teaspoons) active dry yeast
1 tablespoon sugar

Mix together in a large bowl:

2 ³/₄ cups all-purpose flour
2 tablespoons unsalted butter, cut into small pieces, softened
1 teaspoon salt

Make a well in the center and add the warm milk mixture. Mix with a fork or your fingers to make a dough. Transfer to a lightly floured surface and knead for a few seconds, until smooth. Refrigerate the dough for 15 minutes.

Sprinkle the top of the dough with flour and roll into a 15 ¹/₂ x 8-inch rectangle, sprinkling additional flour underneath it as needed to prevent sticking. Position the dough so that one of the short ends is facing you. Cover the upper two-thirds of the dough with the rectangle of butter, leaving a 1-inch border of dough on the sides and at the top. Fold the bottom third of the dough over the butter. Fold the top third of the dough, with the butter on it, down over the first third, as if you were folding a business letter. Press the edges of the dough together on all 3 sides to seal in the butter. Rotate the dough so that the folded edge is on the left and the sealed edge is on the right.

Sprinkle the dough lightly with flour and press it gently with the rolling pin to flatten it slightly. Keeping the short end of the dough facing you, roll into an 18 x 8-inch rectangle. Fold the bottom third up and the top third down again. (This rolling and folding is called a single turn.) Rotate the dough so that the folded edge is on the left and the open edge is on the right (like a book about to be opened). Give the dough one more single turn, rolling it into an 18 x 8-inch rectangle and folding it in thirds. Sprinkle the work surface lightly with flour as needed to prevent the dough from sticking; if at any time the butter gets soft, refrigerate it for 10 to 15 minutes. Mark the dough with 2 imprints to remind yourself that you have given the dough 2 turns. Wrap the dough loosely in plastic and refrigerate for 30 minutes.

Place the dough so the folded edge is on the left and the open edge is on the right, and give it another turn. Rotate and give the dough a final turn. If at any time the butter gets soft, refrigerate it for 10 to 15 minutes. (At this point the dough can be frozen, wrapped in plastic, then aluminum foil, then a plastic bag with the air removed. If frozen, thaw overnight in the refrigerator before proceeding.)

Roll the dough into a 24 x 12-inch rectangle, about ¹/₄ inch thick. Let stand for 5 minutes to relax the gluten and prevent shrinking when cut.

Cut the dough lengthwise into two 24 x 6-inch strips. Refrigerate 1 strip on a baking sheet. Position the remaining rectangle with one long side facing you. Starting from the left, mark the bottom edge of the dough by nicking it with a knife at 4 ¹/₂-inch intervals. Mark the top edge of the dough 2 ¹/₄ inches from the left edge, then continue to mark it at 4 ¹/₂-inch intervals. To cut the dough into triangles, cut from the bottom left corner of the dough to the first mark at the top, then from that mark to the first mark at the bottom, then from the first mark at the bottom to the second mark at the top, and so forth, until you have 9 triangles. Make a ¼-inch-long nick in the middle of the short side of each triangle.

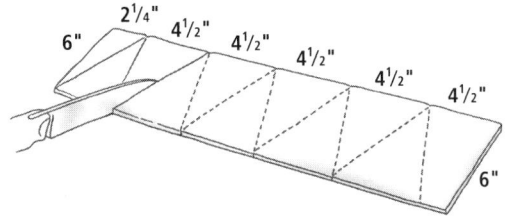

Cutting triangles for croissants

To form a croissant, stretch the short side of a triangle by pulling the corners gently as you begin to roll the stretched edge tightly (but not too tightly) toward the opposite point of the triangle. Finish rolling the croissant so that the point to the triangle is on the bottom of the roll. Shape the other triangles in the same manner. Place the croissants at least 2 inches apart on ungreased baking sheets, curving the ends to form crescent shapes. Repeat the procedure with the second rectangle. (Unbaked croissants can be refrigerated overnight; they will rise partially, for the yeast continues to work slowly in the chilled environment. Let them finish rising at room temperature before baking. They can also be frozen; thaw overnight in the refrigerator before proceeding.)

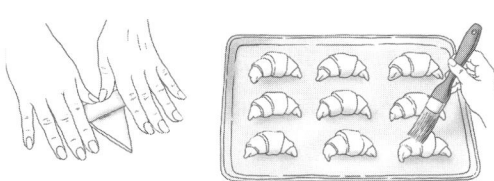

Rolling and brushing a croissant

Cover the croissants with a clean cloth or plastic wrap. Let rise at room temperature until increased in volume by almost half, 1 to 1½ hours.

Position a rack in the lower third of the oven. Preheat the oven to 375°F.

Brush the croissants lightly with:

1 egg, lightly beaten

Bake until golden brown, 20 to 25 minutes. Transfer the croissants to a rack and let cool completely. Croissants are best served the day they are baked, but they may be frozen for 1 month in a sealed plastic bag. Reheat in a preheated 300°F oven for 5 minutes.

RASPBERRY CROISSANTS

Any jam may be used in place of the raspberry jam—try apricot, blueberry, or black currant jam or apple butter. Prepare **Croissants, above.** Place **1½ teaspoons raspberry jam (9 tablespoons total)** ¾ inch from the nick at the wide end of each triangle before rolling up the croissant. On the first roll, pinch the dough around the jam to seal it in.

ALMOND CROISSANTS

Prepare **Croissants, above.** Place **1½ teaspoons almond paste, 877 (9 tablespoons total)** ¾ inch from the nick at the wide end of each triangle before rolling up the croissant. After brushing with the egg wash, sprinkle the tops with **sliced almonds.**

PAIN AU CHOCOLAT
Twenty-four 3 ½-inch-long rolls

Little flaky rolls of croissant pastry filled with dark chocolate are a traditional French *goûter*–teatime or after-school snack.

Have ready:

12 ounces semisweet or bittersweet chocolate, coarsely chopped, or 12 ounces large chocolate chips

Prepare:

Dough for Croissants, 616

Divide in half, and refrigerate one half. Roll the other half into a 16 x 12-inch rectangle. Cut into twelve 4-inch squares. Arrange ½ ounce of the chocolate in a 2-inch-long mound in each square, parallel to and about ½ inch from one edge of the square. Lightly brush the opposite edge of the square with a ½-inch band of:

1 large egg, lightly beaten

Fold the edge of the dough closest to the chocolate over the chocolate and continue to roll the dough up into a cylinder. Place the rolls seam side down at least 2 inches apart on ungreased baking sheets. Repeat with the remaining dough and chocolate.

Let rise and bake as for Croissants, above.

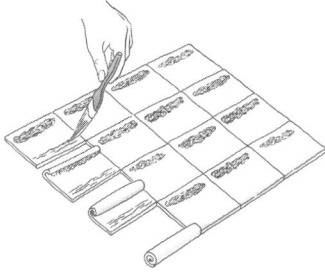

Cutting, filling, and shaping Pains au Chocolat

FILLED SWEET CRESCENTS
About 28 crescents
Prepare:
> **Refrigerator Potato Rolls, 620, or Danish Pastry Dough, 624**

Use for each crescent:
> **1 teaspoon nut or fruit filling, 623
> (generous $1/2$ cup total)**

If using the refrigerator dough, divide the dough into 4 pieces and let rise 30 minutes, or until doubled in size. Roll each piece out to a 9-inch round about $1/4$ inch thick. Cut each circle into 8 wedges. Place the filling in the center of each triangle and roll up like Rugelach, 778. If using Scandinavian Pastry, shape after chilling. Place on greased baking sheets and let rise until doubled in bulk.
Brush the crescents lightly with:
> **French Egg Wash, 799**

Bake in a preheated 375°F oven 18 to 20 minutes. Serve warm, cool on a rack.

HARD ROLLS (VIENNA ROLLS)
Twelve $2^1/4$-inch rolls
These rolls are wonderfully crusty. The beaten egg whites give them a light, soft crumb.
Combine in a large bowl or the bowl of a heavy-duty mixer and let stand until the yeast is dissolved, about 5 minutes:
> **$1/4$ cup warm (105° to 115°F) water
> 1 package ($2^1/4$ teaspoons) active dry yeast**

Add:
> **1 cup warm (105° to 115°F) water
> 2 to $2^1/2$ cups all-purpose flour
> 2 tablespoons vegetable shortening
> 1 tablespoon sugar
> $1^1/4$ teaspoons salt**

Mix by hand or on low speed until thoroughly blended. Beat until soft peaks form:
> **2 large egg whites**

Fold into the dough. Gradually stir in until the dough is moist but no longer sticky:
> **$1^3/4$ to 2 cups all-purpose flour**

Knead for about 7 minutes by hand or with the dough hook on low to medium speed until the dough is smooth and elastic. Transfer the dough to an oiled bowl and turn it once to coat with oil. Cover with plastic wrap and let rise in a warm place (75° to 85°F) until doubled in volume, 1 to $1^1/2$ hours.
Punch down the dough, knead it briefly, and let rise again until doubled, about 1 hour.
Punch down the dough and divide it into 12 pieces. On an unfloured work surface, roll each piece into a ball. Loosely cover the balls of dough with plastic wrap. Lightly dust a baking sheet with:
> **Cornmeal**

Place the rolls 2 inches apart on the baking sheet. Loosely cover with oiled plastic wrap and let rise in a warm place until doubled, about 1 hour.

Set the racks in the middle and bottom of the oven and place a 13 x 9-inch baking pan on the bottom rack. Preheat the oven to 425°F.
Place the rolls on the center rack and immediately pour 2 cups boiling water into the hot baking pan. Bake the rolls until golden brown and crusty, about 20 minutes. Serve freshly baked and warm, or reheat for 4 to 6 minutes in a 400°F oven.

ENGLISH MUFFINS
About twenty 3-inch muffins
These are heavenly when eaten fresh and do not taste at all like store-bought ones. They do begin to resemble them on the second day, however, so instead freeze any leftovers immediately. Muffin rings help them keep their shape; they can be purchased, or you can make them from short cans of fruit or fish—remove the tops and bottoms and thoroughly scrub the rims. English muffins are always baked on a greased griddle.
Stir together in a small bowl and let stand until the yeast is dissolved, 3 to 5 minutes:
> **2 tablespoons warm (105° to 115°F) water
> 1 package ($2^1/4$ teaspoons) active dry yeast**

Combine in a large bowl:
> **1 cup warm (105° to 115°F) water
> $1/2$ cup room temperature (72° to 75°F) milk
> 2 teaspoons sugar
> 1 teaspoon salt**

Stir in the dissolved yeast. Gradually beat in:
> **2 cups sifted all-purpose flour**

Cover the bowl with a clean cloth. Let this sponge rise in a warm place (75° to 85°F) about $1^1/2$ hours, or until it collapses back into the bowl.
Beat in:
> **3 tablespoons butter, softened**

Beat or knead in:
> **2 cups sifted all-purpose flour**

For the final rising, you may put the dough into greased rings on a lightly greased baking sheet, filling them to a depth of no more than $1/2$ inch. Or, place the dough on a board lightly floured or sprinkled with cornmeal. Pat or press the dough to a thickness of about $1/2$ inch, cut into rounds about 3 inches in diameter, and place on the baking sheet. Let rise until doubled in volume.
Generously butter a griddle and heat until hot. Remove the rings, and, working in batches, carefully slip a pancake turner under each muffin ring or rounds of dough and transfer to the griddle. Cook until light brown on the bottom. Turn and cook on the second side. Cool on a rack.
To separate the muffins before toasting, hold 2 forks back to back and pry them open. Butter generously and toast. The uneven browning gives them great charm. Serve with, if desired:
> **(Marmalade)**

CRUMPETS
About 12 crumpets
Crumpets are similar to English muffins except that they are made from a batter rather than a dough. Classically, crumpets are baked in greased muffin rings, but they may also be dropped free-form, as here, in which case they may be called instead pikelets. Crumpets are eaten warm but need not be toasted. They are buttered on the "holey" side, not split.
Follow the recipe for:
   English Muffins, above
omitting the water and using **1 1/2 cups milk.** Reduce the flour to 2 1/2 cups. Mix until smooth, cover, and let stand until the batter rises and then falls, 1 1/2 to 3 hours.
Drop the batter by 1/4-cupfuls onto a moderately hot greased griddle or skillet, making 4-inch cakes. (The cakes will not be even in shape.) Cook until the bottom is lightly browned and the top is bubbly, turn with a spatula, and cook until cooked through, about 2 minutes per side. If not serving at once, wrap and refrigerate; to serve, toast or wrap in foil and reheat in a warm oven.

BAGELS
8 bagels
The classic accompaniment is cream cheese and lox or smoked salmon. But try sprinkling spices, raisins, poppy or sesame seeds, finely chopped nuts, or freeze-dried onions on top of the dough.
Combine in a large bowl or the bowl of a heavy-duty mixer and let stand until the yeast dissolves, about 5 minutes:
   1 cup plus 2 tablespoons warm (105° to 115°F) water
   1 package (2 1/4 teaspoons) active dry yeast
   2 1/2 teaspoons sugar
Stir in:
   1 tablespoon melted vegetable shortening
   1 1/2 teaspoons malt syrup or sugar
   1 3/4 teaspoons salt
   1 cup bread flour
Gradually stir in:
   3 to 3 1/2 cups bread flour
Knead for about 10 minutes by hand or with the dough hook on low to medium speed until the dough is smooth and elastic. Let rest, covered, 15 to 20 minutes.
Punch down the dough and divide into 8 equal pieces. Roll each piece into a rope about 10 inches long, tapering the ends. Wet the ends to help seal, and form into rings, stretching the top end over and around the bottom end and pinching them together underneath. Let rise, covered, on a floured board about 15 minutes, until puffy.
Preheat the oven to 425°F.
Bring to a boil in a large pot:
   4 quarts water
   1 tablespoon malt syrup or sugar
   1/2 teaspoon salt
Drop the rings 4 at a time into the boiling water. As the

bagels surface, turn them over and cook about 45 seconds longer. Skim out and place on an ungreased baking sheet coated with:
   Cornmeal
Sprinkle with toppings of choice. Bake 20 to 25 minutes, turning after 15 minutes, until golden brown and crisp.

PRETZELS
Twelve 5-inch pretzels
A chewy pretzel that is easy to make. These can be stored in an airtight container for up to 3 days.
Combine in a large bowl or the bowl of a heavy-duty mixer and let stand until the yeast is dissolved, about 5 minutes:
   1/2 cup warm (105° to 115°F) water
   1 package (2 1/4 teaspoons) active dry yeast
Add:
   1 1/2 cups all-purpose flour
   1 1/2 cups bread flour
   2 tablespoons butter or margarine, melted
   1 tablespoon sugar
   1/2 teaspoon salt
Mix by hand or on low speed while slowly pouring in:
   1/2 cup warm (105° to 115°F) water
Stir for a minute, adding more flour or water if needed to make a moist but not sticky dough. Knead for about 10 minutes by hand or with the dough hook on low to medium speed until the dough is smooth and elastic. Transfer the dough to an oiled bowl and turn it once to coat with oil. Loosely cover with plastic wrap and let rise in a warm place (75° to 80°F) until doubled in volume, 1 to 1 1/2 hours.
Punch down the dough and divide it into 12 pieces (about 2 ounces each). On an unfloured work surface, roll each piece into a ball. Loosely cover with oiled plastic wrap and let rest for 10 minutes.
Grease 2 baking sheets. Roll each ball into an 18-inch-long rope, working from the center outward and slightly tapering the ends. To form the pretzels, lift the ends of the strip of dough so they meet in front of you and form an oval, but do not join the ends: Lift them and twist them around each other about 3 inches from the end. Gently press one end into the dough at 3 o'clock and the other at 7 o'clock. Place the pretzels on the baking sheets, cover, and let rise in a warm place until nearly doubled in volume, about 35 minutes.
Preheat the oven to 400°F. Bring to a boil in a big pot or deep skillet:
   8 cups water
   2 tablespoons plus 1 teaspoon baking soda
Reduce the heat to maintain a simmer. Using a slotted spoon, gently slide several pretzels at a time into the water. Simmer for 30 seconds, then flip them over and continue to simmer until puffed, about 30 seconds longer. Return to the greased baking sheets. Sprinkle with:
   Coarse salt
Bake until deep golden brown, about 15 minutes.

BREAD STICKS (GRISSINI)

Any bread dough may be used for bread sticks. The dough is given only one rise.

Prepare:

White Bread, 596

Set the racks in the lower and middle levels of the oven and place a baking pan on the lower rack. Preheat the oven to 500°F. Liberally sprinkle 2 baking sheets with:

All-purpose flour, cornmeal, or semolina flour

Use the palm of your hand to flatten the dough into a ½-inch-thick rectangle about 25 x 7 inches. With a knife, cut the dough crosswise into ½-inch-wide strips. Transfer the strips to the baking sheets, leaving about ½ inch between them. They will stretch to the width of the pan, 12 inches, as you transfer them. Brush lightly with:

Water, melted butter, or beaten egg

Sprinkle with:

Coarse salt, seeds, herbs, spices, nuts, or grated cheese

Slide the pans into the oven and immediately pour 2 cups hot or boiling water into the preheated baking pan. Reduce the heat to 400° and bake until well browned, about 18 minutes. Cool completely on a rack.

ABOUT REFRIGERATOR DOUGHS

By "refrigerator," we mean just that—these are not freezer doughs. If it's a freezer product you're after, for best results, bake before freezing. We find the following recipes somewhat limited in use, because ➤ the milk-based ones can be kept chilled only 3 days and the water-based ones 5 days. Yeast action is slowed by the cold, but it does continue, so both more fat and more sugar are needed in refrigerator doughs than in other kinds to keep the yeast potent during the refrigerator period. We find that kneading before storage helps to retain rising power. The advantage of this type of dough, of course, is that you can bake some at once and keep the rest for later.

To store for chilling, ➤ keep the dough in a greased plastic bag or container large enough to allow for some expansion. If it rises in the refrigerator, punch down the dough. Or, place the balled dough in a greased bowl, turn it so the entire surface is evenly coated, cover it tightly with plastic wrap or foil, and weight it down with a plate.

After removing it from the refrigerator, always ➤ rest the dough, covered, 30 minutes. Then ➤ punch it down. To shape or fill, see previous roll recipes and illustrations. Be sure the dough at least doubles in volume after shaping. Allow ample time for rising because of the chilled condition of the dough. To bake, see the individual recipes.

NO-KNEAD REFRIGERATOR ROLLS

Eighteen 2½-inch rolls

Combine and heat until the fat melts:

1 cup milk

6 tablespoons (¾ stick) butter or ⅓ cup vegetable shortening

⅓ cup sugar

1 teaspoon salt

Cool to lukewarm, and pour into the large bowl of a heavy-duty mixer.

Meanwhile, combine in a small bowl and let stand until the yeast is dissolved, about 5 minutes:

½ cup warm (105° to 115°F) water

1 package (2¼ teaspoons) active dry yeast

Beat into the dissolved yeast:

1 large egg

Add to the milk mixture. Add:

1¾ cups all-purpose flour

and beat at medium speed for 2 minutes. Add:

1¾ cups all-purpose flour

and beat until the dough begins to pull away from the sides of the bowl, about 10 minutes. To store for chilling, shape and prepare for baking; see About Refrigerator Doughs, above.

Bake the rolls in a preheated 425°F oven about 15 minutes, until golden brown.

REFRIGERATOR POTATO ROLLS

About forty 2-inch rolls

A sweet dough also entirely suitable for coffee cakes.

Prepare:

1 cup freshly cooked potatoes, passed through a potato ricer or mashed with a fork

Place in a large bowl:

½ cup lard or vegetable shortening

Heat and pour over it:

1 cup milk

Stir until the lard is melted. Let cool to lukewarm.

Meanwhile, combine in a small bowl and let stand until the yeast is dissolved, about 5 minutes:

½ cup warm (105° to 115°F) water

1 package (2¼ teaspoons) active dry yeast

Add the dissolved yeast and the potatoes to the milk mixture. Add:

3 large eggs, beaten

¾ cup sugar

2 teaspoons salt

Beat well. Add:

4 cups all-purpose flour

and beat in thoroughly. Stir in:

1 cup all-purpose flour

or toss the dough onto a board and knead in the flour. To store for chilling, shape and prepare for baking; see About Refrigerator Doughs, above. It may be necessary to add up to 1 cup more flour to the dough to make it workable.

If desired, brush the shaped rolls with

Egg Wash, 601, or heavy cream

Bake in a preheated 425°F oven until golden brown, about 15 minutes.

REFRIGERATOR WHOLE WHEAT ROLLS
About twenty 2-inch rolls

Combine in a small bowl and let stand until the yeast is dissolved, about 5 minutes:

>**1 cup warm (105° to 115°F) water**
>**1 package (2¹/₄ teaspoons) active dry yeast**

Beat in a large bowl until creamy:

>**¹/₃ cup sugar**
>**¹/₄ cup vegetable shortening**

Stir in the yeast mixture. Gradually stir in:

>**1³/₄ cups all-purpose flour**
>**1¹/₂ cups whole wheat flour**
>**1¹/₄ teaspoons salt**

Beat until well blended. To store for chilling, shape and prepare for baking; see About Refrigerator Doughs, above.

Bake the rolls in a preheated 425°F oven until brown, about 12 minutes.

REFRIGERATOR BRAN ROLLS
About forty-eight 2-inch rolls

These are crisp, crunchy, and light.

Combine in a large bowl:

>**1 cup vegetable shortening**
>**³/₄ cup sugar**
>**1¹/₂ to 2 teaspoons salt**

Pour over and stir until the shortening is melted:

>**1 cup boiling water**

Add:

>**1 cup bran or 100% bran cereal**

Let cool to lukewarm. Meanwhile, combine in a small bowl and let stand until the yeast is dissolved, about 5 minutes:

>**1 cup warm (105° to 115°F) water**
>**2 packages (1¹/₂ tablespoons) active dry yeast**

Stir into the bran mixture:

>**2 large eggs, well beaten**

Stir in the dissolved yeast. Gradually add:

>**6 cups all-purpose flour**

Beat well. To store for chilling, shape and prepare for baking; see About Refrigerator Doughs, above.

If the dough forms a dark crust as it stands, knead it into the dough before shaping. Bake the rolls in a preheated 425°F oven until brown, about 15 minutes.

ABOUT YEAST COFFEE CAKES

Holidays are an inspiration to bakers. The Portuguese make an Easter bread, hiding within it hard-cooked eggs, and the Italians, a panettone, a rich bread filled with nuts and fruit.

Remember when you are baking bread and rolls that many of those doughs can be made into coffee cakes and sweet rolls. Try some with the special fillings suggested at the end of this section, 623–624.

PANETTONE (ITALIAN EASTER BREAD)
2 tall round loaves

If baked in greased coffee cans and attractively packaged, this cake makes wonderful gifts.

Combine in a medium bowl and let stand until the yeast is dissolved, about 5 minutes:

>**1 cup warm (105° to 115°F) water**
>**2 packages (1¹/₂ tablespoons) active dry yeast**

Stir in:

>**1 cup all-purpose flour**

Cover this sponge and let rise about 30 minutes in a warm (75° to 85°F) place.

Beat in a large bowl until soft:

>**¹/₂ cup (1 stick) butter**

Gradually add and blend until light and creamy:

>**¹/₂ cup sugar**

Beat in one at a time:

>**2 to 3 large eggs**

Add:

>**1 teaspoon salt**
>**2 teaspoons grated lemon zest**

Beat in the sponge. Gradually beat in:

>**3¹/₂ cups all-purpose flour**

Beat the dough for 5 minutes more. Add, if desired:

>**(1 cup chopped nuts)**
>**(¹/₄ cup golden raisins, candied orange peel, or**
>**chopped candied pineapple)**
>**(2 tablespoons chopped candied citron)**

Cover the bowl with a clean cloth and let the dough rise about 2 hours, or until almost doubled in bulk.

Punch down the dough and divide it in half. Place in 2 greased 9-inch tube pans or greased 6-cup coffee cans and let rise until puffy, about 30 minutes.

Preheat the oven to 350°F.

Lightly brush the tops of the cakes with:

>**Melted butter**

If no fruits or nuts were added to the dough, combine and sprinkle on top:

>**(¹/₂ cup slivered blanched almonds)**
>**(¹/₄ cup sugar)**

Bake until golden, about 30 minutes. If you didn't use the almonds and sugar, spread on, if desired, after the cake has baked and cooled:

>**(Milk or Lemon Glaze, 799)**

YEASTED COFFEE CAKE
1 loaf

A simple and popular multipurpose yeasted coffee cake dough that here is made as a breakfast loaf with a streusel topping.

Combine in a large bowl or the bowl of a heavy-duty mixer and let stand until the yeast is dissolved, about 5 minutes:

>**¹/₄ cup warm (105° to 115°F) water**
>**1 package (2¹/₄ teaspoons) active dry yeast**

Add:

$^{1}/_{2}$ **cup all-purpose or bread flour**
$^{1}/_{3}$ **cup sugar**
$^{1}/_{4}$ **cup milk**
2 large eggs
1 teaspoon vanilla
1 teaspoon salt

Mix by hand or on low speed until blended. Gradually stir in:

2 to 2$^{1}/_{4}$ cups all-purpose or bread flour

Mix for 1 minute, or until the dough comes together. Knead by hand for about 10 minutes or with the dough hook on low to medium speed for 5 to 7 minutes, until the dough is smooth and elastic and no longer sticks to your hands or the bowl. Add:

6 tablespoons ($^{3}/_{4}$ stick) butter, very soft

Vigorously knead in the butter until completely incorporated and the dough is once again smooth.

Place the dough in a large buttered bowl. Cover with plastic wrap and let rise in a warm place (75° to 85°F) until doubled in volume, about 1$^{1}/_{2}$ hours.

Punch down the dough, knead briefly, and refrigerate, covered, until doubled again, 4 to 12 hours.

Butter a 9 x 5-inch loaf pan. Prepare:

$^{2}/_{3}$ **cup Streusel I, 799, or Streusel II, 799**

Punch down the dough and roll out to a 16 x 9-inch rectangle, about $^{1}/_{3}$ inch thick. Brush the surface with:

1$^{1}/_{2}$ teaspoons butter, melted

Sprinkle evenly with half the streusel topping, along with:

($^{1}/_{3}$ cup chopped nuts, such as pecans or walnuts)

Starting from one short side, roll up the dough as you would a jelly roll. Place seam side down in the loaf pan, cover loosely with plastic wrap, and let rise in a warm place until doubled in volume, about 1$^{1}/_{2}$ hours.

Preheat the oven to 375°F. Whisk together and brush over the top of the loaf:

1 egg
A pinch of salt

Sprinkle the remaining streusel topping over the dough. Bake the loaf until golden brown and a knife inserted in the center comes out clean, about 45 minutes. Unmold the loaf onto a rack and let cool.

KNEADED FILLED COFFEE CAKE

2 loaves

Prepare:

Dough for Buttermilk Potato Rolls, 613,
     or Milk Bread, 597

adding an additional:

$^{1}/_{4}$ **cup sugar**

To give the breads an interesting color, use the tiniest smidgen of:

Saffron, 1008

Roll dough as for a Jelly Roll, 735. For a **wreath,** roll 2 pounds of dough out to a 22 x 11-inch rectangle spread with any filling, 623–624, then form, as for Danish Coffeecake, 626. For an **alligator,** roll 1 pound of dough into a

10 x 15-inch rectangle and cut nine 1$^{1}/_{2}$-inch-wide strips on each side. There should be at least 3 inches of space in the center, in which to place filling. To fill, see About Flavorings and Fillings for Coffee Cakes, 623. Lace the strips over the filling, folding the strips in one at a time, alternating sides, being sure to cover the tips of each strip with the strip from the opposing side. Fold the tip of the last strip under the alligator, to hide it. To glaze, see 799.

STOLLEN (CHRISTMAS LOAF)

2 long loaves

Stollen is traditionally served during the Christmas holidays, but many bake it year-round. The shape and folds of the dough are said to represent the folds of the blanket of the baby Jesus. Stollen is similar to brioche, but it has a slightly coarser texture and contains more sugar, as well as nuts and candied fruits to give it a festive note.

Have ready:

6 to 8 cups all-purpose flour

Combine in a medium bowl and let stand until the yeast is dissolved, about 5 minutes:

1$^{1}/_{2}$ cups warm (105° to 115°F) water or milk
2 packages (1$^{1}/_{2}$ tablespoons) active dry yeast

Add 1 cup of the flour. Cover this sponge and let it rest in a warm place until light and foamy, about 1 hour.

Beat in a large bowl until creamy:

1$^{1}/_{2}$ cups (3 sticks) butter, softened

Gradually add and beat until light and creamy:

$^{3}/_{4}$ **cup sugar**

Beat in one at a time:

3 large eggs

Add:

$^{3}/_{4}$ **teaspoon salt**
$^{3}/_{4}$ **teaspoon grated lemon zest**

Add the sponge, then gradually knead in enough flour to make a smooth, elastic dough. Cover and let rise until doubled in volume, 1 to 1$^{1}/_{2}$ hours.

Toss with a little of the flour:

1$^{1}/_{2}$ to 2 cups raisins
1$^{1}/_{2}$ to 2 cups chopped or slivered blanched almonds
($^{1}/_{2}$ cup chopped candied fruits)

Toss the dough onto a floured board. Knead in the fruit and nuts. Divide the dough into 2 equal pieces; cover one piece and set aside. Using a rolling pin, roll the other piece of dough into a $^{1}/_{2}$-inch-thick oval about 16 inches long and 9 inches wide. Do not roll out to the edges of the oval—the edges should be thicker than the center. Brush the top of the dough with half of:

2 tablespoons butter, melted

Fold the dough oval slightly less than half lengthwise so the long edges of the dough are about $^{1}/_{2}$ inch apart. Tuck the two short ends (about 1 inch on each end) underneath the loaf. Place the stollen on a greased baking sheet. Shape the other piece of dough in the same way. Loosely cover both loaves with oiled plastic wrap and let rise in a warm place (75° to 85°F) for about 45 minutes. The dough does not have to fully double in volume; a three-quarter rise is enough.

Position a rack in the center of the oven. Preheat the oven to 350°F.

Bake the loaves until deep golden brown and a knife inserted in the center comes out clean, 50 to 60 minutes. Brush the loaves with:

3 tablespoons butter, melted

Thickly sift over the top:

¼ cup confectioners' sugar

Return to the oven for about 3 minutes. Sift over with:

¼ cup confectioners' sugar

Transfer to a rack to cool.

KUGELHOPF

1 ring

This slightly sweet decorative loaf comes from the Alsace region of France. Kugelhopf is baked in a tall fluted ring mold. An earthenware mold is traditional, but metal or glass molds work just as well. You can also use a plain or fluted tube pan. This makes wonderful breakfast bread.

Place in a small saucepan with enough cold water to cover by ½ inch:

½ cup dried currants

Bring to a boil, then drain well. Transfer the currants to a small bowl and sprinkle with:

2 tablespoons rum or orange juice

Cover and let soak for at least 1 hour, or up to 3 days. Prepare:

Dough for Brioche, 614

Butter a 7- to 8-cup kugelhopf mold or tube pan. Sprinkle the bottom of the mold with:

¼ cup slivered almonds

Or place in the indentations in the bottom of the mold:

Whole almonds

Knead the currants and any unabsorbed liquid into the dough. Press small balls of dough into the bottom of the mold, covering the almonds completely. Press the remaining dough over the top, as even as possible. Cover with oiled plastic wrap and let rise in a warm place (75° to 85°F) until doubled in volume, 1 to 1½ hours.

Preheat the oven to 375°F.

Bake the kugelhopf until golden brown and a knife inserted in the middle of the loaf comes out clean, about 45 minutes. Immediately unmold onto a rack. Dust the top with:

Confectioners' sugar

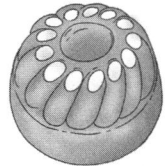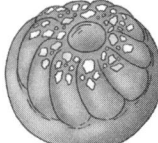

Baked Kugelhopf

Let cool completely. Just before serving, dust a second time with:

Confectioners' sugar

ABOUT FLAVORINGS AND FILLINGS FOR COFFEE CAKES

Crumb mixtures get a considerable flavor boost with the addition of crushed macaroons, almond paste, rolled cake crumbs, or finely ground nuts—especially hazelnuts. Or add pecans, walnuts, almonds, or Brazil nuts. Considerably less effective are finely chopped peanuts, coconut, and cashews.

You may also add distinction to fillings with a small quantity of lemon juice, grated lemon or orange zest, dried currants, finely chopped citron, finely chopped sweet chocolate, or a thin layer of jam or marmalade. Fillings are applied during final shaping and before the last rising. A 9-inch ring needs about 1 cup-plus of filling, individual rolls about 2 teaspoons. For various toppings, glazes, and streusels, see 799–800.

NUT FILLINGS FOR COFFEE CAKES

I. *For one 9-inch ring*

Combine:

½ cup ground hazelnuts or other nuts
½ cup sugar
2 tablespoons finely chopped candied citron
or candied orange peel
2 teaspoons ground cinnamon
½ teaspoon vanilla

Add:

1 large egg, well beaten

Thin with:

Milk

until of the right consistency to spread over the dough.

II. *For one 9-inch ring*

Have ready:

¼ cup chopped blanched almonds,
¼ cup chopped citron
¼ chopped raisins

Melt:

¼ cup (½ stick) butter or 2 tablespoons butter plus
2 tablespoons sour cream

After rolling the dough, spread it with the melted butter and sprinkle with the chopped ingredients and, if desired:

(Sugar)
(Ground cinnamon)

III. *For three 9-inch rings*

You can buy canned almond paste or make it, 877. For each:

10 ounces almond paste

allow:

1 cup sugar
2 large egg whites

Blend these ingredients until smooth in a bowl placed over ice, to keep them cool and to prevent the oil in the almonds from being released.

CRUMB FRUIT FILLING FOR COFFEE CAKES
For one 9-inch ring
Mix well:
> $^3/_4$ cup crushed macaroons or amaretti cookies
> $^1/_2$ cup raisins, chopped dates or prunes, or shredded sweetened coconut
> ($^1/_4$ cup chopped nuts)
> 3 tablespoons butter, melted
> 2 tablespoons sugar

APPLE FILLING FOR COFFEE CAKES
For two 9-inch rings
Combine and boil until the juices are thick and sticky, at least 4 minutes:
> $2^1/_2$ cups chopped peeled apples
> 1 cup packed brown sugar
> 1 cup raisins
> 6 tablespoons ($^3/_4$ stick) butter
> $^1/_2$ teaspoon ground cinnamon
> $^1/_2$ teaspoon salt

Cool slightly before spreading over the dough.

PRUNE OR APRICOT FILLING FOR COFFEE CAKES
For one 9-inch ring
Combine **1 recipe filling for Prune or Apricot Danish, 625,** with **1 tablespoon butter, melted.**

DATE OR FIG FILLING FOR COFFEE CAKES
For one 9-inch ring
Combine in a small saucepan and bring to a simmer, stirring to dissolve the sugar:
> 4 tablespoons ($^1/_2$ stick) butter
> $^1/_3$ cup packed brown sugar

Simmer 2 minutes then remove from the heat and stir in:
> $^3/_4$ cup chopped dates or dried figs
> $^1/_4$ cup almond paste, homemade, 877, or store-bought
> $^1/_2$ teaspoon ground cinnamon
> A grating of nutmeg

Cool slightly before using.

POPPY SEED FILLINGS FOR COFFEE CAKES
I. COCKAIGNE
For one 9-inch ring
For that special occasion.
Grind:
> $^1/_2$ cup poppy seeds

Put the poppy seeds in the top of a double boiler and add:
> $^1/_4$ cup milk

Bring to a boil over direct heat, then remove from the heat and add:
> $^1/_3$ cup packed brown sugar
> 2 tablespoons butter

Put the pan over, not in, boiling water and add:
> 2 large egg yolks

Heat, stirring constantly, until the mixture thickens. Let cool slightly, then add:

> $^1/_3$ cup almond paste, homemade, 877, or store-bought,
> or $^1/_2$ cup ground blanched almonds
> (3 tablespoons chopped candied citron)
> (2 teaspoons fresh lemon juice or 1 teaspoon vanilla)

Cool before using.
II. *For two 9-inch rings*
Mix together well:
> $^3/_4$ cup ground poppy seeds
> $^1/_2$ cup sour cream
> $^1/_4$ cup sugar
> $^1/_4$ cup raisins
> 1 teaspoon grated lemon zest
> $^1/_8$ teaspoon ground cinnamon

III. *For four 9-inch rings*
Grind:
> 2 cups poppy seeds

Mix with.
> 1 large egg
> $^1/_3$ cup honey
> $^1/_4$ cup chopped nuts
> 1 tablespoon fresh lemon juice

CHEESE FILLING FOR COFFEE CAKES
For one 9-inch ring
Put through a ricer or a strainer into a bowl:
> $1^1/_2$ cups ricotta

Add and mix well:
> $^1/_4$ to $^1/_2$ cup raisins
> $^1/_4$ cup sugar
> 1 large egg yolk
> 2 teaspoons grated lemon zest

Beat until stiff but not dry, and fold in:
> 1 large egg white

CHOCOLATE FRUIT FILLING FOR COFFEE CAKES
For two 9-inch rings
Stir together until thoroughly combined:
> $^2/_3$ cup finely chopped walnuts or pecans
> $^2/_3$ cup packed light brown sugar
> $^1/_3$ cup chocolate chips
> 2 tablespoons unsweetened cocoa powder
> 2 tablespoons instant coffee or espresso powder
> 2 teaspoons ground cinnamon
> $^1/_4$ cup dried cranberries or cherries or chopped dried apricots

DANISH PASTRY DOUGH
Enough for about twenty-four 3-inch pastries
This rich butter pastry, a cross between a rich bread and puff pastry, is a revelation, so much better than store-bought Danish as to seem like a different thing altogether. For more information on rolling, see instructions for Food Processor Puff Pastry, 669. Remember in particular to refrigerate the dough if the butter becomes soft or if the

dough is difficult to roll. The ideal temperature for letting the dough rise is between 70° and 80°F.

Danish pastry dough is egg-enriched and somewhat less flaky than croissant dough, but the procedure for making it is quite similar. Bake Danish pastries on unbuttered baking sheets unless you are making filled, rolled, and sliced ones, which are baked on their sides with the filling touching the baking sheet—in this case, buttered pans are essential. Danish pastries are best eaten the day they are baked.

Place on a work surface:

> **1 cup (2 sticks) cold unsalted butter**

Measure:

> **2 tablespoons all-purpose flour**

Sprinkle the butter with a little of the flour and begin to beat it with a rolling pin. Scrape the butter from the work surface and the rolling pin as needed and fold it over itself into a heap. Continue to work the butter until it is a smooth and malleable mass. Knead the rest of the flour into the butter with your hands, working quickly to keep the butter cold. Place the butter on a sheet of plastic wrap and shape it into an 8 x 5½-inch rectangle. Wrap and refrigerate the butter while you make the dough.

Whisk together in a small bowl and let stand until the yeast is dissolved, about 5 minutes:

> **½ cup warm (105° to 115°F) whole milk**
> **1 package (2¼ teaspoons) active dry yeast**
> **1 tablespoon sugar**

Mix together in a large mixing bowl:

> **2 cups plus 2 tablespoons all-purpose flour**
> **2 tablespoons sugar**
> **½ teaspoon salt**
> **½ tablespoon unsalted butter, cut into small pieces, softened**

Make a well in the center and pour the yeast mixture into it. Mix lightly with a fork to form a thin batter in the well. Beat together and add to the well:

> **1 large egg**
> **1 large egg yolk**

Then mix with a fork or your fingers to make a dough. Transfer to a lightly floured work surface and knead for a few seconds, until smooth. Let the dough stand for 5 minutes.

Sprinkle the top of the dough with flour. Roll out into a 14 x 8-inch rectangle, sprinkling additional flour underneath it as needed to prevent sticking. Position the dough so that one of the short ends is facing you. Cover the upper two-thirds of the dough with the rectangle of butter, leaving a 1-inch border of dough on the sides and at the top. Fold the bottom third of the dough over the butter. Fold the top third of the dough, with the butter on it, down over the first third, as if you were folding a business letter. Press the edges of the dough together on all 3 sides to seal in the butter. Rotate the dough so that the folded edge is on the left and the sealed edge is on the right. Sprinkle the dough lightly with flour and press it gently with the rolling pin to flatten it slightly. Keeping the short

end of the rectangle facing you, roll into a 16 x 8-inch rectangle. Fold the bottom third up and the top third down again. (This rolling and folding is called a single turn.) Rotate the dough so that the folded edge is on the left and the open edge is on the right (like a book about to be opened). Give the dough one more single turn, rolling it into a 16 x 8-inch rectangle and folding it in thirds. Sprinkle the work surface lightly with flour as needed to prevent the dough from sticking. If at any time the butter gets soft, refrigerate it for 10 to 15 minutes. Mark the dough with 2 imprints, to remind yourself that you have given the dough 2 turns. Wrap the dough loosely in plastic wrap and refrigerate for 30 minutes.

Give the dough 2 more single turns, always making sure that the folded edge is on the left and the open edge is on the right before beginning the next roll. Make 4 imprints, wrap in plastic, and refrigerate for 30 minutes.

Give the dough a final single turn, wrap, and refrigerate it for at least 30 minutes. (At this point, the dough can be frozen or refrigerated overnight. Before freezing, wrap in plastic, then aluminum foil, then airtight in a plastic bag; thaw overnight in the refrigerator before rolling.)

RASPBERRY DANISH PINWHEELS

Eighteen 3-inch pastries

Roll out into an 18 x 9-inch rectangle:

> **½ recipe Danish Pastry Dough, above**

Cut into eighteen 3-inch squares. Lightly brush the squares with:

> **1 large egg, lightly beaten**

Make a 1½-inch slit from each corner toward the center. Starting at the bottom left, fold one corner of each triangle to the center and press it down, forming a pinwheel. Dollop each center with:

> **1 teaspoon raspberry jam (6 tablespoons total)**

Sprinkle with:

> **Sugar**

Place the pinwheels 2 to 3 inches apart on ungreased baking sheets. Let rise until puffy, 30 to 60 minutes.

Position a rack in the lower third of the oven. Preheat the oven to 375°F.

Bake the pastries until golden brown, 20 to 30 minutes. Remove to a rack and let cool completely.

PRUNE OR APRICOT DANISH

Eighteen 3-inch pastries

Combine in a saucepan and bring to a boil:

> **8 ounces pitted prunes or dried apricots, cut in half**
> **1 cup water or apple cider**
> **¼ cup sugar**
> **Pinch of salt**

Reduce the heat and simmer until the fruit is very soft, 20 to 30 minutes. (Some fruits are drier than others—add more liquid and cook a bit longer if necessary to soften.) Stir in:

2 tablespoons fresh lemon juice
(2 tablespoons Armagnac or Cognac)

Transfer to a blender or food processor and puree. Remove to a small bowl and cool before using.
Prepare:

Raspberry Danish Pinwheels, above

without cutting slits in the dough squares and substituting the prune filling for the jam. Place a scant tablespoon of the filling in the center of each square, gather up the 4 corners of the dough, and pinch together above the filling. Place the pastries 2 to 3 inches apart on an ungreased baking sheet. Let rise until puffy, 30 to 60 minutes.

Position a rack in the lower third of the oven. Preheat the oven to 375°F.

Bake the pastries until golden brown, 20 to 30 minutes. Remove to a rack and let cool completely.

CREAM CHEESE DANISH SPIRALS

Sixteen 3 1/2-inch pastries

Beat in a large bowl until smooth:

6 ounces cream cheese, softened
1/4 cup sugar

Add and stir until blended:

(1 1/2 to 2 teaspoons ground cinnamon)
1 1/2 tablespoons heavy cream

Roll out into a 17 x 12-inch rectangle:

1/2 recipe Danish Pastry Dough, 624

Spread the cream cheese mixture evenly over the dough, leaving a 1/4-inch border on all sides. Roll the dough into a log, starting at one long edge. Place the log seam side down on a buttered baking sheet and freeze for 15 minutes.

Place the log on a cutting board and trim the ends by 1/2 inch. Cut the log into sixteen 1-inch-thick slices, wiping the knife clean between cuts if necessary. Arrange the slices cut side down 2 to 3 inches apart on the baking sheet. Let rise until puffy, 30 to 60 minutes.

Position a rack in the lower third of the oven. Preheat the oven to 375°F.

Lightly brush the pastries with:

1 large egg, beaten

Bake until golden brown, 15 to 20 minutes. Remove to a rack. While the pastries are still hot, stir together and brush over the tops:

6 tablespoons confectioners' sugar
2 teaspoons water

Let cool completely.

DANISH COFFEE CAKE

One 10-inch ring

Scandinavians have among the highest coffee consumption in the world, so it's understandable that they have also created some of the best pastries, especially this light confection, which falls between a rich coffee cake and a rich pastry. If a Fruit Glaze, 800, is to be applied, allow the

pastry to cool and apply the glaze warm; for other glazes, see 799.
Prepare:

1/2 recipe Danish Pastry Dough, 624

Roll the chilled dough out on a slightly floured surface into a rectangle about 29 x 11 inches and about 3/8 inch thick. Trim any folded edges that might keep the dough from rising. Spread it with any rich filling for coffee cake, 623–24, and starting from the short side, roll the dough into a cylinder. Bring the two ends of the roll together, and press to seal using a little water for glue. Using 1 or 2 pancake turners, lift the ring onto a greased baking sheet. With floured scissors held perpendicular to the roll, cut diagonal gashes 1 to 2 inches apart into the upper outer edges of the ring, cutting to within 1 inch of the inner circle. As you cut, turn each partially cut slice flat onto the baking sheet. Brush the top of the dough with:

French Egg Wash, 799

Forming Danish Coffee Cake

being careful not to cover the cut portions, as the glaze could inhibit the rising of the dough. Cover with a clean cloth and let rise until doubled in volume, about 25 minutes.

Preheat the oven to 400°F.

Bake until golden brown, about 25 minutes.

ABOUT QUICK BREADS AND COFFEECAKES

These breads and coffee cakes are delightful, tasty, and deserving of their name. Those made with nuts and fruits keep fairly well, but the plainer breads, such as Sally Lunn, Irish Soda Bread, and the quick coffee cakes, should be served immediately after baking; they fade fairly soon. If you want coffee cakes that keep and reheat well, see the recipes for yeasted coffee cakes, 621–623. Also see Additions to Yeast Doughs, 596, and the Cornell Triple-Rich Flour Formula, 596, to enrich these breads.

Nut and fruit breads are attractive baked in 6-ounce juice cans or miniature loaf pans so that they slice prettily for tea. If you use cans or small loaf pans, do not fill them more than three-quarters full, to allow for expansion of the dough, and bake for less time than a loaf. Quick nut and fruit breads slice better if, once cooled, they are wrapped in foil and refrigerated about 12 hours.

▲ Quick breads are leavened with baking powder and/or baking soda. Both need to be reduced as altitude increases. Baking soda produces carbon dioxide and also neutralizes acidity in the batter. ➤ At high altitudes, the more acidic a batter, the more quickly it will set in the oven's heat—a great advantage. For some recipes, it is best to leave more of a batter's acidity intact by removing a little more baking soda (but don't cut it out) or replacing part of it with baking powder or reworking the balance between the two.

NUT BREAD

One 9 x 5-inch loaf
Grease a 9 x 5-inch loaf pan. Preheat the oven to 350°F. Whisk in a medium bowl until blended:

2 cups all-purpose flour
$^1/_2$ cup sugar or packed brown sugar
2 teaspoons baking powder
1 teaspoon salt

Beat in a separate bowl, until light yellow:

1 large egg

Beat in:

1 cup milk
2 tablespoons butter, melted
($^1/_2$ teaspoon vanilla)

Beat the liquid ingredients into the dry ones until just blended. Fold in:

1$^1/_2$ cups chopped walnuts or pecans

Pour the batter into the greased pan and bake until a toothpick inserted in the center comes out clean, about 40 minutes. Cool slightly, then unmold.

HONEY NUT BREAD

Raisins or dried fruit can be added for texture.
Prepare **Nut Bread, above,** increasing the flour by $^1/_2$ cup and omitting the sugar. Add **$^3/_4$ cup honey** and **$^1/_2$ teaspoon baking soda.**

DATE NUT BREAD

One 9 x 5-inch loaf or four 5$^1/_2$ x 3-inch loaves
Choose relatively dry dates, rather than Medjools, which are too soft here. Position a rack in the lower third of the oven. Preheat the oven to 350°F. Grease one 9 x 5-inch loaf pan or four 5$^1/_2$ x 3-inch loaf pans.
Cut into quarters (sixths if large) and place in a medium bowl:

1$^1/_2$ cups packed pitted dates

Stir in:

1 cup boiling water
1 teaspoon baking soda

Let stand until the mixture is lukewarm, about 20 minutes. Whisk together thoroughly in medium bowl:

1$^2/_3$ cups all-purpose flour

$^1/_2$ teaspoon salt
$^1/_2$ teaspoon baking powder

Whisk together in a large bowl:

2 large eggs
1 cup packed brown sugar
$^1/_4$ cup vegetable oil
1 teaspoon vanilla

Stir in the cooled date mixture. Stir in the flour mixture just until blended. Fold in:

2 cups coarsely chopped walnuts

Scrape the batter into the pan(s) and spread evenly. Bake until a toothpick inserted in the center comes out clean, 35 to 40 minutes for small loaves, 55 to 65 minutes for the large loaf. Let cool in the pan(s) on a rack for 5 to 10 minutes before unmolding to cool completely on the rack.

SALLY LUNN BREAD

One 13 x 9-inch bread
A light sweet bread. For an even lighter one, see Brioche, 614.
Preheat the oven to 425°F. Butter a 13 x 9-inch baking pan. Whisk together in a medium bowl:

2 cups sifted all-purpose flour
2$^1/_4$ teaspoons baking powder
$^3/_4$ teaspoon salt

Combine in a large bowl and beat at medium-high speed until light and fluffy, about 3 minutes:

$^1/_2$ cup vegetable shortening or 10 tablespoons
(1$^1/_4$ sticks) butter, softened
$^1/_2$ cup sugar

Beat in one at a time:

3 large eggs

The mixture will look curdled. On slow speed, add the dry ingredients to the batter in about 3 parts, alternating them with:

1 cup milk

Beat the batter just until it looks smooth. Scrape into the prepared pan. Bake until a toothpick inserted into the center comes out clean or the cake begins to pull away from the sides of the pan, about 30 minutes. Cut the bread into squares. Serve hot.

ORANGE BREAD

Two 8$^1/_2$ x 4$^1/_2$-inch loaves
This is an easily made tea bread. If you want a quick treat, slice it and eat it while hot, with or without lots of good butter. If you intend it for tea sandwiches, bake it in cans; see about Quick Breads, 626. You'll find it easier to slice on the second day.
Preheat the oven to 350°F. Grease two 8$^1/_2$ x 4$^1/_2$-inch loaf pans. Whisk together in a large bowl:

3 cups all-purpose flour
1 tablespoon baking powder
$^1/_2$ teaspoon salt

Stir in:

1 tablespoon grated orange zest

$^1/_2$ to $^3/_4$ cup sugar

using the larger amount of sugar for a more cakelike result.

Beat together in a medium bowl:

1$^1/_4$ cups milk

$^1/_4$ cup orange juice

1 large egg

2 tablespoons melted vegetable shortening

Add, if desired:

(1 cup chopped walnuts or pecans)

($^1/_3$ cup finely chopped cranberries or apricots)

Pour the liquid mixture into the dry ingredients and combine with a few swift strokes. Stir lightly until barely blended. Scrape the batter into the greased loaf pans. Bake about 50 minutes, or until a toothpick inserted in the center comes out clean. Cool slightly, then unmold.

BANANA BREAD COCKAIGNE

One 8$^1/_2$ x 4$^1/_2$-inch loaf

Have all ingredients at room temperature, about 70°F. Preheat the oven to 350°F. Grease an 8$^1/_2$ x 4$^1/_2$-inch loaf pan.

Whisk together:

1$^1/_2$ cups all-purpose flour

1$^1/_2$ teaspoons baking powder

$^1/_2$ teaspoon salt

Beat in a large bowl at medium speed until creamy:

$^2/_3$ cup sugar

$^1/_3$ cup vegetable shortening or 6 tablespoons

($^3/_4$ stick) butter, softened

$^3/_4$ teaspoon grated lemon zest

Beat in:

1 to 2 large eggs, beaten

1 to 1$^1/_4$ cups mashed ripe bananas (2 to 3)

Add the dry ingredients in about 3 parts, beating until smooth after each addition. Fold in, if desired:

($^1/_2$ cup chopped nuts)

($^1/_4$ cup finely chopped dried apricots)

Scrape the batter into the greased pan. Bake the bread about 1 hour, or until a toothpick inserted in the center comes out clean. Cool slightly, then unmold. Cool completely before slicing.

QUICK BANANA WHEAT-GERM BREAD

Prepare **Banana Bread Cockaigne, above,** reducing flour to 1$^1/_4$ cups and adding $^1/_4$ **cup wheat germ.**

PUMPKIN BREAD

One 9 x 5-inch loaf

This loaf can be made with any cooked mashed squash, yams, or sweet potatoes.

Preheat the oven to 350°F. Grease a 9 x 5-inch loaf pan.

Whisk together:

1$^1/_2$ cups all-purpose flour

1 teaspoon baking soda

$^1/_4$ teaspoon baking powder

1 teaspoon salt

1$^1/_2$ teaspoons ground cinnamon

1 teaspoon ground ginger

$^1/_2$ teaspoon grated or ground nutmeg

$^1/_4$ teaspoon ground cloves

Combine in a small bowl:

$^1/_3$ cup water or milk

$^1/_2$ teaspoon vanilla

Beat in a large bowl until fluffy:

6 tablespoons ($^3/_4$ stick) butter, softened,

or $^1/_3$ cup vegetable shortening

1$^1/_3$ cups sugar or 1 cup sugar plus $^1/_3$ cup packed

brown sugar

Beat in one at a time:

2 large eggs

Add and beat on low speed just until blended:

1 cup cooked or canned pumpkin puree

Add the flour mixture in 3 parts, alternating with the milk mixture, beating on low speed or stirring with a rubber spatula until smooth and scraping the sides of the bowl as necessary. Fold in:

$^1/_2$ cup coarsely chopped walnuts or pecans

$^1/_3$ cup raisins or chopped dates

Pour into the prepared pan and spread evenly. Bake until a toothpick inserted in the center comes out clean, about 1 hour. Let cool in the pan on a rack for 5 to 10 minutes before unmolding to cool completely on the rack.

CARROT NUT BREAD

One 9 x 5-inch loaf

Preheat the oven to 350°F. Grease a 9 x 5-inch loaf pan.

Whisk together:

1$^1/_2$ cups all-purpose flour

1 teaspoon baking soda

1 teaspoon baking powder

$^1/_4$ teaspoon ground cinnamon

Blend well in a large bowl:

$^3/_4$ cup sugar

2 large eggs, beaten

$^1/_2$ cup vegetable oil

1 teaspoon vanilla

$^1/_2$ teaspoon salt

Stir in the dry ingredients. Blend in with a few swift strokes:

1$^1/_2$ cups grated carrots

1$^1/_2$ cups ground pecans or walnuts

Scrape the batter into the greased pan. Bake until the bread pulls away from the sides of the pan, about 45 minutes. Cool in the pan on a rack for 10 minutes before unmolding to cool completely on the rack.

SWEET ZUCCHINI BREAD

One 9 x 5-inch loaf

Prepare **Carrot-Nut Bread, above,** reducing the flour to 1$^1/_4$ cups. Replace the carrots with **2 cups grated zucchini, squeezed of excess moisture.**

BEER BREAD

One 8 1/2 x 4 1/2-inch loaf

Serve with hearty soups or stews and mild or strong cheeses. Slices are good toasted, or you can rewarm the whole loaf in the oven for a crisp outer crust. This bread keeps for 2 to 3 days.

Preheat the oven to 400°F. Grease an 8 1/2 x 4 1/2-inch loaf pan.

Whisk together thoroughly in a large bowl:

   1 cup whole wheat flour
   1 cup all-purpose flour
   1/2 cup old-fashioned rolled oats
   2 tablespoons baking powder
   1/2 teaspoon baking soda
   1/2 teaspoon salt

Add:

   1 1/2 cups light or dark beer (but not stout),
       cold or at room temperature, but not flat

Fold just until the dry ingredients are moistened. Scrape the batter into the pan and spread evenly. Bake until a toothpick inserted in the center and all the way to the bottom of the pan comes out clean, 35 to 40 minutes. Let cool in the pan on a rack for 5 to 10 minutes before unmolding to cool completely on the rack.

BEER, CHEESE, AND SCALLION BREAD

Prepare **Beer Bread, above,** adding to the flour mixture **1/2 cup finely diced sharp Cheddar or aged Monterey Jack, 1/4 cup sliced scallions,** and **(2 teaspoons caraway seeds).**

IRISH SODA BREAD

One 8-inch round loaf or 8 1/2 x 4 1/2-inch loaf

When this batter is made with the greater amount of sugar and buttermilk and baked in a loaf pan, it becomes a fine crusty bread that stays moist for 3 to 4 days.

Preheat the oven to 375°F, 350°F if you are baking in a loaf pan. Grease a large baking sheet or an 8 1/2 x 4 1/2-inch loaf pan.

Whisk together thoroughly in a large bowl:

   1 2/3 cups all-purpose flour
   2 tablespoons sugar, or 5 tablespoons for the tea loaf
   1 teaspoon baking powder
   1/2 teaspoon baking soda
   1/2 teaspoon salt

Stir in:

   1 cup raisins
   (2 teaspoons caraway seeds)

Whisk together in another bowl:

   1 large egg
   2/3 cup buttermilk, or 1 cup for the tea loaf
   1/4 cup (1/2 stick) butter, melted and still warm

Add to the flour mixture and stir just until the dry ingredients are moistened. The batter will be stiff but sticky. Scrape the batter onto the baking sheet in a mound 6 to 7 inches in diameter, or scrape it into the loaf pan and spread evenly. Use a sharp knife to slash a large X about 1/2 inch deep on top of the batter.

Bake until golden brown and a toothpick inserted in the center comes out clean, 25 to 30 minutes on the baking sheet, 45 to 50 minutes in the loaf pan. Transfer the round loaf to a rack to cool completely before serving. Or, if using a loaf pan, let cool in the pan on a rack for 5 to 10 minutes before unmolding to cool completely on the rack.

POPPY SEED LOAF

Position a rack in the lower third of the oven. Preheat the oven to 350°F. Grease an 8 1/2 x 4 1/2-inch loaf pan.

Prepare **Irish Soda Bread, above,** using the greater amount of sugar and buttermilk. Substitute **1 tablespoon plus 2 teaspoons poppy seeds** for the raisins and caraway seeds. Scrape the batter into the pan and bake as above, but 35 to 40 minutes.

BROWN BREAD

2 round loaves or 7 1/2 x 3 5/8-inch loaves

Grease two 4-cup molds, such as pudding molds, small heatproof bowls, or 7 1/2 x 3 5/8-inch loaf pans. Have ready a steamer, Dutch oven, or lidded kettle large enough to hold both molds, or 2 smaller pans with lids to hold 1 mold each.

Whisk together thoroughly in a large bowl:

   1 cup yellow cornmeal
   1 cup rye flour
   1 cup whole wheat flour
   2 teaspoons baking soda
   1 teaspoon salt

Whisk together in another bowl:

   2 cups buttermilk
   1 cup chopped raisins
   3/4 cup molasses

Add to the dry ingredients and stir until well blended. Divide the batter between the molds. If the pudding molds have lids and clips, grease the inside of the lids and secure the clips. Otherwise, cover the molds with a double thickness of greased aluminum foil, greased side down, and secure tightly with kitchen string.

Set the molds on a trivet or a folded towel in the steamer. Pour boiling water into the steamer until it reaches halfway up the sides of the molds. Cover the steamer and turn the heat to high. When the water boils, adjust the heat so that the water simmers gently. Steam for about 3 hours, replenishing the water in the steamer as necessary. The bread is done when a toothpick inserted in the center comes out clean.

Transfer the molds to a rack, uncover the breads, and let cool for about 20 minutes before unmolding. Serve warm, or let cool completely on the rack before wrapping to store. To slice without crumbling, use a tough string or dental floss and a sawing motion. The loaves can be reheated in a 300°F oven or slipped back into their molds and resteamed before serving.

QUICK COFFEE CAKE (KUCHEN)
One 9-inch square coffee cake

We prize this coffee cake for a Sunday brunch.

Preheat the oven to 375°F. Grease a 9-inch square baking pan.

Sift together:

1¹⁄₂ cups sifted all-purpose flour
2 teaspoons baking powder
¹⁄₄ teaspoon salt

Beat until creamy in a large bowl with a wooden spoon:

¹⁄₄ cup (¹⁄₂ stick) butter, softened

Gradually add and beat until light and fluffy:

¹⁄₄ to ¹⁄₂ cup sugar

Beat in:

1 large egg
²⁄₃ cup milk

Beat in the dry ingredients. Add:

³⁄₄ teaspoon grated lemon zest or ¹⁄₂ teaspoon vanilla

Stir until smooth. Spread the batter in the greased pan. Cover with:

1¹⁄₄ cups blueberries or cherries tossed with ¹⁄₃ cup
sugar, Streusel, 799, or Honey-Bee Glaze, 799

Bake about 25 minutes if covered with streusel or glaze, 25 to 30 minutes if covered with fruit. Cool on a rack.

QUICK SOUR CREAM COFFEE CAKE
One 9-inch square coffee cake

This cake is wonderfully good and easy to prepare.

Have all ingredients at room temperature, about 70°F. Preheat the oven to 350°F. Grease a 9-inch square baking pan.

Whisk together thoroughly:

1¹⁄₂ cups all-purpose flour
1 cup sugar
2 teaspoons baking powder
¹⁄₂ teaspoon baking soda
¹⁄₄ teaspoon salt

Beat well in a large bowl:

1 cup sour cream
2 large eggs

Add the dry ingredients and beat until just smooth. Overbeating tends to toughen the cake. Spread in the greased pan. Sprinkle with:

Streusel, 799

Bake until a toothpick comes out clean, about 25 minutes. Cool on a rack.

BISHOP'S BREAD

Prepare: **Sour Cream Coffee Cake, above,** adding to the batter **2 ounces unsweetened chocolate, grated, 1 cup chopped dates, and 1 cup chopped nuts.**

CRANBERRY OR APPLE STREUSEL COFFEE CAKE

Prepare **Quick Sour Cream Coffee Cake, above,** increasing the sugar to 1¹⁄₄ cups. If using cranberries, add to the sour cream mixture (**1 tablespoon grated orange zest**). Sprinkle

2¹⁄₂ cups dried cranberries or diced peeled apples over the batter in the pan. Sprinkle the streusel over the fruit. Bake for 40 to 45 minutes. Cool on a rack.

COFFEE CAKE WITH MARBLED FILLING
1 large ring

Grease an 8- to 10-cup fluted tube or Bundt pan. Prepare:

Chocolate Fruit Filling, 624

Prepare:

Batter for Quick Sour Cream Coffee Cake, above

Spoon one-quarter of the batter into the pan and spread evenly. Sprinkle with half of the filling. Top with half of the remaining batter and sprinkle with the remaining filling. Top with the remaining batter. Marble the cake and filling with a small spoon, scooping batter from the bottom of the pan up to the top 5 to 6 times and moving around the tube with each scoop. Spread the surface of the batter evenly.

Bake until a toothpick inserted in the center comes out clean, 45 to 50 minutes. Let cool in the pan on a rack for 5 to 10 minutes. Rotate and tap the pan until the cake is loosened on all sides, and invert the cake onto the rack to cool. Serve warm or at room temperature, sprinkled with:

Confectioners' sugar

CRUMB CAKE
13 x 9-inch coffee cake

Preheat the oven to 325°F. Grease and flour a 13 x 9-inch baking pan.

Whisk together:

1¹⁄₂ cups all-purpose flour
¹⁄₂ cup sugar
2¹⁄₂ teaspoons baking powder
¹⁄₂ teaspoon salt
(¹⁄₂ teaspoon ground cardamon)

Whisk together in a medium bowl until well blended:

1 large egg
¹⁄₂ cup milk
2 tablespoons vegetable oil
2 teaspoons vanilla

Using a rubber spatula, fold in the dry ingredients. Drop the batter in dollops into the prepared pan, smooth the top, and set aside.

Using a rubber spatula, stir together in a medium bowl until well combined:

2¹⁄₂ cups all-purpose flour
(¹⁄₂ cup chopped walnuts or pecans or
    shredded sweetened coconut)
1 cup packed light brown sugar
1 teaspoon ground cinnamon

Pour over this mixture:

1 cup (2 sticks) butter, melted

Toss with a rubber spatula until large crumbs form. Sprinkle the crumbs over the batter. Bake 30 minutes, or until a toothpick inserted in the center comes out clean. Place the pan on a rack and let cool to room temperature.

Sprinkle with:
>   Confectioners' sugar

Cut into 3-inch squares.

DELUXE SUNDAY MORNING COFFEE CAKE
One 10-inch cake

This is a moist coffee cake with a crumbly top. A portion of the dry ingredients becomes the streusel topping, while, with the addition of buttermilk and an egg, the rest is turned into a rich cake.

Have all ingredients at room temperature, about 70°F. Preheat the oven to 350°F. Generously grease the bottom and lightly grease the sides of a 10-inch springform pan. Sprinkle the bottom of the pan with:
>   Dry bread crumbs

and turn lightly to coat. Tap out the excess crumbs. Whisk together in a large bowl until well blended:
>   **2 cups all-purpose flour**
>   **1 cup plus 2 tablespoons sugar**
>   **1 teaspoon salt**

Add and cut in with a whisk until the mixture resembles coarse crumbs:
>   **10 tablespoons (1¼ sticks) butter**

Remove 1 cup of the crumbs to a small bowl and set aside. Add to the mixture in the large bowl and whisk thoroughly:
>   **1 teaspoon baking powder**
>   **½ teaspoon baking soda**

Add:
>   **¾ cup buttermilk or plain yogurt**
>   **1 large egg**
>   **1 teaspoon vanilla**

Whisk vigorously until the batter is smooth and fluffy, 1½ to 2 minutes. (The batter is heavy; if you prefer, beat on medium-high speed for about 1 minute.) Scrape the batter into the prepared pan and smooth the top.

For the streusel topping, add to the reserved crumbs and toss with a fork until blended:
>   **¾ cup walnuts or pecans, finely chopped**
>   **½ cup packed dark brown sugar**
>   **1 teaspoon ground cinnamon**

Sprinkle the crumbs over the batter. Bake until a wooden skewer inserted in the center comes out clean, 50 to 65 minutes. Let cool in the pan on a rack for 5 to 10 minutes. Slide a slim knife around the cake to release it from the pan. Remove the pan sides. Let cool on the rack for 1½ hours before serving.

DELUXE COCONUT CHOCOLATE CHIP COFFEE CAKE

Prepare **Deluxe Sunday Morning Coffee Cake, above,** stirring into the batter **1 cup miniature chocolate chips.** For the streusel topping, reduce the nuts to ½ cup, omit the cinnamon, and add **1 cup lightly packed sweetened flaked dried coconut.**

DELUXE RASPBERRY ALMOND COFFEE CAKE

Prepare **Deluxe Sunday Morning Coffee Cake, above,** adding along with the vanilla **1 teaspoon almond extract.** Scrape the batter into the prepared pan and smooth the top. Stir until smooth and fluid ½ **cup seedless raspberry jam,** then carefully spread over the batter. For the streusel topping, omit the cinnamon and substitute ½ **cup sugar** for the dark brown sugar and ¾ **cup ground almonds** for the chopped walnuts or pecans. Add **1 large egg yolk** and **1 teaspoon almond extract.**

Mix with a fork, then firmly knead the mixture with your fingers until uniform in color. Sprinkle the crumbs over the jam and bake as directed.

SKILLET OR GRIDDLE BREADS

Either Irish Soda Bread, 629, or Skillet Corn Bread, 632, will make acceptable, even good, skillet bread on an open fire, especially over charcoal. But our results on these heats did not compare in quality with those obtained when the same recipes were oven-baked. Elevate the skillet on a rack or grill set over glowing embers and bake the bread covered. The baking must be slow—as long as 1 hour—or the bottom will scorch. If you prefer **Irish Farls,** use the Irish Soda Bread recipe and cut the bread in triangular wedges about 1 inch thick and bake on a griddle heated to about 370°F and lightly rubbed with oil. Allow about 10 minutes for one side; turn and allow 10 minutes more.

ABOUT CORN BREADS

Anyone who grew up on Southern corn bread hankers for a golden brown crust, crunchy edges, and a light but slightly gritty bite. Corn bread is best made with stone-ground cornmeal and baked in a preheated heavy pan to create a golden brown crust. For a very crisp crust, grease the pan well and preheat it in a 425°F oven.

Whether you bake corn muffins, corn sticks, or corn bread, you can vary the cornmeal and flour proportion, within a 2-cup limit, to your own taste. We like 1¼ cups cornmeal to ¾ cup all-purpose flour. You can substitute whole wheat flour for up to half of the all-purpose flour, or substitute honey or molasses for the sugar, mixing it in with the liquid, or omit the sweetener altogether. You can also substitute oil, bacon grease, or other fats for the butter. Fold dry additions, such as chopped nuts, raisins, or shredded cheese, into the batter after it is mixed. Moist ingredients, such as honey, corn kernels, and cooked chile peppers or onions, are mixed with the liquid ingredients. Stir dry ingredients, such as herbs and spices, into the flour mixture.

▲ Corn bread is leavened with baking powder and/or baking soda. Both need to be reduced as altitude increases. Baking soda produces carbon dioxide and also neutralizes acidity in the batter. At high altitudes, the more acidic a batter, the more quickly it will set in the oven's heat—a great advantage. For some recipes, it is best to leave more of a batter's acidity intact by removing a little more baking soda (but don't cut it out) or replacing part of it with baking powder or reworking the balance between the two.

ADDITIONS TO CORN BREAD

Canned chipotle peppers in adobo: 3 to 4 drained, stemmed, and finely chopped or pureed

Jalapeño peppers: 1 to 2 fresh or roasted, 292, peeled and minced

Canned mild green chile peppers—up to one 4-ounce can, drained and diced

Poblano pepper; 1, roasted, 292, peeled, seeded, and diced

Sun-dried tomatoes in oil: 1/2 cup diced

Corn kernels: up to 1 cup fresh or frozen or 1 cup canned creamed corn

Cheddar or Monterey Jack: up to 1 cup grated

Sautéed chopped onions: 1 cup

Crisp-cooked bacon or ham: 1/2 cup diced

Sunflower seeds or roasted pumpkin seeds: 1/2 cup

CORN BREAD, MUFFINS, OR STICKS

One 8-inch square bread, about fifteen 2-inch muffins, or about 20 sticks

Using 2 eggs will make this richer.

Have all ingredients at room temperature, about 70°F. Preheat the oven to 425°F. Grease the pan(s) with butter, oil, or bacon drippings. Place in the oven until sizzling hot. Whisk together in a large bowl:

1 1/4 cups yellow or white cornmeal, preferably stone-ground

3/4 cup all-purpose flour

2 1/2 teaspoons baking powder

1 to 4 tablespoons sugar

3/4 teaspoon salt

Add:

1 or 2 large eggs, beaten

2 to 3 tablespoons melted butter, bacon drippings, or vegetable oil

1 cup milk

Combine with a few rapid strokes. Scrape the batter into the hot pan(s). Bake sticks about 12 minutes, corn bread and muffins 15 to 18 minutes, until nicely browned. Serve immediately.

SKILLET CORN BREAD

One 8 x 8-inch loaf

Prepare **Corn Bread, above,** using whole milk. Pour the batter into a generously greased heavy 10-inch skillet and cook, covered, over very low heat for about 20 minutes, or until done.

BUCKWHEAT CORN BREAD

One 8-inch square bread

Prepare **Corn Bread, above,** substituting for 1/2 cup of the cornmeal 1/2 cup buckwheat flour and adding (1/2 cup hulled sunflower seeds).

SOUTHERN CORN BREAD

One 8-inch square bread or 12 muffins

Southern corn bread is traditionally made with white cornmeal, buttermilk, eggs, leavening, and salt—and little, if any, flour or sugar. Some cooks stir in a tablespoon of bacon fat. The bread is moist and crusty. Rush this bread from oven to table. If preparing muffins, see Corn Bread, Muffins, or Sticks, above.

Preheat the oven to 450°F. Grease a heavy 9-inch ovenproof skillet, preferably cast iron, or an 8-inch square glass baking dish with:

1 tablespoon bacon fat, lard, oil, or vegetable shortening

Whisk together thoroughly in a large bowl:

1 3/4 cups cornmeal, preferably stone-ground white

(1 tablespoon sugar)

1 teaspoon baking powder

1 teaspoon baking soda

1 teaspoon salt

Whisk until foamy in another bowl:

2 large eggs

Whisk in:

2 cups buttermilk

Add to the dry ingredients and whisk just until blended. Place the skillet or pan in the oven and heat until the fat smokes. Pour in the batter all at once.

Bake until the top is browned and the center feels firm when pressed, 20 to 25 minutes. Serve immediately from the pan, cut into wedges or squares, with:

Butter

Leftovers, though dry, are nice enough if wrapped in foil and rewarmed in a low oven.

BUTTERMILK CRACKLING CORN BREAD

One 9- or 10-inch round bread

This corn bread has an almost puddinglike interior, a crunchy top, and golden brown edges.

Preheat the oven to 425°F.

Rinse quickly, then pat dry:

4 ounces fatty salt pork

Slice off and discard the rind, then cut the pork into 1/4-inch dice. (If the pork is too soft to cut easily, freeze it for 30 minutes.) Place in a heavy 9- or 10-inch ovenproof skillet, preferably cast-iron, and cook over medium heat until the fat is rendered and the cracklings are very brown and crisp. Remove from the heat.

Whisk together thoroughly in a large bowl:

3/4 cup cornmeal

3/4 cup all-purpose flour

1 tablespoon sugar

1 1/2 teaspoons baking powder

1/2 teaspoon baking soda

1/2 teaspoon salt

Whisk in another bowl until foamy:

2 large eggs

Whisk in:

1¹/₂ cups buttermilk

Add to the dry ingredients and stir just until moistened. Fold in the cracklings and all but 1 tablespoon of the fat in the skillet. Set the skillet over high heat until the fat smokes. Remove from the heat and pour in the batter all at once.

Bake until a toothpick inserted in the center comes out clean, 15 to 25 minutes. Serve at once, either plain or with:

(Jam or sorghum syrup)

CORN ZEPHYRS COCKAIGNE

About thirty 2¹/₂-inch puffs

In our endless search for the best recipe of its type, we welcomed the offer of a Southern acquaintance to send us the Zephyr recipe she was raving about. When it arrived, it turned out to be word for word our own favorite recipe from JOY. We consider this the highest of compliments. These light-as-air puffs are delicate and delicious with a salad.

Combine in a large saucepan:

1 cup cornmeal, preferably stone-ground white
1 tablespoon lard or vegetable shortening

Pour over:

4 cups boiling water

Add:

1 teaspoon salt

Cook over low heat 30 minutes, stirring frequently. Remove from the heat and lightly butter the top to keep it from crusting. Cool to room temperature.

Preheat the oven to 350°F. Grease a large baking sheet. Beat the cornmeal mixture well. Whip until stiff:

4 large egg whites

Fold them lightly into the cornmeal mixture. Drop the batter from a tablespoon onto the baking sheet. Bake until firm, about 40 minutes.

CORN DODGERS COCKAIGNE

About 24 dodgers

Serve with butter and maple syrup.

Preheat the oven to 400°F. Grease a large baking sheet. Combine in a large bowl:

1 cup cornmeal, preferably stone-ground
1¹/₂ teaspoons sugar
1 teaspoon salt

Pour over the dry ingredients:

1 cup boiling water

Stir well. Beat in until blended:

2 tablespoons butter, softened, or bacon drippings
1 large egg, beaten

Drop the batter from a spoon onto the greased baking sheet. Or dip your hand in cold water, fill with batter, and release the batter "splat" onto the sheet. The hand method was learned from a dear friend Sarah, who, as a child, helped her father make dodgers at the Kentucky Derby. Bake until golden, about 25 minutes.

JONNYCAKES

Ten 3-inch skillet cakes

These corn cakes are crusty on the outside, moist on the inside. Jonnycakes can be eaten at breakfast, with maple syrup or butter and jam. They are also delicious with Pot Roast, 477, with Chicken Fricassee, 432, or topped with a salsa, 571, or corn relish, 948. Use stone-ground cornmeal, and serve the cakes as quickly as possible.

Combine in a large bowl:

1¹/₂ cups stone-ground cornmeal
1 teaspoon salt
1 teaspoon sugar

Pour over slowly, stirring constantly to prevent lumps:

2¹/₄ cups boiling water

Set aside for 10 minutes. Set 2 very large skillets over medium heat. (You can also use a medium-hot griddle, set to about 325°F.) Divide between the skillets.

2 tablespoons butter

When the butter begins to color, add the batter by quarter cupfuls. The cakes should be thick (about ³/₄ inch) and no more than 3 inches across. Smooth the tops lightly with your fingertips if necessary. Let cook at a quiet sizzle, without allowing the butter to become darker than a pale nut brown, until the underside is a very deep golden brown, 6 to 11 minutes. Cut into extremely thin pats:

1 to 1¹/₂ tablespoons butter

Lightly press one pat onto each jonnycake, flip with a spatula, and cook on the other side until deep golden brown, 6 to 11 minutes more. Keep warm in a 200°F oven, and repeat with the remaining batter.

HUSH PUPPIES

About eighteen 2¹/₂-inch puppies

Fishermen used to cook these finger-shaped concoctions on the river bank, along with their catch. Rumor has it that they threw a large number to their clamorous dogs with the admonition, "Hush, puppies!" Please read About Deep-Fat Frying, 1046.

Whisk together in a large bowl:

1 cup cornmeal, preferably stone-ground
¹/₄ to ¹/₂ cup minced onion
1 teaspoon baking powder
¹/₂ teaspoon salt
(¹/₄ teaspoon ground red pepper)

Beat together in a small bowl:

1 large egg
¹/₂ cup milk

Add to the dry ingredients and stir to mix. Form into oblong cakes or pones, about 2 x 4 x ³/₄ inches. Fry in deep fat heated to 370°F until golden brown. Drain on paper towels and serve at once.

ABOUT SPOON BREAD

These corn breads are soft enough to eat with a spoon (or fork). Serve them as a starch with any main dish, such as chicken or ham. For a light meal, sprinkle with grated cheese or add a dollop of sour cream and spicy salsa and serve with a green salad.

CRUSTY SOFT-CENTER SPOON BREAD

4 servings

Using stone-ground cornmeal will result in a more soufflé-like texture.

Preheat the oven to 375°F.

Whisk together in a large bowl:

$^3/_4$ **cup yellow cornmeal, stone-ground if desired**
$^1/_4$ **cup all-purpose flour**
1 tablespoon sugar
1 teaspoon salt
1 teaspoon baking powder

Stir in until well blended:

1 large egg, beaten
1 cup milk

Melt in an 8-inch square baking dish in the oven:

2 tablespoons butter

Pour in the batter. Pour over the top:

$^1/_2$ **cup milk**

Bake 45 minutes, until good and crusty on top.

BUTTERMILK SPOON BREAD

4 servings

Place in a large bowl:

1 cup white cornmeal, stone-ground if desired

Pour over:

1$^1/_2$ cups boiling water

Mix well, and cool slightly.

Preheat the oven to 350°F.

Beat well in a medium bowl:

1 large egg
1 cup buttermilk
1 tablespoon butter, melted
1 teaspoon baking soda
$^3/_4$ **teaspoon salt**

Add to the cornmeal mixture and mix well. Heat a greased 8-inch square baking dish in the oven until hot. Pour in the batter and bake until lightly puffed and set, 30 to 40 minutes. If you wish to keep the top soft, add from time to time, while the bread is baking, a few tablespoons of milk, using in all:

($^1/_2$ cup milk or half-and-half)

This process calls for longer baking, about 1 hour.

ABOUT MUFFINS

Muffin batters are easily made. ➤ To mix, add the liquid ingredients to the dry ones in a few swift strokes. ➤ The mixing should be held to an absolute minimum, a light stirring of from 10 to 20 seconds, which will leave some lumps. The batter should not be mixed to the point of pouring, ribbonlike, from the spoon, but should break in coarse globs. If the batter is beaten too long, the gluten in the flour will develop and toughen it; and the muffins will be coarse and full of tunnels.

Good muffins should be rounded on top, with the grain of the muffin uniform but not fine and the crumb moist. A weary muffin peak is caused by oven heat that is too low, and a wobbly peaked, unsymmetrical shape is caused by oven heat that is too high.

Muffin pans should be greased with vegetable shortening, butter, or nonstick spray, or lined with paper cups. In any case, grease the top surface of the pan if you are making giant muffins with mushrooming tops.

Fill the muffin cups to any level you wish. The standard is about two-thirds full, but you can fill them to the rim or even above the rim for jumbo muffins. Should the dough not fill every muffin cup, put a few tablespoons of water in the empty cups, both to protect the pans and to keep the muffins moist. Batter for 12 standard muffins will make 24 to 32 miniature muffins, but only 6 to 8 jumbo muffins.

Muffin pan sizes vary, and baking times vary with them: a mini muffin will take 10 to 12 minutes, a standard-sized muffin 20 to 25 minutes, and a jumbo muffin 22 to 25 minutes.

Unless otherwise directed in the individual recipe, ➤ bake muffins in a preheated 400°F oven. ➤ If the muffins are left in the tins for a few minutes after coming out of the oven, they will be easier to remove. They are best eaten promptly. If you must reheat them, wrap them loosely in foil and heat about 5 minutes in a preheated 450°F oven.

The richer and sweeter the muffin, the longer it will stay moist. Muffins that contain only 4 tablespoons or less butter or oil are best consumed freshly baked or as soon as possible, for they go stale quickly.

Most muffin batters can be mixed, spooned into the pan, and refrigerated overnight, to be baked in the morning. Muffins can also be frozen before baking or after. To freeze before baking, simply scoop the batter into paper-lined muffin pans and freeze. Then transfer the frozen muffins to a plastic freezer bag, with a note to remind you of the oven temperature and baking time called for in the recipe. To bake, plop the still-frozen muffins into a muffin pan and bake for about 5 minutes longer than specified in the recipe, to compensate for the cold batter. To freeze baked muffins, cool thoroughly, then bag and freeze. To reheat, place the frozen muffins on a baking sheet in a 350°F oven or in a toaster oven for 5 to 10 minutes, until hot. Microwave heating is also effective, but you will not have a crisp crust or crunchy edges.

ADDITIONS TO MUFFINS

Muffins may be enriched by these additions, but have them ready before beginning and beat them in quickly.

I. Use any of the following, alone or in combination:

$^1/_4$ **to** $^1/_2$ **cup chopped nuts, apricots, prunes, dates, or figs**
$^1/_2$ **cup chopped cranberries plus 2 teaspoons grated orange zest**
$^1/_2$ **cup mashed ripe bananas or chopped apples**

½ cup very well drained canned crushed pineapple
6 to 8 slices bacon, cooked and crumbled
II. Cornell Triple-Rich Formula, 596
III. For other suggestions, see Additions to Yeast Doughs, 596.

MUFFINS
12 muffins
Please read About Muffins, above. With this recipe, you can create myriad muffins by adding berries, chopped fresh or dried fruit, or nuts. See Additions to Muffins, above. You can substitute up to 1 cup whole wheat flour or whole wheat pastry flour for an equal measure of all-purpose flour. Note that the liquid ingredient is your choice, from low-fat milk to cream. The flexible amount of butter or oil allows control of the richness with the following advice: Muffins made to be eaten warm from the oven are perfectly delicious with ¼ cup butter or oil. If muffins must be made hours before they will be consumed, or even the day before, you are wise to use ½ cup butter or oil.
Position a rack in the center of the oven. Preheat the oven to 400°F. Grease a standard 12-muffin pan or line with paper liners.
Whisk together thoroughly in a large bowl:
2 cups all-purpose flour
1 tablespoon baking powder
½ teaspoon salt
(¼ teaspoon grated or ground nutmeg)
Whisk together in another bowl:
2 large eggs
1 cup milk or cream
⅔ cup sugar or packed light brown sugar
¼ to ½ cup (½ to 1 stick) butter, melted, or
¼ to ½ cup vegetable oil
1 teaspoon vanilla
Add to the flour mixture and mix together with a few light strokes just until the dry ingredients are moistened. Do not overmix; the batter should not be smooth. Divide the batter among the muffin cups.
Bake until a toothpick inserted in 1 or 2 of the muffins comes out clean, about 17 minutes (or longer for variations with fruit). Let cool for 2 to 3 minutes before removing from the pan. If not serving hot, let cool on a rack. Serve as soon as possible, preferably within a few hours of baking.

SOUR CREAM MUFFINS
Prepare **Muffins, above,** using 4 tablespoons butter, adding ½ **teaspoon baking soda** to the dry ingredients, and substituting **1 cup sour cream, buttermilk, or plain yogurt** for the milk or cream.

LEMON POPPY SEED MUFFINS
Prepare **Muffins, above,** adding 1½ **tablespoons poppy seeds** to the dry ingredients and **1 tablespoon grated lemon zest** to the wet ingredients.

PUMPKIN OR SWEET POTATO MUFFINS
16 muffins
Prepare **Muffins, above,** adding to the dry ingredients ⅓ **cup additional sugar, 1 teaspoon ground cinnamon, and 1 teaspoon grated or ground nutmeg.** Add to the milk mixture **1 cup cooked or canned pumpkin or 1 cup cold mashed sweet potatoes.** Add **(1 cup chopped pecans)** and **(2 teaspoons grated orange zest).**

BLUEBERRY MUFFINS
Prepare **Muffins, above, or Corn Bread, 632,** using ⅓ cup sugar and folding into the batter **1½ cups fresh or unthawed frozen blueberries.** Before baking, sprinkle with **cinnamon sugar, 1019.**

HERB OR ROASTED GARLIC MUFFINS
Prepare **Muffins, above,** folding into the batter **3 tablespoons chopped chives, tarragon, or dill, 1 tablespoon chopped rosemary, or 1 head Roasted Garlic, 277, pulp mashed or chopped, plus the zest of 1 lemon.**

WHOLE WHEAT MUFFINS
12 muffins
Please read About Muffins, 634.
Preheat the oven to 400°F. Grease standard 12-muffin pan or line with paper liners.
Whisk together in a large bowl:
1⅔ cups whole-wheat flour
1 cup all-purpose flour
2 teaspoons baking powder
1¼ teaspoons salt
Beat in a separate bowl:
1 large egg
1¼ cups milk
¼ cup molasses or honey
2 tablespoons melted butter
Add to the dry ingredients with a few swift strokes. Fold in, before the dry ingredients are entirely moist:
(¼ cup chopped dates, raisins,
or roasted pumpkin seeds)
Divide the batter among the muffin cups. Bake 20 to 25 minutes, until a toothpick comes out clean. Let cool for 2 to 3 minutes before removing from the pan. If not serving hot, let cool on a rack. Serve within a few hours of baking.

BRAN MUFFINS
16 muffins
These muffins are rather hefty. Served with cheese, they make excellent picnic companions.
Please read About Muffins, 634. Preheat the oven to 350°F. Grease standard muffin cups or line with paper liners.
Whisk together in a large bowl:
2 cups all-purpose or whole wheat flour
1½ cups oat or wheat bran

2 tablespoons sugar
(1 to 2 tablespoons grated orange zest)
1 1/4 teaspoons baking soda
1/4 teaspoon salt
Beat in another bowl:
2 cups buttermilk
1/2 cup molasses
1 large egg
2 to 4 tablespoons butter, melted
Add to the dry ingredients and combine with a few swift strokes. Fold in, before the dry ingredients are entirely moist:
1 cup chopped walnuts or pecans and raisins,
or 1 cup chopped dates
Divide the batter among the muffin cups. Bake 25 minutes, until a toothpick comes out clean. Let cool for 2 to 3 minutes before removing from the pan. If not serving hot, let cool on a rack. Serve within a few hours of baking.

CHEESE MUFFINS
12 muffins

Please read About Muffins, 634. Preheat the oven to 350°F. Grease a standard 12-muffin pan or line with paper liners.
Whisk together in a medium bowl:
2 1/2 cups all-purpose flour
1 tablespoon baking powder
1 tablespoon sugar
1 teaspoon salt
Stir into the dry ingredients, until all the particles of cheese are separated:
1 cup grated sharp Cheddar (4 ounces)
Beat well in a small bowl:
1 large egg
1 1/4 cups milk
1/4 cup (1/2 stick) butter, melted
Add to the dry ingredients with a few swift strokes. Divide the batter among the muffin cups. Bake for about 15 minutes, until a toothpick comes out clean. Let cool for 2 to 3 minutes before removing from the pan. If not serving hot, let cool on a rack. Serve within a few hours of baking.

APPLE WALNUT MUFFINS
12 muffins

Allowing the apples to render their juices with the sugar and eggs makes tender, flavorful muffins.
Please read About Muffins, 634. Preheat the oven to 400°F. Grease a standard 12-muffin pan or line with paper liners.
Whisk together thoroughly:
1 1/2 cups all-purpose flour
2 teaspoons baking powder
1 teaspoon baking soda
Scant 1/2 teaspoon salt
1 1/2 teaspoons ground cinnamon

Whisk together in a large bowl:
2 large eggs
3/4 cup sugar
Stir in and let stand for 10 minutes:
1 1/2 cups packed coarsely grated or finely chopped peeled apples (about 2 medium), with their juice
Stir in:
5 tablespoons butter, melted
1/2 cup chopped walnuts or pecans
Add the flour mixture and fold just until the dry ingredients are moistened. Do not overmix; the batter should not be smooth. Divide the batter among the muffin cups.
Bake until a toothpick inserted in 1 or 2 of the muffins comes out clean, 14 to 16 minutes. Let cool for 2 to 3 minutes before removing from the pan. If not serving hot, let cool on a rack. Serve as soon as possible, preferably the day they are baked.

BANANA NUT MUFFINS
12 muffins

These muffins are enhanced with walnuts and just enough whole wheat flour or wheat bran for extra texture and flavor. Serve as soon as possible.
Please read About Muffins, 634. Preheat the oven to 375°F. Grease a standard 12-muffin pan or line with paper liners. Whisk together thoroughly:
1 1/2 cups all-purpose flour
1/2 cup whole wheat flour or wheat bran
2 teaspoons baking powder
1/2 teaspoon baking soda
1/4 teaspoon salt
1 teaspoon ground cinnamon
1/8 teaspoon grated or ground nutmeg
Stir in:
2/3 cup coarsely chopped walnuts
Whisk together in a large bowl:
1 large egg
3/4 cup packed light brown sugar
1 1/3 cups mashed ripe bananas (2 to 3)
1/3 cup vegetable oil
1 teaspoon vanilla
Add the flour mixture and fold just until the dry ingredients are moistened. Do not overmix; the batter should not be smooth. Divide the batter among the muffin cups.
Bake until a toothpick inserted in 1 or 2 of the muffins comes out clean, 14 to 16 minutes. Let cool for 2 to 3 minutes before removing from the pan. If not serving hot, let cool on a rack. Serve preferably the day they are baked.

DOUBLE CHOCOLATE MUFFINS
12 muffins

These muffins are mixed like a butter cake—do not substitute oil for the butter.
Please read About Muffins, 634. Preheat the oven to 350°F. Grease a standard 12-muffin pan or line with paper liners.

Melt and let cool:

2 ounces unsweetened chocolate

Whisk together thoroughly:

1 ^{3}/$_4$ cups all-purpose flour

1 teaspoon baking soda

^{1}/$_4$ teaspoon salt

Combine in small bowl:

1 cup buttermilk

1 teaspoon vanilla

Beat in a large bowl until creamy, about 30 seconds:

^{1}/$_2$ cup (1 stick) butter, softened

Gradually add and beat on high speed until lightened in color and texture, 4 to 5 minutes:

1 cup packed light brown sugar

Beat in:

1 large egg

Beat in the chocolate just until blended. Add the flour mixture in 3 parts, alternating with the buttermilk mixture in 2 parts, beating on low speed or stirring with a rubber spatula until smooth and scraping the sides of the bowl as necessary.

Stir in:

1 cup chocolate chips

Divide the batter among the muffin cups. Bake until a toothpick inserted in 1 or 2 of the muffins comes out clean, 25 to 30 minutes. Let cool for 2 to 3 minutes in the pan before removing to cool completely on a rack.

POPOVERS

8 large or 12 medium popovers

Everyone enthusiastically gives us a favorite popover recipe, and all are equally enthusiastic, but contradictory, about baking advice. We prefer a preheated oven, but starting with a cold oven also works.

Have all ingredients at room temperature, about 70°F. Preheat the oven to 450°F. Grease a popover tin, a standard 12-muffin pan, or eight 6-ounce custard cups. If using custard cups, grease them lightly and, depending on what you are serving with the popovers, dust with sugar, flour, or grated Parmesan cheese. This will give the batter something to cling to.

Beat together in a medium bowl just until smooth:

1 cup milk

1 tablespoon butter, melted

1 cup all-purpose flour

^{1}/$_4$ teaspoon salt

Beat in one at a time, but do not overbeat:

2 large eggs, beaten

The batter should be no heavier than whipping cream. Fill the baking cups no more than three-quarters full. Don't overload—too much batter in the pans will give the popovers a muffinlike texture. ➤ Bake at once. After 15 minutes, lower the heat ➤ without peeping, to 350°F and bake about 20 minutes longer. To test for doneness, remove a popover and check to be sure the side walls are firm. If not cooked long enough, the popovers will col-

lapse. You may want to insert a sharp paring knife gently into the popovers to allow the steam to escape after baking. Serve immediately.

CHEESE POPOVERS

Combine ^{1}/$_2$ cup grated sharp Cheddar or Parmesan, ^{1}/$_8$ teaspoon paprika, and a few grains of ground red pepper. Prepare **Batter for Popovers, above.** Pour 1 scant tablespoon of batter into each cup and divide the cheese among the cups. Add the remaining batter. Bake as directed.

YORKSHIRE PUDDING

6 servings

It was customary to cook this old and delicious dish in the pan with the roast, letting the drippings fall upon it. As many of us now cook roast beef in a low oven and no longer have extravagant drippings, we prepare the pudding separately in the hot oven required to puff it up and brown it quickly. Serve it from the dish in which it was baked, cut into squares. It was traditionally served before the meat, but we prefer to substitute the pudding for the usual starch served with the main course.

Have all ingredients at room temperature, about 70°F. Preheat the oven to 400°F. Sift into a bowl:

^{3}/$_4$ cup plus 2 tablespoons all-purpose flour

^{1}/$_2$ teaspoon salt

Make a well in the center, and pour in:

^{1}/$_2$ cup milk

Stir in the milk. Beat in:

2 large eggs, beaten

Add:

^{1}/$_2$ cup water

Beat the batter until large bubbles rise to the surface. (The batter can be covered and refrigerated for 1 hour then beat it again before cooking.) Pour **^{1}/$_4$ inch hot beef drippings or melted butter** into a 9 x 12-inch baking dish or 6 regular muffin cups. Heat the dish or pan in the oven until hot. Pour in the batter and bake for 20 minutes. Reduce the heat to 350°F and bake 10 to 15 minutes longer, until puffed and golden brown. Serve immediately.

ABOUT BISCUITS AND SCONES

So little effort, so good a result: Now, as in the time of the pioneers, biscuits are popular for the speed with which they can be made. A light hand in kneading gives the desired flaky result. The amount of liquid called for in the recipe determines whether the biscuit is a rolled or dropped type. ➤ Cut the shortening into the dry ingredients with a pastry blender or 2 knives until the mixture is the consistency of coarse cornmeal. Make a well in the center of these ingredients. ➤ Pour in all the liquid at once. Stir cautiously until there is no danger of splashing, then stir vigorously until the dough comes away from the sides of the bowl. The time for stirring should be less than 30 seconds.

Turn the dough onto a lightly floured board. ➤ Knead it gently and quickly for 30 seconds or less—just long enough so it is neither knobby nor sticky. If it isn't, or if too much baking soda is used, tiny brown spots will appear on the surface of the baked biscuits. Roll the dough with a lightly floured rolling pin or pat it gently with the palms of your hands until it has the desired thickness—between $1/4$ and $1/2$ inch is right for plain biscuits, $3/4$ inch or more for shortcakes and scones. To cut the dough into rounds, use a biscuit cutter that has been lightly dipped in flour; ➤ do not twist the cutter. There are many other ways to shape biscuit dough. We like square and rectangular shapes because they result in very few scraps.

Rolled biscuits can also be filled like tiny sandwiches: Roll the dough into a square or rectangle $1/4$ inch thick. Cut in half and spread or sprinkle one half with any flavorful sweet or savory mixture, such as jam or preserves, streusel or coffee cake filling, 623–24, nuts and raisins, chutney, pesto or tapenade, anchovy paste, goat cheese, or herbs. Top with the second half of the dough, then cut and bake.

For a breakfast ring, see Quick Drop Biscuits, 639. Make Easter Bunny Biscuits for children, 639. You can also place small rounds of dough on top of a casserole. Or cut the dough into sticks for hors d'oeuvres or fill as for Pinwheels, 625. Use a spatula to place these on the baking sheet.

Scones are sweet, rich biscuits that are usually made with cream as well as butter. Eggs add flavor, rich color, and a slightly cakey texture.

For a golden brown finish, brush the tops of biscuits or scones with milk or butter. Place biscuits 1 inch apart if you like them crusty all over, close together if not. Bake in a ➤ preheated oven 12 to 15 minutes, depending on their thickness.

▲ At high altitude, baking powder biscuits should require no adjustment of the leavening.

MIXING BISCUITS AND SCONES IN A FOOD PROCESSOR

To mix the dough for biscuits or scones in a food processor, cut the butter or shortening into tablespoon-sized pats, cut each pat into 4 cubes, and freeze until hard, 20 to 30 minutes. Pulse the dry ingredients in the food processor to mix thoroughly. Add the frozen butter (or shortening) cubes. For scones or for biscuits with a flaky, layered structure, pulse just until the largest butter pieces are the size of peas and the smallest resemble bread crumbs. For classic fluffy biscuits, continue to pulse until all of the butter pieces are the size of bread crumbs. Add the liquid ingredient(s) and pulse just until the dough comes together as one mass, not longer. Do not allow the butter to form a blended paste with the flour. Turn the dough out onto a lightly floured board and knead a few times. Shape as directed.

ADDITIONS TO BISCUITS AND SCONES

In general, add moist ingredients, such as ham or drained diced chile peppers, with the wet ingredients in the recipe, and add dry ingredients, such as herbs, to the dry ingredients. If in doubt, mix in the flavor ingredient after cutting in the butter and before adding the liquid.
Incorporate into the dough any of the following:
   3 to 6 slices cooked crumbled bacon
   $1/4$ cup sautéed chopped onion
   5 to 6 tablespoons finely chopped ham or prosciutto
   5 to 6 tablespoons finely chopped sun-dried tomatoes
Herbs:
   2 tablespoons finely chopped parsley, sage, or dill
   $1/4$ cup snipped chives
   1 teaspoon minced fresh or $1/2$ to $3/4$ teaspoon crumbled dried rosemary
   $1/3$ to $1/2$ cup grated Parmesan; add to the dry ingredients, reduce the salt slightly, if desired, and bake at 425°F instead of 450°F
   $1/3$ cup crumbled Roquefort; add to the dry ingredients; reduce the salt slightly, if desired, and bake at 425°F
   $3/4$ cup finely shredded Cheddar or Monterey Jack; add after the butter is cut in, reduce the salt slightly, if desired, and bake at 425°F
   $1/4$ to $1/3$ cup drained canned diced green chile peppers; to make chile cheese biscuits, add to Cheddar or Monterey Jack biscuits
   1 cup chopped watercress leaves
Or, before baking, dust the biscuits or scones with:
   Cinnamon sugar
or, just before they are finished, with:
   Grated Parmesan and paprika
Or, press into the top center of each biscuit:
   1 sugar lump
soaked in:
   Orange juice
You can also prepare biscuits like turnovers, using as a filling one of the following:
   1 cup sugared sliced strawberries or whole raspberries or blueberries
   $1/4$ cup nuts, dates, or dried figs
   $1/2$ cup raisins or dried currants
   1 cup cooked ground and seasoned poultry, sausage, ham, or other meat

ROLLED BISCUITS

About twenty-four $1^{1}/2$-inch biscuits
Preheat the oven to 450°F.
Sift together into a large bowl:
   $1^{3}/4$ cups all-purpose flour
   1 tablespoon baking powder
   $1/2$ teaspoon salt
Cut in, using a pastry blender or 2 knives, until the size of small peas:
   4 to 6 tablespoons chilled butter or shortening, or a combination
Make a well in the center. Add all at once:
   $3/4$ cup milk

Stir just until the dough comes away from the sides of the bowl. Turn the dough out onto a lightly floured board. Knead gently and quickly, about 8 to 10 times. Roll out with a lightly floured rolling pin, to between $1/4$ and $1/2$ inch thick. Cut with a $1\frac{1}{2}$-inch biscuit cutter dipped in very little flour, and place on an ungreased baking sheet. If desired, brush the tops with:

(Milk or melted butter)

Bake until lightly browned, 12 to 15 minutes.

CORNMEAL BISCUITS

Prepare **Rolled Biscuits, 638,** reducing the flour to $1\frac{1}{2}$ cups and the baking powder to 2 teaspoons, and adding: $1/2$ **cup cornmeal, 2 tablespoons sugar, and $1/2$ teaspoon baking soda** to the dry ingredients. Substitute $3/4$ **cup buttermilk** for the milk.

QUICK DROP BISCUITS

No kneading or rolling necessary. The biscuits are very palatable but less shapely, unless you drop them into muffin tins. For a breakfast ring, prepare I, below. Form the dough into 12 balls. Roll them in melted butter and place them in a 7-inch fluted tube pan into which you have poured the topping for Sticky Buns, 613.
Bake at 400°F about 25 minutes.

I. Preheat the oven to 450°F.

Prepare **Rolled Biscuits, above,** using **1 cup milk.**
Stir the dough 1 scant minute. Drop walnut-sized dabs of dough from a spoon onto an ungreased baking sheet and bake 12 to 15 minutes, or until lightly browned.

II. DROP BISCUITS WITH OIL

About twenty-four $1\frac{1}{2}$-inch biscuits

When you are obliged to use oil instead of butter, it is preferable to flavor the biscuits highly; see Additions to Biscuits, above.
Preheat the oven to 475°F. Sift into a bowl:

2 cups all-purpose flour
1 tablespoon baking powder
1 teaspoon salt

Add all at once:

$2/3$ **cup milk**
$1/3$ **cup vegetable oil**

Stir with a fork just until the dough readily leaves the sides of the bowl. Drop walnut-sized dabs of dough from a spoon onto an ungreased baking sheet. Bake 10 to 12 minutes.

BUTTERMILK BISCUITS

About twenty-four $1\frac{1}{2}$-inch biscuits

Because of the buttermilk and baking soda, these biscuits are very soft and tender.
Prepare **Rolled Biscuits, above, or Quick Drop Biscuits I, above,** reducing the baking powder to 2 teaspoons and adding $1/2$ **teaspoon baking soda.** Substitute $3/4$ **to 1 cup (depending on the recipe) buttermilk** for the milk.

FLUFFY BISCUITS OR SHORTCAKES

About twenty-four $1\frac{1}{2}$-inch biscuits or
twelve $2\frac{1}{2}$ or 3-inch shortcakes

For other shortcakes, see Index.
Prepare **Rolled Biscuits, 638,** adding **1 tablespoon sugar** to the dry ingredients. For added richness, use **half-and-half** instead of milk. For shortcakes, roll out the dough a scant $3/4$ inch thick and cut $2\frac{1}{2}$-inch squares or 3-inch rounds. After baking, cool and split the biscuits with a fork before filling.

CREAM BISCUITS OR SHORTCAKES

About twenty 2-inch biscuits or 12 shortcakes

Preheat the oven to 450°F.
Whisk together thoroughly in a large bowl:

2 cups all-purpose flour
$2\frac{1}{2}$ teaspoons baking powder
$1/2$ to $3/4$ teaspoon salt

Add all at once:

$1\frac{1}{4}$ cups heavy cream

Mix with a rubber spatula, wooden spoon, or fork just until most of the dry ingredients are moistened. Knead, shape, and bake as for Rolled Biscuits, 638, or Fluffy Biscuits or Shortcakes, above. Serve hot.

WHOLE WHEAT BISCUITS

About twenty $1\frac{1}{2}$-inch biscuits

Preheat the oven to 400°F.
Whisk together thoroughly in a bowl:

1 cup whole wheat flour
$3/4$ cup all-purpose flour
2 teaspoons sugar
2 teaspoons baking powder
$1/2$ teaspoon baking soda
$3/4$ teaspoon salt

Cut with a pastry blender or 2 knives until the consistency of fine crumbs:

$1/3$ cup ($5\frac{1}{3}$ tablespoons) butter or shortening

Stir in with a fork:

1 cup sour cream or buttermilk

Knead, shape, and bake as for Rolled Biscuits, 638. Serve hot.

EASTER BUNNY BISCUITS

Preheat the oven to 425°F.
Prepare:

Dough for Fluffy Biscuits or Shortcakes, above

Roll out the dough to a thickness of $1/2$ inch. Cut the dough with 3 sizes of round cutters: 3 inches, $1\frac{1}{2}$ inches, and about $3/4$ inch. For each bunny, cut 1 large round, 3 medium, and 1 small round. Assemble, using the large biscuit for the body, one of the medium ones for the head, and the small one, rolled into a ball, for the tail. Flatten two of the medium-size biscuits slightly and shape into ovals for the ears. Place the bunnies on a greased baking sheet. Bake about 15 minutes.

BISCUIT STICKS

Prepare **Dough for Rolled Biscuits, 638.** Roll the dough $1/2$ inch thick and cut into 3 x $1/2$-inch sticks. Place the sticks on an ungreased baking sheet and brush with **Melted un- salted butter.** Reduce the baking time slightly. To serve, stack log-cabin fashion.

GRIDDLE BISCUITS

Prepare any rolled biscuit dough, 638–639. To cook, place 1 inch apart on a lightly greased hot griddle. Brown them on one side 5 to 7 minutes, then turn and brown on the other side.

BEATEN BISCUITS

About fifty 1 $1/2$-inch biscuits

I. To win unending gratitude, serve this classic accompani- ment for Kentucky or Virginia ham to any homesick Southerner. In order to break the gluten in the dough and thus ensure a tender, flaky texture, the dough must be thoroughly beaten. This is a labor of love. If you make these often, it might be worth investing in a biscuit ma- chine, available from a bakers' supply company. Or con- sider the food processor version below.

Stir together thoroughly in a large bowl:

> **4 cups all-purpose flour**
> **1 tablespoon sugar**
> **1 teaspoon salt**
> **(1 teaspoon baking powder)**

Cut in with a pastry blender or 2 knives until the consis- tency of cornmeal:

> **$1/4$ cup chilled lard**

Add, stirring to make a stiff dough:

> **Equal parts chilled milk and ice water,**
> **about 1 cup in all**

Beat the dough with a mallet until it crackles, folding it over frequently. This is a long process, requiring 30 min- utes or more. When the dough is smooth, roll it to the thickness of $1/2$ inch and cut it with a floured biscuit cutter. Place the biscuits on an ungreased baking sheet and brush the tops with:

> **Melted butter**

Pierce each biscuit with a fork in 3 places. Bake in a pre- heated 325°F oven until light brown on the bottom and golden brown on top, about 30 minutes.

II. Mixed in the food processor.

About twenty-four 2-inch biscuits

Drier and crisper than the true hand-beaten article, above. Preheat the oven to 325°F.

Combine in a food processor and process for 5 seconds:

> **2 cups all-purpose flour**
> **2 teaspoons sugar**
> **$1/4$ teaspoon baking powder**
> **$1/2$ teaspoon salt**

Add and process until the mixture resembles coarse crumbs, about 10 seconds:

> **6 tablespoons ($3/4$ stick) butter or lard,**
> **cut into small pieces**

Add and process for 3 minutes:

> **$1/2$ cup milk**

The dough will be soft and puttylike, something like melted mozzarella. Wrap in plastic and let rest for 10 min- utes.

On an unfloured surface, roll the dough out to a little more than $1/8$ inch thick. Fold it in half, making 2 layers, and roll lightly to a thickness of about $3/8$ inch. Cut out 2-inch rounds with a biscuit cutter. Knead the scraps together, then roll, fold, and cut in the same manner. Arrange the biscuits on an ungreased baking sheet so they are close to- gether but not touching. Prick all over with a fork.

Bake until the tops are golden brown and the bottoms are deep brown, 30 to 40 minutes. Beaten biscuits can be stored, airtight at room temperature, for up to 3 weeks.

CLASSIC SCONES

8 to 12 scones

Increase the sugar up to $1/4$ cup for a sweeter scone. Preheat the oven to 450°F.

Sift together into a large bowl:

> **$1 3/4$ cups all-purpose flour**
> **$2 1/4$ teaspoons baking powder**
> **1 tablespoon sugar**
> **$1/2$ teaspoon salt**

Cut in, using a pastry blender or 2 knives, until the size of small peas:

> **$1/4$ cup ($1/2$ stick) cold butter**

Beat in a small bowl:

> **2 large eggs**

Reserve 2 tablespoons of the beaten eggs. Beat in to the reminder:

> **$1/3$ cup heavy cream**

Make a well in the dry ingredients. Pour in the liquid and combine with a few swift strokes. Handle the dough as lit- tle as possible. Turn it out onto a lightly floured board. Pat to $3/4$ inch thick. To make the classic wedge shape, pat into an 8-inch round and then cut into 8 to 12 wedges or cut into diamond shapes or as for Biscuit Sticks, above. Place on an ungreased baking sheet. Brush with the reserved egg and sprinkle with:

> **Salt or sugar**

Bake until golden, about 15 minutes. Serve warm or at room temperature.

CREAM SCONES

Heavy cream provides both the fat and the liquid in this simplest of all scone recipes.

Prepare:

> **Classic Scones, above**

omitting the butter and egg and using:

> **$1 1/4$ cups heavy cream**

DRIED FRUIT OR GINGER SCONES

Prepare **Classic Scones** or **Cream Scones, 640,** adding after the eggs and cream $1/2$ **cup dried fruit (blueberries, cranberries, cherries, currants, chopped apricots, or chopped pears)** or $1/4$ **cup finely chopped crystallized ginger (or candied ginger in syrup, drained and patted dry).** If the fruit pieces stick together, lightly toss with 1 teaspoon of the dry ingredients to separate them.

LEMON SCONES

Prepare **Classic Scones** or **Cream Scones, 640,** increasing the sugar by 1 tablespoon and adding **1 tablespoon grated lemon zest** with the egg/cream mixture. Then add $1/4$ **cup chopped best-quality candied lemon peel** or $1/2$ **cup chopped dried apricots, dried blueberries, or slivered almonds.**

CHOCOLATE CHIP ORANGE SCONES

Prepare **Classic Scones** or **Cream Scones, 640,** adding **3 to 4 teaspoons grated orange zest** with the egg/cream mixture and then adding $1/2$ **cup semisweet or white chocolate chips**.

ABOUT USES FOR LEFTOVER BREADS AND CRACKERS

A bread surplus can be put to many good uses—so don't throw a piece away! It can be used for Melba Toast, below, or Crostini, 642; for Stuffings, 532; as a thickener in soups—see Tuscan Bread and Tomato Soup, 132; and for a sauce—see Bread Crumbs, 545. For other uses, see About Crumbs, 960; and don't forget good old Bread Pudding, 822. Many recipes in JOY call for dry bread, cracker, or cake crumbs.

CHEESE OR BUTTER BREAD CUBES

Serve hot as an appetizer. Also good with soup or salads.
I. Preheat the oven to 375°F. Butter a baking sheet.
Beat together:
> **1 large egg**
> **1$1/2$ tablespoons butter, melted**
Cut into cubes of any size:
> **Fresh bread**
Roll the cubes in the egg mixture, then add in:
> **Finely shredded American cheese**
> **Salt and ground red pepper or paprika**
Spread the cubes on the buttered baking sheet and toast until the cheese is melted.
II. Preheat the oven to 375°F.
Combine and mash to a paste:
> **Softened butter**
> **Grated Parmesan**
> **Caraway or celery seeds**
> **Salt**
> **Ground red pepper**
> **(Mustard)**
Cut into cubes of any size:
> **Fresh bread**
Spread with the paste and toast as above.

MELBA CHEESE ROUNDS

Especially good with Onion Soup, 129.
Spread **Melba Toast, below,** lightly with **softened unsalted butter.** Sprinkle generously with **grated Parmesan.**
Just before using, run them under a broiler until toasted. Serve at once, floating one or two on top of the soup.

GARLIC BREAD OR TOASTED BUTTERED BREAD LOAF

Preheat the oven to 350°F. Slice thick or thin to taste, without cutting all the way through (leave the bottom crust intact):
> **A medium loaf of bread or French bread**
Brush the top and sides of each piece with:
> $1/2$ **cup (1 stick) butter, softened or melted**
flavored with, if desired:
> **(A minced clove garlic)**
> **(Herbs: basil, marjoram, oregano, etc.)**
Separate the slices slightly, so that the butter will be evenly distributed. Cover the loaf with foil. Place on a baking sheet and toast in the oven until the top is lightly browned, about 20 minutes. Serve immediately.
You may also mash and chop 2 cloves garlic with a little salt until smooth. Spread a little on each slice. Follow with melted butter as above.

QUICK CINNAMON LOAF

Preheat the oven to 400°F.
Slice without cutting all the way through (leave the bottom crust intact):
> **A loaf of French or Vienna bread**
Combine:
> $1/3$ **cup (5$1/3$ tablespoons) butter, melted**
> $1/3$ **cup packed light brown sugar**
> **2 teaspoons ground cinnamon**
> **A grating of nutmeg**
> $1/4$ **teaspoon grated lemon zest**
Spread the bread with the mixture as for Toasted Buttered Bread Loaf, above. Place on a baking sheet and bake 8 minutes.

CINNAMON TOAST OR STICKS

Preheat the oven to 400°F.
Remove the crusts from bread. Spread the tops of:
> **Thin bread slices**
Spread the tops with the mixture for:
> **Quick Cinnamon Loaf, above**
You may sprinkle the bread with:
> **(Rum)**
Cut into strips, if desired. Place on a baking sheet and toast about 8 minutes. Be sure to toast the bread on all sides. You may also place them under a broiler to crisp them. Applesauce is a good complement to these.

MELBA TOAST

Cut into the thinnest possible slices:
> **White or other bread**

Remove the crusts. Place on a baking sheet and toast in a 250°F oven until crisp and a light golden brown.

CROSTINI

42 to 64 pieces

Crostini are easy and quick. Use leftovers to make croutons.

Preheat the oven to 400°F. Slice into ¼- to ½-inch slices:

2 French bread baguettes, about 3 inches in diameter and 16 inches long

Place the slices on cookie sheets or in a large shallow baking pan and brush one side of each slice with:

5 tablespoons extra virgin olive oil

Bake until lightly browned and toasted, about 6 to 10 minutes. Turn the trays halfway through baking to ensure even toasting. Remove from oven. While still hot, rub each slice with the cut side of:

1 fresh garlic clove, halved crosswise

Serve warm or at room temperature. Leftovers can be wrapped in foil and kept at room temperature for several days, then refreshed briefly in the microwave before using.

HONEY-BUTTER TOAST

Prepare:

Honey Butter, 179

Spread it on:

1 slice of bread

Cover with:

1 slice of bread

Cut the bread into 1-inch strips. Toast the strips on both sides under a broiler. Serve sprinkled with:

Ground cinnamon

ORANGE TOAST

6 toasts

Very nice with tea.

Combine:

Grated zest of 1 orange
¼ cup orange juice
½ cup sugar

Remove the crusts and toast:

6 slices of bread

Spread, while hot, with:

Butter

Cover with the orange mixture. Put in the oven or under a broiler just long enough to brown the tops lightly.

PANCAKES, WAFFLES, FRITTERS, AND DOUGHNUTS

Perhaps no foods lend themselves to more occasions than those in this chapter, which can be served as appetizers; as breakfast, luncheon, or supper treats; or as desserts. What's more, they are an ideal way to glamorize leftover tidbits of cooked meats, fruits, and vegetables. Some people like to cook these delicacies at the table, using auxiliary heat so that they reach the diner in peak condition. Today's cooks have the tableside convenience of nonstick electric waffle irons, skillets or griddles, and crêpe pans; while in the kitchen, both iron and soapstone griddles and skillets still have devoted users.

ABOUT PANCAKES OR GRIDDLE CAKES

No matter what they are called—pancakes, blintzes, crêpes, griddle cakes, or batter cakes—all are simple to mix and make. ➤ There are three equally important things to control in producing pancakes and waffles: the consistency of your batter, the surface of your griddle, and the evenness of its heat. Mix the liquid ingredients quickly into the dry ingredients. ➤ Don't overbeat. Give just enough quick strokes with a whisk to barely moisten the dry ingredients. ➤ Ignore lumps. Superior results are gained with most pancake batters if they are mixed and ➤ rested, covered and refrigerated, for 3 to 6 hours or longer before cooking. The resting period does not apply to recipes that include separately beaten egg whites or to yeast-raised griddle cakes that have the word "raised" in the name. Variation in moisture content of flours, 983, makes it wise to test the batter by cooking a trial pancake first. Adjust the batter ➤ if it is too thick by diluting it with a little water, ➤ or, if too thin, by adding a little flour. You can also use pancake batter for waffles, provided you ➤ add, for each recipe, at least 2 tablespoons of butter or oil to keep the dough from sticking to the griddle.

If your skillet or griddle has a nonstick surface or is soapstone, you may not need to use any fat. Nor should you need to grease any seasoned pan surface if you have at least 2 tablespoons of butter or oil for every cup of liquid in the recipe. If you are using a skillet or crêpe pan, grease it lightly with butter or vegetable oil and continue to do so as needed between batches. ➤ Before cooking, test the griddle by letting a few drops of cold water fall on it. If the water bounces and sputters, the pan is ready to use. If the water just sits and boils, the griddle is not hot enough; the pancakes will spread too much and not rise well. If the water evaporates instantly, the griddle is too hot; see illustration, below.

To ensure a well-rounded cake, spoon, ladle, or pour the batter from the tip of a spoon just a few inches above the pan, being sure to space the batter well apart to allow room for spreading. Make the cakes large or small, as you like. It may be 2 or 3 minutes before they are ready to turn. When bubbles have appeared on the surfaces and are beginning to break, lift the edges of the cake with a spatula to see if the undersides have browned. If they have, slide the spatula under the pancake and turn it. ➤ Turn the cakes only once, and cook only until the second side is done. The second side takes only half as long to cook as the first and will not brown as evenly. Pancakes are best served at once, but if this is not possible, keep them on a baking sheet, layers separated by paper towels, in a 200°F oven.

▲ In high altitudes, decrease the baking powder and/or soda called for in the following recipes by about one-quarter.

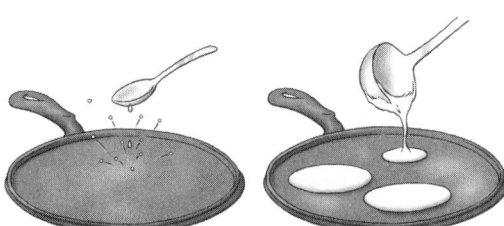

Making pancakes

Pancakes are delicious when stuffed and rolled, or glazed with a sauce and run under the broiler. Try filling them with cooked fruit and cinnamon or season with sautéed chopped onions and, when cooked, top with seafood or creamed chicken. Sweet dessert versions can be made with berries or peaches. For additional garnishes and sauces, see Dessert Sauces, 828.

PANCAKES OR GRIDDLE CAKES
About sixteen 4-inch pancakes
Here is the classic all-American pancake, the basis for seemingly endless variations.
Whisk together in a large bowl:
> 1$\frac{1}{2}$ cups all-purpose flour
> 3 tablespoons sugar
> 1$\frac{3}{4}$ tablespoons baking powder
> 1 teaspoon salt

Combine in another bowl:
> 1$\frac{1}{2}$ cups milk
> 3 tablespoons butter, melted
> 2 eggs
> ($\frac{1}{2}$ teaspoon vanilla extract)

Mix the liquid ingredients quickly into the dry ingredients. To cook, see About Pancakes or Griddle Cakes, 643. Use $\frac{1}{4}$ cup batter for each pancake.

BUTTERMILK PANCAKES
About sixteen 3-inch pancakes
Prepare **Pancakes or Griddle Cakes, above.** Add ½ **teaspoon baking soda** to the dry ingredients. Decrease the **baking powder** to 1 teaspoon. Substitute **buttermilk** for the milk.

ADDITIONS TO PANCAKES
You can incorporate many ingredients, such as finely chopped nuts and dried fruits or wheat germ, soy flour, or flaked bran, into the batter. For best results, let the fruit or cereal rest in the liquid called for in the recipe for about 30 minutes before making up the batter. For other ingredients, gently stir any of the following into the batter after the liquid and dry ingredients have been mixed together:
> 1 cup shredded sharp Cheddar (about 4 ounces)
> $\frac{3}{4}$ cup fresh or unthawed frozen blueberries or raspberries
> $\frac{3}{4}$ cup finely diced ripe bananas
> $\frac{1}{2}$ cup raisins or any finely diced soft dried fruit
> $\frac{1}{2}$ cup finely chopped toasted walnuts or pecans
> $\frac{1}{2}$ cup crumbled cooked bacon
> $\frac{1}{4}$ cup shredded sweetened dried coconut

To cook, see About Pancakes or Griddle Cakes, 643.

SILVER DOLLAR PANCAKES
About thirty 2-inch pancakes
Whisk together in a medium bowl:
> $\frac{1}{2}$ cup all-purpose flour
> 1$\frac{1}{2}$ tablespoons sugar
> $\frac{1}{2}$ teaspoon salt
> $\frac{1}{2}$ teaspoon baking soda

In another bowl, combine:
> 2 large eggs
> One 8-ounce container sour cream ($\frac{3}{4}$ cup plus 2 tablespoons)

Mix the liquid ingredients quickly into the dry ingredients. To cook, see About Pancakes or Griddle Cakes, 643. Use 1 tablespoon for each pancake.

SOURDOUGH PANCAKES
About twenty 4-inch pancakes
Though not a must, an overnight rest takes these tart, moist pancakes from really good to great.
Whisk together in a large bowl:
> $\frac{1}{2}$ cup warm (105° to 115°F) water
> 1 envelope (2$\frac{1}{4}$ teaspoons) active dry yeast

Let stand until the yeast is dissolved, about 5 minutes. Whisk in:
> 1$\frac{1}{2}$ cups warm (105° to 115°F) milk
> 3 tablespoons butter, melted

Add, then whisk until a smooth batter forms:
> 2 cups all-purpose flour
> 3 tablespoons sugar

Cover the bowl tightly with plastic wrap and set in a warm place until the mixture increases in volume by at least half and forms bubbles, about 1 hour. Stir the batter down, then cover and let rise at least 3 hours or overnight in the refrigerator. The batter can be refrigerated for up to 48 hours, but it will become more tangy. When ready to cook, let the batter stand at room temperature for 20 minutes. Stir the batter to deflate, then whisk in:
> 2 eggs
> 1 teaspoon salt

To cook, see About Pancakes or Griddle Cakes, 643.

FOUR-GRAIN FLAPJACKS
About eighteen 4-inch pancakes
Whisk together in a large bowl:
> 1 cup whole wheat flour
> $\frac{3}{4}$ cup all-purpose flour
> $\frac{1}{3}$ cup cornmeal
> $\frac{1}{4}$ cup old-fashioned or quick-cooking rolled oats
> 2 tablespoons sugar
> 2 teaspoons baking powder
> 1 teaspoon salt
> $\frac{1}{2}$ teaspoon baking soda
> ($\frac{1}{2}$ teaspoon ground cinnamon)
> ($\frac{1}{8}$ teaspoon grated or ground nutmeg)

In another bowl, combine:
> 1$\frac{3}{4}$ cups milk
> $\frac{1}{4}$ cup ($\frac{1}{2}$ stick) butter, melted
> $\frac{1}{4}$ cup honey
> 3 eggs

Quickly mix the liquid ingredients into the dry ingredients. To cook, see About Pancakes or Griddle Cakes, 643.

CORNMEAL PANCAKES

About sixteen 4-inch pancakes

I. These tall, golden pancakes have the hearty taste and texture of a corn muffin and a slightly irregular shape. For savory cornmeal pancakes, do not add sweeteners.
Combine in a large bowl:

> **1 cup white or yellow cornmeal**
> **1 to 2 tablespoons honey, maple syrup, or sugar**
> **1 teaspoon salt**

Slowly stir in:

> **1 cup boiling water**

Cover and let stand 10 minutes. Add, then whisk well:

> **$1/2$ cup milk**
> **2 tablespoons butter, melted**
> **2 teaspoons baking powder**

Add and whisk well:

> **1 egg**

Whisk in with a few quick strokes:

> **$1/2$ cup all-purpose flour**

To cook, see About Pancakes or Griddle Cakes, 643. Use 3 tablespoons batter for each pancake.

About twenty 4-inch pancakes

II. These are moist, tender, and slightly sweet. Serve them with maple syrup or honey, either at breakfast or as an accompaniment to ham, pork chops, or fried chicken.
Whisk together thoroughly in a large bowl:

> **$1 1/4$ cups yellow cornmeal**
> **$3/4$ cup all-purpose flour**
> **$1 3/4$ teaspoons baking powder**
> **$3/4$ teaspoon salt**

Whisk together in a medium bowl:

> **$1 2/3$ cups milk**
> **$1/4$ cup ($1/2$ stick) butter, melted**
> **$1/4$ cup maple syrup or honey**
> **2 eggs**

Pour the wet ingredients over the dry ingredients and combine with a few quick strokes of the whisk. Add:

> **($3/4$ cup fresh, thawed frozen, or drained canned corn kernels)**

To cook, see About Pancakes or Griddle Cakes, 643. Use about $1/4$ cup batter for each pancake.

BUCKWHEAT PANCAKES

About eighteen 4-inch pancakes

Whisk together in a large bowl:

> **1 cup buckwheat flour**
> **1 cup all-purpose or whole wheat flour**
> **2 tablespoons sugar**
> **1 teaspoon baking soda**
> **1 teaspoon salt**

In another bowl, combine:

> **2 cups buttermilk**
> **$1/4$ cup ($1/2$ stick) butter, melted**
> **2 egg yolks**

Pour the wet ingredients over the dry ingredients and combine with a few quick strokes of the whisk, leaving the batter slightly lumpy. Beat until stiff but not dry, 978:

> **2 egg whites**

Fold them into the batter just until blended. To cook, see About Pancakes or Griddle Cakes, 643.

RAISED BUCKWHEAT BLINI

About twenty-four $2 1/2$-inch blini

These small yeast-raised pancakes serve as the traditional base for caviar and smoked fish. For best results, cook in cast iron.
Combine in a small saucepan:

> **$3/4$ cup milk**
> **3 tablespoons unsalted butter**

Heat until the butter is melted. Let cool to between 105° and 115°F. Stir in:

> **$1 1/8$ teaspoons active dry yeast**

Let stand 5 minutes, then stir until the yeast is completely dissolved. Whisk together in a large bowl:

> **$1/2$ cup all-purpose flour**
> **$1/2$ cup buckwheat flour**
> **1 tablespoon sugar**
> **$1/2$ teaspoon salt**

Pour the wet ingredients over the dry ingredients and whisk until well combined. Cover tightly with plastic wrap and let rise in a warm place until doubled in volume, about 1 hour. You can make the blini immediately or stir the batter down and refrigerate, covered, for up to 8 hours. If the batter has been refrigerated, let stand at room temperature for 20 minutes before proceeding.
Stir to deflate the batter, then whisk in:

> **2 large eggs**

Let the batter stand 5 minutes. To cook, see About Pancakes or Griddle Cakes, 643. Use a heaping tablespoon of batter for each blini. If the batter becomes puffy, gently stir it down before making more cakes. Serve with:

> **Melted butter and/or sour cream or crème fraîche (Caviar or smoked fish)**

MINI BLINI

About sixty $1 3/4$-inch blini

These make simple, lovely hors d'oeuvres.
Prepare batter for:

> **Raised Buckwheat Blini, above**

To cook, see About Pancakes or Griddle Cakes, 643. Use a heaping teaspoonful of:

> **Butter**

to cook each cake. Top with:

> **A dab of sour cream**
> **$1/2$ teaspoon caviar or small piece of smoked fish**

OATMEAL PANCAKES

About twenty 3¹/₂-inch pancakes
Whisk together in a large bowl:
   ¹/₂ cup all-purpose flour
   1 teaspoon baking powder
   ¹/₂ teaspoon salt
Beat in a separate bowl:
   2 eggs
Stir in:
   1¹/₂ cups cooked oatmeal
   ¹/₂ cup milk or buttermilk
   2 tablespoons melted butter or bacon drippings
Quickly stir this mixture into the dry ingredients. The batter may appear lumpy. To cook, see About Pancakes or Griddle Cakes, 643. Use ¹/₄ cup batter for each cake, lightly stirring the batter periodically to prevent settling.

LEMON PANCAKES

About twelve 4-inch pancakes
Delicious with honey, sweetened sour cream, or crème fraîche, 1014.
Whisk together in a large bowl:
   1 cup all-purpose flour
   ¹/₃ cup sugar
   1¹/₂ teaspoons baking powder
   ¹/₂ teaspoon baking soda
   ¹/₄ teaspoon salt
Combine in another bowl:
   ³/₄ cup sour cream
   ¹/₃ cup milk
   Finely grated zest of 2 lemons
   ¹/₄ cup fresh lemon juice
   3 tablespoons butter, melted
   1 egg
   1¹/₂ teaspoons vanilla extract
Quickly mix the liquid ingredients into the dry ingredients. The batter will be thick and bubbly. To cook, see About Pancakes or Griddle Cakes, 643. Use ¹/₄ cup batter for each pancake.

ABOUT WAFFLES

You don't have to be told how good waffles are with syrup, honey, marmalade, or cooked fruit. They also make attractive and delicious bases for ice cream or savory creamed foods such as Creamed Chicken or Turkey, 445, and Fried Chicken, 429. Most waffle batters are similar to pancake batters and are mixed in the same way. See About Pancakes or Griddle Cakes, 643. Waffle batters are distinct from pancake batters in one way: They are always made with a fair amount of butter or shortening to promote a crisp, light texture and to ensure that the baked waffles will release easily from the iron. The richer the dough, the crisper the waffle. With the butter flavor baked in, there is then no reason for ladling butter on top of the waffle. You can substitute 3 tablespoons vegetable oil for every 4 tablespoons butter. We also suggest ➤

beating egg whites separately for a superbly light result. Since waffles are made from a batter ➤ keep them tender by not overbeating or overmixing the dough.

Electric waffle irons, especially those with nonstick grids, have made making waffles much easier. To use and care for a waffle iron, and season a new one, follow the manufacturers' instructions exactly. ➤ Once conditioned, the grids should never be washed or even wiped with a damp cloth. Instead, flick out crumbs with a dry soft cloth or soft brush. Removable nonstick plates, however, can be washed using a soft cloth or sponge. ➤ Never immerse a waffle iron in water. After use, merely wipe down the outside with a hot soapy damp cloth.

Heat the waffle iron until the indicator shows it is ready to use. If it has been properly seasoned, it will need no greasing, as most waffle batters are heavy in butter. Have the batter in a pitcher, and pour on enough to ➤ cover about two-thirds of the grid surface, or approximately ¹/₂ cup per waffle. Close the lid and wait about 4 minutes. When the waffle is ready, steam will have stopped emerging from the cracks of the iron. If you try to lift the top of the iron and it shows resistance, it probably means the waffle is not quite done. Allow it to cook slightly longer and try again.

Waffles can be kept warm in a 200°F oven by placing them on a rack set on a baking sheet or directly on the oven racks, allowing the air to circulate so that they will remain crisp. Leftover waffles can be cooled and wrapped in plastic and stored in the refrigerator for 2 days or frozen for several months. To reheat, bake them, unthawed, on a rack in a 350°F oven for about 10 minutes, or toast in the toaster at the lowest setting for 5 minutes.

Recipe yields will vary depending on the size of your waffle iron. For example, irons for Belgian waffles, which have very deep plates, will produce only about half as many waffles as conventional waffle irons. The yields of our recipes are based on a standard iron, with a plate divided into 4 x 4¹/₂ x ¹/₂-inch grids.

▲ In high altitudes, decrease the baking powder and/or soda called for in the following recipes by about one-quarter.

WAFFLES

About 6 waffles
We give you three choices for preparing this recipe: Use 4 tablespoons butter for a reduced-fat waffle, 8 tablespoons (1 stick) for a classic light and fluffy waffle, or ¹/₂ pound (2 sticks) for the crunchiest, most delicious waffle imaginable. If serving these with savory food, omit the sugar.
Preheat a waffle iron. Whisk together in a large bowl:
   1³/₄ cups all-purpose flour
   1 tablespoon baking powder
   1 tablespoon sugar
   ¹/₂ teaspoon salt
Thoroughly blend in another bowl:

3 eggs
$^1/_4$ cup to 1 cup ($^1/_2$ to 2 sticks) butter, melted
1$^1/_2$ cups milk

Make a well in the center of the dry ingredients and pour in the wet ingredients. Combine with a few swift strokes of the whisk. If desired, gently stir in one of the:

Additions to Pancakes, 644

To cook, see About Waffles, 646. Serve with:

Maple syrup, honey, chopped fresh fruit, or a dessert sauce, 828

BUTTERMILK WAFFLES

Prepare **Waffles, 646.** Add $^1/_4$ teaspoon baking soda to the dry ingredients. Decrease baking powder to 2 teaspoons. Substitute **buttermilk** for the milk.

CORNMEAL WAFFLES

About 6 waffles

Terrific with syrup and sausages, these can also be cut into wedges and paired with Roast Chicken, 424, Grilled Shrimp, 386, Beef Stew, 479, Fried Chicken, 429. Think of these as flat, crisp corn bread.

Preheat a waffle iron. Whisk together in a large bowl:

1 cup all-purpose flour
1 cup cornmeal
2 teaspoons baking powder
$^3/_4$ teaspoon salt
$^1/_2$ teaspoon baking soda

Whisk together in another bowl:

2 cups buttermilk
5 tablespoons butter, melted
$^1/_4$ cup maple syrup
2 egg yolks

Make a well in the center of the dry ingredients and pour in the wet ingredients. Combine with a few swift strokes of the whisk. Beat until stiff but not dry, 978, then fold into the batter:

2 egg whites

To cook, see About Waffles, 646. Cover about two-thirds of the grid surface.

BACON CORNMEAL WAFFLES

Prepare **Cornmeal Waffles, above.** Cook until crisp **2 to 3 slices thin bacon.** Crumble into the batter or cut into quarters and place 1 piece on each waffle iron section after pouring in the batter.

HONEY BRAN WAFFLES

About 6 waffles

Preheat a waffle iron. Whisk together in a large bowl:

$^3/_4$ cup all-purpose flour
$^3/_4$ cup whole wheat flour
$^1/_2$ cup coarse wheat bran or miller's bran
2 teaspoons baking powder
$^1/_2$ teaspoon salt
$^1/_4$ teaspoon baking soda

Whisk together in another bowl:

1$^1/_2$ cups buttermilk
$^1/_3$ cup honey
$^1/_2$ cup (1 stick) butter, melted
2 eggs
$^1/_2$ teaspoon vanilla extract

Make a well in the center of the dry ingredients and pour in the wet ingredients. Combine with a few swift strokes of the whisk. To cook, see About Waffles, 646.

CHOCOLATE WAFFLES

About 8 waffles

Delectable with vanilla ice cream. These waffles are delicate, so remove them from the iron carefully.

Preheat a waffle iron. Whisk together in a large bowl:

1$^1/_2$ cups sifted all-purpose flour
1$^1/_3$ cups sugar
$^1/_2$ cup unsweetened cocoa powder, sifted if lumpy
2 teaspoons baking powder
$^1/_2$ teaspoon salt

Whisk in a medium bowl until frothy:

2 large eggs

Whisk in:

1 cup milk
$^3/_4$ cup plus 2 tablespoons vegetable oil
1 teaspoon vanilla extract

Add the wet ingredients to the dry ingredients and combine with a few swift strokes of the whisk. To cook, see About Waffles, 646.

BELGIAN WAFFLES

About 12 Belgian waffles

Serve these yeast-raised waffles with Whipped Cream, 754, and sliced strawberries.

Preheat a waffle iron. Whisk together in a large bowl:

3 cups warm (105° to 115°F) milk
1 envelope (2$^1/_4$ teaspoons) active dry yeast

Let stand until the yeast is dissolved, about 5 minutes, then stir until smooth. Whisk in:

$^3/_4$ cup (1$^1/_2$ sticks) butter, melted and cooled to lukewarm
$^1/_2$ cup sugar
3 egg yolks
2 teaspoons vanilla
1$^1/_2$ teaspoon salt

Add in 3 additions, beating with a large spoon until smooth after each addition:

4 cups all-purpose flour

Cover tightly with plastic wrap and let rise at room temperature until doubled in volume, 1 to 1$^1/_2$ hours. Stir to deflate the batter. Beat until soft peaks form, 978, then fold into the batter:

3 egg whites

To cook, see About Waffles, 646. Sprinkle with:

Confectioners' sugar

FRENCH TOAST WAFFLES

6 waffles

Preheat a waffle iron. Whisk together in a large bowl:

3 large eggs
$1/2$ cup milk
2 tablespoons butter, melted
$1/8$ teaspoon salt

Cut to fit the waffle iron grid:

6 slices white sandwich bread

Coat the bread well in the egg mixture. Place on the hot iron, close the lid, and cook until the bread is golden brown.

ABOUT FRENCH TOAST

This favorite breakfast dish is an excellent use of stale bread, although fresh will do. White bread, which is typically used, is dipped into a mixture of milk and egg and then browned in butter. Syrup, powdered sugar, or jam is customarily served on top. The bread may also be cut into rounds with a biscuit cutter.

FRENCH TOAST

8 slices

Whisk together in a shallow bowl:

$2/3$ cup milk or half-and-half
4 eggs
2 tablespoons sugar or maple syrup
1 teaspoon vanilla or 1 tablespoon rum
$1/4$ teaspoon salt

One at a time, soak both sides in the egg mixture:

8 slices white sandwich bread
Butter as needed

Brown the bread on each side in a hot well-buttered skillet. Serve hot sprinkled with:

(Confectioners' sugar)

STUFFED FRENCH TOAST

8 servings

Preheat the oven to 400°F. Lightly butter a large baking sheet. Combine and blend in a large bowl:

8 ounces cream cheese, softened
$1/4$ cup packed light brown sugar
$1/4$ cup honey or maple syrup
1 teaspoon vanilla extract
(Grated zest of $1/2$ orange)
Pinch of ground cinnamon
Pinch of salt

Stir in, if desired:

($1/4$ cup finely chopped walnuts or pecans, toasted, or $1/4$ cup raisins)

Trim the ends and crusts from:

One 1-pound loaf white sandwich bread, unsliced

Cut the loaf into 8 thick slices. Carefully cut into one side of each slice to create a pocket that you can open with your fingers. Spoon an equal amount of the filling into each pocket. Mix in a shallow bowl:

1 cup milk
3 eggs
$1/4$ cup all-purpose flour
3 tablespoons sugar
2 teaspoons baking powder
2 teaspoons vanilla extract
$1/4$ teaspoon salt

One slice at a time, soak the bread in the egg mixture until thoroughly saturated but not falling apart and transfer to a plate before browning. Heat in a large skillet over medium-low heat until the butter has melted:

2 tablespoons butter

Cooking in batches, add the stuffed bread add and brown on both sides. Transfer to the prepared baking sheet. Bake the bread about 6 minutes, until fragrant and golden brown all over. Serve immediately.

BAKED FRENCH TOAST

4 servings

Whisk together in large bowl:

1 cup heavy cream, half-and-half, or milk
6 eggs
$1/4$ cup maple syrup
2 tablespoons light brown sugar
1 teaspoon vanilla extract
$1/4$ teaspoon salt

Trim the crusts from:

8 slices white sandwich bread or Challah, 600

One slice at a time, turn the bread in the egg mixture to coat it, then fit the coated bread into an 8 x 8-inch baking dish, making a double layer. Very gently press the bread with the back of a fork to compress the slices slightly. Cover with plastic wrap pressed directly onto the bread to help it soak up the egg mixture. Refrigerate overnight. Preheat the oven to 400°F. Lightly butter a baking sheet, preferably nonstick. Using a wide spatula—or, if you find it easier, your hands—lift the bread, slice by slice, out of the soaking mixture, allowing the excess liquid to drip back into the pan, and place on the baking sheet. Bake until puffed and golden, 12 to 15 minutes, turning the slices halfway through baking. Serve immediately with:

Maple syrup
(Sliced fresh fruit)

ABOUT CRÊPES

Crêpes are thin, delicate pancakes, and crêpe batter must be mixed until smooth. This is most easily done in a blender, but whisking in a bowl works fine. Cover and let stand at least 30 minutes before cooking. In fact, crêpe batter can be made up to 2 days ahead and refrigerated in a covered container. Before using a refrigerated batter, gently stir and let stand at room temperature for 30 minutes.

Crêpes can be made in a regular crêpe pan, as shown on 649, or in a regular small to medium skillet, preferably nonstick. Crêpes to be filled with savory foods need to be cooked in a large nonstick skillet.

Making crêpes

The skill of making crêpes comes with practice, but sufficient practice is often acquired after a few tries. Place your pan over medium heat and add $1/2$ teaspoon butter. The temperature is right when the butter begins to color, but not smoke. Lift the pan off the heat and, using a ladle or small measuring cup, slowly pour in enough batter to cover the entire bottom with a very thin coating. If you have too much, pour the excess back in the bowl. Quickly tilt and rotate the pan, then return to the heat and cook until the crêpe bubbles and the bottom is lightly browned, 1 to $1^1/2$ minutes. Turn the crêpes with a spatula or with your fingers (to do this, slide the pan off the heat, lift an edge of the crêpe with a knife, then gently hold the edge, pulling the crêpe off the pan, and gently flip it over). Return the pan to heat and cook the second side until browned, but not evenly. Slide the crêpe onto a wax paper–covered plate.

To store the crêpes, cover the plate tightly with plastic wrap and refrigerate up to 24 hours, or wrap the stack in foil, seal in a plastic bag, and freeze up to 1 month. To thaw frozen crêpes, place in the refrigerator for about 12 hours or defrost at room temperature, just long enough to make them soft enough to peel each one off without tearing.

SAVORY OR SWEET CRÊPES
About 12 crêpes
Savory crêpes make an elegant brunch, lunch, or supper dish when rolled around a filling; see the recipes that follow or use some tasty leftovers. Sweet crêpes are generally used to make fancy desserts, such as those on the following pages. However, they may be simply sprinkled with sugar and lemon juice or spread with warmed preserves, then folded into quarters or rolled.
I. SAVORY CRÊPES
Combine in a bowl and mix until smooth:
> **1 cup all-purpose flour**
> **1 cup milk**
> **$1/2$ cup lukewarm water**
> **4 large eggs**
> **$1/4$ cup ($1/2$ stick) butter, melted**
> **$1/2$ teaspoon salt**

Cover with plastic wrap and let stand for 30 minutes, or refrigerate for up to 2 days. To cook, see About Crêpes, 648. Use about $1/4$ cup batter for each crêpe.
II. SWEET CRÊPES
Prepare as above, adding **3 tablespoons sugar** and decreasing the salt to $1/8$ teaspoon.

BUCKWHEAT CRÊPES
About ten 9-inch crêpes
Buckwheat crêpes, a specialty of the Brittany region of France, are larger and a little thicker than regular crêpes with an assertive flavor, thanks to the buckwheat flour. Buckwheat crêpes are typically filled with savory mixtures, such as ham and cheese, below, but also sautéed mushrooms and chopped tomatoes, and are often topped with a fried egg. The batter needs to rest for an hour before cooking.
Combine in a blender until smooth:
> **$1/2$ cup buckwheat flour**
> **$1/2$ cup all-purpose flour**
> **1 cup milk**
> **$3/4$ cup water**
> **3 large eggs**
> **2 tablespoons vegetable oil**
> **1 teaspoon salt**

Scrape down the sides of the container and process until thoroughly blended, about 15 seconds more. Pour the batter into a pitcher or other container with a spout. Cover with plastic wrap and let stand for 1 hour, or refrigerate for up to 1 day. To cook, see About Crêpes, 648. Cook in a 12-inch nonstick skillet, using about $1/3$ cup batter for each crêpe.

FILLED SAVORY CRÊPES
12 crêpes
Preheat the oven to 400°F. Lightly butter a 13 x 9-inch baking dish. Have ready:
> **12 Savory Crêpes, above**
and 4 cups of one of the following:
> **Creamed Mushrooms, 283, omitting porcinis**
> **Creamed Spinach, 305**

Creamed Chicken or Turkey, 445, or
Ham and Cheese

Spread 3 to 4 tablespoons of filling in the center of the pale side of each crêpe, leaving a 1-inch border all around, then roll up the crêpes. Arrange seam side down in a single layer in the prepared baking dish. Brush with:

3 tablespoons butter, melted

Sprinkle with:

$^1/_2$ cup grated Parmesan

Bake until lightly browned, about 20 minutes.

FILLED SWEET CRÊPES

12 crêpes

Preheat the oven to 400°F. Lightly butter a 13 x 9-inch baking dish. Have ready:

12 Sweet Crêpes, 649

and 4 cups of one of the following:

Any poached or sautéed fruit, 212; Pastry Cream, 755, plain or mixed with berries, toasted nuts, 1001, or crushed almond macaroons, 771; Whipped Cream, 973, plain or sweetened and mixed with berries or toasted nuts, 1001; Applesauce, 216; jam or preserves, 927; Lemon Curd, 756; Hot Lemon Sauce, 844; or Chocolate Ganache, 796

Spread 3 to 4 tablespoons of filling in the center of the pale side of each crêpe, leaving a 1-inch border all around, then roll up the crêpes. Arrange seam side down in a single layer in the prepared baking dish. Brush with:

3 tablespoons butter, melted

Sprinkle with:

$^1/_2$ cup grated Parmesan

Bake until lightly browned, about 20 minutes.

HAM AND SPINACH CRÊPES

12 crêpes

Preheat the oven to 400°F. Lightly butter a 13 x 9-inch baking dish. Have ready:

12 Savory Crêpes, 649
12 thin slices ham
Creamed Spinach, 305

Place a ham slice on the pale side of each crêpe. Spread each one with 2 tablespoons spinach, and roll up. Arrange seam side down in the prepared baking dish. Spoon over the top:

Mornay Sauce, 551

Sprinkle with:

$^1/_3$ cup grated Parmesan

Bake until the sauce is lightly browned, about 20 minutes.

CRÊPES WITH CHICKEN, APPLES, AND BLUE CHEESE

12 crêpes

Preheat the oven to 400°F. Lightly butter a 13 x 9-inch baking dish. Have ready:

12 Savory Crêpes, 649
3 cups diced cooked chicken

2 medium apples, peeled, quartered, cored, and cut into thin slices
2 cups White Sauce I, 551
3 ounces Roquefort or other blue cheese, crumbled

Spread 2 to 3 tablespoons of the sauce in the center of the pale side of each crêpe. Place the chicken on the lower third of the crêpes. Top with apples and cheese. Roll up the crêpes and arrange seam side down in the prepared baking dish. Cover with the remaining sauce and cheese, if any. Bake until the sauce is bubbly and lightly browned, about 20 minutes.

CRÊPES SUZETTE

12 crêpes

Have ready:

12 Sweet Crêpes, 649

Place in a large skillet or chafing dish over medium heat:

$^1/_4$ cup ($^1/_2$ stick) butter
(Grated zest of 1 small orange)
$^1/_2$ cup orange juice
$^1/_3$ cup sugar
1 teaspoon fresh lemon juice

Bring to a boil, stirring to melt the sugar, then continue to boil just until slightly thickened, 2 to 3 minutes. Stir in:

2 tablespoons Grand Marnier
2 tablespoons Cognac or other brandy

Return the sauce to a boil and boil for 30 seconds. Using tongs, add the crêpes one at a time to the skillet or chafing dish and soak each in the sauce about 15 seconds, then fold it twice so it will be triangular in shape with the brownest side out. Lay the folded crêpes against the side of the pan while you prepare the rest. When all are folded, arrange the crêpes over the bottom of the skillet and pour over them:

$^1/_2$ cup Grand Marnier

Cook about 15 seconds, spooning the sauce mixture over the crêpes. Then, standing back, carefully ignite with a long lighter or wooden match. Serve still flaming.

CRÊPES WITH CARAMELIZED APPLES

12 crêpes

The cider syrup, which can be refrigerated for a week, is delicious on any pancake or waffle.

Combine in a small saucepan:

1 cup apple cider
3 tablespoons light corn syrup
1 tablespoon light brown sugar
1 tablespoon fresh lemon juice

Simmer over medium heat until the mixture is reduced by half, about 10 minutes. Remove from the heat and swirl in, piece by piece:

2 tablespoons cold unsalted butter, cut into 6 pieces

Cover and set aside at room temperature, up to 6 hours. Melt in a large skillet, preferably nonstick, over high-medium heat:

2 tablespoons unsalted butter

Add and cook, stirring frequently, until the apples start to soften, about 5 minutes:

3 medium Golden Delicious apples (1 to 1¼ pounds), peeled, cored, and cut into 12 wedges each

Sprinkle with:

2 tablespoons sugar

Cook, stirring frequently, until the apples are caramelized, 10 to 15 minutes. Remove from the heat. Preheat the oven to 350°F. Line a large baking sheet with parchment paper. Have ready:

12 Sweet Crêpes, 649
3 tablespoons butter, melted

Brush the crêpes lightly with the butter and arrange on the baking sheet, overlapping as necessary. Bake until warmed through, about 5 minutes. Meanwhile, return the apples and sauce to low heat until warmed. If the sauce separates, whisk to recombine. Serve the crêpes topped with the apples and sauce. Top with:

(Whipped Cream, 973, crème fraîche, 1014, or vanilla ice cream)

CRÊPE CAKE

12 crêpes

For an especially dramatic cake that will serve 10 to 12 people, prepare a double recipe of crêpes. Have ready:

12 Sweet Crêpes, 649

Stack the crêpes like a layer cake on a heatproof platter, spreading each with a thin layer of:

Jelly or jam or Hot Lemon Sauce, 844

Sprinkle the top with:

Sugar

Set aside at room temperature for up to 8 hours. Preheat the oven to 250°F. If you would like to flame the dessert, heat until barely warm, 1055:

(¼ cup brandy or rum)

Pour over the crêpes and, standing back, carefully ignite with a long lighter or wooden match. To serve, place the crêpe cake in the oven until warmed through, about 15 minutes. Cut into wedges. Serve with:

(Whipped Cream, 973)

BLINTZES

About twelve 7½-inch blintzes

Combine in a blender or food processor until smooth:

1 cup all-purpose flour
1 cup milk
3 large eggs
2 tablespoons butter, melted
2 teaspoons sugar
Pinch of salt

Pour the batter into a pitcher or other container with a pouring lip. Cover with plastic wrap and let stand at room temperature for 30 minutes, or refrigerate up to 2 days. To cook, see About Crêpes, 648. Use 3 tablespoons batter for

each blintz, but do not turn the blintzes. Instead, cook until the top is dry and set and the underside is golden.

SWEET CHEESE BLINTZES

12 blintzes

The classic accompaniment to sweet cheese blintzes is Poached Sour Cherries, 212. Also delicious are mixed fresh berries, a warm Dried Fruit Compote, 211, or Applesauce, 216. Cheese blintzes can be made with either small-curd cottage cheese or farmer's cheese. If using cottage cheese, drain it for 1 hour in a sieve set over a bowl. Have ready:

12 Blintzes, above

Combine in a blender or food processor until smooth:

1 pound small-curd cottage cheese, drained, or farmer's cheese
3 ounces cream cheese
2 eggs
2 tablespoons sugar
1 teaspoon vanilla extract
½ teaspoon salt
(Grated zest of ½ orange)

Transfer to a bowl and stir in:

(½ cup raisins)

Spoon 3 tablespoons of the filling onto the center of the unbrowned side of each blintz. Fold sides over, then bottom, and roll up to form a rectangular package. The filled blintzes can be wrapped airtight and frozen for up to 1 month. Thaw in the refrigerator. Heat in a large skillet, preferably nonstick, over medium heat until the butter is melted and the bubbles have subsided:

2 tablespoons butter
1 tablespoon vegetable oil

Add the blintzes, seam side down, to the pan and cook, turning once, until golden brown on both sides. Transfer the blintzes to paper towels to drain for a moment. Serve immediately with:

(Sour cream)

and any other topping or accompaniment of your choice.

BLUEBERRY BLINTZES

6 blintzes

Combine in a medium saucepan:

1 cup fresh or unthawed frozen blueberries
Finely grated zest and juice of ½ lemon
2 tablespoons sugar
(Pinch of ground cinnamon)

Bring to a boil over medium heat, stirring constantly, then continue to boil until the mixture is the consistency of jam. Add:

1 cup fresh or unthawed frozen blueberries

Cook and stir for 1 minute. Transfer to a bowl and let cool to room temperature. Have ready:

6 Blintzes, above

Spoon 2 generous tablespoons of the filling onto the center of the unbrowned side of each blintz. Fold the sides of each blintz around the filling to form a rectangular package. (The filled blintzes can be wrapped airtight and frozen for up to 1 month.) Heat in a large skillet, preferably nonstick, over medium heat until the butter is melted and the bubbles have subsided:

2 tablespoons butter
1 tablespoon vegetable oil

Add the blintzes, seam side down, to the pan and cook, turning once, until golden brown on both sides. Transfer the blintzes to paper towels to drain briefly. Serve immediately with:

Sour cream, Custard Sauce, 846, or Lemon Curd, 756

VIENNESE OR AUSTRIAN CRÊPES (PALATSCHINKEN)

8 rolled pancakes

Combine in a blender or food processor until smooth:

1 cup all-purpose flour
1 cup milk
2 large eggs
3 tablespoons sugar
$1/2$ teaspoon vanilla extract
Pinch of salt

Pour the batter into a pitcher or other container with a pouring lip. Cover with plastic wrap and let stand 30 minutes at room temperature, or refrigerate up to 2 days. To cook, see About Crêpes, 648. Use $1/4$ cup batter for each pancake, making 8 pancakes slightly thicker than crêpes. Cool, then wrap until ready to serve. Preheat the oven to 350°F. Line a large baking sheet with parchment paper. Brush the pancakes lightly with:

2 tablespoons butter, melted

Arrange on the baking sheet, overlapping slightly if necessary. Bake until warmed through, about 5 minutes. Meanwhile, combine in a small saucepan and bring to a boil:

1 cup apricot jam
1 tablespoon Cointreau or Grand Marnier

Remove from the heat. Spread each pancake with 2 tablespoons of the jam mixture and roll up. Transfer to individual plates and sprinkle with:

$1/2$ cup finely chopped walnuts
Confectioners' sugar

Serve with:

(Whipped Cream, 973)

ABOUT OVEN-BAKED PANCAKES

These are pancakes only in the sense that they are cakes cooked in a pan; they bear no resemblance to the usual pancakes. Though they are conventionally classified as desserts, they are quite popular served at breakfast or brunch. All are light, puffy creations and the Austrian Pancake is virtually a soufflé.

DUTCH BABY

2 to 4 servings

Sometimes called a puff pancake, it emerges from the oven puffed and golden, like a giant popover. Sprinkle with confectioners' sugar and serve with fruit preserves or Sautéed Fruit, 214.

Set a rack in the lower third of the oven and preheat the oven to 425°F. Whisk together in a medium bowl:

$1/2$ cup milk
2 large eggs, at room temperature
$1/4$ teaspoon salt

Add and whisk until smooth:

$1/2$ cup all-purpose flour

Melt in a 10-inch cast iron skillet or other ovenproof pan over medium heat:

4 tablespoons ($1/2$ stick) butter

Tilt the pan so that the butter coats the sides. Pour the egg mixture into the skillet and cook, without stirring, for 1 minute. Place the skillet in the oven and bake for 15 minutes without opening the oven door. Lower the heat to 350°F, and bake until the pancake is puffed and richly browned, 10 to 15 minutes longer. Sprinkle with:

Confectioners' sugar

Serve immediately, straight from the skillet, before the pancake falls.

GERMAN PANCAKE (PFANNKUCHEN)

4 servings

Our recipe is based on one by Henrietta Davides, nineteenth-century Germany's greatest cookbook author. Preheat the oven to 400°F.

Combine in a medium bowl:

4 large egg yolks
3 tablespoons sugar
$1/8$ teaspoon salt

Whisk vigorously until thickened and lemon colored, 1 to 2 minutes. Whisk in:

$1/4$ cup milk
$1/4$ cup lukewarm water
Finely grated zest of 1 lemon
($1/4$ teaspoon vanilla extract)

Add and whisk until smooth:

$1/2$ cup cornstarch

Beat until stiff but not dry, 978:

4 large egg whites

Add to the yolk mixture, gently whisking until the whites are incorporated but not deflated; the batter should have the appearance of a light foam. Immediately melt in a 10-inch heavy ovenproof skillet, preferably nonstick, over medium heat:

3 tablespoons butter

When the bubbles have subsided, pour in the batter. Cook until the the pancake, when pried back from the pan with a knife, looks golden brown on the underside, about 2 minutes. Place the pan in the oven and bake until the pancake has puffed and the top feels dry and set when gently touched, about 5 minutes. Immediately slide the pancake onto a serving platter and sprinkle with:

Confectioners' sugar

(Ground cinnamon)

Serve at once, before the pancake falls, and accompany with:

**²/₃ cup warmed apricot or cherry preserves or
Baked Fruit Compote, 213**

AUSTRIAN PANCAKES (NÖCKERLEN)

4 servings

In Salzburg, few visitors fail to indulge in one or more of these souffléed globular puffs. Serve immediately.

Preheat the oven to 350°F. Combine in a medium bowl and whisk until thickened and pale:

2 large egg yolks

1 tablespoon sugar

(¹/₂ teaspoon finely grated lemon zest)

Beat in a large bowl until almost stiff, 978:

3 large egg whites, at room temperature

Gradually beat in:

¹/₄ cup sugar

Beat until the whites are very stiff and shiny, then beat in:

¹/₂ teaspoon vanilla extract

Sift over, then gently fold in with a large rubber spatula:

2 tablespoons all-purpose flour

Gently fold in the egg yolk mixture. Immediately melt in a 12-inch ovenproof skillet over medium-high heat:

2 tablespoons butter

When the butter smells fragrant and is just beginning to color, spoon four 1-cup mounds of the mixture into the skillet, heaping them high and spacing them as far apart as possible. Cook until the pancakes are lightly colored on the bottom, about 3 minutes. Transfer the skillet to the oven and bake the pancakes until lightly brown and puffed but still soft in the center, 10 to 12 minutes. Sprinkle generously with:

Confectioners' sugar

Serve at once. Accompany with:

**(Warmed preserves, Hot Lemon Sauce, 796, or Fresh
Fruit Sauce, 844–853)**

ABOUT DOUGHNUTS, CRULLERS, AND BEIGNETS

When mixing doughnut doughs, have all ingredients at room temperature, and stir the wet and dry ingredients together quickly just until well blended. This prevents the development of gluten in the dough, which would tend to toughen the doughnuts. These doughs are soft and sticky when just mixed, but when chilled for at least 2 hours before cutting, they become firm enough to handle. Unless raised with yeast, these doughs can be refrigerated up to 1 day.

To form doughnuts, roll the dough ¹/₂ inch thick (unless otherwise specified) on a lightly floured work surface or on floured wax paper. In most cases, it is easier to roll the

dough to an even thickness if you divide it in half before rolling, rather than rolling out a large amount at once.

➤ Cut out doughnuts either with a well-floured doughnut cutter, 654, or with 2 sizes of round biscuit or cookie cutters, using a smaller cutter for the doughnut holes. ➤ Our recipes are developed for a 3¹/₂-inch cutter with a 1-inch hole. If you use a smaller cutter, the yield will be greater than that given in the recipe (a 2¹/₂-inch cutter, for example, will yield nearly twice as many doughnuts). Using a spatula, transfer cut doughnuts to a sheet of wax paper that has been generously floured. The doughnuts will soften as they stand, and the flour is needed to prevent the doughnuts from sticking. Press the scraps together, handling them as little and as gently as possible, then roll and cut out more doughnuts. Scraps of scraps will make tough doughnuts, so use these instead to make "holes," which you can either cut or form with your hands.

Allow most cut doughnuts to rest at room temperature for 20 minutes to 1 hour before frying. During this time, the dough will warm up and form a light crust, both of which will reduce the amount of fat that the doughnuts will absorb during frying. This does not apply to yeast-raised doughnuts, which will warm and crust during rising.

Before beginning, ➤ read About Deep-Fat Frying, 1046. Fry the doughnuts in a heavy pot or a deep heavy skillet, using about 3 inches of vegetable oil or melted shortening. Whichever fat you use, it must be fresh, not recycled.

Heat the oil or fat to 375°F. To keep the fat at a constant temperature, ➤ never crowd the fryer. The easiest and safest way to transfer doughnuts to the pot is to ➤ slide them in one at a time using a long metal spatula that has been dipped in the hot fat. Each doughnut takes 1¹/₂ to 2 minutes per side to cook depending on the size. A deep golden brown color is the best indicator of doneness. To be sure that you are gauging doneness correctly, you may wish to cut into one doughnut from the first batch to be sure the inside is done. If it is underdone, the remaining doughnuts from this batch can be returned to the pot and cooked longer. Remove the doughnuts with tongs or with a wooden chopstick inserted through the hole in each one, holding them briefly over the pot to allow excess fat to drip off. Place the cooked doughnuts on a triple layer of paper towels, then immediately turn them to blot fat from the second side.

When the doughnuts cool, dust with powdered, spiced, or flavored sugar, then either roll the doughnuts in sugar on a plate or, one or two at a time, gently shake them with the sugar in a sturdy paper or plastic bag. Both yeast doughnuts and cake can be glazed or iced. See Glazes and Icings, 784.

Homemade doughnuts are best eaten on the day they are made, though they will remain reasonably moist for up to 2 days if stored in a tightly sealed container at room

Rolling and cutting doughnuts

temperature. Doughnuts can also be frozen in a resealable plastic freezer bag for up to 1 month and eaten immediately after thawing.

▲ Recipes for yeast-raised doughnuts require no adjustment at high altitudes. For other doughnuts, reduce the baking powder or baking soda by one-quarter—➤ but do not reduce baking soda to below ¹⁄₂ teaspoon per each cup of buttermilk or sour cream used.

CAKE DOUGHNUTS
About 18 doughnuts
Please read About Doughnuts, Crullers, and Beignets, 653.
Whisk together in a medium bowl until thoroughly mixed:
    4 cups all-purpose flour
    4 teaspoons baking powder
    ³⁄₄ teaspoon ground cinnamon or 1 teaspoon grated lemon zest
    (³⁄₄ teaspoon grated or ground nutmeg)
    ³⁄₄ teaspoon salt
In a large bowl, beat well with an electric mixer:
    2 eggs
Add slowly and beat until thick and creamy:
    ³⁄₄ cup plus 2 tablespoons sugar
On low speed, add and beat until blended:
    ³⁄₄ cup milk
    5 tablespoons butter, melted
Pour the wet ingredients over the dry and mix with a large spoon just until blended. The dough will be soft and sticky. Wrap the dough in plastic and refrigerate at least 2 hours, or up to 24 hours. To roll, cut, rest, and fry, see 653.

YEAST DOUGHNUTS
About 24 doughnuts
If you do not have a heavy-duty mixer, the dough can be mixed by hand using a large wooden spoon.
Please read About Doughnuts, Crullers, and Beignets, 653. Whisk together in the bowl of a heavy-duty mixer:
    1 cup warm (105° to 115°F) water
    2 envelopes (2¹⁄₄ teaspoons each) active dry yeast
Let stand until the yeast is dissolved, about 5 minutes. Add and whisk until smooth:

    1 cup all-purpose flour
Cover the bowl tightly with plastic wrap and let stand at room temperature until bubbly, about 30 minutes. Whisk in:
    ²⁄₃ cup sugar
    ²⁄₃ cup butter, softened
    3 large eggs
    2 teaspoons vanilla extract
    1 teaspoon salt
    (Grated zest of ¹⁄₂ lemon or ¹⁄₄ orange)
Add and beat with the dough hook or paddle at medium-low speed until the dough wraps around the hook or paddle and comes away from the sides of the bowl:
    3¹⁄₂ cups all-purpose flour
Remove the bowl from the mixer. Cover tightly with plastic wrap and let the dough rise at room temperature until tripled in volume, 1¹⁄₂ to 2 hours. Punch the dough down. Wrap it tightly in plastic wrap and enclose in a large plastic bag. Refrigerate for at least 3 hours, or up to 16 hours. The dough will rise slightly and may pop out of the plastic wrap; if it does, the plastic bag should prevent it from developing a crust. To roll, cut, rest, and fry, see 653. Roll the dough out ³⁄₈ inch thick, and let the cut doughnuts rise, uncovered, at room temperature until soft and puffy, about 1 hour. Begin frying the doughnuts as soon as they have risen, or they will overrise and the taste and texture will be impaired.

SOUR CREAM DOUGHNUTS
About 36 doughnuts
Please read About Doughnuts, Crullers, and Beignets, 653.
Beat well in a large bowl:
    3 eggs
Add slowly, beating constantly:
    1¹⁄₄ cups sugar
Stir in:
    1 cup sour cream
Sift together:
    4 cups all-purpose flour
Resift with:
    2 teaspoons baking powder

1 teaspoon baking soda
$^1/_2$ teaspoon ground cinnamon or grated or ground
 nutmeg
$^1/_2$ teaspoon salt

Stir the sifted ingredients into the egg mixture until blended. To roll, cut, rest, and fry, see 653.

BUTTERMILK POTATO DOUGHNUTS
About 20 doughnuts

Please read About Doughnuts, Crullers, and Beignets, 653.
Prepare:

2 cups riced potatoes, 295

Whisk together thoroughly in a medium bowl:

$3^3/_4$ cups all-purpose flour
$2^1/_2$ teaspoons baking powder
1 teaspoon salt
$^1/_2$ teaspoon baking soda
$^1/_4$ teaspoon grated or ground nutmeg or cinnamon

In a large bowl, beat with an electric mixer at high speed until foamy, about 1 minute:

2 eggs

Gradually add and beat until thick and creamy:

$^3/_4$ cup sugar

On slow speed, add and beat until blended:

1 cup buttermilk
$^1/_4$ cup ($^1/_2$ stick) butter, melted
1 teaspoon vanilla

Beat in the potatoes. Using a large spoon, stir in the dry ingredients. The dough will be very soft. Wrap in plastic and refrigerate for at least 2 hours, or up to 24 hours. To roll, cut, rest, and fry, see 653.

CHOCOLATE DOUGHNUTS
About 18 doughnuts

Please read About Doughnuts, Crullers, and Beignets, 653.
Combine in a medium bowl:

$^2/_3$ cup Dutch-processed cocoa powder
$^1/_4$ cup ($^1/_2$ stick) butter, cut into bits

Pour over:

$^2/_3$ cup boiling water

Whisk until smooth, then let stand 5 minutes. Add, whisking until thoroughly blended:

1 cup sugar
$^2/_3$ cup sour cream
2 large eggs
2 teaspoons vanilla extract
1 teaspoon salt
1 teaspoon baking powder
$^1/_2$ teaspoon baking soda

Add:

4 cups sifted all-purpose flour

Stir until the flour is absorbed and a soft dough forms. Wrap the dough in plastic and refrigerate at least 2 hours, or for up to 24 hours. To roll, cut, rest, and fry, see 653.

The doughnuts are cooked through when they have become several shades darker.

CHOCOLATE GLAZED DOUGHNUTS
About 18 doughnuts

Prepare:

Chocolate Doughnuts, above, or Cake Doughnuts, 654

Melt in a saucepan over very low heat or in a double boiler:

**4 ounces semisweet or bittersweet chocolate,
 chopped**
$^1/_4$ cup ($^1/_2$ stick) butter
$^1/_4$ cup water

Remove from the heat and whisk until smooth. Whisk in:

$1^1/_3$ cups confectioners' sugar

Dip one side of each doughnut into the glaze, then place on a rack, glazed side up. Let stand until the glaze is dry, about 1 hour.

DROPPED DOUGHNUTS
About sixty $1^1/_2$-inch balls

Without the characteristic hole, these are lighter in texture. If you dip the spoon into the frying oil before taking up each gob of batter, the doughnuts will slide easily into the pot.
Prepare the dough for either of the following, decreasing the flour by $^1/_2$ cup:

Cake Doughnuts, 654, or Chocolate Doughnuts, above

Cover the dough and set aside at room temperature for 30 minutes. Do not refrigerate. Slide tablespoons of the dough, 5 or 6 at a time, into fat heated to 375°F, and fry about 3 minutes. Drain on paper towels.

JELLY DOUGHNUTS
About 24 doughnuts

Be sure to let these rise until very light and puffy, or air pockets will develop around the jelly centers.
Prepare the dough for:

Yeast Doughnuts, 654

Working with one-quarter of the dough at a time, on a lightly floured work surface, roll the dough a little more than $^1/_8$ inch thick. Cut into rounds (not rings) using a 3- to $3^1/_2$-inch round cookie or biscuit cutter. Gather, roll, and cut the scraps. You should have about 48 rounds altogether. Have ready:

About $^3/_4$ cup jelly or jam

Place a heaping teaspoon of jam or jelly each in the center of half of the rounds. Brush the edges of these filled rounds with:

1 large egg white, lightly beaten

Top each filled round with a plain round of dough and pinch the edges together to seal. Transfer to well-floured wax paper and let rise until light and puffy, about 1 hour. To fry, see About Doughnuts, Crullers, and Beignets, 653.
Dust with:

Confectioners' sugar

HONEY-DIPPED DOUGHNUTS

About 24 doughnuts
Prepare:

> Yeast Doughnuts, 654

Set a wire rack over a baking sheet. Combine in a saucepan:

> One 1-pound box confectioners' sugar (4 cups)
> $^1/_3$ cup honey
> $^1/_4$ cup water

Cook over medium heat, whisking constantly, until the mixture just begins to simmer and is completely smooth. Remove the pan from the heat. Drop the doughnuts into the glaze one at a time, turning to glaze both sides. Using a chopstick or long skewer, transfer the doughnuts to the wire rack. If the glaze stiffens while you are dipping the doughnuts, warm it briefly over low heat. Let the doughnuts stand about 15 minutes, or until the glaze is dry. If possible, apply the glaze while the doughnuts are still warm.

CRULLERS

About 24 crullers
Crullers are richer than doughnuts and, of course, they look different. The first variation makes soft braided crullers and the second yields old-fashioned thin, crunchy crullers. Please read About Deep-Fat Frying, 1046.

I. Whisk together thoroughly in a medium bowl:

> 4 cups sifted all-purpose flour
> (1 teaspoon grated or ground nutmeg)
> $^3/_4$ teaspoon ground cinnamon
> 2 teaspoons baking powder
> $^3/_4$ teaspoon salt

Add:

> $^1/_2$ cup (1 stick) unsalted butter, well softened

Rub with your hands until the butter has completely disappeared into the dry ingredients, without a speck of unblended butter remaining. The mixture should feel soft and slightly greasy and should hold together in a crumbly mass when grasped. Beat in a medium bowl with a mixer at high speed until very foamy:

> 4 large eggs

Gradually, add then beat until thick and creamy:

> $^3/_4$ cup sugar

On low speed, beat in:

> 2 tablespoons milk

Pour the egg mixture over the dry ingredients and stir with a large spoon until a soft dough forms. Wrap the dough in plastic and refrigerate at least 2 hours, or up to 24 hours. Using 1 level tablespoon for each, roll the dough between your hands into about 48 balls. Do not flour the dough; if it becomes too soft to handle, refrigerate it briefly. Place the balls on a baking sheet covered with wax paper, cover with wax paper, and refrigerate for at least 1 hour.

Line a baking sheet with wax paper and sprinkle generously with flour. Work with just a few balls at a time, leaving the rest in the refrigerator. On unfloured wax paper,

roll 2 balls under your palms into 5-inch ropes. Place the ropes side by side, pinch both ends to seal, then twist a few times. Transfer to the prepared baking sheet. Repeat, making 24 crullers. Let stand at room temperature, uncovered, for 30 minutes. To fry, see About Doughnuts, Crullers, and Beignets, 653. Fry, turning periodically, until deep golden brown, 3 to 4 minutes. Drain on a rack or paper towels. Roll the crullers while still warm in:

> (Sugar)

II. Prepare the dough as above, but omit the baking powder and milk. Divide the dough in half (each half equals $1^1/_2$ cups), wrap each half in plastic, and refrigerate at least 2 hours, or up to 24 hours.

Line a baking sheet with wax paper and sprinkle with flour. Work with one half of the dough at a time, leaving the other half in the refrigerator. Generously flour the dough and shape into a rectangle with your hands. Place the dough on a floured strip of wax paper, flour the top of the dough, and roll it into a rectangle 12 inches by 6 inches and about $^1/_4$ inch thick. Using a knife or fluted pastry wheel, cut the dough crosswise into twelve 1-inch-wide strips. Twist each strip, then transfer to the prepared baking sheet. Let stand at room temperature, uncovered, for 1 to 3 hours.

To fry, see About Doughnuts, Crullers, and Beignets, 653. Fry, turning periodically, until deep-golden brown, 3 to 4 minutes. Drain on a rack or paper towels. Dust the cooled crullers generously with:

> Confectioners' sugar

NEW ORLEANS BEIGNETS

About thirty $2^1/_2$-inch beignets
New Orleans is famous for these puffy, crusty treats, which go well with the city's renowned chicory-flavored coffee. Please read About Doughnuts, Crullers, and Beignets, 653. Combine in a large bowl:

> $^3/_4$ cup lukewarm water
> 1 teaspoon active dry yeast

Let stand 5 minutes, then whisk until the yeast is dissolved. Whisk in, blending well:

> $^1/_2$ cup evaporated milk
> $^1/_4$ cup sugar
> 1 egg
> $^1/_2$ teaspoon salt

Add, then beat with a large spoon until a smooth batter forms:

> 2 cups all-purpose flour

Beat in:

> 3 tablespoons butter, softened, or vegetable
> shortening

Beat in thoroughly:

> 2 cups all-purpose flour

Cover the bowl tightly with plastic wrap and refrigerate at least 12 hours, or up to 24 hours. Heat to 365°F in a 9- to 10-inch heavy pot or deep heavy skillet:

> 3 inches vegetable oil or vegetable shortening

Meanwhile, form the beignets (adjust the heat as necessary to maintain the fat at 365°F): Punch the dough down, divide in half, and return one half to the refrigerator. On a lightly floured work surface, roll the other half of the dough $\frac{1}{8}$ inch thick and, using a sharp knife, cut into $2\frac{1}{2}$-inch squares. Then immediately roll and cut the refrigerated dough; do not permit the beignets to rise. Starting with the beignets you cut first, fry, 5 or 6 beignets at a time, until golden brown, 1 to 2 minutes on each side. Drain on paper towels. Dust with:

> **Confectioners' sugar**

Serve as soon as possible, preferably while still warm.

BEIGNETS OR FRENCH FRITTERS
About 28 small beignets

Light as air, these beignets are actually small, deep-fried cream puffs. Serve as a pastry with coffee or as a dessert. Please read About Doughnuts, Crullers, and Beignets, 653. Prepare:

> **Dough for Cream Puff Shells, 669, using 4 large eggs**

Add:

> **(1 teaspoon grated lemon or orange zest)**

Heat to 365°F in a 9- to 10-inch heavy pot or deep heavy skillet:

> **3 inches vegetable oil or vegetable shortening**

Drop level tablespoons of the dough into the fat, adding 6 or 8 at a time. As soon as they are cooked enough on one side, they will turn themselves over. When brown on both sides, 4 to 5 minutes, remove from the fat with a slotted spoon and drain on paper towels. Sprinkle with:

> **Confectioners' sugar**

Serve at once. Dessert beignets may be accompanied with, if desired:

> **(Vanilla Sauce, 850, Clear Lemon Sauce, 844, or**
> **Fresh Fruit Sauce, 844–853)**

ROSETTES
About forty-eight 3 x $\frac{1}{2}$-inch rosettes

Rosettes are shaped with a special long-handled mold. They are fried in deep fat in order to ensure that the mold doesn't touch the bottom of the pot when submerged in the oil. As a rule of thumb, the depth of the fat should be about 3 times the height of the mold. Since only one rosette is fried at one time, a narrow pot and a relatively small amount of fat may be used. Fill the pot with vegetable oil or shortening, being sure to leave headroom to allow for bubbling. See about Deep-Fat Frying, 1046. Whisk in a medium bowl until blended:

> **2 large eggs**
> **1 tablespoon sugar**
> **1 teaspoon vanilla extract**
> **$\frac{1}{4}$ teaspoon salt**

Whisk alternately into the egg mixture:

> **1$\frac{1}{4}$ cups sifted all-purpose flour**
> **1 cup milk**

Pour the batter into a shallow bowl just large enough to dip the iron into. Heat to 365°F in a deep 8-inch heavy pot:

> **2$\frac{1}{2}$ to 3 inches vegetable oil or vegetable shortening**

Dip the iron into the hot fat for 15 seconds, then dip it into the batter, only enough to come halfway up the sides of the iron, and immediately immerse the iron in the fat, being sure not to touch the bottom of the pot. Cook until the rosette is golden brown and crisp, about 30 to 45 seconds. Remove the rosette with a fork or skewer and place hollow side down on paper towels to drain. Dip the iron in the fat again and repeat the process.

Dust the rosettes with:

> **Confectioners' sugar**

ABOUT FRITTERED FOODS

The term fritter is confusingly used to cover three quite different types of food. We think of a plain or true fritter as a delicately flavored batter, heavy in egg, that is deep-fat-fried. While they are not called fritters, crullers and doughnuts, 653, are very closely related to true fritters. The success of these batters depends on the care and skill with which they are mixed and fried.

Don't confuse the fritters mentioned above with certain pan- or shallow-fried mixtures like corn or conch fritters, 272. These are flat and thin, much like a pancake. The term fritter may also refer to meat, fish, vegetable, or fruit, whole or cut into bits, dipped in a batter, dried, and deep-fat fried. In this last type, the fritter batter acts as a protective coating. Other examples of fritterlike foods are Deep-Fried Vegetables, 243, and Croquettes, 659.

Cooked or uncooked foods may be fried in a batter, although ➤ real pork and pork products should always be precooked. To prepare frittered vegetables, use almost any leftover or raw vegetable. Seafood and sliced firm tomatoes are also delectable served this way.

To cook fritters, first read about Deep-Fat Frying, 1046. One at a time, ➤ slide the fritters into the heated fat; if using a spoon, dip the spoon into the hot fat before picking up the fritter. The cooking time depends on the size of the fritter. Fritters smaller than a doughnut containing **precooked foods** require about 2 to 3 minutes at 365° to 375°F. Frittered **uncooked food** of larger sizes are better fried at 350° to 360°F, and will need 5 to 7 minutes. The lower temperature and longer cooking time allows for thorough cooking of the interior of the fritter. Once cooked, fritters are best served immediately.

▲ Batters for deep-fried fritters must be adjusted and the temperature of the fat must be lowered when cooking at high altitudes.

FRITTER AND TEMPURA BATTERS

These are much like simple pancake batters, but they ➤ must have the consistency that makes them stick to the food that is to be fried. Dry the food with paper towels. While not always necessary, a light dusting of flour may help the batter adhere. When the surface of the food is dry, the batter will adhere if it passes this easy test: Hold a generous spoonful of the batter above the mixing bowl. Rather than running from the spoon in a broad shining band (called *au ruban* or a ribbon), the batter should start to run for just about a 1 1/2-inch length, then drop in successive long triangular splats. If the batter proves too thin, stir in a bit more flour. If you have the time, refrigerate the batter, covered, for at least 2 hours, or overnight, then beat until very smooth. This resting period allows a slight fermentation, which breaks down any rubberiness in the batter, a process that is further activated if beer or wine is used in the batter. ➤ If you do not have time to let the batter rest, mix it to smoothness with as few strokes as possible, so as not to build up the gluten in the flour. Batters heavy in egg yolk resist fat penetration during frying. Use whole eggs if you wish, but if you separate them and plan to rest the batter, fold the whites beaten ➤ stiff, but not dry, at the last minute before coating the food. Tempura, one of Japan's many notable exports, is made with a batter that is light and simple and is used to coat chunks of fish and vegetables before deep-frying.

FRITTER BATTER FOR VEGETABLES, MEAT, AND FISH

Enough to coat 2 cups food

Try this beer batter with thin slices of zucchini, eggplant, sweet potato, or pumpkin; whole mushrooms; asparagus spears; scallions; scallops; strips of chicken; or shrimp, shelled, with the tail left on, butterflied. Whisk together in a medium bowl until blended:

   1 cup all-purpose flour
   1 teaspoon salt
   1/4 teaspoon black pepper

Whisk together in another medium bowl until blended:

   2 egg yolks
   1 tablespoon butter

Whisk in:

   3/4 cup beer

Pour the wet ingredients over the dry and whisk just until smooth. If time permits, cover the bowl with plastic wrap and let stand up to 2 hours at room temperature, or up to 12 hours in the refrigerator. If refrigerated, bring the batter to room temperature before proceeding. Beat until stiff but not dry, 978:

   (2 egg whites, at room temperature)

Fold the food gently but thoroughly into the batter. Pat the food dry with paper towels. Heat to 375°F in a heavy 10-inch pot:

   3 inches vegetable oil or vegetable shortening

Drop 3 to 4 pieces of food into the batter at a time and turn gently to coat well, then, using tongs, lift out and drop into the hot fat. Fry until golden brown, 3 to 5 minutes, turning once or twice. Drain on a rack or on paper towels.

TEMPURA BATTER

Enough to coat 4 cups food

Whisk together in a medium bowl until blended:

   1 cup all-purpose flour
   1/2 teaspoon salt
   1/8 teaspoon ground black pepper

In a separate medium bowl, whisk together until blended:

   1 egg
   1 cup cold water

Combine them and mix with a fork just until blended. The batter will be lumpy. Use immediately. Fry as for Fritter Batter, above.

FRUIT FRITTERS

Fritter batter for fruit, like any other batter, profits by resting at least 2 hours after mixing. ➤ Please read Fritter and Tempura Batters, 657.

   It is very important that fruit used in these desserts be ripe but not mushy. Keep fruit slices about 1/2 inch thick. Use apples—cored and cut crosswise—pineapple and orange wedges, halves of canned or stewed apricots, or bananas cut in 3 or 4 diagonal pieces. In season, try fuzzy white elderberry blossoms. Dusted with powdered sugar and sprinkled with kirsch, they are dreamy.

   The fruit is often marinated in advance in a little wine, kirsch, rum, or brandy. This marinade may also be used in the batter, but in this case you must marinate and drain prior to mixing the batter and adjust the amount of liquid to that called for in the recipe. Even beer can be used as a liquid. Both beer and wine help to break down the gluten and make a tender batter. After marination of about 2 hours, be sure to ➤ drain the fruit well and dust it with confectioners' sugar just before immersing it in the batter. To cook, please read Fritter Batter for Fruit, below. Either dust fritters with sugar or serve with a sauce. If a variety of fruits are served in this way, they are called a **Fritto Misto.**

FRITTER BATTER FOR FRUIT

About 8 to 10 servings

This batter can be used either to encase about 2 cups diced fruit or to hold the same amount of small fruits and berries that are mixed directly and gently into it. See Fruit Fritters, above. For a savory batter, omit the sugar.

   I. Whisk together in a medium bowl until blended:

   1 cup all-purpose flour
   2 tablespoons sugar
   1 1/2 teaspoons baking powder
   1/4 teaspoon salt

Add and whisk until the batter is smooth:

   2/3 cup milk
   1 large egg yolk
   1 tablespoon butter, melted, or vegetable oil

Beat until stiff peaks form:

   2 large egg whites, at room temperature

Fold into the batter with a large rubber spatula.

II. Prepare, decreasing the salt to $1/4$ teaspoon and omitting the pepper:

Fritter Batter for Vegetables, Meat and Fish, 658

adding:

1 tablespoon sugar

Pat the fruit dry with paper towels. To help the batter adhere, after patting them dry, you may dust very juicy fruits with:

(All-purpose flour)

BLOOMS IN BATTER

Eating flowers is an age-old custom. If you are an organic gardener and know your flowers, all is well. Otherwise, exercise caution. A lily of the valley, though it looks good enough to eat, is poisonous, and the sprays used on roses and other flowers are lethal not only to pests, but also to you. Wash and drain well any blooms or leaves that you use uncooked as garnish. Please read Fritter and Tempura Batters, 657. Pick:

Unsprayed squash, zucchini, pumpkin, nasturtium, elderberry, lilac, or yucca blossoms

Pick small blossoms from the stems. Arrange the blossoms in a single layer on a baking sheet lined with paper towels if not using immediately. Cover with additional paper towels and refrigerate up to 12 hours. Prepare:

Fritter Batter for Fruit II

Heat to 350°F in a 10-inch pot:

3 inches vegetable oil or vegetable shortening

Dip large blossoms into the batter, or mix 2 cups small blossoms into the batter. Fry large blossoms or 3-tablespoon dollops of small blossoms, a few at a time, until pale golden, 3 to 4 minutes, turning as necessary. Drain on a rack or on paper towels. Dust with:

Confectioners' sugar

DAY LILY FRITTERS

4 servings

Steam until wilted, 2 to 4 minutes, then drain:

12 day lily flowers (unsprayed)

Combine:

1 cup all-purpose flour
Salt and black pepper

Dredge the steamed flowers in the flour. Blend in a medium bowl:

2 egg yolks
$1/2$ cup milk
$1/3$ cup crumbled goat cheese

Beat until stiff but not dry:

2 egg whites

Fold the whites into the yolk mixture. Heat to 350°F in a 10-inch pot:

3 inches vegetable oil or vegetable shortening

Dip the flowers into the batter, then drop into the hot fat and fry, a few at a time, until golden brown, 3 to 4 min-

utes, turning as necessary. Drain on a rack or on paper towels. Season to taste with:

Salt

CORN AND HAM FRITTERS

6 servings

Whisk together in a medium bowl:

$1^1/3$ cups all-purpose flour
2 teaspoons baking powder
$3/4$ teaspoon salt
$3/4$ teaspoon paprika

Whisk together in another medium bowl until well blended:

2 egg yolks
$1/2$ cup milk
$1/2$ cup canned cream-style corn

Pour the wet ingredients over the dry and whisk until barely blended, leaving the batter lumpy. Fold in:

$3/4$ cup minced ham
2 tablespoons minced onion
2 tablespoons minced parsley

Beat until stiff but not dry, 978:

2 large egg whites

Fold the whites into the batter. Heat to 365°F in a heavy 10-inch pot:

3 inches vegetable oil or vegetable shortening

Drop the batter by 3-tablespoon dollops, a few at a time, into the hot oil and fry until golden brown, 3 to 4 minutes. Drain on a rack or paper towels.

ABOUT CROQUETTES

When well made, these fried cakes or balls, whether savory or sweet, are crunchy on the outside, creamy on the inside, and deserving of their status as a classic. Because their cooking time is short—3 to 4 minutes—the recipes nearly always call for minced precooked foods. With shellfish such as oysters and mussels, parboiling is called for. ➤ Beef, poultry, and pork and pork products should always be precooked. You will need about $3/4$ cup of a binding agent—mashed potatoes, heavy White Sauce III, 550, Brown Sauce, 554, or condensed canned cream soup—for each 2 cups of solid foods—minced cooked meat or fish and vegetables. ➤ The solids should never be watery, always well drained. Add enough sauce to the solids so they are bound together, much like meat loaf. Check the mixture to make sure it can be formed into a ball or patty, then spread some croquettes about 1 inch thick in a greased pan. Cover with plastic wrap and chill at least 2 hours in the refrigerator or 1 hour in the freezer.

Set out a shallow dish of flour. Cut the chilled mixture into $1^1/2$- to $2^1/2$-inch squares. Flour your hands, then shape and flour the croquettes one at a time, and coat thoroughly with Breading, 961, if directed in the recipe. ➤ Let the coated croquettes dry on a rack for 30 minutes.

➤ Or, if the mixture is a very soft one, let them dry for 10 minutes, then coat again with the breading. ➤ Should the croquettes not be completely enveloped in the outer coating, the mixture may leak into the oil and cause it to boil over.

Please read about Deep-Fat Frying, 1046, or Pan-Frying, 1048. Immerse the croquettes, a few at a time, in oil heated to 365°F, or pan-fry in olive oil or butter in a cast-iron or other heavy skillet. They should be golden in 2 to 4 minutes unless otherwise indicated. Drain on paper towels. You may hold croquettes briefly on a rack in a 350°F oven before serving. To reheat, once they have cooled, use a 400°F oven.

CHEESE CROQUETTES COCKAIGNE

Melt in a medium saucepan over medium heat:

3 tablespoons butter

Gradually stir in:

$1/4$ cup all-purpose flour

Cook 2 minutes, stirring constantly. Whisk in:

$2/3$ cup milk

Cook, whisking, until very thick, 5 minutes. Reduce the heat to low and stir in:

$1^1/4$ cups grated Swiss or Gruyère (about 5 ounces)
Salt and black pepper to taste
(Pinch of ground red pepper)

Remove from the heat and stir in until blended:

2 egg yolks

Spread the mixture in a greased 8 x 8-inch baking dish. Cover and chill, about 1 hour in the freezer, 2 to 3 hours in the refrigerator. Turn the mixture out onto a work surface and cut into 2-inch squares. To coat and fry, see About Croquettes, 659. Coat and dry twice. Serve with:

Tomato Sauce, 562

SALMON CROQUETTES

16 croquettes

Combine in a medium bowl:

1 pound cooked or canned or pouch salmon,
  bones and skin removed ($1^1/2$ cups)
$1^1/2$ cups coarse mashed potatoes, 295
1 egg, beaten
1 tablespoon chopped parsley
1 tablespoon minced chives
1 tablespoon chopped dill
2 scallions, thinly sliced
$1/4$ teaspoon ground red pepper
Salt to taste

Spread in separate shallow bowls:

2 cups fresh bread crumbs
1 cups all-purpose flour

Whisk together in a third shallow bowl:

3 large eggs

Form balls from $1/4$-cup scoops of mixture. Gently roll each ball in the flour until coated, dip into the beaten egg, and then roll in the bread crumbs until coated on all sides. Set aside on a rack or a plate to dry for 10 minutes.

Heat to 375°F in a deep-fryer or deep heavy pot:

4 inches vegetable oil or vegetable shortening

Gently drop 4 croquettes at a time into the hot fat and fry until deep brown on all sides, 2 minutes. Remove with a slotted spoon and drain on paper towels.

CHICKEN OR TURKEY CROQUETTES

4 servings

Prepare, using 4 tablespoons butter and $1/4$ cup flour:

$1/2$ recipe Velouté Sauce, 552, or 1 recipe
  White Sauce I, 550

Melt in a medium saucepan over medium-low heat:

1 tablespoon unsalted butter

Stir in:

1 cup chopped onion

Cook, stirring often, until crisp-tender, 7 to 10 minutes. Add the sauce and cook for 1 minute. Scrape the sauce into a large bowl. Add and blend thoroughly:

$2^1/2$ cups finely chopped, cooked chicken or turkey
$1/4$ cup chopped parsley
$1/2$ teaspoon white or black pepper
$1/2$ teaspoon dried thyme
$1/8$ teaspoon grated or ground nutmeg
Salt to taste

Press a sheet of plastic wrap directly on the surface of the mixture. Refrigerate until very cold and firm, at least 2 hours. Spread evenly on 2 separate plates:

$1/2$ cup fresh bread crumbs
$1/4$ cup all-purpose flour

Whisk together in a wide shallow bowl:

2 large eggs

Drop a generous $1/4$-cup scoop of the croquette mixture into the flour and gently roll until the rough ball is evenly coated, then roll in the beaten egg, transfer to the bread crumbs, and roll until coated on all sides. As you roll it, shape the croquette into an oval, cylinder, or pyramid. Set on a plate. Repeat with the remaining mixture to make 8 croquettes. Heat to 375°F in a deep-fryer or deep heavy pot:

4 inches vegetable oil or vegetable shortening

Gently drop 4 croquettes at a time into the hot fat and fry, turning, until deep brown on all sides, 3 to 4 minutes. Remove with a slotted spoon and drain on paper towels. Arrange on 4 plates or on a platter and serve with:

Lemon wedges or Whole Cranberry Sauce, 221

PIES AND PASTRIES

At home and abroad, Americans boast about their pies. Our kitchens have never been closed to the variations that have wandered in from across the globe and have provided the basis for seemingly endless regional inventions of our own. Our love affair with these desserts, covered or open, filled with fruit, creamy custards, chocolate, nuts and caramel, ice cream, or airy chiffon, is ongoing. We've also cheerfully welcomed sumptuous tarts, galettes, strudels, turnovers, and profiteroles or éclairs. There is nothing that brightens a kitchen so much as the smell of a pie or pastry baking in the oven. Whether you seek the down-home charm of a cherry pie or are searching for the stylish look of a classic napoleon or a tarte Tartin, these recipes are all approachable and the results far superior to any that you can buy.

ABOUT EQUIPMENT

First, let's consider the elements needed for successful pastry dough for pies, tarts, galettes, and puff pastry. ➤ Having proper equipment will go far in creating praiseworthy pies and pastries.

There are two styles of **rolling pins**—the **standard pin** with handles, and the **pastry pin,** or **French-style.** If you have never rolled out dough before, choose a standard pin of a size and weight you find comfortable. Pastry pins are either thick and uniformly cylindrical or slender and tapered at the ends. Once you get the hang of rolling out dough, you may want a tapered pin for the way it allows you to maneuver the dough to any effect, but sometimes beginners find a pastry pin awkward to work with. Wood is the perfect material for all rolling pins. The hollow metal pins filled with ice water sweat, glass pins are beautiful to

behold but fragile, and marble pins are heavy. Silicone-coated pins, with a nonstick surface, are now available.

Mixing the dough can be accomplished by hand or by machine. A **pastry blender**, with 5 or 6 bowed metal blades for cutting butter into flour, is the best tool for the hand method, but a **food processor** also makes good and speedy dough. Other useful tools include a **ruler**, to measure thickness and diameter of dough; a **fluted pastry wheel** or **pastry jagger** (a pizza wheel works as well), for cutting lattices; a **pastry docker,** which pricks pastry dough for even expansion; and a **metal dough scraper.** For weighting unfilled, or blind-baked, crusts, use **metal pie weights** or uncooked dried beans or rice. Some home bakers cover the edge of a pie with a **metal shield** to prevent overbrowning, but the same benefit can be achieved with strips of aluminum foil shaped into a ring.

Pie pans come in two standard diameters, 9 and 10 inches; the former has a capacity of around $4\frac{1}{2}$ cups, the latter, 6 cups. Glass pie pans produce wonderfully brown, crisp crusts, but heavy metal pans, whether matte, shiny, or black finish, are perfectly acceptable. Do not use a deep-dish glass pie pan for an ordinary pie, because it lacks the flared rim needed to form the edge of the crust.

For tarts, use a **tart pan** with or without fluted sides, measuring $9\frac{1}{2}$ to 10 inches across and about 1 inch deep for 4 to $4\frac{1}{2}$ cups filling, and a tart pan 11 inches in diameter and about 1 inch deep for $4\frac{1}{2}$ to 6 cups filling. To unmold a tart for serving, the pan must be a two-piece affair with a removable bottom.

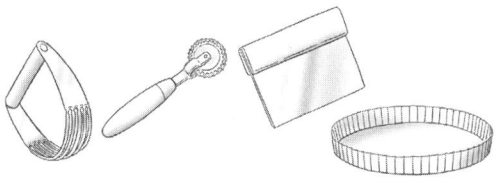

Left to right: Pastry blender, fluted pastry wheel, metal dough scraper, tart pan

Tartlet pans come in a great number of sizes, from $1\frac{1}{2}$-inch miniature pans used to make hors d'oeuvre cases to $4\frac{1}{2}$-inch pans for individual tartlets. They may be of one-piece or two-piece construction; they may have straight or sloping sides; and their sides may be either smooth or fluted. They are made in a variety of shapes. It's best to buy wider, shallow tartlet pans, as crusts tend to lose their shape during baking when formed in deep, narrow pans. Muffin pans, ramekins, and baking cups can be substituted for tartlet pans. You can either line these molds with dough in the usual way, or turn them upside down and line the outside. If you choose the latter, use Cream Cheese Pastry Dough, 666; other doughs have a tendency to melt and split when baked this way.

ABOUT MAKING PASTRY DOUGH

Measure carefully—➤ too much flour toughens pastry; too much liquid makes it soggy; too much shortening makes it greasy and crumbly. For more about measuring ingredients, see 1031. ➤ Handle dough lightly to inhibit excessive development of gluten. The aim is to make a flaky and tender crust.

There are two steps in making pastry dough by hand. **First,** cut the fat into the dry ingredients, usually with a pastry blender, but you can also use your fingers if you have a light touch—don't overwork it or the dough will become dense and greasy. Leave it in firm, separate pieces, some fine and crumblike and the rest the size of peas. **Second,** bind the dough with water. The trick is to add only enough water to make the dough hold together but not so much as to cause excessive gluten to develop, which would produce pastry that is hard or chewy and breadlike. The amount of water required varies and depends on the protein content of the flour, the type of fat used, the degree of blending of fat and flour, and the temperature of the fat and water. As a general rule, the flour and fat mixture should be moistened only to the point where it forms small balls that hold together when pressed with your fingers. If the mixture gathers into a mass on its own, without pressure, it is too wet. However, beginners should probably err on the side of overmoistening, as a very dry dough tends to split or crumble when rolled.

Cutting the fat into the
dry ingredients with a pastry blender

Divide the dough into 2 equal parts, or as directed in the recipe, wrap in plastic, and refrigerate. ➤ Chilling pastry dough up to 12 hours tenderizes it, helps keep it from shrinking during baking, and makes it easier to handle. If the dough has been chilled for longer than 30 minutes, let it stand until it feels firm yet pliable, like modeling clay, when pressed. If it is too cold, the dough will crack around the edges when rolled.

▲ In making pies at high altitudes, where evaporation is greater, you may find that you achieve better results with pastry if you add a trifle more liquid. When baking double-crust apple pies, note that above 7,000 feet, it is nearly impossible to bake through a tall pile of packed apple slices (or other hard fruit) before the crust begins to burn. Since water boils at a lower temperature at higher elevations, it takes a very long time to get enough heat into the fruit to soften it. To remedy this, use soft eating apples instead of green cooking apples, or precook a por-

tion of the apples with sugar and spices on top of the stove, then layer them with thin-sliced raw apples to build up a mound before covering with pastry.

MIXING PASTRY DOUGH USING A FOOD PROCESSOR

Combine the dry ingredients in the food processor and process for 10 seconds. Scatter the butter, shortening, and/or lard (or cream cheese) over the dry ingredients. Pulse in 1- to 2-second bursts until most of the fat is the size of peas. With the machine turned off, drizzle ice water (or cream for cream cheese pastry) evenly over the top. Pulse until no dry patches remain and the dough just begins to clump into small balls. Try to press the dough together with your fingers; if it will not cohere, sprinkle on a bit more ice water (or cream), pulse, and try again. Do not allow the dough to gather into a single mass during processing. Wrap and refrigerate; see About Making Pastry Dough, above.

MIXING PASTRY DOUGH USING AN ELECTRIC MIXER

Basic Pie or Pastry Dough, 665, Deluxe Butter Pie or Pastry Dough, 665, and its variations, as well as Cream Cheese Pastry Dough, 666, can be made with an electric mixer.

Combine the dry ingredients and butter, shortening, lard, and/or cream cheese in a large bowl. Scraping the bowl frequently, beat at medium speed until the mixture is the consistency of coarse crumbs. Add the water and mix until the dough begins to cling to the beaters. Should the dough be too crumbly, incorporate 1 teaspoon to 1 tablespoon water with your hands so that the dough comes together.

ROLLING PASTRY DOUGH

You can roll dough on a pastry cloth, pastry board, marble slab (which retains cold and helps keep the dough from softening) or on a clean smooth countertop. Do not roll dough next to the oven or in a hot corner of the kitchen, or the fat will melt. If the dough becomes too soft during rolling, slide a rimless cookie sheet beneath it, and refrigerate until it firms up.

Lightly flour the work surface. Place the dough in the center of the floured surface and lightly flour it as well. Exerting even pressure on the pin, ➤ roll the dough from the

Rolling pastry dough

center out in all directions, stopping just short of the edge. In order to keep the dough in a circular shape, each stroke should be a quarter-turn or so from the one that preceded it. You can do this by rotating the dough itself or by moving the pin. Be sure to check the dough for sticking by periodically sliding your hand beneath it; scatter a little more flour on the work surface as necessary. Seal cracks and splits by pushing the dough together with your fingers. Patch any holes, tears, or thin spots with dough scraps, dabbing them on one side with cold water and then firmly pressing them, moistened side down, into place. Cover any gaps in the overhang in the same manner.

SHAPING AND TRIMMING DOUGH

Roll the dough into a circle roughly 3 to 4 inches larger than your pan. This will allow plenty of dough with which to construct a rim. To calculate the size by eye, place the pan (right side up for a tart pan, inverted for a pie pan) in the center of the dough. Transfer the rolled dough to the pan by rolling it loosely around the pin, centering the pin over the pan, and then unrolling the dough. If the dough

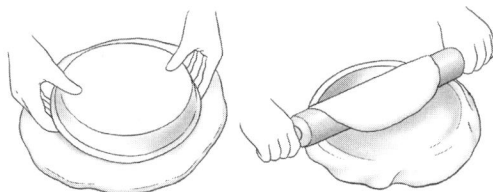

Calculating the size of the pie dough and transferring it to the dish with the rolling pin

is off center, slide your hands under the dough and carefully slide it into position. Ease the dough into the pan loosely and then, using your fingertips or a small scrap of dough, press it firmly into the pan. Trim the edges of the dough with scissors or a small paring knife, leaving an overhang of ¾ inch. Trimmings can be given to kids for "play dough" or baked, sprinkled with sugar and cinnamon. To make top crusts, see below.

ABOUT CRUSTS FOR FILLED PIES

For crusts that are to be baked with fillings, use a pie pan with a wide, preferably channeled, rim to catch any juices.

For a one-crust pie, make a fluted or crimped edge (see below). This edge is important, as it will help to hold the juices in the pie. Do not prick the bottom of the crust. If the filling for the pie is the juicy kind, first brush the bottom crust lightly with the white of an egg, melted butter, or a light sprinkling of flour. Any of these will keep the crust from becoming soggy. Putting a precooked filling in when it is very hot helps too. Tuck the overhanging dough underneath itself to make a doubled rim, then rest the rim on the edge of the pie pan. This edge helps hold the juices in the pie.

To crimp the rim, press it all around with the tines of a fork or the back of a knife. **For a fluted rim,** press your thumb and index finger, held about 1 inch apart, against the outside of the rim, then press a dent in the dough from the inside with the index finger of your other hand. **For a coiled or braided design,** roll dough trimmings into long thin ropes, then twist or braid the ropes to your choosing. Flatten the rim of the piecrust against the edge of the pan, brush with cold water, and press the fancy rope into place.

For a tart, fold the overhanging dough back onto itself, doubling the thickness of the upper part of the crust, and press firmly. Squeeze any noticeably thicker parts of the sides with your fingers to even them, then trim excess dough flush with the top using scissors or a paring knife.

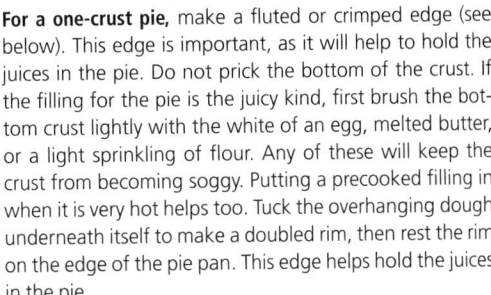

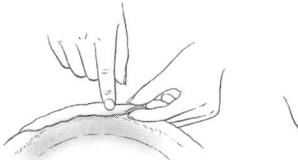

Folding the overhanging dough back onto itself and trimming the excess

For double-crust pies, a flaky pastry dough, such as Basic Pie or Pastry Dough, 665, made with shortening or a combination of butter and shortening, or Deluxe Butter

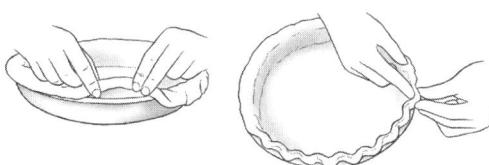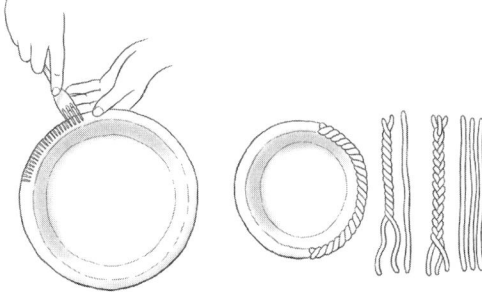

Tucking the overhanging dough underneath itself to make a double layer, forming a fluted rim, crimping the rim, and making coiled rims by twisting or braiding dough ropes and pressing them along the rim of the pan

Pie or Pastry Dough, 665, is best. The basic dough made with lard is particularly good with apple pies and works as well with other fruit pies. Cream Cheese Pastry Dough, 666, is also a good all-purpose dough, though you may find it a bit too tangy with fillings such as tart cherries and rhubarb. If you like, use Cornmeal Pie or Pastry Dough, 665, for blueberry or blackberry pies, or Nutted Pie or Pastry Dough, 665, with stone fruits, such as peaches or cherries. Be aware, however, that these doughs tend to leak during baking. Sweet Pie or Pastry Dough, 665, is not good for covered fruit pies, as it is likely to char during the long baking.

The following directions are for a 9-inch pie. Adjust measurements as necessary for a 10-inch pie. Roll out the bottom crust, fit it into the pan, and trim the overhanging dough to $3/4$ inch all around; see Shaping and Trimming Dough, above. **To make a solid top crust,** cut the rolled dough 1 inch larger than the pan.

Spoon the filling into the bottom crust. Dot the top of the filling with butter if your recipe calls for it. Brush the overhanging edge of the bottom crust with cold water. Place the top crust over the pie. Firmly pinch the edges of both crusts together with your fingers to seal. Trim the doubled edge to an even overhang of $3/4$ inch, then tuck the overhang underneath itself so that the folded edge is flush with the rim of the pie pan. Crimp or flute the edge as for a single-crust pie, above; a high fluted rim will help to contain any juices that bubble through the top crust. To allow the steam to escape during baking, prick it with a fork in several places; or using a sharp paring knife, make three or four 2-inch vents or slashes in the top crust. If you wish, cut scraps of dough into decorative shapes, brush lightly with cold water, and press onto the top crust.

There are many attractive ways to make a lattice. You can cut plain $1/2$-inch-wide strips with a knife or pastry wheel, or you can roll pieces of dough into ropes, if desired, then twist and weave or arrange the plain strips or ropes in a crisscross as described. **To make a plain lattice top** for a 9-inch pie, roll the dough for the top crust into a $13^1/2$-inch round. Cut the dough into 18 strips. Spoon the filling into the bottom crust and brush the edge of the bottom crust with cold water. Place 9 of the dough strips $1/2$ inch apart on top of the pie, then arrange the remaining dough strips over these, either on a diagonal or in a perpendicular crisscross pattern. Trim the lattice strips, leaving at least a $1/4$-inch overhang at each end. Press the strips against the bottom crust. Fold the edge of the bottom crust up, covering the ends of the lattice strips, then crimp or flute the edge, as illustrated below.

To make a woven lattice top for a 9-inch pie, roll the dough for the top crust into a $13^1/2$-inch round. Cut the dough into 18 strips. Spoon the filling into the bottom crust and brush the edge of the bottom crust with cold water. Place 9 of the dough strips $1/2$ inch apart on top of the pie. Fold every other strip halfway back over itself, making the ends meet, then place 1 strip crosswise just

beyond the folded edges, in the center of the pie. Return the folded strips to their original flat position over the perpendicular strip. Fold back the strips that you left flat the first time and place a second strip crosswise just beyond the folded edges. Unfold these strips over the second perpendicular strip. Repeat until you have woven 5 crosswise strips into the lattice, completing one half. Now weave the remaining 4 crosswise strips into the lattice starting on the other side of the center crosswise strip, to complete the other half. Trim the lattice strips, leaving at least a $1/4$-inch overhang at each end. Press the strips against the bottom crust. Fold the edge of the bottom crust up, covering the ends of the lattice strips, then crimp or flute the edge, as illustrated on 663. We like to sprinkle a tablespoon of sugar over the lattice before baking.

It's possible that your raw woven lattice will soften from the juices of the pie filling as you assemble it. You may instead want to weave it, as above, on a cookie sheet, then lay it over the pie just before baking. Chilling the woven lattice for a short period will make the transfer easier.

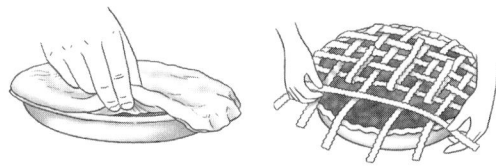

Folding over the excess dough on a double-crust pie and forming a woven lattice

ABOUT BAKING CRUSTS BEFORE FILLING

If the pie shell is to be baked without filling, or as the English say "blind," ➤ prick or "dock" the dough generously with a fork after you have placed it in the pie pan, line with foil, then weight it with dry beans or metal pie weights. This keeps it from buckling and baking unevenly. You can also keep the dough for a pie in place by nesting a pie pan of identical size in the crust. If you use this method, choose a simple crimped rim; the second pan will flatten a fluted or braided rim. This also protects the crust from overbrowning, as does covering the edge of the dough with a strip of aluminum foil. Remove the beans or pebbles a few minutes before the baking period is over. To cut a round for a prebaked top crust, prick it and bake it on a baking sheet.

When making small crusts for individual pies, use an inverted muffin tin or, for deeper shells, inverted custard cups. Cut the rounds of dough $4^1/2$ or $5^1/2$ inches in diameter and fit them over the cups; or, with the help of foil as a support, create your own fancy shape. ➤ Prick the shells before baking. When you fill baked shells, spoon the filling in carefully.

To glaze piecrust, giving it added flavor or color, see 799. Keep in mind that glaze also tends to toughen crusts.

Baking time will vary according to the material from which the pan is made. ➤ If it is ovenproof glass or enamelware, cut the baking time indicated by one-fifth to one-quarter. When pie pans are used, those that are perforated, have lost their shininess, or have a dark color are helpful for producing a well-browned crust.

Unfilled shells, whether for individual or big pies, are baked in a preheated 425°F oven, unless otherwise noted, 15 minutes. Remove foil and weights and bake 5 to 10 minutes longer until golden. Cool before filling.

SUGGESTED ADDITIONS TO CRUSTS
Vary a basic pie or pastry dough for a double crust by adding to the dry ingredients, before mixing, one of the following to enhance your filling:

> **1 to 3 teaspoons poppy or caraway seeds**
> **1 to 3 tablespoons sesame seeds, toasted, 1001**
> **$^1\!/_4$ to $^1\!/_2$ teaspoon ground cinnamon and/or grated or ground nutmeg**
> **2 tablespoons unsweetened cocoa powder**
> **2 tablespoons confectioners' sugar or**
> > **1 tablespoon sugar**

BASIC PIE OR PASTRY DOUGH
One 9- or 10-inch double crust
For a 9-inch single-crust pie, use half the recipe.
Sift together:

> **2$^1\!/_2$ cups all-purpose flour**
> **1$^1\!/_4$ teaspoons salt**

Add:

> **$^3\!/_4$ cup chilled lard or vegetable shortening**
> **3 tablespoons cold unsalted butter**

Cut half of the shortening into the flour mixture with a pastry blender or work it in lightly with the tips of your fingers until it has the consistency of cornmeal. Cut the remaining half into the dough until it is pea-sized. Sprinkle the dough with:

> **6 tablespoons ice water**

Blend the water gently into the dough until it just holds together; you may lift the ingredients with a fork, allowing the moisture to spread. If necessary to hold the ingredients together, add:

> **1 teaspoon to 1 tablespoon ice water**

Divide the dough in half, shape each into a disk, and wrap in plastic wrap. To fill and bake, see individual recipes. For a baked shell, see About Baking Crusts Before Filling, above.

PIE DOUGH COCKAIGNE
One 9- or 10-inch double crust
This dough refrigerates well after baking and reheats to perfection.
Sift together:

> **2$^1\!/_2$ cups all-purpose flour**
> **2 teaspoons sugar**
> **1 teaspoon salt**

Add:

> **6 tablespoons ($^3\!/_4$ stick) cold unsalted butter**
> **$^1\!/_4$ cup chilled vegetable shortening**

Cut half the shortening into the flour mixture until it has the consistency of cornmeal. Cut in the remaining half until it is pea-sized. Sprinkle the dough with:

> **6 tablespoons ice water**

Blend the water gently into the dough until it just holds together; you may lift the ingredients with a fork, allowing the moisture to spread. If necessary to hold the ingredients together, add:

> **1 teaspoon to 1 tablespoon ice water**

Divide the dough in half, shape each into a disk, and wrap in plastic wrap. To fill and bake, see individual recipes. For a baked shell, see About Baking Crusts Before Filling, 664.

DELUXE BUTTER PIE OR PASTRY DOUGH (PÂTE BRISÉE)
One 9- or 10-inch double crust
Prepare **Basic Pie or Pastry Dough, above,** substituting **1 cup (2 sticks) cold unsalted butter** for the vegetable shortening or lard and **$^1\!/_4$ cup chilled vegetable shortening** for the butter.

CORNMEAL PIE OR PASTRY DOUGH
Cornmeal adds both crunch and lightness to crusts. Use this for fresh fruit tarts made with berries, peaches, or nectarines.
Prepare **Deluxe Butter Pie or Pastry Dough, above.** Add **$^1\!/_3$ cup confectioners' sugar** to the dry ingredients and substitute **$^3\!/_4$ cup yellow cornmeal** for **$^3\!/_4$ cup of the flour.**

NUTTED PIE OR PASTRY DOUGH
Prepare **Deluxe Butter Pie or Pastry Dough, above.** Add **$^1\!/_2$ cup finely chopped or coarsely ground walnuts or pecans** and **$^1\!/_3$ cup confectioners' sugar** to the dry ingredients. Add **(1 teaspoon grated lemon zest)** with the nuts.

SWEET PIE OR PASTRY DOUGH (PÂTE SUCRÉE)
This pastry is delicious but burns easily. Use it only for pies and tarts that require little or no baking after being filled, such as Lemon Meringue Pie, 687, and fresh fruit tarts.
Prepare **Deluxe Butter Pie or Pastry Dough, above.** Add **$^3\!/_4$ cup confectioners' sugar** to the dry ingredients.

WHOLE WHEAT PIE OR PASTRY DOUGH
Prepare **Deluxe Butter Pie or Pastry Dough, above.** Add to the dry ingredients **$^1\!/_3$ cup confectioners' sugar** and substitute **1 cup of whole wheat pastry flour** for 1 cup of the all-purpose flour. For extra tenderness, beat **1 large egg yolk** with **$^1\!/_3$ cup ice water** and add it to the dough in place of the 6 tablespoons water.

CREAM CHEESE PASTRY DOUGH

One 9-inch single piecrust or eight 3-inch tart shells

Delicious as tart shells, for turnovers, 695, or as thin wafers served with soup or salad.

Whisk together:

1 cup all-purpose flour
$1/4$ teaspoon salt

Cut until well blended:

$1/2$ cup (1 stick) cold unsalted butter
$4 1/2$ ounces cream cheese

Shape the dough into a disk, wrap in plastic wrap, and refrigerate for at least 12 hours.

To use for tart shells, divide the dough into 8 pieces and shape over inverted muffin tins. Bake at 450°F for about 12 minutes.

To use for wafers, roll and cut the dough into rounds or put it directly into a cookie press without rolling. Before baking, dot with **sesame or poppy seeds.** Bake at 400°F, for 8 to 10 minutes.

RICH EGG TART DOUGH

One $9 1/2$- or 10-inch tart shell or six 3-inch tart shells

There are many versions of this pastry, varying in richness and sweetness. This one makes a very tender dough for fresh fruit fillings. If desired, glaze the fruit with melted and cooled Currant or Apricot Glaze, 800.

Whisk together in a bowl:

1 cup all-purpose flour
2 tablespoons sugar
$1/2$ teaspoon salt

Cut into it, using a pastry blender or the tips of your fingers:

6 tablespoons ($3/4$ stick) unsalted butter, softened

Make a well in the center and add:

1 large egg yolk, lightly beaten
1 tablespoon fresh lemon juice or water
$1/2$ teaspoon vanilla

Stir with your fingers until the dough comes together and no longer adheres to your hands. Shape into a disk, wrap in plastic, and refrigerate for at least 30 minutes. Roll to $1/8$-inch thickness as for pie dough; see 662. Line the tart pans and blind bake, 664, for 7 to 10 minutes. Unmold the pastry shells and cool on a rack. To fill, see individual recipes.

MERINGUE PIE SHELL

One 9-inch or 10-inch piecrust

Pure white, sweet, crisp meringue makes an excellent crust for ice cream and frozen yogurt pies or for tarts made with fresh fruit and whipped cream. Meringue shells can be made in small pans of any size or formed on a baking sheet using a spoon or a pastry bag. Note the long baking—and long storing—time. To cut the sweetness, flavor the meringue with coffee or cocoa. See Soft Meringue Toppings, 797.

Position a rack in the lower third of the oven. Preheat the oven to 225°F. Very generously grease both the inside and the rim of a 9-inch pie pan, preferably glass, with vegetable shortening. Dust the pan with flour, tilt in all directions to coat, and then tap out the excess.

Prepare:

Soft Meringue Topping I or II, 798

Spread the meringue over the bottom and up the sides of the prepared pie pan with the back of a spoon. Bake until the interior of the meringue seems just slightly sticky when probed with the point of a paring knife, $1 1/2$ to 2 hours. Turn off the oven and let the crust cool completely in the oven.

Wrap the crust airtight and store at room temperature for up to a month. If it becomes soft during storage, bake (unwrapped) in a 200°F oven for 1 hour to recrisp.

ABOUT PAT-IN-THE-PAN CRUSTS

This dough is soft and supple, making it very easy to handle and shape. Crumbly and pleasantly crunchy rather than flaky, pat-in-the-pan crusts are always baked before they are filled. Therefore, they cannot be used to make covered fruit pies, though shortbread doughs can be used to good effect in making flat free-form dessert tarts such as crostatas and galettes, 697.

To shape the crust for a pie or tart, pat the dough evenly over the bottom and up the sides of a 9-inch pie pan or a $9 1/2$- or 10-inch two-piece tart pan, or roll it with a rolling pin between sheets of wax paper and flip it into the pan. If making a pie, crimp or flute the rim, 663. To bake, thoroughly prick the sides and bottom of the crust with a fork. Bake in a preheated 425°F oven (400°F for shortbread) until the crust is golden brown, 18 to 22 minutes, pricking the bottom once or twice if it bubbles. If you will be filling the crust with an uncooked mixture that requires further baking, whisk together 1 large egg yolk and a pinch of salt, and brush the warm crust with this glaze, then return to the oven and bake until the glaze sets, 1 to 2 minutes.

This dough will also make eight $3 1/2$-inch tartlet crusts. For tartlets, divide the dough into 8 pieces and press it into molds or shape over inverted muffin tins. If baking "blind," without a filling, bake at 450°F until firm and golden brown, 12 to 15 minutes, pricking the crusts once or twice if they bubble.

PAT-IN-THE-PAN BUTTER DOUGH

One 9-inch single piecrust or $9 1/2$- or 10-inch tart shell or eight $3 1/2$-inch tartlet shells

Whisk together in a bowl or process in a food processor for 10 seconds:

$1 1/2$ cups all-purpose flour
$1/2$ teaspoon salt

Add:

$1/2$ cup (1 stick) unsalted butter, cut into 8 pieces, softened

Mash with the back of a fork or process until the mixture resembles coarse crumbs.

Drizzle over the top:

2 to 3 tablespoons heavy cream

Stir or process until the crumbs look damp and hold together when pinched. To shape and bake, see About Pat-in-the-Pan Crusts, above.

PAT-IN-THE-PAN OIL DOUGH

One 9-inch single piecrust or 9 1/2- or 10-inch tart shell or eight 3 1/2-inch tartlet shells

The oil gives this variation on the above recipe a softer texture, perfect for cream pies, Key Lime Pie, 688, or Lemon Meringue Pie, 687. The shell must be baked before filling.

Whisk together in a medium bowl:

1 1/2 cups all-purpose flour

1 1/2 teaspoons salt

Whisk together in a cup until creamy:

1/2 cup vegetable oil

2 tablespoons cold milk or ice water

Pour the mixture over the flour all at once and stir lightly with a fork until blended. To shape and bake, see About Pat-in-the-Pan Crusts, 666.

PAT-IN-THE-PAN SHORTBREAD DOUGH

One 9-inch single piecrust or 9 1/2- or 10-inch tart shell or eight 3 -inch tartlet shells

When baked, this rich, sweet dough resembles a shortbread cookie. Use it for a cream pie, a lemon tart, a fresh fruit tart with pastry cream, or any other pie or tart with a creamy or buttery filling.

Whisk together in a bowl or process in a food processor for 10 seconds:

1 1/4 cups all-purpose flour

1/3 cup sugar

(1 teaspoon grated lemon zest)

1/4 teaspoon salt

Add:

1/2 cup (1 stick) unsalted butter, cut into

8 pieces, softened if working by hand

Mash with the back of a fork or process until the mixture resembles coarse crumbs. Add:

1 large egg yolk

Mix with a spatula or process just until the dough comes together in a ball. If the dough is too soft and sticky to work with, wrap it and refrigerate for at least 30 minutes (up to 2 days). Grease or butter the bottom of a 9-inch pie pan or 9 1/2- or 10-inch two-piece tart pan or eight 3 1/2-inch tartlet pans. Dust the pans with flour, and tap out the excess. Pat the dough evenly over the bottom and up the sides of the prepared pan. Thoroughly prick the bottom and sides with a fork. Refrigerate for 30 minutes. Preheat the oven to 400°F. Bake until deep golden brown, 18 to 22 minutes for crust, 19 minutes for tartlets. To shape and bake, see About Pat-in-the-Pan Crusts, 666.

PAT-IN-THE-PAN CHEDDAR DOUGH

One 9-inch single piecrust

A classic with apples. Try it with tart fruit fillings, or for savory pastries such as quiche.

Toss together in a bowl:

3/4 cup lightly packed extra-sharp Cheddar, grated

2/3 cup all-purpose flour

1/2 teaspoon salt

6 tablespoons (3/4 stick) cold unsalted butter, cut into

1/4-inch pieces

Cut in the butter and cheese with a pastry blender to the consistency of coarse crumbs, then press together with your fingers and knead in the bowl until a cohesive dough forms. Flatten the dough into a disk, wrap in plastic, and refrigerate until firm but malleable, about 30 minutes. To shape and bake, see About Pat-in-the-Pan Crusts, 666.

ABOUT CRUMB AND NUT CRUSTS

These crusts, mixed and patted into the pan, are a pie-making shortcut. Graham cracker crumbs are the traditional base, but chocolate and vanilla wafers, gingersnaps, and zwieback also make wonderful crumbs for crusts, as do nuts. If you are starting with whole crackers or cookies rather than buying crumbs, grind them in a food processor or put them in a sturdy plastic bag and pulverize them with a rolling pin until fine.

An easy way to shape them is to place the crumb mixture in a pie pan, distributing the crumbs fairly evenly, then press another pie pan of the same diameter firmly into the dough. When the top pan is removed, presto!—a crust of even thickness underneath. Trim any excess that is forced over the top edge, or just pat back into the pan.

Crumb crusts do not need to be baked before filling, ➤ but if used unbaked, the crust must first be frozen for 20 minutes, or the filling will soften it. If baked before filling, they are more crunchy and flavorful; a 350°F oven for 10 to 12 minutes will do the trick. ➤ Cool the baked shell before filling. Nut crusts without any crumbs should not be baked before filling.

Fill the chilled or baked shell with chiffon fillings, Bavarian creams, or mousses, 816, topped with sweetened whipped cream, or with custard or fruit fillings, which may be covered with meringue; see 797.

CRUMB CRUST

One 9- or 10-inch single piecrust and topping

The flavor of the filling should determine which cracker or cookie to crumble.

Put in a bowl, reserving a tablespoon or two for topping, if desired:

1 1/2 cups fine graham cracker, vanilla or chocolate wafer, or gingersnap crumbs

Add and stir until well blended:

1/4 to 1/2 cup sugar, depending on sweetness of the cookies

6 tablespoons (³/₄ stick) unsalted butter, melted and cooled

(1 teaspoon ground cinnamon)

To shape the shell and chill or bake, see About Crumb and Nut Crusts, above. When the pie is filled, scatter reserved crumbs as a topping.

NUT CRUST

One 9- or 10-inch single piecrust

To make this crust in a food processor, combine the nut halves or pieces, butter, sugar, and salt in the processor and pulse until the nuts are finely chopped.

Chop to the consistency of coarse crumbs:

2 cups walnuts or pecans

Combine in a bowl with:

¹/₄ cup (¹/₂ stick) unsalted butter, softened

3 tablespoons sugar

¹/₄ teaspoon salt

Mix with a fork until uniformly moistened. To shape the shell and bake, see About Crumb and Nut Crusts, 667.

ABOUT LAYERED DOUGHS

To make any kind of layered dough—such as Food Processor Puff Pastry, 669, Croissant Dough, 616, or Danish Pastry Dough, 624—a large block of butter is wrapped in the dough like a package, then rolled out and folded, rerolled, and refolded: The idea is to create thin, even layers of butter between distinct layers of dough, rather than integrating dough and butter. For this to work, ➤ the butter and the dough must be similar in temperature and consistency so that they move together at an even pace under the pressure of the rolling pin. If the butter is too cold and hard, the pressure of the rolling pin, instead of extending the butter, may push it through the dough layer, resulting in nonuniform layers. Fortunately, if this happens, it is possible to see and feel the butter cracking in the dough as it is rolled out, enabling you to stop and let the dough rest (and the butter soften a bit) until it can be rolled out smoothly. Butter that is too soft is even worse, as the dough and butter merge under pressure from the rolling pin instead of maintaining their separate identities. If the dough seems squishy and/or the butter oozes from it as you roll, stop and refrigerate it until firm but still pliable. ➤ At no point allow the dough to absorb excess moisture or to dry out.

To roll the dough, flour the work surface, the dough and the rolling pin lightly. Always position the dough with a short edge in front of you. Roll the dough with even pressure to maintain an even thickness: Keeping the pin parallel to the work surface, roll from the center of the dough away from you and then from the center of the dough back toward you, lifting the pin after each roll. (Rolling back and forth without lifting the pin overdevelops the gluten in the dough, making it tough and elastic.) Never roll the pin over the edges of the dough. Roll the dough the long way to the desired length and then adjust the width if necessary. As you roll, keep the corners square, the sides of the dough as straight as possible, and the thickness even. Straighten the sides of the dough occasionally with your hands, as though straightening a stack of papers, or press the sides with a pastry scraper or the rolling pin. If a small area of butter becomes uncovered as you roll the dough, gently pat a little flour over the butter spot, and brush off any excess flour. Brush excess flour from the dough with a dry pastry brush before folding.

The specific folding technique and the number of "turns" (rotating the pastry so that every time you fold it, you are folding a new side) required varies according to the type of pastry you are making. Classic puff pastry is given 3 sets of 2 turns each for a total of 6 turns, and the folding is always in thirds like a business letter; this is called a single fold. Food Processor Puff Pastry, 669, is given 4 turns, but 3 of these employ double folds. Croissant Dough, 616, is given 4 turns with single folds, and Danish Pastry Dough, 624, 5 turns with single folds.

As in all wheat flour doughs, the gluten in the dough is created as the dough is handled or rolled. To avoid excess gluten development, which would make the dough tough, the dough should be rotated after every turn so that the gluten strands are stretched in a different direction with each successive turn. The dough is wrapped in plastic wrap, refrigerated, and allowed to rest for 30 to 60 minutes (depending on which pastry you are making) between turns. The rest period relaxes the gluten strands and lets them adjust to their new length; chilling firms the butter, which helps keep the layers of dough and butter distinct. (Do not allow the butter to turn hard or brittle; if this occurs, let the dough sit on the counter for 10 minutes or so until the butter reaches a pliable state.) Then the finished dough is chilled again after it has been rolled into a sheet, before it is cut into shapes—and often still again just before baking. (See specific instructions in each recipe.) It is surprisingly easy to lose track of how many turns you have given the dough as it rests. To keep count of the turns, make a shallow fingertip imprint in the dough—one for each turn—before refrigerating the dough for each rest period.

ABOUT PUFF PASTRY

Puff pastry is the flakiest pastry imaginable, which is not surprising when you consider that it is made up of hundreds of layers and contains more butter than flour. The tools and equipment required are the same as those needed for piecrusts, 661; a cool marble work surface is ideal, but not essential. To roll puff pastry, see About Layered Doughs, above, and the specific recipes for instructions.

Puff pastry can be cut into a myriad of shapes or sizes and filled to create countless desserts and savory foods, from appetizers to main courses to desserts. Save all puff pastry scraps, trimmings, and unused dough and freeze according to the instructions below. The accumulated scraps can be rolled together once thawed, then folded as if you were giving the dough a single turn before rolling out and using. Rolled scraps of puff pastry are best used for napoleons, twists, mini tarts, palm leaves, or any other pastry for which full height is not crucial.

To cut and dock the dough: After rolling out the dough to the desired thickness, trim the edges and cut into desired shapes. Always cut puff pastry with a sharp knife, pressing straight down through the dough. Dragging the knife prevents the edges of the pastry from rising evenly or to full capacity.

"Docking" (or pricking) is the term for piercing a pastry all over with the tines of a fork, or a spiky tool called a pastry docker, to inhibit the rise but maintain flakiness. Napoleon layers are docked to keep them very thin but still flaky; the centers of patty shells (bouchées) are docked so the sides will rise but the interiors will remain thin. After cutting, except for napoleons, turn the pieces of pastry upside down before docking.

Puff pastry dough can be refrigerated for up to 2 days or frozen for up to 6 months. Wrap in plastic and then aluminum foil, then slip the packets into a sealable plastic bag, pressing out the air before sealing. Before using, thaw frozen pastry, still wrapped, overnight in the refrigerator.

Puff pastry can also be frozen after it is rolled out, either in sheets or cut into shapes. After rolling, chill on a baking sheet until firm; cut into shapes if desired or leave sheets whole, and wrap. Stack cut pieces with wax paper between each layer for wrapping and freezing. For the best rise, bake frozen (unfilled) cut pieces without thawing. If freezing sheets, thaw them overnight in the refrigerator before cutting. Unbaked filled puff pastry shapes such as turnovers can be covered and refrigerated for up to 8 hours before baking.

FOOD PROCESSOR PUFF PASTRY

2 ¾ pounds

In this modernized puff pastry recipe, both the dough and the butter block are mixed in the food processor. It's almost as good as the classic version and takes a fraction of the time.

Pulse to combine in a food processor:
>   **2¹⁄₃ cups all-purpose flour**
>   **1¹⁄₄ teaspoons salt**

Scatter over the flour:
>   **5 tablespoons cold unsalted butter, cut into ¹⁄₂-inch cubes**

Pulse until the mixture resembles coarse crumbs. Drizzle over:
>   **³⁄₄ cup ice water**

Pulse just until the dough begins to come together, 10 to 15 seconds. Scrape the dough onto a sheet of plastic wrap and form it into a 5-inch square. Wrap the dough and refrigerate for 1 hour.

Cut into ¹⁄₂-inch slices and freeze for 2 minutes:
>   **1³⁄₄ cups (3¹⁄₂ sticks) unsalted butter**

Place in the food processor:
>   **1 cup all-purpose flour**

Distribute the butter slices over the flour and pulse just until the mixture looks like fine gravel. Scrape the mixture down from the processor sides and process just until smooth. Scrape onto a sheet of plastic wrap, cover, and shape into a 6-inch square. Wrap and refrigerate while you roll out the dough.

Place the dough square on a lightly floured surface and roll into a 13 x 8-inch rectangle, with an 8-inch side facing you. Brush off the excess flour. Remove the butter package from the refrigerator, unwrap it, and center it on one half of the dough. Fold the dough over the butter, completely covering it. Press the dough together on the 3 open sides. Turn the dough so that the folded edge is on the left, with one of the sealed sides (where the dough was pressed together) on the right, to change the direction of the pastry for the next roll.

Roll the dough package into a 17 x 7¹⁄₂-inch rectangle, keeping a short side facing you. Slide a metal dough scraper or spatula under the bottom third of the dough and fold it up over the center of the dough. Slide the spatula under the top third of the dough and fold it down on top of the first third, as though you were folding a business letter. This rolling and folding is called a single turn. Rotate the dough so that the folded edge is on the left, and roll the dough once more into a 17 x 7¹⁄₂-inch rectangle. This time fold the bottom end up and the top end down to meet in the center (do not overlap), then fold the dough in half, to make 4 layers of dough. This double fold is the second turn. Mark the dough with 2 finger imprints to remind yourself that you have given the dough 2 turns. Wrap the dough and refrigerate for 45 minutes.

With the folded edge on the left, roll the dough out again to 17 x 7¹⁄₂ inches. Make another double fold, for the third turn. Mark with 3 imprints, wrap the dough, and refrigerate for 45 minutes.

Folding puff pastry

Roll the dough out and make another double fold for the fourth turn. Mark the dough with 4 imprints, wrap, and refrigerate for at least 1 hour before using.

ELEPHANT EARS

About forty-eight 3-inch cookies or twenty-four 5 1/2-inch cookies
Have ready:
   1 cup sugar
Lightly sugar a work surface, and roll out into a 12 x 5 1/2-inch rectangle:
   **8 ounces (one 4 1/2 x 1 1/2-inch piece) Food Processor
      Puff Pastry, 669**
Sprinkle about 1/4 cup of the sugar over the dough and roll over it lightly with the rolling pin. With a short end closest to you, fold the dough into thirds, like a business letter. Turn the dough so the folded edge is on the left and roll out into a 13 x 7-inch rectangle, with one short end facing you. Sprinkle about 2 tablespoons sugar over the dough and roll over it lightly with the rolling pin. Fold each long side of the dough over toward the center, leaving a 1/4-inch space in the middle. Lightly brush the top of one folded side with:
   1 large egg white, lightly beaten
Sprinkle the other folded side with about 1 tablespoon sugar. Fold the dough lengthwise in half, so that the sugared surface meets the egg white, and press together. Place the pastry on an ungreased baking sheet. Cover and refrigerate for at least 30 minutes, or wrap airtight and freeze until ready to use.
Position a rack in the lower third of the oven. Preheat the oven to 425°F. Line with parchment paper or silicone liners or generously grease 2 baking sheets.
If the dough is frozen, let it thaw for 5 to 10 minutes before cutting. Spread some of the remaining sugar in a shallow bowl. Transfer the dough to a cutting board, and cut into 1/4-inch slices. Press one cut side of each slice into the sugar, and place the cookies sugar side down and at least 3 inches apart on a baking sheet. If necessary, push each slice back into shape. Sprinkle more sugar over the tops.
Bake one sheet at a time, for 5 minutes, or until the cookies begin to brown around the edges. Turn each cookie over with a spatula and bake until golden brown and caramelized all over, 2 to 5 minutes longer. Watch carefully, for the cookies can burn quickly. Remove to a rack and let cool completely.

PATTY SHELLS (BOUCHÉES)

Bouchées (mouthfuls) are individual patty shells—deep puff pastry shells baked and then filled with sweet or savory fillings. They can be made into much smaller sizes for hors d'oeuvres, when they are called **Petites Bouchées**, or "little mouthfuls."
Prepare:
   Food Processor Puff Pastry, 669

I. SMALL PATTY SHELLS
Eighteen 2-inch shells
Divide the dough into thirds, working with one piece at a time (keep the remainder refrigerated), roll the dough out to a 6 1/2 x 14 inch-rectangle. Using a 2-inch cutter, cut out 12 circles. Arrange 6 rounds upside down on an ungreased or parchment- or silicone-lined baking sheet, about 2 inches apart. Using a 1-inch round cutter, cut out the centers of the remaining 6 rounds to make rings. (Save the centers for another use.) Turn the rings upside down and then position on top of the rounds on the baking sheet. Using the back of a table knife, press an indentation every 1/4-inch around the outside edge of the circles to flute them. With a fork, prick only the centers of the shells, not the rings. Cover and refrigerate while the oven preheats. Preheat the oven to 425°F. Using a sharp knife, score the inside edge of each circle. Bake until puffed and golden brown, about 20 minutes. As soon as the patty shells come from the oven, release the inner circles that were cut from the center of each shell. Remove to a rack to cool.

II. MEDIUM PATTY SHELLS
Six 4-inch shells
Prepare as directed for Small Patty Shells, above, rolling each third of the dough to a 9 x 13-inch rectangle. Cut out the circles using a 4-inch cutter, and use a 2-inch cutter to make the rings. Assemble and bake as directed.

III. LARGE PATTY SHELLS OR VOL-AU-VENT
One 8-inch shell
Prepare as directed for Small Patty Shells, above, dividing the dough in half and rolling each half to a 10-inch square. Cut out 2 circles using an 8-inch cutter, the removable bottom of an 8-inch cake pan, or an 8-inch cake pan, then cut out the center of one with a 6-inch cutter or pan. Assemble as directed. Bake at 425°F for 20 minutes, then reduce the heat to 350°F and continue baking until puffed and golden brown, about 20 minutes.

NAPOLEON (MILLE-FEUILLE)

6 to 8 servings
Could the Emperor conceivably have had these in mind when he contended that "an army marches on its stomach"? A classic napoleon, or *mille-feuille* (literally, a thousand leaves), is made up of 3 layers of puff pastry coated with apricot jam and filled with vanilla pastry cream. Serve the napoleon within a few hours of making it. If you make the napoleons with saved puff pastry scraps, you need not weight the layers during baking.
Prepare and chill:
   Pastry Cream, 755
Roll out to a 17 1/2 x 13 1/2-inch rectangle 1/16 to 1/8 inch thick:
   1/2 recipe Food Processor Puff Pastry, 669
Transfer the pastry to an ungreased sheet. Prick it all over with a fork. Cover and refrigerate for at least 30 minutes, or wrap airtight and freeze until ready to use.
If the dough is frozen, let it thaw for a few minutes before

trimming. Transfer the dough to a cutting board and trim
$1/2$ inch from all the sides to make a 16 x 12-inch rectangle.
Return it to the baking sheet and the refrigerator while the
oven preheats.

Position a rack in the lower third of the oven. Preheat the
oven to 400°F.

Invert a wire rack on the dough to prevent it from rising
high in the oven while baking. Bake until golden brown,
20 to 25 minutes. After the first 10 minutes, remove the
rack and prick the pastry all over, then replace the rack and
finish baking. Remove the rack for the final 2 to 3 minutes
to dry and cook the top layers. Slide the pastry onto a wire
rack and let cool.

Using a sharp serrated knife, saw the pastry gently lengthwise into 3 equal strips. If desired, brush 2 of the strips
with:

(1$1/2$ tablespoons apricot jam, warmed)

Spread half of the pastry cream over one of the (jam-
covered) pastry strips. Place the second (jam-covered)
piece on top and cover with the remaining pastry cream.
Turn the last puff pastry strip upside down and place it
over the pastry cream. Refrigerate until ready to serve, but
no longer than 6 hours.

Use a sharp serrated knife and a sawing motion to cut the
napoleon into individual servings. Dust the top of each
serving with:

Confectioners' sugar

CINNAMON SUGAR STICKS

Prepare **Cheese Straws, 91,** substituting **6 tablespoons
sugar, mixed with 2 teaspoons ground cinnamon** for the
cheese and salt and pepper. Before cutting the strips,
sprinkle the top of the dough with sugar and roll over it
gently to press it in. Cut, twist, and bake as directed, until
light brown, 10 to 15 minutes. These cook faster than the
cheese straws because of the sugar, so watch carefully.

ABOUT CHOUX PASTE (PÂTE À CHOUX)

Choux is French for "cabbages," and these little dollops of
puff paste indeed expand in the oven to resemble tiny cabbage heads. Choux paste can be formed into a variety of
shapes and filled with an even greater variety of fillings
both sweet and savory. It is the basis for cream puffs and
éclairs.

Please don't think of this basic, quite easy paste as
something for adventurous moments only. Use it unsweetened as a base for gnocchi; as a soup garnish; or as
hors d'oeuvre cases. When sweetened, pâte à choux imparts great individuality to the presentation of food. With
a pastry tube, you can make Cream Puffs, 672, elegant
Éclairs, 672, Beignets, 653, Swans, 673, or dainty cases for
preserves or other fillings of your choice. If you fill small
puffs with ice cream or pastry cream and cover them with
a sauce, they become Profiteroles, 673.

Like other pastry doughs, choux paste consists of flour,
butter, and water, but it is cooked on top of the stove be-

fore it is shaped and baked. The cooked paste must be allowed to cool slightly before the eggs are added, to prevent the eggs from cooking prematurely; but if the paste is
too cold when the eggs are added, they will not blend in
smoothly. The finished paste should be shiny, smooth, and
very thick but not stiff. The paste is baked in a hot oven for
the first few minutes to cause quick expansion; the temperature is then reduced to finish the baking and dry out
the hollow shells.

A spoon or a pastry bag will serve to form the different
shapes. Be sure to press the filled bag until you are rid of all
the air in the tube before piping out the paste. Allow
space for expansion around shapes as you squeeze them
onto the baking sheet.

**To form the puffs or the characteristic cabbage-y choux
shape,** hold the tube close to the baking sheet. ➤ Do not
move the tube. Simply let the paste bubble up around it
until the desired size is reached.

To form éclairs, draw the tube along the pan while
pressing, and always finish with a lifting reverse motion.

To form profiteroles or small pastry cups, make 1-inch
balls. The little point made when you lift the bag can be
pressed down with a moistened finger.

For small puffs and éclairs, remove them from the
sheets after baking, poke a small hole in each bottom (or
the ends for éclairs) with a skewer or the tip of a small
knife, and turn them upside down on the sheets or a rack
for drying. For larger shapes and rings, slide a spatula
under the shapes to loosen them, and poke them in a few
places on the sides. Or slice off the tops horizontally, place
the tops upside down on the baking sheet, remove any
soft dough inside, and let the puffs dry and crisp in the
oven. Let the puffs cool on racks.

To fill the puffs, use the holes that you poked and fill the
cooled puffs with pastry cream or whipped cream, or slice
the tops off the puffs. If using pastry cream, fill a pastry
bag fitted with a $1/4$-inch plain tip, or spoon the cream into
open puffs. If using whipped cream, pipe it into open
puffs with a huge star tip for an attractive presentation, or
spoon it in. Whipped cream does not retain its texture if
piped through a small tip.

Once baked and filled, choux pastries should be served
immediately or refrigerated and served within a few
hours. However, unfilled baked shells can be frozen for up
to 1 week in an airtight container.

CHOUX PASTE

About 2$1/2$ cups

Measure:

1 cup all-purpose flour

Combine in a large saucepan:

1 cup water or milk, or $1/2$ cup each water and milk
**$1/2$ cup (1 stick) unsalted butter, cut into
small pieces**
1 tablespoon sugar (only for puffs with sweet fillings)
$1/2$ teaspoon salt

Bring the mixture to a full boil over medium heat. Add the flour all at once and stir vigorously with a wooden spoon. The mixture will look rough at first but it will suddenly become smooth, at which point you should stir faster. The butter may ooze out, which is fine; it simply means that the moisture is evaporating. In a few minutes, the paste will become dry and not cling to the spoon or the sides of the pan, and when the spoon is pressed on it lightly, it will leave a smooth imprint. Do not overcook or overstir at this point, or the dough will fail to puff. Transfer to a bowl and let cool for 5 minutes, stirring occasionally.

Add one at a time by hand, with a wooden spoon, beating rigorously after each addition or on low speed with a mixer:

4 large eggs, at room temperature

Make sure that the paste is smooth each time before adding the next egg. Continue to beat with each egg until the dough is smooth and shiny. The proper consistency has been reached when a small quantity of the dough will stand erect if scooped up on the end of a spoon. The paste can be covered and refrigerated for up to 4 hours; you do not need to bring the paste to room temperature before shaping.

ABOUT FILLINGS FOR CREAM PUFFS AND ÉCLAIRS

Use Whipped Cream, 754, Custards, 755–56, Pastry Cream, 755, or almost any of the fillings for cakes, 755–759. Fill as close to serving time as possible to avoid sogginess. In any case, ➤ remember that cream-based and egg-based fillings must be kept refrigerated. For a marvelous tea-teaser, put in the base of a small puff shell cut in half a layer of:

Whipped cream

Lightly place with the pointed end up:

A strawberry or raspberry

Then cover with the top half of the shell. Or, fill the puffs with:

Soft cream cheese
A dab of bright jelly

For fillings for unsweetened puff shells, see Appetizers and Hors d'Oeuvres, 91.

CREAM PUFFS

15 puffs

These large shells are a very quick way to make an attractive dessert. Fill just before serving, set the tops slightly askew, and dust with confectioners' sugar. Please read About Choux Paste, 671.

Position a rack in the lower third of the oven. Preheat the oven to 400°F.

Prepare:

¹/₂ recipe Choux Paste, 671

Scoop the paste into a pastry bag fitted with a ¹/₂-inch plain tip. Shape the paste into fifteen 2¹/₂-inch-wide 1-inch-high puffs on an ungreased baking sheet, as di-

rected in About Choux Paste. Before baking, lightly sprinkle a few drops of water over the shapes on the pan for a light, airy texture. Bake for 10 minutes. Reduce the heat to 350°F and bake until golden brown and very firm to the touch, about 25 minutes longer. Remove to a rack and let cool completely.

Prepare:

2 cups lightly sweetened whipped cream, flavored or plain, 754–755, or Pastry Cream, vanilla or another flavor, 755

Slice the tops from the puffs and remove any uncooked paste. Fill with the cream, place the tops slightly askew, and dust the puffs with, if desired:

(Confectioners' sugar)

CHOCOLATE ÉCLAIRS

8 to 10 large or 24 miniature éclairs

Please read About Choux Paste, 671.

Position a rack in the lower third of the oven. Preheat the oven to 400°F. Butter and flour a baking sheet if making large éclairs, or have ready 2 unbuttered baking sheets if making miniature éclairs.

Prepare:

Choux Paste, 671

Scoop the paste into a large pastry bag fitted with a 1-inch tip for large éclairs or a ¹/₂-inch tip for miniatures. Shape the paste into 8 to 10 large (5 inches long and 1¹/₂ inches wide) or 24 miniature (2¹/₂ inches long and ¹/₂ inch wide) éclairs, as directed in About Choux Paste. Before baking, lightly sprinkle a few drops of water over the shapes on the pan for a light, airy texture. Bake for 10 minutes. Reduce the heat to 350°F and bake until golden brown and very firm to the touch, about 25 minutes longer, or less for the miniature éclairs. Remove the éclairs to a rack and let cool completely.

Prepare:

2 cups Pastry Cream, 755, lightly sweetened whipped cream, 754, or Custard Chocolate or Coffee Fillings, 756

Fill a pastry bag fitted with a ¹/₄-inch tip with the cream. Poke the pastry tip into the drying hole in each éclair and pipe in the filling. Or cut off the top third of the éclairs with a serrated knife (reserve the lids), remove any uncooked dough, and spoon the filling into the éclairs; this method works best for whipped cream. Dip the top of each éclair (either the whole éclair or the lid) into:

Bittersweet Chocolate Glaze or Frosting, 796, Clear Caramel Glaze, 800, or Chocolate Ganache Glaze or Frosting, 795

Replace the lids on the cut éclairs. Before the glaze sets, garnish with:

(Toasted, 1001, slivered almonds)

Refrigerate the éclairs, until the glaze is set, for up to 3 hours.

PROFITEROLES

24 profiteroles; 6 servings

A profiterole is a miniature cream puff. It can be filled with any sweet or savory mixture, though it is usually associated with dessert. Vanilla ice cream is traditional, but any flavor can be used, such as Whipped Cream, 754.

Position a rack in the lower third of the oven. Preheat the oven to 400°F.

Prepare:

¹/₂ recipe Choux Paste, 671

Scoop the paste into a pastry bag fitted with a ¹/₂-inch plain tip. Shape the paste into 24 profiteroles (1 inch wide and 1 inch high) on an ungreased baking sheet. Before baking, lightly sprinkle a few drops of water over the shapes on the pan for a light, airy texture. Bake for 10 minutes. Reduce the heat to 350°F and bake until golden brown and very firm to the touch, about 25 minutes longer. Remove to a rack and let cool completely.

Prepare:

Chocolate Ganache Glaze or Frosting, 795

Whisk the glaze until smooth. If necessary, thin it with a little:

(Heavy cream)

Keep warm in the top of a double broiler (or reheat in a microwave just before serving). To serve, slice the shells horizontally in half. Remove any uncooked dough. Place a small scoop of:

Ice cream (24 scoops total), or whipped cream

In each bottom half. Cover with the top halves, and place 4 profiteroles on each plate. Drizzle with some of the chocolate glaze. Serve immediately, with the remaining glaze on the side.

CHOUX PASTE SWANS

About 24 swans

Preheat the oven to 400°F.

Prepare:

¹/₂ recipe Choux Paste, 671

Use a small plain tip to pipe out the paste for each head and neck, all in one piece, onto a greased baking sheet. To force a greater quantity of paste for the head, squeeze hard at the inception of the movement, then swing the tube in an arc for the neck, as shown. Be sure your piped dough is of a uniform thickness, or your swans will not bake evenly. For the rest of the swan's anatomy, use an open star tip to form 3-inch-long éclairs, piping them onto

Making Choux Paste Swans

a separate sheet. Before baking, lightly sprinkle a few drops of water over the shapes on the pan for a light, airy texture. Bake for 10 minutes. Reduce the heat to 350°F and bake until golden brown and very firm to the touch, about 25 minutes longer.

Slice off the top of each éclair body; reserve the tops. Just before serving, fill the bottom halves with whipped cream. Remove to a rack to cool completely. Cut the tops lengthwise in half for the wings. Embed them and the neck in the cream filling, bracing the wings somewhat diagonally to steady the neck. Dust the body lightly with confectioners' sugar. Perfect for a little girl's party!

ABOUT STRUDEL

When the last princess slip was freshly beribboned, Janka, the family's Hungarian laundress, sometimes found time to make a treat: She made strudel. Draping the round dining room table with a fresh cloth, she patiently worked flour into it. Neighborhood small-fry gathered on the fringes of the light cast by the Tiffany dome, and their eyes would pop as she rolled the dough, no larger than a softball, into a big thin circle. Then, hands lightly clenched, palms down, working under the sheet of dough and from the center out, she stretched it with the flat planes of her knuckles. She would play it out, so to speak, no so much pulling it as coaxing it with long, even friction, moving round and round the table as she worked.

In our household, the filling was invariably apple. But whether you make strudel dough yourself or buy it, or the similar **phyllo**, there are endless possibilities for "interior decoration": poppy seeds, cherries, ground meat mixtures, cheese, or just pepper worked into the dough. This last makes an excellent hors d'oeuvre pastry.

Janka organized her filling well in advance. Browned bread crumbs, lemon zest grated into sugar, walnuts, currants, very finely sliced apples, almonds, and a small pitcher of melted butter were all set out on a tray. These were strewn alternately over the surface of the dough. Then came the forming of the roll. Using both hands, Janka picked up one side of the cloth and, never actually touching the dough itself, tilted and nudged the cloth and the sheet this way and that until the dough rolled over on itself—jelly-roll fashion—and completely enclosed the filling. Finally she slid the long cylinder onto a greased baking sheet and curved it into a horseshoe. From beginning to end, the process had masterly craftsmanship. Would that we could give you her skill as easily as we give you her recipe.

Do not feel limited by these proportions or materials. See other fillings, 623.

APPLE STRUDEL

10 to 12 servings

The strudel can be formed, wrapped tightly in buttered aluminum foil, and frozen for up to 2 months before baking, but the pastry will lose crispness. Although strudel is best served on the day it is made, you can freeze baked strudel; after thawing, reheat it in a 350°F oven for 15 to 20 minutes.

Cover a table at least 3 feet square with a cloth or sheet. Make sure there is enough room to walk around the table. Do not flour the cloth.

Melt, and set aside in a small bowl:

1/2 cup (1 stick) unsalted butter

Sift together into a large bowl:

1 1/2 cups all-purpose flour
1/2 teaspoon salt

Make a well in the center of the mixture. Whisk together in a small bowl with 1 tablespoon of the melted butter, then pour into the well:

1 large egg
1/3 cup room-temperature water
1 teaspoon cider vinegar

Working from the inside of the well, mix the wet ingredients quickly into the dry ingredients with your fingers or a fork. When all the liquid is incorporated, knead the dough on a lightly floured work surface until it is silky, pliable, and no longer sticky, about 10 minutes. Form the dough into a ball and brush with some of the melted butter. Let rest in a covered bowl in a warm place for 30 to 60 minutes.

Cut into wedges, then cut crosswise into 1/4-inch slices (about 8 cups):

6 medium tart, dry apples, such as Gravenstein, Braeburn, Granny Smith, peeled and cored

Preheat the oven to 350°F.

Toast in a cake pan in the oven until browned, 10 to 15 minutes:

3/4 cup coarse fresh bread crumbs

Remove half of the bread crumbs to a medium bowl. Add and stir together:

1 cup sugar
1/2 cup walnuts, toasted, 1001, and finely chopped
1/3 cup dried currants
1 tablespoon grated lemon zest
2 teaspoons ground cinnamon

Increase the oven temperature to 400°F. Butter a baking sheet.

Roll the dough as thin as possible, then transfer it to the cloth-covered table: Lightly flour the surface only as necessary as you roll the dough; try rolling it without flour. The dough will be soft and responsive to the touch. Remove any rings or bracelets, and drape the edges of the dough over the backs of your hands (palms downward and fingers halfway clenched). Stretch the dough gently at the table, pulling it away from the center and moving your hands apart at the same time. Stretch one section of the dough at a time, and work slowly around the table. Take your time; patience will reward you with a thinner dough. Try not to tear the dough or make holes in it. Stretch the dough into a square 30 to 35 inches on each side, letting it drape over the edges of the table if it is bigger. Anchor each corner of the dough with a small plate if the square

stretches back a bit while you work on the other edges. Trim the thicker edges of dough with scissors and use the trimming to patch any holes. Let the dough dry for 10 minutes so that it will not stick to itself during rolling.

Brush the entire surface of the dough gently with some of the melted butter. Leaving a 3-inch border of dough along one edge, sprinkle the remaining toasted bread crumbs in a strip next to the border, covering one third of the dough. Mix the apples with the sugar mixture. Again leaving the 3-inch border of dough along the edge, spread the apple filling over the crumbs. Fold the 3-inch border over the filling. Pick up one end of the cloth underneath the strudel with both hands, one on either side, and let the strudel roll slowly over onto itself. It should not be tightly rolled. Continue to lift the cloth underneath the strudel and let the strudel roll onto itself to the end. Place the rolled strudel on the prepared baking sheet, curving it into a horseshoe shape.

Brush the strudel with two-thirds of the remaining melted butter. Bake for 20 minutes. Brush with the remaining butter. If necessary, rotate the strudel in the oven for even coloring. Bake until golden brown, 20 to 25 minutes more. Slide onto a rack and let cool.

Dust the strudel with:

Confectioners' sugar

Slice on a diagonal with a serrated knife.

ABOUT PHYLLO

Phyllo, filo, yuka, brik, malsouka—call it what you like— is the tissue-thin pastry used in Greece and much of the Middle East. The simplest of ingredients, flour and water, are so skillfully kneaded, rested, and stretched as almost to defy amateur reproduction.

Phyllo—the name means leaf in Greek—can be made by hand, but we do not recommend it; it is an arduous and tricky process that yields results no better than what is commercially available frozen in most grocery stores or fresh from Greek and Middle Eastern bakeries.

Store-bought phyllo is easy to work, but it is essential to keep the thin sheets from drying out. ➤ If using frozen phyllo, thaw it slowly, without unwrapping, in the refrigerator for several hours, or overnight. Once it is thawed, unwrap the phyllo and remove only the number of sheets required for the recipe; rewrap the remaining sheets in plastic wrap and return them to the refrigerator or freezer. Stack the sheets to be used on a tray or a sheet of plastic wrap, and immediately cover the stack with a sheet of plastic wrap, and cover the wrap with a damp towel. (Do not allow the damp towel to touch the phyllo, or it will dissolve into paste.) A sheet of phyllo left uncovered dries out in just a minute and will crack when you try to use it. Remove from the covered stack only the number of sheets of phyllo immediately called for and quickly re-cover the stack before proceeding.

In recipes calling for these leaves, we have successfully used our strudel dough; see 673. Other recipes using phyllo include Spinach and Feta Triangles, 89, Mushroom Triangles, 88, and Samosas, 89

BAKLAVA
About 30 squares or diamonds
Baklava is popular in Greece and throughout the Middle East. Layered with nuts and drenched in sugar syrup or honey, it is the best known of all phyllo pastries. In Greece, it was originally an Easter specialty, made with 40 layers of pastry representing the 40 days of Lent. Chopped nuts are the traditional filling, but dried fruits, sesame seeds, coconut, or pineapple may be substituted for a nontraditional version.

Preheat the oven to 325°F. Butter a 13 x 9-inch baking pan. Finely chop or coarsely grind:

> **3 cups coarsely chopped nuts (walnuts, pistachios, almonds, and/or pecans), toasted, 1001**

Stir together in a small bowl:

> **¼ cup sugar**
> **1 teaspoon grated lemon zest**
> **½ teaspoon ground cinnamon**

Melt:

> **1 cup (2 sticks) unsalted butter**

Unfold and stack on a work surface:

> **1 pound phyllo dough**

Trim the phyllo into 13 x 9-inch sheets; save the scraps for another use, if desired. Keep the stack covered with plastic wrap and a damp towel. Place 2 phyllo sheets in the baking pan and brush the top sheet evenly with melted butter. Add 2 more sheets and brush with butter, then repeat once more, for a total of 6 sheets. Sprinkle with half of the nuts and then half of the sugar mixture. Cover the filling with 2 phyllo sheets, butter the top sheet, and repeat until there are 6 sheets on top of the filling. Cover with the remaining nuts and sugar mixture. Cover with all of the remaining phyllo sheets, adding them 2 at a time and buttering only the second sheet each time. Brush the top with the remaining butter.

Using a sharp serrated knife, cut through all of the layers to make 2-inch diamonds or squares. This is important, because you will not be able to cut the baklava once it is baked without crushing the pastry; it also allows the syrup to soak in and around each piece.

Bake for 30 minutes. Reduce the oven temperature to 300°F. Continue to bake until the baklava is golden brown, 45 to 60 minutes.

Meanwhile, during the last 30 minutes of baking, combine in a saucepan:

> **1⅓ cups sugar**
> **1⅓ cups water**
> **⅓ cup honey**
> **1 tablespoon fresh lemon juice**
> **Zest of 1 orange—removed in large strips**

Bring the mixture to a gentle boil, stirring to dissolve the sugar, then reduce the heat and simmer, uncovered, for 15 minutes.

Strain the hot syrup and pour evenly over the baked baklava. Let cool completely on a rack at room temperature, at least 4 hours, before serving.

PHYLLO CUPS
6 cups
Individual phyllo cups are versatile. To maintain their crispness, spoon a sweet or savory filling into them just before serving. Unfilled baked phyllo cups can be stored in an airtight container for up to 2 days before using.

Position a rack in the lower third of the oven. Preheat the oven to 350°F. Butter the insides and rims of 6 standard-sized muffin cups.

Melt:

> **¼ cup (½ stick) unsalted butter**

Have ready:

> **¼ cup sugar (for sweet fillings only)**

Unfold and stack, then cover with plastic wrap and a damp towel:

> **4 sheets phyllo dough**

Place 1 sheet of phyllo on a work surface. Brush the sheet evenly with one-quarter of the melted butter and sprinkle 1 tablespoon of the sugar evenly over it. Cover with a second sheet of phyllo and butter and sugar it in the same manner. Repeat with the remaining sheets of phyllo, ending with a layer of butter and sugar.

Cut the stack of phyllo sheets into twelve 4½-inch squares (3 strips down and 4 across). Place a square stack in a muffin cup, easing it in with the backs of your fingers so that it covers half the bottom and rises to hang over the sides of the cup. Ease in a second stack, slightly overlapping the first, to cover the other half of the muffin cup. Repeat to make 5 more phyllo cups.

Bake until the pastry is golden brown, 10 to 15 minutes. Carefully remove from the muffin cups and let cool before filling.

ABOUT FRUIT PIES
A fruit pie is simply fruit baked between two crusts, the upper one of which is a single pastry sheet or a lattice or a streusel topping. Other than the fruit, which may be canned, frozen, dried, precooked, or fresh and raw, the filling usually contains sugar and a thickener such as flour, cornstarch, or quick-cooking tapioca.

We prefer to start with 4 to 5 cups of fresh or cooked fruit, or even more in the case of apples, to ensure that the filling will seem ample and the top crust will not sink. The measuring cup should be leveled, not heaped.

Ideally, the amount of sugar and thickener added to the filling should be adjusted according to the sweetness, acidity, the juiciness of the fruit, and your personal taste. Deciding how much thickener to add is tricky. Technically, each batch requires a different amount of thickening, depending on the variety of fruit and how ripe it is. In general, we lean toward the lesser quantity of thickener when there is a choice given in the recipes: However, if you are partial to pies that slice neatly and are willing to risk a slightly solid filling, add the greater amount of thickener called for.

While flour is still a popular choice for thickening pies, cornstarch and quick-cooking tapioca produce more glossy and clear fillings and a smoother consistency. However, apple pie benefits from the thickening that flour imparts, making the filling more opaque and creamy in appearance, and you may thicken any fruit pie with flour. To read more about starches, see 1016.

Fruit pies should be baked (or frozen; see below) as soon as they are filled and assembled, or the filling will become very juicy and begin to soften the bottom crust. Preheat the oven before beginning, and place the pie on the lowest oven rack to brown and crisp the bottom crust and prevent the upper crust from becoming too dark. Fruit pies made with uncooked fillings are baked at a high temperature for 30 minutes to set the crust, then about 30 minutes more at a moderate temperature to cook the filling. Pies made with precooked fillings are baked at a high temperature throughout, generally for somewhat less time than for those with fresh fruit fillings. Do not declare a pie done until the top has turned a deep, rich brown, almost the color of a hazelnut shell, and thick juices bubble through the steam vents or lattice. Remember that pies glazed with egg, milk, or cream will often brown within the first 30 minutes of baking, long before they are baked through. You can slow, but not stop, the browning process by laying a sheet of aluminum foil loosely over the top crust or by covering the edges of the pie with strips of foil.

If you buy frozen fruits such as peaches, cherries, or berries, choose those that are "individually quick frozen" (IQF) or "dry-packed," meaning they have been processed without sugar and come in loose pieces rather than a block. Follow any recipe calling for fresh fruit, substituting an equal volume of frozen fruit. Separate the pieces, but do not thaw before measuring the fruit. Toss the still-frozen fruit with the other ingredients, doubling the maximum amount of thickening called for, and spoon the filling into the crust at once. (If the fruit is allowed to thaw, it will release a flood of juice and make the crust soggy.) Do not glaze the top crust with sugar or egg, as it would burn during the longer cooking time. Bake the pie at 400°F for 50 minutes, then slip a baking sheet beneath it and bake at 350°F until thick juices bubble through the vents, 25 to 40 minutes more.

Canned fruits, preferably packed in unsweetened juice, make acceptable pies. For Berry or Cherry Pie with Canned or Bottled Fruit, see 677; for Winter Peach Pie, see 677. Otherwise, use the following generic formula.

SUGGESTIONS FOR FRESH OR FROZEN FRUIT PIE

If you don't find the fruit combination you are looking for in the following recipes, perhaps you would like to experiment with fillings for yourself. Use these suggestions as a guide to some good beginnings. If using frozen fruit, do not thaw before measuring.

Mix together one of the following fruit combinations:
> **5 cups sliced fruit or whole berries**
> **3¹/₂ cups sliced peeled pears and 1¹/₂ cups raspberries, cranberries, or raisins**
> **3¹/₂ cups sliced peeled peaches and 1¹/₂ cups blueberries or raspberries**
> **3 cups sliced peeled apples and 2 cups sliced green tomatoes**
> **3¹/₂ cups sliced peeled apples and 1¹/₂ cups raspberries, blackberries, cranberries, or fresh currants**
> **2¹/₂ cups pitted sour cherries or strawberries and 2¹/₂ cups diced rhubarb**
> **4 cups pitted sour or sweet cherries and 1 cup dark raisins**
> **2¹/₂ cups sliced strawberries and 2¹/₂ cups gooseberries**
> **4 cups diced fresh pineapple and 1 cup dark raisins or 2 cups sliced strawberries**

with:
> **³/₄ to 1¹/₄ cups sugar**
> **3 tablespoons quick-cooking tapioca, cornstarch, or all-purpose flour**
> **1 tablespoon strained fresh lemon juice**
> **¹/₈ teaspoon salt**
> **2 to 3 tablespoons unsalted butter, cut into small pieces**

FREEZING FRUIT PIES

Fruit pies, except those made with custard, freeze surprisingly well. For best results, freeze the pies before baking. For additional information, see Freezing Unbaked Pies, 926, and Freezing Baked Pies, 926.

FRESH BERRY PIE

One 9-inch double-crust pie

Please read Rolling Pastry Dough, Shaping and Trimming Dough, and About Crusts for Filled Pies, 662–663.
Line a 9-inch pie pan with:
> **1 recipe Basic Pie or Pastry Dough, 665, Pie Dough Cockaigne, 665, or Deluxe Butter Pie or Pastry Dough, 665, or a double recipe of Cream Cheese Pastry Dough, 666**

Pick over and hull as necessary:
> **5 cups fresh gooseberries, currants, blackberries, raspberries, cut up strawberries, blueberries, huckleberries, or loganberries**
> **(1¹/₂ tablespoons fresh lemon juice)**

Combine:
> **²/₃ to 1 cup sugar, or more to taste**
> **¹/₄ cup all-purpose flour**
> **(¹/₂ teaspoon ground cinnamon)**

If the fruit is juicy, add:
> **(1 tablespoon quick-cooking tapioca)**

Sprinkle this mixture over the berries and stir gently until well blended. Let stand 15 minutes.

Meanwhile, preheat the oven to 450°F. Turn the fruit into the pie shell. Dot with:

1 to 2 tablespoons unsalted butter, cut into small pieces

Cover the pie with a well-pricked or vented top or with a lattice. Bake for 10 minutes. Reduce the heat to 350°F and bake 35 to 40 minutes, or until golden brown. Cool completely on a rack.

BERRY, CHERRY, OR PEACH PIE WITH FROZEN FRUIT

One 9-inch double-crust pie

Please read Rolling Pastry Dough, Shaping and Trimming Dough, and About Crusts for Filled Pies, 662–663. Prepare:

1 recipe Basic Pie or Pastry Dough, 665, Pie Dough Cockaigne, 665, or Deluxe Butter Pie or Pastry Dough, 665, or a double recipe of Cream Cheese Pastry Dough, 666

Line a 9-inch pie pan with half the dough. Defrost only until the fruit separates easily:

5 cups frozen berries, cherries, or peaches

Mix with:

3 tablespoons quick-cooking tapioca
1$^1/_4$ cup sugar
$^1/_8$ teaspoon salt
2 tablespoons unsalted butter, melted

Position a rack in the lower third of the oven and preheat the oven to 450°F. Turn the filling into the pie shell and cover with a pricked or vented top crust or a lattice. Bake for 10 minutes. Reduce the heat to 350°F and bake about 45 minutes, or until golden brown.

BERRY OR CHERRY PIE WITH CANNED OR BOTTLED FRUIT

One 9-inch double-crust pie

Prepare:

1 recipe Basic Pie or Pastry Dough, 665, Pie Dough Cockaigne, 665, or Deluxe Butter Pie or Pastry Dough, 665, or a double recipe of Cream Cheese Pastry Dough, 666

Line a 9-inch pie pan with half the dough. Position a rack in the lower third of the oven. Preheat the oven to 425°F. Pour into a strainer set over a bowl:

3 pounds canned or bottled fruit

Shake the fruit lightly to drain. Measure 3$^1/_2$ cups fruit and $^1/_2$ cup juice and combine in a bowl with:

$^1/_2$ to $^3/_4$ cup sugar
3 tablespoons quick-cooking tapioca or cornstarch
2 tablespoons fresh lemon juice

Let the mixture stand for 15 minutes, then pour into the bottom crust. Dot with:

2 tablespoons unsalted butter, cut into small pieces

Cover with a pricked or vented top crust or a lattice. Bake the pie for 30 minutes.
Slip a baking sheet beneath the pan, reduce the oven temperature to 350°F, and bake until thick juices bubble through the vents, 25 to 35 minutes more. Let cool completely on a rack.

BLUEBERRY PIE

One 9-inch double-crust pie

If you are constructing a lattice, use the greater amount of cornstarch suggested to avoid watery filling that could bubble over the strips.

Please read Rolling Pastry Dough, Shaping and Trimming Dough, and About Crusts for Filled Pies, 662–663. To use frozen blueberries, see page 676. Prepare:

1 recipe Basic Pie or Pastry Dough, 665, Pie Dough Cockaigne, 665, or Deluxe Butter Pie or Pastry Dough, 665, or a double recipe of Cream Cheese Pastry Dough, 666

Line a 9-inch pan with half the dough. Position a rack in the lower third of the oven. Preheat the oven to 425°F. Combine in a bowl and let stand for 15 minutes:

5 cups blueberries, picked over
$^3/_4$ to 1 cup sugar
3$^1/_2$ to 4 tablespoons quick-cooking tapioca or cornstarch
1 tablespoon fresh lemon juice
(1 teaspoon grated lemon zest)
$^1/_8$ teaspoon salt

Pour the mixture into the bottom crust and dot with:

1 to 2 tablespoons unsalted butter, cut into small pieces

Cover with a pricked or vented top crust or a lattice. Bake the pie as directed on 676, about 55 to 65 minutes total. Cool completely on a rack.

FRESH CHERRY PIE

One 9-inch double-crust pie

Tart cherries make the best pie, but ripe Bing cherries will certainly do.

Please read Rolling Pastry Dough, Shaping and Trimming Dough, and About Crusts for Filled Pies, 662–663. Prepare:

1 recipe Basic Pie or Pastry Dough, 665, Pie Dough Cockaigne, 665, or Deluxe Butter Pie or Pastry Dough, 665, or a double recipe of Cream Cheese Pastry Dough, 666

Line a 9-inch pan with half the dough. Position a rack in the lower third of the oven. Preheat the oven to 425°F. Combine in a bowl and let stand for 15 minutes:

5 cups pitted sour or Bing cherries (2 to 2$^1/_2$ pounds)
1$^1/_4$ cups sugar for sour cherries, $^3/_4$ cup for Bing cherries
3 to 3$^1/_2$ tablespoons quick-cooking tapioca or cornstarch
2 tablespoons water
1 tablespoon fresh lemon juice
($^1/_4$ teaspoon almond extract)

Pour the mixture into the bottom crust and dot with:

2 to 3 tablespoons unsalted butter, cut into small pieces

Cover with a pricked or vented top crust or a lattice. Bake as directed on 676, about 55 to 65 minutes total. Cool completely on a rack.

SOUR CREAM CHERRY OR BERRY PIE OR TARTS

One 9-inch single-crust pie or four 3 1/2 inch tarts

Prepare a 9-inch pie shell or four 3 1/2-inch tart shells, using:

Crumb Crust, 668, made with graham crackers

Chill the shell(s). Preheat the oven to 325°F. Beat in a medium bowl:

3 large eggs

Stir in:

3/4 cup sugar
3/4 cup sour cream
2 cups fresh or drained canned cherries or berries

Pour the filling into the chilled shell(s). Bake until the custard is firm, about 1 hour. Serve very hot or very cold.

GLAZED BERRY PIE

One 9-inch single-crust pie

Prepare with a generous high rim.

Line a 9-inch pie pan with:

1/2 recipe of Basic Pie or Pastry Dough, 665, Pat-in-the-Pan Butter Dough, 666, or Crumb Crust, 667, made with graham crackers or vanilla wafers

Bake the crust as directed in About Baking Crusts Before Filling, 664, or About Crumb and Nut Crusts, 667.

Pick over:

6 cups strawberries or red or black raspberries

Hull the strawberries; cut any very large ones in half. Measure 4 cups of berries and put in a large bowl. Puree the remaining 2 cups berries in a blender or food processor.

Whisk together in a medium saucepan:

1 cup sugar
1/4 cup cornstarch
1/8 teaspoon salt

Whisk in:

1/2 cup water

Stir in the pureed berries, along with:

2 tablespoons fresh lemon juice

Bring the mixture to a simmer over medium-high heat, stirring constantly, and cook for 1 minute. Add to the remaining berries, and stir gently to combine. Pour into the crust. Refrigerate the pie for at least 4 hours to set. This pie is best served the day it is made. Serve with:

Whipped cream

APPLE PIE

Call it *à la mode* if you top your pie with ice cream; call it paradise when you have good tart apples.

Please read Rolling Pastry Dough, Shaping and Trimming Dough, and About Crusts for Filled Pies, 662–663.

One 9-inch double-crust pie

I. Prepare:

1 recipe Basic Pie or Pastry Dough, 665, or Deluxe Butter Pie or Pastry Dough, 665

Line a 9-inch pie pan with half the dough. Position a rack in the lower third of the oven. Preheat the oven to 425°F. Peel, core, and slice 1/4 inch thick:

2 1/2 pounds apples (5 to 6 large)

Combine in a bowl with:

3/4 cup sugar
2 to 3 tablespoons all-purpose flour
(1 tablespoon fresh lemon juice)
1/2 teaspoon ground cinnamon
1/8 teaspoon salt

Let stand for 15 minutes, stirring several times, so that the apples soften slightly. Pour the filling into the bottom crust and gently level with the back of a spoon. Dot the top with:

2 tablespoons unsalted butter, cut into small pieces

Cover the pie with the upper crust as directed on page 663–64. Sprinkle with:

2 teaspoons sugar
1/8 teaspoon ground cinnamon

Bake for 30 minutes. Slip a baking sheet under the pie, reduce the oven temperature to 350°F, and bake until the fruit feels just tender when a knife is poked through a steam vent and juices have begun to bubble through the vents, 30 to 45 minutes more. Cool completely on a rack, 3 to 4 hours. If you wish to serve the pie warm, place it in a 350°F oven for about 15 minutes. The pie is best the day it is baked, but it can be kept at room temperature for 2 to 3 days.

One 9-inch double-crust pie

II. In this recipe, the filling is precooked, eliminating any gap between it and the top crust when baked and producing a beautifully full, compact pie that slices like a charm.

Prepare:

1 recipe Basic Pie or Pastry Dough, 665, or Deluxe Butter Pie or Pastry Dough, 665

Line a 9-inch pie pan with half the dough. Peel, core, and slice a little thicker than 1/4 inch:

3 pounds apples (6 to 8 medium-large)

Heat in a very wide skillet or pot over high heat until sizzling and fragrant:

3 tablespoons unsalted butter

Add the apples and toss until glazed with butter. Reduce the heat to medium, cover tightly, and cook, stirring frequently, until the apples are softened on the outside but still slightly crunchy, 5 to 7 minutes. Stir in:

3/4 cup sugar
1/2 teaspoon ground cinnamon
1/8 teaspoon salt

Increase the heat to high and cook the apples at a rapid boil until the juices become thick and syrupy, about 3 minutes. Immediately spread the apples in a thin layer on a baking sheet, and let them cool to room temperature.

Position a rack in the lower third of the oven. Preheat the oven to 350°F. Pour the apple mixture into the bottom crust. Cover with a pricked or vented top crust or a lattice. Bake until the crust is richly browned and the filling has begun to bubble, 30 to 40 minutes. Let cool completely on a rack, 3 to 4 hours.

If you wish to serve the pie warm, place it in a 350°F oven for about 15 minutes. The pie is best if eaten promptly, but it can be kept at room temperature for 2 to 3 days.

One 9-inch single-crust pie

III. Prepare I or II above, using:

> ½ recipe Basic Pie or Pastry Dough, 665, or Deluxe
> Butter Pastry Dough, 665

In place of an upper crust, top with a sprinkling of:

> Streusel, 799

Bake as directed. If the crumb crust starts to become too brown, protect with a foil covering until the apples are tender. Cool completely on a rack.

APPLE TARTLETS

8 tarts

Please read Rolling Pastry Dough, 662.

Position a rack in the lower third of the oven. Preheat the oven to 375°F. Line eight standard muffin cups or individual pie pans with:

> 1 recipe Basic Pie or Pastry Dough, 665, or Deluxe
> Butter Pie or Pastry Dough, 665

Fill with:

> 4 cups thinly sliced peeled apples

Combine and pour over the fruit:

> ½ cup sugar
> 2 eggs, slightly beaten
> 2 tablespoons unsalted butter, melted
> 1 tablespoon fresh lemon juice
> 1 cup heavy cream or ½ cup evaporated milk plus
> ½ cup water
> (½ teaspoon ground cinnamon)
> (⅛ teaspoon grated or ground nutmeg)

Bake for about 40 minutes. Cool completely on a rack.

OPEN-FACED PEACH CUSTARD PIE COCKAIGNE

One 9-inch single-crust pie

Prepare:

> ½ recipe Basic Pie or Pastry Dough, 665

Line a 9-inch pie pan with the dough and bake as directed in About Baking Crusts Before Filling, 664.

Glaze the baked crust with:

> 1 egg yolk, beaten

Position a rack in the lower third of the oven. Preheat the oven to 400°F. Whisk together in a bowl until well blended:

> 1 large egg or 2 large egg yolks
> ⅓ cup sugar
> 6 tablespoons (¾ stick) unsalted butter, melted
> 3 tablespoons all-purpose flour

> ½ teaspoon vanilla
> ¼ teaspoon salt

Arrange in a single layer, cut side down, in the bottom of the crust:

> 3 to 4 fresh peaches, peeled, halved, and pitted, or
> 6 to 8 drained canned peach halves

Pour the egg mixture over the peaches. Bake the pie for 10 minutes. Reduce the oven temperature to 300°F and bake until the custard is brown and crusty on top and appears firmly set in the center when the pan is shaken, about 1 hour longer. Let cool on a rack. Serve warm or at room temperature. The pie can be refrigerated for up to 1 day. If you wish, garnish with:

> (Whipped Cream, 754)

PEACH PIE

One 9-inch double-crust pie

Before beginning, please read Rolling Pastry Dough, Shaping and Trimming Dough, and About Fruit Pies, 675–676. To use frozen peaches, see page 675.

Prepare:

> 1 recipe Basic Pie or Pastry Dough, 665, Deluxe Butter
> Pie or Pastry Dough, 665, or a double recipe of
> Cream Cheese Pastry Dough, 666

Line a 9-inch pie plate with half the dough. Position a rack in the lower third of the oven. Preheat the oven to 425°F. Peel, pit, and slice ¼ thick:

> 2½ pounds peaches

Combine in a bowl with:

> ½ to ¾ cup sugar
> 3 to 3½ tablespoons all-purpose flour, quick-cooking
> tapioca, or cornstarch
> 3 tablespoons fresh lemon juice
> (¼ teaspoon almond extract)
> ⅛ teaspoon salt

Let stand for 15 minutes, stirring occasionally. Pour the filling into the bottom crust and dot with:

> 2 to 3 tablespoons unsalted butter, cut into
> small pieces

Cover the pie with a pricked or vented top crust or a lattice. Lightly brush the top of the pie with:

> Milk or cream

Sprinkle with:

> 2 tablespoons sugar

Bake as directed on 676, 55 to 65 minutes total. Cool completely on a rack.

RHUBARB PIE

One 9-inch double-crust pie

Please read Rolling Pastry Dough, Shaping and Trimming Dough, and About Crusts for Filled Pies, 662–663.

Prepare:

> 1 recipe Basic Pie or Pastry Dough, 665, Deluxe Butter
> Pie or Pastry Dough, 665, or a double recipe of
> Cream Cheese Pastry Dough, 666

Line a 9-inch pie pan with half the dough. Position a rack in the lower third of the oven. Preheat the oven to 425°F. Without peeling, cut into 1-inch lengths:

1³/₄ to 2 pounds rhubarb stalks, trimmed

Measure 5 cups and combine in a bowl with:

1¹/₄ to 1¹/₂ cups sugar, depending on tartness of fruit
¹/₄ cup quick-cooking tapioca or cornstarch
(1 to 2 teaspoons grated orange zest)
¹/₄ teaspoon salt

Let stand for 15 minutes, stirring occasionally.
Pour the filling into the bottom crust and dot with:

2 tablespoons unsalted butter, cut into small pieces

Cover with a pricked or vented top crust or a lattice. Lightly brush the top of the pie with:

Milk or cream

Sprinkle with:

2 teaspoons sugar

Bake for 30 minutes, then lower the heat to 350°F and bake for 25 to 30 minutes more, until the juices are thick and bubbling. Cool completely on a rack.

STRAWBERRY RHUBARB PIE

This tastes more of strawberries than of rhubarb and generally pleases even the rhubarb-wary.

Prepare **Rhubarb Pie, above,** substituting **2¹/₂ cups strawberries, hulled and halved lengthwise,** for 2¹/₂ cups of the rhubarb. Reduce the sugar to 1 cup and omit the orange zest.

CONCORD GRAPE PIE

One 9-inch double-crust pie

Please read Rolling Pastry Dough, Shaping and Trimming Dough, and About Crusts for Filled Pies, 662–663. Use only Concord grapes or a related variety whose skins slip off when pinched.

Prepare:

1 recipe Basic Pie or Pastry Dough, 665, or Deluxe
Butter Pie or Pastry Dough, 665

Line a 9-inch pie pan with half the dough. Rinse, stem, and pick over:

About 2 pounds Concord grapes

Measure 4 cups. One at a time, pinch the grapes to slip off the skins; reserve both skins and pulp. Simmer the pulp in a saucepan over medium heat until the seeds loosen, about 5 minutes. Strain through a coarse sieve into a bowl and discard the seeds. Add the skins to the pulp, then whisk in:

³/₄ to 1 cup sugar
2 tablespoons unsalted butter, cut into bits
1 tablespoon fresh lemon juice
¹/₈ teaspoon salt

Let cool, then whisk in:

2¹/₂ to 3 tablespoons quick-cooking tapioca or
cornstarch (use the greater amount of cornstarch
for a lattice pie)

Position a rack in the lower third of the oven. Preheat the oven to 425°F. Pour the filling into the bottom crust. Cover

with a pricked or vented top crust or a lattice. Brush the top of the pie with:

(1 large egg yolk, beaten with ¹/₈ teaspoon water)

and sprinkle with:

(2 teaspoons sugar)

Bake 55 to 65 minutes total. Cool completely on a rack.

MOCK MINCEMEAT PIE

One 9-inch double-crust pie

This JOY classic originally appeared in the 1931 edition. Please read About Crusts for Filled Pies, 662–663.

Cut into pieces:

1¹/₂ cups seeded raisins

Peel, core, and slice:

4 medium-sized tart apples or a combination of
apples and green tomatoes (3 cups)

Combine the raisins and apples. Add:

Grated rind of 1 orange
Juice of 1 orange (¹/₂ cup)
¹/₂ cup cider or other fruit juice

Cover these ingredients and simmer until the apples are very soft. Stir in until well blended:

³/₄ cup sugar
¹/₄ teaspoon each cinnamon and cloves
2 to 3 tablespoons finely crushed soda crackers

If the apples are dry, use the smaller amount. This mixture will keep for several days. Shortly before using it, add:

(1 tablespoon brandy)

Preheat oven to 450°F. Line a pie pan with:

1 recipe Basic Pie or Pastry Dough, 665, or Deluxe
Butter Pie or Pastry Dough, 665

Fill it with mock mincemeat. Cover with a pricked upper crust or with a lattice. Bake at 450°F for 10 minutes, then reduce heat to 350°F and bake about 20 minutes longer.

RAISIN PIE

One 9-inch double-crust pie

Please read Rolling Pastry Dough, Shaping and Trimming Dough, and About Crusts for Filled Pies, 662–663.

Combine in a medium saucepan and bring to a boil over high heat:

4 cups (1¹/₂ pounds) raisins or 2 cups dark raisins plus
2 cups golden raisins
2¹/₂ cups water

Reduce the heat and simmer gently for 5 minutes. Remove from the heat. Mix thoroughly, then stir into the raisins:

1 cup packed brown sugar
¹/₄ cup all-purpose flour
(³/₄ teaspoon ground cinnamon)
¹/₂ teaspoon salt

Add:

3 tablespoons unsalted butter, cut into bits
1 tablespoon fresh lemon juice or any kind of vinegar

Bring to a simmer over medium heat, stirring constantly, then continue to simmer for 1 minute. Let cool to room temperature. Prepare:

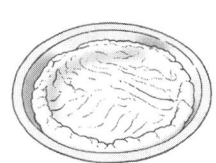 

Forming a pat-in-the-pan pie crust

Forming a pat-in-the-pan tart crust edge

1 recipe Basic Pie or Pastry Dough, 665, Deluxe Butter Pie or Pastry Dough, 665, or a double recipe of Cream Cheese Pastry Dough, 666

Line a 9-inch pie pan with half the dough. Position a rack in the center of the oven. Preheat the oven to 400°F. Turn the filling into the bottom crust. Cover with a pricked or vented top crust or lattice. If you wish, brush the top of the pie with:

(1 large egg yolk, beaten with ¹/₈ teaspoon water)

Bake the pie until the crust is richly browned and the filling is bubbly, 40 to 45 minutes. Let cool completely on a rack. The pie can be stored at room temperature for up to 2 days. Serve accompanied with:

Whipped Cream, 754, or vanilla ice cream

FRESH FRUIT TART
One 9¹/₂- or 10-inch tart

Please read Rolling Pastry Dough and Shaping and Trimming Dough, 662–663, or About Pat-in-the-Pan Crusts, 666. The same formula can also be used for tartlets, but slightly more or less glaze, pastry cream, and fruit may be needed. Line a 9¹/₂- or 10-inch two-piece tart pan with:

¹/₂ recipe Basic Pie or Pastry Dough, 665, or 1 recipe Pat-in-the-Pan Shortbread Dough, 667

Glaze the crust with:

1 large egg yolk

Bake the crust as directed in About Baking Crusts before Filling or the pat-in-the-pan dough recipe. Let cool completely.

To moisture-proof the crust, brush over the bottom:

3 tablespoons currant, raspberry, or strawberry jelly, melted, or 1 tablespoon unsalted butter, softened

Refrigerate the shell for 10 minutes to set the glaze or butter. Spread evenly in the crust:

1 cup Pastry Cream, 755, or Frangipane Pastry Cream, 755

Arrange over the cream in a single layer:

2 cups whole small berries, sliced strawberries, or thinly sliced fruit, such as apricot, kiwi, or mango

If desired, brush the fruit lightly with:

2 to 3 tablespoons jelly, melted

Or, just before serving, dust the tart very lightly with:

Confectioners' sugar

If not serving immediately, store in the refrigerator for no longer than 6 hours.

RASPBERRY STREUSEL TART
One 9¹/₂- or 10-inch tart

Please read Rolling Pastry Dough, Shaping and Trimming Dough, 662–663, or About Pat-in-the-Pan Crusts, 666. You can make this tart with any summer berry or with a mixture of berries.

Line a 9¹/₂- or 10-inch two-piece tart pan with:

¹/₂ recipe Basic Pie or Pastry Dough, 665, or 1 recipe Pat-in-the-Pan Shortbread Dough, 667

Glaze the crust with:

1 large egg yolk

Bake the crust as directed in About Baking Crusts Before Filling, 664, or About Pat-in-the-Pan Crusts, 666. Let cool completely. Position a rack in the center of the oven. Preheat oven to 350°F. Stir together just until combined:

3 cups raspberries or other berries

¹/₂ cup sugar

2 tablespoons cornstarch

1 tablespoon strained fresh lemon juice

Distribute the raspberry mixture evenly in the tart crust. Sprinkle over the berries:

Streusel I, 799

Bake until the streusel has browned and thick juices bubble up near the center, 45 to 60 minutes. Let cool completely on a rack.

TARTE TATIN
One 10- or 11-inch tart

This classic French upside-down apple tart is named for the Tatin sisters, who served it at their hotel in the Loire Valley. The apples are cut into quarters and arranged in circles over the bottom of a skillet containing sugar and melted butter. The apples are cooked over high heat until their juices begin to darken, then covered with a pastry crust and baked. When the tart is turned out of the skillet, the crust becomes a base for concentric circles of caramelized apples, a deep gold, enticing sight.

Prepare the tarts in any deep heavy ovenproof skillet measuring 7 to 8 inches across the bottom and 10 to 11 inches across the top. The filling will not react with cast iron, but you may find a cast-iron skillet heavy to flip when unmolding the tart. Pans made especially for tarte Tatin are available at some cookware stores.

Please read Rolling Pastry Dough, Shaping and Trimming Dough, 662–663, and About Pat-in-the-Pan Crusts, 666.

flip apples

Assembling a tarte Tatin

Prepare:

¹/₂ recipe Deluxe Butter Pie or Pastry Dough, 665

Roll the dough into a 12-inch round, slip a rimless cookie sheet beneath it, and refrigerate.

Position a rack in the upper third of the oven. Preheat the oven to 375°F. Peel, core, and quarter:

6 medium apples (about 3 pounds)

Melt in the skillet (see note above):

¹/₂ cup (1 stick) unsalted butter

Remove from the heat and sprinkle evenly over the bottom:

1 cup sugar

Arrange a ring of apple quarters against the sides of the pan, standing the apples on the thin edge of their cut side so as to fit as many as possible. Fill in the center of the skillet with the remaining apple quarters. (You may have a piece or two of apple left over.) Place the skillet over the highest possible heat and cook until the juices turn from butterscotch to deep amber, 10 to 12 minutes. Remove the skillet from the heat, spear the apples with a fork or the point of a paring knife, and flip them onto their uncooked sides. Return the skillet to high heat and boil 5 minutes more. Remove the skillet from the heat and slide the prepared crust onto the apples. Being careful not to burn your fingers, gently tuck the edges of the dough against the inner sides of the skillet.

Bake the tart until the crust is richly browned, 25 to 35 minutes. Let cool on a rack for 20 minutes.

Loosen the sides of the tart with a knife and invert the tart onto a heatproof serving plate. Return any apples that stick to the skillet to their proper place on top of the tart. Serve immediately, or let stand at room temperature for up to 8 hours. When ready to serve, warm the tart to tepid in an oven heated at the lowest setting.

ABOUT TRANSPARENT PIES

There is a whole galaxy of pie fillings based on brown sugar, molasses, and corn or maple syrup, generally considered a Southern specialty, although they've traveled widely as Chess Pie, a name of unknown origin. These are usually thickened with egg, but sometimes with a crumb mixture or, as in the Pennsylvania Dutch specialty Shoofly Pie, with a flour base, which gives the dessert a cakelike quality. Some cooks cut the sweetness with tart jellies, lemon, or vinegar. Some add butter or cream, spices, nuts,

and/or dried fruits. You may top these pies with crumb mixtures, meringues, whipped cream or icing. To test for doneness, read About Custard and Cream Pies, 684. Store these pies in the refrigerator, but let come to room temperature or warm in a 275°F oven for 15 minutes before serving.

BASIC TRANSPARENT PIE

We have encountered this great Southern favorite at all sorts of gatherings, from fiestas to funerals. There are many variations, but we like to use our recipe for **Pecan Pie, below,** omitting the pecans and replacing the vanilla with **a grating of nutmeg or 1 tablespoon fresh lemon juice.** If you add to the filling or line the crust with ¹/₄ cup of tart jelly, you have **Amber Pie.**

PECAN PIE

One 9-inch single-crust pie

Please read Rolling Pastry Dough and Shaping and Trimming Dough, 662–663.

Made with white sugar and light corn syrup, this has a mild, sweet, buttery flavor. For a dark pecan pie with a caramel-like taste, use light or dark brown sugar and dark corn syrup. Black walnuts instead of pecans make a piquant substitution. Prepare with a generous high rim.

Line a 9-inch pie pan, preferably glass, with:

¹/₂ recipe Basic Pie or Pastry Dough, 665, or Pat-in-the-Pan Butter Dough, 666

Glaze the crust with:

1 large egg yolk

Bake the crust as directed in About Baking Crusts Before Filling, 664, or About Pat-in-the-Pan Crusts, 666. Position a rack in the center of the oven. Preheat the oven to 375°F. Whisk in a large bowl until blended:

4 large eggs

1 cup sugar or packed brown sugar

³/₄ cup light corn syrup

5 tablespoons unsalted butter, melted

1 teaspoon vanilla or 1 tablespoon dark rum

¹/₂ teaspoon salt

Stir in:

2 cups pecans

Pour the filling into the piecrust. Bake until the edges are firm and the center seems set but quivery, like gelatin, when the pan is nudged, 35 to 45 minutes. Let cool on a rack for at least 1 1/2 hours. Serve warm or at room temperature. The pie can be stored in the refrigerator for up to 2 days, but let come to room temperature or warm in a 275°F oven for 15 minutes before serving.

CHOCOLATE CHIP OR CHUNK PECAN PIE

Prepare **Pecan Pie, above,** reducing the pecans to 1 cup and stirring in **1 cup chocolate chips or 2 ounces** *each* **dark, milk, and white chocolate, cut into** 1/4**-inch chunks,** along with the nuts. Bake 35 minutes, or until set. Refrigerate the cooled pie until cold and hard, then slice. To serve, warm the slices in a 275°F oven until the chocolate just begins to soften.

BOURBON PIE

Prepare **Pecan Pie, 682.** Omit the nuts and use **3 tablespoons bourbon whiskey** instead of the vanilla or rum.

SHOOFLY PIE

One 9-inch single-crust pie

Please read Rolling Pastry Dough and Shaping and Trimming Dough, 662–663.

There are both "dry bottom" and "wet bottom" versions of this Pennsylvania Dutch specialty. The dry-bottom pie is almost like soft gingerbread in a crust, while the "wet" one, as in our version, consists of a molasses custard topped with crumbs.

Line a 9-inch pie pan with:

   1/2 **recipe Basic Pie or Pastry Dough, 665, or Pat-in-the-**
      Pan Butter Dough, 666

Bake the crust as directed in About Baking Crusts Before Filling, 664, or About Pat-in-the-Pan Crusts, 666.

Position a rack in the center of the oven. Preheat the oven to 400°F. Combine in a bowl:

   1 cup all-purpose flour
   2/3 **cup packed dark brown sugar**
   5 tablespoons unsalted butter, softened

Mash with a fork or chop with a pastry blender until crumbly. Beat with a large spoon in a separate bowl until blended:

   1 cup light molasses
   1 large egg
   1 teaspoon baking soda

Stir in thoroughly:

   1 cup boiling water

Stir half of the crumb mixture into the molasses mixture, and pour into the prepared crust. Sprinkle the remaining crumb mixture evenly over the top. Bake for 10 minutes. Reduce the oven temperature to 350°F and bake until the edges are firm, 20 to 30 minutes more. Let cool completely on a rack. The pie can be stored at room temperature for up to 3 days. Serve accompanied with:

   Whipped Cream, 754

CHESS PIE

One 9-inch single-crust pie

Please read Rolling Pastry Dough and Shaping and Trimming Dough, 662–663.

Line a 9-inch pie pan with:

   1/2 **recipe Basic Pie or Pastry Dough, 665**

Glaze the crust with:

   1 large egg yolk

Bake the crust as directed in About Baking Crusts Before Filling, 664. Position a rack in the center of the oven. Preheat the oven to 275°F. Warm the piecrust in the oven while you prepare the filling. Whisk in a heatproof bowl just until no yellow streaks remain:

   1 large egg
   4 large egg yolks
   2/3 **cup sugar**
   2/3 **cup packed light brown sugar**
   1/2 **teaspoon salt**

Whisk in:

   2/3 **cup heavy cream or evaporated milk or** 1/3 **cup milk**
      plus 1/3 **cup heavy cream**

Scatter over the top:

   6 tablespoons (3/4 **stick) unsalted butter, cut into**
      small pieces

Bring 1 inch of water to a simmer in a skillet. Set the bowl in the skillet and gently whisk the mixture until shiny and warm to the touch. Stir in:

   (1/2 **to** 3/4 **cup chopped toasted, 1001, walnuts**
      or pecans)

Pour the filling into the crust. Bake until firm, 50 to 65 minutes.

JEFFERSON DAVIS PIE

Prepare **Chess Pie, above.** Add 1/2 **cup chopped dates,** 1/2 **cup raisins,** 1/2 **cup chopped nuts, 1 teaspoon ground cinnamon, 1 teaspoon grated or ground nutmeg,** and 1/2 **teaspoon ground allspice** to the filling mixture before heating it.

BUTTERMILK CHESS PIE

Prepare **Chess Pie, above.** Add 2/3 **cup additional white** sugar and use 2/3 **cup buttermilk** instead of cream or milk. Stir into the filling (1/2 **cup chopped pecans or walnuts**) and (1/2 **cup chopped raisins**). Bake until the center is set when nudged, 35 to 40 minutes.

LEMON CHESS PIE

Prepare **Chess Pie, above.** Substitute 2/3 **cup additional white sugar** for the brown sugar. Omit the salt and add **grated zest of 1 lemon.** Use 1/3 **cup heavy cream plus** 1/3 **cup fresh lemon juice** instead of cream and milk. Stir (1/2 **cup shredded sweetened dried coconut**) into the filling. Reduce baking time to 25 to 40 minutes.

CHESS TARTS

Prepare:

   1 recipe Rich Egg Tart Dough, 666

Line six 3-inch tart shells with the dough and bake as directed in the dough recipe. Reduce oven to 275°F. Fill with the filling for:

Chess Pie, Jefferson Davis Pie, Buttermilk Chess Pie, or Lemon Chess Pie, 683

Bake for 20 minutes. When cool, cover with:

Whipped cream

MAPLE SYRUP PIE

One 9-inch pie

Please read Rolling Pastry Dough and Shaping and Trimming Dough, 662–663.

Preheat the oven to 350°F. Line a 9-inch pie pan with:

¹/₂ recipe Basic Pie or Pastry Dough, 665

Bake as directed in About Baking Crusts Before Filling, 664. Whisk together:

1¹/₂ cups packed brown sugar
2 large eggs
¹/₂ cup heavy cream
¹/₃ cup pure maple syrup
2 teaspoons unsalted butter, melted

Pour into the crust and bake until the center seems set but still quivers, like gelatin, when the pan is nudged, 50 to 60 minutes. Cool completely on a rack. Serve with:

Whipped Cream, 754, sour cream

PEANUT BUTTER PIE

One 10-inch pie

The filling is mousselike and surprisingly subtle in flavor, and the chocolate glaze gives the pie an elegant finished look. Please read About Crumb and Nut Crusts, 667. Prepare and bake in a 10-inch pie pan:

Crumb Crust, 667, made with graham crackers or chocolate wafers

Beat in a large bowl just until smoothly blended:

8 ounces cream cheese, softened
1 cup chunky or smooth peanut butter
¹/₂ cup sugar
2 teaspoons vanilla

Beat in a medium bowl until stiff peaks form:

1 cup cold heavy cream

Using a large rubber spatula, fold half of the whipped cream into the peanut butter mixture to lighten it, then fold in the remaining cream. Spread the mixture evenly in the cooled piecrust. Press a sheet of plastic wrap directly on the surface and refrigerate until firm, about 4 hours. Bring to a boil, stirring, in a saucepan over high heat:

Chocolate Ganache Glaze or Frosting, 795

Let cool to lukewarm, then pour the glaze over the top of the pie and spread evenly. Sprinkle with:

(¹/₃ cup chopped salted peanuts)

Refrigerate for at least 1 hour, or up to 3 days. Serve accompanied with, if desired:

(Whipped Cream, 754)

ABOUT CUSTARD AND CREAM PIES

Like all custards, fillings for custard pies need to be baked at a relatively low temperature to keep from curdling, but the crust tends to become soggy unless the pie is baked at a high heat. The trick is to have both custard and crust hot when the pie is assembled. This allows the custard to set quickly at the comfortably low temperature it favors, and thus the crust does not become soaked. For this to work, use Basic Pie or Pastry Dough, blind-baked, 664, and carefully moisture-proofed after baking with a glaze of beaten egg yolk. To prevent the filling from overcooking and turning grainy around the edges, custard pies must be removed from the oven when the center is still quivery, like gelatin. The filling will continue to cook on stored heat as the pie stands and will thicken further upon cooling.

Because custard and cream pies are highly susceptible to spoilage, refrigerate as soon as they have cooled to room temperature. Serve within a day of baking, or the crust will soften. Custard pies can be served cold, at room temperature, or slightly warmed. Cream pies must be served chilled.

CUSTARD PIE

One 9-inch pie

Preheat oven to 425°F. Building up a high fluted ring, line a 9-inch pie pan, preferably glass, with:

¹/₂ recipe Basic Pie or Pastry Dough, 665

Glaze the crust with:

1 large egg yolk

Prick the bottom and bake the crust for 10 minutes as directed in About Baking Crusts Before Filling, 664. Decrease the oven to 325°F.

If the crust has cooled, warm it in the oven for up to 10 minutes while you prepare the filling. Whisk together in a large bowl just until blended:

3 large eggs
2 to 3 large egg yolks
¹/₂ cup sugar
1 teaspoon vanilla
¹/₈ teaspoon salt

Bring to a simmer in a medium saucepan over medium heat:

2 cups whole milk

Gently whisking all the while, gradually add the milk to the egg mixture. Immediately pour the hot custard into the warm crust. Dust the top with:

(¹/₄ to ¹/₂ teaspoon grated or ground nutmeg)

Bake 25 to 35 minutes. Bake until the center of the custard seems set but quivery, like gelatin, when the pan is nudged. Cool completely on a rack. Serve plain, with sugared fresh fruit, or garnished with:

Sweet Chocolate Curls, 970

CHOCOLATE GLAZED CUSTARD PIE

A great favorite in our grandmother's day and overdue for a revival.

Prepare **Custard Pie, 684,** omitting the nutmeg. Let the pie cool to room temperature. Prepare:

> **Chocolate Ganache Glaze or Frosting, 795**

Let cool slightly, then spread over the top of the pie. Refrigerate until the glaze sets.

VANILLA CREAM PIE

One 9-inch single-crust pie

Please read Rolling Pastry Dough and Shaping and Trimming Dough, 662–663, About Crumb and Nut Crusts, 667, or About Pat-in-the-Pan Crusts, 666.

Line a 9-inch pie pan with:

> **¹/₂ recipe Basic Pie or Pastry Dough, 665, any Pat-in-the-Pan Dough, 666–67, or Crumb Crust, 667**

Bake the crust for 10 minutes as directed in About Baking Crusts Before Filling, 664.

If topping the pie with meringue, reduce heat to 325°F. Whisk in a medium heavy saucepan until well blended:

> **²/₃ cup sugar**
> **¹/₄ cup cornstarch**
> **¹/₄ teaspoon salt**

Gradually whisk in:

> **2¹/₂ cups whole milk**

Vigorously whisk in until no yellow streaks remain:

> **5 large egg yolks**

Reserve the whites if making meringue. Stirring constantly with a heatproof rubber spatula, bring to a simmer over medium heat. Remove from the heat, scrape the corners of the saucepan, and whisk until smooth. Return to the heat and, whisking constantly, bring to a simmer and cook for 1 minute. Off the heat, whisk in:

> **2 to 3 tablespoons unsalted butter, cut into small pieces**
> **1¹/₂ teaspoons vanilla**

Spoon the filling into prepared crust and press a sheet of plastic wrap directly on the surface. If not using a meringue, refrigerate the pie for at least 3 hours to firm the filling. Shortly before serving, remove the plastic wrap and cover the pie with:

> **Whipped Cream, 754**

Or if you are covering the pie with meringue, proceed at once to prepare:

> **Soft Meringue Topping I or II, 798**

Remove the plastic wrap and spread the meringue over the top of the hot pie, anchoring it to the crust rim on all sides. Bake the pie for 20 minutes, let cool completely on a rack, and then refrigerate.

CHOCOLATE CREAM PIE

One 9-inch single-crust pie

Please read About Crumb and Nut Crusts, 667.

I. Chop:

> **2 ounces unsweetened chocolate**

Prepare:

> **Vanilla Cream Pie, above**

increasing the sugar to ³/₄ to 1 cup. Melt the chocolate in the hot milk mixture, then add the egg yolks. Proceed as directed.

II. Fill the piecrust with:

> **¹/₂ recipe Pots de Crème, 804, French Chocolate Mousse, 816, White Chocolate Mousse, 816, or Mocha Filling, 756**

Refrigerate until chilled, or until ready to serve. Garnish with:

> **Whipped Cream, 754**

BANANA CREAM PIE

One 9-inch pie

Please read About Crumb and Nut Crusts, 667.

Prepare the crust and filling for **Vanilla Cream Pie, above.** Cool the filling. Peel and thinly slice **2 to 4 firm ripe bananas (1¹/₂ to 2 cups).** Spoon one-third of the cooled vanilla filling into the pie shell, and scatter half of the bananas over the top. Cover with another third of the filling and then the rest of the bananas. Spread the remaining filling over the top. Proceed as directed.

BUTTERSCOTCH CREAM PIE

One 9-inch single-crust pie

Line a 9-inch pie pan with:

> **Nut Crust, 668, Crumb Crust, 667, or ¹/₂ recipe Basic Pie or Pastry Dough, 665**

Bake the crust as directed in About Crumb and Nut Crusts, 667, or About Baking Crusts Before Filling, 664.

Combine in a medium heavy saucepan and cook over medium heat, stirring, until melted and bubbly, 3 to 5 minutes:

> **6 tablespoons (³/₄ stick) unsalted butter**
> **1 packed cup light brown sugar**

Remove from the heat and gradually stir in:

> **¹/₂ cup heavy cream or evaporated milk**

Do not use regular milk, as it may curdle. If necessary, return briefly to the heat to melt the butterscotch. Let cool slightly. Prepare the filling for:

> **Vanilla Cream Pie, above**

omitting the sugar and reducing the milk to 2 cups. Add the brown sugar mixture along with the milk, and omit the butter. Spoon the filling into the crust and proceed as directed.

COCONUT CREAM PIE

One 9-inch pie

Please read About Crumb and Nut Crusts, 667.

Prepare **Vanilla Cream Pie, above,** adding **1 to 1¹/₃ cups shredded sweetened dried coconut, toasted, 972,** to the filling along with the butter. If desired, reserve 2 to 3 tablespoons of the coconut for sprinkling over the whipped cream or meringue topping. Serve the chilled pie with **(Chocolate Sauce, 847, or Caramel Sauce, 849).**

ABOUT PUMPKIN, SQUASH, AND SWEET POTATO PIES

Pies made from cooked vegetable purees such as pumpkin or sweet potato should be handled in a similar way to custard pies. **To prepare fresh pumpkin or squash puree:** Look for a pie pumpkin—a smaller, sweeter variety with finer-textured flesh than the not so good for cooking jack-o'-lanterns—or squash such as Hubbard, Delicata, Kabocha, or Buttercup. You will need 5 to 6 pounds to make 4 cups of puree, enough for 2 pies. Wash and split the pumpkins into quarters with a cleaver or heavy knife. Cut out the stem, scrape out the stringy pulp, and seeds, and hack into 4-inch pieces. Place the pumpkin rind side down in an oiled roasting pan, cover tightly with aluminum foil, and bake at 325°F until very soft, about 1 1/2 hours. Scrape the flesh free of the rind and puree in a food processor, or force it through a food mill or fine sieve.

If the puree seems loose and wet, pour it into a colander lined with cheesecloth, bring the ends of the cheesecloth up over it, and cover with a cake pan and several large cans. Let the pumpkin drain for 30 to 60 minutes or until it reaches the same consistency as the canned type.

PUMPKIN OR SQUASH PIE

One 9-inch single-crust pie
Please read Rolling Pastry Dough and Shaping and Trimming Dough, 662–663.
Use 3 eggs for a soft, custardy filling, 2 for a firmer pie with a pronounced pumpkin flavor. To prepare this with sweetened condensed milk, substitute **1 1/2 cups sweetened condensed milk** for the heavy cream and do not add white sugar.
I. Position a rack in the center of the oven. Preheat the oven to 425°F. Building up a high fluted rim, line in a 9-inch pie pan with:

> **1/2 recipe Basic Pie or Pastry Dough, 665**

Glaze the crust with:

> **1 large egg yolk**

Bake as directed in About Baking Crusts Before Filling, 664. Decrease the oven to 375°F.
Whisk thoroughly in a large bowl:

> **2 to 3 large eggs (see above)**

Whisk in thoroughly:

> **2 cups cooked pumpkin or squash puree**
> **1 1/2 cups heavy cream or evaporated milk**
> **1/2 cup sugar**
> **1/3 cup packed brown sugar**
> **1 teaspoon ground cinnamon**
> **1 teaspoon ground ginger**
> **1/2 teaspoon grated or ground nutmeg**
> **1/4 teaspoon ground cloves or allspice**
> **1/2 teaspoon salt**

Warm the piecrust in the oven until it is hot to the touch, leaving the filling at room temperature. Pour the pumpkin mixture into the crust and bake 35 to 45 minutes, until firm. Cool completely on a rack. The pie can be refrigerated for up to 1 day. Serve cold or at room temperature, accompanied with:

> **Whipped Cream, 754, flavored with (2 tablespoons bourbon) and/or Hot Brandy Sauce, 852**

II. Follow the directions in I, above, omitting the milk and adding **2 tablespoons molasses** and **1 1/2 cups sour cream.**

SWEET POTATO PIE

Prepare **Pumpkin Pie, above,** substituting **2 cups pureed sweet potatoes, 301,** for the pumpkin.

FUDGE PIE

One 9-inch pie
A crustless pie or cake unexcelled in its delicious and devastatingly rich quality. But do not let a little devastation deter you.
Preheat the oven to 325°F. Grease a 9-inch pie pan.
Cream together:

> **1 cup sugar**
> **1/2 cup (1 stick) unsalted butter**

Beat in:

> **2 large egg yolks**
> **2 ounces unsweetened chocolate, melted and slightly cooled**

Beat in:

> **1/3 cup all-purpose flour**
> **1 teaspoon vanilla**

Stir in:

> **1 cup chopped walnuts or pecans**

Whip until stiff but not dry, 978:

> **2 large egg whites**
> **1/8 teaspoon salt**

Fold into the batter. Pour into the greased pie pan and bake for 30 to 35 minutes. Serve topped with:

> **Ice cream or Whipped Cream, 754**

BITTERSWEET CHOCOLATE TART

One 9 1/2- or 10-inch tart
Best served the day it is baked.
Prepare in a 9 1/2- or 10-inch two-piece tart pan.

> **Pat-in-the-Pan Shortbread Dough, 667**

Position a rack in the lower third of the oven. Preheat the oven to 375°F. Bring to a simmer in a small saucepan:

> **1 cup heavy cream**

Remove from the heat and add:

> **8 ounces bittersweet or semisweet chocolate, finely chopped**

Whisk gently until the chocolate is completely melted and the mixture is smooth, then whisk in:

> **1 large egg, lightly beaten**

Pour the chocolate mixture into the tart shell. Bake until the center seems set but still quivers, like gelatin, when the pan is nudged, 15 to 20 minutes. Let cool on a rack.
Serve slightly warm or at room temperature with:

> **Whipped Cream, 754**

Store in refrigerator.

CHOCOLATE-GLAZED CARAMEL TART

One 9 1/2- or 10-inch tart
Please read Rolling Pastry Dough and Shaping and Trimming Dough, 662–663.

Serve this tart in small slices. It is almost like candy.

Line a 9¹/₂- or 10-inch two-piece tart pan:

¹/₂ recipe Basic Pie or Pastry Dough, 665, or Pat-in-the-Pan Shortbread Dough, 667

Glaze the crust with:

1 large egg yolk

Bake as directed in About Baking Crusts Before Filling, 664, or the shortbread dough recipe. Position a rack in the lower third of the oven. Preheat the oven to 325°F. Place in a medium heavy saucepan:

1¹/₂ cups sugar

Drizzle evenly over the top:

¹/₂ cup water

Place the pan over medium heat and, without stirring, very gently swirl the pan until the sugar dissolves and a clear syrup forms. It is important that the sugar is dissolved before the boil is reached, so slide the pan off and on the burner as necessary. Increase the heat to high and bring the syrup to a rolling boil. Cover the pan tightly and boil for 2 minutes. Uncover the pan and cook until the caramel begins to darken. Again gently swirling the pan, cook until the caramel turns a deep amber. Remove the pan from the heat. Standing back to avoid spatters, pour in:

1¹/₄ cups heavy cream

Stir until smooth. If the caramel remains lumpy, place the saucepan over low heat and stir until smooth. Let cool for 10 minutes. Whisk until frothy in a medium bowl:

1 large egg
1 large egg yolk
1 teaspoon vanilla
¹/₈ teaspoon salt

Gradually whisk in the caramel mixture. Pour the filling into the prepared tart crust. Bake until the edges darken and begin to bubble and the center looks almost set, 45 to 55 minutes. Let cool completely on a rack.

Spread over the caramel filling:

¹/₂ recipe Chocolate Ganache Glaze or Frosting, 795

Sprinkle with:

¹/₂ cup chopped toasted slivered, 1001, almonds

Refrigerate the tart until firm, at least 4 hours, or for up to 2 days. Serve cold with:

Whipped Cream, 754

ABOUT LEMON AND LIME PIES

If you are going to make a fresh lemon or lime pie, it is worth taking the time to grate the zest and squeeze the juice from fresh citrus fruits. Citrus zest, with its pungent oils, is essential to a well-flavored filling, and fresh juice tastes better than frozen or bottled juices, whose flavor is compromised by pasteurization and preservatives.

LEMON MERINGUE PIE

One 9-inch single-crust pie

Please read Rolling Pastry Dough and Shaping and Trimming Dough, 662–663.

Line a 9-inch pie pan with:

¹/₂ recipe Deluxe Butter Pie or Pastry Dough, 665

Bake the crust as directed in About Baking Crusts Before Filling, 664, Combine in a 2- or 3-quart saucepan:

1¹/₂ cups sugar
6 tablespoons cornstarch
¹/₄ teaspoon salt

Gradually blend in until smooth:

¹/₂ cup cold water
¹/₂ cup fresh lemon juice

Add, blending thoroughly:

3 egg yolks, well beaten

Add:

2 tablespoons unsalted butter, cut into small pieces

Stirring constantly, gradually add:

1¹/₂ cups boiling water

Bring to a full boil, stirring gently. Once it begins to thicken, reduce the heat and simmer slowly 1 minute. Remove from the heat and stir in:

1 teaspoon grated lemon zest

Pour into the baked pie shell. Prepare:

Soft Meringue Topping I or II, 798

Spread a band of meringue around the edges of the filling, anchoring it to the crust at all points. Dollop the remaining meringue over the center and smooth the top. Bake for 20 minutes more. Cool completely on a rack, then serve or refrigerate for up to 3 days.

OHIO SHAKER LEMON PIE

One 9-inch double-crust pie

The very tart filling in this favorite consists of paper-thin lemon slices macerated in sugar until tender and sweet. It may sound odd, but don't be afraid—it is as delicious as it is unusual.

Please read Rolling Pastry Dough, Shaping and Trimming Dough, and About Baking Crusts for Filled Pies, 662–663. Grate and reserve the zest from:

2 large lemons

Slice the lemons paper-thin, removing the seeds. Combine the lemon slices and zest in a bowl with:

2 cups sugar
¹/₄ teaspoon salt

Cover and let stand at room temperature for 2 to 24 hours, stirring occasionally, the longer, the better.

Prepare:

1 recipe Basic Pie or Pastry Dough, 665, or Deluxe Butter Pie or Pastry Dough, 665

Line a 9-inch pie pan with half the dough. Position a rack in the lower third of the oven. Preheat the oven to 425°F. Whisk in a large bowl until frothy:

4 large eggs

Whisk in:

¹/₄ cup (¹/₂ stick) unsalted butter, melted
3 tablespoons all-purpose flour

Stir in the lemon mixture. Pour the filling into the bottom crust and level with the back of a spoon. Cover with a pricked or vented top crust or a lattice.

Bake the pie for 30 minutes. Reduce the oven temperature to 350°F and bake until a knife inserted into the center comes out clean, 20 to 30 minutes more. Let cool completely on a rack. The pie can be refrigerated for up to 2 days, but it should be served at room temperature.

LEMON TART

One 9 1/2- or 10-inch tart

Though this classic is simple, it is elegant and richer than other lemon pies and tarts.

Please read Rolling Pastry Dough and Shaping and Trimming Dough, 662–663. Line a 9 1/2- or 10-inch two-piece tart pan with:

> 1/2 **recipe Basic Pie or Pastry Dough, 665, Deluxe**
> **Butter Pie or Pastry Dough, 666, Rich Egg Tart**
> **Dough, 665, or Pat-in-the-Pan Butter Dough, 666**

Glaze the crust with:

> **1 large egg yolk**

Bake as directed in About Baking Crusts Before Filling, 664. Position a rack in the center of the oven. Reduce the heat to 350°F. Combine in a heatproof bowl:

> **1 cup sugar**
> 1/2 **cup (1 stick) unsalted butter, cut into**
> **small pieces**

Bring 1 inch of water to a bare simmer in a skillet. Set the bowl in the skillet and stir until the butter is melted. Remove the bowl from the skillet. Add and beat until no yellow streaks remain:

> **8 large egg yolks**

Stir in:

> 1/2 **cup strained fresh lemon juice (from 2 to 3 lemons)**

Return the bowl to the skillet and, stirring gently, heat the mixture until thickened to the consistency of heavy cream (it will lightly coat a spoon), 6 to 8 minutes. Strain through a fine-mesh sieve into a bowl, then stir in:

> **1 tablespoon grated lemon zest**

Pour the filling into the tart crust. Bake 15 to 20 minutes, until the center is set when jiggled. Let cool completely on a rack. Lightly press a sheet of oiled plastic wrap directly on the filling. The tart can be refrigerated for up to 1 day. Let warm to room temperature before serving. If desired, serve with:

> **(Fresh Raspberry Sauce, 853)**
> **(Whipped Cream, 754)**

KEY LIME PIE

One 9-inch single-crust pie

Please read Rolling Pastry Dough and Shaping and Trimming Dough, 662–663.

This pie owes its distinctive character to the pungent citrus variety native to Florida called the Key lime. Bottled Key lime juice is perfectly acceptable when fresh Key limes are not available.

Line a 9-inch pie pan with:

> 1/2 **recipe Basic Pie or Pastry Dough, 665, or Crumb**
> **Crust, 667, made with graham crackers**

Bake the crust as directed in About Baking Crusts Before Filling, 664, and About Crumb and Nut Crusts, 667
Position a rack in the center of the oven. Preheat the oven to 325°F. Whisk together until well blended:

> **One 15-ounce can sweetened condensed milk**
> **4 large egg yolks**
> 1/2 **cup Key lime juice (12 to 14 Key limes)**
> **(3 to 4 teaspoons grated Key lime zest)**

Pour the filling into the piecrust. If not topping the pie with meringue, bake the pie until the center looks set but quivers when the pan is jiggled, 15 to 17 minutes. Let cool completely on a rack, then refrigerate for up to 1 day. Serve with:

> **Whipped Cream, 754**

If topping the pie with meringue, bake the pie until the filling thickens just enough to support the topping, 5 to 7 minutes, but no longer. Meanwhile, prepare:

> **Soft Meringue Topping I or II, 798**

Spread a band of meringue around the edges of the filling, anchoring it to the crust at all points. Dollop the remaining meringue over the center and smooth the top. Bake for 20 minutes more. Let cool completely on a rack, then refrigerate for up to 1 day.

ABOUT CHIFFON AND MOUSSE PIES

These pies have a light and airy texture imparted by whipped cream, beaten egg whites, or marshmallows. Their lightness creates an impression of dessert without guilt—or nearly so. If the filling is based on a custard sauce stiffened with gelatin, you have a chiffon pie; otherwise the filling is a mousse. The secret is a gentle hand in folding the whipped cream, egg whites, or other aerated mixture into the filling. Mousse pies soften quickly at room temperature and become difficult to slice neatly, so leave them in the refrigerator until just before serving.

Many chiffon pies call for raw egg whites, so please see the note on uncooked eggs, 980. Bavarian Creams, 817–818, and Fruit Whips, 813, can also be served in a baked pie shell, 664.

LEMON OR LIME CHIFFON PIE

One 9-inch single-crust pie

Please read Rolling Pastry Dough and Shaping and Trimming Dough, 662–663.

Line a 9-inch pie pan with:

> 1/2 **recipe Basic Pie or Pastry Dough, 665, or 1 recipe**
> **any Pat-in-the-Pan Dough, 666–667, or Crumb**
> **Crust, 667**

Bake the crust as directed in About Baking Crusts Before Filling, 664, or Pat-in-the-Pan, 666–67, or Crumb Crust recipes, 667–68.

Please see note on uncooked eggs, 980.

Combine in the top of a double boiler:

> 1/2 **cup sugar**
> 2/3 **cup water**
> **4 egg yolks**

1 tablespoon gelatin
$^1/_3$ cup lemon or lime juice

Cook and stir these ingredients over—not in—boiling water until thick. Add:

1 tablespoon grated lemon or lime peel

Chill mixture in refrigerator until it forms little mounds when dropped from a spoon. Whip:

4 egg whites

until stiff, but not dry. Fold in:

$^1/_3$ cup sugar

Fold this mixture lightly in turn into the lemon mixture. Fill the pie crust. Chill until set, which may take several hours.

ORANGE CHIFFON PIE

Follow directions for **Lemon or Lime Chiffon Pie, 688**, substituting **fresh orange juice** for the water and lemon juice in the lemon curd, and **orange zest** for the lemon peel. Use only 1 teaspoon gelatin. Proceed as directed.

STRAWBERRY OR RASPBERRY BAVARIAN PIE

One 9-inch pie

Please read Rolling Pastry Dough and Shaping and Trimming Dough, 662–663.

Line a 9-inch pie pan with:

$^1/_2$ recipe Basic Pie or Pastry Dough, 665

Bake the crust as directed in About Baking Crusts before Filling, 662–663. When cool, fill with:

Bavarian Berry Cream, 818

BLACK BOTTOM PIE

One 10-inch pie

Please read Rolling Pastry Dough, 662, Shaping and Trimming Dough, 663, and About Crumb and Nut Crusts, 667. Line a 10-inch pie pan with:

Crumb Crust, 667, preferably made with gingersnaps

Pour into a small cup:

$^1/_4$ cup cold water

Sprinkle over the top and let stand for 5 minutes:

1$^1/_2$ teaspoons unflavored gelatin

Place in a small bowl:

6 ounces bittersweet or semisweet chocolate, finely chopped, or 1 cup semisweet chocolate chips

Whisk together thoroughly in a medium heavy saucepan:

$^1/_3$ cup sugar
4 teaspoons cornstarch

Gradually whisk in:

2 cups half-and-half or 1 cup milk plus
1 cup heavy cream

Vigorously whisk in until no yellow streaks remain:

4 large egg yolks

Stirring constantly, bring to a simmer over medium heat and cook for 30 seconds. Immediately stir 1 cup of the mixture into the chocolate. Add the softened gelatin to the mixture remaining in the pan and stir for 30 seconds to dissolve the gelatin. Vigorously stir the chocolate mixture

until smooth (if the chocolate fails to melt completely, set the bottom of the bowl in very hot water). Spread the chocolate mixture evenly over the bottom of the piecrust and refrigerate. Stir into the custard in the pan:

2 tablespoons dark rum
2 teaspoons vanilla

Beat in a large bowl until foamy:

3 large egg whites

Add:

$^1/_4$ teaspoon cream of tartar

Continue to beat until soft peaks form, then gradually beat in:

$^1/_3$ cup plus 1 tablespoon sugar

Increase the speed to high and beat until the peaks are stiff and glossy. Gently fold the egg whites into the custard mixture. Spoon the filling over the chocolate mixture in the piecrust. Refrigerate for at least 3 hours, or up to 1 day. Top with:

Whipped Cream, 754

made with:

$^1/_4$ cup confectioners' sugar
$^1/_2$ teaspoon vanilla

If you wish, sprinkle with:

(1 ounce bittersweet or semisweet chocolate, grated or shaved)

The pie can be refrigerated for up to 1 day.

PUMPKIN CHIFFON PIE

One 9-inch pie

Please read Rolling Pastry Dough and Shaping and Trimming Dough, 662–663.

Line a 9-inch pie pan with:

1$^1/_2$ recipe Basic Pie or Pastry Dough, 665, or 1 recipe Crumb Crust, 667, made with graham crackers

Bake the crust as directed in About Baking Crusts Before Filling, 664, or About Crumb and Nut Crusts, 667.

Soak:

1 tablespoon unflavored gelatin

in:

$^1/_4$ cup cold water

Lightly beat in the top of a double boiler:

3 large egg yolks

Add:

$^1/_2$ cup white or packed brown sugar
1$^1/_4$ cups cooked or canned pumpkin
$^1/_2$ cup milk
$^1/_2$ teaspoon salt
$^1/_4$ teaspoon ground cinnamon
$^1/_4$ teaspoon grated or ground nutmeg
$^1/_4$ teaspoon ground ginger

Cook and stir over, not in, boiling water until thickened. Stir in the soaked gelatin until dissolved. Chill until the mixture begins to set.

Whip in a large bowl until stiff but not dry, 978:

3 large egg whites

Gradually beat in:

1/2 **cup sugar**

Fold into the pumpkin mixture and fill the pie shell. Chill several hours to set.

Serve garnished with:

Whipped Cream, 754

ABOUT FRUIT PASTRIES

Here we include cobblers, deep-dish pies, fresh fruit cakes, upside-down cakes, crisps, brown Betties, slumps, grunts, and buckles. Remember that fresh fruit cakes such as kuchen also lend themselves well to baking for individual servings. This family of desserts is based on biscuit or pie dough, dumplings, bread crumbs, or crumbled toppings; the fruit may be cooked under, over, or inside the dough, or between dough layers. A few are adapted from European pastries, but most are American inventions, simple home cooking.

Deep-dish pies should be baked in dishes that are wide and shallow rather than narrow and deep, so that there is enough crust in relation to fruit. Most are best enjoyed the same day as they're made, and they can be reheated in a 350°F oven for 10 to 15 minutes until warm. Serve with ice cream, whipped cream, or with a pitcher of cream to pour on top.

The 10-inch dishes made expressly for deep-dish pies lack the flared rim of ordinary pie pans and are well suited for recipes made with up to 6 cups of fruit. For recipes with more generous fillings, choose a larger glass or ceramic casserole.

Any fruit pie in this chapter can be baked as a deep-dish pie. Since the filling need not be firm enough to slice— deep-dish pies are served with a spoon—you can reduce the thickening by up to half. For the top crust, use a half recipe of any pastry dough, 665–666, or a full recipe of Cream Cheese Pastry Dough, 666. Roll the dough the same shape as and a little wider than the top of the dish, lay it over the filling, and tuck the edges in against the inside of the dish. Cut steam vents in the top. If you wish, sprinkle the crust with sugar or glaze with an egg yolk beaten with 1/8 teaspoon water. Set the pie on a baking sheet and bake in the center of a preheated 375°F oven until the crust is nicely browned and juices bubble through the vents, about 40 to 60 minutes.

Kuchen is the generic German word for cake, but in America it refers specifically to a breakfast pastry or dessert filled with cheese or fruit and usually made from yeast dough. Our streamlined version, however, is raised with baking powder. Before baking, kuchen is sometimes topped with streusel. A **buckle** is another type of cake, with fruit folded into the batter before baking and a generous crumbly streusel topping. The cake buckles, or crumples, in spots from the weight of the topping before the batter sets, creating pockets of caramelized sugar and butter. Buckles may be kept covered at room temperature for up to 2 days or refrigerated for up to 3 days. (Remove from refrigerator 30 minutes before serving or reheat, cov-

ered with aluminum foil, in a 325°F oven until the center is warm, about 20 minutes.)

For a **crisp,** the flour, butter, and sugar are mixed together—like pie dough before the liquid is added—and the mixture scattered over the top of the fruit like a streusel or crumb topping. An approximate ratio of three parts fruit to one part topping makes a perfect crisp. Nobody remembers who Betty was, but a **brown Betty** is both layered and topped with sweet buttered crumbs. The crumbs should be dry, so that they will absorb the juices in the middle and bottom layers and remain crunchy on the top (for homemade bread crumbs, see 960). Another style of Betty blends a pastry-cream custard with the fruit, then layers the mixture with the crumbs.

APPLE PIE WITH CHEDDAR CRUST

One 9- or 10-inch deep dish pie

Prepare:

1/2 **recipe Deluxe Butter Pie or Pastry Dough, 665**

cutting in with the butter:

1 cup shredded Cheddar (about 4 ounces)

Flour the dough lightly, then roll into a 9- or 10-inch round between sheets of wax paper. Slip a cookie sheet beneath the dough and refrigerate until firm, about 30 minutes.

Preheat the oven to 375°F.

Peel, core, and slice 1/4 inch thick:

2 pounds apples (4 medium-large)

Heat over high heat in a very wide skillet (not cast iron) until sizzling and fragrant:

6 tablespoons (3/4 stick) unsalted butter

Add the apples and cook until just tender, 5 to 7 minutes; reduce the heat if the apples begin to color. Stir in:

(1 cup dark raisins)

1/2 **cup chopped walnuts or pecans**

1/2 **cup sugar**

Grated zest of 1 large lemon

Strained juice of 1 large lemon

1/4 **cup brandy or apple cider**

1/2 **teaspoon grated or ground nutmeg**

1/4 **teaspoon ground cinnamon**

1/4 **teaspoon ground cloves**

1/2 **teaspoon salt**

Bring to a boil and boil over medium-high heat, stirring occasionally, until the juices thicken to the consistency of maple syrup. Pour the mixture into a 9- or 10-inch deep-dish pie pan. Peel the top sheet of wax paper off the dough, then flip the dough onto the filling and peel off the bottom sheet. Let the dough soften slightly, then tuck the edges inside the rim of the pan, and cut two 2-inch steam vents.

Place the pie on a baking sheet and bake until the crust is golden brown and the filling is bubbly, 30 to 40 minutes. Let cool slightly before serving.

Accompany with:

Vanilla ice cream

FRESH FRUIT KUCHEN

One 9-inch round kuchen

This cake can be made with apricots, plums, cherries, raspberries, blueberries, or a combination, instead of the peaches or nectarines.

Position a rack in the lower third of the oven. Preheat the oven to 350°F. Grease a 9 x 2-inch round cake pan.

Prepare and set aside:

   Streusel Topping, 799

Peel, pit, and slice, then spread evenly in pan:

   1 pound ripe peaches or nectarines (3 cups sliced)

Whisk together:

   1 cup all-purpose flour
   1¹/₂ teaspoons baking powder
   ¹/₈ teaspoon salt
   (1 teaspoon grated lemon zest)

Beat in a large bowl until fluffy:

   ¹/₂ cup (1 stick) unsalted butter, softened
   ³/₄ cup sugar

Beat in one at a time just until blended:

   2 large eggs

Stir in the flour mixture just until incorporated. Scrape the batter into the pan and spread evenly. Scatter the streusel on top. Bake until the topping is golden brown and a toothpick inserted in the center of the cake (avoiding the fruit) comes out clean, 40 to 45 minutes. Let cool to room temperature on a rack.

BLUEBERRY AND PEACH BUCKLE

One 10-inch round or 9-inch square buckle

Position a rack in the lower third of the oven. Preheat the oven to 350°F. Butter and flour a 10 x 2-inch round cake pan or 9-inch square baking dish.

Prepare:

   Streusel Topping, 799

Halve, pit, and cut into small chunks:

   1 large ripe peach

Combine with:

   1¹/₂ cups blueberries or boysenberries

Whisk together:

   1³/₄ cups all-purpose flour
   2 teaspoons baking powder
   ¹/₂ teaspoon salt

Combine in another bowl and beat until slightly fluffy:

   ¹/₄ cup (¹/₂ stick) unsalted butter, softened
   1 cup sugar
   1 large egg

Gradually beat in:

   ¹/₂ cup milk

Add the flour mixture and stir just until the dry ingredients are moistened and the batter is smooth. Gently fold in the fruit. Spoon into the prepared pan and spread evenly. Sprinkle the topping evenly over the batter. Bake for 50 to 55 minutes, until the top springs back when touched and a toothpick inserted in the center comes out clean. Let cool in the pan on a rack for at least 20 minutes before serving.

APPLE, PEACH, OR PLUM CAKE COCKAIGNE

One 9- or 10-inch cake

An old JOY friend Jane Nickerson, former food editor of the *The New York Times,* suggested using fresh guavas in this dish. Still a family favorite.

Preheat the oven to 425°F. Grease a 9- or 10-inch round cake pan. Sift together into a bowl:

   1 cup all-purpose flour
   1 teaspoon baking powder
   2 tablespoons sugar
   ¹/₄ teaspoon salt

Add:

   1¹/₂ to 3 tablespoons cold unsalted butter

Using a pastry blender or 2 forks, cut the butter into the dry ingredients until the mixture resembles coarse cornmeal. Beat well in a measuring cup:

   1 large egg
   ¹/₂ teaspoon vanilla

Add:

   Enough milk to make ¹/₂ cup

(If the fruit used is very juicy, reduce the liquid by at least 1 tablespoon.) Stir into the flour and butter to make a stiff dough. You may pat the dough into the greased pan with your floured palm, or spread it in part with a spoon and then distribute it evenly by pushing it with the slices of fruit when you add them. Arrange on top of the dough in tight overlapping rows:

   4 cups sliced peeled apples or peaches or sliced plums

Combine and sprinkle over the fruit:

   1 cup white or packed brown sugar
   2 teaspoons ground cinnamon
   3 tablespoon unsalted butter, melted

Bake about 25 minutes, until tester comes out clean. Serve warm.

PINEAPPLE UPSIDE-DOWN CAKE

One 9-inch cake

Traditionally baked in a cast-iron skillet or "spider," this cake was devised to promote canned pineapple. The best variations we know are fresh apricots, peaches, or plums, cut into wedges, or ¹/₂-inch slices of tart apple with a few chopped walnuts between them and ¹/₄ teaspoon cinnamon mixed into the brown sugar topping. For a gooier topping (one of the joys of this cake), you have two options: Either increase the butter in the pan to 6 tablespoons and the brown sugar to 1 cup, or bake the cake in an 8-inch pan and increase only the butter to 4 tablespoons.

Preheat the oven to 350°F. Have ready a 9-inch skillet or a 9 x 2-inch round cake pan.

Drain and place in 1 layer on paper towels to absorb the excess juice:

   7 slices canned unsweetened pineapple (20-ounce can)

Place in the skillet or cake pan:

   3 tablespoons unsalted butter

Place the pan in the oven until the butter is melted, or melt it on the top of the stove. Tilt to coat all sides with butter. The extra butter will settle in the bottom of the pan. Sprinkle evenly over the bottom of the pan:

³/₄ cup packed brown sugar

Place 1 pineapple ring in the center of the pan and arrange 6 more around it. Place any of the following, best side down, in the center of each ring and in the spaces between them:

19 maraschino cherries or 19 pecan halves

Whisk together in a small bowl with a fork:

2 large eggs
2 tablespoons buttermilk
¹/₂ teaspoon vanilla

Whisk together in a mixer bowl or other large bowl:

1 cup all-purpose flour
³/₄ cup sugar
³/₄ teaspoon baking powder
¹/₄ teaspoon baking soda
¹/₄ teaspoon salt

Add:

6 tablespoons (³/₄ stick) unsalted butter, softened
6 tablespoons buttermilk

Beat on low speed just until the flour is moistened, then increase the speed to medium, or high if using a handheld mixer, and beat for exactly 1¹/₂ minutes. The batter will be stiff. Add one-third of the egg mixture at a time, beating for exactly 20 seconds and scraping the bowl after each addition. Scrape the batter over the fruit in the pan and spread evenly. Bake until a toothpick inserted in the cake comes out clean, 35 to 40 minutes. Remove the cake from the oven and tilt the pan in all directions to detach it from the sides of the pan. Let cool for 2 to 3 minutes before unmolding. Invert a serving platter on top of the pan. Cover your hands with oven mitts and turn the cake onto the platter. Lift off the pan. If any fruit or nut pieces are askew, use a fork to push them back into place. If any brown sugar is left in the pan, scrape it up and spoon it over the cake. Serve warm or cool.

APPLE OR FRUIT CRISP

6 to 8 servings

Select a tart, crisp apple to balance the sweetness of the topping. Gravenstein, Pippin, and Braeburn are good choices, but local apples in season may be the best choice of all.

Preheat the oven to 375°F. Have ready an unbuttered 2-inch-deep 2-quart baking dish. Peel, core, and cut into 1-inch chunks:

8 medium apples (about 2¹/₂ pounds)

Or use the same amount of:

Peaches, slightly sugared rhubarb or pitted cherries

Spread evenly in the baking dish.
Combine in a bowl:

³/₄ cup all-purpose flour
³/₄ cup white or packed brown sugar
¹/₂ teaspoon salt

1 to 1¹/₂ teaspoons ground cinnamon
(¹/₄ teaspoon grated or ground nutmeg)

Add:

¹/₂ cup (1 stick) cold unsalted butter, cut into small pieces

Using a pastry blender or 2 knives, cut the butter into the dry ingredients until the mixture resembles coarse bread crumbs. (This may also be done with a mixer or in a food processor, taking care not to blend the butter too thoroughly.) Scatter the topping evenly over the fruit. Bake until the topping is golden brown, the juices are bubbling, and the apples are tender, 50 to 55 minutes. Serve hot or cold with:

Whipped Cream, 754, or sour cream

APPLE ALMOND CRISP

Add **¹/₂ cup sliced almonds,** coarsely crumbled in your hand, with the flour.

QUICK CHERRY CRUNCH

One 9-inch square

A well-flavored, easy cherry dessert.
Butter a 9-inch square pan. Preheat oven to 350°F. Mix and let stand 15 minutes:

¹/₂ cup cherry juice
1¹/₂ tablespoons quick-cooking tapioca

Melt in a large pan:

¹/₂ cup unsalted butter

Mix with:

1 to 1¹/₂ cups packed brown sugar
1 cup all-purpose flour
1 cup quick-cooking oatmeal
¹/₄ teaspoon baking powder
¹/₄ teaspoon salt
¹/₄ teaspoon baking soda

Put half of this mixture into the baking pan. Scatter over it:

2 cups drained canned red cherries

and the juice and tapioca mixture. Cover the fruit with the other half of the pastry mixture. Bake 30 to 35 minutes or until brown.

APPLE BROWN BETTY

One 8-inch square

This also works well with peaches or pears, though the baking time may need to be adjusted.
Preheat the oven to 350°F. Have ready an unbuttered 8-inch square baking dish.
Peel, core, and slice:

1 pound apples (about 3 medium)

Stir together with a fork:

1¹/₂ cups dry bread crumbs
6 tablespoons (³/₄ stick) unsalted butter, melted

Whisk together:

1¹/₄ cups packed dark brown sugar
1 teaspoon ground cinnamon
¹/₄ teaspoon grated or ground nutmeg
¹/₄ teaspoon ground cloves

Have ready:

   5 tablespoons fresh lemon juice

Spread one-third of the crumb mixture evenly in the bottom of the baking dish. Distribute half of the apples in the dish. Sprinkle with half the sugar mixture, and then with:

   1$\frac{1}{2}$ tablespoons of the fresh lemon juice

Continue layering until you have used all the lemon juice and have three layers. Cover the dish with aluminum foil and bake until the apples are tender, about 40 minutes. Uncover the dish, increase the oven temperature to 400°F, and bake until browned, about 15 minutes. Serve warm in bowls with:

   Vanilla Bean Custard Sauce, 846, or vanilla ice cream

ABOUT COBBLERS

A cobbler, first cousin to a deep-dish pie, involves a rich biscuit dough and fruit. While neither tidy nor shapely, it is indisputably delectable, and a great way to get youngsters started on baking. Baked with the fruit either under the dough or occasionally over it, cobblers are usually served with rich cream, or Hard Sauce, 851. Or try warm blackberry cobbler with vanilla ice cream. Although almost any type of fruit or combination of fruits—such as apples, peaches, or plums—may be used, berries are traditional. Unsweetened frozen berries can be substituted when fresh ones are out of season; use them directly from the freezer without thawing, and increase the baking time as needed to cook the dough through.

COBBLER BISCUIT DOUGH

Prepare:

   Dough for Rolled Biscuits, 638, Buttermilk
   Biscuits, 639, or Fluffy Biscuits, 639

Dust the dough with a little flour, then roll or pat it with your hands to the shape of the top of the baking dish and between $\frac{1}{4}$ and $\frac{1}{2}$ inch thick. Cut the dough into circles, squares, rectangles, or wedges, or into 1-inch-wide strips for a lattice, or just trim the edges and leave it whole. You may also gently roll small pieces of the dough into balls, flatten each one slightly, and place on the fruit. If leaving the dough whole, cut 3 small steam vents. Place the biscuit dough on the fruit. Lightly brush the top with:

   1 to 2 tablespoons melted unsalted butter, heavy
   cream, milk, or lightly beaten egg

Sprinkle with:

   2 to 4 teaspoons sugar

Bake as directed in the individual recipe.

CORNMEAL COBBLER BISCUIT DOUGH

Prepare **Cobbler Biscuit Dough, above,** substituting $\frac{1}{3}$ **cup cornmeal** for $\frac{1}{3}$ cup of the flour.

SOUR CREAM COBBLER BISCUIT DOUGH

Prepare **Cobbler Biscuit Dough, above,** substituting a mixture of $\frac{3}{4}$ **teaspoon baking powder** and $\frac{1}{4}$ **teaspoon baking soda** for the baking powder, and a mixture of $\frac{1}{2}$ **cup sour cream** and $\frac{1}{4}$ **cup heavy cream** for the heavy cream or

milk. Whisk the creams together before adding to the flour mixture.

FRUIT AND BERRY COBBLER

6 to 8 servings

Position a rack in the lower third of the oven. Preheat the oven to 375°F. Have ready an unbuttered enameled cast-iron, earthenware, or glass baking dish of about 2-quart capacity and 2 inches deep.

Combine in any combination, equaling about 6 cups:

   Up to 3 pints blueberries, 1$\frac{3}{4}$ pounds ripe peaches,
   pitted and sliced, and/or, 2 cups fresh or unthawed
   frozen raspberries

Combine and toss with the berries:

   $\frac{1}{2}$ cup sugar
   2 tablespoons cornstarch or $\frac{1}{4}$ cup all-purpose flour
   1 teaspoon grated lime zest

Spread evenly in the baking dish. Prepare:

   Any of the Cobbler Biscuit Doughs, above

Roll or pat out and cut into desired shapes or shape into balls as described.

Arrange the dough over the fruit. Brush with a glaze and sprinkle with sugar. Bake until the top is golden brown and the juices have thickened slightly, 45 to 50 minutes. Let cool for 15 minutes before serving.

Serve in shallow bowls with:

   Chilled heavy cream, Whipped Cream, 754,
   or Lemon Sherbet, 838

ABOUT SLUMPS AND GRUNTS

Slumps and **grunts** are steamed fruit topped with dumplings. Grunts are steamed in a mold in a pot of water and inverted when served—somewhat resembling a warm fruit shortcake. Slumps are cooked in a covered saucepan and served dumpling side up in bowls—more like a hot, sweet soup or stew under dumplings. If the grunt is perhaps named for the sound it makes when unmolded, the name "slump" seems to describe the eventual fate of the dumplings. Grunts are best steamed in a soufflé dish, but pudding molds or heatproof bowls work as well; metal molds are not recommended, as they may impart a metallic taste. Cook slumps in stainless steel, enameled cast-iron, or glass saucepans, but make sure the vessel has a tight-fitting lid to contain the steam. If the pan is uncovered before the dumplings are done, they will collapse and be tough.

The origin of **pandowdy** is unknown but may refer to the act of "dowdying" the pastry—slashing or breaking the partially baked crust to submerge it in the juicy filling as it finishes baking.

These desserts are best served right away. If you need to wait 10 minutes or so before serving a slump, cover the saucepan with a clean dish towel, placed under the lid, to absorb excess moisture. Likewise, a grunt can be held in its mold for 30 minutes before unmolding. Serve either dessert in shallow bowls.

APRICOT CHERRY SLUMP

6 to 8 servings

Please read About Slumps and Grunts, 693.

Whisk together thoroughly in a medium bowl:

1¹/₂ cups all-purpose flour
2 teaspoons baking powder
¹/₂ teaspoon salt

Add and stir just until the dry ingredients are moistened:

1 cup milk
¹/₄ cup (¹/₂ stick) unsalted butter, melted

Combine in a large heavy-bottomed saucepan or Dutch oven with a tight-fitting lid and stir until the sugar is dissolved:

1 cup water
¹/₂ cup sugar

Halve and pit:

1 pound ripe apricots (about 8 medium)

Pit:

1 pound Bing cherries

Add the fruit to the sugar water, cover, and bring to a boil over high heat. Reduce the heat and simmer for about 10 minutes; do not lift the lid.

Remove the lid and quickly cover the fruit with spoonfuls of the batter. Replace the lid and simmer over low heat for 20 minutes. Check the dumplings for doneness (look quickly, so that little steam escapes). They should look firm and feel dry to the touch. If not, cover and continue steaming for 5 to 10 minutes more. Serve with:

Whipped Cream, 754, or lemon or vanilla yogurt

BLACKBERRY RASPBERRY GRUNT

6 to 8 servings

Also try this with blueberries or strawberries, in any combination of berries.

Please read About Slumps and Grunts, 693. Butter a 1¹/₂-quart baking dish, such as a soufflé dish or pudding mold. Have ready a covered Dutch oven or pot large enough to hold the soufflé dish or mold with ample room around it.

Toss together:

1 pint raspberries
1 pint blackberries
¹/₂ cup sugar

Pour into the buttered mold and spread evenly. Whisk together thoroughly:

1¹/₄ cups all-purpose flour
2 tablespoons sugar
1¹/₄ teaspoons baking powder
¹/₂ teaspoon salt

Add:

3 tablespoons cold unsalted butter, cut into
**   small pieces**

Using a pastry blender or 2 knives, cut the butter into the dry ingredients until the mixture resembles coarse crumbs. Add:

¹/₂ cup milk

Stir just until the dry ingredients are moistened. Lightly flour your hands and gather the dough into a ball. Knead it gently against the sides of the bowl, turning and pressing any loose pieces into the dough until they adhere. Dust the top and bottom of the dough with a little flour. On a work surface, pat the dough into a round just large enough to cover the top of the fruit. Cover the fruit with the dough. Tear off a piece of aluminum foil large enough to cover the top and reach halfway down the sides of the mold. Butter an area in the center of the foil the same size as the dough. Cover the mold with foil, butter side down, and press the foil against the outside of the mold. Tie a string or fasten a rubber band around the foil to secure it. Place a second piece of foil, folded in half, in the bottom of the Dutch oven. Set the mold on the foil. Place a plate on top of the mold. Cover the pot with a tight-fitting lid and simmer for 1¹/₂ hours, replenishing the water as needed to maintain the water level.

Carefully remove the mold from the Dutch oven. Remove the plate. Cut the string and carefully remove the foil. Run the knife around the biscuit to loosen it from the sides of the dish. Carefully unmold the dessert onto a large platter deep enough to hold the juices. Serve warm.

APPLE OR PEAR PANDOWDY

6 to 8 servings

Serve the pandowdy warm, with heavy cream, whipped cream, vanilla yogurt, or ice cream. To reheat, cover with aluminum foil and warm in a 325°F oven.

Please read About Slumps and Grunts, 693.

Position a rack in the lower third of the oven. Preheat the oven to 400°F. Have ready an unbuttered 8-inch square baking dish. Prepare:

¹/₂ recipe Deluxe Butter Pie or Pastry Dough, 665,
**   or Basic Pie or Pastry Dough, 665**

On a lightly floured surface, roll out the dough into a 9-inch square. Place on a cookie sheet, cover with plastic wrap, and refrigerate while you prepare the filling.

Peel, halve, core, and cut into ¹/₄-inch-thick slices:

2 pounds apples (4 medium) or ripe pears

Combine in a bowl with:

¹/₂ cup maple syrup, molasses, packed brown sugar,
**   or white sugar**
2 tablespoons cornstarch or 3 tablespoons
**   all-purpose flour**
¹/₂ teaspoon ground cinnamon
¹/₄ teaspoon grated or ground nutmeg
¹/₄ teaspoon salt
¹/₈ teaspoon ground allspice

Spread the mixture evenly in the baking pan. Dot with:

2 tablespoons unsalted butter, cut into small pieces

Remove the dough from the refrigerator and let stand for a few minutes, until pliable, then arrange the dough over the top of the apples. Tuck the edges of the dough into the dish. Bake until the top has browned lightly, about 30 minutes.

Remove the dish from the oven, and reduce the oven temperature to 350°F. With a knife, score the crust into 2-inch squares. Baste the crust squares by tilting the pan and spooning the juices over them; or submerge the squares in the juices with the back of a spoon.

Return the dish to the oven and bake until the fruit is tender when pierced with a skewer, the filling has thickened slightly, and the crust is golden brown, about 30 minutes more. Let cool for 15 minutes before serving.

BLUEBERRY PANDOWDY

Prepare **Apple Pandowdy, 694,** using $^1/_2$ recipe Cornmeal Pie or Pastry Dough, 665, for the crust. Substitute **3 pints blueberries, raspberries, or blackberries, or a combination,** for the apples, and use **light brown sugar.** Use $^1/_4$ **teaspoon cinnamon** and omit the nutmeg and allspice. Do not dot the fruit with butter.

CHERRY CLAFOUTI

6 to 8 servings

A clafouti is a simple French country dessert. It is similar to an old American dessert called batter pudding and is made with of a quick batter poured over fresh fruit.

Please read About Slumps and Grunts, 693.

Preheat the oven to 375°F. Butter a 10-inch deep-dish pie pan. Beat in a medium bowl until frothy, about 2 minutes:

   4 large eggs
   $^3/_4$ cup sugar

Add and beat until smooth:

   1 cup milk
   (1 tablespoon Cognac or rum)
   1$^1/_2$ teaspoons vanilla

Stir in:

   $^3/_4$ cup all-purpose flour
   Pinch of salt

Distribute over the bottom of the pie pan:

   1 pound sweet cherries, pitted (frozen cherries, thawed and patted dry, or canned cherries, drained and dried, can be used)

Pour the batter over the cherries, and place the pie pan on a baking sheet. Bake the clafouti for 10 minutes. Reduce the oven temperature to 350°F and bake until the top has puffed (it will sink on cooling) and a toothpick inserted in the center comes out clean, about 35 minutes. Cool for about 20 minutes before serving.

ABOUT FRUIT DUMPLINGS AND TURNOVERS

Any pie dough, puff pastry, or biscuit dough can be used to make fruit dumplings or turnovers. Dumplings are formed by gathering the edges of the dough up around the filling like a purse or pouch; the resulting packets may be baked or boiled. (The texture of baked pastry contrasts particularly nicely with the filling.) Turnovers are made by folding the dough over the filling and can be formed in any size from miniature to large. The dough can be made

well ahead and kept chilled until ready to use. These little "pies" are best eaten the day they are baked.

APPLE DUMPLINGS

6 dumplings

You may substitute jam or preserves for the brown sugar filling.

Please read About Fruit Dumplings and Turnovers, above.

Prepare:

   1 recipe Fluffy or Shortcake Biscuit Dough, 639, Cream Cheese Pastry Dough, 666, or $^1/_2$ recipe Basic Pie or Pastry Dough, 665, or Deluxe Butter Pie or Pastry Dough, 665

Refrigerate at least 30 minutes.

Preheat the oven to 425°F. Generously butter a baking dish with sides large enough to hold the dumplings with 1 to 2 inches between each one, such as an 11 x 7-inch rectangular dish or a 12-inch oval gratin dish. Peel and core:

   6 small apples (about 4 ounces each)

Or peel, halve lengthwise, and core:

   3 large apples (about 8 ounces each)

Mix with a fork in a small bowl until blended:

   $^1/_2$ cup packed dark brown sugar
   1 teaspoon ground cinnamon
   $^1/_4$ teaspoon salt

Add and mix well:

   $^1/_4$ cup ($^1/_2$ stick) unsalted butter, softened

Fill the whole apples with the mixture, and pat any remaining mixture on top of the fruit, or, if using apple halves, fill the hollows with the mixture and reserve any remaining mixture. On a lightly floured surface, roll the dough into an 18 x 12-inch rectangle about $^1/_8$ inch thick. Cut into six 6-inch squares, then roll each square a little larger, into a 7-inch square. Lightly brush with:

   1 egg, lightly beaten

Place an apple in the middle of each square. If using apple halves, place cored side down and spread the remaining sugar mixture over the rounded tops of the apples. For each square, bring the 4 corners of the dough up around the apple and pinch the corners and edges of the dough together. Prick the top of each pastry several times with a fork. Place in the baking dish and bake for 10 minutes. While the dumplings bake, make the syrup. Whisk together in a saucepan:

   1 cup water
   $^1/_2$ cup packed light brown sugar
   1 teaspoon ground cinnamon
   $^1/_4$ teaspoon salt

Add:

   2 tablespoons unsalted butter
   1 small lemon, thinly sliced and seeded

Bring to a boil and boil for 5 minutes. Pour the boiling syrup over the dumplings when they begin to color, 10 to 15 minutes into the cooking time. Reduce the oven temperature to 350°F and bake until the apples are tender when pierced with a small knife or toothpick, 30 to 35 minutes more. Baste the apples with the syrup every 10 minutes or so to form a glaze and flavor the crust. Let cool slightly. Serve warm with:

Heavy cream, softly whipped cream,
or vanilla ice cream

SWEET FRUIT TURNOVERS

To shape these tea pastries, see Filled Cookies, 777
Please read About Fruit Dumplings and Turnovers, 695.
Preheat the oven to 450°F. Prepare:

Food Processor Puff Pastry, 669 or 1 recipe Deluxe
Butter Pie Dough, 665, or Pastry Dough, 665

After cutting the dough into shapes, place in the center of each pastry 1 teaspoonful or more of one of the following fillings:

Well-flavored applesauce
Preserves or jam
Mincemeat, 902
Any Filled Cookie Filling, 777–778

Brush the edges of each turnover lightly with water. Fold the dough over into triangles or half-moons and press the edges to seal. Place 1½ inches apart on greased baking sheets. Brush the tops with:

1 egg yolk, beaten with 2 tablespoons heavy cream

Bake for about 20 minutes, or until golden brown. While they are still warm, dust the pastries with:

Confectioners' sugar

APPLE OR PEAR TURNOVERS

8 turnovers

Cut in half:

1 pound Food Processor Puff Pastry, 669, or 1 recipe
Deluxe Butter Pie or Pastry Dough, 665

Roll each portion of dough into an 11-inch square, about ⅛ inch thick, place on a baking sheet, and refrigerate. Peel, core, and cut into ¼-inch dice:

1 pound apples (about 3), or pears

Toss well with:

¼ cup sugar
1 teaspoon all-purpose flour
½ teaspoon ground cinnamon
¼ teaspoon fresh lemon juice
Pinch of salt

Transfer the pastry squares to a cutting board and trim ½ inch from all sides to make two 10-inch squares. Cut each into four 5-inch squares (or circles if you prefer, using a large cutter). Turn each piece upside down. Spoon the apple mixture, dividing it equally, onto the center of the pastry squares. Lightly brush a ½-inch border on 2 adjacent edges of each pastry square with:

1 large egg, lightly beaten

Form a triangular turnover by folding the dry corner of each square over the apples to the egg-washed corner; press the edges together with the tines of a fork to seal them. Brush the top of each turnover with egg wash, and

cut 3 small slits in the top of each one. Arrange the turnovers at least 1 inch apart on 2 ungreased baking sheets, and refrigerate for about 30 minutes. Position a rack in the lower third of the oven. Preheat the oven to 425°F. Bake the turnovers until they begin to brown, about 15 minutes. Reduce the oven temperature to 350°F and bake until golden, about 20 minutes more. Serve warm.

LINZERTORTE

One 9½-inch torte

Named after the Austrian town of Linz, the traditional linzertorte is a lattice-top tart made with a rich nut crust and filled with raspberry or currant jam. Other jams, preserves, and marmalades can be substituted, as can fruit butters. Linzertorte actually improves in flavor if it stands for 2 to 3 days after baking, and it keeps for at least 1 week.
Whisk thoroughly in a large bowl:

1⅓ cups all-purpose flour
1 cup slivered almonds or whole hazelnuts,
toasted, 1001, and finely ground
½ cup granulated sugar
(1 tablespoon unsweetened cocoa powder)
1 teaspoon ground cinnamon
¼ teaspoon ground cloves
¼ teaspoon salt

Add:

10 tablespoons (1¼ sticks) unsalted butter, softened
2 large egg yolks
Grated zest of 1 lemon

Mix on low speed with an electric mixer until a smooth dough forms. Press the dough into a flat disk, wrap in plastic, and refrigerate for at least 2 hours, or up to 2 days. Let the dough stand at room temperature until malleable but firm, about 30 minutes.
Position a rack in the center of the oven. Preheat the oven to 350°F. Have ready a 9½- or 10-inch two-piece tart pan. Set aside one-quarter of the dough for the lattice. Press the remaining dough evenly into the bottom and up the sides of the tart pan; see 661. Roll the remaining dough between 2 sheets of plastic wrap or wax paper into a 10-inch square. Remove the top sheet of plastic or paper and cut the dough into 8 to 12 strips of equal width. If the strips are too soft to handle, refrigerate or freeze them until firm.
Spread evenly in the crust in the pan:

1 to 1½ cups raspberry jam

The layer of jam should be about ¼ inch thick. Carefully arrange half of the dough strips on the tart at equal distance from each other; pinch the ends onto the crust. Arrange the remaining strips on top at right angles to those beneath, forming a crisscross lattice. If the strips break during handling, simply piece them together; they will fuse during baking.
Bake until the lattice is golden brown, 40 to 45 minutes. Let cool completely on a rack. The torte can be wrapped

airtight, still on the pan bottom, and stored in the refrigerator for up to 1 week or frozen for up to 1 month. Serve at room temperature.

ABOUT GALETTES, CROSTATAS, AND DESSERT PIZZAS

A galette (French) or crostata (Italian) is a free-form tart baked on a cookie sheet rather than a pie or tart pan. Galettes and crostatas may be made with a flat crust of pastry, baked with sweetened fruit on top. Or, if the fruit is juicy, the sides of the pastry can be folded over part of the fruit filling to keep in the juices. To make a dessert pizza, the pastry crust is baked alone and then topped with a layer of jam, sweetened whipped cream or pastry cream, and fresh fruit.

GALETTE DOUGH

There are as many recipes as there are cooks in France for this classic pastry, and even if they could agree on just a few, they'd have to negotiate all over again with the pastry cooks of Italy, who call the free-form flat tart made with the dough a crostata.

Our version of galette dough, which, we hope, will merit majority approval, is a round of Deluxe Butter or Pie Pastry Dough, 665, rolled thick, coated with jam or butter.
➤ Keep the glaze on top surface only, for if it runs over the edges, it will set and prevent the dough from puffing as it should.

An alternative is to use a yeast coffee cake dough. After the last rising, pat it out thin and make a rim by pinching the dough edges all around. Put the fruit in the depression and cover it with a Streusel, 799. Bake as directed for bread. You may, as the cake cools, cover it with Apricot Glaze, 800. Another, we think, delicious solution is simply to bake Apple, Peach, or Plum Cake Cockaigne, 691.

FRUIT GALETTE OR CROSTATA

8 servings

Prepare:

$^1/_2$ **recipe Deluxe Butter Pie or Pastry Dough, 665**

Position a rack in the lower third of the oven. Preheat the oven to 375°F.

Roll the dough into an 11-inch round; see 662. Lift the dough onto a large baking sheet. Leaving a 1-inch border at the edges, spread evenly over the dough:

$^1/_4$ **cup raspberry or other jam**

Fold over the border to form a rim. Toss together gently:

4 medium plums, 2 medium peaches, peeled,
or 2 medium nectarines, pitted and cut into
$^1/_2$**-inch pieces**

($^1/_2$ cup raspberries or blueberries)

2 tablespoons sugar

4 teaspoons all-purpose flour

Distribute the fruit mixture over the jam. Bake until the crust is golden brown and the fruit juices have thickened, 25 to 35 minutes. Serve warm.

APPLE GALETTE OR CROSTATA

8 servings

Prepare:

$^1/_2$ **recipe Deluxe Butter Pie or Pastry Dough, 665**

Position a rack in the lower third of the oven. Preheat the oven to 425°F.

Roll the dough into an 11- to 12-inch round; see 662. Transfer the dough to a baking sheet. Brush the pastry with a thin coat of:

3 tablespoons unsalted butter, melted and
cooled to lukewarm

Reserve the rest of the butter. Sprinkle the pastry with:

1 tablespoon sugar

Peel, core, and slice $^1/_8$ inch thick:

2 large firm apples, such as Golden Delicious

Leaving a 1-inch border at the edges, arrange the apple slices in slightly overlapping concentric rings on the pastry. Fold the border of dough over the edges of the apples. Brush or drizzle all but about 2 teaspoons of the remaining melted butter over the apples. Combine, then sprinkle over the apples:

3 tablespoons sugar

$^1/_8$ **teaspoon ground cinnamon**

Bake until the pastry begins to color, 15 to 20 minutes. Reduce the oven temperature to 350°F and bake until the pastry is golden brown, 5 to 10 minutes more. Brush the apples with the reserved butter, and serve warm or at room temperature.

DESSERT PIZZA

4 to 6 servings

Prepare:

$^1/_2$ **recipe Basic Pie or Pastry Dough, 665, Pie Dough**
Cockaigne, 665, or Deluxe Butter Pie or Pastry
Dough, 665, or 1 recipe Cream Cheese Pastry
Dough, 666

Position a rack in the middle of the oven. Preheat the oven to 400°F.

Roll the dough into a 10-inch circle, 662, and place on a large rimless cookie sheet. Bake until golden brown, about 15 minutes. Let cool completely on a rack.

Spread the pastry with:

$^1/_3$ **cup jam (strawberry or raspberry), $^1/_2$ recipe**
Pastry Cream, 755, or $^1/_2$ cup Whipped Cream, 754

leaving a 1-inch border all around. Arrange over the cream:

2 cups berries (any assortment) or sliced peaches,
plums, or nectarines

Refrigerate until ready to serve. The pizza is best served the day it's made.

CAKES AND CUPCAKES

If you wish to be glamorous, become a cake baker. It is a simple accomplishment, rewarding beyond its desserts! At birthdays and weddings, as well as on other more casual occasions, a cake is frequently the center of interest, and this interest has been known to extend to the cook.

A cake should be a treat to the eye and the palate, but good or bad, it is unfailingly reliable as a conversation piece. Whether you bake a cake as a gift for a friend, bake a batch of cupcakes for a bake sale, or hand a pan of gingerbread over a back fence, the gesture is one of fellowship that adds to your stature and enriches your life. Besides, cake baking is fun. If time is short, whip up a Lightning Cake, 722, which can be eaten warm from the oven, with its baked-on garnish of cinnamon, sugar, and nuts, or Honey Bee Glaze, 799. On more leisurely days, make a perfectly textured Pound Cake, 716, which needs only a dusting of confectioners' sugar to complete it with simple elegance. As a birthday treat, bake a Fresh Coconut Milk Cake Cockaigne, 713, and highlight it with one tactful candle. For other special occasions, you may want to try your hand at a classic Bûche de Noël (Yule Log Cake), 737, or a Black Forest Cake, 733. The fame of many a host or hostess can still be built on "that great cake."

For all these cakes, start with high-quality ingredients. Because a cake baker is unable to taste and correct along the way, you must pay careful attention to ➤ pan sizes, measurements, and the temperature of everything, including the ingredients and ➤ the heat of the oven. ➤ Pay attention also to the physical states you induce by stirring, creaming, and folding. Our drawings and descriptions can do no more than get you off to a flying start. You will learn to recognize the proper "look" of well-creamed butter and eggs, of batter ready for the oven, and of other critical stages in cake making most effectively through practice.

CAKE TYPES

We divide cakes according to their leaveners. If you know what makes them rise, it will help you to safeguard this lifting action during the mixing period. Angel and sponge cakes are sometimes called ➤ foam cakes, because they depend exclusively on the expansion of the vapor trapped in their egg-rich batters for leavening. Egg yolks contain fat, egg whites do not. Consequently, angel cakes are fat-free, ➤ but sponge cakes, though light in texture, contain an appreciable amount of fat by way of their yolk content.

➤ Butter cakes need baking powder for proper leavening. We feel that most cakes in this category are more delicious if butter alone is used as the fat. One exception may be spice cakes, where the strong flavors can overwhelm the taste of butter. If you care to use vegetable shortening, you will trade distinctive flavor for a measure of economy, a spongier texture, and somewhat greater volume.

In cakes made with ➤ melted butter, such as the classic Génoise, 709, the butter is put in last. In cakes made with oils, special mixing procedures are employed to allow the incorporation of air into the batter.

Tortes often depend on egg yolks instead of butter for their fat content and on egg whites for their leavening; ground nuts and bread crumbs replace flour as their base. Our cake recipes are all adjusted in method to the specific demands of the ingredients. So, for success, please follow directions as given.

➤ All these cake types may be frozen, see 702, but will dry out rapidly after thawing.

▲ To bake cakes at high altitude, see 746.

MEASURING AND SIFTING

Nowhere else in cooking is accurate measuring as important as in baking. While some recipes are more forgiving than others, you will not achieve consistently excellent results in cake making with haphazard measurement.

In baking cakes, flour is often sifted before measuring in order to make volume measurement more consistent. Even if the flour package says "presifted," be sure to sift when so directed in a recipe. Before measuring unsifted flour, stir or whisk flour in the bag or container to lighten it. One cup of unsifted all-purpose flour weighs 5 ounces, while 1 cup of sifted all-purpose flour weighs only 4 ounces—a big difference! To measure flour, sifted or unsifted, do not pack the flour into the measuring cup— simply spoon it in lightly and level it by sweeping a knife across the top of the cup. Measure small quantities of dry ingredients, such as leavenings, with measuring spoons, leveling them off. Use clear liquid measuring cups for measuring liquids. Check the level of the liquid at eye level—looking down at the cup will not give accurate results unless using a cup designed to be read from the top down. For more about measuring, see 1031.

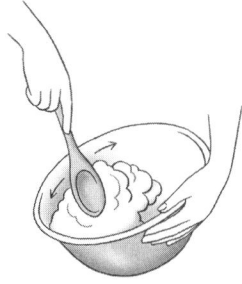

Creaming and mixing cake batter by hand

ABOUT THE TEMPERATURE OF INGREDIENTS

In general, before starting to bake, all ingredients should be at room temperature (68° to 70°F). This is especially important with butter cake recipes, where the butter, liquid, and eggs are intended to form an emulsion during the mixing steps. Emulsions can break or curdle (like a sauce) if some ingredients are colder than the others. When this happens, the batter loses its ability to trap air, and the cake will be heavy.

Butter should still be cool—from 60° to 70°F—but malleable when squeezed, not soft and squishy. Butter that is too soft or melted will not trap air and the batter will collapse with prolonged beating.

Cold eggs do not increase in volume when beaten as much as room-temperature or warm eggs, and when they are too cold, they won't blend smoothly into batters containing large quantities of melted chocolate.

Transform cold dairy products into room-temperature ingredients quickly by judiciously using the microwave, a few seconds at a time, on low power or "defrost." Break eggs and separate the eggs and whites or beat them lightly before microwaving, and stir before checking the temperature each time. Liquids at 68° to 70°F feel quite cool, not warm, to the touch. If you are not sure of what this temperature feels like, an inexpensive instant-read thermometer can be used to verify your judgment. If you don't have a microwave, place whole eggs or a bowl of broken eggs in a bowl of warm water to bring them to room temperature. Do the same for liquids.

MIXING CAKE BATTERS

Whether you mix a cake by hand or with an electric mixer (often you will do both for the same recipe), mixing affects leavening and, therefore, the volume and texture of a cake. Different methods of mixing, creaming, stirring, beating, and folding are used for different ingredients and with different goals.

There are two kinds of mixers, **heavy-duty stand (stationary)** and **hand-held (portable)**. Mixing times and speeds are given for both. Hand-held mixers are fine for most jobs—mixing cake batters, cookie doughs, frostings—but are not effective for stiff doughs. Beaters made of thin wires do a better job of getting into corners, are less likely to become clogged with thick cookie doughs, and whip ingredients more quickly than those with wider blades. Some models come with a whisk attachment for whipping cream. Consider a cordless model if your favorite work space is far from an outlet.

Heavy-duty stand mixers are the best for aerating cake batters or handling larger quantities of frosting; they are best for kneading stiff pastry and bread doughs. Stand mixers usually have one large stationary bowl with a beater that spins. Most come with an open paddle for cake batters, a whisk for whipping egg whites or cream, and a dough hook. We do not recommend a blender or a food processor in place of an electric mixer when making cakes.

Times and speeds are given to provide guidance. However, the most important signals are in the bowl. Learning to bake is learning to recognize when egg yolks and sugar

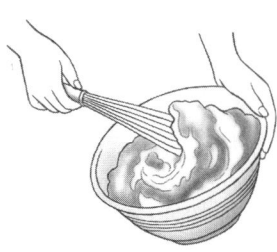

Folding egg whites into cake batter

are "thick and pale yellow" or when butter beaten with sugar has "lightened in color and texture," regardless of the clock or the mixer setting.

➤ Creaming butter and sugar is the essential first step in mixing butter cakes: The butter and sugar are beaten together until the mixture appears lighter in color, smooth, even, and creamy or fluffy, because of the incorporation of air. While creaming the sugar crystals cut air holes in the fat; these holes, or air bubbles, are essential because they will expand with leavening gases during baking, enabling the cake to rise. ➤ Regular granulated sugar, not confectioners' or superfine sugar, must be used. Well-creamed butter and sugar creates the initial structure of the batter, enabling the addition of other ingredients without causing that structure to collapse.

To cream by hand, mash the butter against the side of the bowl with the back of a wooden spoon, using a gliding motion and keeping the butter in a limited area of the bowl rather than spreading it all over. Scrape the mass together as necessary and repeat the gliding motion until the butter is softened. Add the sugar gradually and work the butter and sugar together until the mixture is light in color and smooth, even, and creamy in texture. It will look like sugary frosting. If it looks curdled or frothy, or begins to ooze melted butter, you have worked it too long and the oil in the butter has separated. The result will be a coarse-grained cake. Correct the situation by refrigerating the mixture for 5 to 10 minutes before continuing to beat.

To cream with an electric mixer, beat the butter at low speed for about 30 seconds, until creamy. Add the sugar gradually and beat at high speed until the mixture is light in color, smooth, even, and creamy in texture and resembles a sugary frosting. This usually requires from 3 to 7 minutes, depending on quantities. If using a heavy-duty mixer that offers a choice between a whisk and paddle, use the paddle and beat on medium speed for less time.

Stirring is used to incorporate dry and/or wet ingredients gently but thoroughly into another mixture without overmixing or beating. **To stir by hand,** use a wooden spoon or rubber spatula, begin at the center of the bowl, mixing with a circular motion; widen the circle as the ingredients become blended. Scrape the sides of the bowl from time to time as necessary. The entire operation of adding and blending the dry and liquid ingredients should not take more than 2 minutes. **To stir by machine,** mix at low speed, just until the ingredients are smoothly blended. Do not overmix.

To beat or whip by hand, ➤ use a long, free-swinging, lifting motion that brings the bottom mass constantly to the top, trapping air in the batter and increasing its volume. Use a long, thin or balloon-shaped whisk for beating cream or egg whites; use a wooden spoon or rubber spatula for batters. Whipping is done rapidly, with increasing tempo. Your wrist should move as though you were twirling a lasso, and you should hear the utensil striking the bottom of the bowl with each stroke. For best results

in handling egg whites, use a long, thin whip. For beating cream, use a wider whisk. In choosing an electric mixer, see that the beaters have many wires that are as thin as is consistent with durability.

To beat by machine, beat on medium to high speed until the desired state, smoothness, or volume is reached. If you have a choice of whip or paddle attachment on your mixer, choose the whip for egg whites and cream and the paddle for batters and doughs.

Folding egg whites into a batter is a delicate operation. The object is to blend thoroughly yet not lose any of the air you have incorporated into the ingredients. It is always done by hand, with a large rubber or silicone spatula, rather than with an electric mixer. ➤ To fold, first of all make sure the bowl is large enough. Scoop the beaten whites onto the batter. Use the edge of the spatula to cut down through the middle of the egg whites to the bottom of the bowl. Sweep the spatula up against the side of the bowl, scooping up batter from the bottom of the bowl and bringing it to the top. Repeat the folding stroke, rotating the bowl slightly with the other hand each time you repeat the folding motion until the batter is uniform.

ABOUT CAKE PANS

If you want a thin, evenly browned crust, ➤ sturdy medium-weight aluminum pans with dull surfaces or non-stick finishes are best. Avoid stainless steel, which does not conduct heat evenly. Heavy dark metal and glass pans absorb and hold more heat, resulting in heavier, darker crusts. If you bake in these pans, ➤ reduce the oven temperature by 25 degrees but expect the baking time to be approximately the same. In any case, pan materials affect baking time, so always check cakes early to be safe. When baking layer cakes, use pans with straight sides. Fill no more than one-half to two-thirds full. Loaf and tube pans can be filled a little fuller.

The best results in each recipe will be achieved by using the pan size(s) specified. If you bake in a larger pan, you will have a thinner cake that will bake in less time; if the sides of the pan are too tall, the cake may not brown well. If you bake in a pan that is too small, you will have a coarse-textured cake or one that overflows the pan.

If you do not have a pan that corresponds to the size and shape called for in the recipe, see the chart on page 701 to find a pan with a similar surface or square-inch area, and substitute a pan of that approximate size. A recipe calling for a 9-inch round pan (about 64 square inches) can be baked in an 8-inch square pan (also 64 square inches). ➤ A 9-inch round pan equals only about three-quarters of the capacity of a 9-inch square pan. A recipe that calls for two 9-inch layer pans can be baked in one 13 x 9-inch pan, but it will come out slightly higher than the individual layers (64 inches × 2 is 128 inches, while the 13 x 9-inch pan has an area of 117 inches). Should a square or rectangular pan be too large, you can reduce the size of it with a divider made of folded aluminum foil, as shown. The batter holds

Reducing the pan size with an aluminum foil divider,
weighted on one side

the divider in place on one side. Dried beans or rice can be
used to support the other side.

The texture of butter cakes, especially, varies with the
depth of the batter in the pan. Thin layers baked in separate pans turn out with a lighter texture but are prone to
drying out. The same cakes baked in loaf pans or tube
pans, either plain or fluted, are usually moister and more
velvety but denser. Home bakers are accustomed to dividing batters for layer cakes between 2 or 3 separate shallow
pans. If you prefer a moister, denser texture, you can bake
a layer cake in one 3-inch-tall springform pan of the same
diameter. The finished cake, 2 to 3 inches tall, is then cut
horizontally into thin layers, 753. Remember that the baking time for a deeper cake will be longer.

Pans from different manufacturers differ in exact measurement, and pan capacities vary depending on whether
the pan sides are straight or flared. For the chart pans are
measured across the top between the inside edges. The
capacities are approximate.

ABOUT SPECIAL CAKE PAN SHAPES

Whatever the mood or occasion, there's a cake pan to suit,
with shapes from rabbits to rocket ships. Fill these pans no
more than two-thirds full of batter, bake at the temperature called for, and use the test for doneness described in
the recipe. To determine how much batter to mix for an
oddly shaped pan, first measure the volume with water.
Using a liquid measuring cup, pour water by the cupful
into the pan until it is full to the brim. Then calculate two-
thirds of that amount for your batter. In general, recipes
that call for two 8- or 9-inch round layer pans or an 8- to
10-cup plain or fluted tube pan make 6 to 7 cups of batter.
Recipes that call for three 8- or 9-inch round layer pans
make 8 to 9 cups batter. Recipes that call for a 6-cup fluted

ROUND LAYER CAKE PANS AND SPRINGFORM PANS WITH STRAIGHT SIDES

Size	Surface Area in Square Inches	Capacity
6 x 2 inches	28	$3^3/_4$ cups
8 x 2 inches	50	7 cups
8 x $2^1/_2$- or 8 x 3-inch springform	50	10–11 cups
9 x 2 inches	63	$8^2/_3$ cups
9 x $2^1/_2$- or 9 x 3-inch springform	63	10–12 cups
10 x 2 inches	79	$10^3/_4$ cups
10 x $2^1/_2$- or 10 x 3-inch springform	79	12–14 cups
12 x 2 inches	113	$15^1/_2$ cups
14 x 2 inches	154	21 cups

SQUARE, RECTANGULAR, AND JELLY-ROLL PANS WITH STRAIGHT OR TAPERED SIDES

Size	Surface Area in Square Inches	Capacity
8 x 8 x 2 inches	64	$8^3/_4$ cups
9 x 9 x 2 inches	81	11 cups
11 x 7 x 2 inches	77	8 cups
13 x 9 x 2 inches	117	15 cups
$15^1/_2$ x $10^1/_2$ x 1-inch jelly roll	163	10 cups
17 x $11^1/_2$ x 1-inch jelly roll	201	13 cups

PLAIN AND FLUTED TUBE PANS

Size	Capacity
$6^1/_4$ x $3^1/_4$-inch fluted tube	5 cups
$8^1/_4$ x $3^1/_4$-inch fluted tube	6–7 cups
8 x 4-inch fluted tube	8–10 cups
10 x $3^1/_4$-inch fluted tube	12 cups
9 x 3-inch plain tube	9–10 cups
$9^1/_2$ x $4^1/_4$-inch plain tube (angel cake pan)*	16–17 cups
Conventionally described as 10 x 4-inch plain tube	

LOAF PANS

Size	Capacity
$5^1/_2$ x 3 x 2 inches	2 cups
$7^1/_2$ x $3^3/_4$ x $2^1/_4$ inches	4 cups
$8^1/_2$ x $4^1/_2$ x $2^1/_2$ inches	6 cups
9 x 5 x 3 inches	8 cups
10 x 4 x 3 inches	$7^1/_2$ cups

tube pan yield about 4 cups of batter. Recipes that call for an 8-inch square pan make 4 to 5 cups of batter.

ABOUT PAN PREPARATION

Angel cakes, chiffon cakes, and most sponge cakes and tortes are baked in ungreased pans so that the batter can climb up and cling to the sides of the pan for support during baking and cooling. While most other types of cake are traditionally baked in greased or greased and floured pans, there is no imperative to do so for most layer cakes with flat bottoms and smooth sides. We recommend lining only the pan bottoms with wax or parchment paper. To line with paper, place a pan on top of the parchment or wax paper and trace around the pan with a pencil. Cut out the shape and fit it into an already greased pan. Release the baked cake from the sides of the pan by running a thin knife or metal spatula around the edges of the cake.

Parchment paper does not usually need to be greased. However, pans are sometimes lightly greased before lining with parchment simply to keep the parchment from slipping.

Fluted tube pans and decorative molds are prepared differently. These must be greased and floured carefully, and in all grooves and crevices, so that the cake will release without the aid of a knife, which would damage the cake's surface. The same is true for layer cakes that will not be iced on the sides.

To grease a pan, use solid vegetable shortening—not butter, oil, nonstick cooking spray, or margarine—and apply to the inside of the pan in a thin, even layer with a piece of paper towel, a pastry brush, or your fingers. Butter, oil, nonstick spray, and margarine do not release cakes as well as shortening does. Be sure to use enough shortening. A layer cake pan requires $1\frac{1}{2}$ teaspoons, a small plain or fluted tube pan 1 tablespoon, and a large plain or fluted tube pan 2 tablespoons.

To flour a pan, sprinkle about a tablespoon of flour into the greased pan and tap and rotate the pan until the greased surfaces are evenly coated with the flour. Invert the pan over another pan to be dusted or over the sink and tap out the excess. Do not flour pans for cakes that will be served in the baking pan—flour coatings turn pasty when the cake is left in the pan. To prevent unsightly white edges on a chocolate cake, dust pans with cocoa powder. Use a strainer when applying cocoa powder because it tends to stick and clump in the pan. Hold the strainer over the pan and tap to sprinkle cocoa all over.

If using nonstick pans, follow the manufacturer's instructions; wax or parchment paper can still be used in the bottom. Tube pans should be greased and floured even if they are nonstick and coated. For pan placement in the oven, see 1063.

ABOUT TESTING CAKES FOR DONENESS

Some cakes such as Molten Chocolate Cake, 729, are ready to be removed from the oven when they are still gooey in the center. Most, however, can be tested for doneness with the following methods. Insert a cake tester—such as a thin metal or wooden skewer—in the center of the cake; if it emerges perfectly clean, or with a few moist crumbs, depending on recipe, the cake is done. The cake should be lightly browned and beginning to shrink from the sides of the pan. If pressed lightly with a finger, it should at once spring back into shape, except in very rich cakes and chocolate cakes, which may dent slightly and still be done.

After removing it from the oven, cool the cake briefly in the pan on a rack—plain cakes about 5 minutes, and rich cakes 10 to 15 minutes—and then cool completely out of the pan, on a rack. Turn the pan over a plate or another rack or put a plate on top of the pan and flip gently. For exceptions, see About Angel Cakes, 705, About Sponge Cakes, 706, Génoise, 709, and About Fruit Cakes, 725. If cakes are left in the pan too long, they become soggy and obstinate. Or try setting the pan on a cloth wrung out in hot water. This often helps in removing the cake from the pan.

ABOUT STORING CAKES

Unless a cake requires refrigeration, store it at room temperature under a cake dome or in a cake box. If the cake has been cut, you can press a piece of plastic wrap or wax paper against the cut edges to keep it from drying out. Refrigerated cakes are best stored in airtight plastic containers to keep them from absorbing odors and flavors from other foods. Unless otherwise directed, once removed from the refrigerator, let cakes come to room temperature before serving.

ABOUT FREEZING CAKES

Most cakes can be frozen for 4 to 6 months with little loss of quality. The richer the cake, the better it will retain flavor and texture after freezing and thawing. Thus, butter cakes, cheesecakes, and rich chocolate tortes freeze especially well. Cakes with little or no fat, such as angel cakes, many sponge cakes, and most reduced-fat cakes, dry out and lose quality after 6 to 8 weeks. Spice cakes may diminish in flavor after about 6 weeks in the freezer.

The better a cake is wrapped (the less air there is in the package) and the faster it is frozen, the better results you will have. To this end, chill cakes before freezing, then wrap airtight first in plastic and then in heavy-duty foil or plastic freezer containers or bags for a second barrier.

Thaw cakes without unwrapping or removing them from the freezer container, so that the condensation that forms on any thawing items will collect on the surface of the wrapper or container rather than on the cake. Thaw cakes that are to be served cold in the refrigerator. Thaw cakes that are to be served at room temperature at room temperature.

ABOUT PACKAGED CAKE MIXES

We know that people save time by using mixes—though just how much time is a sobering consideration—but we also know they forfeit flavor. Use mixes if you must, but re-member that, in concocting the mix, everything was con-trived to use ingredients that would keep. Egg whites are used in preference to whole eggs, as the fat from the yolks might turn rancid. For the same reason, nonfat dry milk solids are preferred. Real butter is never used, and choco-late, flavorings, and spices are often artificial. So why not become expert at a few quick cakes and create really top-notch flavor?

If you do use a mix, consider adorning your cake with a homemade filling and frosting. The quickest—and among the best—is Whipped Cream, plain or flavored, 154. A double recipe will nicely fill and frost a 2-layer cake.

▲ Most cake mix packages carry "High Altitude Adjust-ment" notes. Bakers in the mountains often rely on mixes, but are frequently disappointed by their results. In fact, they are developed to work up only to about 6,500 feet. Above that, even following box adjustments, cakes can fall or have a bowl-shaped dip in the center as they cool. Above 8,000 feet you will also find cakes stick to pans de-spite directions, and many have a coarse texture. To rem-edy, above 6,500 feet: **follow box altitude adjustments and** ➤ always grease pans, line with baking parchment or wax paper, grease paper, dust with flour, tap out excess flour. Add 1 to 4 tablespoons flour to strengthen batter. Add 1 to 3 tablespoons water, add 1 teaspoon more vanilla or other flavoring extract. Above 7,000 feet, place baking rack in lower third of oven so cake will receive a little more heat and/or increase baking time 2 to 5 minutes.

ABOUT WEDDING AND OTHER LARGE CAKES

Be sure for any large cake to choose a recipe that can be doubled or tripled successfully; see White Cake I, 711, for guidance. It is surprisingly easy to make a large white cake with three 2-layer tiers for about 75 guests. For up to 25 additional servings, you can make a 2-layer "back-up" sheet cake by baking one additional recipe of the cake in two 13 x 9-inch pans and frosting it with 4 to 5 cups frost-ing. We find that when rather shallow pans are used—not more than 2 inches deep for each layer—the cake bakes more evenly and cuts more attractively. For any large cake, lower the indicated oven temperature by 25°. For more even baking, turn the pans in the oven frequently during the necessarily longer baking period.

To make the cake tiers: Grease and flour the sides of two 12 x 2-inch pans, two 9 x 2-inch pans, and two 6 x 2-inch round pans and line the bottoms with wax or parchment paper. Mix and bake 3 separate recipes of White Cake I, 711: One recipe makes enough batter for one 12-inch layer plus one 6-inch layer or two 9-inch lay-ers. Measure the batter into the pans: about 6 cups for the 12-inch pan, about 4 cups for the 9-inch pans, about 2 cups for the 6-inch pan. Bake the 6-inch layer for 10 to 20 minutes, the 9-inch layers for 25 to 30 minutes, and the 12-inch layer for 40 to 50 minutes. Be sure not to un-derbake the 12-inch layer.

To fill, frost, and decorate a three-tier wedding cake: You'll need 16 cups Swiss Meringue Buttercream, 792, or Quick White Icing I, 793 (4 to 5 cups to fill the layers and 10 to 11 cups to frost the cake and pipe the borders). Make 5 recipes of Swiss Meringue Buttercream, or make 8 recipes of Quick White Icing I, allowing 1 pound confec-tioners' sugar for every 2 recipes.

To fill the layers and assemble the tiers: Layers must be completely cool before assembly. Each tier has 2 cake lay-ers with filling or frosting between them. Slide a rimless cookie sheet under large cake layers to move them with-out cracking. If the layers are not flat, or if the top crust is tough or dry, trim with a serrated knife.

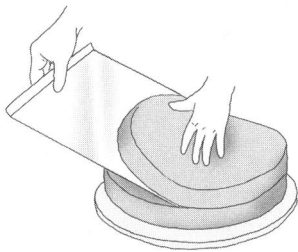

Using a rimless sheet to move large layers

To assemble the 12-inch tier, dab frosting on a 12-inch cardboard cake round to keep the cake from sliding. Cen-ter 1 of the 12-inch layers right side up on the cardboard. Spread with 2 to 2½ cups frosting. Top with the second cake layer, upside down. Spread a very thin crumb coat, 785, a thin layer of frosting or jam over the top and sides of the cake that will cover cracks and secure crumbs. Re-frigerate or put in a cool place so the frosting sets.

Assemble the 9-inch tier on a 9-inch cardboard round, filling the layers with about 1¼ cups frosting and then crumb-coating. Assemble the 6-inch tier on a 6-inch card-board round, filling with about ⅓ cup frosting and then crumb-coating. Refrigerate or put in a cool place.

To frost the tiers: Place 3 or 4 pieces of double-sided ad-hesive tape on the cake plate or presentation board about 4 inches in from the edges. (To make a presentation board, wrap an 18-inch plywood round with florist's foil or foil wrapping paper. Secure the foil to the underside of the board with tape.) Frost the 12-inch tier, either as smoothly as possible or with swirls. A long extra-wide pancake turner with a stiff blade is best for lifting and transferring tiers. Otherwise, slide a sturdy metal spatula under the tier and tilt it up so that you can slide your hands under for support. Lift the tier over the center of the plate or presen-tation board. Set the front edge (farthest from you) down first, 2 inches from the edge of the plate or board. Pivot the cake to the left or right to center it, if necessary, before lowering the back edge. Refrigerate or put in a cool place to set the frosting. Frost the top and sides of the other 2 tiers, and refrigerate or put in a cool place.

To stack the tiers: Cut a circle of wax or parchment paper 7 inches in diameter. Center it on top of the 12-inch tier. Insert a plastic drinking straw straight down into the cake at one edge of the paper circle. Mark the straw at the surface of the frosting, remove it, and cut at the mark to make a support. Cut 5 more identical lengths of plastic straws. Insert the supports into the cake, evenly spaced around the perimeter of the paper circle. Put a generous teaspoon of frosting in the center of the paper circle.

Cut a circle of wax or parchment paper 4 inches in diameter. Center it on top of the 9-inch tier. Mark and cut 4 or 5 drinking straw supports and insert them evenly around the perimeter of the paper circle. Put a small dollop of frosting in the center of the paper circle.

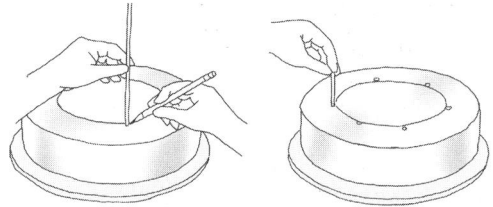

Marking the dowel at the surface
of the frosting and inserting the supports
into the cakes at even intervals

Lift the 9-inch tier with the long pancake turner or your hand and hold it centered over the paper circle on the 12-inch tier. Lower the front edge (opposite you) first, with a friend guiding you if possible. Then, in place of your hand and the spatula, put a small paring knife or the small offset spatula, which will be easier to remove without damaging the frosting, on the lower tier; lower the tier into place. Carefully remove the paring knife.

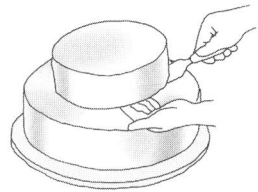

Lowering the 9-inch onto the 12-inch tier

Transfer the 6-inch tier to the center of the 9-inch tier, using the procedure described above. If you are transporting the cake, you may wish to "stake" it for added stability. Cut a length of 1/4-inch wooden dowel slightly shorter than the height of the cake. Whittle a long sharp point in one end, or use a pencil sharpener. Drive the stake straight down into the center of the cake, tapping with a hammer. (You will cover the hole later with decoration.)

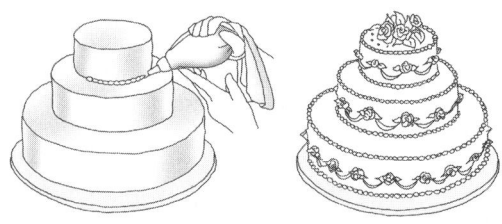

Piping frosting to cover the seams
Completed wedding cake

To decorate the cake: Adjust the consistency of the frosting or buttercream as necessary (see 785) so that it holds a stiff shape when piped. Fit a star tip into a pastry bag and fill the bag no more than half full with buttercream or icing. Pipe a border around the base of the top tier where it meets the tier below. Pipe a similar border to cover the seam between the 9-inch tier and the bottom tier. Refrigerate the cake to set the frosting before decorating. The cake is now ready to decorate with buttercream designs, crystallized flowers, 881, frosted grapes, 881, or ➤ edible flowers, see Fresh flowers for Cakes, 800. For decorating, see 703.

After cutting the first slice, whether the wedding cake is round or rectangular, the cutting begins at the lowest tier. To make the cuts even in depth, run a knife perpendicularly through the bottom layer, where it abuts the second layer. Continue this process at each tier. Cut successive slices until a single cylindrical central core remains, crested by the ornate top. Remove and save this, or *freeze* it for the first anniversary party. Then finish slicing the central core, beginning at the top.

ABOUT FOAM CAKES

Angel cakes, sponge cakes, and chiffon cakes are all foam cakes. They contain a high proportion of eggs or egg whites in relation to other ingredients, and they rely on a foam created by beating eggs or egg whites for their leavening and delicate structure. Leavening comes from the air trapped in the egg foam that gets hot and expands in the oven, aided by the steam produced as the moist batter bakes. Some foam cakes contain baking powder for additional leavening. The creation and handling of the egg foam is critical to the success of any foam cake: Mixing and folding must be done in such a way as to preserve as much air in the foam as possible. Follow the recipe instructions carefully, and review the techniques for beating egg whites, 700, and folding, 700.

The most delicate sponge cakes are often baked in tube pans that are ungreased, so that the batter can cling to the pan sides (and the tube) for support as it rises and as it cools. These cakes are cooled upside down, like angel cakes, see page 705, to set the structure before unmolding. Sturdier sponge cakes are cooled right side up.

ABOUT ANGEL CAKES

Laboratory research in some types of recipes—and no cake has a larger bibliography than angel cake—has become so elaborate as to intimidate home bakers, who can rarely know the exact age of the eggs they use or the precise blend of flour. Yet, working innocently as they must, home bakers can still contrive a glamorous result with surprisingly little care.

Angel cakes have no chemical leaveners such as baking powder or baking soda. The main sources of leavening in angel cake are air and steam, so the volume of air beaten into the egg whites is of supreme importance, as is the care with which other ingredients are folded into them. See Beating Eggs, 978, for the type of bowl and preparation of equipment.

The choice of pan and its careful preparation are essential to good results. Choose an angel cake or tube pan with a removable bottom. Since the batter is light, a central tube gives the cake additional support during baking. ➤ Do not grease or flour the pan. A clean, dry, grease-free pan is essential for the cake to rise properly; wash your pan with detergent before use.

The egg whites should be at least 3 days old, at about 60 to 70°F, and separated just before use. Do not exceed medium speed on either a hand-held or heavy-duty stand mixer; overbeating the whites is the single most common mistake in the production of angel cakes. Unlike the whites in most other meringues, egg whites for angel cakes should be beaten a little short of stiff. The finished batter should be just soft enough to pour, rather than scrape, into the cake pan.

Cream of tartar is used to keep the cake white and to stabilize the egg whites. A portion of the sugar is sifted with the flour to keep the sugar dispersed and prevent clumping as it is folded in. The remaining sugar is beaten into the egg whites. Folding is done by hand with a rubber or silicone spatula. If your mixer bowl is tall and narrow, you will have better results if you transfer the batter to a very large wide bowl just before folding. Do not rush the addition of ingredients. For a review of folding technique, see page 700.

After putting the batter in the pan, draw a thin spatula gently through the batter to burst very large air pockets. Bake on a rack in the lower third of a preheated 350°F oven. When the cake is done, invert immediately and cool upside down in the pan, to prevent it from sinking. Use the feet of the pan to hold it above the surface of the table or prop it higher by resting the tube on a bottle or inverted funnel. Let the cake cool for at least 1½ hours, until it is thoroughly set. Remove it from the pan before storing.

To remove the cake from the pan, slide a thin knife around the cake to detach it from the pan. Using the same procedure, detach the cake from the tube. If the pan has a removable bottom, pull the tube up, to lift the cake from the pan sides. Slide the knife under the cake, to detach it from the bottom. If the pan does not have a removable

bottom, invert the pan and tap it against the counter to loosen the cake. Allow the cake to drop onto a rack, or a serving platter. Let the cake cool completely before frosting or wrapping airtight.

Angel cakes keep well for 2 to 3 days. They do not freeze as well as butter cakes or other sponge cakes; do not count on freezing them for more than a week.

It is best to cut an angel cake with a special cake comb, resembling a fork with several widely spaced long, thin, prongs, or 2 forks inserted back-to-back to pry the cake gently apart. Or use a very sharp serrated knife and a gentle sawing motion, to avoid compacting the tender cake.

To make angel cake for a jelly roll, use 1 recipe for a 10½ x 15½-inch pan, and grease the bottom of the pan. To fill an angel cake, see About Filled Cakes, 730. Fresh berries and whipped cream are natural partners. You also can cut the cake into three or four horizontal layers and fill with Lemon Curd, 756, or mousse, 817, Bavarian cream, ice cream, sorbet, or flavored whipped cream.

ANGEL CAKE
One 10-inch tube cake
A high, very moist, and tender angel cake.
The egg whites should be 60° to 70°F. Preheat the oven to 350°F. Have ready an ungreased 10-inch tube pan.
Sift together 3 times:
 1 cup sifted cake flour
 ¾ cup sugar
 ½ teaspoon salt
Combine in a large bowl, and beat on low speed for 1 minute:
 1½ cups egg whites (about 11 large whites)
 1 tablespoon water
 1 tablespoon fresh lemon juice
 1 teaspoon cream of tartar
 1 teaspoon vanilla
 (¼ teaspoon almond extract)
Increase the speed to medium-high and beat until the mixture increases 4½ to 5 times in volume and resembles a bowl of soft foam. (This takes anywhere from 3 to 5 minutes.) The foam will hold a very soft, moist shape when the beaters are lifted. On medium-high speed, beat in 1 tablespoon at a time, taking 2 to 3 minutes:
 ¾ cup sugar
When all the sugar has been added, the foam will be creamy white and hold soft, moist, glossy peaks that bend over at the points; do not beat until stiff. If the mixer bowl is nearly full, transfer the mixture to a wide 4- to 6-quart bowl for easier folding. Sift a fine layer of the flour mixture (about ¼ cup) evenly over the batter and fold gently with a rubber spatula only until the flour is almost incorporated; do not stir or mix. Repeat 7 more times, folding in the last addition until no traces of flour are visible. Pour the batter into the pan and tilt or spread to level the top. Bake until a cake tester inserted in the center comes out

clean, 35 to 40 minutes. To cool and to unmold, see About Angel Cakes, above.

Over this cake, we like to dribble:

> European Chocolate Icing, 796

thinned a bit by an additional tablespoon of cream. Or try:

> Translucent Sugar Glaze, 799

made with orange or lemon juice.

COFFEE-FLECKED ANGEL CAKE

With a rolling pin or in a coffee grinder, crush **3 tablespoons instant coffee.** Prepare **Angel Cake, 705.** Fold in the coffee with the last addition of flour (the coffee will not disperse completely). Or, for coffee flavoring throughout the cake instead of flecks, replace the water with **3 tablespoons cold extra-strong coffee or espresso.** Serve plain or frost with sweetened whipped cream, 754, or any chocolate icing or glaze, 795–797.

CANDY ANGEL CAKE

With a rolling pin, crush **enough peppermint sticks, sour lemon drops, toffee bars, or peanut butter cups to make** $^1/_3$ **cup.** Prepare **Angel Cake, 705.** Fold the candy in with the last addition of flour. Frost with **Whipped Cream, 754, Boiled White Icing, 790, or Seven-Minute Frosting, 790,** to which you can add more crushed candy.

COCONUT ANGEL CAKE

Prepare **Angel Cake, 705,** adding $^1/_2$ **teaspoon coconut extract** to the unbeaten egg whites. Fold into the batter with the last addition of flour $^1/_2$ **cup shredded sweetened dried coconut.** Frost with **Whipped Cream, 754,** and sprinkle the top with **Shredded sweetened dried coconut.** Or ice with **Quick Lemon Icing, 703, Luscious Orange Icing, 791, or Translucent Sugar Glaze, 799, made with rum.**

LEMON OR ORANGE ANGEL CAKE

Prepare **Angel Cake, 705.** Stir **1 teaspoon grated lemon zest** or **2 tablespoons grated orange zest** into the flour mixture and substitute **1 teaspoon lemon or orange extract** for the almond extract. Frost with **Quick Lemon Icing, 793, Luscious Orange Icing, 791, Translucent Sugar Glaze, 799, made with rum, or Chocolate Ganache Glaze or Frosting, 796.**

COCOA OR EXTRA-CHOCOLATE ANGEL CAKE

Prepare **Angel Cake, 705.** Substitute $^1/_2$ **cup (unsifted) unsweetened cocoa powder, preferably Dutch-process (alkalized)** for $^1/_2$ **cup sifted cake flour** and reducing the lemon juice to 1 teaspoon. Dissolve in the water (**1 teaspoon instant coffee or espresso powder**). For **Extra-Chocolate Angel Cake,** fold into the batter with the last addition of cocoa and flour **2 ounces semisweet or bittersweet chocolate, finely chopped.** Cover the cooled cake with **Chocolate Coating over Boiled White Icing, 790, or Coffee Icing, 793.** Or, for a richer effect, fill with **Whipped Ganache Filling, 759,** and frost with **Bittersweet Chocolate Glaze, 796.** Or fill and frost with **Chocolate Mousse Frosting, 797,** or **Mocha Buttercream, 797,** and sprinkle the top with **chopped pecans.**

NUTTY ANGEL CAKE

Prepare **Angel Cake, 705,** or **Cocoa Angel Cake,** above. Into either batter with the last addition of flour, fold $^3/_4$ **cup chopped or finely ground nuts.** Frost with (**Chocolate Mousse Frosting, 797**).

MARBLE ANGEL CAKE

Two 10-inch tube cakes

Prepare **Angel Cake, 705, and Cocoa Angel Cake,** above. Alternate the batters in 2 ungreased 10-inch tube pans, either by layering the batters or by alternating blobs of each batter into the pan, and then swirl with a knife to marble.

ABOUT SPONGE CAKES

In true sponge cakes, as in angel cakes, the main leavening is air plus steam, so all the suggestions for trapping air given in About Angel Cakes, 705, apply here—with this added admonition: Egg yolks beat to a greater volume if they are at about 70°F. Beat the yolks until light and foamy, then add the sugar gradually, while continuing to beat, until the mixture is pale in color and thick in texture. It has reached proper consistency when a sample dropped from a spoon remains raised for a moment above the rest of the batter and then rather reluctantly settles down to the level in the bowl. An electric mixer is used to beat the egg and sugar mixtures. Then stir in the dry ingredients carefully by hand, using the folding technique described on 700.

For pan preparation and baking, see About Angel Cakes, 705.

True-blue sponge cake enthusiasts scorn baking powder, but it does ensure good volume in the recipe just below. Also included is a sponge cake with no chemical leavening. Any of the flavored angel cakes, 705–706, except cocoa, chocolate, and marble, can be adapted to vary the basic sponge cake.

SPONGE CAKE

I. *Two 8- or 9-inch round layers, one 9-inch round cake, or one 10-inch tube cake*

A very light cake when made with 3 eggs, a moister—and larger—one when made with 6 eggs. Bake a small cake in one or two round pans and use for Boston Cream Pie, 732, or a layer cake; bake a large cake in a tube pan.

Have all ingredients (except the water) at room temperature, about 70°F.

Preheat the oven to 350°F. For a 3-egg cake, line the bottom(s) of two 8 or 9 x 2-inch round cake pans or one 9 x 3-inch springform pan with wax or parchment paper. For a 6-egg cake, have ready an ungreased 10-inch tube pan. Sift together:

1 cup sifted cake flour
1¹/₂ teaspoons baking powder
¹/₄ teaspoon salt

Have ready:

1 cup sugar

Beat in a large bowl at medium-high speed until thickened, about 1 minute:

3 or 6 large egg yolks

Gradually beat in the sugar, then beat 3 minutes longer. Beat in:

¹/₄ cup boiling water

Beat in:

1 teaspoon grated lemon or orange zest
1 tablespoon fresh lemon or orange juice
(1 teaspoon vanilla)
(3 drops anise oil or extract)

At low speed, gradually beat in the sifted ingredients. Using clean beaters in a medium or large bowl beat at medium-high speed until stiff but not dry:

3 or 6 large egg whites
¹/₄ teaspoon cream of tartar

Fold one-quarter of the whites into the batter, then fold in the remaining whites. Scrape the batter into the pan(s) and spread evenly. Bake until the top springs back when lightly pressed and a cake tester inserted in the center comes out clean; about 2 minutes for two round pans, 40 to 50 minutes for a springform or tube pan. To cool and unmold, see About Angel Cakes, 705.

II. One 10-inch tube cake or 10-inch round cake

This sponge cake contains no chemical leavening.

Have all ingredients at room temperature, about 70°F. Preheat the oven to 325°F.

Sift:

1 cup cake flour

Combine in a large bowl and beat on high speed until thick and pale yellow, 2 to 3 minutes:

²/₃ cup sugar
7 large egg yolks
1 teaspoon vanilla

Beat in:

2 tablespoons water or fresh orange juice
(1 teaspoon grated lemon zest)
(1 teaspoon grated orange zest)
¹/₄ teaspoon salt

Sift the flour evenly over the top, but do not mix it in. Using clean beaters, beat in a large bowl on medium speed until soft peaks form:

7 large egg whites
1 tablespoon sugar
¹/₂ teaspoon cream of tartar

Gradually add, beating on high speed:

¹/₃ cup sugar

Beat until the peaks are stiff but not dry. Use a rubber spatula to fold one-quarter of the egg whites into the egg yolk mixture, then fold in the remaining whites. Scrape the batter into a clean, dry, ungreased tube pan or a round cake

pan lined with wax or parchment paper, and spread evenly.

Bake until the top springs back when lightly pressed and a cake tester inserted into the center comes out clean, 40 to 50 minutes. To cool and remove from the pan, see About Angel Cakes, 705.

Serve unadorned or frost with:

Luscious Orange Icing, 791, or Quick Lemon Icing, 793

or serve with:

Strawberries and cream

PASSOVER SPONGE CAKE

One 10-inch tube cake

Have all ingredients at room temperature, about 70°F. Preheat the oven to 350°F.

Whisk together thoroughly:

²/₃ cup matzo meal
¹/₃ cup potato starch
¹/₄ teaspoon salt

Beat in a large bowl on high speed until thick and pale yellow, about 2 minutes:

9 large egg yolks
1 cup sugar

Beat in:

1 teaspoon grated orange zest
1 teaspoon grated lemon zest
¹/₄ cup fresh orange juice
1 tablespoon fresh lemon juice

Gradually add the dry ingredients, beating on low speed just until smooth. Using clean beaters, beat in a large bowl on medium speed until soft peaks form:

9 large egg whites
¹/₂ teaspoon cream of tartar

Gradually add, beating on high speed:

¹/₂ cup sugar

Beat until the peaks are stiff but not dry. Use a rubber spatula to fold one-quarter of the egg whites into the egg yolk mixture, then fold in the remaining whites. Spoon the batter gently into the clean, dry, ungreased tube pan and spread evenly. Bake until the top springs back when lightly pressed and a cake tester inserted into the center comes out clean, 40 to 45 minutes. To cool and remove from the pan, see About Angel Cakes, 705.

PASSOVER NUT SPONGE CAKE

Prepare **Passover Sponge Cake, above,** folding in with the second addition of egg whites **1 cup finely chopped or ground walnuts or pecans.**

CHOCOLATE SPONGE CAKE

One 10-inch tube cake

You can cut this cake into layers, sprinkle the layers with rum or a liqueur of choice, if desired, and spread them with Whipped Ganache Filling, 759. Frost with additional filling or glaze with Bittersweet Chocolate Glaze, 796.

Have all ingredients at room temperature, about 70°F. Preheat the oven to 350°F. Have ready an ungreased 10-inch tube pan. Sift together 3 times, and then return to the sifter:

⅔ cup sifted cake flour
½ cup Dutch-process (alkalized) cocoa powder
¼ teaspoon salt

Combine in a large bowl:

6 large eggs
2 teaspoons vanilla
2 teaspoons instant coffee powder

Beat on high speed until the consistency of softly whipped cream, about 10 minutes. Gradually beat in 1 tablespoon at a time, beating for about 3 minutes in all:

1 cup sugar

Sift about one-fifth of the cocoa mixture over the top and fold in. Sift and fold in the remaining cocoa mixture in 4 more additions. Scrape the batter into the tube pan and spread evenly. Bake until the top springs back when lightly pressed and a cake tester inserted into the center comes out clean, about 45 minutes. To cool and unmold, see About Angel Cakes, 705. Serve plain or with:

Whipped Cream, 754

DAFFODIL CAKE

One 10-inch tube cake

A yellow and white marble cake.
Have all ingredients at room temperature, about 70°F. Preheat the oven to 350°F.
Have ready in 2 separate containers:

¾ cup sifted cake flour
¼ cup plus 2 tablespoons sifted cake flour

Beat in a large bowl at medium-high speed until frothy:

10 large egg whites

Add:

1 teaspoon cream of tartar
½ teaspoon salt

Whip until stiff but not dry. Beating at low speed, gradually add:

1¼ cups sugar

Continue to beat until the egg whites form glossy peaks. Transfer half the mixture to another large bowl. Fold into one half, a little at a time, the ¾ cup sifted flour and:

6 large egg yolks, beaten
Grated zest of 1 orange

Fold into the other half, a little at a time, the remaining sifted flour and:

1 teaspoon vanilla

Place the batters, a cupful or more at a time, in the clean, dry, ungreased tube pan, alternating them. Bake until the top springs back when lightly pressed and a cake tester inserted into the center comes out clean, about 35 minutes. To cool and unmold, see About Angel Cakes, 705.

"THREE MILKS" CAKE (TRES LECHES)

One 9-inch square cake or one 11 x 7-inch cake

This Latin American sponge cake is drenched with a sweet mixture of two types of milk and heavy cream. It is tradi-

tionally topped with sweet soft meringue; replace the meringue with whipped cream, if you prefer.
Have all ingredients at room temperature, about 70°F. Preheat the oven to 350°F (325°F if the baking pan is glass). Grease a 9-inch square pan or an 11 x 7-inch baking pan. Sift together:

1 cup all-purpose flour
2 teaspoons baking powder

Beat in a large bowl on medium speed until soft peaks form:

3 large egg whites
⅛ teaspoon cream of tartar

Gradually add, beating on high speed:

1 cup sugar

Beat in one at a time:

3 large egg yolks

Add one-quarter of the flour mixture at a time, beating on low speed or stirring with a rubber spatula just until incorporated and scraping the sides of the bowl as necessary. Add and beat just until the mixture is smooth and evenly mixed:

¼ cup milk

Scrape the batter into the pan and spread evenly. Bake until the top springs back when lightly pressed and a toothpick inserted into the center comes out clean, 25 to 30 minutes. Let cool in the pan on a rack for 10 minutes. Meanwhile, combine:

½ cup heavy cream
¾ cup evaporated milk
¾ cup plus 2 tablespoons sweetened condensed milk

Leaving the cake in the pan, prick it with a toothpick at 1-inch intervals. Pour the milk mixture slowly over the cake, including the edges and the corners. Let cool, then refrigerate for at least 1 hour, or overnight, before serving. For topping, prepare:

Soft Meringue Topping I or II, 798

To serve, leave the cake in the pan or slide a slim knife around the cake to detach it from the pan, and invert the cake onto a large shallow serving platter with enough of a rim to hold the excess milk that will gradually collect around the cake like a sauce. Spread or pipe that meringue topping over the cake. Cut into squares to serve. Use within 24 hours.

FRENCH SPONGE CAKE (BISCUIT)

Two 9-inch round layers or one 10-inch round cake

Biscuit (bis-KWEE) is a classic air-leavened sponge cake used to make fancy layered cakes. This light, dry-textured cake is meant to be soaked with syrups before being filled with buttercream, mousse, or other filling. This recipe yields two 1-inch layers or one 2-inch layer that can be sliced into 2 or 3 thin layers.
Have all ingredients at room temperature, about 70°F. Preheat the oven to 325°F. Grease and flour the bottom(s) of two 9 x 2-inch round cake pans or one 10-inch springform

pan or line the bottom(s) with wax or parchment paper. (See About Angel Cakes, 705.)

Measure and return to the sifter:

1 cup plus 2 tablespoons sifted cake flour

Beat in a large bowl on high speed until thick and pale yellow, 2 to 3 minutes:

6 large egg yolks
¼ cup sugar
1 teaspoon vanilla

Sift the flour evenly over the top but do not mix it in. Using clean beaters, beat in another large bowl on medium speed until soft peaks form:

6 large egg whites
¼ teaspoon cream of tartar

Gradually add, beating on high speed:

⅓ cup sugar

Beat until the peaks are stiff but not dry. Use a rubber or silicone spatula to fold one-third of the egg whites not quite thoroughly into the egg yolk mixture. Fold in the remaining whites in 2 additions. Scrape the batter into the pan(s) and spread evenly.

Bake until the top springs back when lightly pressed and a toothpick inserted into the center comes out clean, 20 to 25 minutes in cake pans, 35 to 40 minutes in a springform pan. To cool and remove from the pan, see 702.

GÉNOISE

One or two 9-inch layers

Enriched with a little butter, this is a rich, moist cake of Italian origin, and has no equal for versatility—excellent with fruit fillings, as a roll cake with cream fillings, as a foil for a simple glaze or fresh fruit. This recipe makes two 1-inch layers or one 2-inch layer that can be split into 3 or 4 thin layers. Clarified butter gives a superior result, but regular butter will do. You'll need a bit more butter to make ⅓ cup if you clarify it.

Have all ingredients at room temperature, about 70°F. Preheat the oven to 350°F. Grease and flour the bottom(s) of two 9 x 2-inch round cake pans or one 9-inch springform pan or line the bottom(s) with wax or parchment paper.

Sift together 3 times and return to the sifter:

1¼ cups sifted cake flour
¼ cup sugar

Melt in a small saucepan:

⅓ cup (5⅓ tablespoons) unsalted butter, preferably clarified, 963

Set aside. Whisk together in a large heatproof bowl:

6 large eggs
¾ cup sugar

Set the bowl in a skillet of barely simmering water and whisk constantly until the mixture is warm to the touch (about 110°F). Remove the bowl from the heat and beat on high speed until the mixture is lemony-colored, has tripled in volume, and has reached the stage known as **au ruban**—like a continuous flat ribbon when dropped from

a spoon (about 5 minutes in a heavy-duty mixer with the whisk attachment, 10 to 15 minutes with a hand-held mixer). In 3 additions, sift the flour mixture over the top and fold in very gently with a rubber spatula.

Reheat the butter until it is hot and transfer to a medium bowl. Fold about 1½ cups of the egg mixture into the butter until completely incorporated, along with:

1 teaspoon vanilla

Scrape the mixture onto the remaining egg mixture and fold in. Scrape the batter into the pan(s) and spread evenly.

Bake until the cake begins to pull away from the sides of the pan(s) and the top springs back when lightly pressed, about 15 minutes in cake pans, 30 minutes in a springform pan. Let cool in the pan(s) on a rack for 10 minutes. Slide a thin knife around the cake to detach it from the pan(s); remove the side of the springform pan, if using. Invert the cake and remove the paper liner(s), if using. Let cool right side up on the rack.

CHOCOLATE GÉNOISE

Reduce the flour to ½ cup plus 1 tablespoon sifted flour. Sift it together 3 times with **½ cup plus 1 tablespoon unsweetened cocoa powder** and return to the sifter. Do not sift any of the sugar with the flour mixture; instead, whisk together all of the sugar (1 cup total) with the eggs. Proceed as directed.

ABOUT CHIFFON CAKES

With a very light, fluffy, and tender texture, chiffon cakes are less sweet than angel cakes and moister than sponge cakes. Chiffon cakes contain oil instead of shortening or butter. The egg whites and baking powder and/or soda provide leavening. To achieve their light texture, chiffon cakes contain a large amount of sugar and egg, and consequently the calorie content approximates that of butter cakes. The eggs are added separately, as egg yolks and then as stiffly beaten egg whites folded in. The precise mixing method makes chiffon cakes the easiest type of foam cake to master.

Choose an oil that has a neutral flavor. Safflower, canola, corn, and sunflower oils are good choices—but not olive or peanut. Because chiffon cakes are specially formulated, do not try to substitute melted butter or shortening for the oil (and do not substitute oil for butter or shortening in other types of cakes). Since oil does not contribute flavor the way butter does, chiffon cakes need lots of flavor from other ingredients, such as tangy citrus juice and zest, spices, chocolate or cocoa, and/or toasted nuts. You can customize these cakes by changing the flavors—varying the spices, extracts, and citrus zest, changing the liquid from water to fruit juice or coffee, and/or adding finely chopped nuts or miniature chocolate chips.

Remove chiffon cakes from the pan as you would Angel Cake, 705. All chiffon cakes can be served with a simple dusting of confectioners' sugar. To add flavor, drizzle a citrus or liquor sugar glaze, 799, over the cake. Oil keeps chiffon cakes soft even when refrigerated, tender even when frozen. Thus a chiffon cake is a good choice for filling or layering with ice cream. Slice a chiffon cake horizontally into 3 layers and fill with softened ice cream, sorbet, or frozen yogurt. Refreeze for at least several hours, or overnight, before serving with a chocolate or a fruit sauce or with whipped cream and toasted nuts.

CHIFFON CAKE

One 10-inch tube cake or 13 x 9-inch cake

Please read About Chiffon Cakes, 709, and mix exactly as indicated.

Have all ingredients at room temperature, about 70°F. Preheat the oven to 325°F. Have ready an ungreased 10-inch tube pan or a 13 x 9-inch baking pan.

Whisk together thoroughly in a large bowl:

2¼ cups sifted cake flour
1¼ cups sugar
1 tablespoon baking powder
1 teaspoon salt

Add and beat on high speed until smooth:

5 large egg yolks
¾ cup water
½ cup vegetable oil
(1 teaspoon grated lemon zest)
1 teaspoon vanilla

Using clean beaters, beat in another large bowl on medium speed until soft peaks form:

8 large egg whites
½ teaspoon cream of tartar

Gradually add, beating on high speed:

¼ cup sugar

Beat the whites until they're so stiff they begin to lose their gloss. Use a rubber spatula to fold one-quarter of the egg whites into the egg yolk mixture, then fold in the remaining whites. Scrape the batter into the pan and spread evenly. Bake until the top springs back when lightly pressed and a toothpick inserted into the center comes out clean, 55 to 65 minutes, for a tube pan or 30 to 35 minutes for a baking pan. Let the tube cake cool upside down as for Angel Cake, 705; rest the 9 x 13-inch pan on 4 glasses. To unmold, see page 709.

Ice with:

Quick Lemon Icing, 793, or Luscious Orange Icing, 791

or serve with:

Fresh berries and Whipped Cream, 754

ORANGE CHIFFON CAKE

Prepare **Chiffon Cake, above,** substituting for the water and lemon zest **2 tablespoons grated orange zest** and **¾ cup fresh orange juice.** Emphasize the orange flavor by icing with **Luscious Orange Icing, 791,** or use Translucent Sugar Glaze, 799, made with rum.

PUMPKIN CHIFFON CAKE

Ice with 2 recipes of Cream Cheese Frosting, 794, or serve with vanilla ice cream.

Prepare **Chiffon Cake, above.** To the dry ingredients add: **1½ teaspoons ground cinnamon, ¾ teaspoon ground ginger, ½ teaspoon grated or ground nutmeg, and ¼ teaspoon ground cloves.** If you wish, fold in with the second addition of egg whites (**¾ cup finely chopped walnuts or pecans**). Substitute **1¼ cups cooked or canned pumpkin** for the water and omit the lemon zest. Bake until the top springs back when lightly pressed and a toothpick inserted into the center comes out clean, about 1 hour. To cool, see left.

FUDGE CHIFFON CAKE

One 10-inch tube cake

Have all ingredients (except for the water) at room temperature, about 70°F.

Preheat the oven to 325°F. Have ready an ungreased 10-inch tube pan. Whisk together in a medium bowl until smooth:

¾ cup boiling water
½ cup unsweetened cocoa powder
1 tablespoon plus 1 teaspoon instant coffee powder

Let cool, then whisk in:

½ cup vegetable oil
5 large egg yolks
1 teaspoon vanilla

Whisk together thoroughly in a large bowl:

1¾ cups sifted cake flour
1¼ cups sugar
2 teaspoons baking powder
¼ teaspoon baking soda
½ teaspoon salt

Add the cocoa mixture and whisk until smooth. Using clean beaters, beat in another large bowl, on medium speed until soft peaks form:

8 large egg whites
½ teaspoon cream of tartar

Gradually add, beating on high speed:

¼ cup sugar

Beat until the peaks are very stiff. Use a rubber spatula to fold one-quarter of the egg whites into the cocoa mixture, then fold in the remaining whites. Scrape the batter into the pan and spread evenly. Bake until the top springs back when lightly pressed and a toothpick inserted into the center comes out clean, 55 to 65 minutes. Let cool as for Angel Cake, 705. To unmold, see 709. Ice with:

Luscious Orange icing, 791, Quick Mocha Icing, 793, any chocolate frosting, 795–797, or plain or flavored whipped cream, 754–755

ABOUT BUTTER CAKES

Butter cakes are the glory of the American cake repertoire. For flavor and texture, butter is our strong preference, as it has been for generations of bakers back to the eighteenth century, when butter cake began as "pound cake," because it called for a pound each of four ingredients—butter, flour, eggs, and sugar. A lot of experience, a little imagination, and a bit of baking powder have given us lighter and more sophisticated versions of butter cakes ever since.

Have all the ingredients measured, the pans prepared, and the oven preheated, so that the mixing sequence is not interrupted until the cake batter is safely in the pans. ➤ All ingredients should be at 68° to 70°F, or slightly lower—65°F—in a very hot kitchen or climate. Butter at this temperature is pliable but still cool, not melted or squishy. Cold butter will not disperse properly; melted butter will prevent the proper incorporation of air into the batter. (See About the Temperature of Ingredients, 699.)

The butter or shortening is creamed with the sugar, which is added gradually, until lightened in color and texture; this takes from 3 to 10 minutes on medium-high speed, depending on the quantity of ingredients and the type of mixer. (For heavy-duty mixers with a choice of paddle or whisk, use the paddle; the lower times and speeds given in a recipe will apply.) If the recipe calls for whole eggs, they may be creamed from the beginning, with the sugar and butter, but whole eggs or egg yolks are sometimes added to the sugar and butter ➤ gradually so as to preserve the volume and avoid breaking the emulsion of the ingredients. If the eggs are added too fast, or if they are too cold, the emulsion with the butter "breaks" and the mixture looks curdled. If this happens, volume may be lost and the cake may suffer in texture. Turning the mixer briefly to a higher speed can sometimes smooth out the batter and restore the emulsion.

After the eggs are incorporated, the dry ingredients (flour and leavenings, sometimes cocoa and spices) are added in 3 parts, alternating with 2 additions of the wet ingredients (milk or water, or buttermilk, yogurt, or sour cream, and any liquid flavorings). To keep the mixture as stable as possible, start and end with the dry ingredients. Thus, first add one-third of the flour mixture, followed by half of the liquid, then another third of the flour, followed by the rest of the liquid, and then the rest of the flour. Low speed is used for adding the dry and wet ingredients. Scrape the sides of the bowl as necessary to ensure that the batter is smooth. Mix the added ingredients only enough to incorporate; ➤ overmixing during this stage can develop too much gluten in the flour, toughen the cake, and result in too fine a crumb. For this reason, some careful bakers like to mix in the dry and wet ingredients by hand with a rubber spatula. If nuts and other lumpy substances are to be added, fold them in lightly with a fork at the end of the mixing process, or briefly use the low speed on the beater.

If the eggs were separated and only the yolks were added to the beaten butter and sugar, the egg whites are beaten with a little sugar "until stiff but not dry." ➤ The whites are then folded into the batter gently but quickly as

shown on 700. This step provides extra lightness. Be sure ➤ before you begin beating the egg whites that your oven has reached the right temperature and that your pans are greased. To beat egg whites, see 700. Cool for at least 10 minutes before removing from the pan.

To remove it, slide a thin knife around the cake to detach it from the pan. Invert onto a rack. Peel off the wax or parchment paper, and turn right side up to cool. If using a fluted tube pan, rotate and tap the pan against the counter until the cake is loosened on all sides. Invert the cake onto the rack to cool. Unless otherwise noted, let cool completely before wrapping airtight or frosting.

Do not increase or reduce the sugar, eggs, or liquids in these recipes. And do not count on success if you simply add chocolate or cocoa to a batter—this type of alteration may require additional modifications. You can, though, vary other flavorings and extracts or spices to suit your taste. You can fold finely chopped dried fruits, raisins, or nuts, miniature chocolate chips, or grated citrus zest into most butter cake batters.

Any butter cake that is baked in layers can also be baked in a loaf or tube pan, or as a single thick layer, should you wish to serve the cake like a pound cake or tea cake without frosting. As a rule of thumb, fill loaf and tube pans two-thirds to three-quarters full. If you don't know how much batter a recipe yields or which loaf or tube pan to choose, set out pans of several capacities before you start. Scrape the batter into a 4-quart glass measure or a bowl, then select the pan with a capacity of $1\frac{1}{3}$ to $1\frac{1}{2}$ times the liquid measure of the batter. Baking time will be longer than for thin layers. Loaves often take 50 to 60 minutes or longer to bake; cakes baked in 6- to 8-cup fluted tube pans take approximately 40 to 50 minutes, as do layers in 2-inch-deep 8- and 9-inch pans filled two-thirds full. Cakes baked in 9- and 10-inch flat-bottomed tube pans and 12-cup fluted tube pans take close to 1 hour, or more. Use the toothpick test, and check early every time. The texture of cakes baked in deeper pans will be closer grained and more velvety, like moist pound cake, than those baked in thin layers. You can also bake butter cake batter in individual pans or molds, such as cupcake tins, tartlet, or madeleine pans.

Try baked Crunchy Almond Topping, 798, or Broiled Icing, 797, with butter cakes.

WHITE CAKE

I. *Three 8-inch round layers or one 9-inch round cake*

This recipe is amazing, in that it can be multiplied by 8 and still give as good a result as when made in the smaller quantity below. We once saw a wedding cake made from this recipe that contained 130 eggs and was big enough to serve 400 guests. See instructions under About Wedding and Other Large Cakes, 703. This formula is also the classic base for Lady Baltimore Cake, 712, for which, in the good old days, 5 layers were considered none too many.

Have all ingredients at room temperature, about 70°F. Preheat the oven to 375°F. Grease and flour three 8 x 2-inch or 9 x 2-inch round cake pans or line the bottoms with wax or parchment paper. (See About Angel Cakes, 705.)

Whisk together thoroughly in a medium bowl:

3^1/$_2$ cups sifted cake flour
1 tablespoon plus 1 teaspoon baking powder
^{1}/$_2$ teaspoon salt

Combine in a separate bowl or liquid measuring cup:

1 cup milk
1 teaspoon vanilla
(^{1}/$_4$ teaspoon almond extract)

Beat in a large bowl until creamy:

1 cup (2 sticks) unsalted butter

Gradually add and beat until light and fluffy, 3 to 5 minutes:

1^2/$_3$ cups sugar

On low speed, add the flour mixture in 3 parts, alternating with the milk mixture in 2 parts, beating until smooth. Using clean beaters, beat in another large bowl on medium speed until soft peaks form:

8 large egg whites
^{1}/$_2$ teaspoon cream of tartar

Gradually add, beating on high speed:

^{1}/$_3$ cup sugar

Beat until stiff but not dry. Use a rubber spatula to fold one-quarter of the egg whites into the batter, then fold in the remaining whites. Divide the batter among the pans and spread evenly.

Bake until a toothpick inserted into the center comes out clean, about 25 minutes. To cool and remove from the pan, see 702. Spread the cake when cool with your choice of icing, 788–800.

II. This batter, which we use for our Easter Bunny Biscuits, see 639, is enough to fill a 7-cup mold or pan.

Have all ingredients at room temperature, about 70°F. Preheat the oven to 375°F. Grease and flour three 8 x 2-inch or 9 x 2-inch round cake pans or line the bottoms with wax or parchment paper.

Whisk together thoroughly in a medium bowl:

2^1/$_4$ cups sifted cake flour
2^1/$_2$ teaspoons baking powder
^{1}/$_2$ teaspoon salt

Combine in a separate bowl or liquid measure cup:

1 cup milk
1 teaspoon vanilla

Beat in a large bowl on medium-high speed until light and fluffy, about 5 minutes:

1^1/$_4$ cups sugar
^{1}/$_2$ cup (1 stick) unsalted butter

On low speed, add the sifted ingredients in 3 parts, alternating with the milk mixture in 2 parts, beating until smooth. Using clean beaters, beat in another large bowl on medium-high speed until stiff but not dry:

4 large egg whites
^{1}/$_4$ teaspoon cream of tartar

Fold one-quarter of the egg whites into the batter, then fold in the remaining whites. Spread the batter in the prepared pans and bake until a toothpick inserted in the center comes out clean, about 25 minutes. Unmold and cool as for White Cake I. Fill and frost as desired; particularly good choices are:

Luscious Orange Icing, 791, or Quick Chocolate Icing, 794

LADY BALTIMORE CAKE

Prepare **White Cake I, 711.** Let cool. Finely chop **1 cup walnuts or pecans, 6 dried figs,** and **^{1}/$_2$ cup raisins.** Prepare **Seven-Minute White Icing, 790.** Reserve two-thirds of this. Add the nuts, figs, and raisins to the rest, and spread between the layers. Spread the reserved icing over the top and sides.

LEMON COCONUT LAYER CAKE

Prepare **White Cake I, 711.** Let cool. Fill with **Lemon Filling, 756,** or **Lemon Curd, 756.** Cover the top and sides with **Boiled White Icing, 790,** or **Seven-Minute Frosting, 790.** Press into the frosting **1 to 2 cups grated fresh or flaked sweetened dried coconut.**

LANE CAKE

Three 8-inch layers

Emma Rylander Lane published a version of this Southern cake in her 1898 edition of *Some Good Things to Eat.* The addition of pecans, coconut, dates, and cherries—even kumquats—to Mrs. Lane's original filling of yolks, butter, sugar, and raisins is testimony to a cook's natural inclination to embellish and create.

Prepare **White Cake I, 711,** baked as three 8-inch layers. Let cool. Prepare **Lane Cake Filling, 759.** Spread two-thirds of the filling between the cake layers, and cover the top with the remainder. If desired, frost the top and sides with **Boiled White Icing, 790,** or **Seven-Minute Icing, 790.**

For best flavor, store at room temperature in a covered container for 8 to 24 hours before serving.

MARBLE CAKE

One 8- to 10-inch or 9-inch tube cake

This old-fashioned cake is still a great favorite.

Preheat the oven to 350°F. Grease and flour an 8- or 10-inch fluted tube or 9-inch plain tube pan.

Prepare **White Cake II, above,** but before whipping the egg whites, remove half the batter to another bowl. Add to half the batter **1^1/$_2$ ounces unsweetened chocolate, melted and cooled, 1 teaspoon ground cinnamon, a pinch of ground cloves,** and **^{1}/$_8$ teaspoon baking soda.**

Whip the egg whites with the cream of tartar as directed, and fold half into the light and half into the dark batter. Place large spoonfuls of batter in the prepared pan, alternating the batters.

Bake until a toothpick inserted in the center comes out clean, about 45 minutes. Cool in the pan on a rack for 10 minutes, then loosen the sides with a knife, unmold, and cool upside down on the rack.

When cool, spread with:
> Boiled White Icing, 790, or Chocolate Butter Icing, 794.

LADY CAKE
One 10-inch fluted tube cake or 9-inch plain tube cake

Another white cake using egg whites only, this makes a tube or round cake. It is also an excellent batter for Petits Fours, 738. It tastes and looks a lot like a traditional white wedding cake.

Have all ingredients at room temperature, about 70°F. Preheat the oven to 350°F. Grease and flour a 10-inch fluted tube pan or a 9-inch plain tube pan. For Petits Fours, grease the sides of a 13 x 9-inch baking pan, line with parchment paper, and flour the pan.
Whisk together thoroughly in a medium bowl:
> 1³/₄ cups sifted cake flour
> 2 teaspoons baking powder
> ¹/₄ teaspoon salt

Beat in a large bowl until creamy:
> ³/₄ cup (1¹/₂ sticks) unsalted butter

Gradually add and beat until light and fluffy, about 5 minutes:
> 1 cup sugar

Add the flour mixture to the butter mixture in 3 parts, alternating with:
> ¹/₂ cup milk

in 2 parts, beating just until smooth. Add:
> ³/₄ teaspoon almond extract
> Grated zest of 1 lemon

Using clean beaters, beat in a medium bowl until stiff but not dry:
> 3 large egg whites

Fold one-quarter of the whites into the batter, then fold in the remaining whites. Scrape the butter into the pan and spread evenly. Bake until a toothpick inserted into the center comes out clean, about 45 minutes for a tube pan, 28 to 30 minutes for petits fours. Let cool 10 minutes in the pan on a rack, then loosen the sides with a knife, invert onto the rack, and let cool completely upside down. Sprinkle with:
> Confectioners' sugar

or spread with:
> Quick Lemon Icing, 793

FRESH COCONUT MILK CAKE COCKAIGNE
Three 8-inch round layers

Some years ago we gave a pet recipe to a friend who later presented us with the one that follows—best made with fresh coconut. She said that, in her family, whenever a treasured recipe was received, an equally treasured one was given in return. We love this festive adopted child.

Have all ingredients at room temperature, about 70°F. Preheat the oven to 350°F. Grease and flour three 8 x 2-inch round cake pans or line the bottoms with wax or parchment paper.

Prepare, reserving the coconut liquid:
> 1¹/₂ cups grated freshly coconut

Whisk together thoroughly in a bowl:
> 3 cups sifted cake flour
> 1 tablespoon baking powder
> ¹/₂ teaspoon salt

Beat in a large bowl on medium-high speed until creamy:
> ³/₄ cup (1¹/₂ sticks) unsalted butter, softened

Gradually add and beat until very light and fluffy, about 5 minutes:
> 1¹/₂ cups sugar

Beat in:
> 3 large egg yolks

Add:
> ¹/₂ teaspoon vanilla

On low speed, add the flour mixture in 3 parts, alternating with:
> ³/₄ cup coconut milk from a fresh coconut, 972, or canned coconut juice

in 2 parts, beating just until smooth. Stir in ³/₄ cup of the grated coconut. Using clean beaters, beat in a large bowl, at medium-high speed until stiff but not dry:
> 3 large egg whites

Fold one-quarter of the egg whites into the batter, then fold in the remaining whites. Scrape the batter into the pans, smoothing the top. Bake until a toothpick inserted into the center comes out clean, 20 to 25 minutes. To cool and remove from the pan, see 702. Spread between the layers:
> ³/₄ to 1 cup currant, strawberry, or raspberry jelly

Frost the cake with:
> Seven-Minute Sea Foam Icing, 790

Coat the top and sides with the remaining grated coconut.

COCONUT PECAN CAKE
Two 8-inch round layers or one 10-inch fluted tube cake

Have all ingredients at room temperature, about 70°F. Preheat the oven to 350°F. Grease and flour two 8 x 2-inch round cake pans or one 10-inch fluted tube pan, or line the bottoms of the round pans with wax or parchment paper.
Whisk together thoroughly:
> 1¹/₂ cups sifted cake flour
> ³/₄ teaspoon baking soda
> ¹/₄ teaspoon salt

Combine:
> ²/₃ cup buttermilk
> 1 teaspoon vanilla

Beat in a large bowl until creamy, about 30 seconds:
> ¹/₂ cup (1 stick) unsalted butter, softened

Gradually add and beat on high speed until light and fluffy, 4 to 6 minutes:
> 1¹/₃ cups sugar

Beat in one at a time:
> 3 large egg yolks

Turn the mixer to low speed. Add the flour in 3 parts, alternating with the buttermilk mixture in 2 parts, beating until smooth. Stir in:

1 cup sweetened shredded dried coconut
$^2/_3$ cup chopped pecans

Using clean beaters, beat in a large bowl on medium speed until soft peaks form:

3 large egg whites
$^1/_8$ teaspoon cream of tartar

Gradually add, beating on high speed:

$^1/_4$ cup sugar

Beat until the peaks are stiff but not dry. Use a rubber spatula to fold one-quarter of the egg whites into the buttermilk mixture, then fold in the remaining whites. Scrape the batter into the pan(s) and spread evenly.

Bake until a toothpick inserted into the center comes out clean, 30 to 35 minutes in round pans, 55 to 65 minutes in a fluted tube pan. To cool and remove from the pan, see 711. Frost with:

Cream Cheese Frosting, 794

ITALIAN CREAM CAKE

This Southern specialty has nothing whatsoever to do with Italy—it is an all-American buttermilk cake loaded with coconut and pecans and filled and frosted with cream cheese frosting.

Prepare **Coconut Pecan Cake, 713.** Let cool. Prepare 2 recipes **(4 cups) Cream Cheese Frosting, 794**

Cut each cake layer in half horizontally. Fill and frost. Store in a covered container at room temperature or in the refrigerator for up to 24 hours before serving. Remove from the refrigerator at least 1 hour before serving.

BUTTERMILK LAYER CAKE

Two 8- or 9-inch round layers

Preheat the oven to 350°F. Have all ingredients at room temperature, about 70°F. Grease and flour two 9 x 2-inch or 8 x 2-inch round cake pans or line the bottoms with wax or parchment paper.

Whisk together until thoroughly blended:

$2^1/_3$ cups sifted cake flour
$1^1/_2$ teaspoons baking powder
$^1/_2$ teaspoon baking soda
$^1/_4$ teaspoon salt

Beat in a large bowl until creamy

$^3/_4$ cup ($1^1/_2$ sticks) unsalted butter

Gradually add and beat on high speed until light and fluffy, 3 to 5 minutes:

$1^1/_3$ cups sugar

Whisk together, then gradually beat in, taking about 2 minutes:

3 large eggs
1 teaspoon vanilla

Beating at low speed, add the flour mixture in 3 parts, alternating with:

1 cup buttermilk

in 2 parts, beating until smooth and scraping the sides of the bowl as necessary. Divide the batter between the pans and spread evenly. Bake until a toothpick inserted into the center comes out clean, 25 to 30 minutes in 9-inch pans, 30 to 35 minutes in 8-inch pans. To cool and remove from the pan, see 702.

Fill and frost with:

Chocolate frosting, 794, or a double recipe of Cream Cheese Frosting, 794

SOUR CREAM CAKE

Two 8-inch round layers

Have all ingredients at room temperature, about 70°F. Preheat the oven to 375°F. Grease and flour two 8 x 2-inch round cake pans or line the bottoms with wax or parchment paper.

Whisk thoroughly in a bowl:

$1^3/_4$ cups sifted cake flour
$1^3/_4$ teaspoons baking powder
$^1/_4$ teaspoon baking soda
$^1/_4$ teaspoon salt

Beat in a large bowl until creamy:

5 tablespoons unsalted butter

Gradually add and beat until light, 3 to 5 minutes:

1 cup sugar

Beat in:

2 large egg yolks
1 teaspoon vanilla

Add the flour mixture to the butter mixture in 3 parts, alternating with:

1 cup sour cream or plain yogurt

in 2 parts, beating until smooth.

Using clean beaters, beat at in a medium bowl medium-high speed until stiff but not dry:

2 large egg whites
$^1/_8$ teaspoon cream of tartar

Fold one-third of the whites into the batter, then fold in the remaining whites. Scrape the batter into the pans, spreading it evenly.

Bake until a toothpick inserted into the center comes out clean, about 25 minutes. To cool and remove from the pan, see 702.

Fill with:

Almond Fig or Raisin Filling, 758

Frost with:

Boiled White Icing, 790, or Seven-Minute White Icing, 790

FOUR-EGG YELLOW CAKE

Three 8- or 9-inch round layers

This is a slightly modernized version of the old 1-2-3-4 Cake.

Have all ingredients at room temperature, about 70°F. Preheat the oven to 350°F. Grease and flour three 8 x 2-inch or 9 x 2-inch round cake pans or line the bottoms with wax or parchment paper.

Whisk together thoroughly in a bowl:

2²/₃ cups sifted cake flour
2¹/₄ teaspoons baking powder
¹/₂ teaspoon salt

Combine in another bowl or in a liquid measure cup:

1 cup milk
1¹/₂ teaspoons vanilla or 1 teaspoon vanilla
   plus ¹/₂ teaspoon almond extract

Beat in a large bowl until creamy.

1 cup (2 sticks) unsalted butter, softened

Gradually add and beat on high speed until light, 3 to 5 minutes:

1¹/₂ cups sugar

Beat in one at a time:

4 large egg yolks

On low speed, add the flour mixture in 3 parts, alternating with the milk mixture in 2 parts, beating until smooth. Using clean beaters, beat in a large bowl on medium speed until soft peaks form:

4 large egg whites
¹/₄ teaspoon cream of tartar

Gradually add, beating on high speed:

¹/₄ cup sugar

Beat until the peaks are stiff but not dry. Use a rubber spatula to fold one-quarter of the egg whites into the egg yolk mixture, then fold in the remaining whites. Divide the batter among the pans and spread evenly.

Bake until a toothpick inserted into the center comes out clean, 25 to 35 minutes. To cool and remove from the pan, see 702.

COCONUT CAKE

Three 8- or 9-inch round layers or one 10-inch tube cake or two 9 x 5-inch loaf cakes

Prepare **Four-Egg Yellow Cake, 714,** adding to the batter before folding in the egg whites ³/₄ **cup shredded sweetened dried coconut, 1¹/₂ teaspoons grated lemon zest,** and ¹/₄ **teaspoon salt.** Bake in 3 layer pans, as above; or bake in a greased and floured 10-inch tube pan for 55 to 70 minutes or in two 9 x 5-inch loaf pans for about 50 minutes.

EIGHT-YOLK GOLD CAKE

Three 9-inch round layers

Nicely complemented by any orange or chocolate filling or frosting. Use the egg yolks left over from making Angel Cake, 705 or White Cake I, 711.

Preheat the oven to 350°F. Have all ingredients at room temperature, about 70°F. Grease and flour three 9 x 2-inch round cake pans or line the bottoms with wax or parchment paper.

Whisk together thoroughly:

2¹/₂ cups sifted cake flour
2¹/₂ teaspoons baking powder
¹/₄ teaspoon salt

Beat in a large bowl until thick and lemon colored:

8 large egg yolks
1 teaspoon vanilla
1 teaspoon grated lemon zest
1 teaspoon fresh lemon juice

Beat in a large bowl until creamy:

³/₄ **cup (1¹/₂ sticks) unsalted butter**

Gradually add and beat on high speed until light and fluffy, 3 to 5 minutes:

1¹/₄ cups sugar

Beat in the yolk mixture. On low speed, add the flour mixture in 3 parts, alternating with:

³/₄ **cup milk**

in 2 parts, beating until smooth. Divide the batter among the pans and spread evenly. Bake until a toothpick inserted into the center comes out clean, 18 to 20 minutes. To cool and remove from the pan, see 702. Fill and frost with:

Luscious Orange Icing, 791, or any Seven-Minute Icing, 790

or sprinkle with:

Confectioners' sugar

and accompany with:

Fruit and Whipped Cream, 754

ABOUT TWO-PIECE CAKE MOLDS

To prepare a cast-iron mold, see 1066 or follow manufacturer's instructions for preparing a shiny metal mold. Lambs, bunnies, and Santas need firm, compact batters. Save nuts, raisins, etc., for decorations, rather than using them in the batter itself, because these solid ingredients, while they make a cake more interesting, tend to break down the tensile strength of the batter. Ground spices, however, are a good addition.

Preheat the oven to 350°F. Grease the mold, using a pastry brush and being rather lavish, then dust with flour.

Prepare:

Batter for White Cake II, 712

Fill the face side of the mold with batter. (Any leftover batter may be used for cupcakes.) If the mold has steam vents, fill the solid section with the batter to just below the joint. (Using these directions, we have baked successfully in cake molds even when they had no steam vents.) Move a wooden spoon gently through the batter to release any air bubbles; ➤ be careful not to disturb the greased and floured surface of the mold. You may insert wooden toothpicks into your animal's nose and into the ears where they join the head, ➤ but be sure to remove the picks when you cut the cake. Put the lid on the mold, making sure it locks, and tie or wire together so the steam of the rising batter will not force the two sections apart.

Put the mold on a rimmed baking sheet and bake for 40 minutes to 1 hour. Test as you would for any cake, inserting a thin metal skewer or wooden pick through a steam vent.

Cool the cake in the mold on a rack for about 15 minutes. Carefully remove the top of the mold and let cool about 5 minutes more to allow the steam to escape and the cake to firm up a little, then unmold and cool completely on the rack. ➤ Do not try to stand it upright until it is cool. If the cake has constitutional weaknesses, reinforce it with a wooden or metal skewer before icing.

Ice with:

Boiled White Icing, 790, or Seven-Minute
White Icing, 790

Or, as a variation to coat a bunny mold, use:

Caramel Icing, 800

Or, if you are in a hurry, try:

Quick White Icing, 793, or French Icing, 796

Increase the recipes by half for a heavy coat. For woolly or angora effects, press into the icing:

$1/2$ to 1 cup shredded sweetened coconut

To accentuate the features, use:

Raisins, nuts, cherries, and/or gumdrops

Surround your animals with seasonal (edible and unsprayed, of course) flowers. If bunnies or lambs are made for Easter, you may want to confect cake eggs and decorate them with icings of different colors. See Angel Cake Balls, 738.

POUND CAKE

Two 9 x 5-inch loaves or one 10-inch tube

Add the eggs whole to yield the traditional dense pound cake, or separate the yolks and whites for a fluffier texture. Sometimes we add $1/2$ cupful each of candied or dried cherries, chopped, candied pineapple and citron, or nuts and golden raisins to half the batter for a delicious fruit cake.

Have all ingredients at room temperature, about 70°F. Preheat the oven to 325°F. Grease and flour two 9 x 5-inch loaf pans or one 10-inch tube pan, or line the bottom(s) with wax or parchment paper. Beat in a large bowl at medium-high speed for 1 minute:

2 cups (4 sticks) unsalted butter

Gradually add and beat until light, 5 to 7 minutes:

2 cups sugar

Beat in one at a time:

8 or 9 large egg yolks (see note above)

beating well after each addition. Add and beat 1 minute:

2 teaspoons vanilla
(2 tablespoons brandy or 8 drops rosewater)
($1/2$ teaspoon ground mace)

On low speed, add slowly, mixing only until thoroughly blended:

4 cups sifted cake flour

Using clean beaters, beat in a large bowl at medium-high speed until stiff but not dry:

8 or 9 large egg whites
$1/2$ teaspoon cream of tartar
$1/2$ teaspoon salt

Fold one-quarter of the whites into the batter, then fold in the remaining whites. Scrape the batter into the pan(s). Bake the cake until a toothpick inserted into the center comes out clean, about 1 hour for the loaf pans, about

15 minutes longer for a tube pan. Let small loaves cool in the pans on a rack for 10 minutes, a tube cake for 15 minutes. Turn small loaves right side up to cool, let the tube cake cool upside down.

SEED CAKE

A Victorian-era cake that reminds us of the bygone days of antimacassars and aspidistra plants, when seeds were used to flavor cakes instead of extracts.

Prepare **Pound Cake, above.** Add **2 to 4 teaspoons caraway seeds, $1/3$ cup minced candied citron or candied orange peel, and 1 teaspoon grated lemon zest** with the flour.

LIQUOR-SOAKED POUND CAKE

Prepare **Pound Cake, above,** as a 9 x 5-inch loaf. While the cakes are baking, combine in a medium saucepan and bring to a boil over medium heat, stirring until the sugar dissolves, **$2^2/3$ cups sugar, $1^1/3$ cups water, and $2/3$ cup corn syrup.** Boil until the sugar is dissolved, about 1 minute. Let cool, then stir in **$1^1/3$ cup rum, brandy, or other liquor.** Poke holes halfway through the warm cakes with a skewer or fork, spacing $1/2$ inch apart. Pour the syrup over the cakes and let cool before removing from the pan.

LEMON POPPY SEED POUND CAKE

One 8-inch fluted tube cake or $8^1/2$ x $4^1/2$-inch loaf

Have all ingredients at room temperature, about 70°F. Preheat the oven to 350°F. Grease and flour an 6-inch fluted tube pan or an $8^1/2$ x $4^1/2$-inch loaf pan, or line the bottom of the loaf pan with wax or parchment paper.

Whisk together thoroughly in a medium bowl:

3 large eggs
3 tablespoons milk
$1^1/2$ teaspoons vanilla

Whisk together thoroughly in a large bowl:

$1^1/2$ cups sifted cake flour
$3/4$ cup sugar
3 tablespoons poppy seeds
1 tablespoon grated lemon zest
$3/4$ teaspoon baking powder
$1/4$ teaspoon salt

Add half of the egg mixture to the flour mixture, along with:

13 tablespoons (1 stick plus 5 tablespoons)
unsalted butter

Beat on low speed until the dry ingredients are moistened. Increase the speed to high and beat for exactly 1 minute. Scrape the sides of the bowl. Gradually add the remaining egg mixture in 2 parts, beating for 20 seconds after each addition. Scrape the sides of the bowl. Scrape the batter into the pan and spread evenly. Bake until a toothpick inserted into the center comes out clean, 35 to 45 minutes in a fluted tube pan, 55 to 65 minutes in a loaf pan.

Meanwhile, shortly before the cake is done, combine in a small saucepan and stir over low heat until the sugar is dissolved:

¹/₃ cup sugar
¹/₄ cup strained fresh lemon juice

As soon as the cake comes out of the oven, place the pan on a rack, poke the cake all over with a wooden skewer, and brush it with half of the syrup. Let cool in the pan in a rack for 10 minutes.

Slide a slim knife around the cake to detach it from the pan, or tap the sides of the fluted tube pan against the counter to loosen the cake. Invert onto a greased rack and peel off the paper liner, if using. Poke the bottom of the cake with the skewer and brush with some of the syrup. Invert onto another greased rack and brush the remaining syrup over the sides of the cake. Let cool completely, right side up or inverted, on the rack, then wrap airtight and store for at least 24 hours before serving.

SOUR CREAM POUND CAKE

One 10-inch fluted tube or 9-inch tube cake

Stays moist for close to a week.
Have all ingredients at room temperature, about 70°F. Preheat the oven to 325°F. Grease and flour a 10-inch fluted tube pan or 9-inch plain tube pan.
Whisk together until thoroughly blended:

3 cups sifted cake flour
¹/₄ teaspoon baking soda
¹/₄ teaspoon salt

Combine in a small bowl:

1 cup sour cream
2 teaspoons vanilla

Beat in a large bowl until creamy, about 30 seconds:

1 cup (2 sticks) unsalted butter

Gradually add and beat on high speed until light and fluffy, 3 to 5 minutes:

2 cups sugar

Beat in one at a time:

6 large egg yolks

On low speed, add the flour mixture in 3 parts, alternating with the sour cream mixture in 2 parts, beating until smooth and scraping the sides of the bowl with a rubber spatula as necessary. Using clean beaters, beat in a large bowl on medium speed until soft peaks form:

6 large egg whites
¹/₄ teaspoon cream of tartar

Gradually add, beating on high speed:

¹/₂ cup sugar

Beat until the peaks are stiff but not dry. Use a rubber spatula to fold one-quarter of the egg whites into the sour cream mixture, then fold in the remaining whites. Scrape the batter into the pan and spread evenly. Bake until a toothpick inserted into the center comes out clean, 1 hour 10 minutes to 1 hour 20 minutes. Let cool in the pan on a rack for 10 minutes. Slide a thin knife around the cake to detach it from the pan, invert the cake, and let cool right side up on the rack.

RED VELVET CAKE

Two 8- or 9-inch round layers

This smooth and rich chocolate cake has a distinctive red color.
Prepare **Buttermilk Layer Cake, 714.** Add to the flour mixture **1 tablespoon unsweetened cocoa powder.** Add **1 to 3 tablespoons red food coloring** with the first addition of buttermilk. Fill and frost with **a double recipe of Cream Cheese Frosting, 794.** Sprinkle with **(shredded sweetened coconut).**

CHOCOLATE CAKE

One 13-x 9-inch layer

A mild, light chocolate cake known as the "Rombauer Special" first appeared in the 1931 edition of JOY.
Preheat the oven to 350°F.
Have all ingredients at room temperature, about 70°F.
Grease a 13 x 9-inch pan.
Whisk together thoroughly:

1³/₄ cups sifted cake flour
1 tablespoon baking powder
¹/₄ teaspoon salt
(1 teaspoon ground cinnamon)
(¹/₄ teaspoon ground cloves)
(1 cup coarsely chopped walnuts or pecans)

Melt over hot water:

2 ounces unsweetened chocolate

Add:

¹/₃ cup boiling water

In a large bowl, beat at high speed until creamy:

¹/₂ cup (1 stick) unsalted butter

Add and beat until light and fluffy, about 5 minutes:

1¹/₂ cups sugar

Beat in, one at a time:

4 large egg yolks

Add the cooled chocolate mixture. Beating at low speed, add the flour mixture to the butter mixture in 3 parts, alternating with:

¹/₂ cup milk

Beat the batter until smooth after each addition.
Add:

1 teaspoon vanilla

Using clean beaters, in a large bowl, beat at medium-high speed until stiff but not dry:

4 large egg whites

Fold them lightly into the batter. Scrape the batter into the prepared pan and bake until a cake tester inserted in the center comes out clean, about 30 minutes. Place the cake on a rack and let cool in the pan.
Spread with thick:

Chocolate Coating over Boiled White Icing, 790;
    or Chocolate Butter Icing, 793, flavored with
    peppermint extract

DEVIL'S FOOD CAKE COCKAIGNE

One 9-inch layer cake

The best chocolate cake we know of—wonderfully light, but rich and moist.

Have all ingredients at room temperature, about 70°F. Preheat the oven to 350°F. Grease and flour two 9 x 2-inch round cake pans or line the bottoms with wax or parchment paper.

Cook, stirring, in a double boiler over, not in, boiling water, until smooth and thickened:

   4 ounces unsweetened chocolate, chopped
   ¹/₂ cup milk
   1 cup packed light brown sugar
   1 large egg yolk

Remove from the heat and let cool to room temperature. Whisk together thoroughly in a bowl:

   2 cups sifted cake flour
   1 teaspoon baking soda
   ¹/₂ teaspoon salt

Combine in a small bowl:

   ¹/₂ cup milk
   ¹/₄ cup water
   1 teaspoon vanilla

Beat in a large bowl at medium-high speed until creamy, about 30 seconds:

   ¹/₂ cup (1 stick) unsalted butter

Gradually add and beat until light and fluffy, about 5 minutes:

   1 cup sugar

Beat in one at a time:

   2 large egg yolks

On low speed, add the flour to the butter mixture in 3 parts, alternating with the milk mixture in 2 parts, beating until smooth. Stir in the chocolate mixture.

Using clean beaters, beat in a medium bowl at medium-high speed until stiff but not dry:

   2 large egg whites

Fold lightly into the batter. Scrape the batter into the prepared pans, smoothing the top. Bake until a toothpick inserted into the center comes out clean, about 25 minutes. To cool and remove from the pan, see 711.

Fill with:

   Coconut Pecan Filling, 759

Frost with:

   Caramel Icing, 792, or Chocolate Fudge Icing, 791

COCOA DEVIL'S FOOD CAKE

One 9-inch plain tube cake, 10-inch fluted tube cake,
or two 9-inch round layers

For a caramel undertone, try it with half white and half brown sugar. For special occasions, fill with Whipped Ganache Filling, 796, and glaze with Chocolate Ganache Glaze, 796, or Bittersweet Chocolate Glaze, 796.

Have all ingredients at room temperature, about 70°F. Preheat the oven to 350°F. Grease and flour a 9-inch plain tube pan, a 10-inch fluted tube pan, or two 9 x 2-inch

round cake pans, or line the bottoms of the round pans with wax or parchment paper.

Whisk together in a medium bowl:

   2 cups sifted cake flour
   1 teaspoon baking soda
   ¹/₂ teaspoon salt

Whisk together in a separate bowl:

   1 cup sugar
   1 cup buttermilk or yogurt
   ¹/₂ cup nonalkalized cocoa powder
   1 teaspoon vanilla

Beat in a large bowl until creamy, about 30 seconds:

   ¹/₂ cup (1 stick) unsalted butter

Gradually add and beat on high speed until light and fluffy, 3 to 5 minutes:

   1 cup sugar

Beat in one at a time:

   2 large eggs

On low speed, add the flour mixture in 3 parts, alternating with the buttermilk mixture in 2 parts, beating until smooth and scraping the sides of the bowl with a rubber spatula as necessary. Scrape the batter into the pan(s) and spread evenly. Bake until a toothpick inserted into the center comes out clean, 30 to 35 minutes in round pans, 45 to 55 minutes in a tube pan. To cool and remove from the pan, see 711.

Fill and spread with:

   Boiled White Icing, 790, Seven-Minute White
   Icing, 790, or any quick Chocolate Icing, 794

CHOCOLATE MAYONNAISE CAKE

One 13 x 9-inch cake or two 9-inch round layers

So dark, rich, and moist it needs no frosting.

Have all ingredients at room temperature, about 70°F. Preheat the oven to 350°F. Grease and flour a 13 x 9-inch pan or two 9-inch round cake pans, or line the bottoms with wax or parchment paper.

Whisk together into a medium bowl:

   2 cups all-purpose flour
   1 teaspoon baking soda
   ¹/₂ teaspoon baking powder

Melt:

   4 ounces unsweetened chocolate, chopped

Set aside. Beat in a large bowl at medium-high speed until light, about 3 minutes:

   3 large eggs
   1²/₃ cups sugar
   1 teaspoon vanilla

Mix the melted chocolate until smooth with:

   ³/₄ cup mayonnaise

and beat into batter. On low speed, add flour mixture in 3 parts, alternating with:

   1¹/₃ cups water

in 2 additions, beating until smooth. Scrape the batter into the prepared pan(s).

Bake until a toothpick inserted in the center comes out

clean, 30 to 40 minutes. Let the 13 x 9-inch cake cool on a rack in the pan if desired, or to cool and remove from the pan, see 702.

Dust with, if desired:

    (Confectioners' sugar or cocoa)

GERMAN CHOCOLATE CAKE

Three 8- or 9-inch round layers

This well-loved American cake is made with a sweet chocolate invented by a man named German.

Have all ingredients at room temperature, about 70°F. Preheat the oven to 350°F. Grease and flour three 8 x 2-inch or 9 x 2-inch round cake pans or line the bottoms with wax or parchment paper.

Whisk together until thoroughly blended:

    $2^{1}/_{4}$ cups sifted cake flour
    1 teaspoon baking soda
    $^{1}/_{2}$ teaspoon salt

Combine in a small bowl and stir until the chocolate is melted and smooth:

    4 ounces sweet baking chocolate, finely chopped
    $^{1}/_{2}$ cup boiling water

Stir in:

    1 teaspoon vanilla

Have ready:

    1 cup buttermilk or sour cream

Beat in a large bowl until creamy, about 30 seconds:

    1 cup (2 sticks) unsalted butter

Gradually add and beat on high speed until light and fluffy, 4 to 6 minutes:

    $1^{3}/_{4}$ cups sugar

Beat in one at a time:

    4 large egg yolks

On low speed, add the melted chocolate and beat just until incorporated. Add the flour mixture in 3 parts, alternating with the buttermilk or sour cream in 2 parts, beating until smooth and scraping the sides of the bowl with a rubber spatula as necessary.

Using clean beaters, beat in a large bowl on medium speed until soft peaks form:

    4 large egg whites
    $^{1}/_{4}$ teaspoon cream of tartar

Gradually add, beating on high speed:

    $^{1}/_{4}$ cup sugar

Beat until the peaks are stiff but not dry. Use a rubber spatula to fold one-quarter of the egg whites into the egg yolk mixture, then fold in the remaining whites. Divide the batter among the pans and spread evenly.

Bake until a toothpick inserted into the center comes out clean, 25 to 30 minutes in 9-inch pans, 30 to 35 minutes in 8-inch pans. To cool and remove from the pan, see 711. Spread between the layers and over the top, leaving the sides bare:

    (Coconut Pecan Filling, 759)

or fill and frost as desired.

VELVET SPICE CAKE

One 9-inch tube pan or 8- to 10-inch fluted cake

This cake has a very delicate crumb. Its flavor is unequaled among spice cakes.

Have all ingredients at room temperature, about 70°F. Preheat the oven to 350°F. Grease and flour a 9-inch plain tube pan or an 8- or 10-inch fluted tube pan.

Whisk together until thoroughly blended:

    $2^{1}/_{3}$ cups sifted cake flour
    $1^{1}/_{2}$ teaspoons baking powder
    $^{1}/_{2}$ teaspoon baking soda
    1 teaspoon grated or ground nutmeg
    1 teaspoon ground cinnamon
    $^{1}/_{2}$ teaspoon ground cloves
    $^{1}/_{2}$ teaspoon salt

Beat in a large bowl until creamy, about 30 seconds:

    $^{3}/_{4}$ cup ($1^{1}/_{2}$ sticks) unsalted butter

Gradually add and beat on high speed until light and fluffy, 2 to 4 minutes:

    $1^{1}/_{4}$ cups sugar

Beat in one at a time:

    3 large egg yolks

On low speed, add the flour mixture in 3 parts, alternating with:

    $^{3}/_{4}$ cup plus 2 tablespoons yogurt or buttermilk

in 2 parts, beating until smooth and scraping the sides of the bowl with a rubber spatula as necessary.

Using clean beaters, beat in a large bowl on medium speed until soft peaks form:

    3 or 4 large egg whites
    $^{1}/_{8}$ teaspoon cream of tartar

Gradually add, beating on high speed:

    $^{1}/_{4}$ cup sugar

Beat until the peaks are stiff but not dry. Use a rubber spatula to fold one-quarter of the egg whites into the egg yolk mixture, then fold in the remaining whites. Scrape the batter into the pan and spread evenly.

Bake until a toothpick inserted into the center comes out clean, 45 to 55 minutes. To cool and remove from the pan, see 711.

If desired, spread with:

    Chocolate Butter Icing, 794, Boiled White Icing, 790,
        or Seven-Minute Sea Foam Icing, 790

BROWN SUGAR SPICE CAKE

Prepare **Velvet Spice Cake, above,** substituting for the white sugar **$1^{1}/_{2}$ cups packed brown sugar** and adding to the batter **2 to 3 teaspoons grated orange zest.**

BURNT SUGAR CAKE

Two 9-inch round layers

The caramelized flavor is a taste sensation and a JOY classic from 1931.

Have all ingredients at room temperature, about 70°F. Preheat the oven to 375°F. Grease and flour two 9 x 2-inch round pans or line the bottoms with wax or parchment paper.

Caramelize, 856:

¹/₂ cup sugar

and add very slowly, stirring until smooth:

¹/₄ cup boiling water

Cool the syrup until it has the consistency of molasses.

Whisk together until thoroughly blended:

2¹/₂ cups sifted cake flour

2¹/₂ teaspoons baking powder

¹/₄ teaspoon salt

Beat in a large bowl at medium-high speed until creamy:

¹/₂ cup (1 stick) unsalted butter

Gradually add and beat until light and fluffy, about 5 minutes:

1¹/₂ cups sugar

Beat in one at a time:

2 large egg yolks

On low speed, add the flour mixture in 3 parts, alternating with:

1 cup water

in 2 parts, beating until smooth. Beat in:

3 tablespoons of the caramel (reserve the remaining caramel)

1 teaspoon vanilla

Using clean beaters, beat in a medium bowl until stiff but not dry:

2 large egg whites

Fold lightly into the cake batter. Spread the batter in the pans, smoothing the top.

Bake until a toothpick inserted into the center comes out clean, about 25 minutes. To cool and remove from the pan, see 702.

Prepare:

Boiled White Icing, 790, Seven-Minute White Icing, 790, or 2 cups Quick White Icing, 793, flavored with 4 teaspoons of the caramel

in addition to the vanilla. Fill and frost the cake.

(Store any remaining caramel in a closed jar; it will keep indefinitely.)

APPLESAUCE CAKE

One 8-inch square cake, 8-inch fluted tube cake, or 8¹/₂- x 4¹/₂-inch loaf

The 8-inch square pan yields the lightest-textured cake; the loaf is denser. Use white sugar for a more pronounced apple flavor, brown for a stronger spice cake flavor. If someone in your family is allergic to eggs, omit the egg and add 1 teaspoon baking powder in addition to the soda.

Have all ingredients at room temperature, about 70°F. Preheat the oven to 350°F. Grease and flour an 8-inch square baking pan, an 8-inch fluted tube pan, or an 8¹/₂ x 4¹/₂-inch loaf pan, or line the bottom of the square or loaf pan with wax or parchment paper.

Whisk together thoroughly:

1³/₄ cups sifted all-purpose flour

1 teaspoon baking soda

1 teaspoon ground cinnamon

¹/₂ teaspoon ground cloves

(¹/₂ teaspoon ground allspice)

(¹/₄ teaspoon grated or ground nutmeg)

¹/₂ teaspoon salt

Beat in a large bowl until creamy, about 30 seconds:

¹/₂ cup (1 stick) unsalted butter

Gradually add and beat on high speed until lightened in color and texture, 3 to 5 minutes:

1 cup white or packed light brown sugar

Beat in:

1 large egg

On low speed, add the flour mixture in 3 parts, alternating with:

1 cup lightly sweetened or unsweetened thick applesauce

in 2 parts, beating after each addition just until incorporated and scraping the sides of the bowl with a rubber spatula as necessary. Stir in, if desired:

(1 cup finely chopped walnuts or pecans)

(1 cup raisins or dried currants)

Scrape the batter into the pan and spread evenly. Bake until a toothpick inserted into the center comes out clean, 25 to 30 minutes in a square pan, 40 to 45 minutes in a fluted tube pan, 1 hour to 1 hour 10 minutes in a loaf pan. To cool and remove from the pan, see 702.

Frost with:

Caramel Frosting, 792, Quick Butterscotch or Penuche Icing, 794, or Quick Brown Butter Icing, 794

or sprinkle with:

Confectioners' sugar

ROMBAUER JAM CAKE

One 8- to 10-inch fluted tube cake or 9-inch plain tube cake

Have all ingredients at room temperature, about 70°F. Preheat the oven to 350°F. Grease and flour an 8- or 10-inch fluted tube pan or a 9-inch plain tube pan.

Whisk together thoroughly in a bowl:

1¹/₂ cups sifted all-purpose flour

1 teaspoon baking powder

¹/₂ teaspoon baking soda

¹/₂ teaspoon ground cloves

1 teaspoon ground cinnamon

1 teaspoon grated or ground nutmeg

¹/₂ teaspoon salt

Beat in a large bowl until light and fluffy, about 5 minutes:

²/₃ cup packed dark brown sugar

10 tablespoons (1¹/₄ sticks) unsalted butter

Beat in one at a time:

3 large eggs

Beat in:

¹/₄ cup milk

On low speed, beat in the flour mixture until barely blended. Beat in:

$^2/_3$ cup seedless raspberry or blackberry jam

($^1/_2$ cup coarsely chopped walnuts or pecans)

Scrape the batter into the pan, spreading it evenly. Bake until a toothpick inserted in the center comes out clean, about 30 minutes. Let cool in the pan on a rack for 10 minutes, then tap the pan against the countertop to loosen the cake, unmold onto a rack, and let cool upside down. Ice with:

> Brown Sugar Frosting, 794, or Quick Butterscotch
>   (Penuche) Icing, 794

OATMEAL CAKE

One 13 x 9-inch cake

This sweet, moist cake with a broiled topping has a loyal following. Make it a day or two before serving.

Have all ingredients (except the water) at room temperature, about 70°F. Preheat the oven to 350°F. Grease a 9 x 13-inch baking pan.

Combine and let stand for 20 minutes:

> 1 cup old-fashioned rolled oats
> 1$^1/_2$ cups boiling water

Meanwhile, whisk together thoroughly:

> 1$^1/_3$ cups all-purpose flour
> 1 teaspoon baking soda
> 1 teaspoon ground cinnamon
> $^1/_2$ teaspoon grated or ground nutmeg
> $^1/_2$ teaspoon salt

Beat in a medium bowl on high speed until light and fluffy, 4 to 6 minutes:

> $^1/_2$ cup (1 stick) unsalted butter
> 1 cup sugar
> 1 cup packed brown sugar

Beat in:

> 2 large eggs
> 1 teaspoon vanilla

On slow speed, beat in the oat mixture, then the flour mixture. Scrape the batter into the pan and spread evenly. Bake until a toothpick inserted in the center comes out clean, about 30 minutes. Let cool briefly in the pan on a rack. While still warm, ice with:

> A double recipe of Broiled Icing, 797

and broil as directed.

TOMATO SOUP CAKE (MYSTERY CAKE)

One 9-inch square cake

This combination of ingredients makes a surprisingly good cake. But why shouldn't it? The deep secret is tomato, which is, after all, a fruit, and it curiously contains no eggs or milk.

Have all ingredients at room temperature, about 70°F. Preheat the oven to 350°F. Grease a 9-inch square baking pan.

Whisk together thoroughly in a bowl:

> 2 cups sifted all-purpose flour
> 1 teaspoon baking soda
> 1 teaspoon ground cinnamon
> $^1/_2$ teaspoon grated or ground nutmeg
> $^1/_2$ teaspoon ground cloves
> $^1/_2$ teaspoon salt

Beat in a large bowl at high speed until light and fluffy, about 5 minutes:

> $^1/_4$ cup ($^1/_2$ stick) unsalted butter
> 1 cup sugar

On low speed, beat in the flour mixture in 3 parts, alternating with:

> One 10$^3/_4$-ounce can condensed cream of tomato
>   soup

in 2 parts, beating until smooth. Fold in:

> 1 cup chopped walnuts or pecans
> 1 cup raisins

Scrape the batter into the prepared pan, smoothing the top. Bake until a toothpick inserted into the center comes out clean, about 45 minutes. Let the cake cool in the pan on a rack.

Spread with:

> Boiled White Icing, 790, or Cream Cheese Frosting, 794

or dust with:

> Confectioners' sugar

BANANA CAKE COCKAIGNE

Two 9-inch round layers

If served very fresh, this cake is good without icing, just sprinkled with confectioners' sugar.

Have all ingredients at room temperature, about 70°F. Preheat the oven to 350°F. Grease and flour two 9 x 2-inch round cake pans or line the bottoms with wax or parchment paper.

Whisk together thoroughly in a bowl:

> 2$^1/_4$ cups sifted cake flour
> $^3/_4$ teaspoon baking soda
> $^1/_2$ teaspoon baking powder
> $^1/_2$ teaspoon salt

Combine in a bowl:

> 1 cup lightly mashed ripe bananas (about 2 large)
> $^1/_4$ cup plain yogurt or buttermilk
> 1 teaspoon vanilla

Beat in a large bowl until creamy, about 30 seconds:

> $^1/_2$ cup (1 stick) unsalted butter, softened

Gradually add and beat until light and fluffy, about 5 minutes:

> 1 cup plus 2 tablespoons sugar

Beat in one at a time:

> 2 large eggs

On low speed, add the flour mixture in 3 parts, alternating with the banana mixture in 2 parts, beating until smooth. Scrape the batter into the pans, smoothing the top.

Bake until a toothpick inserted into the center comes out clean, about 30 minutes. To cool and remove from the pan, see 711.

Arrange between the layers:

> 2 ripe bananas, sliced

Frost with:

> Boiled White Icing, 790, Seven-Minute White
> Icing, 790

ABOUT QUICK OR ONE-BOWL CAKES

We all want a good cake in a hurry. Quick cakes are great favorites, not only for their ease of preparation but also for their delicious flavors and hearty, satisfying textures. Feel free to make them even when you are not in a hurry, and use them to teach your children to bake. All of these cakes can be mixed in one bowl in a matter of minutes. Many are just as easy to mix by hand as with an electric mixer. Contrary to our usual insistence on sifting before measuring flour, we give unsifted flour measurements here both in order to save a step and because these batters are forgiving.

To mix so-called **one-bowl** cakes made with eggs and butter or solid shortening, usually the flour, baking powder, any spices and cocoa, the fat and two thirds of the liquid are put into a large bowl and beat on medium speed about 2 minutes. Add the rest of the liquid. Add, unbeaten, the whole eggs, yolks, and or whites, as called for, and beat. ➤ Scrape the bowl several times during beating. ➤ Overbeating will reduce the volume and give a too densely grained cake.

LIGHTNING CAKE (BLITZKUCHEN)

One 13 x 9-inch cake or two 8-inch layers

This JOY classic is traditionally baked in a thin layer topped with sugar, nuts, and cinnamon. However, the batter can also be baked in round pans without the topping, and used to make a layer cake.

Have all ingredients at room temperature, about 70°F. Preheat the oven to 375°F. Grease a 13 x 9-inch pan for the tea cake, or grease and flour two 8 x 2-inch round cake pans or line the bottoms with wax or parchment paper.

If you want a wonderful thin tea cake, have ready a topping of:

> $^1/_2$ cup confectioners' sugar
> 1 tablespoon ground cinnamon
> $^1/_4$ to $^1/_2$ cup chopped pecans or sliced almonds

Whisk together in a large bowl:

> $1^3/_4$ cups cake flour or $1^1/_2$ cups all-purpose flour
> 1 cup sugar
> $1^1/_2$ teaspoons baking powder
> $^1/_2$ teaspoon salt

Add and mix for 2 minutes at medium speed:

> 2 large eggs
> $^1/_2$ cup milk
> (1 teaspoon vanilla)

Beat in:

> $^1/_2$ cup (1 stick) unsalted butter, softened

for 1 minute at low speed. Scrape the bowl. Beat for $1^1/_2$ minutes at medium-high speed. Scrape the bowl again and beat for 30 seconds on low speed.

Scrape the batter into the pan(s). If making the tea cake,

sprinkle evenly with the topping. Bake until a toothpick inserted into the center comes out clean, about 20 minutes. Cool the tea cake completely in the pan on a rack. Cool layers in the pans on a rack for 10 minutes, then loosen the sides with a knife, unmold, and cool right side up on the rack.

Fill and frost with:

> Peanut Butter Frosting, 795, or Caramel Frosting, 792

QUICK COCOA CAKE

Two 8-inch round layers

Prepare **Lightning Cake, above, in 2 round pans.** Omit the topping and substitute for $^1/_4$ cup of the flour $^1/_4$ **cup Dutch-processed cocoa powder.**

When cool, fill and frost with **European Chocolate Icing, 796.**

QUICK CARAMEL CAKE

Prepare **Lightning Cake, above, omitting the topping.** Substitute for the white sugar **1 cup packed brown sugar.** You may add to the batter ($^3/_4$ **cup chopped pecans or walnuts**), ($^3/_4$ **cup chopped dates**). Spread the cake when cool with **Caramel Icing, 792.**

CHOCOLATE SHEET CAKE (TEXAS SHEET CAKE)

One 13 x 9-inch cake

Mix this cake by hand and serve from the pan.

Have all ingredients at room temperature, about 70°F. Preheat the oven to 375°F. Grease a 13 x 9-inch pan.

Whisk together in a large bowl until well blended:

> 2 cups sugar
> 2 cups all-purpose flour
> 1 teaspoon baking soda
> $^1/_2$ teaspoon salt

Combine in a medium saucepan and bring to a boil, stirring constantly:

> 1 cup water
> $^1/_2$ cup vegetable oil
> $^1/_2$ cup (1 stick) unsalted butter
> $^1/_2$ cup unsweetened cocoa powder

Pour the hot mixture over the dry ingredients and stir together just until smooth. Let cool slightly, then whisk in:

> 2 large eggs
> $^1/_2$ cup buttermilk
> 1 teaspoon vanilla

Scrape the batter into the pan and spread evenly. Bake until a toothpick inserted in the center comes out clean, 20 to 25 minutes. Let cool in the pan on a rack.

If desired, spread with:

> $1^1/_2$ to 2 cups Quick Mocha Icing, 793,
>   or Quick Chocolate Butter Icing, 794

or sprinkle the top with;

> (1 cup chopped pecans or walnuts)

Or spread with:

> Coffee Whipped Cream, 755, or Mocha Whipped
>   Cream, 755

MISSISSIPPI MUD CAKE

One 13 x 9-inch cake

This easy recipe for a cake chock-full of goodies is a great way to let kids have a turn at baking.

Prepare:

Chocolate Sheet Cake, 722

As soon as the cake comes out of the oven, cover the top evenly with:

3¹/₂ cups miniature marshmallows

Sprinkle the marshmallows with:

1 cup chopped pecans

Return the cake to the oven until the marshmallows soften and puff, 2 to 3 minutes. Remove from the oven and spread over the top:

2 to 3 cups Chocolate Satin Frosting, 796

Spread the frosting gently so as not to dislodge the marshmallows and nuts. Cool the cake on a rack until the topping is set.

DAIRY-FREE CHOCOLATE CAKE

One 8-inch square cake

This is a delightfully simple chocolate cake, whether or not you observe dietary restrictions.

Preheat the oven to 375°F. Grease and flour an 8-inch square baking pan or line the bottom with wax or parchment paper.

Whisk together in a large bowl until well blended:

1¹/₂ cups all-purpose flour
1 cup plus 2 tablespoons sugar
¹/₃ cup plus 1 tablespoon unsweetened cocoa powder
1 teaspoon baking soda
¹/₂ teaspoon salt

Add:

1 cup cold water
¹/₄ cup vegetable oil
1 tablespoon distilled white vinegar
2 teaspoons vanilla

Whisk until smooth. Scrape the batter into the pan and spread evenly.

Bake about 30 minutes, until a cake tester inserted in the center comes out clean. Let cool in the pan on a rack for 10 minutes. Slide a thin knife around the cake to detach it from the pan. Invert the cake and peel off the paper liner, if using. Let cool right side up on the rack.

Serve plain, dusted with:

Confectioners' sugar

or frost with:

Quick Cookie Icing, 800, flavored with rum, brandy, or coffee liqueur

ORANGE RUM CAKE

One 8-inch round cake

This orange cake has the lightness of a sponge cake and the butteriness of a pound cake.

Have all ingredients at room temperature, about 70°F. Preheat the oven to 375°F. Grease and flour an 8 x 2-inch round cake pan or line the bottom with wax or parchment paper.

Melt and let cool:

3 tablespoons unsalted butter

Beat in a large bowl, on high speed until thick and pale yellow, about 4 minutes:

1 cup sugar
3 large eggs
Grated zest of 1 large orange
¹/₈ teaspoon salt

Sift over the top and fold in:

1¹/₄ cups all-purpose flour
1¹/₂ teaspoons baking powder

Stir in the melted butter, along with:

¹/₃ cup heavy cream

Scrape the batter into the pan and spread evenly. Bake until a toothpick inserted into the center comes out clean, 30 to 35 minutes. To cool and remove from the pan, see 711.

Puncture the cake all over with wooden skewer. Spoon over:

¹/₂ cup dark rum

Let cool completely.

Glaze with:

Bittersweet Chocolate Glaze, 796

or dust with:

Confectioners' sugar

ORANGE ALMOND CAKE

Prepare **Crunchy Almond Topping, 798,** in the cake pan before making **Orange Rum Cake, above,** adding to the batter along with the orange zest **¹/₈ teaspoon almond extract.**

APPLE CAKE

One 8-inch square cake

We like tart green apples with the skins left on.

Preheat the oven to 350°F. Grease and flour an 8-inch square baking pan or line the bottom with wax or parchment paper.

Whisk together thoroughly in a large bowl, pinching out any lumps in the brown sugar:

1¹/₂ cups all-purpose flour or 1 cup all-purpose flour plus ¹/₂ cup whole wheat flour
1 cup packed brown sugar
1 teaspoon baking soda
1 teaspoon ground cinnamon
¹/₂ teaspoon ground cloves
¹/₂ teaspoon grated or ground nutmeg
¹/₂ teaspoon salt

Add and stir together until smooth:

1 cup buttermilk
¹/₂ cup vegetable oil
(2 tablespoons rum or brandy)
1 teaspoon vanilla

Stir in:

1 cup chopped apples
$^1/_2$ cup chopped walnuts or pecans

Scrape the batter into the pan and spread evenly. Bake until a toothpick inserted into the center comes out clean, 40 to 45 minutes. Let the cake cool in the pan on a rack, or to cool and remove from the pan, see 702.

Serve warm, plain or with:

Vanilla ice cream

or let cool completely and frost with:

Quick White Icing, 793, or Quick Butterscotch
(Penuche) Icing, 794

CARROT CAKE

Two 9-inch round layers, two 8-inch square layers,
or one 13 x 9-inch cake

Carrot cake is now as American as apple pie. Ours is moist and flavorful enough to enjoy without frosting.

Have all ingredients at room temperature, about 70°F. Preheat the oven to 350°F. Grease and flour two 9 x 2-inch round cake pans, two 8-inch square pans, or one 13 x 9-inch pan or line the bottom(s) with wax or parchment paper.

Whisk together thoroughly in a large bowl:

1$^1/_3$ cups all-purpose flour
1 cup sugar
1$^1/_2$ teaspoon baking soda
1 teaspoon baking powder
1 teaspoon ground cinnamon
$^1/_2$ teaspoon ground cloves
$^1/_2$ teaspoon grated or ground nutmeg
$^1/_2$ teaspoon ground allspice
$^1/_2$ teaspoon salt

Whisk together well in a small bowl, then, using a rubber spatula, stir into the flour mixture until just combined:

$^2/_3$ cup vegetable oil
3 large eggs

Stir in:

1$^1/_2$ cups shredded carrots
1 cup chopped walnuts
(1 cup golden raisins)
($^1/_2$ cup canned crushed pineapple, lightly drained)

Scrape the batter into the pan(s) and spread evenly. Bake until a toothpick inserted into the center comes out clean, 25 to 30 minutes in round or square pans, 30 to 35 minutes in a 13 x 9-inch pan. Let the 13 x 9-inch cake cool in the pan on a rack if desired, or to cool and remove from the pan, see 702.

Cream Cheese Frosting, 794, Quick White Icing, 793,
or Quick Brown Butter Icing, 794

Or sprinkle the sheet cake with:

Confectioners' sugar

GINGERBREAD

One 9-inch square cake

Have all ingredients at room temperature, about 70°F. Preheat the oven to 350°F. Grease and flour a 9-inch square

baking pan or line the bottom with wax or parchment paper.

Whisk together thoroughly:

2$^1/_4$ cups all-purpose flour
1$^1/_2$ teaspoons baking soda
1 teaspoon ground ginger
1 teaspoon ground cinnamon
$^1/_2$ teaspoon salt

Whisk together in a small bowl:

1 cup hot water
$^1/_2$ cup light molasses
$^1/_2$ cup honey

Whisk together in a large bowl:

$^1/_2$ cup (1 stick) unsalted butter, melted and cooled
1 large egg
$^1/_2$ cup sugar

Add the dry and liquid ingredients alternately to the butter mixture, whisking well after each addition. Add, if desired:

(3 tablespoons finely chopped crystallized ginger)

Pour the batter into the prepared pan. Bake until a toothpick inserted into the center comes out clean, about 1 hour. Let the pan cool on a rack for 10 minutes. Let the cake cool in the pan on a rack.

GUY FAWKES DAY CAKE

One 8-inch square cake

Also called **parkin,** this not-too-sweet cake is the traditional gingerbread of northern England. Perfect with a dollop of whipped cream.

Preheat the oven to 350°F. Grease an 8-inch baking pan. In a saucepan, melt and stir together:

$^1/_2$ cup (1 stick) unsalted butter
$^2/_3$ cup molasses

Remove from the heat. Whisk together thoroughly in a large bowl:

1 cup all-purpose flour
$^2/_3$ cup old-fashioned rolled oats
1 tablespoon sugar
1 teaspoon ground ginger
$^1/_4$ teaspoon ground cloves
$^1/_2$ teaspoon salt
$^1/_2$ teaspoon baking soda
(1 teaspoon grated lemon zest)

Add the melted butter mixture to the dry ingredients alternately with:

$^2/_3$ cup milk

Stirring just until the dry ingredients are moist. The batter will be thin. Pour into the pan and bake until the cake begins to pull away from the sides of the pan, about 35 minutes. Let the cake cool in the pan on a rack.

HONEY CAKE

One 13 x 9-inch cake

This version is typical of the Eastern European cake known in Yiddish as *lekach*.

Preheat the oven to 300°F. Grease a 13 x 9-inch glass bak-

ing pan. Combine in a medium saucepan and cook, stirring gently, over low heat until well blended:

1¹/₂ cups honey

1 cup coffee

³/₄ cup vegetable oil

2 teaspoons vanilla

Remove from the heat and set aside to cool. Whisk together thoroughly in a large bowl:

3³/₄ cups all-purpose flour

1¹/₂ teaspoons baking soda

1 teaspoon baking powder

2 teaspoons ground cinnamon

¹/₂ teaspoon ground ginger

(³/₄ cup raisins)

(³/₄ cup chopped walnuts)

Beat in a medium bowl on high speed until thick and pale
yellow, 4 to 5 minutes:

3 large eggs

³/₄ cup sugar

Beat the cooled honey mixture into the eggs. Add the dry
ingredients and beat until well blended. Scrape the batter
into the pan and spread evenly. Bake until a toothpick inserted into the center comes out clean, 40 to 45 minutes.
As soon as the cake is removed from the oven, use a fork
to prick holes all over the surface. Heat to lukewarm:

¹/₄ cup honey

Using a large spoon, pour and spread the honey over the
surface of the cake. Let the cake cool completely in the
pan on a rack before cutting.

ABOUT FRUITCAKES

Many people feel that these cakes improve greatly with
age, though not everyone agrees. When they are well saturated with alcoholic liquors, which raise the spirits and
keep down mold, and are buried in powdered sugar in
tightly closed tins, they have been reported to be enjoyed
as long as twenty-five years after baking.

Fruitcakes are essentially butter cakes with just enough
batter to bind the fruit. If you do not care for the usual candied fruits, replace them with chopped dried fruits such as
apricots, pears, or dates, along with the traditional raisins
or currants. Use oiled scissors to snip candied or dried fruits
rather than trying to cut them up with a knife—a sticky
procedure at best. Do not worry about uniformity in the
sizes of pieces, as the knife that slices the cake will cut any
fruit or nut in its path. If you do like glacéed or candied
fruits, you will be rewarded by spending a little extra on the
best quality, often available from specialty stores. Larger
pieces are usually fresher and better.

Bake fruitcakes in shiny metal pans rather than dark or
glass ones, to prevent excessive browning of the cake and
any fruit pieces that touch the pan during the long, slow
baking period—as long as 3¹/₂ hours. Line the bottoms
and sides of pans with wax, parchment, or brown paper to
further insulate the batter and ensure that the heavy but
fragile cake will emerge from the pan without sticking or
breaking. If you use a tube pan, line the bottom with
paper by cutting a hole to allow for the tube; use wide
strips of paper to line the sides and tube as well. Grease
pans first to hold the paper in place. It is not essential to
grease wax or parchment paper, but greased paper is easier to peel off the cake.

For a 2¹/₂- to 3-pound cake, use two 8¹/₂ x 4¹/₂-inch or
9 x 5-inch loaf pans, which yield cakes that can be cut into
30 or more ¹/₂-inch-thick slices. The amount of batter for
2 loaf pans of either size can be baked in one 10-inch tube
pan; the baking time will be twice as long. Do not overlook the possibility of baking miniature loaves, or using
small fluted molds (up to 6-cup capacity) or disposable
aluminum pans for gifts. Be sure to grease and flour fluted
molds generously, as they cannot be lined with paper. As a
general rule, pans can be filled to within ³/₄ inch of the top,
as fruitcake batters rise very little during baking.

Hot fruitcakes have a tendency to break apart. Let them
cool still in the pan for at least 30 or up to 60 minutes on
a rack before removing them very carefully from the pan.
After removing from the pan, peel off the paper liner, if
any, and allow the cake to cool on the rack.

When the cake is cool, you can puncture it a few times
with a skewer and very slowly pour over it, drop by drop,
up to 1 cup (for a 2¹/₂-pound cake) heated, but not boiling,
liquor—such as brandy, bourbon, rum, or wine—allowing
the cake to absorb the liquid. Be aware, however, that
liquor-soaked fruitcakes, as well as those wrapped in spirit-
soaked cloths (see below), tend to crumble when sliced.

To decorate the cakes with candied fruit or nuts, dip the
undersides of the decorations into a light sugar syrup before applying them, or simply cover the cake with a sugar
syrup glaze and then arrange the fruit or nuts on it.

To store, wrap in plastic wrap and then double-wrap in
aluminum foil. Or, if you prefer, wrap in brandy- or liquor-
soaked linens or cheesecloth and place a heavy-duty resealable plastic bag. Fruitcakes can be stored for about
1 month at room temperature or for at least 6 months in
the refrigerator.

FRUITCAKE COCKAIGNE

Two 8 x 4-inch loaf cakes

The fruits stay light in color in this white pound cake.
Please read About Butter Cakes, 710, and About Fruitcakes, above. Have all ingredients at room temperature,
about 70°F. Preheat the oven to 325°F. Grease two 8¹/₂ x
4¹/₂-inch loaf pans and line the bottoms and sides with
wax or parchment paper or brown paper.
Measure:

4 cups sifted all-purpose flour

Mix ¹/₂ cup of the flour with:

1 cup chopped nuts (preferably slivered almonds)

1 cup golden raisins

**(¹/₂ cup thinly sliced candied citron or candied orange
  or lemon peel)**

(¹/₄ cup candied pineapple)

(¹/₄ cup candied cherries)

(¹/₂ cup shredded sweetened dried coconut)

Whisk together the remaining flour with:

1 teaspoon baking powder

¹/₂ teaspoon salt

Beat in a large bowl until creamy, about 30 seconds:

³/₄ cup (1¹/₂ sticks) unsalted butter

Gradually add, beating on high speed, and beat until light and fluffy, 5 to 7 minutes:

2 cups sugar

Beat in one at a time:

5 large eggs

Beat in:

1 teaspoon vanilla

On low speed, gradually beat in the flour–baking powder mixture until thoroughly combined. Fold in the floured nuts and fruits. Divide the batter between the pans and spread evenly. Bake until a toothpick inserted in the center comes out clean, about 1 hour. To cool and remove from the pan, see 702. To store, see 702.

DARK FRUITCAKE

Four 8¹/₂ x 4¹/₂-inch or 9 x 5-inch loaf cakes
or two 10-inch tube cakes

I. Please read About Butter Cakes, 710, and About Fruit-cakes, 725. This recipe may easily be halved.

Have all ingredients at room temperature, about 70°F. Pre-heat the oven to 275°F. Grease four 8¹/₂ x 4¹/₂-inch or 9 x 5-inch loaf pans or two 10-inch tube pans and line the bottoms and sides with wax or parchment paper.

Have ready:

4 cups sifted all-purpose flour

Reserve 1 cup. Whisk the remainder thoroughly together in a large bowl with:

1 tablespoon ground cinnamon

1 tablespoon ground cloves

1 tablespoon ground allspice

1 tablespoon grated or ground nutmeg

1¹/₂ teaspoons ground mace

1 teaspoon salt

Toss well with the reserved flour in a very large bowl:

2¹/₂ pounds dried currants (8 cups)

2¹/₂ pounds raisins (6²/₃ cups)

1 pound candied citron, diced (3 cups)

1 pound pecans, coarsely chopped (3¹/₂ cups)

Beat in a very large bowl until creamy, about 30 seconds:

2 cups (4 sticks) unsalted butter

Gradually add and beat at medium-high speed until very light and fluffy, 5 to 7 minutes:

2 cups packed dark brown sugar

Beat in one at a time:

12 large egg yolks

Add the flour mixture in 3 parts, alternating with:

¹/₂ cup bourbon or brandy or ¹/₂ cup prune or dark grape juice

¹/₂ cup molasses

Stir in the floured fruits and nuts until well blended. Using clean beaters, beat in a large bowl until stiff but not dry:

12 large egg whites

Fold one-quarter of the whites into the batter, then fold in the remaining whites. Divide the batter among the prepared pans. Bake until the cakes have shrunk slightly from the sides of the pan and a toothpick inserted into the center comes out clean, about 1¹/₂ to 3 hours, depending on pan size. Let cool right side upon a rack. To store, see 725.

II. Some say this is best stored for at least 1 month before serving, but we have enjoyed it fresh as well.

Two 9 x 5-inch loaf cakes or one 10-inch tube cake

Have all ingredients at room temperature, about 70°F. Pre-heat the oven to 300°F. Grease two 9 x 5-inch loaf pans or one 10-inch tube pan and line the bottom and sides with wax or parchment paper.

Sift together:

3 cups all-purpose flour

1 teaspoon baking powder

¹/₂ teaspoon baking soda

¹/₄ teaspoon salt

1 teaspoon ground cinnamon

1 teaspoon grated or ground nutmeg

¹/₂ teaspoon ground mace

¹/₂ teaspoon ground cloves

Beat in a large bowl until creamy, about 30 seconds:

1 cup (2 sticks) unsalted butter

Gradually add and beat on high speed until lightened in color and texture, 3 to 5 minutes:

2 cups packed dark brown sugar

Beat in one at a time, scraping the sides of the bowl as necessary:

6 large eggs

Beat in:

¹/₂ cup molasses

Grated zest and juice of 1 orange

Grated zest and juice of 1 lemon

On low speed, add the flour mixture in 3 parts, alternating with, in 2 parts:

¹/₂ cup brandy

beating just until blended and scraping the sides of the bowl with a rubber spatula as necessary. Stir in:

2¹/₂ cups diced mixed candied fruit (citron, pineapple, cherries, kumquats, and/or orange and lemon peel)

2 cups coarsely chopped walnuts

1¹/₂ cups chopped dates

1¹/₂ cups dried currants (about 1 pound)

1¹/₂ cups golden raisins

Scrape the batter into the pan(s), and spread evenly. Bake until a toothpick inserted in the center comes out clean, about 1¹/₂ hours for loaf cakes, 2¹/₂ to 3 hours for a tube cake. (If the cake is getting too dark on top, tent it loosely with foil for the last 30 to 60 minutes.)

Let cool in the pan on a rack for about 1 hour. Invert the

cake and remove the liner. Let cool right side up on the rack. To store, see 702.

ABOUT TORTES

Many people think of baking nut tortes as unattainably difficult, not realizing that a nut torte is just a sponge cake in which the flour is replaced with dry bread or cake crumbs and nuts ground to a fine meal. The technique for preparing nut tortes is just like that of sponge cakes: Egg yolks and sugar are beaten until thick and pale yellow before flavorings and nuts are added. Stiffly beaten egg whites are folded in, providing most of the leavening, as opposed to baking powder.

Here are some tricks in making nut tortes: ➤ Do not use ground commercial bread crumbs; they are too fine. Prepare your own by crushing dry crustless white bread in a plastic bag using a rolling pin, or in a food processor, 1068. ➤ The nuts must never be ground to the point where they become oily. A small coffee/spice grinder with a sharp blade—or a food processor—will produce the light dry, fluffy nuts needed. Do not grind more than $1/4$ cup at a time.

Because nut tortes are often too delicate in texture to withstand much handling, they are baked in springform pans or tube pans with removeable bottoms. ➤ Never grease the pan. The cakes must rise and cling to the sides of the pans like sponge cakes. Let them cool completely in the pan before removing them from the pan.

To unmold a torte made in a springform pan, slide a thin flexible knife or small metal spatula around the edges of the cake, pressing it against the pan to avoid tearing the torte. If desired, with the cake still in the pan, level the torte by pressing down and compacting the edges with your fingers, so the center and edges are the same height, shown below. Remove the sides of the pan and invert. Remove the paper liner, if using, then turn right side up if desired.

You can leave nut tortes unleveled and pipe or heap whipped cream in the depression. For a more formal presentation, level the torte as above and stencil the top using a doily or hand-cut stencil, 786, or glaze it with a chocolate glaze, 796.

Tortes are delicious plain, with coffee, or they can be soaked in wine, filled with pastry cream, or frosted. And who can possibly object to a whipped cream or fruit sauce garnish?

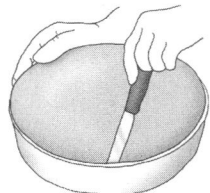 

Removing a torte from a springform pan

ALMOND TORTE COCKAIGNE

Two 8-inch round pans or one 8-inch springform pan

This is the classic German Mandeltorte—a not-too-sweet cake with just a hint of citrus. The extra egg white makes a lighter cake. Please read About Tortes, above.

Have all ingredients at room temperature, about 70°F. Preheat the oven to 325°F. Grease and flour the bottom(s) of two 8 x 2-inch round cake pans or one 8-inch springform pan or line the bottom(s) with wax or parchment paper. Finely grind:

$3/4$ **cup unblanched whole almonds**

Beat in a large bowl, on high speed until thick and pale yellow, about 2 minutes:

$3/4$ **cup sugar**
6 large egg yolks

Stir in the almonds, along with:

$1/2$ **cup toasted or dry white bread crumbs**
Grated zest and juice or 1 lemon or 1 small orange
1 teaspoon ground cinnamon
2 teaspoons almond extract

Using clean beaters, beat in another large bowl on medium speed until soft peaks form:

6 or 7 egg whites
$1/4$ **teaspoon cream of tartar**

Gradually add, beating on high speed:

$1/4$ **cup sugar**

Beat until the peaks are stiff but not dry. Use a rubber spatula to fold one-quarter of the egg whites into the almond mixture, then fold in the remaining whites. Scrape the batter into the pan(s) and spread evenly.

Bake until a toothpick inserted into the center comes out clean, about 20 minutes in round pans, 50 to 55 minutes in a springform pan. Let cool completely in the pan(s) on a rack; the center will sink as it cools. To level and remove from the pan, see About Tortes, above.

Frost (and fill) with:

> Whipped Cream, 754, Coffee Whipped Cream, 755,
> Chocolate Butter Icing, 794, or Bittersweet
> Chocolate Glaze, 796

Or sprinkle with:

> **Confectioners' sugar**

and serve with:

> **Sauce Cockaigne, 847**

Or fill layers with:

> Whipped Cream, 754, a mixture of whipped cream
> and Lemon Curd, 756, or Lemon-Orange
> Custard Filling, 757

and sprinkle with:

> **Confectioners' sugar**

PECAN TORTE

For a richer, moister cake, prepare **Almond Torte Cockaigne, above,** substituting pecans for the almonds.

FLOURLESS MATZO ALMOND TORTE

Prepare **Almond Torte Cockaigne, above,** substituting $1/2$ **cup matzo meal** for the bread crumbs.

HAZELNUT TORTE

One 10-inch springform pan

Toasted hazelnuts will yield a more intense flavor.
Please read About Tortes, 727.
Have all ingredients at room temperature, about 70°F. Preheat the oven to 350°F. Grease and flour the bottom of a 10-inch springform pan or line with wax or parchment paper.
Beat in a large bowl at medium-high speed for 1 minute:

12 large egg yolks

Gradually add and beat well until ingredients are thick and lemon colored:

1 cup sugar

Stir in, blending well:

1 cup hazelnuts, finely ground
1 cup pecans or walnuts, finely ground
(2 tablespoons dry bread crumbs, 545)

Using clean beaters, beat in a large bowl at medium-high speed until stiff but not dry:

8 large egg whites
$1/2$ **teaspoon cream of tartar**

Fold one-quarter of the egg whites into the batter, then fold in the remaining whites. Scrape the batter into the pan.
Bake until a toothpick inserted into the center comes out clean, about 40 minutes. Let cool in the pan on a rack; the center will sink. To level and unmold, see 702.
Serve with:

Whipped cream, flavored with vanilla or sweet sherry

or spread the cake with:

Coffee Icing, 800, or Caramel Icing, 792

CHOCOLATE WALNUT TORTE

One 9-inch cake

Please read About Tortes, 727.
Have all ingredients at room temperature, about 70°F. Preheat the oven to 325°F. Grease and flour the bottom of a 9-inch springform pan or line with wax or parchment paper.
Beat in a large bowl at medium-high speed for 1 minute:

6 large egg yolks

Gradually add, beating until thick and pale:

$3/4$ **cup plus 2 tablespoons sugar**

Stir in, blending well:

$3/4$ **cup chopped walnuts**
$1/2$ **cup finely crushed cracker crumbs**
2 ounces unsweetened chocolate, grated
2 tablespoons brandy or rum
$1/2$ **teaspoon baking powder**
($1/2$ teaspoon ground cinnamon)
($1/4$ teaspoon ground cloves)
($1/4$ teaspoon grated or ground nutmeg)

Using clean beaters, beat in a large bowl at medium-high speed until stiff but not dry:

6 large egg whites
$1/4$ **teaspoon cream of tartar**

Fold one-quarter of the whites into the batter, then fold in the remaining whites. Scrape the batter into the pan.
Bake until a toothpick inserted into the center comes out clean, about 1 hour. Let cool in the pan; the center will sink. To level and unmold, see 702.
Spread with:

**Chocolate Butter Icing, 794, or Bittersweet
    Chocolate Glaze, 796**

or serve with:

Custard Sauce, 846

SACHERTORTE

One 9-inch cake

Frau Sacher, one of the great personalities of Vienna, fed the impoverished Austrian nobility in her famous restaurant long after they had ceased to pay. Today she is remembered throughout the world for her chocolate torte, for which endless recipes, all claiming authenticity, abound. We make no claims but think the following delicious. The extra egg white makes a lighter cake.
Please read About Tortes, 727.
Have all ingredients at room temperature, about 70°F. Preheat the oven to 325°F. Grease and flour the bottom of a 9-inch springform pan or line with wax or parchment paper.
Grate:

6 ounces semisweet or bittersweet chocolate

Beat in a large bowl at medium-high speed until light and creamy about 3 minutes:

$1/2$ **cup sugar**
$1/2$ **cup (1 stick) unsalted butter**

Beat in one at a time:

6 large egg yolks

Add the grated chocolate and:

$3/4$ **cup dry bread crumbs**
$1/4$ **cup finely ground blanched almonds**
$1/4$ **teaspoons salt**

Using clean beaters, beat in a large bowl at medium-high speed until stiff but not dry:

6 or 7 egg whites
$1/2$ **teaspoon cream of tartar**

Fold one-quarter of the whites into the batter, then fold in the remaining whites. Scrape the batter into the pan.
Bake until a toothpick inserted in the center comes out clean, 50 minutes to 1 hour. Let the cake cool completely in the pan on a rack. Remove the sides of the pan and slice the torte horizontally into 2 layers. Should the top be mounded, reverse the layers so the finished cake has a flat top. Spread between the layers:

1 cup apricot jam or preserves

Cover the cake with:

Bittersweet Chocolate Glaze, 796

which should retain its glossy sheen. For a really Viennese effect, garnish each slice with a great gob of *Schlag,* or whipped cream.

ABOUT FLOURLESS CHOCOLATE CAKES

These dense cakes are similar to nut tortes in that the leavening and much of the structure are provided by eggs. All these cakes tend to sink in the center as they cool and remain moister than other cakes. They are ultrarich, not only in eggs and butter but also in chocolate. Choose a fine-quality chocolate, as it is the star ingredient. ➤ To test for doneness, follow the individual recipes, as some of these cakes should be removed from the oven when they are still gooey in the center.

INDIVIDUAL MOLTEN CHOCOLATE CAKES

8 small cakes
Worthy of an elegant dinner party, these flourless, ultra-rich, sauce-in-the-center chocolate cakes are baked in a muffin tin and served warm. You can make the batter ahead, scrape it into the muffin tin, and cover and refrigerate overnight before baking.
Have all ingredients at room temperature, about 70°F. Preheat the oven to 400°F. Butter and sugar 8 muffin cups.
Heat, in the top of a double boiler or in a microwave on medium, stirring often, until melted and smooth:

6 ounces bittersweet or semisweet chocolate, coarsely chopped
6 tablespoons ($^3/_4$ stick) unsalted butter

Remove from the heat and sift in:

$^1/_4$ cup unsweetened cocoa powder

Stir until smooth. Beat in a medium bowl on medium speed until soft peaks form:

4 large egg whites
$^1/_4$ teaspoon cream of tartar

Gradually add, beating on high speed until the peaks are stiff but not dry:

2 tablespoons sugar

Use a rubber spatula to fold one-quarter of the egg whites into the chocolate mixture, then fold in the remaining whites. Fill the muffin cups about three-quarters full. Bake until the cakes are cracked on the top but still gooey in the center, 7 to 8 minutes (a minute or so longer if the batter has been the refrigerated). Let sit for 2 to 3 minutes; the cakes will shrink slightly from the sides of the pan. Place a rack over the cakes and invert to unmold. Serve hot, accompanied with:

Whipped Cream, 754

FLOURLESS CHOCOLATE DECADENCE

One 8-inch round cake
Serve cut into very small wedges with whipped cream and fresh raspberries or Fresh Raspberry Sauce, 853.
Have all ingredients at room temperature, about 70°F. Preheat the oven to 325°F. Grease an 8 x 2-inch round cake pan (not a springform) and line the bottom with wax or parchment paper.

Combine in a large heatproof bowl:

1 pound bittersweet or semisweet chocolate, coarsely chopped
10 tablespoons ($1^1/_4$ sticks) unsalted butter, cut into 10 pieces

Set the bowl in a large skillet of barely simmering water and stir often until the chocolate and butter are warm, melted, and smooth. Remove from the heat and whisk in:

5 large egg yolks

Beat in large bowl on medium speed until soft peaks form:

5 large egg whites
$^1/_4$ teaspoon cream of tartar

Gradually add, beating on high speed until the peaks are stiff but not dry:

1 tablespoon sugar

Use a rubber spatula to fold one-quarter of the egg whites into the chocolate mixture, then fold in the remaining whites. Scrape the batter into the pan and spread evenly. Set the pan in a large shallow baking dish or roasting pan, set the baking dish in the oven, and pour in enough boiling water to reach halfway up the sides of the cake pan. Bake for exactly 30 minutes; the top of the cake will have a thin crust and the interior will still be gooey.
Set the cake pan on a rack to cool completely, then refrigerate until chilled, or overnight. To unmold, slide a thin knife around the cake to detach it from the pan. Invert the cake and peel off the paper liner. Reinvert onto a serving platter. Using a doily or hand-cut stencil, 786, if desired, sprinkle with:

Confectioners' sugar

Store in the refrigerator, but remove 1 hour or more before serving to soften.

CHOCOLATE MOUSSE CAKE

One 8-inch round cake
Only 1 to $1^1/_2$ inches tall, this confection has the texture of mousse, with the intensity of a bittersweet chocolate truffle.
Have all ingredients at room temperature, about 70°F. Preheat the oven to 350°F. Grease the sides of an 8 x 2-inch round cake pan (not a springform) and line the bottom with wax or parchment paper.
Place in a large heatproof bowl:

5 ounces bittersweet or semisweet chocolate, coarsely chopped

Combine in a small heavy saucepan:

$^2/_3$ cup sugar
$^1/_2$ cup Dutch-process (alkalized) cocoa powder
2 tablespoons all-purpose flour

Stir in just enough to make a paste, then stir in the rest:

$^3/_4$ cup milk

Bring to a simmer over medium heat, stirring constantly with a wooden spoon to prevent scorching. Reduce the heat and simmer very gently, stirring constantly, until slightly thickened, about 1 minute. Immediately pour the hot mixture over the chopped chocolate and whisk until the chocolate is melted and the mixture is completely smooth. Whisk in:

2 large egg yolks
1 teaspoon vanilla

Beat in a large bowl on medium speed until soft peaks form:

4 large egg whites
¹⁄₄ teaspoon cream of tartar

Gradually add, beating on high speed until the peaks are stiff but not dry:

¹⁄₄ cup sugar

Use a rubber spatula to fold one-quarter of the egg whites into the chocolate mixture, then fold in the remaining whites. Scrape the batter into the pan and spread evenly. Bake, cool, and unmold as in Flourless Chocolate Decadence, 729.

Using a doily or hand-cut stencil, 786, if desired, sprinkle with:

Confectioners' sugar

Or serve with:

Vanilla ice cream, 831, a berry compote, 839,
Whipped Cream, 754, or Crème Anglaise, 845

Cut with a hot knife.

ABOUT REFRIGERATED FILLED CAKES

We have assembled here some individual recipes that we particularly enjoy serving. We also suggest a number of ways that basic cakes can be combined with fillings. If you must, buy your basic angel and sponge cakes and ice creams. But when you combine them, make a delicious sauce with fresh cream, eggs, or fruit and, most important of all, real vanilla, fresh spices, and quality spirits. The recipes for sponge and angel cakes, 705–706, Genoise, 709, Daffodil Cake, 708, and nut tortes, 727, are all suitable for lining molds. For additional fillings and combinations, see About Cake Fillings, 753.

FILLED ANGEL, CHIFFON, OR SPONGE CAKE

One 10-inch tube cake

Not only delicious but a tour de force. The cake will be easier to handle if baked 1 to 2 days ahead and stored in the baking pan.

Prepare any of the following in a tube pan:

Angel Cake, 705, Chiffon Cake, 710, Sponge
Cake I, 706 (using 6 eggs), Sponge Cake II, 707,
or Daffodil Cake, 708

Have ready a serrated knife or a long piece of thread. Marking the section of cake to be separated with toothpicks, as shown, cut a 1-inch incision at the pick level all around the cake. Then slice through or, if using a thread, hold it taut and with a sawing motion cut the 1-inch high section free. Reserve this top slice for the lid.

Then start to cut a smooth-rimmed channel in the remaining section, to receive the filling. Allow for 1-inch walls by making 2 circular, vertical incisions to within 1 inch of the base. To remove the cake loosened by these incisions, insert your knife diagonally from the top of the inside of the outer rim to the base cut of the inner rim, and continue to cut diagonally all around through the channel core. Then reverse the action and repeat the cut from the top of the inside of the inner rim to the base cut of the outer rim. These two cuts will bisect each other in an X and give you 3 loose triangular sections that are easily removed. The fourth triangle still attached at the base is then cut free 1 inch from the base of the cake. A curved knife, like a grapefruit knife, is a help here.

Prepare:

Any Bavarian pastry cream, 817–18, or Chocolate
Mousse, 816

If desired, some of the cake cut from the channel area can be shredded and mixed with the filling. Ladle the filling of your choice into the channel as shown, below. Replace the lid. Combine in a large bowl and beat until stiff:

1¹⁄₂ to 2 cups cold heavy cream
¹⁄₂ cup confectioners' sugar
¹⁄₂ teaspoon vanilla

Top the cake with the whipped cream or icing. Refrigerate at least 8 hours, or up to 24 hours. Dust with:

Toasted nuts, 1001
Shredded coconut or Praliné, 972

LEMON ICEBOX CAKE

One 8-inch cake

This JOY classic from 1931 is light and sweet.

Please read About Egg Safety, 978. Line an 8-inch bowl or soufflé dish with waxed paper or plastic wrap, letting the sides over hang the bowl. Line the sides and bottom with:

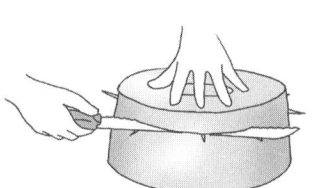

Making a filled cake

Slices of Sponge Cake, 706, or Angel Cake, 705

Mix together:

Zest of 1 lemon

1 cup sugar

Beat in a large bowl until creamy:

¹⁄₂ cup (1 stick) unsalted butter

Gradually add the sugar, beating until lemon colored. Beat in one at a time:

4 large egg yolks

Beat in:

3 tablespoons fresh lemon juice

Using clean beaters, beat in a large bowl until stiff but not dry:

4 large egg whites

¹⁄₈ teaspoon salt

Fold one-quarter of the egg whites into the butter mixture, then fold in the remaining whites. Fold in:

¹⁄₄ cup apricot pulp, stewed apricots put through a ricer, or drained canned crushed pineapple

Put some of the custard in the bowl, then add a layer of cake slices, then more custard, and lastly a layer of cake. Cover and refrigerate for at least 12 hours. Invert the cake onto a serving plate. Whip until stiff:

1 cup cold heavy cream

Fold in:

¹⁄₄ cup confectioners' sugar

¹⁄₂ teaspoon vanilla

Spread the cream over the cake.

STRAWBERRY ICEBOX CAKE

Line a bowl as for **Lemon Icebox Cake, 730.** Fill it in layers alternating with cake and **Strawberry Bavarian, 818.** Chill for about 6 hours. Unfold and garnish with **Whipped Cream, 754 and whole berries.**

MOCHA ICE CREAM CAKE

One 10-inch cake

Cut:

Angel Cake, 705

into 4 horizontal layers and store in the freezer for 30 minutes. Soften:

2 quarts Mocha Ice Cream, 832

Divide softened ice cream into three 1-cup portion and one 4¹⁄₂-cup portion and freeze until ready to use. Chop:

Three 5-ounce sweet chocolate and almond bars

Spread 1 cup ice cream between each of the layers and sprinkle ¹⁄₃ of the chopped chocolate on the ice cream, then cover the cake with the remainder of the ice cream. Freeze at least 6 hours, preferably overnight, to set. Soften the cake in the refrigerator for 20 minutes before serving.

SICILIAN CASSATA

One 8-inch cake

Cassata is Sicily's special-occasion cake. The lightest of sponge cakes is flavored with sweet rum syrup and filled with ricotta cheese studded with spicy candied citron, cinnamon, and vanilla. The whole cake is enveloped in sheets of marzipan and gilded with candied fruits.

Prepare:

Sponge Sheet Cake, 735

Have ready an 8-inch springform pan. Puree in a food processor until perfectly smooth, 3 to 4 minutes:

2 pounds whole-milk ricotta

Add and pulse until combined:

1 cup confectioners' sugar

²⁄₃ cup finely chopped candied citron or candied orange peel

1 teaspoon vanilla

(¹⁄₄ teaspoon ground cinnamon)

Cut two 8-inch round layers and two 13 x 1¹⁄₂-inch strips from the cooled sponge cake. Brush generously with:

¹⁄₄ cup rum

Place 1 cake layer, moist side up, in the bottom of the springform pan. Line the sides of the pan with the strips, moist sides facing in. Trim the strips to fit snugly, and cut level with the pan rim. Scrape the ricotta filling into the pan and spread evenly. Place the second cake layer, moist side down, on top of the filling. Press to level. Cover the pan and refrigerate for at least 2 hours, or overnight. Remove the pan and invert the cake onto a serving platter (or leave it on the pan bottom). Refrigerate until needed. Combine in a small saucepan and bring to a simmer:

²⁄₃ cup apricot jam

3 tablespoons water

Strain. Knead until smooth and pliable:

14 ounces marzipan, homemade, 877, or store-bought

Use a rolling pin to roll a little less than half of the marzipan between 2 sheets of wax paper into a smooth 9¹⁄₂-inch round; to avoid creases, peel off and reposition the wax paper now and then. Brush the top and sides of the cake generously with the warm apricot glaze. Center the marzipan, best side facing up, on top of the cake, smoothing the surface and pressing the edges over and against the sides of the cake. Roll the remaining marzipan into a rough 8 x 12-inch rectangle. Cut 4 neat strips, each 7 inches long and exactly as wide as the cake is tall. One by one, press the strips smoothly against the sides of the cake, overlapping the edges neatly. Arrange on top of the cake in a geometric pattern:

Candied fruit

sticking the fruit in place with a little apricot jam or light corn syrup. Refrigerate for at least 2 hours, or up to 8 hours before serving.

MOORS' HEADS (MOHRENKÖPFE)

Twelve 3-inch square cakes

These Moors' Heads, along with Individual Nut Tarts, 778, and Macaroon Jam Tarts, 779, were specialties of a famous St. Louis bakery, now extinct, and these cakes graced a thousand kaffeeklatsches. While the true Mohrenköpf is baked in a special half-round mold, then

filled and the halves joined, the full taste effect can be achieved by the following method.
Prepare:

Génoise, 709

Using a 17 x 12-inch pan, cut the cooled cake lengthwise into four equal strips, about 3 inches wide.
Make a "sandwich" filling of:

2 cups Whipped Cream, 754, flavored with 1 teaspoon rum or amaretto as desired
1/2 cup hazelnuts, toasted peeled, 1001, and finely chopped

Spread two strips evenly with the whipped cream mixture and cover with the remaining strips, making two long "sandwiches." Ice with:

European Chocolate Icing, 796, or Bittersweet Chocolate Glaze, 796

Allow icing to firm, then cut each strip crosswise into 6 equal pieces.

POPPY SEED CUSTARD CAKE COCKAIGNE

One 9-inch layer cake
A delightful filled tea cake.
Have all ingredients at room temperature, about 70°F.
Combine in a small bowl and soak 2 hours:

3/4 cup milk
2/3 cup poppy seeds

Preheat the oven to 375°F. Grease and flour or line with parchment paper two 9 x 2-inch round cake pans.
Whisk together thoroughly in a bowl:

2 cups sifted cake flour
2 1/2 teaspoons baking powder
1/2 teaspoon salt

Add to the poppy seed–milk mixture:

1/4 cup milk
1 teaspoon vanilla

Beat in a large bowl at medium-high speed until creamy, about 30 seconds:

11 tablespoons (1 stick plus 3 tablespoons) unsalted butter, softened

Gradually add and beat until light and fluffy, about 5 minutes:

1 1/2 cups sugar

On low speed, add the dry ingredients in 3 parts, alternating with the liquid ingredients in 2 parts and beating until blended. Using clean beaters, beat in a large bowl, at medium-high speed until stiff but not dry:

4 large egg whites
1/4 teaspoon cream of tartar

Fold one-quarter of the whites into the batter, then fold in the remaining batter. Scrape the batter into the pans, smoothing the top. Bake until a toothpick inserted into the center comes out clean, about 20 minutes. Let cool in the pans on a rack for 10 minutes, then loosen the sides with a knife, unmold, and let cool right side up on the racks. Fill with:

Lemon Pastry Cream, 756

Dust with:

Confectioners' sugar

ORANGE-FILLED CAKE

Three 9-inch round layers
Have all ingredients at room temperature, about 70°F. Preheat the oven to 375°F. Grease and flour three 9 x 2-inch round cake pans or line the bottoms with wax or parchment paper.
Whisk together thoroughly in a bowl:

3 cups sifted cake flour
3 1/2 teaspoons baking powder
3/4 teaspoon salt

Combine in another bowl or a glass measure:

1/2 cup orange juice
1/2 cup water
2 tablespoons fresh lemon juice

Grate:

Zest of 1 orange

into:

1 1/2 cups sugar

in a large bowl. Add and beat at medium-high speed until light and fluffy, about 5 minutes:

3/4 cup (1 1/2 sticks) unsalted butter

Beat in one at a time:

3 large eggs

On slow speed, add the flour mixture in 3 parts, alternating with the liquid ingredients in 2 parts and beating until smooth. Scrape the batter into the pans, smoothing the top.
Bake until a toothpick inverted into the center comes out clean, about 30 minutes. Let cool in the pans on a rack for 10 minutes. Loosen the sides with a knife, invert the cake, and peel off the paper liners, if using. Let cool right side up on the racks.
Brush the layers with:

Orange juice

Spread between the layers:

Orange Cream Filling, 757

Frost with:

1 to 2 cups Luscious Orange Icing, 791, or Whipped Cream, 754, flavored with orange liqueur

BOSTON CREAM PIE

Two 8- or 9-inch layers
Traditionally called a pie because the layers were originally baked in pie plates, this is really a 2-layer cake. It may be made with sponge cake or plain butter cake.
Have ready 2 layers of:

Sponge Cake I, 706, Four Egg Yellow Cake, 714, or Buttermilk Layer Cake, 714

Fill with:

About 1 1/2 cups Pastry Cream, 755

Leave the sides exposed, but cover the top with:

Chocolate Butter Icing, 794

BLACK FOREST CAKE

One 9-inch layer cake

If you want to fill this cake with a less sweet filling than the traditional whipped cream, substitute 3 cups crème fraîche for 2 cups of the heavy cream. Divide the sugar and whip separately.

Prepare:

> **One 9-inch Chocolate Génoise, 736, cut into 3 layers**

Combine:

> **$1/2$ cup Moistening Syrup, 759**
> **$1/4$ cup kirsch**

Thaw and drain:

> **Two 10- to 12-ounce packages frozen cherries, preferably unsweetened**

Combine in a small bowl:

> **6 ounces bittersweet or semisweet chocolate, finely chopped**
> **$1/4$ cup boiling water**

Stir until the chocolate is melted and the mixture is smooth. Place 1 cake layer on a cardboard cake round or the bottom of a 9-inch springform pan. Brush liberally with kirsch syrup.

Whip in a large bowl until soft peaks form:

> **4 cups cold heavy cream or crème fraîche**
> **4 to 5 tablespoons sugar**
> **2 teaspoons vanilla**

Fold $1/3$ cup of the whipped cream into the chocolate mixture, then fold in another $1/2$ cup. Immediately spread the chocolate cream over the moistened cake. Moisten the top of another layer with syrup and place it moist side down on the chocolate cream. Press to level. Moisten the top of the layer. Arrange a single layer of cherries without packing them tightly, on top; you will have some cherries left over. Spread about 2 cups of whipped cream over and between the cherries. Moisten the last cake layer and place it moist side down on the cherries and cream; press gently to level. Refrigerate the cake, as well as the remaining whipped cream and cherries, until firm, at least 30 minutes.

Frost the top and sides of the cake with the remaining whipped cream. Use a pastry bag fitted with a large star tip to pipe 12 to 16 whipped cream rosettes or a border of whipped cream around the top edge of the cake. Blot the remaining cherries dry and place 1 on each rosette. Decorate the center of the cake with:

> **Chocolate shavings**

Refrigerate for at least 12 hours, or up to 24 hours, before serving.

CHOCOLATE RASPBERRY CREAM CAKE

Prepare **Black Forest Cake, above.** Substitute: **two 5-ounce cartons (about $2^1/2$ cups) fresh raspberries** for the cherries and **$1/4$ cup framboise (raspberry eau-de-vie)** for the kirsch. Or substitute **$3/4$ cup raspberry liqueur** for the kirsch mixture.

ABOUT SHORTCAKES

It is difficult to imagine a more classic American dessert than shortcake. Shortcakes may be made with split biscuits or scones or with layers of sponge cake. They are filled with sugared fresh fruit and topped with lots of whipped cream. A number of doughs will work well for shortcake. For traditional shortcakes, choose Fluffy or Shortcake Biscuits, 639, Cream Biscuits, 639, or Cream Scones, 640. For a contemporary twist, try Cornmeal Biscuits, 639. Roll any biscuit dough a scant $3/4$ inch thick; if any thinner, it will not rise enough to split easily. Sponge Cake Sheet, 735, or Génoise Sheet, 736 also make a great shortcake. For 8 shortcakes, cut the sheet into 16 squares, rounds, hearts, or other shapes and stack them in pairs with fruit in between.

You can use any berries or sliced peaches or nectarines; you can also substitute chilled or hot stewed fruit for the fresh fruit and sugar. Whipped and lightly sweetened crème fraîche or a combination of one-third sour cream and two-thirds heavy cream can be substituted for the plain whipped cream. The fruit and cream can be prepared up to 2 hours ahead of serving. Leave the fruit at room temperature; keep the cream chilled. The cream will separate slightly in the refrigerator but will reblend if given a few swift whiskings.

STRAWBERRY SHORTCAKE

8 shortcakes

Prepare:

> **Eight Fluffy or Shortcake Biscuits, 639, 3-inch Cream Biscuits, 639, or Cream Scones, 640, dough patted or rolled $3/4$ inch thick before cutting, or 16 squares or rounds of sponge cake, 706**

Wash, pat dry, and hull:

> **3 pints strawberries**

Crush one-quarter of the berries in a bowl with a potato masher or fork. Slice the remainder. Combine the sliced and crushed berries with:

> **$1/4$ cup sugar, or more to taste**

Just before serving, reheat the biscuits or scones in a 250°F oven for 10 minutes. (Do not heat sponge cake, if using.) Meanwhile, prepare:

> **$1^1/2$ recipes Whipped Cream, 754**

Split each warm biscuit horizontally in half with a fork. Place the bottom of each biscuit (or a layer of sponge cake) on each of 8 dessert plates. Spoon the berry mixture over and top with the biscuit tops or another layer of cake. Spoon a generous dollop of cream on top of each shortcake. Serve immediately.

ABOUT SAVARINS AND BABAS

The same feather-light yeast-raised dough is used for savarins and babas, but the shapes are different, and babas contain raisins or currants. Savarins, which can be large or small, may be baked in individual doughnut-shaped molds or in large savarin molds or fluted tube pans. Babas are baked in individual cup-shaped molds. Savarins and babas are thoroughly soaked in a sugar syrup and doused with rum or other spirits. The finished product is deliciously moist. A flavorful dark rum from Martinique or Jamaica is traditional, but babas and savarins also can be flavored with any fruit brandies such as kirsch, Poire Williams, framboise, or mirabelle.

SAVARIN

One 8-inch fluted tube cake

Combine in a large bowl or the bowl of a heavy-duty mixer and let stand until the yeast is dissolved, about 5 minutes:

1 package (2^1/$_4$ teaspoons) active dry yeast
^{3}/$_4$ cup warm (105° to 115°F) water

Add:

1^1/$_3$ cups all-purpose or bread flour
1 tablespoon sugar
^{1}/$_2$ teaspoon salt

Mix until blended. Gradually stir in:

2 large eggs, lightly beaten
1^1/$_3$ cups all-purpose or bread flour

Mix until the dough comes together, about 2 minutes. Knead by hand for 10 minutes or with the dough hook for about 6 minutes, until the dough is smooth and elastic and no longer sticks to your hands or the bowl. Gradually knead in:

^{1}/$_4$ cup (^{1}/$_2$ stick) unsalted butter, melted and cooled

Continue to knead until the butter is completely incorporated and the dough is soft and pliable. Place the dough in an oiled large bowl, cover with plastic wrap, and let rest in a warm place (75° to 80°F) about 15 minutes. Lightly oil a savarin mold or a 8-inch fluted tube pan (oil is used because butter can pit the surface of the savarin). Gently place the dough in the mold, spreading it with your fingers so it fills the mold evenly. Cover with plastic wrap and let rise in a warm place (75° to 85°F) until doubled in volume, about 1 hour.

Preheat the oven to 350°F. Place the pan on a baking sheet and bake until the savarin is golden brown all over, including the sides, and a knife inserted in the center comes out clean, about 45 minutes. Immediately unmold the savarin onto a rack and let cool completely. (The savarin can be stored in a well-sealed plastic bag for up to 4 days in the refrigerator or up to 2 weeks in the freezer.)

When you are ready to serve the savarin, soak it with a light simple syrup. To make the syrup, bring to a boil in a saucepan, stirring to dissolve the sugar:

1 cup sugar
2 cups water
Grated zest of ^{1}/$_2$ lemon
(1 vanilla bean, split)

Remove from the heat. If not using a vanilla bean, stir in:

(1 teaspoon vanilla)

Place a rack on a baking sheet. Place the savarin on a plate and ladle the hot syrup over the top (which was the bottom as it baked) until the entire savarin is well soaked with

the syrup. The syrup must be hot so the savarin can quickly absorb it without becoming soggy or losing its shape; the syrup that runs off can be rewarmed and ladled over the cake again. Let the thoroughly moistened savarin drain for about 10 minutes. Brush it with:

^{1}/$_2$ cup dark rum or fruit brandy

If desired, lightly glaze with:

(Strained warmed apricot jam)

Just before serving, fill the center of the savarin with:

Whipped Cream, 754

Top with:

Strawberries or other fresh or macerated fruits

BABA AU RHUM

12 babas

Place in a small saucepan with enough cold water to cover by ^{1}/$_2$ inch:

^{1}/$_2$ cup dried currants or raisins

Bring to a boil, then drain well. Transfer to a small bowl and sprinkle with:

^{1}/$_4$ cup rum

Cover and let soak for at least 30 minutes, or up to 3 days. Prepare:

Dough for Savarin, above

kneading the drained currants into the dough just after the butter. This can be done by hand or with the dough hook. Let rest in a warm place (75° to 80°F) for about 15 minutes.

Lightly oil 12 traditional baba molds or the 12 cups of a standard muffin tin. Divide the dough into 12 pieces and fill each cup. Cover loosely with oiled plastic wrap and let rise in a warm place until the dough has doubled in bulk and fills the molds, about 30 minutes.

Preheat the oven to 350°F. Bake until golden brown and a knife inserted in the center comes out clean, about 30 minutes. Steep the cooled babas in syrup as for Savarin. Serve the soaked babas plain, or fill by cutting them horizontally in half and spreading the bottom layer with:

(Whipped Cream, 754, or Pastry Cream, 755)

Cover with the top baba layers. If desired, brush the tops with:

(Strained warmed apricot jam)

And decorate with:

(Almonds and/or candied fruits)

ABOUT ROLL CAKES

Almost any foam cake can be made into a sheet for roll cakes simply by spreading the batter in a 17^1/$_2$ x 11^1/$_2$ x 1-inch or 10^1/$_2$ x 15^1/$_2$ x 1-inch pan and baking it. Grease the baking sheet and always line with wax or parchment paper. Bake for just 10 to 15 minutes. In addition to the classic sponge, chiffon, and angel cake batters, rolled cakes can be made using flourless chocolate batters that resemble thin soufflé cakes.

Thin cake sheets have a reputation for burning on the edges and for cracking when rolled. To avoid, spread the batter evenly all the way to the edges of the pan. Edges that are too thin burn before the rest of the cake is done. If the batter is ¹/₂ inch deep in the center of the pan, it should reach ¹/₂ inch up the sides of the pan all around as well. An offset spatula is the best tool for spreading batters evenly in shallow pans. Cake sheets crack while rolling if they are overbaked and dry; thin cake sheets become overbaked and dry much faster than thick sheets. Test early, and take the cake out of the oven as soon as the top springs back when lightly pressed or the cake meets the test specified in the recipe. A properly baked cake sheet can be allowed to cool flat, even in the pan, and still remain flexible enough to roll.

ROLLING A CAKE SHEET

Here is how to roll a cooled cake sheet tightly so it keeps a nice round shape. Before filling any cake sheet, let it cool completely, and transfer the cake to a sheet of aluminum foil (not wax paper or plastic wrap) as described in the individual recipe.

Rolled cakes, like sleeping bags, must be rolled tightly at the beginning to ensure a compact shape at the finish. Starting at a short end, fold and press an inch or so of the cake firmly up over the filling to get started. Keep these first turns tight; cracking will diminish as the diameter of the roll increases. Use the sheet of foil under the cake to help roll the cake. Once the cake is rolled, use two hands to move the roll carefully back to the center of the foil. Wrap the back of the foil over the cake so that it overlaps the front portion of foil, covering the roll completely. Place the edge of a baking sheet on top of the foil right in front of the long end of the cake roll facing you, and tighten the cake roll by pressing the baking sheet at an angle toward the counter while you grasp the bottom sheet of foil, shown below. Then wrap the tightened cake roll in the foil and fold the ends. Refrigerate to firm the roll before unwrapping and serving.

Tightening the cake roll

SPONGE CAKE SHEET

One 17 x 11-inch sheet for an 11-inch roll

A delightfully tender, moist, close-grained sponge that rolls beautifully without cracking.

Have all ingredients at room temperature, about 70°F. Pre-

heat the oven to 400°F. Grease a 17¹/₂ x 11¹/₂-inch rimmed baking sheet and line the bottom with wax or parchment paper.

Measure and return to the sifter:

   ³/₄ cup sifted cake flour

Heat in a small saucepan until the butter is melted:

   ¹/₄ cup milk
   3 tablespoons unsalted butter

Combine in a large bowl and beat until light-colored, tripled in volume, and the consistency of softly whipped cream (about 5 minutes in a heavy-duty mixer with the whisk attachment, 7 to 10 minutes with a hand-held mixer):

   ³/₄ cup sugar
   5 large eggs

Beat in:

   1 teaspoon baking powder

Reheat the butter and milk until steaming hot. In 3 additions, sift the flour mixture over the top of the egg mixture and fold in. Add the hot milk mixture all at once and fold in until well combined. Scrape the batter into the pan and spread evenly. Bake until the top is golden brown and springs back when lightly pressed, 8 to 10 minutes. While the cake is still hot, run a knife along the edges to release it from the pan. Immediately invert the cake onto a sheet of aluminum foil on top of a sheet pan or cutting board and remove the pan. Let the cake cool completely before peeling off the paper liner. Peel off the paper liner. Lift the pan and the foil and place the cake right side up onto another inverted pan lined with a sheet of foil, with the first sheet of foil still stuck on top. Peel off the top sheet of foil, removing the brown "skin" from the cake as you do so. Spread the cake with 1¹/₂ to 2 cups filling. Roll, see Rolling a Cake Sheet, above, wrap, and refrigerate for at least 1 hour, until firm.

If desired, frost, or sift over the cake before serving:

   (Confectioners' sugar)

JELLY ROLL

One 15 x 10-inch sheet, for a 10-inch roll

This is our standard roll cake. The batter can also be baked in two 8-inch round layer pans.

Have all ingredients at room temperature, about 70°F. Preheat the oven to 375°F. Grease a 15¹/₂ x 10¹/₂ x 1-inch rimmed baking sheet and line the bottom with wax or parchment paper.

Whisk together thoroughly in a bowl:

   ³/₄ cup sifted cake flour
   ³/₄ teaspoon baking powder
   ¹/₂ teaspoon salt

Beat in a large bowl at medium-high speed for 1 minute:

   4 large egg yolks

Gradually add and beat until pale and thick:

   ¹/₂ cup sugar

On low speed, gradually add the flour, beating until smooth.

Using clean beaters, beat in a large bowl at medium-high speed until soft peaks form:

4 large egg whites
$1/4$ teaspoon cream of tartar

Slowly add and beat until stiff but not dry:

$1/4$ cup sugar

Using a rubber spatula, fold one-quarter of the whites into the batter, then fold in the remaining whites. If desired, fold in:

($1/2$ cup finely chopped nuts)

Scrape the batter into the pan and spread evenly. Bake until the top is golden brown and springs back when lightly pressed, 10 to 12 minutes. Run a knife along the edges to release the cake from the pan. Invert the cake onto a sheet of aluminum foil that has been sprinkled with:

Confectioners' sugar

Let the cake cool completely before peeling off the paper. Fill with:

About $3/4$ cup jam or jelly, such as raspberry, blackberry, or apricot

Roll, see Rolling a Cake Sheet, 735. Wrap, and refrigerate as for Sponge Cake Sheet, 735.

CHIFFON CAKE SHEET

One 17 x 11-inch sheet, for an 11-inch roll

Preheat the oven to 325°F. Grease a $17^1/2$ x $11^1/2$ x 1-inch rimmed baking sheet and line the bottom with wax or parchment paper. Prepare:

$1/2$ recipe batter for any chiffon cake, 709–710

Scrape the batter into the pan and spread evenly. Bake until the top is pale golden and springs back when lightly pressed, about 15 minutes. Run a knife along the edges to release the cake from the pan. Invert the cake onto a sheet of aluminum foil that has been sprinkled with:

Confectioners' sugar

Let the cake cool completely before peeling off the paper liner. Spread the cake with $1^1/2$ to 2 cups desired filling. Roll, see Rolling a Cake Sheet, 735, wrap, and refrigerate for at least 1 hour, until firm. If desired, frost, or sift over the cake before serving:

(Confectioners' sugar)

ANGEL CAKE SHEET

One 15 x 10-inch sheet for a 10-inch roll

Angel cake becomes very dense when rolled.
Preheat the oven to 350°F. Grease a $15^1/2$ x $10^1/2$ x 1-inch rimmed baking sheet or standard jelly roll pan and line the bottom with wax or parchment paper. Prepare:

$1/2$ recipe batter for Angel Cake, 705

Scrape the batter into the pan and spread evenly. Bake until the top springs back when lightly pressed, about 15 minutes.
Run a knife along the edges to release the cake from the pan. Invert the cake onto a sheet of wax paper and re-

move the pan and paper liner. Lift the wax paper and turn the cake right side up onto a sheet of aluminum foil. Peel off the paper liner.
Spread the cake with $1^1/2$ to 2 cups desired filling. Roll, see Rolling a Cake Sheet, 735, wrap, and refrigerate for at least 1 hour, until firm.
If desired, frost, or sift over the cake before serving:

(Confectioners' sugar)

GÉNOISE OR CHOCOLATE GÉNOISE SHEET

One 17 x 11-inch sheet, for an 11-inch roll

You can also cut this sheet into four pieces to make a rectangular layer cake.
Preheat the oven to 350°F. Grease a $17^1/2$ x $11^1/2$ x 1-inch rimmed baking sheet and line the bottom with wax or parchment paper. Prepare:

Batter for Génoise, 709, or Chocolate Génoise, 709

Scrape the batter into the pan and spread evenly. Bake until the top springs back when lightly pressed, 15 to 20 minutes. While the cake is still warm, run a knife along the edges to release it from the pan. Immediately invert the cake onto a sheet of aluminum foil and remove the pan. Let the cake cool completely before peeling off the paper liner. The cake will stick to the foil as it cools.
Peel off the paper liner. Lift the foil and turn the cake right side up onto another sheet of foil, with the first sheet of foil still stuck on top. Peel off the top sheet of foil, removing the "skin" from the cake as you do so.
Brush the cake with:

$1/2$ cup Moistening Syrup, 759, flavored with
2 to 5 tablespoons liquor or liqueur

Spread it with $1^1/2$ to 2 cups desired filling. Roll, see Rolling a Cake Sheet, 735, wrap, and refrigerate for at least 1 hour, until firm.
If desired, frost, or sift over the cake before serving:

(Confectioners' sugar)

CREAM ROLL

One 11-inch roll

Prepare **Sponge Cake Sheet, 735, Chiffon Cake Sheet, above, or Génoise Sheet, above.** Spread the cooled sheet with **2 to $2^1/2$ cups lightly sweetened plain or flavored whipped cream, $1^1/2$ to 2 cups Pastry Cream, 755, or Ginger Fruit Filling, 758.** Roll, see Rolling a Cake Sheet, 735, wrap, and refrigerate for at least 1 hour, or until firm. If desired, frost, or sift **confectioners' sugar** over the cake before serving.

LEMON ROLL

One 11-inch roll

This is especially delicious with an angel cake sheet, which, conveniently, yields surplus yolks for the filling.
Prepare **Sponge Cake Sheet, 735, Chiffon Cake Sheet, across, or Génoise Sheet, above.** Spread the cooled sheet with **Lemon Filling, 756, or Lemon Curd, 756.** Roll, see Rolling a Cake Sheet, 735, wrap, and refrigerate for at

least 1 hour, or until firm. If desired, frost, or sift **confectioners' sugar** over the cake before serving.

CHOCOLATE-FILLED ROLL

One 10- or 11-inch roll

Prepare **Sponge Cake Sheet, 735, Chiffon Cake Sheet, 736, Angel Cake Sheet, 736, or Génoise Sheet, 736.** Spread the cooled sheet with **2 cups (for the Angel Cake Sheet) or 3 cups Whipped Chocolate Ganache, 759, Cocoa Whipped Cream, 755, or Mocha Whipped Cream, 755, or 1½ to 2 cups Chocolate Buttercream, 755, Chocolate Custard Filling, 756, or Mocha Filling, 756.** Roll, see Rolling a Cake Sheet, 735, wrap, and refrigerate for 1 to 2 hours, until firm, or up to 24 hours. Dust with **Cocoa powder or confectioners' sugar.**

BÛCHE DE NOËL (YULE LOG CAKE)

One 11-inch roll

This makes a stunning holiday centerpiece. Instead of buttercream, try Whipped Ganache Filling and Frosting, 759.

Prepare:

> **Sponge Cake Sheet, 735, or Chocolate Génoise Sponge Sheet, 736**
>
> **3 cups Classic Buttercream, 792, or Swiss Meringue Buttercream, 792**

Flavor 1⅔ cups of the buttercream with:

> **1½ teaspoons instant espresso or coffee powder dissolved in 1 teaspoon water or to taste, or**
> **1 teaspoon vanilla**

Combine in a medium bowl:

> **8 to 9 ounces bittersweet or semisweet chocolate, finely chopped**
> **⅓ cup boiling water**

Stir until the chocolate is melted and the mixture is smooth. Stir into the remaining plain buttercream. Refrigerate until needed. Combine:

> **½ cup Moistening Syrup, 759**
> **¼ to ⅓ cup brandy or rum**

Place the sponge sheet right side up on a large sheet of aluminum foil. Brush generously with the syrup. Spread with the buttercream. Starting at a short edge and using the foil to help roll, roll up the cake tightly, see 735, and wrap in the foil. For easiest handling, freeze for at least 3 hours until semifrozen. It will keep, frozen, for up to 3 months.

When ready to decorate, let the chocolate buttercream come to room temperature and stir until smooth. Spread most of the buttercream roughly over the cake roll, and texture it with a fork to look like tree bark. Use a sharp knife dipped in hot water to cut a 2-inch slice from each end of the roll. Set the cake roll on a serving plate. Place the reserved slices on either side of the cake roll to resemble stumps, using the remaining buttercream to cover the joints. If serving immediately, decorate the log with:

> **Meringue Mushrooms, 741**

Refrigerate for up to 48 hours before serving (mushrooms on the bûche may soften—keep extras in an airtight container at room temperature to decorate just before serving). Remove the bûche from the refrigerator 2 to 3 hours before serving for the best flavor and texture.

ABOUT CUPCAKES AND MINIATURE CAKES

You can transform any cake batter into cupcakes by baking it in muffin pans lined with paper liners or pans that are greased and floured (even for sponge and angel cake batters, which are normally baked in ungreased pans). Paper liners are easy and neat; they also keep cupcakes moist and fresh longer. Children enjoy eating cupcakes that have been baked in flat-bottomed ice cream cones (set the cones on a baking sheet before baking).

Fill muffin cups or plain ice cream cones about two-thirds full and bake at 350°F. Baking time is usually 18 to 25 minutes. It is always best to check early and watch carefully. Bake until the tops spring back when pressed and a toothpick inserted into the center of a cupcake comes out clean. Let cool in the pan for about 5 minutes before unmolding.

You can also transform rich butter cake batters into sophisticated miniature cakes, to be eaten like cookies. Bake in small decorative molds such as round or rectangular tartlet pans or madeleine molds. Grease and flour the molds and fill them about half full. Baking time will be about 10 minutes, more or less, depending on the size of the molds. Serve sprinkled with confectioners' sugar or glaze with Translucent Sugar Glaze, 799, made with rum, or Quick Lemon Icing, 793, and serve with coffee or tea.

Choose any icing or frosting for cupcakes. Stiff or creamy icings can be spread with a small knife or spatula. To apply a chocolate glaze, hold cupcakes upside down and dip the tops. For a pointed swirl on top, dip into a soft, fluffy topping such as Seven-Minute Frosting, 790, and twist as you lift and turn the cupcake right side up.

For children, decorate cupcakes with faces, using raisins, nuts, and/or candies for the features. Or stick a small inexpensive plastic doll in each cupcake up to its waist and frost the cakes to resemble fancy ball gowns or tutus. Use candies, colored sugars, or jimmies for sequins and jewels. For a children's party activity, supply a variety of decorations and let each child create his or her own miniature cake.

YELLOW CUPCAKES

About 18 cupcakes

For baking and frosting cupcakes, see About Cupcakes and Miniature Cakes, above.

Preheat the oven to 350°F. Prepare **batter for Eight Yolk Gold Cake, 715, Lightning Cake, 722, or Four-Egg Yellow Cake, 714,** adding **(1 cup chopped raisins or currants).** Bake until golden, 18 to 25 minutes. When cool, sprinkle the cupcakes with **confectioners' sugar.**

SPONGE CUPCAKES
About 20 cupcakes

For baking and frosting cupcakes, see About Cupcakes and Miniature Cakes, 737.

Preheat the oven to 350°F. Prepare **batter for Sponge Cake I, 706**. Bake 18 to 25 minutes. When cool, sprinkle the cupcakes with **confectioners' sugar**.

ANGEL CUPCAKES OR BALLS
About 40 cupcakes

For baking and frosting cupcakes, see About Cupcakes and Miniature Cakes, 737. Preheat the oven to 350°F. Prepare **batter for Angel Cake, 705, or any flavored angel cake, 705–706**. Bake about 20 minutes. When cool, split the cupcakes horizontally and fill them; see about Filled Cakes, 753, and About Tortes, 727, for suggestions. For a luxurious tea cake, ice with a soft icing and roll in chopped nuts or sweetened chopped shredded coconut.

CHOCOLATE CUPCAKES
About 24 cupcakes

For baking and frosting cupcakes, see About Cupcakes and Miniature Cakes, 737. Preheat the oven to 350°F. Prepare **batter for Devil's Food Cake Cockaigne, 718**. When cool, spread the cupcakes with **Quick White Icing, 793, Chocolate Butter Icing, 794, or Coffee Icing, 793**.

CARAMEL CUPCAKES
About 20 cupcakes

For baking and frosting cupcakes, see About Cupcakes and Miniature Cakes, 737. Preheat the oven to 350°F. Prepare **batter for Quick Caramel Cake, 722**. When cool, spread with **Caramel Icing, 792, or Quick Butterscotch or Penuche Icing, 794**.

SOUR CREAM SPICE CUPCAKES
About 18 cupcakes

For baking and frosting cupcakes, see About Cupcakes and Miniature Cakes, 737. Preheat the oven to 350°F. Prepare **batter for Sour Cream Cake, 714**. Add: **$1/2$ teaspoon ground cinnamon and $1/4$ teaspoon ground cloves** to the dry ingredients and substituting **1 cup packed brown sugar** for the white sugar. Fold into the finished batter **$3/4$ cup chopped walnuts or pecans**. Bake 15 minutes. Serve plain or iced.

JAM CUPCAKES
About 20 cupcakes

For baking and frosting cupcakes, see About Cupcakes and Miniature Cakes, 737. Preheat the oven to 350°F. Prepare **batter for Rombauer Jam Cake, 720**. Spread the cool cupcakes with **Quick Butterscotch (Penuche) Icing, 794**.

COCONUT CUPCAKES
About 36 cupcakes

For baking and frosting cupcakes, see About Cupcakes and Miniature Cakes, 737. Preheat the oven to 350°F. Pre-pare **batter for Coconut Loaf Cake, 715**, omitting the lemon. When cool, spread with, **Seven-Minute Frosting with Toasted Coconut, 790**.

BLACK BOTTOM CUPCAKES
18 cupcakes

For baking and frosting cupcakes, see About Cupcakes and Miniature Cakes, 737. Moist, dark chocolate cup-cakes with a heart of cream cheese and chocolate chips. Have all ingredients at room temperature, about 70°F. Preheat the oven to 350°F. Beat in a medium bowl until smooth:

> **8 ounces cream cheese, softened**
> **$1/3$ cup sugar**

Add and beat until smooth:

> **1 large egg**

Stir in:

> **1 cup chocolate chips**

Whisk together thoroughly in a large bowl:

> **$1 1/2$ cups all-purpose flour**
> **1 cup sugar**
> **$1/4$ cup nonalkalized cocoa powder**
> **1 teaspoon baking soda**
> **$1/2$ teaspoon salt**

Add:

> **1 cup water**
> **$1/3$ cup vegetable oil**
> **1 tablespoon distilled white vinegar**
> **1 teaspoon vanilla**

Stir with a rubber spatula just until smooth. Fill the muffin cups about half full. Place a heaping tablespoon of the cream cheese mixture in the center of each. Bake until a toothpick inserted into the cakey part of a cupcake comes out clean, 20 to 25 minutes. Remove from the pan and let cool completely on a rack before frosting or sprinkling with powdered sugar.

PETITS FOURS
About eighty 1-inch squares

Traditional petits fours are made of small cubes of white cake, pound cake, or sponge cake split and filled with jam and iced with white, pink, and green fondant. However, if you are willing to experiment, you can create interesting and elegant petits fours from almost any cake, filling, and frosting you choose.

Prepare:

> **Batter for Sponge Sheet Cake, 735, Génoise or Chocolate Génoise Sheet, 736, Lady Cake, 713, or Pound Cake, 716**

Bake in a 13 x 9-inch baking pan lined with wax or parchment paper and floured, at the temperature recommended for the cake; baking time will be 28 to 30 minutes. Bake just until the top of the cake springs back when lightly pressed and a toothpick inserted into a few places comes out clean. Let cool completely in the pan on a rack before filling and frosting.

Cut the finished cake crosswise in half and spread one of the halves with:

1 cup jam, heated and strained or pureed for easy spreading, or a filling or buttercream of your choice, 753

Stack the layers, with the uncoated piece on top. If the finished cake is 1 inch or more tall, cut it into three large pieces to make it easier to handle, then cut each piece horizontally into two layers with a serrated knife before filling. (If the cake is rich, you don't have to split and fill it—simply cut and glaze it.) Cakes filled with jam should be weighted: Place the filled cakes on a cookie sheet and cover the top and sides with plastic wrap. Place a second cookie sheet on top and weight with canned goods to level and compact the layers so they will not come apart when cut into small shapes. Refrigerate for several hours, until firm, or wrap and freeze for up to 3 months.

To cut and glaze the petits fours: If desired, first brush hot strained preserves over the filled cakes and top with a ⅛-inch-thick layer of rolled marzipan, 877. Génoise cakes are best when brushed with Moistening Syrup, 759. Cut the cake into small squares or bars with a sharp serrated knife; 1-inch squares will yield the classic two-bite-size cake. Or, with cookie or canapé cutters, cut the cake into small squares or diamonds, rounds or hearts, or other shapes. (This may yield larger—and therefore fewer— petits fours.)

If you have not covered the cake with preserves and marzipan, you can brush the top and sides of each cut shape with hot preserves now, or spread a thin coat of buttercream on the tops and sides. Refrigerate to set the coating before glazing.

Place the cakes 1 inch apart on a wire grid or a rack set on a baking sheet. Spoon Bittersweet Chocolate Glaze, 796, Chocolate Ganache Glaze, 796, or Fondant Icing, 791, over each one, shown above (you will need 4 pounds of fondant to coat 80 petits fours). For detailed instructions, see Fondant Icing, 791. Chill or let stand to set the coating. Once the glaze or fondant is set, you can decorate the petits fours with pieces of candied violets or rose petals, candied fruits, dragées, sliced almonds, or pistachios. Or pipe dainty designs with melted chocolate or

Glazing petits fours

tinted fondant. If you like, serve in pleated paper cups. Petits fours can be completed up to 24 hours in advance.

MADELEINES
About 20 tea cakes

It was Proust's fortuitous nibble of a madeleine with tea that awakened from the subconscious the sensitive recollections of his childhood in a French provincial town—and from there, the long pageant of *Remembrance of Things Past.*

These buttery French tea cakes, something between a sponge cake and a butter cake in texture, are traditionally baked in scallop-shaped madeleine molds, but you can use miniature muffin tins or small tartlet pans in any shape.

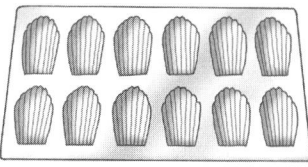

Madeleine pan

Have all ingredients at room temperature, about 70°F. Sift together and then return to the sifter:

1½ cups sifted cake flour
½ teaspoon baking powder
¼ teaspoon salt

Mash and beat in a medium bowl with a wooden spoon or rubber spatula until the consistency of mayonnaise:

¾ cup (1½ sticks) unsalted butter, cut into small pieces

Warm the bowl by dipping it into hot water if necessary to hasten the softening of the butter. Beat in a large bowl on high speed until thick and pale yellow, 2 to 5 minutes:

3 large eggs
1 large egg yolk
¾ cup sugar
1½ teaspoons vanilla

Sift the flour mixture over the top and fold in with a rubber spatula. Fold a dollop of the egg mixture into the butter, then scrape the butter mixture back into the remaining egg mixture and fold together. Let rest for at least 30 minutes.

Preheat the oven to 450°F. Using the melted butter, generously grease 1 or 2 madeleine pans with 12 molds each. Fill the molds three-quarters full; set any remaining batter aside. Bake until the cakes are golden on the top and golden brown around the edges, 8 to 10 minutes. Immediately loosen each cake with the tip of a slim knife and unmold onto a rack to cool. If necessary, wipe the molds clean and let cool, rebutter them, and bake with the remaining batter. These are best the day they are made but they can be stored in an airtight container for a day or two.

LADYFINGERS

Thirty-six 4-inch ladyfingers

These light sponge fingers are a delicious nibble, but most find their way into refrigerator desserts such as Tiramisù, 819, or Charlotte Russe, 818.

Preheat the oven to 350°F. Grease and flour 2 large baking sheets or line the bottoms with parchment paper.

Prepare:

Batter for French Sponge Cake (Biscuit), 708

Scrape the batter into a large pastry bag fitted with a ⁵/₈-inch plain tip. Pipe 4-inch fingers at least 1 inch apart on the baking sheets. Sift lightly over the ladyfingers:

Confectioners' sugar

Bake until golden brown, 10 to 15 minutes. Transfer the ladyfingers to a rack, or slide the parchment paper onto the rack, and cool completely. Store in an airtight container.

ABOUT MERINGUE PASTE

In the broadest sense, the term "meringue" refers to any baked or unbaked mixture of beaten egg whites with sugar. Raw meringue is folded into cake batters, mousses, Bavarian creams, sauces, pancakes, soufflés, and other mixtures that need an infusion of air or lightness. As all meringues and variations are based on beaten egg whites, see 978 for the proper beating technique.

Here, however, we are concerned with baked meringue. Baked meringues can be crisp and dry throughout, crisp on the outside and marshmallowy within, or dry with a cakelike texture. They may be plain, flavored, or nutted. Dacquoise, 741, also called Japonaise, Broyage, and Succès, is a crisp sheet of meringue with ground nuts and often a little flour or cornstarch. Meringue and Dacquoise are used as cake layers, on their own or alternated with thin sponge or génoise layers. Filled and frosted with buttercream, these make elegant layer cakes such as Fresh Strawberry Dacquoise, 741. Meringue is also used to make cookies, 771, meringue mushrooms, and meringue pie shell, 666.

Meringues are crisp or soft depending upon the ratio of sugar to egg whites and the temperature at which the meringue is baked. The eggs should be at room temperature. For most uses, ingredients and proportions do not vary. For every 4 large egg whites use 1 cup of sugar. Meringues are baked in a very low oven (200° to 225°F) for as long as 2 hours, to dry them completely without browning or coloring. Then they are left to cool in the turned-off oven to ensure dryness; an overnight rest in an oven with a pilot light is the sure way to get perfect meringues. The same meringue base baked at 275°F for half the time is crisp on the outside and marhmallowy within. We encounter these types of meringues garnished with whipped cream and fruit. (Soft meringue toppings, 740, and soft dry nut meringue cake layers are made with about half as much sugar and baked at higher temperatures for shorter periods of time.)

Crisp dry meringue keeps for several weeks in airtight containers. Do not refrigerate or freeze.

Crisp baked meringue shells or layers to be filled with whipped cream, custard, mousses, or any other moist fillings should be filled just before serving if they are to remain crisp. Meringues filled with ice cream or frozen desserts are called meringues glacées. These can be filled in advance and returned to the freezer for up to 4 days until serving; freezing protects the meringues from disintegration. Crisp meringue or dacquoise layers layered with buttercreams retain much of their crispness because the high fat content of the buttercream protects the layers from moisture.

ABOUT FORMING AND BAKING MERINGUES AND DACQUOISE

To form individual meringues: Drop 12 shapely 3-inch dollops of meringue onto the prepared baking sheet with a spoon.

To form layers with a spatula: Divide the meringue evenly among the traced circles and spread with a spatula, making sure that the thickness of the meringue is as uniform as possible. Neaten the edges of each circle by tracing around them with your finger.

To form meringue layers with a pastry bag: Scrape the meringue into a large pastry bag fitted with a ³/₈- to ¹/₂-inch plain tip. Starting in the center of each circle, pipe a widening spiral of meringue until each circle is covered with a coiled rope of meringue.

Bake for 1¹/₂ to 2 hours. To check, Remove a test shape from the oven and let it cool for 5 minutes. If it is dry and crisp to the bite, then similarly sized meringues are done. Larger meringues can also be tested by probing with the tip of a sharp paring knife. If the center of the meringue seems only slightly sticky, it will crisp as it cools. If meringue kisses are to be filled, you can make a depression in the flat side of each one with your finger while they are still slightly sticky inside and return them to the oven. If in doubt, bake for the full 2 hours, or even a little longer. Leave the meringues in the turned-off oven to cool. If not using immediately, store airtight. Meringue layers are fragile. Cut the excess parchment paper from around each one and store still attached to the paper for protection. To remove it from the parchment, slide a slender metal spatula under each layer.

MERINGUE

Two 8- or 9-inch rounds or three 7-inch rounds or twelve 3-inch meringues

Have all ingredients at room temperature, about 70°F. Preheat the oven to 225°F. Line cookie sheets with parchment paper for free-form meringues or individual meringue shells. Or, for layers, trace two 8- or 9-inch or three 7-inch circles on the parchment, leaving an inch between them, and turn it upside down so that the tracing shows through but cannot transfer to the meringue.

I. Beat in a large bowl on medium speed until soft peaks form:

4 large egg whites (about $^1/_2$ cup)
(1 teaspoon vanilla)
$^1/_2$ teaspoon cream of tartar

Very gradually add, 1 tablespoon at a time, beating on high speed:

1 cup superfine sugar

Beat until the meringue holds very stiff peaks. Shape and bake as directed in About Forming and Baking Meringues and Dacquoise, 740, or in the individual recipe.

II. Prepare:

Meringue I, 740

reducing the superfine sugar to $^2/_3$ cup. After beating it in, sift:

$^2/_3$ cup confectioners' sugar

over the meringue and fold in with a rubber spatula.

WARM-METHOD MERINGUE

Use this method for either Meringue I or II, 740. Whisk together the egg whites, superfine sugar, cream of tartar, and vanilla, if using, in a large heatproof bowl. Set the bowl in a skillet of gently simmering water and whisk until the whites are warm, not hot, to the touch (110° to 115°F). Remove the bowl from the skillet and beat on high speed until the whites are stiff. If making Meringue II fold in the confectioners' sugar.

COFFEE-FLAVORED MERINGUE

Prepare **Meringue I or II, 740**. Stir **2$^1/_2$ teaspoons instant espresso powder or pulverized instant coffee** into the superfine sugar before adding it to the egg whites.

COCOA MERINGUE

Prepare **Meringue II, 740**. Sift **3 tablespoons unsweetened cocoa powder** with the confectioners' sugar before folding it into the meringue.

MERINGUE MUSHROOMS

48 to 60 mushrooms

It is best to use the warm method when preparing the meringue for these mushrooms, as it will hold its shape longer while you pipe the caps and stems.

Preheat the oven to 200°F. Line 2 baking sheets with parchment paper. Prepare:

Meringue I or II, 740, using the Warm Method, above

Scrape the meringue into a large pastry bag fitted with a $^1/_2$-inch plain tip. Pipe thin pointed "kiss" shapes about 1 inch tall onto the baking sheets to make stems. Pipe round button shapes to make mushroom caps. Use a lightly moistened or damp finger to smooth the tops of the caps if necessary. Dust lightly with:

Unsweetened cocoa powder

Bake until crisp and completely dry, about 2 hours. Let cool in the turned-off oven. Melt:

2 ounces semisweet or bittersweet chocolate, coarsely chopped

Use a sharp knife to cut off and discard the pointed ends of the meringue stems. Spread a little melted chocolate on the flat side of each meringue mushroom cap and attach the stems while the chocolate is still soft. Let stand until the chocolate is set. The mushrooms can be stored in an airtight container for up to 4 weeks.

DACQUOISE

Two 8- or 9-inch rounds or three 7-inch rounds

See About Meringue Paste, 740. Use $^1/_2$ to $^3/_4$ cup nuts, depending on how much nut flavor you wish.

Have all ingredients at room temperature, about 70°F. Preheat the oven to 200°F. Line cookie sheets with parchment paper. Trace two 8- or 9-inch or three 7-inch circles on the parchment, leaving at least an inch between them, and turn it upside down so that the tracing shows through but cannot transfer to the meringue. Combine in a food processor:

$^1/_2$ to $^3/_4$ cup nuts (whole or pieces)
$^1/_3$ cup superfine sugar
1 tablespoon cornstarch

Pulse until the mixture has the consistency of fine cornmeal; do not overprocess, or the nuts will become oily. Beat in a large bowl on medium speed until soft peaks form:

4 large egg whites (about $^1/_2$ cup)
$^1/_2$ teaspoon cream of tartar

Very gradually add, 1 tablespoon at a time, beating on high speed:

$^1/_2$ cup superfine sugar

Beat until the meringue holds very stiff peaks. Fold in the nut mixture. Shape and bake the layers as directed in About Forming and Baking Meringues and Dacquoise, 740.

FRESH STRAWBERRY MERINGUE OR DACQUOISE WITH WHIPPED CREAM AND CHOCOLATE

One 9-inch cake

Crunchy and creamy, sweet and tart, this is a grand dessert. Have your way with it: Vary the nuts in the dacquoise, omit the chocolate coating on the layers, and/or substitute whole raspberries for the sliced strawberries. For a singularly American twist, try bananas and cream between layers of peanut dacquoise, topped with chocolate-dipped strawberries.

Prepare:

Three 9-inch layers (from 1$^1/_2$ recipes) Meringue I or II, 740, or Dacquoise, above, made with almonds

Choose 12 of the best-looking berries from:

2 pints strawberries, hulled

Dip them halfway into:

1 cup Bittersweet Chocolate Glaze, 796

Set on a cookie sheet lined with wax or parchment paper and refrigerate. Spread both sides of each meringue or dacquoise layer with the remaining glaze. Set the coated layers on wax or parchment paper and refrigerate to set the chocolate. Slice the remaining strawberries. Whip until thickened:

2 cups heavy cream or crème fraîche

Add and beat just until almost stiff:

1 to 2 tablespoons sugar

1 teaspoon vanilla

Fold the sliced berries into 2 cups of the whipped cream. Spread 1 chocolate-coated layer with about half of the strawberry filling. Top with a second layer. Spread with the remaining filling. Top with the third layer. Frost the top and sides of the stack with the plain whipped cream. Press into the sides:

¾ cup sliced blanched almonds, toasted, 1001

If there is any cream remaining, use a pastry bag fitted with a medium star tip to pipe a border of rosettes around the top edge of the cake. Decorate the top with the chocolate-coated strawberries. Refrigerate for 2 to 4 hours before serving.

ABOUT CHEESECAKES

The two main cheesecake camps are cream cheese and ricotta or curd-style cheese. Then there are fans of creamy versus dry, dense versus light. Factions exist as well for and against different types of crust (or any crust at all), toppings other than sour cream, any flavors other than plain. We offer several kinds so you and your guests can choose—and then probably, keep arguing.

Cheesecakes are really very rich cheese and egg custards, not cakes at all. As such, they require low heat and proper timing to avoid the big cheesecake faults: cracking, shrinkage, and overbaking around the edges. ➤ Overmixing is the culprit in some cases, but most of the time the causes are baking too long or at too high a temperature and/or cooling too quickly. To make matters worse, cracking and shrinking do not become obvious until the cheesecake is out of the oven and cooling.

The remedy for most cheesecake problems is to ➤ keep baking temperatures low (300° to 325°F, with some exceptions), to check the accuracy of your oven, and to learn to take the cake out of the oven when it is still jiggly in the center. ➤ Remember that cheesecakes do not set until completely cool or even chilled. Cool a cheesecake slowly on the counter with a large bowl or pot inverted over it to keep the environment warm and moist. We also take care to grease the sides of the pan before filling it so that the cake lets go of the pan as it cools and shrinks instead of cracking in the center. Baking the cheesecake in a water bath, see below, is also a powerful weapon against all cheesecake faults.

MIXING CHEESECAKES

If your mixer offers the choice of paddle versus whisk, use the paddle to achieve the best-textured cake. Cheesecake batter must be well mixed but not overbeaten. If too much air is beaten into a cheesecake batter, the cake will puff like a soufflé as it bakes and then fall dramatically and

crack as it cools. More extreme overbeating—which most often happens in the food processor—results in thin, dense batters that may not rise.

The food processor is the best possible tool for transforming cottage cheese, ricotta cheese, and other curd cheeses into perfectly smooth purees when appropriate. Process for a full 3 to 4 minutes, scraping the sides of the bowl and the blade several times. This is much easier and more effective than the traditional method of forcing curd cheeses through a fine sieve. We rarely use the processor for mixing cream cheese and other ingredients, however, as overprocessing can break down the cheese and produce a thin, heavy batter that does not rise at all. When we use the processor, we add the cream cheese—very well softened—last, so that it blends quickly with the other ingredients.

Lumps in the batter mar a good cheesecake; to avoid them, have the cream cheese at room temperature, or soften it in the microwave (20 to 30 seconds on high for an 8-ounce package) before beating. If you start with cold cream cheese, you are more likely to overbeat the cheese while trying to eliminate the lumps. For most recipes, beating the cream cheese with the sugar is the last chance you have to remove lumps. Once eggs and other liquid ingredients are added, any lumps in the cheese are likely to remain there. The sides of the bowl and the beaters should be scraped frequently during all stages of mixing, as the stiffer cheese mixture clinging to the beaters or bowl will not blend with the thinner mixture after the eggs and liquids are added. If the recipe calls for whipped cream or beaten egg whites, these are always folded in last, and by hand.

BAKING CHEESECAKES

The traditional method: Moderate to low heat results in smooth cheesecakes without cracking, as long as the batter is mixed properly, the oven temperature is accurate, the baker's timing is impeccable, and the cooling is slow. Cheesecake with crusts on the bottom and sides work best with this method because the crust tends to insulate the batter. Alas, having so many variables, this method is the trickiest, and it can yield cracked and overbaked cheesecakes.

The New York method: A low-heat method, this takes some of the guesswork out of the hands of the baker. The cake goes into the oven at 500°F for 15 minutes, then oven temperature is reduced to 200°F for about an hour more of baking, and finally the cake is left in the turned-off oven with the door ajar. Remarkably, this yields a cheesecake with a golden brown surface and a dry or creamy smooth interior, depending on the recipe.

The water-bath method: Placing the cake pan in a pan of hot water when it goes into the oven insulates the cake pan from extreme heat and allows the center and the edges of the cheesecake to cook at about the same rate. It almost guarantees that the cake will be as creamy around the sides as it is in the center, and it promotes a gentle, even rise with very little shrinkage. The water bath is very forgiving: even 10 minutes of extra baking are unlikely to damage the texture of the cake. We have never seen a cracked cake emerge from a water bath.

You may ask why we do not recommend baking all cakes in the water bath. But cheesecake crusts do not emerge as crisp if baked in a water bath, and some cheesecake lovers demand a certain dense, dry, creamy texture and intense cheese flavor that cannot be produced with a water bath. To each cheesecake maven his or her own, and *vive la différence*!

To bake in a water bath, if you are using a springform pan, you must first wrap the bottom and sides in foil to prevent water from seeping into the seams and soaking the cake. Set the pan on a wide sheet of heavy-duty aluminum foil. Fold the foil up, against the sides of the pan, making sure there are no rips or holes. To be safe, you may wish to use a double layer of foil. For the water bath, choose a baking dish or roasting pan that is at least 3 inches wider but no deeper than the pan. Put a kettle of water on to boil when you preheat the oven. After filling the cheesecake pan, set it in the baking dish. Slide the oven rack partway out and set the baking dish on it. Carefully pour boiling water around the cheesecake pan to a depth of about 1 inch. Slide the oven rack back gently to avoid sloshing.

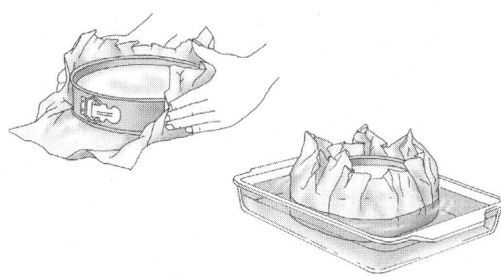

The water-bath method

If you use a solid cake pan, line the bottom with a round of wax or parchment paper and grease the sides (there is no need to wrap the pan in foil). Bake in the water bath as described. Cool and then chill the cake completely before unmolding.

UNMOLDING AND SERVING CHEESECAKES

Cheesecakes baked in springform pans can be unmolded while still slightly warm, but they are less fragile if chilled first. If the cake has pulled away cleanly from the sides of the pan, simply release the spring and carefully remove the pan side. Otherwise, slide a thin knife blade around the sides of the cake to detach it from the pan, pressing the blade against the pan to avoid tearing the cake, before releasing and removing the side. Serve the cake directly on

the pan bottom, or chill it thoroughly before attempting to transfer it to a serving platter or cardboard cake circle.

To unmold a cheesecake baked in a solid pan, cover the top of the pan with tightly stretched plastic wrap. Place a piece of cardboard or a lightweight baking sheet on top of the plastic wrap. Invert the pan and cardboard and rap the edge of the pan gently until the cheesecake is released. Remove the pan and peel off the paper liner. Place a cake circle or serving plate on the cake and carefully invert the cake so that it is right side up. Remove the plastic wrap.

The flavor and texture of all cheesecakes profit by ➤ thorough chilling before serving, for at least 24 hours, or, preferably, 48 hours; longer chilling intensifies the cheese flavor and the density of the cake. Store cheesecakes, covered, in the refrigerator. Remove an hour or so before serving to bring out the flavor and soften the texture.

ADDITIONS TO CHEESECAKE

Specialty cheesecakes come in every conceivable flavor, and anyone who can make a plain cheesecake can invent a fancy new one. Start by varying the crust with nuts or spices. Toppings beyond sour cream can include Bittersweet Chocolate Glaze, 796, Lemon Curd, 756, caramel sauce, crushed toasted or caramelized nuts, fresh fruit, or preserves. Fold into plain cheesecake batter fresh berries rolled in sugar, liquor-soaked raisins or chopped dried fruit, minced crystallized ginger, caramelized nuts, or bits of drained chestnuts in syrup, or layer or fold in broken chocolate cookies or cubed brownies. You can flavor batters with nut pastes or praline powder, cocoa or instant coffee powder, citrus zest, or liquor. Marble them with Lemon Curd, 756, or Orange Curd, 756, preserves, or sweetened chestnut puree. You can substitute brown sugar or maple sugar for a portion of the white sugar and add nuts and a little bourbon for a praline caramel effect. You can bake almost any cheesecake with or without a crust, and you can alter the texture of a conventional cheesecake by baking it in a water bath or by trying the New York method.

CHEESECAKE COCKAIGNE

12 to 16 servings
One of the simplest and best. This old-fashioned sour cream-topped cake, only about 1¼ inches tall, tastes wonderfully homemade.
Prepare and bake in a 10-inch springform pan:
  Crumb Crust, 667, made with graham crackers
Have all ingredients at room temperature, about 70°F. Preheat the oven to 300°F. Beat in a medium bowl until creamy, about 30 seconds:
  1½ pounds (three 8-ounce packages) cream cheese
Gradually beat in:
  1 cup sugar
  1 teaspoon vanilla or ¼ teaspoon almond extract
Beat in one at a time just until incorporated, scraping the sides of the bowl and the beaters after each addition:

3 large eggs

Scrape the batter into the crust and smooth the top. Place on a cookie sheet. Bake until the center just barely jiggles when the pan is tapped, 45 to 55 minutes. Let cool in the pan on a rack for at least 1 hour. Combine and spread over the cake:

1 cup sour cream
¼ cup sugar
1 tablespoon vanilla
⅛ teaspoon salt

Let cool completely in the pan on a rack before unmolding, see 743. Cover and refrigerate for at least 3 hours, preferably 24 hours, before serving. Serve with:

Fresh strawberries

NEW YORK–STYLE CHEESECAKE

15 to 20 servings

Do not be afraid of the extreme oven temperature—the surface of the cake will be golden, with a creamy interior. Preheat the oven to 400°F. Lightly grease a 9-inch springform pan. Prepare the dough for:

Shortbread Crust, 667

Press one-third of the dough, or slightly less, over the bottom of the pan as evenly as possible. Prick the dough all over with a fork. Bake until the crust is light golden brown, 10 to 15 minutes. Let cool completely on a rack. Press the remaining dough about ⅛ inch thick around the sides of the pan, making sure that it is attached to the bottom crust all around. Brush the bottom and sides of the crust with:

1 egg white, well beaten

Refrigerate the crust if you are not filling it right away. Have all the ingredients at room temperature, about 70°F. Preheat the oven to 500°F.

Beat in a large bowl until smooth and creamy, about 30 seconds:

2½ pounds (five 8-ounce packages) cream cheese

Scrape the sides of the bowl and the beaters well. Gradually add and beat until smooth and creamy, 1 to 2 minutes:

1¾ cups sugar
(up to 3 tablespoons all-purpose flour, if you prefer a denser texture)

Beat in:

1 teaspoon grated lemon zest
½ teaspoon vanilla

Beat in one at a time just until incorporated, scraping the sides of the bowl and the beaters after each addition:

5 large eggs
2 large egg yolks

On low speed, beat in:

½ cup heavy cream

Scrape the batter into the crust and smooth the top. Bake for 15 minutes at 500°F, then reduce the oven temperature to 200°F and bake for 1 hour more. Turn the oven off, prop the oven door ajar with the handle of a wooden spoon, and let the cake cool in the oven for 30 minutes. Remove to a rack and let cool completely in the pan before unmolding, see page 743. Cover and refrigerate for at least 6 hours, preferably 24 hours, before serving. The cheese flavor is even more intense after 48 hours.

CREAMY WATER-BATH CHEESECAKE

12 to 16 servings

Baking in a water bath yields an ultracreamy cheesecake with a texture that is consistent from the edges to the center. You can bake any crustless cheesecake this way.

Have all ingredients at room temperature, about 70°F. Preheat the oven to 325°F.

Coat the bottom and sides of a 9-inch springform pan with:

1 tablespoon unsalted butter

Sprinkle with:

¼ cup graham cracker crumbs

Tilt and tap the pan to spread the crumbs evenly over the bottom and sides. Beat in a large bowl just until smooth, 30 to 60 seconds:

2 pounds (four 8-ounce packages) cream cheese

Scrape the sides of the bowl and the beaters well. Gradually add and beat until smooth and creamy, 1 to 2 minutes:

1⅓ cups sugar

Beat in one at a time just until incorporated, scraping the sides of the bowl and the beaters after each addition:

4 large eggs

Add and beat on low speed just until mixed:

¼ cup heavy cream
¼ cup sour cream
2 teaspoons vanilla
1 teaspoon grated lemon zest

Scrape the batter into the pan and smooth the top. Set the pan on a length of wide heavy-duty aluminum foil. Fold the foil carefully up against the sides of the pan without tearing it. Set the pan in a large baking dish or roasting pan. Set the baking dish in the oven and pour in enough boiling water to reach halfway up the sides of the cheesecake pan. Bake until the edges of the cheesecake look set but the center jiggles slightly when the pan is tapped, 55 to 60 minutes. Turn off the oven, prop the door ajar with the handle of a wooden spoon, and let the cake cool in the oven for 1 hour. Remove to a rack and let cool completely in the pan before unmolding, see 743. Cover and refrigerate for at least 6 hours, preferably 24 hours, before serving.

FRESH RASPBERRY WATER-BATH CHEESECAKE

Roll ½ pint raspberries gently in **2 tablespoons sugar, or enough to coat.** Prepare the batter for **Creamy Water-Bath Cheesecake, above,** and scrape three-quarters of it into the pan. Sprinkle the sugared berries over the top, scrape in the remaining batter, and smooth the top. Rap the pan on the counter to eliminate any bubbles. Bake as directed. After refrigerating, spread the top with **1 cup sour cream** and arrange **½ to 1 pint raspberries** on top.

RICOTTA CHEESECAKE

10 to 12 servings

For the creamiest and best cheesecake of all, buy whole-milk ricotta. If you use part-skim ricotta, you can make it creamier by processing it for 3 to 4 minutes in a food processor or pressing it through a fine sieve.

Grease one 9-inch springform pan. Prepare:

Pat-in-the-Pan Butter Dough, 666

Press the dough into the pan so that it comes a bit more than halfway up the sides of the pan. (The dough can also be rolled out $1/8$ inch thick with a rolling pin and fitted into the pan.) Refrigerate for at least 30 minutes.

Preheat the oven to 400°F. Prick the dough with a fork and press a sheet of aluminum foil over the bottom and up the sides of the pan. Fill with rice or pie weights and bake for about 15 minutes. Carefully remove the foil and weights and bake until the crust is golden brown, about 15 minutes more. Let cool completely in the pan on a rack. Patch any cracks or holes with scraps of dough before filling.

Have all ingredients at room temperature, about 70°F. Preheat the oven to 375°F. Toss together:

3 tablespoons pine nuts, toasted, 1001

2 tablespoons chopped blanched almonds, toasted, 1001

(2 tablespoons chopped candied citron or candied orange or lemon peel)

(2 tablespoons chocolate chips)

1 tablespoon all-purpose flour

Beat in a large bowl on high speed until thick and pale yellow, 1 to 2 minutes:

4 large eggs

1 cup sugar

1$1/2$ teaspoons vanilla

Stir in:

3 cups whole-milk or part-skim ricotta cheese

Stir in the nut mixture. Scrape the batter into the crust and smooth the top. Bake for 30 minutes, reduce the oven temperature to 325°F, and bake until a knife inserted about 2 inches from the edge of the cake comes out clean, 20 to 25 minutes more. The center will be softer and the cake will seem too jiggly, but it will set after it has cooled. Remove to a rack and let cool completely in the pan on a rack before unmolding (see 743). Cover and refrigerate for at least 6 hours, preferably 24 hours, before serving.

CHOCOLATE CHEESECAKE

12 to 16 servings

Richer than rich; for chocolate lovers only.

Prepare and bake in a 9-inch springform or cake pan:

Crumb Crust, 667, made with chocolate wafers

Let cool. Have all ingredients at room temperature, about 70°F. Place a loaf pan or cake pan filled with water on the bottom rack of the oven to moisten the air. Preheat the oven to 350°F. Place in a small bowl:

8 ounces bittersweet or semisweet chocolate, finely chopped

Add:

$1/3$ cup boiling water

Stir until the chocolate is melted and smooth. Beat in a large bowl just until smooth, 30 to 60 seconds:

1 pound (two 8-ounce packages) cream cheese

Scrape the sides of the bowl and the beaters well. Gradually add and beat until smooth and creamy, 1 to 2 minutes:

$2/3$ cup sugar

1 teaspoon vanilla

Beat in one at a time just until incorporated, scraping the sides of the bowl and the beaters after each addition:

3 large eggs

Beat in:

2 cups sour cream

1 tablespoon unsweetened cocoa powder

Add the warm chocolate mixture and beat on low speed just until well blended. Scrape the batter into the crust and smooth the top. Place on a baking sheet and bake until the edges of the cake have puffed but the center still looks moist and jiggles when the pan is tapped, 40 to 45 minutes. Turn the oven off, prop the door ajar with the handle of a wooden spoon, and let the cake cool in the oven for 1 hour. Remove to a rack and let cool completely in the pan before unmolding, see 743. Cover and refrigerate for at least 6 hours, preferably 24 hours, before serving. The flavors are even more intense after 48 hours.

PUMPKIN CHEESECAKE

10 to 12 servings

Warm fall pumpkin pie spices in a rich cheesecake.

Prepare and bake in an 8-inch springform or cake pan:

Crumb Crust, 667, made with graham crackers, or Nut Crust, 668, made with pecans

Let cool. Have all ingredients at room temperature, about 70°F. Place a loaf pan or cake pan filled with hot water in the oven to moisten the air. Preheat the oven to 350°F. Combine in a small bowl:

$2/3$ cup packed brown sugar

$3/4$ teaspoon ground cinnamon

$1/4$ teaspoon ground cloves

$1/4$ teaspoon ground ginger

$1/8$ teaspoon grated or ground nutmeg

Beat in a large bowl just until smooth, 30 to 60 seconds:

1 pound (two 8-ounce packages) cream cheese

Scrape the sides of the bowl and the beaters well. Gradually add the sugar mixture and beat until smooth and creamy, 1 to 2 minutes. Beat in one at a time until well blended, scraping the sides of the bowl and the beaters after each addition:

2 large eggs

2 large egg yolks

Add and beat in just until mixed:

1 cup canned or cooked pumpkin

Scrape the batter into the crust and smooth the top. Set the pan on a baking sheet. Bake for 30 minutes at 350°F, then reduce the oven temperature to 325°F and bake until the edges of the cheesecake are puffed but the center still looks moist and jiggles when the pan is tapped, 10 to 15 minutes more. Meanwhile, whisk together until well blended:

1¹/₂ cups sour cream
¹/₃ cup packed light brown sugar
1 teaspoon vanilla

Scrape on top of the hot cake and smooth with a spatula. Return to the oven for 7 minutes. Remove the pan to a rack and cover the pan and rack with a large inverted bowl or pot so that the cake cools slowly. Let cool completely before unmolding, see 743. Cover and refrigerate for at least 6 hours, preferably 24 hours, before serving.

▲ ABOUT HIGH-ALTITUDE CAKE BAKING

Cakes baked at high altitudes are subject to pixielike variations that often defy general rules. Cakes begin to react strongly to atmospheric changes at elevations around 3,000 feet above sea level and changes grow more intense as elevation increases: Cakes may rise fast, then fall flat, or cool with a bowl-shaped depression in the center. They may crust over on top and have a wet sodden center or a coarse and heavy crumb. They may overflow the pan or stick to it.

Remedies? The only real rule is, alas, that there is no rule. There are some adjustment guidelines, but each recipe requires its own individual changes. To adapt your favorite sea-level recipes, read the explanation below, then launch forth on your own, keeping records at first until you know what gives you the greatest success.

There are three main factors to consider at high altitudes: First, ➤ the higher in elevation you go above sea level, the less the air pressure, so leavening gases (air, carbon dioxide, water vapor) in baked goods can, and do, expand more quickly. In most recipes, baking powder and/or baking soda must be reduced or rebalanced for proper rise. ➤ Acidity helps a batter set in the heat of the oven, so sometimes you need to reduce the amount of baking soda (which neutralizes the acidity of certain ingredients) more than you would expect in order to leave some of the batter's acidity intact. ➤ Buttermilk is preferred to regular milk above 5,000 feet, because it provides acidity as well as contributing to moisture, richness, and tenderness. (Powdered buttermilk can be used, but liquid is preferable; to substitute regular milk for liquid buttermilk, blend 3 tablespoons of plain yogurt into 1 cup of milk.) With reduced air pressure, whipped egg whites tend to rise spectacularly and then fall flat unless beaten with special care (see below). Sometimes adding an extra egg will improve a sea-level recipe by contributing moisture and strength, but too many whites can dry out a batter, so use caution. For best results, follow our high-altitude recipes exactly as written.

Second, ➤ the higher the elevation, the lower the boiling point of water (see table, 1056). This makes it is harder to deliver enough heat to the center of dense wet cake batter to make it rise. Every 500-foot increase in altitude causes the boiling point of water to drop about 1°F. ➤ The higher the elevation, the longer it takes to bake some cakes and the longer it takes to cook foods in or over liquid; custards take longer to set, cornstarch takes longer to gelatinize and thicken.

When baking cakes, sometimes it is advisable to raise the oven temperature by about 25 degrees. However, this can cause the cake to crust over on top before the center bakes through—the solution then is to lower the temperature and bake longer. ➤ An easy fix for loaf cakes and tea breads is to replace the traditional loaf pan with a tube pan in order to deliver heat to the batter's center.

Third, ➤ the higher the altitude, the faster liquids and moisture evaporate, leaving behind higher concentrations of sugar and fat. Excess sugar coarsens a cake's texture. Excesses of both sugar and fat reduce the strength of gluten in wheat flour, leaving a weakened structure that can cause a cake to fall. ➤ At high altitudes, many recipes call for reducing the sugar, and some butter-rich recipes also need a slight reduction in fat. ➤ Be sure to use the type of flour called for in a high-altitude recipe: All-purpose flour is often used instead of cake flour because its slightly higher protein content contributes to a stronger batter structure, preventing the cake from collapsing when it cools.

Other atmospheric factors also affect baking. Humidity is a wild card at every altitude. Along with changes in atmospheric pressure, humidity affects the evaporation rate of exposed food surfaces. ➤ The higher you go, the dryer the air, and the more quickly surfaces (of baked goods, your skin, your coffee) dry out and cool off. Baked meringues stay crisp longer, but other baked goods grow stale quickly.

Dryer air in mountainous elevations means that ➤ flour often needs more liquid blended into it (although it is primarily the type of flour that governs water requirements—high-protein flour absorbs more liquid than all-purpose flour, which absorbs more water than cake flour). Higher, dryer air also means less molecules of moisture carrying tastes and flavors to your nose and mouth; the higher the altitude, the weaker may be your perception of flavors in baked goods. ➤ For more intense taste, add a little more salt and flavoring extract.

At high altitudes always double-wrap baked goods airtight as soon as they are completely cool. For freezing, double-wrap airtight, then wrap again with heavy-duty foil or place in a freezer-weight self-sealing plastic bag.

Directions for every elevation work approximately 1,500 feet above and below that elevation. For example, recipes for 7,000 feet work up to about 8,500 feet.

SPECIAL TECHNIQUES FOR HIGH-ALTITUDE BAKING

Ingredients: Before baking, have all ingredients, including eggs, at room temperature (about 70°F). Butter should be soft, easily pressed.

Pans and pan preparation: Be sure to use the size of pan called for in the recipe. Batter can overflow an undersized pan or bake up thin and hard in an oversized pan. If unsure, fill the pan a scant three-quarters full to leave room for rising.

At high altitudes, pan preparation is especially critical. "Grease" means coating the bottom and sides of the baking pan with solid vegetable shortening or nonstick vegetable spray. To dust a greased pan with flour, sift or shake on a light coating of flour, tap the pan edge to evenly distribute flour then invert and tap pan bottom to knock out excess flour.

From sea level to 5,000 feet, grease layer or loaf pans, then line with wax or parchment paper. Rectangular baking pans are greased and floured but not lined, when cakes baked in these pans are cut and served from the pan. Angel food cake pans are never greased; after baking, these cakes are inverted to cool upside down on the pan's legs or placed over the neck of a wine bottle. Some sponge cakes use ungreased pans, others need pans that are greated and floured. Follow the recipe carefully. Cupcake pans at this elevation are greased and sometimes floured, but not lined.

Pan preparation at and above 7,000 feet, baked goods are much more likely to stick to the pan, ➤ so always take special care to generously grease the pans. Line with baking parchment, then grease the parchment, dust with flour, and tap out excess flour. Around 10,000 feet, as extra insurance against sticking in very decorative Bundt pans, you can press a ring of parchment or foil into the bottom of the greased pan before regreasing and flouring. At 10,000 feet, cupcake pans also need generous greasing and flouring, or use paper or foil liners.

Beating egg whites: At altitudes above 3,000 feet, you do *not* want stiff peaks; whip the whites on high speed just until you begin to see beater tracks on the surface. At this point, start watching carefully until you have whites that are smooth, glossy, and form soft, gently droopy peaks when the beaters are lifted. Soft peaks have room to expand and hold shape when baked. At high altitudes, stiff peaks are overwhipped—as they expand when baked, they will burst and the baked goods will collapse. See Whipping Egg Whites, 978.

Removing excess air bubbles before baking: To remove excess air bubbles from thick buttery batters, tap the bottom of the pan(s) sharply on the counter once or twice before setting them in the oven. For sponge cake or angel cake batters leavened with whipped whites, draw a knife blade once through the batter just before baking.

Testing doneness: Follow baking times for your elevation in the recipes; test at the earliest time, and bake just until a cake tester in center comes out clean. At this point, the cake top will be risen, feel springy to the touch, and in some cases, will have begun to shrink slightly from the pan sides.

Cooling and unmolding cakes: Unless otherwise directed in a recipe, all baked goods should be left to cool in their pans on a wire rack at least 10 to 15 minutes (fluted tube or big tube cakes need about 25 minutes, or until the bottom of the pan is comfortable to touch) before unmolding; if unmolded too soon, cakes may stick to the pans. For layers and sheet cakes, run a thin knife between the cake and pan sides to release the cake; for tube pans, also run the knife around the tube. Top the cake with a flat plate, rack, or a cardboard cake round (preferably foil-covered), invert, remove the pan, and peel off the paper liner, if used. Cool completely. Always wrap cooled cakes to retain moisture.

Baking cupcakes: Fill the cups a scant three-quarters full with batter. (If there are empty cups in pan, put a little water in them.)

GENERAL HIGH-ALTITUDE CAKE-BAKING ADJUSTMENT GUIDELINES

Directions for every elevation work approximately 1,500 feet above and below that elevation. Each recipe requires specific adjustments. These general guidelines will give you a point from which to begin your own changes for a sea level recipe.

From sea level to about 2,500 feet, no adjustments to sea-level recipes are necessary. As you near 3,000 feet, some cakes benefit from raising the oven temperature 25 degrees. Whip egg whites only to soft peaks. Ingredients may (but not always) need adjusting. If the baked results are disappointing, try these adjustments: Increase each cup of flour by 1 tablespoon. Reduce each teaspoon of baking powder or baking soda by $1/8$ teaspoon. Reduce each cup of sugar by 1 tablespoon. Increase each cup of liquid by up to 2 tablespoons.

The recipes in this section are written for 5,000 feet, with adjustments given for higher altitudes. At around 5,000 feet, as indicated in the recipes, many cakes benefit from raising the oven temperature by 25 degrees. You may need to increase each cup of flour by 0 up to 2 tablespoons. Reduce each teaspoon of baking powder or baking soda by $1/8$ to $1/4$ teaspoon. You may also reduce each cup of sugar by 0 to 2 tablespoons. Increase each cup of liquid by 2 to 4 tablespoons.

At around 7,000 feet, some cakes (though not all) benefit from baking at moderate heat (say 350°F) for a slightly longer baking time, rather than raising the heat. Increase each cup of flour by 3 to 4 tablespoons; reduce each teaspoon of baking powder or baking soda by $1/4$ to $1/2$ teaspoon; reduce each cup of sugar by 2 to 4 tablespoons; and increase each cup of liquid by 3 to 4 tablespoons.

At around 10,000 feet, increase each cup of flour by 2 to 4 tablespoons; reduce each teaspoon of baking powder or baking soda by $1/2$ to $2/3$ teaspoon; reduce each cup of sugar by 3 to 4 tablespoons; and increase each cup of liquid by 3 to 4 tablespoons. In very rich cakes, reduce each cup of fat by 1 to 2 tablespoons.

▲ HIGH-ALTITUDE CLASSIC 1-2-3-4 CAKE (OR CUPCAKES)

Two 9-inch round layers, or one 13 x 9-inch cake,
or about twenty-four 2³/₄-inch cupcakes

This easy-to-remember formula was originally designed—at sea level—for reliability: 1 cup butter, 2 cups sugar,

3 cups flour, 4 eggs. At higher elevations, because adjustments are needed, the numbers and proportions change, as you can see below. You can vary the flavor, keeping the vanilla, by adding orange, lemon, or almond extract.

Please read About High-Altitude Cake Baking, 746, and About Butter Cakes, 710. This recipe is designed for baking at 5,000 feet. If baking at 7,000 feet, reduce the oven heat to 350°F. Add 2 tablespoons flour, reduce the sugar by 1 tablespoon sugar, and add 2 tablespoons buttermilk. Bake layers for 22 to 27 minutes, a sheet cake for 30 to 32 minutes, or cupcakes for 22 to 25 minutes. At 10,000 feet, preheat the oven to 375°F, then reduce the heat to bake at 350°F. Add 2 tablespoons flour and 3 tablespoons plus 1 teaspoon buttermilk; reduce the baking powder by $1/2$ teaspoon and the sugar by 1 tablespoons. Bake layers for 28 to 30 minutes, sheet cake for 30 to 35 minute, or cupcakes for 28 to 30 minutes.

Preheat the oven to 375°F. Prepare two 9-inch round cake pans, one 13 x 9-inch baking pan, or two 12-cup muffin pans as directed for your altitude, 746.

Whisk together thoroughly:

> **3 cups plus 1 tablespoon sifted all-purpose flour**
> **2 teaspoons baking powder**
> $3/4$ **teaspoon salt**

Combine in a large bowl and beat until well blended:

> **1 cup (2 sticks) unsalted butter, softened**
> **2 cups minus 1 tablespoon sugar**
> **2 teaspoons vanilla**
> **(1 teaspoon almond or other extract)**

Scrape down the bowl and beat for 1 minute. Add 2 or 3 at a time, beating well after each addition:

> **5 large eggs**

Scrape down the bowl. (Don't worry if the batter looks curdled.) On low speed, add the flour mixture in 2 parts, alternating with:

> **1 cup plus 2 tablespoons buttermilk**

in 2 parts, blending well. Then beat on high speed for about 1 minute or until the batter is smooth and creamy. Divide the batter between the round pans or scrape into the baking pan; or, for cupcakes, fill the cups a scant three-quarters. Bake layers for 22 to 25 minutes, the sheet cake for 30 to 33 minutes, or cupcakes for 20 to 22 minutes, or until a toothpick inserted in the center comes out clean. Cool the cake in the pans on a rack for about 15 minutes, then unmold as directed, 747, and cool completely. (The sheet cake can be served from the pan.)

▲ HIGH-ALTITUDE ANGEL CAKE

One 10-inch tube cake

With a melt-in-your-mouth tender crumb, this is truly the food of angels.

This recipe is designed for baking at 5,000 to 7,000 feet. If baking at 10,000 feet, reduce the oven heat to 350°F. Add 2 tablespoons flour, $1/2$ teaspoon cream of tartar, and 1 more teaspoon almond or orange extract, if using. Bake for 30 to 35 minutes.

Please read About High-Altitude Cake Baking, 746, and About Angel Cakes, 705. Have all ingredients at room temperature, about 70°F. Preheat the oven to 375°F. Have ready an ungreased 10-inch tube pan.

Sift together and return to the sifter:

> **1 cup plus 2 tablespoons sifted cake flour**
> $1/2$ **cup sifted confectioners' sugar**

Beat in large bowl until foamy:

> $1^{1}/2$ **cups egg whites (10 to 13 large whites)**
> $1^{1}/2$ **teaspoons cream of tartar**
> $1/2$ **teaspoon salt**

Gradually add and beat on high speed until arrow soft, slightly droopy peaks form:

> $3/4$ **cup sugar preferably superfine**

Fold in:

> **2 teaspoons vanilla extract**
> **(1 teaspoon almond or orange extract)**
> **2 tablespoons water**

Add the dry ingredients one-quarter at a time, sifting them over the whites and gently folding them in, until no flour is visible. Scoop the batter into the tube pan. Cut through the batter once with knife to burst any large air bubbles. Bake until a cake tester inserted in the center comes out clean, 25 to 30 minutes. To cool and unmold, see About Angel Cakes, 705. Top cake with a little sifted:

> **Confectioners' sugar**

▲ HIGH-ALTITUDE CHOCOLATE ANGEL CAKE

Prepare **High-Altitude Angel Cake, above,** reducing the cake flour to 1 cup and adding $1/4$ **cup sifted unsweetened cocoa powder, preferably Dutch-process.** Increase the superfine or granulated sugar by $1/4$ cup.

▲ HIGH-ALTITUDE COCONUT ANGEL CAKE

Prepare **High-Altitude Angel Cake, above,** using the vanilla and, if desired, almond extract and adding $1^{1}/2$ **teaspoons coconut extract**. Measure about 2 tablespoons of the sifted flour-sugar mixture into a small bowl and toss with $1/3$ **cup lightly packed shredded sweetened coconut.** Fold coconut-flour into whites along with sifted flour.

▲ HIGH-ALTITUDE WHITE CAKE

Two 8- or 9-inch round layers

The batter rises higher in 8-inch pans than in 9-inch pans, but the latter is fine if you don't mind a cake with 1-inch-high layers.

Please read About High-Altitude Cake Baking, 746, and About Butter Cakes, 710. This recipe is designed for baking at 5,000 feet. If baking at 7,000 feet, preheat the oven to 350°F. Reduce the baking powder by $1/4$ teaspoon and the sugar creamed with the butter by 2 tablespoons. Add $1/4$ teaspoon cream of tartar, replace the milk with buttermilk and increase by $1^{1}/2$ tablespoons. Bake about 25 minutes. At 10,000 feet, bake at 375°F. Use a blend of $1^{1}/4$ cups plus 1 tablespoon sifted cake flour and $1^{1}/4$ cups plus 1 tablespoon sifted all-purpose flour. Reduce the baking powder by $\frac{1}{4}$ teaspoon, the butter by 1 tablespoon, and the sugar creamed with butter by $\frac{1}{4}$ cup. Add $\frac{1}{4}$ teaspoon salt, $\frac{1}{4}$ teaspoon cream of tartar, and $\frac{1}{2}$ teaspoon each vanilla and almond extract. Replace the milk with buttermilk and increase by $\frac{1}{4}$ cup. Bake about 27 minutes. Preheat the oven to 375°F. Prepare two 8- or 9-inch round cake pans as directed for your altitude, 746.

Whisk together thoroughly:

$2\frac{1}{2}$ cups sifted cake flour
$1\frac{1}{2}$ teaspoons baking powder
$\frac{1}{4}$ teaspoon salt

Beat in a large bowl until foamy:

4 large egg whites
$\frac{1}{4}$ teaspoon cream of tartar

Gradually add and beat on high speed until soft, slightly droopy peaks form:

$\frac{1}{3}$ cup sugar

Set aside. Beat in another large bowl (no need to wash beaters) until well blended:

$\frac{1}{2}$ cup (1 stick) unsalted butter
1 cup sugar
1 teaspoon vanilla extract
(1 teaspoon almond or other extract)

On low speed, add the flour mixture in 3 parts, alternating with:

$1\frac{1}{4}$ cups milk

in 2 parts, down scraping the bowl after each addition. Beat on high about 30 seconds, until smooth and creamy. Gently fold the whites by hand into the batter in 3 additions, until flour is no longer visible. Divide the batter between the pans. Bake until a cake tester inserted in the center comes out clean, 25 to 27 minutes. Cool in the pans on a rack for 10 to 15 minutes, then invert the cake and remove the paper liners, if using. Let cool completely.

▲ HIGH-ALTITUDE FUDGE CAKE

Two 9-inch round layers, or one 13 x 9-inch cake, or about twenty-four $2\frac{3}{4}$-inch cupcakes

With a rich chocolate flavor and moist tender crumb, this is a good recipe for layer or sheet cakes or cupcakes. Unsweetened chocolate gives a slightly deeper chocolate flavor but you can also use semisweet chocolate morsels.

Please read About High-Altitude Cake Baking, 746, and About Butter Cakes, 710. This recipe is designed for baking at 5,000 feet. If baking at 7,000 feet, replace the cake flour with all-purpose flour and reduce the baking powder by $\frac{1}{2}$ teaspoon. Replace the regular milk with buttermilk and increase it by 1 tablespoon. Reduce the sugar beaten into the whites to 2 tablespoons. Bake layers or a sheet cake for 35 to 40 minutes, cupcakes for 15 to 20 minutes. At 10,000 feet, replace the cake flour with all-purpose flour and increase by 1 tablespoon, reduce the baking powder by $\frac{3}{4}$ teaspoon. If using unsweetened chocolate, reduce sugar beaten with butter by $\frac{1}{2}$ cup; if using semisweet chocolate, reduce it by $\frac{3}{4}$ cup. Replace the milk with buttermilk and increase it by 2 tablespoons. Bake lay-

ers about 33 minutes, a sheet cake about 42 minutes, or cupcakes 25 minutes.

Have all ingredients at room temperature, about 70°F. Preheat the oven to 350°F. Prepare two 9-inch round cake pans, one 13 x 9-inch baking pan, or two $2\frac{3}{4}$-inch 12-cup muffin pans as directed for your altitude, 746. Melt:

4 ounces unsweetened chocolate, chopped,
or 1 cup chocolate chips

Whisk together thoroughly:

2 cups sifted cake flour
2 teaspoons baking powder
$\frac{1}{2}$ teaspoon salt

Beat in a large bowl until foamy:

3 large egg whites
$\frac{1}{4}$ teaspoon cream of tartar

Gradually add and beat on high speed until soft, slightly droopy peaks form:

$\frac{1}{4}$ cup sugar

Set aside. Beat in another large bowl (no need to wash beaters) until light and fluffy:

$\frac{1}{2}$ cup (1 stick) unsalted butter
2 cups sugar (reduce to $1\frac{1}{2}$ cups if using chocolate chips)
2 teaspoons vanilla

Scrape down the bowl and beat a few seconds longer. Beat in, blending well:

3 large egg yolks

Beat in the melted chocolate. Scrape down the bowl. On low speed, add in 3 parts, alternating with the flour mixture:

$1\frac{1}{2}$ cups milk

in 2 parts, scraping down the bowl and beating well after each addition. Gently fold in the whites by hand in 3 additions until the batter no longer looks streaky.

Divide the batter between the round pans or scrape into the baking pan; or, for cupcakes, fill cups a scant three-quarters full. Bake layers or a sheet 35 to 40 minutes, cupcakes 15 to 20 minutes, or until a cake tester inserted in the center comes out clean. Cool in the pan(s) on a wire rack for 10 to 15 minutes. Then unmold as directed, 747, and cool completely. (The sheet cake can be served from the pan.)

▲ HIGH-ALTITUDE TWO-EGG CAKE

Two 8-inch round layers

With its sweet moist crumb, this easy-to-make cake is an old-fashioned favorite.

Please read About High-Altitude Cake Baking, 746, and About Butter Cakes, 710. This recipe is designed for baking at 5,000 feet. At 7,000 feet, reduce the oven heat to 350°F. Add 1 tablespoon flour, reduce the baking powder by $\frac{1}{4}$ teaspoon and the sugar by 2 tablespoons. Replace the regular milk with buttermilk and increase it by 1 tablespoon. Bake about 25 minutes. At 10,000 feet, preheat the oven to 375°F, then reduce the heat to bake at 350°F. Add 2 tablespoons flour and $\frac{1}{2}$ teaspoon vanilla. Replace the milk with buttermilk and increase it by 2 tablespoons. Reduce the baking powder by $^1/_2$ teaspoon and the sugar by 3 tablespoons. Bake 23 to 25 minutes.

Preheat the oven to 375°. Prepare two 8-inch round cake pans as directed for your altitude, 746.

Whisk together thoroughly:

2 cups sifted cake flour
1$^1/_2$ teaspoons baking powder
$^1/_2$ teaspoon salt

Beat together in a large bowl until light and fluffy, scraping down the bowl once or twice:

$^1/_2$ cup (1 stick) unsalted butter
1 cup sugar
1 teaspoon vanilla extract

Add and mix thoroughly:

2 large eggs

Scrape down the bowl, and beat until hard. Add the flour mixture in 3 parts, alternating with:

$^3/_4$ cup plus 1 tablespoon milk

in 2 parts, scraping down the bowl after each addition. Beat until smooth, thick, and creamy. Scrape the batter into the pans. Bake until a toothpick inserted in the center comes out clean, 22 to 25 minutes. Cool in the pans on a rack for about 15 minutes, then unmold as directed, 747, and cool completely.

▲ HIGH-ALTITUDE SPICE CAKE

This recipe is designed for baking at 5,000 feet. At 7,000 feet, replace milk with **buttermilk** and add 1 more tablespoon. At 10,000 feet, replace milk with **buttermilk** and add 1 more tablespoon. Add $^1/_4$ teaspoon more cinnamon, nutmeg, and ginger.

Prepare **High Altitude Two-Egg Cake, 750,** observing the adjustments for the altitude at which you are baking. Add to the dry ingredients before whisking: **1 teaspoon ground cinnamon, 1 teaspoon grated or ground nutmeg, 1 teaspoon ground ginger, $^1/_4$ teaspoon ground cloves, 1 tablespoon sifted unsweetened cocoa powder, and (pinch of ground red pepper, or to taste).**

▲ HIGH-ALTITUDE SPONGE CAKE

One 10-inch fluted tube cake

This citrus-scented cake blends orange and lemon to enhance the flavor.

Please read About High-Altitude Cake Baking, 746, and About Butter Cakes, 710. This recipe is for baking at 5,000 through 7,000 feet. At 10,000 feet, reduce the oven heat to 350°F. Reduce the butter by 2 tablespoons, use only 7 yolks, and reduce the sugar beaten into the yolks by 2 tablespoons. Increase the flour by 2$^1/_3$ tablespoons flour and the cream of tartar by $^1/_2$ teaspoon. Bake 25 to 30 minutes, then (without cooling first) immediately invert onto a rack, unmold, and cool completely.

Preheat the oven to 375°F. Grease a 10-inch fluted tube pan generously and dust with flour; tap out excess flour.

Melt:

3 tablespoons unsalted butter

Pour into a medium bowl. When cool, stir in:

1$^1/_2$ tablespoons grated lemon zest
1 tablespoon grated orange zest
$^1/_4$ cup fresh lemon juice
2 teaspoons lemon extract
1 teaspoon vanilla

Sift together and return to the sifter:

1$^1/_4$ cups plus 1 tablespoon sifted cake flour
$^1/_2$ teaspoon salt

Beat in a large bowl until foamy:

7 large egg whites
$^1/_2$ teaspoon cream of tartar

Gradually add and beat on high speed until soft, slightly droopy peaks form:

$^1/_2$ cup sugar

Set aside. Beat in another large bowl (no need to wash beaters) on high speed until the batter is thick and a pale lemony color and forms a continuous flat ribbon when dropped from the beaters:

8 large egg yolks
$^1/_2$ cup sugar

Fold about one-quarter of the whipped whites into the batter. Alternately sift on the flour and fold it in, alternating with all but about 1$^1/_2$ cups of the whites. Stir the melted butter–lemon juice mixture, and fold this into the remaining whites; try to maintain volume in the whites while blending in the liquid. Fold the lemon mixture into the yolk batter; make sure no liquid pools in the bottom of the bowl. Scoop the batter into the pan and carefully, without touching the pan, cut once through the batter with a knife to release any large air bubbles. Bake until a cake tester in the center inserted comes out clean, 20 to 25 minutes. Cool the cake in the pan on a rack for about 10 minutes, then run a knife between the cake sides and tube, top with a plate, invert, and unmold. Cool completely.

Just before serving, sprinkle with:

Confectioners' sugar

Slice with a serrated knife.

▲ HIGH-ALTITUDE CARROT CAKE

One 9$^1/_2$- to 10-inch fluted tube or plain tube cake

The best-ever carrot cake—not too sweet, and packed with nutritious nuts, raisins, and sunflower seeds. Top it with a simple dusting of confectioners' sugar, or spread with the traditional Cream Cheese Frosting, 794.

Please read About High-Altitude Cake Baking, 746, and About Baking Butter Cakes, 710. This recipe is designed for baking at 5,000 feet. If baking at 7,000 feet, reduce the oven heat to 350°F. Reduce the sugar by $^1/_4$ cup; add 2 tablespoons flour and $^1/_4$ teaspoon ginger. Bake for 35 to 40 minutes. At 10,000 feet, preheat the oven to 375°F, then reduce the heat to bake at 350°F. Reduce the oil by $^1/_4$ cup, the sugar by $^1/_2$ cup, and the baking soda by

¼ teaspoon. Add 1 large egg plus 1 yolk, ¼ cup flour, and ¼ teaspoon each nutmeg and ginger. Bake for 55 to 58 minutes.

Have all ingredients at room temperature, about 70°F. Preheat the oven to 375°F. Prepare a 9½- to 10-inch fluted tube or tube pan as directed for your altitude, 746.

Toss together:

> 3 cups grated carrots
> 1 cup chopped walnuts
> (¼ cup sunflower seeds)
> (⅓ cup raisins or dried currants)
> ¼ cup wheat germ or wheat or oat bran

Whisk together in a large bowl:

> 1½ cups vegetable oil
> 2 cups sugar
> 6 large eggs
> 2 teaspoons vanilla

Place a large strainer over the bowl and measure into it:

> 2 cups plus 1 tablespoon sifted all-purpose flour
> 1½ teaspoons baking soda
> 1 teaspoon salt
> 2 teaspoons ground cinnamon
> ¾ teaspoon grated or ground nutmeg
> ½ teaspoon ground ginger
> ½ teaspoon ground allspice

Stir the dry ingredients into the oil-egg mixture and blend well. Stir in the nut-fruit mixture. Scoop the batter into the pan and bake until a toothpick inserted in the center comes out clean, 42 to 45 minutes. Cool the cake in the pan on a rack for about 25 minutes, or until the pan bottom is almost comfortable to touch. Unmold as directed, 747, and cool completely.

▲ HIGH ALTITUDE PEACH-PECAN UPSIDE-DOWN CAKE

One 9- or 10-inch round cake

This delicious peach variation on traditional pineapple upside-down cake has a lightly spiced cake and buttery honey-cardamom sauce. Fresh or whole frozen raspberries can be substituted for the nuts. Replace the peaches with nectarines, or use fresh or canned apricots, pears, apples, or whole frozen berries.

Please read About High-Altitude Cake Baking, 746, and About Butter Cakes, 710.

This recipe is for baking at 5,000 feet. If baking at 7,000 feet, reduce the oven heat to 325°F and bake 40 minutes. At 10,000 feet, bake at 350°F. Use only 5 tablespoons butter in the topping and reduce the sugar by 1 tablespoon. Reduce the sugar in the batter by 2 tablespoons plus 2 teaspoons and the baking powder by ½ teaspoon; add 2 tablespoons flour and ¼ teaspoon salt. Bake about 45 to 48 minutes.

Have all ingredients at room temperature, about 70°F. Preheat the oven to 350°F.

Have ready:

> 3 or 4 medium to large peaches, peeled, 208, halved, pitted, and sliced (about 30 slices), 30 frozen (or partially thawed) peach slices, or 30 canned peach slices (from two 15-ounce cans in light syrup), drained on paper towels

Combine in a 10-inch ovenproof skillet or a 9 x 2-inch round cake pan and stir over medium heat until the butter is melted:

> 5 tablespoons unsalted butter
> ⅔ cup packed light brown sugar (or slightly less if fruit is very juicy)

Add, stirring until smooth and just beginning to bubble:

> ¼ cup honey
> ¼ teaspoon grated or ground nutmeg
> ¼ teaspoon ground cardamom or ginger
> Pinch of salt

Remove from the heat. Arrange the peach slices in the syrup in a pinwheel pattern. Tuck in around the peaches:

> ½ cup pecan halves or pieces

Set aside. Whisk together thoroughly:

> 1½ cups unsifted all-purpose flour
> 1½ teaspoons baking powder
> ¼ teaspoon salt
> 1 teaspoon ground cardamom
> 1½ teaspoons ground ginger
> ½ teaspoon ground cinnamon
> ½ teaspoon grated or ground nutmeg

Beat together in large bowl:

> ⅓ cup (5⅓ tablespoons) unsalted butter, melted
> ½ cup sugar
> ¼ cup honey
> 2 large eggs
> 1 teaspoon vanilla
> ⅓ cup buttermilk

Add the flour mixture and stir well to blend. Spoon the batter over the fruit in the pan. (Don't worry if the batter looks skimpy; it spreads as it bakes.) Set the pan on a cookie sheet and bake 35 to 40 minutes, until a cake tester set in the center comes out clean or with a few moist crumbs. Cool the cake in the pan on a rack for about 5 minutes, or until the juices stop bubbling. Cover the cake with a serving plate that has a lip to catch the sauce, and invert with a sharp downward shake. Lift off the pan and reposition any fruit stuck to the pan. Cool about 5 minutes, and serve warm, with:

> (Whipped Cream, 754)

▲ HIGH-ALTITUDE SOUR CREAM STREUSEL COFFEE CAKE

A 9- to 9½-inch fluted tube cake

This rich moist cake, layered with crunchy cinnamon-nut crumbs is wonderfully satisfying served with hot coffee or tea. It's everyone's favorite at a brunch or picnic, and tastes even better the day after it is baked.

Please read About High-Altitude Cake Baking, 746, and

About Butter Cakes, 710. This recipe is designed for baking at 5,000 feet. If baking at 7,000 feet, reduce the oven temperature to 350°F. Add 2½ tablespoons milk or buttermilk, and bake for 50 to 55 minutes. At 10,000 feet, reduce the oven temperature to 350°F. Add 3 tablespoons flour, 1 tablespoon sugar, and 2 tablespoons plus 1 teaspoon milk or buttermilk. Bake 55 to 58 minutes.

Have all ingredients at room temperature, about 70°F. Preheat the oven to 375°F. Prepare a 9- to 9½-inch fluted tube pan as directed for your altitude, 746.

Set aside:

   ¼ cup chopped walnuts

Combine:

   ¾ cup chopped walnuts
   ⅓ cup sugar
   ¾ teaspoon ground cinnamon

Whisk together thoroughly:

   3 cups sifted all-purpose flour
   1 teaspoon baking powder
   ½ teaspoon baking soda
   1 teaspoon salt

Beat in a large bowl until well blended:

   ¾ cup (1½ sticks) unsalted butter
   1¼ cups sugar
   2 teaspoons vanilla

Scrape down the sides of the bowl and the beaters and beat for 1 minute. Add 2 or 3 at a time, beating well after each addition:

   5 large eggs

Scrape down the bowl, and beat in:

   1½ cups sour cream
   3 tablespoons milk or buttermilk

On low speed, gradually add the flour mixture. Scrape down the bowl and beat just until smooth, thick, and creamy; don't overbeat. Sprinkle the reserved ¼ cup chopped walnuts over the bottom of the prepared baking pan. Spoon about 2 cups batter over the nuts, covering them completely. Sprinkle on about half the cinnamon nut crumbs, taking care not to spread them quite to the pan edges. Top with about 2 more cups of batter, add the remaining crumbs, and top with remaining batter.

Bake until a toothpick inserted in the center comes out clean, 45 to 50 minutes. Cool the cake in the pan on a rack for about 25 minutes, or until the pan feels comfortable to touch before unmolding, 747, and cooling completely. The nuts will be on the top.

▲ HIGH-ALTITUDE GINGERBREAD

A 9-inch square cake

This moist, tender gingerbread has a wonderfully spicy kick. Serious ginger lovers can also add the grated fresh ginger.

   Please read About High-Altitude at Cake Baking, 746, and About Baking Butter Cakes, 710.

   This recipe is for baking at 5,000 feet. If baking at 7,000 feet, reduce the oven heat to 350°F. Add ¼ teaspoon salt

and the increased hot water by 2 tablespoons. Bake 40 to 45 minutes. At 10,000 feet, bake at 375°F. Omit the baking powder and reduce the baking soda by ¼ teaspoon and the sugar by 2 tablespoons. Bake 42 to 45 minutes.

Have all ingredients at room temperature, about 70°F. Preheat the oven to 375°F. Prepare a 9-inch square baking pan as directed for your altitude, 746.

Whisk together thoroughly:

   2½ cups sifted all-purpose flour
   ¾ teaspoon baking soda
   ½ teaspoon baking powder
   ½ teaspoon salt
   1½ tablespoons ground ginger
   1 teaspoon ground cinnamon
   ½ teaspoon grated or ground nutmeg
   ¼ teaspoon black or white pepper

Beat in a large bowl until well blended:

   ½ cup (1 stick) unsalted butter
   ½ cup plus 2 tablespoons sugar

Add one at a time, beating well after each addition:

   2 large eggs

Scrape down the sides of the bowl and the beaters, and beat in:

   ⅔ cup sour cream
   (1 tablespoon peeled grated fresh ginger)

Combine in a 2-cup measure and stir until dissolved:

   ½ cup unsulphured molasses
   1 cup very hot water

On lowest speed, add the flour mixture in 4 parts, alternating with the molasses mixture in 3 parts, scraping down the bowl after each addition and beating until smooth. The batter will be quite runny. Pour the batter into the pan and bake until a toothpick inserted in the center comes out clean about 38 to 40 minutes. Cool in the pan on a rack. Serve from pan, topped with:

   (Whipped Cream, 754)

▲ HIGH-ALTITUDE CHOCOLATE SPONGE ROLL

10 one 15 x 10-inch sheet, for a 10-inch roll

Fill this cake with your favorite preserves, sweetened whipped cream, or any buttercream icing. For Christmas, this can be made into a Bûche de Noël, 737.

   Please read About High-Altitude Cake Baking, 746, and About Roll Cakes 734. Note: At sea level, this recipe is made with Dutch-processed cocoa, but at 5,000 feet and above, the slightly more acidic quality of nonalkalined (natural) cocoa, gives best results.

   This recipe is designed for baking at 5,000 feet. If baking at 7,000 feet, and ½ teaspoon cream of tartar. Bake for 9 to 10 minutes. At 10,000 feet, reduce the oven heat to 350°F. Add 1 tablespoon flour, reduce the baking powder by ⅛ teaspoon, and increase the cream of tartar by ¾ teaspoon. Bake for 9 to 10 minutes.

Have all ingredients at room temperature, about 70°F. Preheat the oven to 375°F. Grease a 10 x 15-inch rimmed baking sheet, line with wax or parchment paper, generously grease the paper, and dust with flour. (This recipe will also work with an 11 x 17 x 1-inch pan, but the cake will be slightly thinner pan.)

Whisk together thoroughly:

> **$1/4$ cup sifted cake flour**
> **$1/4$ cup nonalkalized cocoa powder, sifted**
> **$1/2$ teaspoon baking powder**
> **$1/4$ teaspoon salt**

Beat in a large bowl until foamy:

> **6 large egg whites**
> **$1/4$ teaspoon cream of tartar**

Gradually add and beat on high speed until soft, slightly droopy peaks form:

> **3 tablespoons sugar**

Set aside. Beat in another large bowl (no need to wash beaters) on high speed until the batter is thick and a pale lemony color and forms a continuous flat ribbon falling back on itself when dropped from the beaters:

> **6 large egg yolks**
> **$1/2$ teaspoon vanilla**
> **3 tablespoons sugar**

Fold in about one-third of the whites. Sprinkle about $1/4$ of the cocoa-flour mixture onto the batter and fold in with a light touch to avoid losing volume. Repeat, alternately folding in whites and flour mixture; don't worry if there are still a few streaks of white.

Scoop the batter into the pan and spread it evenly. Bake until the top is springy to the touch and a toothpick inserted in the center comes out clean, 5 to 7 minutes; don't overbake, or cake will be dry.

Meanwhile, sift onto a clean tea towel in an area the size of the baking pan:

> **$1/3$ cup nonalkalized cocoa powder**

As soon as the cake is baked, invert the pan over the cocoa, lift off the pan, and peel off the paper liner. With a serrated knife, trim off scant $1/8$-inch strips of the crusty cake edges. Leave the cake flat until it cools completely, then spread with the desired filling, roll, see 735, wrap, and refrigerate for at least 1 hour, or until firm. If not filling immediately, wrap tightly in plastic wrap to prevent it from drying out.

ABOUT CAKE FILLINGS

With some exceptions, cake fillings are less sweet than icings or frostings. They offer a creamy texture in contrast to the cake itself. Fillings are often starch-based, or like some puddings, or thickened with eggs, like lemon curd or custard. For acidic fillings such as lemon, almost all the ingredients are combined and cooked over direct heat, because the acid in the lemon juice protects the eggs from curdling even when the mixture simmers. With less-acidic fillings thickened with cornstarch or flour, the starch, sugar, and eggs are beaten together before being cooked with a hot liquid. The starch protects the eggs from curdling as the filling cooks.

We cook most fillings over direct heat rather than in the once-favored double boiler. Use heavy-bottomed pans and a whisk to help prevent burning or lumps. If the mixture contains citrus juice, be sure to use a stainless steel or other nonreactive pan. We recommend straining the finished mixture to remove any tiny bits of cooked egg white. Pay attention to the timing and heating details of any filling made with cornstarch or flour: Overcooking or overbeating can result in a thin filling. Undercooking may leave a starchy taste, or the filling may turn watery from the breakdown of starch caused by insufficiently cooked eggs.

Egg safety is an issue in cooking custards. To avoid spoilage and salmonella contaminations, be sure to scrape the finished cooked filling into a clean container (not one that has the remains of raw eggs in it), using a clean rubber spatula. Most custard-style fillings should be used within a day or two. Lemon curd can be kept refrigerated for up to 1 week. Cakes filled with pastry cream and other custards thickened with flour or cornstarch can be frozen, but such creams and custards should not be frozen in containers, as they may turn watery and grainy when thawed.

In addition to Whipped Ganache Filling, 759, you can also use Chocolate Ganache as a filling (see Chocolate Ganache and Other Rich Chocolate Frostings and Glazes, 796).

FILLING A LAYER CAKE

Cakes should be completely cool before being trimmed, cut, and filled. Warm cake layers melt fillings and cause layers to slip and slide.

To cut a single cake or layers horizontally into thinner layers: If the cake is just baked and very tender, first place it in the freezer for 20 minutes. Set the cake on a cardboard round, a piece of aluminum foil, or a decorating turntable or lazy Susan. If the cake is not level, trim it now (see below). Cut a notch down one side of the cake so that you can line up the layers when you assemble the cake.

To divide a cake or layer, place one hand flat on top of the cake. Hold the blade of a long serrated knife against the side of the cake where you wish to cut it. Turn the cake counterclockwise (clockwise if you are left-handed) while you saw a shallow groove all around the cake, always at an equal distance from the top of the cake so the layer will be even. Do not try to cut all the way through the cake the first time around. After you have cut the groove, continue to rotate the cake while cutting deeper and deeper into the groove until the layer is free. Alternatively, once the groove is cut, wrap a length of strong thread or dental floss around the groove, cross the ends in front, and pull them until the layer is cut through. Slide a piece of cardboard or a cookie sheet under the new layer and lift and set it aside. Repeat if necessary.

To cope with dome-shaped layers or trim layers: Some cakes may be slightly domed on top. In assembling a layer cake, the bottom and middle layers are usually placed dome side down and the top placed dome side up. If the

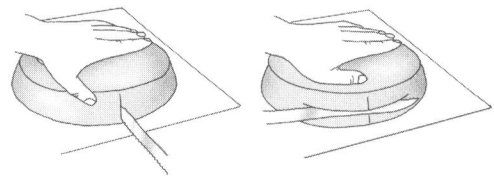

Cutting a single cake into layers

domes are very pronounced, trim them level and place all the layers upside down, since it is easier to spread frosting on an uncut surface.

Creating a base for the cake: A cardboard cake round or springform pan bottom the same diameter as the cake allows you to move the cake safely after you have completed it, simply by sliding a metal spatula underneath it and lifting; anchor the cake to the base with a dab of frosting. Otherwise, assemble and frost the cake directly on the serving platter. Slide wide strips of wax or parchment paper under the edges of the cake on all 4 sides to keep the platter clean. Remove the strips after the cake is frosted.

Using the right amount of filling: The amount of filling used for a particular cake depends on the style of cake and the richness of the filling. Fluffy frostings and whipped cream are spread thicker than denser buttercreams. The buttercream between multiple thin layers should be spread less than $1/8$ inch thick (only $1/3$ cup of buttercream between 8-inch layers, $1/3$ to $1/2$ cup between 9-inch layers). Fillings between thicker cake layers can be spread up to $1/4$ inch thick (up to 1 cup between layers). In other words, if the layers are thin, spread the filling thin; if the layers are thicker, spread the filling thicker. Each time you set a layer in place, make sure it is centered on the layer beneath it and line up the notch if cut layers, sliding it as necessary.

Regard these as general guidelines; consider your own taste as well as the flavor, richness, and sweetness of the cake layers and the frosting. Whipped cream and Seven-Minute frostings are quite fluffy, and you can use the higher suggested amounts—or even more. For rich chocolate glazes or buttercreams in European-style cakes with thin layers, work with the smaller amounts and count on having some left over as well.

Filling for each layer:
For 8- or 9-inch layers: $1/2$ to 1 cup
For a $17 1/2$ x $11 1/2$-inch jelly roll: $1 1/2$ to 3 cups
For frosting:
For a 13 x 9-inch sheet: $1 1/2$ to 3 cups

WHIPPED CREAM

Cream must have a fat content of at least 30 percent to hold a stable, unseparated foam when whipped; for optimal stability, a fat content of 36 percent or more is preferable. Both 30 and 36 percent cream are usually available, the former sold as "medium" cream and the latter as "heavy." Confusingly, cream with a fat content of either

30 or 36 percent may be labeled either "whipping" or "heavy." Our advice is simply to choose the heaviest cream available.

The cream must be cold, or the fat will melt and the cream will refuse to aerate, thicken, and expand. When the weather is hot, it is a good idea to put the bowl and the beaters in the freezer for 5 minutes before beating. If your kitchen is very warm, set the bottom of the bowl of cream in ice water as you beat. Cream can be whipped by hand using a large balloon whisk, but it is certainly easier to use an electric mixer instead. To whip cream, see 973.

Perfectly whipped cream—billowy and stiff but still smooth—is frequently on its way to becoming butter by the time one has frosted or filled a cake with it, spread it over a cake sheet for a jelly roll, or forced it through a pastry bag to make rosettes. This is because any manipulation of whipped cream, including stirring, spreading, or forcing it through a small opening, has the same result as continuing to beat it. The solution is to underwhip any cream to be used as a frosting, filling, or piped decoration. It is also advisable to underwhip cream whenever it must be refrigerated for several hours before use; then whisk the cream briefly to the desired consistency just before use, to reincorporate any liquid that may have separated from it. A cake frosted or filled with whipped cream is best served the day it is made.

SWEETENED WHIPPED CREAM
2 to 2 $1/2$ cups
Beat in a chilled bowl with chilled beaters at high or medium-high speed until thickened:
   1 cup cold heavy cream
If desired, add and beat to the desired consistency:
   (2 teaspoons to 2 tablespoons sugar, 1 to 4
      tablespoons confectioners' sugar,
      or 2 teaspoons honey)
   ($1/2$ teaspoon vanilla)
Use immediately or to store, see 753.

STABILIZED WHIPPED CREAM
Heavy cream can be used to fill or frost a cake, even a day in advance, without adding a stabilizer. Gelatin added to whipped cream gives it a firmer, mousselike texture and keeps it from weeping. It must still be stored in the refrigerator, but it will hold up longer on a buffet table, and you can fill or frost a cake with it a day in advance without worry.

Pour **1 tablespoon cold water** into a heatproof cup. Sprinkle with $1/2$ **teaspoon unflavored gelatin.** Let the gelatin soften, without stirring, for 5 minutes. Place the cup in a pan of simmering water until the gelatin is melted and the liquid is clear. Let cool to room temperature. Prepare **Sweetened Whipped Cream, above,** adding the cooled (but not cold) gelatin mixture while you beat as the cream begins to thicken. Stabilized whipped cream can be flavored according to the variations below, but do so as soon as possible—before the gelatin sets. To store, see 754.

COFFEE WHIPPED CREAM

Prepare **Sweetened Whipped Cream, 754,** adding **2 teaspoons instant coffee or espresso powder** to the cream with the vanilla. Use about 2 tablespoons sugar, or to taste.

LIQUOR-FLAVORED WHIPPED CREAM

Prepare **Sweetened Whipped Cream, 754,** adding **1 to 1^1/$_2$ tablespoons liquor** to the cream with the sugar.

COCOA WHIPPED CREAM

Prepare **Sweetened Whipped Cream, 754,** combining a small amount of the cream and the vanilla, if using, with ^{1}/$_3$ **cup sifted confectioners' sugar, 3 tablespoons Dutch-process cocoa powder,** and ^{1}/$_8$ **teaspoon salt.** Stir in the remaining cream and beat as directed, omitting the additional sugar.

MOCHA WHIPPED CREAM

Prepare **Sweetened Whipped Cream, 754,** combining a small amount of the cream and the vanilla, if using, with **2 teaspoons instant coffee or espresso powder** and **2 tablespoons Dutch-process cocoa powder.** Stir in the remaining cream and beat as directed, using 2 to 3 tablespoons sugar.

WHIPPED CREAM FILLING WITH NUTS, FRUIT, CANDY, OR COOKIES

If you are folding in wet ingredients, such as a fruit puree, consider using Stabilized Whipped Cream, above. Prepare but do not beat quite as stiff:

Whipped Cream, 754

Fold in any of the following:

- ^{1}/$_2$ **cup chopped nuts—walnuts, pecans, pistachios, hazelnuts, or almonds**
- ^{1}/$_2$ **cup toasted, 1001, or untoasted shredded sweetened coconut (mixed with 1 tablespoon rum)**
- ^{1}/$_4$ **cup praline paste (mixed with 1 tablespoon complementary liqueur)**
- ^{1}/$_2$ **cup jam or marmalade**
- ^{1}/$_2$ **cup fresh, frozen, or canned fruit puree (mixed with 2 tablespoons kirsch or a complementary liqueur)**
- ^{3}/$_4$ **cup drained chopped fresh fruit (reserve ^{1}/$_4$ cup of perfect berries or fruit slices for garnish)**
- ^{1}/$_2$ **cup crushed or chopped candy, such as peppermint, toffee, nut brittle, or peanut butter cups**
- ^{1}/$_2$ **cup crushed chocolate wafer or sandwich cookies**

PASTRY CREAM (CRÈME PÂTISSERIE)

About 2 cups

This is the vanilla custard filling for many cakes as well as Boston Cream Pie, 732, éclairs, fresh fruit tarts, and countless other desserts. You can add 1 to 2 tablespoons liqueur to any variation of this custard along with the vanilla, if desired. For a lighter but richer filling, fold ^{1}/$_4$ to ^{3}/$_4$ cup Whipped Cream, 754, into this or any of the variations that follow.

I. VANILLA

Beat in a medium bowl on high speed until thick and pale yellow, about 2 minutes:

> ^{1}/$_3$ **cup sugar**
> **2 tablespoons all-purpose flour**
> **2 tablespoons cornstarch**
> **4 large egg yolks**

Meanwhile, combine in a medium saucepan and bring to a simmer:

> **1^1/$_3$ cups milk**
> **(1 vanilla bean, split)**

Remove the vanilla bean if you used it, and discard. Gradually pour about one-third of the hot milk into the egg mixture, whisking to combine. Scrape the egg mixture back into the pan and cook over low to medium heat, whisking constantly and scraping the bottom and corners of the pan to prevent scorching, until the custard is thickened and beginning to bubble. Then continue to cook, whisking, for 45 to 60 seconds. Using a clean spatula, scrape the custard into a clean bowl. If you did not use the vanilla bean, stir in:

> **(^{3}/$_4$ teaspoon vanilla)**

Cover the surface of the custard with a piece of wax or parchment paper to prevent a skin from forming. Let cool, then refrigerate before using. This keeps, refrigerated, for up to 2 days.

II. CHOCOLATE

Prepare **Pastry Cream, above.** Fold **3 to 5 ounces semisweet or bittersweet chocolate, finely chopped** into the hot custard. Stir gently just until the chocolate is melted and well blended.

III. COFFEE

Prepare **Pastry Cream, above.** Stir into the hot milk **2 to 3 teaspoons instant coffee or espresso powder.**

IV. BANANA

Prepare **Pastry Cream, above.** Stir into the hot custard **1 to 2 tablespoons rum.** Just before using, fold **2 or more bananas, thinly sliced** into the cold custard.

V. FRANGIPANE

Prepare **Pastry Cream, above,** folding into the hot custard ^{1}/$_3$ **cup ground blanched almonds** and ^{1}/$_8$ **to ^{1}/$_4$ teaspoon almond extract.** Or, just before using, fold ^{1}/$_3$ **cup crushed almond macaroons** and **(2 to 3 teaspoons minced candied orange peel)** into the cold custard.

VI. BUTTERSCOTCH

Prepare **Pastry Cream, above.** Substitute **brown sugar** for the sugar and add **a pinch of salt.**

BUTTERSCOTCH FILLING

About 2 cups

Prepare **Butterscotch Cream Pie Filling, 755,** using in all **1^1/$_2$ cups milk.**

CHOCOLATE CUSTARD FILLING
About 1 1/2 cups

Combine in a medium heavy saucepan:

1 cup milk
1/4 cup heavy cream
2 ounces unsweetened chocolate, finely chopped

Cook, stirring occasionally, over medium-low heat until the chocolate is melted and the mixture begins to simmer. Meanwhile, in a medium bowl, beat on high speed until thick and pale yellow, about 1 minute:

1/3 cup sugar
1 tablespoon cornstarch
1 tablespoon all-purpose flour
2 large egg yolks
1/8 teaspoon salt

Gradually pour about one-quarter of the hot chocolate mixture into the egg mixture, whisking to combine. Scrape the egg mixture back into the pan and cook over medium heat, whisking constantly and scraping the bottom and corners of the pan to prevent scorching, until the mixture is thickened and begins to bubble. Then continue to cook, whisking, for about 1 1/2 minutes. Using a clean spatula, scrape the filling into a clean bowl and stir in:

1 teaspoon vanilla

Cover the surface of the filling with a piece of wax or parchment paper to prevent a skin from forming and refrigerate to thicken. This keeps, refrigerated, for up to 2 days.

MOCHA FILLING
About 1 2/3 cups

Coffee lovers will appreciate the pronounced mocha flavor in this dark chocolate custard, which has the texture of thick pudding.

Combine in a medium heavy saucepan:

3/4 cup extra-strong coffee
1/3 cup heavy cream
1 ounce unsweetened chocolate, finely chopped

Cook, stirring occasionally, over medium-low heat until the chocolate is melted and the mixture begins to simmer. Meanwhile, in a medium bowl, beat on high speed until thick and pale yellow, about 1 minute:

3/4 cup sugar
1 1/2 tablespoons cornstarch
1/8 teaspoon salt
3 large egg yolks or 1 large egg plus 1 large egg yolk

Gradually pour about one-quarter of the hot chocolate mixture into the egg mixture, whisking to combine. Scrape the egg mixture back into the pan and cook over over medium heat, whisking constantly and scraping the bottom and corners of the pan to prevent scorching until the mixture is thickened and begins to bubble. Then continue to cook, whisking, for about 1 1/2 minutes. Using a clean spatula, scrape the filling into a clean bowl. Cover the surface of the filling with a piece of wax or parchment paper, cool, then refrigerate to thicken. This keeps, refrigerated, for up to 2 days.

LEMON FILLING
About 1 1/3 cups

Thickened with cornstarch, this has the taste and texture of lemon meringue pie filling.

Whisk together in a small stainless steel or enamel saucepan:

3/4 cup sugar
2 tablespoons cornstarch
1/8 teaspoon salt
Grated zest of 1/2 lemon
1/2 cup water or orange juice
1/4 cup strained fresh lemon juice
3 large egg yolks or 1 large egg plus 1 large egg yolk

Add:

1 tablespoon unsalted butter

Cook over medium heat, whisking constantly and scraping the bottom and corners of the pan to prevent scorching, until the mixture comes to a simmer and thickens. Then continue to cook, whisking briskly, for about 30 seconds. Using a spatula, scrape and strain the filling into a medium-mesh sieve set over a bowl. Cover the surface of the filling with a piece of wax or parchment paper, cool, then refrigerate to thicken. Stir gently if necessary before using; do not beat. This keeps, refrigerated, for up to 2 days.

LEMON CURD
About 1 2/3 cups

Tarter and tangier than Lemon Filling, above, this makes a sensational filling for sponge rolls or Angel Cake, 705. You can also swirl it into a plain cheesecake.

Whisk together in a medium stainless steel or enamel saucepan until light in color:

3 large eggs
1/3 cup sugar
Grated zest of 1 lemon

Add:

1/2 cup strained fresh lemon juice
6 tablespoons (3/4 stick) unsalted butter, cut into small pieces

Cook, whisking, over medium heat until the butter is melted. Then whisk constantly until the mixture is thickened and simmers gently for a few seconds. Using a spatula, scrape the filling into a medium-mesh sieve set over a bowl and strain the filling into the bowl. Stir in:

1/2 teaspoon vanilla

Let cool, cover, and refrigerate to thicken. This keeps, refrigerated, for about 1 week.

ORANGE CURD
About 1 2/3 cups

Blood oranges, if you can get them, are sensational in this filling.

Whisk together in a medium stainless steel or enamel saucepan, until light in color:

8 large egg yolks or 2 large eggs plus 4 large eggs

²/₃ cup sugar
Grated zest of 1¹/₂ oranges
Add:
¹/₂ cup strained fresh lemon juice
10 tablespoons (1¹/₄ sticks) unsalted butter, cut into
small pieces
Cook, whisking, over medium heat until the butter is melted. Then whisk constantly until the mixture is thickened and simmers gently for a few seconds. Using a spatula, scrape the filling into a medium-mesh sieve set over a bowl and strain the filling into the bowl. Let cool, cover, and refrigerate to thicken. This keeps, refrigerated, for about 1 week.

ORANGE CUSTARD FILLING
About 1¹/₂ cups
Whisk together in a medium saucepan until well blended:
¹/₃ cup sugar
¹/₃ cup all-purpose flour
¹/₄ teaspoon salt
Whisk in until smooth:
1 cup milk
Whisk in:
¹/₂ cup orange juice
Cook over medium heat, whisking constantly until the mixture comes to a boil and then continue to cook, whisking briskly, 1 minute. Remove from heat.
Whisk in a small bowl until frothy:
1 large egg
Whisk about a one-third of the sauce into the egg. Return this mixture to the pan. Continue to cook, whisking, until the filling begins to simmer and thickens. Let cool, cover, and refrigerate to thicken. This keeps, refrigerated, for about 1 week.

LEMON-ORANGE CUSTARD FILLING
About 1 cup
Whisk together in a small stainless steel or enamel saucepan:
Grated zest of ¹/₂ lemon
Grated zest of ¹/₄ orange
¹/₂ cup fresh orange juice
3 tablespoons fresh lemon juice
3 tablespoons water
¹/₃ cup sugar
2 tablespoons all-purpose flour
¹/₈ teaspoon salt
3 large egg yolks or 1 large egg plus 1 large egg yolk
Cook over medium heat, whisking constantly and scraping the bottom and corners of the pan to prevent scorching, until the mixture is thickened and begins to bubble. Then continue to cook, whisking briskly, for about 1 minute. Using a spatula, scrape the filling into a medium-mesh sieve set over a bowl and stain the filling into the bowl. Cover the surface of the filling with a piece of wax or parchment paper and refrigerate to thicken. Stir gently

if necessary before using; do not beat. This keeps, refrigerated, for up to 2 days.

APRICOT CUSTARD FILLING
About 1¹/₂ cups
Combine in a small saucepan and simmer gently for 25 minutes:
¹/₂ cup gently packed dried apricots
1 cup water
Stir in:
1 tablespoon sugar
Simmer until the liquid is reduced to a glaze, 3 to 5 minutes. Puree the mixture in a food processor until smooth. Prepare:
Lemon-Orange Custard Filling, above
Stir the apricot puree into the hot filling.

ORANGE CREAM FILLING
About 2¹/₂ cups
Soak:
1 teaspoon unflavored gelatin
in:
1 tablespoon cold water
for about 5 minutes. Meanwhile, combine in a medium saucepan and whisk until well blended:
³/₄ cup sugar
2 tablespoons cornstarch
2 tablespoons all-purpose flour
Whisk in:
³/₄ cup hot water
Cook over medium heat, whisking constantly, until the mixture comes to a boil. Add:
1 tablespoon unsalted butter
Meanwhile, beat in a small bowl
2 large egg yolks
Whisk about one-third of the cornstarch mixture into the egg yolks, then pour back into the saucepan. Cook, stirring, until the custard begins to simmer and thickens. Add the soaked gelatin, and whisk until dissolved. Remove from the heat. Scrape the filling into a bowl and stir in:
Grated zest of 1 orange
3 tablespoons fresh orange juice
3 tablespoons fresh lemon juice
Cover the surface of the custard with a sheet of plastic wrap, and refrigerate until cool but not cold and set, 15 to 30 minutes. Beat until stiff peaks form:
¹/₂ cup heavy cream
Fold the cream into the custard. Refrigerate 1 hour, then spread on the cake before the gelatin sets. If spreading between the layers of a cake, ice with:
Luscious Orange Icing, 791

CHOPPED FRUIT FILLING
About 1³/₄ cups
I. Combine in the top of a double boiler and cook over, not in, boiling water, stirring, until the sugar dissolves:

$^3/_4$ **cup evaporated milk**
$^1/_4$ **cup water**
$^3/_4$ **cup sugar**
$^1/_8$ **teaspoon salt**
Add and cook until thick:
$^1/_4$ **cup finely chopped dates**
$^1/_4$ **cup finely chopped dried figs**
Cool, then add:
$^1/_2$ **cup chopped nuts**
1 teaspoon vanilla
II. *About 2 cups*
Combine in a small saucepan and simmer gently for 25 minutes:
$^1/_2$ **cup gently packed dried apricots**
1 cup water
Raise the heat to high and boil until nearly all the liquid has evaporated. Puree in a food processor. Return the mixture to the saucepan. Stir in:
$^2/_3$ **cup sugar**
Cook over low heat until it thickens, about 3 minutes. Remove from the heat and add:
2 tablespoons grated orange zest
2 tablespoons fresh orange juice
$^3/_4$ **cup chopped raisins**
$^1/_4$ **cup chopped dates or dried figs**

GINGER FRUIT FILLING
About 1 $^1/_2$ cups
Mix well in a small saucepan and cook over medium heat, stirring constantly, until the mixture comes to a simmer and thickens:
1 cup canned pineapple juice
$^1/_4$ **cup confectioners' sugar**
3 tablespoons cornstarch
$^1/_4$ **teaspoon salt**
Cook about 1 minute longer. Remove from the heat and add:
$^1/_2$ **cup mashed banana**
$^1/_2$ **cup drained canned crushed pineapple**
Return to the heat stirring gently, and cook 2 minutes. Add:
3 tablespoons finely chopped crystallized ginger
1 teaspoon vanilla
($^1/_4$ cup slivered almonds)
Transfer the filling to a bowl, cover the surface with plastic wrap, and refrigerate until cold before using.

CHOCOLATE FRUIT FILLING
About 2 cups
Stir together until thoroughly combined:
$^2/_3$ **cup finely chopped walnuts or pecans**
$^2/_3$ **cup packed light brown sugar**
$^1/_3$ **cup chocolate chips**
2 tablespoons unsweetened cocoa powder
2 tablespoons instant coffee or espresso powder
2 teaspoons ground cinnamon

$^1/_4$ **cup dried cranberries, cherries, or chopped dried apricots**
Let cool before using. This keeps, refrigerated, for about 1 week. Soften at room temperature before using.

ALMOND AND FIG OR RAISIN FILLING
About 1 $^1/_2$ cups
Stir together in a small saucepan until well blended:
$^1/_2$ **cup sugar**
2 tablespoons all-purpose flour
Stir in:
1 tablespoon grated orange zest
$^1/_2$ **cup orange juice**
$^1/_2$ **cup water**
1 $^1/_2$ cups finely chopped or ground dried figs or raisins
$^1/_8$ **teaspoon salt**
Bring to a simmer over medium heat, stirring, and simmer 5 minutes, stirring constantly. Remove from the heat and stir in:
$^3/_4$ **cup slivered almonds, toasted, 1001**
$^1/_2$ **teaspoon vanilla**
Let cool before using. This keeps, refrigerated, for about 1 week. Soften at room temperature before using.

TOASTED WALNUT OR PECAN FILLING
About 1 $^1/_2$ cups
Brown sugar and toasted nuts make a superb filling.
Combine in a small saucepan:
1 cup packed light brown sugar
$^1/_4$ **cup ($^1/_2$ stick) unsalted butter, cut into small pieces**
2 tablespoons water
$^1/_4$ **teaspoon salt**
Cook over low heat, whisking, until the butter is melted and the mixture begins to simmer. Remove from the heat and whisk in:
2 large egg yolks
Return to low heat and cook, whisking constantly, until thickened, 1 to 2 minutes. Remove from the heat and stir in:
1 $^1/_2$ cups chopped toasted, 1001, walnuts or pecans
Let cool before using. This keeps, refrigerated, for about 1 week. Soften at room temperature before using.

ALMOND OR HAZELNUT CUSTARD FILLING
About 1 $^1/_2$ cups
Combine in the top of a double boiler and cook over, not in, boiling water, stirring, until slightly thickened:
1 cup sugar
1 cup sour cream
1 tablespoon all-purpose flour
Meanwhile, beat in a small bowl:
1 large egg
Whisk about one-third of the sour cream mixture into the egg, then scrape into a bowl and stir in:
1 cup ground blanched or unblanched almonds or hazelnuts

Return it to the double boiler. Stir and cook the custard until thick.

> **1 cup ground blanched or unblanched almonds or hazelnuts**

When the custard is cool, add:

> $\frac{1}{2}$ **teaspoon vanilla or 1 tablespoon almond or hazelnut liqueur**

COCONUT PECAN FILLING

About 3 $\frac{1}{4}$ cups

Sweet and delicious, this is the traditional German Chocolate Cake, 719, filling and topping. The sides of the cake are left unfrosted.

Combine in a medium saucepan:

> **1 cup sugar**
> **1 cup evaporated milk or heavy cream**
> **3 large egg yolks**
> $\frac{1}{2}$ **cup (1 stick) unsalted butter, cut into small pieces**

Cook over medium heat, stirring constantly, until the mixture is thickened and bubbling gently around the edges. Reduce the heat to low and cook, stirring, for 1 to 2 minutes more. Remove from the heat and stir in:

> $1\frac{1}{3}$ **cups flaked sweetened dried coconut**
> $1\frac{1}{3}$ **cups chopped pecans**

Let cool until spreadable. This keeps, refrigerated, for about 1 week. Soften at room temperature before using.

LANE CAKE FILLING

About 2 $\frac{1}{4}$ cups

Whisk together in a medium heavy saucepan:

> **8 large egg yolks**
> **1 cup sugar**
> $\frac{1}{8}$ **teaspoon salt**
> $\frac{1}{2}$ **cup bourbon**
> $\frac{1}{2}$ **cup (1 stick) unsalted butter, cut into small pieces**

Cook over medium-low heat, stirring constantly, until the mixture is thickened enough to coat the back of a spoon, about 10 minutes. Remove from the heat and stir in:

> **1 cup pecans, finely chopped**
> $\frac{3}{4}$ **cup shredded sweetened dried coconut**
> $\frac{3}{4}$ **cup raisins, finely chopped**
> $\frac{1}{2}$ **cup chopped dates or raisins**
> (**$\frac{1}{4}$ cup chopped maraschino cherries**)
> $\frac{1}{4}$ **teaspoon grated or ground nutmeg**

Let cool before using. This keeps, refrigerated, for about 1 week. Soften at room temperature before using.

WHIPPED GANACHE FILLING

About 1 $\frac{1}{2}$ cups

This is a light-colored but rich and creamy chocolate filling. Double the recipe to fill a 17 $\frac{1}{2}$ x 11$\frac{1}{2}$-inch jelly-roll sheet generously. If you whip it until it is too stiff, warm the spat-ula with hot water to help in spreading. Start this at least several hours in advance.

Bring to a boil in a medium saucepan:

> **1 cup heavy cream**

Remove from the heat and whisk in:

> **4 ounces bittersweet or semisweet chocolate, finely chopped**

Cover and let stand for 10 minutes. With a rubber spatula, stir the mixture until perfectly smooth, scraping the bottom of the pan to be sure all of the chocolate is melted. Cover and chill for at least several hours. (The ganache can be refrigerated for up to 5 days or frozen for up to 6 months.) To use, beat on low to medium speed just until the ganache is thickened and begins to hold a shape; do not overbeat. Use immediately.

WHIPPED WHITE CHOCOLATE OR MILK CHOCOLATE FILLING

Prepare **Whipped Ganache Filling, above,** substituting **white or milk chocolate** for the bittersweet or semisweet chocolate.

MOCHA GANACHE FILLING

Prepare Whipped Ganache Filling, above, substituting **milk chocolate** and add **2 teaspoons instant coffee powder** to the cream with the chocolate.

MOISTENING SYRUP

About 1 cup

Use this to dilute and sweeten liqueurs for moistening cake layers, such as Génoise, 709, before filling and frosting. A lighter syrup can be made using equal parts sugar and water.

Combine in a small saucepan:

> **1 cup sugar**
> $\frac{2}{3}$ **cup water**

Cook, stirring gently, over low heat just until the sugar is dissolved; the syrup does not have to come to a simmer. Remove from the heat and let cool, uncovered, before using. This keeps in a covered jar for up to 3 weeks at room temperature or up to 6 months refrigerated.

LEMON SYRUP

Prepare **Moistening Syrup, above,** substituting $\frac{2}{3}$ **cup fresh lemon juice** for the water. Heat the mixture just until the sugar is dissolved. Simmering mars the lemon flavor. As soon as the cake comes out of the oven, place the pan on a rack, poke the cake all over with a wooden skewer, and brush it with half of the syrup. Let the cool in the pan for 10 minutes. Unmold and invert the cake onto a greased rack. Poke the bottom of the cake with the skewer and brush with some of the syrup. Turn the cake right side up on the rack and brush with the remaining syrup. Let the cake cool completely, then wrap and store for at least 24 hours before serving.

COOKIES AND BARS

Cookies are as American as baseball and apple pie. We are proud to boast that the chocolate chip cookie is also a famous American original. Cookies are the traditional after-school snack, as well as the midnight munchies children leave for Santa on Christmas Eve.

ABOUT MIXING AND DECORATING COOKIES

The mixing of cookie dough is usually quick and easy. Some ingredients are stirred together; some are creamed to combine, 700, and others are blended like pastry, 662. For best results, follow the instructions in each recipe. Unless otherwise specified, it's best to let butter, eggs, nuts, and any other ingredients warm almost to room temperature. And once you add the flour to the wet ingredients in a recipe, don't overbeat the dough: This can result in tough cookies.

While nothing compares to the flavor of a cookie made entirely with butter, we understand that dietary or budget constraints must be taken into account at times. ➤ When substituting for butter, you will achieve the best flavor by replacing up to $1/2$ of the butter with the same amount of regular stick margarine or solid vegetable shortening. ➤ If you must avoid butter altogether, use the same quantity of quality stick margarine or butter-flavored shortening for the best flavor. Because the creamy, rich flavor of shortbread and butter cookies depend on butter, we do not recommend substituting margarine or shortening in those recipes. ➤ Steer clear of reduced-fat tub margarines and spreads when making cookies. Their high water content causes the cookies to be soft and puffy.

You may want to combine different flours. If you do, ➤ be sure to see the note on flour substitutions, 984. Our recipes call for all-purpose flour, and you can use bleached or unbleached. Keep in mind that ➤ too much flour makes cookies tough and dry; too little makes them spread and lose their shape. It is possible to use all whole wheat flour in the recipe, but expect the cookies to be dense and a bit dry. Richly flavored cookies made with molasses, chocolate, or peanut butter produce the best whole wheat cookies. If you are interested in substituting honey or other sugars, read Sugars, Solid, 1018, and Sugars, Liquid, 1018.

In recipes with additions to the cookie dough such as nuts, dried fruits, or chocolate chips, changes in these ingredients are easy. Experimentation is the best teacher. Try substituting dried fruit for nuts, nuts for dried fruit, or a combination of both. If you have a favorite type of nut, use it instead of the one called for. The same goes for extracts, chocolate chips, or coconut. ➤ Do be careful not to go over the total cup volume called for in the recipe, and that your other measurements are accurate.

We've always liked the idea of decorations that provide a clue to a cookie's flavor—a sprinkling of cinnamon and sugar to advertise a hint of spices, for example, or a few coconut shreds to signal a coconut filling. Whatever you choose for decoration, it is best to keep it simple.

To ensure that nonpareils and other garnishes will stay on top of cookies, press them firmly into the dough before baking (use a wide-bladed spatula if the cookies are flat), or decorate the cookies after baking, securing such garnishes with Royal Icing, 789.

ABOUT BAKING COOKIES

Always preheat the oven 20 minutes before baking. If you use a convection oven to bake cookies, set it 25° lower than the recipes call for or follow the manufacturer's instructions. Choose a medium-to-heavy-gauge baking sheet. A pan with high sides deflects the heat and makes the cookies hard to remove. The very best aluminum sheets have a shiny baking surface and specially dulled bottoms to produce even browning. If you have only thin dark sheets, you can place a second empty sheet under the first while baking, for insulation.

Unless the recipe specifies otherwise, grease cookie sheets with butter, shortening, or a coating of nonstick cooking spray, or use parchment or silicone liners. Some cookies—such as shortbread and others that have a high amount of fat, for instance—can be baked on ungreased sheets. A few, such as meringue kisses and others with a large proportion of egg whites and little or no fat, will stick to the cookie sheet so they will not lose their shape. ➤ Always fill the baking sheet, placing cookies of equal size and thickness at least 1 inch apart, or as directed. If you haven't enough dough for your last baking to fill the baking sheet, turn a small baking pan or a pie pan upside down and use it to bake the last batch.

Unless otherwise directed, bake only 1 sheet of cookies at a time, on the center oven rack. Rotate the sheet halfway through for even baking. Because many factors can affect baking time, you will find a range of suggested times in our recipes. ➤ Set your timer to the minimum time specified. If necessary, reset it and bake again for the additional time. It takes only a matter of moments for cookies to bake too long or burn (especially cookies containing molasses or brown sugar).

Within 2 to 3 minutes after cookies have finished baking, use a wide, thin-bladed spatula to lift the cookies and ➤ place them on racks to cool. If cookies cool and stick to the sheet, return them to the oven for a few minutes to heat and soften again. Between batches, cookie sheets should be cooled and wiped with a dry paper towel. If you have one or two extra baking sheets on hand, you'll work more efficiently by rotating them.

▲ BAKING COOKIES AT HIGH ALTITUDES

Between sea level and 3,000 feet, simple sugar cookies may not require any adjustments, but many types begin to show changes related to altitude. At 5,000 feet and above—as you rise in elevation and atmospheric pressure decreases—cookies tend to spread more, get thinner, tougher, or overcrisp. To control spread, strengthen batter by adding a little flour and/or decreasing sugar. Also slightly reduce baking powder, baking soda, or cream of tartar. Oven temperature can be raised 15 to 25 degrees in some cases, though other cookies benefit from longer baking at moderate temperature; there is no single fix. If texture is too dry, add a tablespoon or more liquid or another egg yolk or a little dark corn syrup. In high dry air, cookies stale quickly and must be stored airtight as soon as they are completely cooled.

STORING BAKED COOKIES

Keep cookies in tightly covered plastic storage containers, cookie tins, or resealable plastic bags. Pack each type of cookie in its own container, to prevent the mingling of flavors, and changes in moisture content. Most cookies can be stored at room temperature for 1 to 2 weeks.

Cookies and bars tend to dry out or go limp if not properly stored. ➤ Never put cookies in any kind of container until they have cooled completely. Warm cookies will produce steam, which will cause the entire batch to soften, and eventually to spoil. And if the cookies have been iced, be sure to let the icing set and dry completely before storing them. To restore freshness, they can be heated briefly before serving.

Most cookies freeze well for a month if packed airtight. Brownies, chocolate chip and sugar cookies, and thin crispy varieties freeze particularly well. If freezing bar cookies, freeze them uncut, then cut into servings when partially thawed. Cookies should be frozen without icing or decorations. Allow them to defrost completely before sugar-coating, glazing, or frosting. When setting cookies out to thaw, it is best to partially unwrap them so they can breathe and condensation won't build up.

If you want to eat frozen cookies right away, lay them on baking sheets and warm in a preheated 300°F oven for a few minutes. Homemade and even store-bought cookies can be recrisped this way. When setting cookies out to thaw, it is best to partially unwrap them so they can breathe and condensation won't build up.

Cookies that have dried out and hardened can also be refreshed by placing a piece of apple in the container of cookies. Close the lid tightly, and in a day or two, the cookies will have softened.

ABOUT STORING COOKIE DOUGH

Because cookie dough can be refrigerated or frozen successfully, cookies are a baker's dream come true, especially the baker with limited time. Dough for rolled, shaped, or drop cookies can be made ahead and stored in the refrigerator for up to 3 days or in the freezer for 2 months. Whether you are freezing or refrigerating dough, use the following guidelines to wrap it for storage.

Dough can be frozen or refrigerated with or without rolling, dropping, or shaping. Be sure to store each type of dough individually in its own airtight container or wrapping in batch sizes. If you want to roll and cut cookies beforehand, put them on trays in the freezer until hard, then package for freezing or refrigeration. If you want to cut them afterward, make a roll of the dough and wrap it in airtight plastic or containers in batch sizes. Drop cookie dough can be frozen as unshaped dough or in ready-to-bake balls. Store bar cookies covered tightly in the container in which they will be baked. To bake frozen cookie dough, simply use the temperature as directed in the recipe, and add a few minutes if needed.

ABOUT PACKAGING COOKIES FOR SHIPPING AND GIFT GIVING

If you are sending cookies to out-of-towners, the best choices are small to medium-size cookies that are at least $1/4$ inch thick and firm in consistency, or bar cookies. More delicate varieties can be shipped successfully if they are packed in tins or sturdy plastic boxes with crumpled wax or parchment paper to protect them. Extremely thin, brittle cookies and tender, crumbly ones do not travel well, nor do cookies with sticky glazes or with moist fillings or glazes. Meringue kisses and other eggwhite cookies are also an unwise choice.

After placing the cookies in durable rigid containers, pack them in larger boxes filled with foam "peanuts," plastic bubble wrap, crumpled newspaper, or as we used to, popcorn, to cushion the goodies from bumps and knocks. As added insurance that the cookies will arrive at their destination unbroken, consider shipping by air.

Cookie tins, ceramic cookie jars, clear glass storage jars, and decorative wooden boxes all make a gift of home-baked cookies more special. Secure loose lids by tying the containers up with ribbons. If you have sewing skills, you can also present cookies in fabric sacks tied with ribbon or fancy twist-ties made with wire ribbon. (Slip a plastic bag, cut down to size, inside for an airtight liner.) Small, dainty cookies can be tucked into colored candy papers or mini cupcake cups in flat candy boxes. For a special touch, when you tie the ribbon around the gift bag or box, secure a cookie cutter in the bow, and include the recipe.

ABOUT CHRISTMAS COOKIES AND COOKIE ORNAMENTS

Christmas and cookies are inseparable. Stars, angels, bells, trees, and the beloved St. Nick are all time-honored shapes for holiday treats. You may already have a collection of cookie cutters that you use at this special time of year, or you may cut your own shapes.

To prepare a cookie for hanging as an ornament, use the end of a straw to cut a hole through the uncooked shaped dough. Be sure the hole is far enough from the top so that it is strong enough not to break the cookie when it hangs. When the cookie is fully baked and cooled, loop ribbon, string, or lace trim through the hole and tie. If you want a decoration for the table or mantelpiece, the gingerbread house, 781–783, is charming, and a perfect project to do with the kids.

ABOUT BARS OR SQUARES

The quickest and most easily produced cookies are squares and bars. Bake them in greased pans at least 1¹/₂ inches deep. ➤ Pay close attention to the size of the pan called for in each recipe—variations will throw off the baking time and the thickness of the batter in the pan affects texture. A too-large pan will give a dry, brittle result. A pan smaller than indicated in the recipes will give a cakey result—not a chewy one.

For easy removal after baking, line the pan with greased foil, leaving enough overhang on two opposite sides or ends to use as handles. The cooled slab can be lifted from the pan to a board for cutting, making cleanup easy as well. Cool bars completely before cutting with a knife into bars, squares, or triangles. To prepare filled bars, line a 13 x 9-inch pan with two-thirds of the dough, spread the filling over it, see Filled Cookies, 777, and cover the filling with the remaining dough. We suggest using muffin tins for individual servings or pie pans to make larger, festive rounds to be the base for ice cream. See the chart of comparative pan sizes on 700.

BROWNIES COCKAIGNE

About 30 brownies

Almost everyone wants to make this classic American confection. This recipe has appeared in JOY since the original 1931 edition. Brownies may vary greatly in richness and contain anywhere from 1¹/₂ cups of butter and 5 ounces of chocolate to 2 tablespoons of butter and 2 ounces of chocolate for every cup of flour. If you want them chewy and moist, use a 13 x 9-inch pan; if cakey, a 9 x 9-inch pan.

Preheat the oven to 350°F. Grease a baking pan lined with foil, 1052. Melt in a small saucepan:
> ¹/₂ **cup (1 stick) unsalted butter**
> **4 ounces unsweetened chocolate**

Let cool. If you don't, your brownies will be heavy and dry. Beat until light in color and foamy in texture:
> **4 large eggs**
> ¹/₄ **teaspoon salt**

Gradually add and continue beating until thick:
> **2 cups sugar**
> **1 teaspoon vanilla**

With a few swift strokes, stir in the cooled chocolate mixture just until combined. Even if you are using an electric mixer, switch to a wooden spoon for this. Stir in just until combined:
> **1 cup all-purpose flour**

Gently stir in, if desired:
> **(1 cup chopped pecans)**

Scrape batter into the prepared pan. Bake about 25 minutes. Cool completely in the pan on a rack. Garnish with:
> **Whipped Cream, 754, ice cream, 828,**
> **or an icing, 784–800**

BOOK CLUB BROWNIES

About 30 brownies

Prepare **Brownies Cockaigne, above,** reducing the sugar to 1³/₄ cups. Whisk into the flour ¹/₂ **teaspoon baking powder** before adding the sugar. Bake until a toothpick inserted near the center comes out almost clean, about 35 minutes.

BUTTERSCOTCH BROWNIES OR BLONDIES

Sixteen 2-inch squares

Preheat the oven to 350°F. Grease an 8-inch square baking pan lined with foil, 1052. Whisk together thoroughly:
> **1 cup all-purpose flour**
> ¹/₄ **teaspoon baking powder**
> ¹/₈ **teaspoon baking soda**
> ¹/₈ **teaspoon salt**

In a large heavy saucepan, melt, then boil, stirring constantly, until light golden brown, about 4 minutes:
> ¹/₂ **cup (1 stick) unsalted butter**

Remove from the heat and stir in until well blended:
> ²/₃ **cup packed light brown sugar**
> ¹/₄ **cup sugar**

Let cool to barely warm. Stir in until well combined:
> **1 large egg**
> **1 large egg yolk**
> **1 tablespoon light corn syrup**
> **1¹/₂ teaspoons vanilla**

Stir in flour mixture and, if desired:
> **(1 cup chopped, toasted pecans, 1001, 1 cup chocolate**
> **chips, or ²/₃ cup shredded sweetened coconut)**

Scrape into the pan. Bake until the top is golden brown and a toothpick inserted in the center comes out clean, 25 to 30 minutes. Cool completely in the pan on a rack.

CHEESECAKE BROWNIES

Twelve 2-inch squares

Preheat the oven to 350°F. Grease an 8-inch square baking pan lined with foil, 1052. Whisk together:

1 cup all-purpose flour
¼ teaspoon baking soda
¼ teaspoon salt

Melt in a large heavy saucepan over very low heat, stirring until smooth:

6 ounces bittersweet or semisweet chocolate,
**   coarsely chopped**
¼ cup (½ stick) unsalted butter

Remove from the heat and let cool until barely warm, then stir in until well blended:

⅔ cup sugar
2½ teaspoons vanilla

Beat in one at a time until well combined:

2 large eggs

Stir in:

2 tablespoons light corn syrup

Stir in the flour mixture until well blended.

Spread the batter evenly into the baking pan. Bake for 12 minutes. Meanwhile, beat in a large bowl until well blended and smooth:

12 ounces cream cheese, softened
½ cup sugar
2 tablespoons unsalted butter, melted
1 large egg
1 teaspoon vanilla

Spread the cream cheese topping evenly over the chocolate layer. Reduce the oven temperature to 325°F and bake until the cheesecake layer is just tinged with brown and beginning to crack on top and a toothpick inserted in the center comes out clean but still moist and fudgy at the bottom, about 36 minutes. Cool completely in the pan on a rack. Refrigerate until well chilled before cutting into squares. Serve at room temperature.

CHOCOLATE-GLAZED TOFFEE BARS

Twenty-four 2⅔ x 1-inch bars

A chewy brown sugar–pecan toffee layer spread over shortbread and topped with chocolate. These bars are best made a day ahead.

Preheat the oven to 350°F. Grease an 8-inch square baking pan lined with foil. Whisk together in a bowl:

⅔ cup all-purpose flour
1½ tablespoons sugar
⅛ teaspoon salt

Add:

¼ cup (½ stick) cold unsalted butter,
**   cut into small pieces**

Using a pastry blender or your fingertips, cut in the butter until the mixture resembles fine crumbs. Sprinkle over the top and stir in to blend:

2 teaspoons milk

Knead until the milk is evenly distributed and the crumbs

begin to hold together. (Or, pulse the dry ingredients and butter in a food processor just until the mixture resembles coarse crumbs; be careful not to overprocess. A bit at a time, add the milk, pulsing until the crumbs begin to hold together.) Press the dough firmly into the bottom of the pan to form a smooth, even layer. Bake the dough for 12 minutes. Set aside on a rack.

Combine in a medium heavy saucepan and bring to a boil over medium heat, stirring frequently:

5 tablespoons unsalted butter, cut into pieces
½ cup packed light brown sugar
2 tablespoons clover or other mild honey
1 tablespoon milk
⅛ teaspoon salt

Boil, uncovered, for 3 minutes. Remove from the heat and stir in:

1½ cups toasted chopped pecans, 1001
1 teaspoon vanilla

Spread the mixture evenly over the baked crust. Bake until the crumb mixture is bubbly, golden brown, and just slightly darker at the edges, 17 to 20 minutes, remove the pan to a rack and sprinkle over the top:

¼ cup semisweet or bittersweet chocolate chips

Let stand until the chocolate chips partially melt, then smooth with a table knife to spread the chocolate; the surface will not be completely covered with chocolate. Sprinkle over the top:

2 tablespoons finely chopped pecans

Let the chocolate cool until beginning to set but still slightly soft. Cut into bars, then let cool completely in the pan before removing the bars.

CHRISTMAS CHOCOLATE BARS COCKAIGNE

Fifty-four 2 x 1-inch bars

Preheat the oven to 350°F. Grease a 13 x 9-inch baking pan lined with foil. Whisk together:

1½ cups all-purpose flour
½ teaspoon baking soda
½ teaspoon salt
1½ teaspoons ground cinnamon
¾ teaspoon ground cloves
¼ teaspoon ground allspice

Beat in a large bowl until thick and pale:

3 large eggs
1⅓ cups packed brown sugar

Add the flour mixture in 2 parts, alternately with:

¼ cup honey or molasses

Stir in:

1¼ cups mixed dried cherries, golden raisins, and
**   chopped blanched almonds**
2 ounces unsweetened chocolate, finely chopped

Spread the batter evenly into the greased pan. Bake about 20 minutes, until set. Place the pan on a rack. While the bars are still warm, spread evenly with:

Lemon Glaze, 799

Let stand until bars are cool and the glaze is set.

CHOCOLATE OAT BARS

Fifty-four 2 x 1-inch bars

Preheat the oven to 350°F. Grease a 13 x 9-inch baking pan lined with foil. Beat together in a large bowl:

³/₄ cup (1¹/₂ sticks) unsalted butter, softened
1¹/₂ cups packed brown sugar

Beat in:

1 large egg
1 large egg yolk
1¹/₂ teaspoons vanilla

Set aside. Whisk together in a bowl:

1³/₄ cups all-purpose flour
³/₄ teaspoon baking soda
³/₄ teaspoon salt

Stir in:

2¹/₄ cups old-fashioned rolled oats

Combine in a medium saucepan and stir over low heat until smooth:

1¹/₂ cups semisweet chocolate chips
1¹/₄ cups sweetened condensed milk
1¹/₂ tablespoons unsalted butter
Pinch of salt

Stir in:

³/₄ teaspoon vanilla
³/₄ cup chopped walnuts or pecans

Remove from the heat. Stir the flour mixture into the egg mixture. Pat about two-thirds of it into the baking pan. Pour the chocolate mixture over all, then dot with the remaining batter. Bake about 25 minutes. Cool completely in the pan on a rack.

RASPBERRY STREUSEL BARS

Twenty 2¹/₂ x 2¹/₈-inch bars

Preheat the oven to 375°F. Grease a 13 x 9-inch baking pan lined with foil. Whisk together in a bowl:

2 cups all-purpose flour
¹/₄ cup sugar
¹/₄ teaspoon salt

Add:

**³/₄ cup (1¹/₂ sticks) cold unsalted butter, cut into
    small pieces**

Using a pastry blender or your fingertips, cut in the butter until the mixture resembles fine crumbs. Stir together:

3 tablespoons milk
1 teaspoon almond extract

Sprinkle over the flour mixture. Lightly stir to blend, then knead until the dough begins to hold together. (Alternatively, pulse dry ingredients and butter in a food processor just until the mixture resembles coarse crumbs; be careful not to overprocess. Slowly add the milk mixture, pulsing until the dough begins to hold together.) Press the dough evenly into the baking pan. Bake until barely firm in the center, 12 to 15 minutes. Set the pan on a rack (leave the oven on) and spread evenly over the hot crust:

1 cup seedless raspberry jam

Whisk together in a bowl:

1³/₄ cups all-purpose flour
²/₃ cup sugar
¹/₄ teaspoon salt
¹/₂ teaspoon ground cinnamon

Add:

**¹/₂ cup (1 stick) cold unsalted butter, cut into
    small pieces**

Using a pastry blender or your fingertips, cut in the butter until the mixture is well blended. (Or, combine the flour, sugar, cinnamon, and salt in a food processor, sprinkle the butter over the top, and process until well blended. Turn out into a bowl.) Using a fork, stir in:

³/₄ cup sliced (blanched or unblanched) almonds
¹/₂ cup old-fashioned rolled oats

Beat together lightly:

1 large egg
2 tablespoons milk

Stir into the flour mixture until the streusel is moistened and forms small clumps. Sprinkle the streusel evenly over the raspberry jam, breaking up any large clumps with a fork or your fingertips. Bake until the streusel is nicely browned and the raspberry mixture is bubbly, 25 to 30 minutes. Cool completely in the pan on a rack.

PECAN OR ANGEL SLICES

Twelve 2³/₄ x 2¹/₃-inch bars

Many a copy of JOY has been sold on the strength of this recipe. One fan says her family is sure these are the cakes St. Peter gives little children at the Gates of Heaven, to get them over the first pangs of homesickness.

Preheat the oven to 350°F. Grease a 9 x 9-inch baking pan lined with foil. Beat in a medium bowl until well blended:

¹/₄ cup (¹/₂ stick) unsalted butter, softened
2 tablespoons sugar
1 large egg yolk
¹/₄ teaspoon vanilla

Stir in until well blended and smooth:

³/₄ cup all-purpose flour

Press the dough evenly into the baking pan. Bake for 10 minutes. Meanwhile, beat in a medium bowl until well combined:

2 large eggs
1 cup packed light brown sugar
1¹/₂ tablespoons all-purpose flour
¹/₄ teaspoon baking powder
¹/₈ teaspoon salt
1¹/₂ teaspoons vanilla

Stir in:

1¹/₂ cups chopped toasted, 1001, pecans or walnuts
**1 cup flaked or shredded sweetened coconut, lightly
    toasted, 972**

Spread the mixture evenly over the hot baked crust. Bake until the top is firm and golden brown and a toothpick inserted in the center comes out slightly wet, 20 to 25 minutes. Set the pan on a rack. If desired, while the bars are still warm, spread evenly with:

(Lemon Glaze, 799)
Let stand until the bars are cool and the glaze is set.

NUT BARS
Fifty-four 2 x 1-inch bars
Preheat the oven to 350°F. Grease a 13 x 9-inch baking pan lined with foil. Beat in a bowl until blended:
- 1/2 cup (1 stick) unsalted butter, softened
- 1/4 cup sugar

Beat in:
- 1 large egg
- 1/2 teaspoon vanilla

Whisk together:
- 1 1/4 cups all-purpose flour
- 1/8 teaspoon salt

Add in about 3 parts to the butter mixture, blending well. Press the dough evenly into the baking pan. Bake about 15 minutes. Meanwhile, beat in a medium heavy saucepan until they begin to froth:
- 4 large egg whites

Stir in:
- 2 1/4 cups finely chopped pecans
- 1 cup sugar
- 1 1/2 teaspoons ground cinnamon

Cook over low heat, stirring until sugar has dissolved. Increase the heat slightly and cook, stirring, until the mixture leaves the sides of the pan; remove it from the heat before it is dry. Spread the nut mixture over the hot crust. Bake until slightly puffed, about 15 minutes. Cool in the pan on a rack.

DATE BARS COCKAIGNE
Twenty-four 2 1/2 x 2-inch bars
Preheat the oven to 325°F. Grease a 13 x 9-inch baking pan lined with foil. Whisk together:
- 1/2 cup old-fashioned rolled oats
- 3 tablespoons all-purpose flour
- 1/4 teaspoon baking powder
- Pinch of salt
- 3/4 teaspoon ground cinnamon
- 1/4 teaspoon ground allspice
- Pinch of ground cloves

Beat in a large bowl until blended:
- 1/3 cup (5 1/3 tablespoons) unsalted butter, softened
- 1/3 cup packed brown sugar

Add and beat well:
- 1 large egg yolk
- 4 1/2 tablespoons milk
- 3/4 cup chopped dates
- 3/4 cup chopped pecans
- Grated zest and juice of 1/2 lemon

Stir in the flour mixture until blended.
Spread evenly into the baking pan. Bake 15 to 18 minutes, or until the dough begins to pull away from the sides of the pan. Set the pan on a rack. If desired, while the bars are still warm, spread evenly with:

(Lemon Glaze, 799)
Let stand until the bars are completely cool and the glaze is set.

ENERGY BARS
Eighteen 3 x 1 1/2-inch bars
Preheat the oven to 350°F. Grease a 9 x 9-inch square baking pan lined with foil. Combine in a medium bowl:
- 1 1/2 cups packed dried fruit (apricots, pitted dates, raisins, figs, cherries, and/or cranberries), coarsely chopped
- 1 cup old-fashioned rolled oats
- 3/4 cup all-purpose flour
- 1 cup packed dark brown sugar
- 1/2 cup chopped walnuts, pecans, hazelnuts, almonds
- 1/4 teaspoon salt
- 3/4 teaspoon ground cinnamon

Add and stir until well blended:
- 3/4 cup (1 1/2 sticks) unsalted butter, melted
- 1 1/2 teaspoons vanilla

Press the mixture into the pan. Bake until top is golden brown, 35 to 40 minutes. Cool in the pan on a rack.

LEMON CURD BARS
Eighteen 3 x 2-inch bars
Preheat the oven to 325°F. Whisk together in a bowl:
- 1 1/2 cups all-purpose flour
- 1/4 cup confectioners' sugar
- Pinch of salt

Add:
- 3/4 cup (1 1/2 sticks) cold unsalted butter, cut into small pieces

Using a pastry blender or your fingertips, cut in the butter until the mixture is the size of small peas. Press the dough into the bottom and 3/4 inch up the sides of an ungreased 13 x 9-inch baking pan. Bake until golden brown, 25 to 30 minutes. Transfer the pan to a rack and reduce the oven temperature to 300°F.
Whisk together in a large bowl until well combined:
- 6 large eggs
- 3 cups sugar

Stir in:
- Grated zest of 1 lemon
- 1 cup plus 2 tablespoons fresh lemon juice (from about 5 lemons)

Sift over the top and stir in until well blended and smooth:
- 1/2 cup all-purpose flour

Pour the batter over the baked crust. Bake about 35 minutes, until the topping is set. Cool in the pan on a rack.

LEBKUCHEN (GERMAN HONEY BARS)
Fifty-four 2 x 1-inch bars
These honey bars will keep 6 months in a tightly closed tin, especially if, as my great-grandmother used to say with a twinkle, "locked up." If a crisper bar is desired, substitute carbonate of ammonia, 958, for the baking powder and

soda; use 1 teaspoon carbonate of ammonia dissolved in 2 tablespoons warm water, rum, or wine.

Preheat the oven to 350°F. Grease a 13 x 9-inch baking pan lined with foil. Combine in a large saucepan and cook, stirring, until the butter is melted:

>**²/₃ cup honey or molasses**
>**¹/₃ cup sugar**
>**1¹/₂ tablespoons unsalted butter**

Remove from heat. Whisk together, and stir in:

>**1 cup all-purpose flour**
>**¹/₂ teaspoon baking powder**
>**¹/₄ teaspoon baking soda**
>**Pinch of salt**

Stir in:

>**¹/₂ cup chopped blanched almonds**
>**2 tablespoons chopped candied citron**
>**2 tablespoons chopped candied orange or lemon peel**
>**1 teaspoon ground cinnamon**
>**¹/₄ teaspoon ground cardamom**
>**¹/₈ teaspoon ground ginger**
>**Pinch of ground cloves**

Stir in:

>**1 cup all-purpose flour**

The dough should be sticky to the touch. Press evenly into the baking pan. Bake about 25 minutes, until golden brown. Set the pan on a rack. If desired, while the bars are still warm spread evenly with:

>**(Lemon Glaze, 799)**

Let stand until cool and the glaze is set.

ABOUT DROP COOKIES

Unless otherwise indicated, the dough should be dropped from a measuring teaspoon or tablespoon. This is for the sake of precision, as it helps ensure that recipe yields and baking times are accurate. Drop cookie doughs vary in texture. Some fall easily from the spoon and flatten into wafers in baking. Stiffer doughs need a push with a finger or a second spoon to release them.

When chilled, these doughs may be formed into balls and flattened between your palms. First dampen your hands or dust them with flour or confectioners' sugar, or, if the cookies are a chocolate or other dark dough, with cocoa. To flatten the balls, use the bottom of a glass that has been lightly greased or dusted with flour, confectioners' sugar, or cocoa, or use a spatula dipped in ice water.

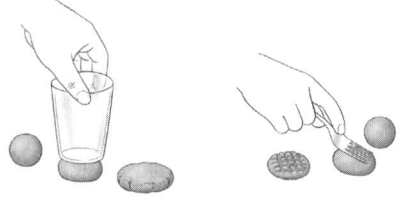

Two ways to flatten drop cookies

To give a crisscross effect, score them in lines with a fork dipped in flour.

Grease cookie sheets with butter, shortening, or non-stick cooking spray, or use parchment paper or silicone liners. Unless otherwise directed, drop cookies should be cooled on the baking sheets about 1 to 2 minutes before transferring them to a rack to cool completely. Please see About Baking Cookies, 760.

DROP BUTTER WAFERS
About forty-eight 2-inch wafers

Preheat the oven to 375°F. Grease or line 2 cookie sheets. Beat in a medium bowl until light and fluffy:

>**¹/₂ cup (1 stick) unsalted butter, softened**
>**¹/₂ cup sugar**

Beat in:

>**1 large egg**
>**1 teaspoon vanilla**
>**¹/₄ teaspoon grated lemon zest**
>**³/₄ cup sifted cake flour**
>**Pinch of salt**
>**(1¹/₂ tablespoons poppy seeds or 1 teaspoon grated orange zest)**

Drop the cookies from a teaspoon 1 inch apart onto the cookie sheets. Bake, 1 sheet at a time, until the edges brown, about 7 minutes. Let stand briefly, then remove to a rack to cool.

SUGAR DROP COOKIES
About sixty 2¹/₂-inch cookies

Preheat the oven to 375°. Lightly grease or line 2 cookie sheets.

Sift together:

>**2¹/₂ cups all-purpose flour**
>**1¹/₂ teaspoons baking powder**
>**³/₄ teaspoon salt**
>**¹/₄ teaspoon ground cinnamon or ¹/₂ teaspoon grated or ground nutmeg**

Combine and mix to blend in a large bowl:

>**1 cup sugar**
>**³/₄ cup vegetable oil**

Add one at a time, beating well after each addition:

>**2 large eggs**

Add:

>**1 teaspoon vanilla**

Add the flour mixture and beat well.

Shape the dough into ¹/₂-inch balls, dip the balls in:

>**Sugar**

and place about 1 inch apart on the cookie sheets, or flatten the balls, above. Then sprinkle with sugar. Bake, 1 sheet at a time, about 10 to 12 minutes, until golden brown. Let stand briefly, then remove to a rack to cool.

CHOCOLATE CHIP COOKIES
About thirty-six 2¹/₂-inch cookies

This recipe is a JOY classic, appearing in the book since the 1943 wartime edition.

Preheat the oven to 375°F. Grease or line 2 cookie sheets. Whisk together:

1 cup plus 2 tablespoons all-purpose flour
1/2 teaspoon baking soda

Beat in a large bowl until well blended:

1/2 cup (1 stick) unsalted butter, softened
1/2 cup sugar
1/2 cup packed light brown sugar

Add and beat until well combined:

1 large egg
1/4 teaspoon salt
1 1/2 teaspoons vanilla

Stir in the flour mixture until well blended and smooth. Stir in:

1 cup chocolate chips
(3/4 cup chopped walnuts or pecans)

Drop the dough by heaping teaspoonfuls about 2 inches apart onto the cookie sheets. Bake, 1 sheet at a time, until the cookies are just slightly colored on top and the edges are brown, 8 to 10 minutes. Let stand briefly, then remove to a rack to cool.

CRISP CHOCOLATE CHIP COOKIES

Prepare **Chocolate Chip Cookies, above,** mixing the brown sugars and using a total of 1 cup sugar. Add an additional **2 tablespoons all-purpose flour.** Bake about 13 to 15 minutes, until golden brown.

GINGERSNAPS

About forty 2 1/4-inch cookies

For crunchy cookies, overbake slightly; for more tender ones, underbake by a minute or two.
Preheat the oven to 350°F. Grease or line 2 cookie sheets. Whisk together:

1 3/4 cups all-purpose flour
3/4 teaspoon baking powder
1/4 teaspoon baking soda
Pinch of salt
2 1/2 teaspoons ground ginger
1 teaspoon ground cinnamon
1/8 teaspoon ground cloves

Beat in a large bowl until very fluffy:

6 tablespoons (3/4 stick) unsalted butter, softened
3/4 cup sugar

Add and beat until well combined:

1 large egg
1/4 cup dark molasses
1/4 teaspoon finely grated lemon or orange zest
1 teaspoon fresh lemon juice

Stir in the flour mixture until blended. Form the dough into 3/4-inch balls and arrange about 1 1/2 inches apart on the cookie sheets. Bake, 1 sheet at a time, about 12 minutes. The cookies will flatten and develop a crinkled surface as they bake. Let stand briefly, then remove to a rack to cool.

WHITE CHOCOLATE MACADAMIA MONSTERS

Fourteen 5-inch cookies or twenty-four 2 1/2-inch cookies

For regular-sized cookies, drop by heaping measuring teaspoonfuls 1 1/2 inches apart and bake for 13 to 15 minutes.
Preheat the oven to 350°F. Grease or line 2 cookie sheets. Whisk together:

2 1/2 cups all-purpose flour
1 teaspoon baking soda
1/4 teaspoon salt

Beat in a large bowl until light and fluffy:

1 cup (2 sticks) unsalted butter, softened
1 1/3 cups sugar
2/3 cup packed dark brown sugar

Beat in one at a time:

2 large eggs
1 teaspoon vanilla

Stir in the dry ingredients. Stir in:

1 cup coarsely chopped macadamia nuts (about 4 ounces)
1 cup coarsely chopped white chocolate (about 4 ounces)

Using a 1/3-cup measure, drop the dough about 3 inches apart onto the cookie sheets. Bake, 1 sheet at a time, until golden brown, 18 to 20 minutes. Let stand briefly. Then remove to a rack to cool.

PEANUT BUTTER COOKIES

About sixty 1 1/2-inch cookies

For those who dote on peanut butter cookies, try these rich and crumbly ones. This is another JOY classic.
Preheat the oven to 375°F. Grease or line 2 cookie sheets. Whisk together:

1 1/2 cups all-purpose flour
1/2 teaspoon baking soda

Beat in a large bowl until well blended:

1/3 cup (5 1/3 tablespoons) unsalted butter, softened
1/2 cup sugar
1/2 cup packed brown sugar

Beat in:

1 large egg
1 cup peanut butter (smooth or chunky)
1/2 teaspoon vanilla

Stir in the flour mixture until blended. Shape into 1-inch balls and arrange about 2 inches apart on the cookie sheets. Press flat with a fork, as shown on 766. Bake, 1 sheet at a time, about 10 to 12 minutes. Let stand briefly, then remove to a rack to cool.

OATMEAL RAISIN COOKIES

About forty-eight 3-inch cookies

Preheat the oven to 350°F. Grease or line 2 cookie sheets. Whisk together:

1 3/4 cups all-purpose flour
3/4 teaspoon baking soda
3/4 teaspoon baking powder

$\frac{1}{2}$ teaspoon salt
$\frac{1}{2}$ teaspoon ground cinnamon
$\frac{1}{2}$ teaspoon grated or ground nutmeg
Beat in a large bowl until well blended:
1 cup (2 sticks) unsalted butter, softened
$\frac{1}{4}$ **cup sugar**
1$\frac{1}{2}$ cups packed brown sugar
2 large eggs
2$\frac{1}{2}$ teaspoons vanilla
Stir in the flour mixture. Stir in:
1 cup raisins, chopped
3$\frac{1}{2}$ cups old-fashioned rolled oats
($\frac{3}{4}$ cup chopped walnuts)
Shape the dough into generous 1$\frac{1}{2}$-inch balls and place about 2 inches apart on the cookie sheets. Flatten the balls into $\frac{1}{2}$-inch-thick rounds. Bake, 1 sheet at a time, until the cookies are lightly browned all over, 12 to 14 minutes. Let stand briefly, then remove to a rack to cool.

OATMEAL CHOCOLATE CHIP COOKIES
Prepare **Oatmeal Raisin Cookies, above,** omitting the cinnamon and nutmeg, substituting for the raisins **1 cup chocolate chips.**

SNICKERDOODLES
About thirty-six 3-inch cookies
Preheat the oven to 350°F. Grease or line 2 cookie sheets.
Whisk until well blended:
2 cups all-purpose flour
2 teaspoons cream of tartar
1 teaspoon baking soda
$\frac{1}{4}$ **teaspoon salt**
Beat in a large bowl:
1 cup (2 sticks) unsalted butter, softened
1$\frac{1}{2}$ cups sugar
Add and beat until well combined:
2 large eggs
Stir in the flour mixture. Combine:
$\frac{1}{4}$ **cup sugar**
4 teaspoons ground cinnamon
Shape the dough into 1$\frac{1}{4}$-inch balls, roll in the cinnamon sugar, and arrange about 2$\frac{3}{4}$ inches apart on the cookie sheets. Bake, 1 sheet at a time, until the cookies are light golden brown at the edges, 12 to 14 minutes. Let stand briefly, then remove to a rack to cool.

PEPPERNUTS (PFEFFERNÜSSE)
About sixty 1-inch cookies
Whisk together:
1 cup plus 1 tablespoon all-purpose flour
$\frac{1}{4}$ **teaspoon baking powder**
$\frac{1}{8}$ **teaspoon baking soda**
$\frac{1}{8}$ **teaspoon salt**
1 teaspoon ground cinnamon
$\frac{1}{2}$ **teaspoon ground cardamom**
$\frac{1}{4}$ **teaspoon ground cloves**

$\frac{1}{4}$ teaspoon grated or ground nutmeg
$\frac{1}{8}$ teaspoon black pepper
Beat in a large bowl until very fluffy:
$\frac{1}{4}$ **cup ($\frac{1}{2}$ stick) unsalted butter, softened**
$\frac{1}{2}$ **cup sugar**
Add and beat until well combined:
1 large egg yolk
Stir in:
$\frac{1}{4}$ **cup slivered almonds, finely chopped**
$\frac{1}{4}$ **cup finely chopped candied orange peel**
1 teaspoon finely grated lemon zest
Stir the flour mixture alternately with:
3 tablespoons molasses
3 tablespoons brandy
Cover and refrigerate the dough for at least 8 hours, or up to 2 days, to allow the flavors to blend. Preheat the oven to 350°F. Grease or line 2 cookie sheets. Shape the dough into $\frac{3}{4}$-inch balls and arrange about 1 inch apart on the cookie sheets. Bake, 1 sheet at a time, until the cookies are lightly browned, 12 to 14 minutes. Let cool briefly, then roll the still-warm cookies in:
$\frac{1}{2}$ to $\frac{2}{3}$ **cup confectioners' sugar**
Remove to a rack to cool.

MEXICAN WEDDING CAKES
About sixty 1$\frac{1}{4}$-inch cookies
Preheat the oven to 350°F. Grease or line 2 cookie sheets.
Beat in a large bowl until well blended:
1 cup (2 sticks) unsalted butter, softened
$\frac{1}{2}$ **cup confectioners' sugar**
$\frac{1}{4}$ **teaspoon salt**
2 teaspoons vanilla
Stir in:
1 cup pecans, toasted, 1001, and finely ground
Stir in until well blended:
2 cups all-purpose flour
Shape into 1-inch balls and arrange about 1$\frac{1}{4}$ inches apart on the cookie sheets. Bake, 1 sheet at a time, until the cookies are lightly browned, 12 to 15 minutes. Let stand briefly. Then remove to a rack to cool. Roll the cooled cookies in:
$\frac{3}{4}$ **cup confectioners' sugar**

ABOUT NUT DROP COOKIES
The following recipes have in common a brown sugar and egg base, so ➤ don't try to bake them in hot, humid weather. To grind nuts, please see Nuts, 1000.

Most of these cookies are fragile, but if made small and baked on a greased cookie sheet or a silicone liner, as directed, they are easy to remove intact. ➤ Should they harden on the pan, return the baking sheet to the oven for a moment before trying to remove them. See About Baking Cookies, 760.

PECAN PUFFS
About forty 1 1/2-inch balls
Rich and devastating.
Preheat the oven to 300°F. Beat until soft:

1/2 cup (1 stick) unsalted butter

Add and blend until creamy:

2 tablespoons sugar

Add:

1 teaspoon vanilla

Measure, then grind in a nut grinder:

1 cup pecan meats

Sift before measuring:

1 cup cake flour

Stir the pecans and the flour into the butter mixture. Roll the dough into small balls. Place balls on a greased cookie sheet and bake about 30 minutes. Roll while hot in:

Confectioners' sugar

To glaze, put the sheet back into the oven for a minute. Cool and serve.

SESAME SEED (BENNE SEED) WAFERS
About forty-two 2 1/4-inch cookies
Benne, an African word for "sesame," is still used in the South, particularly South Carolina. Benne seed wafers are so nutty tasting that people often think they contain peanuts. Be sure to buy white sesame seeds. Read About Nut Drop Cookies, 768.
Preheat the oven to 375°F. Grease and flour 2 cookie sheets, or use parchment paper or silicone liners. Whisk together:

1 1/2 cups all-purpose flour
1/3 cup white sesame seeds, toasted, 1011
1 1/4 teaspoons baking powder
1/2 teaspoon baking soda
1/4 teaspoon salt

Beat in a large bowl until blended:

1/2 cup (1 stick) unsalted butter, softened
3/4 cup packed light brown sugar

Add and beat until combined:

1 large egg
1 1/2 teaspoons vanilla

Stir in the flour mixture. Pull off pieces of the dough and roll between your palms into 1-inch balls. Dip the tops of the balls into:

1/2 cup white sesame seeds, toasted, or 1 cup chopped pecans

and place the balls, seeded side up, about 2 inches apart on the cookie sheets. Gently flatten the balls into 1 1/2-inch rounds. Bake, 1 sheet at a time, until the cookies are just lightly browned at the edges, 6 to 8 minutes. Let stand briefly. Then remove to a rack to cool.

FLOURLESS NUT BALLS
About thirty-six 1 1/4-balls
Read about Nut Drop Cookies, 768. Preheat the oven to 325°F. Generously grease 2 cookie sheets.

Grind in a nut grinder, 1001, or food processor:

1 1/2 cups almonds or pecans
Pinch of salt

Combine in a saucepan with:

1 cup firmly packed brown sugar
1 large egg white
1 1/2 teaspoons unsalted butter

Stir over low heat until well blended. Let cool. Shape the dough into small balls. If the dough is hard to handle, dust your hands with a little confectioners' sugar. Place the cookies about 2 inches apart on the cookie sheets. Bake 30 to 40 minutes. Cool on the sheet on a rack. Ice the cooled cookies with:

Lemon Glaze, 799, or a chocolate icing, 796–797

NUTTY DRIED FRUIT DROPS
About twenty 2 1/2-inch cookies
Preheat the oven to 350°F. Grease or line 2 cookie sheets. Beat in a large bowl until blended:

2 large egg whites
1/2 cup packed light brown sugar
Pinch of salt
1 teaspoon vanilla

Stir in:

1 1/2 cups chopped almonds, pecans, and/or walnuts
1 1/2 cups chopped mixed assorted dried fruit (apricots, raisins, dates, cherries, and/or cranberries)

Drop by heaping tablespoonfuls about 1 1/2 inches apart onto the cookie sheets. Bake, 1 sheet at a time, until golden brown, 10 to 12 minutes. Let stand briefly, then remove to a rack to cool.

PECAN LACE
About forty-eight 3-inch wafers
Much of the appeal of these see-through wafers is in their brittle, caramelized texture, so be sure to make them on a dry day.
Preheat the oven to 375°F. Grease or line 2 cookie sheets. Melt in a medium saucepan:

6 tablespoons (1 1/4 sticks) unsalted butter

Simmer the butter gently, stirring occasionally, until the solids on the bottom of the pan turn light brown, 3 to 4 minutes. Remove from the heat and stir in until blended:

1 cup packed light brown sugar
1/4 cup light corn syrup
1 tablespoon milk
1/4 teaspoon salt

Stir in until combined:

1 1/2 cups old-fashioned rolled oats
1/2 cup finely chopped toasted pecans, 1001
2 tablespoons all-purpose flour
2 teaspoons vanilla

Drop by teaspoonfuls about 3 1/2 inches apart onto the cookie sheets. Bake, 1 sheet at a time, until the cookies are lightly browned, 12 to 14 minutes. Let stand briefly, then remove to a rack to cool.

FLORENTINES COCKAIGNE
About fifteen 3-inch cookies

These cookies were one of Mom's favorites. She considered them "the height of elegance."

Preheat the oven to 350°F. Line 2 cookie sheets with parchment paper, silicone liners, or aluminum foil. Toss together until the fruit is separated:

    1¼ **cups packed chopped mixed candied fruit**
    ½ **cup all-purpose flour**

Combine in a food processor with:

    ¼ **cup packed light brown sugar**
    ¼ **cup honey**
    ½ **teaspoon vanilla**
    ½ **cup slivered almonds**
    ⅛ **teaspoon salt**

Pulse until the fruit and nuts are about ¼ inch in size. Add:

    ¼ **cup (½ stick) unsalted butter, melted**

Process briefly, until the fruit and nuts are about ⅛ inch in size. Remove to a bowl. Shape into 1-inch balls and place about 3 inches apart on the cookie sheets. Flatten the balls to 2½ inches. Bake, 1 sheet at a time, until golden brown, about 7 to 9 minutes. Let the cookies cool slightly, then turn onto a rack and coat the bottoms with:

    4 ounces bittersweet or semisweet chocolate, melted

GINGER THINS
About three hundred ¾-inch wafers

These little cakes will be the size of a quarter when baked. Preheat the oven to 325°F. Grease or line 2 cookie sheets. Sift together:

    1½ **cups all-purpose flour**
    ½ **teaspoon baking soda**
    ¼ **teaspoon salt**
    ½ **teaspoon ground cloves**
    ½ **teaspoon ground cinnamon**
    ½ **teaspoon ground ginger**

Beat in a large bowl until light and fluffy:

    ¾ **cup (1½ sticks) unsalted butter, softened**
    1 **cup packed brown sugar**
    1 **large egg, beaten**
    ¼ **cup molasses**

Stir in the dry ingredients until smooth. Drop ⅛-teaspoon dots of dough 1 inch apart onto the cookie sheets. Bake, 1 sheet at a time, 5 to 6 minutes. Cool on a rack. The cooled cookies will snap off if you twist the sheets slightly.

MOLASSES COOKIES MOLDOW
About forty-two 2-inch cookies

This recipe came to JOY from our publisher. These cookies are one of her favorites, and the recipe is from her sister-in-law, Gay Moldow.

Beat in a large bowl until light and fluffy:

    ¾ **cup (1½ sticks) margarine or unsalted butter**
    1 **cup sugar or packed brown sugar**

Beat in until well blended:

    2 cups sifted all-purpose flour
    ½ **teaspoon salt**
    2 teaspoons ground cinnamon
    1 teaspoon ground cloves
    1 teaspoon ground ginger
    1 large egg
    ¼ **cup molasses**
    1 teaspoon baking soda

The dough will be soft. Refrigerate until firm enough to handle, about 2 hours. Preheat the oven to 350°F. Grease or line 2 cookie sheets or line with parchment paper. Shape the dough into 1-inch balls, roll in:

    Sugar

and place 2 inches apart on the cookie sheets. Bake, 1 sheet at a time, until firm, about 8 minutes. Let stand briefly. Then remove to a rack to cool.

HERMITS
About forty 2-inch cookies

Preheat the oven to 375°F. Grease or line 2 cookie sheets. Whisk until blended:

    1⅓ **cups all-purpose flour**
    ¼ **teaspoon baking soda**
    Pinch of salt
    ¾ **teaspoon ground cinnamon**
    ½ **teaspoon ground cloves**

Beat in a large bowl until creamy:

    ½ **cup (1 stick) unsalted butter, softened**
    1 **cup packed light brown sugar**

Beat in:

    1 large egg
    ½ **cup sour cream or buttermilk**

Add the flour mixture and beat until smooth. Stir in:

    ½ **cup chopped raisins, dried dates, figs,**
        or dried apricots, or candied citron
    ¼ **cup chopped hickory or other nuts**
    (¼ **cup shredded sweetened coconut)**

Drop the dough by teaspoonfuls about 3 inches apart onto the cookie sheets. Bake, 1 sheet at a time, until the cookies are browned, 10 minutes. Let stand briefly, then remove to a rack to cool.

ORANGE MARMALADE DROPS
About thirty-six 2-inch cookies

The marmalade for this chewy cookie should be quite tart. Preheat the oven to 375°F. Grease or line 2 cookie sheets. Whisk together:

    1½ **cups all-purpose flour**
    1¼ **teaspoons baking powder**
    Pinch of salt

Beat in a medium bowl until well blended:

    ⅓ **cup (5⅓ tablespoons) unsalted butter, softened**
    ⅔ **cup sugar**

Beat in:

    1 large egg
    6 tablespoons tart orange marmalade

Stir in the flour mixture until well blended. Drop by teaspoonfuls about 2 inches apart onto the cookie sheets. Bake, 1 sheet at a time, until the cookies are golden brown, 8 to 10 minutes. Let stand briefly, then remove to a rack to cool.

BUTTERSCOTCH NUT COOKIES
About thirty 1 1/2-inch cookies
Preheat the oven to 375°F. Grease or line 2 cookie sheets. Prepare **dough for Butterscotch Blondies, 762,** adding **2 tablespoons all-purpose flour** and **(1 cup chopped, toasted, 1001, pecans, 1 cup chocolate chips, or 2/3 cup shredded sweetened coconut).** Drop the dough by heaping teaspoonfuls about 2 inches apart onto the cookie sheets. Bake until the cookies are slightly browned on top, 8 to 10 minutes. Let stand briefly, then remove to a rack to cool.

ALMOND MACAROONS
About thirty 1 3/4-inch cookies
Combine in a food processor and process or mix together until finely crumbled:
   7 ounces almond paste
   1 cup confectioners' sugar
   Pinch of salt
With the machine running, slowly add and process until the mixture is smooth, about 1 minute:
   3 large egg whites
   (1/4 teaspoon almond extract)
Transfer the mixture to a large heavy saucepan and cook, stirring constantly, over medium heat until slightly thickened, about 4 minutes. Remove to a bowl and refrigerate until cooled and slightly firm, 20 to 30 minutes. Preheat the oven to 350°F. Grease or line 2 cookie sheets. Drop the batter by heaping teaspoonfuls about 2 inches apart onto the cookie sheets. Bake, 1 sheet at a time, until the cookies are tinged with brown, 15 to 17 minutes. Let stand briefly, then remove to a rack to cool.

COCONUT MACAROONS
About thirty-six 1 1/2-inch cookies
Preheat the oven to 325°F. Grease or line 2 cookie sheets. Stir together in a large bowl until combined:
   2/3 cup sweetened condensed milk
   1 large egg white
   1 1/2 teaspoons vanilla
   1/8 teaspoon salt
Stir in until blended:
   3 1/2 cups flaked or shredded sweetened coconut
Drop the dough by tablespoonfuls about 2 inches apart onto the cookie sheets. Bake, 1 sheet at a time, until golden brown, 20 to 24 minutes. Let stand briefly, then remove to a rack to cool.

CHOCOLATE COCONUT MACAROONS
Prepare the recipe for **Coconut Macaroons, above.** In a small saucepan, combine **3 tablespoons unsweetened cocoa powder or 1 ounce unsweetened chocolate, chopped,** with the condensed milk. Heat over low heat, stirring until the cocoa is dissolved or the chocolate is melted. Let cool before proceeding as directed.

MERINGUE KISSES
About thirty-six 1 1/2-inch cookies
You can bake these cookies 2 sheets at the same time. Preheat the oven to 225°F. Line 2 cookie sheets with parchment paper or leave ungreased. Beat in a medium bowl on low speed until foamy:
   3 large egg whites
   1/4 teaspoon cream of tartar
   1/8 teaspoon salt
Increase the speed to high and beat until the egg whites just begin to form soft peaks. Gradually add, beating until well combined:
   3/4 cup sugar
Reduce the speed to low and add:
   3/4 teaspoon vanilla
   (1/4 teaspoon almond extract)
Beat until the meringue is glossy and stands in very stiff peaks. Using a pastry bag fitted with a 1/2-inch open star tip or a heavy-duty zipper-topped plastic bag with a bottom corner snipped off, pipe the batter into 1 1/4-inch kisses about 1 inch apart on the cookie sheets. (Or, drop heaping teaspoonfuls of batter in peaked mounds.) Bake for 45 minutes rotating the sheets and switching positions halfway through baking. Turn the heat off and let the cookies stand in the oven for 30 minutes, or until cool.

COCOA MERINGUE KISSES
Prepare **Meringue Kisses, above.** Along with the sugar, add **3 tablespoons unsweetened cocoa powder,** then shape and bake as directed.

NUTTY MERINGUE KISSES
Prepare **Meringue Kisses, above,** folding in **3/4 cup finely chopped pecans, almonds, pistachios, or skinned hazelnuts** into the batter.

ABOUT ROLLED, MOLDED, AND SHAPED COOKIES
Aunties and grandmothers who roll cookies for and with children are scarce these days. But shaping cookies is such fun that children should be encouraged to learn to make them for themselves. Inexperienced bakers often ruin rolled cookies by adding too much flour in the rolling process; use as little extra flour as possible. To prevent most cookie doughs from sticking to your work surface and rolling pin, ➤ chill the dough at least 1 hour before rolling it, and dust the surface with confectioners' sugar instead of flour. Divide the dough into thirds or quarters, shape into disks, and wrap in plastic. The dough can be refrigerated for up to 2 days or frozen up to 1 month.

When cutting or shaping cookies, ➤ try to keep them all about the same size and thickness so that they will bake evenly. And remember that if you choose to make cookies larger or smaller than the recipe specifies, the amount of spreading, the baking time, and the recipe yield may vary. Use cutters dipped in flour, and handle the dough as little as possible.

Other cookies are formed by hand, with molds, presses, or other special equipment. To shape dough into balls, use a small ice cream scoop or lightly floured hands, and handle the dough as little as possible. If the dough is very soft or sticky, refrigerate it for a few minutes.

A pastry bag fitted with a metal tip can be used to shape a variety of cookies. The dough must be soft enough to be squeezed through the tip. A cookie press can also be used, but the dough ➤ must be chilled and slightly firm or the dough won't squeeze out neatly. See the dough recipe for use in a press, 775. Traditional cookie molds can also be used for firm dough like shortbread and Springerle; ➤ they must be well oiled and floured to ensure easy removal.

A roller cutter also speeds cookie cutting. Two time-saving devices are an old French one of dovetailed hearts and diamonds, and a wheel cutter, which spins out the shapes with great rapidity. Amusing cutters lurk in antique shops and contemporary cookware stores.

ROLL COOKIES
About forty 2-inch cookies
Remarkable for its handling quality, this dough can be shaped into crusts for filled cookies or tarts, as well as cut into intricate patterns.
Cream together:
   $^1/_2$ cup white or brown sugar
   $^1/_2$ cup (1 stick) unsalted butter, softened
Beat in:
   1 teaspoon vanilla
   2 eggs
   $2^1/_2$ cups sifted all-purpose flour
   2 teaspoons baking powder
   $^1/_2$ teaspoons salt
Chill the dough 3 to 4 hours before rolling. Preheat the oven to 375°. To roll and cut, see About Rolled, Molded, and Shaped Cookies, above. Place cookies on a greased or lined cookie sheet. You may decorate them with:
   (Colored sprinkles, cinnamon, sugar, or decorating sugar)
   ($^1/_2$ nutmeat or a candied cherry)
Bake 7 to 12 minutes.

RICH ROLL COOKIES
About thirty-six 2- to 3-inch cookies
Just what they are called—and delicious.
Beat in a large bowl until creamy:
   1 cup (2 sticks) unsalted butter, softened
   $^2/_3$ cup sugar

Add and beat until combined:
   1 large egg
   $^1/_4$ teaspoon baking powder
   $^1/_4$ teaspoon salt
   $1^1/_2$ teaspoons vanilla extract or almond extract
Stir in until blended:
   $2^1/_2$ cups all-purpose flour
Divide the dough into thirds or quarters, shape into disks, and wrap in plastic. Refrigerate until firm enough to roll. Preheat the oven to 350°F. Grease or line 2 cookie sheets. Working with 1 portion of dough at a time, roll out to $^1/_4$ inch thick. Cut out cookies using 2- or 3-inch cutters and arrange about 1 inch apart on the cookie sheets. Reroll and cut the scraps. If desired, sprinkle the cookies very lightly with:
   (Colored sprinkles, decorating sugar, or nonpareils)
Bake, 1 sheet at a time, until the cookies are lightly colored on top and slightly darker at the edges, 10 to 12 minutes. Let stand briefly, then remove to a rack to cool. If desired, decorate the cooled cookies with:
   (Royal Icing, 789)

SAND TARTS
About eighty $1^1/_2$-inch cookies
When touring in Normandy we met up with a famous local specialty, which, curiously enough, proved to be our very own sand tarts.
Sift:
   3 cups all-purpose flour
Resift with:
   $^1/_4$ teaspoon salt
Beat in a large bowl until creamy:
   $^3/_4$ cup ($1^1/_2$ sticks) unsalted butter, softened
Gradually add and beat until light and fluffy:
   $1^1/_4$ cups sifted sugar
Beat in:
   1 large egg
   1 large egg yolk
   1 teaspoon vanilla
   1 teaspoon grated lemon zest
Gradually stir in the flour until well blended; the last of the flour may have to be kneaded in by hand. Divide the dough into thirds or quarters, shape into disks, and wrap in plastic. Chill for several hours.
Preheat the oven to 400°F. Grease or line 2 cookie sheets. Working with 1 portion of the dough at a time, roll until very thin. Using a $1^1/_2$-inch fluted or plain round cutter, cut out cookies and place about $1^1/_2$ inches apart on the cookie sheets. Brush the tops of the cookies with:
   1 large egg white, beaten
Sprinkle generously with:
   Sugar
Place in the center of each:
   ($^1/_2$ blanched almond)
Bake, 1 sheet at a time, about 8 minutes, until golden. Let stand briefly, then remove to a rack to cool.

BROWN SUGAR SAND TARTS

Prepare Sand Tarts, 772, and substitute **1¹/₃ cups packed brown sugar** for the sugar.

MORAVIAN MOLASSES THINS

About sixty-five 2¹/₂-inch cookies

These paper-thin cookies are traditional in American communities settled by Moravian immigrants from central Europe.

Whisk together:

1 cup all-purpose flour
¹/₂ teaspoon baking soda
Pinch of salt
1¹/₂ teaspoons ground cinnamon
1 teaspoon ground ginger
¹/₂ teaspoon ground cloves
¹/₄ teaspoon ground cardamom

Beat in a medium bowl until blended:

¹/₃ cup molasses
¹/₄ cup vegetable shortening or good-quality lard
¹/₂ cup packed dark brown sugar
1 teaspoon vanilla

Stir in the flour mixture, then knead until smooth. Divide the dough into thirds, shape into disks, and wrap in plastic. Let stand at room temperature for at least 6 hours or, preferably, 12 hours. (The dough can also be refrigerated for up to 4 days; return to room temperature before using.) Preheat the oven to 300°F. Grease or line 2 cookie sheets. Working with 1 portion of the dough at a time, roll as thin as possible (about ¹/₈ inch). Cut out the cookies using a 2¹/₄-inch fluted or plain round cutter and arrange about 1 inch apart on the cookie sheets. Bake, 1 sheet at a time, until the edges of the cookies are just barely browned, 6 to 9 minutes, depending on the thickness; don't overbake, or the cookies will be bitter. Let stand briefly, then remove to a rack to cool.

GINGERBREAD MEN

Twenty 4-inch ginger men

Prepare:

¹/₂ recipe Gingerbread Dough, 781

Divide the dough in half, shape into disks, and wrap in plastic. Let stand at room temperature for at least 2 hours, or up to 8 hours. The dough can also be refrigerated for up to 4 days; return to room temperature before using. Preheat the oven to 375°F. Grease or line 2 cookie sheets. Working with 1 portion of the dough at a time, roll out to ¹/₄ inch thick. Cut out cookies using a 4- or 5-inch-tall gingerbread boy or girl cutter and arrange about 1¹/₂ inches apart on the cookie sheets. Decorate, if desired, with:

(Raisins and/or red hots for eyes and buttons)

Bake, 1 sheet at a time, until the edges of the cookies have just barely darkened, 7 to 10 minutes. While they are still warm, spread evenly with:

Lemon Glaze, 799

Let stand briefly, then remove to a rack to cool. Decorate the cooled cookies with:

Royal Icing, 789

Apply the icing with a wooden pick or a small knife for additional garnishes—caps, hair, mustaches, belts, etc.

Forming gingerbread men

VIENNESE CRESCENTS

About forty-eight 2¹/₄-inch cookies

Preheat the oven to 350°F. Grease or line 2 cookie sheets.

Beat in a large bowl until creamy:

1 cup (2 sticks) unsalted butter, softened

Add and beat until well combined:

³/₄ cup confectioners' sugar

Beat in:

1 cup ground walnuts or blanched almonds
2 teaspoons vanilla
(1 teaspoon cinnamon)

Stir in until well blended:

2 cups all-purpose flour

Chill the dough. If using a crescent cookie cutter, roll the dough to the thickness of ¹/₄ inch. If shaping into crescents, roll 1-tablespoon pieces of dough into short ropes to shape. Arrange about ¹/₄ inch apart on the cookie sheets. Bake until crescents begin to brown, 13 to 15 minutes. Let stand briefly, then remove to a rack to cool. Roll the cooled cookies in:

²/₃ cup confectioners' sugar

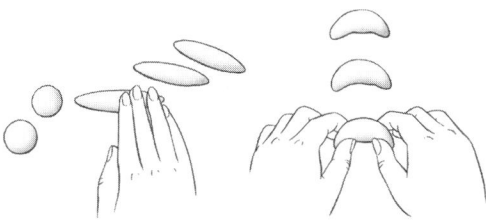

Rolling and shaping Viennese crescents

LETTER COOKIES

About 50 initials or thin 1¹/₂-inch-long cookies

These cookies use up leftover yolks, have strength, and make excellent shells for nut or jam tarts. We have used

them for engagement parties and, of course, they can be a delicious way to teach the alphabet as well as baking skills to children.
Beat in a large bowl until blended:

   $1/2$ **cup (1 stick) unsalted butter, softened**
   $1/2$ **cup sugar**
   $1/4$ **teaspoon salt**
Beat in:

   $1/4$ **teaspoon grated lemon zest**
   $3/4$ **teaspoon fresh lemon juice**
   4 large egg yolks
Stir in:

   2 cups all-purpose flour
Divide dough into thirds or quarters, shape into disks, and wrap in plastic. Refrigerate for at least 1 hour. Preheat the oven to 375°F. Grease or line 2 cookie sheets. Working with 1 disk at a time, roll the dough into 3-inch sticks $1/4$ inch in diameter. Shape these into letters and arrange about $1/2$ inches apart on the cookie sheets. Brush the cookies with:

   1 egg yolk, beaten
Then sprinkle lightly with:

   (Colored sprinkles, decorating sugar, or nonpareils)
Bake, 1 sheet at a time, until the cookies are golden brown, 6 to 10 minutes, depending on the shape. Let stand briefly, then remove to a rack to cool.

ALMOND PRETZELS (MANDELPLÄTTCHEN)

Forty-eight 3-inch pretzels
Whisk together:

   $2^1/2$ **cups all-purpose flour**
   1 teaspoon baking powder
   Pinch of salt
   2 teaspoons ground cinnamon
   (1 teaspoon grated lemon zest)
Beat in a large bowl until blended:

   1 cup (2 sticks) unsalted butter, softened
   1 cup sugar
Beat in:

   2 large eggs
   1 large egg yolk
   $1/4$ **cup sour cream**
   1 teaspoon vanilla
   ($1/4$ teaspoon almond extract)
Stir in the flour mixture. Divide the dough in half, shape into disks, and wrap in plastic. Refrigerate until firm enough to handle, about 2 hours.
Preheat the oven to 375°F. Grease or line 2 cookie sheets. Working with 1 disk at a time, divide dough into 24 equal pieces. Shape into long thin rolls, twist into pretzel shapes, and arrange about 2 inches apart on the cookie sheets. Brush the pretzels with:

   1 egg yolk, beaten
Sprinkle the tops with:

   Chopped blanched almonds
   Sugar

Bake, 1 sheet at a time, until the edges are tinged with brown, 10 to 12 minutes. Let stand briefly, then remove to a rack to cool.

BISCOTTI

About forty-two 3 x $1/2$-inch biscotti
Preheat the oven to 375°F. Grease or line a cookie sheet. Whisk together:

   $3^1/3$ **cups all-purpose flour**
   $2^1/2$ **teaspoons baking powder**
   $1/2$ **teaspoon salt**
Beat in a large bowl until blended:

   $1/4$ **cup corn or canola oil**
   $1^1/4$ **cups sugar**
   2 large eggs
   2 large egg whites
   1 teaspoon finely grated lemon zest
   $1/2$ **teaspoon finely grated orange zest**
   1 teaspoon anise or almond extract
   1 teaspoon vanilla
Stir in the flour mixture until blended. Divide dough in half. Shape each half into a smooth 11 x $1^1/2$-inch log by wrapping the log in plastic and rolling it back and forth until smooth, or by shaping it with lightly floured hands. Arrange the logs as far apart from one another as possible on the cookie sheet and press to flatten slightly. Bake for 25 minutes. Remove the sheet to a rack.
When the logs are cool enough to handle, carefully transfer to a cutting board and cut on a slight diagonal into $3/8$-inch-thick slices. Lay the slices flat on the sheet, return to the oven, and bake for 10 minutes. Turn the slices over and bake until lightly browned, 5 to 10 minutes more. Transfer the biscotti to racks to cool.

CINNAMON STARS

About thirty-six $1^1/2$-inch stars
Deservedly one of the most popular decorative Christmas cookies. The dough can also be shaped into 1-inch balls and flattened slightly.
Preheat the oven to 300°F. Grease or line 2 cookie sheets. Whip to medium-firm peaks, 978, in a large bowl:

   3 large egg whites
   $1/8$ **teaspoon salt**
Gradually beat in:

   $1^1/3$ **cups confectioners' sugar**
   $1^1/4$ **teaspoons ground cinnamon**
   $1/2$ **teaspoon grated lemon zest**
Beat until stiff and glossy. Remove one-third of the mixture to another bowl. Fold into the remainder:

   $2^1/3$ **cups whole unblanched almonds, finely ground**
Dust a work surface lightly with confectioners' sugar. Pat the dough out to a thickness of $1/3$ inch; it is too delicate to roll. If it sticks, dust your palms with confectioners' sugar. Cut using a $1^1/2$-inch star cutter. Arrange on the cookie sheets about $1^1/2$ inches apart. Brush the tops with the reserved egg white mixture. Bake until the tops look dry and

slightly crackled, about 20 minutes. Let stand briefly, then remove to a rack to cool.

SPRINGERLE
About thirty assorted 2- to 4-inch cookies
This recipe produces the well-known German anise cakes, which are stamped with a wooden mold or roller into quaint little designs and figures. If you have no mold, cut the dough into ³/₄ x 2¹/₂-inch bars. For a more pronounced anise flavor, add 1 to 2 teaspoons anise seeds to the storage container.
Whisk together:
   3¹/₄ cups all-purpose flour
   ¹/₄ teaspoon baking powder
Beat in a large bowl:
   4 large eggs
Add and beat until blended:
   1²/₃ cups sugar
   1 teaspoon finely grated lemon zest
   1 teaspoon anise extract
Stir in the flour mixture until well blended. Grease or line 2 cookie sheets. Sprinkle a clean work surface with:
   ¹/₄ cup all-purpose flour
Turn out the dough onto the work surface and sprinkle with a little more flour. Knead in enough flour to firm the dough and make it manageable. Divide the dough in half and wrap one half in plastic (do not refrigerate). Roll out the remaining dough to ¹/₄ inch thick. Lightly dust a Springerle carved rolling pin or cookie mold with flour; tap off the excess. Firmly roll the rolling pin over the dough to imprint designs, or press the molds firmly into the dough, then lift off. Cut the designs apart using a pastry wheel or sharp knife and arrange about ¹/₂ inch apart on the cookie sheets. Set the cookies aside, uncovered, for 10 to 12 hours. Preheat the oven to 300°F. If desired, sprinkle the cookies with:
   (2 to 3 tablespoons whole or crushed anise seeds)
Bake until the cookies are almost firm but not colored, 18 to 25 minutes. Let stand briefly. Transfer to a rack to cool.

SPEKULATIUS
About twenty-eight 2 x 4-inch thin cookies
A rich cookie of Danish origin, pressed with carved wooden molds into Santa and Christmas symbols.
Work as for pie dough, until the particles are like coarse cornmeal:
   ²/₃ cup unsalted butter
   1 cup flour
Cream:
   1 egg
with:
   ¹/₂ cup firmly packed brown sugar
Add:
   ¹/₈ teaspoon cloves or ¹/₁₆ teaspoon cardamom
   1 teaspoon cinnamon
Combine the egg and butter mixtures well. Spread the dough on a 14 x 17-inch baking sheet. Let it rest, chilled, for 12 hours.
Preheat the oven to 350°F. Stamp the figures with the floured molds. Bake about 10 minutes or until done.

COOKIE-PRESS OR SPRITZ COOKIES
About sixty 2-inch cookies
Some spritz cookies are soft and tender to the point of being cakelike, but these are crisp-tender. They may be made with a pastry bag or a cookie press.
Sift together:
   2¹/₄ cups all-purpose flour
   ¹/₂ teaspoon salt
Cream together:
   ³/₄ cup sugar
   1 cup (2 sticks) unsalted butter
Add:
   2 egg yolks
   1 teaspoon vanilla or almond extract
Stir in the flour. Beat well, then chill. Put dough through cookie press onto an ungreased cookie sheet. The dough should be pliable, but if it becomes too soft, rechill it slightly. Bake about 10 minutes in a 350°F oven until lightly browned.

SCOTCH SHORTBREAD
Twenty-four 2 ²/₃ x 1-inch bars
If desired, substitute ¹/₃ cup rice flour or cornstarch for an equal amount of the all-purpose flour, which produces an especially crumbly and tender shortbread.
Preheat the oven to 300°F. Beat in a large bowl:
   ³/₄ cup (1¹/₂ sticks) unsalted butter, softened
   ¹/₄ cup confectioners' sugar
   ¹/₄ cup sugar
   ¹/₄ teaspoon salt
Stir in:
   1¹/₂ cups all-purpose flour
Lightly knead until blended. Press the dough evenly into the bottom of an ungreased 8-inch square baking pan or a rectangular shortbread mold. If baking in a pan, pierce the dough deeply with a fork all over in a decorative pattern. Sprinkle with, if desired:
   (1 to 2 teaspoons sugar)
Bake until the shortbread is lightly browned and darker at the edges, 45 to 50 minutes. Immediately cut into bars while still warm, then cool in the pan or on a rack.

CHOCOLATE SHORTBREAD
Fifteen 3 x 2¹/₂-inch bars
The late, beloved Mildred Kroll used to make this version of shortbread as a snack for her kids when they went off to college.
Preheat the oven to 300°F. Beat in a bowl until fluffy:
   1 cup (2 sticks) unsalted butter, softened
   ¹/₂ cup superfine sugar
   ¹/₄ teaspoon salt
Stir in until blended:

3 ounces semisweet or bittersweet chocolate, melted and cooled slightly

Gently stir in:

2 cups all-purpose flour

Press the dough evenly into the bottom of an ungreased 13 x 9-inch baking pan. Bake until the top is firm when lightly pressed and a toothpick inserted in the center comes out clean, about 40 minutes. Remove the pan to a rack and let cool until barely warm. Cut into bars and transfer to a rack to cool.

ABOUT ICEBOX COOKIES

In the 1950s, Mom renamed these cookies "refrigerator cookies" but most of us still think of them as "icebox cookies," just as my grandmother called them in the first JOY, in 1931.

An advantage of these doughs is that ➤ they can all be baked as drop cookies, 766, without chilling, if you want to make up a batch immediately. After mixing the dough, form it into a 2-inch-diameter roll on a piece of parchment or wax paper, in which you wrap it securely. Chill the roll 4 to 12 hours, after which time it can be very thinly sliced with a sharp knife. You may hasten the chilling by placing the roll in the freezer.

Whole nuts may be combined with the dough or used to garnish the cookies, or the entire roll of dough may be rolled in chopped nuts so as to make a border when the cookies are cut. Two sheets of differently colored dough may be rolled together, as shown below. When sliced, these become pinwheel cookies.

Bake the refrigerated cookies on a greased or lined cookie sheet in a 375°F oven for 8 to 10 minutes unless otherwise directed in the recipes.

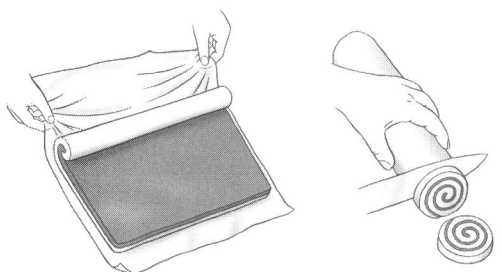

Making Pinwheel Icebox Cookies

VANILLA ICEBOX COOKIES

About forty-two 2 1/2-inch cookies

This dough also makes a good filled cookie, or rich drop cookie, see About Drop Cookies, 766, or About Filled Cookies, 777.

Whisk together:

1 1/2 cups all-purpose flour
1 1/2 teaspoons baking powder
1/4 teaspoon salt

Beat in a large bowl until fluffy:

10 tablespoons (1 1/4 sticks) unsalted butter, softened
2/3 cup sugar

Add and beat until combined:

1 large egg
2 teaspoons vanilla
(1/4 teaspoon finely grated lemon zest)

Stir in the flour mixture until blended. Shape the dough into an even 11-inch-long log. Read About Icebox Cookies, above. Refrigerate or freeze until firm.

Preheat the oven to 375°F. Grease or line 2 cookie sheets. Cut the log into 3/16-inch-thick slices and arrange about 2 inches apart on the cookie sheets. Bake, 1 sheet at a time, until the cookies are lightly browned, 8 to 10 minutes. The longer the baking time, the crisper the cookies. Let stand briefly, then remove to a rack to cool.

BUTTERSCOTCH ICEBOX COOKIES

Prepare **Vanilla Icebox Cookies, above,** omitting the lemon zest and substituting for the white sugar **1 cup packed dark brown sugar.** Add along with the flour mixture **1 cup chopped nuts.**

CHOCOLATE CHIP ICEBOX COOKIES

40 to 48 cookies

Prepare **Vanilla Icebox Cookies, above,** omitting the lemon zest and substituting for 1/3 cup of the sugar **1/3 cup packed light brown sugar.** Add **1 cup mini chocolate chips** along with the flour mixture.

CHOCOLATE ICEBOX COOKIES

Prepare **Vanilla Icebox Cookies, above,** omitting the lemon zest. Add **4 ounces bittersweet or semisweet chocolate, melted,** and **(1 tablespoon brandy or rum)** with the sugar.

PINWHEEL ICEBOX COOKIES

Prepare **Vanilla Icebox Cookies, above,** omitting the lemon zest. Divide the dough in half. Knead into half the dough **2 ounces bittersweet or semisweet chocolate, melted.** If the dough is soft, chill until firm. Roll the white and brown dough separately into equal sized 1/8-inch-thick rectangles, left. Place the dark dough on the light dough and roll up like a jelly roll.

COFFEE ICEBOX COOKIES

Prepare **Vanilla Icebox Cookies, above,** omitting the lemon zest. Substitute for the sugar **3/4 cup firmly packed brown sugar.** Mix in a small bowl, and add with the sugar **1 tablespoon coffee liqueur** and **1 tablespoon instant espresso or finely ground coffee.**

CREAM CHEESE ICEBOX COOKIES

About forty-two 2 1/4-inch cookies

Whisk together:

2 cups all-purpose flour
1/2 teaspoon baking powder

$^1/_8$ teaspoon baking soda

$^1/_2$ teaspoon salt

Beat in a large bowl until fluffy:

11 tablespoons unsalted butter, softened

3 ounces cream cheese, softened

1 cup sugar

Beat in:

1 large egg

1 teaspoon vanilla

($^1/_4$ teaspoon finely grated lemon zest)

Stir in the flour mixture until blended. Refrigerate until slightly firm, about 1 hour. Shape the dough into a 12-inch log. Read About Icebox Cookies, 776. Refrigerate or freeze until very firm. Preheat the oven to 375°F. Grease or line 2 cookie sheets. Cut the log into $^3/_{16}$-inch-thick slices and arrange about 2 inches apart on the cookie sheets. Before baking, sprinkle the tops with:

(Decorative sugar, cinnamon sugar, or nonpareils)

Bake, 1 sheet at time, until the cookies are browned at the edges, 10 to 12 minutes. Let stand briefly. Then remove to a rack to cool.

MOLASSES CRISPS COCKAIGNE

About forty-eight 3-inch cookies

Bring to a boil in a medium saucepan:

$^1/_4$ cup molasses

Remove from the heat, add, and beat until blended:

2 tablespoons sugar

3 tablespoons unsalted butter

1$^1/_2$ teaspoons milk

1$^1/_4$ cups all-purpose flour

$^1/_4$ teaspoon baking powder

$^1/_4$ teaspoon salt

1 teaspoon ground cinnamon

$^1/_4$ teaspoon grated or ground nutmeg

$^1/_4$ teaspoon ground cloves

Shape into a 3$^1/_2$-inch-long log. Read About Icebox Cookies, 776. Refrigerate or freeze until very firm. Preheat the oven to 325°F. Grease or line 2 cookie sheets. Cut the log into $^1/_{16}$-inch-thick slices and arrange 1 inch apart on the cookie sheets. Using lightly floured fingertips, pat the cookies as necessary until paper thin. Press into the center of each cookie:

A pecan half or blanched almond

Bake, 1 sheet at a time, 10 to 12 minutes. Let stand briefly, then remove to a rack to cool.

ABOUT FILLED COOKIES

Fillings can be anything from jam tucked in the indentations of thumbprint cookie to thin chocolate mints sandwiched between golden wafers. Since there is so much variety in the shaping, handling, and baking of filled cookies, not many general rules apply. Simply follow the directions in each recipe and study the illustrations, below, for inspiration.

FILLED COOKIES

About forty 2- to 3-inch cookies

Prepare:

Dough for Rich Roll Cookies, 772, Vanilla Icebox Cookies, 776, or Roll Cookies, 772

Form the dough into 1-inch balls and make an imprint with your thumb to hold a filling as shown on the left, below. Or roll the dough thin and cut into rounds. For a turnover, use a single round of dough and less than a tablespoon of filling; fold over and seal the edges firmly by pressing them with a floured fork. A closed tart takes 2 rounds of dough. Place a tablespoon of filling on one and cover with the other, then seal. For a see-through tart, cut out the top with a doughnut cutter, then seal the outer edges in the same way. Here are 4 basic fillings.

I. RAISIN, FIG, OR DATE FILLING

Combine in a small heavy saucepan and bring to a boil:

1 cup chopped raisins or dried figs or dates

6 tablespoons sugar

5 tablespoons water

$^1/_2$ teaspoon grated lemon zest

2 teaspoons fresh lemon juice

2 teaspoons unsalted butter

$^1/_8$ teaspoon salt

Boil, stirring, until thickened. Cool before using.

II. APRICOT-ORANGE FILLING

Combine in a small heavy saucepan and bring to a boil:

1 cup dried apricots, chopped

$^1/_3$ cup sugar

2 tablespoons finely grated orange zest

$^1/_4$ cup orange juice

($^1/_2$ cup chopped raisins)

Boil, stirring, until thickened. Cool before using.

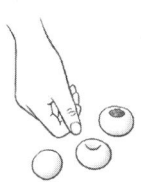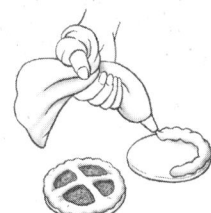

Filled cookies

III. COCONUT FILLING
Combine:
> **1 large egg, slightly beaten**
> **$^1/_2$ cup packed brown sugar**
> **1 tablespoon all-purpose flour**
> **1$^1/_2$ cups flaked or chopped shredded sweetened coconut**

IV. USE DRAINED MINCEMEAT, 902.

RUGELACH
About 30 rolled rugelach or 16 large or 32 small crescents
Use jam or preserves—not jelly. The dough can be refrigerated for up to 1 week or packed airtight and frozen for up to 1 month.

Beat in a large bowl until blended:
> **1 cup (2 sticks) unsalted butter, softened**
> **6 ounces cream cheese, softened**

Add and beat until blended:
> **2$^1/_4$ cups all-purpose flour**

Divide the dough into thirds. Flatten into 6 x 4-inch rectangles if making rolled rugelach, or into 6-inch disks if making crescents. Wrap in plastic and refrigerate for at least 1 hour.

Preheat the oven to 350°F. Grease or line a large baking sheet with parchment paper. Whisk together:
> **$^1/_3$ cup sugar**
> **Pinch of salt**
> **1 teaspoon ground cinnamon**

Work with 1 portion of dough at a time, leaving the remainder refrigerated. Generously flour the work surface and the top of the dough.

For rolled rugelach: Roll each portion into a 16 x 10-inch rectangle about $^1/_8$ inch thick. Brush the excess flour from the top and bottom of the dough and work surface, and turn the long edge of the rectangle so it faces you. Leaving a $^1/_4$-inch border, spread each rectangle with:
> **$^1/_4$ cup raspberry jam or apricot preserves ($^3/_4$ cup total)**

Place in a line along the edge of the jam on the side nearest you:
> **$^1/_4$ cup raisins or chocolate chips ($^3/_4$ cup total)**

Sprinkle the rest of the jam with 2 teaspoons of the cinnamon sugar and:
> **2$^1/_2$ tablespoons ground walnuts ($^1/_2$ cup total)**

Roll the dough, starting at the edge nearest you, gently tucking and tightening it as you go. Turn the roll seam side down. Cut into 1$^1/_2$-inch-thick slices, and arrange about 1 inch apart on the prepared cookie sheet.

For crescent rugelach: Roll each portion into a circle about 14 inches in diameter and $^1/_8$ inch thick. Spread the jam in a thin layer, leaving a $^1/_4$-inch border; then sprinkle entire surface with raisins, cinnamon sugar, and ground nuts. Cut the circle into wedges like a pizza, creating 8 (for large cookies) or 16 (for small cookies) triangles, as shown above. Roll each one up from the wide end to the point, tucking the point under. Place seam side down on the pre-

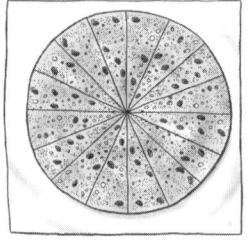
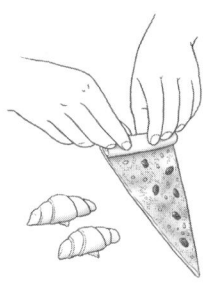

Making crescent rugelach

pared cookie sheet. Sprinkle each cookie with $^1/_8$ teaspoon of the remaining cinnamon sugar. Bake until the bottoms are lightly browned, about 25 minutes. Let stand briefly, then remove to a rack to cool.

INDIVIDUAL NUT TARTS
10 to 12 tarts
Prepare and chill 12 hours:
> **Dough for Vanilla Icebox Cookies, 776**

Preheat the oven to 350°F. Lightly grease the bottoms of 12 muffin cups. Pat or roll the dough thin and cut circles with a cookie cutter to line shallow muffin pans. Beat in a large bowl:
> **3 large egg yolks**
> **1 cup sugar**
> **$^1/_4$ teaspoon salt**

Stir in:
> **1 cup blanched almonds or other nuts, ground**
> **1$^1/_2$ tablespoons fresh lemon juice**

Beat until stiff but not dry, 978:
> **3 large egg whites**

If desired, place in the bottom of each tart shell:
> **(1 teaspoon Apricot Glaze, 800, $^1/_4$ cup total)**

Fill the tart shells with the nut and egg mixture. Bake about 20 minutes. Cool in pans on racks.

JELLY TOTS
About forty-two 1$^1/_2$-inch cookies
You may call these **thimble cookies, deep-well cookies,** or **pits of love**—the last borrowed, of course, from the French—but a rose by any other name. . . .
Prepare:
> **Dough for Roll Cookies, 772**

Roll dough into a ball. Wrap and chill it briefly for easier handling. Preheat the oven to 375°F. Grease or line 2 cookie sheets. Form the dough into 1-inch balls. Roll them in:
> **Sugar**

Or, for a fancier cookie, roll in:
> **1 egg white, slightly beaten**

and then in:
> **1 cup finely chopped nuts**

Place the cookies about 1 inch apart on greased or lined cookie sheets. Bake, 1 sheet at a time, for 5 minutes. Depress the center of each cookie with a thimble or your thumb, 777. Continue baking until lightly brown, about 8 minutes. Let stand briefly. When cool, fill the center of each cookie with:

> **Strawberry preserves, jelly or jam, a candied cherry, a pecan half, or a dab of icing, 788**

MACAROON JAM TARTS

About fourteen 2-inch cookies
The star of stars.
Beat in a medium bowl until creamy:

> **$1/2$ cup (1 stick) unsalted butter, softened**
> **2 tablespoons sugar**

Beat in:

> **1 large egg yolk**
> **$1^1/2$ teaspoons fresh lemon juice**
> **$1/2$ teaspoon grated lemon zest**

Gradually stir in until blended:

> **$1^1/2$ cups all-purpose flour**
> **Pinch of salt**

alternately with:

> **2 tablespoons cold water**

Shape the dough into a disk, wrap in plastic, and refrigerate for 12 hours.
Preheat the oven to 325°F. Grease or line 2 cookie sheets. Roll out the dough $1/8$ inch thick. Using a round cookie cutter, cut into 3-inch rounds, and place on the cookie sheets about 1 inch apart. Whip in a medium bowl until foamy:

> **3 large egg whites**

Gradually beat in and beat until stiff but not dry, 978:

> **$1^1/3$ cups confectioners' sugar**
> **1 teaspoon vanilla**

Fold in:

> **8 ounces blanched almonds, ground**

Place the mixture around the edges of each cookie, making a $3/4$-inch border, and, if you like, add two crossed lines on top, 777. Use a pastry bag, a spatula, or a spoon. Bake 20 minutes or until done. When cool, fill centers with:

> **A thick jam**

DREI AUGEN

About thirty-six 1 $1/2$-inch sandwich cookies
Drei Augen means "three eyes" in German—the "eyes" are the small holes in the top cookies revealing the jelly within.
Whisk together thoroughly:

> **$2^1/2$ cups all-purpose flour**
> **$1/2$ cup unblanched whole almonds, finely ground**
> **Pinch of salt**
> **1 teaspoon ground cinnamon**

Beat in a large bowl until blended:

> **$1^1/4$ cups ($2^1/2$ sticks) unsalted butter, softened**
> **$2/3$ cup sugar**

Stir in the flour mixture until blended. Divide the dough into thirds. Place each portion between 2 large sheets of wax or parchment paper and roll to $1/8$ inch thick, lifting the paper and lightly flouring the dough as needed. Leaving the paper in place, stack the rolled dough on a baking sheet and refrigerate for at least 1 hour, or until firm.
Preheat the oven to 350°F. Grease or line 2 cookie sheets. Work with 1 portion of dough at a time (leave the remainder refrigerated): Gently peel away the top sheet of paper, and use a $1^1/2$-inch cutter to cut out rounds. Then use the small end of a $3/8$-inch plain pastry tip or a straw to cut out 3 small holes in half of the rounds. Arrange on the cookie sheets about $1^1/2$ inches apart, placing the top and bottom cookies on separate sheets. Bake until the cookies are pale golden, 10 to 15 minutes. Let stand briefly, then remove to a rack to cool.
Boil for 2 minutes:

> **$3/4$ cup red currant jelly**

Cool to lukewarm.
Sift over the cooled cut-out cookies:

> **1 cup confectioners' sugar**

Turn over the solid cookies so the bottom is up. Spoon $1/4$ teaspoon of the cooled jelly onto each solid cookie, then top with a cut-out cookie. Press lightly so the jelly fills in the holes.

LINZER HEARTS

Prepare **Drei Augen, above,** using a heart-shaped cutter to omit the holes. Substitute **$3/4$ cup seedless raspberry preserves** for the red currant jelly.

ABOUT CURLED COOKIES

Some curled cookies are simply dropped onto the cookie sheet; others require a special iron. In either case, they are very elegant—whether they make a tube or cornucopia or are just partially curled after being shaped over a rolling pin or wooden spoon handle while still warm. ➤ Filled just before serving, they make a complete dessert. Use flavored whipped cream fillings, 754, Chocolate Ganache, 759, or sweetened cream cheese. Serve them as teacakes with a contrasting buttercream filling, 792. For a festive look, dip the end of the rolled cookies in:

> **Ground pistachios, chocolate sprinkles, or melted dark or white chocolate**

SCANDINAVIAN KRUMKAKES

To make these fabulously thin wafers, you will need the inexpensive krumkake iron, which fits over a gas or electric burner and is always used over moderate heat. Electric krumkake irons are also available. The iron should be lightly rubbed with unsalted butter before beginning each batch, but after that initial greasing, nothing more is required. The batter needs a preliminary testing, as it is quite variable, depending on the flour, so do not add all the flour called for in the recipe to start. Test the batter for consistency by baking 1 teaspoonful first: The iron is geared to use 1 tablespoon of batter for each wafer, and it should spread easily over the whole surface but not run over the sides when the top is pressed down. If the batter is too thin,

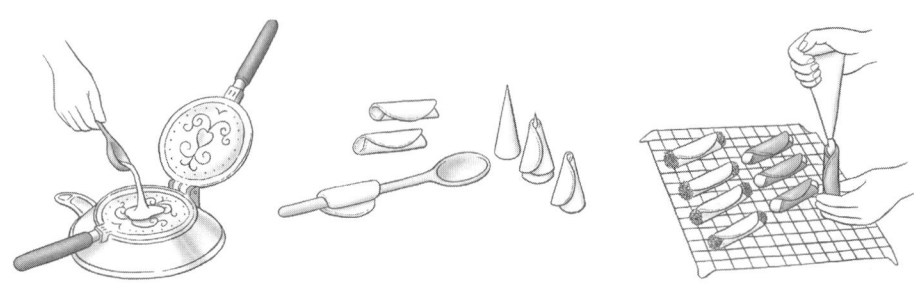

Making krumkakes

add more flour. Should any batter drip over, lift the iron off its frame and cut off the excess batter along the edge with a knife. Cook each wafer about 2 minutes on each side, or until barely colored. As soon as you remove it from the iron, roll it up on a wooden spoon handle or cone form, as illustrated. When cool, fill the cookies. Or you may prefer to leave these cookies flat to use as sandwich cookies; see Frankfurter Oblaten, below. For a toasted sesame seed effect, a JOY fan suggests sprinkling ¼ teaspoon sesame seeds over the batter each time before closing the iron. For filling suggestions, see About Curled Cookies, 779.

I. BUTTER KRUMKAKES
About thirty 5-inch wafers

A teenage neighbor recommends an ice cream filling. We like sour cream with a spot of tart jelly, or a flavored whipped cream, 754–755.

Beat in a medium bowl until light:

2 large eggs

Slowly add and beat until pale:

²/₃ cup sugar

Slowly add:

½ cup (1 stick) unsalted butter, melted and cooled
1 teaspoon vanilla

Stir in until well blended:

Up to 1³/₄ cups all-purpose flour

To bake, form, and fill, see above.

II. LEMON KRUMKAKES
About thirty 5-inch wafers

Prepare **Butter Krumkakes, above,** adding ³/₄ **teaspoon grated lemon zest** along with the sugar. To bake, form and, fill, see above.

III. ALMOND KRUMKAKES
About thirty 5-inch wafers

Prepare **Butter Krumkakes, above,** adding **3 tablespoons ground almonds** along with the sugar. Then add ¼ **teaspoon almond extract** along with the vanilla. To bake, form, and fill, see above.

FRANKFURTER OBLATEN

Prepare **Butter, Lemon, or Almond Krumkakes, above,** leaving the cookies flat. Sandwich pairs of cookies, filled with a thin layer of **Flavored Basic Fondant, 866,** or uncooked **Fondant, 867.**

ICE CREAM CONES (GAUFRETTES)
10 large or 20 small cones

If made on a krumkake iron, as shown above left, this dough can be rolled into delicious thin-walled cones or molded over small ramekins for ice cream bowls. If made on a rectangular waffled gaufrette iron, they will become the typical French honeycombed wafer or gaufrette so often served with wine or ices. The Italians know them as *pizzelle,* and you can also use a pizzelle iron.

Preheat the iron as directed. Beat in a medium bowl until stiff but not dry, 978:

2 large egg whites

Gradually fold in:

³/₄ cup confectioners' sugar
¹/₈ teaspoon salt
¹/₄ teaspoon vanilla

Fold in:

¹/₂ cup all-purpose flour

Stir in gently:

¹/₄ cup (¹/₂ stick) unsalted butter, melted and cooled

Put 1 tablespoon batter into the preheated iron. After about 1¹/₂ minutes, turn the iron if necessary and cook the second side until beige in color. Remove and use flat or shape over upside-down ramekins, or form a cone, above. When cool, fill and serve. Or serve plain in the French fashion, as described above.

FORTUNE COOKIES
About 24 cookies

These cookies and Almond Krumkakes, above, may be made into a Western version of fortune cookies for a party. Print the fortunes on thin strips of papers.

Preheat the oven to 350°F. Line 2 cookie sheets with silicone liners or parchment paper. Combine in a medium bowl, stirring:

3 large egg whites
²/₃ cup sugar
¹/₈ teaspoon salt

Stir in one at a time, beating until blended after each addition:

¹/₂ cup (1 stick) unsalted butter, melted and cooled slightly
¹/₂ cup all-purpose flour

(¹/₃ cup finely ground blanched almonds)
**¹/₄ teaspoon vanilla or 1¹/₂ teaspoons fresh
    lemon juice**

Drop by tablespoonfuls about 4 inches apart onto the cookie sheets. Bake until the edges are golden brown, about 10 minutes. Turn over one cookie at a time, place a fortune in the center, letting part of the paper stick out, and fold the cookie in half. Pinch closed and lift the cookie and bring the corners together to make a C shape. Set on a rack to cool.

BRANDY SNAPS
About twenty 3 ¹/₂-inch cookies

Preheat the oven to 300°F. Combine in a medium heavy saucepan, stirring over low heat until the butter is melted and the mixture is smooth:

**¹/₂ cup (1 stick) unsalted butter
¹/₂ cup sugar or ¹/₄ cup sugar plus ¹/₄ cup packed
    maple sugar
¹/₃ cup molasses
Pinch of salt
¹/₂ teaspoon ground cinnamon
¹/₄ teaspoon ground ginger
¹/₂ teaspoon grated lemon or orange zest**

Remove from the heat and stir in:

**1 cup all-purpose flour
2 teaspoons brandy**

Cool until firm enough to shape. Roll into ³/₄-inch balls and arrange about 2 inches apart on ungreased or parchment-lined cookie sheets (do not use silicone liners). Bake, 1 sheet at a time, until browned on the edges, 12 to 15 minutes. Remove the sheet to a rack and let stand for 2 or 3 minutes, then roll up each cookie on the handle of a wooden spoon. If some of the wafers cool too much to shape, return the sheet to the oven briefly to warm and soften them.

TUILES (FRENCH ALMOND WAFERS)
About thirty 3-inch wafers

Almost paper-thin, with a subtle almond flavor, tuiles are curled by being draped, while still warm and pliable, over a rolling pin or glass bottles until cool and firm. The most challenging step is removing them from the cookie sheet. The trick is to work quickly using a wide spatula with a very thin blade.

Preheat the oven to 350°F. Generously grease or line 2 cookie sheets or line with parchment paper or silicone liners. Have ready several rolling pins or bottles about the same size to shape the wafers.

Coarsely chop and set aside:

¹/₂ to ²/₃ cup sliced almonds blanched or unblanched

Whisk together in a medium bowl until frothy:

**2 large egg whites
¹/₈ teaspoon salt
¹/₃ cup plus 1 tablespoon sugar
¹/₂ teaspoon vanilla**

(¹/₄ teaspoon almond extract)

Gradually whisk in:

¹/₂ cup cake flour, sifted

Whisk in until well blended and smooth:

**5 tablespoons unsalted butter, melted and
    cooled slightly**

Drop by heaping measuring tablespoonfuls about 3 inches apart onto the cookie sheets. Using a small metal spatula, work in a circular motion, spreading each portion into a 3-inch round. Sprinkle with the nuts.

Bake until golden brown around the edges, 6 to 9 minutes. Remove the sheet to a rack and let stand for a few seconds. Working quickly, lay the cookies, bottom side down, over the rolling pins or bottles, and let cool completely. If some of the wafers cool too quickly to shape them, return the sheet to the oven briefly to warm and soften them.

GINGERBREAD HOUSE
*One gingerbread house, about 5 ¹/₂ inches wide by 7 inches
high on a 9-inch square base, plus 10 to 15 cookies*

Connecticut cookbook author and baking teacher Susan G. Purdy has been using this recipe to make festive gingerbread houses with adult-child teams for more than thirty years, and at home, with her daughter, Cassandra (now a chef). Make this a family holiday tradition in your home too. The gingerbread can be baked up to a week in advance of assembling.

In a medium (2-quart) saucepan, melt:

1 cup (2 sticks) butter or margarine

Add and stir over low heat until the sugar is dissolved and the mixture no longer feels gritty:

**1 cup sugar
1 cup unsulphured molasses**

Remove from the heat and set aside to cool to lukewarm. In a large bowl, whisk together:

**4¹/₂ cups all-purpose flour
1 teaspoon baking soda
1 teaspoon salt
1 tablespoon ground ginger
1 teaspoon ground cinnamon
1 teaspoon grated or ground nutmeg**

Make a well in the center of the dry ingredients, pour in the lukewarm butter mixture, and beat to blend everything together. Work in:

¹/₂ cup all-purpose flour

beating until the dough forms a ball and pulls away from the sides of the bowl:

Remove the dough from the bowl and knead 3 or 4 times on the counter, until smooth and pliable. Wrap well and refrigerate until dough is thoroughly cool. (The dough can be prepared several days in advance.)

After refrigerating, if the dough feels too soft to roll out, work in a tiny bit more flour.

To make the pattern pieces: Copy the pattern pieces onto stiff cardboard and cut them out. You should have 7 pieces: 2 sides, 1 front and 1 back, 2 roof panels, and 1 base. Rub flour over both sides of the pattern pieces to prevent the dough from sticking to them.

To cut out and bake the gingerbread house: Position the racks to divide the oven into thirds. Preheat the oven to 350°F.

With a lightly floured rolling pin, roll out about one-third of the dough directly on an ungreased cookie sheet, preferably with only 1 raised edge, to about ¼ inch thick. Lightly dust the dough with flour. Position as many pattern pieces as will fit comfortably on top of the rolled dough, leaving about ¾ inch between them to allow for spreading during baking. Cut around the patterns with a sharp paring knife. Remove the pattern pieces. Peel away the dough between the cut pieces and gather the scraps together to reroll. Repeat with a second and third cookie sheet if needed, using the remaining dough and cutting out all the pieces. Cut around, but do not lift out, the windows and the front door (if they are removed now, the shapes will warp). Roll out the scraps and use cookie cutters or a paring knife to cut out gingerbread people, fence posts, animals, and other designs.

Bake the gingerbread pieces 12 to 15 minutes, or until the color darkens slightly and the pieces feel nearly stiff; they will firm completely as they cool. (Note: If the pieces are not crisp when completely cool, return them to the oven and bake a few minutes longer).

As soon as they come from the oven, set the cookie sheets on a heatproof surface and immediately, while the dough is still hot, place the pattern pieces on the corresponding pieces of hot gingerbread. One at a time, place a pot holder over each shape, to protect your hands, and cut around each pattern with a paring knife (trimming all the house edges will make them fit together neatly). Lift off and save the scraps for decorations. Cut out and remove the door and windows. While the dough is still warm, you can cut each window in half to make shutters. Once the shapes are rigid but still slightly warm, use a broad spatula to transfer them to wire racks to cool completely. Store them flat on a tray or in a sturdy box in a cool, dry place until ready to assemble.

To assemble the house: Prepare:

    A double or triple recipe of Royal Icing, 789

The house will require 2 to 6 cups icing, depending on the style of the decorations. Leave about half the icing in the bowl for assembling the house, and use the rest for decorations. Scoop the remaining icing into cups or small bowls, mixing in:

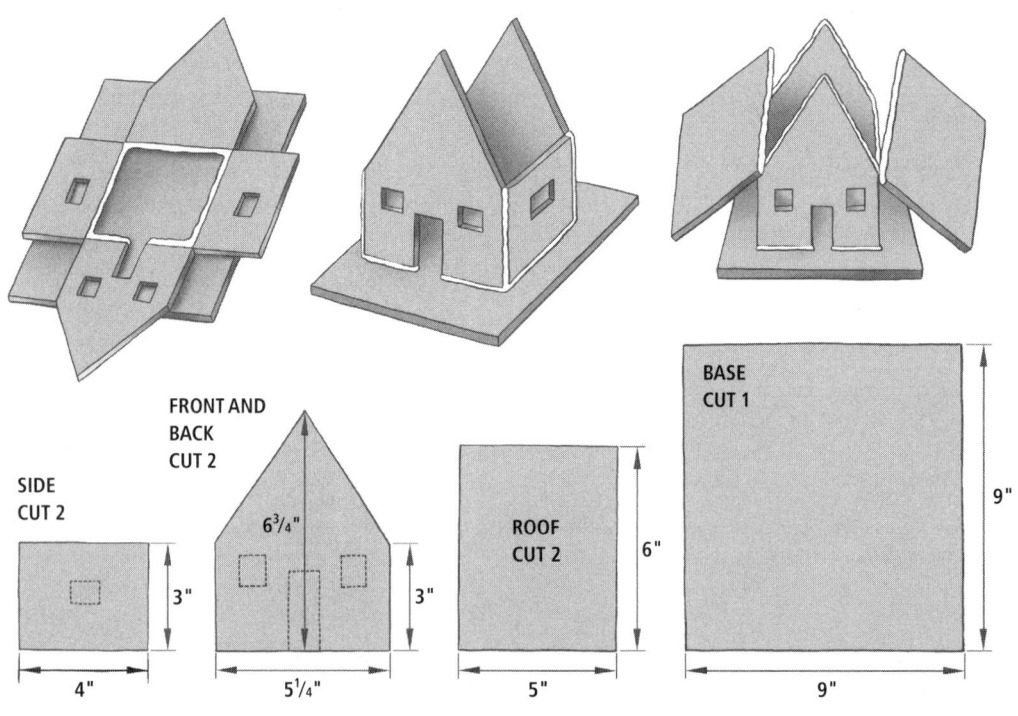

FRONT AND BACK
CUT 2

SIDE
CUT 2

ROOF
CUT 2

BASE
CUT 1

6¾"

3"   3"   6"   9"

4"   5¼"   5"   9"

CUT WINDOWS AND DOOR IN FRONT ONLY

Blueprints for a gingerbread house

Drops of vegetable food coloring

Immediately cover the bowls of icing with plastic wrap so they don't dry out; keep tightly covered when you are not using the icing.

Set the gingerbread base right side up on a tray. (The right side of each piece is the side facing up when baked.) Center the front, back, and side pieces, right side down, on top of the base, with the bottom corners touching. The dark lines in the center mark the "foundation" of the house.

Place some of the white icing in a pastry bag fitted with a plain ¼- to ½-inch tip or a plastic bag with a ¼-inch hole cut in one corner, and pipe out a thick ½-inch-deep line of icing around the foundation lines. One at a time, lift the side pieces into place and, with the pastry bag or your fingertip, pipe or spread a generous line of icing along both side edges of each piece. Repeat with the front and back pieces, icing their side edges and standing them up in the foundation icing next to the sides. Gently press all the iced edges of the house together. If the icing is thick enough, the house should now stand up unaided. If it is wobbly, support it on all 4 sides with jars or cans until the icing dries, 1 hour to overnight, depending on the humidity. Do not attempt to add the roof until the icing is dry and the structure feels solid. Note: Don't worry if the icing shows, especially along the seam joints, as it will be covered with "icicles" or other decorations.

To attach the roof: Spread icing generously along the top edges of each house piece and along one long edge of each roof panel. Press the roof panels in place, touching each other at the peak. Use your fingertip to smooth all the joints where the pieces meet; add extra icing if necessary for stability. If the roof panels droop, support them with jars or cans until the icing sets. Don't decorate the roof until the icing is set, or the weight of the decorations may cause it to collapse.

To decorate the house: Use icing to glue on the window shutters and position the front door ajar. Using icing as glue, decorate the house with:

> **Jelly beans, gumdrops, candy-coated chocolate pieces, nonpareils, jellied wintergreen leaves, hard round peppermint candies, candy canes, silver dragées, cinnamon red hots, colored sugar wafers, ring-shaped hard candies, caramels, "stone" candies, mini shredded wheat cereal, toasted oat cereal, red shoestring licorice, marshmallows, mini pretzels and pretzel rods, colored sugars, sunflower and pumpkin seeds, dried fruits, raisins, and/or nuts**

Make a chimney from flat candies glued together with icing and stacked up on the roof ridge line. To prevent sticking, oil the scissors before cutting soft candies. After the shutters, door, and chimney are in place, add a little water to some of the white icing, making it runny enough to drip. Use the pastry bag to pipe drippy icicles along the edges of the roof. For snow, sift over the top of the house and the base a light dusting of:

> **Confectioners' sugar**

ICINGS, TOPPINGS, AND GLAZES

Icings, toppings, and glazes are the party clothes that transform simple cakes into celebrations: birthday cakes, bake sale treats, wedding extravaganzas, and memorable party desserts. These mixtures add moisture, creaminess, flavor, visual appeal, and, of course, the opportunity to personalize your efforts. The creative possibilities are nearly endless, as well as great fun. While we offer guidelines, we encourage you to experiment with combinations that strike your fancy.

In general, richer, denser frostings and glazes are used sparingly and spread thinner. Fluffy mixtures, such as whipped cream, are used more lavishly. Pay attention to flavor, sweetness, creaminess, and density when creating cake and frosting combinations. Complement or contrast the flavor, texture, and richness of a cake. Devil's Food Cake Cockaigne glazed with Bittersweet Chocolate Glaze amply demonstrates the sublime results to be had by layering and reinforcing the same flavor. A tangy lemon cake with chocolate icing is equally impressive for its sharp contrast of flavors.

Balance is the name of the game. Because it is so light in texture, whipped cream is an extraordinary partner for a variety of cakes, from the richest chocolate torte to the lightest sponge cake. Cakes made with as many as six thin layers of light génoise or meringue are typically paired with a very rich buttercream, spread ultrathin. Nut tortes and flourless chocolate cakes are so rich that frosting is often unnecessary, but a thin cloak of rich chocolate glaze or a dollop of whipped cream adds a touch of glamour.

Classic layer cakes feature thicker layers of cake covered generously with frosting. These frostings, however, are not especially rich. Fluffy frostings, such as Boiled White Icing, 790, and Seven-Minute White Icing, 790, have a marshmallowy texture and are very sweet. Quick confectioners' sugar icings taste buttery and are easy to prepare. Gossamer-thin confectioners' sugar glazes add sweetness and flavor to angel cakes, chiffon cakes, and sponge cakes without overwhelming them. Recipes in the cookie chapter, 760, suggest special icings. Use your imagination to pair classic flavors such as raspberry and chocolate or strawberry and vanilla when making your own match of icing to cookie.

ABOUT ICING A CAKE

When icing a cake, if you are working directly on the serving platter, you can keep the platter clean by tucking narrow overlapping strips of wax paper or foil just under the cake, extending out to the edges of the platter; remove them as the icing sets. If you are using a turntable or another work surface, you can place several strips of sturdy paper or foil on it projecting beyond the cake on all sides. After the cake has been iced, lift it by the paper strips onto the serving platter; pull out the strips and discard. When filling and icing a cake, the layers should be turned upside down for a flatter but rougher surface. If the cake is uneven, you may want to trim it slightly.

Use about a quarter to a third of the total icing as filling between the layers. Then, depending on the consistency of your icing, either pour it over the top and smooth with a spatula, spreading evenly on the sides, or slather the icing around the sides and then apply to the top. The back of a spoon can be used to make peaks and valleys.

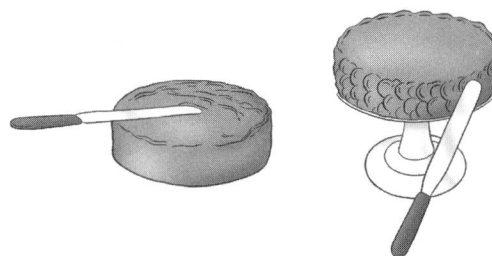

The spatula enables you to apply a smooth
or textured frosting

Refrigeration is a point to consider when pairing cakes with frostings. Sponge cakes, chiffon cakes, and angel cakes do not harden in the refrigerator, so they are compatible with frostings that require refrigeration, such as whipped cream or buttercreams. Any cake frosted with buttercream should be removed from the refrigerator an hour or more in advance of serving to restore its creamy glory. Butter cakes and rich chocolate tortes are diminished by refrigeration; flavor and fragrance are lost, and their velvety-rich and creamy textures harden. Should you pair one of these cakes with an icing that requires refrigeration, try to frost it at the last minute, or remove the chilled cake from the refrigerator well in advance of serving. Quick confectioners' sugar icings do not require refrigeration, which makes them especially compatible with butter cakes.

ICING YIELDS

Yields in these icing and filling recipes are given in cups, so you can mix or match your choice according to the size of your cake. For comparative pan sizes and areas, see 701. For fluffy frostings, choose the greater amounts; for butter icings the lesser.

For information about fillings, see 753.

Top and sides only

For a 1-layer 8- or 9-inch cake: 1 to $1^{1}/_{2}$ cups
For a 2-layer 8- or 9-inch cake: $1^{1}/_{2}$ to $2^{2}/_{3}$ cups
For a 3-layer 8- or 9-inch cake: $2^{1}/_{4}$ to 3 cups
For a 13 x 9-inch sheet: $2^{1}/_{2}$ to 3 cups
For a $9^{1}/_{2}$ x $5^{1}/_{2}$ x 3-inch loaf cake: 1 to $1^{1}/_{2}$ cups
For a 16 x 5 x 4-inch loaf cake: 2 to $2^{1}/_{2}$ cups
For a 9- or 10-inch tube cake: 3 cups
For glazing a 9- or 10-inch cake: 1 cup
For 12 cupcake tops: $1^{1}/_{2}$ cups

Tops, sides, and filling

For a 2-layer 8- or 9-inch cake: 2 to 3 cups
For a 3-layer 8- or 9-inch cake: 3 to 4 cups
For glazing a 9- or 10-inch cake: 1 cup
For filling a 10 x 15-inch roll: 2 cups

EQUIPMENT

Bakers have different tools that they swear by. A **stainless steel spatula with a narrow 8-inch blade** is an excellent all-purpose tool for spreading frostings on cakes. The spatula enables you to spread a frosting smooth or to decorate with swirls or with raised spikes; it also facilitates the spreading of poured chocolate glazes. A **cake comb** or **serrated knife** enables you to texture the sides and/or top of a cake. Perhaps not surprisingly, a perfectly smooth coat of frosting is the hardest texture to master. If you are determined to learn this technique, it is useful to acquire a **decorating turntable** or a **lazy Susan** to rotate the cake, holding the spatula steady as you smooth the frosting.

Any frosting or icing that is smooth and holds a shape can be piped with a **pastry bag** fitted with a **decorative pastry tip.** Practice piping on the back of a cake pan.

Confectioners' sugar icings and buttercreams should be stirred briskly with a **rubber spatula** before use and then from time to time to eliminate air bubbles and keep the icing smooth.

ADJUSTING THE CONSISTENCY OF FROSTINGS

The consistency of the frosting is critical to achieving the effect you want. Frosting that is too thick or stiff will tear the cake and pull up crumbs. Frosting that is too thin will collapse into a puddle when piped and may even slide off the cake. Modify the consistency of the frosting according to need. Frostings rich in butter or chocolate can be softened or stiffened by placing the bowl in a pan of either warm or ice water and stirring to the desired consistency. Treat confectioners' sugar icings the same way, or beat in extra liquid a few drops at a time to soften, powdered sugar to stiffen.

Whipped cream frosting works a little differently; do not try to soften or stiffen it once it is made, and do not warm the spatula as you work, or you will break down the cream. When you are frosting with whipped cream (or whipped ganache), underwhip the cream slightly. Spreading and smoothing the cream as you frost the cake will stiffen it adequately. If the cream is stiff before you begin, your finished frosting will look and taste overbeaten and grainy. See Decorative Treatments for Cake Icing, below.

DEALING WITH CRUMBS IN THE FROSTING

Brush loose crumbs from the cake layers as necessary while you work. If a stiff frosting is tearing the cake and causing crumbs, adjust the consistency as directed above. Keep crumbs from "contaminating" the frosting in the bowl by scraping the spatula against another container each time before dipping it back into the frosting. Or divide the frosting between two bowls and work out of one for the crumb coat (see below), saving the other for the final frosting.

"CRUMB-COATING" AND FINISHING THE CAKE

To keep crumbs from marring the finished frosting or glaze, seal the cake by first spreading a very thin coating of frosting, the crumb coat, all over to smooth the surface and secure any crumbs. It is fine to use frosting "contaminated" with crumbs for the crumb coat. Some cakes are sealed with hot strained jam or preserves; heat 2 cups jam or preserves, strain through a sieve, and use immediately. You can refrigerate the cake for a few minutes to set the crumb coat before the final frosting. For chocolate butter glazes and ganaches, cool the glaze to the consistency of frosting for the crumb coat, then gently warm the remaining glaze to the correct temperature and fluidity for glazing.

Use a clean, crumb-free spatula for the final frosting, and spread the cake with a final attractive coat of frosting, smooth or in swirls as desired. You can texture the sides as directed on 784, or coat with chopped nuts, or use the back of a spoon to make peaks and valleys in the frosting—see page 786 for decorating techniques.

DECORATIVE TREATMENTS FOR CAKE ICING

TO TEXTURE THE TOP AND SIDES OF A FROSTED CAKE

While the frosting is still soft, dip a cake comb or serrated knife in hot water and wipe it dry. Hold it gently against the side of the cake at a 45-degree angle and, if you are using a turntable or lazy Susan, rotate it slowly while holding the comb or knife steady; otherwise, gently sweep it around the sides of the cake.

TO STENCIL THE TOP OF A CAKE

This is a good, quick decorative effect on any cake—plain or frosted. Refrigerate the cake to firm the frosting if used. Use a paper doily, or make a hand-cut stencil: Fold a round of wax or parchment paper slightly larger than the surface of the cake into eights or sixteenths and cut out small shapes along the folds (as for snowflakes). The shapes need not be specific or symmetrical. The advantage of a hand-cut stencil is that the cutouts will be larger and more distinct than those of a lace doily and thus the design will show up better. No special design talent is necessary, and you can even enlist children to do the cutting. Flatten the stencil under a phone book if necessary before using. Place the doily or stencil on top of the cake and use a fine-mesh sieve to sift a thin, even coating of confectioners' sugar or cocoa over it and to fill the interstices with the cocoa sugar. Use both hands to lift it carefully off the cake, in a straight upward motion without disturbing the pattern. Stencil cakes shortly before serving: the design will fade as the sugar or cocoa is absorbed by the frosting.

Stenciling the top of a cake

TO USE A PASTRY BAG

For piping borders, rosettes, stars, or other larger motifs with frostings, buttercream, or whipped cream, several types of cloth, plastic, or disposable pastry bags are available. If you choose cloth, be sure to use it with the ragged fabric seam outside. Several metal tips with different shapes are included in pastry bag kits. See illustrations, 787. The most useful have a rose, star, and plain tip.

HOW TO MAKE YOUR OWN DECORATING BAG

Using parchment or heavy bond paper, cut a rectangle about 11 x 15 inches. Fold the paper diagonally in half as shown on the left, 787. Keep the folded edge away from you. Roll the paper from the right side into a cornucopia with a tight point at the center of the long fold, as seen in the upper right, then continue to roll the paper until the cornucopia is complete. Turn it with the seam up toward

you and the point away from you. The seam should lie in direct line with the point of one of the highest peaks of the

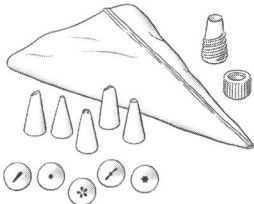

Pastry bag, tips, and coupler

bag, so that by when you fold the peaks outward and away from you, you stabilize the shape of the cornucopia and the seam. This is shown by the two upright bags illustrated. If you could see through the lower one, you would find the hollow cone ready to receive the icing. The upright bag on the right shows the final double fold that tightly closes the top of the filled bag. The peaks have been turned inside to help make the cornucopia leakproof at the top when pressure is applied. Before filling, press the tip of the paper cone flat and cut off the end. If you plan to use a metal tip from your pastry bag kit, be sure the opening is large enough to hold the tip but not so large that it will slip through under pressure. If you plan to use the tip of the paper cone itself rather than a metal tip to make the designs, make a separate paper cone for each "tip": Cut the tip straight across to make a small round opening; clip it with a single notch for a star tip, or with a double notch for a rose tip.

Frostings to be piped should be stiff enough to hold a crisp shape. Stir them with a rubber spatula until smooth before filling the bag. Whipped cream should be slightly underwhipped before piping, as forcing it through the bag will stiffen it further; stiffly whipped cream will come out of a pastry bag looking grainy and overbeaten. For best results, avoid piping whipped cream through a tip smaller than $1/4$ inch.

If using several colors for decoration, divide the icing among several small bowls and tint with paste or liquid food coloring. ➤ Keep the bowls covered with plastic wrap. Never fill a pastry bag more than two-thirds full. For colors that are needed only in small quantities, use smaller bags. Use a small spatula to push the icing well down into the point of the bag. Before you begin, press the bag to equalize the icing and to force any air bubbles toward the tip, so that they will not destroy the smoothness of your decorations.

Practice making and filling bags. Then apply the icing on an inverted cake pan. For practice, the icing can be scraped off repeatedly and reused. Make patterns like script writing doodles until you have achieved some ease. ➤ Experiment with the feel of the bag until you can sustain the pressure evenly for linear effects and use varying

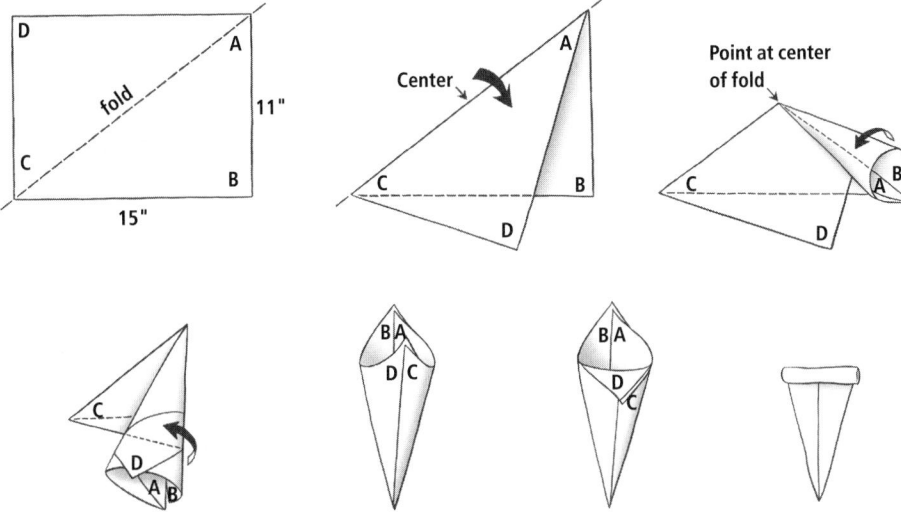

Making your own decorating bag

force for borders, petals, and leaves. Using your dominant hand, you may draw with the bag as freely as you would with a pencil or brush.

Now you are ready to pipe designs. It is helpful if the cake is on a turntable or lazy Susan. In any case, when working on the sides, try to have the cake just above elbow level. Pressure and movement ➤ are controlled by your writing hand. ➤ Your other hand is used only for steadying. As shown in the sketch below, grasp the bag lightly but firmly in the palm of your hand ➤ with your thumb resting on top, leaving your fingers free to press the bag as you turn your hand and wrist to form designs. Sometimes you will rest the bag in a scissorlike V of your first two fingers; at other times you will merely guide the bag as shown in the second-to-last figure. As you use up the icing, refold the bag at the top, pushing the icing down.

Icing designs are the result of three factors: the angle of the bag and tip with respect to the surface of the cake, the timing and pressure of the squeeze, and the direction and speed of the stroke or movement. The bag and tip are held at either a 45-degree angle to the surface of the cake or a 90-degree angle (meaning the bag is held straight up as you pipe on top of the cake). Start to squeeze the bag a split second before starting to move the tip, and stop squeezing a split second before coming to a stop. If your designs trail off with an extra tail, it is because you are continuing to squeeze as you finish the stroke. The amount of squeezing before you begin to move the tip determines how full and fanned out the shape will be at the start. If you decrease pressure as you finish the stroke, it tapers off.

If you have trouble getting the shape, try altering any of these three variables. Practice is really the only way. There are two inexpensive and sturdy mixtures that can be used

over and over again to practice piping. You can mix instant mashed potatoes with water to the desired consistency. As you practice, adjust the consistency of the potatoes with water as needed. Alternatively, make practice buttercream by beating 4 cups (1 pound) confectioners sugar into 1½ cups vegetable shortening mixed with 2 tablespoons water and 1 tablespoon corn syrup.

As in any work of art, the concept should make you forget technique. Make a sketch first of what you want to do, or have it clearly in mind. The patterns shown on 786 are conventional ones; try them, and then develop your own style. We remember a cake that Alexander Calder did for a family friend—complete with mobile and showing a clarity of line so characteristic of his talent.

It is a great temptation when decorating cakes to overload them. Try out some asymmetrical compositions. Partially bind the top and sides of the cake with garlands, and remember to leave plenty of undecorated space to set them off. At first you may want to make some of the more complicated designs separately on a piece of wax paper and let them dry before applying them to the cake. For those items made separately, let the icing stiffen on the paper, then gently peel off the paper, and use a little reserved icing as adhesive to fix it to the cake.

TO PIPE FILIGREE OR WRITE IN SCRIPT

The best mixtures for fine piping are Royal Icing, 789, and plain melted chocolate (thinned if necessary with drops of flavorless vegetable oil). Use a paper cone made of wax or parchment paper, shown above. Or use a small resealable plastic bag. After filling, fold over and roll up the open end of the paper cone (like a toothpaste tube) or gather up and twist the plastic bag, forcing the frosting toward a bottom corner. Snip the end to make a tiny opening for

Holding the pastry bag to pipe designs

piping. Test the size of the opening by practicing on a plate or waxed paper; snip the opening larger if necessary.

ABOUT ICING SMALL CAKES AND COOKIES

There are a number of ways to ice and garnish small cakes quickly. **I.** Place on a hot cupcake small bits of semisweet or sweet chocolate. Spread as they melt. **II.** Just before removing cookies from the oven, put on each one a mint-flavored chocolate candy wafer and return the cookie sheet to the oven until the wafer melts. **III.** To ice cupcakes or leaf cookies, dip them quickly into any soft icing. Swirl the cakes. **IV.** For cupcakes, sift confectioners' sugar over them through a small fine-mesh sieve. **V.** Or ice as for Petits Fours, 791.

Icing cupcakes

ABOUT DECORATIVE ICINGS

You have a choice of three fine icing for decorating: Decorative Icing, below, Creamy Decorating Icing, below, and Royal Icing, 789. In any case, apply a crumb coat to the cake, 785. Allow it to set in the refrigerator. Finish the cake with a smooth layer of frosting, though Royal Icing should be used only for decoration. ➤ For Decorative Icing and Royal Icing, you may use a spatula dipped in tepid water for a glossy finish. ➤ Allow the base coat to dry.

DECORATIVE ICING (TWICE-COOKED ICING)
About 1 ³/₄ cups

This keeps a long time without hardening if tightly covered with plastic wrap. Please read About Boiled Icings, 789, and

have all your equipment and ingredients ready before you begin. Tartaric acid can be purchased from Internet retailers. Combine in a small saucepan and stir until the sugar is dissolved, then bring to a boil over medium heat without stirring:

1 cup sugar
¹/₂ cup water

Meanwhile, beat at medium-high speed in a large bowl until stiff but not dry:

2 large egg whites
¹/₈ teaspoon salt

Add very slowly, beating constantly:

3 tablespoons sugar

Meanwhile, pour an inch or so of water into a large saucepan and bring to a simmer. When the sugar syrup begins to fall in heavy drops from a spoon, about 230°F, add a small quantity of it to the eggs and sugar, beating constantly. Repeat this process, adding the syrup to the eggs in 4 or 5 parts and beating constantly. If these additions are properly timed, the last of the syrup will have reached the thread stage by the time you use it.

Set the bowl over the saucepan of water; the bowl should be over, not in, the water. When the water in the pan begins to boil, add to the icing:

¹/₈ teaspoon baking powder
¹/₈ teaspoon cream of tartar

Continue to beat the icing until it sticks to the sides and the bottom of the bowl and forms stiff peaks. Remove from the heat. Place as much as is required for the cake decoration—usually about one-third—in a small bowl. Cover it loosely with wax paper. To the remainder, add:

1 teaspoon or more hot water

thinning it to the right consistency for spreading. Beat it well and frost the cake. To decorate, see About Decorative Icings, above.

CREAMY DECORATING ICING
Enough to frost and lightly decorate a 9-inch layer

A highly manageable icing for intricate, precise decorations that keeps well if stored tightly covered.

Sift into a large bowl:

1 pound (4 cups) confectioners' sugar

Add and mix well with an electric mixer:

$^1/_2$ cup vegetable shortening

2 to 4 tablespoons milk or heavy or light cream

1 teaspoon vanilla or $^1/_2$ teaspoon vanilla and
$^1/_2$ teaspoon almond extract

Continue beating until icing is smooth. It will be slightly stiff. Add more liquid for the proper consistency for making decorations.

ROYAL OR QUICK DECORATIVE ICING

About 2 cups

This icing will become very hard. To avoid the naturally grayish tone that develops during preparation, add to portions that you want to keep white a slight amount of blue vegetable coloring. Do not use blue in any icing that you plan to color yellow, orange or any other pale, warm tint.

Sift:

$^1/_8$ teaspoon cream of tartar

$3^1/_2$ cups confectioners' sugar

Beat until stiff, but not dry:

2 large egg whites at room temperature

Gradually add the sifted sugar and:

2 tablespoons lemon juice

until it is of a good consistency to spread. Cover with a damp cloth until ready to use.

To apply as piping or for decorative effects, see About Decorative Icings, 788. Should you want the icing stiffer, add a little more sifted sugar. To make it softer, thin it very, very gradually with lemon juice, more egg white or water.

ROYAL ICING

$^3/_4$ cup

This decorative icing dries hard like plaster and is pure white unless tinted with food coloring. Made with a bit less sugar, it is still spreadable (or you can add a little water); otherwise, it is stiff enough to pipe and makes beautiful filigree, lace, tiny dots, and string work on wedding cakes. The icing is mostly sugar and not especially delicious, though it is used to ice certain traditional wedding (and other) cakes. Our advice is to use it only when decoration is more important than taste and/or in very small quantities. Royal Icing is usually made by beating confectioners' sugar into raw egg whites, above. In this version, the egg whites are heated to 160°F as a safeguard against salmonella bacteria; it is a simple process. We also give a variation made with powdered egg whites that does not require heat.

Avoid making Royal Icing on humid days. Be sure that any container or utensils that comes in contact with the icing is grease-free, and do not store the icing in a plastic container. While working, keep the bowl of icing covered with a damp dish towel and, when not piping, cover the tip of the icing bag as well to prevent drying.

I. ROYAL ICING MADE WITH FRESH EGG WHITES

Stir together in a microwave-safe bowl until thoroughly combined:

1 large egg white

$^1/_3$ cup confectioners' sugar

Microwave on high until the mixture reaches 160°F on a thermometer (it should not exceed 175°F), 30 to 60 seconds. If you need to take more than one temperature reading, wash the thermometer thoroughly or dip it into a mug of boiling water before taking additional readings.

Add and beat on high speed until the icing is cool and holds stiff peaks:

$^2/_3$ cup confectioners' sugar, or as needed

If the icing is not stiff enough, add more sugar.

Color, if desired, with liquid, powdered, or paste food coloring; the color will intensify as the icing stands. The icing can be stored in a covered container for up to 3 days; press a piece of wax or parchment paper directly against the surface to prevent drying. The icing can be rebeaten if necessary. To pipe, use a small pastry bag fitted with a fine tip, or cut off the corner of a sealable plastic bag or the tip of a parchment paper cone.

II. ROYAL ICING MADE WITH POWDERED EGG WHITES

Beat together in a medium bowl until stiff peaks form:

$1^1/_3$ cups confectioners' sugar

1 tablespoon powdered egg whites

2 tablespoons water

Color if desired with liquid, paste powdered food coloring. Use and store as directed above. Tightly covered, this keeps for up to 2 weeks.

ABOUT BOILED ICINGS

Just as in candy making, success with boiled icing depends on favorable weather and recognizing certain stages in preparing sugar syrup; see 855. If the icing is too soft or too hard, take the corrective steps suggested below. ➤ Never ruin a good cake with a doubtful icing.

Boiled white icing is based on Italian meringue—essentially egg whites that are cooked by ➤ gradually beating a hot sugar syrup into them.

When using boiled icing, the cake must be completely cooled before the icing is applied. ➤ Have all utensils absolutely free of grease, and the egg whites ➤ absolutely free of yolk and at room temperature. You must start with stiffly whipped whites stabilized with cream of tartar (see Egg Whites, 978).

Cook the syrup to 238° to 240°F, the soft-ball stage; see 856. Then dip the bottom of the pan in cold water for 1 second to stop the cooking. Hold the pan of very hot, but not bubbling, syrup above the bowl and let it drop in a slow, gradual thin stream onto the whites as you beat them. As the egg whites are cooked by the hot syrup, the beating will increase the volume of the icing. By the time the syrup is used up, you should have a creamy mass almost ready for spreading. At this point, beat in the flavoring of your choice, or add any of the stabilizers—a few drops of lemon juice or vinegar, a pinch of cream of tartar, or a teaspoon or two of light corn syrup. These help to keep the icing from sugaring and becoming gritty. Then continue to beat until the icing cools to room temperature. It is ready to use. ➤ Do not scrape the bowl if the icing on the bowl sides or bottom seems gummy or gritty.

If the syrup was not boiled long enough and the icing is somewhat runny, beat it in strong sunlight. If this doesn't do the trick, place the icing in the top of a double boiler or in a heatproof bowl ➤ over, not in, boiling water and beat until it reaches the right consistency. As this stratagem always thickens the icing but also makes it sandy, use it only as a last resort. If the syrup was overcooked and the icing is too stiff to spread, a teaspoon or two of boiling water or a few drops of lemon juice will restore it. If raisins, nuts, zest, or other ingredients are to be added to the icing, wait until the last moment to incorporate them. They contain oil or acid that will thin the icing.

▲ Above 5,000 feet, the lower boiling point of water at higher elevations means there will be greater evaporation of moisture; when cooking Boiled White Icing over direct heat, keep a careful watch on temperatures and see 857, (High Altitude Temperature Adjustments for cooking sugar syrup). If using a double boiler, it will take longer to beat the whites into a stiff, stable foam. Seven-Minute Icing can go fast on direct heat or take up to 15 minutes, depending on your altitude, when whipped in a double boiler.

BOILED WHITE ICING
About 3 ²/₃ cups

Stir in a small heavy saucepan until the sugar is dissolved, then bring to a boil over high heat:

1 cup sugar
¹/₂ cup water

In the meantime, beat in a large mixer bowl at medium-high speed until stiff:

3 large egg whites
¹/₈ teaspoon cream of tartar

Turn the heat down to low, cover, and simmer to allow the steam to wash down any sugar crystals on the sides of the pan. Turn the mixer down to the lowest speed and continue to beat. Uncover the syrup and cook to about 230°F, the soft-ball stage.

When the syrup reaches the correct temperature, dip the bottom of the pan in cold water for 1 second to stop the cooking. Beating the whites at high speed, add the syrup in a thin stream, whipping constantly. Add:

1 teaspoon vanilla

Continue to beat at high speed until the icing has cooled, about 4 minutes. Lower the speed to medium and beat 1 more minute. Use at once.

SEVEN-MINUTE WHITE ICING
About 3 cups

A very fluffy, delightful icing that is similar to Boiled White Icing, above.

Combine in the top of a large double boiler or a heatproof bowl and beat until thoroughly blended:

3 large egg whites
1¹/₂ cups sugar

¹/₃ cup cold water
1 tablespoon light corn syrup
¹/₄ teaspoon cream of tartar

Set over rapidly boiling water. Beat constantly with a hand-held mixer at medium-high speed, or with a wire whisk, until the mixture stands in stiff peaks, 7 minutes. Remove from the heat. Add:

1 teaspoon vanilla

Continue beating until the icing is cooled to room temperature. You may add to it at this point:

(¹/₂ cup chopped nuts or grated coconut, sweetened, or 1 stick peppermint candy, crushed)

Use at once.

SEVEN-MINUTE LEMON ICING

For the liquid, use **3 tablespoons water plus 2 to 3 tablespoons fresh lemon juice.** When the icing is stiff and cooled, add **¹/₄ teaspoon grated lemon zest.**

SEVEN-MINUTE ORANGE ICING

Substitute **¹/₄ cup fresh orange juice and 1 tablespoon fresh lemon juice** for the water, and add **¹/₂ teaspoon grated orange zest** when the icing is stiff and cooled.

SEVEN-MINUTE SEAFOAM ICING

Substitute **1¹/₃ cups packed brown sugar** for the white sugar. If desired, add **¹/₂ teaspoon maple, walnut, or pecan extract** along with the vanilla.

CHOCOLATE COATING FOR FLUFFY WHITE ICING
About ¹/₃ cup

The supreme touch to something that is already good.

Frost a cake with **Boiled White Icing, above, or Seven-Minute White Icing, above,** then apply the chocolate coating (make sure the surface is smooth.) This may be done as soon as the white icing is spread. This coating is always thin when applied, and it hardens more rapidly if refrigerated. It is not recommended for use in damp hot weather. Melt:

4 ounces semisweet or bittersweet chocolate

Cool, then spread with a broad knife or spatula over the frosted cake. Allow several hours for the coating to set, or refrigerate to harden it more quickly.

FLUFFY RAISIN OR RAISIN-NUT ICING
About 4 cups

Add pistachios to make a classic JOY icing, used in the 1931 edition.

Chop **1 cup raisins or ¹/₂ cup raisins and ¹/₂ cup nuts.**

Prepare **Boiled White Icing, above, or Seven-Minute White Icing, above.** Add raisins (and nuts) at the last minute, or sprinkle them onto the top of the cake and spread the icing over them.

FLUFFY NUT OR COCONUT ICING

To make a nut or coconut coating, press **about 1 cup chopped nuts or fresh coconut, dried shredded or grated** gently into the frosted cake.

Frost the cake with **Boiled White Icing, 790,** or **Seven-Minute White Icing, 790.** While the icing is still soft, hold the cake on the plate, in the palm of your nonwriting hand and, cupping your other hand to the curve of the cake, apply coconut or nuts to the icing as shown. Have a bowl underneath to catch the reusable excess.

Coating the sides of a cake with nuts

LUSCIOUS ORANGE ICING

About 4 cups

Please read About Boiled Icings, 789. Stir in a small heavy saucepan until the sugar is dissolved, then bring to a boil over high heat:

>   **1 cup sugar**
>   **$^1/_2$ cup water**
>   **1 tablespoon light corn syrup**

In the meantime, beat in a large mixer bowl at medium-high speed until stiff:

>   **3 large egg whites**
>   **$^1/_8$ teaspoon cream of tartar**

Turn the heat down to low, cover, and simmer to allow the steam to wash down any crystals that may have formed on the sides of the pan. Turn the mixer down to the lowest speed and continue to beat. Uncover the syrup and cook to 238° to 240°F, the soft-ball stage. Dip the bottom of the saucepan in cold water for 1 second to stop the cooking. Beating the whites at high speed, add the syrup in a slow, thin stream. Beat for 10 minutes, until cooled. Add:

>   **$^1/_4$ cup confectioners' sugar**
>   **1 teaspoon grated orange zest**
>   **1 tablespoon fresh orange juice or $^3/_4$ teaspoon vanilla**

Beat the icing to a spreading consistency and use immediately.

ABOUT FONDANT ICING

Fondant Icing is fondant candy warmed and thinned to pouring or spreading consistency (see About Fondant, 866, and Basic Fondant, 866). Properly applied, it makes a satiny finish on petits fours and cakes. The temperature and consistency of the fondant is important, as is the preparation of the items to be glazed. It takes a little practice to apply fondant perfectly.

For best results, warm the fondant very gently in a heat-proof bowl set in a skillet of 110°F water; reheat the water as necessary on the stove to maintain the temperature. Stir the fondant gently, to avoid creating air bubbles, with a rubber spatula, until it reaches a temperature between 98° and 105°F. Stir in food coloring, if desired, and flavor to taste with extracts, lemon juice, instant espresso powder dissolved in a few teaspoons of water, liqueurs, or the like. If necessary, thin the fondant judiciously with warm water until it is the desired consistency—thinner for pouring over small sweets such as petits fours, thicker for spreading on the tops of cakes. You can test the fondant on a spare piece of cake or a cookie.

Fondant will not hide cracks, unevenness, crumbs, or other imperfections, so cakes and petits fours must be neat and smooth before the fondant is applied. A smooth thin coat of buttercream or hot apricot glaze spread or brushed on the top and sides of each item is the usual preparation. Chill or freeze (briefly) the items to be coated with fondant so that the surface is firm and the fondant will set quickly.

To store fondant, cover the surface with plastic wrap. It keeps for up to 1 week at room temperature or up to 6 months refrigerated.

TO COVER PETITS FOURS OR OTHER PASTRIES WITH FONDANT

Line them up, with spaces between them, on a wire grid or rack set on a baking sheet to catch the excess, which can be scraped up and reused as long as it is crumb free. Warm the fondant as directed above, then pour it with a small pitcher, or use a spoon. If it is necessary to spread the fondant with a spatula, do so with a quick, sure stroke, as the fondant glazes over quickly and should not be re-worked. You can also spear petits fours or other small items from the bottom with a fork and dip them into the fondant to coat. Apply any decorations while the fondant is still wet. If you have only a very few cakes to frost, place them one at a time on a slotted pancake turner or spoon held over the pan and ice them individually.

CHOCOLATE FUDGE FROSTING

About 2 $^1/_2$ cups

On any chocolate layer cake, old-fashioned fudge frosting fits the bill. This is also quite tasty on cookies and dough-nuts.

Prepare **Chocolate Walnut Fudge, 863,** omitting the walnuts or reserving them to sprinkle on top of the cake. In the final stage of beating, when the fudge begins to thicken and lose its sheen, beat in **1 tablespoon half-and-half** just until blended. Use a rubber spatula to scrape down and stir in the frosting from the sides and bottom of the bowl, then let the frosting stand and stiffen for 4 to 5 minutes before correcting the consistency. Adjust, if necessary, by stirring in a little more **half-and-half** 1 teaspoon at a time, until the perfect spreading consistency is obtained. Use immediately, or cover the surface with plastic wrap. This keeps for about 1 week at room temperature or about 3 weeks refrigerated; or freeze for up to 6 months. Soften and stir until smooth before using.

CARAMEL FROSTING
About 3 cups

The flavor of brown sugar is a divine partner for Banana Cake, 721, or any spice cake. If desired, top the frosted cake with chopped nuts.
Combine in a medium heavy saucepan and stir until the sugar is dissolved:

2 cups packed brown sugar
1 cup heavy cream or $^1/_2$ cup (1 stick) unsalted butter, cut into small pieces, plus $^1/_2$ cup milk

Cook about 3 minutes, washing down any crystals on the sides of the pan with a wet pastry brush. Cook, without stirring, to 238° to 240°F (soft-ball stage). Remove from the heat, and float on top:

3 tablespoons unsalted butter

Cool, without stirring, to 110°F, about 45 minutes. Add:

1 teaspoon vanilla

Beat the icing until cool, thick, and creamy. If it becomes too heavy, thin it with a little:

(Heavy cream or milk)

until it is of spreading consistency. Use immediately, or cover the surface with plastic wrap. This keeps for up to 1 week at room temperature or about 3 weeks refrigerated; or freeze for up to 6 months. Soften and stir until smooth before using.

CLASSIC BUTTERCREAM
About 3 cups

Have all the ingredients at room temperature, 68° to 70°F. Combine in a medium heavy saucepan and cook, stirring, over medium heat until the mixture begins to simmer:

1 cup sugar
$^1/_2$ cup water
$^1/_4$ teaspoon cream of tartar

Stop stirring, cover, and simmer for 2 minutes to dissolve the sugar. Uncover and wash any sugar crystals from the sides of the pan with a wet pastry brush. Cook, uncovered, until the syrup registers 238°F (soft-ball stage) on a candy thermometer.
Meanwhile, fill a wide deep skillet with 1 inch of water and bring to a simmer. Place in a medium heatproof bowl and beat on high speed until thick and pale yellow:

2 large eggs or 5 large egg yolks

Just before the syrup is ready, begin beating the eggs again on medium speed. Beating constantly, pour the hot syrup in a thin steady stream into the eggs, being careful to avoid the beaters. Set the bowl in the skillet of simmering water and stir constantly with a whisk until the mixture registers 160°F on an instant-read thermometer. Remove from the heat. Wash the beaters, and beat the hot mixture

until it cools to room temperature. Beat in 1 tablespoon at a time:

$1^1/_2$ cups (3 sticks) unsalted butter, softened

beating until the buttercream is smooth and spreadable. If the mixture looks curdled at any time, simply continue beating until smooth. If the butter is added too quickly, the mixture may become soupy; refrigerate it briefly, then resume beating.
This keeps, refrigerated, for up to 6 days; or freeze for up to 6 months. To soften chilled or frozen buttercream, break it into chunks with a fork and place in a heatproof bowl in a pan of barely simmering water, or soften in a microwave on low at 15- to 30-second intervals, until some of the buttercream begins to melt. Stir with a rubber spatula until the buttercream is smooth and spreadable. If you oversoften it, you will have to refrigerate it again and re-soften it again.

SWISS MERINGUE BUTTERCREAM
3 to 3 $^1/_2$ cups

This egg white buttercream is the easiest of the classic French buttercreams because it does not require a cooked syrup. A hand-held electric mixer is necessary. Use a stainless steel bowl, rather than glass or crockery, to ensure that the meringue is adequately heated. Be sure to rinse the stem of the thermometer in the simmering skillet water between readings, to avoid contaminating the egg whites. Have the butter and egg whites at room temperature, 68° to 70°F.
Whisk together in a large stainless steel bowl:

4 large egg whites
$^3/_4$ cup sugar
2 tablespoons water
$^1/_4$ teaspoon cream of tartar

Set the bowl in a wide deep skillet filled with about 1 inch of simmering water. Make sure the water level is at least as high as the depth of the egg whites in the bowl. Beat the whites on low speed until the mixture reaches 140°F on an instant-read thermometer. Do not stop beating while the bowl is in the skillet, or the egg whites will overcook. If you cannot hold the thermometer stem in the egg whites while continuing to beat, remove the bowl from the skillet just to read the thermometer, then immediately return the bowl to the skillet. Beat on high speed just until the mixture reaches 160°F, 2 to 4 minutes. Remove the bowl from the skillet and add:

1 teaspoon vanilla

Beat on high speed for 3 to 5 more minutes, to cool. The meringue should hold glossy peaks. Beat in another large bowl until creamy, about 30 seconds:

$1^1/_2$ cups (3 sticks) unsalted butter, softened

Beat a large dollop of the meringue into the butter until well combined. Continue to beat in about half of the meringue in large dollops. Scrape the remaining meringue into the mixture and beat until smooth and fluffy. Beat in:

(1 to 2 tablespoons liqueur)

This keeps, refrigerated, for up to 6 days; or freeze for up to 6 months. Soften as for Classic Buttercream, above.

COFFEE BUTTERCREAM

3 to 3 1/2 cups

Dissolve **1 tablespoon instant coffee or espresso powder** in 1 1/2 teaspoons water. Stir most of the mixture into **Classic Buttercream, 792,** or **Swiss Meringue Buttercream, 792,** then add the rest as desired, to taste.

MOCHA BUTTERCREAM

Melt **2 ounces bittersweet or semisweet chocolate, chopped,** and let cool to lukewarm. Stir into **Coffee Buttercream, above,** along with **2 tablespoons coffee liqueur,** if desired.

CHOCOLATE BUTTERCREAM

About 4 1/2 cups

Melt **8 to 12 ounces semisweet or bittersweet chocolate, chopped,** with **1 tablespoon water for each 2 ounces chocolate.** Let cool to lukewarm. Using a rubber spatula, stir into **Classic Buttercream, 792,** or **Swiss Meringue Buttercream, 792,** along with **(2 or more tablespoons rum, brandy, or liqueur).**

PRALINE OR NUT BUTTERCREAM

3 to 3 1/2 cups

Stir 1/3 to 1/2 **cup nut or praline paste, chopped toasted, 1001, nuts, or sweetened or unsweetened canned chestnut puree** into **Classic Buttercream, 792,** or **Swiss Meringue Buttercream, 792.** Stir in **(1 to 2 tablespoons liqueur).**

ORANGE BUTTERCREAM

3 to 3 1/2 cups

Stir **2 tablespoons grated orange zest, 1 teaspoon grated lemon zest,** and **1 to 2 tablespoons orange liqueur** into **Classic Buttercream, 792,** or **Swiss Meringue Buttercream, 792.**

LEMON BUTTERCREAM

3 to 3 1/2 cups

Stir **4 teaspoons grated lemon zest** into **Classic Buttercream, 792,** or **Swiss Meringue Buttercream, 792.** Or stir in **Lemon Curd, 756,** to taste.

LIQUOR-FLAVORED BUTTERCREAM

3 to 3 1/2 cups

Gradually stir **up to** 1/2 **cup liquor** into **Classic Buttercream, 792,** or **Swiss Meringue Buttercream, 792.** The addition of the liquid will make the buttercream less stable: If the mixture begins to separate, stir briskly with a rubber spatula until smooth. If this fails, beat in: 1/4 **to** 1/2 **cup (**1/2 **to 1 stick) unsalted butter, softened.**

ABOUT QUICK ICINGS

These classic icings are sweet, flavorful, not too rich, and quick to prepare. The basic formula is easily remembered:

➤ 1/2 cup (1 stick) of butter to 4 cups (1 pound) confectioners' sugar and just enough liquid to get the consistency you want. The quickest method entails beating softened butter with the sifted sugar, gradually adding liquids and flavorings until the desired consistency is obtained.

Often the consistency of confectioners' sugar icings is adjusted by adding more sugar to thicken or more liquid to thin. But since an icing of this type tends to thicken on its own if left undisturbed for a few minutes, and certainly if stirred over a bowl of ice water, we try one or both of these methods before adding more sugar, which can diminish the flavor and the texture of the icing as well. Make these icings just before using. To store, cover the surface of the icing with plastic wrap. This keeps for up to 3 days at room temperature or up to 3 weeks refrigerated; or freeze for up to 6 months. Soften and stir or beat until smooth before using. Icings containing cream cheese keep, refrigerated, for about 1 week; or freeze for up to 3 months. Soften and stir until smooth before using.

QUICK WHITE ICING

About 2 cups

The quickest icing of all.

Combine in a medium bowl and beat together on medium speed:

   4 cups (1 pound) confectioners' sugar, sifted
   1/2 **cup (1 stick) unsalted butter, softened**

Add and beat until smooth:

   4 to 6 tablespoons milk, dry sherry, rum, or coffee
   2 teaspoons vanilla
   1/4 **teaspoon salt**

To correct the consistency, see above.

QUICK LEMON ICING

A very subtle flavor may be obtained by coarsely grating the rind of an orange or lemon, wrapping the rind in a piece of cheesecloth, and wringing the citrus oils onto the sugar before it is blended. Stir the oils into the sugar and allow it to stand 15 minutes or more.

Add the **grated zest of 1 lemon** to the confectioners' sugar mixture and use **1 to 2 tablespoons fresh lemon juice, plus milk as needed for the liquid.**

QUICK ORANGE ICING

Add the **grated zest of 1 small orange** to the confectioners' sugar mixture and use **4 to 6 tablespoons fresh orange juice** for the liquid.

QUICK MOCHA ICING

Reduce the confectioners' sugar to 1 2/3 cups and add **2 tablespoons unsweetened cocoa powder and 1 teaspoon**

instant coffee or espresso powder to the mixture. Use water for the liquid.

QUICK BUTTERSCOTCH (PENUCHE) ICING
About 1 ½ cups
This icing is a pale coffee color with a creamy brown sugar flavor.
Heat, stirring, in the top of a double boiler until smooth:
   ¼ cup (½ stick) unsalted butter
   ½ cup packed brown sugar
   ⅛ teaspoon salt
   ⅓ cup light cream or evaporated milk
Remove from the heat and let cool for about 5 minutes. Gradually add, beating until spreadable:
   3 cups confectioners' sugar, sifted
   ½ teaspoon vanilla or 1 teaspoon rum
If the icing seems thin, set the pan in a larger pan of ice water and beat until spreadable. If necessary, add more:
   (Confectioners' sugar)
Stir in:
   (½ cup chopped walnuts or pecans)

QUICK CHOCOLATE BUTTER ICING
About 1 ¼ cups
Melt in the top of a double boiler or a heatproof bowl:
   3 ounces unsweetened chocolate, coarsely chopped
   3 tablespoons unsalted butter
Remove from the heat and stir in:
   ¼ cup hot coffee, cream, or milk
   1 teaspoon vanilla
Gradually add, beating until spreadable:
   2 cups confectioners' sugar, sifted, or to taste

QUICK BROWN BUTTER ICING
About ¾ cup
The flavor of brown butter enhances plain butter cakes and spice cakes. The icing has little golden brown flecks in it. Make it just before using.
Melt in a medium skillet over medium heat:
   6 tablespoons (¾ stick) unsalted butter
Heat, stirring constantly, until deep golden. Gradually whisk in:
   1 ¼ cups confectioners' sugar, sifted
   1 teaspoon vanilla
Scrape into a bowl and beat until smooth and spreadable; do not attempt to thin with liquid. Use immediately.

COCONUT PECAN ICING
About 2 ½ cups
Combine in a pan:
   ⅔ cup sugar
   ⅔ cup evaporated milk
   2 egg yolks
   6 tablespoons (¾ stick) unsalted butter
   ½ teaspoon vanilla
Cook and stir constantly over low heat about 10 minutes

or until the egg thickens. Do not boil. Remove from heat and add:
   1 ½ cups flaked coconut
   ⅔ to 1 cup chopped pecans

QUICK MAPLE ICING
About 1 cup
Beat together in a medium bowl:
   2 cups confectioners' sugar, sifted
   1 tablespoon unsalted butter, softened
   ¼ teaspoon salt
   ½ teaspoon vanilla
Add, beating until spreadable:
   About ½ cup pure maple syrup

CREAM CHEESE FROSTING
About 2 cups
There are two secrets to making perfectly smooth cream cheese frosting with enough body to swirl onto a cake or pipe through a pastry bag: Do not overbeat, and use cold—not softened—cream cheese. Have the butter, if using it, at room temperature, and sift the confectioners' sugar after measuring.
   Feel free to vary the amount of confectioners' sugar to suit your taste: we have seen recipes with as little as 1 teaspoon and as much as ½ cup sugar per ounce of cream cheese.
I. FOOD PROCESSOR METHOD
The fastest method of all.
Combine in a food processor and pulse just until smooth and creamy:
   8 ounces cold cream cheese
   (6 tablespoons [¾ stick] unsalted butter, softened)
   2 teaspoons vanilla
   3 cups confectioners' sugar, sifted
If the frosting is too stiff, pulse for a few seconds longer; do not overprocess. If desired, stir in additional flavoring to taste, such as:
   (Grated lemon or orange zest, ground cinnamon, or liqueur)
II. ELECTRIC MIXER METHOD
Beat in a medium bowl at low speed just until blended:
   8 ounces cold cream cheese
   (5 tablespoons unsalted butter, softened)
   2 teaspoons vanilla
Add one-third at a time and beat just until smooth and the desired consistency:
   1 pound (4 cups) confectioners' sugar, sifted
If the frosting is too stiff, beat for a few seconds longer; do not overbeat. If desired, stir in additional flavoring to taste, such as:
   (Grated lemon or orange zest, ground cinnamon, or liqueur)

CHOCOLATE CREAM CHEESE FROSTING
About 2 ⅔ cups
Melt **5 ounces semisweet or bittersweet chocolate, chopped,** with **3 tablespoons water or coffee,** stirring often until smooth. Let cool to lukewarm, then stir into the frosting.

PEANUT BUTTER FROSTING
About 2 cups
Stir in chopped peanuts to taste, or sprinkle them over the finished cake, if desired. Try this as a filling for any cake frosted or glazed with chocolate. Have the cream cheese cold. The butter can be cold, but it's better to have it at room temperature, 68° to 70°F.
Beat in a medium bowl just until blended:
>   **½ cup smooth peanut butter**
>   **3 ounces cold cream cheese**
>   **1½ tablespoons unsalted butter, softened**
>   **1 teaspoon vanilla**
>   **3 tablespoons cream or milk**
>   **(1 to 2 tablespoons bourbon or rum)**
Add one-third at a time and beat just until smooth and the desired consistency is reached:
>   **2⅔ cups confectioners' sugar, sifted**
If the frosting is too stiff, add, but do not overbeat:
>   **1 to 2 tablespoons cream, milk, or liquor,**
>   **or as needed**

ABOUT CHOCOLATE GANACHE AND OTHER RICH CHOCOLATE FROSTINGS AND GLAZES
The sleek, rich chocolate coating on a torte is apt to be chocolate ganache, as is the center of a rich chocolate truffle. *Ganache* is a French term that refers to any combination of chocolate and cream. Butter and, occasionally, eggs or egg yolks, may be included; butter used in place of cream makes a variant of ganache. Ganaches are versatile, used as fillings, frostings, and glazes. Often the very same recipe is a pourable glaze at 85°F and spreadable when cooled to room temperature. Ganache is simple and quick to make, smooth on the tongue, and rich in flavor.

TO COAT A CAKE OR TORTE WITH CHOCOLATE GLAZE
Unlike lavishly spread frostings, which cover a multitude of imperfections on the surface of a cake, a poured chocolate glaze reveals all of them—from lopsided shapes to earthquakes cracks. There are two great secrets to a perfectly glazed chocolate cake or torte: the preparation of the cake shape and surface and the temperature at which the cake is stored and the glaze is poured.
    The cake must be level. Trim sponge or butter cakes if necessary. Level chocolate or nut tortes that have a characteristic sunken center by pressing the edges and inverting the cake as directed on page 727. Place the cake on a rigid base such as a cardboard round or the bottom of a springform pan so that the glaze will not crack or buckle when the cake is moved.
    The cake surface must be smooth before glazing. In some classic European desserts, a coat of hot strained apricot or red currant jam is used to seal the cake or torte before glazing. An even more effective technique is to frost the cake thinly with a little chocolate glaze that has been cooled to the consistency of frosting. As with frosted cakes, this is called crumb-coating, 785, the cake, because it smooths the surface, patches up cracks, and secures loose crumbs. Room-temperature cakes should be crumb-coated at room temperature, and cakes that must be refrigerated or are to be served cold should be well chilled before crumb-coating. Once crumb-coated, a room-temperature cake should be refrigerated for 5 to 10 minutes to set the crumb coat slightly without chilling the cake; then remove the cake from the refrigerator even if you are not ready to glaze it. A cake to be served cold should be refrigerated until you are ready to glaze it.
    To glaze the cake, place it on a rack over a cookie sheet or on a lazy Susan or decorating turntable. Reheat the remaining glaze just until it is pourable (about 85°F). If it is too cool, it will immediately turn dull; if it is too warm, it will pour off the cake before coating it thickly enough. Pour the glaze onto the top of the cake and use a metal spatula to coat the top and sides completely, as shown below. Gaps in coverage can be fixed by dipping the spatula or a finger into the excess glaze on the turntable or cookie sheet and touching the bare spot. Avoid spreading the glaze as it dries—this will dull the surface and cause streaks. The glaze on a cold cake will start to set immediately, so you must work quickly. For a room-temperature cake, let the glaze set naturally at room temperature; do not refrigerate the cake at any time. For cold cakes, return them to the refrigerator immediately after glazing and leave there until needed—which can be just before serving or up to 2 hours in advance of serving, depending on the nature of the cake.
    In short, dull, mottled, or streaked glazes are caused by glazes poured at the wrong temperature or by cakes at the wrong temperature before or after glazing. Following

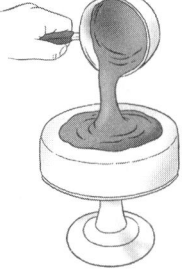

Pouring a glaze in the center of the cake and
spreading it with a spatula

these instructions will ensure gleaming, mirror-smooth glazed cakes.

Most chocolate ganache will keep in the refrigerator for a specified amount of time or freeze for up to 3 to 6 months. Soften and stir until smooth before use.

CHOCOLATE GANACHE GLAZE OR FROSTING
About 1 1/2 cups

Bring to a boil in a small saucepan:

> 3/4 **cup heavy cream**

Remove from the heat and add:

> 8 **ounces semisweet or bittersweet chocolate, finely chopped**

Stir until most of the chocolate is melted. Cover and let stand for 10 minutes, then stir or whisk very gently until completely smooth. Stir in:

> **(1 tablespoon liqueur, or more to taste)**

For a pourable glaze, let stand at room temperature, stirring occasionally, until the ganache cools to about 85°F. For frosting, let stand until spreadable. If the ganache becomes too stiff, set the pan in a larger pan of hot water and stir until softened; or remelt and then cool to 85° to 95°F for use as a glaze. This keeps for up to 3 days at room temperature or up to 1 week refrigerated.

BITTERSWEET CHOCOLATE GLAZE OR FROSTING
About 1 cup

A very sophisticated glaze or frosting to use on rich chocolate or nut tortes. For an even more bittersweet effect, substitute 1 ounce unsweetened chocolate for 1 ounce of the bittersweet or semisweet chocolate.

Heat in the top of a double boiler or in a microwave on medium, stirring often, just until the chocolate is melted and smooth:

> 6 **ounces bittersweet or semisweet chocolate, coarsely chopped**
> 1/3 **cup water, coffee, or milk**
> **(Pinch of salt)**

Remove from the heat. With a rubber spatula, stir in 2 or 3 pieces at a time:

> 6 **tablespoons (3/4 stick) unsalted butter, cut into small pieces**

Continue to stir—do not beat—until perfectly smooth. Stir in:

> **(1 to 2 tablespoons liqueur)**

For a pourable glaze, let stand at room temperature, stirring occasionally, until the mixture cools to 90°F. For frosting, let stand until spreadable. If the frosting becomes too stiff, set the pan in a larger pan of hot water and stir gently with a rubber spatula; or remelt and then cool to 90°F for use as a glaze. This keeps for up to 3 days at room temperature or up to 3 weeks refrigerated.

EUROPEAN CHOCOLATE ICING
About 2/3 cup

A letter from a homesick American bride made us realize that familiar tastes abroad can have an accent as foreign as English words spoken by other nationals. Where to get bitter chocolate for icing to make it taste the way she thought it should. Chef James Gregory, who was a friend of mom's, made her feel almost at home with this semisweet answer. Double or triple this recipe if you are frosting a cake.

Melt in the top of a double boiler over, not in, boiling water:

> 4 **ounces bittersweet chocolate, chopped**
> 1 **tablespoon unsalted butter**

Remove from heat. Add and beat well:

> 1/3 **cup heavy cream**

Add, stirring, until the desired sweetness is reached and the icing is smooth:

> 1 **cup confectioners' sugar, sifted, or to taste**
> 1 **teaspoon vanilla**

Drizzle or spread while warm.

CHOCOLATE SATIN FROSTING
About 3 cups

Both kids and adults love this shiny dark sweet chocolate frosting, which is easily made in a food processor. Keep any extra in a jar in the refrigerator and melt it for a quick ice cream sauce, or spread it on graham crackers or cookies.

Break or cut into 1/2-ounce pieces:

> 6 **ounces unsweetened chocolate**

Bring to a boil in a small saucepan:

> 1 **cup evaporated milk or heavy cream**

Remove from the heat and add the chocolate, without stirring. Cover and let stand for exactly 10 minutes. Scrape into a food processor or blender and add:

> 1 1/2 **cups sugar**
> 6 **tablespoons (3/4 stick) unsalted butter, cut into small pieces**
> 1 **teaspoon vanilla**

Process until the mixture is perfectly smooth, 1 minute or more. Transfer to a bowl. If necessary, let stand for a few minutes (longer if you used cream), until thickened to the desired spreading consistency. This keeps, refrigerated, for up to 1 week if made with cream, or about 3 weeks if made with evaporated milk.

CHOCOLATE SOUR CREAM FROSTING
About 2 cups

Very bittersweet and glossy. Use this to fill and frost any chocolate butter cake. Prepare just before using.

Melt, stirring often, in the top of a double boiler or in a microwave on medium:

> 10 **ounces bittersweet or semisweet chocolate, coarsely chopped**

Remove from the heat and stir in—do not beat—just until combined:

1 cup sour cream

Use immediately. If the frosting becomes too stiff or loses its gloss at any time, set the pan in a larger pan of hot water for a few seconds and stir to soften. This keeps, refrigerated, for up to 1 week.

WHITE CHOCOLATE FROSTING

Prepare **Chocolate Sour Cream Frosting, 796,** substituting **10 ounces white chocolate** for the bittersweet or semisweet chocolate.

CHOCOLATE MOUSSE FROSTING

About 3 ¹/₂ cups

This frosting has an appealing mousselike texture. Try it between layers of any angel cake, 705, a moist sponge cake, 706–709, or a devil's food cake, 718.

Whisk together in a medium heatproof bowl, preferably stainless steel:

2 large eggs
2 cups confectioners' sugar, sifted
¹/₂ cup milk, coffee, or water
¹/₈ teaspoon salt

Set the bowl in a large skillet of barely simmering water and heat, stirring constantly, until the mixture registers 160°F on an instant-read thermometer. Remove from the heat and stir in:

4 ounces unsweetened chocolate, finely chopped
6 tablespoons (³/₄ stick) unsalted butter, cut into
small pieces
1 teaspoon vanilla

Stir until the chocolate and butter are melted and the mixture is smooth. Set the bowl in a larger bowl of ice water and beat on high speed until the frosting holds a shape. This keeps, refrigerated, for up to 4 days.

MOCHA GLAZE OR FROSTING

About 1 ¹/₃ cups

This glaze makes a grand topping for almost any cake. Place in a small bowl:

9 ounces milk chocolate, finely chopped

Combine in a medium saucepan and bring to a simmer:

²/₃ cup heavy cream
1 tablespoon light corn syrup
1 tablespoon instant coffee or espresso powder
(¹/₈ teaspoon ground cinnamon)

Immediately pour over the chocolate. Stir until the chocolate is melted and the mixture is smooth. For a glaze, let cool just to 100°F. To use as a frosting, let cool to room temperature, and stir with a wooden spoon or rubber spatula until spreadable. If the frosting becomes too stiff, set the pan in a larger pan of hot water and stir gently with a rubber spatula; or remelt and then cool to 100°F for use as a glaze. This keeps for up to 3 days at room temperature or up to 3 weeks refrigerated.

HARD-SAUCE TOPPING

About 1 cup

Soften **Hard Sauce, 851, made with brandy** slightly in a heatproof bowl set over simmering water. Apply in a thin layer to any cooled cake, cookie or bar, or coffee cake.

BAKED ICING

Enough for an 8-inch square cake

This icing is baked with the cake. Use it on a thin cake only, one that will require 25 minutes of baking or less—such as a spice or ginger cake or coffee cake.

Preheat the oven to 375°F, or as indicated in the cake recipe.

Beat in a small bowl until stiff but not dry:

1 large egg white
¹/₈ teaspoon salt

Slowly beat in:

¹/₂ cup packed dark brown sugar.

For a chocolate icing, fold in:

(2 tablespoons unsweetened cocoa powder)

Gently spread the icing over the cake batter. Sprinkle it with:

¹/₄ cup chopped nuts

Bake the cake as indicated in the recipe.

BROILED ICING

Enough for an 8 x 8-inch square cake; about 1 cup

Spread on a cake or coffee cake, or on cookies, while still warm.

Preheat the broiler. Combine, stirring until smooth:

²/₃ cup packed brown sugar
3 tablespoons unsalted butter, melted
3 tablespoons heavy cream
¹/₈ teaspoon salt
¹/₂ cup shredded sweetened coconut or chopped nuts

Spread on the cake, and broil 3 to 5 inches below the heating element until the icing is bubbly all over the surface; take care that it does not burn.

ABOUT SOFT MERINGUE TOPPINGS

Few things are as disappointing or as frustrating to a home baker as a meringue pie topping that weeps and puddles, and few kitchen conundrums have inspired as much theorizing and contradictory advice in the pages of cookbooks. In truth, undissolved sugar in the meringue, though often blamed, has little to do with this sad condition, and humid weather, another common suspect, has even less. The real culprit is egg white, with its characteristic sensitivity to heat. Most recipes direct you to spread the meringue over a cool or lukewarm filling and then brown the topping in an oven for up to 20 minutes. The problem with this procedure is that it leaves the egg whites nearly raw along the bottom, where they meet the tepid filling, but scorching hot on top, where they are exposed to the oven's heat. The undercooked part of the meringue simply melts as the pie stands, resulting in that infamous slippery puddle between filling and topping. Meanwhile, the overheated meringue on the surface breaks down and curdles, just like an overcooked custard, and weeps those unsightly beads of sticky syrup.

The melting of the meringue along the bottom is easily prevented by simply having the filling hot, not warm, when you apply the meringue, so that the bottom of the meringue cooks in the heat of the filling. If the filling has cooled before you are ready to apply the meringue, slip the pie into the oven for 5 minutes before you top it. Ideally, you will think to do this before you have finished preparing the meringue, because meringue does not like to sit once it is ready.

The overheating of the surface of the meringue and the resulting beading is a more complex problem. Heating meringue over hot water, as one does in the making of a Swiss meringue, 790, or Seven-Minute White Icing, 790, serves to stabilize it and make it less prone to weeping. However, heated meringue tastes dry and sticky and tends to develop a leathery skin when further baked. A better solution, we think, is to stabilize the meringue with a cooked cornstarch paste, as indicated for Soft Meringue Topping I, below. Of course, the making of the paste entails an extra step that you may not have time to dispatch. So if you can live with a few beads, by all means use Soft Meringue Topping II, which is made in the conventional manner.

When applying meringue to a pie or pudding, ➤ spread a band of topping around the edge of the crust or dish before you fill in the center. If you cover the center first, you are likely to displace some of the filling and cause it to spill over. ➤ If it does not adhere well to the edges at all points, it may pull away during baking. Be especially careful to heed this advice when spreading meringue over a partially cooked and still-liquid filling, as in the making of Chess Pie, 683, or Key Lime Pie, 688. When applying meringue to a crustless pudding, spread the topping to the edge of the dish. That said, this may not prevent shrinking, especially if the dish is greased.

Meringue safety: If you wish to be certain that any possible pathogens in the egg whites have been killed, you must heat the meringue to 160°F. Follow the recipes as written, being sure that your pie filling is piping hot when you spread on the topping. After 20 minutes of baking, carefully insert an instant-read thermometer sideways into the center of the meringue. If the temperature is shy of the mark, bake the meringue a little longer. Be careful, though, not to go much beyond 165°F, or the meringue will begin to break down even if stabilized by cornstarch.

If you are concerned about meringue and egg safety for a dessert that isn't baked for long, such as Banana Pudding, 807, or Baked Alaska, 843, use pasteurized egg whites, 977.

SOFT MERINGUE TOPPING

I. *Enough to cover one 9-inch pie; about $^3/_4$ cup*

Because it is stabilized by the cornstarch, this meringue topping will not weep, leak, or deflate, even when refrigerated for several days. Since your filling should be piping hot when the meringue is applied, measure out your ingredients and prepare the cornstarch paste before you embark on the filling.

Mix thoroughly in a small saucepan:

    1 tablespoon cornstarch
    1 tablespoon sugar

Gradually stir in, making a smooth, runny paste:

    $^1/_3$ cup water

Bring to a boil over medium heat, stirring briskly all the while, then boil for 15 seconds. Remove the thick paste from the heat and cover. Beat in a clean grease-free glass or metal bowl until foamy:

    4 large egg whites, at room temperature

Add and beat until soft peaks form:

    $^1/_2$ teaspoon vanilla
    $^1/_4$ teaspoon cream of tartar

Very gradually beat in:

    $^1/_2$ cup sugar, preferably superfine

Beat on high speed until the peaks are very stiff and glossy but not dry. Reduce the speed to very low and beat in the cornstarch paste 1 tablespoon at a time. When all the paste is incorporated, increase the speed to medium and beat for 10 seconds. Spread over a hot pie filling (or pudding) as described above. Bake as directed in the recipe.

II. *Enough to cover one 9-inch pie; about $^3/_4$ cup*

This conventional soft meringue topping is more quickly made than I but is not as stable. It is best served the day it is made. Measure out the meringue ingredients before you start to make the filling.

Please read About Soft Meringue Topping, above. Beat in a clean grease-free glass or metal bowl on medium speed until foamy:

    4 large egg whites, at room temperature

Add and beat until soft peaks form:

    $^1/_4$ teaspoon cream of tartar

Very gradually beat in:

    $^1/_2$ cup sugar, preferably superfine

Beat on high speed until the peaks are stiff and glossy but not dry. Beat in:

    $^1/_2$ teaspoon vanilla

Spread over the hot filling (or pudding) as described above. Bake as directed in the recipe.

CRUNCHY ALMOND TOPPING

About 1 $^1/_3$ cups

This topping is really a crust, which bakes with the cake and becomes a topping after the cake is inverted and unmolded.

Preheat the oven to 325°F. Toast in a small pan or pie pan until lightly browned, 5 to 10 minutes:

    $^1/_3$ cup sliced blanched almonds

Let cool. Grease the cake pan liberally with:

2 teaspoons unsalted butter, softened

Press the toasted nuts into the butter on the bottom and sides of the pan. Sprinkle with:

2 to 3 teaspoons sugar

Mix the cake batter, and carefully pour into the pan. Bake and unmold as directed.

STREUSEL AND TOPPINGS APPLIED BEFORE BAKING

I. STREUSEL TOPPING

²/₃ to ³/₄ cup

Prepare:

Any coffee cake dough, 621–631

After spreading the dough with butter, combine:

¹/₃ cup sugar

2 tablespoons all-purpose or rice flour

2 tablespoons unsalted butter

Blend these ingredients until crumbly. Add:

¹/₂ teaspoon ground cinnamon

(¹/₄ to ¹/₂ cup chopped nuts)

Sprinkle the crumbs and nuts, if using, over the dough and bake as directed.

II. HONEY-BEE GLAZE

For two 9-inch square cakes

Spread this glaze on coffee cakes just before baking. Combine in a small saucepan and bring to a boil over low heat, stirring to dissolve the sugar:

¹/₂ cup sugar

¹/₄ cup milk

¹/₄ cup (¹/₂ stick) unsalted butter

¹/₄ cup honey

¹/₂ cup chopped nuts

Use immediately.

GLAZES APPLIED BEFORE OR DURING BAKING

I. To give color to a yeast dough or pastry, brush before baking with:

Milk or butter or a combination of milk and sugar

II. FRENCH EGG WASH

To give color and gloss to yeast dough or pastry, brush before baking with:

1 egg yolk, beaten with 1 to 2 tablespoons water or milk

III. To sparkle a glaze, sprinkle before baking with:

Sugar

IV. For a clear glaze, just before the pastry has finished baking, brush with:

¹/₄ cup sugar

dissolved in:

¹/₄ cup hot water or strong hot coffee

(¹/₂ teaspoon ground cinnamon)

Return to the oven to finish baking.

GLAZES APPLIED AFTER BAKING

Just after these glazes are applied, decorate the cake, sweet bread, or pastry with whole or half nuts or dried or candied fruits, if desired. When it dries, the glaze will hold the decorations in place on cakes and sweet breads.

I. MILK GLAZE

About ¹/₃ cup

This can be used as a substitute for fondant on small cakes such as petits fours.

Beat together until smooth:

¹/₂ cup confectioners' sugar, sifted

2 teaspoons hot milk

¹/₄ teaspoon vanilla

II. LEMON GLAZE

About ¹/₂ cup; enough to lightly glaze four 8-inch square cakes

This glaze should be spread on warm cakes or Christmas cookies. It has a fine consistency for imbedding decorative nuts and fruits.

Beat together until smooth:

1¹/₄ cups confectioners' sugar, sifted

¹/₄ cup fresh lemon, orange, or lime juice

1 teaspoon vanilla

III. HONEY GLAZE

About ¹/₃ cup

Combine in a small saucepan and bring to a boil:

¹/₄ cup honey

2 tablespoons sugar

1 tablespoon unsalted butter

IV. WHIPPED CREAM CHEESE TOPPING

About ¹/₃ cup

Combine in a blender and blend until smooth:

3 ounces cream cheese

1 tablespoon heavy cream

¹/₂ teaspoon vanilla

Blend in well:

3 tablespoons confectioners' sugar

V. LIQUEUR GLAZE

About ²/₃ cup

Beat together until smooth:

2 cups sifted confectioners' sugar

3 tablespoons liqueur

2 tablespoons unsalted butter, melted

Spread over cakes or cookies.

TRANSLUCENT SUGAR GLAZE

About ¹/₂ cup

This glaze gives loaf and tube cakes a slightly shiny crust and a bit of extra sweetness. Or try it on cookies. Double the recipe for a large tube or fluted tube cake.

Stir together briskly until thoroughly combined:

1 cup confectioners' sugar, sifted

(¹/₂ teaspoon grated orange or lemon zest)

2 to 3 tablespoons water, liquor, fresh lemon juice, or coffee

(¹/₄ teaspoon vanilla)

Use immediately. Brush or use a spoon to drizzle over the cake.

QUICK COOKIE ICING
About 1 cup

This is good for children's cookie making. It can be tinted with food coloring and kept in small cups to be spread on gingerbread or sugar cookies. Mix up a thick batch for piping out of sealable plastic bags (cut off one bottom corner).

Stir together in a medium bowl until smooth:

4 cups (1 pound) confectioners' sugar, sifted
3 to 4 tablespoons water

Adjust the consistency as necessary with more:

Confectioners' sugar or water

Color as desired. To store, cover the surface of the icing with plastic wrap. This keeps for up to 4 days at room temperature or about 1 month refrigerated.

QUICK LEMON ICING FOR COOKIES

Substitute **3 to 4 tablespoons fresh lemon juice** for the water.

GLAZES FOR FRUIT PIES, TARTS, AND COFFEE CAKES
I. APRICOT, PEACH, OR RASPBERRY GLAZE
About 4 1/2 cups

For baked pastries, the simplest glazes are melted preserves or jellies such as currant, quince, or apple. This recipe makes a large amount, but it is a useful glaze to keep on hand in the refrigerator.

Combine in a medium heavy saucepan:

3 cups strained apricots, peaches, or raspberries
1 cup sugar
1 cup light corn syrup

Cook, stirring, until the sugar is dissolved. While the mixture is still warm, glaze the cooled pastry.

II. FRUIT GLAZE
Enough for glazing 3 cups berries or fruit

The butter will keep the glaze supple.

Boil to the jelly stage, 927, then strain:

1 cup sugar
1 cup cleaned peeled fruit of your choice
2 medium apples, peeled, cored, and chopped
(A little red vegetable coloring)
1/4 cup water
(1 tablespoon unsalted butter)

Cool until the glaze is about to set, then pour it or spread it over the fruit to be glazed.

III. STRAWBERRY GLAZE
Enough for one 9-inch fruit pie or tart or six 3 1/2-inch tarts

Puree in a food processor:

3 cups halved strawberries

Strain through a fine sieve into a medium saucepan. Add:

1/3 cup sugar
1 tablespoon fresh lemon juice
1 tablespoon cornstarch
(A little red food coloring)

Stir and bring to a boil over low heat until thick and transparent, about 1 minute. Cool and spread over the fruit to be glazed.

IV. THICKENED FRUIT GLAZE

Glaze may also be made of canned fruit syrups or jellies. Cornstarch will give a smooth glaze, arrowroot a more transparent and sticky one.

Boil the syrup or jelly until thick. For each 1/2 cup, add:

1 teaspoon cornstarch or arrowroot

blended with:

1 tablespoon sugar

CLEAR CARAMEL GLAZE
About 1 cup

This brittle topping is used on many European cakes.

Combine in a small heavy saucepan over medium-high heat:

1 cup sugar
1/3 cup water

Bring to a boil, swirling the pan until the sugar dissolves. Then boil undisturbed until the caramel is light amber and has reached a temperature of about 310°F. Spread it at once with a hot spatula. If you work quickly, you may score it in patterns for easier cutting later; use a knife dipped in butter.

FRESH FLOWERS FOR CAKES

Cake decorations can be made from edible flowers, if you are sure ➤ they were not sprayed. Choose delicately colored open-petaled flowers such as hollyhocks, chamomile, nasturtiums, pansies, and violets. Field daisies and African daisies hold up well. ➤ Beware of flowers like lilies of the valley or Star of Bethlehem, which are poisonous. Remove the stamens. Cut off all but 3/4 inch of the stems. Arrange the flowers on the iced cake just before serving it. If desired, place a small candle in the center of each one.

DESSERTS

Featured here are custards and flans, ethereal soufflés, and puffy meringues. Cornstarch, rice, and tapioca puddings transport us happily back to our childhoods. A family we know had a cook who always urged the children to eat sparingly of the main course, so as to leave a little room for the "hereafter." Desserts can indeed be heavenly. They also give the hostess a chance to build a focal point for a buffet, such as gelatin molds, from simple fruit jells to those chock full of suspended fruit, nuts, and other sweets. There are soft, airy mousses, Bavarian creams, and their close relatives, charlottes, in which the mousse is tucked behind ladyfingers or cake, and cakelike baked and steamed puddings. Finally you will find here a guide to constructing a cheese course sure to please any guest, as well as a delectable cheese-based dessert. For other desserts, remember Frozen Desserts, 828, and Fruit Compotes, 211, and Cheese Spreads, 698. See also Cakes, 698, Pies and Pastries, 661, Fruits, 208, Fruit Fondue, 848, Crêpes and Beignets, 653, Pancakes, 643, and Waffles, 208.

ABOUT CUSTARDS

To prepare custards in ways that enhance their charm, keep in mind that the technique and basic ingredients are the same whether preparing a simple cup custard or a crisp-crusted crème brûlée. Remember these universal rules: ➤ Heat eggs and milk or cream just to the point where they set and become perfectly smooth and creamy. If the custard exceeds a certain temperature, the egg proteins will shrivel into tiny lumps, giving the custard a hard, dry, grainy consistency.

For baked custard, simply whip the ingredients together well and pour them into custard cups. We prefer glazed ceramic ramekins or cups. A **water bath,** below, also known as a **bain-marie,** is the cook's principal means of managing heat during the cooking of custards. Baking a dish of custard in a larger pan of water partially insulates the custard from the oven's heat and thereby protects it from overcooking. To bake custards in a water bath, choose a pan large enough to accommodate the cups comfortably. They should not touch one another or the pan sides. Set a cake rack in the pan or cover the pan bottom with a dish towel or several layers of paper towels; the rack or towel(s) will prevent the custards from coming into direct contact with the hot pan bottom. Arrange the custards in the prepared pan, place the pan on a rack in a preheated 325°F oven, and immediately pour enough scalding-hot tap water into the pan to come one-half to two-thirds of the way up the sides of the custard dishes. By pouring the water into the pan after setting the pan in the oven, you are able to keep the pan steady and prevent splashing water into the custards.

To test for doneness, ➤ gently shake a cup, and remove the custard from the oven as soon as the center appears quivery, like firm gelatin. Or insert a knife ➤ near the edge of the cup; if the blade comes out clean, the custard will be set all the way through when cooled—there is sufficient stored heat in the cups to finish the cooking process. Remove the custards from the pan and cool on a rack. ➤ Test them at the centers. If they are as

Baking custard in a water bath

well done as at the edges, set the cups in ice water at once to stop further cooking.

For softer top-of-the-stove custards and custard sauces, use very low heat or a double boiler, cooking ➤ over, not in, boiling water. Too high heat will toughen and shrink the albumen in the eggs and keep it from holding the liquid in suspension as it should. Beat the eggs well. You can also **temper,** 646, the eggs by gradually adding the hot liquid to them, and stirring constantly. Cook until the custard reaches 175°F on an instant-read thermometer and is thick enough to coat a spoon, and running a finger across the spoon leaves a trail. Remove from the heat and strain, if desired, then continue stirring to release steam. If the steam is allowed to condense, it may make the custard watery. Should you have reason to believe that the custard has become too hot, turn it into a chilled bowl and whisk it quickly, or put it in the blender at high speed to cool rapidly. ➤ Always store custards or custard-based dishes covered in the refrigerator, as they are highly susceptible to bacterial activity even though they may give no evidence of spoilage.

Cream, whole milk, low-fat milk, and skim milk are interchangeable in any custard recipe, though, of course, a custard made with skim milk will not be as thick, rich, or dense as one made with heavy cream. As for eggs, a good rule of thumb is that 1 whole egg has roughly the same thickening power as $2\frac{1}{2}$ egg yolks or $1\frac{1}{2}$ egg whites (or 3 tablespoons). If you want to make your custard lean, be sure to use the maximum amount of sugar called for. Sugar promotes tenderness in custards, and its sweetness partially compensates for the loss of flavor resulting from the reduction of fat. ➤ Lean custards cook more quickly than rich ones.

BOILED CUSTARD

$2\frac{1}{4}$ cups; 4 servings

This confection is badly named, because ➤ it must not be permitted to boil at any time. It is never as firm as baked custard but is more like a thin custard sauce, delicious served with Floating Islands, 805.

Lightly beat in a medium bowl:

4 large egg yolks

Whisk in:

$\frac{1}{4}$ cup sugar
$\frac{1}{8}$ teaspoon salt

Heat in a medium saucepan until bubbles form around the edges:

2 cups milk

Slowly whisk the hot milk into the egg yolks and sugar. Return this mixture to the saucepan over low heat. Using a heatproof rubber spatula or a wooden spoon, stir the sauce gently but constantly, sweeping the entire pan bottom and reaching into the corners. As soon as the custard is thickened enough to coat the back of a spoon and reaches 175°F on an instant-read thermometer, pour it into a bowl and let cool at room temperature. As it cools, stir periodically to prevent a skin from forming. Add before chilling thoroughly:

1 teaspoon vanilla, rum, or dry sherry, or a little grated lemon zest

Refrigerate until chilled. Serve in individual cups, bowls, or spoon over fruit or cake.

RICH CUSTARD

6 to 8 servings

This resembles a thick custard sauce and can be served with steamed or baked puddings.

Combine in a medium saucepan:

$\frac{3}{4}$ cup sugar
2 tablespoons cornstarch
$\frac{1}{8}$ teaspoon salt

Gradually whisk in:

2 cups half-and-half
4 large egg yolks, well beaten
2 tablespoons unsalted butter, cut into pieces

Whisking constantly, bring to a boil over medium-low heat, and boil for 1 minute. Remove from the heat and immediately stir in:

$1\frac{1}{2}$ teaspoons vanilla

Pour into a bowl, cover with plastic wrap, and chill. Whip to firm peaks:

$\frac{1}{2}$ cup cold heavy cream

Fold into the chilled custard.

BAKED OR CUP CUSTARD

5 servings

Delicious served in solitary glory. This can be readied for the oven in only a few minutes.

Preheat the oven to 325°F.

Whisk in a medium bowl just until blended:

3 large eggs
$\frac{1}{3}$ to $\frac{1}{2}$ cup sugar
$\frac{1}{8}$ teaspoon salt

Heat in a small saucepan just until steaming:

2 cups milk

Gradually whisk the hot milk into the egg mixture, and stir gently until the sugar is dissolved. If you wish, strain the mixture through a fine-mesh sieve into a bowl or large measure with a pouring lip. Stir in:

$\frac{3}{4}$ teaspoon vanilla or seeds scraped from one 1-inch piece vanilla bean

Pour into five 6-ounce custard cups or ramekins. Dust with, if desired:

(Grated or ground nutmeg)

Bake the custards in a water bath, 801, until set but still quivery in the center when the cups are shaken, 40 to 60 minutes. Remove from the water bath and let cool for 30 minutes, then cover each one tightly with plastic wrap and refrigerate until cold. If desired, serve with:

(Pure maple syrup, berries, Caramel Syrup, 849, or a fruit sauce, 852–853)

CARAMEL CUSTARD

5 servings

Proceed as for **Baked or Cup Custard, above**, omitting the sugar; heat the milk but do not combine yet with the eggs and salt.

To prepare the caramel, heat $\frac{3}{4}$ **cup sugar** in a heavy saucepan over medium heat. Stir gently until the sugar is dissolved and the syrup is clear. The mixture should not boil until the sugar is completely dissolved. Increase the heat to high, cover the saucepan tightly, and boil the syrup for 2 minutes. Uncover the saucepan and continue to boil until the caramel begins to darken around the edges. Gently swirl the pan until the caramel turns deep amber. Immediately remove from the heat and add **2 tablespoons very hot water.** Stir to mix, then add the warm milk. Return

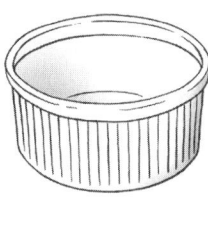
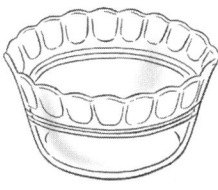

Ovenproof ramekin and custard cups

the pan to low heat to dissolve the caramel, stirring frequently. Add the milk to the eggs as above, and add flavorings as desired. Proceed as directed.

FLAN (CRÈME CARAMEL)

8 servings

Flan is the preeminent dessert of Spain and Latin America. It is also a favorite in France, where it is known as crème caramel. Flan is a baked egg custard with caramel in its bottom. The custard is turned out of its baking dish and served upside-down. Allow time to chill the baked custards thoroughly.

Preheat the oven to 325°F. Have ready eight 6-ounce custard cups or ramekins or a 2- to 2$\frac{1}{2}$-quart soufflé dish.

Combine in a small heavy saucepan:

> $\frac{3}{4}$ **cup sugar**
> $\frac{1}{4}$ **cup water**

Cook over medium heat without stirring, very gently swirling the pan, until the sugar is dissolved. ➤ The mixture should not boil until the sugar is dissolved, so slide the pan off and on the burner as necessary. Increase the heat to high and bring the syrup to a rolling boil; cover the pan tightly and boil for 2 minutes. Uncover the pan and cook until the caramel begins to darken. Gently stir once again and cook until the caramel turns deep amber.

Quickly pour the caramel into the cups or soufflé dish. Using a pot holder, immediately tilt the cups or dish to spread the caramel over the bottom and halfway up the sides. Whisk in a large bowl just until blended:

> **5 large eggs or 4 large eggs plus 2 large egg yolks**
> $\frac{3}{4}$ **cup sugar**
> $\frac{1}{8}$ **teaspoon salt**

Heat in a medium saucepan just until steaming:

> **3 cups whole milk**

Gradually whisk the milk into the egg mixture and stir gently until the sugar is dissolved. If you wish, strain the mixture through a fine-mesh sieve into a bowl or large measure with a pouring lip. Stir in:

> $\frac{3}{4}$ **teaspoon vanilla**

Pour into the caramel-lined cups or dish. Bake in a water bath, 801, until firmly set in the center, 40 to 60 minutes for individual cups, 1 to 1$\frac{1}{2}$ hours for a single dish. Cool

on a rack, then refrigerate for at least 4 hours, or up to 2 days. Cover individual cups tightly with plastic wrap before refrigerating. To unmold, dip the cups or dish briefly in hot water, loosen the edges of the flan with a knife, and invert onto individual plates or a large plate (the plate for a large flan must be either broad or deep to catch all the caramel).

FLAN WITH CONDENSED MILK

8 servings

In Latin America, a type of flan is made by simmering milk and sugar until reduced to a thick cream, then adding eggs. Since the cooking of the milk and sugar takes as long as an hour, many prefer to make this with sweetened condensed milk.

Preheat the oven to 325°F. Coat eight 6-ounce custard cups or ramekins or a single 2- to 2$\frac{1}{2}$-quart mold with caramel as directed for **Flan, above.** Combine in a saucepan:

> **One 14-ounce can sweetened condensed milk**
> **1$\frac{1}{2}$ cups water**
> **Zest of $\frac{1}{2}$ lime, removed in large strips**
> **1 cinnamon stick**
> **Pinch of salt**

Bring to a boil, then reduce the heat and simmer gently for 5 minutes. Remove from the heat, cover, and let stand until just warm. Strain the mixture through a sieve into a bowl or large measure with a pouring lip.

Whisk in a large bowl just until blended:

> **4 large eggs**
> **3 large egg yolks**
> $\frac{3}{4}$ **teaspoon vanilla**

Gradually whisk in the milk mixture. Pour into the caramel-lined cups or dish. Bake in a water bath, 801, until firmly set in the center, 40 to 55 minutes for individual cups, 50 to 70 minutes for a single dish. Cool and unmold as for Flan, above.

CRÈME BRÛLÉE

4 to 6 servings

Crème brûlée is famous for its hard, caramelized sugar glaze. The caramel crust can be achieved many ways. You can cover the custards with liquid caramel, which quickly hardens into a hard glaze, or sprinkle the custards with sugar and melt the sugar under the broiler or with a propane torch.

Heat almost to a simmer:

> **2 cups heavy cream**

Stir with a wooden spoon in a medium bowl just until blended:

> **8 large egg yolks or 4 large eggs**
> $\frac{1}{2}$ **cup sugar**

Gradually stir in the cream. Strain through a fine-mesh sieve into a bowl or a large measure with a pouring lip. Stir in:

> $\frac{3}{4}$ **teaspoon vanilla**

Pour into four 6-ounce or six 4-ounce custard cups or ramekins and place in a water bath, 801. Set the pan in the oven and set the oven temperature at 325°F. Bake until the custards are set but still slightly quivery in the center when the cups are gently shaken, 30 to 35 minutes. Remove the custards from the water bath and let cool to room temperature.

Cover each one tightly with plastic wrap and refrigerate for at least 8 hours, or up to 2 days. Shortly before serving, gently blot any liquid that has formed on the surface of the custards with the paper towels, then caramelize using one of the methods below.

CARAMEL GLAZE

For best results, the custards should be very cold before glazing.

I. This method yields a hard, glossy, candylike glaze. The glaze may be applied to the custards up to 4 hours ahead without softening.

Combine in a small heavy saucepan:

$^3/_4$ **cup sugar**
$^1/_4$ **cup water**

Cook over medium heat, without stirring, very gently swirling, until the sugar is dissolved. ➤ Do not let the mixture boil until the sugar is dissolved. Increase the heat to high and bring the syrup to a rolling boil; cover the pan tightly and boil for 2 minutes. Uncover the pan and cook until the caramel begins to darken. Gently stir once again and cook until the caramel turns deep amber.

Dip the bottom of the pan briefly in cold water, then immediately spoon a tablespoon of the hot caramel over one of the custards and tilt the mold to cover the surface evenly. Glaze the remaining custards in the same manner. If the caramel continues to darken as you proceed, briefly dip the pan again in cold water. Or, if the caramel becomes too thick to pour, stir it over low heat to liquefy it. Refrigerate the custards for at least 30 minutes, or up to 4 hours.

II. This method yields a delicate, brittle crust. The crust must be applied within an hour of serving, or it will begin to melt. If your broiler isn't very hot or you can't get the custards very close to it, broil the custards in an oven-proof pan of ice water to prevent them from cooking.

Adjust the rack so that the tops of the custards will be about 2 inches from the broiler heating element. If your rack cannot be set high enough, elevate the custards on an inverted roasting pan. Preheat the broiler for 10 minutes. Sprinkle evenly over the top of each custard:

2 to 3 teaspoons granulated light brown sugar

Or force through a sieve evenly over the top of each custard:

3 to 4 teaspoons packed regular light brown sugar

The coating should be $^1/_{16}$ to $^1/_8$ inch. Arrange the custards on a baking sheet or in a large pan of ice water and place under the broiler. Broil until the sugar melts and bubbles, turning the pan and/or moving the custards around if some cook more quickly than others. Some sugar will re-

main unmelted and some spots will char; this is part of the charm. Serve at once, or refrigerate for up to 1 hour.

III. This glaze is thinner and more delicate than I and harder, glossier, and more transparent than II.

Sprinkle evenly over the surface of each custard:

$1^1/_2$ **to 2 teaspoons sugar**

The coating should be $^1/_{16}$ to $^1/_8$ inch. Caramelize the sugar with a propane torch, holding the flame about 2 inches above the surface of each custard. Slowly rotate it to melt and color the sugar as evenly as possible.

MAPLE CRÈME BRÛLÉE

Prepare **Crème Brûlée, 803**, substituting $^2/_3$ **cup pure maple syrup** for the sugar.

RASPBERRY CRÈME BRÛLÉE

Prepare **Crème Brûlée, 803**, placing **4 raspberries (16 to 24 total)** in each cup before pouring in the custard.

VANILLA POTS DE CRÈME

6 servings

This cup custard is rich because it is made with egg yolks instead of whole eggs. Pots de crème are named for the individual lidded porcelain jars, or *pots*, in which they are traditionally baked.

Preheat the oven to 325°F.

Whisk in a medium bowl just until blended:

6 large egg yolks
$^1/_3$ **to $^1/_2$ cup sugar**

Bring just to a simmer in a small saucepan:

Pots de crème cup

2 cups whole milk or half-and-half

Gradually whisk into the egg yolk mixture. Strain through a fine-mesh sieve into a bowl or large measure with a pouring lip. Skim off any foam with a spoon. Stir in:

1 teaspoon vanilla

Pour the mixture into 6 pot de crème cups or 4-ounce ramekins. Put the lids on the cups or cover each ramekin tightly with a piece of aluminum foil to prevent a skin from forming. Bake in a water bath, 801, until set but still quivery in the center when the cups are shaken, 40 to 50 minutes. Remove the custards from the water bath and let cool for 30 minutes, then refrigerate for at least 2 hours before serving. If using pot de crème cups, serve with the lids on.

COFFEE POTS DE CRÈME

Prepare **Vanilla Pots de Crème, above**, using $^1/_2$ cup sugar, and add **4 teaspoons instant coffee powder or 1 tablespoon instant espresso powder** to the hot milk.

CHOCOLATE POTS DE CRÈME

I. *8 servings*

Although the classic technique calls for baking, the consistency is simpler to control by this top-of-the-stove method.

Combine in the top of a double boiler:

2 cups milk or cream or 1 cup milk plus
    1 cup heavy cream
5 to 8 ounces bittersweet or semisweet chocolate,
    finely chopped
(2 tablespoons sugar)

Cook, stirring, over, not in, boiling water until the chocolate melts and the milk comes to just under a simmer. Meanwhile, beat lightly in a medium bowl:

6 large egg yolks, at room temperature

Before adding the eggs to the hot milk mixture, temper them by gradually stirring about $\frac{1}{2}$ cup of the hot milk mixture into the eggs, then stir the eggs into the mixture in the double boiler. Add:

1 teaspoon vanilla or grated zest of 1 orange

Continue to stir until the custard very thickly coats the back of a spoon and running your finger across the spoon leaves a trail. Strain the custard, if desired, and pour into 8 pot de crème cups or 4-ounce ramekins. Cool uncovered until no longer steaming, then cover and refrigerate for at least 6 hours, or overnight.

II. *4 servings*

This is quickly made.

Blend together in a blender or in a bowl with a whisk:

$\frac{3}{4}$ **cup chocolate chips**
$\frac{3}{4}$ **cup milk, heated until very hot**

When the chocolate is melted, add and blend or whisk well:

1 large egg, lightly beaten

Pour into 4 pot de crème cups or 4-ounce ramekins. Chill for at least 8 hours, or overnight. Serve garnished with, if desired:

(Whipped Cream, 754)

FLOATING ISLANDS

4 servings

Countless desserts are known as floating islands, or snowy eggs—*îles flottantes* or *oeufs à la neige* in French. All consist of some sort of puffy confection, typically a meringue, floated on a liquid custard or other dessert sauce. In most floating islands, caramel, jelly, fruit, or a fruit puree is also involved, most commonly as a garnish or drizzle, but sometimes as an ingredient in the puffs themselves.

Separate:

4 large eggs

Put the whites in a large bowl; reserve the yolks. Whip the whites until stiff. Gradually beat in:

$\frac{2}{3}$ **cup sugar**

Bring to just under a simmer in a large skillet:

2 cups milk

Drop the meringue mixture from a tablespoon into 4 mounds on the milk. Poach them gently, without letting the milk boil, for about 4 minutes, turning them once. Lift them out carefully with a skimmer and place a towel beneath the skimmer and meringue to dry up the excess milk.

Use the milk and the reserved egg yolks to make:

Boiled Custard, 802, or any custard sauce, 845–846

Pour into a wide bowl and place the meringues on top. Refrigerate until chilled. If desired, just before serving drizzle over the tops of the islands:

(Caramelized Sugar I, 1019)

ABOUT SPONGE CUSTARDS

From a fan came a drawing of an elaborate mold and the question, "Can you tell me how my great-aunt used to make a dessert that had a spongy bottom and a clear quivery top?" Her aunt's creation must have been an unmolded baked sponge custard. The batter holds together when put into the baking dish, but then magically divides during cooking into a quivery layer of custard on the bottom and a light and spongy cake on top. If you serve it in the dish, the sponge will form a decorative top; or you may unmold it. If you prefer a meringue-like quality rather than a spongy one, reserve $\frac{1}{4}$ cup of the sugar to beat slowly into the stiff egg whites before folding them into the egg yolk mixture.

LEMON SPONGE CUSTARD

6 servings

Please read About Sponge Custards, above. Preheat the oven to 325°F. Lightly butter a 9 x 2-inch round cake pan or six 6-ounce custard cups or ramekins.

Combine in a medium bowl and mash together with the back of a wooden spoon:

$\frac{2}{3}$ **cup sugar**
2 tablespoons unsalted butter, softened
$\frac{1}{8}$ **teaspoon salt**

Beat in:

3 large egg yolks

Add and mix until smooth:

3 tablespoons all-purpose flour

Gradually beat in:

2 to 3 teaspoons grated lemon zest
$\frac{1}{4}$ **cup strained fresh lemon juice**

Stir in:

1 cup whole milk

Beat in a large bowl on medium-high speed until stiff but not dry:

4 large egg whites, at room temperature

Gently whisk the whites into the milk mixture, blending just until no large lumps of whites remain. Ladle (do not pour) the batter into the prepared pan or cups; it may reach the top. Bake in a water bath, 801, until the tops are puffed and golden brown and spring back when pressed lightly with a finger, 30 to 40 minutes for both small and large custards. Let stand for 10 minutes in the water bath. Serve warm, at room temperature, or chilled, in the mold(s) or turned out. If you wish, accompany with:

Fresh Raspberry Sauce, 853, or Whipped Cream, 754

ORANGE SPONGE CUSTARD

Prepare **Lemon Sponge Custard, 805,** substituting **the grated zest of 1 orange** for the lemon zest. Reduce the lemon juice to 2 tablespoons, and add ¼ **cup strained fresh orange juice.**

ZABAGLIONE

4 servings

Zabaglione is an Italian dessert made by ➤ whisking egg yolks, sugar, and Marsala in a double boiler over hot water until the mixture thickens into a foamy cream that is served as soon as it is made. *Sabayon* is the French name for zabaglione and a term that designates a range of desserts and sauces, both savory and sweet. Success hinges on heating these mixtures slowly to a temperature of 160°F. If warmed too quickly, the foam will not thicken properly or acquire maximum volume. If overheated, it will become heavy and sticky and eventually curdle. Heating is best done in a double boiler. If your double boiler is wider than 6 inches, be sure to use very gentle heat, as the mixture will be spread thin and thus be especially prone to overcooking.

Madeira and sherry or dry white wine and a little Cointreau can be used in place of the Marsala. For sweet sabayon sauces, see 847.

Combine in the top of a double boiler, off the heat:

> **4 large egg yolks**
> ¼ **cup sugar**

Whisk vigorously until thick and pale yellow. Whisking constantly, gradually add:

> ½ **cup dry Marsala**

Scrape the sides of the double boiler clean with a rubber spatula, then set ➤ over, not in, very gently simmering water. Whisking constantly, heat the zabaglione to 160°F (insert an instant-read thermometer in the center, off the heat), by which point it will have increased several times in volume and become thick enough to mound very softly on a spoon. The cooking should take 5 to 10 minutes. If the zabaglione appears to be heating too quickly, periodically remove it from the water and whisk vigorously to cool. For a lighter zabaglione, beat until stiff peaks form:

> **4 large egg whites**

and fold into the warm custard. Spoon into cups or stemmed glasses and serve immediately.

ABOUT CORNSTARCH PUDDINGS

To most, pudding means a creamy thick dessert in one of three flavors: vanilla, butterscotch, or chocolate. This beloved treat is made by cooking milk, sugar, cornstarch, and sometimes eggs together until thickened into a smooth, satiny cream. It is as simple as it is delicious, and enduringly memorable.

To avoid lumping and scorching, the two most common problems, prepare cornstarch puddings in a heavy-bottomed saucepan, which will provide gentle, even heat. The best stirring implement is a large, heatproof rubber or silicone spatula, which easily reaches the bottom, sides, and corners of the saucepan; the next best alternative is a wooden spoon or a long narrow whisk. In mixing the pudding, be sure to first dissolve the cornstarch thoroughly in a small amount of the liquid, forming a lump-free runny paste, before adding the remaining liquid. Cooking is carried out in two distinct phases: first over medium-high heat and then over low. During the higher-heat phase, stir the pudding in slow, sweeping circles, keeping the bottom, sides, and corners of the saucepan scraped clean so that hot pudding from the outer part of the pan is constantly swept into the cooler center. When the pudding begins to thicken, immediately turn the heat down as low as possible—if using an electric stove, slide the pan off the heat briefly to allow the burner to cool—and begin stirring the pudding in quick little circles, rotating the spatula, spoon, or whisk all around the pan. The pudding may look a little lumpy at this point, but if you stir fast enough, the lumps will soon smooth out. Bring the pudding to a sputtering simmer and then, still stirring, let it simmer for 1 full minute to cook the starch completely. Pour the pudding into a bowl or cups at once before it has a chance to congeal.

Pudding can be served from a single large dish or in individual cups. To prevent a skin from forming, press a piece of plastic wrap directly onto the surface of the warm pudding before chilling. If you wish to serve the pudding unmolded, ➤ use individual cups rather than a large mold, since pudding is rather soft and could split or warp when turned out if formed in a large size. If making unmolded puddings, first coat the cups with vegetable oil spray or wipe them with a paper towel dipped in a mild vegetable oil. Spoon in the pudding, then chill for at least 4 hours. To unmold, invert each pudding over a plate and let it drop out. For a special presentation, individual puddings may be encased in ladyfingers or cake and unmolded as for charlottes; see 814.

Finally, many of our readers have wondered why, on occasion, their puddings, after having thickened properly in the saucepan, suddenly thin out. This dismaying mystery has to do with the nature of cornstarch bonds, which are surprisingly fragile, especially once the pudding has begun to cool. If the bonds break, your pudding turns to soup. To avoid this, ➤ do not beat, blend, or strain the pudding once you have taken it off the stove, even if it has lumped and ➤ if using eggs, be sure to bring your mixture to a boil and heat thoroughly after adding the eggs to prevent an enzyme in the eggs from breaking the cornstarch bonds. Just pour it quickly, before it has a chance to cool and stiffen, into the serving dish and let it set undisturbed. And midnight snackers be warned: If you help yourself to a few spoonfuls of pudding from a fully set mold and then try to smooth the spot over, the pudding will betray your deed by liquefying.

VANILLA PUDDING
4 servings

Have ready a 3-cup bowl or four 5- to 6-ounce cups or ramekins. If unmolding the pudding, oil the small molds. Mix thoroughly in a medium heavy saucepan:

   $^1/_4$ **cup sugar**
   3 tablespoons cornstarch
   $^1/_8$ **teaspoon salt**

Gradually stir in, making a smooth, runny paste:

   $^1/_4$ **cup milk**

Whisk in:

   $1^3/_4$ **cups milk**

Stirring constantly, heat over medium heat until the mixture just comes to the simmer. Remove from the heat and stir $^1/_2$ cup of the milk mixture slowly into:

   1 large egg, well beaten

Stir this back into the milk mixture, bring to a boil over medium heat, and continue to cook for 1 minute, stirring constantly. Remove from the heat. Stir in:

   $^1/_2$ **teaspoon vanilla**

Pour the pudding into the bowl or cups, then press plastic wrap directly onto the surface. Refrigerate for at least 2 hours, 4 hours if unmolding, or up to 2 days.

BUTTERSCOTCH PUDDING
4 servings

Have ready a 3-cup bowl or mold or four 5- to 6-ounce cups or ramekins. If unmolding the pudding, oil the small molds.

Melt in a small heavy saucepan over low heat:

   3 tablespoons unsalted butter

Stir in:

   $^1/_3$ **cup packed dark brown sugar**

Cook, stirring, until melted and bubbly. Gradually stir in:

   $^1/_2$ **cup heavy cream**

Stir over low heat until the butterscotch is dissolved. Add and stir until blended:

   $1^1/_4$ **cups whole milk**
   $^1/_8$ **teaspoon salt**

Remove from the heat. Mix until smooth:

   3 tablespoons cornstarch
   $^1/_4$ **cup milk**

Stir slowly into the milk mixture. Cook, stirring constantly, over medium-high heat until the mixture just comes to a simmer. Reduce the heat to low; stirring briskly, bring to a simmer and cook for 1 minute. Remove from the heat, and stir in:

   1 teaspoon vanilla

Finish and store as for Vanilla Pudding, above.

OLD-FASHIONED CHOCOLATE PUDDING
4 servings

Have ready a 3-cup bowl or mold or four 5- to 6-ounce cups or ramekins. If unmolding the pudding, oil the small molds.

Combine in a medium heavy saucepan:

   $1^3/_4$ **cups milk**
   $^1/_2$ **cup sugar**
   2 ounces unsweetened chocolate, chopped
   $^1/_8$ **teaspoon salt**

Heat over medium-low heat, stirring occasionally, until the chocolate is melted. Mix together until smooth:

   3 tablespoons cornstarch
   $^1/_4$ **cup milk**

Stir slowly into the hot milk mixture. Stirring constantly, heat over medium heat until the mixture just comes to a simmer. Reduce the heat to low, stirring briskly, bring to a simmer, and continue to cook for 1 minute. Remove from the heat, and stir in:

   1 teaspoon vanilla

Finish and store as for Vanilla Pudding, above.

BANANA PUDDING
8 to 10 servings

Mix together thoroughly in a medium heavy saucepan:

   $^2/_3$ **cup sugar**
   3 tablespoons cornstarch
   $^1/_8$ **teaspoon salt**

Gradually stir in, making sure to dissolve the cornstarch:

   3 cups whole milk

Whisk in thoroughly:

   3 or 4 large egg yolks

Add:

   2 to 3 tablespoons unsalted butter, cut into pieces

Stirring constantly, heat over medium heat until the mixture just comes to a simmer. Reduce the heat to low; stirring briskly, bring to a simmer and cook for 2 minutes. Remove from the heat, and stir in:

   $1^1/_2$ **teaspoons vanilla**

Press plastic wrap directly onto the surface of the pudding and set aside. Have ready:

   60 to 70 vanilla wafers

Peel and slice $^1/_4$ inch thick:

   4 to 5 ripe, firm large bananas

Line the bottom and sides of a 2- to $2^1/_2$-quart dish with the wafers. Cover with half the pudding and bananas. Arrange a layer of wafers over the top, then cover with the remaining pudding and bananas. Spoon pudding over any exposed bananas to prevent browning. Press plastic wrap directly onto the surface of the pudding and refrigerate for at least 4 hours. Just before serving, cover with:

   Whipped Cream, 754

BANANA PUDDING WITH MERINGUE

Have $^1/_2$ **recipe Soft Meringue Topping I or II, 740,** and $^1/_4$ **to** $^1/_2$ **cup finely crushed vanilla wafers** ready before cooking **Banana Pudding, above.** Preheat the oven to 425°F. Form the pudding layers as quickly as possible, using a heat-proof dish. Scatter a thin, even layer of the crushed cookies over the hot pudding. Spread the meringue topping over the hot pudding, being sure it adheres to the cookies lining the sides of the dish. Brown the meringue in the oven for 5 minutes. Let cool to room temperature, then refrigerate for at least 2 hours, or up to 24 hours. The longer the pudding is chilled, the softer the cookies become.

COCONUT MILK PUDDING (TREMBLÈQUE)

8 servings

A creamy coconut pudding that "trembles" when turned out of the mold.

Grease a 1½-quart soufflé dish or mold. Combine in a heavy saucepan:

4½ cups canned unsweetened coconut milk
½ cup sugar
¼ teaspoon salt

Heat over medium-low heat, stirring, until the sugar is dissolved.

Mix together until smooth:

½ cup canned unsweetened coconut milk
½ cup cornstarch

Stir slowly into the hot coconut milk mixture. Stirring constantly, heat over medium heat until the mixture just comes to a simmer. Reduce the heat to low and continue to cook for 1 minute, stirring constantly. Pour the pudding into the prepared dish, then press plastic wrap directly onto the surface. Refrigerate for at least 12 hours.

Invert onto a plate and unmold. Garnish with:

Cut-up fresh tropical fruits (such as pineapple, papaya, and mango)
A fresh fruit sauce, 853

FRIED CREAM (CRÈME FRITE)

Sixteen 1-inch squares

Please ➤ read about Deep-Fat Frying, 1046.

Butter an 8 x 2-inch square baking pan. Place in a saucepan:

2 cups milk
(½ vanilla bean, split lengthwise in half)
(1 cinnamon stick)

Bring to a boil, then remove from the heat. Beat well in a medium bowl:

3 large egg yolks

Beat in:

¼ cup sugar
¼ cup cornstarch
1 tablespoon all-purpose flour
⅛ teaspoon salt

Remove the vanilla bean, if using, from the milk and scrape the seeds into the milk. Discard the bean (and cinnamon stick). Gradually stir about ½ cup of the milk into the egg yolk mixture, then return this mixture to the saucepan. Stir in:

1 tablespoon unsalted butter, softened

Return the pan to the heat, bring to a boil, and boil 30 seconds; it will be very thick. If you did not use the vanilla bean and cinnamon stick, stir in:

1 teaspoon vanilla
¼ teaspoon ground cinnamon

Pour the cream into the prepared pan. Chill for at least 8 hours, or overnight.

Cut the cream into 1-inch squares. Beat in a shallow bowl:

3 large eggs

Spread on a plate:

Fine dried cake, gingerbread, or bread crumbs

Dip the pieces of cream in the crumbs, then in eggs, and again in the crumbs. Fry in deep fat heated to 370°F until golden brown. Drain on paper towels and roll in:

(Vanilla sugar, 1019, made with confectioners' sugar)

Serve at once, sprinkled with:

Rum

Or serve with:

A fruit sauce, 853, maple syrup, or fresh fruit

ABOUT DESSERT SOUFFLÉS

If you have never made a soufflé, ➤ please read About Soufflés, 203. Soufflés have a reputation for difficulty, but it's undeserved—they are actually quite easy to prepare. Like their savory counterparts, dessert soufflés are made by folding stiffly beaten egg whites into a thick, flavorful base. In traditional recipes, this base is a pastry cream, but in more contemporary recipes, the base may be nuts, a fruit puree, or even simply fruit juice mixed with egg yolks and sugar. For fruit and nut soufflés, the proper beating of the egg whites and the right baking temperatures are especially important. If the egg whites are under- or overbeaten or the baking heat is too high, the soufflé will have the look and texture of old leather. If mixed and baked with care, though, these ingredients result in a delicacy and strength that remind us of dandelion seed puffs just before they blow.

To prepare a mold for a sweet soufflé: Brush the mold with a thick coat of softened, not melted, butter, then sprinkle generously with sugar. Tilt the mold in all directions to spread the sugar evenly, then invert the mold and tap out the excess sugar. When prepared in a properly coated mold, a soufflé will rise tall, straight, and even and, even better, it will emerge from the oven with a delightfully crunchy, lightly caramelized crust.

A well-cooked soufflé should be firmly set but still moist and creamy in the center, not dry. At the minimum estimated baking time, open the oven door slightly and peek in. If the soufflé has risen about 2½ inches and is deep golden brown on top, you can assume that it has set firm enough not to fall when tested. First, touch the top of the soufflé lightly with your hand. If it feels firm, the soufflé may well be cooked through. To be sure, insert a thin skewer at a 45-degree angle through the side of the soufflé into the center. Remove the soufflé when the skewer comes out dry, or, if you prefer a creamy center, just slightly moist with a bit of thick batter adhering. If it comes out wet, the soufflé needs to be baked longer. A baked soufflé will stay fully risen for at least a minute or two, giving you plenty of time to rush it to the table.

If desired, after bringing the soufflé to the table, open a slit in the top of the soufflé with 2 forks held back to back and pour in custard sauce. Or, if serving individual soufflés, slit open and tuck a chocolate truffle into each.

To glaze a soufflé, dust it with confectioners' sugar 2 or 3 minutes before it is done. The soufflé should have ➤ doubled in height and be firm before the sugar is applied. Watch it closely with the oven door partially open. The glaze will remain fairly shiny when the soufflé is served.

Pay careful attention to the size of the dish called for, as this affects the lightness and volume of the result. A 1½-quart or 7-inch dish should serve 3 to 4, a 9-inch or 2-quart dish, 6 to 8.

Cold dessert soufflés are based on gelatin mousses or Bavarians, see 814.

VANILLA SOUFFLÉ

6 to 8 servings

You may use 2 vanilla beans in place of the vanilla extract. Split them lengthwise and scrape the seeds into the hot cream and sugar, add the beans, and let stand, covered, for 30 minutes. Remove the beans, return to a boil, and continue with the recipe as directed.

Prepare a 9-inch or 2-quart soufflé mold. ➤ Please read About Dessert Soufflés, 808. ➤ Position a rack in the lower third of the oven. Preheat the oven to 375°F.

Melt in a medium saucepan over medium heat:

3 tablespoons unsalted butter

Whisk in until smooth:

2 tablespoons all-purpose flour

Cook, stirring, for 1 minute. Remove from the heat and stir in:

1 cup heavy cream
⅓ cup sugar

Bring to a boil, whisking constantly, and remove from the heat. Whisk in a large bowl until well blended:

4 large egg yolks

Very gradually whisk in the cream mixture, then stir in:

5 teaspoons vanilla

Beat in another large bowl on medium speed until foamy:

5 large egg whites, at room temperature

Add and beat until soft peaks form:

½ teaspoon cream of tartar
⅛ teaspoon salt

Increase the speed to high and beat until the peaks are stiff but not dry. Using a large rubber spatula, gently stir one-quarter of the egg whites into the egg yolk mixture, then fold in the remaining whites. Turn the batter into the prepared soufflé mold and smooth the top.

Bake until the soufflé is well risen and the top is deep golden brown, 25 to 30 minutes. Serve at once with:

Any custard, 845–846, sabayon, 847, or hot butter-and-egg sauce, 852

GRAND MARNIER SOUFFLÉ

Prepare **Vanilla Soufflé, above,** adding the **grated zest of 1 large orange** to the cream and sugar before bringing to a boil. Replace the vanilla with **3 tablespoons Grand Marnier.** Serve with **Orange Liqueur Sauce, 852, or Custard Sauce, 846.**

CHOCOLATE SOUFFLÉ

3 to 4 servings

Unlike most chocolate soufflés, this is made without milk or starch. It is light yet moist, with an exceptional chocolate taste.

Position a rack in the lower third of the oven. Preheat the oven to 375°F. Prepare a 7-inch or 1½-quart soufflé mold. Please read About Dessert Soufflés, 808.

Combine in a heatproof bowl:

6 ounces semisweet or bittersweet chocolate, chopped
6 tablespoons (¾ stick) unsalted butter
2 tablespoons rum, coffee, or water

Set the bowl in a skillet of ➤ hot, but not simmering, water and stir until the mixture is smooth. Let cool for 10 minutes, then whisk in:

3 large egg yolks

Beat in a large bowl on medium speed until foamy:

4 large egg whites, at room temperature

Add and beat on high speed until soft peaks form:

¼ teaspoon cream of tartar

Gradually beat in:

¼ cup sugar

Beat until the peaks are stiff but not dry. Using a large rubber spatula, stir one-third of the egg whites into the chocolate mixture, then fold in the remaining whites. Pour the batter into the prepared soufflé mold and smooth the top. (The soufflé can be set aside at room temperature, covered with an inverted bowl, for up to 1 hour; or cover with plastic wrap and refrigerate for up to 24 hours before baking.)

Bake until the soufflé is risen and set, 25 to 30 minutes. Serve at once.

LEMON SOUFFLÉ

6 to 8 servings

Position a rack in the lower ➤ third of the oven. Preheat the oven to 375°F. Prepare a 9-inch or 2-quart soufflé mold. Please ➤ read About Dessert Soufflés, 808.

Melt in a medium saucepan over medium heat:

3 tablespoons unsalted butter

Whisk in until smooth:

¼ cup all-purpose flour

Cook, stirring, for 1 minute. Remove from the heat and stir in:

1 cup half-and-half or ½ cup whole milk and ½ cup heavy cream
½ cup sugar
Grated zest of 2 lemons

Bring just to a boil, whisking constantly, and remove from the heat. Whisk in a large bowl until slightly thickened:

5 large egg yolks

Very gradually whisk in the cream mixture, then stir in:

1/3 cup strained fresh lemon juice

Beat in another large bowl on medium speed until foamy:

6 large egg whites, at room temperature

Add and beat until soft peaks form:

1/2 teaspoon cream of tartar

1/8 teaspoon salt

Increase the speed to high and beat until the peaks are stiff but not dry. Using a large rubber spatula, gently stir one-quarter of the egg whites into the egg yolk mixture, then fold in the remaining whites. Turn the batter into the prepared soufflé mold and smooth the top.

Bake until the soufflé is well risen and the top is deep golden brown, 25 to 30 minutes. Serve at once with:

Rich Hot Lemon Sauce, 844, or Lemon Sabayon, 847

FRESH FRUIT SOUFFLÉ

3 to 4 servings

Position a rack in the lower third of the oven. Preheat the oven to 375°F. Prepare a 7-inch or 1 1/2-quart soufflé mold. Please ➤ read About Dessert Soufflés, 808.

Place in a large bowl:

1 1/2 cups mashed ripe fruit: peeled apricots, peeled nectarines, peeled peaches or plums, raspberries, or strawberries

Add:

4 large egg yolks, beaten

4 to 6 tablespoons sugar

1 to 2 tablespoons fresh lemon juice

1 tablespoon grated orange zest

1/8 teaspoon salt

Beat until stiff but not dry:

4 large egg whites

Stir about one-quarter of the whites into the fruit mixture, then fold in the remaining whites. Turn the batter into the prepared soufflé mold and smooth the top.

Bake until the soufflé is well risen and the top is deep golden brown, 25 to 30 minutes. Serve at once with:

Heavy cream

SOUR CREAM APPLE CAKE SOUFFLÉ COCKAIGNE

8 servings

The specialty of my great-grandmother who came from Lübeck, Germany.

Peel, core, and thinly slice:

4 apples

Melt in a large heavy skillet:

4 tablespoons (1/2 stick) unsalted butter

Add the apples and cook over medium heat, stirring often, until tender, about 5 minutes; do not let them brown. Reduce the heat to low. Combine and pour over the apples:

8 large egg yolks, beaten

1 cup sugar, or more if the apples are very tart

1/2 cup sour cream

(1/2 cup sliced blanched almonds)

2 tablespoons all-purpose flour

Grated zest and juice of 1 lemon

Stir until thickened. Remove to a large bowl and cool. Preheat the oven to 325°F. Grease a 9 x 13-inch baking dish. Whip in a large bowl until stiff but not dry:

8 large egg whites

Gently fold into the apple mixture. Spread in the prepared dish. Combine and sprinkle over the top:

2 tablespoons dry bread crumbs

2 tablespoons slivered almonds

2 tablespoons sugar

1 1/2 teaspoons ground cinnamon

Bake until the top is a deep golden brown and springs back when pressed, about 45 minutes. The cake may be served hot, but it is best very cold, covered with:

Whipped Cream, 754, flavored with vanilla

ABOUT GELATIN DESSERTS

These desserts vary greatly in texture. Easiest to prepare are the clear gelatins, to which you may add fruit and nuts. If you add pureed fruits, you lose clarity at once, and the dessert bears some similarity to a mousse, 814. When gelatins are allowed to set partially and are then beaten or combined with beaten egg whites or cream, they are known as **whips, sponges,** or **snows.** ➤ If the gelatin is not sufficiently chilled before whipping or before adding the egg white, it may revert to a clear jelly. We describe in Sponge Custard, 805, a method whereby you can get a jellied effect in the bottom of the mold and a custard on top. ➤ For more detail about working with gelatin, see About Gelatin, 987.

To chill gelatin until it is thick enough to hold other ingredients, refrigerate, stirring frequently and scraping down the sides of the dish, until it is the consistency of unbeaten egg whites and falls from a spoon in sheets. This can take as little as 30 minutes and as long as 1 1/2 hours, depending on the mixture and the temperature of your refrigerator. To thicken the gelatin more quickly, set the bowl in a larger bowl of ice and water and begin to stir at the first sign of congealing. If you inadvertently let the gelatin set, simply melt it over gently simmering water and start again.

Certain fruits, ➤ such as fresh pineapple, kiwi, peaches, figs, mango, and papaya, contain an enzyme that prevents gelatin from setting. These fruits must be cooked first in a sugar syrup until completely tender to make them safe to use in gelatin. Canned pineapple is precooked and does not pose a problem. Marshmallows, nuts, and pieces of fruit are traditional and much-loved additions to gelatin desserts.

A word of caution: ➤ Some of these desserts contain uncooked egg whites. If this is a concern, see About Egg Safety, 980, or prepare instead some of the desserts we describe in which the egg whites are cooked, like meringues, custards, and ice cream.

For very rich gelatin desserts, see Bavarians, 817, and Mousses, 814. Although gelatins without cream or eggs must be refrigerated, ➤ they cannot be frozen. But Bavarians and mousses, with gelatin as a stabilizer, rich in cream and eggs, may be solidified and then stored in the freezer ➤ for no longer than 3 to 4 days. The gelatin in these desserts prevents the formation of coarse crystals and results in a lovely smooth texture.

Almost any bowl that splays outward is suitable for a gelatin dessert mold. Be sure the slanted sides allow the mold to slide out easily when inverted. For straight-sided desserts, use a springform pan. **To prepare a mold for a gelatin dessert,** in most cases, rinse the mold with water and shake out the excess, then pour in the gelatin mixture. Some recipes advise lightly coating the mold with vegetable oil. Gelatin desserts usually become firm within 3 to 4 hours of refrigeration. Small desserts set in simple molds may be unmolded at this point. Gelatin terrines and large gelatins made in tall or intricate molds should be refrigerated for at least 8 hours, and preferably up to 1 day. Gelatin continues to stiffen over a 24-hour period.

To unmold, dip the mold into a sink filled with very hot tap water. Dip metal molds for no longer than a couple of seconds; thick molds of glass or ceramic may need to be dipped for up to 10 seconds before they release. Invert a plate over the top of the mold and then turn both over together. If the dessert is reluctant, tilt the mold up slightly at one side and pry a little part of the top away from the mold with a knife. Quickly withdraw the knife as soon as the dessert begins to descend. Desserts set in ring, heart, or star molds are less likely to end up rumpled if you lightly oil the top—which will become the bottom—before unmolding.

Gelatin desserts are delicious served with custard or fruit sauces, whipped or unwhipped cream, even milk. Pour the sauce over individual servings before serving, or pass a pitcher of the accompaniment at the table.

LEMON GELATIN
4 servings
Pour into a bowl:
   3 tablespoons cold water
Sprinkle over the top:
   1 envelope (2$^1/_4$ teaspoons) unflavored gelatin
Let stand 5 minutes. Add and stir to dissolve the gelatin:
   1$^1/_3$ cups boiling water
Add and stir until dissolved:
   $^3/_4$ to 1 cup sugar
   $^1/_4$ teaspoon salt
Add:
   $^1/_3$ cup fresh lemon juice
Pour the mixture into a wet 3- to 4-cup mold, 803. Refrigerate until set, about 4 hours. If desired, when the mixture is set to the thickness of unbeaten egg whites, stir in:
   (1 teaspoon grated lemon zest)

Unmold and serve with:
   Whipped Cream, 754, or Custard Sauce, 846

ORANGE GELATIN
4 servings
Pour into a bowl:
   3 tablespoons cold water
Sprinkle over the top:
   1 envelope (2$^1/_4$ teaspoons) unflavored gelatin
Let stand 5 minutes. Add and stir to dissolve the gelatin:
   $^1/_3$ cup boiling water
Add and stir until dissolved:
   $^1/_2$ cup sugar
   $^1/_4$ teaspoon salt
Add:
   1$^1/_3$ cups fresh orange juice
   5 tablespoons fresh lemon juice
Pour the mixture into a wet 3- to 4-cup mold, 803. Refrigerate until set, about 4 hours. If desired, when the mixture is set to the thickness of unbeaten egg whites, stir in:
   (1$^1/_2$ teaspoons grated orange zest)
Unmold and serve with:
   Whipped Cream, 754, or Custard Sauce, 846

FRUIT MOLDED INTO LEMON OR ORANGE GELATIN
4 servings
Prepare **Lemon or Orange Gelatin, above.** Chill the gelatin in a bowl until it is the thickness of unbeaten egg whites. Stir in up to 1$^1/_2$ cups total:
   Cooked or raw fruit, well drained
   (Nuts)
   (Marshmallows, cut into quarters)
Fresh pineapple must be cooked before it is added to any gelatin mixture. Pour the mixture into a wet 3- to 4-cup mold, 803. Refrigerate until set, about 4 hours, before serving.

PINEAPPLE GELATIN
8 servings
Note that fresh pineapple must be poached before it is added to any gelatin.
Pour into a bowl:
   1 cup cold water
Sprinkle over the top:
   2 envelopes (4$^1/_2$ tablespoons) unflavored gelatin
Let stand 5 minutes. Add and stir to dissolve the gelatin:
   1$^1/_2$ cups boiling pineapple juice
   1 cup boiling water
Add and stir until dissolved:
   $^3/_4$ cup sugar
   $^1/_8$ teaspoon salt
Chill the gelatin in a bowl until it is the thickness of unbeaten egg whites. Stir in:
   2$^1/_2$ cups drained canned crushed pineapple
   3 tablespoons fresh lemon juice

Pour the mixture into a wet 4-cup mold, 811. Refrigerate until set, about 4 hours. Unmold and serve with:

> Custard Sauce, 846

FRUIT GELATIN
4 servings

Pour into a small bowl:

> 3 tablespoons cold water

Sprinkle over the top:

> 1 envelope (2¼ teaspoons) unflavored gelatin

Let stand 5 minutes.

Meanwhile, bring to a simmer in a medium saucepan:

> 2 cups cranberry, grape, or apple juice
> (1 to 3 tablespoons sugar)

Remove from the heat, add the softened gelatin, and stir 1 minute to dissolve the gelatin thoroughly. Set the bottom of the saucepan in a bowl of cold water and let the gelatin cool to lukewarm.

Prepare:

> 1 to 1½ cups fruit, such as thinly sliced apples, sliced strawberries, or whole blueberries or raspberries

For a dessert with fruit on the top, divide the fruit among wet, 6-ounce bowls or cups, 803, or place it in a wet 4-cup mold, and ladle the gelatin over. If you want the fruit suspended in the dessert, chill the gelatin in a bowl until it is the thickness of unbeaten egg whites. Then stir in the fruit and pour the gelatin into the wet mold(s). Refrigerate until set, about 4 hours.

Unmold and serve with, if desired:

> (Milk or cream)

QUICK FRUIT GELATIN
4 servings

Whisk together in a small bowl until the gelatin is dissolved:

> One 3-ounce package fruit-flavored gelatin
> 1 cup boiling water

Chill rapidly by adding:

> One 6-ounce can frozen fruit juice (not pineapple)

Pour into 4 sherbet glasses. Refrigerate until set, about 4 hours.

RASPBERRY TEA GELATIN
4 to 6 servings

English breakfast tea makes a uniquely refreshing gelatin, welcome on a hot day.

Gently whisk together in a medium bowl until the gelatin is dissolved:

> One 3-ounce package raspberry gelatin
> 2 cups scalding-hot English breakfast tea

Refrigerate until the gelatin is the thickness of unbeaten egg whites, 1 to 1½ hours.

Fold in:

> 1 cup raspberries

Pour the mixture into a wet 4-cup bowl or mold, 803. Refrigerate until set, about 4 hours.

Unmold, or serve from the bowl.

CHERRY MARSHMALLOW NUT GELATIN
4 to 6 servings

Gently whisk together in a medium bowl until the gelatin is dissolved:

> One 3-ounce package cherry or other red gelatin
> 1 cup boiling water

Stir in:

> 1 cup club soda

Refrigerate until the gelatin is the thickness of unbeaten egg whites, 1 to 1½ hours.

Fold in:

> ⅔ cup halved pitted fresh cherries or well-drained and halved canned sweet cherries
> 3 tablespoons chopped unblanched almonds
> ½ cup miniature marshmallows

Pour the mixture into a wet 3- to 4-cup bowl or mold, 803. Refrigerate until set, about 4 hours.

Unmold and serve with, if desired:

> (Whipped Cream, 754)

STAINED GLASS GELATIN
8 to 12 servings

Among the most spectacular of all contemporary gelatin creations. Each serving resembles a pane of stained glass. If you mound this gelatin in a 10-inch crumb crust, 667, you will have a Stained Glass Pie, plus enough extra filling for a separate small mold.

Lightly oil three 8-inch square baking pans. Prepare separately according to the package instructions:

> One 3-ounce package lime gelatin
> One 3-ounce package cherry gelatin
> One 3-ounce package orange gelatin

Pour the gelatins into the pans and refrigerate until firmly set, about 4 hours. Cut the gelatin into ½-inch cubes, then return, still in the pans, to the refrigerator.

Gently whisk together in a large bowl until the gelatin dissolves:

> One 3-ounce package lemon gelatin
> 1 cup boiling water

Stir in:

> ½ cup cold water

Refrigerate until the gelatin is the thickness of unbeaten egg whites.

Grease a 13 x 9-inch baking pan. Beat until stiff peaks form:

> 1 cup cold heavy cream

Fold the cream into the lemon gelatin, then gently fold in the gelatin cubes. Turn at once into the oiled baking pan. Refrigerate until set, about 4 hours.

Serve with, if desired:

> (Whipped Cream, 754)

BLANCMANGE
6 servings

"Blancmange" is simply a fancy name for vanilla cornstarch pudding.

Process in a food processor until tiny moist clumps form, about 3 minutes:

1 cup slivered blanched almonds

$^1/_4$ cup sugar

With the machine running, slowly add:

1$^1/_4$ cups boiling water

Scrape down the sides of the bowl and process for 30 seconds longer. Let steep for 3 minutes. Set a sieve over a bowl, line the sieve with dampened cheesecloth, and pour in the almond mixture. Let the almond milk drip through for 45 minutes. Use a spoon to press as much of the liquid out of the almonds as you can before discarding the solids. Pour the almond milk into a large measure and add enough to make exactly 1$^3/_4$ cups liquid:

About $^3/_4$ cup whole milk

Pour into a bowl. Stir together in a small heatproof cup:

$^1/_4$ cup heavy cream

1 envelope (2$^1/_4$ teaspoons) unflavored gelatin

Let stand for 5 minutes to soften. Meanwhile, lightly oil six 4- to 6-ounce custard cups or ramekins. Set the cup with the gelatin in a skillet of barely simmering water and stir gently over low heat until the mixture is thick and foamy, and the gelatin has dissolved, about 3 minutes. Thoroughly stir the gelatin mixture into the almond milk. Stir in:

$^1/_2$ teaspoon almond extract

(4 drops rose water)

Divide the blancmange among the prepared cups. Refrigerate until set, about 4 hours. If not serving at once, press plastic wrap directly onto the surface and refrigerate for up to 3 days. Unmold onto plates and serve with:

Fresh raspberries and/or sliced peaches

PANNA COTTA

6 servings

Like blancmange, Italian panna cotta, or cooked cream, is a rich but light, smooth gelatin cream. Mold panna cotta in small ramekins or custard cups, then serve it turned out with a fruit sauce, fresh fruit, or both.

Lightly oil six 4- to 6-ounce custard cups or ramekins. Pour into a small bowl:

3 tablespoons cold water

Sprinkle over the top:

1 envelope (2$^1/_4$ teaspoons) unflavored gelatin

Let stand for 5 minutes to soften. Meanwhile, combine in a saucepan:

1$^1/_2$ cups heavy cream

1 cup whole milk or buttermilk

$^1/_2$ cup sugar

(1 vanilla bean, split lengthwise)

Bring to a boil, stirring, over medium-high heat. Remove from the heat and remove the vanilla bean, if using. Add softened gelatin and stir for 1 minute until completely dissolved. Stir in:

1 teaspoon vanilla, if not using vanilla bean

($^1/_2$ teaspoon almond extract)

Pour into the prepared cups and refrigerate until firmly set, about 4 hours. If not serving at once, press plastic wrap directly onto the surface of each cream and refrigerate for up to 3 days.

Unmold onto plates and serve with:

Kumquat Compote, 225, or sliced fresh fruit and/or fruit sauce, 853

MOLDED CUSTARD

8 servings

This creamy, vanilla-flavored gelatin dessert is also known as **Spanish Cream** or Persian Cream.

Oil a 4- to 5-cup mold or bowl or eight 4-ounce ramekins. Pour into a heavy saucepan:

3 cups milk

Sprinkle over it:

1 envelope (2$^1/_4$ teaspoons) unflavored gelatin

$^1/_2$ cup sugar

Let stand 5 minutes, then place over low heat and stir until the milk is hot and the sugar and gelatin are dissolved. Beat in a medium bowl:

3 large egg yolks

$^1/_4$ teaspoon salt

Slowly whisk in the hot milk mixture. Return this mixture to the saucepan over low heat. Using a heatproof rubber spatula or a wooden spoon, ➤ stir gently but constantly, sweeping the entire pan bottom and reaching into the corners. As soon as the mixture is thickened enough to coat the back of a spoon, remove from the heat. Add:

1 teaspoon vanilla

If you want a molded custard all of one texture, add to the hot gelatin mixture:

3 large egg whites, stiffly beaten

If you prefer a clear jellied base with an opaque layer at the top of the mold, cool the gelatin mixture slightly before adding the whites. In either case, turn the mixture into the prepared mold(s). Chill until set, about 6 hours.

Unmold and serve with:

Sliced fresh fruit or fruit sauce, 853

Nuts or coconut, toasted, 1001

FRUIT WHIP

8 servings

Fruit whips look as good as they taste—light and airy, with a pretty swirl of color. Oranges, raspberries, peaches, strawberries, apricots, prunes, etc.—raw, cooked, or canned, crushed or pureed in a food processor or blender—may be used alone or in combination. Fresh pineapple must be cooked before being added to any gelatin mixture.

Stir together:

$^3/_4$ cup plus 2 tablespoons sugar

1 teaspoon grated lemon zest

Pour into a bowl:

$^1/_4$ cup cold water

Sprinkle over the top, using the larger amount if the fruit is very juicy:

1 tablespoon unflavored gelatin

Let stand 5 minutes, then stir in until the gelatin is dissolved:

$1/4$ cup boiling water

Stir in the sugar mixture until dissolved. Add:

1 cup crushed or pureed fruit

3 tablespoons fresh lemon juice

Place the bowl in a larger bowl of ice water and chill until the gelatin is the thickness of unbeaten egg whites. Whip or beat the mixture until frothy. Whip until stiff peaks form:

4 large egg whites

Whip the egg whites into the gelatin mixture until the mixture holds its shape.

Pour into a wet 1-quart mold, 803. Refrigerate until set, about 4 hours.

Serve with:

Cream or Custard Sauce, 846

PINEAPPLE SNOW

8 servings

Pour into a bowl:

$1/4$ cup cold water

Sprinkle over the top:

1 envelope ($2^1/4$ teaspoons) unflavored gelatin

Meanwhile, combine in a saucepan and bring to a boil, stirring to dissolve the sugar:

One 20-ounce can crushed pineapple or

2 cups cooked fresh pineapple

1 cup sugar

$1/8$ teaspoon salt

Add the softened gelatin, remove from the heat, and stir until the gelatin is dissolved. Pour into a bowl and refrigerate until the gelatin is the thickness of unbeaten egg whites.

Whip to stiff peaks in a large bowl:

1 cup cold heavy cream

Add:

$1/2$ teaspoon vanilla

Fold in the pineapple mixture. Pour the mixture into a wet 5-cup mold, 803. Refrigerate until set, about 4 hours. Unmold and garnish with:

(Coconut, toasted, 1001, and mandarin oranges) or

(Pistachio nuts and maraschino cherries)

SNOW PUDDING

6 servings

An ideal summer dessert.

Pour into a medium bowl:

$1/4$ cup cold water

Sprinkle over the top:

1 envelope ($2^1/4$ teaspoons) unflavored gelatin

Let stand 5 minutes. Add and stir to dissolve the gelatin:

1 cup boiling water

Add and stir until the sugar is dissolved:

$1/2$ cup sugar

1 teaspoon finely grated lemon zest

$1/3$ cup fresh lemon juice

Refrigerate until the gelatin is the thickness of unbeaten egg whites.

Whip to stiff peaks in a large bowl:

3 large egg whites

$1/8$ teaspoon salt

While beating, pour in the gelatin mixture. Continue to beat until well blended. Pour the pudding into a serving bowl. Refrigerate until set, about 4 hours.

Serve with:

Boiled Custard, 802, a fruit sauce, 853,

or fresh fruit

ABOUT MOUSSES, BAVARIAN CREAMS, AND CHARLOTTES

These are all soft, light, airy desserts made with beaten egg whites or whipped cream. **Mousse** means froth or foam in French. Any dessert or savory dish that has a frothy or foamy texture may be dubbed a mousse. Mousse made with gelatin is firm enough to be unmolded.

A **Bavarian cream** is a specific kind of mousse composed of two elements: a gelatin-thickened custard, which gives the dessert its firmness and stability, and whipped cream and, sometimes, beaten egg whites, which make the dessert light in texture. When set in a towering, crenulated mold and turned out onto a polished silver tray, a Bavarian makes a spectacular finale for a formal dinner party.

A **charlotte** consists of a mousse corseted in ladyfingers or slices of cake or jelly roll and served unmolded. The filling can be any mousse or pudding, but the best choices are those that are very firm, such as Bavarians and others made with gelatin. It is important to distinguish between this type of charlotte and another: a stiff fruit puree, typically apple, encased in buttered bread strips and baked.

Classically only a mousse is served in a dish, but we have long presented Bavarians and charlottes in dishes as well. A single large dessert is shown to best advantage in a cut-glass bowl, or it can be spooned into chocolate cups, 830, for a luxurious effect; sherbet glasses, wine goblets, and champagne flutes make especially pretty dessert presentations.

A "cold soufflé" is in fact simply a mousse—most often a Bavarian cream—molded in such a way that it rises above the rim of the serving dish and so resembles a baked soufflé. Choose either a single large soufflé dish or individual ramekins with a total capacity about one-third less than the volume of the dessert. Fold a sheet of wax or parchment paper lengthwise in half (or, for small dishes, into quarters), then wrap it around the dish and fasten securely in place with kitchen string, a rubber band, or tape, making a collar. Oil the inside of the collar, then fill the mold at least 1 inch above the rim. At serving time, unfas-

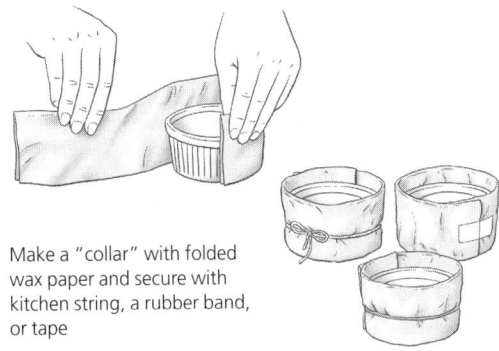

Make a "collar" with folded wax paper and secure with kitchen string, a rubber band, or tape

ten and carefully peel off the collar, thereby creating a cap like that of a true soufflé.

When unmolded, mousses and Bavarians are a thrilling sight on the table. For a large dessert, use a soufflé dish, loaf pan, mixing bowl, charlotte mold or a ring, heart, star, or other mold. One of the favorite shapes for Bavarians is a melon mold. Coat the mold with neutral vegetable oil or cooking spray or rinse with cold water before filling. Refrigerate individual desserts for 3 to 4 hours and large desserts for at least 4 hours, but preferably 12 to 24 hours if formed in high, narrow, or complex molds. To unmold, see About Gelatin Desserts, 810. Or see About Preparing Dessert Molds, below, for preparing and unmolding a charlotte.

All of these are delicious served with custard or fruit sauces or with whipped cream. You may pass a sauce separately at the table to allow diners to serve themselves. Or, for a dressier presentation, unmold the desserts onto individual plates and pour a sauce around the base of each.

PREPARING CHARLOTTE OR DESSERT MOLDS

For the classic charlotte consisting of mousse encased in ladyfingers or cake or for any dessert, you will need a mold with a flat bottom and straight or only slightly sloping sides. The traditional charlotte mold is shaped like a fez and has little heart-shaped handles. Charlotte molds come in a variety of sizes. For most of our recipes, you will need one that measures about 7 inches across the top when unmolded and has a capacity of 2 to 2$^1/_2$ quarts. Our charlottes can also be prepared in 9 x 5-inch loaf pans, 2- to 2$^1/_2$-quart soufflé dishes, 8-inch square baking pans, 9 x 2-inch round cake pans, or 8 x 3-inch springform pans.

The simplest cake linings are made with thin sheets of Génoise, 709, Biscuit, 708, or Sponge Sheet II, 735. Arrange long strips of cake along the inside of the mold and line the bottom with a single large piece cut to fit. You may also use filled jelly-roll slices, 735, or macaroons, 771. The most common lining is ladyfingers: Depending on your mold and on how you choose to line it, you will need 18 to 36 moist, pliable 3- to 4-inch ladyfingers, either homemade, 740, or good-quality store-bought. Do not use the hard, dry, crunchy ladyfingers often used for tiramisù; they are difficult to trim without crumbling.

To prepare the mold, lightly oil the interior, line the bottom with wax or parchment paper, and oil the paper as well. Snugly line the sides with ladyfingers or cake, standing the ladyfingers on end, with their curved sides against the mold. For a shallow mold, cut the ladyfingers in half and arrange them cut ends up. If you make the ladyfingers yourself, pipe them close together (about $^1/_4$ inch apart) on the baking sheet so that they fuse during baking, then simply fit a strip of ladyfingers into the mold. Brush the ladyfingers with simple Moistening Syrup, 759, or the syrup specified in the recipe.

Now you must decide what to do about the bottom of the mold—which is to say, the eventual top of the dessert. If you are using a charlotte mold, soufflé dish, or other deep round mold, the top is prettiest when left bare and adorned after the dessert is turned out with rosettes of whipped cream, each decorated with, for example, a coffee bean, a candied violet, or chocolate shavings. If you are working with a shallow mold, you will probably want the top of the dessert to be covered. For square and rectangular molds, arrange the ladyfingers over the bottom of the mold in rows, trimming as necessary. The traditional design for round molds is a sort of daisy, with a circle in the center and petals all around. To make the petals, trim ladyfingers into teardrop shapes, using kitchen shears or a paring knife. Arrange the petals flat side up, with their pointed ends in toward the center; some of the petals will require further trimming to fit together neatly. When you have filled in the periphery, cut a circle from another ladyfinger and place it in the middle. If you are proficient with a pastry bag, you can pipe ladyfinger batter into a top that will fit your mold exactly. Pipe the batter as a daisy, in coils, or in any other design that appeals to you, see 786.

Lining a charlotte mold with filled jelly roll slices

To unmold a charlotte is quite simple with a charlotte mold. If using a stainless steel or glass bowl 1$^1/_2$ to 2 quarts in volume, dip the bowl into warm water for a few seconds, place a plate over the bowl, and flip both over.

You do not have to cover the top (which will be, after unmolding, the bottom) with ladyfingers, but if you have ladyfingers to spare, it is a good idea to do so: Charlottes that rest on a solid base are more stable and make neater slices than those with unlined bottoms. Trim the ladyfingers as necessary to make a neat fit. Use the leftover scraps from lining the bottom and sides of the mold as well.

Arrange the ladyfingers, flat side up, inside the tops of the ladyfingers lining the sides of the mold. Then trim the side lining flush with the bottom. If you have any Moistening Syrup left over, brush it over the bottom lining.

Charlottes can also be made in individual sizes. Oil eight to ten 8-ounce soufflé ramekins or small charlotte molds and line with wax or parchment paper as above. Line the sides with ladyfingers that have been cut crosswise in half; leave both bottom and top bare.

CHOCOLATE MOUSSE

8 servings

The director of a boys' camp in Maine once told us about the crestfallen faces in the dining room when it turned out that the "moose" promised for evening dessert had emerged from the pages of JOY instead of from the woods.

Heat 1 inch of water in a large skillet over low heat until bubbles form along the bottom; adjust the heat to maintain the water at this temperature. Combine in a large heatproof bowl:

6 ounces semisweet or bittersweet chocolate, chopped

3 tablespoons unsalted butter

2 tablespoons liquor, liqueur, coffee, or water

(1 teaspoon vanilla, if using water)

Set the bowl in the water bath and stir until the chocolate is melted. Remove from the water and set aside. Whisk together thoroughly in another heatproof bowl:

3 large egg yolks

3 tablespoons coffee or water

3 tablespoons sugar

Set the bowl in the water bath and, whisking constantly, heat the mixture until thick and puffy, like marshmallow sauce. Remove from the water bath and whisk thoroughly into the melted chocolate. Let cool to room temperature. Beat in a large bowl until foamy:

3 large egg whites, at room temperature

Add and beat until soft peaks form:

$1/4$ teaspoon cream of tartar

Gradually beat in:

$1/4$ cup sugar

Increase the speed to high and beat until the peaks are stiff but not dry. Using a large rubber spatula, stir one-quarter of the egg whites into the chocolate mixture to lighten it, then gently fold in the remaining whites. Beat in a small bowl until soft peaks form:

$1/2$ cup cold heavy cream

Gently but thoroughly fold the cream into the chocolate mixture. Turn into a 5-cup bowl or eight 6-ounce cups. Refrigerate for at least 4 hours, or up to 24 hours. Serve with:

Whipped Cream, 754

If you wish, sprinkle with:

(1 ounce semisweet or bittersweet chocolate, grated)

CHOCOLATE MOUSSE WITH GELATIN

8 servings

When stiffened with a small amount of gelatin, chocolate mousse can be set in a mold and unmolded or used as a filling for a chocolate charlotte or a mousse cake.

Pour **3 tablespoons cold coffee or water** into a small cup. Sprinkle **$1/2$ teaspoons unflavored gelatin** over the top. Let stand for 5 minutes. Prepare **Chocolate Mousse, above,** substituting the gelatin mixture for the 3 tablespoons plain coffee or water added to the egg yolks. Be sure to fold the whipped whites and cream in very thoroughly. If you want to unmold the mousse, be sure to oil the mold or bowl in which the mousse will set. Refrigerate at least 6 hours.

WHITE CHOCOLATE MOUSSE WITH TOASTED ALMONDS

6 to 8 servings

This mousse is firm enough to be unmolded or used in a charlotte, yet soft and creamy on the tongue.

If you wish to turn out the dessert, lightly oil six to eight 4- to 6-ounce stemmed glasses, ramekins, or bowls or one 2-quart mold.

Chop into $1/8$-inch bits:

$1/3$ cup slivered blanched almonds, toasted, 1001

Chop into the same-sized bits:

1 to 2 ounces white chocolate

Combine with the almonds and set aside. Measure into a small bowl:

3 tablespoons cold water

Sprinkle over the top:

$3/4$ teaspoon unflavored gelatin

Let stand 5 minutes. Very finely chop with a sharp knife or pulverize to a crumblike consistency in a food processor:

8 ounces white chocolate

If chopped, turn the chocolate into a bowl; if processed, leave in the work bowl of the machine. Bring to a rolling boil in a small saucepan:

$1/2$ cup heavy cream

Remove from the heat, add the softened gelatin, and stir for 30 seconds to dissolve the gelatin. Immediately pour this mixture over the chocolate and whisk or process just until smooth. Pour into a bowl if necessary and refrigerate until the gelatin is the consistency of unbeaten egg whites.

Beat until stiff enough to hold a firm shape on a spoon:

1 cup cold heavy cream

Fold the cream into the white chocolate mixture, then gently fold in the almond mixture. Turn into the glasses or mold and refrigerate for 2 hours, or at least 4 hours if unmolding. If you wish, decorate with:

(1 to 2 ounces white chocolate, grated)

and serve with:

(Fresh Raspberry Sauce, 853)

CHOCOLATE TERRINE

12 to 16 servings

Made like a chocolate mousse, this loaf of pure chocolate is cut into slices and served with a sauce. It also makes a delicious and very sturdy charlotte filling. The terrine can be tightly wrapped and frozen for up to 1 month. Let stand at room temperature for 1 hour before slicing and serving.

Lightly oil an 8½ x 4½-inch loaf pan and line with plastic wrap, pressing it firmly into the corners and against the sides. Oil the plastic as well.

Heat 1 inch of water in a large saucepan until simmering. Combine in a large heatproof bowl and stir over, not in, the simmering water until melted and smooth:

> **1 pound bittersweet or semisweet chocolate, chopped**
> **1 cup (2 sticks) unsalted butter, cut into chunks**

Remove from the saucepan and set aside. Whisk together in a large heatproof bowl:

> **8 large egg yolks**
> **¹/₃ cup cooled strong coffee or ¹/₄ cup water plus**
>   **1¹/₂ tablespoons liquor or liqueur**
> **¹/₂ cup sugar**

Set the bowl over the saucepan. Whisking constantly, heat the mixture until thick, puffy, and shiny, like marshmallow sauce, at least 10 minutes. Remove from the water bath and whisk in the chocolate mixture until thoroughly combined. (The mixture will deflate and look something like shiny chocolate mayonnaise.) If there is any sign of separation, whisk in cold water, 1 teaspoon at a time, until the mixture smoothes out.

Beat in a large bowl on medium speed until frothy:

> **4 large egg whites, at room temperature**

Add and beat until soft but definite peaks form:

> **¹/₄ teaspoon cream of tartar**

Gradually sprinkle in:

> **1 tablespoon sugar**

Increase the speed to high and beat until the peaks are stiff but not dry. Using a large rubber spatula, fold the egg whites into the chocolate mixture. Turn the mixture into the prepared pan and cover with plastic wrap. Refrigerate for at least 8 hours.

Remove the plastic from the top, invert the terrine onto a serving plate, and peel off the plastic liner. Cut crosswise into slices and serve with:

> **Coffee Custard Sauce, 846, or Custard Sauce, 846,**
>   **and/or Fresh Raspberry Sauce, 853**

COLD LEMON SOUFFLÉ OR BAVARIAN CREAM

8 servings

This can be used as a charlotte filling.

Please read About Mousses, Bavarian Creams, and Charlottes, 824.

If making a cold soufflé, tie paper collars around eight 6-ounce ramekins or one 1¹/₂-quart soufflé dish. For a Bavarian cream, oil eight 8-ounce custard cups or ramekins or a 2¹/₂-quart charlotte or other mold. Combine in a medium bowl:

> **1 tablespoon grated lemon zest**
> **¹/₂ cup cold strained fresh lemon juice**

Sprinkle over the top:

> **1 envelope (2¹/₄ teaspoons) unflavored gelatin**

Let stand 5 minutes.

Whisk in a large bowl just until combined:

> **5 large egg yolks**
> **¹/₃ cup sugar**

Heat in a medium heavy saucepan:

> **1 cup whole milk**

Gradually whisk the hot milk into the egg yolks, then return this mixture to the saucepan. Cook, gently stirring, over very low heat until the mixture is thickened enough to coat the back of a spoon and reaches 175°F on an instant-read thermometer. Immediately pour the hot custard over the gelatin mixture and stir to completely dissolve the gelatin. Strain into a large bowl; set the bowl in a pan of cool water and stir until the custard is no longer warm and has thickened slightly. Beat in a large bowl on medium speed until soft peaks form:

> **3 large egg whites, at room temperature**

Gradually beat in:

> **¹/₃ cup plus 1 tablespoon sugar**

Increase the speed to high and beat until the peaks are stiff but not dry. If the custard has stiffened, whisk until smooth. Whisk in one-third of the egg whites, then gently fold in the remaining whites.

Beat until soft peaks form:

> **³/₄ cup cold heavy cream**

Gently fold the cream into the egg white mixture. Turn into the prepared mold(s). Refrigerate the soufflé for at least 4 hours or the Bavarians for 8 to 12 hours.

Untie the collar(s) from the soufflé(s) or unmold the Bavarian(s) onto plates. Decorate the soufflé(s) with:

> **Whipped cream**

Or serve with:

> **Whipped Cream, 754, Fresh Raspberry Sauce, 853, or**
>   **Custard Sauce, 846**

COLD ORANGE SOUFFLÉ OR BAVARIAN CREAM

Combine **2 tablespoons grated orange zest** and **1¹/₂ cups strained fresh orange juice** in a small nonreactive saucepan and simmer until reduced to just under ¹/₂ cup.

Let cool completely, then add **1 tablespoon strained fresh lemon juice.** Substitute the orange reduction for the lemon zest and juice, and proceed as directed for **Cold Lemon Soufflé or Bavarian Cream, above.**

COLD LIME SOUFFLÉ OR BAVARIAN CREAM

Prepare **Cold Lemon Soufflé or Bavarian Cream, above,** substituting **1 tablespoon grated lime zest** and ¹/₂ **cup strained fresh lime juice** for the lemon juice and zest. If you wish, add **1 drop green food coloring** when whipping the cream.

CHOCOLATE OR COFFEE BAVARIAN CREAM
8 servings

Without eggs, this and the recipe that follows are not classic but are nevertheless quite good.
Pour into a bowl:

3 tablespoons cold milk

Sprinkle over the top:

1 envelope (2$^{1}/_{4}$ teaspoons) unflavored gelatin

Bring to just under a simmer:

1$^{1}/_{2}$ cups milk or $^{1}/_{2}$ cup milk plus 1 cup heavy cream

Remove from the heat and add, stirring to dissolve the sugar:

4 ounces bittersweet or semisweet chocolate, finely chopped, or 1 tablespoon instant coffee powder
$^{1}/_{4}$ to $^{1}/_{3}$ cup sugar
$^{1}/_{8}$ teaspoon salt

Stir in the gelatin until dissolved. Stir in:

1 teaspoon vanilla
($^{1}/_{4}$ teaspoon almond extract)

Chill until the gelatin is the thickness of unbeaten egg whites.
Whisk the gelatin mixture until fluffy. Beat until stiff peaks form:

1 cup cold heavy cream

Fold the cream into the gelatin mixture. Pour into a wet or lightly oiled 4-cup mold. Or, if desired, alternate the cream in layers (use a 5- to 6-cup mold) with:

(6 crumbled macaroons or ladyfingers, soaked in rum or dry sherry, and $^{1}/_{2}$ cup ground nuts, preferably almonds)

Chill at least 8 hours if you plan to unmold the cream.
Serve with:

Whole or crushed berries or sliced fresh fruit and Whipped Cream, 754

BAVARIAN BERRY CREAM
8 servings

Not a classic Bavarian but more of a firm fool, 210, this makes a delicious summer treat as is, or it can be used in a charlotte.
Crush in a large bowl:

1 quart strawberries, hulled, or raspberries

Add:

$^{1}/_{2}$ cup sugar

Let stand 30 minutes.
Pour into a small bowl:

3 tablespoons cold water

Sprinkle over the top:

2 teaspoons unflavored gelatin

Let stand 5 minutes. Add and stir to dissolve the gelatin:

3 tablespoons boiling water

Stir into the berries. You may add:

(1 tablespoon fresh lemon juice)

Chill the gelatin until it is the thickness of unbeaten egg whites.
Whip until firm peaks form:

1 cup cold heavy cream

Gently fold into the berry mixture. Pour into a lightly oiled or wet 1$^{1}/_{2}$-quart mold. Refrigerate for 8 hours if you plan to unmold the cream.
Serve with:

Strawberry, 853, or fruit sauce, 853

CHARLOTTE RUSSE
8 to 10 servings

True charlotte russe is rich vanilla cream molded in ladyfingers. This dessert is always served with a light fruit sauce.
Line a 2- to 2$^{1}/_{2}$-quart mold as described in Preparing Charlotte or Dessert Molds, 815, with:

18 to 36 ladyfingers, homemade, 740, or store-bought

Stir over low heat until smooth:

$^{1}/_{2}$ cup seedless raspberry jam
3 tablespoons raspberry liqueur or water

Brush the syrup over the ladyfinger lining. The ladyfingers should be thoroughly soaked, but if they threaten to flop over before all the syrup has been used, reserve the remaining syrup for any ladyfingers you will use for the top.
Pour into the top of a double boiler:

3 tablespoons cold water

Sprinkle over the top:

1$^{1}/_{2}$ teaspoons unflavored gelatin

Let stand 5 minutes, then whisk in:

6 large egg yolks
$^{1}/_{2}$ cup sugar

Set the top of the double boiler over, not in, simmering water and, whisking constantly, heat the mixture until thick and puffy, like marshmallow sauce. (If you are concerned about eating uncooked eggs, periodically insert an instant-read thermometer for 15 seconds, off the heat, until the mixture reaches 160°F.) Set the double boiler top in cold water and, whisking now and then, cool to room temperature. Pour into a large bowl and stir in:

2 tablespoons brandy, Cognac, or water
2 teaspoons vanilla

Beat in a large bowl on medium speed until light and fluffy:

4 tablespoons ($^{1}/_{2}$ stick) unsalted butter, softened
$^{1}/_{4}$ cup sugar
$^{1}/_{8}$ teaspoon salt

Beat in the egg yolk mixture by heaping tablespoons.
Beat in a large bowl until stiff peaks form:

1$^{1}/_{2}$ cups cold heavy cream

Using a rubber spatula, stir $^{1}/_{2}$ cup of the cream into the egg yolk mixture, then gently fold in the remaining cream. Turn the mixture into the prepared mold. Cover the top with additional ladyfingers, if you have them, and brush with any remaining syrup. Refrigerate for at least 8 hours, or up to 3 days. Invert the charlotte onto a plate and un-mold, 815. Serve with:

Fresh Raspberry Sauce, 853, or Cherries Jubilee, 826

CHOCOLATE CHARLOTTE

8 servings

Line a 2- to 2¹/₂-quart mold as described in Preparing Charlotte or Dessert Molds, 815, with:

18 to 36 ladyfingers, homemade, 740 or store-bought, Génoise, 709, Biscuit, 708, or Sponge Sheet II, 735

Stir together in a small bowl until the sugar is dissolved:

¹/₄ cup hot water or coffee

2 tablespoons sugar

Let cool to lukewarm. Stir in:

¹/₄ cup liquor, liqueur, or coffee, to flavor the mousse

Or, if the mousse is to be flavored simply with vanilla, double the hot water and sugar above and add:

(1 tablespoon vanilla)

Brush this sugar syrup onto the ladyfinger lining. Prepare:

Chocolate Mousse with Gelatin, 816

If you wish, fold in:

(¹/₂ cup chopped nuts, toasted, 1001)

Fill the lined mold with the mousse. Cover the top with additional ladyfingers, if you have them, then brush with any remaining syrup. Refrigerate for at least 6 hours, or up to 3 days. Invert the charlotte onto a plate and unmold, 815. Serve with:

Whipped Cream, 754, Coffee Custard Sauce, 846, or a chocolate sauce, 847

COFFEE CHARLOTTE

6 servings

Prepare **Chocolate Charlotte, above,** substituting **Coffee Bavarian Cream, 818,** for the chocolate mousse. Serve with **Custard Sauce, 846,** flavored with rum, or **Chocolate Sauce, 847.**

TIRAMISÙ

10 to 12 servings

Tiramisù is Italian for "pick me up"—and how could ladyfingers soaked in espresso and brandy and slathered with sweetened Marsala-laced mascarpone fail to do so? This is best served 1 to 4 hours after it is prepared. Have ready:

24 ladyfingers, homemade, 740, or store-bought, or Génoise, 709, baked in two 8-inch square pans

Preheat the oven to 350°F.

If using the génoise, use only 1¹/₂ layers: Cut the whole layer into 8 strips and the half layer into 4; reserve the remainder for another use. Cut all the strips in half. Arrange the ladyfingers or génoise strips on a baking sheet. Bake until golden brown and crisp, 8 to 10 minutes. Let cool. Meanwhile, beat on high speed in a medium heatproof bowl until thick and pale yellow, about 2 minutes:

5 large egg yolks

¹/₃ cup sugar

Whisk in:

¹/₃ cup sweet Marsala

1 tablespoon water

Set the bowl in a skillet of barely simmering water and whisk or beat on low speed until the mixture reaches 160°F. Remove the bowl from the water and let cool for about 15 minutes.

Combine in a large bowl and beat until soft peaks form:

12 to 14 ounces mascarpone, softened

¹/₂ cup heavy cream

2 teaspoons vanilla

Fold in the cooled egg yolk mixture.

Combine in a shallow dish:

1¹/₂ cups cooled espresso or extra-strong coffee

2 to 3 tablespoons rum or brandy

2 to 3 tablespoons sugar

Have ready:

4 ounces bittersweet or semisweet chocolate, grated

Dip half of the ladyfingers or génoise strips into the espresso mixture and arrange in a 2- to 3-quart serving bowl, leaving a little space between them. Spread half of the mascarpone filling over and between the ladyfingers or génoise strips. Sprinkle with half of the grated chocolate. Dip the remaining ladyfingers or génoise strips into the remaining espresso mixture and arrange on top. Spread the remaining filling over and between them, and sprinkle with the remaining chocolate. Sift over the top:

1 tablespoon unsweetened cocoa powder

Cover and refrigerate for at least 1 hour, or up to 24 hours before serving.

TRIFLE

12 to 14 servings

Traditionally this English dessert features vanilla custard and raspberries. However, you can use fresh, frozen, or canned fruit; omit the wine in favor of coffee or fruit juice or puree; and/or add amaretti crumbs or chopped chocolate. Prepare:

Custard Sauce, 846

using:

9 large egg yolks

³/₄ cup sugar

1¹/₂ cups whole milk

1¹/₂ cups heavy cream

Refrigerate until cold.

Have ready:

24 to 30 ladyfingers, homemade, 740, or store-bought, Génoise, 709, or any sponge cake, cut into pieces of any size

¹/₂ to ³/₄ cup preserves

2 cups berries or sliced fruit

¹/₄ cup sliced or slivered blanched almonds, toasted, 1001

Arrange half of the ladyfingers or cake pieces in the bottom of a 2- to 3-quart serving bowl. (If the bowl is glass, make sure that each layer of ingredients touches the sides

of the bowl so that the contrasting layers can be seen.)
Sprinkle with:

2 to 4 tablespoons sweet wine (such as sherry,
Muscat, Marsala, or Sauternes), brandy, or rum

Spread with half the preserves. Sprinkle with half of the
berries or fruit. Top with half of the custard, and sprinkle
with half the nuts. Repeat the assembly with the remaining ladyfingers or cake pieces, more liquor, and the remaining preserves, fruit, and custard.

Whip until nearly stiff:

$^3/_4$ cup cold heavy cream
2 to 3 teaspoons sugar
$^1/_2$ teaspoon vanilla

Spread the cream or pipe it decoratively on top of the trifle. Sprinkle with the remaining nuts. Cover and refrigerate for at least 3 hours, or, preferably, up to 24 hours
before serving.

ABOUT RICE PUDDING

Short- and medium-grain white rices are high in starch
and thus give puddings an especially smooth and creamy
texture, but avoid Arborio rice, a very starchy medium-
grain rice used for making risotto; it does not make good
puddings. Long-grain rice makes good rice pudding as
long as it has not been "converted" or otherwise precooked (as in "instant" rice). Do experiment with specialty
long-grain rices, such as basmati and jasmine rice. Each
will impart its own characteristic flavor. See About Rice,
354. Rice puddings are enhanced by spices such as nutmeg, anise, cloves, or cinnamon. Serve with toppings such
as toasted nuts or coconut or crushed brittle; fruit sauces
or compotes; or sauces flavored with chocolate, coffee,
vanilla, caramel, or maple.

BAKED RICE PUDDING

6 to 8 servings

Preheat the oven to 325°F. Butter a 1$^1/_2$-quart shallow baking dish or six 6-ounce custard cups or ramekins. If desired, coat the bottom and sides with:

(Fine cake or cookie crumbs)

Place in a large bowl:

2 cups cooked short- or medium-grain white rice

Combine and beat until well blended:

1$^1/_3$ cups milk
2 large eggs
6 tablespoons sugar or packed brown sugar
2 tablespoons unsalted butter, softened
1 to 1$^1/_2$ teaspoons vanilla (use the smaller amount if
using lemon)
$^1/_8$ teaspoon salt

Add to the rice, along with, if desired:

($^1/_3$ cup raisins or chopped dates)
($^1/_2$ teaspoon grated lemon zest)
(1 teaspoon fresh lemon juice)

Stir lightly with a fork to combine. Spread the rice in the
prepared dish or ramekins and top with more crumbs;

bake until a knife inserted in the center comes out clean,
about 40 minutes for the large pudding or 25 minutes for
the smaller puddings. Serve warm with:

Cream or a fresh fruit sauce, 853

RICE PUDDING BRÛLÉE

Prepare individual **Baked Rice Puddings, above.** Refrigerate
until cold, then cover with **Caramel Glaze I, II, or III, 804.**

STOVETOP RICE PUDDING

6 to 8 servings

Combine in a large heavy saucepan:

$^3/_4$ cup medium- or long-grain white rice, 354
1$^1/_2$ cups water
Heaping $^1/_4$ teaspoon salt

Bring to a simmer over medium-high heat, then reduce
the heat to low, cover, and simmer until the water has
been absorbed, about 15 minutes. Stir in:

4 cups whole milk
$^1/_2$ cup sugar

Cook, uncovered, over medium heat for about 30 minutes, stirring frequently, especially toward the end of
cooking. The pudding is done when the rice and milk have
made a thick porridge. Do not overcook.

Remove from the heat, and stir in:

$^1/_2$ teaspoon vanilla

Spoon into a serving bowl or six 5- to 6-ounce custard
cups or ramekins. Press plastic wrap directly onto the surface to prevent a skin from forming. Serve warm, at room
temperature, or cold. If you wish, sprinkle with:

(Ground cinnamon)

The pudding can be accompanied with:

(Whipped Cream, 754, or a fruit sauce, 853)

TAPIOCA CUSTARD

4 to 6 servings

Please read about tapioca, 1017.

Use the greater amount of tapioca if you like a thick custard or if you are not adding egg. Using light or dark
brown sugar adds a hint of butterscotch.

Whisk together thoroughly in a heavy saucepan:

2$^1/_2$ cups milk
$^1/_3$ cup sugar or $^1/_2$ cup packed brown sugar
3 to 4 tablespoons quick-cooking tapioca
$^1/_8$ teaspoon salt

Let stand for 10 minutes, then slowly bring to a simmer
over medium heat, stirring constantly. Simmer, stirring, for
2 minutes. If desired, gradually whisk about half of the
pudding into:

(1 or 2 large eggs, well beaten)

Thoroughly stir this mixture into the remaining pudding.
Cook, stirring, over low heat just until you see the first sign
of thickening, about 3 minutes. Remove from the heat
and stir in:

1 teaspoon vanilla

Let cool in the saucepan for 30 minutes; the pudding will

thicken considerably. Spoon into cups or bowls. Serve warm or chilled. If you wish, accompany with:

> (Whipped Cream, 754, or a fruit sauce, 853)
>
> (Cream, fresh berries, crushed or canned fruit, or chocolate sauce, 847)

BAKED PEARL TAPIOCA PUDDING

8 servings

Please read about tapioca, 1017.

Combine in a bowl:

> $1/2$ cup tapioca
>
> 1 cup milk

Cover and refrigerate overnight.

Transfer the tapioca and milk to a heavy saucepan and stir in:

> 3 cups milk

Bring to a boil over medium-high heat, then reduce the heat to low and simmer, stirring frequently, until the mixture is translucent and beginning to thicken, about 12 minutes. Remove to a large bowl, and cool.

Preheat the oven to 325°F. Grease a $2^{1}/2$- to 3-quart baking dish. Beat together:

> 5 large egg yolks
>
> $3/4$ cup sugar
>
> Grated zest of 1 lemon and juice of $1/2$ lemon, or $1^{1}/2$ teaspoons vanilla

Stir into the tapioca mixture. Beat until stiff but not dry:

> 5 large egg whites

Fold into the tapioca mixture, and pour into the prepared baking dish. Bake about 40 minutes, until the top is puffed and golden brown and the pudding jiggles when the dish is lightly shaken. Serve hot or cold with, if desired, a sauce such as:

> (Hot Fruit Sauce, 844)

COCONUT TAPIOCA PUDDING

6 servings

Please read about tapioca, 1017.

This pudding is exceptionally good when made with pearl tapioca, however, you can substitute quick-cooking tapioca: Reduce the amount of tapioca to $1/3$ cup, soak it for only 10 minutes, and cook the pudding for just 2 minutes at a rolling boil.

Combine in a large heavy saucepan:

> $2/3$ cup pearl tapioca
>
> $2^{3}/4$ cups whole milk

Cover and refrigerate for at least 8 hours, or overnight.

Stir into the tapioca:

> One $14^{1}/2$-ounce can unsweetened coconut milk
>
> 2 tablespoons sugar
>
> $1/8$ teaspoon salt

Bring to a simmer over medium-high heat, then reduce the heat and gently simmer, stirring constantly, until the pearls are translucent and no longer gritty, about 15 minutes. Be careful not to overcook the pudding, or it will be sticky. Remove from the heat.

Whisk in a small bowl until frothy:

> 1 large egg

Gradually whisk in 1 cup of the hot pudding. Whisk this mixture into the remaining pudding in the pan and let stand for 5 minutes, covered. (The pudding will still be hot enough to cook the egg.) Just before serving, stir in:

> $2/3$ cup shredded coconut, toasted, 1001

Transfer to a bowl or individual cups and sprinkle with:

> Toasted coconut

Serve warm with:

> Fresh fruit or a fruit sauce, 853

FARINA PUDDING

4 to 6 servings

Farina is a meal made from hard wheat; see 986. Try this creamy pudding for a finicky breakfaster or serve as a dessert. Do not use a farina labeled "instant" for this recipe. If egg whites are used, see About Egg Safety, 980.

Combine in a heavy saucepan and bring to a boil, stirring to dissolve the sugar:

> 2 cups milk
>
> $1/4$ cup sugar

Stir in:

> $1/4$ cup farina

Cook over low heat, stirring frequently, until thick, about 5 minutes. Add and stir until melted:

> 1 tablespoon unsalted butter

Remove from the heat. Beat in one at a time:

> 2 large egg yolks

Pour into a bowl and cool, then add:

> 1 teaspoon vanilla
>
> ($3/4$ teaspoon ground cinnamon)
>
> ($1/2$ teaspoon grated lemon zest)

For a lighter pudding, whip until stiff but not dry:

> (2 large egg whites)

Fold into the farina mixture. If serving as a dessert, serve cold with:

> Whipped Cream, 754, a fruit sauce, 853, or crushed sweetened berries
>
> (Walnuts or pecans, toasted, 1001)

ROTE GRÜTZE

4 servings

Long popular in our family, this German fruit pudding is usually made with raspberry juice. Strawberries, cherries, or black currants may be used, but our favorite base is a combination of raspberry and strawberry juice, which may be strengthened with raspberry jelly or red wine. In winter, a wonderfully fresh taste may be obtained if you cook frozen raspberries and strawberries and strain off the juice.

I. Bring to a boil in a heavy saucepan:

> 2 cups fruit juice

Sweeten to taste with:

> $1/2$ to $3/4$ cup sugar

Season with:

> $1/8$ teaspoon salt

Stir in:

3 to 4 tablespoons farina

Simmer over low heat, stirring constantly, until thickened, 5 to 10 minutes. Pour into individual serving dishes. Cover tightly with plastic wrap and chill until very cold. Serve with:

Whipped Cream, 754, Custard Sauce, 846, or diced fresh fruit

II. Substitute **2½ tablespoons quick-cooking tapioca** for the farina.

ABOUT BREAD PUDDING

Bread pudding is an efficient way to transform stale bread into a considerable variety of delicious desserts. Bread puddings are baked custards, so those that are rich in eggs turn grainy and watery unless baked in a water bath. Those made with enough bread to soak up the custard do not need to be baked in a water bath.

Bread puddings may be made with virtually any bread or roll except quick breads, like biscuits or muffins, that are leavened by baking powder or baking soda. Egg breads such as challah or brioche produce bread puddings with a light texture. Many of the recipes use generous quantities of cream and egg yolks, but these ingredients, too, should be regarded as flexible. Cream can always be replaced by half-and-half or even whole milk, and each 3 egg yolks can be replaced by 1 whole egg. We like to add raisins, chopped dried apricots, toasted nuts, 1001, chocolate chips, grated orange or lemon zest, or a few tablespoons of bourbon, brandy, or rum. Bread puddings are best served warm and are especially good served with cream, milk, or sauces, as suggested in the recipes below. Most bread puddings can be made 2 to 3 days in advance of serving and reheated in a 300° or 325°F oven for about 15 to 30 minutes.

BREAD PUDDING

8 servings

Butter a 2-quart baking dish. Trim the crusts and cut into ½-inch cubes:

12 to 16 ounces sliced white bread, stale but not hard

You should have 4 to 5 lightly packed cups. Spread the bread in the prepared baking dish, then scatter over the top, if desired:

(¾ cup raisins or other dried fruit)

Whisk together thoroughly in a bowl:

4 large eggs
3 cups whole milk
¾ cup sugar
1 teaspoon vanilla
¾ teaspoon ground cinnamon
¼ teaspoon grated or ground nutmeg
Pinch of salt

Pour the mixture over the bread and let stand for 30 minutes, periodically pressing the bread down with a spatula to help it absorb the liquid. Preheat the oven to 350°F.

Bake the pudding in a water bath, 801, until a knife inserted in the center comes out clean, 55 minutes to 1 hour. Serve warm with:

Whipped Cream, 754, milk, or cream

NEW ORLEANS BREAD PUDDING

10 to 12 servings

Spread over the bottom of a 13 x 9-inch baking dish, preferably glass:

3 tablespoons unsalted butter, softened

Cut into ½-inch-thick slices:

1¼ pounds French or Italian bread (1½ to 2 loaves)

Arrange the slices almost upright in tightly spaced rows in the prepared dish. Tuck between the slices:

1 cup raisins

Whisk in a large bowl until frothy:

3 large eggs
4 cups whole milk
2 cups sugar
2 tablespoons vanilla
1 teaspoon ground cinnamon

Pour the liquid over the bread and let stand for 1 hour, pressing down now and then with a spatula to wet the tops of the slices. Preheat the oven to 375°F. Bake the pudding until the top is puffed and lightly browned, about 1 hour. Cover with:

Southern Whiskey Sauce, 852

Let cool on a rack for 30 to 60 minutes, then cut into squares and serve.

CHOCOLATE BREAD PUDDING

10 to 12 servings

Extravagant and luscious.

Cut into ½-inch-thick slices:

1 pound challah, brioche, or other light egg bread

Taking care to preserve as much of the bread as possible, trim off and discard the crusts. Cut the bread into ½-inch cubes, making 6 to 7 cups.

Bring to a boil in a heavy saucepan, stirring to dissolve the sugar:

1 cup heavy cream
¾ cup sugar
⅛ teaspoon salt

Remove from the heat and add:

12 ounces bittersweet or semisweet chocolate, chopped

Let stand for 2 minutes, then whisk until smooth.

Whisk together thoroughly in a large bowl:

2 large eggs
2 large egg yolks

Add:

2 cups whole milk
1 tablespoon vanilla

Whisk in the chocolate mixture, then stir in the bread cubes. Let stand for 1 to 2 hours, gently stirring and pressing the bread down now and then with a spatula to help it absorb the liquid.

Preheat the oven to 325°F. Generously butter a shallow 2-quart baking dish. Pour the pudding mixture into the prepared baking dish and smooth the top. Bake in a water bath, 801, until the center feels firm when pressed, 55 to 65 minutes.

Let cool for 45 minutes, then serve with:

> Southern Whiskey Sauce, 852, or Warm White Chocolate Sauce, 848

ABOUT BAKED PUDDINGS

These desserts are firmer and more substantial than cornstarch puddings, because they contain a high proportion of flour, bread crumbs, grains, or some other starch. Baked puddings can be served cold or hot, and they can be prepared in advance and reheated at serving time. While not obligatory, a sauce or accompaniment such as Southern Whiskey Sauce, 852, or a custard, 846, lemon, 844, or foamy sauce, 851, is traditional with most baked puddings.

COTTAGE PUDDING

8 to 10 servings

Preheat the oven to 375°F. Grease a 9-inch square baking pan. Prepare the batter for:

> Lightning Cake, 722

If desired, spread over the bottom of the prepared pan:

> (1 cup marmalade, heated until liquified)

Pour the batter carefully over the marmalade, or spread it in the pan. Bake until a toothpick inserted in the center comes out clean and the top springs back when pressed, about 40 minutes.

Cut into squares, and serve warm with:

> Hot Lemon Sauce, 844, or Hot Chocolate Sauce, 847

PERSIMMON BUTTERMILK PUDDING

8 servings

A soft pudding with an old-fashioned flavor. Be sure to use very ripe, mushy persimmons, see 233.

Preheat the oven to 400°F. Butter a shallow 3-quart baking dish. Cut lengthwise in half:

> 4 to 6 very ripe large persimmons

Remove any seeds, then scrape the pulp free from the skins with a teaspoon. Puree the pulp in a blender or food processor. If it looks stringy, force it through a sieve with the back of a spoon. Measure 1 1/2 cups pulp.

Whisk in a large bowl until light:

> 4 large eggs

Whisk in the persimmon pulp, then whisk in:

> 2 1/2 cups buttermilk
> 1/4 cup (1/2 stick) unsalted butter, melted

Whisk together thoroughly in a separate bowl:

> 1 1/2 cups sugar
> 1 1/2 cups all-purpose flour
> 1 1/2 teaspoons baking powder

> 1 1/2 teaspoons baking soda
> 1/2 teaspoon ground cinnamon
> 1/2 teaspoon grated or ground nutmeg
> 1/2 teaspoon salt

Add the dry ingredients to the persimmon mixture and whisk until well blended. Pour the batter into the prepared dish. Bake until the top is deep golden brown and springs back when lightly pressed, about 50 minutes.

Serve the pudding warm or cold with:

> Whipped Cream, 754, Rich Hot Lemon Sauce, 844, or a foamy sauce, 851

PUMPKIN BUTTERMILK PUDDING

Prepare **Persimmon Buttermilk Pudding, above**, substituting **1 1/2 cups canned pumpkin puree** for the persimmon pulp. Serve with **Hot Brandy Sauce, 852, Whipped Cream, 973**, or vanilla ice cream.

INDIAN PUDDING

6 to 8 servings

A truly warming dessert, with a taste and texture somewhat like pumpkin pie.

Preheat the oven to 325°F. Generously butter a heavy 1 1/2- to 2-quart baking dish.

Measure into a large heavy saucepan:

> 2/3 cup cornmeal

Stir in, very gradually at first to prevent lumps:

> 4 cups whole milk

Stirring constantly, bring to a boil over medium-high heat. Reduce the heat to low and simmer, stirring frequently, until thick, about 5 minutes. Remove from the heat and whisk in:

> 1/3 cup sugar
> 1/4 cup molasses
> 2 large eggs
> 2 tablespoons unsalted butter, cut into pieces
> 1 teaspoon ground cinnamon
> 1/2 teaspoon ground ginger
> 1/8 teaspoon grated or ground nutmeg
> 1 teaspoon vanilla
> 1/8 teaspoon salt

Turn the pudding into the prepared dish. Bake in a water bath, 801, until the center looks firm but still slightly quivery when the dish is shaken, about 1 hour 10 minutes. A dark crust will form on top. Serve warm or cold with:

> Vanilla ice cream or cream

STICKY TOFFEE PUDDING

8 servings

Preheat the oven to 350°F. Butter and flour eight 6-ounce ramekins or a 9 x 2-inch square baking pan.

Combine in a small saucepan:

> 1 1/2 cups pitted dates, coarsely chopped
> 1 1/2 cups water

Bring to a boil, then reduce the heat and simmer, uncovered, for 5 minutes. Remove from the heat and stir in:

1¼ teaspoons baking soda

Set aside. Whisk together in a small bowl:

2 cups all-purpose flour
¼ teaspoon baking powder

Beat in a large bowl on high speed until lightened in color and fluffy:

1¼ cups packed light brown sugar
6 tablespoons (¾ stick) unsalted butter, softened

Beat in one at a time:

3 large eggs

Beat in:

1½ teaspoons vanilla

Gradually add the flour mixture, beating on low just until mixed. Stir in the date mixture until just combined. Pour into the prepared dish(es). If using ramekins, put them on a baking sheet. Bake until the pudding is a deep golden brown and a skewer comes out moist but clean, 20 to 25 minutes for ramekins, about 35 minutes for a single large dish. Cool on a rack for 10 minutes. Run a knife around the edge of the dish(es), then turn out the pudding(s) and invert onto the rack, right side up, to cool slightly. Serve warm, each serving covered generously with warm:

Butterscotch Sauce, 849

ABOUT STEAMED PUDDINGS

Steaming is an efficient cooking method for many puddings; most importantly, it's also good at retaining flavor. Some of these taste much like cake, while others have moist, soufflé like textures. Once there were many fruited suet puddings—which were dense, moist, and compact, something like soft fruitcake—but today only plum, or Christmas, pudding remains familiar.

If you do not have a pudding basin—a deep bowl of heatproof ceramic—you may use any heatproof bowl with equally good results. The deep 4- to 5-quart metal bowls for heavy-duty mixers are good for steaming large puddings. Grease these and all other metal bowls especially well, as the puddings are more prone to sticking to metal than to glass or ceramic. Some specialty cookware stores sell fancy pudding molds. These are usually a tube design and come with a cover that snaps on tightly, shown below. Only plum pudding or other very firm puddings should be prepared in such molds. Lighter, more fragile steamed puddings, such as Chocolate Feather Pudding, will stick hopelessly and may collapse (or, worse, explode) if cooked tightly covered.

To steam a pudding, find a pot large enough to hold the pudding basin or bowl comfortably. If you are steaming several small plum puddings, a covered turkey roaster, set over two burners, is convenient. (Puddings must be steamed ➤ in simmering water, which rules out a double boiler.) To insulate the bottom of the pudding, set a trivet, rack, or folded dish towel in the bottom of your pot. Place the pudding in the pot, then pour in enough *boiling* water to reach halfway to two-thirds the way up the sides of the

pudding bowl. Bring the water to a boil over high heat, then turn the heat down to a brisk simmer. Cover the pot tightly and steam the pudding until done, checking the pot every 30 minutes and replenishing with boiling water as needed. When removing the cooked pudding from the pot, protect your hands with oven or silicone mitts.

▲ In high altitudes, reduce the leavening for these puddings by half.

STEAMED CHOCOLATE FEATHER PUDDING

8 to 10 servings

Reminiscent of a chocolate soufflé, but more substantial.
Preheat the oven to 350°F.
Spread on a baking sheet:

1 cup fine dry bread crumbs

Toast, stirring 2 or 3 times, until lightly golden, about 3 minutes. Let cool completely.

Very generously butter a 2-quart heatproof bowl or pudding basin. Sprinkle the inside of the bowl with 2 tablespoons of the crumbs, tilting to coat.
Combine in a large heatproof bowl:

8 ounces bittersweet or semisweet chocolate, chopped
½ cup heavy cream
4 tablespoons (½ stick) unsalted butter
2 tablespoons dark rum or strong coffee

Set the bowl in a skillet of almost simmering water and stir until the mixture is smooth. Remove from the heat and whisk in:

6 large egg yolks
1 tablespoon vanilla

Beat in a large bowl on medium speed until foamy:

6 large egg whites, at room temperature

Add and beat until soft peaks form:

½ teaspoon cream of tartar

Gradually beat in:

½ cup sugar

Increase the speed to high and beat until the peaks are stiff and glossy. Using a large rubber spatula, fold the egg whites into the chocolate mixture. Sprinkle the remaining bread crumbs over the top, along with:

2 tablespoons all-purpose flour

Fold until the crumbs and flour are incorporated. Turn the batter into the prepared mold and cover with an inverted plate. Set a rack or folded towel in the bottom of a pot large enough to hold the pudding comfortably. Set the pudding inside and pour enough boiling water into the pot to come halfway up the sides of the mold. Bring the water to a brisk simmer over medium-high heat and tightly cover the pot. Replenishing the water as needed, steam the pudding until the top has flattened and the center feels firm, about 1¼ hours. Turn off the heat and let the pudding stand in the covered pot for 15 minutes. Invert the pudding onto a platter and serve with:

**Whipped Cream, 754, Hot or Cold Foamy Sauce,
851–852, or Caramel Cream Sauce, 849**

STEAMED CARAMEL PUDDING

10 to 12 servings

This is an updated version of a very special Rombauer family pudding that has appeared in JOY since the original 1931 edition. Light as a feather but intense in flavor, and very handsome.

Preheat the oven to 350°F.

Spread on a baking sheet:

> **2 cups slivered blanched almonds**

Toast, stirring 2 or 3 times, until golden brown, 5 to 7 minutes. Let cool completely, then grind in a food processor until fine but not at all oily.

Generously butter a 4-quart heatproof bowl or pudding basin. Sprinkle the inside of the bowl with 3 tablespoons of the almonds, tilting to coat.

Prepare a caramel as directed in Caramel Custard, 802, using:

> **1¹⁄₂ cups sugar**
> **3 tablespoons very hot water**

Stir in until smooth:

> **1 cup heavy cream**
> **6 tablespoons (³⁄₄ stick) unsalted butter, cut in pieces**

If necessary, heat briefly over low heat to melt the caramel, stirring until smooth. Transfer the caramel to a large bowl and let cool to lukewarm. Beat the remaining ground almonds into the caramel, along with:

> **6 large egg yolks**
> **¹⁄₃ cup all-purpose flour**
> **1 tablespoon vanilla**
> **1 teaspoon almond extract**
> **³⁄₄ teaspoon salt**

Beat in a large bowl on medium speed until foamy:

> **6 large egg whites, at room temperature**

Add:

> **¹⁄₂ teaspoon cream of tartar**

Beat until soft peaks form, then increase the speed to high and beat until the peaks are stiff but not dry. Using a large rubber spatula, stir one-quarter of the egg whites into the caramel mixture to lighten it, then gently but thoroughly fold in the rest. Turn the batter into the prepared mold and cover the top with an inverted plate or cake pan. (The uncooked pudding can be refrigerated for up to 4 hours before steaming.)

Set a rack or folded towel in the bottom of a pot large enough to hold the pudding comfortably. Set the pudding inside and pour enough boiling water into the pot to come halfway up the sides of the mold. Bring the water to a brisk simmer and cover the pot tightly. Replenishing the water as needed, steam the pudding until a skewer inserted in the center comes out with only a few moist crumbs clinging to it, about 2 hours. Turn off the heat and let the pudding stand in the covered pot for 15 minutes. Invert the pudding onto a platter and serve with:

> **Whipped Cream, 754**

STEAMED PLUM PUDDING

1 large or 2 or 3 small puddings; 12 to 16 servings

A festive Christmas dish that needs patience in the making. The ➤ slow cooking is necessary so that the suet melts before the flour particles expand. If cooked too fast, the pudding will be hard. Many cooks set aside a calm day early in the holiday season for this project, for the pudding will only improve and mature while stored. There are no plums in plum pudding. The English, who created it, called most dried fruits plums.

To make a single large pudding, use a 3-quart pudding mold, a 3-quart pudding basin, or a deep heatproof glass or ceramic bowl with a capacity of 3 to 3¹⁄₂ quarts. To make smaller puddings, use 2 or 3 molds, basins, and/or baking dishes with a total capacity of 3 to 4 quarts.

Very generously grease the mold(s) with vegetable shortening. Divide in half and coarsely chop one half:

> **2²⁄₃ cups raisins**

Combine all the raisins in a large heavy saucepan with:

> **2 cups dried currants**
> **2 cups water**

Cover tightly and simmer gently for 20 minutes; then uncover and cook, stirring, until nearly all the liquid has evaporated. Let cool to room temperature, at least 2 hours. Combine in a bowl:

> **1¹⁄₂ cups all-purpose flour**
> **8 ounces ground or finely chopped beef suet, 1018**

Rub together lightly with your hands just until the suet particles are separated. Add:

> **1 cup firmly packed dark brown sugar**
> **1¹⁄₂ teaspoons ground cinnamon**
> **1¹⁄₂ teaspoons ground ginger**
> **¹⁄₂ teaspoon ground cloves**
> **¹⁄₂ teaspoon salt**

Rub together just until blended. Whisk together thoroughly in a separate bowl:

> **4 large eggs**
> **¹⁄₃ cup brandy or Cognac**
> **¹⁄₃ cup cream sherry**

Stir into the flour mixture, then stir in the raisin mixture and:

> **(¹⁄₂ cup finely chopped dates)**
> **(¹⁄₂ cup finely chopped candied citron)**

Pour the batter into the prepared mold(s), leaving at least 1 inch of headspace for expansion. If you are using a fancy pudding mold with a cover, grease the inside of the cover and snap it in place. Otherwise, crimp a sheet of aluminum foil over the rim of each mold allowing little or no overhang down the sides, and cover with an inverted plate.

Set a rack or folded dish towel in the bottom of a large pot and set the mold(s) on top. Pour enough boiling water into the pot to come two-thirds of the way up the sides of the mold(s). Cover the pot tightly. Bring the water to a boil over high heat, then adjust the heat to maintain a brisk simmer. Replenishing the pot with boiling water as necessary, steam a single large pudding for 6 to 7 hours, 2 smaller puddings for 4 to 5 hours, or 3 small puddings for 3 to 4 hours. When done, the pudding should be very dark in color nearly to the center. At this point, a large pudding can be kept warm in the covered pot, with the heat off, for 3 hours; smaller puddings for about 1 1/2 hours.

Remove the pudding(s) and let stand at room temperature for 20 minutes, then invert onto a platter. If you wish to flame the pudding, warm to barely lukewarm in a small saucepan:

1/2 cup brandy or Cognac

Drizzle the liquor over the pudding and then, standing back, ignite with a long wooden match. Serve with:

Custard Sauce, 846, Hot Wine or Plum Pudding Sauce, 852, Fluffy Hard Sauce, 841, or Hot Foamy Sauce, 851

To store the pudding, cool to room temperature in the mold(s) then turn out. Wrap first in plastic, then in aluminum foil; refrigerate for up to 1 month (the pudding will become softer, darker, and more flavorful with age). To reheat, return the pudding to its original mold, well greased, and steam again in briskly simmering water for 1 1/2 to 2 hours for a large pudding, about 1 hour for smaller puddings, or until a knife inserted in the center for 15 seconds comes out hot.

ABOUT PANCAKE AND WAFFLE DESSERTS

There are a delicious handful of recipes in the Pancake and Waffle chapter that make sweet endings to a meal: Crêpes Suzette, 650, Crêpes with Caramelized Apples, 650, Crêpe Cake, 651, and Palatschinken, 652, a traditional Hungarian dessert. Don't be limited to just these, however, for any pancake or waffle can be dressed up and served for dessert.

Serve any of the following:

Chocolate Waffles, 647
Belgian Waffles, 647
Waffles, 646
Dutch Baby, 652
German Pancakes, 652
Austrian Pancakes, 653
Basic Pancakes, 644

topped with any of the following:

Sour cream or crème fraîche
Whipped Cream, 754
Sweetened Butters, 851
Strawberry or other preserves
Chocolate Sauce, 847
Chocolate Custard Sauce, 846
Coffee Custard Sauce, 846
Hard Sauce, 851
Southern Whiskey Sauce, 852
Butterscotch Sauce, 849
Maple Syrup Sauce, 850
Cherries Jubilee, below
Any fresh fruit sauce, 853
Ice cream

and garnished with any of the following:

Chocolate or butterscotch chips
Sliced fresh fruit
Nuts or coconut, toasted, 1001

COEUR À LA CRÈME

8 servings

When the fruit is prime, this very simple dessert is as good as any elaborate concoction we know. If you have the traditional heart-shaped molds with perforated bottoms, line them with dampened cheesecloth and drain the cream directly in the molds for 24 hours.

Have ready in a large bowl:

1 cup sour cream or Whipped Cream, 754

Beat until soft:

1 pound cream cheese
2 tablespoons heavy cream
1/8 teaspoon salt

Fold the cheese into the cream. Place in a sieve lined with moistened cheesecloth and set over a bowl to drain in the refrigerator for 24 hours. Divide the cheese among 8 small ramekins or other molds and refrigerate 1 hour.

Unmold and serve with:

Stem-on strawberries, raspberries, or other fresh fruit or Fresh Strawberry Sauce, 853

CHERRIES JUBILEE

About 1 cup

If you do not wish to ignite the brandy, you may simply soak the cherries in it well ahead of time. If you flambé, be sure that the fruit is at room temperature and the brandy warm, see 1055. Other preserved fruits may be substituted for the cherries.

Heat in a small saucepan:

1 cup bottled pitted Bing or other cherries

Add:

1/4 cup brandy, slightly warmed

Standing back, carefully ignite the brandy with a long wooden match. When the flame has died down, add:

2 tablespoons kirsch

Serve hot on or with:

Charlotte Russe, 818, Crêpes, 648, any cake, 698–759, Chocolate Mousse, 816, or White Chocolate Mousse, 816

BANANAS FOSTER

4 servings

If you enjoy chafing-dish cooking, prepare this at the table before your guests.

Peel and cut lengthwise in half:

4 firm ripe bananas

Cut each half into 4 pieces. Melt in a large heavy skillet:

2 tablespoons butter

Place the bananas in the skillet cut side down. Cook over low heat, turning once, for about 5 minutes per side, just until fork-tender—do not overcook. Sprinkle with:

3 tablespoons light brown sugar

$1/4$ teaspoon ground cinnamon

$1/8$ teaspoon grated or ground nutmeg

Transfer the bananas to a heatproof serving dish and arrange in a single layer. Add to the skillet:

$1/2$ cup dark rum

(1 tablespoon brandy)

Use a spatula to loosen the caramelized bits while the spirits heat over medium heat. When they are hot, carefully ignite with a long wooden match, then pour over the bananas. Spoon over:

Vanilla ice cream

THE CHEESE COURSE

The cheese course may be served after the main course or after a salad that follows the main course. Cheese may also be served following the sweet or instead of one, with a suitable dessert fruit such as apples, pears, grapes, or dried figs or other dried fruit. ➤ Cheeses should always be served at room temperature. Any that are best when *coulant,* or runny, should be removed from the refrigerator 3 to 6 hours before serving.

Bread or crackers are served on a separate tray. This can be simply good French bread or a country-style loaf; thick slices of toasted whole-grain bread or pumpernickel; slices of walnut or artisan raisin bread; an array of good-quality mild-tasting crackers (the mild English round ones called water biscuits are good with blues and other strong cheeses); or the thin crisp oat-based crackers called oatcakes. Softened butter is usually served with a cheese course. Unsalted toasted or freshly shelled nuts, roasted chestnuts, or sliced celery or fennel are pleasant accessories. Other accompaniments enhance cheese by contrasting it, usually with something tangy or sweet. Try pairing relishes such as ploughman's pickle, Italian *mostarda,* or fruit-based chutneys with sharp Cheddar; *membrillo,* or quince paste, with Spanish or goat cheese; and fig preserves with any hard aged sharp cheese.

An ideal cheese plate should include ➤ no more than 3 or 4 cheeses. Generally, these should be of different types:

for instance, one fresh goat cheese; one soft fermented cheese, such as Brie, Camembert, or Pont-l'Evêque—the rind, incidentally, is edible; one blue-veined cheese—the classics are Roquefort from France, Gorgonzola from Italy, and Stilton from England, but there are many others, including some splendid American blue cheeses; and one firm cheese, such as farmhouse Cheddar, Caerphilly, good-quality provolone, Gruyère, Gouda, or Manchego. Alternately, a single cheese may be served: irregular chunks of crumbly Parmigiano-Reggiano, drizzled with balsamic vinegar, for example, or a ripe whole Brie, or a cylinder of Stilton soft enough to be scooped out with a spoon.

Although chunks of Parmigiano-Reggiano may be picked up in the fingers and nibbled, ➤ a small knife is proper for almost every other kind of cheese. Butter knives are appropriate for fresh and/or very ripe soft cheeses; if you don't have smaller versions of your dinner knives, use the dinner knives. Cheese is usually spread or placed on bread or crackers, but you may want to offer diners small forks so that they have the option of eating bits of cheese by themselves.

Red wine is the traditional accompaniment to cheese, though almost as a default—often being the same red wine that has accompanied the main course. Slightly sweet white wine goes very well with certain kinds of cheese—fresh goat cheese, for instance—and quite sweet wines often complement blue cheeses and other strong cheeses—Sauternes with Roquefort, for example, or port with Stilton. See Wine and Cheese, 51.

An acquaintance used to maintain that there were three stages of maturity for Brie: firm, soft, and "Quick, Mabel, it's heading out the door!" In fact, there is a perfect point of ripeness (or rather there are several perfect points, depending on individual taste) for every cheese, and the watchful storage of cheese until it reaches its optimum condition—which the French call *affinage,* or refining—is a complicated art. ➤ Unless you're going to serve it the day you buy it, cheese should be stored, loosely wrapped in foil or waxed paper, in the refrigerator.

FROZEN DESSERTS
AND SWEET SAUCES

ABOUT ICE CREAM

It is rumored that ice cream may have been invented in ancient China, perfected in Italy, and further refined in France. But one thing is for sure, it was America, from the time of the colonies, that made it such a popular dessert. Every time the science of refrigeration advanced, ice cream tailgated along right behind it. The biggest breakthrough came in the 1840s, when an American woman, Nancy Johnson, invented a small hand-cranked ice cream maker. Still, anyone could make it at home, and ice cream parties became the fashion. The crowning moment for ice cream came at the 1904 World's Fair in St. Louis, with the introduction of the ice cream cone: 50 booths sold 5,000 gallons of ice cream a day, a jump start for ice cream that has never run down. Still, the tune we can all recall and kids still listen for is the tinny tinkle of the ice cream truck: the anthem of summer, childhood, and good cheer.

In recent years, high-quality electric freezers have proliferated, proving that homemade ice cream is still best. And though we have hundreds of concoctions at our disposal, the pure flavors of vanilla, chocolate, and fresh fruit are still hard to beat. Ice cream is based on either an eggless "syrup" of heated cream, milk, and sugar or a thick egg custard, both commonly referred to as the ice cream "base." The first type is known as **Philadelphia-style ice cream,** the second as custard-style or **French-style** ice cream. The natural emulsifiers in eggs preserve the fine texture of custard-style ice cream; see About Custards, 801. Philadelphia-style ice cream is ➤ best eaten soon after freezing and may become icy or grainy in as little as 24 hours.

Ice creams can be flavored by a technique known as **in-**

fusing: The liquid in the recipe is heated with a flavoring, such as lemon zest, a vanilla bean, ground nuts, or coconut. Just as the mixture begins to boil, the pan is removed from the heat, covered, and allowed to stand, or **steep,** for about 30 minutes, then strained out before the liquid is put into the ice cream maker.

There are two distinct freezing techniques. **Churned,** or **stir-frozen** desserts employ hand-cranked or electric machines that incorporate air into the mixture and break up ice crystals to produce a smooth consistency. **Still-frozen desserts,** 840, are made by placing the mixture in a mold in the freezer and allowing it to freeze completely, without stirring or using any special equipment. These desserts usually require an emulsifying ingredient to ensure their smoothness.

ABOUT CHURN-FREEZING

Churned, or stir-frozen, desserts, including most kinds of ice cream, sherbets, frozen yogurts, and sorbets, require an ice cream maker capable of producing subzero temperatures, because the sugar in the various mixtures lowers the freezing point of the liquids from 32° to around 26°F. There are three general types of ice cream makers: hand-cranked machines, frozen-canister models, and electric machines with a built-in cooling unit.

Hand-cranked ice cream makers consist of a metal canister, into which the chilled ice cream mixture is poured, set in a larger container filled with ice and salt (the brine). The stirring mechanism, turned by hand or an electric motor, controls the dasher or paddle inside the canister. The salt lowers the temperature of the brine well below 32°F, chilling the metal canister and freezing the mixture inside. Hand-cranked ice cream makers allow you to control the freezing temperature by adjusting the amount of salt you add, and they tend to have a capacity of at least 2 quarts, thus permitting a large quantity of ice cream to be made at one time. These machines make the process as much fun as the eating, and children love to watch, even assisting with the cranking and, in the end, licking the dasher clean.

To pack the freezer, allow 4 parts crushed ice to 1 part coarse rock salt. Pack about one-third of the freezer container with ice and add layers of salt and ice around the container until it is full. Allow to stand about 3 minutes before you start turning—slowly at first, about 40 revolutions a minute, until a slight pull is felt, then triple speed for 5 or 6 minutes. If any additions such as fruit or nuts are to be made, do so at this point. Then add more ice and salt as necessary, and taper off the churning to about 80 revolutions a minute. The ice cream should be ready in 10 to 20 minutes, depending on quantity. To remove the dasher, pour off the salt water in the freezer container and wipe off the lid. Remove the dasher carefully, making sure that no salt or water gets into the canister.

The ice cream should be smooth when frozen. ➤ If it proves granular, you used too much salt in the packing mixture, overfilled the inner container with the mixture, or turned too rapidly.

Frozen-canister ice cream makers are inexpensive and feature a smaller metal canister, usually about an inch thick and hollow, with a coolant in its walls. The coolant's temperature is lowered by keeping the canister overnight (or longer) in the freezer. The canister is then fitted into a plastic shell and filled with the ice cream mixture. Most frozen-canister models call for the dasher to be turned every few minutes, but constant stirring is best and results in a better texture. Some frozen-canister machines have an electric stirring mechanism. Although slow, these devices are simple enough to be operated by children and are fine for light, occasional use. Most have a capacity of 1 to 1½ quarts, and the metal canister needs 12 hours to chill between uses, which means you can make only one batch of ice cream a day.

Electric ice cream makers with built-in cooling units are both reliable and efficient. These countertop machines are quite heavy and are about the size of a small microwave oven. The freezing mechanism is turned on to cool the unit, the ice cream mixture is poured into a metal bowl in the machine, and the dasher is activated. These machines can produce batches of 1 to 1½ quarts in approximately 25 minutes, and the texture is excellent—ice cream is always silky smooth, sorbets are never icy. Successive batches can be frozen with little downtime, and some can be run almost continuously. These are the most expensive ice cream makers, but if you make ice cream often, they are a worthwhile investment.

No matter what kind of ice cream maker you use, there are a number of general rules to follow when stir-freezing or churning a frozen dessert. ➤ Remember that all types of freezers are affected by ambient conditions. On a hot summer's day, the temperature of the brine in the hand-cranked type is likely to rise more quickly and therefore require more salt. Frozen-canister units and electric machines work more efficiently when you aim a fan at the freezer.

➤ Make the cream or custard mixture for ice cream a full day ahead and refrigerate for improved flavor and texture.

➤ Fill the canister no more than three-quarters full to allow room for expansion. If you wish to ➤ add fruits, nuts, or candy, wait until the mixture is almost frozen before adding them.

When the machine has finished its work, the ice cream, though frozen, will still be comparatively soft. Most ice creams taste best at this stage. If you want a firmer consistency—to scoop into cones, for example—transfer the mixture to a plastic container with a tight-fitting lid and place it in the freezer for an hour or so to set.

ABOUT STORING AND SERVING ICE CREAM AND OTHER FROZEN DESSERTS

The ➤ more heavy cream the mixture contains, the longer it will keep; and ➤ a mixture that was heated during preparation will keep longer than one that wasn't. If possible, store ice cream in an upright or chest freezer. If keeping in a refrigerator's freezer, place the ice cream in the center or coldest section. To prevent ice crystals from forming during storage, eliminate air pockets when you pack the ice cream into the freezer container, level the top, and cover with plastic wrap or wax paper before you snap on the lid. If the ice cream is too hard to scoop directly from the freezer, allow it to soften on a refrigerator shelf for 20 to 30 minutes, on a kitchen counter for up to 10 minutes, or in a microwave oven for 15 to 20 seconds on low power. Melting and refreezing causes ice crystals to form.

It is difficult to prevent the development of large ice crystals during storage in sorbets, sherbets, and other reduced-fat frozen desserts. They will turn icy after a short time. If this happens, chop the dessert into small pieces and puree in a food processor. If the puree becomes too slushy, return the machine to the freezer for an hour.

The shovel scoop shown below is useful for serving Snow Cream, 838, as well as for packing frozen desserts in general and for serving them attractively on a plate in thin slabs. A spring-release scoop, also shown, turns out uniform ball shapes or scoops. Wet in hot water between dips.

Spring-release and shovel ice cream scoop

Ice cream can be served in a variety of visually appealing and delicious ways. **To marbleize,** layer two kinds of soft ice cream or other frozen dessert in a shallow storage container, alternating ½-inch-thick layers of each one. Freeze the layered mixture until firm enough to scoop. When you draw the scoop through the layers, the ice cream will have a marbleized effect. Marbleize two flavors of the same type of frozen dessert, such as vanilla and coffee ice creams, peach and raspberry sorbets, or strawberry and banana frozen yogurts. Or mix and match styles and textures, such as toasted coconut ice cream and mango sorbet, cranberry sherbert and lime sorbet, or vanilla ice cream and hazelnut gelato.

To ripple, use about ½ cup sauce to 1 quart ice cream or other frozen dessert. Alternate ½-inch-thick layers of ice soft cream with ⅛-inch-thick layers of sauce (Chocolate Sauce, 847, Caramel Sauce, 849, Butterscotch Sauce,

849, Marshmallow Sauce, 850, Melba Sauce, 845, or fruit jam, for example) in a storage container, then draw the handle of a wooden spoon through the mixture several times, until the sauce is threaded throughout the ice cream. Freeze until firm enough to scoop. Some good rippled combinations are Pumpkin Spice Ice Cream with caramel, Vanilla Frozen Yogurt with chocolate, and Chocolate Ice Cream with apricot or raspberry jam.

FROZEN ORANGE OR LEMON SURPRISE

This dessert can be made well in advance. Arrange on a shallow tray of cracked ice, just before the guests are served to use as a centerpiece or table decoration.
Cut a slice off the top of:

Navel oranges or thick-skinned lemons

about one-quarter of the way down to serve as lids. Slice a small piece off the bottom of each fruit so it will stand upright. Keep the lids and bottoms matched until ready to fill. Hollow out the pulp from both bottoms and lids. Place the shells and lids on a baking sheet and freeze for 2 hours. Remove and fill with:

Fruit sorbet, sherbet, or granita

or a combination of:

Fruit sorbet
Ice cream
Partially frozen raspberries, sliced peaches
   or strawberries
A touch of liqueur

Return to the freezer for another 2 hours.
Allow about 30 minutes or more to soften before serving. To serve, place the tops on the shells at a slight angle. If desired, garnish the cases with fresh green unsprayed citrus leaves or other nontoxic leaves stuck in the lids and around the bases.

CHOCOLATE CUPS

8 to 10 cups

If the chocolate is at the correct temperature, it will take only one dip to evenly coat a balloon; too cold, the coating will be too thick; too hot, and the balloon will likely need more than one dip. Keep leftover chocolate to fill any holes in the cups.
Line a baking sheet with parchment paper or a silicone liner. Inflate to about 5 inches in diameter:

8 to 10 small balloons

Temper, 857, and pour into a bowl slightly larger than the balloons:

1 pound bittersweet or semisweet chocolate

Dip the bottom third to half of one balloon into the chocolate, moving it from side to side to coat evenly. Lift the balloon and allow the excess chocolate to drip off, then place, dipped end down, on the baking sheet. Repeat with remaining balloons and chocolate. Refrigerate until set, about 30 minutes. Prick each balloon with a pin to release the air and gently peel the deflated balloon from the chocolate cup. Holes can be patched with the remaining

chocolate. Return the bowls to the refrigerator until ready to serve.

ICE CREAM SANDWICHES

For each sandwich, spoon partially softened ice cream between two cookies, then refreeze. Some favorite combinations are:

> Chocolate Chip Cookies, 766, and Vanilla Ice
>   Cream, 831, or French Vanilla Ice Cream, 831
> Chocolate Cookies, 767, and Peppermint Stick
>   Ice Cream, 832
> Macadamia Monsters, 767, and Coffee Ice Cream, 832
> Coconut Macaroons, 771, and Pineapple Ice Milk, 834

Roll the sides in:

> Coconut, toasted, 1001
> Chocolate or multicolored sprinkles
> Miniature chocolate chips or mini candy-coated
>   chocolate pieces

ICE CREAM CAKE ROLLS

See also Mocha Ice Cream Cake, 731, and Ideas for Chiffon Cake, 710. This works best when the ice cream has just been churned.
Prepare:

Sponge Cake Sheet, 735

Fill with:

Any freshly made ice cream, 831–834

Roll and freeze until firm. Let stand at room temperature for 5 to 10 minutes before slicing, and serve with, if desired:

(Chocolate Sauce, 847, Caramel Sauce, 849,
   or any fruit sauce, 844–853)
(Whipped Cream, 754)
(Nuts, toasted, 1001, and fresh fruit)

ICE CREAM PIE

Do not be limited by the combinations here. You can mix any ice cream with these crusts.
I. Prepare, bake, cool, and freeze until very cold, at least 20 minutes:

Meringue Pie Shell, 666, or Crumb Crust, 667

Fill with:

Vanilla Ice Cream, 831, French Vanilla Ice Cream, 831,
   or Butter Pecan Ice Cream, 833

Top with:

Hot Fudge Sauce, 847, Caramel Sauce, 849,
   Butterscotch Sauce, 849, or Marshmallow
   Sauce, 850

Freeze until firm, about 1 hour.
II. Prepare, bake, cool, and freeze until very cold, at least 20 minutes:

Crumb Crust, 667, made with chocolate cookies

Fill with:

Mint Chocolate Chip Ice Cream, 831

Top with:

(Hot Fudge Sauce, 847)

Freeze until firm, about 1 hour. Serve with:

Whipped Cream, 754

III. Prepare, bake, cool, and freeze until very cold, at least 20 minutes:

Nut Crust, 668

Fill with:

Pumpkin Spice Ice Cream, 833

Top with, if desired:

(Caramel Sauce, 849)

Freeze until firm, about 1 hour. If not topped with caramel sauce, serve with:

(Hot Buttered Maple Sauce, 852)

GARNISHES AND ADDITIONS TO ICE CREAM

You may also add to ice cream, when it is in an almost frozen state, allowing the following amounts per quart:

1 cup chopped toasted nuts, 1001

1 cup finely crushed Peanut Brittle, 872

$^1/_2$ to $^3/_4$ cup crushed Praline, 876

2 tablespoons chopped preserved or stem ginger with 1 tablespoon of the syrup

1 cup crushed amaretti or Almond Macaroons, 771, plus 2 tablespoons sherry or liqueur

1 cup crumbled chocolate sandwich cookies

1 cup crumbled gingersnaps

3 to 4 ounces bittersweet, semisweet, milk, or white chocolate, finely chopped, or $^2/_3$ to 1 cup chocolate chips

$^2/_3$ to 1 cup butterscotch chips

$^2/_3$ to 1 cup candy-coated chocolate pieces

1 cup chopped Dark Chocolate Truffles, 858

$^1/_2$ to $^3/_4$ cup crushed espresso beans

1 cup chopped English Toffee, 873, or toffee bars

1 cup chopped peanut butter cups

$^1/_2$ to $^2/_3$ cup crushed peppermint candy

1 cup chopped chocolate-covered almonds or peanuts

To garnish ice cream, add just before serving:

Sweet sauces, 844–853

Chopped nuts or shredded sweetened coconut

Chopped candied citrus peel or candied fruits

Chocolate or multicolored sprinkles

Shaved or chopped semisweet or bittersweet chocolate

Marzipan fruits or rosettes

Candied violets

Fill any of the following with small scoops of homemade ice cream, sorbet, or gelato:

Chocolate Cups, 830

Tuiles, 781, shaped into cups

Phyllo Cups, 675

Serve sorbets, sherbets, and granitas in:

Frozen Orange or Lemon Surprise, 830

VANILLA ICE CREAM

1 quart

Combine in a medium saucepan:

1 cup heavy cream

$^3/_4$ cup sugar

$^1/_8$ teaspoon salt

Split lengthwise in half:

(1 vanilla bean)

Scrape the seeds into the cream mixture, then add the bean. Bring to a simmer over medium-low heat, stirring to dissolve the sugar. Pour into a bowl and stir in:

2 cups heavy cream

1 cup whole milk

$1^1/_2$ to 2 teaspoons vanilla (if not using vanilla bean)

Refrigerate until cold, overnight if possible. Remove the vanilla bean, if used, pour the mixture into an ice cream maker, and freeze as directed.

Serve with:

Cherries Jubilee, 844, a heavy liqueur, or a chocolate sauce, 847–848

FRENCH VANILLA ICE CREAM

About 1 quart

Combine in a medium saucepan and bring to a simmer over medium-low heat, stirring to dissolve the sugar:

$1^1/_2$ cups whole milk

$^3/_4$ cup sugar

$^1/_8$ teaspoon salt

Beat together in a bowl:

2 or 3 large egg yolks

Slowly stir about $^1/_2$ cup of the hot milk mixture into the beaten egg yolks. Then stir the egg mixture into the milk. Cook over low heat, stirring constantly, until the custard reaches 175°F on a thermometer and coats the back of a spoon. Do not allow the mixture to boil. Strain, if desired. Transfer to a bowl and refrigerate until cold. Stir in:

2 cups heavy cream

1 tablespoon vanilla

Pour into an ice cream maker and freeze as directed.

MINT CHOCOLATE CHIP ICE CREAM

About 1 $^1/_2$ quarts

Though optional, crème de menthe adds a second level of mint flavor, a softer texture, and a pretty pale green color. Prepare **French Vanilla Ice Cream, above.** Bring the milk, sugar, and salt to a simmer as directed, and stir in **1 cup chopped mint.** Remove the pan from the heat, cover, and let steep for 30 minutes. Strain the mixture into a clean saucepan, pressing firmly to extract all the liquid; discard the mint. Bring the milk back to a simmer and proceed as directed, omitting the vanilla. If desired, instead add **1 to 2 tablespoons crème de menthe.** When the ice cream is almost frozen, stir in **3 to 4 ounces bittersweet or semisweet chocolate, chopped.**

COFFEE ICE CREAM

About 1 quart

Prepare **French Vanilla Ice Cream, 831.** Bring the milk, sugar, and salt to a simmer as directed, and add ¼ **cup crushed or coarsely ground coffee beans.** Remove from the heat, cover, and steep for 30 minutes. Strain into a clean saucepan; discard the coffee beans. Bring the milk back to a simmer and proceed with the recipe as directed, omitting the vanilla.

RUM RAISIN ICE CREAM

About 1 quart

Prepare **French Vanilla Ice Cream, 831.**

Before making the ice cream mixture, gently warm ½ **cup dark rum** and ¾ **cup raisins** in a saucepan. Remove from the heat, cover, and steep for 20 minutes. Drain the raisins, reserving both the rum and raisins. Substitute the rum for the vanilla. When the ice cream is almost frozen, add the raisins. Because of its alcohol content, this ice cream will need to chill for several hours before it is firm.

GREEN TEA ICE CREAM

About 1 quart

Green tea gives this ice cream a light, herbal flavor. We recommend loose tea, but you can use 6 tea bags, in which case there's no need to strain the milk.

Prepare **French Vanilla Ice Cream, 831.** Bring the milk, sugar, and salt to a simmer as directed, and add **2 tablespoons green tea leaves.** Remove from the heat, cover, and steep for 15 minutes. Strain into a clean saucepan, pressing firmly to extract all the liquid; discard the tea leaves. Bring the milk back to a simmer and proceed as directed, omitting the vanilla.

CARAMEL ICE CREAM

5 cups

Combine in a small heavy saucepan:

   ¾ **cup sugar**
   ¼ **cup water**

Set over medium-high heat and swirl the saucepan gently until the sugar is dissolved and the syrup is clear. Don't let the syrup boil until the sugar is completely dissolved. Increase the heat to high, cover, and boil for 2 minutes. Uncover and continue to boil until it begins to darken around the edges. Gently stir the pan until the caramel turns deep amber.

Heat the milk, sugar, and salt as directed in:

   Vanilla Ice Cream, 831, or French Vanilla
      Ice Cream, 831

When the caramel is ready, remove from the heat and immediately stir in the warm milk until thoroughly blended. If the caramel hardens, place the pan over low heat and stir until it softens and blends with the cream. Remove from the heat and proceed as directed. Reduce the vanilla extract, if using, to 1 teaspoon.

PEPPERMINT STICK ICE CREAM

About 1 ½ quarts

Very finely grind or crush:

   8 ounces peppermint stick candy

Place in a medium bowl and add:

   2 cups whole milk

Cover and refrigerate for 12 hours. Stir the milk mixture well, then add:

   2 cups heavy cream

Refrigerate until cold. Pour into ice cream maker and freeze as directed. Serve with:

   Shaved sweet chocolate, 970, or Chocolate Sauce
      Cockaigne, 847

CHOCOLATE ICE CREAM

5 cups

Combine in a medium saucepan and bring to a simmer over medium-low heat, stirring occasionally to dissolve the sugar:

   2 cups whole milk
   ½ **cup sugar**

Combine and whisk in a medium bowl:

   4 large egg yolks
   ¼ **cup sugar**

Whisk in:

   ⅓ **cup Dutch-process cocoa powder**

Slowly pour about half the hot milk mixture into the eggs, whisking constantly. Pour this mixture back into the saucepan and cook over low heat, stirring constantly, until the custard reaches 175°F on a thermometer and coats the back of a wooden spoon. Do not allow the mixture to boil. Remove the pan from the heat and strain the custard through a fine sieve into a bowl. Stir in:

   1 cup heavy cream
   1 teaspoon vanilla

Refrigerate until cold. Pour into an ice cream maker and freeze as directed.

ROCKY ROAD ICE CREAM

Prepare **Chocolate Ice Cream, above.** When the ice cream is almost frozen, stir in **1 cup miniature marshmallows** and ½ **cup chopped toasted walnuts or almonds, 1001.**

PISTACHIO ICE CREAM

About 1 quart

If you like green pistachio ice cream, add **1 or 2 drops of green food coloring** after the almond extract. A pretty Christmas dessert served in a meringue shell, 666, garnished with whipped cream and cherries.

Finely grind in food processor, but not to a paste:

   1⅓ **cups shelled unsalted pistachio nuts, toasted, 1001**

Set aside. Combine in a medium saucepan:

   2¼ **cups heavy cream**
   2 cups whole milk
   1 cup sugar

Bring to a simmer over medium-low heat, stirring to dissolve the sugar. Stir in the ground nuts. Remove from the heat, cover, and steep for 30 minutes. Strain into a medium bowl, pressing firmly to extract all the liquid; discard the nuts. Add:

1 teaspoon vanilla
$^1/_2$ teaspoon almond extract

Refrigerate until cold. Pour into an ice cream maker and freeze as directed.

BUTTER PECAN ICE CREAM

About 1 quart

If the nuts are salted, a very special piquancy results.
Combine in a saucepan and bring to a boil, stirring to dissolve the sugar:

1 cup packed light brown sugar
$^1/_2$ cup water
$^1/_8$ teaspoon salt

Boil the syrup for 2 minutes. Meanwhile, beat together in a medium bowl:

2 large eggs

Slowly beat in the syrup. Cook in a double boiler over, not in, boiling water, stirring constantly, until the mixture reaches 175°F and coats the back of a spoon. Do not allow the mixture to boil. Add and stir until melted:

2 tablespoons unsalted butter

Strain into a medium bowl, then refrigerate until cold. Add:

1 cup whole milk
1 teaspoon vanilla extract
(1 tablespoon sherry)

Beat until soft peaks form:

1 cup heavy cream

Fold it into the egg mixture. Pour into an ice cream maker and freeze as directed. When the ice cream is almost frozen, add:

$^1/_2$ cup chopped toasted pecans, 1001

COCONUT ICE CREAM

About 1 quart

Combine in a medium saucepan and bring to a simmer over medium-low heat, stirring to dissolve the sugar:

$^3/_4$ cup whole milk
$^3/_4$ cup unsweetened coconut milk
$^1/_2$ cup sugar
$^1/_8$ teaspoon salt

Stir in:

2 cups shredded sweetened coconut toasted, 972

Remove from the heat, cover, and steep for 30 minutes. Strain the milk into a clean saucepan, pressing firmly on the coconut to extract all liquid. Discard all but $^3/_4$ cup of the coconut, and stir back into the milk. Bring to a simmer over medium-low heat. Beat together in a bowl:

2 or 3 large egg yolks

Slowly stir in about $^1/_2$ cup of the milk mixture, then stir the egg mixture into the rest of the milk. Cook over low heat, stirring constantly, until the custard reaches 175°F on a

thermometer and coats the back of a spoon. Do not allow the mixture to boil. Transfer to a bowl and refrigerate until cold. Stir in:

2 cups heavy cream

Pour into an ice cream maker and freeze as directed.

PUMPKIN SPICE ICE CREAM

1 $^1/_2$ quarts

Combine in a medium saucepan and bring to a simmer over medium-low heat, stirring occasionally to dissolve the sugar:

1 $^1/_2$ cups whole milk
$^1/_4$ cup sugar
$^1/_2$ teaspoon ground cinnamon
$^1/_2$ teaspoon ground ginger
Pinch of grated or ground nutmeg

Beat together in a medium bowl:

4 large egg yolks
$^1/_2$ cup sugar

Slowly stir in half the hot milk mixture, then pour this mixture back into rest of the milk. Cook over low heat, stirring constantly, until the custard reaches 175°F on a thermometer and coats the back of a spoon. Do not allow the mixture to boil. Remove the pan from the heat and strain the custard through a fine sieve into a bowl. Stir in:

1 $^1/_4$ cups heavy cream
1 cup cooked or canned pumpkin puree
1 teaspoon vanilla

Refrigerate until cold. Pour into an ice cream maker and freeze as directed.

PEACH, APRICOT, MANGO, OR NECTARINE ICE CREAM

About 2 quarts

Peel, pit, and puree in a food processor:

2 pounds very ripe peaches, apricots, mangoes, or nectarines

Pour into a medium bowl and stir in:

1 teaspoon fresh lemon juice
$^1/_2$ teaspoon vanilla
$^1/_2$ cup sugar
Pinch of salt

Refrigerate until the sugar is dissolved, stirring occasionally.
Combine in a bowl and stir to dissolve the sugar:

1 $^1/_2$ cups heavy cream
$^1/_2$ cup whole milk
$^1/_3$ cup sugar

Pour into an ice cream maker and freeze as directed. When the ice cream is almost frozen, add the fruit mixture.

STRAWBERRY ICE CREAM

2 quarts

Combine in a food processor:

1 quart strawberries, hulled and sliced
$^3/_4$ cup sugar
1 teaspoon vanilla

Pulse 2 to 3 times, just until the fruit is crushed. Transfer to a bowl and refrigerate for 1 hour. Add:

  2 cups heavy cream
  1 cup whole milk

Stir until the sugar is dissolved, 2 to 3 minutes. Pour into an ice cream maker and freeze as directed.

BLACKBERRY OR RASPBERRY ICE CREAM
1 quart
Combine in a food processor:

  1 pint blackberries or raspberries
  $1/2$ cup sugar
  1 teaspoon vanilla

Pulse 2 to 3 times, just until the fruit is crushed. Transfer to a bowl and refrigerate for 1 hour. Strain the mixture through a fine sieve, pressing firmly to extract all the berry juices; discard the seeds. Add:

  $1/2$ cup whole milk
  $1 1/2$ cups heavy cream

Stir until the sugar is dissolved, 2 to 3 minutes. Pour into an ice cream maker and freeze as directed.

ORANGE ICE MILK
2 quarts
Before there was ice cream, there was undoubtedly ice milk; in some Asian countries, it still prevails.
Combine in a bowl and stir until the sugar is dissolved:

  $1 1/2$ teaspoons grated orange zest
  $1 1/2$ cups sugar
  $1 1/2$ cups fresh orange juice
  $1/4$ cup fresh lemon juice
  ($3/4$ cup mashed bananas: about $1 1/2$ bananas)

Stir these ingredients gradually into:

  4 cups very cold whole milk

If the milk looks slightly curdled, it will not affect the texture of the ice milk. Pour into an ice cream maker and freeze as directed.

PINEAPPLE ICE MILK
$1 1/2$ quarts
Combine in a bowl and stir until the sugar is dissolved:

  1 cup unsweetened pineapple juice
  1 cup sugar
  1 teaspoon grated lemon zest
  $1/4$ cup fresh lemon juice
  $1/8$ teaspoon salt
  $3/4$ cup drained canned crushed pineapple

Stir these ingredients slowly into:

  4 cups very cold whole milk

Pour into an ice cream maker and freeze as directed.

ABOUT GELATO
Although *gelato* is the Italian word for ice cream, here the term has come to mean a specific churned or stir-frozen variety with an intense flavor and dense texture. Gelato is generally lower in butterfat and can become icy at lower temperatures, therefore it is best served at around 15°F. Let gelato stand at room temperature for 5 to 10 minutes before scooping, or serve it straight from the ice cream maker, when it is at its best.

HAZELNUT GELATO
About 1 quart
Toast 8 to 10 minutes in a 350° oven, stirring occasionally. Wrap the nuts in a clean kitchen towel and rub vigorously to remove as much of the skins as possible.
Finely grind in a food processor, but not to a paste:

  2 cups toasted hazelnuts, 1001

Bring just to a simmer in a medium saucepan:

  3 cups whole milk

Add the nuts. Remove from the heat, cover, and steep for 30 minutes. Strain the milk into a clean saucepan, pressing firmly to extract as much liquid as possible; discard the nuts. Add:

  $1/2$ cup sugar

Bring to a simmer over medium-low heat, stirring occasionally to dissolve the sugar. Meanwhile, beat together in a medium bowl:

  6 large egg yolks
  $1/4$ cup sugar

Slowly stir in about half the hot milk mixture into the eggs, then stir the egg mixture into the rest of the milk. Cook over low heat, stirring constantly, until the custard reaches 175°F on a thermometer and coats the back of a spoon. Do not allow the mixture to boil. Strain the custard through a fine sieve into a bowl. Stir in:

  $1/4$ cup heavy cream
  $1/4$ teaspoon vanilla
  (1 tablespoon Frangelico or other hazelnut liqueur)

Refrigerate until cold. Pour into an ice cream maker and freeze as directed.

CHOCOLATE HAZELNUT GELATO (GIANDUJA)
Prepare **Hazelnut Gelato, above,** beating $1/4$ cup **Dutch-processed cocoa powder** into the egg yolk mixture before adding the hot milk.

ABOUT FROZEN YOGURT
Frozen yogurt is made with a mixture of drained yogurt, whole milk or cream, sugar, flavorings, and gelatin. Gelatin improves the texture of stored frozen yogurt. Plain low-fat yogurt works best in our recipes, as does flavoring the yogurt yourself. Because excess water can contribute to iciness, it's important to drain off some of the yogurt's liquid. Spoon the yogurt into a fine-mesh sieve suspended over a measuring cup, refrigerate, and allow the liquid to slowly drip out of the yogurt, about 2 hours.

As with other frozen desserts, add ingredients such as chopped nuts, chocolate chips, raisins, or crumbled cookies when the freezing is almost completed. About $3/4$ cup of additions of your choice is enough for one batch.

If you want homemade frozen yogurt to approximate the texture of commercial soft-serve yogurt, serve it fresh out of the ice cream maker. Once it has been frozen for a few hours, it will become firm. Some tang is desirable, but if you want to tame the acidic flavor of the yogurt, add an extra ¼ cup sugar.

VANILLA FROZEN YOGURT

5 cups

Spoon into a fine-mesh sieve set over a large measuring cup:

2 cups plain low-fat yogurt

Scrape the yogurt into a medium bowl; discard the liquid. Sprinkle:

1 envelope (2¼ teaspoons) unflavored gelatin

over:

¼ cup whole milk

in a small cup. Let stand for 10 minutes to soften. Combine in a medium saucepan:

1½ cups whole milk

¾ cup sugar

Split lengthwise in half:

(½ vanilla bean)

Scrape the seeds into the milk mixture. Add the bean and bring just to a simmer over low heat, stirring occasionally to dissolve the sugar. Remove from the heat and let cool for 5 minutes, then add the gelatin and milk mixture, stirring until the gelatin dissolves completely. Let cool to room temperature.

Gently whisk the gelatin mixture into the drained yogurt. Stir in:

1½ teaspoons vanilla (if not using vanilla bean)

Refrigerate until cold. Remove the vanilla bean if you used it, pour into an ice cream maker, and freeze as directed.

CHOCOLATE FROZEN YOGURT

Prepare **Vanilla Frozen Yogurt, above,** omitting the vanilla bean and adding ½ **cup Dutch-processed cocoa powder** to the hot milk mixture; whisk until smooth. Proceed as directed, adding the vanilla extract.

STRAWBERRY FROZEN YOGURT

About 5 cups

Spoon into a fine-mesh sieve set over a large measuring cup:

2 cups plain low-fat yogurt

Refrigerate until ½ cup liquid has drained off, about 2 hours, then scrape the yogurt into a medium bowl; discard the liquid.

Place in a food processor:

1 pint strawberries, hulled and sliced

Pulse 2 to 3 times, just until the fruit is crushed; do not puree. Transfer to a bowl and stir in:

¼ to ⅓ cup sugar, to taste

1 teaspoon vanilla

Pinch of salt

Cover and let stand at room temperature for 1 hour. Sprinkle:

1 envelope (2¼ teaspoons) unflavored gelatin

over:

¼ cup whole milk

in a small cup. Let stand for 10 minutes to soften. Combine in a medium saucepan:

¾ cup whole milk

¼ cup plus 2 tablespoons sugar

Bring just to a simmer, stirring occasionally to dissolve the sugar. Remove from the heat and let cool for 5 minutes, then add the gelatin mixture, stirring until it dissolves completely. Let cool to room temperature.

Gently whisk the milk and strawberry mixtures into the drained yogurt. Refrigerate until cold. Pour into an ice cream maker and freeze as directed.

ABOUT SORBET

Sorbet is a churned or stir-frozen mixture of fresh fruit juice or puree, combined with sugar, and sometimes a little alcohol, resulting in a frozen dessert with an intense fruit flavor. ➤ For a more complex flavor, substitute orange juice or lemonade for the water.

Like other churned desserts, sorbet will be soft when it comes out of the ice cream machine. A few hours in the freezer will harden it somewhat, but sorbet should be scoopable right from the freezer, without softening. The key to this consistency is the amount of sugar (and alcohol, if used), which lowers the freezing point of the fruit mixture and prevents it from getting too hard.

Traditionally the first step in making a sorbet is to prepare a simple syrup by boiling equal amounts of sugar and water for 5 minutes (or microwaving on high for 2 to 3 minutes), cooling, and adding two parts fruit juice or puree, but most recipes here are lower in water and sometimes sugar, which results in a truer fruit flavor. Less sugar and water affect the long-term storage of sorbet, so these recipes are best served the day they are made. The sweetness of fresh fruits varies, so taste the sorbet before freezing. ➤ It should taste a little too sweet, as freezing dulls both the fruit and sugar flavors. If extra sweetness is needed, add extra sugar a tablespoon at a time, stirring until completely dissolved.

You'll get a lighter-textured sorbet when you use juice rather than puree. Whether you use juice or puree, ½ cup sugar for each cup of fruit juice or puree is sometimes too sweet. Lemon juice, up to 1 tablespoon per cup of fruit, keeps sorbets made with sweet fruits from becoming cloying. Alcohol intensifies fruit flavor and helps ensure a soft texture. A liqueur whose flavor complements the fruit is a good choice in most recipes, but unflavored vodka may be used instead.

Sorbets are beautiful served as Frozen Orange or Lemon Surprise, see 830.

RASPBERRY SORBET

5 cups

Combine in a small saucepan:

1 cup sugar

$^1/_2$ cup water

Bring just to a simmer, stirring occasionally to dissolve the sugar. Set aside to cool. Puree:

1$^1/_2$ pints raspberries

Strain through a fine-mesh sieve into a medium bowl, pressing firmly to extract as much juice as possible; discard the seeds. Stir in:

1 tablespoon fresh lemon juice

(1 tablespoon framboise)

Add the cooled sugar syrup and stir to blend thoroughly. Refrigerate until cold. Taste and add more sugar if needed, stirring until the sugar is completely dissolved, 2 to 3 minutes. Pour into an ice cream maker and freeze as directed.

BLACKBERRY SORBET

Prepare **Raspberry Sorbet, above,** substituting **1$^1/_2$ pints blackberries** for the raspberries. Add the **framboise,** if desired, or substitute **kirsch.**

BLUEBERRY SORBET

Prepare **Raspberry Sorbet, above,** substituting **2$^1/_2$ cups blueberries** for the raspberries. Increase the lemon juice to 2 tablespoons. If desired, substitute **crème de cassis or kirsch** for the framboise.

STRAWBERRY SORBET

Prepare **Raspberry Sorbet, above,** substituting **1 pound strawberries, hulled and sliced,** for the raspberries. If desired, substitute **kirsch or amaretto** for the framboise.

MANGO SORBET

Prepare **Raspberry Sorbet, above,** substituting **3 ripe medium mangoes, peeled and pitted** for the raspberries. Reduce the sugar to $^3/_4$ cup. Substitute **2 tablespoons fresh lime juice** for the lemon juice, and, if desired, substitute **Grand Marnier or tequila** for the framboise.

PEACH SORBET

Prepare **Raspberry Sorbet, above,** substituting **1$^1/_2$ pounds soft, ripe peaches, peeled, and pitted** for the raspberries. Increase the lemon juice to 2 tablespoons and add it to the peaches before they are pureed. Taste the mixture after chilling, and add more lemon juice if needed. If desired, substitute **amaretto or peach brandy** for the framboise.

LEMON SORBET

2$^1/_3$ cups

Fresh lemon juice and strips of lemon zest are essential for this recipe. If you have access to Meyer lemons, 224, this sorbet will highlight their sweetness.

Combine in a small saucepan:

1$^1/_2$ cups water

1$^1/_4$ cups sugar

Zest of 1 lemon, removed in strips, 223

Bring to a boil over medium heat, stirring occasionally to dissolve the sugar. Stir in:

($^1/_2$ cup chopped mint, rosemary, lavender, or thyme sprigs)

Remove the pan from the heat, cover, and steep until the flavor is strong, 20 to 40 minutes. Strain into a medium bowl. Stir in:

$^1/_2$ cup fresh lemon juice

(1 tablespoon lemon vodka)

Refrigerate until cold. Taste and add more sugar if needed, stirring until the sugar is completely dissolved, 2 to 3 minutes. Pour into an ice cream maker and freeze as directed.

LIME SORBET

Prepare **Lemon Sorbet, above,** substituting $^1/_2$ cup fresh **lime juice** for the lemon juice and, if desired, **tequila** for the lemon vodka.

ORANGE SORBET

2$^2/_3$ cups

Combine in a small saucepan:

$^1/_2$ cup fresh orange juice

1 cup sugar

Zest of 1 medium orange, removed in strips, 223

Heat over medium heat, stirring, just until the sugar is dissolved. Do not boil. Remove the pan from the heat, cover, and steep for 15 minutes. Strain into a medium bowl. Stir in:

1$^1/_2$ cups fresh orange juice

1 tablespoon fresh lemon juice

(1 tablespoon Grand Marnier or orange juice)

Refrigerate until cold. Taste and add more sugar if needed, stirring until the sugar is completely dissolved, 2 to 3 minutes. Pour into an ice cream maker and freeze as directed.

PINK GRAPEFRUIT SORBET

Pink grapefruits are sweeter than white ones, though still tart enough to make this pale pink sorbet supremely appealing.

Prepare **Orange Sorbet, above,** omitting the lemon juice and substituting **the zest of 1 pink grapefruit** and $^1/_2$ cup **fresh pink grapefruit juice** for the orange juice and zest. If desired, substitute **tequila** for the Grand Marnier.

WATERMELON SORBET

Make watermelon juice by removing the rind and seeds from **2$^1/_2$ pounds red or yellow watermelon.** Puree until smooth, then strain through a fine-mesh sieve; discard the pulp. Prepare **Orange Sorbet, above,** omitting the orange zest and substituting 2 cups of watermelon juice for the orange juice. Increase the lemon juice to 2 tablespoons and, substitute **Campari or vodka** for the Grand Marnier.

ROSEMARY SORBET

5 cups

Herb sorbets are often served between courses to cleanse the palate. They also make refreshing light desserts, accompanied by fresh fruit or a slice of apple tart. Instead of rosemary, try basil, thyme, or mint. Fresh herbs vary greatly in intensity; taste as they steep in the sugar syrup, remembering that their flavor should be quite strong, since freezing mellows their flavor.

Combine in a medium saucepan:

>   **2$^1/_4$ cups water**
>   **$^1/_2$ cup sugar**

Bring to a boil, stirring occasionally to dissolve the sugar. Stir in:

>   **$^1/_2$ cup chopped fresh rosemary sprigs**

Remove the pan from the heat, cover, and steep until the flavor is strong, 20 to 40 minutes. Strain into a bowl; discard the rosemary. Refrigerate until cold. Pour into an ice cream maker and freeze as directed.

INSTANT SORBET

This is a quick and easy ice dessert that doesn't require an ice cream maker. The secret is **canned fruit** in heavy syrup. The higher proportion of sugar in the heavy syrup means the texture of the sorbet is soft and creamy even after a couple of days in the freezer. The flavor is not identical to scratch sorbet, but this is a handy trick when you need a dessert in a pinch. Fruit in a light syrup can be used, but the final texture will be icier. Canned fruit with pits needs to be pitted before using.

These brightly colored and refreshing sorbets are enhanced when combined. Freeze two or three different types of sorbets, then layer them in clear glasses. You can include layers of plain yogurt between the fruit layers to add extra tang. Try cherries and peaches, blueberries and peaches, raspberries and mangoes, strawberries and pineapple, cherries and blueberries, and blueberries, peaches, and raspberries. A 15- to 16-ounce can will yield 1$^1/_2$ to 1$^3/_4$ cups frozen sorbet; layer the frozen fruit from two cans of this size for 6 to 8 servings.

Puree in a food processor or blender:

>   **One 15- to 16-ounce can fruit in heavy syrup,**
>   **undrained**

Pour the puree into a plastic freezer bag and freeze overnight. Repeat with as many different fruits as desired. Stir well to mix, then freeze overnight:

>   **(Plain yogurt)**

When ready to serve, remove the fruit from the bag, slice into pieces, and place in the food processor. Add:

>   **(2 to 3 teaspoons liqueur)**

Pulse until the mixture is almost smooth—some chunks of frozen fruit should remain. Scrape down the sides once or twice. Repeat with each frozen puree. Layer the fruit sorbets in clear parfait glasses or wineglasses, alternating with the frozen yogurt, if using. Top with:

>   **(Whipped Cream, 754)**

ABOUT SHERBET

Sherbet is a churned or stir-frozen dessert made from a mixture of whole milk, sugar, fruit juice and/or fruit puree, flavorings, and sometimes gelatin. Gelatin is the key to smooth, creamy sherbets. The gelatin granules swell and prevent the ice crystals from becoming large. After the gelatin is soaked in cold water, it is added to a base of juice and sugar that has been heated just until the sugar dissolves. ➤ Do not let the base come to a boil.

As the gelatin sherbet base cools, it may begin to set and become lumpy. Don't worry—it will smooth out when churned. As with ice cream, sherbet emerges from the ice cream maker fairly soft. Freeze it for several hours if you prefer it firm. Sherbet is best served at around 20°F, so soften it slightly before serving, as described in About Storing and Serving Ice Cream and Other Frozen Desserts, 829.

Sherbets and ices, 838, are excellent with fruits—fresh, poached, preserved, or candied. They are delectable when served in fruit shells, see Frozen Orange or Lemon Surprise, 830.

RASPBERRY OR STRAWBERRY SHERBET

5 cups

Sprinkle:

>   **1 teaspoon unflavored gelatin**

over:

>   **1 tablespoon cold water**

in a small cup. Let stand for 10 minutes to soften. Combine in a small saucepan and bring to a boil, stirring to dissolve the sugar:

>   **1 cup water or $^1/_2$ cup water plus**
>   **$^1/_2$ cup pineapple juice**
>   **$^3/_4$ to 1 cup sugar, to taste**

Cover and boil 5 minutes without stirring. Add:

>   **1 to 2 tablespoons fresh lemon juice**

Dissolve the gelatin in the heated syrup. Refrigerate until cold. Puree in a food processor:

>   **1 quart strawberries, hulled, or raspberries**

Strain through a fine-mesh sieve into a bowl. Stir in the gelatin mixture. Pour into an ice cream maker and freeze as directed.

ORANGE SHERBET

5 cups

Sprinkle:

>   **1 envelope (2$^1/_4$ teaspoons) unflavored gelatin**

over:

>   **$^1/_4$ cup cold water**

in a small cup. Let stand for 10 minutes to soften. Combine in a medium saucepan:

>   **Zest of 1 orange, removed in strips, 223**
>   **1$^3/_4$ cups fresh orange juice**
>   **$^3/_4$ cup sugar**

Bring to a simmer, stirring occasionally to dissolve the

sugar. Strain through a sieve into a bowl; discard the zest. Add the gelatin, stirring until it is completely dissolved. Stir in:

1 cup whole milk

Refrigerate until cold. Pour into an ice cream maker and freeze as directed.

LEMON SHERBET
5 cups

Prepare **Orange Sherbet, 837,** substituting **the zest of 1 lemon** for the orange zest and **³/₄ cup fresh lemon juice and 1¹/₄ cups water** for the orange juice. Increase the sugar to 1 cup.

LIME SHERBET
5 cups

Prepare **Orange Sherbet, 837,** substituting **the zest of 1 lime** for the orange zest. Substitute **¹/₂ cup fresh lime juice and 1¹/₄ cups water** for the orange juice. Increase the sugar to 1 cup.

CRANBERRY SHERBET
5 cups

Try this tart sherbet as a palate cleanser. Frozen cranberries may be used here—do not thaw. (A standard 12-ounce bag yields 3 cups cranberries, so buy two and freeze the leftovers for another use.)
Sprinkle:

1 envelope (2¹/₄ teaspoons) unflavored gelatin

over:

¹/₄ cup water

in a small cup. Let stand 10 minutes to soften. Combine in a medium saucepan:

4¹/₂ cups cranberries
1¹/₂ cups water

Bring to a simmer and cook over medium heat until the berries have popped, about 10 minutes. Let cool slightly. Puree the cranberry mixture in a blender or food processor until smooth. Strain through a fine-mesh sieve into a bowl, pressing firmly to extract as much juice as possible; discard the pulp. Combine in a small saucepan:

¹/₂ cup water
1¹/₂ cups sugar

Heat, to dissolve the sugar. Stir into the cranberry puree. Add the gelatin, stirring until completely dissolved. Stir in:

1 cup whole milk

Refrigerate until cold. Pour into an ice cream maker and freeze.

ICE POPS

Pour these mixtures into 3-ounce plastic or paper cups or molds made especially for freezing homemade ice pops. When the mixture has begun to solidify, insert a wooden craft stick into each for a handle. Freeze until completely solid. Unmold by briefly running the outside of the cups or molds under hot water.

I. *Eight 3-ounce pops*
Stir well:

2 cups pureed fresh, frozen, or canned fruit, such as pineapple, berries, mango, peaches, or watermelon
1 cup fresh orange juice
2 tablespoons sugar

Freeze and unmold as described above.

II. *Eight 3-ounce pops*
Stir well:

1 cup plus 2 tablespoons fresh orange juice
1¹/₂ cups plain yogurt
¹/₃ cup sugar
³/₄ teaspoon vanilla

Freeze and unmold as described above.

III. *Ten 3-ounce pops*
Stir well:

One 12-ounce can frozen juice concentrate, such as orange, pineapple, apple, cranberry, or fruit punch
2 cups plain yogurt
¹/₃ cup sugar
¹/₃ cup pineapple or other juice

Freeze and unmold as described above.

SNOW CREAM

After the first two hours of snowfall, snow is clean and usable for this favorite childhood treat. Do not use snow gathered off the ground.
In a chilled bowl, place:

Clean fresh snow

Drizzle over it:

Sweetened fruit juice or maple syrup

Or, for a gallon of snow, stir in:

1 cup heavy cream
³/₄ cup sugar
¹/₂ teaspoon vanilla

ABOUT GRANITA OR ICES

Granita is the Italian word for a dessert ice, made from a sugar-syrup base flavored with coffee, fruit juice, or fruit puree that is frozen solid, then scraped or shaved to produce its characteristically coarse texture of ice crystals. Granitas, ices, or glacés contain less sugar than sorbets and should taste strongly of their flavoring.

Classic granita is still-frozen. The base is poured into a 13 x 9-inch stainless steel pan or freezer tray in the freezer for 30 minutes. Cover with plastic wrap. ➤ Every 30 minutes, scrape the mixture with a large spoon or fork as it hardens in the freezer, stirring the frozen crystals from the edges of the pan back into the liquid, loosening and breaking up frozen crystals. Repeat until the mixture is frozen and creamy, about 3 hours total. As soon as the granita has properly solidified, it should be scooped into individual bowls or goblets and served immediately. If you start the granita several hours before dinner, the timing should work.

For less work, try ➤ the food processor or blender

method. Pour the mixture into two ice cube trays and freeze at least 3 hours. (The cubes can be transferred to a resealable plastic freezer bag and frozen for up to 1 week.) Just before serving, puree the cubes in a food processor. Process only as many cubes at a time as will fit in a single layer in the bowl, and pulse 10 to 12 times, or until the granita is smooth. The granita can become slushy if pureed too long.

BERRY GRANITA

2¹/₂ cups
Prepare:
   Simple Syrup, 835
using:
   ¹/₂ cup water
   ¹/₂ cup sugar, or to taste
Let cool. Puree in a food processor or blender:
   4 cups berries, hulled if necessary and sliced if large
Strain through a fine-mesh sieve into a bowl; discard the seeds or skins. Stir the puree into the cooled syrup. Refrigerate until cold. Freeze as described above.

ESPRESSO GRANITA

3 cups
A classic Italian dessert, served with unsweetened whipped cream. Very strong brewed coffee may be used in place of the espresso.
Combine in a medium bowl:
   2 cups hot espresso
   ¹/₄ to ¹/₂ cup sugar
   (1 tablespoon amaretto, Frangelico, or sambuca)
Stir until the sugar is dissolved, then refrigerate until cold. Freeze as described above.

CAFFE LATTE GRANITA

3 cups
Prepare **Espresso Granita, above,** substituting **1 cup hot whole milk** for 1 cup of the espresso.

LEMON GRANITA

2 cups
Combine in a small saucepan:
   1¹/₂ cups water
   ¹/₂ cup sugar
   Zest of 1 lemon, removed in strips, 223
Bring to a boil over medium heat, stirring occasionally to dissolve the sugar, then boil 5 minutes. Remove the pan from the heat, cover, and let steep for 15 minutes.
Strain into a medium bowl; discard the zest. Let cool to room temperature, then stir in:
   ¹/₂ cup fresh lemon juice
Refrigerate until cold, then freeze as described above.

LIME GRANITA

2 cups
Prepare **Lemon Granita, above,** substituting **the zest of 1 lime** and **¹/₂ cup fresh lime juice** for the lemon.

PINK GRAPEFRUIT GRANITA

2 cups
Prepare **Lemon Granita, above,** substituting **the zest of 1 pink grapefruit** and **¹/₂ cup fresh pink grapefruit juice** for the lemon. Reduce the water to ¹/₂ cup and the sugar to ¹/₃ cup.

ABOUT ICE CREAM PARFAITS AND ICE CREAM SUNDAES

Ice cream parfaits are made by layering several different flavors of ice creams and sauces in tall, clear parfait glasses or wineglasses. Ice cream parfaits may include syrups, liqueurs, fruits, nuts, and whipped cream or consist only of a layering of different ice creams and sauces. When making parfaits, ➤ chill the glasses in the freezer for 30 minutes. Once you have assembled the parfaits, serve right away, or freeze until ready to serve. You may freeze parfaits made with fudge, caramel, marshmallow, or butterscotch sauce until firm. Parfaits with a fruit sauce or chopped fruit are best eaten right away, but may be frozen 1 to 2 hours. Increasing the sugar in fruit sauces by half will help prevent the sauce from completely freezing. If you have frozen a fruit parfait, let it mellow in the refrigerator for 15 to 20 minutes or at room temperature for 5 to 10 minutes before serving.

An **ice cream sundae** is made using any combination of ice cream and sauce, or with assorted ice creams and sauces in one dish. The most popular toppings are nuts, syrups, and whipped cream, but fruit is also delicious. Don't forget the cherry on top.

CHOCOLATE, VANILLA, AND COFFEE PARFAIT

One serving
Place in the bottom of a glass:
   1 scoop Coffee Ice Cream, 832
Top with:
   2 to 4 tablespoons Hot Fudge Sauce, 847
Add:
   1 scoop Vanilla Ice Cream, 831, French Vanilla Ice Cream, 831, or Vanilla Frozen Yogurt, 835
Top with:
   2 to 4 tablespoons Butterscotch Sauce, 849
Add:
   1 scoop Chocolate Ice Cream, 832, or Chocolate Frozen Yogurt, 835
Top with:
   2 to 4 tablespoons Marshmallow Sauce, 850

BERRY PARFAIT

One serving
Place in the bottom of a glass:
   1 scoop Blueberry Sorbet, 836
Top with:
   ¹/₄ cup raspberries

2 to 4 tablespoons Fresh Raspberry Sauce, 853,
or Melba Sauce, 844
Add:
1 scoop Raspberry Sorbet, 836
Top with:
1/4 cup blueberries
2 to 4 tablespoons Fresh Raspberry Sauce, 853,
or Melba Sauce, 844
Add:
1 scoop Blueberry Sorbet, 836
Top with:
1/4 cup raspberries
2 to 4 tablespoons Fresh Raspberry Sauce, 853,
or Melba Sauce, 844

WINTER PARFAIT

One serving

Place in the bottom of a glass:
1 scoop Chocolate Ice Cream, 832
Top with:
2 to 4 tablespoons Mocha Sauce, 848
Add:
1 scoop Butter Pecan Ice Cream, 833
Top with:
2 to 4 tablespoons Caramel Sauce, 849
Add:
1 scoop Coffee Ice Cream, 832
Top with:
2 to 4 tablespoons Cherries Jubilee, 826,
or Cherry Sauce, 844
Whipped Cream, 754

HOT FUDGE SUNDAE

One serving

Place in a dessert glass or bowl:
3 scoops Vanilla Ice Cream, 831, French Vanilla Ice
Cream, 831, or Peppermint Stick Ice Cream, 832
Top with:
2 to 4 tablespoons Hot Fudge Sauce, 847
Drizzle over the top:
2 to 4 tablespoons Marshmallow Sauce, 850
Top with:
Whipped cream
2 tablespoons chopped toasted nuts, 1001
1 maraschino cherry

BANANA SPLIT

One serving

Place on their sides on each side of an oblong dish:
1 banana, split lengthwise in half
Place in between the banana halves:
1 scoop Vanilla Ice Cream, 831
1 scoop Chocolate Ice Cream, 832
1 scoop Strawberry Ice Cream, 833
Spoon one of the following over each scoop of ice cream:

2 tablespoons Chocolate Sauce Cockaigne, 847,
or 2 tablespoons Fresh Strawberry Sauce, 853
2 tablespoons Butterscotch Sauce, 849
2 tablespoons Marshmallow Sauce, 850
Top with:
Whipped Cream, 754
Scatter over the top:
(2 tablespoons chopped nuts, toasted, 1001)
Top with:
1 maraschino cherry

ABOUT STILL-FROZEN DESSERTS

Still-frozen desserts are made by allowing the mixture to freeze without stirring or using any special equipment. Still-frozen desserts ➤ need an emulsifying agent—heavy cream, egg yolks, gelatin, cornstarch, or corn syrup—to keep large ice crystals from forming during the freezing process. Count on a very different texture in these still-frozen desserts from those made by churning. Whipping the cream to soft peaks and freezing the mixture as quickly as possible can help reduce iciness. The whipped cream and any solids such as nuts and candied fruits are incorporated when the rest of the mixture is very well chilled or partially frozen, and liqueurs are usually added almost at the end of the freezing period.

Freeze these desserts in molds and unmold as for **bombes,** 842. Or form into individual **parfaits,** frozen in and served from tall parfait glasses, goblets, or wineglasses. You may freeze the mixtures in bowls or trays, then add other ingredients to the mixtures or layer them with fruits and sauces in parfait glasses or goblets. When serving, top them with freshly whipped cream and a cherry. ➤ Do not store more than 24 hours if you want a satisfactory texture.

Semifreddi are frozen mousses usually made with a custard or egg base, lightened with whipped cream, and molded in a loaf pan or individual goblets. **Frozen soufflés** are not baked and don't actually rise. Instead, a frozen soufflé is made to look like a soufflé—towering out of a mold—and, like a classic baked soufflé, it is dusted with confectioners' sugar or adorned with berries or a berry sauce, shaved chocolate or a chocolate sauce, unsalted toasted nuts, and/or decorative dollops of whipped cream.

FROZEN STRAWBERRY OR RASPBERRY MOUSSE

6 servings

Prepare:
Bavarian Berry Cream, 818
using:
1 cup sugar
Pour into a 1 1/2-quart mold or 6 individual parfait glasses and freeze until firm, about 6 hours for a single mold or 3 hours for glasses.
Top with:

Whipped Cream, 754
Fresh berries

FROZEN FRUIT MOUSSE

12 to 14 servings

Prepare:

 **2 cups crushed peaches, apricots, bananas,
 or strawberries, or pureed blackberries
 or red raspberries, strained**

Stir in:

 ³/₄ to 1 cup confectioners' sugar
 ¹/₈ teaspoon salt

Sprinkle:

 1¹/₂ teaspoons unflavored gelatin

over:

 2 tablespoons cold water

in a small cup. Let stand 10 minutes to soften. Dissolve the gelatin in:

 ¹/₄ cup boiling water

Cool, then add:

 2 tablespoons fresh lemon juice

Stir into the fruit mixture. Whip to soft peaks:

 2 cups heavy cream

Fold into the fruit and gelatin mixture. Transfer to a 2-quart mold and freeze until firm, about 8 hours. Let stand for 30 minutes after unmolding.

COFFEE PARFAIT

6 to 8 servings

Combine in the top of a double boiler:

 ²/₃ cup sugar
 2 tablespoons cornstarch
 ¹/₈ teaspoon salt

Stir in:

 2 tablespoons whole milk
 2 large egg yolks, beaten
 1 cup espresso or very strong coffee

Stir and cook in a double boiler until the custard coats the back of a spoon. Pour into a bowl and refrigerate until cold. Whip to soft peaks:

 1¹/₂ cups heavy cream

Fold into the coffee mixture. Divide among parfait glasses and freeze for at least 4 to 5 hours. If frozen longer, let stand at room temperature for 5 to 10 minutes before serving topped with:

 Whipped Cream, 754
 (Grated chocolate)

HAZELNUT SEMIFREDDO

6 servings

Preheat the oven to 350°F.

Spread on a baking sheet:

 2 cups hazelnuts

Toast until fragrant, stirring occasionally. Immediately transfer the nuts to a clean kitchen towel. Wrap the nuts in the towel and rub vigorously to remove as much of the skins as possible. Let cool completely.

Reserve 6 hazelnuts for garnish. Finely grind in a food processor the remaining nuts, but not to a paste. Bring almost to a simmer in a medium saucepan:

 3 cups whole milk

Stir in the ground nuts. Remove the pan from the heat, cover, and steep for 30 minutes. Strain the milk into a bowl, pressing on the nuts to extract as much liquid as possible. Discard the nuts, and return the milk to the saucepan. Add:

 ¹/₃ cup sugar

Bring to a simmer, stirring occasionally to dissolve the sugar. Beat in a medium bowl:

 4 large egg yolks
 ¹/₂ cup sugar

Slowly pour half the hot milk mixture into the eggs, whisking. Pour this mixture back into the saucepan and cook over low heat, stirring constantly with a wooden spoon, until the custard reaches 175°F on a thermometer and coats the back of a spoon. Do not allow the mixture to boil. Remove the pan from the heat and strain the custard through a fine sieve into a large bowl. Chill thoroughly. Whip to soft peaks:

 1 cup heavy cream

Gently stir one-quarter of the whipped cream into the chilled custard, then fold in the remaining cream. Spoon the mixture into 6 individual goblets. Place plastic wrap directly on the surface of the custards. Freeze until firm, at least 3 hours. Garnish each goblet with a hazelnut. Serve immediately.

CHOCOLATE SEMIFREDDO

12 to 18 servings

For a dramatic increase in flavor, substitute brandy or Frangelico for the water.

Line a 9 x 5-inch loaf pan with plastic wrap, allowing the excess to hang over the edges. Beat in the bowl of a stand mixer on medium-high speed, 2 to 3 minutes:

 4 large eggs

Combine in a small saucepan:

 ¹/₄ cup water
 ³/₄ cup sugar

Simmer over medium heat until the syrup is clear. With the mixer running on medium-high speed, slowly add the hot sugar syrup to the eggs, pouring it down the side of the bowl. Place the bowl over, not in, a saucepan of simmering water, and heat the egg mixture, whisking constantly to prevent curdling, to 160°F, 2 to 4 minutes. Remove from the heat and beat on high speed until light and fluffy and cooled to room temperature, 5 to 10 minutes. Gently fold in:

 6 ounces bittersweet or semisweet chocolate, melted
 1 teaspoon vanilla

Whip to soft peaks:

 1 cup heavy cream

Gently fold the cream into chocolate mixture. Pour into the prepared pan and place plastic wrap directly on the surface. Freeze until firm, at least 8 hours.

Remove the plastic covering and unmold the semifreddo onto a serving platter. Peel away plastic wrap, slice, and serve immediately.

ESPRESSO SEMIFREDDO

Prepare **Chocolate Semifreddo, 841,** omitting the melted chocolate. Dissolve **1 tablespoon instant espresso powder** in **1 teaspoon hot water,** and gently fold this into the cooled egg mixture with the vanilla.

SPUMONI

8 to 10 servings

Authentic Italian *spumone* is essentially an unmolded bombe, 842, usually with a center of soft semifreddo or pastry cream, often flavored with amaretti and studded with candied fruit.

Line a 9 x 5-inch loaf pan with plastic wrap, allowing the excess to hang over the edges. Spread evenly in the pan:

2 cups Chocolate Ice Cream, 832, softened

Freeze until firm enough to hold the next layer, about 30 minutes. Spread evenly on top of the first layer:

2 cups Pistachio Ice Cream, 832, softened

Freeze as for the first layer. Finish with a layer of:

2 cups Strawberry Ice Cream, 833, softened

Freeze until hard, at least 2 hours. Unmold and remove the plastic wrap. Slice and serve with:

Whipped Cream, 754
(Chocolate Sauce, 847)

FROZEN GRAND MARNIER SOUFFLÉ

6 servings

This soufflé may be made with any liqueur, such as Cointreau, Triple Sec, Kahlúa, or Drambuie; with good Scotch or Irish whiskey; or with an unsweetened fruit-based eau-de-vie, such as framboise or poire Williams.

Prepare collars, 815, for six 4-ounce ramekins or one 1-quart mold. Beat in the bowl of a stand mixer on medium-high until thick and pale yellow, 2 to 3 minutes:

5 large egg yolks

Combine in a small saucepan:

¼ cup water
½ cup sugar

Simmer over medium heat until the syrup is clear. Continue to cook until the sugar reaches 243°F on a candy thermometer. With the mixer on medium-high speed, immediately add the hot sugar syrup to the eggs, pouring it down the side of the bowl. Beat in:

¼ cup Grand Marnier

Place the bowl over, not in, a saucepan of simmering water. Heat the egg mixture, whisking constantly to prevent curdling, to 160°F, 3 to 5 minutes. Remove from the heat, leaving the pan of water at a gentle simmer. Beat on high until the mixture is light and fluffy and cooled to room temperature, 5 to 10 minutes.

Combine in a medium bowl:

4 large egg whites
½ cup sugar
2 tablespoons water
¼ teaspoon cream of tartar

Place the bowl over, not in, the simmering water. Heat to 160°F, whisking constantly to keep the whites moving, but not to whip them. Remove from the heat and beat on high until the whites are cool and form soft peaks.

Gently stir one-quarter of the whites into the cooled egg yolk mixture, then fold in the remaining whites. Whip to soft peaks:

½ cup heavy cream

Fold the cream into the soufflé mixture. Fill the molds to the top of the collars, smoothing the surface. Cover with plastic wrap and freeze at least 3 hours. To serve, remove the collars and dust the tops with:

Confectioners' sugar

FROZEN BERRY SOUFFLÉ

6 servings

Do not overwork the mixture when folding in the puree and whipped cream, or it may separate.

Prepare collars, 815, for six 4-ounce ramekins or one 1½-quart mold. Combine in a medium bowl:

4 large egg whites
⅔ cup sugar
2 tablespoons water
¼ teaspoon cream of tartar

Place the bowl over, not in, a saucepan of simmering water. Heat to 160°F, whisking constantly to keep the whites moving, but not to whip them. Remove from the heat and beat on high speed until the whites are cool and form soft peaks. Fold in:

1 cup strained berry puree (from 2 to 2½ cups sliced or small whole berries, fresh or frozen)

Whip until soft peaks form:

1 cup heavy cream

To prevent separating gently stir one-quarter of the whipped cream into the berry mixture, then fold in the remaining cream. Fill the molds to the top of the collars, smoothing the surface. Cover with plastic wrap and freeze at least 3 hours.

To serve, remove the collars and dust the tops with:

Confectioners' sugar

ABOUT BOMBES

In our family, a richly loaded bombe betokened festivity—its array of flavors tantalizingly on display as it was sliced was the burst of glory that topped off a dinner party. A **bombe** is a molded still-frozen dessert layered with different flavors of ice cream, frozen yogurt, semifreddo, sherbet, or sorbet and made in a variety of molds—all of which you have in your kitchen. Bombes are traditionally made with still-frozen desserts, but churned, stir-frozen, or store bought ice creams and sorbets may be used.

Most bombes consist of one or two outside layers and one center layer. Use flavors and textures that will complement one another. Combine ice cream with a sorbet or a sherbet with a semifreddo. Avoid granitas because of their icy crystals. Stir in chopped candies, cookies, or nuts as well, or add crunchy morsels between layers.

Choose a mold made of stainless steel or tin; glass molds are difficult to unmold. The oval mold with ridges or a melon mold are classic, but a loaf pan, bowl-shaped mold, charlotte mold, gelatin mold, or springform pan will work as well. Chill the mold in the freezer for 30 minutes before filling. If using homemade churned or stir-frozen ice cream or sorbet, make the bases ahead, then churn each one as needed so that you will be assured of a soft, easy-to-spread consistency, or soften frozen ice cream in the refrigerator until it is spreadable. Spread to a thickness of ³/₄ to 1 inch, one layer at a time, into the mold. ➤ Each layer must be thoroughly frozen before the next layer is added. Use the back of a serving spoon and pack the ice cream firmly and evenly so there are no air pockets.

After the mold is filled, it must be frozen until solid, at least 6 hours, or up to 24 hours. ➤ But they do not keep much longer than this and are best made in the morning and served that same day or the next.

To unmold a bombe, ➤ invert onto a chilled plate or platter. Place a hot wet dish towel over the mold for 30 seconds, then give the platter a rap on the counter to release the bombe. Once the bombe is unmolded, immediately place back in the freezer to firm the outside layer. To slice, let soften in the refrigerator for 20 to 30 minutes before serving. You also may cut into slices using a sharp knife and arrange on a platter; rinse the knife in hot water and dry between each slice. Let the slices stand in the refrigerator for 5 to 10 minutes and then serve. A bombe is best when just beginning to melt slightly.

Bombes are especially festive when decorated with and/or accompanied by fresh berries, Fruit Sauce, 845, or whipped cream.

Here are some good combinations. The first in each list is the outside layer:

French Vanilla Ice Cream, 831, and Strawberry
    Sorbet, 836
Chocolate Ice Cream, 832, and Caramel Ice Cream, 832
Chocolate Ice Cream, 832, and Coffee Ice Cream, 832
Pumpkin Spice Ice Cream, 833, and Orange Sherbet,
    836, or Orange Sorbet, 837
Pistachio Ice Cream, 832, and Cranberry Sherbet, 838,
    or Raspberry Sherbet, 837
Apricot Ice Cream, 833, and Strawberry Sorbet, 836
Vanilla Ice Cream, 831, and Peach Sorbet, 836
Coconut Ice Cream, 833, and Mango Ice
    Cream, 833, Mango Sorbet, 836, or Pineapple Ice
    Milk, 834
French Vanilla Ice Cream, 831, Chocolate Ice Cream,
    832, and Orange Sherbet, 836

BAKED ALASKA
10 to 16 servings
Miraculously, a little cake on the bottom and a covering of soft meringue is enough to insulate ice cream while the topping is browned in a hot oven. This marvelous construction is a tour de force, always a gala finale to a meal. Though it needs last-minute preparation it isn't very difficult to make. There are individual or large oven-proof pans and also dishes made especially for this dessert. You may also build a similar "cake case" in an oval heatproof dish. A layer of brownies can be substituted for the cake if assembled with hard ice cream less than an hour before topping and browning.
Place a layer of:
    Génoise, 709, Angel, 705, or Sponge Cake, 706
at least ¹/₂ inch thick and slightly larger than the base of the ice cream being used on a foil-lined baking sheet. Sprinkle it lightly with:
    (Rum or brandy)
Position on top of the cake:
    A 1¹/₂-pint to ¹/₂-gallon brick of ice cream, frozen solid
Or, for a dome- or melon-shaped Baked Alaska, before placing the ice cream on the cake, soften it slightly and mold it in a bowl or melon-shaped mold lined with plastic wrap. Freeze solid, then transfer the ice cream to the cake.
The ice cream can be topped with a second ¹/₂-inch-thick layer of:
    (Génoise, Angel, or Sponge Cake)
Freeze until needed.
Preheat the oven to 450°F. Prepare:
    A double recipe of Soft Meringue Topping I or II, 798
Cover the dessert with the meringue so the surface is entirely coated to at least a ³/₄-inch thickness, bringing the meringue right down to the surface of the dish. Swirl the topping decoratively with the back of a spoon, or reserve some of the meringue in a pastry bag and pipe on fluted edges and patterns. Bake 5 minutes, watching carefully, to lightly brown the meringue.Serve immediately, with:
    (Warm Chocolate Sauce, 847, or Caramel Sauce, 849)

BISCUIT TORTONI OR MACAROON BOMBE
6 servings
Combine in a medium bowl:
    ³/₄ cup crushed amaretti or Almond Macaroons, 771
    ³/₄ cup heavy cream
    ¹/₄ cup sifted confectioners' sugar
    A few grains of salt
Let stand 1 hour. Whip to soft peaks:
    1 cup heavy cream
Fold in the macaroon mixture and:
    1 teaspoon vanilla
Divide among 12 paper muffin cups set in a muffin tin or on a baking sheet. Before freezing or when partly frozen, decorate the tops with:

Unsalted toasted almonds (about 1 tablespoon
  per dessert; ³/₄ cup total)
(Candied cherries)

Freeze until firm, about 3¹/₂ hours.

ABOUT SWEET SAUCES

Serving a sauce with dessert can be the luxurious extra touch that makes it memorable. Unless the sauce will complement the dessert, omit it. Create a provocative but pleasing contrast between dessert and sauce. For example, try pairing mousse, custard, ice cream, or other creamy desserts with a tart fruit sauce or a bitter chocolate or dark caramel sauce. With a light fruit dessert or gelatin, consider a creamy but light-tasting sauce, such as whipped cream or sabayon, 846. Cakes, bread puddings, baked puddings, and other desserts that are firm and dry take well to sauces that soak in. You need not, however, always strive for contrast. A rich chocolate bread pudding or chocolate cake is divine with an equally rich caramel, white chocolate, or Southern whiskey sauce. And plum pudding, perhaps the richest dessert of all, is always accompanied with very buttery sauces, such as Hard Sauce, 851, Hot Wine Sauce, 852, or Hot Foamy Sauce, 851.

Dessert sauces have distinct family lines similar to those of their unsweetened counterparts. ➤ Don't overbeat cream bases or cream garnishes. ➤ Cook egg sauces over, not in, boiling water. ➤ Be sure that sauces thickened with flour and cornstarch are free from lumps, and cook them thoroughly to avoid any raw taste. ➤ In preparing heavy syrups, guard against crystallization; see 855.

ABOUT COOKED FRUIT SAUCES

These sauces are thicker and, if made with butter, richer than the uncooked fruit sauces, or coulis, 853; they are usually served hot. Some of these make good low-fat alternatives to whipped cream or custard sauce on hot puddings and cakes.

HOT LEMON SAUCE

1¹/₃ cups

This hot butter-and-egg sauce, 852, is traditional with gingerbread, pound cake, and angel cake. It is also delicious with desserts containing apples, blueberries, peaches, bananas, or coconut.
Combine in a small heavy saucepan:

  ²/₃ **cup sugar**
  Grated zest of 1 lemon
  ¹/₄ **cup strained fresh lemon juice**
  2 tablespoons water

Whisk in until thoroughly blended:

  3 large egg yolks

Add:

  ¹/₂ **cup (1 stick) unsalted butter, cut into pieces**

Set over low heat. Stirring constantly but gently, bring to a simmer and cook until thickened, about 1 minute. Strain through a fine-mesh sieve. Serve at once, or let cool, then

cover and refrigerate for up to 3 days. Reheat over low heat, stirring.

HOT LIME SAUCE

Especially good with banana or coconut desserts.
Prepare **Hot Lemon Sauce, above,** substituting **the grated zest of 1 lime** and ¹/₄ **cup strained fresh lime juice** for the lemon.

CLEAR LEMON SAUCE

1¹/₂ cups

This is a pleasant alternative to Hot Lemon Sauce, above.
Combine in a small heavy saucepan and stir thoroughly:

  ¹/₂ **cup sugar**
  1 tablespoon cornstarch

Stir in until well blended:

  1 cup water or unsweetened apple juice
  Grated zest of 1 lemon
  ¹/₄ **cup strained fresh lemon juice**
  Pinch of salt

Bring to a boil over medium-high heat. Reduce to low and cook, stirring constantly, until thickened, about 10 minutes. Stir in:

  (3 tablespoons unsalted butter, cut into pieces)

Serve the sauce at once, or let cool. Cover and refrigerate for up to 1 week. Reheat over low heat, stirring.

CLEAR LIME SAUCE

Prepare **Clear Lemon Sauce, above,** using **water,** not apple juice, and substituting **the grated zest of 1 lime** and ¹/₄ **cup strained fresh lime juice** for the lemon.

CHERRY SAUCE

2 cups

Serve over vanilla or chocolate ice cream. For a nonalcoholic cherry sauce, see Hot Blueberry Sauce, 845.
Place in a medium bowl:

  **1 pound fresh sweet red cherries, such as Bing,
    or well-drained canned or bottled sweet cherries,
    halved and pitted**

Sprinkle with:

  ¹/₃ **to ¹/₂ cup kirsch or cherry cordial**

Cover and let stand 30 minutes, up to 3 hours or more, stirring occasionally. Combine the cherries and:

  ³/₄ **cup sugar**
  3 tablespoons strained fresh lemon juice

in a heavy skillet set over medium-high heat. Bring to a boil and cook until the juices are red and syrupy, about 5 minutes. Add:

  ¹/₂ **cup brandy**

Standing back, carefully ignite with a long match. Let the flames die off, then continue to boil to a thick, syrupy sauce. If serving the sauce with a warm or room-temperature dessert, stir in until incorporated:

  (3 to 6 tablespoons unsalted butter)

Boil until thickened again. Turn off the heat and stir in:

  2 tablespoons kirsch or cherry cordial

Serve at once, or let cool. Cover and refrigerate for up to 3 days. If making ahead, reheat and add kirsch just before serving.

MELBA SAUCE

1 1/2 cups

Use for Peach Melba on pound cake, angel food cake, or even plain yogurt.

Puree in a blender or food processor:

> **1 1/2 pints raspberries or 15 ounces frozen dry-pack raspberries, thawed**

Push the pulp through a fine-mesh sieve, pressing firmly, scraping the inside of the sieve clear of seeds. You should have 1 cup strained pulp. Combine in a heavy saucepan with:

> **1/2 cup currant jelly**

Bring to a simmer over medium-low heat. Mix and add:

> **1/2 cup sugar**
> **1 teaspoon cornstarch**
> **1/8 teaspoon salt**

Simmer until the foam dies down and the surface is glassy, about 10 minutes. Cool and chill before using.

HOT BLUEBERRY SAUCE

About 2 cups

Lovely over vanilla ice cream, pound cake, hot biscuits, or corn bread. Make with cherries for a simple, nonalcoholic Cherry Sauce, 844.

Combine in a stainless steel skillet:

> **1 pint blueberries or 12 ounces frozen dry-pack blueberries, frozen or thawed**
> **1/3 cup sugar**
> **3 tablespoons fresh lemon juice, strained**

Cook over medium-high heat, stirring, until the berries release their juices. Stir to a smooth paste:

> **1 tablespoon water**
> **1 1/2 teaspoons cornstarch**

Briskly stir the cornstarch mixture into the berries and cook until thickened, about 1 minute. If using the sauce with warm or room-temperature food, stir in:

> **(1 to 2 tablespoons unsalted butter)**

Serve at once, or let cool. Cover and refrigerate for up to 3 days. Reheat over low heat.

BUTTERED CIDER SAUCE

Scant 1 cup

A delicious and unusual sauce. Terrific on gingerbread, pumpkin pie, fruit crisps, or even spooned over roast pork. Without peeling or coring, chop into 1/4-inch pieces:

> **1 large Granny Smith or other firm apple**

Melt in a medium heavy saucepan:

> **1 tablespoon unsalted butter**

Add the chopped apple and cook over medium heat, stirring occasionally, until softened, about 5 minutes. Add:

> **1 1/2 cups cider or unsweetened apple juice**
> **1/4 cup sugar**
> **1/4 cup honey**

Simmer until the apple pieces are translucent, about 15 minutes. Strain into a bowl. Return the liquid to the saucepan. Force the apple pulp through the sieve. Discard the skin and core. Stir the apple pulp into the liquid and boil rapidly over high heat, stirring, until reduced to about 1 cup. Remove from the heat and stir in:

> **3 tablespoons unsalted butter, softened**
> **1/4 teaspoon grated or ground nutmeg**
> **1/8 teaspoon salt**

When the butter is melted, add:

> **(2 tablespoons brandy, applejack, or Calvados)**

Serve at once, or let cool. Cover and refrigerate for up to 1 week. Reheat over low heat.

FRUIT SAUCE

1 1/4 cups; 2 1/4 cups with fruit

Serve with ice cream, spice or pound cake, or over plain cheesecake. If you omit the crushed fruit, this can serve as a hot **Quick Chocolate Fondue Sauce, 848,** for fruits or bits of cake.

Combine in a medium saucepan:

> **1 cup unsweetened fruit juice**
> **1/2 to 3/4 cup sugar, to taste**
> **1 tablespoon cornstarch or 2 tablespoons all-purpose flour**

Cook, stirring, over low heat, until thickened, about 6 minutes. Remove from the heat. Stir in:

> **2 teaspoons fresh lemon juice**
> **(2 tablespoons unsalted butter)**

Add:

> **(1 cup crushed fresh or cooked fruit)**

Flavor with:

> **2 teaspoons sherry or liqueur**

Serve cold or hot.

COCONUT DULCIE

4 1/2 cups

Like a coconut jam, this is good over rice or fruit puddings. Turn it into a sauce by combining with a puree of tart fruit such as guava and currant.

In a large saucepan, bring to a simmer over medium heat, stirring until the sugar is dissolved:

> **4 cups water**
> **3 cups sugar**
> **1/2 cup corn syrup**

Cook until the syrup reaches 220°F on a candy thermometer. Add:

> **Freshly grated meat of 1 coconut, 972, or 1 cup shredded coconut**

Cook slowly until the mixture thickens and again reaches 220°F, about 40 minutes.

Pour into sterilized jars and seal, 890, or cool and pack into airtight containers and freeze for up to 3 months.

ABOUT CUSTARD SAUCE (CRÈME ANGLAISE)

Although made from the same basic ingredients as crème brûlée, flan, and other dessert custards, custard sauce has a very different consistency, because the sauce is prepared on top of the stove and is stirred constantly. The stirring disrupts the bonding of the eggs, resulting in a liquid rather than semisolid custard. A custard sauce can be made with milk alone, but do consider enriching the sauce with cream when it is to accompany poached fruit or a gelatin dessert.

Custard sauce must be heated to about 175°F in order to thicken. At this point it will be thick enough to coat the back of a spoon—lightly if made with milk alone and fairly heavily if made in part with cream—and running a finger across the back of the spoon will leave a clean line. One of the first signs that the sauce is about to thicken is the dissipation of the foam on top—the sauce will acquire body and a slight sheen. You can return the sauce to the heat if it seems too thin, but remember that the sauce will thicken when cold.

Use a heavy pan that will diffuse the heat evenly. Stir with a heatproof rubber spatula or wooden spoon, over very low heat. Stir constantly but *gently* as the sauce heats, sweeping the entire pan bottom and reaching into the corners of the pan. Hard stirring damages the egg bonds and yields a runny sauce. If the sauce becomes grainy and dull as you stir, signs that it has begun to overheat, immediately pour it through a fine-mesh sieve. A slightly overcooked sauce will still be delicious, even if not entirely smooth. Processing it in a blender will partially restore its creaminess.

CUSTARD SAUCE (CRÈME ANGLAISE)

2 ⅔ cups
Prepare:
  Boiled Custard, 802
using:
  5 large egg yolks
  ⅓ to ½ cup sugar
  2 cups whole milk, 1 cup whole milk plus 1 cup light
    or heavy cream, or 2 cups half-and-half
Proceed as directed. If desired, pour the sauce through a sieve before adding the vanilla. Serve warm or cold. If serving cold, let the sauce chill thoroughly before covering. Condensation will cause it to thin. The sauce can be covered and refrigerated for up to 3 days. To reheat, set the container of sauce on a double boiler over warm (165°F) water and stir until warmed through.

VANILLA BEAN CUSTARD SAUCE

Prepare **Custard Sauce, above.** Before heating the milk or cream, cut **1 vanilla bean** lengthwise in half. Scrape out the seeds and add them along with the pod halves to the milk. Bring to a simmer. Remove from the heat, cover, and steep for 15 minutes. Rewarm the milk, then proceed with the recipe, using ½ **teaspoon vanilla.** Strain out the seeds and pod halves when cooled.

COFFEE CUSTARD SAUCE

Prepare **Custard Sauce, above,** using **1 cup coffee or espresso** and **1 cup light or heavy cream** in place of the milk. If desired, add **1 to 2 tablespoons coffee liqueur** to the sauce.

CHOCOLATE CUSTARD SAUCE

2 cups
Heat in a heavy medium saucepan, stirring, until the chocolate is melted:
  2 cups whole milk
  2 ounces unsweetened chocolate, chopped
Meanwhile, beat well in a medium bowl:
  4 large egg yolks
  ¾ cup sugar
  ⅛ teaspoon salt
Slowly whisk the hot milk into the egg yolks and sugar. Return this mixture to the saucepan, set over medium-low heat. Stir the sauce gently but constantly, until the custard reaches 175°F on a thermometer and coats the back of a spoon. Immediately pour the sauce into a bowl. Strain, if desired. As it cools, stir to release the steam. Stir in:
  1 teaspoon vanilla
Serve hot or cold, over puddings, ice cream, or filled cream puffs.

FRUIT CUSTARD SAUCE

2 ⅓ cups
Beat in a medium bowl until creamy:
  ¼ cup (½ stick) unsalted butter, softened
Gradually add and beat until fluffy:
  ¾ cup sugar
Beat in one at a time:
  2 large eggs
One or 2 extra eggs will add richness.
Heat in a medium heavy saucepan until bubbles form around the edges:
  1 cup whole milk
Slowly whisk the milk into the eggs and sugar. Return this mixture to the saucepan, set over low heat until the custard reaches 175°F on a thermometer and coats the back of a spoon. Immediately, pour the sauce through a sieve, if desired, into a bowl and let cool. As it cools, stir to release the steam. Let cool for 10 minutes, stirring periodically. Stir in:
  1 teaspoon vanilla
  Pinch of grated or ground nutmeg
Fold in:
  1 cup whole small or sliced large berries, sliced
    peaches, pineapple chunks, or tangerine or ruby
    red grapefruit sections, 223

ABOUT SABAYONS

The cooking of these light, delectable egg foams is discussed on page 806. *Zabaglione,* the Italian name for sabayon, is always served freshly made and hot. Sabayon sauces, however, may be prepared ahead and served at room temperature or, if they contain whipped cream, cold. ➤ If you want to prepare a sabayon ahead, set the pan of sauce in ice water immediately after cooking and whisk gently until it has cooled to room temperature—otherwise it will deflate. A sabayon will also deflate if stirred or disturbed when ice cold, so ➤ be sure to bring a refrigerated sabayon to room temperature before pouring it into a sauceboat or spreading it on fruit for a gratin. Sabayons are not reheatable. However, once the sauce has reached room temperature, it can be set in a bowl of luke-warm water for 10 minutes to warm slightly.

SABAYON WITH WHITE WINE OR ORANGE LIQUEUR

2 cups

Prepare in a double boiler:

    Zabaglione, 806

replacing the Marsala with:

    $1/2$ cup sweet white wine or $1/4$ cup orange liqueur plus $1/4$ cup water

Serve at once, or set the top of the double boiler in ice water and gently whisk the sauce until cool to the touch. Cover and refrigerate for up to 1 day. Let the chilled sauce stand at room temperature for at least 2 hours before pouring it into a sauceboat or spreading on a fruit gratin, cake, or over fruit.

LEMON SABAYON

2 cups

Grand on a lemon soufflé, 809, especially when freshly made and spooned on piping hot. Also good with almond tart or cake, or berries served fresh or in a gratin.

Whisk together vigorously in the top of a double boiler until slightly thickened:

    2 large eggs
    2 large egg yolks
    $1/3$ cup plus 1 tablespoon sugar

Whisking constantly, slowly add:

    $1/4$ cup water
    3 tablespoons strained fresh lemon juice
    Grated zest of 1 lemon

Cook as for Zabaglione, 806.

COLD SABAYON SAUCE

3 cups

This sauce—unlike—the classic version will keep for several days in the refrigerator. Use it over fresh fruits.

Combine in the top of a double boiler:

    4 large egg yolks
    $3/4$ cup sugar
    $3/4$ cup dry sherry or other dry wine

Whisk over boiling water until very thick. Set the top of the double boiler in ice water and gently whisk the sauce until cold. Add:

    $1/4$ cup heavy cream, lightly whipped

Serve at once, or refrigerate until ready to serve.

ABOUT CHOCOLATE SAUCES

Chocolate sauces are best made from high-quality chocolate—deep and rich in flavor and smooth on the tongue. Whether made with dark, milk, or white chocolate, many chocolate sauces are part of the family known as **ganache,** which means that their basic ingredients are chocolate and cream. One notable exception is hot fudge sauce, which is actually a sugar syrup with chocolate added.

CHOCOLATE SAUCE COCKAIGNE

$1 1/2$ cups

Dreamy on vanilla, coffee, or chocolate ice cream.

Melt in the top of a double boiler over, not in, boiling water:

    3 ounces unsweetened chocolate, chopped

Combine, then stir into the chocolate:

    1 large egg, well beaten
    $3/4$ cup evaporated milk
    1 cup sugar

Cook, stirring frequently, until the sauce reaches 160°F on a thermometer, about 20 minutes. Remove from heat and beat with a hand mixer 1 minute or whisk until well blended. Stir in:

    1 teaspoon vanilla
    ($1/4$ teaspoon ground cinnamon)

Cool and serve. Cover and refrigerate for up to 3 days.

CHOCOLATE SAUCE

1 cup

To make in a food processor, grind the chocolate to crumbs and then, with the motor running, add the simmering cream mixture. By the time the last of the cream has been added, the chocolate will be melted and the sauce will be smooth.

Combine in a medium heavy saucepan:

    $1/2$ cup light cream or $1/4$ cup heavy cream plus $1/4$ cup whole milk
    1 to 2 tablespoons sugar
    1 tablespoon unsalted butter

Bring to a rolling boil, stirring constantly. Remove from the heat and immediately add:

    4 ounces semisweet or bittersweet chocolate, finely chopped

Let stand for 1 minute, then whisk until smooth. Whisk in:

    1 teaspoon vanilla or 1 tablespoon dark rum or Cognac

Serve warm or cold; thin with water as needed. Cover and refrigerate for up to 2 weeks. Reheat over low heat, whisking in a little hot water if the sauce looks oily.

HOT FUDGE SAUCE

$2 1/2$ cups

This sauce becomes firm and chewy when served over ice cream. Vanilla ice cream is classic, but peppermint, coffee, strawberry, and chocolate ice cream are delicious too. Be sure that your ice cream is frozen hard.

Mix in a large heavy saucepan:

> 1/2 cup sugar
> 1/4 cup unsweetened cocoa powder
> 1/4 teaspoon salt

Whisk in until well blended:

> 1/2 cup water

Bring to a simmer over medium-high heat. Remove from the heat and whisk in:

> 1 cup heavy cream
> 1 cup light corn syrup
> 1/4 teaspoon distilled white vinegar
> 2 ounces semisweet or bittersweet chocolate, coarsely chopped

Return to medium-high heat and boil. Whisk frequently, until the bubbles become small and the syrup is thick and sticky (about 225°F on a candy thermometer), 5 to 8 minutes. Remove from the heat and add:

> 2 ounces semisweet or bittersweet chocolate, finely chopped
> 1/4 cup (1/2 stick) unsalted butter, softened
> 1 tablespoon vanilla

Whisk until smooth. Serve at once, or let cool. Cover and refrigerate for up to 2 weeks. Reheat in a heavy saucepan over low heat.

MOCHA SAUCE

1 1/2 cups

This dark mocha sauce is wonderful with chocolate mousse.

Combine in a small heavy saucepan:

> 2/3 cup espresso or strong coffee
> 3 tablespoons sugar

Cook, stirring, over very low heat until the sugar is dissolved and the mixture is steaming hot. Add:

> 8 ounces semisweet or bittersweet chocolate, finely chopped

Whisk until the chocolate is melted and the sauce is smooth. Remove from the heat and whisk in:

> 2 tablespoons unsalted butter, softened

Serve at once. Cool, cover, and refrigerate for up to 2 weeks. Reheat over low heat, adding a little warm water if the sauce becomes oily.

CHOCOLATE MINT SAUCE

1 1/2 cups

Melt in a double boiler over boiling water:

> One 13-ounce bag chocolate peppermint creams, chopped

Add:

> 1/3 cup heavy cream

Stir well until smooth.
Serve warm over ice cream.

CHOCOLATE CARAMEL SAUCE

About 1 1/2 cups

Prepare:

> Caramel Sauce, 849

using:

> 1/4 cup (1/2 stick) unsalted butter
> 1 teaspoon vanilla

Add after the cream is incorporated and stir until melted:

> 3 ounces bittersweet or semisweet chocolate, finely chopped

Serve warm, or cool and roll in cocoa to make chocolate caramel truffles.

WARM WHITE CHOCOLATE SAUCE

About 1 1/2 cups

White chocolate will turn into a solid mass if overheated, so monitor the temperature of the water bath carefully. Place a skillet of water over low heat and heat just until the water is hot enough to steam, about 145°F. Combine in a heatproof bowl:

> 8 ounces white chocolate, coarsely chopped or broken into small pieces
> 6 tablespoons (3/4 stick) unsalted butter, cut into pieces
> 1/3 cup heavy cream

Set the bowl in the water bath and stir until the chocolate is melted. Remove from the heat and stir vigorously until smooth. Serve at once, or cool, then cover and refrigerate for up to 2 weeks. Reheat by setting the sauce in hot water, as above, and stir until thin.

WARM MILK CHOCOLATE SAUCE

Prepare **Warm White Chocolate Sauce, above,** substituting **8 ounces milk chocolate** for the white chocolate.

QUICK CHOCOLATE FONDUE SAUCE

Use for dipping fruit—pieces of pineapple, banana, or orange—or small squares of cake.

I. *1 2/3 cups*

Combine in a saucepan. Stir over low heat until smooth:

> 1 1/2 cups chocolate chips
> 3/4 cup evaporated milk
> (4 to 5 large marshmallows or 1/2 cup mini marshmallows)

Keep warm in a fondue pot, 110.

II. *1 1/2 cups*

Heat in a saucepan over medium-low heat until warm:

> 3/4 cup whole milk, light or heavy cream, coffee, or sherry

Add and cook over low heat, stirring until smooth:

> 4 ounces unsweetened chocolate, chopped
> 1 cup sugar
> 1 teaspoon vanilla or rum
> 1/4 teaspoon salt

Keep warm in a fondue pot.

ABOUT CARAMEL AND BUTTERSCOTCH SAUCES

Caramel is simply sugar cooked to the point where it melts and then begins to burn. Old cookbooks refer to it, appropriately enough, as burnt sugar. **Butterscotch** is similar, except that butter is added to the sugar as it caramelizes, resulting in the characteristic deep, nutty taste. To convert caramel and butterscotch into sauces, a mixture of butter and cream, and/or water or other liquid is added while the syrup is still hot—otherwise, the syrup, once cooled, will become a hard candy.

Many professional chefs make caramel by stirring dry sugar in a pot over a flame. Home cooks, however, find the process easier when the sugar is first mixed with water. ➤ It is important that the sugar be fully dissolved before the syrup is allowed to boil: Otherwise, the sugar may recrystallize once it reaches 238°F, leaving the cook with a white rock in the pan. (Actually, if the cook breaks the rock up with a spoon and continues cooking, caramel will eventually ensue.) As the syrup approaches the caramelization point, the bubbles in the saucepan will become smaller and quieter. Then, around the edges of the pan, the first signs of darkening will appear. Begin swirling the pan by the handle to disperse these hotter areas of syrup toward the cooler center. Continue to cook the syrup until it becomes a deep amber color, but stop before it becomes reddish or mahogany. If overcooked, the syrup will taste bitter and salty. Remove the syrup from the heat and immediately add the butter and cream, or water or other liquid to stop the cooking. Be prepared for the caramel to sputter and foam. If adding water, as in Caramel Syrup, below, stand back to prevent yourself from being spattered. Stir the sauce briskly. If some of the caramel refuses to melt, set the pan over low heat and stir until the sauce smooths out. Reheat sauces in a microwave or a double boiler.

CARAMEL SAUCE
1 ½ cups

Combine in a small heavy saucepan:
   ¼ cup water
   1 cup sugar
Set over medium-high heat and stir gently until the sugar is dissolved and the syrup is clear. Avoid letting the syrup boil until the sugar is completely dissolved. Increase the heat to high, cover the saucepan, and boil the syrup for 2 minutes. Uncover and continue to boil the syrup until it begins to darken around the edges. Gently stir until the syrup turns deep amber. Remove from the heat and add:
   ½ cup (1 stick) unsalted butter, cut into pieces
Gently stir until the butter is incorporated. Stir in:
   ½ cup heavy cream
If the sauce becomes lumpy, set the pan over low heat and stir until smooth. Remove from the heat and stir in:
   1 teaspoon vanilla
   Pinch of salt
Serve warm or at room temperature. Cover and refrigerate for up to 1 month. Reheat in a double boiler or in a heavy saucepan over very low heat, adding a bit of water if too thick.

CARAMEL SYRUP
About ¾ cup

Adding water to hot caramel yields a thick syrup that is irresistible on ice cream, custard, or broiled, poached, or sautéed fruit.

Prepare **Caramel Sauce, above,** omitting the butter and cream. Instead, combine the sugar and water and caramelize as directed, then remove from the heat and standing back, add **⅓ cup water.** Stir until smooth. If the caramel remains lumpy, stir briefly over low heat. Remove from the heat and add the vanilla and salt. Serve at once or let cool. Cover and refrigerate for up to 6 months. Reheat over low heat, stirring in a little water if needed.

CARAMEL CREAM SAUCE
1 cup

Combine in a double boiler and stir over boiling water until melted:
   8 ounces Caramels, 864
   5 tablespoons heavy cream or whole milk, or as needed
Add more cream to reach the desired consistency.

BUTTERSCOTCH SAUCE
1 ½ cups

The old-fashioned favorite is made with virtually the same ingredients as caramel sauce but cooked in a different way. Either version below may be stored in the refrigerator for up to 1 month.

I. Cook, stirring, in a medium heavy saucepan over medium-low heat until butter is melted and mixture is combined:
   ½ cup (1 stick) unsalted butter
   ¼ cup water
   2 tablespoons light corn syrup
Add:
   1 cup sugar
Stir until dissolved. Increase the heat to medium-high and, without stirring, boil the mixture until it begins to color around the edges, 4 to 8 minutes. Continue to stir until the mixture turns a light brown. Remove from the heat and, standing back, pour in:
   ½ cup heavy cream
Stir until smooth. If the sauce remains lumpy, stir briefly over low heat. Remove from the heat and stir in:
   1 teaspoon vanilla
   ⅛ teaspoon salt
Serve at once, or let cool, then cover and refrigerate. Reheat in a double boiler.

II. An easier version with delicious results.
Cook, stirring, over medium-low heat in a medium heavy saucepan:
   ⅔ cup light corn syrup
   1 cup packed brown sugar
   ¼ cup (½ stick) unsalted butter
   ⅛ teaspoon salt

Stir to dissolve sugar. Increase heat to medium-high and, without stirring, boil until as thick as corn syrup, about 3 minutes. Let cool slightly. Add:

²/₃ cup heavy cream

Serve the sauce hot or cold. Reheat in a double boiler.

BROWN SUGAR BUTTER SAUCE

Generous 2 cups

Combine in a medium saucepan:

1 cup packed brown sugar
¹/₄ cup (¹/₂ stick) unsalted butter, softened

Using a hand-held mixer, beat on high speed until thoroughly blended. Gradually beat in:

1 cup warm half-and-half or light cream

Stir over low heat until the mixture comes to a boil. Remove from the heat and add:

¹/₄ cup bourbon, brandy, or rum

Stir until smooth. Stir in:

(¹/₃ cup chopped nuts)

Serve over bread pudding or a fresh tropical fruit salad.

MAPLE SYRUP SAUCE

³/₄ cup

Good with hot steamed or baked puddings or waffles. Heat in a small saucepan over low heat without boiling:

¹/₂ cup pure maple syrup

Add:

¹/₂ teaspoon grated lemon zest
¹/₄ teaspoon grated or ground nutmeg or ¹/₈ teaspoon ground ginger or cloves
(2 to 3 tablespoons chopped nuts)

Cool, chill, and serve cold. To serve hot, stir into the warm sauce:

1 to 2 tablespoons unsalted butter

VANILLA SAUCE

About 1 ¹/₄ cups

Combine in a small heavy saucepan:

¹/₄ cup sugar
1 tablespoon cornstarch
1 cup water

Cook over low heat, stirring, until as thick as heavy cream, about 10 minutes. Remove from the heat. Stir in until smooth:

2 to 3 tablespoons unsalted butter
¹/₈ teaspoon salt
Seeds scraped from a 2-inch length of vanilla bean, 1022

Serve warm or at room temperature.

RUM SAUCE

Serve over bread pudding.
Prepare **Vanilla Sauce, above,** replacing the vanilla bean with **2 tablespoons rum.**

MARSHMALLOW SAUCE

6 cups

Wonderful on a hot fudge sundae, sorbets, gelatin desserts, and chocolate cake.
Combine in a medium heavy saucepan:

¹/₃ cup water
²/₃ cup sugar

Stirring, bring to a rolling boil. Remove from the heat and immediately add:

20 large marshmallows

Stir gently until the marshmallows are melted. Stir in:

1 teaspoon vanilla

Cover and set aside. Proceed at once to make a water bath. Heat 1 inch of water in a large skillet over very low heat until it reaches 155° to 160°F and keep at this temperature. Combine in a heatproof bowl, stirring to dissolve the cream of tartar:

3 tablespoons water
¹/₄ teaspoon cream of tartar

Whisk in thoroughly:

3 large egg whites
¹/₃ cup sugar

Set the bowl in the water bath and, whisking frequently, heat the mixture to 140°F. Whisk gently to maintain the mixture between 140°F and 155°F for 5 minutes.
Remove the bowl from the water bath and, beat the egg white mixture on high speed until the bottom of the bowl no longer feels warm, 4 to 8 minutes. Add the marshmallow mixture and beat for 30 seconds more. Use at once, or cool and cover tightly and refrigerate for up to 2 weeks.

SWEETENED BUTTERS

I. CINNAMON BUTTER

³/₄ cup

Beat together until well combined:

6 tablespoons (³/₄ stick) unsalted butter, softened
1 cup sifted confectioners' sugar
1¹/₂ teaspoons ground cinnamon

Cover and chill before using.

II. HONEY BUTTER

About 1¹/₂ cups

Beat until fluffy:

1 cup (2 sticks) unsalted butter, softened

Stir in:

¹/₃ cup honey

Cover and chill before using.

III. RASPBERRY BUTTER

About 1 cup

Puree in a food processor or blender:

³/₄ cup raspberries

Push through a sieve; discard the seeds. Combine the pulp using a food processor, blender, or a hand-mixer with:

¹/₂ cup (1 stick) unsalted butter, softened
3 tablespoons sifted confectioners' sugar

Combine well. Serve at room temperature on pancakes, waffles or toast.

IV. See Butter Sauce for Crêpes Suzette, 650.

SOUR CREAM SAUCE
About 1 1/2 cups
Use as a dressing for berries, or combine berries with it and serve over cake or fruit gelatin.
Combine:
 1 cup sour cream
 1/2 cup packed brown sugar
 (1 cup berries)
 (1/2 teaspoon vanilla)

SOUR CREAM WHIPPED TOPPING
About 2 2/3 cups; 8 to 12 servings
Combine in a medium bowl:
 1 cup cold heavy cream
 1/2 cup cold sour cream
Beat on high speed until soft but definite peaks form. Use at once, over a warm fruit tart, or cover and refrigerate for up to 1 day.

ABOUT HARD SAUCE
Hard sauce is a mixture of confectioners' sugar, butter, and spirits, usually brandy or dark rum, or other flavorings such as vanilla or orange juice. Classic **hard sauce** is, as the name implies, a hard cake of butter and sugar that can be cut with a knife. An attractive way to serve hard sauce on cold cakes or puddings is to chill it and slice it with a small fancy cutter—or to put it through the individual butter mold. Hard sauce can also be whipped into a fluffy cream like a buttercream frosting. See Fluffy Hard Sauce, below.

HARD SAUCE
Generous 3/4 cup
A classic accompaniment to Plum Pudding, 825.
Beat in a medium bowl until creamy:
 5 tablespoons butter, softened
Gradually add:
 1 cup confectioners' sugar, sifted
Beat until well blended and fluffy. Add:
 1 teaspoon vanilla or 1 tablespoon coffee, rum,
  whiskey, brandy, or fresh lemon juice
 1/8 teaspoon salt
beating until very smooth. Chill thoroughly before using.

FLUFFY HARD SAUCE
3 3/4 cups
Combine in large bowl:
 1 cup (2 sticks) unsalted butter, softened
 3 cups confectioners' sugar, sifted
 2 teaspoons vanilla
 1/2 teaspoon grated or ground nutmeg
Beat on high speed until light and fluffy but thick enough to hold a firm shape, 6 to 10 minutes. Beating, slowly add:
 1/4 cup brandy, Cognac, dark rum, or orange juice

For a nonalcoholic sauce, add:
 (Grated zest of 1 orange)
Use at once, or cover and refrigerate for up to 3 days. Soften the cold sauce at room temperature until spreadable before serving, or it may deflate and thin out.

BROWN SUGAR HARD SAUCE
2 1/3 cups
Serve with Plum Pudding, 825, pound cake, apple crisp, or plum or peach crumble.
Beat in a medium bowl until fluffy:
 1/2 cup (1 stick) unsalted butter, softened
Gradually add:
 1 1/2 cups packed brown sugar
Beat until well blended. Slowly beat in:
 1/3 cup heavy cream
Beat in, drop by drop:
 2 tablespoons dry white wine or 1 teaspoon vanilla
Cover and chill well before using. Garnish with:
 (1/4 cup chopped nuts)

ABOUT FOAMY SAUCES
In our grandmothers' day, foamy sauces were the most fashionable for hot puddings. These sauces are thick foams that melt when spooned onto hot desserts. **Hot foamy sauces** are made with butter and whipped over boiling water until they thicken and foam. They must be finished just before serving. **Cold foamy sauces** are thick custards made frothy by the addition of whipped cream or meringue. Less special than their hot counterparts, they taste much the same and are more convenient, since they can be prepared up to several days ahead.

HOT FOAMY SAUCE
1 cup
A very dressy accompaniment to Persimmon Buttermilk Pudding, 823, Plum Pudding, 825, or any bread pudding. This recipe can easily be doubled.
Combine in the top of a double boiler:
 6 tablespoons (3/4 stick) unsalted butter, softened
 1 1/4 cups confectioners' sugar
 1/4 teaspoon grated or ground nutmeg
 1/4 teaspoon salt
Beat with a hand mixer on medium-high speed until fluffy, 5 to 10 minutes. Whisk together in a spouted measuring cup:
 1 large egg, at room temperature
 2 tablespoons brandy or Cognac
  or 2 teaspoons vanilla
With the mixer running, pour the egg mixture into the butter mixture in a slow, steady stream. At this point, you may cover the mixture and set aside at room temperature for up to 1 hour or refrigerate for up to 3 days. Bring to room temperature before proceeding. Pour a few inches of water into the double-boiler base, and boil. Set the top pan in place. Whisk in:
 2 tablespoons boiling water

Whisking constantly or beating on medium speed, heat the sauce until it reaches 160°F and thickens into a light foam. Serve immediately.

COLD FOAMY SAUCE

1 ¼ cups

Delectable with Steamed Chocolate Pudding, 824, Chocolate Bread Pudding, 822, or warm chocolate cake. This recipe can easily be doubled.

Whisk thoroughly in the top of a double boiler:

1 large egg
½ cup sugar

Pour a few inches of water into the double-boiler base and boil. Set the top on and, whisking or beating constantly, heat until the mixture thickens and reaches 160°F. Remove the top from the base and add:

2 tablespoons brandy, Cognac, or dark rum
½ teaspoon vanilla

Beat on high speed until the bottom of the pan no longer feels warm. In a small bowl, beat on medium-high speed until stiff peaks form:

½ cup cold heavy cream

Gently fold the cream into the egg mixture. Use at once, or cover and refrigerate for up to 3 days. The sauce will separate slightly upon standing; gently fold to recombine.

ABOUT HOT BUTTER-AND-EGG SAUCES

Brought from England by the first colonists, these buttery liquid custards were America's original hot dessert sauces. They are actually custards, but because their main ingredients are sugar and butter rather than milk or cream, they are translucent and syrupy. When made ahead and reheated, these sauces often separate or become slightly sugary. These problems are easily remedied by removing the sauce from the heat and whisking in a little warm water.

SOUTHERN WHISKEY SAUCE

About 1 ½ cups

For a milder sauce, replace up to half the whiskey with water; for a very potent sauce, replace the water with whiskey.

Melt in a small heavy saucepan over low heat:

½ cup (1 stick) unsalted butter

Stir in:

1 cup sugar
¼ cup bourbon or other whiskey
2 tablespoons water
¼ teaspoon grated or ground nutmeg
⅛ teaspoon salt

Cook, stirring, until the sugar is dissolved. Remove from the heat. Whisk in a medium bowl until frothy:

1 large egg

Slowly whisk butter sauce into the egg, then return this mixture to the saucepan. Set over medium heat and, stirring gently, bring to a simmer. Cook until thickened, about 1 minute. Serve at once, or set aside at room temperature

for up to 1 hour. Cool, cover, and refrigerate for up to 3 days. Reheat over low heat, stirring; if the sauce separates, remove from the heat and whisk in a little warm water.

HOT BRANDY SAUCE

Thanksgiving will never be the same once you try this on pumpkin pie.

Prepare **Southern Whiskey Sauce, above,** substituting **¼ cup brandy or Cognac** for the bourbon.

HOT BROWN SUGAR SAUCE

A nonalcoholic alternative to traditional whiskey sauce.

Prepare **Southern Whiskey Sauce, above,** substituting **1 cup packed light brown sugar** for the sugar, omitting the bourbon, and increasing the water to ⅓ cup. When the sauce is done, remove from the heat and stir in **1 tablespoon vanilla.**

ORANGE LIQUEUR SAUCE

1 ¾ cups

Lovely with any chocolate or orange dessert, especially soufflés.

Combine in a small heavy saucepan:

⅔ cup sugar
⅓ cup Grand Marnier or other orange liqueur
⅓ cup heavy cream

Whisk in until thoroughly blended:

3 large egg yolks

Add:

½ cup (1 stick) unsalted butter, cut into pieces

Set over low heat. Stirring constantly, cook the sauce until thick enough to coat the spatula; do not let the sauce simmer. Strain the sauce through a fine-mesh sieve. Serve at once, or let cool, cover, and refrigerate for up to 3 days. Reheat over low heat or over hot water. If the sauce separates, remove from the heat and whisk in a little hot water.

HOT WINE OR PLUM PUDDING SAUCE

Generous 2 ⅓ cups

Combine in the top of a double boiler:

½ cup (1 stick) unsalted butter, softened
1 cup sugar

Using a hand mixer, beat on medium-high speed until fluffy and lightened in color. Beat in:

2 large eggs, beaten

Beat in:

¾ cup dry sherry or Madeira
1 teaspoon grated lemon rest
(¼ teaspoon grated or ground nutmeg)

The sauce may look curdled at this point, but will smooth out once cooked. Cook over boiling water, beating constantly, until the sauce reaches 160°F, about 5 minutes.

HOT BUTTERED MAPLE SAUCE

1 ⅓ cups

For a delicious dessert, put a scoop of vanilla ice cream on a waffle and top with this sauce.

Combine in a medium heavy saucepan:

1 cup pure maple syrup

¹/₃ cup sugar

Stirring constantly, bring to a boil and cook until the last drop of sauce that falls from the spoon makes a short thread. Remove from the heat and add:

6 tablespoons (³/₄ stick) unsalted butter, cut into pieces

2 tablespoons water

¹/₈ teaspoon salt

Stir briskly until the butter is melted and the sauce is thick and creamy. Whisk in a medium bowl until light and frothy:

1 large egg

Slowly whisk the hot maple syrup mixture into the egg. Rinse out the saucepan, making sure to dissolve any sugar crystals, then dry the pan thoroughly. Return the sauce to the pan and cook, stirring constantly, over medium heat until the sauce comes to a simmer and is thickened. Stir in:

(¹/₄ cup chopped pecans or walnuts)

Serve at once, or let cool, cover, and refrigerate for up to 3 days. Reheat over low heat, stirring; if it separates, remove from the heat and whisk in a little hot water.

ABOUT UNCOOKED FRUIT SAUCES (COULIS)

Smooth, seedless purees of uncooked berries and other fruits today are often called by their French name *coulis,* which means strained juice. These lovely sauces are very easy to make, fresh in flavor, and vivid in color. Frozen fruit works as well as fresh, but be sure to use dry-pack frozen fruit, which usually is sold in a plastic bag, not fruit that has been prepared with a syrup.

FRESH RASPBERRY SAUCE (RASPBERRY COULIS)

About 1 cup

Puree in a blender or food processor:

1 pint raspberries or 12 ounces frozen dry-pack raspberries, thawed

3 tablespoons sugar, or more to taste

2 teaspoons strained fresh lemon juice, or more to taste

Use a flexible rubber spatula to push the pulp through a fine-mesh sieve into a bowl. Press firmly and periodically scrape the inside of the sieve clear of seeds, which will otherwise plug up the holes. Do not waste any of the precious pulp. Continue to press until you are left with just a heaping tablespoon of stiff, clumped-together seeds. Taste,

then stir in a little more sugar or lemon juice if needed. Serve, at room temperature or chilled. Cover and refrigerate for up to 3 days.

FRESH STRAWBERRY SAUCE (STRAWBERRY COULIS)

About 1¹/₂ cups

If using pale, underripe fresh berries, the sugar and lemon juice may need to be doubled.

Puree in a blender or food processor:

1 pint strawberries or 12 ounces frozen dry-pack strawberries, thawed

3 tablespoons sugar, or more to taste

1 tablespoon strained fresh lemon juice, or more to taste

Do not strain. Taste, adjust sugar or lemon juice if needed. Serve, at room temperature or chilled. Cover and refrigerate for up to 3 days.

FRESH BLUEBERRY SAUCE (BLUEBERRY COULIS)

About 1 ¹/₄ cups

Because blueberries are high in pectin, a jelling agent, this sauce will thicken upon standing. Whisk and thin, if necessary, with water before serving.

Puree in a blender or food processor:

1 pint blueberries or 12 ounces dry-pack blueberries, thawed

3 tablespoons sugar, or more to taste

1 tablespoon strained fresh lemon juice, or more to taste

Strain through a fine-mesh sieve. Taste, adjust sugar or lemon juice if needed. Serve, at room temperature or chilled. Cover and refrigerate for up to 3 days.

FRESH MANGO SAUCE (MANGO COULIS)

About 1 ¹/₄ cups

An unusual sauce with a tropical accent. Especially nice with banana and coconut desserts.

Prepare:

1 large soft but not mushy mango, ¹/₂-inch dice

Puree in a blender or food processor with:

2 tablespoons sugar, or more to taste

2 tablespoons water

1 tablespoon strained fresh lime or lemon juice

If needed, thin with a bit more water and adjust sugar. Serve, at room temperature or chilled. Cover and refrigerate for up to 3 days.

CANDIES AND CONFECTIONS

The fudge pot is responsible for many an early stirring of culinary curiosity and the beginnings of a good cook, so there's reason to be pleased if your children take an interest in the sweeter side of kitchen life. On the other hand, candy making is hardly child's play. Though some types of candy can be made easily by any supervised child, most candy making is a craft, if not an art—and most candy recipes require a considerable degree of patience, time, attention, and practice. Being well prepared is important with any kind of cooking, but it is absolutely vital in candy making.

Before beginning, make sure you have all the ingredients and equipment you need. Read through the recipe to see if there are any steps that must be done in advance, such as toasting nuts or preparing a pan, or any special techniques described elsewhere that you'll need to read first. Also, before beginning to work with sugar, make sure all your equipment and utensils are very clean, to help prevent crystallization, 855.

Accurate measurements are essential in candy making. See About Measuring, 1031.

To avoid a mess, ➤ always choose large, heavy-bottomed pans with a capacity of three to four times the volumes of the ingredients to leave plenty of room for boiling up; overflows can be dangerous. Don't use lined or nickel-coated copper pans, as these materials can react with milk products and acid, and the high temperature of the syrups can melt nickel. ➤ To keep from burning yourself, use a long wooden spoon or heat-resistant silicone spatula that will not heat up during the prolonged cooking time.

One final basic counsel: Watch the weather report and altitude. Heat, humidity, and how high above sea level your kitchen is all play important roles in obtaining the best results when making candy. On humid days, candy must cook longer, to a temperature at least 2 degrees higher than on dry days. And you should dip chocolates or make cooked fondant, hard candy, divinity, nougat, taffy, and any candy that requires drying time on a rack only when it's cool and dry.

▲ Altitude also affects the cooking of candy syrups; see About Candy-Thermometer Temperatures, 855.

ABOUT EQUIPMENT

Having the right equipment simplifies candy making. Most of what you'll need is probably already in your kitchen, but you may want to purchase some specialty items. Here is a list of such special equipment, with some essential tools of a more conventional sort. **Candy and truffle dippers** are made of a stiff metal loop and wooden handle or a single piece of molded plastic. Make your own dipping tool, if you wish, by breaking out the two middle tines of a plastic fork. **Cutters** such as small cookie or aspic cutters can be used to cut candy. A **double boiler** melts chocolate without scorching it. The top pan must fit snugly into the lower one so that steam or sputtering water won't mix with the chocolate and ruin it. A double boiler can be improvised with a saucepan and a stainless steel or heatproof glass bowl.

Candy scraper, offset spatula,
double boiler, candy and truffle dippers

Those who make candy frequently will do well to provide themselves for the finishing step with a **marble slab** of generous proportions. For candies that require rapid cooling, this material absorbs heat quickly and evenly, but not so rapidly as to hasten crystallization. The next best base is a heavy stoneware platter or a flat pan elevated on a cooling rack so that air can circulate around it. Surfaces should be buttered in advance, except in making fondant.

A **candy scraper** or bench knife, a flat sheet of metal with a handle, is a great multipurpose tool. Use it to move, scrape, and divide warm masses of candy and dough.

For making molded candies, inexpensive plastic **molds** in a multitude of designs and sizes are available. For solid candies, buy shallow sheets with multiple cups. For filled candies, 860, buy two-part molds with clips; these come in simple shapes like balls or eggs, as well as fancy and seasonal shapes. Bar molds for making candy bars, 861, are also available. ➤ Do not use any abrasives when cleaning those molds, as chocolate will stick to a scratched surface. **Offset spatulas (offset palette knives)** have long, angled, flexible blades. These are particularly useful for such tasks as spreading chocolate on a marble slab. **Parchment paper (baking or silicone paper),** treated nonstick sheets of paper, is for lining baking sheets and making piping cones. **Silicone liners** are excellent for easy cooling and removal of candies from baking sheets. There are several types of pastry bags. **Piping bags and tips,** for piping out truffle mixtures and candy fillings, are long canvas or plastic bags; 12- and 14-inch bags are the most practical, with a set of plain round tips and a ½-inch opening. (Wash and dry the bags thoroughly after each use to prevent them from souring.) **Parchment paper pastry cones** are for piping candy and truffle mixtures and filling chocolate molds. You can make these yourself, 786, or buy the paper precut. **Zip-top plastic bags** are an alternative to parchment or canvas bags. Fill a plastic sandwich or storage bag no more than two-thirds full with the piping mixture, seal the top, and then cut a small hole in one bottom corner; squeeze the mixture through the hole.

For brushing down the sides of the pan to avoid crystallization when melting sugar, use a **pastry brush** with natural (not plastic) bristles, or a **metal bend scraper.** A **pastry scraper (bowl scraper),** made of thin and flexible plastic, is used for tempering chocolate and for scraping mixtures from bowls. **Thermometers** are essential for gauging the temperature of sugar syrups and chocolate. **Candy thermometers** are designed for reading the stages of cooked sugar in at least 2-degree gradations between 100° and 400°F. **Chocolate thermometers** are calibrated in 1-degree gradations between 40° and 130°F for more precise measurements. **Thermometers** can be used when tempering chocolate only if they are calibrated in 1-degree gradations. Never use a metal spoon for candy making, as the metal gets very hot. Instead, use **long-handled wooden** or **silicone spoons.**

ABOUT CRYSTALLIZATION

One of the greatest frustrations in candy making comes when a smooth, promising candy syrup turns with lightning speed into a dense, grainy mass. This is often caused by sugar crystals that have formed on the sides of the pan being stirred down into the syrup, where they multiply rapidly. Here are several ways to prevent this from happening. ➤ If the recipe calls for butter, grease the sides of the pan with some of it before putting in the other ingredients. ➤ As the syrup cooks, wash down any crystals on the sides of the pan with a natural-bristle (not plastic) pastry brush dipped into hot water. It may be necessary to wash down the sides of the pan more than once if the syrup is boiling violently. ➤ Avoid stirring the syrup once it begins to boil. (The rare exceptions to this rule are noted in individual recipes.) ➤ If you use the ice-cold water test, be sure to use an impeccably clean wooden spoon. If you detect the beginnings of crystallization, ➤ add a small quan-

tity of water to the pan and begin the cooking process over again.

When pouring or molding the finished syrup, ➤ avoid scraping the dregs from the pan. The crystallization rate of the syrup nearest the bottom of the pan, which has been exposed to the greatest heat, is faster than that of the free-flowing syrup from the upper portion. Adding the former to the latter can cause the entire batch to crystallize.

ABOUT CANDY-THERMOMETER TEMPERATURES

An accurate candy thermometer is simply a thermometer designed for reading the stages of cooked sugar in at least 2-degree gradations between 100° and 400°F (top-of-the-line models have gradations of 1 degree and range from 20°F to 500°F). An instant-read thermometer is not accurate enough for most candy making.

To test a candy thermometer for accuracy, put it in a saucepan of water and gradually, to avoid breaking the thermometer, bring the water to a rolling boil. It should register 212°F. If there is any variation, add or subtract the number of degrees necessary to correct its reading when using it. If the reading is off by more than 5 degrees, or if you can see gaps in the mercury, replace the thermometer. Test the thermometer periodically, and always test it if you happen to drop it.

To use the thermometer, warm it by placing it in hot water before inserting it into the sugar syrup or candy to prevent the thermometer from breaking and the syrup from crystallizing. When inserting it, be careful not to let the bulb touch the pan bottom. Many thermometers clip to the side of the pan. Keep it from rolling around in the syrup, for this can trigger crystallization, and have a spoon ready when you remove the thermometer to catch any syrup drops that might fall back into the pan, for the same reason. Clean the thermometer by letting it stand in warm water. If syrup or chocolate is allowed to dry on the thermometer bulb, you won't get an accurate temperature reading.

The temperature of candy rises slowly to 220°F, then seems to hover there forever, but it will take off in a spurt, so pay attention. The temperature will level off again at about 230°F and about every 10 degrees thereafter. For best accuracy, read the thermometer at eye level (which of course means some gymnastics on your part), with the instrument slanted slightly to one side (be careful not to get your face too close to the pan, as hot syrup can sometimes splatter). For safekeeping, hang thermometers rather than storing them in a drawer.

THE STAGES OF COOKED SUGAR SYRUP

If you don't have a thermometer, practice can make you an expert in recognizing the subtle differences in color, bubbling, and threading that reveal crucial temperatures. Always remove the pan from the heat while testing so as not to overcook, as a few extra degrees can bring the candy up into the next stage. Use fresh chilled water for each test.

Most experienced candy makers use both a thermometer and the chilled water test. Exact temperature as measured by a thermometer is a useful guide, but a candy that is ready at 250°F one day may need to be 3 degrees higher the next day: Room temperature, humidity, even the moisture content of granulated sugar can all make a difference. To perform the chilled water test, use a clean wooden or silicone (not metal) spoon to drop a small quantity of candy syrup—less than a teaspoonful—into a small container of chilled (not ice) water. Quickly gather the syrup between your fingers. The temperature to which the sugar has been cooked can be identified by the way the syrup reacts; see below. As the water heats and evaporates, the concentration of sugar in the syrup rises, and the higher the concentration of sugar, the harder the mixture will be upon cooling. Thus chewy candy, like caramel, is cooked to a lower temperature than that of the crunchy type, like toffee. The stages of cooking describe the temperature range for each one, the visual characteristics of each, and a few of the candies that are cooked to that stage. If you're a novice candy maker, you may want to practice by cooking a sugar syrup to each stage, then testing it in cold water so you'll know what to look for when making an actual candy.

Because testing will take several minutes, we recommend removing the pan from the heat, remembering that doing so cools the syrup and can delay the cooking; if you're an old hand, leave the pan on the heat, as a few seconds won't make much difference.

PEARL—220° to 222°F
Runs off a spoon in drops.
Jelly, 927, Icing, 784

THREAD—Begins at 230°F
Makes a brittle thread that runs off the end of spoon.
Decorative spun sugar

BLOW/SOUFFLÉ—220° to 234°F
Makes a loose thread.
Rock Candy, 875

SOFT BALL—Begins at 234°F
A small quantity of syrup dropped into chilled water forms a limp, sticky ball that flattens when removed from the water and rolled between the fingers.
Fudge, 862, Caramel Corn, 866, Fondant, 866, Opera Creams, 868, Cream Pull Candy, 871, Peppermint Wafers, 867

FIRM BALL—244° to 248°F
The ball will hold its shape and will not flatten unless pressed with fingers.
Caramels, 864, Halvah, 878, Marshmallows, 869, Marzipan, 877

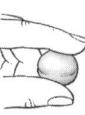

HARD BALL—250° to 266°F
The ball is more rigid but is still pliable.
Divinity, 869, Pulled Mints, 871, Taffy, 870

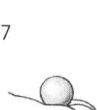

SOFT CRACK—270° to 290°F
Drop a small quantity of syrup into chilled water. It will separate into hard threads, which, when removed from the water, will bend.
Nougat, 868, Taffy, 870, Popcorn with White Sugar Syrup, 866

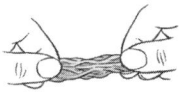

HARD CRACK—300° to 310°F
The syrup separates into threads that are hard and brittle.
Butterscotch, 874, Coffee Drops, 874, nut brittles, 872–873, Lollipops, 875

CARAMELIZED SUGAR

310° to 338°F
Syrup changes from honey colored to light brown
Sesame Seed Brittle, 873

356°F
Syrup turns a medium brown color
Praline, 876, Nougat, 868, spun sugar, caramel cages

374°F
Syrup turns a dark brown color
Coloring agent for sauces

410°F
Black Jack: the syrup turns black and then decomposes
None

Cooked sugar sticks tenaciously to any surface it touches, but it cleans up neatly with hot water and patience. Once the syrup has been poured from the pan, immediately fill the pan with hot water and add any sticky utensils. Let sit for 30 minutes, then wash both pan and utensils well with hot soapy water. In the case of caramel, which can be particularly sticky, fill the pan with hot water, add the utensils, and bring the water to a boil over medium heat before rinsing out. You may need to do this several times to dissolve particularly troublesome caramel spots.

▲ As with baking, altitude can make a difference in candy making. If you live above sea level, cook candy syrups 1 degree lower than indicated in the following recipe for each increase of 500 feet above sea level. For instance, if you're making fudge, which needs to cook to a minimum of 234°F, your syrup should "fudge" at about 230°F at 2,000 feet, or at about 224°F at 5,000 feet.

ABOUT WRAPPING CANDY

To protect candy and preserve its freshness, precut squares of colored foil and cellophane are best for wrapping hard candies, taffies, and caramels. For fun, make candy chains by cutting two long narrow strips of cellophane or plastic wrap, then laying out pieces of candy, generously spaced, along one strip and placing the other on top. Seal in the candy by twisting the strip sausage fashion; these can be cut apart later into individually wrapped candies. Candy chains make colorful Christmas tree decorations.

For holding soft finished candies so they can be handled easily, and for serving candies attractively, buy paper, foil, or cellophane cups. The latter two won't absorb oil from the candies. Chocolates and other oily candies may leave an oily residue in the paper cups. Candy cups come in several sizes; the most useful is 1 1/2 inches in diameter.

ABOUT SERVING AND STORING CANDY

Most candies taste best at room temperature. Most chocolate candies usually keep up to 3 weeks, stored in an airtight container, in the refrigerator and can be frozen for up to 2 months. In the refrigerator, place them away from strong-flavored foods, because chocolate easily absorbs other flavors, even when covered. To freeze, pack candies between layers of wax paper in an airtight container and wrap the container in several layers of aluminum foil. Chocolate truffles, truffle cups, molded candies, fudge, marzipan candies, and other shaped or cut candies are easy to serve in paper candy cups. Some hard candies, such as brittles and toffees, may be too large to fit in candy cups and are better arranged free-form on the serving platter—perhaps on top of a grease-resistant doily, available in cake and candy supply stores.

Hard candies, caramels, taffies, and divinity will stay fresh and keep their texture best when individually wrapped and stored in airtight containers at room temperature for no longer than 3 weeks. Do not refrigerate, because they are highly hygroscopic—meaning they will absorb moisture and become soft and crumbly.

If you have refrigerated your candies, be sure to let them stand at room temperature for at least 20 minutes before serving. Defrost frozen candies in the refrigerator for at least 24 hours before serving, then let them stand at room temperature for at least 20 minutes longer. (Remember that sudden changes in temperature can cause chocolate coating to crack and discolor.)

ABOUT TEMPERING CHOCOLATE

To melt chocolate, see 970.

Tempering is a process of heating and cooling melted chocolate to specific temperatures so that the finished chocolate has a glossy surface, a smooth texture, and a nice snap. The seed method relies on a larger piece of chocolate being put in the melted chocolate to lower the temperature. The piece or pieces are then removed so the temperature will rise again, creating "tempered" chocolate when it dries. Chocolate is in that condition when it leaves the factory, and with proper handling and storage, it should still be in temper when purchased. Once you melt the chocolate, however, tempering is recommended if you want to dip confections, mold shapes, and make fanciful decorations; tempering is not required when melted chocolate is used as an ingredient in a recipe. To verify the temperature of your chocolate, you will need a chocolate thermometer, 855, or a thermometer calibrated in 1-degree gradations. Be careful not to let the thermometer bulb touch the bottom of the pan, or your temperature reading will be off. **To temper chocolate by the seeding method,** set aside:

4 ounces of chocolate cut into 1-inch chunks or grated
Grate or chop into small pieces about:
1 pound high-quality unsweetened, bittersweet, semisweet, milk, or white chocolate
Melt it very slowly in the top of double boiler over, not in, simmering water. (If you don't have a double boiler, a stainless steel bowl over a pot of water works just as well.) Stir the chocolate until its temperature reaches 105° to 115°F. (If you do not stir constantly at temperatures over 100°F, the cocoa butter will separate out.) Transfer the chocolate to another bowl and cool to 100°F. Add the reserved chocolate chunks and stir until the temperature cools to a maximum of 86°F for milk and white chocolates and 90°F for dark, unsweetened, or bittersweet chocolate. Then remove the unmelted chunks, place them on a baking sheet lined with wax or parchment paper or a silicone liner, and refrigerate until dry; they are reusable. The chocolate is now in temper and ready to be tested as below and used.

To temper chocolate using the marble slab method, melt the chocolate as directed above, then remove the top of the double boiler or bowl from the water and wipe the bottom dry to avoid contaminating the chocolate with water. Pour about two-thirds of the chocolate onto a marble slab. With a metal scraper and an offset spatula, spread the chocolate out in a thin layer and quickly scrape it back together into a mass, working it back and forth several times to cool it. Return this cooled chocolate to the bowl with the remaining melted chocolate and stir it in to remelt. Repeat this process several times until the chocolate cools to 85°F. Place the bowl of chocolate over simmering water again and heat it to 88°F.

To test tempered chocolate, place a dab of the chocolate on a piece of wax paper and chill for 3 minutes. If it is dry to the touch and evenly glossy, the chocolate is ready to use. **To maintain the temper in a bowl of chocolate over an extended period,** place it in a pan of water up to 2 degrees warmer than the maximum temperatures allowed for tempered dark, milk, or white chocolates (90°F for dark, 88°F for milk and white chocolates), depending on the type you are using. Or microwave as necessary in 5-second increments until warm. Be careful; if you exceed the maximum temperatures, you will "break" the chocolate's temper and have to begin again.

DARK CHOCOLATE TRUFFLES

About 1 ½ pounds; about 80 pieces

Named whimsically after the savory black truffle, these candies have centers of plain or flavored ganache, a mixture of chocolate and cream. The ganache centers are dipped in chocolate or coated with a variety of ingredients; see across. Ganache, 795, will keep, refrigerated, up to 1 month, and, frozen, 3 months. Truffles are one of the easiest chocolate candies to make. Use the best-quality chocolate you can afford.

Chop into tiny pieces and place in a medium mixing bowl:

    12 ounces bittersweet or semisweet chocolate

Heat to just under a simmer in a small saucepan over medium heat:

    1¼ cups heavy cream

Pour the hot cream all at once over the chocolate and stir gently until the mixture is smooth and thoroughly blended. Cool to room temperature, stirring occasionally, then refrigerate for 3 to 4 hours, until the ganache is thick and quite stiff. Line a baking sheet with wax or parchment paper or a silicone liner and refrigerate until cold. Use a melon baller or pastry bag fitted with a ½-inch plain round tip to scoop or pipe out balls of ganache about ¾ inch in diameter onto the chilled baking sheet. Cover loosely with plastic wrap and refrigerate until firm, about 2 hours. When firm, roll the balls between your palms to smooth them out. Return to the baking sheet and freeze the truffle centers until ready to dip in a chocolate coating as below or coat, across.

DIPPED CHOCOLATE TRUFFLES

Temper, 857:

    1 pound high-quality bittersweet or
      semisweet chocolate

Before dipping into chocolate, be sure the centers are about 70°F. Otherwise the chocolate may streak with gray. Using a fork or a candy dipper, 854, dip the centers, one by one, in batches, keeping the remaining centers in the freezer while working. Coat the centers one at a time in a small quantity of the chocolate. Lift them out with the fork onto a ¼-inch wire mesh rack set over a pan or tray to catch chocolate drippings, which may be remelted and reused. Place on a baking sheet lined with wax or parchment paper or a silicone liner. Cover and refrigerate until set, about 20 minutes, then place the truffles in paper candy cups. Serve the truffles right away, or store between layers of wax paper or parchment in an airtight container in the refrigerator for up to 3 weeks or in the freezer for up to 2 months. If frozen, defrost for 24 hours in the refrigerator. Remove the truffles from the refrigerator 30 to 45 minutes before serving.

MICROWAVE CHOCOLATE TRUFFLE CENTERS

Chop into small pieces and place in a 1-quart microwavable glass bowl:

    10 ounces bittersweet or semisweet chocolate

Add:

    ¾ cup heavy cream

Heat in a microwave oven on High in 30-second increments until melted and smooth (1½ to 2½ minutes total). Add:

    ¼ cup (½ stick) unsalted butter, cut into
      small pieces

Stir until the butter is melted and thoroughly absorbed. Cool and chill the mixture and dip the centers as for **Dark Chocolate Truffles, above.** Then form centers as directed.

COATED CHOCOLATE TRUFFLES

Coating the centers in cocoa powder, sugar, coconut, or nuts rather than dipping them in chocolate is a simple, delicious method of coating truffles. Cocoa, meant to suggest the earth that clings to real truffles when they are dug, is traditional in France.

Form and chill the truffle centers as for **Dark Chocolate Truffles, above.** Place the centers on a pan lined with wax or parchment paper or a silicone liner. Have ready another lined pan. Spread in a pie plate or shallow bowl one or more of the following:

    1 cup sifted unsweetened cocoa powder
    1 cup sifted unsweetened cocoa powder,
      mixed with 2 teaspoons ground cinnamon
    1 cup confectioners' sugar, sifted
    1 cup shredded sweetened coconut, toasted, 972
    1 cup nuts, toasted, 1001, finely chopped

Drop one center into the bowl of cocoa or other coating, shake the bowl to coat it. Lift the truffle out and place it on the lined pan. Repeat with the remaining centers, then place the truffles in paper candy cups and serve or store as directed above in Dipped Chocolate Truffles, above.

MILK CHOCOLATE TRUFFLES

About 1 pound; about 54 pieces

Substitute **12 ounces milk chocolate** for the dark chocolate in **Dark Chocolate Truffles, above,** and reduce the amount of cream to ½ cup. Place the chocolate and cream in the top of a double boiler or a stainless steel bowl over hot, not boiling, water and stir frequently until the chocolate is melted and smooth. Cool and chill, then proceed as directed.

WHITE CHOCOLATE TRUFFLES
About 1 pound; about 54 pieces

Substitute **12 ounces white chocolate** for the dark chocolate in **Dark Chocolate Truffles, 858,** and reduce the amount of cream to ½ cup. Place the white chocolate and cream in the top of a double boiler or a stainless steel bowl over hot, not boiling, water and stir frequently until the chocolate is melted and smooth. Cool and chill, then proceed as directed.

NUTTY CHOCOLATE TRUFFLES

Prepare **Dark Chocolate Truffles, Milk Chocolate Truffles, or White Chocolate Truffles, 858–859.** Add ⅔ **cup almonds, hazelnuts, pecans, walnuts, macadamia nuts, pistachio nuts, or pine nuts, toasted, 1001, and very finely chopped,** to the chocolate and cream mixture and stir thoroughly. Cool, then chill the chocolate and cream mixture for 1 hour. Stir well to distribute the chopped nuts, then chill for another 2 to 3 hours. Form the centers and dip as directed. Before the coating chocolate sets, decorate the top of each tuffle with a nut to match the filling. Or roll the truffles in the same finely chopped nut as in the filling.

CHOCOLATE TRUFFLES WITH LIQUEUR

Reduce the cream in the **Dark Chocolate Truffles, 858,** to 1 cup. Add ¼ **cup port, rum, Cognac, framboise, kirsch, Grand Marnier, or other liqueur** to the warm chocolate and cream mixture and stir thoroughly. Cool and chill the chocolate and cream mixture, then proceed as directed.

MOCHA TRUFFLES

Prepare **Dark Chocolate Truffles, Milk Chocolate Truffles, or White Chocolate Truffles, 858–859.** Dissolve **1 tablespoon plus 2 teaspoons instant espresso powder** in **2 tablespoons warm water,** and stir thoroughly into the warm chocolate and cream mixture. Cool and chill the mixture, then proceed as directed. If desired, before the coating chocolate sets, decorate the top of each truffle with a coffee bean.

TRUFFLE CUPS
About 1½ pounds; about 75 pieces

Truffle cups are made from the same chocolate and cream mixture used for truffle centers. The mixture is piped into 1-inch pleated foil candy cups, placed in mini muffin tins or on a baking sheet, and frozen until set.
Prepare the chocolate and cream mixture for **Dark Chocolate Truffles** or any of the variations, 858–859, about 30 minutes at room temperature. Set aside until thick but not stiff.
Fill a pastry bag fitted with a plain round tip and pipe the mixture to the top of each candy cup. Lightly tap the cups on the work surface to release air bubbles. If you like, decorate each with **1 whole or half nut or sliver of dried, candied, or crystallized fruit** to match the filling. Place in the freezer for 20 minutes to set.

Peel away the foil cups to show the pleated design. Serve or store as directed.

DARK CHOCOLATE BARK
About 1¼ pounds

A simple chocolate candy to make, which is said to resemble tree bark. Chocolate bark usually has two ingredients: tempered chocolate and nuts or dried, candied, or crystallized fruit. Bark is ideal for using up bits of leftover chocolate. Any amount of chocolate may be used, as long as the proportion of chocolate to nuts remains the same as below.
Line a baking sheet with aluminum foil. Temper, 857:
 1 pound bittersweet or semisweet chocolate
Stir in:
 **2 cups unblanched almonds or other nuts,
 toasted, 1001, and coarsely chopped**
Coat the nuts thoroughly, then spread the mixture about ¼ inch thick on the lined baking sheet. Tap the pan on the work surface to release any air bubbles.
Refrigerate until firm, about 15 minutes. Then let stand in a cool place for 30 minutes to 1 hour to set completely. Holding the chocolate with the foil to avoid getting fingerprints on it, break it into two bite-sized irregular shapes. If the bark is too hard to break with your hands, place a sheet of foil on top and hit it with a wooden spoon. To store, see 857.

MILK CHOCOLATE BARK

Pecans contrast vividly with the mild flavor of milk chocolate.
Prepare **Dark Chocolate Bark, above,** substituting **1 pound milk chocolate** for the dark chocolate and using **pecans.**

WHITE CHOCOLATE BARK

For an all-white candy, use pine nuts; for a green-and-white one, use pistachios.
Prepare **Dark Chocolate Bark, above,** substituting **1 pound white chocolate** for the dark chocolate and using **1½ cups skinned pistachio nuts or pine nuts.**

FRUITED CHOCOLATE BARK

Of all combinations of chocolate and fruit, our favorite is bittersweet chocolate with crystallized ginger.
Prepare **Dark Chocolate Bark, Milk Chocolate Bark, or White Chocolate Bark, above,** substituting **2 cups finely chopped dried, candied, or crystallized fruit or ginger** for the nuts.

SMALL SOLID CHOCOLATES
About 1 pound; about 32 pieces

Before beginning, you may want to polish your molds with a cotton cloth or makeup-removal pads; this will lower the incidence of air bubbles.
Temper, 857:

1 pound high-quality bittersweet, semisweet, milk, or white chocolate

Spread the chocolate over the top of the mold with an off-set spatula. Lightly tap the mold on the work surface to release any air bubbles. Scrape any excess chocolate into an empty bowl.

Place the mold on a baking sheet in the freezer for about 15 minutes to set.

The chocolates are ready to unmold when they have shrunk somewhat from the sides of the molds. Invert the mold over a wax paper–lined plate or pan and twist it slightly (like an ice cube tray) to release the chocolates. They should come out easily. If not, return to the freezer for 10 minutes more and try again. Serve or store as directed, 859.

LARGE SOLID CHOCOLATES

About 1 pound

Temper, 857:

1 pound high-quality bittersweet, semisweet, milk or white chocolate

For each chocolate, clip the halves of a chocolate mold together, then hold the mold with the opening facing up. Pour the chocolate into the mold to fill it. Rap the mold on the work surface to release any air bubbles.

Place the mold in the freezer with the opening up to set the chocolate, about 30 minutes.

Remove the mold from the freezer and let it stand at room temperature for 10 minutes. Remove the clips from the sides of the mold and carefully remove the mold from the chocolate. Serve or store as directed, 859.

HOLLOW CHOCOLATES

About 1 pound

Temper, 857:

1 pound high-quality bittersweet, semisweet, milk, or white chocolate

Spread the chocolate over the top of each half of the mold and scrape the excess into an empty bowl with an offset spatula. Lightly tap the mold on the work surface to release any air bubbles. Let the mold sit for up to 2 minutes, or until the edges of the chocolate start to look as if they are setting and turn dull in color.

Invert the mold onto a rack set over an empty bowl and let the still-melted chocolate drip from the mold for 3 to 5 minutes. Repeat this process several times, until the desired thickness of chocolate is obtained.

Place the mold on a baking sheet in the freezer to set for 30 minutes.

Gently unmold the chocolate, taking care not to crack it; turning it out onto a clean kitchen towel will help reduce the odds of cracking. Spread melted chocolate around the edges of each half and hold the 2 halves of the molded chocolate together for 1 to 2 minutes to seal them. Serve or store as directed, 859.

CHOCOLATE NUT BONBONS

About 1¼ pounds; about 55 small bonbons

These candies resemble ice cream bonbons, but instead of ice cream, their center is a voluptuous chocolate truffle filling surrounding a toasted whole nut.

Chop into very tiny pieces and place in a medium bowl:

12 ounces bittersweet or semisweet chocolate

Bring just to a boil in a small saucepan over medium heat:

1 cup heavy cream

Pour the hot cream over the chocolate, and shake the bowl gently to cover the chocolate completely with cream. Let stand for 2 to 3 minutes, then stir gently with a rubber spatula until the chocolate and cream mixture is smooth and thoroughly blended.

Stir in until thoroughly mixed:

½ cup nuts, toasted, 1001, and finely chopped

Cool to room temperature, until thickened but still soft enough to pipe. Temper, 857:

1½ pounds high-quality bittersweet or semisweet chocolate

Fill as for Hollow Molded Chocolates, above. Hollow out the molds by turning them upside down on a rack set over an empty bowl for 5 minutes to let the excess chocolate drip out.

Turn the molds right side up and let them stand 3 to 4 minutes, just to set the chocolate. Drop into each cup:

1 whole toasted nut (about ¾ cup total)

Use a parchment paper cone or a plastic zip-top bag, 855, with a ½-inch opening to pipe the thickened chocolate and cream mixture into the molds, filling each one three-quarters full. Then pipe the remaining tempered chocolate into the molds, filling them to the top. Alternatively, gently spread the tempered chocolate across the top of the molds and scrape the excess into an empty bowl with an offset spatula. Clean off the edges of each mold if needed.

Place the molds on a baking sheet in the freezer for about 30 minutes to set the chocolate.

See unmolding, 860. Serve or store as directed, 859.

PEANUT BUTTER CUPS

About 1 pound; about 24 cups

One of the most addictive of chocolate candies. Be sure to stir the peanut butter before using in case the oil has separated. Milk chocolate is traditional, but bittersweet, semisweet, or white chocolate may be substituted.

Have ready two 11- or 12-cup candy molds with 1½-inch fluted paper cups. Or sit fluted foil cups in a mold or mini muffin pan. Make 3 parchment paper pastry cones or use plastic zip-top bags, 855.

Temper, 857:

1 pound milk chocolate

Pour half of the chocolate into 1 of the parchment paper cones or plastic bags. Snip off a ¼-inch opening at the tip of the cone or from a bottom corner of the bag and pipe

chocolate into each cup, filling it about one-third full. Let set for 8 to 10 minutes.
Fill the second parchment paper cone or plastic bag with:

¾ cup natural or regular smooth peanut butter, at room temperature

Snip off a ½-inch opening and pipe peanut butter into the center of each chocolate cup, filling them no more than three-quarters full. Be careful not to pipe the peanut butter to the edges of the mold, or the chocolate will not seal around it. Fill the third parchment paper cone or plastic bag with the remaining chocolate, snip off a ¼-inch opening, and pipe chocolate into each cup, filling it to the top. Tilt the mold as necessary so the chocolate completely fills in any spaces. Alternatively, use an offset spatula to spread the chocolate across the top of the mold and scrape the excess into an empty bowl. Lightly tap the filled molds on the work surface to release any air bubbles.
Place the molds on a baking sheet and chill in the freezer for 20 minutes to set the chocolate.
See unmolding, 860. Serve or store as directed, 859.

DARK CHOCOLATE CANDY BARS WITH NUTS

About 1 pound; twelve 5 x 2-inch bars
These bars may be personalized by varying the size or shape of the molds, the type of chocolate, and the nuts.
Temper, 857:

1 pound high-quality bittersweet or semisweet chocolate

Stir in:

¾ cup blanched almonds or other nuts, toasted, 1001, and coarsely chopped

Pour the mixture into twelve 5 x 2-inch bar-shaped molds. When the molds are full, gently shake them to spread the chocolate evenly. Tap lightly on the work surface to remove any air bubbles.
Place the molds on a baking sheet and chill in the freezer for 20 minutes to set the chocolate.
See unmolding, 860. Wrap the bars individually in silver or colored foil. Store as directed, 859.

JOY OF COCONUT

About 1½ pounds; about 24 bonbons or 18 small bars
You won't be able to tell these candies from the popular store-bought coconut-and-almond candy bar, except that the ingredients for this version are fewer and easier to pronounce. The coconut filling is prepared in a microwave oven. If you don't have a microwave, dry the coconut in the oven without browning, see toasting coconut, 972, and heat the corn syrup on top of the stove. If you opt to use sweetened coconut, keep in mind that it will take considerably longer than unsweetened coconut to absorb the corn syrup.
Toast, 972, in a microwave-safe pie plate:

2½ cups shredded unsweetened coconut

Pour into a microwave-safe cup:

¾ cup light corn syrup

Heat in the microwave on High for 1 to 2 minutes, until steaming but not boiling. Pour over the coconut and stir well. Let stand for 1 hour or until the coconut has absorbed the corn syrup. Line a baking sheet with parchment paper or a silicone liner. With hands dipped in cold water, shape the coconut into bonbons or 2½ x 1-inch bars and place on the lined sheet. If the coconut is sticky, wet your hands frequently.
Top each candy with:

1 unblanched whole almond (18 to 24 total)

Temper, 857:

12 ounces high-quality milk chocolate

Use 2 forks or a candy dipper to coat the candies with the chocolate, then gently shake off the excess chocolate and return the dipped candy to the baking sheet. Place in the refrigerator for 30 minutes to set the chocolate. Let the candies stand at room temperature for 10 minutes, then place each bonbon in a paper candy cup to serve. Store as directed, 859.

DARK CHOCOLATE CLUSTERS

About 1 pound; about twenty-five 1-inch clusters
There are countless variations on this popular, easy-to-make candy, some of which appear below.
Line a baking sheet with wax or parchment paper or a silicone liner. Temper, 857:

8 ounces high-quality bittersweet or semisweet chocolate

Stir together:

1 cup dried apricots, finely chopped
1 cup walnuts, toasted, 1001, and coarsely chopped

Blend this mixture into the chocolate and stir to coat completely. Spoon out 1-inch clusters onto the lined baking sheet. Chill the clusters in the freezer for 20 minutes to set the chocolate. Place each cluster in a paper candy cup to serve. Store as directed, 859.

GINGERED CHOCOLATE CLUSTERS

Prepare **Dark Chocolate Clusters, above,** substituting **1 cup crystallized ginger, finely chopped,** for the dried apricots and **1 cup macadamia nuts, toasted, 1001, and coarsely chopped,** for the walnuts.

MILK CHOCOLATE CLUSTERS

Prepare **Dark Chocolate Clusters, above,** substituting **8 ounces high-quality milk chocolate** for the dark chocolate. Substitute **1 cup dried cherries, finely chopped,** for the apricots and **1 cup pecans, coarsely chopped and toasted, 1001,** for the walnuts.

WHITE CHOCOLATE CLUSTERS

Prepare **Dark Chocolate Clusters, above,** substituting **8 ounces high-quality white chocolate** for the dark chocolate. Substitute **1 cup candied orange peel, finely chopped,** and **1 cup blanched almonds, coarsely chopped, toasted, 1001,** for the walnuts.

ABOUT FUDGE

Fudge is a semisoft candy made from a cooked sugar syrup enriched with cream or butter. In the innocent days of the late nineteenth century, fudge making was a collegiate craze and a somewhat competitive after-school pursuit, and it has always been one of our favorite confections. Although it can be tricky to make, the technique is easily mastered if you follow a few simple rules.

Use caution. ➤ Fudge can overcook in just the time it takes to retrieve the correct spatula. Fudge must be cooked slowly over medium heat to the soft-ball stage (234° to 240°F). Resist the temptation to raise the heat in an effort to quicken the process, as this often results in a scorched flavor and overly grainy texture. Remember, though, that the soft-ball stage only begins at 234°F; professional candy makers expect their fudge to come in at 238°F, but on occasion, on a very humid day, for instance, it can refuse to ball until the syrup is as hot as 242°F. It is also important to stir the sugar mixture until the sugar is dissolved. Then cover the pan or brush down the sides of the pan with a natural or silicone-bristle pastry brush dipped in warm water a couple of times as the mixture comes to a boil. Alternatively, you can cover the pan and allow steam to wash down the sides; be very careful when removing the lid, as the hot liquid may splatter when the lid is lifted. Once the fudge starts to boil, let it cook ➤ undisturbed until it reaches the proper temperature or balls, or you run the risk of spoiling the batch. For an old-fashioned grainy fudge, start stirring the moment you take the pan off the heat. For a smooth, creamy fudge, let the syrup mixture cool to 110°F first before stirring.

To cool fudge: The best way to hasten cooling is to place the pan in a second pan of cold water or in a sink with just enough cold water to come about an inch up the sides of the fudge pan. Let it cool until you can comfortably touch the bottom of the pan with your hand. Alternatively, pour the syrup onto a marble slab or baking sheet sprinkled with cold water. The advantage of marble is that it absorbs heat evenly and quickly—but not too quickly. (A 24 x 18-inch slab will hold up to 2 pounds of fudge.) If you pour the mixture out, be careful not to scrape the bottom of the pan, as the sugar mixture on the bottom, cooked to a higher temperature than the rest, could crystallize the rest of the batch.

When the fudge has cooled to 110°F, transfer the mixture to the bowl of a heavy-duty mixer and beat it with the paddle attachment on low speed for 8 to 15 minutes. As soon as it thickens, loses its sheen, and begins to hold peaks, pour the fudge into a buttered pan. If you're making chocolate fudge, ➤ watch it very carefully—if you neglect it for a moment, it may thicken too much and become hard and unworkable.

Fudge may also be mixed by hand; this takes a bit of elbow grease but is safer for beginners. If you've cooled the mixture on a marble slab or baking sheet, work it with the candy scraper on the slab. If it's still in the pan, stir it with a wooden spoon, using gentle, almost lazy motions, in a figure-eight pattern, covering the entire bottom of the pan. As soon as the fudge thickens and starts to lose its sheen, pour it into a buttered pan.

After 2 hours, while the fudge is still semisoft, score it with a sharp knife and chill until set.

The flavor of fudge matures after a day or so, and the texture improves. Don't wait too long to enjoy it, though: If stored longer than 10 days at room temperature or 1 month in the refrigerator, it will develop white spots, known as bloom. These won't affect the flavor, but they give it an unappetizing look. Like all candies, fudge tastes best served at room temperature.

Fudge is very versatile, and it can be flavored with many things besides chocolate; maple syrup and peanut butter are particularly popular. Any of the fudges in this chapter may be made into candy centers. Either score and chill as directed, then shape each piece into a ball and dip in tempered chocolate, 857, or beat the fudge until quite thick, knead it, and shape it into balls, then dip the balls into tempered chocolate.

FUDGE COCKAIGNE

About 1 ¼ pounds; 52 pieces
Please read About Fudge, above. Bring to a boil in a large heavy saucepan:

1 cup minus 1 tablespoon milk

Remove from the heat and stir in until the sugar is dissolved:

2 cups sugar

⅛ teaspoon salt

2 ounces unsweetened chocolate, grated

Bring to a boil and cook 5 minutes, washing down any sugar crystals that may have formed on the sides of the pan with a pastry brush dipped in warm water. Reduce the heat, place a warmed candy thermometer in the pan, and cook, without stirring, to 234°F, the soft-ball stage. When nearing 234°F, there will be a fine overall bubbling with, simultaneously, a coarser pattern, as though the fine bubbled areas were being pulled down for quilting into the coarser ones. Remove from the heat without jostling or stirring.

Cool the fudge to 110°F. You may hasten this process by placing the pan in a large pan of cold water until the bottom of the pan has cooled.

Add:

2 to 4 tablespoons unsalted butter

Stir in:

1 teaspoon vanilla

Beat until it thickens and begins to lose its sheen. At this point, the drip from the spoon, when you flip it over, holds its shape against the bottom of the spoon. Quickly stir in:

½ to 1 cup chopped nuts

Pour the fudge into a buttered 8-inch square pan. Cut into squares before it hardens.

WHITE FUDGE COCKAIGNE

About 1 1/2 pounds; 64 pieces

Please read About Fudge, 862. Combine in a large heavy saucepan and cook over medium heat, stirring, until the sugar is dissolved:

2 1/2 cups sugar
1/2 cup sour cream
1/4 cup milk
1 tablespoon light corn syrup
1/4 teaspoon salt

After the mixture begins to boil, cook for 2 to 3 minutes, washing down any sugar crystals that may have formed on the sides of the pan with a pastry brush dipped in warm water. Reduce the heat, place a warmed candy thermometer in the pan, and cook, without stirring, to 234°F, the soft-ball stage.

Pour at once into an electric mixer bowl; do not scrape the pan. Float on top, but do not stir in (stirring at this point can cause graininess):

2 tablespoons unsalted butter, softened
1 teaspoon vanilla

Let cool to room temperature, in about 1 hour. Beat the fudge until it begins to lose its gloss. Quickly beat in, if desired:

(3/4 cup chopped nuts)
(1/4 cup finely chopped dried apricots, cranberries, or cherries)

Pour into an 8-inch square buttered pan and let harden, then cut into squares.

CHOCOLATE WALNUT FUDGE

About 1 1/2 pounds; 64 pieces

This fudge is smooth and creamy.

Please read About Fudge, 862. Combine in a large heavy saucepan:

2 cups sugar
1/8 teaspoon salt
1/2 cup half-and-half
1/2 cup heavy cream
1/4 cup light corn syrup

Stir over low heat until the sugar is dissolved, about 5 minutes. Bring to a boil and cook, without stirring, for 1 minute. Brush down the sides of the pan with a pastry brush dipped in warm water to remove any sugar crystals that may have formed, and remove from the heat. Stir in until melted and completely smooth:

6 ounces bittersweet or semisweet chocolate, chopped

Brush down the sides of the pan again, then set the pan over medium heat, place a warmed candy thermometer in the pan, and cook the mixture, without stirring, until it reaches 234°F, the soft-ball stage. Remove from the heat.

Float on top, but do not stir in (stirring at this point can cause graininess):

2 tablespoons unsalted butter, softened
1 teaspoon vanilla

Cool the candy to 110°F by placing the bottom of the pan in cold water to stop the cooking. Alternatively, pour it out onto a marble slab or baking sheet (inverted over a rack) sprinkled with cold water, without scraping the bottom of the pan.

When it is cool, stir the fudge in the pan with a wooden spoon or work it on the slab with a candy scraper just until it "snaps" and begins to lose its sheen. Or transfer the cooled fudge to the bowl of a heavy-duty mixer. Using the paddle attachment, beat the fudge on low speed until it begins to thicken and lose its sheen, 5 to 10 minutes. Watch the mixture carefully or it may thicken too much and become unworkable.

Stir in:

1 to 1 1/2 cups English or black walnuts, coarsely chopped

Turn the fudge out into an 8-inch square pan lined with buttered foil that extends over the sides. Smooth the top with an offset or rubber spatula, dipping it in hot water as needed. Let stand for at least 1 hour.

Use a large heavy knife to score the fudge into 1-inch squares. Cover and refrigerate for at least 24 hours.

Remove the fudge from the pan and peel off the foil. Use the knife to finish cutting the fudge into squares. Serve in paper candy cups. Or store as directed, 859.

MAPLE WALNUT FUDGE

About 1 1/2 pounds; 64 pieces

Please read About Fudge, 862. Combine in a large heavy saucepan:

1 cup half-and-half
3/4 cup maple syrup
1/2 cup heavy cream
3 cups sugar
1/4 cup dark corn syrup
1/8 teaspoon salt

Stir over low heat until the sugar is dissolved, about 5 minutes, then brush down the sides of the pan with a pastry brush dipped in warm water. Raise the heat to medium, place a warmed candy thermometer in the pan, and cook the mixture, without stirring, until it reaches 234°F, the soft-ball stage. Remove from the heat. Float on top, but do not stir in (stirring at this point can cause graininess):

3 tablespoons unsalted butter, softened
2 teaspoons vanilla

To cool, see Dark Chocolate Walnut Fudge, above. Fold in:

1 1/2 to 2 cups walnuts, coarsely chopped

Let set and store as directed, 859.

PEANUT BUTTER FUDGE

About 1½ pounds; 64 pieces

Have ready an 8-inch square pan buttered on the bottom. In a large saucepan, combine:

1¼ cups (2½ sticks) unsalted butter
1¼ cups smooth peanut butter

Cook over medium heat until mixture comes to a boil. Remove from heat and add:

Pinch salt
1½ teaspoons vanilla
(¼ teaspoon maple extract)

Stir in:

4½ cups confectioners' sugar, sifted

Mix well to combine. Pour mixture into buttered pan. Cover fudge directly with a piece of plastic wrap. Chill until firm.

CHOCOLATE-DIPPED FUDGE

About 100 pieces

Prepare any recipe for **fudge, 862–864.** Cool for 1 hour, then score the fudge into ¾-inch squares. After it has chilled for 2 hours, finish cutting the squares, and roll each one between your palms to shape them into balls. Temper, 857, **8 ounces high-quality bittersweet, semisweet, milk, or white chocolate.** Dip the fudge centers as directed on 858.

ABOUT CARAMEL CANDIES

Caramels are based on sugar, corn syrup and/or honey, milk and/or cream, and butter. Their characteristic flavor comes from the caramelization of the sugar, but additions such as chocolate, coffee, citrus zest, and nuts are welcome. Caramels are cooked slowly over medium heat to the firm-ball stage (244° to 248°F). Resist the temptation to raise the heat to quicken the process, as this can result in a scorched flavor and grainy texture. The temperature to which the caramels are cooked determines their ultimate texture: The higher the temperature, the firmer they are. The length of cooking determines their flavor and color: The longer they cook, the more their flavor develops and their color deepens. Patience is the key. It can take from 25 to 45 minutes, depending on the quantity, to cook a batch of caramels.

To cook caramels, stir the sugar mixture gently for the first few minutes, until the sugar is dissolved, then wash down the sides of the pan a couple of times with a pastry brush dipped in warm water. Use a long-handled wooden spoon or silicone spatula to stir the mixture frequently as it cooks. As it nears the end, it will thicken and must be stirred more often to keep it from burning. When you turn the mixture out into an 8-inch square pan lined with aluminum foil that extends over the sides, take care not to scrape the bottom of the pan, as the bottom portion of the mixture will be hotter and have a different texture than the rest of the batch. To set and cut, the caramels need to stand at room temperature anywhere from a few hours to overnight before cutting, because they will be sticky if cut too soon. **To set and cut,** immediately pour the mixture, without stirring, into an 8-inch square pan lined with oiled aluminum foil that extends over the sides. Let set until partially firm, about 30 minutes, then score into 1-inch squares by pressing down with an oiled knife. When completely firm, anywhere from 4 to 12 hours later, invert the candy onto a cutting board and peel away the foil. Oil a sharp heavy knife or Chinese cleaver and cut along score lines using a light sawing motion.

To store, wrap the caramels individually in cellophane squares or wax paper, or store them between layers of cellophane or wax paper in an airtight container. They keep well at room temperature for about 1 week.

BUTTERSCOTCH CARAMELS

About 1¼ pounds; 64 pieces

Brown sugar and dark corn syrup combine to produce a deep butterscotch flavor that's so good it once solicited a marriage proposal. Cutting this recipe in half yields an ideal filling for Turtles, 865.

Please read About Caramel Candies, above. Combine in a large heavy saucepan over low heat:

1 cup (2 sticks) unsalted butter, cut into pieces
2¼ cups packed light brown sugar
⅛ teaspoon salt
½ cup dark corn syrup
¼ cup light corn syrup

Stir over low heat until the sugar is dissolved, about 5 minutes, then wash down the sides of the pan with a pastry brush dipped in warm water. Place a warmed candy thermometer in the pan and cook over medium heat, stirring constantly, until the mixture comes to a boil. Wash down any sugar crystals that have formed on the sides. Wash the thermometer. Bring to a boil and continue to cook to 244°F, the firm-ball stage, about 25 minutes. Remove the pan from the heat.

With a clean wooden spoon, very gradually stir in:

1 cup heavy cream

Bring to a boil, then wash down the sides of the pan again. Place a warmed candy thermometer in the pan and cook, stirring frequently, until the mixture reaches 245°F; do not allow the temperature to rise much higher, or the caramels will become very hard, almost toffeelike, upon cooling. Remove the pan from the heat. With a clean wooden spoon, quickly stir in:

2 teaspoons vanilla

Let stand for several hours, until it sets and isn't sticky. To set, cut, and store, see About Caramel Candies, above.

CREAM CARAMELS

About 2 pounds; 64 pieces

These are old-fashioned golden-brown caramels that practically dissolve in your mouth. They contain butter and cream and are among the richest candies of all.

Please read About Caramel Candies, 864. Combine in a large heavy saucepan or Dutch oven:

>**2 cups sugar**
>**2 cups dark corn syrup**
>**1 cup (2 sticks) unsalted butter; cut into pieces**
>**1 cup heavy cream**

Stir over low heat until the sugar is dissolved, about 5 minutes, then wash down the sides of the pan with a pastry brush dipped in warm water. Place a warmed candy thermometer in the pan and cook the mixture over medium heat, stirring constantly, until it comes to a boil. Wash down any crystals that form on the sides. Bring the ingredients to a boil and continue to cook to 244°F, in the firmball stage (about 25 minutes). Remove the pan from the heat. With a clean wooden spoon, very gradually stir in:

>**1 cup heavy cream**

Be careful, as the mixture will bubble furiously. Return to the heat and bring back to the firm-ball stage, at least 245°F. To set, cut, wrap, and store, see About Caramel Candies, 864.

CHOCOLATE CREAM CARAMELS

About 1 pound

Please read About Caramel Candies, 864. In a large heavy saucepan or Dutch oven, stir over high heat until the sugar is dissolved:

>**1 cup sugar**
>**³/₄ cup light corn syrup**
>**¹/₄ teaspoon salt**
>**¹/₂ cup heavy cream**

Bring to 234°F, the soft-ball stage, over moderate heat, stirring constantly.
Add:

>**1 cup heavy cream**

Cook candy until it again reaches the soft-ball stage, 234°F, stirring occasionally.
Remove from the heat and add:

>**3 ounces unsweetened chocolate, finely chopped**

Pour into a buttered 8-inch square pan and follow instructions on how to set and cut, 864. Do not scrape the bottom of the saucepan. Let stand until firm, about 3 hours. Invert the candy onto a board and cut into squares.

SPICED CARAMEL NUTS COCKAIGNE

About 1 pound

Have ready:

>**Blanched almonds, hazelnuts, or pecans (about ¹/₂ to**
>**³/₄ cup total), toasted, 1001**

Prepare **Chocolate Cream Caramels, above.** Once the sugar has dissolved, add **1 teaspoon ground cinnamon.** When the candy has almost reached the hard-ball stage, 250°F, remove it from the heat and spread to a ¹/₄-inch thickness on a marble slab, 854. Score the candy into 1-inch squares. Place a whole toasted nut on each square. Let stand briefly. Before the caramel hardens, enclose each nut in its candy square, shaping it around the nut.

TURTLES

About 2 pounds; 35 pieces

Lightly grease 2 baking sheets or line them with silicone liners. Arrange on the sheets in groups of 4:

>**2 cups pecan halves**

Combine in a medium heavy saucepan:

>**1 cup heavy cream**
>**¹/₂ cup light corn syrup**
>**³/₄ cup packed light brown sugar**
>**2 tablespoons unsalted butter**

Bring to a boil over low heat, stirring to dissolve the sugar, then wash down the sides of the pan with a pastry brush dipped in warm water. Place a warmed candy thermometer in the pan and cook, stirring frequently, until the mixture reaches 246°F, the firm-ball stage. Remove from the heat.
Quickly stir in with a clean wooden spoon:

>**2 teaspoons vanilla**

Transfer the mixture to a small mixing bowl or a loaf pan lined with lightly oiled foil (for easy cleanup) to cool slightly, about 5 minutes.
Working quickly so that the caramel does not harden, and using a greased spoon, spoon 1 tablespoon caramel over the center of each pecan group. Let the caramel cool for 30 minutes, then loosen each candy from the pan.
Temper, 857, or melt:

>**6 ounces high-quality semisweet or milk chocolate**

Spoon a level teaspoon of chocolate over each caramel candy. Refrigerate for 20 minutes to set the chocolate.
Store the candies between layers of wax paper in an airtight container at room temperature for 10 days or in the refrigerator for up to 3 weeks. Serve at room temperature.

ABOUT CANDIED POPCORN

Kernels of popcorn have been found in the remains of Central American settlements dating back almost 7,000 years, but candied popcorn is a modern-day treat. A half cup of unpopped corn equals about 4 cups popped. If using an electric popper, follow the manufacturer's instructions. ➤ Microwave popcorn, though fine for snacking, is too fragile for popcorn balls.

To candy popcorn, prepare any of the syrups that follow, then pour it over the popped corn. Stir gently with a wooden spoon until the corn is well coated, then turn it out onto a cookie sheet lined with parchment paper.

When the corn is cool enough to handle, lightly butter your fingers and separate the corn into individual kernels or press into balls or lollipops (with an embedded loop of thick string or a wooden stick). Candied popcorn can also be shaped into Christmas decorations or molded into other forms in a buttered or well-oiled cake pan. Press the corn tightly into every corner of the mold after coating it with syrup. You can also color popcorn, using paste food coloring.

Candied popcorn keeps well in an airtight container for about 10 days.

CARAMEL CORN
About 6 cups
This is the sticky-sweet confection of the circus and board-walk. Use this syrup if you want to add peanuts to the popcorn. Please read About Candied Popcorn, 865.
Pop:

³/₄ cup popcorn, 865 (6 cups popped corn)

Melt in a medium heavy saucepan:

1¹/₂ tablespoons unsalted butter

Add:

1¹/₂ cups packed light brown sugar

6 tablespoons water

Stir over low heat until the sugar is dissolved. Bring to a boil over medium heat, then wash down the sides of the pan with a pastry brush dipped in warm water. Place a warmed candy thermometer in the pan and cook, without stirring, to 234°F, the soft-ball stage. Pour over the popcorn.

POPCORN WITH WHITE SUGAR SYRUP
About 6 cups
Less sweet, more tangy than the version above. Please read About Candied Popcorn, 865.
Pop:

³/₄ cup popcorn, 865 (6 cups popped corn)

Combine in a medium heavy saucepan:

²/₃ cup sugar

¹/₂ cup water

2¹/₂ tablespoons light corn syrup

¹/₈ teaspoon salt

¹/₄ teaspoon white vinegar

Stir over low heat until the sugar is dissolved. Bring to a boil over medium heat, then wash down the sides of the pan with a pastry brush dipped in warm water. Place a warmed candy thermometer in the pan and cook, without stirring, until it reaches the high end of the soft-crack stage, about 290°F. Working quickly, pour over the pop-corn.

ABOUT FONDANT
Fondant is a candy itself, and it is also used to make other candies, either as filling or as coating. Fondant centers can be dipped in chocolate, and melted fondant can be an icing, to be poured over pastries and confections (especially the little cakes called Petits Fours, 738). Fondant is made from water, sugar, and cream of tartar or corn syrup. You can enrich it by using milk or cream in place of the water, or by substituting brown sugar for part of the white sugar. Fondant is cooked to the soft-ball stage (234° to 242°F). If cooked to a higher temperature, it will become too firm to handle upon cooling. One of the charms of fondant is that a batch can be made and ripened and then used over a period of weeks, with varying flavors, colors, and shapes to suit the occasion. Fondant also lends itself to variations during cooking. You can replace the water in the recipe with strong coffee, or half white and half maple sugar.

The key to a successful fondant is controlling the crystallization of the sugar—controlling, not preventing, because this mixture must crystallize, but in a predictable manner. After bringing the syrup to a boil, you must brush down any sugar clinging to the sides of the pan with a pastry brush dipped in warm water. At this stage, let the syrup cook without stirring. See About Crystallization, 855. After cooking, pour the sugar syrup onto a nonporous surface, such as a large marble slab, baking sheet, or stainless steel counter, lightly sprinkled with water. ➤ Don't scrape out the bottom of the pan, for the sugar there will have a different texture. Let the fondant cool undisturbed. When it has cooled, work the fondant with a candy scraper by lifting and folding, always from the outer edges to the center. It will go through several stages as you work it, from clear to cloudy to opaque to very white. Once it thickens and becomes white in color, knead it by hand until it is smooth and pliable. If the fondant is to be melted down, it can be used immediately; otherwise, it needs to ripen for 24 hours.

To ripen fondant, form it into a ball, let it cool completely to room temperature, and seal it tightly in plastic wrap or in a resealable plastic bag. Fondant may be stored in the refrigerator indefinitely, but be sure to bring it to room temperature, covered, before using.

To dip candy centers in fondant, liquefy the fondant in the top of a double boiler or a heatproof bowl over barely simmering water, stirring frequently and making sure that the temperature doesn't rise above 140°F. Remove the double boiler from the heat, but keep the fondant over the water to keep it liquid. Drop a candy center into the fondant and turn to coat it completely. Lift out the candy using a candy dipper or fork, let the excess drip off, and place it on a wax paper–lined plate. Refrigerate the dipped candies for 15 to 20 minutes to firm up.

For instructions on covering petits fours or other pastries with fondant, see 791.

BASIC FONDANT
About 1¹/₄ pounds
Please read About Fondant, above. Combine in a large heavy saucepan:

1 cup water

3 cups sugar

Bring to a boil, stirring occasionally, until the sugar is dissolved. Sprinkle in:

¹/₄ teaspoon cream of tartar

This may make the syrup boil up, so be ready to stir with a long-handled wooden spoon. Brush down sugar clinging to the sides of the pan with a pastry brush dipped in warm water. Insert a warmed candy thermometer into the boiling syrup and cook, without stirring, to 234°F, the soft-ball stage. Immediately pour the syrup onto a nonporous surface, such as a marble slab or a baking sheet sprinkled with cold water, tilting the pan away from you. Do not scrape the bottom of the pan. Let the syrup cool for 20 to

30 minutes (the mixture will be thicker on a baking sheet and may take up to 30 minutes longer to cool). When you can place your hand over the fondant and feel no heat rising, test a corner by touching it with a fingertip. If it holds the indentation, it is ready to work.

Use a candy scraper or a metal spatula to work the syrup by lifting and folding, always from the edges to the center. Continue to do this until the syrup turns opaque and white and the mass becomes thickened but pliable. At this stage, knead it well with your hands, dusting them with confectioners' sugar. Gather the fondant into a ball, then push it outward with the heel of your hand. Draw it back in with a candy scraper and repeat the process until the surface is smooth and creamy-looking. Tightly cover the ball with plastic wrap or place it in a resealable plastic bag. Cool to room temperature before sealing the bag. Let the fondant ripen in a cool place overnight; it gets better day by day. To keep the fondant for several weeks or months, store it in the refrigerator.

If you accidentally overcook the fondant, and it becomes too hard to knead, cook it again: Place it in the top of a double boiler over simmering water, add $2/3$ cup hot water, and cook, stirring constantly, until it has thoroughly liquefied. Then pour it into a clean heavy saucepan and heat it to the boiling point again. Wash down the sides of the pan with a pastry brush dipped in warm water, place a warmed candy thermometer in the pan, and cook the mixture, uncovered and without stirring, to 234°F, the soft-ball stage. Cool, stir, and knead as above. When ready to use the fondant, have at hand:

Confectioners' sugar, for dusting the work surface

To color fondant, place it on a work surface dusted with confectioners' sugar. Make several slashes in the fondant and use a toothpick to dot in a few drops of paste food coloring. One-eighth teaspoon will create vivid color in this recipe. Knead and fold the fondant to distribute the color evenly. To flavor fondant, work in the flavoring the same way. You may want to use a stand mixer fitted with a dough hook, then knead by hand. Use one of the following:

1 to 2 teaspoons vanilla, almond extract, rose water, or orange flower water
3 to 5 drops peppermint or anise oil
1 tablespoon Grand Marnier, kirsch, framboise, or other liqueur
2 teaspoons grated orange or lemon zest
$1/2$ cup shredded or flaked sweetened coconut
2 to 4 ounces bittersweet, semisweet, milk, or white chocolate, melted and cooled
$1/3$ cup peanut or hazelnut butter
$1/2$ cup almonds or walnuts, toasted, 1001, and chopped
$1/3$ cup finely chopped dried cherries, candied orange peel, or candied ginger

To shape the fondant, be sure it is at room temperature. Dust the work surface generously with confectioners' sugar. You may find it easier to work with half of the fon-

dant at one time. Form it into a long cylinder by rolling it under your palms, then cut into candy-size pieces, or mold it into shapes.

To use liquid fondant, heat it in the top of a double boiler set over barely simmering water. If it is too thick, add 1 tablespoon hot water at a time and stir until the proper consistency is reached. Be careful not to heat the fondant over 140°F or it will be too stiff.

To cover pastries or petits fours with fondant, see 791.

UNCOOKED FONDANT
About 1 $1/2$ pounds; about seventy-five 1-inch balls

This uncooked version of fondant for candies or candy centers is very fast and foolproof, but not quite as creamy as the cooked variety. It can be colored or flavored in the same way. Kids love to model this fondant (or Marzipan, 877) into pumpkins, turkeys, Christmas trees, or other shapes. The texture is like that of clay—but it tastes a lot better!

Beat in a large bowl until soft:
$1/2$ cup (1 stick) unsalted butter
$3/4$ teaspoon vanilla
$1/4$ teaspoon salt
(1 teaspoon almond extract, $1/2$ teaspoon mint extract, or $1/2$ teaspoon orange or lemon extract)
Add very slowly and beat until very light:
$2/3$ cup sweetened condensed milk
Add cup by cup:
5 cups confectioners' sugar, sifted
Dust a work surface with:
1 cup confectioners' sugar, sifted
Turn the fondant out onto the work surface and work in the sugar. Shape it into 1-inch balls. Raisins, nuts, or bits of candied fruit may be used as centers. Refrigerate the balls to harden.

CHOCOLATE-DIPPED FONDANT
"Candy," as Dorothy Parker, reminded us, "is dandy." But the chocolate-coated balls are nothing short of seditious. Prepare **Basic Fondant, or Uncooked Fondant, above,** flavoring it as desired. Shape into 1-inch balls and set aside. Temper, 857, **1 pound high-quality bittersweet, semisweet, milk, or white chocolate.** Dip the fondant into the chocolate as described in Dipped Chocolate Truffle, 858.

PEPPERMINT WAFERS
About 1 pound; about thirty-six 1-inch wafers

In the days of teas and genteel luncheons, hostesses would decorate and/or initial these fondant wafers. If you'd like to revive that custom, see About Decorative Icings, 858. For an even richer, fuller-flavored candy, replace half the granulated sugar with light brown sugar.

Combine in a large heavy saucepan over medium heat:
$2 1/2$ cups sugar
1 cup heavy cream
2 tablespoons unsalted butter, cut into small pieces

Stir until the sugar is dissolved, then add:

$1/4$ teaspoon cream of tartar

Continue as for Basic Fondant, 866, to cook and cool. Place the fondant in the top of a double boiler over barely simmering water and stir just until it is warm to the touch and the mixture flows easily from the spoon, add water if necessary. Do not allow the temperature to rise above 140°F, or the mixture will become too thick. Remove from the heat. Combine:

1 tablespoon unsalted butter, softened
10 drops peppermint oil

Add to the fondant and stir until smooth. If desired, add:

(A few dots of green paste food coloring)

Line a baking sheet with parchment or wax paper and lightly dust with:

Sifted confectioners' sugar

Drop the mixture from a teaspoon onto the sheet, using a second teaspoon to push it off if necessary. Flatten any peaks by tapping them down lightly with a moistened fingertip. If the fondant stiffens before all the patties are formed, return it to the double boiler and warm until melted again. As soon as the patties are firm, 5 to 10 minutes, dip a small offset spatula in warm water, and shaking off the excess, carefully loosen the edges of the patties, and then run the spatula underneath them. Turn them over and place on a second lined baking sheet. Let dry until very firm to the touch and no traces of moisture are evident. Temper, 857:

1 pound high-quality bittersweet, semisweet, milk, or white chocolate

Dip the mint patties in the chocolate as described on 858. Place the candies in paper candy cups. Store between layers of wax paper in an airtight container at room temperature for up to 10 days or in the refrigerator for up to 2 months. Serve at room temperature.

OPERA CREAMS (OR CENTERS)

About $1^1/4$ pounds; sixty-four 1-inch squares

Opera creams are a tan variation of fondant, originally created for operagoers during the Victorian era. Chewing in public was frowned on in those days, and these melt-in-your-mouth morsels allowed opera buffs to indulge their sweet tooth unobtrusively during performances. Opera creams are often dipped in chocolate.

Place in a large heavy saucepan:

2 cups sugar
$3/4$ cup heavy cream
1 cup whole milk
2 tablespoons light corn syrup
$1/8$ teaspoon salt

Bring to boil over low heat, stirring until the sugar is dissolved. Brush down the sides of the pan with a pastry brush dipped in warm water. Cook over low heat, stirring occasionally to prevent scorching, until the mixture turns medium-tan in color and reaches 234°F, the soft-ball

stage. This process will take about 30 to 35 minutes—do not turn up the heat to quicken the cooking. The mixture will appear to be separated at first, but it will come together as the cooking continues. Pour the mixture into the bowl of a heavy-duty mixer, and cool to 110°F. Add:

1 teaspoon vanilla

Beat the mixture with the paddle attachment on medium speed until it thickens, looks creamy, and has lost some of its sheen. Pour onto a very lightly oiled baking sheet. Knead lightly until the candy becomes firm and holds its shape, then pat into an 8-inch square, about $1/4$ inch thick. Let the opera cream sit uncovered in the pan overnight to ripen.

The next day, cut into 1-inch squares using a lightly oiled knife. Place in paper candy cups, serve at room temperature.

If you want to dip the opera creams in chocolate, temper, 857:

8 ounces high-quality bittersweet or semisweet chocolate

Dip the centers as directed on 858.

Place in an airtight container, and store in the refrigerator for up to 1 month.

ABOUT NOUGAT

Nougat is a chewy nut candy, sometimes with added candied fruit, made from a cooked sugar syrup combined with stiffly whipped egg whites. Nougat is traditionally pressed between layers of edible rice paper, called *ostia* in Italian or *Oblaten* in German. Ostia and Oblaten are available in some supermarkets and gourmet stores, in Asian markets, in cake decorating and candy supply stores, and by mail or through the Internet from candy supply sources. Edible wheat paper can also be used. Aluminum foil may be used as a substitute, but it must be removed before serving.

Nougat is very sensitive to humidity, which turns it soft and soggy, so make it on a dry day.

CLASSIC NOUGAT

About $1^1/4$ pounds; twenty-four $2^1/2$ x 1-inch bars

This recipe calls for almonds and pistachios, but the same quantity of blanched hazelnuts and/or walnuts may be substituted.

Please read About Nougat, above. Line an 8-inch square pan with edible rice paper or well-buttered aluminum foil. Combine in a small heavy saucepan:

$1/2$ cup water
$1^1/2$ cups sugar
$1^1/4$ cup light corn syrup

Place over low heat and stir with a long-handled wooden spoon until the sugar dissolves. Bring to a boil, washing down the sides of the pan with a pastry brush dipped in warm water. Place a warmed candy thermometer in the pan, raise the heat to medium, and cook, without stirring, to 275°F, the soft-crack stage.

Meanwhile, place in the bowl of a heavy-duty mixer fitted with the whisk attachment:

2 large egg whites, at room temperature

Turn the mixer to low and beat the egg whites slowly while the sugar syrup is cooking. As the syrup nears the soft-crack stage, turn up the mixer speed, so that the egg whites reach stiff peaks at the same time that the syrup reaches 275°F.

With the mixer on high, add the syrup to the beaten whites in a slow, steady stream, being careful to avoid the whisk. Continue to beat for 10 to 12 minutes, until warm but no longer hot.

Beat in:

2 tablespoons softened unsalted butter, cut into small pieces

Remove the nougat from the mixer and fold in:

1 cup sliced almonds, lightly toasted, 1001

$^1/_2$ cup skinned pistachio nuts, toasted, 1001

($^1/_2$ cup chopped dried or candied cherries or candied orange peel)

Spread the mixture evenly in the prepared pan—you may need to use your hands to spread it evenly. Cover the top with another layer of edible paper, then place a second 8-inch square pan on top and press lightly to even out the mixture and make the edible paper adhere.

Fill the top pan with cans or other heavy weights, and let stand overnight at room temperature.

Remove the top pan and weights, run a thin knife around the edges of the pan to loosen the nougat, and invert onto a cutting board. With a lightly oiled knife, cut into bars. Wrap each bar in cellophane or plastic wrap. Store in an airtight container at room temperature for 1 week or in the refrigerator for up to 3 weeks. Serve at room temperature.

DIVINITY

About 1 $^1/_2$ pounds; about thirty 1 $^1/_2$-inch rounds

Divinity is a classic Southern candy related to Marshmallows, below, and Nougat, 868. Divinity has a reputation for being difficult to make, but it's actually very easy if you have a heavy-duty electric mixer—and work on a dry day. **Sea Foam** is simply divinity made with brown sugar in place of white and dark corn syrup in place of light. For a delightful and spirited Southern touch in either recipe, plump the raisins in $^1/_3$ cup sherry over low heat. Drain off any excess sherry and cool the raisins before adding them to the candy.

Bring to a boil in a large heavy saucepan over medium heat:

$^1/_2$ cup water

$^1/_2$ cup light corn syrup

Add:

2 cups sugar

Bring to a boil, stirring until the sugar has dissolved. Wash down any sugar crystals that may have formed on the sides of the pan with a pastry brush dipped in warm water.

Place a warmed candy thermometer in the pan and cook over medium heat, without stirring, to 250° to 255°F, the hard-ball stage.

Meanwhile, place in the bowl of a heavy-duty mixer fitted with the whisk attachment:

2 large egg whites, at room temperature

Beat the whites at medium speed just until they hold their shape.

With the mixer going, pour the syrup slowly over the egg whites in a thin, steady stream, being careful to avoid the beater. As the whites increase in volume, you may add the syrup more quickly and beat faster. Beat on medium speed for 12 to 15 minutes, or until the mixture is thick, fluffy, and cooled somewhat.

Fold in:

1 cup chopped pecans or walnuts

1 cup golden raisins

1 teaspoon vanilla

Drop the mixture by spoonfuls onto a lightly greased baking sheet, forming 1 $^1/_2$-inch rounds. You may need to use a second spoon to help push the sticky mixture onto the pan. Let cool.

Divinity dries out quickly and does not store well. Store between layers of wax paper in an airtight container at room temperature for several days.

MARSHMALLOWS

About 1 $^1/_4$ pounds; 108 1-inch squares

Homemade marshmallows are very different from store-bought ones, better than you can imagine. Don't attempt to make marshmallows unless you have a heavy-duty mixer to handle the beating for you.

Combine in a medium bowl:

$^1/_4$ cup cornstarch

$^1/_4$ cup confectioners' sugar

Dust a lightly oiled 9 x 13-inch baking pan with some of the mixture. Reserve the remaining mixture.

Pour into the bowl of a heavy-duty mixer:

$^1/_2$ cup water

Sprinkle over the water:

4 envelopes (3 tablespoons) unflavored gelatin

Let stand 5 minutes to soften the gelatin, then place the bowl over a pot of simmering water for 2 to 3 minutes, just until the gelatin dissolves. Set aside on the mixer stand fitted with the whisk attachment if you have one.

Combine in a large heavy saucepan:

2 cups sugar

$^3/_4$ cup light corn syrup

$^1/_2$ cup water

$^1/_4$ teaspoon salt

Bring to a boil over low heat, stirring with a long-handled wooden spoon until the sugar is dissolved, if necessary. Wash down the sides of the pan with a pastry brush dipped in warm water. Place a warmed candy thermometer in the pan, raise the heat to high, and cook, without stirring, to 244° to 246°F, the firm-ball stage. Do not allow the temperature to rise any higher, or the marshmallows will be tough. Remove from the heat.

With the mixer running at medium speed, slowly pour the syrup into the gelatin in a thin, steady stream, being careful to avoid the whisk. Do not scrape the pan. Then beat for about 10 to 15 minutes, until the mixture is thick and fluffy but still warm and thin enough to pour. Add:

   2 tablespoons vanilla

Transfer the mixture to the prepared pan. Cool completely, then cover very loosely with aluminum foil and let dry for 4 to 6 hours, or until firm enough to cut.

Remove the marshmallows from the pan and cut into 1-inch squares (or smaller to float in cocoa), using kitchen scissors dusted with:

   Cornstarch

Dust the marshmallows with the remaining confectioners' sugar mixture. Store between layers of wax paper in an airtight container at room temperature.

ABOUT TAFFY

If you hanker to re-create an old-time candy pull, be sure you have a stout pair of arms. However, should you decide to make taffy pulling a frequent practice, you may find that a candy hook is well worth the investment. The hook is normally placed at least 6 feet from the floor. The rope of candy is thrown over it repeatedly, and gravity does the rest.

When the syrup for taffy has cooked to the indicated temperature ➤ pour it slowly onto an oiled marble slab or oiled and chilled baking sheet. ➤ Hold the pouring edge of the pan away from you and only a few inches above the slab, so you won't be spattered with the dangerously hot syrup. Allow the syrup to cool briefly. ➤ This is the moment to flavor the taffy. Because of the great heat, use flavoring essences based on essential oils. See About Hard Candies, 872. Sprinkle these over the hot syrup. Go easy, as they are very strong. If chocolate is to be added, grate it onto the hot syrup poured onto the buttered slab. Nuts, fruits, and coconut can be worked in during the pulling process.

Using a candy scraper, or a metal spatula, begin to work the syrup into a central mass, turning it and working it until it is cool enough to handle with your oiled fingertips. ➤ Take care in picking up the mass. It may have cooled on the surface and still be hot enough to burn as you press down into it. Taffy cooked to 270°F should be pulled near a source of heat so it doesn't stiffen. When you can gather it up, start pulling it with your fingertips, allowing a spread of about 18 inches between your hands, then fold it back on itself. Repeat this motion rhythmically. As the mass changes from a somewhat sticky side-whiskered affair to a glistening crystal ribbon, start twisting, while folding and pulling. ➤ Pull until the ridges of the twist begin to hold their shape. The candy will become opaque, firm, and elastic but will retain its satiny finish. Depending on the cooking, the weather, and your pulling skill, this process may last from 5 to 20 minutes.

Have ready ➤ a surface dusted with confectioners' sugar or cornstarch. Form the taffy into a ball in your hands and press it into a narrow point at the fingertip end. Grasping the narrow point in one hand, pull it away from the rest of the ball so you have a long rope about $^3/_4$ inch thick and let the rope fall out onto the dusted board like a snake. With well-buttered kitchen scissors, cut into segments of the size you prefer. Let cool.

If you do not want to wrap the candies separately, put the taffy into a tightly covered tin, dusting and all. Some taffies, especially those heavy in cream, will, of their own accord, turn from a pulled chewy consistency to a creamy one. This happens sometimes a few minutes after cutting, sometimes as long as 12 hours later. After creaming takes place, be sure to wrap the taffies in foil and store them in a closed tin, because in that state they will dry out readily with exposure to air.

VANILLA TAFFY

About 12 ounces; about 60 pieces

This is the classic taffy, which can be flavored in myriad ways—with chocolate, coconut, candied citrus peel, or chopped nuts, for instance. This is also the one to use for an old-fashioned taffy pull: Divide family and friends into teams and see who can finish pulling the candy first. For children, such events are the stuff of memory.

Please read About Taffy, above. Combine in a medium heavy saucepan:

   1 cup sugar
   $^1/_4$ cup water
   $^1/_4$ cup light corn syrup

Stir over low heat until the sugar is dissolved. Wash down the sides of the pan with a pastry brush dipped in warm water. Place a warmed candy thermometer in the pan, raise the heat to medium-high, and cook, uncovered, without stirring, to 265°F, the high end of the hard-ball stage. (For a softer taffy, cook the mixture to 250°F; for a firmer texture, cook to 270°F in the soft-crack stage.)

Remove from the heat and quickly stir in with a wooden spoon until completely absorbed:

   2 tablespoons unsalted butter, softened
   1 tablespoon distilled white vinegar
   2 teaspoons vanilla

Carefully pour the syrup onto an oiled marble slab or chilled and oiled rimmed baking sheet. Do not scrape the saucepan. Allow the mixture to sit 3 to 5 minutes, until cooled somewhat. If you wish to add a flavoring oil, sprinkle it over the mixture at this point. With a sturdy scraper or spatula, start to fold the edges of the mixture into the center. Keep scraping and folding until the mixture is cool enough to handle. Then gather it up into a ball with oiled or buttered fingertips and begin pulling, folding, and twisting until the taffy is opaque and firm and holds thin ridges.

Dust a work surface with:

   Confectioners' sugar or cornstarch

Form the taffy into a long $^3/_4$-inch-thick rope, letting it fall

onto the work surface. Cut into 1-inch pieces with buttered kitchen scissors.
To store, see About Taffy, 870.

CHOCOLATE TAFFY
Prepare **Vanilla Taffy, 870,** cooking the syrup only to 258°F; the addition of chocolate will harden the final mixture considerably. After pouring the syrup onto the baking sheet, sprinkle **3 ounces bittersweet, semisweet, or milk chocolate, grated,** over it. Proceed as directed.

COCONUT TAFFY
Prepare **Vanilla Taffy, 870.** After pouring the syrup onto the baking sheet, sprinkle ²/₃ **cup shredded sweetened coconut, lightly toasted, 972,** over it. Proceed as directed, but because the addition of coconut can cause the taffy to break in the center when stretched too far, pull the taffy only to 8 to 12 inches before folding it back on itself.

SALTWATER TAFFY
About 1 ¹/₂ pounds; about 60 pieces
This famous taffy is a specialty of the New Jersey shore, where it was traditionally made with seawater. Unlike other taffies, the saltwater variety never becomes creamy. This has to do not with the salt it contains but with the glycerin that's added, and with the temperature to which it's cooked—lower than for other taffies. Edible glycerine is available at candy supply stores.
Combine in a large heavy saucepan:

> **2 cups sugar**
> **1¹/₂ cups water**
> **1 cup light corn syrup**
> **1 teaspoon salt**
> **1 tablespoon edible glycerin**

Stir over low heat until the sugar is dissolved. Wash down the sides of the pan with a pastry brush dipped in warm water. Bring to a boil and place a warmed candy thermometer in the pan. Raise the heat to medium-high, and cook, without stirring, to 250°F, the hard-ball stage. Remove from the heat.
Add:

> **2 tablespoons unsalted butter**

Stir until it has melted entirely. Carefully pour the syrup onto an oiled marble slab or chilled and oiled rimmed baking sheet. Do not scrape the saucepan. If you want to make different flavors of taffy, pour the syrup into separate pools on the slab or pan. Flavor and color with any of these (chocolate will color the taffy as well as flavor it):

> **Cinnamon oil and red paste food coloring**
> **Citrus or banana oil and yellow paste food coloring**
> **Peppermint or spearmint oil and green paste**
>   **food coloring**
> **Grated bittersweet, semisweet, or milk chocolate**

Let the syrup cool until heat no longer rises from it and an indentation holds when it is pressed with a fingertip. Using a candy scraper, bring the syrup into a mass, lifting, turning, and folding it. When it is cool enough to handle,

gather it up with oiled or buttered fingertips into a ball and begin pulling, folding, and twisting it until it is opaque, firm, and elastic and holds its ridges.
Dust a work surface with:

> **Confectioners' sugar or cornstarch**

Form the taffy into a long ³/₄-inch-thick rope, letting it fall onto the work surface. Cut into 1-inch pieces with buttered scissors. These taffies will remain chewy and sticky, and they love to stick to one another. See About Taffy, 870, for wrapping and storage.

PULLED MINTS
About 1 pound; about 40 pieces
These are like the old-fashioned little mint cushions.
Bring to a boil in a large heavy-bottomed saucepan:

> **1 cup water**

Add and stir until the sugar is dissolved:

> **2 cups sugar**
> **¹/₄ teaspoon cream of tartar**

Wash down the sides of the pan with a pastry brush dipped in warm water. Cook over medium heat until the syrup comes to a boil, then wash down the sides of the pan again. Place a warmed candy thermometer in the pan, raise the heat to medium-high, and cook, without stirring, to about 262°F, the hard-ball stage (for a firmer texture, cook to 270°F, the soft-crack stage). Remove from the heat. Carefully pour the syrup onto an oiled marble slab or chilled and oiled rimmed baking sheet. Do not scrape the saucepan.
Using an eye dropper or toothpick dipped in the oil, sprinkle with:

> **6 to 8 drops peppermint oil**

Do not stir the oil into the mixture. Let the syrup cool until heat no longer rises from it and an indentation holds when it is pressed with a fingertip. Using a candy scraper, bring the syrup into a mass, lifting, turning, and folding it. When it is cool enough to handle, gather it up with oiled or buttered fingertips into a ball and begin pulling, folding, and twisting it until it is opaque, firm, and elastic and holds its ridges.
Dust a work surface with:

> **Confectioners' sugar or cornstarch**

Form the taffy into a long ³/₄-inch-thick rope, letting it fall onto the work surface. Cut into 1-inch pieces with buttered scissors. For these mints to cream, place between layers of wax paper in an airtight container; this could take 30 minutes to as long as overnight.
Once the candies have creamed, wrap individually in cellophane and store in an airtight container at room temperature.

CREAM PULL CANDY
About 1 ¹/₂ pounds; about 60 pieces
This is a tender, buttery cross between a caramel and a taffy. It is a temperamental candy, and is not to be tried in hot or humid weather.

Bring to a boil in a large heavy saucepan:

1 cup water

Add and stir until the sugar is dissolved:

3 cups sugar
$1/2$ teaspoon salt
$1/8$ teaspoon baking soda

Wash down the sides of the pan with a pastry brush dipped in warm water, and bring the syrup to a boil. Place a warmed candy thermometer in the pan, raise the heat, and cook, without stirring, to 234° to 238°F, the soft-ball stage.

Reduce the heat, but do not allow the temperature of the syrup to drop below 225°F. Add by the teaspoonful to avoid rapidly changing the consistency, but do not stir in:

1 cup heavy cream
$1/4$ cup ($1/2$ stick) unsalted butter, cut into small bits

Cook over medium heat, without stirring, to several degrees above hard-ball stage, about 257°F. Remove from the heat.

Carefully pour the syrup onto an oiled marble slab or chilled and oiled rimmed baking sheet, using a sweeping motion to allow the syrup to spread. Do not scrape the saucepan. Let the syrup cool until heat no longer rises from it and an indentation holds when it is pressed with a fingertip. Using a candy scraper, bring the syrup into a mass, lifting, turning, and folding it. When it is cool enough to handle, gather it up with oiled or buttered fingertips into a ball and begin pulling, folding, and twisting it until it is opaque, firm, and elastic and holds its ridges. It will still be slightly warm, but do not continue to pull, or the mass may crystallize and harden.

Dust a work surface with:

Confectioners' sugar or cornstarch

Form the candy into a long $3/4$-inch-thick rope, letting it fall onto the work surface. Cut into 1-inch pieces with buttered kitchen scissors. For these candies to cream, place between layers of wax paper in an airtight container; this could take 30 minutes to as long as overnight.

Once the candies have creamed, wrap individually in cellophane and store in an airtight container at room temperature.

ABOUT HARD CANDIES

Among the specialties classified as hard candies are brittle, toffee, nut crunch, butterscotch, and lollipops. All are cooked to high temperatures, mostly the hard-crack stage (300° to 310°F). Some are cooked to an even higher temperature, to light caramel (about 320°F). Humidity is no friend of hard candies—you may need to cook the sugar syrup as much as 10 degrees higher to compensate under such conditions, so we recommend that you don't even try to make hard candies on a rainy day.

Always cook the syrup for hard candies in a heavy-bottomed saucepan, stirring with a long-handled wooden spoon or heat-resistant silicone spatula until the sugar is dissolved and the mixture boils. Wash down the sides of

the pan with a pastry brush dipped in water a few times as the mixture cooks to help prevent crystallization. If the recipe calls for glycerin, make sure the bottle does not say "for external use only"; you want edible glycerin. Once the syrup comes to a boil, stop stirring, and cook the candies fast over high heat so they keep their clear color and don't crystallize. Once the mixture is cooked, pour it onto an oiled marble slab or chilled and oiled rimmed baking sheet, pouring away from you and holding the pan close to the surface so that you won't be splattered with the hot mixture. Unless otherwise instructed, don't scrape out the bottom of the saucepan.

To flavor the candies, use the concentrated oils that have been developed specifically for hard candies. Their flavor can stand up to the high heat of the syrups, whereas the flavor of an alcohol extract would be dissipated by the heat. Use paste food coloring for lollipops and other colored hard candies.

Wrap hard candies in squares of cellophane or plastic wrap when they are cool and store them in an airtight container at room temperature. Hard candies absorb moisture easily from the air and turn sticky or soft and crumbly but, if well-sealed, will keep for 2 to 3 weeks.

PEANUT BRITTLE

About 1 $1/4$ pounds

In the South, peanut brittle is sometimes called groundnut candy, *groundnut* being another word for peanuts. Like taffy, this opaque brittle needs to be pulled; this is done while it's hot, with buttered fingertips. Many brittle connoisseurs use raw nuts, which cook in the syrup; others prefer the roasted kind. Substitute other nuts for the peanuts or use a combination, if you like. Rub salted peanuts between towels to reduce the salt flavor in the candy. This candy gets better with age.

Combine in a large heavy saucepan:

2 cups sugar
1 cup light corn syrup
$1/2$ cup water
$1/4$ teaspoon cream of tartar

Bring to a boil over low heat, stirring until the sugar is dissolved. Wash down the sides of the pan with a pastry brush dipped in warm water. Place a warmed candy thermometer in the pan and raise the heat, without stirring, to 265°F, the hard-ball stage.

Remove from the heat and quickly stir in with a wooden spoon:

3 tablespoons unsalted butter, cut into small pieces
$1/4$ teaspoon baking soda

Return to the heat and cook, without stirring, to 300°F, the hard-crack stage. Add:

2 cups Spanish peanuts, pecans, or chopped brazil nuts, or a combination, toasted, 1001

Stir, using a lightly oiled clean wooden spoon or silicone spatula, to completely coat the nuts with the syrup. Remove from the heat. Quickly stir in:

1 teaspoon vanilla

Carefully pour out onto an oiled marble slab, an oiled and chilled rimmed baking sheet, a silicone liner, or well-greased aluminum foil; you can scrape the saucepan to get every bit out, but work fast. Spread the mixture out quickly with a lightly oiled wooden spoon, and let stand for 2 to 5 minutes.

Loosen the mixture with an oiled offset spatula. Wearing generously buttered plastic gloves, pull and stretch the brittle by lifting it with the spatula while gently pulling it with the other hand until it is very thin. If it firms up before it can be completely stretched, reheat by holding the pan 6 to 8 inches over a medium flame until softened enough to resume stretching. Let cool completely.

Break the brittle into pieces. Store between layers of wax paper in an airtight container at room temperature for up to 1 month.

SCOTCH TOFFEE
About 1 1/2 pounds

This old-style Southern candy uses chopped blanched almonds instead of peanuts and adds chocolate.

Coat a 10 x 15-inch rimmed baking sheet with:

2 tablespoons unsalted butter, softened

Prepare:

Peanut Brittle, 872

substituting:

2 cups chopped blanched almonds

for the peanuts. After stirring the nuts into the hot sugar syrup, pour the mixture onto the prepared pan. Use an oiled offset spatula to spread the brittle out until it reaches the corners of the pan. Let it cool for 5 to 10 minutes.

Melt in the top of a double boiler over hot water:

4 ounces bittersweet or semisweet chocolate

Pour half the chocolate on top of the brittle and spread it out to cover completely. Sprinkle with:

**1/2 cup blanched almonds, toasted, 1001,
and finely chopped**

Refrigerate the candy for 10 minutes to set the chocolate. Invert the candy onto a large piece of wax paper and spread with the remaining chocolate, rewarmed if necessary. Sprinkle with:

1/2 cup almonds, toasted, 1001, and finely chopped

Refrigerate the candy again to set the chocolate.

Break the toffee into pieces. Store between layers of wax paper in an airtight container at room temperature for up to 1 month.

SESAME SEED BRITTLE
About 1 1/2 pounds

This Southern specialty is packed with benne or sesame seeds.

Combine in a large heavy saucepan:

1 1/2 cups sugar
3/4 cup light corn syrup
1/4 cup (1/2 stick) unsalted butter, softened

Stir over low heat until the sugar is dissolved. Wash down the sides of the pan with a pastry brush dipped in warm water. Place a warmed candy thermometer in the pan, bring the mixture to a boil, and cook, without stirring, to 330°F, the light-caramel stage.

Remove from the heat and use a lightly oiled wooden spoon to quickly stir in:

2 cups sesame seeds, toasted, 1011

Then stir in:

1 1/2 teaspoons vanilla

Carefully pour the mixture out onto a marble slab, an oiled baking sheet, or well-greased aluminum foil. Spread it out thin with the wooden spoon. Let cool completely.

Break the brittle into pieces. Store between layers of wax paper in an airtight container at room temperature for up to 1 month.

ENGLISH TOFFEE
About 1 1/2 pounds

Though toffee is harder than taffy, it is still chewy and sticky—which is why a friend calls it "the dentist's special."

Line a 13 x 9-inch pan with a silicone liner or heavy-duty aluminum foil, leaving a 2-inch overhang of foil at the two narrow ends of the pan. Coat the foil with nonstick spray.

Combine in a large heavy saucepan:

1 3/4 cups sugar
1 cup heavy cream
1/2 cup (1 stick) unsalted butter
1/8 teaspoon cream of tartar

Stir over low heat until the sugar is dissolved. Wash down the sides of the pan with a pastry brush dipped in warm water. Bring to a boil and boil for 3 minutes. Place a warmed candy thermometer in the pan and cook, stirring frequently, to about 280°F, the soft-crack stage. The syrup will be light-colored and thick.

Remove from the heat and stir in with a wooden spoon:

2 teaspoons vanilla or 1 tablespoon dark rum

Pour the candy into the prepared pan and cool 3 minutes. Sprinkle the hot toffee with:

**4 ounces bittersweet, semisweet, or milk chocolate,
finely chopped or grated**

Let stand for 1 to 2 minutes, then spread the chocolate evenly across the toffee with a small offset spatula. Sprinkle on top:

1/2 cup almonds, toasted, 1001, and finely chopped

Refrigerate the toffee for 20 minutes to set the chocolate. Break the toffee into pieces. Store between layers of wax paper in an airtight container at room temperature for up to 1 month.

BUTTERCRUNCH
About 2 1/2 pounds

Line a 13 x 9-inch pan with a silicone baking liner or heavy-duty aluminum foil, leaving a 2-inch overhang of foil at the two narrow ends of the pan. Coat the foil with nonstick spray.

Combine in a large heavy saucepan:

2^1/$_3$ cups sugar
^{3}/$_4$ cup (1^1/$_2$ sticks) unsalted butter, cut into chunks
^{1}/$_4$ cup light corn syrup
2 tablespoons water
^{1}/$_2$ teaspoon salt

Bring to a boil over high heat, stirring until the sugar dissolves. Wash down the sides of the pan with a pastry brush dipped in warm water. Turn the heat down to maintain a simmer and cook, stirring gently with a wooden spoon, to about 320°F, the light-caramel stage. Stir in:

1^1/$_4$ cups slivered almonds, toasted, 1001
1^1/$_4$ cups coarsely chopped pecans or walnuts, toasted, 1001

Continue cooking until the almonds turn a rich caramel brown, about 3 minutes. Be careful not to burn the mixture.

Remove from the heat and immediately stir in:

2 teaspoons vanilla

Working quickly, before the mixture begins to harden, spread it evenly in the prepared pan with the back of the spoon. Let cool completely, about 1 hour. Pour over the toffee:

8 ounces bittersweet or semisweet chocolate, melted

Pour and spread evenly with a spatula or table knife. Immediately, sprinkle with:

1 cup finely chopped toasted, 1001, nuts—half almonds and half walnuts or pecans, or another proportion

Pat lightly with your fingertips to embed the nuts in the chocolate, without submerging them. Refrigerate until the chocolate is set.

Break the buttercrunch into pieces. Store between layers of wax paper, in an airtight container at cool room temperature for up to 3 weeks.

BUTTERSCOTCH

About 1 ^{1}/$_4$ pounds; about 80 pieces

Butterscotch begins to solidify immediately after it's cooked and so may be scored or shaped before it cools. Work quickly for best results. If butterscotch sits long enough uncovered, it will absorb moisture from the air and turn slightly chewy—though this is unlikely to happen with a family of candy lovers.

Line and grease a 13 x 9-inch pan as for English Toffee, 873.

Combine in a large heavy saucepan:

2 cups sugar
^{2}/$_3$ cup dark corn syrup
^{1}/$_4$ cup water
^{1}/$_4$ cup heavy cream

Stir over low heat until the sugar is dissolved. Wash down the sides of the pan with a pastry brush dipped in warm water. Raise the heat to medium-high and stir constantly until the mixture comes to a boil. Place a warmed candy thermometer in the pan and cook, stirring frequently, to 300°F, the hard-crack stage.

Pour the candy into the prepared pan. Do not scrape the bottom of the saucepan. Let cool for 3 to 4 minutes.

Score the candy into 1-inch pieces with a buttered knife. Let cool completely.

Break the butterscotch into pieces along the scored lines. Wrap each piece in cellophane, or store between layers of wax paper in an airtight container at room temperature for up to 1 month.

COFFEE DROPS

About 1 ^{1}/$_4$ pounds, 80 pieces

Don't try these addictive little morsels if you have a loose filling.

Lightly coat a baking sheet with nonstick spray or arrange individual ^{3}/$_4$-inch foil candy cups on a baking sheet. Combine:

^{1}/$_4$ cup instant coffee powder
3 tablespoon water
1 tablespoon cider vinegar or other mild vinegar
^{1}/$_2$ teaspoon edible glycerin

Prepare:

Butterscotch, above

As soon as you remove the pan from the heat, sprinkle the coffee essence over the surface of the syrup and then stir in thoroughly but gently with a wooden spoon. Drop the syrup from the edge of the spoon into ^{3}/$_4$-inch patties onto the baking sheet, or drop into the foil cups.

When cool, wrap the patties individually in cellophane. Store in an airtight container at room temperature for up to 1 month.

MEXICAN ORANGE DROPS

About 2 pounds

Heat:

1 cup evaporated milk

Meanwhile, melt in a deep saucepan:

1 cup sugar

When the sugar is a rich brown, slowly stir in:

^{1}/$_4$ cup boiling water or orange juice

Add the hot milk. Add and stir until dissolved:

2 cups sugar
^{1}/$_4$ teaspoon salt

Bring to a boil, cover, and cook 3 minutes, or until the steam washes down any crystals on the sides of the pan. Reduce the heat to low and cook, uncovered, without stirring, to 234°F, the soft-ball stage. Add:

Grated zest of 2 oranges

Let cool.

Beat the mixture until creamy. Stir in:

1 cup chopped nuts

Drop the candy from a spoon onto a foil-lined baking sheet. When cool, wrap the drops individually in cellophane. Store in an airtight container at room temperature for up to 1 month.

LOLLIPOPS

About 1 ½ pounds; about twenty-four 1-tablespoon-sized lollipops

A lollipop may be just a lump of hard candy on the end of a stick, but what a versatile lump! You can make it in an infinite number of flavors, colors, sizes, and shapes—not just flat or ball-shaped, but formed in cast-iron or plastic molds (available from candy supply shops and Internet retailers) into candy canes, Santa Clauses, Easter Bunnies, and more.

To flavor lollipops, be sure to use the very concentrated essential flavoring oils, not alcohol-based extracts, which would dissipate too fast in the hot syrup. You can stick to classic lollipop flavors such as cherry, lime, lemon, and orange, or opt for more unusual ones, like cinnamon or anise. To color lollipops, use paste food coloring rather than liquid colorings.

Lightly coat the lollipop molds with nonstick spray and insert the sticks. Or, for free-form candies, lightly oil a marble slab or baking sheet and line up lollipop sticks with ample space between them.

Bring to a boil in a large heavy saucepan:

> **1 cup water**

Remove from the heat. Add:

> **2 cups sugar**
> **³/₄ cup light corn syrup**
> **1 tablespoon unsalted butter**

Stir gently over low heat until the sugar is dissolved. Wash down the sides of the pan with a pastry brush dipped in warm water. Place a warmed candy thermometer in the pan, raise the heat to high, and cook, without stirring, to 300°F, the hard-crack stage. Remove from the heat and stir in any flavoring and/or coloring with a long-handled wooden spoon. Flavor suggestions include:

> **¹/₄ teaspoon peppermint or cinnamon oil**
> **¹/₂ teaspoon orange, lime, or spearmint oil**
> **¹/₈ teaspoon anise oil**

To color the lollipops, stir in:

> **3 or 4 dots of paste food coloring**

If you are using molds, fill them immediately with the hot syrup. If you are making free-form lollipops, let the syrup cool to 230° to 240°F, then drop a tablespoonful of the mixture over the top of each lollipop stick.

As soon as the lollipops are firm and cool, wrap individually in cellophane. Store in an airtight container at room temperature for up to 1 month.

ROCK CANDY

About 1 pound

Rock candy looks like sparkling, sugary diamonds. Serve it broken into small pieces and piled high in an open bowl at a party or as a sophisticated-looking sugar for coffee. Or dye the sugar with red or green food coloring and use the strings as Christmas decorations or as part of a holiday centerpiece.

Punch 7 or 8 holes ¹/₂ inch up 2 opposite sides of an 8-inch square aluminum foil pan, and lace about 7 strings from one side to the other. Place the laced pan in a larger pan at

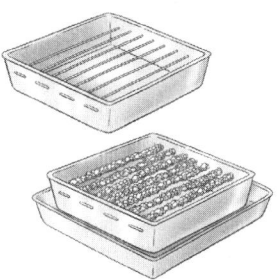

Making rock candy

least 1 inch deep to catch leaking syrup. Combine in a medium heavy saucepan:

> **2¹/₂ cups sugar**
> **1 cup water**
> **Pinch of cream of tartar**

Stir over low heat to dissolve the sugar. Wash down the sides of the pan with a pastry brush dipped in warm water. Place a warmed candy thermometer in the pan, raise the heat to medium, and cook, without stirring, until the mixture reaches 250°F, the hard-ball stage. Remove from the heat and, if desired, quickly stir in with a wooden spoon:

> **(3 or 4 dots paste food coloring)**

Carefully pour the syrup into the laced pan. Do not scrape the bottom of the saucepan. The syrup should come ¹/₂ to ³/₄ inch over the strings. Cover the pan with a piece of plastic wrap, so that you can see what's happening without jostling the pan. Place in a warm, dry, draft-free place, such as an oven. Watch and wait. Within 36 to 48 hours, you should see crystallization begin. When all the syrup has crystallized, lift out the laced pan. This can take days. Cut the strings and dislodge the rock candy from the pan. Put on a baking sheet in a 200°F oven to dry. Use the strings as decorations or remove the candy and store in an airtight container at room temperature.

ABOUT PRALINE AND PENUCHE

Two distinct candies go under the praline name. The one pronounced "PRAH-leen" is a patty-shaped pecan candy from New Orleans. The French "PRAY-leen" is a clear nut brittle made with almonds or hazelnuts and pulverized for use in various confections. New Orleans pralines have an unmistakable grain that comes from beating the sugar mixture while it's warm; that and the city's notorious humidity have resulted in a softer, more fudgelike candy than the French brittle. New Orleans pralines are cooked to the soft-ball stage, about 236°F. French praline is cooked to a much higher temperature, the medium-caramel stage, about 356°F.

Penuche has a taste similar to that of New Orleans pralines, but it is more often cut into squares, like fudge, while pralines are made into patties.

PECAN BUTTERMILK PRALINES

About forty-two 2-inch pieces

Preheat the oven to 350°F.

Spread in a baking pan and toast in the oven, stirring occasionally, until very lightly browned, 5 to 8 minutes:

2 cups pecan halves or pieces

Set aside to cool. Line a baking sheet with wax paper, a silicone liner, or lightly buttered aluminum foil.

Combine in a large heavy saucepan:

2 cups sugar
$\frac{1}{2}$ cup packed light brown sugar
1 teaspoon baking soda
Pinch of salt
1 cup buttermilk

Stir over low heat with a long-handled wooden spoon until the sugar is dissolved. Wash down the sides of the pan with a pastry brush dipped in warm water. Add:

$\frac{1}{4}$ cup ($\frac{1}{2}$ stick) unsalted butter, cut into
small pieces and softened

Stir to melt the butter completely. Raise the heat to medium, place a warmed candy thermometer in the pan, and cook, without stirring, until the mixture reaches 236°F, the soft-ball stage. Remove from the heat.

Quickly stir in the toasted pecans and:

1 teaspoon vanilla

Beat with a wooden spoon for about 1 minute, or until the mixture begins to thicken and become opaque. Drop tablespoonfuls onto a baking sheet lined with wax paper, a silicone liner, or lightly buttered aluminum foil, forming patties about 2 inches in diameter. Let the pralines stand until completely cool, about 30 minutes.

Store between layers of wax paper in an airtight container for up to 3 days.

PRALINE

About $\frac{1}{2}$ pound

A mixture of equal parts almonds and hazelnuts is traditionally used for this recipe, but other nuts may be substituted. Praline is used not only as an ingredient in other confections, but also as a garnish for desserts. It is often sprinkled over vanilla ice cream, and can be mixed into frostings and baked goods.

Coat a 9 x 13-inch rimmed baking sheet with nonstick vegetable spray. Combine in a small heavy saucepan:

1 cup sugar
$\frac{1}{2}$ cup water
$\frac{1}{8}$ teaspoon cream of tartar

Stir over low heat until the sugar is dissolved. Wash down the sides of the pan with a pastry brush dipped in warm water. Bring to a boil. Place a warmed candy thermometer in the pan, raise the heat to medium-high, and cook, with-

out stirring, until the mixture reaches 356°F, the medium-caramel stage.

Add and stir quickly with a wooden spoon to coat the nuts completely with the caramel:

1 cup blanched whole almonds or hazelnuts, or a
combination of the two, lightly toasted, 1001

Immediately turn out onto the prepared pan. Let cool completely.

Break the praline into small pieces. Crush with a rolling pin or pulverize in a food processor to make **Praline Powder.** Store in an airtight container in the freezer for up to 1 year.

PENUCHE

About 1 pound; 64 pieces

Penuche, whose name comes from the Mexican Spanish word for raw sugar, is simply fudge made with brown sugar—which gives it a rich molasses-like flavor and a grainy texture. Pecans are traditional in penuche, but coconut is also good.

Combine in a large heavy saucepan:

3 cups packed light brown sugar
$\frac{1}{8}$ teaspoon salt
$\frac{1}{2}$ cup half-and-half
$\frac{1}{2}$ cup heavy cream

Stir over low heat until the sugar is dissolved, about 5 minutes. Brush down the sides of the pan with a pastry brush dipped in warm water. Raise the heat to medium, place a warmed candy thermometer in the pan, and cook, without stirring, until the mixture reaches 238°F, the soft-ball stage. Remove from the heat.

Add but do not stir in (stirring at this point can cause graininess):

2 tablespoons unsalted butter
1 teaspoon vanilla

Cool to 110°F; see 863. Then fold in:

1 cup pecans, roughly chopped
(1 cup shredded sweetened coconut)

Proceed as for Chocolate Walnut Fudge, 863. Let set and store as directed, 857.

ABOUT ALMOND PASTE AND MARZIPAN

Almond paste and marzipan are both made from a mixture of finely ground almonds and sugar. The distinction between the two is a fine one: Almond paste has a higher proportion of nuts to sugar and is uncooked; marzipan is made with a cooked sugar syrup. Almond paste tends to be slightly grainier and stickier than marzipan, which is very smooth and pliable. Traditionally both sweet and bitter almonds are used in these mixtures. However, bitter almonds, which contain harmful hydrocyanic acid, are banned in the United States. To compensate for the milder taste of sweet almonds, we add a dose of almond extract, which is actually made from bitter almond oil. Both marzipan and almond paste can be colored and flavored by kneading in the colorings and flavorings.

ALMOND PASTE

About 1 pound

The high proportion of nuts to sugar makes this paste a good choice for flavoring cake batters and for the centers of bonbons; or use it to stuff the cavities of dried fruits. Before the advent of the food processor and heavy-duty mixer, this was a time-consuming confection. This recipe can be doubled and processed in a large-capacity food processor or in batches.

Combine in the bowl of a food processor:

  $1^1/_2$ **cups blanched whole almonds**
  $^3/_4$ **cup confectioners' sugar**
  $^1/_2$ **cup sugar**

Process until the nuts are very finely ground. Add:

  $^1/_4$ **cup light corn syrup**
  $^1/_2$ **teaspoon almond extract**

Process until the mixture is thoroughly blended and moist enough to hold together when pressed in your hand. If it seems a bit dry, add a teaspoon or so of water and process to combine.

Remove the paste from the processor and knead several times, just to bring the paste together, on a surface dusted with:

  Confectioners' sugar

The paste is now ready for use. Or store at room temperature, wrapped tightly in plastic, for 1 week; for long-term storage, refrigerate for up to 4 weeks, or freeze for up to 3 months. Bring to room temperature before using. If the paste seems very hard, knead in by hand, or in the bowl of a heavy-duty mixer fitted with the paddle attachment, a little:

  Corn syrup (or liquid flavoring such as rose or orange flower water or fruit or nut liqueur)

MARZIPAN

About 1 $^1/_2$ pounds

Marzipan is often molded into shapes such as fruits, flowers, birds, and lambs. Disks, balls, and logs of flavored marzipan can be dipped in chocolate, and marzipan half-moons and other shapes are often filled with dense, mild-flavored preserves. Modeling marzipan into various forms either with your hands or in molds is great fun. Paint molded forms with food coloring; ordinary liquid food coloring will do in this case.

Combine in the bowl of a food processor:

  $1^1/_2$ **cups blanched whole almonds**
  $1^1/_4$ **cups confectioners' sugar**

Process until the nuts are very finely ground. Leave the nuts in the processor. Combine in a large heavy saucepan:

  $1^3/_4$ **cups sugar**
  $^1/_4$ **cup light corn syrup**
  $^1/_4$ **cup water**

Stir over low heat with a wooden spoon until the sugar is dissolved. Wash down the sides of the pan with a pastry brush dipped in warm water. Raise the heat to medium,

place a warmed candy thermometer in the pan, and cook, without stirring the mixture, until it reaches 244°F, the firm-ball stage.

Remove from the heat, turn on the food processor, and immediately pour in the sugar syrup. Grind to a fine paste, then add:

  $1^1/_2$ **teaspoons almond extract**

Pulse to blend, then remove the paste to a medium bowl that has been lightly coated with nonstick vegetable spray. The mixture will be runny, but it will thicken as it cools. Place a damp kitchen towel over the top to keep the paste from drying out, and allow to cool.

The marzipan is now ready for use. If you like, knead in a few drops of paste food coloring or a little extra flavoring, such as rose or orange flower water or a fruit liqueur. Marzipan can be stored at room temperature, tightly wrapped in plastic and in an airtight container, for 2 to 3 months. It can also be frozen for up to 6 months. Thaw and bring to room temperature before using.

Marzipan shapes can be formed by hand or using the decorative plastic molds used for chocolate. Coat the mold lightly with nonstick spray. Pinch off pieces of marzipan, knead for a moment to make them pliable and smooth, and press into the mold. Use a small sharp knife to trim any excess so that the marzipan is level with the surface of the mold (be careful not to scratch the decorative depressions of the mold). Turn the mold over and rap sharply on the counter—the marzipan pieces should fall out; if not, gently prod them out with the tip of a knife.

Kids are great at modeling free-form shapes and enjoy making fanciful creatures and surreal fruits. Shape marzipan by hand just as you would modeling clay, but use a tiny dab of light corn syrup to affix one shape to another. Use whole cloves for fruit stems or the rough side of a grater to create the stippled skin of an orange—just look in your kitchen cupboards for inspiration. Marzipan can also be rolled out on a surface dusted with confectioners' sugar and cut into various shapes with miniature cookie cutters or the tip of a small knife.

To paint molded marzipan, use regular liquid food coloring. Place a few tablespoons of clear liqueur (such as kirsch, framboise, or grappa) in a small bowl or cup and add the food coloring little by little until you like the color. Prepare as many colors as you like in this manner. Use a tiny watercolor brush to paint the marzipan. Let dry for 1 hour, then lightly glaze the candy for a sparkling finish and to help preserve its moistness.

To make the glaze, combine in a small saucepan:

  $^1/_3$ **cup water**
  $^1/_3$ **cup light corn syrup**

Bring just to a boil, then remove from the heat. While the glaze is still hot, lightly brush the candies with the glaze. Let stand for 30 minutes, or until completely dry. Store in an airtight container at cool room temperature or in the refrigerator for up to 1 month.

HALVAH

About one hundred 1-inch pieces

A mixture of tahini (sesame paste), 1021, and sugar syrup cooked to the firm-ball stage creates a dense, chewy, nutty-tasting candy.

Combine in a medium heavy saucepan:

   1³/₄ cups sugar
   ¹/₂ cup honey
   ¹/₂ cup water

Stir gently over low heat until the sugar is dissolved. Wash down the sides of the pan with a pastry brush dipped in warm water, then bring to a boil. Place a warmed candy thermometer in the pan and cook, without stirring, to 246° to 248°F, the firm-ball stage.

Meanwhile, place in the bowl of a heavy-duty mixer fitted with the whisk attachment:

   One 16-ounce jar or can tahini (sesame paste, preferably lightly roasted)

Beat on medium speed with the paddle attachment until smooth.

With the mixer running, pour the hot syrup into the tahini in a thin, steady stream, being careful to avoid the whisk. When all the syrup has been added and the mixture is smooth, add:

   ¹/₂ teaspoon ground cinnamon
   ¹/₈ teaspoon ground cloves
   1¹/₂ teaspoons vanilla

Blend well, then add:

   1 cup sesame seeds, toasted, 1011

Turn the mixture into an 9 x 13-inch pan lightly coated with nonstick spray, and use a spatula to smooth and level the top. Cool completely.

Turn the halvah out onto a cutting board and cut into 1-inch squares with a lightly oiled knife. Store at room temperature between layers of wax paper in an airtight container for up to 3 months.

FRUIT JELLIES

Sixty-four 1-inch squares

Packed with the bright flavor of fruit, these jewel-colored candies are a welcome change from chocolate. Almost any fresh or thawed frozen fruit may be used, and two or more fruits may be combined.

Line an 8-inch square baking pan with lightly greased wax or parchment paper or a silicone liner. Place in a medium heavy-bottomed saucepan:

   3 cups fresh or thawed frozen raspberries, halved strawberries, blackberries, or blueberries

Cook the berries over medium heat until they release their juices, about 5 minutes. Strain the berries through a fine-mesh strainer into a medium bowl, pressing against them with a rubber spatula. Measure out ²/₃ cup puree and save the remainder for another use.

Stir into the puree:

   2 tablespoons fresh lemon juice

Sprinkle over:

   4 envelopes (3 tablespoons) unflavored gelatin

Stir into the mixture, then set aside to allow the gelatin to soften.

Combine in a large heavy saucepan:

   1 cup water
   3 cups sugar

Cook over medium heat, stirring with a long-handled wooden spoon, until the sugar dissolves. Brush down the sides of the pan with a pastry brush dipped in warm water. Raise the heat to high, place a warmed candy thermometer in the pan, and cook, without stirring, to 236°F, the soft-ball stage. Remove from the heat and add the gelatin mixture, stirring until the gelatin is completely dissolved.

Return the pan to the heat and cook, stirring constantly, to 224°F. Immediately pour the jelly into the prepared pan. Let the jelly sit at room temperature for 12 hours before cutting it.

Invert the candy onto a cutting board and peel off the paper. Use a sharp heavy knife to cut the candy into 1-inch squares. Roll or dip the jellies in:

   ³/₄ to 1 cup superfine sugar

coating them completely. Spread out on wax paper to air-dry. Place in paper candy cups. Store between layers of wax paper in an airtight container for up to 1 week at room temperature or up to 2 weeks in the refrigerator. Serve at room temperature.

CITRUS FRUIT JELLIES

Prepare **Fruit Jellies, above,** substituting **²/₃ cup fresh lemon, lime, orange, tangerine, or grapefruit juice** for the berry puree.

QUINCE PASTE

5 to 6 cups

You'll find this delicacy wherever quinces grow—often served with soft fresh cheese. It takes patience to prepare the fruit pulp and then cook it down with sugar until it turns into a translucent coral-colored jelly, but you can shave some time off the process with the help of a microwave oven; see below. Similar fruit pastes can be made with guavas, apples (use a variety that's tart but not too juicy), apricots, or peaches; you may want to use slightly less sugar for these fruits.

Combine in a large pot with water to cover:

   5 pounds quinces (about 10), scrubbed
   3 to 4 lemons, scrubbed and sliced

Bring to a boil and cook, uncovered, until the quinces are tender, about 30 minutes. Drain and discard the lemon slices.

When the quinces are cool enough to handle, quarter and core the fruit. If you will be pureeing it in a food processor, first peel the fruit. Puree using a food mill or a food processor.

Put the puree in a large heavy pot or Dutch oven. Stir in:

   6 cups sugar
   Juice of 5 lemons (about ³/₄ cup)

Bring to a boil, then reduce the heat and simmer until the mixture is very thick and shiny and comes away from the side of the pan, at least 1 hour—it is not unusual for this to take up to 2 hours. Stir with a long-handled wooden spoon, at first just from time to time and then more and more frequently; you must stir constantly during the last 15 to 20 minutes of cooking, or the much-thickened paste will stick to the pot and scorch. Test the paste by dropping a spoonful on a plate to see if it holds its shape.

Oil individual molds or a rimmed baking sheet and spoon in the paste, spreading it evenly. Let stand at room temperature (or in an oven with a pilot light) until the paste shrinks from the sides of the molds and is no longer sticky to the touch. This can take anywhere from 1 day to 1 week, depending on the humidity.

Invert the paste onto a wire rack covered with wax paper and air-dry until the other side is no longer sticky.

If the paste was made in a pan, cut into 2 x 1-inch bars. Store, lightly covered with wax paper, at room temperature for 1 month. After that, store between layers of wax paper in an airtight container at room temperature indefinitely.

OREGON DELIGHT
Sixty-four 1-inch squares

These are similar to the famous confections known as Aplets and Cotlets—a West Coast version of Turkish delight. For a more Middle Eastern flavor, substitute unsweetened pomegranate juice for the apple or apricot juice and add a teaspoon of rose water. Almonds, pistachios, or macadamia nuts would also be nice in place of the walnuts.

Place in a small bowl:

   1/2 cup apple or unsweetened apricot juice

Sprinkle over:

   4 envelopes (3 tablespoons) unflavored gelatin

Set aside to allow the gelatin to soften.

Whisk together in a small bowl until smooth:

   1/4 cup plus 2 tablespoons cornstarch
   2 tablespoons fresh lemon juice
   2 tablespoons fresh lime juice

Combine in a large heavy saucepan:

   2 1/2 cups apple or unsweetened apricot juice
   1 1/3 cups sugar

Bring to a boil, stirring with a long-handled wooden spoon to dissolve the sugar, then cook for 15 minutes to reduce and concentrate the juice.

Remove from the heat, add the gelatin mixture, and stir until the gelatin has completely dissolved. Return to the heat, add the citrus and cornstarch mixture, and bring to a boil. Boil, stirring constantly, for 10 minutes. The mixture will be very thick.

Stir in:

   1 cup walnuts, toasted, 1001, and chopped

Remove from the heat. Rinse an 8-inch square baking pan with cold water, and shake to remove the excess water.

Pour in the juice mixture, and let the jelly harden for at least 12 hours, or overnight.

Use a lightly oiled knife to cut the jelly into 1-inch squares. Remove from the pan with a small offset spatula. Toss the squares in:

   1/2 cup cornstarch

Coating them completely. Place in fluted candy cups. Store in an airtight container at room temperature for 1 week or for up to 3 weeks in the refrigerator. Serve at room temperature.

STUFFED DRIED FRUITS
About 1 1/4 pounds

Stuffed fruits keep well and can be prepared well in advance for entertaining, or to have on hand for unexpected guests.

Steam over hot water until soft, 5 to 10 minutes:

   1 pound (3 cups) dried pitted dates, figs, or prunes

As each piece of fruit softens and becomes malleable, remove, one by one, with tongs. Stuff each fruit with a level 1/2 teaspoon of one of the following:

   Basic Fondant, 866, or Uncooked Fondant, 867,
       flavored with almond extract
   Almond Paste, 877, or Marzipan, 877
   Nuts, toasted, 1001, whole or finely chopped

Roll the stuffed fruit in one of the following:

   Superfine sugar or sifted confectioners' sugar
   Finely grated sweetened or unsweetened coconut
   Finely ground nuts

Place each fruit in a paper candy cup. Store between layers of wax paper in an airtight container in the refrigerator for up to 1 month. Serve at room temperature.

BOURBON BALLS
About sixty 1-inch balls

Many of our readers don't think it's Christmas without this cherished JOY classic. These get even better as they age. Try them with rum, too.

Sift together into a medium bowl:

   1 cup confectioners' sugar
   2 tablespoons unsweetened cocoa powder

Whisk together in a small bowl until well mixed:

   1/4 cup bourbon or dark rum
   2 tablespoons light corn syrup

Stir into the cocoa mixture and set aside. Combine:

   2 1/2 cups vanilla wafer crumbs
   1 cup coarsely chopped pecans

Stir into the cocoa mixture.

Roll the mixture into balls between your palms (the balls do not have to be even). Roll in:

   1/2 cup confectioners' sugar

Place in fluted candy cups. Store between layers of wax paper in an airtight container at room temperature for up to 3 weeks.

HEAVENLY HASH
About 1¼ pounds

At least a child's idea of heavenly!

Line a 9-inch square baking pan with wax paper. Melt:

1 pound milk chocolate

Pour half the chocolate into the lined pan. Sprinkle over:

12 large or 48 miniature marshmallows, diced

1 cup nuts, chopped

Pour the rest of the chocolate over the top. Cool.

Break the candy into pieces. Store between layers of wax paper in an airtight container in the refrigerator for up to 3 weeks. Serve at room temperature.

CANDIED APPLES
5 candied apples

Combine in a medium heavy saucepan:

2 cups sugar

⅔ cup light corn syrup

1 cup water

(1 cinnamon stick)

Cook, stirring, over medium heat until the sugar has dissolved. Bring to a boil. Cover and cook for about 3 minutes, until the steam has washed down any crystals on the sides of the pan. Uncover and cook, without stirring, nearly to the hard-crack stage, 290°F.

Meanwhile, insert a wooden skewer in the stem end of each of:

5 medium apples, washed and dried

Remove the cinnamon stick from the syrup if used. Add:

A few drops of red food coloring

Transfer to the top of a double boiler over, not in, boiling water. Working quickly, dip the apples, turning to coat, and stand them on a metal flower holder on wax paper or a silicone liner to harden, see below. Or, to make these lollipops easier to handle after dipping, dust the tops with finely chopped nuts or with sweetened puffed dry cereal, and stand on a piece of foil. Or arrange a trefoil decoration of 3 pecan or walnut halves on the top of each and stand on the foil.

Making Candied and Caramel Apples

CARAMEL APPLES
5 caramel apples

For a quick version, unwrap and melt over low heat one pound caramels.

Insert a wooden skewer in the stem end of each of:

5 medium apples, washed and dried

Place in the top of a double boiler over simmering water:

½ recipe (1 pound) Cream Caramels, 864

2 tablespoons water

Heat and stir until the caramels melt into a smooth coating. Dip the skewered apples into the sauce, twirling them until completely coated. Dry as above. If refrigerated, they will harden in a few minutes.

CANDIED ORANGE SLICES
About 36 slices

Sugar-glazed citrus slices are an old Mediterranean tradition. Half-moons or chunks of fresh pineapple may be treated the same way.

Cut crosswise into ⅜-inch-thick slices, discarding the ends:

3 large seedless navel oranges

Combine in a large heavy pot or a Dutch oven:

4½ cups sugar

4 cups water

Using a long-handled wooden spoon, stir over low heat to dissolve the sugar. Raise the heat to medium and bring just to a boil. Brush down the sides of the pan with a pastry brush dipped in warm water.

Meanwhile, place the orange slices loosely overlapping on a rack that will fit into the pan, and attach strings to it for easy removal. Lower it into the pan. Press a round of parchment or wax paper on top. Bring the syrup slowly back to a simmer. Let simmer—do not boil—for 10 to 15 minutes, until the slices are translucent and soft. Remove the pan from the heat and let the oranges steep, covered, at room temperature for 24 hours.

Using the string, lift out the rack with the fruit onto a rimmed baking sheet and let drain for 30 minutes to 1 hour.

Transfer the fruit to paper towels and leave until dry, 3 to 5 hours. The surface of the slices should be completely dry and hard.

Store between layers of wax paper in an airtight container at room temperature for up to 1 week or refrigerate for up to 3 weeks.

CANDIED CITRUS PEEL
About 2 cups

Candied citrus peel can be nibbled on its own or dipped into chocolate, and it makes a bright, flavorful addition to other desserts: For instance, it can be finely chopped and folded into cheesecake, gingerbread batter, even ice cream. This recipe is easily doubled.

Scrub:

3 oranges, 2 grapefruit, or 6 lemons

Remove the peel in large strips, place in a saucepan, and add cold water to cover. Bring to a simmer and simmer for 30 minutes. Drain, cover with cold water again, and simmer until tender. Drain and rinse under cold water. Remove any remaining pulp or stringy white pith by scraping it away with a spoon. Cut the peel into strips 2 inches long and ¼ inch wide.

Combine in a large heavy saucepan:

> **1 cup sugar**
> **3 tablespoons light corn syrup**
> **¾ cup water**

Stir over low heat until the sugar has dissolved. Wash down the sides of the pan with a pastry brush dipped in warm water. Add the fruit peel and cook very gently over low heat until most of the syrup has been absorbed. Remove from the heat, cover, and let stand overnight.

Bring to a simmer again, then let cool a little and drain. Spread several thicknesses of paper towels on a countertop and spread over them:

> **1 cup sugar**

Roll the peel in the sugar until well coated. Transfer to a sheet of wax paper and let air-dry for at least 1 hour.

To dip the peel in chocolate, temper, 857:

> **4 ounces high-quality bittersweet or**
> **semisweet chocolate**

Holding each strip of peel at one end, dip into the melted chocolate. Transfer to another sheet of wax paper and let dry until the chocolate is set. Store between layers of wax paper in an airtight container in the refrigerator for up to 4 months.

CANDIED GINGER

About 1 pound; about 3 cups

Serve candied ginger as a confection, unadorned or with its ends dipped in chocolate or fondant, or as an ingredient in other candies or desserts. Fresh young ginger, which has very thin, almost transparent, pink-tinged skin, is essential for this recipe; the fibrous, brown-skinned more mature sort toughens during prolonged cooking. Young ginger can often be found at Asian markets.

Peel and trim:

> **1¼ pounds fresh young ginger**

Cut crosswise into ⅛-inch slices. If you choose, cut the slices into thin slivers.

Place in a medium heavy saucepan and add water to cover generously. Bring to a boil, then reduce the heat and simmer, stirring occasionally, until the ginger is tender when pierced with a fork, 30 to 40 minutes. Drain.

Combine in the saucepan:

> **2 cups sugar**
> **2 cups water**

Stir over low heat with a long-handled wooden spoon until the sugar is dissolved, about 5 minutes. Wash down the sides of the pan with a pastry brush dipped in warm water. Raise the heat to medium-high, bring to boil, and

add the ginger. Reduce the heat to maintain a low simmer and cook, stirring occasionally, until the liquid has nearly boiled away, 1½ to 2 hours.

Drain the ginger and arrange on a baking sheet lined with parchment paper or a silicone liner. Let dry overnight. Or, if you would like to coat the ginger with sugar, toss with:

> **Superfine sugar**

while still lukewarm, then dry as directed.

Store in an airtight container at room temperature for up to 1 year.

CRYSTALLIZED FLOWERS

Real blossoms encased in a sheer, sparkling coat of sugar make an elegant decoration for cakes or almost any other kind of dessert. Not just any flowers can be used, however: Some species are toxic (among others, delphinium, foxglove, and lily-of-the-valley should be avoided), and even edible flowers may be rendered toxic by pesticides or preservatives. To avoid toxic species, check with a local gardening or nursery supply store or the local agricultural extension office, or consult a current botanical reference book. And stay away from flower-shop blossoms, which are almost always sprayed or treated with something you shouldn't ingest. A good source for edible flowers is a farmers' market, but be sure to ask the farmer if they are organic and untreated. Edible flowers are also now sold in some supermarkets and specialty produce markets. Of course, the best source is your own garden, where you can be sure that they're untreated and can pick them at their optimum point, just as they blossom. Whatever their source, make sure the flowers are clean and dry. This technique also works to frost red or green seedless grapes with a sparkly sugar coating.

Place in a small bowl:

> **Pasteurized powdered egg whites**

Stir in just enough water to form a thin paste; (do not beat the white, as froth is undesirable).

Spread on a small plate:

> **Superfine or granulated sugar**

Hold the flower (or petal or leaf) to be candied with tweezers and using a small watercolor brush, lightly coat the entire surface of the petal with the egg white. Hold the flower over the plate of sugar and gently spoon sugar over it, allowing the excess sugar to fall back onto the plate. It is imperative that you cover every surface with egg white and sugar, for exposed surfaces will decompose—if you missed a spot, simply touch it up with the brush and a little more sugar. Then, holding the flower over the plate, gently tap the tweezers on the side of the plate (or with your finger) to knock off excess sugar.

Set the flower on a baking sheet lined with parchment paper or a silicone liner and continue with the remaining flowers. When you have finished, check the candied blossoms for any spots that may need touching up.

Set the baking sheet in a warm, dry place to dry for several days, turning the flowers (or petals or leaves) once a day to ensure that they dry evenly (this is especially important with whole flowers, for their weight can prevent moisture from evaporating from the bottom). When the flowers are very dry, they will be crisp.

Store them between layers of parchment paper in an airtight container in a cool, dry spot. If dried and stored properly, these will keep at least 3 months, even up to 6 months or more.

PASTILLAGE (GUM PASTE)
About 3 cups

A favorite mixture for decorations, especially on wedding cakes, pastillage makes lovely molded leaves and flowers. The shapes are separately formed and held together later with Quick Decorative Icing, 789. Gum paste can be rolled out like piecrust, but never roll more at a time than you plan to shape immediately, because it dries rapidly and will become cracked and grainy. Powdered gum tragacanth can be ordered by mail or through Internet retailers.

Combine in the top of a double boiler over, not in, boiling water:

1 tablespoon unflavored gelatin

$^1/_2$ cup water
1 tablespoon powdered gum tragacanth
1 teaspoon cream of tartar

Stir until the gelatin is dissolved. To keep the paste white, add:

1 or 2 drops liquid blue food coloring

Mix and knead the mixture with:

4 cups confectioners' sugar

Once the sugar is incorporated, if you wish, separate the mixture into portions and knead in various food colorings. Place the paste in a bowl (or bowls), covered with a damp cloth, and let it rest at least 30 minutes.

When you are ready to use the paste, dust a board, a rolling pin, and your hands with:

Cornstarch

Roll only as much paste as you will use immediately to the desired thickness. Cut into shapes. Allow large flat shapes to dry on the cornstarch-dusted board for at least 24 hours; dust the top surfaces of the shapes with cornstarch too. Petals, leaves, and other shapes should be stored in cornstarch until dried and you are ready to use them.

KEEPING AND STORING FOOD

As modern living moves many of us farther and farther from primary sources of food, we more easily take for granted the marvels of modern packaging. Gone is the close awareness of growth and decay, of the fragile balance between the heat that halts enzymatic growth and the chill that retards decomposition, of the interaction between humidity and ventilation that discourages molds. No matter what method of preservation we investigate—freezing, canning, salting, smoking, drying, preserving, or storing— we still find intricate reactions at work, confronting us with the very same problems that have faced conservers from time immemorial. In the following chapters we give you the safest methods we have found to keep food from season to season. In carrying out these procedures, you will experience almost complete success, but unexpected contingencies may lead to a rare and potentially dangerous failure. Such failures may occur in commercial packaging as well. ➤ Whenever foods show the slightest signs of spoilage, such as leaking packages, off odors, mold, bubbling or unnaturally cloudy liquids, bulging or rusty cans, or liquid that spurts out when a can is opened, please accept the best advice we know: **If in doubt, throw it out.** Do not taste even the smallest bit of the contents.

The following chapters discuss how best to freeze, can, dry, salt, smoke, and otherwise preserve foods for which we, as cooks, must assume the responsibility of safe preparation. Of all these processes, whether home or commercial, freezing—if its time limitations are observed—seems to give us superior flavor and nutritive values, and canning is next best, generally, in both flavor and nutrition but wins in superior long-term keeping qualities.

In addition to freezing, canning, drying, smoking, and salting foods, there are more recent processes capable of extending shelf life. Commercial **dehydration** equipment is capable of removing 98 percent of the moisture from a food, as opposed to the 25 to 30 percent extracted in home drying. Some commercially dehydrated foods include nonfat dried milk and powdered eggs, as well as dried soup and cake mixes and dehydrated grains, fruits, and vegetables. Some claim they are good for 15 years if properly packaged and kept at proper temperatures. A safer estimate seems to be closer to 5 years.

Compare commercially dehydrated foods with the bulkier freeze-dried for which exorbitant storage claims are also made. **Freeze-dried foods** are created when food that is sliced or processed is immersed in or sprayed with a preserving agent, then frozen, placed in a vacuum chamber, and heated. As the ice crystals in the frozen food melt, they are "vacuumed" away, but the cellular structure of the food remains, lightweight, porous, and ready for quick reconstitution.

Irradiated foods have been passed through an irradiation field. The food never comes in contact with radioactive material, and the dose is not strong enough to disintegrate the nucleus of even one atom of a food molecule. The amount of radiation normally used destroys most but not necessarily all microorganisms present. Irradiation is generally used to extend the shelf life of certain foods, but hospitals may use it to process food for those with compromised immune systems. Loss of nutrients is less than or about the same as in cooking and freezing. Irradiation does produce chemical changes in food. Irradiated food cannot be recognized by sight, smell, taste, or feel. In the United States, irradiated foods must be labeled as such. The FDA, along with independent scientific studies in Denmark, Sweden, the United Kingdom, and Canada, has reaffirmed the safety of food irradiation.

Most disease-causing **bacteria** grow best on low-acid foods—which means almost everything but fruit. Taking into consideration the temperatures and speed at which bacteria grow, food scientists have given us the 2-hour rule: ➤ Foods susceptible to bacterial contamination should not be left at temperatures between 40° and 140°F for more than 2 hours. That means from the market's refrigerator to yours, from your refrigerator to the dinner table (and back again), or from your refrigerator to a picnic.

Among common food-borne bacteria, **Salmonellae** survive but remain inactive from freezing temperature up to 39°F; ➤ they are destroyed when heated to 165°F. Make sure foods are cooked through. **Staphylococci** react to temperatures similarly, but the toxin—a substance produced by living cells or organisms, also called staphylococcus—it produces is destroyed only by long boiling at 240°F. **Clostridium botulinum** grow best between 70° and 110°F; the bacterial cell form is destroyed at 212°F, but ➤ the deadly spore form is not destroyed until held at 240°F or above. These spores are the usual form found on food, so great care is needed to prevent them from becoming a problem in low-acid foods—such as green beans, corn, beets, and asparagus—canned at home, see 888. Extra-high temperatures, found only in a steam-pressure canner, must be used for low-acid foods.

Enzymes develop flavor, texture, color, and nutrients—but once a plant reaches maturity, enzymes have no regulator that says, "Stop!" In continuing to work after they're needed, enzymes destroy vitamins, skew flavors, soften cell walls, and darken colors. ➤ Temperatures below freezing slow down enzymes considerably. Above freezing, enzyme activity about doubles for every 20 degrees of rise in temperature. Most activity stops above 170°F, though some enzymes won't give up until they're boiled.

Molds are the primary spoilers of plant foods, invading plant tissue when it has been damaged, or settling on food where mold is already growing. Avoid gashed or bruised fruits and vegetables in the market. Should one of these foods be accidentally damaged in the kitchen, prepare and serve as soon as possible. Keep leafy vegetables moist, and delicate fruits and vegetables dry. Do not crowd or bump fruits and vegetables in storing. Should you discover that mold has developed on a food, discard it immediately. Molds are ➤ inactive below freezing and start to grow above freezing, with maximum activity between 50° and 100°F. Molds are destroyed at temperatures between 140° and 190°F. **Yeasts** cause the natural sugars in fresh fruits and vegetables to ferment, rendering these foods unpalatable, though not unsafe. Yeasts behave identically to molds under the same temperatures.

STOCKING THE KITCHEN

For pots and pans and all the other cooking equipment so necessary for a well-equipped kitchen, see 1061, and the illustrations of equipment at the point of use in recipes. Use the following list to ensure that your kitchen is well stocked with a set of basic supplies. Try to buy products that are package-dated: There is no way otherwise to tell how long food has been on a shelf or even before that in a storage warehouse. And be wary of packages bought in places or shops where turnover may be slow.

REFRIGERATOR
Butter or margarine
Carrots
Catsup
Celery
Cheese
Cream cheese
Eggs
Fresh herbs
Heavy or whipping cream
Horseradish
Jellies or jams
Lemons
Maple syrup

Mayonnaise
Milk
Mustard
Sour cream
Yeast
Yogurt

PANTRY
Almond extract
Anchovies
Applesauce
Baking powder
Baking soda
Bread

Broth
Brown sugar
Canned beans
Canned fruits
Capers
Cereal
Chili sauce
Chocolate chips
Chocolate, semisweet
Chocolate, unsweetened
Chopped green chiles
Chopped pimientos
Cocoa powder
Coconut
Coffee
Condensed cream soups
Corn syrup
Cornmeal
Cornstarch
Crackers
Cream of tartar
Dried beans, lentils, split
   peas
Dried bread crumbs
Dried fruit
Dried pasta
Egg noodles
Flour
Fruit juices
Garlic
Gelatin, unflavored
Grits
Honey
Hot pepper sauce
Instant tapioca
Milk, evaporated
Milk, sweetened
   condensed
Nonstick cooking spray
Oatmeal
Oil, olive
Oil, vegetable
Olives
Onions
Onion soup mix
Pancake syrup
Peanut butter
Pickles
Potatoes
Raisins
Rice
Salmon and tuna, canned
   or pouched
Salsa
Soy or tamari sauce
Sugar, brown

Sugar, confectioners'
Sugar, granulated
Tea
Tomato paste
Tomato puree
Tomato sauce
Tomatoes, diced or
   crushed
Tomatoes, whole
Vanilla extract
Vegetable shortening
Vinegar, balsamic
Vinegar, cider
Vinegar, red wine
Vinegar, rice
Worcestershire sauce

HERBS AND SPICES
Allspice, ground and whole
Basil
Bay leaves
Caraway seeds
Cayenne pepper
Celery seeds
Chili powder
Chives
Cinnamon, ground and
   sticks
Cloves, ground and whole
Coarse salt
Crystallized ginger
Cumin, ground
Curry powder
Dill, seed and weed
Fennel seeds
Garlic, fresh
Ginger, ground
Iodized salt
Mace
Marjoram
Mustard, dry powder and
   seeds
Nutmeg, ground and
   whole
Oregano
Paprika
Peppercorns
Pickling spice
Poppy seeds
Red pepper flakes
Rosemary
Rubbed sage
Sesame seeds
Tarragon
Thyme
Turmeric

ABOUT STORING FOODS

Here are some general guidelines for the length of time to store foods. For best quality, we assume you will give the food optimum packaging and storing conditions. If your pantry is often warmer than 70°F, the storage time will be shorter than stated. If temperatures are lower than 70°F but still above freezing, the permissible storage period for most of these items is longer.

Follow a system of rotation so that new foods are placed at the back of shelves and older purchases are used from the front for the day-to-day needs of the household.

➤ About 5 years: dehydrated foods if properly packaged.

➤ About 2 years: salt, sugar, whole pepper.

➤ About 18 months: canned meat, poultry, and vegetables—except sauerkraut and tomatoes—alone or mixed with cereal products. Canned fruit—except citrus fruits and juices and berries. Dried legumes, if stored in stainless steel or aluminum containers, and freeze-dried foods if properly packaged.

➤ About 12 months: canned fish, hydrogenated fats and oils, flour, ready-to-eat dry cereals stored in stainless or aluminum containers, uncooked cereal in original container, canned nuts, instant puddings, instant dry cream and bouillon products, baking soda and baking powder.

➤ About 6 months: evaporated milk, nonfat dry whole milk in metal containers, condensed meat and beef soups, dried fruits in metal containers, canned citrus fruits and juices, canned berries. To store water, see 1027.

THE REFRIGERATOR

At temperatures below 40°F, the activity of elements that can spoil food slows down or may be halted. ➤ The main compartment of your refrigerator should register 35° to 40°F, with the meat drawer just above the freezing point of 32°F. The overall goal is to keep all food temperatures at 40°F or below. The coldest place in the main compartment differs in each model (use an appliance thermometer to find it), but it's usually at the back of the top shelf; when the freezing unit is inside the refrigerator, the shelf closest to it is the coldest place. The warmest place in any refrigerator is the shelves on the door, which are exposed to warm air every time the door is opened. The less often you open the door, the more economically and efficiently the refrigerator will operate. Try to remove what you need in one trip.

Do not crowd foods in the refrigerator or allow them to touch the interior walls anywhere, as the cold air must circulate to do its job. Keep the most perishable foods front and center, where you can see them and remember to use them. Place heavy foods on the strongest shelf, and make sure one food doesn't spill potentially harmful substances onto another. Store raw foods under cooked foods, and raw meats and poultry on the bottom shelf or in the meat drawer. Place raw meat, poultry, and fish in pans so their juices cannot drip onto fruits and vegetables or other uncooked foods.

How long food will keep in the refrigerator has a great deal to do with how it has been packaged. Refrigerated air has a drying effect, and foods need to be protected from it. Refrigerate everything that's not already packaged, except fruits and vegetables, in storage containers with lids or in heavy-duty sealable plastic bags. Place the food in the container and fill the container as full as possible to displace the air.

Fruits and vegetables need air and are best stored in a moist environment—the crisper or produce drawer. Crispers are most efficient when at least two-thirds full. If your refrigerator has no crisper, or the crisper is full, store fruits and vegetables in their perforated plastic produce bags. To keep fresh herbs or any vegetable with a stalk, such as asparagus, crisp, put their stems in a jar of water and tent the leaves or tops with a plastic food bag. This gives them water and oxygen but shields them from drying air. Set the jar in a place where it is not likely to be knocked over.

If it will be used in not much more than a day, meat can be refrigerated as it came from the market. For optimum quality, wrap fresh fish in plastic wrap, lay it on crushed ice, and serve the same day. Place live shellfish on a bed of ice and serve within hours. Opened packages of luncheon meats and hot dogs should be rewrapped in plastic wrap and used within a few days. Buy and store dairy products in opaque containers, which must always be tightly closed to keep out odors. Wrap all cheeses in an inner layer of wax or parchment paper and an outer layer of plastic wrap. Discard any moldy dairy products (except cheese with natural molds) *without tasting*. Store eggs in the coldest part of the refrigerator. For long keeping, refrigerate oils, including olive (nut oils are particularly perishable); allow them to return to room temperature before using. Pure maple syrup and fruit syrups must be kept refrigerated.

Once a can of food has been opened, transfer any leftovers to a glass jar or plastic storage container. Do not store in the opened metal can: exposed to air, the metal can affect the color and flavor of the food.

Modern home refrigerators have the capacity to cool food rapidly, but very hot food or a large quantity of warm food should be cooled to room temperature before refrigerating, otherwise it will raise the temperature of the interior. This may warm the already cooled stored foods in the refrigerator to an unsafe level. Putting a small amount of loosely covered, moderately hot food in the refrigerator—a custard sauce, for instance—won't do any harm.

Keep your refrigerator clean. Get in the habit of wiping off containers with a damp cloth before they go in. If something spills, clean it up at once, or the dry air will dehydrate it quickly, making it hard to remove. If there has been moldy food in any part of the refrigerator, wash the surfaces down with a dilute solution of bleach, 1069. We recommend regularly checking all the foods for spoilage, giving a baking soda wash to the shelves, and carefully drying all the surfaces with a clean cloth. Excess moisture is an invitation to mold. An opened box of baking soda helps keep your refrigerator smelling fresh.

THE PANTRY

Store any staples that are not refrigerated in the darkest, driest area you have, preferably with a constant temperature of no more than 70°F. The food should be on a rotating system: Place new food at the back of cupboard shelves and use older purchases from the front for the day-to-day needs of the household. Keep all packages tightly closed. If you have the benefit of a cool place, as described below, keep all appropriate foods there.

Before the advent of the icebox and then the refrigerator, food was kept in a larder—a cool, airy cupboard or closet. Whenever possible, the larder was set against a north wall, the coldest in the house. Depending on ventilation, air flow, and climate, temperatures in the larder usually stayed below the low 60s, even on a hot summer day. If you have "a cool place," we mean one with conditions resembling those of a larder, with a temperature ranging from 55° to 65°F, use it to store: bread for daily use; bananas, citrus fruits, tomatoes, pineapples, and melons; eggplants, rutabagas, avocados, onions, garlic, shallots, potatoes, sweet potatoes, winter squash, and pumpkin; unshelled nuts; dried foods; tea; cocoa; sugar; chocolate; flours (except whole-grain); crackers; dry bread crumbs; olive oil (for comparatively short periods); vegetable shortening; vinegars; honey, molasses, corn syrup, sorghum, and pancake syrups; Worcestershire and hot pepper sauces; gelatin and pudding mixes; flavoring extracts; nonfat dry milk; canned goods; corked opened bottles of wine (for 1 day); and jars of herbs and spices. All fruits and vegetables must be whole; once they're cut, refrigerate them.

All foods such as flours, crackers, and bread must be wrapped to protect them from dust and insects. Except for fruits and vegetables and canned goods, the shelf life of all these foods will increase significantly if they are kept in tightly closed containers. In cool weather, yeast breads are best wrapped in aluminum foil or a sealable plastic bag and stored in a cool, dark place. In hot, humid weather, bread is prone to mold and so can be refrigerated, wrapped in foil or loose plastic, although it may dry out a bit.

Since heat rises, an improvised cool place can be a low cupboard under your kitchen counter. If you have a few cubic feet of free space against a northern wall not far from the kitchen, consider turning it into a mini larder. Close it off from the adjacent warm area with a thick door, vented at the top. If possible, fit the area with shelves of slate or marble, for maximum cooling.

ABOUT VACUUM-PACKING

Home vacuum-sealing machines are available today with an assortment of bag sizes, rolls of plastic to make your own bags, and canisters. To approximate vacuum-sealing of food without buying such an appliance, use zippered sealable plastic bags. Zip the bag closed up to the last inch or so. Holding the bag at the point where it is closed, plunge the bag into cool water until all is submerged except the inch you are holding above the water. You will see the bag collapse against the food as the water pressure forces out the air; you may even hear a slight sound as the air is expelled. Now slowly zip the bag closed while sinking that part, too, below the water. Very little air, if any, will be left inside.

WINTERING OVER FRESH PRODUCE

The earliest agricultural societies realized how urgent it was to protect seed grains from deterioration between harvest and planting time, and they developed many ingenious storing methods for protecting them against rodents, rain, insect infestation, and decay. The same enemies plagued them that plague us in our effort to winter over fresh produce: to find areas cool enough to stave off enzymatic action and ventilated sufficiently to prevent decay. **Root cellars** with stone walls and earthen floors are still the most practical solution if the climate is not too cold, too damp, or too dry, since they allow easy access and adequate space in which to segregate fruits from vegetables. When floors and walls are of concrete, produce must be stored away from these surfaces to prevent mildew. Should a basement area be heated, through proximity to a furnace or otherwise, steps must be taken to compensate for this situation; but the precautions necessary depend on so many individual factors that they cannot be spelled out here.

The latest possible mature crops are best for any wintering over, but they should not be overripe. Harvest them on a dry day. Most crops for storage do best if allowed to cool in the field overnight. There are some exceptions: For example, onions need about a week after harvesting to attain regular storage status. With root vegetables like carrots, beets, rutabagas, and kohlrabi, be sure to leave on an inch of the tops, discarding the rest.

Unbruised and unblemished produce—no other—may then be stored, for the most part at temperatures between 35° and 40°F. Sweet potatoes and yams respond best to somewhat higher temperatures—40° to 50°F. They need moderately dry storage, while late cabbage, potatoes, pumpkins, winter squash, root crops, hard apples, and pears require moderately moist conditions. Some people prefer to wash vegetables before storing; other refrain, from fear of vitamin loss. In any case, ➤ the surface of the produce should be dry before storage. It can be insulated and kept at more even temperatures if packed in dry sand or sawdust, although we have heard complaints that sand imparts off flavors. Fruits such as apples and pears may be wrapped separately in paper to keep down contact spoilage from any unnoticed bruises. Whatever material is used, packing should be relegated to the compost heap after one season's use.

Outdoor storage in reinforced sod-house mounds is tricky wherever temperatures average 30°F or higher. In climates where the ground freezes, if the mound does not have an insulated entry door, it should be kept small, because, once opened, the earth covering cannot be made cold-impervious again. Should this happen, all produce should be removed and used quickly and/or, if suitable, refrigerated. Mounds should be located in well-drained areas with a drainage trench dug around the outside. Line the mound bottom with at least 6 inches of straw or dry leaves. To protect the produce from rodents, place over the base insulation a piece of hardware cloth, which can be shaped up against the sides of the conelike pile of vegetables or fruits you will be placing on it. ➤ Never store fruits and vegetables in the same mound. Then cover the hole with about 6 inches of straw or dry leaves. Shape over this a 6-inch layer of earth, leaving at the top of the cone a chimneylike opening that will allow sufficient ventilation even when filled with straw and weighted down with a piece of board or metal held in place by a rock. Finally, cover the sides of the produce cone with one more layer of leaves or straw as further insulation and erosion control.

You may prefer pit rather than mound storage. In a well-drained shady area, dig a hole deep enough to accommodate an 18 by 30-inch section of ceramic tile set on a hardware-cloth base, insulating the base beforehand with a layer of straw or dry leaves. Put in the produce. After filling the tile, keep it covered with a thick layer of straw and an outer one of soil and straw, and proceed to make a chimney in the center as described above. Dig a drainage ditch around the finished mound. Whether you use a mound or a pit, if you are in snow country, mark the location of your storage area with a tall pole.

The simplest method of all for storing root vegetable crops, of course, is to leave them in the ground where they were grown and cover them with 15 to 18 inches of straw. This mulch applied on late crops just before frost should keep the ground from freezing hard. Again mark your rows with tall poles and keep a plan of your planting. It is surprising how easy it is to lose the location of the storage rows once the tops have shrunk in colder weather or are snow covered.

CANNING, SALTING, SMOKING, AND DRYING

It is a thrill to possess shelves well stocked with home-canned food. In fact, you will find their inspection—often surreptitious—and the pleasure of serving the fruits of your labor comparable only to a clear conscience or a very becoming hat.

ABOUT CANNING

Canning is not always a simple procedure, but with our instructions we hope to make it more simple for you. ➤ We suggest that your first attempt be a small batch, perhaps no more than six or eight jars. The following section will give you a quick walk through the canning process, and then this chapter will detail each and every step, equipment and utensils, and safety precautions. In fact, you must carry a clear conscience right with you through the processing itself, making absolutely sure that the food you keep is safe to eat. Great care must be exercised in the canning of all foods to avoid spoilage.

Today canning is easy (though it can be fairly time consuming) and—as long as you follow the canning guidelines outlined here in accordance with the USDA's latest *Complete Guide to Home Canning*—absolutely safe. Read the information in this chapter carefully before beginning your home-canning project. ▲ If you live in a high-altitude area (above 1,000 feet above sea level), adjust sterilizing and processing times accordingly for maximum safety; see High-Altitude Canning, 891.

The term **canning** is somewhat misleading, since most "putting up" of food at home is done in specially designed glass jars rather than metal cans. Raw or cooked food is packed into the jars with enough liquid to elimi-nate most air space. The jars are then heated, or processed, in one of two types of canners. Processing kills the microorganisms and enzymes that are in all fresh foods and eventually cause them to spoil. Of special concern is the killing of microorganisms that could make someone sick if they survived an inadequate process.

Processing also forces air from the jars. As the processed jars cool, excess air is expelled, resulting in a **vacuum seal.** This all-important seal keeps the foods free from bacteria that might otherwise enter the jars, contaminate the contents, and cause illness. If you are planning to do a lot of canning, especially of low-acid foods, invest in a pressure canner; they are available for less than $100 and can save hours of processing time.

CANNING CAUTIONS

Great care must be exercised in the canning of any food. Always follow the directions and processing methods and times in the recipes in this book. ➤ Be extra-cautious when canning nonacid or low-acid foods, such as berries, plums, and almost all vegetables, to prevent the development of the potentially lethal botulism toxin. Because the spores of the bacteria *Clostridium botulinum* that produces the toxin may resist 212°F—the temperature of boiling water—even after many hours, low-acid foods must be processed in a steam-pressure canner at a temperature of 240°F.

How can botulism be detected in canned foods? That can prove to be difficult, since it may be present even if no odor, gas, color change, or softness in food texture is discovered. ➤ The first indicator of any spoilage to look for is a broken seal or bulging lid. However, botulism toxin can be present without any signs if low-acid food is not processed correctly. A sealed jar is not a guarantee of safety either; how the food in the jar was prepared and heated is just as important. Become familiar with the guidelines in Checking for Spoilage, 892, and ➤ never test suspicious canned food by tasting it. The safest rule of thumb is **when in doubt, throw it out.**

CANNING EQUIPMENT
BOILING-WATER CANNERS
These are are readily available in kitchen and hardware stores, but any large pot will do, as long as it's large enough to accomodate 6 to 8 jars and is at least 2½ inches taller than the jars—1 inch to accommodate the boiling water covering the jars, 1 inch to allow for the splashing water as it boils, and ½ inch for the rack placed under the jars. The pot should fit over just one burner, although the bottom may be several inches wider than the burner. (If a large pan is set over two burners, the jars in the middle may not receive adequate heat.) For gas burners, the bottom of the pot can be "corrugated"; for electric burners, it must be flat. The pan lid must be either tight-fitting or heavy enough to stay in place over briskly boiling water.

Boiling-water canner

STEAM-PRESSURE CANNERS

These canners are more complicated and expensive than boiling-water canners, but they are essential for canning low-acid foods safely. Read the manufacturer's instructions that come with the canner. A steam-pressure canner has a locking cover that allows the steam generated inside to build pressure and reach temperatures of 240° to 250°F, below. Fitted into the cover is a vent and either a weighted pressure gauge or a dial-pressure gauge; some steam-pressure canners have both gauges. The pressure inside a canner is controlled manually by regulating the heat of the burner.

A **weighted gauge** regulates the pressure inside the canner by allowing small amounts of steam to escape each time the gauge rocks or whistles during processing. These gauges are reliable and trouble free. Their only disadvantage is that they offer fewer options at altitudes above 1,000 feet, because the only choices are 10 pounds pressure or going all the way to 15 pounds at any altitude over 1,000 feet. ➤ All pressure canners should be kept at full steam for 10 minutes before applying the weight.

A **dial gauge,** on the other hand, gives you a precise reading of the pressure inside the canner at any altitude. Dial gauges must be checked annually for accuracy; many county cooperative extension advisers have equipment to check the accuracy of the gauge. Otherwise, check with hardware stores in your area. If your gauge registers more than 2 pounds higher at 5, 10, or 15 pounds pressure, order a new one.

Only buy a canner that was made after 1970 and bears the Underwriter's Laboratory (UL) seal of approval. We don't recommend antique or hand-me-down canners that predate 1970. The USDA says that to be considered a canner, the pot should hold at least 4 quart jars. Otherwise, it is too small to use as a canner. Smaller pressure cookers are unsafe for canning. Always thoroughly check and clean the canner according to the manufacturer's instructions before each use, and store it with the cover on upside down in a cool, dry place with crumpled paper towels inside to help absorb moisture and odors that might develop during storage.

JARS

The only jars recommended for home canning are mason-type jars manufactured in the United States specifically for canning. Made of tempered glass, these jars are designed to withstand the intense heat of processing (and the extreme cold of freezing). Canning jars may be reused, as long as they are in perfect condition, do not have uneven rims, and are free of chips, cracks, nicks, and scratches. Lids should be used only once.

Jars used for commercially canned foods are intended to be used only once and are unsuitable for home canning. Antique and decorative canning jars, as tempting as they may be, should be avoided because they may be improperly tempered or brittle or have flaws that will cause them to break in processing.

Canning jars come in standard sizes ranging from half-pints to quarts. Half-gallon jars are also available but are difficult to handle; we avoid them for anything but very acidic juices. There are no currently supported processes for any other types of foods in half-gallon jars. Canning jars may be wide- or narrow-mouthed. Widemouthed jars are easier to fill and empty.

LIDS AND RINGS

Canning jars are sealed with two-piece vacuum lids consisting of a lid and a metal ring. Use lids only once; rings may be reused until they start to rust or warp. Read the manufacturer's instructions, as there may be small differences in design and use. Older domed glass lids and other bail-type or spring-lock lids, one-piece metal lids, and old-fashioned porcelain-lined zinc lids are no longer recommended.

UTENSILS

A jar lifter, for removing jars from the canner, and long tongs or a lid wand to pick up lids from very hot water are essential for safe canning. Some canners use an oven mitt or hot pad to remove the jars. Several other items will prove to be vital: a jar funnel, to keep rims clean when filling jars; a long, thin, nonmetallic spatula to remove air bubbles from filled jars; a timer; pot holders; and clean towels. For hot-packing foods, you will need a wide, heavy-bottomed stainless steel or other nonreactive saucepan to cook foods evenly and to prevent discoloration.

Also useful for preparing food for canning are a candy thermometer, paring knife, chef's knife, vegetable peeler,

Steam-pressure canner

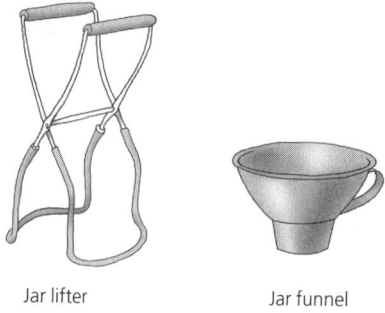

Jar lifter   Jar funnel

slotted spoon, cup-sized ladle, large strainer, set of meas-uring cups and spoons, cutting board, blanching basket, cooling rack, large colander, small mortar and pestle, food mill, 10-pound kitchen scale, and permanent marker for marking jars.

PREPARING JARS FOR CANNING

The first step in any canning project is to wash the canning jars, new lids, and metal rings in hot soapy water or the dishwasher, then rinse them thoroughly. Food that will be processed for less than 10 minutes—all jellies and some juices—must go into sterilized jars.

To sterilize jars, place them upright in the canner, cover them with hot water, and boil fairly vigorously for 10 min-utes at altitudes of 1,000 feet or less. ▲ At higher eleva-tions, boil 1 additional minute for each 1,000 feet. Leave the jars in the hot water until needed. They can be left for several hours, but in that case bring to a boil again before filling.

Pour boiling water over the lids in a bowl to soften the sealing compound and sterilize. The lids must be hot when they go on the jars, but do not boil them, or you may ruin the seal. Follow the manufacturer's instructions that come with the lids.

PACKING JARS

There are two basic techniques for packing jars: **cold- or raw-pack** and **hot-pack.** ➤ With the raw-pack method, hot jars are filled with raw or only partially cooked food and covered with boiling liquid; they begin their process-ing in hot, not boiling, water.

The ➤ hot-pack method involves filling hot jars with hot precooked food and adding boiling liquid. Preheating improves the quality of foods to be canned by forcing air from them. More food then fits in the jar, pieces are less likely to float, colors and flavors retain their brightness longer, and fewer nutrients are lost to oxidation. ➤ The hot-pack method should always be used for unsweetened fruit and is strongly recommended for all foods processed in a boiling-water bath and for most foods processed in a steam-pressure canner.

With both methods of filling jars, ➤ pack the foods firmly, but not so tightly that the produce is crushed. Pack halves and slices of fruit or vegetables in overlapping lay-ers for the best fit.

Always pack solids first then add the boiling liquid. **Headspace,** the pocket of air between the top of the food in the jar and the underside of the rim, allows room for food to expand as it heats in processing. ➤ Pack fruits and acid vegetables to within ½ inch of jar tops. ➤ Lima beans, dried beans, peas, corn, and other low-acid foods, which swell considerably more than other vegetables, plus meats canned under pressure, should be packed loosely to within 1 inch of jar tops. Add boiling liquid to completely cover the food solids, but leave headroom for expansion above the liquid, as indicated in individual recipes. You may add salt to meats and vegetables at the rate of 1 tea-spoon per quart.

Fill jars of fruit with sugar syrup, 893, to within ½ inch of the top. ▲ No adjustment of headspace is required for high altitudes.

If food for a hot-pack falls below a simmer as you fill the jars, bring it back to a boil. If the last jar is only partially filled, refrigerate or freeze it and eat the contents within a few days.

Before putting on lids, ➤ make sure that any air that may be trapped in the liquid is expelled. Run a long thin spatula down between the inside of the jar and the pro-duce, changing the position of the contents enough to re-lease any trapped air. Then carefully wipe the top of the jar before lidding. Set on the lids and screw the rings on firmly, but ➤ stop turning when you feel resistance.

ADDITIVES

Salt is optional in most canning. It adds flavor but has no effect on preservation, except when used in large quanti-ties in pickling or fermenting. Salt can be added directly to the jars before applying the lids. For some hot-packed foods, salt may be added during cooking. Do not can with iodized salt or salt substitutes—the heat of canning may turn them bitter. Use canning or pickling salt to avoid dis-coloration or precipitation from additives that may be present in other salts.

Acid is called for in some canning recipes because it acts as a preservative and can enhance the flavor and color of some foods. When using lemon juice to boost acid content, use only commercially bottled or frozen juice—its acidity is constant, whereas that of fresh juice varies. Citric acid is de-rived from citrus fruits. It is found in crystal form as "sour salt" in the kosher foods section at the grocery store. Unlike lemon juice, it adds tang without clouding the liquid.

Use a high-grade **vinegar** with a content of at least 5 percent acetic acid (sometimes labeled 50 grain). Cider vinegar and distilled white vinegar are both recom-mended.

BOILING-WATER CANNING

The boiling-water method is used for high-acid fruits and brined and pickled vegetables. Unless your canner has a jar rack that will securely hold the jars, place a rack in the bottom of the kettle to keep the jars from touching the canner or each other. Leave a 2-inch space between them. Fill the canner half full with hot water and heat to 140°F for raw-packed foods, 180°F for hot-packed. Have a pot of boiling water on hand to top off the kettle once the jars are loaded. Lower the filled and capped jars into the canner on the rack, allowing space for the boiling water to circulate. Add or remove boiling water so the level is at least 2 inches above the jars. Cover, raise the heat to high, and bring the water to a rolling boil. Set a timer for the required processing time from the moment the water boils, noting any adjustment for altitude, right. Check the water level periodically, and keep a kettle of boiling water handy in case the water falls below 1 inch above the jars.

STEAM-PRESSURE CANNING

Pressure canning ➤ at a temperature of 240°F at sea level is the only method recommended for nonacid fruits, vegetables, fish, and meats. Detailed directions for the use of a steam-pressure canner are furnished by the manufacturer and should be followed carefully—especially with regards to the checking of the gauge.

Place a rack in the bottom of the canner. Then add 2 to 3 inches of hot water and, if desired, 2 tablespoons of white vinegar to help prevent staining on the canner and jars. Lower the filled and capped jars into the canner with a jar lifter or tongs, allowing space for the steam to circulate. Fit on the lid and lock securely, leaving the vent wide open. Raise the heat to high, and when steam begins to escape, let it vent for 10 minutes, or longer at ▲ high altitude, right. After this venting, close the vent and bring the canner up to pressure.

With a weighted gauge, use the appropriate number of weights, or marked setting, consulting the manufacturer's instructions to learn how your weight should behave when full pressure is reached. With a dial gauge, bring the pressure to 2 to 3 pounds below the goal over high heat, then turn the heat down to medium until the correct pressure is reached. With either type of gauge, ▲ be sure to adjust for higher altitudes, right. Start timing the moment the recommended pressure has been reached. Always monitor the pressure gauge. You can hear the rocking of a weighted gauge, but a dial gauge must be watched.

Should the pressure drop below your target at all, ➤ you must regain the full recommended pressure and then start timing again from the beginning. If the pressure goes past the optimum point, reduce the heat a little. ➤ Turning the burner up and down, producing big fluctuations of pressure, can draw food out of the jars and ruin the seals. Try to keep the pressure from exceeding 15 pounds.

When ➤ the timer rings, turn off the heat. Remove the canner from the burner. Let the canner cool until the pressure registers 0—depending on the amount of pressure and size of the canner, this may take up to an hour. Then

open the vent or remove the weight. Wait a few minutes more before removing the lid. This cool-down period is calculated into processing time, and shortened or sudden cooling may result in spoilage and broken jars.

PROCESSING TIMES

The length of time required to process food is determined by the density of the food, how it is packed, the volume and shape of the jars, the method of processing, and the altitude. ▲ See High-Altitude Canning, below.

When using jars smaller than a pint, follow the recommended time for pint jars unless a time is given for the smaller jars. Quarts often require extra time. Follow the processing time given in each recipe.

▲ HIGH-ALTITUDE CANNING

Canning recipes have been formulated for sea level. At higher altitudes, the temperature of both boiling water and steam is lower. ➤ This means that, in order to can foods safely, the processing time must be increased when boiling-water canning and the pressure must be increased when steam-pressure canning.

BOILING-WATTER, CANNING

1,001–3,000 feet, add 5 minutes
3,001–6,000 feet, add 10 minutes
6,001–8,000 feet, add 15 minutes
8,001–10,000 feet, add 20 minutes

STEAM-PRESSURE CANNING

Use the timing given for sea level but make the following adjustments in pounds of pressure:

Dial Gauge
0–2,000 feet: 11 pounds
2,001–4,000 feet: 12 pounds
4,001–6,000 feet: 13 pounds
6,001–8,000 feet: 14 pounds
8,001–10,000 feet: 15 pounds

Weighted Gauge
0–1,000 feet: 10 pounds
1,001–10,000 feet: 15 pounds

COOLING THE JARS

After processing (and, if pressure-canning, depressurizing), immediately use a jar lifter, tongs, or oven mitt to remove the jars from the canner and set them upright on a cloth, a board, newspapers, or a rack. (Leaving hot jars in the canner can induce spoilage.) Place the jars with at least an inch between them to allow air circulation, but do not put them in front of an open window or in a draft. (Food that has been pressure-canned will continue to boil vigorously in the jars for a short time, but that will stop as it cools.)

Do not tighten the metal rings at this point, as this could damage the sealing compound and ruin the seal. As each jar cools, you should hear a hollow popping sound, indicating that the vacuum has pulled the lid down into place. Let the jars stand at room temperature for 12 to 24 hours before testing the seals.

TESTING THE SEALS

Remove the metal rings and check to see if the lids curve down slightly. Then press the center of each lid: It should not move. If the lid depresses and pops back up, the seal has failed. Or, test-seal the metal tops by ➤ tapping the lids lightly with a metal spoon or knife. A ringing note indicates a safe seal. If the contents touch the inner side of the lid, the sound may be dull but not hollow. ➤ If the note is both dull and hollow, reprocessing with a new lid is in order. Or, if you prefer, use the food right away.

Jars that did not seal properly should be refrigerated at once, then either served within a few days, frozen immediately (if the jar has at least 1½ inches headspace in the jar to allow for expansion), or reprocessed within 24 hours of the original processing.

To reprocess, first remove the lid and discard it. Check the rim of the jar where the lid sits for any small nicks that may have caused the seal to fail. Prepare a new lid, and a new jar if necessary, for processing. Process the same way, for the same amount of time, watching each step closely to try to determine what went wrong. Reprocessed food will be somewhat diminished in quality.

SEALING, LABELING, AND STORING CANNED GOODS

Before storing your jars, remove the metal rings and wipe the jars clean with a damp cloth. This prevents problems later on with corroded or stubborn metal rings and also lets you check to see whether any food is caught between the lid and rim. If you see food on the rim but the seal is secure, simply mark the jar and serve it sooner rather than later. ➤ Be sure to leave the jars upright and undisturbed for 12 hours. ➤ Do not tighten caps after jars have cooled. While the jars are still hot after sealing, you may see active bubbling going on. This is merely continued boiling caused by the lowered boiling point produced by the vacuum in the jar; it will cease as the contents cool.

Label and ➤ store jars in a cool, dark, airy place. Storage temperatures between 45° and 60°F maintain good color and are generally suitable for all properly heat-processed foods. Label each lid with a permanent marker indicating the date of canning, variety of food, and batch number, if there is more than one batch—which will be useful if a storage problem later develops. ➤ For best results, use within a year. After a year, chemical changes will begin to diminish the taste, appearance, and nutritional value of canned foods.

Keep jars of home-canned foods in a clean, cool (between 40° and 70°F), dark, dry spot. ➤ Dampness can corrode the lids and seals. Heat from a radiator, stove, furnace, or the sun will cause spoilage. Do not store jars at temperatures over 95°F. If the storage place is likely to approach freezing temperatures, wrap the jars in newspapers, set them in heavy cartons, and cover with newspapers and blankets.

RULES FOR SAFE CANNING

Before you start your canning project, read through your recipe twice and collect the necessary ingredients, equipment, and utensils. Follow the recipes in this book to the letter. They adhere to USDA guidelines.

Be meticulously clean. ➤ Make sure everything that touches the food to be canned is spotless. Wash food thoroughly to remove contaminants. ➤ Measure and cut food according to the recipe. Don't improvise. Can only as the recipe directs, and do not use a mixture of foods or substitutions. Improvisation and safe canning are incompatible.

Do not can pureed low-acid foods, such as ➤ vegetables, bananas, figs, ripe mangoes, or papayas, and do not thicken liquids with flour or cornstarch before canning. The density of pureed or thickened food makes it difficult for the heat to penetrate the contents of the jar. Puree or thicken canned foods just before serving, if desired.

Prepare ➤ only as many jars as will fit in the canner in one load. Larger canners of both types can accommodate two layers of half-pint jars. Straddle one jar on top of two, staggering them. A jar or cake rack set between the layers is helpful.

Remember to dress for safety. ➤ Wear long sleeves or use oven mitts that can absorb an unexpected burst of steam. Long sleeves should be tight to the arm, however, not loose enough to fall into pans or catch fire.

CHECKING FOR SPOILAGE

Before serving home-canned food, inspect for spoilage. Make sure that the lids are tight and that each is still depressed at the center, indicating a good seal. If any of the following indications of spoilage is evident, **do not taste the food,** and immediately follow the directions given under Handling Contaminated Food and Jars, 893.

Before opening the jar, check to see if: the lid is swollen or no longer depressed in the center; there are streaks of dried food on the outside that originate at the top of the jar; there is mold on the outside of the jar; bubbles are rising in the jar; liquid or food is seeping from the jar; the color of the food is unnatural, or much darker than it ought to be; or the liquid is unnaturally cloudy. **Do not open** if you see any of these signs of spoilage.

When opening a properly sealed jar, you should hear a reassuring "whoosh" as you pry off the lid. Sniff for unnatural or disagreeable (cheesy or sour) odors; look for spurting liquid, gas, or other signs of fermentation; check for mold—any color, even tiny flecks—on the surface of the food and under the lid; and examine the food with a fork for sliminess or other unnatural texture. Discard the jar without tasting as directed below if any of these are apparent. Sometimes, however, the top of canned fruit darkens because there is too much headspace and the fruit is sitting above the level of the liquid. This is harmless if there are no other signs of spoilage. Likewise, dark deposits on the underside of the lid are corrosion from acids and salts and are harmless.

HANDLING CONTAMINATED FOOD AND JARS

Treat any jar with any of the above conditions as though it contained botulism toxins. **Do not taste!**

Handle the jar so no part of it comes in contact with a surface that may later touch food. If the lid of the jar is still sealed, wrap the jar in a heavy garbage bag and place in a garbage container with a tight-fitting cover.

If the jar is unsealed, open, or leaking, you must detoxify the food before disposing of it, to be certain that no child, pet, or unwary wild animal is accidentally poisoned.

You may want to wear plastic or rubber gloves. Carefully lay the jar on its side in your canner. Wash your hands thoroughly. Without splashing, add water to cover the jar by at least 1 inch. Cover the pot and boil for 30 minutes. **The food has now been detoxified, but it remains inedible.** When cool, wrap the jar in a heavy garbage bag and dispose of it in a garbage can with a tight-fitting lid. The food and water can be put down the garbage disposal or drained and discarded.

Prepare a solution of 1 part chlorine bleach to 5 parts water, and use it to thoroughly wash anything—including your clothing and hands—that may have come in contact with the jar and its contents before you detoxified it. Wet surfaces and equipment with the solution and let stand for 5 minutes before rinsing. Wrap sponges, cloths, or other materials you used in cleaning in a garbage bag and discard. Wash your hands again.

UNSAFE CANNING METHODS

Over the years, many unsafe canning practices have developed. No matter what your grandmother may tell you, **do not:** can without heat-processing (the so-called open-kettle method); steam-can without pressurization; or process jars in an oven, a microwave, a slow-cooker, or a dishwasher, or under the sun. Do not use aspirin and so-called canning powders as preservatives in lieu of processing correctly; and don't mix foods in one jar without a proven recipe.

ABOUT CANNING FRUIT

Fruit can be canned in water, fruit juice, or sugar syrup, with slightly different results.

When fruit is canned in plain water, the texture softens and the color diminishes within months. A little sweetening helps canned fruit retain color, flavor, and shape, but too much sugar can overwhelm a fruit's natural flavors. We recommend adding the least amount of sugar you find palatable.

Sucralose is a sugar substitute that can withstand the heat of canning and be substituted to taste for sugar. It will not provide the protection to texture and color that sugar often does in the canning of fruits, but it will sweeten the food. If you prefer to use other sugar substitutes, can the fruit without them and then add the sweetener when serving.

A **light sugar syrup** is very close to the natural sweetness of most fruits and will preserve the quality of the fruit without adding much more than a tablespoon of sugar to each pint jar. Syrup made with white sugar is the most common. The sugar's lack of color and flavors brings the natural flavors of the fruit into sharp focus.

Brown sugar has caramelized undertones that complement some fruits. **Mild honey** or **light corn syrup** can be used to replace one-third to one-half the sugar in the syrup, but be aware that honey has its own flavor and that corn syrup is supersweet.

Another sweetening possibility is unsweetened (but naturally sweet) **apple or white grape juice,** which may be used in place of a light sugar syrup. ➤ Putting up fruit in its own juice is also permissible as long as the juice is finely strained and is no thicker than the thickest syrup recommended.

SUGAR SYRUP FOR CANNING FRUITS

Percent Sugar	Intensity of Sweetness	Measure of Sugar to Make 1 Quart Syrup
10	**Very light:** close to the natural sweetness of most fruits	Heaping $1/3$ cup
20	**Light:** satisfying with sweet fruits	Heaping $3/4$ cup
30	**Medium:** perfect for most tart-sweet fruits	$1 1/4$ cups
40	**Heavy:** needed only for very tart fruits	About $1 2/3$ cups
50	**Very heavy:** cloying	2 cups

Prepare the syrup before you prepare the fruit, so the syrup will be ready when the fruit is. Place the sugar in a quart measuring cup or pitcher. Add enough cold water to make 1 quart and stir until the sugar is dissolved. Allow about $3/4$ cup to 1 cup finished sugar syrup per pint of fruit.

PREPARING THE FRUIT

Unless otherwise specified, select firm fruit of perfect quality at its peak of ripeness. ➤ The pieces should be as similar in size as possible. Wash thoroughly by scrubbing sturdy fruits with a brush under cold running water and shaking berries and other delicate fruits in a colander in several changes of cool water. Rinse fruits after peeling as well.

ANTIBROWNING SOLUTIONS FOR CANNING FRUITS

To prevent light-colored fruits from discoloring after being cut, give the pieces a quick soak (10 to 20 minutes) in a solution prepared according to one of the following methods:

1. Crush and dissolve six 500-mg tablets vitamin C, ascorbic acid, in 1 gallon water, or

2. Use a commercial antibrowning product, following the manufacturer's instructions, or

3. Dissolve 1 teaspoon citric acid or lemon juice in 1 gallon water. Vitamin C, ascorbic acid, is most effective with the largest number of fruits. Always drain fruits—but do not rinse—before canning with the desired liquid.

4. Or, prepare a solution of 2 tablespoons salt and 2 tablespoons vinegar to 1 gallon water. Do not leave the fruit in the solution longer than 20 minutes, and ➤ rinse before packing.

APPROXIMATE YIELD OF COMMON FRUITS

	Pounds per Quart Jar	Quart Jars per Bushel or Crate
Apples	2$\frac{1}{2}$ to 3	16 to 20
Apricots	2 to 2$\frac{1}{2}$	7 to 11
Berries	1$\frac{1}{2}$ to 3	12 to 18
Cherries	2 to 2$\frac{1}{2}$	(unpitted) 22 to 32
Peaches	2 to 3	18 to 24
Pears	2 to 3	20 to 25
Plums	1$\frac{1}{2}$ to 2$\frac{1}{2}$	24 to 30
Tomatoes	2$\frac{1}{2}$ to 3$\frac{1}{2}$	15 to 20

BOILING THE FRUIT

Place the prepared fruit, without crowding, in a wide shallow saucepan on a burner. In a separate pan, bring the desired liquid to a boil and pour it over the fruit to cover. Turn the heat to high and, when the liquid starts to boil, set the timer according to the recipe. Stir frequently.

GUIDE TO CANNING FRUITS

Please read About Canning, 888, before proceeding. We note superior canning varieties for each fruit as a guide only; other varieties also can successfully. Hot-pack all fruits except grapefruit and mangoes. Use half-pint, 12-ounce, pint, or quart jars. Processing times are the same for all sizes of jars unless otherwise noted and are calculated for sea level. To adjust for higher altitudes, see 891.

APPLES

Apples are excellent for canning. Select crisp, juicy apples, a mix of sweet and tart. *Recommended liquid:* Water or 10- to 30-percent sugar syrup, 893, made with up to one-third mild honey.

Wash, peel, and core; slice into $\frac{1}{4}$-inch-thick wedges. Place slices in an antibrowning solution, above, as they are cut. Drain.

Boil gently in the desired liquid (a little cinnamon, allspice, or nutmeg can be added) for 5 minutes. Pack the hot apples into hot jars, and add the hot cooking liquid, leaving $\frac{1}{2}$-inch headspace, 890. Process for 20 minutes. See Boiling-Water Canning, 888.

APPLESAUCE

Recommended liquid: Water.

Prepare the apples as above, peeling only if desired. Place in a pan with just enough water to keep the apples from sticking (about $\frac{1}{2}$ to 1 cup water per quart of sliced apples). Heat quickly over high heat and cook, stirring frequently, until tender, 5 to 20 minutes. Mash or puree; sweeten to taste, if desired. A little cinnamon, allspice, or nutmeg can be added. Bring to a rolling boil and ladle hot into hot jars, leaving $\frac{1}{2}$-inch headspace, 890. Process for 15 minutes (20 minutes for quarts), 891.

APRICOTS, NECTARINES, AND PEACHES

Cling peaches hold their shape best. *Recommended liquid:* White grape juice or 10- to 30-percent sugar syrup, 893.

Dip peaches in boiling water; slip off the skins. Wash apricots and nectarines well—peeling apricots is optional; do not peel nectarines. Cut the fruits in half and remove the pits. If desired, scrape the red from the cavities—it darkens in canning. For easy packing, cut large halves crosswise into 4 wedges. Place the fruit in an antibrowning solution, above, as you cut. Drain.

Place the fruit in a pan without crowding, cover with the desired liquid, and bring to a boil. Ladle the hot fruit into hot jars, packing the halves in layers, cut side down. Add the hot liquid, leaving $\frac{1}{2}$-inch headspace, 890. Process for 20 minutes (25 minutes for quarts), 891.

BERRIES

All canned berries soften, but their flavors remain delicious. They are especially good as a light dessert topping for cakes, ice cream, and waffles. Superior canning varieties are blackberries, blueberries, boysenberries, currants, dewberries, elderberries, gooseberries, huckleberries, loganberries, mulberries, black and red raspberries, strawberries, and youngberries. *Recommended liquid:* Sweetened juice and water, 893.

Working with 1 to 2 quarts of berries at a time, stem, wash, drain, and hull as needed. Halve any strawberries that are much larger than the rest. In a shallow bowl, mix $\frac{1}{2}$ cup sugar with each quart fruit. Let stand in a cool place for 2 hours, stirring occasionally.

Place the berries, without crowding, in a large heavy skillet over high heat. Stir gently until the syrup comes to a simmer, or until tight-skinned berries glisten, indicating that most of the sugar has dissolved. Ladle the hot berries into hot jars and add boiling water as needed, leaving 1/2-inch headspace, 890. Process for 15 minutes (strawberries for just 10 minutes), 891.

CHERRIES

Sweet and tart cherries are both excellent canned, and then are perfect in pie fillings. *Recommended liquid:* Water, apple juice, or white grape juice, or 30-percent sugar syrup, 893.

Stem and wash. Cherries retain their color and shape best when unpitted, but they may be pitted. To prevent unpitted cherries from splitting, prick each cherry with a clean pin. Place in an antibrowning solution, 894, as prepared. Drain.

In a pan without crowding, combine 1/2 cup desired liquid with each quart of cherries and quickly bring to a boil. Using a slotted spoon, pack the hot cherries into hot jars, and add the hot liquid, leaving 1/2-inch headspace, 890. Process for 15 minutes (20 minutes for quarts), 891.

CRANBERRIES

Although they are firmer when frozen, canned cranberries make a delicious sauce for poultry and meat. *Recommended liquid:* 40-percent sugar syrup, 893.

Stem and wash. Bring the syrup to a boil, add the berries, and boil for 3 minutes, stirring frequently. Using a slotted spoon, pack the hot cranberries into hot jars, and add the boiling syrup, leaving 1/2-inch headspace, 890. Process for 15 minutes, 891.

CRANBERRY SAUCE, JELLIED

The classic accompaniment to Thanksgiving turkey, this is also wonderful served chilled for dessert. Slice and top with whipped cream and chopped walnuts. *Recommended liquid:* Water.

Stem and wash. In a pan without crowding, mix each quart of berries with 1 cup water. Cook until soft, then press through a sieve. For each original quart berries, stir in 3 cups sugar. Boil for 3 minutes, stirring. Ladle the hot sauce into hot widemouthed jars, leaving 1/2-inch headspace, 890. Process for 15 minutes, 891.

FIGS

Canned figs have a beautiful appearance and an excellent texture, but their flavor can fade. Select firm fruits without splits. Acid must be added, because figs have only borderline acidity. *Recommended liquid:* 20-percent sugar syrup, 893, made with up to one-third mild honey.

Do not stem or peel. Wash. Cover with water and boil gently for 2 minutes; drain.

Bring the syrup to a boil, add the figs, and boil gently for 5 minutes. Pack the hot figs in hot jars. Add 1/4 teaspoon citric acid or 1 tablespoon bottled lemon juice to each pint jar, or twice this amount to each quart jar. Add the hot cooking liquid, leaving 1/2-inch headspace, 890. Process for 45 minutes (50 minutes for quarts), 891.

FRUIT PUREES AND BABY FOOD

Puree any fruit except bananas, cantaloupe and other melons, coconut, figs, mangoes, and papayas, which are insufficiently acidic. (Do not can pureed tomatoes by these directions.) If necessary, sweeten the fruit puree to taste with sugar or honey. **If making a fruit puree for baby food, however, do not use honey,** as it can cause botulism in babies and children under one year of age. *Recommended liquid:* Water.

Stem, wash, pit, peel, and/or core the fruit as needed. Place in an antibrowning solution, 894. Drain.

Crush slightly or chop. Mix in a pan with 1 cup hot water for each quart of fruit. Cook slowly until soft, stirring frequently. Press through a sieve, or puree using the fine blade of a food mill. Sweeten to taste. If using honey, bring to a boil, stirring. If using sugar, boil until the sugar dissolves. Ladle the hot puree into hot half-pint or pint jars, leaving 1/4-inch headspace, 890, Process for 15 minutes, 891.

GRAPES

Superior canning varieties are Flame, Glenora, Reliance, seedless Concord, and Thompson. *Recommended liquid:* 10- to 20-percent sugar syrup, 893.

Select tight-skinned seedless grapes, ideally picked 2 weeks before the peak of ripeness. Wash and stem. Place in an antibrowning solution, 894. Bring the syrup to a boil in one pot and 1 gallon of water to a boil in a separate pot. Drain the grapes, put in a blanching basket or a sieve, and dip in the boiling water for 30 seconds. Drain. Pack the hot grapes into hot jars and add the hot syrup, leaving 1/2-inch headspace, 890. Process for 10 minutes, 891.

LOQUATS

Tasting of apricot, pear, and orange, loquat pieces are good in winter fruit cups and sauces. *Recommended liquid:* 20-percent sugar syrup, 893.

Wash, remove the stem and blossom ends, halve, and remove the seeds. Boil gently for 3 to 5 minutes. Pack the hot fruit in hot jars, and add the hot syrup, leaving 1/2-inch headspace, 890. Process for 15 minutes (20 minutes for quarts), 891.

MANGOES, GREEN

Raw-pack, 890, only borderline acidity of ripe mangoes makes it important that acid be added and that only firm, green mangoes be canned by these directions. *Recommended liquid:* 20- to 30-percent sugar syrup, 893.

Select firm green mangoes. **Caution:** Handling green mangoes may irritate the skin of some people in the same way as poison ivy (they belong to the same plant family). To avoid this reaction, wear plastic gloves while working with raw green mangoes, and do not touch your face, lips, or eyes after touching or cutting green mangoes until you wash your hands and the cutting surfaces carefully.

Wash and score the skin lengthwise in quarters to pull off the peel. Cut the flesh from either side of the large pit into ¼-inch-thick slices. Do not use overly fibrous pieces of fruit. Place the fruit slices in enough syrup in a saucepan to cover the fruit. Bring to a boil and cook 2 minutes.

Using a slotted spoon, pack the hot fruit into hot jars. Add ¼ teaspoon citric acid or 1 tablespoon bottled lemon juice to each pint jar, or twice this amount to each quart jar. Return the syrup to a full boil and add to the jars, leaving ½-inch headspace, 890. Process for 15 minutes (20 minutes for quarts), 891.

ORANGES, MANDARINS, GRAPEFRUITS, AND POMELOS

Raw-pack only. The flavor of oranges canned alone is not the best. Try canning with equal parts of grapefruit. *Recommended liquid:* 10- to 30-percent sugar syrup, 893.

Wash, peel, and cut off the white pith. Cut between segments, if possible, and discard the seeds and membrane.

Bring the desired liquid to a boil. Pack the fruit into hot jars. Add the hot liquid, leaving ½-inch headspace, 890. Process for 10 minutes, 891.

PAPAYAS

The texture and color of canned papayas are excellent, and the flavor is intensified. Papayas have borderline acidity, making it necessary to add acid. *Recommended liquid:* 20- to 30-percent sugar syrup, 893.

Wash and peel. Halve, remove the seeds, and cut the fruit into ½-inch cubes. Place in the syrup in a saucepan without crowding and bring to a simmer. Cook gently for 2 to 3 minutes.

Using a slotted spoon, pack the hot fruit into hot jars. Add ¼ teaspoon citric acid or 1 tablespoon bottled lemon juice to each pint jar, or twice this amount to each quart jar. Add the hot syrup, leaving ½-inch headspace, 890. Process for 15 minutes (20 minutes for quarts), 891.

PEACHES

See Apricots, Nectarines, and Peaches, 894.

PEARS

One of the most successfully canned of all foods. Large pieces are rich in flavor and not too soft. Superior canning varieties are Bartlett, Clapp's Favorite, Duchess, Kieffer, and Moonglow. *Recommended liquid:* Water, apple juice, or white grape juice, or 10- to 30-percent sugar syrup, 893.

Wash and peel. Halve or quarter and core. Place in an antibrowning solution, 894. Drain.

Boil gently in the desired liquid for 5 minutes. Pack the hot pears into hot jars. Add the hot liquid, leaving ½-inch headspace, 890. Process for 20 minutes (25 minutes for quarts), 891.

PINEAPPLE

Recommended liquid: Water, pineapple juice, or 10 to 30-percent sugar syrup, 893, made with up to one-third mild honey.

Wash, then remove the peel and eyes. Quarter lengthwise and slice out the core. Cut into ½-inch-thick slices or

wedges or 1-inch chunks. Simmer in the desired liquid for 10 minutes.

Using a slotted spoon, pack the hot fruit into hot jars. Add the hot liquid, leaving ½-inch headspace, 890. Process for 15 minutes (20 minutes for quarts), 891.

PLUMS

Superior canning varieties are Burbank, Early Italian, Fellemberg, Greengage, Italian Prune, Laroda, Mount Royal, Nubiana, Santa Rosa, Satsuma, Seneca, Stanley, and Victoria; also wild plums. *Recommended liquid:* Water or 20- to 30-percent sugar syrup, 893.

Stem and wash. Most plums are best canned whole. Prick skins with a fork to prevent bursting. Boil gently for 2 minutes in the desired liquid, then cover the pan and let stand for 20 to 30 minutes.

Ladle the hot plums into hot jars. Add the syrup, leaving ½-inch headspace, 890. Process for 20 minutes (25 minutes for quarts), 891.

RHUBARB, STEWED

Recommended liquid: The fruit's own juice or water.

Select tender bright red stalks. Discard the leaves and green parts. Wash and cut into 1-inch pieces. In a large pan without crowding, combine each quart of chopped rhubarb with ½ to 1 cup sugar. Let stand in a cool place until the juices flow, but no more than 4 hours, stirring occasionally.

Slowly bring to a boil. Using a slotted spoon, pack the hot fruit into hot jars. Add boiling water if needed, leaving ½-inch headspace, 890. Process for 15 minutes, 891.

CANNING FRUIT JUICES

Canning fruit juices is practically as simple and every bit as safe as canning whole fruits. Besides the fact that they are intensely delicious and nutritious, home-canned juices can be sweetened to your taste. Select fully ripe but firm fruit. A juice extractor makes quick work of juicing; if you don't have one, simmer the cut-up fruit according to the recommendation in each recipe and strain it through a jelly bag or a colander lined with 4 layers of damp cheesecloth. For the clearest juice, refrigerate the strained juice for 24 hours, then pour off the clear juice, leaving the sediment behind, and strain it again through a damp coffee filter.

Pour the strained juice into a heavy-bottomed saucepan, set over low heat, and add sugar to taste, if desired. Stir without simmering until the sugar is dissolved. Raise the heat to high and cook, stirring frequently, until the juice almost boils. Overcooking or boiling fresh juice deteriorates the flavor and nutrients, and we recommend temperatures no higher than 190°F. Pour the hot juice immediately into hot pint or quart jars, observing the headspace noted in the recipe. Juices that will be processed for less than 10 minutes must go into sterilized jars. Adjust the lids and process according to the directions for canning high-acid foods in a boiling-water canner, 888. Cooking and processing times for clear fruit juices are brief because liquid absorbs heat much faster than whole foods.

Please read Canning Cautions, 888, and Rules for Safe Canning, 892, before proceeding. Unless otherwise noted, all juices are hot-packed in any size jar with a ¼-inch headspace.

Processing times are the same for all jar sizes and are calculated for sea level. ➤ To adjust for higher altitudes, see 891.

APPLE JUICE
Combine very juicy apples, both sweet and sharp.

Wash and remove the stem and blossom ends. Use a juice extractor or fruit press, or finely chop the fruit in a food processor. Simmer until soft. Strain, heat the juice to 190°F, and pour into hot sterilized jars, leaving ¼-inch headspace, 890. Process for 5 minutes, 891.

APPLE CIDER
Use a blend of three or more varieties of firm, ripe apples, making sure to balance the sweet apples against those that are acid. Because crab apples are astringent, use them in small proportions.

Use raw-pack only. After putting apples through a cider mill or fruit press, strain and put into hot, sterile jars. Process 30 minutes in a hot-water bath at 185°F.

APRICOT, NECTARINE, OR PEACH NECTAR
Excellent quality. Can in pint jars only.

Wash, pit, and coarsely chop. Use a juice extractor. Or in a pan without crowding, mix 1 cup boiling water with each quart chopped fruit. Cook at below a simmer until soft, stirring frequently, and press through a strainer, or puree using the fine blade of a food mill. Add 1 or 2 tablespoons bottled lemon juice per quart of nectar. Sweeten to taste. Immediately pour the hot nectar into hot jars, leaving ¼-inch headspace, 890. Process for 15 minutes, 891.

BERRY, CHERRY, OR CURRANT JUICE
True flavor and color. Use sweet or tart varieties.

Wash, stem, and crush berries; or wash, stem, pit, and chop cherries. Use a juice extractor. Or cook at below a simmer until soft, crushing and stirring frequently; add water as needed to prevent sticking. Strain and heat to 190°F. Sweeten to taste. Immediately pour the juice into hot jars, leaving ½-inch headspace, 890. Process for 15 minutes, 891.

CRANBERRY JUICE
Much fresher tasting than commercially canned juice.

Wash, stem, and pick over, discarding softened or discolored berries. Mix equal measures of berries and water in a pan without crowding. Quickly bring to a boil, then reduce the heat and cook at below a simmer until all the berries have popped. Strain and heat to 190°F. Sweeten to

taste. Immediately pour the juice into hot jars, leaving ¼-inch headspace, 890. Process for 15 minutes, 891.

GRAPE JUICE
Remove large stems. Wash. Use a juice extractor. Or cover with boiling water in a pan and cook at below a simmer until soft, crushing frequently; avoid crushing the seeds (they are bitter), whether extracting with a juicer or when cooked. Strain. Refrigerate the strained juice overnight, then pour off the clear juice from the sediment. (This is essential for grape juice—otherwise, tartrate crystals will form in the juice.) Strain again and heat to 190°F. Sweeten to taste. Immediately pour the juice into hot sterilized jars, leaving ¼-inch headspace, 890. Process for 5 minutes, 891.

GRAPEFRUIT OR GRAPEFRUIT-ORANGE JUICE
For a grapefruit-orange blend, use equal amounts of each juice. Use varieties as indicated for canning fruit, 896.

Wash. Halve and extract the juice. Strain and sweeten to taste. In a double boiler, heat to 190°F and hold for 5 minutes at 190°F. Immediately pour the juice into hot jars, leaving ¼-inch headspace, 890. Process for 15 minutes, 891.

PLUM JUICE
Superior canning varieties are Au Producer, Elephant Heart, Pipestone, Red Heart, Satsuma, and Waneta.

Wash, pit, and chop. Use a juice extractor. Or, in a pan without crowding, mix 1 quart water with each quart chopped fruit and cook below a simmer until soft, stirring frequently. Strain and heat to 190°F. Sweeten to taste. Pour the juice into hot jars, leaving ¼-inch headspace, 890. Process for 15 minutes, 891.

RHUBARB JUICE
This makes a tangy summer cooler. Use varieties as indicated for canning fruit, 896. Select tender bright red stalks. Discard the leaves and green parts. Do not peel. Chop. Combine each quart chopped rhubarb with ½ cup sugar and let stand in a cool place, stirring occasionally, until the juices flow, but no more than 4 hours.

Use a juice extractor. Or, in a pan, mix 1 quart water with each 5 quarts fruit. Heat quickly until the water just begins to boil. Strain and heat to 190°F. Immediately pour the juice into hot jars, leaving ¼-inch headspace, 890. Process for 15 minutes, 891.

ABOUT CANNING TOMATOES
Tomatoes are the all-time favorite fruit for home canning. They're abundant in their season, extremely versatile to use, and easy to can.

Tomatoes can be processed by either the boiling-water or steam-pressure method. While the boiling-water method gives good results, we recommend steam-pressure canning for better flavor and nutritional value. Select perfect, firm, ripe—not overripe—tomatoes without soft spots, bruises, mold, or broken skin. Do not can tomatoes from dead or frost-killed vines. Wash until the rinsing water is clear. Peel according to the techniques below. Green tomatoes can safely be canned following any recommendations for ripe tomatoes. Cherry and grape tomatoes do not can successfully.

Tomatoes have unpredictable acid levels; this is true even of old-fashioned varieties with a high-acid reputation. To be safe, add acid to ripe tomatoes (it isn't necessary for green tomatoes or tomatillos). We prefer citric acid for its lack of flavor, but bottled lemon juice or, in a pinch, 1/4 cup of 5 percent–acidity cider vinegar per quart jar can also be used (though the flavor of tomatoes canned with the latter is an acquired taste). A little sugar can be blended into the tomatoes to balance tartness, if necessary, but do not add vegetables or other ingredients that would lower the level of acid. A single small washed fresh herb leaf, like sweet basil, is acceptable; its flavor will intensify with time.

Tomatillos are small, tart, husk-covered green orbs used widely in Mexican cooking. Though only distantly related to tomatoes, they are canned by the same methods and with equal ease and success.

HOW TO PEEL TOMATOES

1. If you are canning large quantities of tomatoes, place in a single layer in a roasting pan and cover with boiling water. Wait until cool and slip skins off and cut out the stems and any blemishes or green areas that are on the tomatoes.

2. If only canning a few tomatoes, you can peel as follows: Using a small sharp knife, cut a shallow X in the skin at the bottom of each tomato—do not cut into the flesh. Ease the tomatoes one by one into a pot of boiling water. Leave ripe tomatoes in for about 15 seconds, barely ripe tomatoes in for twice as long. Lift out with a slotted spoon and drop into a bowl of ice water to stop the cooking.

3. If the recipe can use a touch of smoky flavor, hold each tomato on a long-handled fork over a gas burner, turning it until the skin splits. Do not plunge in water, but peel as directed below. All green, bruised, or brown spots must be removed.

4. Pull off the skin with the tip of the knife. If the skin sticks, return the tomato to the boiling water for another 10 seconds.

Please ➤ read the directions for safe and proper canning, 888–893, and About Canning Tomatoes, 897, before proceeding. Hot-pack all forms of tomatoes in pint or quart jars. After packing, add 1/4 teaspoon citric acid or 1 tablespoon bottled lemon juice to each pint jar, twice this amount to each quart jar. Processing times are calculated for sea level. ▲ To adjust for higher altitudes, see 891.

TOMATOES, CRUSHED

Wash, peel, and cut out the cores. Trim away any bruised or discolored portions and quarter. ➤ Do not prepare any more tomatoes than can fit in one canner load at a time. Working quickly once the tomatoes are cut, place only one layer of tomatoes in a large pan. Set over high heat and crush with a potato masher or pestle to prevent sticking, then stir until boiling. If desired, sprinkle with salt as you go. Gradually add the remaining pieces, stirring constantly—no need to crush. When all the tomatoes have been added, boil gently for 5 minutes, stirring frequently.

Pack the hot tomatoes into hot jars, leaving 1/2-inch headspace, 890. Add acid to each jar, as above. Process pints for 35 minutes in a boiling water canner, quarts for 45 minutes; or process either for 15 minutes in a steam-pressure canner, 891.

TOMATOES PACKED IN WATER

This process is ➤ only for tomatoes packed in water. For other methods of packing whole, halved, or quartered tomatoes, consult the USDA's *Complete Guide to Home Canning*.

Wash, peel, and cut out the cores. To can whole tomatoes, select small meaty ones of uniform size. To can halves, cut the tomatoes on a plate to catch the juice. Put in a pan without crowding, add the juices and water to cover, and boil gently for 5 minutes.

Pack the hot tomatoes into hot jars. Add acid, as above, and salt to taste. Add the hot cooking liquid, leaving 1/2-inch headspace, 890. Process pints for 40 minutes in a boiling-water canner, quarts for 45 minutes; or process either for 10 minutes in a steam-pressure canner, 891.

TOMATO JUICE OR SOUP

Wash, stem, and trim off bruised or discolored portions. To prevent the juice from separating, quarter only about 1 pound of the tomatoes, on a plate to catch the juice. Place in a pan over high heat and crush the tomatoes with a potato masher or pestle as they come to a boil. Boil constantly and vigorously while slowly adding and crushing the rest of the tomatoes and juices. The mixture should maintain a boil all the time. If desired, sprinkle with salt as you go. When all the tomatoes have been added, simmer for 5 minutes, stirring frequently.

Press while hot through a sieve or food mill and return to the pan. Quickly boil the juice, and immediately fill hot jars, leaving 1/2-inch headspace, 890. Add acid to each jar, as above. Process pints for 35 minutes in a boiling-water canner, quarts for 40 minutes; or process either for 15 minutes in a steam-pressure canner, 891.

Do not thicken or add cream for soup. If desired, this must be done after opening jars, at the time of serving.

TOMATO-VEGETABLE JUICE OR SOUP

Use tomato varieties as indicated for juice or soup, above. Weigh the tomatoes, then wash, stem, trim, quarter, and crush and boil as for juice, above. For every 5½ pounds tomatoes, blend in up to, but no more than, ¾ cup finely chopped mixed carrots, celery, onions, and/or bell or chili peppers. Simmer for 20 minutes, stirring frequently.

Press while hot through a sieve or food mill and return to the pan; discard the vegetables. Rapidly bring the juice to a boil and immediately fill hot jars, leaving ½-inch headspace, 890. Add acid to each jar, as above. Process pints for 35 minutes in a boiling-water canner, quarts for 40 minutes; or process either for 15 minutes in a steam-pressure canner, 891.

Do not thicken or add cream for soup. If desired, this must be done after opening jars, at the time of serving.

TOMATO PUREE
Use tomato varieties as indicated for juice or soup, above. Wash, prepare, cook, and strain tomatoes as for juice, above. Simmer in a large stockpot, stirring frequently, until reduced to the desired consistency. Fill hot jars with the hot sauce, leaving ½-inch headspace, 890. Add acid, as above. Process pints for 35 minutes in a boiling-water canner, quarts for 40 minutes; or process either for 15 minutes in a steam-pressure canner, 891.

TOMATILLOS
Tomatillos have a consistently high acid level and do not need any added acid.

Select firm underripe fruit. Peel off and discard the husks, then rinse off the sticky covering. Run a clean needle all the way through each fruit to prevent bursting.

Prepare as for whole tomatoes in water, above; leave ½-inch headspace, 890. Process pints for 40 minutes in a boiling-water canner, quarts for 45 minutes; or process either for 10 minutes in a steam-pressure canner, 891.

ABOUT CANNING VEGETABLES
The most important thing to keep in mind when canning vegetables is that they are low in acid, making them highly susceptible to the growth of harmful bacteria, and therefore ➤ must be steam-pressure processed, 889.

The following vegetables are better pickled, frozen, or eaten fresh and ➤ **should not be canned:** artichokes, broccoli, Brussels sprouts, cabbage, cauliflower, cucumbers, eggplant, endive, chicory, lettuce and other salad greens, and any root vegetables not mentioned in this chapter.

Select ripe but firm vegetables of good quality, as close to the same size as possible. Reject any with soft spots, bruises, mold, or broken skin. Scrub sturdy vegetables, such as carrots, potatoes, and squashes, under cold running water until clean. Shake and stir small but firm vegetables, such as shelled peas, in a colander under cold running water. Rinse delicate vegetables, such as greens, in several changes of tepid water until the water is free of sand and impurities. Rinse vegetables after peeling or shelling as well.

Most vegetables for canning are improved by brief pre-cooking. Place the prepared vegetables, without crowding, in a wide shallow pan on a burner. Pour enough boiling salted water over them to cover, turn the heat to high, and start timing when the liquid starts to boil. Some vegetables are topped off in the jars with the cooking liquid, while others benefit from the addition of fresh boiling water. Certain vegetables are more apt to be loaded with potential contaminants, which are best tossed out with the cooking liquid.

APPROXIMATE YIELD OF COMMON VEGETABLES		
Raw Vegetable	Pounds per Quart Jar	Quart Jars per Bushel
Beans, lima, in the pod	4 to 5	6 to 8
Beans, snap	1½ to 2	15 to 20
Beets	2½ to 3	17 to 20
Carrots	2½ to 3	16 to 20
Corn cut off cob	7 ears	8
Greens	2 to 3	6 to 9
Okra	1½ to 2	17
Peas in the pod	2 to 2½	5 to 10
Squash, summer	2 to 2½	16 to 20
Sweet potatoes	2½ to 3	18 to 22
Tomatoes	2½ to 3½	15 to 20

Please read the directions for safe and proper canning, 888–893, before proceeding. Hot-pack all vegetables with 1-inch headspace, 890, in half-pint, 12-ounce, pint, or quart jars except where otherwise noted. Processing times are calculated for sea level. Adjust for higher altitudes, 891. We note superior canning varieties for vegetables as a guide only; other varieties can successfully as well.

ASPARAGUS
Select thick, tight-tipped spears. Wash. For whole stalks, cut 1 inch shorter than the height of the jars. For pieces, remove the tough skin and ends and cut into 1-inch lengths. Boil gently for 2 to 3 minutes. Loosely pack the hot asparagus into hot jars, whole stalks tips up, and add the boiling cooking liquid, leaving 1-inch headspace, 890. Process for 30 minutes (40 minutes for quarts) in a steam-pressure canner, 891.

BEANS, GREEN, SNAP, OR WAX
Select crisp, tender, meaty pods. Wash. Remove the tips and any strings. Leave whole, or snap, or cut into uniform pieces. Boil gently for 5 minutes. Loosely pack the hot beans into hot jars, standing whole beans on end. Add the boiling cooking liquid, leaving 1-inch headspace, 890. Process for 20 minutes 25 minutes for quarts in a steam-pressure canner, 891.

BEANS AND PEAS, FRESH

Select plump, tender pods. Shell and wash thoroughly. Sort sizes, if necessary. Boil gently for 3 minutes. Loosely pack the hot beans into hot jars and add the boiling cooking liquid (if canning fresh kidney beans, use fresh boiling water to cover instead of the cooking liquid), leaving 1-inch headspace, 890. For black-eyed, crowder, and field peas, leave 1 1/2-inches headspace in quart jars. Process for 40 minutes (50 minutes for quarts) in a steam-pressure canner, 891.

BEETS

Superior canning varieties are Big Red, Detroit Dark Red, Detroit Supreme, Formanava, Little Ball, Pacemaker III, Red Ace, and Ruby Queen.

Select crisp beets up to 3 inches in diameter. Wash and trim, leaving 1 inch of the roots and stems. Boil gently just until the skins slip off, 25 to 30 minutes. Trim the roots and stems flush with the beets and remove the skins. Baby (1- to 2-inch) beets may be left whole. Cut tender young beets into 1-inch chunks, larger older beets into 1/2-inch cubes or slices. Pack the hot beets into hot jars, adding 1/4 teaspoon salt per pint. Add fresh boiling water, leaving 1-inch headspace, 890. Process for 30 minutes (35 minutes for quarts) in a steam-pressure canner, 891.

CARROTS

Select sweet, crisp young carrots up to 1 1/4 inches in diameter. Wash, peel, and wash again. Cut into 1/2-inch-thick sticks or 1/2-inch slices or chunks. Boil gently for 5 minutes. Pack the hot carrots into hot jars and add the boiling cooking liquid, leaving 1-inch headspace, 890. Process for 25 minutes (30 minutes for quarts) in a steam-pressure canner, 891.

CORN, WHOLE-KERNEL

Home-canned corn is crisp and sweet. Supersweet or underripe kernels may turn brown, but this is not harmful. Remove the husks and silks. Wash the corn. Drop into boiling water and boil for 3 minutes. Cut the kernels from the cobs at about three-quarters the depth of the kernels. Do not scrape the cob—the cob material will cloud the jars and add starch that can create a food safety hazard.

In a pan, mix 1 cup boiling water (salted to taste) with every 4 cups kernels and bring to a boil. Simmer for 5 minutes. Pack the hot kernels into hot jars and add the boiling cooking liquid, leaving 1-inch headspace, 890. Process for 55 minutes (1 hour 25 minutes for quarts) in a steam-pressure canner, 891.

CORN, CREAM-STYLE

Only use pint jars or smaller, because the mixture is so dense.

Remove the silks and husks and wash the corn. Drop into boiling water and boil for 4 minutes. Cut the kernels

from the cobs at half the depth of the kernels. Scrape off the remaining kernels and "milk" with a table knife, but do not include any cob material.

In a pan, mix half as much boiling salted water as corn and scrapings. Bring to a boil, stirring. Ladle the hot mixture into hot jars, leaving 1-inch headspace, 890. Process half-pints (only) for 1 hour 25 minutes in a steam-pressure canner, 891.

GREENS

The flavor of canned greens is true but the texture soft, making them perfect for soups. A mix gives best results.

Select freshly harvested crisp, very thick leaves. Wash. Cut off any roots, tough ribs, and stems; leave tender ribs and stems. Drop about 2 quarts at a time into a blanching basket or colander in boiling water—handle with long tongs—and boil until well wilted, 3 to 5 minutes. Loosely drop the drained leaves into hot jars, adding 1/4 teaspoon each citric acid and salt per quart. Add fresh boiling water, leaving 1-inch headspace, 890. Process for 1 hour 10 minutes (1 1/2 hours for quarts) in a steam-pressure canner, 891.

MUSHROOMS

This method produces delicious canned mushrooms. **Caution: Do not can wild mushrooms!** Use only pint jars or smaller.

Select unblemished 1- to 1 1/2-inch in diameter commercial mushrooms heavy for their size, with tightly closed caps. Trim off the stems flush with the caps. Soak the caps in cold water for 10 minutes. Wash in fresh water. Cover with cold water and boil gently for 5 minutes. Pack the hot mushrooms into hot jars, adding 1 crushed 500-mg vitamin C tablet (ascorbic acid) and 1/4 teaspoon salt per pint. Add fresh boiling water, leaving 1-inch headspace, 890. Process half-pints or pints (only) for 45 minutes in a steam-pressure canner, 891.

OKRA

Canned whole okra pods are soft but not slimy, and the flavor is excellent.

Select young, tender pods. Wash and leave whole. Boil gently for 2 minutes. Pack the hot pods upright into hot jars and add the hot cooking liquid, leaving 1-inch headspace, 890. Process for 25 minutes (40 minutes for quarts) in a steam-pressure canner, 891.

ONIONS, BOILING/PEARL

The texture of canned onions is soft, but the flavor is good. Lightly brown in oil before serving—but never before canning.

Select sweet onions of uniform size, up to 1 inch in diameter. Wash and peel, cutting a shallow X in the base of each. Boil gently for 5 minutes. Pack the hot onions into hot jars and add the boiling cooking liquid, leaving 1-inch headspace, 890. Process for 40 minutes in a steam-pressure canner, 891.

PEAS, GREEN
Use pint jars or smaller, or the peas will overcook.

Using young, tender small to medium sweet peas. Shell as for fresh beans and peas, but bring to a rolling boil and boil for 2 minutes. Pack as for fresh beans and peas, leaving 1-inch headspace, 890.

Process for 40 minutes in a steam-pressure canner, 891.

PEPPERS
Can only peppers with extra-thick walls—the rest are too soft. Use only pint jars or smaller.

Select crisp, meaty peppers of any color. Wash, roast, 292, and peel the peppers. Remove the cores and seeds. Leave small peppers whole, slashing twice lengthwise with a knife. Quarter or flatten large peppers. Fit the peppers into hot jars, adding $1/4$ teaspoon salt per pint. Add boiling water, leaving 1-inch headspace, 890. Process half-pints and pints (only) for 35 minutes in a steam-pressure canner, 891.

POTATOES
Canned potatoes are firm and sweet.

Select firm, new waxy potatoes. Leave whole if up to 1 inch in diameter, or cut larger potatoes in half. Wash, peel, and wash again. Cut if desired. Gently boil $1/2$-inch pieces for 2 minutes; boil larger pieces and whole potatoes for 10 minutes. Pack the hot potatoes into hot jars. Add salt to taste and fresh boiling water, leaving 1-inch headspace, 890. Process for 35 minutes (40 minutes for quarts) in a steam-pressure canner, 891.

Note: Potatoes stored below 45°F may discolor in jars, but this is harmless.

POTATOES, SWEET
Caution: Do not mash or puree pieces, or the product may be unsafe to eat.

Select tubers up to 2 inches wide, with waxy flesh (left whole, 3 to 4 will fit in a quart jar). Prepare 20-percent sugar syrup, 893. Wash the potatoes. Boil gently, or steam until the skins loosen, about 15 minutes. Peel. Fit the hot sweet potatoes into hot quart jars, adding $1/2$ teaspoon salt. Add the boiling syrup, leaving 1-inch headspace, 890. Process for $1^1/2$ hours in a steam-pressure canner, 891.

SQUASH, WINTER AND PUMPKIN
Can only cubed squash. Do not mash or puree before canning. Serve mashed with butter and nutmeg.

Select small squashes or pumpkins with hard rinds and sweet, dry, thick, fine-grained (not stringy) flesh. Wash and peel. Cut crosswise into 1-inch slices. Remove the seeds and fibers, then cut into 1-inch cubes. Boil gently for 2 minutes. Pack the hot squash into hot jars, and add boil-

ing cooking liquid, leaving 1-inch headspace, 890. Process for 55 minutes ($1^1/2$ hours for quarts) in a steam-pressure canner, 891.

SUCCOTASH
This traditional American dish cans well. The tomato is optional.

Use freshly shelled lima beans and freshly cut whole corn kernels (and, if desired, tomatoes as directed for crushing, 898), and prepare as directed for each vegetable, 900. In a pan, combine 4 parts lima beans, 3 parts corn, and, if using, 2 parts crushed tomatoes. Boil gently for 5 minutes. Pack the hot mixture into hot jars and add the boiling cooking liquid, leaving 1-inch headspace, 890. Process for 1 hour (1 hour 25 minutes for quarts) in a steam-pressure canner, 891.

TURNIPS
Sweet, crisp young turnips remain tasty and firm when canned. Superior canning varieties are Market Express, Purple Top White Globe, and Tokyo Cross.

Select tender young turnips no more than 3 inches in diameter. Wash thoroughly and peel. Cut into 1-inch cubes, or slice. Boil gently for 5 minutes. Pack the hot turnips into hot jars and add the boiling cooking liquid, leaving 1-inch headspace, 890. Process for 30 minutes (35 minutes for quarts) in a steam-pressure canner, 891.

ABOUT CANNING MEAT, POULTRY, GAME, AND FISH

The canning of meats, poultry, and game at home can be both a safe and more convenient procedure than the old-fashioned methods of preservation by salting and smoking. However, most people prefer freezing as an even more satisfactory method. Freezing is also the recommended alternative for preserving fish and for better retention of flavor and food value. For safe serving of home-canned meat products, process all these foods in a steam-pressure canner. Make sure that the temperature reaches at least 240°F during processing, using an accurate gauge on your pressure canner, and making any necessary altitude adjustments, 891.

It is best to can only fresh, not brined or salted, meats. For brined or salted meats, smoking is a more satisfactory method of preserving than canning. To butcher meat for canning, see About Preparing Game, 523.

As the packing of cooked meats involves cooking them first and processing them the same length of time as for raw-packed meats, we prefer the raw-pack method. ➤ Please read the directions for safe and proper canning. To **raw-pack fresh meats and poultry,** first prepare the jars, 890. Cut the meat from the bones. (Use the bones and scraps to prepare Stock, 114.) For chicken, separate the pieces at the joints. ➤ Trim the fat carefully from both meats and poultry, as it could cause the meat to have a strong flavor after canning. ➤ Do not soak the meat. Cut meats against the grain into 1-inch strips or chunks. Pack into the hot prepared jars. ➤ Do not add liquid. ➤ Never use a thickened gravy, as it is unsafe for the canning process. You may add 1 teaspoon salt to each quart for seasoning. Allow 1-inch headspace for meat pieces and 1¼-inch headspace for poultry, 890. Wipe off the tops and threads of jars before applying lids. Process in a dial-gauge steam-pressure canner at 11 pounds pressure or in a weighted-gauge pressure canner at 10 pounds pressure if you live below 1,000 feet altitude. ➤ Adjust for higher altitudes, see 891. Process 1 hour 15 minutes for pints, 1½ hours for quarts. Let the canner cool to 0 pounds pressure naturally, 891. To remove the jars from the canner, cool, test the seals, and store, see 892.

Liquids cook out of meat and poultry during processing. Sometimes there is not enough after processing and some pieces are no longer covered by liquid. These pieces may darken and dry out somewhat in storage, so use those jars first.

PRECOOKING AND PACKING MEATS AND POULTRY FOR CANNING

Roast or ground meat browned loosely or shaped into patties, links, or small meatballs may be canned. Use beef, veal, lamb, pork, goat, bear, or venison.

To **hot-pack fresh meats,** roast in a preheated oven 350°F. Cut the meat into pieces about 1 pound each. Remove the bones, gristle, and all surface fat. Place in uncovered roasting pans and roast until the red or pink color of the meat has almost disappeared in the center, 20 to 40 minutes. Cut the meat into pieces small enough to fit the jars. ➤ Pack tightly, while still hot, into prepared hot jars. ➤ Skim the fat from the drippings if using in covering liquid for jars. Add enough boiling water or stock to the drippings to cover the meat in the jars, leaving 1-inch headspace, 890. ➤ Never use a thickened gravy. Remove any trapped air, 890, adjust the liquid level if needed, and ➤ wipe off the tops and threads of jars, being careful to remove any fat. Adjust the lids and process in a dial-gauge pressure canner at 11 pounds pressure or in a weighted-gauge pressure canner at 10 pounds pressure if you live below 1,000 feet altitude. ➤ To adjust for higher altitudes, see 891. Process 1 hour 15 minutes for pints, 1½ hours for quarts. ➤ Let the canner cool to 0 pounds pressure naturally, 891. To remove the jars from the canner, cool, test the seals, and store, see 892.

To stew meat, cut into uniform pieces, drop into boiling water, and simmer 12 to 20 minutes, or until the raw color has disappeared at the center. Tongue should be simmered about 45 minutes, or until the skin can be removed. After stewing, cut the meat into smaller pieces. Remove the fat and gristle, then pack tightly in jars and cover with the boiling broth, leaving 1-inch headspace. You may add 1 to 2 teaspoons salt to each quart jar for seasoning. Remove air bubbles, 890, and wipe the jar rims carefully.

Pint jars are preferable to larger jars to ensure the heat penetrates more readily to the center of the food.

Ground meats or sausage may be shaped into small patties or balls; cased sausage links should be 3 to 4 inches long. Cook until lightly browned. Ground meat may also be sautéed without shaping. Remove excess fat after precooking these ground meats. Hot-pack, as above.

Adjust the lids and process in a dial-gauge pressure canner at 11 pounds pressure or in a weighted-gauge pressure canner at 10 pounds pressure if you live below 1,000 feet altitude. ➤ To adjust for higher altitudes, see 891. Process 1 hour 15 minutes for pints, 1½ hours for quarts. ➤ Let the canner cool to 0 pounds pressure naturally, 891. To remove the jars from the canner, cool, test the seals, and store, see 892.

To precook chicken, simmer meaty pieces, with fat removed, in stock or broth until medium done. Fill the prepared hot jars with the pieces and cover with boiling broth, leaving 1¼-inch headspace, 890. You may add 1 to 2 teaspoons salt to each quart jar for seasoning. Remove air bubbles, 890, and wipe the jar rims carefully.

Adjust the lids and process in a dial-gauge pressure canner at 11 pounds pressure or in a weighted-gauge pressure canner at 10 pounds pressure if you live below 1,000 feet altitude. ➤ To adjust for higher altitudes, see 891. ➤ **For chicken with bones,** process 65 minutes for pints, 1 hour 15 minutes for quarts. ➤ **For chicken without bones,** process 1 hour 15 minutes for pints, 1½ hours for quarts. Gizzards and hearts may be canned together, in boiling chicken broth to cover, but should be packed separate from the meat. Process in pint jars for 1 hour 15 minutes. ➤ Let the canner cool to 0 pounds pressure naturally, 891. To remove the jars from canner, cool, test the seals, and store, see 892.

MINCEMEAT

This is enough filling for 20 pies. Some of our fans make this recipe for Christmas gifts. It is best if prepared at least 2 weeks before using. Please read the directions for safe and proper canning, 888–893.
Prepare:
9 quarts sliced peeled and cored apples
Combine in a large pot with:
4 pounds lean beef, chopped
2 pounds beef suet, chopped
3 pounds (7 cups) sugar
2 quarts apple cider
4 pounds raisins
3 pounds dried currants
1½ pounds candied citron, chopped
8 ounces candied orange peel, chopped
8 ounces candied lemon peel, chopped
Grated zest and juice of 1 lemon
1 tablespoon ground cinnamon
1 tablespoon ground mace

1 tablespoon ground cloves
1 teaspoon salt
1 teaspoon black pepper
2 whole nutmeg, grated
4 quarts sour cherries, with their juice
1 pound nuts, broken or chopped
(1 teaspoon ground coriander)

Simmer ingredients about 2 hours, stirring frequently to prevent scorching. Ladle into prepared hot quart jars, 890, allowing 1/2-inch headspace, 890. Remove any trapped air, 890, adjust the headspace if needed, and wipe off the tops and threads of jars. Adjust the lids and process in a dial-gauge pressure canner at 11 pounds pressure or in a weighted-gauge pressure canner at 10 pounds pressure if you live below 1,000 feet altitude. To adjust for higher altitudes, see 891. Process 1 1/2 hours. Let the canner cool to 0 pounds pressure naturally, 891. To remove the jars from the canner, cool, test the seals, and store, see 892. Before serving, season with:

Brandy

ABOUT SAUSAGE MAKING

There are three main types of sausage: fresh, or country; cooked, lightly cured; and, partially dried, or dry, sausage—all described more fully on 515. The preparation for all three types requires using the freshest meat or game combinations and preferably hard fatback when called for. Best flavor results from grinders with blades that cut and chop rather than grind and crush, as a typical home meat grinder does. Special grinders to do the job are available through specialty stores such as butchers' supply houses and catalogs and food-service equipment suppliers, as well as the Internet. If you plan to make sausage regularly, or in any volume, invest in an electric machine. Butchers' supply sources and specialty catalogs are also the place to find hand or electric stuffers and sausage casings, unless you live in an area where they may be sold in grocery stores.

For home use, we do not recommend plastic casings because they are impervious to moisture and may allow the growth of hazardous bacteria. ➤ To avoid trichinosis, a parasitic infection, see 523.

Natural casings made from hog, sheep, or cattle intestines are preferred because they are edible. More important, they shrink during smoking and adhere to the meat as it dehydrates. Hog casings, which are usually preferred by the home sausage maker, are very permeable to smoke and moisture. They work very well for Polish and breakfast-type sausages. Fibrous casings are stronger and more suitable for summer sausage and similar products. Collagen casings have the benefits of both natural and fibrous casings and are ready to slide onto a stuffer. They are primarily for products like fresh pork sausage and pepperoni sticks. They are permeable and will shrink, so they can be used for dry sausages.

Casings come in different diameters for different sausage products, usually from 1 to 4 inches around. Smaller ones are good for link sausages, while larger ones are suitable for bolognas, salami, and luncheon loaves.

If natural casings come dry-salted, the salt must be flushed away before they are used. If the casings come in a brine, they do not need desalting and washing. ➤ All casings should be kept refrigerated until ready to use. Do not freeze unless the manufacturer states that it will not harm the casings. Follow the manufacturer's directions for desalting the casings, or use the following procedure. Handle the casings with great care, as they are very long and tangle easily. ➤ Separate the bundles of casing and soak in lukewarm water at least 30 minutes. Then run cold water through each unraveled casing to remove excess salt.

Fibrous casings should be soaked before using for at least 30 minutes, or up to, but no longer than, 4 hours in 80° to 100°F water. If your fibrous casings do not come "pre-stuck," puncture with a knife point or pin to prevent air pockets in the finished sausage.

Throughout the sausage-making processes, ingredients must be kept chilled for safety and quality. Wash your hands before beginning and after each task. Start with clean equipment and be sure all surfaces that will be in contact with ingredients are clean. Sanitize surfaces and equipment before and after work with a solution of 1 tablespoon chlorine bleach per gallon of water. Allow to air-dry. Any marination of meats should be done in the refrigerator.

Keep meat as cold as possible during grinding and mixing. ➤ Work in small batches, up to 25 pounds, for even distribution of ingredients, unless you have special large-volume equipment. The usual procedure is to grind the meats to the desired consistency, mix in the other ingredients, and then perform a final grind to distribute everything evenly. Successful filling depends on the consistency of the sausage mix. If it seems dry, work a little wine or water into the seasoned chopped meat.

Not all sausage has to be stuffed; it can also be formed into patties or left in bulk. If stuffing, the trick is to keep air from being trapped in the casings. In forcing air out, continuous gentle handling is necessary to avoid too much tension and formation of kinking as the casings fill.

Slip the open end of the casing onto the horn of the stuffer. Put some meat through the stuffing horn until it is filled. After forcing just a little meat from the end of the horn, pull 1 or 2 inches of casing over the end and knot it. Continue filling the casing to the desired lengths. If you will be twisting the casing to tie off links, you need to fill a little loosely and allow enough space for twisting without breaking the casing. Links may also be formed by tying the casing with clean cotton butcher or kitchen string as you fill each link. Make the final tie so tight that some of the meat is forced out of the end.

If you will be smoking your links, cut the last tie, leaving enough extra string to make a loop for hanging. Stuffed sausages may be kept refrigerated for use as fresh sausage, smoked uncooked, or smoked and cooked before refrigerating. Dry-cured sausage does not require refrigeration.

DRY SUMMER SAUSAGE

A great favorite in hot climates. Though it is made in winter, is called summer sausage because it holds over through the next spring and summer.
Cut into 2-inch cubes:

6 pounds boneless beef chuck
2 pounds boneless lean pork

Soak the meat in a 10-percent brine, 962, in a glass, enamel, or stone crock. Weight the meat with a plate held in place with a clean brick or stone, making sure the meat is continually covered with brine. Keep refrigerated at 35°F, stirring every 2 or 3 days.

Remove the meat after 8 to 12 days. Rinse briefly in cold water, dry, and refrigerate at 35°F on a stainless mesh rack. After 4 more hours, when the meat is well dried and chilled, cut into pieces that will fit your grinder. Add to the ground meat and grind again:

2 pounds hard fatback

Season with:

3 tablespoons salt
$\frac{1}{2}$ teaspoon ground cloves
1 teaspoon ground ginger
1 teaspoon grated or ground nutmeg
1 teaspoon ground coriander
2 teaspoons white pepper
2 cups dry red wine or water

To stuff, hang, smoke, and age, see Sausage Making, 903.

ABOUT BRINING AND DRY-CURING MEAT, GAME, AND POULTRY

There are two chief ways to salt meats at home: brining, see Corned Beef, below, and dry-curing. When meat is soaked in a brine, the temperature must be very carefully controlled to prevent foodborne disease. Dry-cured meats are more tolerant of fluctuating temperatures during processing than those treated with brine. Ideally, the curing and storing of meats should take place at 36° to 38°F. A mixture of curing ingredients, such as salt, sugar, and sodium nitrite and/or nitrate, is added and the meat is cured for days in this mixture.

DRY-CURED HAM

To dry-cure, allow the meat to cool as rapidly as possible after butchering. Carcasses should be chilled to 40°F or below before being cut. That temperature should be maintained until time of purchase or use. Rub the meat with the following salt-cure mixture, being sure to coat the entire surface well. Put the rubbed meat into a sterilized crock, being careful not to disturb the salt coating. Cover with a loose-fitting lid or cheesecloth.

For every 10 pounds of meat, make a mixture of:

1 cup salt
$\frac{1}{4}$ cup sugar
2 teaspoons Prague Powder No. 2 or Instacure No. 2

with:

(2 bay leaves)
(2 coriander seeds)
(3 whole cloves)
(6 black peppercorns)

crushed in a mortar.

To ensure effective salt-penetration, cure the salted meat for $1\frac{1}{2}$ days per pound of meat. Do not let the temperature go below 36°F, or it will slow the curing process; do not let the temperature go above 40°F, or the meat could sour. It is best to remain between 36° and 38°F. After 7 days, turn the meat. If it is no longer completely covered with the salt, apply a second application. Be sure to write down the dates when the meat is placed in the cure and when it should be turned as well as removed from the cure.

When the prescribed time is up, the meat should be placed in clean cold water, more than 70°F for 1 hour to dissolve surface salts and make it receptive to smoking. Scrub well and then dry for at least 14 days at 50° to 60°F to allow the cure to equalize. Smoking gives that wonderful "country" taste to dry-cured and brined foods. If it is not to be smoked, wrap each piece of meat individually, first in clean muslin, then in layers of heavy paper. Hang in a cool, well-ventilated room. Age ham for 45 to 180 days at 75° to 95°F and a relative humidity of 55 to 65%. Use an exhaust fan to limit mold growth and prevent excessive drying.

CORNED BEEF

This salted beef has nothing to do with corn but got its name in Anglo-Saxon times when a granular salt the size of a kernel of wheat—"corn" to a Briton—was used to process it.
To corn, combine, stirring to dissolve the salt and sugar:

4 quarts hot water
2 cups coarse salt
$\frac{1}{4}$ cup sugar
2 tablespoons pickling spices
$1\frac{1}{2}$ teaspoons Prague Powder No. 2 or Instacure No. 2

Let cool, then pour over:

One 5-pound piece of beef brisket or tongue

in a deep enameled pot or stoneware jar. Add:

3 garlic cloves

Weight the meat to keep it submerged, and cover the pot. Cure in the refrigerator 3 weeks, turning the meat every 5 days. To cook corned beef, see 484.

SALT (OR PICKLED) PORK

Known as white bacon in some parts of the country, salt pork may be sliced and used as bacon, but it is more often used for seasoning vegetables or for larding roasts.

Please read About Pickling Equipment, 943. Cut into pieces 6 inches square:

Fatback or other thin pieces of pork fat

Rub each square well all over with:

Pickling salt, 1009

Pack the salted pork tightly into a sterilized crock and let stand 12 hours in the refrigerator.

For each 25 pounds of meat, mix the following brine:

2¹⁄₂ pounds kosher salt
¹⁄₂ ounce Prague Powder No. 2 or Instacure No. 2
4 quarts boiling water

Let cool completely, then pour the brine over the meat to cover. Refrigerate the pork, weighted and covered at 35° to 38°F, until ready to use. Use within 3 weeks.

JERKY

Use jerky when backpacking or for high-protein snacking. This chewy, well-flavored item is a great extravagance, for you will end up with only ¹⁄₄ to ¹⁄₃ by weight of the amount of meat you started with. Good cuts of meat to use for jerky include round or flank steak, rump roast, brisket, and cross rib. Highly marbled and fatty cuts of meat will not dry as well and cause flavor problems.

Raw meats can be contaminated with microorganisms that cause disease. For safe handling of meat and poultry, wash your hands and equipment well before starting. Keep meat and poultry refrigerated until ready to begin. If thawing frozen meat, do so in the refrigerator, not on the counter. Pork or wild game should be treated to kill the Trichinella parasite before it is sliced and marinated. Freeze the meats in pieces that are 6 inches thick or less at 0°F or below for at least 30 days.

There have been several notable outbreaks involving *Salmonella* and *E. coli* O157:H7 bacteria in home-dried jerky. ➤ The risk can be decreased by allowing the internal temperature of the meat to reach 160°F, but it is important to do it in such a way as to prevent case-hardening; see 908. Two methods can be used: heating the meat strips in marinade before drying or heating the dried jerky strips in an oven after the drying process is completed. When the strips are heated in a marinade before drying, the jerky is different from what most people are used to. Both methods require the use of an instant-read thermometer to ensure safety. An electric dehydrator with an adjustable thermostat is preferred for drying jerky at home.

Preheat the oven or a food dehydrator to at least 140°F for at least 15 minutes. Slice lean meat on the bias into strips 6 inches long, 3 inches wide, and ¹⁄₈ to ➤ no more than ¹⁄₄ inch thick. Cutting across the grain makes the jerky easier to chew or reconstitute in stews. Partially freezing the meat ahead of time makes it easier to slice. Cut away pieces of fat and any muscle membrane left on the meat.

The meat strips may be seasoned with salt or pepper or marinated. Marinating may take from 1 to 24 hours and

should be done in the refrigerator. If they have been marinated, drain the meat strips on clean paper towels before placing on racks.

If heating jerky in the marinade prior to drying, bring the strips and marinade to a boil after marination. Boil for 5 minutes before draining the strips again, as above. ➤ It is important that the meat strips reach at least 160°F before draining. ➤ If you do not do this step, you will need to heat the dried jerky strips in an oven after drying (see below).

Place the drained strips in single layers on drying racks so the pieces do not touch each other. Dry the meat on racks in the oven or dehydrator for 10 to 14 hours, until the pieces are dry enough to crack but not break when bent. ➤ The jerky must be very dry, or bacteria will grow. Let it cool slightly before testing by bending. When it is dry enough, cool completely, pat off the surface oil with clean paper towels, and store in a cool area.

If the meat strips were not heated in a marinade before drying, heat the dried jerky in an oven preheated to 275°F before packaging. Place the jerky on a baking sheet so the pieces do not touch or overlap. ➤ Heat the jerky until the strips reach at least 160°F. For strips originally cut ¹⁄₄ inch or less, this should take 10 minutes. After the strips cool, pat off the surface oil with clean paper towels again if needed.

Store jerky in airtight freezer-weight plastic bags or a jar with a tight-fitting lid. Vacuum-packing works well because ➤ the more air left in the storage container, the more off flavors and rancidity will occur. Be sure to label and date your packages. Store in a cool, dry, dark place, or refrigerate or freeze for longest storage. ➤ Properly dried jerky will keep only about 2 weeks at cool room temperature, 3 months in the refrigerator, and up to 1 year in the freezer. ➤ If any mold forms, discard the package of jerky.

PREPARING ROE FOR CAVIAR

Remove from very fresh fish as soon as possible:

Roe

Tear the egg masses into small pieces. Work them through a ¹⁄₄-inch or finer sieve to free the eggs from the membrane. Place them for 15 to 20 minutes in a cold-water brine made of:

1 cup plus 2 tablespoons pickling salt, 1008,
per quart of cold water

If you use a salinometer, the reading should be 28.3. There should be twice as much brine as roe in volume. Remove from the liquid and drain thoroughly in a strainer for about 1 hour; keep refrigerated during this operation.

Place the drained roe in an airtight nonmetal container and store at 34°F for 1 to 2 months. Remove, drain, repack, and store at 0°F in the freezer until ready to use.

ABOUT SMOKING FOOD

Smoking is a method of heating food indirectly in the presence of a fire. Smoking can be done in a covered grill or in a "smoker," a specialized piece of outdoor equipment.

For instructions on how to build an indirect fire in a grill, see 1057. Follow the manufacturer's directions for using a gas or electric outdoor smoker. The most satisfactory smoke flavor is obtained by using mesquite, oak, hickory, maple, apple, or other fruitwood, or any other hardwood. ➤ Never use green or resinous wood. Soak the chips in water to prevent flare-ups.

Food may be either cold-smoked or hot-smoked. **Cold-smoking** will preserve food if combined with brining or curing of the meat before smoking. It does not cook food and is unsafe without prior curing. Cold-smoking is fundamentally a drying process in which brined foods, 904, such as meat, game, poultry, or wildfowl are smoked for anywhere from 24 hours to as long as 3 weeks. Smoking time depends on the size of the food being processed and the steadiness of the temperature in the smoking chamber. ➤ Cold-smoking is done at low temperatures, at least 80°F but rarely exceeding 90° to 100°F. Because these temperatures are in the zone where bacteria grow best, cold-smoking should only be used with meats that are cured. To prepare cured meat for any smoking process, first dry out under refrigeration and wipe the surface dry. Dry-cured hams should be hung for at least 14 days in temperatures between 50° and 60°F to allow the cure to equalize before smoking. Individual taste and final moisture content determine how long to smoke meats, but general guidelines suggest up to 72 hours for a ham, 60 hours for a pork shoulder, and 45 hours for a thinner piece of meat like bacon. Food has been sufficiently smoked if it has lost at least one-quarter of its weight during the process; country hams will have an even lower final moisture content, and a 35 percent shrinkage in weight is common for these hams. Because food safety must be carefully managed when cold-smoking at these temperatures, careful monitoring of temperatures and moisture loss by weight is essential. It should be done in a carefully managed smokehouse or smoker with a thermometer to measure the temperature inside the unit.

After cold-smoking and then hanging until cool in a room or area with temperatures not exceeding 60°F (for large pieces this sometimes takes a week or longer, depending on weather), the food is ready for storing. Should any salt crystals have accumulated on the surface, wipe them off, as this crystallization will attract moisture and cause spoilage. Dry-cured sausage will continue to lose moisture unless covered. If you intend to eat the sausage right away, a loose plastic bag will do. For longer storage, it should be vacuum-sealed and refrigerated.

Unlike cold-smoking, **hot-smoking,** which cooks the food, does not produce enough drying to ensure safe storage or preservation qualities. Hot-smoking is done much more slowly and at a lower temperature than grilling. Less tender cuts of meat such as pork shoulder, beef brisket, or spareribs benefit from a long, slow cooking time and the natural smoke flavor that permeates the meat. Hot-smoking may be done for as short a time as 2 or 3 hours,

or for as long as 10 hours, depending on the type and size of the food being smoked. ➤ A general guideline is 1 to 1½ hours in the smoker per pound of meat. Hot-smoking usually involves a smoker temperature of 225° to 300°F. A thermometer for measuring the temperature inside the smoker is important to ensure that this temperature range is maintained. ➤ Meat and poultry need to be cooked to a safe internal temperature, see 423. Use a food thermometer to check the internal temperature.

After hot-smoking, the food should be eaten at once. If it is not to be served immediately, the food should be cut into smaller portions or chunks and refrigerated without delay. Discard any hot-smoked food that is left out of refrigeration for more than 2 hours, or for more than 1 hour if the ambient temperature is above 90°F. Use refrigerated smoked meat and poultry within 4 days. If you plan to use the product at a later time, freeze at 0°F after cooling and packaging for freezer storage.

PASTRAMI

To convert Corned Beef, 904, to pastrami, the meat must be smoked.

You may also wish to experiment with a more elaborate marinade, substituting **2 quarts red wine vinegar** for half the water and adding one or more of the following:

> **(2 tablespoon ground ginger)**
> **(1 tablespoon ground coriander)**
> **(1 tablespoon paprika)**
> **(1 teaspoon black pepper)**

After marination, commercial pastrami is cooked entirely by hot-smoking, at 320°F for 6 to 7 hours. Because the relatively high heat required is hard to maintain in domestic appliances, we have a friend who produces pastrami by attaching the marinated meat to a continuously revolving rotisserie and smoking it outdoors over his barbecue grill, using plenty of charcoal and oak and hickory chips. This procedure takes about 10 hours.

SMOKING FOWL AND COOKING SMOKED FOWL

To prepare wild game birds for smoking, bleed, cool rapidly and pluck, clean, 453, and rinse quickly but thoroughly in running cold water.

Dry-cure, 904, or prepare a basic brine of 1 pound brown sugar, 2 pounds noniodized salt, and 3 gallons water. Chicken and game birds should be steeped in the brine 24 to 48 hours, depending on size; ducks and geese for about 3 days; and a 12- to 20-pound turkey for 5 days. Cover the brining bird(s) with a weighted plate and keep refrigerated, checking during the process to make sure they are brine-covered at all times.

After curing or brining, soak the poultry in fresh cold water for 30 minutes to 2 hours. Wipe well, and further dry by hanging for at least 3 hours in a 38°F temperature.

If you wish to serve the fowl at once, roast in a preheated 350°F oven for about three-quarters of the usual roasting time, then remove to a smoker and flavor by hot-smoking at 225°F until the skin takes on a pleasing rich color. The meat will retain a certain redness; it is done when with a gentle twisting you can turn the leg of the fowl in the socket and the thickest part of the meat has reached an internal temperature of at least 165°F. Birds to be cold-smoked must be brined first; see 904. After smoking and before the final cooking, they should be steamed for about 10 minutes to remove excess salt.

Smoked poultry must be refrigerated. It will keep for 3 to 4 weeks at 35° to 40°F. Discard if mold develops. Although not our favorite recommendation, smoked poultry may be frozen up to 6 months, after that, you may get a stale, off flavor.

SMOKING FISH

Like meat, poultry, wild fowl, and game, fish smoked without following proper salting and cooking procedures can be the source of foodborne disease, including the possibly deadly botulism. To safely store smoked fish without refrigeration, you must: heat the fish to at least 160°F internal temperature maintained for at least 30 minutes, and then salt or brine the fish long enough to make sure there is enough salt content in the finished product. ➤ Use fresh fish with a high fat or oil content for smoking. Small fish under 3 pounds should be headed and gutted after cleaning, 394, before brining. Fish over 3 pounds are best filleted, 394, with the skin left on. Clean all fish thoroughly, removing blood, slime, and harmful bacteria. ➤ Even, uniform-sized pieces of fish will help ensure more even salt absorption during brining. Keep the fish as cool as possible, but only freeze once. Thaw frozen fish in the refrigerator. ➤ Do not let more than 1 or 2 hours elapse after cleaning and before smoking.

Fish must first be brined before smoking, as for fowl, above. A basic brine of 1 cup salt to 7 cups water will salt 2 to 3 pounds of fish. Fish under 4 ounces need 30 minutes; from 1 to 2 pounds, 2 hours; and 4 to 5 pounds, 5 hours. Immediately after brining, rinse the fish quickly in cold water. Dry off carefully and then dry further, either hung or racked, in a minimum temperature of 38°F and, in any case, protected from insects. A smokehouse with low heat, 80° to 90°F, and no smoke, with the doors open, could be used for drying before smoking.

Place the fish or fillets ➤ on oiled racks, skin side down, during the entire smoking period. It is best to split small whole fish open down the belly and, before hanging them in the smoker, to insert small pointed clean wooden wedges into the chest cavity to keep it and the split edges below from touching and closing off circulation as the fish smokes. Cook the fish to at least 160°F for at least a 30-minute period sometime during the smoking process, which should provide 200° to 225°F oven temperatures. A typical process should bring the fish to over 160°F internal temperature within 6 to 8 hours. It is best to wait 3 to 5 hours before elevating the fish to the 160°F internal

temperature, as it is easier after much of the moisture is gone. Additional smoking and drying can be done after the 30 minutes at 160°F internal temperature. Always keep the fish temperature above 140°F to prevent growth of harmful bacteria. If your smokehouse cannot provide 200° to 225°F oven temperatures, the fish can be moved to a kitchen oven for the final cooking. In any case, never wait longer than 6 to 8 hours for the essential 30 minutes over 160°F internal temperature.

If you do not eat your fish immediately, it is essential to store it in the refrigerator at below 38°F. Mold growth can be retarded by packaging in a porous material such as cloth or paper towel that prevents sweating inside an airtight package. For storage longer than 2 weeks, tightly wrap or vacuum-pack and freeze.

ABOUT DRYING FOOD

Though it's an age-old custom, few climates lend themselves ideally to sun-drying food. Today's modern electric dehydrators provide a much more satisfactory environment for drying high-quality items. Many foods are more suited to canning and freezing for preservation, but when harvests are heavy, drying is an option for numerous choices. And when storage space is limited, dried foods demand only one-third to one-sixth as much space. Although there is some vitamin loss due to heat during drying, dried fruits that are eaten without moisture reconstitution have greater caloric value, weight for weight, than fresh or otherwise processed fruits. In order to prevent the growth of spoilage organisms, such as the bacteria, molds, and yeasts that are present in all foods, at least 80 percent of the water must be removed from fruit and about 90 percent from vegetables, which are less acidic. To dry herbs, see 991. Meat and fish require even greater moisture removal; see Jerky, 905.

Drying is accomplished by a combination of processes, such as recommended pretreatments of steam- or water-blanching, 1054; sulfuring, or pretreating with sulfiting compounds; and salting, 904, most often in the case of meats and fish, before final drying by the sun or other heat. Home methods rarely achieve the same texture as produced by commercial drying methods, in which spoilage and sometimes moisture content are also controlled by other means, such as sulfuring or additives.

Blanching, 1054, which stops enzymatic action, discourages oxidation changes during storage and ➤ is necessary for most vegetables; it is recommended for some fruits but is optional for most. We recommend blanching for best quality. Whether or not you blanch fruits, wash all produce well first in cold water. To remove coatings on fruits such as apricots, nectarines, plums, and blueberries, you may place the fruit in a colander and dip it into rapidly boiling water for about 35 seconds. This dipping should also be done for small fruits to be dried whole, such as blueberries, cherries, and grapes, to allow cracking of the skins and prevent case-hardening (described below) during drying. The blanching times given for freezing vegetables or fruits can be used to prepare for drying.

Drying needs to be done quickly enough to prevent spoilage organisms from growing during the process, but the heat of the dryer should rarely go over 140°F. The heating of food must not be so rapid that the outside of the food hardens in a way to inhibit the release of moisture from the center. This is known as **case-hardening,** and it can result in spoiled food during storage.

For the most consistent drying, purchase an electric dehydrator with a good fan to circulate air throughout the unit and a thermostat to set the air temperature. An electric or gas oven can be used if a temperature no higher than 140°F can be maintained with the door slightly open. It is possible to make your own drying cabinet, shown below, which includes a heat source, such as a hot plate, and venting.

Venting in the drying cabinet is provided by a 2-inch-wide, 12-inch-long screened slot near the top at the sides of the cabinet. In order to allow air intake at the base, the hinged door has a long 2-inch-high slot at the base. Line

Drying cabinet

the cabinet wall and door to the height of the food with aluminum building paper. Diffused heat is achieved by suspending a metal sheet on brackets as a lower shelf over the heating element as shown. In both oven and cabinet drying, keep the bottom tray of food 6 to 8 inches from the heat source. In both cases, also, a small electric fan outside the oven door or blowing past the cabinet intake vent at the base will help keep air circulating. Trays used in the regular oven or drying cabinet need to be racks of food-safe material, such as stainless steel screening, plastic or nylon mesh, or cake racks on cookie sheets. Finally, the dimensions of the trays should be 3 to 4 inches less than the interior of the oven or cabinet to allow for air circulation.

As in all food processing, drying demands the utmost attention to cleanliness and selection of high-quality produce, showing no signs of spoilage or decay. All foods should be cut or sliced as evenly and thinly as practical to hasten drying. Pieces should be loosely placed on the drying trays in single layers, without touching or overlapping. If drying outdoors, the sides of the trays should be at least

2 inches high so cheesecloth or sheeting can be used as a covering to protect from insects and airborne contaminants without touching the food.

Sun-drying should only be attempted with fruits, because of their acid content, and where a minimum temperature of 85°F with low humidity is achieved during the day. This process takes longer than an electric dehydrator because the fruit must be ➤ brought inside at sundown, as cool night air or dew will condense and add moisture back to the food. Special equipment for sun-drying can be fashioned with a glass cold frame to intensify the heat, as shown below.

Be sure to provide screening strips top and bottom for ventilation. The equipment itself should be light enough to be shifted during the day to catch the most sun, and the food on the trays should be turned every hour. With full sun, most foods should dry by this method in about 2 days—again, if the humidity is low. With any of these units, it is best to place a thermometer on the lowest rack to make sure the temperature does not exceed 140°F. If new loads of food are put in while other food is still drying, it is best to place them on the top rack, where the heat is apt to be less intense. ➤ No food should be dried outdoors in air-polluted areas.

Whether drying in an electric dehydrator, oven, or drying cabinet or outdoors, testing for doneness is a multi-staged affair. Let the pieces cool a little off the tray before testing. ➤ Fruits are considered dry enough when they are leathery and produce no moisture when cut and squeezed. If a piece is folded in half, it should not stick to itself. These will not be as moist as many dried fruits you buy, because additives, and sometimes sulfur dioxide, are used to protect them from spoilage with higher moisture contents. ➤ Vegetables are ready when they are brittle or crisp; they seemingly would shatter if hit with a hammer. They should rattle when stirred on the trays. When testing dryness, remove a few pieces and let them cool before making a final judgment.

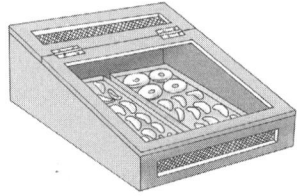

Cold frame

After drying to the appropriate doneness, condition fruits to distribute the remaining moisture evenly, as well as to make sure they are really dry enough for storage. Loosely pack the cooled, dry fruit in glass jars or plastic containers with tight lids. Let them stand at room temperature for 7 to 10 days. Shake daily to separate and mix the pieces. If condensation develops, keep the fruit in the refrigerator or return to the dehydrator and dry some more; it is too moist for long-term room storage.

Foods dried outdoors should also be pasteurized before storage. Preheat the oven to 160° to 175°F. Put the pieces in a single layer on baking sheets or in a shallow pan. Heat for 30 minutes. Cool the fruit on paper towels.

Package dried foods in plastic storage bags and then place in airtight containers, such as glass jars or freezer boxes. Heavy-duty plastic bags are acceptable but not as good for long-term storage and keeping moisture out. Label and date the containers. ➤ Dried fruits will keep for 4 to 12 months, depending on the amount of retained moisture, pretreatments, temperature, and exposure to light. Dried fruits generally keep longer than vegetables.

Many dried fruits make the perfect snack just out of the package. However, for many uses, you will want to reconstitute dried fruits first; see 907. To reconstitute most dried vegetables, cover with cold water until almost restored to their original texture. Use the soaking water to cook the vegetables. ➤ Don't soak greens; cover with boiling water and simmer until tender.

FRUIT LEATHER

Fruit leather is a sheet of pureed fruit that has been dried. Fresh fruits that make excellent leathers are apples, apricots, berries, sweet cherries, nectarines, peaches, pears, pineapples, and plums. An electric dehydrator is the easiest way to dry a fruit leather: Drying can also be done in the oven. Cover a drying tray or baking sheet with plastic freezer wrap, extending it over the edges. Make sure the baking sheet or tray has edges to prevent spilling the puree. Your electric dehydrator may come with special plastic liners for trays for making leathers. Keep in mind that fruit will become sweeter once it is dried. One cup puree will make 2 to 3 servings; 2 cups of puree will cover a 12- by 17-inch baking sheet.

Wash, peel, trim, and seed or pit:

Ripe or slightly overripe fruit

Place the fruit in a saucepan and cook, stirring, over low heat, until a candy thermometer registers 190°F.

Let cool thoroughly, then puree in a blender, food processor, or food mill; strain, if necessary to make a fine, smooth, fairly liquid puree. If the puree is very thick, thin it with:

Fruit juice

Add:

$\frac{1}{2}$ teaspoon ascorbic acid (vitamin C) or 2 tablespoons lemon juice per each 2 cups of fruit

If the fruit needs sweetening or additional flavor, add:

1 to 2 tablespoons corn syrup, honey, sugar, or lemon or orange juice per each 2 cups of fruit

Corn syrup prevents the formation of crystals, so it is best for long storage; artificial sweeteners can also be used. Spread the puree evenly on the tray, or baking sheet $\frac{1}{8}$ inch thick in the center and $\frac{1}{4}$ inch thick around the edges. Dry in the dehydrator or oven at 140°F. If using an oven, check the temperature periodically with an oven thermometer so it does not get too hot. If necessary, the oven can be turned off for short intervals to reduce the temperature.

Leathers take from 4 to 10 hours to dry; test frequently for dryness. The fruit is ready when the sheet is leathery and not sticky. Touch it in several places—there should be no indentation left. The leather should peel easily from the plastic wrap or tray liner. While it is still warm, roll up jelly-roll fashion in the plastic wrap. If desired, use scissors to cut the roll into serving pieces. Cool completely, then pack in airtight containers. Store in a cool, dark, dry place; for longer keeping, refrigerate or freeze.

DRYING CHILE PEPPERS

Chile peppers keep well when dried and are handy for use in many of your favorite dishes.

To dry green chile peppers, wash and dry. Wear gloves if necessary, and peel the peppers: Loosen the skins by cutting a slit in the skin of each and rotate over a gas flame for 6 to 8 minutes or broil, or scald in boiling water. Then peel and split the chiles; remove the seeds and stem. Place on dryer trays and dry in a dehydrator or on a baking sheet in the oven at 140°F until crisp, brittle, and medium green.

To dry red chile peppers, wash and dry. These peppers may be left whole if small; otherwise, slice. Blanch in boiling water for 4 minutes, if desired, to stop the rotting process. Place on dryer trays and dry in a dehydrator or oven at 140°F until shriveled, dark red, and a little flexible.

Drying peppers may take 12 to 24 hours. Cool dried peppers completely and pack in airtight containers. Store in a cool, dark, dry place.

DRYING TOMATOES

Steam or dip tomatoes in boiling water for 30 to 60 seconds so the skins will crack.

Immediately place in ice water to loosen the skins, and slip the peels off. Slice into $\frac{1}{2}$-inch-thick rounds. Dip for 10 minutes into a solution of:

1 teaspoon citric acid per each quart of water

Place on dryer trays and dry in a dehydrator or oven at 140°F until crisp. This may take 6 to 24 hours. Cool completely and pack in airtight containers.

FREEZING

Home freezing is a comparatively easy and time-saving method of food preservation, making it the most convenient type of short- and long-term preserving. However, those who simply toss any type of food into the freezer and expect excellent results most likely will be disappointed. ➤ High-quality food only comes out if high-quality food goes in. Other important factors also help determine the resulting quality. Foods to be frozen must be given ➤ quick, careful preparation. They must be ➤ sealed in moisture- and vapor-proof packaging and kept at ➤ a constant 0°F or lower temperature for best quality. Freezer temperatures that fluctuate above and back to 0°F or below will draw moisture from the food, resulting in loss of quality and nutritive value. Finally, of course, the food must be properly thawed and cooked.

Meats, fish, poultry, fruits, and precooked foods readily freeze. Vegetables, because of the need for blanching, require more time and attention during preparation. Even so, ➤ freezing can take a third to half the amount of time and labor involved in canning and a fresher flavor can be obtained in most foods by freezing instead of canning. The yields of produce preserved by either method are about the same; see 894, 899.

ENSURING QUALITY IN FROZEN FOOD

Quality cannot be created in the freezing process itself. Fruit should be ripe but still firm. Vegetables should be garden fresh, tender, young, and unwilted. It is best to freeze produce within hours of harvest, if not immediately. Because horticultural and crop scientists are frequently testing and researching the characteristics of fruit and vegetables to improve some aspect or another, if you are planning to freeze large quantities of food, ➤ it is best to consult your county agricultural extension agent about the best varieties to grow and buy in your locale.

The retention of nutritional values and flavors depends on the speed with which food is processed after harvesting. From then on, ➤ it must be kept at the coldest temperatures, so that enzymatic activities as well as microbial action are held to a minimum. Freezing halts the action of bacteria, molds, and yeasts only temporarily; when the food thaws and warms up again, these organisms can recover and be contaminants to worry about in the food again; see The Freezing Process, 911.

The economics of keeping a well-stocked freezer can be negated if it is used for miserly hoarding. Diligent planning and rotating of foods stored there is needed. Foods stored too long will lose their quality and eventually even their desirability. ➤ Avoid bargain frozen foods that have been kept a long time in the stores; they have already lost vitamins and flavor, and transferring them to your freezer will only create a loss of yet more quality. ➤ Even if you do not raise produce in your garden for preservation, you may profit when markets are glutted with fresh food specials.

Avoid practices that cause the temperatures in your freezer to warm up and damage the stored food. ➤ Neither overload your freezer, ➤ nor add more than 3 pounds food for each cubic foot of freezer space during any 24-hour period. If you are preparing a quantity of fresh foods to be frozen, the temperature control for the freezer should be put at the coldest setting several hours before loading the new foods. If necessary, cool the food before freezing. ➤ Until new packages of freshly prepared food are frozen, keep them on shelves in the coldest spot, as indicated by the freezer manufacturer. Do not stack unfrozen foods on top of each other; instead, spread them out until frozen and reorganize later if necessary.

Some foods simply do not hold up to freezing. For example, freezing will ruin gelatins, mayonnaise, and many meringues. Cooked pastas and rice, if frozen plain, will turn mushy and develop a warmed-over taste. Milk sauces may separate or even curdle, as will sour cream, custards, and cream fillings. Vegetables that have a very high water content will show a significant change in texture upon thawing, becoming quite limp and waterlogged. These include lettuce, celery, cabbage, cucumbers, endive, and radishes.

POWER OUTAGES

If you receive warning that a brownout or blackout is possible in your area, turn the freezer to its coldest setting. ➤ If it is not opened, a fully packed freezer will usually keep food safely frozen for about 2 days without electricity. Food in a half-full freezer may last for 1 day. In a sparsely filled freezer, quickly pack everything close together, then close the door and keep it closed.

If it appears the power will be off longer than the food will stay frozen, if possible, get some dry ice (look under

"Ice" in the Yellow Pages), which is carbon dioxide frozen to lower than –100°F. A 10-pound block will maintain 20 pounds of frozen food for 24 hours. Work quickly and safely with dry ice. Open windows and doors to let fumes escape as it goes in the freezer, wear superthick gloves to prevent frostbite (never touch dry ice with your bare hands), and wrap each piece in several thicknesses of newspaper. If the freezer isn't full, consolidate the packages, stacking them tightly and leaving space on top for the ice. Set heavy cardboard on top of the food and lay the ice on the cardboard. Close the door and cover the freezer with blankets or other insulation, but leave the freezer vents clear.

When the power comes back on, quickly check the food, without unwrapping it if possible. ➤ If the food is refrigerated-cold (40°F or lower) or if you can feel or see ice crystals, see When to Refreeze, 914. ➤ If the food is at room temperature and you do not know whether it has been that warm for more than 2 hours, discard it without tasting. Low-acid foods in particular can smell fine but be harboring dangerous organisms. When discarding potentially dangerous food, wrap it so no person or animal can ingest it.

THE FREEZING PROCESS
Food freezes in a sort of chain reaction. The water in the open spaces between cells freezes first. Next, these frozen sections pull water out of the cells, and then that freezes. With less water to dilute them, salts and enzymes in the cells are so concentrated that they weaken membranes, and ice crystals form in the empty spaces in the cells. When food is frozen fast, the crystals that form, both in the cells and between them, are many and tiny. ➤ Tiny crystals do a minimum of damage to cell structure and result in thawed food with the finest texture. Sugar is added to uncooked fruit in freezing not just to sweeten it but to stiffen cell walls and to keep crystals small. When food is frozen slowly, on the other hand, large needlelike crystals form (this also happens when food is partially thawed and refrozen several times). Large crystals puncture membranes and cell walls and result in thawed food with a coarse texture. ➤ It is important to freeze food as fast as possible, but every food has its own freezing point. Pure water freezes at 32°F, but some foods do not freeze until they reach temperatures as low as 25°F.

It is important to remember that microorganisms are not destroyed by freezing the way they are in the canning process. Bacteria, molds, and yeasts are, for the most part, merely held at bay. Enzymes are not inactivated—they merely slow down (some activity continues even at –100°F), causing colors and vitamins to deteriorate. Enzymes are inactivated by boiling temperatures, however, which is why all vegetables and some fruits are heated to a boil before freezing. Unfortunately, it is not feasible to do this with other foods. While freezing does not destroy microorganisms, it can destroy other organisms. The parasite

in pork that causes trichinosis is killed if held at 5°F for 20 days, for example, and Japanese sushi chefs commonly freeze their fish at –4°F for 7 days, or in a blast freezer before serving, to destroy any parasites it might contain.

ABOUT FREEZERS
If buying a new freezer, choose it with regard to how much food you expect to store in it on average for the next twenty years, the amount of floor space you have available to accommodate it, and its cost both to purchase and to run. Most experts suggest allowing 6 cubic feet of space per person to be fed. On average, 1 cubic foot of usable space holds about 35 pounds of frozen food. A secondhand freezer can be a good investment if it was manufactured after January 1, 1993; this was the date after which freezers had to meet energy efficiency standards, making them less expensive to operate and friendlier to the environment. Following are the available freezer types. Make sure the freezer will maintain 0°F or less.

If you have the space, a **chest freezer** is the best choice. Chests hold more food per cubic foot, lose less cold air when opened, and cost less to purchase and to operate in the long run. Make sure the one you choose has lift-out or sliding baskets, and before you buy it, try lifting a package weighing 15 to 20 pounds—the weight of a holiday turkey—out from the bottom.

The most convenient to load and unload is an **upright freezer,** and it is the most economical in terms of floor space. But an upright freezer is also the most costly to purchase and to run, and each time the door is opened, a considerable amount of cold air is lost. The freezer section of a **refrigerator with a bottom freezer** may offer nearly half the space of the refrigerator section. It is more economical to run than one with a top freezer (cold air settles to the bottom, so less is lost when the door is opened), but drawers can be heavy to pull out when full. On average, a **refrigerator with a top freezer** gives about 40 percent as much freezer space as refrigerator space. Placement is convenient, especially for tall people, because you can easily see the contents.

A **side-by-side refrigerator-freezer** provides a little less than half as much freezer space as refrigerator space. In some models, the compartment is divided in two, so only half the freezer loses cold air when you add or remove an item. However, the narrow shape means it does not accommodate standard baking sheets and large platters, which can be a nuisance when tray freezing or quick-chilling pastry dough and other foods.

Because a **freezer compartment inside the refrigerator** lacks the insulation of a separate heavy door, this sort of freezer cannot provide adequate cold for long-term storing. However, these refrigerators are rarely seen today and should only be used as a last resort. Restrict the use of this type of freezer compartment to ice cubes and to small packages of food to be used within a few days.

Frost-free freezers should not need to be defrosted, but

always wipe visible spills off surfaces immediately. All freezers should be cleaned out once a year by removing the food and wiping them out with a solution of baking soda and water. Keep frozen food in the refrigerator or in coolers while cleaning the freezer. When finished, rinse, dry, and replace the food.

PACKAGING MATERIALS

The way food is wrapped for freezing is crucial. Wrapping materials must be without flavors or odors of their own, nonabsorbent, and as impervious as possible to moisture and air. Select the material according to the size and shape of the food and the length of time you expect to keep it.

There are many types of rigid freezer containers. **Can-or-freeze jars** made of tempered glass are excellent. ➤ Look for jars labeled on the carton as "suitable for freezing." If you don't have the carton, only use jars with wide mouths and straight sides, and in sizes up to 1½ pints. Canning jars with shoulders are not practical for freezing. Food expands when it freezes and typically moves upward in the container. This may cause enough stress at the rounded shoulder area to result in breakage. If convenience in defrosting is a priority, use plastic containers that can go directly from freezer to microwave—but remember to remove any freezer tape. (Caution: Glass jars of frozen food may break in a microwave and could crack during freezer storage. Should the glass crack, remove it immediately from the freezer discarding the jar and its contents.

Plastic freezer containers come in sizes ranging from half-pints to half-gallons. ➤ Select shapes that allow the cold to penetrate quickly to the center of the food—e.g., a long, shallow rectangle instead of a cube, or a tall, narrow oblong instead of a thick column. Should the plastic become brittle or show the start of a crack, remove the container from freezer duty.

Delicate objects that need protection from breakage can be well wrapped, then set inside a heavily waxed dairy carton or a coffee can topped with its lid before being placed inside a glass or plastic container. (By themselves, these cartons and coffee cans are not adequate vapor and moisture barriers for freezing.) ➤ An obvious advantage to rigid containers is that they can be reused. A disadvantage is that all the air cannot be forced out, and trapped air is destructive, as it draws moisture from the food, forming frost—made from irreplaceable juices of the food itself.

Some glass, plastics, ceramics, and contemporary materials can tolerate extreme temperatures at both ends of the thermometer. ➤ Use the same containers for freezing, thawing, and cooking only when specifically labeled as safe for all three operations. Such containers are time-savers, but if the material from which they're made is thick, freezing may be relatively slow.

Plastic wrap used for freezing must have the word "freezer" on the box. Wraps designed for the microwave will also work in the freezer. No matter whether the shiny side is in or out, **heavy-duty aluminum foil** makes an incomparable air and moisture barrier, but it tears easily. **Freezer wrap** is paper, plastic, or foil formulated (and labeled) for the freezer. **Freezer paper** is paper coated or laminated with plastic. ➤ Food should be placed on the plastic–shiny side, and the package should be sealed with freezer tape. This is best for baked goods and other foods that dry out rapidly. **Plastic freezer bags** are available in many sizes and shapes, from half pint to 2 gallons. Small quantities spread flat in these bags will freeze fastest, thereby yielding the highest quality when thawed. ➤ Do not freeze food in garbage or lawn-and-leaf bags, as these contain chemicals and are not acceptable for food storage.

Freezer boil-in-bags are specialty bags made of extra-heavy plastic. Food can be frozen in them, then thawed and heated in a pan of boiling water. These bags must be heat-sealed with a special appliance; the best models remove air from the bag before sealing, so that the food is vacuum-packed. Although these bags are expensive and not always reusable, results are often superior, particularly for vegetables. Blanch vegetables according to the instructions that come with the appliance.

COOLING, PACKING, AND FREEZING

If you do not cool food sufficiently before freezing, the outside edges may freeze hard, but the interior may not cool quickly enough to prevent spoilage. For optimum quality, ➤ food must go from preparation to freezer as fast as possible. For fastest cooling of fully cooked foods, cut large chunks into smaller pieces, then spread the food in quantities of 8 cups or less in aluminum or stainless steel containers no more than 2 inches deep (glass and plastic are poor thermal conductors), place the containers uncovered in a pan or sink, surround with ice water (more ice than water is important), and stir every 15 minutes, replacing the ice as needed. In 3 hours, hot food will cool to about 40°F. Pack and freeze. For instructions on cooling blanched foods, see page 1054.

Remember that freezing does not destroy microorganisms. It is important to ➤ have very clean working conditions as you prepare your food, or you will increase the contamination level on the foods to be dealt with as they come out of the freezer. Wash your hands and equipment well before starting. Wash all produce well, with agitation and lots of cold running water (both before and after peeling if done). Keep meat, poultry, seafoods, and any perishable ingredients such as dairy products and cheeses refrigerated at 40°F until ready to begin.

Unless the recipe says otherwise, it is not necessary to leave headspace when freezing dry food. ➤ If the food is liquid at room temperature, leave a ¼- to ½-inch headspace in rigid plastic containers; a ½-inch headspace in widemouthed pint glass jars; ¾ inch below the zipper in 1-pint freezer bags, or 1 to 2 inches or more in larger bags; and about ¼ inch in cube trays. Leave 1½ inches for juices.

To make pieces of food easy to remove individually from a package, they can first be partially frozen on a tray, or **tray-frozen,** before packing dry (without sugar, syrups or covering liquids for fruits). This works well with whole or halved strawberries, small whole berries, sliced peaches, melon balls, and prepared cuts of many vegetables. The prepared food is spread in a single layer on clean shallow trays and frozen until firm, then the pieces are promptly packaged dry—with no headspace needed—and put back in the freezer. Pieces will remain loose and can be removed a little at a time. ➤ Check the pieces on the tray frequently after the first hour. Long exposure before packaging will result in loss of moisture. **To prepare fruits for tray-freezing,** wash, trim or peel if needed, and remove excess moisture before laying out on trays with some space between pieces; do not overlap. **To prepare vegetables for tray-freezing,** wash, trim and cut pieces to size for blanching, blanch, cool, and drain. Then spread in a single layer, without overlap.

To fill a plastic freezer bag with a mixture containing liquid, set the bag in a bowl of about the same volume and ladle in the food; ➤ a canning funnel helps. Leave a $^3/_4$-inch headspace below the seal in small bags, a 1- to 2-inch headspace in large bags. ➤ Expel practically all the air from plastic bags: If zipper style, close the opening to within $^1/_2$ inch of one end; with nonzipper bags, gather the bag at the neck about 1 inch above the food. Have ready a deep pot of cool water; holding the bag at the unzipped corner, or fairly tightly at the neck, slowly push the bag underwater, being careful not to let any water enter. As the bag sinks, pressure will force out the air and the bag will flatten. Removing the bag from the water, zip the opening closed, or twist the neck of the bag and tie with a twist tie below your hand but about $^1/_2$ inch above the food (to allow expansion space). ➤ Do not reuse plastic freezer bags; washing them may weaken the seams or zipper or cause a pinhole opening. Alternatively, use a vacuum-packaging appliance according to the manufacturer's directions. ➤ Use only the plastic wrap or bags sold for that appliance.

As you fill **rigid freezer containers** with solid food, push the food down with a thin metal spatula or knife to force out air pockets. After filling, wipe the rim clean. Then cover and push down on the plastic lid, forcing out as much air as possible.

The drugstore wrap is a method advocated by many county extension offices. ➤ Use plastic wrap to cushion anything that protrudes—a bone, the leg of a gingerbread man—before wrapping the whole. ➤ The drugstore wrap, which both presses out and locks out air, should be used with freezer wrap. ➤ Place the food in the center of a sheet of freezer wrap just large enough to make the two folds described below. If the food is oversized, ➤ tape

Combining several servings of food into one package

two pieces of wrap together, folding the seam over and taping along the edge. Bring the two longest sides together over the food. Fold the edges over by $^1/_2$ to 1 inch and crease. Bring the seam down, pressing it flat against the top of the food. Fold the corners of each end of the wrap toward the center, making a triangle, then press out the air while folding the triangle's tip down flat, toward the package, press the end up flat against the package, and tape securely. After wrapping, for maximum protection, place the package in a plastic freezer bag and force out all the air. To pack several flat items in one package, separate each with two squares of wrap. For quick freezing, keep the height of the stack under 3 inches. Drugstore-wrap the whole stack in a sheet, then place in a plastic freezer wrap bag and freeze.

Should several servings of meat, cookies, or other small items be combined in each package, they will separate more easily when two thicknesses of moisture-proof paper are placed between each 2 units, as shown on the left below, or when they are slid into folded foil, as shown on the right below, before the outside wrapping is put on. ➤ Package foods in convenient serving or meal-sized quantities.

To label, use a waterproof felt-tip pen and write directly on the package or paper label or on top of a reusable container. ➤ Write the contents and number of servings, and in addition to—or instead of—the date

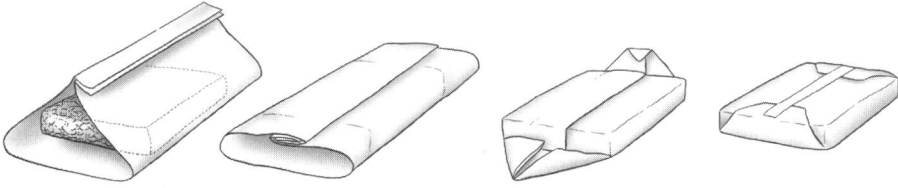

The drugstore wrap

frozen, note the last month (and year) when the food will still be of good quality. ➤ Keep a master record of freezing dates, as well as poundage of meats and number of portions of other foods.

HOW LONG TO KEEP FOODS FROZEN

Each frozen food has a life span during which, when thawed, it will be as close as possible to the quality of the fresh item. ➤ Once that time is up, the food continues to be safe to eat but becomes less and less palatable and nutritious. Cooked foods keep a shorter time than raw foods. When exposed to air over a long period of time, fat in food turns rancid. ➤ You may find our storage-limit recommendations short compared to others, but we believe in eating food that meets optimum standards for flavor and texture.

When prepared with prime ingredients and not too much salt or fat, commercially frozen foods can be of superior quality, because they are **flash-frozen**—far faster than we can manage in a home freezer. For the same reason, they will also store a bit longer than comparable home-frozen items. Commercially frozen foods carry expiration dates, but these are usually in code. You can contact the manufacturer to decode the expiration dates on packages. If they are items you use frequently, keep a record of the symbols.

THAWING FROZEN FOOD

Defrosted food is more perishable than fresh food. Freezing, remember, only puts most microorganisms to sleep; the minute food starts to thaw, the spoilers revive. This is why ➤ it is dangerous to defrost food at room temperature: Do not do it. At 40°F and above, microorganisms multiply rapidly. As soon as raw food, except fruit, has thawed, by whatever method, cook it immediately. Do not thaw, then refrigerate, food before cooking it. There are three acceptable ways to defrost frozen food; all will ensure that the raw or cooked frozen food is safe to eat.

To thaw in the refrigerator, place the still-wrapped package or the container in the refrigerator, preferably where air can circulate around it. ➤ Place raw meat, poultry, or fish in a pan to catch drippings (they can carry harmful bacteria), and put it on the lowest shelf. Allow 24 to 48 hours for defrosting, turning the package every 12 hours or so. Breaded frozen food should be defrosted out of all wrappings, so that moisture doesn't form on its surface and make the coating soggy.

To thaw in a microwave, defrost small to medium amounts of food in a microwave on the automatic defrosting cycle, or according to the manufacturer's instructions. Food can be microwave-defrosted while still in its plastic freezer bag, but ➤ first open a corner of the bag for a vent. After the defrosting is finished, transfer the food to a microwave-safe dish for cooking. In cooking, ➤ bring all microwaved foods to the usual finished temperature, or to at least 165°F, whichever is highest. Rotate

or stir partway through the cooking, and check the final temperature in several places with a thermometer. Let stand, covered, for 2 minutes before serving if the food is, or contains, meat, poultry, or fish.

Thawing while cooking brings frozen food through the thawing process straight to its desired finished temperature in one continuous action. It is the best method for most vegetables and some fruits, for if they are allowed to defrost before cooking, juices from the frozen foods' cells may flow freely from them, resulting in a watery texture, and reduced flavor and nutrition. ➤ Be sure to allow extra cooking time, and taste the food frequently to make sure it is cooked through.

WHEN TO REFREEZE

The following foods can safely be refrozen: certain foods ➤ containing ice crystals and feeling refrigerator-cold; sauces without dairy products; cooked meat and poultry; vegetables, fruits, juices, fruit juice concentrates; thawed foods; uncooked grains, flours, dried beans, and pasta; nuts; all baked goods except those with fillings or frostings based on dairy products.

The following should not be refrozen, but can be cooked and served immediately: foods containing ice crystals and feeling refrigerator-cold that are cooked combination dishes (casseroles, soups, stews) and sauces, particularly those containing meat or dairy products; unbaked fruit pies; thawed foods that, to your certain knowledge, have been at room temperature for no more than 2 hours, including meat, poultry, fish, fruits, and vegetables. ➤ The following must be discarded *without tasting*: ice cream and frozen yogurt; food with an off odor or appearance; or thawed food that has been at room temperature for more than 2 hours.

The quality of food frozen a second time is always compromised. Partial thawing and refreezing creates larger ice crystals, which gives a coarser texture. It is difficult to know how long refrozen food will keep, so plan to serve it as soon as possible, and prepare with extra attention. Meat, poultry, and fish that have been commercially frozen, then thawed at the market the day of purchase, are safe to refreeze and quality may not suffer. Commercial freezing is so fast there is far less damage to the cells.

ABOUT FREEZING FRUITS

Unless directed otherwise, ➤ choose sound, firm ripe fruit. The good parts of bruised and blemished fruit can be saved and used for a puree. Consult the chart, 209, for the peak season for each fruit. Fruit will be at its least expensive during this period because it is most plentiful, and it will probably have the best flavor.

Before freezing fruit, refrigerate it until chilled; cold tissue retains juices better. Unless it was homegrown without pesticides, wash the fruit quickly but thoroughly by placing it in a colander and rinsing it with several changes of ice-cold water. Shake off the water, then spread the fruit on thick towels to absorb as much moisture as possible, working gently to avoid crushing or bruising the fruit. Prepare for freezing immediately, exactly as you would if serving it: stemming, hulling, peeling, pitting, coring, and so on. If the fruit varies considerably in size, sort or cut it up uniformly so pieces in a package will freeze and thaw in about the same time.

ANTIBROWNING SOLUTION FOR FREEZING

The enzymes in the flesh of many fruits oxidize, causing the fruit to turn brown upon exposure to air. Discolored fruit remains perfectly edible, but its appearance may be unappetizing. ➤ Cutting up fruit quickly and getting it into the freezer fast may keep air from discoloring it, but the fruit will darken as it defrosts. An antibrowning solution will prevent discoloration from start to finish. When preparing a large quantity of light-colored fruit, such as those listed below, you can prevent discoloration ➤ by holding the peeled and cut fruit in a solution of $1/2$ teaspoon or 1,500 mg ascorbic acid per 2 quarts water as you work. Ascorbic acid is available in powder form from a pharmacy, or you can finely crush tablets of vitamin C, a form of ascorbic acid. Pure ascorbic acid is most commonly used, because it is the most effective long-term antioxidant for freezing. If the fruit will be served raw after thawing, it is also desirable to add ascorbic acid to the packed fruit. Either sprinkle an antibrowning solution over it before freezing or add the solution to the syrup or fruit juice.

In either case, ➤ measure and dissolve the powder in a little cold water before adding. The fruits listed below are those that tend to darken most easily. For each fruit, ➤ add the given amount of pure ascorbic acid or crushed vitamin C to 4 cups sugar syrup, 212, fruit juice, or water. Alternative antioxidants are listed below.

Apples: $1/2$ teaspoon pure ascorbic acid or 1,500 mg vitamin C
Apricots: $3/4$ teaspoon pure ascorbic acid or 2,250 mg vitamin C
Bananas: 2 teaspoons pure ascorbic acid or 6,000 mg vitamin C
Cherries: $1/2$ teaspoon pure ascorbic acid or 1,500 mg vitamin C
Figs: $3/4$ teaspoon pure ascorbic acid or 2,250 mg vitamin C
Melons: $1/4$ teaspoon pure ascorbic acid or 750 mg vitamin C
Nectarines: 1 teaspoon pure ascorbic acid or 3,000 mg vitamin C
Peaches: 1 teaspoon pure ascorbic acid or 3,000 mg vitamin C
Pears: $3/4$ teaspoon pure ascorbic acid or 2,250 mg vitamin C
Plums: $1/2$ teaspoon pure ascorbic acid or 1,500 mg vitamin C

Also available are commercial ascorbic acid mixtures (found with the canning supplies at the market), containing sugar and sometimes citric acid; follow the directions on the label. Citric acid and lemon and lime juice also prevent oxidation, but they are less effective, so more is required—which may alter the flavor of the fruit. They are best used as a temporary method of preventing browning. Drain the fruit before freezing.

Steam-blanching, 1055, is recommended as an alternative for preventing discoloration of apple and pear slices, $1 1/2$ to 2 minutes; rhubarb, 1 minute; and apricots, $1/2$ minute. Chill the blanched fruit in ice water before packing.

PACKING FRUIT FOR FREEZING

Freeze fruit by the method suited to your tastes and to the way you plan to serve it after defrosting.

Dry Pack (raw and unsweetened): For preserves, cooked desserts, pies, purees, or fruit sauces, raw fruit can be frozen whole or cut up. ➤ Add an antibrowning solution if necessary: For every 4 cups of fruit, dissolve the amount of ascorbic acid or vitamin C listed above in 3 tablespoons cold water and sprinkle over the fruit. Tray-freeze, 913, then pack into plastic freezer bags, shaking down the pieces to pack closely. Return to the freezer. Because the enzymes have not been inactivated, fruit frozen by this method will be very soft and juicy when thawed. Dry-packed frozen fruit holds its quality in the freezer the shortest time; after 1 month, it will deteriorate rapidly.

To puree, cook the thawed fruit, such as peaches, just enough to release the juice and flavor, or cook the fruit, such as apples, until thoroughly soft, then puree. Use as a topping or sauce, or combine with milk and a little ice and whirl in a blender to make a milk shake. Note: Fruit too ripe for canning is delicious frozen and prepared this way.

Sugar Pack (medium sweetened): For cooked desserts, pies, purees, and fruit sauces. This method is best for juicy fruits. ➤ Before sugaring, treat with an antibrowning solution if necessary: For every 4 cups of fruit, dissolve the amount of ascorbic acid or vitamin C listed above in 3 tablespoons cold water and sprinkle over the fruit. Add the required amount of sugar to the fruit and toss until sugar coats each piece. Some prefer to stir until part or all of the sugar is dissolved, feeling it will better plump the fruit; the sugar needs liquid in which to dissolve, so dissolved sugar means juice has been drawn from the fruit. Either method works well. Pack the fruit immediately into plastic freezer bags or rigid freezer containers, or tray-freeze, 913, then pack and return to the freezer. Shake the bags to pack the pieces closely. Fruit frozen by this method keeps almost as long as fruit frozen in syrup, 212, and thaws faster than syrup- or dry-packed frozen fruit. Add any thawed juice to other juices for drinking.

Juice Pack (unsweetened): For cooked desserts, fruit frozen by this method defrosts with especially true flavor and is superior to fruit frozen in water. It is rarely as plump as sugar-pack frozen fruit, however, and takes longer to thaw. Pack whole fruit or cut-up pieces into plastic freezer bags or rigid freezer containers and cover with juice of the same or a complementary fruit, allowing from $^1/_3$ to $^1/_2$ cup liquid for every 2 cups fruit. The juice can be raw or cooked. ➤ Add an antibrowning solution if necessary: For every 4 cups of fruit, dissolve the amount of ascorbic acid or vitamin C listed on 915 in 3 tablespoons cold water and sprinkle over the fruit. A piece of crumpled wax paper pressed on top of the fruit in the headspace will keep the fruit submerged. Seal and freeze. The thawed juice can be mixed with other juices to make punch.

Juice Pack (sweetened with nonnutritive sweetener): The manufacturers of these products provide instructions for freezing.

Syrup Pack (sweetened): For uncooked desserts and garnishes, ➤ a fruit's flavor, shape, and texture are preserved best and for the longest time when the fruit is cut up and packed in a sugar syrup, 212. Make a syrup that balances the fruit's tartness—usually 20-percent for sweet fruits, 30-percent for tart fruits, or 40-percent for very sour fruits. You can use the fruit's own juice—or a complementary fruit juice—instead of water, if you like. If you enjoy the distinctive flavor of brown sugar, honey, corn syrup, or pure maple syrup, one or more can replace one-quarter the sugar. ➤ Caution: If a baby under 1 year old will be eating the fruit, do not use honey, as it may contain botulism spores that the infant's digestive system cannot handle. ➤ Chill the syrup thoroughly, ➤ adding any antibrowning solution just before using; see 915. Generally the best technique for the syrup pack is to add about $^1/_2$ cup syrup to a rigid 1-pint freezer container (though this amount may range from $^1/_3$ cup to 1 cup, depending on the density and shape of the pieces), then add the fruit directly, pressing it down and covering it with additional syrup. A piece of crumpled wax paper pressed on top of the fruit in the headspace will keep the pieces submerged. Seal and freeze. The thawed syrup can be used to poach fruit.

Pectin Syrup Pack (lightly sweetened): For cooked or uncooked desserts, this method gives body to fruit without much sugar. To make 2 cups pectin syrup, blend 1 box regular powdered pectin with 1 cup water in a small saucepan. Stirring constantly, bring to a boil over high heat and boil for 1 minute. Turn off the heat and add $^1/_2$ cup sugar. Stir until the sugar is dissolved, then remove from the heat and pour into a 2-cup glass measure. Stir in enough cold water to make 2 cups, then chill thoroughly. ➤ Add antibrowning solution if necessary: For every 4 cups of fruit, dissolve the amount of ascorbic acid or vitamin C listed on 915 in 3 tablespoons cold water and sprinkle over the syrup. Pack immediately as for syrup pack, above, and freeze. Whisk the thawed syrup with other juices for drinking.

GUIDE TO FREEZING FRUITS

Have your equipment and packaging materials ready to go. Make sure all containers are washed and dried. They can already be labeled and dated, if preferred. The storage time for optimum quality is indicated with the name of the fruits below. The following fruits do not retain good quality after freezing: cherimoyas, kumquats, prickly pears, sapotes, star fruit, and tamarind. Preserve them by other methods.

APPLES (6 MONTHS)
Leave unpeeled, if desired. Core and cut into $^1/_4$-inch-thick slices. If planning to use for pie, water-blanch, 1054, the slices for 2 minutes, then cool quickly, and drain. *Freezing options:* dry pack; sugar pack using $^1/_2$ cup sugar to 4 cups fruit; 40-percent syrup pack; juice pack.

APRICOTS (6 MONTHS)
Peel the fruit, or water-blanch, 1054, for 30 seconds. Cool quickly, and drain. Halve and pit. Slice, if desired. *Freezing options:* dry pack; sugar pack using $^1/_2$ cup sugar to 4 cups fruit; 40-percent syrup pack; juice pack.

BANANAS (1 MONTH)
The defrosted fruit is good if not stored for too long. Peel just before tray-freezing, 913. Freeze whole or sliced, dipping in antibrowning solution, 915, first. *Freezing options:* dry pack.

BLACKBERRIES, BOYSENBERRIES, DEWBERRIES, LOGANBERRIES, AND YOUNGBERRIES (6 MONTHS)
Leave whole; do not wash berries for dry pack. *Freezing options:* dry pack; sugar pack using $^3/_4$ cup sugar to 4 cups fruit; 20- to 40-percent syrup pack.

BLUEBERRIES, ELDERBERRIES, AND HUCKLEBERRIES (6 MONTHS)
Leave whole; do not wash berries for dry pack. *Freezing options:* dry pack; sugar pack using $^1/_2$ cup sugar to 4 cups fruit; 20- to 40-percent syrup pack.

CHERRIES (6 MONTHS)
Stem and pit. *Freezing options:* dry pack; sugar pack using $^2/_3$ cup sugar to 4 cups fruit for sweet cherries, $^3/_4$ cup sugar to 4 cups fruit for tart cherries; 40-percent syrup pack for sweet cherries, 50-percent syrup pack for tart cherries; juice pack; pectin syrup pack.

CITRUS FRUITS (GRAPEFRUITS, ORANGES, MANDARINS, POMELOS, AND UGLI FRUIT) (6 MONTHS)
Do not freeze navel oranges. Peel and slice other citrus fruits, or slice into segments, removing the membranes and seeds. Pack into glass jars. *Freezing options:* dry pack; 40-percent syrup pack; juice pack; pectin syrup pack.

COCONUT (3 MONTHS)
Shred the meat, 971. *Freezing options:* Pack into glass jars and cover with coconut liquid, 971; dry pack the shreds in plastic freezer bags; sugar pack using $^1/_2$ cup sugar to 4 cups coconut.

CRANBERRIES (6 MONTHS)
Leave whole; do not wash berries for dry pack. *Freezing options:* dry pack; 50-percent syrup pack.

CURRANTS, DRIED, AND RAISINS (6 MONTHS)
Freezing options: dry pack.

CURRANTS, FRESH (6 MONTHS)
Freezing options: dry pack; sugar pack using $3/4$ cup sugar to 4 cups fruit; 50-percent syrup pack.

DATES (6 MONTHS)
Split lengthwise and remove the pits. *Freezing options:* dry pack.

FEIJOA (6 MONTHS)
Halve, scoop out the pulp, and mash. *Freezing options:* Add sugar to taste to the mashed pulp and pack into rigid freezer containers.

FIGS (6 MONTHS)
Leave whole; peel, if desired. *Freezing options:* dry pack; sugar pack using $3/4$ cup sugar to 4 cups fruit; 40-percent syrup pack; juice pack.

FRUITS, DRIED (APRICOTS, BERRIES, CHERRIES, PEACHES, PINEAPPLES, AND PRUNES) (12 MONTHS)
Freezing options: dry pack.

GINGER, FRESH (2 WEEKS)
Select small, fresh rhizomes with thin skins. Dry pack or tray-freeze, then pack into plastic freezer bags. Grate, slice, or chop without thawing.

GOOSEBERRIES (6 MONTHS)
Trim, if desired. *Freezing options:* dry pack; juice pack.

GRAPES (6 MONTHS)
Leave whole. *Freezing options:* dry pack; 40-percent syrup pack; juice pack.

GUAVAS (6 MONTHS)
Guavas must be fully ripe. Leave whole and unpeeled. *Freezing options:* dry pack.

KIWIFRUIT (6 MONTHS)
Peel and cut into $1/4$-inch slices. *Freezing options:* dry pack.

LEMONS AND LIMES (6 MONTHS)
The defrosted fruit is excellent for juicing and can be sliced for garnish. Leave whole. *Freezing options:* dry pack.

LONGANS (6 MONTHS)
Freezing options: Dry pack whole and serve partially frozen, or peel and seed and freeze in a 30-percent syrup pack.

LOQUATS (6 MONTHS)
Prepare and cook as usual. *Freezing options:* 40-percent syrup pack.

MANGOES (6 MONTHS)
Peel, pit, and slice. *Freezing options:* dry pack; sugar pack using $1/3$ cup sugar to 1 cup fruit; 30-percent syrup pack.

MELONS (CANTALOUPES, CASABAS, CRENSHAWS, HONEYDEW, PERSIAN MELONS, AND WATERMELONS) (6 MONTHS)
Remove the seeds and rind and cut into $3/4$-inch cubes or balls. Serve partially thawed. *Freezing options:* dry pack; 20-percent syrup pack.

NECTARINES (6 MONTHS)
Leave unpeeled. Halve and pit. Quarter or slice, if desired. *Freezing options:* sugar pack using $1/3$ to $2/3$ cup sugar to 4 cups fruit; 20-percent syrup pack; juice pack.

PAPAYAS (6 MONTHS)
Peel and slice. Freeze and serve as for Melons, above.

PASSION FRUIT (3 MONTHS)
Passion fruit must be fully ripe. Leave whole. *Freezing options:* dry pack.

PEACHES (6 MONTHS)
Peel or water-blanch, 1054. Halve and pit. Quarter or slice, if desired. *Freezing options:* sugar pack using $1/3$ to $2/3$ cup sugar to 4 cups fruit; 20-percent syrup pack; juice pack.

PEARS (6 MONTHS)
Pears are better canned than frozen, but if you do freeze them, avoid mealy ones. Peel and halve, quarter, or slice. Heat in simmering sugar syrup, 893, or juice for 1 to 2 minutes; let cool. *Freezing options:* 40-percent sugar syrup; juice pack.

PERSIMMONS (6 MONTHS)
Leave whole. *Freezing options:* dry pack.

PINEAPPLE (6 MONTHS)
Peel, core, and cut up as desired. *Freezing options:* dry pack.

PLUMS (6 MONTHS)
Plums are better canned than frozen. To freeze, leave whole or halve, pit, and cut into pieces. *Freezing options:* dry pack; 50-percent syrup pack; juice pack.

QUINCES (6 MONTHS)
Prepare and freeze as for Apples, 916.

RASPBERRIES (6 MONTHS)
Leave whole; do not wash berries for dry-pack. *Freezing options:* dry pack; sugar pack using $3/4$ cup sugar to 4 cups fruit; 40-percent syrup pack; juice pack.

RHUBARB (6 MONTHS)
Cut the trimmed stalks into desired lengths (be sure to remove all leaves; they are poisonous). *Freezing options:* dry pack; 40-percent syrup pack; juice pack.

STRAWBERRIES (6 MONTHS)
Wash and remove the hulls. Leave whole for dry pack, or slice if desired for other freezing methods and dry well before freezing. *Freezing options:* dry pack; sugar pack using $3/4$ cup sugar to 4 cups fruit; 50-percent syrup pack; juice pack; pectin syrup pack.

SERVING FROZEN FRUIT

Keep fruits sealed in their packages while they defrost to help preserve color and vitamin C, then use as soon as defrosted, as thawed fruit deteriorates rapidly. When using for pies, tarts, upside-down cakes, cobblers, puddings, and ices, or for folding into batter, thaw fruits just enough to measure accurately. Many berries make finer jelly when frozen, because the juices flow freely. ➤ To serve uncooked, partially thaw fruits and berries, as they retain their quality—and most of the juices—when still slightly icy. Frozen berries can be fully thawed and used for sauces and flavorings, where their taste is superb and the juices are an asset. Use crushed or pureed fruits as fillings or toppings or in ice cream or ices—or cook into fruit butter or jam.

FREEZING FRUIT PUREES

Fruits such as plums, prunes, avocados, papayas, mangoes, persimmons, and melons freeze better in pureed form if uncooked. To puree, use a food mill, 122. Applesauce is one of the most delicious of frozen cooked purees, especially if made with early apples. Cooked purees should be used within 4 months. All fruit purees may, if necessary, be packaged without sugar. Otherwise, allow about 1 cup of sugar per pound of fruit. Fruit sauces or cobbler fillings made from seedy berries, especially blackberries, are smoother if the frozen berries are broken apart and put, unthawed, through a food mill, using a fine blade.

FREEZING JUICES

Of fruit ciders and juices, apple, raspberry, plum, cherry, and grape freeze most satisfactorily. To retain good color, add $\frac{1}{2}$ teaspoon ascorbic acid, 894, or 2 teaspoons lemon juice to each gallon of cherry or apple juice. Cherries, plums, prunes, and grapes have a better flavor if slightly cooked before juicing, to extract some of the flavor from the skin. Peaches for juice can be steamed, 897, to 150°F to keep the color clear without tasting cooked. Raspberries are best if the whole berries are mixed with 1 pound or 2 to $2\frac{1}{4}$ cups sugar to every 10 pounds of fruit and frozen; extract the juice when ready to use. When freezing citrus juices, add $\frac{1}{2}$ teaspoon ascorbic acid, 894, or 2 teaspoons lemon juice per gallon.

Whole fruits can also be dry-pack frozen, 915, then juiced. ➤ Fruit for jelly can be frozen unsweetened and the juice extracted later without cooking. To make the jelly, proceed as usual, see 927.

For fresh-tasting tomato juice from the freezer, wash and core ripe sweet tomatoes, but do not peel. Coarsely chop and simmer for about 5 minutes. Puree and strain, let cool, and pack into rigid freezer containers; leaving at least 1 inch headspace in the container; freeze.

ABOUT FREEZING VEGETABLES

Most vegetables take well to freezing. If they are garden fresh and properly processed, their taste, when served, is excellent. ➤ Choose young, tender vegetables. Starchy ones such as peas, corn, and lima beans are best when slightly immature.

Consult 240–319 for the peak season for each vegetable, at which time it will be at its least expensive and have the best flavor.

If not prepared and frozen at once to retain their freshness, vegetables must be kept chilled between harvesting and processing. If broccoli or cauliflower is straight from the garden or field, soak for 30 minutes in a solution of 2 tablespoons salt to 1 gallon water. Rinse well and drain.

If the vegetables are to be blanched before freezing, rinse in cold water as you normally would for cooking. If the vegetables will be frozen without blanching, wash in ice water as necessary. Stem and remove the peel as necessary and directed, as if you are preparing to cook the vegetables. ➤ Vegetables will blanch, freeze, and later cook most evenly when sizes are uniform, so sort and cut up as necessary. Better food values and flavor are retained if the vegetables are not shredded. Bell peppers do not need to be blanched before freezing if they are diced after removing seeds and membranes. Tray-freeze them, 913, before packing. For other cuts, blanching is best for long storage.

It is best to fully cook before freezing such vegetables as pumpkin, squash, and sweet potatoes. Mushrooms may be sautéed before freezing by melting 1 tablespoon butter in an uncovered pan and cooking 2 cups sliced or small whole mushrooms for about 3 minutes. Cool and freeze immediately. Frozen tomatoes are not good served raw, but tomatoes for stewing or seasoning can be scalded 2 minutes to loosen the skins, if desired, then cored and packed for the freezer without any additional heating. Cook before serving.

Freezing raw: Thawed unblanched vegetables are very soft and their juices flow freely, which is fine for vegetables and herbs to be used as seasoning. If you have an abundance of ripe tomatoes, for instance, they can go from vine to freezer with no more preparation than a rinse. Quality will decline after about 4 weeks, so plan to use by then, or before in soups or stews. When thawing, be careful to reserve the juices, as these contain valuable nutrients and flavor.

BLANCHING VEGETABLES

The enzymes that cause plant tissues to deteriorate are not completely destroyed by freezing, but a brief boiling or steaming will slow down or even stop the process. For the finest quality, ➤ every vegetable you plan to keep frozen for more than a month and then serve on its own should be blanched before freezing. In addition to destroying enzymes and surface microorganisms, blanching brightens colors and shrinks vegetables slightly, so they pack more compactly. There are three methods of blanching vegetables:

Immersion in boiling water, **water-blanching,** gives the fastest penetration of heat, is most effective against enzymes and microorganisms, and takes the least time. For water-blanching, bring 4 quarts unsalted water to a boil in a large pot with a tight-fitting lid. Place 8 ounces leafy greens or 16 ounces other vegetables in a blanching basket, or tie up in a big square of cheesecloth. Submerge the vegetables completely in the water, cover tightly, and set the timer. Keep the heat on high. The water should return to a boil immediately. If it does not, start your timer when the water is boiling again; next time, use more boiling water or fewer vegetables.

Lift the lid and shake the basket or swish the bag a couple of times for even penetration of heat. Remove the vegetables from the water and begin to cool (see below) the instant the timer rings.

For **steam-blanching,** bring 2 to 3 inches of water to a rolling boil in a large saucepan with a tight-fitting lid. ➤ Arrange the vegetables in a single layer in a wire basket and set the basket above the water. ➤ Cover tightly, keeping the heat on high. When steam starts to escape, set the timer. Lift the lid and shake the basket a few times for even penetration of steam. Remove the vegetables from the heat and begin to cool (see below) the instant the timer rings. Steam-blanched vegetables offer fresher flavor and preserve water-soluble C and B vitamins, but ➤ steaming takes longer than boiling-water blanching.

A reliable way of **microwave-blanching** vegetables is to follow the instructions in your operating guide. If blanching instructions are not included, telephone the manufacturer's customer service number and request the information you need. ➤ Microwave-blanching is controversial: Optimally, the results are superior in flavor and retain more water-soluble vitamins. However, not all enzymes may be inactivated, which may result in vegetables with poor quality after a few months. Also, with too much heat, the vegetables cook, losing color, flavor, and nutrients; with too little, enzymes are actually stimulated rather than inactivated, which is worse than not blanching at all.

Cool vegetables immediately after blanching to stop further softening of tissues. If your tap water is cold (50°F or less), let it run over the vegetables. If not, plunge them into ice water, using about 1 pound of ice per pound of vegetables. ➤ Cooling should take about the same length of time as blanching. When they have cooled, lift the vegetables out and drain well: Spread them on thick towels and cover them with more towels to absorb as much moisture as possible. Gently pat dry. ➤ Excess moisture can cause a loss of quality in freezing.

Pack blanched vegetables into plastic freezer bags or rigid freezer containers and freeze immediately, or tray-freeze, 913, then pack when frozen. Do not season, and make sure you leave sufficient headspace, 890.

GUIDE TO FREEZING VEGETABLES

Please read About Freezing Vegetables, 918, before proceeding. Select the freshest, most tender vegetables available at the peak of their season and prepare them as quickly as possible. Vegetables can be packed in plastic freezer bags or rigid freezer containers, according to their size and shape. When freezer boil-in-bags are mentioned, it is because they give especially good results for that form of that vegetable. The storage time for optimum quality is indicated with the name of the vegetables below.

The following vegetables do not retain good quality after freezing; preserve them by other methods: cardoons, cassava, daikon and other radishes, Jerusalem artichokes, jicama, kelp, lettuces and other salad greens, olives, salsify, sorrel, sprouts, taro root, truffles, and water chestnuts.

AMARANTH GREENS (4 MONTHS)
Prepare and freeze as for Greens, 920.

ARTICHOKES, GLOBE; HEARTS (4 MONTHS)
Select artichokes whose leaves are tight. Trim down to the heart, 247. Water-blanch for 7 minutes. Cool quickly, drain, and tray-freeze, then pack into rigid freezer containers and freeze.

ASIAN GREENS (4 MONTHS)
Prepare and freeze as for Greens, 920.

ASPARAGUS (4 MONTHS)
Select tender young spears. Prepare for cooking, 249, then water-blanch and freeze in boil-in-bags. Or water-blanch thin stalks for 2 minutes, medium stalks for 3 minutes, thick stalks for 4 minutes; add 1½ minutes to each for steam-blanching. Cool quickly, drain, pack into plastic freezer bags, and freeze.

AVOCADOS (2 MONTHS)
If pureed, avocados will not darken when frozen; otherwise they will. Select unblemished, slightly soft fruits. Peel, pit, and puree. Add ¼ teaspoon ascorbic acid, 894, for every 4 cups of puree or 1 tablespoon fresh lemon juice for every 2 avocados to prevent darkening. In preparation for avocado ice cream, also add 1 cup sugar per 4 cups puree. Quickly pack into rigid freezer containers and freeze.

BEANS, LIMA AND OTHER SHELL BEANS (4 MONTHS)
Select pods whose beans are plump but not hard. Shell and sort by size. Water-blanch small beans for 2 minutes, medium beans for 3 minutes, large beans for 4 minutes; add 1 minute to each for steam-blanching. Cool quickly, drain, and tray-freeze, then pack into plastic freezer bags and return to the freezer.

BEANS, PEAS, AND LEGUMES, DRIED (1 YEAR)
Best stored in a cool, dry place, but these can be frozen. Do not blanch.

BEANS, SNAP (4 MONTHS)
Ideal snap beans for freezing have crisp, thin pods up to 4 inches long, with barely visible seeds. Trim and, if necessary, string, but do not halve. Water-blanch for 3 minutes, or steam-blanch for 5 minutes; fleshy Italian beans require 30 seconds longer. Cool quickly, drain, pack into plastic freezer bags, and freeze. Some cooks prefer to freeze snap

beans raw, simply trimmed and packed into plastic freezer bags.

BEANS, SOY AND FAVA (4 MONTHS)
Select tender pods whose beans are developed but not hard. Water-blanch for 4 to 5 minutes, depending on size and tenderness. Cool quickly, push out the beans, rinse, and drain. Pack into plastic freezer bags and freeze.

BEETS (6 MONTHS)
Most beets are canned or pickled, but very young beets are good frozen. Select unblemished small, tender beets of uniform color. Beets must be fully cooked for freezing; they turn grainy if frozen raw. Prepare and cook whole and unpeeled, then peel and cool quickly. Tray-freeze, then pack into plastic freezer bags, and return to the freezer.

BEET GREENS (4 MONTHS)
Prepare and freeze as for Greens, below.

BROCCOLI (6 MONTHS)
Select young broccoli, choosing tender but crisp stalks with tight buds on compact heads. Prepare the buds and stalks in inch-size pieces for servings. Water-blanch for 3 minutes, or steam-blanch for 5 minutes. Cool quickly, drain, pack into plastic freezer bags, and freeze. Frozen broccoli is best when partially thawed before cooking.

BRUSSELS SPROUTS (6 MONTHS)
Select firm small to medium heads. Prepare for cooking, 241, then sort for size. Water-blanch small heads for 3 minutes or medium heads for 4 minutes; add 2 minutes to each for steam-blanching. Cool quickly, drain, pack into plastic freezer bags, and freeze.

CABBAGE AND CHINESE CABBAGE (4 MONTHS)
Most thawed cabbage is watery and of poor quality. If it's essential to freeze cabbage, select crisp, firm heads, and look for crisp unblemished leaves in Chinese cabbage. Prepare solid heads for serving, 262. Cut into wedges or shred coarsely. Water-blanch wedges for 3 minutes or shreds for 1 1/2 minutes; add 1/2 minute or 1 minute, respectively, for steam-blanching. Cool quickly, drain, pack into plastic freezer bags, and freeze. Outer cabbage leaves (for soups or stuffed cabbage) can be stacked and frozen in plastic bags without blanching.

CARROTS (6 MONTHS)
Mashed cooked carrots have the truest flavor and best texture after thawing, but cooked carrots in a butter-and-sugar glaze also freeze well. Select and peel sweet, tender, (not baby), coreless carrots. To freeze in pieces, water-blanch and freeze in boil-in-bags. Or water-blanch small whole carrots for 5 minutes or 1/4-inch rounds and dice for 2 minutes; add 3 minutes and 1 minute, respectively, for steam-blanching. Cool quickly, drain, and tray-freeze. When solid, pack into plastic freezer bags and return to the freezer. To freeze pureed carrots, first cook as for Mashed Carrots, 266. Puree cooked carrots. Season lightly, cool quickly, pack into rigid freezer containers, and freeze. Thaw in the refrigerator.

CAULIFLOWER (6 MONTHS)
Prepare and freeze as for Broccoli, above.

CELERY (6 MONTHS)
Select tender, stringless stalks. Prepare for cooking, 241, cutting into 1/4-inch slices. Chop the leaves and freeze as for herbs, 918. Water-blanch for 2 minutes or steam-blanch for 3 minutes. Cool quickly, drain, pack into plastic freezer bags, and freeze. Raw celery freezes well in gelatin salads, 173.

CHAYOTE (6 MONTHS)
While best enjoyed fresh, chayote with tender skins may be frozen. Select those that are unblemished and very firm. Prepare for cooking, 269, removing the seed but not peeling. Cut into 1/2-inch dice. Water-blanch for 2 minutes. Cool quickly, drain, pack into plastic freezer bags, and freeze.

CORN (6 MONTHS)
Husk, remove the silks, trim the ends, and rinse the ears. For corn on the cob, water-blanch and freeze in boil-in-bags, or water-blanch the ears (up to 1 1/4 inches in diameter, 7 minutes; up to 1 1/2 inches in diameter, 9 minutes; larger ears, 11 minutes; add 3, 4, or 5 minutes, respectively, for steam-blanching). Drain and cool quickly and completely. Drain and pack into plastic freezer bags and freeze. Thaw completely before heating. It is also possible to simply remove the silks from the ears and freeze the ears in their husks without blanching; place in plastic freezer bags and freeze. For cream-style kernels, water-blanch the ears for 4 minutes or steam-blanch for 6 minutes. Cool quickly, and drain. Cut and scrape the kernels and juices from the cobs. Pack into rigid freezer containers and freeze.

COWPEAS/SOUTHERN PEAS AND BLACK-EYED PEAS (4 MONTHS)
Prepare as for lima beans, 252, water-blanching small peas for 1 minute, large peas for 2 minutes.

GREENS (4 MONTHS)
Select young leaves, ideally with tender stems. Prepare for cooking, removing any tough ribs and stems but retaining those that are tender. Water-blanch—1 to 2 pounds at a time—collards and tough mustard greens for 3 minutes, more tender leaves for 2 minutes. Or stir-fry over high heat until the leaves are wilted, 2 to 3 minutes. Cool quickly, drain, and pack into boil-in-bags or rigid freezer containers with the water that clings to the leaves. Freeze. Frozen greens are best when partially thawed before cooking.

KALE (4 MONTHS)
Prepare and freeze as for Greens, above.

KOHLRABI (6 MONTHS)

Select tender, not fibrous, stems. Prepare for cooking, 279, then cut into $1/2$-inch dice. Water-blanch for 2 minutes. Cool quickly, drain, pack into rigid freezer containers, and freeze.

LEEKS (6 MONTHS)

Prepare for cooking, 280, then chop and freeze as for Onions, below.

MUSHROOMS (4 MONTHS)

Mushrooms change texture after freezing and so can be used only in cooking, although their flavor remains fresh. Rinse well, trim, pat dry, and process immediately, as the mushrooms will darken quickly. Small mushrooms can be frozen whole; cut large caps into $1/4$-inch slices. Steam-blanched or sautéed mushrooms will keep longer. Soak first in an antibrowning solution of $1/2$ teaspoon ascorbic acid, 1 teaspoon fresh lemon juice, or $1 1/2$ teaspoons citric acid, 890, per 2 cups water. Steam-blanch whole large mushrooms for 5 minutes, buttons or large quarters for $3 1/2$ minutes, slices for 3 minutes. Cool quickly, and drain. Or cook the mushrooms in butter in a skillet over high heat until almost cooked. Set the pan in ice water to cool. Pack in their cooking juice in rigid freezer containers and freeze.

OKRA (6 MONTHS)

Tender young okra freezes well as long as the pods are not cut. Wash, then sort by size. Water-blanch pods under 4 inches for 3 minutes, longer pods for 5 minutes; add 2 or 3 minutes, respectively, for steam-blanching. Cool quickly, and drain. Tray-freeze and pack into plastic freezer bags, or pack directly into freezer bags.

ONIONS (1 MONTH)

To freeze chopped scallions and mature onions, wash, and trim, and cut the tender parts crosswise into $1/4$-inch-thick slices or chop. Tray-freeze, tightly covered in a double thickness of plastic freezer wrap. Wrap in $1/2$-cup packages in plastic freezer wrap, then place in doubled plastic freezer bags, to contain the pungent odor.

PARSNIPS (6 MONTHS)

Prepare and freeze as for Turnips, 922.

PEAS, SNAP AND SNOW (6 MONTHS)

These are among the most successfully frozen vegetables. Prepare for cooking, 290. Water-blanch small pods for $1 1/2$ minutes or large pods for 2 minutes; add 2 minutes each for steam-blanching. Cool quickly, drain, and tray-freeze, then, pack into plastic freezer bags and return to the freezer.

PEAS, GREEN (6 MONTHS)

Choose pods containing tender young peas. After washing the pods, shell and sort the peas by size. Immediately, as the skins will start to toughen, water-blanch, and freeze in a boil-in-bag. Or water-blanch small peas for 2 minutes or large peas for 3 minutes; add 2 minutes each for steam blanching. Cool quickly, drain, and pack into plastic freezer bags.

PEPPERS, BELL AND CHILE (6 MONTHS)

Select crisp, thick-walled peppers. Bell peppers can be, and chile peppers should be, dry-pack frozen, 915, without blanching. For longest keeping, water-blanch bell pepper halves for 3 minutes or rings and strips for 2 minutes; add 1 minute each for steam-blanching. Cool quickly, drain, and tray-freeze, then pack into plastic freezer bags. Wrap bell peppers as for chopped onions, above. Chile peppers can be roasted and peeled, 292. Tray-freeze, then pack into plastic freezer bags or rigid freezer containers and return to the freezer.

POTATOES

Baked Stuffed Potatoes, 297, French Fries, 299, and Hash Browns, 298, freeze very well. Blanched potatoes do not.

BROCCOLI RABE (4 MONTHS)

Also called broccoli raab, broccoli di rape, or rapini. Select stalks with tender leaves and tight sprouts, or no sprouts. Discard the heavy stalks and prepare the leaves and sprouts for serving, 298. Continue as for Greens, 920.

RUTABAGAS (4 MONTHS)

Select tender medium young roots. Peel and cook until tender, then mash for the best quality. Pack into rigid freezer containers and freeze.

SCALLIONS

Prepare and freeze as for Onions, above.

SHALLOTS (1 MONTH)

Prepare and freeze as for Onions, above.

SPINACH (4 MONTHS)

Select tender young leaves with tender stems. Prepare and freeze as for Greens, 920.

SQUASH, SPAGHETTI (6 MONTHS)

Select a mature squash with a hard rind. Halve and bake, cut side down, in a baking dish at 350°F until tender. Remove the seeds, then use a fork to pull out the strands. Cool quickly, then pack into rigid freezer containers and freeze.

SQUASH, SUMMER (6 MONTHS)

Select small firm but tender squashes. Cut into $1/2$-inch-thick slices, and water-blanch and freeze in boil-in-bags. Or water-blanch for 3 minutes. Cool quickly, drain, pack into plastic freezer bags, and freeze. Some cooks cut zucchini into long shreds, water-blanch for 1 to 2 minutes, and freeze. This saves a step when preparing zucchini breads and cakes. Thaw the shreds enough to squeeze out the excess moisture before measuring.

SQUASH, WINTER AND PUMPKIN (6 MONTHS)

Select fully mature squashes with hard rinds and fine, dry pulp. Wash, cut into manageable pieces, and bake at 350°F until tender. Remove the seeds, scrape the pulp from the rind, and mash or puree. Sweeten to taste, if to be used for desserts. Cool quickly, pack into rigid freezer containers, and freeze.

SWEET POTATOES (2 WEEKS)

Select medium bright-colored tubers that have been cured for at least 1 week. Scrub and bake, unpeeled, at 350°F until almost tender. Let cool and peel, then place for 5 seconds in an antibrowning solution of $\frac{1}{4}$ cup fresh lemon juice per 2 cups cold water. For whole potatoes, drain, wrap individually in freezer foil, and freeze. To serve, place frozen and still wrapped, on a baking sheet in a 350°F oven and bake until hot. Or, for slices, after peeling, cut into $\frac{1}{2}$-inch-thick slices. Pack into plastic freezer bags and freeze. For candied sweets, after dipping and draining the slices in the antibrowning solution, dredge each piece in white or light brown sugar. Tray-freeze, then pack into plastic freezer bags and return to the freezer. Mashed or pureed sweet potatoes freeze very well. Bake unpeeled as above, but until thoroughly cooked. Halve, remove the flesh from the skins, and mash or puree. To keep the color, mix in 2 tablespoons fresh orange or lemon juice for every 4 cups of potatoes. Pack into rigid freezer containers and freeze.

SWISS CHARD (4 MONTHS)

Cut the leafy sides from the ribs, reserving the ribs for another purpose. Prepare for cooking, 920, then continue as for Greens, 920.

TOMATILLOS (6 MONTHS)

Select firm tomatillos with papery husks. Remove the husks, place the tomatillos in a pan, and cover with water or unsalted broth. Cover and simmer until tender. Cool quickly, pack into rigid freezer containers, and freeze.

TOMATOES, GREEN (4 MONTHS)

Select firm, shiny green fruit. Wash, core, and cut into $\frac{1}{4}$-inch-thick slices. Pack into rigid freezer containers ➤ with freezer paper between the slices. Freeze.

TOMATOES, RIPE (1 MONTH)

Select firm but ripe tomatoes. Whole unpeeled tomatoes can be dry-pack frozen, 915. (To peel while frozen, run under cool water, and the skins will slip off.) Or cook and puree the tomatoes. To save space, simmer the puree, uncovered, until thick, or until reduced to a paste. Cool quickly, pour into rigid freezer containers, and freeze. Or, prepare stewed tomatoes, 312, cool quickly, pack into rigid freezer containers, and freeze.

TURNIP GREENS (4 MONTHS)

Prepare and freeze as for Greens, 920.

TURNIPS (4 MONTHS)

When thawed, frozen turnips have fair to good quality diced, and good quality when mashed. Select tender young turnips. Prepare for cooking, 314, then slice or cut into small dice. Water-blanch for 2 minutes. Cool quickly, drain, and pack into plastic freezer bags. Or cook the turnips until tender and mash; cool quickly, then pack into rigid freezer containers and freeze.

VEGETABLES, PUREED AND MASHED

Carrots, parsnips, potatoes, pumpkins, rutabagas, summer squashes, sweet potatoes, turnips, and winter squashes all have better texture when frozen cooked and mashed or pureed than when frozen in any other form. Trim and simmer, steam, or bake until soft. Mash, process in a food processor, or puree through a food mill, being careful not to incorporate air. Two tablespoons fresh lemon or orange juice can be added to every 4 cups orange-colored vegetables to keep the puree from darkening. Pack purees into rigid freezer containers, using a fork to tamp lightly to prevent pockets of air. Potato puree can be packed into baked potato shells, covered with melted cheese, and tray-frozen. Wrap individually when solid and pack into plastic freezer bags. Thick purees can be formed into patties or balls, brushed with melted butter, and tray-frozen. When solid, pack into rigid freezer containers with 2 pieces of freezer paper between each layer, gently pressing out the air.

THAWING AND COOKING FROZEN VEGETABLES

As a rule, ➤ cook frozen vegetables without thawing. Steaming best preserves nutrients and flavor. Use as little water as possible (and save the water for soup). Break a block of vegetables into chunks and arrange them in a single layer in a steamer, so heat can penetrate rapidly and evenly. Remove frozen pureed or mashed vegetables from the container and place in a dish in a steamer. Most frozen vegetables will cook in from one-third to one-half the time of their fresh equivalents. When using frozen vegetables in a recipe calling for fresh, shorten their cooking time—for example, add them to stews during the last minutes of cooking. To cook in water, spread frozen chunks in a heavy skillet in which they just fit. Add as little boiling water as possible, about $\frac{1}{4}$ to $\frac{1}{2}$ cup per 2 cups vegetables. You may need as much as $\frac{1}{2}$ cup water for cauliflower and soybeans and 1 cup for lima beans. Cover and bring to a boil over high heat, then reduce the heat and simmer until the vegetables are tender. Whether cooking in steam or water, frequently break up the frozen chunks with a fork until defrosted. Take care not to overcook. For maximum nutrients, serve immediately. Frozen vegetables may also be heated unthawed in the microwave just before serving or using in recipes.

FREEZING MEAT, GAME, POULTRY, FISH, AND SEAFOOD

Meats, both domestic and wild-game, should be divided into meal-sized quantities for packaging. For best quality, freeze store-bought meats, poultry, fish, and seafood as soon as you get them home. When it comes time to cook them, prepare them as if they were fresh.

The same advice for all frozen produce applies to the choice of meats: Watch quality. Freezing at low temperatures does not induce enough change to make tough meats tender. If you usually buy high-quality cuts over the counter, make sure you can trust your source that sells in quantity for freezing.

Selecting and Preparing: ➤ Choose lean, tender meat (fat has a short storage life), and stock up when prices go down. Freeze poultry and game birds whole or in parts, but always freeze innards separately, and ➤ do not stuff a whole bird before freezing (the stuffing can spoil). Leave the skin on birds—it's good protection. Chill poultry and birds thoroughly before freezing, allowing 2 days for a whole turkey. Freeze livers, kidneys, hearts, and tongue uncooked; freeze sweetbreads and tripe cooked.

Generally, fish weighing 2 pounds or less before cleaning should be frozen whole. To avoid a mushy texture when cooked, cut fish fillets at least $^1/_4$ inch thick. Wash and clean all shellfish, squid, and octopus. Clams, oysters, and scallops can be frozen live in the shell or shucked. Steam mussels open and remove their meat. Boil crabs for 5 minutes, cool quickly, and freeze meaty pieces in the shell. Freeze lobster cooked in the shell. For longest storage life, freeze shrimp raw in their shells, with heads removed.

Packaging: Please read Cooling, Packing, and Freezing, 912, noting particularly the drugstore wrap, 913. Wrap all these foods unseasoned, as seasonings deteriorate. ➤ Remove all visible fat from meat, game, and poultry. The larger the piece, the longer it can be frozen. On the other hand, the smaller the piece, the faster it freezes and thaws, retaining quality and saving time. Wrap large cuts individually with the drugstore wrap. Flat shapes such as steaks, chops, patties, and pieces of fish and poultry can be wrapped individually or in a stack. For storing less than 2 weeks, most meats, all fresh poultry, crab and lobster pieces, live clams, live oysters, shucked mussels, and shrimp can be frozen in plastic freezer bags with the air expelled, 913. ➤ For long-term storage, overwrap the bag, drugstore fashion, in freezer foil or paper. Pork, sausage in casings, and variety meats should be tightly wrapped in plastic freezer wrap or plastic freezer bags, then overwrapped the same way. Smoked and pickled meats, poultry, and fish should be double- or triple-wrapped to keep their odors from reaching other foods. Market-wrapped meats, poultry, and fish—either sealed airtight in heavy butcher paper or in a tray in plastic freezer wrap with no air around the food—can be frozen as is only for up to 1 week. If the food is on a tray that is not vacuum-packed, so there is air around it, remove and repackage as for longer-term storage.

Fish and shellfish must be chilled from the time they're caught to the time they're frozen. To preserve quality, just before freezing, dip lean fish, 413, for 20 to 30 seconds in a brine of $^1/_4$ cup salt (without additives) to 4 cups cold water with 2 tablespoons pure ascorbic acid, 894. For freezing for just a week or two, drugstore-wrap in plastic freezer wrap. For longer storage of small to medium whole fish, steaks, and fillets, give them an ice glaze: Dip in ice water, then tray-freeze until the water is frozen. Repeat the dipping and freezing until the pieces are glazed with ice $^1/_8$- to $^1/_4$-inch thick. Drugstore-wrap pieces in freezer wrap, or place in plastic freezer bags—either way, place 2 pieces of freezer wrap between pieces. The following are best packed in rigid freezer containers, leaving a $^1/_2$-inch headspace: shucked clams, shucked scallops, shucked oysters with their liquor, and squid and octopus covered with water.

THAWING AND COOKING FROZEN MEAT, GAME, POULTRY, FISH, AND SHELLFISH

Most frozen meats, game, poultry, and fish can be cooked thawed or unthawed. ➤ Cooking unthawed meat can take $1^1/_2$ times as long as cooking it fresh. ➤ When roasting, never use an oven temperature lower than 325°F, and keep the temperature constant. When broiling unthawed meat, place it at least 5 to 6 inches below the heat source. Pan-broiling thin cuts of meat—chops, for example—will take about $1^1/_4$ times as long as cooking thawed meat. ➤ Variety meats, foods to be cooked in breading or dredging, all seafood except shrimp, and poultry to be stuffed must be thawed completely. Shrimp only needs thawing if it is to be deep-fried. Unless they will be simmered, poultry and game birds are best when thawed before cooking.

These foods must be thawed in the refrigerator at 40°F or lower. Keep wrapped and place on a tray or in a pan to catch dripping juices or liquids. Place below any cooked or ready-to-eat foods in the refrigerator. Slow thawing of meat and poultry helps retain juiciness (add any thawing juices to the cooking pan). These foods can also be thawed in a microwave oven. ➤ Marinade can be added to thawing meat and poultry in a plastic freezer bag. Meat thawed to the point where the center is soft but a few ice crystals are visible on the surface usually tastes best and has the best texture after cooking. Slowly thawed fish loses less juice and is more delicate when cooked than quickly thawed fish.

FREEZING AND THAWING EGGS

Eggs must be removed from the shell before freezing. For short periods, shelled eggs may be frozen individually in an ice-cube tray, then packed and stored. Usually, however, yolks and whites are stored separately. The whites may be packed in small tightly sealed one-recipe-sized containers, perhaps in the exact amount for a favorite angel cake. ➤ Yolks should be stabilized, or they will become pasty and hard to mix after freezing. If yolks are to be used for unsweetened food, add 1 teaspoon salt to each 2 cups; if for desserts, add 1 tablespoon sugar, honey, or corn syrup to each 2 cups. Label the yolks accordingly. You will need about 10 whole eggs, 16 whites, or 24 yolks for each pint container. To use, ➤ thaw in the refrigerator for 8 to 10 hours.

If you prefer to package whole eggs, stir $1^1/_2$ teaspoons sugar or corn syrup or 1 teaspoon salt into each pint, depending on how you will be using them, incorporating as little air as possible. When packing, allow $\frac{1}{2}$-inch headspace, 890, for expansion during freezing. Thaw all eggs before using in recipes. For each whole egg, use 3 tablespoons thawed whole eggs. To reconstitute a whole egg from separately packed whites and yolks, allow $1\frac{1}{3}$ tablespoons yolk and 2 tablespoons white.

FREEZING BUTTER, CREAM, AND MILK

Unsalted butter freezes well for 6 months, but 3 months should be the limit of storage for salted butter. ➤ Cream may be frozen for up to 2 months. When thawed, the uses for heavy cream are limited mainly to making frozen desserts and using small amounts in vegetables and casseroles. Its whipping quality will be impaired, its oil rises on contact with coffee, and the texture is unsatisfactory for use with cereals. If you are making ice cream or frozen desserts, 828, for the freezer, choose a recipe that calls for heating the cream first. It is not advisable to freeze sour cream. ➤ Freeze milk for only 1 month.

To use, ➤ thaw butter about 3 hours on a refrigerator shelf and milk or cream about 4 hours.

FREEZING CHEESES

Hard and Cheddar cheeses may be frozen for up to 4 months. Cream cheese becomes crumbly when frozen but can be used as an ingredient in sandwiches or dips. Thaw about 3 hours on a refrigerator shelf.

FREEZING PRECOOKED FOODS

The frozen precooked meal, for better or for worse, is a reality. Labor can be saved by baking several pies, cakes, or batches of bread at one session and storing the extras or by doubling a casserole recipe and freezing half. Prepare school lunches in advance. Frozen sandwiches in the lunchbox will be thawed by lunchtime and will keep other foods cool. We urge you, though, to read about the kinds of products suitable for freezing, 910, and to remember ➤ to cool the cooked dishes you plan to freeze through and through before you pack them. If you do not cool them sufficiently, the outside edges may freeze hard and the interior may not cool quickly enough to prevent spoilage. ➤ Also, do not try to freeze too much at one time, for overloading your freezer raises the temperature to the detriment of your already stored frozen foods. Be just as careful with packaging cooked foods, 912, as with raw ones. Try to use them within 1 month, and when reheating, be sure to thaw properly or reheat slowly.

Fried foods almost without exception tend to rancidity, toughness, and dryness when frozen. No appreciable time is gained by freezing such starchy foods as macaroni, noodles, or rice. Prepare main dishes as usual, following your favorite recipes. But, in all instances, undercook the vegetables involved, as they will receive further cooking during reheating for serving.

Perhaps the most important thing to consider in precooking frozen foods is not to overcook foods that are to be reheated later. Milk sauces sometimes curdle and separate, so stirring while reheating, otherwise discouraged, will be necessary. Potatoes in casseroles will be waterlogged and mealy. Avoid sauces based on egg. Celery and cabbage may alter flavors and become limp and waterlogged. ➤ Season carefully. Peppers, cloves, garlic, and onion tend to become strong or bitter; celery seasoning becomes stronger. Some herbs tend to become stronger, while others wash out, as does salt. Curry may acquire a musty, off flavor. In all cases, season lightly before freezing; adjustments can be made when reheating or serving.

Reheat stews and creamed dishes in a saucepan over low heat or in the oven at 350°F in a baking dish. Stir as little as possible. Allow $1\frac{1}{2}$ times as long as normal to heat a frozen casserole at the usual temperature. Bake frozen meat pies into a 350°F to 375°F oven until browned. Thaw croquettes or ➤ any breaded food that is to be sautéed or deep-fried ➤ uncovered and refrigerated, so that moisture does not form. If the food is already fried, thaw ➤ uncovered and refrigerated, and bake in a 400°F oven. ➤ Reheat all meat and/or vegetable dishes to an internal food temperature of at least 165°F before serving.

FREEZING CANAPÉS AND SANDWICHES

Canapés and sandwiches should not be stored longer than a few weeks. Make them up quickly to keep the bread from drying out. Be sure to spread all bread well and to make the fillings rather heavy in fats, so that the bread will not become saturated. Or you may prefer to prepare and freeze sandwich spreads for use later with fresh bread. As a corollary, bread for canapés can be cut into fancy shapes, frozen and then thawed slightly just before spreading. ➤ In choosing recipes for fillings, avoid mayonnaise and boiled salad dressings, hard-cooked egg whites, jellies and all crisp salad materials. Garnishes like cress, parsley, tomato and cucumber cannot be frozen, so add these the last moment before serving.

You may freeze canapés on trays first or wrap them carefully and then freeze them. In either case, keep the different kinds separated from one another and away from the interior walls of the freezer, as this contact makes the bread soggy. Canapés and sandwiches should always be thawed in the wrappings. They take from 1 to 2 hours to thaw on a refrigerator shelf and from 15 to 45 minutes at room temperature—depending on size.

FREEZING SOUPS

Soups are an excellent candidate for freezing. To freeze soups, prepare them as usual, then chill rapidly over ice water. Store in any containers suitable for liquids, allowing headspace of $\frac{1}{2}$ inch in pint and 1 inch in quart containers. For concentrated meat or fish stock, the stock should be simmered until reduced to one-half or one-third its original quantity, see About Soup Stock, 114. This is the most space-saving soup to store. You may freeze them, if you like, in ice-cube trays, for additions to gravy and sauces, then put the frozen cubes in plastic bags and seal. Another way to freeze liquids is to use a sealed plastic bag inserted in a coffee can with a plastic lid. When the liquid is frozen solid, remove it from the can. If a soup or chowder calls for potato, it is preferable to add freshly cooked potato just before serving. If you do freeze the potato, undercook it. Fish and meat stock thawed and combined in a blender with fresh vegetables make delicate soups in short order. To serve frozen soups, bring them to a boil in a saucepan—unless they are thick or have a cream base, in which case a double boiler or very low heat is necessary. For cold soups, thaw until liquid and serve still chilled.

FREEZING SALAD INGREDIENTS
The materials that the word salad brings to mind—fresh crisp greens, tomatoes, cucumbers and aspics—are impossible to freeze, but some of the foods traditionally served with them freeze well and will shorten salad preparation time. For instance, frozen precooked meats, poultry, and fish—whole, diced, or sliced and covered with concentrated stocks—are welcome ingredients for a salad when thawed and drained. Precooked green beans, evenly sized and unsliced, may be packaged, frozen, and later coated with French dressing. And almost any fruit mixture, excluding pears, may be frozen for use in fruit salads later. If using bananas, freeze slices separately.

COOK FOR A DAY, EAT FOR A WEEK
By spending a well-planned day in the kitchen, then properly cooling and freezing the cooked food, you can stock the freezer with a wide variety of home-prepared meals. Planning and preparing food in this fashion is a true convenience for busy families and individuals and is economically wise as well. When planning the menu, take advantage of sale items, bulk quantities, and seasonal bargains. The resulting meals will be both nutritious and delicious. See menus, 24, for a list of recipes from JOY that will work well for this plan.

To prepare food for the week, focus your menus on ingredients and dishes that keep as much of their taste, texture, and nutritive value when frozen as possible. Good candidates are soups and stews; casseroles; pasta sauces; cooked fruits, vegetables, meats, and poultry; savory and sweet pies; cakes; and cookies. Use this chapter as a guide when selecting foods. Before you start to cook, select your recipes and have on hand all ingredients necessary for the recipes. Also necessary to have on hand are the freezing tools of choice: plastic freezer bags, freezer boil-in-bags, rigid freezing containers, freezer wrap and foil, and, to mark each package's contents and freezing date, a waterproof felt-tip pen or paper labels. See 912 for more tips on freezer containers, and 913 for wrapping and packaging food for freezing. Quickly cool, and freeze the cooked food in individual or family-sized portions. Docu-

ment each meal on a master chart of the freezer inventory, and keep it by the refrigerator. Then thaw the meals in the refrigerator according to when they are to be consumed. A frozen meal can be supplemented with a fresh fruit or green salad, and the meal is complete.

FREEZING UNBAKED PASTRY, COOKIES, AND DOUGHS
Doughs, batters, and unbaked pastry on the whole respond less favorably to freezing than do the finished products, though cookie and pie doughs are exceptions to this rule. ➤ We do not recommend freezing cake batters; all leaveners are highly variable under frozen storage, particularly those incorporated into moister doughs.

Unbaked yeast bread dough is most acceptable if frozen for only a week or 10 days. It is made up in the usual way, see 591, kneaded, and allowed to rise once until doubled in bulk, then kneaded again and shaped before packaging into loaves no more than 2 inches thick. Thin loaves, of course, will thaw much faster than thick ones. "Serve soon" would be a timelier suggestion, because thawed and baked bread dough dries out very rapidly. Frozen bread dough is a notable exception to the rule that frozen foods are best when slowly thawed: Place the dough in a 250°F oven for 45 minutes, then bake it as usual, cool, and serve. Partially baked breads in the brown-and-serve category may be put into the oven without thawing.

Unbaked dough for yeast rolls should not be frozen for more than 1 week. See Milk Rolls, 611. Follow the procedure for frozen dough, above. Grease all roll surfaces; tray-freeze them 2 to 4 hours on trays set away from the walls of the freezer, and package within 24 hours after freezing. Or, wrap the rolls before freezing, separating them with sheets of moisture and vapor-proof material such as plastic wrap or resealable plastic bags. To serve, unwrap the rolls, cover with a cloth, and put them in a warm place to rise until doubled in bulk, 2 to 4 hours. Bake as usual.

Unbaked biscuits may also be frozen on trays or packaged before freezing. They, too, rise well and thaw quickly if rolled thin. Thaw them, wrapped, at room temperature for 1 hour and bake as usual.

Pastries heavy in fat, like pies, tarts, filled rings, and rich cookies, whether frozen baked or unbaked, come through frozen storage rather well. If you want to cut cookies before freezing, tray-freeze them, 913, then package for freezing. If you want to cut them after freezing, make a roll of the dough, wrap it in moisture and vapor-proof material in batch sizes, and seal. These uncooked cookie doughs keep about 2 months. Bake the cookies in a 350° to 375°F oven 10 to 12 minutes.

FREEZING BAKED PASTRY, CAKES, COOKIES, AND DOUGHS

Baked doughs are quicker and easier to freeze than raw doughs and, generally speaking, yield more satisfactory results. Careful packaging is essential. ➤ Always plan to thaw just the amount of baked articles needed, for they will dry out rapidly after having been frozen. But though they do not keep the longest, their flavor remains truer.

Precooked pastries heavy in fats are the most successful "freezers" of all, but their storage limit is about 2 to 3 months. Baked yeast bread and rolls have the longest storage potential—6 months or more—but they begin to lose flavor after 2 months. Bake all of these in the usual way and, before packaging, let them cool for 3 hours. If frozen bread is to be used for toast, it is not necessary to thaw it. Otherwise thaw it still wrapped, at room temperature, for 2 to 3 hours before serving. Freshen it in a 300°F oven for 20 minutes.

Baked cakes will keep 2 to 3 months if unfrosted, but only 1 month if frosted. Filled cakes tend to sogginess, and any filling with an egg base should not be frozen. Actually, it is a better policy to wait and add any filling just before serving. Spice cake should not be stored for over 6 weeks, as the flavors change in the freezing process; use a minimum of spices and omit the cloves. If frosted cakes are to be frozen, use icings with a confectioners'-sugar-and-butter base. Brown sugar icings and those containing egg whites or syrups tend to crystallize and freeze poorly. Boiled frosting becomes sticky on thawing.

Do not wrap any iced cakes until the icing has been well firmed by chilling, unwrapped, in the freezer. Place waxed paper over iced portions before putting on the outer wrap and sealing. Protect cakes with an extra carton to avoid crushing. Thaw them, unwrapped, in a covered cake container at room temperature for 2 hours before serving.

If cookies are baked before freezing, plan to use in 1 to 2 months for best quality. Bake as usual, then cool and pack tightly, separating each layer with moisture- and vapor-proof material. To avoid breakage, place in an extra carton after wrapping. Let the cookies thaw, wrapped, in the refrigerator. ➤ Freshen them in a 350°F oven for a few minutes.

FREEZING UNBAKED PIES

Use foil pans, or pans you can spare, so your pies can be frozen and then baked in the same container. You will get better results with frozen piecrust if it has ➤ a high fat content. Piecrust may be frozen ready for rolling or may be rolled out ready to be put in the pan; ➤ unrolled dough must be handled while it is still chilled so it will remain tender. Freeze unfilled shells in the pan, then remove and stack them in a box before wrapping, or store them, wrapped, in disposable foil pans. Bake, without thawing,

at 425°F 12 to 15 minutes. If making pies for freezing, brush the inside of the bottom crust with egg wash to keep it from becoming soggy before filling. Brush the top crust with egg wash too, but do not prick until ready to bake. ➤ Never use water, egg, or milk for glazing.

The best pie fillings for freezing are fresh fruits or mincemeat, and their storage limit is 4 to 6 months. For best flavor, use pumpkin pies within 4 weeks. Fruits such as peaches, apples, and apricots, which darken on exposure to air, should be treated with ascorbic acid, 894. The fillings for unbaked pies should have about 1½ times more cornstarch or tapioca than usual; or, if possible, use waxy starches; see 1017. ➤ Never freeze a cream or custard pie.

Freeze the pie before wrapping if the filling is a wobbly one. Then wrap tightly. Seal, and protect against the weight of other objects in the freezer until frozen hard.

To bake, remove the wrapping, cut vent holes in the top crust, and place the pie unthawed on the lowest shelf of a 450°F preheated oven for 15 to 20 minutes. Reduce heat to 375°F until done, about 1 hour in all.

FREEZING BAKED PIES

Please read Freezing Unbaked Pies, above. Use foil pans or containers you are willing to spare, so the ➤ pie can be cooked, stored, and reheated in the same pan. Cool completely after baking, then wrap in freezer plastic wrap, 912, and seal.

If you are freezing any precooked fillings with starch, be sure to ➤ cook them very thoroughly and, if possible, use waxy starches, 1017. ➤ Never freeze a baked cream or custard pie, and do not freeze pie meringue. Chiffon pies can be frozen in a baked shell if, before freezing, the filling has at least ½ cup of whipping cream incorporated into it. ➤ Thaw unwrapped and refrigerated. Garnish with whipped cream before serving, if desired.

Thaw a baked pie in the refrigerator if it is to be served cold. If it is to be served hot, let stand at room temperature for 15 minutes, then heat in a 350°F preheated oven until warm, about 30 to 40 minutes.

Unfilled baked pie shells are one of the most convenient of all frozen items, ready for filling with quiche batters, creamed foods such as potpie filling, or fruit fillings. Freeze the pie shells unwrapped in the pans, then remove and stack them in a box before wrapping; or store them wrapped in disposable foil pans.

FREEZING DRIED FRUITS AND NUTS

Dried fruits and nuts can be successfully frozen whole, chopped, or ground for 6 to 7 months. Wrap them in convenient quantities, taking the usual precautions to expel air from the packages.

JELLIES AND PRESERVES

An afternoon spent putting up jams, jellies, fruit butters, or other sweet preserves may seem like a throwback to another time—and it is. It is also very satisfying, a way to expand your pantry, to savor the taste of seasonal fruit year-round, and to make old-fashioned, thoughtful gifts, better than anything manufactured commercially.

Jellies, jams, preserves, conserves, marmalades, fruit butters, and jellied fruit sauces are all based on the principle of cooking and preserving fruit with a sweetener—sugar, honey, or fruit juice. But what are the differences among them?

Jelly has great clarity. Two cooking processes are involved. First, the juice alone is extracted from the fruit. Then only that portion thin and clear enough to drip through a cloth is cooked with sugar until ➤ sufficiently firm to hold its shape. It is never stiff and never gummy. ➤ **Jams, butters,** and **jellied fruit sauces** are purees of progressively increasing density. ➤ **Preserves, marmalades,** and **conserves** are bits of fruit cooked to a translucent state in heavy syrup. These and the **jams,** all of which need only one cooking, take patience and ➤ careful stirring, so that they reduce without scorching.

EQUIPMENT

Get your equipment ready before you begin to cook the jelly, jam, or preserves. In addition to standard cutting, measuring, and mixing equipment, the most important tool is a heavy wide, shallow 8- to 10-quart pan with a flat bottom. Heavy-duty nonstick versions work well, but any nonreactive surface is fine. Stay away from uncoated aluminum, copper, iron, thin enamel, or galvanized pots. Long-handled utensils are helpful, such as a wide silicone

cooking spatula, a large stainless steel spoon, a whisk, a skimmer, a 4- to 8-ounce ladle (preferably with a spout), and a 1-inch-wide pastry brush with natural bristles, to wash down sugar crystals. You may also find a fine-mesh strainer, colander, ruler, timer, and/or jar funnel helpful. To can jars, use a large, wide, deep pot for a boiling-water canner, sterilized canning jars without nicks or cracks, metal rings and new lids (shown on 889), and a jar lifter (shown on 890). A jelly bag (shown on 93) is preferable for straining juice for jelly. However, 4 layers of clean cheese-cloth may also be used. For microwave cooking, use a 2-quart glass measuring cup. Also helpful are a food processor, kitchen scale (10-pound capacity), candy thermometer, food mill, potato masher or large pestle, cherry pitter, citrus juicer, and zester.

SELECTING FRUIT

Choose only the freshest and most flavorful fruit. The only true test is to smell and taste—if the fruit lacks full flavor, your results will disappoint. ➤ Slightly underripe to firm but ripe fruit is ideal. Overly ripe fruit can lead to problems with texture and spoilage. When the fruit you want is out of season, a wise choice is to buy unsweetened frozen fruits.

The recipes here mostly call for fruits by weight because that is the most accurate measure. ➤ Frozen fruit, however, contains an excess of water and should be measured by volume after briefly thawing. Remove as little from the fresh fruit as possible, peeling the skin when the recipe directs and cutting away any bruised or unsound spots. In all the recipes, it is essential to rinse all fruits and remove all seeds before you begin.

PECTIN

Pectin, found in the skin, seeds, and flesh of fruit, is a natural substance that reacts with sugar and acid to form a thick jell. Fruits are rated as having high or low pectin content (see Pectin Content of Fruits, 928). ➤ High pectin content is crucial for the success of jellies, marmalades, and jellied fruit sauces. Pectin content is less important for softer-textured jams, conserves, and fruit butters. Unfortunately, natural pectin can be fickle depending on climate and the variety and ripeness of the fruit. As fruit ripens, pectin breaks down, which is why barely ripe fruits are preferable. Prolonged cooking also deteriorates pectin, making it important not to exceed the recommended cooking times. When jelling is especially important—such as for jellies—we recommend testing for pectin, opposite. If your fruit does not have enough pectin for jelly, use commercial pectin and follow the package directions.

An easy way to make firm preserves with a low-pectin fruit is to combine the fruit with an equal amount of grated tart apples, which contain a large quantity of pectin. Grating the apples will ensure that they cook quickly and thicken the preserves without affecting the flavor or texture of the dominant fruit.

We recommend ➤ using **commercial pectin**—a liquid

or powdered substance derived primarily from apple pomace or citrus peels—only in jelly recipes made with very low-pectin fruits. Some recipes using commercial pectin require too much sugar for our tastes, and the high level of sugar can overwhelm the flavor of the fruit. Liquid and powdered pectin are not interchangeable in recipes. The order of combining and cooking ingredients depends on the type of pectin used.

PECTIN CONTENT OF FRUITS

Fruits should be barely ripe to firm-ripe.

High-Pectin Fruits: tart apples; crab apples; cranberries; currants; gooseberries; Concord, Muscadine, and Scuppernong grapes; lemons; loganberries; bitter oranges; Damson and other tart plums (not Italian); and quinces.

Low-Pectin Fruits: apricots, blackberries, blueberries, cherries, elderberries, figs, all grapes except those listed above, huckleberries, guavas, nectarines, peaches, pears, pineapples, pomegranates, raspberries, rhubarb, sweet and Italian plums, and strawberries.

How to test for pectin: Pectin content cannot be determined by taste. ➤ Since pectin is essential for well-set jellies, we recommend testing extracted fruit juice for pectin. There are two ways of determining the pectin content of the juice. The first, the alcohol test, is closer to a scientific experiment, while the second involves making a small sample of jelly.

Alcohol Test: After extracting the juice from the fruit (see Extracting the Juice, 930), thoroughly blend 1 teaspoon of the cooled cooked juice with 1 tablespoon rubbing alcohol. ➤ **The alcohol mixture is inedible; do not taste!** If a single gelatinous mass forms that can be picked up with a fork, there is ample pectin for jelly, marmalade, and jellied fruit sauces. Use $3/4$ to 1 cup sugar for 1 cup fruit or juice.

If the mixture separates into 2 or 3 masses, use $2/3$ cup sugar per cup of fruit or juice. If numerous masses form, make preserves that do not need to jell, using half as much sugar as fruit or juice; or add commercial pectin to make jelled preserves. On rare occasions, inexplicably, a pectin-rich juice does not react with the alcohol, which is why the second test may be more practical.

Small Jelly Sample Test: After extracting the juice (refer to Extracting the Juice, 930), bring $1/3$ cup of strained juice to a simmer in a small pan. Stir in $1/4$ cup sugar. Boil to the jelling point, 929, using the quick-chill test on 929.

Adjust the lemon juice if needed, making calculations for the entire recipe, then add the remaining juice and proceed. When in doubt, use a little more sugar, adding fresh citrus juice to balance the sweetness.

If the sample will not jell, discard the test and use the rest of the fruit juice in a recipe with commercial pectin.

ACID

Unlike pectin, the acid content of a fruit is easily determined by taste. If the fruit tastes as tart as a green apple, a sour plum, or rhubarb, there is sufficient acid to thicken the preserves, given the proper proportions of pectin and sugar. For fruits slightly less tart than these, such as tart cherries, elderberries, table grapes, and sweet plums, ➤ add $1/4$ tablespoon bottled lemon juice per cup of fruit or juice in the pan before cooking. For low-acid fruits, including sweet apples, sweet cherries, figs, nectarines, peaches, pears, and strawberries, add 1 tablespoon bottled lemon juice per cup. Alternatively, add orange juice to the uncooked fruit until it just barely begins to taste of orange. In addition to the juice's role in helping preserves set, a few drops of lemon or orange juice perk up the flavor of the fruit. ➤ Keep in mind that underripe and just-ripe fruits are highest in acid. Citrus peel also enhances the flavor of sweet preserves, but it must be simmered in a little water until tender before it is added. Once tender, drain the peel and add it to the fruit; save the pectin-rich simmering water to add to the preserves when possible.

SUGAR AND OTHER SWEETENERS

The role of sugar goes beyond that of a sweetener in making jellies and jams. It preserves the fruit by inhibiting the growth of bacteria. ➤ Decreasing the sugar in a recipe can drastically reduce shelf life. In addition, sugar reacts with the pectin to set jellies and jams. High-pectin fruits yield the best-set jellies, but only in the presence of enough sugar. The more pectin in a mixture, the more sugar needed and the firmer the jelly.

It takes very little sugar to bring out a fruit's flavor. Finding the right amount of sugar is a balancing act. Less sugar means less preserves and they will keep for a shorter time, but the fruit flavors will be brighter. White sugar has a neutral taste that does not compete with the flavors of the fresh fruit.

Sometimes jars of preserves end up with grainy crystals that multiply and ultimately solidify the contents. ➤ Prevent this by using a pastry brush dipped in water to dissolve any sugar clinging to the sides of the pan during cooking. If there is sugar on the sides of the pan when the cooking is done, carefully remove it with a damp cloth before ladling out the preserves.

For a deeper, fuller flavor, substitute brown sugar for up to one-quarter of the white sugar in a recipe. Alternatively, up to half the sugar in any recipe without commercial pectin may be replaced with mild honey. Some manufacturers of commercial pectin allow the substitution of light corn syrup for up to one-quarter of the sugar. ➤ Keep in mind that honey is sweeter and stronger flavored than sugar. Corn syrup is also very sweet, but is neutral tasting. Another alternative is fruit juice. Apple juice is a favorite because of its relatively neutral flavor and high pectin content.

Nonnutritive, artificial sweeteners work only in thick jams and fruit butters, which don't rely on the sugar's interaction with pectin to set. Keep in mind that ➤ anything made with any sort of nonnutritive sweetener will lack the preserving power of sugar and will need to be processed in a water bath, 890, for 15 minutes. Follow the manufacturer's directions on substituting for sugar, or follow the suggested amounts in packages of commercial pectin.

JELLED PRESERVES

Jellies, marmalades, jams, and some preserves and conserves, while they range from firm to soft and almost runny, are all based on the principle of boiling sweetened fruit or juice until enough moisture has evaporated and the pectin, acid, and sugar have concentrated. This point is referred to as **the jelling point** and is ➤ best reached by rapid boiling, because the elements that make preserves jell—pectin, sugar, and acid—interact most effectively over intense heat (prolonged cooking at lower temperatures deteriorates pectin). Rapid boiling also tends to keep jellies clearer than slow-cooking, while retaining the flavor of fresh fruit.

This chapter is about small-batch making. ➤ Do not double the amounts in recipes; doubled recipes will not always jell properly.

BOILING PRESERVES

Choose a heavy, large, wide pan. ➤ We recommend cooking the fruit in batches of 2 to 2½ pounds or less per pan. Cook rapidly over high heat to retain the flavor and pectin of the fruit.

Jellied products tend to foam dramatically when boiled. Any additive, such as honey, will cause even more foam. For clear jellies, skim the foam throughout the cooking process.

THE JELLING POINT

This is the moment of truth when everything comes together and when, once cooled, the preserves will jell. The jelling point is unpredictable, so it is a good idea to start testing for it early and often while cooking, as described below. A good visual indicator is when, after boiling high and foamy in the pan, the mixture settles and its surface is suddenly covered with furiously boiling small bubbles.

There are three reliable tests for the jelling point in jams and jellies made without commercial pectin: the spoon test, the temperature test, and the quick-chill test. ➤ They are best used in conjunction with one another, especially if you are making jam or jelly for the first time. Most experienced jam and jelly makers, however, come to rely on just one test. Whichever you choose, be certain the mixture has reached the consistency you want before you declare it ready.

The spoon test works best for jellies but is also effective for all but the thickest fruit purees. Scoop up a little boiling syrup or some of the thinnest part of the fruit mixture with a cool, dry stainless steel spoon. Raise it over the pot, but out of the steam, then turn it so that the syrup falls back into the pan from the spoon's side. At first the drip will be light and syrupy. As the syrup continues to cook and thick-

ens, 2 large drops will form along the spoon's edge. ➤ When the drips slide together and fall as one, jelling has begun. For a tender-firm set, wait until these drops are heavy. When the drips glide together and hang off the edge of the spoon a moment before dropping, **the sheeting stage** has been reached, and this will make as firm a jell as the pectin can give.

In **the temperature test,** we use temperature as an indication the jelling point is near, then finish with the quick-chill test. ➤ Use a candy thermometer. Traditionally, the jelling point is 8 to 10 degrees higher than the boiling point of water, which is 212°F. So, at sea level, the jelling point is 220°F to 222°F. (For higher elevations, see High-Altitude Preserving, 930.) These temperatures are based on ¾ cup sugar for each 1 cup fruit and result in a moderately firm jell. For a very soft jell, stop cooking at 2 to 3 degrees lower. For a very firm jell, boil to 3 to 4 degrees higher.

The quick-chill test is a bit more involved, but it is the surest test because you actually see how the finished product will jell. We recommend using the temperature or spoon test as an indication of progress and then, as the preserves begin to settle, trying the quick-chill test. Before you start cooking, place a couple of saucers in the freezer or set a small metal bowl in a larger bowl of ice water. ➤ Remove the pan from the heat each time you do this test, or the preserves may overcook. Drop a small amount of syrup onto a chilled saucer and return it to the freezer, or drop the sample into the icy bowl. After about 3 minutes, pull a finger through the center of the chilled preserves. ➤ For a soft set, the sides should glide back together slowly. For a tender-firm set, the sides should not move and the surface should wrinkle when gently pushed.

Once the desired consistency has been reached, ➤ immediately remove the pan from the heat. Undercooked preserves can be cooked again until set—you can remove the pan from the heat as many times as necessary and quality will not be affected—but overcooked preserves are usually lost. All jellied products will be thicker after cooling and will continue to set for 1 to 3 weeks.

PUTTING UP PRESERVES

There are three ways of keeping homemade preserves. Based on how long you want to keep the product, choose refrigeration, freezing, or canning.

Refrigeration: Refrigeration is the simplest method, but it also means the shortest storage time. Pour the hot preserves into sterilized jars (see Canning, below), cover, cool, and refrigerate. ➤ The shelf life of refrigerated preserves depends on the amount of sugar in the recipe—preserves made with one-half to two-thirds as much sugar as fruit will keep in the refrigerator for at least 2 to 3 weeks. Those made with equal amounts of sugar and fruit will last for 2 months or more.

Freezing: Cooked jelled preserves do not freeze well. All other preserves will keep for 6 months packed in freezer containers. ➤ Leave ½-inch headspace in containers, 890; leave the same headspace in freezer bags, but force out the air. Label with the contents and the date frozen.

Canning: Please read the directions for safe and proper boiling-water canning, 890–891. The best method for storing preserves is to pour them into sterilized small canning jars. ➤ Half-pints are preferred and you will rarely want to use a jar larger than a pint. ➤ Use metal rings and new flat lids, leaving ¼-inch headspace, unless otherwise noted in the recipe. ➤ Process in a boiling-water canner for 5 to 15 minutes, according to the recipe.

Make sure ➤ jars are free of nicks or cracks. While the jars and undamaged metal rings can be reused, use new flat lids each time. See Equipment, 927. Wash in hot soapy water and rinse well. ➤ Preserves that will be processed for less than 10 minutes, such as jellies, must go into sterilized jars.

To sterilize the jars, place a rack in the bottom of the canning kettle and fill it with hot water. Lower the jars into the kettle—be sure they are all covered and filled with water—and boil for 10 minutes at altitudes of 1,000 feet or less ➤ (at higher altitudes, boil 1 additional minute for each 1,000 feet). Leave the jars in the kettle until needed. ➤ Prepare the lids and metal rings, 889, according to manufacturer's directions. Do not boil them, or you may ruin their ability to seal.

When ready to fill the jars, lift them out one at a time, pouring the hot water back into the pan, and stand upright on a clean dish towel.

Ladle or pour the hot preserves into the hot jars, leaving ¼-inch headspace, 890, unless otherwise noted in the recipe. ➤ Wipe the rims clean with a damp paper towel and set on the lids. Screw on the rings and, using the jar lifter, lower the jars into the kettle filled with hot water. Be sure the water covers the lids and bring to a boil. Process for the time directed. ➤ See Processing Canned Foods, 891. Carefully remove the jars with the jar lifter and set them on a clean towel to cool. ➤ See Cooling the Jars, 891. When the seal is formed and the jars are cool, dry completely. Write the name of the product and the date on the lid with a permanent marker. See Storing Canned Goods, 892.

Discard preserves that exhibit any of the following: mold (rare in unopened canned preserves, inevitable at some point in refrigerated preserves), fermentation, or bubbling. See Checking for Spoilage, 892, and Handling Contaminated Food and Jars, 893.

Once opened, all preserves need to be refrigerated. To slow the growth of mold, minimize the time the jar stays open or out of the refrigerator. Molds are in the air and will contaminate your preserves each time they are exposed.

▲ HIGH-ALTITUDE PRESERVING

Jelling-point temperatures as altitude increases:

1,000 feet	218° to 220°F
2,000 feet	216° to 218°F
3,000 feet	214° to 216°F
4,000 feet	212° to 214°F
5,000 feet	211° to 212°F
6,000 feet	209° to 211°F
7,000 feet	207° to 209°F
8,000 feet	205° to 207°F

Increased processing times:
  1,000 to 6,000 feet, add 5 minutes
  6,001+ feet, add 10 minutes

ABOUT MAKING JELLY

A good jelly is a bright, clear, tender-set jell made from strained fruit juice, wine, spirits, or even herb infusions. Two cooking processes are involved. First, juice is extracted from nearly every part of the fruit. Then, after the juice has settled for at least 12 hours, or overnight, it is boiled with sugar until firm enough to hold its shape when cold. Picture-perfect jelly takes time to make and is more dependent on just the right proportions of pectin, sugar, and acid than any other type of preserves.

PREPARING THE FRUIT

When selecting fruits for jelly, in general, ➤ mix one-quarter slightly underripe to firm but ripe fruit for pectin and three-quarters firm but ripe fruit for flavor. With medium- and low-pectin fruits, 928, however, pectin must always be added, so use fully ripe fruit for the deepest flavor. Wash and chop hard fruits such as apples into small (¼-inch) bits and mash soft fruits. Skins, cores, and seeds should not be removed, because they contribute pectin and/or flavor and will be strained out in the end. Thick stems are the only parts to trim away.

EXTRACTING THE JUICE

Place the prepared fruit in a heavy, large, wide, shallow pan—the wider it is, the more efficiently the fruit will cook. Water may be necessary to prevent scorching, or to produce juice from firm fruits, such as apples and quinces, but add only as much as needed. ➤ When a recipe says "cover" with water, just barely cover—never float—the fruit. Cover the pan and bring to a boil over high heat, lifting the lid and mashing and stirring the fruit frequently. Turn down the heat and simmer until the fruit is thoroughly soft, mashing and stirring frequently. ➤ To preserve the pectin, do not boil rapidly and do not cook longer than called for in the recipe.

To strain the juice, ➤ we recommend you use a ready-made jelly bag, which consists of a three-prong steel frame fitted with a cloth or nylon sack. Some models come with a shallow bowl that hooks onto the frame under the sack. Wash or replace the jelly bag after every use, according to the manufacturer's instructions.

If you do not have a jelly bag, use the following method: Wet and wring out 4 layers of clean cheesecloth. Lay the cloth in a colander set inside a deep bowl and ladle or pour in the contents of the pan. The bag or colander should be left to drip for 3 to 4 hours—rarely more than a spoonful of extra juice will come after that. ➤ For clear jelly, do not squeeze the bag or press the fruit against the cheesecloth. For maximum yield but cloudy and possibly bitter jelly, squeeze out all the juice. When the dripping stops, you can gently press the bag to flatten it, and then let the pulp in the center drip. For the clearest jelly, strain the juice a second time, using fresh wet cloths, and do not squeeze. All the juice for a jelly must be cloth-strained, including any added citrus juices. Line a small strainer with a moist cloth and pour the juices through it into the pan.

Straining the juice with a ready-made jelly bag and a colander lined with cheesecloth

After straining, ➤ all juices profit from settling. This settling is essential for grape juice, to avoid tartrate crystals that might otherwise form later in the jar. Pour into a glass container and let stand undisturbed in the refrigerator. After 12 to 24 hours, carefully pour off the clear juice (discard the sediment). If desired, the juice may now be frozen to use at a more convenient time.

VARYING FRUIT JUICE YIELDS

Occasionally a fruit will yield much less juice than expected, usually because the fruit was dry. (This can happen particularly with apples.) If your juice is very thick, blend in water until it has the consistency and taste of a natural juice. Or, if the juice is not thick enough, return the fruit pulp to a pan with some water and repeat the cooking and straining steps.

COOKING JELLY

Please read the directions for safe and proper canning, 888–909, and Making Jelly, above, before proceeding. The yield for jelly generally equals the amount of strained fruit juice so have the right number of jars ready. Have a thermometer and chilled saucers on hand for the quick-chill test, 929.

Measure the juice into a heavy shallow saucepan. ➤ The syrup will boil up high, so use a pan at least 4 times taller than the syrup is deep. Bring the juice to a simmer

oven high heat. Remove the pan from the heat. Add the sugar **(1)** and any lemon juice called for and mix thoroughly. ➤ Use a wet pastry brush to wash down any sugar from the sides of the pan **(2)**. Return the pan to the heat and boil rapidly, stirring constantly. ➤ When the syrup thickens noticeably, start testing for a jell, 928 **(3)**. If a skin forms while the pan is off the heat waiting for the quick-chill test, whisk to break it up and blend it back in. When the syrup reaches the jelling point, ➤ immediately remove from the heat and then skim off any foam.

Pour the hot jelly into ➤ hot sterilized ½-pint jars, leaving ¼-inch headspace, 890. Process in a boiling-water canner for 5 minutes, 890. Jelly may be refrigerated, but it does not freeze well.

DECORATIVE TOUCHES

A large bay leaf, a curl of citrus zest, a cinnamon stick, a spray of rose hips, a sprig of herb, or a dried red chile—one of these set in the jar before the hot jelly is poured in lifts the jelly from special to superb. Choose garnishes whose flavors blend well with the jelly. Wash and dry garnishes well. If the garnish floats, occasionally turn the jar gently once it has sealed and thoroughly cooled until the object is where you want it. Do not turn it upside down as the jelly thickens—you do not want jelly to stick to the lid.

TROUBLESHOOTING

If the canned jelly is runny or too soft, first remember that some mixtures do not fully set for 2 weeks. Refrigerate to make firmer. Alternatively, the surest way of fixing runny jelly is to boil it again with a mixture of 1 tablespoon sugar, 1 tablespoon water, and 1 teaspoon powdered pectin for each cup of jelly—cooking no more than 1 quart at a time. Melt the soft jelly by slowing warming if necessary. Bring the sugar, water, and pectin mixture to a boil over high heat, stirring constantly. Add the runny or melted jelly, bring to a full boil, and boil for just 30 seconds, stirring constantly. Remove from the heat, skim off any foam, and pour into sterilized jars. Or, easiest of all, label runny jelly as syrup and use as a topping or meat glaze.

JELLY BAG BUTTER

If, after dripping juice, the pulp in the bag is still flavorful and does not contain seeds or tough bits of peel, put it in a heavy shallow pan, stir in apple juice until the pulp is the consistency of applesauce, and simmer, stirring frequently, until thick. Put through a food mill, then return to the heat and sweeten to taste with sugar, brown sugar, or honey. Simmer down to fruit-butter thickness, adding a few sweet spices, if desired. For a recipe, see 936.

RED OR WHITE CURRANT JELLY
About three ½-pint jars

This very old technique makes exquisite jelly. No water is added, and the jelly is only lightly cooked. Spread on breads or use as a glaze, or with white meats. Do not can this jelly, but refrigerate after it sets. It may keep as long as 6 months before opening.

Please read Making Jelly, 930, and Putting Up Preserves, 929.

Wash and drain, then thoroughly crush in a large heavy saucepan:

3 pounds stemmed or 3³/₄ pounds unstemmed red or white currants

Cover and bring to a boil, then turn the heat to low and simmer until colorless, about 10 minutes, mashing frequently. Strain, 930.

For each cup of juice, add:

³/₄ to 1 cup sugar

Boil rapidly, stirring constantly, to the jelling point, 929. Pour into hot sterilized ¹/₂-pint jars, put on the lids and rings and set on a towel or rack. Cool, then refrigerate.

BLACK RASPBERRY AND GOOSEBERRY JELLY

About five ¹/₂-pint jars

Please read Making Jelly, 930, and Putting Up Preserves, 929.

Wash and drain all the fruit.

Combine in a saucepan and simmer until soft, stirring and mashing the fruit.

4 quarts black raspberries
¹/₄ cup water

Place in a separate saucepan and simmer until soft:

2 quarts gooseberries or about 2 cups sliced green apples (with peel and core)
¹/₂ cup water

Combine the fruits and strain, 930. Bring juice to a boil. For each cup of juice, add:

³/₄ to 1 cup sugar

Boil rapidly, stirring frequently, to the jelling point, 929. Remove from the heat and skim off any foam. Pour the hot jelly into hot sterilized jars, leaving ¹/₄-inch headspace, 890. Process for 5 minutes, 890.

BLACKBERRY JELLY

About three ¹/₂-pint jars

Almost any sort of blackberry works for this jelly, but boysenberries, loganberries, marionberries, and olallieberries work especially well. One form of blackberry or another is in season from June through mid-September. No water is added to this pure berry jelly, and there is just enough sugar to firm it up. Please read Making Jelly, 930, and Putting Up Preserves, 929.

Wash and drain, then thoroughly crush in a large heavy saucepan:

4 pounds blackberries

Cover and bring to a boil, stirring to prevent sticking. Reduce the heat and simmer until soupy, about 10 minutes, mashing frequently. Strain, 929, transfer the juice to a glass container, and refrigerate until the sediment has settled.

Pour the clear juice into a measuring cup, leaving the sediment behind. For each cup of juice, add:

³/₄ cup sugar

Boil rapidly, stirring frequently, to the jelling point, 929. Remove from the heat and skim off any foam. Pour the hot jelly into hot sterilized ¹/₂-pint jars, leaving ¹/₄-inch headspace, 890. Process for 5 minutes, 890.

GRAPE JELLY

Prepare **Blackberry Jelly, above,** substituting **Concord, Muscadine, or Scuppernong grapes** for the blackberries. Wash, drain, and stem, then thoroughly crush the grapes in the pan. Cook, then press out the juice in a colander. Let the sediment settle as directed above, then strain the clear juice through a cloth to eliminate tartrate crystals. Use 1 cup sugar for each cup of juice.

APPLE OR CRAB APPLE JELLY

About four ¹/₂-pint jars

This delicately flavored jelly is invaluable for its versatility. Use it as a glaze for chicken or pork, to glaze a fruit tart, or to serve over pancakes. Choose aromatic apples such as Gravenstein, Wealthy, or Cox's Orange Pippin, when available. All crab apples are excellent. They are extra rich in pectin and have a full, spicy flavor. Please read Making Jelly, 930, and Putting Up Preserves, 929.

Wash, remove stems and chop into ¹/₄-inch pieces:

3 pounds unpeeled green apples or crisp crab apples

Place in a large heavy saucepan with:

3 cups water

Cover and bring to a boil, then reduce the heat and simmer, mashing and stirring frequently, until the fruit is thoroughly soft, 20 to 25 minutes for apples, 20 to 30 minutes for crab apples. Strain, 929. Expect about 1 quart juice; add water if necessary.

For each cup of clear juice, add:

1 cup sugar

Stir in:

2 tablespoons bottled lemon juice

Boil rapidly, stirring frequently, to the jelling point, 929. Remove from the heat and skim off any foam. Pour the hot jelly into hot sterilized ¹/₂-pint jars, leaving ¹/₄-inch headspace, 890. Process for 5 minutes, 890.

GUAVA JELLY

About three ¹/₂-pint jars

Please read About Guavas, 228.

Prepare **Apple or Crab Apple Jelly, above,** substituting **3 pounds slightly underripe guavas** for the apples. Simmer until soft, about 30 minutes. Strain twice, 929. In place of the lemon juice, use **2 tablespoons lime juice.**

QUINCE JELLY

About three ¹/₂-pint jars

Rich in pectin and delicate in flavor, quinces are excellent fruit for jelly-making. Prepare **Apple or Crab Apple Jelly,**

above, using **3¹/₂ pounds quinces, stemmed,** and **7 cups
water.** Simmer about 30 minutes.

TART PLUM JELLY
About three ¹/₂-pint jars
Plum juice is rich and needs water.
Prepare **Apple or Crab Apple Jelly, above,** using **12 ounces
plums** and **1²/₃ to 3¹/₄ cups water, depending on the thickness of the juice.** Simmer for 15 to 20 minutes. Omit the
lemon juice.

HERB OR SCENTED JELLY
Prepare **Apple or Crab Apple Jelly, above.** While the jelly
simmers, bruise the leaves and bind together with kitchen
twine **a bunch of mint, basil, tarragon, thyme, lemon verbena, or unsprayed rose geranium leaves.** After testing for
jelling but before removing the jelly from the heat, hold
the stem ends and pass the leaves through the jelly repeatedly until the desired strength of flavoring is reached. If
desired, add a small amount of **food coloring.** Remove
from heat, skim off any foam, and proceed as directed.

PARADISE JELLY
About seven ¹/₂-pint jars
This delicate jelly with its exquisite rose color is a family favorite and was included in every edition of JOY from 1931
to 1975. Less sugar makes a darker, fruitier jelly. Please
read Making Jelly, 930, and Putting Up Preserves, 929.
Cut into ¹/₄-inch pieces, then place in two separate large
heavy saucepans:

    3 pounds unpeeled green apples
    1¹/₂ pounds quinces

Add to the apples:

    3 cups water

Add to the quinces:

    3¹/₂ cups water

Combine in another saucepan:

    **8 ounces cranberries, picked over, washed,
        and coarsely chopped**
    ²/₃ cup water

Bring each pan to a boil, then reduce the heat and simmer
until the fruit is thoroughly soft: cranberries, about 10
minutes; apples and quinces, about 25 minutes. Strain,
929.
Combine the juices, then divide the juice in half. For each
cup of clear juice, add:

    1 cup sugar

Cook in 2 batches: Boil rapidly, stirring frequently, to the
jelling point, 929. Remove from the heat and skim off any
foam. Combine the batches, and pour the hot jelly into
hot sterilized ¹/₂-pint jars, leaving ¹/₄-inch headspace, 890.
Process for 5 minutes, 890.

HOT PEPPER JELLY
About three ¹/₂-pint jars
The balanced hot and sweet flavors are delicious with corn
bread, or as a glaze for sautéed chicken and pork. Ripe red

peppers give the jelly a translucent orange-red appearance.
Please read Making Jelly, 930, and Putting Up Preserves,
929.
Wash, drain, and mince or grind, in a food processor or
meat grinder:

    1 pound ripe sweet red bell peppers
    **8 ounces jalapeño peppers (remove seeds, if desired,
        to make them less hot)**

Combine the peppers and their juices in a large heavy
saucepan with:

    1¹/₂ cups white wine vinegar

Stir and bring to a boil, then reduce to a simmer over
medium heat, then simmer until the peppers are thoroughly soft, 10 to 12 minutes. Strain, 929. Expect about
2 cups of juice; add water if necessary.
Return the juice to the saucepan, and add:

    2¹/₂ cups sugar

Bring to a boil, stirring constantly. Add:

    6 tablespoons liquid pectin, 927

Boil hard for 1 minute. Remove from the heat and skim off
any foam. Pour the hot jelly into hot sterilized ¹/₂-pint jars,
leaving ¹/₄-inch headspace, 890. Process for 5 minutes,
890.

MINT JELLY
About four ¹/₂-pint jars
The classic accompaniment to roast lamb. Make this jelly
in the summer when mint is plentiful and aromatic. The
two mints we commonly use for cooking are peppermint
and spearmint. Please read Making Jelly, 930, and Putting
Up Preserves, 929.
Wash and dry, then place in a large heavy saucepan and
thoroughly crush:

    1¹/₂ cups packed mint leaves

Add:

    1¹/₂ cups apple juice
    ¹/₂ cup bottled lemon juice

Bring to a boil over high heat. Remove from the heat,
cover, and let stand for 10 minutes.
Strain, 929. Expect about 1³/₄ cups of juice; add water if
necessary. Return the mint juice to the saucepan, and add:

    3¹/₂ cups sugar
    (4 drops green food coloring)
    ³/₄ teaspoon salt

Bring to a boil, stirring constantly. Add:

    6 tablespoons liquid pectin

Boil hard for 1 minute. Remove from the heat and skim
off any foam. Pour the hot jelly into hot sterilized ¹/₂-pint
jars, leaving ¹/₄-inch headspace, 890. Process for 5 minutes, 890.

PRICKLY PEAR JELLY
About five ¹/₂-pint jars

Please read About Prickly Pears, 236, Making Jelly, 930, and Putting Up Preserves, 929. Wear gloves and wash and slice in half:

4¹/₂ pounds ripe prickly pears, halved

With the tip of a spoon, scrape the pulp into a large heavy saucepan. Mash thoroughly, then blend in:

1 cup water

Bring to a boil, stirring frequently, then remove from the heat. Strain, 929. You'll need 3 cups juice; if there is more, simmer it down to 3 cups.

Pour the juice into a large heavy saucepan and add:

6 tablespoons strained lime juice

2 tablespoons strained orange juice

One 1.75-ounce package powdered pectin
(5 tablespoons)

Stir and bring to a rolling boil over high heat. Mix in:

4 cups sugar

Stirring constantly, return to a rolling boil, and boil according to the package directions. Pour the hot jelly into hot sterilized ¹/₂-pint jars, leaving ¹/₄-inch headspace, 890. Process for 5 minutes, 890.

LEMON JELLY
About six ¹/₂-pint jars

This has a fine jelly consistency with the taste of lemon marmalade. Spread it on hot breads, or serve as an unusual condiment for savory dishes. Please read Making Jelly, 930, and Putting Up Preserves, 929.

Wash and quarter, then finely chop in a food processor:

2 pounds unpeeled lemons

8 ounces unpeeled oranges

Combine in a large heavy saucepan with:

7¹/₂ cups water

Bring to a boil, then reduce the heat, cover, and simmer 1¹/₄ hours, stirring occasionally. Strain, 929.

For each cup of clear juice, add:

¹/₂ cup sugar

Cook in 2 batches. Boil rapidly, stirring frequently, to the jelling point, 929. Remove from the heat and skim off any foam. Combine the batches and pour the hot jelly into hot sterilized ¹/₂-pint jars, leaving ¹/₄-inch headspace, 890. Process for 5 minutes, 890.

SAVORY LEMON JELLY
About six ¹/₂-pint jars

Prepare: **Lemon Jelly, above,** blending one of the following into each jar of jelly just before sealing.

To serve with fish:

1¹/₂ teaspoons fennel seeds

To serve with chicken:

2 teaspoons finely grated peeled fresh ginger

To serve with beef:

¹/₂ teaspoon crushed red pepper flakes

To serve with lamb:

Three 3¹/₂-inch sprigs rosemary, washed and dried

To serve with pork:

1 teaspoon cumin seeds

To serve with vegetables:

¹/₂ to 1 teaspoon white pepper

ABOUT MAKING JAM

Jam contains lightly jelled whole, crushed, or ground fruit. It is the simplest and most forgiving of sweet preserves to make and is economical as it uses the fruit pulp. There is a lot of leeway in consistency, and most fruits need little preparation. Use firm but ripe fruit sliced or chopped ¹/₄ to ¹/₂ inch thick unless otherwise noted.

Please read the directions for safe and proper canning, 888–909, before proceeding.

RED RED STRAWBERRY JAM
About four ¹/₂-pint jars

Please see Making Jelly, 930, and Putting Up Preserves, 929.

Wash, dry well, and hull:

1 quart strawberries

Put them into a very heavy 10-inch pot, cutting into a few of the berries to release a little juice. Cover with:

4 cups sugar

Stir the mixture very gently with a plastic or wooden spoon over low heat until it has "juiced up." Then raise the heat to medium and stop stirring. When the whole is a bubbling mass, set your timer for 15 minutes—17 if the berries are very ripe. From this point do not disturb, but you may take your spoon and streak it slowly through the bottom to make sure there is no sticking. When the timer rings, tilt the pot. You should see in the liquid at the bottom a tendency to set. Slide the pot off the heat. Allow the berries to cool uncovered. Then stir in:

(Juice of ¹/₂ lemon or 2 tablespoons bottled
lemon juice)

Ladle into sterilized ¹/₂-pint jars, 890. Refrigerate.

BLUEBERRY JAM
About four ¹/₂-pint jars

If blueberries are picked early in the day and are only half ripe, at the red instead of blue stage, the result is a jam far more flavorful than usual—almost like one made with Scandinavian lingonberries. Please read Making Jelly, 930, Making Jam, above, and Putting Up Preserves, 929.

Pick through, wash, and stem:

2 pounds blueberries

Remove, then put them in a heavy stainless steel pan. Crush the bottom layer. If desired, add:

(¹/₂ cup water)

Cook over medium heat, simmering until the berries are almost tender. Add for each cup of blueberries:

³/₄ to 1 cup sugar

Boil rapidly, stirring frequently, to the jelling point, 929. Remove from the heat and skim off any foam. Ladle into hot ½-pint jars. Leaving ¼-inch headspace, 890. Process for 10 minutes, 890.

SPICED PEAR JAM WITH PINEAPPLE
About four 1-pint jars or eight ½-pint jars
As it is hard to gauge the acidity of the pears used, taste the jam as it cooks, and add sugar or lemon juice as needed. Please read Making Jelly, 930, Making Jam, 934, and Putting Up Preserves, 929.
Wash, peel, and core:
   3 pounds firm Barlett, Kieffer, or Seckel pears
Wash well:
   1 orange
   1 lemon
Halve and remove the seeds. Put all the fruit through a grinder, using a coarse blade, or pulse in a food processor. Save the juices, then add them to the pulp, in a heavy 10-inch pan, along with:
   1 cup canned crushed pineapple
   4 to 5 cups sugar
Tie in a square of cheesecloth and add:
   3 or 4 whole cloves
   2 cinnamon sticks
   A 1-inch piece fresh ginger, washed and peeled
Simmer about 30 minutes, stirring frequently, to the jelling point, 929. Remove from the heat, take out the spice bag, and skim off any foam. Ladle into hot jars, leaving ¼-inch headspace, 890. Process for 10 minutes, 890.

BERRY JAM
About five ½-pint jars
Please read Making Jelly, 930, Making Jam, 934, and Putting Up Preserves, 929.
Peel, core, and finely grate:
   8 ounces tart green apples
Mix with:
   2 pounds blackberries, cranberries, loganberries, elderberries, or raspberries, washed and stemmed
   1 tablespoon orange juice
   3 cups sugar
In a heavy 10-inch pan, cook, crushing one-quarter of the berries in the pan (do not crush raspberries). Boil rapidly, stirring frequently, to the jelling point, 929. Remove from the heat and skim off any foam. Ladle into hot ½-pint jars, leaving ¼-inch headspace, 890. Process for 10 minutes, 890.

GOOSEBERRY JAM
About three ½-pint jars
Prepare **Berry Jam, above,** omitting the apples and using **2 pounds gooseberries.** If available, cook with **6 elderflowers tied in a cloth.** Squeeze their syrup into the jam, then discard the flowers.

FIVE-FRUIT JAM COCKAIGNE
About nine ½-pint jars
Please read Making Jelly, 930, Making Jam, 934, and Putting Up Preserves, 929.
Wash and stem, hull, or pit as necessary, placing each fruit in its own bowl:
   1 pound strawberries
   1½ pounds red currants
   1 pound sweet cherries
   1 pound gooseberries
   1 pound raspberries
Put the strawberries in one pan, the currants and cherries in another, and the gooseberries and raspberries in a third pan. Lightly crush all but the gooseberries and raspberries. Measure:
   7 cups sugar
Mix 1 cup of the sugar with the strawberries and 3 cups sugar with the fruits in each of the remaining pans. Bring each pan to a boil, stirring frequently, and boil rapidly, stirring, to the jelling point, 929. Remove from the heat and skim off any foam. Combine the jams and ladle into hot ½-pint jars, leaving ¼-inch headspace, 890. Process for 10 minutes, 890.

SEEDLESS RED GRAPE JAM
About five ½-pint jars
This jam is a boon for those who don't have access to Concord and Muscadine grapes.
Please read Making Jelly, 930, Making Jam, 934, and Putting Up Preserves, 929.
Stem:
   3 pounds Red Flame seedless grapes
Mix with:
   2½ cups sugar
Steep, 937.
Strain the grape syrup into a large saucepan, reserving the grapes. Add to the pan:
   ¼ cup bottled lemon juice
Slowly bring the syrup to a boil, then boil rapidly until it falls from a spoon in 2 heavy drops, 929. Stir in the grapes. Boil rapidly, stirring frequently, to the jelling point, 929. Remove from the heat and skim off any foam. Ladle into a hot ½-pint jars, leaving ¼-inch headspace, 890. Process for 10 minutes, 890.

PLUM JAM
About four ½-pint jars
Please read About Plums, 235. Juicy greengages, damsons, mirabelles, and many wild plums make excellent jam. Leave the skin on for maximum flavor and nutrients. Please read Making Jelly, 930, Making Jam, 934, and Putting Up Preserves, 929.
Wash, stem, halve, and pit:
   2 pounds plums

Halve large plums once more. Mix in a large saucepan with:

2¹/₂ cups sugar
¹/₄ cup bottled lemon juice

Lightly crush, then bring to a boil, stirring frequently, to the jelling point, 929. Remove from the heat and skim off any foam. Ladle into hot ¹/₂-pint jars, leaving ¹/₄-inch headspace, 890. Process for 10 minutes, 890.

NATURALLY SWEETENED PEAR AND GRAPE JAM

About three ¹/₂-pint jars

You must use high-pectin grapes (Concord, Muscadine, or Scuppernong) in this recipe. Please read Making Jelly, 930, Making Jam, 934, and Putting Up Preserves, 929. Wash:

6 pounds high-pectin grapes (see note above),
  preferably dark-skinned

Mash while bringing to a simmer. Remove from the heat and strain through a sieve into a bowl, pressing out all the juice; discard the stems and seeds.

Pour the juice into a large saucepan and boil down to 3 cups, skimming often.

Meanwhile, wash, core, and cut into 1-inch-wide slices:

2 pounds pears

Add to the juice in the saucepan. Simmer, stirring frequently, until the pears are tender, about 15 minutes, then boil rapidly, stirring frequently, to the jelling point, 929. Remove from the heat and skim off any foam. Ladle into hot ¹/₂-pint jars, leaving ¹/₄-inch headspace, 890. Process for 10 minutes, 890.

GOLDEN CHERRY TOMATO AND GINGER JAM

About three ¹/₂-pint jars

These golden preserves are almost tropical. Serve as a condiment or jam. Please read Making Jelly, 930, Making Jam, 934, and Putting Up Preserves, 929. Wash and slice in half, catching the juice:

2 pounds yellow or orange cherry tomatoes
  or plum tomatoes

If using plum tomatoes, quarter them. Combine in a bowl with:

2 cups sugar

Steep, 937.

Wash the ginger and lemons. Peel and slice in thin strips:

4 ounces fresh ginger

Strain the tomato syrup into a large saucepan, reserving the tomatoes. Add the ginger and:

Finely grated zest and juice of 8 ounces lemons

Slowly bring the syrup to a boil, then boil rapidly until it falls from a spoon in heavy drops, 929. Blend in the tomatoes. Boil rapidly, stirring frequently, to jelling point, 929. Remove from the heat and skim off any foam. Ladle into hot ¹/₂-pint jars, leaving ¹/₄-inch headspace, 890. Process for 10 minutes, 890.

MAKING FRUIT BUTTER

Fruit butters are purees that are cooked slowly and thickened by the evaporation of water, resulting in deeply concentrated fruit flavors. They earn their name for their smooth, spreadable consistency. Born of thrift, fruit butters contain the least added sugar of all preserves. They are often accented with spices. ➤ The challenge in making fruit butters is to cook them slowly for several hours without scorching. For the best flavor, begin by cooking the whole fruit, much as for jelly. ➤ Put it through a food mill to remove the inedible parts and slowly simmer the strained pulp until it becomes thick enough to mound on a spoon. Fruits can be cooked in the oven in both stages. ➤ Please read the directions for safe and proper canning, 888–899, before proceeding. Pack hot fruit butters into hot half-pint or pint jars, leaving ¹/₄-inch headspace, 890, and process in a boiling-water canner, 890, as directed in the recipes.

BAKED APPLE BUTTER

About eight ¹/₂-pint jars

This is the easiest, and perhaps finest, apple butter of all. Please read Making Fruit Butter, above, and Putting Up Preserves, 929.

Wash, stem, and quarter:

6 pounds unpeeled cooking apples, such as
  Cortland and Macoun

Combine in a large heavy saucepan with:

8 cups apple juice

Cover and simmer, stirring occasionally, until the apples are soft, about 1¹/₂ hours.

Preheat the oven to 200°F.

Pass the apples through a food mill or medium-mesh sieve. Return to the pan, and add:

Grated zest and juice of 1 lemon
1¹/₄ cups sugar (half may be packed brown sugar)
1¹/₂ teaspoons ground cinnamon
³/₄ teaspoon ground cloves
¹/₄ teaspoon ground allspice

Slowly bring to a boil, stirring frequently. Stir in, if desired:

(¹/₂ cup port or dry red wine)

Pour three-quarters of the puree into a deep baking dish, reserving the rest. Bake, uncovered, until thick enough to mound on a spoon, about 10 hours. As the mixture shrinks, stir in the reserved puree, and continue baking until entire mixture is very hot.

Pack the hot fruit butter into hot ¹/₂-pint jars, leaving ¹/₄-inch headspace, 890. Process for 15 minutes, 890.

NATURALLY SWEETENED APPLE BUTTER

Try Gala, Golden Delicious, or Northern Spy for this pure apple variation. Prepare **Baked Apple Butter, above,** using sweet cooking apples and omitting the sugar. Replace the wine with **¹/₂ cup thawed frozen unsweetened apple juice concentrate.** When the puree is thick, stir in **a pinch of salt.**

MICROWAVE FRUIT BUTTER
About four ¹/₂-pint jars

Fruit butter cooked in a microwave oven is lighter in color and flavor than baked. For this butter, finely puree the fruit pulp left in the jelly bag after making jelly, 930. ➤ Please read Making Fruit Butter, above, and Putting Up Preserves, 929.

Microwave mixtures may spatter and expand in volume when very hot to boiling. Use at least a 2-quart container for heating, and use extreme caution when you stir or move the container with the heated mixture.

Mix together thoroughly in a microwave-safe container:

    3³/₄ cups pureed fruit pulp
    ³/₄ cup mild honey
    1 tablespoon bottled lemon juice
    2³/₄ teaspoons ground cinnamon
    ³/₄ teaspoon ground mace or grated or
        ground nutmeg

Cover with wax paper, place in the microwave, and cook on high until nearly thick enough to mound up on a spoon, stirring every 5 minutes. If desired, add:

    (About 1 tablespoon brandy)

Pack the hot fruit butter into hot ¹/₂-pint jars, leaving ¹/₄-inch headspace, 890. Process for 10 minutes, 890.

ABOUT MAKING PRESERVES

Although we use the term "preserves" to refer to the entire category of foods in this chapter—including fruit butter, jams, jellies, conserves, marmalades, and jellied fruit sauces to be more exact, preserves are defined as bits of fruit cooked to a translucent state in a heavy syrup, similar to jam, but chunkier. Preserves are found in two styles. In one, the fruit is close together and thick enough to spread. In the other, more European style, the fruit is runny in a light syrup. Those preserves may drip off the toast, but their flavor is very fresh. Runny preserves are perfect for spooning over pancakes and waffles, ice cream, yogurts, puddings, and even cakes.

Whichever style you choose, use your finest fruits to make preserves. Fruits for preserves can be just ripe to fully ripe, since jelling is less important.

STEEPING AND PLUMPING

Because of their unique texture, ➤ preserves benefit from both **steeping** and **plumping** the fruit before canning. Gently mix the raw fruit and sugar in a nonreactive bowl until all the sugar has dissolved, cover the fruit mixture, and let steep in a cool place for up to 4 hours (or in the refrigerator for up to 24 hours).

Cook the preserves as outlined in Boiling Preserves, 929. You may process and can the preserves as soon as they reach the jelling point, 929, or pour them into a shallow dish, cover loosely, and plump overnight in the refrigerator. Plumping is optional, but we recommend this step to ensure tender fruit that will not float in the syrup in the jars. The next day, return the preserves to a rolling boil before canning.

STRAWBERRY PRESERVES
About four ¹/₂-pint jars

Please read Making Preserves, above, and Putting Up Preserves, 929.
Hull:

    2 pounds firm but ripe strawberries

Place in a bowl and crush half the berries if desired. Gently mix with:

    3 cups sugar

Steep, above. Stir in:

    ¹/₄ cup bottled lemon juice

In a heavy 10-inch pan, boil rapidly, stirring frequently, to the jelling point, 929. Remove from the heat and skim off any foam.

Plump overnight, above. Return the preserves to a boil before ladling into hot ¹/₂-pint jars, leaving ¹/₄-inch headspace, 890. Process for 10 minutes, 890.

APRICOT PRESERVES
About six ¹/₂-pint jars

Please read Making Preserves, above, and Putting Up Preserves, 929.
Pull apart on the seam line:

    5 pounds unpeeled sweet firm but ripe apricots

Place in a bowl and gently mix with:

    6 cups of sugar

Steep, above. Stir in:

    ¹/₄ cup bottled lemon juice
    ¹/₄ cup orange juice

In a heavy 10-inch pan, cook in 2 batches: Boil rapidly, stirring frequently, to the jelling point, 929. Remove from the heat and skim off any foam. Combine the batches and plump overnight, above.

Return the preserves to a boil before ladling into hot ¹/₂-pint jars, leaving ¹/₄-inch headspace, 890. Process for 10 minutes, 890.

PEACH OR NECTARINE PRESERVES

Use the tastiest fruit you can find. Prepare **Apricot Preserves, above,** substituting **5 pounds peaches or nectarines** for the apricots. Peel, pit, and slice ¹/₄ inch thick, and proceed as above.

STRAWBERRY AND PINEAPPLE PRESERVES
About four ¹/₂-pint jars

Please read Making Preserves, above, and Putting Up Preserves, 929.
Wash and hull:

    About 1¹/₂ pounds firm but ripe strawberries

Combine and plump overnight, above:

    4 cups of the berries (reserve any extra for
        another use)
    4 cups sugar

1 cup canned crushed pineapple
Grated zest and juice of $^1/_2$ lemon

Bring to a boil, stirring frequently, then reduce the heat and simmer until thickened, about 20 minutes. Remove from the heat and skim off any foam. Ladle into $^1/_2$-pint hot jars, leaving $^1/_4$-inch headspace, 890. Process for 10 minutes, 890.

STRAWBERRY AND RHUBARB PRESERVES

About five $^1/_2$-pint jars

Please read Making Preserves, 937, and Putting Up Preserves, 929.

Wash, trim, and cut into $^1/_2$-inch pieces:

About 12 ounces rhubarb

Combine 2 cups of the rhubarb (reserve any extra for another use) in a bowl with:

4 cups sugar

Steep, 937, 12 hours in the refrigerator.
Wash and hull:

1 quart strawberries

Quickly bring the rhubarb mixture to a boil. Add the strawberries. Return to a boil, stirring frequently, then reduce the heat and simmer, stirring, until thickened, about 15 minutes, continuing to stir until thickened. Remove from heat and skim off any foam. Plump overnight, above. Return the preserves to a boil, then ladle into hot $^1/_2$-pint jars, leaving $^1/_4$-inch headspace, 890. Process for 10 minutes, 890.

DAMSON, ITALIAN PLUM, OR GREENGAGE PRESERVES

Please read Making Preserves, 937, and Putting Up Preserves, 929.

Wash, halve, and pit:

Damsons, Italian plums, or greengages

Combine in a bowl with an equal amount, pound for pound, of:

Sugar

(If fruit is very sweet, 12 ounces sugar per pound of fruit will suffice.) Cover and steep, 937, 12 hours in the refrigerator.

Quickly bring the preserves to a boil, then reduce the heat and simmer until the syrup thickens. Plump, 937, overnight. Return the preserves to a boil, then ladle into hot $^1/_2$-pint jars, leaving $^1/_4$-inch headspace, 890. Process for 10 minutes, 890.

QUINCE PRESERVES

Please read Making Preserves, 937, and Putting Up Preserves, 929.

Scrub:

Quinces

Slice them into eighths, core, and peel, reserving the fruit, and put the peelings in a pan with just enough water to cover. For each quart of liquid, add:

1 lemon, washed, sliced, and seeded
1 orange, washed, sliced, and seeded

Simmer until the peelings are soft. Strain the liquid in a pot. Weigh the quince slices and add them. Weigh the same quantity of:

Sugar

and set aside. Bring the quince slices to a boil and add the sugar. Bring to a boil again. Reduce the heat and simmer until the fruit is tender. Plump, 937, overnight. Return the preserves to a boil. Using a slotted spoon, pack the fruit into hot $^1/_2$-pint jars. Continue to reduce the syrup until thick. Cover the fruit with the reduced syrup, leaving $^1/_4$-inch headspace, 890. Process for 10 minutes, 890.

HARVEST PRESERVES

Wash, core, peel, or pit, and quarter equal parts of **tart apples, pears, and plums.** Prepare as for **Quince Preserves, above.**

TOMATO PRESERVES

About three $^1/_2$-pint jars

Yellow tomatoes may be used with especially fine results. Please read Making Preserves, 937, and Putting Up Preserves, 929.

Peel, 311:

1 pound tomatoes

Combine in a bowl with:

$2^1/_4$ to $2^1/_2$ cups sugar (1 pound)

Let steep, 937, 12 hours in the refrigerator.

Drain the juice from the tomatoes; set the tomatoes aside. Boil the juice rapidly, stirring frequently, to the jelling point, 929. Add the tomatoes and:

Grated zest and juice of 1 or 2 lemons, washed, thinly sliced, and seeded
2 ounces preserved ginger slices or 1 cinnamon stick

Return to a boil, stirring frequently, then reduce the heat and simmer, stirring, until thickened. Plump, 937, overnight. Return the preserves to a boil, then ladle into hot $^1/_2$-pint jars, leaving $^1/_4$-inch headspace, 890. Process for 10 minutes, 890.

FIG PRESERVES

About four $^1/_2$-pint jars

Excellent as a glaze for red meats. If their skins are tough, cover the figs with boiling water and let stand for 10 minutes, then proceed.

Please read Making Preserves, 937, and Putting Up Preserves, 929.

Wash, stem, and quarter lengthwise:

2 pounds firm but ripe figs

Gently mix in a bowl with:

2 cups packed light brown sugar

Steep, 937. Stir in:

$^1/_4$ cup thawed frozen unsweetened apple juice concentrate

Simmer until the fig peels are soft, 25 to 30 minutes. Stir in:

$^1/_4$ cup bottled lemon juice
2 tablespoons orange juice

Boil rapidly, stirring frequently, to the jelling point, 929. Remove from the heat and skim off any foam. Stir in:

$^1/_8$ teaspoon ground cinnamon

Plump overnight, 937.

Return the preserves to a boil before ladling into hot $^1/_2$-pint jars leaving $^1/_4$-inch headspace, 890. Process for 10 minutes, 890.

KUMQUAT PRESERVES

About six $^1/_2$-pint jars

Please read Making Preserves, 937, and Putting Up Preserves, 929.

Weigh and wash:

3 pounds kumquats or calamondins

Peel and reserve the pulp. Cover the peel with cold water and simmer until tender. (If you do not like the bitter taste, drain several times during this process and replace with fresh water.) Drain and thinly slice or grind the peel in a meat grinder or food processor. Meanwhile, cover the pulp with 3 cups water and simmer 30 minutes. Strain the juice into a saucepan (discard the pulp) and add:

3 cups water

Measure for each cup of juice:

$^3/_4$ cup sugar

Heat the juice, then stir in the sugar until dissolved. Add the peel and boil rapidly, stirring frequently, to the jelling point, 929. Remove from the heat and skim off any foam. Plump, 937, overnight. Return the preserves to a boil, then ladle into hot $^1/_2$-pint jars, leaving $^1/_4$-inch headspace, 890. Process for 10 minutes, 890.

ABOUT MAKING CONSERVES

Conserves resemble thick preserves in consistency but, rather than spread them, you eat them with a fork or spoon. They often contain a mixture of fruits, usually one of them citrus, and special touches like raisins, nuts, coconut, or ginger. Conserves can be served as a condiment for poultry and meat or stirred into softened ice cream.

Citrus fruits, used in conserves, are often chilled to make slicing easier. Because conserves are dense with rich ingredients that easily scorch, most are simmered over low heat to the jelling point, 929, or until thick. ➤ Stir these mixtures carefully, especially toward the end. After adding the sugar, it is important to stir and simmer until the sugar has completely dissolved. To test for the jelling point, use the quick-chill test, 929, ➤ when the mixture has become noticeably thick. If the fruit is cooked but the syrup is too thin, remove the fruit with a slotted spoon, set it aside, and simmer the syrup to the desired thickness. When the syrup reaches the jelling point, immediately remove the pan from the heat and return the fruit to the syrup.

Please read the directions for safe and proper canning, 888–899, before proceeding. Pack the hot fruit into hot jars, leaving $^1/_4$-inch headspace, 890. Process in a boiling-water canner for 15 minutes, 890, or as directed in the recipes.

PEACH CONSERVES

About eight $^1/_2$-pint jars

A rich accompaniment for dark meats and spicy dishes. Please read Making Conserves, above, and Putting Up Preserves, 929.

Wash and remove the zest with a peeler:

1 large orange

1 small lemon

Peel, then chop the zest and pulp, discarding the seeds. Wash, peel, pit, and cut into 1-inch chunks:

3 pounds firm but ripe peaches

Gently mix all the fruits in a large heavy saucepan. Stir in:

8 ounces golden raisins (2 cups)

$3^1/_2$ cups sugar

Bring to a boil, then reduce the heat and simmer, stirring frequently, until thick, about 1 hour. Stir in:

4 ounces (1 cup) pecan pieces, toasted, 1001

Cook for 5 minutes. Remove from the heat and add:

$^1/_4$ cup bourbon

Ladle the hot conserves into hot $^1/_2$-pint jars, leaving $^1/_4$-inch headspace, 890. Process for 15 minutes, 890.

BLUE PLUM CONSERVES

About nine $^1/_2$-pint jars

Serve alongside pork and white meat poultry.

Prepare **Peach Conserves, above,** substituting **3 pounds blue (or any) plums** for the peaches. Add **10 ounces dark raisins,** and for the golden raisins use **$3^3/_4$ cups sugar.** Substitute **4 ounces walnut pieces, toasted, 1001,** for the pecans and **$^1/_4$ cup hot brandy** for the bourbon. Simmering time is about $1^1/_4$ hours.

CRANBERRY CONSERVES

About six $^1/_2$-pint jars

Besides the obvious turkey, this is also very good with roast pork. Please read Making Conserves, above, and Putting Up Preserves, 929.

Chill, then wash well, cut lengthwise in half, and slice very thin, removing any seeds:

12 ounces unpeeled oranges

Place, with their juice, in a small skillet, along with:

$^1/_2$ cup apple cider

Cover and simmer until the orange peel is soft, 15 to 20 minutes.

Meanwhile, wash, peel, core, and cut into $^1/_2$-inch chunks (to make $1^1/_2$ cups):

1 pound fresh pineapple

Pick over and wash:

1 pound cranberries

Combine all the fruits in a large saucepan with:

4 cups sugar

$^1/_2$ cup bottled lemon juice

1 teaspoon ground cinnamon

$^1/_2$ teaspoon whole cloves

Bring to a boil, then reduce the heat and simmer, stirring frequently, until thick, about 45 minutes.

Ladle the hot conserves into hot $^1/_2$-pint jars, leaving $^1/_4$-inch headspace, 890. Process for 15 minutes, 890.

CHRISTMAS CONSERVES

About nine $^1/_2$-pint jars

Make these colorful conserves with fruits of the holiday season.

Please read Making Conserves, 939, and Putting Up Preserves, 929.

Chill, then wash well, cut into quarters, slice very thin, removing any seeds:

12 ounces unpeeled oranges

Chill, then wash well and slice into the thinnest possible rounds, removing any seeds:

12 ounces unpeeled limes

Wash and cut in half lengthwise (ignore the seeds, they will cook to tender):

12 ounces kumquats

Cover the fruits with cold water in a saucepan and simmer, covered, until the citrus peel is soft, about 15 minutes. Drain the fruit and combine with:

3 cups sugar

in a saucepan. Rapidly boil until the slices are translucent and the mixture is thick, about 35 minutes.

Meanwhile, wash, peel, quarter, core, and slice lengthwise $^1/_2$ inch thick, dropping the pieces into cold water to keep them from darkening:

12 ounces tart apples
12 ounces firm but ripe pears
12 ounces ripe quinces (if unavailable, use 1$^1/_4$ pounds
   apples and 1 pound pears total)

Combine in a large heavy saucepan:

3 cups sugar
5 cups water

Stir over low heat until the sugar dissolves, then cover and bring the syrup to a simmer. Drain the apple mixture and add it to the syrup. Simmer for 15 minutes.

Add the citrus fruit to the apple mixture, and mix in:

12 ounces cranberries, picked over and washed

Return to a boil. Remove from the heat, cover, and let stand for 5 minutes, then stir.

Ladle the hot conserves into hot $^1/_2$-pint jars, leaving $^1/_4$-inch headspace, 890. Process for 15 minutes, 890.

SPICED RHUBARB CONSERVES

About five $^1/_2$-pint jars

Serve these spicy, tart conserves slightly warmed with rich poultry or meat.

Please read Making Conserves, 939, and Putting Up Preserves, 929.

Chill, then wash well and slice very thin, removing any seeds:

8 ounces unpeeled oranges
4 ounces unpeeled lemons

Peel, then cut into slivers:

1 ounce fresh ginger

Combine the citrus fruit, with its juice, and the ginger in a small saucepan with:

1 cup apple cider

Cover and simmer until the citrus peel is soft, about 15 minutes.

Meanwhile, wash, trim, and cut into 1-inch pieces:

1 pound slender red rhubarb

Combine the citrus mixture and rhubarb in a large heavy saucepan, along with:

$^1/_2$ cup golden raisins
$^1/_2$ teaspoon ground cinnamon
$^1/_4$ teaspoon ground mace
3$^1/_4$ cups sugar

Bring to a boil, then reduce the heat and simmer, stirring frequently, until thick, about 40 minutes. (The conserves will thicken further once cool.)

Ladle the hot conserves into hot $^1/_2$-pint jars, leaving $^1/_4$-inch headspace, 890. Process for 15 minutes, 890.

SWEET CHERRY CONSERVES

About eight $^1/_2$-pint jars

Please read Making Conserves, 939, and Putting Up Preserves, 929.

Wash and cut into very thin slices; discarding any seeds:

2 oranges

Barely cover with water in a large saucepan, about $^1/_4$ cup. Cook until very tender.

Wash, stem, pit and add:

1 quart sweet cherries

Add:

6 tablespoons bottled lemon juice
3$^1/_2$ cups sugar
$^3/_4$ teaspoon ground cinnamon
(6 whole cloves, tied in a cheesecloth bag)

Simmer the conserves, stirring frequently, until thick and clear. Discard the spice bag, if using. Ladle the hot conserves into hot $^1/_2$-pint jars, leaving $^1/_4$-inch headspace, 890. Process for 15 minutes, 890.

ABOUT MAKING MARMALADE

Marmalade is best described as a soft fruit jelly containing small pieces of fruit—most often citrus peel—suspended in the transparent jelly. Like jam, there is leeway in marmalade—it can be soft or firm—but like jelly, the juice should be clear and the pectin and acid contents high. Because the syrup of citrus marmalade jells, ➤ cooking is the same as for jelly. ➤ Please read the directions for safe and proper canning, 888–899, before proceeding. Pour hot marmalades into hot, sterilized jars, leaving $^1/_4$-inch headspace, 890, and process in a boiling-water canner for 10 minutes, 890.

PREPARING CITRUS FRUITS FOR MARMALADE

Choose citrus that is heavy for its size—it will be the juiciest. The color of the rind has no bearing on the interior quality. When blood oranges are available, their garnet color makes gorgeous marmalade. As other uncommon citrus come along—limequats, pomelos, ugli fruit—try them in place of bitter oranges in Bitter Orange Marmalade, below.

➤ Chilling citrus makes it easier to slice very thin. ➤ Use a stainless steel knife (carbon steel reacts with acid and stains the fruit). The center of a citrus fruit is tough; remove it for better marmalade. Begin by washing the fruits and slicing in half, then use clean scissors to snip around the white area just outside where the points of the segments meet. Snip all the way down, then lift out the center, and flick out the seeds. Since seeds and centers are rich in pectin, tie them in a single layer of cheesecloth and add the bag to the fruit. At the end of the cooking, squeeze the juice from the bag and blend it into the marmalade.

➤ The spongy white pith just under the colored citrus peel is where most of the pectin lies, so always include some in marmalade. End slices that are pure peel and pit are best cut into strips the thickness of the other pieces.

➤ Tenderizing citrus peel is crucial to marmalade. Soak the prepared fruit and peel in water in the refrigerator overnight. The next day, cover and simmer until the peel is thoroughly tender—from 15 minutes to more than an hour, depending on the size and thickness of the fruit slices. To test, ➤ cut a piece against the side of the pan with the edge of a wooden or plastic spoon—it should instantly fall in half if done.

BITTER ORANGE MARMALADE

About ten ¹/₂-pint jars

Please read About Oranges, 225. In winter, look for bitter Seville oranges or blood oranges, or make sweet orange marmalade with 1¹/₂ pounds sweet oranges and 1 pound lemons. For amber marmalade, use half brown sugar. Please read Making Marmalade, 940, and Putting Up Preserves, 929.

Chill, then wash, halve crosswise, snip out tough centers, and thinly slice, removing any seeds:

2 pounds unpeeled bitter oranges
8 ounces unpeeled lemons

Combine in a bowl, with their juice, and add:

8 cups water

Cover and let stand overnight in the refrigerator.
Simmer with the water until the citrus peel is tender. Add:

6¹/₂ cups sugar

Divide the mixture in half and cook in 2 batches: Boil rapidly, stirring frequently, to the jelling point, 929. Remove from the heat and skim off any foam. Combine the batches, then pack into hot ¹/₂-pint jars, leaving ¹/₄-inch headspace, 890. Process for 10 minutes, 890.

FOUR-CITRUS MARMALADE

About eight ¹/₂-pint jars

Please read Making Marmalade, 940, and Putting Up Preserves, 929.

Wash:

1¹/₂ pounds grapefruit, preferably ruby
1 pound sweet oranges
8 ounces tender-skinned limes (Bears if possible)
8 ounces lemons

Cut off the peel with ¹/₈ inch of the pith; set the fruit aside. Chop the peel into ¹/₄-inch pieces by hand, or in a food processor. Combine the peel and

2 cups water

in a saucepan and simmer until the peel is soft, 5 to 10 minutes.

Meanwhile, cut off and discard the remaining white pith from the fruit. Cut the fruit in half and remove the centers and seeds. Chop the pulp into ¹/₄-inch pieces. Mix the peel and pulp in a bowl with:

4 cups water

Cover and let stand overnight in the refrigerator.
Add to the fruit:

5¹/₂ cups sugar

Divide the mixture in half and cook in 2 batches: Boil rapidly, stirring frequently, to the jelling point, 929. Remove from the heat and skim off any foam. Combine the batches, then pack into hot ¹/₂-pint jars, leaving ¹/₄-inch headspace, 890. Process for 10 minutes, 890.

LIME MARMALADE

About three ¹/₂-pint jars

Wash and cut the thin outer rind from **6 small limes** and **3 lemons**. Prepare **Four-Citrus Marmalade, above,** substituting the trimmed limes and lemons for the fruits, seeding and cutting them as directed, then proceeding as above.

GINGER MARMALADE

About four ¹/₂-pint jars

Spread these invigorating preserves on English muffins or rich meats, or stir into marinades and sauces. Select ginger that is not stringy. Adding the sugar in 2 stages helps plump the ginger. Please read Making Marmalade, 940, and Putting Up Preserves, 929.

Wash, then peel, thinly slice, and finely chop:

2 pounds fresh ginger

Combine in a large heavy saucepan with:

12 cups water

Bring to a boil, then reduce the heat and simmer, stirring occasionally, until the ginger is softened, about 2 hours. Stir in:

1¹/₄ cups apple cider
5 tablespoons bottled lemon juice
5 tablespoons light corn syrup

Stir in:

3 cups sugar

and boil gently for 15 minutes. Let stand in a bowl and refrigerate overnight.
Bring to a simmer and add:

1 cup sugar

Simmer, stirring often, until the spoon cuts a path through the marmalade, 45 minutes to 1 hour.

Pack the hot marmalade into hot $1/2$-pint jars, leaving $1/4$-inch headspace, 890. Process for 10 minutes, 890.

ABOUT MAKING JELLIED FRUIT SAUCES

Jellied fruit sauces are made, like fruit butter, from thick fruit purees, but they rely on pectin for their luscious firm texture. These dense preserves, also called fruit cheese, are aged for 6 to 24 months after canning and then un-molded and sliced—much like the familiar canned jellied cranberry sauce. The flavor is incomparable.

It's best to age jellied fruit sauces for at least 6 months before serving—their flavor develops for up to 2 years, and the preserves keep at their best for up to 3 years. To serve, run a table knife around the inside of the jar, being careful not to damage the glass, shake out the preserves, and slice $1/2$ inch thick. Studded with chopped almonds and sur-rounded with port or cream, these make a superb dessert.

Please read the directions for safe and proper canning, 888–899, before proceeding. The trick to these preserves is boiling the puree rapidly to develop the pectin. When boiling, the puree will erupt, so wear an apron, tight long sleeves, and protective glasses. Stir constantly with a long-handled spoon, scraping around the edges of the pan and thoroughly across every inch of the bottom. The preserves are ready if you can see the bottom of the pan when you pull a spoon through the center of the puree.

Lightly oiling or spraying the insides of the sterilized jars with a neutral-tasting vegetable oil will help the jellied fruit slide out of the jars. Fill the jars, leaving $1/2$-inch head-space, 890, and process in a boiling-water canner, 890, for 15 minutes (the longer processing time is needed to pene-trate these dense preserves).

JELLIED DAMSON SAUCE

About five 1-pint jars

For a quick and excellent dessert, top the sliced sauce with chopped almonds and a dollop of whipped cream. The method used here also works well with other tart plums, as well as with tart green apples, barely ripe quinces, cran-berries, and tart blackberries. Use $1^{1}/_{2}$ cups sugar per pound of puree.

Preheat the oven to 275°F. Brush or spray the insides of sterilized, 890, and cooled widemouthed straight-sided pint jars with:

   Vegetable oil

Wash, stem, and place in a $4^{1}/_{2}$-quart crock or earthen-ware baking dish, or in 2 large bowls:

   6 pounds Damson plums

Cover and bake until simmering and syrupy, about $2^{1}/_{2}$ hours. Push the hot pulp through a food mill or a colander with a pestle or plastic spoon; discard the pits. Measure and divide in half:

   8 cups sugar

Cook the puree in 2 batches: Bring the puree to a simmer in a wide, heavy 7- to 8-quart saucepan over low heat. Add half the sugar to each batch. When the sugar dis-solves, boil over high heat, stirring, until you can see the bottom of the pan when you pull a spoon through the center of the puree, about 9 to 10 minutes. Pour the hot preserves into the prepared jars, leaving $1/2$-inch head-space, 890. See Putting Up Preserves, 929. If desired, press into the top of each jar before sealing:

   (1 fresh bay leaf, washed and dried, about 5 total)

Process for 15 minutes, 890.

NESSELRODE SAUCE

3 cups

Combine and stir well:

   $3/4$ **cup chopped maraschino cherries**
   $1/3$ **cup chopped citron or orange peel**

Add:

   1 cup orange marmalade
   $1/2$ **cup coarsely chopped candied ginger**
   2 tablespoons maraschino cherry juice
   1 cup chopped Boiled Chestnuts, 270,
      or jarred peeled chestnuts
   $1/2$ **cup or more rum, to make the sauce**
      of a good consistency

Place in jars and seal. Rest for 2 weeks before serving.

PICKLES AND RELISHES

Peter Piper proved a pretty pampered pepper picker, picking peppers pickled as he did. The rest of us, less privileged, have to pick our produce and process it promptly ourselves. Pickling can be accomplished in several ways, some of them a bit lengthy, but none of them difficult. Though a considerable number of vitamins and minerals leach away into liquid residue during the pickling process, pickling remains a piquant flavor-booster and an important method of food preservation.

In spite of the fact that our mothers never did it, it is now a recommended practice to subject pickles and relishes to ➤ a boiling-water bath, 890.

EQUIPMENT

Please read the directions for safe and proper canning, 890–893. ➤ Do not use utensils made of materials that react with acid—that includes aluminum, brass, copper, galvanized or zinc-coated metal, and cast iron. For simmering food, use stainless steel or unchipped enamel. A large deep heavy skillet—roughly 11¾ inches x 2¼ inches deep—or an 8- to 10-quart stockpot will accommodate most ingredients in these recipes for simmering. For crock-curing—steeping food in acidic ingredients—crocks, jars, pots, bowls, and buckets of uncracked stoneware, unchipped enamel, glass, stainless steel, and food-grade plastic are the only containers safe to use. Allow 1 gallon in volume for every 5 pounds of food. This guarantees several inches of essential air space between the food and the top of the container.

For stirring and for transferring the pickles, use a long-handled stainless steel, enamel-covered, or slotted plastic or heatproof silicone spoon or a glass measuring cup. Pack pickles in unflawed hot glass canning jars with two-piece lids, unless otherwise indicated.

A crinkle-edge cutter leaves more surface area exposed to the vinegar solution, in addition to making the slices more interesting. Crinkle-edge cutters are available at cookware stores. All equipment should be absolutely clean and grease-free.

PICKLING INGREDIENTS

For best results, it is ➤ imperative that vegetables and fruit for pickling are in prime condition. Gardeners should harvest ingredients no more than 24 hours in advance. If cucumbers have been held longer, they tend to become hollow during processing.

Select the freshest fruits and vegetables available, perfectly ripe and without a trace of mold or blemishes. The importance of freshness cannot be overemphasized. If pickling cannot be started within 24 hours of harvest, refrigerate the food and use as soon as possible. If fruit or vegetables are very firm or slightly unripe, ➤ be sure to cook them a little longer so brine can permeate to their centers. This will help keep the food from floating to the tops of the jars later and will also discourage spoilage.

Many fruits and vegetables are unpredictable in terms of size, weight, and yield. One pound of Seckel pears may fill a quart jar, a pint jar, or even less. Prepare to be flexible. Especially when pickled whole, the short varieties of cucumbers bred specifically for pickling give superior results. Their tissues absorb brine and sustain processing without excessive softening. Very long cucumbers such as Asian "burpless" or English hothouse do not have a good texture when pickled or canned.

Standard pickle length is 4 inches. For tiny gherkins and cornichons, choose varieties bred to be harvested around 1½ inches long, although some pickling cucumbers are successful when harvested smaller. Small, rounded West Indian gherkins absorb brine and syrup like sponges and make prize pickles. Misshapen cucumbers or those that float when washed (being hollow) can be used in relishes. ➤ When washing fruits and vegetables, scrub particularly around the stems, blossom ends, and crevices—these are hiding places for bacteria.

Specific instructions for preparing produce are in the recipes; however, ➤ keep in mind that the blossom end of cucumbers contains an enzyme that may soften pickles, so ➤ slice ¹⁄₁₆ inch off that end (if you are not sure which end that is, trim both ends). Also, when pickling chile peppers whole, slash them through once or twice with a thin knife, so the vinegar solution can seep inside. For other whole pickles, ⅛ to ¼ inch of stem may be retained after scrubbing well.

➤ Acid inhibits the growth of harmful and destructive microorganisms. For safety's sake, ➤ it is essential to use a high-grade vinegar with a content of at least 5 percent acetic acid (sometimes labeled 50 grain). Cider vinegar and distilled white vinegar are both recommended. Cider vinegar is preferred for its mellow fruity flavor, but its color will darken the pickle over time. Distilled white vinegar is clear and ideal for most quick pickling, but it is sharp. Occasionally, for smoothness, we blend the two vinegars or add bottled lemon juice, which is dependably high in acid. If a recipe's vinegar solution seems strong for your taste, remember that it will mellow with curing. ➤ **Never reduce the proportion of vinegar called for in a recipe.**

Balsamic and malt vinegars may contain 6 percent acetic acid and, if they are labeled with this amount of acid, are effective in pickling. However, because their flavors may overwhelm the flavor of the food being pickled, it is best to mix them with cider or distilled white vinegar. Most vinegars made from wine, fruit, and rice have 4.3 percent acetic acid and are not acidic enough. ➤ If the label does not give the vinegar's acid content, do not use it for pickling. ➤ And do not use homemade vinegars, because their acid content is unknown.

➤ Water used should be soft; see 1026. If the water contains iron or sulfur compounds, the pickles will become dark. If soft tap water is unavailable, either use distilled water or boil the water for 15 minutes, cover, and let stand for 24 hours. Skim off any scum on top, then carefully pour off the clear water, leaving the sediment behind. Add 1 tablespoon 5 percent acetic-acid vinegar to each gallon before using.

➤ Salt is the primary preservative in long-brining or fermenting. In these procedures, the salt level is essential for safety as well as successful fermentation. For long-brining or fermentation as well as short-brining or quick-pickling, ➤ use only **pickling salt** or **canning salt,** which do not contain additives that cloud the vinegar solution. Do not use kosher salt, which varies in density, or iodized salt, which can darken pickles. Do not use "light" or reduced-sodium salts.

➤ Sugar flavors food, intensifies color, and helps plump and firm fruits and vegetables. It also nourishes beneficial bacteria produced while the food is curing. Brown sugar lends caramel color and flavor. Artificial sweeteners can be used in quick-pickling or short-brining, but they do not actually contribute to the preserving process. Follow the manufacturer's directions when substituting these for sugar.

Spices should be ➤ both fresh and whole to hold up best in pickling. Ground spices will cloud the vinegar solution, although sometimes it is worth sacrificing clarity for intensity of flavor. Bay leaves are especially potent—simmer 1 or 2 in the vinegar solution, then remove before canning. Mustard seed is commonly used in pickling, adding both flavor and texture. Yellow, brown, and black mustard seeds are interchangeable in these recipes. Ground turmeric is a favorite pickler's spice because a very small amount brightens the color of the brine. For example, corn relish without turmeric is pale—with turmeric, it glows. **Mixed pickling spice,** readily purchased in grocery stores, is generally a ground blend of mustard seeds, cin-

namon, ginger, bay leaves, pepper, allspice, caraway seeds, cloves, mace, and cardamom. These and other whole spices are often tied in a cloth bag for easy removal before canning.

In old-fashioned recipes, alum and pickling lime were sometimes added to ensure crisp pickles. The calcium in pickling lime (also known as slaked lime or calcium hydroxide) does make pickles firm, but it can also make them bitter, and rinsing them several times before serving is a nuisance. ➤ Too much alum can be unsafe and is no longer recommended. When today's techniques and fresh prime ingredients are used, pickles can be crisp without chemicals.

Our favorite crisping technique is to ➤ place a 2- to 3-inch layer of crushed or cubed ice over vegetables while they are brining. This aids crispness and helps keep pieces from breaking when they are heated. A wet towel between the ice and the foods lets the cold through but eliminates the necessity of having to pick ice out of the food at the end. Add more ice as needed.

Fine crisping agents are also grown in the wild: The leaves of grapevines (especially Scuppernong), cherry trees, black currant bushes, and oak trees contain a substance that blocks enzymes from softening vegetables—particularly cucumbers. Thoroughly wash unsprayed leaves and layer them with the cucumbers during brining, then discard the leaves.

RULES FOR SAFE PICKLING

Many old-fashioned recipes have been dropped from revised editions of cookbooks because the recipes do not conform to modern safety guidelines. Although putting up pickles is simple, the pickling process is actually extraordinarily complex, and potential harm can come from improvising.

Clostridium botulinum is a dangerous bacterium that flourishes in moist, airless, low-acid, room-temperature environments. It seems impossible that a pickled food can be low-acid, but that can happen if a low-acid food has not been permeated by enough vinegar of the correct strength. To be safe, only use tested, up-to-date pickling recipes, such as those in this chapter, and follow them to the letter.

PICKLING METHODS

There are two basic methods of introducing acid to food, or pickling. In the **direct method**—called quick-pickling or short-brining—the food is simply covered with vinegar, and that is that. Sometimes there is a short soak in salt and ice or a salt solution for the vegetables before they are pickled. This brining period is sufficiently long to draw out moisture ➤ but not long enough to induce fermentation. It is helpful for increasing the uptake of the vinegar solution into the food and sometimes for crisping. ➤ Preservation of the pickles occurs from the vinegar solution and subsequent canning.

Foods most commonly quick-pickled are fruits and vegetables. Vinegars used for quick-pickling are cider vinegar and distilled white vinegar, both containing 5 percent pure acetic acid. The flavor of quick pickles is fresh and sharp, but it will mellow after a few weeks. Fruit and sweet vegetable pickles have sugar mixed with their acid for a sweet-tangy taste.

In the **indirect method**—often called salting, long-brining, fermentation, or curing—➤ vinegar is not required, because the food creates its own acid. The pickling begins by salting directly or by brining (brine is salt in liquid, normally water, and usually in high concentration). ➤ Just enough salt is used to keep harmful microorganisms at bay while allowing the bacteria that cause fermentation to multiply. ➤ Do not reduce the amount of salt in fermenting, long-brining, or curing, as it is essential to safety and the success of the fermentation. Fermentation produces lactic acid, the ultimate preserver, and can take weeks, even months. Slowly developed, the flavors of these pickled foods are deep and rich. Crock-cured pickles and sauerkraut are prepared this way.

PUTTING UP PICKLES

There are two ways of keeping or storing homemade pickles—refrigeration and canning. You can refrigerate any quick pickle without processing the jar in a boiling-water bath, but the jars should still be sterilized, 890. Unprocessed pickles and opened processed pickles will keep from 2 to 4 weeks in the refrigerator, perhaps longer. Few pickles freeze well.

Whether canning pickles by the direct or indirect method, ➤ pickles need to be canned in a boiling-water bath if they are to be stored out of the refrigerator. ➤ Please read the directions for safe and proper canning, 888–893, before proceeding.

➤ Pickles processed for less than 10 minutes must go into sterilized jars, see About Pickling Equipment, 943. Unless otherwise noted, pack hot pickles and liquid into hot jars, see Preparing Jars for Canning, 890.

A pint jar, preferably widemouthed, is ideal for pickles, because the vinegar solution and the heat in processing can evenly reach each piece and tapered-mouth jars may be more difficult to pack. A pint jar holds 2 cups pickles plus 3/4 to 1 cup vinegar solution. Do not alter or experiment with processing times and jar sizes. Also, if a jar is only partially filled, do not process. Instead, refrigerate and eat the contents within 2 to 4 weeks.

Some recipes call for packing the prepared produce into the jars as a raw-pack, 890, then adding a hot, spicy vinegar solution to cover them. Other recipes call for simmering or cooking the produce for a while in the vinegar solution before filling the jars, and some recipes refer to plumping overnight.

When it is time to pack jars, put the pieces of food into the prepared hot jars first, leaving room for at least 1/2-inch headspace. Then ➤ cover the solids with the boiling-hot vinegar solution, ➤ leaving 1/2-inch headspace. Remove air bubbles, 890, and wipe the rims and threads of the jar with a clean, damp cloth before applying the lids. Process in boiling water for the length of time specified in the recipe.

Relishes and finely chopped vegetables or fruits may be put into the jars together with the liquid. Always make sure liquid completely covers all the food at the top of the jar, or it will discolor and dry out in storage.

The ➤ flavor of almost all pickled produce is improved if it is stored for 6 weeks before using. ➤ Keep an eye on your pickles after you have stored them away in a dark, dry, cool place where they cannot freeze. If you detect evidence of fermentation, a bulging lid, leakage, or other signs of spoilage, 892, ➤ do not even taste the product. Destroy it; see 893.

YELLOW CUCUMBER PICKLES
About seven 1-pint jars
This recipe is adapted from the 1931 edition of JOY. Use large, mature cucumbers that have yellowed on the vine. Serve these pickles chilled with meat. Please read about pickling, 943–945.
Wash and peel:
  15 pounds large yellow pickling cucumbers
Halve lengthwise, scrape out the seeds, and cut into 2 1/2 x 1 1/2 x 3/4-inch strips.
Make a brine of:
  5 1/2 quarts water
  2 cups pickling or canning salt, 944
Stir until the salt is dissolved, then pour over the cucumber strips in a large bowl. Place a plate on the cucumbers to keep them submerged and refrigerate for 12 hours.
Drain, rinse, and drain again. Place in each hot pint jar (double the amounts for quarts):
  Two 1/3-inch cubes peeled horseradish
  One 1/4-inch piece red chile pepper
  2 sprigs seeded dill flowers
  1 1/2 teaspoons mustard seeds
    (about 3 1/2 tablespoons total)
  2 white peppercorns (about 14 total)
Combine in a saucepan and bring to a boil, stirring until the sugar is dissolved:
  6 cups cider vinegar
  3/4 cup water
  1/4 cup sugar
Divide between 2 or 3 large skillets. Add the cucumber strips and return just to a boil—do not cook longer, or the cucumbers will soften. Pack into hot pint or quart jars and add the hot vinegar solution, leaving 1/2-inch headspace. See Canning Pickles, above. Process pints for 10 minutes, quarts for 15 minutes, above.

SWEET-AND-SOUR SPICED GHERKINS

About six 1-pint jars

Please read about pickling, 943–945.

Wash:

5 pounds 1$\frac{1}{2}$- to 2-inch gherkins or pickling cucumbers

Slice $\frac{1}{16}$ inch from the blossom ends, but leave $\frac{1}{4}$ inch of the stems.

Combine in a large bowl:

3 quarts water

1 cup pickling or canning salt, 944

Stir until the salt is dissolved, then add the cucumbers. Place a plate on the cucumbers to keep them submerged and refrigerate for 24 hours.

Drain, cover the cucumbers with boiling water, and quickly drain again. Pack into hot pint jars. Heat in a saucepan, stirring until the sugar is dissolved:

4 cups cider vinegar

2$\frac{3}{4}$ cups sugar

Tie in a moist square of cheesecloth and add to the saucepan:

2 tablespoons mixed pickling spices

Two 2-inch cinnamon sticks, broken

$\frac{1}{4}$ teaspoon whole cloves

Bring just to a boil and remove the spice bag. Add the hot vinegar solution to the jars, leaving $\frac{1}{2}$-inch headspace. See Putting Up Pickles, 945. Process for 10 minutes, 945.

BREAD-AND-BUTTER PICKLES

About five 1-pint jars

These probably got their name because they livened up so many sandwiches. This recipe offers stovetop or microwave cooking options.

Please read about pickling, 943–945.

Wash, then slice $\frac{1}{8}$ inch from each end of:

2$\frac{1}{2}$ pounds pickling cucumbers

Cut into $\frac{1}{4}$-inch-thick slices. Peel, and cut the same way:

1 pound 2- to 2$\frac{1}{2}$-inch onions

Combine the cucumbers and onions in a large bowl, along with:

3 tablespoons pickling or canning salt

Mix well to dissolve the salt. Cover with a clean wet towel, then top with 2 inches of ice. Refrigerate for 3 to 4 hours. Discard the ice; drain the vegetables, rinse, and drain again. Combine in a 4-quart or larger microwave-safe bowl (or a pot if using the stovetop):

2 cups distilled white vinegar

2 cups sugar

1 tablespoon mustard seeds

(1 teaspoon crushed red pepper flakes)

$\frac{3}{4}$ teaspoon celery seeds

$\frac{3}{4}$ teaspoon turmeric

$\frac{1}{4}$ teaspoon ground cloves

Stir until the sugar is dissolved. Cover with waxed paper and microwave on high (or cook uncovered on a burner) until the syrup boils. Add the vegetables, stir to mix, and

microwave on medium high (or heat) until the syrup just begins to boil. Using a slotted spoon, pack the hot slices into hot pint jars and then add the hot syrup, leaving $\frac{1}{2}$-inch headspace. See Putting Up Pickles, 945. Process for 10 minutes, 945.

LOW-SALT SWEET CUCUMBER SLICES

About four 1-pint jars

Please read about pickling, 943–945.

Wash and trim $\frac{1}{8}$ inch from each end of:

2 pounds 3- to 4-inch pickling cucumbers

Cut into $\frac{1}{4}$-inch-thick slices.

Combine in a saucepan:

1$\frac{2}{3}$ cups distilled white vinegar

3 cups sugar

1 tablespoon whole allspice berries

1 tablespoon celery seeds

$\frac{1}{4}$ teaspoon turmeric

Cook, stirring, over medium heat until the sugar is dissolved. Turn off the heat and cover the syrup. Combine in a large deep skillet:

4 cups distilled white vinegar

$\frac{1}{2}$ cup sugar

1 tablespoon mustard seeds

1 tablespoon pickling or canning salt, 944

Stir to dissolve sugar. Add the cucumbers and simmer just until their green turns from bright to dull, 5 to 7 minutes, stirring frequently—do not let the slices soften. Meanwhile, bring the syrup to a boil.

Drain the slices, discarding the liquid. Using a slotted spoon, pack the slices into hot pint jars and then add the hot syrup, leaving $\frac{1}{2}$-inch headspace. See Putting Up Pickles, 945. Process for 10 minutes, 945.

PICKLED GHERKINS (CORNICHONS)

About eight 1-pint jars

Please read about pickling, 943–945.

Wash:

5$\frac{1}{2}$ pounds 1$\frac{1}{4}$- to 1$\frac{1}{2}$-inch long pickling cucumbers, or gherkins

Cut a thin slice from the blossom ends, but leave $\frac{1}{4}$ inch of the stems. (If using standard-sized cucumbers, slice crosswise every 1$\frac{1}{2}$ inches, then quarter lengthwise.)

Make a brine of:

8 cups water

$\frac{1}{2}$ cup pickling or canning salt, 944

Stir until the salt is dissolved, and pour over the cucumbers in a large bowl. Place a plate on the cucumbers to keep them submerged and let stand at room temperature for 12 hours.

Drain, rinse, and drain again. Pat dry with a clean towel. Tightly pack the cucumbers into hot pint or quart jars, adding to each pint (double the amounts for quarts):

A few sprigs of tarragon (1 bunch total)

($\frac{1}{2}$ teaspoon mustard seeds; about 4 teaspoons total)

5 whole white peppercorns (about 40 total)

Combine in a saucepan and bring just to a boil, stirring until the salt is dissolved:

5¼ cups cider vinegar

4¼ cups water

⅓ cup pickling or canning salt

Pour over the cucumbers in the jars, leaving ½-inch headspace. See Putting Up Pickles, 945. Process pints for 10 minutes, quarts for 15 minutes, 945. For true cornichon flavor, cure 1 month before serving.

QUICK DILL PICKLES

About six 1-pint jars

Because the brine is weaker and the curing more rapid than for traditional pickles, these are best enjoyed within a few months.

Please read about pickling, 943–945.

Wash:

4 pounds 4-inch pickling cucumbers

Halve lengthwise and pack into hot pint jars. (Cut longer cucumbers into 4-inch pieces, and fill the spaces in the jars with the scraps.) Combine in a saucepan and bring just to a boil, stirring until the salt is dissolved:

3 cups cider vinegar

2¼ cups water

¼ cup pickling or canning salt, 944

Place in each jar:

1 garlic clove, peeled (about 6 garlic cloves total)

1 teaspoon dill seeds (about 2 tablespoons total)

1 teaspoon mixed pickling spice
  (about 2 tablespoons total)

6 whole black peppercorns (about 36 total)

Add the hot vinegar solution, leaving ½-inch headspace. See Putting Up Pickles, 945. Process for 10 minutes, 945.

MUSTARD PICKLE (CHOW-CHOW)

About ten 1-pint jars

Another *Joy* original, this recipe appeared in the 1931 edition. Chow-chow can be served as a creamy relish or a crunchy cool sauce. Please read about pickling, 943–945. Wash all the vegetables well. Remove a thin slice from each end, then slice crosswise ¼-inch thick:

2 pounds unpeeled 4-inch pickling cucumbers

Stir together until the salt is dissolved:

5 cups cold water

½ cup pickling or canning salt, 944

Pour over the cucumbers in a large bowl. Place a plate on the cucumbers to keep them submerged and refrigerate for 12 hours.

For the sauce, combine and stir until the sugar is dissolved:

2½ quarts cider vinegar

2½ cups sugar

Whisk together in a medium bowl until smooth:

1½ cups all-purpose flour

6 tablespoons dry mustard

1½ tablespoons turmeric

3 tablespoons celery seeds

Slowly whisk in about 2 cups of the vinegar mixture until smooth. Bring the remaining vinegar mixture to a simmer in a large saucepan over low heat. Slowly whisk in the flour mixture. Cook, whisking constantly, until smooth and simmering. Remove from the heat, cover, and reserve. Core or trim and cut into ½-inch pieces or dice:

1½ pounds firm green tomatoes

1½ pounds green bell peppers

1 pound tender young snap peas, trimmed

You should have about 3 quarts. Combine the vegetables in a large saucepan with:

1½ pounds tender cauliflower, cut into
  bite-sized florets

Blanch for 1 minute in boiling water, peel, and then add to the vegetables:

8 ounces pearl onions

Pour boiling salted water (1 teaspoon salt to every 1 quart water) over the vegetables to cover. Return to a boil, then drain thoroughly. Thoroughly drain the cucumbers, add them to the vegetables, and stir together well. Heat the mustard sauce to boiling and stir into the hot vegetables. Season with:

Pickling or canning salt to taste

Pack the hot mixture into hot pint jars, leaving ½-inch headspace. See Putting Up Pickles, 945. Process for 15 minutes, 945.

PICCALILLI

About five 1-pint jars

Two generations ago, many Americans thought piccalilli was the only relish. It was certainly the most popular. Please read about pickling, 943–945.

Wash:

5 pounds small pickling cucumbers

Remove a thin slice from each end and chop. Combine in a large bowl with:

1⅓ pounds green bell peppers, chopped

1⅓ pounds onions, chopped

Stir together in another bowl until the salt is dissolved:

10 cups cool water

1 cup pickling or canning salt, 944

Add the brine to the vegetables. Place a plate on the vegetables to keep them submerged and refrigerate for 12 hours.

Drain the vegetables well, but do not rinse. Combine in a large saucepan or pot and bring just to a boil, stirring until the sugar is dissolved:

4 cups cider vinegar

4 cups sugar

Tie in a moist square of cheesecloth and add to the saucepan:

3 tablespoons mixed pickling spice

1½ teaspoons celery seeds

1½ teaspoons mustard seeds

Add the drained vegetables and return to a boil. Stir in, if desired:

(1 tablespoon plus 2 teaspoons crushed red
    pepper flakes)

Discard the spice bag. Using a slotted spoon, pack the hot vegetables into hot pint jars and then add the hot liquid, leaving 1/2-inch headspace. See Putting Up Pickles, 945. Process for 15 minutes, 945.

GREEN TOMATO RELISH

About six 1-pint jars

Please read about pickling, 943–945.
Wash all the vegetables. Combine in a large bowl:

8 pounds green tomatoes, thinly sliced
2³/₄ pounds onions, thinly sliced

Sprinkle with:

1/2 cup pickling or canning salt, 944

Stir together well, cover, and refrigerate for 12 hours. Rinse the vegetables in cold water and drain. Combine in a large saucepan or pot and bring to a boil, stirring until the sugar is dissolved:

6 cups cider vinegar
2 pounds brown sugar

Stir in:

2 pounds green bell peppers, sliced
1 pound red bell peppers, diced
6 garlic cloves, minced
1 tablespoon dry mustard
1¹/₂ teaspoons salt

Add the tomatoes and onions and stir together well. Tie in a moist square of cheesecloth and add to the saucepan:

1 tablespoon whole cloves
1 tablespoon ground ginger
1¹/₂ teaspoons celery seeds
1 cinnamon stick, broken

Simmer, stirring often, until the tomatoes are translucent, about 1 hour. Discard the spice bag.
Using a slotted spoon, pack the hot vegetables into hot pint jars and then add the hot liquid, leaving 1/2-inch headspace. See Putting Up Pickles, 945. Process for 15 minutes, 945.

GREEN TOMATO PICKLE

About six 1-pint jars

Please read about pickling, 943–945.
Wash all the vegetables. Cut into thin slices:

4 quarts green tomatoes

Place in a large bowl and add:

3 pounds onions, thinly sliced

Sprinkle with:

1/2 cup pickling or canning salt, 944

Stir together well, cover, and refrigerate for 12 hours. Rinse the vegetables in cold water and drain.
Bring to a boil in a large pot:

6 cups cider vinegar

Seed, remove membranes, and add:

2¹/₂ pounds green bell peppers, thinly sliced

1 pound red bell peppers, diced
6 garlic cloves, minced
2 pounds brown sugar
1 tablespoon dry mustard
1¹/₂ teaspoons salt

Add the tomatoes and onions. Tie in a moist square of cheesecloth and add to the pan:

1 tablespoon whole cloves
1 cinnamon stick, broken
1 tablespoon ground ginger
1¹/₂ teaspoons celery seeds

Simmer until tomatoes are translucent, about 1 hour, stirring frequently. Discard the spice bag.
Using a slotted spoon, pack the vegetables into hot pint jars. Add the hot liquid, leaving 1/2-inch headspace. See Putting Up Pickles, 945. Process for 10 minutes, 945.

TART CORN RELISH

About ten 1-pint jars

Please read About Pickling Equipment, 943, and About Pickling Ingredients, 943.
Husk and remove the silks and wash:

18 medium ears yellow or bicolor corn

Cook in boiling salted water (1 teaspoon salt to every 1 quart water) for 5 minutes. Drain, cool in cold water, and drain again; pat dry. Cut the kernels from the cobs, without scraping, into a very large bowl. Chop and then add:

8 ounces green bell peppers
1 pound red bell peppers
4 ounces mild green chile peppers, seeded
1¹/₂ pounds red onions
12 ounces green or red cabbage

Stir in:

5 cups cider vinegar
1 cup sugar
1 cup water
1/2 cup bottled lemon juice
3 tablespoons chopped fresh dill or
    1¹/₂ teaspoons dried dill
2 tablespoons pickling or canning salt, 944
2 teaspoons yellow mustard seeds
2 teaspoons turmeric
1 teaspoon celery seeds

Mix until well blended. Whisk until smooth in a small bowl:

1 cup water
1/2 cup all-purpose flour

Divide the vegetables between 2 large pots (or cook in 2 batches if necessary). Bring to a boil over high heat, then reduce the heat and simmer, stirring often, for 10 minutes. Stir half the flour mixture into each pot, and cook, stirring, until the mixture thickens. Cook for 10 minutes more, stirring often.
Pack the hot mixture into hot pint jars, leaving 1/2-inch headspace. See Putting Up Pickles, 945. Process for 15 minutes, 945.

CORN AND TOMATO RELISH

About 3 1/2 cups

This relish, based on the piccalillis or pickle relishes of the American South, goes particularly well with pork. If you wish, you can use thawed frozen corn, but be sure to use only good-quality, ripe tomatoes.

Husk, remove the silks, and wash:

3 ears corn

Cook in boiling salted water to cover for 1 minute, then drain, and cut off the kernels. Place the corn kernels in a small bowl, along with:

2 ripe tomatoes, finely diced
1 small red onion, finely diced
1/4 cup diced sweet pickles
1/2 cup cider vinegar
1 tablespoon sugar
1 tablespoon celery seeds
Salt and cracked black peppercorns to taste

Mix together well, cover, and refrigerate until ready to serve. This relish will keep, covered and refrigerated, for 4 to 5 days.

RED ONION MARMALADE

About 2 cups

Onion marmalade is wonderful with roasted or braised meats.

Combine in a medium nonreactive saucepan over low heat:

3 1/2 large red onions, halved and cut into
  1/4-inch-thick slices
1/3 cup dry red wine
1/3 cup red wine vinegar
1/4 cup packed light brown sugar
1/4 cup mild honey

Cook, stirring, until the sugar is dissolved, then simmer, stirring often, until the consistency of marmalade, about 30 minutes.

Stir in:

1 tablespoon orange juice
1 tablespoon lemon juice

Continue to cook, stirring, until the juices are absorbed. Let cool, then cover and refrigerate for up to 3 weeks. Serve at room temperature.

PICKLED DILLED BEANS

About one 1-pint jar

Please read About Pickling Equipment, 943, and About Pickling Ingredients, 943. This recipe is easily doubled or tripled.

Wash and trim (the pieces should be no more than 4 inches long):

8 ounces plump green beans

Place in a hot clean pint jar:

3 to 6 sprigs fresh dill or 2 1/2 tablespoons dill seeds
(1 garlic clove, peeled)
(1 teaspoon crushed red pepper flakes or
  1/4 teaspoon ground red pepper)

Closely pack the beans upright in the jar. Combine in a saucepan and bring to a boil:

1/2 cup distilled white vinegar
1/2 cup water
1 tablespoon pickling or canning salt, 944

Pour the hot vinegar solution into the jar, leaving 1/2-inch headspace, 945. See Putting Up Pickles, 945. Process for 10 minutes, 945.

PICKLED RED OR GOLDEN BEETS

About three 1-pint jars

Please read About Pickling Equipment, 943, and About Pickling Ingredients, 943.

Wash, then trim the tops and roots to 1 inch:

1 1/2 to 2 1/2 pounds red or golden beets of
  uniform size (1 to 2 1/2 inches wide)

Place in a saucepan, cover with boiling water, and simmer just until tender. Drain, discarding the liquid. Remove the stems, roots, and skins. Leave baby beets under 1 1/2 inches whole. Cut large beets into 1/4-inch-thick slices.

Peel and thinly slice:

6 ounces 2- to 2 1/2-inch onions, preferably white

Combine in a large deep skillet and bring to a boil, stirring until the sugar is dissolved:

2 cups cider vinegar
1/4 cup bottled lemon juice
3/4 cup water
2/3 cup sugar
2 teaspoons whole black peppercorns
3/4 teaspoon pickling or canning salt, 944

Add the beets and onions and simmer for 5 minutes, stirring often. During the last minute, stir in:

1/3 cup finely chopped lovage or other fresh herb

Using a slotted spoon, pack the vegetables into hot pint jars, and then add the hot vinegar solution, leaving 1/2-inch headspace. See Putting Up Pickles, 945. Process for 30 minutes, 945.

PICKLED WATERMELON RIND

Eight to ten 1-pint jars

An American invention, crunchy and refreshing. Please read About Pickling Equipment, 943, and About Pickling Ingredients, 943.

Wash, then cut lengthwise into eighths:

20 pounds slightly underripe watermelons
  with thick, firm rinds

Scrape out all but a thin line of flesh (it will not get crisp), then peel off the outer green skin. Refrigerate the watermelon flesh for another use. Cut the rind into 1-inch-wide diamonds or squares or stamp out with a 1-inch-wide cookie cutter. Blanch in boiling water until the pieces are tender yet slightly crisp at the center when pierced with a skewer, about 10 minutes—do not overcook. Drain and place in a large bowl.

Combine in a large deep skillet and bring just to a boil, stirring until the sugar is dissolved:

7 cups sugar

2 cups distilled white vinegar

$1/2$ teaspoon oil of cinnamon

$1/4$ teaspoon oil of cloves

Pour the syrup over the rind, just covering it. Cover and plump in the refrigerator overnight, 937.

The next day, drain the syrup back into the pan, bring just to a boil, and pour again over the rind. Cover and plump overnight as before.

The third day, bring the syrup and rind to a boil. Using a slotted spoon, pack the hot rind into hot pint jars, then add the hot syrup, leaving $1/2$-inch headspace. See Putting Up Pickles, 945. The flavor of this pickle may be varied by placing in each jar:

(1 star anise; 8 to 10 total)

(1 to 2 teaspoons chopped preserved ginger or candied lemon peel; about 3 to 6 tablespoons total)

Process for 10 minutes, 945.

CRANBERRY-PICKLED PEARS

About two 1-pint jars

The flesh of whole Seckel and Forelle pears turns a beautiful color in this recipe. Core before adding to the syrup if using hard 2-inch pears such as Asian pears. If using hard large pears, quarter, core, and simmer in water for 10 to 15 minutes before adding to the syrup. Please read about pickling, 943–945.

Wash and pick over:

$1^1/2$ pounds cranberries

Combine the berries in a large deep skillet that will just accommodate the pears with:

$2^1/4$ cups cider vinegar

3 cups packed light brown sugar

$1/8$ teaspoon pickling or canning salt, 944

Cook, stirring, over medium heat until the sugar is dissolved, then simmer for 10 minutes. Strain the syrup through a fine-mesh sieve back into the pan, pressing the juice from the berries, and return it to the pan. Tie in a square of moist cheesecloth and add to the saucepan:

12 whole allspice berries

Two 2-inch cinnamon sticks

$1/2$ teaspoon whole cloves

Wash:

2 pounds small firm but ripe pears of uniform size

Peel, remove the blossom ends but leave the stems on, and place in an antibrowning solution, 894. Drain the pears. Return the syrup to a boil and add the pears. Simmer, constantly pushing the pears under the syrup with a wooden spoon until just tender, 15 to 25 minutes; do not overcook. Pour into a shallow dish, cover loosely with wax paper, and place in the refrigerator overnight.

Bring the pears and syrup to a simmer, stirring. Remove the spice bag. Using tongs or slotted spoon, pack the hot pears tightly into hot pint jars, then add the hot syrup,

leaving $1/2$-inch headspace. See Putting Up Pickles, 945. Process for 20 minutes, 945.

PICKLED PEACHES

About twelve 1-pint jars

Another classic from the first edition of JOY. Tree-ripened peaches produce the fullest flavor. Please read about pickling, 943–945.

Wash:

16 pounds small clingstone peaches

Peel and place in an antibrowning solution, 894. Drain, and press into each peach, spacing them evenly:

3 whole cloves

Combine in a large pot and bring to a boil, stirring until the sugar is dissolved:

8 cups cider vinegar

12 cups sugar

Simmer for 5 minutes. Skim, then add:

Six 2-inch cinnamon sticks, tied in a square of cheesecloth

Drain the peaches. Return the syrup to a boil and add the peaches. Simmer until just tender enough to be pierced with a thin skewer, about 5 minutes—do not overcook. Pour into a shallow dish. Cover loosely with wax paper, and place in the refrigerator overnight.

Bring the peaches and syrup to a boil, stirring. Remove the spice bag. Using a slotted spoon, pack the hot peaches into hot pint jars, then add the hot syrup, leaving $1/2$-inch headspace. See Putting Up Pickles, 945. Process for 20 minutes, 945.

CURRIED APRICOT CHUTNEY

About two 1-pint jars

Please read about pickling, 943–945.

Combine in a large saucepan and simmer for 30 minutes:

2 cups water

2 cups chopped dried apricots (one 11-ounce package)

$3/4$ cup finely chopped onion

$1/4$ cup sugar

Meanwhile, combine in a small pan and cook for 5 minutes:

$1^1/2$ cups cider vinegar

1 teaspoon ground ginger

$1^1/2$ to $2^1/2$ teaspoons curry powder

1 cinnamon stick

$1/2$ teaspoon pickling or canning salt, 944

Remove the cinnamon stick if desired, and add before combining the spiced vinegar mixture to the apricots. Stir in:

2 cups golden raisins

Pack the hot chutney into hot pint jars, leaving $1/2$-inch headspace. See Putting Up Pickles, 945. Process for 10 minutes, 945.

APPLE OR GREEN TOMATO CHUTNEY

About three 1-pint jars

Please read about pickling, 943–945.

Wash the fruit and peppers, if using.

Combine in a large saucepan:

1 lemon, seeded and chopped

1 garlic clove, chopped

5 cups chopped peeled firm apples or peeled, 951, firm green tomatoes

2¹/₄ cups packed brown sugar

1¹/₂ cups raisins

3 ounces preserved ginger, chopped, or ¹/₄ cup chopped peeled fresh ginger

1¹/₂ teaspoons pickling or canning salt, 944

¹/₄ teaspoon ground red pepper

2 cups cider vinegar

(2 red bell peppers, chopped)

Simmer, stirring frequently, at least 2 hours, or until the sauce has thickened. Pack the hot chutney into hot pint jars, leaving ¹/₂-inch headspace. See Putting Up Pickles, 945. Process for 15 minutes.

CHILI SAUCE

About eight 1-pint jars

Please read about pickling, 943–945.

Wash the vegetables.

Grind together in batches through the medium blade of a food mill, or chop medium-fine in a food processor:

6 red bell peppers, coarsely chopped

6 large onions, coarsely chopped

Put in a large pot and stir in:

14 pounds ripe tomatoes, peeled, 951, seeded, and chopped

3 cups cider vinegar

2 cups packed light brown sugar

2 tablespoons pickling or canning salt, 944

1 tablespoon black pepper

1 tablespoon ground allspice

1 teaspoon ground cloves

1 teaspoon ground ginger

1 teaspoon ground cinnamon

1 teaspoon grated or ground nutmeg

1 teaspoon celery seeds

Stir to blend thoroughly, then bring to a boil over medium heat. Simmer, stirring often to prevent scorching, until thick, about 3 hours. Adjust the seasonings to taste.

Pack the hot sauce into hot pint jars, leaving ¹/₂-inch headspace. See Putting Up Pickles, 945. Process for 15 minutes, 945.

ABOUT CATSUP

We got our catsup from the British in the nineteenth century, and they got theirs from the Far East long before. The word catsup is derived from the Malay word for "taste."

No other food so familiar to Americans seems to have so many spellings. In the beginning, catsups resembled today's unsweetened Asian seasoning sauces—thin, sharp, and dark. Some were concocted from tomato juice, but many were based on mushrooms, walnuts, anchovies, or oysters. Mushroom Catsup, 952, an English sauce, gives a sense of the early catsup.

TOMATO CATSUP

About ten 1-pint jars

One taste of homemade catsup and you will understand why it is worth taking the time to prepare it. Please read About Pickling Equipment, 943, and About Pickling Ingredients, 943.

Wash all the vegetables.

Combine in a large pot:

14 pounds ripe tomatoes, peeled, 951, seeded, and chopped

8 medium onions, sliced

2 red bell peppers, diced

Simmer over medium heat, stirring occasionally, until very soft.

Puree through the medium blade of a food mill or push through a coarse-mesh strainer, then return to the pot. Stir in:

³/₄ cup packed light brown sugar

¹/₂ teaspoon dry mustard

Tie in a square of cheesecloth and add to the tomato mixture:

1 cinnamon stick

1 tablespoon whole allspice berries

1 tablespoon whole cloves

1 tablespoon ground mace

1 tablespoon celery seeds

1 tablespoon whole black peppercorns

2 bay leaves

1 garlic clove, peeled

Bring to a rolling boil, then reduce to a simmer. Cook until the sauce is reduced by half, stirring often to prevent scorching. Remove and discard the spice bag. Stir in:

2 cups cider vinegar

Pickling or canning salt to taste

(Ground red pepper to taste)

Reduce the heat and simmer, stirring almost constantly, for 10 minutes. Pack the hot catsup into hot pint jars, leaving ¹/₈-inch headspace. See Putting Up Pickles, 945. Process for 15 minutes, 945.

BLENDER TOMATO CATSUP

About nine 1-pint jars

Please read about pickling, 943–945.

Wash all vegetables.

Process in small batches in a blender or food processor until pureed, about 5 seconds each batch:

24 pounds ripe tomatoes, peeled, seeded, and
quartered
2 pounds onions, quartered
1 pound red bell peppers, cut into strips
1 pound green bell peppers, cut into strips

Stir together well in a large pot and bring to a boil, stirring often, over medium heat. Reduce the heat slightly and boil gently, stirring often and thoroughly, for 1 hour. Stir in:

9 cups cider vinegar
9 cups sugar
$1/4$ cup pickling or canning salt, 944

Tie in a cheesecloth bag and add to the tomato mixture:

3 tablespoons dry mustard
$1^1/2$ tablespoons whole allspice berries
$1^1/2$ tablespoons paprika
$1^1/2$ tablespoons whole cloves
2 cinnamon sticks

Boil gently, stirring often, until the mixture is reduced by half and mounds up on a spoon with no separation of liquid and solids.

Remove and discard the spice bag. Pack the hot catsup into hot pint jars, leaving $1/8$-inch headspace. See Putting Up Pickles, 945. Process for 15 minutes, 945.

RED ONION–GARLIC CATSUP

About three $1/2$-pint jars

The rich, deep, robust flavors of this catsup are perfect with steak or roast beef. Please read about pickling, 943–945.

Wash all the vegetables.
Heat in a large deep skillet over medium heat:

$1/3$ cup olive oil

Add and cook, stirring often, until well browned, 10 to 20 minutes:

5 large red onions, thinly sliced

Stir in and cook until the garlic and ginger are softened, about 3 minutes:

$1/4$ cup minced garlic
1 tablespoon minced peeled fresh ginger
1 medium ripe tomato, finely diced

Add:

1 teaspoon hot pepper sauce, or to taste
5 tablespoons Worcestershire sauce
$1/2$ cup molasses
$3/4$ cup cider vinegar
1 teaspoon ground allspice

Reduce the heat to low and cook, stirring occasionally, until slightly thickened, about 15 minutes. Remove from the heat and season with:

Salt and black pepper to taste

Let cool to room temperature.
Once the mixture has cooled, puree it in a blender or food processor. Serve warm or cold.

MUSHROOM CATSUP

About three $1/2$-pint jars

This English condiment is thin, pungent, and deeply flavored.

Please read About Pickling Equipment, 943, and About Pickling Ingredients, 943.
Wash and coarsely chop:

4 pounds mushrooms, preferably cremini

Spread out on a large rimmed baking sheet lined with wax paper, and sprinkle with:

7 tablespoons kosher salt

Cover and refrigerate, stirring occasionally, for 2 to 3 days. Drain the mushrooms and rinse well. Combine in a large saucepan with:

1 cup red wine vinegar
$2/3$ cup cider vinegar
1 medium red onion, finely chopped
1 garlic clove, finely chopped
$1/2$ teaspoon black pepper
$1/4$ teaspoon ground ginger
$1/4$ teaspoon ground allspice
$1/4$ teaspoon grated or ground nutmeg

Bring to a boil, then reduce the heat and simmer uncovered, stirring often, until very fragrant and flavorful, about 30 minutes.

Strain into a clean saucepan, pressing out all the liquid. Bring to a simmer, then strain through a sieve lined with a dampened cheesecloth. Pack the hot catsup into hot $1/2$-pint jars, leaving $1/8$-inch headspace. See Putting Up Pickles, 945. Process for 15 minutes, 945.

PICKLED GINGER

1 quart

Please read about pickling, 943–945. Peel and slice thinly:

1 pound ginger (2 large roots)

Combine with:

$1^1/2$ teaspoons salt

Pack into a quart container. Bring to a boil in a large saucepan over medium-high heat:

$1^1/4$ cups rice vinegar
$1/2$ cup sugar
$1/2$ cup mirin

Pour warm liquid over the ginger. Let cool, cover, and refrigerate for at least 1 week and up to two months.

PICKLED HORSERADISH

About two $1/2$-pint jars

Please read about pickling, 943–945.
Wash well in hot water:

12 ounces fresh horseradish

Scrape off the skin. Have ready in a glass or stainless steel bowl a combination of:

1 cup vinegar
$1/2$ teaspoon salt

Grate, mince, or blend the horseradish, and combine with

the vinegar mixture. Pack into sterilized jars, 890, and store in the refrigerator.

WALNUT CATSUP
About 3 ¹/₂ quarts
Please read About Pickling Equipment, 943, and About Pickling Ingredients, 943.

Pick and bruise:

100 immature green English walnuts

still so soft they can be pierced through with a needle. Put them into a crock with:

2 quarts vinegar
6 ounces salt

Cover, mash, and stir daily for 8 days. Drain the liquid and put it into an enamel or stainless steel pan with:

4 ounces finely chopped anchovies
12 finely chopped shallots or 1 garlic clove, chopped
¹/₂ cup grated fresh horseradish
¹/₂ teaspoon *each* mace, nutmeg, ginger, whole cloves, and peppercorns

Cover and bring mixture to a boil, then simmer gently about 40 minutes. Filter, cool, and add:

2 cups Port

Pour into sterile glass bottles. Cork well. Cover the corks with wax. Store in a cool, dry place.

WORCESTERSHIRE SAUCE
About 5 half-pints
Put into a jug:

1 quart cider vinegar
6 tablespoons Walnut Catsup, above
5 tablespoons essence of anchovies or 2 ounces finely chopped anchovies
A pinch of cayenne
1 teaspoon salt
1 tablespoon sugar

Cork and shake 4 times daily for 2 weeks. Strain into sterile bottles. Cork tightly and store in a cool place.

ABOUT FERMENTING VEGETABLES
Dill pickles, sauerkraut, and some olives have their distinctive taste from undergoing a fermentation process. Fruits and vegetables may not ferment at all below 60°F; for the unrefrigerated brining of vegetables, 60° to 65°F will produce the highest quality, and fermentation will take between 4 and 6 weeks. For safety's sake, food must be completely covered with a vinegar solution or brine. Quick-pickling vegetables at room temperature—70° to 75°F—will take 3 to 4 weeks. The pickle will be good, but not as good as at the lower temperature. Above 80°F, the pickle will be too soft or may spoil. **Caution:** If, in the process of fermenting, the food becomes soft or slimy or develops a disagreeable odor, discard it without tasting according to the directions on 893.

All food in brine must be weighted so it will stay submerged in the brine and ferment properly. One very simple method of making a weight to use in long-brining is to place a large sealable plastic freezer bag inside another. Fill the inside bag with pickling brine and close both bags securely. (It's important to fill the bag with brine instead of water so that if the bags leak or break, the brine will not be diluted.) Place on top of the food in the crock. Use enough weight to sink the food 1 to 2 inches beneath the brine. The bag (or bags) must completely cover and submerge the food to prevent the formation of scum.

If not using filled plastic bags, cover the food with wet clean muslin or cheesecloth, tucking the cloth against the sides of the container. Place a clean dry plate on top of the cloth—it should just fit inside the container. Set tightly capped clean water-filled jars on top of the plate. Check for scum every day. If any does form, remove it from the surface and around the sides of the crock.

As a precaution, use only plastic, silicone, wood, or stainless steel implements when stirring or retrieving pickling foods—and use tongs instead of your hands. Even the cleanest of hands can spread bacteria. A spotless heavy bath towel to cover the crock at room temperature will keep out dust, insects, and other contaminants. A tight-fitting heavy lid is best for a container in the refrigerator.

CROCK-CURED DILL PICKLES
About three 1-quart jars
Although fully cured pickles take weeks, after only about 1 week, pickles are called "new dill," and, to many, are at their prime. This recipe fills a 1-gallon crock. The leaves add crunch but are not essential. Please read about pickling, 943–945, and About Fermenting Vegetables, above. Wash:

4 pounds 4-inch pickling cucumbers

Slice ¹/₁₆ inch from the blossom ends but leave ¹/₄ inch of the stems. Wash and pat dry:

(8 cups unsprayed grape or cherry leaves)
4 to 6 sprigs dill

Wash, peel, and thinly slice:

2 to 6 large garlic cloves

Measure:

1 tablespoon to ¹/₃ cup mixed pickling spice, according to taste

Loosely layer the leaves, if using, and seasonings with the cucumbers in a 1-gallon crock, leaving space for air between the cucumbers. Start and end with the leaves and seasonings. Combine in a large bowl, stirring until the salt is dissolved:

8 cups water
¹/₂ cup pickling or canning salt, 944
¹/₄ cup cider vinegar

Pour over the cucumbers. Weight to keep the cucumbers submerged and cover. Check for scum daily, and stir every 2 to 3 days. Test after 1 week to see if the pickles are to your taste. New dills—ready when their color has changed from bright green to dull yellowish green—should be tightly packed into hot sterilized jars, covered with brine, and refrigerated. Fully fermented pickles may be refrigerated in the crock and will keep for 4 to 6 months. Promptly remove any surface scum and mold on refrigerated pickles, or they will quickly spoil.

Pour the brine into a saucepan, bring slowly to a boil, and simmer for 5 minutes. Pack the pickles into hot jars and add the hot brine, leaving 1/2-inch headspace. See Putting Up Pickles, 945. Process pints for 10 minutes, quarts for 15 minutes, 945.

SAUERKRAUT

About 1 quart

Fabulous to eat and an adventure to make, home-cured sauerkraut has little in common with its factory-made counterpart. Prepare 5 pounds cabbage at a time. Please read about pickling, 943–945, and About Fermenting Vegetables, 953.

Remove the outer leaves, wash well under cold running water, and drain:

5 pounds firm mature cabbage—any but Savoy

Quarter and remove the cores. Thinly slice the cabbage and place in a large bowl along with:

3 tablespoons pickling or canning salt

Mix well, then let stand a few minutes to wilt (this makes packing easier). Pack firmly and evenly in a stoneware crock or other suitable container. Press down with a spoon until the juice rises to the surface. If, after pressing, the juice does not rise above the shreds, make a brine of:

1 1/2 tablespoons pickling or canning salt
per each 4 cups water

Bring to a boil, cool, and then add to the crock. Weight to keep the cabbage submerged and cover, as above. The next day, the presence of gas bubbles will indicate that fermentation has begun. Check the cabbage once or twice a week. If scum develops, remove it immediately, or the kraut will spoil. When the bubbles stop, in 3 to 6 weeks, fermentation is complete.

Fully fermented sauerkraut keeps in a covered jar in the refrigerator for several months, as long as the cabbage is always completely covered by liquid. For longer keeping, bring the kraut and liquid slowly to a boil, stirring frequently. Firmly pack the kraut into hot jars, then add the hot brine solution, leaving 1/2-inch headspace, See Putting Up Pickles, 945. Process pints for 10 minutes, quarts for 15 minutes, 945.

SALT-CURED BLACK OLIVES

One pound of olives makes about 1 pint

You may choose to rinse some of the salt off the olives before serving.

Line a slatted wooden box with clean burlap and set it on a tarp (dark tannin from the olives will stain). Wash, then pat dry, handling carefully:

Uncured fully ripe small dark olives

Place a single layer of olives in the box. Sprinkle with a layer of:

Food-grade rock salt

The salt should just cover the olives. Continue layering the olives and salt, finishing with salt. Cover the box with burlap and let stand for 24 hours in a bright, airy place out of full sun.

Wearing rubber gloves, use your hand to gently but thoroughly mix the olives and salt every day or two—the olives can spoil if this is not done faithfully. They will be ready in about 4 to 6 weeks.

Remove the olives from the salt, brushing it off. (Do not wash off the salt, as what remains helps preserve the olives.) Pack them into sterilized jars. See Putting up Pickles, 945. Add to each:

(1 fresh bay leaf)
(White pepper to taste)
Olive oil to cover

Cover tightly and store in a cool, dark place.

PICKLED PEPPERS

About seven 1-pint jars

Please read about pickling, 943–945, and About Fermenting Vegetables, 953.

Banana, Hungarian, and jalapeño peppers work well in this recipe. Wear gloves when handling hot peppers, or wash your hands thoroughly with soap and water before touching your face.

Wash:

4 pounds long hot red, green, or yellow chile peppers
3 pounds mixed red and green bell peppers

Blanch in boiling water or blister under the broiler in order to loosen the skin. Cool and peel off the skin. Small peppers can be left whole, but slash 2 to 4 slits in each and flatten. Quarter large peppers. Fill hot pint jars with the peppers, leaving 1/2-inch headspace. Combine in a large saucepan and bring to a boil, then reduce the heat and simmer 10 minutes:

5 cups distilled white vinegar
1 cup water
4 teaspoons pickling or canning salt
2 tablespoons sugar
2 garlic cloves, peeled

Remove the garlic. Pour the hot pickling liquid over the peppers in the jars, leaving 1/2-inch headspace. See Putting Up Pickles, 945. Process for 10 minutes, 945.

ABOUT PRESERVING IN SPIRITS

Spirits (alcoholic beverages) keep food the way vinegar does, by basically knocking out the spoilers. Fruits preserved in spirits are spooned over ice cream or used in puddings and compotes. The syrup is strained into a bottle and used to flavor fruits and desserts, and, of course, sipped in cordial glasses. Brandy or an eau-de-vie (a fruit brandy) is traditional abroad, but in this country, there is no reason not to use bourbon. Recipes for three approaches to preserving fruits in spirits are found below.

Peaches, cherries, and apricots are the examples, but equally successful are small whole plums and peeled small whole pears. In all cases, the fruit darkens; this does not mean that the process has gone wrong. The fruit will hold its flavor for a year or so, then gradually fade; the spirits will keep virtually forever. Jars for these mixtures do not need to be sterilized because of the alcohol content; however, they should be scrupulously clean and it would not hurt to scald or immerse in boiling water. A cool storage temperature is essential.

BRANDIED PEACHES

One pound of peaches makes about 1 pint

Please read Preserving in Spirits, above.
Weigh:

Small firm but ripe peaches

Prepare a syrup in a large heavy saucepan, combining for every 1 pound fruit:

1 cup sugar

1 cup water

Wash and peel the peaches; leave whole. Add the peaches to the syrup and simmer 5 minutes. Using a slotted spoon, pack the peaches into hot pint jars, leaving $1/2$-inch headspace. Pour into each jar:

2 to 4 tablespoons brandy

Bring the syrup to a boil and pour over the fruit in the jars, leaving $1/2$-inch headspace. See Putting Up Pickles, 945. Process for 15 minutes, 945. Store in a cool, dark place for 3 months before using.

BRANDIED CHERRIES

One pound of cherries makes about 1 pint

This old French recipe is the easiest method of preserving summer fruits.
Please read Preserving in Spirits, above.
Snip the stems down to $1/2$ inch, then wash and weigh:

Plump, ripe sweet cherries

For every 1 pound of fruit, measure:

Heaping $1/2$ cup sugar

Layer the fruit and sugar in pint jars. Leaving $1/4$-inch headspace, fill the jars with:

**Brandy, kirsch, framboise, grappa, vodka,
or bourbon**

Cap tightly, wrap in brown paper, and let stand in a cool, dark place for 7 to 8 weeks before serving. For the first month or so, occasionally rock the jars back and forth to help the sugar dissolve and to distribute the flavors.

BRANDIED APRICOTS

One pound of apricots makes about 1 pint

These fruits have a mild brandy flavor, because the brandy is diluted with water. As a result, potential contaminants must be destroyed before putting the jars away. Lightly cook the fruit, then process the filled jars in a boiling-water canner, 888. If you prefer a stronger spirit flavor, use $1 1/2$ cups sugar for every 1 cup water. After poaching the fruit, boil down the syrup until it is the consistency of maple syrup, then cover the fruit with equal parts syrup and brandy. Please read Preserving in Spirits, 954.
Wash and weigh:

Firm but ripe apricots of the same size

Blanch and peel. Prepare syrup in a large heavy saucepan, combining for every 1 pound fruit:

1 cup sugar

1 cup water

Bring to a boil, stirring until the sugar is dissolved. Add the apricots and simmer until barely tender when tested with a thin skewer, about 5 minutes. Using a slotted spoon, pack into hot pint jars, then pour the simmering syrup over the fruit, filling the jars three-quarters full. Add, leaving $1/4$-inch headspace:

Brandy, kirsch, framboise, vodka, or bourbon

Process for 10 minutes, 945. Let stand in a cool, dark place for at least 1 month before serving.

KNOW YOUR INGREDIENTS

Modern cooks are confronted with an immense abundance—we have more ingredients to cook with than ever before. If a recipe calls for vanilla or paprika or strawberries in winter, we're unfazed, knowing they're a walk or short drive away. Staples present an even larger cornucopia of choices: How would you like your milk, beans, nuts, herbs, cheese, chocolate, or butter—whole, low-fat, nonfat, dried, fresh, canned, chopped, roasted, shredded, grated, sliced, blended with something that's better for you, lightened, softened, or substituted? Just ask.

Where do all these possibilities fit into your kitchen? What qualities make them work and which must you compensate for? Can you mix, match, and triumph?

Many of the most basic cooking ingredients are so familiar, so constantly used, that their characteristics are sometimes taken for granted even by experienced cooks, while their peculiarities are often simply ignored by beginners. Yet success in cooking depends largely on becoming fully aware of how both common and uncommon ingredients react. Here we focus on the key elements—from water to weather—to see just what they contribute to the cooking process. With the knowledge gained in this chapter and the chapter on cooking methods and techniques, 1011, plus the information keyed by arrows and referenced into our recipes at the point of use, we assure you a continuous and steady progress to becoming a better cook.

UNDERSTANDING FLAVORS AND SEASONINGS

"Season to taste." How that time-tested direction stimulates the born cook! We know that seasonings, spices, herbs, and condiments can complement and compliment food, but it is our own sense of taste that composes the symphony. Just how does it do so? The anatomy of taste is differentiated among five basic sensations: sweet, sour, salty, bitter, and umami (a unique taste first named in 1908, often described as savory and meaty). When we taste things, they pass so quickly over our taste buds and the tongue that a fast sequence of flavors results, like an arpeggio or a chord. When we were young, lollipops were their sweetest—not without reason, because senses dull with age, and our taste buds were more impressionable then. Not only were we told to gulp our medicines fast, but we took them iced to reduce their impact. On the other hand, to taste normally sweet, the ice cream we freeze must be sugared more than warm foods. It is relished more, too, when taken in small amounts and held in the mouth momentarily before swallowing. Heat seems to affect sourness and saltiness too: Lemon seems less acid when the tea is hottest, and soup seems saltier when hot than when cold. The best time to judge for salt adjustment is when food is just below 98°F.

But sweet, sour, bitter, salty, and umami are only basic foundation tastes. The pleasures of the complex and subtle structure built up from them, which we casually refer to as "flavor," are due much more to the sense of smell than to the sense of taste. Try tasting food while holding your nose, and you will notice that a full and characteristic flavor is realized only when the breath is expelled through your nostrils. Since foods must be in solution for their flavors to be fully appreciated, texture plays a large part both directly and as contrast. Flavors that stand out in liquid may grow duller rather than sharper if some gumlike substance such as tragacanth or agar is used as a thickener. The peppers and ginger, because of their nonvolatile components, leave a somewhat painful burning sensation, along with a pleasant glow and tingle. In contrast, mint has the power to cool because of its high menthol content. Types of seasoning modify one another. Salt, for example, can make sugar less cloying and tone down acidity. As a corollary, sugar or vinegar may reduce saltiness. Ginger, brandy, or sherry can lessen "gaminess" or strong flavor in fish and wildfowl while bringing a comforting warmth. Salt, pepper, and parsley act as catalysts for other flavors. A reminder: Prolonged drinking before or smoking during a meal tends to desensitize all the pathways along which food is appreciated.

The history of seasonings is an ironical one. Back in medieval days, the spice routes to the Orient were fiercely contested, for spices were essential to make the poorly preserved foods of Europe palatable. Nowadays, many foods in our Western world are so overrefined or processed that seasonings are needed to make them interesting enough to eat! The infinite interplay among taste, aroma, and texture combined with hereditary and national preferences defies exact classification, and only the familiar remains acceptable to the majority of people. Try setting your sails for new courses on this endlessly fascinating sea of taste.

When adding seasoning, the greatest care must be used to enhance the natural or previously acquired flavor of the food. The role of seasoning is to bring out the best in the material, not to stifle or to smother it with heavy off-key trappings. First and best, of course, even before seasoning, are the built-in flavors of food grown in rich soils or from animals that have been nourished on flavor-inducing vegetation. Examples are the famous sea-marsh–grazed lamb of France, the heather-nibbling grouse of Scotland, and our own peach-fed Southern pigs or northern game birds after they have taken their fill of juniper or other aromatic berries. Next come the flavors accentuated by heat: in the browning of meats or glazes; in the essential roasting of coffee and cocoa beans; in the toasting of nuts, seeds, and breads; and in the highly treasured osmazome, as a gourmet calls it, which is present in rich meat broths; as well as in the blending of taste achieved generally through slow cooking.

Soy sauce, Worcestershire, catsups, hot pepper sauces, and other such condiments can mask or enhance other flavors. We find them useful as flavor accents and we indicate suitable quantities as components in various sauces.

Then there are the flavors induced by fermentation and bacterial activity, as in wines and cheeses; those created by distillation in extract and liqueurs; and those brought about by smoking, 905, brining, 962, or marination, 584. Intensification of flavor in foods can be by purely mechanical means, too: the cracking or toasting of seeds like those of cumin, coriander, anise, caraway, and poppy to release their essential oils, the sources of aroma. This is also true during the mincing of herbs and the crushing of spices in a mortar. Keep kitchen shears handy to quickly add bits of flavorful ingredients such as herbs, celery, bacon, and peppers to food. In seasoning recipes to which unseasoned or mildly seasoned foods are added, be sure to retaste after adding them. Perhaps most important, ➤ heat seasoned food with great care, since certain spices like cayenne, paprika and curry blends scorch easily, and others become bitter if overheated.

FLAVOR BASES AS SEASONING

Many recipes begin with creating a flavor base to form a foundation for a dish such as soup, a sauce, stew, or roast. This flavorful mixture is an essential starting point, made by cooking in butter, olive oil, or lard a mix of aromatic vegetables such as onions, garlic, celery, carrots, and onion. Sometimes the aromatic vegetables are removed from the fat and don't appear in the finished dish—they just flavor the fat. These flavor bases vary in their ingredients in various cuisines. The first step in a stir-fry, 1048, for example, is to cook garlic or ginger in hot oil, while in parts of Africa, chopped onions and garlic are sautéed in peanut oil with chile peppers. For some classic flavor bases, see Mirepoix, 998, and Sofrito, 1013.

ACIDULATED WATER

Easily made, water with a slight acid content has many uses in cooking, mostly for keeping cut fruits and vegetable from turning brown during food preparation. Four methods for making acidulated water follow.

I. Add **1 tablespoon cider or distilled white vinegar** to each **1 quart of water**.

II. Add **2 tablespoons cider or distilled white vinegar or 3 tablespoons lemon juice** and, if desired, **1 teaspoon salt** to each **1 quart of water**.

III. Add **½ cup wine** to each quart of water.

IV. Also see Anti-Browning Solutions for Canning, 894, for Freezing, 915, and for Fresh Fruit, 209.

ALLSPICE

Allspice berries, also known as Jamaica pepper, are sold whole or ground. Despite the common misconception, allspice is not a blend of spices, but within its single small reddish-brown berry lies a mixture of cinnamon, clove, nutmeg, and juniper berry flavors. Use allspice anywhere from soup to nuts, alone or in a combination with other spices.

Allspice, or *pimento,* and the red chile pepper called a *pimiento* are similar in their spelling. *Pimiento* is reserved for the name of peppers of the *Capsicum* family, see 1006, and *pimento,* or the botanical name, *Pimenta dioica,* is for allspice only.

ALMONDS

Almonds are available in the shell or shelled; toasted with skins on; and blanched, with skins removed. They are also available sliced, slivered, or whole. Look for plump smooth kernels, and buy in the shell for reasons of economy and optimal freshness. Almonds may be ground to make tortes and marzipan and almond paste, or slivered for toppings. As a garnish, see below. Almonds may also be eaten while green and soft with cheese and wine. **Marcona almonds** are large flat nuts with a more intense flavor than regular almonds. They are native to Spain and are increasingly available. **Bitter almonds** are used as a flavoring and in some classic European recipes, but they are not available in the United States because they contain the poison prussic acid. They are processed, however, and sold in almond extract and almond-flavored liqueurs.

ALMOND (AMANDINE) GARNISH
About ½ cup
This garnish is a classic. It glorifies the most commonplace dish. As a variation on almonds for a vegetable garnish, try roasted pumpkin, squash, or sesame seeds.
Melt in a small skillet:
   ¼ cup (½ stick) butter
Add and stir over low heat until the nuts are lightly browned:
   ¼ cup sliced almonds
   Salt to taste

ANCHOVIES

Anchovies are tiny fish that have been filleted, salted, and canned, rolled or flat, in oil. Discreetly added to food, they add a piquant flavor, the source of which is most difficult to trace. About ⅛ teaspoon diced anchovy to 1 cup of sauce will do the trick, or ⅛ teaspoon anchovy paste. Sold in tubes, **anchovy paste** is a mixture of mashed anchovies, spices, vinegar, and water and is convenient when only a small quantity of anchovy is needed. The paste is less strong in flavor and apt to be saltier than the anchovy fillets, which may be treated in several ways.

I. For use in a salad or canapés or to eat uncooked, reduce the saltiness by soaking anchovies in cold water or milk 30 minutes. Drain and dry on paper towels before using.

II. For use in a sauce, soak anchovies in warm water 5 to 10 minutes. Drain and pat dry before using. Anchovies are sometimes used as lardoons to season meats, see 464.

ANCHOVY PESTO

Use as a spread on crostini.
Crush together:

1 anchovy fillet
2 tablespoons grated Parmesan

Combine with an equal amount of:

Butter

ANGELICA

The leaves of this slightly licorice-flavored plant are candied as a garnish for desserts, 880. The seeds may be added to pastry, the young tips to rhubarb or gooseberries.

Angelica archangelica grows 4 to 8 feet tall. It dies after blooming but is perennial if blooming is inhibited. The seeds must be fresh, the soil moist, and the locale shady.

ANISE

Anise has subtle licorice overtones. Use the seeds in Springerle, 775, and the oil as flavoring in sponge cake. Or try star anise, 1016, in watermelon-rind pickle. To release the full flavor, crush anise seeds in a mortar and pestle, or place them in a heavy plastic bag and crush with a rolling pin. *Pimpinella anisum* grows to 3 feet. Because of the long taproot, transplant into light rich soil when the seedlings are young. See also Star Anise, 1016.

ANNATTO (ACHIOTE)

Annatto or achiote seeds from the annatto tree are commonly used in Mexican, Caribbean, and South American cooking. They are available whole or ground. Because of its yellow-orange hue, annatto, or *Bixa orellana,* is often used as a substitute for saffron, to add color to rice. Annatto seeds have no flavor, but food manufacturers frequently rely on the vivid color in the coloring of cheese and margarine. The color of the seeds can be rendered in cooking oil by simmering ½ cup of seeds in 1 cup vegetable oil for 10 to 15 minutes. Strain out the seeds and store the oil in the refrigerator for up to 1 month.

ARROWROOT

See Starches, 1016.

BAKER'S AMMONIA

Baker's ammonia, the forerunner of our modern and more stable chemical leaveners, is also known as **ammonium bicarbonate, carbonate of ammonia,** and **hartshorn.** Used for years in Europe to produce long-lasting crisp cookies, it is sold as a fine powder, often at drugstores or from Internet retailers. Buy only small amounts as it evaporates quickly if not very tightly contained. It is sifted with the dry ingredients or dissolved in a warm liquid such as water, rum, or wine. The uncooked dough or batter containing baker's ammonia should not be eaten. Substitute it for the baking powder and baking soda called for in cookie and cake recipes.

BAKING POWDER

Baking powder is a ready-made combination of baking soda, 959, and various liquid- and heat-responsive acid salts such as tartaric acid (cream of tartar), monocalcium phosphate, sodium acid pyrophosphate, or sodium aluminum sulfate.

There are three main kinds of baking powders: double-acting, phosphate and tartrate, or single-acting baking powder. Typically, the ➤ type is specified on the label. In all of them there must be an acid and an alkaline material that react separately in the presence of moisture to form a gas—carbon dioxide—which takes the form of tiny bubbles in a dough or batter. In baking, these quickly expand the batter, which is then set by the heat to make a light-textured crumb. Before measuring any of these leaveners, stir and break up any lumps, and use a dry measuring spoon.

Most commercial baking powders are double-acting, meaning that one acid starts to work in the cold batter or dough and action of the other acid is held in reserve until the batter reaches a certain temperature, usually 140°F. This two-phase reaction ensures additional push during the later stages of baking, usually producing a taller, lighter product.

If you doubt the effectiveness of any baking powder, ➤ test by mixing 1 teaspoon baking powder with ⅓ cup hot water. Use the baking powder only if it bubbles enthusiastically.

Just in case you run out of baking powder, you can mix up a homemade version of single-acting baking powder: For each teaspoon of baking powder called for in the recipe, mix together ½ teaspoon cream of tartar, ⅓ teaspoon baking soda, and ⅛ teaspoon salt. After adding the above mixture, do not delay putting the batter into the oven. ➤ And don't try to store this mixture, it has poor keeping qualities.

▲ Because of the decrease in barometric pressure at high altitudes, carbon dioxide gas expands more quickly and thus has greater leavening action. For this reason, the amount of baking powder should be decreased if you are using a sea-level recipe. Or select recipes designed especially for high altitudes; see 1056.

DOUBLE-ACTING BAKING POWDER

Sometimes referred to as ➤ combination baking powder, this is the type of baking powder specified in this book. These powders typically use sodium aluminum sulfate and monocalcium phosphate as the acid ingredients. They too start work in the cold dough or batter, but the great rising impact does not begin until the dough contacts the heat from the hot oven.

PHOSPHATE BAKING POWDER

Phosphate baking powders use monocalcium phosphate or sodium acid pyrophosphate, or a combination of these, as the acid ingredient. They are somewhat slower in reaction and give up a significant part of their carbon dioxide in the cold dough or batter. The remainder is released when the mixture is baked. Phosphate baking powders are aluminum-free.

TARTRATE BAKING POWDER

In single-acting tartrate baking powders, baking soda is combined with tartaric acid or a combination of cream of tartar and tartaric acid. They are the quickest in reaction time, giving off carbon dioxide the moment they are combined with liquid. Therefore, if you are using this kind, be sure to ➤ have the oven preheated and mix the batter quickly so that not much gas escapes from the dough or batter before the cells can become heat-hardened in their expanded form. Especially ➤ avoid using tartrate powder for doughs and batters that are to be stored in the refrigerator or frozen before baking.

BAKING SODA (SODIUM BICARBONATE)

Used alone, baking soda has no leavening properties. But used in combination with acidic ingredients such as buttermilk, sour milk, yogurt, sour cream, or molasses, baking soda gives one of the very tenderest crumbs. This bubbly reaction is the essence of chemical leavening. The carbon dioxide pushes against the batter, causing it to expand as it simultaneously bakes and sets. If timed correctly, the baked item reaches its maximum size at the same time the starches gelatinize and the gluten proteins set. The result is a fully leavened bread or cake. If the batter is too thin to hold the rise, though, it will collapse before it can set. If the leaven is activated early, the batter will fall before it can set. The reaction of the soda with the acid is essentially the same as that which takes place when the two ingredients in baking powder meet moisture, so always mix the baking soda with the dry ingredients first. A single-acting leavener activated when the soda and acid combine in the wet batter, baking soda begins producing carbon dioxide immediately; batters containing it should be baked as soon as possible.

The proportion of baking soda to sour milk or buttermilk is usually ➤ 1 teaspoon soda to 1 cup milk and 4 cups flour. For more details about soda and sour milk or cream reactions, see 1014.

Chocolate, honey, citrus juice, and corn syrup are not acidic enough to be the only source of acid, so some recipes with these acid ingredients may call for both baking powder and baking soda. If they do, use about 1/4 teaspoon baking soda and 1 teaspoon baking powder for each 1 cup flour. A smaller amount of baking soda is used for neutralizing the acid ingredients in the recipe, while the main leavening action is left to the baking powder. The amounts of baking powder per cup of flour suggested above are not for high altitudes.

To substitute baking soda for baking powder, see Substitutions, 1037.

▲ At high altitudes, baking soda is usually decreased as for baking powder, 958, though sometimes, to increase the acidity of the batter—an advantage at high altitudes—the balance of the two is adjusted to use more baking powder than soda.

BASILS

Not without reason called "the royal herb" (l'herbe royale), these versatile leaves have a great affinity for tomatoes, fish, and egg dishes, but they are good in almost all savory dishes. They darken quickly after cutting, and they should be added to hot foods at the end of cooking. Serve them as they do in Italy, in a bouquet of sprigs set in water in a small vase and used at the table to flavor food. Be sure to try Pesto, 569, with pasta.

Various basils are used in Asian cuisines. Most of these basils have a clovelike flavor that is more pronounced than in the Mediterranean basils. Thai cuisine uses cultivars of two different species: holy basil, *Ocimum sanctum,* and Thai basil, *Ocimum basilicum.* Sweet basil, *Ocimum basilicum,* which grows to 2 feet, dries poorly and should never be dried in heat above 110°F. It roots in water in a few days. Make cuttings and transplant into rich soil in small pots before the first frost, which will surely kill the tender foliage. It is worth keeping at least one potted plant over the winter to supply that fresh basil flavor until the new crop is ready. *Ocimum minimum,* dwarf bush basil, less than 1 foot tall, is the sweetest and mildest in flavor and the best for house culture.

To chiffonade or make ribbon cuts of basil, see 1071. To make basil oil, see 590.

BAY LEAVES

Always use bay leaves, fresh or dry, with discretion—and do not crumble or crush before adding to the pot; leave them whole for easy removal. Use them not only in stuffings, but also in stocks, sauces, and marinades; in the cooking of vegetables and meats; and in a Bouquet Garni, 960. Dry the leaves in August. ➤ Do not confuse the leaves of the edible bay laurel tree, *Laurus nobilis,* highly aromatic when bruised, with those of the poisonous *Prunus laurocerasus,* the cherry laurel or English laurel leaf of our gardens, which is high in prussic acid, or cyanide. More commonly sold as bay leaves is California laurel, or *Umbellularia californica,* which is similar to bay laurel but has a stronger flavor. ➤ Always remove the bay leaves after the cooking process is complete.

BEECHNUTS
A real treat—but you'll have to beat the squirrels and blue-jays. Beechnuts are not harvested commercially.

BLACK BEAN SAUCE
Made from soybeans, this is an essential ingredient in many dishes in China. You can find it as whole bean sauce, which has a unique texture, or as ground bean sauce, which tends to be saltier. All types of bean sauces can be stored indefinitely, tightly covered, in the refrigerator.

BONITO FLAKES
Also called katsuobushi and smoky fish flakes, bonito flakes are dried, salted, fermented fish flakes. They are a Japanese ingredient used in broths for flavoring. The flakes keep indefinitely stored in a pantry.

BORAGE
Borage is only good fresh; its flavor vanishes as it dries. Use the fuzzy leaves, in moderation, wherever you want to add a cucumber flavor to soups, fish sauces, or salads. The choice blue starlike blooms are beautiful floated in punches and lemonades, or used as a garnish. Young borage can be cooked like spinach. *Borago officinalis,* which self-seeds, causing it to return the next summer, grows to $2\frac{1}{2}$ feet even in poor soil.

BOUQUET GARNI
A bouquet garni is a combination of herbs, vegetables, and occasionally spices bundled in cheesecloth or tied with a string and used to flavor soup, stock, and sauces. They are removed before serving.
I. Bunch together:

    3 or 4 sprigs parsley
    $\frac{1}{3}$ to $\frac{1}{2}$ bay leaf
    2 sprigs thyme
    (1 leek, white portion only)
    (2 cloves)

To make removal easier, you may place them inside:
    (Several overlapping celery ribs or leek greens)
and bind tightly with kitchen string.
II. If you cannot get fresh herbs, wrap dried herbs, coarsely crumbled but not powdered, in 4-inch squares of cheesecloth tied into pouches. Store in a tightly covered container up to 1 month.
Allow for 12 bags:

    2 tablespoons dried parsley
    1 tablespoon dried thyme
    1 tablespoon dried marjoram
    2 bay leaves
    2 tablespoons dried celery leaves

BRAZIL NUTS
Brazil nuts are large, long nuts—twice the size of a cashew or almond. They may be eaten whole, or to slice these large kernels, cover the shelled nuts with cold water, bring slowly to a boil, and simmer 5 minutes. Drain. Slice lengthwise, or make curls with a vegetable slicer. You may also toast the slices at 350°F for about 12 minutes.

BREAD CRUMBS
When reading a recipe, note what kind of bread crumbs are called for. The results are very different depending on whether they are dry, fresh, or browned or buttered. Finely crushed cracker crumbs, cake crumbs, or cornflakes and corn or potato chip crumbs are sometimes used in place of bread crumbs in breading and in au gratins, see 961. Store bread ends and leftover slices in the freezer and use to make crumbs (or croutons) when needed.

BROWNED OR BUTTERED BREAD CRUMBS
Use dry bread crumbs, below. Season with salt, allowing $\frac{1}{2}$ teaspoon for each cup of bread crumbs. Brown them slowly in $\frac{1}{4}$ cup (4 tablespoons) butter. Use at once. You may season with bits of crumbled cooked bacon, chopped nuts, grated cheese, ground or crumbled dried herbs, garlic or onion powder, salt or pepper. Cook until the butter is absorbed and the crumbs are golden brown.

DRY CRUMBS
Dry crumbs are made from dry bread, corn bread, crackers, or cake. If the bread or cake is not sufficiently dry, crisp on a baking sheet in a 200°F oven for 1 to 2 hours before making crumbs; do not let color. To make a small quantity of crumbs, grind them in a rotary hand grater, as shown, or use a food processor, pulsing several times to achieve the desired texture. Or place in a closed zip-top bag and crush with a rolling pin or mallet. To toast the crumbs, spread on a baking sheet and bake in a 375°F oven for 10 to 15 minutes. ➤ Measure dry crumbs as you would sugar, 1018, by spooning the crumbs into a measuring cup and then leveling off the top with the back of a knife. Store dry bread crumbs in an airtight container in a cool, dry place.

Grinding bread crumbs in a rotary hand grater

JAPANESE-STYLE DRY CRUMBS (PANKO)

Panko, Japanese-style dry bread crumbs, available in specialty or Asian markets, have a coarse texture and are desirable for coating foods with larger crumbs that stay crisp. Cracker crumbs or crushed melba toast is a good substitute if panko is unavailable.

SOFT OR FRESH BREAD CRUMBS

Use fresh bread. You may crumble it lightly with your fingers but a safer way to retain the light texture desired in such crumbs is to gingerly pull the bread apart with a fork, or to pulse in a food processor until the crumbs have reached the desired texture. ➤ To measure soft bread crumbs, pile them lightly into a cup; do not pack them down unless the recipe calls for soaking these fresh crumbs in water, milk, or stock and pressing the moisture out before using. When they naturally compact, use at once. ➤ One slice of bread yields about ½ cup fresh crumbs.

BREADING, FLOURING, AND CRUMBING FOODS

When **dredging**, or lightly covering, food with flour or crumbs or enrobing it with a more elaborately "bound" coating, the main thing to remember is that ➤ you want a thin, even, and unbroken covering that adheres. The food should be at about room temperature and ➤ dry. For fish fillets, shrimp, meat, or any food with a moist surface, it is essential to pat it dry first and then dredge or coat it.

To prepare a simple breading, ➤ use flour, fine bread crumbs, or cornmeal. Cornmeal gives the firmest coating. If the food is not fragile, simply put a small quantity of the seasoned coating material in a paper or plastic bag with the food you want to cover, and shake. You will find this method gives a very even, quick, and economical coating. Or prepare Seasoned Flour or Crumbs, below.

Coating food in a bag

AU GRATIN

"Au gratin" is a term that, in America, is usually associated with cheese. But the term may refer to any light but thorough topping of fine fresh or dry bread crumbs or even crushed cornflakes, cracker crumbs, or finely ground nuts on scalloped dishes or casseroles. These dishes, usually combinations of cooked shellfish, fish, meats, vegetables, or eggs, bound by a sauce and served in the dish in which they were cooked, are then browned in the oven or under the broiler to form a crisp golden crust. Set the casserole dish or baking dish on a piece of foil, shiny side down to deflect the heat, or just set it on a baking sheet.

I. Sprinkle:

> **Dry bread crumbs**

in a light but thorough covering over the food. Bake in a 350° to 375°F oven until a crisp, golden brown crust forms. Or place the dish in a preheated broiler 3 inches below the source of heat.

II. Place:

> **Dry bread crumbs**
> **(Paprika—about ½ teaspoon per cup)**
> **Dots of butter**

in a light but thorough covering over the food. Bake in a 350°F oven to produce a crisp golden crust. Or run the dish under a preheated broiler 5 inches from the source of heat.

III. Completely cover the food with:

> **Dry bread crumbs**
> **(Paprika—about ½ teaspoon per cup)**
> **Dots of butter**
> **Grated Cheddar, Romano, or Parmesan**

Place the dish in a preheated 350°F oven or under the broiler 5 inches below the source of heat, and broil until a glazed golden crust is created.

BOUND BREADING OR COATING

This is an excellent coating for panfried or deep-fried foods and creates a more adhesive breading than dry crumbs.

Begin by wiping the food dry. Have ready a shallow bowl of:

> **Seasoned Flour, below**

Combine in a second shallow bowl:

> **1 egg, slightly beaten**
> **2 to 3 teaspoons water or milk**
> **(2 teaspoons vegetable oil)**

Stir together with a fork, 10 or 12 gentle strokes. Do not let the egg get bubbly, as this would make the coating uneven. Place in a third bowl:

> **¾ cup Seasoned Crumbs for Breading, below, or other crumbs**

Dredge each piece of food in the flour: Toss it lightly from one palm to the other, patting it gently all over, and shake off any excess flour, as shown. Then, using or "dirtying" only one hand, slide the flour-coated food through the egg mixture, making sure the entire surface is coated; allow any excess moisture to drip off. Then, using the same hand, place the food in the crumb-lined bowl. See that the crumbs adhere evenly to all the edges of the food as well as to its larger surfaces. If you see any vacant

Applying bound breading or coating

places, sprinkle a few crumbs onto them. Pat on any excess crumbs that might fall off and brown too rapidly, thus discoloring the frying fat. ➤ Place on a rack to dry for about 20 minutes before frying. ➤ Do not chill the food before frying, as that would tend to make it absorb an undue amount of fat.

SEASONED FLOUR OR CRUMBS FOR BREADING
I. Mix:

> 1 cup all-purpose flour, fine dry bread crumbs,
>   or finely crushed cornflakes
> 1 teaspoon salt
> ¹/₄ teaspoon black pepper or ¹/₂ teaspoon paprika
> (¹/₈ teaspoon ground ginger or grated or ground
>   nutmeg)

II. Mix:

> 1 cup fine dry bread crumbs or crushed cornflakes
>   or crackers
> 3 tablespoons grated Parmesan
> ¹/₂ teaspoon dried herbs, such as thyme, basil, chives,
>   savory, or tarragon, or a pinch of rosemary

BRINE

Brine is a solution of salt and water; it has two uses in cooking. Brines for pickling and vegetables draw the natural sugars and moisture from foods, thus protecting them against spoilage bacteria. A **10-percent brine,** about the strongest used in food processing, is made by dissolving 1¹/₂ cups pickling salt in 1 gallon of liquid, or 6 tablespoons salt per quart of liquid. During brining, as more liquid continues to be drawn from fruits and vegetables, the brine may be weakened. Always allow about 2 gallons of 10-percent brine plus enough food to fill a 4-gallon jar. ➤ A rule of thumb to test for 10-percent brine is that it will float a 2-ounce large egg so the shell just breaks the surface of the liquid.

Brines also enhance the juiciness and moisture content of pork, poultry, and shellfish. The ratio is either 1 cup table salt or 2 cups kosher salt in 1 gallon water, or for a smaller quantity, ¹/₄ cup table salt or ¹/₂ cup kosher salt per quart of water. ➤ Place the food in a plastic or glass container, cover the food with the brine, and soak **pork chops** for 4 hours, **extra-large shrimp** for 30 minutes, **turkey breast** for 4 to 6 hours, **whole chicken** 3 to 4 hours, and cut-up **chicken pieces** 2 hours. Discard brine after use. For more information, see About Brining Poultry, 421.

BURNET

Burnet is sometimes called salad burnet—in fact, Italians say that salad without burnet is like love without a woman. This herb has a haunting cucumberish flavor. It does not dry well, but it keeps green in the garden all winter long and can be plucked at any time. Pick the center leaves; the older ones are tough and bitter. Use the leaves, or soak the seeds in vinegar for use in salads. A hardy evergreen perennial growing to 2 feet, *Poterium sanguisorba* is almost fernlike in habit and is easy to germinate in any well-drained soil in sun.

BUTTER

Many of the recipes in this book call for **unsalted sweet butter**—Grade A butter made from sweet cream, with no added salt. Sometimes the amount of butter listed in a single recipe is given as a range. In such instances, the lesser amount will give you a good result, and the larger quantity may produce a superlative one.

All butter is made from fresh cream and, in the United States, by law must have a fat content of at least 80 percent. Richer, or European-style, butters have a fat content of up to 86 percent: The remaining 14 to 20 percent is largely water, with some milk solids. Small amounts of salt are sometimes added for flavor or for preservative action. **Salted butter** may be purchased or made at home, 963, from sweet or soured cream. It keeps longer than unsalted butter because of the addition of salt, but the salt does change the flavor slightly. Although the salt content does vary by brand, 1 stick of salted butter generally contains about ³/₈ teaspoon salt. Without the addition of the color that manufacturers sometimes add, butter is very pale rather than the warm "butter yellow" to which we are accustomed.

In accordance with labeling restrictions, **light or "lite" butter** has 50 percent less fat than regular butter. Because of the high water content, light butter is inappropriate for cooking and baking and is only useful as a spread.

The same bacteria that give buttermilk its velvety thickness and tang are added to the cream for **cultured butter.** The culture, typically lactic acid, causes the cream to ferment just enough to give it a faint tartness and for some a more pronounced, distinct flavor.

Whipped butter is butter that is whipped while nitrogen gas or air is injected, usually up to 60 percent of the total volume—1 cup whipped butter weighs two-thirds as much as 1 cup traditional butter. The fat content is still 80 percent *by weight*.

The word "creamery," which sometimes appears on butter packages, is a hangover from the days when cream went to a place called a creamery to be processed. The word now carries no standard or type significance—it's just meant to be reassuring!

All ➤ butter should be stored in the refrigerator and kept tightly covered to prevent absorption of other food flavors. It is preferable to use store-bought butter, whether salted or unsalted, within 1 week of the date stamped on the package. You can freeze butter for up to 6 months.

Butter stored at room temperature can become rancid. There are specially designed containers, known as butter bells or butter keepers, that make it possible to store butter at room temperature for a longer time. To use, pack the butter into the lid cup and add an inch of water to the base. When the lid cup is in place on the base, the water creates an airtight seal, keeping the butter fresher without refrigeration.

➤ One pound of butter equals 2 cups. When the pound is wrapped as sticks or quarters, each stick equals 8 tablespoons or $1/2$ cup.

To substitute butter for other fats, see 1037. While these substitutions are satisfactory in cooking, flavor and nutritional factors are not necessarily similar. For flavored butters, see 557. For nut butters, see 178.

CHURNED BUTTER

Most of us have inadvertently turned small quantities of cream into butter in an electric mixer or blender. We may even have imitated churning by flipping a carton of cream rhythmically in a figure-eight motion. To make larger quantities of butter use a churn and keep the cream between 55° to 60°F during the entire butter making process. A higher temperature will produce a greasy consistency; a lower one, a brittle, tallowy one. A gallon of heavy cream should yield about 3 pounds of butter.

Use cream with at least 30-percent fat content, fill a sterile churn one-third to half full. Depending on the quantity, the butter should "make" within 15 to 40 minutes of churning. We used to visit a neighbor while she churned and we were amazed at how much slower the process was in threatening or stormy weather. The cream usually stays foamy during the first half of churning. By and by, it will begin to look like cornmeal mush. At this point, proceed cautiously. It then grows to corn-kernel size. Stop churning. Drain off and measure the liquid, or buttermilk. Rinse the butter twice with as much 50° to 70°F water as you have buttermilk. If you want to salt the butter, use $1\frac{1}{2}$ teaspoons salt per 1 pound butter, folding

the salt into the butter with a wet paddle. Mold or shape into rolls, then wrap in parchment paper or foil. To store, see Butter, above.

CLARIFIED OR DRAWN BUTTER

Clarified butter is butter that has had its water and milk solids removed. It keeps about three times longer than butter, does not burn when used in high-heat cooking methods such as sautéing, and has a pure clean flavor. To make clarified butter, see 557. When chilled, clarified butter becomes grainy. It should not be used as a spread, only in cooking.

Ghee, a primary fat used in the cuisine of India and South Asia, is cooked longer than clarified butter, so the milk solids in the butter are lightly browned, imparting a nutty flavor. Originally a staple in warm climates with no refrigeration, ghee can be stored in an airtight container for 6 to 8 months in the refrigerator. Because it is further refined than clarified butter, the smoke point of ghee is high enough for high-heat cooking methods such as deep-fat frying. To make ghee, see 557.

BLENDER BUTTER

3 ounces

Chill the blender container. Blend at high speed about 15 seconds:

1 cup cold heavy cream

or until the cream coats the blades. Add:

$1/2$ cup ice water

Continue to blend at high speed until the butter rises to the surface. Strain off the butter. Press out any additional moisture; mold and chill. If desired, reserve the liquid residue or "buttermilk," covered and refrigerated, for another use; it is not rich enough to substitute for buttermilk.

HAND-MADE BUTTER

6 ounces

Butter is only as good as the cream from which it is made. Cool the cream and keep it at about 55°F during the entire butter-making process.

Refrigerate a large clean 1-quart glass jar with a tight-fitting lid for at least 1 hour. Pour into the cold jar:

2 cups cold heavy cream

Tightly secure the lid and shake as hard as possible until chunks of butter start to form, 15 to 30 minutes. Pour into a strainer set over a bowl. The chunks in the strainer are butter, and the liquid in the bowl is buttermilk.

Pour the buttermilk into a clean container, cover, refrigerate, and reserve for another use. Immediately turn the butter into a clean bowl and cover with very cold water, then pour into a strainer, discarding the liquid. Rinse the butter with very cold water until the water runs clear. Work it with a wooden spoon or rubber spatula to press out any remaining liquid. If desired, fold into the butter $1/2$ to $3/4$ teaspoon of salt. to the butter, folding it in with the wooden spoon.

Transfer the butter to a clean container pressing with a

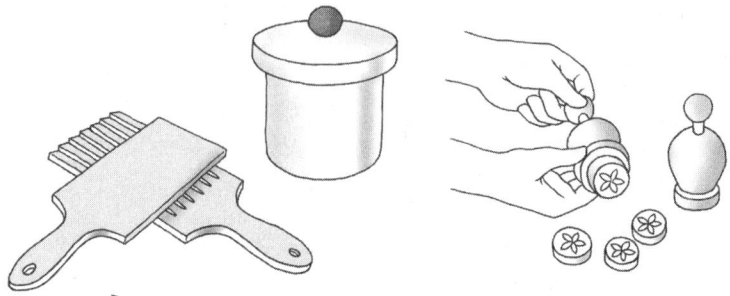

Corrugated wooden paddles, butter crock, butter plunger

wooden spoon or spatula to dispel any air bubbles. The butter may be molded or rolled, then wrapped in parchment paper or foil. To store, see Butter, 963.

MOLDING AND SHAPING BUTTER

Such a delicious staple deserves an attractive presentation. Try using a butter curler. It is our favorite because the light $\frac{1}{8}$-inch-thick shells are decorative and of just the right texture for spreading. Dip the curler into warm water before pulling it lightly over firm butter. If the butter is too cold, the curls will crack. Put the curls at once into cold water and store in the refrigerator until ready, then drain and serve. The same procedure will keep intact butter balls and the molds described below.

Butter for molding is first cut into $\frac{1}{2}$-inch-thick slices. It is most easily molded with a plunger, or, if formed into balls, with a pair of corrugated wooden paddles. Use the paddles so their striations form a crisscross pattern. Then treat as for butter curls, above. Both types of utensils must be conditioned for use by pouring over them a generous stream of boiling water, then submerging them in ice water.

For an easier, if less elegant, way to make butter balls, try melon ballers, which come in various sizes. Dip the baller first into hot water. Scoop out the butter ball and drop it into a dish of ice water. Serve the balls piled on a rack over ice. Another attractive way to serve butter is in small clay crocks. Our favorite is the butter keeper that fits into a base that holds ice water. Or you may decorate evenly cut squares of butter with tiny herb leaves or flowers, lightly pressed into the surface with the fingertips.

BUTTERMILK

See Sour Milks and Creams, 1013.

CANE SYRUP

Cane syrup is a thick syrup made from the evaporated and concentrated sap of sugarcane. Delicious on hot biscuits, it can be substituted as for Molasses, 998.

CAPERS AND CAPERLIKE BUDS AND SEEDS

The bulletlike unopened buds of the caper bush, which taste like tiny sharp gherkins, are typically sold in a brine but are sometimes salted; the former should be drained, the latter rinsed and drained. Use them as a salty-sour enhancement, especially in Tartar Sauce with fish, and wherever you want to add a piquant note to food. Capers can range in size from that of a tiny peppercorn to as large as the tip of your little finger. The smallest capers are labeled "nonpareil." Also pickled are immature or mature seeds and buds of *Tropaeolum minus* or *majus,* a nasturtium, and the buds of *Caltha palustris,* marsh marigold. Similar in use are fermented black beans, 982, and the pickled green seeds of *Martynia proboscidea juisieui,* an annual growing to $2\frac{1}{2}$ feet, with dramatic flowers and an evil horned pod. *Capparis spinosa* is a 3-foot perennial shrub of southern Europe. ➤ Do not confuse it with the mole plant or caper spurge, *Euphorbia lathyrum,* which is poisonous.

CARAWAY

Use the leaves of this herb sparingly in soups and stews. The seeds are classic additions to rye breads, cheeses, stews, marinades, cabbage, sauerkraut, turnips, and onions. They are the basic flavoring of the colorless liqueur kümmel. When adding the seeds to soups or stews, put them in a cheesecloth bag and add for the last 30 minutes of cooking only, as protracted heating makes them bitter. Crush them to release their flavor before adding to vegetables or salads. *Carum carvi,* a flower that looks like Queen Anne's lace, is an easily grown biennial that reaches 2 feet in the second year, when the seeds develop.

CARDAMOM

Cardamom, *Elettaria cardamomum,* is a pod, consisting of an outer shell with little flavor and tiny seeds inside with intense flavor. The pods may be green or white. Some spice merchants like the pods paper white, so they bleach the green pods, turning not just the pods white, but also blunting the spice's color and intensity. Grind the seeds of cardamom only as needed, for otherwise the aromatic loss is great. Use as for cinnamon and cloves, alone or in combination. Cardamom is delicious in coffee. The bigger, more round brown cardamom pod *Amomum cardamomum,* is used whole in barbecue sauces and pickles. Black cardamom, *Amomum subulatum,* is yet another different type and has its own unique, smoky flavor.

CASHEWS

Cashews have an edible, fleshy fruit covering (the "cashew apple") that can be eaten fresh, cooked, or fermented. But between this edible outside shell and the kernel we know as a cashew is a very irritating toxic oil, related to the oils in poison ivy, that must be removed or destroyed by heat—thus cashews are never sold in the shell. Make cashew butter as for Peanut Butter, 1006. For baking, use untoasted cashews. Because of their relatively high starch content, cashews work better than most nuts as a thickener in stews, soups, and some desserts containing milk.

CELERY

The tender leaves of the celery you grow or buy can be used fresh or dried in almost all savory foods. **Celery salt** is a powdered form of the edible tender leaf combined with salt. The **celery seeds** sold for flavoring are not those of the plant we grow for stalks, but those of smallage, or wild celery, a plant grown specifically for the seeds. The seeds, either whole or ground, have a powerful flavor and must be used sparingly: whole in stocks, court bouillon, pickles, and salads; or ground in salad dressings, seafood dishes, or vegetables. *Apium graveolens* needs rich, moist soil. It may be grown in mounds of dirt, thus blanching the celery, due to lack of sunlight. For celery as a vegetable, see 268, and for celeriac, see 268.

CHAMOMILE

Chamomile is famous as a herbal tea or a tisane, 465. A small quantity is occasionally put into beef stock. It is the very yellow center of the flower that is most prized, although at times the fresh leaves are used as well. The apple-scented petals of this tiny daisy are removed after the flower is dried. *Anthemis nobilis,* a creeping perennial, grows to 6 inches in dry, light soil.

CHEESE

We heartily agree with author Clifton Fadiman, who once called cheese "milk's leap to immortality." A bit of cheese as garnish, topping, or dessert not only enlivens the taste of the recipe or meal but often adds proteins that make a dish nutritionally satisfying as well. No two types of cheese are exactly alike. Different cheeses are heat-sensitive in different ways, and individual recipes reflect their special properties. Moreover, many cheeses depend on skillful aging and careful storage for their flavor and cooking quality.

Cheese is a substance constantly in the process of change. In some climates, certain hard cheeses are aged and improve for years, but the cook without access to mountain caves must settle for paying the cheesemaker a premium. Soft cheeses, such as fresh mozzarella and fresh goat cheese, are best soon after they are made. Cheeses do not freeze well, and they should be refrigerated only on a short-term basis.

Cheeses should be bought in small amounts at their peak of ripeness and served promptly. Cheese continues to ripen until it is eaten. Some cheeses are packaged in a specially designed plastic wrap that allows them to breathe. After serving, wrap leftover cheese in parchment paper; it is more permeable than plastic wrap or aluminum foil. Store in the cheese or vegetable compartment of your refrigerator. These drawers are designed to provide extra humidity, which is ideal for storing cheese. If you use a resealable zip-top bag, close the zipper only partway to keep in the moisture while the cheese continues to breathe. Never take cheese directly from the refrigerator to the table. Room temperature is the best temperature for serving cheese. At higher temperatures, the butterfat risks melting and sweating out of the cheese.

MAKING SEMI-HARD AND HARD CHEESES

There are many variables but, generally, the harder and more frequently you press and drain the cheese during processing, the firmer the cheese will become. Except for the cheese press, which can be improvised as described below, semi-hard and hard cheeses can be made using regular sterile household equipment suggested in making soft cheeses, below. Mold-ripened cheeses like Roquefort and blue which show a mold pattern throughout are specially impregnated with a bacillus during aging and are beyond the skills of most household operations. **Cheddaring** of cheese calls for still another cooking operation and elaborate cutting and layering of the cheese, as well as aging up to 3 years for a sharp Cheddar.

HOMEMADE CHEESE

1½ pounds

If you plan on aging the cheese, make larger wheels to keep it from drying out.

Pour into a large stainless steel or enamel pan:

    1 gallon whole milk or goat's or sheep's milk

Add and stir well:

    3 tablespoons buttermilk

If you use goat's or sheep's milk, you may need to double the amount of buttermilk. Cover and let stand at room temperature for at least 4 but not longer than 12 hours. If you care to color the cheese, dissolve:

    (A coloring tablet based on malt—available from cheese-making suppliers)

well in:

    2 tablespoons water

Place the pan of prepared milk in a larger pan of hot water and slowly bring up the heat until the temperature of the milk is 86°F. If you are coloring the cheese, stir in the liquid color thoroughly at this time.

Meanwhile, prepare a coagulant by thoroughly dissolving:

    1 household rennet tablet (available from cheese-making suppliers)

in:

2 tablespoons cold water

Allow the milk to reach 88° to 90°F before stirring in the rennet solution. Continue stirring about 1 minute, then remove the pan from the hot water and allow the mixture to stand, covered, 30 minutes to 1 hour. It should coagulate during this period. To test for the proper degree of coagulation, insert your well-washed finger into the curd at an angle, as if to lift some out. If the curd breaks cleanly over your finger, it is ready for cutting.

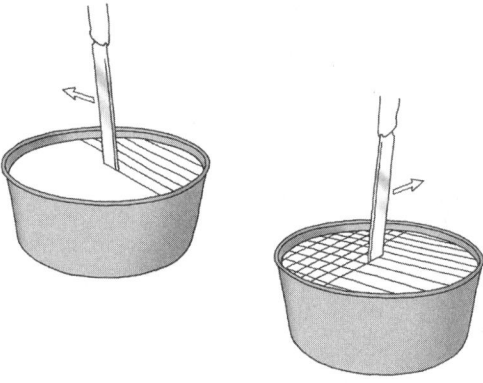

Cutting the curds lengthwise and crosswise

Cut the curd lengthwise and crosswise at $1/2$-inch intervals, as shown above, using a long stainless steel curd cutter or a stainless steel knife. Then cut diagonally at a 45-degree angle as shown. These repeated cuts will divide the curd into small, even bits. If these cuts are carefully made from the top to the bottom of the pan, there should be no large lumps when you start to work the curd with your hand. Should there be some, however, cut them now with the curd cutter rather than smashing them between your fingers. For 15 minutes, work the curd with one well-washed hand, using slow movements around the edges and up through the curd from the bottom to top, letting the portion you bring to the surface each time gently recede into the mass. The curds will begin to shrink in size as they separate from the yellowish whey. Cook the curd a second time by returning the pan to its hot water bath and

slowly bringing the curds and whey to 102°F over a 20- to 30-minute period.

Hold at 102°F for 30 to 40 minutes longer, stirring gently with a long wooden spoon every 3 to 5 minutes. The curd is ready for firming when it forms a loose mass in your hand. The individual curds will be of wheat-grain size and the entire mass will look like eggs scrambled over too high heat.

To firm the curd, remove the pan from the hot water and let the curds-and-whey mixture stand, covered, 1 hour. During this period, stir every 5 to 10 minutes.

To drain the curd, line a colander with several thicknesses of cheesecloth that are large enough so the ends hang well over the sides of the colander, and set over a bowl or sink. Pour the curds and whey into the lined colander, and drain off the whey by lifting the curds in the cloth and rolling the mass from one side of the cloth to the other. Now set the drained curd, still in the cloth, in the colander again. If desired, you may work into it with your well-washed hand:

(About 5 teaspoons salt)

Form the curd into a ball within the cloth and squeeze out as much whey as possible. Knot the cheesecloth around the ball to form a bag you can hang from your sink faucet, and let the cheese drain another 20 minutes.

Just before pressing, you may add flavorings such as:

2 tablespoons caraway seeds, crushed black peppercorns, or cumin seeds; 2 to 4 tablespoons finely chopped chiles or fresh herbs such as dill, basil, or sage; or $1/2$ cup whole or sliced almonds, walnuts, or hazelnuts

Now prepare to press the cheese. As pressing is a drippy business, confine your activities to the sink area. If you have no press, improvise one by cutting a 7- to 8-inch-deep rim from a round plastic container about 4 to 5 inches in diameter. Place it on a plate, as shown below. You will also need two 1-inch-thick oak disks, just smaller in diameter than the mold, and bricks for weighting them down. This will be your mold. Line it with a 15-inch square of boiled muslin or cheesecloth. After heaping the curds into the lined mold, fold the muslin or cheesecloth over the top so all the curds are wrapped. Put on one disk and weight it down with the bricks. As the whey rises and runs or is poured off and the curds con-

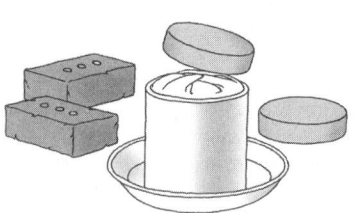

Pressing cheese

tract, place the second disk under the bricks to allow pressure to continue.

During the next 20 minutes, increase the pressure by gradually adding weight with extra bricks. Be careful to add weight only to the point at which whey, and not curds, escapes. Then let the cheese rest in the press 12 to 24 hours in a cool place.

Remove the cheese from the press, unfold the muslin, and place the cheese on a rack. Allow to air, unwrapped, again in a cool place for from 12 to 36 hours.

This so-called new cheese is bland in flavor and suitable for cheese spread recipes, 76, and for some dessert cheeses, 827. To age this new cheese and allow it to develop its full flavor, when the exterior is absolutely dry, dip it into a thin coat of cheese wax, available from cheese-making suppliers, to seal off the air and prevent mold. Date the wrapping with a label. Refrigerate on a rack where the temperature drops no lower than 35°F or in the vegetable crisper, where the temperature is about 40°F. Temperatures above 55°F cause the cheese to spoil. Flavor will develop within 2 weeks to 2 months or longer.

If any surface mold has formed, wipe it off; or if it has penetrated the cheese, cut it out.

MAKING UNRIPENED SOFT CHEESES

Time was when milk was allowed to rest in a warm place until it soured and curdled, or clabbered, and then the curds and whey—the cloudy liquid—were separated by draining through a cloth bag. When the curds were firm to the touch, they were refrigerated for several hours, after which they could be beaten with cream until smooth to make cottage cheese.

Although cheese is made in a variety of textures, flavors, and colors, most cheese making starts with the same ingredients—milk, rennet, 1007, and a dose of starter bacteria to acidify the milk, create flavors, modify texture, and in some cases to grow blue or green molds as desired.

The milk used in cheese can vary in its source (goat, cow, or sheep) and in whether the milk is raw or pasteurized. In the United States, any cheese made from raw milk must be aged at least 60 days; it is illegal to sell soft raw milk cheeses that have been aged less than 60 days. In countries such as France, Switzerland, and Italy, the European Union regulates the production of traditional raw milk cheeses, and some of those cheeses cannot be imported into the U.S.

In our recipes, we use pasteurized milk, which, unfortunately means that some of the bacteria and enzymes that make cheese so flavorful have been killed.

Have ready: a dairy thermometer, a long wooden spoon, a large pan, a rack, and cheesecloth or a China cap strainer, or chinoise, right, for dripping the cheese. A long stainless knife is needed for cutting the curd. Or, if you make soft cheese often, ➤ make yourself a curd cutter of a stainless steel wire looped into an elongated U, with the

arms about 1 to 2 inches apart and deep enough to fit the pan in which you develop the curd. Follow the recipes as written below. When the curd is ready, cut through it with your cutter, lengthwise and crosswise of the pan as shown on 966. Then cut from the bottom of the pan horizontally at 1-inch intervals to form cheese-curd cubes. Proceed as described in the recipe.

Store these cheeses refrigerated. ➤ Do not keep more than 4 or 5 days. Serve garnished with:

> **Chopped chives, basil, or tarragon**
> **Chopped olives or nuts**

or use as a base for hors d'oeuvres and dips and to fill tomato cases. Or use in:

> **Coeurs à la Crème, 826**

To make Paneer, a fresh Indian cheese, see 306.

COTTAGE CHEESE
About 1 ½ pounds

A wide variety of cottage cheeses is commercially available today. The different types have varying milk fat contents and curd sizes. **Small-** and **large-curds cottage cheeses** are named based on curd size. The curd size affects only texture, not the flavor of the cheese. **Creamed cottage cheese** has been combined with cream so as to have the approximate fat value of whole milk. Low-fat cottage cheese is also available. **Hoop cheese** is, like cottage cheese, made of skimmed milk but it is more acidic because the curd is not washed. Hoop cheese may be difficult to find in retail establishments today. **Farmer's cheese** may have been made with whole milk, but the curd has been pressed sufficiently to remove moisture, and the cheese can be sliced.

Please read about Making Unripened Soft Cheeses, above. It is important to use skim milk, or the cream is lost when the whey is removed.

Pour into a large deep saucepan:

> **1 gallon skim milk, at room temperature**

Stir in:

> **½ cup buttermilk**

Let stand at room temperature until clabbered, 1014, 12 to 14 hours. Cube the curd as described, 1014. Let rest 10 minutes. Add:

> **8 cups warm water (98° to 100°F)**

Set the pan on a rack in a larger pan of water and heat until the curd reaches 98° to 100°F. Hold at this temperature, not higher, 30 minutes to 1 hour; stir gently every 5 minutes, or the curd will toughen. Do not break the curd. As the whey, or clear liquid, separates from the

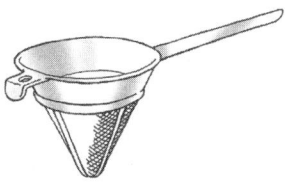

China cap strainer or chinoise

curds, the curds will settle. To test for doneness, squeeze them: They should break clean between your fingers and, when pressed, should not leave a semifluid milky residue. Gently pour the curds and whey into a China cap or chinois, 967, or a very fine mesh strainer. If desired, rinse the curds with:

(Cold water)

to minimize the acidic flavor. Let drain in a cool place until the whey or liquid stops dripping, but not so long that the surface of the cheese becomes dry looking. To make creamed cottage cheese, combine the cheese curds with:

(Heavy cream)

To serve or store, see Making Unripened Soft Cheeses, above.

CREAM CHEESE
About 1 1/2 pounds

Cream cheese is a white, soft, unripened cheese made from cow's milk. Two types of cream cheese are commercially available. Regular cream cheese is soft and mild tasting with at least 33 percent fat. Neufchâtel is a cream cheese with a lower fat content. This homemade version has the tang of store-bought cream cheese but is much softer in texture. Note that the recipe takes several days to complete. Please read Making Unripened Soft Cheeses, 967.

Combine and heat to 85°F in a large deep pan:

1 gallon whole milk
1/2 cup buttermilk

Dissolve:

1/4 to 1/2 household rennet tablets (available from cheese-making suppliers)

thoroughly in:

1/4 cup cold water

Add to the milk, which should be at 85°F, and stir well for 1 minute. Put the pan into a larger one of warm water and maintain the milk at 80° to 85°F until whey covers the surface and the curds break clean from the sides of the bowl when it is tipped; this may take as long as 24 hours. Scoop the curds with a ladle or large spoon into a colander—do not pour—lined with several layers of cheesecloth that has been moistened and wrung out and set over a bowl. Cover the curds with a layer of cheesecloth, then wrap the bowl in plastic wrap. Refrigerate overnight. Drain off any excess whey. Stir in:

1 1/2 teaspoon salt
(Heavy cream)

To serve or store, see Making Unripened Soft Cheeses, above.

CHERVIL

One of the famous *fines herbes*, 982, chervil is more delicate and ferny than parsley. The leaf is used with chicken, veal, omelets, green salad, and spinach, as garnish; in Vinaigrette, 572; and always in the making of a Béarnaise Sauce, 561. It is one of the herbs it pays to grow—for

when dried at even as low a temperature as 90°F, it is practically without flavor. *Anthriscus cerefolium* is a self-sowing annual that grows to 2 feet. It needs some shade to keep it from turning purplish and toughening. Sow in place from April to September—do not transplant, as this forces bolting or rapid growth and premature seed production.

CHESTNUTS

Chestnuts are frequently used in stuffing for poultry, especially in turkey and goose for Thanksgiving and Christmas, and are traditionally combined with Brussels sprouts and red cabbage. One of our more knowing friends insists that if navy beans are substituted for chestnuts in desserts strongly laced with coffee or almond paste, one cannot tell the difference. We haven't tried this, but it may be worth a try. Chestnuts are available fresh in the fall and winter. During other times of the year, they can be purchased canned, bottled, vacuum-packed, and dried. Before they are eaten, fresh chestnuts must be either roasted or boiled, then shelled and the inner covering removed.

To shell and peel chestnuts, make 2 gashes in an X on their flat side with a sharp pointed knife. (The outer shell may come off when you do this, but the inner skin will still protect the kernel.) Place the nuts in a pan over high heat and drizzle oil or butter over them—1 teaspoon to 1 pound of nuts. Shake them until coated, then place in a 400°F oven until the shell and inner brown skin start to peel and can be easily removed. The inside skin is bitter, and must be peeled off while still warm.

Or, if you are using the chestnuts in a recipe calling for boiled chestnuts, they can be covered with boiling water, simmered 15 to 25 minutes, and drained, after which the shell and skin may be removed. Or put on a paper plate and cook in a microwave oven on high power until the skins begin to peel back.

The meats may then be tender enough to be put through a food mill. If not, again cover with boiling water and cook until tender. **To boil, bake, or steam chestnuts,** see 269. **To roast,** see 71.

To reconstitute dried chestnuts, soak overnight in water to cover. Rinse and pick over. Simmer until they are puffed up and tender. ➤ Substitute them for cooked fresh chestnuts, cup for cup.

Fresh chestnuts are quite perishable due to their high moisture content. Keep covered in the refrigerator, and use quickly. Allow about 1 1/2 pounds in the shell for 1 pound shelled chestnuts. Thirty-five to 40 fairly large whole chestnuts make about 2 1/2 cups peeled. For the many uses of chestnuts, see Index.

CHILI POWDER
About 1/4 cup

I. A chili blend may be based on a combination of spices as varied as cumin, coriander, oregano, black pepper, cloves, and ground chile peppers. Or it may be made up quickly from a combination of:

3 tablespoons paprika
1 tablespoon turmeric
$^1/_8$ teaspoon ground red pepper

But, no matter how simple or how complex the mix, use with it plenty of:

Minced garlic

To heighten the flavor of food seasoned with chili powder, simmer the food at least 15 minutes after adding the seasonings.

About $^1/_2$ cup

II. Based on ground dried chiles, this blend is used to flavor Southwestern dishes. It is as individual as the person who prepares it. Sometimes it is very dark, sometimes a rusty red. Use store-bought ground chiles or, to grind your own chile peppers, see 1007.

Combine and toast in a skillet over low heat for 2 minutes, or until fragrant:

5 tablespoons ground mild chile peppers,
    such as New Mexico, pasilla, or ancho
2 tablespoons dried oregano
$1^1/_2$ tablespoons ground cumin
$^1/_2$ teaspoon ground red pepper, or to taste

CHIVES

See Onions, 1002.

CHOCOLATE AND COCOA

Another gift from America to the rest of the world, and perhaps the most well traveled, chocolate and cocoa come from evergreen trees of the genus *Theobroma*, which translates to "food of the gods." Cocoa beans grow inside the pod of a cocoa tree. The manufacture of the two is identical up to the moment when the chocolate liquor is extracted from the nibs, or hulled beans, and molded into solid cakes. The nibs are rich in cocoa butter, a cream-colored, natural vegetable fat that melts during the grinding process, producing a dark brown, fluid mass called chocolate liquor—the primary ingredient in all forms of chocolate (except white chocolate). If much of the fat, or cocoa butter, is removed from the cakes, they can be ground into powder. If additional cocoa butter is added to the cakes, they can be made into various types of chocolate. Cocoa butter is remarkable for the fact that, under normal storage conditions, it will keep for years without becoming rancid.

Unsweetened chocolate is pure chocolate with no added ingredients. It contains nearly equal parts cocoa butter and cocoa solids, the meat of the cocoa bean, which is why it imparts such a deep, rich chocolate flavor. Unsweetened chocolate is always combined with sugar and other ingredients to make cakes, brownies, frostings, and fudges.

Bittersweet or semisweet chocolates are made of at least 35% chocolate liquor, cocoa butter, sugar, vanilla or vanillin, and lecithin. Bittersweet bars usually have a deeper chocolate flavor than those labeled "semisweet," and they are apt to be less sweet, but the amount of sugar they contain is not regulated. These chocolates may be used interchangeably in most recipes, but their differences can affect the flavor, texture, and appearance of the finished product. Bittersweet is good for icings, sauces, fillings and candy dipping because of its sheen when tempered and melted.

Milk chocolate, a favorite eating chocolate, is the sweetest of the sweet chocolates. It is lighter in color and less intensely chocolate flavored than semisweet or bittersweet chocolate because it contains less chocolate liquor and at least 3.39 percent cocoa butter and 12 percent milk solids. Milk chocolate is rarely used for baking, because of its high sugar content and heat-sensitive milk solids; it is best in candy, icings, pies, and puddings.

White chocolate resembles milk chocolate in composition but it contains no chocolate liquor, which is why it is ivory, not brown. The cocoa butter it contains gives it a very mild milk-chocolate flavor and a creamy mouthfeel. It has a short shelf life and can easily become rancid, so buy small quantities. White chocolate is used when a delicate chocolate flavor is desired in cheesecakes, light-textured cakes, mousses, and icings.

German's sweet chocolate refers not to the country but to a very canny person, Samuel German, who realized there was a greater profit if the sugar was already added to the chocolate when it was sold. It is traditionally used in German Chocolate Cake, 719.

Couverture, which means coating or covering, is a term used to identify dark, milk, and white chocolates of the highest quality. Couvertures contain a high percentage of cocoa solids and have a deep, rich flavor and a smooth, creamy texture. When tempered, 857, couverture maintains a smooth, glossy shine. Use couverture to enrobe pieces of candy in a thin coating of chocolate, to mold shapes, and to dip strawberries.

Chocolate chips, which come in various flavors and sizes, are formulated to withstand normal oven heat and to hold their shape in baked desserts, even though the fat they contain is fully melted. For that reason, they should not be substituted for bar chocolates in recipes that require melted chocolate.

Another type of chocolate is known as **coating** or **compound chocolate.** It is chocolate that has had part or all of the cocoa butter replaced with other fats. It does not have the full flavor of real chocolate, but it is less expensive and does not require tempering.

For best results in baking, use the type of chocolate specified in the recipe. All chocolates do not taste the same, and we encourage cooks to try different brands of baking chocolate and to experiment with other chocolates instead of the standard squares of baking chocolate.

Cocoa powder is pulverized partially defatted chocolate liquor that contains 10 to 12 percent cocoa butter and no sugar. Two types of cocoa are available in supermarkets. **Unsweetened** or **nonalkalized cocoa powder** is light in color and somewhat acidic, with a strong, assertive chocolate flavor. In baking recipes that call for baking soda, it is important to use nonalkalized cocoa powder. **Dutch-process,** or **alkalized, cocoa powder** has a small quantity of alkali introduced during processing to neutralize the acidity, producing a darker cocoa that is milder in taste. When shopping for Dutch-processed cocoa, look on the label or in the ingredient list, which should specify Dutch-process (alkalized) or European-style.

In some baking recipes, ➤ cocoa powders can react differently, so we recommend using the type of cocoa specified in the recipe. In recipes where the choice of cocoa powder is simply a matter of taste, we simply call for unsweetened cocoa powder. Do not confuse cocoa powder with **instant cocoa,** which usually contains 80 percent sugar, is precooked, and has an emulsifier added to make it dissolve readily in either a hot or a cold liquid.

For details about cocoa and chocolate as a beverage, see 35. For tempering and dipping chocolate, see 857. ➤ Should you be allergic to chocolate, try carob, 984, which tastes almost like chocolate, although not as strongly flavored.

Ideally, chocolate should be stored in a cool place away from heat and direct sunlight, at 55° to 65°F with a humidity of less than 50 percent. Fluctuations in temperatures may cause a gray cast, or "bloom," to appear on the chocolate, a superficial flaw that will disappear when the chocolate is melted. Under optimum conditions, dark chocolate will last at least 1 year, milk chocolate 10 months, and white chocolate 8 months.

An entire square of baking chocolate equals 1 ounce. One cup of semisweet chocolate chips is 6 ounces by weight.

For substitution and equivalents of chocolate and cocoa, see 1031. ➤ It is easy to substitute cocoa for chocolate in sauces: Just use 1 tablespoon butter and 3 tablespoons cocoa for each ounce of chocolate. In baking, it is wiser to choose recipes written either for cocoa or for chocolate, as cocoa has a flourlike quality that must be compensated for if chocolate is substituted, or the cake texture will be compromised. In cakes and cookies, baking soda is often added to give chocolate a ruddy tone.

When it is grated or chopped, chocolate moves around a lot due to static electricity—use a large cutting board or grate into a large bowl to control the mess. **To grate chocolate,** slightly chill it (do not refrigerate for long, as condensation will damage the chocolate) and shave or grate it in a rotary grinder, 960, or a food processor. Have a big bowl ready to receive it—or you may be annoyed by its flighty dynamism. **To make chocolate curls or shavings,** hold a wrapped square of chocolate in your hand to warm it slightly. Unwrap and shave chocolate with long thin strokes at a 45-degree angle using a vegetable peeler or a small sharp knife. **To chop chocolate,** use a large, dry cutting board and a large knife. Start chopping away at the chocolate from a corner of the bar or piece. Then chop as for nuts, 1001.

Chocolate is heat-sensitive and burns easily, especially when melted alone. White chocolate is the most delicate of all. Chocolate can separate at temperatures over 130°F, so do not heat dark chocolate over 120°F or milk and white chocolates over 110°F. Containers and stirring utensils must be clean and perfectly dry, and stray drops of water or condensation must not be allowed to touch the chocolate. Small amounts of water may cause melted chocolate to "seize." When this happens, the chocolate loses its gloss and become grainy instead of melting smoothly. If this should happen, add for each ounce of chocolate ½ teaspoon or more of vegetable shortening—not butter—to reliquify the chocolate.

To **melt chocolate on the stovetop,** chop it into almond-sized pieces with a sharp dry knife. Place one-third of it in the top of a double boiler or in a heatproof bowl that fits snugly over a saucepan. Fill the bottom pan with enough tap hot water (130°F) to touch the bottom of the top bowl, but not so much as to allow the bowl to float, and set it on top. Avoid splashing water into the chocolate. Start stirring with a rubber spatula when the chocolate around the edges begins to liquefy. Gradually add the rest of the chocolate. When the chocolate is nearly melted, carefully lift the bowl of chocolate from the water, dry the bottom, and continue stirring the chocolate until it is smooth and shiny.

To **melt chocolate in a microwave oven,** fill a dry microwave-safe dish no more than half full with chopped chocolate; you can melt up to 8 ounces at a time. Do not cover. Heat bittersweet or semisweet chocolate on medium power (50 percent); use low power (30 percent) for milk and white chocolates. Heat in 20-second increments, stirring after each 20 seconds and rotating the dish if your microwave doesn't have a turntable. Remember that chocolate holds its shape when melted in the microwave, so stir even if it appears firm. If necessary, continue heating in increasingly shorter increments at the appropriate power level until most of the chocolate is melted, then stir until the chocolate is smooth and shiny. ➤ Cool chocolate to about 80°F before adding it to cake, cookie, or pudding mixtures.

CILANTRO
See Coriander, 972.

CINNAMON
True cinnamon, *Cinnamomum zeylanicum* or *C. verum,* is the bark of a tree that flourishes in Sri Lanka along the Malabar coast. It is extremely mild whether rolled into a tight quill or stick or in powdered form. Most of the so-called cinnamon on the market is really cassia, *Cinnamomum cassia.* This is a similar bark that is sometimes quilled, or formed as though a short scroll were rolled

Citrus garnishes and zest

from both ends and left with its center portion flat. It has slightly bitter and hot overtones compared to the warm, sweet, aromatic true cinnamon. The best forms of cassia come from China, Vietnam, and Indonesia. Use the stick form of either of these spices in hot chocolate, mulled wine, fruit compotes, and pickles. We need hardly suggest trying ground cinnamon with sugar on buttered toast, dusting it on cookie tops, or incorporating it into desserts and baked items but consider also its use in small quantities in stews, sauces, rubs, marinades, or seafood.

CITRUS ZESTS, JUICES, AND GARNISHES

What better name than "zest" could be found for the gratings of the colorful outer coatings of lemons, oranges, tangerines, and limes—those always available, valuable, and yet somehow not fully appreciated ingredients! Zest is the very quality they add to baked items, stuffings, sauces, soups, meats, and desserts. ➤ Zest must, however, be used with a light touch. If you keep an easily cleaned zester or rasp-type zester, 223, you will be amazed at the subtlety you can add quickly to your seasoning. Wash the citrus fruit and remove only the colored portions of the citrus skins; the white beneath is bitter.

To prepare citrus peels for fruit sauces or candy, remove just the colored portion of the peel with a sharp paring knife, a vegetable peeler, or a special channel zester tool, shown above. Blanch in boiling water for 3 minutes, until limp. Rinse in cold water. Shred the thin pieces of peel if necessary and resimmer in the sauce, or simply proceed with the recipe.

Citrus zest is more intense in flavor than juice because of its heavy oil concentration. Fold it into frostings or icings, for instance, when the initial mixing is finished, so as not to disturb the texture of the zest. Another way to get this flavorful oily residue is to grate the zest coarsely, place in a piece of cheesecloth, and wring the oils onto the sugar called for in a recipe. Let stand about 15 minutes before using. For longer storage, the zest can be dried and stored in an airtight container and the peel candied; see 880.

We are very much in favor of the frequent use of small quantities of fresh citrus juices to bring out and enliven the flavors of meat, fish, poultry, and even vegetables, especially in salt-free diets where these flavors can stand in for the omitted salt. Use them as a substitute for vinegar wherever delicacy is wanted. ➤ To get the greatest amount of juice out of citrus fruit, roll the whole fruit on a hard surface, gently but firmly pressing it with your palm while rolling, before cutting. Lemons and limes can be juiced quickly by squeezing the juice through a small sieve or by holding the cut side of the citrus fruit against the palm of your hand and squeezing firmly. If the fruit is held properly, the seeds will be trapped. Lemon juice can be stored for later use. Pour fresh lemon juice into ice cube trays and freeze, then store the cubes in heavy plastic bags in the freezer.

It is ➤ only the fresh zest and juice of citrus fruits that hold the really magic seasoning power, but, if you must substitute, the following are approximations: 1 teaspoon grated zest = 2 tablespoons fresh juice = 1 teaspoon dried zest = $\frac{1}{2}$ teaspoon extract = 2 teaspoons grated candied peel.

To use lemons as garnishes, ➤ cut them, as shown, in an attractive fashion.

Keep on hand Citrus-Flavored Sugar, 1019, for flavoring drinks and sauces.

CLOVES

The spicy, rich red, dried, unopened bud of the clove tree, *Syzygium aromaticum,* contains so much oil that you can squeeze it out with a fingernail. Because its flavor is so strong, the heads of the cloves are sometimes removed so the seasoning will be milder. These milder portions are often what is ground into the powdered form of cloves. Before serving a dish cooked with whole cloves, always remove them. The best cloves come from Madagascar and Indonesia. Use in curries, in stewed fruits and marmalades; in chutneys, pickles, and marinades; and, in small quantities, with onions and meats. Cloves are especially good with ham, as well as in spiced braised stews. An onion stuck with 3 or 4 cloves is a classic addition to stocks and stews. Oil of clove is available for use cooking and flavoring light-colored foods, but watch out for its terrific pungency.

COCONUTS AND COCONUT MILK

If you live in coconut country, you know the delight of using the flower sap as well as the green and the mature fruit of this graceful palm. In cooking, you may substitute its "milk," "cream," and "butter" for dairy products. However, be aware that this exchange is not an equal one nutritionally, because coconut is much lower in protein. ➤ Coconut products are very sensitive to high heat. For this reason they are added to hot sauces at the last minute. They are especially treasured in preparing curries and delicate fish and fruit dishes.

The first thing to do with a coconut, of course, is to get at it. Lacking power tools, you can drop the large whole fruit onto a rock-hard substance. If it doesn't crack open enough so that the husk pulls away, use your trusty ax. Out comes a fiber-covered nut. Shake it. A sloshing noise means that the nut is fresh and that you can count on some watery liquid, erroneously referred to as milk. If the husked coconut is green, the top can be lopped off with a large heavy knife or a machete. The liquid within is clear, and the greenish jellylike pulp makes ideal food for small children. To open the harder shell of the mature nut, pierce the three shiny black dots that form a monkey face at the peak. Use a strong ice pick, and hammer it in. Reserve the drained liquid under refrigeration, and be certain to use within 24 hours or freeze it. Tap the nut briskly all over with a hammer. It usually splits lengthwise, and these halves can be used as containers for serving hot or cold food.

You may also open the shell with heat. To do so, place the undrained husked coconut in a preheated 325°F oven for 15 to 20 minutes. ➤ Do not overcook, as this destroys the flavor. Remove from the oven and cool until the nut can be handled. Wrap it in a heavy cloth to prevent any pieces from flying off, then crack it with hammer taps. ➤ Have a bowl ready to catch watery liquid.

Coconut milk and cream, very rich in fat, are made from the grated firm, mature white meat of the nut. The grating is sometimes done while the meat is still in the shell. Or you may leave the thin brown skin on and use it to protect your fingers as you hand grate. Use a vegetable peeler to remove the skin. Once the skin is removed, cut the meat into small chunks and chop in the blender, no more than $1/2$ cup at a time. Add $1/4$ cup hot water to make coconut milk, or hot milk to make coconut cream. Then strain and measure. If more milk or cream is needed than results, add more hot water, reblend, and strain again.

Another technique is to heat the grated coconut meat in its own natural liquid ➤ just to the boiling point, then remove it from the heat and cool. You can also pour boiling water or milk over grated coconut and add the natural liquid—allowing in all about 1 pint liquid for a medium coconut. In either case, when the mixture has cooled, the coconut is drained through two thicknesses of cheesecloth and the meat, retained in the cloth, is squeezed and kneaded until dry. The drained liquid is allowed to set, refrigerated; it solidifies into a cold butter and can be taken off in one piece. When the "cream" rises, it is skimmed off and refrigerated.

Grated fresh coconut may be soaked 6 hours refriger-

ated in milk to cover and then drained before use. This gives it about the same moisture content as the canned, shredded, or flaked types—for which it may, of course, be substituted.

Coconut milk is also available canned. If desired, you can obtain coconut cream by letting canned coconut milk settle, then skimming off the thick coconut cream that rises to the top. Don't confuse coconut milk or coconut cream with **cream of coconut,** which is a rich, thick, and cloyingly sweet canned liquid, commonly used in mixed drinks, especially Piña Coladas, 61. Coconut milk and cream of coconut are not interchangeable in recipes.

Coconut "butter," or the oil of the coconut meat, is usually solid at room temperature. Though vegetable in origin, it contains saturated fatty acids. It is made from chilled coconut cream—also very rich in fat—by beating with a rotary beater or in a blender. When the solid mass rises, force any excess water out of it with the back of a spoon.

To use the coconut that remains from making coconut "butter," make **polvo de amor,** or "dust of love." Use it as a garnish for breakfast foods and desserts, or as a chutney. Brown slowly in a heavy pan over low heat:

1 cup strained coconut pulp
2 tablespoons sugar

When it is a very light brown, turn off the heat, and continue browning in the residual heat left in the pan and the coconut itself.

To toast grated or shredded coconut in the oven, spread it in a thin layer on a baking sheet and heat about 10 minutes in a preheated 325°F oven. Stir frequently. For a dessert or a spread made from grated coconut, see Coconut Dulcie, 972. **To toast coconut in the microwave,** spread in a thin layer in microwave safe dish or pie pan. Microwave on high power in 30-second bursts, stirring after each 30 seconds and rotating the dish if it is not on a turntable. When done, the coconut should be crumbly when rubbed with your finger.

To substitute flaked for grated coconut, ➤ use $1 1/3$ cups firmly packed for 1 cup grated.

COMFREY

A healing herb—its name comes from a Latin word that means a knitting together—comfrey makes a popular herbal tea or tisane, 35. Use its young leaves sparingly, raw, in salads, or cook them as for spinach, cutting the leaves before the plant blooms. *Symphytum officinale* is a hardy perennial growing to 3 feet, preferring rich, friable lime soil and moisture and shade. Propagate in spring by dividing its long white roots.

CORIANDER

Both the seeds and leaf of this herb have culinary uses. Many of us identify the flavor of the seed with gingerbread, apple pie, sausages, and pickles or as an ingredient of curry powders. The seed is used whole or ground and benefits from toasting, 1011, before use. We also know **cilantro,** another name for the green leaves of the plant, the world's most widely consumed fresh herb. The fresh leaves are also known as Chinese parsley, although it is not related to parsley. It is called kothamille in Sri Lanka, or dhania in India, where the somewhat fetid odor and soapy taste are much treasured. Use the leaves only—no stems—whole or lightly chopped in pea or chicken soups and in stews, scatter them over roasts; or use them in a court bouillon for clams. Cilantro loses its aroma quickly when heated, so for this reason use as a garnish or stir in at the end when preparing hot foods or use in uncooked dishes such as salads, salsas or dips. The flavor is less pungent when dried. *Coriandrum sativum,* a 12- to 18-inch plant, grows in moderately heavy soil and, while needing drainage, can take some moisture.

CORNSTARCH

See Starches, 1016.

CORN SYRUP

Corn syrup is generally used in canning, desserts, sweet sauces, and jelly making. Available in light and dark forms, the dark having a slight molasses flavor. ➤ In this book, the term "corn syrup" applies to the light type. If called for, the stronger-tasting dark is specified. ➤ For the same amount of sweetening power, you must substitute 2 cups corn syrup for 1 cup sugar. In cooking, for best results ➤ never use corn syrup to replace more than half the amount of sugar called for. In baking, you are taking a chance in substituting corn syrup. But if you must, for each 2 cups of sugar in the recipe, reduce the liquid called for—other than the syrup—by ¼ cup. For example: suppose you are baking a cake that calls for 2 cups of sugar. "Maximum syrup tolerance" here would be 1 cup sugar, 2 cups syrup. And for each 2 cups of sugar originally called for, you would reduce the other liquid ingredients by ¼ cup. It is composed of glucose and fructose sugars.

COSTMARY

Used sparingly in sauces, soups, and stuffings, costmary is sometimes substituted for mint but has bitter overtones. *Chrysanthemum balsamita,* a perennial, also known as alecost, grows to 4 feet and is not particular as to soil.

CREAM

Cream is the fat that slowly rises to the surface of fresh unhomogenized whole milk on standing. The longer the milk stands, the richer the cream becomes, as outlined below. Today these uncultured, or "sweet," creams (as opposed to cultured creams or "sour" cream) are sold in pasteurized and ultrapasteurized forms. Ultrapasteurized creams have a longer shelf life, but traditional pasteurized creams have better flavor, whip up fluffier, and hold their whipped state longer.

CRÈME CHANTILLY

The French equivalent of our Whipped Cream.

CRÈME FRAÎCHE

See Sour Milks and Creams, 1013.

HALF-AND-HALF CREAM

A mixture of milk and cream, half-and-half is frequently homogenized. It contains 10½ percent to 18 percent fat.

HEAVY OR WHIPPING CREAM

Cream that is labeled **heavy cream,** or sometimes *heavy whipping cream,* contains at least 36 percent fat and is the richest cream available in most stores. **Whipping cream** contains 30 to 36 percent fat. Unwhipped, these enrich sauces and soups and are used for making ice cream. Whipped and sweetened, they generally frost or garnish desserts. Heavy cream whips and mounds the best. While ultrapasteurized creams have a longer shelf life, traditional pasteurized creams usually have a better flavor, whip up fluffier, and hold their whipped state longer.

LIGHT CREAM, COFFEE, OR TABLE CREAM

These creams contain between 18 percent and 30 percent fat. They do not whip well, unless gelatin is added, 974.

WHIPPED CREAM

Whipping cream expands to twice its volume by the incorporation of air. For optimal results, cream must have a fat content of at least 30 percent, and preferably 36 percent, to create a stable unseparated foam. For best results, the bowl, whisk or beaters, and cream should all be ➤ chilled in the refrigerator at least 2 hours or in the freezer for 10 minutes before whipping, so that the fat stays firm during whipping rather than becoming oily from the friction involved. ➤ In a hot kitchen, beat over ice. If the cream is warmer than 45°F, it may, on beating, quickly turn to butter. ➤ Never overwhip.

Cream can be whipped by hand using a large balloon whisk, but it is certainly easier to use an electric mixer. ➤ **To beat cream** with an electric mixer, beat on medium-high speed until the chilled cream begins to thicken. Add any sugar or flavorings in a steady stream. Lower the speed—and watch like a hawk. Stop beating when the cream is just stiff enough to hold itself up. Be careful not to beat too long, as the cream may get grainy and soupy, with butter particles forming. We like our cream whipped just to the point where it falls in large globs and soft peaks, but still carries a gloss. This is a state almost comparable to the ➤ stiff but not dry peaks of beaten egg white. It is possible to use it in this desirably delicate state only if it is prepared the last second before serving.

➤ Do not try to whip cream in a blender. A food processor with the regular steel blade can be used to whip cream. Fill the bowl less than half full so the cream level remains below the top of the blade, or the cream may leak out.

Process for just a few seconds, until the cream stiffens and the surface rises in a doughnut-like curve. Be very careful to avoid overbeating, as food processors tend to heat up their contents, which will hasten the forming of butter.

It does help, if the cream is to be flavored, to mix in a small quantity of confectioners' sugar, as the cornstarch in the sugar acts as a stabilizer. For interesting ways to flavor whipped cream, see 755.

If whipped cream is to be used decoratively, whip the cream until very stiff, almost to the point where the cream molecules are about to become buttery. Should the cream be whipped too far and threaten to turn to butter, whip in 2 or more tablespoons of additional cream or evaporated milk and continue to beat. Cream at the stiff-peaks stage may be piped through a pastry tube for decorating. ➤ To freeze small decorative garnishes, shape them on foil. Freeze them uncovered on the foil, wrap when firm, and return to the freezer for future use. It is also advisable to underwhip cream whenever it must be refrigerated for several hours before use, then whisk the cream briefly to the desired consistency just before use to reincorporate any liquid that may have separated.

WHIPPED CREAM SUBSTITUTES

First, let us say there are really no very satisfactory substitutes for whipped cream, but the following makeshifts are sometimes used. It is often wise to add vanilla, 1 teaspoon per cup, or one of the other flavors suggested for Whipped Cream, 755, to mask the inferior flavor and texture of these substitutes.

I.

About 2 cups

Soak:

   1 or 1¹/₂ teaspoons unflavored gelatin

depending on heaviness of the cream desired, in:

   2 tablespoons apple juice

until softened, about 5 minutes. Dissolve thoroughly in:

   ¹/₂ cup scalded, 997, light cream

Add:

   1 cup light cream
   1 tablespoon confectioners' sugar

Refrigerate, stirring from time to time. During the early part of the 4 to 6 hours needed to chill properly, add:

   ¹/₂ teaspoon vanilla

Beat as for whipped cream, about 5 to 7 minutes.

II.

About 3 cups

If partially frozen, evaporated milk whips well to about 3 times its original volume, but then must be used immediately.

Chill for about 12 hours and pour into a small bowl:

   One 12-ounce can evaporated milk

Place the beaters or whisk in the bowl along with the milk and freeze until ice crystals form around the edges, about 30 minutes. Beat on high speed for 2 minutes or until very frothy. Gradually add:

   (¹/₄ to ¹/₂ cup confectioners' sugar)
   1 teaspoon vanilla

Continue beating for 2 minutes, or until stiff. Serve immediately.

CROUTONS

These dried or fried seasoned bread morsels come in all sizes. They are made by cutting bread into cubes or slices, coating with oil or butter, if desired, and then sautéing or toasting. As coarse crumbs, they are an attractive garnish for noodles, dumplings, or spätzle. In small dice, they add crunch and heft to salads and soups. Place larger toasts under game or a chop to soak up the juices. Croutons made from thin slices of bread, also known as crostini or croûtes, are perfect for spreads and pâtés.

I. Dice or thinly slice bread, fresh or dry, and sauté it in butter or olive oil until evenly brown. Or butter slices of bread, dice, and brown them in a 375°F oven.

II. *6 cups*

Preheat the oven to 425°F. Toss together on a baking sheet:

   6 thick slices French bread, cut into 1-inch cubes
   3 tablespoons extra-virgin olive oil

Bake, shaking the pan once or twice, until the croutons are golden brown, about 10 minutes.

III. *2 cups*

Preheat the oven to 350°F. Toss together on a baking sheet:

   2 cups ¹/₂-inch cubes corn bread (from about
      2 large pieces)
   2 tablespoons olive oil

Bake, shaking the pan once or twice, until golden, about 10 minutes. Transfer to a plate and let cool.

IV. After 2 cups croutons have been sautéed or browned in the oven, drop them while still hot into a bag containing:

   1 teaspoon salt
   1 teaspoon paprika
   2 to 4 tablespoons finely grated Parmesan
      or very finely minced herbs

Close the bag and shake it until the croutons are evenly coated. Add them to hot soup or use on a salad.

V. Use for soup, noodles, or Caesar salad.

Cut into ¹/₂-inch cubes or ¹/₄-inch slices:

   Bread

Sauté in:

   Hot butter or olive oil

to which you may add:

   (Minced garlic or grated onion)

Stir the cubes gently or shake the skillet until they are coated. Sprinkle with:

   Grated cheese or minced herbs

VI. Use these for stuffings and poultry dressings.

Cut into cubes:

   Bread or corn bread

Place on a baking sheet and dry in a 200°F oven, stirring occasionally, for 1 to 2 hours until dry and golden brown.

CUMIN

The flavor of cumin is classic in the foods of Mexico, India, and North Africa, as well as in cheese, eggs, beans, rice, chili, sauerkraut, and unleavened bread. The seeds can be used ground or whole in marinades, chili powders, and tomato sauces, and are one of the principal ingredients of a curry powder. Toasting, 1001, enhances the flavor of the seeds. *Cuminum cymimum,* or *Cuminum odorum,* an annual growing to 1 foot, needs near-tropical conditions for good growth.

CURRY LEAVES

Curry (or kari) leaves are the leaves of the kari plant, *Chalcas koenigii,* used to flavor the cooking of southern and southwestern India. Fresh curry leaves are sold at Indian specialty stores. You may substitute dried leaves, but their flavor is much less pungent.

CURRY POWDER AND PASTE

We think of curry, which is really a highly seasoned sauce, mainly as a powder sitting in the pantry ready to be added when foods need a lift. But curry powders, which are a blend of spices and not a single spice, called masalas in India, are as individual as the cook making the dish. They are best when the spices are freshly ground or incorporated into a paste with onion, garlic, fruits, and vegetables as commonplace as apples and carrots or as exotic as tamarind and pomegranate.

In either powder or paste form, the curry has a more developed flavor when cooked in some type of fat, such as in ghee, 963, a clarified butter, or olive oil. Curries should be specially blended for each kind of dish: a dry one for coating meat; a sour one for marinated meats; and other mixtures for chicken, lamb or mutton, rice, beans, vegetables, and fish. They range in strength from the fiercely hot curries of Madras to the mild ones of Indonesia. The mixtures below give you an idea of their variety and extent. Amounts to use per portion are a matter of tolerance. Choose beer, a tart limeade, or a yogurt drink as a beverage with curried foods. When making up the dish, use plenty of garlic and onion and, if possible, coconut milk, 972, especially in Thai curries, 589.

I.

1 tablespoon ground ginger
1 tablespoon ground coriander
1 tablespoon ground cardamom
1 teaspoon ground red pepper
3 tablespoons turmeric

II.

²/₃ cup cumin seeds
²/₃ cup ground coriander
¹/₂ cup ground turmeric
¹/₃ cup *each* fenugreek and cardamom seeds

¹/₃ cup whole black peppercorns
4¹/₂ tablespoons poppy seeds
4 teaspoons mustard seeds
2 tablespoons ground ginger
¹/₂ cup red pepper flakes
4 tablespoons ground cinnamon

III.

4 tablespoons *each* turmeric and ground coriander
4¹/₂ tablespoons ground cumin
2 tablespoons ground ginger
1¹/₂ tablespoons whole black peppercorns
1 tablespoon red pepper flakes
1 tablespoon fennel seed
1¹/₂ teaspoons ground mustard
1 teaspoon *each* poppy seeds, ground cloves, ground mace

IV. MADRAS CURRY POWDER

About 1 ¹/₃ cups

Combine in a dry skillet and toast over medium heat until fragrant and a shade darker, about 4 minutes:

6 tablespoons coriander seeds
¹/₄ cup cumin seeds
3 tablespoons *chana dal* (yellow split peas)
1 tablespoon black peppercorns
1 tablespoon black mustard seeds
5 dried red chile peppers
(10 fresh or dried curry leaves)

Combine with:

2 tablespoons fenugreek seeds

Grind to a powder in batches in a spice mill or coffee grinder. Mix well with:

3 tablespoons turmeric

Store in an airtight container in a cool place.

V. GARAM MASALA, see 987

DEVIL SEASONING

About ³/₄ cup

We have chosen Soyer's universal devil seasoning from Alexis Soyer's *Culinary Campaign,* a fabulous account of the Crimean War, through which this first British celebrity chef cooked his way with abandon. No one brought more conviction to his work, whether improving the diet of the British armed forces, cooking at the Reform Club, or remolding the cooking habits of the English working classes—which he attempted through his *Shilling Cook Book.* The original recipe called for a tablespoon of red pepper. We have changed it to a small pinch, for in Soyer's day cayenne was baked into a sort of bread and then ground, making it about the same strength as a mild paprika.

Combine:

1 tablespoon dry mustard
¹/₄ cup chile or cider vinegar
1 tablespoon prepared horseradish
2 shallots, finely chopped
1 teaspoon salt

A pinch of ground red pepper
$^1/_2$ teaspoon black pepper
1 teaspoon sugar
(2 teaspoons chopped chile peppers)

Rub on meat or poultry before grilling. Soyer's instructions are to "broil slowly at first and end as near as possible to the Pandemonium Fire."

DILL

Both the seeds and leaves of this feathery, pungent, and slightly bitter plant are used in sour cream, fish, bean, cucumber, and cabbage dishes as well as in potato salad, on new potatoes, and, of course, in dill pickles, 947. If making a dill butter sauce, do not brown the butter. Dried dill leaves or fronds are sold as dill weed. The seeds are also good in vinegar, and the leaves make a lovely garnish. *Anethum graveolens,* an annual, grows to 3 feet and self-sows. Pull up plants when flower heads brown, and dry over paper so that the easily shattered seeds are not lost. The tender flower heads can be used just like the leaves; they are particularly appealing in a jar of pickles.

DRIED SHRIMP

Mildly salty, with a fragrant aroma, dried shrimp are used in Asian cuisines as a flavoring. Add to stir-fries, noodle dishes, sauces, and soups. They are sold in packets either whole or powdered; store in a sealed container in a cool place. To reconstitute, soak in warm water.

EGGS AND EGG PRODUCTS

Nothing stimulates the practiced cook's imagination or the nutritionist's enthusiasm like a good fresh egg, for eggs contain all the balanced nutrients from which a complete organism develops. Eggs transform cake batters and bread doughs by providing a structural framework for leaveners, thicken custards and make them smooth, bind meat loaves and bread dressings, and help produce smooth, rich ice creams. They emulsify sauces, hollandaise, and mayonnaise; clarify or enrich soups; glaze rolls; insulate pie doughs against sogginess; create glorious meringues and soufflés; and make ideal brunch, lunch, and quick or emergency meals.

Because fresh eggs do all these things better than old eggs and because there is no comparison in taste and texture between the two, ➤ always buy the very best quality you can find. It doesn't matter if their yolks are light or dark or if their shells are white or brown. While there is no test, except tasting, for good flavor, ➤ the relative freshness of eggs may be determined by placing them in a bowl of cold water. Those that float are not usable. You can also break an egg into a clean bowl and smell it. An old egg will smell like damp grass or straw and will taint any delicate or pure egg dishes. Unshelled onto a plate, as shown, 977, ➤ a truly fresh egg has a yolk that domes up and stays up and a thick, translucent white containing two twisted ropelike strands of material, called the chalazae, which anchor the yolk in place. This is usable, as are the red flecks or blood spots that sometimes appear on the yolk. Blood spots are not harmful. Remove them with the tip of a knife, if desired, when using the egg in a light-colored sauce or dessert.

Strange as it may seem after stressing the purchase of fresh eggs, we now tack on an amendment! ➤ Do not use eggs fresher than 3 days old for hard-cooked eggs. If you do, hard-cooked eggs will be difficult to peel. ➤ Never use a doubtful egg with any odor or discoloration, especially one that is cracked, for that is one way salmonella, 980, enters the egg. The shell naturally protects an egg, and if it is cracked or damaged, the contents will deteriorate rapidly; eggs that are cracked, damaged, or have dirty shells should not be used.

Eggs should be bought and measured by weight, but tradition is against this sensible approach. ➤ Unless otherwise stated, we assume in this book that you are using 2-ounce eggs. These are known as "large." However, eggs of any size may be used for preparations such as fried, boiled, or poached—when the size of the egg has

EGG SIZES AND EQUIVALENTS

Use this chart when replacing the large eggs called for in recipes with eggs of another size. The amounts in parentheses are the weights of each egg in the shell.

Large (2 ounces)	Jumbo (2$^1/_2$ ounces)	Extra-Large (2$^1/_4$ ounces)	Medium (1$^3/_4$ ounces)	Small (1$^1/_2$ ounces)
1	1	1	1	1
2	2	2	3	3
3	2	3	3	4
4	3	4	5	5
5	4	4	6	7
6	5	5	7	8

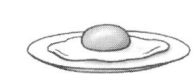

The domed yolk of a fresh egg

2 large eggs or 3 medium eggs equal $\frac{1}{2}$ cup

no effect on the overall recipe. The typical serving size is 1 to 2 eggs per person. For recipes such as soufflés, custards, and cakes that depend on an exact number of large eggs, use the Egg Sizes and Weights chart, 976, to substitute smaller or larger eggs.

Store-bought eggs should carry a Grade A or Grade AA stamp as well as date of grading and freshness code. Grade AA and Grade A are the top two classifications of the USDA's voluntary system for indicating an egg's quality. These grades have no bearing on size or freshness. Rather, both indicate eggs that had high, round yolks and firm, thick whites when they were first laid. While eggs graded AA are a bit more shapely, the difference between the two grades is slight, and with age, no matter what its grade, any egg yolk will flatten out and the white will turn watery. If in doubt about size, weigh or measure them. The yolk of a 2-ounce egg is just about 1 tablespoon plus a teaspoon; the white, about 2 tablespoons. For more equivalents, see 976 and 977. To realize how great a difference egg size has on volume, notice below that 2 large eggs give you about $\frac{1}{2}$ cup, but it takes 3 medium eggs to fill that same $\frac{1}{2}$ cup. Sometimes it is convenient or necessary to weight or measure eggs out of the shell. When you reduce a recipe and want to use only part of an egg, beat the egg slightly and measure about $1\frac{1}{2}$ tablespoons for half an egg and about 1 tablespoon for one-third or use the following approximate conversions:

1 large egg white = about 1 ounce = about 2 tablespoons
1 large egg yolk = about $\frac{1}{2}$ ounce = about 1 tablespoon

Don't expect the same texture or flavor from eggs of other poultry or fowl, from duck to ostrich (one of the latter, by the way, will serve 24 for brunch). In using offbeat eggs, be very sure of freshness. To freeze and thaw eggs, see 923. A number of egg products available on the market are described below.

EGG SUBSTITUTE

Most egg substitutes are 98 to 99 percent egg whites and thus lack both the cholesterol content and the yolk-rich taste of whole eggs. Because egg whites are apt to dry out when cooked, cook egg substitutes gently; and add seasonings such as hot sauce or chopped fresh herbs for flavor.

Another way to reduce the fat and cholesterol and still retain some of the taste of a whole egg is to substitute egg whites for up to half of the whole eggs in a recipe. Figure $1\frac{1}{2}$ egg whites (or a scant 3 tablespoons) for every whole egg you omit.

HOMEMADE EGG SUBSTITUTE
About 1 $\frac{1}{2}$ cups

About $\frac{1}{4}$ cup of this mixture is the equivalent volume of 1 whole large egg.
Gently mix together:
   12 large egg whites
   1 tablespoon vegetable oil
   $\frac{1}{4}$ teaspoon salt
For a more egglike color, add:
   6 drops yellow food coloring

LIQUID EGG WHITES AND YOLKS

Egg whites and yolks are sold separately as a pasteurized product packaged in pourable containers. They are convenient for recipes using uncooked egg whites or egg yolks. Because they are pasteurized, the beating time for meringues made with liquid egg whites may be longer than the beating time given in the recipe.

LIQUID WHOLE EGGS

These are pasteurized whole eggs. The pasteurization process destroys any harmful bacteria that may be present in the eggs. Useful for recipes using uncooked whole eggs. Unopened containers will last as long as 3 months under proper refrigeration.

MERINGUE POWDER

Meringue powder is dried egg whites with the addition of sugar and thickeners. To make a meringue, add water to the powder and whip it. Meringue powder is pasteurized, so it is useful when making uncooked meringues. It also has a long shelf life. For fresh egg meringues, see 740.

PASTEURIZED WHOLE EGGS

Pasteurized whole eggs in the shell have been heat-treated to destroy bacteria; this process does not cook the eggs. The shells are stamped to signify that the eggs have been pasteurized. These are more expensive than regular shell eggs, but are a good alternative for use in raw or partially cooked egg recipes. They can also be used in any egg dishes just like eggs that are not pasteurized.

POWDERED EGG WHITES

Some pasteurized powdered egg whites contain no other ingredients, while others contain additives to help build volume and stabilize the foam when beating egg whites. These freeze-dried egg whites have a very long shelf life and do not require refrigeration. They are simply blended with water to produce liquid egg whites, which makes them convenient to use.

POWDERED WHOLE EGGS

Dried eggs are a convenience when fresh eggs are unavailable. Because of bacterial dangers, they must always be used in recipes that call for thorough cooking, unless a large percentage of acid is indicated. Store at room temperature, and refrigerate after opening. To reconstitute the equivalent of 3 fresh eggs, sift $1/2$ cup whole egg powder over $1/2$ cup water and whip until smooth. To substitute for 1 egg, use $2 1/2$ tablespoons egg powder to $2 1/2$ tablespoons water. Beat until smooth. ➤ Use within 5 minutes after combining. You may instead add the egg powder to the dry ingredients, and the water to the rest of the liquid called for in the recipe.

BEATING EGGS

To attempt to describe the beating of egg whites is almost as cheeky as advising how to lead a happy life. But, because the success of a dish may rest entirely on this operation, we go into it in some detail. ➤ To beat whole eggs to their greatest volume, have them at 65° to 75°F. Before adding them to batters and doughs, beat whole eggs and yolks together, unless otherwise directed in the recipe, until they are light in color and texture. ➤ To warm eggs to room temperature, place the eggs in a bowl of hot tap water for 5 minutes.

For some recipes, whole eggs and yolks profit by as much as 5 minutes or more of beating in the electric mixer and will increase up to six times their original volume.

When beating egg whites, to get the greatest volume, ➤ see that the egg whites are properly separated and at 65° to 75°F. ➤ Choose a large deep bowl, 979, in which to beat egg whites. Be sure the bowl is not aluminum, which will gray the eggs, or plastic, which in spite of careful washing may retain a slight film of grease, deterring volume development. The French dote on copper—but if cream of tartar is used to give a more stable and tender foam, its acid will turn the eggs greenish in a copper bowl.

The lightness of the beating stroke and the whisk used make an appreciable difference in building up the air capacity of egg-white cells. ➤ Choose as a beater a long, many-thin-wired whisk. ➤ Be sure that bowl, beater, and scraper are absolutely free of grease—if made of plastic the equipment may not be greaseproof. To clean them, use a detergent or a combination of lemon juice and vinegar. Rinse completely and dry carefully.

If you are going to use the whites in baking, have the oven preheated. Start beating only when all other ingredients are mixed and ready.

To beat egg whites with an electric mixer, use a whip attachment if available. The beating will not take as long as when done by hand, but the tests for readiness are the same. We do not recommend the use of a blender, immersion blender, or food processor (unless fitted with a whipping device) for beating egg whites.

To beat egg whites by hand, be prepared to give about 300 strokes in 2 minutes to beat 2 egg whites. You can expect $2 1/2$ to 4 times the volume you start with. Begin slowly and lightly with a very relaxed wrist motion and beat steadily until the egg whites lose their yellowish translucency and become foamy. Then gradually increase the beating tempo. Beat without stopping ➤ until the whites are airy and stand in peaks that are firm but still soft and elastic.

In recipes for meringues and in some cakes, a portion of the sugar, about 1 teaspoon per egg, is beaten into the egg whites once they are foamy. Although this reduces volume slightly and means a longer beating period, it does give a much more upstanding foam.

From start to finish, there should be no stopping until that state is reached that is best described as ➤ stiff, but not dry. Another test for readiness is the rate of flow when the bowl is tipped. The egg whites when whipped stiff are not fluid and do not move. Some cooks use the inverted bowl test in which the whites cling dramatically to the bottom of the upside-down bowl, a sign, unfortunately, that the eggs may have been beaten a bit too long and are as a consequence too dry. Although they may have greater volume, their cells will not stretch to capacity in baking without breaking down.

Folding in egg whites should always be a manual operation rather than a mechanical one, since it is essential, again, to retain as much air in the whites as possible. ➤ Working both quickly and gently, the goal is to incorporate the lighter mixture into the heavier one, combining the two substances with two separate movements. With a large rubber spatula, first use a sharp, clean action, bringing the spatula down to the bottom of the bowl, as though cutting a cake. Then, with a lifting motion, envelop the whites by bringing the heavier substance up from the bottom of the bowl. Repeat these slicing and lifting motions alternately, turning the bowl as you work, trying meanwhile not to break down the beaten whites.

COOKING EGGS

It is possible, on a hot summer day, "they" say, to fry an egg on the sidewalk. We do not recommend this particular activity; we mention it to remind you that eggs cook quickly over any kind of heat—beginning to thicken at 150°F. When heated, an egg's remarkable transformation from a thin, runny liquid into a firm, opaque food is the result of a simple process. When eggs are heated, their proteins begin to unravel and bond with one another. At relatively low temperatures, the proteins remain loose and supple, allowing the egg to set while remaining moist and tender. At high temperature and with long cooking, however, the proteins fuse into a hard, tough mass. In the case of plain cooked eggs, such as fried, poached, or hard-boiled, the result is a rubbery white and a dry, crumbly yolk. In the case of custards, quiches, and egg-thickened sauces and soups, the result is a curdled state where the eggs take on a grainy, watery consistency. Be doubly careful, then, ➤ with all egg dishes, not to use excessive heat and not to prolong the cooking period.

Cream, butter, and cheese are especially welcome in egg dishes not only because they add richness, but also because their fat protects the egg's proteins and counteracts the tendency to curdle. Only prior precautions, however, will produce smooth egg-enhanced sauces or egg dishes. For, once the protein of the egg has shrunk, it can no longer hold moisture in suspension, and the results are bound to be watery. If you are combining eggs with a hot mixture, condition them first by using a technique called **tempering.** To temper, whisk a small quantity of the hot mixture into the beaten eggs. Then add the eggs to the remaining hot mixture. Often at this point in egg cookery—if you are preparing a soufflé base or thickening a soup, sauce, or custard with yolks—there is enough stored heat in the pan to do the necessary cooking.

If you are going to cook an egg yolk and sugar mixture, beat the eggs, add the sugar, and continue to beat until the mixture runs in a broad ribbon from the side of the spoon. When this stage has been reached, the eggs will cook without curdling.

Now, armed with two more secrets, you can expect real magic from the rich, complete, and tasty protein that is tidily packed inside an eggshell. In baking and in making omelets or scrambled eggs, remember that eggs will give better texture and volume if they are at about room temperature at the outset. Also remember that because egg yolks are almost one-third fat, you can count on some slight thickening action as eggs cool in a pudding or sauce.

SEPARATING EGGS

You have heard about the cook who couldn't boil an egg, but there are some who can't even break or separate one. Here's how: Separating eggs can be done with an egg separator or by hand. To use an egg separator, place the device on the rim of a cup or small bowl. Crack the egg carefully into the center. The white will run through the horizontal slits around the sides into the container below, while the yolk will sit in the depression of the separator. Or

have 3 bowls ready, as sketched. Holding an egg in one hand, tap the center of the side of the egg lightly yet sharply on a flat surface, such as the countertop, making an even break. Then hold the egg in both hands, with the break on the upper side. Hold it over the center of a small bowl and tip it so that the wider end is down. Hold the edges of the break with your thumbs, and widen the break by pulling the edges apart until the eggshell is broken in half. As you do this, some of the egg white will flow into the bowl underneath, but the yolk and the rest of the egg white will remain in the lower half of the shell. Pour the remaining egg back and forth from one half-shell to the other, letting some more of the white flow into the bowl each time until only the yolk remains in the shell. During this shifting process, you will be able to tell quickly, with each egg in turn, if there is any discoloration or off odor. Discard any dubious egg before it is put with the yolks on the left or with the whites in the large bowl on the right. Should the yolk shatter during breaking, you can try to remove yolk particles from the white with the corner of a paper towel moistened in cold water. Should you fail to clear the yolk entirely from the white, keep that egg (yolk and white) for another use, because the slightest fat from the yolk will lessen the volume of the beaten whites and perceptibly change the texture.

STORING EGGS

The storage of eggs is simple if you follow a few basic rules. ➤ Keep them in their original container in the back on a colder (lower) shelf of the refrigerator (not on the door) where a constant, colder temperature is maintained. ➤ Foods containing raw or partially cooked eggs—like homemade mayonnaise and custards in which the eggs are raw or only slightly cooked—should be kept covered, under refrigeration, and away from strong-smelling foods such as cut garlic and onions and pungent cheeses as they absorb odors easily.

To store egg whites, place them in an airtight container and do refrigerate for no longer than 1 week. Then ➤ use them only in recipes that call for cooking. To store unbroken egg yolks, cover them with a little cold water to prevent them from drying out, cover, and refrigerate. Drain

Separating eggs and beating egg whites

the water before using. ➤ The egg yolks should only be used in recipes that call for cooking. Raw yolks may be stored up to 2 days, or, if poached in water until firm, for a few days longer. For other uses of extra whites or yolks, see, 994.

Before we leave this subject, we pull out of our hat a conjurer's trick. Should you have any doubts about which eggs in your refrigerator are hard-cooked and which are not, a quick test is to twirl them on their pointed ends. Hard-cooked eggs will spin like a top; others will simply topple over.

And a hint about washing egg-soiled dishes. Start with cold water, which releases, rather than glues on, the protein. Rub egg-stained silver with salt if polish is not handy.

ABOUT EGG SAFETY

The bacteria *Salmonella enteritidis,* which can cause illness, is occasionally found in raw eggs, even uncracked eggs. While the risk remains extremely low (it is estimated that 1 in 10,000 eggs is infected, and even infected eggs may not cause problems if properly stored and cooked), we recommend handling eggs carefully, particularly when cooking for young children, the elderly, pregnant women, or anyone with a compromised immune system. Buy refrigerated eggs and store them in your own refrigerator as quickly as possible. Never use a doubtful egg. When cracking or separating eggs, make sure that the fresh egg never touches the exterior of the shell, which is more apt to carry contamination. Before and after handling eggs, wash your hands and any utensils or equipment that may have come into contact with either the shell or the contents.

When eggs are cooked, either alone or combined with other ingredients, to a temperature of 140°F for 3$\frac{1}{2}$ to 5 minutes or 160°F for only seconds, all harmful bacteria will be killed. An instant-read thermometer with a thin probe is the easiest way to check the temperature of many dishes. For preparations of eggs on their own—fried or poached eggs, for example—you can use your eyes. Egg whites firm and begin to set at 150°F, and yolks begin to thicken at 150°F and set at 158°F. Eggs have reached the safe zone when the white is set and the yolk is just starting to firm but may remain runny in the center. For whole-egg dishes such as scrambled eggs or omelets, the mixed eggs will set at around 165°F—well above the safety margin. The addition of other ingredients, especially fat, will raise the temperature at which eggs set, meaning scrambled eggs made with additional cream and/or butter will stay soft and moist at higher temperatures, making them both safe and succulent. For dishes like casseroles and quiches, the eggs are sufficiently cooked when a knife inserted in the center comes out clean.

Of greater concern to some are a number of classic recipes that depend on raw or lightly cooked eggs— among them mayonnaise, dessert mousses, eggnog, and Caesar salad. Some cooks now substitute pasteurized liquid eggs or dried egg whites. The liquid eggs most closely resemble fresh eggs and are only slightly less efficient than fresh eggs for emulsifying or beating purposes. Dried whites are best for lightly cooked meringues. Some cooks refuse to compromise and continue using fresh eggs, raw or lightly cooked, without incident. If you are of this school, minimize risk by using the freshest eggs possible and storing them at temperatures below 40°F. It is essential to serve cooked egg dishes immediately or to chill them quickly and then refrigerate and to store any dish containing raw eggs in the refrigerator before cooking.

EPAZOTE

With a penetrating herb-like aroma, *Chenopodium ambrosioides* is a member of the same family as quinoa and spinach. It is frequently used in Mexican soups and in stews such as posole, 351.

EXTRACTS AND FLAVORINGS

There are a number of extracts other than vanilla from berries, spices, citrus fruits, nuts, chocolate, liqueurs, and coffee. They add a hint of flavor and are to be used sparingly—a little goes a long way. Other flavorings for cooking and baking include **grenadine,** made from the juice of pomegranates, and **rose and orange water,** both sweetened distillations used in Middle Eastern cooking. ➤ We do not recommend nonalcoholic liqueur flavorings. They may be more dilute in flavor, although less expensive. For the best, true-flavored extracts, look for the word "pure" on the label.

FATS IN COOKING

Nothing reveals the particular quality of a national or regional cuisine so unmistakably as the fat on which it is based. Bacon arouses memories of our South, olive oil evokes Mediterranean cooking, and different types of butter summon up memories of fine meals around the globe. Not only flavors but food textures change with the use of different fats, whose characteristics are as individual as their tastes.

Let's look at the versatility of fat in cooking. Fats, when used with discretion and skill, have the power to absorb flavors and to envelop gluten strands and "shorten" them into a more tender structure. Fats also form the emulsifying agent in gravies and mayonnaise and can act as a preservative when coating some food, such as confit, 451. And butter creates a beautiful brown color in breads and pastries.

Fats are derived from animal sources (butter and lard) and vegetable sources (solid vegetable shortening, as well as grain, seed, and nut oils). Fats for cooking, of course, include both solid fats and liquid oils. ➤ Fats are solid at about room temperature. ➤ Oils remain liquid at those temperatures, but they may become solidified when refrigerated. Many scorn fats for their calories and saturated and trans fats for their effect on our health. For more about the properties of fat, see 5.

CLARIFYING FATS

To clarify fats that have been used in frying and to rid them of burned food particles and other impurities, ➤ heat them slowly until warm. You may add to the warming fat 4 to 5 slices of potato per cup of fat to help absorb unwanted flavors. When the potato is quite brown, or when the fat is just melted, strain the warm fat through cheesecloth. ➤ Store refrigerated. To clarify butter, see 963.

MEASURING FATS

There is no mystery involved in measuring oils or sticks of butter, margarine, or shortening. For oils, use a standard liquid measuring cup and measuring spoons. For sticks of butter, margarine, or shortening, cut them using the premeasured marks on the wrapper.

There are two methods for measuring bulk fats such as solid shortening, blocks of butter, or tub margarine or butter. One is the displacement method. If you want $1/2$ cup fat, fill a 1-cup liquid measuring cup with $1/2$ cup water. Add the fat in pieces or chunks until the water is pushed up and reaches the 1-cup mark. The amount of fat in the container will then be equal to $1/2$ cup. Pour off the water.

Measuring bulk fats

Some people prefer to use a set of dry measuring cups, especially when measuring solid shortening. But if you use them, rinse the measuring cup with warm water, then push the solid shortening down well into the bottom of these measures, or a considerable air space may be left, which will make your measurement inaccurate.

REMOVING EXCESS SALT FROM FATS

To remove excess salt from bacon or salt pork before use in delicate braises and ragouts or in larding, 464, cut into pieces as directed in the individual recipes. Then parblanch, 1054. Put it in a heavy pan, cover it with ➤ cold water, and bring the water slowly to a boil. Reduce the heat and ➤ simmer, uncovered, 3 to 10 minutes. Allow the longer time if the dice are as big as 1 x 1 x $1/2$ inch. Drain and use.

To remove salt from cooking butter, heat it slowly, to avoid browning it. Skim it. Allow it to cool in the pan, and remove the fat cake. Any sediment and moisture should be in the bottom of the pan. Clarified butter is used in a number of ways, especially in cooking where a slower browning is wanted, or in making hollandaise or Béarnaise Sauce, 561.

RENDERING FATS

Rendering, or "trying out," meat is the process of extracting and purifying solid fat from animal products. It improves the quality by removing all connective tissue, possible impurities, and moisture, and can easily be done at home. Begin by trimming the fat from the meat and cutting it into small pieces. Do not worry if there are a few bits of skin or meat attached—these can be strained out after rendering. The two methods for rendering, dry rendering and wet rendering, produce slightly different results. Wet-rendered fat is pure and bland tasting, while dry-rendered fat tends to have a more savory flavor and a darker color. Dry-rendering occurs any time you cook bacon or ground meat. The fat that appears in the pan as the meat cooks may be collected and used as a cooking fat. Dry-rendered fat will also smoke or burn at a lower temperature than wet-rendered fat. Dry-rendering is the first step of many meat soups and stews: Toss a few bits of bacon, beef trimmings, or chicken fat into a pot, heat it until the fat melts, and then proceed to add the other ingredients. Dry-rendering may also be done in a 350°F oven.

Wet-rendering is generally reserved for times when you have saved a large amount of fat to be rendered at a later time. Dice the trimmed fat and heat it ➤ very slowly with a small quantity of water in a heavy pan. You may speed up this process by pressing the fat with the back of a spoon or potato masher. When the fat is liquid and still fairly warm, strain it through cheesecloth and store it ➤ refrigerated. The browned connective tissues left in the strainer—known as **cracklings**—may be kept for flavoring cooked dried beans, green beans, or any dish that you would season with bacon or a ham hock.

DRIPPINGS

Drippings are fats that are rendered in the process of cooking meats or poultry. When making gravies, they are desirable in reinforcing the flavors of the meat from which they come, as we all learn with the Thanksgiving turkey, saving the pan drippings to make gravy. Lamb and mutton drippings are strongly flavored and should be used with great discretion. Bacon grease is often stored for use in corn breads and meat piecrusts and for flavoring other dishes where salt pork may be called for. ➤ All these fats should be clarified, above, before storage in the refrigerator, to improve their keeping qualities. The natural desire to keep a container handy at the back of the stove to receive and reuse these drippings should be curbed! Exposed to varying degrees of warmth, these are subject to quick spoilage.

To ➤ substitute drippings for butter, use 15 percent to 20 percent less drippings.

PORK FAT

Pork fat is used both fresh and salted. Salt pork, which comes from the flank, is used to line Pâtés for Lardoons, 464, and for Barding, 455. Fresh pork fat is used as an ingredient in stuffings and sausages and in pâté mixtures. ➤ To remove excess salt from salt pork, see 981.

POULTRY FATS

Fats from chickens, turkeys, ducks, and geese are highly regarded for many cooking applications. When rendered from the fat around the kidneys or from the abdominal cavity, they are firm, bland, and light in color. From other sources, such as skimmed broth or roasting, the rendered fat is likely to be soft, grainy, and darker in color. ➤ Store covered in the refrigerator. To substitute, use $3/4$ cup rendered and clarified poultry fat for 1 cup butter.

FENNEL

The leaves, or feather-like fronds, of Florence fennel and the seeds and fronds of sweet fennel can be used interchangeably where a slightly vigorous aniselike flavor is wanted. In flavoring, both the leaves and seeds are used—as for dill, 976—especially with fatty fish and rice and potatoes, as well as in sausages, with lentils, and in fruit dishes with apples and pears. Fish is sometimes cooked over fennel fronds. In sauces, do not let the leaves cook long enough to wilt. The fronds do not retain flavor in drying. *Foeniculum vulgare dulce* and its variant, bronze fennel, are self-sowing and grow wild or cultivated to 5 feet. They do not produce bulbs for eating. *F. vulgare azoricum*, Florence fennel, or *finocchio*, produces a bulb that is used as a vegetable, 276.

FENUGREEK

Fenugreek has the same odor as celery but a more bitter flavor. Popular as a herbal tea or tisane, 35, it is also used in many North African dishes, including Ethiopian berbere. It constitutes one of the main ingredients of Indian curries and is the base of artificial maple flavor. *Trigonella foenumgraecum*, which grows to 1 or 2 feet, needs well-drained loam.

FERMENTED BLACK BEANS

Fermented black beans are soybeans that are partially decomposed by means of a special mold, then dried and sometimes salted. Black beans have a pleasing winelike flavor and when used properly, are a wonderful complement to seafood and meats. Rinsing black beans is recommended except in recipes where their saltiness is desired. Add the beans and taste before adding other seasonings. Depending on the dish, black beans should be chopped lightly or crushed with the side of a large knife. Sometimes flavored with bits of ginger and orange peel, black beans are sold in plastic packages. After opening, store in a covered jar in a cool, dark place. They will keep indefinitely.

FINES HERBES

The French term connotes a delicate blend of fresh herbs suitable for savory sauces, soups, and cheese and savory egg dishes. Use equal parts of parsley, tarragon, chives, and chervil—although some other mild herbs such as thyme may be allowed to creep in. These mixed herbs, minced with a sharp knife and added ➤ at the last minute to the food being cooked, give up their essential oils but retain a lovely freshness. The blend is also available dried in most supermarkets.

FISH SAUCE

A staple of Southeast Asian cooking and a relative of the ancient Roman sauce garum, fish sauce has many different names. Called *nuoc nam* in Vietnam, *nam pla* in Thailand, *patis* in the Phillipines, *sauce de poisson* in France, and *shottsuru* in Japan, fish sauce is produced by packing fish, usually anchovies, in crocks or barrels, covering them with salt, and allowing them to ferment over a period of 6 months to a year. The resulting tea-colored liquid is drained off, filtered, and bottled. As with olive oil, the first pressing (in this case siphoning), from which flows a clear amber liquid, is most highly prized. Fish sauce has an extremely pungent, salty flavor. It is used as a seasoning, condiment, or dipping sauce. It keeps indefinitely in a cool, dark place. Replace if it crystallizes or darkens in color.

FIVE-SPICE POWDER

This pungent, slightly sweet mixture of ground spices is available ready-mixed, or make your own. The mix sometimes contains cardamon or ginger, and black peppercorns can be substituted for the Szechuan peppercorns. Use sparingly when preparing roasted meats or poultry. Grind into a powder equal amounts of:

> **Star anise, fennel seeds, Szechuan peppercorns, whole cloves, and broken or crushed cinnamon sticks**

Store in an airtight container.

FLAVORED OILS

See About Flavored Oils, 590.

FLOURS

We have become so accustomed to bleached white flour that we forget earlier cooks knew only whole-kernel or whole-grain flours. These were not the so-called whole wheat flour of our commercial world, but those with the whole grain, which includes the germ. Many flours in general use today lack both the germ and bran. The nutritious, tasty germ is usually removed in modern milling because flours made with it are harder both to mill and to keep. After the removal of the outer coats and germ, our flours may be "enriched." ➤ Enriched flour contains some of the many ingredients known to have been removed in milling. You may further fortify your enriched all-purpose flour by combining it with some of the flours described below, which may have as much as sixteen times the protein value of wheat along with other important substances lacking in the wheat and rye flours we commonly use. If you are interested in these grain components, you can search the USDA National Nutrient Database online: www.nal.usda.gov/fnic/foodcomp/search.

Flours must meet rigid government specifications and, when manufactured, must contain not more than 15 percent moisture. Keep flour in clean, airtight containers and store in a cool place. Varying protein content affects the way flours "handle," so some recipes for breads and pastries may read, for example, "$2\frac{1}{2}$ to $2\frac{3}{4}$ cups flour." If they do, ➤ measure the smaller amount of flour first, then add enough of, or even more than, the remaining flour, until the dough begins to clean the sides of the bowl, or as otherwise indicated. In order to aerate the flour, remove lumps and possible impurities, and separate the flour granules, we sometimes recommend sifting white flours for cakes and cookies. But neither white flours nor coarser flours nor cornmeal need be sifted for bread making.

For various ways to use flours as thickeners, see 544.

MEASURING FLOURS

It is particularly important that flour is not packed when measuring it. Before measuring, stir the flour in the bag or canister to incorporate some air. Spoon the flour lightly into the cup so that it overflows the rim, then level it off by gently sweeping a straight-sided knife, as shown opposite, across the top of the cup. ➤ Never try to level the flour by shaking the cup.

If a recipe calls for sifted flour, ➤ there is an easy way to sift and measure the flour neatly and quickly. Cut two 12-inch squares of parchment paper, foil, or wax paper. Sift the flour onto the first square, as shown. Rest your sifter on the side of the second square. Pick up the first sheet and curve it into a slide from which the flour can funnel itself into the measuring cup, which should be a dry measuring cup. For very accurate measuring, cups de-

Measuring flour

signed for $\frac{1}{4}$, $\frac{1}{3}$ and $\frac{1}{2}$ are also desirable. Choose the cup that is the correct measure for the quantity you want. When the measure is filled, level the flour by running a knife across the top of the cup. ➤ Never try to level the flour contents by shaking the cup, as this just repacks the sifted flour. Now you are ready to resift the flour with the other dry ingredients. Between siftings, move the sifter to the empty sheet and funnel the dry ingredients of the other sheet into the sifter top; as you did in measuring the flour in the center illustration.

Always remember the important fact that ➤ flours can vary more than 20 percent in their ability to absorb moisture, depending on the type of wheat from which they were milled and the protein content of the flour. The more protein a flour contains, the more water it absorbs. For this reason, even the most accurate measurement may not always result in unqualified success. If the flour used has a different protein content from the flour used in the recipe testing, the batter or dough can be much wetter or drier than the recipe intends. For more about the protein content of flour, see Flours, Wheat, 985.

Read About Flour Substitutions, 1040.

FLOURS, NONWHEAT

Some of the following nonwheat flours can be used alone. But in any bread recipe that fails to call for any wheat flour,

Sifting flour, measuring sifting, resift with other dry ingredients

you must expect a marked difference in texture, as the gluten formed from wheat flour and water has a unique elastic quality. The gluten-forming proteins in wheat are activated when the flour is both moistened and handled, at which time the gluten is said to "develop." The flour is then able to absorb as much as 200 times its weight in moisture. In discussing nonwheat flours, some of which are richer in overall protein content than wheat, we give the closest substitutions we have been able to find, but ➤ we advise, if possible, using at least 1 cup wheat flour for every 2 cups other flour, or a very heavy dough will result. For increased protein content, we suggest the use of Cornell Triple-Rich Formula, 596, or vital wheat gluten, 987.

Coarse flours need not be sifted before measuring. They do need more leavening than wheat types. ➤ Allow $2^1/_2$ teaspoons baking powder for every cup of coarse flour.

BARLEY FLOUR

To substitute, use $1/_2$ cup barley flour for 1 cup all-purpose flour.

BEAN FLOUR

Dried beans can be ground into a flour for use in making gluten-free baked products. ➤ Substitute 4 to 5 cups bean flour for 1 cup all-purpose flour.

BUCKWHEAT FLOUR

Buckwheat flour, which has a high protein content, is best used in the proportion of $1/_4$ cup buckwheat to $3/_4$ cup all-purpose flour for good texture and robust flavor.

CAROB FLOUR OR POWDER

A chocolate-flavored flour milled from the carob tree pod, which is also known as Saint John's bread. A nutritious substitute for chocolate for the allergic, it is low in fat and delicious in its own right.

To add to batters or doughs, allow $1/_8$ to $1/_4$ cup carob flour plus $7/_8$ to $3/_4$ cup all-purpose flour for every cup of flour. ➤ To substitute for chocolate, 3 tablespoons of carob flour plus 2 tablespoons liquid equals 1 ounce unsweetened chocolate. Reduce the sugar, as it is naturally sweet.

CORN FLOUR

Yellow or white corn may be milled into corn flour, or the flour may be a by-product in the making of cornmeal. Use in baking for added corn flavor, mixing corn flour with other flours. Do not confuse corn flour with **masa harina,** which is a yellow or white flour made from dried hominy, 349, and used in making corn tortillas and tamales.

CORNMEAL

There is little difference in the nutritional or baking properties of yellow and white cornmeal. Stone-ground cornmeal not only retains the germ but has a superior corn flavor. Cornmeals can be used alone in Corn Dodgers Cockaigne, 633, or mixed with other flours in quick and

yeast corn breads. Self-rising cornmeal contains the correct proportion of leaveners and salt and can be successfully used in recipes developed for self-rising cornmeal. ➤ If a recipe calls for self-rising cornmeal and you want to make your own, add $1^1/_2$ teaspoons baking powder and $1/_2$ teaspoon salt per each cup of cornmeal.

COTTONSEED FLOUR

With at least four times the protein value of wheat, cottonseed flour is used to enrich breads. ➤ Substitute 2 tablespoons cottonseed flour for 2 tablespoons of the flour in each 1 cup of all-purpose flour.

NUT MEAL

Finely ground nuts, or nut meal are used as a flour substitute in many cakes; see 727.

OAT FLOUR

Oats are ground to different consistencies and can be combined with wheat flours. Use $1/_3$ cup per each $2/_3$ cup flour. Oat flour works especially well in cookies and quick breads.

PEANUT FLOUR

Peanut flour contains at least 16 times the protein value of wheat. Substitute 2 tablespoons peanut flour for 2 tablespoons all-purpose flour per each cup of flour.

POTATO FLOUR

Made from whole cooked potatoes that have been dried and ground, potato flour is used chiefly in soups, gravies, breads, and cakes, in combination with other flours, or alone in Sponge Cakes. Potato flour is different from potato starch, 1017. To avoid lumping in cake batters, blend it with the sugar before mixing, or cream it with the shortening before adding a liquid. In bread recipes, it gives a moist slow-staling loaf. ➤ In baking, substitute $1/_2$ cup plus 2 tablespoons potato flour for 1 cup all-purpose flour. ➤ To use as a thickener, substitute 1 tablespoon potato flour for 2 tablespoons all-purpose flour.

RICE FLOUR (NONWAXY)

Nonwaxy rice flour makes a dense but delicately textured cake in recipes heavy in egg, and it is useful for making gluten-free bread. For recipes using rice flour, see Index. ➤ Substitute 1 cup minus 2 tablespoons rice flour for 1 cup all-purpose flour. In baking, do not mistakenly use sweet rice flour (waxy rice flour), 1017, which is a thickener or starch, not a flour.

ROLLED OATS

These are separate flakes formed by rolling toasted hulled whole oat kernels, or groats, and steaming them. The thinness of the flake determines whether they are regular or quick-cooking oats. Rolled oats are popular for adding flavor and texture to cookies. Steel-cut oats are made by passing the groats or kernels through special cutting machines. ➤ Substitute $1^1/_3$ cups rolled oats for 1 cup all-purpose flour. Or, to combine with wheat flour for breads, use ⅓ cup oats for each cup flour. To cook oats as a grain, see 366–367.

RYE FLOUR

In most rye bread recipes, white rye flour is combined with varying proportions of all-purpose flour or vital wheat gluten, 318, because rye flour proteins provide stickiness but lack gluten-forming proteins. Breads made largely with rye flour are moist and compact and usually call for a sourdough leavener, or, if using dry yeast, to mix the rye flour with all-purpose flour. ➤ Substitute 1¼ cups rye flour for 1 cup all-purpose flour. Medium rye flour is a darker rye flour than white because it contains more of the whole rye grain components.

RYE MEAL

Rye meal is coarsely ground whole-rye flour. ➤ Substitute 1 cup rye meal for 1 cup all-purpose flour. See Rye Flour, above.

SORGHUM FLOUR

Gluten free and ground from the large yellow or white grain of sorghum. Also called **milo maize,** this flour is often used to add flavor in gluten-free baking, and is used in addition to flour in cookies, cakes, and bread. Available from online retailers and in some supermarkets and most health food stores.

SOY FLOUR

Soy flour may be made from very lightly toasted soybeans or from raw soybeans. It has both a high protein and a high fat content. A low-fat version made of beans from which the fat has been largely expressed is also available. Because of the high fat content, soy flour is not mixed with the dry ingredients but is creamed with the shortening or blended with the liquids. Stir before measuring. You may substitute ➤ 2 tablespoons of soy flour for 2 tablespoons of the all-purpose flour in each cup of flour. But if you like the flavor, substitute it for up to 20 percent of the weight of the flour in the recipe. Soy flour causes heavy browning of the crust, so reduce baking temperatures by about 25°F.

SPELT FLOUR

Ground from an ancient grain, a cousin of wheat, spelt is not well tolerated by most individuals with gluten sensitivity because it contains gluten-forming proteins. It can be used interchangeably with wheat flour.

FLOURS, WHEAT

To understand wheat flour, we must first understand the wheat kernel. Most grains are similar in their structure to the wheat kernel sketched in enlarged cross section, 344. The outer, or bran, layers contain, with the germ—indicated by the darker swirl on the right—most of the grain's vitamins and minerals. The germ is only 2 percent of the entire kernel, but it contains the highest-grade protein and all of the fat. The endosperm is largely starch, with some protein—different from, but complementary to the protein of the germ. The outer coatings and the germ—small though they are compared with the whole kernel—are of unchallenged importance in content and irreplaceable in flavor.

Stone-ground flours contain the whole grain. These flours deteriorate faster because of the presence of the high-oil-content germ. Refined flours without the germ or bran will stay fresher longer. Try to buy quantities of flour you can use within 2 months. Store in a cool, dry place, and refrigerate whole-grain flours.

When water is added to wheat flour and stirred, two proteins occurring separately in the flour, glutenin and gliadin, interact with the water and each other to form elastic sheets of gluten. Wheat is the only grain that has substantial amounts of glutenin and gliadin. Gluten can never be developed except in the presence of moisture and when the dough or batter is worked or agitated, as in kneading. The more of these proteins a flour contains, the more water it absorbs.

If a recipe specifies cake flour or bread flour, the cook can simply use the appropriate flour and get reliable results, because the protein content of bread and cake flours are consistent. However, if a recipe calls for all-purpose flour, there can be considerable variables, as the protein content of all-purpose flours runs from 8-plus grams of protein per cup (8 percent) to 13 grams per cup (13 percent). Southern all-purpose flours are on the low end, 8 to 9 grams per cup, and have a protein content closer to cake flour, while New England and Canadian flours are on the high end, with about 13 grams, and have a protein content more like bread flour. National brands of all-purpose flour are in the middle, with about 12 grams of protein per cup. The grams per cup and the percent protein are frequently similar numbers but they are different measures of protein content.

Flour labels used to give the protein content in grams per cup. Unfortunately, the government changed the portion size to ¼ cup and applied a round-off rule. So, nearly every flour says 3 grams per ¼ cup, which means nothing. In actuality, all-purpose flour can run from about 9 grams per cup (8 to 9 percent) to about 14 grams per cup (12 to 14 percent).

Flours with a higher protein content make doughs and batters with more of the elastic gluten, which is ideal for the leavening of yeast. Yeast oozes out a liquid that releases carbon dioxide and alcohol into the air bubbles in the dough. This inflates the bubbles, making the batter or dough rise. The structure created by the gluten holds the released carbon dioxide and expands as more and more carbon dioxide is released. A flour with a high protein content is perfect for the gentle inflating action of yeast.

On the other hand, flours with a lower protein content are better for doughs and batters, such as for quick breads, cakes, pancakes, and biscuits, that contain the chemical leaveners baking powder or baking soda. These leaveners produce smaller, finer carbon dioxide bubbles. Strong doughs with a large amount of gluten hold down and interfere with the tiny bubbles created with chemical leavening. Baking powder and baking soda leavenings also work best with mixing procedures that aerate the fat.

If you **need a wheat-flour-allergy substitute,** keep this mixture on hand for use in gravies and some quick breads, pancakes, and biscuits. Sift together 6 times $^1\!/_2$ **cup cornstarch** and $^1\!/_2$ **cup of any of the following:** potato flour, soy flour, or rice flour. If you use this combination for baking, you will need to add **2 teaspoons baking powder** for each cup of the flour mixture. ➤ If using cornstarch or rice flour in baking, be sure to avoid waxy types.

ALL-PURPOSE FLOUR

All-purpose flour is typically milled from a blend of hard (higher-protein) and soft (lower-protein) wheat flours, but as mentioned above, the protein content of these flours can vary. The presence of more gluten-forming proteins in hard-wheat flours may result in a rather elastic and porous product. ➤ Bleached and unbleached all-purpose flour can be used interchangeably, but unbleached usually has a higher protein content than bleached flour.

Some labels indicate where the flour was milled. Northern or Canadian all-purpose flours generally have a higher protein content. When a yeast bread recipe calls for all-purpose flour, choose a brand of flour milled in the northern United States or Canada. Some of the all-purpose flours milled in the southern United States are closer to cake flour in texture and in protein content. When a recipe using chemical leavening calls for all-purpose flour, choose an all-purpose flour that is milled in the southern United States or a national brand of flour. These contain a lower-protein content. ➤ In most recipes you may substitute $1^1\!/_8$ cups plus 2 tablespoons cake flour for 1 cup of all-purpose flour.

Cooked grains may be ➤ substituted in some bread recipes for all-purpose flour in these proportions: 1 cup cooked cereal or grain for $^1\!/_4$ cup flour. But you must also cut the liquid in the recipe by 1 cup for each cup of cooked cereal used. To mix, stir the cooked cereal into the remaining liquid before combining with the other ingredients.

BRAN FLOUR

Ground from the bran portion of the kernel, bran flour often gives a dry result unless you soften the bran first, by allowing the wet bread mixture, minus the yeast or baking powder, to stand for 8 hours or so. Bran flours are usually mixed with some all-purpose flour and used to add fiber to bread.

BREAD FLOUR

Widely available, bread flour is highly desirable for bread making because of its high protein content; it is sometimes called "high-gluten" flour. The gluten-forming proteins give elasticity to dough and allow it to expand and hold the gas liberated by the yeast. Bread flour feels al-

most granular or gritty when rubbed between the fingers. Although the term is not technically correct, many bakers refer to high-protein or bread flour as "high-gluten" flour. Flour in actuality does not contain gluten. It contains two proteins, glutenin and gliadin, that form gluten when mixed with water and kneaded. For further discussion of the protein content of flour, see 985.

CAKE FLOUR

Cake flour, made from soft, lower-protein wheat, is more finely ground than all-purpose flour, and in the U.S. is chlorinated, which causes it to absorb more water and also aids in the distribution of the fat and the air bubbles for a finer-textured cake. Although you will not get the same result, in emergencies you may ➤ substitute 1 cup minus 2 tablespoons sifted all-purpose flour for 1 cup cake flour.

CRACKED WHEAT

When the wheat kernel is cut rather than ground, cracked wheat results. Because wheat milled in this fashion gives up little of its starch as a binder, it must be mixed with all-purpose or whole wheat flour when used in baking. It adds a nutty texture and crunch to bread doughs. Sometimes we prefer cooking it, 362, before adding it to the flour mixture.

FARINA

A creamy-colored, granular, protein-rich flour made from hard wheat other than durum, farina has had the bran and most of the germ removed. In this book it is used in Farina Balls, a type of dumpling, and is commonly eaten as a hot breakfast cereal.

INSTANT FLOUR

A specialty formulated granulated flour most often used for gravies and sauces, 544, instant flour readily dissolves into liquids without lumps. ➤ Instant flour should not be substituted for all-purpose flour, but it can be used in place of pastry flour.

PASTRY FLOUR

A soft, finely milled low-protein flour, pastry flour is similar to cake flour, although it is usually not chlorinated. Available from online retailers and in specialty markets, it is best used for pastries and quick breads. Whole wheat pastry flour is also available if you desire a soft, finely milled whole-grain flour. ➤ You may substitute $^2\!/_3$ cup all-purpose flour and $^1\!/_3$ cup cake flour for 1 cup pastry flour.

RYE FLOUR

See 985.

SELF-RISING FLOUR

Self-rising flour contains the correct amounts of leaveners and salt for baking. Many bakers do not like to use this type of flour because the leaveners may have lost potency. While most often used for quick breads, biscuits, and pancakes, self-rising flour is not recommended for pastries, as it results in a spongy, rather than flaky, texture. It is also not recommended for making bread, but if you must use it, omit the salt called for in the recipe. ➤ If a recipe calls for self-rising flour and you want to make your own, add 1½ teaspoons baking powder and ½ teaspoon salt per cup of all-purpose flour.

SEMOLINA
A creamy-colored, granular wheat flour used commercially for making dry pasta. Durum wheat is a high-protein wheat from which most semolina is ground, and produces superior pasta because of its high protein content. If homemade pastas and noodles fail to hold their shape no matter how carefully you have prepared and cooked them, the trouble probably lies in the lower protein content of the all-purpose flour most cooks use. Semolina is available from specialty markets and online retailers.

TRITICALE FLOUR
A nutritious sweet-tasting flour that comes from a hybrid of durum wheat, hard red winter wheat, and rye. Although the flour is higher in protein than all-purpose wheat flour, it is low in gluten-forming proteins and so should be mixed with higher-protein flours for bread making. Use the grain as sprouts, 1011, or cook as for Rye Flour, see 985.

VITAL WHEAT GLUTEN OR GLUTEN FLOUR
This is a starch-free high-protein flour made by washing the starch from hard wheat flour. The residue is then dried and ground. It may contain up to 50 grams protein per cup and is used as an additive in bread. See Breads, 591. Vital wheat gluten can be added to other flours that are lower in gluten-forming proteins such as rye, soy, and rice to produce a better-leavened loaf.

WHEAT GERM
Wheat germ adds flavor, texture, and fiber to doughs. It must be refrigerated after opening. You may ➤ substitute ⅓ cup wheat germ and ⅔ cup all-purpose flour for 1 cup of the all-purpose flour in a recipe. For flavor, wheat germ is best very slightly toasted before combining it with the dough. It is now available toasted or untoasted.

WHOLE WHEAT OR WHOLE-GRAIN FLOUR
Whole wheat flour retains the bran and germ and thus the original vitamins, mineral salts, and fats of the whole wheat kernel. Whether coarsely or finely milled, the entire wheat kernel is ground to create this flour. ➤ You may substitute 1 cup very finely milled whole wheat flour for 1 cup all-purpose flour. If using coarsely ground whole wheat flour, substitute 1 cup plus 2 tablespoons for 1 cup of all-purpose flour. This should be stirred lightly rather than sifted before measuring. Bread made with 100 percent whole wheat flour can be very heavy because the gluten-forming capacity of the wheat is reduced due to the presence of bran and germ. To remedy this, use a mixture of whole wheat flour and bread flour, or use 1 or 2 tablespoons of vital wheat gluten, left, per 1 cup of whole wheat flour, or consider using whole wheat pastry flour, a lower protein wheat flour that contains the germ and the bran portion of the wheat kernels, to produce a well-leavened loaf.

GALANGAL
Related to ginger, galangals come in two forms. The large rhizome, **greater galangal,** looks like pale yellow ginger etched with thin crosswise stripes. In Thailand, its hot, ginger-pepper, sour flavor is preferred to that of ginger. The texture is woody; pieces are thinly sliced (to be left, uneaten, on the plate) or finely pounded or grated for use in cooking. Select and store as for Ginger, 988. **Lesser galangal** is a smaller rhizome with orange-red flesh and a stronger flavor. It is an ingredient in some bitters, liqueurs, and beers; in China, lesser galangal infusions are used medicinally. It is rarely available fresh.

GARAM MASALA
About 1 cup
This is a traditional all-purpose spice blend characterizing the flavor of Indian dishes, including tandoori food.
Put in a heavy plastic bag and smash with a rolling pin until lightly crushed:
   ½ **cup green or black cardamom pods**
Break open the pods and pull out the tiny seeds. Discard the pods and combine the seeds with:
   ⅓ **cup whole cloves**
   Scant ¼ cup cumin seeds
   Scant ¼ cup black peppercorns
   5 hefty (about ⅓ inch thick) cinnamon sticks
Grind the mixture to a powder in batches in a spice mill or coffee grinder. Store in an airtight container in a cool place.

GARLIC
See Onions, 1003.

GELATIN
Gelatin is full of tricks. It can turn liquids into solids to produce gala dessert and salad molds. It makes sophisticated meringues and mousses and the simple marshmallow. It gives a smoother texture to frozen desserts, cheesecakes, chiffon pies, jellies, and cold soups, and it thickens cold sauces and glazes. In sponge and whipped desserts, it doubles the volume.

Gelatin is extracted from the bones, skin, hooves, and body tissues of animals, yielding a protein-rich but flavorless and colorless substance. To get the most nourishment out of gelatin, add nuts, fruit, meat, fish, or milk to enrich its nutritional value. To get the most allure, ➤ never use too much, because the result will be rubbery and unpleasant. Finished gelatin should be quivery, not rigid, when jostled. It is compatible with almost all foods ➤ except fresh or frozen pineapple, papaya, peaches, kiwi, figs, honeydew, mango, and ginger. All these contain enzymes that break down gelatin, and inhibit jelling. To use one of these fruits in gelatin, cook it or use canned fruit, for precooking the fruit kills the enzymes.

Gelatin dishes must, of course, be refrigerated until ready to use. And, when served for a buffet, they are best presented on chilled trays. While gelatin must be kept cold, it should ➤ never be frozen unless the fat content of the recipe is very high—as in certain ice creams.

Gelatin's power to displace moisture is due to its strength, or "bloom." In household gelatins this is rated at 150 and means that the contents of 1 envelope or packet of unflavored gelatin, or $2\frac{1}{4}$ teaspoons, can set about 2 cups of liquid. Gelatin is sold ready to use in packets of granules, but it also comes in sheets, called leaf or sheet gelatin. For equivalents, see 1041. The most delicate fish and meat aspics are made with stocks, which naturally contain gelatin, because they are made from bones, skin, and fish heads.

High sugar concentrations and boiling retard gelatinization and reduce its setting power. Unless a recipe is exceedingly acid, 1 envelope ($2\frac{1}{4}$ teaspoons) of gelatin to 2 cups of liquid should produce a consistency firm enough to unmold after 2 hours of chilling—if the gelatin is a clear one. But if the gelatin has fruits, vegetables, herbs, cream, sour cream, or nuts added to it, it will need 4 hours of chilling. Also, allow proportionately more jelling time for large molds, as opposed to individual batches. If you prefer a less firm texture, use 1 envelope ($2\frac{1}{4}$ teaspoons) of gelatin and $2\frac{1}{4}$ to $2\frac{1}{2}$ cups liquid. These gelatins will not mold but are delightful when served in cups as individual portions. If you are ➤ doubling a gelatin recipe that calls for 2 cups of liquid, use only $3\frac{3}{4}$ cups in the doubled recipe.

For basic gelatin aspic recipes, see 174. For Gelatin Desserts, see 810.

MIXING GELATIN

I. Sprinkle 1 envelope ($2\frac{1}{4}$ teaspoons) gelatin over $\frac{1}{4}$ cup cold water and, ➤ without stirring, let it soak about 5 minutes until it has absorbed the water and is translucent. Bring $1\frac{3}{4}$ to 2 cups stock, fruit juice, milk, wine, or water just to a boil, combine with the soaked gelatin, and stir until dissolved.

Cool the gelatin over a bowl of cracked ice or in the refrigerator—but not in the freezer, as a gummy look is apt to develop, and the surface will crack miserably. It is interesting that gelatins that are slow to jell are also slow to break down when they are removed from the refrigerator, but any gelatin will begin to weep if exposed too long to high temperatures.

II. If you do not want to subject the liquid in the recipe to high heat or reduce its flavor, use a double boiler: Sprinkle 1 envelope ($2\frac{1}{4}$ teaspoons) gelatin over $\frac{1}{4}$ cup cold water, let it soak, and then dissolve ➤ over, not in, boiling water. Add $1\frac{3}{4}$ to 2 cups room-temperature liquid to the dissolved gelatin and stir well.

III. If you are in a hurry and are making a gelatin that calls for 1 cup water and 1 cup stock or fruit juice, you can prepare the gelatin as in I above, boiling the cup of stock or fruit juice and then stirring about 8 large or 10 small ice cubes into the hot liquid to cool it. Stir the cubes constantly for 2 to 3 minutes, then remove the unmelted ice. Let the mixture stand 3 to 5 minutes. Incorporate the fruit or other solids called for, and pour into the mold.

IV. For an even faster gelatin with frozen fruits, see Fruit Whip, 813.

GERANIUMS

Sweet-scented many-flavored geranium leaves are used in pound cake, jellies, and compotes, or, for added elegance in formal entertaining, floated in finger bowls. Use a lime-scented leaf in custards or an apple-flavored one in baked apples. For lime flavor, try *Pelargonium nervosum;* for apple, *P. odoratissimum;* for mint, *P. tomentosum;* and for rose, *P. graveolens.* These geraniums are tender but grow well in pots under ordinary household conditions.

GINGER

The rhizome of the bold perennial *Zingiber officinale*—with the most heavenly scented lily—must be harvested at just the right time, or it becomes woody and fibrous. Whole fresh ginger should have smooth skin and be a uniformly buff color. Select firm, heavy pieces. If fresh and firm, ginger will keep for about a week on the counter; refrigerated in a plastic bag, it will keep about 3 weeks. Or you may wash fresh ginger, cover it with sherry, and keep refrigerated. It really tastes best sliced thin and sautéed in oil to extract the flavor. To use in recipes, peel, grate, slice, or mash. Ginger is easily peeled with a vegetable peeler, or even by scraping off the skin with the edge of a spoon. Thinly sliced ginger can be added to stews or rubbed like garlic over poultry or fish. Do not use fresh ginger in gelatin salads; it wrecks the jelling capacity of gelatin.

Dried ginger be cut into $\frac{1}{2}$-inch cubes and steeped for several hours in a marinade or in cold water, after which the liquid can be used as seasoning. Dried ginger is available from spice retailers and online sources. Boiled and preserved in syrup, it becomes **stem ginger,** a milder form that is delicious in desserts, chopped fine and used with or without its syrup; it is worth trying with bananas, tomatoes, squash, onions and sweet potatoes. **Pickled ginger,** 952, thinly sliced fresh ginger preserved in seasoned rice vinegar, is used as a condiment or side dish, most freqently with sushi. It is sold both dyed pink and in its natural buff color. **Candied ginger,** 884, may be used in baked goods and desserts. This form can, in a pinch, be washed of its sugar and substituted for fresh ginger. We all know the value of dried ground ginger for flavoring baked items. ➤ Equivalent flavoring strengths of the various forms are:

½ teaspoon ground equals 1 to 2 teaspoons thinly sliced preserved equals 2 tablespoons syrup.

GOLDEN SYRUP AND TREACLE

A residual molasses, golden syrup, sometimes called **refiner's syrup**, is clarified and decolorized, which makes it mild in flavor. It can be used as a topping for ice cream, pancakes, waffles, or breads, or as a sweetener for a variety of baked goods. ➤ Substitute cup for cup for corn syrup. Treacle (a British term for molasses) is a darker and heavier residual molasses than golden syrup. Neither can be substituted for molasses.

GRAINS OF PARADISE

Also known as Guinea pepper, melegueta pepper, and alligator pepper, grains of paradise are spicy, warm, and a little on the bitter side, with a zesty flavor reminiscent of pepper, coriander, and cardamom. Terrific on vegetables, and a good substitute for black pepper. The seeds not only are used to flavor food, but can be chewed on cold days to warm the body. *Aframomum melegueta* produces a poppylike pods that each contain about 50 of the cube-shaped seeds. Try adding it to Middle Eastern lamb or eggplant dishes.

GREMOLATA

3 tablespoons
A mixture of seasonings used for osso buco, sauces, pan gravies, and roasted or grilled meats.
Mix:
    2 tablespoons finely chopped parsley
    2 garlic cloves, minced
    2 teaspoons grated lemon zest
Sprinkle this mixture on during the last 5 minutes of cooking.

GUM TRAGACANTH

Gum tragacanth is used in some icings for pliability and in commercially prepared salad dressings to add body. Use from 1 to 4 grams of powder for each cup liquid, depending on the thickness desired.

HARISSA

The familiar red sauce of Moroccan cooking, harissa is made from a blend of chile peppers, garlic, and olive oil. Commonly served with couscous, harissa is often passed at the table as a seasoning. Available in ethnic or specialty markets; or, for a homemade version, see 569.

HAZELNUTS AND FILBERTS

Hazelnuts have a distinctive, somewhat perfumed sophisticated flavor, which pairs particularly well with chocolate. Filberts are the cultivated versions of our native hazelnuts.

HERBS

Confucius refused to eat anything not in season. Anyone who has tasted the difference between foods flavored with fresh rather than dried herbs knows how wise he was. Fresh herbs cannot always be bought at the market but most can be easily grown. For more information on specific herbs, see individual entries.

CHIFFONADE OF FRESH HERBS

A chiffonade is a thin ribbon cut of herb, used to season or garnish food. Chiffonade works beautifully with most broad or long-leafed herbs, especially chives, basil, and flat-leaf parsley. One of our very favorite ways to brighten up a bowl of soup or season a grilled fish fillet or fresh tomato salad is to use a freshly gathered or store-bought bouquet of tender herbs, which we chiffonade and use liberally. See also Chiffonade of Herbs for Soup, 150, and the technique for cutting chiffonade, 1071.

GROWING CULINARY HERBS

We encourage you to exercise your green thumb at least on those herbs whose oils deteriorate or almost disappear in drying: Chervil, borage, burnet, and summer savory suffer the greatest losses. And the mainstays—cilantro, chives, tarragon, parsley, and basil—can never in their dry form begin to approach the quality of their fresh counterparts. Even the flavor of fresh sage, when discreetly used, is much more delicate, complementary, and interesting.

You might like to duplicate the sequences of plantings shown on 990: In the end section is sage, followed by tarragon, parsley, dwarf basil, and thyme, all partitioned by chives. Or you may prefer partitions of clipped lavender or fernlike burnet, which, with the sage and thyme end sections, will give your garden in winter an indication of form. We have tried growing herbs in many patterns. Since most herbs are sun lovers, need air, and dislike competition, bed layouts such as those shown at center and below it suit them well.

Proper and good drainage, whether secured by boxing or simply by the selection of terraced ground, is a primary consideration in herb growing. The upper and lower sketches show raised beds, the upper crescent-shaped held high by old granite street cobbles, the lower by flue liners, which also provide containment for rampant aggressors like the mints. Shown in the partially sunken flue liners are squares of mints, calendulas, and nasturtiums and a combination of chives and parsley—all edible yet colorful. You might also try other annual or deciduous squares, or use alternate evergreen and deciduous herbs, again to allow for some winter form. Try placing the liners in Greek fret designs or any pattern that adapts to your space.

You may prefer to use squared beds. A 15- to 24-inch square area for each of most culinary herbs is more than enough to supply a busy kitchen. Sometimes, if we want only a single specimen—for instance, a sage or a lavender—we keep it pruned to a central shrub and use the edges around it for smaller plants. And sometimes we repeat a color accent—like the gray of sage or lavender—to unify the whole complex of squares. A more elegant so-

Mom's culinary herb garden at Cockaigne in the early 1970s

lution is to use millstones or other large round stones, which also reflect the heat most herbs thrive on and which make ideal access points for the gardener to weed from. A millstone also gives the surrounding herbs freedom to spread over its edges, as well as over the flat stones that define the bed. Here in the centers are a pot of rosemary and a dwarf pepper plant, although a cherry tomato plant on a trellis would give more height to the layout. Chamomiles and thymes are shown as bordering plants, but any of the dwarf creepers, like dwarf savories, could be used. Also to be considered, though not for patterned beds, are the unruly tousle-headed giants, the dills; the

fennels, lovage, and sorrel; the floppy borage and scraggly corianders; and anises, sesames, and mustards. If these mavericks are grown in unregimented fashion, borage, dill, fennel, chervil, coriander, and parsley will self-sow. These all have less stability of condition, as well as of structure, and will profit by a background of fencing or a south-facing house wall, which not only protects but lends unity to the plantings. These plants are always problems for the neat-minded, as are the treasured onion family, shown on 1003 and 1005, for with the exception of chives, they die back and yellow after ripening.

If you haven't room for the extended layouts shown on

990, try setting out a few pots of annuals on your patio. Some evergreen perennials will weather the winter in a strawberry jar or pot. To prepare a jar for herbs, fill with a mixture of one-third rich, friable soil and two-thirds sand. Try the thymes, sweet marjoram, burnet, and chervil on the shady side. You can dwarf fennel, borage, and sage by root confinement. Replace the coarse marjorams with the healing herb dittany of Crete, and replace coarse mints with the tiny Corsican mint or *Mentha requienii*—both tender perennials.

Pots can be used, too, for growing herbs indoors in sunny windows. We have had moderate success with rosemary, sweet marjoram, the basils, chives, the thymes, lemon verbena, and scented geranium—all from late-summer cuttings—and with dill and bronze fennel from seed. If you plan on bringing plants indoors, pot them up in late August and put them in a partially shaded area. Bring them in before frost. Tarragon dug after cold-weather dormancy and potted up indoors may show 6 inches of green within 10 days. A small potted sweet bay is both decorative and useful. ➤ But most houseplant herbs deteriorate in flavor, just as hothouse tomatoes do.

We find that the various thymes, pot marjoram, and winter savories flourish in a rock garden. Treat them with neglect, and reap them for 20 years. But we also find that in areas of the U.S. with hot summers and variable winters, sage, burnet, and tarragon are more apt to hold over in well-enriched garden soil. Most perennial herbs also hold over better if they have been clipped to about two-thirds their height several times during the season prior to early August. If they are creepers like thymes, bob them back at the base as well. Follow each clipping with a dose of liquid manure or other fertilizer. If the herbs are evergreen varieties, treat them to a thorough watering prior to the first killing frosts.

HARVESTING, DRYING, AND FREEZING HERBS AND SPICES

Our instinctive inclination toward the cultivation and use of herbs and our longing for a year-round supply put us in good company across the centuries: Alcuin, Charlemagne's tutor, called herbs "the friends of physicians and the praise of cooks." Which brings us to the matters of harvesting, drying, and freezing of herbs—processes to adopt to keep your kitchen in steady supply.

The first rule of harvesting herbs is to clip constantly through July; never allow the plants to reach the blossoming stage. Later heavy clipping may weaken perennials such as thyme, oregano, and marjoram—not allowing recovery of the plant before winter. Unless otherwise indicated in the individual notes on cultivation, herbs should be harvested ➤ just before their flowers emerge. At this time, when they are budding up, the leaves are at their most aromatic. Herbs are remarkably free from insect pests and should be grown where they will not be sprayed. Nonetheless, to rinse the herbs of any dirt, gently spray them with water the day before harvesting. Pick

early the next morning, as soon as the dew on the leaves has dried. If necessary, pat the leaves dry, taking care not to bruise the delicate foliage.

Because most fresh herbs are perishable, careful storage is crucial. Store bunches in the refrigerator, their stems in water, if possible. Pack loose leaves and flowers in plastic bags in the refrigerator crisper. If there is excess moisture in the leaves, lay a dry paper towel in the bag and place the leaves on top. A little moisture helps keep plant parts fresh, but too much promotes decay.

Fresh leaves and seeds that have good flavor after drying include anise seeds, sweet basil, bay laurel, caraway seeds, celery seeds, dill seeds, fennel seeds, juniper berries, marjoram, mint, mustard seeds, oregano, poppy seeds, rosemary, sage, summer savory, tarragon, and thyme. After gathering herbs, you may tie them together in skimpy bunches with cotton string and hang upside down in small bunches until dry. Alternatively, place each bunch upside down inside a large paper bag well punctured with air holes. Tie the neck of the bag tight and hang the bag, with the leaves facing down, in a warm, airy place. The bag keeps light from degrading the leaves and flowers and catches any seeds that pop. You can expect about 1 pound dry herbs for every 8 pounds freshly gathered. The location traditionally recommended is a cool, airy attic or a shady breezeway. Or room-dry herbs, at temperatures preferably below 90°F. This is preferable to oven-drying, for even when the oven is preheated as low as possible and the herbs inserted the moment the temperature drops below 90°F, their flavor is weakened. And for thick-leaved varieties, the oven process may have to be repeated several times until the herbs are bone-dry.

To ➤ test for dryness before packaging, put a few of the brittle sprigs or leaves in a tightly sealed glass jar and watch for condensation, mold development, or discoloration. This is especially important with basil. ➤ Store dried herbs and spices in tightly closed glass jars in a cool, dark, dry place. Should they show signs of visible insect activity, discard them.

You may want to strip the leaves from the stems before drying or freezing herbs. If drying seeds, collect them in paper, rather than plastic, bags, and let them dry thoroughly before packing in glass jars. ➤ Dried herbs retain their flavor best if pulverized with a mortar and pestle, below, just before using. To grind and toast spices, see 1016.

Mortar and pestle, and mezzaluna

You may also freeze herbs. If you do, use them before defrosting—in the same proportion as for fresh herbs. They are too limp for garnishes. Some herbs, like chives, get slimy when frozen, ➤ so to freeze chives, first par-blanch, 1054, for 10 seconds, plunge into ice water for 1 minute, and dry between towels. Freeze herbs individually in recipe-sized packets for seasoning a salad dressing or a batch of stew, or freeze mixed Bouquets Garnis, 960, for soups and sauces. You can freeze leafy herbs such as basil and parsley by mincing washed herbs, and packing into ice cube trays, and filling the spaces with water. Freeze, then pop out the cubes and store in airtight freezer containers. To use, drop the frozen cubes of herbs into soups or stews.

To preserve herbs by salting, see 1009. The herbs and the salt, which will have become savory, will be ready to use within 2 weeks. To make basil oil, see 590.

USING HERBS

Handy as an herb chart might seem, we have refrained from compiling one, because some herbs are overpowering, and it is difficult to indicate in a general way the amounts to use. Suitable quantities of herbs are given in the individual recipes. Let us add that the delicately flavored herbs should be placed in sauces and soups only toward the end of preparation . And, once again, ➤ keep in mind that there are times when a large measurement of herbs can transform a dish.

Below we set down detailed characteristics and helpful horticultural tips for each culinary herb. Some of these readily grown herbs yield an edible seed that is also used in cooking—dill, 976, coriander, 972, and fennel, 982, for example. While these seeds are technically spices, we include them here because of how readily these plants can be grown in an herb garden.

To familiarize yourself with herb flavors, some "lazy day," when you feel experimental, blend 8 ounces grated mild Cheddar with 2 tablespoons sour cream and 2 tablespoons vodka. The vodka, although it can be an optional ingredient, will dissolve unique components of the herbs' flavor into the spread. Divide the mixture into small portions and add to each an herb or herb combination. Label the cheese samples as you mix them. Let them rest for about an hour to develop flavor. Then have a tasting party with your spouse or friends.

To substitute dried herbs for fresh, use $^1/_3$ teaspoon powdered or 1 teaspoon crushed for every tablespoon chopped fresh herbs. ➤ To reconstitute dried herbs and develop their flavors, soak them in some liquid you can incorporate in the recipe—water, stock, milk, lemon juice, wine, olive oil, or vinegar—for 10 minutes to one hour before using. Or simmer them in butter. In cooking, place nonpowdered dry herbs in a cheesecloth bag or a metal tea ball for subsequent easy removal. For herb blends, see 1009.

HERBES DE PROVENCE
See Lavender, 993.

HICKORY NUTS AND BUTTERNUTS
Hickory and butternuts are rich native American nuts, like pecans. They never need blanching.

HOISIN SAUCE
This dark, thick Chinese sauce is made from soybeans and is almost always sweet, garlicky, and spicy. It has the anise flavor of five-spice powder and is peppered with a little dried chile. Once opened, store in the refrigerator.

HONEY
Humanity owes bees a debt of considerable gratitude for providing us with honey for thousands of years. We know hundreds of varieties of this wonderful sweetener, and there are probably many more. Most honey is named after the principal nectar source and the varying flavors it provides: thyme, tupelo, and orange blossom, to name just a few. Different honeys are easily distinguished from one another, but those from the same type of plant can taste markedly different when the plant is grown on different soils and in different climates. Honeys range in color from almost white to amber to dark brown. As a rule of thumb, the lighter the color, the milder the flavor. This valuable ingredient has long been treasured because of its preservative qualities owing to its high sugar content and an antimold enzyme. It is cherished by cooks for the chewy texture and the browner color it gives to cakes, cookies, and bread doughs. It is composed chiefly of fructose and glucose.

Honey is both mass-produced and available from small or artisanal producers. It is sold in two basic forms: comb and extracted. Extracted honey may be found in liquid or cream (crystallized) form, and the latter may be labeled "creamed," "candied," "fondant," "spun," or "spread."

When cooking with honey, warm the honey or add it to the other liquids called for to make mixing more uniform. To measure honey, oil the measuring cup or spoon so the honey will slip out easily; or measure the shortening first, then the honey in the same measuring cup.

As honey has greater sweetening power than sugar, we prefer to substitute 1 cup honey for $1^1/_4$ cups sugar and to reduce the liquid in the recipe by $^1/_4$ cup. Too much honey in a recipe may cause too brown a product. To neutralize the acidity of honey—unless buttermilk, yogurt, or sour cream is called for in the recipe—add a mere pinch of baking soda. If honey is substituted in jams, jellies, or candies, a higher temperature must be used in cooking. For candies, more persistent beating is needed and careful storage required against absorption of atmospheric moisture.

Honey is best stored covered in a dry place at room temperature. If it becomes crystallized, it can easily be reliquified by setting the opened jar in a pan of ➤ warm water until the crystals are melted or by heating the honey in a microwave oven on low power. ➤ Children under a year old should not be given honey, as it is a suspected source of infant botulism.

HOREHOUND

The woolly leaves of the horehound plant, more licoricey than licorice, are made into an extract that is combined with sugar into an old-fashioned candy. *Marrubium vulgare,* a perennial that grows to 3 feet, flourishes in poor soil.

HORSERADISH

Horseradish is a long cream-colored tapered root. Along with coriander, nettle, horehound, and lettuce, it is one of the five bitter herbs of Passover seders. As the flavor can be overpowering, like very strong radishes, use sparingly. Use it fresh for best flavor. To prevent it from darkening, grate the peeled fresh root into lemon juice or cider vinegar. The ground dried form must be ➤ reconstituted no more than 30 minutes before serving, for once the powder is mixed, its volatile oils are dissipated. To prepare the dried ground root in an excellent sauce for cold beef, soak 1 tablespoon dried horseradish in 2 tablespoons of water and add $1/2$ cup heavy cream. Dried horseradish is also used to make powdered wasabi, 1026. Whether fresh, reconstituted, or jarred—in this book the term for the latter is "prepared horseradish"—use all horseradish promptly to avoid loss of volatile oils and development of intense bitterness. Horseradish is prized for use with Boiled Beef, 478, Baked Ham, 507, pot-au-feu, 136, roast beef, 470, and other rich meats; in cocktail sauces and potato salad; and with cold meats, fish, and shellfish.

To prepare fresh horseradish sauce, place about 1 pound diced peeled horseradish in a food processor. Process until finely chopped, then pour in cider vinegar until the mixture is of a spreadable consistency. Add salt and a few tablespoons sugar, to taste. This keeps several months in the refrigerator. When the root is not in season (early spring), prepared horseradish sauce can be found in the grocery deli or dairy case. *Armoracia rusticana,* a perennial growing to 2 feet, is propagated from pieces of root and demands rich, moist soil. You may store roots in moist sand for winter use. See Wasabi, 1026.

HYSSOP

The leaves of this minty, spicy, somewhat bitter herb are used sparingly in salads and with fruits. The dried flowers are used in soups and herbal teas or tisanes, 35. *Hyssopus officinalis,* a perennial that grows to 2 feet, prefers dry, calcareous soil. It looks like a small rosemary plant with soft green leaves.

JUNIPER BERRIES

The berries from *Juniperus communis* are prized for seasoning game, meat, cabbage, and bean dishes. Three to 6 berries per serving suffice. In fact, $1/2$ teaspoon of these berries soaked for several hours in a marinade—or cooked long in a stew—gives a flavoring equivalent to $1/4$ cup gin, to which these berries lend their aroma. If not available, a splash of gin is a good substitute.

LARD

Lard, which is rendered pork fat, is softer, sweeter, and oilier than butter, margarine, and other solid shortenings. **Leaf lard** is a superior type. It comes from the layered fat around the kidneys, rather than from trimmings and incidental fatty areas. Due to the more crystalline structure of this lard, it can be cut into flour to create a wonderfully flaky texture in biscuits and pastry crusts, although this same crystalline character handicaps it for cake baking. Lard sold in bulk or package form has been bleached, hydrogenated, refined, and/or emulsified. ➤ All lards should be stored covered preferably in the refrigerator. Pure lard (99 percent fat) is highly valued as a cooking oil because it has a high smoke point. Because of the low turnover in some stores, it may be difficult to find fresh lard. Ethnic markets can be a good choice. To ➤ substitute lard for butter in cooking and baking, use 15 percent to 20 percent less lard than butter.

LAVENDER

The leaves and flowers of this highly aromatic plant give a bitter pungency to salads. We use lavender most often as a sachet, but it is used in increasingly inventive ways as a seasoning, particularly in the classic mixture **Herbes de Provence,** where lavender is mixed with thyme, rosemary, basil, savory, marjoram, and fennel. Blossoms of varieties of *Lavandula dentate, L. angustifolia,* and *L. stoechas* are used in chutneys, confections, sauces, and as a garnish. Its grayness lends a lovely accent to the herb garden. Grown from cuttings or seed, *L. vera,* a perennial growing to 4 feet, prefers dry lime soil and a warm climate.

LEAVENERS

We are all so accustomed to light breads and cakes that we seldom question how they got that way or the part that leaveners play.

Where does this rising power lie? First, in any baking, the steam converted from the moisture in the batter or dough may account for 30 to 80 percent of the expansion of that batter or dough. The greater amount is characteristic of popovers, 637, and cakes rich in egg white. To encourage the generation of this easily lost asset, ➤ always preheat the oven.

We usually think of leaveners as baking powders, 958, baking soda, 959, and yeast, 1028 all of which form a gas that becomes a major force in rising. We tend to forget the importance of the mechanical incorporation of air from which rising power also comes. To give a boost to the chemical reactions, be sure you know how to cream fat and sugar, 700; how to fold and mix batters, 700; how to beat eggs, 978; and, especially, how to beat egg whites to that state called "stiff but not dry," 978.

LEEKS

See Onions, 1002.

LEFTOVERS

The minister's bride set her luncheon casserole down with a flourish and waited for grace. "It seems to me," murmured her husband, "that I have blessed a good deal of this material before."

Leftovers can, of course, stand for simple repetition, but they can also stimulate a cook's ingenuity. For our part, we feel positively blessed when we have a tidy store of them garnered away in the refrigerator. So often they give a needed fillip to a dish we are making from scratch. Sometimes they combine to make a vegetable soufflé or to dress up an omelet. And how often they turn a can of soup into a real delicacy!

One secret we have learned is to limit the number of leftover ingredients we are working with so that they retain some semblance of identity. If there is too much of a mishmash, the flavors simply cancel each other out—as well as the appetite.

Another secret is to watch leftovers for color. Freshen them up by presenting them with the more positive accents of tomatoes or bright greens, or with a color-contrasting sauce.

Still another secret is to be careful that you create some contrast in texture. When leftover mixtures are soft, contrast can be achieved by adding minced celery or peppers, nuts, water chestnuts, crisp bacon, or herbs.

Consult the Index under the category you wish to use, or try one of the following suggestions:

See About Uses for Ready-Baked and Leftover Breads, Cakes, and Crackers, 641. Also see About Crumbs, 960, and About Bread Stuffing, 532.

For ways to use cooked grains and pastas, see About Pasta Salads, 171, About Grain and Rice Salads, 171, or About Garnishes for Soups, 150. Also see About Croquettes, 659, and Frittatas, 202.

See About Stocks, 114, and About Poultry and Meat Soups, 134, for uses of bones, and for meat, fowl, fish, and vegetable trimmings.

For cooked meat, fish, and vegetable leftovers, see Brunch, Lunch, and Supper Dishes, 95, mousses, soufflés, timbales, meat pies; Cases for Food, 111; and About Stuffed Vegetables, 244.

For cooked potatoes, use in Shepherd's Pie, 102, or see About Leftover Potatoes, 300.

Use leftover gravies and savory sauces with vegetables, pastas, meats, hot sandwiches, and About Hash, 107.

For cheese, see Soufflés, Timbales, Sauces, and Au Gratin, 961.

For egg yolks, see About Sponge Cakes, 706, Eight-Yolk Gold Cake, 715, salad dressings, custards. Use hard-cooked yolks in sauces or riced as a garnish for creamed spinach, 305, or as insulation for piecrust, 663.

For egg whites, see Angel and White Cakes, 705 and 711; meringues of all kinds; Fruit Whip, 813; hot and cold dessert soufflés, 808; icings, 784; and for breading, 961, and Eggs in a Nest, 199.

For citrus peels, see Candies and Confections, 854, and zest, 971.

For buttermilk, see About Soup, 122, and Sour Milks and Creams, 101.

For fruit juices, see fruit drinks or gelatins. Or use as the liquid in cakes and custards, for basting meat, for sauces, or for fruit salad dressings.

For leftover coffee, see About Coffee Drinks, 32, and mocha desserts and dessert sauces.

LEMON BALM

Use the lemony leaves for herbal tea or tisane or as a garnish in fruit punch or fruit soups and fruit salads. *Melissa officinalis,* a perennial that reaches $2^1/_2$ feet, grows in sun in any soil.

LEMONGRASS

Lemongrass is a staple in Southeast Asian cooking. Sold dried or fresh in Asian markets and some supermarkets, the gray-green stalks are nearly 2 feet in length and resembles a fibrous scallion. In cooking it is valued for the flavor it imparts rather than the substance it adds. Only the bulblike 6- to 8-inch base is used. After trimming off the top, peel away the layer of tough outer leaves, revealing the inner "heart." Not as exotic as one might think, *Cymbopogon citratus* is a thrill to grow. The plant grows to about 2 to 3 feet around and 6 feet tall, and it thrives in sunshine and moisture.

LEMON VERBENA

With its very strong lemon flavor and aroma, some feel lemon verbena is better reserved for sachets or closets than for food. However, we find small amounts desirable as a lemon substitute in drinks and herbal teas or tisanes. *Aloysia triphylla* is a tender perennial growing to 5 feet; it does well in pots.

LILY BUDS

Also known as golden needles and tiger lilies, dried lily buds are the unopened flowers of day lilies. Hot-and-Sour Soup, 131, features lily buds. When purchasing lily buds, look for ones that are pale in color and not brittle. Store them in a jar in a cool, dry place. Before using, you may need to cut off about a quarter inch at the bottom to get rid of the woody stem. Soak in warm water before use.

LOVAGE

The leaves of this bold herb, whose stems can be candied like angelica, 958, or blanched and eaten like celery, are often used as a celery substitute with stews, tomato sauces, poultry, and stuffings. The seeds are sometimes pickled like capers. *Levisticum officinale,* a perennial that grows to 8 feet, is not particular as to soil; it is best divided in the spring.

MACADAMIA NUTS

Use macadamias, exotic, nutritious, larger-than-most, 1-inch-round nuts roasted or unroasted, in recipes calling for nuts, or as cocktail snacks or substitutes for water chestnuts. Their very hard shells and proneness to rancidity means most are sold shelled, in vacuum-packed cans or bottles. If found in the shell, to crack, try wrapping each one in heavy cloth and hammering it on a very hard surface. **To roast,** spread the shelled nuts in a shallow pan and heat in a 250°F oven 12 to 15 minutes, stirring often. Salt lightly and store refrigerated in an airtight container.

MACE

See Nutmeg and Mace, 1000.

MALT SYRUP

This is a liquid sweetener made from sprouted barley. It is dark brown in color and thick and sticky in consistency, like molasses. Sometimes called barley malt syrup, it may contain rice syrup or corn malt in addition to the barley malt. It has a mild sweet flavor and is frequently used in breads and desserts.

MAPLE SYRUP

By law pure maple syrup must weigh not less than 11 pounds to the gallon. The syrup is largely sucrose with some invert sugar. U.S. grades of maple syrup are: AA or Fancy is light in color, with the mildest flavor; Grade A is amber in color and mellow in flavor; Grade B has a hearty maple flavor and is darker in color than Grade A. Grade C is molasses-like, dark and strong.

Although it is often stored at room temperature, maple syrup is best stored in the refrigerator after opening, to inhibit mold growth. If mold develops, discard the syrup. Should the syrup crystallize, set the container in hot water; the syrup will quickly become liquid and smooth again.

To substitute maple syrup for sugar in cooking, generally use only ¾ cup for each cup of sugar. ➤ To substitute the syrup for sugar in baking, use the same proportions, but reduce the other liquid called for by about 3 tablespoons for every cup of syrup substituted. One pint of maple syrup has the same sweetening power as 1 pound of maple sugar.

Maple-flavored syrups contain a small amount of pure maple syrup but are primarily an inexpensive syrup such as corn syrup. They are less expensive than pure maple syrup, but it is best not to substitute them for pure maple syrup in cooking or baking. They are for topping pancakes and waffles. **Pancake syrup** is artificially flavored and colored corn syrup.

Maple, that choicest of all syrups, is yours for the taking, with no harm to the trees that produce it. Collecting, however, is simpler than processing, for you will get only about 1 part syrup from about 40 to 50 parts of sap. The sugar maple, *Acer saccharum,* gives the sweetest sap. The best months are late February, March, and early April, when night temperatures are around 20°F and daytime around 45°F. Trees with a diameter of 12 to 18 inches can be hung with one bucket; above 18 inches, use two buckets. The taps can be on any area of the trunk from 2 to 5 feet above the ground; if made late in the season, they should be on the north-facing side of the tree. With a ⁷⁄₁₆-inch bit, bore a hold diagonally upward 2 to 3 inches. Insert a sap spout with a bucket hook attached, as shown below. Hammer the spout in gently but firmly so as not to split the bark, which would cause a leaky taphole. If your bucket has a rim, make a small incision in the bucket beneath the rim so the bucket will be almost flush against the tree. Or use a special plastic collecting bag.

Tapping maple syrup with a sap spout and bucket

Empty the buckets as they fill and strain the clear sap through a fine-mesh strainer into sterile containers. Boil as soon as possible to limit growth of microorganisms. If you are unable to boil right away, store the sap under refrigeration. (During cold weather you will probably not be bothered with microbial development at tapholes or in buckets.) Sap runs clear and usable until the buds begin to swell. When an unpleasant odor and slight discoloration warns you that the season is over, pull the taps.

When you have collected enough sap, it is advisable to start boiling it in shallow pans out of doors, as it is not recommended to complete the boiling-off process in an indoor kitchen. At first there is no danger of scorching the syrup, because of its great water content, but later there is danger of its boiling over. Maple sap, like water, boils at 212°F. It becomes syrup at 219°F. Adjust the temperature, therefore, according to the barometric pressure that day. ▲ At higher altitudes, adjust the temperature according to the boiling point of water at your altitude and the barometric pressure the day of the boil.

Before storing maple syrup, and while it is still hot, filter it through a cheesecloth-lined colander to rid it of sugar sand, a malate of lime. Pour into sterilized, 890, containers, and reheat if necessary. If sealed at 180°F, the syrup will remain sterile for a year or more.

MARGARINE

Margarines, like butter, must by law contain a minimum of 80 percent fat—the rest being water, milk solids, and sometimes salt or other flavorings. Almost all margarines are enriched with added vitamins and color, to try to make them comparable to butter. Margarines today are usually emulsions of milk and refined vegetable oils, some of which may be hydrogenated and contain trans fats, 5. Also, some may have added animal fats. Check the label. ➤ Regular stick margarines, because of their similar moisture content, may be substituted for butter, weight for weight or measure for measure, but they produce textures somewhat different from butter in both cooking and baking and lack the desirable butter flavor. Margarine is perishable and must be kept covered under refrigeration. Tub margarine, whipped margarine, and diet margarine will not produce satisfactory results when substituted for butter or regular stick margarine in baking. Limit their use to the table, as a spread on bread or toast, or as a flavor enhancer for cooked vegetables.

MARIGOLDS

The dried centers of pot marigolds are sometimes used as a color substitute for saffron, and the young leaves can be used in salads to add a slight bitterness. The petals are used only when the recipe calls for cooking, as in stews.

Calendula officinalis is not particular as to soil and grows to 15 inches. Gem marigolds, *Tagetes tenuifolia,* differ with a citrus-tarragon flavor to their petals. Flowers of either type should not have been sprayed if harvested for culinary use.

MARJORAMS AND OREGANOS

These, whether bold sweet marjoram, Turkish oregano, or Mexican oregano, are all pungent and all part of the *Origanum* family. While similar in their uses, they are not quite the same in their growth habits. Use them in sausages, stews, and tomato sauces, and dishes; with lamb, pork, chicken and goose; in omelets, eggs, pizzas sauces, chilies, and cream cheeses; with all of the cabbage family and with green beans; and in minestrone and mock turtle soups. And, of course, don't fail to try them fresh and finely chopped for salads. There is great horticultural confusion in regard to the oreganos of commerce, and seeds ordered under the genus *Origanum* vary enormously. *Origanum vulgare* and *O. onite,* or pot marjoram, are hardly perennials growing to 2 feet. *Origanum marjorana,* sweet marjoram used for cooking, is a tender perennial growing about a foot high; it prefers alkaline soil.

MILK AND CREAM

"Drink your milk" has been a time-worn admonition at many an American family table, for the high nutritional value of milk is an accepted fact. The most important consideration when buying milk is the sell-by date on the container. Milk is as perishable as it is valuable. Always buy the freshest milk you can find and ➤ keep it refrigerated at about 40°F at all times. Although milk may last up to 7 days after the sell-by date, a significant amount of flavor and body may be lost before then. Buy milk in opaque containers rather than glass to protect it from the oxidizing effects of sunlight and fluorescent light.

In this book ➤ the word "milk" means pasteurized whole milk unless otherwise specified. Such milk contains about 87 percent water, 4 percent milk fat, 3 percent protein, 5 percent lactose or carbohydrate, and 1 percent minerals.

MILK AND CREAM SUBSTITUTIONS

Sometimes it may be necessary to substitute milk for cream, but if the substitution is made for baking, a different texture will result unless the fat content of the cream is compensated for. ➤ For 1 cup light cream, use $3/4$ cup plus 2 tablespoons milk and 3 tablespoons butter. For 1 cup heavy cream, use $3/4$ cup milk and $1/3$ cup ($5 1/3$ tablespoons) butter. (This substitution, of course, will not whip.)

PASTEURIZATION AND HOMOGENIZATION OF MILK AND CREAM

Milk and cream sold in interstate commerce must by law be pasteurized. Pasteurization, a carefully controlled heating and cooling process, effectively eliminates the possibility of many dreaded milk-borne diseases that the sanitary handling of raw milk, no matter how scrupulously carried out, cannot always achieve. Most milk in this country is also homogenized, a mechanical process that shatters the fat particles so that they remain uniformly dispersed throughout the milk, preventing them from rising to the top to form a layer of cream.

It is still possible to find milk that has not been homogenized or even milk that has not been pasteurized in areas where it is legal to sell raw milk. Dairies that sell raw milk are frequently inspected and certified, and the milk carries a warning label. Some say raw milk is more healthful than commercial pasteurized milk because raw milk contains active enzymes that help with digestion and absorption of nutrients. Many cheese makers prefer raw milk, since pasteurization diminishes the cheese's flavor potential and homogenization gives cheese a waxy texture. However, it's illegal to sell raw milk in many states.

In 1994, the government approved the use of Bovine Growth Hormone (BGH) to stimulate cows to produce more milk. It is still undetermined what the effects are on people who drink milk produced by cows that have been given these hormones, but no serious health risks are anticipated. If you wish to avoid BGH, buy certified organic milk.

Raw milk or cream may be pasteurized at home.

Arrange sterilized heatproof glass jars on a rack in a deep kettle. Allow an inch or two of headroom when you pour the raw milk or cream into the jars. Fill the kettle with water until it comes above the fill line of the jars. ➤ Put a sterile dairy thermometer (available at a dairy supply store or from Internet retailers) in one of the jars. ➤ Heat the water and, when the thermometer registers 145°F, hold the heat at that temperature for 30 minutes. ➤ Cool the water rapidly until the milk is between 50 and 40°F. ➤ Refrigerate, covered, at once.

SCALDING MILK

Today scalding milk is employed more often to hasten or improve a cooking process than to destroy bacteria. Scalding is that point at which milk begins to come up to a light froth, just as it reaches about 180°F. In practice, we usually rely on the age-old visual test for scalding—milk is scalded ➤ when tiny bubbles form around the edges of the pan. Heating may be either over direct heat or in the top of a double boiler ➤ over, not in, boiling water. Before heating milk for scalding, it is a help in later cleaning to rinse out the pan with cold water.

DRY OR POWDERED MILK

Dry milk powders are pasteurized milk particles, air-dried to eliminate most of their moisture. In whole dry-milk form, they contain not less than 26 percent fat, and in nonfat dry milk form, about $1\frac{1}{2}$ percent fat. Dry whole milk should always be stored in the refrigerator. Once opened, all dry milks should be refrigerated in an airtight container. Discard them if they acquire any off flavors. Dry milk is handy in emergencies and for camping.

To ➤ reconstitute whole or skim dry milk, follow the package instructions, or use 3 to 4 tablespoons powdered milk to 1 cup of water—which will make slightly more than a cup of fresh whole or skim milk in volume, and its equivalent in nutrition. For the best flavor, reconstitute at least 2 hours before using and refrigerate.

Dry milk powders are useful in adding protein, calcium, and calories to the diet, but they need special handling. They scorch easily, requiring lower cooking and baking temperatures. To avoid scorching gravies and sauces made with dry milk, use a double boiler or very low heat. When preparing sauces, do not add more than 3 tablespoons of milk solids to each cup of liquid. To avoid lumping, mix the milk solids first with the flour and then with the melted fat or oil off the heat, then add the warm, not hot, liquid gradually.

For cooked breakfast cereals, add 3 tablespoons dry milk solids to each $\frac{1}{2}$ cup of dry cereal before cooking, then use the same amount of water or milk called for in the recipe. For cocoas, custards, and puddings, add 3 tablespoons dry milk powder for each 1 cup of liquid called for in the recipe. In baking, mix dry milk powder with the flour ingredients, see Cornell Triple-Rich Formula, 596, but be careful never to add more than $\frac{1}{4}$ cup of milk solids for

each cup of flour, or the dough will have poor rising properties and the crumb will be too dense.

To substitute reconstituted dry skim milk in recipes requiring whole milk, add about 2 teaspoons butter for each 1 cup reconstituted dry skim milk.

EVAPORATED MILK

Evaporated milk is whole, reduced-fat, or fat-free milk that has 50 percent of its moisture content removed; it is sealed in cans and heat sterilized. It has a slightly caramelized taste due to the processing. The cans come in $5\frac{1}{3}$-ounce and 12-ounce sizes. To make it flow easily from the can, punch 2 holes near the rim at opposite sides of the top. Any leftover contents should be poured into another container, covered, and refrigerated. Once opened, the milk should be stored as fresh milk. Reconstitute by adding an equal amount of water to the evaporated milk. ➤ To whip, see Whipped Cream Substitute II, 974.

FAT-FREE OR SKIM MILK

Also called nonfat milk, these milks have only $\frac{1}{2}$ percent or less fat but all the protein and mineral value of whole milk. Skim milk is bluish white in color and lacks much of the body and flavor of whole milk. Skim milk is fortified with vitamins A and sometimes D.

FILLED MILK

This imitation milk is composed of milk in which vegetable oil replaces the fat. Filled whole milk has approximately the same texture and caloric value as whole milk but is not its nutritional equivalent.

FLAVORED MILKS

Chocolate and other flavored milks may contain chocolate syrups, fruit juices, fruit flavorings, or other flavorings as well as extra sugar or sweeteners, so while they may offer the same nutrients as regular milk, they are likely to have added calories.

GOAT'S MILK

Goats produce milk that is whiter and richer-tasting than cow's milk, with a similar nutritional content. Although it is slightly lower in cholesterol, goat's milk actually contains more fat than cow's milk. The fat molecules in goat's milk are relatively small, so it does not need to be homogenized. Goat's milk is not available in lower-fat varieties, nor is it fortified with vitamin D, as commercial cow's milk is. Those who are lactose-intolerant and/or allergic to cow's milk protein need to avoid goat's milk as well.

LACTOSE-REDUCED MILK

Many adults, especially those of non-European ancestry, find it difficult to digest lactose, the principal sugar in milk. They experience bloating and gas after consuming fresh milk products. Milk can be treated with an enzyme that splits each lactose molecule into two simpler sugars, glucose and galactose, making it easier to digest. Lactose-reduced milk tastes sweeter than regular milk but is equal in nutritional value.

REDUCED-FAT/LOW-FAT MILK

Low-fat milks have some but not all of the fat removed. They are labeled according to the percentage of fat by weight: 2 percent, 1 percent, or $\frac{1}{2}$ percent. These milks have the same protein and lactose content as whole milk. Low-fat milks are fortified with vitamin A and sometimes vitamin D to compensate for the vitamins lost when the fat is removed. Low-fat milk can be made at home by mixing equal parts of whole milk and fat-free milk.

SWEETENED CONDENSED MILK

The process, used as early as Civil War days, involved in making condensed milk reduces the water content of whole or skim milk by about half and adds sugar. A 14-ounce can contains the equivalent of $2\frac{1}{2}$ cups milk plus $\frac{1}{2}$ cup sugar. Once opened, any leftovers should be poured into another container, covered, and refrigerated. Because of the high sugar content, condensed milk will keep somewhat longer after opening than will evaporated milk. It is popular for use in making caramel sauce, pies, and bars.

WHOLE MILK

A fresh, fluid homogenized milk that typically contains at least 3.25 percent fat, and at least 8.25 percent protein, lactose, and minerals. Whole milk may be fortified with vitamins A and D.

MINTS

We all know peppermint and spearmint, but the genus *Mentha* includes numerous distinct species. There are many worth trying, such as the curly varieties and apple, orange, and pineapple mint. These are less penetrating but equally refreshing. Use any of them in fruit cups, coleslaw, and cream cheeses; peas, zucchini, lamb, and veal; with chocolate combinations; as a dessert garnish; in teas; and, of course, in jellies and juleps. The leaves, fresh or candied, see 881, make attractive garnishes. If using fresh leaves, $\frac{1}{4}$ to $\frac{1}{2}$ teaspoon—minced just before using—is usually enough per serving. Follow the recipes. In the form of mint oil, a drop is often too much—so go easy. Peppermint leaves are considered superior for drying; pick the leaves before the plant flowers. All of the following grow rampant in sun or partial shade, and even in dry, but preferably moist, soil: *Mentha viridis,* perhaps the most peppery of all; *M. piperita,* the peppermint we know best; *M. spicata,* or spearmint, and its preferred form, *M. crispa;* and the woolly apple mint, *M. rotundifolia,* frosted in appearance and fine for a drink garnish. All mints are perennials and easily raised from root divisions. They reach $1\frac{1}{2}$ to 3 feet. Plant them in areas confined by metal or rock edgings sunk at least 6 inches deep to keep them from invading less sturdy neighbors in the herb garden. Keep them pruned, to have bushy tops for beverage garnishes. If your growing area is confined, try *Mentha requienii,* or Corsican mint—a tiny-leaved plant only 1 inch high, as discreet as a moss. Incidentally, field mice hate mint odor and will stay away from any plant near which it is scattered.

MIREPOIX

About $\frac{2}{3}$ cup

This term refers to a blend of vegetables—diced in mirepoix, minced in **matignon.** In Italy, the mixture, made with olive oil in place of butter, is referred to as **soffrito,** and it may also include fennel, leeks, garlic, and chopped herbs such as parsley. Always made just before use, these blends are an essential starting point of many sauces, 542, and may be used either as a base or as a seasoning for roasting and braising meats and poultry, making soups, or for flavoring shellfish. To make a white mirepoix, for light-colored dishes, substitute the white part of a leek for the carrot. Dice:

> **1 carrot**
> **1 onion**
> **1 rib celery**

Add:

> **1 bay leaf**
> **1 sprig thyme**
> **(1 tablespoon minced raw ham or bacon)**

Simmer in:

> **1 tablespoon butter**

until the vegetables are soft. If desired, deglaze, 1055, the pan with:

> **(Madeira)**

MISO

Miso is a fermented soybean paste used to season and thicken sauces, marinades, and salad dressings and, most commonly, to prepare broth for Miso Soup, 125. Miso varies in strength but is always salty; use about 1 tablespoon miso to season 4 cups liquid or food and always blend the paste with a few tablespoons of the liquid before stirring it into the rest of the dish. Intense heat destroys the healthful enzyme in miso, so, when appropriate, add it at the end of cooking and avoid boiling. It comes in a variety of colors, from white to yellow to red, and textures, smooth or chunky, depending on the length of fermentation and the addition of grains such as barley or rice. It is commonly characterized as white, sweet, and mild (*shiro* in Japanese); medium golden or tan in color (*chu*); or pungent, dark red, or brown (*aka*)—which is good for marinades and should not be cooked for a long time. As a general rule, the darker the miso, the longer it has been fermented and the stronger and saltier it will taste. Lighter miso, fermented for a shorter period, is sweeter; barley miso is earthy and well aged. Refrigerate miso in a covered container, and use it within a few months for best flavor.

MOLASSES

High in iron, molasses adds a rich, earthy taste to breads, cakes, and cookies. Molasses is a by-product of sugar making. The juice from sugarcane or sugar beets is boiled down to a dark, thick liquid. By adding moisture, it improves the storage qualities of breads and cakes. "Molasses" in this book means unsulfured or light molasses; some recipes specify dark molasses.

Unsulfured molasses is made from the juice of sugarcane or sugar beets, and sulfur was not used in the processing. **Sulfured molasses** is a by-product of sugar making; the sulfur fumes used in the manufacturing of sugar are retained as sulfur in the molasses. Light molasses results from the first boiling of the sugarcane syrup. Dark molasses is a product of the second boiling. **Blackstrap molasses** is essentially the bitter residue of a third boiling in which more sugar crystals are extracted but in which minerals such as iron remain.

Since molasses is not as sweet as sugar, use 1 cup molasses for each ³⁄₄ cup sugar. Molasses should not replace more than half the amount of sugar called for in the recipe. ➤ Because of its acid content, add ¹⁄₂ teaspoon baking soda for each cup molasses added, and omit or use half the baking powder called for. Reduce the other liquid in the recipe by 5 tablespoons for each cup of molasses used.

MSG (MONOSODIUM GLUTAMATE)

MSG is a flavor enhancer that may be extracted from grains, sugarcane and its by-products, or beets. MSG is also present in tofu and soy sauce. Long part of Chinese cooking, it is sometimes used in this country, especially in commercially processed foods, because of its power to intensify some flavors. It seems to have no effect on eggs or sweets. It can modify the acidity of tomatoes, the earthiness of potatoes, and the rawness of onions and eggplant. It acts as a blending agent for mixed spices used in meat and fish cookery. It is soluble in water but not in fat, ➤ so, if you do use it, add it to the liquid ingredients. While it accentuates the saltiness of some foods, just as wine does, it lessens the saltiness of others. ➤ We detect a certain deadening similarity in foods flavored with monosodium glutamate and prefer, if a meat or vegetable is prime, to let its own choice character shine through unassisted.

MSG has a reputation for causing an allergic reaction with untoward physical side effects in some people who have consumed a large dose, perhaps on an empty stomach.

MUSHROOMS AS SEASONING

The mushroom family contributes one of the most coveted of all tastes. ➤ Never discard stems, and particularly not skins, for it is here that the greatest amount of flavor lies. Even the scrapings of their rarefied cousins, truffles, are sold at a good price and can be cooked to form pungent garnishes. To give more flavor into canned mushrooms, sauté them in butter. Consider also, for seasoning, dried or powdered mushrooms. And for a classic mushroom seasoning, see Duxelles, 284.

White button mushrooms, *Agaricus bisporus,* are the variety most commonly found in supermarkets, although portobellos and cremini are also readily available. Some mushrooms, especially morels, black trumpet, shiitake, and porcini (cèpes), become more flavorful as they dry, but they must be kept free of moisture while drying, so as not to mold.

To ➤ dry mushrooms for storage, select fresh, firm specimens. You may rinse them, then dry in a low oven; or simply place them on a screen or thread them on a string to sun-dry. When thoroughly dry, put in tightly sealed sterile glass jars. Keep from all moisture until ready to use.

For mushroom types and a further discussion of mushrooms, see 281. Mushroom spores are often sold in brick form for home culture.

MUSTARD

Mustard fanciers will argue the merits of a mild champagne-based or Dijon type or a Louisiana mix against the sharp English or the fiery Jamaican or Chinese mustards. There are many ways to prepare mustards from dry mustard, which is the dry residue left after the oil is expressed from the seeds. But the freshness of the mix is an important factor. The flavor changes rapidly once moisture is added, or once a bottle of prepared mustard is opened. Try keeping it fresh by putting a slice of lemon on top before closing the lid; the lemon needs renewal about once a week. Commercial mustards, with their blends of flour and spices—often heavy in turmeric to color them—may be based on water, wine, or vinegar. Dry mustard can be added advantageously in small quantities to cheese, seasoned flour, chicken, or pot roasts and to sauces, hot or cold. Mustard is classic with cold meats and for use in pickles—both ground and as seed. ➤ In this book, "prepared mustard" indicates the store-bought, saucelike mustard, not mustard powder or seed. It has about one-third to one-half the strength of dry mustard. Preparing your own mustard from whole or ground seeds is a cooking adventure—and a source of gifts from your kitchen. Somehow, homemade mustard is even more impressive to most people than homemade preserves, although it is far easier to prepare. Mustards have good keeping power in the refrigerator, and they mellow with time.

MUSTARD SEEDS

White, or yellow, mustard seeds come from *Sinapis alba* or *Brassica hirta.* These spicy but somewhat sweet seeds are readily available in supermarkets. Most seeds of this type are ground into dried mustard powder or blended into prepared mustard. Brown mustard seeds come from *B. juncea,* both self-seeding and growing to 3 feet. They are smaller and hotter than white seeds. Either type of seed can be toasted, 1001, using a small amount of oil or butter in the skillet. Tiny black mustard seeds come from *B. nigra* and are the most pungent. Whole mustard seeds can be used in rubs or marinades. The seeds soften, yielding their pungent flavor. If seeds are desired, plants can tolerate poor soil. If leaves are to be used as a vegetable, *Brassica nigra, Sinapsis alba* and *Brassica juncea* should be grown in rich soil.

COOKED HOT MUSTARD
¹/₂ cup
Place in a heatproof glass bowl or double boiler:
> **2 ounces (10¹/₂ tablespoons) dry mustard**
Pour over:
> **Boiling water to cover**
Set over, not in, rapidly boiling water. Before covering, see that the mustard has been stirred into a paste but is still covered with the hot liquid, and drain off any excess water. Cover and cook for 15 minutes.
Thin if necessary with:
> **Warm water or vegetable oil**
You can add:
> **(1 teaspoon sugar)**
> **(¹/₄ to ¹/₂ teaspoon salt)**
For a brightly colored mustard, add:
> **(¹/₄ teaspoon ground turmeric)**
Place in a jar and let cool, uncovered, for 1 to 2 hours. Cap tightly. Keep this mustard at room temperature, not refrigerated, for up to 2 weeks.

GRAINY MUSTARD
1 cup
This mellows and improves after a couple of days.
Combine in a bowl:
> **5 tablespoons whole yellow mustard seeds**
> **¹/₃ cup dry white wine**
> **¹/₃ cup white wine vinegar**
> **(1¹/₂ teaspoons grated onion)**
> **¹/₂ teaspoon salt**
> **¹/₂ teaspoon sugar**
> **¹/₄ teaspoon white pepper**
Cover and refrigerate overnight. Process in a blender until blended but still grainy. Store, covered and refrigerated, for up to 3 weeks.

UNCOOKED HOT MUSTARD
¹/₂ cup
Catch-in-the-throat Chinese and German mustards may seem mysterious, but they are no more complicated than blending dry mustard to a paste with a cold liquid such as water, flat beer, or vinegar. The liquid gives these mustards character. Use high-quality dry mustard for best results. Use this mustard as is, or add one of the various flavorings recommended below. It is very sharp when freshly made, but mellows and improves over time; we suggest refrigerating it, covered, for several days before serving it. This is wonderful spread on cold meat sandwiches, particularly roast beef, corned beef, or cold pork.
Combine in a bowl:
> **¹/₂ cup dry mustard**
> **2 tablespoons dry white wine**
> **2 tablespoons cider vinegar**

> **2 tablespoons water**
> **1 teaspoon salt**
> **¹/₂ teaspoon white pepper**
Let stand for 2 hours, then stir well again. Cover and refrigerate until ready to use. This will keep, covered and refrigerated, for 2 to 3 weeks.

IDEAS FOR FLAVORING MUSTARD
Stir one of the following into **Uncooked Hot Mustard,** above.
> **¹/₄ cup dried fruit (such as nectarines, apricots, or plums), plumped, 937, and finely diced, plus 1 tablespoon honey, or to taste**
> **¹/₄ cup minced or finely snipped herbs (such as tarragon, rosemary, thyme, or chives) plus 1¹/₂ teaspoons brown sugar**
> **1 tablespoon fresh lemon juice plus 1¹/₂ teaspoons ground coriander**
> **¹/₂ teaspoon *each* ground cloves, grated or ground nutmeg, and ground cinnamon**
> **1¹/₂ teaspoons drained prepared horseradish plus ¹/₂ teaspoon dill seeds**
> **Finely minced garlic to taste**
> **¹/₂ teaspoon minced shallots**

NASTURTIUM
Nasturtium flowers, seeds, and leaves are all used as flavorings. The unsprayed leaves and lovely orange and yellow flowers are good in salads and the pickled pods often replace capers. The unsprayed *Tropaeolum* are best picked just as soon as the blossom drops and prepared at once. *T. major* vines to 6 feet; *T. minus* grows to 9 inches.

NUTMEG AND MACE
The flavors of nutmeg and mace are so closely allied because they come from the same tough-husked fruit of *Myristica fragrans.* When opened, it has a lacy coating, which is dried and occasionally used whole in cooking fruits or desserts or ground into **mace.** Mace is traditional in cake doughnuts and meat dishes. The hard inner kernel is the **nutmeg.** Use it sparingly but often, and, for full flavor, grind nutmeg with a nutmeg grinder that merely needs a twist—like a pepper mill—or use a rasp-type grater. Try it not only in baked items but also in spinach, with veal, on French toast—and always with Eggnog, 66.
➤ One whole nutmeg, grated, equals 2 to 3 teaspoons ground nutmeg.

NUTS
Whether they are seeds, like pecans and walnuts; fruits, like lychees; or actually legumes, like peanuts, nuts contain protein and fats. Except for chestnuts, 968, and cashews, 965, they contain very little starch. It is for their oils, which carry the flavor and nutrition, and for the textural contrast they add to recipes that we treasure them so much. The reason they are often listed as an optional ingredient in our recipes is because most recipes will be OK

without them; extraordinary with. Except for green almonds and pickled green walnuts, nearly all nuts are eaten ripe. For information on specific nuts, see individual entries.

Because nuts are high in oils, the best way to store them is in their shells. The shells protect them from light, heat, moisture, and exposure to air—factors that tend to cause rancidity.

The difference in the keeping time for shelled nuts may range from 2 months at room temperature to as long as 1 year in a freezer. If nuts are already shelled, store them tightly covered in a cool, dark, dry place or in the freezer. Unsalted nuts have longer storage life than salted ones, which tend to turn rancid more quickly. Some nuts, like pecans and Brazil nuts, have stubborn husks and are more easily shelled if boiling water is poured over them and they are allowed to stand in it 15 to 20 minutes. Be sure to discard any nuts that are moldy, shriveled or dry, as they may prove bitter or rancid.

As a rough rule, ➤ 1 pound of nuts in the shell yields about 8 ounces shelled. For more detailed yields, see 1042.

BLANCHING NUTS

In addition to the tough outer shell, some nuts like hazelnuts and almonds have a thin inner skin that may need removing, as it can taste bitter. If so, just before using, pour boiling water over the shelled nuts. For large quantities, you may have to let them stand briefly, only about 1 minute at the most. ➤ The briefer the time, the better. Drain. Pour cold water over the nuts to stop further heating and drain again. Pinch or rub off the skins.

For peanuts, hazelnuts, and pistachios, you may prefer to remove the skin by roasting in a 350°F oven for 10 to 20 minutes and then vigorously rub the nuts together in a dish towel to loosen the covering. This can be done when the nuts are hot or cold.

CHOPPING NUTS

If rather large pieces of nuts are needed, simply break nuts like pecans and walnuts with your fingers. For finer pieces, use a knife or the tool called a **mezzaluna,** 991, or chop as described here. ➤ It is easier if the nuts are moist and warm and if the knife is sharp. Gather the nuts in a circle with a diameter as wide as the knife blade. Grasp the knife

Chopping nuts

at the top at both ends. Rock the blade briskly from point to hilt, gradually turning the knife toward you in a semicircle. Gather the chopped bits together and repeat the rocking until the bits are as fine as you want them. Nuts may also be chopped in a food processor, using short pulses. ➤ Process no more than 2 cups at a time, and use caution not to overprocess, lest you end up with nut butter.

GRINDING NUTS

To grind nuts, ➤ use a special drum grinder—one that shreds or grates them sharply to keep them dry, rather than a type that will crush them and release their oils. Grind small quantities at a time. The light, dry, fluffy particles that result often become an ingredient in nut tortes, 727. We also find that a dry food processor bowl fitted with a sharp dry blade does a fine job of pulverizing nuts without turning them oily or pasty—but, again, be careful not to overprocess. A blender is not as effective in grinding or chopping nuts. But if that is your only choice, pulverize only $1/4$ cup at a time, making sure the container and blade are dry before you start. There are some times, however, as when making nut butters and pastes, a blender is used.

Toasted nuts should be cooled completely before being ground. It is the volume of nuts after grating or grinding that should be measured, not the quantity of nuts you start with.

Peanut butter is so popular that it has overshadowed the making and use of other nut butters. Try grinding almonds, pecans, cashews, or walnuts into fresh nut butter, 178. These are so rich they need no additional oil. Use $1/4$ to $1/2$ teaspoon salt for every cup of nuts.

SALTING NUTS

To salt nuts, coat a bowl with whipped egg white, butter, or olive oil, add the nuts, and shake them until they are coated. If you salt before cooking, allow no more than $1/2$ teaspoon salt to 1 cup nuts. Spread the nuts on a baking sheet and heat in a 250°F oven about 10 to 15 minutes, stirring frequently to achieve even browning. A more rapid way is to heat in a heavy skillet 2 tablespoons oil for every cup of nuts. Add the nuts and stir constantly about 3 minutes. Drain on paper towels, salt, and serve. For more recipes for seasoned nuts, see 70.

TOASTING NUTS

Toasting nuts crisps them and enhances their flavor. Toasted nuts can have quite an impact on the flavor of a dish, so it is well worth the few extra minutes to do so. **To toast nuts in the oven:** Spread them on an ungreased baking sheet and toast in a 325°F oven for 5 to 7 minutes, depending on the size of the nuts, checking and stirring often to prevent burning. **To toast nuts on the stovetop:** Place them in a dry skillet over medium heat and cook, stirring or shaking the pan frequently to prevent burning, until they just begin to release their fragrance, about 4 minutes. To avoid loss of flavor and toughening, do not overtoast, as nuts tend to darken and become crisper as they cool; be sure to remove them from the heat when they begin to cook but haven't darkened, as they will continue to cook for a minute or two after removal from the heat, and transfer the hot nuts to a plate or a cool baking sheet immediately after toasting. They can be chopped with a knife while still warm, but let them cool completely before processing them in a food processor or blender. **To toast nuts in a microwave oven,** place them on a microwave safe dish. Cook uncovered on high power for 2 to 4 minutes, stirring occasionally and rotating the dish if necessary. The nuts will be very aromatic and feel hot to the touch, but they should not brown. Toasted nuts can be stored, covered, in a cool, dry place for up to 2 weeks.

OLIVE OIL

Olive oils are like wines in the way their flavors are affected by the soils in which they grew. Greek, Spanish, or Italian—try them all and find your favorite. Olive oil is cheaper by the gallon, but, as it is susceptible to rancidity—especially the cold-press type—when exposed to light and air, it should always be decanted into smaller containers. Store in a cool, dark place.

Olive oils are graded according to how much acidity they contain and whether they are processed with or without solvents. The oil obtained from the first pressing of the olives is the only olive oil that can be classified as extra-virgin or virgin. **Extra-virgin olive oils** are premium. They are the first cold-pressed oils, processed without the application of heat or solvents. They are the lowest in acid of all olive oils, a desirable characteristic. Their color ranges from gold to deep green, but color is no indication of quality. Clouded, unfiltered oils are prized by many for their fuller flavor. While the words "extra-virgin" on the label may guarantee fruity, pronounced flavor, they do not guarantee a good-tasting oil. If at all possible, sample before buying. Because it is the most expensive, it is best to use extra-virgin olive oil for dishes in which olive oil will not be heated, such as in vinaigrettes or as a condiment. Heating olive oil will cause it to lose some of its flavor, so it is best to use a lower quality olive oil for cooking.

Virgin olive oil, also a first-pressed oil and processed without heat or chemicals, has a higher acid content than extra-virgin oil. With a flavor and character more subdued than extra-virgin oil, virgin oil is an excellent substitute for extra-virgin oil when budget considerations are necessary. It is also more versatile, because it can be used in cooking but still has enough flavor for salads and for use as a condiment. **Olive oil,** sometimes labeled "pure" olive oil, is a blended oil made from refined olive oil (extracted with pressure, heat, solvents, and or chemicals) and virgin olive oil, from which it gains color and flavor. It has a higher smoke point than virgin or extra-virgin, making it an excellent choice for cooking. **"Light" olive oil** is a marketing title describing refined olive oils that are mild or light in taste or color. Despite the name, the calorie content is the same as all other olive oils—120 calories per tablespoon.

OLIVES

To classify olives as being simply green or black would not do justice to the wealth of varieties available. Fresh olives are bitter due to the compound oleuropein, present in olive skin; olives are processed, or "cured," to make them suitable for eating. Green olives are picked unripe and black olives are picked ripe. To reduce the saltiness of dried or pickled olives, store them in olive oil that you can later use to make vinaigrettes.

Brine-, oil-, and water-cured olives have a moist-looking exterior and a smooth, shiny skin; salt- or dry-cured olives look wrinkled and shriveled. The flavor of each variety of olive depends upon its ripeness, where it is grown, and the type of processing it undergoes. While the grading and typing of olives is taken very seriously by the processors, what should matter most to the cook is that size or color does not necessarily have anything to do with quality.

Buy olives that are uniform in color and free of surface blemishes and white spots. Explore the delicious array of Greek, Italian, French, Spanish, Middle Eastern, and California olives to find what best satisfies your palate.

Keep bulk-purchased olives in the refrigerator for up to several weeks. Canned or bottled olives can be kept unopened in the pantry for up to 2 years but should be refrigerated when opened.

ONIONS

Never since our first encounter with the host of alliums in a bulb catalog have these lilies lost their allure for us as food or flower—from the thinnest chive to the enormous *Allium schubertii,* or fireworks alium, with its choicest florets held captive within a flowered cage like a large sparkler. This is a plea not only to use a variety of onions in your cooking, but to grow the perennial ones so you will always have them on hand. To cook onions as vegetables, see 285. Nothing can add such subtlety to a dish, yet none is more abused in the cooking than onions. And when we say onions, we mean any of the alliums we list below. We indicate their use in individual recipes. Use bulb onions fresh or dry, the green tops of onions or leeks in making soups and court bouillon. And don't forget that ➤ a touch of onion freshly added to canned or frozen vegetables and soups often disguises the canned taste and varies the expected one.

High heat and too long a cooking period can bring out the worst features. ➤ If you scorch onions, they will be bitter. ➤ Yet onions must be cooked long enough to get rid of any rawness. If you want them to taste mild in soups or in delicate stews, the flavor of the dish can be improved and the onion odor lessened during cooking if you will follow this procedure. ➤ If they are 1 inch in diameter, parblanch, 285, the onions 5 minutes, before adding them to the soup or stew. If you want them ➤ mild in sautéing, cook them only until translucent—tender but not flabby. If you want them ➤ penetrating, sauté until golden; if ➤ all-pervasive, brown them very slowly, as for an onion

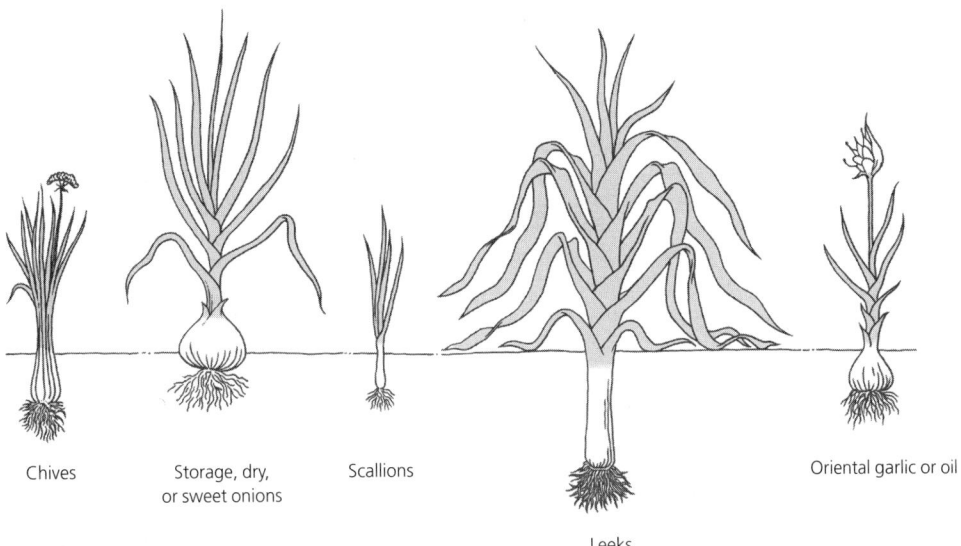

Chives   Storage, dry,   Scallions   Oriental garlic or oil
                or sweet onions

                                                        Leeks

soup, 129, or a Lyonnaise, 555. To give color and flavor to a pot-au-feu, see 136.

In cooking, onions are frequently chopped or minced fine. A number of ways exist to make this process less tearful; see 286. When you haven't time to sauté an onion properly but do not want a raw taste in cold dishes, hot sauces, or dressings, use ➤ onion juice. Ream a cut onion on a lemon juicer, or scrape the cut center of the onion with the edge of a spoon.

To make onions milder when serving them in salads, first soak them in milk. Or put slices in a bowl and pour boiling water over them. Let stand 30 to 40 minutes. Drain, then soak them briefly in cold water with a few ice cubes to crisp. Drain and serve.

To rid your breath of onion traces, eat raw parsley. Onion odor on the hands can be rubbed off with salt, vinegar, or lemon juice. For onion scent on pots, moisten them, sprinkle generously with salt, and let stand, then rinse with very hot water.

All onions are of easy culture. They prefer sandy, moist, rich earth, with shallow planting in full sun. Dry, or storage, onions should all be sun-dried a few days after being dug up. You may braid the tops so the bulbs can be hung in clusters for even airing during storage. If trimming off the tops, do not cut too close to the neck of the bulb. ➤ Store all onions in a cool, dark, dry, well-ventilated place.

CHIVES

Although chives are considered an herb, we group them here with the *Allium* family to which they belong botanically and in flavor. Only the delicate freshly cut leaves are used. Combine with soft white cheeses and with eggs, or use in green sauces. Cut and add them to hot and cold food just before serving to preserve their crisp texture and unique flavor. Chives are easiest to snip into small pieces with a sharp pair of kitchen scissors or shears. ➤ Do not put chives in any uncooked dish you plan storing even as long as overnight, as they get unpleasantly strong.

To keep plants of *Allium schoenoprasum* looking well, cut a few of the thin tubular leaves low rather than bobbing the top, which will brown where cut. Remember that, like all bulbs, chives rely for plant renewal strength on the leaves—so don't cut any one plant more than 3 or 4 times a season. The leaves are tenderer after each cutting. Also keep the blooms picked low so the tougher stem does not get mixed with the leaves when you use them and so you are not bothered with seeding. About 3 to 6 small bulbs set in humus-filled soil in the fall will make a good cluster 8 to 10 inches high by the following summer. A slightly larger variety, *A. sibericum,* with thicker leaves, is also hardy.

GARLIC

This is perhaps the most controversial, yet potentially one of the most delicious additions to food. The nineteenth-century French novelist Balzac, a formidable gastronome, recommended that even the cook should be rubbed with it! We couldn't live without it. If you are fond of it ➤ keep a check on the amount used, for tolerance to it may grow apace, to the discomfort of your friends. The bulb at the base of the plant is the treasure. Note the scalloped form of the bulb, indicating the cloves within an outer skin.

Learn to place slivers of garlic in meat before cooking it; to rub a salad bowl lightly with a cut clove; or to make chapons, 157. Drop a peeled garlic clove into a vinaigrette 24 hours before serving, but do not leave it in longer, as it will deteriorate. Add a small squeeze of garlic juice to sauces. This is easy to do with a garlic press, a handy kitchen utensil. Should you not own a press, use the back of a spoon or fork against a small bowl, or a mortar and pestle, to crush garlic with salt. The salt softens the bulb almost at once. If you drop a whole clove into a liquid for seasoning, ➤ be sure to strain it out before serving. When cooking, ➤ never allow garlic to brown. Always use fresh garlic. Powdered and salt forms tend to have rancid overtones. ➤ To blanch garlic, drop unpeeled cloves into boiling water for 2 minutes. Drain, peel, and simmer slowly in butter about 15 minutes. Mince the blanched, buttered garlic and add to sauces if a more mellow flavor is desired. To roast garlic, see 277.

True garlic plants, which grow 1 to 3 feet high, are not hardy. Plant bulbs of *Allium sativum* in light soil in March. They should be ready for lifting in later July. Be sure to sun-dry the cloves until the outer skin is white and parched.

Elephant garlic is the source of much confusion. Elephant garlic—*Allium ampeloprasum*—is more closely related to the leek than to ordinary garlic. The bulbs are very large and can weigh over a pound. A single clove of elephant garlic can be as large as a whole bulb of ordinary garlic. Due to its size, many assume it must be more strongly flavored. In fact, the opposite is true. Elephant garlic is much less intense and sweeter. When buying elephant garlic, follow the same guidelines as for ordinary garlic: look for heads that are firm with plenty of dry, papery covering. When cooking with elephant garlic, remember that it is *not* a substitute for ordinary garlic. Instead it is used where a subtle hint of garlic is wanted without overpowering the rest of the food. Elephant garlic is often served raw in salads or sliced and sautéed in butter (be careful, it browns very quickly and can turn bitter). It's also frequently used to give a hint of flavor to soups.

GARLIC CHIVES

This is a coarser plant, about 15 inches high, whose flatter, somewhat stronger leaves are used like chives, above. The charming starry, honeyed white bloom cluster of this perennial can be used as a decorative garnish, or the flowers sprinkled over salads. Cultivate *Allium tuberosum* as for chives.

LEEKS

The leek, the beloved French *poireau,* is king of the soup onions. It also lends itself well to braising. This biennial, *Allium ampeloprasum* var. *porrum* grows its first year with an elongated root and closely interlaced foliage. Leeks are often planted in a dirt hill, sheltering them from sunlight in an effort to keep them white. This practice traps grit unless the leeks are grown with a paper collar. Be sure to rid them of this grit by washing well, 280. They are choice the first year. A leek with a tough, hollow stem—from which the glorious silver-green bloom has been cut from the center of the foliage—and a more bulbous form at the base is in its second year and will prove too tough to eat. However, the green portion can be utilized in soups and seasonings. To prepare leeks, see 280.

RAMPS OR WILD LEEKS

Around the bulbs of *Allium tricoccum* revolve many American folk festivals. Growing only in the springtime and at relatively high altitudes, these and the strong field garlic in your lawn—*Allium vineale*—make a wonderful accompaniment, sautéed lightly in butter, to scrambled eggs and panfried small fish. Uncooked, they are an interesting flavor experience, especially when consumed with smoked meats.

ROCAMBOLE

This hardy plant has a beautiful glaucous leaf and an entrancing pointed bud carried on a furled stem. Its unwinding is a source of great pleasure to watch. The edible bulbs that bunch at the top are indistinguishable in taste and form from the tender garlic described above. Cultivate *Allium sorodoprasum* as for chives.

SCALLIONS

Use scallion greens, also known as fresh spring onions, as a soup flavoring or use in salsas and stir-fries. The thin white bulb portion with about 4 inches of leaf can be braised as for leeks, 280, and they are eaten raw by self-assertive people. Scallions are the thinnings of *Allium cepa* plantings or are grown from seeds sown close together and harvested before the bulb develops its characteristic shape.

SHALLOTS

The shallot, queen of the sauce onions, is not hardy but well worth growing. Shallot flavor is perhaps closer to garlic than to onions, and although it has a much greater delicacy, it must still be used with discretion. Shallots are indispensable in Bercy Butter, 559, and Mignonette Sauce, 568, where they should be minced simultaneously with the herbs. They taste especially good in wine cookery. In sautéing them, mince fine so as not to subject them to too much heat. ➤ Never let them brown, as they become bitter. ➤ Substitute 3 to 4 shallots for 1 medium onion. To roast or cook shallots as a vegetable, see 304.

Allium cepa var. *ascalomicum,* always grown from sets, should be put in, barely covered, in the early spring. They should be harvested by late June, when the leaves are no longer upright—carving in at the neck—but not yet turning in color. Allow them to dry off on the ground for several days and then braid the leaves so the shallots can be hung in strands in a dry place for use as wanted.

STORAGE OR DRY ONIONS AND SWEET ONIONS

These *cepa* types are the onions most available in the market; they vary greatly in flavor, color, and shape. Good raw and mild in cooking are the big yellow or white Bermudas or the sweet onions such as Vidalias or Walla Wallas. Red onions are a favorite garnish on hamburgers and in salads. They mush somewhat in cooking, so if you want a mild red cooker, try the rounder, more elongated Italian red onions. Pearl onions, including the kind you find in the bottom of your Gibson cocktail, are cluster sowings of *cepa* varieties.

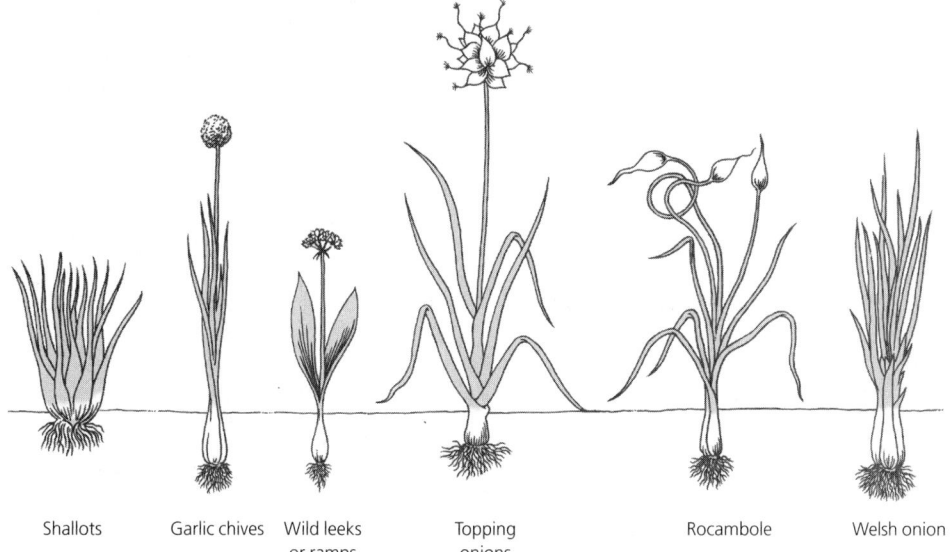

Shallots   Garlic chives   Wild leeks   Topping   Rocambole   Welsh onion
or ramps   onions

Allium cepa types are biennials; they are planted in sets in February and harvested in July when the browning leaves have died down. Sweet onions have a high water content and don't store well. To cook onions as a vegetable, see 285.

TOPPING ONIONS

Use these as you would any medium-sharp onion. *Allium catawissa,* unlike dry onions purchased in markets, is a perennial. It has a fibrous root system, and the onions develop early in the season at the top of the blooming stock. In fact, some even begin to sprout there too, and, in turn, produce more onions at the top of the second sprout the same season. The nonsprouting bulblets can be kept for planting the following August or the next spring. The original plants may also be separated. There is really no excuse for not trying anything that easy. These are similar to the so-called Egyptian topping onion—*A. cepa viviparum*—which, surprisingly, does not grow in Egypt; it is hardy and has a usable bulb at the base as well.

WELSH ONIONS

These can be used as a substitute for scallions. *Allium fistulosum,* known also as the **Japanese bunching onion,** is usually homegrown.

OREGANO

See Marjorams and Oreganos, 996.

OYSTER SAUCE

A staple of Chinese and Filipino cuisines, oyster sauce was originally made from oysters, water, and salt. Now it may contain added cornstarch and caramel color, to improve its appearance and to thicken liquids when used in stir-frying. When buying oyster sauce, avoid the less-expensive vari-

eties, which contain fewer oysters and more cornstarch. Once opened, store it in the refrigerator.

PAPRIKA

See Sweet and Chile Peppers, 1006.

PARSLEYS

These plants—roots, stems, and leaves—have a high vitamin A content. They are flavorful in themselves but also valuable as an agent for blending the flavors of other herbs, and they have the power to destroy the scent of garlic and onion. There is practically no salad, meat, or soup in which they cannot be used. But they should be handled with discretion, particularly the **Hamburg parsley,** also called **parsley root** or **turnip-rooted parsley.** These roots are sometimes cooked as for Parsnips, 289.

There are numerous varieties of **curly parsley,** varying in strength. When mincing or deep-frying, remove the florets or leaves from the more strongly scented stems. The stems are used in white stocks and sauces for their strength of flavor and because they do not color the sauce, as does the leaf. **Flat-leaf** or **Italian parsley** is preferred by some for its richer, stronger taste and its ability to hold up to heat in cooking. Curly *Petroselinum crispum,* flat-leaf *P. crispum neapolitanum,* and **Hamburg Parsley** (*P. hortense*) are the parsleys seen most frequently in the markets. Biennials, they grow to about 1 foot in rich loamy soil and sun. As they often bolt, or tend to go to seed prematurely, and too early during the second season, they are best treated as annuals. To grow from seed, soak in water to cover about 24 hours. The flat-leaf type is better for fall use, as its leaves shed the snow and stay green longer. *Petroselinum carum,* a coarser-growing, heavier-rooted biennial, grows to 3 feet. Soak seeds as described above.

PERSILLADE
¾ cup

From *persil*, the French word for "parsley," persillade is a mixture of chopped parsley and garlic that is sprinkled on food toward the end of cooking to add flavor and color. Add bread crumbs to form a crust for fish fillets, rack of lamb, or broiled shrimp.

Mix together:

½ cup chopped parsley
1 tablespoon minced garlic
(⅓ cup fresh bread crumbs)
2 tablespoons olive oil, or enough to make a paste

PEANUTS

Peanuts, actually underground legumes—also called groundnuts or goobers—are high in protein. Peanuts are best eaten right after roasting or boiling. To roast raw peanuts in the shell, roast in a 300°F oven 30 to 45 minutes, or 20 to 30 minutes if shelled. Turn them frequently to avoid scorching. Check for doneness by removing the shells. The inner skins are pleasantly flavored. But little is gained by home-roasting, as the steam process used commercially for roasting peanuts in the shell gives superior results. Boiled peanuts are usually served as a snack, but they may also be substituted for dried cooked beans. To boil peanuts, place 2 to 3 pounds of fresh green or raw peanuts and 1½ cups salt in a large stockpot, cover with water, and bring to a boil. Simmer for at least 1 hour and up to 3 hours. To check for doneness, pull a few peanuts out of the pot and open them. When soft, they are done. If they are not salty enough, leave them in the salted water and turn off the heat. When cooked, drain and serve immediately. ➤ Discard any peanuts that are moldy.

PEANUT BUTTER

Federal regulations require commercial peanut butter to contain 90 percent shelled roasted ground peanuts, with additions of no more than 10 percent of salt, sweeteners, and oil. If you are smart, you will make your own full-bodied peanut butter.

Put in the bowl of a food processor:

Roasted or salted peanuts

For each cup of peanuts, add:

1½ to 2 tablespoons safflower or canola oil

Process until smooth. If the nuts are unsalted, add:

About ½ teaspoon salt per cup of nuts, or to taste

PECANS

A native American nut from a variety of hickory tree, pecans are one of the nuts heaviest in fat, with sometimes as much as 75 percent fat. The high fat content can lead to rapid rancidity. For this reason, store in the freezer.

PEPPERCORNS

All peppercorns come from the berry cluster of a leafy green vine, *Piper nigrum*, the master spice. Green peppercorns are the unripe berry of the vine. They have a mild fresh flavor and are delicious chopped and creamed with butter as a seasoning or stirred into light sauces. The soft green berries can be preserved in vinegar in jars, although some are shipped in their plump green state. **Black peppercorns** are fermented green berries that are dried, becoming hard, wrinkled, and dark brown to black. Their flavor is rich and spicy, especially if the berries are Malabar or Tellicherry peppercorns. If left on the vine, green berries ripen to red. **White peppercorns** are produced from this fully ripe red berry. The dark outer shell is buffed off, revealing a gray inner core. White pepper has the hottest flavor, and it is the preferred pepper for light-colored foods and sauces (unless a color contrast is wanted). The flavor of white peppercorns also holds up better in sausages and canned meats. Try combining equal parts black and white peppercorns in a mill; you will have the aromatic qualities of the black and the strength of the white.

Peppercorns add different flavors to a dish, depending on how they are ground. Used whole to flavor soups and other long-cooking mixtures, their flavor is discreet; tie the peppercorns in a cheesecloth bag, then remove them before serving. When they are freshly crushed with a mortar and pestle or spice grinder, most of their oils are retained and the flavor is pungent. Crushed or cracked pepper, used in *poivrade* dishes such as Steak au Poivre, 474, is wonderful pressed into meats before grilling or sprinkled over fish and meats before serving. Use cracked peppercorns when a bold, assertive taste is desired. **To crack peppercorns,** place them in a zip-top plastic bag and crack them with a rolling pin or a meat mallet. Ground pepper is always best freshly ground. Pepper remarkably manages to strengthen food flavors without masking them as some other spices do.

Pepper is not just for savory foods. Sneak a pinch into cookies such as Pfeffernüsse, 768, cakes, and fruit dishes, or try freshly ground black pepper on strawberries.

For ground red, or cayenne, pepper, see 1007.

PEPPERS, SWEET AND CHILE

These plants of the *Capsicum* family are rich in vitamins A and C. They are also said to have bacteria-deterrent and antioxidant qualities that can extend the keeping periods of fats, meats, and casseroles made with them. Native to the Americas, they are very different from peppercorns. The *Capsicums* all have this in common: The ➤ mid-rib or placenta that runs down the middle of the chile produces and secretes an irritating substance called capsaicin. This mid-rib should always be removed if you are using fresh chile peppers. The condiments made from the dried peppers may or may not include the mid-rib or the seeds. ➤ To roast and peel fresh peppers, see 292. See various types on 291.

The sweet bell peppers, variety *C. annuum*, have been known to be misnamed "mangoes" in the market in the

Midwest. These 4- to 5-inch-long peppers, both green and, in their more ripened state, red, purple, or yellow, are used for stuffing and are diced for flavoring.

Also to this general type belong the bonnet peppers, *C. tetragona,* from which **paprikas** are ground. The mild or sweet types are seeded and dried and deprived of their mid-rib before grinding. Hot paprika is prepared with sweet peppers whose flesh contains more heat; some seeds and mid-ribs may be added. Most paprikas are blends that fall between mild, sweet, and hot. The best paprika has long come from Hungary, where paprika making is an important culinary tradition. Paprika is sensitive to heat and should be added toward the end of the cooking period. If added to broiled food for color, paprika browns when scorched.

The hot peppers, *C. annuum* var. *longum,* include most of the chile peppers, and come in many colors, from chartreuse green to yellow to red. There are hundreds of crosses, and in the endless regional recipes for chili or mole powder, as many as 6 or 8 varieties of *Capsicum* will be indicated: ancho, pasillo, chipotle, etc., 291.

Any variety of dried chiles can be ground into a powder at home. ➤ **To grind dried chile peppers,** remove the stem and seeds. Use a spice grinder or coffee mill. Use caution not to inhale the fumes or dust while grinding, as it can be quite irritating to the eyes and nose.

Ground cayenne pepper, which comes from *C. annuum L.,* is often adulterated or replaced commercially by *C. frutescens,* a small red, dried treeberry, or *C. croton annuum,* known also as bird peppers. ➤ Cayenne is very hot, so it should be used only in the smallest pinches. Very hot too are the red clustered *C. fasciculatum* varieties, with fruit over 6 inches long, for which the seeds are supposed to have come from Tabasco in Mexico. Now grown in southern Louisiana, they constitute the base for the famous hot pepper sauces, see 1021, which are often matured 2 to 3 years. ➤ Use gloves when seeding any hot pepper to avoid skin irritation. Red pepper, not so hot as cayenne, is ground from this type. A popular ground pure chile used in Mexican cooking is ancho chile powder.

To prepare dried chile peppers, see 909. For other *Capsicum* recipes see Chili Powder, 968, Chile Vinegar, and About Peppers, 1024.

PINE NUTS

Known as *piñon* in Spain or *pignoli* in Italy, these small, ivory-colored seeds are harvested from inside the pinecone of several varieties of pine trees. There are two main varieties, the slender Mediterranean or Italian pine nut, which has a delicate, sweet flavor, and the triangular Chinese pine nut, which has a pungent pine flavor. Pine nuts are used in sweet and savory dishes, and as a garnish. Both varieties are high in fat, so to prevent them from turning rancid, store in an airtight container in the refrigerator or freezer. These nuts are good in Pesto Sauce, 569, as a garnish on salads, and in Dolmas, 82.

PISTACHIO NUTS

These nuts, beloved for their green color and haunting flavor, are often used in stuffings, confections, sausages or pâtés. To skin, spread on baking sheets and heat at 400°F for 4 minutes. Cool and pinch or rub off the skins.

QUATRE ÉPICES (SPICE PARISIENNE)

This mixture is a favorite for stews and sweets. It may vary in ingredients according to the will of the *épicier* or the whim of his customer, and frequently contains more than four spices. Antoine Carême, the famous French chef who is considered the father of haute cuisine, concocted a formula for **épices composées** that included dried thyme, bay leaves, basil, sage, a little coriander, and mace, and—at the end—the addition of one-third part ground pepper. Store these in an airtight container.

I. Mix:
- **1 teaspoon ground cloves**
- **1 teaspoon grated or ground nutmeg**
- **1 teaspoon ground ginger**
- **1 tablespoon ground cinnamon**

II. Mix:
- **1 teaspoon white pepper**
- **$1/2$ teaspoon grated or ground nutmeg**
- **$1/2$ teaspoon ground ginger or cinnamon**
- **$1/4$ teaspoon ground cloves**

RAS EL HANOUT
About $1/2$ cup

This Moroccan spice mix typically contains many different elements, from seeds, leaves, flowers, roots, and bark to Spanish fly beetle, a supposed aphrodisiac. It is usually added by the pinch or half teaspoon to stews of meat and poultry and to couscous dishes. Here is our version, without the Spanish fly.

Mix together thoroughly:
- **2 tablespoons ground ginger**
- **2 teaspoons black pepper**
- **2 teaspoons ground allspice**
- **2 teaspoons grated or ground nutmeg**
- **2 teaspoons ground mace**
- **2 teaspoons ground cardamom**
- **2 teaspoons ground cinnamon**
- **2 teaspoons turmeric**
- **1 teaspoon ground coriander**
- **$1/4$ teaspoon ground cloves**
- **$1/4$ teaspoon ground red pepper**

RENNET

Rennet, an extract from the lining of the fourth stomach of calves (now bioengineered), is the coagulant in cheese making. A Greek pharmacologist, Dioscorides, once said that rennet had the power to join things that were dispersed and to disperse things that came together. No chemist these days dares match such a claim! Available in tablet or liquid form from cheese-making suppliers.

ROSEMARY

The stiff resinous leaves of this shrub are extremely pungent—rosemary is not a subtle herb. Because the leaves are tough, be sure to chop the herb fine. The leaves dry well. In marinades, for which this flavoring is popular, allow about $\frac{1}{4}$ to $\frac{1}{2}$ teaspoon fresh for 4 servings, or follow the recipes as directed. Use the lightly crushed leaves with lamb, pork, duck, partridge, rabbit, capon, veal peas, and spinach, and on foccacia and pizza. A perennial, *Rosmarinus officinalis,* depending on the variety, grows from 2 to 6 feet and tolerates drought and lean soil, but it is not hardy in the North, where nighttime temperatures dip below 10°F. It grows well in pots for indoor winter use in cold climates.

RUE

Ruta graveolens, a handsome gray-green perennial, grows to 3 feet and prefers alkaline soil. This herb is sometimes suggested as a flavoring for fruit or claret cups. As many people are allergic to its irritant qualities, which produce symptoms comparable to poison ivy, we do not recommend its use.

SAFFRON

The golden orange stigmas of the autumn crocus are used to provide extraordinary fragrance, golden color, and aromatic flavor in cakes, breads, and dressings and are classic in rice dishes such as paella, 358, Risottos, 360, and in Bouillabaisse, 142. Even a ➤ small amount of saffron has an overpoweringly medicinal flavor, so use only as directed in the recipes. Two or three stigmas too many, and the dish turns bitter. If using saffron mainly for color, make an infusion with the saffron and as much liquid as you can use in the recipe. The more liquid, the farther the flavor will carry in the recipe. For baking just $\frac{1}{4}$ teaspoon mixed in 2 tablespoons of hot water will suffice for 5 to 6 cups of flour; or use as directed in the recipe. Use only about $\frac{1}{8}$ to $\frac{1}{4}$ teaspoon in 2 tablespoons hot water or white wine to season 6 to 8 servings of a sauce. *Crocus sativus* grows in mellow soil. As with all bulbous plants, the foliage of this fall-blooming bulb must be allowed to ripen fully if the plant is to prosper.

SAGE

"The young sow wild oats; the old grow sage." Sage is perhaps one of the best known and loved of all American seasonings. Use for meats such as pork, especially in sausages, and for duck, goose, and rabbit. Sage is also used in cheese and chowders and, of course, in poultry stuffings. The flavor of the freshly chopped tender leaves will be more powerful than that of the dried, which loses much of its volatile oil. Dried sage is available as "rubbed" or "ground" in the supermarket; rubbed is more coarse and will lose its oils and aroma less rapidly. If harvesting your own crop, dry carefully, 991, as the leaves are thick and mold easily. Always use sage sparingly. *Salvia officinalis,* a perennial, grows to 2 feet and should be cut back after blooming. But prune lightly, and only on new growth. Many hybrids exist and dwarf forms are available.

SALT PORK AND BACON AS SEASONING

Salt pork and bacon give an interesting fillip or embellishment to many foods, such as salads, soups, stews, and cooked beans. They are often blanched, 981, to remove excess salt. Although they may be used interchangeably, the flavors are quite distinct. Used as a garnish, the rendered bits are called **cracklings, lardons,** or **grattons.** Dice:

> **Salt pork or bacon**

Dry-render it, 981, in a skillet until it has released the fat and is brown and crisp. Or render in a very low oven until golden brown.

SALTS

Salt may be the ultimate culinary multitasker. The power of salt to heighten the flavor of other foods is its greatest culinary asset. This is true even in candy making, when a pinch of salt often brings out a confection's characteristic best, and with uncooked food, as when salt is sprinkled on citrus fruits. Its differing effects on different cooked foods are complex. It speeds up cooking time: Green beans get tender 10 percent faster if cooked in salted water. It draws the moisture from meats and fish in cooking processes. It toughens eggs. And it must be used cautiously in bread making, as too much inhibits the growth of yeast and adversely affects gluten formation. For the effects of salt water on cooking, see 1026.

The diverse properties of salt have provoked arguments, from time to time, as to just when this very important ingredient should be added when cooking. It must, of course, be used very sparingly, if at all, at the start of any cooking in which liquids will be greatly evaporated—such as the making of soups, stocks, and sauces. But small quantities of salt added early to soups and stews will help in clarification. It is good practice to sear grilled, broiled, or roasted meat after adding salt, to enhance flavor. And since it is almost impossible to get rid of excess salt in cooked foods—although occasionally a touch of sugar will make them more palatable—the amount must be calculated with care.

We know from long experience that the flavor-enhancing power of salt is most effective if it is added judiciously near the end of the cooking process.

Salt occurs within foods in varying amounts, animal sources having a higher salt content than vegetables. Seafood, especially shellfish, is heavier in salt than freshwater fish. Of course, pickled, cured, and corned meats and sausages; broths, catsups, and extracts; brine-processed frozen fish, sardines, herring, and anchovies; as well as canned soups, unless labeled "low or reduced sodium," and canned fish and meats are all high in salt. Do watch your salting arm when dealing with any of these foods, and in cooking artichokes, beets, carrots, celery, chard, kale, spinach, dandelion greens, endive, and corn—all of which are naturally more salty than most other vegetables. Also be cautious with dates, coconut, and molasses.

The interplay of salt and water is essential to life itself. The maintenance of a proper salt balance is vital to the human body and different in every individual. Those for whom a low- or no-sodium diet has been recommended by a physician may replace the missing flavor by the skillful use of herbs, spices, lemon juice, and wine. Such individuals should also be aware of the salt or sodium content of softened water. ➤ Salt's powers of preservation made possible our ancestors' survival in the waters, wastes, and wilderness through which they forged the world's great trade routes. While its use in preserving food became much less important with the advent of refrigeration, it is surprising how much we still depend on it: in food processing of various kinds; in the curing of meats; in the brining and pickling of vegetables; in freezing ice cream; and even, now and then, for heating oysters and baking potatoes.

In food preservation, the action of salt is twofold. First draws moisture out of the food by osmosis, a process whereby the moisture moves in or out of the food to equalize the concentration of salt, thus discouraging the microorganisms which are always more active in moist than in dry food. Then, the brine, 962, formed by the salt and moisture in combination further prevents or retards the growth of surface microorganisms. To cook salted meats, see 506. To remove excess salt from bacon and salt pork, see 981; from anchovies, 413.

Various kinds of salt are mentioned in this book. When the word "salt" is used without qualification, it means ➤ table salt. ➤ To keep it freeflowing, put a few grains of rice in the salt shaker or saltcellar.

COARSE SALT

Coarse salt is not a specific type of salt, but a reference to the size of the salt grain. It can refer to either sea salt or kosher salt. While a fine-grained salt is frequently used in cooking, coarse salt is preferred for frosting the rims of a cocktail glass, 55, making a salt crust for fish or meat, 399, and creating a bed for oysters, 371. Some also prefer to use coarse salt in cooking because it's easy to pinch and sprinkle with the fingers.

HERB SALTS

I. Blend in a mortar or pulverize in a food processor for 3 or 4 minutes:

> **1 cup iodized salt or 1$\frac{1}{2}$ cups kosher salt**
> **1$\frac{1}{2}$ cups pounded fresh herbs**

Spread the mixture on a baking sheet. Preheat the oven to 200°F, then turn it off. Place the pan in the oven and allow the herb mixture to dry.
II. You may also preserve fresh herbs by salting them in a covered baking dish or glass bowl, alternating $\frac{1}{2}$-inch layers of salt with $\frac{1}{2}$-inch layers of herbs; begin and end with

slightly heavier salt layers. After a few weeks, the salt will take on the flavor of the herbs you have chosen to combine and will be ready for use. Any herbs that remain green may also be used.

IODIZED SALT

Iodized salt is table salt with added iodine. It is recommended for certain regions where the water and soil lack iodine, an essential trace element. Essentially all salt sold at the supermarket is iodized, and the label will say "iodized."

KOSHER SALT

A coarse-grained salt free of additives, kosher salt is used by cooks because of its texture, lack of impurities, and the way it readily dissolves. It is also used in kosher preparation of meat. Because of the larger crystal size, when substituting kosher salt for table salt, it is necessary to use up to 1$\frac{1}{2}$ to 2 times more kosher salt than specified. It is often served sprinkled over meats after carving and just before serving, so that it does not have time to melt completely in the juices of the meat. It is also sprinkled over rolls, pretzels, and bread before baking as a sparkling garnish.

PICKLING SALT

Pickling salt is a pure salt free of additives that might cloud a brine made for pickling. It is available in both granulated and flake forms, which may be substituted pound for pound. But, if measuring by volume, for every cup of granulated pickling salt, use about 1$\frac{1}{2}$ cups flake pickling salt.

ROCK SALT

Rock salt is a nonedible unrefined variety of salt that is used in combination with ice for the freezing of ice cream made in an electric or hand-cranked paddle-style ice cream maker. It is used as a base for baking potatoes or oysters on the half-shell.

SEA SALT

A squarish-grained coarse or finely ground salt obtained from the evaporation of sea water, with natural iodine and other minerals. More expensive than traditional salt, it is very flavorful and should be applied with a light touch. There are individual differences in sea salts from different bodies of water. ➤ Do not confuse coarse sea salt with rock salt or kosher salt.

SEASONED SALTS

Commercial seasoning salts are usually a combination of salts, spices, and at times even MSG (monosodium glutamate); check the label. In using flavoring salts, be sure to taste the food before adding any additional salt. Make your own with the following formulas.
I.

> **$\frac{1}{2}$ cup plus 2 tablespoons salt**
> **5 tablespoons white pepper**
> **3 tablespoons black pepper**
> **1 teaspoon ground red pepper**

1 teaspoon *each* grated or ground nutmeg,
    ground cloves, ground cinnamon, sage,
    marjoram, and rosemary

II.
    ¹/₄ cup salt
    1 tablespoon sugar
    1 tablespoon paprika
    1 teaspoon *each* ground mace, celery salt, grated or
       ground nutmeg, curry powder, garlic powder,
       onion powder, and dry mustard

SMOKED SALTS

Hickory wood smoke and other scented smokes have
been purified of tars and are chemically bound to smoked
salts by an electrical charge. Use as an ingredient in dry
rubs, 587, or sprinkled on cooked meats, fish, vegetables,
and in some soups where a smoky flavor is desired. Available in some supermarkets, in specialty stores, or from online retailers. Or make your own mixture, below.

SMOKY SALT MIXTURE

About ³/₄ cup

Used as a paste or rub for grilled meats or as a table condiment for grilled meats.
Combine:
    1 teaspoon smoked salt
    ¹/₂ cup catsup
    ¹/₄ cup olive oil
    2 tablespoons prepared mustard

SOUR SALT

Also called citric acid, sour salt is sometimes used to replace lemon flavoring or to prevent discoloration in fruits
or canned foods, and sometimes used in sausage making,
pickling, and canning. A very small pinch has tartness
equivalent to a few squeezes of fresh lemon or lime juice,
but the sour salt doesn't have a fruit flavor. Available in
some supermarkets that sell kosher foods, sold with canning supplies, or from specialty markets and online retailers.

TABLE SALT

Table salt is a finely grained freeflowing type, about 99
percent sodium chloride.

VEGETABLE SALTS

Vegetable salts are sodium chloride with added vegetable
extracts, such as celery and onion. They add saltiness to
food in addition to the flavor of the vegetable extract. If
you use them, cut down on the amount of salt called for in
the recipe.

SALT SUBSTITUTES

Salt substitutes are chloride salts in which sodium is replaced by calcium, potassium, or ammonia. Because they
contain higher levels of other electrolytes in place of the
sodium, they should be used only on the advice of a physician. **Salt-free seasoning blends,** different from a salt substitute, are a tasty alternative to salt and salt substitutes

because they are sodium free and free of the replacement
electrolytes. Fresh lemon juice, chopped fresh herbs, and
vinegar all make delicious sodium-free enhancements to
food as well. See Citrus Zests, Juices, and Garnishes, 971,
and Chiffonade of Fresh Herbs, 989.

SAVORIES

The leaves of **winter savory** are used in stews, stuffings,
and meat loaves. *Satureja montana,* winter savory, is a
rather resinous perennial evergreen sub-shrub that grows
to 18 inches and tolerates lean soil. **Summer savory** is a
much more delicately flavored herb and has many more
uses. It is classic in green beans and green bean salad; in
horseradish sauce and lentil soup; and even in deviled
eggs. It is also used with fatty fish, roast pork, potatoes,
and tomatoes, and in vinaigrettes. *Satureja hortensis,*
which grows to 18 inches, needs light, well-composted
soil.

SCALLIONS

See Onions, 1002.

SEAWEED

Vegetables from the sea are quite popular in Japanese cuisine. These are edible forms of red or brown algae, traditionally used in soups and salads, as a thickener, and as a
wrap for sushi. Seaweed is prized for its mineral-like flavor
and high nutritional value. Store in a cool, dry place,
tightly sealed once opened.

AGAR

Agar, or agar-agar, is a dried seaweed that looks like transparent noodles. It is also available as a powder. Its jell
strength is not easily destroyed by heat or acid. For aspics
or jelled desserts, allow 1 teaspoon agar for each cup of
liquid. Soften by first soaking in ¹/₄ cup cold liquid, then
dissolve in ³/₄ cup hot liquid. To avoid a weedy odor and
flavor, be sure the agar you buy is highly purified. To use as
a salad garnish, soak the strands for 2 hours, changing the
water 2 or 3 times. Cut into 2-inch lengths before serving.

CARRAGEEN OR IRISH MOSS

Carrageen, like agar, needs to be well purified if a weedy
odor and flavor is to be avoided. Carrageenan is derived
from Irish moss and is used as an emulsifier, stabilizer, and
thickener in a variety of foods. Allow 1 ounce of powder
per cup of liquid, depending on how stiff a jell is needed.
Prepare as for agar, above. Heat to 140°F to dissolve, and
remember ➤ it becomes thin in the presence of acid.

KELP (KOMBU)

This brown seaweed is sold under the Japanese name
dashi kombu. A 6-ounce package of dried kombu yields
enough to make about 6 batches of dashi, a beloved Japanese broth, for 4 to 6 people. The whitish coating on
kombu is normal; it should never be washed, or it will lose
flavor. Used dried or fresh, it may be served as a vegetable,
used as a soup base, or in Dashi, 119, or in salads; it is

sometimes fried. Dried kombu keeps indefinitely in a tightly sealed container.

NORI
Nori, also called laver, are paper-thin sheets of dried seaweed used to wrap sushi. Available toasted or untoasted, nori can be stored in the freezer, and the sheets thaw very quickly.

WAKAME
Wakame is sold dried and packaged, sometimes labeled *ito wakame*. After reconstituting the dried leaves of this seaweed are briefly cooked in miso soups or used to make salads. To reconstitute, soak in tepid water for 20 minutes. If the stems are present, tear off and discard.

SEEDS
Sunflower, pumpkin, buckwheat, barley, and **squash seeds,** all flavorful and nutritious, should be hulled before eating or using in recipes. **To toast,** see the general rule under Nuts, 1000. However, to roast **soybeans,** soak ¼ cup beans overnight, refrigerated, in a cup of water. Drain and dry thoroughly. Roast in a shallow pan for about 2 hours in a 200°F oven, then put pan under broiler to brown the soybeans. Use as is, or season and mix with oil.

Poppy seeds come from *Papaver somniferum,* the opium poppy, but the seed has no narcotic properties. The most desirable come from Holland and are a slate-blue color. The seeds are best when roasted or steamed and crushed just before use in cooking, so their full flavor is released. If poppy seeds are one of your favorite flavors, it is worth getting a special hand mill for grinding them. Use poppy seeds, both whole and ground, in baked items, and sprinkle them on buttered egg noodles.

Sesame, or **benne, seeds** are a favorite topping for breads, cookies, and vegetables and are available in three types: brown, white, or black. Black sesame seeds are more flavorful and aromatic than white or brown seeds. The nutty flavor of the brown or white seeds is strongest when they are lightly toasted about 20 minutes in a 350°F oven, stirring frequently. Sesame seeds may be made into an oily paste called tahini; see 1021. With cooked chickpeas, tahini forms the base for Hummus, 74. Toasted sesame oil from the seeds is desirable in salads and as a condiment, 1023. For other seeds, see About Spices, 1015, and About Herbs, 989.

SPROUTING SEEDS, GRAINS, AND BEANS
Imagine having fresh garden greens growing in your kitchen all year long. No digging, no weeding, no sweating. Sprouting seeds, grains, and beans produces by far the most nutritious addition to the diet in relation to their cost. The sprouting action greatly increases the already rich vitamin and enzyme content, and their flavor and texture are distinctive. Add them to stir-fried dishes or to soups and stews just before serving, but for best results serve them raw, hulls and all, as a garnish on salads or sandwiches.

Sprouting is a very simple procedure: You start with dormant seeds, add water, and they are brought to life by the water they absorb. The yields are astonishing. ➤ Seeds yield between 2 and 8 times their original weight in sprouts. ➤ **Beans** such as lentils, peas, garbanzos, adzuki; **larger seeds** like almond, pumpkin, hulled sunflower, peanut; and **grains** such as wheat, rye, oats, barley, kamut, spelt yield about 2 times their dry seed weight in sprouts. The one exception is mung beans, which can grow 3 to 4 times their original weight. ➤ **Small seeds** vary; brassica seeds (broccoli, radish, mustard, cabbage) will grow between 4 and 5 times their weight. **Leafy sprout seeds** such as alfalfa and clover can grow as much as 8 times their original weight—2 heaping tablespoons will fill a quart-sized sprouter in 5 to 6 days.

Most sprouts develop in 3 to 5 days, and in most cases, within 36 hours. Mung and soybeans may take 6 to 8 days. Beans can be used at that point or rinsed and drained again (every 8 to 12 hours). Taste them at every rinse-and-drain session to decide when you most enjoy the flavor. But don't delay too long. The sprouts will turn into plants eventually—a lentil, pea, or garbanzo sprout will produce a main stem, in addition to the sprout (taproot) after several days. Typically, the smaller they are, the more tender. When growing small seeds like alfalfa, clover, brassicas, and fenugreek, it is common to grow them 4 to 6 days.

If you cannot rinse and drain the sprouts at least twice daily, it is beneficial to purchase a sprouting device that compensates for the rinsing and draining. Our favorite commercial sprouter is a 1-quart plastic container, engineered to maximize air circulation and regulate moisture. A wide-mouth 1-quart jar with a meshlike cover made from nylons or cheesecloth or commercial screw-on strainer lid is also quite effective. Avoid automatic sprouting devices; they can produce inconsistent crops and require too much time to clean to make them time-efficient. These and other sprouting devices as well as a wide variety of seeds are readily available online, and in some health food stores.

SPROUTED SEEDS
About ½ pound sprouts
Avoid potato and tomato seeds, which, when sprouting, are poisonous, and fava and lima beans, which are extremely toxic raw. Use or buy seeds, preferably organically grown, that have not been chemically pretreated for agricultural purposes. Remove any damaged or moldy seeds.

In a 1-quart sprouting device or 1-quart wide-mouth jar, rinse by swirling the seeds in cold water, drain, then soak for 8 to 12 hours one of the following:

> **2 tablespoons small seeds, alfalfa, clover, or leafy sprout blend**
> **3 tablespoons small seeds, broccoli, other brassica, or fenugreek**

4 tablespoons medium to large allium seeds (onion,
    garlic chive, or leek)
$1/2$ cup beans, grains, or seeds
covered with:
    Twice as much cool water as seed
Too much water is fine because the seeds will absorb only
what they can. Some seeds sprout better if soaked for less
time—for example, hulled sunflowers and pumpkins
sprout better when soaked for 1 to 2 hours.

Next morning, make sure the lid of the sprouting device
is securely closed, or, if using a jar, cover the top with nylon
mesh or cheesecloth attached to the jar by screwing the
ring over the cloth or nylon or securing it with a rubber
band, or screw on the straining lid. Drain, then rinse thoroughly once or twice with cool water, swishing the jar
around to give all the seeds a good bath. Drain all of the
water out by shaking and spinning your jar or sprouting
device vigorously. If using a jar, shake the seeds to spread
over a larger area on the glass, and ➤ store the jar on its
side at a slight angle, propping up the bottom. This allows
the excess water to drain out, while also allowing air circulation. It is important to rinse your sprouts 2 to 3 times
daily with cool water, and to drain them thoroughly after
every rinse. ➤ Continue to rinse and drain every 8 to 12
hours for as long as you grow your sprouts. ➤ Grow your
sprouts anywhere out of direct sunlight, such as on your
kitchen counter. They will absorb light when they have
leaves, and the leaves will turn green. Direct sunlight will
"cook" your sprouts, causing them to spoil.

If you care to remove the hulls, stir the sprouts in a bowl
of cold water until the husks rise. Skim them off and drain
the sprouts thoroughly. If not served at once, refrigerate in
a sealed plastic bag with a paper towel in the bottom.
Some sprouts will keep for several weeks in the refrigerator, but fresh is always best, so try to grow only what you
need and eat what you grow. ➤ If refrigerating, it is essential that your sprouts be dry to the touch. We suggest
not refrigerating the sprouts until 12 hours after their last
rinse and drain cycle. Sprouts can be frozen, but considerable nutritive value is lost.

SPROUTED MICROGREENS

Growing microgreens is an age-old English custom. The
sprouts, so tiny-leaved, are reminiscent of a little garden
for a dollhouse. Certain seeds, such as cress, brown mustard, arugula, flax, and chia form a gel-like sack when they
contact water. They are called mucilaginous, and cannot be sprouted in the conventional method detailed
above.

To grow microgreens, thoroughly moisten a planting
medium—anything that can retain moisture is acceptable—**soil, vermiculite, fabric, or microgreen-specific
medium**—and scatter the seeds in a thin layer on top.
Keep the medium and seeds moist by watering regularly
for 7 to 14 days. When sprouted, leave the sprouts on the
germinating surface. Keep them moist and exposed to

light until the two small leaves are green and about $1/8$ inch
long. Harvest by cutting the stems just above the planting
medium, rinse, pat dry, and serve. Microgreens are not
only delicious, but a beautiful garnish for salads and sandwiches. They store poorly once harvested. They can be refrigerated in a sealed plastic bag when dry to the touch,
but they will wilt quickly.

A famous tea sandwich hails to us from England combining sprouts of garden cress, *Lepidium sativum*, with
sprouts of mustard, *Brassica nigra* or *Sinapsis alba*. To have
them ready simultaneously, sow the mustard 4 days later
than the cress, as it germinates more rapidly. Serve scattered on very thin, lightly sweet-buttered rounds of bread.

SHALLOTS
See Onions, 1002.

SHICHIMI, OR SEVEN-SPICE MIX
Shichimi togarashi in Japanese means "seven flavor chile
pepper." Coarse ground red chile peppers are frequently
mixed with orange peel, sesame and poppy seeds, hemp
seeds, and nori to create an Asian seasoning mixture used
to flavor noodle dishes, miso and other soups, and rice.

SHORTENING
Vegetable shortenings, called shortening because of their
ability to "shorten" gluten strands in baked goods, creating a flaky crust. They are white or yellow usually tasteless
or butter-flavored fats. Frequently these have a polyunsat-
urated-oil base—soybean, corn, cottonseed, or peanut—
that is refined, deodorized, and ➤ hydrogenated.
Hydrogenation adds hydrogen molecules and solidifies
the liquid vegetable oils, absorbing the oxygen in their free
fatty acids and converting them to fats that are solid at
room temperature. Hydrogenation also creates trans fatty
acids that have recently come under great scrutiny because of the health risks they pose; see 5. Shortenings free
of trans fats are available and can be successfully used in
baking or frying.

Sometimes solid shortening may have some added animal fats or saturated vegetable fats such as coconut oil or
palm oil. There may also be additions of emulsifiers, yellow
coloring, and sometimes butter flavor to shortenings.
These and the nitrogen incorporated into them make
these shortenings appropriate for baking: They add a
greater volume than that achieved with other solid fats
like butter, and they create a softer, spongier texture. If
color, flavor, or other fats have been added to any of these
products, the label will list any additions.

Vegetable shortening ➤ may be stored covered at
room temperature or refrigerated. ➤ To substitute solid
shortening for butter, you can replace cup or volume measure for measure, as the water content in the butter will
equal the air in the shortening. ➤ If substituting weight
for weight, use 15 percent to 20 percent less shortening
than butter, because shortening weighs less for a given

volume than butter. ➤ To measure solid shortening, see Measuring Fats, 981.

SOFRITO (SEASONED LARD)

Called sofrito in the Caribbean (not to be confused with the Italian soffrito; see Mirepoix, 998), this yellow lard is gets its color from annatto seeds. Sofrito is made in advance of use and is stored in the refrigerator, in a sealed container.

Wash, drain, and melt uncovered over slow heat in a heavy pan, stirring occasionally:

1 pound salt pork, diced

Remove from heat and strain the lard into another heavy pan. Wash and drain:

¼ pound annatto seeds

Add them to the lard and heat slowly for about 5 minutes, then strain the colored lard into a large heavy pot. Grind in a food processor and add:

1 pound cured ham
1 pound green bell peppers, cores, seeds, and membranes removed
4 ounces chile peppers, seeds and membranes removed
1 pound onions

Mash in a mortar and add:

15 cilantro leaves
1 tablespoon oregano leaves

Place in a small tea ball:

6 garlic cloves, peeled

Add to the lard mixture. Bring to a simmer and simmer over low heat, stirring frequently, for about 30 minutes. Cool then remove the garlic. Store covered and refrigerated.

SORGHUM

Sorghum is a large grass, and the liquid sweetener of the same name is a syrup produced from the juice of this grass. Also called sorghum molasses, it is thinner and sourer in flavor than sugar cane molasses. Sorghum can be substituted as for Molasses, 998.

SORREL

The elongated leaves of the sorrel plant are quite high in oxalic acid and taste quite sour, adding acidity to food. Sorrel is used in small amounts to flavor soups, 150, or sauces, or combined in small quantities with other vegetables. It is also used as a garnish for goose or pork. The young leaves may be pounded in a mortar with sugar and vinegar to make a tart sauce. *Rumex acetosa* species grow to 3 feet. For culinary use, the so-called French sorrel, *R. scutatus*, is preferred.

SOUR MILKS AND CREAMS

The longevity of people in certain cultures in Eastern Europe, Scandinavia, and western Asia is often attributed to their diet of sour and fermented milks. The friendly bacteria, or probiotics, such as *Lactobacillus fermentum, L.*

casei, and *L. brevis* in these milks settle in the intestines, where they break down the milk sugar into lactic acid, and where some are reported to stimulate beneficial growth in the intestinal flora and boost the body's immune response. Some food producers now add additional probiotic bacteria to cultured dairy products to achieve the same desirable effects.

Known by many names—including **yogurt, 1029, koumiss,** and **kefir**—cultured and fermented milks are made from milk inoculated with various bacilli that create differences in acidity, flavor, and content. When yeast cells are also present—as in koumiss and kefir—fermentation takes place, resulting in mild alcoholic content as well. Starters to make these products are available at health food stores and come with full directions. These starters often produce more stable or reliable results than inoculation with yogurt or kefir, because yogurt or kefir has been exposed to airborne contaminants and their bacillus count may have been weakened through pasteurization.

Soured milks and creams also play an important part in cooking. The presence of lactic acid gives them all a tenderer curd, and this in turn makes for a more tender crumb in baking and a smoother texture in sauces. In sauces, they also contribute a slightly acid flavor that is highly prized. ➤ Be sure to add these milks and creams at the very end of cooking, and off the heat or over very low heat. If not, they will curdle. Stir constantly but gently. In bread making, just heat until warm. In any sour cream recipes, use salt sparingly, as salting also tends to cause curdling. Soured milks do not freeze well.

Milks and creams may be allowed to sour naturally, but yogurt and today's commercial buttermilk are processed by means of specially introduced bacterial cultures. In this book, for reasons of safety, we recommend making yogurt, 1029, or sour milk, 1014, only from milks and creams that have been pasteurized—and for best results, use only the freshest.

BUTTERMILK

Originally buttermilk was the liquid residue left after making butter. Today it is usually made commercially from pasteurized skim or low-fat milk to which a culture is added to develop the flavor and acidity, and to produce a heavier consistency and thicker body than that of the milk from which it is made. Buttermilk differs nutritionally from milk mainly in its greater amount of lactic acid. Commercial buttermilk may have added cream or butter particles. In older recipes calling for sour milk, substitute buttermilk.

Powdered buttermilk, sometimes called cultured buttermilk blend, is readily available in supermarkets. When it is used in recipes that call for liquid sour milk or buttermilk, the specified amount of powder is blended with dry ingredients, and then water equal to the volume of the buttermilk called for in the recipe is added to the liquids. Refrigerate after opening.

Or make buttermilk yourself.

1 quart

Combine:

> **1 quart skim milk, at room temperature**
> **¹/₂ cup buttermilk, at room temperature**
> **¹/₈ teaspoon salt**

Stir well and cover. Let stand at room temperature until clabbered, below. Stir until smooth. Refrigerate before serving. Store as for fresh milk.

CLOTTED OR DEVONSHIRE CREAM

This is an English specialty made from certified unpasteurized cream; clotted cream contains about 60 percent fat. In winter, let fresh unpasteurized cream stand 12 hours in a heatproof dish; in summer, about 6 hours. Then put the cream on low heat—the lower, the better. It must never boil, as this would coagulate the protein and ruin the cream. When small rings or undulations form on the surface, the cream is sufficiently hot; this heating will sterilize the cream. Remove at once from the heat and refrigerate at least 12 hours. Then skim the thick, clotted cream from the surface and serve it very cold as a garnish for berries or fresh fruit, or serve on scones or with cake.

CRÈME FRAÎCHE

Crème fraîche results from a specific method of cream production in which cream with a fat content of 30 percent or higher is allowed to thicken and mature until its flavor is somewhat similar to sour cream but more nutty than acidic. It tolerates higher temperatures in cooking than sour cream before it curdles. You can flavor homemade crème fraîche with vanilla and sweeten it lightly to taste, whip it, and, generally, substitute it for heavy cream. For best results, don't use ultrapasteurized cream.

1 cup

I. Mix together:

> **1 cup heavy cream**
> **1 teaspoon buttermilk**

Heat to 85°F. Pour into a jar, shake, and let stand at between 60° and 85°F until thickened, 12 to 48 hours. Do not allow it to stand so long that the flavor becomes acidic or ammonia-like. (If you multiply the recipe, the culturing time may be longer.) Stir gently, cover, and refrigerate until ready to use. It will thicken further when chilled. Crème fraîche keeps, refrigerated, for up to 3 weeks.

1¹/₂ cups

II. A slightly thicker version.

Combine:

> **1 cup heavy cream**
> **¹/₄ cup plus 2 tablespoons buttermilk**
> **2 tablespoons yogurt**

Proceed as for I.

SOUR CREAM

Sour cream is made by adding a bacterial culture to cream and incubating it until the lactose is converted to lactic acid. The cultured cream is then packaged, chilled, and aged for 12 to 48 hours. Sour cream is available in full-fat, low-fat, and fat-free versions where dried milk proteins and starches replace the fat. Many uses for this smooth cultured cream are suggested in this book. You can also try making sour cream yourself.

2 cups

The cream you use must contain at least 20 percent fat content and may contain more—the heavier the better for the texture of the end product. Always add sour cream at the end of cooking process over low heat and stir gently to avoid curdling. Do not overstir.

Place in a quart glass jar:

> **1 cup light cream**

Add:

> **5 teaspoons cultured buttermilk (not homemade)**

Cover the jar and shake vigorously. Stir in:

> **1 cup light cream**

Cover the jar and allow this mixture to stand at 75° to 80°F for 24 hours. The sour cream may then be used at once, although storage under refrigeration for another 24 hours makes a finer product. It does not freeze well.

SOUR CREAM SUBSTITUTE

If low-fat or fat-free sour cream is not available, try this substitute, to be used only in uncooked dressings or for garnish.

Mix for 2 or 3 seconds in a food processor:

> **1 cup smooth cottage cheese**
> **¹/₃ cup buttermilk**
> **1 tablespoon lime or lemon juice**

SOUR MILK

This is unpasteurized whole or skim milk that has been allowed to sour naturally. ➤ Pasteurized milk will not sour, but simply spoil. Therefore, in old recipes that call for sour milk, use buttermilk. Or you may sour milk another way; see Sour Milk Substitutes, below.

SOUR MILK SUBSTITUTES

If a recipe for baking specifies sour or buttermilk and only regular milk is available, you can substitute milk that you make sour with the addition of an acidic ingredient. ➤ Using the same amount of total liquid called for in the recipe, place in the bottom of a 1-cup measuring cup:

> **1 tablespoon lemon juice or distilled white vinegar**

Then fill with:

> **Milk or the equivalent amount of reconstituted**
> **evaporated milk or dried whole-milk powder**

Stir and let the mixture stand about 5 minutes, until it begins to clabber. Clabber, much like cultured buttermilk or yogurt, is milk that has soured to the stage of a firm curd but not to a separation of the whey. Be sure to add the baking soda to the dry, not the liquid, ingredients. For every teaspoon of baking powder called for in the recipe, use ¹/₄ teaspoon baking soda plus ¹/₂ cup sour milk or buttermilk, or ¹/₄ teaspoon baking soda and ¹/₂ tablespoon vinegar or lemon juice plus enough milk to make ¹/₂ cup. For other substitutions, see 1042.

In baking, you may interchange sweet milk and baking powder with sour milk and baking soda.

SOY MILK

See About Vegetable and Nut Milks, 1022.

SOY SAUCE

Soy sauce is a naturally fermented product made in several steps and aged up to 2 years. Typically, roasted soybean meal and a lightly ground grain, usually wheat, are mixed with an *Aspergillis* mold starter; the resulting culture takes a few days to grow. Brine is then added to the fermented meal, along with a *Lactobacillus* starter and yeast, and the mash is aged slowly. When the producer determines that it is ready, the soy sauce is strained and bottled. Asian soy sauces, which are naturally fermented, are preferable to domestic types, which are produced by chemical means, tend to be more bitter and salty due to additives, and may also include corn syrup or caramel and monosodium glutamate, 999.

The Chinese invented soy sauce, and the Japanese learned the technology from them. The Chinese use both **light** and **dark soy sauces.** The latter is aged longer and toward the end of the processing is mixed with molasses, which gives it a dark caramel hue. Think of them as red and white wine, since as a rule, dark soy sauce flavors (and colors) heartier dishes, particularly those with red meat, whereas light soy sauce is used with seafood, vegetables, soups, and in dipping sauces.

The technique of aging and fermenting is the same for Japanese and Chinese soy sauces, but as a rule Japanese soy sauce *(shoyu)* contains more wheat and is thus a little sweeter and less salty. Standard in Japanese cooking is what they call dark soy sauce, which is labeled simply soy sauce, *shoyu,* or *koi-kuchi shoyu.* This sauce, on a Chinese scale of dark to light, would fall on the light end, and in a pinch could be substituted for light soy. The Japanese also market low-sodium soy sauces. As with salt, however, it is better to cut back on the amount of this most fundamental seasoning than to use an altered version of it.

The Japanese term *tamari* has been misapplied to Japanese-style soy sauces of varying quality. True tamari, rare even in Japan, is a rich, dark soy sauce brewed without wheat. It is a remnant of the ancient soy sauce methods learned from the Chinese. *Tonkatsu* sauce is a dark spicy Japanese sauce that is soybean-based. It is sweetened through the addition of tomatoes and fruit. This sauce is a favorite for barbecuing or for adding flavor to breaded fried fish and vegetables. It should be kept in a cool, dark place; although it does not spoil, it may lose some flavor after several months.

SPICES

Perhaps our interest in spices is the greater because of our descent from a sailing family, not in New England, but in the old Hansa town of Lübeck, where ships with their cargoes anchored at the wharves on the Trave. The spices were stored in warehouses on the floors above the merchants' living quarters. For informaton on specific spices, see individual entries.

Spices, indeed, bring all the world together. Like wines and cheese, their individuality is intense and their identification with places a vivid one. Spices are derived from the bark, pods, buds, fruits, roots, or seeds of plants and trees. Herbs, 989, on the other hand, are the leafy portions or stems of plants. We associate the best bay leaves with Turkey; the best true cinnamon with Sri Lanka; the best red hot peppers with Louisiana. And there have been lively controversies over the relative merits of Spanish and Hungarian paprika, and of Mexican and Madagascar vanilla beans. Pepper, like salt, because of its preservative qualities, has been at times worth its weight in gold.

Long before the first New England farm wife bought a wooden nutmeg, spice traders have known ways to camouflage their wares. We are lucky today that both government agencies and trade associations work hard to develop and maintain high standards for these relatively costly and still most important condiments.

Since spices are used in small quantities, we recommend that you purchase from impeccable sources. We also suggest that ➤ if you are using ground spices, they should be replenished at least every year, as they tend to lose strength rapidly. Always check the sell-by dates, and be sure to date your own jars when you fill them. Store spices in tightly covered containers made of glass, metal, or tin and in as dark and cool an area as your kitchen offers. But have them handy! Their discriminating use will elevate the flavor of many a dish to a memorable height.

In cooking, wrap whole spices in a cheesecloth pouch or put them in a stainless metal tea ball so you can remove them more easily when the dish is done. ➤ Do not overboil spices, in particular pepper and caraway, as they become bitter. And do not use high heat for paprika or curry, for they scorch easily.

Some spices are available as distilled essences or extracts, like oil of cinnamon, anise oil, or oil of cloves. These concentrated pungent additives are valuable for imparting the essence of the spice without adding the spice itself. They are sold in small quantities, and available from spice merchants or online retailers, for use in careful amounts, as directed. Delicious in light Fruit Butters, 936, or Pickles, 943, or baked goods such as cakes, and cookies, their flavor does not last as long as that of whole spices cooked with the food. See also Extracts and Flavorings, 980.

In frozen foods, the flavors of spices do not hold up well. In ➤ quantity cooking, if you are enlarging recipes, spice to taste rather than to measure. In our recipes, we suggest amounts considered pleasurable by the average person. You may wish to use more or less than we indicate.

The depth of flavor is terrific when spices are freshly

ground, and whole spices keep infinitely better than ground ones. For centuries, cooks have used stone, wood, earthenware, brass, or ceramic mortars and a matching round pestle to crush spices, herbs, and nuts. A marble mortar, 991, is easy to clean and won't absorb flavors or odors. For best flavor, **grind spices** as needed in a mortar and pestle or a spice mill or a dedicated electric coffee grinder. Some spices, like peppercorns or coriander seeds, can be coarsely cracked by placing them in a heavy plastic bag and rolling over the bag with a rolling pin. The flavor of whole seeds is intensified when toasted first. **To toast spices,** use a dry skillet and shake the seeds over medium heat until they release an intense aroma.

SPROUTS

See Sprouting Seeds, Grains, and Beans, 1011.

STAR ANISE

Star anise, *Illicium verum,* imported from China, comes from a tree that belongs to the magnolia family. These striking eight-pointed pods are one of the few spices used in Chinese cooking. Because of its more intense flavor and higher essential oil content, star anise is used as a licorice flavoring more often then aniseed, 958. The Chinese use star anise in much the same way they use cinnamon, and sometimes in conjunction with it, whole, in meat and poultry dishes. It is also one of the components of five-spice powder. The Vietnamese add star anise pods to the beef soup called Pho Ba, 137.

STARCHES

Before cooking with starches, it is necessary to know a little about the science and the source of starches. All naturally occurring starches, whether from a grain, root, or tuber, contain a mix of two basic starches: a long straight-chain starch called **amylase** and a short branched-chain starch called **amylopectin.** A starch's characteristics and how it reacts in cooking varies according to the proportions of these components found in the starch. For cooks, Mother Nature simplified this. All the grain starches share the same characteristics, and all the root starches share the same characteristics; potato starch, which comes from a tuber, not a root, has characteristics somewhere in between the grain and root starches.

Grain starches, such as flours ground from wheat, corn, or oats, contain a relatively high amount (about 26 percent) of amylase (long straight-chain starch). They are clear when hot but cloudy when cold. The mixtures they thicken set up enough to slice with a knife, but they become spongy and leak watery fluid if frozen and thawed. They thicken at around 190°F and can be kept hot without damage, but the mixtures do thin out if stirred once cool and firmly set. Sauces made with flour are opaque hot or cold because flour contains things other than starch.

Root starches, such as tapioca and arrowroot contain less amylase than grain starches, and a higher ratio of amylopectin. **Waxy starches** from corn or rice contain up to 99 percent amylopectin (short branched-chain starch). Root and waxy starches are crystal clear hot or cold, and are thickest when hot, at their jell temperature. They thin a little when cooled, although they set up in a thick, clear, glossy coating that may not be firm enough to cut. They freeze and thaw nicely without change and thicken at a lower temperature than grain starches—140° to 160°F. Use caution, ➤ because these starches thin when vigorously stirred, hot or cool.

Asian markets sell many types of starches. Arrowroot, potato starch, sweet rice flour, tapioca starch (the powder), and wheat starch are available at a fraction of their cost in regular grocery stores.

HOW STARCH WORKS

As starch solutions are heated, starch granules soak up liquid, swell to many times their original size, and finally pop. When they pop, starch rushes out into the solution and thickening occurs. This thickening begins with grain starches around 190°F and continues to boiling. With root starches, thickening begins at much lower temperatures, 140° to 160°F.

Since the big balloonlike starch granule is part of the thickening, excessive stirring can thin a starch sauce. A few words of caution when working with starches: ➤ Starch needs to be dispersed grain by grain using a method such as a slurry, 544, a roux, 543, or Beurre Manié, 545, to prevent lumping. ➤ To avoid overthickening, starches should be brought to a gentle boil before you decide whether they are thick enough. ➤ Starches will not swell and thicken if there is too much acid or sugar present. This is why lemon meringue pie filling is frequently thickened with just the starch, sugar, and water and the lemon juice stirred in after it has thickened. ➤ Stirring after the starch has completely cooled and set will thin the dish.

ARROWROOT

A popular base for cream sauces and clear glazes, arrowroot, is cooked by the same method as cornstarch, but ➤ substitutes in the amount of 1½ teaspoons arrowroot to 1 tablespoon flour. To ensure an attractive consistency when arrowroot glaze is used on cold acid fruits, dissolve 1½ teaspoons gelatin in 1 tablespoon cold water and add it to the hot glaze. Spoon the cooled glaze over the chilled fruit and keep cold until you serve.

CORNSTARCH

A starch from the endosperm of corn, this is a valuable thickener. ➤ Substitute 1 tablespoon plus 1 teaspoon cornstarch for 2 tablespoon all-purpose flour.

Few things are more discouraging than the lumps cornstarch can form or the raw taste that results if it is badly handled or insufficiently cooked. Here is what we have learned about handling cornstarch more easily:

Use very gentle heat or a double boiler. In recipes calling for sugar, avoid lumping by mixing the cornstarch, sugar, and salt together just before gradually adding the ➤ cold liquid. In recipes without sugar, mix the cornstarch with some cold water to make a slurry, or paste. Whisk this paste gradually into the ➤ hot, but not boiling, liquid.

Because cornstarch produces a clear jelled filling—as do tapioca and arrowroot—use it for thickening very acidic fruits, because it keeps its thickening power better than flour in the presence of acid. But if it is ➤ overcooked, it loses its thickening power very quickly, regardless of the presence or absence of acid. These facts account for the countless letters we get on pie fillings. In the extra special care cooks lavish on fillings, they are apt to overcook or overbeat them after cooking. Be very careful to check the cooking stages described below.

Other causes for breakdown of thickening may come from too high a percentage of sugar in the recipe. Also, tests have shown that ➤ the material from which the pan is made has a direct result on the thickening quality and the success of unmolding cornstarch-based puddings. Metals that distribute heat evenly, such as stainless steel, are superior to heatproof glass. However, glass does work well when, with stirring, cornstarch is thickened in the microwave.

But let's get on with the cooking. Once the cornstarch is properly added to the liquid, dispersed either in sugar or in a slurry or paste, it goes through a few different cooking periods. During the first period over low heat, ➤ constant, gentle stirring is necessary to keep the mixture free from lumps and to hold the starch particles in suspension until gelatinization takes place and the mixture thickens. In this time, the mixture should have reached at least the 190°F temperature that is essential for proper thickening.

If eggs are added, use the tempering method, the essential way for eggs or egg yolks to meet hot liquid. The eggs are well beaten first. A portion of the hot mixture is added to the eggs very gradually, then it is returned to the original mass, which has ➤ been removed from the heat temporarily. ➤ The stirring is less constant and extremely gentle during this period. Return to the heat and, if it's going to be refrigerated any longer than two hours, ➤ it is important to bring the entire mass of pudding or pie filling back to a full boil—it will be thick and large bubbles will burst open throughout the mixture, not just at the edges. Use a flat-bottom spatula, scraping the pan as you stir. The high temperature kills alpha-amylase, an enzyme present in eggs that if allowed to live would turn the pudding or pie filling to soup overnight. The pudding should thicken much more in cooling.

If using, have ready molds rinsed with cold water. Stir the mixture very gently into them—releasing the steam, which would condense and thin the mixture. Cool for about 30 minutes at room temperature. For successful unmolding, refrigerate individual molds for 1 to 2 hours; larger molds, 6 to 12 hours.

▲ Above 5,000 feet, cornstarch needs to cook longer before it thickens or gelatinizes, so fillings and puddings thickened with cornstarch take longer to cook; for maxi-mum gelatization, cook cornstarch mixtures over direct heat, stirring constantly.

POTATO STARCH

Potato starch is a tuber starch, extracted from the flesh of a white potato, that is dried and ground. Used to thicken, it creates a clear jell. It has the highest thickening potential of all the starches—a little goes a long way. Most large grocery stores carry potato starch, but it may be sold with matzo meal and other kosher ingredients, rather than with other starches.

SWEET RICE FLOUR (WAXY STARCH)

Also known as mochi, mochik, or glutinous rice flour, waxy rice flours are used in making sauces, confections, and Asian desserts. Their remarkable stabilizing powers prevent the separation of frozen gravies and sauces when reheated, and they are also much less likely to lump. Don't confuse with rice flour, 984.

TAPIOCA AND SAGO

Similar in uses, tapioca is processed from the Brazilian cassava root and sago from certain Indian palms. Cassava is poisonous until heated; heat releases the hydrocyanic acid. Sago and the so-called pearl tapioca, so named because it resembles pearls, must both be soaked before use. Soak 1/4 cup of the pearls in 1/2 cup water or milk; it should be completely absorbed—if it isn't, the pearls are too old to use. ➤ Pearl tapioca loses its thickening capacity when stored for a prolonged period. There is no way to know the condition until it's soaked or cooked. If you have already embarked on mixing the recipe, and you realize the thickening powers of the pearl tapioca are weak, you can substitute rice in equal parts for pearl tapioca. Pearl tapioca is available in some specialty food stores and Asian markets. Most supermarkets carry quick-cooking tapioca, a pre-cooked form that comes in tiny granules and is used to make tapioca custard or pudding, 820, and thicken fruit pies. ➤ To substitute quick-cooking or instant tapioca for pearl tapioca, allow 1 1/2 to 2 tablespoons of this finer form for 4 tablespoons of the pearl. ➤ As a thickener, substitute 1 tablespoon quick-cooking tapioca for 1 tablespoon flour.

TAPIOCA FLOUR

Like waxy rice and waxy corn starches, tapioca flour is an effective thickener for sauces and fruit fillings that will be frozen. Tapioca-based sauces and fillings thaw without breaking down and becoming watery, as flour-thickened sauces do after freezing.

To use in freezing, ➤ substitute 1 tablespoon tapioca flour for 2 1/2 tablespoons all-purpose flour to 1 cup liquid. ➤ In nonfrozen sauces, substitute 1 1/2 teaspoons tapioca flour for 1 tablespoon all-purpose flour.

Tapioca flour is also popular for making very clear glazes. Cook the tapioca and fruit juice or water only to the boiling point. ➤ Beware of overcooking, or the tapioca will become stringy; ➤ never boil. When the first bubbles begin to break through the surface, remove the pan from the heat at once. The mixture will look thin and milky. Let it stand 2 or 3 minutes. Stir. Wait 2 or 3 minutes longer, and stir again. If the recipe calls for butter, stir it in at this time. After 10 to 15 minutes more of undisturbed cooling, the glaze should be thick enough to glaze food.

WAXY CORNSTARCH

This is not traditional cornstarch but one of the waxy starches made from specific varieties of corn. They are revolutionizing frozen sauces and fillings with their great stabilizing powers, ➤ but they are not to be used in baking. For thickening, ➤ substitute 1 tablespoon waxy cornstarch for 1 tablespoon all-purpose flour.

SUET

A solid, light-colored fat obtained from around the kidney or loin area of beef or mutton, used in the preparation of Mincemeat, 902, steamed puddings, 824, and haggis. True beef suet is best obtained from a butcher; it is not the same as suet sold for bird feeding. Buy at least 10 ounces suet to yield 8 ounces cleaned. Cut away and discard any parts that are reddish or that look dried out, then crumble what remains between your fingers and remove any pieces of tough filament. A certain amount of fine, papery filament will remain. To chop, separate the pieces of suet and freeze solid in preparation for chopping. For plum pudding, 825, the suet must be chopped to a very fine consistency, but it must not be allowed to melt and become pasty. If you work quickly, you will have no trouble doing this with a large chef's knife. Alternatively, you can grind the suet in a food processor fitted with a metal blade, being careful not to overprocess. Extra suet can be sealed in an airtight plastic bag and frozen for up to 6 months.

SUGARS, LIQUID

There are a number of factors to contend with in substituting liquid for solid sweeteners: Their sweetening powers vary quite a bit; their greater moisture content has to be taken into account; and those that are acidic, such as molasses or honey, need neutralizing by the addition of baking soda. To measure liquid sugars, lightly spray the measuring container first with nonstick vegetable spray, or lightly coat the inside with vegetable shortening or oil. This will cause the liquid sugar to slip out easily without adhering to the sides of the measuring cup. Then pour or spoon these sticky ingredients into the measure, just to the level mark. ➤ Never dip a measuring cup into the honey or syrup container, for the added amount clinging to the outside may make your recipe too sweet or too liquid. For information about specific sugars, see individual entries.

SUGARS, SOLID

Most of our cooking is done with sugars derived from sugarcane or sugar beets. Both are so similar in their cooking reactions and taste that only the label gives us the clue to their source. But the various grinds of solid sugars affect not only their comparative volumes but also their sweetening powers well. Liquid sweeteners, such as honey, corn syrup, and molasses react very differently in cooking and baking combinations. Whichever type you use, more is needed to sweeten food or drinks.

Among other things, sugars, like fats, give tenderness to doughs. In small amounts, they speed up the working of yeast. However, too much sugar during proofing, 593, will inhibit yeast activity. Sugar in bread, rolls, and muffins produces a golden brown crust. Small pinches are added to some vegetables, such as caramelized onions, to enhance their flavor.

Sugars, whether solid or liquid, are not interchangeable. For a quick comparison of sugar weights and volumes, see 1032. Many baking recipes call for sifting confectioners' sugar before measuring. To measure any sugar except brown sugar, 1018, fill a dry measuring cup with a scoop to overflowing, taking care not to shake down the contents to even it, then level off the top with the straight edge of a knife, as shown for flour on 983.

In ➤ substituting liquid for dry sweeteners, an adjustment in other liquid ingredients must be made, especially in baking, as discussed in Sugars, Liquid, above.

BROWN AND BARBADOS SUGAR

Brown sugar is a moister cane or beet sugar with added molasses. It is available in light or dark—the latter more strongly flavored with molasses. As both types harden and lump easily, keep brown sugar in a tightly covered container or in a tightly closed plastic bag. If the sugar should become hard or lumpy, place it in a dish, cover with plastic wrap, and microwave on high for 30-second intervals, using a fork to break up the sugar. Or place in a resealable plastic bag, add half an apple or a slice of bread to the bag, seal, and let stand. Remove the apple when the sugar softens. Or push the sugar through a strainer, forcing the lumps out with the back of a spoon. ➤ In this book, if neither light nor dark brown sugar is specified, either type can be used. Use dark brown sugar when a stronger flavor or darker color is wanted.

To measure brown sugar, pack it firmly into the measuring cup and level it by pressing with the palm of your hand. Then unmold it, sandcastle-like, as shown. ➤ To

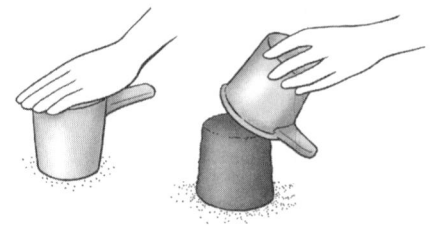

Measuring brown sugar

substitute brown sugar for granulated sugar, use 1 cup firmly packed brown sugar for each cup granulated sugar.

Pourable **granulated brown sugar** is also widely available. Depending on the brand, it may not be as sweet, so be sure you know what you are buying and follow the directions on the package when using in recipes.

Barbados sugar, also called **Muscovado,** is a moist light to dark brown sugar with a strong molasses taste, and a coarse grain. Like turbinado sugar, 1020, it is a partially refined raw sugar. ➤ Substitute cup for cup for light or dark brown sugar.

CARAMELIZED SUGAR

A marvelous flavoring that can be made in several ways. While its caramel flavor is strong, the sweetening power of the sugar used is reduced by about one-half.

I. For Hard Glazes

Place in a small heavy saucepan:

$^3/_4$ **cup sugar**

Drizzle evenly over the top:

$^1/_4$ **cup water**

Place the pan over medium heat and, without stirring, very gently swirl the pan until a clear syrup forms. It is important that the sugar dissolves and the syrup clarifies before it boils, so slide the pan on and off the burner as necessary. Increase the heat to high and bring the syrup to a rolling boil. Cover the pan tightly and boil for 2 minutes. Uncover the pan and cook the syrup until it begins to darken. Gently swirl the pan once again, and cook the syrup until it turns a deep amber.

Store the syrup tightly covered at room temperature. The syrup hardens on standing, but if stored in a heat-proof jar, is easily melted by heating the jar gently in hot water.

Should the sugar burn, use it for coloring, below.

II. For Coloring

Caramelized sugar will keep indefinitely if stored at room temperature. This can be used to replace the more highly seasoned commercial gravy colorings. The intense heat under which it is processed destroys all sweetening power. Melt in a very heavy large nonreactive pan over high heat:

1 cup sugar

Stir constantly until it is burned smoke-colored to black, about 10 minutes. Remove from the heat and let cool. ➤ Quick addition of water to intensely hot sugar, which is well over 300°F, can be explosive and very dangerous. When cool, add almost drop by drop:

1 cup hot water

Stir over low heat until the burnt sugar becomes a thin dark liquid.

CHINESE ROCK SUGAR

Made from refined sugarcane juice and used as a sweetener for various Chinese desserts, and soups, this sugar is sold in lumps and is available in Asian markets. It is usually crushed or broken into small pieces before use.

COLORED SUGAR

You can use a combination of colors to customize your hue. Place a large bowl:

1 cup regular or coarse sugar

Sprinkle:

10 to 12 drops food coloring

over the surface of the sugar. Whisk to blend the color evenly. Pour into an even layer onto a baking sheet or flat surface and let dry, about 3 hours.

CONFECTIONERS' SUGAR

Confectioners' sugar, also called powdered sugar, is a bright white powdery sugar. Its finest form, known as 10X, is the type sold packaged at most markets. Confectioners' sugar is the counterpart of the English **icing sugar.** In order to lessen lumping, a small quantity of cornstarch is added to the sugar during processing. If it does lump, sift it. Measure confectioners' sugar as you would flour, 983. Sometimes the cornstarch gives uncooked icings a raw flavor. If desired, before spreading this kind of mixture, you can heat it for about 10 minutes ➤ over boiling water; see 789. ➤ Do not try to substitute confectioners' sugar for granulated in baking—its dense texture gives a different crumb to cakes. In other uses, substitute $1^3/_4$ cups confectioners' for each 1 cup granulated.

CORN SUGAR

Corn sugar is a crystallized dextrose obtained by hydrolyzing cornstarch with acid. Corn sugar is used in home beer-brewing operations.

FLAVORED SUGARS

Keep these on hand for quick flavoring.

I. CINNAMON SUGAR

Mix 1 cup sugar with 2 tablespoons ground cinnamon. Use for buttered toast, for coffee cake, and as a yogurt topping.

II. CITRUS-FLAVORED SUGAR

We find this extremely useful and delicious in custards and desserts. Mix 1 to 2 tablespoons grated lemon, orange, or lime zest for every cup of sugar. Let stand, covered, in a cool place, for 5 to 7 days before using.

III. VANILLA SUGAR

Add 1 to 2 vanilla beans for each 2 cups of granulated or confectioners' sugar, and store tightly sealed in a canister. You may crush the beans with a few tablespoons of sugar before adding them to the rest of the sugar. Sift the sugar before using, then return the vanilla to the canister, replace it with new sugar, and use until the beans lose their flavoring power. Use in hot cereals, on cookies, and in hot coffee or cocoa.

GRANULATED SUGAR

In this book, when the word "sugar" appears, it means granulated white sugar—beet sugar or cane sugar, both being 99.5 percent pure sucrose. Granulated sugar can be used for almost every purpose, even for meringues. En-

glish granulated sugar is too coarse for this, and their **castor sugar,** closer to our superfine sugar, is used instead. **Coarse or decorating sugar** is large-crystal granulated sugar and may be clear, white, or tinted colors; see 1019.
➤ One pound of granulated sugar equals approximately 2 cups.

LUMP SUGAR AND SUGAR CUBES

Lump sugar and sugar cubes are granulated sugar molded or cut into convenient rectangles or cubes for use in hot drinks. Rock Candy Crystals, 875, make an interesting stand-in for lump sugar and, when separated or crushed, a sparkling garnish for frosted cakes.

MAPLE SUGAR

Made from evaporation of maple sap or syrup boiled until most of the liquid has evaporated, maple sugar has a distinctive, strong, sweet taste. Because of its high cost, it is often reserved for flavoring. As it dissolves slowly, grate or shave it before combining it with other ingredients. ➤ In substituting, allow about $1/2$ cup maple sugar for each cup of granulated sugar.

RAW AND TURBINADO SUGARS

Raw sugar is processed from sugarcane, and the USDA notes that it is "unfit for direct use as an food ingredient because of the impurities it ordinarily contains." However, **turbinado sugar** and Barbados sugar, 1018, are partially refined raw sugars (refined in a turbine, thus the name). With coarse, beige crystals that contain the molasses portion of the sugar, turbinado sugar is closest in character to the yellow or brownish **Demerara sugar** often called for in English recipes. ➤ Substitute cup for cup for granulated sugar, but be aware of its heavier molasses flavor.

SUPERFINE SUGAR

Also called bar or berry sugar, superfine sugar is a finer grind of granulated sugar. It is still coarse enough that the individual crystals are easily discernible. Because it dissolves readily, it is used in meringues and for sweetening fruits, cold mixtures, and cocktails and drinks. The crystals are too small for creaming with butter in making cakes, cookies, or in any baking where the sugar crystals must "cut" into the butter. If it becomes lumpy, put the sugar in a plastic bag and use a rolling pin to crush the lumps. Make superfine sugar at home with a food processor, pulsing granulated sugar until fine and powderlike. ➤ Superfine sugar can be substituted cup for cup for granulated sugar where appropriate.

SUGAR SUBSTITUTES

Some sugar substitutes can be used in cooking or baking, according to the manufacturer directions. However, they do not give the same texture and color in baking as do true sugars and should be used only in recipes especially developed for them. There is some reason to question the systemic effects of all noncaloric sweeteners, but several have been given government approval for use. **Saccharin** is a synthetic sweetener commonly used at the table. It is 300 times sweeter than sucrose (granulated sugar), but it does have a slightly metallic aftertaste. It does not contribute any calories, because it is not metabolized in the body. Saccharin should not be cooked, as it becomes bitter when heated. **Aspartame** is marketed for commercial use and is found in breakfast cereals, soft drinks, desserts, and candy. It is also available as a powder for use in the home. Although technically considered a nutritive sweetener, contributing 4 calories per gram, aspartame is 200 times sweeter than sugar and very little is needed to achieve sweetness. Therefore, its caloric contribution is negligible. It is digested and metabolized the same way as other protein foods. ➤ People diagnosed with phenylketonuria (PKU), a rare hereditary disease, who need to limit phenylalanine intake should restrict aspartame in their diet. **Sucralose** is available as a multipurpose sweetener. A white crystalline powder made from sugar, sucralose is 400 to 800 times sweeter than granulated sugar. It is stable when subjected to heat, and it can be used in a variety of hot and cold drinks, pastries and baked goods, and frozen and canned fruits and vegetables. Its chemical structure is very close to that of sucrose. **Acesulfame-K** is found in beverages, fruit spreads, baked goods, dessert bases, tabletop sweeteners, hard candies, chewing gum, and breath fresheners. It is 200 times sweeter than sugar. People who are on a potassium-restricted diet or have sulfa-antibiotic based allergies should discuss its use with a physician.

SWEET CICELY

The green seeds and fresh leaves of this soft, ferny plant may be used as a garnish for salads or cold vegetables. Use the seeds in cakes, candies, and liqueurs. *Myrrhis odorata,* a perennial growing to 3 feet, prefers partial shade and rich moist soil.

SWEET WOODRUFF OR WALDMEISTER

The beautiful dark green starlike whorled fresh leaves of this plant are floated in May Wine, 66, or in other cold punches, but they should not be left in longer than about 30 minutes. The plants emit a strong odor of freshly mown hay when the foliage is crushed or cut. Their aromatic intensity increases when dried. *Asperula odorata,* which grows to 1 foot, makes a charming ground cover in shady locations.

SZECHUAN PEPPERCORNS

These dried reddish-brown berries are not related to black peppercorns or chile peppers. They have a clean, spicy fragrance that has made them popular in Chinese cooking. "Seasoned oil"—made by heating Szechuan peppercorns in peanut oil until they blacken, then straining the oil and discarding the peppercorns—makes a wonderful cooking oil for stir-fried dishes, or it may be used for dressing Chinese salads. To toast, see 969. Also popular is a seasoned salt made with Szechuan pepper, an easy way to add the flavor of this spice to any dish; see below. It is a popular accompaniment to roasted pork or duck, and try it on salads or eggs.

SZECHUAN-PEPPER SALT
About ⅓ cup
Combine in a dry skillet and toast over medium heat, shaking the pan, until the peppercorns begin to smoke:

    2 tablespoons Szechuan peppercorns
    3 tablespoons kosher salt
    1 teaspoon white peppercorns

Transfer to a mortar or spice grinder and grind to a coarse powder.

TABASCO® SAUCE
This uniquely American flavoring is made from Tabasco peppers, vinegar, and salt and aged in charred oak barrels previously used in the production of bourbon and reused for this fiery sauce. ➤ Go easy at first—a few drops may be too much. Use in soups, cocktail sauce, piquant sauces, or wherever food needs a drop of fire.

TAHINI
Like fresh peanut butter, this sesame seed paste will keep, refrigerated, in a tightly covered container for several months. Stir before use if the oil separates.
Preheat the oven to 350°F. Spread on a baking sheet:

    4 cups white sesame seeds

Bake, shaking frequently, until fragrant, 8 to 10 minutes, do not brown. Cool. Put the seeds in a blender or food processor. Add:

    ¼ cup vegetable oil, or as needed

Process to a smooth paste, about 3 minutes. Add more oil if necessary to bring the paste to a thick pouring consistency.

TAPIOCA
See Starches, 1016.

TARRAGONS
Called *estragon* by the French, this herb, when fresh, is one of the luxuries of cooking. The flavor, chemically identical to that of anise, is somewhat lost in drying, when the leaf vein stiffens, and it does not resoften in cooking. So, if the dry leaf is used, it must be carefully strained out before the food is served. To avoid the need for straining and to retain flavor better than by drying, we hold tarragon in vinegar and remove the leaves as needed. Do not crowd the vinegar bottle, allowing about 3 tablespoons of leaves to 1 quart vinegar, 1024. This gives enough acid to keep the leaves from spoiling. Always keep them well immersed. Although tarragon is too pungent to be cooked in soups, it is good added to practically everything else: eggs, mushrooms, tomatoes, sweetbreads, mustard, tartar sauce, and fish or chicken. And it is essential in a Béarnaise sauce. Tarragon is of the mix Fines Herbes, 982. True tar-ragon, *Artemisia dracunculus,* is perennial. As it seldom sets seed, it is propagated by cuttings, or by divisions pulled—not cut—from the emerging shoots in early March. A less desirable form, because of its lack of flavor and harshness, called Russian tarragon, *A. dracunculoides,* can be grown from seed.

THYMES
The tiny leaves of thymes may be used with almost any meat or vegetable, roasted poultry, lamb, veal, pork, and rabbit; in Creole dishes and gumbos; in brown sauces; for pickled beets, pasta sauces, and tomatoes; and with fatty fish, stews, and stuffings. They are frequently found in stocks as a part of a Bouquet Garni, 960. Fresh thyme makes a lovely garnish for hors d'oeuvres and canapés. The leaves dry very well. Caraway-scented thyme, or *Thymus herba-barona* is traditional with a beef round roast or a baron of beef.

There are so many charming varieties of *Thymus,* and their flavors are so varied, that a collection of them makes a garden in itself. The narrow-leaf French or garden thyme, *Thymus vulgaris,* with its upright habit and gray-green balsamic foliage, and the glistening, small-bushed, strongly scented lemon variety—*T. serpyllum citriodorus*—are the thymes most frequently found in the market. Thymes, which grow best in sun, are perennial, persisting for years among rocks. Prune after blooming.

TOMATOES AS SEASONING
Whether fresh, canned, cooked, or pureed, or as paste or sauce—and even as soup—the tomato weaves its way into innumerable dishes. To get the flavor without too much moisture, cut fresh tomatoes crosswise in half and squeeze to release extra moisture and seeds. Peel before using, and seed if desired as shown on 311. Canned and cooked tomatoes are best drained, and sometimes strained so that the tasty, pulpy part is forced through the sieve, leaving only the skin and seeds to discard. When making substitutions for purees, pastes, and catsups, be sure to compensate for moisture differences and to allow for the variations in strength of flavor. Before modern canning methods were available, tomatoes were dried for use when fresh tomatoes were not available. These dried vessels of concentrated flavor are still popular in antipasto, dips, and spreads, or as a flavor booster for sauce. To make your own dried tomatoes, see 709.

ITALIAN TOMATO PASTE
This flavorful paste is oven- or sun-dried and then rolled into balls. To use, it is diluted in a little boiling water or stock and added to sauces and soups. Fine in spaghetti and noodle dishes, as a dressing for cooked vegetables or salads, and as an addition to salad dressings.
Combine in a large pot:

    6 quarts ripe plum or Italian tomatoes,
        washed and sliced

1 large rib celery with some leaves, cut up

$3/4$ cup chopped onion

3 tablespoons minced fresh herbs or 1 tablespoon
  dried herbs: basil, thyme, marjoram, or oregano

$3/4$ teaspoon whole black peppercorns

12 whole cloves

1 tablespoon salt

One 2-inch cinnamon stick

(1 garlic clove, minced)

Bring to a simmer and simmer gently until the tomatoes are soft, stirring frequently. Strain through a fine sieve, pressing on the vegetables with the back of a wooden spoon. Simmer the pulp over, not in, boiling water or over direct very low heat, with the use of a heat diffuser, 1062, if necessary to prevent burning. Stir frequently. After several hours, when the pulp is thick and reduced by about half, spread the paste to a depth of $1/2$ inch on moist plates. Make short cuts into the paste to let air penetrate. Place the paste in the sun or in a 200°F oven to dry. When the paste is so dry that it retains it shape, roll it into balls. Store refrigerated in airtight sterile jars.

TOMATO PASTE (OR VELVET)
About $3/4$ cup

This makes a relish or a fine addition to sauces.
Wash, then mash:

6 large ripe tomatoes

Melt in the top of a double boiler:

2 tablespoons butter

Add the tomatoes and:

1 teaspoon brown sugar

$1/4$ teaspoon paprika

$3/4$ teaspoon salt

Cook over, not in boiling water, stirring occasionally, until the consistency of a thick paste. Put the paste through a strainer. Store refrigerated.

TURMERIC

Turmeric, an Indian rhizome of *Curcuma longa*—is somewhat bitter when dried and ground, and its rather acrid fugitive or musky fragrance warms the mouth, so it must be used with discretion. It contains the highly prized antioxidant curcumin. Its golden color gives the underlying tone to blended curry powders and to certain pickles. In small quantities, turmeric is used as a food coloring, often replacing the far more expensive saffron.

VANILLA

The long, thin vanilla bean is a pod from a climbing orchid vine. When the bean is picked, it has no flavor. After curing for several months, tiny fragrant crystals called vanillin are secreted in the pod's lining. Eventually the aroma of the crystals fills the inside of the pod as crystals cover the outside. The pod wrinkles and turns chocolate brown. Vanilla extract is prepared by macerating the beans in a 35-percent alcohol solution. ➤ Beware of synthetic vanil-

las, whose cheap flavor is instantly detected. To retain its greatest flavor, add the extract only when food is cooling. Try 2 parts vanilla to 1 part almond flavoring—a great Viennese favorite. Or try keeping vanilla beans in brandy and using the flavored brandy as a seasoning.

If you are curious about the little dark specks in vanilla ice cream, these are the seeds scraped from the vanilla bean. The pod is slit open lengthwise, and the black specks of seeds are scraped out with the tip of a knife. Allow the seeds scraped from about 1 inch of a vanilla bean for 1 teaspoon vanilla extract. For another way to use vanilla, see Vanilla Sugar, 1019.

Vanilla paste is made from vanilla extract and finely ground vanilla beans, suspended in a thick liquid. It adds extraordinary flavor to whipped cream, crème brûlée, and other recipes where the flavor and appearance of vanilla bean is desired. ➤ One teaspoon of the paste is equivalent to 1 teaspoon of vanilla extract or $1 1/2$ inches of a vanilla bean.

VEGETABLE AND NUT MILKS

These are all valuable nutritionally, but not comparable to animal milks, as their protein is of lower biologic value and their vitamin content is different. These are, however, a boon to those who are lactose-intolerant and to vegans.

ALMOND MILK
1 cup

Combine in a food processor and process to tiny, moist clumps, about 3 minutes:

1 cup slivered blanched almonds

$1/4$ cup sugar

With the machine running, slowly pour in:

$1 1/4$ cups boiling water

(2 tablespoons orange water)

Scrape down the sides of the work bowl and process for 30 seconds longer. Let steep for 3 minutes. Set a sieve over a bowl, line the sieve with dampened cheesecloth, and pour in the almond mixture. Let the almond milk drip through for 45 minutes, then use a spoon to press as much of the liquid out of the almonds as you can before discarding the debris. Refrigerate.

NUT MILK

Almond and walnut milks have long been known in Europe. Native Americans used hickory and pecan milk. These rather fragilely flavored milks, as well as coconut milk, are a great delicacy in sauces and puddings. ➤ They are as perishable as cow's milk and in storage and cooking should be treated like Coconut Milk, 972.

As nuts vary in weight, to substitute other nuts in the recipe for almond milk above, look up the measurement equivalent for almonds, and blanch the nuts if necessary. Nut milks are often used instead of milk in desserts, with sugar added. If using for sauces other than dessert sauces, you may use stock as your liquid base.

SOY MILK

Soy milk is the creamy "milk" of whole soybeans. With its unique nutty flavor and considerable nutritional value, soy milk can be used in a variety of ways. It can be served hot or cold and is often sweetened or flavored. Prepared soy milk is widely available. Unopened aseptically packaged soy milk can be stored at room temperature for several months. Once opened, refrigerate it. Soy milk stays fresh for about 5 days.

Plain unfortified soy milk is an excellent source of high-quality protein, most B-vitamins, and iron. Brands of soy milk that are fortified with vitamins and minerals can be good sources of calcium and vitamin D, and vitamin B_{12}. Free of milk sugar or lactose, soy milk is a good choice for lactose-intolerant individuals as well as for those allergic to cow's milk. A number of "lite" soy milks, with reduced fat content, are also available. Soy milk is not intended for infant feeding, but it can be enjoyed by children over the age of 1.

6 cups

This soy milk is naturally sweet and rich. To flavor it, add a vanilla bean while the milk is simmering and discard it after the milk has cooled. The chilled milk can also be sweetened with honey. To prepare the milk, use a blender with a metal, glass, or heatproof plastic container and lid; if the container is glass, warm it with hot water before using to prevent cracking.

Soak, 253:

> **1 cup dried soybeans, picked over and rinsed**

in:

> **5 cups cold water**

Drain and divide the soybeans into 3 equal portions. Process 1 portion of the soybeans at high speed in a blender with:

> **$^{3}/_{4}$ cup boiling water**

Continue processing until the mixture is smooth, about 1 minute. Remove to a sieve or colander lined with several layers of cheesecloth and set over a large bowl. Repeat the procedure 2 times with the remaining soybeans and add more boiling water. Mash the soybean pulp, or *okara* ("honorable pulp" in Japanese) against the side of the sieve with a wooden spoon to extract as much liquid as possible. Gather the cheesecloth around the bean pulp and squeeze to extract the remaining liquid. Remove the soy milk to a large saucepan. Cook over medium-high heat, stirring constantly, until the mixture foams up, then remove from the heat and let stand for 1 minute. Return the saucepan to the burner, reduce the heat, and simmer gently for 10 minutes, stirring often. Remove from the heat and let cool, stirring occasionally to prevent a film from forming on the top. (If a film does form, the soy milk can be strained.)

Measure the soy milk and add water, if necessary, to make 6 cups. Refrigerate the soy milk for up to 5 days, or freeze for up to 1 month. (Thawed soy milk may need to be whipped in a blender or food processor to restore its smoothness.) If you plan to make tofu, or bean curd, 316, you can use the milk at once, while still hot.

VEGETABLE OILS

Vegetable oils are pressed from various seeds, fruits, and nuts. Nutrients are best retained by cold-press processes. In cold-pressing, the seeds, fruits, or nuts are crushed and then pressed using minimal pressure and heat. Oils extracted in this way retain their natural flavors and textures.

Vegetable oils include **corn, cottonseed, grapeseed, soybean, canola, safflower, sunflower, peanut, coconut,** and **palm oil.** These oils when further refined and deodorized are difficult to distinguish from one another by flavor and odor. With the exception of coconut and palm kernel oil, most vegetable oils contain a large amount of monounsaturated and polyunsaturated fatty acids. Coconut and palm oils contain large amounts of saturated fatty acids. To read more about fats and fatty acids, see Nutrition, 4.

Toasted nut oils such as walnut, almond, sesame, and macadamia have an intense flavor and cannot stand up to intense heat. They are best used as a condiment, as a seasoning sprinkled over cooked food, or as an ingredient in sauces, salad dressings, or marinades. Buy in small quantities.

When cooking with any oil, avoid heating it to the point where it begins to smoke—the smoke signals that the oil has reached the highest safe temperature, or its **smoke point.** Every oil has its own unique smoke point. Once an oil reaches its smoke point, it starts to smoke and break down, possibly producing acrid gases. All cooking should be done below the smoke point of the oil used. An oil's smoke point is determined by its fatty-acid content. Safflower, cottonseed, grapeseed, peanut, and canola oil have the highest smoke points and are suitable for high-heat cooking processes like deep-frying or sautéeing. Avoid cooking with metals that can cause oils to oxidize, such as copper, brass, or bronze; opt for stainless steel instead.

Store oils in airtight containers in a cool, dark place. Keep cold-pressed and toasted nut oils in the refrigerator. Refrigeration does not affect the flavor, but if the oil clouds or "winterizes," it will return to its clear and liquid state at room temperature. To prevent "winterization" of refrigerated oils and to have the oil readily available for cooking, decant a small amount of each into a bottle or closed container and keep the rest refrigerated. ➤ Discard any oil that smells rancid, fishy, or musty or that starts to foam, darken, or smoke excessively when heated. Discard any oil that has smoked, has darkened, or does not bubble when food is added. For a discussion and recipes for flavored oils, see 590.

Oils are 100 percent fat, so they ➤ must be reduced by 15 percent to 20 percent when substituted for butter, either by weight or by volume measure. However, there are additional complications when substituting them for solid fats, especially in baking; see 709. So in this book, ➤ when oil can be used in baking recipes, it is specifically indicated and the proper amounts and procedures are given.

VINEGAR

In most cases the product of two stages of fermentation, vinegar can be made from almost any liquid. In the first fermentation, the action of yeast converts the sugar to alcohol; in the second, bacteria convert the alcohol to acetic acid. Vinegars are made from fruit or grains.

Whether a vinegar is sharp, rich, or mellow makes a tremendous difference in cooking. ➤ All vinegars are corrosive—with a 4 to 6 percent acidity—so be sure to prepare pickled or marinated foods or those dressed with a vinaigrette in glass, enamel, or stainless steel bowls or vessels. Keep away from copper, zinc, aluminum, and galvanized or iron ware. Store in glass with cork or plastic tops.

BALSAMIC VINEGAR

Balsamic vinegar falls into two categories. Traditional balsamic vinegars are made from the juice of white grapes and only in the provinces of Modena and Reggio in northern Italy. Depending on their age, they can be very expensive. By law this balsamic contains no added wine vinegar. Its guarantee of authenticity is the word *tradizionale* on its label. It is aged 12 years for *vecchio* (old), and 25 years for *extra vecchio*. Use traditional balsamic as an intense sauce or condiment, by the drop, on finished dishes or with fresh fruit such as strawberries or watermelon.

Commercial balsamic vinegar can be produced anywhere and is usually made with a wine vinegar to which caramel coloring is added. The quality varies, as no regulations govern its production. Use in marinades, in dressings, and cooked in recipes.

CIDER VINEGAR

Cider vinegar results from the fermentation of the juice of apples. Sometimes labeled apple cider vinegar, these full-bodied vinegars usually have 5 percent acetic acid. They are frequently used in pickling, 943.

DISTILLED WHITE VINEGAR

Based on dilute distilled alcohol fermented to a 5 percent acetic acid content, white vinegar is used in pickling when the pickle must remain light in color.

HERB VINEGARS

Herb vinegars are commercially available but easily made at home. Use cider or wine vinegar for best results. Individual herbs like tarragon or rosemary are choice, or develop your favorite herb combinations—allowing approximately 3 tablespoons fresh herb leaves per quart of vinegar. The reason for this caution is that if too much vegetable matter is used, the vinegar's preservative strength may not be strong enough to prevent botulism, 888. If using garlic, crush it and leave it in the jar only 24 hours, then remove it. After 2 to 4 weeks of steeping, filter the vinegar through cheesecloth, rebottle it in sterilized containers, and keep tightly sealed.

MALT VINEGAR

Malt vinegars are the fermentations of an infusion of barley malt or corn, rye, or oats whose starch has been converted by malt. Unlike other vinegars, malt vinegar is most often used as a condiment, traditionally with fish and chips.

RICE VINEGAR

Much of the rice vinegar produced is made from fermented rice wine. Sometimes called rice wine vinegar, it is pleasant but weaker in acid content—4 percent—and thus milder in flavor than other vinegars. **Seasoned rice vinegar** contains added sugar and salt; it can be used to season sushi rice, 359. Because of its lower acid content, rice vinegar is not recommended for pickling. **Chinese black vinegar** is very popular in southern China, where Chinkiang vinegar, the best of the black rice vinegars, is produced. Usually made with rice, although millet, wheat, or sorghum may be used instead, it is dark in color, with a deep, almost smoky flavor. One word of warning: The quality of black rice vinegars varies greatly. Black rice vinegar works well in braised dishes and as a dipping sauce. Balsamic vinegar is a good, but possibly more expensive, substitute.

SHERRY VINEGAR

Sweet or cream sherries are fermented to create a specialized wine vinegar much like a cross between balsamic and red wine vinegar. These vinegars are sometimes fermented and aged in oak barrels.

WINE VINEGAR

The three most common types of wine vinegar are **red wine vinegar, white wine vinegar,** and **champagne vinegar.** Each has an acetic acid content of about 7 percent. Red is strongest in flavor, champagne the lightest; all are excellent for vinaigrettes or marinades. Wine vinegars are not recommended for pickling but are good for making herb and spice vinegars. If you plan to make vinegars in quantity for gifts, please mix in small batches. Some wine vinegars "mother," forming a wispy residue at the bottom of the bottle. This is harmless, and can be strained or filtered from the vinegar.

CHILE VINEGAR
2 cups

You can make a really fiery French dressing with this. Steep:

    1 ounce dried chiles

in:

    1 pint vinegar

for 10 days. Shake daily. Then strain and store in well-sealed sterilized bottles, 930.

GARLIC VINEGAR

1 cup

Use in dressings or sauces.

Heat to just below the boiling point:

1 cup wine vinegar

Add:

4 garlic cloves, halved

After 24 hours, remove the garlic and place the vinegar in a sterilized glass bottle, 930. Cork tightly.

GINGER VINEGAR

About 1 cup

Combine:

1 cup cider vinegar

Four 1-inch pieces fresh or dried ginger

2 tablespoons sugar

Strain after 1 week-and store in a well-sealed sterilized bottle, 930.

FRESH HERB VINEGAR

Makes 12 quarts

A quantity recipe that serves well for making gifts. Be sure all vegetables are washed and herbs rinsed and dried well.

Heat slowly to just below the boiling point:

12 quarts cider or white wine vinegar

Wash and add:

24 whole black peppercorns

12 shallots, sliced

$^3/_4$ cup tarragon

8 sprigs rosemary

8 sprigs thyme

4 branches winter savory

1 sprig chervil

1 celery root, scrubbed but not peeled and sliced

$^1/_2$ cup parsley sprigs

(1 parsley root, scrubbed and sliced)

Bottle these ingredients. After 2 weeks, strain the vinegar through cheesecloth. Place in sterilized bottles, 930, and seal tightly.

QUICK HERB VINEGAR

About 1 cup

Combine:

1 cup wine or cider vinegar

1 teaspoon crushed dried herbs: basil, tarragon, etc.

You may use this at once in a vinaigrette. If desired, add and then remove within 24 hours:

($^1/_2$ garlic clove)

Shortly before serving, add:

2 tablespoons chopped parsley

1 tablespoon chopped chives

RED RASPBERRY VINEGAR COCKAIGNE

4 cups

Somewhat surprisingly, this makes a marvelously refreshing summer drink served over crushed ice. See Raspberry or Blackberry Shrub, 38.

Put into a large enamel or stainless steel pan:

2 quarts ripe red raspberries

Cover them with:

4 cups cider vinegar

Let stand covered in a cool place about 48 hours. Strain the liquid and use it to cover another:

2 quarts ripe red raspberries

Let stand 48 hours, then strain and measure the liquid into an enamel or stainless steel saucepan. Add an equal quantity, or slightly less, of:

Sugar

Bring to a boil and simmer 10 minutes. Skim and cool. Store in well-sealed sterilized bottles, 930.

SPICED VINEGAR

About 6 quarts

An excellent, if deceptive, mixture. It tastes like a delicious blend of herbs, but it is flavored with spices, whole or ground.

Combine and heat slowly until just under the boiling point, stirring to dissolve the sugar:

6 quarts cider vinegar

2 cups sugar

6 tablespoons whole black peppercorns

$^1/_4$ cup whole cloves

$^1/_4$ cup allspice berries

$^1/_4$ cup mustard seeds

$^1/_4$ cup minced peeled fresh or ground ginger

3 tablespoons celery seeds

3 tablespoons turmeric

2 tablespoons ground mace

Place these ingredients in a covered noncorrosive container. Add:

4 or more garlic cloves

After 24 hours, remove the garlic. Allow the other ingredients to steep 3 weeks. Filter the vinegar and pour into sterilized glass bottles, 930. Seal tightly.

TARRAGON OR BURNET VINEGAR

About 2 cups

This makes a strong infusion that may be diluted later with more vinegar.

Wash, then dry well:

1$^1/_2$ tablespoons fresh tarragon or burnet leaves

Bruise them slightly, and add to:

2 cups warmed cider vinegar

2 whole cloves

1 garlic clove, halved

Place in a covered jar. After 24 hours, remove the garlic. After 2 weeks, strain, and store the vinegar in well-sealed sterilized bottles, 930.

WALNUTS

Walnuts are rich and flavorful and high in beneficial omega-3 fatty acids. Blanching for 3 minutes rids them of an acid that some people find indigestible. Then dry and toast, 1001. The English, or Persian, walnut and the American, or black, walnut are perhaps the most familiar varieties. Walnuts have a crisp texture, and the flavor of the English walnut is much milder than the distinctively flavored black walnut. For black walnuts, hull at once after harvesting. The shell is extremely hard to open, most often requiring a hammer to crack.

WASABI

Also called Japanese horseradish, this perennial herb is native to Japan. Unrelated to horseradish, *Wasabia japonica* belongs to the same family as mustard and broccoli. It grows in moist ground by running water, such as a stream. The root harvested from the plant is grated much like horseradish, 993, and traditionally used in Japanese cooking. Fresh wasabi is becoming more widely available in Asian markets and is now grown in some parts of the Northwest. Fresh wasabi root has a pungent flavor. Gently peel with a vegetable peeler or paring knife, remove the knots, and grate in a circular motion on the finest side of a box grater or ginger grater. Store any unused wasabi root wrapped in damp paper towels in the refrigerator.

More widely available than the fresh root is **powdered wasabi.** Powdered wasabi may not contain any wasabi root—it is typically made from dried ground horseradish or mustard powder, tinted green. It shares little with fresh wasabi except for the strong, sharp flavor. To reconstitute, mix with equal parts warm water. Stir and allow to sit for 15 minutes to develop its flavor. Once rehydrated, it can be shaped into small green lumps and served with soy sauce as the traditional condiment for sushi. Once a package of wasabi is opened, its potency deteriorates quickly, so buy in small quantities and use quickly. To make a wasabi sauce, soak 1 tablespoon wasabi powder in 2 tablespoons water and add ½ cup heavy cream.

WATER

The United States has one of the safest water supplies in the world. As long as tap water runs clear, plentiful, hot and cold, and reasonably pleasant in taste, few of us worry about its purity. Yet, though water is basic, and certainly essential, it is not necessarily simple; it can vary from place to place, depending on the source water and the treatment it receives. And the water with which we cook is relevant to the results we achieve in our kitchens.

Water hardness is related to various combinations of salts present in the water. Should you be interested in finding out what type of water you have, call your local water company or health department. ➤ Soft water contains little or no dissolved salts of calcium or magnesium and is best for most cooking and baking. However, very soft water will make yeast doughs soggy and sticky. ➤ Hard water contains an appreciable quantity of dissolved minerals. Artificially softened waters will affect flavor, toughen legumes and fruits, extend the cooking time of green beans, and shrivel pickles. They will also markedly alter the color of vegetables in the cabbage family and turn onions,

cauliflower, potatoes, and rice yellow. If your water is hard, cooking these vegetables à blanc, 467, is a superior method of preparation. Alkaline waters have a strengthening effect on gluten, as well as increasing its gas-retaining properties—and, consequently, the size of the loaf.

There are a number of ways by which the hardness in water may be reduced: Passing the water through an ion-exchange apparatus, or a water filter mounted under the sink or on the faucet, or using water pitcher with a built-in filter that contains counteractive chemicals may be helpful, but most such systems principally exchange sodium for calcium compounds and are more effective in treating water used in the general household rather than water used in cooking. If the salts happen to consist of bicarbonates of calcium and magnesium, boiling the water for 20 or 30 minutes will cause them to precipitate. But if the water originally contains large amounts of sulfates, boiling it will increase hardness rather than reduce it, because the sulfates are concentrated by evaporation. ➤ Should you have hard or soft water that affects your cooking and baking outcomes in an undesirable way, keep a few gallons of bottled water in the pantry to assure that your cooking results will be successful.

Some older recipes may recommend long soaking of certain foods in water, but we do not recommend this: Fruits, salad greens, and vegetables should be washed as quickly as possible. Soaking leaches out water-soluble vitamins. ➤ Because of this leaching action, some cooks save soaking and cooking waters whenever possible, to use in household stocks, 114, unless they have bitter or off flavors, or unless discarding is specified in a given recipe.

In this book, when the word ➤ "water" appears in a recipe, we assume tap water that has a temperature of 60° to 80°F. ➤ If hotter or colder water is needed, it is specified.

Occasionally recipes indicate ➤ water by weight, where 16 fluid ounces of water also weighs 16 ounces or 1 pound. In that case use 1 tablespoon for ½ ounce, 1 cup for 8 ounces, 2 cups for 1 pound.

▲ The boiling temperature of water at sea level—212°F—is increased in direct proportion to the amount of water-soluble substance(s) dissolved in it. The amount of salt or sugar added in cooking is not enough to change the normal sea-level boiling point. For boiling temperatures at high altitudes, see 1056.

EMERGENCY WATER PURIFICATION

These are temporary water disinfecting methods recommended during an emergency for obtaining potable water for drinking or to use for cooking. In using or storing water, be sure of two things: That the source from which you get it is uncontaminated, and that the vessels you store it in are sterile. The color of water has nothing to do with its purity. Because disease germs are more often derived from animal than from vegetable matter, a brown swamp water may be purer than a blue lake water.

For **water storage,** use food-grade plastic bottles or glass with tight-fitting screw-on lids. Soda bottles and water, juice, or punch containers all work. Avoid plastic milk jugs, because it may be hard to remove residual milk sugars and proteins, allowing bacteria to grow. Store glass bottles surrounded by and separated from each other by packing material. Inspect the stored water periodically and replace any that is cloudy. ➤ Allow for each person, for drinking, a minimum of 7 gallons for each 2-week period; and for personal cleanliness, another 7 gallons. Allow at least 2 quarts (eight 8-ounce glasses) or 8 cups of water each day. Allow more for hot climates and for children, pregnant woman, and the elderly or ill. Allow 1 quart per day for each cat or dog.

If you are in doubt as to the purity of water, treat it in one of the following ways:

I. Boil the water vigorously for 5 minutes; add an extra minute for each 1,000 feet of elevation. Boiled water tastes flat, but it can be improved in flavor if aerated by pouring it a number of times from one clean vessel to another.

II. Use water purification tablets containing iodine or chlorine, in the dosage recommended on the label. These are available at sporting and camping supply stores, as are portable water purifiers.

III. Add to ➤ clear water, allowing 8 drops or ⅛ teaspoon per gallon, any liquid household bleach without added fragrances, soaps, or other additives that contains sodium hypochlorite in 5.25 percent solution. The label should give you this information. ➤ If the water is cloudy, increase the amount to 16 drops or ¼ teaspoon per gallon. ➤ In either case, stir and allow the water to stand for 30 minutes after adding the bleach. ➤ The water should have a distinct chlorine taste and odor. This is a sign of safety, and if you do not detect it by smell, add another dose of bleach and wait 15 minutes. If the chlorine odor is still not present, the chlorine may have weakened through age, and the water is not safe.

WATER CHESTNUTS

There are two types of water chestnut—both of which are crisp and delicious. In one type, the shell grows together into a horn at one end; the other is bulbous. Use water chestnuts in Appetizers and Hors d'Oeuvres, 69, Vegetables, 240, and Salads, 152.

WINE AND SPIRITS IN COOKING

There is no doubt that adding wine to food can, in many instances, create a welcome extra dimension. Sometimes its contribution is richness, sometimes aroma; often it is an additional depth of flavor; and much of the time it is all of these combined. Other alcoholic beverages, notably some spirits and beer, can also occasionally enhance our cooking when used judiciously. Throughout this book, there are numerous examples in recipes. Here we provide some general principles, ideas, and techniques.

What kind of wine to use? ➤ The wine you choose need not be a very old or expensive one, but it should be good enough to be drunk with pleasure for its own sake. Dry red and white table wines are most commonly used, but a good dry rosé is also acceptable in light dishes. Avoid wine labeled "cooking wine," as it's usually heavily salted—the basic rule should always be, "if it's not fit to drink, it's not fit to cook with." Wine left over a day or two after opening, which may have lost its prime freshness but is still palatable, is a good candidate for the pot. ➤ To extend its usefulness and reduce the amount of oxygen it comes into contact with, pour the wine from its original bottle into a smaller bottle or jar, close tightly, and store it in the refrigerator. It will keep for up to a week. In general, keep wine away from very tart or very piquantly seasoned foods, unless you are using it in a marinade, 584.

How much wine to use? Never add so much as to overbalance or drown out the characteristic flavor of the food itself. ➤ Count the wine as part of any given sum total of liquid ingredients, not as an extra. For casseroles, stews, and braised meats, some cooks warm the wine before adding, so as not to interrupt simmering. In meat or poultry recipes that call for both wine and bacon or salt pork, watch out for a too salty flavor: Season to taste ➤ at the end of cooking. Wines may be reduced to increase their flavoring power and to avoid overdilution in sauce making: 1 cup of wine will reduce to about ¼ cup in 10 minutes of strong, uncovered simmering.

Some myths have built up around wine in the kitchen. There has long been an assumption that a wine marinade tenderizes meat, but in fact it primarily flavors and moistens it—meat cooked briefly after marinating may seem more tender because it retains a bit of that moisture. The alcohol in wine is also sometimes a concern. ➤ However, the boiling point of alcohol is much lower than that of water, and almost all the alcohol evaporates fairly rapidly over heat, leaving only a minuscule amount—another good reason, besides an improvement in flavor, for heating the wine before adding it to a recipe.

When to add the wine? For sauces, where the distinctiveness of the wine is desirable, the usual idea is to add a small amount near the end of cooking. This especially applies to fortified wines, such as port, sherry, Madeira, and Marsala, where 2 or 3 tablespoons is equivalent in flavoring strength to about ½ cup dry red or white wine. Or, the wine itself can become a sauce by deglazing; see Sauces, 542. Simply add ¼ cup of wine to the pan in which the meat, poultry, or vegetables have been cooked, turn up the heat, and scrape up browned bits from the bottom of the pan.

For stews and braises, the best time to add wine is after the meat and vegetables have been browned or initially cooked and flavored with herbs, spices, or other seasonings. A wine's varietal character and complexity cooks away (another good reason not to use expensive wine), but what survives is a somewhat mellowed basic wine character and flavor, and some richness—a good beginning.

While you may boil wine to reduce it, ➤ never raise the heat to above a simmer when cooking food in wine. ➤ To avoid curdling or separation, wine should always be added beforehand in any recipes which include milk, cream, or eggs. The wine should be reduced slightly and the milk, cream, or eggs added off the heat. If the dish cannot be served at once, it may be kept warm in a double boiler ➤ over, not in, boiling water.

Just as there is no need to use expensive or otherwise exalted wine in cooking, there is also no need to adhere to old-fashioned basic assumptions. Exceptions not only prove the rule, they often improve it. We encourage defiance and initiative in combinations when cooking with wine. Chicken cooked with white wine may be delicious, but so is coq au vin, made with a dry red. Salmon or tuna poached in red wine is a stunning dish, and lamb stew simmered with white wine is fine indeed. One consideration to keep in mind when rule bending is color—for example, Eggs Poached in Red Wine, 197, is a classic French dish, but its deep purple hue can be a little startling at first sight.

Spirits, liqueurs, and cordials are most frequently used in flavoring desserts, lightly cooked if cooked at all, and added in moderation. The pronounced flavor of most types of whiskey means they must be used judiciously. Rum provides a spirituous aroma and flavor without being intrusive, and the relative lightness of brandy also makes it a good candidate. A spectacular use of spirits in cooking is flambéing—sometimes done at midpoint in preparation and sometimes as a final flourish in the dining room. ➤ Flambéing is surefire only if the liquor to be ignited, as well as the food, is first warmed, see 1055. To flambé fruits, see 215.

Beer and cider also have their virtues in cooking, especially if the beer is flat and the cider hard. As a cooking liquid, beer features in such classics as the beef stew known as Belgian Beef Stew (Carbonnade Flamande), 480, as well as Steak and Kidney Pie, 483, and both beverages add lightness and flavor to various doughs and batters, such as Beer Bread, 629. You will find them indicated in recipes where their use is appropriate.

Various forms of rice wine are frequently used in cooking. Sake, a Japanese rice wine processed by fermentation, is more like beer than wine. Any brand of sake is suitable for use in cooking except those labeled "cooking wine," which are made from inferior rice wines and may contain additives. Sake also removes strong odors in cooking. When looking for a substitute, try pale dry sherry, white wine, or dry vermouth.

Mirin, sometimes called sweet sake, is a very sweet Japanese rice wine with added sugar. Buy *hon-mirin,* which is naturally brewed and contains natural sugars, if you can find it. *Aji-mirin* is sweetened with corn syrup and may contain other additives. Shaoxing wine, a Chinese rice wine, has been made, it is said, for more than 2,000 years.

Glutinous rice, yeast, and local waters give this amber-colored beverage its unique flavor. Sometimes aged in earthenware vessels and in underground cellars, the finest varieties are aged a century or more. Like sake, Shaoxing is served warm as a beverage, and is vital to Chinese cooking. Because it is similar in color and alcohol content to sherry, dry sherry is a good substitute.

WORCESTERSHIRE SAUCE

This dark, flavorful sauce is claimed as original by the English, but it was originally developed in India. The name is derived from the location where it was first bottled, Worcester, England. Its roots are said to be Roman and it is similar to their **garum,** an ancient Roman fish sauce, see 982, with an anchovy base. To make homemade Worcestershire Sauce, see 953. Worcestershire sauce is used as a table condiment, in meat and meat-based gravies, soups, and cocktails. It adds a sharp, tangy flavor and dark color.

YEAST

Yeasts are tiny single celled living organisms with approximately 3,200 billion cells to the pound—and not one is exactly like another. They feed on sugars and produce alcohol and carbon dioxide—the "riser" in batters and doughs. But you may prefer, as we do, to accept a Mexican attitude toward yeast doughs. They call them *almas,* or souls, because they seem so spirited.

When flour is mixed with water to form a dough that is then kept in a warm place, the **wild yeasts** coming from the air and in the flour will start working and form a sourdough. Enzymes in the flour convert the wheat starch into the sugar on which the yeast feeds, making alcohol and carbon dioxide. Organic acids and other fragrant compounds that are created give the sour effect. Sourdoughs, 602, are products of this primitive bacterial ferment—it is so primitive that sourdoughs are recorded in Egyptian history in 4000 B.C. This leavened bread has been called the first "convenience" food, as its yeast content gives it excellent keeping quality.

For other types of bread, a store-bought yeast—active dry, instant or quick-rise, and compressed yeasts—is added to the dough. These yeasts are activated at different temperatures; see below. Temperatures and the amount of food available limit the life span of yeast. Its force, therefore, can be easily computed. One-half ounce of active dry yeast raises 4 cups of flour in $1^1/_2$ to 2 hours; 1 ounce active dry yeast raises 28 cups of flour in about 7 hours. For speedier rising, you can add some additional yeast, but be aware that this often affects the flavor of the dough and causes a porous texture in the baked product. Small quantities of sugar also speed yeast activity, but too much will inhibit it—you may have noticed that it takes very sweet doughs longer to rise. As salt also inhibits yeast, ➤ never use heavily salted water for dissolving yeast. In very hot weather or kitchen conditions, after the yeast is dissolved and added to the flour, salt may be added in small quantities to control too rapid fermentation.

Yeast doughs are allowed to rise at least once to improve the texture, but if doughs are allowed to overexpand, the yeast can use up its food. Then, there is little rising power left for the baking period, when it is most needed.

For different methods of incorporating yeast into doughs, read about Mixing Bread Dough, 592. Liquids added to yeast, either alone or in combination, include water, which brings out the wheat flavor and makes a crisp crust, and skim milk, which not only adds to the nutritive value but also gives a softer crumb. The fat in whole milk tends to coat the yeast and prevent its proper softening. Potato water, left over from boiling potatoes, may also be used, but it hastens the action of the yeast and gives a somewhat coarser, moister texture to dough. Both milk and potato water somewhat increase the storage time of bread.

To produce the best yeast bread, you must give the dough time to rise slowly; the entire process can take up to 4 to 5 hours before baking. If you use 1 package active dry yeast to 1 1/2 cups liquid and the temperature is right, you can count on about 2 hours or more for the first rising; 1 hour or more for the second; and 1 hour for rising in the pans or on the baking sheet. You may increase the yeast content in any recipe and reduce your rising time considerably. Successful quick recipes are based on instant or quick-rise yeast. In our opinion, if you are using yeast, you might as well work for the superlative result that comes from the slower process.

ACTIVE DRY YEAST

This granular form of yeast is sold in airtight moisture-proof 1/4-ounce packages measuring 2 1/4 teaspoons and is also sold in 4-ounce jars. Active dry yeast has a longer shelf life than compressed yeast. It comes dated and, if stored in a cool place, will keep for several months or somewhat longer in the refrigerator, and indefinitely in the freezer. Greater heat and more moisture than compressed or fresh yeast are needed to activate it. We recommend that you test, or proof, the yeast to make sure it is "alive" ➤ by using approximately 1/4 cup warm water (105° to 115°F) to dissolve it, and ➤ decrease the liquid called for in the recipe by that amount. To dissolve it readily, sprinkle the yeast granules on the surface of the water. It may also be mixed with the dry ingredients in the mixer method, 592, and activated by using 120° to 130°F liquid. To enhance proofing, add small quantities of flour and sugar.

To ➤ substitute active dry yeast for compressed yeast, use 1 package (2 1/4 teaspoons) active dry yeast for each 0.6-ounce cake of compressed yeast. To substitute active dry yeast for instant or quick-rise yeast, use the same amount, and be sure to proof or rehydrate active dry yeast.

BREWER'S OR NUTRITIONAL YEAST

Brewer's yeast, a dry yeast available at health food stores, has no leavening power. It is used to add nutritive value to foods. It may be added to breads in the proportion of 1 to 3 teaspoons per 1 cup of flour without affecting flavor or texture adversely.

COMPRESSED (FRESH) YEAST

Compressed yeast, also called fresh yeast, is yeast with a high moisture content. This living organism, dependent on definite temperature ranges, begins to activate at about 50°F ➤ and is at its best between 78° and 82°F. It begins to die around 120°F and is useless for baking above 143°F. Cakes of compressed yeast typically weigh about 0.6 ounce, although it comes in larger sizes as well. Compressed yeast must be kept refrigerated.

If you can't find it at the supermarket, it can be purchased from a bakery supply company, online retailer, or catalog. If bought fresh, it will keep about 2 weeks. Frozen, it will keep for 2 months; take out only what is needed and let it defrost overnight in the refrigerator. When fresh yeast is at its best, it is a light grayish-tan in color. It crumbles readily, breaks with a clean edge, and smells pleasantly aromatic. When old, it becomes brownish in color. To test for freshness, cream a small quantity of yeast with an equal amount of sugar. It should become liquid at once. Crumble compressed yeast and dissolve in warm liquid at 70° to 80°F for about 5 minutes before combining with the other ingredients called for in the recipes.

To substitute fresh yeast for active dry or quick-rise, use one 0.6-ounce cake for each package active dry or quick-rise yeast.

INSTANT OR QUICK-RISE YEAST

Also labeled as "quick acting" or "rapid rise," this type of active dry yeast is sold in packets, and cuts rising times dramatically, sometimes in half.

The main advantage of instant yeast it that it can be added directly to the dry ingredients without rehydration or proofing, making it more convenient than active dry yeast. Instant yeast is 25 percent stronger than active dry yeast. To substitute for active dry yeast, use the same amount of instant or quick-rise yeast.

YOGURT

A cultured and fermented milk, yogurt is available in whole, low-fat, and nonfat varieties, depending on the milk from which it is made. It is sold plain or sweetened and flavored and may use natural or artificial sweeteners; check the label. Keep refrigerated at or below 40°F. It generally keeps for 10 days after the sell-by date. For more about sour milks and creams, see 1013.

HOMEMADE YOGURT

Like yeast, the activator in yogurt is a living organism sensitive to temperatures. For consistent results, test the milk temperature with a thermometer. Yogurt has the added idiosyncrasy that it doesn't care to be jostled while growing, so place all your equipment where you can leave it undisturbed. If you use one of the many electric devices for quick yogurt making, follow the directions carefully.

We make yogurt successfully using either an insulated picnic cooler or an oven warmed to 100°F, keeping the yogurt at a temperature at which the bacteria will "work." Have ready and keep warm enough sterilized glass jars, 930, to hold the amount of milk you are preparing.

For the first batch, you will need a starter. Buy a container of plain yogurt, get a small quantity from a friend, or buy a package of yogurt culture from a health food store. Use the milk of your choice, from skim to half-and-half richness.

2 cups

Heat to 180°F, or almost boiling:

2 cups milk

Cool it to between 105° and 110°F. Stir thoroughly into the milk:

**1 package yogurt culture or 2 to 3 tablespoons
room-temperature plain yogurt**

Pour into jars. Do not allow the milk to register less than 106°F when it is in the jars. Cover the jars at once. Place them in the warmed oven or insulated cooler. Milk with added yogurt should reach a custardy consistency in 3 to 4 hours; milk with a yogurt culture may take 7 to 8 hours. Check every half hour, and refrigerate when the custardy consistency is reached. Reserve from this first batch a small quantity to use for another batch. Homemade yogurt in general will keep 6 to 7 days, but yogurt should preferably be not older than 5 days when used as a starter.

You may wonder why so little starter is used and think that a little more will produce a better result: It won't. The bacillus, if crowded, gives a sour, watery product. But if the culture has sufficient space or room to "work," it will be rich, mild, and creamy. If your yogurt does not coagulate within 8 hours, it may be because the temperature of the milk was too high and the culture was destroyed, or because your culture was a poor one. Always remember, ➤ don't eat every drop of your most recent batch. Keep 2 to 3 tablespoons to form the starter for the next one.

To incorporate fruit, ➤ put warm, sweetened crushed fruit in the bottom of the jars before adding the milk.

When using yogurt in cooking, ➤ fold gently into other ingredients, as beating will break down its texture.

YOGURT CHEESE
About ½ cup

Use it as a substitute for sour cream, for topping mashed potatoes, or spreading on toast or using as a base for dips. Line a strainer or colander with cheesecloth or a coffee filter and set over a bowl. Spoon in:

1 cup plain yogurt

Cover with plastic wrap and refrigerate at least 6 hours, or overnight; discard the liquid. You can keep yogurt cheese in the refrigerator for up to a week. Pour off any liquid that accumulates.

ABOUT COLOR IN FOOD

When cooking, resist the impulse to add color from little bottles or to retain it by the use of chemicals like soda. Instead, determine, in general, to maintain whatever color is inherent in the food itself and to heighten it by skillful cooking and effective contrast.

First begin with the selection of fresh well-grown foods, properly washed, dried, and trimmed, then prepared according to the "pointers" in our individual recipes. ➤ Choose utensils made of materials suitable to the foods cooked in them; see 1065. If you have done so and are still unhappy with the results, check the kind of water you are using; see 1026. ➤ Never overcook foods: Nothing so irrevocably dulls the kitchen palette.

Here are some further ways to keep foods colorful: The color of soups and sauces is built into them by the way their stocks are made; see 114. During the making of meat and poultry stocks, a gray foam rises to the surface. The color and clarity of the stock will be least affected if the scum is removed during cooking and the stock is cooked uncovered. Meats, if light, maintain better color if the scum is also removed during cooking. If dark, their color will be improved by browning, by greasing during roasting or broiling, or by glazing or flambéing. Grilled fish and light meats profit in color by a prior dusting of paprika. Vent stews by the use of poaching paper, 1050.

Cook variety meats—or vegetables or fruits that discolor on exposure to air—in slightly acidulated water, 957, or à blanc, 467. But first sprinkle the cut surfaces of such foods with a little lemon juice. Or use an AntiBrowning Solution, 209, to prevent the discoloration of fresh fruits peeled slightly in advance of serving. And keep in mind that color in all foods is enhanced if they are not held hot and covered after cooking. To keep green vegetables bright during cooking, see 242.

Foods served in light sauces may be gratinéed, 961, or glazed, 582. And sauces may be garnished with herb chiffonades, 989; tomato concasse, 563, or diced red pepper; lobster coral, 382; Lobster Butter, 559; egg yolks; saffron; meat glaze; mushrooms, and browned flour.

If you are faced with really listless-looking vegetables, a green coloring additive may be very quickly made up in a blender: Use spinach, parsley, or watercress mixed with a small quantity of stock.

Breads and pastries develop beautiful crust color not only through the use of dairy products or honey in their dough, but by the discreet addition of butter or oil. The absolute best source of color in a crust comes from a small amount of corn syrup in the dough. Color may also be improved just before baking by brushing with butter, egg-glazing, or sugar-coating, 799.

As to color combinations and color contrasts, no one can lay down hard-and-fast rules, except to say that they need not be spectacular. Even so simple a combination as light and dark lettuces in a salad—or an accent of cress—will make for substantially greater interest. The occasional use of edible garnishes—suggestions for which are scattered throughout this book—is also helpful. Do consider, too, the total background: dishes and tableware, table surface, linens, and decor are all part and parcel of satisfactory and colorful food presentation.

Artificial food colorings are available in liquid, paste, or gel form. Widely available at supermarkets and kitchen supply stores, these colorings can tint foods in all colors of the rainbow and more—black, gray, silver, and gold. Used frequently for decorating cakes, cookies, and even in Red Velvet Cake, 717, these colorings usually produce vibrant, vivid colors. A small amount typically goes a long way. A paste- or gel-based coloring is less likely than a liquid coloring to dilute or liquefy a frosting or glaze. ➤ Be aware that recent research indicates that some people are highly allergic to artificial colorings.

ABOUT WEATHER

Weather—humid or dry, hot or cold—plays an important part in cooking. When its role is decisive, it is so noted in individual recipes. Let's review just a few instances: Damp weather will greatly affect sugars after food is cooked—as in meringues—and during candy making, 854. Cold and heat have both positive and negative effects on the creaming of butter and sugars, 699, and on success with Puff Pastry, 669, or the rising of bread, 593. Threatening weather will even delay the "making" of butter, 963, and Mayonnaise, 578. It is evident that Mark Twain was wrong when he complained that nobody did anything about the weather: The circumspect cook takes account of its vagaries and acts accordingly.

ABOUT MEASURING

The importance of careful measuring, especially in baking, cannot be overestimated. Every kitchen needs three kinds of measuring tools. Measuring spoons are designed to measure small quantities of dry or wet ingredients; look for sets that include spoons for $1/4$, $1/2$, and 1 teaspoon, as well as 1 tablespoon. Dry measuring cups are designed for measuring flour, 983, sugar, 1018, brown sugar, 1018, bulk fats, 98, and other dry ingredients. Standard sets include measures for $1/4$, $1/3$, $1/2$, and 1 cup. Glass or clear plastic cups for liquid measuring have their measurements marked on the side of the device. Look for cups with easy to read lines. A 1- or 2-cup measure with lines for every $1/8$ cup (for every ounce) is a good size for small jobs, while a 4-cup measure with less precision is good for large quantities. ➤ Do not use liquid measuring cups for dry ingredients, as the results will not be accurate.

Weighing fruits, vegetables, and meats can mean the difference between success and failure in many recipes. And many bakers like to use a scale to measure their baking ingredients. Kitchen scales are either mechanical,

functioning much like a bathroom scale, or compact and electronic, with a digital readout. For either type of scale, look for a feature that allows a reset of the scale to zero after the bowl is on the scale. If you use or intend to use European recipes frequently, a gram/ounce scale is a necessity.

All recipes in this book are ➤ based on standard U.S. containers: the 8-ounce cup and a tablespoon that takes exactly 16 level fillings to fill that cup. We suggest that you test the size of the tablespoon you select for this purpose, because those on sale frequently do not meet standard specifications.

All our recipes, in turn, are based on level measurements—most hedgers, like "heaping" or "scant," were weeded out of our instructions years ago. Until you are experienced, we strongly urge you to make a fetish of the level standard measure.

To prove how very careful measurement affects quantity, conduct this simple experiment: Dip a standard spoon into flour or baking powder and then level its contents with a knife. Don't shake. Then scoop up a heaping spoonful of the same ingredients, without leveling. You will find that lighter materials, if casually taken, often triple or quadruple the amount called for in the recipes. We're willing to bet that cooks who pride themselves on using nothing but their intuition as a guide to quantity are "old hands" who, for years, have used the same bowls, cups, and spoons, the same stove; and even the same brands of staples—and who, in addition, get more than their share of lucky breaks. Like as not, too, they don't mind variations in their product.

Accuracy in ➤ measuring basic ingredients is especially necessary in baking and when using recipes that include gelatin. ➤ For dry ingredients, use a cup that measures 1 cup even—with a flush rim for leveling. ➤ No shortcuts should be taken if the recipe requires the sifting of flour. If they are, the outcome is chancy, to say the least. In fact, sifting after measurement will improve the texture of all cakes. Sifting salt, leaveners, and spices with the flour ensures even distribution.

The measurement of what we might call side ingredients, such as flavorings and spices, is important too, but here much depends on individual taste, to say nothing of the age of the spices, and amounts may vary considerably without risking failure.

ABOUT SUBSTITUTIONS AND EQUIVALENTS

You're a new cook and you run out of granulated sugar. Don't think this doesn't happen to old cooks too! So you just substitute confectioners' sugar. And when the cake is not so sweet as it should be and the texture is horrid, you wonder what happened.

Good recipes and the reasonable use of standard measures allow you to cook well without knowing that it takes about 2 cups of sugar or butter to make a pound but that you would need about 4 cups of all-purpose flour for a pound. This you discover fast enough if you leave the United States, for almost everyone else cooks by weight, not volume.

Let's look at a few lucky volume-weight relationships that for the moment protect you, as a new cook, from the menace of that old dragon mathematics—and his allies, physics, chemistry, and semantics. Here are some of our victorious, if homely, weapons, tested in many a battle with these old tricksters.

By weight, if not quite by volume, 2 tablespoons butter equals 2 tablespoons butter, melted. But don't try to incorporate this positive knowledge into a cake without reading About Butter Cakes, 710.

By weight, 1 cup 36-percent heavy cream equals 1 cup 36-percent cream, whipped. By volume, 1 cup 36-percent heavy cream equals about 2 cups 36-percent cream, whipped. ➤ If a recipe calls for whipped cream, you need the airier, drier texture that results from whipping.

Let's take a closer look at sugars.

1 cup granulated weighs about 7 ounces
1 cup confectioners' sugar weighs about 4 ounces
1 cup packed brown sugar weighs about 7½ ounces
1 cup molasses, honey, or corn syrup weighs
    12 ounces

These are only differences in weight. But you also have to reckon with changes in sweetening power and in texture, and—in the case of molasses and honey—with liquids that also have an acid factor. And don't forget about taste, that most important element of all.

When any of the foregoing ingredients are called for in a recipe, the recipe is written to take care of inequalities. But if you are substituting in emergencies, say, sugar for molasses, please read Molasses, 998, first. Some substitutions work fairly well, others only under special circumstances. ➤ And never expect to get the same results from a friend's recipe if she uses one kind of shortening and you use another. Your product may be better or worse than hers, but it won't be the same.

Before leaving you to delve into the tables that follow, we introduce our ➤ multiply-and-conquer principle for fractions.

You are preparing only one-third of a given recipe. The recipe calls for ⅓ cup of flour: ⅓ cup of flour equals 5⅓ tablespoons. 1 tablespoon equals 3 teaspoons. So 5⅓ tablespoons equals 16 teaspoons, and, finally, 16 teaspoons divided by 3—you are working for one-third of the recipe, remember?—gives you 5⅓ teaspoons. Now, maybe you can get this result by leaving out some of these steps, but we can't.

Here is another tried-and-true kitchen formula—one for proportions. You want to make your grandmother's fruit cake, which has a yield of 11 pounds. You'd like only 3 pounds. The recipe calls for 10 cups of flour. How much flour should you use for 3 pounds of cake? Make yourself

a formula in simple proportion: 11 pounds of cake is to 3 pounds of cake as 10 cups of flour is to ?, or X cups of flour: i.e., 11 : 3 = 10 : X. Multiply the end factors—11 x X—and the inside factors—3 x 10—to get 11 X = 30. Divide 30 by 11 to find that X = 2⁸/₁₁, or approximately 2¾ cups. If you are in any doubt that ⁸/₁₁ is close to ¾, divide 8 by 11, finding the decimal closest to the standard measure. It is worth going through the same reducing process for the other basic ingredients such as egg, liquid, and fruit, so the cake will hold together. Approximate the spices.

But one more caution in changing recipes. ➤ Don't decrease or enlarge recipes by dividing or multiplying by any number larger than 4—purists recommend 2. This sounds and is mysterious. But the fact remains that recipes are just not indefinitely expandable or shrinkable.

TABLES OF EQUIVALENTS AND CONVERSIONS

It is most unfortunate that in U.S. measuring systems, the same word can have two meanings. For instance, an ounce may mean ¹/₁₆ of a pound or ¹/₁₆ of a pint, but the former is strictly a weight measure and the latter a volume measure. See the difference, for example, in the weights of cups of different kinds of sugar above. Except in three instances—water, whole milk, and whole eggs—a fluid ounce and an ounce of weight are two completely different quantities. Perhaps for this reason most foreign cooks measure solid ingredients by weight. If you intend to use European recipes frequently, a gram/ounce scale, 1031, is a necessity.

UNITED STATES MEASUREMENTS

All these equivalents are based on United States "fluid" or volume measure. This measure is used not only for liquids such as water and milk, but also for materials such as flour, sugar, and shortening, since the volume measure for these is customary in the United States.

LIQUID-MEASURE VOLUME EQUIVALENTS

For U.S.–metric fluid volume, see 1034.

A few grains	=	Less than ⅛ teaspoon
60 drops	=	1 teaspoon
1 teaspoon	=	⅓ tablespoon
1 tablespoon	=	3 teaspoons
2 tablespoons	=	1 ounce
4 tablespoons	=	¼ cup or 2 ounces
5⅓ tablespoons	=	⅓ cup or 2⅔ ounces
8 tablespoons	=	½ cup or 4 ounces
16 tablespoons	=	1 cup or 8 ounces
⅜ cup	=	¼ cup plus 2 tablespoons
⅝ cup	=	½ cup plus 2 tablespoons
⅞ cup	=	¾ cup plus 2 tablespoons
1 cup	=	½ pint or 8 fluid ounces
2 cups	=	1 pint or 16 fluid ounces

1 gill (liquid)	=	$^{1}/_{2}$ cup or 4 fluid ounces
1 pint (liquid)	=	4 gills or 16 fluid ounces
1 quart (liquid)	=	2 pints or 4 cups
1 gallon (liquid)	=	4 quarts

LINEAR MEASURES

For equipment comparison.

1 centimeter	=	0.394 inch
1 inch	=	2.54 centimeters
1 meter	=	39.37 inches

DRY-MEASURE VOLUME EQUIVALENTS

Dry measures are used for raw fruits and vegetables when dealing with fairly large quantities. Be careful not to confuse dry measure pints and quarts with liquid measure pints and quarts. The former are about «1/6» larger than the latter.

	Dry pints	Dry quarts	Pecks	Bushels	Liters
1 Dry Pint	1	$^{1}/_{2}$	$^{1}/_{16}$	$^{1}/_{64}$	.55
1 Dry Quart	2	1	$^{1}/_{8}$	$^{1}/_{32}$	1.1
1 Peck	16	8	1	$^{1}/_{4}$	8.8
1 Bushel	64	32	4	1	35.23
1 Liter	1.82	0.91	0.114	0.028	1

COMMON CAN SIZES

The following chart lists common can sizes and the volume measures they typically hold.

Can	Fluid Ounces	Cups
Number 10	104.9	13
Number 5	56.6	7
Number 3	33.5	4.25
Number 3 cylinder	49.6	6
Number 2$^{1}/_{2}$ square	31.0	4
Number 2$^{1}/_{2}$	28.6	3.5
Number 2	19.7	2.5
Number 303	16.2	2
Number 300	14.6	1.8
Number 211	13.0	1.6
12-ounce vacuum	12	1.5
Number 1 picnic	10.5	1.3
8-ounce	8.3	1
6-ounce	5.8	0.75
4-ounce	4.1	0.5
2$^{1}/_{2}$-ounce	2.5	0.25

AVERAGE FROZEN FOOD PACKAGES

Vegetables	8 to 16 oz.
Fruits	10 to 16 oz.
Canned frozen fruits	13$^{1}/_{2}$ to 16 oz.
Frozen juice concentrates	6 oz.

COMPARATIVE U.S. AND BRITISH MEASUREMENTS

Many British, or "Imperial," units of measurements have the same names as U.S. units, but not all are identical. In general, weights are equivalent but volumes are not. The most important difference for the cook, and one we were slow to realize until we had had consistent failures using English recipes with American measures, is noted below.

Also, the variable sizes of the British teaspoon and tablespoon created a further problem. Confronted with our dilemma, a British friend laughed and told us that there were no standard household British teaspoons and tablespoons. Her own teaspoons and tablespoons had been in the family since the fifteenth century and fit the family recipes perfectly. As a result the best we can recommend is experimentation. Below are differences between U.S. and British measuring cups:

An 8-ounce U.S. measuring cup = 16 U.S. tablespoons or 48 U.S. teaspoons.

A 10-ounce British measuring cup = 1 English breakfast cup or 2 Imperial English gills of 5 Imperial ounces each or 20$^{4}/_{5}$ U.S. tablespoons, or 62$^{1}/_{2}$ U.S. teaspoons.

ABOUT METRIC CONVERSION

These tables, which convert by both weight and volume, are handy if you want to translate American or British recipes into metric measures.

The charts, 1034–1036, compare common kitchen measures from metric to American Standard and vice versa. To use, we give the following example: To determine the equivalent number of U.S. cups in a recipe that calls for 500 milliliters of liquid, look at the U.S.–Metric Fluid Volume chart. Find 1 milliliter in the left column; follow across to cups to find 0.004. Multiply 500 by 0.004, and you will get the answer—2 cups.

U.S.–METRIC FLUID VOLUME

	Fluid Drams	Tea-spoons	Table-spoons	Fluid Ounces	¼ Cups	(Gills) ½ Cups	Cups	Fluid Pints	Fluid Quarts	Gallons	Milli-liters	Liters
1 Fluid Dram	1	¾	¼	⅛ .125	1/16 .0625	.03125	.0156	.0078	.0039	1/1024	3.70	.0037
1 Tea-spoon	1⅓	1	⅓	⅙	1/12	1/24	1/48	1/96	1/192	1/768	5	.005
1 Table-spoon	4	3	1	½	¼	⅛	1/16	1/32	1/64	1/256	15	.015
1 Fluid Ounce	8	6	2	1	½	¼	⅛	1/16	1/32	1/128	29.56	.030
¼ Cup	16	12	4	2	1	½	¼	⅛	1/16	1/64	59.125	.059
½ Cup (Gill)	32	24	8	4	2	1	½	¼	⅛	1/32	118.25	.118
1 Cup	64	48	16	8	4	2	1	½	¼	1/16	236	.236
1 Fluid Pint	128	96	32	16	8	4	2	1	½	⅛	473	.473
1 Fluid Quart	256	192	64	32	16	8	4	2	1	¼	946	.946
1 Gallon	1024	768	256	128	64	32	16	8	4	1	3785.4	3.785
1 Milli-liter	.27	.203 ⅕	.067	.034	.017	.008	.004	.002	.001	.0003	1	.001 1/1000
1 Liter	270.5	203.04	67.68	33.814	16.906	8.453	4.227	2.113	1.057	.264	1000	1

U.S. METRIC MASS (WEIGHT)

	Grains	Drams	Ounces	Pounds	Milligrams	Grams	Kilograms
1 Grain	1	.037	.002	$1/7000$	64.7	.064	.0006
1 Dram	27.34	1	$1/16$	$1/256$	1770	1.77	.002
1 Ounce	437.5	16	1	$1/16$	2835	28.35	.028
1 Pound	7000	256	16	1	"Lots and lots"	454	.454
1 Milligram	.015	.0006	$1/29{,}000$	1/"lots and lots"	1	.001	.000001
1 Gram	15.43	.565	.035	.002	1000	1	.001
1 Kilogram	15,430	564.97	35.2	2.2	1,000,000	1000	1

BRITISH–METRIC FLUID VOLUME

The British are presently using the metric system, but if you wish to use English recipes written before the early 1970s, you may find these tables a great help.

	Fluid Drams	Fluid Ounces	$1/4$ Cups	$1/2$ Cups (Gills)	Cups	Fluid Pints	Fluid Quarts	Milliliters	Liters
1 Fluid Dram	1	$1/8$	$1/20$ .05	$1/40$ .025	$1/80$ .0125	$1/160$ .017	$1/320$ .003	3.55	.0035
1 Fluid Ounce	8	1	$2/5$ .4	$1/5$ .2	$1/10$	$1/20$ .05	$1/40$ .025	28.4	.028
$1/4$ Cup	20	2.5	1	$1/2$	$1/4$	$1/8$	$1/16$	71	.07
$1/2$ Cup (1 Gill)	40	5	2	1	$1/2$	$1/4$	$1/8$	142	.14
1 Cup	80	10	4	2	1	$1/2$	$1/4$	284	.28
1 Fluid Pint	160	20	8	4	2	1	$1/2$	568	.57
1 Fluid Quart	320	40	16	8	4	2	1	1136	1.13
1 Milliliter	.28	.035	.014	.007	.0035	.0018	.0009	1	.001 $1/1000$
1 Liter	281.5	35.19	14.08	7.04	3.52	1.76	.88	1000	1

APPROXIMATE TEMPERATURE EQUIVALENTS

	Fahrenheit	Celsius
Coldest area of freezer	−10°	−23°
Freezer	0°	−18°
Water Freezes	32°	0°
Water simmers	115°	46°
Water scalds	130°	54°
Water boils (at sea level)	212°	100°
Soft ball	234°	112°
Firm ball	244°	118°
Hard ball	250°	121°
Very low oven	250°–275°	121°–135°
Low oven	300°–325°	149°–163°
Moderate oven	350°–375°	177°–191°
Hot oven	400°–425°	204°–218°
Very hot oven	450°–475°	232°–246°
Extremely hot oven	500°–525°	260°–274°
Broil	*See Broiling,* 1046	

To convert Fahrenheit into Celsius, subtract 32, multiply by 5, divide by 9. To convert Celsius into Fahrenheit, go in reverse: Multiply by 9, divide by 5, add 32.

100°C x 9 = 900°
900° ÷ 5 = 180°
180° + 32 = 212°F

USDA RECOMMENDED COOKING TEMPERATURES

Eggs and Egg Dishes

Eggs	Cook until yolk and white are firm
Egg dishes	160°F

Ground Meat and Meat Mixtures

Turkey and chicken	165°F
Veal, beef, lamb, and pork	160°F

Fresh Beef, Veal, and Lamb

Medium-rare	145°F
Medium	160°F
Well-done	170°F

Fresh Pork

Medium	160°F
Well-done	170°F

Poultry

Chicken, whole	180°F
Turkey, whole	180°F
Poultry breasts, roasted	170°F
Poultry thighs and wings	180°F
Stuffing (cooked alone or in bird)	165°F
Duck or goose, whole	180°F

Ham

Fresh (raw)	160°F
Precooked (to reheat)	140°F

Fish

Well-done	145°F

Leftovers and Casseroles — 165°F

EQUIVALENTS AND SUBSTITUTIONS FOR COMMON INGREDIENTS
Also check "Abouts" for individual items; see Index for further information.

Almonds		
in the shell	3$\frac{1}{2}$ lb.	1 lb. shelled
unblanched, whole	6 oz.	1 cup
unblanched, ground	1 lb.	2$\frac{2}{3}$ cups
unblanched, slivered	1 lb.	5$\frac{2}{3}$ cups
blanched, whole	5$\frac{1}{3}$ oz.	1 cup
blanched, slivered	4 oz.	1 cup
Apples	1 lb. or 3 to 4 medium	3 to 4 cups peeled, cored, and sliced
	3$\frac{1}{2}$ to 4 lb. raw	1 lb. dried
	About 10 apples	1 lb. dried
Apricots, fresh	5$\frac{1}{2}$ lb.	1 lb. dried
	1 lb. or 12 to 14 medium	2$\frac{1}{2}$ cups sliced or 2 cups chopped
Apricots, dried	1 lb.	3$\frac{1}{4}$ cups
Apricots, cooked and drained	1 lb.	3 cups
Arrowroot (as a thickener)	1$\frac{1}{2}$ teaspoons	1 tablespoon all-purpose flour
	2 teaspoons	1 tablespoon cornstarch
Asparagus	1 lb.	20 medium spears
Avocados	1 lb. or 2 medium	2 cups diced or 1 cup mashed
Bacon	16 oz. package	16 to 20 slices
	8 slices cooked	$\frac{1}{2}$ cup crumbled
Baker's ammonia or ammonium carbonate	$\frac{3}{4}$ teaspoon ground	1 teaspoon baking soda
Baking powder	1 teaspoon	$\frac{1}{4}$ teaspoon baking soda plus $\frac{5}{8}$ teaspoon cream of tartar
	1 teaspoon	$\frac{1}{4}$ teaspoon baking soda plus $\frac{1}{2}$ cup buttermilk or yogurt
	1 teaspoon	$\frac{1}{4}$ teaspoon baking soda plus $\frac{1}{4}$ to $\frac{1}{2}$ cup molasses
double-acting	1 teaspoon	1$\frac{1}{2}$ teaspoons phosphate or tartrate baking powder
Bananas	1 lb. or 3 to 4 medium	1$\frac{3}{4}$ cups mashed
Beans, black-eyed peas, fresh	1 lb. in the shell	1$\frac{1}{2}$ cups shelled
Beans, fava, fresh	1 lb. in the shell	$\frac{3}{4}$ cup shelled
Beans, green, fresh	1 lb. or 3 cups	2$\frac{1}{2}$ cups cooked
Beans, kidney, dried	1 lb. or 2$\frac{1}{2}$ cups	6 cups cooked
Beans, lima, fresh	1 lb. in the pod	1 cup shelled
Beans, lima, dried	1 lb. or 2$\frac{1}{2}$ cups	6 cups cooked
Beans, navy, dried	8 ounces or 1 cup	2$\frac{1}{2}$ cups cooked
Beef, cooked	1 lb.	3 cups minced
Beef, uncooked	1 lb.	2 cups ground
Beets	1 lb.	2 cups cubed or sliced
Blackberries	1 lb.	2 cups
Blueberries	1 lb.	3 cups
Brazil nuts	2 lb. in the shell	1 lb. shelled or about 3 cups
Bread crumbs, dry	$\frac{1}{4}$ cup	1 slice bread
soft	$\frac{1}{2}$ cup	1 slice bread

Broccoli	1 lb.	4 cups chopped
Broth	10½ oz. can	1¼ cups
	14½ oz. can	1¾ cups
	48 to 49½ oz. can	6 cups
Brussels sprouts	1 lb.	2½ cups
Bulgur	1 lb. or 2½ cups	6 cups cooked
Butter		
1 stick	4 oz.	½ cup or 8 tablespoons
4 sticks	1 lb.	2 cups
	1 cup	1 cup margarine
		¾ cup plus 1 to 2 tablespoons clarified bacon fat or drippings
		¾ cup clarified chicken fat
		¾ cup plus 2 tablespoons lard or vegetable seed or nut oil, solid, or liquid
	8 oz.	7.3 oz. shortening; see 1012
Butter, whipped	1 lb.	3 cups
Buttermilk	1 cup	1 cup plain yogurt
Cabbage	8 oz. chopped	3 cups packed
	1 lb.	4½ cups shredded
Cane syrup, see Sugars, Liquid, 1018		
Cape gooseberries	1 lb. trimmed	3 cups
Carob powder	3 tablespoons plus 2 tablespoons water	1 oz. chocolate
Carrots, without tops	1 lb.	3 cups shredded or 2½ cups diced
Cauliflower	1 lb.	4 cups chopped
Celery	1 lb.	2½ cups chopped
Cheese, grated	1 lb.	4 cups
Cheese, shredded	4 oz.	1 cup
Cheese, blue	4 oz.	1 cup crumbled
Cheese, cottage	8 oz.	1 cup
	12 oz.	1½ cups
Cheese, cream	3 oz.	6 tablespoons
	8 oz.	1 cup
Cherimoya	1 large	2 cups peeled and cubed
Cherries	1 lb.	2 to 3 cups unpitted, 2½ cups pitted, or 2 cups chopped
Chestnuts	35 to 40 large	2½ cups peeled
	1½ lb. in shell	1 lb. shelled
Chocolate	1 oz.	¼ cup grated
Chocolate, semisweet	6 oz.	6 tablespoons unsweetened cocoa powder plus 7 tablespoons sugar plus ¼ cup vegetable shortening
	1⅔ oz. semisweet chocolate	1 oz. unsweetened plus 4 teaspoons sugar
Chocolate, unsweetened	1 oz.	3 tablespoons unsweetened cocoa powder plus 1 tablespoon butter or other fat

	1 oz.	3 tablespoons carob powder plus 2 tablespoons water
Chocolate chips	6 oz.	1 cup
Cocoa powder	1 lb.	4 cups
Coconut, fresh, finely grated	3$\frac{1}{2}$ oz.	1 cup
Coconut, grated	1 cup	1$\frac{1}{3}$ cups flaked
Coconut, flaked	3$\frac{1}{2}$ oz.	1$\frac{1}{3}$ cups
Coconut	1 tablespoon chopped dried	1$\frac{1}{2}$ tablespoons grated fresh
	1 medium	3 cups grated fresh
	1 lb.	5 cups shredded unsweetened
	1 lb.	4 cups shredded sweetened
Coconut milk (see 972)	1 cup	1 cup milk
Coconut cream (see 972)	1 cup	1 cup cream
Coffee	1 lb.	40 to 50 6-oz. cups
Coffee, instant or powdered	2 oz.	25 6-oz. cups
Coffee, freeze-dried	4 oz.	About 60 6-oz. cups
Corn	1 medium ear	$\frac{1}{2}$ cup kernels
Corn syrup, see Sugars, Liquid, 1018		
Cornmeal	1 lb.	3 cups
	1 cup uncooked	4 to 4$\frac{1}{2}$ cups cooked
Cornstarch, see Starches, 1016		
Cracker crumbs	$\frac{3}{4}$ cup	1 cup dry bread crumbs
Crackers	24 buttery-round	1 cup crumbs
	15 graham	1 cup crumbs
	30 saltines	1 cup crumbs
Cranberries	1 lb.	4 cups
	12 oz. package	3 cups
Cream, half-and-half	1 cup	1$\frac{1}{2}$ tablespoons butter plus about $\frac{3}{4}$ cup plus 2 tablespoons milk or $\frac{1}{2}$ cup light cream plus $\frac{1}{2}$ cup milk
Cream, light	1 cup	3 tablespoons butter plus about $\frac{3}{4}$ plus 2 tablespoons cup milk
Cream, heavy (36 percent fat)	1 cup	$\frac{1}{3}$ cup butter plus about $\frac{3}{4}$ cup milk
	1 cup	2 to 2$\frac{1}{2}$ cups whipped
Cream, sour	1 cup	$\frac{1}{3}$ cup butter plus $\frac{3}{4}$ cup buttermilk or yogurt
Currants, dried	1 lb.	3 cups
Currants, fresh	1 lb. unstemmed	About 3$\frac{1}{4}$ cups, 2$\frac{2}{3}$ cups stemmed, or 1$\frac{1}{4}$ cups juice
Damson plums	1 lb.	2$\frac{1}{2}$ cups coarsely chopped
Dates	1 lb.	2$\frac{1}{2}$ cups pitted
Eggplant	1 lb.	5 cups cubed
Eggs		
jumbo	4	About 1 cup
extra-large	4	About 1 cup
large	5	About 1 cup
medium	5	About 1 cup
small	6	About 1 cup

Eggs, dried, sifted	1 lb.	5¼ cups
	2½ tablespoons, beaten with	1 whole egg
	2½ tablespoons water	
Eggs, frozen	1 lb.	1¾ cups plus 2 tablespoons
Egg whites		
jumbo	5	About 1 cup
extra-large	6	About 1 cup
large	7	About 1 cup
medium	8	About 1 cup
small	9	About 1 cup
Egg whites, dried, sifted	1 tablespoon plus	1 large egg white
	2 tablespoons water	
Egg whites, frozen	2 tablespoons thawed	1 large egg white
Egg yolks, for thickening	2 yolks	1 large egg
Egg yolks		
jumbo	11	About 1 cup
extra large	12	About 1 cup
large	14	About 1 cup
medium	16	About 1 cup
small	18	About 1 cup
Egg yolks, dried, sifted	1½ tablespoons plus	1 egg yolk
	1 tablespoon water	
Egg yolks, frozen	3½ teaspoons thawed	1 large egg yolk
Eggs, bantam	1	⅔ oz.
Eggs, duck	1	3 oz.
Eggs, goose	1	8 to 10 oz.
Eggs, dried	1 lb.	2⅔ cups chopped
Feijoa	8 to 10 medium	1 cup pulp
Figs, fresh	1 lb. or 12 medium	About 4 cups
Filberts or hazelnuts	2¼ lb. in the shell	1 lb. or 3⅓ cups shelled
Flour, bread	1 lb.	4 cups
Flour, cake	1 lb.	3¾ cups
	1 cup sifted	¾ cup plus 2 tablespoons sifted all-purpose
Flour, self-rising	1 cup	1 cup sifted all-purpose plus 1½ teaspoons baking powder and ½ teaspoon salt
Flour, all-purpose	1 lb.	4 cups
	4 cups	3½ cups cracked wheat
	1 cup	1 cup cornmeal
		½ cup plus 2 tablespoons potato flour
		1 cup minus 2 tablespoons rice flour
		1¼ cups rye flour
		¾ cup plus 1 tablespoon gluten flour
	5 lb. bag	20 cups
Flour, whole-grain or whole wheat	1 lb.	3¾ to 4 cups finely milled
Flour and starches for thickening	1 tablespoon all-purpose flour	1½ teaspoons cornstarch, potato starch, rice starch, or arrowroot
		1 tablespoon quick-cooking tapioca
		1 tablespoon waxy rice flour

		1 tablespoon waxy corn flour
	1½ teaspoons all-purpose flour	1 tablespoon browned flour, 544
Fruit, glacéed	1 lb.	About 1½ cups
Garlic	1 small clove	⅛ teaspoon powder, ¼ teaspoon granulated, or ½ teaspoon minced
Gelatin	¼-oz. envelope	About 2¼ teaspoons
	¼-oz. envelope	4 sheets gelatin (4 x 9 inches)
Gelatin for 2 cups liquid	¼-oz. envelope	About 2¼ teaspoons
Ginger	1 tablespoon crystallized, washed of sugar, or 1 tablespoon minced fresh	⅛ teaspoon ground
Gooseberries	1 lb. trimmed	3 cups
Grapefruit	1 medium	1¼ cups juice or 1 cup sections 10 to 12 tablespoons juice
Grapes	1 lb.	3 cups seeded and halved
	1 lb. stemmed	About 3 cups
Greens, fresh	1 lb.	10 cups chopped
Grits	1 lb. or 2 cups	3 cups cooked
Guava	1 (2 to 3 oz.)	About ½ cup sliced
Hazelnuts	2¼ lb. in the shell	1 lb. shelled; 3⅓ cups
Herbs, see 989	⅓ to ½ teaspoon dried	1 tablespoon chopped fresh
Honey, see Sugars, Liquid, 1018	1 lb.	1⅓ cups
	1 cup	1¼ cups sugar plus ¼ cup liquid
Horseradish, fresh	1 tablespoon grated	2 tablespoons prepared
Horseradish, dried	6 tablespoons grated	10 tablespoons prepared
Kiwis	1 lb. or 4 large	1½ cups sliced
Lard	1 lb.	2 cups
Lemons	1	2 to 3 tablespoons juice, 1 to 1½ teaspoons grated zest
	1 teaspoon juice	½ teaspoon vinegar
	1 teaspoon grated zest	½ teaspoon lemon extract
	1 lb. or 4 to 6 medium	1 cup juice, ¼ cup grated zest
Lentils	1 lb. or 2¼ cups	5 cups cooked
Lettuce	1 lb.	10 cups bite-sized pieces
Limes	1	1½ to 2 tablespoons juice
	1 lb. or 8 medium	About ¾ cup juice
Macaroni	1 lb.	4 cups uncooked
	1 cup	2 to 2¼ cups cooked
Mandarins	1 lb. (4 small, 3 medium, or 2 large)	2 cups sections
Mango	1 medium	1 cup peeled and sliced
Maple sugar, grated	1 tablespoon packed	1 tablespoon white
	½ cup packed	1 cup maple syrup
Maple syrup, see Sugars, Liquid, 1018		
Marshmallows	16 large or 160 miniature	1 cup
Meat, ground	1 lb.	2 cups uncooked
Melons	1 lb.	3 cups cubed

Milk, whole	1 cup	½ cup evaporated plus ½ cup water
		¼ cup dry whole milk powder plus ¾ cup plus 2 tablespoons water
		1 cup reconstituted nonfat dry milk plus 2½ teaspoon butter or margarine
		1 cup soy or almond milk
		1 cup fruit juice or 1 cup potato water (for baking)
	1 cup	1 cup water plus 1½ teaspoons butter
	1 quart	1 quart skim milk plus 3 table-spoons cream
Milk, skim	1 cup	⅓ cup nonfat dry milk powder plus about ¾ cup water
Milk, whole dry powder	1 lb.	14 cups reconstituted
Milk, nonfat dry powder	1 lb.	About 5 quarts reconstituted
Milk, to sour	1 cup	Add 1 tablespoon vinegar or lemon juice to 1 cup minus 1 tablespoon milk and let stand 5 minutes

Molasses, *see* Sugars, Liquid, 1018

Mushrooms	8 oz. or about 3 cups whole	About 1 cup cooked sliced
Mushrooms, canned	6 oz. drained	8 oz. fresh
Mushrooms, dried	3 oz., reconstituted	1 lb. fresh
Mustard	1 teaspoon dry	1 tablespoon prepared mustard
Nectarines	1 lb. or 3 to 4 medium	2 cups sliced or 2½ cups chopped
Noodles	1 lb.	6 to 8 cups cooked
Noodles, 1-inch pieces	1 cup	About 1¼ cups cooked
Nuts, *see individual nuts*	1 lb. in the shell	8 oz. shelled (a bit less for heavier nuts, a bit more for lighter ones)
Oatmeal	1 lb.	5⅓ cups
	1 cup	1¾ cups cooked
Oats, rolled	1 lb. or 6¼ cups	8 cups cooked
Oil	1 lb. fat	2 cups
Okra	1 lb.	4½ cups sliced
Onions		
Onions, pearl	1 lb.	3¾ cups (unpeeled)
Onions, white	1 lb.	2½ cups chopped or 2½ cups sliced
Orange	1 medium	4 to 6 tablespoons juice, 2 to 3 tablespoons grated zest ¾ cup diced
Papayas	1 lb.	1¼ to 1½ cups peeled and sliced
Parsnips	1 lb.	2½ cups sliced
Peaches	1 lb. or 3 to 4 medium	2 cups sliced
Peanuts	1½ lb. in the shell	1 lb. shelled or about 3 cups
Peanut Butter	18 oz. jar	2 cups
Pears	1 lb. or 3 to 4 medium	2 cups sliced
Peas, fresh	1 lb. in the shell	1 cup shelled

Peas, dried, split	1 lb. or 2$\frac{1}{4}$ cups	5 cups cooked
Pecans	2$\frac{1}{2}$ lb. in the shell	1 lb. shelled or about 4$\frac{1}{4}$ cups
Peppers, bell	6 oz. or 1 large	1 cup diced
Persimmons	1 lb.	$\frac{3}{4}$ cup diced
Pineapple, fresh	1 medium	3$\frac{1}{2}$ cups diced or 4 cups sliced
Pistachios, shelled	1 lb.	3$\frac{2}{3}$ cups
Plums	1 lb.	2 cups quartered
Pomegranate	1 average	$\frac{1}{2}$ cup pulpy seeds
Pomelo	1 medium	1$\frac{1}{4}$ cups juice or 1 cup sections
Potatoes	1 lb. or 3 medium	3$\frac{1}{2}$ to 4 cups raw sliced or diced, 2$\frac{1}{2}$ cups cooked, or 1$\frac{3}{4}$ cups mashed cooked
Prickly pear	1 large	$\frac{1}{4}$ to $\frac{1}{3}$ cup peeled and sliced or pureed
Prunes	1 lb. unpitted 1 lb. cooked and drained	2$\frac{1}{4}$ cups pitted 2 cups
Pumpkin	1 lb.	2$\frac{1}{2}$ cups cubed or 1$\frac{3}{4}$ cups cooked and mashed
Quinces	1 lb. or 3 medium	4 cups chopped peeled
Radishes	4 oz.	1 cup sliced
Raisins	1 lb.	About 2$\frac{3}{4}$ cups
Raspberries	1 lb.	3 cups
Rennet	1 tablet	1 tablespoon liquid rennet
Rhubarb	1 lb.	2 cups cooked
Rice Rice, instant	1 lb. or 2 cups 2 cups	About 6 cups cooked 4 cups cooked
Rutabaga	1 lb.	2$\frac{1}{4}$ cups cubed
Scallions	4 oz.	1$\frac{1}{4}$ cups sliced
Shallots	1 medium 1 lb.	2 tablespoons chopped About 2 cups chopped
Shortening, vegetable sticks	16 oz. 1 stick	2$\frac{1}{2}$ cups 1 cup
Sorghum molasses	1 lb.	1$\frac{1}{3}$ cups
Spaghetti Spaghetti, 2-inch pieces Spaghetti, 12-inch pieces	1 lb. 1 cup dry 1 lb. dry	7 to 8 cups cooked About 1$\frac{3}{4}$ cups cooked About 6$\frac{1}{2}$ cups cooked
Squash, summer Squash, winter	1 lb. 1 lb. 12 oz. frozen	2$\frac{1}{2}$ cups sliced 2$\frac{1}{2}$ cups cubed or 1$\frac{3}{4}$ cups cooked and mashed 1$\frac{1}{2}$ cups mashed
Starfruit	1 lb.	1$\frac{1}{2}$ cups sliced
Strawberries	1 quart 1 lb.	4 cups sliced 3 cups whole or 2 cups chopped or sliced

Sugar, in baking, *see* Sugars, Solid, 1018, and Sugars, Liquid, 1018

Sugar, white	1 lb.	2 cups
Sugar, brown	1 lb.	2¼ cups packed
	1 cup	1 cup granulated sugar
Sugar, superfine	1 cup	1 cup granulated sugar
Sugar, confectioners'	1 lb.	3½ to 4 cups
	1¾ cups	1 cup granulated sugar
Sweetener—noncaloric solution	⅛ teaspoon	1 teaspoon sugar
Tapioca	1½ to 2 tablespoons quick-cooking	¼ cup pearl, soaked
Tapioca, for thickening	1 tablespoon quick-cooking	1 tablespoon all-purpose flour
Tea	1 lb.	125 cups, brewed
Tomatoes	1 cup packed	½ cup tomato sauce plus ½ cup water
	1 lb. or 2 medium	1 to 1½ cups peeled, seeded, and diced
	1 lb. or 2 medium	2 cups chopped
Tomatoes, cherry	1 lb.	2 cups
Tomato juice	1 cup	½ cup tomato sauce plus ½ cup water
Tomato sauce	2 cups	¾ cup tomato paste plus 1 cup water
Turnips	1 lb.	2½ cups cubed
Walnuts, English	2 to 2½ lb. in the shell	1 lb. shelled or about 4½ cups
Walnuts, black	5½ lb. in the shell	1 lb. shelled or about 3 cups broken
Water	1 lb.	1 pint
Watermelon	16 lb.	5 to 6 lb. pickled rind
Watermelon rind	1 lb.	About 4 cups chopped or 2 cups pickled
Wheat germ	12 oz.	3 cups
Yeast, compressed	1 cake (⅗ oz.)	1 package active dry
Yeast, active dry	1 package	2¼ teaspoons
Yogurt	1 cup	1 cup buttermilk

COOKING METHODS AND TECHNIQUES

It's a familiar story now, but well worth repeating: A hard-boiled professional cook, when asked for some elementary advice by an ambitious beginning cook, tersely replied, "Stand facing the stove." While our first cooking lesson would substitute the gradual approach, it is true that somewhere along the line, in perhaps 95 out of 100 kitchen sequences, heat will have been applied, and this has been so from ages past.

There can be no more useful reminder for all of us than that paying attention to cooking basics, and taking nothing for granted, will take any cook a long way toward success. People who say, "I can't boil water," are usually surprised to find that they can—perhaps even moving quickly on to cooking an egg—once they're prepared. Professional cooks call it *mise en place,* a French term translated as "everything in its place." The next step begins, of course, not with fancy gadgets or exotic ingredients, but with deciding on heat.

We have tried throughout our book, but especially in this chapter, to identify and explain the various types of cooking heat, to tell you simply and clearly how these heats are initiated, controlled, and stopped in order to ensure the highest nutritive value and the best flavor, texture, and color. We have tried also to indicate which techniques will bring cooked food to the table in that ideal state of readiness. Here we sum up the key processes.

Asking a cook why food is heated at all is like asking an architect why humans do not live in caves. The obvious answer is that it tastes better that way. There are other reasons too: Cooking seals in natural juices, extracts and enhances flavors, improves sometimes unfavorable tex-

tures, destroys unwanted microorganisms, and makes many foods more digestible and less allergenic.

Let us consider first how heat is transferred to food, whether in air or in moisture, in fat, or through a pan. The results can be quite astonishingly different. Cooking heats are generally known as **dry** or **moist,** with quite a few variations in each.

ABOUT DRY-HEAT COOKING METHODS

Truly dry heats are achieved in a number of ways. They usually involve the transfer of heat from above or below the food, or from dry heat surrounding the food. Grilling over coals or gas is one example; broiling, baking, and roasting in an oven are others. When we say "barbecue," we may be referring either to Pit Cooking, 1057, in which case we refer to a moist-heat process, or to the dry-heat process of low, slow cooking over a fire. Parenthetically, the word "barbecue" has been traced back by some philologists to the Spanish *barbacoa,* a raised platform for cooking, but we like to think of it, with other authorities, as originating among the French settlers in Florida, who roasted the native goats whole, *de barbe en queue*—from beard to tail. Some further remarks on barbecuing can be found later in this chapter; see Outdoor Cooking, 1056.

Oddly, deep-fat frying is actually another kind of dry-heat cooking. Here the heat is transferred not only by the hot oil or fat used as a cooking medium, but by the moisture in the food itself, some of the steam from the food juices being forced out into the fat (as bubbles) and then into the air. Among dry-heat cooking methods done in a pan, sautéing uses the smallest amount of fat. Pan-broiling and panfrying are successive steps beyond sautéing and away from the driest heat. In pan-broiling and panfrying, the food gives off a greater amount of rendered fat than in sautéing and absorbs a larger share of it. In doing so, it gives up proportionately more of its juices. To keep both panfried and pan-broiled foods at their best, excess fat should be poured off during cooking.

Among dry-heat processes that may be described as "partial" are planking and flambéing, or flaming. Either way, the food is heated beforehand, and these processes simply give it its finishing touch before the food is served.

BAKING AND ROASTING

Baking is a dry-heat cooking method where heat surrounds the food. In addition to the reflected and radiant heat of the oven, heat is transferred from the pan to the food and may be further diffused by the use of parchment paper pan liners, temporary foil covers, or a dusting of flour between food and pan bottom. Even though, in baking, some moisture is released from the food and continues to circulate as warm steam in the closed oven, this process is still considered dry. The technique is the same whether you are using a conventional oven or a convection oven, although the circulating air of a convection oven gives the most even results.

Roasting is a term synonymous with baking, where the food is surrounded by dry heat. Roasting in front of a hot fire is one of the oldest forms of cooking and the one from which all forms of roasting spring. Roasting is almost always done uncovered and perhaps at a higher heat than baking. To promote browning when roasting use a shallow, uncovered roasting pan, and do not add liquid. Setting meats and poultry on a rack during roasting keeps them from steaming in their own juices.

▲ At high altitudes, use a slightly higher temperature when roasting.

BROILING

Whether you broil in an oven or grill over a hot fire, the principle is identical. The heat is radiant, direct, and intense, and the process differs from roasting or baking in that only one side of the food at a time is exposed to the heating source. Generally you will want to broil or grill foods that are inherently tender, relatively lean, and not too thick—chicken breasts, hamburger patties, and fish fillets are perfect candidates. To read more about grilling, see 1057.

Like baking and roasting, broiling depends for its effectiveness on proper ventilation. In the great majority of household ranges, you are given limited selectivity in broiling temperatures, and individual variations in wattage as well as venting capacity make it necessary that you become familiar with the special requirements of your own equipment. Some ranges, for example, must be preheated before broiling can begin; in others, broiler heat is almost instantaneous. In some electric ranges, broiling takes place with the oven door ajar; in others, the door may, or even must, be kept closed.

When the heat indicator on a household range is turned to the broil position, the temperature is around 550°F or slightly above and should remain constant. If you really want to match the results you admire in some restaurant cooking, you may have to consider buying one of the professional ranges now available for installation in home kitchens, which can deliver much higher heat than standard home equipment.

Under the limitations of the household range, ➤ much of the temperature control in broiling is determined by the placement of the oven rack. It is usually adjusted so that there is a 3-inch space between the heat source and the top of the food. ➤ To lower the broiling heat for browning delicate dishes or for cooking thick cuts of meat—where the heat must have time to penetrate deeply without charring—lower the broiling rack to make a 4- to 6-inch space between the food and heating element. For details on broiling and pan-broiling meats, see 465; poultry and wildfowl, 426 and 453; fish, 402; and vegetables, 240.

DEEP-FAT FRYING

Done with care, a great number of delicacies can emerge from hot oil crisp on the outside, moist within, and not at all greasy. Pieces of fish, shellfish, poultry, and meat, as well as vegetables, fruits, breads, and pastries, can be deep-fried. Although intensely hot, the process is brief, so the food must already be tender. To add a crunchy coating or to protect the most fragile items, many foods are battered or otherwise coated before frying. Most important, the secret is hot oil.

Deep-fat frying, like a number of other accomplishments in cooking, is an art in itself—an art in which experience is the best teacher. However, even a novice who follows our instructions to the letter can succeed in preparing delicious food fried without excessive fat absorption. Remember that fat absorption increases with cooking time and with the amount of surface exposed to the fat.

Equipment need not be elaborate, for equally good French-fried potatoes can come out of a black iron kettle and from the latest-model electric fryer. This is not to underestimate the value of the fryer, which offers the convenience of a built-in thermostat, but any deep kettle or saucepan, preferably a heavy one, serves nicely for deep-frying. If you choose a self-contained covered electric fryer, look for one with a dial that automatically opens the lid, to avoid burns from the steam. Higher wattage will ensure quick preheating and recovery time. For a 3- or 4-quart kettle or fryer, use about 3 pounds of fat. It isn't wise to try to skimp on the amount, for there must always be enough to cover the food and to permit it to move freely in the kettle. ➤ There must be also be room for the quick bubbling up of the fat that always occurs in deep-frying potatoes, onions, and other foods with high moisture content. ➤ Never fill any container more than half full with fat or more than the quantity specified by the manufacturer. ➤ Remember also to heat the fat gradually and uncovered so that any moisture in it will have evaporated by the time it reaches the required temperature.

The kettle or pot should have a flat bottom so that it sits firmly on the heating unit. Keep the handle turned toward the back of the stove to avoid knocking against it. A short handle is desirable, to avoid the danger of accidentally overturning the pot of hot fat and causing a small conflagration. In case fat should catch fire, always have a metal lid handy to drop over the pot. You may also smother the flame with salt or baking soda. ➤ Never use water, as this will only spread the fire.

For frying certain types of food, such as doughnuts and fritters, where bubbling is not a problem, a heavy skillet or an electric skillet is sometimes preferred to a deep pot or kettle because of the wider surface, which allows more pieces to be fried at one time.

A wire basket or wire skimmer is practically a necessity for successful results in frying any quantity of small-sized material. The food is raised and lowered more easily and uniform browning is assured.

Nothing is more important in deep-frying than the proper temperature. As that wise old gourmet Alexandre

Dumas so aptly put it, the food must be "surprised" by the hot fat, to give it the crusty, golden coating so characteristic and so desirable. The proper temperature in most instances is 365°F, as easy to remember as the number of days in a year.

For judging the temperature of the fat, use a deep-fat frying thermometer that clips onto the side of the pot. The thermometer must read temperatures up to 400°F. If using a glass thermometer, warm the thermometer in a bowl of hot water to lessen the chance of breakage, but ➤ never plunge it into the fat without wiping it thoroughly dry.

If you don't have a thermometer, a simple test for temperature can be made with a small cube of bread about 1 inch square. When you think the fat is hot enough, drop in the bread cube and count slowly to 60, or use a timer set for 60 seconds. If the cube browns in this time, the fat is around 365°F. Some foods—souffléed potatoes, for instance—may require higher or lower temperatures, but this is always noted in the specific recipes.

Above all, ➤ do not wait for the fat to smoke before adding the food. Not only is this hard on the fat, since smoke indicates that it is breaking down and may be spoiled for reuse, but the crust that forms on the food is likely to be too brown before the food is cooked through, and it will be burned on the surface but raw inside. On the other hand, food added to fat that isn't hot enough to form a crust immediately will tend to become grease-soaked. After frying each batch, ➤ let the temperature come up again to the required heat, so that you continue to "surprise" each additional batch. ➤ Skim out bits of food or crumbs frequently as they collect in the fat during frying. If allowed to remain, they can induce foaming, discolor the fat, and affect the flavor of the food. Have ready a tray and a supply of paper towels on which to drain the cooked food and so rid it of excess fat before serving.

Fresh, clear oil will produce superior results, but oil can also be carefully recycled and reused. After frying, when the fat has cooled and become safe to handle, strain it through a fine-mesh strainer or folded cheesecloth to remove all extraneous particles, then store it well covered and refrigerated for future use. To clarify fats before reusing, see 981. ➤ We recommend exercising great caution in recycling oil, because the smoke point, 1023, of the oil may have been reduced to a point at which the oil will smoke or worse yet, flame up, when heated again for frying. Adding some fresh fat for each new frying can materially lengthen the life of the fat, but sometimes after only one use, it may be no longer satisfactory to fry in.

Solid vegetable shortening, lard, and liquid vegetable oils such as peanut, corn, canola, safflower, and soybean are favorites for deep-frying. Except for lard, which has a characteristic odor and flavor, these fats are bland and very similar in appearance and composition. Most of them are 100 percent vegetable in origin. These all have smoke points well above those needed for deep-frying. For more detail, see About Oils, 1043. ➤ Butter and margarine are not suitable for deep-frying, because of their low smoke points.

For special purposes and in certain circumstances, chicken and goose fat may be rendered for frying, as can be veal, pork and suet, or beef kidney fat. These tend to have low smoke points, but when handled with care, they can produce acceptable fried foods. If it seems desirable, the smoke point of these animal fats can be raised to the required limit by blending them with any one of the cooking oils. To render these fats, see 981.

For good results, the food to be fried must be properly prepared. ➤ So that they will all cook in the same length of time, pieces should be uniform in size and preferably not thicker than 1½ inches. Small pieces, obviously, will cook through faster than large ones. It is difficult to give precise advice here about the length of cooking. When in doubt, remove one piece and try for doneness. Raw foods, ➤ especially wet ones, should be patted dry with paper towels before cooking to remove excess surface moisture. This will reduce the amount of bubbling when the food is introduced into the fat.

Whenever possible, foods should be room temperature and as dry as possible when added to hot oil. ➤ Always immerse them gently, using long-handled tongs or a slotted spoon or a frying basket. ➤ Dip utensils into hot fat first, so that the food will release quickly without sticking. And have a pan or dish ready in which to rest the utensils when they come dripping from the fat. When adding a batch of raw food, always lower the basket gradually so that you can observe the amount of bubbling and be ready to lift it up if it looks as though the fat might go over the top. Do not try to put too many pieces in at one time: Fry several small batches rather than one large one. The cooked food may be kept hot on a paper towel– or brown paper–lined pan in an oven set at very low heat—150° to 200°F.

Certain types of food, such as croquettes, eggplant, and fish, need special coating for proper browning and crust formation. For Breading, see 961. The coating may be flour, cornmeal, or finely crushed bread crumbs or crackers. Or it may be a fritter batter, 658, an egg and crumb mixture, or even a pastry envelope. Whatever it is, it should cover the surface evenly. Foods to be coated with batter—shrimp, for instance, or vegetables—should be thoroughly dried beforehand.

Doughnuts, fritters, and other foods made from a batter need no extra coating, as the egg-starch mixture browns nicely by itself when lowered into the hot fat. Many cooks do not realize that ➤ the richer a dough or batter mixture, the more fat it will absorb during frying. By adding even a little too much shortening or sugar to the mix, a doughnut may become too rich and end up greasy. A fritter may simply disintegrate in the hot fat, or a too rich batter slide off onion rings altogether.

Frozen foods already breaded and deep-fried need only defrosting and reheating in the oven. They should be defrosted unwrapped to avoid the formation of surface moisture that would interfere with the crisping of the outer coating. Uncooked frozen foods that are to be coated should be patted dry after defrosting, and the coating applied as usual.

▲ When deep-fat frying at high altitudes, you will find that the lower boiling point of water within moist food requires that the temperature of the cooking oil be lower. This will prevent the food from browning excessively on the outside while remaining undercooked on the inside. The reduction in oil temperature varies according to the food to be fried, but a rough guide is to lower the frying temperature by about 3 degrees for every increase of 1,000 feet in elevation.

SAUTÉING

The French word *sauter* literally means "to jump," and this is just about what happens to the food you cook by sautéing. The cooking is done in an ➤ open pan that is kept in motion by shaking the handle so that the food moves in the pan. The process is rapid, the food is usually thin or minced, and the ➤ heat must be kept up from the moment cooking starts until the food is tender.

There are other requirements too. The pan and the ➤ small quantity of fat used must be hot enough when the food is added to sear the food at once, and to prevent sticking. The food should be cut to a uniform thickness and size and be dry on the surface. If the food is too cold, it will lower the heat, and if it is wet, it will not brown properly. Worst of all, steam will form and the food will not properly brown. To ensure a dry surface, food is frequently floured or breaded, see 961, prior to cooking. ➤ Steam will also form if the pan is crowded. There must be space between the pieces of food you are sautéing, or it will steam, not brown.

For the best sauté, use Clarified Butter, 963, or a combination of 3 parts butter and 4 parts oil. When the fat reaches the point of fragrance, but is not smoking, add the food; the handsomest or presentation side goes into the pan first. Do not add so much food at a time as to reduce the heat in the pan. To keep the food from too-quick browning, agitate the pan frequently. Too much turning of the food delays the quickness of heating. But food with a bound breading, especially if the coating has not been allowed to dry long enough before cooking, may steam. In this case, turning will help to release some of that steam more rapidly. Meat not floured or breaded is browned or cooked on one side until the juices come up to the surface of the exposed side, then turned and browned on the other side. Proceed in the same way for fish, keeping in mind that the cooking time is apt to be considerably shorter. Generally meat or fish is cooked through when the juices rise to the surface of the cooked side. The exception is rare-cooked meat, which is done as soon as it has firmed slightly. Fish should be turned as soon as the bottom half appears opaque, 1 to 4 minutes depending

on thickness. If breaded pieces fail to brown, turn up the heat and, if necessary, add more fat to the pan. During cooking, you may need to reduce the heat on the second side.

Though many call regular skillets sauté pans, true sauté pans have straight, not flaring, sides. Sauté pans are excellent for cooking dishes that contain a considerable quantity of sauce or other liquid. Since what you sauté may then be braised, 1051, as well, buy a pan with a lid if possible. Materials that diffuse heat evenly are preferable, as is a handle that is ovenproof and doesn't retain heat.

To serve sautéed food with a sauce, remove the food from the pan and keep it warm on a hot serving dish. Quickly deglaze, 1055, the delicious residue in the sauté pan—unless you have been cooking a strongly flavored fish—with stock or wine. Reduce the sauce and pour it over the sautéed food. ➤ If you heat or keep sautéed food hot in a sauce, you will steam it.

PANFRYING

Panfrying is similar to sautéing, but is generally used for larger pieces of food such as pieces of bone-in chicken, or thick pork chops. Because the food is in larger pieces, the heat is lower and a greater amount of fat is used. The food is not tossed or "jumped" as in sautéing. Turning the food at least once ensures the most even cooking.

STIR-FRYING

In classic stir-frying, the food is always bite-sized, the stirring is ceaseless, and the heat is extremely high. In fact, it may be hard to get the heat high enough on some home stoves to achieve this classic technique. In anywhere from 3 to 8 minutes, depending on the ingredients, you will have tender but still crunchy vegetables and thin strips of fresh-tasting meat—for immediate consumption.

Familiarize yourself with the recipe before beginning, since you may not have time to stop and read once you are in action. Have all ingredients prepared and measured and within easy reach. Undercook rather than overcook—you can always return food to the heat.

A 12- to 14-inch wok is ideal, but you can stir-fry beautifully in a skillet as long as it is heavy and large—the largest your burner will accommodate. The pan must be capable of being heated empty over the highest heat without damage. On gas burners, either a round- or a flat-bottomed wok will work but may need to be stabilized with a special ring-shaped holder; for all other burners, a flat-bottomed wok is preferable. Always heat the empty wok (or skillet) until it just begins to smoke, then add the oil and tip the wok to coat it before proceeding with the recipe.

Preparing the food is the longest part of this procedure. If the meat is cooked along with vegetables—a typical practice—it is uniformly sliced to a thickness of about $1/8$ inch and partially cooked first, until red changes to bright pink. Then it is removed and reserved for addition later to the half-cooked vegetables for final cooking. For further details about vegetable stir-frying, see 242; for meats, see 476.

PAN-BROILING

In pan-broiling, a dry pan becomes the direct heat source. A well-seasoned cast-iron skillet, a griddle, or a sauté pan without a nonstick coating is thoroughly heated first. Then the food, such as a piece of meat or fish, is laid into the hot pan. When it is browned on one side, turn and cook on the other. If fat accumulates in the pan, pour it off, to keep the food from frying rather than broiling.

Blackening, associated with Cajun cooking, is a unique kind of pan-broiling that sears highly seasoned surfaces so intensely that they form a crust. This method produces an enormous amount of smoke, so cook in a well-ventilated area. A very hot burner on top of the stove or over a hot gas or charcoal grill will give you sufficient heat. To blacken food, heat a dry cast-iron skillet (no other) over very high heat until extremely hot, 5 to 10 minutes—when a white film is just beginning to appear in the center. Dip the food in melted butter, coating it thoroughly, then generously coat it all over with Cajun Dry Rub, 587. At once, lay the food in the skillet and drizzle the top with a little more butter (be careful, as it usually flares up). When a crust has formed on the bottom, in about 2 to 3 minutes, turn the food with a spatula and moisten again with butter. Blacken until done, about 2 to 6 minutes more, depending on the thickness of the food you are cooking. Do not try to cook beef past medium—the exterior will burn and be bitter. After each pass, wipe the skillet completely clean with a thick cotton cloth.

SKEWER COOKING

From a marshmallow impaled on a stick to the most delicate bay scallops, skewer-grilled food never seems to lose its charm. A most important first step is to ➤ choose items that will cook at the same rate of speed, or to make the proper adjustments if they do not. When the meat, poultry, or fish selected is a quick-cooking one, see that the onions, peppers, or other more resistant vegetables that will alternate with it are precooked, so that the food will all be done at the same time. Or, should the meat need relatively longer cooking, skewer delicate alternates like tomatoes and mushrooms separately and mingle meat and vegetables when serving. Protect delicate meats such as liver with a wrapping of thinly sliced bacon.

Choose skewers, whether of metal or wood, that are either square or oval so that as the food softens in cooking, it will not slip when you turn the skewers. ➤ Soak wood skewers in water for an hour before using.

If using a grill, grease or oil the rack and place the skewered food over medium heat. Turn the skewers often. Food grilled in this way may take anywhere from 6 to 12 minutes. If cooking skewers in an oven, broil on a greased baking sheet about 3 inches from the source of heat. You may, of course, use the skewer element on a rotis-serie; for more details about rotisserie and spit-cooking, see 1059.

Should you decide to precook any sort of skewered food, you may do so on the skewers themselves in a skillet—provided, of course, the skewers are no longer than the pan bottom.

ABOUT MOIST-HEAT COOKING METHODS

The moist-heat category has an abundance of processes, magnified by a further abundance of variations. Luckily, most of them are quite forgiving, so we approach them with pleasure rather than apprehension. There are complete ones like boiling, pressure-cooking, scalding, simmering, poaching, stewing, fricasseeing, braising, cooking in wraps, double-boiler cookery, and steaming. Just as with dry heats, there are partial moist-heat processes, like those in blanching and slow cooking. Also, a number are neither simply moist nor dry, but a combination of both. Some stews, for example, may be begun in a pan by browning, though others, like the Irish variety of stew, never see the inside of a skillet. Similarly, a braise, a fricassee, and a "smother" may all, like a browned stew, have their origins in dry-heat sautéing and are then finished by cooking in a little stock or other liquid.

BOILING

Discussing this process tempts us to mention stews again, in connection with an old adage, "A stew boiled is a stew spoiled." And we may point out that the same sentiment can be applied to almost every other kind of food. While recipes often call for foods to be brought to the boiling point—that is, in liquid that has reached 212°F and is vigorously bubbling or "rolling"—or to be plunged into boiling water, they hardly ever demand boiling for a protracted period. Even "hard-boiled" eggs should only be simmered.

Quick evaporation—seldom advisable except in parboiling—is one of the few justifications for keeping a food at boiling point. When evaporating, never boil covered, as steam will condense on the lid and fall back into the pot, thereby reducing the amount of liquid very little, if at all.

Adding foods to boiling water will lower the temperature unless the quantity of water is at least three times as much as will cover the food, to offset the drop in temperature. Such compensation is recommended in Blanching, 1054, and in the cooking of some grains, vegetables, and pastas. When the pores of food are to be sealed, it may be plunged into rapidly boiling liquid, after which the temperature is usually reduced to a simmer.

SIMMERING

Cooking food in simmering liquid is one of the most important methods of cooking with moist heat. The temperatures used range from about 140° to 185°F. Simmering protects fragile foods and tenderizes tough ones. The French say a simmer "makes the pot smile." When food is simmering, bubbles come gently to the surface and barely seem to break. It is the heat best used for soups (uncovered); for soups, stews, braises, pot roasts, and fricassees (covered); and for food prepared à l'étouffée, 1051 (covered).

POACHING

Poaching is a kind of moist-heat cooking that we associate mostly with eggs, but its range is much wider. The principle of poaching never varies: The heat source is a calm liquid just under the boiling point, with nary a bubble breaking the surface; a distinguishing feature of the process is the basting or self-basting that is constant during the cooking period.

When an egg is properly poached, it is floated in the poaching water and then either basted with the liquid or covered with a lid so that steam accumulates above it to perform a self-basting action. Because the egg cooks in just a few minutes, the lid does not result in the formation of excess steam. In poaching meat or fish, where the cooking period is longer, trapped steam may become too heavy. For these and delicate foods, therefore, a lid is not recommended. Instead, a poaching paper, see below, should be substituted.

A poaching paper permits excess steam to escape through its small top vent and around the sides. The narrow vent also maintains better color in the food than when air is excluded altogether—as in other more tightly confined moist-heat processes, such as braising or stewing. ➤ **To make a poaching paper,** cut a square of parchment paper, a little larger than the diameter of the pan you wish to cover. Fold it into quarters and roll it diagonally: Begin at the folded tip, as sketched. Hold it over the pan to determine the radius, then snip off the part projecting beyond the edge of the pan. Cut a tiny piece off the pointed tip to form a vent. When you unfold the paper, you will have a circle just the area of your pan, with a hole at its center. Place it over the food to provide a self-baster.

If the cooking process is a short one, or if the food to be cooked is in small units, the liquid may be simmering when the food is added. If the food is large, like a whole chicken, the food is added to cold water and the water brought to

a simmer ➤ uncovered. The liquid may then be skimmed and the poaching paper applied. If the liquid reduces too much during the cooking process, it must be replenished. This type of poaching is often miscalled boiling or stewing.

If you plan to serve the food cold, remove the pan from the heat when the food is on the brink of being done, then let it stand in the liquid until cool. This method makes chicken perfect for chicken salad.

STEAMING

Steaming is one of the gentlest ways to cook vegetables, plump dried fruit, release salt from smoked meat, and to perfectly cook fish and prepare vegetables for freezing. The even, moist heat of the steam—not the simmering water—envelops the food, allowing it to retain most of it natural juices and nutrients. Water is the most common steaming medium, though using broth, beer, wine, or other herb-infused liquids is an easy way to add flavor.

Ready-made stovetop steamers come in many sizes, shapes, metals, and prices, from the collapsible kind and the shallow insert of a spaghetti pot to the asparagus steamer and the whole-fish–sized oval stainless steel steamer. Chinese tiered bamboo steamers are beautiful, but set in a wok as they were meant to be (they come with a top but not a bottom), they have to be watched so their rims do not burn. Rinse with hot water after each use and dry thoroughly before storing in a well-ventilated place. The multitiered aluminum or lightweight stainless steel steamers are more desirable and can be used more easily. Either type has the capacity for steaming a complete meal on one burner. The food that needs the most heat goes on the lowest tier, and the food that needs the least heat goes on top.

Always keep the water level an inch or so below the bottom of the steamer. It is also best to keep most foods an inch or so from the steamer sides. If the food will not render juices—vegetables, for example—it goes in the steamer directly. If the food is juicy, steam it in a shallow bowl or deep plate, to capture all the juices. If you are steaming fish or vegetables, add very thin slices of highly flavored foods, such as ginger, onions, celery, and/or fennel to the tier above the fish so that their juices drip down and flavor the fish.

  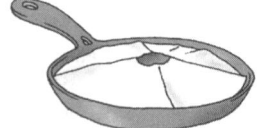

Cutting a poaching paper lid

Steam over moderate heat. A trick that will alert you to dwindling water is to put two or three marbles or coins in the bottom of your steamer. They will make a racket until the water is gone; silence means it is time to add water.

Remember that steam is scalding hot—and deceptive, since you cannot see all of it. ➤ Always lift the lid away from you, protecting your hands and arms from the steam.

BRAISING AND STEWING

When **braising,** a tight lid is essential, and it is usually done with one food—meat, fish, or vegetable—and with a small amount of liquid. Generous quantities of butter, fat, or oil may be used and sometimes—but not always—a small amount of stock; the steam from the stock, as well as from the juice from the food, condenses on the lid and supplies a measure of continuous basting. The very slow cooking goes on in about a 300°F oven and develops a bare simmer, condensing the food juices into a delicious residue. After the food is removed, the residue, degreased if necessary and then deglazed, becomes the sauce for the dish. This method of cooking is also sometimes called cooking **à l'étouffée.** We also refer to this method as pot-roasting when large pieces of meat, up to 4 or 5 pounds, are braised.

Braised dishes can be prepared in a Dutch oven. A Dutch oven is a heavy covered pot, frequently made of cast iron or enameled cast iron. It holds heat well, cooks evenly, can go from stovetop to oven, and can be used in hearth cooking, 1059.

Dutch oven and camp-style Dutch oven
with hook to lift lid

Stewing involves browning smaller pieces of meat, poultry, or fish, then simmering them with vegetables or other ingredients in enough liquid to cover in a closed or partly closed pot, either in the oven or on the stovetop, or in a slow cooker.

SLOW COOKING

If a long cooking or heating period is needed for certain foods, there is an advantage in using a slow cooking method, typically using a special piece of equipment called a slow cooker. The slow cooker "watches the pot," stretches time, retains nutrients, saves fuel, keeps the kitchen cool, doesn't need monitoring, and cooks many foods from chili to soups and stews to spaghetti sauce. The cooking insert is surrounded by a material that is a non-conductor of heat. Food is placed in the slow cooker insert and the heat is turned to the desired temperature. The food continues to cook and the cooking temperature is maintained. For more about slow cooking and slow cookers, see 99.

▲ For every 1,000 feet above 4,000 feet, allow 1 hour more on low or 30 minutes on high.

WRAP COOKERY

Wrapping food before exposing it to direct heat is almost as old as cooking itself. Many cultures to this day surround pieces of food with various materials to tenderize them and to protect them from burning. In the Caribbean, petate mats serve this tenderizing purpose, just as papaya leaves do in the Pacific Islands. One of the most mouthwatering sights we've ever seen was in a documentary of an Indonesian tribe on the move. When mealtime came, everyone, from oldster to tot, stopped to devise a case for cooking his or her food in the coals—an intricately folded leaf, a stoppered section of bamboo, a reed basket. You knew at once that in each "case" the steam produced would give the special flavor and succulence to the food. Early Native Americans baked fish, small animals, and birds in clay. Drawn but not skinned, the animal was completely packaged in mud and bedded in coals—for up to several hours if the size required it. Removal of the clay brought along with it skin and feathers, leaving the skinned game ready to eat. To bake fish in clay, see 1052.

More sophisticated techniques of exploiting the wrap principle are the dough-encased meat turnovers of English kiln workers and the esteemed French *en croûte,* as in Beef Wellington, 468, and *en papilotte,* 1052, methods in which pastry and paper are the respective casings. And one could consider the prized product of a New England clambake, 375—with seaweed the incomparable flavoring agent—as a glorified example of wrap cookery. But in any true wrap cookery, the enclosing material allows some steam to escape. If you use aluminum foil to wrap the food, 1052, remember that the food is actually steamed and will be far removed in taste and texture from food cooked either by direct heat or in a less impervious wrapping.

LEAF WRAPPINGS

Some fresh, unblemished green leaves, such as lettuce, cabbage, grape, and papaya, create a flavorful and edible wrap for food, while banana leaves, palm leaves, and corn husks only furnish protection during cooking. Preparation of suitable leaves and the wrapping and timing of the food for cooking are described below.

As a rule, leaf-wrapped bundles have deeper flavor the day after cooking, and they reheat beautifully, because the leaves hold in their moisture. When you are collecting or buying leaves for wrapping, get extras; some will tear, and you may have more filling than you thought. Use any extra leaves to line the cooking dish or place extra leaves between the layers of bundles, or cover everything with leaves during cooking for added flavor.

Cabbage leaves: Cut out the core from a head of cabbage deep enough to start a separation of the very outer leaves. Drop the head in boiling water for 5 to 10 minutes. This will loosen 3 or 4 leaves. Dip again and continue to remove the loosened leaves. Wrap a meat mixture in the leaves. Either tie the leaf packet, or place it seam side down in the pot or steamer. Cook as follows.

I. Melt in a Dutch oven or other heavy pot:

2 tablespoons butter

Add:

2 cups boiling water or stock

Put the packets in a single layer in the bottom of the pot. Place a heavy heatproof plate on top of the food as a weight. If the filling is uncooked, bring to a simmer, then reduce heat and simmer packets, ➤ covered, 1 to 1½ hours. If the filling is precooked, 10 minutes is enough to heat the packets through.

II. If the packets are tied, they may be dropped into simmering broth and cooked, ➤ covered, gently until done; see timing above.

III. Or steam the tied packets in a vegetable steamer; see timing above.

Lettuce leaves: Blanch them very briefly in boiling water. Drain, dry, and fill. Wrap as for cabbage leaves and cook as for I or III. The leaves are not strong enough to cook as for II.

Fresh grape leaves: For Dolmas, see 82. Drop young pale-green leaves into boiling water and blanch until the color darkens, about 4 to 5 minutes. Remove the leaves and drain them on a rack. Should you have to use large leaves, remove the tough part of the central rib. Place shiny side down on a board. Roll the filling into ¾-inch balls; if the filling is of rice, use no more than 2 teaspoons, as the rice will swell. Set a mound of stuffing near the broad bottom of a leaf and fold over the left and right segments, as shown, 82, then roll up to form a packet. Cook as directed in I above, placing the packets seam side down.

Canned grape leaves: Place briefly in hot water to separate, then drain and dry. Fill and cook as for fresh grape leaves.

Papaya leaves: Cover with cold water and bring ➤ just to a boil, uncovered, to remove any bitterness. Drain. Plunge into boiling water to cover and ➤ simmer, uncovered, until tender. Fill and cook as for III, above.

Banana leaves: Cut away the central rib and carefully tear into sections about 10 inches square by pulling along the veins. Sponge off on both sides with cold water, al-

ways keeping the action along the leaf veins. Dry gently with paper towels. Center the filling as for Tamales, 351, but fold first against the veining, and then secure the loose ends by folding them up and securing them with string. Cook as for III, above.

Corn husks: Place in a pot of boiling water, remove from the heat, and allow to stand 30 to 45 minutes before draining. To wrap food, overlap 2 or 3 corn husks. Fold one side over slightly past the center and then overlap from the other side, as shown. Fold over the ends, overlapping them, and tie with string. For Tamales, see 351.

BAKING FISH IN CLAY

Scoop out of the ground a hole about twice as big as the fish you are going to cook. Either wet and tamp the ground or line the area with stones; see 1057. Prepare a bed of coals in the pit, and lay more flat stones on top of the coals to heat for 1 to 2 hours. After cleaning the fish, season the cavity with onions or herbs or wipe with lemon. Close openings so that mud cannot get inside. Have ready a batch of "mud-pie" clay, preferably blue clay, with which to encase the fish. Continue to lay on layers of clay until the covering is 1½ to 2 inches thick. Clear away the top rocks and the coals from the pit, place the "clay fish" on the hot lining stones, and cover with earth and then the hot stones you set aside. Rebuild the fire over all and cook 1 to 3 hours, depending on the size of the fish; a 2½- to 3-pound fish will take about 2 hours. When it is done, uncover and crack open the clay mold. Skin and scales, head and tail, all will come off with the mold, revealing a delicious result. Needless to say, serve at once with corn roasted in the husks, 271.

FOIL COOKERY

Aluminum foil solves many kitchen problems. An effortless way to cook food is to wrap it, butcher-wrap style, in heavy-duty foil, with the shiny side in, but if you cook food wrapped in foil, please consider the following: Foil is impervious to air and moisture from the outside. Therefore, it traps all the moisture released from the food during the cooking period. So, even if the heat is dry, like that of an oven, the result will always be a steamed food, never a roasted or browned one. Since the foil also has high insulating qualities, foil-wrapped food will require ➤ longer cooking periods at the same temperatures indicated for non-foil cookery.

You may be willing to pay for both the foil and extra heat needed to enjoy the convenience of, for example, the practically effortless Pot Roast described on 477. If you are cooking outdoors, see about Grilling Vegetables, 243, and the comments in Outdoor Cooking, 1056, for foil wrapping is an invaluable technique for the grill.

COOKING EN PAPILLOTE

This is a delightful way to prepare delicate quick-cooking foods, such as fish fillets or shellfish and vegetables in a light sauce. The dish, served in the parchment paper in which it was cooked, retains the aromas until ready to eat. As the food heats, some of the unwanted steam it generates evaporates through the paper. Just the same, the paper rises and puffs as heating progresses, putting considerable strain on the folded seam—so note the following directions and sketches carefully.

To make a papillote: Fold a piece of parchment paper, ➤ not foil, of appropriate size crosswise in half. Starting at the folded edge, cut a half-heart shape, so that when the paper is unfolded the full heart shape materializes, as shown below.

Be generous in cutting, allowing almost twice again as much paper as the size of the object to be enclosed. Place the food near the fold, but not too near. Turn the filled paper with the folded edge toward you. Holding the edges of the paper together, make a fold in a small section of the rim. Crease it with your fingers and fold it over again. Hold down this double fold with the fingers of one hand and, with the other, start a slightly overlapping and then again double overlapping fold. Each double fold should overlap the previous one. Repeat this folding, creasing, and folding around the entire rim, finishing off at the pointed end of the heart with a tight twist of the parchment, locking the whole in place.

Making a papillote

Butter the paper well. Place the papillote in a buttered ovenproof dish and cook as directed. When serving, snip about three-fourths of the paper on the curved edge just next to the fold to reveal the lovely food and release the aroma.

Because of the varied composition of the paper, we do not recommend the brown paper bag of the supermarket type as a substitute for parchment paper.

DOUBLE-BOILER COOKING

For those foods that can be quickly ruined beyond hope of resurrection if heated over direct heat even for a short period—especially those containing egg, cream, or chocolate—we recommend the use of a double boiler. A double boiler is made of two nesting pans. The food to be cooked is placed in the top insert. Sometimes the food may be started over direct heat in the top of the double boiler and finished ➤ over, not in, boiling water. To prevent the water in the bottom pan from boiling over, add no more than an inch of water (it should not touch the bottom of

the upper container), and heat the water only to a gentle simmer.

For sauces, we like a double boiler that is rather wide. Deep, narrow vessels tend to overheat the sauce at the bottom, even when it is stirred, if it is held for any time at all. ➤ The material of which the upper portion of the double boiler is made is very important. If it is too thin, it will transmit heat too fast. If it is too thick, it will absorb and retain too much heat.

If you do not have a double boiler, choose any heat-resistant bowl that rests snugly on one of your saucepans, leaving 2 to 3 inches between the bottom of the bowl and the bottom of the pan. For years we made magnificent hollandaise in a stoneware bowl that fit over the base of an aluminum double boiler. It was a completely effortless procedure. Then the bowl broke, and the magic fled.

PRESSURE-COOKING

We often wonder what is done with the moments saved by the purchase and preparation of convenience foods. Something, we assume, of major importance, to compensate for their secondhand flavor. For the cook who is in a hurry but who still hankers after taste and nutritional value, we offer the pressure cooker as a kind of consolation prize.

No matter how high the heat source, boiling in water can never produce a temperature over 212°F. But because in pressure-cooking a great volume of steam is trapped under a locked lid, heat as high as 250°F can be maintained at a gauge reading 15 pounds of pressure. Some home pressure cookers are geared to a range of 3¾ to 20 pounds, but 15 pounds is commonly used. Cooking at 15 pounds pressure takes only about one-third the total time—from putting the lid on the pressure cooker through the final release of pressure—that it takes to cook food in conventional ways at boiling temperatures. Timing varies with each pressure cooker, so consult your manual.

In pressure-cooking vegetables over short periods at these higher temperatures, more than time is saved, and nutrients and flavor are also preserved. See Pressure-Cooking and Pressure-Steaming Vegetables, 243. If pressure-cooking meats and soups, however, the higher heats involved tend both to toughen the protein and to affect flavor adversely. Therefore, we recommend this method only when time is more important to you than choice results.

In the canning ➤ of all nonacid foods, the higher heat of pressure cooking with a pressure canner is essential to kill unwanted organisms; see 889.

A pressure cooker is nothing more than a large heavy saucepan with a lid that locks in place. The locked-on lid enables the pan to trap the steam from the boiling liquid, creating a superheated pressure that speeds along the cooking. Without its lid, a pressure cooker is merely a saucepan. The "new" generation of pressure cookers have stationary regulators that replace the old jiggle-top regulators. Pressure cookers can be made from aluminum or stainless steel, and if stainless steel is layered with copper or aluminum, the heat is very well conducted and the pan will not react easily with foods.

The newer pressure cookers are extremely safe, and cooking with a pressure cooker is not dangerous if you follow common-sense guidelines. It is essential in any pressure-cooking to know your equipment well. ➤ Follow the manufacturer's directions to the letter, observing the following general principles: ➤ Never fill a pressure cooker with more food than two-thirds to three-quarters full, depending on your model. Consult the manual. ➤ Be sure to put the required amount of liquid into the cooker. ➤ Season lightly, as there is less liquid to dilute the flavor than in other types of cooking. If you have a timer, use it. If not, watch the time carefully, as overcooking occurs very quickly.

The cover must not be removed until all the steam is out of the pressure cooker. Here again, handle your particular type of appliance exactly as you are instructed. ➤ If the cover is difficult to remove, do not force it; there is still steam in the container, which will be exhausted if you wait a few minutes.

When you are adapting recipes designed for conventional methods, you can use less liquid, because there will be no evaporation. Vegetables contain considerable moisture, so when you pressure-cook them (or stews with vegetables), you may add as little as $1/2$ cup water to the pot—the minimum to produce steam.

Dried beans and dried whole (not split) green or yellow peas must be presoaked before going into the pressure cooker. If using a jiggle-top cooker, *always* add 1 tablespoon oil per cup of dried beans to control the foaming; if using a cooker with a stationary pressure regulator, the oil may be optional. Again, consult your owner's manual.

When cooking rice and dried beans (or soups or stews that include rice or dried beans), do not fill the cooker more than half full, since both rice and beans expand.

Always ➤ consult your manual if you are considering cooking foods that foam, froth, or sputter, since they might clog the vent. These include applesauce, cranberries, rhubarb, pearl barley, split peas, soup mixes containing dried vegetables, any form of noodles or pasta, and oatmeal or other cereals. Fresh fruit is generally too fragile for this cooking method, but reconstituted dried fruits, custards, and bread and rice puddings do beautifully in the pressure cooker.

PRESSURE-COOKING AT HIGH ALTITUDES

▲ To reach the same boiling temperature at high altitudes as at sea level, the pressure in the cooker must be increased by 1 pound for every 2,000 feet above sea level, and the cooking time under pressure should be increased by 5 percent for every 1,000 feet after 2,000 feet above sea level. At sea level, the pressure cooker is normally set to 15 pounds. At higher altitudes (5,000 feet and above),

15 pounds pressure will not raise the boiling temperature to as high a point as it does at sea level, and the gauges of most home pressure cookers do not go above 15 pounds. To compensate, it is necessary to lengthen the cooking time recommended for sea level, or the gauge from your pressure cooker may be sent to the manufacturer and adjusted to the proper weight for the altitude at which you live. When pressure-cooking at altitudes over 2,000 feet, the cooking time should be increased. Increase cooking times 5 percent for every 1,000 feet above 2,000 feet. Increase cooking times as follows:

3,000 ft: 5 percent
4,000 ft: 10 percent
5,000 ft: 15 percent
6,000 ft: 20 percent
7,000 ft: 25 percent
8,000 ft: 30 percent

For additional details about high-altitude pressure-cooking, see Vegetables, 245, Meat, 462, and Canning, 888.

ABOUT PARTIAL-HEAT PROCESSES

Certain processes involve heating but are not in themselves complete methods of cooking. They extend from the driest, like toasting, which adds color and flavor, to complete immersion, as in steeping, which may plump foods or remove unwanted flavors.

BLANCHING AND PARBOILING

These terms are among the most carelessly used in a cook's vocabulary. To introduce some order into traditional confusion, we differentiate among four different types of blanching.

Blanching I: This means pouring boiling water over food to remove outer coverings, as in loosening the brown hulls of almonds or hazelnuts or making the skins of peaches and tomatoes easier to peel. This process is also used to soften herbs and vegetables for more flexible and longer-lived decoration.

Blanching II, or Parblanching: This involves placing food to be blanched in ➤ a large quantity of cold water, bringing it slowly to a boil, uncovered, and simmering it for the length of time specified for blanching. Following this hot bath, the food is drained, plunged quickly into cold water to firm it and to arrest further cooking, and then finished as directed in the recipe. This is the process used to leach excess water from tongue, cured ham, or salt pork and to remove excess blood or strong flavor from variety meats. The cold-water plunge after blanching effectively firms the protein in the most fragile variety meats, like sweetbreads.

Blanching III, or Parboiling: This means that food is plunged into ➤ a large quantity of rapidly boiling water—adding it a little at a time so as not to disturb the boiling—and then boiled for the period indicated in the recipe. The purpose of this particular kind of blanching, or parboiling, may be to set color or—by partial dehydration—to help preserve nutrients and to firm the tissues of vegetables. If further cooking follows immediately, the blanched food need not be chilled as above, merely drained. Should an interval elapse before final cooking and serving, use the cold-water plunge, drain, and store the food refrigerated.

Blanching vegetables in this way preparatory to canning or freezing is described in greater detail on 899. Small amounts of vegetables or fruits are plunged into ➤ boiling water just long enough to retard enzymatic action and to shrink them for more economical packaging. Then the vegetables are drained and quickly plunged into ice water so that the cooking is arrested at once.

Blanching IV, Steam-blanching or Parsteaming: Similar to steaming, 1050, but of shorter duration. An alternate method for food to be frozen or canned is described on 899.

REDUCING LIQUIDS

Reducing is the process of boiling down a liquid to thicken the consistency and to intensify and concentrate the flavors: Wine, heavy cream, stock, or a sauce is evaporated and condensed over lively heat. Season the reduction only after it reaches the desired thickness, or it may be overseasoned or salty. A so-called double consommé is made by reduction, the final product being half the original in volume. Naturally, reducing applies only to sauces or liquids made without added egg, which would curdle during the cooking process. Those that have a cream or flour base must be watched and stirred often to avoid scorching as they reduce. For further details, see Reducing Sauces, 545.

PLANKING OR PLANK-ROASTING

Why bother with planking? One reason is the attractive appearance of a planked piece of meat or fish. Another reason is the delicious flavor a hardwood slab can give to the food. Plank-roasting, a traditional technique that calls for cooking directly on a wooden board—over a fire, or today, under the broiler or on a backyard grill—was favored by Native Americans of the Pacific Northwest. This method infuses the food with the flavor of wood smoke and helps it retain its shape and stay moist.

You can buy boards especially for plank cooking, sold with grilling supplies, or you can use a piece of untreated "construction grade" wood, which you can find at most lumber yards, ideally about 1/2 inch thick. For most grills, the optimal size is 6 to 8 inches wide by 10 to 12 inches long. Western cedar is the traditional choice, as it does contribute a distinctive flavor, but any fragrant hardwood (such as cherry, apple, maple, or hickory) is acceptable. Avoid soft or resinous woods such as poplar, birch, pine, and fir.

Before cooking, soak the wood in cold water (a roasting pan is good for this) for at least 6 hours, or overnight. Weight the plank with cans or bricks to keep it under the water. Avoid reusing wood for plank cooking unless it's only lightly charred.

FLAMBÉING OR FLAMING

Flambéing is always a dramatic moment in the meal, sometimes a tragicomic one if you manage to get only a mere flicker. Flambéing, or flaming, is a technique of quickly enveloping a dish in flames by igniting a small amount of heated liquor poured over it. To avoid anticlimax, remember that both ➤ the food to be flamed and the brandy or liqueur used in flambéing should be warm—but well under the boiling point. For meat, do not attempt this process with less than 1 ounce of liquor per serving. For nonsweet food served from a chafing dish, pour the warmed liquor over the surface of the food and ignite by touching the edge of the pan with the flame of a match or taper. For hot desserts, sprinkle the top with granulated sugar, add the warm liqueur, and ignite as above. Or ignite brandy-dipped sugar cubes. To flambé fruits, see 215.

SCALDING

As the term is used in this book, scalding means heating to a temperature of about 185°F, or just below boiling. You will find this process discussed in relation to Milk, 997, or Cream the foods for which it is most frequently used.

DEGLAZING

Deglazing is a technique for dissolving, with wine, stock, or other liquid, the tasty browned bits left in the roasting pan or skillet in which you have cooked meat, poultry, or fish. To deglaze, tilt the pan or skillet and degrease, or skim off excess fat from any juices with a spoon. Add a generous splash of stock, wine, or water and gently cook for a few minutes, stirring and scraping up the precious residue from the bottom and sides of the pan.

SWEATING

To release the flavor from finely chopped aromatic vegetables such as onions, garlic, shallots, carrots, and celery, for example, before they are simmered in a sauce, stew, or braise, they are sweated—gently cooked in a small amount of butter, oil, broth, or stock in a covered pan over low to medium heat. After a few minutes—when the vegetables are tender but not browned and their juices have been released—they are ready.

BROWNING

As a preliminary cooking technique, browning meats and vegetables is generally achieved by quick broiling, sautéing, pan-broiling, or even grilling. The term **searing** specifically refers to browning food, especially meat, over intense high heat. The goal is to add another layer of flavor before continuing with the recipe. As a finishing technique, browning a dish in an oven or under a broiler adds flavor, texture, and eye appeal. When the focus is browning sugar (either natural or added), we use the word **caramelizing.**

GRATINÉING

This partial cooking technique means creating a golden crust by covering the surface of a dish with bread crumbs and/or grated cheese and browning it in the oven or under the broiler. Dishes prepared this way are referred to as "au gratin," or simply "gratin." See 961 for more tips on gratinéing.

▲ HIGH-ALTITUDE COOKING

Cooking in mountainous country is an art in itself. In our experience, there is practically nothing you can do at sea level that you cannot do at a mile high. In a high-altitude kitchen, you must compensate for the effects of thinner, drier air.

If high altitudes are new to you, watch for the high-altitude cooking symbol ▲, which will give you formulas for adjusting ingredients or temperatures. Roasting may require slightly more heat than at sea level. Adjustments required in using sea-level baking recipes at high altitude are indicated as necessary for each baking category. For basic theory and adjustments for cakes and many other baked goods at high altitude, read About High-Altitude Cake Baking, 746. For specially designed high-altitude cake recipes, see pages 747–753. For yeast breads, see Breads, 594.

If these hints are not sufficiently specialized for your area, write the Consumer and Family Sciences department of your state college, or call your county extension agent for more information. If you are doing any pressure-cooking, the accuracy of the gauge is vital. These agencies can also tell you where to have gauges tested.

Any cooking process involving liquid will be proportionately lengthened as altitude increases. The chart below shows the boiling point of water at different levels. The higher the elevation, the lower the temperature at which water boils. Approximate temperatures are based on the U.S. Standard Atmosphere.

Sea level	212°F	100°C
2,000 feet	208.5°F	98.06°C
3,000 feet	206°F	97.06°C
5,000 feet	203.2°F	95.11°C
7,000 feet	199.8°F	93.22°C
7,500 feet	198.9°F	92.72°C
10,000 feet	194.7°F	90.39°C
15,000 feet	185°F	85°C

OUTDOOR COOKING OR COOKING WITH FIRE

Cooking outdoors may involve all kinds of heat, but it works best when you stick to simple methods. As soon as cookouts get complicated, the whole party—in our perhaps jaundiced opinion—will do better to move back into the kitchen, where equipment is handy and the controls positive and effects less problematic.

Speaking of easy outdoor cooking devices, we once went on a picnic with some friends. Our host, toward suppertime, made crisscross fires just big enough for each individual steak. First he set up log-cabin–like cribs about four layers high using sticks approximately 1 inch thick. In each of these he laid a handful of dry leaves and fine brush. On top of the cribs, he continued to build for about 3 inches an additional structure of pencil-like twigs. When, after firing, the wood had been reduced to a rectangular framework of glowing rods, he unlimbered some thin steaks from a cooler and, to our consternation, laid them calmly and directly on the embers. In a few moments he removed them with tongs, shook off whatever coals had adhered, turned the steaks over, and repeated the process on the other side. They were delicious.

There is no law, of course, against availing oneself of ready-made instead of improvised cooking gear, and as much of it as the traffic will bear. There are even available various solar-heat cookers, but it is suggested that they be given homeside tryouts in advance. Various solid fuels based on hexamethylenetetramine can be purchased in granular form, in bulk, from a chemical supply house, or in tablets at outfitters. This fuel is adequate only for emergencies or when traveling light. For long-cooking camp foods, gas is the preferred fuel. Propane gas stoves are easy to use but do not work so well at very low temperatures.

For campers, alfresco cooking is a necessity rather than a pleasant indulgence. But fires in wilderness areas carry for the builder perhaps the greatest responsibility. Before starting your fire, dig or scrape a narrow trench around the area to stop roots under the fire pit from catching fire and smoldering, sometimes for days, then suddenly bursting into flame many yards away. Through the duration of the fire, watch for sparks on surrounding vegetation.

To start a wood fire, collect a few small dead branches with the twigs attached and break up the branches into categories, beginning with matchstick thickness, then pencil thickness, then thumb size and larger. Make a loose untidy pile about 3 or 4 inches high of the smallest size, thrust a burning match into the center, and, as it blazes up, slowly add the next thickness, and then the thumb size. Add fuel on the downwind side of the fire, and remember to let it breathe—air is as important as fuel! Hardwoods smoke less and provide much more heat than do most softwoods. Those preferred are oak, beech, maple, and ash, then the evergreens. Beech wood will burn green; aspen will not burn at all. If the wood is wet, split it; the interior portions are usually drier, and if a fire is started and is hot, it will use all but soaking-wet wood—albeit with a great deal of smoke. Take a tip from Native Americans and keep your fire small: It takes less wood for cooking, it is less bothersome and cozier, and in winter it is easier to cuddle up to for warmth.

Never leave a fire untended. Be sure to watch for overhead branches as fire hazards. When you finally leave a fire, drown it, mix it with mud, stir into it nonvegetation-carrying dirt, stomp on it, mix it with snow or sand, and leave it ➤ dead.

Before bringing any sort of cooking container into close

contact with a wood fire, remember to cover the pan's undersurface with a film of soap or detergent. This precaution will greatly facilitate the removal of soot later, when the pan is cleaned.

PIT COOKING

Pit cooking employs hot rocks buried in a pit to cook large quantities of food. It is the most glamorous of all primitive cooking types because it is so largely associated with picturesque places, hearty group effort, and holiday spirit. Dig a pit not less than 2 feet deep, 3 feet across, and 4 feet long. If pit cooking is more than occasional, and the locale does not vary, you may find it more convenient to build a surface pit by constructing a hollow rectangle of concrete blocks about the same height as a true pit is deep.

In the pit, build and light a substantial bonfire of hardwood deadfall or driftwood. Hickory, beech, maple, and oak are prime for this purpose. Mesquite charcoal can also be used to heat the pit. The next step is to put in the bonfire about 40 medium-sized flat rocks; ➤ never use shale or rocks from a stream bed as these may explode when heated. Tend the fire carefully and fan if necessary, because the fire may be oxygen deprived. When the fire has completely burned down and the rocks are red hot—this should take not less than 2 hours—rake out and remove unburned wood with a shovel or tongs. Spread the hot rocks over the bottom of the pit. Add a 2-inch layer of fresh leaves—grape, beech, pawpaw, fresh grass, or banana—or of corn husks or seaweed for a shore dinner. You can also add handfuls of aromatic herbs. Some pit roasters sprinkle a quart or so of water over the leaves to increase the amount of steam.

On the bed of packed foliage, arrange the elements of your meal: fish, cuts of meat, green peppers, onions, corn in its husk, unpeeled potatoes, acorn squash. Pile over them a second layer of green leafage, then a second grouping of food, and finally a third layer of green leafage. Cap off the stratification with the remaining hot rocks, layers of wet burlap, and then a tarpaulin or canvas cover and 4 inches of the earth or sand excavated from the pit to insulate the cooking chamber. How long cooking will take depends, of course, on what's cooking—maximum time will probably be required for a small pig: Calculate about 30 minutes per pound and always check with a thermometer to ensure that the center of the meat has reached 170°F.

The whole pit-cookery operation, whether it is carried out on the beach or in the woods, has a distinctly adventurous character. Periodic tests for doneness performed on the foods closest to the edge of the pit are an essential part of the process. In lifting the tarp and in removing it altogether when you are ready to serve, be extremely careful not to get food fouled up with sand or earth or to burn yourself from the quick release of steam and heat.

A modified form of pit cookery is described in About Smoking Food, 905. For shore dinners, with seaweed as filler, wire mesh is often placed over at least one layer to better support small crustaceans, clams, and oysters. For details of a Clambake, see 375.

GRILLING

Far and away the most popular technique for outdoor cookery involves direct heat from charcoal or gas below the food.

The central fact about grilling is that it is generally a dry-heat cooking method, which involves cooking relatively tender foods quickly over a hot fire. When food is exposed to the direct heat of the flames, a seared crust develops on its exterior. Tender cuts of meat such as beef, pork, or lamb grill beautifully, as do shrimp, scallops, lobster, and firm-textured fish such as tuna, salmon, swordfish, and mahimahi.

Most outdoor grills fall into one of two categories: open or covered. Open grills range in size and portability from the simple small hibachi to large built-in units. An open grill is most useful if it has a heavy grate (to transfer heat and give beautiful grill marks) and an adjustable firebox or grate (to help control the intensity of heat).

Covered grills come in many styles, but the covered kettle grill ranks high. Neither the charcoal grate on which the coals rest nor the cooking grate is adjustable, and the most popular units were designed to be used with the lid, to reduce the possibility of flare-ups and to speed cooking by circulating heat around the food.

Gas grills have come a long way, most notably in burning fuel more efficiently and in their ability to achieve the higher temperatures crucial for a delectable brown crust.

Equipment for a full-scale grilling operation should include a **hinged wire basket** with a long handle—especially desirable for grilling fish and vegetables; a **grill brush;** a metal fork with a heatproof handle; a **long-handled spatula;** a **pair of long tongs;** a long-handled heatproof **basting brush;** a **cutting board; skewers**—these must be nonrusting ➤ and sharp-pointed; a **roll of heavy-duty aluminum foil;** a supply of **pot holders** or a couple of pairs of **heavy-duty mitts;** a **pail of water** and, with it, a flare-up quencher such as a **spray-bottle filled with water,** a bucket of sand, or perhaps even a **fire extinguisher;** a **bellows** or a fan to encourage the embers; a black iron pot or **Dutch oven** for burgoos, stews, or beans; a skillet or two; and, if you plan to grill whole poultry or a beef or pork roast, you will need also a baster, and a **thermometer.**

"Stovetop grills"—a variety of metal grid that fits over a stove burner, equipped with a pan to catch dripping grease—can get hot enough to grill indoors. A grill pan, or specialized skillet with ridges across the bottom, produces ridge marks that appear similar to char marks from a charcoal or gas grill; the rendered fat drips down into the ridges of the pan, keeping the meat out of the fat. If you want to grill inside and you have a fireplace, see Fireplace or Hearth Cooking, 1059.

Grilling has become synonymous with the little pillow-shaped charcoal briquettes available in every supermarket. They are a combination of charcoal, sawdust, powdered scrap lumber, starch, and additives that can impart unpleasant flavors to the food. Hardwood lump charcoal is worth seeking out in grocery stores and hardware and specialty stores. These hardwood chunks light more easily, give heat that is more responsive, and burn cleaner and hotter than briquettes.

A wide variety of wood chips on the market, including oak, mesquite, cherry, hickory, and apple, can be added to glowing charcoal—or to a gas grill, encased in a smoker box—to give a smokier, wood-fired flavor. But unless the food spends more than a few minutes on the grill, the smoke from the chips will have little time to penetrate the food. Before use, soak wood chips in water and add a few at a time during the cooking period.

To start a fire in a grill, crumple several sheets of newspaper in the bottom of the grill, set the grate in place over the newspapers, and lay several handfuls of twigs or kindling on the grate. Top the twigs with a rather loose tepee-shaped arrangement of slightly larger twigs (or several handfuls of charcoal, if that is your fuel of choice) and light the newspaper. When the wood or charcoal is well lit—about 5 minutes for wood, 15 minutes for charcoal—add additional fuel.

If the fuel is charcoal, you can start the fire with an electric coil starter instead of paper and twigs. These electrical coils, attached to a power cord by means of a plastic handle, are reliable and consistent. To use a coil fire starter, remove the cooking grill and place the starter right on the fire grate. Mound charcoal on top of the starter and plug it into a grounded outlet. As the element becomes red hot, it will ignite the charcoal that is in contact with it. At this point, you can unplug the starter and remove it; the hot coals will ignite the others. To prolong the life of your electric starter, don't let it cool down in the fire; instead, remove it as soon as the coals are lit, unplug it, and set it aside on a fire-proof surface, out of reach of children, until it is cool. Another alternative is the chimney starter, also known as a flue starter, a paragon of efficiency, reliability, and economy. It is basically a sheet metal cylinder, open at both ends, with a grid set inside the flue several inches from the bottom. Fill the bottom section with crumpled newspaper, then fill the top with charcoal and light the newspaper. When the charcoal is red hot, dump it out and put as much additional charcoal as you want on top of it.

To ready fuel for an extended firing period, arrange an extra circle of charcoal around the edge. As the center of your fire burns to embers, these may be pushed inward.

Whatever lighting method you use, light the fire far enough in advance to ensure an even, flameless fire of the proper temperature (15 to 40 minutes, depending on your fuel). Allow enough time for the fuel to get fiery red and then die down. ➤ When the charcoal is covered with fine white ash, you are ready to begin cooking. Flick off the ash, which acts as insulation.

Judging the heat of a fire is strictly a matter of manual training. Hold your hand above the grill at about the same distance from the coals that the food will be while cooking, and count. When you have to pull your hand away, the count will tell you the heat level.

High	2 counts
Medium high	4 counts
Medium	6 counts
Medium low	8 counts
Low	10 counts

For safety's sake, ➤ always set your grill on level ground in the largest possible open space, away from walls, wooden fences, overhanging eaves or tree branches, or anything else that might easily catch fire. ➤ Keep toddlers well away from the grill, and do not let older children run or play too close to the grilling area. ➤ If using charcoal-fired equipment, do so with adequate ventilation, where the carbon monoxide fumes can be carried off completely. ➤ Never use charcoal grills in a house, tent, cabin, garage, or other enclosed area—insufficient ventilation may prove fatal. Never light the fire with gasoline, and never spray lighter fluid onto lit coals. Remember, a fire goes out without oxygen, so that fires in covered grills can be extinguished by closing the lid and vents.

What food should be cooked out of doors or on a grill? Just as we recommend simple cooking equipment in the open, so we now urge simple outdoor menus. Do remember to protect your meat and the other foods against insects. For menu suggestions, see 21.

Pan-broiled and pan-cooked food may be prepared on a grill outdoors. For grilling vegetables, see 243. For cooking on skewers, see 1049.

Steaks and chops are extraordinarily well suited to grilling. ➤ Avoid excessively thick cuts: 1½ inches should be the limit for individual servings. ➤ Choose well-marbled meat, 462—but by this we do not mean meat that has a rim or collar of fat. On the contrary, it is important ➤ to trim off all excess fat before grilling to reduce the risk of flare-ups, which can carry greasy smoke and ash to the meat. Also, cut through encircling sinew—being careful not to slice into the meat itself—so that the meat will not curl up under the high heat which initiates its cooking. Grease the grill first with some of the meat fat or with a vegetable oil. ➤ To sear the meat, place the grill grate close to the coals before laying the meat on it, or use a bellows to increase the heat momentarily.

Searing to create flavor is even more tedious in grilling than in pan- or oven-broiling, because of the heat of the fire. After searing, you may need to raise the grill grate to about 3 inches from the fire and cook the meat until done. No specific time schedule for doneness can be set up, because so much depends not only on the degree of heat itself, but on the age of the animal and the age of the meat, the nature of the cut and, of course, individual preference. However, here are a few things to keep in mind: Just as in any meat cookery, large cuts take, pound for pound, proportionately less cooking time than smaller ones. If the cut is large, testing for doneness with an instant-read thermometer is safer than testing with a knife or fork or with your thumb, 467. We would like to spare you the ordeal of an old friend of ours whose enthusiasm for outdoor grilling is repeatedly dampened by his wife's low-voiced but grim injunction: "Remember, Orville, medium-burned, not well-burned."

SPIT AND ROTISSERIE COOKING

These are best for very small or large fowl; for roasts, like leg of lamb; and for other chunky cuts of meat. Consult the directions that come with your equipment to determine maximum weight, which will probably be in the neighborhood of 10 pounds for roasts and up to 15 for whole birds. Smaller birds should be strung transversely on the spit, larger ones head to tail along the spit's axis, as illustrated.

For spareribs, get your butcher to cut them in half crosswise, forming two long strips. Prebake or parboil them in the kitchen and then string them like an accordion on your outdoor spit, as shown. Poultry and certain other types of meat must be trussed, 421, before spit-cooking. Especially if they are heavy or of irregular shape, it is necessary, while attaching them to the skewer, to determine their approximate center of gravity so that they balance well in turning. Poultry on a spit should be carefully coated in advance with melted butter or cooking oil. You may baste with butter or oil during the cooking period, but ➤ do not apply any barbecue sauce until the last 15 to 20 minutes of cooking. For Barbecue Sauces, see 586.

Remember that because of the high heat of spit-

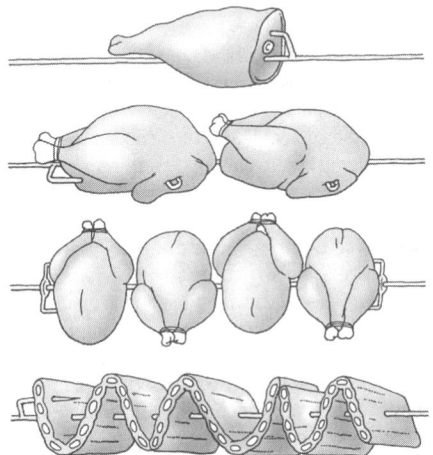

Cooking lamb, poultry, and spareribs on a spit

roasting, the weight losses due to shrinkage can be great and flare-ups from dripping fat frequent. (In hearth cooking, 1061, spit-roasting is done in front of a fire, not over it, thus avoiding too strong a heat and any flare-ups.) Flare-ups can be avoided in part by careful trimming of excess fat. Some short flare-ups may be desired for browning; unwanted ones can be doused with a spritz of water from a spray bottle.

GRILL-ROASTING/INDIRECT GRILLING

In this hybrid method, large cuts of meat like legs of lamb or whole fish or poultry, such as whole chickens or turkeys, are roasted by the indirect heat of the fire in a covered grill. Build a fire in your grill in the usual manner, then push all the coals to one side. If desired, place a drip pan on the other side to collect the juices and fill the cooking kettle with the steam from aromatic liquids. When you put the food on the cooking grate, place it over the side that has no coals, over the drip pan if you are using one, making sure no portion of the item you are cooking is directly over the fire. Then set the grill cover in place. Adjust the vents as necessary to maintain the temperature between 250° and 300°F; an oven thermometer set close to the food will help you determine the temperature.

BARBECUING

While grilling is quick and hot, barbecuing is slow and low. Barbecuing involves cooking whole pigs or lambs or one of the large, tougher cuts of meat such as beef brisket or pork shoulder on a rack or revolving spit with hot coals of a wood fire. The temperature is usually kept at around 220°F. The slow cooking causes the meat's connective tissues, called collagen, to dissolve into tenderness. Because of the moisture in the enclosed space, barbecuing resembles the moist-heat method of pot-roasting, transforming tough meat into a tender, smoke-tinged treat.

Since the meat spends many hours in contact with smoky hot air, only a live fire can impart the proper taste. As fuel, charcoal briquettes will do in a pinch, but hardwood charcoal is better, and the top choice is hardwood logs, particularly oak, hickory, mesquite, or any fruitwood.

To approximate true barbecue using a backyard grill, set up the grill as you would for indirect grilling, above. Let the fire burn down to a medium-low heat. Cover the coals with a foil-wrapped packet of wood chips, as you would for smoking, 905. Add a handful of charcoal or wood chunks every 20 to 30 minutes.

SMOKING

See About Smoking Food, 905.

FIREPLACE OR HEARTH COOKING

Hearth cooking can be as simple as roasting a hot dog on the end of a fork, tossing an onion onto the embers, or setting a stockpot in front of the fire. ➤ As a general rule, traditional masonry fireplaces (without inserts) that are safe for burning wood fires are safe for cooking. The fireplace can work as a stovetop, slow cooker, griddle, grill, rotisserie, or oven. With practice, you will discover that the heat in your fireplace has a greater dynamic range than that of the kitchen stove and is easily controlled for cooking. As with any new cooking method, experiment with single dishes and work up to complete meals. Try hearth cooking for part of your holiday meals, and it will quickly become a tradition in your family. It is a hobby that brings great pleasure and delicious results.

COOKING ON THE HEARTH

Hearth cooking is done many ways: in the radiant heat of the fire, on a stand above embers, directly on the embers, in hot ashes, and over flames. ➤ The firebox is the area under the chimney where the fire burns and embers collect. The hearth extension or hearth is the portion of the fireplace that extends into the room and is where you will do a lot of your cooking. ➤ When cooking with embers on the hearth, keep a strong fire in the fireplace to pull fumes and grilling smoke up the chimney. If the chimney isn't drawing well, try opening a window. Keep embers within the first 8 inches of the hearth and toward the center of the fireplace opening. Always follow standard fireplace safety practices, and observe all relevant cautions applicable to cooking on a grill or campfire. Never use more than a couple of fireplace-shovel scoops of embers on the hearth at one time. Immediately shovel embers back into the fireplace once they are no longer being used for cooking.

When building a fire for hearth cooking, leave 2 to 6 inches of ash from previous fires on the fireplace floor. In lieu of metal andirons or a metal grate, position two logs, like andirons, parallel to each other, and then build your fire as you usually do, adding wood as needed to maintain a steady heat. Aged, dry hardwood is preferred for cooking. ➤ Do not use wood that is wet, rotten, that has been treated with paint or chemicals, or that is manufactured from synthetic materials.

The radiant heat projected outward from the flames or glowing embers is the hearth's most steady and reliable heat source. Remember that a change in distance of even 1 or 2 inches from the embers or flames makes a significant difference in the heat and rate of cooking. Control the heat by moving the food closer to or farther from the fire. ➤ When a long period of cooking in a pot is called for, rely on radiant heat falling on the side of the pot rather than on heat from underneath. ➤ When cooking directly on embers in the firebox, control the heat by dusting them with ashes to cool them down, or fanning them to make them hotter.

Overall, food cooks at about the same rate as it does using conventional methods. To paraphrase an eighteenth-century English cookbook author, the hotter the fire, the faster it roasts, and the cooler the fire, the slower it roasts. For example, a 12-pound turkey can be roasted in not much more than 2 hours using a hot fire

and keeping it fed. If your food is taking too long to cook, chances are your fire is too small. ➤ For the most predictable results, bring all foods, including meats, to room temperature before cooking on the hearth.

➤ Equipment needs are simple: the standard fireplace shovel, a pair of long-handled tongs, two ordinary bricks, the cookware you use in your kitchen, and a small metal grill rack. For those who are interested, specialized hearth cooking equipment can be found via the Internet, and iron cookware is available in many hardware and outdoor stores.

Using Radiant Heat: Recipes that include a lot of liquid are cooked by placing the pot, bean pot, or saucepan on the hearth near the fire. The pot simmers on the side closest to the flames. ➤ Control the heat by moving the pot closer to or farther from the fire, and stir as needed. If you place it right up against the ashes in the fireplace, you may shovel embers around the base of the pot for additional heat.

Baking food wrapped in foil, 1052; sturdy leaves, such as banana, 1052; or paper, *en papillote,* 1052, is another hearth-cooking method that takes advantage of the fire's radiant heat. The method is especially suited for fish, poultry, and ground meat, wrapped in oiled paper or foil with herbs and vegetables. ➤ Wrap the packet tightly, place a few inches from the fire on the hearth, or on the ashes beside the fire, and turn as needed. A hot dog, slices of steak or chicken, or a piece of bread can be grilled in front of the fire on the end of a fork. Whole or filleted fish can be roasted if tied to an untreated wooden plank first soaked in water, and then propped up in front of the fire. A red-hot fireplace shovel held close will melt cheese on a sandwich.

Cooking on Embers: The most spectacular flavors generated by hearth cooking are from one of the easiest techniques to master—baking directly on embers. Onions, eggplant, and bell peppers are perfect for this. Place the vegetables on the hottest embers a few inches from the fire, and turn with long-handled tongs as needed until the outsides are charred black and the flesh soft. When done, take out of the fireplace, let cool, and then remove the burned outer layer.

You can also cook a steak on the embers. ➤ Be sure to pat the meat dry before placing it on the embers so ashes will not stick. Whole fish, like trout, or fish fillets such as that of salmon, can be cooked on embers (skin side down for fillets). The skin chars, but the flesh remains moist. ➤ Turn whole fish with a spatula or long-handled tongs. ➤ Control the heat by dusting the embers with ashes to cool them down or fanning them to make them hotter.

Cooking in Hot Ashes: Anything buried in hot ashes bakes as it would in an oven. Foods can be cooked wrapped, 1051, or unwrapped. Use the fireplace shovel to mix ashes and embers together in a pile beside the fire, starting with a half-and-half mix of ashes and embers. With practice, you will develop a sense of how hot the ashes are. Dense root vegetables, such as potatoes, turnips, and beets, are easily baked unwrapped in ashes, as are roasts, such as beef brisket and pork loin. Rub the meat with flour to dry its surface before baking in the ashes. Ashes that stick to meat can usually be brushed off; otherwise, rinse briefly in warm water. Firm breads, such as those made of cornmeal, can also be baked directly in hot ashes, or wrapped in cabbage leaves. If you surround a pot of beans with hot ashes at night before going to bed, they will be cooked in the morning.

Cooking on a Stand Above Embers: To fry an egg, sauté vegetables, grill fish, cook kebabs, or any food that requires heat from below, position the cookware or grill over the embers on a stand that is about 2½ inches high. Two bricks laid on their sides close to the fire work perfectly. Shovel one layer of embers about 1 inch deep between them, set your pan on the bricks, and then add a sprinkling of embers as needed to maintain cooking temperature.

Boeuf Bourguignonne, 479, and Beef Pot Roast, 477, are examples of dishes that first need heat from below to brown the ingredients and then are cooked slowly, covered, at a simmer. In your kitchen, these recipes often start on the stovetop and end in the oven. On the hearth, they begin with embers underneath for a burst of high heat, followed by long cooking by radiant heat on the side of the pot.

When you want to brown the top of a dish—as for Lasagna, 340, or Au Gratin Potatoes, 297—or bake Cornbread, 641, or Irish Soda Bread, 629, no piece of cookware is more versatile than a camp-style Dutch oven: an iron pot with three short legs, a flat lid with a lip to hold embers, and an iron hook to lift the lid, see 1051. Heat falls on the side of the Dutch oven, and embers can be placed underneath and on the lid. ➤ Use the iron hook to lift the lid to check on cooking progress. ➤ A single shovelful of embers underneath is often sufficient for baked goods, while you usually need to refresh embers on the lid. If the food is not browned when ready to serve, add fresh embers to the lid and cook for another few minutes.

Roasting Meat in Front of the Fire: There is no roast, chicken, turkey, or duck, 447, like one cooked in front of an open fire. Electric spits can be modified for use on the hearth, and clockwork spits can be purchased. ➤ Meat and poultry brought to room temperature just before roasting cook more evenly than meats that are cold. ➤ The meat should turn above the hearth over a drip pan and be about 6 inches from the fire in the fireplace. In a deep fireplace, build the fire more forward than you usually do.

An ancient, wonderful, and inexpensive alternative to using a spit is roasting meat on a string. Meat hanging on a string turns in front of the fire first in one direction, and then the other, requiring only an occasional nudge from the cook. Hang a hook from the ceiling, the underside of the mantel, or the mantel's edge, and tie a length of cot-

Hearth cooking and roasting meat on a string

ton string to the hook. ➤ The longer and thinner the string, the longer the meat turns without being nudged—as long as 10 minutes. Never use synthetic fiber. It takes experimenting to get the right diameter of string, and the right length, but the string can be saved and used many times. Make a single loop, or tie a small loop on either end of the single strand. To prepare the meat to hang, put a skewer through the top and another skewer through the bottom third of the roast. ➤ Cut a 14-inch length of string, tie loops at either end, and attach them to the skewers, like the handle of a purse. When you hold the meat by this string handle, it should hang straight down. If it doesn't, reposition the skewer to rebalance the meat. ➤ When you bring the meat to the hearth, detach one end of the string handle from the skewer, slip it through the loop in the bottom of the long string, and then slip it back onto the skewer. Let the meat down so the string bears its weight and hangs above the hearth 4 inches above a drip pan and about 6 inches from the fire. ➤ About halfway through the cooking time, flip the roast over by moving the handle to the other skewer for even cooking. ➤ For most of the cooking time the fire should be hot enough that you can barely hold your hand where the roast is turning.

Cooking over Flames: If your fireplace is equipped with a crane, a metal arm that lets you hang pots over the flames, you can cook over the fire. ➤ Heat is controlled by swinging the arm closer to or farther from the fire and by using hooks of different lengths to adjust the distance from the pot to the fire. This method is most appropriate for use in very large fireplaces, for boiling water, and when preparing food in such large quantities that the cooking pot is too heavy to lift.

ABOUT INDOOR COOKING EQUIPMENT

Certain cooking effects we admire cannot be duplicated in the average American kitchen. This is true of the quick, intense, short-lived fires and the huge woks that are essential to Chinese stir-frying; the very low, long-retained-heat chamber called *étuve* in old French kitchens—ideal for drying out meringues or for simmering foods in covered pots; and, for that matter, the seaweed-smother that gives that authentic touch to lobsters pit-cooked at the shore. Conditions like these may be approximated in cooking on modern ranges, but never completely reproduced.

If you grew up using gas for cooking fuel, you appreciate its dynamic flexibility of control. If your experience has been with electric ranges, you value the evenness of their broiling heat and the stored warmth of their surface units. Microwave ovens are popular because of their ability to reduce heating time to a fraction of its former length; see 1063.

Whatever your source of cooking heat, learn thoroughly the characteristics of your range. Find out, for example, if the broiling element needs preheating and if broiling in the oven requires an open or a closed door.

In purchasing, consider the safety value of controls. If located along the front of a range, they may be dangerous to small children. If at the rear, they may be obstructed by tall pots or cause accidents by bringing hands and clothing too close to the burners. Pay particular attention, also, to the quality of oven insulation in any range you plan to buy, and to its venting characteristics.

The heating elements on many ranges and cooktops cannot maintain the very low temperature needed for slowly simmering a sauce for an extended period of time. A heat diffuser, below, will mute the heat and disperse it evenly over the bottom of the pot—an important feature if your pot is fairly lightweight. Look for heat diffusers that are sturdy enough not to warp and the appropriate size for your cooking element.

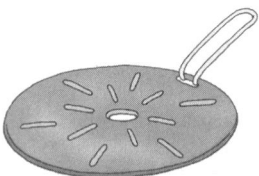

Heat diffuser

For loading ovens, we make the following suggestions: ➤ Place the oven racks where you want them before heating, not after. To brown a casserole, place the pan—briefly—close under the broiler, as shown, 1063. Few cooks realize the importance of air circulation in conventional ovens: Overcrowding results in uneven baking. Make sure that the pans or baking sheets you are using fit on the oven shelf comfortably, with at least 2 inches of space between them as well as between the pans and oven walls. Don't use two shelves if you can avoid it, but if you must, stagger the pans as shown second from the left. For a discussion of heat and pan size relationships, see 700.

In convection ovens, a built-in fan circulates the hot air around the oven cavity. Because the air is moving, the heat is efficiently conducted to the food from all sides, so it cooks evenly and sometimes faster than in conventional ovens. Convection ovens are often equipped with three or more racks on which baked goods can be placed, and the baking is even because of the air movement.

For cake baking in general, the best position for the pan(s) is just above center. But for angel food cakes, tortes, or soufflés, the best placement is below center, as shown, for often, in most ovens, the slight heat provided by a top element is enough to set the surface of a soufflé if it is set too close, preventing a rise in the soufflé.

Some commercial ovens feature devices for introducing moisture into an oven as needed. In the home range, a practical substitute, should the recipe require it, is a shallow pan partially filled with water, as shown on the right.

When baking, set the oven dial to the desired temperature. If there is no indicator light to inform you when the temperature is reached, preheat for 10 to 15 minutes. Insert the pans as quickly as possible. Try not to peek until the time is up—or almost up.

Don't try to speed things up by setting the thermostat higher than the recipe indicates. You will get better results at the specified temperature. And don't, incidentally, press an oven into service as a kitchen heater. This will throw the thermostat out of calibration. Ovens vary, however, and even under normal use, thermostats may need frequent adjustment—at least once every 12 or 14 months. Invest in an oven thermometer to keep an eye on the temperature accuracy.

Keep in mind that a clean oven will maintain temperature and reflect heat more accurately than a dirty one. When buying a new range, you will want to consider a self-cleaning oven.

As for the range top or cooktop, here again, as with its interior, familiarity breeds assurance. Questions about its use are answered in the literature that comes with the equipment. If you are confronted with a range for which printed instructions are lacking, or if special problems arise, call the manufacturer or the appliance store where you purchased the equipment.

In using gas burners, watch the relation of the flame to the pan. ➤ The flame should never come closer than ¹/₂ inch to the outer edges of the pan bottom.

Before using a specialized utensil such as a wok or any utensil that would concentrate unusual heat onto the surface of a range, check with the manufacturer as to its practicality. Some one-piece flat-surface cooktops have their own cookware engineered to fit the heating areas exactly; the pots and pans are flat-bottomed so that no heat is lost. Other flat-surface tops use any type of flat-bottomed cookware. Another one-piece flat-surface cooktop has magnetic coils beneath that leave the cook-

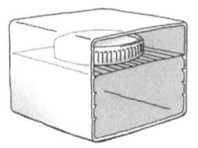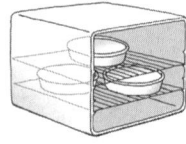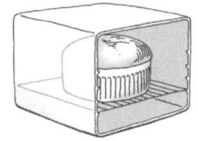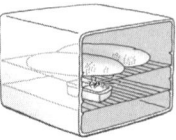

Proper oven placement for broiling or browning, and baking casseroles, cakes, soufflés, and breads

ing surface cool. Energy is generated only in the magnetic pans in which the cooking is done.

A toaster oven is a popular all-in-one appliance that can in various circumstances stand in for an oven, toaster, and even a broiler. Toaster ovens may be all some people want or need on a hot summer day, or in a small kitchen when only countertop appliances will fit. They are good for reheating foods but not for baking anything delicate, because of the sometimes imprecise thermostat and temperature controls.

Also called contact grills, countertop grills are inexpensive electric appliances that come in a range of shapes and sizes and are prized for their convenience and speed. Whatever you cook is ready twice as fast as in a sauté pan, because heat penetrates the food directly from both sides once you close the lid. Speed makes countertop grills ideal for weeknight suppers. For the best results and even cooking, start with food that's a relatively even thickness, such as boneless poultry, steaks, burgers, and fish fillets.

MICROWAVE COOKING

Our experience with the microwave oven has followed a familiar contemporary pattern: inadequate response to great expectations. Once we thought of it as the champion time-saver that would allow us, on long summer afternoons, to prolong to the very last minute the joys of gardening, or of tennis, or beachcombing with the children, before returning to the kitchen and putting dinner together in a flash. Now we know its limitations. Even microwave's most obvious advantage—defrosting and then reheating frozen foods—has proved of limited value, and in any case, it takes care of only an inconsequential fraction of our cooking schedule. Because no matter what particular microwave you own, you may have to be on hand during much of the reheating period—to rotate the dish, to alternate cooking and withdrawal so that the outside of the food will not overcook before the center thaws, or to stir the food intermittently and so vary the heating impact.

The microwave is one of the most misunderstood appliances in the kitchen. There are a few basic facts to keep in mind: It is not a substitute for the stovetop and oven. It does *not* cook foods from the inside out. It cooks some things very well, but it cannot be used for all of your cooking needs.

In a microwave oven, electricity is converted into microwaves and the waves are spread throughout the oven cavity via a revolving "stirrer fan" in the oven. With a tight-sealing door, today's ovens are well within safety standards. Microwaves can penetrate glass, ceramic, paper, and plastic, but they are deflected by metal, which is why microwave oven interiors are lined with metal.

When these aimless, fat little waves are scattered about the oven cavity, they behave like billiard balls gone awry, bouncing off the walls and careening about until they land on something moist—water or food. At that point, the waves will penetrate only $3/4$ to $1^1/_2$ inches deep, but in so doing, they cause the water molecules they touch to vibrate, causing friction and thus producing heat. Once the water molecules are moving about, the food cooks by simple conduction, from the outside to the inside. Microwaves are the energy source, but the cooking process is the equal of what happens to food in a skillet over a burner or in the cavity of a hot oven: The heat is conducted from the outside of the food to the interior. But it is the excited molecules that transfer the heat to the center of the food, rather than a heat source below or above it.

Cooking fresh foods by microwave is also not without disappointments, especially when one compares the eating quality or appearance with that of more conventionally cooked foods. Timing may vary greatly from that prescribed in the manuals of microwave instruction, and almost all types of food tend to toughen. Meats dry out and lose more nutrients than when roasted by conventional methods. Microwave-baked cakes turn out coarse in texture and over-moist, with pallid tops. If milk or milk mixtures are heated or cooked in a microwave oven, they must be constantly watched, as they tend to boil over very quickly.

Browning—which in many traditional cooking processes is responsible for both the flavor and the aesthetic pleasure of the food—is not really achievable with microwave equipment. Attempts through the use of special browning dishes or pre- and post-browning techniques with a unit combining conventional electric heat may help, but they often complicate procedures or add to the cooking time so that the microwave cooking period may be longer than that of a traditional method.

Microwaving does have virtues, though. Ingredients that have a high water content—most vegetables, virtually all greens, fish, and fruits—can be quickly cooked in a microwave oven. They will have a steamed quality to them, but without the excess moisture steam might leave behind. Fresh sweet corn cooks in seconds, artichokes in minutes, and a winter squash or baked potato requires only a fraction of the time it takes in an oven or steamer. Wilted spinach salads—from cooking the bacon to finishing the dish—are ready to eat in moments. Peeling tomatoes or peaches is simple after a few seconds in the microwave, and, for melting cheese or chocolate or butter, nothing could be tidier.

In addition, microwaving fruits and vegetables preserves more nutrients than practically any other cooking method because you use little or no nutrient-leaching water and because the microwave cooks faster than any other method. Defrosting in a microwave is healthful too, because it is fast—no meat or poultry sitting at room temperature encouraging bacteria to grow. Also, less butter, oil, or other fat is required for microwave cooking, because these ingredients are used solely as flavorings, rather than to prevent sticking.

It is very tricky to adapt a conventionally cooked recipe to microwave cooking. The surest way is to find a microwave recipe that is comparable and use it for a model. Take all microwave recipe cooking times with a grain of salt. The oven's wattage makes a difference; the higher the wattage, the faster the oven cooks. You can always put food back, but you cannot undo overcooking—and the microwave can overcook in a wink. There is no simple formula for adjusting time according to wattage, since minor fluctuations in voltage at your plug can also make a difference; have your microwave oven on a dedicated circuit. The oven's age is another factor in determining timing; an older oven may have not only lower wattage but also decreased efficiency from repeated usage.

Care must be exercised in choosing the material on which food is microwave-cooked. The molecular structure of glass, some plastics, ungreased white paper, and some ceramics is such that energy input is not impaired; the food cooked in or on such materials absorbs the waves without adverse effects on them or on the oven. But don't use any plastic containers that are not labeled microwave safe. A simple test for any nonplastic cookware suitability is to fill a 1-cup glass measure with water. Set the water and the empty cookware in the oven and heat for 1 minute. If the water comes out hot, and the vessel is still cool, you can cook in it. If the vessel is lukewarm, you risk breakage; and if the vessel is hot, never use it in the microwave oven. In any event, ➤ metal or metal-trimmed dishes must be avoided, as they cause an arcing interaction with the oven walls. Wire twist ties and metal handles can also cause arcing, so use caution.

It is true that microwave ovens do not heat up the kitchen, and that the cookware indicated above remains cool during the cooking procedure itself, almost all heat being absorbed by the food. But at the end of the cooking period the hot food very quickly transfers its heat to the dish, and—especially if the dish is quite full—pot holders may be necessary to remove it. Lids or wrappings should be cautiously removed to avoid steam burns.

Covering keeps moisture in foods from evaporating too rapidly, thus helping the microwaves cook more evenly. Plastic wrap is routinely recommended for covering food in the microwave, particularly when abundant steam is needed for tenderizing and speeding the cooking along. But higher temperatures and prolonged contact with food—especially foods with high fat and sugar content—increase chances that the plastic will melt. When plastic wrap is called for, always leave an inch or more of space between the food and the wrap. And only use plastic wraps that are clearly labeled safe for the microwave; ones not labeled as such may contain many plasticizers, which cause the plastic to melt quickly and possibly transfer unwanted chemicals to the food.

Because of the buildup of steam, never tightly seal a dish with plastic wrap. If a recipe directs you to cover tightly during cooking, use a microwave-safe lid. If using plastic wrap, give the steam a way out: Fold back an edge about an inch. ➤ When removing a lid or wrap, lift it from the side away from you to avoid the escaping steam, which can easily burn you. When neither trapping steam nor absorbing moisture is your goal (say, when microwaving a plate of leftovers), lay a sheet of wax paper on top of the dish. ➤ Paper towels and napkins are good for covering foods that may splatter, such as melting butter. To melt chocolate in the microwave, see 970.

When reheating in the microwave, it is especially important to turn and/or stir the food two or three times, to ensure even distribution of heat and avoid overcooking in spots. To heat bread, rolls, muffins, and sweet rolls, loosely wrap in a paper napkin and microwave in 5-second increments until the bread is warm—no further. Bread warmed in the microwave acquires an unpleasant rubbery texture as soon as it cools, and no amount of toasting can change it. For a whole plate of food, arrange thicker pieces toward the rim of the plate and quick-to-heat pieces toward the center. Cover with wax paper and heat in 1-minute increments. Meat sliced about $1/4$ inch thick reheats best. Slices covered with gravy should be covered with wax paper; slices without gravy should be covered with a paper towel. Heat on medium power in increments of 30 seconds. ➤ Be especially watchful with small portions of food; they can easily overcook and burn. If a doughnut or a Danish has a jelly center, be careful when you bite into it—sugar attracts the waves, remember, and that jelly can be scalding hot and cause painful burns.

Never heat food in closed jars. Never heat fats and oils or try to deep-fry in the microwave—fat is a magnet for the little waves and can quickly overheat. ➤ Do not process food for canning in the microwave. Do not use a conventional meat thermometer—the metal will cause arcing. Pop popcorn only in bags or poppers designed for the microwave.

There are many other safety factors one must keep aware of. To avoid danger, door mechanism and switches should be in perfect working order. Air filters must be clean and the oven interior unpitted. Any sign of irregularity should be occasion enough for a service call.

There are available countertop and built-in combination microwave and conventional ovens that dispel some of the disadvantages described above.

None of these pieces of equipment is apt to bring to the average household cook the freedom dreamt of via a kitchen robot, for heat is a subtle medium that for best results will always demand intelligent human attention.

So, all things considered—and at the risk of being put down as unadventurous or just plain not with it—we still prefer conventional techniques over those of microwave cookery. We find them less demanding, more flexible, and productive of more nutritious and appealing food.

THE TIME ELEMENT IN COOKING

How long to heat food? There are many answers. They lie in the interactions between the heat source, the equipment, and the medium—air, liquid, or fat.

Consider the following rates of heat transferal: A dough that bakes at 400°F or steams at 212°F for 20 minutes will cook in deep fat heated to 400°F in 3 minutes. A hot hard-cooked egg will cool off in 5 minutes if plunged into ice water but will need 20 minutes to cool in 32°F air. A vegetable that will cook in 20 minutes in boiling water (212°F) will need only 2 minutes steaming under 15 pounds pressure at 250°F.

In timing, a great deal also depends on the freshness of food, especially of vegetables; on the aging and fat content of meat; and on the size of the food. Large, thick objects like roasts need lower heat and a longer cooking period than do cutlets to allow the heat to penetrate deep into the center. The amount of surface area is also a factor, as you learn from experience with whole compared to diced vegetables.

Still another determinant is the reflective and absorptive quality of the pan used. Recent tests have shown that an entire hour can be cut from the roasting time of a 10- or 12-pound turkey if it is cooked in a dark pan that absorbs heat rather than in a shiny metal one that reflects it. And we have discussed elsewhere, 1052, the insulative qualities of foil when used in wrap-cooking. Personal preference affects timing, of course, as well as the idiosyncrasies of equipment. Placement in the oven, 1046, makes a difference, and so does the temperature of food at the onset of heating.

For all these reasons it is with some trepidation that we have indicated cooking periods in our individual recipes. We know from our fan mail that timing is among the most worrisome of all problems for the beginning cook. Therefore, if our timing and yours do not jibe, we beg you to look for solutions in the facts we have set down above before you take pen or keyboard in hand.

HOLDING AND REHEATING FOOD

Everyone knows that food that is held hot or reheated is not so tasty or nutritious as that served immediately after preparation. Unfortunately, laggards and leftovers are frequently a cook's fate. Here, then, are a few hints on the best procedures.

There are three ways to reheat dishes that are apt to curdle when subjected to direct high temperatures—these include au gratin, egg, and creamed dishes, as well as any other dish rich in fat. One way is to put them in a moderate to low oven in a container of hot water about two-thirds the depth of the cooking pan. Or place a cookie sheet or a piece of foil—under the pan shiny side down—so that the heat is deflected. The latter suggestion is particularly handy to avoid overbrowning when reheating pies or coffee cakes. A third way is to reheat cream- and egg-sauced foods in a double boiler ➤ over—not in—boiling water. To retain color in reheated vegetables partially cover the vegetables.

If reheating roasted meat, slice it paper thin and put it on heated plates just before pouring over it boiling-hot gravy. ➤ Any other method of reheating will toughen it and make it taste old.

To reheat deep-fried foods, spread them on a rack, on a baking sheet ➤ uncovered, in a 250°F oven.

To hold pancakes, place them on and between clean cloth towels on a baking sheet in a 200°F oven.

To reheat casseroles, make certain the baking dish is ovenproof and can withstand rapid temperature changes before placing it in a 325°F oven directly from the refrigerator or freezer.

To reheat creamed or clear soups, heat to boiling point and serve immediately.

Other devices that hold foods for short periods include warming drawers, electrically controlled trays, the age-old chafing dish, and the bain-marie or water-bath, 890. None of these should be used for a protracted period, however, if you hope to preserve real flavor and avoid bacterial growth. ➤ Holding temperatures for hot food should be above 140°F, or for cold food under 40°F. "Keep hot foods hot and cold foods cold."

ABOUT UTENSILS

The material of which kitchen utensils are made, as well as their sizes and shapes, can determine success or failure in cooking. So, in this book we often not only caution about too high heat, but warn against using it with lightweight pans. The latter may develop hot spots and cause sticking, or they may require an undue amount of stirring to prevent scorching. ➤ Choose a pan, then, of fairly heavy gauge—not so heavy as to make for difficult handling, but heavy enough to diffuse heat evenly. Note, too, that some utensils are **flame- or heat-proof,** meaning that they can be used on direct heat—except for heatproof glass—and **bakeware,** which is designed for oven use only.

ALUMINUM

The advantage here is very good heat diffusion, but aluminum—no matter how expensive—will pit. And it not only tends to become discolored itself but can adversely affect the color of some foods, such as eggs, tomatoes, leafy greens, and wine. If you buy untreated or uncoated aluminum cookware, choose the heaviest-gauge aluminum you can find. Don't clean aluminum pans with harsh soaps, alkalis, or abrasives. To remove discoloration, boil in the pans for 5 to 10 minutes a solution of 2 teaspoons cream of tartar to 4 cups water.

Aluminum manufacturers have found ways to anodize or electrochemically treat the surfaces of their pans. Anodized aluminum pans have a harder cooking surface that does not react with most ingredients as untreated aluminum does, and they are stronger yet still lightweight.

COPPER

Best in heavier gauges, copper gives a quick, even heat distribution if kept clean. But ➤ unless the surfaces contacting the food are well tinned or lined with stainless steel, the pan will be affected by acids and can be toxic. To polish the exterior, keep handy a squeeze bottle filled with a vinegar-and-salt mixture. Place some on a cloth and rub the discolored copper until bright, then rinse in hot water.

If your copper is lined with tin, remember that the tin has problems of its own. Tin will melt at temperatures above 425°F, so these pans are unsuitable for high-heat cooking methods such as deep-fat frying. Use caution so as not to scratch the tin lining, and don't clean it with abrasive cleaners. Treat with care, as you would a nonstick surface. Copper that is lined with tin will periodically require retinning. Copper pans that are lined with stainless steel rather than tin are easier to maintain, since stainless steel will not melt, wear away, or need relining.

STAINLESS STEEL

This metal is completely nonreactive with food and it stays shiny and new looking even after considerable use. It is affordable and is the easiest material of all to keep clean. Its poor heat conductivity is usually offset by thinning down the gauge or thickness of the steel, but this causes hot spots to develop and food cooked in it is apt to burn easily. Stainless steel with an inner core of aluminum or copper has increased heat conduction and diffusion and makes one of the most desirable utensils for surface cooking.

CAST IRON

Heavy but low in conductivity, cast iron rusts easily and can discolor acidic foods. To treat new commercially preseasoned skillets or Dutch ovens, simply wash with soapy water, rinse, and dry. Coat lightly with unsalted vegetable oil or shortening, and just before using, wipe with paper towels. To season an iron skillet, scour and wash with ➤ hand soap—not detergent. Dry, then coat with unsalted shortening and place in a 350°F oven for about 2 hours. Cast-iron is recommended for Hearth Cooking, 1059.

ENAMELED CAST IRON

This is cast iron that has been coated with a porcelain enamel finish. The enameling slows down heat conduction to a small degree, but it makes the cooking surface impervious to reaction with foods. Enameled cast iron is heavy and can crack or chip if mishandled. It is also marked by metal utensils; only wooden, plastic, or silicone hand tools should be used.

TEMPERED GLASS

This type of glass has been treated to be stable at extreme temperatures. Though it is ideal for microwave cooking and in baking, it is a poor heat conductor. The glass is apt to chip and crack.

EARTHENWARE

While a poor conductor of heat, glazed or unglazed earthenware or clay holds heat well and doesn't discolor foods. But it is heavy and breaks easily with sudden temperature changes. New or recently produced earthenware is made with lead-free glazes. Older or antique earthenware most likely has lead in the glaze and should not be used for cooking. To season an unglazed earthenware or clay casserole, fill one-third full with water and set in a large bowl of water. Let sit and soak until it stops bubbling, about 5 minutes. This type of cookware is recommended for Hearth Cooking, 1059. ➤ To avoid cracking, never set a clay dish directly on a heating element.

TINWARE

This is a good conductor of heat but is apt to mar, and it rusts quickly. It turns dark after use and is affected by acid foods.

SILICONE

Utensils, all kinds of cookware, and pan liners or baking mats are manufactured from food-grade silicone. Silicone is ovenproof, withstanding temperatures from −40°F up to 500°F. It can go from freezer to oven; conducts heat evenly; cools quickly; doesn't rust, chip, or break; and is dishwasher-, freezer-, and microwave-safe. Because silicone is flexible as well as nonstick, you can turn out cakes and muffins from silicone pans with just a twist of the pan—like ice cubes.

NONSTICK PANS AND COATING

Nonstick pans are a delight to people suddenly put on fat-free diets. The soapstone griddle is age-old. Newer equipment with nonstick silicone and fluorocarbon resin surfaces can withstand temperatures up to 450°F. These surfaces do not affect heat distribution but will help to keep food from sticking; when cooking eggs or breaded fish and meat, you may need added fat. As some surfaces scratch easily, use only plastic, silicone, or wooden utensils. More recently, nonstick coatings that will last a very long time have been applied to stainless steel pans—in fact, some manufacturers are offering warranties of several years on the durability of the nonstick surface.

Even an inexpensive aluminum skillet with a nonstick coating has its virtues: It is lightweight, highly conductive, relatively strong, impervious to reactions with foods, inexpensive, relatively difficult to damage, and will wash up with the swipe of a sponge.

One caution: The Environmental Protection Agency recently drafted an assessment of the risk posed by PFOA, or perfluorooctanoic acid, known as C-8, a material commonly used in nonstick cookware, on the human body. Early studies point to it as a possible human carcinogen. ➤ If you use nonstick pans, it is important that you keep abreast of this and future studies concerning its safety.

PLASTICS
There are some plastics that can stand relatively high heat but not heat high enough for cooking or ➤ even hot liquids, which may dissolve the plastic and seriously burn the cook. Many storage containers, funnels, and other kitchen utensils should not even be washed in water over 140°F. Others are ruined by oil and grease. The surfaces of all plastic utensils retain some grease, ➤ so don't try to whip egg whites in a plastic bowl; see 978.

CHOOSING COOKWARE
You may wonder after reading these pros and cons what utensil materials to choose. Fortunately, there are a number of brands of cookware with good flat bottoms made of alloys that take advantage of the superior diffusion of aluminum, the quick conductivity of copper, and the noncorrodible quality of stainless steel. But while we are speaking of combinations of metals, let us say that ➤ pots of cast iron and copper (even tin-lined) must not be covered with aluminum foil if the food to be cooked is very acid, as the foil can be dissolved into it. In fact, it is usually best to avoid dissimilar metal pots and lids when cooking any very acid foods. And in the final analysis, you may still prefer a heavy cast-iron Dutch oven, enameled or not, or an earthenware casserole for stews.

Don't invest in large pan sets of a single material until you know what your preference really is. And be sure the pot handles are metal-reinforced at the seam and will stay cool during the cooking process.

When you cook, choose a pan that fits the size of the burner. This correlation gives better cooking results and is more economical. Be certain, too, that the lid, if the process calls for one, is tight-fitting. ➤ Be sure the cooking pan is appropriate in size to its contents. Especially in braising, the relation of pan size to contents is vital; see 466.

In baking, pans must also be of appropriate size. Round pans will give you more even browning, while square pans tend to cause heavier browning at the corners. Note, too, that shiny metal baking pans deflect heat and that dark metal or glass ones both catch and hold the heat more. ➤ Therefore, food baked in glass or dark pans needs at least a 25°F reduction in the oven temperatures given in

our recipes. While dark metal materials may brown cookies too rapidly, they will ensure better browning for pies and puff pastes. If fuel is for some reason scarce, a great saving can be effected by the use of these heat-retaining pans.

In pan-broiling or when using a stovetop griddle pan, utensils should be brought up slowly to cooking temperature. ➤ As a general rule, unless blackening, 1049, do not place a pan over high heat unless it has fat or liquid in it.

Should you scorch food by some unlucky chance, the scorched taste is greatly lessened by plunging the pan first into cold water before transferring the food to a clean container. To clean scorched pots, except those coated with silicone or a similar material, use a nylon pouf or a nylon brush with a built-in detergent container. If that is not sufficient, soak overnight with some detergent in the water. If that still isn't enough, bring to a boil in the scorched pot 1 teaspoon washing soda or cream of tartar for each quart of water.

BASIC KITCHEN EQUIPMENT
We all enjoy working in an attractive environment. One of the key features for that is also the most utilitarian: good-looking, easily cleaned kitchen surfaces. When setting up a kitchen, combine practicality with aesthetics. Crosscut or laminated wood chopping blocks can harbor harmful bacteria and so will need frequent cleaning. Stone and some synthetic surfaces can dull knife edges or, by their hardness, cause breakages. It is hard but wise to toss out slightly crazed or chipped pottery—or you can always relegate it to the flower department. Choose equipment with shapes that are free from grooves and seams that could catch food, and select materials that are impervious to acids and rust.

A man once summed up his wife's life with the epitaph, "She died of things." It might have happened to any of us. We are constantly encouraged to buy the latest gadget that will absolutely, positively make kitchen life sublime. No kitchen can ever have enough space at convenient levels to take care of even a normal array of equipment. So think hard before you buy so much as an extra spatula.

Get pans that nest. If you can't resist a bulky cake pan, see that it hangs on an out-of-the-way pegboard panel, or make it a decorative feature for an odd unused nook. Buy square rather than round canisters for economical use of storage space. Keep canisters with spices and staples in alphabetical arrangement for quick identification. And place these close to the areas where you will be using them most.

Kitchens today are fairly scientifically laid out. Most people are aware that a big kitchen is a time and energy waster, and that a U-shape or a triangular relationship of sink, stove, and refrigerator—with their accompanying work spaces—is a step saver. We may have to live with the kitchens we have, but it pays to think about your work habits. See if you can make them more efficient.

Well-designed, nonrusting hand tools save your towels and your temper. The following is a reasonably comprehensive basic equipment list for which illustrations can be found as noted.

Cooking Equipment
4 saucepans of assorted sizes with lids
12-inch sauté pan with lid
Small lightweight skillet with a nonstick surface
Large stewing or soup kettle
Stockpot
Double boiler
6- to 8-quart Dutch oven or other lidded enameled pot
Pressure cooker
Deep-fat frying equipment
3 strainers
Collapsible steamer
Colander
Coffeemaker
China teapot and teakettle
Thermometer
Griddle
Roasting pan with rack
Small baking dish
Large baking dish
Set of mixing bowls
Set of metal measuring cups
8-ounce liquid-measure glass cup
Set of measuring spoons
Large and small metal spoons
Wooden spoons
Offset spatula
Food mill
Potato masher or potato ricer
Salad bowl
Ladle
Carving fork
Small kitchen fork
Paring knife
Serrated knife
Slicing or carving knives
Chef's knife
Kitchen shears
Grapefruit knife
Cutting board
Knife sharpener
Four-sided box grater
Rotary grater and rasp-style grater
Tongs
Vegetable peeler
Rubber or silicone spatula
Kitchen scale
Citrus juicer
Food processor
Electric mixer
Blender

Trivets
Bottle opener
Corkscrew
Can opener
Nutcracker
Salt shaker and pepper grinder
Pot holders

Baking Equipment
Deep-fat-frying and candy thermometer
Three 9-inch round cake pans
Two 9-inch square cake pans
Two 9 x 4-inch loaf or bread pans
2 cooling racks
Muffin tins
2 pie pans
2 cookie sheets
Jelly-roll pan or rimmed baking sheet
6 custard cups or ramekins
9-inch or 10-inch plain or fluted tube pan
13 x 9-inch baking pan
8-inch soufflé dish
Mold for steaming
Sugar or flour scoop
Funnel
Sifter
Doughnut cutter
Biscuit cutter
Pastry blender
Pastry board
Silicone baking liner
Pastry brush
Vegetable brush
Rolling pin
Pastry cloth and cover for rolling pin
Pancake turner
Apple corer
Ice cream freezer
Waffle iron
Cake tester

Other Useful Accessories
4 or more canisters
Cake cover and carrier
Dish drainer
Toaster
Bucket
Wax paper and parchment paper
Zip-top plastic storage bags
Aluminum foil
Dishpan
12 cotton dishtowels
4 dishcloths

Other small kitchen amenities for which we are enduringly grateful are those extensions of power like lid lifters and jar unscrewers, the nylon brush–topped detergent dispenser, pot holders, waste baskets, storage containers, and paper towels.

We end these lists with a reminder: ➤ Always clean off the tops before opening cans, as they may be dusty or may have been sprayed with poisonous insecticides while in the store. Also in opening a can, ➤ avoid metal slivers by starting beyond the side seam and stopping before you cut through it.

ABOUT KNIVES

Without a doubt, the most important tool in the kitchen, next to a copy of this book, is a sharp knife. You can cook over a campfire, in a fireplace, in a oven, or on a grill, but if you can't get to the interior of an acorn squash, or carve a roast, or chop an onion, you can't cook.

Modern knives are generally made from steel alloys. Carbon steel is easy to sharpen and maintains a very sharp edge. However, it has to be properly maintained to prevent rust. Stainless steel never rusts and is used in many knives, from inexpensive to expensive. Stainless steel knives are very durable, but they dull easily and are more difficult to sharpen. High-carbon stainless steel is a better option, as it combines the durability of stainless steel with the sharpness of carbon steel. Each knife manufacturer relies on a different formula to produce what they consider to be the best balance of materials for the best performance and durability.

Traditionally knives were made by a process called hot drop forging: Steel was superheated, dropped into a mold, and then shaped by hand. Since this process is quite costly, many manufacturers now rely on a cheaper process called stamping, in which long sheets of steel are fed through a cookie cutter–type machine that punches out blade after blade. The best forged knives are superior to the best stamped knives, but there are many quality levels in both categories.

A big variable in knife design is the handle. Modern technology has expanded the options beyond the traditional wood. Molded plastic handles are popular now, although some feel that wood provides a surer grip. However, the choice of handles is really a matter of personal preference and comfort.

Not surprisingly, the best knives tend to carry the highest price tags—but don't judge solely by price. Hold the knife, test its grip and its weight to make sure it feels comfortable and balanced in your hand. Knives with a full tang (the portion of the blade that extends into the handle) usually feel the most balanced.

In addition to a good knife, you will need a good-quality **cutting board.** Cutting boards are made of wood or plastic. All cutting boards, regardless of the material, can harbor bacteria in nicks and gouges. Wash all boards with hot soapy water after every use, and occasionally soak or scrub them in a light chlorine bleach solution made with 2 teaspoons of bleach per quart of water. After soaking or scrubbing for several minutes, rinse the board thoroughly with fresh water, then rub with vinegar or lemon juice to remove any chlorine odor. It is a good idea to keep a couple of cutting boards on hand—one for raw beef, poultry, and other uncooked meats and another board for chopping foods that will be not be cooked, such as fruit, lettuce, bread, and vegetables. Boards made of synthetic material wash well and are long lasting. Wood boards are prone to splitting and staining, but are preferred by many for its warmth and beauty. Glass cutting boards are not recommended because they can dull the edge on a knife.

TYPES OF KNIVES

How many knives are enough? That really depends on your budget and how you cook. In a basic kitchen setup, most cooks need a paring knife, a chef's knife, a serrated knife, and a pair of kitchen shears. Other knives are useful, especially a slicing (carving) knife for turkey, chicken, roast beef, or ham.

Chef's knives: By far the most useful knife, the chef's knife can chop vegetables, mince herbs, slice fruits, and do much more. The curved blade of most chef's knives allows you to rock the blade against the cutting board when mincing herbs or garlic. Standard sizes for the blade length are 6, 8, 10, and 12 inches. Six-inch blades are too small for many tasks, while the 12-inch blade may be impractical because it is too long—unless you have particularly large hands and like the larger size. We recommend a blade length of 8 to 10 inches as the most practical for an all-purpose chef's knife.

Paring knives: The blade of a paring knife has a shape similar to that of a chef's knife, but it is smaller, thinner, and slightly less curved. It is relatively short, and it may be more flexible than a chef's knife. Paring knives are meant for preparing "smaller" foods and more detailed cutting than a chef's knife can handle, such as trimming fruit or finely dicing a shallot. Foods prepared or cut "in the air" also usually require a paring knife—such as peeling potatoes, quartering an apple, or slicing chunks of carrot into a pot of soup.

Serrated knives: Designed to cut through foods with a tough exterior and soft interior, such as tomatoes and bread, serrated knives are often called bread knives. This is one type of knife that can be made of stainless steel with no carbon added, since serrated edges cannot be sharpened. When it no longer does a good job of cutting—though that may take a while—you'll have to buy a new knife. Choose a moderately priced knife with an 8- or 10-inch blade, and look for one that is medium, not heavy, weight, as you don't want the knife squashing the food it's cutting.

Boning knives: Given the fact that supermarkets and butchers do most of the work, these knives are less important in the kitchen than they were years ago. But if you want to bone chicken breasts or a leg of lamb yourself, a boning knife is indispensable. Boning knives are flexible, meant to cut around bones and to cut the tendons and cartilage to release the meat from the bone. The blade must be pointed, sharp, and narrow, to get into tight spots. Smaller, more flexible blades are designed for filleting fish and boning small birds. Larger, more rigid knives are better for boning larger cuts of meat, such as a leg of lamb.

Cleavers: Available in a variety of shapes and sizes, cleavers are suited for every task from heavy butchering to fine vegetable slicing. An all-purpose size usually has a blade about 8 x 4 inches. If you are uncomfortable with a chef's knife, you may feel more in control with a cleaver because of the broad shape and heavier weight of the blade, when chopping, cutting, and mincing. An extra attraction is that the wide flat blade is excellent for mashing garlic and for scooping up vegetables after they are chopped.

Slicing (carving) knives: Slicers are long, thin, very sharp knives that are usually used to carve cooked meat. Most slicers have a full tang to offset the length of the blade. Buy one with an 8- or 10-inch blade and a blunt or pointed tip. If you frequently slice softer foods, like smoked salmon, a scalloped-edge slicing knife makes sense. The scalloped edge helps minimize friction against the food, thus preventing tearing.

Kitchen shears: For trimming poultry, snipping herbs, or opening a food package, kitchen shears are indispensable. Look for shears with blades that twist apart for cleaning. Like knives, the best shears are made from high-carbon stainless steel.

HANDLING KNIVES

There are two basic ways to hold a knife. In the handle grip, all four fingers are wrapped around the handle and the thumb is placed on the metal spine where the blade joins the handle. In the blade grip, the back of the knife blade is held between the thumb and index finger and the remaining three fingers are wrapped around the handle. The handle grip is preferred by cooks with small hands. The blade grip is better for cooks whose hands are too large to wrap four fingers comfortably under the handle. The blade grip requires more strength in the wrists, but it can provide a better sense of control, since the hand is farther forward on the blade. Both grips are safe if executed properly, so choose one based on comfort.

CARING FOR KNIVES

Since knives are used so frequently, it is important that they be close and safely at hand. Several solutions exist: knife blocks, wall-mounted magnetic holders, and wooden drawer inserts, to name just a few. We do not recommend washing knives in the dishwasher. The repeated heating affects the blade, and soon the knife will neither take nor hold a sharp edge.

SHARPENING KNIVES

A dull knife is a lazy servant that requires you to do more than your share of the work. A sharp knife allows for neater slices, permits greater precision, and requires less cutting pressure—meaning you are less likely to cut or slice a finger.

For sharpening knives, the standard is a sharpening stone. A good stone measures 6 to 10 inches in length and has a coarse side and a fine side. Place the stone in front of you, parallel to the edge of the countertop. Lay the knife against the stone, first on the coarse side, at a 15- to 20-degree angle and draw it in a curved sweeping motion toward you, as shown, first on one side of the knife, then on the other side—10 times for each side. Then turn the stone over to the fine side, increase the angle of the blade slightly, and repeat. Be sure to clean from the blade the grit and the metal you will have removed from the stone.

The final stage, steeling, or "trueing" the blade, does not sharpen the knife, but merely smooths out tiny nicks in the edge of the blade. Steeling should be part of everyday knife maintenance to help keep the blade as sharp as possible. There are many methods for steeling. One of the easiest is to hold the piece of equipment called a steel perpendicular to the cutting board, resting the metal tip on the board. Starting with the heel of the knife at the tip of the steel, gradually pull the knife back and up toward your body as you slide it up the length of the steel. By the time you have reached the top, the blade should be almost in contact with the steel's handle. ➤ The entire blade should pass over the steel. Repeat this motion, alternating from one side of the steel to the other and making sure to keep the blade at a 15- to 20-degree angle to the steel. Four or five strokes on either side is enough to true the edge. When finished, wipe the steel and knife with a damp cloth.

If you get in the habit of sharpening your knife at frequent intervals, you will find that chopping, slicing, and

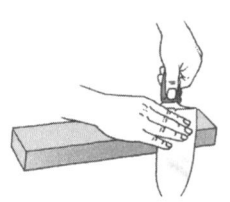 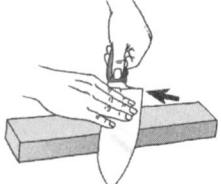 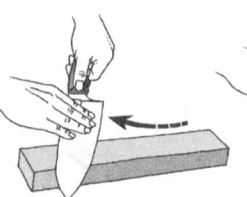 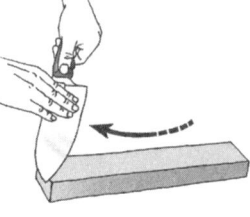

Sharpening a knife with a sharpening stone

carving will go incredibly faster, and you will have a truly useful, extremely snappy servant at your command.

Electric knife sharpeners have great appeal for some cooks. These mechanical sharpeners take the guesswork out of knife sharpening. Most have two or three slots to run the knife through. Pass the knife through the slots, and a rotating sharpening disk does the work while magnets hold the blade at the correct angle for sharpening.

ABOUT KNIFE CUTS

Cooking requires the skillful use of a sharp knife for cutting meats, chopping herbs, and preparing fresh vegetables. Learning basic knife cuts and acquiring skill in making these cuts will form the base for many culinary preparations.

Cutting most food begins with slicing. Many chopping and slicing devices are available, but nothing can replace a relaxed skilled wrist and a sharp knife. Practice with soft food items like mushrooms, or with bread, which is yielding and not slippery when placed on the cutting board. Work up to an onion or potato, each of which can be resistant and evasive. When slicing any food item, the point of the knife is never lifted from the cutting board; instead it acts as a pivot point. The cutting edge, in turn, is never lifted above the joints of the fingers that hold the food, as shown, 1070. The handle of the knife is raised high enough to be eased gently up and down, its wide blade guided by the knuckles of the hand that holds and guides the food being cut. When guiding the food, keep your fingers safely turned under, so only the first joints of the hand are exposed to the blade of the knife. As the slicing progresses, the holding hand inches a slow retreat, without releasing its grasp on the object.

Cutting or chopping an onion "chef's style" gives control of the size of the pieces to the cook and keeps the pieces from scattering all over the cutting board, shown and described, 286.

To peel and mince garlic, see About Garlic, 276.

To chiffonade, or cut a leafy herb or leafy green into thin ribbons or fine shreds, stack the leaves one on top of the other and roll tightly into a cylinder, like a cigar. Slice the cylinders of leaves crosswise into thin strips.

To mince, first roughly chop the herb or food item. Gather the herb or food in a circle on the cutting board as wide as the knife blade. Grasp the knife at the top and the handle. Mince the chopped food, using a rocking motion—keeping the tip of the knife on the cutting board and moving the handle up and down. Stop every few strokes and use the blade of the knife to draw the food pieces back into a neat pile before continuing. Scrape off the food that has stuck to the side of the knife blade too. Continue until the food is cut into very fine pieces.

We also suggest reading about Preparing Vegetables for Cooking, 241. Illustrations and instructions are included there for **slicing,** or making uniformly shaped cross cuts; for **dicing,** or cutting the food into cubes; and for making **batonette** or **julienne** matchstick cuts.

ABOUT BURNS

In the foregoing pages we have supplied, among other information, enough facts to keep our readers from ever burning the food they heat. Now a few safeguards against burning the cook—and what to do should such an emergency occur.

Choose a range on which the burners or grates are level with the surrounding platform so pots cannot tip.

Use pots and pans that are well balanced and steady when empty. Be sure handles are not so heavy that the pan will tip, or so long that they can catch on a sleeve.

Put boiling liquids at the back of the stove, and turn the handles of all pots so they are out of reach of small children.

In panfrying, keep a colander handy to place over the pan should the fat begin to sputter.

Never throw water on a grease fire. Cover the fire with salt or baking soda, or if the area is a small one, cover with a metal lid.

When deep-fat frying, please note the precautions on 1046–1048.

Keep heavy pot holders and metal tongs near the range for removing hot objects and hot foods.

Check that your hands or the pot holders or any cloths you use are not damp when touching or wiping hot handles or lids or electrical equipment.

Should you get an extensive or painful burn, seek immediate help from your physician or the emergency room of your local hospital. Lie down, remain calm, and keep warm until skilled help is available. Call 911 for serious burns.

The first aid treatment of the burn itself is much the same for large or small burns. Loosen clothing or other material over or near the burn and remove it, but take care not to cut or remove the burned skin or any material adhering to the burned surface. If blisters appear, they should not be broken or cut.

Submerge the burned area in cold water or apply cold water as soon as possible after injury for up to 1 or 2 hours. This will help to relieve the pain. Then apply a dry sterile gauze dressing as a protective bandage. If sterile gauze is not readily available, clean linen can be used.

Larger burns should be covered by a clean sheet for protection and comfort until medical help is provided. Do not use antiseptic preparations, ointments, sprays, butter, or home remedies on the burn, since these substances may interfere with treatment.

Any individual with a face burn should be observed continuously to make sure he or she is breathing normally and not going into shock.

After first aid treatment has been administered, further medical care should be under the direction of a physician.

STAIN REMOVAL

We give here a partial list of removal instructions for those stains most encountered in the kitchen and dining room. These directions are for natural linens and cotton. If wool or synthetic fibers are involved, avoid hot water and bleaches. For other stains, we recommend consulting other books about homemaking or laundry.

Alcoholic beverages: Sponge the stain with cool water or soak for 30 minutes or longer. Wash with soap or detergent. For red wine, soak in cold water immediately, then wash as soon as possible.

Butter, margarine, oil, or mayonnaise: Regular washing will remove some stains; others will need to have soap or detergent rubbed into the stain, then be rinsed with warm water. For large stains, use a commercial grease solvent and follow the manufacturer's directions.

Catsup and chili sauces: See Alcoholic beverages, above.

Chocolate and cream: Sponge with cool water or soak for 30 minutes or longer. Rub gently with soap and rinse. If the stain remains, apply a commercial grease solvent.

Coffee and tea: Boiling water poured from a height of 2 feet is good for fresh stains: Stretch the stained material over a bowl, and ➤ be very careful not to scald yourself.

Fruit, fruit juice, and wine: Use boiling water as for Coffee, above; or try bleaching in the sun after moistening with lemon juice and salt.

Lipstick: Apply undiluted detergent to the stain, rub well, and rinse. Repeat if necessary.

Mustard: See Lipstick, above.

Soft Drinks: See Alcoholic beverages and wine, above.

Wax or paraffin: Scrape the cloth to remove the hardened wax, then place blotting paper or facial tissues both over and under the cloth and press gently with a warm iron. Sponge with a commercial grease solvent.

INDEX

"Knowledge," said Samuel Johnson, "is of two kinds. We know a subject ourselves, or we know where we can find information on it." Below we put into your hands the second kind of knowledge—a kitchen-door key that will help you to open up the first.

We begin this book with a History of the Joy of Cooking, and a discussion on nutrition. Then the book divides into three sections—the recipe chapters, chapters about keeping food, and JOY's encyclopedia reference chapters: Know Your Ingredients and Cooking Methods and Techniques, which are banded to put them at your fingertips.

Our index is simple and basic, but contains bonus entries (in bolded type) which we hope you find useful such as: ethnic cuisines, cooking terms, quick recipes, casseroles, charts, and high-altitude, children, and so many more! JOY Classics will point you to 75 years of beloved recipes from1931–1975; the Family Favorites list shows you recipes we cook often; and Becker recipes are dishes created by Ethan. If you are looking for illustrations, check the index for boldface numbers. And be sure to also read Ethan's note about using this book on page xvii.

As your familiarize yourself with JOY, you will need the index less and less and will become, in the fullest sense of Samuel Johnson's words, a know-it-all. Meanwhile, happy hunting and happy cooking.

Note: **Bold** headings indicate topics of special interest. **Bold** page numbers indicate illustrations.

A
abalone
    about, 379
    sautéed, 379
à blanc, 467
acerolas, 238, **238**
Acesulfame-K, 1020
achiote (annatto), 958
acid
    acidulated water, 957
    antibrowning solutions, 894, 915
    folic, 6
    in jellies and preserves, 928
acorn squash, 307
    baked acorn, with pear and apple, 309
active dry yeast, 1029
additives, 9
    for canning, 890
adzuki beans, 254
African horned cucumbers, 239, **239**
African pheasant, 451
afternoon teas, 17
    menus for, 21
agar, 1010
aglio e olio (spaghetti with garlic and oil), 327
aïoli (garlic mayonnaise), 581–582
a jus, about making, 471
Alaska cod, 416
albacore, 417
Albariño, 47
alcohol. see also beer; cocktails and party drinks; wine
    in flambéing (flaming), 215, 1055
    nutrition and, 6
al dente, 320
ale, 51–52
ale glass, **52**
à l'étouffée, 1051

alliums, broad-leaf, 1004, **1005**
all-purpose flour, 591
all-purpose potatoes, 294
allspice, 957
allumette vegetables, 241
almond(s), 957
    apple crisp, 692
    croissants, 617
    cucumber sauce, 565–566
    custard filling, 758–759
    and fig filling, 758
    flourless matzo torte, 728
    garnish (amandine), 957
    ginger cream cheese spread, 179
    krumkakes, 780
    macaroons, 771
    milk, 1022
    orange cake, 723
    pretzels (mandelplättchen), 774
    and raisin filling, 758
    raspberry coffee cake, deluxe, 631
    rice stuffing with raisins, Middle eastern spices and, 539–540
    toasted, white chocolate mousse with, 816
    toppings, crunchy, 798–799
    torte, Cockaigne, 727
    wafers, French (tuiles), 781
almond paste, 876, 877
amandine (almond) garnish, 957
amanita mushrooms, 282
amaranth, 155, **155**
    about, 346
    greens, freezing, 919
    with mushrooms, 346
    preparing, 364 (chart)
    with tomatoes, 346
ambrosia (fruit salad), 210
ambrosia (herb), 155

American cucumbers, 272
American dory, 414
American lobsters, 382, **382**
American medium-grain rice, 360
Americano, 57
American persimmon, 233
American potato salad, 168
American shad, 416
ammonia, baker's, 958
Anaheim peppers, 291
ancho chiles, 291, 292
anchovy(ies), 413
    butter, 558–559
    dressing, 574
    paste, 958
    pesto, 958
    sauce, 552
    toasts, 87
andalouse sauce, 580
angel balls, 738
angel cakes, 705–706
    about, 704, 705
    candy, 706
    cocoa, 706
    coconut, 706
    coffee-flecked, 706
    extra-chocolate, 706
    as fat free, 698
    filled, 730
    high-altitude, 748
        chocolate, 748
        coconut, 748
    leaveners for, 698
    lemon, 706
    marble, 706
    nutty, 706
    orange, 706
    sheet, 736
angel cupcakes, 738

angel hair pasta, 321
angelica, 155, 958
angel slices, 764–765
angels on horseback, 84–85
anglerfish, 415
anise, 155, 958
anisette, 63
Anjou pears, 232
annatto (achiote), 958
antelope, 527
antibrowning solutions
  for canned fruits, 894
  for frozen fruits, 915
antipasto, about, 80
Apalachicola oysters, 371
appetizers and hors d'oeuvres, 69–94. *see also* salad(s)
  antipasto, 80
  canapés, 86–88
    anchovy toasts, 87
    beef tenderloin canapés, 87
    bruschetta with tomatoes and basil, 88
    cheese puff canapés, 87
    ham biscuits, 87–88
    marinated herring on toast, 87
    open-faced tea sandwiches (canapés), 86–89
    pork tenderloin canapés, 87
    smoked salmon canapés, 87
    turkey biscuits with chutney butter, 88
  caviar, 86
    Texas, 73
  cheese
    balls, 75–76
    canapés, puff, 87
    cip, hot chorizo and cheese, 73
    dip, beer cheese in a bread bowl, 73
    mozzarella, marinated, 77
    mozzarella sticks, fried, 77
    pesto cheesecake, 76
    platters, 70
    quesadillas, 77
    spread, chutney, 76
    spread, liptauer cheese, 76
    spread with blue cheese walnuts, 73
    wafers, quick, 91–92
  chicken
    Buffalo chicken wings, 80
    chicken satay with peanut sauce, 81–82
    fingers, 80–81
    lemon rosemary chicken on skewers, 80
  chicken liver
    mousse, 81
    rumaki, 83
  chips, 94
  crackers and bread, 93–94
    bagel chips, 93
    pita chips, 93
    potato chips, 94
    quick cheese wafers, 91–92
    root vegetable chips, 94
    Saratoga chips, 94
    soda crackers, 93–94
    tortilla chips, 94
  dips and spreads, 71–77, 78
    baba ghanoush (roasted eggplant dip), 74–75
    baked artichoke dip, 74
    beer cheese dip in a bread bowl, 73

blue cheese spread with walnuts, 76
    cheddar cheese ball, 75
    chutney cheese spread, 76
    clam dip, 72
    cream cheese ball, 75
    eggplant caviar, 75
    garlic cheese spread, 76
    guacamole, 72–73
    honey yogurt dip, 78
    hot chorizo and cheese dip, 73
    hot crab dip, 74
    hummus (chickpea and tahini dip), 74
    liptauer cheese spread, 76
    marinated goat cheese with fresh thyme, 77
    pesto cheesecake, 76
    red onion dip, 72
    roasted garlic and Parmesan spread, 76
    Roquefort cheese balls, 76
    salmon mousse, 85
    salmon pâté, 85
    seven-layer dip, 74
    shrimp dip, 72
    sour cream dip, 72
    sour cream dip, Becker, 72
    spinach dip in a bread bowl, 73
    tapenade (olive caper paste), 75
    taramasalata, 75
    Texas caviar, 73
    white bean dip with rosemary and garlic, 73
  egg rolls, 92
  fried mozzarella sticks, 77
  fried wontons, 93
  fruit platters, 77–78
  marinated mozzarella, 77
  meat
    beef and scallion rolls (negi maki), 83
    beef satay with peanut sauce, 81–82
    beef tenderloin canapés, 87
    cocktail meatballs, 82
    five-spice ribs, 81
    ham biscuits, 87–88
    pork tenderloin canapés, 87
    steak tartare, 82–83
  nachos, 77
  nuts and seeds, 70–71
    crisp spicy pecans, 70–71
    curried nuts, 70
    roasted, 70
    roasted chestnuts, 71
    rosemary and brown sugar, 70
    toasted pumpkin seeds, 71
    toasted squash seeds, 71
    toasted sunflower seeds, 71
  olives
    about, 71
    Spanish-style marinated, 71
  party platters, 69–70, 77–78
  pastry, 88–93
    Brie baked in pastry, 92
    cheese puffs (gougères), 91
    cocktail tartlets, 90
    miniature quiches, 90
    miniature tartlet shells, 90
    miniature turnovers, 90–91
    mushroom triangles, 88
    pigs in a blanket, 91
    puff pastry cheese straws, 91–92
    quick cheese straws, 91–92
    quick cheese wafers, 91–92

samosas with ground beef, 89–90
    samosas with potatoes and peas, 89
    spinach and feta triangles, 89
    stuffed choux puffs, 91
  piroshki, party, 89
  popcorn, 71
  pot stickers, 93
  salami rolls, 83
  seafood, 83–86
    anchovy toasts, 87
    angels on horseback, 84–85
    baked honey shrimp, 84
    beer-batter shrimp, 84
    broiled shrimp Cockaigne, 84
    Cajun popcorn shrimp, 84
    clams casino, 85
    coconut shrimp, 84
    grilled shrimp Cockaigne, 84
    marinated herring on toast, 87
    oysters casino, 85
    oysters Rockefeller, 85
    salmon mousse, 85
    salmon pâté, 85
    shellfish cocktail, 370–371
    smoked salmon canapés, 87
    smoked salmon rolls, 85–86
    smoked trout on cucumber rounds, 86
  stuffed grape leaves (dolmas), 82, **82**
  summer rolls, 92–93
  turkey
    biscuits with chutney butter, 88
    smoked turkey and arugula rolls, 83
  vegetables
    bagna cauda, 78
    broiled stuffed mushrooms Cockaigne, 78–79
    crispy potato skins, 79–80
    crudités, 78
    marinated green beans, 78
    marinated mushrooms, 78
    new potatoes stuffed with sour cream and caviar, 79
    stuffed celery, 79
    stuffed raw vegetables, 79
appetizer wines, 50
apple(s), 215–217. *see also* apple juice; applesauce; cider
  about, 215–216
  almond crisp, 692
  apple butter
    baked, 936
    naturally sweetened, 936–937
  and bacon, sautéed, 216
  baked, 216–217
    acorn squash with pear and, 309
    butternut squash with sausage and, 309
    stuffed with sausage, 217
  brown betty, 692–693
  cake, 723–724
    Cockaigne, 691
    sour cream cake soufflés Cockaigne, 810
  candied, 880
  canning, 894
  caramel, 880
  and cherry bread stuffing, 534
  chutney, 951
  crêpes
    with caramelized apples, 650–651
    with chicken, blue cheese and, 650
  crisp, 692

crostata, 697
dressing, 537
 with prunes, 537
dumplings, 695
filling for coffee cakes, 624
freezing, 916
galette, 697
granola, three-grain cinnamon, 353
and herring, 412
honey, 216
and horseradish sauce, Bavarian, 566
jelly, 932
muffins, with walnuts, 636
omelets, filled souffléd, 203
pandowdy, 694–695
pheasant braised with, 458
pie, 678–679
 with cheddar crust, 690
rings, 216
salad
 with carrot and horseradish, 167
 with tart greens and pecans, 158
 Waldorf, 169
sausage, with chicken, 516
strudel, 673–674
stuffing
 bread stuffing with sausage and, 533
 with sweet potatoes, 538
sweet potatoes and, 302, 538
tartlets, 679
turnovers, 696
types, 215–216
-watermelon-celery splash, 39
apple cider vinegar, 1024
apple corer, **215,** 216
Applejack, 62
apple juice
 canning, 897
apple pears, 233
applesauce, 216
 cake, 720
 canning, 894
 seasoned, 216
apricot(s), 217
 brandied, 955
 canning, 894
 cherry slump, 694
 cooked dried, 217
 curried, chutney, 950
 custard filling, 757
 Danish, 625–626
 dipping sauce, 570
 dressing, 540, 575
 dried, couscous stuffing with pistachios and, 539
 filling for coffee cakes, 624
 freezing, 916
 glaze, 800
 ice cream, 833
 nectar, canning, 897
 orange filled cookies, 777
 peeling, 208–209
 preserves, 937
 sauce, spicy, 217
Arborio rice, 354, 360
arctic char, 413
armadillo, 525
Armagnac, 62
armored car, 63
aromatic rice, 354
arrowroot, 544, 1016
arroz con pollo (chicken and rice), 435

artichoke(s), 247–249. *see also* Jerusalem artichoke
 about, 247
 baby, peas and braised, 248
 dip, baked, 74
 fried, 248
 frittata for a crowd, 202
 hearts, 248
  freezing, 919
  salad, 165
 pizza with olives, prosciutto and, 191
 stuffed, 172, 248
 trimming of uncooked, **247**
 uncored, 247–248
arugula, 153
Asiago cheese, 322
Asian eggplants, 273
Asian greens
 freezing, 919
 and whole herbs, 158
Asian menus, 22
Asian noodles, 320, 330–334
Asian pears, 233
Asian radishes, 303
asopao de pollo, 135
asparagus, 249
 about, 249
 canning, 899
 fettuccine with salmon and, 327
 freezing, 919
 with orange and hazelnuts, 250
 roasted, 250
 sesame salad, 165
 soup, cream of, 144
 stir-fried, 250
 timbales, 206–207
 tips Cockaigne, creamed eggs with, 195
 warm barley and mushroom salad, 347
Aspartame, 1020
aspics, 174–175
 about, 174
 basic savory, 174
 tomato, 174
Asti Spumante, 50
Atlantic halibut, 414
Atlantic mackerel, 415
au gratin, 961
au ruban, 658
avgolemono (Greek lemon soup), 124
avgolemono sauce (lemon egg sauce), 561–562
avocado(s)
 about, 218
 and citrus salad, 166
 cups, 172–173
 cutting, 218
 freezing, 919
 guacamole, 72–73
 lobster cocktail, 371
 and mango salad, 166
 salads, 165–166
 salsa, 571–572
 and shrimp tostadas, 189
 soup
  with chicken and tomato soup, 135
  cold, 146
 spinach salad with grapefruit, orange and, 159–160
 and turkey wraps, 187
 vinaigrette, 573

B
baba(s)
 about, 733–734
 au rhum, 734
baba ghanoush (roasted eggplant dip), 74–75
baby food
 canning, 895
baby greens, 155
backpacking menu suggestions, 26–27
backyard entertaining, 17. *see also* barbecue; grilling
 menus for, 21
bacon, 506
 about, 508
 baked, 508
 baked beans with, 255
 BLT sandwich, 180
 broiled, 508–509
 cornmeal waffles, 647
 microwaved, 509
 to oven broil, 508
 sautéed, 508
  apples and, 216
 as seasoning, 1008
 spinach salad with seared shrimp and, 163
 stuffing for fish, 536
bagels, 619
 chips, 93
 and lox, 184
bagna cauda, 78
bags, plastic
 for freezing, 912
baguette
 forming of, **601**
baked Alaska, 843
baker's ammonia, 958
baking, 1045–1046. *see also* high-altitude cooking and baking
 accuracy, importance of, 698
 cheesecakes, methods of, 742–743
 creaming butter, 700
 folding egg whites, **699,** 700
 measuring and sifting, 698
 mixing batters, **699,** 699–700
 potatoes, 294
 stirring and whipping, 700
 temperature of ingredients, 699
baking powder, 958–959
 double-acting, 959
 in high-altitude cooking, 958–959
 phosphate, 959
 tartrate, 959
baking soda
 in high-altitude cooking and baking, 627, 959
baklava, 675
baldpate duck, 455
Baldwin apples, 216
Balkan marinade, 585
balsamic vinegar, 1024
bamboo shoots, 250
banana(s), 218–219
 about, 218
 baked, 218
 bread, Cockaigne, 628
 cake, Cockaigne, 721–722
 chocolate-dipped, 218
 cream pie, 685
 Foster, 826–827
 freezing, 916
 frozen, 218

banana(s) (*cont.*)
  honey-grilled, 218–219
  nut muffins, 636
  pudding
    with meringue, 807–808
  puddings, 807
  wheat germ bread, quick, 628
banana peppers, 291
banana split, 840
banana squash, 307
band-tail pigeon, 459
Barbados cherries, 238
Barbaresco, 48
barbecue, 1059
  backyard, 17
  burgers, 510
  dry rub, Southern, 587–588
  of meat, 467
  spareribs, 505
barbecue sauce
  about, 586
  broiled scallops with, 387
  broiled shrimp with, 387
  country-style ribs baked in, 505
  grilled scallops with, 387
  grilled shrimp with, 387
  mustard, Ray's, 586
  North Carolina-style, 587
  for poultry, 586–587
  Western North Carolina-style, 587
Barbera, 49
barding, of wildfowl, 455
barley, 346–347, 1011
  about, 346
  flour, 984
  grits, 346
  preparing, 364 (chart)
  "risotto" with mushrooms, 347
  soup
    beef, 136
    chicken, 125–126
    mushroom, 131
  types, 346
  warm, mushroom and asparagus salad, 347
Barolo, 48
bars. *see also* cookies
  chocolate-glazed toffee, 763
  chocolate oat, 764
  Christmas chocolate, Cockaigne, 763
  date, Cockaigne, 765
  energy, 765
  German honey (lebkuchen), 765–766
  lemon curd, 765
  nut, 765
  raspberry streusel bars, 764
Bartlett pears, 232
basil, 155, 959
  oil, 590
  pesto, 569
  prosciutto, and mozzarella panini, 181
  vinaigrette, 573
basmati rice, 354
bass, 413
basters, 466
batido
  papaya-mango, 40
batters, 592
  cake, mixing, 699–700
  fritter, 657–658
  storing muffin, 634
  tempura, 658
battonet vegetables, 241

Bavarian cream
  about, 814
  berry, 818
  chocolate, 818
  coffee, 818
  lemon, 817
  lime, 817–818
  orange, 817
  serving and presentation, 814–815,
    815
bay leaves, 959–960
bay scallops, 378
bean curd, 315
bean(s), dried, 253–259. *see also* bean
    sprouts; black-eyed peas; *specific*
    beans and legumes
  baked, 255
    with bacon, 255
  boiled, 254
  burgers, veggie, 107
  burritos, 103–104
  canning, 899–900
  cassoulet, 496
  chili with meat and, 513
  flour, 984
  freezing, 920
  gratin, with tomato, sausage and, 97
  pasta and (pasta e fagioli), 329
  refried (frijoles refritos), 254
  and rice cakes, 106–107
  salads, 170–171
    black bean, 170
    chickpea, 170
    three-bean, 171
  serving size, 10
  soup, 133–134
    black bean, 133–134
    Mediterranean white bean, 133
    U.S. Senate, 133
    with vegetables (garbure), 131
  tacos, 189
  types, 253–254
  white bean dip with rosemary and
    garlic, 73
bean(s), fresh. *see also* green bean(s) *and*
    specific types
  about, 250
  canning, 900
  freezing, 919–920
  green, pickled, 949
  shell beans, 252–253
  types, 250
bean sprouts, 1011–1012
  stir-fried, 253
  types, 253
bear
  about, 530–531
  braised, 530–531
bear claws, 614, **614**
béarnaise sauce, 561
  about, 560
  blender, 561
  fresh herb, 561
Beaujolais, 49
beaver, 525
béchamel, 550–551
Becker bloody bull shot, 57
Becker recipes (Ethan's creations)
  barbecued shrimp, 386
  blender gazpacho, 147
  bloody bull shot, 57
  brussels sprouts, 262
  buffalo burgers, 531

burgers, 510
  chicken marinade, 585
  chicken soup, 134
  cocktail sauce, 568
  coleslaw, 161
  duxelles, 284
  express stock, 120
  five-minute polenta rustica, 349
  gyro sandwich, 188
  lamb patties, 511
  Mongolian beef, 477
  pork hash, 108
  pork marinade, 585
  portobello pizzas, 282
  quick miso soup, 125
  rice and noodle pilaf, 355
  sour cream dip, 72
  tuna salad, 164
  venison medallions, 529
beechnuts, 960
beef, 470–485. *see also* beef, roast;
    corned beef; meat *for general*
    information; steak; *specific cuts*
  about, 470–471
  boiled (boeuf bouilli), 478–479
  bottom sirloin, roast, 471
  braciole, 483
  broth, 121
  chipped, with gravy, 112
  chow fun, 331–332
  chuck roast in foil, 481–482
  consommé, broth on the rocks, 38
  cooking cubes, strips and tips of,
    476
  cuts for stew, 479
  cuts of, 470, 472–473
  enchiladas, 104
  eye of round, butterflied, 471
  eye of round, roast, 471
  fondue, 110–111
  ground. *see* ground beef
  hash with gravy, old-fashioned, 108
  kebabs, 494
  Kentucky burgoo, 484
  Mongolian, Becker, 477
  New England boiled dinner, 484–485
  paupiettes, 483
  potpie, 103
  pot roast, 477
  prime rib for a crowd, 471–472
  rib roast, standing, 471–472
  roast, 470–471
    boneless, 470
    carving, **470,** 470–471
    hash, 107
    sandwich, 177
    sandwich, hot, 182
    Yorkshire pudding, 637
  rolls, 483
  Rouladen, 483
  roulades, 483
  salad
    taco, 163
    Thai, 163
  satay with peanut sauce, 81–82
  sauerbraten, 478
  and scallion rolls (negi maki), 83
  short ribs, 482
  soup
    with barley, 136
    French simmered, and vegetables
      (pot-au-feu), 136–137
    Vietnamese noodle (pho bo), 137

steak cuts of. see steak
steak tartare, 82–83
stock
    brown, 117
    household, 117
strip sirloin, roast, for a crowd, 471
Stroganoff, 476
sukiyaki, 476–477
tacos, ground, 188–189
top round roast, 471
top round roast, butterflied, 471
tostadas with black beans, 189–190
and vegetable stir-fry, 476
Wellington, 468–469
beef brisket. see brisket
beef daube (beef stew with mustard,
        herbs, and white wine), 480
beef fillets
    about, 472
    broiled, 474
    grilled, 472, 474
    roasted, 472
beef stew, 479
    Belgian
        (carbonnade flamande), 480
    French (boeuf bourguignonne),
        479–480
    with mustard, herbs, and white wine
        (beef daube), 480
    quick, 148–149
beef tenderloin
    canapés, 87
    grilled, 472
    roasted, 472
beef tongue, 518
    about, 520
    boiled, 520
    pickled, 520
    smoked, 520
beer
    about, 51–52
    batter shrimp, 84
    bread, 629
        cheese, and scallion, 629
    cheese dip in a bread bowl, 73
    glasses and mugs, **52**
    lager-style, 51
    marinade, 585
    mop, 587
    wassail, 68
beer mug, **52**
beer stein, **52**
beet(s), 258–259
    baked or roasted, 259
    canning, 900
    -carrot-grape juice, 39
    freezing, 920
    greens, 154, 277, 278
        freezing, 920
    pickled, 949
    salad
        creamy, 166
        pickled, 166
    soup
        borscht, 129, 138, 149
        jellied, 127
    in sour cream, 259
    steamed or boiled, 259
    sweet-and-sour (Harvard), 259
beignets. see also doughnut(s)
    New Orleans, 656–657
Belgian waffles, 647
Bellini, 53

bell pepper(s), 291, 1006–1007. see also
        red pepper(s)
    corn bread stuffing with sausage and,
        535
    freezing, 921
    onions and, 292
    pizza with mushrooms, onion and, 191
    and sausage sub, 184
    stuffed, 293
        about, 292–293
        with rice, 293
Belon oysters, 371
Benedictine spread, 179
benne seeds (sesame seeds), 1011
    brittle, 873
    sesame chicken, 432
    wafers, 769
Bermuda onions, 286
berry(ies), 219–223. see also specific
        berries
    about, 219
    Bavarian cream, 818
    canning, 894–895
    Cockaigne, 219
    cones, 219, **219**
    freezing, 916
    fresh self-garnished, 219
    and fruit cobbler, 693
    granita, 839
    jam, 935
    juice, canning, 897
    parfait, 839–840
    pie
        with canned or bottled fruit, 677
        fresh, 676–677
        with frozen fruit, 677
        glazed, 678
    soufflé, frozen, 842
    sour cream tarts, 678
    substitutions for, 209
    syrup, 43
between the sheets, 63
beurre manié (kneaded butter), 545
beurre meunière (lemon butter), 557
beurre noisette (brown butter), 557
beurres composés (flavored butters),
        558–560
beverages, 28–43. see also drinks; names
        of specific beverages
    chocolate and cocoa, 35–37
    coffee, 28–34
    ice cream drinks and smoothies, 39–40
    juice and fruit, 37–39
    low-calorie, 6
    party. see cocktails and party drinks
    soft drinks, 43
    sugar syrup for, 43
    tea, 33–35
Bibb lettuce, 152
bigarade sauce, 448
bigeye tuna, 417
billi-bi (cream of mussel soup), 140
Bing cherries, 223
Bintje potatoes, 294
biscotti, 774
biscuits. see also scones
    about, 637–638
    additions to, 638
    beaten, 640
    buttermilk, 639
    cornmeal, 639
    cream, 639
    Easter bunny, 639

fluffy, 639
food processor mixing for, 638
griddle, 640
ham, 87–88
high-altitude baking, 638
    with oil, drop, 639
quick drop, 639
rolled, 638–639
sausage gravy for, 547
shortcakes, 639
sticks, 640
tortoni, 843–844
turkey, with chutney butter, 88
whole wheat, 639
Bismarck herring, 415
bison (buffalo), 531
bisque, 127, 139
    lobster, 140
    oyster, 141
bistro salad, 160
bitter ale, 52
bitter oranges, 225
    marmalade, 941
black bean(s), 254
    Brazilian, 256
    chicken, turkey, or beef tostadas with,
        189–190
    chili, venison, 529
    fermented, 982
    salad, 170
    sauce, 960
    sauce, Asian, 570–571
    soup, 133–134
    tacos, 189
blackberry(ies)
    about, 220
    flummery, 221
    ice cream, 834
    jelly, 932
    pie, 676
    raspberry grunt, 694
    shrub, 38
    sorbet, 836
black bottom cupcakes, 738
black cod, 416
black currants, 222
black drum, 414
black duck, 455
blackening, 1049
black-eyed peas, 254
    freezing, 920
    greens and, 256–257
    hoppin' John, 356
    Texas caviar, 73
blackfish, 413
black forest cake, 733
black olives
    and chicken with rice salad, 171
    salt-cured, 954
    white pizza with carmelized onions,
        rosemary and, 192
black pepper
    fish steaks, seared and crusted with,
        409
    peppercorn(s), 1006
        Szechuan, 1020–1021
    sauce (sauce poivrade), 556
    steak, with cream sauce (steak au
        poivre), 474
    vinaigrette, 573
    vodka, 58
black radishes, 303
black rice, 354

black Russian, 58
black salsify, 304
black sea bass, 413
black truffles, 284–285
black trumpet mushrooms, 281
black velvet, 53
Blanc de Blancs, 49
Blanc de Noirs, 49
blanching, 1054–1055
    of vegetables, 918–919
blancmange, 812–813
blanquette de veau (white veal stew),
    489
blended juices
    about, 38–39
blended whiskey, 59
blenders, 122. see also mixers
    hand-held immersion, 122, **122**
    pastry, 661, **661,** 661–662
blini
    mini, 645
    raised buckwheat, 645
blintzes, 651. see also crêpes
    blueberry, 651–652
    sweet cheese, 651
blitzkuchen (lightning cake), 722
bloaters, 415
blondies, 762
blood oranges, 225
bloody Maria, 57
bloody Mary, 57
blowfish, 413
BLT, 180
blueberry(ies)
    about, 220
    blintzes, 651–652
    cobbler, 693
    coulis, 853
    jam, 934–935
    muffins, 635
    pandowdy, 695
    and peach buckle, 691
    pie, 677
    sauce, hot, 845
    sorbet, 836
    syrup, fresh, 220
blue cheese
    crêpes with chicken, apples and, 650
    grilled venison chops with caraway
        butter and, 529
    miniature turnovers with carmelized
        onions and, 91
    -Parmesan soufflé, 204
    salad dressing, creamy, 576
    spread with walnuts, 76
    vinaigrette, 573
blue cornmeal, 348
blue crabs, 379–381
bluefin tuna, 417
bluefish, 413
    barbecue-rubbed grilled, 404
bluegills, 415
blue plum conserves, 939
Blue Point oysters, 371
blushing bunny, 112
boar
    about, 530
    chops, lemon-rosemary, 530
bobwhite quail, 459
boeuf à la mode (French pot roast), 478
boeuf bouilli (boiled beef), 478–479
boeuf bourguignonne (French beef stew),
    479–480

boiling, 1049
    potatoes, 294
boiling points of water, 1056
boiling water canning, 890–891
    equipment for, 888
bok choy, 153, **153,** 262
    stir-fried, with mushrooms, 264
bolete mushrooms, 282
bombes, 840
    about, 842–843
    decoration of, 843
    macaroon, 843–844
    molds for, 843
    suggested combinations for, 843
bonbons
    chocolate nut, 860
bonito, 417
    flakes, 960
borage, 960
borlotti beans, 254
borscht (beet soup), 129
    blender, 149
    with meat, 138
    Rombauer, 149
Bosc pears, 232
Boston butt ham, 506
Boston cream pie, 732
Boston lettuce, 152, **152**
bouchées (patty shells), 670
boudin blanc (white sausage), 516–517
bouillabaisse, 142
bound breading or coating, 961, **962**
bouquet garni, 960
bourbon
    balls, 879
    glaze, 583
    pie, 683
    whiskey, 59
bowle, 66
bow ties
    kasha with (kasha varnishkes), 347–348
boysenberries, 220
Braeburn apples, 215
brains, 518, 519–520
braising, 1051
    fish, 399–400
    meat, 466, 467
    vegetables, 243, 246, 248, 281
bran
    honey waffles, 647
    muffins, 635–636
    rolls, refrigerator, 621
brandied fruits, 955
brandy cocktails and drinks, 39, 62–63,
    65, 67
brandy sauce, hot, 852
brandy snaps, 781
brandy snifter, **53**
branzino, 413
bratwurst, 515
braunschweiger sandwich, 183
Brazilian chocolate, 36
Brazil nuts, 960
bread(s), 591–642. see also muffin(s);
        yeast rolls and buns
    about, 93
    bagels, 619
    banana, Cockaigne, 628
    beer, 629
    beer, cheese, and scallion, 629
    biscuits. see biscuits
    bishop's, 630
    brown, 629

buttermilk potato, 600
buttermilk spoon, 634
carrot nut, 628
cases for dishes in cream sauce, 111
challah, 600–601, **601**
cheese, 598
cheese popovers, 637
cinnamon raisin, 597–598
cinnamon sticks, 641
cinnamon toast, 641
cooling and storing, 596
corn. see corn bread
corn tortillas, 609
cracked-wheat, 599–600
crostini, 642
crust on, 595
crusty soft-center spoon, 634
cubes, butter, 641
cubes, cheese, 641
date nut, 627
dill batter loaf, 598–599
dough. see yeast dough
English muffins, 618
fast white, 597
flour tortillas, 608–609
focaccia, 607
French, 601
garlic, 641
griddle, 631
herb, 598
high-altitude baking, 594, 627
honey-butter toast, 642
honey nut, 627
hot cross buns, 610
Italian Easter (panettone), 621
leftover, uses for, 641
loaf, toasted buttered, 641
melba cheese rounds, 641
melba toast, 641–642
milk, 597
mixed starter, 602
naan, 608
nut, 627
oat, Cockaigne, 600
orange, 627–628
pain au chocolat, 617
pita, 607–608
pizza dough, 607
popovers, 637
poppy seed loaf, 629
pretzels, 619
pumpkin, 628
quick, 626–630
    about, 626–627
    banana wheat-germ, 628
    cinnamon loaf, 641
rolls. see yeast rolls and buns
rustic
    French, 603–604
    sourdough, 604
rye
    all-rye-flour, 605
    sourdough, 605
    with a sponge starter, 605–606
salad
    pita, 159
    with tomato (panzanella), 169
Sally Lunn, 627
salt-risen, 606–607
for sandwiches, 177
scones. see scones
scoring loaf, 595, **595**
shaping pan baked, **594,** 594–595, **595**

skillet, 631
soda, Irish, 629
sopapillas, 608
with soups, 150
sourdough, 601–604
sponge starter, 602
spoon, 633–634
sticks (grissini), 620
sweet zucchini, 628
tea sandwiches on sweet, 186
testing for doneness, 595–596
Tuscan loaf, 606
white, 596–597
    made with a mixed starter, 605
    made with a sponge starter, 604
whole wheat, 599. see whole wheat,
    bread
    made with mixed starter, 605
Yorkshire pudding, 637
bread-and-butter pickles, 946
bread bowl
    beer cheese dip in, 73
    spinach dip in, 73
bread crumb(s)
    browned or buttered, 960
    coating, 961–962
        fried clams with, 377
        fried oysters with, 377
        fried scallops with, 377
        fried shrimp with, 377
        seasoned, broiled fish fillets with,
        404
    dry, 960, **960**
    egg noodles with garlic and, 330
    grinding, **960**
    Japanese-style (panko), 961
    and parsley stuffing for fish, 535–536
    seasoned, 404, 962
    soft or fresh, 961
    as thickener, 545
bread flour, 591
breadfruit, 238, **238,** 259–260
breading
    of foods, **961,** 961–962
bread pudding, 822–823
    about, 822
    chocolate, 822–823
    New Orleans, 822
breakfast
    casseroles (stratas), 98
    cereals and grains, reheating, 348
    menus for, 23
    smoothie, 40
bream, 415
breasting out
    of birds, 454
Breton Sound oysters, 371
brewer's yeast, 1029
Brie, baked in pastry, 92
brine, brining, 421, 443, 904, 962
brioche, 614–615, **615**
    à tete (topped brioche), 615, **615**
    au chocolat, 615
    sectioned loaf, 615–616
brisket
    beef, with sauerkraut, 481
    dry rub, beef, 588
    smoked, 481
    sweet-and-sour, 481
broad beans, 254
broad chicory, 154
broccoli, 260–261
    cheese casserole, 261

deep-fried, 260
freezing, 920
soufflé, 205
soup, cream of, 144
steamed, 260
stir-fry, 260–261
timbales, 206
white pizza with chicken and, 192
broccoli rabe, 154, 261
    freezing, 921
    garlic braised, 261
    orecchiette sausage and, 329
broiling, 1046
Bronx, 56
broth
    about, 121
    beef, 121
    chicken, 121
    clam, 121
    .fondue, 111
    mushroom, 121
    on the rocks, 38
    vegetable, 121
brown ale, 52
brown betties
    about, 690
    apple, 692–693
brownies
    book club, 762
    butterscotch, 762
    cheesecake, 763
    Cockaigne, 762
browning, 1055
brown rice, 354
    salad with dates and oranges, 171
    wheat berries and, 345
brown sugar, **1018,** 1018–1019. see also
    sugar
    butter sauce, 850
    glaze, 583
    hard sauce, 851
    and rosemary nuts, 70
    rum glaze, 583
    sand tarts cookies, 772
    sauce, hot, 852
    spice cake, 719
brown trout, 417
brunch, 15
    menus for, 23
brunoise vegetables, 241
bruschetta with tomatoes and basil,
    88
brussels sprouts, 261–262
    Becker, 262
    with chestnuts, 261–262
    freezing, 920
Brut, 49
bucatini pasta, **321**
bûche de noël (Yule log cake), 737
buckles, 690–691
    about, 690
    blueberry and peach, 691
buckwheat
    about, 347
    blini, raised, 645
    corn bread, 632
    crêpes, 649
    flour, 984
    kasha, 347
    pancakes, 645
    pilaf, 348
    preparing, 364 (chart)
    seeds, 1011

buffalo (bison)
    about, 531
    burgers, Becker, 531
    rib roast with orange molasses glaze,
        531
Buffalo chicken wings, 80
buffets, 15
    wedding, menus for, 21
bufflehead duck, 455
bulb-type basters, 466
bulgur
    about, 362
    cabbage rolls stuffed with kasha and,
        348
    preparing, 365 (chart)
    tabbouleh, 362
bullhead, 413, 415
bullshot, 57
bunching onions, 286
buns. see muffin(s); yeast rolls and buns
burdock, 262
burgers. see hamburgers
Burgundy
    sauce (sauce bourguignonne), 549
burnet, 962
burns
    about, 1071
burritos
    bean, 103–104
    chicken, 104
    con carne, 104
burr mill grinders, 29–30, **30**
butter, 962–964, 963–964. see also butter
        cakes; butter sauce(s)
    anchovy, 558–559
    apple, 936–937
    bercy, 559
    blender, 963
    bread cubes, 641
    caviar, 559
    chile, roast guinea hen with, 451–452
    chocolate icing, quick, 794
    churned, 963
    cinnamon, 850
    clarified, 557, 963
    creaming of, 700
    cultured, 962–963
    curried macadamia, 179
    dough, pat-in-the-pan, 666–667
    drawn, 557, 963
    drop wafer, 766
    dumplings (butterklösse), 335
    fettuccine with cheese and, 325
    flavored (beurres composés), 558–560
    freezing, 924
    garlic, 559
    ghee, 557, 963
    green, 559–560
    hand-made, **964**
    honey, 179, 850
    kneaded (beurre manié), 545
    krumkakes, 780
    lemon and parsley, 559
    light, 962
    lobster, 559
    molding and shaping, 964
    nut, 178–179, 558
    orange, 559
    raspberry, 850–851
    rosemary pecan, 179
    salted, 962
    in sauces, 545
    savory walnut, 178–179

butter (*cont.*)
  shrimp, 559
  snail, 559
  sweetened, 850–851
  toast, honey, 642
  unsalted sweet, 962
  whipped, 963
butter cakes, 710–725
  about, 710–711
  incorporation of ingredients, 711
  as layer cakes, 711
  leaveners for, 698
  preparation for, 711
  temperature of ingredients for, 711
  testing for doneness, 711
buttercream icing
  chocolate, 793
  classic, 792
  coffee, 793
  lemon, 793
  liquor-flavored, 793
  meringue, Swiss, 792–793
  mocha, 793
  nut, 793
  orange, 793
  praline, 793
butter crock, **964**
buttercrunch candy, 873–874
buttercrunch lettuce, 152
buttercup squash, 307
Butterfinger potatoes, 294
butterfish, 413, 416
butterhead lettuce, 152
butterklösse (butter dumplings), 335
buttermilk, 1013–1014
  biscuits, 639
  chess pie, 683
  crackling corn bread, 632–633
  honey dressing for fruit salad, 578
  layer cake, 714
  marinade, 585
  pancakes, 644
  pecan pralines, 876
  persimmon pudding, 823
  potato bread, 600
  potato doughnuts, 655
  potato rolls, 613
  pumpkin pudding, 823
  rolls (fan-tans), 611–612, **612**
  spoon bread, 634
  waffles, 647
butternuts, 992
butternut squash, 307
  baked, stuffed with sausage and
    apples, 309
  soup, 129
butter paddles, wooden, **964**
butter pecan ice cream, 833
butter plunger, **964**
butter sauce(s), 557–560
  black, 557
    panfried skate with, 408–409
  brown (beurre noisette), 557
    egg noodles with nuts and, 330
  brown butter, 557–558
  brown sugar, 850
  herbed, 558
  lemon, 557, 558
  walnut, 558
  white butter (beurre blanc), 558
butterscotch
  brownies, 762
  cake filling, 755–756

candies, 874
caramels, 864
cream pie, 685
icebox cookies, 776
icing, quick, 794
nut cookies, 771
puddings, 807
sauce, 849–850

C
cabbage, 262–265. *see also* coleslaw;
    sauerkraut
  about, 262
  creamed, 263
  freezing, 920
  potatoes, ham and, 263
  red, 153, **153**
    braised, 264
    in salads, 153, 156
  sautéed, 263
  soup, 130
  types, 262
cabbage rolls
  stuffed, 263–264, **264**
  stuffed with kasha and bulgur, 348
Cabernet Sauvignon, 47
cactus pad(s), 265
  salad, roasted, 265
cactus pears. *see* prickly pears
Caesar salad, 159
café au lait, 31
café diablo, 32
caffè latte, 31
  granita, 839
caffè macchiato, 31
Cajun/Creole/New Orleans, 22
Cajun/Creole/New Orleans cuisine
  bananas Foster, 826
  Becker barbecued shrimp, 386
  beignets, 656
  blackened fish steaks or fillets, 409
  bread pudding, 822
  brown roux, 543
  café au lait, 31
  cajun dry rub, 587
  cajun popcorn shrimp, 84
  chicken étouffée, 436
  chicken gumbo, 136
  chicken jambalaya, 356–357
  file powder, 544
  muffeletta, 181
  oyster po' boy, 185
  pecan buttermilk pralines, 876
  red beans and rice, 256
  seafood gumbo, 141
  shrimp or crawfish étouffée, 388
  tasso, 507
  turtle soup, 391
Cajun popcorn shrimp, 84
cake(s), 698–736. *see also* baking;
    cupcakes; *specific types of cakes*
  angel, 705–706
  angel cake sheet, 736
  apple, 723–724
  apple, Cockaigne, 691
  applesauce, 720
  baba au rhum, 734
  banana, Cockaigne, 721–722
  biscuit (French sponge), 708–709
  black forest, 733
  Boston cream pie, 732
  brown sugar spice, 719
  burnt sugar, 719–720

butter, 710–725
buttermilk layer, 714
candy angel, 706
carrot, 724
  high-altitude, 750–751
celebration/multi-tiered
  about, 703–704
  filling and assembling, **703,**
    703–704, **704**
  frosting tiers, 703–704
  making tiers for, 703
cheese. *see* cheesecake(s)
chiffon, 709–710, 730, 736
chocolate, 717
chocolate-filled roll, 737
chocolate Génoise, 709
chocolate Génoise sheet, 736
chocolate mayonnaise, 718–719
chocolate mousse, 729–730
chocolate raspberry cream, 733
chocolate sheet, 722
coating ganache, 795, **795**
cocoa devil's food, 718
cocoa or extra-chocolate angel, 706
coconut, 715
coconut angel, 706
coconut pecan, 713–714
coffee. *see* coffee cakes
coffee-flecked angel, 706
cream roll, 736
crêpes, 651
crumb, 630–631
cupcakes, 737–738
daffodil, 708
dairy-free chocolate, 723
decorating. *see also* frosting; icing
  flowers for, 800
  multi-tiered cakes, 704, **704**
  stenciling tops, 786, **786**
devil's food, Cockaigne, 718
eight-yolk gold, 715
filled, **730**. *see also* cake fillings
flourless chocolate decadence, 729
foam, 704–710
foam, filled, 730
freezing, 702
fresh coconut milk, Cockaigne, 713
fruit. *see* fruitcakes
Génoise, 709
Génoise sheet, 736
German chocolate, 719
Guy Fawkes Day, 724
high-altitude
  angel, 748
  carrot, 750–751
  chocolate angel, 748
  chocolate sponge roll, 752–753
  classic 1–2–3–4, 747–748
  coconut angel, 748
  fudge, 749
  gingerbread, 752
  peach-pecan upside-down, 751
  spice, 750
  sponge, 750
  two-egg, 749–750
  white, 748–749
honey, 724–725
ice cream, mocha, 731
individual molten chocolate, 729
Italian cream, 714
jelly roll, 735–736
kuchen, fresh, 691
lady, 713

lady Baltimore, 712
ladyfingers, 740
lane, 712
layer, filling of, 753–754
leaveners for, 698
lemon coconut layer, 712
lemon icebox, 730–731
lemon or orange angel, 706
lemon poppy seed pound, 716–717
lemon roll, 736–737
lightning (blitzkuchen), 722
liquor-soaked pound, 716
madeleines, 739
marble, 712–713
marble angel, 706
Mississippi mud, 723
mixing batters for, **699,** 699–700
molds, two-piece, 715–716
Moors' head (mohrenköpfe), 731–732
mystery, 721
nut coating on, **791**
nutty angel, 706
oatmeal, 721
orange almond, 723
orange-filled, 732
orange rum, 723
packaged mixes for, 702–703
Passover nut sponge, 707
Passover sponge, 707
peach, Cockaigne, 691
peach-pecan upside-down, high-
    altitude, 751
petits fours, 738–739, **739**
pineapple upside-down, 691–692
plum, Cockaigne, 691
poppy seed custard, Cockaigne, 732
pound, 716
quick caramel, 722
quick cocoa, 722
quick or one-bowl, 722–725
red velvet, 717
refrigerated filled, **730,** 730–733
roll, 734–737
rolls, ice cream, 830
Rombauer jam, 720–721
savarins, 733–734
seed, 716
sheet, 735–736
shortcakes, 733
Sicilian cassata, 731
sour cream, 714
sour cream pound, 717
sponge, 698, 706–709
storing, 698, 702, 784–785
strawberry icebox, 731
strawberry shortcake, 733
Texas sheet, 722
"three milks" (tres leches), 708
tomato soup, 721
types, 698
vegan, 723
velvet spice, 719
wedding, 703–704
white, 711–712
yellow, four-egg, 714–715
Yule log (bûche de noël), 737
cake comb, 785
cake doughnuts, 654
cake fillings
    almond and fig or raisin, 758
    almond or hazelnut custard, 758–759
    amount of filling, 754
    apricot custard, 757

butterscotch, 755–756
chocolate custard, 756
chocolate fruit, 758
chopped fruit, 757–758
cocoa whipped cream, 755
coconut pecan, 759
coffee cake, 624
coffee whipped cream, 755
crème pâtisserie, 755
ginger fruit, 758
lane, 759
lemon, 756
lemon curd, 756
lemon-orange custard, 757
lemon syrup, 759
liquor-flavored whipped cream, 755
mocha, 756
mocha ganache, 795
mocha whipped cream, 755
moistening syrup, 759
orange cream, 757
orange curd, 756–757
orange custard, 757
pastry cream, 755
stabilized whipped cream, 754–755
sweetened whipped cream, 754
toasted walnut or pecan, 758
whipped cream, 754
whipped cream, with nuts, fruit, candy,
    or cookies, 755
whipped ganache, 795
whipped white chocolate or milk
    chocolate, 759
cake pans, 700–702
    preparing, 702
    sizing of, 700–701, **701, 702**
calamari, 399
caldo verde (Portuguese greens soup), 139
calf's liver, 518
calico macaroni salad, 172
calicos, 378
California halibut, 414
California quail, 459
Calimyrnas figs, 227
callaloo
    Caribbean, 141
calories, 6
    on food labels, 7
Calvados, 62
calzones, 190–193
Campari cocktail, 57
Canadian bacon, 508
Canadian whiskey, 59
canapés (open-faced tea sandwiches),
    86–89
    freezing, 924
Canary melons, 230
candies and confections
    almond paste, 877
    angel cake, 706
    apples, 880
    basic fondant, 866–867
    bourbon balls, 879
    buttercrunch, 873–874
    butterscotch, 874
    butterscotch caramels, 864
    caramel apples, 880
    caramel corn, 866
    chocolate cream caramels, 865
    chocolate-dipped fondant, 867
    chocolate-dipped fudge, 864
    chocolate nut bonbons, 860
    chocolate taffy, 871

chocolate truffles with liqueur, 859
chocolate walnut fudge, 863
citrus fruit jellies, 878
citrus peel, 880–881
classic nougat, 868–869
coated chocolate truffles, 858
coconut taffy, 871
coffee drops, 874
cooked sugar syrup in, 855–856
cooking and kitchen safety, 854, 870
cream caramels, 864–865
cream pull candy, 871–872
crystallization of, 855
crystallized flowers, 881–882
crystallized grapes, 881
dark chocolate bark, 859
dark chocolate candy bars with nuts,
    861
dark chocolate clusters, 861
dark chocolate truffles, 858
dipped chocolate truffles, 858
divinity, 869
English toffee, 873
equipment for, 854
fruited chocolate bark, 859
fruit jellies, 878
fudge Cockaigne, 862–863
ginger, 881
gingered chocolate clusters, 861
gum paste, 882
halvah, 878
hard, 872
heavenly hash, 880
hollow chocolates, 860
joy of coconut, 861
large solid chocolates, 860
lollipops, 875
making, 855–856
maple walnut fudge, 863
marshmallows, 869–870
marzipan, 877
Mexican orange drops, 874–875
microwave chocolate truffle centers,
    858
milk chocolate bark, 859
milk chocolate clusters, 861
milk chocolate truffles, 858
mocha truffles, 859
molds for, 854
nutty chocolate truffles, 859
opera creams (or centers), 868
orange slices, 880
Oregon delight, 879
pastillage, 882
peanut brittle, 872–873
peanut butter cups, 860–861
peanut butter fudge, 864
pecan buttermilk pralines, 876
penuche, 876
peppermint wafers, 867–868
popcorn with white sugar syrup, 866
praline, 876
pulled mints, 871
quince paste, 878–879
rock, 875
saltwater taffy, 871
Scotch toffee, 873
serving and storing, 857
sesame seed brittle, 873
small solid chocolates, 859–860
spiced caramel nuts Cockaigne, 865
stuffed dried fruits, 879
testing for doneness, 856

candies and confections (*cont.*)
  thermometer temperatures for, 855
  truffle cups, 859
  turtles, 865
  uncooked fondant, 867
  vanilla taffy, 870–871
  whipped cream filling with, 755
  white chocolate bark, 859
  white chocolate clusters, 861–862
  white chocolate truffles, 859
  white fudge Cockaigne, 863
  wrapping of, 857
candy bars. see candies and confections
candy dippers, 854
candy scraper, 854
caneberries, 220–221
cane syrup, 964
canned ham, 506
cannellini (white beans), 254
  dip with rosemary and garlic, 73
  soup, Mediterranean, 133
cannelloni, 340
canning, 888–902
  acid, 890
  additives, 890
  baby food, 895
  beans, 899–900
  boiling-water method, 888–889,
    890–891
  equipment for, 888–890, **889, 890**
  fish, 901–902
  fruit, 893–896
  fruit juices, 896–897
  game, 901–902
  high-altitude, 888, 890, 891
  jars
    cooling, 891–892
    packing, 890
    selecting, 889
    testing seals, 892
  jellies and preserves, 930
  meat, 901–902
  poultry, 901–902
  processing times, 891
  safety in, 888, 892–893
  spoilage in, 892–893
  steam-pressure method, 889, 891
  sucralose in, 893
  syrups for, 893
  tomatoes, 897–899
  vegetable chart, 899
  vegetables, 899–901
  yield
    fruit chart, 894
cantaloupes, 230
cape gooseberries, 238, **238**
capellini pasta, **321**
capers, 964
  sauce, 554
caponata (eggplant relish), 275
cappuccino, 31
carambolas, 238, **238**
caramel
  apples, 880
  buns (schnecken), 613
  cake, quick, 722
  chocolate sauce, 848
  corn, 866
  cream sauce, 849
  cupcakes, 738
  custard, 802–803
  frosting, 792
  glaze, clear, 800

glaze for custard, 804
ice cream, 832
pudding, steamed, 825
sauce, 849
syrup, 849
tart
  chocolate-glazed, 686–687
caramel candies
  about, 864
  butterscotch, 864
  chocolate cream, 865
  cream, 864–865
  nuts Cockaigne, spiced, 865
  turtles, 865
caramelized sugar, 856–857, 1019
caramelizing, 1055
caraway, 155, 964
  butter, grilled venison chops with blue
    cheese and, 529
  salad dressing, creamy, 577
carbohydrates, 5
  good *vs.* bad, 5
  total, on food labels, 8
carbonnade flamande (Belgian beef stew),
  480
cardamom, 964–965
cardoons, 265–266
Caribbean callaloo, 141
caribou, 527
Carnaroli rice, 360
carob, flour, 984
carp, 413
carrageen, 1010
carrageenan, 1010
carrot(s), 266–267
  about, 266
  braised, 266
  canning, 900
  freezing, 920
  glazed, 266
  -grape-beet juice, 39
  nut bread, 628
  peas and, 290
  puree, 266
  and raisin salad, 166
  roasted, 267
  salad
    with apple and horseradish, 167
    with edamame and rice vinegar
      dressing, 167
  soufflé, 205
  soup, cream of, 144
  stir-fried Napa cabbage and, 264
  -tomato-celery cooler, 39
  vichy, 266
carrot cake, 724
  high-altitude, 750–751
carving
  roast beef, **470,** 470–471
casaba melons, 230
cascabel peppers, 292
case-hardening, 908
cashews, 965
  spiced vegetable pilaf with, 355
cassava, 315
casserole(s)
  au gratin potatoes, 297
  baked macaroni and cheese, 326
  baked manicotti or jumbo shells, 339
  bean, tomato, and sausage gratin, 97
  beef pot pie, 103
  breakfast (stratas), 98
  broccoli cheese, 261

candied sweet potatoes, 302
cannelloni, 340
chicken or turkey potpie, 103
chicken rice, 96
chicken tamale pie, 102
cornbread tamale pie, 102
corn pudding, 271
creamed pearl onions, 287
croque monsieur, 98
green bean, 251
hamburger pie, 101
hot chicken salad, 106
King Ranch chicken, 96
lasagne, 340
lasagne bolognese, 340
leftover pasta, 323
macaroni and cheese for a crowd,
  326
moussaka, 274
mushroom-walnut noodle kugel, 336
pastitsio, 336
quick chicken rice, 96
quick tuna, 96
quick turkey tetrazzini, 96
roasted vegetable lasagne, 340
salmon, potatoes, and spinach, 97
sauteed cabbage, 263
scalloped potatoes, 296
scalloped tomatoes, 313
summer squash, 307
sweet noodle kugel, 337
sweet potatoes and apples, 302
tuna-vegetable, 97
turkey tetrazzini, 96
cassoulet, 496
caterers
  working with, 18
catfish, 413
catsup
  blender tomato, 951–952
  mushroom, 952
  red onion-garlic, 952
  tomato, 951
  walnut, 953
cauliflower, 267–268
  about, 267
  freezing, 920
  mashed, 267
  potato curry and, 267–268
  scalloped, 267
  soufflé, 205
  soup
    cream of, 144
    quick cream of, 149
  steamed, 267
  timbales, 206
cavatelli pasta, **321**
caviar, 86
  butter, 559
  mock
    eggplant, 75
    Texas, 73
  new potatoes stuffed with sour cream
    and, 79
  preparing, 905
  sauce, 568
cayenne peppers, 291
  ground, 1007
celeriac. see celery root
celery, 153, **153,** 965
  apple-watermelon splash, 39
  carrot-tomato cooler, 39
  cooked, 268

freezing, 920
stuffed, 79
celery cabbage, 262
celery root
    about, 268
    baked, 269
    mashed, 268–269
    rémoulade, 167
    soup, 144
    steamed, 268
celery seed
    dressing, 574
celtuce, 153, **153**
centerpieces, 11
cèpe mushrooms, 282
cephalopods, 369
cerimans, 238, **238**
chai, 34
challah, 600–601, **601**
chamomile, 965
Champagne, 49–50
    cocktail, 53
    mignonette sauce, 568
    mimosa, 53
    punch, 65
    sauce, 553
Champagne glasses, **53,** 54, **55**
champagne vinegar, 1024
Chandler grapefruit, 226
channel cat, 413
channel knife, 54, **54**
channel sole, 416–417
chanterelle mushrooms, 281
chapon, 157
chard, 277
    creamy pasta with tomatoes and,
        328–329
    freezing, 921
Chardonnay, 46
charlottes
    about, 814
    chocolate, 819
    coffee, 819
    preparing, 815, **815**
    russe, 818–819
    sizes, 816
    unmolding, 815
charmoula (Moroccan herb paste),
    589–590
charts
    alcoholic drink measures, 55
    boiling point of water, 1056
    can sizes, 1033
    equivalants
        substitutions for common
            ingredients, 1037–1044
    equivalents
        conversions, 1032–1033
        dry-measure, 1033
        egg sizes, 976
        linear measures, 1033
        liquid-measure volume, 1032
        metric, 1033–1035
        temperature, 1036
        U.S.-British, 1033, 1035
    frozen food packages, 1033
    fruits
        canning yields, 894
        seasonal, 209
    grains, cooking, 364–368
    icing yields, 785
    jelling point of preserves at high
        altitudes, 930

pan capacity, 701
party trays, 70
pasta shapes, 321
serving sizes, 10
substitutions
    healthy, 8
    salad greens, 155–156
sugar syrup
    for canning fruits, 893
    stages in candy-making, 856
    temperature, 1036
    for meat after carry-over cooking,
        467
    USDA recommended, 1036
vegetables
    canning yields, 899
chayote
    about, 269
    boiled, 269
    freezing, 920
    Louisiana-style, 269
cheddar cheese
    balls, 75
    dough
        apple pie with cheddar cheese crust,
            690
        pat-in-the-pan, 667
    soup, 146
    Welsh rarebit, 112
cheese, 965–968. see also appetizers and
        hors d'oeuvres; specific cheeses
    and-herb-filled souffléd omelets, 203
    baked chiles rellenos with, 293
    balls, 75–76
    beer, and scallion bread, 629
    beer dip in a bread bowl, 73
    board, 70
    bread, 598
    bread cubes, 641
    broccoli casserole, 261
    and chicken filling for stuffed pasta,
        338
    and chicken tamales, 351–352
    chile corn squares, 272
    coney, 185
    cottage, making, **967,** 967–968
    cream, making, 968
    crisp, 158
        mixed greens with, 159
    croquettes, Cockaigne, 660
    custard
        flan, 110
        pie, 110
    dessert course, 827
    dog, 185
    enchiladas, 104
    farmer's, making, 967–968
    fettuccine with butter and, 325
    filling for coffee cakes, 624
    filling for stuffed pasta, 337
    fondue, 110
    freezing, 924
    grits
        baked, 350
        souffléd, 350
    and ham soufflé, 204
    hard and semi-hard, making, 965–967,
        966
    hoop, making, 967–968
    and hot chorizo dip, 73
    macaroni and. see macaroni, and
        cheese
    muffins, 636

for pasta, 322
platters, 70
popovers, 637
and potato filling for pierogi, 341–342
puffs
    canapés, 87
    gougères, 91
    quesadillas, 77
    quiche, 109
    rolls, 613
    sandwich, 178
        grilled, 180
    sauce
        creamy microwave, 551
        soft, making, 967
        soufflé Cockaigne, 204
        soup, quick, 149
    spread
        blue cheese with walnuts, 76
        chutney, 76
        garlic, 76
        Liptauer, 76
        roasted garlic and Parmesan, 76
        squash blossoms stuffed with herbs
            and, 309–310
    straws
        puff pastry, 91
        quick, 91–92
    toast, 182
    toppings or fillings for pizza or
        calzones, 191
    wafers, quick, 91–92
    wine and, 51
cheeseburgers, 510. see also hamburgers
cheesecake(s)
    additions to, 743
    baking methods, 742–743
    brownies, 763
    chocolate, 745
    Cockaigne, 743–744
    common problems with, 742
    creamy water-bath, 744
    fresh raspberry water-bath, 744
    mixing of, 742
    New York-style, 744
    pesto, 76
    pumpkin, 745–746
    ricotta, 745
    unmolding and serving, 743, **743**
    water-bath, 744
chef's salad, 162
cherimoyas, 238, **239**
cherry(ies)
    about, 223
    and apple bread stuffing, 534
    apricot slump, 694
    brandied, 955
    canning, 895
    chocolate smoothie, 40
    clafouti, 695
    conserves, 940
    crisp, 692
    crunch pie, quick, 692
    freezing, 916
    jubilee, 826
    juice, canning, 897
    macerated, with herbs, 223
    marshmallow nut gelatin, 812
    pie
        with canned or bottled fruit, 677
        fresh, 677–678
    poached, 223
    sauce, 565, 844

cherry(ies) (*cont.*)
  soup, 148
  sour, 223
    and red wine pan sauce, 548–549
  sour cream tarts, 678
  sweet, 223
    conserves, 940
  types, 223
cherry belle radishes, 303
cherry peppers, 291
cherry pitter, **223**
cherrystone clams, 374
cherry tomatoes. *see* tomato(es)
chervil, 155, 968
chess pie
  buttermilk, 683
  lemon, 683
chess tarts, 683–684
chestnut(s), 968. *see also* water chestnuts
  about, 269–270
  boiled, 270
  bread stuffing with dried fruit and, 533
  brussels sprouts with, 261–262
  dressing, 537
  roasted, 71
  soup, 144
Chianti, 48–49
chicken, 423–440. *see also* chicken
        breasts; chicken liver(s); poultry
        for general information
  about, 423
  à la king, 112–113
    quick, 113
  and apple sausage, 516
  ash-roasted, hobo packs, 429
  baked
    chili-garlic chicken, 426
    ginger spice, 426
    Thai curry, 426
  Basque, 434
  braised, about, 430–431
  broiled
    about, 426
    barbecued, 426
    lemon garlic, 427
    teriyaki, 426–427
  broiler/fryer, 423
  broth, 121
    on the rocks, 38
  burritos, 104
  cacciatore, 433
  casserole, King Ranch, 96
  and cheese filling for stuffed pasta, 338
  and cheese tamales, 351–352
  chili hash with sweet potatoes, 108
  chili verde, 435–436
  Cordon Bleu, 437–438
  country captain, 434
  couscous with lemon, olives and, 363
  creamed
    about, 445
    quick, 446
  crêpes with chicken, blue cheese,
        apples and, 650
  croquettes, 660
  curry, 105, 434
    coconut, 431
  divan, 112
  and dumplings, 432
  enchiladas, 104
  étouffée, 436
  fajitas, 190
  farce, 541

fingers, 80–81, 430
fricassee, 432
  about, 431
  with sweet potato, 100
fried, 429–430
  about, 429
  extra crispy, 430
grilled, 427–428
  lemon, 428
  pasta salad with, 172
ground, 423
  about, 445
  patties, 511
gumbo, 136
Jamaican jerk, 428
jambalaya, 356–357
kebabs, 427–428
Kiev, **438**, 438–439
lemon grilled, 428
lemon rosemary, on skewers, 80
livers. *see* chicken liver(s)
loaf, ground, 445
lo mein, 331
Marengo, 433–434
marinade, Becker, 585
meatballs, 445
noodle soup, 125
oven-fried, with cornmeal crust, 430
panfried, 429
paprika (paprikás csirke), 431–432
parmigiana, 437
parts, using broiler/fryer for, 423
piccata, 436–437
poached, 423–424
potpie, 103
and rice (arroz con pollo), 435
rice casserole, 96
  quick, 96
roast, 424
  with 40 cloves of garlic, 425
  stuffed under the skin, 424–425,
        425
  with stuffing, 424
  turned, 424
roasters, 423
salads, 163–164
  with black olives with rice salad, 171
  Chinese, 164
  curried, 164
  hot, 106
  variations on, 164
sandwich
  deviled, 180
  salad, 178, 180
  sliced, 178
satay with peanut sauce, 81–82
sautéed, 429
sesame, 432
soup
  with avocado and tomato, 135
  Becker, 134–135
  cock-a-leekie, 135
  rice, 135
  rice or barley, 125–126
  Thai, with coconut, 135
stews, about, 431
stir-fried garlic, 439–440
stock, 117
stuffed boned, 446
sweet-and-sour, 105
tacos, shredded, 189
tagine with chickpeas, 435
tamale pie, 102

tandoori, 428
thighs, ash-roasted, 428
tostadas with black beans, 189–190
trussing of, **421**
types, 423
white pizza broccoli and, 192
whole
  butterflying, 419–420, **420**
  cutlets or strips, 420
  grill roasted, 427
wings, Buffalo, 80
chicken breasts
  baked on a bed of mushrooms,
        425–426
  boneless, skinless, 436–440
    about, 436
    baked stuffed, 439
    baked stuffed Sicilian-style, 439
    Mediterranean, baked in foil, 439
    sautéed, 436
    sautéed breaded, 437
  boning, **420**, 420–421
    cutlets or strips, 420
    sautéed stuffed, 438
    sautéed with mushroom sauce, 437
chicken-fried steak, 475
chicken liver(s)
  fried, 440
  mousse, 81
  pâté, 440
    maison, 518
  rumaki, 83
  sautéed, 440
chickpea(s), 254
  chicken tagine with, 435
  curried, with vegetables, 257
  falafel sandwich, 188
  hummus, 74
  oven-roasted, 257
  salad, 170
chiffon cake
  about, 704, 709–710
  filled, 730
  fudge, 710
  orange, 710
  pumpkin, 710
  roll, 736
  sheet, 736
chiffon pie
  about, 688
  lemon, 688–689
  lime, 688–689
  orange, 689
  pumpkin, 689
children
  berry cones, **219**
  burns, 1071
  chicken fingers, 80–81, 430
  chocolate-dipped
        bananas, 218
  chocolate satin frosting, 796
  Christmas cookies and cookie
        ornaments, 762
  churn freezing, ice cream, 828
  coloring Easter eggs, 207
  dinner for family and friends, 24
  egg safety, 980
  eggs in a basket, 196
  family meals, 16
  frozen bananas, 218
  fruit cups, 172, 210
  fruit purees and baby food, 895
  grill safety, 1058

honey (infant botulism), 993
kitchen safety, 1062. *see also* cooking
    and kitchen safety
letter cookies, 773–774
oranges for, 225
parties for, 15–16
party menus for, 23
pie dough trimmings, 663
pigs in a blanket, 91
quick cookie icing, 800
recipes
    banana snow, 218
    Becker brussels sprouts, 262
    caramel apples, 880
    cupcakes and miniature cakes, 737
    Easter bunny biscuits, 639
    fruit leather, 909
    gingerbread house, 781
    heavenly hash, 880
    hot dogs, 185
    ice cream sandwiches, 830
    Mississippi mud cake, 723
    pizza with tomato sauce and
        mozzarella, 191
    quick chocolate fondue sauce, 848
    quick hot cocoa, 36
    quick lemonade or limeade, 41
    quick or one bowl cakes, 722
    Shirley Temple, 64
    stovetop macaroni and cheese,
        325
    stromboli, 193
    vanilla taffy, 870
    Waldorf salad, 169
rolled, molded and shaped cookies for,
    771–776
snow cream, 838
soft drinks, about, 43
stenciling top of cake, 786
vegetarian diet for, 8–9
virgin cocktails for, 57, 61, 63–64
water storage requirements, 1027
Chilean sea bass, 414
chile pepper(s), 291–293, 1006–1007. *see*
    also bell pepper(s); *specific*
    peppers
about, 291
butter, roast guinea hen with, 451
canning, 901
cayenne, ground, 1007
corn bread stuffing with cumin and,
    535
corn squares with cheese and, 272
dried
    about, 292
    drying process, 909
    grinding, 1007
    rehydrating, 293
dry rub, 587
freezing, 921
glaze, chipotle, 583–584
jelly, 933
oil, 590
paste with garlic and, 589
pickled, 954
rice stuffing with chorizo and, 539
roasting, about, 292
sauce
    harissa, 569–570
    nuoc cham, 570
    with parsley, 567
    Thai chile-lime dipping, 570
types, 291–292

chile peppers(s)
    sauce
        salsa, 571–572
Chiles de Arbol peppers, 292
chiles rellenos
    baked, with cheese, 293
chiles verdes, 291
chile vinegar, 1024
chili
    burgers, 510
    cheese coney dog, 15
    chicken verde, 435–436
    Cockaigne, Cincinnati, 514
    con carne, 513
    garlic chicken
        baked, 426
    Macleid's Rockcastle, 513–515
    with meat and beans, 513
    Ohio farmhouse sausage, 514
    paste
        broiled scallops with, 387
        broiled shrimp with, 387
        grilled scallops with, 387
        grilled shrimp with, 387
    picadillo, 514
    powder, 968–969
    sauce, 951
    vegetarian, 254
        slow-cooker, 101
    venison black bean, 529
chimichurri, 566
china capstrainer, **967,** 968
Chincoteague oysters, 371
Chinese black vinegar, 1024
Chinese cabbage, 153, **153,** 262
    freezing, 920
Chinese cuisine
    beef and vegetable stir-fry, 476
    black bean sauce, 570
    black vinegar, 1024
    broccoli stir-fry, 260
    cabbage, 153
    chicken lo mein, 331
    chicken salad, 164
    chop suey or chow mein, 105
    egg noodles, 330
    egg rolls, 92
    fermented black beans, 982
    fortune cookies, 780
    grilled duck breast with hoisin ginger
        sauce, 449
    grilled or broiled shrimp with hoisin
        sauce, 387
    hoisin sauce, 992
    home-smoked squab, 452
    jujube, 239
    Mongolian hot pot, 137
    moo shu tempeh, 317
    oyster sauce, 1005
    plum, peach, or apricot dipping sauce,
        570
    roast duck, 448
    rock sugar, 1019
    sauce for vegetables, 557
    Shaoxing wine, 1028
    soy sauce, 1015
    spicy peanut sesame noodles, 332
    spicy slaw, 161
    spicy Szechuan noodles, 332
    sticky rice, 354
    stir-fried bok choy with mushrooms,
        264
    stir-fried garlic chicken, 439

sweet-and-sour sauce, 564
Szechuan peppercorns, 1020
uncooked hot mustard, 1000
Chinese dates, 239, **239**
Chinese egg noodles, 330
Chinese parsley (cilantro). *see* cilantro
    (Chinese parsley)
Chinook, 416
chipotles, 291, 292
    mayonnaise, 580
    pepper glaze, 583–584
    roasted tomato salsa, 572
chipped beef and gravy, 112
chips, 243
    bagel, 93
    fish and, 410
    pita, 93
    potato, 94
    root vegetable, 94
    Saratoga, 94
    tortilla, 94
        nachos, 77
        soup, 132–133
chitterlings, 521–522
    sautéed, 522
chives, 155, 1003, **1003**
    egg noodles with sour cream and,
        330
chocolate, 969–970. *see also* chocolate
        beverages; chocolate, white
    alcoholic drinks, 42
    bark, 859
    bars Cockaigne
        Christmas, 763
    Bavarian cream, 818
    Brazilian, 36
    bread pudding, 822–823
    brioche au chocolat, 615
    buttercream icing, 793
    butter icing, quick, 794
    cakes, 717
        angel cake, extra, 706
        angel cake, high-altitude,
            748
        black forest, 733
        dairy-free, 723
        flourless, 729–730
        Génoise sheet cakes, 736
        German, 718–719
        individual molten, 729
        Mississippi mud, 723
        mousse, 729–730
        raspberry cream, 733
        sponge, 707–708
        sponge roll, high-altitude, 752–
            753
    candy bars with nuts, 861
    charlotte, 819
    cheesecakes, 745
    chopping, 970
    clusters, 861
    coating for fluffy white icing, 790
    coconut macaroons, 771
    coffee cake filling with fruit, 624
    cream caramels, 865
    cream cheese frosting, 794
    cream pie, 685
    cupcakes, 738
        black bottom, 738
    cups, 830
    curls, 970
    custard filling, 756
    custard sauce, 846

chocolate (*cont.*)
  dipped
    bananas, 218
    fondant, 867
    fudge, 864
    strawberries, 220
  doughnuts, 655
    glazed, 655
  éclairs, 672
  feather pudding, steamed, 824
  -filled roll, 737
  filling, whipped, 759
  flourless decadence, 729
  fresh strawberry dacquoise with
      whipped cream and, 741–742
  fresh strawberry meringue with
      whipped cream and, 741–742
  frosting, 796
  frozen yogurt, 835
  fruited, bark, 859
  fruit filling, 758
  fruit filling for coffee cakes, 624
  fudge frosting, 791–792
  Génoise, 709
  gingered, clusters, 861
  glaze, bittersweet, 796
  glazed caramel tart, 686–687
  glazed custard pie, 684–685
  -glazed toffee bars, 763
  grating, 970
  hazelnut gelato (gianduja), 834
  icebox cookies, 776
  ice cream, 832
  icing, European, 796
  mayonnaise cake, 718–719
  melting, 970
  mousse, 816
  mousse frosting, 797
  mousse with gelatin, 816
  muffins, double chocolate, 636–637
  nut bonbons, 860
  oat bars, 764
  pie, black bottom, 689
  pots de crème, 804–805
  pudding, old-fashioned, 807
  raspberry cream cake, 733
  satin frosting, 796
  sauce. *see* chocolate sauce
  semifreddo, 841–842
  sheet cake, 722
  shortbread, 775–776
  soufflé, 809
  sour cream frosting, 796–797
  taffy, 871
  tart, bittersweet, 686
  tempering of, 857–858
  terrine, 817
  truffle centers, microwave, 858
  truffles, 858–859
  types of, 970
  vanilla, and coffee parfait, 839
  waffles, 647
  walnut fudge, 863
  walnut torte, 728
chocolate,
  frosting, bittersweet, 796
chocolate beverages, 35–37. *see also*
    cocoa; hot chocolate
  cherry smoothie, 40
  egg cream, 37
  iced, 37
  kai, 37
  milkshake, 39

chocolate chip
  coconut coffee cake, deluxe, 631
  cookies, 766–767
  cookies, crisp, 767
  icebox cookies, 776
  mint ice cream, 831
  oatmeal cookies, 768
  orange scones, 641
  pie, 683
chocolate ganache
  about, 795
  glaze, 796
chocolates
  hollow, 859–860
  large solid, 860
  small solid, 859–860
chocolate sauce, 847–848
  about, 847
  caramel, 848
  Cockaigne, 847
  fondue, 848
  hot fudge, 847–848
  mint, 848
  warm white, 848
chocolate, white
  bark, 859
  clusters, 861–862
  filling, whipped, 759
  frosting, 797
  macadamia monsters, 767
  mousse with toasted almonds, 816
cholesterol, 5, 6
chop suey, 104–105
chorizo, 515
  and cheese dip, hot, 73
  rice stuffing with hot chile peppers and,
    539
choux paste (pâte à choux), 671–672
  choux puffs, stuffed, 91
  swans, 673, **673**
chow-chow (mustard pickles), 947
chowder, 140
  clam
    Manhattan, 142–143
    New England, 142
    Rhode Island, 143
  corn, 143
    quick tomato, 149
  fish, 143
  salmon, 143
chowder clams, 374
chow mein, 104–105
Christmas
  menus for, 19
Christmas conserves, 940
Christmas melons, 230
Christmas recipes
  bourbon balls, 879
  bourbon or rum soaked fruitcake, 725
  brandy snaps, 781
  candied popcorn decoration, 865
  chocolate bars Cockaigne, 763
  cinnamon stars, 774
  conserves, 940
  cooked eggnog, 66
  cookie ornaments, 762
  dark fruitcake, 726
  date bars Cockaigne, 765
  drei augen, 779
  eggnog, 66
  flourless nut balls, 769
  gingerbread house, 781
  gingerbread men, 773

  glögg, 67
  lebkuchen, 765
  Mexican wedding cakes, 768
  mincemeat, 902
  mock mince pie, 680
  mulled cider, 68
  pecan or angel slices, 764
  peppernuts, 768
  rich roll cookies, 772
  roasted chestnuts, 71
  spekulatius, 775
  springerle, 775
  steamed plum pudding, 825
  stollen, 622
  syllabub, 67
  Viennese crescents, 773
  wassail, 68
  Yule log, 737
christophene, 269
chukar partridge, 458
churn freezing, ice cream, 828–829
chutney
  apple, 951
  butter, turkey biscuits with, 88
  cheese spread, 76
  curried apricot, 950
  curried tropical, 219
  gooseberry, 222
  green tomato, 951
  nut cream cheese spread, 180
  turkey burgers, 445
cider
  canning, 897
  mulled (alcoholic), 68
  mulled (nonalcoholic), 38
  sauce, buttered, 845
cider vinegar, 1024
cilantro (Chinese parsley), 155, 972–
    973
  mangoes with, 229
Cinco de Mayo
  menus for, 20
cinnamon, 970–971
  butter, 850
  granola, three-grain apple, 353
  loaf, quick, 641
  raisin bread, 597–598
  stars, 774–775
  sticks, 641
  sugar, 1019
  toast, 641
cipolline onions, 286
citrons, 224
citrus, 223–226
  about, 223–224
  and avocado salad, 166
  freezing, 916
  fruit jellies, 878
  juice medley, 38
  in marmalade, 940–941
  peel, candied, 880–881
  salad, 224
  sectioning, 223–224, **224**
  substitutions for, 209
  vodka, 58
  zests and garnishes, 55, 971, **971**
citrus hand press, **223**
citrus reamer, **223**
clafouti, cherry, 695
clam(s), 369
  broiled, on the half-shell, 375
  broth, 121
  casino, 85

chowder
    Manhattan, 142–143
    New England, 142
    Rhode Island, 143
dip, 72
fresh, white pizza with garlic and, 192
fried
    with bread crumb coating, 377
    with cornmeal coating, 377
    with cracker coating, 377
pot, Thai, 376
roll, 183
sauce
    red, linguine with, 328
    white, linguine with, 328
shucking, **374,** 374–375
soft-shell, **374,** 374–375
steamed, 375
stir-fried, with oyster sauce, 376
tempura, 377
types, 374–375
clambake, 375–376
clarifying fats, 981
clay, baking, 1052
clear soups, 123–127
    about, 123
    garnishes for, 150
cleaver, 464
clementines, 225
clingstone peaches, 231
clotted cream, 1014
clove pinks, 155
cloves, 971
club sandwich, 180
clusters
    chocolate, dark, 861
    gingered chocolate, 861
    milk chocolate, 861
    white chocolate, 861–862
coarse salt, 1009
cobbler
    about, 693
    biscuit dough, 693
    fruit and berry, 693
cobb salad, 162
cock-a-leekie, 135
cockles, 374
cocktail avocados, 218
cocktail glasses, 54, **55**
cocktail meatballs, 82
cocktail parties, 16
    menus for, 22–23
cocktails and party drinks, 40–43, 52–68,
    64–68. *see also* beverages;
    specific cocktails
    about, 40, 54–55, 64–65
    Becker bloody bull shot, 57
    Bellini, 53
    black Russian, 58
    black velvet, 53
    bloody Mary, 57
    bowle, 66
    brandy, 62–63
    Bronx, 56
    Champagne, 53
    Champagne punch, 65
    citrus vodka, 58
    cocomoka cold, 42
    cocomoka hot, 42
    coconut extravaganza, 64
    coffee, 32–33
    cooked eggnog, 66–67
    cordial and liqueur, 63

cosmopolitan, 58
Cuba libre, 60
daiquiri, 60
decorative ice mold for, 65
eggnog, 66
Fish House punch, 65
frozen daiquiri, 60–61
frozen margarita, 62
fuzzy navel, 63
garnishes for, 55
gimlet, 56
gin, 55–57, 59
gin and tonic, 56
gin cocktail, 56
gin fizz, 56
glassware, 54, **55**
glögg, 67
grapefruit herb margarita, 62
grasshopper, 63
greyhound, 58
grog, 61
Harvey wallbanger, 58
highball, 59
hot buttered rum, 61
hot toddy, 60
ice for, 55
Joy tea, 58
Kir, 52–53
Long Island iced tea, 61
Lynchburg lemonade, 60
Madras, 58
mai tai, 61
Manhattan, 59
margarita, 62
martinis, 56
May wine, 66
measurements for, 55
mimosa, 53
mint julep, 60
Moscow mule, 58
mudslide, 63
mulled cider, 68
mulled wine, 67
Negroni, 57
the Nikolashka, 63
nonalcoholic, 40–42, 57, 61, 63–64
old-fashioned, 59
orange blossom, 56
Pimm's cup, 57
piña colada, 61
pineapple tropic, 64
pink lady, 57
planter's punch, 61, 66
Rhine wine cup, 66
rickey, 59
rock shandy, 64
rum, 59, 60–61
rusty nail, 60
salty dog, 58
sangría, 65
Sazerac, 60
Scarlett O'Hara, 63
screwdriver, 57
seabreeze, 58
shandy, 53
sidecar, 63
Singapore sling, 57
stinger, 63
syllabub, 67
tequila, 57, 61–62
tequila shots, 62
tequila sunrise, 62
Tom and Jerry, 67

Tom Collins, 56
virgin, 57, 61, 63–64
vodka, 56, 57–58
wassail, 68
whiskey, 58–60
whiskey or brandy cup, 65
whiskey sour, 59
white Russian, 58
white wine spritzer, 53
wine and beer, 52–53
cocktail sauce
    Becker, 568
cocktail shellfish, 370–371
cocktail tartlets, 90
cocoa. see also chocolate
    about, 35
    angel cake, 706
    cake, quick, 722
    devil's food cake, 718
    egg cream, 37
    hot, 35–36
    meringue kisses, 771
    meringues, 741
    powder, 35
        types, 969–970
    quick hot, 36
    spiced hot, 36
    syrup, 36
    whipped cream, 755
cocomoka
    cold, 42
    hot, 42
coconut, 971–972
    about, 226
    angel cake, 706
        high-altitude, 748
    cake, 715
    chicken curry, 431
    chocolate chip coffee cake, deluxe, 631
    chocolate macaroons, 771
    crab cocktail, 370–371
    cream pie, 685
    cupcakes, 738
    dulcie, 845
    extravaganza, 64
    filled cookies, 778
    freezing, 916
    ice cream, 833
    Italian cream cake, 714
    joy of, 861
    lemon layer cake, 712
    lime salad, 226
    macaroons, 771
    pecan cake, 713–714
    pecan filling, 759
    pecan icing, 794
    rice, 357
    shrimp, 84
    shrimp, vanilla, 388
    taffy, 871
    tapioca pudding, 821
    and Thai chicken soup, 135
coconut milk
    about, 971–972
    beef satay with peanut sauce, 81
    cake, fresh coconut milk cake
        Cockaigne, 713
    Caribbean callaloo, 141
    curry
        cauliflower and potato curry,
            267–268
        chicken or turkey, 105
        coconut chicken, 431

coconut milk (*cont.*)
  ice cream, coconut, 833
  Indonesian rice table (rijsttafel), 358
  Jamaican rice and peas, 356
  pudding
    coconut milk (tremblèque), 808
    coconut tapioca, 821
  rice, coconut, 357
  shellfish
    crab coconut cocktail, 370
    vanilla coconut shrimp, 388
  smoothies
    papaya, 40
    papaya coconut, 40
    tropical, 40
  soup
    mulligatawny soup, 136
    Thai chicken and coconut, 135
cocozelle squash, 306
cod, 414, 416
  boulangère, 399
  codfish balls, 412
  codfish cakes, 412
coddled eggs, 194–195
coeurs à la crème, 826
coffee
  Bavarian cream, 818
  buttercream icing, 793
  custard sauce, 846
  drops, 874
  flavored meringues, 741
  flecked angel cake, 706
  icebox cookies, 776
  ice cream, 832
  pots de crème, 804
  rubs, with spice, 588
  vanilla, and chocolate parfait, 839
coffee cake
  high-altitude
    sour cream streusel coffee, 751–752
coffee cakes. *see also* Danish; yeast coffee
    cakes
  cranberry or apple streusel, 630
  cream cheese Danish spirals, 626
  crumb cake, 630–631
  Danish, 626, **626**
  deluxe coconut chocolate chip, 631
  deluxe raspberry almond, 631
  deluxe Sunday morning, 631
  fillings and flavoring
    about, 623
    apple filling, 624
    apricot, 624
    cheese filling, 624
    chocolate fruit filling, 624
    crumb fruit-filling, 624
    date filling, 624
    fig filling, 624
    with marbled filling, 630
    nut fillings, 623
    poppy seed fillings, 624
    prune, 624
  glazes, 800
  Italian Easter bread, 621
  kneaded filled, 622
  kugelhopf, 623, **623**
  panettone, 621
  prune or apricot Danish, 625–626
  quick
    about, 626–627
    kuchen, 630
    sour cream, 630
  raspberry Danish pinwheels, 625

Stollen (Christmas loaf), 622–623
  yeasted, 621–622
coffee, coffee drinks, 6, 28–34
  about, 28
  alcohol in, 32–33, 42
  arabica *vs.* robusta, 28
  brewing, 28–29, **29**
  café diablo, 32
  charlotte, 819
  drip, 30
  espresso, 31
  flavored, 32
  at formal dinners, 14
  French press pot, 30
  frozen, 33
  grinding and storing beans for, 29–30,
    30
  iced, 32–33
  at informal dinners, 15
  instant, 31
  Middle Eastern, 31–32
  percolated, 30
  in quantity, 31
  steeped, 30–31
  Turkish, 31–32
  vacuum-method, 30
  Viennese-iced, 33
coffee filters
  gold screen, 28
coffee pots, 28–29, **29**, 31
  Cognac, 62
coho, 416
colcannon (mashed potatoes with
    cabbage and scallions), 296
cold frame, **908**
cold soups, 146–147
coleslaw, 161–162
  Becker, 161
  creamy, 161
  creamy dressing for, 578
  hot slaw, 161–162
  spicy Chinese slaw, 161
  tangy, 161
collards, collard greens, **115,** 277
collins glasses, 54, **55**
color
  in food, about, 1030–1031
  retaining, in vegetables, 241–242
combination salads, 162–165
comfrey, 972
Comice pears, 232
compote(s)
  dried fruit, 211
  fig, with lemon and ginger, 227
  fresh fruit, baked, 213
  kumquat, 225
compôte composée, 209
"compressed" yeast, 591
compressed (fresh) yeast, 1029
conch, 369
  about, 390–391
  salad, 391
conchiglie pasta, **321**
concord grapes, 227
condiments
  for party platters, 70
confections. *see* candies and confections
confit
  goose, 451
conserves
  cherry, 940
  Christmas, 940
  cranberry, 939–940

making, 939
  peach, 939
  plum, 939
  rhubarb, 940
consommé, 123–124
  brunoise, 124
  madrilene, 124
contaminated food
  handling, 893
convenience foods. *see* store-bought and
    convenience foods
conversions
  tables for, 1032–1036
cook for a day, eat for a week
  freezing for, 925
  menus, 25
cookies
  almond macaroons, 771
  almond pretzels (mandelplättchen),
    774
  angel slices, 764–765
  baking, 760–761
  bar. *see* bars
  bar and square, about, 762
  biscotti, 774
  book club brownies, 762
  brandy snaps, 781
  brownies Cockaigne, 762
  brown sugar sand tarts, 773
  butterscotch brownies or blondies, 762
  butterscotch icebox, 776
  butterscotch nut, 771
  cheesecake brownies, 763
  chocolate chip, 766–767
  chocolate chip icebox, 776
  chocolate coconut macaroons, 771
  chocolate icebox, 776
  chocolate shortbread, 775–776
  Christmas, 762
  cinnamon stars, 774–775
  cocoa meringue kisses, 771
  coconut macaroons, 771
  coffee icebox, 776
  cream cheese icebox, 776–777
  crisp chocolate chip, 767
  curled, 779–781
  dough, additions to, 760
  drei augen, 779
  drop, 766–771
  filled, **777,** 777–779
  florentines Cockaigne, 770
  flourless nut balls, 769
  fortune, 780–781
  Frankfurter oblaten, 780
  freezing, 925–926
  gingerbread house, 781–783, **782**
  gingerbread men, 773, **773**
  gingersnaps, 767
  ginger thins, 770
  hermits, 770
  high altitude, about, 761
  icebox, 776–777
  ice cream cones (gaufrettes), 780
  icing, quick, 800
  individual nut tarts, 778
  jelly tots, 778–779
  letters, 773–774
  linzer hearts, 779
  macaroon jam tarts, 779
  meringue kisses, 771
  Mexican wedding cakes, 768
  mixing and decorating, 760
  molasses crisps Cockaigne, 777

molasses, Moldow, 770
molded, 771
Moravian molasses thins, 773
nut drop cookies, 768–771
nutty dried fruit drops, 769
nutty meringue kisses, 771
oatmeal chocolate chip, 768
oatmeal raisin, 767–768
orange marmalade, 770–771
as ornaments, 762
packaging as gifts, 761–762
peanut butter, 767
pecan lace, 769
pecan puffs, 769
pecan slices, 764–765
peppernuts (pfeffernüsse), 768
pinwheel icebox, 776
press, 775
quick lemon icing for, 800
rich roll, 772
roll, 772
rolled, 771
rolled, molded and shaped, 771–776
rugelach, 778, **778**
sand tarts, 772
Scandinavian krumkakes, 779–780,
    780
Scotch shortbread, 775
sesame seed wafers, 769
shaped, 771
shipping, 761–762
snickerdoodles, 768
speculatus, 775
spingerle, 775
spritz, 775
storing
    baked, 761
    dough for, 761
tuiles (French almond wafers), 781
vanilla icebox, 776
Viennese crescents, 773
whipped cream filling with, 755
white chocolate macadamia monsters,
    767
cooking and kitchen safety. see also food
        safety
    burns, 1071
    candies, 854
    deep-fat frying, 1046–1048
    fondue safety, 110
    freezer power outages, 918
    grilling, 1058–1059
    hearth cooking, 1060–1061
    knives, handling, 1070–1071
    microwaves, 1064
    non-stick pans, 1067
    packaging materials, 912
    power outages, frozen food and, 918
    pressure cooking, 1053–1054
    stoves, 1062
    taffy, 870
cooking clubs, 17
    menus for, 22
cooking methods and techniques,
        1045–1072
    dry-heat, 1045–1049
    fireplace (hearth), 1059–1061, **1061**
    at high-altitude. see high-altitude
            cooking and baking
    for holding and reheating food, 1065
    microwave, 1063–1065
    moist-heat, 1049–1054
    outdoor, 1056–1059

partial-heat, 1054–1056
    time element in, 1065
cooking terms
    à la mode, 678
    al dente, 171, 320
    au gratin, 961
    baking, 1045
    baking fish in clay, 1052
    barbecuing, 1059
    basting, 466
    beating, 978
    blackening, 1049
    a blanc, 467, 480
    blanching, 1054
    boiling, 1049
    braising, 1051
    broiling, 1046
    browning, 1055
    caramelizing, 1055
    carry-over cooking, 467
    cooking en papillote, 1052
    creaming sugar and fat, 699, **700**
    deep-fat frying, 1046
    deglazing, 1055
    degreasing, 123, 546
    double-boiler cooking, 1053
    embers, cooking on, 1060
    embers, cooking over, 1061
    fire-roasting, 1061
    flambéing or flaming, 1055
    foil cookery, 1052
    folding, 978, **979**
    garnishing, 1031
    gratinéing, 961, 1056
    grilling, 1057
    grill-roasting, 1059
    grinding, 29, 464, 903, 960, 1001,
            1007
    hearth cooking, 1059
    hot ashes, cooking in, 1060
    larding, 564
    leaf wrapping, 1051
    a l'étouffée, 1051
    marinating, 584
    measuring
        about, 1031
        baking, 698
        fats, 981
        flour, 983
        sugar, **1018**
    microwave cooking, 1063
    mincing, 1071
    pan broiling, 1049
    panfrying, 1048
    parboiling, 1054
    pit cooking, 1057
    planking or plank-roasting, 1055
    poaching, 1050
    pressure cooking, 1053
    puréeing, 215
    radiant heat, 1060
    ragout, 531
    reducing liquids, 1055
    reheating food, 1065
    roasting, 1045
    rotisserie cooking, 1059
    sautéing, 1048
    scalding, 1055
    searing. see browning
    simmering, 1049
    skewer cooking, 1049
    slow cooking, 1051
    smoking, 905

spit cooking, 1059
    stand or rest, 467
    steaming, 1055
    sweating, 1055
    timing, 1065
    trussing, 521
    whipping, 973
    wrap cookery, 1051
cooking with fire, 1056
cookware
    about, 1065–1067
    choosing, 1067
cooler, 59
coots, 459
coq au vin, 431
coquilles St. Jacques au gratin (sea scallop
        gratin), 378–379
coral, 382
cordial and liqueur cocktails, 63
coriander, 972–973
corkscrews, 54, **54**
corn, 270–272
    about, 270
    canning, 900
    caramel, 866
    chowder, 143
        quick tomato, 149
    on the cob, 270–271
    creamed, 271
    flour, 984
    freezing, 920
    fritters
        fresh, 272
        with ham, 659
    grilled or roasted, 271
    pudding, 271
        additions to, 271
        souffléd, 271
    relish, 948
    removing kernels from, **270**
    salad, 152
    salsa, 571–572
    sautéed (fried), 271
    soufflé, 205
    squares, cheese-chile, 272
    and tomato relish, 949
    and tomato salad, Dee's, 272
corn bread, 631–634
    about, 631–632
    additions to, 632
    buckwheat, 632
    buttermilk crackling, 632–633
    dodgers Cockaigne, 633
    high altitudes baking, 631–632
    hush puppies, 633
    johnnycakes, 633
    muffins, 632
    skillet, 632
    Southern, 632
    spoon bread, 633–634
    sticks, 632
    stuffing, 534–535
    tamale pie, 102
    zephyrs Cockaigne, 633
corn dogs, 185
corned beef, 484, 904
    corning process, 904
    hash, 107
    hash, red flannel, 485
    sandwich
        Reuben, 181
        triple-decker, with pastrami,
                182–183

cornichon cucumbers, 282
cornichons (pickled gherkins), 946–947
Cornish hens. see also poultry for general information
about, 440–441
broiled, 441
glazed stuffed, 441
grilled, in spicy port marinade, 441
roast, 441
cornmeal, 348–350. see also polenta
about, 348–349
biscuits, 639
coating
fried clams with, 377
fried scallops with, 377
fried shrimp with, 377
oven-fried chicken, 430
cobbler biscuit dough, 693
dumplings, 334–335
flour, 984
mush, 349
pancakes, 645
pastry dough, 665
pie dough, 665
types, 348
waffles, 647
and bacon, 647
cornstarch, 544, 1016–1017
in high-altitude cooking, 1017
waxy, 1018
corn syrup, 973
corn tortillas, 609
corn whiskey, 59
Cortland apples, 215
cosmopolitan, 58
costmary, 973
cottage cheese
egg noodles with, 330
making, **967**, 967–968
cottage pie, 102
cottonseed
flour, 984
coulis (uncooked fruit sauces), 853
blueberry, 853
mango, 853
raspberry, 853
strawberry, 853
countertop grills, 1063
count neck clams, 374
country ham, 506
country sausage, 516
court bouillon, 120–121
Louisiana, 141
cousa squash, 306
couscous, 262–263
about, 362
with chicken, lemon and olives, 363
Israeli, 363
with pine nuts and raisins, 362
preparing, 365 (chart)
stuffing with dried apricots and pistachios, 539
cowpeas, 254
freezing, 920
crab apple(s)
jelly, 932
crab, crabmeat, 369, 379–381. see also soft-shell crabs
about, 379–380
cakes, 381
coconut cocktail, 370–371
crab Louis, 162–163
dip, hot, 74

imitation (surimi), 391
male and female, **379**
parboiling live, 379–380
soufflé, 206
soup
Charleston, 140
steamed, 381
strata, 98
stuffing, for fish, 536
sushi rolls, 359, **360**
types, 379–380
crabs, crabmeat
softshell, 374–375, 380–381
cracked wheat, 986
about, 362
bread, 599–600
cracker
crumbs, seasoned, 962
cracker(s)
about, 93
appetizer, 93–94
coating
fried clams with, 377
fried oyster with, 377
fried scallop with, 377
fried shrimp with, 377
leftover, uses for, 641
cracklings, 508
cranberry(ies), 221–222
about, 221
canning, 895
Collins, 64
conserves, 939–940
freezing, 916
glaze, 583
juice, 38
hot, 38
-mango punch, 41
relish
cooked, 221–222
uncooked, 222
salad
molded, 175
sauce
additions to, 221–222
canning, 895
jellied, 221
whole berry, 221
sherbet, 838
cranberry beans, 250, 254
crappies, 415
crawfish. see crayfish (crawfish)
crayfish (crawfish), 369, 382
about, 389
boiled, 389
étoufée, 388–389
cream, 973–974
biscuits, 639
caramels, 864–865
chocolate, 865
clotted (Devonshire), 1014
freezing, 924
fried, 808
homogenization of, 996
horseradish, 565
(chantilly) mayonnaise, 580
opera, 868
pasteurization of, 996
pulled candy, 871–872
Russian horseradish, 581
sauce, 553
scones, 640
shortcakes, 639

sour, 1013–1015
substitutions, 996
as thickener, 545
types, 973
whipped, 973–974
substitutes, 974
cream cake
chocolate raspberry, 733
Italian, 714
cream cheese
ball, 75
blintzes, sweet, 651
chocolate frosting, 794
Danish spirals, 626
dressing for fruit salad, 578
frosting, 794
icebox cookies, 776–777
making, 968
mayonnaise, 580
pastry dough, 666
spreads, 179–180
almond ginger, 179
chutney nut, 180
cucumber, 179
orange pecan, 179
topping, whipped, 799
vinaigrette, 578
creamed mushrooms on toast, 112
cream filling
orange, 757
cream pies
about, 684
banana, 685
butterscotch, 685
chocolate, 685
coconut, 685
vanilla, 685
cream puffs
about fillings for, 672
cream roll, 736
cream sauce
about dishes in, 111
bread and pastry cases for dishes in, 111
peppered steak with, 474
white sauce (béchamel), 550–551
cream soup. see soup(s), cream
creamy slaw, 161
dressing for, 578
crème brûlée, 803–804
maple, 804
raspberry, 804
crème caramel (flan), 803
crème chantilly, 973
crème de cacao, 63
crème de cassis, 63
crème de menthe, 63
crème fraîche, 1014
as thickener, 545
crème frite (fried cream), 808
crème patisserie (pastry cream), 755
cremini mushrooms, 281
Crenshaw melons, 230
crêpe pan, 648
crêpes. see also blintzes; pancakes
about, 648–649, **649**
buckwheat, 649
cake, 651
with caramelized apples, 650–651
with chicken, apples, and blue cheese, 650
ham and spinach, 650
making, 649, **649**

savory, 649–650
storing, 649
suzette, 650
sweet, 649–650
Viennese or Austrian (palatschinken), 652
crescent rolls
sweet filled, 618
crescents
Viennese, 773
cresses, 153, **153**
crisps
about, 690
apple, 692
apple almond, 692
fruit, 692
croaker, 414
crock-cured dill pickles, 953
croissants, 616–617, **617**
almond, 617
pain au chocolat, 617, **617**
raspberry, 617
croque madame sandwich, 181
croque monsieur casserole, 98
croque monsieur sandwich, 181
croquettes
about, 659–660
cheese, Cockaigne, 660
chicken, 660
frying, 660
preparing, 659
salmon, 660
turkey, 660
crostata, apple, 697
crostini, 642
croutons, 974–975
as addition to green salads, 157
soup, 151
crowd-size recipes
artichoke frittata, 202
baked ham, 507
bean, tomato, and sausage gratin, 97
beef rib roast or prime rib, 471–472
casseroles, about, 95
caterers, working with, 18
chicken salad, 163–164
country ham, 507
creamy macaroni salad, 172
eggs baked in a muffin tin, 199
enlarging recipes, 1032
frozen daiquiri, 60
ham biscuits, 87
hearty meat ragu, 101
hot chicken salad, 106
macaroni and cheese, 326
matzo brei, 199
poached eggs for a crowd, 197
pork shoulder with mustard rosemary sauce, 99
quick turkey gravy, 547
roast fresh ham or leg of pork, 499–500
roast strip sirloin, 471
roast turkey, 442
tea for a crowd, 34
tea sandwiches, 185–186
turkey salad, 163–164
turned roast turkey, 442
crudités, 78
crullers, 656. see also doughnut(s)
crumb cake, 630–631
crumbing foods, **961,** 961–962

crumpets, 619
crunch
dumplings, 695
grunt, 693–694
kuchen, 691
leather, 909
pandowdy, 694
slump, 693–694
crustaceans, 369
crusts
bread, 595
pie. see pie crust
Cuba libre, 60
Cuban sandwich, 181
cucumber(s)
about, 272–273
almond sauce, 565–566
cocktail with pineapple and, 39
cooked, 273
cream cheese spread, 179
cups, 173, **173**
low-salt sweet, slices, 946
mangoes and, 229
marinated, 167
mousse, 175–176
rounds, smoked trout on, 86
salad, 167
creamy, 167
soup, cold, 147
types, 272
yellow, pickling, 945
cumin, 975
corn bread stuffing with hot chile peppers and, 535
seeds, lentil and rice pilaf with toasted, 355
cupcakes
about, 737
angel, or balls, 738
black bottom, 738
caramel, 738
chocolate, 738
coconut, 738
high-altitude 1–2–3–4, 747–748
icing, 788, **788**
jam, 738
sour cream spice, 738
sponge, 738
yellow, 737
curaçao, 63
curing and pickling fish, 411
curled cookies, 779–781
about, 779
curlews, 459
curly cress, 153
curly endive, **153,** 153–154
curly leaf spinach, **155**
curly parsley, 289, 1005
currant(s)
about, 222
dried, 211
freezing, 917
jelly, 931–932
juice, canning, 897
plumping of, 211
sauce, red, 222
types, 222
curry, curried
cauliflower and potato, 267–268
chicken, 105, 434
Thai baked, 426
chicken salad, 164
chickpeas with vegetables, 257

coconut chicken, 431
dressing for fruit salad, 578
eggs, 195
goat, Jamaican, 509
lamb, with tomato, 497
macadamia butter, 179
mayonnaise, 580
meat, 105
nuts, 70
paste
red, 589
Thai green, 589
sauce, 553
tropical chutney, 219
turkey, 105
turkey salad, 164
curry leaves, 975
curry powder and paste, 975
Cushaw squash, 307
cusk, 414
custard(s), 801–806. see also crème brûlée; pots de crème
about, 801–802
baked, 802
boiled, 802
cake Cockaigne, poppy seed, 732
caramel, 802–803
caramel glaze, 804
containers for, 801, **801**
crème brûlée, 803–804
cup, 802
filling
almond, 758–759
apricot, 757
chocolate, 756
hazelnut, 758–759
lemon orange, 757
orange, 757
fillings
vanilla, 755
molded, 813
pie, 684
chocolate glazed, 684–685
rich, 802
sauce (crème anglaise)
about, 845–846
chocolate, 846
coffee, 846
fruit, 846
vanilla bean, 846
sponge, 805–806
storing, 802
tapioca, 820–821
testing for doneness, 801
timbales, basic, 206
vanilla, 846
zabaglione, 806
custard apples, 238
cutlets or strips
poultry, **420,** 420–421
cutters, 854
cutthroat trout, 417
cutting boards, 1069
cuttlefish, 369, **389,** 389–390

D
dacquoise, 741
fresh strawberry, with whipped cream and chocolate, 741–742
daikon radishes, 303
daiquiri, 60
frozen, 60–61
grenadine, 60

dairy products. *see also specific dairy products*
    freezing, 924
    homogenization, 996
    pasteurization, 996–997
    serving size, 10
dal (Indian lentil puree), 258
Damson plums, 235
    sauce, jellied, 942
dandelion greens, **153,** 154
Danish. *see also* coffee cakes
    apricot, 625–626
    baking, 625
    coffee cake, 626, **626**
    pastry dough for, 624–625
    pinwheels, raspberry, 625
    prune, 625–626
    spirals, cream cheese, 626
dasheen taro, 310
dashi, 119
    Japanese noodles in, 333
date(s), 226–227
    about, 226
    bars, Cockaigne, 765
    brown rice salad with oranges and, 171
    cookies, filled, 777
    filling for coffee cakes, 624
    freezing, 917
    nut bread, 627
    stuffed, 226–227
    types, 226
day lily fritters, 659
decorating turntable, 785
deep-frying, 1046–1048
    doughnut, 653
    fish, 409–410
    fritters, 659
    high-altitude, 657, 1048
    mushrooms, 284
    onion rings, 288
    parsley, 289
    plantains, 294
    potatoes, French fries, 243, 299–300
    sweet potatoes, 302
    turkey, 443–444
    vegetables, 243
    zucchini, 308
deer. *see also* venison
    types, 527
deglazing, 582, 1055
Deglet Noor dates, 226
dehydration
    of food, 883
delicious apples, 215
Denver omelet, 202–203
dessert(s). *see also* sauce(s), dessert; *specific desserts*
    cheese course for, 827
    fondue, 110
    frozen. *see also* ice cream
        gelato, 834
        ice pops, 838
        ices, 838–839
        lemon surprise, 830
        orange surprise, 830
        parfaits, 839–840
        sauces for, 844–853
        sherbets, 837–838
        snow cream, 838
        sorbets, 835–837
        still-frozen, about, 840
        yogurts, 834–835

gelatin, 810–814
    pizza, 697
dessert sauce(s), 844–853
    brown sugar butter, 850
    buttered cider, 845
    butterscotch, 848–850
    caramel, 848–849
    cherry, 844
    chocolate, 847–848
    chocolate caramel, 848
    chocolate Cockaigne, 847
    chocolate fondue, 848
    chocolate mint, 848
    clear lemon, 844
    clear lime, 844
    foamy, 851–852
    fresh blueberry, 853
    fresh mango, 853
    fresh raspberry, 853
    fresh strawberry, 853
    fruit, fresh, 853
    fruit, jellied, 942
    hard, 851
    hot blueberry, 845
    hot brandy, 852
    hot brown sugar, 852
    hot butter-and-egg, about, 852
    hot buttered maple, 852–853
    hot fudge, 847–848
    hot lemon, 844
    hot lime, 844
    hot wine, 852
    jellied Damson, 942
    maple syrup, 850
    marshmallow, 850
    melba, 845
    mocha, 848
    nesselrode, 942
    orange liqueur, 852
    plum pudding, 852
    prickly pear, with melon, 236
    rum, 850
    sour cream, 851
    southern whiskey, 852
    vanilla, 850
    warm white chocolate, 848
dessert wines, 50
deviled chicken spread, 180
deviled eggs, 195
    Pop's, 195
deviled ham spread, 180
devil seasoning, 975–976
Devonshire cream, 1014
dial gauge, 889
diamondback terrapin, 391
dicing vegetables, 241, **241**
diets
    healthy substitutions and, 8
    vegetarian, 8–9
    weight-loss, 7
dijon
    dressing, creamy, 577
dill, 155, 976
    batter loaf, 598–599
    dilled beans, pickled, 953
    green beans with onions, tomatoes and, 251–252
    mustard sauce, Scandinavian, 566
    pickles
        crock-cured, 953–954
        quick, 947

dining
    formal, 13–14, 24
    informal, 14–15, 24
dip(s), 71–75
    about, 71–72
    baba ghanoush, 74–75
    baked artichoke, 74
    chickpea and tahini, 74
    chorizo and cheese, hot, 73
    clam, 72
    crab, hot, 74
    eggplant caviar, 75
    eggplant, roasted, 74–75
    honey yogurt, 78
    hummus, 74
    red onion, 72
    seven-layer, 74
    shrimp, 72
    sour cream, 72
        Becker, 72
    spinach, in a bread bowl, 73
    Texas caviar, 73
    white bean, with rosemary and garlic, 73
dipping sauce
    apricot, 570
    commercial, 564
    honey mustard, 566
    peach, 570
    peanut, 570
    plum, 570
    tamarind, 237–238
    Thai chile-lime, 570
dirty martini, 56
distilled white vinegar, 1024
ditaline pasta, **321**
divinity, 869
dofu, 315
Dolcetto, 49
Dolly Varden, 413
dolmas (stuffed grape leaves), 82, **82**
dolphinfish, 415
dorado, 415
dory, 414
double-boilers, 854, 1053
dough
    biscuit
        cobbler, 693
        cornmeal cobbler, 693
        sour cream cobbler, 693
    bread
        mixing, 592
        yeast, 591–596
    cookie, additions to, 760
    folding, 668
    freezing, 925–926
    galette, 697
    layered, 668
    pastry. *see* pastry dough; pie crust
    pat-in-the-pan butter, 666–667
    pat-in-the-pan cheddar, 667
    pat-in-the-pan oil, 667
    pat-in-the-pan shortbread, 667
    pie, 665–668
    pizza, 607
    refrigerator, about, 620
    rich egg tart, 666
    storing cookie, 761
dough hook, 593
doughnut(s), 653–657
    about, 653–654
    beignets or French fritters, 657
    buttermilk potato, 655

cake, 654
chocolate, 655
chocolate glazed, 655
crullers, 656
dropped, 655
forming and shaping, 653, **654**
frying and heating, 653
high-altitude adjustments, 654
honey-dipped, 656
jelly, 655
New Orleans beignets, 656–657
rosettes, 657
sour cream, 654–655
storing, 653–654
yeast, 654
doughnut cutter, **653**
dough scraper, metal, 661, **661**
dover sole, 416–417
doves, 418, 460–461
and noodles, 461
wild, 459
and wild rice pilau, 461
drei augen, 779
dressing. see also salad dressing; stuffing
apple, 537
apple and prune, 537
apricot, 540–541
chestnut, 537
dry, 535
onion and sage, 537
oyster, for fish, 536
prune, 540–541
sausage, 537
seafood, 536
wild rice
for game, 540
and porcini, 540
dried fruit. see also currant(s); raisin(s);
specific dried fruit
apricots
cooked, 217
couscous stuffing with pistachios
and, 539
dressing, 540–541
compote, 211
cooking, 211
dressing, prune, 540–541
drops, nutty, 769
drying process, 909
filling
with chocolate, 758
with chopped fruit, 757–758
with ginger, 758
freezing, 917, 926
fruit-nut pemmican, 212
plumping, 211
scones, 641
stuffed, 879
stuffing
with chestnuts and, 533
with couscous and pistachios, 539
with rice, almonds, and Middle
Eastern spices, 539–40
with toasted nuts and, 533
wheat berries with sautéed onions and,
362
dried rice noodles, 330
drinks
alcoholic. see cocktails and party
drinks
garnishes for, 55
glassware for, 12, **12**, 13, **53**, 54, **55**
nonalcoholic. see beverages

party. see cocktails and party drinks
soda, 6, 39–40
soft, 43
drippings, 981
drop cookies, 766–771
about, 766
butter wafer, 766
flattening, **766**
nut, 768–771
nutty dried fruit, 769
orange marmalade, 770–771
sugar, 766
drugstore wrapping method, 913, **913**
drum, 414
dry-heat cooking methods, 1045–1049
drying
about, 907–909
chile peppers, 909
fruit, 909
herb, 991
mushrooms, 999
tomatoes, 909
drying cabinet, **908**
dry jack cheese, 322
dry Manhattan, 59
dry onions, 286
dry rubs, 587–588
duck, 446–449. see also poultry for
general information; wild
ducks
about, 446–447
breasts
grilled, with hoisin ginger sauce,
449
pan-seared, 448–449
pan-seared, with fig and red wine
sauce, 449
fricassee, black, 455–456
parts, about, 448
roast, 447
à l'orange (bigarade), 448
Chinese, 448
crispy, 447
crispy, with quick orange sauce,
447–448
fruit and honey glazed, 448
roasting, about, 447
types, 446–447
dumplings, 334–336
about, 334
apple, 695
butter (butterklösse), 335
chicken and, 432
cornmeal, 334–335
filled, 341–343
fruit, about, 695–696
potato (kartoffelklösse), 335
dungeness crabs, 380
durians, 238, **239**
dutch oven, **1051**
dutch oven cooking
braising, 466–467, 1051
cast iron, 1066
cookware selection, 1067
grilling, 1057–1059
hearth, 1060–1061
pot roasting, 466–467
stewing, 466–467, 1051
stocks, meat and poultry, 114
duxelles, 284
Becker, 284
dwarf bananas, 218
dye, Easter egg, 207

E
Early Richmond cherries, 223
Easter
eggs, coloring, 207
menus for, 20
Eastern European cuisine
bagel and lox, 184
beef Stroganoff, 476
beets in sour cream, 259
borscht, 129
borscht with meat, 138
bowties with kasha (kasha varnishkes),
347
braised pork with sauerkraut, 501
brisket and sauerkraut, 481
butter dumplings (butterclosse), 335
challah, 600–601
cherry soup, 148
chicken Kiev, 438
chicken paprika, 431
clear caramel glaze, 800
European chocolate icing, 796
gefilte fish, 401
honey cake, 724
Hungarian goulash, 480
liptauer cheese spread, 76
matzo ball soup, 126
palatschinken, 652
paprika sauce (sauce hongroise), 553
pierogi, 341
potato dumplings (kartoffelklosse), 335
rugelach, 778
Russian dressing, 576
Russian horseradish cream, 581
sachertorte, 728
strawberries Romanoff, 220
sweet noodle kugel, 337
vareniki, 341
Eastern European menus, 22
Eastern oysters, 371
eaux-de-vie, 62
éclairs
about fillings for, 672
chocolate, 672
choux paste in form of, 671
écrevisses. see crayfish (crawfish)
edamame
about, 252
and carrot salad with rice vinegar
dressing, 167
edible flowers. see flowers, edible
edit pie crust
pat-in-the-pan, 666–667, **681**
eel, 414
egg(s). see also egg dishes
beating, 978, **979**
folding in, 978
freezing and thawing, 923–924
pasteurized whole, 977
safety of, 66, 798, 976–980, 980
separating, 979, **979**
sizes and equivalents chart, 976
storing, 979–980
substitutes, 977
substitutes, homemade, 977
tempering, 542, 979
whites. see egg whites
whole, powdered, 978
yolks of, as thickener, 544–545
egg cream, 37
egg dishes, 194–207. see also egg(s);
omelets; soufflés
about, 976–980, **977**

egg dishes (cont.)
  baked, 199
    additions to, 199
    in a muffin tin, 199
  in a basket, 196
  coddled, 194–195
  cooking, 978–979
  creamed
    with asparagus tips Cockaigne, 195
    au gratin, 195
  deviled or stuffed, 195
    Pop's, 195
  drop soup, 124
  fried, 196
    sandwiches, 183–184
  garlic soup with, 124–125
  yellow cake with four eggs, 714–715
egg(s), egg dishes
  hard-boiled, 194
    Easter eggs, coloring, 207
  hollandaise sauce, quick whole,
    560–561
  huevos rancheros, 196
  lemon sauce (avgolemono sauce),
    561–562
  in a nest, 199–200
  poached, 196–198
  salad, 164
  sandwich
    egg salad, 178
    fried egg, 183–184
    western, 184
  scotch, 195–196
  scrambled, 198
    additions to, 198
    matzo brei, 199
    Scotch woodcock, 198
  shirred, 199
  soft-boiled, 194
  soup, Italian Parmesan and, 124
  tart dough, rich, 666
  -thickened velouté (sauce allemande),
    554
eggnog, 66
  cooked, 66–67
egg noodles, 320, 329–330
  about, 320
  boiled, 325
  with brown butter and nuts, 330
  buttered, 329
  with cottage cheese, 330
  fresh, 325
  with garlic and bread crumbs, 330
  Pennsylvania Dutch, 325
  with sour cream and chives, 330
eggplant(s), 273–275
  about, 273
  dips
    baba ghanoush (roasted eggplant
      dip), 74–75
    caviar, 75
  fried, 273
  moussaka, 274–275
  Parmigiana, 273–274
  pizza with mushrooms, sun-dried
    tomatoes and grilled, 191
  ratatouille Provençale, 274
  relish, 275
  roasted whole, 274
  slices, baked, 273
  types, 273
egg rolls, 92
egg wash, French, 799

egg whites
  beating, at high altitudes, 747
  folding, **699,** 700
  fresh, royal icing made with, 789
  omelet, 201
  powdered, 977
    royal icing made with, 789
  uncooked
    in gelatin desserts, 810–811
    safety with, 798, 810–811
Eiswein (ice wine), 50
elbow macaroni, **321**
elderberry(ies), 155, 222–223
  about, 222
  vinegar, 222–223
electric drip coffeemakers, 28
electric juice extractors, 39
electric mixer
  for cake batters, 699
  creaming butter with, 700
  kneading bread dough with, 592
  mixing bread dough with, 592
  mixing pastry dough with, 662
electric rice cookers, 354
elephant ears, 670
elephant garlic, 276, 1004
Elephant Heart plums, 235
elk, 527
emmer wheat, 362
Empire apples, 215
emu, 418
  about, 453
  fillets, 453
emulsions, 578–579
enchiladas, 104
en croûte
  cooking meat, 468
endive, 153, 275–276
  about, 275
  Belgian, 153
    au gratin, 275–276
  curly, **153,** 153–154
  salad
    with pear and walnut, 170
    with walnut, 160
English muffin, 618
  pizza, 182
English runner beans, 250
English short ribs, 482
English zucchini squash, 306
enoki mushrooms, 282
entertaining, 11–18
  afternoon teas, 17
  brunches, 15
  buffets, 15
  candles, 11
  children's parties, 15–16
  cocktail parties and open houses, 16
  cooking for large parties and, 17–18
  family meals, 16
  final note on, 18
  formal dining and, 13–14, 24
  glassware for, 12, **12,** 13
  informal dining and, 14–15
  lunches, 16–17
  menus for, 11, 13, 14
  outdoor, 17
  seating for, 12–13
  supper and cooking clubs, 17
  table decor for, 11–12
  table setting for, 12, **12, 13, 14**
  working with a caterer and, 18
epazote, 155, 980

equipment. see also cooking and kitchen
    safety
  about indoor cooking, 1061–1063
  candy making, 854
  for canning, 888–890
  grilling, 1057
  icing cakes, 784–785
  jellies and preserves, 927
  kitchen, basic, 1067–1069
  mixers and blenders, 122, 592,
    661–662, 699–700
  pickling, 927
  pie/pastry, 661–663
equivalents
  about, 1031–1032
  for common ingredients, 1037–1044
  of measure, tables for, 1032–1036
escabèche (pickled fish), 411–412
escarole, 154, **154**
  about, 275
espresso
  about, 31
  granita, 839
  preparing, 31
  semifreddo, 842
espresso machines, 29, **29,** 31
étouffée, shrimp or crawfish, 388
eulachon, 416
European broad beans, 250
European cucumbers, 272
European flat oysters, 371
European lobsters, 382
evaporated milk
  whipped, 974
express fish stock, 120
extracts and flavorings, 980

F
fajitas, 190
  chicken, 190
  shrimp, 190
  steak, 190
falafel sandwich, 188
family favorites (favorites of the JOY
    family)
  black pepper vodka, 58
  blender hollandaise, 560
  burgers, 510
  buttermilk pancakes, 644
  caramelized onions, 287
  Charleston crab soup, 140
  chicken, avocado, and tomato soup,
    135
  chicken Marengo, 433
  chicken marinade, 585
  cold vichyssoise, 130
  corn and tomato salad, 272
  cornbread, 632
  corn pudding, 271
  cream of mushroom soup, 144
  cream scones, 640
  duxelles, 284
  eggnog, 66
  French coq au vin, 431
  garlic herb paste, 589
  garlic soup with eggs, 124
  German meatballs (konigsberger klops),
    512
  gin and tonic, 56
  gravlax, 411
  green goddess dressing, 576
  grilled mushrooms, 283
  guacamole, 72

iced hibiscus tea, 35
lemon meringue pie, 687
Macleid's Rockcastle chili, 513
mustard barbecue sauce, 586
Nikolashka, 63
Oregon shrimp salad, 163
parsley chile sauce, 567
party piroshki, 89
pecan or angel slices, 765
Pop's deviled eggs, 195
Portuguese greens soup (caldo verde), 139
puttanesca sauce, 563
quick tuna casserole, 96
roasted asparagus, 250
roasted garlic and Parmesan spread, 76
roasted garlic soup, 125
roasted tomato-chipotle salsa, 572
sausage gravy for biscuits, 547
Scotch eggs, 195
seafood gumbo, 141
slow-roasted tomatoes, 312
smoked turkey and arugula rolls, 83
South Carolina skillet shrimp, 385
Southern cornbread, 632
spaghetti carbonara, 329
spicy Chinese slaw, 161
sprouting seed, grains and beans, 1011
steak au poivre, 474
tea vodka, 58
uncored artichokes, 247
white cake I, 711
white gazpacho, 147
family meals, 16
menus for, 25
farfalle, **321**
farfalle pasta, **321**
farina, 986
balls Cockaigne, 334
pudding, 821
farro
about, 362
preparing, 368 (chart)
fatback, 508
Father's Day
menus for, 20
fats
clarifying, 981
in cooking, 980–982
measuring, 981, **981**
pork, 982, 993
poultry, 982
removing excess salt from, 981
rendering, 981
fats, dietary, 5
on food labels, 7, 8
fattoush, 159
fava beans, 250
mashed, 255–256
Roman-style, 253
feijoas, 238–239, **239**
freezing, 917
feldsalat, 152
fennel, 276, 982
fronds, 155
roasted, 276
and sausage stuffing, 541
fenugreek, 982
fermented food
black beans, 982
vegetables, 953
feta
dressing, 576–577

spinach and feta triangles, 89
white pizza with fresh tomatoes, basil and feta cheese, 191
fettuccine, **321**
Alfredo, 327
with butter and cheese, 325
with fresh herbs, 326
with salmon and asparagus, 327
fiber, dietary, 5
fiddlehead ferns, 276
field peas, 254
field salad with fresh herbs, 158
fig(s)
and almond filling, 758
baked, with ricotta, 227
canning, 895
compote with lemon and ginger, 227
filled cookies, 777
filling for coffee cakes, 624
grilled or broiled, with prosciutto, 227
preserves, 938
and red wine sauce, pan-seared duck breasts with, 449
types, 227
filberts. see hazelnuts
filé powder, 544
filled cakes, **730**
filled cookies, **777**, 777–779
filleting
fish, 395, **395**
fillings. see cake fillings
filter cone method, 28, **29**
fine cornmeal, 348
fines herbes, 982
finger bananas, 218
finger bowls, 14
fingerling potatoes, 294
finnan haddie, 414
creamed, 412
fire, fireplace cooking methods, 1056–1061, **1061**
fish, 393–417. see also fish fillets; fish steaks; seafood; specific types
bacon stuffing for, 536
baked, baking, 396
in clay, 1052
in a covered dish, 399
in foil, 399
in salt, 399
braising, 399–400
broiling, 402–406
cakes, Thai, 410–411
and chips, 410
chowder, 143
cold, serving cooked, 396
commonly cooked, 413–417
curing and pickling, 411
deep-fried, 409–410
filleting, 395, **395**
freezing, 922–923
fritter batter for, 658
frozen, 393–394
thawing and cooking, 923
green herb dressing for, 536–537
grilling, 402–406
kebabs, 405
loaf, 106
marinated deep-fried, 410
mercury and pesticide levels in, 393
microwaving, 402
oyster dressing for, 536
en papillote, 398–399
pickled (escabèche), 411–412

plank-roasted, 406
poached, poaching, 399–400
preparation for cooking, 394–395
purchasing and storing, 393
reduction of cooking liquid for, 400
roasting, 396, 402–406
sandwich, grilled or fried, 178
sauce, 982
sautéing and panfrying, 406–407
serving size, 10
slicing steaks from, 394, **394**
smoking, 907
soups, 139–143
steaming, 399–400
stuffing
parsley and bread crumb, 535–536
preparation for, 394
tacos, grilled, 189
test for doneness, 395–396
warm, keeping sauced, 396
whole
boning cooked, 396–397
braised with red wine sauce, 401
broiled, 403
broiled with bacon, 403
cleaning, 394, **394, 395**
filleting, 395, **395**
grilled, 403
grilled with bacon, 403
panfried, 407
roasted stuffed, 397
serving, **396,** 396–397
fishermen's soups, 139
fish fillets
blackened, 409
broiled
with herbs, 404
with lemon, 403–404
with seasoned bread crumbs, 404
with tomatoes and herbs, 406
deep-fried, Southern-style, 409–410
filleting, 395, **395**
molded filled (paupiettes), 398
panfried, 407
breaded, 407–408
spice-crusted, 407–408
roasted
high-heat, 398
slow-roasted, 398
in white wine, 397
skinning, 395
sole florentine, 402
Fish House punch, 65
fish steaks
blackened, 409
broiled, 404
grilled, 404
with tomato-olive relish, 404
panfried, 407
poached in white wine, 400–401
seared pepper-crusted, 409
teriyaki-grilled, 405–406
fish stock, 118
express, 120
five-spice powder, 982
five-spice ribs, 81
flageolet beans, 250, 254
flambéing (flaming), 1055
fruit, 215
flaming (flambéing), 1055
flan, 803
with condensed milk, 803
roasted garlic, 207

flanken short ribs, 482
flank steak, 474–475, 482
flat-leaf parsley, 1005
flat-leaf spinach, **155**
flavor(s)
    bases, 957
    understanding, 956–957
floating islands, 805
floats, ice cream, 39
florentines
    Cockaigne, 770
flounder, 414
    fillets, marinated, 408
    Pacific, 416
    summer, 414
flour, 982–987
    bread, 986
    browned, for gravies, 544
    cake, 986
    Cornell triple-rich formula, 596
    gluten, 923, 987
    instant, 986
    measuring, 698, 983, **983**
    nonwheat, 983–985
    pastry, 986
    rice, 591
    self-rising, 986–987
    semolina, 923, 986
    sifting, 698, 983, **983**
    sweet rice, 1017
    tapioca, 1017–1018
    as thickener, 123, 544
    tortillas, 608–609
    triticale, 361–362, 368 (chart), 923, 987
    types, 591
    vital wheat gluten, 987
    wheat, 985–987
    whole-grain, 987
    whole wheat, 591, 987
flouring foods, **961,** 961–962
flourless recipes
    chocolate cakes, about, 729
    chocolate decadence, 729
    matzo almond torte, 728
    nut balls, 769
    white sauce, 511
flowers
    as centerpiece, 11
    edible, 155, 800, 1000
        for cakes, 800
        crystallized, 881
        frittered, 659
        squash blossoms, 309–310
fluids, nutrition and, 6
fluke, 414
flying fish, 416
flying mocha monkey, 40
foam cakes, 704–710
focaccia bread, 607
foie gras, 449–450
    about, 449
    pan seared, 449–450
foil, aluminum
    cooking with, 1052
    for freezing, 912
folding
    of egg whites, **699,** 700
    of pastry dough, 668
folic acid, 6
fondant
    about, 866
    basic, 866–867
    chocolate-dipped, 867

icing, 791–793
    about, 791
    on pastries, 791
    uncooked, 867
    work surface for, 867
fondue
    about, 110
    beef, 110–111
    broth, 111
    cheese, 110
    chocolate sauce, 848
    desserts, 110, 848
food coloring dye, for Easter eggs, 207
food labels, reading, **7,** 7–8
food mill, 122, **122**
food processors, 122, 593, 661
    mixing pastry dough with, 662
    puff pastry, 669
food safety
    about, 9
    additives, 9
    bovine spongiform encephalopathy, 519
    canning, 888, 893, 901–902
        sweet potatoes, 901
    caramelized sugar, 1019
    cooking in quantity, 17–18
    cooking temperatures, USDA, 1036
    custards
        cake fillings, 753
        cooking and storing, 753, 802
    doughnuts, 653
    eggnog, cooked, 66
    eggs and egg products, 798, 976–980
    ferns, 276
    fish and shellfish
        curing and pickling, 411
        pollutants, 393
        raw shellfish, 370
    frozen foods
        power outages, 918
        thawing, 914
    hearth cooking, 1060–1061
    honey (infant botulism), 916
    jerky, 905
    low acid foods, 888
    marinades, 584
    mayonnaise, 168, 579
    meat, 463
        canning, 901–902
        game, 523–524
        ground meat and hamburger, 509
        jerky, 905
        mincing, grinding, pounding, and macerating, 464
        sausage, 515, 903
        steak tartare, 82
    meringue, 798
    milks and creams, sour, 1013
    mushrooms, wild, 282
    oils, flavored, 590
    pasta, 320
    pâte, 517
    pickling, 943–945
    potato salad, 168
    poultry, 418–419
    refreezing foods, 914
    royal icing, 789
    salads
        potato, 168
        transporting, 157
    salt-preserved lemons, 224
    smoking food, 905–907

stocks, 115
storing food, 883–884
stuffing, 423, 442
sweet potatoes, canning, 901
tofu, 315
vegetables
    wild greens, 156
vegetables, fermenting, 953
water, 1026–1027
    backpacking water supply, 27
    baking in a water bath, 743
forks, 12, **12, 14**
fork-tender, 467
fortune cookies, 780–781
four-citrus marmalade, 941
fowl
    smoking, 906–907
Frankfurter oblaten, 780
free-range poultry, 418
freestone peaches, 231
freeze-drying, 883
freezing, 910–926. *see also* frozen foods
    butter, 924
    cakes, 926
    canapés, 924
    cheese, 924
    cook for a day, eat for a week, 925
    cookies, 925–926
    cooling food before, 912
    cream, 924
    dough, 925–926
    dried fruits, 926
    eggs, 923–924
    fish, 922–923
    freezers, about, 911–912
    fruit juice, 918
    fruits, 914–918
    game, 922–923
    home-cooked meals, 925
    jellies and preserves, 929–930
    meat, 922–923
    milk, 924
    nuts, 926
    packaging materials for, 912
    packing food for, 912–914, **913**
    pastry, 925–926
    pies, 926
    poultry, 922–923
    power outages and, 910–911
    precooked dishes, 924
    process of, 911
    quality in, 910
    salad ingredients, 925
    sandwiches, 924
    seafood, 922–923
    soups, 924–925
    vegetables, 918–922
French breakfast radishes, 303
French cuisine
    aïoli (garlic mayonnaise), 581–582
    beef daube, 480
    beignets or French fritters, 657
    boeuf à la mode, 478
    boeuf bouilli, 478
    boeuf bourguignonne, 479–480
    brandied cherries, 955
    brioche au chocolat, 615
    cassoulet, 496
    cherry clafouti, 695
    choux paste (pâte a choux), 671–672
    coeur a la crème, 826
    coq au vin, 431
    coulis, 853

cream cheese mayonnaise, 580
crème brûlée, 803–804
crème chantilly, 973
crème frite, 808
crème pâtisserie, 755
crêpes, 648–650
croque monsieur, 181
duxelles, 284
eclairs, 672
fines herbes, 982
flan (crème caramel), 803
foie gras, 449–450
fondue, 110–111
French bread, 181
French chocolate mousse, 816
French icing, 795–796
French onion soup, 129
French parsnips, 289
French sponge cake (biscuit),
    708–709
French toast, 648
galettes, 697
ganache, 795–796
gaufrettes, 780
génoise, 709
lapin a la moutarde, 526
leeks vinaigrette, 280
madeleines, 739
mille-feuille, 670
mousse, 814–816
omelets, 200–201
pâté maison, 518
persillade, 1006
pistou, 569
pot-au-feu, 136
pots de crème, 804
praline and penuche, 875–876
quatre epices (spice Parisienne),
    1007
rabbit à la mode, 525
rémoulade sauce, 581
salmi of squab, 452
sauteed kidneys with mustard, 520
soufflés, 203–206
tarte tatin, 681–682
tremblèque, 808
tuiles (French almond wafers), 781
veal francese, 487
vin brûle, 67
French endive, 153
French fries, 243
    never-fail, 299–300
French onion soup, 129–130
French press (plunger) pots, 28–29, **29**
    preparing, 30
French toast
    baked, 648
    stuffed, 648
    waffles, 648
freshwater turtles, 391
Friar plums, 235
fricassee
    black duck, 455–456
    chicken, 432
    rabbit, 525
    turkey, 432
fried eggs, 196
    additions to, 196
    sandwich, 183–184
frijoles refritos (refried beans), 254
frisée, 153, 154
frittata, 202
    artichoke, for a crowd, 202

fritters, frittered foods, 657–659
    batters, 657–658
        for fish, 658
        for fruit, 658–659
        for meat, 658
        for vegetables, 658
    corn
        fresh, 272
        and ham, 659
    day lily, 659
    flowers as, 659
    French, 657
    fruit, 658–659
    garnish, 151
    high-altitude adjustments for, 657
fritto misto, 243, 658
frog legs
    about, 392
    braised, 392
    deep fried, 392
    preparing, 392
frosted glasses, 55
frosting. see also icing
    caramel, 792
    chocolate, 796
        bittersweet, 796
        cream cheese, 795
        fudge, 791–792
        mousse, 797
        satin, 796
        sour cream, 796–797
    consistency, adjusting, 785
    cream cheese, 794, 795
    crumbs in, 785
    mocha, 797
    peanut butter, 795
    white chocolate, 797
frozen foods. see also freezing
    bargains, avoiding, 910
    brunch, lunch, and supper dishes,
        95–113
    deep-fat frying, 1047–1048
    eggs, 923–924
    fish and shellfish
        thawing and cooking, 923
    flash freezing, commercial, 914
    food packages, 1033 (chart)
    freezers
        about, 911–912
        power outages, 918
    freezers, about
    fruit, 210–211, 914–915
        cranberries, 221
        high-altitude cooking, 245
        in pies, 675–676
        selecting jellies and preserves, 927
        serving, 918
        soups, 147
    game
        thawing and cooking, 923
    juice concentrates, 37
    meat
        thawing and cooking, 923
    phyllo, 674
    poultry
        thawing and cooking, 418–419,
            463, 923
    pressure cooking, 245
    quality in, 910
    refreezing, 914
    serving sizes, 10 (chart)
    shelf life of, 914
    soups, 122, 147

substitutions, healthy, 8 (chart)
thawing, 418–419, 914, 922–924
vegetables, 244–245
    cooking, 244–245, 922
    high-altitude cooking, 245
    thawing and cooking, 922
fruit(s), 208–239. see also specific fruits
    baked
        additions to, 213–214
        blanching, 208–209
        brown betty, 692
        brûlé, 214
        buckle, 691
        butter, 936
            microwaved, 937
        cakes. see fruitcakes
        candied or glacéed, 211
        canned, 210–211
            canning process, 893–896
        chocolate bark, fruited, 859
        clafouti, 695
        cobbler with berries, 693
        cooked
            about, 212
            spiced syrup, 212
        crisp, 692
        crostata, 697
        crunch, 692
        custard sauce, 846
        dried. see dried fruit
        flambéed, 215
        fool, cooked, 210
        fresh, 208–210
            about, 208–210
            antibrowning solution for,
                209–210
            buying and selecting, 208
            compote, baked, 213
            cups, 172, 210
            fool, 210
            macédoine of, 210
            peeling, 208
            ripening shipped, 208
            seasonal guide to, 209
            soufflé, 810
            spiced syrup, 212
            tart, 681
            washing, 208
        fritters, 658–659
        frozen, 210–211
            freezing process, 914–918
            thawing and serving, 918
        galette, 697
        gelatin, 812
        glaze, 800
        grilled or broiled, 214–215
            about, 214
            kebabs, 214
        and honey glazed roast duck, 448
        jellies, 878
        kefir, 40
        in lemon gelatin, 811
        milk shake, 40
        mousse, frozen, 841
        in orange gelatin, 811
        party platters, 78–79
        pastries, about, 690
        plugged, 64
        poached, 212–213
        puréed, 215
            canning, 895
            freezing, 918
            garnishes for, 215

fruit(s) *(cont.)*
salads. *see* fruit salad
salsa, 572
sauce. *see* fruit sauce(s)
sautéed
lychees, 214, 216
with meat, 214–215, 216
serving size, 10
sodas, 39
soup, winter, 147–148
substitutions for, 209
syrup, 43
toppings or fillings for pizza or
calzones, 190
tropical exotic, 238–239
turnovers, 696
whipped cream filling with,
755
whips, 813–814
wintering over, 886–887
fruitcakes, 725–727
Cockaigne, 725–726
dark, 726–727
fruit juice
canning, 896–897
freezing, 918
juices and beverages, 37–39
fruit leather, 909
fruit pies, 675–682. *see also specific*
fruits
about, 675–676
baking, 676
canned fruit in, 676
filling, 675–676
freezing, 676
frozen fruit in, 676
glazes, 800
suggestions for, 676
thickeners, 675–676
fruit platters, 70
about, 77–78
fruit punch, 42
for 50 people, 42
strawberry, 42
fruit salad, 169–170, 210
about, 169
ambrosia, 210
dressings for, 578
gelatin, 175
mayonnaise for, 581
winter, 224
fruit sauce(s), 845
about cooked, 844
Damson, jellied, 942
jellied, 942
uncooked (coulis), 853
frying. *see* deep-frying; panfrying;
sautéing; stir-frying
fudge. *see also* hot fudge
cake
chiffon, 710
high-altitude, 749
candy, 862–864
chocolate frosting, 791–792
pie, 686
Fuerte avocados, 218
fugu, 413
Fuji apples, 215
Fumé Blanc, 46
fumet, 118–119
fusilli pasta, **321**
Fuyu persimmons, 233
fuzzy navel, 63

G
gadwall duck, 455
Gala apples, 215
galangal, 987
galantine of turkey, 446
galette, fruit, 697
gallinules, 459
Gambel's quail, 459
game, 523–531. *see also specific meats*
brining and dry-curing, 904
buying, 523
cooked marinade for, 585
cooking, 524
field-dressing, 524
freezing, 922–923
large, 527–531
preparing, 523–524
stock, 118
thawing and cooking, 923
wild rice dressing for, 540
game birds, small. *see also specific game*
birds
about, 459
braised, 460
broiled, 460
roasted, 460
skewered, 460
ganache
about, 795
chocolate sauces, 36, 847
filling
mocha, 759
whipped, 759
for hot chocolate, 36
truffles, dark chocolate, 858
garam masala, 987
garbanzo beans, 254
garbure (bean soup with vegetables), 131
garden cress, 153
garlic, 155, 276–277, **1003**, 1003–1004
about, 276–277
as addition to green salads, 157–158
bread, 641
broccoli rabe, braised, 261
butter, 559
catsup, red onion-, 952
cheese spread, 76
chicken
baked chili, 426
chicken, broiled with lemon, 427
chicken with 40 cloves of, 425
stir-fried, 439–440
chile spice paste, 589
egg noodles with bread crumbs and,
330
flan, roasted, 207
greens sautéed with, 278
herb paste, Mediterranean, 589
mayonnaise
aïoli, 581–582
with potatoes, 582
red pepper (rouille), 582
pizza, white, with fresh clams and, 192
roasted, 277
muffins, 635
Parmesan cheese spread, 76
salad dressing, 575
soup, 125
sauce with walnuts, 568–569
soup
with eggs (sopa de ajo), 124–125
with roasted garlic, 125
vinegar, 1025

garlic chives, 155, 1004, **1005**
garnish(es)
citrus, 55, 971, **971**
cookie, 760
drinks, alcoholic, 55
fritter, 151
ice cream, 831
juice and fruit beverage, 37
party tray, 70
pureed fruits, 215
soup, 150
spinach, 305
gaufrettes (ice cream cones), 780
gazpacho, 146–147
Becker blender, 147
white, 147
gefilte fish, 401–402
gelatin, 987–988
cherry marshmallow nut, 812
chocolate mousse with, 816
fruit, 812
lemon, 811
fruit molded into, 811
mixing, 988
molded salads, 173–176
orange, 811
fruit molded into, 811
pineapple, 811–812
quick fruit, 812
raspberry tea, 812
stained glass, 812
gelatin desserts, 810–814. *see also* snows;
whips; *specific gelatins*
about, 810–811
fruit selection for, 810
preparing, 810
uncooked egg whites in, 810
unmolding and serving, 811
gelato
about, 834
chocolate hazelnut, 834
hazelnut, 834
genips, 239, **239**
Génoise, 709
chocolate, 709
sheet cakes, 736
geoduck clams, 374
geraniums, 988
German cuisine
almond torte Cockaigne (mandeltorte),
727
apple and horseradish sauce, 566
apple strudel, 673
Black Forest cake, 733
braised red cabbage, 264
breaded veal cutlets (Wiener schnitzel),
487
buttermilk dumplings (butterklosse),
335
drei augen, 779
frankfurter oblaten, 780
fresh egg noodles, 325
fresh fruit kuchen, 691
German-fried potatoes, leftover, 300
German hot dog, 185
German pancake (pfannkuchen), 652
German potato salad, 168
himmel und erde, 313
hot slaw, 184
kolatchen, 612
Lebkuchen (German honey bars), 765
lightning cake (blitzkuchen), 722
paprika schnitzel (or cutlet), 487

Pennsylvania Dutch egg noodles, 325
potato dumplings (kartoffelklosse), 335
rote grutze, 821
Rouladen, 483
sauerbraten, 478
sauerkraut, 265
Schneken, 613
sour cream apple cake soufflé
    Cockaigne, 810
spätzle, 335
springerle, 775
stollen, 622
uncooked hot mustard, 1000
Weiner schnitzel a la Holstein, 487
German dog, 185
Gewürztraminer, 47
ghee, 557, 963
gherkins
    pickled (cornichons), 946–947
    sweet-and-sour spiced, 946
gianduja (chocolate hazelnut gelato), 834
giblets, 444
    bread stuffing with, 534
    gravy, 546–547
    roast stuffed goose with, 450–451
Gibson, 56
gimlet, 56
gin
    cocktails and drinks, 55–57, 59
    pheasant braised with juniper and, 457
ginger, 988–989
    almond cream cheese spread, 179
    candied, 881
    dressing
        Japanese steakhouse, 575
        lemongrass, 575
    fig compote with lemon and, 227
    freezing, 917
    fruit filling, 758
    jam, golden cherry tomato and, 936
    marmalade, 941–942
    and orange sauce, 549
    pickled, 952
        grilled tuna with soy sauce, wasabi
            and, 405
    scones, 641
    soup with melon, 148
    soy sauce, 571
    -soy vinaigrette, grilled whole red
        snapper with, 403
    spice, baked chicken, 426
    spice paste, Asian, 589
    thins, 770
    vinegar, 1025
gingerbread, 724
    Guy Fawkes Day cake, 724
    high-altitude, 752
    house, 781–783, **782**
    men, 773, **773**
gingersnaps, 767
girolle mushrooms, 281
glassware, 12, **12,** 13
    for beer, **52**
    for cocktails and party drinks, 54, **55**
    frosting of, 55
    for wine, **53**
glazes
    about, 582
    applied after baking, 799
    applied before or during baking, 799
    apricot, 800
    bittersweet chocolate, 796
    bourbon, 583

brown sugar, 583
caramel, for custard, 804
chipotle pepper, 583–584
chocolate ganache, 796
    about, 795–796
clear caramel, 800
cranberry, 583
French egg wash, 799
fruit, 800
    thickened, 800
for fruit pies, tarts, and coffee cakes,
    800
ham, 582
honey, 583, 799
lemon, 799
liqueurs, 799
marmalade, 583
meat, 117
milk, 799
mocha, 797
mustard, 583
orange molasses, 583
peach, 800
pineapple, 583
raspberry, 800
reduction, 116
rum-brown sugar, 583
savory, 582
strawberry, 800
translucent sugar, 799–800
globe onions, 286
glögg, 67
gluten, 318, 923
gluten flour, 923
gnocci, **321**
    potato, 335
goat, 509
    about wild, 529–530
    Jamaican curried, 509
    roast mountain, 530
goat cheese
    dressing, 577
    marinated, with fresh thyme, 77
    and mesclun, baked, 160–161
    quiche with tomato and, 109
    and walnut soufflé, 205
    watermelon and, 230
    white pizza with portobello mushrooms
        and, 192
gohan (Japanese rice), 359
golden delicious apples, 215
golden-eye duck, 455
golden glow salad, 175
golden syrup, 989
golden trout, 417
Goldgelber, 154
gold screen filters, 28
Good King Henry, 154, **154**
goose, 418, 450–451. see also poultry for
        general information
    about, 450
    confit, 451
    roasting
        about, 447
        stuffed, with giblet gravy, 450–451
    scalding, 450
    stuffing, 450
gooseberry(ies)
    about, 222
    chutney, 222
    freezing, 917
    jam, 935
    jelly, black raspberry and, 932

gorgonzola
    cheese course, 827
    Mornay sauce (cheese sauce), 551
    pasta, addition to, 322
    on pizza, 191
    salads
        endive and walnut salad, 160
        pear, walnut and endive, 170
gougères, 91
goulash
    Hungarian (pirkilt), 480–481
grades of meat, 462–463, 509
grain(s), 344–368. see also specific grains
    breakfast cereals and, 346
    buying and storing, 344, 346
    combining, 345
    flavoring, 345
    preparing, 345, 364–368 (chart)
    presoaking, 344–345
    refined, substitutions for, 8
    reheating, 346
    salads, 171, 347, 361, 362, 363
    serving, 346
    serving size, 10
    sprouting, 1011–1012
    toasting, 345
    whole, as substitutes, 8
grains of paradise, 989
Grana Padano cheese, 322
Grand Marnier
    soufflé, 809
    souffléd omelets, 203
    soufflé, frozen, 842
granita, 838–839
    berry, 839
    caffè latte, 839
    espresso, 839
    lemon, 839
    lime, 839
    pink grapefruit, 839
Granny Smith apples, 215
granola, 353
    breakfast smoothie, 40
    three-grain apple cinnamon, 353
Granos onions, 286
grape(s)
    about, 227–228
    -beet-carrot juice, 39
    canning, 895
    crystallized, 881
    freezing, 917
    jam
        with pear, naturally sweetened,
            936
        seedless red, 935
    jelly, 932
    juice, canning, 897
    pickled, 228
    pie, Concord, 680
    sausages and, 228
    types, 227–228
grapefruit
    about, 225–226
    broiled, 226
    canning, 896
    cups, chilled, 226
    granita, pink grapefruit, 839
    herb margarita, 62
    juice, canning, 897
    -pineapple juice, 38
    sorbet, pink grapefruit, 836
    spinach salad with avocado, orange
        and, 159–160

grapefruit (*cont.*)
  sweetened, 226
  types, 225–226
grape leaves
  stuffed (dolmas), 82, **82**
grappa, 62
grasshopper, 63
graters, 542
gratinéing, 1056
Gravenstein apples, 216
gravlax (cured salmon), 411
gravy, 546–549
  about, 546
  giblet, 546–547
  herb, 547–548
  meat, 546
  with orange, rosemary and leeks, 548
  poultry, 546
  quick turkey, 547
  red wine and sour cherry, 548–549
  sausage, for biscuits, 547
  sweet-sour orange, 548
  for wildfowl, 547
grayling, 413
gray sole, 414
Great Northern beans, 254
  dip with rosemary and garlic, 73
  soup, Mediterranean white bean, 133
Greek cuisine
  baklava, 675
  feta dressing, 576
  Greek salad, 159
  gyro sandwich, 188
  lamb kebabs, 494
  lemon egg sauce (avgolemono sauce), 561
  lemon soup (avgolemono), 124
  moussaka, 274
  pastitsio, 336
  phyllo cups, 675
  potato garlic mayonnaise (skordalia), 582
  spinach and feta triangles, 89
  stuffed grape leaves (dolmas), 82
  tzatsiki, 567
Greek menus, 22
green(s). *see also* salad green(s); *specific types*
  about cultivated, 277
  Asian, and whole herbs, 158
  black-eyed peas and, 256–257
  canning, 900
  deribbing, 245, **245**
  freezing, 920
  lentil soup with, 134
  mixed, with cheese crisp, 159
  sautéed with garlic, 278
  shellfish stew with mushrooms and, 369–370
  soup
    Caribbean callaloo, 141
    greens for, 150–151
    Portuguese, 139
  Southern-style, 277–278
  wild, 156, 278–279
  wilted, 160
    spinach, 305–306
    tagliatelle with, 328
  young leafy, 154–155
green bean(s), 250–251
  additions to, 251
  casserole, 251
  marinated, 78

  with onions, tomatoes and dill, 251–252
  potatoes, and smoked meat, 251
green cabbage, **153**
green chiles, 291
greengage plums, 235
green garlic, 276
green goddess dressing, 576
green leaf lettuce, 152, **152**
green onions, 286
green pea(s), 290–291
  soup, 130
green posole, 351
green salad, 158
green tea, 33
  ice cream, 832
gremolata, 989
grenadine, 980
greyhound, 58
griddle breads, 631
griddle cakes, 644
grilling, 1057–1059
  chicken, 427
  equipment, 1057
  fruit, 214
  indirect (grill-roasting), 1059
  meat, 467
  roasting, 1059
  safety tips, 1058–1059
  skewer cooking, 1049. *see also* kebabs
  vegetables, 243–244
Grimes Golden apples, 216
grinders
  coffee, 29–30, **30**
grissini (bread sticks), 620
grits
  about, 349
  baked cheese, 350
  barley, 346
  low country cream-style, 350
  preparing, 365 (chart)
  shrimp and, 350
  souffléd cheese, 350
groats
  oat, 353
grog, 61
ground beef, 509–510. *see also* hamburgers; meatballs
  labeling and grades of, 509
  meat loaf, 511–512
    sandwich, 183
  with potatoes and spices (keema alu), 515
  samosas with, 89–90
  tacos, 188–189
ground cherries, 238
ground round, 509–510
groupers, 413
grouse, 418, 458–459
  baked marinated, 458–459
  roasted, 458
    sharptail, 459
  types, 458–459
grunts
  about, 693
  blackberry raspberry, 694
guacamole, 72–73
guajillo peppers, 292
guava(s)
  about, 228
  freezing, 917
  jelly, 932
  in light rum syrup, 228

guest participation
  menus with, 26
guinea hen, 418, 451
  roast, with chile butter, 451–452
gum
  paste, 882
  tragacanth, 989
gumbo
  chicken, 136
  seafood, 141
Guy Fawkes Day cake, 724
gyro sandwich, Becker, 188

H
habanero peppers, 291
Hachiya persimmons, 233
haddock, 414
hake, 414
halal meat, 463
half and half, 973
Half Moon hummus, 74
Half Moon pomosa, 53
halibut, 414
halvah, 878
ham. *see also* pork
  about, 506
  baked, 507
  biscuits, 87–88
  cabbage, potatoes and, 263
  cakes with pineapple and sweet potatoes, 106
  and corn fritters, 659
  country, 507
  crêpes with spinach, 650
  desalting, 506
  dry-cured, 904
  glazing, 582
  loaf, 106
  roast fresh, 499–500
  salad, 164
  sandwich, 178
    deviled, 180
  size and shape, 506
  soufflé with cheese, 204
  steak
    broiled, 507–508
    country, with red-eye gravy, 508
  and vegetable strata, 98
hamachi, 415
hamburger pie, 101
hamburgers, 510. *see also* ground beef
  about, 509
  barbecue, 510
  Becker, 510
  Becker buffalo, 531
  cheeseburgers, 510
  chili, 510
  chutney turkey, 445
  patty melt, 510
  sloppy Joe, 510–511
  venison, 528
Hamburg parsley, 289, 1005
ham dressing
  for turkey, 535
ham hocks, 507
hand-held immersion blender, 122, **122**
hand-held mixer
  for cake batters, 699
hangtown fry, 202
hard-boiled eggs, 194
  Easter eggs, coloring, 207
hard clams, 374
hard roe, 416

hard sauce, 851
about, 851
brown sugar, 851
fluffy, 851
hard-shell clams, **374,** 374–375
hard-shell crabs, 379–380
boiled, 381
cleaning, 379, **380**
poached, 381
hare
about, 525
jugged (hasenpfeffer), 525–526
haricots verts, 250
harissa, 569–570, 989
Hartshorn, 958
harvest preserves, 938
Harvey wallbanger, 58
hasenpfeffer (jugged hare), 525–526
hash, 107–108
about, 107
beef
with gravy, old-fashioned, 108
roast, 107
chicken chili, with sweet potatoes, 108
corned beef, 107
red flannel, 485
heavenly, 880
lamb, with gravy
old-fashioned, 108
pork, Becker, 108
turkey chili, with sweet potatoes, 108
Hass avocados, 218
hazelnuts, 989
asparagus with orange and, 250
chocolate gelato, 834
chocolate torte, 728
custard filling, 758–759
gelato, 834
semifreddo, 841
head cabbage, 262
heart, 518
about, 520
baked stuffed, 520–521
hearth cooking methods, 1059–1061,
1061
hearts of palm, 288–289
salad, 167
hearty meat ragù, 101
heat diffuser, 1062, **1062**
heavy cream, 973
heirloom potatoes, 294
herb(s), 155, 989–992
-and-cheese-filled souffléd omelets,
203
beef stew with mustard, white wine
and, 480
broiled fish fillets with, 404
broiled fish fillets with tomatoes and,
406
butter sauce, 558
drying, 991
fresh
béarnaise sauce, 561
chiffonade, 989
drying, 991
fettuccine with, 326
field salad with, 158
vinaigrette, 572
garlic paste, Mediterranean, 589
grapefruit margarita, 62
gravy, 547–548
green, mayonnaise with, 580
growing, 989–991, **990**

harvesting, 991
harvesting, drying, and freezing,
991
in jellies, 933
lemonade or limeade, 41
muffins, 635
pasta, 324
paste, Moroccan (charmoula), 589–590
pork sausage, 516
in salad, 155
salsify with, 304
for soups, 150–151
squash blossoms stuffed with cheese
and, 309–310
syrup, 43
toppings or fillings for pizza or
calzones, 191
using, 992
vinegar, 1025
whole, Asian greens and, 158
yogurt dressing, 577
herbal teas (tisanes)
about, 35
iced hibiscus, 35
herb dressing
green, for fish, 536–537
green, for poultry, 536–537
herbes de provence, 993
herb garden, at Cockaigne, **990**
herb vinegar, 1024
hermits, 770
herring, 414–415, 416
and apples, 412
marinated, on toast, 87
salad, 165
salt, potatoes and, 412
hibiscus iced tea, 35
hickory nut(s), 992
high-altitude cooking and baking
(watch for ▲ symbol)
baking powder in baking, 958–959
baking soda in baking, 627, 959
beating egg whites in baking, 747
biscuits, 638
boiling point of water, 790, 1056
bread, 594, 596
cakes, 746–747
carrot, 750
chocolate angel, 748
chocolate sponge roll, 752–753
classic 1–2–3–4, 747–748
coconut angel, 748
cooling and unmolding, 747
flour used in, 746
fudge, 749
general adjustment guidelines,
747
gingerbread, 752
leavening gases in, 746
peach-pecan upside-down, 751
sour cream streusel coffee,
751–752
spice, 750
sponge, 750
storing, 746
two-egg, 749–750
white, 748–749
canning, 888, 891
cookies, 761
corn breads, 631–632
cornstarch in, 1016
cupcakes, 747
deep-fat frying, 657, 1048

doughnuts, 654
dried legumes, 254
evaporation point in, 746
frittered foods, 657
general adjustment guidelines, 747
ingredient preparation, 746
jellies and preserves, 930
maple syrup, 995
packaged cake mixes, 702–703
pancakes, 643
pans and pan preparation, 746–747
pies, 662
pressure-cooking, 1054
quick breads, 627
rising of dough, 594
roasting, 462, 1046
steamed puddings, 824
storing goods, 746
testing for doneness, 747
vegetables, 245
waffles, 646
yeasts for, 594
highball, 59
highball glasses, 54, **55**
History of *Joy of Cooking*
1931 edition, 1–2
1936 edition, 1
1943 wartime edition, 1, 102, 766
1946 edition, 2
1950's work on JOY, 2
1963 edition, 2
1975 edition, 2, xi
1997 edition, 3
2006 anniversary edition, 3, xii-xiii
Becker, Ethan, 3
Becker, John (husband of Marion), 2
Becker, Marion Rombauer, 1–3
Becker, Mark, 3
Becker, Susan Cope, 3
Child, Julia, ix, xi
Cockaigne, 2
Gourmet revolution, 2
Green, Maggie, xi-xii
Half Moon, xvii
Hunstein, Elsa and family, xi
Rombauer, Irma von Starkloff, 1–2
Streamlined Cooking, 101
hoisin sauce, 992
broiled scallops with, 387
broiled shrimp with, 387
grilled scallops with, 387
grilled shrimp with, 387
holding
of food, 1065
holiday dinners
menus for, 19–21
hollandaise sauce, 560–561
hominy
about, 348–349
baked, 350–351
preparing, 365 (chart)
homogenization
of milk and cream, 996
honey, 992–993
apples, 216
bars, German, 765
bran waffles, 647
butter, 179, 850
-butter toast, 642
cake, 724–725
dipped doughnuts, 656
dressing for fruit salad, 578
and fruit glazed roast duck, 448

honey (*cont.*)
  glaze, 799
    for meat, 583
    for onions, 583
  grilled bananas, 218–219
  mustard
    dipping sauce, 566
    vinaigrette, 573
  nut bread, 627
  poppy seed dressing, 574
  shrimp, baked, 84
  yogurt dip, 78
honeydew melons, 230
hoppin' John, 356
horehound, 993
horned melons, 239
horns of plenty mushrooms, 281
hors d'oeuvres. *see* appetizers and hors
    d'oeuvres
horseradish, 993
  and apple sauce, Bavarian, 566
  carrot, and apple salad, 167
  cream, 565
  cream, Russian, 581
  dressing, creamy, 578
  pickled, 952–953
  sauce, 552
  tomatillo sauce, 568
  vinaigrette, 573
horse's neck, 59
hot-and-sour soup, 131–132
hot chocolate
  ganache for, 36
  quick, 36
  spiced, 36
hot cocoa, 35–36
hot dogs, 185
hot fudge
  ice cream sundae, 840
  sauce, 847–848
hot pepper jelly, 933
hot slaw, 161–162
hot toddy, 60
household beef stock, 117
household poultry stock, 118
Hubbard squash, 307
huevos rancheros, 196
hulled barley, 346
hull-less barley, 346
hummus (chickpea and tahini dip), 74
  Half Moon, 74
Hungarian partridge, 458
hurricane glasses, 54, **55**
hush puppies, 633
hyssop, 155, 993

I

ice
  about, 55
  cubes, decorative or flavored, 37
  mold, decorative, 65
iceberg lettuce, 152, **152**
  cleaning, 156
icebox cakes
  lemon, 730–731
  strawberry, 731
icebox cookies, 776–777
ice cream. *see also* gelato; ice milk; yogurt,
    frozen
  about, 828
  additions to, 831
  apricot, 833
  blackberry, 834

butter pecan, 833
cake rolls, 830
caramel, 832
chocolate, 832
coconut, 833
coffee, 832
cones (gaufrettes), 780
drinks recipes, 39–40
flavoring techniques for, 828
float, 39
freezing techniques for, 828
French vanilla, 831
garnishes, 831
green tea, 832
mango, 833
marbelized, 829
mint chocolate chip, 831
nectarine, 833
parfaits
  about, 839
  berry, 839–840
  chocolate, vanilla and coffee, 839
  winter, 840
peach, 833
peppermint stick, 832
Philadelphia-style *vs.* French-style, 828
pie, 830–831
pistachio, 832–833
pumpkin spice, 833
raspberry, 834
to ripple, 829–830
rocky road, 832
rum raisin, 832
sandwiches, 830
serving, 829
soda, 39
storing, 829
strawberry, 833–834
sundae, hot fudge, 840
vanilla, 831
ice cream makers, 828–829
ice cream scoop, 829
iced chocolate, 37
iced coffee, 32–33
iced tea, 34–35
  with alcohol/mock tea
    Joy tea, 58
    Long Island, 46
    rum tea, 61
  with cold water, 35
  flavored, 35
  hibiscus, 35
  sweet Southern, 34
ice milk
  orange, 834
  pineapple, 834
ice pops, 838
ices, 838–839
ice wine (Eiswein), 50
icicle radishes, 303
icing
  applied before baking, 799
  applied before or during baking, 799
  baked, 797
  boiled, 789–791
    white, 790
  broiled, 797
  buttercream
    chocolate, 793
    classic, 792
    coffee, 793
    lemon, 793
    liquor-flavored, 793

    mocha, 793
    orange, 793
    praline or nut, 793
  chocolate coating for fluffy white, 790
  chocolate ganache and glazes, **795,**
    795–796
  coconut pecan, 794
  creamy decorative, 788–789
  crunchy almond toppings, 798–799
  of cupcakes, 788, **788**
  decorative, 785–788
  density of, 784
  equipment for, 784–785
  European chocolate, 796
  fluffy
    nut or coconut, 791
    raisin, 790
  fondant, 791
  for gingerbread house, 782–783
  hard-sauce topping, 797
  of layer cakes, 784
  luscious orange, 791
  meringue
    soft meringue toppings, 797–798
    Swiss meringue buttercream,
      792–793
  penuche, 794
  for piped filigree or writing, 787–788,
    788
  quick
    brown butter, 794
    butterscotch, 794
    chocolate butter, 794
    cookie, 800
    decorative, 789
    lemon, 793
    lemon, for cookies, 800
    maple, 794
    mocha, 793–794
    orange, 793
    white, 793
  raisin-nut, 790
  royal, 789
    with fresh egg whites, 789
    with powdered egg whites, 789
  seven minute
    seafoam, 790
    white, 790
  seven-minute
    lemon, 790
    orange, 790
  small cakes and cookies, 788
  twice-cooked, 788
  yields of, 785
Idaho potatoes, 294
Ida Red apples, 216
Indian cuisine
  apple or green tomato chutney, 951
  cauliflower and potato curry, 267
  chicken curry, 434
  chicken or turkey curry, 105
  coconut chicken curry, 431
  coconut rice, 357
  curried apricot chutney, 950
  curried chickpeas with vegetables, 257
  curry mayonnaise, 580
  curry powder and paste, 975
  curry sauce, 553
  dal, 258
  garam masala, 987
  ground beef with potatoes and spices
    (keema alu), 515
  lamb curry with tomato, 497

Madras curry powder, 975
mango lassi, 40
meat curry, 105
naan, 608
raita, 567
rice pilaf with basmati rice, 355
saag paneer, 306
somosas with ground beef, 89
somosas with potatoes and peas, 89
tandoori chicken, 428
tandoori marinade, 584
yogurt or buttermilk marinade, 585
Indian menus, 22
India pale ale (pale ale), 52
indoor cooking
    equipment for, 1061–1063
indoor grills, 1057
ingredients
    stocking basic, 884
insalata Caprese (tomato and mozzarella
    salad), 169
instant grits, 349
instant or quick-rise yeast, 1029
instant rice, 354
instant yeast, 591
invitations
    for formal dinners, 13
iodized salt, 1009
Irish coffee, 32
Irish moss, 1010
irradiation
    of food, 883
Italian cuisine
    almond macaroons, 771
    antipasto, 80
    apple galette or crostata, 697
    bagna cauda, 78
    beef braciole, 483
    boneless roast pork Florentine, 499
    braised veal shanks (osso bucco), 489
    bruschetta with tomatoes and basil, 88
    Campari cocktail, 57
    cappuccino, 31
    chicken cacciatore, 433
    chicken Parmigiana, 437
    cold veal in tuna sauce (vitello tonnato
        freddo), 486
    damson, Italian plum, or greengage
        preserves, 938
    eggplant parmagiana, 273
    eggplant relish (caponata), 275
    espresso, 31
    espresso granita, 839
    fava beans Roman-style, 253
    focaccia, 607
    fried artichokes, 248
    fritto misto, 243
    fruit galette or crostata, 697
    gelato, 834
    granitas, 838–839
    grappa, 62
    Italian bread stuffing, 533
    Italian cream cake, 714
    Italian meatballs, 513
    Italian tomato paste, 1021
    lemon granita, 839
        with biscotti, 774
    panettone (Italian Easter bread), 621
    panna cotta, 813
    Parmesan and egg soup (stracciatella),
        124
    pizza, calzone, and stromboli, 190–193
    poached figs in heavy syrup, 212

pork braised in milk, 501
pot roast (stracotto), 477
proscuitto, mozzarella, and basil panini,
    181
risotto Milanese, 360
Rombauer Italian rice (risotto), 354
sautéed veal cutlet (scaloppine), 486
shrimp scampi, 386
Soave wine, 46
spumoni, 842
squash blossoms stuffed with cheese
    and herbs, 309
tiramisu, 819
Tuscan beans, 255
veal marsala, 486
veal piccata, 486
veal saltimbocca, 486
zabaglione, 806
Italian meatballs, 513
Italian menus, 22
Italian parsley, 1005

J
jack fish, 415
jackfruit, 238
Jack O'Lantern mushrooms, 281
jalapeño peppers, 291
jam
    berry, 935
    blueberry, 934–935
    cake, Rombauer, 720–721
    cupcakes, 738
    filled souffléd omelets, 203
    five-fruit, Cockaigne, 935
    golden cherry tomato and ginger, 936
    grape and pear, naturally sweetened,
        936
    grape, seedless red, 935
    macaroon tarts, 779
    making, 934
    plum, 935–936
    spiced pear, with pineapple, 935
    strawberry, 934
Jamaican coffee, 32
Jamaican jerk chicken, 428
jambalaya
    chicken, 356–357
Japanese buckwheat noodles, 330–331
Japanese cucumbers, 272
Japanese cuisine
    beef and scallion rolls (negi maki), 83
    bonito flakes, 960
    burdock, 262
    cold soba noodles, 333
    daikon, 303
    dashi, 119
    dry crumbs (panko), 961
    edamame and carrot salad with rice
        vinegar, 167
    ginger soy sauce, 571
    grilled tuna with pickled ginger, soy
        sauce, and wasabi, 405
    kelp (kombu), 1010
    komatsuna, 155
    mirin, 1028
    miso, 998
    mizuna, 154
    moon viewing noodles, 333
    noodles in broth, 333
    noodles in dashi, 333
    pickled ginger, 952
    plain rice (gohan), 359
    rolled sushi (maki-zushi), 359

sake, 50, 1028
shichimi (seven-spice mix), 1012
shrimp, scallops, squid, clams, or
    oysters tempura, 377
shrimp tempura, 388
soba (buckwheat noodles), 330
soy sauce (shoyu), 1015
steakhouse ginger dressing, 575
sukiyaki, 476
sushi rice (shari), 359
tamari, 1015
tempura batter, 658
teriyaki grilled fish steaks, 405
teriyaki marinade, 586
tofu, 315
udon, 331
wasabi, 1026
wasabi soy sauce, 571
Japanese rice, 354
Japanese udon, 331
jar funnel, **890**
jar lifter, **890**
jars
    can-or-freeze, 912
jars, for canning
    cooling, 891–892
    preparing and packing, 890
    sealing and storing, 892
    selecting, 889
jasmine rice, 354
jellied soups, 127
    beet, 127
    tomato, 127
jellies and preserves, 927–942
    about, 927
    acid in, 928
    apricot, 937
    boiling in, 929
    canning, 930
    citrus fruit, 878
    equipment for, 927
    fig, 938
    freezing, 929–930
    fruit, 878
    high-altitudes preparation, 930
    jelling point, 929
    kumquat, 938
    making, 937
    nectarine, 937
    peach, 937
    pectin, 927–928
    pineapple and strawberry, 937–938
    plum, 938
    quince, 932–933, 938
    rhubarb and strawberry, 938
    selecting fruit for, 927
    steeping and plumping fruit for, 937
    storing, 929–930
    strawberry, 937
        and pineapple, 937–938
        and rhubarb, 938
    sugar and sweeteners in, 928–929
    tomato, 938
jelling point, 929
jelly
    apple, 932
    blackberry, 932
    black raspberry and gooseberry, 932
    cooking, 931
    currant, 931–932
    decorative touches for, 931
    doughnuts, 655
    grape, 932

jelly *(cont.)*
  guava, 932
  herb, 933
  hot pepper, 933
  juice extraction for, 930–931, **931**
  lemon, 934
  mint, 932
  paradise, 933
  plum, 933
  preparing fruit for, 930
  prickly pear, 934
  quince, 932–933, 938
  roll cake, 735–736
  scented, 933
  tots, 778–779
  troubleshooting, 931
jelly bag, 930–931, **931**
  butter, 931
jerky, 905
Jerusalem artichoke, 249
jicama, 279
  salad, 167–168
jiggers, two-sided, 54, **54**
johnnycakes, 633
Johnny Marzetti spaghetti pie, 95
Jonagold apples, 216
Jonathan apples, 216
JOY classics (JOY recipes 1931–1975)
  blender borscht, 149
  bourbon balls, 879
  brownies Cockaigne, 762
  burnt sugar cake, 719
  chicken Marengo, 433
  chicken tamale pie, 102
  chocolate cake, 717
  chocolate cake "Rombauer Special," 717
  chocolate chip cookies, 766–767
  chop suey or chow mein, 104
  club sandwich, 180
  country captain, 434
  egg drop soup, 124
  European chocolate icing, 796
  fluffy raisin or raisin-nut icing, 790
  gin cocktail, 56
  hamburger pie, 121
  lemon icebox cake, 730
  lightning cake (Blitzkuchen), 722
  mock mincemeat pie, 680
  mustard pickle (chow-chow), 947
  paradise jelly, 933
  peanut butter cookies, 767
  pecan or angel slices, 764
  pimento cheese, 179
  Rombauer borscht, 149
  Rombauer Italian ice, 354
  Rombauer Italian rice, 354
  Rombauer jam cake, 720
  sauerbraten, 478
  shrimp wiggle, 113
  steamed caramel pudding, 825
  strawberries Rombauer, 220
  white bread, 596
  yellow cucumber pickles, 945
Joy tea, 58
juices and fruit beverages, 6
  about, 37
  blended, 38–39
  canning, 896–897
  combinations, 38
  recipes for, 37–39
jujubes, 239, **239**

julienne vegetables, 241, **241**
jumbo shells
  baked, 339–340
juniper berries, 993
  pheasant braised with gin and, 457

K
kai, 37
kaki persimmons, 233
kale, **155,** 277
  freezing, 920
  and potato gratin, 278
kamikaze, 58
kamut, 362
  preparing, 365 (chart)
kartoffelklösse (potato dumplings), 335
kasha, 347. *see also* buckwheat
  bow ties with (kasha varnishkes), 347–348
  cabbage rolls stuffed with bulgur and, 348
  preparing, 366 (chart)
Katahdin potatoes, 294
kebabs
  about, 493–494
  beef, 494
  chicken, 427–428
  fish, 405
  fruit, 214
  lamb, 494
kedgeree, 412–413
keema alu (ground beef with potatoes and spices), 515
kefir, 1013
  fruit, 40
kelp (kombu), 1010–1011
Kelsey plums, 235
Kentucky burgoo, 484
Kennebec potatoes, 294
key limes, 224
  pie, 688
Khadrawy dates, 226
kid. *see* goat
kidney beans, 254
kidneys, 518
  about, 519
  pie, steak and, 483–484
  preparation for boiling, 519–520
  sautéed, with mustard, 520
kielbasa, 515
king crabs, 380
king mackerel, 415
king salmon, 416
kippered herring, 415
kir, 52–53
Kirby cucumbers, 282
kir royale, 53
kitchen safety. *see* cooking and kitchen safety
kiwanos, 239, **239**
kiwifruit, 228–229
  about, 228
  freezing, 917
  shrimp salad, 228
kneading
  yeast dough, 592–593, **593**
knife cuts
  about, 1071
  descriptions of, 1071
knives, 12, **12, 13**
  about, 1069–1071
  caring for, 1070
  handling, 1070, 1071

sharpening, **1070,** 1070–1071
  types of, 1069–1070
knucklebones, 518
kohlrabi, 279–280
  freezing, 921
kolatchen, 612
komatsuna, 155
kombu (kelp), 1010–1011
königsberger klops (German meatballs), 512
kosher meat, 463
kosher salt, 1009
koumiss, 1013
kreplach soup, 126, **126**
krumkakes, Scandinavian, 779–780, **780**
  almond, 780
  butter, 780
  lemon, 780
kuchen
  about, 690
  fresh fruit, 691
  quick coffee cake, 630
kugel
  mushroom walnut, 336–337
  sweet, 337
kugelhopf, 623, **623**
Kumamoto oysters, 371
kümmel, 63
kumquat(s), 225
  compote, 225
  preserves, 938

L
Labrusca grapes, 227
ladyfingers, 740
lamb, 489–497. *see also* meat *for general information;* sheep
  about, 489–490
  chops
    about, 492–493
    broiled, 493
    grilled, 493
    sautéed, 493
  curry with tomato, 497
  cuts of, 490, **490,** 492–493
  ground, patties, 511
  hash with gravy, old-fashioned, 108
  kebabs, 494
  leg
    broiled butterflied, 491–492
    carving, 490, **491**
    grilled butterflied, 491–492
    roast, 490–491
    stuffed butterflied, 491
  loin
    roasted, 492
  patties, Becker, 511
  rack of
    roasted, 492
  sandich, Becker gyro, 188
  shanks, braised, 495
  shepherd's pie, 102–103
  shoulder
    braised, 494–495
    braised stuffed, 495
  shoulder chops, braised, 493
  stews and braises
    about, 494
    stew (navarin printanière), 495–496
  stock, 118
lamb's lettuce, 152
langouste lobsters, 382

lapin à la moutarde (rabbit with mustard), 526
lard, 993
   seasoned (sofrito), 1013
larding
   about, 464
larding needles, 464
lardoons, **464,** 464–465
   preparing, 464
largemouth bass, 413
lasagne, **321,** 340
   Bolognese, 340
   roasted vegetable, 340–341
lassi
   mango, 40
lavender, 155, 993
lazy Susan, 785
leaveners, 993–994
lebkuchen (German honey bars), 765–766
leek(s), **1003,** 1004
   about, 280
   braised, 280
   creamy, 280
   freezing, 921
   pan sauce with orange, rosemary and, 548
   soup, potato, 130
   tart, 109
   vinaigrette, 280
   wild, 1004, **1005**
leftovers, 994
   breads, uses for, 641
   pasta, 322–323
   potatoes. see potato(es), leftover
   rice, uses for, 357
leftovers
   beans
      bean and rice cakes, 106
      bean burritos, 103
      veggie bean burgers, 107
   breads
      frittered foods, 657
      savory or sweet crêpes, 649
      uses for breads and crackers, 641–642, 960
      waffles, 646
   cans, 885, 998, 1098
   Champagne, 553
   chocolate, dark chocolate bark, 859
   eggs
      angel cake, 705
      letter cookies, 773
      soufflés, 203
   family meals, 16
   as fillings for omelets, 201
   fish
      fish loaf, 106
   grains
      fried rice, 357
      salads, 171
      spoon bread, 633
   meat and poultry
      beef or pork enchiladas, 104
      brown onion sauce (sauce Lyonnaise), 555
      burritos con carne, 104
      casseroles, 95–98
      chicken burritos, 104
      chicken chile verde, 435
      chicken enchiladas, 104
      chicken or turkey curry, 105
      chicken or turkey potpie, 103
      chop suey or chow mein, 104

corned beef, 484
creamed chicken or turkey, 445
croquettes, 659
enchiladas verdes, 104
ham cakes with pineapple and sweet potatoes, 106
ham loaf, 106
hash, 107–108
hot chicken salad, 106
hot roast beef sandwich, 182
Italian pot roast (stracotto), 477
meat curry, 105
sweet-and-sour pork, chicken, or turkey, 105
turkey, 442
turkey tetrazzini, 96
pasta
   about, 322–323
   baked dishes, 336–337
   fillings, 337
   frittata, 202
   salads, 171–172
   turkey tetrazzini, 96
reheating, 467, 1064, 1065
safety, 9, 1036
   in soups, 122, 148
   in stock making, 116–122
   thickeners for soups, 123
vegetables
   about, 245
   asparagus timbales, 206
   duchess potatoes, 300
   mashed potato stuffing, 537
   potatoes, 300–301
   puffed potatoes, 299
legume(s), dried, 253–259. see also bean(s), dried
   about, 253–254
   cooking, 253–254
Lemhi Russet potatoes, 294
lemon(s), 155, 224–225
   about, 224
   angel cake, 706
   Bavarian cream, 817
   broiled fish fillets with, 403–404
   buttercream icing, 793
   butter sauce (lemon beurre blanc), 558
   butter, with parsley, 559
   coconut layer cake, 712
   couscous with chicken, olives and, 363
   curd, 756
   curd bars, 765
   egg sauce (avgolemono sauce), 561–562
   fig compote with ginger and, 227
   filling, 756
   freezing, 917
   garlic chicken, broiled, 427
   gelatin, 811
      fruit molded into, 811
   glaze, 799
   granita, 839
   grilled chicken, 427–428
   icebox cake, 730–731
   icing
      for cookies, quick, 800
      quick, 793
      seven minute, 790
jelly, 934
krumkakes, 780
marinade, 584

meringue pie, 687
orange custard filling, 757
oregano vinaigrette, 573
pancakes, 646
and parsley butter (maître d'hôtel butter), 559
pie
   chiffon, 688–689
   meringue, 687
   Ohio Shaker, 687–688
poppy seed muffins, 635
poppy seed pound cake, 716–717
roll cake, 736–737
rosemary
   boar chops, 530
   chicken on skewers, 80
sabayon, 847
salt-preserved, 224–225
sauce
   clear, 844
   hot, 844
scones, 641
sherbet, 838
sole, 414
sorbet, 836
soufflé, 809–810
   cold, 817
soup, Greek (avgolemono), 124
sponge custards, 805
surprise, frozen, 830
syrup, 43, 759
tart, 688
lemonade
   herbed, 41
   old-fashioned, 40–41
   for 100 people, 41
   pink, 41
   quick, 41
lemon balm, 155, 994
lemongrass, 994
   ginger dressing, 575
lemon verbena, 994
lentil(s), 254, 257–258
   about, 257
   braised, with sausage, 258
   and potato salad, warm, 171
   puree, Indian (dal), 258
   and rice pilaf with toasted cumin seeds, 355
lentil soup, 134
   with greens, 134
   with sausage and potato, 134
lettuce
   braised, 281
   cooked, 281
   drying loose, 156
   salad greens, 152
   substitutes for, 155
lids and rings
   for canning, 889
light cream, 973
light veal stock, 117
lily buds, 994
lima beans, 250, 252–253
   mushrooms and, 252–253
lime(s)
   about, 224
   Bavarian cream, 817
   coconut salad, 226
   freezing, 917
   granita, 839
   marmalade, 941
   -orange juice, 38

lime(s) *(cont.)*
  pie
    about, 687
    chiffon, 688–689
    key lime, 688
  sauce
    clear, 844
    hot, 844
    Thai chile-lime dipping, 570
  sherbet, 838
  sorbet, 836
  soufflé, cold, 817–818
  syrup, 43
  types, 224
  vinaigrette, 573
    with parsley, 573
limeade
  herbed, 41
  old-fashioned, 40–41
  quick, 41
Limestone lettuce, 152
ling cod, 415
linguine
  with red clam sauce, 328
  with white clam sauce, 328
linzer hearts, 779
linzertorte, 696–697
liptauer cheese spread, 76
liqueur
  sabayon with orange, 847
liqueur(s)
  chocolate truffles with, 859
  cordial and liqueur cocktails, 63
  glaze, 799
  sauce, orange, 852
litchies. *see* lychees
littleneck clams, 374
liver, 518. *see also* chicken liver(s)
  about, 518
  calf's, sautéed, 518
  and onions, 519
  pâté maison, 518
  preparation for cooking, 518
lobster(s), 369, 382–385
  about, 382–383
  Americaine (Armoricaine), 384
  avocado cocktail, 371
  baked stuffed, 384
  bisque, 140
  boiled, 383
  broiled, 383–384
  butter, 559
  cocktail, 370
  grilled, 383–384
  imitation (surimi), 391
  killing without cooking, **383**
  live, storing, 382
  mousse, 176
  Newburg, 385
  poached, 383
  removing meat from, 383, **383**
  roll, 183
  salad, 165
    vinaigrette, 162
  steamed, 383
  thermidor, 384–385
  types, 382, **382**
  whole, 382–383
loganberries, 220
lollipops, 875
London broil, 474–475
longans, freezing, 917
long-grain rice, 354

Long Island duck, 446
Long Island iced tea, 61
longneck clams, 374
loose-leaf lettuce, 152
loosemeat sandwich, 510–511
loquats, 239, **239**
  canning, 895
  freezing, 917
lotte, 415
lotus root
  about, 281
  stir-fried, 281
lovage, 155, 994–995
lox
  bagels and, 184
lunch, 16–17
  formal, 17
  menus for, 23–24
  sit-down, 16–17
lychees
  about, 229
  sautéed, 229
Lynchburg lemonade, 60
Lyonnaise sauce (brown onion sauce), 555

M
macadamia(s), 995
  butter, curried, 179
  monsters, white chocolate, 767
macaroni
  and cheese
    baked, 326
    for a crowd, 326
    stovetop, 325–326
  salad
    calico, 172
    creamy, for a crowd, 172
macaroons
  almond, 771
  bombe, 843–844
  chocolate coconut, 771
  coconut, 771
  jam tarts, 779
mace, 1000
mâche, 152, **152**
mackerel, 415
Mackie, the, 112
Macoun apples, 215
Madeira sauce, 555
madeleines, 739
Madras, 58
madras curry powder, 975
Mad River oysters, 371
mahimahi, 415
mahogany clams, 374
main-course salads, 162–165. *see also*
    specific salads
mai tai, 61
maître d'hôtel butter (lemon and parsley
  butter), 559
maki-zushi (rolled sushi), 359–360
Mako shark, 416
Makrut limes, 224
Malbec, 49
mallards, 446, 455
mallets, 464
Malpeque oysters, 371
malt liquor, 52
malt syrup, 995
malt vinegar, 1024
mamoncillos, 239, **239**
Mandarin oranges, 225
mandelplättchen (almond pretzels), 774

mandolines, **295**
mango(es)
  about, 229
  and avocado salad, 166
  with cilantro, 229
  coulis, 853
  -cranberry punch, 41
  cucumbers and, 229
  freezing, 917
  green, canning, 895–896
  ice cream, 833
  lassi, 40
  -papaya batido, 40
  peeling and dicing, **229**
  sorbet, 836
mangosteens, 239, **239**
Manhattan, 59
Manhattan clam chowder, 142–143
manicotti
  baked, 339–340
Manila clams, 374
manioc, 315
maple
  crème brûlée, 804
  icing, quick, 794
  -roasted quail, spicy, 460
  sauce
    hot buttered, 852–853
  sugar, 1020
  walnut fudge, 863
maple syrup, 995–996
  making, 995–996
  pie, 684
  sap spout and bucket, **995**
  sauce, 850
marble slab, 854
  in tempering chocolate, 857–858
marc, 62
marchand de vin (mushroom wine sauce),
    555–556
Marcona almonds, 957
Marenne oysters, 371
margarine, 996
margarita, 62
  frozen, 62
  grapefruit herb, 62
margarita glasses, 54, **55**
marigolds, 996
marinade, 584–586
  about, 584
  Balkan, 585
  beer, 585
  buttermilk, 585
  chicken, Becker, 585
  cooked, for game, 585
  lemon, 584
  pork, Becker, 585–586
  red wine, 584
  storing, 584
  tandoori, 584–585
  teriyaki, 586
  timing of, 584
  for vegetables, 584
  yogurt, 585
marionberries, 220
marjoram, 155, 996
marlin, 415
marmalade
  bitter orange, 941
  four-citrus, 941
  ginger, 941–942
  glaze, 583
  lime, 941

making, 940–941
orange drops, 770–771
red onion, 567, 949
marrow, 306, 518
about, 522
and red wine sauce, 555
Marsala
veal, 486
marshmallows, 869–870
cherry nut gelatin, 812
sauce, 850
martini, 56
martini glasses, 54, **55**
marzipan, 877
about, 876
masa, 349
masa harina, 349
matchsticks vegetables, 241
matignon, 998
matjes, 415
matzo
almond flourless torte, 728
ball soup, 126
brei, 199
gefilte fish, 401–402
Passover sponge cake, 707
Maui onions, 286
mayonnaise, 578–581
about, 578–579
blender, 579
cake, chocolate, 718–719
chipotle, 580
cream (chantilly), 580
cream cheese, 580
curry, 580
flavored, 578–579
for fruit salad, 581
garlic, 581–582
with green herbs, 580
grilled salmon fillets with, 406
making, 579
mustard, 580
potato garlic, 582
safety, 168, 579
souffléd, 580–581
tomato and red pepper, 580
variations on store bought, 579
watercress, 581
yogurt, 579
May wine, 66
McIntosh apples, 215
meals, home-cooked
freezing, 925
measurements
conversion tables for, 1032–1036
measuring
about, 1031
in baking, 698
baking powder, 958
conversion tables
equivalents and conversions, 1032–1033
U.S.-British measures, 1032
dry crumbs, 960
dry ingredients, 1031
fats, 981
flour, 983
honey, 992
liquids, 1031
pan shapes, special, 701
salt, Kosher, 1009
sugars
brown, 1018–1019

liquid, 1018
solid, 1018–1019
tools, 1031
meat, 462–522. *see also* beef; lamb; pork;
veal
barbecuing, 467
basting, 466
bony cuts, 463
borscht with, 138
braising, 466, 467
brining, about, 904
broiling, 465
browning, 465, 467
chili with beans and, 513
curry, 105
cuts. *see* meat cuts
dry-curing, about, 904
dry-heat cooking methods, 463
en croûte cooking, 468
filling for stuffed pasta, 338
freezing, 922–923
fritter batter for, 658
frozen, thawing and cooking, 923
glaze, 117
honey glaze, 583
grades and buying, 462–463, 509
grass-fed, 463
gravy, 546
grilling, 467
grinding, 464
larding, 464–465
loaf. *see* meat loaf
macerating, 464
marinating, 463
mincing, 464
moist-heat cooking methods, 463
"natural" on label, 463
"organic" on label, 463
pan-broiling, 465
panfrying, 464
party platters, 70
pot-roasting, 466–467
pounding, 464
reheating cooked, 469–470
roasting, 465–466
roasting browned, 467
sautéed fruit with, 214–215, 216
sautéing, 465
seasoning, 463
serving sizes, 10, 463
smoked, green beans, potatoes and,
251
and spinach filling for stuffed pasta,
338
stewing, 466, 467
stocks, 114–115
storing cooked, 469
storing uncooked, 463
timing and doneness, 467–468
tomato sauce, 563–564
toppings or fillings for pizza or
calzones, 190
tough, cooking, 464
trimmed, 463
variety meats, about, 518
meatballs
about, 511–512
chicken, 445
cocktail, 82
German (königsberger klops), 512
Italian, 513
sandwich, 184
for soup, 151

Swedish, 513
with tomato sauce, 564
turkey, 445
meat cuts. *see also specific cuts and meats*
about, 470
bony, 463
economical use of large, 470
meat loaf, 512
about, 511–512
additions to, 512
sandwich, 183
meat pastries, 469
meat pie
toppings for, 469
Medjool dates, 226
medlars, 229
melba sauce, 845
Melogold grapefruit, 226
melon(s). *see also specific melons*
about, 229–230
baskets, 230, **230**
cups, 170
freezing, 917
-orange juice, 39
with prickly pear sauce, 236
prosciutto and, 230
soup, winter, 129
soup with ginger and, 148
substitutions for, 209
types, 230
melon baller, **229**
membrillo (quince paste), 236–237,
878–879
menus, 19–27
Asian, 22
backpacking, 26–27
breakfasts and brunches, 23
children's parties, 23
Christmas, 19
Cinco de Mayo, 20
cocktail parties, 22–23
cook for a day, eat for a week, 25
dinner for family and friends, 24
for dinner with family and friends,
24
Easter, 20
Eastern European, 22
for entertaining, 11, 13, 14
Father's Day, 20
formal dining, 13, 24
Greek, 22
with guest participation, 26
holiday dinners, 19–21
Indian, 22
informal dining, 14
Italian, 22
lunches, 23–24
Middle Eastern, 22
Mother's Day, 20
New Orleans, 22
New Year's Day, 20
New Year's Eve, 19–20
outdoor entertaining ideas, 21
for party platters, 23
Passover, 20
picnic, 21
special occasions, 21–22
St. Patrick's Day, 20
Super Bowl, 21
for supper and cooking clubs, 22
for Thanksgiving, 19
for 30-minute recipes, 25–26
for Valentine's Day, 20

menus (*cont.*)
   vegetarian, 21–22
   for wedding buffets, 21
meringue(s), 740–741
   application to pies, 798
   buttercream icing, Swiss, 792–793
   cocoa, 741
   coffee-flavored, 741
   dacquoise, 741
   floating islands, 805
   forming and baking, 740
   fresh strawberry, with whipped cream
      and chocolate, 741–742
   kisses, 771
      cocoa, 771
      nutty, 771
   lemon pie, 687
   mushrooms, 741
   paste, 740
   pie shell, 666
   powder, 977
   safety, 798
   storing, 740
   toppings, 797–798
   warm-method, 741
Merlot, 47
mesclun, 155
   baked goat cheese and, 160–161
Mexican dog, 185
Mexican/Tex-Mex cuisine
   bean burritos, 103
   black bean tacos, 189
   cheese enchiladas, 104
   cheese quesadillas, 77
   chicken and cheese tamales, 351
   chicken and rice (arroz con pollo), 435
   chicken chili verde, 20
   chicken enchiladas, 104
   chicken rice soup (asopao de pollo),
      135
   chicken, turkey, or beef tostadas with
      black beans, 189
   Cinco de Mayo menu, 20
   corn, tomato, and avocado salsa, 572
   corn tortillas, 609
   enchiladas verdes, 104
   flour tortillas, 608
   green posole, 351
   grilled fish tacos, 189
   grilled shrimp tacos, 189
   ground beef tacos, 188
   guacamole, 72
   hot sauce, 566
   huevos rancheros, 196
   pork enchiladas, 104
   refried beans (frijoles refritos), 254
   roasted cactus pad salad, 265
   roasted-tomato chipotle salsa, 572
   salsa fresca, 571
   shredded chicken tacos, 189
   shredded pork tacos, 189
   shrimp and avocado tostadas, 189
   shrimp fajitas, 190
   steak fajitas, 190
   tomatillo salsa (salsa verde cruda), 571
Mexican wedding cakes, 768
Meyer lemons, 224
mezcal, 61–62
mezzaluna, **991**
Michihli cabbage, 262
microgreens, growing, 1012
microwave cooking
   about, 1063–1065

bacon, 509
blanching, 919
cheese sauce, 551
chocolate
   melting, 970
   truffle centers, 858
fish, 402
fruit butter, 937
safety tips, 1064
toasting coconut, 972
vegetables, 243, 305
Middle Eastern cuisine
   baba ghanoush, 74
   braised lamb shanks, 495
   couscous stuffing with dried apricots
      and pistachios, 539
   couscous with chicken, lemon and
      olive, 363
   couscous with pine nuts and raisins,
      362
   falafel sandwich, 188
   harissa, 989
   hummus, 74
   Israeli couscous pilaf, 363
   lamb kebabs, 494
   Moroccan herb paste (charmoula), 589
   Moroccan-style vegetable stew, 246
   Persian rice, 357
   pita bread, 607
   pita salad (fattoush), 159
   ras el hanout, 1007
   rice pilaf, 355
   roasted rack of lamb with Moroccan
      spice rub, 492
   tabbouleh, 362
Middle Eastern menus, 22
milk. *see also* buttermilk
   about, 996
   almond, 1022
   bread, 597
   condensed, flan with, 803
   dry, 997
   freezing, 924
   glaze, 799
   homogenization, 996–997
   nut, 1022
   pasteurization, 996–997
   pork braised in, 501
   scalding, 997
   sour, 1013–1015
   soy, 1023
   steaming, 31
   substitutions for, 996
      sour milk, 1014–1015
   types, 997–998
milk shake, 39
   flying mocha monkey, 40
   fruit, 40
milk toast, 146
milkweed pods, sautéed, 279
mille-feuille (Napoleon), 670–671
millet
   about, 352
   cakes with Parmesan and dried
      tomatoes, 352–353
   preparing, 366 (chart)
milt, 416
mimosa, 53
mincemeat, 902
   filled cookies, 778
   pie, mock, 680
minerals, 6
   on food labels, 8

miner's lettuce, 154, **154**
minestrone, 128
Minneola oranges, 225
mint, 155, 998
   chocolate chip ice cream, 831
   chocolate sauce, 848
   jelly, 932
   julep, 60
   pulled, 871
   sauce, 565
Mirabelles plums, 235
mirepoix, 998
mirliton, 269
miso, 998
miso soup, 125
   Becker quick, 125
Mission figs, 227
Mississippi mud cake, 723
mitsuba, 155
mixed pickling spice, 944
mixed starters, 601
   about, 601, 602
   white bread made with, 605
   whole wheat bread made with, 605
mixers. *see also* blenders
   for cake batters, 699–700
   creaming butter with, 700
   electric, 662, 699
   hand-held, 699
   for kneading bread dough, 593
   for mixing bread dough, 592
   pastry dough, 662
mizuna, 154, **154**
mocha
   buttercream icing, 793
   filling, 756
   flying mocha monkey, 40
   frosting, 797
   ganache filling, 795
   glaze, 797
   ice cream cake, 731
   icing, quick, 793–794
   truffles, 859
   whipped cream, 755
mock turtle soup, 138
mohrenköpfe (Moors' head cake),
      731–732
moist-heat cooking methods, 1049–1054
mojo, 566
moka pots, 29, **29**, 31
molasses, 998–999
   cookies, Moldow, 770
   crisp, Cockaigne, 777
   orange glaze, 583
      Buffalo rib roast with, 531
   pie, shoofly, 683
   pomegranate, 236
   thins, Moravian, 773
molded salads, 173–176
mole
   red, 549–550
      turkey in, 444
mollusks, 369
Mongolian hot pot, 137
monkfish, 415
monosodium glutamate (MSG), 999
monounsaturated fats, 5
monsteras, 238, **238**
Monte Cristo, 181
Montmorency cherries, 223
mooli radishes, 303
moo shu
   tempeh, 317

mops, mopping sauce. *see also* barbecue
    sauce
    about, 586
    basic, 587
    beer, 587
Moravian molasses thins, 773
Morello cherries, 223
morel mushrooms, 282
Mornay sauce, 551
mortar and pestle, **991**
Moscow mule, 58
Mother's Day
    menus for, 20
moulard duck, 447
Mountain quail, 459
mountain spinach, 154
moussaka, 274–275
mousse
    about, 814
    cake, chocolate, 729–730
    chocolate, 816
    frozen fruit, 841
    frozen raspberry, 840–841
    frozen strawberry, 840–841
    savory, 175–176. *see also* timbales
        chicken liver, 81
        cucumber, 176
        lobster, 176
        salmon, 85
    serving and presenting, 814–815, **815**
mousseline sauce, 561
mozzarella
    marinated, 77
    panini with prosciutto, basil and, 181
    pizza with tomato sauce and, 191
    sticks, fried, 77
    and tomato salad, 169
MSG (monosodium glutamate), 999
muddlers, muddling, 54, **54,** 55
mudslide, 63
muesli, 353
muffin(s), 634–637
    about, 634
    additions to, 634–635
    apple walnut, 636
    banana nut, 636
    blueberry, 635
    bran, 635–636
    cheese, 636
    cheese popovers, 637
    corn bread, 632
    double chocolate, 636–637
    English, 618
        pizza, 182
    herb, 635
    lemon poppy seed, 635
    popovers, 637
    pumpkin, 635
    roasted garlic, 635
    sour cream, 635
    storing, 634
    sweet potato, 635
    whole wheat, 635
muffuletta, 181–182
mulato chiles, 292
mulberry(ies)
    about, 222
mullet, 415
mulligatawny soup, 136
multivitamins, 6
mung bean sprouts, 253
muscadine grapes, 227–228
Muscovy duck, 447

musellunge, 415
mushroom(s), 281–284. *see also specific*
    mushrooms
    about, 281–282
    amaranth with, 346
    broiled stuffed
        caps, 284
        Cockaigne, 78–79
    broth, 121
    brown rice baked with, 355
    canning, 900
    catsup, 952
    chicken breasts baked on a bed of,
        425–426
    creamed, 283
        on toast, 112
    deep-fried, 284
    dressing with rice, 540
    drying, 999
    duxelles, 284
    filling for stuffed pasta, 337–338
    freezing, 921
    grilled, 283
    lima beans and, 252–253
    marinated, 78
    meringues, 741
    peas and, 290
    pizza
        with peppers, onion and, 191
        portobello, Becker, 282
        with sausage, pepperoni and, 191
        with sun-dried tomatoes, grilled
            eggplant and, 191
    ragout, 283–284
    risotto with, 361
    "risotto" with barley, 347
    sauce
        chicken breasts sautéed with, 437
        quick, 557
        wine sauce (marchand de vin),
            555–556
    sauerkraut filling for pierogi, 342
    and sausage strata, 98
    sautéed, 283
        wild rice with, 363
    as seasoning, 999
    soufflé, 205
    soup
        with barley, 131
        cream of, 144–145
        quick cream of, 149
        with scallion, 145
    stir-fried bok choy with, 264
    stuffing
        bread and, 533
        with spinach and ground meat, 538
    timbales, 206
    triangles, 88
    types, 281–282
    walnut noodle kugel, 336–337
    warm barley and asparagus salad, 347
    wild, foraging for, 282
    wild rice with sautéed, 363
muskmelons, 230
muskrat, 525
mussels, 369, 373–374
    about, 373
    beard on, 373, **373**
    butter and baked, 374
    cleaning, 373, **373**
    grilled, 374
    removal of sand from, 373
    steamed, 373–374

    stir-fried, with oyster sauce, 376
    storing, 373
    test for freshness, 373
mustard, 155, 999–1000
    beef stew with herbs, white wine and,
        480
    cooked hot, 1000
    flavoring ideas, 1000
    glaze, 583
    grainy, 1000
    honey vinaigrette, 573
    ideas for flavoring, 1000
    mayonnaise, 580
    paste, 589
    rabbit with, 526
    sauce, 552
        barbecue, Ray's, 586
        cold, 566
        dill, Scandinavian, 566
        dipping, with honey, 566
        sweet-and-sour, 564–565
    seeds, 999–1000
    uncooked hot, 1000
mustard greens, 154, 277
mustard pickles (chow-chow), 947
mustard spinach, 155
Mutsu/Crispin apples, 215
mutton. *see* lamb

N
naan
    bread, 608
nachos, 77
Napa cabbage, 153, **153,** 262
    carrots and stir-fried, 264
napkins, 11–12
Napoleon (mille-feuille), 670–671
nasturtium, 155, 1000
native American plums, 235
navarin printanière (lamb stew), 495–496
navel oranges, 225
navy beans, 254
Neapolitan coffee pots, 29, **29**
nectarine(s), 232
    about, 232
    canning, 894
    freezing, 917
    glazed, 232
    ice cream, 833
    nectar, canning, 897
    peeling, 208–209
    preserves, 937
negi maki (beef and scallion rolls), 83
Negroamaro, 49
Negroni, 57
Nero d'Avola, 49
Nesselrode sauce, 942
Newburg sauce, 561
New England clam chowder, 142
New Mexico chile, 291
New Mexico peppers, 292
new potatoes, 294
Newtown/Pippin apples, 215
New Year's Day
    menus for, 20
New Year's Eve
    menus for, 19–20
New Year's soups, 146
Nikolashka, the, 63
niña colada, 61
nöckerlen (Austrian pancakes), 653
noisette vegetables, 241
nonorganic foods, 9

noodle(s). *see also* egg noodles; pasta; *specific noodles*
  Asian, 320, 330–334
  baked, about, 336
  and doves, 461
  Japanese, in broth, 333
  Japanese, in dashi, 333
  kugel
    mushroom walnut, 336–337
    sweet, 337
  moon-viewing, 333
  and rice pilaf, Becker, 355
  soup
    beef, Vietnamese, 137
    chicken, 125
  spicy peanut sesame, 332
  spicy Szechuan, 332–333
nopales, 265
nori, 1011
Northern lobsters, 382, **382**
Northern pike, 415
Northern Spy apples, 215
nougat
  about, 868
  classic, 868–869
nuoc cham, 570
nut(s), 1000–1002. *see also specific nuts*
  as addition to green salads, 157
  angel cake, 706
  balls, flourless, 769
  banana muffins, 636
  blanching, 1001
  bread, 627
  buttercream icing, 793
  butters, 178–179, 558
  butterscotch cookies, 771
  caramel Cockaigne, spiced, 865
  carrot bread, 628
  cherry marshmallow gelatin, 812
  chocolate bonbons, 860
  chocolate truffles, 859
  chopping, 1001
  chutney cream cheese spreads, 180
  coating cakes with, **791**
  curried, 70
  date bread, 627
  drop cookies, 768–771
  egg noodles with brown butter and, 330
  fillings
    for coffee cakes, 623
    whipped cream, with nuts, 755
  freezing, 926
  ground
    grinding process, 1001
    as thickener, 545
  honey bread, 627
  icing, fluffy, 791
  meal, 984
  meringue kisses, 771
  milk of, 1022
  nutty dried fruit drops, 769
  oils of, 1023
  pastry dough, 665
  pie crust, 668
  pie dough, 665
  raisin icing, 790
  roasted, 70
  rosemary and brown sugar, 70
  salting, 1001
  serving size, 10
  tarts, individual, 778

toasted
  bread stuffing with dried fruit and, 533
  toasting process, 1001–1002
nutmegs, 230, 1000
nutrition, 4–10
  additives and, 9
  alcohol and, 6
  calories and, 6
  carbohydrates and, 5
  fats and, 5
  fluids and, 6
  food labels and, **7**, 7–8
  food safety and, 9
  future of food and, 9–10
  guidelines for, 4–5, 7
  healthy substitutions and, 8
  nonorganic and organic foods and, 9
  protein and, 5–6
  vegetarian diets and, 8–9
  vitamins and minerals and, 6
  weight management and, 7

O

oak leaf lettuce, 152, **152**
oats, oatmeal
  about, 353
  bread Cockaigne, 600
  cake, 721
  cookies
    chocolate bars, 764
    chocolate chip, 768
    raisin, 767–768
  flour, 984
  pancakes, 646
  preparing, 366–367 (chart)
  rolled, 353, 984–985
  rolls, 614
  types, 353
oblong radicchio, **154**
octopus, 369, **389**, 389–390
offset spatulas, 855
oil(s)
  basil, 590
  chile, 590
  dough, pat-in-the-pan, 667
  drop biscuits with, 639
  flavored, about, 590
  olive, 1002
  orange, 590
  smoke point, 1025
  toasted nut, 1023
  vegetable, 1023–1024
okra
  about, 285
  canning, 900
  freezing, 921
  fried, 285
  gumbo
    chicken, 136
    seafood, 141
  stewed, 285
old-fashioned, 59
  glasses, 54, **55**
olivade, 75
olive(s), 1002
  about, 71
  black
    and chicken with rice salad, 171
    salt-cured, 954
    white pizza with carmelized onions, rosemary and, 192
  caper paste (tapenade), 75

  couscous with chicken, lemon and, 363
  Mediterranean short ribs with, 99–100
  pizza with prosciutto, artichokes and, 191
  Spanish-style marinated, 71
  tapenade (olive caper paste), 75
  tomato relish, grilled fish steaks with, 404
olive oil, 1002
olivette vegetables, 241
Olympia oysters, 371
omega-3 fats, 5
omelets, 200–203. *see also* frittata; soufflés
  about, 200
  egg white, 201
  fillings, 200, 201
  firm, 200, 201
  French, **200**, 200–201
  hangtown fry, 202
  potato (tortilla Española), 203
  souffléd, 200, 203
    apple-filled, 203
    Grand Marnier, 203
    jam-filled, 203
    savory cheese-and-herb-filled, 203
  Spanish, 201
  western or Denver, 202–203
onion(s), 285–288, 1002–1005, **1003, 1005**
  about, 285–286
  baked
    stuffed with sausage, 288
    whole, oven- or fire-, 287
  browning, 286
  bunching, 286
  canning, 900–901
  carmelized, 287
    miniature turnovers with blue cheese and, 91
    white pizza with black olives, rosemary and, 192
  catsup, with garlic and red onions, 952
  creamed pearl, 287
  dicing, 286, **286**
  dip, red onion, 72
  dry, 296
  freezing, 921
  green beans with tomatoes and, 251
  green peppers and, 292
  grilled sweet, 287
  honey glaze for, 583
  liver and, 519
  marmalade, red onion, 949
  and orange salad, 168
  peas with prosciutto and, 291
  pizza
    with Italian sausage and, 191
    with mushrooms, peppers and, 191
  rings, French-fried, 288
  and sage dressing, 537
  sauce
    brown (sauce lyonnaise), 555
    sauce soubise, 551–552
  sautéed, 287
    wheat berries with dried fruits and, 362
  scalloped, with cheese, 288
  soup
    cream of, 145
    French, 129–130
  steamed, 286
  storing, 286, **1003,** 1004–1005

sweating, 286
sweet, 286, **1003, 1004**–1005
topping, 1005, **1005**
types, 286, 1002–115
open houses, 16
opera creams, 868
opossum, 524–525
orache, 154, **154**
orange(s)
about, 225
asparagus with hazelnuts and, 250
blossoms, 56
bread, 627–628
butter, 559
cake
with almonds, 723
angel, 706
chiffon, 710
filled, 732
rum, 723
canning, 896
cookies
apricot filled, 777
marmalade drops, 770–771
curd, 756–757
drops, Mexican, 874–875
filling
Bavarian cream, 817
cream, 757
custard, 757
custard, with lemon, 757
gelatin, 811
ice milk, 834
icing
buttercream, 793
luscious, 791
quick, 793
seven minute, 790
juice
broth on the rocks, 38
with lime, 38
with melon, 39
with tomato, 37
liqueur, sabayon with, 847
marmalade, 941
molasses glaze, 583
Buffalo rib roast with, 531
oil, 590
pecan cream cheese spread, 179
pie, chiffon, 689
salad
with brown rice, dates and, 171
with onion, 168
pineapple gelatin, 175
spinach, with avocado, grapefruit
and, 159–160
sauce
crispy roast duck with quick,
447–448
with ginger, 549
liqueur, 852
pan, sweet-sour, 548
pan, with rosemary, leeks and,
548
scones, with chocolate chips and,
641
sherbet, 837–838
slices, candied, 880
sorbet, 836
soufflé, cold, 817
sponge custards, 806
surprise, frozen, 830
in syrup, 225

toast, 642
types, 225
water, 980
orange roughy, 415
orato, 415
Orblanco grapefruit, 226
orecchiette pasta, **321**
with sausage and broccoli rabe, 329
oregano, 155, 996
lemon vinaigrette, 573
Oregon truffles, 285
organic foods, 9
poultry, 418
organ meat, about, 518
orzo pasta, **321**
spicy seafood stew with, 100
Oso Sweet onions, 286
ostrich, 418
about, 453
fillets, 453
outdoor cooking. see also barbecue;
grilling
about, 1063
backpacking menus, 26
outdoor entertaining, 17
menus for, 21
oven
rack placement of food in, 1062,
1063
oxtail(s), 518
braised, 521
soup, 137–138
stew, 521
oyster(s), 369
about, 371–372
angels on horseback, 84–85
baked, on the half-shell, 372
bisque, 141
broiled, 372
casino, 85
creamed, 373
dressing for fish, 536
fried
with bread crumb coating, 377
breaded, 372
with cornmeal coating, 377
with cracker coating, 377
grilled, 372
on the half-shell, 372
hangtown fry, 202
mignonette sauce, 568
po'boy, 185
Rockefeller, 85
scalloped, 373
shucking, **371,** 371–372
stew, 140–141
storing, in shell, 372
stuffing
bread, 533
corn bread, 535
tempura, 377
types, 371
oyster mushrooms, 282
oysters, 371–373
oyster sauce, 552, 1005
stir-fried clams with, 376
stir-fried mussels with, 376

P

Pacific butter clams, 374
Pacific flounder, 416
Pacific halibut, 414
Pacific oysters, 371

Pacific pompano, 413
pad Thai, 332
paglia e fieno (straw and hay), 326–327
pain au chocolat, 617, **617**
pak choi, 153, 262
palatschinken (Viennese or Austrian
crêpes), 652
pale ale (India Pale Ale), 52
paloise sauces, 561
pan(s)
cake, 700–702
muffin, 634
nonstick, safety of, 1067
pastry, 661
pie, 661
sizes and capacities, 701
tart, 661, **661**
tartlet, 661
pan-broiling, 1049
of meat, 465
pancakes, 643–646. see also crêpes
about, 643–644
additions to, 644
Austrian (nöckerlen), 653
blini
mini, 645
raised buckwheat, 645
buckwheat, 645
buttermilk, 644
cornmeal, 645
desserts, 826
Dutch baby, 652
filled, 644
four-grain flapjacks, 644–645
German (pfannkuchen), 652–653
high-altitude adjustments for, 643
lemon, 646
making, 643, **643**
oatmeal, 646
oven-baked, 652
pans for, 643
silver dollar, 644
sourdough, 644
pancetta, 508
pandowdy
about, 693
apple, 694–695
blueberry, 695
pear, 694–695
panettone (Italian Easter bread), 621
panfish, 415
panfrying, 429, 1048
of fish, 406–407
of meat, 465
panini
prosciutto, mozzarella, and basil, 181
panko, 961
panna cotta, 813
pantry
food storage in, 886
panzanella (bread and tomato salad),
169
papaya(s), 230–231
about, 230
canning, 896
coconut smoothie, 40
freezing, 917
-mango batido, 40
salad, green, 231
sautéed, 231
paper
cover for poaching, 1050, **1050**
freezer, 912

paper (*cont.*)
  parchment, 855
    French en papillote cooking, 1051
    en papillote cooking, 398–399,
      1052–1053, **1053**
en papillote cooking, 398–399, 1051,
  1052–1053, **1053**
pappa al pomadoro (Tuscan bread and
  tomato soup), 132
pappardelle, **321**
  with grilled tomato sauce, 329
paprika, 1007
  chicken, 431–432
  cutlet, 487–488
  sauce (sauce hongroise), 553
  schnitzel, 487–488
paprikás csirke (chicken paprika), 431–432
paradise jelly, 933
parblanching, 1054
parboiled rice, 354
parboiling, 1054–1055
parchment paper, 855
parfaits
  ice cream
    about, 839
    berry, 839–840
    chocolate, vanilla and coffee, 839
    winter, 840
  whipped cream, coffee, 841
Parisienne sauce, 580
Parmesan, 322
  cheese crisp, 158
  Italian soup with egg and (stracciatella),
    124
  millet cakes with dried tomatoes and,
    352–353
  salad dressing, creamy, 578
  soufflé with blue cheese, 204
  spread with roasted garlic and, 76
  vinaigrette, 574
Parmigiano-Reggiano cheese, 322
Parsienne vegetables, 241
parsley, 155, 1005–1006
  about, 289
  and bread crumb stuffing for fish, 535
  butter, with lemon, 559
  -chile sauce, 567
  deep-fried, 289
  types, 1005
  vinaigrette, with lime, 573
parsnips, 289–290
  about, 289
  freezing, 921
  glazed, 289
  oven-braised, 289
  puree, 289–290
parsteaming, 1055
partial-heat cooking methods
  about, 1054–1056
partial heat-cooking methods
  en croûte, 468
parties. *see also* appetizers and hors
    d'oeuvres; *specific holidays*
  children's, 15–16, 23
  cocktail, 16, 22–23
  drinks for. *see* beer; beverages;
    cocktails and party drinks; wine
  food platters for, 23, 69–70
  large parties, 17–18
  menus, special occasion, 21–22
  open houses, 16
  potlucks, 15
  tailgating, 17

partridge, 418. *see also* grouse
  baked marinated, 458–459
party platters, 69–70
  cheese, 70
  condiments and garnishes for, 70
  crudités, 78
  fruit, 70, 77
  meat, 70
  menu for, 23
  quantities for, 70
party trays. *see* party platters
pasilla peppers, 292
passion fruit
  about, 231
  freezing, 917
Passover
  menus for, 20
Passover sponge cake, 707
pasta. *see also specific pastas*
  about, 320
  additions to, 322
  and beans (pasta e fagioli), 329
  cheese for, about, 322
  cooking
    about, 320–321
    baked, 336, 339–340
    boiled, 325
  creamy, with chard and tomatoes,
    328–329
  dried, 320
  fresh
    making and storing, **323,** 323–324
  herb, 324
  Johnny Marzetti spaghetti pie, 95
  leftover
    about, 322–323
    casserole, 323
    pan-fried, 323
  machines, 323, **323**
  primavera, 327
  salads, 171–172
  sauce
    about, 321
    commercially prepared, 322
    matching to pasta, 321
    suggested, 321–322
  shapes, illustrated, **321**
  spinach, 324
  stuffed, 337–340
    about, 337
    baked, 339–340
    boiled, 337
    chicken soup with, 126
    fillings, 337–339
    fillings, cheese, 337
    fillings, chicken and cheese, 338
    fillings, meat, 338
    fillings, meat and spinach, 338
    fillings, mushroom, 337–338
    fillings, winter squash, 338–339
    ravioli, **339**
    shumai, **343**
    tortellini, **339**
    wontons, **342**
  types, illustrated, **321, 339, 342, 343**
  whole wheat, 325
paste(s)
  about, 587
  Asian ginger spice, 589
  chile garlic spice, 589
  gum, 882
  harissa, 569–570
  Jamaican jerk, 588

  Mediterranean garlic herb, 589
  Moroccan herb, 589–590
  mustard, 589
  quince, 236–237, 878–879
  red curry, 589
  tapenade (olive caper paste), 75
  Thai green curry, 589
  tomato, 1021–1022
pasteurization, of milk and cream,
  996–997
pastillage (gum paste), 882
pastitsio, 336
pastrami
  and corned beef triple-decker
    sandwich, 182–183
  making, 906
pastries, 670. *see also* pie(s); tart(s);
    tartlets
  baklava, 675
  choux paste, 671–672
  choux paste swans, 673, **673**
  cinnamon sugar sticks, 671
  cream puffs, 672
  dough for. *see* pastry dough; puff
    pastry
  dumplings
    about, 695
    apple, 695–696
  éclairs, chocolate, 672
  elephant ears, 670
  fondant icing on, 791
  freezing, 925–926
  Napoleon (mille-feuille), 670–671
  party foods, 88
  patty shells (bouchées), 670
  phyllo cups, 675
  profiteroles, 673
  savory
    miniature turnovers, 90–91
  strudel, apple, 673–674
  sweet fruit turnovers, 696
  turnovers
    about, 695
    apple, 696
    miniature, savory, 90–91
    pear, 696
    sweet fruit, 696
pastry bags, 785
  making your own, 786, **787**
  use of, 786–788
pastry blender, 661, **661**
pastry brush, 855
pastry cases
  for dishes in cream sauce, 111
pastry cones, 855
pastry cream (crème patisserie), 755
pastry docker, 661
pastry dough. *see also* dough; pie crust
  about making, 661
  basic, 665
  choux paste (pâte à choux),
    671–672
  cornmeal, 665
  cream cheese, 666
  croissant, 616
  cutting fat into, 662, **662**
  Danish, 624–625
  deluxe butter, 665
  folding, 668
  freezing, 925
  layered, 668
  mixing, 662
  nut, 665

puff, 668–670
  cutting and docking, 669
  food processor, 669–670
  shaping and folding, 668–669, **669**
  storing, 669
  rolling, **662**, 662–663
  shaping and trimming, 663, **663**
  sweet, 665
  whole wheat, 665
pastry jagger, 661
pastry pans, 661
pastry tip, 785
pastry wheel, fluted, 661, **661**
Patagonian toothfish, 414
pâte
  about, 517
  chicken liver, 440
pâté
  maison, 518
  salmon, 85
pâte à choux (choux paste), 671–672
  for éclairs, 671
  filling of, 671
  for profiteroles, 671
patty melt, 510
pattypan squash, 306
paupiettes (molded filled fish fillets), 398
pawpaw(s)
  about, 231
  pudding, 231
pea(s). see also black-eyed peas; pea
    shoots; snap peas; snow peas;
    specific peas
  baby artichokes and, braised, 248
  carrots and, 290
  green, 290
    canning, 901
    freezing, 921
  mushrooms and, 290
  with prosciutto and onions, 291
  puree of, 290
  rice and
    Jamaican, 356
    risi e bisi, 361
  salad, three-pea, 168
  samosas with potatoes and, 89
  soup, green, 130
  split, 253
    soup, 253
peach(es)
  about, 231–232
  baked stuffed, 232
  brandied, 955
  buckle with blueberry and, 691
  cake
    Cockaigne, 691
    pecan upside-down, high-altitude, 751
  canning, 894
  conserves, 939
  dipping sauce, 570
  filled, 232
  freezing, 917
  glaze, 800
  ice cream, 833
  melba sauce, 845
  nectar, canning, 897
  peeling, 208–209
  pie, 679
    custard, Cockaigne, 679
    with frozen fruit, 677
  preserves, 937

sorbet, 836
types, 231
peanut(s), 1006. see also peanut butter
  brittle, 872–873
  dipping sauce, 570
  flour, 984
  sesame noodles, spicy, 332
  soup, Georgia, 134
  stew, sweet potato and, 302–303
peanut butter, 1006
  cookies, 767
  cups, 860–861
  frosting, 795
  fudge, 864
  pie, 684
  sandwich, 178
peanut sauce, 81–82
pear(s)
  about, 232–233
  baked acorn squash with apple and, 309
  cactus. see prickly pears
  canning, 896
  cranberry-pickled, 950
  freezing, 917
  jam
    with grapes, naturally sweetened, 936
    with pineapple, 935
  pandowdy, 694–695
  poached
    poaching process, 232
    in red wine, 233
  salad, with walnut, endive and, 170
  stuffed, 233
  turnovers, 696
  types, 232–233
pearl barley, 346
  preparing, 364 (chart)
pearl onions, 286
pearls, 241
pea shoots, 155, **155,** 290
pecan(s), 1006
  butter, with rosemary, 179
  cake
    with coconut, 713–714
    peach upside-down, high-altitude, 751
  crisp spicy, 70–71
  filling, 758
    with coconut, 759
  ice cream, butter pecan, 833
  icing, with coconut, 794
  lace, 769
  pie, 682–683
    chunk, 683
  pralines, buttermilk, 876
  puffs, 769
  salad, with tart greens with apples and, 158
  slices, 764–765
  spread, orange cream cheese, 179
  torte, 727
pecan rice, Louisiana, 354
Pecorino cheese, 322
Pecorino Romano cheese, 322
pectin, in jellies and preserves, 927–928
Pekin duck, 446
penne, **321**
  with vodka sauce, 328
penuche, 875, 876
peperoncini peppers, 291

pepper(s). see bell pepper(s); chile
    pepper(s); red pepper(s)
peppercorn(s), 1006. see also black pepper
  Szechuan, 1020–1021
peppermint
  stick ice cream, 832
  wafers, 867–868
peppernuts (pfeffernüsse), 768
pepperoni, 515
  pizza, 191
  pizza with mushrooms, sausage and, 191
pepper pot, 139
pequín chiles, 292
perch, 415
perfect Manhattan, 59
périgourdine sauce, 555
périgueux sauce, 555
perilla (shiso), 155
Perlette grapes, 227
Persian limes, 224
Persian melons, 230
persillade, 1006
  broiled scallops with, 387
  broiled shrimp with, 387
  grilled scallops with, 387
  grilled shrimp with, 387
persimmons, **235**
  about, 233
  buttermilk pudding, 823
  freezing, 917
  sautéed, 233
  types, 233
  in vinaigrette, 233
Peruvian Blue potatoes, 294
pesto
  anchovy, 958
  cheesecake, 76
  miniature turnovers with sun-dried
    tomatoes and, 90
  pasta salad with, 172
  sauce, 569
  sun-dried tomato, 569
petits fours, 738–739, **739**
  fondant icing on, 791
pewter cups, 54, **55**
pfannkuchen (German pancakes), 652–653
pfeffernüsse (peppernuts), 768
pheasant, 418
  about, 457
  braised with apples, 458
  braised with gin and juniper, 457
  roast, 457
Philly cheese steak, 184–185
pho bo (Vietnamese beef noodle soup), 137
phyllo, 673
  about, 674–675
  cups, 675
  handling of, 674
  store bought, 674
picada, 569
picadillo, 514
piccalilli, 947–948
pickles
  salt, 1069
pickles, pickled. see also relish
  beets, 949
    salad, 166
  bread-and-butter, 946
  canning, 945
  cornichons (gherkins), 946–947

pickles, pickled (*cont.*)
  cucumber slices, low-salt sweet, 946
  dill
    crock-cured, 953
    dilled beans, 949
    quick, 947
  fish, 411
  gherkins (cornichons), 946–947
  gherkins, sweet-and-sour spiced, 946
  ginger, 952
  grapes, 228
  green tomato, 948
  horseradish, 952–953
  mustard (chow-chow), 947
  peaches, 950
  pear(s), cranberry-, 950
  peppers, chile, 954
  piccalilli, 947–948
  pickling process
    equipment, 943
    ingredients, 943–944
    methods, 944–945
    safety, 944
    storing, 945
    vinegar, 944
  pork, 904–905
  watermelon rind, 949–950
  yellow cucumber, 945
pickling salt, 1009
picnics, 17
  menus for, 21
pico de gallo, 571
pie(s). *see also* pie crust; quiches; tart(s),
    tartlets
  apple, 678–679
    with cheddar crust, 690
    galette, 697
  banana cream, 685
  berry
    with canned or bottled fruit, 677
    fresh, 676–677
    with frozen fruit, 677
    glazed, 678
    sour cream, 678
  blueberry, 677
  Boston cream, 732
  bourbon, 683
  buttermilk chess, 683
  butterscotch cream, 685
  cherry
    with canned or bottled fruit, 677
    fresh, 677–678
    with frozen fruit, 677
    sour cream, 678
  chess, 683
  chiffon, 688–689
  chocolate
    black bottom, 689
    chip, 683
    chunk pecan, 683
    cream, 685
    fudge, 686
    glazed custard, 684–685
  coconut cream, 685
  Concord grape, 680
  cream, 684–685
    about, 684
    banana, 685
    butterscotch, 685
    chocolate, 685
    coconut, 685
    vanilla, 685
  custard, 684–685

deep dish fruit, 690
dough for. *see* pie crust, dough
    recipes
freezing, 926
fruit, 675–682
glazed berry, 678
high-altitude baking, 662
ice cream, 830–831
Jefferson Davis, 683
key lime, 688
lemon
  about, 687
  chess, 683
  chiffon, 688–689
  meringue, 687
  Ohio shaker, 687–688
lime
  about, 687
  chiffon, 688–689
  key lime, 688
maple syrup, 684
mincemeat, mock, 680
mousse, 688
orange chiffon, 689
peach, 679
  custard, Cockaigne, 679
  with frozen fruit, 677
peanut butter, 684
pecan, 682–683
pumpkin, 686
  chiffon, 689–690
raisin, 680–681
raspberry Bavarian, 689
rhubarb, 679–680
savory, 101–103, 108–110
  cheese custard, 110
  kidney, 483–484
  leek, 109
  meat, 469
  potpie, 103
  quiche, 108–109
shoofly, 683
sour cream cherry or berry, 678
squash, 686
strawberry
  Bavarian, 689
  rhubarb, 680
sweet potato, 686
transparent, 682–684
vanilla cream, 685
pie crust
  additions to, 665
  baking, before filling, 664–665
  crumb, 667–668
  for double-crust pies, 663–665, **664**
  dough recipes. *see also* pastry dough
    basic, 665
    Cockaigne, 665
    cornmeal, 665
    deluxe butter, 665
    nut, 665
    sweet, 665
    whole wheat, 665
  for filled pies, 663–665
  glazing, 664
  meringue, 666
  nut, 667, 668
  for one-crust pies, 663
  rims
    braided design, 663
    coiled design, 663, **663**
    crimped, 663, **663**
    fluted, 663, **663**

shaping and sizing, **663,** 663–664
  for tarts, 663
  tops
    plain lattice, 664
    solid, 664
    woven lattice, 664, **664**
pie pans, 661
pierogi, 341
  potato and cheese filling for, 341–342
  sauerkraut mushroom filling for, 342
pie shell, meringue, 666
pie weights, metal, 661
pigeon(s), 418, 452, 459–461
pigeonneau, 452
pig, roast suckling, 500–501
pigs in a blanket, 91
pike, 415
Pilsner glass, **52**
pimento cheese spread, 179
pimiento peppers, 291
Pimm's cup, 57
piña colada, 61
pineapple
  peeling and serving, **234**
pineapple(s)
  about, 234
  canning, 896
  cup, fresh, 234
  filled, 234
  freezing, 917
  gelatin, 811–812
  glaze, 583
  ice milk, 834
  juice, 39
    cocktail with cucumber and, 39
    with grapefruit, 38
  orange gelatin salad, 175
  preserves, with strawberry, 937–938
  punch, 41
  sliced, 234, **234**
  snow, 814
  spiced pear jam with, 935
  tidbits, 234
  tropic, 64
  upside-down cake, 691–692
pineapple guavas, 238–239
pine nut(s), 1007
  couscous with raisins and, 362
pink daiquiri, 60
pink grapefruit. *see also* grapefruit
  granita, 839
  sorbet, 836
pink lady, 57
Pink Lady apples, 216
Pinot Grigio, 46
Pinot Gris, 46
Pinot Noir, 48
pintail duck, 455
pinto beans, 254
pinwheel
  icebox cookies, 776, **776**
  sandwiches, **187**
pirkilt (Hungarian goulash), 480–481
piroshki, party, 89
pismo, 374
pistachios, 1007
  couscous stuffing with dried apricots
    and, 539
  ice cream, 832–833
pistou, 569
pita bread, 607–608
  chips, 93
  salad, 159

sandwiches, 188
  about, 187
  Becker gyro sandwich, 188
  falafel sandwich, 188
pit cooking, 1057
pizza, 190–192
  about, 190
  Becker portobello, 282–283
  dessert, 697
  dough, 607
  English muffin, 182
  grilled, 192
  with grilled eggplant, mushrooms, and
    sun-dried tomatoes, 191
  with Italian sausage and onion, 191
  margherita, 191
  with mushrooms, peppers, and onion,
    191
  with mushrooms, sausage, and
    pepperoni, 191
  pepperoni, 191
  with prosciutto, artichokes, and olives,
    191
  Seattle, 191
  with tomato sauce and mozzarella, 191
  toppings or fillings for, 190–191
  white
    with carmelized onions, black olives,
      and rosemary, 192
    with chicken and broccoli, 192
    with fresh clams and garlic, 192
    with fresh tomatoes, basil and feta
      cheese, 191
    with portobello mushrooms and
      goat cheese, 192
    with potatoes and sage, 192
    with spicy shrimp and roasted red
      peppers, 192
placemats, 11
planking (plank-roasting), 406, 1055
plantain(s), 293–294
  about, 293
  deep-fried (tostones), 294
  slices, golden sautéed, 294
planter's punch, 61, 66
plastic wrap
  for freezing, 912
plugged fruit, 64
plum(s)
  about, 235
  cake, Cockaigne, 691
  canning, 896
  conserves, 939
  freezing, 917
  jam, 935–936
  jelly, 933
  juice, canning, 897
  peeling, 208–209
  preserves, 938
  pudding
    sauce, 852
    steamed, 825–826
  sauce
    dipping, 570
    jellied Damson, 942
  types, 235, **235**
plum sauce, wine, 235
plunger(s)
  butter, 964
  French press coffee, **29**
  French press coffee pots, 28–29, 30
poaching, 1050
  cherries, 223

chicken/turkey, 423
eggs, 196–198
fish, 399
fruit, 212–213
hard-shell crabs, 381
lobster, 383
paper cover for, 1050, **1050**
pears, 233
quenelle, 401
rhubarb, 237
poblano peppers, 291
poi, 310
polenta. see also cornmeal
  baked, 349
  fried, 349–350
  rustica, Becker five-minute, 349
  soft, 349
  toasted, 349–350
pollack, 414
polyunsaturated fats, 5
pome fruits
  substitutions for, 209
pomegranate(s), **235,** 235–236
  about, 235
  molasses, 236
  sunburst punch, 41
Pomelo grapefruits, 225–226. see also
  grapefruit
  canning, 896
pommes anglaise (boiled potatoes), 295
pommes Anna (potatoes Anna), 298, **298**
pompano, 415
popcorn, 71
  candied, 865–866
  savory additions, 71
  with white sugar syrup, 866
popcorn shrimp, Cajun, 84
popovers, 637
  cheese, 637
poppy seed(s), 1011
  custard cake Cockaigne, 732
  filling for coffee cakes, 624
  -honey dressing, 574
  lemon muffins, 635
  lemon pound cake, 716–717
  loaf, 629
  noodles, 329
porcini, 282
  and wild rice dressing, 540
porcupine, 524–525
porgy fish, 415
pork. see also bacon; ham; meat for
  general information; prosciutto;
  rib(s); sausage
  about, 497–498
  adobo, 502
  braised
    braising and stewing process, 501
    in milk, 501
    with sauerkraut, 501
    with Caribbean-style red bean stew,
      255
  chops, 504
    about, 503–504
    braised stuffed, Cockaigne, 504
    breaded, 504
  cooking, 497
  crown roast, 498–499
    stuffing for, 539
  Cuban sandwich, 181
  cutlets
    about, 503–504
    breaded, 504

cuts of, 497, **497**
enchiladas, 104
fats, 982, 993
goetta, 517
ground, stuffing with spinach,
    mushroom and, 538
hash, Becker, 108
hocks, stewed, 508
leg of, roast fresh, 499–500
loin roast, bone-in, 498
marinade, Becker, 585–586
neck bones, stewed, 508
Orloff Cockaigne, 499
pickled, 904–905
pulled, 500
ribs. see also rib(s)
  about, 505
roast
  boneless, 498
  boneless, Florentine, 499
  picnic shoulder, Latin, 501–502
  sandwich, 177
  suckling pig, 500–501
salt, 904–905
  as seasoning, 1008
sausage, herbed, 516
scrapple, 517
shoulder with mustard and rosemary
    sauce, 99
shumai, 343
steaks, about, 503–504
sweet-and-sour, 105, 504–505
tacos, shredded, 189
tenderloin
  about, 502–503
  canapés, 87
  country-fried with gravy, 503
  grilled, 503
  pan-roasted, 503
port, 50
porter, 52
Portion Distortion, 10
port marinade
  spicy, grilled Cornish hens in, 441
portobello(s), 282
  pizza, Becker, 282–283
  white pizza with goat cheese and, 192
Portuguese greens soup (caldo verde), 139
potages, 127
potato(es), 294–301. see also sweet
    potato(es); specific potatoes
  about, 294–295
  Anna (pommes Anna), 298
  au gratin, 297
  baked, 297
  boiled
    new potatoes, 295
    pommes Anglaise, 295
  bread, with buttermilk, 600
  browned or Franconia, 297–298
  cabbage, ham and, 263
  canning, 901
  casserole, with salmon and spinach, 97
  chantilly, 296
  chips, 94
  creamed, 296
  croquettes, 300
  with curry and cauliflower, 267–268
  doughnuts, with buttermilk, 655
  duchess, 300
  dumplings (kartoffelklösse), 335
  flour, 984
  freezing, 921

potato(es) (*cont.*)
French fries, 243, 299–300
garlic mayonnaise (skordalia), 582
gnocci, 335
with green beans, and smoked meat, 251
ground beef with spices and, 515
hash brown, 298
and kale gratin, 278
leftover, 300–301
about, 300
au gratin, 301
baked potato soup, 130
cakes, 301
German-fried, 300
O'Brien, 300–301
mashed, 295–296
additions to, 296
with cabbage and scallion (colcannon), 296
stuffing, 537–538
O'Brien, 300
omelet (tortilla Española), 203
oven "French-fried," 300
pan-broiled grated, 298–299
pancakes, 298
pan-fried or Lyonnaise, 297
pierogi filling with cheese and, 341–342
riced, 295
rolls
with buttermilk, 613
refrigerator, 620
salad, 168–169
American, 168
German, 168–169
warm, with lentils, 171
salted herring and, 412
samosas with peas and, 89
scalloped, 296–297
shoestring, 300
skins, crispy, 79–80
snow, 295
souffléd or puffed potato(es), 299, **299**
soup
baked, 130
with leeks, 130
with lentils and sausage, 134
vichyssoise, 130
starch, 1017
stuffed with sour cream and caviar, 79
sweet. *see* sweet potato(es)
twice-baked, 297
types, 294
white pizza with sage and, 192
potato starch, 544
pot-au-feu (French simmered beef and vegetables), 136–137
pot barley, 346
potlucks, 15
potpies, 103
pot roast
beef, 477
French (boeuf à la mode), 478
Italian (stracotto), 477–478
pot-roasting process for meat, 466–467
pots de crème, **804**
chocolate, 804–805
coffee, 804
vanilla, 804
pot stickers, 93
poule-au-pot, 136

poulette
sauce, 554
poultry, 418–451. *see also* chicken; Cornish hens; duck; goose; squab; wildfowl
barbecue sauce for, 586–587
breasts, preparing boneless, skinless, 420
brining, 421, 443, 904
buying, 418
carving, **421,** 421–422
cooking, 423
dry-curing, 904
fats, 982
free-range, 418
freezing, 922–923
frozen, thawing and cooking, 923
gravy, 546
green herb dressing for, 536–537
organic, 418
parts
baking and roasting, 423
cutting up, **419,** 419–421, **420**
roasting, 422–423
serving size, 10
stock, 114–115, 117
brown, 118
household, 118
storing and safe handling, 418–419
stuffing and trussing, 421, **421**
test for doneness, 423
thawing, 418–419
whole
boning, **420,** 420–421
butterflying, 420, **420**
cutting into parts, 419–421
splitting, 420
pound cake, 716
lemon poppy seed, 716
liquor soaked, 716
sour cream, 717
powdered buttermilk, 1013
power outages
and frozen foods, 910–911
prairie chicken, 458
roasted, 459
pralines, 876
buttercream icing, 793
candies, 875–876
pecan buttermilk, 876
prawns, 385
precooked dishes
freezing, 924
pregnancy, 6
preserves. *see* jellies and preserves
pressure-cooking, 1053–1054
in canning, 889, 891
high-altitude, 1054
vegetables, 243, 245
pretzels, 619
almond, 774
prickly pears, **235**
about, 236
jelly, 934
sauce, melon with, 236
prime rib, 471–472
Primitivo, 48
profiteroles, 673
choux paste in form of, 671
proof, 593–594
propeller-blade grinders, 29, **30**
prosciutto, 506–507
grilled or boiled figs with, 227

melon and, 230
mozzarella, and basil panini, 181
peas with onions and, 291
pizza with artichokes, olives and, 191
Prosecco, 50
protein, 5–6
complete, 6
on food labels, 8
package, 6
Provençal vegetable soup (soupe au pistou), 128
prune(s). *see also* plum(s)
and apple dressing, 537
braised marinated rabbit with, 526
Danish, 625–626
dressing, 540–541
filling for coffee cakes, 624
stewed, 235
prune plums, 235
ptarmigan, 458
roasted, 459
puddings. *see also* bread pudding; rice pudding
baked
about, 823
pearl tapioca, 821
banana, 807
with meringue, 807–808
butterscotch, 807
chocolate, old-fashioned, 807
coconut milk, 808
corn, 271
additions to, 271
souffléd, 271
cornstarch, 806–808
cottage, 823
farina, 821
Indian, 823
pawpaw, 231
persimmon buttermilk, 823
pumpkin buttermilk, 823
snow, 814
steamed
about, 824
caramel, 825
chocolate feather, 824
plum, 825–826
sticky toffee, 823–824
tapioca, 820–821
vanilla, 807
puffball mushrooms, 282
puffer fish, 413
puff pastry. *see also* pastry dough, puff
beef Wellington, 468–469
Brie baked in pastry, 92
cheese straws, 91–92
piroshki, party, 89
pump espresso machines, 29, **29,** 31
pumpkin
bread, 628
cake, chiffon, 710
canning, 901
cheesecakes, 745–746
freezing, 921
ice cream, spice, 833
muffins, 635
pie, 686
pie, chiffon, 689–690
pudding, buttermilk, 823
seeds, 1011
soup, 129
pumpkin seeds, toasted, 71

punch
  alcoholic, 66–68
    bowle, 66
    Champagne, 65
    eggnog, 66–67
    Fish House, 65
    May wine, 66
    mulled cider, 68
    mulled wine, 67
    planter's, 66
    Rhine wine cup, 66
    sangria, 65
    Tom and Jerry, 67
    wassail, 68
    whiskey or brandy cup, 65
  cranberry-mango, 41
  fruit, 42
    for 50 people, 42
  gala tomato, 42
  glasses or cups, 54, **55**
  pineapple, 41
  pomegranate sunburst, 41
  strawberry, 42
  watermelon, 41
purees
  baby food, 895
  equipment for, 122, **122**
  fruit
    about, 215
    applesauce, 216
    baby food, 895
    freezing, 918
    raspberry, 221
  lentil (dal), 258
  soups, 127–128
  as thickener, 545
  tomato, canning, 899
  vegetable
    about, 244
    carrot, 266
    freezing, 922
    pea, 290
    root vegetable, 245–246, 303–304,
      314
    rutabaga, 303–304
    turnip, 314
purslane, 154, **154**
  soup, cream of, 145–146

Q
quail, 418
  about, 459
  spicy maple-roasted, 460
  types, 459
quatre épices (spice Parisienne),
  1007
Queen Anne cherries, 223
quenelle, poached, 401
quesadillas, cheese, 77
quiches
  about, 108
  additions to, 109
  cheese, 109
  Lorraine, 108–109
  miniature, 90
  tomato and goat cheese, 109
quick
  bean burritos, 105
  Becker express stock, 120
  chicken enchiladas, 104
  chicken or turkey curry, 105
  cold avocado soup, 146
  coleslaw, about, 161

dishes using cooked meats, poultry, fish
  or beans, 103
express fish stock, 120
grapes and sausages, 228
iced chocolate, 37
instant coffee, 31
instant flour, 986
instant sorbet, 837
instant yeast, 1029
ligtning cake, 722
meat curry, 105
New England clam chowder, 142
quick-cooking couscous, 365
quick tomato aspic, 174
quick tuna casserole, 96
South Carolina skillet shrimp, 385
spiced hot chocolate, 36
30 minute meals, 25
quick-cooking grits, 349
quick-rising yeast, 591
quince(s), 236–237, **237**
  about, 236
  baked, 236
  freezing, 917
  jelly, 932–933
  paste (membrillo), 236–237, 878–879
  preserves, 938
quinoa
  about, 353
  pilaf, 353
  preparing, 367 (chart)

R
rabbit, 524, 525–527
  about, 525
  braised marinated, with prunes, 526
  dressing and cutting, 525
  fricassee of, 525
  with mustard (lapin à la moutarde), 526
  and sausage, casseroled, 526–527
  sautéed, 525
rabbit à la mode, 525
raccoon, 525
rack of lamb, 492
radiant heat, 1060
radicchio, 154, **154**
  about, 275
  braised, 276
  rosso, 154
radishes
  about, 303
  red, with scallions, 303
  types, 303
rails, 459, 460–461
rainbow smelt, 416
rainbow trout, 417
Rainier cherries, 223
raisin(s), 211
  and almond filling, 758
  and carrot salad, 166
  cinnamon bread, 597–598
  couscous with pine nuts and, 362
  filled cookies, 777
  freezing, 917
  icing, fluffy, 790
  nut icing, 790
  oatmeal cookies, 767–768
  pie, 680–681
  plumping of, 211
  rice stuffing with almonds, Middle
    eastern spices and, 539–540
  rum ice cream, 832
  sauce, 565

raita (Indian yogurt sauce), 567–568
ramps, 1004, **1005**
ranch dressing, 576
rapunzel mâche, 152
ras el hanout, 1007
raspberry(ies), 220–221
  about, 220
  Bavarian pie, 689
  butter, 850–851
  cheese cake, creamy water-bath, 744
  chocolate cream cake, 733
  cobbler, 693
  coffee cake, deluxe almond, 631
  coulis, 853
  crème brûlée, 804
  croissants, 617
  Danish pinwheels, 625
  freezing, 917
  glaze, 800
  grunt with blackberry and, 694
  ice cream, 834
  jelly, black raspberry and gooseberry,
    932
  melba sauce, 845
  mignonette sauce, 568
  mousse, frozen, 840–841
  peaches filled with, 232
  pie, 676
  puree, 221
  sherbet, 837
  shrub, 38
  sorbet, 836
  streusel bars, 764
  streusel tart, 681
  syrup, 221
  tea gelatin, 812
  vinegar, 1025
rasp grater, **223**
ratatouille Provençale, 274
ravioli, 339, **339**
ray, 416
razor, 374
red bananas, 218
red bean(s), 254
  rice and, 256
  stew, pork with Caribbean-style, 255
red cabbage, 153, **153**. see also cabbage
  braised, 264
red channel fish, 414
red currants, 222
Red Delicious apples, 215
red drum, 414
redfish, 414
Red Flame grapes, 227
Red Gold potatoes, 294
redhead duck, 455
red leaf lettuce, 152, **152**
red mullet, 415
red onion(s), 286. see also onion(s)
  dip, 72
  garlic catsup, 952
  marmalade, 567
red pepper(s). see also bell pepper(s)
  garlic mayonnaise (rouille), 582
  mayonnaise with tomato and, 580
  roasted, dressing, 574–575
    rye berry salad with, 361
  roasted, pizza with spicy shrimp and,
    192
  roasted, sauce, 549
  roasted, soup, 132
red red strawberry jam, 934
red rice, 354

red romaine lettuce, 153
red snapper, 416
    whole, grilled with ginger-soy
        vinaigrette, 403
Red Tip lettuce, 152
reductions, 1055
    of glazes, 116
    of sauces, 545
    of stocks, 116
red wine, 47–49
    with cheese course, 827
    eggs en meurette, 197–198
    marinade, 584
    pears poached in, 233
    sauce
        braised whole fish in, 401
        with figs, pan-seared duck breasts,
            449
        marrow (sauce bordelaise), 555
        with mushrooms, 555–556
        with plums, 235
        sauce bourguignonne, 548
        sour cherry pan sauce, 548–549
red wine vinegar, 1024
refreezing food, 914
refrigerator
    food storage in, 885–886
refrigerator cookies. see icebox cookies
refrigerator rolls, 620–621
reheating
    of food, 1065
    of grains, 346
    of meat, 469–470
    of vegetables, 245
relish
    corn and tomato, 949
    eggplant, 275
    green tomato, 948
    rhubarb, 237
    tart corn, 948
rémoulade sauce, 581
rendering fats, 981
rennet, 1007
Reuben sandwich, 181
Rhine wine cup, 66
Rhode Island clam chowder, 143
Rhode Island Greening apples, 216
rhubarb, **237**
    about, 237
    canning, 896
    conserves, 940
    crisp, 692
    freezing, 917
    juice, canning, 897
    pie, 679–680
    poached, 237
    preparing, 237
    preserves, with strawberry, 938
    relish, 237
rib(s)
    baby back, 505
    barbecued spareribs, 505
    beef short ribs, 482
    country-style, baked in barbecue sauce,
        505
    five-spice, 81
    pork, about, 505
    prime rib, 471–472
ribbon sandwiches, 186–187, **187**
rice, 354–362. see also rice pudding;
    risotto; specific type of rice
    bean and rice cakes, 106–107
    brown, baked with mushrooms, 355

casserole
    chicken, 96
    quick chicken, 96
chicken and, 96, 435
coconut, 357
cooking, 354
flour, 984
fried, 357
hoppin' John, 356
Indonesian rice table (rijsttafel), 358
Jamaican peas and, 356
leftover, fried rice from, 357
parboiled, 354
peas and (risi e bisi), 361
Persian, 357
pilaf, 355
    with cashews, spiced, 355
    with lentils and toasted cumin seeds,
        355
    with noodles, Becker, 355
plain Japanese (gohan), 359
preparing, 367 (chart)
    steaming methods, 354
red beans and, 256
Rombauer Italian, 354
salads, 171
soup
    chicken, 125–126, 135
    Spanish, 356
stuffing
    with almonds, raisins, and Middle
        eastern spices, 539–540
    with chorizo and hot chile peppers,
        539
sushi (shari), 359
types, 354, 360
white, baked, 354
rice flour, 591
rice pudding, 820
ricers, **295**
rice vinegar, 1024
rickey, 59
ricotta, 322
    baked figs with, 227
    cheesecakes, 745
    spinach
        stuffing, 538–539
Riesling, 46, 50
rigatoni pasta, **321**
rimming (glassware), 55
ring-neck duck, 455
Rioja, 49
risi e bisi (rice and peas), 361
risotto. see also rice
    about, 360
    in bianco, 360
    Milanese, 360–361
    with mushrooms, 361
    preparing, 360
roast beef. see beef, roast
roasting, 1045–1046
    fish, 396
    in front of the fire, **1061**
    garlic, 277
    at high altitudes, 1046
    meat, 465–466
    planking (plank-roasting), 406, 1055
    poultry, 422–423
    vegetable, 244
roasting rack, 465
Rob Roy, 59
rocambole, 1004, **1005**
rock bass, 415

rock candy, 875, **875**
rock crabs, 380
rocket, 153
rockfish, 413, 416
rock lobsters, 382, **382**
rock salt, 1009
rock shandy, 64
roe, 382, 905. see also caviar
    shad, 405, 416
    taramasalata, 75
roll cakes, 734–737
    about, 734–735
    chocolate-filled, 737
    cream, 736
    jelly, 735–736
    lemon, 736–737
    tightening, 735, **735**
roll cookies, 772
rolled barley, 346, 364 (chart)
rolled oats, 353
rolled rye, 361
rolled sandwiches, 187
rolling pins, 661
rollmops, 415
rolls. see muffin(s); yeast rolls and buns
romaine lettuce, 153, **153**
Romano beans, 250
Romano cheese, 322
Rome Beauty apples, 215
root cellars, 886–887
root vegetable(s)
    braise, 246
    chips, 94
    glazed, 245
    puree, 245–246
    and seitan stew, 319
Roquefort. see also blue cheese
    cheese ball, 76
    vinaigrette, 573
rose, 155
rose hip soup, 148
rosemary, 155, 1008
    and brown sugar nuts, 70
    cream sauce, woodcock in, 461
    pan sauce with leeks, orange and,
        548
    pecan butter, 179
    sorbet, 836
    white pizza with carmelized onions,
        black olives and, 192
rosés, 49
rosettes, 657
rose water, 980
rote grütze, 821–822
rotisserie cooking, 1059
rouille (red pepper garlic mayonnaise),
    582
round radicchio, **154**
roux, 543–544
Roy Rogers, 64
rubs. see dry rubs
rubs, dry, 587–588
Ruby Seedless grapes, 227
ruddy duck, 455
ruddy Mary, 57
rue, 1008
ruffed grouse, 458
rugelach, 778, **778**
rum
    baba au rhum, 734
    brown sugar glaze, 583
    fruitcake soaked in, 725
    orange cake with, 723

pound cake soaked in, 716
raisin ice cream, 832
sauce, 850
syrup, guavas in, 228
rumaki, 83
rum cocktails and drinks, 59–61, 66–67, 67
Russet Burbank potatoes, 294
russet potatoes, 294
Russian Banana potatoes, 294
rusty nail, 60
rutabaga, 303–304
about, 303
boiled, 303
freezing, 921
puree, 303–304
rye, 361
about, 361
berries
preparing, 368 (chart)
salad with roasted red pepper dressing, 361
bread
all-rye flour, 605
sourdough, 605
with sponge starter, 605–606
flour, 985
meal, 985
pilaf, 361
rolls, 614
rye whiskey, 59

S
saag paneer, 306
sabayons
about, 846–847
lemon, 847
with orange liqueur, 847
sauce, cold, 847
with white wine, 847
sablefish, 416
Saccharin, 1020
safety. see cooking and kitchen safety; food safety
safety, food, 9, 883
in canning, 888, 892–893
uncooked egg whites, 798, 810–811
saffron
about, 1008
bouillabaisse, 142
braised lamb shoulder, 494
chicken and rice (arroz con pollo), 435
coffee cake, kneaded filled, 622
couscous with chicken, lemon, and olives, 363
curry sauce, 553
mashed potatoes, addition to, 296
Moroccan herb paste, 589–590
paella, seafood and sausage, 358
Persian rice, 357
picada, 569
Provençal vegetable soup (soupe au pistou), 128
risotto Milanese, 360–361
Rombauer Italian rice, 354
sage, 155, 1008
and onion dressing, 537
white pizza with potatoes and, 192
sage grouse, 458
sago, 1017
St. Patrick's Day
menus for, 20

sake, 50
salad(s), 152–176. see also coleslaw; salad dressing; salad greens
artichoke
hearts, 165
stuffed, 172
asparagus sesame, 165
aspic
basic savory, 174
tomato, 174
avocado
about, 165–166
and citrus, 166
cups, 172–173
and mango, 166
bean, 170–171
black bean, 170
chickpea, 170
three-bean, 170
beet
creamy, 166
pickled, 166
bistro, 160
bread
pita, 159
and tomato, 169
Caesar, 159
carrot
with apple and horseradish, 167
with edamame rice vinegar dressing, 167
with raisins, 166
celery root rémoulade, 167
chef's, 162
chicken or turkey, 163–164
Chinese, 164
curried, 164
hot, 106
variations on, 164
cobb, 162
coconut lime, 226
combination, 162–165
conch, 391
corn and tomato, Dee's, 272
crab Louis, 162–163
cucumber
creamy, 167
cups, 173, **173**
marinated, 167
mousse, 175–176
dressing of, 156–157
edamame and carrot, with rice vinegar dressing, 167
egg, 164
endive and walnut, 160
freezing ingredients for, 925
fruit, 169–170
citrus, 224
fresh, 210
gelatin, 175
winter, 224
grain and rice, 171
brown rice, with dates and oranges, 171
rice, with chicken and black olives, 171
rye berry, with roasted red pepper dressing, 361
tabbouleh, 362
warm barley, mushroom, and asparagus, 347
wild rice, with sausage, 171
Greek, 159

green, 158
additions, 157–158
Asian greens and whole herbs, 158
baked goat cheese and mesclun, 160–161
field, with fresh herbs, 158
mixed greens with cheese crisp, 159
pear, walnut, and endive, 170
tart green, 158
tart greens with apple and pecans, 158
wilted greens, 160
green papaya, 231
ham, 164
hearts of palm, 167
herring, 165
jicama, 167–168
lentil and potato, warm, 171
lobster, 165
mousse, 176
vinaigrette, 162
main-course, 162–165
molded, 173–176
aspic, basic savory, 174
aspic, tomato, 174
cranberry, 175
fruit, 175
golden glow, 175
pineapple, orange gelatin, 175
orange and onion, 168
pasta, 171–172
calico macaroni, 172
creamy macaroni, for a crowd, 172
with grilled chicken, 172
with pesto, 172
with shrimp, 172
potato, 168–169
American, 168
German, 168–169
warm, with lentil, 171
roasted cactus pad, 265
seafood, 165
shrimp, 165
with kiwi, 228–229
Oregon, 163
spinach, 159
with grapefruit, orange, and avocado, 159–160
with seared shrimp and bacon, 163
taco, 163
Thai beef, 163
three-pea, 168
tofu, 317
tomato, 169
aspic, 174
with bread (panzanella), 169
cold stuffed, 173
and mozzarella, 169
tuna, 164
Becker, 164–165
salade Niçoise, 162
vegetable, 165–169
Waldorf, 169
warm or wilted, 160
watermelon, spicy, 170
whelk, 391
salad bowls, 157
salad burnet, 155
salad dressing. see also vinaigrette
about, 572
anchovy, 574
apricot, 575
boiled, 577

salad dressing (*cont.*)
   buttermilk honey, for fruit salad, 578
   celery seed, 574
   cream cheese, for fruit salad, 578
   creamy blue cheese, 576
   creamy caraway, 577
   creamy dijon, 577
   creamy, for coleslaw, 578
   creamy Parmesan, 578
   curry, for fruit salad, 578
   dressing a salad, 156–157
   feta, 576–577
   for fruit salads, 578
   ginger
     Japanese steakhouse, 575
     lemongrass, 575
   goat cheese, 577
   green goddess, 576
   honey, for fruit salad, 578
   horseradish, creamy, 578
   Lorenzo, 574
   Midwest cream, 577
   poppy seed-honey, 574
   ranch, 576
   roasted garlic, 575
   roasted red pepper, 574–575
   Russian, 576
   Southwest, 573
   tahini, 576
   tangerine shallot, 575
   Thousand Island, 576
   yogurt
     for fruit salad, 578
     herb, 577
salade Niçoise, 162
salad greens, 152–156. *see also* green(s); lettuce
   about, 152–156
   cleaning, 156
   foraging for wild, 156
   packaged, 156
   preparing, 156
   substitutions for, 155–156
salami, 515
   rolls, 83
salmi
   of squab, 452
salmon, 416
   casserole, with potato and spinach, 97
   chowder, 143
   croquettes, 660
   cured (gravlax), 411
   fettuccine with asparagus and, 327
   fillets grilled with mayonnaise, 406
   mousse, 85
   pâté, 85
   poached, 400
   roasted, whole, 397
   smoked
     bagels and lox, 184
     canapés, 87
     eggs with, 198
     rolls, 85–86
salmon roe, 416
salsa, 571–572
   about, 571
   avocado, 571–572
   corn, 571–572
   fresca, 571
   fruit, 572
   roasted tomato-chipotle, 572

tomatillo, 571
tomato, 571–572
verde (green sauce), 567
salsify
   about, 304
   with herbs, 304
salt(s), 6, 1008–1010
   fish baked in, 399
   risen bread, 606–607
   seasoned, 1009–1010
   smoky, mixture, 1010
   substitutes for, 8, 1010
salt cod, 414
salt pork, 508
   as seasoning, 1008
saltwater
   taffy, 871
salty dog, 58
samosas
   with ground beef, 89–90
   with potatoes and peas, 89
sand tarts, 772
   brown sugar, 772
sandwich(es), 177–187. *see also* wrap(s)
   bagels and lox, 184
   Becker gyro, 188
   BLT, 180
   braunschweiger, 183
   bread for, 177
   cheese, 178
   cheese toast, 182
   chicken or turkey
     salad, 178, 180
     sliced, 178
   clam roll, 183
   club, 180
   corn dogs, 185
   croque madame, 181
   croque monsieur, 181
   Cuban, 181
   deviled ham or chicken spread, 180
   egg
     fried, 183–184
     salad, 178
     western, 184
   falafel, 188
   fillings and dressings, 177–178
   freezing, 924
   fried soft-shell crab, 183
   grilled cheese, 180
   ham, 178
   hamburgers. *see* hamburgers
   hot Brown, 182
   hot dogs, 185
   ice cream, 830
   lobster roll, 183
   loosemeat, 510–511
   loose meat, 510–511
   meatball, 184
   meat loaf, 183
   mixed veggie, 183
   Monte Cristo, 181
   muffuletta, 181–182
   oyster po'boy, 185
   panini, with prosciutto, mozzarella, and basil, 181
   pastrami and corned beef triple-decker, 182–183
   peanut butter, 178
   Philly cheese steak, 184–185
   pita, 188
   preparation and keeping of, 177
   Reuben, 181

roast beef, 177
   hot, 182
roast pork, 177
sausage and pepper sub, 184
sliced chicken or turkey, 178
sloppy Joe, 510–511
submarine or hero, 184
tea, 185–188
tuna melt, 182
tuna salad, 178
twin, 180–181
vegetable, 178
waffle, 180
sangría, 65
Santa Claus melons, 230
Santa Rosa plums, 235
sapodillas, 239, **239**
sapotes, 239
Saratoga chips, 94
sardine(s), 416
   toast, 412
Satsuma oranges, 225
saturated fats, 5
sauce(s), savory, 542–590. *see also* barbecue sauce; butter sauce(s); dessert sauce(s); dressing; glazes; gravy; marinade; salad dressing; tomato sauce
   allemande (egg-thickened velouté), 554
   amatriciana, 563
   anchovy, 552
   apple and horseradish, Bavarian, 566
   Asian black bean, 570–571
   Asian sweet-and-sour, 564
   béarnaise, 560
   bigarade, 448
   black bean, 960
   black bean, Asian, 570–571
   Bolognese, 564
   bordelaise (red wine and marrow), 555
   brown, 554–556, 557
     about, 554
     onion, 555
   brown butter crumb (sauce polonaise), 557–558
   Burgundy, 549
   butter, 557–560
   caper, 554
   caviar, 568
   Champagne, 553
   Champagne, mignonette, 568
   chasseur (hunter's sauce), 555
   cheese, creamy microwave, 551
   cherry, 565
   chili, 951
   chimichurri, 566
   Chinese-style, for vegetables, 557
   cocktail, Becker, 568
   cold mustard, 566
   cream, 553
   cucumber almond, 565–566
   curry, 553
   demi-glace, 554
   egg-thickened, about
     about, 560
   English Cumberland, 565
   fish, 982
   garlic and walnut, 568–569
   green (salsa verde), 567
   hoisin, 992
   hollandaise, 560–561
   hongroise (paprika sauce), 553

horseradish, 552
hunter's (sauce chasseur), 555
Indian yogurt, 567–568
ingredients for, 543
keeping, 543
lemon egg, 561–562
Louis, 581
Lyonnaise (brown onion sauce), 555
Madeira, 555
marinara, 562
Mexican hot, 566–567
mignonette, 568
mint, 565
mojo, 566
Mornay, 551
mousseline, 561
mushroom, 557
mushroom wine, 555–556
mustard, 552
    Scandinavian, with dill, 566
    sweet-and-sour, 564–565
Newburg, 561
nuoc cham, 570
onion, 551–552
orange and ginger, 549
oyster, 552, 1005
paloise, 561
paprika, 553
Parisienne, 580
parsley-chile, 567
pasta, 321–322
peanut, 81–82
pepper, 556
périgueux, 555
pesto, 569
picada, 569
piquant, 556
pistou, 569
poivrade (pepper sauce), 556
polonaise (brown butter crumb sauce),
    557–558
poulette, 554
puttanesca, 563
in quantity, 543
quick, 556–557
raisin, 565
raspberry mignonette, 568
ravigote, 553
red wine and marrow, 555
rémoulade, 581
roasted red pepper, 549
roasted tomatillo spinach, 568
sauce bourguignonne, 549
serving, 545–546
shrimp, 552
soy. see soy sauce
spicy apricot, 217
tabasco, 1021
table, 564
tartar, 581
Thai hot (nam prik), 570
thickeners for, 543–545
tuna, 567
tzatziki, 567
utensils for, 542–543
velouté, 552–553
white, 550–551
white wine, 552, 553
Worcestershire, 953, 1028
sauerbraten, 478
sauerkraut, 265, 954
    beef brisket with, 481
    mushroom filling for pierogi, 342

pork braised with, 501
stuffing for wildfowl, 539
sausage. see also specific types
    about, 515–516
    apple, chicken and, 516
    baked apples stuffed with, 217
    baked butternut squash with apples
        and, 309
    baked onions stuffed with, 288
    balls for soup, 151
    boiled, 517
    braised lentils with, 258
    bread stuffing with apples and, 533
    chili, Ohio farmhouse, 514
    corn bread stuffing with bell peppers
        and, 535
    country, 516
    cured, 515
    dressing, 537
    dry summer, 904
    and fennel stuffing, 541
    grapes and, 228
    gravy for biscuits, 547
    herbed pork, 516
    Italian, pizza with onion and, 191
    lentil soup with potato and, 134
    making, 515–516, 903–904
    and mushroom strata, 98
    orecchiette with broccoli rabe and,
        329
    pan-broiled, 517
    and pepper sub, 184
    pizza with mushrooms, pepperoni and,
        191
    precooked, 515
    and rabbit, casseroled, 526–527
    and seafood paella, 358–359
    and sweet potato stuffing, 538
    white (boudin blanc), 516–517
    with wild rice salad, 171
sautéing, 1048
    fish, 406–407
    meat, 465
Sauternes, 50
Sauvignon Blanc, 46
savarin(s), about, 733–734
savories, 155, 1010
    aspic, basic, 174
    pies, about, 101
Savoy cabbage, 153, **153,** 262
Sazerac, 60
scalding, 450, 1055
    milk, 997
scallion(s), 286, **1003,** 1004
    and beef rolls, 83
    cheese, and beer bread, 629
    freezing, 921
    and mushroom soup, 145
    red radishes with, 303
scallop(s), 369, 377–379
    about, 377–378
    au gratin (coquilles St. Jacques au
        gratin), 378–379
    broiled, 386
        with barbecue sauce, 387
        Basque-style, 387
        with chili paste, 387
        with hoisin sauce, 387
        with persillade, 387
    calicos, 378
    fried
        with bread crumb coating, 377
        with cracker coating, 377

grilled, 386
    with barbecue sauce, 387
    Basque-style, 387
    with chili paste, 387
    with hoisin sauce, 387
    with persillade, 387
meunière, 378
poached, 378
preparing, 377–378
sea, 378–379
seviche, 370
in the shell, 377
tempura, 377
test for freshness, 378
types, 378
scarlet runner beans, 254
Scarlett O'Hara, 63
scaup canvasbacks, 455
scented geranium, 155
schnecken (caramel buns), 613
scones
    about, 637–638
    additions to, 638
    chocolate chip orange, 641
    classic, 640
    cream, 640
    dried fruit, 641
    food processor mixing for, 638
    ginger, 641
    lemon, 641
scorzonera salsify, 304
Scotch
    about, 59
    single-malt, 59
Scotch barley, 346
    preparing, 364 (chart)
Scotch bonnet peppers, 291
Scotch broth, 139
Scotch eggs, 195–196
Scotch old-fashioned, 59
Scotch shortbread, 775
Scotch woodcock, 198
scrapers, 855
screwdriver, 57
scup, 415
Scuppernong grapes, 227–228
sea bass, 413
sea bream, 415
seabreeze, 58
sea clams, 374
seafood. see also fish; shellfish; specific
        seafood
    divan, 112
    dressing, 536
    freezing, 922–923
    frozen, thawing and cooking,
        923
    gumbo, 141
    party foods, 83–86
    salad, 165
    and sausage paella, 358–359
    serving size, 10
    shumai, 343
    soups, 139–143
    stew
        spicy, 100
        spicy with orzo, 100
    toppings or fillings for pizza or
        calzones, 190
sea salt, 1009
sea scallops, 378–379
seasoned flour or crumbs, 962
seasoned salts, 1009–1010

seasonings, understanding, 956–957
sea squab, 413
seating, 12–13
sea trout, 417
Seattle pizza, 191
sea urchin roe, 416
seaweed, 1010–1011
    sushi, 359–360
Seckel pears, 232
seed(s), 1011. *see also specific seeds*
    as addition to green salads, 157
    cake, 716
    sprouting, 1011–1012
    toasting, 1011
seedless red grape jam, 935
seitan, 318–319
    stew and root vegetables, 319
semifreddo, 840
    chocolate, 841–842
    espresso, 842
    hazelnut, 841
Semillon, 47
semolina, 923, 986
serrano ham, 507
serrano peppers, 291
serving sizes, 7, 10
sesame seed(s), 1011
    brittle, 873
    sesame chicken, 432
    wafers, 769
seviche, 411
    scallop, 370
    shrimp, 370
Seville oranges, 225
shad, 416
shaddock grapefruit, 225–226
shad roe, 416
    about, 405
    broiled, 405
shallot(s), 1004, **1005**
    about, 304
    crispy, 304
    freezing, 921
    roasted, 304
    tangerine dressing, 575
shandy, 53
shari (sushi rice), 359
shark, 416
sharpening stone, **1070**
sharptail grouse, 458
shears, kitchen, 542
she-crab soup, 140
sheep
    wild, about, 529–530
    roast bighorn, 530
sheep sorrel, 156
shell beans, fresh, 252–253
shellfish, 369–392. *see also specific shellfish*
    cocktail, 370–371
    cooking liquids for, 371
    fried, with flour coating, 376–377
    mixed, in tomato sauce, 369
    raw, about, 370
    stew, with mushrooms and greens, 369–370
shepherd's pie, 102–103
sherbet, 837–838. *see also* sorbet
    about, 837
    cranberry, 838
    lemon, 838
    lime, 838
    orange, 837–838

raspberry, 837
strawberry, 837
sherry, 50
    vinaigrette, 573–574
    wassail, 68
sherry vinegar, 1024
shichimi (seven-spice) mix, 1012
shield and baste roasting, 422
shiitake mushrooms, 282
    barley "risotto" with mushrooms, 347
    chicken breasts baked on a bed of mushrooms, 425
    creamed mushrooms, 283
    grilled mushrooms, 283
    mushroom triangles, 88
    sauerkraut and mushroom filling, 342
    sausage and mushroom strata, 98
    sautéed mushrooms, 283
    as seasoning, 999
    stir-fried bok choy with mushrooms, 264
Shiraz, 48
Shirley Temple, 64
shoofly pie, 683
shortbread
    chocolate, 775–776
    dough, pat-in-the-pan, 667
    Scotch, 775
shortcakes, 733
    cream, 639
    fluffy, 639
    strawberry, 733
shortening, 591, 1012–1013
short-grain rice, 354
short ribs
    braised, 482–483
    with olives, Mediterranean, 99–100
shoveler duck, 455
shrimp, 369, 385–389
    about, 385
    and avocado tostadas, 189
    baked honey, 84
    baked stuffed jumbo, 388
    Becker barbecued, 386
    beer-batter, 84
    boiled, no-fail, 385–386
    broiled, 386
        Basque-style, 387
        with chili paste, 387
        with hoisin sauce, 387
        with persillade, 387
    butter, 559
    butterflying, 385, **385**
    Cajun popcorn, 84
    Cockaigne, grilled or broiled, 84
    cocktail, 370
    coconut, 84
        vanilla, 388
    deep-fried, 387–388
    deveining of, 385
    dip, 72
    dried, 976
    étouffée, 388–389
    fajitas, 190
    fried
        in batter, 388
        with bread crumb coating, 377
        with cornmeal coating, 377
        with cracker coating, 377
        deep-fried, 387–388
    grilled, 386
        with barbecue sauce, 387
        Basque-style, 387

with chili paste, 387
with hoisin sauce, 387
with persillade, 387
and grits, 350
peeling, 385, **385**
salad, 165
    with kiwi, 228–229
    Oregon, 163
    pasta, 172
sauce (sauce nantua), 552
scampi, 386
seared, spinach with bacon and, 163
seviche, 370
South Carolina skillet, 385
spicy, white pizza with roasted red peppers and, 192
stock, 119
tacos, grilled, 189
tempura, 377, 388
test for freshness, 385
wiggle, 113
shrub
    blackberry, 38
    raspberry, 38
shumai, **343**
shungiku, 155
Sicilian salad, 168
sidecar, 63
silicone liners, 855
silicone spoons, 855
silver cups, 54, **55**
silver fizz, 56
silver mullet, 415
silver salmon, 416
simmering, 1049–1050
simple syrup. *see* sugar syrup
Singapore sling, 57
sirloin, ground, 509
skate, 416
    panfried, with black butter, 408–409
skewer cooking, 1049. *see also* kebabs
    lemon rosemary chicken on skewers, 80
    satay with peanut sauce, 81–82
skillet breads, 631
    corn, 632
skipjack, 417
skordalia (potato garlic mayonnaise), 582
slab bacon, 508
slaw. *see* coleslaw
sloppy Joe, 510–511
slow-cooker food, 99–101
    about, 99
    fricassee with chicken and sweet potato, 100
    meat, 466–467
    meat ragù, hearty, 101
    pork shoulder with mustard and rosemary sauce, 99
    short ribs with olives, Mediterranean, 99–100
    stew, spicy seafood, 100
    stock, 118
    vegetarian chili, 101
slow cooking
    high altitude, 1051
slumps
    about, 693
    apricot cherry, 694
slurry, 544
smallmouth bass, 413
small red radishes, 303
smelts, 411, 416, 417
    breaded, 408

Smithfield ham, 506
smoked salmon
    canapés, 87
    eggs with, 198
    rolls, 85–86
smoke point, 1023
smoking food, 905–906
smoky salt mixture, 1010
smoothies
    about, 39
    recipes for, 40
snail(s), 369
    about, 391
    butter, 559
    cooking, 391–392
snap beans, 250
snap peas, 290
    freezing, 921
    salad, three-pea, 168
snapper, 416
snapping turtles, 391
snaps
    brandy, 781
    ginger-, 767
snickerdoodles, 768
snipe, 418, 459, 460–461
snow crabs, 380
snow cream, 838
snow peas, 290
    freezing, 921
    stir-fried, 290–291
snows, 810
    pineapple, 814
    pudding, 814
Soave, 46
soba noodles, 330–331
    cold, 333
    spicy, 333–334
sockeye, 416
soda(s)
    fruit, 39
    ice cream, 39
    low-calorie, 6
    regular, 6, 43
soda bread
    Irish, 629
soda crackers, 93–94
sodium, 6
    on food labels, 8
soffrito (mirepoix), 998
sofrito (seasoned lard), 1013
soft-boiled eggs, 194
soft drinks, 43. see also soda(s)
soft roe, 416
soft-shell clams, **374,** 374–375
    baked, 375
soft-shell crabs, 374
    broiled, 381
    cleaning, 380
    deep-fried, 380
    grilled, 381
    preparing, 380
    roasted, 381
    sandwich, fried, 183
sole, 414, 416–417
    dugléré, 397–398
    florentine, fillets, 402
sopa de ajo (garlic soup with eggs),
    124–125
sopapillas, 608
sorbet, 835–837. see also sherbet
    about, 835
    blackberry, 836

blueberry, 836
    instant, 837
    lemon, 836
    lime, 836
    mango, 836
    orange, 836
    peach, 836
    pink grapefruit, 836
    raspberry, 836
    rosemary, 837
    strawberry, 836
    watermelon, 836
sorghum, 1013
    flour, 985
Sorinaw cherries, 223
sorrel, 154, **154,** 304–305, 1013
souffléd omelets. see omelets, souffléd
soufflés, 203–206
    blue cheese-Parmesan, 204
    broccoli or cauliflower, 205
    carrot, 205
    cheese, Cockaigne, 204
    corn, 205
    crab or tuna, 206
    dessert, 808–810
        about, 808–809
        chocolate, 809
        fresh fruit, 810
        frozen, 840, 842
        Grand Marnier, 809, 842
        lemon, 809–810
        lemon, cold, 817
        lime, cold, 817–818
        orange, cold, 817
        sour cream apple cake, Cockaigne,
          810
        vanilla, 809
    goat cheese and walnut, 205
    ham and cheese, 204
    mushroom, 205
    spinach, 205
    sweet potato, 205–206
soup(s), 114–151. see also stocks
    about, 122
    baked potato, 130
    bean
        bean with vegetables (garbure),
          131
        black bean, 133–134
        Mediterranean white bean, 133
        U.S. Senate bean, 133
    Becker blender gazpacho, 147
    Becker chicken, 134–135
    beef barley, 136
    borscht, 129
        blender, 149
        with meat, 138
        Rombauer, 149
    bouillabaisse, 142
    breads to serve with, 150
    butternut squash, 129
    cabbage, 130
    Caribbean callaloo, 141
    Charleston crab, 140
    cheddar cheese, 146
    cherry, 148
    chicken, avocado, and tomato, 135
    chicken gumbo, 136
    chicken noodle, 125
    chicken rice, 135
    chicken rice or barley, 125–126
    clear, 123–127
    cock-a-leekie, 135

    cold, 146–147
        avocado, 146
        cucumber, 147
    coloring, 122
    consommé, 123–124
    consommé brunoise, 124
    consommé madrilene, 124
    corn chowder, 143
    court bouillon, 120–121
        Louisiana, 141
    cream, 127, 143–146
        asparagus, 144
        broccoli, 144
        carrot, 144
        cauliflower, 144
        cauliflower, quick, 149
        celery root, 144
        chestnut, 144
        mushroom, 144–145
        mushroom, quick, 149
        mussel, 140
        onion, 145
        purslane, 145–146
        scallion and mushroom, 145
        spinach, 145
        tomato, 144
        watercress, 145–146
    croutons, 151
    egg drop, 124
    fish and seafood, 139–143
    fish chowder, 143
    freezing, 924–925
    French onion, 129–130
    fruit, 147–148
    garlic with eggs, 124–125
    garnishes for, 150–151
    gazpacho, 146–147
    Georgia peanut, 134
    ginger melon, 148
    Greek lemon, 124
    green pea, 130
    herbs and greens for, 150–151
    hot-and-sour, 131–132
    Italian Parmesan and egg, 124
    jellied, 127
    kreplach, 126
    lentil, 134
        with greens, 134
        with sausage and potato, 134
    lobster bisque, 140
    Manhattan clam chowder, 142–143
    matzo ball, 126
    meatballs for, 151
    milk toast, 146
    minestrone, 128
    miso, 125
    mock turtle, 138
    Mongolian hot pot, 137
    mulligatawny, 136
    mushroom barley, 131
    New England clam chowder, 142
    New Year's, 146
    oxtail, 137–138
    oyster bisque, 141
    oyster stew, 140–141
    pepper pot, 139
    Portuguese greens, 139
    potato leek, 130
    pot-au-feu, 136–137
    poultry and meat, 134–139
    Provençal vegetable (soupe au pistou),
        128
    pumpkin, 129

soup(s) (cont.)
  quick
    Becker miso, 125
    beef stew, 148–149
    cheese, 149
    Cockaigne, 148–150
    cream of cauliflower, 149
    cream of mushroom, 149
    fresh tomato cream, 149–150
    tomato corn chowder, 149
  removing fat from, 123
  Rhode Island clam chowder, 143
  roasted garlic, 125
  roasted red pepper, 132
  rose hip, 148
  salmon chowder, 143
  sausage balls for, 151
  Scotch broth, 139
  seafood gumbo, 141
  seasoning, 122–123
  she-crab, 140
  split pea, 134
  Thai chicken and coconut, 135
  thick, 127–133
  thickeners for, 123
  tomato, 132
    canning, 898
  tortilla, 132–133
  turtle, 391
  Tuscan bread and tomato, 132
  vegetable (soupe paysanne), 128
  vegetable stew, 131
  vichyssoise, 130
  Vietnamese beef noodle, 137
  white gazpacho, 147
  winter fruit, 147
  winter melon, 129
  wonton, 126–127
soupe au pistou (Provençal vegetable
  soup), 128
soupe paysanne (vegetable soup), 128
sour cherry(ies), 223
  and red wine pan sauce, 548–549
sour cream, 1014
  apple cake soufflés Cockaigne, 810
  berry tarts, 678
  cake, 714
  cherry tarts, 678
  chocolate frosting, 796–797
  cobbler biscuit dough, 693
  coffee cake, quick, 630
  dip, 72
  doughnuts, 654–655
  egg noodles with chives and, 330
  muffins, 635
  new potatoes stuffed with caviar and,
    79
  pound cake, 717
  rolls, 611, **611**
  sauce, 851
  spice cupcakes, 738
  streusel cake, high-altitude,
    751–752
  substitute for, 1014
  whipped topping, 851
sourdough
  bread, rustic, 604
  pancakes, 644
  rye bread, 605
  starters, 601–604
sour milks and creams, 1013–1015
sour salt, 1009
soursops, 28

Southern cuisine
  baby back ribs, 505
  barbecued spareribs, 505
  basic transparent pie, 682
  beaten biscuits, 640
  black-eyed peas and greens, 256
  Brunswick stew, 432
  buttermilk biscuits, 639
  buttermilk crackling corn bread, 632
  chicken and dumplings, 432
  corn bread, 34
  corn dodgers Cockaigne, 633
  cornmeal dumplings, 134
  corn zephyrs Cockaigne, 633
  country ham steak with red-eye gravy,
    508
  cucumber cream cheese spread
    (benedictine), 179
  deep-fried fillets, 409
  divinity, 869
  fried chicken, 429
  Georgia peanut soup, 134
  greens, 277
  hot Brown, 182
  iced tea, 34
  Italian cream cake, 714
  Kentucky burgoo, 484
  lane cake, 712
  low country cream-style grits, 350
  mint julep, 60
  Mississippi mud cake, 723
  North Carolina-style barbecue sauce,
    587
  pecan pie, 682
  pulled pork, 500
  red beans and rice, 256
  sausage gravy, 547
  Scarlett O'Hara, 63
  Scotch toffee, 873
  sesame seed brittle, 873
  sesame seed (benne seed) wafers, 769
  shrimp and grits, 350
  smoked brisket, 481
  South Carolina skillet shrimp, 385
  Southern barbecue dry rub, 587
  twice-baked sweet potatoes, 302
  western North Carolina barbecue
    sauce, 587
  whiskey sauce, 852
soybeans, 250, 254. see also edamame;
  tofu
  curd, 316
  flour, 985
  fresh, 252
  roasting, 1011
  sprouts, 253
  textured soy protein (TSP), 318
soy milk, 1023
soy sauce, 1015
  ginger, 571
  -ginger vinaigrette, grilled whole red
    snapper with, 403
  grilled tuna with pickled ginger, wasabi
    and, 405
  wasabi, 571
spaghetti, **321**
  carbonara, 329
  chicken lo mein, 331
  Cincinnati chili Cockaigne, 514
  with garlic and oil (aglio e olio), 327
  Johnny Marzetti spaghetti pie, 95
  linguine with white clam sauce, 328
  spicy peanut sesame noodles, 332

  spicy szechuan noodles, 332
  turkey tetrazzini, 96
spaghetti squash, 307
Spanish mackerel, 415
Spanish omelet, 201
Spanish onions, 286
spareribs
  barbecue, 505
sparkling wines, 49–50
spatulas, 542, 784, **784**, 785
  offset, 855
spätzle, 335–336
special occasion menus, 21–22
spelt, 362
  flour, 985
  preparing, 368 (chart)
spice(s), 1015–1016. see also specific
  spices
  harvesting, drying, and freezing, 991
  parisienne (quatre épices), 1007
  seven, (shichimi) mix, 1012
spice cake
  brown sugar, 719
  high-altitude, 750
  leaveners for, 698
  velvet, 719
spinach, 154, **155**, 305–306
  about, 305
  boiled, 305
  casserole, with salmon and potato, 97
  creamed, 305
  curly leaf, **155**
  dip in a bread bowl, 73
  and feta triangles, 89
  freezing, 921
  and ham crêpes, 650
  and meat filling for stuffed pasta, 338
  mushroom and ground meat stuffing,
    538
  panned or Sicilian, 306
  pasta, 324
  ricotta
    stuffing, 538–539
  roasted tomatillo sauce, 568
  saag paneer, 306
  salad, 159
    with grapefruit, orange, and
      avocado, 159–160
    with seared shrimp and bacon, 163
  with seared shrimp and bacon, 163
  soufflé, 205
  soup, cream of, 145
  timbales, 206
  vinaigrette, 573
  wilted, 305–306
spingerle, 775
spiny lobsters, 382, **382**
spiral cut ham, 506
spirits
  in cooking, 1027–1028
  preserving fruits in, 954–955
spit cooking, 1059
Spitzenburg apples, 215–216
split peas, 253
  soup, 134
spoilage
  in canning, 892–893
  in food, 883–884
sponge cake, 706–709
  about, 704, 706
  chocolate, 707–708
  chocolate roll, high-altitude, 752–753
  daffodil, 708

filled, 730
French, 708–709
high-altitude, 750
leaveners for, 698
Passover, 707
Passover nut, 707
sheet, 735
sponge cupcakes, 738
sponge custards, 805–806
lemon, 805
orange, 806
sponge starters, 601–606
rye bread with, 605–606
white bread made with, 604
spoon bread, 633–634
buttermilk, 634
crusty soft-center, 634
spoon mustard, 154
spoons, 12, **12, 14,** 542
measuring, 542
spotfin fish, 414
spot fish, 414
spotted sea trout, 417
spread(s)
almond ginger cream cheese, 179
blue cheese with walnuts, 76
chicken or ham salad, 180
chutney cheese, 76
chutney nut cream cheese, 180
cream cheese, 179–180
cucumber cream cheese, 179
deviled ham or chicken, 180
garlic cheese, 76
liptauer cheese, 76
orange pecan cream cheese, 179
pimento cheese, 179
roasted garlic and Parmesan, 76
tea sandwiches with, 186
spring mix greens, 155
spring onions, 286
spritzer, white wine, 53
sprouts, 155, 253, 1011–1012
spruce grouse, 458
spumoni, 842
Spygold apples, 215
squab, 418. *see also* poultry *for general information*
about, 452
broiled, 452
broilers, 423
grilled, 452
home-smoked Chinese-style, 452–453
salmi of, 452
squash, 306–310. *see also* summer squash; winter squash; *specific squash*
about, 306–307
spaghetti, freezing, 921
squash blossoms, 309–310
about, 309
stuffed with cheese and herbs, 309–310
squash seeds
toasted, 71
squid, 369, **389**
about, 389–390
cleaning, 390, **390**
grilled, 390
storing, 389
stuffed, 390
tempura, 377
squirrel, 524–525
stain removal, 1072

star anise, 1016
starch, 5
starch(es), 1016–1018
star fruit, 238, **238**
Stayman Winesap apples, 216
steak
about cuts of, 472–473
broiled, 473–474
broiled fillet of, 474
chicken-fried, 475
Diane, 475
fajitas, 190
fish. *see* fish steaks
flank, broiled, 474–475
flank, with dressing, 482
grilled, 473–474
grilled fillet of, 474
and kidney pie, 483–484
London broil, 474–475
pan-broiled, 474
peppered, with cream sauce (steak au poivre), 474
Philly cheese, 184–185
plank, 475
sautéed, 475
Swiss, 482
tartare, 82–83
venison, 528–529
wraps, 187
steak au poivre (peppered steak with cream sauce), 474
steam blanching, 1055
steam-blanching, 919
"steamers," 374
steaming, 1050–1051
of fish, 399–400
steam-pressure canning, 891
equipment for, 889
steelhead trout, 417
steeped coffee, 30–31
steeping
of ice cream, 828
stenciling
top of cake, 786, **786**
stew(s)
beef, 479
Belgian, 480
stewing, 1051
Brunswick, 432–433
Irish, 496
lamb, 495–496
of meat, 466, 467
Moroccan-style vegetable, 246–247
oxtail, 521
oyster, 140–141
quick beef, 148–149
spicy seafood, 100
veal (blanquette de veau), 489
vegetable, 131
stinger, 63
stir-frozen
of ice cream, 828
stir-frying, 260–261, 1048–1049
bean sprouts, 253
beef and vegetable, 476
bok choy with mushrooms, 264
broccoli stir-fry, 260–261
carrots and Napa cabbage, 264
chicken with garlic, 439–440
clams with oyster sauce, 376
lotus root, 281
mussels with oyster sauce, 376
snow peas, 290–291

vegetable, 242
water chestnut, 314–315
yard-long beans, 252
stocks
about, 114
Becker express, 120
brown beef, 117
brown poultry stock, 118
chicken, 117
clarifying, 116
court bouillon, 120–121
court bouillon, Louisiana, 141
dashi, 119
express fish, 120
fish, 118
fumet, 118–119
game, 118
household
beef, 117
poultry, 118
lamb, 118
light veal, 117
meat, 114–115
meat glaze, 117
poultry, 114–115, 117, 118
reduction, 116
rich vegetable, 119–120
seasoning, 115
shrimp, 119
slow-cooker, 118
store bought, 120
straining and storing, **115,** 115–116
vegetable, 119–120
Stollen (Christmas loaf), 622–623
stone crabs, 380
stone fruits. *see also specific stone fruits*
substitutions for, 209
stone-ground grits, 349
storage onions, 286
store-bought and convenience foods
bagels, 113
berry or cherry pie with canned or bottled fruit, 677
canned and frozen fruits, 210
canned beans, 254
canned hams, 506
canned vegetables, 242, 245
can sizes, 1033 (chart)
commercially prepared foods, 11
dried eggs, 978
dried fruits, 211
frozen food packages, 1033 (chart)
frozen vegetables, cooking, 344, 922
ground meats, 509
juices and beverages, 57, 64
mayonnaise, 579
mustard, 999
pectin, 927, 928
phyllo, 674
pie with frozen fruit, 677
pomegranate juice, 235
puffed pastry, 109, 111, 112, 569
stocks and broths, 120
tofu, 315–316
yeast, 1028
stout, 52
stovetop metal drip pots, 28, **29**
stracciatella (Italian Parmesan and egg soup), 124
stracotto (Italian pot roast), 477–478
straightneck yellow squash, 306
strainers, 54, **54**

strata
about, 98
baked French toast, 648
crab, 98
ham and vegetable, 98
sausage and mushrooms, 98
straw and hay (paglia e fieno),
326–327
strawberry(ies), 219–220
about, 219–220
Bavarian pie, 689
chocolate-dipped, 220
coulis, 853
dacquoise, with whipped cream and
chocolate, 741–742
freezing, 917
fresh, variations on, 220
frozen yogurt, 835
fruit punch, 42
glaze, 800
hulling, **219,** 220
icebox cake, 731
ice cream, 833–834
jam, 934
meringue, with whipped cream and
chocolate, 741–742
mousse, frozen, 840–841
preserves, 937
pineapple and, 937–938
rhubarb pie, 680
Romanoff, 220
Rombauer, 220
sherbet, 837
shortcake, 733
smoothie, 40
sorbet, 836
streusel tart
raspberry, 681
striped bass, 413
striped mullet, 415
strip sirloin
roast, for a crowd, 471
stromboli, 190, 193
strudel
about, 673
apple, 673–674
filling for, 673
stuffing, 532–541. see also dressing
bacon, for fish, 536
bread
about, 532
apple and cherry, 534
with chestnuts and dried fruit, 533
with giblets, 534
Italian, 533–534
with mushrooms, 533
with oysters, 533
with sausage and apples, 533
with toasted nuts and dried fruit,
533
chicken farce, 541
corn bread
basic, 534–535
with cumin and hot chile peppers,
535
with oysters, 535
with sausage and bell peppers,
535
crabmeat, for fish, 536
for crown roast of pork, 539
dry dressing, 535
mashed potato, 537–538
parsley and bread crumb, for fish, 535

rice
with almonds, raisins, and Middle
eastern spices, 539–540
with chorizo and hot chile peppers,
539
roast chicken with, 424
sauerkraut, for wildfowl, 539
sausage and fennel, 541
spinach
mushroom and ground meat, 538
with ricotta, 538–539
sweet potato
and apple, 538
and sausage, 538
submarine sandwich, 184
sausage and pepper, 184
substitutions
about, 1031–1032
for common ingredients,
1037–1044
healthy, 8
succotash, 272
canning, 901
Sucralose, 1020
sucralose
in canning, 893
suet, 1018
sugar, 5
Barbados, 1018
brown. see brown sugar
cake, burnt sugar, 719–720
caramelized, 856–857, 1019
Chinese rock, 1019
cinnamon, 1019
citrus-flavored, 1019
colored, 1019
confectioner's, 1019
corn, 1019
flavored, 1019
glaze, translucent, 799–800
granulated, 1019–1020
granulated brown, 1019
in jellies and preserves, 928–929
liquid, 1018
lump, 1019
maple, 1020
measuring, 1018
muscovado, 1019
raw, 1020
solid, 1018–1020
stages of cooked, 855–856
substitutes for, 1020
sugar cubes, 1020
superfine, 1020
turbinado, 1020
vanilla, 1019
sugar apples, 238
sugar syrup
about, 43
for canning, 893
recipes for, 43
stages of cooked, 855–856
sukiyaki, 476–477
summer flounder, 414
summer melons, 230
summer rolls, 92–93
summer squash, 306–308
about, 306–307
casserole, 307
deep-fried zucchini, 308
freezing, 921
ratatouille Provençale, 274
sautéed, 308

steamed, 307
stuffed baked, 308
zucchini bread, sweet, 628
summer truffles, 285
sunchoke, 249
sunfish, 415
sunflower seeds, 1011
toasted, 71
Super Bowl party menus, 21
supper clubs, 17
menus for, 22
surf clams, 374
surimi (imitation crab and lobster),
391
surprise, frozen lemon, 830
sushi
crab rolls, 359, 360, **360**
rolled (maki-zushi), 359–360
tuna rolls, 359–360, **360**
vegetable rolls, 359–360, **360**
sushi rice (shari), 359
sweating, 1055
Swedish meatballs, 513
sweetbreads, 518
cooking, 519
sweet cherry(ies), 223
conserves, 940
sweet cicely, 155, 1020
sweet corn, 348
sweeteners. see also sugar
in jellies and preserves, 928–929
Sweet Imperial onions, 286
sweet Manhattan, 59
sweet onions, 286
sweet potato(es), 301–303
about, 301
apples and, 302
baked, 301–301
boiled, 301
candied, 302
canning, 901
chicken chili hash with, 108
deep-fried, 302
freezing, 922
fricassee with chicken, 100
mashed, 301
muffins, 635
and peanut stew, 302–303
pie, 686
soufflé, 205–206
stuffing
with apple, 538
with sausage, 538
turkey chili hash with, 108
twice-baked, 302
sweet rice flour, 1017
sweetsops, 238
sweet tea spreads, 179–180
sweet woodruff (waldmeister), 1020
Swiss chard. see chard
swordfish, 417
syllabub, 67
Syrah, 48
syrup. see also sauce(s); sugar syrup
berry, 43
blueberry, 220
raspberry, 221
cane, 964
caramel, 849
cocoa, 36
corn, 973
fruit, 43
golden, 989

herb, 43
lemon, 43, 759
lime, 43
malt, 995
maple, 995–996
moistening, 759
oranges in, 225
refiner's, 989
simple, 43
spiced, 43
for canned fruits, 212
for fresh fruits, 212
Szechuan peppercorns, 1020–1021
Szechuan-pepper salt, 1021
Szechuan-style "hacked" tempeh, 318

T
tabasco peppers, 291
tabasco sauce, 1021
tabbouleh, 362
table decor, 11–12
table radishes, 303
table salt, 1009
table setting, 12, **12, 13, 14**
taco(s), 188–189
about, 188
black bean, 189
grilled fish, 189
grilled shrimp, 189
ground beef, 188–189
salads, 163
shredded chicken, 189
shredded pork, 189
taffy
about, 870
chocolate, 871
coconut, 871
saltwater, 871
vanilla, 870–871
tagliatelle, **321**
with wilted greens, 328
tahini, 1021
baba ghanoush (roasted eggplant dip), 74
falafel sandwich, 188
halvah, 878
hummus, 74
Half Moon, 74
salad dressing, 576
sesame chicken, 432
tailgating, 17
tamales, **352**
chicken and cheese, 351–352
tamari, 1015. see also soy sauce
tamarillos, 239, **239**
tamarinds, **237,** 237–238
about, 237
dipping sauce, 237–238
tandoori
chicken, 428
marinade, 584–585
tangelo oranges, 225
tangerine(s), 225
shallot dressing, 575
Tangor oranges, 225
tangy coleslaw, 161
tapenade (olive caper paste), 75
tapioca, 1017
custard, 820–821
flour, 544, 1017–1018
pudding, baked pearl, 821
pudding, coconut, 821
taramasalata, 75

taro
about, 310
cakes, 310
dasheen, 310
tarragon, 155, 1021
vinegar, 1025
tartar sauce, 581
spicy, 581
tarte Tatin, 681–682, **682**
tart green(s)
with apple and pecans, 158
salad, 158
tartlet pans, 661
tart pans, 661, **661**
tart(s), tartlets. see also pie(s)
apple, 679
bittersweet chocolate, 686
chess, 683–684
chocolate-glazed caramel, 686–687
fresh fruit, 681
glazes for, 800
individual nut, 778
leek, 109
lemon, 688
linzertorte, 696–697
pastry dough, 663
rich egg, 666
raspberry streusel, 681
shells, 90
sour cream cherry or berry, 678
tarte Tatin, 681–682, **682**
tasso, 507
tatsoi, 154, **155**
tautog, 413
tayberries, 220
tea, 6, 33–35
about, 33
with alcohol
tea vodka, 58
with alcohol/mock tea
Joy tea, 58
Long Island iced tea, 61
rum tea, 61
balls, **34**
brewing, 33–34
chai, 34
herbal, 35
iced, 34–35
raspberry gelatin, 812
spiced, 34
tea, afternoon, 17
menus for, 21
teal duck, 455
tea sandwiches, 185–188
about, 185–186
hearty, 186
open-faced (canapés), 86–89
shaped, 186
with spreads, 186
on sweet bread, 186
tea vodka, 58
teff
about, 361
preparing, 368 (chart)
tempeh
about, 317
moo shu, 317
Szechuan-style "hacked," 318
Temple oranges, 225
tempura, 243
batters, 657–658
clams, 377

oysters, 377
scallops, 377
shrimp, 377, 388
squid, 377
Tennessee whiskey, 59
tequila, tequila cocktails, 61–62
about, 61–62
bloody Maria, 57
frozen margarita, 62
grapefruit herb margarita, 62
margarita, 62
shots, 62
sunrise, 62
teriyaki
marinade, 586
terrine
chocolate, 817
testing for doneness
beef steak, 473
bread, 595–596
cakes, 702
candies and confections, 856
fish, 395–396
meat, 467–468
pot roast, 467
poultry, 423
turkey, 442
wildfowl, 453
Texas caviar, 73
Texas sheet cake, 722
Texas Spring Sweet onions, 286
Texmati rice, 354
Tex-Mex style dinner loaf, 318
textured soy protein (TSP), 318
textured vegetable protein (TVP), 318
Thai cuisine
beef salad, 163
beef satay with peanut sauce, 81
black rice, 354
chicken and coconut soup, 135
chile-lime dipping sauce, 570
clam pot, 376
curry baked chicken, 426
fish cakes, 410
fish sauce, 982
five-spice ribs, 81
ginger lemongrass dressing, 575
green papaya salad, 231
holy basil, 959
hot sauce (nam prik), 570
lemongrass, 994
pad thai, 332
peanut dipping sauce, 570
vinaigrette, 575
Thai peppers, 291
Thanksgiving menus, 19
thawing
of frozen food, 914
thermometers
candy, 855
chocolate, 855
instant-read, 467
meat, 467–468
for poultry, pop-up, 442
thick soups, 127–133
garnishes for, 150
30-minute recipes, 25–26
Thompson seedless grapes, 227
Thousand Island dressing, 576
Thuringer, 515
thyme, 155, 1021
tilapia, 417
tilefish, 417

timbales. see also mousse, savory
  about, 206
  asparagus, 206–207
  basic custard, 206
  mushroom, 206
  spinach, broccoli or cauliflower, 206
tiramisù, 819
tisanes (herbal tea), 35
toast(s)
  anchovy, 87
  baskets, 111
  cheese, 182
  cinnamon, 641
  creamed mushrooms on, 112
  French. see French toast
  honey-butter, 642
  melba, 641–642
  orange, 642
  sardine, 412
toaster oven, 1063
toasts
  bruschetta with tomatoes and basil, 88
  crostini, 642
  garlic, 641
tobiko, 416
toffee
  bars, chocolate-glazed, 763
  English, 873
  pudding, sticky, 823–824
  Scotch, 873
tofu, 315–317
  about, 315
  burgers, 316–317
  curd, 316
  salad, 317
  smoked, 316
Tokay, 50
tomalley, 382
Tom and Jerry, 67
tomatillo(s), 310–311
  canning, 899
  freezing, 922
  horseradish
    sauce, 568
  roasted, spinach sauce, 568
  salsa (salsa verde cruda), 571
tomato(es), 311–313
  about, 311
  as addition to green salads, 157
  amaranth with, 346
  aspic, 174
  and bread salad, 169
  broiled, 312
  broiled fish fillets with herbs and, 406
  canning, about, 897–898
  catsup, 951–952
  celery-carrot cooler, 39
  cherry tomato and ginger jam, golden, 936
  cold stuffed, 173
  corn and, relish, 949
  creamy pasta with chard and, 328–329
  creole, 312–313
  dried, millet cakes with Parmesan and, 352–353
  drying, 909
  freezing, 922
  and goat cheese quiche, 109
  green
    chutney, 951
    fried, 312
    pickles, 948
    relish, 948

green beans with onions, dill and, 251–252
  hot stuffed, 313
  juice, 37
    broth on the rocks, 38
    with orange juice, 37
  lamb curry with, 497
  olive relish
    grilled fish steaks with, 404
  peeling, 311, **311**, 898
  pizza with mushrooms, grilled eggplant and sun-dried, 191
  preserves, 938
  Provençale, 312
  punch, gala, 42
  and red pepper mayonnaise (andalouse sauce), 580
  roasted, chipotle salsa, 572
  salad, 169
    with corn, Dee's, 272
    with mozzarella (insalata Caprese), 169
  salsa, 571–572
  scalloped, 313
  as seasoning, 1021–1022
  slow-roasted, 312
  soup
    with avocado and chicken, 135
    corn chowder, quick, 149
    cream soup, quick fresh, 149–150
  stewed, 312
  sundried, pesto
    miniature turnovers with, 90
  sun-dried, pesto, 569
tomato juice
  canning, 898
tomato paste, 1022
  Italian, 1021–1022
tomato puree
  canning, 899
tomato sauce, 562–564
  about, 562
  amatriciana, 563
  Bolognese, 564
  concassé, 563
  fresh, 563
  grilled, 563
    pappardelle with, 329
  meat, 563–564
  with meatballs, 564
  pizza with mozzarella and, 191
  puttanesca, 563
  quick, 562–563
  shellfish mixed in, 369
  sun-dried, 562
tomato soup, 132
  cake, 721
  canning, 898
  cream of, 144
  jellied, 127
  Tuscan bread and, 132
Tom Collins, 56
tongue, 518
  about, 520
  boiled beef, 520
  pickled beef, 520
  smoked beef, 520
top neck clams, 374
toppings. see icing
tortellini, 339, **339**
tortes, 698, 727–729
  almond, Cockaigne, 727
  chocolate walnut, 728

flourless matzo almond torte, 728
  leaveners for, 698
  pecan, 727
  sachertorte, 728–729
  serving of, 727
  tricks for nut, 727
  unmolding of, 727, **727**
tortilla(s). see also wrap(s)
  burritos, 103–104
  corn, 609
  flour, 608–609
  heating and frying, 188
  quesadillas, cheese, 77
  tacos, 188–189
  tostadas, 188, 189–190
tortilla chips, 94
  nachos, 77
  soup, 132–133
tortilla Española (potato omelet), 203
tostadas, 188, 189–190
  with black beans, chicken, turkey, or beef, 189–190
  shrimp and avocado, 189
tostones, 294
trans fats, 5
treacle, 989
tree tomatoes, 239, **239**
tremblèque (coconut milk pudding), 808
tres leches ("three milks") cake, 708
Treviso radicchio, 154
trifle, 819–820
tripe, 518
  about, 521
  pepper pot, 139
  Spanish-style, 521
triticale, 923
  about, 361–362
  preparing, 368 (chart)
tropical juice, 39
tropical smoothie, 40
trout, 417
  brook, meunière, 408
  grilled whole, stuffed with pesto, 403
  smoked on cucumber rounds, 86
true salsify, 304
truffles (confection), 858–859
truffles (fungus), 284–285
trumpets of death mushrooms, 281
TSP (textured soy protein), 318
tubetti pasta, **321**
tuiles (French almond wafers), 781
tuna, 417
  casserole, quick, 96–97
  grilled, with pickled ginger, soy sauce and wasabi, 405
  melt, 182
  salad, 164
    Becker, 164–165
    salade Niçoise, 162
  salad sandwich, 178
  sauce, 567
    cold veal in, 486
  soufflé, 206
  sushi rolls, 359–360, **360**
  vegetable casserole, 97
turban squash, 307
turbot, 417
turkey, 418, 441–446. see also poultry for general information; wild turkey
  about, 441–442
  and avocado wraps, 187
  biscuits with chutney butter, 88

breast, roast, 444
burgers, chutney, 445
chili hash with sweet potatoes, 108
creamed
    about, 445
    quick, 446
croquettes, 660
curry, 105
deep-fried, 443–444
divan, 112
fresh, 418
    vs. frozen, 441–442
fricassee, 432
galantine of, 446
gravy, quick, 547
grill-roasted brined, 443
ground
    about, 445
    availability of, 423
    burgers, chutney, 445
ham dressing for, 535
loaf, ground, 445
meatballs, 445
parts
    about, 444
        about, 444
        cooking, 444
poached, 423–424
pop-up thermometers with, 442
potpie, 103
in red mole, 444
roast, 442
    breast, 444
    brined, 443
    turned, 442–443
salads, 163–164
    curried, 164
sandwich
    salad, 178, 180
    sliced, 178
self-basting, 442
smoked, and arugula rolls, 83
sweet-and-sour, 105
test for doneness, 442
tetrazzini, 96
    quick, 96
tostadas with black beans, 189–190
weight of, 441
Turkish coffee, 31–32
turmeric, 1022
turned roasting, 422–423
turnip(s)
    about, 313–314
    braised, 314
    canning, 901
    cooked, 314
    freezing, 922
    greens, 154
    puree, 314
turnip greens, 277
    freezing, 922
turnip-rooted parsley
    rooted parsley, 289
turnovers
    about fruit, 695
    apple, 696
    miniature, 90–91
        with carmelized onions and blue
            cheese, 91
        with sun-dried tomatoes and pesto,
            90
    pear, 696
turtle beans, 254

turtles, 865
    about, 391
    types, 391
turtle soup, 391
    mock, 138
Tuscan loaf, 606
TVP (textured vegetable protein), 318
twin sandwich, 180–181
tzatziki, 567

U
udon, 331
ugli fruits, 225
uni, 416
unsaturated fats, 5
    substitutes for, 8
upland cress, 153
U.S. Senate bean soup, 133
utensils
    for canning, 889–890
    choosing, 1067
    materials used to make, 1065–1067
    for sauces, 542–543

V
vacuum brewers, 29, **29**
    preparing, 30
vacuum-packing
    of food, 886
vacuum seals
    in canning, 888
Valencia oranges, 225
Valentine's Day menus, 20
Valpolicella, 49
vanilla, 1022
    chocolate, and coffee parfait, 839
    coconut shrimp, 388
    cream pie, 685
    frozen yogurt, 835
    icebox cookies, 776
    ice cream, 831
        French, 831
    pots de crème, 804
    puddings, 807
    sauce, 846, 850
    soufflé, 809
vanilla bean
    custard sauce, 846
vareniki, 341
veal, 485–489. *see also* meat *for general
        information*
    about, 485
    braised, 488, 489
    chops
        about, 488
        grilled, 488
        sautéed, 488–489
    cold, in tuna sauce (vitello tonnato
            freddo), 486
    Cordon Bleu, 488
    cutlets
        about, 486
        breaded (wiener schnitzel), 487
        paprika, 487–488
        sautéed, 486
    cuts of, **485,** 486, 488
        for stews, 489
    francese (veal dorato), 487
    ground
        patties, 511
        spinach, mushroom and ground
            meat stuffing, 538
    Marsala, 486

medallions
    about, 488
parmigiana, 487
piccata, 486
roast, 485
saltimbocca, 486–487
scallops
    about, 486
    scallopine, sautéed, 486
schnitzel, paprika, 487–488
shanks, braised (osso bucco), 489
shoulder chops, braised, 488
stew (blanquette de veau), 489
stock, 117
stock, light, 117
stuffed roasted, 485
vegan cake, (dairy free chocolate),
    723
vegetable(s), 240–319. *see also
        specific vegetables*
    à la Grecque, 246
    baby, 240
    and beef stir-fry, 476
    blanching, 918–919
    boiling, 242
    braising, 243
    broth, 121
    buttered and sauced, about, 244
    canning
        about, 899
        by type, 899–901
    Chinese-style sauce for, 557
    cups, 172–173
    curried chickpeas with, 257
    deep-frying, 243
    fermenting, about, 953
    foraging for, 240
    freezing, 918–922
    fritter batter for, 658
    frozen
        cooking, 244–245
        thawing and cooking, 922
    grilling, 243–244
    growing garden, 240
    high-altitude cooking for, 245
    marinades for, 584
    mashed and pureed, about, 244
    methods of cooking, 241–244
    microwaving of, 243
    as party food, 78–80
    preparing, 241–242
    pressure-cooking, 243
    raw
        as addition to green salads, 157
        crudités, 78
        freezing, 918
        stuffed, 79
    reheated and canned, 245
    for a roast, 244
    roasted, lasagne, 340–341
    roasting, 244
    salads, 165–169
    sandwich, 178
        mixed, 183
    serving size, 10
    soup (soupe paysanne), 128
    steaming, 242
    stew, 131
        Moroccan-style, 246–247
    stir-frying, 242, 260–261
    stock, 119–120
        rich, 119–120
    storing, 240–241

vegetable(s) (*cont.*)
  stuffed
    about, 244
    raw, 79
  sushi rolls, 359–360, **360**
  toppings or fillings for pizza or
    calzones, 190
  tuna casserole with, 97
  wintering over, 886–887
  wontons, 342
  wraps, grilled, 187–188
vegetable oil, 1023–1024
vegetarian chili, 254
  slow-cooker, 101
vegetarian cuisine. *see also* fruit(s);
      grain(s); salad(s); vegetable(s)
  baked cheese grits, 350
  bean curd, 315
  bell peppers stuffed with rice, 293
  breakfast cereal and grains, 346
  creamy pasta with chard and tomatoes,
    328
  curried chickpeas with vegetables, 257
  diet, vegetarian, 8, 21–22, 28–29, 31
  dofu, 315
  gazpacho, 146
  Israeli couscous pilaf, 363
  lentil and rice pilaf with toasted cumin
    seeds, 355
  millet cakes with Parmesan and dried
    tomatoes, 352
  moo shu tempeh, 317
  Moroccan-style vegetable stew, 246
  mushroom barley soup, 131
  peas and carrots, 290
  portobello pizzas, 282
  raita (Indian yogurt sauce), 567–568
  risotto with mushrooms, 361
  roasted vegetable lasagne, 340
  root vegetable and seitan stew, 319
  rye berry salad with roasted red pepper
    dressing, 361
  sauerkraut, 265
  smoked tofu, 316
  stuffed grape leaves (dolmas), 82
  Szechuan-style hacked tempeh, 318
  tagliatelle with wilted greens, 328
  Tex-Mex style dinner loaf, 318
  tofu burgers, 316
  tofu or soybean curd, 316
  tofu salad, 317
  tofu, tempeh, and vegetarian proteins,
    315–319
  tomato goat cheese quiche, 109
  Tuscan bread and tomato soup, 132
  TVP (textured vegetable protein), 318
  vegetarian chili, 254
  white bean dip with rosemary and
    garlic, 73
  wonton soup, 126
veggie bean burgers, 107
veggie sandwich, mixed, 183
velouté
  egg-thickened, 554
  sauce, 552–553
  soup, 127
venison, 527–529
  about, 527
  black bean chili, 529
  burger, 528
  chops
    grilled, with blue cheese and
      caraway butter, 529

cooking, 527
  medallions, Becker, 529
  pot roast, 528
  roasted leg of, 528
  steaks, sautéed, 528–529
vermicelli, **321**
vermouth cassis, 59
Vialone Namo rice, 360
vichyssoise, 130
Vidalia onions, 286
Viennese coffee, iced, 33
Viennese crescents, 773
Vietnamese beef noodle soup, 137
vinaigrette, 572. *see also* salad
    dressing
  about, 572
  avocado, 573
  basil, 573
  black pepper, 573
  blue cheese, 573
  cream cheese, 578
  dressings
    vs., 572
  fresh herb, 572
  honey mustard, 573
  horseradish, 573
  leeks, 280
  lemon oregano, 573
  lime, 573
  lobster salad, 162
  Parmesan, 574
  parsley lime, 573
  persimmons in, 233
  Roquefort, 573
  sherry, 573–574
  spicy walnut, 574
  spinach, 573
  sweet-and-sour, 574
  Thai, 575
  watercress, 573
vin brûle, 67
vinegar(s), 1024–1025
  carrot and edamame salad with rice
    vinegar dressing, 167
  chile, 1024
  elderberry, 222–223
  fresh herb, 1025
  garlic, 1025
  ginger, 1025
  in pickling, 944
  quick herb, 1025
  red raspberry, Cockaigne, 1025
  spiced, 1025
  tarragon, 1025
  types, 1024–1025
Viognier, 47
violets, 155
virgin, 415
virgin cocktails, 63–64
  about, 63
  cranberry Collins, 64
  daiquiri, 61
  niña colada, 61
  rock shandy, 64
  Shirley Temple, 64
  Virgin Mary, 57
vitamin(s), 6
  on food labels, 8
  vitamin B12, for vegetarians, 8
  vitamin D, 5, 6
vitello tonnato freddo (cold veal in tuna
    sauce), 486
vodka sauce, penne with, 328

vodka, vodka cocktails, 56, 57–58
  about, 57
  Becker bloody bull shot, 57
  black pepper, 58
  black Russian, 58
  bloody Mary, 57
  bullshot, 57
  citrus, 58
  Collins, 56
  cosmopolitan, 58
  flavored, 58
  gimlet, 56
  greyhound, 58
  Harvey Wallbanger, 58
  Joy tea, 58
  kamikaze, 58
  Madras, 58
  martini, 56
  Moscow mule, 58
  salty dog, 58
  screwdriver, 57
  seabreeze, 58
  tea, 58
  tonic, 56
  white Russian, 58

W
waffle(s), 646–648
  about, 646
  bacon cornmeal, 647
  Belgian, 647
  buttermilk, 647
  chocolate, 647
  cornmeal, 647
  desserts
    about, 826
  French toast, 648
  high-altitude adjustments for, 646
  honey bran, 647
  sandwich, 180
waffle iron, 646
waiter's corkscrew, 54, **54**
wakame, 1011
waldmeister (sweet woodruff), 1020
Waldorf salad, 169
Walla Walla onions, 286
Walleye, 415
walnut(s), 1025
  apple muffins, 636
  blue cheese spread with, 76
  butter, 558
    savory, 178–179
  catsup, 953
  chocolate fudge, 863
  chocolate torte, 728
  and endive salad, 160
  filling, toasted, 758
  and garlic sauce, 568–569
  and goat cheese soufflé, 205
  maple fudge, 863
  mushroom noodle kugel, 336–337
  pear, and endive salad, 170
  vinaigrette, spicy, 574
  vinegar, 1025
wasabi, 1026
  grilled tuna with pickled ginger, soy
    sauce and, 405
  soy sauce, 571
wassail, 68
water, 1026–1027
  acidulated, 957
  boiling point at high altitude, 1056
  boiling points at various altitudes, 746

drinking, 6
emergency purification of, 1026–1027
evaporation point at high altitude, 746
for ice, 55
orange, 980
rose, 980
safety, 1026–1027
    backpacking water supply, 27
    baking in a water bath, 743
for tea, 33
water-bath
    for cheesecakes, 744
    for custards, 801, **803**
water-blanching, 918–919
water chestnuts, 314–315, 1027
    about, 314
    stir-fried, 314–315
watercress, 153, **153,** 315
    mayonnaise, 581
    soup, cream of, 145–146
    vinaigrette, 573
watermelon, 230
    basket, **230**
    -celery-apple splash, 39
    goat cheese and, 230
    pickled rind of, 949–950
    plugged, 64
    punch, 41
    salad, spicy, 170
    sorbet, 836
wax beans, 250
waxy starches
    sweet rice flour, 1017
    waxy cornstarch, 1018
weakfish, 417
weather
    power outages, 910–911
weather and cooking, about, 1031
wedding buffets
    menus for, 21
wedding cakes
    about, 703–704
Wehani rice, 354
weight management, 7
Wellfleet oysters, 371
Welsh rarebit, 112
Westcott Bay oysters, 371
West Indian cherries, 238
Westphalian ham, 506
wheat
    cracked, 986
    flour, 987
    types, 362
    whole. see whole wheat
wheat beer, 52
wheat beers, 52
wheat berries
    about, 362
    brown rice and, 345
    preparing, 368 (chart)
    with sautéed onions and dried fruits,
        362
wheat germ, 987
    banana bread, quick, 628
wheat gluten, 318, 923
wheat meat, 318
whelk. see conch
whipped cream
    as cake filling, 754
    cocoa, 755
    filling
        with candies, 755
        with cookies, 755

with fruit, 755
with nuts, 755
fresh strawberry dacquoise with
    chocolate and, 741–742
fresh strawberry meringue with
    chocolate and, 741–742
liquor-flavored, 755
mocha, 755
parfaits, coffee, 841
sweetened, 754
whipping cream, 973
whips, 810
    fruit, 813–814
    sponges, 810
whiskey cocktails and drinks, 58–60,
    65–67
whiskey sauce, Southern, 852
whisks, 542, 700
whitebait, 411
    smelt, 416, 417
white beans, 254
    dip with rosemary and garlic, 73
    soup, Mediterranean white bean, 133
white button mushrooms, 281
white chile (chicken chile verde), 435–436
white cornmeal, 348
white currants, 222
white eggplants, 273
whitefish, 417
white gazpacho, 147
white onions, 286
white rice, 354
white Russian, 58
white sauce (béchamel), 550–551
white truffles, 284–285
white wine, 46–47
    beef stew with mustard, herbs and, 480
    fish fillets roasted in, 397
    fish steaks poached in, 400–401
    sabayon with, 847
    sauce, 553
        for fish, 552
    spritzer, 53
whiting, 414
whole barley, 346
whole wheat
    biscuits, 639
    bread, 599
        Cockaigne, 599
        fast, 599
        made with mixed starter, 605
        sandwich, 599
        sprouted, 599
        sugar-free, 599
    flour, 591
    muffins, 635
    pasta, 325
    pastry dough, 665
    pie dough, 665
    rolls, 614
        refrigerator, 621
widgeon, 455
wiener schnitzel (breaded veal cutlet), 487
    á la Holstein, 487
wild doves, 459
wild ducks, 418
    about, 455
    roast, 455
    types, 455
wildfowl, 418, 451–461. see also poultry
    about, 453–454
    barding of, 455
    buying, 453

cooking, 455
drawing and dressing, 454
field dressing, 453–454
gravy, 547
hunting, 453
plucking and singeing of, 454
potted, 457
preparing, 453–454, 454
preparing whole, 454
sauerkraut stuffing for, 539
test for doneness, 453
wild goose, braised, 456
wild greens
    about, 278
    cooking, 278–279
    foraging for, 156
wild mint, 156
wild mushrooms, foraging for, 282
wild pheasant, 457–458
wild quail, 459
wild rice, 354
    about, 363
    dressing for game, 540
    pilau, doves and, 461
    and porcini dressing, 540
    preparing, 368 (chart)
    salad with sausage, 171
    with sautéed mushrooms, 363
wild roots, cooking, 279
wild shoots, cooking, 279
wild turkey
    about, 456
    braised, 456
    roasted in a baking bag, 456
wilted greens, 160
    spinach, 305–306
wine, 44–53. see also specific wines
    about, 44–45
    appetizer, 50
    cheese and, 51
    in cooking, 1027–1028
    dessert, 50
    food and, 45–46
    fruit and other grape, 50
    glassware for, **53**
    May, 66
    mulled, 67
    red. see red wine
    rosés, 49
    sangria, 65
    sauce, hot, 852
    sauce, mushroom, 555–556
    sparkling, 49–50
    temperature for, 50–51
    vocabulary of, 45
    white. see white wine
wine vinegar, 1024
winter cress, 156
winter fish, 414
winter fruit soup, 147
wintering over fresh produce, 886–887
winter melon, 230
    soup, 129
Winter Nellis pears, 232
winter squash, 307
    about, 307
    baked, 308
    canning, 901
    filling for stuffed pasta, 338–339
    freezing, 921
    mashed, 308–309
    pie, 686
    seeds, toasted, 1011

witloof chicory, 153
wolffish, 417
wontons, 342, **342**
    fried, 93
    soup, 126–127
    vegetable, 342
woodchuck, 524–525
woodcock, 418, 459
    about, 461
    in rosemary cream sauce, 461
wood duck, 455
wood mushrooms, 282
Worcestershire sauce, 953, 1028
wrap(s), 187–188
    fillings and dressings for, 177–178
    steak, 187
    turkey and avocado, 187
wrap cookery, 351–352, 398–399,
        1051–1053
    leaf wrappings, 1051–1052
wrap, freezer, 912

Y

yams. see also sweet potato(es)
    about, 301
yard-long beans, 250
    stir-fried, 252
yeast, 591, 1028–1029
    in food spoilage, 884
    types, 591
yeast breads. see also bread(s); yeast
        dough; yeast rolls and buns
    about, 591–592
    starters for, 601–603
yeast coffee cakes, 621–623. see also
        coffee cakes
    about, 621
yeast dough
    additions to, 596
    in high altitude cooking, 594, 596
    kneading, 592–593, **593**
    mixing, 592

    proofing, 593–594
    rising, **593,** 593–594
    scoring, 595
    shaping, 594, **594**
yeast rolls and buns, 609–623
    almond croissants, 617
    bear claws, 614, **614**
    brioche, 614–615, **615**
    brioche à tete, 615, **615**
    brioche au chocolat, 615
    buttermilk, 611–612, **612**
    buttermilk potato, 613
    caramel, 613
    cheese, 613
    cloverleaf, 610, **610**
    croissants, 616–617, **617**
    crumpets, 619
    doughnuts, 654
    fan-tans, 611–612, **612**
    filled pinwheel, **612,** 612–613
    filled sweet crescents, 618
    hard, 618
    hot cross, 610
    joined finger, 610–611, **611**
    kolatchen, 612
    no-knead light, 609–610
    no-knead refrigerator, 620
    oat, 614
    overnight, 612
    palm leaf, 611, **611**
    Parker House, 610, **610**
    raspberry croissants, 617
    refrigerator bran, 621
    refrigerator potato, 620
    rye, 614
    sectioned brioche loaf, 615–616
    sour cream, 611, **611**
    sticky, **613,** 613–614
    topped brioche, 615
    Vienna, 618
    whole wheat, 614, 621
yellow cornmeal, 348

yellow crookneck squash, 306
Yellow Finn potatoes, 294
yellowfin tuna, 417
yellow onions, 286
yellow perch, 415
yellowtail pompano, 415
yellowtail snapper, 416
yogurt, 1013, 1029–1030
    dip, honey, 78
    drained or yogurt cheese,
        1030
    dressing for fruit salad, 578
    frozen
        about, 834–835
        chocolate, 835
        strawberry, 835
        vanilla, 835
    herb dressing, 577
    marinade, 585
    mayonnaise, 579
    sauce, Indian (raita), 567–568
Yorkshire pudding, 637
youngberries, 220
yuca
    about, 315
    with citrus and garlic, 315
Yukon Gold potatoes, 294
Yule log (bûche de noël), 737

Z

zabaglione, 806
zest
    citrus, 971, **971**
zester, 54, **54,** 542
Zinfandel, 47–48
    white, 49
ziti, **321**
zucchini, 306. see also summer
        squash
    bread, sweet, 628
    deep-fried, 308
    ratatouille Provençale, 274